Baseball
Prospectus
2014

Baseball Prospectus 2014

THE ESSENTIAL GUIDE TO THE 2014 SEASON

EDITED BY SAM MILLER AND JASON WOJCIECHOWSKI

R.J. Anderson • Bill Baer • Craig Brown • Ken Funck • Ryan Ghan • Craig Goldstein • Chris Jaffe • Andrew Koo • Ben Lindbergh • Rob McQuown • Ian Miller • Jack Moore • Adam J. Morris • Tommy Rancel • Daniel Rathman • Bret Sayre • Adam Sobsey • Paul Sporer • Matt Sussman • Doug Thorburn • Will Woods • Geoff Young

WILEY

Wiley General Trade, an imprint of Turner Publishing Company
424 Church Street • Suite 2240 • Nashville, Tennessee 37219
445 Park Avenue • 9th Floor • New York, New York 10022
www.turnerpublishing.com

For general information about our other products and services, please contact Ingram Publisher Services at (866) 400-5351.

Library of Congress Cataloging-in-Publication Data:

ISBN 978-1-118-45923-2 (pbk); 978-1-118-45926-3 (ebk)

Printed in the United States of America

10 9 8 7 6 5 4 3 2

CONTENTS

Foreword

By Gabe Kapler, retired MLB player, Fox Sports 1 MLB analyst

Every morning when I rise and read the Baseball Prospectus Newsletter over a cup of coffee and a plate full of farm fresh scrambled eggs and mushrooms, I'm reminded how lucky I am. I'm grateful for the culinary experience of course, but just as importantly, for the opportunity to digest content that has encouraged me for quite some time now to think about the sport I love in a deeper, more thorough fashion.

Most baseball fans still get their sports news from the morning newspaper—or, more accurately, some online adaptation of the morning newspaper—with an RBIs-and-Ws type of approach to the game. In doing so, these fans are missing an opportunity to truly connect with what happened in each game, and to understand what's likely to happen in the next one. Folks who actually make decisions in the sport—the game within the game—are utilizing different, more advanced, and ever-changing metrics. They're evaluating players, teams and other executives in ways that a box score and a wire report can no longer decode. Baseball Prospectus is not just a slightly smarter newspaper. It's the window into the world of these executives. In fact, many of the front office minds I'm alluding to use Baseball Prospectus as a resource or as a jumping-off point to formulate ideas.

In 2007, just before I embarked on a season as minor-league manager in the Red Sox' system, Boston General Manager Ben Cherington gave me a study on the sacrifice bunt and how it was being misused at the major-league level. I laid down 20 sacrifice bunts in my playing career; being able and willing to do the little things contributed to my consistent employment as a player. It would have been very easy for me to discard Cherington's information. That would have been an ego-driven approach, based on the rigid belief that because I played the game at a high level, I had little left to learn.

Many players have chosen that route. Executives in the game (like Cherington) have moved on from old-school statistics to newer metrics when it comes to player analysis, yet most of the players themselves have not. But that stance would have left me stagnant while more open-minded individuals continued their growth. We shouldn't want to be left behind, and I'm driven not to be. In my quest, I'm led by the ingenuity and substance of publications like the one you hold.

I am now a sponge dabbing at BP's content. Because I know that I need assistance, I'm able to learn from Baseball Prospectus why FIP is often a better indicator of a pitcher's future performance than WHIP; about which Rule 5 draftees (I'm talking about you, Brian Moran) are most likely to stick with their new clubs and make an impact; I can confidently make predictions about the coming season, thanks to BP's game simulators. But, more importantly, I've discovered something bigger about baseball knowledge: I've learned that finding good teammates who can inspire intellectual growth is essential. You can only attempt to master baseball by listening intently, by absorbing and by never thinking you've got it licked.

After my eggs and mushrooms over BP's morning newsletter, I work out to BP's Effectively Wild podcast, with Sam Miller and Ben Lindbergh. It's an odd choice—what could be invigorating about these guys' informative nonsense, right?—but I laugh and sweat along with them, and am moved not just by the content but the deliberate, thoughtful delivery. The information is unique and intricate, as is all of BP's content. My opinion and intelligence as a reader is respected—and not just because I was a mediocre MLB baseball player for a long time. Quite simply, I feel like if I was in the room with these guys, I'd be included in the discussion.

Like the podcast and the web site, the book you hold in your hand makes content king. The writing style is thoughtfully unapologetic, open-mindedly direct.

Most importantly, it's refreshingly counter to what else is out there.

Preface

Just before the 1996 season began, just before Mariano Rivera the failed starter with a 5.51 ERA turned into Mariano Rivera the greatest relief pitcher of all time, *Baseball Prospectus* sent out its first preseason annual, 51 words of which were devoted to Rivera: "Skinny swingman who has good control of the corners of the strike zone. His K rate seemed to jump up a little as of late, and if that's development rather than a fluke, this kid could really be something special. Looks way too skinny to be durable, but you never know."

Considering Rivera's pedigree—low-bonus signee out of a country that had never produced an All-Star pitcher; 26-year-old already confined to relief work; never appeared on a top-100 prospects list; as yet no fall-to-your-knees-and-weep cut fastball—you have to give that 1996 author an awful lot of credit. The comment nails Rivera's strength (the ability to avoid the middle of the plate) and his weakness (he wouldn't hold up as a starter), but what leaps out is the borderline prescient "could really be something special." Naturally, the comment doesn't predict two exceptional, game-changing decades, but who ever can?

This year sees the 19th *Baseball Prospectus* player comment for Rivera. Each year, his story changed a bit: We called him "quite possibly the most important player in the game" in 1997 but worried that "something very bad is happening" in 1999, were "skeptical" that "a pitcher [can] survive on one pitch [even] if that one pitch is perhaps the best in baseball" in 2000, called it "patently absurd" when folks wanted to save him room in the Hall of Fame in 2001, conceded in 2004 that "Rivera is, without question, the best one-pitch pitcher ever," regretted that by 2006 there were no longer "any superlatives left with which to garland Rivera," found one we'd missed by calling him "the closest thing baseball has to Fred Astaire" in 2009, called the "obvious first-ballot Hall of Famer" "beyond encomiums" (which is itself arguably an encomium) in 2011, and, finally, this year, find ourselves getting misty in an uncharacteristically sentimental sendoff.

Of course, this isn't a book about Rivera; we invoke him as synecdoche. All these comments, ever changing, ever adapting, always attempting to learn from themselves, don't just give us a chronology of one great career. They give us a chronology of the great career of *Baseball Prospectus* itself.

There's a simplicity to that first Rivera comment. Facts, judgment. In the years that follow, the tone gets more incisive, the judgments more certain. As baseball's amateur sabermetricians consolidated their findings during an extraordinary period of research, they could quite fairly claim authority arising from being years ahead of the sport's conventional wisdom.

In 2000, the word "I" disappears. Sabermetrics had coalesced from a collection of message board denizens into a semi-organized movement (political, religious, ideological, revolutionary), and the comments began to reflect the growth of a new conventional wisdom—one based on data, one upending the sport.

By the end of the decade, sabermetrics was no longer upending the sport; it was intrinsic in the sport. The comments became self-aware. One revisited all the superlatives that had been bestowed on Rivera in BP comments through the years. (Sound familiar?) Another tweaked a classic piece of sabermetric jargon (coined by John Sickels) to turn a joke about Rivera's encroaching fragility: "Rivera is slowly turning into the world's greatest variation on the LOOGY, the CLOOGY (CLoser Only Occasionally Guy)."

Always learning, always changing. So what is the state of BP writing in 2014, for Rivera's final comment? It incorporates scouting far more than BP did in the culture-war years. The input of BP's sizeable scouting bureau should be apparent in comments about prospects. Where scouts were once (unfairly) a punchline in sabermetric circles, we now appreciate that good information comes from a variety of sources and disciplines, and good conclusions come from incorporating all of them. (And scouting, it should be said, grows to use new data and tools as well. It was not *so* long ago that old-school scouts came to games equipped only with their eyes and scorned these new kids with their radar guns and stopwatches.)

BP is also not as snarky as the early years. Back then, sabermetrics were outside the game, marginalized while entrenched baseball executives often operated with incomplete information and poor processes. The former isn't true at all anymore (no fewer than three BP staffers have been hired by teams since last year's Annual) and the latter can be confined to a few stubborn cases, if that. That's not to say teams don't make mistakes, or that we don't mock them as mercilessly as the situation calls for. It means merely that we start with the presumption of competence, not idiocy, and we appreciate that teams have access to information we don't.

Absence of snark does not mean absence of humor: We guarantee you no fewer than 500 jokes in this book. (We'll give you one in this paragraph for free.) Baseball remains an awkward game, an absurd game, a game that gives us hours of down time to appreciate that awkwardness and absurdity. It's a game with the best names, the highest-hiked pants, the strangest injuries, the most aggressively anachronistic scribes and the most self-serious rigidity to mock. It also has the Marlins.

Finally, we promise you good writing. We—the editors of this book—are both decidedly second-generation BPers. We discovered *Baseball Prospectus* in our formative years and have bookshelves bent under the weight of previous Annuals. We learned to write and we learned to think from reading these books, and we consider the form something unique and special. All of that goes for nearly everybody who contributed to this year's Annual. A great deal of effort has gone into stocking this book with the best writers and the best writing possible.

To that end, and prompted by our obligation to be as critical of ourselves as we are of others, we've made one big change to this year's book. For the first time, the essays are bylined. As you'll see from those bylines, we've gone outside our immediate BP family to build a staff of amazing writers bringing a bevy of styles and perspectives to the essays. We have announcers and beat writers, bloggers and book authors, even a few writers who have made their names in fields other than baseball. We were elated when each of the 30 said "yes," and we gave them latitude to approach the essays in whatever style they felt best. This is a more demanding assignment than it might seem, but they flourished with that freedom.

We're immensely proud of the book you're holding, we're proud to continue the distinguished tradition established by the 18 Annuals that came before and, most of all, we're proud to be part of the extraordinarily talented and dedicated BP family that comes together to make this book a reality. The authors on the title page and above the essays are only the beginning. The book would, quite simply, not exist without Rob McQuown taking charge on technical issues, the stats backbone created and shepherded by Colin Wyers (who was rudely stolen from us midprocess by the Astros) and Harry Pavlidis, and the general leadership of Dave Pease and Joe Hamrahi, who have quietly steered BP from a rude upstart kicking up an outsider fuss to a force to be reckoned with. Bill Skelton, Ryan Lind, Andrew Koo and Stuart Wallace provided valuable assistance, as did Jason Parks and his scouting team, as did Dan Brooks and BrooksBaseball.net, as did Eric Nelson and his expert steering.

The book and the site owe debts of gratitude to many others who help us grow and improve: Cory Schwartz, Jeff Volk, Dinn Mann, Marissa Fish and Jim Jenks at MLB Advanced Media; Jerry Ford, Brad Clement, Patrick Ebert, Darron Sutton, Steve Griffin, Tyson Kim, Jason Gerst, Todd Gold, David Rawnsley, Kendall Rogers, Taylor McCollough, Frankie Piliere and Allan Simpson at Perfect Game USA; Mike Ferrin, Chris Eno, Olivia Branco and Zach Wilt at SiriusXM; A.J. Hinch, John Coppolella, Michael Girsch, Dan Kantrovitz, Jon Daniels, Don Welke, Ned Colletti, Brian Minniti, Adam Cromie, Jeff Luhnow, Kevin Goldstein, Mike Fast, Sig Mejdal, John Tumminia, Dennis Sheehan, Chris Calo, Mike Groopman, Jeff Evans, Dustin Morse, Steve Grande, Shannon Forde and John Dever with MLB teams; and Dan Evans, Blake Rhodes, Gary Gillette, Pete Palmer, Kevin Kerrane, Jason Martinez, C.J. Nitkowski, Ken Rosenthal, Chuck Fox, Shaun Clancy, Angela Parker, Erica Brooks, Amanda Rykoff, Bill Mitchell, District Lines and Yardbarker.

But you opened this book for the words themselves, not our words about the words. Go.

Sam Miller & Jason Wojciechowski
December 26, 2013

Statistical Introduction

Why don't you get your nose out of those numbers and watch a game?

It's a false dilemma, of course. I would wager that Baseball Prospectus readers watch more games than the typical fan. They also probably pay better attention when they do. The numbers do not replace observation, they supplement it. Having the numbers allows you to learn things not readily seen by mere watching, and to keep up on many more players than any one person could on their own.

So this book doesn't ask you to choose between the two. Instead, we combine numerical analysis with the observations of a lot of very bright people. They won't always agree. Just as the eyes don't always see what the numbers do, the reverse can be true. In order to get the most out of this book, however, it helps to understand the numbers we're presenting and why.

Offense

The core of our offense measurements is True Average, which attempts to quantify everything a player does at the plate—hitting for power, taking walks, striking out and even "productive" outs—and scale it to batting average. A player with a TAv of .260 is average, .300 exceptional, .200 rather awful.

True Average also accounts for the context a player performs in. That means we adjust it based on the mix of parks a player plays in. Also, rather than use a blanket park adjustment for every player on a team, a player who plays a disproportionate amount of his games at home will see that reflected in his numbers. We also adjust based upon league quality: The average player in the AL is better than the average player in the NL, and True Average accounts for this.

Because hitting runs isn't the entirety of scoring runs, we also look at a player's Baserunning Runs. BRR accounts for the value of a player's ability to steal bases, of course, but also accounts for his ability to go first to third on a single, or advance on a fly ball.

Defense

Defense is a much thornier issue. The general move in the sabermetric community has been toward stats based on zone data, where human stringers record the type of batted ball (grounder, liner, fly ball) and its presumed landing location. That data is used to compile expected outs for comparing a fielder's actual performance.

The trouble with zone data is twofold. First, unlike the sorts of data that we use in the calculation of the statistics you see in this book, zone data wasn't made publicly available; the data was recorded by commercial data providers who kept the raw data private, only disclosing it to a select few who paid for it. Second, as we've seen the field of zone-based defensive analysis open up—more data and more metrics based upon that data coming to light—we see that the conclusions of zone-based defensive metrics don't hold up to outside scrutiny. Different data providers can come to very different conclusions about the same events. And even two metrics based upon the same data set can come to radically different conclusions based upon their starting assumptions—assumptions that haven't been tested, using methods that can't be duplicated or verified by outside analysts.

The quality of the fielder can bias the data: Zone-based fielding metrics will tend to attribute more expected outs to good fielders than bad fielders, irrespective of the distribution of batted balls. Scorers who work in parks with high press boxes will tend to score more line drives than scorers who work in parks with low press boxes.

Our FRAA incorporates play-by-play data, allowing us to study the issue of defense at a granular level, without resorting to the sorts of subjective data used in some other fielding metrics. We count how many plays a player made, as well as expected plays for the average player at that position based upon a pitcher's estimated groundball tendencies and the handedness of the batter. There are also adjustments for park and the base-out situations.

Pitching

Of course, how we measure fielding influences how we measure pitching.

Most sabermetric analysis of pitching has been inspired by Voros McCracken, who stated, "There is little if any difference among major-league pitchers in their ability to prevent hits on balls hit in the field of play." When first published, this statement was extremely controversial, but later research has by-and-large validated it. McCracken (and others) went forth from that finding to come up with a variety of defense-independent pitching measures.

The trouble is that many efforts to separate pitching from fielding have ended up separating pitching from pitching—looking at only a handful of variables (typically walks, strikeouts, and home runs—the "three true outcomes") in isolation from the situation in which they occurred. What we've done instead is take a pitcher's actual results—not just what happened, but when it happened—and adjust it for the quality of a pitcher's defensive support, as measured by FRAA.

Applying FRAA to pitchers in this sense is easier than applying it to fielders. We don't have to worry about figuring out which fielder is responsible for making an out, only identifying the likelihood of an out being made. So there is far less uncertainty here than there is in fielding analysis.

Note that Fair RA means exactly that, , not his earned runs allowed per game. Looking only at earned runs tends over time to overrate three kinds of pitchers:

1. Pitchers who play in parks where scorers hand out more errors. Looking at error rates between parks tells us scorers differ significantly in how likely they are to score any given play as an error (as opposed to an infield hit);
2. Groundball pitchers, because a substantial proportion of errors occur on groundballs; and
3. Pitchers who aren't very good. Good pitchers tend to allow fewer unearned runs than bad pitchers, because good pitchers have more ways to get out of jams than bad pitchers. They're more likely to get a strikeout to end the inning, and less likely to give up a home run.

For a metric that provides a more forward-looking perspective, we have Fielding Independent Pitching, a metric developed independently by Tom Tango and Clay Dreslough that says what a pitcher's expected ERA would be given his walks, strikeouts, and homeruns allowed. FIP is attempting to answer a different question than Fair RA; instead of saying how well a pitcher performed, it tells us how much of a pitcher's performance we think is due to things the pitcher has direct control over. Over time, we see pitchers who consistently over- or underperform their FIPs through some skill that isn't picked up by the rather limited components. FIP may be useful in identifying pitchers who were "lucky" or "unlucky," but some caution must be exercised.

Projection

Of course, many of you aren't turning to this book just for a look at what a player has done, but a look at what a player is going to do—the PECOTA projections.

PECOTA, initially developed by Nate Silver (who has moved on to greater fame as a political analyst), consists of three parts:

1. Major league equivalencies, to allow us to use minor-league stats to project how a player will perform in the majors;
2. Baseline forecasts, which use weighted averages and regression to the mean to produce an estimate of a player's true talent level; and
3. A career path adjustment, which incorporates information on how comparable players' stats changed over time.

Now that we've gone over the stats, let's go over what's in the book.

The Team Prospectus

The bulk of this book comprises team chapters, with one for each of the 30 major-league franchises. On the first page of each chapter, you will be greeted by a box laying out some key statistics for each team.

2013 W-L is exactly as it sounds, the unadjusted tally of wins and losses. Pythag tallies wins and losses on an adjusted basis by taking the runs scored per game (RS/G) and allowed (RA/G) by a team in a season and running them through a version of Bill James' Pythagorean formula refined and developed by David Smyth and Brandon Heipp called "Pythagenpat."

A team's runs scored is accompanied by True Average and Baserunning Runs to give a picture of how a team scores its runs. In terms of run-prevention ability, we present a team's

TAv against, FIP, and Defensive Efficiency Rating, which is its rate of balls in play turned into outs.

Then we have several measures not directly related to on-field performance. B-Age and P-Age tell us the average age of a team's batters and pitchers, respectively. Salary tells us how much the team cost to put on the field, and Doug Pappas' Marginal Dollars per Marginal Win (M$/MW) tells us how much bang for the buck a team got out of its payroll.

This year we're expanding the annual's coverage of injuries. We count up the number of disabled-list days a team has, as well as the estimated WARP that a team lost in those DL days, to quantify the impact of the specific players who were out of commission.

Position Players

After a bylined opening essay about teach team, each chapter moves onto the player comments, which are written by the Baseball Prospectus team. Each player is listed with the major-league team with which he was employed as of December 25, 2013, meaning that free agents who changed teams after that date will be listed under their previous employer. As an example, take a look at the winter's big offseason prize, Robinson Cano.

The player-specific sections begin with biographical information before moving onto the column headers and actual data. The column headers begin with more standard information like year, team, level (majors or minors, and which level of the minors), and the raw, untranslated tallies found on the back of a baseball card: PA (Plate Appearances), R (Runs), 2B (doubles), 3B (triples), HR (home runs), RBI (runs batted in), BB (walks), SO (strikeouts), SB (stolen bases), and CS (caught stealing).

Following those are the untranslated triple-slash rate statistics: batting average (AVG), on base percentage (OBP), and slugging percentage (SLG). Their "slash" nickname is derived from the occasional presentation of slash-delimitation, such as noting that Cano hit .314/.383/.516. The slash line is followed by True Average (TAv), which rolls all those things and more into one easy-to-digest number.

BABIP stands for Batting Average on Balls in Play, and is meant to show how well a hitter did when he put the ball in

play. An especially low or high BABIP may mean a hitter was especially lucky or unlucky. However, line drive hitters will tend to have especially high BABIPs from season to season; so will speedy hitters who are able to beat out more grounders for base hits.

Next is Baserunning Runs (BRR) which, as mentioned earlier, covers all sorts of baserunning accomplishments, not just stolen bases. Then comes Fielding Runs Above Average; for historical stats, we have the number of games played at each position in parenthesis.

The last column is Wins Above Replacement Player. WARP combines a player's batting runs above average (derived from a player's True Average), BRR, FRAA, an adjustment based upon position played, and a credit for plate appearances based upon the difference between the "replacement level" (derived from looking at the quality of players added to a team's roster after the start of the season) and the league average.

Pitchers

Now let's look at how pitchers are presented, looking at the American League's reigning Cy Young:

The first line and the YEAR, TM, LVL, and AGE columns are the same as in the hitter's example above. The next set of columns—W (Wins), L (Losses), SV (Saves), G (Games pitched), GS (Games Started), IP (Innings Pitched), H (Hits), HR, BB, SO, BB9, SO9—are the actual, unadjusted cumulative stats compiled by the pitcher during each season.

Next is GB%, which is the percentage of all batted balls that were hit on the ground including both outs and hits. The average GB% for a major league pitcher in 2007 was about 45%; a pitcher with a GB% anywhere north of 50% can be considered a good groundball pitcher. As mentioned above, this is based upon the observation of human stringers and can be skewed based upon a number of factors. We've included the number as a guide, but please approach it skeptically.

BABIP is the same statistic as for batters, but often tells you more in the case of pitchers, since most pitchers have very little control over their batting average on balls in play. A high BABIP is most likely due to a poor defense or bad luck

Robinson Cano   2B
Born: **10/22/1982** Age: **31**
Bats: **L** Throws: **R** Height: **6' 0"**
Weight: **210** Breakout: **0%**
Improve: **42%** Collapse: **1%**
Attrition: **1%** MLB: **99%**
Comparables:
Chase Utley, Aramis Ramirez, Vladimir Guerrero

YEAR	TEAM	LVL	AGE	PA	R	2B	3B	HR	RBI	BB	SO	SB	CS	AVG/OBP/SLG	TAv	BABIP	BRR	FRAA	WARP
2011	NYA	MLB	28	681	104	46	7	28	118	38	96	8	2	.302/.349/.533	.306	.316	2.8	2B(157): 6.0	6.0
2012	NYA	MLB	29	697	105	48	1	33	94	61	96	3	2	.313/.379/.550	.319	.326	-1.6	2B(154): 6.3	6.9
2013	NYA	MLB	30	681	81	41	0	27	107	65	85	7	1	.314/.383/.516	.324	.327	-0.9	2B(153): -1.8, SS(1): -0.0	6.3
2014	SEA	MLB	31	643	77	40	2	21	87	45	88	5	2	.297/.352/.482	.307	.320	-0.7	2B 2, SS -0	5.4

rather than a pitcher's own abilities, and may be a good indicator of a potential rebound. A typical league-average BABIP is around .295–.300.

WHIP and ERA are common to most fans, with the former measuring the number of walks and hits allowed on a per-inning basis while the latter prorates runs allowed on a nine innings basis. Neither is translated or adjusted in any way.

Fair RA (FRA) has been gone into in some depth above, and is the basis of WARP for pitchers. Incorporating play-by-play data allows us to set different replacement levels for starting pitchers and relievers. Relief pitchers have several advantages over starters: they can give their best effort on every pitch, and hitters have fewer chances to pick up on what they're doing. That means that it's significantly easier to find decent replacements for relief pitchers than it is for starting pitchers, and that's reflected in the replacement level for each.

We also credit starters for pitching deeper into games and "saving the pen"—a starting pitcher who's able to go deep in to a game (while pitching effectively) allows a manager to keep his worst relievers in the pen and bring his best relievers out to preserve a lead.

All of this means that WARP values for relief pitchers (especially closers) will seem lower than what we've seen in the past—and may conflict with how we feel about relief aces coming in and "saving" the game. Saves give extra credit to the closer for what his teammates did to put him in a save spot to begin with; WARP is incapable of feeling excitement over a successful save, and judges them dispassionately.

PECOTA

Both pitchers and hitters have PECOTA projections for next season, as well as a set of biographical details that describe the performance of that player's comparable players according to PECOTA.

The 2014 line is the PECOTA projection for the player at the date we went to press. Note that the player is projected into the league and park context as indicated by his team abbreviation. All PECOTAs represent a player's projected major league performance. The numbers beneath the player's name—Breakout, Improve, Collapse, and Attrition—are also a part of PECOTA. These estimate the likelihood of changes in performance relative to a player's previously established level of production, based upon the performance of the comparable players:

- Breakout Rate is the percent chance that a player's production will improve by at least 20 percent relative to the weighted average of his performance over his most recent seasons.
- Improve Rate is the percent chance that a player's production will improve at all relative to his baseline performance. A player who is expected to perform just the same as he has in the recent past will have an Improve Rate of 50 percent.
- Collapse Rate is the percent chance that a position player's equivalent runs produced per PA will decline by at least 25 percent relative to his baseline performance over his past three seasons.
- Attrition Rate operates on playing time rather than performance. Specifically, it measures the likelihood that a player's playing time will decrease by at least 50 percent relative to his established level.

Breakout Rate and Collapse Rate can sometimes be counterintuitive for players who have already experienced a radical change in their performance levels. It's also worth noting that the projected decline in a given player's rate performances might not be indicative of an expected decline in underlying ability or skill, but rather something of an anticipated correction following a breakout season. MLB% is the percentage of similar players who played at the major league level in the relevant season.

The final pieces of information, are his three highest scoring comparable players as determined by PECOTA. Occasionally, a player's top comparables will not be representative of the larger sample that PECOTA uses. All comparables represent a snapshot of how the listed player was performing at the same age as the current player, so if a 23-year-old hitter is compared to Sammy Sosa, he's actually being compared to a 23-year-old Sammy Sosa, not the decrepit Orioles version of Sosa, nor to Sosa's career as a whole.

Managers

Each team chapter ends with a manager's comment and data breaking down his tactical tendencies. Though it's often difficult to isolate a manager's contribution to a team, comparing specific data modeled after well-documented

---

Max Scherzer

Born: 7/27/1984 Age: 29
Bats: R Throws: R Height: 6' 3'' Weight: 220
Breakout: 16% Improve: 42% Collapse: 30%
Attrition: 3% MLB: 97%

Comparables:
Jake Peavy, Josh Beckett, Tim Lincecum

YEAR	TEAM	LVL	AGE	W	L	SV	G	GS	IP	H	HR	BB	SO	BB9	SO9	GB%	BABIP	WHIP	ERA	FIP	FRA	WARP
2011	DET	MLB	26	15	9	0	33	33	195	207	29	56	174	2.6	8.0	42%	.315	1.35	4.43	4.18	4.74	2.1
2012	DET	MLB	27	16	7	0	32	32	187²	179	23	60	231	2.9	11.1	38%	.334	1.27	3.74	3.22	3.50	4.4
2013	DET	MLB	28	21	3	0	32	32	214¹	152	18	56	240	2.4	10.1	38%	.259	0.97	2.90	2.77	3.23	4.6
2014	DET	MLB	29	11	9	0	28	28	173¹	157	19	52	182	2.7	9.4	42%	.302	1.20	3.41	3.62	3.71	2.6

plays and styles to the league average helps determine what a manager likes to do, even if we are still unable to translate that information into actual wins and losses.

Following the year, team and the actual record, Pythag +/- lets us know by how many games the team under- or over-performed its Pythagenpat record. That isn't necessarily a reflection of the manager, but it does tell us how well a team performed compared to a somewhat less noisy assessment of the underlying talent.

Pitching staff usage follows, first with AVG PC reporting the average pitch count of his starting pitchers; 100+P and 120+P track the number of games in which the starters exceeded certain pitch thresholds. QS is the number of quality starts —a start of at least six innings and with no more than three runs allowed —that a manager received from his starting pitchers. BQS is Blown Quality Starts, a Baseball Prospectus stat that measures games in which the starter delivered a quality start through six innings before losing it in the seventh inning or later. That said, a Blown Quality Start is not necessarily an indictment of a manager's abilities or tactics —a number of factors, ranging from excellent offensive support to extremely poor bullpen support, can lead a manager to leave his starter in a game after he's thrown six quality innings. Conversely, the decision by a manager to "bank" quality starts by restricting his starters to only six innings can have downsides as well, as it increases the bullpen's workload and gives it more opportunities to blow games in which the starter was cruising.

The next stats in the manager table tally how many pitching changes a manager made over the course of the season (REL) and how many times the reliever called upon didn't allow any runners, his own or inherited, to score (REL w Zero R). Bequeathed runners also count against REL w Zero R, meaning that relievers who exit with runners on that subsequently score prevent a manager from "padding" his tally here. Concluding the pitching section, IBB is simply the number of intentional walks the manager ordered during the given season, which can be a mark of managerial strategy so long as outlying intentional-walk recipients such as Miguel Cabrera are accounted for.

Managers do more than manage pitchers, however; their usage of a bench can lead to added or lost performance. Subs lets us know the number of defensive replacements the manager employed throughout the regular season, while PH, PH avg, and PH HR report the offensive statistics of pinch-hitters called upon. We then turn to the so-called small-ball tactics, starting with the running game. The manager's aggressiveness on the bases is broken down by successful steals of second and third base (SB2, SB3) and times caught (CS2, CS3). We also provide the number of sacrifices a team attempted (SAC Att) and their success rate (SAC %). Be sure to keep in mind the differences between leagues as NL sacrifice attempts are greatly inflated by the fact that pitchers bat. To correct for this, we list the number of times a manager got a successful sacrifice from a position paler (POS SAC), which allows for comparisons between the two leagues. We finish up with Squeeze, which counts the number of successful squeeze plays the team executed over the season. Finally, we have a couple of statistics that attempt to measure the manager's hit-and-run tactics. Swing is the number of times a hitter swung at a pitch while the runners were in motion, while In Play reflects how many times hitters swung and made contact while those runners were off to the races. Granted, swings on steal attempts do not always translate to hit-and-run attempts, but managers who greatly deviate from the average can be assumed to be staunch proponents or opponents of the strategy.

PECOTA Leaderboards

As a result of the way it weights previous seasons, PECOTA can tend to appear bullish on players coming off a bad year and bearish on players coming off a great year. And because we list the 50% percentile projections–the middle of the range the system thinks this player is capable of producing–it rarely predicts any player will hit 40 home runs or strike out 200 batters. At the end of this book, though, we've ranked the top players according to their projections. It's often as helpful to know who the system thinks will be the top second baseman as what his actual stats are likely to be.

MANAGER: JOHN GIBBONS

YEAR	TEAM	W-L	Pythag +/-	Avg PC	100+ P	120+ P	QS	BQS	REL	REL w Zero R	IBB	PH	PH Avg	PH HR	SB2	CS2	SB3	CS3	SAC Att	SAC %	POS SAC	Squeeze	Swing	In Play
2013	TOR	74-88	0	92.3	56	1	67	6	487	391	33	102	.220	3	87	38	25	3	44	65.9%	26	0	353	99

Arizona Diamondbacks

By Nick Piecoro

For at least the past decade, baseball has been moving toward an age of uniformity. Front offices have gotten smarter, they've gotten smarter in a lot of the same ways and they all seem to be using those smarts in ways that are readily apparent. Every year, fewer teams make crazy decisions. Both sides of most trades seem defensible to the reasonable onlooker. Prospects are more properly valued, perhaps to the point of being overvalued. Managers' in-game styles are becoming harder to differentiate.

This is all true for the vast majority of baseball's 30 teams. The Arizona Diamondbacks do not appear to reside within the vast majority. This makes them a fascinating team to follow. It also can make them a confusing team to follow. It's not that the Diamondbacks aren't as smart as everybody else—that may or may not be the case, the same as with any of the other 29 clubs—it's that they seem to give exactly zero effs about whether everyone *thinks* they are.

They often seem to trade players when their values are at the lowest, and they don't seem to care if they get back pennies on the dollar so long as they land the guys they want. They did it with Justin Upton and Trevor Bauer and Chris Young two offseasons ago and with Ian Kennedy during last season and then with Tyler Skaggs and Adam Eaton in December. They've become known as the team that values character over talent. Their in-game management can be unusual, too, evidenced by their atrocious stolen-base success rate; while the rest of baseball has become more calculating on the bases, the Diamondbacks have become more reckless.

They enter 2014 at something of an organizational crossroads. They have finished exactly .500 each of the past two seasons—one more and they'll officially be "threediocre"— leading club ownership to decline 2015 and 2016 contract options for General Manager Kevin Towers and manager Kirk Gibson. Owner Ken Kendrick told MLB.com that "it's important for them to go out and prove themselves once again."

Their leadership's potential lame-duck status will frame everything that happens with the Diamondbacks in 2014. And that means things could get even more interesting than normal. Already, the Diamondbacks can be sort of emo as an organization, starting at the top with Kendrick, an outspoken owner who sounds like a fan when he goes on local radio shows and complains about his team. Then there's Towers, who proudly embraces his nickname of "Gunslinger," which former Padres owner Jeff Moorad bestowed upon him pejoratively for his lack of a "strategic approach." The Diamondbacks tend to act swiftly and decisively in most respects, but particularly when it comes to jettisoning an underperforming player they're tired of watching struggle.

It can, in fact, be hard to find strategy in some of the Gunslinger's moves. One day, he pulled the trigger on an Upton trade that would have netted him a package of prospects had Upton not exercised his no-trade clause. Two weeks later, instead of getting a younger, cheaper collection of players, Towers dealt Upton for a package fronted by a 29-year-old infielder one year away from free agency. In June 2011, the Diamondbacks drafted Bauer and gushed about him, eccentricities and all, saying they wouldn't ask him to change a thing. Eighteen months later, the club dealt Bauer, who was pretty much exactly the guy he made himself out to be. That brings us to Didi Gregorius, the shortstop the Diamondbacks acquired for Bauer whom Towers said reminded him of a young Derek Jeter. A year later, Gregorius' name was popping up in trade rumors. One year they're talking about wanting to get a more contact-oriented lineup that's less dependent on power and the next they're looking to land a power bat.

DIAMONDBACKS PROSPECTUS
2013 W-L: 81-81, 2nd in NL West

Pythag	.493	16th	DER	.705	15th
RS/G	4.23	14th	B-Age	27.9	12th
RA/G	4.29	20th	P-Age	26.9	5th
TAv	.251	23rd	Salary	$90.3	17th
BRR	-9.75	28th	M$/MW	$2.37	12th
TAv-P	.267	18th	DL Days	859	13th
FIP	4.02	22nd	$ on DL	18%	19th

	Runs	HR/RH	HR/LH	Runs/RH	Runs/LH
Three-Year Park Factors	103	105	101	107	102

Top Hitter WARP	7.48 (Paul Goldschmidt)
Top Pitcher WARP	2.54 (Patrick Corbin)
Top Prospect	Archie Bradley

"They're like *Sybil*, you know, the story about the schizophrenic lady," a rival executive said. "You don't know what they're going to do. What exactly is the thought process there? There's areas where they have interesting players and have a surplus, but what's the plan to bring it into balance?"

Executives with other teams often are surprised by the moves the Diamondbacks make, many of which seem based on the whole character-over-talent thing. To be clear, it's not that the Diamondbacks don't have talented players. They do. And "character" doesn't tell the whole story. It's that they want guys who play the game a certain way. They want gritty dirtballs. They want guys that are more Lenny Dykstra than Garret Anderson. They want guys who play more like the way their manager played. It's what prompted Towers, during a radio interview in October, to say he wanted his pitchers to own the inner half of the plate, adding that he wanted them to operate with an "eye for an eye" mentality. Like we said, they're a little emo.

Of course, the Diamondbacks aren't the only club that occasionally makes people scratch their heads. The Philadelphia Phillies do this often. So do the San Francisco Giants and the Kansas City Royals. But some of the Diamondbacks' moves make folks wonder about the way they reach their decisions. Take their acquisition of reliever Heath Bell in October 2012. The Diamondbacks agreed to take on $13 million of the remaining $21 million on Bell's contract. Were Bell a free agent coming off his ugly year with the Marlins, does he get anywhere near $13 million? Of course not. And yet somehow the Diamondbacks thought this was a fair deal, making you wonder about the process being employed. Was there a person in the room banging on the table, wondering why they're about to do that deal? Do they have too many like-minded executives? Are people afraid to speak up in the room? Do they even have a room?

In fairness, many of the moves that are widely panned in the moment by the baseball twitterati are actually more than defensible after the fact. A year later, the Upton trade doesn't look like the disaster many had predicted—although they did go into the offseason looking for more power—and Gregorius probably has more value than Bauer. Just because the Diamondbacks appear to change directions like a pinball doesn't mean they're always going in the wrong direction. Everyone knows how unpredictable and fast-changing baseball can be. Maybe Towers, with his *Blink*-like ability to make spur-of-the-moment decisions, actually benefits from his lack of sticktoitiveness. Instead of stubbornly waiting around for a player he had believed in to perform, Towers isn't afraid to go straight to Plan B.

"He can put a deal together very, very quickly," said a scout with an American League team. "He's far more flexible than our guy is. We move very slowly. I don't know if that's right or wrong. Andrew Friedman is the same way. He's slow with everything. That's why they make all their deals in the offseason."

Towers' time in Arizona includes some definite high points. His bullpen makeover was a big reason the Diamondbacks won the division in 2011. His acquisition of Aaron Hill looks like a stroke of genius; Hill's .862 OPS with the Diamondbacks is the 19th-best in the majors since the trade, better than Carlos Beltran, Shin-Soo Choo, Billy Butler. Towers acquired highly effective groundball machine Brad Ziegler for next to nothing. And last spring Towers smartly extended Paul Goldschmidt, giving the slugging first baseman a deal that would have cost perhaps $100 million more had he waited another year.

But some of his quickly conceived deals haven't worked out great for the Diamondbacks. They went from pursuing Hiroki Kuroda to signing Jason Kubel seemingly overnight, the Kubel deal being finalized while Towers was vacationing with his wife in Bruges. A year later, they signed outfielder Cody Ross, getting a deal in place literally the day after the team first made contact with him. Kubel was designated for assignment in the second year of his deal. After a slow start offensively, Ross had begun to turn his season around when he went down with a scary hip injury in August. With no recent injury comps in baseball, people were left wondering if he'll return to anything close to the player he was before.

Kubel and Ross were just two of several Diamondbacks players to see their value take a significant hit in 2013. Catcher Miguel Montero regressed both offensively and defensively. Starting pitchers Trevor Cahill and Brandon McCarthy battled injuries and ineffectiveness. Kennedy pitched his way out of town. Skaggs' velocity remained AWOL.

And yet the Diamondbacks were still kind of/sort of in the hunt for the playoffs. Granted, their version of "contention" only existed thanks to the dual wild card era, but still. Goldschmidt nearly won the MVP. Patrick Corbin pitched like an ace for most of the year. Wade Miley had another solid year. And they could argue that the Great Grit Experiment might have been a success had everyone stayed healthy, namely Adam Eaton and Hill, two of their projected top-of-the-order hitters who missed big chunks of the season.

So, yeah, it wasn't all bad. And if a few things go their way next season—Mark Trumbo rakes, the bullpen and rotation improve, etc.—the Diamondbacks might be able to get on the right side of the .500 mark again. For years, the Diamondbacks survived in the National League West with a mid-range payroll in part because their competition was too broke to do anything but dumpster dive. But with the Dodgers nouveau riche, the Diamondbacks' task has become tougher, particularly this year, with their budget tighter and their need to win more immediate. It raises questions, such as: Will that desperation to win—and thus preserve Towers and Gibson's jobs—lead to deals with long-term value inequality? Or did we already see examples of that when Skaggs and Eaton were dealt for Trumbo or when third base prospect Matt Davidson was unloaded for reliever Addison Reed?

It sure seems as though Gibson is on thin ice. The team remade his coaching staff—to what extent he was on board with the changes is unclear—and there's a sense that a sluggish start could mean trouble for him. His players don't seem crazy about him, but that could just be the sort of hot/cold treatment that runs parallel to a team's win/loss record. Some say he doesn't communicate well enough and that he juggles his lineup too frequently. But when it comes to the latter charge, a manager who constantly changes his lineup is a mad genius when he's winning or a micromanaging tinkerer when he's losing.

Gibson's insistence on aggressive baserunning despite continued failure from his players has been strange. Even stranger have been the comments from the front office about him. In August, Kendrick said Gibson was "relatively new as a big-league manager." Gibson has 3 1/2 years experience as a manager—more time on the job than John

Farrell—plus another six as a bench coach, not to mention his 17-year playing career. In their own estimation, the Diamondbacks have underachieved relative to expectations for two consecutive seasons. They've already swapped out the majority of Gibson's original 2011 coaching staff, meaning that if things go awry again there aren't many places left to assign blame—or at least argue that a new voice is needed—other than the manager himself.

But in the end, it's not the worst time to be a Diamondbacks fan. You can dream. Maybe Goldschmidt repeats. Maybe Archie Bradley becomes the next Jose Fernandez, maybe Matt Stites and Jake Barrett the next Carlos Martinez and Trevor Rosenthal. Maybe everyone stays healthy and the lineup grits and grinds its way to the postseason. But if these things don't happen, change might be afoot. Either way, they'll be an interesting team to follow. They always are. Even if they don't always make sense—or, rather, especially if they don't make sense.

Nick Piecoro has been the Diamondbacks beat writer for The Arizona Republic since 2007.

HITTERS

Henry Blanco C
Born: 8/29/1971 Age: 42
Bats: R Throws: R Height: 5' 11"
Weight: 220 Breakout: 0%
Improve: 17% Collapse: 21%
Attrition: 35% MLB: 59%

Comparables:
Walker Cooper, Carlton Fisk, Hal McRae

YEAR	TEAM	LVL	AGE	PA	R	2B	3B	HR	RBI	BB	SO	SB	CS	AVG/OBP/SLG	TAv	BABIP	BRR	FRAA	WARP
2011	ARI	MLB	39	112	12	3	1	8	12	12	21	0	1	.250/.330/.540	.297	.239	-0.1	C(37): -0.6	1.0
2012	ARI	MLB	40	67	6	3	0	1	7	3	18	1	0	.188/.224/.281	.196	.244	0.1	C(21): 0.5	0.0
2013	SEA	MLB	41	107	8	2	0	3	14	10	26	0	0	.125/.215/.240	.176	.134	0.5	C(34): -0.6	-0.5
2013	TOR	MLB	41	43	3	3	0	0	0	4	10	0	0	.184/.262/.263	.157	.250	0.1	C(13): 0.0	-0.3
2014	ARI	MLB	42	250	24	10	0	6	24	21	55	1	0	.211/.278/.334	.226	.250	-0.4	C -1	0.2

Jamie Quirk. Jim Dwyer. Val Picinich. These are the names Blanco, the forever backup catcher, is chasing. The accomplishment? Each of the trio appeared in a record 18 major-league seasons without ever accruing more than 360 plate appearances. Blanco achieved his 16th such season with reserve duty in Seattle and Toronto in 2013. He was awful with the lumber for a second consecutive season, but he offered a competent mitt behind the plate and threw out six of 19 attempted basestealers. Blanco signed up for another year of emergency duty, this time in Arizona, and Quirk and Dwyer (but not Picinich, RIP) will undoubtedly be watching nervously.

Tony Campana CF
Born: 5/30/1986 Age: 28
Bats: L Throws: L Height: 5' 8"
Weight: 165 Breakout: 2%
Improve: 24% Collapse: 9%
Attrition: 19% MLB: 53%

Comparables:
Jarrod Dyson, Eric Young, Josh Anderson

YEAR	TEAM	LVL	AGE	PA	R	2B	3B	HR	RBI	BB	SO	SB	CS	AVG/OBP/SLG	TAv	BABIP	BRR	FRAA	WARP
2011	IOW	AAA	25	129	27	8	2	0	9	6	23	8	1	.342/.383/.442	.274	.423	1.9	CF(17): -2.0, LF(1): -0.0	0.3
2011	CHN	MLB	25	155	24	3	0	1	6	8	30	24	2	.259/.303/.301	.220	.321	4.2	LF(35): 0.1, CF(29): -0.6	0.3
2012	IOW	AAA	26	165	24	2	1	1	4	12	34	18	7	.280/.338/.329	.261	.358	3.6	CF(27): -0.7, LF(9): 1.4	0.8
2012	CHN	MLB	26	192	26	6	0	0	5	11	43	30	3	.264/.308/.299	.230	.351	3.8	CF(55): -1.7, LF(11): -0.0	0.2
2013	RNO	AAA	27	391	65	11	6	1	29	34	77	32	8	.293/.354/.368	.256	.371	1	CF(70): -3.2, LF(35): 1.0	0.7
2013	ARI	MLB	27	54	10	0	1	0	0	8	14	8	2	.261/.370/.304	.261	.375	-0.4	CF(8): -1.0, LF(2): 0.0	0.0
2014	ARI	MLB	28	250	32	8	2	1	15	16	57	22	5	.254/.305/.318	.231	.320	2.7	CF -2, LF 1	0.1

During one April at-bat in Triple-A, Campana stole second, third and home. That was the moment baseball reached its Tony Campanian nexus. After briefly poking his head into the Diamondbacks' outfield in July, he returned for good in late August to backfill Cody Ross' roster spot; wisely, his manager used him infrequently. A small sample did reveal a better walk rate, and if he can get on base by any means—including asking the pitcher nicely—then that speed can finally be put to good use. Otherwise, he's limited to full-time pinch-runner, still a cool thing because speed is neat.

Eric Chavez   3B

Born: 12/7/1977 Age: 36
Bats: L Throws: R Height: 6' 1''
Weight: 215 Breakout: 0%
Improve: 20% Collapse: 17%
Attrition: 25% MLB: 76%

Comparables:
Bobby Bonilla, Graig Nettles, Johnny Bench

YEAR	TEAM	LVL	AGE	PA	R	2B	3B	HR	RBI	BB	SO	SB	CS	AVG/OBP/SLG	TAv	BABIP	BRR	FRAA	WARP
2011	TAM	A+	33	23	4	2	0	1	3	2	4	0	0	.333/.391/.571	.324	.375	0		0.0
2011	NYA	MLB	33	175	16	7	1	2	26	14	34	0	0	.262/.320/.356	.238	.320	0.3	3B(42): 0.1, 1B(3): -0.0	0.3
2012	NYA	MLB	34	313	36	12	0	16	37	30	59	0	0	.281/.348/.496	.292	.300	-1.1	3B(64): 0.2, 1B(10): 0.2	1.8
2013	ARI	MLB	35	254	28	14	2	9	44	19	45	1	0	.281/.332/.478	.284	.307	-0.5	3B(52): 0.5, 1B(6): -0.1	1.3
2014	ARI	MLB	36	252	26	11	1	7	29	20	51	0	0	.252/.311/.398	.258	.300	-0.3	3B -0, 1B -0	0.5

One theory for Chavez's late-career resurgence as a productive part-timer: The real Eric Chavez had a career-ending injury whilst a rogue Eric Chavez impersonator slipped in to fill the void. He had the impression down so well he almost perfectly mimicked his career batting lines, and even went to the disabled list twice like the real Chavez would. That is dedication. This theory breaks down when you factor in that Chavez broke up Yusmeiro Petit's perfect game bid with two outs in the ninth—a real Eric Chavez impersonator would want to lay low.

Paul Goldschmidt   1B

Born: 9/10/1987 Age: 26
Bats: R Throws: R Height: 6' 3''
Weight: 245 Breakout: 4%
Improve: 48% Collapse: 1%
Attrition: 5% MLB: 100%

Comparables:
Miguel Cabrera, Prince Fielder, Joey Votto

YEAR	TEAM	LVL	AGE	PA	R	2B	3B	HR	RBI	BB	SO	SB	CS	AVG/OBP/SLG	TAv	BABIP	BRR	FRAA	WARP
2011	MOB	AA	23	457	84	21	3	30	94	82	92	9	3	.306/.435/.626	.344	.331	3	1B(71): 2.0	3.7
2011	ARI	MLB	23	177	28	9	1	8	26	20	53	4	0	.250/.333/.474	.289	.323	1.4	1B(43): -2.3	0.8
2012	ARI	MLB	24	587	82	43	1	20	82	60	130	18	3	.286/.359/.490	.307	.340	2.2	1B(139): -2.8	3.4
2013	ARI	MLB	25	710	103	36	3	36	125	99	145	15	7	.302/.401/.551	.325	.343	-0.3	1B(159): 15.9	7.5
2014	ARI	MLB	26	642	90	35	1	29	94	78	142	14	4	.278/.367/.499	.309	.320	0.1	1B 3	4.2

The last time the league's home run leader hit 36 or fewer—as Goldy did—was 1992, when Fred McGriff smacked 35. Goldschmidt is a little beefier than McGriff, with more speed, a better glove, and … okay forget that comparison. While not a defensive wizard, Goldschmidt stayed wildly active, with 150 more putouts than the next closest first baseman. Factor in his RBI and total base crowns and Goldschmidt emerged as a reliable Big Bat. The big difference in his offense, besides improved patience, was doing righties as mercilessly as he has always done lefties. A shrewd extension will keep him under team control until 2019 when, at just 31 years old, he should still be providing valuable middle-of-the-order muscle.

Tuffy Gosewisch   C

Born: 8/17/1983 Age: 30
Bats: R Throws: R Height: 5' 11''
Weight: 180 Breakout: 3%
Improve: 10% Collapse: 8%
Attrition: 17% MLB: 23%

Comparables:
Gustavo Molina, Wil Nieves, Steve Torrealba

YEAR	TEAM	LVL	AGE	PA	R	2B	3B	HR	RBI	BB	SO	SB	CS	AVG/OBP/SLG	TAv	BABIP	BRR	FRAA	WARP
2011	REA	AA	27	406	41	19	0	13	66	20	61	4	6	.247/.295/.404	.232	.259	-5.2	C(84): 2.5	0.4
2012	LEH	AAA	28	228	22	13	0	4	20	9	42	0	0	.192/.241/.310	.198	.220	-1.1	C(59): 0.8, LF(1): -0.0	-0.6
2012	LVG	AAA	28	97	9	8	1	1	8	9	17	0	1	.277/.365/.434	.254	.333	-1.1	C(23): 0.2, LF(1): -0.0	0.4
2013	RNO	AAA	29	272	30	20	1	7	33	17	40	1	1	.284/.327/.456	.264	.309	-0.8	C(68): -1.7	1.6
2013	ARI	MLB	29	47	1	2	0	0	3	0	8	0	0	.178/.174/.222	.146	.211	-0.1	C(13): -0.2	-0.4
2014	ARI	MLB	30	250	21	12	0	5	23	11	48	1	1	.217/.258/.333	.217	.250	-0.6	C 1, LF -0	0.1

All the talent in the world will bring a player to the big leagues. Barring that, some luck can be substituted. Gosewisch, the longtime Phillies farmhand who signed with his hometown Diamondbacks after the 2012 season, falls into the latter category; he's a classic Triple-A talent whose fortune was twinned with the misfortune of Miguel Montero's ailing back. He has always shown MLB-caliber defense in the minors, throwing out more than half of Triple-A basestealers in 2013 and allowing no passed balls. His hitting will make that his default assignment, but as long as he wants to lurk, he'll be ready when injury befalls a major-league catcher.

Didi Gregorius   SS

Born: 2/18/1990 Age: 24
Bats: L Throws: R Height: 6' 1''
Weight: 185 Breakout: 4%
Improve: 31% Collapse: 10%
Attrition: 20% MLB: 78%

Comparables:
Alcides Escobar, Stephen Drew, Steve Lombardozzi

YEAR	TEAM	LVL	AGE	PA	R	2B	3B	HR	RBI	BB	SO	SB	CS	AVG/OBP/SLG	TAv	BABIP	BRR	FRAA	WARP
2011	BAK	A+	21	203	30	12	1	5	28	10	25	8	8	.303/.333/.457	.285	.323	-0.2	SS(36): 0.9	1.2
2011	CAR	AA	21	160	18	6	3	2	16	9	25	3	2	.270/.312/.392	.322	.314	0.3	SS(4): 0.1	0.3
2012	PEN	AA	22	359	45	11	8	1	31	29	49	3	4	.278/.344/.373	.267	.323	-2.7	SS(80): -14.9	0.0
2012	LOU	AAA	22	202	25	10	3	6	23	12	31	0	2	.243/.288/.427	.243	.262	1.5	SS(42): -1.6, 2B(3): 0.1	0.6
2012	CIN	MLB	22	21	1	0	0	0	2	0	5	0	0	.300/.300/.300	.229	.400	0.3	SS(6): -0.4	0.0
2013	RNO	AAA	23	33	7	2	0	2	2	2	1	1	0	.387/.424/.645	.332	.357	-0.6	SS(1): 0.2	0.3
2013	ARI	MLB	23	404	47	16	3	7	28	37	65	0	2	.252/.332/.373	.262	.290	-4.5	SS(100): -6.9	0.3
2014	ARI	MLB	24	374	41	16	3	6	34	23	62	2	2	.256/.307/.379	.252	.290	-0.6	SS -8, 2B -0	0.4

Dutch shortstops are the new trendy Apple innovation in baseball, which makes Didi Gregorius the iPad mini. He's not a defensive metric breaker like Andrelton Simmons or a great offensive hope like Xander Bogaerts, but he does provide a little of both worlds, his name is fun to say and he's USB compatible. Like many rookies before him, he arrived with a flash before the league adjusted; from June onward, Gregorius hit .218/.311/.298. The glove still fits, especially with a groundball staff like Arizona's, but there are better options offensively at short, even if their names are not as uproarious as Gregorius.

Aaron Hill   2B

Born: 3/21/1982 Age: 32
Bats: R Throws: R Height: 5' 11"
Weight: 205 Breakout: 0%
Improve: 42% Collapse: 2%
Attrition: 8% MLB: 95%

Comparables:
Brandon Phillips, Mark Ellis, Orlando Hudson

YEAR	TEAM	LVL	AGE	PA	R	2B	3B	HR	RBI	BB	SO	SB	CS	AVG/OBP/SLG	TAv	BABIP	BRR	FRAA	WARP
2011	ARI	MLB	29	142	23	12	2	2	16	12	19	5	4	.315/.386/.492	.305	.356	1.5	2B(33): 2.2	1.4
2011	TOR	MLB	29	429	38	15	1	6	45	23	53	16	3	.225/.270/.313	.213	.242	-1.4	2B(104): -5.1	-1.6
2012	ARI	MLB	30	668	93	44	6	26	85	52	86	14	5	.302/.360/.522	.297	.317	-0.3	2B(153): 23.2	6.8
2013	RNO	AAA	31	26	8	1	1	0	6	1	3	0	0	.375/.385/.500	.281	.409	0.1	2B(6): 0.7	0.2
2013	ARI	MLB	31	362	45	21	1	11	41	29	48	1	4	.291/.356/.462	.288	.312	-0.1	2B(84): -0.8	1.8
2014	ARI	MLB	32	405	52	20	1	13	44	28	57	6	3	.258/.315/.421	.268	.270	-0.4	2B 4	2.1

Fresh off a three-year, $35-million extension, Hill fit right in with the 2013 Diamondbacks team motto ("Ow, That Hurts!") when an April pitch fractured his hand, forcing him to the pine for two months. Once he returned to the lineup he solidified the position, mostly with wood but also some leather. Gone may be his heydays of hitting 25 home runs a year and two cycles in a month, but in an organization teeming with middle infielders, the veteran's starting job is secure, provided his hands are fully attached and functional.

Kila Ka'aihue   1B

Born: 3/29/1984 Age: 30
Bats: L Throws: R Height: 6' 4"
Weight: 235 Breakout: 2%
Improve: 16% Collapse: 7%
Attrition: 12% MLB: 38%

Comparables:
Jason Botts, Ryan Shealy, Juan Miranda

YEAR	TEAM	LVL	AGE	PA	R	2B	3B	HR	RBI	BB	SO	SB	CS	AVG/OBP/SLG	TAv	BABIP	BRR	FRAA	WARP
2011	OMA	AAA	27	388	43	19	0	11	65	57	81	1	1	.272/.379/.433	.283	.325	-0.3	1B(30): -2.3	0.7
2011	KCA	MLB	27	96	6	4	0	2	6	12	26	0	0	.195/.295/.317	.228	.255	0.7	1B(19): -0.7	-0.2
2012	SAC	AAA	28	305	44	16	0	15	52	44	60	1	1	.256/.367/.496	.299	.273	1.8	1B(22): 0.6, LF(9): -0.1	1.8
2012	OAK	MLB	28	139	13	9	0	4	14	10	28	1	0	.234/.295/.398	.248	.271	-0.1	1B(22): -0.8	-0.1
2013	RNO	AAA	29	235	38	9	1	16	50	38	41	0	1	.312/.426/.620	.339	.319	-2.2	1B(49): 1.7	2.4
2014	ARI	MLB	30	250	31	10	0	10	34	35	55	0	0	.238/.346/.429	.281	.270	-0.5	1B -1, LF -0	0.7

Ka'aihue, naturally, had the PCL's sixth-best OPS, but a Goldschmidt-sized roadblock to the majors ultimately led him to invoke his opt-out clause and sign with the Hiroshima Toyo Carp. If the level of play in Japan is, as they say, somewhere between Triple-A and the majors, then Ka'aihue may have finally found his home planet.

Alfredo Marte   RF

Born: 3/31/1989 Age: 25
Bats: R Throws: R Height: 5' 11"
Weight: 195 Breakout: 3%
Improve: 8% Collapse: 7%
Attrition: 18% MLB: 24%

Comparables:
Josh Kroeger, Seth Smith, Delwyn Young

YEAR	TEAM	LVL	AGE	PA	R	2B	3B	HR	RBI	BB	SO	SB	CS	AVG/OBP/SLG	TAv	BABIP	BRR	FRAA	WARP
2011	VIS	A+	22	250	35	15	3	7	33	14	43	5	0	.299/.344/.479	.269	.342	2.1	RF(42): -2.9, LF(3): 0.0	0.4
2011	MOB	AA	22	49	4	1	0	1	6	4	10	1	0	.233/.306/.326	.202	.273	-0.7	RF(7): 1.0, LF(1): 0.1	-0.1
2012	MOB	AA	23	446	68	25	3	20	75	34	72	6	6	.294/.363/.523	.298	.314	2.7	RF(102): 3.2, CF(5): 0.5	3.5
2013	RNO	AAA	24	343	37	24	1	7	48	22	63	2	1	.280/.335/.431	.261	.327	0.9	RF(84): 8.8	1.4
2013	ARI	MLB	24	48	4	3	0	0	4	4	12	0	0	.186/.271/.256	.203	.258	0.5	LF(9): -0.6, RF(1): 0.0	-0.2
2014	ARI	MLB	25	250	25	12	1	7	30	12	53	1	0	.243/.288/.397	.249	.280	-0.4	RF 2, LF 0	0.5

When Cody Ross and Adam Eaton both broke camp broken down, Alfredo "For The Last Time I'm Not Andy" Marte became the de facto fourth outfielder on the Diamondbacks' Opening Day roster. He struggled at the plate and was eventually sent down as team health improved. His 2012 Double-A numbers might have been too good to be true, which explains how his Triple-A numbers turned out to be "just right," according to noted baseball scout Goldilocks. He's still young enough to improve and contend for a 25-man spot, but this time he'll have to earn it.

Miguel Montero   C

Born: 7/9/1983 Age: 30
Bats: L Throws: R Height: 5' 11"
Weight: 210 Breakout: 3%
Improve: 54% Collapse: 4%
Attrition: 8% MLB: 94%

Comparables:
Johnny Romano, Geovany Soto, Gary Carter

YEAR	TEAM	LVL	AGE	PA	R	2B	3B	HR	RBI	BB	SO	SB	CS	AVG/OBP/SLG	TAv	BABIP	BRR	FRAA	WARP
2011	ARI	MLB	27	553	65	36	1	18	86	47	97	1	1	.282/.351/.469	.284	.317	-2	C(134): 1.8	4.1
2012	ARI	MLB	28	573	65	25	2	15	88	73	130	0	0	.286/.391/.438	.296	.362	-5.9	C(139): 2.2	4.6
2013	ARI	MLB	29	475	44	14	0	11	42	51	110	0	0	.230/.318/.344	.240	.282	-2	C(112): 0.5	0.9
2014	ARI	MLB	30	469	51	23	0	13	56	46	96	0	0	.262/.341/.413	.276	.310	-1	C 1	3.0

Disasters in Arizona usually mean dust storms or missing windshield covers, but Montero's 2013 season might also qualify. He missed nearly a month on the disabled list, posted career lows across his hitting page, led the league in passed balls and finished second in wild pitches allowed. Montero had a fantastic 2012 season but, in retrospect, some of the causes of the 2013 collapse were already flashing: He was making contact less often and hitting more groundballs instead of flies. When his BABIP bubble popped last year, the rest of his numbers fell to earth, too. Optimistically, one might chalk up his replacement-level 2013 to first-year-lucrative-contract jitters, but a) that's not really a thing and b) that excuse won't hold for much longer.

Chris Owings SS
Born: 8/12/1991 Age: 22
Bats: R Throws: R Height: 5' 10"
Weight: 180 Breakout: 2%
Improve: 13% Collapse: 4%
Attrition: 10% MLB: 21%

Comparables:
Alcides Escobar, Chris Nelson, Hector Gomez

YEAR	TEAM	LVL	AGE	PA	R	2B	3B	HR	RBI	BB	SO	SB	CS	AVG/OBP/SLG	TAv	BABIP	BRR	FRAA	WARP
2011	VIS	A+	19	555	67	29	6	11	50	15	130	10	4	.246/.274/.388	.235	.305	0.8	SS(89): 10.2, LF(1): -0.1	1.6
2012	VIS	A+	20	257	51	16	2	11	24	13	63	8	3	.324/.362/.544	.317	.399	1.4	SS(55): 1.1	3.1
2012	MOB	AA	20	310	35	10	3	6	28	11	69	4	3	.263/.291/.377	.231	.324	-0.2	SS(67): 6.5	1.1
2013	RNO	AAA	21	575	104	31	8	12	81	22	99	20	7	.330/.359/.482	.272	.386	6.3	SS(111): 8.7, 2B(11): -0.8	4.2
2013	ARI	MLB	21	61	5	5	0	0	5	6	10	2	0	.291/.361/.382	.254	.356	-0.9	SS(13): -0.6, 2B(3): 0.2	0.0
2014	ARI	MLB	22	250	26	12	1	5	22	6	59	4	1	.250/.268/.368	.231	.310	0.1	SS 3, 2B -0	0.6

Last year we wrote about his tendency to swing and miss, hinting at a make-or-break year. So does Chris Owings read BP? Consider it made. He thrived in Triple-A, winning the Pacific Coast League MVP by leading in total bases, cutting down his strikeouts and sizably boosting his average. He's not a walker so much as a pepperer, spraying the ball for extra bases. A September call-up teased all of this ability, and in a situation where no one shortstop stands out as the answer, Owings could split time between short and second if he doesn't take full ownership of the starting job.

Gerardo Parra CF
Born: 5/6/1987 Age: 27
Bats: L Throws: L Height: 5' 11"
Weight: 200 Breakout: 2%
Improve: 43% Collapse: 5%
Attrition: 15% MLB: 92%

Comparables:
Magglio Ordonez, Rudy Pemberton, Jackie Jensen

YEAR	TEAM	LVL	AGE	PA	R	2B	3B	HR	RBI	BB	SO	SB	CS	AVG/OBP/SLG	TAv	BABIP	BRR	FRAA	WARP
2011	ARI	MLB	24	493	55	20	8	8	46	43	82	15	1	.292/.357/.427	.280	.342	0.8	LF(125): 14.7, RF(14): 0.3	3.8
2012	ARI	MLB	25	430	58	21	2	7	36	33	77	15	9	.273/.335/.392	.260	.323	2.9	CF(48): -2.7, LF(47): 0.4	1.5
2013	ARI	MLB	26	663	79	43	4	10	48	48	100	10	10	.268/.323/.403	.257	.305	0.8	RF(123): 9.7, CF(33): 1.6	3.7
2014	ARI	MLB	27	576	69	29	5	9	51	42	97	12	7	.273/.328/.394	.261	.320	-0.4	CF -3, LF 1	1.4

Injuries to outfield teammates created an opportunity for The Man With The Golden Arm, a career fourth outfielder who netted 17 outfield assists—a six-year National League high—in full-time play. By Defensive Runs Saved, he was the best defensive right fielder in history, a claim FRAA won't make but still fun to say out loud with a flourish. His offense blends into the ocean of average major-league baseball players, save for the abnormally high number of doubles, which could be because he doesn't have to run on Gerardo Parra's arm. His numbers have stayed consistent enough that the right field job should be a lock for him. Or left. Or maybe even center. Just not all three. Too much ground to cover.

Cliff Pennington SS
Born: 6/15/1984 Age: 30
Bats: B Throws: R Height: 5' 10"
Weight: 195 Breakout: 3%
Improve: 43% Collapse: 4%
Attrition: 10% MLB: 88%

Comparables:
Chris Burke, Jason Bartlett, Brendan Ryan

YEAR	TEAM	LVL	AGE	PA	R	2B	3B	HR	RBI	BB	SO	SB	CS	AVG/OBP/SLG	TAv	BABIP	BRR	FRAA	WARP
2011	OAK	MLB	27	570	57	26	2	8	58	42	104	14	9	.264/.319/.369	.255	.314	-1.3	SS(147): -11.9	0.8
2012	OAK	MLB	28	462	50	18	2	6	28	35	90	15	6	.215/.278/.311	.233	.259	2.9	SS(93): 6.4, 2B(32): 3.2	1.8
2013	ARI	MLB	29	299	25	13	1	1	18	26	54	2	0	.242/.310/.309	.233	.298	3	SS(51): 2.0, 2B(29): 0.5	0.9
2014	ARI	MLB	30	315	33	15	2	4	27	26	59	9	3	.248/.314/.356	.247	.290	0.5	SS 1, 2B 1	1.1

There were a couple differences between Pennington and teammate Didi Gregorius at shortstop. For one, Pennington is six years older and remembers more retro television shows. His paycheck is also larger, and will continue to be: he's due $3.25 million this year. Thirdly, any semblance of hitting showed up only after the eighth inning. Pennington hit .377 during those frames (including .477 in extras, with two walkoff hits), .208 all other times. Other than that, the powerless offense and admirable glovework nearly bordered on plagiarism. It's difficult to tell who copied off whom, although Pennington was here first.

A.J. Pollock   CF

Born: **12/5/1987** Age: **26**
Bats: **R** Throws: **R** Height: **6' 1"**
Weight: **195** Breakout: **5%**
Improve: **45%** Collapse: **11%**
Attrition: **29%** MLB: **81%**

Comparables:
Angel Pagan, Josh Anderson, Alejandro De Aza

YEAR	TEAM	LVL	AGE	PA	R	2B	3B	HR	RBI	BB	SO	SB	CS	AVG/OBP/SLG	TAv	BABIP	BRR	FRAA	WARP
2011	MOB	AA	23	608	103	41	5	8	73	44	86	36	7	.307/.357/.444	.274	.346	0.8	CF(94): -4.1, RF(5): 0.2	1.6
2012	RNO	AAA	24	471	65	25	3	3	52	32	52	21	8	.318/.369/.411	.261	.353	3.4	CF(63): 2.6, RF(29): -0.5	1.6
2012	ARI	MLB	24	93	8	4	1	2	8	9	11	1	2	.247/.315/.395	.253	.257	-1.5	CF(14): 0.7, LF(7): 0.4	0.2
2013	ARI	MLB	25	482	64	28	5	8	38	33	82	12	3	.269/.322/.409	.259	.314	2.8	CF(110): -3.0, LF(7): -0.4	1.4
2014	ARI	MLB	26	432	50	22	3	5	35	26	73	14	4	.260/.307/.369	.248	.300	1.1	CF 0, RF 0	0.8

Between the otherworldly Mike Trout and World Series bench player Mike Carp, everybody wants a piece of the fishing action. True to his marine namesake, Pollock isn't a flashy fish but got the job done in a pinch, since he was one of the few Arizonans who didn't take a trip to Disabled List Lane, earning the center field job almost by default. Not that he didn't play well; he did. That and his health and the removal by trade of Adam Eaton will greatly assist Pollock's cause to keep his starting job.

Martin Prado   LF

Born: **10/27/1983** Age: **30**
Bats: **R** Throws: **R** Height: **6' 1"**
Weight: **190** Breakout: **2%**
Improve: **39%** Collapse: **4%**
Attrition: **8%** MLB: **97%**

Comparables:
Bill Madlock, George Kell, Alberto Callaspo

YEAR	TEAM	LVL	AGE	PA	R	2B	3B	HR	RBI	BB	SO	SB	CS	AVG/OBP/SLG	TAv	BABIP	BRR	FRAA	WARP
2011	GWN	AAA	27	20	2	0	0	0	1	3	5	0	0	.176/.300/.176	.122	.250	0	LF(1): -0.1	-0.1
2011	ATL	MLB	27	590	66	26	2	13	57	34	52	4	8	.260/.302/.385	.251	.266	-1	LF(100): -2.7, 3B(41): 4.9	1.2
2012	ATL	MLB	28	690	81	42	6	10	70	58	69	17	4	.301/.359/.438	.286	.322	1.4	LF(119): -8.7, 3B(25): -1.1	3.3
2013	ARI	MLB	29	664	70	36	2	14	82	47	53	3	5	.282/.333/.417	.264	.288	-5.6	3B(113): -0.6, 2B(32): -3.5	1.2
2014	ARI	MLB	30	629	75	36	2	13	62	44	67	7	4	.281/.331/.417	.274	.300	-1.3	LF -5, 3B 2	1.9

The longtime Braves utilityman became the face of the Justin Upton deal (although the prospects were arguably the real haul) and was rewarded prior to the season with a sweet four-year extension. For this he may draw an unjust comparison to Upton (his extension was similar to the money owed Upton, no less), but they are diametrically different players. Prado is an elite contact hitter living by the BABIP gods' streaky grace, a versatile fielder with solid reputations at second, third and left, and a high-volume vendor of "intangibles." All of this will keep him in the lineup for 150 games a year.

Cody Ross   RF

Born: **12/23/1980** Age: **33**
Bats: **R** Throws: **L** Height: **5' 10"**
Weight: **195** Breakout: **0%**
Improve: **27%** Collapse: **12%**
Attrition: **8%** MLB: **96%**

Comparables:
Benny Ayala, Leon Wagner, Dusty Baker

YEAR	TEAM	LVL	AGE	PA	R	2B	3B	HR	RBI	BB	SO	SB	CS	AVG/OBP/SLG	TAv	BABIP	BRR	FRAA	WARP
2011	SFN	MLB	30	461	54	25	0	14	52	49	96	5	2	.240/.325/.405	.275	.279	-0.3	LF(83): 2.6, RF(35): -0.5	1.6
2012	BOS	MLB	31	528	70	34	1	22	81	42	129	2	3	.267/.326/.481	.289	.317	0.2	RF(96): 0.0, LF(22): -2.4	2.4
2013	ARI	MLB	32	351	33	17	1	8	38	25	50	3	2	.278/.331/.413	.267	.303	-0.7	LF(46): -0.7, RF(44): 4.1	1.4
2014	ARI	MLB	33	370	40	19	1	11	45	27	76	3	2	.254/.314/.416	.265	.300	-0.6	RF 2, LF -1	0.9

At long last, America's lovable bald-headed good luck charm and dramatic dinger dwarf finally got his multi-year contract. He provided the Diamondbacks exceptional, error-free outfield defense, and he was on an offensive tear (.321/.365/.538 from July 1st) before breaking his hip in a freak injury suffered while running out a routine grounder in August. Estimates put him out until the middle of spring training, but with any hip injury, a full recovery needs to be seen to be believed. That casts some doubt on his outfield mobility, and on his ability to hop, skip or cartwheel down the first base line whenever he hits a long fly ball.

Stryker Trahan   C

Born: **4/25/1994** Age: **20**
Bats: **L** Throws: **R** Height: **6' 1"**
Weight: **215** Breakout: **0%**
Improve: **0%** Collapse: **0%**
Attrition: **0%** MLB: **0%**

Comparables:
Wilin Rosario, Brandon Snyder, Kyle Skipworth

YEAR	TEAM	LVL	AGE	PA	R	2B	3B	HR	RBI	BB	SO	SB	CS	AVG/OBP/SLG	TAv	BABIP	BRR	FRAA	WARP
2014	ARI	MLB	20	250	20	8	1	5	24	18	79	0	0	.185/.244/.293	.198	.250	-0.3	C -0	-0.7

Just try finding a purer baseball name than Stryker. As the youngest full-timer on his short-season squad, Trahan led Missoula in home runs while throwing out 40 percent of attempted basestealers. He's a thick, strong catcher with more athleticism than one expects out of his position and dimensions. The major blemish is his inability to hold on to pitches, but they don't not call him Catchandthrow Trahan for nothing.

Mark Trumbo LF

Born: 1/16/1986 Age: 28
Bats: R Throws: R Height: 6' 4"
Weight: 235 Breakout: 4%
Improve: 55% Collapse: 3%
Attrition: 11% MLB: 94%

Comparables:
Mike Jacobs, Allen Craig, Juan Gonzalez

YEAR	TEAM	LVL	AGE	PA	R	2B	3B	HR	RBI	BB	SO	SB	CS	AVG/OBP/SLG	TAv	BABIP	BRR	FRAA	WARP
2011	ANA	MLB	25	573	65	31	1	29	87	25	120	9	4	.254/.291/.477	.275	.274	1.3	1B(149): 2.1, RF(10): -0.1	2.2
2012	ANA	MLB	26	586	66	19	3	32	95	36	153	4	5	.268/.317/.491	.286	.316	-3.3	LF(66): -1.0, RF(35): -2.6	1.6
2013	ANA	MLB	27	678	85	30	2	34	100	54	184	5	2	.234/.294/.453	.274	.273	-3.5	1B(123): 6.3, RF(19): -0.4	2.0
2014	ARI	MLB	28	619	79	28	2	31	94	44	153	5	3	.255/.309/.477	.281	.290	-0.9	LF 3, RF -0	2.9

In an environment of decreasing offense, Trumbo is a rare power broker who brings above-average thump into game action. He is a true fastball hitter, as more than half of his 95 career home runs have come on a variation of the heater. Typical for players of his ilk, he swings and misses, with off-speed and breaking balls giving him trouble. He has not taken to walks as much as others who fit the same profile, but does show incremental improvement in plate discipline measures. A hulking right-handed batter, he feasts on southpaws, but his power still plays up against fellow righties. After being penciled in as an outfielder-slash-designated hitter when the season began, Albert Pujols' foot injury allowed him to primarily play first base, where he has been more than capable. In Arizona now, designated hitting and first base are both off the table, so pray for range.

Matt Tuiasosopo LF

Born: 5/10/1986 Age: 28
Bats: R Throws: R Height: 6' 2"
Weight: 225 Breakout: 2%
Improve: 14% Collapse: 14%
Attrition: 26% MLB: 44%

Comparables:
Chip Ambres, Daniel Nava, Chris Dickerson

YEAR	TEAM	LVL	AGE	PA	R	2B	3B	HR	RBI	BB	SO	SB	CS	AVG/OBP/SLG	TAv	BABIP	BRR	FRAA	WARP
2011	TAC	AAA	25	526	73	20	6	14	77	75	132	11	2	.226/.341/.394	.250	.284	1.6	1B(50): -3.6, LF(17): 2.2	-0.2
2012	BUF	AAA	26	481	47	14	0	12	57	51	117	3	4	.242/.329/.361	.246	.305	-1.8	3B(70): -1.7, RF(41): 2.5	0.5
2013	DET	MLB	27	191	26	7	0	7	30	25	57	0	0	.244/.351/.415	.290	.330	-3.4	LF(63): 5.2, 1B(13): -0.1	0.9
2014	ARI	MLB	28	250	26	9	0	7	28	28	72	1	1	.218/.313/.360	.253	.290	-0.4	LF 2, 3B -0	0.5

Tuiasosopo was Detroit's assigned lefty-killing bench bat, a complement to Andy Dirks out in left field. So of course he put up a .216/.336/.371 line against southpaws while hitting .313/.389/.521 against righties. It was his first real opportunity since a herky-jerk 2010 campaign, and he acquitted himself well enough to extend a career that was on death's door. Still, he's a right-handed bat without defensive value and his only real skill is drawing ball four. The Tigers lost confidence in him after a hitless September, and he didn't make the postseason roster.

PITCHERS

Chase Anderson

Born: 11/30/1987 Age: 26
Bats: R Throws: R Height: 6' 0" Weight: 185
Breakout: 64% Improve: 90% Collapse: 6%
Attrition: 70% MLB: 27%

Comparables:
Tony Watson, Steven Wright, Josh Zeid

YEAR	TEAM	LVL	AGE	W	L	SV	G	GS	IP	H	HR	BB	SO	BB9	SO9	GB%	BABIP	WHIP	ERA	FIP	FRA	WARP
2011	VIS	A+	23	1	1	0	3	3	13¹	14	1	1	20	0.7	13.5	70%	.526	1.12	5.40	2.38	5.63	0.1
2012	MOB	AA	24	5	4	0	21	21	104	91	9	25	97	2.2	8.4	45%	.297	1.12	2.86	3.36	4.28	1.5
2013	RNO	AAA	25	4	7	0	26	13	88	107	11	33	80	3.4	8.2	36%	.352	1.59	5.73	4.54	4.83	1.2
2014	ARI	MLB	26	4	4	0	22	10	83¹	82	10	27	65	3.0	7.1	41%	.302	1.31	4.33	4.30	4.71	0.1

Added to the 40-man roster after impressing in the 2012 Arizona Fall League, Anderson spent the Triple-A season taking his punches until the manager threw in the towel and demoted him to the bullpen. His strikeout, walk and homer rates all went in wrong directions; a .350 BABIP didn't help him, and a .376/.422/.592 line with runners on base didn't, either. Righthanders slugged .547 against him. His fabled changeup still makes scouts salivate in their sleep, but there are better things in life than waking up in a puddle of drool.

Archie Bradley

Born: 8/10/1992 Age: 21
Bats: R Throws: R Height: 6' 4" Weight: 225
Breakout: 40% Improve: 81% Collapse: 6%
Attrition: 34% MLB: 31%

Comparables:
Chris Tillman, Scott Elbert, Yovani Gallardo

YEAR	TEAM	LVL	AGE	W	L	SV	G	GS	IP	H	HR	BB	SO	BB9	SO9	GB%	BABIP	WHIP	ERA	FIP	FRA	WARP
2012	SBN	A	19	12	6	0	27	27	136	87	6	84	152	5.6	10.1	57%	.248	1.26	3.84	3.87	4.54	1.4
2013	VIS	A+	20	2	0	0	5	5	28²	22	1	10	43	3.1	13.5	44%	.362	1.12	1.26	2.48	2.41	1.2
2013	MOB	AA	20	12	5	0	21	21	123¹	93	5	59	119	4.3	8.7	46%	.287	1.23	1.97	3.04	3.70	1.6
2014	ARI	MLB	21	7	8	0	23	23	125	108	12	67	114	4.8	8.2	47%	.297	1.40	4.25	4.38	4.62	0.4

No pressure or anything, but Bradley will enter 2014 as one of the heavenliest pitching prospects to follow immediate aces Jose Fernandez, Matt Harvey and Shelby Miller to the majors. He was already near the top of the lists when he orchestrated a lights-out August—1.17 ERA in six starts with a 1.02 WHIP. That didn't earn him a call-up, and it's unlikely to earn him a spot in Arizona's rotation out of camp: in September, Kevin Towers acknowledged the organizational view that Bradley still needs to incorporate his secondary pitches more, rather than ride his swing-and-miss fastball. But while his walk rate remains a little sketchy, everything else is pointing toward Bradley making a start in the big leagues sometime this season; if he's not a top-of-the-line starter immediately, it won't take long.

Charles Brewer
Born: 4/7/1988 Age: 26
Bats: R Throws: R Height: 6' 3" Weight: 205
Breakout: 45% Improve: 71% Collapse: 22%
Attrition: 76% MLB: 42%
Comparables:
Hector Ambriz, Phil Irwin, Sam LeCure

YEAR	TEAM	LVL	AGE	W	L	SV	G	GS	IP	H	HR	BB	SO	BB9	SO9	GB%	BABIP	WHIP	ERA	FIP	FRA	WARP
2011	MOB	AA	23	5	1	0	11	11	52^1	48	2	19	48	3.3	8.3	45%	.336	1.28	2.58	3.17	3.56	1.1
2012	MOB	AA	24	0	0	0	3	3	17^1	19	2	2	13	1.0	6.8	48%	.315	1.21	4.15	3.49	4.62	0.1
2012	RNO	AAA	24	11	7	0	24	24	133^2	177	26	34	104	2.3	7.0	43%	.345	1.58	5.99	5.47	6.53	0.8
2013	RNO	AAA	25	5	12	0	25	22	139^2	158	13	43	107	2.8	6.9	51%	.337	1.44	4.90	4.36	5.17	1.9
2013	ARI	MLB	25	0	0	0	4	0	6	8	0	2	5	3.0	7.5	45%	.400	1.67	3.00	2.35	2.44	0.2
2014	ARI	MLB	26	7	7	0	26	21	131^2	133	16	39	97	2.7	6.6	46%	.304	1.31	4.34	4.33	4.71	0.2

This is the story of a Triple-A pitcher who struggled so much the team decided to call him up. That's how it works, right? Brewer sliced down his homer rate in the Pacific Coast Wiffle Ball League, enough to become the de facto "we just need someone" call-up in June. In a baseball prospect universe where scouts and fans visually lionize prospects as potential Hall of Famers, Brewer is a rational person's pitcher: He'll contend for spot starts and perhaps a back-end rotation gig. Maybe he'll surprise you, maybe he won't. Such is life, and such is Charles Brewer.

Trevor Cahill
Born: 3/1/1988 Age: 26
Bats: R Throws: R Height: 6' 4" Weight: 220
Breakout: 11% Improve: 46% Collapse: 22%
Attrition: 16% MLB: 92%
Comparables:
Gustavo Chacin, Joe Blanton, Jon Garland

YEAR	TEAM	LVL	AGE	W	L	SV	G	GS	IP	H	HR	BB	SO	BB9	SO9	GB%	BABIP	WHIP	ERA	FIP	FRA	WARP
2011	OAK	MLB	23	12	14	0	34	34	207^2	214	19	82	147	3.6	6.4	57%	.303	1.43	4.16	4.14	5.15	-0.2
2012	ARI	MLB	24	13	12	0	32	32	200	184	16	74	156	3.3	7.0	62%	.299	1.29	3.78	3.89	4.95	0.6
2013	RNO	AAA	25	0	2	0	3	3	16^2	16	3	9	13	4.9	7.0	59%	.286	1.50	5.94	5.97	7.14	-0.2
2013	ARI	MLB	25	8	10	0	26	25	146^2	143	13	65	102	4.0	6.3	56%	.300	1.42	3.99	4.23	5.24	-0.1
2014	ARI	MLB	26	9	9	0	26	26	151	138	16	53	106	3.2	6.3	56%	.285	1.26	3.91	4.36	4.24	1.0

If he is the type of character to hold grudges against whole months, Cahill is saving a bullet for June: A perfectly nice season was strewn asunder with five poor starts and a sixth which featured a line drive to his hip, sidelining him for a month. Month-by-month ERAs: 2.84, 2.91, 9.85, (inactive), 3.22, 2.28. Cahill went into the offseason intent on cleaning up the finish to his delivery, which will help him maintain command while preventing the line drives off his body.

Josh Collmenter
Born: 2/7/1986 Age: 28
Bats: R Throws: R Height: 6' 4" Weight: 235
Breakout: 23% Improve: 53% Collapse: 19%
Attrition: 31% MLB: 80%
Comparables:
Randy Wells, Josh Outman, Joe Saunders

YEAR	TEAM	LVL	AGE	W	L	SV	G	GS	IP	H	HR	BB	SO	BB9	SO9	GB%	BABIP	WHIP	ERA	FIP	FRA	WARP
2011	ARI	MLB	25	10	10	0	31	24	154^1	137	17	28	100	1.6	5.8	35%	.256	1.07	3.38	3.77	4.00	1.6
2012	ARI	MLB	26	5	3	0	28	11	90^1	92	13	22	80	2.2	8.0	39%	.320	1.26	3.69	3.97	4.50	0.9
2013	ARI	MLB	27	5	5	0	49	0	92	79	8	33	85	3.2	8.3	35%	.283	1.22	3.13	3.44	3.00	1.9
2014	ARI	MLB	28	4	3	0	26	8	80^2	73	9	23	64	2.6	7.1	40%	.289	1.20	3.48	4.01	3.78	1.0

As the D'backs broke the record for most innings played in a season, Collmenter and his hatchet-style delivery ascended to cult status with his exemplary long-relief work. In fact, he (along with the Twins' Anthony Swarzak) became the first player in at least 20 years to throw 90 or more innings in 50 or fewer appearances without a start. He relies on changing speeds between a high-80s cutter and high-70s changeup, and his repertoire is prone to neither strikeouts or grounders, so the idea of Josh Collmenter, Starting Pitcher no longer seems feasible. He can, however, devour multiple late innings when called upon, which inevitably happens more often than the best laid plans.

Patrick Corbin
Born: 7/19/1989 Age: 24
Bats: L Throws: L Height: 6' 2" Weight: 185
Breakout: 26% Improve: 67% Collapse: 20%
Attrition: 24% MLB: 90%
Comparables:
Derek Holland, Dallas Braden, Matt Garza

YEAR	TEAM	LVL	AGE	W	L	SV	G	GS	IP	H	HR	BB	SO	BB9	SO9	GB%	BABIP	WHIP	ERA	FIP	FRA	WARP
2011	MOB	AA	21	9	8	0	26	26	160^1	172	15	40	142	2.2	8.0	48%	.333	1.32	4.21	3.72	4.18	2.2
2012	MOB	AA	22	2	0	0	4	4	27	22	0	8	25	2.7	8.3	48%	.324	1.11	1.67	2.29	2.40	0.9
2012	RNO	AAA	22	3	2	0	9	9	52^1	57	4	15	55	2.6	9.5	51%	.351	1.38	3.44	3.47	4.31	1.3
2012	ARI	MLB	22	6	8	1	22	17	107	117	14	25	86	2.1	7.2	45%	.308	1.33	4.54	4.04	4.54	0.8
2013	ARI	MLB	23	14	8	0	32	32	208^1	189	19	54	178	2.3	7.7	48%	.288	1.17	3.41	3.40	4.13	2.5
2014	ARI	MLB	24	11	10	0	30	30	174	165	19	46	143	2.4	7.4	47%	.300	1.21	3.72	3.88	4.04	1.6

Perhaps it was for the best Arizona didn't reach the playoffs, because many of their young pitchers tapped out their reserves in September. Corbin, who logged 170 pro innings in 2012, was no exception, eclipsing the 200-inning mark. A surprising (but deserving) All-Star, the control lefty was shelled in the final two months with an ERA on the wrong side of six. Before that he had pitched like an ace for four months, but Corbin is more suited for a No. 2 role; put him and Clayton Kershaw in a lineup and ask hitters to identify the bad man who made them look silly, and Corbin walks out a free man. He can go deep into games, occasionally completing one, and should continue to hit his spots and keep that walk rate fresh and low.

Eury De La Rosa
Born: 2/24/1990 Age: 24
Bats: L Throws: L Height: 5' 9" Weight: 165
Breakout: 47% Improve: 74% Collapse: 12%
Attrition: 51% MLB: 20%
Comparables:
Rich Thompson, Jose Mijares, Greg Holland

YEAR	TEAM	LVL	AGE	W	L	SV	G	GS	IP	H	HR	BB	SO	BB9	SO9	GB%	BABIP	WHIP	ERA	FIP	FRA	WARP
2011	SBN	A	21	1	0	0	10	39	0	53	36	3	13	51	2.2	8.7	44%	.294	0.92	1.36	3.19	4.51	0.1
2012	MOB	AA	22	4	4	8	53	0	63^1	47	3	17	68	2.4	9.7	35%	.280	1.01	2.84	2.51	3.57	1.1
2013	RNO	AAA	23	3	5	0	44	0	49^2	52	6	27	49	4.9	8.9	44%	.326	1.59	5.26	4.92	5.46	0.5
2013	ARI	MLB	23	0	1	0	19	0	14^2	13	5	5	16	3.1	9.8	39%	.222	1.23	7.36	6.29	7.54	-0.4
2014	ARI	MLB	24	2	1	0	48	0	59	54	7	24	52	3.6	7.9	44%	.295	1.32	4.13	4.32	4.49	0.1

He may share a shirt and mitt size with Tim Collins, but that's where the similarities end. The tiny left-hander throws about 90 mph with a multitude of secondary pitches, and earned major-league time mostly because Arizona was chucking whole handfuls of southpaws at the fridge hoping somebody would stick. If De La Rosa pitched against an actual refrigerator, he could get away with throwing average stuff over the middle of the plate. Alas, De La Rosa did not pitch against refrigerators.

Randall Delgado
Born: 2/9/1990 Age: 24
Bats: R Throws: R Height: 6' 3" Weight: 200
Breakout: 26% Improve: 58% Collapse: 23%
Attrition: 33% MLB: 83%
Comparables:
Jason Hammel, Jon Niese, Jo-Jo Reyes

YEAR	TEAM	LVL	AGE	W	L	SV	G	GS	IP	H	HR	BB	SO	BB9	SO9	GB%	BABIP	WHIP	ERA	FIP	FRA	WARP
2011	MIS	AA	21	5	5	0	21	21	117^1	116	11	46	110	3.5	8.4	46%	.358	1.38	3.84	3.93	4.90	0.4
2011	GWN	AAA	21	2	2	0	4	4	21^2	19	4	11	25	4.6	10.4	47%	.296	1.38	4.15	4.85	7.92	-0.2
2011	ATL	MLB	21	1	1	0	7	7	35	29	5	14	18	3.6	4.6	37%	.220	1.23	2.83	5.11	5.80	-0.4
2012	GWN	AAA	22	4	3	0	8	8	44^1	47	6	21	51	4.3	10.4	44%	.354	1.53	4.06	4.11	5.25	0.2
2012	ATL	MLB	22	4	9	0	18	17	92^2	89	8	42	76	4.1	7.4	50%	.307	1.41	4.37	4.11	4.59	0.8
2013	RNO	AAA	23	2	5	0	13	13	64	69	9	35	57	4.9	8.0	54%	.331	1.62	5.91	5.44	6.91	0.0
2013	ARI	MLB	23	5	7	0	20	19	116^1	116	24	23	79	1.8	6.1	42%	.272	1.19	4.26	4.96	5.42	-0.5
2014	ARI	MLB	24	8	9	0	26	26	143	138	20	56	114	3.5	7.2	46%	.294	1.35	4.55	4.74	4.95	-0.2

What an odd year. After joining the Diamondbacks in the Justin Upton trade, he broke camp in Triple-A, battling command issues. After his call-up, he saw his walk rate halve. But instead of missing his spots wide, he was missing down the middle of the zone, and those mistakes flew. He actually allowed more dingers than free passes, just the 29th time in history that happened to a pitcher who threw more than 100 innings in a season. (Let's call this The Lieber, given Jon Lieber did it three times.) The high point was Delgado's three-hit shutout in which he also had two hits at the plate. The results are spotty, but the makeup is there for Delgado to contend for a starting job in 2014.

Will Harris
Born: 8/28/1984 Age: 29
Bats: R Throws: R Height: 6' 4" Weight: 225
Breakout: 21% Improve: 38% Collapse: 44%
Attrition: 47% MLB: 72%
Comparables:
Chris Schroder, Jason Motte, Mitch Stetter

YEAR	TEAM	LVL	AGE	W	L	SV	G	GS	IP	H	HR	BB	SO	BB9	SO9	GB%	BABIP	WHIP	ERA	FIP	FRA	WARP
2011	MOD	A+	26	3	2	0	33	0	47	45	4	21	55	4.0	10.5	47%	.281	1.40	5.55	4.06	3.70	0.9
2012	TUL	AA	27	2	1	1	31	0	34^1	26	2	12	46	3.1	12.1	54%	.304	1.11	2.62	2.49	3.12	0.8
2012	CSP	AAA	27	2	0	0	13	0	17^2	9	0	1	20	0.5	10.2	63%	.220	0.57	1.02	1.57	2.74	0.6
2012	COL	MLB	27	1	1	0	20	0	17^2	27	3	6	19	3.1	9.7	35%	.407	1.87	8.15	4.38	6.21	-0.1
2013	RNO	AAA	28	0	0	2	12	0	11^2	12	1	6	23	4.6	17.7	31%	.440	1.54	4.63	2.28	2.46	0.5
2013	ARI	MLB	28	4	1	0	61	0	52^2	50	3	15	53	2.6	9.1	49%	.326	1.23	2.91	2.72	3.21	0.7
2014	ARI	MLB	29	3	1	1	58	0	60^1	51	6	19	64	2.8	9.5	48%	.306	1.17	3.22	3.39	3.50	0.9

Sometimes kids get chosen last in pickup baseball, but no amount of adolescent rejection prepares a player for the dreaded waiver wire hot potato game. Harris was selected off waivers by Oakland from Colorado to begin the season, only three days later to be claimed by Arizona and stuffed into Triple-A before finally being called up in May. A dismally forgettable 2012 season was quickly washed away as Harris started mixing in his curve more often and punching out a batter per inning to become the fourth-most called-upon pitcher in the Diamondbacks' bullpen. A pitcher of his breed who can keep the white sphere in the ballpark will always have room on a competitive team's bullpen, even if it takes a while for him to land there.

David Hernandez
Born: 5/13/1985 Age: 29
Bats: R Throws: R Height: 6' 3" Weight: 230
Breakout: 40% Improve: 59% Collapse: 28%
Attrition: 12% MLB: 90%

Comparables:
Kevin Gregg, Sean Marshall, Mike Hartley

YEAR	TEAM	LVL	AGE	W	L	SV	G	GS	IP	H	HR	BB	SO	BB9	SO9	GB%	BABIP	WHIP	ERA	FIP	FRA	WARP
2011	ARI	MLB	26	5	3	11	74	0	69¹	49	4	30	77	3.9	10.0	34%	.249	1.14	3.38	2.91	3.73	0.8
2012	ARI	MLB	27	2	3	4	72	0	68¹	48	4	22	98	2.9	12.9	30%	.291	1.02	2.50	2.13	2.70	1.8
2013	ARI	MLB	28	5	6	2	62	0	62¹	50	10	24	66	3.5	9.5	34%	.253	1.19	4.48	4.34	4.39	0.3
2014	ARI	MLB	29	4	2	3	58	2	66	53	7	26	69	3.5	9.5	34%	.283	1.19	3.42	3.75	3.72	0.8

In previous years, Hernandez was a trendy, underground pick to close games, because the guy who never failed as a full-time closer is always the popular candidate. But in a year when the Diamondbacks dropped fliers onto Maricopa County looking for volunteers to shut down the ninth inning, a struggling Hernandez missed his window. He now profiles more as a set-up specialist due to his crippling fear of lefties, who last year hit eight dingers off him in 125 plate appearances as he ditched his changeup. Splits don't get saves, but there's no shame in staring down three right-handers in a late inning.

Daniel Hudson
Born: 3/9/1987 Age: 27
Bats: R Throws: R Height: 6' 3" Weight: 225
Breakout: 19% Improve: 60% Collapse: 29%
Attrition: 14% MLB: 88%

Comparables:
Wade Davis, Clay Buchholz, Tom Gorzelanny

YEAR	TEAM	LVL	AGE	W	L	SV	G	GS	IP	H	HR	BB	SO	BB9	SO9	GB%	BABIP	WHIP	ERA	FIP	FRA	WARP
2011	ARI	MLB	24	16	12	0	33	33	222	217	17	50	169	2.0	6.9	41%	.295	1.20	3.49	3.25	3.99	2.1
2012	ARI	MLB	25	3	2	0	9	9	45¹	62	9	12	37	2.4	7.3	39%	.367	1.63	7.35	4.88	6.07	-0.3
2014	ARI	MLB	27	2	2	0	6	6	39	34	4	10	33	2.4	7.7	42%	.289	1.14	3.34	3.68	3.63	0.5

Admittedly, the worst thing that can happen after a Tommy John surgery is for the arm to be amputated. This has thankfully never happened. The second-worst is for the UCL to tear again, which is what befell Hudson after his first rehab start in June. Another trip to the surgeon (and the Diamondbacks' non-tender) blurs Hudson's future: He has been adamant in interviews that his pitching career will continue, but the realistic outlook for him means if he does return to the majors with a healthy elbow, it will probably not be as a starter.

Matt Langwell
Born: 5/6/1986 Age: 28
Bats: R Throws: R Height: 6' 2" Weight: 220
Breakout: 29% Improve: 42% Collapse: 48%
Attrition: 83% MLB: 19%

Comparables:
Mark Worrell, Devon Lowery, Jim Miller

YEAR	TEAM	LVL	AGE	W	L	SV	G	GS	IP	H	HR	BB	SO	BB9	SO9	GB%	BABIP	WHIP	ERA	FIP	FRA	WARP
2011	AKR	AA	25	4	1	3	36	1	50²	43	4	20	54	3.6	9.6	43%	.275	1.24	2.66	3.61	4.23	0.4
2011	COH	AAA	25	1	0	0	12	0	18	19	1	8	17	4.0	8.5	55%	.273	1.50	4.00	3.74	1.93	0.3
2012	AKR	AA	26	0	0	3	10	0	14¹	10	0	5	18	3.1	11.3	43%	.333	1.05	0.63	1.74	2.18	0.4
2012	COH	AAA	26	4	0	0	32	0	54²	49	0	22	63	3.6	10.4	44%	.340	1.30	3.29	2.44	3.03	1.4
2013	COH	AAA	27	3	4	2	42	1	60¹	54	1	19	52	2.8	7.8	42%	.301	1.21	2.24	2.89	3.51	1.0
2013	CLE	MLB	27	1	0	0	5	0	5¹	5	1	2	6	3.4	10.1	27%	.286	1.31	5.06	4.39	6.35	-0.1
2013	ARI	MLB	27	0	0	0	8	0	8²	8	1	5	6	5.2	6.2	41%	.269	1.50	5.19	5.21	6.18	-0.1
2014	ARI	MLB	28	2	1	0	47	0	66²	61	6	25	57	3.3	7.7	43%	.300	1.28	3.81	3.92	4.14	0.4

Langwell was mostly an unknown commodity before the season, as the former 11th-round pick out of Rice University cut his teeth in the minors for five seasons, mostly as a set-up man. He kept posting good numbers, pumping up his K/9 rate until it topped 10 in 2012. His fastball doesn't go much faster than 92 but his delivery has a hint of deception. After seeing time in the Indians' bullpen he was flipped to Arizona for a month of Jason Kubel; the Diamondbacks gave up on their prize quickly, and he was dropped from the 40-man just after the season ended.

Brandon McCarthy
Born: 7/7/1983 Age: 30
Bats: R Throws: R Height: 6' 7" Weight: 200
Breakout: 15% Improve: 47% Collapse: 20%
Attrition: 10% MLB: 83%

Comparables:
Jeff Karstens, Jeff Niemann, Joe Saunders

YEAR	TEAM	LVL	AGE	W	L	SV	G	GS	IP	H	HR	BB	SO	BB9	SO9	GB%	BABIP	WHIP	ERA	FIP	FRA	WARP
2011	STO	A+	27	1	0	0	2	2	10	7	0	0	8	0.0	7.2	59%	.235	0.70	0.00	2.35	2.81	0.2
2011	OAK	MLB	27	9	9	0	25	25	170²	168	11	25	123	1.3	6.5	48%	.296	1.13	3.32	2.90	3.60	2.6
2012	OAK	MLB	28	8	6	0	18	18	111	115	10	24	73	1.9	5.9	43%	.295	1.25	3.24	3.71	3.98	1.3
2013	RNO	AAA	29	0	0	0	2	2	10¹	15	2	3	4	2.6	3.5	56%	.308	1.74	6.97	6.47	7.58	-0.1
2013	ARI	MLB	29	5	11	0	22	22	135	161	13	21	76	1.4	5.1	50%	.321	1.35	4.53	3.72	4.35	0.7
2014	ARI	MLB	30	8	7	0	21	21	127²	124	12	26	89	1.8	6.3	45%	.299	1.17	3.62	3.73	3.93	1.3

McCarthy has to be one of the top athletes on the Internet. He continually leads the majors in Value Over Replacement Tweeter. Scouts love the way he microblogs and connects with fans: He has an idiosyncratic sense of humor that falls off the table to some and blows right by others. He adeptly shuts down obnoxious fans and has plus-plus sensibilities on social issues. His laugh-to-word ratio continues to improve every year and he has no trouble in his splits against sportswriters and media personalities. In his spare time McCarthy plays the sport of baseball and is good enough to stay in most starting rotations, though it takes a bit too much out of him, physically.

Wade Miley

Born: 11/13/1986 Age: 27
Bats: L Throws: L Height: 6' 0" Weight: 220
Breakout: 30% Improve: 77% Collapse: 16%
Attrition: 24% MLB: 79%

Comparables:
Clayton Richard, Jeff Karstens, Dana Eveland

YEAR	TEAM	LVL	AGE	W	L	SV	G	GS	IP	H	HR	BB	SO	BB9	SO9	GB%	BABIP	WHIP	ERA	FIP	FRA	WARP
2011	MOB	AA	24	4	2	0	14	14	75¹	74	6	28	46	3.3	5.5	52%	.299	1.35	4.78	4.36	5.58	0.0
2011	RNO	AAA	24	4	1	0	8	8	54¹	53	4	16	56	2.7	9.3	57%	.304	1.27	3.64	3.56	3.60	0.6
2011	ARI	MLB	24	4	2	0	8	7	40	48	6	18	25	4.1	5.6	48%	.317	1.65	4.50	5.04	5.75	-0.3
2012	ARI	MLB	25	16	11	0	32	29	194²	193	14	37	144	1.7	6.7	44%	.296	1.18	3.33	3.19	3.90	2.7
2013	ARI	MLB	26	10	10	0	33	33	202²	201	21	66	147	2.9	6.5	53%	.298	1.32	3.55	3.95	4.81	0.0
2014	ARI	MLB	27	10	10	0	28	28	169	170	18	53	113	2.8	6.0	51%	.303	1.32	4.20	4.26	4.56	0.4

Miley was never the extreme strike thrower that he appeared to be in a virtuoso 2012 performance, and regression snapped like a whip: He nearly doubled his walks, did double his HBPs and more than doubled his wild pitches. Lefties also reached base on singles at a much better rate, though it could be a BABIPmonster prank. On the bright side, his groundball rate went up, helping him escape peril with more double plays, and 203 innings from a lefty starter will buy a lot of automobiles. Take his first two years, perhaps split the difference, and that's what his 2014 profile should look like: a contact-inducing lefty who'd work at the back of a rotation for most teams.

Joe Paterson

Born: 5/19/1986 Age: 28
Bats: R Throws: L Height: 6' 1" Weight: 210
Breakout: 39% Improve: 55% Collapse: 30%
Attrition: 66% MLB: 44%

Comparables:
Carlos Muniz, Roy Corcoran, Chris Leroux

YEAR	TEAM	LVL	AGE	W	L	SV	G	GS	IP	H	HR	BB	SO	BB9	SO9	GB%	BABIP	WHIP	ERA	FIP	FRA	WARP
2011	ARI	MLB	25	0	3	1	62	0	34	28	1	15	28	4.0	7.4	55%	.267	1.26	2.91	3.41	4.49	0.0
2012	RNO	AAA	26	2	2	2	48	0	43¹	41	7	16	40	3.3	8.3	50%	.277	1.32	4.15	5.30	6.73	0.1
2012	ARI	MLB	26	0	0	0	6	0	2²	15	2	3	0	10.1	0.0	50%	.650	6.75	37.12	16.26	11.47	-0.3
2013	RNO	AAA	27	3	1	1	48	0	52¹	40	2	15	53	2.6	9.1	47%	.286	1.05	1.89	3.13	3.39	1.5
2013	ARI	MLB	27	0	0	0	2	0	2¹	2	0	2	2	0.0	7.7	33%	.333	0.86	3.86	5.16	5.30	0.0
2014	ARI	MLB	28	3	1	1	50	0	46²	41	4	17	40	3.2	7.7	49%	.293	1.24	3.66	3.89	3.98	0.4

Here are two examples of bad places to be buried on a major-league depth chart: lefty specialist and underwear washer. At least the latter can request to instead wash shirts or go to law school, but what's a LOOGY qualified to do but LOOG? Paterson had to fight for time behind Tony Sipp and Joe Thatcher in Arizona. After a miserable brief appearance in 2012, Paterson was stuck in Triple-A in 2013, except for a cameo in the Diamondbacks' bullpen in June. For what it's worth, he hogtied lefties at both levels to a .144/.204/.196 line, and he is just one eye-opening spring training from rising to the top in a heavy cream soup of side-swiping left-handed options. Interesting sidebar: "Joe Paterson" is an anagram for "Joe Paterno's."

J.J. Putz

Born: 2/22/1977 Age: 37
Bats: R Throws: R Height: 6' 5" Weight: 250
Breakout: 17% Improve: 39% Collapse: 30%
Attrition: 9% MLB: 86%

Comparables:
Joe Nathan, Al Reyes, Arthur Rhodes

YEAR	TEAM	LVL	AGE	W	L	SV	G	GS	IP	H	HR	BB	SO	BB9	SO9	GB%	BABIP	WHIP	ERA	FIP	FRA	WARP
2011	ARI	MLB	34	2	2	45	60	0	58	41	4	12	61	1.9	9.5	44%	.247	0.91	2.17	2.51	3.31	0.9
2012	ARI	MLB	35	1	5	32	57	0	54¹	45	4	11	65	1.8	10.8	46%	.304	1.03	2.82	2.42	3.07	1.1
2013	ARI	MLB	36	3	1	6	40	0	34¹	26	4	17	38	4.5	10.0	51%	.272	1.25	2.36	3.81	3.96	0.3
2014	ARI	MLB	37	2	1	16	42	0	39¹	31	3	12	42	2.8	9.5	46%	.290	1.09	2.80	3.00	3.04	0.8

Putz has taken an impromptu trip to the disabled list every year since 2008 and last year was no exception, except that he double-dipped. (It's okay: He had enough personal days stored up.) In all, he missed more than two months of the season, leaving behind a revolving door of sadness to Arizona's ninth innings. Before his first injury in May, he had converted five saves in nine chances, with enough walks to make the dog nauseous. His slowing fastball will drop him from the ranks of highly desirable closers, but his split-finger still has enough ferocious bite to keep him as a high-leverage option, provided he can throw strikes.

Addison Reed

Born: 12/27/1988 Age: 25
Bats: L Throws: R Height: 6' 4" Weight: 220
Breakout: 27% Improve: 50% Collapse: 27%
Attrition: 15% MLB: 90%

Comparables:
Drew Storen, Bill Bray, Fernando Cabrera

YEAR	TEAM	LVL	AGE	W	L	SV	G	GS	IP	H	HR	BB	SO	BB9	SO9	GB%	BABIP	WHIP	ERA	FIP	FRA	WARP
2011	WNS	A+	22	2	0	1	15	0	28¹	21	1	4	39	1.3	12.4	61%	.385	0.88	1.59	1.57	1.54	0.5
2011	BIR	AA	22	0	1	2	13	0	20²	10	0	6	33	2.6	14.4	33%	.267	0.77	0.87	1.13	1.90	0.6
2011	CHR	AAA	22	0	0	2	11	0	21¹	8	2	3	28	1.3	11.8	29%	.154	0.52	1.27	2.25	3.24	0.3
2011	CHA	MLB	22	0	0	0	6	0	7¹	10	1	1	12	1.2	14.7	20%	.474	1.50	3.68	1.97	3.33	0.2
2012	CHA	MLB	23	3	2	29	62	0	55	57	6	18	54	2.9	8.8	33%	.323	1.36	4.75	3.59	4.07	0.8
2013	CHA	MLB	24	5	4	40	68	0	71¹	56	6	23	72	2.9	9.1	35%	.260	1.11	3.79	3.20	3.38	1.1
2014	ARI	MLB	25	3	1	30	54	0	64	52	5	18	68	2.5	9.6	37%	.296	1.09	2.85	2.98	3.10	1.2

You would think the closer for a last-place team would fidget his way through a light workload, but the anemic White Sox offense provided so few blowout leads that Reed managed to save 40 of Chicago's 63 wins. The big righty lives off his mid-90s gas but has improved his off-speed stuff, generating plenty of swing-and-miss with his slider and changeup last year. His velocity dropped as the team's somnambulant season trudged on, especially in a series of disastrous September outings, but that isn't likely to be a long-term concern. Reed can be comfortably slotted into the second-tier of ninth-inning firebreathers. In another time, Kevin Towers would have been the GM who created "Addison Reed: Closer" rather than the one who traded a top-100 prospect to acquire him.

Matt Reynolds
Born: 10/2/1984 Age: 29
Bats: L Throws: L Height: 6' 5" Weight: 240
Breakout: 25% Improve: 50% Collapse: 27%
Attrition: 28% MLB: 71%
Comparables:
Shawn Kelley, Henry Owens, Jensen Lewis

YEAR	TEAM	LVL	AGE	W	L	SV	G	GS	IP	H	HR	BB	SO	BB9	SO9	GB%	BABIP	WHIP	ERA	FIP	FRA	WARP
2011	COL	MLB	26	1	2	0	73	0	50²	48	10	18	50	3.2	8.9	39%	.280	1.30	4.09	4.65	4.53	0.2
2012	COL	MLB	27	3	1	0	71	0	57¹	65	11	17	51	2.7	8.0	42%	.329	1.43	4.40	4.74	5.18	0.3
2013	ARI	MLB	28	0	2	2	30	0	27¹	25	2	5	23	1.6	7.6	40%	.291	1.10	1.98	2.95	3.03	0.5
2014	ARI	MLB	29	2	1	1	45	0	39	33	4	11	38	2.5	8.8	45%	.294	1.13	3.33	3.49	3.62	0.5

The bad news is a UCL tear means Reynolds will likely miss the entire 2014 season while rehabbing from Tommy John surgery. Here's the good news: When and if he returns as a 30-year-old reliever, he won't be a simple LOOGY, as he has been limited to in previous years. Once the former Colorado farmhand was flipped to Arizona for Ryan Wheeler in the 2012 offseason, Reynolds started trusting his split-finger against righties while better mixing his changeup into counts, keeping righties off balance and producing big outs in late innings. It's uncertain if flying cars will be around for 2015, but lefties who can pitch to righties should still be in demand by then.

Alex Sanabia
Born: 9/8/1988 Age: 25
Bats: R Throws: R Height: 6' 2" Weight: 210
Breakout: 31% Improve: 55% Collapse: 29%
Attrition: 46% MLB: 82%
Comparables:
Tim Stauffer, Jeff Karstens, Jeanmar Gomez

YEAR	TEAM	LVL	AGE	W	L	SV	G	GS	IP	H	HR	BB	SO	BB9	SO9	GB%	BABIP	WHIP	ERA	FIP	FRA	WARP
2011	JUP	A+	22	0	2	0	2	2	11	13	2	0	1	0.0	0.8	43%	.182	1.18	5.73	5.84	7.56	-0.2
2011	NWO	AAA	22	0	3	0	4	4	21²	35	4	3	13	1.2	5.4	—	.387	1.75	7.89	5.68	6.17	0.0
2011	FLO	MLB	22	0	0	0	3	2	11	13	2	3	8	2.5	6.5	32%	.314	1.45	3.27	4.72	3.99	0.1
2012	NWO	AAA	23	6	7	0	17	17	88²	92	11	24	63	2.4	6.4	42%	.294	1.31	4.06	4.74	5.03	0.9
2013	MIA	MLB	24	3	7	0	10	10	55¹	69	10	25	31	4.1	5.0	38%	.337	1.70	4.88	5.82	5.65	-0.6
2014	ARI	MLB	25	3	4	0	10	10	55¹	56	7	17	33	2.8	5.3	42%	.290	1.31	4.41	4.73	4.80	0.0

The thing about a 40-man roster: You can't have more than 40 guys on it. Sanabia is living proof that there is some number of faulty starters too high for even the Marlins to handle, and he was squeezed off (and plucked by Arizona) in October. As someone with fringe-average stuff across the board, Sanabia has little room for error in his control, which evaded him last year. His 10 percent walk rate was his highest since he was a 17-year-old in the Gulf Coast League. He already had low strikeout rates and below-average groundball skills, so that left a guy with a pickoff move. A groin strain in May, which sidelined him for the remainder of the season, not only saved him from erasing all of the positive career WARP he has saved from 2010, but it also allowed the Marlins to move Nathan Eovaldi into the rotation without actually having to make a decision.

Tony Sipp
Born: 7/12/1983 Age: 30
Bats: L Throws: L Height: 6' 0" Weight: 190
Breakout: 23% Improve: 50% Collapse: 36%
Attrition: 13% MLB: 90%
Comparables:
Jorge Julio, John Hudek, David Riske

YEAR	TEAM	LVL	AGE	W	L	SV	G	GS	IP	H	HR	BB	SO	BB9	SO9	GB%	BABIP	WHIP	ERA	FIP	FRA	WARP
2011	CLE	MLB	27	6	3	0	69	0	62¹	45	10	24	57	3.5	8.2	28%	.219	1.11	3.03	4.47	5.30	0.0
2012	CLE	MLB	28	1	2	1	63	0	55	47	9	23	51	3.8	8.3	37%	.255	1.27	4.42	4.63	5.22	-0.2
2013	RNO	AAA	29	1	0	1	9	0	10	3	0	5	12	4.5	10.8	41%	.136	0.80	0.00	2.67	1.80	0.4
2013	ARI	MLB	29	3	2	0	56	0	37²	35	6	22	42	5.3	10.0	28%	.284	1.51	4.78	4.85	4.23	0.2
2014	ARI	MLB	30	3	1	1	55	0	47	37	6	21	49	4.1	9.5	36%	.278	1.25	3.73	4.20	4.06	0.4

After being involved in that wacky nine-player, three-team trade between the Indians, Reds and Diamondbacks, Sipp was supposed to be for Arizona the same effective lefty he was in Cleveland—although his career splits never suggested he was actually better against lefties. Instead, he wasn't great against anybody, and the walk issues that he seemed to have overcome resurfaced. Arizona designated him for assignment at the beginning of August, he took his minor-league stint like a champ, and he returned in September to the big-league club. His stuff continues to miss bats, but also the strike zone, which is enough of a tantalizing mixed bag for a club to try him again, and again.

Zeke Spruill

Born: 9/11/1989 Age: 24
Bats: R Throws: R Height: 6' 5" Weight: 190
Breakout: 62% Improve: 78% Collapse: 9%
Attrition: 67% MLB: 22%

Comparables:
Brandon Cumpton, Mike Ekstrom, Anthony Ortega

YEAR	TEAM	LVL	AGE	W	L	SV	G	GS	IP	H	HR	BB	SO	BB9	SO9	GB%	BABIP	WHIP	ERA	FIP	FRA	WARP
2011	LYN	A+	21	7	9	0	20	20	129²	108	7	23	92	1.6	6.4	56%	.249	1.01	3.19	3.23	5.20	-0.1
2011	MIS	AA	21	3	2	0	7	7	45	45	3	17	16	3.4	3.2	37%	.176	1.38	3.20	4.93	11.49	-0.2
2012	MIS	AA	22	9	11	0	27	27	161²	158	8	46	106	2.6	5.9	51%	.302	1.26	3.67	3.44	4.54	0.6
2013	MOB	AA	23	0	3	0	5	5	31²	24	0	12	20	3.4	5.7	53%	.273	1.14	1.42	2.79	3.52	0.4
2013	RNO	AAA	23	6	5	0	16	16	92	98	8	33	48	3.2	4.7	53%	.299	1.42	4.21	4.83	5.98	0.7
2013	ARI	MLB	23	0	2	0	6	2	11¹	17	3	5	9	4.0	7.1	41%	.361	1.94	5.56	6.46	5.19	0.0
2014	ARI	MLB	24	7	8	0	23	23	120	127	15	40	63	3.0	4.7	50%	.297	1.39	4.83	4.94	5.24	-0.5

It's always an auspicious year for a player when he begins in Double-A and makes it to the majors. That's what happened to Spruill, the string-bean sinkerballer who was hauled to the Diamondbacks in the mega Justin Upton deal. After a successful June tour of duty in the bullpen, the roster ran out of space and he returned to the Triple-A rotation. He then made two big-league starts in August—neither of them very memorable—and finished the season back in Triple-A. Chipped from the mold of Rick Porcello, if he can continue to hammer the bottom half of the zone with that sinker he will act as valuable starting pitching depth in 2014, or perhaps break camp as a pitch-to-contact reliever.

Matt Stites

Born: 5/28/1990 Age: 24
Bats: L Throws: R Height: 5' 11" Weight: 170
Breakout: 20% Improve: 50% Collapse: 28%
Attrition: 58% MLB: 18%

Comparables:
Rob Delaney, C.C. Lee, Mark Melancon

YEAR	TEAM	LVL	AGE	W	L	SV	G	GS	IP	H	HR	BB	SO	BB9	SO9	GB%	BABIP	WHIP	ERA	FIP	FRA	WARP
2011	EUG	A-	21	4	0	5	24	0	32²	14	1	8	36	2.2	9.9	45%	.178	0.67	1.93	2.63	3.52	0.5
2012	FTW	A	22	2	0	13	42	0	48²	25	4	3	60	0.6	11.1	34%	.196	0.58	0.74	2.20	3.00	1.2
2013	SAN	AA	23	2	2	14	46	0	52	37	6	8	51	1.4	8.8	47%	.228	0.87	2.08	3.11	4.14	0.4
2014	ARI	MLB	24	2	1	2	37	0	43²	39	5	13	39	2.8	8.0	41%	.290	1.19	3.70	3.87	4.02	0.4

The latest undersized right-hander to dominate the low minors as a late-drafted strike-throwing reliever, Matt Stites stands out for a few reasons: he passed the Double-A test; he flashes high-90s heat; and bullpen diviner Kevin Towers acquired him, in the Ian Kennedy trade. An emergency appendectomy last summer kept him from making his debut in the Arizona organization, but once he does he'll move fast.

Joe Thatcher

Born: 10/4/1981 Age: 32
Bats: L Throws: L Height: 6' 2" Weight: 230
Breakout: 29% Improve: 53% Collapse: 26%
Attrition: 6% MLB: 92%

Comparables:
Heath Bell, Michael Wuertz, Scott Williamson

YEAR	TEAM	LVL	AGE	W	L	SV	G	GS	IP	H	HR	BB	SO	BB9	SO9	GB%	BABIP	WHIP	ERA	FIP	FRA	WARP
2011	SDN	MLB	29	0	0	0	18	0	10	8	1	7	9	6.3	8.1	43%	.259	1.50	4.50	4.59	4.73	-0.2
2012	SDN	MLB	30	1	4	1	55	0	31²	30	2	14	39	4.0	11.1	43%	.346	1.39	3.41	3.10	2.25	0.5
2013	ARI	MLB	31	0	1	0	22	0	9¹	12	1	6	7	5.8	6.8	23%	.379	1.93	6.75	4.84	3.64	0.0
2013	SDN	MLB	31	3	1	0	50	0	30	28	3	4	29	1.2	8.7	44%	.298	1.07	2.10	2.89	3.63	0.2
2014	ARI	MLB	32	4	2	2	68	0	38²	32	3	12	41	2.8	9.6	47%	.305	1.14	3.03	3.14	3.29	0.7

After seven fruitful years in the Padres' bullpen, Thatcher was suddenly shipped to Arizona in the Ian Kennedy deal, and for years scholars will debate why. Perhaps it was to locate a replacement for the struggling Tony Sipp, but Thatcher accidentally mimicked Sipp's results, struggling to command the strike zone in the last two months while for some reason throwing nearly 80 percent fastballs (he's usually around 70 percent) when his slider is a quality swing-and-miss pitch. Don't look too much into the two-month sample size—his delivery and track record will keep him in use as a seasoned silencer of southpaws.

Brad Ziegler

Born: 10/10/1979 Age: 34
Bats: R Throws: R Height: 6' 4" Weight: 210
Breakout: 14% Improve: 36% Collapse: 35%
Attrition: 10% MLB: 88%

Comparables:
Mark Eichhorn, Matt Guerrier, Dave Smith

YEAR	TEAM	LVL	AGE	W	L	SV	G	GS	IP	H	HR	BB	SO	BB9	SO9	GB%	BABIP	WHIP	ERA	FIP	FRA	WARP
2011	ARI	MLB	31	0	0	0	23	0	20²	15	0	6	15	2.6	6.5	65%	.263	1.02	1.74	2.41	3.39	0.2
2011	OAK	MLB	31	3	2	1	43	0	37²	38	0	13	29	3.1	6.9	72%	.328	1.35	2.39	2.64	3.13	0.6
2012	ARI	MLB	32	6	1	0	77	0	68²	54	2	21	42	2.8	5.5	76%	.264	1.09	2.49	3.25	4.89	0.0
2013	ARI	MLB	33	8	1	13	78	0	73	61	3	22	44	2.7	5.4	71%	.261	1.14	2.22	3.38	4.28	0.3
2014	ARI	MLB	34	4	2	3	70	0	64	57	4	21	45	2.9	6.4	63%	.295	1.22	3.39	3.68	3.69	0.8

For years Brad Ziegler, America's favorite sidearming groundball automaton, has drawn comparisons to Chad Bradford, and rightly so considering his Oakland upbringing. Yet three years in Arizona have not produced nearly enough comps to Byung-Hyun Kim. For the first time since his rookie year, Ziggy was given the opportunity to close, but then again this was Arizona so your uncle also had some save opportunities. Among all the candidates, he was the most consistently effective in the ninth. How's that for a Kim comparison?

LINEOUTS

HITTERS

PLAYER	TEAM	LVL	AGE	PA	R	2B	3B	HR	RBI	BB	SO	SB-CS	AVG/OBP/SLG	TAv	BABIP	BRR	FRAA	WARP
SS N. Ahmed	MOB	AA	23	538	58	21	5	4	46	33	72	26-7	.236/.288/.324	.231	.266	1.3	SS(133): 21.5, 2B(2): -0.2	3.0
CF K. Broxton	MOB	AA	23	372	40	13	3	8	41	30	116	5-1	.231/.296/.359	.239	.325	1.8	CF(48): 1.8, RF(35): -3.4	0.1
3B B. Drury	SBN	A	20	583	78	51	4	15	85	47	92	1-1	.302/.362/.500	.308	.340	-3.8	3B(108): 4.1	4.9
1B E. Hinske	ARI	MLB	35	58	2	3	0	1	6	6	17	0-0	.173/.259/.288	.193	.235	0	1B(6): -0.0	-0.3
LF B. Jacobs	SLM	A+	22	337	44	24	0	11	44	33	88	10-4	.244/.334/.440	.253	.308	-0.5	LF(59): 0.9, CF(9): -0.4	0.6
	BIR	AA	22	176	13	8	0	2	22	11	50	2-3	.237/.291/.327	.233	.321	0.2	LF(35): 0.4	0.0
1B M. Jacobs	RNO	AAA	32	364	53	17	0	18	65	31	68	0-0	.304/.365/.520	.282	.335	1.7	1B(79): 4.8	1.5
	OAX	AAA	32	150	23	8	0	10	30	19	35	0-0	.275/.367/.565	.310	.293	—	—	—
C B. Lalli	NAS	AAA	30	311	36	14	0	11	35	22	68	0-0	.282/.334/.447	.270	.335	-1.3	C(56): -2.3, 1B(14): 0.1	0.8
	MIL	MLB	30	24	1	0	0	0	2	0	7	0-0	.125/.125/.125	.082	.176	0	1B(5): -0.3, C(1): -0.0	-0.5
3B J. Lamb	VIS	A+	22	283	44	20	0	13	47	48	70	0-0	.303/.424/.558	.331	.380	-0.1	3B(55): -2.3	2.8
1B D. Palka	YAK	A-	21	55	10	1	2	2	10	7	16	1-0	.340/.418/.574	.385	.467	0.8	1B(10): 1.3	1.0
C M. Perez	SBN	A	20	178	20	12	2	2	14	14	55	0-0	.247/.303/.383	.245	.355	-2.4	C(39): -0.4	0.3
	VIS	A+	20	193	21	9	0	5	24	11	78	1-1	.173/.223/.307	.191	.265	2.1	C(42): -0.7	-0.3
LF J. Rivera	RNO	AAA	34	383	46	17	1	10	58	17	30	2-1	.304/.345/.440	.259	.309	-1.1	LF(75): -5.3, 1B(20): 1.2	0.0

The third shortstop acquired in Arizona's no-hit-shortstop binge of 2012, **Nick Ahmed** got one year older but no closer to the big leagues in 2013. ⊘ Toolsy third-rounder **Keon Broxton** lost his power stroke, quit stealing bases, moved from center field to the corners and was kicked off the 40-man roster. "Just wait 'til next year!" he tells people, when they ask him when *X-Men: Days Of Future Past* is coming out. ⊘ The low-minors contribution to the Justin Upton deal, **Brandon Drury** doubled his homer and walk rates and plumped up his batting average, easing concerns about spotty defense. ⊘ **Eric Hinske** (58 plate appearances in 52 games) was used almost exclusively as a pinch-hitter, except for one game in which he served as brawl fodder against the Dodgers. He'll be the Cubs' first base coach this year, but if your fantasy league is deep enough go ahead and draft him anyway. ⊘ **Brandon Jacobs** has power and speed but his long, contact-averse swing sabotages it, while his popgun arm limits him to left field. The Diamondbacks, his third organization, picked him up in the Mark Trumbo trade. ⊘ In 2009 **Mike Jacobs** won Kansas City's first base job over Kila Ka'aihue; four years later, Jacobs was plucked from the Mexican League to replace Ka'aihue at Reno. His minor-league slug numbers remain steady but his age does not. ⊘ Prorate **Blake Lalli**'s career over the course of an entire season and he'd be worth about nine wins below replacement. Guess who'll never get to play an entire season. ⊘ **Jake Lamb** sheared minor-league pitching, missed two months with a hamate injury, then returned and hit a bunch more. He demonstrated power and patience from the left side, a sassy recipe for big-league futures. ⊘ Toolsy second-round shortstop **Jose Munoz** has now made 46 errors in 98 games, generous low-minors scorekeepers and all. Thankfully, he's got third-base power. ⊘ A third-round pick from a top college program, **Daniel Palka** has mouth-watering power, reads pitches well and would advance quickly if Arizona's first-base situation didn't assure he'll be trying to learn a new position. ⊘ **Michael Perez**'s bat got him downgraded from the California to the Midwest League in late June, but he continued to clean up the crime-ridden basepaths with his trusty throwing arm. ⊘ While you were resting in your favorite chair or bathtub, **Juan Rivera** was busting his keister at Triple-A Reno. Probably time for that keister to find a favorite chair or bathtub. ⊘ "Raw" is the keyword for second-rounder **Justin Williams**, a long-term project—he's younger than Shaggy's *Boombastic*—who has tons of power but is unrefined in every aspect of the game.

PITCHERS

PLAYER	TEAM	LVL	AGE	W	L	SV	IP	H	HR	BB	SO	BB9	SO9	GB%	BABIP	WHIP	ERA	FIP	FRA	WARP
J. Barrett	VIS	A+	21	2	1	15	27¹	21	2	9	37	3.0	12.2	49%	.284	1.10	1.98	3.33	3.66	0.7
	MOB	AA	21	1	1	14	24²	18	2	3	22	1.1	8.0	47%	.232	0.85	0.36	2.55	3.64	0.3
A. Blair	SBN	A	21	0	2	0	17²	19	0	4	13	2.0	6.6	45%	.328	1.30	3.57	2.72	3.25	0.4
	YAK	A-	21	1	1	0	31	25	2	13	28	3.8	8.1	42%	.280	1.23	2.90	3.80	4.68	0.2
A. Chafin	VIS	A+	23	3	1	0	31	32	1	14	32	4.1	9.3	47%	.341	1.48	4.65	3.48	4.18	0.8
	MOB	AA	23	10	7	0	126¹	118	5	41	87	2.9	6.2	52%	.299	1.26	2.85	3.09	4.24	0.6
E. Marshall	RNO	AAA	23	3	6	3	58	75	2	30	59	4.7	9.2	60%	.415	1.81	4.34	3.79	4.85	0.9
A. Meo	VIS	A+	23	1	1	0	22²	25	2	22	22	8.7	8.7	51%	.377	2.07	7.54	6.15	6.14	0.1
	MOB	AA	23	0	4	0	35¹	31	6	25	17	6.4	4.3	36%	.258	1.58	6.37	6.96	8.77	-1.1
B. Shipley	SBN	A	21	0	1	0	20²	14	2	8	16	3.5	7.0	46%	.218	1.06	2.61	4.35	4.92	0.1
	YAK	A-	21	0	2	0	19	30	1	6	24	2.8	11.4	43%	.475	1.89	7.58	2.58	3.65	0.5

Just a year after the Diamondbacks popped **Jake Barrett** in the third round, he was mowing down Double-A batters, closing the season with a 20-inning scoreless streak that will earn him an honest audition in spring training. ⊘ The highest draft pick in Marshall University's history, the book on **Aaron Blair** is the fabulous tale of a young man who solves mysteries with low-90s stuff and decent command. ⊘ Kent State alumnus **Andrew Chafin** blossomed into an effective pitch-to-mostly-contact lefty, capping his season with a six-hit shutout in the minor-league playoffs to earn some clutchy street cred. ⊘ Once thought to be a speedy promotion to the majors, **Evan Marshall** just keeps inching. After a full season in Triple-A, his mid-90s fastball should get a chance this year to show major-league hitters how wild it has gotten. ⊘ There are many paths to the same summit, but even more paths to no summit at all. **Anthony Meo** found one of the latter, starting 2013 as a Double-A starter and finishing as a High-A reliever with as many walks as strikeouts. ⊘ **Felipe Perez** shunned UCLA to sign with Arizona. It won't get him on the dean's list, but with two complete games and a minuscule walk rate, who needs college? ⊘ Fifteenth overall pick **Braden Shipley** had a bad case of the BABIPs in short-season ball, but his command improved after Arizona promoted him to the Midwest League and stretched him out as a starter.

MANAGER: KIRK GIBSON

YEAR	TEAM	W-L	Pythag +/-	Avg PC	100+ P	120+ P	QS	BQS	REL	REL w Zero R	IBB	PH	PH Avg	PH HR	SB2	CS2	SB3	CS3	SAC Att	SAC %	POS SAC	Squeeze	Swing	In Play
2011	ARI	94-68	1	96.9	80	0	90	6	463	375	16	248	.206	5	117	53	16	2	96	52.1%	18	3	306	79
2012	ARI	81-81	1	95.2	63	3	85	5	461	382	18	225	.234	3	79	47	14	4	96	63.5%	15	2	281	72
2013	ARI	81-81	0	95.1	59	0	87	4	527	432	42	275	.215	3	52	36	10	5	82	61.0%	20	0	277	77

Maybe it's just me or maybe it's just a lazy stereotype, but I'd imagine a redass manager to be the sort of guy to try to grind it out for every last run; the sort of guy who will play small-ball more than most. But Kirk Gibson hates the sacrifice bunt. His Diamondbacks typically rank near the bottom of the National League at it, as they did in 2013. Only the Cubs had fewer.

He will, on the other hand, put on the steal sign, but he might want to reconsider—his teams have a terrible success rate at it. He took over Arizona in mid-2010, and a club that had 45 steals in 58 attempts without him went 41 for 69 with him. From 2011 to 2013, Arizona has the second worst success rate on the bases. Oh, and they've been getting worse, too. They ranked dead last in 2013, after finishing second worst in 2012.

Arizona issued more intentional walks in 2013 than in 2011 and 2012 combined.

In Gibson's three full seasons, Arizona has been the best defensive team in baseball according to Defensive Runs Saved, saving 163 runs above average. There are just five teams with even half that many.

Gibson doesn't make many in-game substitutions for his position players. Arizona had the most position player complete games in the NL in 2011 and 2012, and ranked fourth in 2013.

Atlanta Braves

By Mark Smith

We know two things about the 2014 Atlanta Braves: They're young, and they aren't under team control for much longer.

Per Baseball-Reference, the Braves had the second-youngest position players and the fourth-youngest pitchers in baseball in 2013; the only younger teams were the Astros, Marlins, White Sox and Cardinals. That young core produced, using *BP*'s numbers, the sixth-most batter and third-most pitcher value. That young core boasts a variety of All Star-caliber players under the age of 27: Andrelton Simmons, Jason Heyward, Freddie Freeman, Justin Upton, Mike Minor, Julio Teheran and Craig Kimbrel. That young core also has B.J. Upton—hey, he'll rebound, okay? Okay? OKAY?—Alex Wood, Brandon Beachy, Kris Medlen, Jordan Walden and David Carpenter, useful young assets, if a level below the first group. That young core should be favorites in the NL East in 2014. But that young core's window is rapidly closing.

While good young players across the league are being signed to extensions with regularity to the point of routine, the Braves have not signed their obviously talented young players to similar contracts, either of their own volition or because the players have refused the offers. It's the tension of the relationship between the team and the pre-free agency player. Both the team and the player have the same primary aim—winning—but they have opposing secondary aims. The team wants the most talent for the cheapest price at the lowest possible risk while the player balances personal security against the possibility of maximizing his earning potential. Although teams are frequently blamed for not signing good young players, there are millions of powerful reasons for those players to refuse to sign extensions that cover free agent seasons.

The Braves have either been reluctant or unlucky with their recent crop of youngsters. The last time they extended

a player before he reached free agency was immediately after trading for Dan Uggla during the 2010-11 offseason, when they extended ... Dan Uggla. The last time the Braves extended a homegrown player before he reached free agency was when they signed Brian McCann to a six-year deal in March 2007, just before his second full season. (On the other hand, it was reported that Jeff Francoeur received the same contract offer as his good friend McCann but turned it down.)

vSince the McCann contract, the Braves have been unable to come to an agreement on extensions with any of their young players. (This inability to extend likely contributed to Martin Prado being traded before the 2013 season.) But signing at least some of their young core is probably (hopefully?) near the top of the Braves' to-do list in the near future. If they do not, their window to win is going to close awfully fast.

Of those players mentioned above, Jason Heyward, Justin Upton and Kris Medlen can leave in two seasons, and Freddie Freeman, Craig Kimbrel, Brandon Beachy and Jordan Walden can be free agents after three. By process of elimination, that leaves Andrelton Simmons, Mike Minor, Julio Teheran and David Carpenter as the remaining core. That's a good, enviable collection of talent, but it needs supplements, and there don't appear to be many coming from the minors.

In the current minor-league system, just two players have present Top 100-type talent: Christian Bethancourt and Lucas Sims. Bethancourt is a defensive whiz behind the plate, but he has offensive issues; this adds up to the kind of player who ranks in the 80s or 90s. Sims, a pitcher, is the jewel of the system, but he's only 20 and due for High-A next season. There are several other intriguing prospects—Edward Salcedo, Tommy La Stella, Joey

BRAVES PROSPECTUS
2013 W-L: 96-66, 1st in NL East

Pythag	.601	4th	DER	.708	9th
RS/G	4.25	13th	B-Age	26.7	2nd
RA/G	3.38	1st	P-Age	27.3	7th
TAv	.263	11th	Salary	$90	18th
BRR	-7.72	26th	M$/MW	$1.62	5th
TAv-P	.251	2nd	DL Days	1337	27th
FIP	3.41	5th	$ on DL	22%	23rd

	Runs	HR/RH	HR/LH	Runs/RH	Runs/LH
Three-Year Park Factors	100	99	107	99	108

Top Hitter WARP	5.40 (Andrelton Simmons)
Top Pitcher WARP	1.88 (Julio Teheran)
Top Prospect	Lucas Sims

Terdoslavich, Kyle Kubitza, Jose Peraza, Mauricio Cabrera, recent first-rounder Jason Hursh—but only Peraza has an All-Star ceiling.

Deciding which of the potential free agents to sign and how much to sign them for isn't an exact science. It's easy to say, "I want to keep Heyward around for forever and ever," but there's an unspoken qualifier: "depending on how much he's asking for." Even though those asking prices are unknown, there is a solid set of precedents built from the recent slew of extensions that can give us a feel for the market.

Start with Freddie Freeman. Several young first basemen have signed recently, with Allen Craig, Anthony Rizzo and Paul Goldschmidt all agreeing to extensions early in 2013. Figure 1 shows how their contracts match up with Freeman's upcoming years. (Note that for Rizzo, "Arb1" is really his second year of arbitration eligibility because he is lined up to be a Super Two player after 2014.)

.285/.358/.466 total, including a coming-out party in 2013 (.319/.396/.501), on his way to 7.1 WARP.

Freeman is younger and has a track record of success, which, as a general rule of thumb, should mean more money. (Obligatory mention of the new national television contracts transforming the economic landscape of the game here.) When negotiations begin for Freeman's future (and it's possible that those negotiations will have concluded by the time you are reading this), he could easily ask for more than $50 million for the next five seasons. Considering Freeman's age when he reaches free agency, Mark Teixeira's eight-year, $180 million contract may represent a starting point if Freeman hits the open market. (Teixeira was 29 in his first season of free agency.) The Braves would have to offer enough money to dissuade Freeman from waiting in hopes of landing a stuff-that-dreams-are-made-of nine-figure deal.

Player	Arb1 age	Contract yrs	Millions	Arb1 $	Arb2 $	Arb3 $	FA1 $	FA2 $	4-year $	5-year $
Anthony Rizzo	26	7	41	5	7	7	11	14.5 (opt)	30	44.5
Paul Goldschmidt	27	5	32	3	5.75	8.75	11	14.5 (opt)	28.6	43.1
Allen Craig	29	5	31	2.75	5.5	9	11	13 (opt)	28.3	41.3

The market precedent seems clear for the next five years of Freeman's career: $28 to $30 million and a club option at $13 to $14.5 million. Freeman doesn't *have* to sign away these years of his career for that amount of money, but agents and teams often use comparable contracts to negotiate. Is Freeman comparable?

Age is the obvious place to start. Freeman heads into his first arbitration season at 24, easily younger than any of his three comparables. Rizzo is the next-youngest of the three, and he's two years older than Freeman in terms of age-at-service-time. When the comparables reach their free agent years, they'll be in the last years of their physical peaks or, particularly in the case of Craig, well in the decline phase. Freeman will be heading *into* his peak.

All that ain't nothin' but a number, so we should look at other numbers too. Going into the day he signed his extension, Anthony Rizzo had played in parts of three seasons and hit .255/.333/.437. Allen Craig had hit .300/.348/.515, also across three seasons, but his defense was poor enough that this added up to just 3.8 WARP. And Paul Goldschmidt, he of the MVP-caliber 2013, hadn't yet fully blossomed, hitting .278/.353/.487 for 3.9 WARP in about a season and a quarter. Freeman has three full seasons under his belt and has hit

Jason Heyward's situation represents many of the same problems for the Braves. A list of similar contracts is in Figure 2. (Adam Jones' second-year arbitration salary came on a one-year contract. He signed his extension covering his last year of arbitration plus five years of free agency three months later.)

In addition to those three, Jay Bruce (six years, $51 million) and Justin Upton (six years, $51.25 million) have signed similar extensions themselves. Like Freeman, Heyward is incredibly young for this point in his career: At age 24 in his second arbitration season, he's set to hit free agency at 26, with visions of Alex Rodriguez (who was 25 in his first season in Texas) surely dancing in his head. Heyward hasn't performed at that level, of course, but he played at a four-WARP pace in 2013 while missing time with two flukes (appendicitis and a broken jaw). If he had reached that level, his career WARP figures would go: 4.0, 0.6, 5.9, 4.0. If that's Heyward's established level and if he's hitting free agency at the beginning of his peak, it's awfully easy to start doing dollars-per-win math and pondering a 10-year, $250 million contract if the Braves let him get there. Conservatively. Which means that it could take something like 10 years and $170 million to get a deal done now.

Player	Arb2 age	Contract yrs	Millions	Arb2 $	Arb3 $	FA1 $	FA2 $	FA3 $	4-year $	5-year $
Adam Jones	26	6	85.5	6.15	8.5	13	13	16	40.65	56.65
Andrew McCutchen	27	6	51.5	7.25	10	13	14	14.5 (opt)	44.25	58.75
Carlos Gonzalez	27	7	80	7.5	10.5	16	17	20	51	71

Player	TC2 age	Contract yrs	Millions	TC2 $	TC3 $	Arb1 $	Arb2 $	Arb3 $	Pre-FA $
Elvis Andrus	21	3	14.4	0.42	0.45	2.38	4.8	6.48	15.27
Starlin Castro	22	7	60	0.57	5	5	6	7	23.57
Alcides Escobar	24	4	10.5	0.43	1	3	3	3	10.43

Andrelton Simmons is the newest addition to the list of young Braves the team might look to extend. Figure 3 is a list of comparable contracts. ("TC" stands for "team control" and refers to the years in which a team can normally renew the player's contract for the league-minimum.)

Simmons will likely be a Super Two player in the 2014-15 offseason, as Starlin Castro was, though unlike Freeman and Heyward, Simmons is behind in the aging game—he'll be heading into his age-25 season. Andrus is Simmons' most comparable player in terms of performance, as they share penchants for good defense while leaving something to be desired on the offensive side. Figure 3, of course, only shows the $14.4 million Andrus was paid to buy out his arbitration years, making no mention of the $15 million *per season* he'll be paid beginning in 2015 (and continuing in seeming perpetuity). Simmons plays otherworldly defense, but he doesn't have the same track record that his aforementioned teammates do. Still, you can handwave a bit, figuring that Simmons is older than Andrus but there's been inflation since then, so at a rough estimate, it might take $15 to $20 million to buy out the remainder of his pre-free agency seasons and another $15 million per season after that to keep Simmons long-term.

A word on Craig Kimbrel. History is littered with reasons not to give relievers long-term contracts, but Kimbrel's plausible claim on the "Best Closer in Baseball" title means that it's at least under consideration. Jonathan Papelbon is probably the best comparable pitcher at this point in Kimbrel's career, and he made $6.25, $9.35 and $12 million before signing the four-year, $50 million free-agent contract the Phillies spent this offseason regretting. A five-year, $57 million extension for Kimbrel, who is three years from free agency, would not be unreasonable.

Totaling these four contracts, the Braves could find themselves committing more than $400 million in one offseason. Of course, they don't have to extend all four, but they aren't in an enviable bargaining position with any of them, so narrowing the pool to one or two or three doesn't get the team all that far. All four players are young and talented, which is exactly what any team wants on its team right now, but that also means they have a lot of leverage and can forego any offer the Braves present.

New television contracts have changed the amount of money teams are willing and able to spend for a win, and the number of impact free agents has dwindled as the number of extensions has increased. Those are all advantages for Freeman, Heyward, Kimbrel and Simmons. The extensions suggested here are based on pre-bubble precedent, so in baseball's present uncharted waters, it's likely that the suggestions are substantially too conservative.

So again the tension. The Braves look primed for another big year in 2014 because of an amazing young core, but that young core may not be around much longer if the team can't overcome the substantial pressures of the new TV contracts and the lure of what All-Star players headed into their primes can make on the open market.

Formerly a Braves intern, Mark Smith now just obsesses over them on Twitter and Talking Chop.

HITTERS

Christian Bethancourt C

Born: 9/2/1991 Age: 22
Bats: R Throws: R Height: 6' 2"
Weight: 215 Breakout: 1%
Improve: 5% Collapse: 8%
Attrition: 10% MLB: 14%

Comparables:
Tony Cruz, Angel Salome, Tim Federowicz

YEAR	TEAM	LVL	AGE	PA	R	2B	3B	HR	RBI	BB	SO	SB	CS	AVG/OBP/SLG	TAv	BABIP	BRR	FRAA	WARP
2011	ROM	A	19	235	25	10	3	4	33	8	27	6	3	.303/.323/.430	.278	.323	2.5	C(40): 0.8	1.4
2011	LYN	A+	19	175	11	6	0	1	20	3	35	3	2	.271/.277/.325	.204	.328	1.3	C(30): -0.5	-0.2
2012	MIS	AA	20	288	30	5	1	2	26	11	45	8	6	.243/.275/.291	.229	.281	-2	C(69): 2.5	0.3
2013	MIS	AA	21	388	42	21	0	12	45	16	57	11	7	.277/.305/.436	.273	.294	-0.4	C(85): 0.8	2.4
2013	ATL	MLB	21	1	0	0	0	0	0	0	1	0	0	.000/.000/.000	.053	—	0		0.0
2014	ATL	MLB	22	250	26	10	1	5	22	4	52	4	2	.242/.254/.355	.223	.280	-0.3	C 1	0.2

Bevourt had his best offensive season since Rookie ball in 2009—when he was the same age as high school juniors—thanks to career-high marks in doubles and home runs. While he has pull-side power and good hand-eye coordination, a raw approach limits his offensive ceiling. On the bright side, Bethancourt's defensive game is such that he won't have to hit much to provide value. He's always had the necessary physical tools to post elite pop times, but his improved leadership and receiving skills help round out the package. The Braves rewarded him with a major-league debut in their 162nd game. Bethancourt is going to be on a big-league roster for a long time, likely beginning this season.

Todd Cunningham CF

Born: 3/20/1989 Age: 25
Bats: B Throws: R Height: 6' 0"
Weight: 200 Breakout: 4%
Improve: 21% Collapse: 7%
Attrition: 25% MLB: 34%

Comparables:
Logan Schafer, Shane Robinson, Clay Timpner

YEAR	TEAM	LVL	AGE	PA	R	2B	3B	HR	RBI	BB	SO	SB	CS	AVG/OBP/SLG	TAv	BABIP	BRR	FRAA	WARP
2011	LYN	A+	22	386	59	12	4	4	20	33	47	14	6	.257/.348/.353	.263	.289	4.3	CF(61): -1.8, LF(9): -0.4	1.2
2012	MIS	AA	23	519	77	23	6	3	51	38	51	24	8	.309/.364/.403	.291	.340	5.3	CF(97): -11.7, RF(17): -1.0	2.9
2013	GWN	AAA	24	487	60	13	5	2	38	41	62	20	7	.265/.342/.333	.244	.305	3.6	CF(110): -1.1, RF(3): 0.4	1.4
2013	ATL	MLB	24	8	2	0	0	0	0	0	3	0	0	.250/.250/.250	.150	.400	-0.1	LF(5): -0.1, RF(2): -0.0	-0.1
2014	ATL	MLB	25	250	28	9	2	3	19	15	40	6	2	.256/.308/.348	.245	.290	0.4	CF -3, RF -0	0.1

Drafted with the compensatory pick for losing Mike Gonzalez, Cunningham sipped his first cup of coffee last season. Known as a grinder, he can play each outfield position and has a decent bat, albeit one empty of power. Unfortunately, he didn't show his exceptional contact skills during his time in Triple-A, which impeded his progress toward a permanent big-league gig. In an ideal world, Cunningham becomes a second-division starter. Far more likely, however, that the switch-hitter fills a reserve role.

Ryan Doumit C

Born: 4/3/1981 Age: 33
Bats: B Throws: R Height: 6' 1"
Weight: 220 Breakout: 0%
Improve: 31% Collapse: 7%
Attrition: 17% MLB: 88%

Comparables:
Daryle Ward, Eric Chavez, Kevin Millar

YEAR	TEAM	LVL	AGE	PA	R	2B	3B	HR	RBI	BB	SO	SB	CS	AVG/OBP/SLG	TAv	BABIP	BRR	FRAA	WARP
2011	IND	AAA	30	31	4	1	1	0	3	4	4	0	0	.231/.355/.346	.267	.273	0.2	C(2): -0.0	0.0
2011	PIT	MLB	30	236	17	12	1	8	30	16	35	0	1	.303/.353/.477	.295	.331	-2.6	C(60): 0.1	1.5
2012	MIN	MLB	31	528	56	34	1	18	75	29	98	0	0	.275/.320/.461	.268	.306	1.7	C(59): 0.2, LF(16): 1.2	2.0
2013	MIN	MLB	32	538	49	28	1	14	55	48	99	1	0	.247/.314/.396	.264	.282	-0.8	C(43): 0.2, RF(32): -1.3	1.5
2014	ATL	MLB	33	503	51	24	1	14	58	37	102	1	0	.246/.306/.391	.257	.290	-0.9	C 1, RF -1	1.3

Doumit's modest combination of patience and power remains capable of producing numbers like last year's league-average .260 TAv. Not bad for a catcher, but whatever value Doumit produces at the plate, he gives most if not all of it back with his work behind it. The former Pirate generally keeps the ball from hitting the backstop and isn't completely helpless in controlling the running game, but now that PITCHf/x allows us to start quantifying the effect of pitch framing, it turns out that Doumit loses more net strikes for his pitchers than any catcher in the league. Although he only started 43 games behind the dish, our own Max Marchi estimates Doumit's sloppy receiving cost his pitchers approximately 20 runs, or two wins, last season. That's almost inconceivably bad on a per-pitch basis, making Doumit far more valuable to fantasy baseball teams than real ones. An August concussion kept him from donning the mask down the stretch last season, and any hope he'd be exiled to DH went poof with a December trade to Atlanta.

Freddie Freeman 1B

Born: 9/12/1989 Age: 24
Bats: L Throws: R Height: 6' 5"
Weight: 225 Breakout: 3%
Improve: 63% Collapse: 3%
Attrition: 2% MLB: 100%

Comparables:
Prince Fielder, Billy Butler, John Mayberry

YEAR	TEAM	LVL	AGE	PA	R	2B	3B	HR	RBI	BB	SO	SB	CS	AVG/OBP/SLG	TAv	BABIP	BRR	FRAA	WARP
2011	ATL	MLB	21	635	67	32	0	21	76	53	142	4	4	.282/.346/.448	.286	.339	-2.1	1B(156): -5.1	1.2
2012	ATL	MLB	22	620	91	33	2	23	94	64	129	2	0	.259/.340/.456	.284	.295	1.9	1B(146): -7.2	1.6
2013	ATL	MLB	23	629	89	27	2	23	109	66	121	1	0	.319/.396/.501	.324	.371	-2.6	1B(147): 2.1	5.0
2014	ATL	MLB	24	591	71	29	1	21	79	53	123	2	1	.279/.350/.457	.296	.330	-1.1	1B -2	2.4

Captain Marvel Jr. had his finest offensive season to date and posted new high marks across the slash stats. Naturally, that must come with a note about his unsustainable BABIP; it's as unavoidable as it is banal, but here we go: The odds of the slug-footed first baseman continuing to see more than 37 percent of his batted balls drop for hits are slim. Still, Freeman is a solid player capable of hitting for a decent average, drawing some walks, and adding a fair amount of doubles and homers. Depending on how you view Freeman's defense, he's either a top-10 first baseman or close to it.

Evan Gattis C

Born: 8/18/1986 Age: 27
Bats: R Throws: R Height: 6' 4"
Weight: 230 Breakout: 7%
Improve: 39% Collapse: 12%
Attrition: 20% MLB: 80%

Comparables:
Allen Craig, Scott Hairston, John Bowker

YEAR	TEAM	LVL	AGE	PA	R	2B	3B	HR	RBI	BB	SO	SB	CS	AVG/OBP/SLG	TAv	BABIP	BRR	FRAA	WARP
2011	ROM	A		24	377	58	24	2	22	71	25	53	2	4	.322/.386/.601	.325	.328	-0.1	C(46): -0.5, 1B(6): 0.3	3.2
2012	LYN	A+		25	94	14	7	0	9	29	10	12	1	1	.385/.468/.821	.412	.356	-0.5	C(10): 0.0, LF(3): -0.1	1.9
2012	MIS	AA		25	207	24	13	4	9	37	20	29	1	1	.258/.343/.522	.275	.262	0.2	LF(30): -1.3, C(17): -0.4	0.7
2013	GWN	AAA		26	22	1	4	0	1	1	0	4	0	0	.333/.364/.667	.344	.375	-0.6	LF(1): -0.1, C(1): -0.0	0.2
2013	ATL	MLB		26	382	44	21	0	21	65	21	81	0	0	.243/.291/.480	.271	.255	0.6	LF(48): -0.9, C(42): 0.7	2.0
2014	ATL	MLB		27	324	39	16	1	17	50	18	67	0	0	.253/.303/.481	.282	.270	-0.6	C 0, LF -2	1.6

It's better for a player's rep to start hot and go cold than to start cold and get hot. Gattis—or El Oso Blanco, as the kids call him—is proof: He homered 12 times through May then slumped for three months, thanks in part to a strained oblique and in part to a 30 percent whiff rate on non-fastballs. Yet Gattis continued to receive playing time, and was thus able to redeem himself with a strong finish. He lacks a true defensive home, as he split time between left field and catcher, and he might be overexposed as an everyday player. Gattis will continue to provide value in a part-time role thanks to his raw power and "versatility."

Jason Heyward RF

Born: 8/9/1989 Age: 24
Bats: L Throws: L Height: 6' 5"
Weight: 240 Breakout: 1%
Improve: 54% Collapse: 6%
Attrition: 6% MLB: 100%

Comparables:
Jack Clark, Jeremy Hermida, Al Kaline

YEAR	TEAM	LVL	AGE	PA	R	2B	3B	HR	RBI	BB	SO	SB	CS	AVG/OBP/SLG	TAv	BABIP	BRR	FRAA	WARP
2011	ATL	MLB	21	454	50	18	2	14	42	51	93	9	2	.227/.319/.389	.261	.260	-0.6	RF(122): 3.0	0.9
2012	ATL	MLB	22	651	93	30	6	27	82	58	152	21	8	.269/.335/.479	.296	.319	7.2	RF(154): 15.5, CF(2): -0.1	6.3
2013	GWN	AAA	23	26	1	1	0	0	6	4	7	1	0	.300/.423/.350	.308	.429	0	RF(3): 0.3	0.2
2013	ATL	MLB	23	440	67	22	1	14	38	48	73	2	4	.254/.349/.427	.280	.281	1.2	RF(86): 7.6, CF(20): -0.6	2.7
2014	ATL	MLB	24	458	57	20	2	16	58	51	96	9	4	.256/.345/.434	.290	.300	-0.3	RF 7, CF -0	3.0

Boy, does time fly. We're now four seasons into Heyward's big-league career, and there's no denying he's a quality player: an above-average hitter and a good enough defender that the Braves trusted him to play center field down the stretch and into the postseason. But something feels off. Maybe it's the injuries—not all of which were his fault or any indication of brittleness—or perhaps it's the inconsistent power production. Heyward just isn't the superstar he was supposed to become. When we're let down because a prospect turns into a very good player, it's time to reconsider the expectations we build for the next talented youngster.

Paul Janish SS

Born: 10/12/1982 Age: 31
Bats: R Throws: R Height: 6' 2"
Weight: 200 Breakout: 0%
Improve: 29% Collapse: 12%
Attrition: 19% MLB: 88%

Comparables:
Eric Bruntlett, Alex Arias, Scott Fletcher

YEAR	TEAM	LVL	AGE	PA	R	2B	3B	HR	RBI	BB	SO	SB	CS	AVG/OBP/SLG	TAv	BABIP	BRR	FRAA	WARP
2011	LOU	AAA	28	53	9	2	0	1	3	7	4	1	0	.256/.377/.372	.198	.256	0.4	SS(9): -0.6	-0.1
2011	CIN	MLB	28	366	27	14	1	0	23	18	46	3	2	.214/.259/.262	.205	.244	-0.2	SS(103): 6.0, 3B(8): -0.6	0.0
2012	LOU	AAA	29	194	27	12	1	4	11	20	26	0	1	.237/.332/.391	.257	.259	1.7	SS(43): -3.6, 3B(3): 0.1	0.6
2012	ATL	MLB	29	186	18	6	1	0	9	17	30	1	0	.186/.269/.234	.198	.226	1.1	SS(55): 5.8	0.4
2013	GWN	AAA	30	152	11	5	0	0	12	13	32	0	0	.207/.285/.244	.204	.269	-0.3	SS(41): 2.2	-0.1
2013	ATL	MLB	30	45	7	2	0	0	2	3	11	0	0	.171/.222/.220	.159	.226	-0.1	3B(36): 0.4, 2B(9): -0.4	-0.3
2014	ATL	MLB	31	250	21	11	0	2	19	19	41	1	1	.215/.285/.294	.224	.250	-0.5	SS 2, 2B -1	0.3

A lack of opportunity is the only thing keeping Janish from a run at Mario Mendoza's career numbers. A talented defender and miserable hitter, he's the kind of player you can afford to carry only with a firm resolve to avoid playing him. That, we now know, is true even in Triple-A, where Janish had his team's second-earliest birthdate but worst slugging percentage. Now on the wrong side of 30, this will probably be his final book appearance.

Chris Johnson 3B

Born: 10/1/1984 Age: 29
Bats: R Throws: R Height: 6' 3"
Weight: 220 Breakout: 4%
Improve: 46% Collapse: 4%
Attrition: 9% MLB: 93%

Comparables:
David Freese, Wilson Betemit, Kevin Kouzmanoff

YEAR	TEAM	LVL	AGE	PA	R	2B	3B	HR	RBI	BB	SO	SB	CS	AVG/OBP/SLG	TAv	BABIP	BRR	FRAA	WARP
2011	OKL	AAA	26	94	18	7	0	4	15	10	25	1	1	.272/.372/.506	.257	.346	0.1	3B(12): -1.2	0.1
2011	HOU	MLB	26	405	32	21	3	7	42	16	97	2	2	.251/.291/.378	.246	.317	-1.1	3B(101): -10.2	-0.5
2012	ARI	MLB	27	160	12	7	2	7	35	8	40	1	0	.286/.321/.503	.282	.340	-2.6	3B(39): -2.4	0.2
2012	HOU	MLB	27	368	36	21	3	8	41	23	92	4	1	.279/.329/.428	.263	.360	-1	3B(88): -9.1, 1B(6): 0.6	0.1
2013	ATL	MLB	28	547	54	34	0	12	68	29	116	0	0	.321/.358/.457	.283	.394	2.3	3B(125): -3.8, 1B(12): 0.6	2.9
2014	ATL	MLB	29	510	52	27	2	13	60	26	124	2	1	.271/.312/.417	.266	.340	-0.6	3B -11, 1B 1	0.4

Perhaps we should call it the Chris Johnson Trade. Always known for his line-drive tendencies, Johnson posted his best offensive season in years. Beyond the flashy BABIP, there was some real progress here: He cut into his strikeout rate by a fair margin, from 25 percent to 21. Granted, Johnson's power also went down, but he never relied on home runs for his production, anyway. The Braves were wise to let him play his game without forcing him to conform to positional archetypes.

Elliot Johnson SS

Born: 3/9/1984 Age: 30
Bats: B Throws: R Height: 6' 1"
Weight: 190 Breakout: 2%
Improve: 46% Collapse: 10%
Attrition: 17% MLB: 96%

Comparables:
Charlie Neal, Damion Easley, Kazuo Matsui

YEAR	TEAM	LVL	AGE	PA	R	2B	3B	HR	RBI	BB	SO	SB	CS	AVG/OBP/SLG	TAv	BABIP	BRR	FRAA	WARP
2011	TBA	MLB	27	181	20	7	2	4	17	14	53	6	7	.194/.257/.338	.222	.260	-1.7	SS(52): 0.3, 2B(9): 0.2	-0.3
2012	TBA	MLB	28	331	32	10	2	6	33	24	84	18	6	.242/.304/.350	.253	.316	-0.1	SS(100): -2.5, 2B(13): 0.4	0.7
2013	KCA	MLB	29	173	19	2	1	2	9	8	49	14	0	.179/.218/.241	.183	.243	3	2B(57): -0.8, SS(8): -0.0	-0.6
2013	ATL	MLB	29	102	8	5	2	0	10	8	18	8	2	.261/.317/.359	.249	.320	-0.8	2B(17): 0.1, LF(7): 0.2	0.0
2014	ATL	MLB	30	270	31	9	2	4	22	19	72	16	5	.224/.282/.329	.231	.290	1.7	SS -1, 2B -0	0.3

The last player named in the Wil Myers-James Shields trade was the first to leave his new team. Atlanta plucked Johnson off waivers from the Royals in late August, and he played well enough to start at second base during the postseason. Billed as a switch-hitting utility infielder, Johnson strikes out too often for a player with limited power. Like most bipeds, he was a defensive upgrade over Dan Uggla, though he lacks the arm to play the left side of the infield and, at times, resembles Brooks Conrad. His stint in Atlanta is about as good as it's going to get.

Reed Johnson RF

Born: 12/8/1976 Age: 37
Bats: R Throws: R Height: 5' 10"
Weight: 180 Breakout: 3%
Improve: 17% Collapse: 11%
Attrition: 17% MLB: 77%

Comparables:
Lee Lacy, Hank Bauer, George Hendrick

YEAR	TEAM	LVL	AGE	PA	R	2B	3B	HR	RBI	BB	SO	SB	CS	AVG/OBP/SLG	TAv	BABIP	BRR	FRAA	WARP
2011	CHN	MLB	34	266	33	22	1	5	28	5	63	2	1	.309/.348/.467	.290	.394	0.4	RF(44): 1.4, LF(27): -0.5	1.3
2012	ATL	MLB	35	105	7	5	0	0	4	3	18	0	1	.270/.305/.320	.242	.329	-1.4	LF(19): -0.7, CF(10): -0.9	-0.2
2012	CHN	MLB	35	183	23	9	3	3	16	10	43	2	1	.302/.355/.444	.278	.390	0.3	RF(24): 0.1, CF(22): -0.0	0.8
2013	ATL	MLB	36	136	13	7	1	1	11	6	32	0	0	.244/.311/.341	.233	.322	0.2	RF(15): 0.5, CF(12): -0.2	0.0
2014	ATL	MLB	37	250	26	13	1	3	21	10	58	2	1	.254/.302/.358	.248	.320	-0.4	RF 0, CF -2	0.2

How far can a great clubhouse reputation take a player once his tangibles disappear? Johnson failed to perform when the Braves acquired him in July 2012, and failed again after re-upping on a one-year deal. Typically a passable platoon outfielder, Johnson found himself mismatched more often than he should be, though it's not as though he mashed lefties when he did face them. He missed time with Achilles tendinitis, giving him DL trips in six of the past seven seasons, and his biggest hit came against Carlos Gomez during a scrum. In spite of all the signs suggesting he's done, Johnson could get another shot because of his firm handshake.

Tommy La Stella 2B

Born: 1/31/1989 Age: 25
Bats: L Throws: R Height: 5' 11"
Weight: 185 Breakout: 1%
Improve: 6% Collapse: 18%
Attrition: 32% MLB: 44%

Comparables:
Jarrett Hoffpauir, Eric Sogard, Scott Sizemore

YEAR	TEAM	LVL	AGE	PA	R	2B	3B	HR	RBI	BB	SO	SB	CS	AVG/OBP/SLG	TAv	BABIP	BRR	FRAA	WARP
2011	ROM	A	22	270	46	13	5	9	40	26	28	2	2	.328/.401/.543	.309	.337	0.9	2B(52): -1.8	1.9
2012	LYN	A+	23	358	43	22	5	5	56	36	24	13	2	.302/.386/.460	.314	.305	-0.3	2B(75): -6.5	2.7
2013	LYN	A+	24	29	7	1	0	1	4	8	1	1	1	.550/.690/.750	.488	.556	0.9	2B(3): 0.1	0.9
2013	MIS	AA	24	324	32	21	2	4	41	37	34	7	1	.343/.422/.473	.339	.380	-1.8	2B(73): -3.2	3.1
2014	ATL	MLB	25	250	25	12	1	4	27	21	39	1	0	.269/.337/.392	.271	.300	-0.2	2B -3	0.7

If the editors allowed it, this comment would be four words long: La Stella can hit. Unfortunately, like La Stella's detractors, they require more. The little man's bat control and plate discipline are above reproach, but the rest of his game is questionable; his arm and wheels receive below-average grades, and he's a passable second baseman only because of his fundamentals and motor. Now 25, La Stella is working with a thin margin of error; once he gets the chance, he'll need to do what he always does to stick around.

Gerald Laird C

Born: 11/13/1979 Age: 34
Bats: R Throws: R Height: 6' 1"
Weight: 225 Breakout: 0%
Improve: 16% Collapse: 17%
Attrition: 23% MLB: 83%

Comparables:
Jerry Grote, Del Crandall, Clyde Kluttz

YEAR	TEAM	LVL	AGE	PA	R	2B	3B	HR	RBI	BB	SO	SB	CS	AVG/OBP/SLG	TAv	BABIP	BRR	FRAA	WARP
2011	SLN	MLB	31	108	11	7	1	1	12	9	19	1	1	.232/.302/.358	.232	.276	-2	C(31): 0.4, 1B(1): -0.0	-0.2
2012	DET	MLB	32	191	24	8	1	2	11	14	21	0	0	.282/.337/.374	.249	.309	0.5	C(56): 0.1	0.7
2013	ATL	MLB	33	141	12	8	0	1	13	14	23	1	1	.281/.367/.372	.280	.337	-1.1	C(40): 0.2	0.9
2014	ATL	MLB	34	250	23	11	1	2	20	20	44	2	1	.231/.300/.319	.232	.270	-0.3	C 1, 1B 0	0.5

Signed to replace David Ross as backup backstop, Laird seldom played, thanks to Evan Gattis' early-season breakout. When Laird was in the lineup, he outhit the league-average catcher, running his streak of seasons with above-average production to a career-high two. His caught stealing rate doubled, thanks to a more attentive pitching staff than the one he handled in Detroit, providing a lesson on the shortcomings associated with the metric's usage. Laird might fall short of perfect backup catcher status, but he gets the job done.

Ernesto Mejia 1B

Born: 12/2/1985 Age: 28
Bats: R Throws: R Height: 6' 5"
Weight: 245 Breakout: 1%
Improve: 11% Collapse: 10%
Attrition: 22% MLB: 29%

Comparables:
Joe Koshansky, Randy Ruiz, Steven Hill

YEAR	TEAM	LVL	AGE	PA	R	2B	3B	HR	RBI	BB	SO	SB	CS	AVG/OBP/SLG	TAv	BABIP	BRR	FRAA	WARP
2011	MIS	AA	25	573	82	37	1	26	99	58	156	4	3	.297/.375/.531	.315	.377	-0.6	1B(37): -1.7	0.9
2012	GWN	AAA	26	559	73	32	1	24	92	34	132	10	4	.296/.347/.502	.278	.355	-1.4	1B(95): 4.9	2.0
2013	GWN	AAA	27	551	58	35	1	28	83	48	152	8	2	.249/.323/.497	.278	.298	-5.9	1B(124): -2.4, 3B(1): -0.0	0.9
2014	ATL	MLB	28	250	30	12	0	11	35	16	75	2	1	.243/.297/.447	.269	.310	-0.2	1B -0	0.5

Mejia is a large mammal who bears an unmistakable facial resemblance to Albert Pujols. The similarities end there. Mejia has impressive raw strength, but has struggled with contact throughout his minor-league career due to his long limbs and swing. His size is a negative defensively and on the basepaths, limiting his plausible value. The Braves turned elsewhere when they needed a stand-in for the injured Freddie Freeman, which tells you all you need to know about their thoughts on Mejia's chances of succeeding in the bigs. He's a Quad-A slugger until he proves otherwise.

Tyler Pastornicky SS

Born: 12/13/1989 Age: 24
Bats: R Throws: R Height: 5' 11"
Weight: 190 Breakout: 3%
Improve: 22% Collapse: 7%
Attrition: 13% MLB: 51%

Comparables:
Steve Lombardozzi, Alexi Amarista, Erick Aybar

YEAR	TEAM	LVL	AGE	PA	R	2B	3B	HR	RBI	BB	SO	SB	CS	AVG/OBP/SLG	TAv	BABIP	BRR	FRAA	WARP
2011	MIS	AA	21	395	50	13	5	6	36	24	34	20	8	.299/.345/.414	.200	.315	-0.8	SS(28): -0.4	-0.3
2011	GWN	AAA	21	117	15	2	0	1	9	8	11	7	3	.365/.407/.413	.288	.398	-1.3	SS(10): 0.0	0.2
2012	GWN	AAA	22	167	15	15	1	1	20	11	21	3	3	.268/.317/.399	.256	.301	0.4	SS(29): -2.1, 2B(9): -1.4	0.2
2012	ATL	MLB	22	188	21	6	1	2	13	10	32	2	0	.243/.287/.325	.229	.287	1.4	SS(47): -4.5, 2B(3): 0.1	-0.2
2013	GWN	AAA	23	320	42	13	2	4	28	27	47	9	2	.292/.354/.392	.258	.335	-1.4	2B(59): -1.3, SS(7): 0.6	0.6
2013	ATL	MLB	23	33	5	1	0	0	0	1	5	0	0	.300/.323/.333	.240	.360	0.5	2B(6): -0.2, SS(1): -0.0	0.1
2014	ATL	MLB	24	250	29	10	1	3	20	15	42	8	3	.253/.299/.351	.240	.290	0.3	SS -2, 2B -2	0.1

It feels like far more than 24 months ago that Pastornicky was the Braves' Opening Day shortstop and a Rookie of the Year sleeper candidate; the 24-year-old's future is now mostly an afterthought in Atlanta. His chances of grabbing a bench spot took a shot when he tore his ACL in an August collision with a teammate, and his expected recovery by spring training doesn't guarantee him playing time. The club likes his athleticism, bat-to-ball skills, on-base ability and baseball intellect, but his weak arm prevents him from making the tough plays on the left side, limiting his utility. He's a good bet to stick around for a while on someone's bench, but it might not be Atlanta's.

Ramiro Pena SS

Born: 7/18/1985 Age: 28
Bats: B Throws: R Height: 5' 11"
Weight: 185 Breakout: 4%
Improve: 19% Collapse: 6%
Attrition: 13% MLB: 41%

Comparables:
Terry Tiffee, Alberto Gonzalez, Diory Hernandez

YEAR	TEAM	LVL	AGE	PA	R	2B	3B	HR	RBI	BB	SO	SB	CS	AVG/OBP/SLG	TAv	BABIP	BRR	FRAA	WARP
2011	SWB	AAA	25	231	27	12	1	4	18	20	35	3	2	.273/.339/.397	.264	.312	-0.4	SS(40): 0.7, 2B(5): 0.3	0.9
2011	NYA	MLB	25	46	5	0	0	1	4	2	11	0	0	.100/.159/.175	.172	.103	0.9	3B(13): 0.6, 2B(7): -0.1	0.1
2012	SWB	AAA	26	404	40	13	3	2	29	34	74	1	3	.258/.325/.328	.249	.317	-1.1	SS(69): 7.4, 2B(18): -1.9	1.4
2012	NYA	MLB	26	4	0	0	0	0	0	0	0	0	0	.250/.250/.250	.180	.250	0.2	SS(1): 0.1	0.0
2013	ATL	MLB	27	107	14	5	1	3	12	8	18	0	2	.278/.330/.443	.291	.312	-0.4	3B(32): 0.4, 2B(10): -0.4	0.8
2014	ATL	MLB	28	250	23	9	1	3	21	17	48	2	1	.242/.295/.333	.237	.290	-0.4	SS 1, 3B 1	0.5

The Braves surprised us when they signed "Derek Jeter's Glove" to a big-league deal, but Pena's bat actually produced a bit of thunder before he tore his labrum in June. The timing was a shame, as Dan Uggla's struggles would have opened the door for more playing time. Instead, Pena is left playing the what-if game with the rest of us. The smart money is on Pena failing to repeat in 2014, though anytime a player nearly triples his extra-base-hit rate it's worth noting. Should his bat return to its old ways, Pena will still help a team as a defensive sub.

Jose Peraza SS

Born: 4/30/1994 Age: 20
Bats: R Throws: R Height: 6' 0"
Weight: 165 Breakout: 1%
Improve: 5% Collapse: 0%
Attrition: 1% MLB: 5%

Comparables:
Carlos Triunfel, Tyler Pastornicky, Freddy Galvis

YEAR	TEAM	LVL	AGE	PA	R	2B	3B	HR	RBI	BB	SO	SB	CS	AVG/OBP/SLG	TAv	BABIP	BRR	FRAA	WARP
2013	ROM	A	19	504	72	18	8	1	47	34	64	64	15	.288/.341/.371	.275	.328	7	SS(104): 20.4	5.6
2014	ATL	MLB	20	250	28	8	2	2	15	10	51	15	4	.231/.263/.300	.211	.280	1.7	SS 8	0.8

With most teenage shortstops, teams simply hope for a little stick and some promise of sticking at the position long term. Peraza is a different case: He's a plus runner and thrower, with advanced instincts and motions on defense. Offensively, he shows a projectable hit tool and a mature approach. Numbers mean little at this stage in his development, but success outside of the complex leagues is nice to see, and so is the Braves' willingness to challenge him.

Jordan Schafer CF

Born: 9/4/1986 Age: 27
Bats: L Throws: L Height: 6' 1"
Weight: 190 Breakout: 7%
Improve: 40% Collapse: 5%
Attrition: 24% MLB: 85%

Comparables:
Jim Landis, Rick Miller, Shane Mack

YEAR	TEAM	LVL	AGE	PA	R	2B	3B	HR	RBI	BB	SO	SB	CS	AVG/OBP/SLG	TAv	BABIP	BRR	FRAA	WARP
2011	GWN	AAA	24	186	21	8	0	1	21	14	28	6	3	.256/.309/.323	.230	.297	0.6	CF(11): 2.8, RF(1): 0.0	0.3
2011	OKL	AAA	24	22	4	2	0	0	3	2	5	3	1	.500/.545/.600	.541	.667	0.1	CF(2): -0.1	0.3
2011	ATL	MLB	24	219	32	6	3	1	7	18	42	15	4	.240/.307/.316	.240	.301	1.4	CF(51): 0.2	0.3
2011	HOU	MLB	24	118	14	4	0	1	6	10	28	7	0	.245/.314/.311	.234	.321	2.2	CF(28): 0.5	0.3
2012	HOU	MLB	25	360	40	10	2	4	23	36	106	27	9	.211/.297/.294	.227	.304	4.2	CF(87): -3.7	-0.2
2013	GWN	AAA	26	33	0	2	0	0	2	1	4	0	0	.062/.091/.125	.056	.071	0	CF(5): 0.1	-0.5
2013	ATL	MLB	26	265	32	8	3	3	21	29	73	22	6	.247/.331/.346	.251	.348	1.4	CF(30): 0.3, RF(29): 1.5	0.6
2014	ATL	MLB	27	274	36	9	1	3	18	26	73	18	5	.225/.301/.315	.233	.300	1.7	CF 1, RF 1	0.4

Schafer rejoined the Braves a year and change after departing via the Michael Bourn trade. Although the Steve Finley comparisons from his past remained overzealous, he added value with his glove, legs and career-best .265/.355/.380 line against right-handed pitchers. Schafer's overall numbers took a hit due to utter incompetence against same-sided pitching, but he showed enough to stick around as a fourth or fifth outfielder. That's more than anyone would have said a year ago.

Andrelton Simmons SS

Born: 9/4/1989 Age: 24
Bats: R Throws: R Height: 6' 2"
Weight: 170 Breakout: 4%
Improve: 51% Collapse: 8%
Attrition: 15% MLB: 94%

Comparables:
Aaron Hill, Dustin Pedroia, Asdrubal Cabrera

YEAR	TEAM	LVL	AGE	PA	R	2B	3B	HR	RBI	BB	SO	SB	CS	AVG/OBP/SLG	TAv	BABIP	BRR	FRAA	WARP
2011	LYN	A+	21	570	69	35	6	1	52	29	43	26	18	.311/.351/.408	.273	.334	-0.6	SS(110): 13.1	4.5
2012	MIS	AA	22	203	29	9	2	3	21	20	20	10	2	.293/.372/.420	.290	.314	-0.7	SS(44): 6.8	2.2
2012	ATL	MLB	22	182	17	8	2	3	19	12	21	1	0	.289/.335/.416	.265	.310	1.9	SS(49): 7.5	1.8
2013	ATL	MLB	23	658	76	27	6	17	59	40	55	6	5	.248/.296/.396	.257	.247	-1	SS(156): 26.5	5.4
2014	ATL	MLB	24	548	64	24	4	11	51	31	60	10	5	.264/.308/.393	.261	.280	-0.3	SS 22	4.7

Hands down the best defensive shortstop in baseball, Simmons has an incredible arm, great footwork, soft hands and an uncanny feel for pre-pitch adjustments. It's a package that makes him playable regardless of what he does at the plate. Better for the Braves, Simmons is not an automatic out. At 23, he had baseball's fourth-lowest strikeout rate, and he upped his power production enough to outslug the league-average shortstop. Nobody is confusing Simmons' offensive game for Troy Tulowitzki's, but mere offensive adequacy makes him one of the best players in baseball.

Joe Terdoslavich 1B

Born: 9/9/1988 Age: 25
Bats: B Throws: R Height: 6' 0"
Weight: 200 Breakout: 3%
Improve: 13% Collapse: 9%
Attrition: 21% MLB: 33%

Comparables:
Brett Carroll, Josh Kroeger, Bronson Sardinha

YEAR	TEAM	LVL	AGE	PA	R	2B	3B	HR	RBI	BB	SO	SB	CS	AVG/OBP/SLG	TAv	BABIP	BRR	FRAA	WARP
2011	LYN	A+	22	536	72	52	2	20	82	41	107	2	0	.286/.341/.526	.293	.324	-0.7	1B(90): 1.8, 3B(2): -0.2	2.5
2012	MIS	AA	23	333	43	24	5	5	51	27	62	4	0	.315/.372/.480	.317	.377	-1.2	1B(68): 3.6, 3B(6): -0.4	2.7
2012	GWN	AAA	23	215	19	4	0	4	20	19	50	3	0	.180/.252/.263	.190	.220	2.3	3B(50): -2.4	-1.0
2013	GWN	AAA	24	351	48	24	1	18	58	23	65	3	6	.318/.359/.567	.308	.344	-0.4	RF(66): -6.6, 1B(8): -0.9	1.8
2013	ATL	MLB	24	92	11	4	0	0	4	12	24	1	0	.215/.315/.266	.230	.304	0.3	LF(13): 0.2, 1B(6): 0.1	0.0
2014	ATL	MLB	25	250	26	13	1	8	30	16	61	1	1	.247/.295/.408	.256	.300	-0.4	1B 0, RF -2	0.1

Terdoslavich lived through another summer of defensive homelessness, as the Braves canceled his third-base experiment and tasked him with learning the other corner positions instead. The truth is he's not a talented defender no matter where he plays. To complicate matters further, he struggled to make contact during his big-league stay. If Terdoslavich adjusts to top-level pitching he has a chance to become a useful bat off the bench. Anything less and he's a Quad-A player in the making.

Dan Uggla 2B

Born: 3/11/1980 Age: 34
Bats: R Throws: R Height: 5' 11"
Weight: 205 Breakout: 0%
Improve: 35% Collapse: 7%
Attrition: 14% MLB: 90%

Comparables:
Bobby Grich, Jeff Kent, Ron Cey

YEAR	TEAM	LVL	AGE	PA	R	2B	3B	HR	RBI	BB	SO	SB	CS	AVG/OBP/SLG	TAv	BABIP	BRR	FRAA	WARP
2011	ATL	MLB	31	672	88	22	1	36	82	62	156	1	3	.233/.311/.453	.276	.253	1.9	2B(159): -3.6	2.9
2012	ATL	MLB	32	630	86	29	0	19	78	94	168	4	3	.220/.348/.384	.272	.283	0.5	2B(152): 14.6	4.0
2013	ATL	MLB	33	537	60	10	3	22	55	77	171	2	0	.179/.309/.362	.252	.225	-3.8	2B(133): -12.9	-0.9
2014	ATL	MLB	34	524	63	18	0	22	69	63	137	2	1	.223/.323/.408	.272	.270	-1	2B -3	2.0

Uggla's contract has two years and $26 million remaining. That doesn't sound too bad, except Uggla bottomed out in 2013. He struck out a career-high 32 percent of the time and his isolated power finished below .200 for the second season in a row. It's tough for any player to add value when he's fanning that often; it's downright impossible for a poor defender without elite power. He hit .099/.287/.129 after the trade deadline, and the Braves were disillusioned enough to leave him off the postseason roster. Only PECOTA (with an admirably long memory) is still optimistic about those next two years.

B.J. Upton CF

Born: 8/21/1984 Age: 29
Bats: R Throws: R Height: 6' 3"
Weight: 185 Breakout: 2%
Improve: 45% Collapse: 2%
Attrition: 12% MLB: 93%

Comparables:
Dwayne Hosey, Lloyd Moseby, Chris Young

YEAR	TEAM	LVL	AGE	PA	R	2B	3B	HR	RBI	BB	SO	SB	CS	AVG/OBP/SLG	TAv	BABIP	BRR	FRAA	WARP
2011	TBA	MLB	26	640	82	27	4	23	81	71	161	36	12	.243/.331/.429	.272	.298	2.3	CF(151): 1.5	3.2
2012	TBA	MLB	27	633	79	29	3	28	78	45	169	31	6	.246/.298/.454	.274	.294	2.9	CF(142): -9.7	2.2
2013	ATL	MLB	28	446	30	14	0	9	26	44	151	12	5	.184/.268/.289	.212	.266	-1.8	CF(118): -10.8	-2.1
2014	ATL	MLB	29	460	57	21	2	13	50	44	128	23	7	.230/.305/.385	.256	.300	2	CF -4	1.0

Is it too early to start an Uggla-like countdown for Upton's deal? (Just four more years.) The Braves signed Upton expecting an athletic center fielder with a strong blend of power and speed. What they received in Year One was a center fielder with severe contact issues, limited pop and a career-worst success rate on stolen bases. The Braves tweaked and tweaked some more but nothing took; after appearing with a head-cocked grin on the cover of Sports Illustrated's playoffs preview issue, Upton didn't start a game in October.

Justin Upton RF

Born: 8/25/1987 Age: 26
Bats: R Throws: R Height: 6' 2"
Weight: 205 Breakout: 3%
Improve: 49% Collapse: 2%
Attrition: 7% MLB: 100%

Comparables:
Barry Bonds, Kal Daniels, Joe Charboneau

YEAR	TEAM	LVL	AGE	PA	R	2B	3B	HR	RBI	BB	SO	SB	CS	AVG/OBP/SLG	TAv	BABIP	BRR	FRAA	WARP
2011	ARI	MLB	23	674	105	39	5	31	88	59	126	21	9	.289/.369/.529	.316	.319	2.3	RF(159): 4.1	5.6
2012	ARI	MLB	24	628	107	24	4	17	67	63	121	18	8	.280/.355/.430	.279	.327	0.5	RF(149): 10.6	3.6
2013	ATL	MLB	25	643	94	27	2	27	70	75	161	8	1	.263/.354/.464	.293	.321	2.9	LF(108): 4.5, RF(54): -0.9	3.9
2014	ATL	MLB	26	601	79	26	2	23	80	60	137	14	5	.271/.350/.458	.295	.320	0.2	RF 3, LF 2	3.9

From a broad perspective, Upton had a fine season. Those who experienced his brilliant April, in which he homered 12 times, were left wanting, though. Upton went from a certain MVP candidate through a month to not making the All-Star Game; that tells you everything about how poorly he played from May through July. An eight-homer August helped his numbers regain respectability, but the Braves can probably sympathize with the Diamondbacks, who found Upton too streaky for their liking.

PITCHERS

Luis Avilan

Born: 7/19/1989 Age: 24
Bats: L Throws: L Height: 6' 2" Weight: 195
Breakout: 37% Improve: 55% Collapse: 24%
Attrition: 40% MLB: 67%

Comparables:
Davis Romero, Craig Hansen, Wes Littleton

YEAR	TEAM	LVL	AGE	W	L	SV	G	GS	IP	H	HR	BB	SO	BB9	SO9	GB%	BABIP	WHIP	ERA	FIP	FRA	WARP
2011	MIS	AA	21	4	8	1	36	13	106¹	113	10	36	78	3.0	6.6	40%	.340	1.40	4.57	4.30	4.44	0.3
2012	MIS	AA	22	3	6	1	16	12	61¹	50	7	31	55	4.5	8.1	50%	.263	1.32	3.23	4.40	5.67	-0.2
2012	ATL	MLB	22	1	0	0	31	0	36	27	1	10	33	2.5	8.2	46%	.280	1.03	2.00	2.58	2.82	0.7
2013	ATL	MLB	23	5	0	0	75	0	65	40	1	22	38	3.0	5.3	58%	.204	0.95	1.52	3.25	3.66	0.5
2014	ATL	MLB	24	3	2	0	41	4	60	53	6	24	45	3.5	6.7	46%	.281	1.28	3.85	4.32	4.18	0.3

Avilan's first full season in the majors exceeded expectations. The well-built southpaw's stuff—a mid-90s sinker and mid-70s curveball—was not only effective against all batters, but also difficult to elevate, as he finished the season having allowed only one home run. He swapped out a changeup for increased reliance on that sinker, which he now throws four of every five pitches. There are some sustainability concerns here: in exchange for all those groundballs, his strikeout and walk ratios went in the wrong direction, and no matter what he throws he'll likely yield more than one homer per season. Still, he'll be helpful even in non-LOOGY relief.

Luis Ayala

Born: 1/12/1978 Age: 36
Bats: R Throws: R Height: 6' 2" Weight: 175
Breakout: 30% Improve: 56% Collapse: 34%
Attrition: 9% MLB: 55%

Comparables:
Masa Kobayashi, D.J. Carrasco, John Bale

YEAR	TEAM	LVL	AGE	W	L	SV	G	GS	IP	H	HR	BB	SO	BB9	SO9	GB%	BABIP	WHIP	ERA	FIP	FRA	WARP
2011	NYA	MLB	33	2	2	0	52	0	56	51	5	20	39	3.2	6.3	52%	.282	1.27	2.09	4.22	5.27	0.1
2012	BAL	MLB	34	5	5	1	66	0	75	81	7	14	51	1.7	6.1	50%	.300	1.27	2.64	3.62	3.94	1.1
2013	BAL	MLB	35	1	0	0	2	0	2	4	1	0	2	0.0	9.0	50%	.429	2.00	9.00	7.58	12.03	-0.2
2013	ATL	MLB	35	1	1	0	37	0	31	34	1	13	20	3.8	5.8	60%	.333	1.52	2.90	3.41	3.30	0.4
2014	ATL	MLB	36	2	1	1	42	0	46²	46	4	14	34	2.7	6.6	49%	.305	1.27	4.02	3.89	4.37	0.1

Ayala continued his late-career resurgence with the Braves, his seventh team in six years. He lost three months last year due to what was called anxiety disorder, as he was dealing with high blood pressure. Once Ayala returned he appeared no worse for the wear: He generated a career-best groundball rate thanks to a high-80s sinker that now plays a large role in his repertoire, along with a mid-80s cutter and general craftiness. Expect him to find work in middle relief until his arm gives out, again.

Brandon Beachy

Born: 9/3/1986 Age: 27
Bats: R Throws: R Height: 6' 3" Weight: 215
Breakout: 24% Improve: 63% Collapse: 21%
Attrition: 12% MLB: 89%

Comparables:
Rich Hill, Edinson Volquez, J.P. Howell

YEAR	TEAM	LVL	AGE	W	L	SV	G	GS	IP	H	HR	BB	SO	BB9	SO9	GB%	BABIP	WHIP	ERA	FIP	FRA	WARP
2011	ATL	MLB	24	7	3	0	25	25	141²	125	16	46	169	2.9	10.7	34%	.309	1.21	3.68	3.16	3.60	2.3
2012	ATL	MLB	25	5	5	0	13	13	81	49	6	29	68	3.2	7.6	41%	.203	0.96	2.00	3.53	4.13	0.9
2013	GWN	AAA	26	1	4	0	7	7	30	23	3	18	26	5.4	7.8	39%	.244	1.37	3.00	4.57	5.39	0.1
2013	ATL	MLB	26	2	1	0	5	5	30	27	5	4	23	1.2	6.9	43%	.256	1.03	4.50	4.05	4.57	0.1
2014	ATL	MLB	27	3	3	0	17	8	62²	52	6	19	60	2.8	8.6	40%	.287	1.14	3.17	3.52	3.44	1.0

Beachy missed the first half while recovering from Tommy John surgery. He returned in late July, started five games, then returned to the disabled list with additional elbow issues. The bad news is Beachy needed another elbow operation. The good is that it was a relatively minor procedure, done to clean up loose bodies that were causing irritation. Beachy should be ready when spring rolls around, and perhaps now he can answer whether he's a middle-of-the-rotation starter or something more.

Mauricio Cabrera

Born: 9/22/1993 Age: 20
Bats: R Throws: R Height: 6' 2" Weight: 180
Breakout: 0% Improve: 0% Collapse: 0%
Attrition: 0% MLB: 0%

Comparables:
Chaz Roe, Brett Marshall, Jeurys Familia

YEAR	TEAM	LVL	AGE	W	L	SV	G	GS	IP	H	HR	BB	SO	BB9	SO9	GB%	BABIP	WHIP	ERA	FIP	FRA	WARP
2013	ROM	A	19	3	8	0	24	24	131¹	118	3	71	107	4.9	7.3	51%	.298	1.44	4.18	3.91	5.01	0.2
2014	ATL	MLB	20	5	8	0	20	20	103	108	12	60	62	5.3	5.5	46%	.304	1.63	5.53	5.47	6.01	-1.4

Fish swim, birds fly and the Braves develop pitching; each is a means for survival in this cruel world. That's why nobody's betting against the 20-year-old Cabrera's development, even knowing what we do about pitcher attrition rates. A high-six-figures international signee in 2010, Cabrera provides his instructors with enviable raw material: a potential plus-plus fastball, plus changeup and adequate breaking ball—along with better-than-anticipated feel for the craft. The production is not as good as desired, but Cabrera's upside is too great to ignore.

David Carpenter

Born: 7/15/1985 Age: 28
Bats: R Throws: R Height: 6' 2" Weight: 215
Breakout: 30% Improve: 51% Collapse: 38%
Attrition: 33% MLB: 60%

Comparables:
Matt Hensley, Jack Taschner, Rocky Cherry

YEAR	TEAM	LVL	AGE	W	L	SV	G	GS	IP	H	HR	BB	SO	BB9	SO9	GB%	BABIP	WHIP	ERA	FIP	FRA	WARP
2011	CCH	AA	25	0	1	5	14	0	14	14	4	3	17	1.9	10.9	36%	.143	1.21	4.50	5.73	3.46	0.2
2011	OKL	AAA	25	0	0	9	19	0	19	15	0	6	21	2.8	9.9	27%	.364	1.11	0.00	2.52	1.00	0.2
2011	HOU	MLB	25	1	3	1	34	0	27²	28	3	13	29	4.2	9.4	45%	.320	1.48	2.93	4.15	4.51	0.1
2012	LVG	AAA	26	0	1	1	16	0	17²	15	1	7	19	3.6	9.7	43%	.292	1.25	3.57	3.61	4.23	0.3
2012	TOR	MLB	26	0	0	0	3	0	2²	8	1	2	4	6.8	13.5	54%	.583	3.75	30.38	8.30	6.92	-0.1
2012	HOU	MLB	26	0	2	0	30	0	29²	43	4	14	27	4.2	8.2	41%	.419	1.92	6.07	4.59	4.59	0.1
2013	GWN	AAA	27	1	2	0	6	0	15¹	17	1	4	11	2.3	6.5	55%	.348	1.37	3.52	3.60	5.43	0.0
2013	ATL	MLB	27	4	1	0	56	0	65²	45	5	20	74	2.7	10.1	39%	.261	0.99	1.78	2.81	3.38	0.9
2014	ATL	MLB	28	3	1	0	60	0	66¹	59	7	25	65	3.3	8.9	41%	.307	1.26	3.68	3.88	4.01	0.4

There are two ways to consider Carpenter's trip through organized baseball. You could focus on the negative: Four teams gave up on him before he joined Atlanta. Or the positive: Four teams valued him before he joined Atlanta. Whatever the case, Carpenter is finally making good. Like most converted position players, the former catcher could always bring the heat, but he showed a surprising touch of craft by keeping his walk rate in check and flashing a developing changeup. If the control holds, he could be a set-up man.

Scott Downs

Born: 3/17/1976 Age: 38
Bats: L Throws: L Height: 6' 2" Weight: 220
Breakout: 28% Improve: 50% Collapse: 30%
Attrition: 11% MLB: 76%

Comparables:
Salomon Torres, Larry Andersen, Francisco Cordero

YEAR	TEAM	LVL	AGE	W	L	SV	G	GS	IP	H	HR	BB	SO	BB9	SO9	GB%	BABIP	WHIP	ERA	FIP	FRA	WARP
2011	ANA	MLB	35	6	3	1	60	0	53²	39	3	15	35	2.5	5.9	64%	.218	1.01	1.34	3.32	4.25	0.4
2012	ANA	MLB	36	1	1	9	57	0	45²	43	3	17	32	3.4	6.3	61%	.282	1.31	3.15	3.62	4.51	0.1
2013	ATL	MLB	37	2	1	0	25	0	14	19	0	8	15	5.1	9.6	68%	.432	1.93	3.86	2.59	2.17	0.4
2013	ANA	MLB	37	2	3	0	43	0	29¹	26	1	11	22	3.4	6.8	63%	.291	1.26	1.84	3.35	3.47	0.3
2014	ATL	MLB	38	3	1	3	51	0	41²	37	3	13	34	2.8	7.3	59%	.292	1.20	3.29	3.49	3.58	0.5

The Braves snagged Downs from the Angels around the deadline for Cory Rasmus. It was a great fit on paper, but one that didn't translate to results. After holding lefties to a sub-.500 OPS as an Angel, Downs allowed a .367/.457/.433 line to his prey as a Brave, and was left off the postseason roster as a result. Such is the danger of importing LOOGYs for inherently limited samples. Proven left-handed relievers can work forever if they want, and Downs signed with the White Sox, delaying for another year the decision to put his cleats away and spend more time being injured by his family.

Gavin Floyd

Born: 1/27/1983 Age: 31
Bats: R Throws: R Height: 6' 6" Weight: 235
Breakout: 16% Improve: 42% Collapse: 25%
Attrition: 14% MLB: 94%

Comparables:
Kevin Millwood, Chris Carpenter, John Lackey

YEAR	TEAM	LVL	AGE	W	L	SV	G	GS	IP	H	HR	BB	SO	BB9	SO9	GB%	BABIP	WHIP	ERA	FIP	FRA	WARP
2011	CHA	MLB	28	12	13	0	31	30	193²	180	22	45	151	2.1	7.0	46%	.278	1.16	4.37	3.85	4.47	2.1
2012	CHA	MLB	29	12	11	0	29	29	168	166	22	63	144	3.4	7.7	48%	.299	1.36	4.29	4.41	5.00	1.3
2013	CHA	MLB	30	0	4	0	5	5	24¹	27	4	12	25	4.4	9.2	51%	.343	1.60	5.18	4.64	4.84	0.1
2014	ATL	MLB	31	3	3	0	8	8	49¹	44	4	13	43	2.4	7.8	45%	.301	1.16	3.39	3.40	3.69	0.6

After nearly five full seasons of consistent health and inconsistent results, Floyd lost parts of 2012 to a sore elbow, got off to a rocky start last season, broke down in late April and underwent Tommy John surgery in May. There's never a good time to get hurt, but the timing was especially bad for Floyd as he was in his walk year and pitching for his next contract. Give him credit: He reportedly turned down two years and $20 million from Baltimore to sign a one-year, $4 million contract with Atlanta in December. He's unlikely to return before May, but if he comes back strong he'll be very expensive next winter, and future generations of Floyds will be ever thankful.

Cory Gearrin

Born: 4/14/1986 Age: 28
Bats: R Throws: R Height: 6' 3" Weight: 200
Breakout: 29% Improve: 49% Collapse: 37%
Attrition: 50% MLB: 54%

Comparables:
Josh Kinney, Chris Hatcher, Matt Smith

YEAR	TEAM	LVL	AGE	W	L	SV	G	GS	IP	H	HR	BB	SO	BB9	SO9	GB%	BABIP	WHIP	ERA	FIP	FRA	WARP
2011	GWN	AAA	25	4	1	4	35	0	50	42	0	20	60	3.6	10.8	59%	.314	1.24	1.80	2.22	2.30	0.6
2011	ATL	MLB	25	1	1	0	18	0	18¹	17	0	12	25	5.9	12.3	61%	.370	1.58	7.85	2.56	3.26	0.2
2012	GWN	AAA	26	3	3	9	39	0	54²	43	0	22	66	3.6	10.9	66%	.314	1.19	2.30	2.06	3.68	0.9
2012	ATL	MLB	26	0	0	0	22	0	20	17	1	5	20	2.2	9.0	58%	.308	1.10	1.80	2.84	3.91	0.2
2013	ATL	MLB	27	2	1	1	37	0	31	30	2	16	23	4.6	6.7	53%	.326	1.48	3.77	4.31	4.93	-0.1
2014	ATL	MLB	28	2	1	1	31	0	38¹	32	3	15	37	3.4	8.8	54%	.299	1.21	3.40	3.61	3.70	0.4

When the Braves let Peter Moylan walk last offseason, the expectation was that Gearrin would take over as the groundball-getting right-handed specialist. But Gearrin fought control problems early, and—the appeal of groundball specialists being to end rallies, not egg them on—was demoted in early July. He never did pitch for Gwinnett, and eventually hit the DL with arm fatigue and shoulder tendonitis. Gearrin will get another chance to establish himself as the new Moylan—albeit without the Australian flavor—in 2014.

J.R. Graham

Born: 1/14/1990 Age: 24
Bats: R Throws: R Height: 5' 10" Weight: 195
Breakout: 47% Improve: 68% Collapse: 25%
Attrition: 64% MLB: 24%

Comparables:
Cesar Valdez, Steven Shell, David Phelps

YEAR	TEAM	LVL	AGE	W	L	SV	G	GS	IP	H	HR	BB	SO	BB9	SO9	GB%	BABIP	WHIP	ERA	FIP	FRA	WARP
2012	LYN	A+	22	9	1	0	17	17	102²	88	6	17	68	1.5	6.0	59%	.269	1.02	2.63	3.38	4.72	0.5
2012	MIS	AA	22	3	1	0	9	9	45¹	35	2	17	42	3.4	8.3	56%	.277	1.15	3.18	3.12	3.95	0.6
2013	MIS	AA	23	1	3	0	8	8	35²	39	0	10	28	2.5	7.1	67%	.358	1.37	4.04	2.18	3.14	0.7
2014	ATL	MLB	24	2	3	0	10	7	47²	48	5	17	32	3.1	6.0	54%	.302	1.35	4.34	4.39	4.72	-0.0

Graham, who entered the season as the Braves' no. 2 prospect, is short. That means his durability must testify under oath and with full immunity in order to be trusted, and even then it's iffy. He shows good athleticism, a plus-plus fastball and a plus slider that he can add to or subtract from. But a strained shoulder ended his season in May, raising more doubts, and his ability to endure a big-league workload will remain questioned until he has a few 200-inning seasons on his record.

David Hale

Born: 9/27/1987 Age: 26
Bats: R Throws: R Height: 6' 2" Weight: 205
Breakout: 49% Improve: 85% Collapse: 15%
Attrition: 74% MLB: 17%

Comparables:
Ryan Mattheus, Bryan Morris, Chris Carpenter

YEAR	TEAM	LVL	AGE	W	L	SV	G	GS	IP	H	HR	BB	SO	BB9	SO9	GB%	BABIP	WHIP	ERA	FIP	FRA	WARP
2011	LYN	A+	23	4	6	0	28	13	101	106	9	30	86	2.7	7.7	51%	.313	1.35	4.10	3.87	5.26	0.0
2012	MIS	AA	24	8	4	0	27	27	145²	121	11	67	124	4.1	7.7	47%	.273	1.29	3.77	4.01	5.31	-0.4
2013	GWN	AAA	25	6	9	0	22	20	114²	123	8	36	77	2.8	6.0	53%	.314	1.39	3.22	3.89	4.91	0.3
2013	ATL	MLB	25	1	0	0	2	2	11	11	0	1	14	0.8	11.5	60%	.367	1.09	0.82	0.75	0.97	0.6
2014	ATL	MLB	26	5	6	0	27	15	113²	115	13	46	79	3.6	6.3	49%	.304	1.42	4.75	4.69	5.16	-0.6

It's not often a Princeton graduate reaches the majors, and Hale's two starts make him the school's first pitching alumnus to debut since Ross Ohlendorf in 2007. In addition to a three-pitch mix that includes a low-90s fastball, Hale features drop-and-drive mechanics and a closed delivery. He's got a chance to develop into a back-of-the-rotation starter, but the Braves might have tipped their hand on his future when they carried him as a reliever in the postseason.

Jason Hursh

Born: 10/2/1991 Age: 22
Bats: R Throws: R Height: 6' 3" Weight: 190
Breakout: 100% Improve: 100% Collapse: 0%
Attrition: 0% MLB: 1%

Comparables:
Esmil Rogers, Jared Hughes, Jordan Smith

YEAR	TEAM	LVL	AGE	W	L	SV	G	GS	IP	H	HR	BB	SO	BB9	SO9	GB%	BABIP	WHIP	ERA	FIP	FRA	WARP
2013	ROM	A	21	1	1	0	9	9	27	20	1	10	15	3.3	5.0	63%	.235	1.11	0.67	4.07	5.04	0.3
2014	ATL	MLB	22	2	3	0	9	9	35	39	5	17	18	4.4	4.6	49%	.306	1.60	5.58	5.67	6.06	-0.4

For the fifth time in six drafts, the Braves selected a pitcher with their top pick. Hursh attended Oklahoma State, where he impressed Gerald Turner—the same scout who unearthed Andrelton Simmons and Evan Gattis—with a quality fastball and strike-throwing tendencies. Though his mechanics and secondary offerings remain unrefined, there is enough polish to anticipate a quick big-league arrival, similar to those of Mike Minor and Alex Wood. Astute observers who notice the scar on Hursh's elbow should rest easy: The Braves believe his arm is fresher than the normal draftee due to the time off. They also think he could become a middle-of-the-rotation starter.

Juan Jaime
Born: 8/2/1987 Age: 26
Bats: R Throws: R Height: 6' 2" Weight: 235
Breakout: 44% Improve: 53% Collapse: 44%
Attrition: 76% MLB: 27%

Comparables:
Kevin Whelan, Robert Coello, John Gaub

YEAR	TEAM	LVL	AGE	W	L	SV	G	GS	IP	H	HR	BB	SO	BB9	SO9	GB%	BABIP	WHIP	ERA	FIP	FRA	WARP
2012	LYN	A+	24	1	3	18	42	0	51¹	31	4	33	73	5.8	12.8	36%	.257	1.25	3.16	3.72	4.07	0.7
2013	MIS	AA	25	2	5	0	35	0	42	30	1	28	70	6.0	15.0	31%	.345	1.38	4.07	2.25	2.28	1.2
2014	ATL	MLB	26	2	1	2	34	0	40²	32	4	23	51	5.1	11.2	38%	.307	1.34	3.74	3.82	4.07	0.2

Jaime is a 26-year-old career middle-reliever with plus-plus velocity and large strikeout and walk rates. Add in his extreme flyball ways and infielders can retire to the dugout during his half innings. Sounds typical, except for one little thing: He's never pitched above Double-A, and it feels as though Jaime has been in development for as long as Jay Electronica's album. The questions about both are less about whether we'll ever experience the finished product, and more about whether we'll be satisfied with it after the wait. Probably not.

Craig Kimbrel
Born: 5/28/1988 Age: 26
Bats: R Throws: R Height: 5' 11" Weight: 205
Breakout: 29% Improve: 57% Collapse: 21%
Attrition: 8% MLB: 91%

Comparables:
Sean Doolittle, Jonathan Broxton, Francisco Rodriguez

YEAR	TEAM	LVL	AGE	W	L	SV	G	GS	IP	H	HR	BB	SO	BB9	SO9	GB%	BABIP	WHIP	ERA	FIP	FRA	WARP
2011	ATL	MLB	23	4	3	46	79	0	77	48	3	32	127	3.7	14.8	45%	.315	1.04	2.10	1.49	2.18	2.1
2012	ATL	MLB	24	3	1	42	63	0	62²	27	3	14	116	2.0	16.7	49%	.250	0.65	1.01	0.82	1.41	2.2
2013	ATL	MLB	25	4	3	50	68	0	67	39	4	20	98	2.7	13.2	47%	.263	0.88	1.21	1.90	2.06	1.9
2014	ATL	MLB	26	3	2	47	58	0	59¹	32	3	24	94	3.6	14.2	48%	.287	0.94	1.58	1.90	1.72	2.1

Picking one stat to define Kimbrel's season is tough to do, but here's our best try: He was more likely to strike out the side (10 times) than allow multiple hits in an inning (seven times). While his whiff rate dropped a touch and he found the strike zone a shade less often, he also had a four-month stretch in which he allowed one run. The best closer in baseball is just that dominant, so dominant that the only thing that can stop him from owning the league for the next decade is injury. For now, just sit back and enjoy as hitters flail at the upper-90s heat and devastating curve, and as Kimbrel puts up stats that even Mariano Rivera never did.

Paul Maholm
Born: 6/25/1982 Age: 32
Bats: L Throws: L Height: 6' 2" Weight: 220
Breakout: 12% Improve: 46% Collapse: 32%
Attrition: 14% MLB: 89%

Comparables:
Joe Saunders, Kevin Correia, Jason Johnson

YEAR	TEAM	LVL	AGE	W	L	SV	G	GS	IP	H	HR	BB	SO	BB9	SO9	GB%	BABIP	WHIP	ERA	FIP	FRA	WARP
2011	PIT	MLB	29	6	14	0	26	26	162¹	160	11	50	97	2.8	5.4	50%	.293	1.29	3.66	3.75	4.43	0.8
2012	ATL	MLB	30	4	5	0	11	11	68²	63	8	19	59	2.5	7.7	53%	.285	1.19	3.54	3.81	4.44	0.4
2012	CHN	MLB	30	9	6	0	21	20	120¹	115	12	34	81	2.5	6.1	50%	.290	1.24	3.74	4.18	4.79	0.4
2013	ATL	MLB	31	10	11	0	26	26	153	169	17	47	105	2.8	6.2	53%	.315	1.41	4.41	4.21	4.71	0.2
2014	ATL	MLB	32	8	9	0	24	24	142²	144	13	41	98	2.6	6.1	52%	.309	1.29	4.23	4.01	4.60	0.1

Maholm appeared en route to another solid season, with three scoreless starts to begin the year and decent numbers across the board in the first half. But then the second half came and brought with it elbow and wrist issues. Maholm started just seven times after the break, and underwhelmed by allowing 47 hits in 37 innings, an unprofitable prelude to free agency. He's a capable no. 4 starter when healthy, the kind who gives quality starts in half his appearances.

Cody Martin
Born: 9/4/1989 Age: 24
Bats: R Throws: R Height: 6' 2" Weight: 225
Breakout: 37% Improve: 67% Collapse: 25%
Attrition: 55% MLB: 50%

Comparables:
Boof Bonser, Matt Maloney, Brad Mills

YEAR	TEAM	LVL	AGE	W	L	SV	G	GS	IP	H	HR	BB	SO	BB9	SO9	GB%	BABIP	WHIP	ERA	FIP	FRA	WARP
2011	ROM	A	21	1	0	6	14	0	24¹	18	2	4	35	1.5	12.9	37%	.295	0.90	1.48	2.34	3.65	0.4
2012	LYN	A+	22	12	7	0	22	19	107¹	93	7	34	123	2.9	10.3	40%	.314	1.18	2.93	3.09	3.50	2.3
2013	MIS	AA	23	3	3	0	16	11	67	63	3	27	71	3.6	9.5	42%	.333	1.34	2.82	2.58	2.84	1.6
2013	GWN	AAA	23	3	4	1	13	11	69²	59	6	31	66	4.0	8.5	42%	.283	1.29	3.49	3.85	4.69	0.4
2014	ATL	MLB	24	6	6	1	29	17	115	104	12	46	111	3.6	8.7	40%	.305	1.30	3.91	3.91	4.25	0.6

Back in the 1980s, the Braves had a minor-league pitcher named Chuck Martin. Cody is Chuck's son, though his prospects extend beyond the minors. Don't be fooled by the command-and-control righty's ace-like stats so far; he projects as a back-of-the-rotation starter. His armory includes a solid-average fastball, a plus cutter and an average curveball and changeup. Unsurprisingly given his bloodlines, Martin has a good feel for pitching. He also has experience as a closer. Expect him to earn father-son bragging rights in 2014, with his big-league role to be determined.

Kris Medlen

Born: 10/7/1985 Age: 28
Bats: B Throws: R Height: 5' 10" Weight: 190
Breakout: 22% Improve: 53% Collapse: 23%
Attrition: 3% MLB: 94%

Comparables:
James Shields, Josh Johnson, Jered Weaver

YEAR	TEAM	LVL	AGE	W	L	SV	G	GS	IP	H	HR	BB	SO	BB9	SO9	GB%	BABIP	WHIP	ERA	FIP	FRA	WARP
2011	ATL	MLB	25	0	0	0	2	0	2¹	1	0	0	2	0.0	7.7	33%	.167	0.43	0.00	1.28	2.65	0.0
2012	GWN	AAA	26	0	2	0	3	3	13¹	15	2	6	12	4.1	8.1	35%	.342	1.58	4.72	4.88	5.76	-0.1
2012	ATL	MLB	26	10	1	1	50	12	138	103	6	23	120	1.5	7.8	54%	.261	0.91	1.57	2.46	3.30	2.5
2013	ATL	MLB	27	15	12	0	32	31	197	194	18	47	157	2.1	7.2	45%	.306	1.22	3.11	3.45	4.10	1.7
2014	ATL	MLB	28	10	7	0	42	22	166¹	144	15	37	145	2.0	7.8	46%	.295	1.09	3.02	3.34	3.29	2.8

Okay, so Medlen didn't repeat his gaudy numbers from 2012. What he did do was put together a season that shows he can handle the physicality that comes with taking the mound every fifth day in the majors. Medlen's numbers weren't too bad, anyway, and he repeated one aspect of 2012 by dominating down the stretch, with a 1.37 ERA and beefed up peripherals in his final nine starts. He's equipped with more pitching know-how than stuff, but it comes in an athletic package. Medlen is not Greg Maddux—nobody is—but he has now established that he's a legitimate starter in a playoff rotation.

Mike Minor

Born: 12/26/1987 Age: 26
Bats: R Throws: L Height: 6' 4" Weight: 205
Breakout: 29% Improve: 58% Collapse: 18%
Attrition: 15% MLB: 96%

Comparables:
Tommy Hanson, Ian Snell, Jered Weaver

YEAR	TEAM	LVL	AGE	W	L	SV	G	GS	IP	H	HR	BB	SO	BB9	SO9	GB%	BABIP	WHIP	ERA	FIP	FRA	WARP
2011	GWN	AAA	23	4	5	0	16	16	100²	93	12	27	99	2.4	8.9	39%	.244	1.19	3.13	3.68	5.80	-0.2
2011	ATL	MLB	23	5	3	0	15	15	82²	93	7	30	77	3.3	8.4	37%	.364	1.49	4.14	3.36	3.80	1.2
2012	ATL	MLB	24	11	10	0	30	30	179¹	151	26	56	145	2.8	7.3	37%	.254	1.15	4.12	4.42	5.07	0.5
2013	ATL	MLB	25	13	9	0	32	32	204²	177	22	46	181	2.0	8.0	35%	.275	1.09	3.21	3.34	4.07	1.8
2014	ATL	MLB	26	10	9	0	30	30	168	147	19	47	156	2.5	8.3	39%	.292	1.15	3.42	3.70	3.71	2.1

Once thought of as an overdraft, Minor turned in his best big-league season to date in 2013. He improved on his strikeout and walk rates, and his home-run rate remained manageable despite extreme fly-ball tendencies. Minor was the lone Braves pitcher to top 200 innings, and while he's not good enough to earn the ace distinction—and there's not really an extra gear here—he is a durable above-average starter who would be welcome in any team's rotation. Expect more of the same in 2014.

Aaron Northcraft

Born: 5/28/1990 Age: 24
Bats: R Throws: R Height: 6' 4" Weight: 230
Breakout: 64% Improve: 74% Collapse: 12%
Attrition: 47% MLB: 25%

Comparables:
Ricky Romero, Mitchell Boggs, Drake Britton

YEAR	TEAM	LVL	AGE	W	L	SV	G	GS	IP	H	HR	BB	SO	BB9	SO9	GB%	BABIP	WHIP	ERA	FIP	FRA	WARP
2011	ROM	A	21	7	8	0	23	19	113¹	108	8	41	88	3.3	7.0	53%	.274	1.31	3.34	4.30	5.67	0.4
2012	LYN	A+	22	10	11	0	27	27	151²	143	4	53	160	3.1	9.5	62%	.328	1.29	3.98	2.82	4.45	1.2
2013	MIS	AA	23	8	8	0	26	26	137	124	7	51	121	3.4	7.9	57%	.303	1.28	3.42	3.23	4.81	-0.3
2014	ATL	MLB	24	6	8	0	24	20	118¹	119	13	53	88	4.0	6.7	53%	.308	1.46	4.83	4.70	5.25	-0.7

The problem with Northcraft is that nobody's sure whether he's destined to be a starter or a reliever. His body is large and looks like it belongs to a starter, but his delivery includes a lowered arm slot that makes him prone to platoon abuse. The indecision extends to his arsenal: Northcraft throws a low-90s sinker and a decent slider, but his changeup is still fringy. If he remains in the rotation then he's looking at a back-end ceiling. With a move to the bullpen he could become a useful middle-leverage reliever at least.

Lucas Sims

Born: 5/10/1994 Age: 20
Bats: R Throws: R Height: 6' 2" Weight: 195
Breakout: 50% Improve: 92% Collapse: 8%
Attrition: 64% MLB: 8%

Comparables:
Chris Tillman, Zach Braddock, Trevor Cahill

YEAR	TEAM	LVL	AGE	W	L	SV	G	GS	IP	H	HR	BB	SO	BB9	SO9	GB%	BABIP	WHIP	ERA	FIP	FRA	WARP
2013	ROM	A	19	12	4	0	28	18	116²	83	3	46	134	3.5	10.3	43%	.284	1.11	2.62	3.09	3.47	2.0
2014	ATL	MLB	20	4	5	0	21	14	87²	81	9	44	78	4.5	8.0	42%	.303	1.41	4.47	4.46	4.85	-0.1

A few drafts ago the Braves changed their first-round focus from Georgia preps to collegiate arms, with a concentration on southpaws. They returned to their roots in 2012 by picking Sims, an athletic right-hander with polish and upside, and a graduate of a local high school. Sims has a plus fastball, which can move into the mid-90s with life, and the best curveball in the system. He needs to improve his command and his changeup, but he could move more quickly than the usual teenage pitcher. In a perfect world, Sims develops into a no. 2 starter.

Julio Teheran

Born: 1/27/1991 Age: 23
Bats: R Throws: R Height: 6' 2" Weight: 175
Breakout: 33% Improve: 72% Collapse: 13%
Attrition: 41% MLB: 73%

Comparables:
Carlos Villanueva, Scott Mathieson, Ryan Feierabend

YEAR	TEAM	LVL	AGE	W	L	SV	G	GS	IP	H	HR	BB	SO	BB9	SO9	GB%	BABIP	WHIP	ERA	FIP	FRA	WARP
2011	GWN	AAA	20	15	3	0	25	24	144²	123	5	48	122	3.0	7.6	39%	.268	1.18	2.55	3.10	4.42	0.5
2011	ATL	MLB	20	1	1	0	5	3	19²	21	4	8	10	3.7	4.6	27%	.267	1.47	5.03	5.84	6.10	-0.3
2012	GWN	AAA	21	7	9	0	26	26	131	146	18	43	97	3.0	6.7	36%	.316	1.44	5.08	4.79	5.50	0.2
2012	ATL	MLB	21	0	0	0	2	1	6¹	5	0	1	5	1.4	7.1	12%	.312	0.95	5.68	2.03	2.45	0.2
2013	ATL	MLB	22	14	8	0	30	30	185²	173	22	45	170	2.2	8.2	39%	.295	1.17	3.20	3.67	4.04	1.9
2014	ATL	MLB	23	9	9	0	28	28	149²	139	19	46	127	2.8	7.6	39%	.294	1.24	3.98	4.28	4.33	0.8

Teheran's first full season in the majors was a success. Some struggles early on were forgiven and forgotten by the time he nearly no-hit the Pirates in early June; from there it was smooth sailing as he started 19 more games and tallied 85 more strikeouts than walks. Although Teheran couldn't find the grip on his changeup, he did make strides with his slider, and the pitch became his go-to secondary offering. Earlier visions of a potential ace were overzealous, but Teheran is a smart, athletic pitcher who can be a no. 2 starter for a long time to come.

Anthony Varvaro

Born: 10/31/1984 Age: 29
Bats: R Throws: R Height: 6' 0" Weight: 195
Breakout: 24% Improve: 36% Collapse: 53%
Attrition: 52% MLB: 47%

Comparables:
Mitch Stetter, Rocky Cherry, Mark Malaska

YEAR	TEAM	LVL	AGE	W	L	SV	G	GS	IP	H	HR	BB	SO	BB9	SO9	GB%	BABIP	WHIP	ERA	FIP	FRA	WARP
2011	GWN	AAA	26	2	8	1	38	0	59	37	3	35	69	5.3	10.5	45%	.359	1.22	2.90	3.44	2.95	0.4
2011	ATL	MLB	26	0	2	0	18	0	24	15	3	11	23	4.1	8.6	35%	.203	1.08	2.62	4.08	4.62	0.0
2012	GWN	AAA	27	0	2	6	33	1	44¹	39	1	24	47	4.9	9.5	41%	.311	1.42	2.23	3.02	2.74	1.2
2012	ATL	MLB	27	1	1	0	12	0	16²	16	2	9	21	4.9	11.3	42%	.341	1.50	5.40	4.16	3.88	0.2
2013	ATL	MLB	28	3	1	1	62	0	73¹	68	3	25	43	3.1	5.3	48%	.277	1.27	2.82	3.44	3.53	0.7
2014	ATL	MLB	29	3	1	1	50	0	63	53	5	30	59	4.3	8.4	43%	.290	1.32	3.65	3.89	3.96	0.5

For years, it's been assumed Varvaro would crack a big-league bullpen one day. One day, as it turned out, was 2013. The New York native stayed healthy and made the most of his opportunity, flinging mid-90s fastballs, groundball-inducing curves and the occasional changeup at hitters en route to an unheralded successful season. Varvaro's stuff didn't result in a ton of strikeouts, but as long as he continues to keep his fly balls in the park—particularly against lefties, who slugged .281 against him—he's a keeper.

Jordan Walden

Born: 11/16/1987 Age: 26
Bats: R Throws: R Height: 6' 5" Weight: 235
Breakout: 46% Improve: 64% Collapse: 16%
Attrition: 19% MLB: 76%

Comparables:
Ramon Ramirez, David Aardsma, Renyel Pinto

YEAR	TEAM	LVL	AGE	W	L	SV	G	GS	IP	H	HR	BB	SO	BB9	SO9	GB%	BABIP	WHIP	ERA	FIP	FRA	WARP
2011	ANA	MLB	23	5	5	32	62	0	60¹	49	3	26	67	3.9	10.0	47%	.295	1.24	2.98	2.83	3.14	1.0
2012	ANA	MLB	24	3	2	1	45	0	39	35	3	18	48	4.2	11.1	40%	.311	1.36	3.46	2.97	3.60	0.6
2013	ATL	MLB	25	4	3	1	50	0	47	39	4	14	54	2.7	10.3	33%	.292	1.13	3.45	2.79	2.51	1.1
2014	ATL	MLB	26	2	1	1	43	0	42	36	4	16	46	3.5	9.8	48%	.312	1.25	3.45	3.44	3.75	0.4

During his time with the Angels, Walden developed a reputation for inconsistency. In his first season with the Braves, there was a consistency: He pitched well when he was healthy, and not well when he wasn't. Now that he sits mid-90s with his fastball instead of 98, Walden has his walks under control, along with a changeup that was years in development. But he missed time early in the season with shoulder inflammation and late in the year with a strained groin. The latter injury caused him to struggle down the stretch, and marked the point where Braves fans stopped trusting their non-Kimbrel bullpen options. If healthy, who knows, perhaps Walden is on the mound in Game Four instead of David Carpenter.

Alex Wood

Born: 1/12/1991 Age: 23
Bats: R Throws: L Height: 6' 4" Weight: 215
Breakout: 30% Improve: 75% Collapse: 13%
Attrition: 28% MLB: 89%

Comparables:
Matt Garza, Michael Pineda, Derek Holland

YEAR	TEAM	LVL	AGE	W	L	SV	G	GS	IP	H	HR	BB	SO	BB9	SO9	GB%	BABIP	WHIP	ERA	FIP	FRA	WARP
2012	ROM	A	21	4	3	0	13	13	52²	39	1	14	52	2.4	8.9	62%	.277	1.01	2.22	2.76	3.92	1.2
2013	MIS	AA	22	4	2	0	10	10	57	41	1	15	57	2.4	9.0	54%	.267	0.98	1.26	1.98	2.79	1.3
2013	ATL	MLB	22	3	3	0	31	11	77²	76	3	27	77	3.1	8.9	49%	.348	1.33	3.13	2.62	3.06	1.5
2014	ATL	MLB	23	6	5	0	32	17	106	94	8	34	99	2.9	8.4	50%	.304	1.20	3.40	3.33	3.70	1.3

Wood soaked up his first taste of big-league life last season, and in the process enlivened the arguments surrounding his future role. One camp believes he's qualified to start—with his goodish numbers 11 times through the rotation as proof—while the other camp points to his unorthodox mechanics as unfit for the workload of triple-digit pitch counts. The Braves didn't commit either way, though they have enough starting pitching depth to move Wood to the 'pen without regretting it. If he repeats his 2.08 ERA and 4.6 K/BB ratio as a reliever, they really won't regret it.

LINEOUTS

HITTERS

PLAYER	TEAM	LVL	AGE	PA	R	2B	3B	HR	RBI	BB	SO	SB-CS	AVG/OBP/SLG	TAv	BABIP	BRR	FRAA	WARP
LF J. Constanza	GWN	AAA	29	373	39	7	3	0	17	29	49	21-9	.276/.332/.314	.242	.322	-0.8	LF(72): 6.8, CF(7): 0.2	0.5
	ATL	MLB	29	31	2	0	0	0	3	0	5	0-3	.258/.258/.258	.178	.308	-1.4	LF(9): 0.2, CF(2): -0.2	-0.3
LF J. Elander	ROM	A	22	310	47	22	3	11	61	29	61	6-2	.318/.381/.536	.329	.373	-1.4	LF(65): -4.0	2.3
	LYN	A+	22	252	28	12	0	4	32	26	48	3-1	.262/.345/.371	.258	.316	-1.1	LF(51): -5.5	-0.4
2B P. Gosselin	MIS	AA	24	241	27	10	1	1	23	12	31	5-1	.243/.291/.312	.244	.275	0.4	2B(35): 6.4, LF(16): -1.1	0.5
	GWN	AAA	24	228	17	4	1	2	15	12	38	1-0	.266/.308/.324	.234	.315	1.3	2B(46): 5.1, LF(4): 0.2	0.6
	ATL	MLB	24	7	2	0	0	0	0	1	2	0-0	.333/.429/.333	.258	.500	0.2	2B(3): -0.0	0.0
SS T. Greene	GWN	AAA	29	48	8	4	0	1	4	3	7	0-0	.333/.417/.500	.323	.382	-0.7	SS(7): 0.1, 2B(5): -0.1	0.3
	CHR	AAA	29	226	26	10	2	3	27	15	66	10-3	.240/.295/.351	.235	.338	1.3	RF(18): -2.6, LF(14): -0.9	-0.5
	CHA	MLB	29	57	7	2	1	1	3	3	19	0-0	.222/.263/.352	.222	.324	-0.5	2B(19): -1.0	-0.2
LF R. Hefflinger	LYN	A+	23	307	44	17	1	21	52	22	71	1-1	.286/.339/.579	.297	.309	-2.5	LF(51): -8.0	0.9
	MIS	AA	23	207	19	8	1	6	25	15	64	2-1	.170/.227/.319	.201	.213	0.2	LF(45): -1.7	-1.1
3B K. Kubitza	LYN	A+	22	527	75	28	6	12	57	80	132	8-16	.260/.380/.434	.283	.344	-2.9	3B(125): -1.2	2.8
C S. Lerud	LEH	AAA	28	219	20	8	0	3	21	35	50	1-0	.217/.353/.311	.249	.283	-1.1	C(59): -1.2	0.8
	PHI	MLB	28	5	0	0	0	0	0	0	4	0-0	.000/.000/.000	.015	.000	0	C(5): -0.0	-0.1
CF M. Lipka	LYN	A+	21	571	76	29	7	5	40	29	107	37-14	.251/.305/.362	.233	.307	9.3	CF(128): -14.1	-0.4
3B E. Salcedo	MIS	AA	21	518	52	22	2	12	55	44	111	20-10	.239/.304/.372	.260	.287	-0.4	3B(115): 6.0	2.4

Panamanian teenager **Johan Camargo** is a big-time sleeper. When he's awake he plays the left side of the infield and hits for a good average. ⊘ **Jose Constanza** spent a third season in the majors only because he's really fast, which makes it hard for him to slow down and appreciate the scenery. ⊘ Catcher-turned-outfielder **Josh Elander** can hit, but his limited defensive profile leaves him out in left field on the diamond, and out in left field as a prospect. ⊘ Always hailed as a smart player, **Philip Gosselin** reached the majors when the Braves needed an emergency infielder, but he's unlikely to become more than an organizational player. ⊘ **Tyler Greene** couldn't find playing time with the Astros or White Sox, so what chance did he have with the Braves? ⊘ **Robby Hefflinger** might have the best raw power in the system, though its application is hampered by severe contact issues. ⊘ Former third-rounder **Kyle Kubitza**—complete with solid power and a strong arm—improved his numbers while moving up a level, but the strikeouts remain a concern. ⊘ **Steven Lerud** is organizational filler with very little upside, though his ability to work counts and draw walks is admirable. ⊘ Speedy center fielder **Matt Lipka** announced his breakout party with a loud May, but nobody attended after a stinky second half. ⊘ Venezuelan teenager **Victor Reyes** batted .321 over his first two pro seasons, and he should add power with physical maturation. ⊘ **Edward Salcedo** passed the Double-A test with a C-minus: his performance improved but underwhelmed. Time and tools remain on his side.

PITCHERS

PLAYER	TEAM	LVL	AGE	W	L	SV	IP	H	HR	BB	SO	BB9	SO9	GB%	BABIP	WHIP	ERA	FIP	FRA	WARP
F. Garcia	NOR	AAA	36	8	3	0	82^1	73	10	15	61	1.6	6.7	44%	.262	1.07	2.84	3.85	4.53	0.4
	BAL	MLB	36	3	5	0	53	60	16	12	26	2.0	4.4	42%	.259	1.36	5.77	6.75	7.33	-0.9
	ATL	MLB	36	1	2	0	27^1	23	2	5	20	1.6	6.6	49%	.274	1.02	1.65	3.06	3.03	0.5
M. Lamm	MIS	AA	25	3	3	10	45^2	39	2	21	48	4.1	9.5	38%	.314	1.31	2.56	2.83	3.38	0.4
	GWN	AAA	25	3	3	0	22^1	22	0	15	22	6.0	8.9	39%	.333	1.66	3.63	3.52	3.76	0.4
K. Loe	GWN	AAA	31	4	4	2	76^1	76	3	17	37	2.0	4.4	59%	.281	1.22	3.07	3.49	5.14	0.1
	SEA	MLB	31	1	1	0	6^2	11	6	1	3	1.4	4.1	37%	.238	1.80	10.80	14.33	12.86	-0.5
	CHN	MLB	31	0	0	0	8^1	12	3	4	4	4.3	4.3	61%	.321	1.92	5.40	8.18	7.52	-0.3
	ATL	MLB	31	1	2	0	11^2	17	2	5	8	3.9	6.2	51%	.359	1.89	6.17	5.16	5.26	0.0
C. Martinez	ATL	MLB	31	0	0	0	2^1	5	0	0	0	0.0	0.0	55%	.455	2.14	7.71	3.02	3.41	0.0
E. O'Flaherty	ATL	MLB	28	3	0	0	18	12	2	5	11	2.5	5.5	59%	.192	0.94	2.50	4.08	4.63	0.0
D. Rodriguez	GWN	AAA	28	3	3	0	53	49	3	38	55	6.5	9.3	43%	.326	1.64	5.77	4.19	5.22	0.3
I. Thomas	MIS	AA	26	7	8	1	104^1	72	7	37	123	3.2	10.6	43%	.253	1.04	2.76	2.52	4.33	1.1
J. Venters	ATL	MLB	27	5	4	0	58^2	61	6	28	69	4.3	10.6	64%	.359	1.52	3.22	3.80	3.81	0.5

Sweaty **Freddy Garcia** is no longer a passable big-league starter, which means he's got five or six more seasons in him, tops. ⊘ Former sixth-rounder **Mark Lamm** has a good fastball-slider combination and pitches from a lower release point, which means ROOGY potential. ⊘ **Kameron Loe** conducted an experiment to find out which teams really believe extreme home-run rates regress to the mean. ⊘ So much for **Cristhian Martinez**'s rubber arm; he went under the knife for shoulder surgery in July. The early prognosis had him back by spring, team TBA. ⊘ **Luis Merejo** is a short teenage southpaw with a good feel for the craft and a potential plus fastball. ⊘ Lefty specialist extraordinaire **Eric O'Flaherty** underwent Tommy John surgery in May. ⊘ Atlanta found **Daniel Rodriguez** in Mexico and sent him and his sinker-curveball combination straight to Triple-A, to the delight of International League hitters. ⊘ The Braves signed **Ian Thomas** from the independent York Revolution on the strength of his changeup, deceptive delivery and opposition to taxation without representation. ⊘ **Andry Ubiera** is a young, small power pitcher who works with a lively low-to-mid-90s fastball and flashes a plus curveball. He could become somebody. ⊘ Top-tier set-up man **Jonny Venters** tried rest and rehab but ended up on the surgeon's table in May, undergoing his second elbow surgery.

MANAGER: FREDI GONZALEZ

YEAR	TEAM	W-L	Pythag +/-	Avg PC	100+ P	120+ P	QS	BQS	REL	REL w Zero R	IBB	PH	PH Avg	PH HR	SB2	CS2	SB3	CS3	SAC Att	SAC %	POS SAC	Squeeze	Swing	In Play
2011	ATL	89-73	1	95.9	56	0	86	3	510	435	73	257	.175	8	71	40	6	1	115	65.2%	34	2	289	86
2012	ATL	94-68	1	93.3	53	1	79	3	460	404	40	249	.158	4	83	25	17	5	85	62.4%	18	3	288	93
2013	ATL	96-66	1	95.3	48	1	102	5	466	422	35	213	.247	6	60	28	4	2	99	58.6%	21	3	241	76

More than any other manager, Fredi Gonzalez's teams feature the Three True Outcomes: home runs, walks and strikeouts. In his three-year tenure in Atlanta, Braves batters have drawn the most walks in the NL, belted the fourth most homers and have the second highest strikeout total. Under Gonzalez, the Braves have averaged 1,311 strikeouts a year. Prior to his arrival, the franchise record for whiffs in a season was 1,169.

It was a similar story in his days with the Marlins. In the three full seasons he ran the team, they were first in the National League in Ks, third in homers ... and way back in 11th in walks. But five out of six high rankings ain't bad. Gonzalez's Marlins averaged 1,310 strikeouts a season—practically identical to what his Braves have done. Without Gonzalez, they have just one season ever with over 1,250 Ks.

Gonzalez loves his set lineups. His main eight starters gobbled up 70 percent of Atlanta's plate appearances in 2013. That's good for fifth in the league, which is impressive given that Brian McCann and Jason Heyward both missed extensive time. Fifth place is the lowest Gonzalez has ever ranked in percentage of PA taken by his starters.

The Braves' bullpen had an overall ERA of 2.45, the best the franchise has had since the Deadball Era. It's the best by any team since the 2003 Dodgers (maybe the best bullpen ever) also had a 2.45 mark.

Baltimore Orioles

By Ben Lindbergh

No franchise has had a more confusing start to the two-thousand-teens than the Orioles. We aren't used to seeing a long-time loser get good all of a sudden; in most cases, a team on the upswing has a transition season when the core begins to come together and the record approaches respectability, giving us time to slow our steady stream of snark. By the following spring, we're mentally prepared for the breakthrough, when the rebuilding effort fully flowers and the team becomes a perennial contender (at least until aging and entropy restart the cycle).

On the surface, at least, Baltimore went about this backwards. Without much warning, the Orioles improved from 69 wins and last place in 2011 to 93 wins and a wild card berth in 2012. And just when we'd come to terms with how wrong we'd been to dismiss them, they slipped to 85 wins and third place in 2013.

Because the O's haven't followed a typical trajectory over the past three years, we can't extrapolate along the same path to pinpoint their position in 2014 and beyond. In other words, it's hard to fit Baltimore into a box. Are they a young team on the rise, destined to return to their 2012 heights with the current core? Are they already past their prime, having squandered their one chance at a pennant? Or are they stuck somewhere in the middle, equipped with enough talent to stay in the picture, but not enough to win without every ball bouncing their way?

The first step toward answering that question is stripping out luck. The 2012 Orioles had a historic 29-9 record in one-run games, which allowed them to outplay their run differential. Sabermetrically inclined analysts attributed that one-run success largely to luck, while others gave credit to Buck Showalter and a tenacious bullpen. However it happened, it wasn't repeatable: In 2013, with the same manager and most of the same

relievers, the Orioles went 20-31 in one-run games. The regression the statheads predicted all year in 2012 finally came to pass.

Look only at the Orioles' predicted record based on runs scored and runs allowed (Figure 1), though, and it's clear that that one-run regression wasn't indicative of a decline in their overall performance.

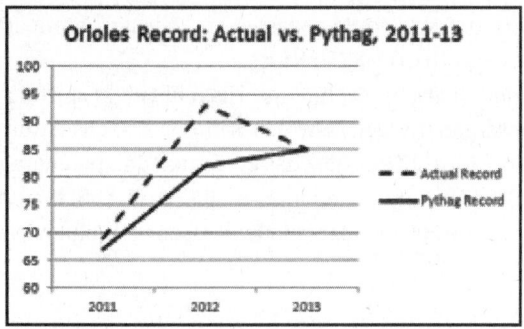

Both the actual and the Pythagorean records agreed: t team. But unlike the line representing their actual record, the Pythagorean line makes 85 wins look like progress—another small step forward instead of a big step back. (Encouragingly, the team's average attendance—up over 4,500 fans per game from 2011 to 2012, and another 2,500 last season—merchandise sales, and TV ratings have exhibited a similar trend.)

So how has Baltimore been taking those steps? It's tempting to attribute the gains to Dan Duquette's most salient characteristic as a general manager: constant tinkering. Duquette treats his Triple-A team as an extension of the active roster and castoffs from other organizations as Orioles-in-waiting. Over the past two seasons, Baltimore has led baseball in contracts selected, the technical term for calling up a minor-league player who isn't already on the 40-man roster. (See Figure 2.)

ORIOLES PROSPECTUS
2013 W-L: 85-77, 3rd in AL East

Pythag	.523	13th	DER	.709	6th
RS/G	4.60	5th	B-Age	27.7	8th
RA/G	4.38	22nd	P-Age	27.7	10th
TAv	.272	7th	Salary	$92.2	16th
BRR	4.3	10th	M$/MW	$2.16	10th
TAv-P	.272	24th	DL Days	1060	19th
FIP	4.35	29th	$ on DL	18%	19th

	Runs	HR/RH	HR/LH	Runs/RH	Runs/LH
Three-Year Park Factors	99	98	108	101	106

Top Hitter WARP	6.97 (Chris Davis)
Top Pitcher WARP	1.52 (Wei-Yin Chen)
Top Prospect	Kevin Gausman

Most Contracts Selected, 2012–13

Team	Contracts Selected	Wins
Orioles	39	178
Mets	37	148
Blue Jays	36	147
Astros	34	106
Phillies	34	154
Padres	32	152
Cubs	31	127
Marlins	30	131
Angels	28	167
Twins	28	132

One thing about that table stands out immediately: this is not a strong group of teams. The nine non-Orioles clubs in that top 10 have averaged 70 wins across those two seasons. The five teams with the fewest contracts selected—the Dodgers, Rays, Tigers, Nationals and Athletics—combined for eight playoff appearances.

The correlation between contracts selected and team wins over the same span was -0.49—the more contracts a team selected, the fewer games it was likely to win. That's not because bringing up players from the minors is, in itself, a bad thing. But more replacements means the team had more vacancies, and more vacancies means it had more injuries and/or underperforming players. *That* leads to fewer wins. The Orioles are employing by choice a strategy that bad teams employ by necessity.

So is Baltimore's contract selection spree responsible for their success? Not really. There have been instances in which Duquette's willingness to dip into the system have helped the Orioles: his aggressive call-up of Manny Machado and the contributions of Miguel Gonzalez and Steve Johnson in 2012, the return of Steve Pearce last season. He's also salvaged value from players who have run out of rope with their previous organizations. Since signing with the Orioles as a free agent after his release from the Pittsburgh Pirates, Nate McLouth has produced 3.2 WARP. Gonzalez has totaled 2.4 since his December 2011 release from the Red Sox. Jason Hammel and Matt Lindstrom gave the O's a good return for Jeremy Guthrie. And when Wilson Betemit and Nolan Reimold spent much of last season on the disabled list, Duquette cobbled together decent DH production out of the likes of Pearce and Danny Valencia.

But not all of Duquette's low-budget pickups have worked so well. The Orioles got very little out of Rule 5 find Ryan Flaherty and waiver addition Alexi Casilla during Brian Roberts' absence last season; Freddy Garcia crashed and burned; Nick Johnson, Endy Chavez and Lew Ford had little left in 2012. Duquette has managed to avoid the excessive impatience that led to self-inflicted mistakes during his Boston days, but when you make as many moves as he does, you're bound to get burned by a few. All told, the contributions of

players whose contracts were selected totals -1.8 WARP. The alternative might have been worse—the team has lost 2,324 games to injury over the past two seasons, sixth-most in the majors, so they've had some holes to fill—and maybe the knowledge that no one on the roster was nailed down had some motivational benefits. But it's not really the moves on the margins that have transformed the sad-sack O's into a competitive team.

Although it wasn't easy to tell at the time, Duquette inherited a productive core from his predecessor, Andy MacPhail, when he was hired in November 2011. Over three quarters of the Orioles' WARP in their surprise 2012 season came from players who predated Duquette. And the percentage of WARP produced by pre-Duquette players only went up in the new GM's second season. (Figures 3 and 4.)

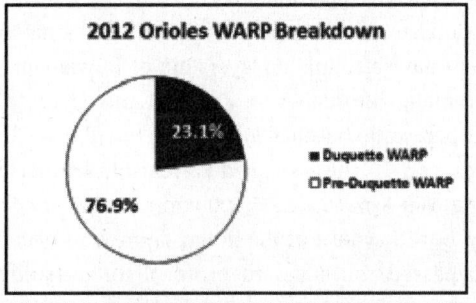

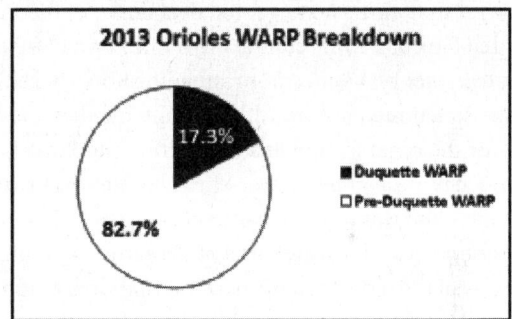

It was MacPhail who acquired Chris Davis, Tommy Hunter, Adam Jones, Chris Tillman and J.J. Hardy in three lopsided trades from 2008 to 2011, costing the Orioles only three-plus seasons of Koji Uehara and Erik Bedard (neither of whom were of much use to them at the time). Those five players combined for nearly 12 WARP in 2013. Manny Machado, Dylan Bundy and Jonathan Schoop were drafted under MacPhail, Matt Wieters under Mike Flanagan, Nick Markakis under Flanagan and Jim Beattie, and Jim Johnson under Syd Thrift. None of this recounting is intended to denigrate the job done by Duquette; it's not as if any GM can (or should) completely remake his roster right out of the gate. But the seeds of the successful Orioles had already sprouted on that decidedly unsuccessful 2011 team, which some of the executives who declined (or even declined to interview for) the GM job might not have realized.

Duquette's task, then, has been to curate and supplement the talent left to him by previous regimes. He's done so in part by making a valiant attempt to expand the Orioles' reach on the international market, an area in which they lagged far behind before he took over. Less than a month after his own introduction, he brought on veteran scouting executive Fred Ferreira to serve as international scouting director, then installed former Brewers and Red Sox colleague Ray Poitevint as executive director of international baseball. The hiring of former major leaguer Nelson Norman (who had previously worked for Duquette in Montreal and Boston) as director of Dominican baseball operations in March 2013 completed a restructuring of the international staff. Under Ferreira's guidance, the Orioles have become more active in traditional international markets while also attempting to become trendsetters in untapped areas. The O's were one of four organizations with two Dominican Summer League teams in 2013, and last November, Ferreira signed 16-year-old right-hander Olelky Peralta to a $325,000 bonus, believed to be the largest the organization has ever dispensed to a Dominican amateur.

The Orioles have also inked players out of Taiwan, Japan, Korea, Guatemala, Mexico, New Zealand and Cuba, and scouted in other exotic baseball locales like Brazil and Costa Rica. In February 2012, the O's signed 17-year-old Korean left-hander Seong-Min Kim to a $575,000 contract that shocked the industry, both because of the dollar figure and because Baltimore bypassed the standard protocol for pursuing a Korean player in their haste to get the deal done. In the fallout from that faux pas, Kim's contract was voided and Orioles scouts were (in theory) banned from attending Korea Baseball Association-sanctioned events. Although the incident was a black eye for the organization, it signaled that the Birds had become much more aggressive. Wei-Yin Chen, Henry Urrutia, and Gonzalez (who was actually spotted in Mexico by Ferreira before Duquette hired him) are some of the earliest and most visible results of the organization's new international emphasis, but they won't be the biggest or the last. Duquette's search for unmined markets reinforces his reputation as a forward thinker, as does his December 2011 formation of a modest analytics department led by Sarah Gelles.

Duquette will need all the creativity and scouting/analytical insight his new staff can supply to address the most obvious obstacle in the Orioles' way: a lack of impact pitching. Baltimore failed to find quality starting pitching in MacPhail's four full seasons at the helm. While Duquette has done a better job with his bullpen, his starters have struggled. (See Figure 5.) The trades he's made for experienced arms like Hammel, Scott Feldman and Bud Norris have helped, but building an effective top-to-bottom rotation out of arms other organizations deemed expendable is a tall order. The Orioles need homegrown help.

Orioles Pitching Woes, 2008–11 and 2012–13

Category	2008–11	2012–13
Starter ERA (Rank)	5.23 (30th)	4.49 (24th)
Starter FIP	5.08 (30th)	4.57 (27th)
Reliever ERA	4.50 (29th)	3.25 (8th)
Reliever FIP	4.47 (30th)	3.71 (15th)

Chris Tillman's success in the second half of last season was a start; even so, the O's entered the offseason with Tillman, Gonzalez, Chen and Norris ticketed for a rotation without an ace or even a solid no. 2 starter. It's too soon to judge the Duquette regime's performance in the draft, although picking the right amateurs wasn't his strength with the Red Sox. The Orioles need someone from the group of Bundy, Kevin Gausman and Hunter Harvey (each of whom is a Top 50 prospect in Jason Parks' rankings; the Royals are the only other team that can boast that kind of minor-league pitching talent) to mature quickly and take over the top spot.

Alternatively, Duquette could try to do something dramatic. One tactic we haven't seen him try with the Orioles (as we go to press) is make the big move. There's precedent for major signings in his previous stops. In *Mind Game*, our 2005 book on how the Red Sox won the '04 World Series, we wrote, "Duquette's success was predicated on buttressing his core talent with low-cost acquisitions, whether through trades, waiver claims, or inventive signings." Sounds familiar, so far. But then we went on: "Due to his success with low-cost/high-performance players, Duquette often had money left over to grab the big fish." There's the missing element.

The O's shelled out a long-term extension for Adam Jones in 2012, but Duquette hasn't gone outside the organization to reel in a player on the level of Pedro Martinez, Manny Ramirez or even Johnny Damon, all of whom he acquired as Boston's GM. The Orioles haven't been among baseball's biggest spenders for years, but back in 1998, they led the league with a cumulative player price tag over $70 million. If owner Peter Angelos has it in him to pony up the cash again in the short term—in addition to the extensions it would take to keep the team's other stars in uniform after 2015—the O's could use their payroll to keep pace with their AL East Rivals and build on their firm, 85-win foundation. Otherwise, Duquette and the Orioles will have to prove they've put their drafting difficulties behind them—or just keep pulling productive players out of hats.

Ben Lindbergh is the editor-in-chief of Baseball Prospectus, *a contributor to* Grantland *and MLB Network's Clubhouse Confidential, and the co-host of Effectively Wild, the BP daily podcast.*

HITTERS

Wilson Betemit 3B
Born: 11/2/1981 Age: 32
Bats: B Throws: R Height: 6' 2"
Weight: 220 Breakout: 5%
Improve: 25% Collapse: 18%
Attrition: 16% MLB: 76%

Comparables:
Laynce Nix, Craig Wilson, Matthew Lecroy

YEAR	TEAM	LVL	AGE	PA	R	2B	3B	HR	RBI	BB	SO	SB	CS	AVG/OBP/SLG	TAv	BABIP	BRR	FRAA	WARP
2011	DET	MLB	29	133	11	7	3	5	19	11	47	1	0	.292/.346/.525	.306	.429	-0.9	3B(40): -0.2	0.9
2011	KCA	MLB	29	226	29	15	1	3	27	20	58	3	1	.281/.341/.409	.255	.372	-0.3	3B(47): 0.9, 1B(3): 0.2	0.6
2012	BAL	MLB	30	376	41	19	0	12	40	31	103	0	1	.261/.322/.422	.262	.336	0	3B(75): -4.4, 1B(15): -0.8	0.5
2013	BOW	AA	31	21	1	0	0	0	3	4	4	0	0	.353/.476/.353	.282	.462	-0.9		0.0
2013	BAL	MLB	31	10	0	0	0	0	0	0	3	0	0	.000/.000/.000	.032	.000	0	1B(1): -0.0	-0.3
2014	BAL	MLB	32	250	26	12	1	7	29	22	70	1	0	.243/.311/.397	.258	.320	-0.4	3B -1, 1B 0	0.3

A knee injury cost Betemit the overwhelming bulk of his 2013 season. The 32-year-old designated hitter nominally switch-hits, but the best way to draw value from his bat is to never ever ever let him face a lefty—his career split against lefties is downright pitcherrific. Betemit's positional flexibility is the same as yours: He can stand around and muse about the great philosophical debates of our day anywhere on the field. Catching and throwing the baseball is an entirely different question.

Alexi Casilla 2B
Born: 7/20/1984 Age: 29
Bats: B Throws: R Height: 5' 9"
Weight: 170 Breakout: 4%
Improve: 47% Collapse: 6%
Attrition: 10% MLB: 98%

Comparables:
Chris Getz, Steve Sax, Andy Stankiewicz

YEAR	TEAM	LVL	AGE	PA	R	2B	3B	HR	RBI	BB	SO	SB	CS	AVG/OBP/SLG	TAv	BABIP	BRR	FRAA	WARP
2011	MIN	MLB	26	365	52	21	4	2	21	28	45	15	4	.260/.322/.368	.252	.294	2.1	2B(56): 4.7, SS(36): 1.4	2.0
2012	MIN	MLB	27	326	33	17	2	1	30	16	52	21	1	.241/.282/.321	.218	.283	0.6	2B(96): -1.7, 3B(4): 0.1	-0.3
2013	BAL	MLB	28	125	15	4	1	1	10	9	20	9	2	.214/.268/.295	.230	.247	-1.3	2B(51): -0.6, SS(2): 0.0	-0.2
2014	BAL	MLB	29	250	27	11	2	3	20	18	38	13	2	.243/.302/.341	.239	.280	1.7	2B 0, SS 0	0.6

Casilla has seen a rapid decline in production from his 2010-11 peak as a league-average hitter. There was a time when he appeared to be an everyday second baseman in the making, but his last two seasons at the dish would have been difficult to tolerate even if he were playing shortstop. There is always room *somewhere* for a utility infielder, but for Casilla, "somewhere" might be the International or Pacific Coast League. Still, no matter what happens from here on out, nobody can ever take away Casilla's black ink—he led the league in sacrifices in 2008 despite playing fewer than 100 games.

Chris Davis 1B
Born: 3/17/1986 Age: 28
Bats: L Throws: R Height: 6' 3"
Weight: 230 Breakout: 3%
Improve: 54% Collapse: 0%
Attrition: 3% MLB: 96%

Comparables:
Nate Colbert, Carlos Delgado, Cliff Johnson

YEAR	TEAM	LVL	AGE	PA	R	2B	3B	HR	RBI	BB	SO	SB	CS	AVG/OBP/SLG	TAv	BABIP	BRR	FRAA	WARP
2011	ROU	AAA	25	210	39	14	1	24	66	11	58	1	0	.368/.405/.824	.306	.412	-0.1	LF(2): 0.0, 3B(1): -0.0	0.1
2011	BAL	MLB	25	129	16	9	0	2	13	6	39	1	0	.276/.310/.398	.262	.390	-0.9	3B(17): -2.2, 1B(16): 0.6	0.1
2011	TEX	MLB	25	81	9	3	0	3	6	5	24	0	0	.250/.296/.408	.248	.327	-1.4	1B(15): -0.6, 3B(9): -0.1	-0.2
2012	BAL	MLB	26	562	75	20	0	33	85	37	169	2	3	.270/.326/.501	.282	.335	0.7	1B(38): 1.7, RF(30): 1.5	2.4
2013	BAL	MLB	27	673	103	42	1	53	138	72	199	4	1	.286/.370/.634	.358	.336	1.9	1B(155): -9.8	7.0
2014	BAL	MLB	28	610	78	29	0	30	92	49	186	3	1	.259/.324/.478	.286	.330	-1.1	1B -2, RF 0	2.0

The 2012 and 2013 seasons from Davis are why teams repeatedly give chances to players with obvious tools who have yet to put them into action at the big-league level. No one from the Orioles' front office would pretend they saw *this* level of production coming, but his elite power isn't often available, especially in a trade for a reliever (even a very good reliever like Koji Uehara). It was worth being wary of Davis's high BABIP for a while, but at this point, as you can see in his PECOTA line, he's hit the ball hard for long enough that it's time to believe it's truly a skill. Davis also got much better on the outer third of the zone, giving him power to all fields. The whiff rate is still scary, but a sampling of the names around Davis' on a contact percentage leaderboard show how hard it is to draw conclusions solely from that number: Giancarlo Stanton and Mark Reynolds miss slightly more often than Davis; Adam Dunn and Brandon Moss slightly less.

Chris Dickerson CF
Born: 4/10/1982 Age: 32
Bats: L Throws: L Height: 6' 4"
Weight: 230 Breakout: 4%
Improve: 16% Collapse: 9%
Attrition: 15% MLB: 45%

Comparables:
Mike Jacobs, Ryan Shealy, Josh Phelps

YEAR	TEAM	LVL	AGE	PA	R	2B	3B	HR	RBI	BB	SO	SB	CS	AVG/OBP/SLG	TAv	BABIP	BRR	FRAA	WARP
2011	SWB	AAA	29	247	33	10	1	2	16	30	63	18	4	.241/.341/.325	.241	.331	1.9	CF(27): 0.4, LF(12): 1.7	0.7
2011	NYA	MLB	29	55	9	2	0	1	7	2	17	4	0	.260/.296/.360	.261	.364	0.5	RF(42): -0.0, LF(14): -0.1	0.2
2012	SWB	AAA	30	321	57	24	4	7	25	49	73	17	3	.316/.417/.515	.329	.403	4.5	CF(40): 2.4, RF(13): 0.3	3.8
2012	NYA	MLB	30	17	5	0	0	2	5	3	6	3	0	.286/.412/.714	.346	.286	-0.1	LF(18): -0.3, RF(5): -0.1	0.2
2013	NOR	AAA	31	160	24	7	2	2	8	21	35	1	1	.243/.350/.368	.254	.310	1.4	RF(16): 1.1, CF(12): -0.1	0.5
2013	BAL	MLB	31	109	17	5	0	4	13	4	36	5	1	.238/.266/.400	.247	.323	0.7	LF(17): 0.2, RF(6): 0.3	0.2
2014	BAL	MLB	32	250	32	10	1	5	22	25	68	10	2	.243/.323/.367	.257	.320	1.1	CF 1, RF 0	0.7

Confining your best work of the year to an early-season 12-game stretch can sometimes breed undue expectations. Dickerson did just that in part-time play in May: His four home runs and 1.029 OPS in 35 plate appearances that month fooled some into believing he might be ready for the long side of a platoon. The team wasn't convinced, however, and continued limiting his exposure. Dickerson barely filled the role of a fifth outfielder the rest of the way, much less a reliable platoon partner. Look for him to log his eighth season in Triple-A, serving as a 26th man, waiting, hopefully not too forlornly, for the phone to ring.

Ryan Flaherty   **2B**
Born: 7/27/1986 Age: 27
Bats: L Throws: R Height: 6' 3"
Weight: 210 Breakout: 5%
Improve: 37% Collapse: 15%
Attrition: 22% MLB: 80%
Comparables:
Luke Hughes, Jayson Nix, Andy Marte

YEAR	TEAM	LVL	AGE	PA	R	2B	3B	HR	RBI	BB	SO	SB	CS	AVG/OBP/SLG	TAv	BABIP	BRR	FRAA	WARP
2011	TEN	AA	24	344	52	20	2	14	66	40	55	4	6	.305/.384/.523	.303	.332	0.5	2B(26): -1.1, LF(15): -0.5	1.8
2011	IOW	AAA	24	186	22	11	1	5	22	10	44	1	0	.237/.277/.399	.230	.288	-0.7	2B(22): -1.9, 3B(10): 0.4	-0.1
2012	NOR	AAA	25	41	5	1	1	2	3	2	9	0	0	.289/.341/.526	.292	.333	0.2	LF(3): 0.5, 2B(2): 0.0	0.3
2012	BAL	MLB	25	167	15	2	1	6	19	6	43	1	0	.216/.258/.359	.222	.257	-0.6	2B(28): 0.2, 3B(17): -0.3	-0.5
2013	NOR	AAA	26	35	4	1	0	2	5	1	8	0	0	.265/.286/.471	.287	.292	0.5	2B(8): -0.4	0.1
2013	BAL	MLB	26	271	28	11	0	10	27	19	62	2	0	.224/.293/.390	.247	.259	0.6	2B(65): -0.8, SS(9): -0.3	0.1
2014	BAL	MLB	27	250	28	10	1	9	30	15	61	1	1	.234/.287/.404	.249	.270	-0.3	2B -1, 3B -0	0.4

The health, or complete and utter lack thereof, of Brian Roberts has led to the Orioles giving more playing time to this Rule 5 pickup than they originally intended after selecting him from the Cubs before 2012. Flaherty is not merely a utility infielder, either, having seen time everywhere but center field and behind the plate. (He is reportedly the team's emergency catcher, too. For what that's worth. (Hint: _____.)) Teams can and do get worse production from their reserve infielders (and not infrequently from their starters—hey there Starlin Castro!), so Flaherty is useful even if his hitting stays static. PECOTA doesn't see it happening, but another small bump in his TAv would make him a legitimate asset.

J.J. Hardy   **SS**
Born: 8/19/1982 Age: 31
Bats: R Throws: R Height: 6' 1"
Weight: 190 Breakout: 0%
Improve: 36% Collapse: 2%
Attrition: 5% MLB: 91%
Comparables:
Alvin Dark, Alexei Ramirez, Edgar Renteria

YEAR	TEAM	LVL	AGE	PA	R	2B	3B	HR	RBI	BB	SO	SB	CS	AVG/OBP/SLG	TAv	BABIP	BRR	FRAA	WARP
2011	BAL	MLB	28	567	76	27	0	30	80	31	92	0	0	.269/.310/.491	.272	.273	1.5	SS(129): 8.1	4.0
2012	BAL	MLB	29	713	85	30	2	22	68	38	106	0	0	.238/.282/.389	.229	.253	0.9	SS(158): 21.0	3.1
2013	BAL	MLB	30	644	66	27	0	25	76	38	73	2	1	.263/.306/.433	.268	.263	-3.8	SS(159): -12.6	1.5
2014	BAL	MLB	31	619	73	25	1	20	69	39	98	1	0	.245/.295/.401	.253	.260	-1.1	SS 3	2.4

Strong defense at a difficult position significantly lowers the offensive bar. Hardy is never going to get on base at a high rate, but his grown-ass-man power leads to league-average offensive production that easily clears that bar. Hardy notched a second Gold Glove in 2013 despite decline in his defensive metrics (though it's worth noting that DRS and UZR saw the drop-off as much less steep than FRAA did) and hit the trifecta with an All-Star bid and Silver Slugger award. Camden Yards does inflate homers, but Hardy's home/road splits show no reason for alarm, as 36 of his 77 homers the last three years have come on the road.

Josh Hart   **CF**
Born: 10/2/1994 Age: 19
Bats: L Throws: L Height: 6' 1"
Weight: 180 Breakout: 0%
Improve: 0% Collapse: 0%
Attrition: 0% MLB: 0%
Comparables:
Xavier Avery, Austin Jackson, Che-Hsuan Lin

YEAR	TEAM	LVL	AGE	PA	R	2B	3B	HR	RBI	BB	SO	SB	CS	AVG/OBP/SLG	TAv	BABIP	BRR	FRAA	WARP
2014	BAL	MLB	19	250	24	8	0	3	15	12	74	6	2	.184/.226/.254	.179	.250	0.4	CF 5	-0.8

Despite ugly overall numbers in a short sample split over two levels, Hart showed flashes of what made him the 37th-overall pick in 2013: speed and approach. At his best, Hart can draw walks, slap the ball around and then use his speed to get extra hits and terrorize pitchers once he's on base. He doesn't even project to have gap power, let alone the ability to leave the yard, but leveraging his speed on both sides of the ball could carry him to the majors. His deep reservoir of athleticism gives him a legitimate chance of reaching his ceiling.

Adam Jones   **CF**
Born: 8/1/1985 Age: 28
Bats: R Throws: R Height: 6' 3"
Weight: 225 Breakout: 1%
Improve: 41% Collapse: 2%
Attrition: 2% MLB: 99%
Comparables:
Ellis Burks, George Hendrick, Andre Dawson

YEAR	TEAM	LVL	AGE	PA	R	2B	3B	HR	RBI	BB	SO	SB	CS	AVG/OBP/SLG	TAv	BABIP	BRR	FRAA	WARP
2011	BAL	MLB	25	618	68	26	2	25	83	29	113	12	4	.280/.319/.466	.279	.304	2.7	CF(148): -1.5	3.9
2012	BAL	MLB	26	697	103	39	3	32	82	34	126	16	7	.287/.334/.505	.289	.313	2	CF(162): 15.5	6.4
2013	BAL	MLB	27	689	100	35	1	33	108	25	136	14	3	.285/.318/.493	.294	.314	2.2	CF(156): -18.4	3.0
2014	BAL	MLB	28	649	81	29	2	26	88	32	126	13	5	.274/.319/.457	.283	.310	0.1	CF 2	3.6

The *Moneyball* era ushered in a necessary focus on the importance of walks, but their importance can be (and for a while probably was) overstated. That kind of thinking understates the value of someone like Jones who has exactly one season with a walk rate north of 5 percent, yet has established himself among the top outfielders in the game. His power development has more than made up for the on-base deficiency, making him an above-average center fielder even if you don't believe in his defense—and if you do, he's a flat-out stud. Still in the midst of his prime, it is not inconceivable that Jones could still improve his skills (strike-zone command, maybe) while maintaining the physical advantages of youth. Which is to say that an MVP award is not out of the question.

David Lough RF
Born: 1/20/1986 Age: 28
Bats: L Throws: L Height: 5' 11"
Weight: 180 Breakout: 1%
Improve: 18% Collapse: 14%
Attrition: 23% MLB: 44%
Comparables:
Shane Costa, Alex Romero, Alexis Gomez

YEAR	TEAM	LVL	AGE	PA	R	2B	3B	HR	RBI	BB	SO	SB	CS	AVG/OBP/SLG	TAv	BABIP	BRR	FRAA	WARP
2011	OMA	AAA	25	516	87	26	11	9	65	36	49	14	8	.318/.367/.482	.283	.335	-0.6	LF(63): 1.5, RF(8): -1.1	1.6
2012	OMA	AAA	26	544	69	19	11	10	69	25	65	26	4	.275/.317/.420	.260	.296	5.2	RF(70): 13.2, CF(38): 3.5	3.3
2012	KCA	MLB	26	65	9	2	1	0	2	4	9	1	0	.237/.292/.305	.210	.275	-0.1	CF(12): -0.2, RF(5): -0.6	-0.2
2013	OMA	AAA	27	172	29	6	3	3	17	11	21	5	5	.338/.391/.474	.326	.374	-0.6	LF(30): 1.7, CF(9): -0.6	1.9
2013	KCA	MLB	27	335	35	17	4	5	33	10	52	5	2	.286/.311/.413	.274	.326	-0.1	RF(74): -3.9, LF(15): 1.1	1.0
2014	BAL	MLB	28	352	35	14	4	6	36	14	56	9	3	.257/.293/.383	.246	.280	0.8	RF 1, LF 1	0.6

With Jeff Francoeur doing Jeff Francoeur things, and prized prospect Wil Myers doing Wil Myers things for Tampa instead, the Royals had to turn to Plan C for right field. With his below-average hit tool and lack of power, Lough profiles more as a fourth outfielder. He doesn't display a platoon split. His lack of power won't play as a regular in the corner, and while he wasn't the root cause of his team's offensive struggles, he was a symptom of a poor plan on offense. The Orioles, who added Lough in the Danny Valencia trade, won't miss a beat with him on defense, so there is value here. Just not on an everyday basis.

Manny Machado 3B
Born: 7/6/1992 Age: 21
Bats: R Throws: R Height: 6' 2"
Weight: 180 Breakout: 5%
Improve: 36% Collapse: 9%
Attrition: 19% MLB: 68%
Comparables:
Ryan Zimmerman, Lonnie Chisenhall, Starlin Castro

YEAR	TEAM	LVL	AGE	PA	R	2B	3B	HR	RBI	BB	SO	SB	CS	AVG/OBP/SLG	TAv	BABIP	BRR	FRAA	WARP
2011	DEL	A	18	170	24	8	2	6	24	23	25	3	1	.276/.376/.483	.302	.296	0.5	SS(29): 1.6	1.5
2011	FRD	A+	18	260	24	12	3	5	26	22	48	8	5	.245/.308/.384	.260	.286	1.4	SS(55): -2.6	1.0
2012	BOW	AA	19	459	60	26	5	11	59	48	70	13	4	.266/.352/.438	.281	.297	1	SS(104): -7.7, 3B(2): -0.0	2.4
2012	BAL	MLB	19	202	24	8	3	7	26	9	38	2	0	.262/.294/.445	.256	.293	-0.1	3B(51): 0.9	0.6
2013	BAL	MLB	20	710	88	51	3	14	71	29	113	6	7	.283/.314/.432	.268	.322	0.7	3B(156): 28.4	6.0
2014	BAL	MLB	21	621	65	34	4	16	72	34	111	7	4	.264/.307/.418	.264	.300	-0.5	3B 14, SS -2	3.3

A great whoosh of sadness was released across the league when Machado tore up his left knee in September, requiring reconstructive surgery. It wasn't quite Mariano Rivera-level (the 21-year-old hasn't built *that* kind of equity in baseball fandom), but not every major injury meets the kind of legitimate nationwide concern elicited by the sight of Machado being carted off on a stretcher. It speaks to the excitement of watching Machado play. The young phenom essentially logged a full season, led the league in doubles (though he finished 16 away from the major-league record after an early-season scorching run had Earl Webb's name on every tongue) and earned a Gold Glove for his indisputably brilliant play at the hot corner. Medicine has come a long way since Mickey Mantle's day, so while we'll hold our breath every time Machado falls down, there's every reason to think that in the long run, he'll be fine.

Adrian Marin SS
Born: 3/8/1994 Age: 20
Bats: R Throws: R Height: 6' 0"
Weight: 165 Breakout: 0%
Improve: 1% Collapse: 0%
Attrition: 0% MLB: 1%
Comparables:
Tim Beckham, Eduardo Escobar, Hector Gomez

YEAR	TEAM	LVL	AGE	PA	R	2B	3B	HR	RBI	BB	SO	SB	CS	AVG/OBP/SLG	TAv	BABIP	BRR	FRAA	WARP
2012	DEL	A	18	23	5	0	0	0	2	1	2	2	0	.286/.348/.286	.234	.316	0	SS(6): 0.3	0.2
2013	DEL	A	19	422	30	19	2	4	48	23	90	11	4	.265/.311/.356	.260	.333	0.7	SS(108): 0.1	1.8
2014	BAL	MLB	20	250	19	9	1	3	21	8	65	1	0	.214/.242/.298	.199	.280	-0.3	SS -0	-0.6

Marin has neither a standout tool nor any glaring flaws. The reports on his defense at short are mixed, but if he can remain there then he could find himself traded out of an organization flush with talent at the position. Any other position would call for Marin to step up his offensive game, which isn't impossible: He has a capable foundation with a modicum of pop, a solid approach and quality bat-to-ball skills.

Nick Markakis — RF

Born: 11/17/1983 Age: 30
Bats: L Throws: L Height: 6' 1"
Weight: 190 Breakout: 0%
Improve: 42% Collapse: 5%
Attrition: 6% MLB: 98%

Comparables:
Harvey Kuenn, Floyd Robinson, Terry Puhl

YEAR	TEAM	LVL	AGE	PA	R	2B	3B	HR	RBI	BB	SO	SB	CS	AVG/OBP/SLG	TAv	BABIP	BRR	FRAA	WARP
2011	BAL	MLB	27	716	72	31	1	15	73	62	75	12	3	.284/.351/.406	.266	.300	0.3	RF(157): -3.0, 1B(3): 0.0	1.5
2012	BAL	MLB	28	471	59	28	3	13	54	42	51	1	1	.298/.363/.471	.285	.310	0.4	RF(102): -2.7	1.8
2013	BAL	MLB	29	700	89	24	0	10	59	55	76	1	2	.271/.329/.356	.255	.291	1.9	RF(155): 0.8	1.2
2014	BAL	MLB	30	613	73	30	1	12	59	54	80	4	2	.274/.340/.399	.271	.300	-0.9	RF -5, 1B 0	1.2

It's hard to look at Markakis' career path without twinges of disappointment and the memory of futures long since passed. He fell flat last year in easily the worst season of his career, but it wasn't a cliff-dive—Markakis has been heading this direction for a long time. He was a slightly above-average player in his first two seasons before making his name with a legitimate star-level season at 24, posting 5.3 WARP. He hit for average, took walks, had pop, added value on the bases and played decent enough defense. He was 24. Life is good, and a long career and many riches awaited.

Life is cruel. The walks have fallen back, the pop is gone and, just to pile on, a broken hamate followed by a broken thumb cut short his best offensive season in years in 2012. Suddenly he's 30 and his $15 million salary feels like a drag. There's almost no way the Orioles pick up his 2015 option ($17.5 million) and without a serious bounce back, he'll be hustling for that "he's okay" money in the free-agent market instead of the nine figures he'd surely have cracked had his career continued on its 2006-2008 trajectory. Somehow, he's never even made an All-Star team.

Chris Marrero — 1B

Born: 7/2/1988 Age: 25
Bats: R Throws: R Height: 6' 3"
Weight: 230 Breakout: 6%
Improve: 17% Collapse: 2%
Attrition: 18% MLB: 27%

Comparables:
David Cooper, Matt Hague, Jordan Brown

YEAR	TEAM	LVL	AGE	PA	R	2B	3B	HR	RBI	BB	SO	SB	CS	AVG/OBP/SLG	TAv	BABIP	BRR	FRAA	WARP
2011	SYR	AAA	22	546	59	30	0	14	69	58	97	3	2	.300/.375/.449	.289	.349	1.8	1B(108): 3.5	2.7
2011	WAS	MLB	22	117	6	5	0	0	10	4	27	0	0	.248/.274/.294	.219	.318	-0.7	1B(31): -0.1	-0.6
2012	HAR	AA	23	23	2	2	0	1	3	0	3	0	0	.273/.304/.500	.266	.278	0.6	1B(3): -0.2	0.1
2012	SYR	AAA	23	144	13	6	1	0	12	16	28	0	0	.244/.333/.307	.228	.313	-0.2	1B(31): -0.9	-0.6
2013	SYR	AAA	24	450	48	17	2	11	59	36	67	0	1	.270/.331/.402	.254	.297	-1.7	1B(95): -5.0	-0.6
2013	WAS	MLB	24	16	0	0	0	0	1	0	4	0	0	.125/.125/.125	.094	.167	0	1B(3): 0.1	-0.2
2014	BAL	MLB	25	250	25	11	0	6	28	19	49	0	0	.254/.313/.385	.257	.300	-0.5	1B -1	0.1

A first-round pick in a front-loaded draft that produced Evan Longoria, Clayton Kershaw, Tim Lincecum and Max Scherzer, Chris Marrero represents the unlucky side of the prospect penny. The Florida prep product has always had patience at the plate, and has recently done well to limit the holes in his swing, but in doing so has sacrificed the little bit of power that he had. Add in less-than-ideal bat speed and it's unlikely that Marrero will ever develop the thump necessary for an offense-first position. Unfortunately, a rough ankle fracture in 2008 and surgery on his hamstring in 2011 assure that his only escape from playing first base is via the dugout.

Michael Ohlman — C

Born: 12/14/1990 Age: 23
Bats: R Throws: R Height: 6' 4"
Weight: 205 Breakout: 3%
Improve: 5% Collapse: 2%
Attrition: 6% MLB: 6%

Comparables:
Chris Parmelee, Lucas Duda, Shane Peterson

YEAR	TEAM	LVL	AGE	PA	R	2B	3B	HR	RBI	BB	SO	SB	CS	AVG/OBP/SLG	TAv	BABIP	BRR	FRAA	WARP
2011	DEL	A	20	431	38	15	2	4	51	48	96	1	2	.224/.320/.307	.245	.289	-0.9	C(64): -0.8	-0.2
2012	DEL	A	21	209	27	16	2	2	28	33	27	0	1	.304/.411/.456	.317	.342	-0.4	C(14): -0.1	1.7
2013	FRD	A+	22	424	61	29	4	13	53	56	93	5	0	.313/.410/.524	.313	.389	-2.1	C(46): 0.2	3.5
2014	BAL	MLB	23	250	23	10	1	5	25	23	65	0	0	.227/.300/.345	.240	.290	-0.4	C -0, 1B 0	0.2

A late bloomer, Ohlman did nothing of import during his first two and a half seasons; a suspension for drug abuse was his only headline. Perhaps the time off served as a wakeup call, though, because Ohlman returned to put up an .868 OPS in the final 51 games of 2012. Forget using 2013 to show it was real: Ohlman blew way past real, exploding with a massive season despite a slow start, including a missed month due to a shoulder injury stemming from a car accident early in the spring. Ohlman's defense is suspect, but if the bat lives up to its potential, he can sustain value even with a change in positions.

Steve Pearce 1B

Born: 4/13/1983 Age: 31
Bats: R Throws: R Height: 5' 11"
Weight: 210 Breakout: 0%
Improve: 26% Collapse: 10%
Attrition: 24% MLB: 72%

Comparables:
Andy Phillips, Dan Johnson, John Rodriguez

YEAR	TEAM	LVL	AGE	PA	R	2B	3B	HR	RBI	BB	SO	SB	CS	AVG/OBP/SLG	TAv	BABIP	BRR	FRAA	WARP
2011	IND	AAA	28	30	5	2	0	3	6	0	9	0	0	.267/.267/.633	.196	.278	-1	RF(1): -0.2, 1B(1): -0.0	-0.2
2011	PIT	MLB	28	105	8	2	0	1	10	7	21	0	0	.202/.260/.255	.191	.243	-0.4	1B(16): 0.3, 3B(10): -0.4	-0.7
2012	SWB	AAA	29	227	37	15	0	11	30	29	33	3	1	.318/.419/.568	.337	.336	-0.6	1B(48): -0.1, 3B(3): 0.1	2.2
2012	NYA	MLB	29	30	6	0	0	1	4	5	8	0	0	.160/.300/.280	.221	.188	0.2	1B(9): 0.2	-0.1
2012	BAL	MLB	29	83	8	4	0	3	14	8	17	0	1	.254/.321/.437	.282	.283	0.1	LF(20): 0.0, RF(9): -0.5	0.4
2012	HOU	MLB	29	75	2	4	0	1	8	7	16	1	1	.254/.347/.349	.246	.327	0.1	RF(10): -1.0, 1B(10): -0.6	-0.3
2013	BAL	MLB	30	138	14	7	0	4	13	15	25	1	0	.261/.362/.420	.301	.300	-0.7	LF(15): -0.4, 1B(13): -0.2	0.7
2014	BAL	MLB	31	250	28	12	1	7	30	27	51	2	1	.244/.333/.405	.271	.280	-0.4	1B 0, LF -0	0.6

After a 2012 in which Pearce changed organizations six different times, including twice apiece to the Yankees and Orioles, 2013 might have been as relaxing and anxiety-free as baseball gets for the ex-Pirate: no waivers, no releases, no trades. Pearce did lose two months to left wrist tendinitis, but the disabled list is nothing compared to being claimed and then waived by the Astros. He'll still mash a lefty if you let him, but there aren't enough lefties in the league to get rich doing so. Not to be confused with the British equestrian painter, New Mexico Congressman or owner of Soft Cell's first record label. (You'd be surprised.)

Francisco Peguero RF

Born: 6/1/1988 Age: 26
Bats: R Throws: R Height: 6' 0"
Weight: 190 Breakout: 0%
Improve: 3% Collapse: 3%
Attrition: 9% MLB: 11%

Comparables:
Nick Stavinoha, Drew T Anderson, Juan Perez

YEAR	TEAM	LVL	AGE	PA	R	2B	3B	HR	RBI	BB	SO	SB	CS	AVG/OBP/SLG	TAv	BABIP	BRR	FRAA	WARP
2011	SJO	A+	23	76	12	2	0	2	9	7	8	4	0	.324/.387/.441	.315	.345	0.2	CF(3): 0.1, RF(2): -0.1	0.3
2011	RIC	AA	23	296	34	12	6	5	37	5	45	8	1	.309/.318/.446	.293	.346	0.1	RF(47): -0.0, CF(3): 0.6	1.3
2012	FRE	AAA	24	476	46	20	10	5	68	15	82	1	0	.272/.297/.394	.235	.319	-2	RF(80): 16.3, CF(27): 0.2	1.0
2012	SFN	MLB	24	16	6	0	0	0	0	0	7	3	0	.188/.188/.188	.136	.333	0	LF(8): 0.2, RF(2): 0.3	-0.1
2013	FRE	AAA	25	288	38	12	2	3	30	13	51	3	0	.316/.354/.408	.260	.381	2.5	RF(36): 1.8, LF(33): -1.2	1.0
2013	SFN	MLB	25	30	4	1	0	1	1	1	2	2	0	.207/.233/.345	.186	.192	-1.1	LF(13): 0.4, RF(2): -0.0	-0.2
2014	BAL	MLB	26	250	21	10	2	4	25	6	52	2	0	.248/.269/.358	.230	.300	0.3	RF 3, LF 0	0.1

Peguero has long been regarded as a guy you could dream on, with raw ability and tools that, in the best possible case, could make him a star. Eight years into his pro career, though, Peguero is having trouble even cracking the big-league roster. MLB granted Peguero a fourth option for 2013, which allowed the Giants to assign him to Triple-A Fresno (again), where he hit .316/.354/.408 and played solid outfield defense. MLB doesn't grant fifth options, though, so now he's Baltimore's to dream on.

Cord Phelps 2B

Born: 1/23/1987 Age: 27
Bats: B Throws: R Height: 6' 1"
Weight: 210 Breakout: 5%
Improve: 18% Collapse: 15%
Attrition: 20% MLB: 43%

Comparables:
Matt Downs, Tug Hulett, Drew Sutton

YEAR	TEAM	LVL	AGE	PA	R	2B	3B	HR	RBI	BB	SO	SB	CS	AVG/OBP/SLG	TAv	BABIP	BRR	FRAA	WARP
2011	COH	AAA	24	434	51	25	4	14	63	51	89	3	6	.294/.376/.492	.301	.348	-1.5	2B(15): 0.3, SS(15): -0.9	0.9
2011	CLE	MLB	24	80	10	2	1	1	6	8	17	1	0	.155/.241/.254	.190	.189	0.7	2B(20): -2.3	-0.5
2012	COH	AAA	25	582	82	34	3	16	62	71	94	9	4	.276/.368/.451	.271	.311	-2	2B(132): -12.3	0.9
2012	CLE	MLB	25	34	2	0	0	1	5	1	10	0	0	.212/.235/.303	.204	.273	0.1	2B(5): -0.3, 3B(1): -0.0	-0.1
2013	COH	AAA	26	287	29	16	1	9	46	27	49	4	3	.267/.333/.443	.271	.295	0.3	2B(39): -1.4, 1B(14): -0.3	0.9
2013	CLE	MLB	26	9	0	0	0	0	0	0	2	0	0	.000/.000/.000	.017	.000	0	2B(3): -0.4	-0.3
2014	BAL	MLB	27	250	26	12	1	7	29	23	49	2	1	.243/.313/.395	.259	.280	-0.3	2B -4, LF -0	0.3

Opportunities have been scarce for Phelps, stuck behind Jason Kipnis without the arm to play regularly on the left side of the infield. He's got a career .838 OPS in 1,576 Triple-A plate appearances, and it's very likely he'd be an above-average offensive second baseman given a chance, but then they never called Cleveland the Land of Opportunity. They never called Baltimore that, either—the Orioles claimed him, then outrighted him to Triple-A two weeks later. Did they ever call Norfolk the Land of Opportunity?

Nolan Reimold LF

Born: 10/12/1983 Age: 30
Bats: R Throws: R Height: 6' 4"
Weight: 205 Breakout: 1%
Improve: 32% Collapse: 2%
Attrition: 9% MLB: 78%

Comparables:
Ryan Spilborghs, Fred Lewis, Chris Duncan

YEAR	TEAM	LVL	AGE	PA	R	2B	3B	HR	RBI	BB	SO	SB	CS	AVG/OBP/SLG	TAv	BABIP	BRR	FRAA	WARP
2011	NOR	AAA	27	161	16	6	0	6	22	18	43	2	1	.237/.329/.410	.273	.293	-0.5	LF(28): 3.5	0.7
2011	BAL	MLB	27	305	40	10	3	13	45	28	57	7	2	.247/.328/.453	.279	.264	0.3	LF(73): 2.6, RF(8): -0.4	1.6
2012	BAL	MLB	28	69	10	6	0	5	10	2	14	1	0	.313/.333/.627	.317	.333	0.8	LF(15): 0.2	0.6
2013	BOW	AA	29	51	3	0	1	1	5	4	13	0	0	.196/.255/.304	.201	.242	0	LF(7): -0.2	-0.3
2013	BAL	MLB	29	140	17	3	0	5	12	10	41	0	1	.195/.250/.336	.226	.238	1.3	LF(11): 0.7	-0.3
2014	BAL	MLB	30	250	31	9	1	9	30	25	54	3	1	.241/.325/.412	.272	.280	-0.1	LF 1, RF -0	0.9

After some promising work through his first three seasons, Reimold has seen his career completely derailed by a serious neck injury that sidelined him in both 2012 and 2013. Surgery to fuse two of his vertebrae in July (and how was *your* July?) is said to be the fix, especially with six months to rest and rehabilitate afterward, but matters of the neck and spine are always tenuous, so it's a wait-and-see process. At full health he is a legitimate power bat who won't make you put a bag over your head when he plays left field, though his best position remains DH.

Brian Roberts   2B

Born: **10/9/1977** Age: **36**
Bats: **B** Throws: **R** Height: **5' 9"**
Weight: **175** Breakout: **0%**
Improve: **31%** Collapse: **9%**
Attrition: **18%** MLB: **67%**

Comparables:
Mark Ellis, Adam Kennedy, Frank Menechino

YEAR	TEAM	LVL	AGE	PA	R	2B	3B	HR	RBI	BB	SO	SB	CS	AVG/OBP/SLG	TAv	BABIP	BRR	FRAA	WARP
2011	BAL	MLB	33	178	18	7	1	3	19	12	21	6	1	.221/.273/.331	.214	.236	2.2	2B(39): -0.5	-0.1
2012	BOW	AA	34	21	4	3	0	1	3	4	3	0	0	.250/.381/.625	.344	.231	-0.1	2B(7): -0.1	0.3
2012	NOR	AAA	34	23	2	2	0	0	1	2	4	0	0	.238/.304/.333	.220	.294	0.2	2B(5): -0.2	0.0
2012	BAL	MLB	34	74	2	0	0	0	5	5	12	1	1	.182/.233/.182	.181	.214	-0.3	2B(17): -1.0	-0.6
2013	BAL	MLB	35	296	33	12	1	8	39	26	44	3	1	.249/.312/.392	.269	.267	-1.7	2B(60): 3.9	1.1
2014	BAL	MLB	36	250	30	13	0	4	22	23	43	6	2	.245/.315/.363	.249	.280	0.2	2B -2	0.3

The discussion on Roberts begins and ends with his health record, as myriad injuries have limited the once-excellent second baseman to just 192 games (30 percent of the schedule) in the last four seasons. Knee, hip, groin and concussion have been the culprits, so it's not one particular injury or even one particular area of his body. Now 36, the outlook isn't great. The injuries have not only robbed him of playing time but have conspired with time to sap his skill, yielding a well below-average stat line when you sum up the last four years. (See also his PECOTA projection.) On the plus side, Roberts was on the field for the final three months of the 2013 season. It's something!

Jonathan Schoop   2B

Born: **10/16/1991** Age: **22**
Bats: **R** Throws: **R** Height: **6' 2"**
Weight: **210** Breakout: **4%**
Improve: **16%** Collapse: **10%**
Attrition: **22%** MLB: **29%**

Comparables:
Adrian Cardenas, Travis Denker, Luis Valbuena

YEAR	TEAM	LVL	AGE	PA	R	2B	3B	HR	RBI	BB	SO	SB	CS	AVG/OBP/SLG	TAv	BABIP	BRR	FRAA	WARP
2011	DEL	A	19	238	45	12	3	8	34	20	32	6	4	.316/.376/.514	.297	.337	0.2	SS(31): 2.7, 3B(16): -0.6	2.2
2011	FRD	A+	19	329	37	12	2	5	37	22	44	6	3	.271/.329/.375	.264	.304	0.2	2B(56): 0.2, SS(9): 1.4	1.1
2012	BOW	AA	20	555	68	24	1	14	56	50	103	5	3	.245/.324/.386	.254	.282	-2.7	2B(88): -2.0, SS(39): -5.0	0.4
2013	NOR	AAA	21	289	30	11	0	9	34	13	55	1	2	.256/.301/.396	.247	.290	0.1	2B(48): -0.1, SS(20): 2.8	0.7
2013	BAL	MLB	21	15	5	0	0	1	1	1	2	0	0	.286/.333/.500	.257	.273	0	2B(4): -0.4	0.0
2014	BAL	MLB	22	250	28	10	1	7	26	13	53	0	0	.236/.284/.375	.242	.270	-0.5	2B -1, SS -0	0.3

Schoop doesn't have one particularly loud tool, but the sum of his work on both sides of the ball should yield a positive player, someone in the mold of Daniel Murphy with a little less offense but better glove-work. A back injury derailed his season for two months in mid-May, so he probably isn't ready for a full-time spot in the majors on Opening Day. He's got time in a physical sense, as he's still just 22, but the Orioles purchased his contract in the winter of 2012, so he's already burned one option year.

Henry Urrutia   RF

Born: **2/13/1987** Age: **27**
Bats: **L** Throws: **R** Height: **6' 5"**
Weight: **200** Breakout: **5%**
Improve: **22%** Collapse: **11%**
Attrition: **20%** MLB: **50%**

Comparables:
Delwyn Young, Jeff Fiorentino, Brandon Guyer

YEAR	TEAM	LVL	AGE	PA	R	2B	3B	HR	RBI	BB	SO	SB	CS	AVG/OBP/SLG	TAv	BABIP	BRR	FRAA	WARP
2013	BOW	AA	26	224	33	16	0	7	37	24	36	1	1	.365/.433/.550	.350	.420	-2.2	RF(45): -2.1, LF(4): -0.3	2.0
2013	NOR	AAA	26	123	16	5	1	2	13	8	15	0	0	.316/.358/.430	.285	.347	-0.6	RF(17): -2.2, LF(11): 1.3	0.7
2013	BAL	MLB	26	58	5	0	1	0	2	0	11	0	0	.276/.276/.310	.219	.340	-0.8	LF(2): -0.0	-0.3
2014	BAL	MLB	27	250	25	11	1	6	29	15	46	0	0	.278/.322/.411	.268	.320	-0.4	RF -3, LF 1	0.4

The Cuban import is about 87 percent leg, but his bat packs a real punch. It is hard to get too excited over the numbers he amassed in Double- and Triple-A last year given that he's 26, but they shouldn't be completely ignored, either. His biggest issues came against off-speed stuff, a common issue for newcomers, so the Orioles sent him to the Arizona Fall League for extra reps. His best defensive position is—hey look a bird! No? No bird? Could've sworn there was a bird. Anyway, the bat carries real potential even without any expectation of further physical growth. The Orioles' roster doesn't have a David Ortiz type currently, so Urrutia doesn't need to be squeezed onto the field.

Christian Walker   1B

Born: 3/28/1991 Age: 23
Bats: R Throws: R Height: 6' 0"
Weight: 220 Breakout: 2%
Improve: 3% Collapse: 1%
Attrition: 4% MLB: 4%

Comparables:
John Jaso, Shane Peterson, Mitch Moreland

YEAR	TEAM	LVL	AGE	PA	R	2B	3B	HR	RBI	BB	SO	SB	CS	AVG/OBP/SLG	TAv	BABIP	BRR	FRAA	WARP
2012	ABE	A-	21	93	12	5	0	2	9	10	14	2	1	.284/.376/.420	.313	.323	1	1B(17): 0.8	0.8
2013	DEL	A	22	131	19	5	0	3	20	11	16	0	3	.353/.420/.474	.345	.388	-1.9	1B(29): 4.3	1.6
2013	FRD	A+	22	239	25	17	0	8	35	17	41	2	0	.288/.343/.479	.283	.318	-1	1B(52): -2.1	0.5
2013	BOW	AA	22	69	7	5	0	0	1	6	10	0	0	.242/.319/.323	.266	.288	-1.6	1B(14): -0.5	-0.1
2014	BAL	MLB	23	250	23	11	0	6	28	13	53	0	0	.243/.288/.371	.243	.280	-0.6	1B 1	-0.1

Walker moved through two levels before graduating to Double-A in 2013, where you could say he was underwhelming or you could more correctly say that 69 plate appearances is about the silliest sample you could look at. Walker's season numbers would look sharp were he not a first baseman, but given his position, he didn't flash nearly enough power to be a big-time prospect. Nor does he have enough defense at first to be a poor man's Olerud type, that guy with a high average and elite defense who can be hidden on a team that draws its power from elsewhere on the diamond. Walker will need to improve something about himself to convince anyone he can make an impact. Which really just means that he's human.

Jemile Weeks   2B

Born: 1/26/1987 Age: 27
Bats: B Throws: R Height: 5' 9"
Weight: 160 Breakout: 4%
Improve: 37% Collapse: 8%
Attrition: 21% MLB: 83%

Comparables:
Russ Adams, Chris Getz, Ryan Theriot

YEAR	TEAM	LVL	AGE	PA	R	2B	3B	HR	RBI	BB	SO	SB	CS	AVG/OBP/SLG	TAv	BABIP	BRR	FRAA	WARP
2011	SAC	AAA	24	217	30	6	4	3	22	29	32	10	4	.321/.417/.446	.280	.373	0.3	2B(11): 1.3	0.4
2011	OAK	MLB	24	437	50	26	8	2	36	21	62	22	11	.303/.340/.421	.286	.350	1.3	2B(96): 4.1	2.9
2012	SAC	AAA	25	51	5	4	0	0	10	6	8	1	0	.333/.412/.422	.283	.405	0	2B(10): -0.4	0.2
2012	OAK	MLB	25	511	54	15	8	2	20	50	70	16	5	.221/.305/.304	.232	.256	-2.1	2B(113): -10.0	-1.0
2013	SAC	AAA	26	614	96	19	10	4	40	80	99	17	2	.271/.376/.369	.275	.328	1.9	2B(45): -5.3, CF(25): 0.5	2.1
2013	OAK	MLB	26	9	3	0	0	0	0	0	5	0	0	.111/.111/.111	.170	.250	0.2	2B(4): 0.0, CF(2): 0.0	0.0
2014	BAL	MLB	27	250	29	10	3	3	20	22	42	7	2	.256/.326/.366	.254	.300	0.7	2B -1, SS -0	0.6

Weeks never recovered from 2012's late-season banishment to Triple-A, returning to the level for 2013 and not resurfacing until rosters expanded in September. He demonstrated speed and efficiency on the basepaths in Sacramento, but the rest of his offensive game failed to mature. Weeks spent time at shortstop and in center field in an effort to increase his appeal for a big-league job, elements which may be necessary for the former first-rounder to stick given the complete devolution of his already modest pop. The luster is off his star potential, but Weeks still has the physical ability to carve out a career as a useful player at the highest level. He should have more opportunity to do so in Baltimore after the Orioles acquired him for Jim Johnson.

Matt Wieters   C

Born: 5/21/1986 Age: 28
Bats: B Throws: R Height: 6' 5"
Weight: 240 Breakout: 1%
Improve: 41% Collapse: 4%
Attrition: 7% MLB: 98%

Comparables:
Miguel Montero, Don Pavletich, Chris Snyder

YEAR	TEAM	LVL	AGE	PA	R	2B	3B	HR	RBI	BB	SO	SB	CS	AVG/OBP/SLG	TAv	BABIP	BRR	FRAA	WARP
2011	BAL	MLB	25	551	72	28	0	22	68	48	84	1	0	.262/.328/.450	.263	.276	-2.2	C(132): 3.1, 1B(1): -0.1	3.2
2012	BAL	MLB	26	593	67	27	1	23	83	60	112	3	0	.249/.329/.435	.265	.274	-5.6	C(134): -2.3	2.4
2013	BAL	MLB	27	579	59	29	0	22	79	43	104	2	0	.235/.287/.417	.262	.247	0.7	C(140): 0.7	3.1
2014	BAL	MLB	28	547	60	25	1	18	68	49	104	2	0	.250/.318/.412	.265	.280	-0.8	C 0, 1B -0	2.8

Remember when Wieters' base hits were going to end world hunger and usher in a new era of shared prosperity for all? That … hasn't exactly happened. Which isn't to say he's been a failure! Wieters has been a league-average hitter (i.e. above average for his position) and an elite defender and game-caller, so it's hard to call him a disappointment in any objective sense, but we'll probably never shake the history, the Hall of Fame expectations, the Matt Wieters Facts. The major problem back in real life is that he has a big platoon split despite nominally being a switch-hitter, and the weak side of that split is against righties. Giving up switch-hitting has surely occurred to the team and Wieters by this point, but that's pretty much the end of our list of ideas. "Hit better," we say, while noting that a small improvement from the left side could push Wieters from above average to perpetual All-Star very quickly.

PITCHERS

Brad Brach
Born: 4/12/1986 Age: **28**
Bats: **R** Throws: **R** Height: **6' 6"** Weight: **215**
Breakout: **37%** Improve: **59%** Collapse: **29%**
Attrition: **35%** MLB: **61%**

Comparables:
Juan Salas, Jesse Carlson, Craig Breslow

YEAR	TEAM	LVL	AGE	W	L	SV	G	GS	IP	H	HR	BB	SO	BB9	SO9	GB%	BABIP	WHIP	ERA	FIP	FRA	WARP
2011	SAN	AA	25	2	2	2	23	42	0	44	32	3	5	64	1.0	13.1	33%	.304	0.84	2.25	1.83	2.64	1.2
2011	TUC	AAA	25	1	3	11	25	0	27²	28	1	7	30	2.3	9.8	47%	.342	1.27	3.90	2.84	3.29	0.9
2011	SDN	MLB	25	0	2	0	9	0	7	9	0	7	11	9.0	14.1	26%	.474	2.29	5.14	3.28	2.66	0.1
2012	SDN	MLB	26	2	4	0	67	0	66²	50	11	33	75	4.5	10.1	34%	.242	1.25	3.78	4.61	4.60	-0.3
2013	TUC	AAA	27	4	3	3	33	0	44¹	43	5	14	44	2.8	8.9	39%	.311	1.29	2.84	4.13	3.88	0.9
2013	SDN	MLB	27	1	0	0	33	0	31	36	3	19	31	5.5	9.0	39%	.384	1.77	3.19	4.12	4.44	0.0
2014	BAL	MLB	28	3	1	0	62	0	66	60	9	24	68	3.3	9.3	39%	.295	1.27	3.61	4.22	3.92	0.7

Brach's 10.8 strikeouts per nine in the minors looks sexy—enough so that Baltimore traded for him in November—but his funky delivery fools fewer hitters at the highest level. His career 1.8 walks per nine in the minors has ballooned to 5.1 in the big leagues. This restricts the effectiveness of his low-90s fastball, and mid-80s slider and splitter (the latter being a true strikeout pitch). He and Padres manager Bud Black agreed that confidence was an issue last year, with Brach admitting after one of his demotions that "you have to be at the top of your game, and I'm not."

Zach Britton
Born: 12/22/1987 Age: **26**
Bats: **L** Throws: **L** Height: **6' 3"** Weight: **195**
Breakout: **46%** Improve: **72%** Collapse: **18%**
Attrition: **20%** MLB: **82%**

Comparables:
Clayton Richard, Ross Detwiler, Wade Miley

YEAR	TEAM	LVL	AGE	W	L	SV	G	GS	IP	H	HR	BB	SO	BB9	SO9	GB%	BABIP	WHIP	ERA	FIP	FRA	WARP
2011	BOW	AA	23	0	2	0	3	3	11²	14	3	2	15	1.5	11.6	44%	.355	1.37	5.40	4.95	7.07	-0.3
2011	BAL	MLB	23	11	11	0	28	28	154¹	162	12	62	97	3.6	5.7	55%	.305	1.45	4.61	4.04	5.09	0.9
2012	BOW	AA	24	1	0	0	2	2	12	8	0	3	11	2.2	8.2	73%	.242	0.92	0.75	2.37	3.61	0.2
2012	NOR	AAA	24	4	2	0	9	9	51¹	49	5	20	37	3.5	6.5	56%	.278	1.34	4.91	4.15	5.67	-0.4
2012	BAL	MLB	24	5	3	0	12	11	60¹	61	6	32	53	4.8	7.9	61%	.311	1.54	5.07	4.27	5.26	0.4
2013	NOR	AAA	25	6	5	0	19	19	103¹	112	5	46	75	4.0	6.5	63%	.324	1.53	4.27	3.86	5.51	-0.4
2013	BAL	MLB	25	2	3	0	8	7	40	52	4	17	18	3.8	4.1	59%	.338	1.73	4.95	4.83	5.13	0.0
2014	BAL	MLB	26	7	8	0	23	23	124²	130	13	51	86	3.7	6.2	59%	.301	1.45	4.53	4.65	4.92	0.1

Britton is an elite groundballer and little else. There is great wiggle on his pitches, but he can't consistently command anything but his breaking ball, leading to too many hits and walks. His 20 percent strikeout rate from 2012 proved to be a mirage as he couldn't even maintain it in the minors, let alone during a 40-inning spell with the Orioles. The one-time top-flight prospect has seen his stock tumble a bit every year and a transition to the bullpen, where he can focus on the sinker-slider combination, might be the next step. As a lefty he is sure to get at least 58 more chances if things don't work out with the Orioles.

Dylan Bundy
Born: 11/15/1992 Age: **21**
Bats: **B** Throws: **R** Height: **6' 1"** Weight: **195**
Breakout: **36%** Improve: **76%** Collapse: **10%**
Attrition: **44%** MLB: **37%**

Comparables:
Shelby Miller, Danny Duffy, Chad Billingsley

YEAR	TEAM	LVL	AGE	W	L	SV	G	GS	IP	H	HR	BB	SO	BB9	SO9	GB%	BABIP	WHIP	ERA	FIP	FRA	WARP
2012	DEL	A	19	1	0	0	8	8	30	5	0	2	40	0.6	12.0	51%	.091	0.23	0.00	1.31	2.53	1.1
2012	FRD	A+	19	6	3	0	12	12	57	48	5	18	66	2.8	10.4	36%	.312	1.16	2.84	3.21	3.35	1.4
2012	BOW	AA	19	2	0	0	3	3	16²	14	1	8	13	4.3	7.0	46%	.265	1.32	3.24	3.86	4.38	0.1
2012	BAL	MLB	19	0	0	0	2	0	1²	1	0	1	0	5.4	0.0	20%	.200	1.20	0.00	4.85	6.60	0.0
2014	BAL	MLB	21	2	2	0	8	8	35¹	33	4	15	32	3.7	8.1	42%	.292	1.34	4.05	4.36	4.40	0.3

In just two years as a pro, Bundy has run the gamut of emotions as a young pitcher. The no. 4 overall pick from 2011 did not yield an earned run in his first professional stop, making it through eight starts and 30 innings with the 0.00 ERA before a promotion to High-A. In that same season he reached Double-A and then skipped to the majors for a quick stint. Sky-high prospect rankings in the 2012-13 offseason were the obvious (and correct) result. Then came the dreaded elbow soreness, leading eventually to Tommy John surgery. As gut-wrenching as that feeling was, Bundy will come out the other end as a 21-year-old with a pinch of MLB experience under his belt already. No surgery comes with guarantees, but the future remains bright.

Wei-Yin Chen
Born: 7/21/1985 Age: **28**
Bats: **L** Throws: **L** Height: **6' 0"** Weight: **195**
Breakout: **19%** Improve: **62%** Collapse: **21%**
Attrition: **5%** MLB: **90%**

Comparables:
Jeff Francis, Odalis Perez, Dave Bush

YEAR	TEAM	LVL	AGE	W	L	SV	G	GS	IP	H	HR	BB	SO	BB9	SO9	GB%	BABIP	WHIP	ERA	FIP	FRA	WARP
2012	BAL	MLB	26	12	11	0	32	32	192²	186	29	57	154	2.7	7.2	39%	.274	1.26	4.02	4.37	5.02	1.1
2013	BOW	AA	27	1	0	0	2	2	12	9	0	2	8	1.5	6.0	50%	.265	0.92	3.00	2.49	3.35	0.3
2013	BAL	MLB	27	7	7	0	23	23	137	142	17	39	104	2.6	6.8	36%	.305	1.32	4.07	4.07	4.10	1.5
2014	BAL	MLB	28	8	8	0	22	22	135²	133	17	38	107	2.5	7.1	39%	.289	1.25	3.86	4.28	4.20	1.2

Chen has become a solid mid-rotation option for the Orioles since coming over from Taiwan. He was pacing toward an excellent season in 2013 despite missing two months in the middle, but wore down in the home stretch, raising his ERA nearly a full run in his final seven starts. He doesn't have overwhelming stuff, but he pounds the zone effectively and misses a fair number of bats. A fly-ball pitcher, Chen might be a more ideal fit in a cavernous stadium, but he has actually fared slightly better in Camden Yards, so there's little reason to expect him to magically improve if he winds up elsewhere.

Zachary Davies

Born: 2/7/1993 Age: 21
Bats: R Throws: R Height: 6' 0" Weight: 150
Breakout: 45% Improve: 57% Collapse: 27%
Attrition: 47% MLB: 15%

Comparables:
Patrick Corbin, Vance Worley, John Danks

YEAR	TEAM	LVL	AGE	W	L	SV	G	GS	IP	H	HR	BB	SO	BB9	SO9	GB%	BABIP	WHIP	ERA	FIP	FRA	WARP
2012	DEL	A	19	5	7	1	25	17	114¹	109	11	46	91	3.6	7.2	55%	.294	1.36	3.86	4.52	5.31	0.7
2013	FRD	A+	20	7	9	0	26	26	148²	145	10	38	132	2.3	8.0	52%	.310	1.23	3.69	3.28	4.12	2.8
2014	BAL	MLB	21	5	7	0	25	18	116¹	130	17	48	72	3.7	5.6	49%	.300	1.52	5.13	5.36	5.58	-0.7

Seen as an arm on the rise coming into 2013, Davies fulfilled that label with a strong effort at High-A. He improved the command and control of his modest arsenal, something he will have to continue doing if he is going to excel in the upper levels and eventually the major leagues. The first thing most notice about Davies is his size—if he doesn't fill out some on his six-foot frame, then he will continue to be doubted even if the performance sings. He didn't wane late, closing out with a 24 percent strikeout rate and 4.6 strikeout-to-walk ratio over the final two months of the season.

Kevin Gausman

Born: 1/6/1991 Age: 23
Bats: R Throws: R Height: 6' 3" Weight: 190
Breakout: 29% Improve: 75% Collapse: 11%
Attrition: 31% MLB: 82%

Comparables:
Brian Matusz, Derek Holland, Johnny Cueto

YEAR	TEAM	LVL	AGE	W	L	SV	G	GS	IP	H	HR	BB	SO	BB9	SO9	GB%	BABIP	WHIP	ERA	FIP	FRA	WARP
2013	BOW	AA	22	2	4	0	8	8	46¹	44	3	5	49	1.0	9.5	54%	.313	1.06	3.11	2.57	2.73	1.5
2013	NOR	AAA	22	1	2	0	8	7	35²	36	1	9	33	2.3	8.3	48%	.354	1.26	4.04	2.56	3.81	0.7
2013	BAL	MLB	22	3	5	0	20	5	47²	51	8	13	49	2.5	9.3	44%	.333	1.34	5.66	4.02	4.68	0.4
2014	BAL	MLB	23	5	5	0	26	15	94	92	12	23	85	2.2	8.1	46%	.303	1.22	3.75	4.00	4.08	1.0

Each year there will be a handful of rookies who realign everyone's notion of just how tough the major leagues truly are the first time around. The Jose Fernandezes and Bryce Harpers of the world skew everything and make it look easy, but it really isn't. Not at all. Gausman showed as much in 2013. He steamrolled Double-A for the first month and a half with nearly 10 strikeouts for every walk. This earned him a trip to the majors, where he promptly posted a 7.66 ERA and allowed seven home runs in five starts. A good run at Triple-A and a solid relief stint in Baltimore capped the year in better fashion, but Gausman serves as a reminder that minor-league dominance doesn't guarantee instant success at the top. The top-of-the-rotation outlook on the 23-year-old is virtually undimmed.

Miguel Gonzalez

Born: 5/27/1984 Age: 30
Bats: R Throws: R Height: 6' 1" Weight: 170
Breakout: 22% Improve: 40% Collapse: 33%
Attrition: 28% MLB: 66%

Comparables:
Jeremy Guthrie, Shawn Hill, Brian Duensing

YEAR	TEAM	LVL	AGE	W	L	SV	G	GS	IP	H	HR	BB	SO	BB9	SO9	GB%	BABIP	WHIP	ERA	FIP	FRA	WARP
2011	PME	AA	27	0	5	0	15	6	46²	55	4	19	45	3.7	8.7	25%	.304	1.59	6.17	4.27	5.99	0.0
2012	NOR	AAA	28	3	2	1	14	6	44²	22	1	10	53	2.0	10.7	42%	.208	0.72	1.61	1.75	3.28	1.1
2012	BAL	MLB	28	9	4	0	18	15	105¹	92	13	35	77	3.0	6.6	37%	.260	1.21	3.25	4.33	4.47	1.1
2013	BAL	MLB	29	11	8	0	30	28	171¹	157	24	53	120	2.8	6.3	41%	.260	1.23	3.78	4.48	4.92	0.5
2014	BAL	MLB	30	8	9	0	26	26	143¹	135	18	45	105	2.8	6.6	40%	.277	1.26	3.85	4.56	4.18	1.4

Gonzalez backed up his stunning major-league debut with essentially a repeat performance. His ERA jumped some, but he added 66 innings to his bottom line and continues to impress considering his path to the majors, the highlights of which are: undrafted free agent; Rule 5 pick; Tommy John surgery; didn't sign a 2012 contract until May 29th. His one major flaw is the long ball, but as a back-end starter the Orioles have to be thrilled with their scrap heap acquisition. Stories like Gonzalez's are what make baseball great, and Baltimore pretty good.

Jason Hammel

Born: 9/2/1982 Age: 31
Bats: R Throws: R Height: 6' 6" Weight: 225
Breakout: 10% Improve: 42% Collapse: 25%
Attrition: 23% MLB: 90%

Comparables:
Brad Penny, Gil Meche, Paul Maholm

YEAR	TEAM	LVL	AGE	W	L	SV	G	GS	IP	H	HR	BB	SO	BB9	SO9	GB%	BABIP	WHIP	ERA	FIP	FRA	WARP
2011	COL	MLB	28	7	13	1	32	27	170¹	175	21	68	94	3.6	5.0	43%	.286	1.43	4.76	4.80	5.54	0.0
2012	BAL	MLB	29	8	6	0	20	20	118	104	9	42	113	3.2	8.6	54%	.291	1.24	3.43	3.24	3.64	2.5
2013	BAL	MLB	30	7	8	1	26	23	139¹	155	22	48	96	3.1	6.2	42%	.303	1.46	4.97	4.96	5.18	-0.2
2014	BAL	MLB	31	7	8	0	22	22	126¹	129	15	37	94	2.7	6.7	46%	.299	1.32	4.15	4.39	4.51	0.7

Can Hammel just decide if he's going to be good or not? After some sharp skills paired with poor results in his mid-20s with the Rockies, he appeared to be a diamond in the rough before the deterioration of his component numbers made him seem to be a plain old pebble in 2011. Then came 2012 in Baltimore and suddenly those earlier Colorado skills didn't seem completely fraudulent, though some of the joy was tempered by a problematic right knee. Still, let's buy that stock! But oh no, there's that rusty pebble again in 2013. Is the sinker from 2012 gone? Was it a lingering knee problem, or perhaps the elbow he strained in late July was an indication of a larger issue? Does anyone know what a rusty pebble is? These questions *will* be answered during Hammel's 2014 season. (Unless they're not.)

Hunter Harvey

Born: 12/9/1994 Age: 19
Bats: R Throws: R Height: 6' 3" Weight: 175
Breakout: 0% Improve: 0% Collapse: 0%
Attrition: 0% MLB: 0%

Comparables:
Jenrry Mejia, J.C. Ramirez, Dellin Betances

YEAR	TEAM	LVL	AGE	W	L	SV	G	GS	IP	H	HR	BB	SO	BB9	SO9	GB%	BABIP	WHIP	ERA	FIP	FRA	WARP
2013	ABE	A-	18	0	1	0	3	3	12	11	0	4	15	3.0	11.2	68%	.355	1.25	2.25	1.60	2.71	0.3
2014	BAL	MLB	19	2	3	0	8	8	32²	36	5	19	21	5.3	5.9	46%	.306	1.71	5.85	5.96	6.36	-0.4

The Orioles were thrilled to land Harvey as the 22nd overall pick in the 2013 draft. He carries major league lineage as Bryan Harvey's son, but also plenty of talent and projectability on his own. He impressed beyond his draft-day scouting report in a 25-inning taste of professional pitching, fanning 33 of the 100 batters he faced with a strong fastball-curveball combination. (He sprinkled a changeup in at times.) The control and pure pitching skill are particularly impressive for a big high school arm. Pitchers always have room for two things: improving execution and Jello. Harvey is advanced and could move quicker than many prep pitchers, but he's still 18 and not far removed from pitching to tiny overmatched children.

Liam Hendriks

Born: 2/10/1989 Age: 25
Bats: R Throws: R Height: 6' 1" Weight: 205
Breakout: 33% Improve: 54% Collapse: 21%
Attrition: 39% MLB: 76%

Comparables:
Junichi Tazawa, Zach McAllister, Jeanmar Gomez

YEAR	TEAM	LVL	AGE	W	L	SV	G	GS	IP	H	HR	BB	SO	BB9	SO9	GB%	BABIP	WHIP	ERA	FIP	FRA	WARP
2011	NBR	AA	22	8	2	0	16	15	90	85	5	18	81	1.8	8.1	44%	.323	1.14	2.70	3.03	3.91	0.9
2011	ROC	AAA	22	4	4	0	9	9	49¹	52	0	3	30	0.5	5.5	47%	.307	1.11	4.56	2.32	4.08	0.5
2011	MIN	MLB	22	0	2	0	4	4	23¹	29	3	6	16	2.3	6.2	47%	.347	1.50	6.17	4.13	4.91	0.1
2012	ROC	AAA	23	9	3	0	16	16	106¹	76	5	28	82	2.4	6.9	46%	.240	0.98	2.20	3.04	4.20	0.9
2012	MIN	MLB	23	1	8	0	16	16	85¹	106	17	26	50	2.7	5.3	42%	.313	1.55	5.59	5.52	5.93	-0.3
2013	ROC	AAA	24	4	8	0	16	16	98¹	115	9	15	62	1.4	5.7	45%	.324	1.32	4.67	3.68	5.02	0.4
2013	MIN	MLB	24	1	3	0	10	8	47¹	67	10	14	34	2.7	6.5	38%	.350	1.71	6.85	5.46	5.58	-0.2
2014	BAL	MLB	25	8	9	0	24	24	137¹	148	19	34	91	2.2	5.9	46%	.299	1.32	4.46	4.65	4.85	0.2

Hendriks has recently spent several years alternating between disastrous stints with the Twins and dominant stretches in the minors, so he opted to shake up the pattern last year by stinking up the joint in Triple-A as well. Known for—get this—his outstanding control, the young Aussie fills the zone with a fastball that reaches 90 and two slurvy breaking balls, but big league hitters know where to find them and frequently launch them into orbit. He was waived and claimed twice between the time we started this book and the time it went to press. Odds are decent it happened again before it got into your hands.

Tommy Hunter

Born: 7/3/1986 Age: 27
Bats: R Throws: R Height: 6' 3" Weight: 250
Breakout: 22% Improve: 57% Collapse: 23%
Attrition: 19% MLB: 84%

Comparables:
Andy Sonnanstine, Jason Davis, Shawn Hill

YEAR	TEAM	LVL	AGE	W	L	SV	G	GS	IP	H	HR	BB	SO	BB9	SO9	GB%	BABIP	WHIP	ERA	FIP	FRA	WARP
2011	ROU	AAA	24	2	2	1	8	5	26²	37	2	3	16	1.0	5.4	62%	.286	1.50	5.06	4.01	3.05	0.2
2011	BAL	MLB	24	3	3	0	12	11	69¹	88	11	10	35	1.3	4.5	41%	.314	1.41	5.06	4.72	4.95	0.4
2011	TEX	MLB	24	1	1	0	8	0	15¹	12	1	5	10	2.9	5.9	57%	.239	1.11	2.93	3.58	4.06	0.3
2012	BOW	AA	25	1	0	1	2	1	10	3	0	1	6	0.9	5.4	59%	.111	0.40	0.00	2.30	3.83	0.1
2012	NOR	AAA	25	2	1	0	3	3	19¹	20	2	5	14	2.3	6.5	53%	.305	1.29	4.66	3.83	4.38	0.1
2012	BAL	MLB	25	7	8	0	33	20	133²	161	32	27	77	1.8	5.2	48%	.296	1.41	5.45	5.70	6.46	-1.1
2013	BAL	MLB	26	6	5	4	68	0	86¹	71	11	14	68	1.5	7.1	41%	.249	0.98	2.81	3.71	4.07	0.6
2014	BAL	MLB	27	4	4	0	27	11	83²	86	13	19	52	2.0	5.6	45%	.282	1.26	4.17	4.89	4.53	0.4

Hunter is a great illustration of why starting is so much harder than relieving. That is not a groundbreaking notion, but it helps to refresh our examples from time to time. Hunter spent the large majority of his time in the rotation in 2012 and posted a 5.45 ERA with modest component stats. He shifted into the bullpen for the entire 2013 season and not only fared better, but was an actual weapon armed with a 97 mph fastball that helped lead to a 20 percent strikeout rate, his first season above the league average. The next hurdle for Hunter is taming lefties. If he can find something to consistently thwart them, he could become a closer candidate in his late 20s.

Steve Johnson
Born: 8/31/1987 Age: 26
Bats: R Throws: R Height: 6' 1" Weight: 220
Breakout: 38% Improve: 49% Collapse: 34%
Attrition: 67% MLB: 52%

Comparables:
J.A. Happ, Brad Mills, Joel Carreno

YEAR	TEAM	LVL	AGE	W	L	SV	G	GS	IP	H	HR	BB	SO	BB9	SO9	GB%	BABIP	WHIP	ERA	FIP	FRA	WARP
2011	BOW	AA	23	5	1	0	10	10	58¹	40	7	15	59	2.3	9.1	28%	.203	0.94	2.16	3.82	3.66	0.4
2011	NOR	AAA	23	2	7	0	17	17	87¹	101	7	47	63	4.8	6.5	29%	.335	1.69	5.56	4.59	5.13	0.0
2012	NOR	AAA	24	4	8	0	19	14	91¹	66	7	31	86	3.1	8.5	30%	.244	1.06	2.86	3.49	4.93	0.3
2012	BAL	MLB	24	4	0	0	12	4	38¹	23	4	18	46	4.2	10.8	26%	.229	1.07	2.11	3.41	4.57	0.3
2013	NOR	AAA	25	2	3	0	10	8	46	40	4	17	52	3.3	10.2	35%	.308	1.24	4.11	3.18	3.56	0.8
2013	BAL	MLB	25	1	1	0	9	1	15²	14	2	13	20	7.5	11.5	28%	.316	1.72	7.47	4.67	4.21	0.2
2014	BAL	MLB	26	3	4	0	18	10	67¹	63	10	32	58	4.3	7.7	31%	.282	1.42	4.52	5.14	4.92	0.1

If 2012 was like an alternate Baltimore universe where everything turned out happy—Hamsterdam worked; Wallace was just out fishing, yum yum let's eat this fish!—then 2013 was a cold dose of this reality for regression candidates like Johnson. If he was a bit too fortunate in his small sample of 2012, he was equally unfortunate in his small sample of 2013, though neither sample should be boiled down solely to luck. He still missed bats (more of them in 2013, in fact), but the warts (control, extreme balls-in-the-air syndrome) overwhelmed the whiffs. Johnson hasn't pitched enough at the big-league level to know what he is, but there is some intrigue, despite his total lack of velocity, based on his recent Triple-A work.

Branden Kline
Born: 9/29/1991 Age: 22
Bats: R Throws: R Height: 6' 3" Weight: 195
Breakout: 100% Improve: 100% Collapse: 0%
Attrition: 0% MLB: 2%

Comparables:
Preston Guilmet, Dan Jennings, Joe Savery

YEAR	TEAM	LVL	AGE	W	L	SV	G	GS	IP	H	HR	BB	SO	BB9	SO9	GB%	BABIP	WHIP	ERA	FIP	FRA	WARP
2012	ABE	A-	20	0	0	0	4	4	12	12	1	4	12	3.0	9.0	47%	.355	1.33	4.50	3.42	3.58	0.2
2013	DEL	A	21	1	2	0	7	7	35¹	41	4	14	32	3.6	8.2	50%	.339	1.56	5.86	4.50	5.48	-0.2
2014	BAL	MLB	22	1	3	0	7	7	32¹	39	5	17	18	4.7	4.9	45%	.307	1.71	6.07	5.98	6.60	-0.5

The second-round pick from 2012 had his season cut short by ankle surgery in May. On the plus side, he bookended his season with two of his best starts, tossing six scoreless innings in his season opener and striking out 13 in his finale. Kline was sent to Arizona for the Fall League to log some innings and make up for the lost injury time. Most slot Kline's future in the bullpen, but there is still a chance that he develops into a starter—if he is a starter, he won't be much more than a back-end one. Reports from the AFL were that Kline's stuff (which includes a low-90s fastball) did not play up in short stints as much as one would hope.

Brian Matusz
Born: 2/11/1987 Age: 27
Bats: L Throws: L Height: 6' 4" Weight: 200
Breakout: 24% Improve: 70% Collapse: 21%
Attrition: 18% MLB: 85%

Comparables:
Manny Parra, Jason Hammel, Luke Hochevar

YEAR	TEAM	LVL	AGE	W	L	SV	G	GS	IP	H	HR	BB	SO	BB9	SO9	GB%	BABIP	WHIP	ERA	FIP	FRA	WARP
2011	NOR	AAA	24	2	3	0	9	9	54²	51	4	19	41	3.1	6.8	43%	.317	1.28	3.46	3.84	4.11	0.5
2011	BAL	MLB	24	1	9	0	12	12	49²	81	18	24	38	4.3	6.9	28%	.382	2.11	10.69	7.69	8.15	-1.2
2012	NOR	AAA	25	2	1	1	10	6	47	43	2	15	32	2.9	6.1	43%	.281	1.23	4.21	3.31	4.65	0.2
2012	BAL	MLB	25	6	10	0	34	16	98	112	15	41	81	3.8	7.4	42%	.322	1.56	4.87	4.64	4.75	0.7
2013	BAL	MLB	26	2	1	0	65	0	51	43	3	16	50	2.8	8.8	40%	.292	1.16	3.53	2.94	3.52	0.6
2014	BAL	MLB	27	3	3	0	32	7	57²	59	8	20	48	3.2	7.4	40%	.301	1.37	4.36	4.58	4.74	0.1

It was evident by the end of 2012 that Matusz was just about done as a starter and positioned to become a useful back-of-the-bullpen piece. He couldn't get deep into games and right-handers were obliterating him, but once Baltimore made him a lefty-killer out of the bullpen the numbers turned around significantly. Matusz wasn't exactly a LOOGY, with half of his appearances totaling at least an inning, but he also improved against righties, earning the extra work. He still hasn't figured them out by any stretch, but his right-handed slugging allowed tumbled from .537 to .372. Matusz is essentially a mirror image of Tommy Hunter—if he can figure out opposite-hand hitters he opens up the possibility of becoming a ninth-inning stopper.

Bud Norris
Born: 3/2/1985 Age: 29
Bats: R Throws: R Height: 6' 0" Weight: 220
Breakout: 28% Improve: 49% Collapse: 26%
Attrition: 12% MLB: 77%

Comparables:
Tom Gorzelanny, Ian Snell, Felipe Paulino

YEAR	TEAM	LVL	AGE	W	L	SV	G	GS	IP	H	HR	BB	SO	BB9	SO9	GB%	BABIP	WHIP	ERA	FIP	FRA	WARP
2011	HOU	MLB	26	6	11	0	31	31	186	177	24	70	176	3.4	8.5	41%	.306	1.33	3.77	3.99	4.32	1.3
2012	HOU	MLB	27	7	13	0	29	29	168¹	165	23	66	165	3.5	8.8	39%	.312	1.37	4.65	4.27	4.45	1.5
2013	HOU	MLB	28	6	9	0	21	21	126	135	11	43	90	3.1	6.4	41%	.316	1.41	3.93	3.90	3.98	1.8
2013	BAL	MLB	28	4	3	0	11	9	50²	61	6	24	57	4.3	10.1	44%	.387	1.68	4.80	3.84	3.31	1.1
2014	BAL	MLB	29	8	10	0	26	26	150²	151	20	60	135	3.6	8.1	43%	.305	1.40	4.49	4.57	4.88	0.1

The Orioles may have been expecting more from Norris when they acquired him in a mid-2013 trade, but the simple fact is he can only get righties out. He has nothing for lefties except fat, juicy meatballs ready to be clubbed over fences across the league. Last year was the worst yet, with an .889 OPS against lefties fueled by 16 home runs allowed. With Baltimore built to continue contending right now, you have to wonder how much leash Norris will have, particularly given that platoon weakness is so easily exploited by opposing managers.

Darren O'Day
Born: 10/22/1982 Age: 31
Bats: R Throws: R Height: 6' 4" Weight: 220
Breakout: 23% Improve: 48% Collapse: 28%
Attrition: 9% MLB: 83%
Comparables:
Ryan Madson, Bobby Jenks, Nick Masset

YEAR	TEAM	LVL	AGE	W	L	SV	G	GS	IP	H	HR	BB	SO	BB9	SO9	GB%	BABIP	WHIP	ERA	FIP	FRA	WARP
2011	ROU	AAA	28	1	0	1	17	1	20¹	16	2	4	26	1.8	11.5	65%	.300	0.98	2.21	3.39	3.72	0.1
2011	TEX	MLB	28	0	1	0	16	0	16²	17	7	5	18	2.7	9.7	37%	.238	1.32	5.40	7.62	7.17	-0.1
2012	BAL	MLB	29	7	1	0	69	0	67	49	6	14	69	1.9	9.3	36%	.253	0.94	2.28	2.91	3.05	1.3
2013	BAL	MLB	30	5	3	2	68	0	62	47	7	15	59	2.2	8.6	40%	.250	1.00	2.18	3.61	4.12	0.5
2014	BAL	MLB	31	3	1	2	58	0	54	45	6	13	51	2.2	8.5	44%	.270	1.08	2.99	3.74	3.25	1.0

As he continues to log under-the-radar brilliant innings year after year, it's hard not to think O'Day will someday stumble into the ninth inning for the Red Sox and become a playoff hero. Maybe O'Day isn't the next Koji Uehara, but there are similar levels of underappreciation. O'Day has struggled with a sharp platoon split against lefties in two of the past three seasons, tied directly to his vulnerability to the home run, a death knell for closers and one reason he has yet to earn a shot at the role. His lack of velocity and extreme release point might contribute to a sense that he's a trick pitcher always a day away from being figured out. Alas, if all he does is log another handful of seasons dominating righties with sporadic success against lefties, he will still be an A O'Day.

Eduardo Rodriguez
Born: 4/7/1993 Age: 21
Bats: L Throws: L Height: 6' 2" Weight: 200
Breakout: 60% Improve: 72% Collapse: 15%
Attrition: 61% MLB: 21%
Comparables:
Jhoulys Chacin, Ian Krol, Vance Worley

YEAR	TEAM	LVL	AGE	W	L	SV	G	GS	IP	H	HR	BB	SO	BB9	SO9	GB%	BABIP	WHIP	ERA	FIP	FRA	WARP
2012	DEL	A	19	5	7	0	22	22	107	103	4	30	73	2.5	6.1	53%	.289	1.24	3.70	3.68	5.12	0.8
2013	FRD	A+	20	6	4	0	14	14	85¹	78	4	25	66	2.6	7.0	48%	.292	1.21	2.85	3.36	4.18	1.6
2013	BOW	AA	20	4	3	0	11	11	59²	53	5	24	59	3.6	8.9	42%	.296	1.29	4.22	3.74	3.77	1.3
2014	BAL	MLB	21	3	5	0	24	12	114	123	15	46	68	3.6	5.3	46%	.295	1.48	4.98	5.21	5.42	-0.5

One of the biggest reasons that you can't examine stats alone to project prospects is age/level disparity. Take Rodriguez. No one is going to be knocked over by a 4.22 ERA at Double-A, but the 20-year-old lefty was one of the youngest players at the level. When you factor in his strikeout-per-inning rate and plus command, all of a sudden he is markedly more intriguing. Building on his big season, the Orioles sent Rodriguez to the Arizona Fall League, extending his career-high workload and perhaps hoping to prepare him for a big season between Double- and Triple-A in 2013. With some graduation in the upper tiers of the organization, Rodriguez has a chance to jump another rung up the prospect ladder.

Francisco Rodriguez
Born: 1/7/1982 Age: 32
Bats: R Throws: R Height: 6' 0" Weight: 195
Breakout: 26% Improve: 48% Collapse: 28%
Attrition: 5% MLB: 96%
Comparables:
J.J. Putz, Roberto Hernandez, Rafael Betancourt

YEAR	TEAM	LVL	AGE	W	L	SV	G	GS	IP	H	HR	BB	SO	BB9	SO9	GB%	BABIP	WHIP	ERA	FIP	FRA	WARP
2011	MIL	MLB	29	4	0	0	31	0	29	23	1	10	33	3.1	10.2	51%	.293	1.14	1.86	2.20	2.55	0.7
2011	NYN	MLB	29	2	2	23	42	0	42²	44	3	16	46	3.4	9.7	53%	.342	1.41	3.16	3.02	3.34	0.6
2012	MIL	MLB	30	2	7	3	78	0	72	65	8	31	72	3.9	9.0	42%	.294	1.33	4.38	3.87	4.56	0.4
2013	BAL	MLB	31	2	1	0	23	0	22	25	5	5	28	2.0	11.5	48%	.351	1.36	4.50	4.30	4.09	0.2
2013	MIL	MLB	31	1	1	10	25	0	24²	17	2	9	26	3.3	9.5	34%	.250	1.05	1.09	3.06	3.04	0.5
2014	BAL	MLB	32	3	1	3	48	0	47¹	40	5	18	51	3.4	9.7	44%	.289	1.22	3.25	3.72	3.53	0.7

The variance tied to relievers is evident, but that doesn't mean that the shifts in utility don't still surprise us from time to time. The Artist Formerly Known as K-Rod, Now Known As "Where'd He Play This Year?" illuminates the point: His 2012 performance was seen as the beginning of the end thanks to mediocre component rates, but 30 years old turned out to be a bit early to sharpen the nails for his coffin. Rodriguez's results with the Brewers were markedly better than as an Oriole, but the numbers above paint a mixed picture, with better whiffs, grounders and walks as an Oriole but fewer homers as a Brewer. The 100-point BABIP difference also jumps out. Rodriguez's velocity has held steady since 2010 and he's shifted to a slightly slower, slightly bigger breaking curve. Don't be surprised if there is at least one more 25-save season in his arm.

Stephen Tarpley
Born: 2/17/1993 Age: 21
Bats: R Throws: L Height: 6' 1" Weight: 180
Breakout: 0% Improve: 0% Collapse: 0%
Attrition: 0% MLB: 0%
Comparables:
Elvin Ramirez, Kyle Drabek, Blake Wood

YEAR	TEAM	LVL	AGE	W	L	SV	G	GS	IP	H	HR	BB	SO	BB9	SO9	GB%	BABIP	WHIP	ERA	FIP	FRA	WARP
2014	BAL	MLB	21	1	3	0	8	8	31²	38	5	20	18	5.8	5.1	45%	.310	1.84	6.46	6.45	7.02	-0.6

The Orioles are no doubt thrilled with the early returns on their third-round lefty, even acknowledging that 21 innings is nothing. Talent isn't the question with Tarpley, though: His elite velocity from the left side got him drafted back in 2011 and netted him a scholarship to Southern Cal, but he left after just a year, fueling questions about his makeup. Can he use this impressive professional debut as a springboard to outrun the off-the-field questions and stay on the path toward fulfilling his high ceiling? That will be the primary focus in 2014, with the development of his breaking pitches and changeup—all tabbed as no worse than average, with the slider showing plus potential—almost secondary.

Chris Tillman
Born: 4/15/1988 Age: 26
Bats: R Throws: R Height: 6' 5" Weight: 210
Breakout: 36% Improve: 68% Collapse: 19%
Attrition: 19% MLB: 95%

Comparables:
Homer Bailey, Boof Bonser, Scott Baker

YEAR	TEAM	LVL	AGE	W	L	SV	G	GS	IP	H	HR	BB	SO	BB9	SO9	GB%	BABIP	WHIP	ERA	FIP	FRA	WARP
2011	NOR	AAA	23	3	6	0	15	15	76¹	77	17	38	54	4.5	6.4	39%	.295	1.51	5.19	6.29	6.36	-0.6
2011	BAL	MLB	23	3	5	0	13	13	62	77	5	25	46	3.6	6.7	41%	.348	1.65	5.52	4.03	4.43	0.8
2012	NOR	AAA	24	8	8	0	16	15	89¹	85	5	30	92	3.0	9.3	51%	.323	1.29	3.63	2.93	3.93	1.0
2012	BAL	MLB	24	9	3	0	15	15	86	66	12	24	66	2.5	6.9	35%	.221	1.05	2.93	4.20	4.45	0.8
2013	BAL	MLB	25	16	7	0	33	33	206¹	184	33	68	179	3.0	7.8	41%	.269	1.22	3.71	4.45	4.58	1.2
2014	BAL	MLB	26	10	11	0	30	30	169	164	24	57	135	3.1	7.2	40%	.286	1.31	4.08	4.68	4.43	1.1

Tillman's 2013 was a success, especially for an organization that has been dying to develop a quality starting pitcher. He's not an original Oriole, but they acquired him before he reached the high minors as part of the Erik Bedard deal, giving them a real hand in his development. His 2012 ERA was flashy but it came in just 86 innings and the BABIP and strikeout rate were low enough to cause some alarm, so 2013 serves as a sort of confirmation that he's probably pretty good. It feels like Tillman has been around forever because of his inclusion in a high-profile trade *six* years ago, but he is still just 26 and not yet a complete product. He needs to alleviate his home run problem or his ceiling will linger around the mid-rotation level, but this might just be the cost of doing business as a fly-ball pitcher in Baltimore.

Tsuyoshi Wada
Born: 2/21/1981 Age: 33
Bats: L Throws: L Height: 5' 11" Weight: 180
Breakout: 38% Improve: 63% Collapse: 37%
Attrition: 46% MLB: 8%

Comparables:
Adam Pettyjohn, Matt Kinney, Dan Reichert

YEAR	TEAM	LVL	AGE	W	L	SV	G	GS	IP	H	HR	BB	SO	BB9	SO9	GB%	BABIP	WHIP	ERA	FIP	FRA	WARP
2013	NOR	AAA	32	5	6	0	19	19	102²	112	9	35	80	3.1	7.0	39%	.328	1.43	4.03	3.93	4.95	0.4
2014	BAL	MLB	33	4	5	0	11	11	72¹	80	10	27	48	3.4	5.9	41%	.304	1.48	5.05	5.09	5.49	-0.5

Well that didn't work. Wada spent all of 2013 at Triple-A after undergoing Tommy John surgery in May 2012. The lefty's two-year, $8 million contract thus expired without him throwing a single pitch in the major leagues. Baltimore, you'll be surprised to hear, declined his $5 million option just after the season ended. It is a requirement that *Baseball Prospectus* comments about Wada use the phrase "crafty lefty," so there you go.

Ryan Webb
Born: 2/5/1986 Age: 28
Bats: R Throws: R Height: 6' 6" Weight: 245
Breakout: 29% Improve: 51% Collapse: 26%
Attrition: 15% MLB: 73%

Comparables:
Cla Meredith, Todd Coffey, Tony Pena

YEAR	TEAM	LVL	AGE	W	L	SV	G	GS	IP	H	HR	BB	SO	BB9	SO9	GB%	BABIP	WHIP	ERA	FIP	FRA	WARP
2011	FLO	MLB	25	2	4	0	53	0	50²	48	2	20	31	3.6	5.5	62%	.291	1.34	3.20	3.59	4.61	-0.2
2012	MIA	MLB	26	4	3	0	65	0	60¹	72	2	20	44	3.0	6.6	52%	.355	1.52	4.03	3.30	3.18	0.8
2013	MIA	MLB	27	2	6	0	66	0	80¹	70	5	27	54	3.0	6.0	58%	.267	1.21	2.91	3.57	3.87	0.4
2014	BAL	MLB	28	3	1	1	59	0	64¹	66	6	20	46	2.9	6.4	52%	.301	1.34	4.07	4.12	4.43	0.3

The big sinkerballer was the hardest working man in the Marlins' bullpen during the 2013 season, and while that doesn't exactly make him James Brown, it did make him an arbitration risk and, consequently, Marlins non-tender. Still a predominantly sinker-slider pitcher, Webb was more effective against left-handed batters this year—partly due to his willingness to not go to his below-average changeup as much. He did see a precipitous decline in velocity, as he averaged 93 mph on his sinker—more than a mile and a half lower than any previous year—though strikeouts have never been a big part of his game. Webb, like a much more famous pitcher he shares a surname with, derives his value by keeping his infielders busy, with a 57 percent career groundball rate. That'll play well this year in front of J.J. Hardy and Manny Machado.

Tyler Wilson
Born: 9/25/1989 Age: 24
Bats: R Throws: R Height: 6' 2" Weight: 185
Breakout: 51% Improve: 84% Collapse: 8%
Attrition: 53% MLB: 28%

Comparables:
Greg Smith, Todd Redmond, Brandon Workman

YEAR	TEAM	LVL	AGE	W	L	SV	G	GS	IP	H	HR	BB	SO	BB9	SO9	GB%	BABIP	WHIP	ERA	FIP	FRA	WARP
2011	ABE	A-	21	0	0	0	6	6	30	19	4	4	24	1.2	7.2	57%	.184	0.77	2.10	4.00	4.50	0.1
2012	DEL	A	22	3	3	0	6	6	32	30	4	11	29	3.1	8.2	53%	.295	1.28	5.06	4.52	5.32	0.3
2012	FRD	A+	22	7	7	0	19	19	111	95	12	19	114	1.5	9.2	43%	.285	1.03	3.49	3.41	3.97	1.9
2013	FRD	A+	23	1	1	0	11	11	62¹	57	4	25	48	3.6	6.9	44%	.285	1.32	4.48	3.89	4.80	0.7
2013	BOW	AA	23	7	5	0	16	16	89¹	85	13	22	70	2.2	7.1	35%	.270	1.20	3.83	4.45	5.25	0.3
2014	BAL	MLB	24	7	9	0	23	23	126¹	133	20	42	86	3.0	6.1	41%	.288	1.39	4.69	5.17	5.10	-0.1

Plugging away two levels at a time, Wilson took a second tour of High-A before getting promoted to Double-A and putting up solid results without overpowering stuff. A control artist type, Wilson has never been one to give up free passes and even though his walk rate was a career-worst in 2013, his 7.4 percent rate is not alarming in a vacuum. Homers have always been an issue and Wilson was something of a launching pad with Bowie. He can't afford to miss with his 88 to 91 mph fastball—command is imperative if that's all the heat you've got. Look for him to repeat Double-A, at least to start the year.

Mike Wright
Born: 1/3/1990 Age: 24
Bats: R Throws: R Height: 6' 6" Weight: 215
Breakout: 46% Improve: 83% Collapse: 15%
Attrition: 72% MLB: 39%
Comparables:
Brandon Workman, Juan Nicasio, Tommy Milone

YEAR	TEAM	LVL	AGE	W	L	SV	G	GS	IP	H	HR	BB	SO	BB9	SO9	GB%	BABIP	WHIP	ERA	FIP	FRA	WARP
2011	DEL	A	21	1	1	0	4	1	13²	21	3	4	12	2.6	7.9	54%	.333	1.83	10.54	5.94	5.09	-0.1
2011	ABE	A-	21	2	1	0	7	7	31	29	3	6	29	1.7	8.4	58%	.338	1.13	3.77	3.43	4.05	0.4
2012	FRD	A+	22	5	2	0	8	8	46¹	47	3	5	35	1.0	6.8	45%	.310	1.12	2.91	3.10	3.46	0.9
2012	BOW	AA	22	5	3	0	12	12	62¹	71	7	17	45	2.5	6.5	52%	.328	1.41	4.91	4.18	5.04	0.3
2013	BOW	AA	23	11	3	0	26	26	143²	152	9	39	136	2.4	8.5	44%	.332	1.33	3.26	3.27	3.44	3.6
2014	BAL	MLB	24	6	8	0	28	22	123	137	17	36	83	2.6	6.1	45%	.306	1.40	4.71	4.80	5.12	-0.0

Wright was solid in his repeat turn around Double-A—this time with a full season's worth of innings—posting his best ERA as a pro yet. It wasn't without flaws, though: His component numbers didn't show any real improvement, and his strikeout-to-walk ratio was a career worst (albeit still healthy at 3.5:1). His command didn't advance in line with the ERA improvement, either. He continues to pepper the zone with solid stuff, but misses too many spots, resulting in too many hits. Worse yet, his ground-ball rate, once an asset, dropped off. There is still upside, though it's modest: fourth starter, good reliever, that type of thing.

LINEOUTS

HITTERS

PLAYER	TEAM	LVL	AGE	PA	R	2B	3B	HR	RBI	BB	SO	SB-CS	AVG/OBP/SLG	TAv	BABIP	BRR	FRAA	WARP
LF J. Borbon	IOW	AAA	27	86	10	5	0	0	1	12	15	5-1	.260/.360/.329	.260	.322	-0.5	LF(14): -2.4, RF(3): 0.0	-0.1
	TEX	MLB	27	1	1	0	0	0	0	0	0	0-0	.000/.000/.000	.001	.000	0		0.0
	CHN	MLB	27	117	10	3	1	1	3	12	22	7-1	.202/.284/.279	.220	.247	0.5	CF(12): 0.1, LF(9): -0.1	0.0
C S. Clevenger	ABE	A-	27	20	4	0	0	0	1	2	0	0-0	.389/.450/.389	.352	.389	-0.3	C(3): -0.0, 1B(2): 0.1	0.2
	IOW	AAA	27	61	14	5	0	3	11	9	7	0-0	.327/.426/.596	.374	.333	-0.5	C(11): 0.1, 1B(2): 0.1	0.8
	NOR	AAA	27	82	12	2	0	2	11	10	9	0-0	.324/.402/.437	.290	.344	-1	C(11): -0.0, 1B(8): -0.1	0.4
	BAL	MLB	27	15	1	1	0	0	2	0	2	0-0	.267/.267/.333	.195	.308	0	C(4): -0.1	-0.1
	CHN	MLB	27	9	1	0	0	0	0	1	3	0-0	.125/.222/.125	.155	.200	0.4	3B(2): 0.0	0.0
CF G. Davis	FRD	A+	21	410	42	17	3	2	32	43	74	19-7	.234/.316/.313	.232	.288	-0.1	CF(91): -4.0, LF(4): -0.1	-0.7
RF L. Ford	BOW	AA	36	75	13	9	0	3	10	6	9	0-0	.258/.347/.530	.309	.259	0.4	RF(9): 0.8, LF(1): 0.0	0.7
	NOR	AAA	36	51	8	3	0	2	4	2	4	0-0	.170/.196/.362	.179	.140	0.6	RF(4): -0.3	-0.3
C C. Joseph	BOW	AA	27	570	74	31	2	22	97	39	92	4-2	.299/.346/.494	.302	.321	0.8	C(64): 0.7, LF(16): -1.5	4.0
C J. Monell	FRE	AAA	27	481	71	27	2	20	64	59	105	6-3	.275/.364/.494	.297	.319	0.3	C(48): 1.0, 1B(47): 0.5	3.0
	SFN	MLB	27	9	2	0	0	0	1	0	3	0-0	.125/.222/.125	.230	.200	0	C(1): -0.0	0.0
C C. Robinson	NOR	AAA	29	113	9	4	0	0	5	4	24	0-0	.241/.268/.278	.204	.310	-0.5	C(27): -0.1, 1B(1): 0.0	-0.4
	TUC	AAA	29	142	20	5	0	0	17	3	18	2-2	.316/.338/.353	.256	.362	0.2	C(39): 1.5	0.6
	SDN	MLB	29	12	1	0	0	1	3	0	3	0-0	.167/.167/.417	.218	.125	0	C(2): -0.0	0.0
CF T. Robinson	BOW	AA	25	228	34	15	1	6	28	24	55	12-4	.271/.348/.447	.289	.345	-2.5	CF(45): -0.8, LF(8): -0.2	1.1
	NOR	AAA	25	201	28	5	0	5	15	22	60	9-2	.220/.307/.333	.251	.304	0.5	LF(35): -1.7, CF(10): -0.0	0.0
C C. Snyder	SLC	AAA	32	86	14	6	0	7	21	6	22	0-1	.342/.388/.684	.350	.400	-1.7	C(9): 0.5	0.9
	NOR	AAA	32	200	16	8	0	6	24	17	47	0-0	.243/.305/.387	.241	.292	-2.6	C(47): -0.9	0.0
	BAL	MLB	32	24	0	0	0	0	1	4	7	0-0	.100/.250/.100	.155	.154	-0.6	C(8): -0.0	-0.1
C T. Teagarden	BAL	MLB	29	62	3	2	0	2	5	1	18	0-1	.167/.180/.300	.162	.200	-0.1	C(23): 0.1	-0.3
3B H. Veloz	ABE	A-	19	224	17	7	1	5	27	17	70	4-2	.213/.277/.332	.245	.292	-0.4	3B(54): -3.0, 1B(1): -0.0	0.2

April waiver claim **Julio Borbon** frustrated his new employers during a summer filled with serial out making, bad defense and mental gaffes, reaffirming his status as a slappy fifth outfielder who doesn't reach base enough to take advantage of his speed. ⏣ **Steve Clevenger** has now strained each oblique in the last two seasons, costing him a total of three and a half months. His strong work from the high minors has yet to translate into anything meaningful, but he's yet to earn a meaningful sample of playing time, either. ⊘ **Glynn Davis**, an undrafted speedster, is a legitimate center fielder with a decent approach at the plate, but zero power, as the remarkable .066 ISO he has compiled in the low minors shows. ⊘ Remember when **Lew Ford** played in the majors in 2012 after not appearing since 2007? That was neat! ⊘ **Caleb Joseph** had a big season, but the reality check is that he did so at 27 and in his fourth year at Double-A, so the upside remains "bench guy." ⊘ **Johnny Monell** Sr. played pro ball for 17 seasons and never got a cup of coffee, but Junior did his old man proud when he was called up by the Giants this September. He doesn't figure to be in San Francisco's plans at the big-league level, especially now that he's with Baltimore. ⊘ Before taking Arizona's Eury De La Rosa deep last September, journeyman catcher **Chris Robinson** hadn't homered since July 17, 2011, while with the Iowa Cubs; apparently he didn't find De La Rosa too hard to handle. ⊘ A disastrous 2013 for **Trayvon Robinson** resulted in a backslide from Triple-A to Double-A. He doesn't make enough contact to succeed in the majors and isn't good enough in center field to even be a defensive replacement. ⊘ **Chris Snyder** had a good OBP over 34 games in 2011, which counts as a stellar resume in the pool of third catchers hanging around in Triple-A for a shot. ⊘ Remember when **Taylor Teagarden** was part of the must-not-trade throng of catchers in Texas? Hope he does, because memories are all he's got left at this point. ⊘ Signed as a 16-year-old in 2010, **Hector Veloz** has raw power to build on, but he remains a long way out and scouts are skeptical about whether he can stick at third.

PITCHERS

PLAYER	TEAM	LVL	AGE	W	L	SV	IP	H	HR	BB	SO	BB9	SO9	GB%	BABIP	WHIP	ERA	FIP	FRA	WARP
N. Additon	MEM	AAA	25	9	7	0	131²	117	15	38	117	2.6	8.0	38%	.272	1.18	4.10	4.21	4.61	0.9
T. Alderson	ALT	AA	24	1	0	2	13²	4	0	2	17	1.3	11.2	61%	.143	0.44	1.32	1.27	1.85	0.5
	IND	AAA	24	3	1	0	42	40	5	10	38	2.1	8.1	51%	.294	1.19	2.79	3.66	4.69	0.1
	NOR	AAA	24	1	2	0	33	39	4	10	26	2.7	7.1	44%	.337	1.48	6.27	4.11	4.76	0.0
M. Belfiore	NOR	AAA	24	2	1	1	76¹	81	8	29	82	3.4	9.7	41%	.348	1.44	3.18	3.60	4.35	0.7
	BAL	MLB	24	0	0	0	1¹	3	2	1	0	6.8	0.0	33%	.250	3.00	13.50	24.83	37.71	-0.3
T. Berry	FRD	A+	22	11	7	0	152	156	13	40	119	2.4	7.0	47%	.310	1.29	3.85	3.84	4.61	2.1
P. Bridwell	DEL	A	21	8	9	0	142²	141	9	59	144	3.7	9.1	42%	.322	1.40	4.73	3.71	4.98	0.4
Z. Clark	FRD	A+	29	1	7	0	44¹	51	3	42	20	8.5	4.1	50%	.312	2.10	9.74	6.91	9.38	-1.1
	BOW	AA	29	1	4	0	24	32	2	20	17	7.5	6.4	57%	.375	2.17	8.62	5.74	6.44	-0.3
	NOR	AAA	29	1	2	0	25²	30	1	7	20	2.5	7.0	62%	.341	1.44	4.56	3.09	4.37	0.3
	BAL	MLB	29	0	0	0	1²	3	0	2	1	10.8	5.4	43%	.429	3.00	16.20	5.48	4.26	0.0
E. Escalona	COL	MLB	26	1	4	0	46	52	8	14	34	2.7	6.7	38%	.308	1.43	5.67	4.85	6.06	-0.4
J. Gurka	BOW	AA	25	2	2	4	39²	35	2	18	46	4.1	10.4	46%	.337	1.34	2.95	3.47	3.30	0.9
T. Howard	FRD	A+	23	3	2	1	88	87	6	25	72	2.6	7.4	48%	.301	1.27	3.48	3.55	4.81	1.6
T. McFarland	BAL	MLB	24	4	1	0	74²	83	7	28	58	3.4	7.0	60%	.319	1.49	4.22	3.87	4.76	0.2
T. Patton	BAL	MLB	27	2	0	0	56	57	8	16	42	2.6	6.8	48%	.295	1.30	3.70	4.45	4.92	0.0
J. Rauch	MIA	MLB	34	1	2	0	16²	23	1	7	15	3.8	8.1	48%	.400	1.80	7.56	3.44	3.49	0.2
L. Rutledge	DEL	A	22	4	3	1	43¹	28	1	16	45	3.3	9.3	66%	.252	1.02	1.45	2.95	3.17	0.7
	FRD	A+	22	1	0	0	12²	18	1	7	15	5.0	10.7	41%	.425	1.97	7.82	3.90	4.26	0.2
J. Stinson	NOR	AAA	25	7	6	0	131	126	11	54	87	3.7	6.0	47%	.293	1.37	3.78	4.30	5.01	0.0
	BAL	MLB	25	0	0	0	17	10	4	3	12	1.6	6.4	47%	.140	0.76	3.18	5.43	5.73	0.0
B. Wager	DEL	A	22	2	3	0	54	56	1	14	41	2.3	6.8	64%	.320	1.30	4.33	3.04	5.01	-0.1
	FRD	A+	22	3	10	0	86	93	5	32	57	3.3	6.0	59%	.315	1.45	5.23	4.28	5.75	0.2

With a capable performance over 315 innings at Triple-A there is good chance that **Nick Additon**, the 1,418th overall pick in 2006, makes the majors at some point in 2014, which is an upset victory regardless of how he performs. ⊘ A former top 100 prospect, **Tim Alderson** is now rebuilding his stock as a full-time reliever, but without overpowering velocity from the right side, his curveball is the key to his success. ⊘ **Michael Belfiore** is looking at a LOOGY ceiling, which is pretty gross when you start building that mental image. ⊘ **Tim Berry**'s second turn around High-A produced almost a carbon copy season as the lefty appears to be tracking toward a future in the bullpen with a useful fastball-curve combo. ⊘ Though still raw, **Parker Bridwell** took a step forward while repeating A-ball. His secondary pitches all need work, but he sliced an ugly 2012 home run rate in half with marked improvements in his command. ⊘ **Zach Clark** has 24 different stops in his eight-year minor-league career, all in the Orioles organization. He's 30 and he doesn't throw very hard. ⊘ As a Rockie, **Edgmer Escalona** was somehow even worse away from Coors Field, which had to just kill his manager. ⊘ **Jason Gurka**'s heater-curve pair could give him a career as a lefty-killer, and the book isn't closed on his changeup, the development of which could upgrade him to a full-inning role. ⊘ **Trent Howard** has been yoyoed between the rotation and bullpen throughout his career, but he'll likely end up in the latter with decent velocity and an improving curveball. ⊘ After 74 league-average innings out of the bullpen, it is hard to label **T.J. McFarland** as anything other than a Rule 5 success, though he was awfully hittable. ⊘ **Troy Patton**'s home run and walk rates have been going the wrong way the last three years, and he'll miss the first 25 games after a second positive amphetamine test. ⊘ **Jon Rauch**'s 2013 ERA passed his height. Even if he were Tim Collins, that would not be great. ⊘ **Lex Rutledge** has a power fastball from the left side and, frankly, he'd better if he's going to do justice to the terrifically badass name "Lex." ⊘ When you allow more homers than walks in a season, you've either done something weird or pitched a very small sample of innings; left as an exercise to the reader is which category **Josh Stinson** fits. ⊘ **Brady Wager** is a sinker/slider righty with a very nice groundball rate who's a reasonable *wager* to make the big leagues, at least in a relief role. (Oh, hush. He's the last guy in the chapter.)

MANAGER: BUCK SHOWALTER

YEAR	TEAM	W-L	Pythag +/-	Avg PC	100+ P	120+ P	QS	BQS	REL	REL w Zero R	IBB	PH	PH Avg	PH HR	SB2	CS2	SB3	CS3	SAC Att	SAC %	POS SAC	Squeeze	Swing	In Play
2011	BAL	69-93	0	91.8	50	0	60	6	478	351	42	57	.309	1	74	20	7	5	41	58.5%	23	2	309	97
2012	BAL	93-69	1	95.6	66	1	78	6	492	415	36	69	.161	0	55	21	3	8	51	74.5%	34	1	282	102
2013	BAL	85-77	1	95.9	75	0	78	5	473	380	32	65	.143	0	70	26	9	2	39	69.2%	23	0	236	68

Buck Showalter used to be one of the game's all-time great opponents of small ball. His 2005 Rangers still hold the record for fewest sacrifice hits in a season, with nine. But, for whatever reason, Buck has bucked his own trend in Baltimore. His Orioles were second in sacrifice hits in 2012. In 2013 they fell back to the pack—but even being in the pack is unusual for Showalter. His teams still typically don't steal very much, but even there Showalter is closing in on the mean. The 2013 Orioles attempted 108 steals, the most by one of Showalter's squads since his days in Arizona.

In other ways, Showalter's teams are the same as they used to be. The Orioles had the highest isolated power in the game last year. That's the third time a Showalter team has topped the league in that stat, and the ninth time one of his squads has finished in the top four.

Showalter's starting nine position players accounted for 82.3 percent of the team's PA, the most by any team in 2013.

Boston Red Sox

By Alex Speier

"There is a set of advantages that have to do with material resources, and there is a set that have to do with the absence of material resources and the reason underdogs win as often as they do is that the latter are sometimes every bit the equal of the former. For some reason, this is a very difficult lesson for us to learn. We have I think a very rigid and limited definition of what an advantage is. We think of things as helpful that actually aren't, and think of other things as unhelpful that are."

—Malcolm Gladwell, *David and Goliath*

Why must Goliath stick to a Goliath's game? What happens if a team armed with tremendous material resources ignores the players whom it is "supposed" to sign, and instead competes for the same players sought by those who lack material resources? This was the case study offered by the 2013 Red Sox, with not merely memorable but also startling results.

The Red Sox' one-year transformation from a 69-win catastrophe to a World Series winner represents one of the most fascinating reversals in baseball history. There are few instances of big-market teams so rapidly repudiating their own operating philosophies, and even fewer of teams so rapidly identifying a successful alternative.

From 2009 to 2011, the Red Sox—tempted by what seemed like their tremendous proximity to a championship—slowly took on one megacontract after another that seemed out of place with the team's proclivities of the previous seven offseasons. In just under a year, they signed John Lackey to a five-year, $82.5 million deal, extended Josh Beckett for four years and $68 million, traded for Adrian Gonzalez and agreed to the parameters of a seven-year, $154 million extension and signed Carl Crawford to a seven-year, $142 million deal.

These were Goliath moves, with Goliath consequences. By 2012, all four players were underperforming their expectations dramatically, and the Sox proved vulnerable both to the bigger Goliaths (the Yankees) and the more nimble, less elephantine smaller-market competitors from Tampa Bay to Oakland. The Sox were cumbersome, their considerable financial resources maxed in a fashion that made the consequences of injuries to regulars drastic. Either a punch to the face from a larger foe or a well-targeted slingshot from a smaller one could topple the club. The Sox suffered plenty of each.

With roughly $75 million tied up in four players who were being paid like superstars without performing at such a level, the Sox were in a terrible place. Their payroll was functionally maxed out, preventing the team from acquiring players who could compensate for the injuries and underperformances of regulars. Given the need to get under the luxury tax threshold of $189 million in 2014 (a pursuit intended not so much to avoid the tax as to get back millions in revenue sharing), the Red Sox faced a very real possibility of being in a bad, bad place with their roster construction for years.

When the Dodgers liberated the Red Sox from their three most cumbersome contracts (Gonzalez, Crawford and Beckett) in one swoop, the Sox were more than happy to endure the miserable end of the 2012 season in order to have a chance to start over. And start over they did, without repeating the sins of their recent past.

Instead of concentrating their resources in big-ticket items, the Red Sox steered clear of free agents who required the sacrifice of a draft pick and/or a massive long-term commitment of five or more years. The team never moved beyond the fringes pursuing Zack Greinke, Josh Hamilton or Anibal Sanchez, instead building its 2013 roster (after re-signing David Ortiz to a two-year, $26 million deal) through seven free agent signings of one to three years.

RED SOX PROSPECTUS
2013 W-L: 97-65, 1st in AL East

Pythag	.622	2nd	DER	.706	11th
RS/G	5.27	1st	B-Age	29.7	26th
RA/G	4.05	13th	P-Age	30.0	28th
TAv	.287	1st	Salary	$150.7	4th
BRR	1.11	14th	M$/MW	$2.84	16th
TAv-P	.261	13th	DL Days	1041	18th
FIP	3.87	16th	$ on DL	17%	16th

	Runs	HR/RH	HR/LH	Runs/RH	Runs/LH
Three-Year Park Factors	101	87	81	101	101

Top Hitter WARP	5.23 (Shane Victorino)
Top Pitcher WARP	2.85 (Jon Lester)
Top Prospect	Xander Bogaerts

Drumroll: Shane Victorino: three years, $39 million; Ryan Dempster: two years, $26.5 million; Stephen Drew: one year, $9.5 million; Jonny Gomes, two years, $10 million; Mike Napoli: one year, $5 million (with incentives that pushed the deal to $13 million); Koji Uehara: one year, $4.25 million; David Ross: two years, $6.2 million.

The team outbid the Rays for Ross (their first signing), the Athletics for Gomes (their second signing), the Indians for Victorino, the Royals for Dempster ... all while identifying players who a) had identifiable on-field value; b) did not cost the team a draft pick, meaning that at no point did the present compromise the future; and c) came with formidable clubhouse credentials that, in combination with the firing of Bobby Valentine and hiring of John Farrell, would permit the team to replace the dizzying and contentious environment of 2012 with restored commitment to nightly preparation.

The result? Uehara jumping into Ross' arms with the organization's third championship in 10 seasons.

That recap glosses over quite a bit, and in fairness the success of the approach couldn't be predicted (and very well might not be possible to replicate with the same group of players under the same circumstances). Indeed, Sox officials gleefully acknowledged that they, too, were damn near as surprised as the fans who had dismissed most of the free agent signings as inadequate and/or cheap.

(One team official chuckled in the last days of the season that the near-universal reaction to the signings of Ross and Gomes to kick off the offseason was, "What the **** are they doing?")

While the Sox avoided using the terminology of "the bridge"—the desperately misunderstood metaphor for the team's effort to sign veterans who could win while buying time for prospects to develop—it was precisely what 2013 was supposed to be. It was a year of restoration that had some chance of modest success (perhaps even a trip to the postseason if everything broke right), but that was meant to bring the franchise closer to what GM Ben Cherington kept describing as "the next great Red Sox team." It was a lofty ideal with an unspecified timeframe, a private acknowledgment that modest gains in 2013 could set the stage for significant ones by 2014, when prospects like Jackie Bradley Jr. and Xander Bogaerts and Allen Webster and Matt Barnes might bring Cherington's goal closer to fruition.

The Sox' internal preseason projections pegged the team's likeliest outcome as 86 wins, with a roughly 30 percent chance of winning 90 or more (meaning contention) and odds little better than one in a hundred that the team would get to its eventual 97-win outcome. When they clinched the AL East, team chairman Tom Werner acknowledged that "we're all in a bit of shock. I had a projection but it was less than this."

He wasn't alone. So what now? Given that a year that was expected to serve as a prelude instead became a pinnacle, do the Red Sox—even at a time when they represent a portrait of organizational health—have anywhere to go but down?

It's an open question, but it's clear that the team will rely on a different formula to try to replicate the results. Consider the clash between projections and reality, and all that had to go right to make it happen. Ortiz, whom the Sox thought would sit one or two games a week in deference to a 2012-ending Achilles injury, instead remained a constant and a force in the middle of the order, hitting .309/.395/.564 in 600 plate appearances and reclaiming October as his personal showcase month. Shane Victorino—despite a succession of injuries that forced him to abandon switch-hitting and instead hit exclusively right-handed in August—shed his disappointing 2012 campaign to post the second-best WARP of his career, and became the first player ever to drive in the go-ahead run in each of three postseason clinchers. Uehara defied his reputation of fragility to make history, recording the lowest WHIP ever while becoming the first pitcher ever to punch out at least 100 batters and walk fewer than 10. Mike Napoli, Jonny Gomes, Ryan Dempster and Stephen Drew all performed roughly to their career track records.

In other words, the Sox got performances that were either in line with or dramatically exceeded the expectations they'd set entering the year. The health of Uehara, Ortiz and Napoli (whose deal was renegotiated from three years to one after the discovery of a degenerative hip condition) proved better than most best-case projections. That health made the Red Sox an incredibly deep team: Mike Carp became a valuable reserve who was never asked to assume a larger role. Daniel Nava enjoyed a breakthrough in part because he could be used largely in a platoon capacity. The Sox were able to create impactful depth almost entirely through players who were not in the organization in 2012.

The Red Sox are staying committed to a depth model rather than a superstar model (or, at least, a resource-exhausting superstar model), but they hope to change the source of that depth. As the postseason performances of both Xander Bogaerts and Brandon Workman suggested, the Sox believe the end of the bridge is nigh, with impact performers ready to emerge from a loaded prospect crop.

Bogaerts certainly appears ready to be a big leaguer, with potential superstardom awaiting him. Workman is a big-league-ready depth option in the bullpen or rotation. The team believes Bradley is good enough to play in the majors now. Others—the prized arms acquired from the Dodgers in 2012 (Allen Webster and Rubby De La Rosa), projected Pawtucket starters Anthony Ranaudo and Matt Barnes, Double-A left-hander Henry Owens, catcher Christian Vazquez, etc.—are close.

That wealth of upper-levels talent underscores that the Red Sox' successes of 2013 were not limited to the big-league club. The player development system also had an impressive year, building the foundation to make that success sustainable—altering the complexion of the depth that proved such a great asset this past year by tapping into a different, less volatile source.

Or, at least, that's the easy-to-reach conclusion at the end of 2013. The reality is that even now, with the organization seemingly positioned well for years to come, it would be foolhardy to take for granted what the Sox accomplished this past year, or their likelihood of remaining atop the baseball world.

If hubris is a temptation, then the Red Sox need look no further than their 2007 championship club, a loaded team that offered a glimpse in the World Series of what appeared to be a title-worthy foundation for years to come. Rookies Dustin Pedroia and Jacoby Ellsbury ran amok while Jon Lester gave a glimpse of potential greatness with a strong performance in the World Series clincher—less than two months after rookie Clay Buchholz had thrown a no-hitter.

After that title, Sox officials wrestled with the question of whether the team was more likely to achieve a dynasty by keeping its full ensemble of prospects intact or by trading Ellsbury and Lester (along with Justin Masterson and Jed Lowrie) for Johan Santana. Yet but for the improbable championship run of 2013 the core of Ellsbury, Lester and Pedroia never would have played in the World Series again. With the benefit of hindsight, such dialogue appears less than flattering

(though it's worth noting that the Sox *did* reach Game 7 of the ALCS in 2008), even if its basis was understandable.

And now? At a time when team officials hope they are on the verge of achieving the sustainable vision for the Next Great Red Sox Team, they are mindful of the unlikely and somewhat unplanned arrival of a great Red Sox team in 2013, a team whose extraordinary collective success might represent the team's most dramatic forecasting whiff.

Even so, the team believes in the merits of the methods it followed, and appears determined to avoid falling back into the Goliath trap. The willingness to avoid getting drawn into a bidding war with the Yankees on Ellsbury offers evidence of that approach. "We still prefer shorter to longer-term contracts. We have a presumption against really long-term contracts," said team president and CEO Larry Lucchino. "A lot of things we did last year proved to be successful, at least in the short term, so I think we're going to behave accordingly going forward."

Will that net another championship, or at least perennial aspirations for division titles? It remains to be seen. But at a time when the market is exploding with megadeals, if the Red Sox prove successful by forgoing the most expensive free agents in favor of modest free agent deals that address a range of deficiencies, then the startling turnaround of 2013 could become the model for other clubs going forward.

Alex Speier is the Red Sox beat writer for WEEI.com.

HITTERS

Mookie Betts   2B
Born: **10/7/1992** Age: **21**
Bats: **R** Throws: **R** Height: **5' 9"**
Weight: **156** Breakout: **3%**
Improve: **15%** Collapse: **0%**
Attrition: **6%** MLB: **19%**

Comparables:
Alexi Amarista, Jonathan Schoop, Johnny Giavotella

YEAR	TEAM	LVL	AGE	PA	R	2B	3B	HR	RBI	BB	SO	SB	CS	AVG/OBP/SLG	TAv	BABIP	BRR	FRAA	WARP
2012	LOW	A-	19	292	34	8	1	0	31	32	30	20	4	.267/.352/.307	.293	.298	2.2	2B(58): 1.0, SS(13): 1.5	2.5
2013	GRN	A	20	340	63	24	1	8	26	58	40	18	2	.296/.418/.477	.329	.322	4.7	2B(76): -4.0	3.4
2013	SLM	A+	20	211	30	12	3	7	39	23	17	20	2	.341/.414/.551	.331	.346	3	2B(50): 7.1	3.5
2014	BOS	MLB	21	250	27	12	1	5	26	23	42	6	1	.257/.328/.380	.260	.290	0.5	2B 1, SS 0	1.1

Betts began 2013 in a more-passive-than-patient funk, but once things clicked and he started swinging at the right offerings, all he did was hit. Following a promotion to High-A, Betts batted .341 with power and patience while striking out—wait for it—17 times in 211 plate appearances, or just 8 percent of the time. Did we mention he's just 20, and did this *after* a promotion? He was also successful on 90 percent of the 42 steals he attempted and played a quality keystone, all of which likely means he'll begin 2014 at Double-A in his age-21 season. The question is whether the 156-pound Betts continues to hit for power, but the bat speed is there thanks to his wrists, and his eye and approach are points in his favor.

Xander Bogaerts   SS
Born: **10/1/1992** Age: **21**
Bats: **R** Throws: **R** Height: **6' 3"**
Weight: **185** Breakout: **8%**
Improve: **22%** Collapse: **2%**
Attrition: **13%** MLB: **34%**

Comparables:
Reid Brignac, Joel Guzman, Eric Hosmer

YEAR	TEAM	LVL	AGE	PA	R	2B	3B	HR	RBI	BB	SO	SB	CS	AVG/OBP/SLG	TAv	BABIP	BRR	FRAA	WARP
2011	GRN	A	18	296	38	14	2	16	45	25	71	1	3	.260/.324/.509	.256	.291	0.4	SS(28): 6.7	1.0
2012	SLM	A+	19	435	59	27	3	15	64	43	85	4	4	.302/.378/.505	.305	.353	-2	SS(98): -7.1	3.2
2012	PME	AA	19	97	12	10	0	5	17	1	21	1	1	.326/.351/.598	.329	.373	-1.4	SS(21): 2.8	1.2
2013	PME	AA	20	259	40	12	6	6	35	35	51	5	1	.311/.407/.502	.324	.378	1.9	SS(47): -3.1	2.4
2013	PAW	AAA	20	256	32	11	0	9	32	28	44	2	2	.284/.369/.453	.285	.320	1.5	SS(49): -5.9, 3B(10): -0.7	1.2
2013	BOS	MLB	20	50	7	2	0	1	5	5	13	1	0	.250/.320/.364	.300	.323	1.1	3B(9): -0.4, SS(8): 0.9	0.5
2014	BOS	MLB	21	250	27	12	1	7	31	20	59	1	0	.262/.324/.426	.274	.320	-0.3	SS -1, 3B -0	1.2

There is nothing more exciting in baseball than possibility. Bogaerts, just 21 years old, is nothing *but* possibility. Despite his youth, he vanquished Double-A in short order, then did the same to Triple-A pitching before earning the call to the majors. While he barely played before October came, he looked like a veteran of huge, high-leverage, bright-spotlight moments when it counted, drawing key walks and scoring runs when the Red Sox needed them most. It's this adjustment to his competition, to his environment, that makes the possibility of Bogaerts so enticing. It's easy to believe that he can become whatever fans, analysts and scouts have dreamed for him, because the talent, the baseball IQ and the work ethic are all strong in this one.

Jackie Bradley CF

Born: 4/19/1990 Age: 24
Bats: L Throws: R Height: 5' 10"
Weight: 195 Breakout: 1%
Improve: 24% Collapse: 15%
Attrition: 22% MLB: 63%

Comparables:
Ryan Kalish, Desmond Jennings, Carlos Quentin

YEAR	TEAM	LVL	AGE	PA	R	2B	3B	HR	RBI	BB	SO	SB	CS	AVG/OBP/SLG	TAv	BABIP	BRR	FRAA	WARP
2011	LOW	A-	21	25	5	0	0	0	0	4	5	0	2	.190/.320/.190	.190	.250	0.1	CF(4): -0.5	-0.1
2012	SLM	A+	22	304	53	26	2	3	34	52	40	16	6	.359/.480/.526	.362	.407	0.3	CF(66): 1.5, RF(1): -0.1	4.4
2012	PME	AA	22	271	37	16	2	6	29	35	49	8	3	.271/.373/.437	.294	.316	-2.4	CF(48): -0.0	1.5
2013	PAW	AAA	23	374	57	26	3	10	35	41	75	7	7	.275/.374/.469	.302	.331	0.1	CF(58): 3.0, RF(7): 0.4	3.3
2013	BOS	MLB	23	107	18	5	0	3	10	10	31	2	0	.189/.280/.337	.236	.246	-2.2	CF(19): 0.5, LF(14): -0.1	-0.3
2014	BOS	MLB	24	250	31	14	1	5	24	26	55	4	2	.254/.342/.398	.273	.310	-0.3	CF 1, LF 0	1.1

Bradley's huge spring gave the uninitiated the wrong impression, as he's not a power-hitting center fielder who will perfectly replace Jacoby Ellsbury. Bradley plays Gold Glove-caliber defense, but he's not a burner on the basepaths, and his game is more about patience and walks than anything. This isn't a bad thing, as he's the kind of player who could make an all-star team or two in his day. While he needs to work on hitting low, inside fastballs, he's a complete enough package to start in the majors on Opening Day, and that's all Boston needs at this early stage of his career.

Bryce Brentz RF

Born: 12/30/1988 Age: 25
Bats: R Throws: R Height: 6' 0"
Weight: 190 Breakout: 4%
Improve: 10% Collapse: 3%
Attrition: 15% MLB: 21%

Comparables:
Jai Miller, Jeremy Moore, Brad Snyder

YEAR	TEAM	LVL	AGE	PA	R	2B	3B	HR	RBI	BB	SO	SB	CS	AVG/OBP/SLG	TAv	BABIP	BRR	FRAA	WARP
2011	GRN	A	22	186	43	10	3	11	36	14	35	2	2	.359/.414/.647	.301	.403	-0.3	RF(15): -0.7	0.4
2011	SLM	A+	22	321	48	15	1	19	58	26	80	1	1	.274/.336/.531	.251	.311	1	RF(29): 1.0	0.1
2012	PME	AA	23	504	62	30	1	17	76	40	130	7	5	.296/.355/.478	.291	.377	-2.2	RF(83): -2.3	1.9
2013	PAW	AAA	24	349	36	16	1	17	56	20	86	1	0	.264/.312/.475	.264	.309	0.1	RF(55): -3.4, LF(14): -0.3	0.5
2014	BOS	MLB	25	250	26	12	0	9	32	13	71	1	0	.249/.291/.418	.255	.320	-0.5	RF -1, LF -0	0.1

If things go right for Brentz in 2014, he could grow up to be a cost-controlled Jonny Gomes, mashing lefties and putting baseballs over the wall with ease. He's a better defender than Gomes, too, as he has a serious arm that could keep him in right, but range-wise is likely a better fit for left field. However, Brentz lacks what makes Gomes tolerable against same-handed pitching: He is nearly bereft of viable plate discipline. He whiffed 25 percent of the time at Triple-A, with free passes coming in just 6 percent of plate appearances. For an offense-first corner outfielder who will be 25, that's problematic.

Dan Butler C

Born: 10/17/1986 Age: 27
Bats: R Throws: R Height: 5' 10"
Weight: 210 Breakout: 3%
Improve: 9% Collapse: 6%
Attrition: 18% MLB: 30%

Comparables:
Robinson Chirinos, Johnny Monell, Landon Powell

YEAR	TEAM	LVL	AGE	PA	R	2B	3B	HR	RBI	BB	SO	SB	CS	AVG/OBP/SLG	TAv	BABIP	BRR	FRAA	WARP
2011	SLM	A+	24	369	39	20	0	11	66	45	56	4	1	.247/.350/.417	.283	.264	0.6	C(35): 1.0	1.4
2011	PME	AA	24	76	4	5	0	0	2	9	11	0	0	.212/.316/.288	.311	.255	-0.7	C(13): 0.7	0.6
2012	PME	AA	25	285	29	14	2	6	26	31	42	0	0	.251/.351/.397	.263	.281	0.5	C(72): -1.1	1.3
2012	PAW	AAA	25	83	8	5	0	3	11	9	20	0	0	.233/.313/.425	.258	.275	0.3	C(22): -0.2	0.6
2013	PAW	AAA	26	323	32	19	0	14	45	34	59	1	1	.262/.350/.479	.284	.284	-0.9	C(72): -0.0	2.4
2014	BOS	MLB	27	250	26	13	1	7	30	22	50	0	0	.241/.318/.400	.261	.280	-0.4	C 0	1.1

The Red Sox thought enough of Butler to add him to the 40-man last winter, but when the Sox were down to Jarrod Saltalamacchia after David Ross' concussion(s), Butler never got the call to show what he could do. Instead, Boston called up Ryan Lavarnway, then tried their hardest to avoid using him. Butler also didn't receive a September call-up, despite batting .262/.350/.479 in his first extended Triple-A stint, with Lavarnway once again promoted. Butler's defense isn't perfect, but he has the reputation of a capable staff handler, and is the superior backstop to Lavarnway by leaps and bounds. Butler has the potential to be a major-league backup, and if things go awry with 2014's catchers, maybe the Sox will give him the chance to show it this time around.

Mike Carp LF
Born: 6/30/1986 Age: 28
Bats: L Throws: R Height: 6' 2"
Weight: 210 Breakout: 4%
Improve: 34% Collapse: 13%
Attrition: 30% MLB: 72%

Comparables:
John Bowker, Brandon Moss, Scott Hairston

YEAR	TEAM	LVL	AGE	PA	R	2B	3B	HR	RBI	BB	SO	SB	CS	AVG/OBP/SLG	TAv	BABIP	BRR	FRAA	WARP
2011	TAC	AAA	25	286	55	14	0	21	64	28	50	6	2	.343/.411/.649	.342	.355	0.4	LF(32): -0.2, 1B(3): 0.5	2.6
2011	SEA	MLB	25	313	27	17	1	12	46	19	81	0	2	.276/.326/.466	.279	.343	-2.1	1B(34): -0.8, LF(27): -0.0	0.8
2012	TAC	AAA	26	154	13	8	0	2	17	12	31	1	3	.223/.286/.324	.210	.269	-0.8	1B(10): -0.2, 1B(3): 0.0	-0.8
2012	SEA	MLB	26	189	17	6	0	5	20	21	46	1	0	.213/.312/.341	.241	.263	-1.2	LF(24): 1.0, 1B(23): -0.1	-0.1
2013	BOS	MLB	27	243	34	18	2	9	43	22	67	1	0	.296/.362/.523	.322	.385	-0.5	LF(41): -1.7, 1B(29): -1.0	1.6
2014	BOS	MLB	28	250	28	12	1	9	32	22	59	1	1	.252/.325/.430	.274	.300	-0.5	LF 0, 1B 0	0.8

Carp was a late-spring addition to the roster for first base and left field insurance purposes, courtesy of a Mariners team that decided Jason Bay was a better use of a roster spot. Free from Safeco and an organization that has ruined more hitters than it has developed over the last few years, Carp resurrected his career by splitting time between a bench role and pinch-hitting duty. The .385 BABIP is the obvious concern, especially with strikeouts in 28 percent of his plate appearances, but as far as a bench piece with some pop goes, the Sox could be in a worse situation than hoping Carp doesn't completely regress.

Garin Cecchini 3B
Born: 4/20/1991 Age: 23
Bats: L Throws: R Height: 6' 2"
Weight: 200 Breakout: 3%
Improve: 14% Collapse: 2%
Attrition: 11% MLB: 22%

Comparables:
Logan Forsythe, Jesus Guzman, Matt Tuiasosopo

YEAR	TEAM	LVL	AGE	PA	R	2B	3B	HR	RBI	BB	SO	SB	CS	AVG/OBP/SLG	TAv	BABIP	BRR	FRAA	WARP
2011	LOW	A-	20	133	21	12	1	3	23	17	19	12	2	.298/.398/.500	.335	.337	-1	3B(22): -0.3	1.0
2012	GRN	A	21	526	84	38	4	4	62	61	90	51	6	.305/.394/.433	.277	.371	6.8	3B(99): -2.9	3.0
2013	SLM	A+	22	262	44	19	4	5	33	43	34	15	7	.350/.469/.547	.349	.400	2.2	3B(59): -8.2	2.9
2013	PME	AA	22	295	36	14	3	2	28	51	52	8	2	.296/.420/.404	.312	.367	0.6	3B(44): 3.4	3.2
2014	BOS	MLB	23	250	26	12	1	2	22	27	55	8	2	.253/.338/.352	.256	.320	0.6	3B -2	0.4

Don't pay attention to Cecchini's High-A numbers, as they don't tell you what he's about. He's a patient—but not overly passive—hitter who won't sell out for power and puts the ball in play consistently while drawing frequent walks. Some of the free passes will vanish as he advances, but if he can stay within his plan and learn to drive the ball with regularity, the bat should play where it's needed. It's unfair to say he—or anyone—is the next Kevin Youkilis, but that *idea*, where power is borne out of a high-quality approach, fits the bill. Plus, it's fitting to have a Roman god of walks borrow from the Greek one. Just how much power is the real question, and the answer is likely tied to that Youkilisian ideal of balanced patience with proper doses of aggression.

Stephen Drew SS
Born: 3/16/1983 Age: 31
Bats: L Throws: R Height: 6' 0"
Weight: 190 Breakout: 0%
Improve: 38% Collapse: 3%
Attrition: 5% MLB: 89%

Comparables:
Jhonny Peralta, Roy Smalley, Carlos Guillen

YEAR	TEAM	LVL	AGE	PA	R	2B	3B	HR	RBI	BB	SO	SB	CS	AVG/OBP/SLG	TAv	BABIP	BRR	FRAA	WARP
2011	ARI	MLB	28	354	44	21	5	5	45	30	74	4	4	.252/.317/.396	.261	.313	1.4	SS(84): -2.5	1.4
2012	RNO	AAA	29	40	6	1	1	2	5	4	6	0	0	.250/.325/.500	.283	.250	-0.8	SS(9): -0.8	0.1
2012	ARI	MLB	29	155	17	8	1	2	12	19	35	0	1	.193/.290/.311	.225	.242	0.3	SS(36): -3.7	-0.4
2012	OAK	MLB	29	172	21	5	0	5	16	18	41	1	1	.250/.326/.382	.270	.306	-0.5	SS(39): -0.5	0.8
2013	PME	AA	30	23	1	2	0	1	4	2	4	0	0	.200/.261/.450	.297	.188	-0.3	SS(5): -0.4	0.1
2013	BOS	MLB	30	501	57	29	8	13	67	54	124	6	0	.253/.333/.443	.282	.320	-0.4	SS(124): -4.6	2.9
2014	BOS	MLB	31	445	47	23	5	8	45	42	90	5	2	.250/.321/.397	.262	.300	0.1	SS -4	1.6

Drew was in a tough spot coming into 2013 thanks to the fractured ankle that cost him half of both 2011 and 2012. The Red Sox had a need, though, and Drew, a Scott Boras client, had a desire to rebuild his value on a short-term deal. A spring training concussion slowed his debut as well as his bat, but by year's end he was one of the better shortstops in the game, both at the plate and in the field. With his ankle further removed from injury, Drew's defense was arguably at its best, as he combined experience, natural skill and the positioning his once-gimpy state had forced him to learn. (FRAA sees him about the same way it always has, while other public defensive metrics kept up their long trend of extreme variance.) While his skills will slip as he ages, he has a head start on knowing how to prolong his defensive relevance, if nothing else.

Jonny Gomes LF
Born: 11/22/1980 Age: 33
Bats: R Throws: R Height: 6' 1"
Weight: 230 Breakout: 1%
Improve: 28% Collapse: 7%
Attrition: 16% MLB: 93%

Comparables:
Jason Bay, Ryan Ludwick, Josh Willingham

YEAR	TEAM	LVL	AGE	PA	R	2B	3B	HR	RBI	BB	SO	SB	CS	AVG/OBP/SLG	TAv	BABIP	BRR	FRAA	WARP
2011	CIN	MLB	30	265	30	8	0	11	31	38	74	5	3	.211/.336/.399	.278	.255	-3.5	LF(54): -0.8	0.8
2011	WAS	MLB	30	107	11	4	1	3	12	10	31	2	0	.204/.299/.366	.247	.267	1.3	LF(19): 0.1, RF(11): 0.1	0.4
2012	OAK	MLB	31	333	46	10	0	18	47	44	104	3	1	.262/.377/.491	.318	.348	-1.7	LF(39): 0.4, RF(3): 0.3	2.3
2013	BOS	MLB	32	366	49	17	0	13	52	43	89	1	0	.247/.344/.426	.283	.298	2.5	LF(98): -5.3, RF(4): 0.0	1.7
2014	BOS	MLB	33	337	40	15	1	12	43	33	91	3	1	.241/.329/.420	.273	.300	-0.4	LF -3, RF -0	0.8

Gomes didn't benefit from Fenway's Green Monster as expected, but there is still one year of his deal left. Strangely, Gomes also didn't mash lefties to the degree his career suggested he should. Despite this, he still managed an above-average line, and even hit right-handers to the tune of .258/341/.404 in addition to his duties as team mascot and resident helmet-punter. Maybe 2014 will be the year he crushes lefties and puts dents in the Monster with regularity, but even at his 2013 levels, the Sox should still be pleased with the Daniel Nava/Gomes platoon in left.

Alex Hassan   LF

Born: 4/1/1988 Age: 26
Bats: R Throws: R Height: 6' 3''
Weight: 220 Breakout: 4%
Improve: 21% Collapse: 11%
Attrition: 22% MLB: 38%

Comparables:
Mike Baxter, Bronson Sardinha, Cole Gillespie

YEAR	TEAM	LVL	AGE	PA	R	2B	3B	HR	RBI	BB	SO	SB	CS	AVG/OBP/SLG	TAv	BABIP	BRR	FRAA	WARP
2011	PME	AA	23	545	75	34	1	13	64	76	79	8	2	.291/.404/.456	.303	.326	0	LF(35): 0.4, CF(5): -0.4	1.6
2012	PAW	AAA	24	380	39	13	0	7	46	55	70	1	1	.256/.377/.365	.282	.305	-3.9	LF(60): 3.8, RF(30): -0.9	1.6
2013	GRN	A	25	33	4	2	0	0	7	10	2	0	0	.478/.636/.565	.455	.524	0.2	LF(4): 0.2	0.8
2013	PAW	AAA	25	225	26	14	0	4	28	36	50	0	1	.321/.431/.460	.309	.418	-0.8	RF(30): -1.1, 1B(10): -0.3	1.2
2014	BOS	MLB	26	250	26	12	0	4	25	32	52	1	0	.257/.361/.374	.275	.320	-0.5	LF -0, RF -1	0.7

Hassan seemed an odd choice for 40-man inclusion before 2013, but the Red Sox believed that, with on-base skills as rare and expensive as they are, it was a small price to pay for the chance that he develops some power. Last summer, Hassan utilized his new swing, in which he replaced his toe tap with a high leg kick in order to improve his timing and—for the first time as a pro—consistently use his legs to drive the ball farther and more often. Injuries limited the time he was on the field, but when he did play, Hassan made the Sox look smart for entrusting a precious roster spot to an unknown quantity. His development isn't finished, but for the first time there is real promise.

Jonathan Herrera   SS

Born: 11/3/1984 Age: 29
Bats: B Throws: R Height: 5' 9''
Weight: 180 Breakout: 3%
Improve: 46% Collapse: 9%
Attrition: 18% MLB: 97%

Comparables:
Paul Janish, Brendan Ryan, Mark Loretta

YEAR	TEAM	LVL	AGE	PA	R	2B	3B	HR	RBI	BB	SO	SB	CS	AVG/OBP/SLG	TAv	BABIP	BRR	FRAA	WARP
2011	COL	MLB	26	320	28	5	1	3	14	28	40	4	4	.242/.313/.299	.231	.273	-0.7	2B(62): 0.2, SS(21): -0.4	-0.2
2012	COL	MLB	27	251	29	9	1	3	12	16	39	4	1	.262/.317/.351	.227	.306	1	SS(42): -1.3, 2B(19): -0.2	-0.2
2013	COL	MLB	28	215	16	7	2	1	16	14	24	3	2	.292/.336/.364	.238	.326	0.2	SS(42): -3.5, 2B(22): 0.9	-0.2
2014	BOS	MLB	29	250	26	9	1	2	18	19	37	3	2	.249/.310/.320	.233	.280	-0.3	SS -1, 2B 1	0.2

For a fourth consecutive year, Herrera enjoyed a season as Colorado's plug-and-play utilityman. He logged at least 10 games at shortstop, second base and third base and even threw in a pair of games in left field for good measure. His fatal flaw at the plate remains the same—no power, even with Coors Field's nudge—but his versatility in the field makes him an ideal bench player, especially at pre-free agency prices. His only elite tool is his contact ability, however, and without anything else, he stands little chance of breaking into a starting role.

Ryan Lavarnway   C

Born: 8/7/1987 Age: 26
Bats: R Throws: R Height: 6' 4''
Weight: 240 Breakout: 5%
Improve: 26% Collapse: 18%
Attrition: 21% MLB: 69%

Comparables:
J.R. Towles, Ryan Garko, Welington Castillo

YEAR	TEAM	LVL	AGE	PA	R	2B	3B	HR	RBI	BB	SO	SB	CS	AVG/OBP/SLG	TAv	BABIP	BRR	FRAA	WARP
2011	PME	AA	23	239	35	5	0	14	38	25	47	0	0	.284/.360/.510	.255	.298	-0.3	C(8): 0.0	0.1
2011	PAW	AAA	23	264	40	18	0	18	55	32	60	1	1	.295/.390/.612	.357	.327	-2.7	C(31): -0.2	3.2
2011	BOS	MLB	23	43	5	2	0	2	8	4	10	0	0	.231/.302/.436	.275	.259	-0.4	C(8): 0.1	0.1
2012	PAW	AAA	24	367	52	22	0	8	43	40	62	1	0	.295/.376/.439	.286	.340	-6	C(80): -0.2	2.4
2012	BOS	MLB	24	166	11	8	0	2	12	11	41	0	0	.157/.211/.248	.172	.196	-0.1	C(28): -0.2	-1.2
2013	PAW	AAA	25	214	23	9	0	3	24	25	25	0	0	.250/.346/.350	.240	.268	-2.8	C(43): -0.1	0.3
2013	BOS	MLB	25	82	8	7	0	1	14	2	17	0	0	.299/.329/.429	.269	.367	-0.1	C(22): -0.3	0.3
2014	BOS	MLB	26	250	26	14	0	7	29	22	51	0	0	.255/.326/.407	.267	.300	-0.5	C -0	1.1

Lavarnway posted a .100 isolated power at Pawtucket in his third go at the level, just two seasons removed from a 32-homer campaign. Even prior to 2013 there were concerns his bat was too slow and exploitable against big-league pitching, and since his offense was supposed to carry him behind the plate, he's running out of reasons to remain on the roster. Lavarnway's defense has improved, but he still doesn't move fast or well enough behind the plate, visibly stabs at pitches rather than frame them effectively, and the lack of use he saw while David Ross sat on the disabled list speaks to how little the Red Sox trust his handling of the pitching staff. With Christian Vazquez and Dan Butler at Triple-A, and Blake Swihart behind them at Double-A, Lavarnway's time might be up in Boston.

Manuel Margot — CF

Born: 9/28/1994 Age: 19
Bats: R Throws: R Height: 5' 11"
Weight: 170 Breakout: 0%
Improve: 0% Collapse: 0%
Attrition: 0% MLB: 0%

Comparables: Aaron Hicks, Che-Hsuan Lin, Andrew McCutchen

YEAR	TEAM	LVL	AGE	PA	R	2B	3B	HR	RBI	BB	SO	SB	CS	AVG/OBP/SLG	TAv	BABIP	BRR	FRAA	WARP
2013	LOW	A-	18	216	29	8	2	1	21	22	40	18	8	.270/.346/.351	.283	.333	2.9	CF(47): 10.5	2.4
2014	BOS	MLB	19	250	27	9	1	2	16	15	61	10	4	.213/.263/.297	.207	.270	0.6	CF 4, RF 0	-0.1

Margot's line doesn't light up the page—unless your Kindle has that function, anyway—but it's impressive in its subtlety. A .270/.346/.351 slash shouldn't catch your eye, but when it comes from an 18-year-old in the New York-Penn League, where your average position player is 21, with college experience, and the owner of a .242/.313/.338 line, there's reason to stop and look. Margot's potential also helps, as it's expected he'll develop more power. Even if he doesn't, his defense, speed and line-drive swing should make him a valuable outfielder near the top of a big-league lineup some day. It helps, too, that Margot is open to waiting for a pitch to drive. Once he's better at recognizing said pitches, the offense should come.

Deven Marrero — SS

Born: 8/25/1990 Age: 23
Bats: R Throws: R Height: 6' 1"
Weight: 195 Breakout: 1%
Improve: 5% Collapse: 0%
Attrition: 4% MLB: 5%

Comparables: Ryan Jackson, Jed Lowrie, Nick Noonan

YEAR	TEAM	LVL	AGE	PA	R	2B	3B	HR	RBI	BB	SO	SB	CS	AVG/OBP/SLG	TAv	BABIP	BRR	FRAA	WARP
2012	LOW	A-	21	284	45	14	3	2	24	34	48	24	6	.268/.358/.374	.290	.325	2.3	SS(29): 1.0	2.0
2013	SLM	A+	22	376	50	20	0	2	21	42	60	21	2	.256/.341/.334	.238	.307	-0.5	SS(85): 5.2	1.3
2013	PME	AA	22	85	7	0	0	0	5	10	16	6	0	.236/.321/.236	.229	.293	1.9	SS(19): 4.4	0.8
2014	BOS	MLB	23	250	26	11	1	2	16	20	56	8	1	.221/.283/.293	.214	.280	0.7	SS 5	0.5

Marrero's glove is going to make him a major-league shortstop. It's advanced enough that it's speeding the 2012 first-rounder through the minors, dragging his bat behind. Considering his position, he wasn't *bad* at the plate at High-A, and he's a plus on the bases, but he also didn't solve things enough to breed confidence for his Double-A debut. The walks are a good thing, especially when you consider he's keeping strikeouts down in the process of earning them, but even shortstop power wasn't there last summer. He's likely to stick at Double-A for some time now while he figures things out, especially if he remains in the Sox organization, where Xander Bogaerts is set up to be the shortstop of the present and future.

Will Middlebrooks — 3B

Born: 9/9/1988 Age: 25
Bats: R Throws: R Height: 6' 3"
Weight: 220 Breakout: 3%
Improve: 55% Collapse: 8%
Attrition: 16% MLB: 95%

Comparables: Ian Stewart, Pedro Alvarez, Chris Davis

YEAR	TEAM	LVL	AGE	PA	R	2B	3B	HR	RBI	BB	SO	SB	CS	AVG/OBP/SLG	TAv	BABIP	BRR	FRAA	WARP
2011	PME	AA	22	397	54	25	1	18	80	21	95	6	0	.302/.345/.520	.346	.363	-0.1	3B(30): -2.5	1.4
2011	PAW	AAA	22	60	4	0	0	2	8	3	18	3	1	.161/.200/.268	.164	.189	0.5	3B(14): -0.2	-0.5
2012	PAW	AAA	23	100	18	3	1	9	27	7	18	3	1	.333/.380/.677	.374	.333	-1.6	3B(24): -2.2	1.3
2012	BOS	MLB	23	286	34	14	0	15	54	13	70	4	1	.288/.325/.509	.279	.335	-0.2	3B(72): 4.0	1.8
2013	PAW	AAA	24	196	25	5	0	10	35	16	38	1	0	.268/.327/.464	.272	.288	-0.2	3B(40): 3.6	1.2
2013	BOS	MLB	24	374	41	18	0	17	49	20	98	3	1	.227/.271/.425	.240	.263	1.5	3B(92): -0.8, 2B(2): 0.0	0.8
2014	BOS	MLB	25	375	47	17	1	18	55	20	92	4	1	.261/.304/.465	.274	.300	-0.1	3B 0, 1B 0	1.5

Middlebrooks' struggles could have been avoided had he bothered to prepare for the league's adjustment to him, but he made it clear in the spring he knew what he was doing. He was wrong, but he was also publicly and appropriately humbled by a demotion to Triple-A. The Sox made themselves clear, stating that his return to the majors was not about numbers, but instead knowing what's expected of him in terms of approach. He returned with a more aggressive—but smarter—look at the plate, one where he took control of plate appearances more often to his benefit, and batted .276/.329/.476 with eight homers and a lessened punchout rate from his August promotion onward. There will still be bumps in the road, as happens with his style, but so long as the lesson sticks, he'll do his job well.

Mike Napoli — 1B

Born: 10/31/1981 Age: 32
Bats: R Throws: R Height: 6' 0"
Weight: 220 Breakout: 0%
Improve: 25% Collapse: 4%
Attrition: 12% MLB: 100%

Comparables: Ryan Howard, Ken Phelps, Richie Sexson

YEAR	TEAM	LVL	AGE	PA	R	2B	3B	HR	RBI	BB	SO	SB	CS	AVG/OBP/SLG	TAv	BABIP	BRR	FRAA	WARP
2011	TEX	MLB	29	432	72	25	0	30	75	58	85	4	2	.320/.414/.631	.353	.344	-1.8	C(61): 0.4, 1B(35): -1.3	5.2
2012	TEX	MLB	30	417	53	9	2	24	56	56	125	1	0	.227/.343/.469	.286	.273	0.5	C(72): 1.1, 1B(28): -0.5	2.6
2013	BOS	MLB	31	578	79	38	2	23	92	73	187	1	1	.259/.360/.482	.294	.367	-0.3	1B(131): 3.2	2.7
2014	BOS	MLB	32	511	66	25	1	23	75	58	143	2	1	.253/.347/.475	.295	.320	-0.8	1B 2, C 0	3.0

Napoli and the Sox agreed to a three-year, $39 million contract, but when his physical turned up avascular necrosis, a degenerative hip condition, it was thrown out the window. ("Necro" is never a prefix you want associated with your body.) The two sides negotiated a one-year deal with incentives instead, and Napoli achieved them all by avoiding the DL. In fact, his hip is stronger now than it was, likely due to leaving catching in his past to play first base full-time—a high-quality first, at that. His prize? The recovery this winter of the two lost contract years, and at a higher average annual value to boot. Napoli is going to strike out, and often, but it's the product of an approach that causes him to see more pitches than anyone else, and in turn leads to lengthy homers. So long as his bat stays quick enough for two more years, the Red Sox will get what they paid for.

Daniel Nava   LF
Born: 2/22/1983 Age: 31
Bats: B Throws: L Height: 5' 11"
Weight: 200 Breakout: 1%
Improve: 31% Collapse: 11%
Attrition: 19% MLB: 80%

Comparables:
Ryan Spilborghs, Mitch Maier, Terrmel Sledge

YEAR	TEAM	LVL	AGE	PA	R	2B	3B	HR	RBI	BB	SO	SB	CS	AVG/OBP/SLG	TAv	BABIP	BRR	FRAA	WARP
2011	PAW	AAA	28	522	69	27	2	10	48	70	88	10	3	.268/.372/.406	.272	.311	1.1	LF(82): 1.9, RF(4): -0.2	1.6
2012	PAW	AAA	29	120	20	7	1	4	18	16	15	1	1	.313/.425/.525	.355	.333	-0.2	LF(16): -0.5, RF(3): 0.1	1.3
2012	BOS	MLB	29	317	38	21	0	6	33	37	63	3	0	.243/.352/.390	.268	.295	2.2	LF(76): -5.6, RF(4): -0.1	0.9
2013	BOS	MLB	30	536	77	29	0	12	66	51	93	0	2	.303/.385/.445	.309	.352	-2.1	RF(69): -4.6, LF(63): -2.0	2.8
2014	BOS	MLB	31	474	50	26	1	8	50	48	94	3	1	.262/.353/.391	.274	.320	-0.8	LF -3, RF -2	1.2

Healthy and not filling in for a more established player for the first time in his career, Nava finished fifth in the American League among qualifiers in on-base percentage, flanked by teammate David Ortiz and MVP-candidate Josh Donaldson. His season-long production verified the belief that a wrist cyst was his downfall in 2012, rather than just the league catching up to a story we all so desperately wanted to be good and true. The Sox love Nava's attitude and clubhouse presence in addition to that OBP—especially on a roster soon to be inundated with kids—and believe his versatility is vital to their roster construction in the present and future. He has the patience and plate smarts to bat leadoff against right-handers now that Jacoby Ellsbury has skipped town, and the Sox would be remiss were they to avoid that obvious fit.

David Ortiz   1B
Born: 11/18/1975 Age: 38
Bats: L Throws: L Height: 6' 4"
Weight: 250 Breakout: 0%
Improve: 10% Collapse: 8%
Attrition: 11% MLB: 80%

Comparables:
Carlos Delgado, Frank Robinson, Rafael Palmeiro

YEAR	TEAM	LVL	AGE	PA	R	2B	3B	HR	RBI	BB	SO	SB	CS	AVG/OBP/SLG	TAv	BABIP	BRR	FRAA	WARP
2011	BOS	MLB	35	605	84	40	1	29	96	78	83	1	1	.309/.398/.554	.307	.321	-5.1	1B(2): -0.1	3.1
2012	BOS	MLB	36	383	65	26	0	23	60	56	51	0	1	.318/.415/.611	.343	.316	-3.1	1B(7): 0.1	3.4
2013	BOS	MLB	37	600	84	38	2	30	103	76	88	4	0	.309/.395/.564	.332	.321	-2.2	1B(6): -0.4	4.9
2014	BOS	MLB	38	523	67	29	1	22	76	63	100	2	1	.269/.359/.482	.299	.300	-0.9	1B -0	2.8

What is there to say about David Ortiz at this point? Big Papi is an icon in the baseball world, and inexplicably still one of the great hitters in the game, despite looking like he was winding down four or five years ago. He came back from an Achilles injury to post one of the greatest offensive seasons for a 37-year-old in history, and that was before he hit .688/.760/1.188 in the World Series. He called his two-homer game against David Price in the ALDS, and even wore an incredible, stylish suit to the clubhouse, stating he knew he needed it for the post-game interview that would follow his achievement. The man wears a quarter-million dollar necklace *during* games, and chugged a rare, $100,000 bottle of champagne after winning the World Series and MVP honors. Ortiz is more than a baseball player: He's a genuine character, an individual, and a presence in a game that too frequently tries to hide those attributes. No one knows when this ride is going to end, but the where should be in upstate New York.

Dustin Pedroia   2B
Born: 8/17/1983 Age: 30
Bats: R Throws: R Height: 5' 8"
Weight: 165 Breakout: 2%
Improve: 40% Collapse: 2%
Attrition: 4% MLB: 98%

Comparables:
Roberto Alomar, Ian Kinsler, Joe Morgan

YEAR	TEAM	LVL	AGE	PA	R	2B	3B	HR	RBI	BB	SO	SB	CS	AVG/OBP/SLG	TAv	BABIP	BRR	FRAA	WARP
2011	BOS	MLB	27	731	102	37	3	21	91	86	85	26	8	.307/.387/.474	.295	.325	1.4	2B(159): 1.9	5.1
2012	BOS	MLB	28	623	81	39	3	15	65	48	60	20	6	.290/.347/.449	.281	.300	-0.9	2B(139): -10.5	2.0
2013	BOS	MLB	29	724	91	42	2	9	84	73	75	17	5	.301/.372/.415	.289	.326	-1.4	2B(160): 4.4	4.5
2014	BOS	MLB	30	660	77	39	2	12	72	66	70	19	6	.288/.361/.425	.287	.310	0.5	2B -5	3.7

There are two items from 2013 that tell you just about everything you need to know about Pedroia. The first came on Opening Day, when he tore the ulnar collateral ligament in his thumb against the Yankees. Pedroia refused surgery once doctors told him he wouldn't cause further damage by playing, and that his level of play depended on his pain tolerance: Pedroia would finish with his third-best season by WARP while missing just two games. The second item is the extension he signed mid-season: Pedroia agreed to an eight-year, $110 million deal. When asked about the money he left on the table, Pedroia said, "I want to make sure the team I'm on wins more games than the other team's second baseman." (He probably meant "than the other second baseman's team," but dammit, Jim, he's a ballplayer, not an English professor.) The extraordinarily team-friendly annual price of his contract, combined with his continuous excellence, makes that dream a realistic possibility.

A.J. Pierzynski   C

Born: 12/30/1976 Age: 37
Bats: L Throws: R Height: 6' 3"
Weight: 235 Breakout: 1%
Improve: 20% Collapse: 9%
Attrition: 18% MLB: 73%

Comparables:
Ramon Hernandez, Rod Barajas, Henry Blanco

YEAR	TEAM	LVL	AGE	PA	R	2B	3B	HR	RBI	BB	SO	SB	CS	AVG/OBP/SLG	TAv	BABIP	BRR	FRAA	WARP
2011	CHA	MLB	34	500	38	29	1	8	48	23	33	0	0	.287/.323/.405	.248	.291	-2.7	C(120): -0.8	0.6
2012	CHA	MLB	35	520	68	18	4	27	77	28	78	0	0	.278/.326/.501	.278	.280	-3.1	C(126): -2.3	2.7
2013	TEX	MLB	36	529	48	24	1	17	70	11	76	1	1	.272/.297/.425	.262	.288	-2.8	C(119): -1.2	1.8
2014	BOS	MLB	37	496	45	26	2	10	54	17	63	1	1	.269/.300/.392	.248	.290	-0.9	C -1	1.4

On the surface, this was your run-of-the-mill A.J. Pierzynski season: decent average, no walks, homer total in the teens, 130-something games played, bad defense, praise for handling pitchers. Basically, the same season Pierzynski has been putting up since he became a major-league starting catcher at the beginning of the 21st century, the type of consistency that leads one to start poking around for a strangely aging painting in his attic. However, lines and wrinkles are showing. Pierzynski spent time on the disabled list for the second time in three years, and his hacktastic approach at the plate grew even more extreme than usual. Not only did Pierzynski draw just nine unintentional walks all season, he got worse as the year went on, drawing only two in 298 plate appearances from July 1st on. He's still steady enough to merit a one-year deal from a team (like the Red Sox, it turns out) looking for a one-year catcher, but the career low in OBP is a sign that his broadcast career might be here sooner than later.

David Ross   C

Born: 3/19/1977 Age: 37
Bats: R Throws: R Height: 6' 2"
Weight: 230 Breakout: 2%
Improve: 20% Collapse: 6%
Attrition: 20% MLB: 73%

Comparables:
Jason Varitek, Joe Ferguson, Greg Vaughn

YEAR	TEAM	LVL	AGE	PA	R	2B	3B	HR	RBI	BB	SO	SB	CS	AVG/OBP/SLG	TAv	BABIP	BRR	FRAA	WARP
2011	ATL	MLB	34	170	14	7	0	6	23	16	51	0	1	.263/.333/.428	.277	.358	-3.2	C(49): 0.8	1.0
2012	ATL	MLB	35	196	18	7	0	9	23	18	60	1	0	.256/.321/.449	.274	.330	-1.7	C(54): -0.0	1.1
2013	BOS	MLB	36	116	11	5	0	4	10	11	42	1	0	.216/.298/.382	.240	.321	0	C(36): -0.2	0.5
2014	BOS	MLB	37	250	28	12	1	7	29	25	73	1	0	.238/.318/.399	.259	.320	-0.4	C 1	1.3

Ross was signed not just to back up Jarrod Saltalamacchia, but also to—whether through osmosis or more direct lessons—help Salty improve behind the plate. As Red Sox pitchers bothered to praise Saltalamacchia's game preparation for the first time since he joined the organization in 2010, Ross likely did his job there. A pair of concussions kept Ross' contributions mostly off the field, though, and he was never quite right at the plate, even if he did have nine extra-base hits in just 116 plate appearances. Defensively, he was exactly what Boston wanted when they signed him, and his work in keeping Jon Lester—who admits he sometimes loses focus when frustrated—on point in the second half and in the postseason was worth the two-year deal on its own.

Blake Swihart   C

Born: 4/3/1992 Age: 22
Bats: B Throws: R Height: 6' 1"
Weight: 175 Breakout: 4%
Improve: 4% Collapse: 4%
Attrition: 7% MLB: 8%

Comparables:
Josmil Pinto, Michael McKenry, J.R. Murphy

YEAR	TEAM	LVL	AGE	PA	R	2B	3B	HR	RBI	BB	SO	SB	CS	AVG/OBP/SLG	TAv	BABIP	BRR	FRAA	WARP
2012	GRN	A	20	378	44	17	4	7	53	26	68	6	2	.262/.307/.395	.255	.300	0.4	C(66): -1.1	1.0
2013	SLM	A+	21	422	45	29	7	2	42	41	63	7	8	.298/.366/.428	.271	.350	-6.9	C(101): 2.6	2.4
2014	BOS	MLB	22	250	19	12	2	2	22	13	58	1	0	.232/.271/.327	.219	.290	-0.3	C 0	0.1

The switch-hitting Swihart shot past his career high in games caught by jumping from 66 to 101, and did so while increasing extra-base hits, adding walks and chopping his strikeout rate despite moving from Low- to High-A. He wasn't bad from the left side, posting a .279/.352/.404 line there, but it's against lefties where he did the real damage, to the tune of .367/.419/.519—there's time still to balance those slashes out, given he'll be all of 22 at Double-A to begin 2014. Defensively, Swihart has already made strides and has attainable room to grow, thanks to high marks for his work ethic and makeup. A catcher who can be above average both at the plate and behind it might not look sexy, but there's loads of value there.

Christian Vazquez   C

Born: 8/21/1990 Age: 23
Bats: R Throws: R Height: 5' 9"
Weight: 195 Breakout: 2%
Improve: 19% Collapse: 0%
Attrition: 10% MLB: 27%

Comparables:
Russell Martin, Jason Castro, Bryan Anderson

YEAR	TEAM	LVL	AGE	PA	R	2B	3B	HR	RBI	BB	SO	SB	CS	AVG/OBP/SLG	TAv	BABIP	BRR	FRAA	WARP
2011	GRN	A	20	444	71	27	3	18	84	43	84	1	1	.283/.358/.505	.306	.316	-1.2	C(38): 0.7	1.8
2012	SLM	A+	21	342	43	17	0	7	41	40	70	2	2	.266/.360/.396	.274	.326	-0.8	C(76): 1.5	2.8
2012	PME	AA	21	82	11	4	0	0	5	8	9	0	0	.205/.280/.260	.192	.231	0.7	C(20): 0.3	-0.3
2013	PME	AA	22	399	48	19	1	5	48	47	44	7	5	.289/.376/.395	.285	.316	1.2	C(93): 0.7	3.7
2014	BOS	MLB	23	250	23	12	0	4	25	22	49	1	0	.240/.310/.349	.242	.290	-0.5	C 1	0.8

Blake Swihart deservedly gets the attention, but Vazquez has a real chance to be much better as a major-league backstop than as a prospect. Vazquez's pop times are off-the-charts ridiculous, scouts and his coaches laud him for his precocious handling of the pitching staff and the Brothers Molina think enough of him to include him in their offseason training in Puerto Rico. While Vazquez could thrive as an all-defense backup, he has real offensive skills. Vazquez is patient, and while his defense has pushed him through the system faster than his bat would have liked, he batted .289/.376/.395 with more walks than strikeouts at Double-A. As Vazquez adjusts slowly to new levels, a full season at Triple-A is key to having him ready for 2015 and the potential hole behind the plate in Boston.

Shane Victorino CF

Born: 11/30/1980 Age: 33
Bats: B Throws: R Height: 5' 9"
Weight: 190 Breakout: 2%
Improve: 34% Collapse: 3%
Attrition: 5% MLB: 96%

Comparables:
David DeJesus, Tony Gwynn, Rusty Staub

YEAR	TEAM	LVL	AGE	PA	R	2B	3B	HR	RBI	BB	SO	SB	CS	AVG/OBP/SLG	TAv	BABIP	BRR	FRAA	WARP
2011	PHI	MLB	30	586	95	27	16	17	61	55	63	19	3	.279/.355/.491	.314	.292	5.4	CF(130): 5.1	6.2
2012	LAN	MLB	31	235	26	12	2	2	15	18	31	15	2	.245/.316/.351	.260	.278	0.4	LF(48): 6.1, CF(8): 0.0	1.3
2012	PHI	MLB	31	431	46	17	5	9	40	35	49	24	4	.261/.324/.401	.266	.278	1.9	CF(101): -0.8	1.9
2013	BOS	MLB	32	532	82	26	2	15	61	25	75	21	3	.294/.351/.451	.292	.321	-0.6	RF(110): 20.8, CF(15): 0.5	5.2
2014	BOS	MLB	33	527	69	25	7	10	50	40	67	23	4	.270/.334/.419	.272	.290	3.2	CF -1, RF 10	3.4

Victorino spent 2013 proving 2012 was a blip in an otherwise stellar, if late-blooming, career. The full-time shift to a corner was a boon to The Man They Call Shane's defense, as he's just old enough that center field shouldn't be his everyday gig, but he's still more than capable of handling even Fenway's sizable right field. He produced on the bases and in the batter's box as well, and when an ailing hamstring caused him to bat right-handed exclusively, he became a monster at the plate: Victorino batted .301/.379/.497 with *22* hit by pitches from August 4th onward. The plan is to switch-hit again in 2014, but that seems like a mistake, unless the goal is to avoid breaking every bone in his ribs, arm and thigh, anyway.

PITCHERS

Burke Badenhop

Born: 2/8/1983 Age: 31
Bats: R Throws: R Height: 6' 5" Weight: 220
Breakout: 35% Improve: 57% Collapse: 29%
Attrition: 15% MLB: 84%

Comparables:
Geoff Geary, Rafael Perez, Matt Lindstrom

YEAR	TEAM	LVL	AGE	W	L	SV	G	GS	IP	H	HR	BB	SO	BB9	SO9	GB%	BABIP	WHIP	ERA	FIP	FRA	WARP
2011	NWO	AAA	28	1	1	1	11	0	14²	20	1	7	10	4.3	6.1	75%	.500	1.84	6.75	4.94	2.51	0.1
2011	FLO	MLB	28	2	3	1	50	0	63²	65	1	24	51	3.4	7.2	60%	.330	1.40	4.10	2.92	3.12	1.1
2012	TBA	MLB	29	3	2	0	66	0	62¹	63	6	12	42	1.7	6.1	55%	.284	1.20	3.03	3.58	4.32	0.4
2013	MIL	MLB	30	2	3	1	63	0	62¹	62	6	12	42	1.7	6.1	56%	.292	1.19	3.47	3.50	4.39	0.3
2014	BOS	MLB	31	2	1	1	45	0	50¹	52	4	14	34	2.5	6.0	55%	.304	1.32	4.02	3.94	4.37	0.3

Badenhop's unimpressive stuff has kept him away from closer and set-up roles throughout his six-year career, but his sinker can be a very valuable pitch to a manager. Badenhop sported a 56 percent groundball rate for Milwaukee, a big reason he entered nearly a third of his appearances with runners on. He induced seven double plays, second-most among Milwaukee's full-time relievers. Badenhop lives in the high 80s with his sinker and likely won't see much late-inning work as a result, but he'll serve a distinct purpose in Boston's bullpen this year.

Andrew Bailey

Born: 5/31/1984 Age: 30
Bats: R Throws: R Height: 6' 3" Weight: 240
Breakout: 30% Improve: 51% Collapse: 29%
Attrition: 11% MLB: 94%

Comparables:
Robb Nen, Dan Wheeler, Bobby Jenks

YEAR	TEAM	LVL	AGE	W	L	SV	G	GS	IP	H	HR	BB	SO	BB9	SO9	GB%	BABIP	WHIP	ERA	FIP	FRA	WARP
2011	OAK	MLB	27	0	4	24	42	0	41²	34	3	12	41	2.6	8.9	38%	.272	1.10	3.24	2.89	2.90	1.0
2012	BOS	MLB	28	1	1	6	19	0	15¹	21	2	8	14	4.7	8.2	33%	.380	1.89	7.04	4.48	5.39	0.0
2013	BOS	MLB	29	3	1	8	30	0	28²	23	7	12	39	3.8	12.2	29%	.276	1.22	3.77	4.78	5.12	0.0
2014	BOS	MLB	30	2	1	11	37	0	36²	32	3	11	39	2.8	9.5	41%	.293	1.17	3.07	3.18	3.34	0.7

It was another disappointing campaign for Bailey, one that ended with a non-tender. It was—depressingly—a step up from his 2012, however. Sure, Bailey hit the disabled list multiple times, with his season ending due to a shoulder capsule tear that required surgery, but when he managed to take the mound there were flashes of the pitcher the Sox thought they were trading for. He gave up the odd homer here and there on the days his arm wasn't right, as his velocity was less than it needed to be in those appearances, but the 39 strikeouts in 28 innings were a sign not all was lost. When he returns in the middle of 2014, the hope will be that swing-and-miss magic survived his procedure.

Trey Ball

Born: 6/27/1994 Age: 20
Bats: L Throws: L Height: 6' 6" Weight: 185
Breakout: 0% Improve: 0% Collapse: 0%
Attrition: 0% MLB: 0%

Comparables:
Zach Britton, Jhoulys Chacin, Brandon Maurer

YEAR	TEAM	LVL	AGE	W	L	SV	G	GS	IP	H	HR	BB	SO	BB9	SO9	GB%	BABIP	WHIP	ERA	FIP	FRA	WARP
2014	BOS	MLB	20	1	3	0	7	7	30¹	40	4	21	12	6.3	3.6	43%	.321	2.01	7.30	6.65	7.93	-0.8

Unlike most high schoolers, the seventh-overall pick in the 2013 draft wasn't allowed to throw a curveball regularly, as Ball's father imposed a changeup on him instead. That was a blessing for more than just health, as Ball's change is more refined than it has any right to be at his tender age, and his curve still looks to be a quality pitch despite its newness. Ball was the top southpaw available in his class, and while the 6-foot-6 southpaw needs to add to his 190 pound frame, he won't even turn 20 until June. Velocity should be attached to that growth: He already tops out in the mid-90s and sits in the lower portion, so more might be what puts him over the edge. There are scouts who think Ball profiles better as an outfielder, but that might be a testament to his athleticism and raw baseball talent more than any Sox mistake.

Matt Barnes
Born: 6/17/1990 Age: 24
Bats: R Throws: R Height: 6' 4" Weight: 205
Breakout: 42% Improve: 71% Collapse: 24%
Attrition: 56% MLB: 50%

Comparables:
Matt Maloney, James Paxton, Boof Bonser

YEAR	TEAM	LVL	AGE	W	L	SV	G	GS	IP	H	HR	BB	SO	BB9	SO9	GB%	BABIP	WHIP	ERA	FIP	FRA	WARP
2012	GRN	A	22	2	0	0	5	5	26²	12	0	4	42	1.4	14.2	60%	.240	0.60	0.34	0.99	1.43	1.3
2012	SLM	A+	22	5	5	0	20	20	93	85	6	25	91	2.4	8.8	47%	.312	1.18	3.58	3.33	4.05	1.5
2013	PME	AA	23	5	10	0	24	24	108	112	11	46	135	3.8	11.2	46%	.356	1.46	4.33	3.54	3.51	2.9
2014	BOS	MLB	24	6	7	0	21	21	99¹	99	11	40	97	3.6	8.8	46%	.318	1.40	4.33	4.13	4.71	0.6

Barnes' 2013 season looks like a failure next to his more attractive past, but he progressed, and that's what matters. The 2011 first-rounder has a promising curveball and changeup, but disposed of low-minors opposition almost entirely with his plus fastball, as pitchers with plus heat in the lower levels tend to do. Double-A was the first challenge for his raw secondary offerings: He scuffled in the first half, but dominated from mid-July on, racking up a 2.30 ERA with 54 strikeouts against 20 walks in his final 43 innings. There's work to be done with his curve and change, and the walks need to come down, but the season ended on a high note with Barnes promoted to Triple-A to face competition that will force that education upon him. If he takes notes, there's a future in the middle of a big-league rotation for him.

Craig Breslow
Born: 8/8/1980 Age: 33
Bats: L Throws: L Height: 6' 1" Weight: 190
Breakout: 21% Improve: 40% Collapse: 33%
Attrition: 13% MLB: 88%

Comparables:
Matt Wise, Brandon Lyon, LaTroy Hawkins

YEAR	TEAM	LVL	AGE	W	L	SV	G	GS	IP	H	HR	BB	SO	BB9	SO9	GB%	BABIP	WHIP	ERA	FIP	FRA	WARP
2011	OAK	MLB	30	0	2	0	67	0	59¹	69	4	21	44	3.2	6.7	40%	.344	1.52	3.79	3.62	3.63	0.8
2012	ARI	MLB	31	2	0	0	40	0	43¹	38	5	13	42	2.7	8.7	44%	.274	1.18	2.70	3.67	4.14	0.4
2012	BOS	MLB	31	1	0	0	23	0	20	14	0	9	19	4.1	8.6	52%	.269	1.15	2.70	2.65	3.06	0.4
2013	BOS	MLB	32	5	2	0	61	0	59²	49	3	18	33	2.7	5.0	45%	.254	1.12	1.81	3.63	3.97	0.5
2014	BOS	MLB	33	3	1	1	54	0	52²	49	5	19	43	3.3	7.5	40%	.289	1.30	3.82	4.11	4.16	0.5

Breslow, who we are obligated to tell you has a degree in molecular biophysics and biochemistry from Yale, was one of 2012's few bright points, as the Red Sox acquired him for Matt Albers and change at the trade deadline. This became apparent in 2013, when Breslow stepped up as the primary lefty in the 'pen following Andrew Miller's ankle-related demise. Expecting a repeat of Breslow's career-best ERA is foolish, but it's worth pointing out that he has a history of outpitching those pesky run estimators. The 2013 plunge in strikeout rate raises alarm bells, but relievers are tough to judge—in the end, it was just 59 innings. Breslow's stuff still looked strong, and so long as his World Series hiccup was just that, there is little to worry about.

Drake Britton
Born: 5/22/1989 Age: 25
Bats: L Throws: L Height: 6' 2" Weight: 215
Breakout: 32% Improve: 62% Collapse: 14%
Attrition: 59% MLB: 50%

Comparables:
Jimmy Barthmaier, P.J. Walters, Lance Broadway

YEAR	TEAM	LVL	AGE	W	L	SV	G	GS	IP	H	HR	BB	SO	BB9	SO9	GB%	BABIP	WHIP	ERA	FIP	FRA	WARP
2011	SLM	A+	22	1	13	0	26	26	97²	111	12	55	89	5.1	8.2	47%	.373	1.70	6.91	4.88	5.66	-0.2
2012	SLM	A+	23	3	5	0	10	8	45	42	5	19	42	3.8	8.4	51%	.282	1.36	5.80	4.50	5.12	0.0
2012	PME	AA	23	4	7	0	16	16	84²	86	3	38	76	4.0	8.1	49%	.331	1.46	3.72	3.25	4.01	1.3
2013	PME	AA	24	7	6	0	17	16	97¹	94	5	36	80	3.3	7.4	48%	.310	1.34	3.51	3.52	4.19	1.7
2013	BOS	MLB	24	1	1	0	18	0	21	21	1	7	17	3.0	7.3	47%	.339	1.33	3.86	3.08	3.91	0.2
2014	BOS	MLB	25	5	7	0	25	17	102¹	113	10	48	76	4.3	6.7	45%	.317	1.57	5.06	4.63	5.50	-0.4

Britton drove 111 in a 45 mph zone during spring training, resulting in a DUI, but thankfully, no one was hurt as a result of his actions. One hopes this freebie was the only one he needed to realize the enormity of the mistake he made, and that knowing will keep him from a similar transgression in the future. As for his mound work, Britton's minor-league numbers have always screamed future reliever, even if Boston kept him starting as long as possible, as their organizational philosophy dictates. The team pushed him to the majors after a brief Triple-A pit stop and Britton responded with solid emergency work. There's small-sample weirdness in his 21 innings, with lefties killing him via BABIP, but ignore that: His future is grounders and lefties whiffing, and his overall success will be tied to how many right-handers he's forced to face.

Clay Buchholz

Born: 8/14/1984 Age: 29
Bats: L Throws: R Height: 6' 3" Weight: 190
Breakout: 23% Improve: 47% Collapse: 18%
Attrition: 8% MLB: 95%

Comparables:
Gavin Floyd, Anibal Sanchez, Josh Johnson

YEAR	TEAM	LVL	AGE	W	L	SV	G	GS	IP	H	HR	BB	SO	BB9	SO9	GB%	BABIP	WHIP	ERA	FIP	FRA	WARP
2011	BOS	MLB	26	6	3	0	14	14	82²	76	10	31	60	3.4	6.5	51%	.264	1.29	3.48	4.38	4.68	0.9
2012	BOS	MLB	27	11	8	0	29	29	189¹	187	25	64	129	3.0	6.1	49%	.284	1.33	4.56	4.60	5.53	0.1
2013	BOS	MLB	28	12	1	0	16	16	108¹	75	4	36	96	3.0	8.0	49%	.254	1.02	1.74	2.81	3.53	1.8
2014	BOS	MLB	29	7	6	0	17	17	105²	97	9	37	80	3.1	6.8	49%	.283	1.26	3.55	4.04	3.86	1.4

Baseball Prospectus devotees might recall adulation for Clay Buchholz following his 2010 campaign, in which he posted a 2.33 ERA. "Buchholz may never post a 2.33 ERA again, but he does have ace potential," we wrote, with the potential living in the possibility of an evolving arsenal. Fast-forward to 2013: When Buchholz was on the mound, ace is what we got. Even if you don't think he's quite *that* good going forward, Buchholz owns a 3.15 ERA since 2010 despite one of baseball's toughest pitching environments. The issue is the missed time. In 2011, it was a stress fracture in his spine. It took him a month-plus to get right before posting a 3.59 ERA over his final 150 innings in 2012. In 2013, shoulder bursitis pushed him out from June into September. He gutted it out in the postseason, and reports are that he's set for 2014. If he can stay healthy, then Buchholz is that ace we thought we saw a few years back.

Ty Buttrey

Born: 3/31/1993 Age: 21
Bats: L Throws: R Height: 6' 6" Weight: 230
Breakout: 0% Improve: 0% Collapse: 0%
Attrition: 0% MLB: 0%

Comparables:
Daniel Webb, Jared Hughes, Danny Salazar

YEAR	TEAM	LVL	AGE	W	L	SV	G	GS	IP	H	HR	BB	SO	BB9	SO9	GB%	BABIP	WHIP	ERA	FIP	FRA	WARP
2013	LOW	A-	20	4	3	0	13	13	61	54	0	21	35	3.1	5.2	46%	.280	1.23	2.21	3.23	4.07	0.4
2014	BOS	MLB	21	2	5	0	17	13	38	50	5	22	13	5.3	3.0	43%	.317	1.91	6.92	6.36	7.52	-0.8

Buttrey could end up the most productive member of Boston's 2012 draft class. He failed to miss bats often at short-season Lowell, but he has three pitches—a low-90s fastball, a knuckle curve in the 70s, and an improving changeup—and the body—6-foot-6 and 230 pounds despite just exiting his teen years—to get prospect hounds drooling. He had mid-90s velocity before he was drafted, and he'll need that to return to keep the interest going. Improvement to his command would also be advised lest he be shuffled off to a bullpen someday. There is inning-eating, mid-rotation potential here, though, and he's far too young and inexperienced to dismiss. Mike Judge fans would be forgiven for hoping the Sox can someday team him up with Blake Beavan.

Rubby De La Rosa

Born: 3/4/1989 Age: 25
Bats: R Throws: R Height: 6' 1" Weight: 205
Breakout: 42% Improve: 63% Collapse: 21%
Attrition: 29% MLB: 84%

Comparables:
Tyson Ross, Franklin Morales, Tyler Clippard

YEAR	TEAM	LVL	AGE	W	L	SV	G	GS	IP	H	HR	BB	SO	BB9	SO9	GB%	BABIP	WHIP	ERA	FIP	FRA	WARP
2011	CHT	AA	22	2	2	0	8	8	40	30	1	19	52	4.3	11.7	25%	.375	1.23	2.92	2.61	0.74	0.3
2011	LAN	MLB	22	4	5	0	13	10	60²	54	6	31	60	4.6	8.9	49%	.305	1.40	3.71	3.83	4.79	-0.2
2012	LAN	MLB	23	0	0	0	1	0	0²	0	0	2	0	27.0	0.0	%	.000	3.00	27.00	12.14	13.83	-0.1
2013	PAW	AAA	24	3	3	0	24	20	80¹	65	9	48	76	5.4	8.5	45%	.265	1.41	4.26	4.82	5.24	0.3
2013	BOS	MLB	24	0	2	0	11	0	11¹	15	2	2	6	1.6	4.8	48%	.325	1.50	5.56	5.63	6.02	-0.1
2014	BOS	MLB	25	3	4	0	19	11	66²	67	7	33	54	4.5	7.3	49%	.302	1.49	4.67	4.72	5.07	0.0

For many organizations, trying to get De La Rosa to start would be Priority Number One: He has already pitched with some success in the majors, and his repertoire—mid-90s two-seamer, four-seam, slider and change—is legitimate enough to believe he could thrive in the role. The problem is the lost year of development to Tommy John, and 2013's attempt to ramp up the right-hander's workload once more. Should he remain with the Sox between now and the time you read this, relief might be his 2014 role in order to shorten his path to the majors. With his command issues, it could be the role of choice for him, anyway, and worth the switch if he stakes claim to future high-leverage spots, as many scouts believe he could and should.

Ryan Dempster

Born: 5/3/1977 Age: 37
Bats: R Throws: R Height: 6' 2" Weight: 215
Breakout: 6% Improve: 36% Collapse: 26%
Attrition: 12% MLB: 80%

Comparables:
Jim Bunning, Jerry Koosman, Connie Johnson

YEAR	TEAM	LVL	AGE	W	L	SV	G	GS	IP	H	HR	BB	SO	BB9	SO9	GB%	BABIP	WHIP	ERA	FIP	FRA	WARP
2011	CHN	MLB	34	10	14	0	34	34	202¹	211	23	82	191	3.6	8.5	45%	.335	1.45	4.80	3.87	4.61	1.8
2012	TEX	MLB	35	7	3	0	12	12	69	74	10	25	70	3.3	9.1	47%	.330	1.43	5.09	4.03	4.45	0.8
2012	CHN	MLB	35	5	5	0	16	16	104	81	9	27	83	2.3	7.2	44%	.251	1.04	2.25	3.47	3.72	1.7
2013	BOS	MLB	36	8	9	0	32	29	171¹	170	26	79	157	4.1	8.2	43%	.296	1.45	4.57	4.70	4.87	0.6
2014	BOS	MLB	37	9	9	0	26	26	150	149	17	57	135	3.4	8.1	47%	.307	1.37	4.29	4.24	4.66	0.6

Dempster's 2013 was spoiled by an on-again, off-again groin injury, but he did his job for a Red Sox squad that, while flush with young pitching, was lacking in *prepared* young pitching. Dempster held on in the rotation for 29 starts even as he pitched just a hair of above replacement level. That sounds dire, but consider that it allowed Allen Webster and his bloated ERA to head back to Rhode Island, limited time spent with the Steven Wright Knuckleball Experience and let the team move Brandon Workman to the bullpen after the trade deadline while using Dempster as the bridge to the return of Clay Buchholz. Granted, Dempster's $13 million price tag was high for a security blanket, but sometimes what you need in a relationship is for the other person just to be there.

Felix Doubront
Born: 10/23/1987 Age: 26
Bats: L Throws: L Height: 6' 2" Weight: 225
Breakout: 35% Improve: 69% Collapse: 17%
Attrition: 20% MLB: 93%
Comparables:
Homer Bailey, Boof Bonser, Luke Hochevar

YEAR	TEAM	LVL	AGE	W	L	SV	G	GS	IP	H	HR	BB	SO	BB9	SO9	GB%	BABIP	WHIP	ERA	FIP	FRA	WARP
2011	PAW	AAA	23	2	5	0	18	16	70¹	65	10	26	61	3.3	7.8	46%	.288	1.29	4.22	4.54	5.92	-0.4
2011	BOS	MLB	23	0	0	1	11	0	10¹	12	1	8	6	7.0	5.2	46%	.344	1.94	6.10	5.48	7.37	-0.2
2012	BOS	MLB	24	11	10	0	29	29	161	162	24	71	167	4.0	9.3	45%	.313	1.45	4.86	4.33	4.66	1.5
2013	BOS	MLB	25	11	6	0	29	27	162¹	161	13	71	139	3.9	7.7	47%	.311	1.43	4.32	3.81	4.28	1.6
2014	BOS	MLB	26	8	9	0	27	27	140	141	15	59	122	3.8	7.8	45%	.310	1.43	4.50	4.38	4.89	0.4

Doubront thrived as a starter, limiting opponents to a .250/.326/.379 line with a 3.87 ERA. He was blasted as a reliever, though, with 11 of his 78 runs on the season allowed in just 6 ⅔ innings. When it was clear Doubront wouldn't start in October, he admitted to not knowing how to prepare for relief mentally, and, awkwardly, showed little interest in finding out. Someone (possibly Farrell-shaped) must have explained it all in a calm but forceful voice before the calendar flipped: Doubront allowed one run in seven postseason relief innings. (And isn't that why you go to the trouble to hire John Farrell?) Doubront doesn't have *serious* makeup problems, but that relief oddity combined with his tendency to show up to camp out of shape every other year is something to watch. The talent is undeniable, so if he can continue to improve his efficiency as he did post-May in 2013, his future in Boston will be secure.

Joel Hanrahan
Born: 10/6/1981 Age: 32
Bats: R Throws: R Height: 6' 4" Weight: 250
Breakout: 26% Improve: 48% Collapse: 26%
Attrition: 5% MLB: 93%
Comparables:
Kyle Farnsworth, Matt Thornton, Kiko Calero

YEAR	TEAM	LVL	AGE	W	L	SV	G	GS	IP	H	HR	BB	SO	BB9	SO9	GB%	BABIP	WHIP	ERA	FIP	FRA	WARP
2011	PIT	MLB	29	1	4	40	70	0	68²	56	1	16	61	2.1	8.0	54%	.282	1.05	1.83	2.15	3.01	1.2
2012	PIT	MLB	30	5	2	36	63	0	59²	40	8	36	67	5.4	10.1	40%	.225	1.27	2.72	4.49	3.42	0.5
2013	BOS	MLB	31	0	1	4	9	0	7¹	10	4	6	5	7.4	6.1	39%	.273	2.18	9.82	11.26	11.24	-0.4
2014	BOS	MLB	32	2	1	20	37	0	35²	31	3	15	41	3.8	10.3	42%	.308	1.29	3.48	3.43	3.79	0.5

Hanrahan's acquisition went about as well as Andrew Bailey's in 2012, as the closer hit the disabled list a couple of times before permanent residence in early May en route to Tommy John surgery. The obvious irony is that Hanrahan was picked up because Bailey's health was in question. When fit, Hanrahan is great—that's why the Sox acquired him to begin with, you know. In his 229 innings with the Pirates, he posted a 2.59 ERA and struck out 265 batters. Even a limited post-surgery version of that pitcher could help a bullpen once he's available.

Brian Johnson
Born: 12/7/1990 Age: 23
Bats: L Throws: L Height: 6' 3" Weight: 225
Breakout: 61% Improve: 75% Collapse: 20%
Attrition: 63% MLB: 20%
Comparables:
Yoervis Medina, Glen Perkins, Billy Buckner

YEAR	TEAM	LVL	AGE	W	L	SV	G	GS	IP	H	HR	BB	SO	BB9	SO9	GB%	BABIP	WHIP	ERA	FIP	FRA	WARP
2013	GRN	A	22	1	6	0	15	15	69	50	4	28	69	3.7	9.0	47%	.251	1.13	2.87	3.63	4.38	1.0
2013	SLM	A+	22	1	0	0	2	2	11	9	0	5	8	4.1	6.5	59%	.281	1.27	1.64	3.26	4.09	0.2
2014	BOS	MLB	23	3	5	0	13	13	55	61	7	29	37	4.7	6.0	47%	.309	1.63	5.46	5.39	5.94	-0.4

A shoulder injury cut out the middle of Johnson's season, but when the 2012 first-rounder made it to the mound, he was productive and earned a promotion from Low-A to High-A. Before the interruptions, it was believed Johnson, a polished lefty with College World Series experience, would shoot through the system as a high-floor, low-ceiling type with a future in the back end of a big-league rotation, powered by a low-to-mid-90s fastball with both sink and tail as well as a change and curve that project as average. If he can avoid another DL stint for the first couple of months of 2014, he'll be back on track and maybe even in Double-A before you know it. He has a very good chance to be the best baseballing Brian Johnson ever—the only prior Brian Johnson had just 1.1 WARP for his career.

John Lackey
Born: 10/23/1978 Age: 35
Bats: R Throws: R Height: 6' 6" Weight: 235
Breakout: 23% Improve: 47% Collapse: 18%
Attrition: 12% MLB: 89%
Comparables:
Kevin Millwood, Esteban Loaiza, Cory Lidle

YEAR	TEAM	LVL	AGE	W	L	SV	G	GS	IP	H	HR	BB	SO	BB9	SO9	GB%	BABIP	WHIP	ERA	FIP	FRA	WARP
2011	BOS	MLB	32	12	12	0	28	28	160	203	20	56	108	3.2	6.1	42%	.340	1.62	6.41	4.74	5.21	0.8
2013	BOS	MLB	34	10	13	0	29	29	189¹	179	26	40	161	1.9	7.7	48%	.281	1.16	3.52	3.89	4.33	1.7
2014	BOS	MLB	35	8	8	0	21	21	130²	138	14	37	98	2.6	6.8	46%	.310	1.34	4.33	4.23	4.71	0.4

Lackey's 2011 was reviled in the moment, but when it was learned he had pitched through an elbow tear with no one to take his place, Sox fans softened. (Well, sort of.) Boston's 2012, which

Lackey was not a part of, also helped: Red Sox Nation no longer needed to invent demons to rally against, as 2012 had introduced them to frightening, tangible enemies of good baseball. Armed with a more accepting outlook from the experience of fates worse than 90-win campaigns and just-miss playoff seasons, fans began to appreciate Lackey, who had returned from his 18-month absence with his velocity, sinker and strike-throwing prowess intact. The three combined to produce one of the better seasons in his career. Now, he's a World Series hero and a recognized anchor in a strong rotation. Double-fist a couple of beers in his honor.

Jon Lester
Born: 1/7/1984 Age: 30
Bats: L Throws: L Height: 6' 4" Weight: 240
Breakout: 11% Improve: 39% Collapse: 30%
Attrition: 14% MLB: 97%
Comparables:
John Lackey, Erik Bedard, Josh Beckett

YEAR	TEAM	LVL	AGE	W	L	SV	G	GS	IP	H	HR	BB	SO	BB9	SO9	GB%	BABIP	WHIP	ERA	FIP	FRA	WARP
2011	BOS	MLB	27	15	9	0	31	31	191²	166	20	75	182	3.5	8.5	51%	.286	1.26	3.47	3.86	4.58	2.4
2012	BOS	MLB	28	9	14	0	33	33	205¹	216	25	68	166	3.0	7.3	51%	.313	1.38	4.82	4.06	5.07	1.4
2013	BOS	MLB	29	15	8	0	33	33	213¹	209	19	67	177	2.8	7.5	46%	.301	1.29	3.75	3.61	4.03	2.8
2014	BOS	MLB	30	12	10	0	30	30	187	172	16	62	177	3.0	8.5	48%	.303	1.25	3.50	3.61	3.80	2.6

While 2012 was worrisome for the normally reliable Lester, it also offered hints to his future. His final 13 starts of the year featured a pitcher focusing more on location, grounders and inducing weaker contact rather than the southpaw who blew heat past opposing hitters in his younger years. That carried over into 2013 and his reunion with former pitching coach John Farrell, and culminated in a fantastic postseason run where Lester allowed just six runs in 34 innings. In between, he produced a more dominant year than his ERA suggests: Of Lester's 89 earned runs, 17 came in a three-start stretch in June when his mechanics slipped. If the other 30 starts are the fairer indication, the old Lester hasn't vanished—he's evolved.

Andrew Miller
Born: 5/21/1985 Age: 29
Bats: L Throws: L Height: 6' 7" Weight: 210
Breakout: 31% Improve: 63% Collapse: 26%
Attrition: 31% MLB: 53%
Comparables:
J.A. Happ, Wil Ledezma, Kason Gabbard

YEAR	TEAM	LVL	AGE	W	L	SV	G	GS	IP	H	HR	BB	SO	BB9	SO9	GB%	BABIP	WHIP	ERA	FIP	FRA	WARP
2011	PAW	AAA	26	3	3	0	13	12	65²	42	2	35	61	4.8	8.4	49%	.225	1.17	2.47	3.51	4.40	0.3
2011	BOS	MLB	26	6	3	0	17	12	65	77	8	41	50	5.7	6.9	49%	.332	1.82	5.54	5.15	5.46	0.4
2012	PAW	AAA	27	0	0	1	10	0	11	4	1	14	23	11.5	18.8	53%	.214	1.64	5.73	4.25	4.76	0.0
2012	BOS	MLB	27	3	2	0	53	0	40¹	28	3	20	51	4.5	11.4	43%	.269	1.19	3.35	3.12	3.45	0.6
2013	BOS	MLB	28	1	2	0	37	0	30²	25	3	17	48	5.0	14.1	57%	.338	1.37	2.64	3.08	4.02	0.2
2014	BOS	MLB	29	2	2	0	16	5	33	33	3	20	30	5.5	8.1	50%	.316	1.63	5.17	4.62	5.62	-0.2

Bobby Valentine left few positives behind from his year at the helm of the Sox, but the changes to Miller's mechanics were unarguably productive. Inconsistency in his delivery was the issue, so it was simplified: He pitched exclusively from the stretch, used a shortened stride to ease his leg through his motion and replaced his loopy curve with a tighter, devastating slider variant. The results were surprising and immediate, and he improved so much in 2013 that his season-ending ankle injury was considered what had been unthinkable roughly a year before: a bullpen-debilitating blow. In his 71 relief innings with these mechanics, Miller has struck out 99 batters, death-murder-killed nearly every lefty he's come up against, and even limited the production of right-handers to .209/.345/.330. With his career thus rescued, he should rejoin a stacked Boston bullpen in 2014.

Edward Mujica
Born: 5/10/1984 Age: 30
Bats: R Throws: R Height: 6' 3" Weight: 225
Breakout: 34% Improve: 57% Collapse: 27%
Attrition: 13% MLB: 89%
Comparables:
Gabe White, Rod Beck, Joe Sambito

YEAR	TEAM	LVL	AGE	W	L	SV	G	GS	IP	H	HR	BB	SO	BB9	SO9	GB%	BABIP	WHIP	ERA	FIP	FRA	WARP
2011	FLO	MLB	27	9	6	0	67	0	76	64	7	14	63	1.7	7.5	51%	.273	1.03	2.96	3.17	4.02	0.3
2012	MIA	MLB	28	0	3	2	41	0	39	36	6	9	26	2.1	6.0	53%	.252	1.15	4.38	4.57	5.70	-0.4
2012	SLN	MLB	28	0	0	0	29	0	26¹	20	1	3	21	1.0	7.2	50%	.268	0.87	1.03	2.38	3.70	0.3
2013	SLN	MLB	29	2	1	37	65	0	64²	60	9	5	46	0.7	6.4	46%	.263	1.01	2.78	3.69	3.81	0.6
2014	BOS	MLB	30	3	1	11	53	0	56	54	7	8	45	1.3	7.2	43%	.290	1.11	3.44	3.81	3.74	0.8

Mujica is a check mark in the "closers are made, not born" column. The journeyman reliever transitioned brilliantly into the role, taking his control-oriented approach to another level with a barely-there 2 percent walk rate that made his otherwise modest 18 percent strikeout rate markedly more tolerable. With several safety nets in place, the Cardinals acted swiftly in September when a dead arm period and balky back limited Mujica's effectiveness, replacing him with Trevor Rosenthal. Still, a 37-save season added sizzle to Mujica's resume and surely contributed to his two-year deal with the Red Sox. Even in a set-up role, he provides peace of mind to traditional-minded managers (read: all of them).

Henry Owens

Born: **7/21/1992** Age: **21**
Bats: **L** Throws: **L** Height: **6' 6"** Weight: **205**
Breakout: **40%** Improve: **72%** Collapse: **18%**
Attrition: **32%** MLB: **28%**

Comparables:
Trevor Bauer, Jake McGee, Chris Tillman

YEAR	TEAM	LVL	AGE	W	L	SV	G	GS	IP	H	HR	BB	SO	BB9	SO9	GB%	BABIP	WHIP	ERA	FIP	FRA	WARP
2012	GRN	A	19	12	5	0	23	22	101²	100	10	47	130	4.2	11.5	38%	.350	1.45	4.87	3.86	3.81	3.0
2013	SLM	A+	20	8	5	0	20	20	104²	66	6	53	123	4.6	10.6	45%	.249	1.14	2.92	3.46	4.28	2.1
2013	PME	AA	20	3	1	0	6	6	30¹	18	3	15	46	4.5	13.6	29%	.254	1.09	1.78	3.26	3.67	0.7
2014	BOS	MLB	21	6	7	0	23	23	105²	98	12	56	113	4.8	9.6	40%	.308	1.45	4.33	4.41	4.70	0.6

The 6-foot-6 Owens was what you'd expect as a 19-year-old lanky lefty in 2012, mixing brilliant performances with starts where his mechanics refused to repeat and the strike zone all but vanished. The 2011 supplemental pick added 15 pounds of much-needed bulk before 2013, however, and saw his command and consistency improve. He then waved goodbye to High-A following 19 ⅓ consecutive no-hit innings. In addition to the weight, Owens also revamped his curveball grip so that he could use the same arm speed for that pitch as he does for his fastball and changeup: In essence, the opposition sees a 67 to 72 mph offering come in at an arm angle that looks like it's delivering 92. Owens will likely begin 2014 with a return to Double-A, where he's already flashed small-sample ridiculousness.

Jake Peavy

Born: **5/31/1981** Age: **33**
Bats: **R** Throws: **R** Height: **6' 1"** Weight: **195**
Breakout: **11%** Improve: **44%** Collapse: **28%**
Attrition: **19%** MLB: **88%**

Comparables:
Josh Beckett, Johan Santana, Kelvim Escobar

YEAR	TEAM	LVL	AGE	W	L	SV	G	GS	IP	H	HR	BB	SO	BB9	SO9	GB%	BABIP	WHIP	ERA	FIP	FRA	WARP
2011	CHR	AAA	30	1	1	0	4	4	24²	21	3	1	26	0.4	9.5	42%	.286	0.89	3.65	2.83	4.02	0.3
2011	CHA	MLB	30	7	7	0	19	18	111²	117	10	24	95	1.9	7.7	40%	.317	1.26	4.92	3.25	4.01	2.1
2012	CHA	MLB	31	11	12	0	32	32	219	191	27	49	194	2.0	8.0	37%	.273	1.10	3.37	3.69	4.41	2.5
2013	CHA	MLB	32	8	4	0	13	13	80	74	14	17	76	1.9	8.6	37%	.271	1.14	4.28	4.13	4.72	0.4
2013	BOS	MLB	32	4	1	0	10	10	64²	56	6	19	45	2.6	6.3	30%	.259	1.16	4.04	3.82	3.99	0.8
2014	BOS	MLB	33	9	7	0	23	23	137¹	131	14	33	122	2.2	8.0	41%	.298	1.20	3.45	3.65	3.75	2.1

The difference between the 2013 Red Sox and the previous two iterations is illustrated by Peavy. Before 2011's deadline, Boston only had the financial flexibility and prospects to acquire the oft-injured Erik Bedard to bolster their playoff hopes. In 2012, they couldn't even manage that, as Theo Epstein's legacy included a bloated budget. Post-Punto trade, however, with Ben Cherington's more fiscally responsible moves on hand, Peavy was an easy acquisition for both the farm and the payroll. His contributions won't end in 2013, either, as he's under contract for this season. He was standard Peavy in 2013, slinging the ball for strikes more often than not, allowing flies but also missing bats. As back-end starters go, you could do far worse.

Anthony Ranaudo

Born: **9/9/1989** Age: **24**
Bats: **R** Throws: **R** Height: **6' 7"** Weight: **230**
Breakout: **27%** Improve: **52%** Collapse: **46%**
Attrition: **71%** MLB: **35%**

Comparables:
Humberto Sanchez, Blake Wood, Cesar Carrillo

YEAR	TEAM	LVL	AGE	W	L	SV	G	GS	IP	H	HR	BB	SO	BB9	SO9	GB%	BABIP	WHIP	ERA	FIP	FRA	WARP
2011	GRN	A	21	4	1	0	10	10	46	35	4	16	50	3.1	9.8	49%	.333	1.11	3.33	3.79	3.07	0.5
2011	SLM	A+	21	5	5	0	16	16	81	80	6	30	67	3.3	7.4	53%	.315	1.36	4.33	3.98	4.11	0.4
2012	PME	AA	22	1	3	0	9	9	37²	41	4	27	27	6.5	6.5	36%	.311	1.81	6.69	5.54	6.46	-0.3
2013	PME	AA	23	8	4	0	19	19	109²	80	9	40	106	3.3	8.7	44%	.250	1.09	2.95	3.63	3.87	2.0
2013	PAW	AAA	23	3	1	0	6	5	30¹	32	1	7	21	2.1	6.2	46%	.320	1.29	2.97	2.94	3.95	0.5
2014	BOS	MLB	24	5	7	0	18	18	98²	102	11	43	70	3.9	6.4	44%	.303	1.47	4.70	4.82	5.10	-0.0

Ranaudo was a forgotten prospect, mostly because no one wanted to remember his 2012: A groin injury delayed his debut, and upon his return, he forgot to bring his mechanics. This past season was different, though, with Ranaudo's velocity jumping back to a consistent 92 to 94 mph, his plus curveball once again the hammer it needs to be, and his changeup ... well, he threw it. Projections that he'll wind up in the bullpen have quieted down once more, with Ranaudo finishing 2013 one step from the majors as a starter. The consensus ceiling is mid-rotation, but there are scouts who think he's a number two if he can stay healthy and keep his mechanics from slipping. That's an if about as large as his 6-foot-7 frame, at least until he shows he can do it again.

Teddy Stankiewicz

Born: **11/25/1993** Age: **20**
Bats: **R** Throws: **R** Height: **6' 4"** Weight: **200**
Breakout: **0%** Improve: **0%** Collapse: **0%**
Attrition: **0%** MLB: **0%**

Comparables:
Brett Marshall, Alberto Cabrera, Liam Hendriks

YEAR	TEAM	LVL	AGE	W	L	SV	G	GS	IP	H	HR	BB	SO	BB9	SO9	GB%	BABIP	WHIP	ERA	FIP	FRA	WARP
2013	LOW	A-	19	0	0	0	9	9	19²	17	1	2	15	0.9	6.9	48%	.271	0.97	2.29	2.69	3.88	0.3
2014	BOS	MLB	20	1	3	0	9	9	31²	40	4	18	15	5.0	4.3	45%	.316	1.80	6.41	5.91	6.96	-0.5

Stankiewicz was drafted out of junior college by the Sox in 2013 after declining to sign with the Mets out of high school. That extra year of amateur ball gave him a leg up on the similarly aged competition of short-season ball, helping Stanky (sorry) retire the opposition with ease despite unimpressive strikeout numbers. Strikeouts could come his way with time, as his low-90s fastball is complemented by a curveball with plus potential and a change that sits about 10 mph below his heater. The second-round selection projects as yet another mid-rotation arm for Boston, and given his youth, there's no need to rush his development. Thanks to his brief college stint and a loaded Low-A rotation he might jump to High-A anyway.

Junichi Tazawa
Born: 6/6/1986 Age: 28
Bats: R Throws: R Height: 5' 11" Weight: 200
Breakout: 47% Improve: 58% Collapse: 28%
Attrition: 29% MLB: 71%
Comparables:
Andrew Bailey, Rafael Perez, Nick Masset

YEAR	TEAM	LVL	AGE	W	L	SV	G	GS	IP	H	HR	BB	SO	BB9	SO9	GB%	BABIP	WHIP	ERA	FIP	FRA	WARP
2011	SLM	A+	25	0	1	0	6	6	19¹	20	4	6	13	2.8	6.1	36%	.222	1.34	6.05	5.97	5.00	0.1
2011	PME	AA	25	3	2	0	8	2	23	20	3	7	27	2.7	10.6	33%	.357	1.17	4.70	3.93	2.75	0.2
2011	PAW	AAA	25	1	1	0	8	0	14¹	14	1	3	19	1.9	11.9	45%	.321	1.19	2.51	2.12	3.18	0.3
2011	BOS	MLB	25	0	0	0	3	0	3	3	1	1	4	3.0	12.0	12%	.286	1.33	6.00	5.73	3.58	0.1
2012	PAW	AAA	26	3	2	4	25	0	42¹	34	2	17	56	3.6	11.9	49%	.308	1.20	2.55	2.33	3.18	0.9
2012	BOS	MLB	26	1	1	1	37	0	44	37	1	5	45	1.0	9.2	49%	.303	0.95	1.43	1.77	2.68	1.1
2013	BOS	MLB	27	5	4	0	71	0	68¹	70	9	12	72	1.6	9.5	35%	.321	1.20	3.16	3.25	3.37	1.1
2014	BOS	MLB	28	3	1	1	52	0	61²	61	6	16	57	2.3	8.3	42%	.309	1.24	3.73	3.58	4.05	0.6

No one outside of Boston noticed that former starter Tazawa added explosive and previously unseen velocity as a reliever in 2012 because the Red Sox were an unwatchable dumpster fire during the season's final two months. His ability to throw strikes didn't go unnoticed in the offseason once someone swept away the ash, though, and Tazawa was penciled in as a key member of the bullpen. While he didn't keep the sub-two ERA, he still punched out six times more batters than he walked, and is now part of a bullpen featuring a foursome (Tazawa, Uehara, Badenhop, Mujica) that combined for 30 unintentional walks in 269 innings last year.

Matt Thornton
Born: 9/15/1976 Age: 37
Bats: L Throws: L Height: 6' 6" Weight: 235
Breakout: 19% Improve: 43% Collapse: 32%
Attrition: 9% MLB: 84%
Comparables:
Joe Nathan, Arthur Rhodes, Francisco Cordero

YEAR	TEAM	LVL	AGE	W	L	SV	G	GS	IP	H	HR	BB	SO	BB9	SO9	GB%	BABIP	WHIP	ERA	FIP	FRA	WARP
2011	CHA	MLB	34	2	5	3	62	0	59²	60	3	21	63	3.2	9.5	49%	.326	1.36	3.32	2.66	2.77	1.7
2012	CHA	MLB	35	4	10	3	74	0	65	63	4	17	53	2.4	7.3	55%	.317	1.23	3.46	3.14	4.41	0.6
2013	BOS	MLB	36	0	1	0	20	0	15¹	22	0	5	9	2.9	5.3	61%	.386	1.76	3.52	2.88	3.76	0.2
2013	CHA	MLB	36	0	3	0	40	0	28	25	4	10	21	3.2	6.8	45%	.266	1.25	3.86	4.72	4.51	-0.1
2014	BOS	MLB	37	3	1	1	47	0	42	39	3	13	43	2.7	9.2	48%	.314	1.22	3.16	3.15	3.43	0.7

Thornton was brought in from the White Sox after Andrew Miller went down, with the hopes he would have something in the tank for a contending team desperate for lefty relief help. Instead, his strikeouts slipped even further, and by year's end he had allowed nearly one-third of his inherited baserunners to score, blighting what looked like a useful campaign on the surface. Drake Britton ended up pitching more key lefty-centric frames down the stretch, a change accelerated by Thornton's early August abdomen strain. Thornton might be useful to a team short on lefties—the Yankees—but it's unlikely the 37-year-old will be the force he was at the start of the decade.

Koji Uehara
Born: 4/3/1975 Age: 39
Bats: R Throws: R Height: 6' 2" Weight: 195
Breakout: 16% Improve: 39% Collapse: 34%
Attrition: 11% MLB: 76%
Comparables:
Billy Wagner, Trevor Hoffman, Dennis Eckersley

YEAR	TEAM	LVL	AGE	W	L	SV	G	GS	IP	H	HR	BB	SO	BB9	SO9	GB%	BABIP	WHIP	ERA	FIP	FRA	WARP
2011	BAL	MLB	36	1	1	0	43	0	47	25	6	8	62	1.5	11.9	31%	.194	0.70	1.72	2.59	3.29	0.9
2011	TEX	MLB	36	1	2	0	22	0	18	13	5	1	23	0.5	11.5	36%	.200	0.78	4.00	4.28	4.23	0.1
2012	TEX	MLB	37	0	0	1	37	0	36	20	4	3	43	0.8	10.8	34%	.203	0.64	1.75	2.35	3.74	0.6
2013	BOS	MLB	38	4	1	21	73	0	74¹	33	5	9	101	1.1	12.2	42%	.188	0.57	1.09	1.64	2.13	2.1
2014	BOS	MLB	39	3	1	6	53	0	53²	42	5	10	62	1.6	10.4	36%	.282	0.97	2.25	2.76	2.45	1.6

Uehara's history of injury kept his price down, allowing the Sox to stash him as depth on the cheap behind Andrew Bailey and Joel Hanrahan. When both went down, the Sox installed Koji as stopper; it's nigh impossible to overstate the impact. Uehara struck out over 11 times as many batters as he walked, retired 37 in a row at one point (a hidden perfect game and then some), and limited opponents to a single run and no walks in 13 postseason innings. As a reliever, Uehara has thrown 219 innings with a 1.93 ERA, 284 strikeouts and 23 unintentional walks, and he somehow had his best year ever as a 38-year-old. Those aren't Mariano Rivera credentials—no one has those—but in this post-Mo world, Uehara might be the closest the game has to offer, at least until he too does the unthinkable and leaves us behind.

Brayan Villarreal

Born: 5/10/1987 Age: 27
Bats: R Throws: R Height: 6' 0" Weight: 170
Breakout: 35% Improve: 60% Collapse: 17%
Attrition: 43% MLB: 58%

Comparables:
Nick Hagadone, Mike Dunn, Scott Mathieson

YEAR	TEAM	LVL	AGE	W	L	SV	G	GS	IP	H	HR	BB	SO	BB9	SO9	GB%	BABIP	WHIP	ERA	FIP	FRA	WARP
2011	TOL	AAA	24	3	5	0	17	10	66	65	6	29	40	4.0	5.5	43%	.303	1.42	5.05	5.02	6.19	-0.5
2011	DET	MLB	24	1	1	0	16	0	16	21	3	10	14	5.6	7.9	42%	.367	1.94	6.75	5.62	6.70	-0.2
2012	TOL	AAA	25	0	0	1	8	0	14	5	1	7	22	4.5	14.1	71%	.200	0.86	1.29	2.66	2.63	0.4
2012	DET	MLB	25	3	5	0	50	0	54²	38	3	28	66	4.6	10.9	32%	.276	1.21	2.63	2.94	3.47	1.0
2013	TOL	AAA	26	2	2	1	28	0	34¹	26	0	26	41	6.8	10.7	49%	.321	1.51	3.15	3.35	4.08	0.3
2013	BOS	MLB	26	0	0	0	1	0	0	0	0	1	0	0.0	0.0	—	—	0.00	0.00	0.00	4.57	-0.1
2013	DET	MLB	26	0	2	0	7	0	4¹	8	1	8	6	16.6	12.5	50%	.538	3.69	20.77	8.84	8.79	-0.2
2014	BOS	MLB	27	2	1	0	30	2	43²	41	5	23	42	4.7	8.8	42%	.306	1.46	4.52	4.70	4.92	0.0

You don't have to look far to see the upside of Villarreal. That's not some metaphorical, thoughtful thing, either; there is literally an impressive stat line directly above where your eyes are now. Wedged right beneath it is the wild downside of the fireballing right-hander, and that's where things get iffy. The Red Sox acquired Villarreal and his inconsistency as a throw-in to the three-team swap that netted them Jake Peavy. He's out of options, so he's a few awful walks away from designation for assignment, especially given John Farrell's preference for relievers who throw strikes. In a less stacked 'pen, he might get a shot at holding his roster spot, but he could easily be elsewhere by the time you read this.

Allen Webster

Born: 2/10/1990 Age: 24
Bats: R Throws: R Height: 6' 2" Weight: 190
Breakout: 41% Improve: 65% Collapse: 26%
Attrition: 55% MLB: 46%

Comparables:
Lance Broadway, Josh Outman, Casey Crosby

YEAR	TEAM	LVL	AGE	W	L	SV	G	GS	IP	H	HR	BB	SO	BB9	SO9	GB%	BABIP	WHIP	ERA	FIP	FRA	WARP
2011	RCU	A+	21	5	2	0	9	9	54	46	2	21	62	3.5	10.3	47%	.281	1.24	2.33	3.53	3.20	0.4
2011	CHT	AA	21	6	3	0	18	17	91	101	7	36	73	3.6	7.2	56%	.326	1.51	5.04	4.15	5.46	0.1
2012	CHT	AA	22	6	8	0	27	22	121²	120	1	57	117	4.2	8.7	58%	.342	1.45	3.55	3.15	4.13	2.0
2013	PAW	AAA	23	8	4	0	21	21	105	71	9	43	116	3.7	9.9	51%	.246	1.09	3.60	3.80	4.21	1.3
2013	BOS	MLB	23	1	2	0	8	7	30¹	37	7	18	23	5.3	6.8	44%	.316	1.81	8.60	6.54	7.21	-0.5
2014	BOS	MLB	24	6	8	0	22	22	111	118	12	51	86	4.2	7.0	49%	.310	1.52	5.05	4.86	5.49	-0.4

Webster looked ready for the majors early in the season, but the chasm between Triple-A and the majors was on display in his spot starts. There were flashes of his ability to overpower the opposition with a combination of velocity, sink and swing-and-miss secondary stuff, but he had not mastered the art of pitching. Webster was still a thrower, and it wasn't until the second half of 2013, when he became more aggressive and focused on location, that "future major-league starter" became more realistic than "bullpen piece." Webster should have 2014 to put the finishing touches on this development, as, barring catastrophe, the Sox won't need him in the rotation until 2015.

Alex Wilson

Born: 11/3/1986 Age: 27
Bats: R Throws: R Height: 6' 0" Weight: 215
Breakout: 52% Improve: 64% Collapse: 19%
Attrition: 56% MLB: 44%

Comparables:
Tony Watson, Hayden Penn, P.J. Walters

YEAR	TEAM	LVL	AGE	W	L	SV	G	GS	IP	H	HR	BB	SO	BB9	SO9	GB%	BABIP	WHIP	ERA	FIP	FRA	WARP
2011	PME	AA	24	9	4	0	21	21	112	103	8	37	99	3.0	8.0	53%	.261	1.25	3.05	3.59	6.23	-0.2
2011	PAW	AAA	24	1	0	0	4	4	21	19	2	7	24	3.0	10.3	41%	.304	1.24	3.43	3.19	4.00	0.3
2012	PAW	AAA	25	5	3	1	40	3	72²	76	3	33	78	4.1	9.7	45%	.353	1.50	3.72	2.91	3.65	1.2
2013	PAW	AAA	26	3	1	0	14	0	17	17	2	5	16	2.6	8.5	42%	.312	1.29	3.71	3.73	3.95	0.2
2013	BOS	MLB	26	1	1	0	26	0	27²	34	0	14	22	4.6	7.2	31%	.378	1.73	4.88	3.11	3.35	0.4
2014	BOS	MLB	27	2	1	0	28	2	43	47	5	18	34	3.8	7.1	42%	.317	1.52	4.95	4.60	5.38	-0.2

Wilson's career path went from promising to disappointing in one season. He had unexpectedly thrived in the minor leagues as a starter until the Red Sox converted him to relief full-time in 2012, but he hasn't taken to the role as hoped. His velocity never ticked up as expected and he might walk too many batters for that to be okay in the majors. Thumb soreness on his throwing hand cost him the last three months of the regular season and the playoffs, and the slew of bullpen acquisitions likely means a return trip to Triple-A. Now 27, Wilson has his work cut out for him to be more than an up-and-down option.

Brandon Workman

Born: 8/13/1988 Age: 25
Bats: R Throws: R Height: 6' 4" Weight: 195
Breakout: 32% Improve: 63% Collapse: 16%
Attrition: 41% MLB: 76%

Comparables:
Wade LeBlanc, Juan Nicasio, Christian Friedrich

YEAR	TEAM	LVL	AGE	W	L	SV	G	GS	IP	H	HR	BB	SO	BB9	SO9	GB%	BABIP	WHIP	ERA	FIP	FRA	WARP
2011	GRN	A	22	6	7	0	26	26	131	128	10	33	115	2.3	7.9	44%	.331	1.23	3.71	3.63	4.58	0.9
2012	SLM	A+	23	7	7	0	20	20	113²	104	10	20	107	1.6	8.5	47%	.297	1.09	3.40	3.20	4.45	1.2
2012	PME	AA	23	3	1	0	5	5	25	23	2	5	23	1.8	8.3	38%	.296	1.12	3.96	3.00	4.00	0.4
2013	PME	AA	24	5	1	0	11	10	65²	51	6	17	74	2.3	10.1	36%	.281	1.04	3.43	3.08	3.10	1.7
2013	PAW	AAA	24	3	1	0	6	6	35¹	39	6	13	34	3.3	8.7	42%	.340	1.47	2.80	4.76	4.45	0.4
2013	BOS	MLB	24	6	3	0	20	3	41²	44	5	15	47	3.2	10.2	41%	.345	1.42	4.97	3.46	3.48	0.7
2014	BOS	MLB	25	6	6	1	30	16	118	123	15	38	101	2.9	7.7	42%	.312	1.37	4.36	4.31	4.74	0.4

Workman's ascent is the fulfillment of his best-case-scenario, as he had the body and the arm to become a mid-rotation starter in the majors, but dreaming that dream on draft day and seeing it in action are two very different things. His stat line from the bigs doesn't jump off the page, but he was also adjusting to a relief role for the first time in his career, on the fly, because that's where Boston's need was. Command is the question for the tall righty: If he can keep his fastball down in the zone with regularity, he won't give up the homers and cheap hits that are a threat to his future as a starter. The Sox believe his future is as a mid-rotation workhorse, and they'll give him every opportunity to prove them wrong.

Steven Wright

Born: 8/30/1984 Age: 29
Bats: R Throws: R Height: 6' 1'' Weight: 220
Breakout: 31% Improve: 59% Collapse: 32%
Attrition: 75% MLB: 9%

Comparables:
Jimmy Barthmaier, Steve Watkins, Philip Barzilla

YEAR	TEAM	LVL	AGE	W	L	SV	G	GS	IP	H	HR	BB	SO	BB9	SO9	GB%	BABIP	WHIP	ERA	FIP	FRA	WARP
2011	LKC	A	26	1	2	0	9	9	46	48	3	24	33	4.7	6.5	46%	.500	1.57	3.13	4.53	7.68	-0.2
2011	KIN	A+	26	1	2	0	7	4	38^1	47	7	16	27	3.8	6.3	39%	.331	1.64	4.46	5.53	6.69	-0.5
2011	AKR	AA	26	2	4	0	8	7	46^2	47	8	28	35	5.4	6.8	51%	.288	1.61	5.98	6.26	6.36	-0.6
2012	AKR	AA	27	9	6	0	20	20	115^2	86	8	62	101	4.8	7.9	51%	.250	1.28	2.49	4.09	5.44	-0.4
2012	PAW	AAA	27	0	1	0	4	4	20	19	1	5	16	2.2	7.2	46%	.281	1.20	3.15	3.26	3.08	0.5
2013	PAW	AAA	28	8	7	0	24	24	135^1	130	10	65	99	4.3	6.6	53%	.294	1.44	3.46	4.23	5.29	-0.2
2013	BOS	MLB	28	2	0	0	4	1	13^1	12	0	9	10	6.1	6.8	39%	.308	1.58	5.40	3.83	4.30	0.1
2014	BOS	MLB	29	5	6	0	37	16	123^1	135	14	58	80	4.2	5.8	45%	.307	1.57	5.15	5.09	5.60	-0.8

Trying to guess a knuckleballer's future is pointless. It's the one style of pitch and pitcher where major-league results are all that matter. In Wright's case, he showed a lot of potential—whenever Ryan Lavarnway wasn't setting passed balls records and extending innings, anyway—or at least enough to justify his 40-man presence. The Sox could be forgiven if they kept him in the loaded Pawtucket rotation and pushed someone else to relief because, while you can't predict what a knuckler is going to be, the upside is obvious. That said, he has shown he can be effective as a bullpen option against lineups sitting fastball, and his potential as a long reliever or swingman make him a useful asset to stash.

LINEOUTS

HITTERS

PLAYER	TEAM	LVL	AGE	PA	R	2B	3B	HR	RBI	BB	SO	SB-CS	AVG/OBP/SLG	TAv	BABIP	BRR	FRAA	WARP
2B S. Coyle	GRN	A	21	28	4	3	0	1	4	3	9	0-1	.320/.393/.560	.282	.467	-0.4	2B(5): -0.3	0.1
	SLM	A+	21	224	41	9	1	14	28	24	65	11-0	.241/.321/.513	.286	.275	4.2	2B(36): -0.6	1.7
2B B. Holt	PAW	AAA	25	329	35	6	0	3	24	30	54	8-3	.258/.327/.309	.244	.303	-0.1	2B(44): -4.0, SS(32): -1.8	-0.2
	BOS	MLB	25	72	9	2	0	0	11	7	4	1-0	.203/.275/.237	.230	.207	0.7	3B(20): -0.9, 2B(5): 0.0	0.0
SS T. Lin	LOW	A-	19	261	34	9	2	1	20	28	59	12-4	.226/.312/.296	.247	.298	4.5	SS(58): 8.1	2.2
2B M. McCoy	BUF	AAA	32	430	50	15	1	4	22	59	68	29-7	.245/.357/.327	.249	.293	2.2	2B(34): -2.0, SS(31): 3.9	1.2
SS J. McDonald	IND	AAA	38	37	5	1	0	0	1	2	3	1-0	.265/.324/.294	.214	.290	0.3	SS(6): 0.3, 2B(4): -0.0	0.0
	CLE	MLB	38	8	2	0	0	0	0	1	1	0-0	.000/.125/.000	.091	.000	0.2	3B(8): -0.0	0.0
	BOS	MLB	38	9	1	0	0	0	0	1	3	0-0	.250/.333/.250	.248	.400	0	2B(6): -0.3	0.0
	PHI	MLB	38	25	5	0	0	1	3	1	4	0-0	.174/.208/.304	.185	.167	-0.5	3B(8): 0.2, SS(6): 0.1	-0.1
	PIT	MLB	38	35	0	1	0	0	1	3	8	0-0	.065/.171/.097	.129	.087	0	SS(13): -0.6, 2B(4): 0.1	-0.5
CF H. Ramos	SLM	A+	21	540	69	27	7	12	55	55	100	11-12	.252/.330/.416	.260	.291	-6.2	CF(104): -7.7, RF(21): 0.1	0.5
1B B. Snyder	PAW	AAA	26	277	37	16	1	10	37	20	69	3-1	.261/.332/.454	.272	.322	-0.9	1B(41): 1.7, 3B(25): 1.2	1.1
	BOS	MLB	26	52	5	3	0	2	7	0	16	0-0	.180/.212/.360	.200	.219	-1.1	3B(17): 0.5, 1B(6): 0.1	-0.3

Second baseman **Sean Coyle** can hit the ball far, but making contact is the question that will define his career. Injuries limited his 2013, and Coyle was passed by Mookie Betts on the depth chart, but he's a capable defender with a big-league ceiling just the same. ⊘ Boston selected **Jon Denney** in 2013's third round, impressing draft prognosticators who felt that was late. Denney's defense behind the plate is a question, but his bat is such that some believe he could move to left field, and others first base, depending on how slow he ends up. ⊘ Acquired with Joel Hanrahan, **Brock Holt** could have a future as a big-league utility infielder, but 2013 was an inauspicious start. You have to root for a guy who acknowledges the inherent "STEVE HOLT!" joke potential in his name, so consider us hopeful. ⊘ **Ryan Kalish** was non-tendered after missing the year recovering from neck surgery; in the last three seasons, he's played just 93 games. ⊘ In 2010, **Tzu-Wei Lin** signed with the Yankees as a 16-year-old before reneging after his country's Baseball Association raised a stink about him not finishing high school. Two years later, he joined Boston for a significantly larger bonus and is now a defense-first shortstop who largely held his own against older competition in the New York-Penn League. ⊘ **Nick Longhi** managed a $440,000 signing bonus after dropping to the 30th round due to signability concerns; he's got a classic "big-time power undermined by contact woes" profile. ⊘ The Blue Jays saw Mark DeRosa standing all alone on the dance floor and completely forgot about **Mike McCoy**. ⊘ **John McDonald** played for four teams in 2013. Yep. ⊘ **Henry Ramos** split his time between soccer and baseball right up until he was drafted in 2010. The switch-hitter has shown flashes of power potential and a strong arm anchors his defense. ⊘ Now recovered from a 2012 ACL tear, **Wendell Rijo's** pro debut featured stolen bases, few strikeouts and a nice walk rate. ⊘ **Brandon Snyder** served as corner depth in 2013 and got a shot at third while Will Middlebrooks worked through his issues; any role bigger than that spells trouble.

PITCHERS

PLAYER	TEAM	LVL	AGE	W	L	SV	IP	H	HR	BB	SO	BB9	SO9	GB%	BABIP	WHIP	ERA	FIP	FRA	WARP
J. Callahan	LOW	A-	18	5	1	0	59²	48	4	17	54	2.6	8.1	31%	.272	1.09	3.92	3.11	4.44	0.2
L. Diaz	GRN	A	21	7	4	0	88	74	5	20	86	2.0	8.8	47%	.283	1.07	2.05	3.05	3.99	1.5
	SLM	A+	21	2	0	0	13	11	0	4	8	2.8	5.5	40%	.275	1.15	1.38	3.04	4.63	0.1
S. Gomez	GRN	A	19	1	3	0	27¹	21	2	10	25	3.3	8.2	28%	.271	1.13	2.96	4.03	4.01	0.3
	LOW	A-	19	3	1	0	50²	40	2	14	55	2.5	9.8	43%	.292	1.07	1.60	2.39	2.26	1.3
J. Haley	GRN	A	22	7	11	0	124²	97	10	74	124	5.3	9.0	41%	.274	1.37	3.68	4.32	5.16	0.7
C. Kukuk	GRN	A	20	4	13	1	107	77	5	81	113	6.8	9.5	51%	.256	1.48	4.63	4.28	5.07	0.6
T. Layne	TUC	AAA	28	2	4	0	46	49	1	27	41	5.3	8.0	51%	.345	1.65	4.50	4.09	4.44	0.7
	SDN	MLB	28	0	2	0	8²	10	1	5	6	5.2	6.2	54%	.360	1.73	2.08	5.56	6.39	-0.2
P. Light	GRN	A	22	1	4	0	28¹	44	4	14	28	4.4	8.9	47%	.417	2.05	8.89	4.93	5.68	0.1
C. Littrell	LOW	A-	21	0	3	0	31	28	0	10	30	2.9	8.7	43%	.315	1.23	1.74	2.23	3.16	0.7
D. McGrath	LOW	A-	18	3	3	0	33¹	29	2	13	35	3.5	9.4	44%	.314	1.26	4.86	3.04	4.26	0.3
S. Mercedes	LOW	A-	21	2	2	1	63¹	62	2	17	57	2.4	8.1	60%	.333	1.25	3.13	2.61	4.44	0.6
N. Ramirez	SLM	A+	23	2	1	1	47	41	0	9	44	1.7	8.4	53%	.328	1.06	2.11	2.31	3.38	1.1
	PME	AA	23	1	1	5	28²	22	4	8	31	2.5	9.7	56%	.265	1.05	2.83	4.02	4.31	0.3

The youngest hurler in the New York-Penn League, lefty **Jamie Callahan** retired 36 of the 37 batters he faced in a two-start July stretch, striking out 17 of them. That dominance belies his development, however, as he still needs a reliable third pitch and was raw enough to get thrashed more than once. ⊘ The changeup and slider of right-hander **Luis Diaz** took leaps forward, but they don't project as high-quality offerings. The numbers are pretty—especially the jump in strikeouts—and he was just 21, but he profiles as a reliever. ⊘ **Sergio Gomez** is as raw as they come. He finished his 2013 campaign with success at Low-A, though, so if the velocity comes with growth and a breaking ball develops, he'll be worth watching. ⊘ **Justin Haley**, who for now is all fastball, walked 37 batters in his first 42 innings, but by August that was a distant memory replaced by strikeouts and a healthy K/BB ratio. ⊘ Another tall, youthful lefty with low-90s velocity and a quality breaking ball, **Cody Kukuk's** action items are a consistent release point, a refined changeup and a final ruling in the Best Joke About My Last Name contest. ⊘ After a surprising 2012 campaign that ended with him in the Padres' bullpen, **Tommy Layne** got hit hard in spring training and spent most of the summer at Tucson, where he finally solved right-handed hitters but not Fermat's Last Theorem. ⊘ **Pat Light's** potential is evident, but he is raw and his future lies in relief, where his mid-90s heat should pair nicely with a slider that still needs focused development. ⊘ Southpaw and fifth-round pick **Corey Littrell** could skip to High-A from short-season ball thanks to polish and a deep repertoire, including a changeup, bender and cutter. ⊘ Australian teenager **Daniel McGrath** wrecked Rookie ball lineups en route to a New York-Penn promotion in his pro debut despite only reaching the upper 80s with his fastball. That's expected to improve. ⊘ **Simon Mercedes'** mid-90s fastball combines with a yakker that misses bats, and while his command needs work, that's almost to be expected when you're 21 and throwing fire. ⊘ Right-hander **Myles Smith** is relatively new to pitching, so occurrences like velocity spikes (up to the mid-90s in 2013) are not unusual. The hope is that mound experience will help his command take a similar leap forward. ⊘ Homers are a potential concern for **Noe Ramirez**, even after getting through High-A without allowing one in 47 innings.

MANAGER: JOHN FARRELL

YEAR	TEAM	W-L	Pythag +/–	Avg PC	100+ P	120+ P	QS	BQS	REL	REL w Zero R	IBB	PH	PH Avg	PH HR	SB2	CS2	SB3	CS3	SAC Att	SAC %	POS SAC	Squeeze	Swing	In Play
2012	TOR	73-89	0	91.9	52	0	74	3	495	396	20	80	.205	1	89	31	33	8	67	49.3%	32	3	406	138
2011	TOR	81-81	0	97.7	81	4	81	3	474	383	28	58	.185	0	98	43	32	6	54	57.4%	31	2	372	103
2013	BOS	97-65	1	100.0	88	5	95	6	450	355	10	81	.235	6	104	17	17	2	38	63.2%	21	0	336	104

Trivia question: Can you name the last former Blue Jays manager prior to John Farrell to ever get hired by another team? Answer: Jimy Williams, who managed in Toronto in the 1980s. As it happens, he was also hired by Boston, in the late 1990s.

Last year, Boston was 123 for 142 in stolen base opportunities, the best success rate by any team in AL history. It helps having three great baserunners in Jacob Ellsbury (52 for 56 in stolen base attempts), Shane Victorino (21 for 24) and Dustin Pedroia (17 for 22). But even the rest of the team was pretty good: 33 for 40. That's a nice feature on the resume of new Boston skipper John Farrell, and first-year first base coach Arnie Beyeler.

Chicago White Sox

By Ken Funck

Sometimes it's not how *much* you lose that defines your season, but *how* you lose. Instead of battling the Tigers for primacy in the American League Central, as they had in 2012 with essentially the same cast of characters, the White Sox fell 22 games back in the standings last year and plummeted to the bottom of the division. As dispiriting as their performance was in the standings, it may have been even worse on an aesthetic level, with Sox fans tempted to pull out their ticket stubs to make sure they had paid for admittance to a baseball game, not a live performance of Mr. Bean. The Sox committed 121 errors, continually ran into outs on the basepaths, blew late leads, scored the fewest runs in the league and elicited a career-high 853 "dadgummits" and several hours of frustrated dead air from announcer Hawk Harrelson. (See Figure 1.) One of the myriad low points came in September when ESPN revealed their Future Power Rankings, based on how their experts scored each organization's current and future talent, finances and management. The White Sox clocked in at no. 29. Right behind the Marlins at 28. Ouch.

Misery Category	Total	AL Rank	Worst Team
Errors	125	2nd	Astros
Unearned Runs Allowed	11.1%	1st	White Sox
Baserunning Outs Per PA	0.019	T-3rd	Astros
Lost When Winning/Tied After 7 Innings	32.2%	2nd	Astros
Fewest Runs Scored	598	1st	White Sox
Baserunners Stranded	73%	3rd	Twins
Dadgummits	853	1st	White Sox

Why are baseball analysts seemingly so down on Chicago's future? After all, this is a franchise that won a World Series less than a decade ago, has remained reasonably competitive for years and isn't noticeably hamstrung by a lack of financial resources. The Sox have ranked among the top 10 in team payroll seven of the last eight seasons. Rick Hahn may only be entering his second season as general manager, but he worked closely with former honcho Kenny Williams for years and his fingerprints can be found all over the organization's longstanding record of success.

Despite all this, Chicago's perceived future ranks so poorly because they are currently deficient in the most important category of all: talent, both on the big league roster and in the minor-league pipeline. Last year's tailspin didn't seem like a fluke, one of those seasons where every key veteran randomly has an off year or half the rotation spends time on the disabled list, pointing toward a quick rebound. Instead, the Sox' collapse was in large part due to an anemic offense filled with aging players whose careers have likely reached their expiration date (Paul Konerko and Adam Dunn), veterans who have hit their modest peaks (Alejandro De Aza and Alexei Ramirez) and disappointing not-quite-youngsters who have never made good on their promise and perhaps never will (Gordon Beckham, Dayan Viciedo, Tyler Flowers). Underpinning this is a farm system that has long been considered one of the weakest in baseball, due primarily to a series of unproductive and penurious drafts. Taken together, it's easy to see why analysts look at the Sox and wonder where the young, cost-controlled players that are the lifeblood of baseball's middle class are going to come from, and mark them down accordingly.

None of this is news to White Sox management, which has made improving the farm system and adding young talent a top priority, with some success. Hahn likes to point out that the White Sox have done a better job with their recent drafts, noting that players taken by the Sox between 2008 and 2011 have produced a higher WAR total than any other team's draftees. While our WARP metric ranks the White Sox fifth (behind the Nats, Giants, Cardinals and ~~Mike Trout~~ Angels), it's still a

WHITE SOX PROSPECTUS
2013 W-L: 63-99, 5th in AL Central

Pythag	.414	25th	DER	.706	11th
RS/G	3.69	29th	B-Age	29.3	23rd
RA/G	4.46	23rd	P-Age	26.7	2nd
TAv	.251	23rd	Salary	$107.4	14th
BRR	-15.13	29th	M$/MW	$7.32	30th
TAv-P	.270	21st	DL Days	702	10th
FIP	4.16	26th	$ on DL	18%	19th

	Runs	HR/RH	HR/LH	Runs/RH	Runs/LH
Three-Year Park Factors	99	91	102	99	105

Top Hitter WARP	3.20 (Alejandro De Aza)
Top Pitcher WARP	3.95 (Chris Sale)
Top Prospect	Eric Johnson

fair point. Beckham, ace starter Chris Sale, departed closer Addison Reed and oft-injured Diamondbacks hurler Daniel Hudson were all drafted by the White Sox and quickly provided major league value. Our own prospect mavens have started giving the system better grades for its depth, if not for its Twins-like stockpile of future superstars—there is no Byron Buxton or Miguel Sano in the Sox organization, but it's a start.

Such improvements are certainly welcome, but it will take time for the Sox to overcome the string of fallow drafts that occurred from 2001, when Williams took over as GM, through 2007. During those seven seasons, the White Sox drafted players that have since earned a total of 44.8 WARP in the major leagues. (See Figure 2.) Only Cleveland had less productive drafts during those years; the average team drafted players that earned twice as much WARP as the White Sox' draftees.

What's more, a series of prospects-for-vets trades aimed at keeping Chicago on top after its 2005 championship meant very little of that production occurred in White Sox laundry, and playing transactional connect-the-dots doesn't draw many flattering pictures. The chain of custody for outfielders Chris Young and Ryan Sweeney and pitcher Gio Gonzalez passes through Javier Vazquez to the disappointing Flowers, and through Nick Swisher to Wilson Betemit to bupkis. Only the challenge trade of pitcher Brandon McCarthy for John Danks worked out significantly in Chicago's favor, and of all the players in their 2001 to 2007 draft classes, only hurlers Hector Santiago and Nate Jones toiled for the White Sox last year.

WARP Produced by Draft Class

Draft Year	White Sox	Average Team
2001	10.4	17.0
2002	5.1	19.0
2003	8.4	14.2
2004	14.2	12.8
2005	2.3	15.5
2006	2.5	10.5
2007	2.0	5.7
2008	8.9	4.3
2009	-0.7	4.4
2010	12.1	1.6
2011	0.1	0.4
2012	0.0	0.1
Total 2001–07	44.8	94.7
Total 2008–12	20.5	10.7

Even more notable has been the inability of the organization to draft and keep top-flight batting talent. The last homegrown Sox hitter to post a three-win season was third baseman Joe Crede in 2006; since then, there have been 209 such seasons for other clubs, but none for the South Siders. The next hitter from their 2001 to 2007 draft classes that posts a two-win season for the Sox will be the first, and only Chris Getz and Josh Fields have earned even a single win for their original organization. In a word, that's craptacular.

This combination of poor drafts and win-now moves caused the White Sox to become less reliant on homegrown talent than any team in the league. (See Figure 3.) In the five years leading up to their 2005 World Series title, the Sox received approximately 30 percent of their production from home-drafted players, right in line with the rest of the league. Since then, the league has increased to 39 percent, but the Sox have gotten only 19 percent of their total WARP during the 2006-2013 seasons from players the club drafted and developed. Only Cleveland (17 percent) has gotten less out of its drafted players than the Sox over the past eight years.

Percent of Team WARP from Team Draftees

Season	White Sox	Average Team
2001	35	30
2002	33	30
2003	22	32
2004	32	27
2005	28	30
2006	20	33
2007	14	38
2008	14	40
2009	21	42
2010	12	42
2011	18	42
2012	19	37
2013	44	42
Total 2001–05	30	30
Total 2006–13	19	39

Unable to fill roster holes from within, the organization has been forced to try other approaches. We've lauded the Sox in the past for their creativity and boldness in adding talent to their big-league roster and staying competitive. They've had success acquiring and rehabilitating other clubs' post-hype prospects, such as Danks, Gavin Floyd, Carlos Quentin and Matt Thornton. They've won challenge trades. They've signed players from Cuba. They've acquired top-end talent that others have shied away from due to injuries (Jake Peavy) or toxic contracts (Alex Rios). They've added low-cost, high-upside veterans in-season. Such admirable flexibility and gambler's nerve has helped make the White Sox perpetual contenders in a mediocre division. However, such creativity works best as an add-on, not an alternative. Despite the widening pipeline of players from the Caribbean, South America and the Far East, fully 76 percent of all WARP in the major leagues last year was earned by players who had been selected and signed through the First-Year Player Draft. Ignore it at your peril. For several years in the mid-Aughties, the White Sox seemingly did ignore it—or at least gave it short shrift—using every method but the draft to fill out their roster. That bill came due last summer, and the Sox paid with 99 losses.

During his first year on the job, Hahn has responded by beefing up the club's international scouting department, watching over a draft that brought in well-regarded shortstop Tim Anderson and pitcher Tyler Danish and signing massive Dominican teenager Micker Zapata. He's engineered deadline trades of Peavy and Rios for toolsy outfielder Avisail Garcia and shortstop tyro Leury Garcia, and injected youth into the lineup by swapping out Reed and Santiago for outfield spark-plug Adam Eaton and potential power bat Matt Davidson. If you saw that task list blowing down Michigan Avenue, you might think it had fallen out of Theo Epstein's pocket. Yet Hahn has been careful not to use the word "rebuild," preferring the term "retool." Unlike the Cubs, who haven't been coy about their focus on the future at the expense of the present, the White Sox have always been skittish about entering a season without any hope of competing in their division. An Astros-style tear-down isn't in the cards, and the Sox will once again cross their fingers and hope against hope that they can cobble together enough offense to help their solid starting pitching and strain towards the edges of contention.

Unfortunately, the club is not likely to get much more out of last year's lineup holdovers. Garcia may grow into a star right fielder one day, but his ceiling is that of Rios, the man he's essentially replacing—that's not a net improvement over last year. Viciedo might still have time on his side, but if he doesn't change his approach, the young Cuban's raw power will never be enough to overcome his unbridled hackery—and how often does that happen, anyway? The upper reaches of the minor-league system remain devoid of impact bats. Thus the Sox once again went off-menu and boldly ordered up another exotic dish, slugger Jose Abreu. Known for his mature approach, bunyanesque power and ridiculous numbers in Cuba's Serie Nacional, Abreu signed the richest contract in White Sox club history last fall. He's a risk, of course, but if he's nothing more than a league-average first baseman, he'll not only be worth the money, he'll be a big step up from the disastrous production the Sox received from Paul Konerko last year. In the pantheon of White Sox gambles, this one feels like a mundane $10 bet on red.

If Abreu, Eaton and Davidson can jumpstart the lineup, and Sale stays healthy, and Danks rounds back into form in his second season back from surgery, and Jose Quintana continues to function as an honest-to-goodness second starter, and rookie Erik Johnson can hold his own at the back end of the rotation, and a catcher emerges who isn't a complete Replacement Level Killer, the White Sox will have a chance. More realistically, since there's virtually no way all those things are going to happen, they can sell the idea that they have a chance. That, along with a few more runs and a tad fewer head-scratching moments on the basepaths and in the field, will keep casual fans interested while the front office goes about the difficult, painstaking work of building a system and laying a sustainable foundation for long-term success. Things shouldn't get any worse in the loss column this year, but the Sox may suffer through another losing season. That's okay. Sometimes it's not how *much* you improve that defines your season, but *how* you improve.

Ken Funck is an author of Baseball Prospectus, *and has contributed to the* Baseball Prospectus *annual since 2010.*

HITTERS

			YEAR	TEAM	LVL	AGE	PA	R	2B	3B	HR	RBI	BB	SO	SB	CS	AVG/OBP/SLG	TAv	BABIP	BRR	FRAA	WARP
Jose Abreu	1B		2014	—	—	—	—	—	—	—	—	—	—	—	—	—	—	—	—	—	—	—

Jose Abreu 1B
Born: 1/29/1987 Age: 26
Bats: R Throws: R Height: 6' 2"
Weight: 258

Abreu signed a franchise-record $68 million contract to move from Cuba's Serie Nacional to the American League and add a little thump to the anemic White Sox lineup—a risky move even for a franchise well acquainted with rolling the dice. Few question the massive slugger's raw power or approach, but some believe his video game statistics were produced by feasting on the bottom tiers of Cuban pitching and mask a swing that can be tamed by well-placed fastballs on the inner half. Of course that's true of most major-league batsmen, but since Abreu's size limits his role to that of base-clogging first baseman/DH, he has a higher offensive bar to clear than most. The Sox feel the presence of fellow Cubans Alexei Ramirez and Dayan Viciedo will help ease his transition, and if GM Rick Hahn—who quoted Abreu's impressive Davenport Translations at the introductory presser—is right about his bat, the Sox will have found the slugging heart of their order for the rest of the decade.

			YEAR	TEAM	LVL	AGE	PA	R	2B	3B	HR	RBI	BB	SO	SB	CS	AVG/OBP/SLG	TAv	BABIP	BRR	FRAA	WARP
Tim Anderson	SS		2013	KAN	A	20	301	45	10	5	1	21	23	78	24	4	.277/.348/.363	.272	.384	6.3	SS(63): 2.8	2.6
			2014	CHA	MLB	21	250	26	8	1	2	16	14	73	8	2	.209/.260/.282	.203	.290	0.8	SS 2	-0.1

Tim Anderson SS
Born: 6/23/1993 Age: 21
Bats: R Throws: R Height: 6' 1"
Weight: 180 Breakout: 0%
Improve: 1% Collapse: 0%
Attrition: 1% MLB: 1%

Comparables:
Marcus Semien, Ian Desmond, Jonathan Villar

Long-time readers should never be surprised when we describe a top White Sox draftee as "fast, toolsy and raw." The South Siders nabbed Anderson in the first round last summer, and the East Central Community College shortstop held his own in his pro debut. Blessed with blazing speed and a quick bat that presages eventual power, Anderson was a multi-sport athlete who only recently focused on baseball and needs some rough edges sanded away, especially in the field. Some question whether he'll stick at shortstop, where his fringe-average arm may become a liability, though center field is a viable backup plan. Anderson also whiffed in more than a quarter of his plate appearances. Long-time readers should never be surprised when we describe a top White Sox draftee as "needing to make more contact, or all the tools in the world won't be able to build a major-league career."

Gordon Beckham 2B
Born: 9/16/1986 Age: 27
Bats: R Throws: R Height: 6' 0"
Weight: 190 Breakout: 2%
Improve: 54% Collapse: 5%
Attrition: 8% MLB: 94%
Comparables:
Aaron Hill, Jose Vidro, Bill Selby

YEAR	TEAM	LVL	AGE	PA	R	2B	3B	HR	RBI	BB	SO	SB	CS	AVG/OBP/SLG	TAv	BABIP	BRR	FRAA	WARP
2011	CHA	MLB	24	557	60	23	0	10	44	35	111	5	3	.230/.296/.337	.240	.276	0.3	2B(149): 6.7	0.8
2012	CHA	MLB	25	582	62	24	0	16	60	40	89	5	4	.234/.296/.371	.242	.254	-0.8	2B(149): -0.4	0.5
2013	CHR	AAA	26	38	7	2	0	0	5	2	6	0	0	.333/.368/.389	.264	.400	0.7	2B(5): 0.2, SS(2): 0.3	0.3
2013	CHA	MLB	26	408	46	22	1	5	24	28	56	5	1	.267/.322/.372	.260	.299	1.3	2B(103): -4.0, SS(2): -0.1	0.8
2014	CHA	MLB	27	424	45	21	0	9	43	30	73	4	2	.250/.313/.377	.257	.280	-0.8	2B -0, SS 0	1.2

After losing most of April and May to a broken hamate bone, Beckham returned with a different stance and a different approach, and wound up producing different results. Alas, "different" and "better" are not synonyms. The former phenom made more contact, lowered his whiff rate and raised his batting average and on-base percentage, but a corresponding loss of home run power and a deep season-ending slump left him no more valuable than he's ever been. Optimists might be justified in attributing last season's power outage to the lingering effects of an injured hand, but after four straight years of disappointment, even Dr. Pangloss has jumped off Beckham's bandwagon. Expect his defense to improve after a season-long case of the glove vapors, but a punchless Beckham is merely a placeholder, not a star.

Jordan Danks CF
Born: 8/7/1986 Age: 27
Bats: L Throws: R Height: 6' 4"
Weight: 210 Breakout: 8%
Improve: 27% Collapse: 12%
Attrition: 26% MLB: 56%
Comparables:
Justin Maxwell, Ryan Spilborghs, Ryan Raburn

YEAR	TEAM	LVL	AGE	PA	R	2B	3B	HR	RBI	BB	SO	SB	CS	AVG/OBP/SLG	TAv	BABIP	BRR	FRAA	WARP
2011	CHR	AAA	24	535	65	24	6	14	65	57	155	18	4	.257/.344/.425	.253	.356	2.6	CF(107): 5.6, RF(1): -0.0	1.7
2012	CHR	AAA	25	264	37	17	1	8	30	44	66	6	3	.317/.428/.514	.335	.418	-0.5	CF(59): -1.1, RF(4): -0.1	2.9
2012	CHA	MLB	25	75	12	1	0	1	4	6	16	3	1	.224/.280/.284	.206	.269	-0.5	LF(21): 0.1, CF(14): -0.3	-0.3
2013	CHR	AAA	26	238	35	9	2	6	26	26	57	3	1	.279/.363/.428	.287	.356	0.8	CF(22): -3.5, LF(20): 1.7	0.8
2013	CHA	MLB	26	179	15	7	0	5	12	18	57	7	2	.231/.313/.369	.250	.327	-0.7	CF(47): -2.2, RF(20): 0.1	-0.3
2014	CHA	MLB	27	250	28	9	1	7	28	26	69	5	2	.243/.324/.383	.259	.320	0.2	CF -2, RF 0	0.5

Like so many prospects in the White Sox' system, Danks has a graceful athleticism that gives him the look of a big-time player, but has always been undone by what our partners at Brooks Baseball term "a disastrously high likelihood to swing and miss." It's not a question of approach, as Danks displays a solid batting eye, but a consistent tendency to swing through hittable pitches has kept him from developing into a potent lefty stick. Still, his .260/.340/.407 line down the stretch last summer earned Danks a look-see this spring, and given his solid defense and occasional pop, he's ready to embark on a useful career as a fourth outfielder.

Matt Davidson 3B
Born: 3/26/1991 Age: 23
Bats: R Throws: R Height: 6' 2"
Weight: 225 Breakout: 1%
Improve: 17% Collapse: 2%
Attrition: 13% MLB: 44%
Comparables:
Josh Bell, Brandon Wood, Alex Liddi

YEAR	TEAM	LVL	AGE	PA	R	2B	3B	HR	RBI	BB	SO	SB	CS	AVG/OBP/SLG	TAv	BABIP	BRR	FRAA	WARP
2011	VIS	A+	20	606	93	39	1	20	106	52	147	0	1	.277/.348/.465	.294	.340	-1.8	1B(49): 0.5, 3B(43): -2.8	2.5
2012	MOB	AA	21	576	81	28	2	23	76	69	126	3	4	.261/.367/.469	.297	.304	-5.2	3B(127): -2.7	3.3
2013	RNO	AAA	22	500	55	32	3	17	74	46	134	1	0	.280/.350/.481	.264	.359	-2.6	3B(108): -0.7	1.5
2013	ARI	MLB	22	87	8	6	0	3	12	10	24	0	1	.237/.333/.434	.258	.306	-0.8	3B(20): -2.0	-0.2
2014	CHA	MLB	23	250	26	11	0	9	31	19	70	0	0	.231/.297/.399	.253	.290	-0.6	3B -2, 1B 0	0.2

Anybody trying to predict the upcoming Rookie of the Year chase realizes a big part of the prediction involves guaranteed playing time; if Davidson is given an opportunity for 130 games at third base, he'll be in the running. During his call-up in Arizona he showed he can put solid contact on the ball and pull it for extra bases, even against right-handers. His game is ready for the big leagues, and a December trade to Chicago relocated him from perhaps the worst depth chart for his positional abilities to perhaps the best. Now can we talk about why in the world you're trying to predict the upcoming Rookie of the Year chase?

Alejandro De Aza LF
Born: 4/11/1984 Age: 30
Bats: L Throws: L Height: 6' 0"
Weight: 190 Breakout: 2%
Improve: 27% Collapse: 7%
Attrition: 12% MLB: 82%
Comparables:
Ryan Spilborghs, Rajai Davis, Chris Duffy

YEAR	TEAM	LVL	AGE	PA	R	2B	3B	HR	RBI	BB	SO	SB	CS	AVG/OBP/SLG	TAv	BABIP	BRR	FRAA	WARP
2011	CHR	AAA	27	435	64	29	5	9	37	33	72	22	11	.322/.378/.494	.298	.373	1.2	LF(61): 0.1, CF(8): -0.1	2.6
2011	CHA	MLB	27	171	29	11	3	4	23	17	34	12	5	.329/.400/.520	.340	.404	1.6	RF(31): 0.7, CF(19): 1.4	2.2
2012	CHR	AAA	28	21	3	1	0	1	2	1	3	0	0	.250/.286/.450	.248	.250	0.9	CF(3): 0.0	0.1
2012	CHA	MLB	28	585	81	29	6	9	50	47	109	26	12	.281/.349/.410	.271	.339	2.9	CF(125): 4.7, LF(11): 0.1	3.0
2013	CHA	MLB	29	675	84	27	4	17	62	50	147	20	8	.264/.323/.405	.266	.318	1.8	CF(107): 5.6, LF(79): 1.3	3.2
2014	CHA	MLB	30	619	81	30	4	11	56	48	124	24	10	.270/.334/.401	.270	.320	0.7	LF 3, CF 0	2.5

De Aza featured prominently in Sox fans' nightmares last summer, as a cavalcade of errors (8), pickoffs (6), and basepath outs (11)—all of which would have been worst in an Astros-free Junior Circuit—made him a poster child for the club's season-long struggles. As painful as that might have been to watch, it shouldn't obscure the fact that De Aza was the most valuable offensive player on the South Side last season. While his batting average and on-base percentage dipped slightly, his power increased and his final slash stats pretty much nailed the average for both leadoff hitters and center fielders. Even his baserunning and defense graded out as positives despite those memorable blunders, after taking into account the extra bases he took and his range in the center pasture. De Aza isn't a star, but an average major leaguer at his peak two years shy of free agency is an asset. If he can keep his head in the game and continue to launch double-digits bombs, he'll be a bargain.

Adam Dunn   1B

Born: 11/9/1979 Age: 34
Bats: L Throws: R Height: 6' 6"
Weight: 285 Breakout: 0%
Improve: 22% Collapse: 7%
Attrition: 17% MLB: 89%

Comparables:
Carlos Pena, Jose Canseco, Russell Branyan

YEAR	TEAM	LVL	AGE	PA	R	2B	3B	HR	RBI	BB	SO	SB	CS	AVG/OBP/SLG	TAv	BABIP	BRR	FRAA	WARP
2011	CHA	MLB	31	496	36	16	0	11	42	75	177	0	1	.159/.292/.277	.216	.240	-6.5	1B(35): -2.3, RF(2): -0.1	-2.7
2012	CHA	MLB	32	649	87	19	0	41	96	105	222	2	1	.204/.333/.468	.283	.246	-2.4	1B(52): -0.9, LF(5): 0.1	1.8
2013	CHA	MLB	33	607	60	15	0	34	86	76	189	1	1	.219/.320/.442	.281	.266	-5.7	1B(71): -2.0, LF(3): -0.1	1.2
2014	CHA	MLB	34	579	74	19	0	28	83	81	189	1	1	.214/.328/.425	.274	.280	-1.3	1B -3, LF -0	1.2

Dunn continues to make history, though not in the way Sox fans would like. Last year in these pages, we described how Dunn's 2012 season was perhaps the least valuable for players hitting 40-plus home runs in the postwar era. Now that Dunn has lost a little more of his power, we're able to report that he's coming off one of history's least valuable 30-plus home run seasons—only Dave Kingman and Tony Armas have posted seasons with more home runs and a lower VORP than Dunn's 2013 campaign. He can still draw a few walks and launch a few bombs, but this is Dunn's new normal, and there's virtually no chance he'll be worth the $15 million he'll earn in the last year of his last big-money contract. His main role in baseball going forward is to be held up as a straw man by indignant fans who completely misunderstood the message of *Moneyball*.

Adam Eaton   CF

Born: 12/6/1988 Age: 25
Bats: L Throws: L Height: 5' 8"
Weight: 185 Breakout: 6%
Improve: 41% Collapse: 7%
Attrition: 37% MLB: 80%

Comparables:
Brett Gardner, Denard Span, Chris Denorfia

YEAR	TEAM	LVL	AGE	PA	R	2B	3B	HR	RBI	BB	SO	SB	CS	AVG/OBP/SLG	TAv	BABIP	BRR	FRAA	WARP
2011	VIS	A+	22	301	54	15	3	6	39	42	41	24	8	.332/.455/.492	.344	.379	2.8	CF(30): 1.6, RF(11): 0.5	3.1
2011	MOB	AA	22	255	31	7	4	4	28	30	35	10	6	.302/.409/.429	.314	.345	-1.9	RF(34): 3.9, CF(7): 0.3	1.7
2012	MOB	AA	23	51	11	1	0	0	3	6	8	6	1	.300/.451/.325	.302	.375	1.3	CF(11): -0.3	0.7
2012	RNO	AAA	23	562	119	46	5	7	45	53	68	38	10	.381/.456/.539	.322	.432	4.6	CF(82): 2.0, RF(29): 2.7	6.5
2012	ARI	MLB	23	103	19	3	2	2	5	14	15	2	3	.259/.382/.412	.292	.294	2	CF(21): -2.7, LF(1): -0.0	0.6
2013	VIS	A+	24	64	12	3	0	1	6	10	6	8	1	.321/.438/.434	.298	.348	1.8	CF(4): -0.2	0.5
2013	RNO	AAA	24	40	5	2	0	1	5	3	8	0	0	.143/.225/.286	.180	.148	-0.7	CF(2): 0.0	-0.4
2013	ARI	MLB	24	277	40	10	4	3	22	17	44	5	2	.252/.314/.360	.239	.294	2.1	LF(35): -1.3, CF(30): -4.6	-0.3
2014	CHA	MLB	25	315	41	13	2	5	26	27	53	14	4	.274/.353/.383	.274	.320	0.8	CF -3, LF -1	1.1

Labeled as a potential fourth outfielder for the past two years, Eaton had a fighting chance at a starting job for Arizona, then missed more than 100 games with a left elbow sprain. When he finally returned, he split time at center and left in a Diamondbacks outfield that had trouble locating three starters that stood out. (Although, next to the 5-foot-8 Eaton, everybody else stands out.) So after a year of promise, his grade remains incomplete and he still is a fine candidate to play anywhere in the outfield. After the White Sox rescued him from a crowded Arizona roster, "anywhere" now means South Side.

Jacob Elmore   2B

Born: 6/15/1987 Age: 27
Bats: R Throws: R Height: 5' 9"
Weight: 185 Breakout: 3%
Improve: 15% Collapse: 8%
Attrition: 17% MLB: 42%

Comparables:
Eric Sogard, Callix Crabbe, Jeff Keppinger

YEAR	TEAM	LVL	AGE	PA	R	2B	3B	HR	RBI	BB	SO	SB	CS	AVG/OBP/SLG	TAv	BABIP	BRR	FRAA	WARP
2011	MOB	AA	24	458	58	19	1	3	41	54	65	15	11	.270/.362/.349	.285	.309	3.1	2B(82): 7.7, SS(3): -0.1	2.8
2012	RNO	AAA	25	511	95	30	9	1	73	74	54	32	8	.344/.442/.465	.301	.386	-0.2	SS(60): -4.0, 2B(39): -1.3	3.7
2012	ARI	MLB	25	73	1	4	0	0	7	5	6	0	0	.191/.247/.250	.186	.210	0.7	SS(17): 0.5, 2B(5): 0.1	0.0
2013	OKL	AAA	26	310	42	13	4	5	30	31	37	16	6	.299/.382/.433	.297	.328	-0.1	2B(54): 5.7, LF(7): 0.4	3.1
2013	HOU	MLB	26	136	16	4	0	2	6	13	20	1	6	.242/.313/.325	.237	.273	0.1	SS(20): -0.3, 2B(12): 0.9	0.2
2014	CHA	MLB	27	250	30	10	1	2	19	24	39	9	4	.255/.335/.344	.258	.290	0	2B 1, SS -1	0.9

A former 34th-round pick made (relatively) good, Elmore's value to a team is tied to his defensive flexibility. After his midseason call-up from Triple-A Oklahoma City, he was the designated super-*duper* utilityman for the Astros, mostly playing the middle infield, but logging at least one inning at every position, including pitching a perfect inning against the Rangers. Elmore will take a walk, but he doesn't muster much power out of his small frame and the Astros let him free on waivers. At the very least, he's fodder for inspirational speeches and gives all the 5-foot-9 dudes hope that someday they, too, can make it to The Show.

Tyler Flowers   C

Born: 1/24/1986 Age: 28
Bats: R Throws: R Height: 6' 4"
Weight: 245 Breakout: 3%
Improve: 26% Collapse: 15%
Attrition: 35% MLB: 67%

Comparables:
Kelly Shoppach, Jason Botts, Taylor Teagarden

YEAR	TEAM	LVL	AGE	PA	R	2B	3B	HR	RBI	BB	SO	SB	CS	AVG/OBP/SLG	TAv	BABIP	BRR	FRAA	WARP
2011	CHR	AAA	25	270	36	8	0	15	32	39	84	2	0	.261/.390/.500	.286	.350	-1.4	C(53): -0.8	1.4
2011	CHA	MLB	25	129	13	5	1	5	16	14	38	0	1	.209/.310/.409	.259	.261	0.2	C(31): -0.3, 1B(3): 0.2	0.6
2012	CHA	MLB	26	153	19	6	0	7	13	12	56	2	1	.213/.296/.412	.232	.301	-0.4	C(49): -0.8, 1B(2): -0.1	0.1
2013	CHA	MLB	27	275	24	11	0	10	24	14	94	0	1	.195/.247/.355	.212	.261	-1	C(84): 0.8	-0.2
2014	CHA	MLB	28	250	30	10	0	9	30	28	80	1	0	.214/.315/.390	.259	.290	-0.4	C -0, 1B 0	1.1

The White Sox anointed Flowers as their new starter behind the dish going into 2013, but his roll-out was nearly as inauspicious as HealthCare.gov. He did manage to punish enough mistakes to launch double-digit home runs in only a half-season of games, but struck out in over a third of his plate appearances, started losing playing time to rookie Josh Phegley in July and ended his season with September shoulder surgery. Flowers admitted his shoulder had bothered him since spring training, so it's possible his bat might rebound, but his contact rate was abysmal even when healthy. The Sox like his game-calling skills so he might stick around as a backup, but T-Flow isn't likely to get another shot at starting on Opening Day.

Avisail Garcia   RF

Born: 6/12/1991 Age: 23
Bats: R Throws: R Height: 6' 4"
Weight: 240 Breakout: 3%
Improve: 34% Collapse: 5%
Attrition: 19% MLB: 59%

Comparables:
Felix Pie, Starling Marte, Aaron Cunningham

YEAR	TEAM	LVL	AGE	PA	R	2B	3B	HR	RBI	BB	SO	SB	CS	AVG/OBP/SLG	TAv	BABIP	BRR	FRAA	WARP
2011	LAK	A+	20	515	53	16	6	11	56	18	132	14	5	.264/.297/.389	.257	.339	-0.2	RF(92): -6.0	0.1
2012	LAK	A+	21	287	47	8	5	8	36	11	57	14	4	.289/.324/.447	.267	.335	1.8	RF(62): 2.3, CF(3): 0.2	1.4
2012	ERI	AA	21	226	31	9	3	6	22	7	38	9	4	.312/.345/.465	.274	.357	1.5	CF(44): 1.1, RF(9): 0.5	1.3
2012	DET	MLB	21	51	7	0	0	0	3	3	10	0	2	.319/.373/.319	.241	.405	0.1	RF(18): -0.5, CF(2): -0.0	0.0
2013	LAK	A+	22	28	9	0	2	1	4	4	1	2	0	.417/.500/.708	.393	.409	0.7	RF(2): 0.0, CF(2): -0.1	0.5
2013	TOL	AAA	22	156	23	7	1	5	23	8	32	4	2	.374/.410/.537	.342	.455	0.6	CF(25): 0.2, RF(6): -0.6	1.8
2013	CHR	AAA	22	32	6	0	1	1	9	4	4	0	0	.370/.469/.556	.387	.409	-0.4	CF(7): -0.6	0.4
2013	CHA	MLB	22	168	19	4	2	5	21	5	38	3	2	.304/.327/.447	.272	.370	-1.1	RF(36): -2.2, CF(8): -0.6	0.1
2013	DET	MLB	22	88	12	3	1	2	10	4	21	0	1	.241/.273/.373	.246	.295	0.3	CF(23): -0.6, RF(5): 0.1	-0.1
2014	CHA	MLB	23	293	31	9	2	8	34	9	70	5	2	.270/.298/.405	.259	.330	0.3	RF -1, CF -1	0.4

Chicago's prize from the Jake Peavy deadline deal, Garcia is a toolsy outfielder who raked last year in Triple-A and impressed during his two-month stint at The Cell, but his offensive game still needs a lot of polish. On the plus side, the young Venezuelan is an excellent defensive right fielder with a strong arm, decent speed and a frame that screams "power potential." However, Garcia has never met a pitch he doesn't like, rarely walks and when he does make contact his groundball rate matches those of slap-merchants Michael Bourn, Jose Iglesias and Elvis Andrus. If he learns to get some loft and make more contact he could turn into a bulkier approximation of Alex Rios, with a smidge more power and a bit less speed. Garcia's no sure thing, but there's plenty here to dream on.

Leury Garcia   SS

Born: 3/18/1991 Age: 23
Bats: B Throws: R Height: 5' 7"
Weight: 160 Breakout: 9%
Improve: 27% Collapse: 6%
Attrition: 22% MLB: 40%

Comparables:
Eduardo Escobar, Dee Gordon, Jeff Bianchi

YEAR	TEAM	LVL	AGE	PA	R	2B	3B	HR	RBI	BB	SO	SB	CS	AVG/OBP/SLG	TAv	BABIP	BRR	FRAA	WARP
2011	MYR	A+	20	482	65	19	5	3	38	28	100	30	12	.256/.306/.342	.233	.324	7.3	SS(97): 1.9	1.2
2012	FRI	AA	21	416	55	12	11	2	30	22	79	31	7	.292/.337/.398	.277	.361	4.7	2B(57): 9.5, SS(39): -0.7	3.5
2013	ROU	AAA	22	208	31	8	4	4	19	14	53	12	4	.264/.314/.409	.257	.346	1.8	SS(42): 3.5, CF(5): -0.4	1.6
2013	CHR	AAA	22	32	3	1	0	0	1	1	8	3	0	.267/.312/.300	.209	.364	0.2	2B(5): 0.0, SS(2): -0.1	-0.1
2013	TEX	MLB	22	57	8	0	1	0	1	3	16	1	0	.192/.236/.231	.187	.278	0.4	2B(12): 0.3, SS(4): 0.2	-0.2
2013	CHA	MLB	22	54	2	1	0	0	1	4	18	6	2	.204/.259/.224	.200	.312	0.2	2B(9): 0.2, CF(6): -0.1	-0.1
2014	CHA	MLB	23	250	28	8	3	2	17	11	63	12	3	.237/.273/.324	.221	.300	1.5	SS 1, 2B 3	0.4

The lesser-known of Chicago's trade deadline Garcias, Leury is a switch-hitting fireplug with speed to burn and top-shelf defensive chops. He shows great instincts, tremendous range and a cannon arm at shortstop, and can be a plus glove all over the diamond, but his bat is an open question. Only 5-foot-7, he's shown little power and doesn't draw enough walks or make enough contact to hit at the top of the order, limiting his offensive potential. Still, given his speed and defensive versatility Garcia is primed to carve out a long career as a utilityman and occasional glove-first shortstop.

Conor Gillaspie 3B

Born: 7/18/1987 Age: 26
Bats: L Throws: R Height: 6' 1"
Weight: 205 Breakout: 6%
Improve: 34% Collapse: 9%
Attrition: 19% MLB: 63%

Comparables:
Michael Morse, Taylor Green, Andy Marte

YEAR	TEAM	LVL	AGE	PA	R	2B	3B	HR	RBI	BB	SO	SB	CS	AVG/OBP/SLG	TAv	BABIP	BRR	FRAA	WARP
2011	FRE	AAA	23	503	63	22	6	11	61	66	79	9	9	.297/.389/.453	.290	.339	-1.9	3B(92): 3.2, 1B(7): 0.8	3.0
2011	SFN	MLB	23	21	2	0	0	1	2	2	1	0	0	.263/.333/.421	.298	.235	0	3B(4): -0.2	0.2
2012	FRE	AAA	24	465	60	18	3	14	49	41	54	0	0	.281/.345/.441	.272	.291	-0.6	3B(81): -1.5, 1B(20): 0.2	1.6
2012	SFN	MLB	24	20	2	1	0	0	2	0	2	0	0	.150/.150/.200	.122	.167	0	3B(5): -0.3	-0.3
2013	CHA	MLB	25	452	46	14	3	13	40	37	79	0	1	.245/.305/.390	.259	.270	-1.4	3B(113): 1.3, 1B(12): 0.6	1.6
2014	CHA	MLB	26	394	40	14	2	10	45	33	67	2	1	.245/.309/.383	.253	.270	-0.6	3B -2, 1B 1	0.5

Gillaspie came to Chicago last spring in a minor trade and turned into one of the happiest stories of the White Sox' season, which is somewhat akin to being the most upbeat episode of *The Walking Dead*. In the wake of Jeff Keppinger's season-long face-plant, Gillaspie emerged as a reasonably serviceable third baseman—his .260 TAv against right-handed pitchers is exactly league average, and you can't get more reasonably serviceable than that. Gillaspie makes contact, draws a few walks, boots more grounders than he should and lacks the power bat you'd want from a corner infielder, making him not only reasonably serviceable but eminently fungible.

Courtney Hawkins CF

Born: 11/12/1993 Age: 20
Bats: R Throws: R Height: 6' 3"
Weight: 220 Breakout: 2%
Improve: 2% Collapse: 0%
Attrition: 2% MLB: 2%

Comparables:
Greg Halman, Marcell Ozuna, Carlos Peguero

YEAR	TEAM	LVL	AGE	PA	R	2B	3B	HR	RBI	BB	SO	SB	CS	AVG/OBP/SLG	TAv	BABIP	BRR	FRAA	WARP
2012	KAN	A	18	72	11	5	2	4	15	4	17	3	2	.308/.352/.631	.329	.356	0	CF(16): -0.6	0.7
2013	WNS	A+	19	425	48	16	3	19	62	29	160	10	5	.178/.249/.384	.216	.236	1.7	CF(100): 2.3	-0.7
2014	CHA	MLB	20	250	25	7	1	9	29	10	95	3	1	.187/.227/.344	.208	.260	-0.1	CF 0, LF 0	-0.6

The Sox challenged the 19-year-old Hawkins with a High-A assignment for his full-season debut, and the young Texan struggled through a nightmarish year at the plate. Hawkins rarely walks and struck out in nearly 40 percent of his plate appearances, helplessly waving at breaking pitches in the dirt and swinging through mediocre fastballs. When he does make contact—especially against southpaws—Hawkins can dent scoreboards, but he may need to completely retool his long swing to make enough contact to have a career. With his thick lower half and average speed, most scouts expect an eventual move to right field, where expectations for his bat will be even higher. Raw power like his is a rare commodity, so the organization will give him plenty of time to refine his approach, but right now Hawkins just looks overmatched.

Jeff Keppinger 2B

Born: 4/21/1980 Age: 34
Bats: R Throws: R Height: 6' 0"
Weight: 185 Breakout: 2%
Improve: 21% Collapse: 8%
Attrition: 15% MLB: 90%

Comparables:
Placido Polanco, Mark Loretta, Red Schoendienst

YEAR	TEAM	LVL	AGE	PA	R	2B	3B	HR	RBI	BB	SO	SB	CS	AVG/OBP/SLG	TAv	BABIP	BRR	FRAA	WARP
2011	OKL	AAA	31	30	2	0	0	0	1	0	0	0	0	.250/.241/.250	.245	.241	0	2B(2): 0.1	0.0
2011	HOU	MLB	31	169	22	9	0	4	20	4	7	0	1	.307/.320/.436	.257	.299	0.3	2B(38): 1.2	0.7
2011	SFN	MLB	31	230	17	11	0	2	15	8	17	0	0	.255/.285/.333	.230	.266	-1.5	2B(55): -2.5	-0.6
2012	DUR	AAA	32	25	4	1	0	0	1	4	2	0	0	.286/.400/.333	.309	.316	-0.5	3B(2): -0.0, 1B(1): 0.0	0.1
2012	TBA	MLB	32	418	46	15	1	9	40	24	31	1	0	.325/.367/.439	.289	.332	-0.6	3B(50): -0.5, 2B(27): 0.2	2.3
2013	CHA	MLB	33	451	38	13	1	4	40	20	41	0	1	.253/.283/.317	.230	.269	-2.5	2B(45): 0.9, 3B(41): -0.0	-0.2
2014	CHA	MLB	34	419	38	17	1	6	41	25	36	1	1	.272/.318/.365	.253	.280	-0.9	2B 1, 3B -1	0.8

Keppinger cashed in on a career year with the Rays by signing a three-year, $12 million deal to man third base on the South Side last spring, and it didn't take long for the Sox to experience buyer's remorse. A contact whiz who eschews the Three True Outcomes, Keppinger's production is consistently inconsistent, depending on how many balls happen to fall in. Last season he usually hit 'em where they was, launching more lazy fly balls and fewer well-placed grounders—his batting average dropped 60 points, taking all of his value with it. Keppinger can be adequate at the hot corner, isn't quite disastrous at second base and usually punishes lefties, so he can again provide value as a versatile bench bat or platoon infielder whenever the BABIP gremlins grow tired of him.

Paul Konerko 1B

Born: 3/5/1976 Age: 38
Bats: R Throws: R Height: 6' 2"
Weight: 220 Breakout: 0%
Improve: 11% Collapse: 13%
Attrition: 17% MLB: 79%

Comparables:
George Brett, Tommy Henrich, Rafael Palmeiro

YEAR	TEAM	LVL	AGE	PA	R	2B	3B	HR	RBI	BB	SO	SB	CS	AVG/OBP/SLG	TAv	BABIP	BRR	FRAA	WARP
2011	CHA	MLB	35	639	69	25	0	31	105	77	89	1	1	.300/.388/.517	.314	.304	-6	1B(111): -8.8	2.8
2012	CHA	MLB	36	598	66	22	0	26	75	56	83	0	0	.298/.371/.486	.293	.312	-3	1B(105): -6.2	1.7
2013	CHA	MLB	37	520	41	16	0	12	54	45	74	0	0	.244/.313/.355	.246	.265	-6.1	1B(76): -1.1	-1.0
2014	CHA	MLB	38	506	61	19	0	19	68	48	83	0	0	.269/.344/.441	.286	.290	-1.1	1B -3	1.5

It was bound to happen eventually, but that didn't make it any easier to watch. After wobbling down the stretch in 2012, Konerko's wheels fell off last season, as persistent back woes and a slowing bat contributed to a disastrous season at the plate. The longtime Sox captain is still a battler but when he gets his pitch he can no longer sting it, resulting in numerous fly outs that used to reach the bleachers. Sure, his balky back could improve this year, but his creaky joints are another year older, making him likely to provide more value in the clubhouse than in the lineup. He's a future candidate for both the managerial and Hall of Fame fraternities, and in what is likely to be his final season this year a legion of grateful Sox fans will get to thank him for the ride.

Jared Mitchell CF
Born: 10/13/1988 Age: 25
Bats: L Throws: L Height: 6' 0"
Weight: 205 Breakout: 1%
Improve: 3% Collapse: 3%
Attrition: 8% MLB: 10%

Comparables:
Jordan Danks, Brandon Boggs, Melky Mesa

YEAR	TEAM	LVL	AGE	PA	R	2B	3B	HR	RBI	BB	SO	SB	CS	AVG/OBP/SLG	TAv	BABIP	BRR	FRAA	WARP
2011	WNS	A+	22	541	74	31	8	9	58	52	183	14	6	.222/.304/.377	.206	.336	-1.8	CF(55): -2.7	-1.2
2012	BIR	AA	23	408	51	13	12	10	54	62	126	20	5	.240/.368/.440	.294	.350	0.5	CF(80): 1.1, LF(7): -1.2	2.6
2012	CHR	AAA	23	141	18	11	1	1	13	16	53	1	1	.231/.329/.364	.258	.397	1.7	LF(21): -0.3, CF(15): -2.0	0.2
2013	BIR	AA	24	291	23	6	2	5	20	41	96	13	5	.174/.297/.275	.215	.260	-0.4	LF(34): 2.8, CF(32): 0.7	-0.3
2013	CHR	AAA	24	65	7	2	0	0	3	10	27	4	1	.132/.277/.170	.198	.259	0.4	CF(11): -0.5, LF(3): 0.0	-0.4
2014	CHA	MLB	25	250	30	7	2	5	20	27	92	7	2	.186/.279/.308	.219	.280	0.8	CF -1, LF 0	-0.4

Mitchell's career has been emblematic of Chicago's developmental woes, as a combination of injury and acute whiffitis has kept the club's 2009 top pick from converting any of his drool-worthy athleticism into production between the lines. He's a true center fielder with speed, power potential and the ability to work a walk, but Mitchell spent another long season fighting nagging injuries and striking out in more than a third of his plate appearances. A nice run in the Arizona Fall League has some believing Mitchell is primed to turn things around, but until the 25-year-old proves he can make solid contact against pitchers his own age in a fair run environment, color us skeptical.

Josh Phegley C
Born: 2/12/1988 Age: 26
Bats: R Throws: R Height: 5' 10"
Weight: 220 Breakout: 3%
Improve: 10% Collapse: 19%
Attrition: 19% MLB: 38%

Comparables:
Guillermo Quiroz, Edwin Bellorin, Curtis Thigpen

YEAR	TEAM	LVL	AGE	PA	R	2B	3B	HR	RBI	BB	SO	SB	CS	AVG/OBP/SLG	TAv	BABIP	BRR	FRAA	WARP
2011	BIR	AA	23	394	43	21	2	7	50	23	61	1	2	.242/.292/.368	.260	.271	-2.7	C(61): -0.6	1.2
2011	CHR	AAA	23	90	9	4	0	2	6	8	18	0	0	.241/.326/.367	.247	.288	-0.1	C(19): -0.2	0.2
2012	CHR	AAA	24	421	40	22	1	6	48	20	60	3	0	.266/.306/.373	.233	.299	-0.2	C(96): 2.4	1.1
2013	CHR	AAA	25	258	39	18	1	15	41	15	38	1	1	.316/.368/.597	.329	.317	-1.5	C(60): 2.3	3.7
2013	CHA	MLB	25	213	14	7	0	4	22	5	41	2	0	.206/.223/.299	.196	.236	-0.7	C(64): 0.5, 2B(1): -0.0	-0.5
2014	CHA	MLB	26	250	24	11	0	7	29	10	44	0	0	.246/.282/.387	.243	.270	-0.4	C 1	0.8

A power-packed half-season in Triple-A earned Phegley his big-league shot last July, and the young catcher came out with guns a-blazin', launching three home runs in his first five games. Then reality, briefly pre-occupied while changing cell phone providers, took notice, and Phegley posted a .206/.223/.299 line the rest of the way. Pitchers quickly learned to take advantage of his aggressive approach, as Phegley walked less and offered at more pitches outside the strike zone than any player not named Pierzynski, and without the former Sox catcher's contact skills. Still, Phegley's power is real, he has a strong arm and he's worked hard to become adequate behind the dish. If he can learn to lay off pitches he can't handle, Phegley has a chance to meet the modest offensive expectations of a major-league catcher.

Alexei Ramirez SS
Born: 9/22/1981 Age: 32
Bats: R Throws: R Height: 6' 2"
Weight: 180 Breakout: 0%
Improve: 40% Collapse: 7%
Attrition: 7% MLB: 97%

Comparables:
Alvin Dark, Cristian Guzman, Julio Lugo

YEAR	TEAM	LVL	AGE	PA	R	2B	3B	HR	RBI	BB	SO	SB	CS	AVG/OBP/SLG	TAv	BABIP	BRR	FRAA	WARP
2011	CHA	MLB	29	684	81	31	2	15	70	51	84	7	5	.269/.328/.399	.251	.288	1.4	SS(155): 7.3	3.0
2012	CHA	MLB	30	621	59	24	4	9	73	16	77	20	7	.265/.287/.364	.229	.290	1.4	SS(158): 8.0	1.6
2013	CHA	MLB	31	674	68	39	2	6	48	26	68	30	9	.284/.313/.380	.254	.309	1.6	SS(158): -3.2	2.4
2014	CHA	MLB	32	623	73	26	2	10	53	31	81	18	7	.265/.304/.367	.248	.290	0.4	SS 3	2.4

Ramirez remains essentially the same player he's been throughout his White Sox career: a durable, fast, rangy, error-prone shortstop with a solid bat for the position and a chronic aversion to ball four. He rebounded somewhat at the plate last season after a subpar 2012, making a little more contact and stealing 30 bases, but his continued exchange of home runs for doubles highlights the slow, steady decline of his power numbers. Ramirez also paced the Junior Circuit with 22 errors, a recurring issue that each year becomes harder to hide behind his subtly declining range. Already 32, Ramirez is on the down slope but his continued health, athleticism, instincts and gap power will keep him from being a lineup drag for at least a few more years.

Carlos Sanchez 2B

Born: 6/29/1992 Age: 22
Bats: B Throws: R Height: 5' 11"
Weight: 195 Breakout: 2%
Improve: 8% Collapse: 5%
Attrition: 13% MLB: 18%

Comparables:
Cesar Hernandez, DJ LeMahieu, Tony Abreu

YEAR	TEAM	LVL	AGE	PA	R	2B	3B	HR	RBI	BB	SO	SB	CS	AVG/OBP/SLG	TAv	BABIP	BRR	FRAA	WARP
2011	KAN	A	19	294	44	10	1	1	27	15	49	7	8	.288/.341/.345	.261	.349	1.3	2B(50): -1.8, SS(10): -2.5	0.7
2012	WNS	A+	20	416	58	14	6	1	42	31	64	19	10	.315/.374/.395	.277	.373	-1	SS(47): -0.5, 2B(45): -0.2	1.9
2012	BIR	AA	20	133	17	9	1	0	13	10	22	7	5	.370/.424/.462	.340	.449	-1.3	2B(14): -0.6, SS(11): 1.5	1.4
2012	CHR	AAA	20	39	4	2	0	0	1	0	6	0	0	.256/.256/.308	.207	.303	0.1	SS(10): -0.4, 2B(1): -0.1	-0.2
2013	CHR	AAA	21	479	50	20	2	0	28	29	76	16	7	.241/.293/.296	.220	.290	-1.9	2B(61): -2.2, SS(52): 0.4	-1.2
2014	CHA	MLB	22	250	26	9	1	2	17	12	48	5	3	.249/.290/.318	.229	.300	-0.3	2B -1, SS -1	0.0

Sanchez cut a wide swath in 2012 by hitting .323/.378/.403 over three minor-league stops, showing off a vacuum glove, a mature approach and solid contact skills. His prospect sheen has been dulled by a rough year at the plate, but there's still plenty to like here. Sanchez kept his walk and strikeout rates relatively steady despite spending a full season in Triple-A in his age-20 season, but lost nearly 100 points of BABIP (from .384 to .290). Not all of this was luck—facing more advanced pitchers backed by better fielders led to softer contact and more outs—but his true talent likely lies somewhere in between. His power rivals Juan Pierre's and his arm might be stretched for everyday work at shortstop, but a switch-hitting middle infielder who makes contact and draws a few walks can always find work on a major-league bench.

Marcus Semien SS

Born: 9/17/1990 Age: 23
Bats: R Throws: R Height: 6' 1"
Weight: 190 Breakout: 3%
Improve: 24% Collapse: 4%
Attrition: 18% MLB: 44%

Comparables:
Josh Rodriguez, Brad Miller, Danny Espinosa

YEAR	TEAM	LVL	AGE	PA	R	2B	3B	HR	RBI	BB	SO	SB	CS	AVG/OBP/SLG	TAv	BABIP	BRR	FRAA	WARP
2011	KAN	A	20	262	35	15	2	3	26	22	53	3	4	.253/.320/.376	.244	.312	0.6	SS(52): 2.4, 2B(4): -0.3	0.8
2012	WNS	A+	21	487	80	31	5	14	59	55	97	11	5	.273/.362/.471	.299	.323	-1.5	SS(80): -7.6, 2B(24): 0.2	3.5
2013	BIR	AA	22	484	90	21	5	15	49	84	66	20	5	.290/.420/.483	.329	.317	2.9	SS(47): 3.3, 2B(41): -2.7	5.9
2013	CHR	AAA	22	142	20	11	1	4	17	14	24	4	0	.264/.338/.464	.275	.293	-0.9	SS(25): -3.9, 3B(6): 0.8	0.5
2013	CHA	MLB	22	71	7	4	0	2	7	1	22	2	2	.261/.268/.406	.266	.348	-0.6	3B(17): 0.1, SS(3): 0.5	0.3
2014	CHA	MLB	23	250	31	10	1	7	25	25	55	3	1	.243/.321/.391	.263	.290	-0.1	SS -1, 2B -0	0.9

One of the few White Sox farmhands with enough on-base ability to hit at the top of the lineup, Semien earned Southern League MVP honors last summer and impressed the big club during a short September call-up. Lacking the range or arm to be a viable everyday shortstop, Semien would be a good defensive fit at second base, where his mature approach, quick bat and gap power would play nicely. Most scouts expect the home run pop he showed in Double-A to wilt under the bright lights of The Cell, so while Semien's glove could handle the hot corner his bat likely lacks the juice to be an asset there. Still, the former Cal product profiles as at least a solid utility option going forward, and in an organization this bereft of Show-ready talent that's cause for celebration.

Trayce Thompson CF

Born: 3/15/1991 Age: 23
Bats: R Throws: R Height: 6' 3"
Weight: 215 Breakout: 2%
Improve: 10% Collapse: 2%
Attrition: 7% MLB: 18%

Comparables:
Kirk Nieuwenhuis, Brett Jackson, Corey Brown

YEAR	TEAM	LVL	AGE	PA	R	2B	3B	HR	RBI	BB	SO	SB	CS	AVG/OBP/SLG	TAv	BABIP	BRR	FRAA	WARP
2011	KAN	A	20	597	95	36	2	24	87	60	172	8	4	.241/.329/.457	.270	.309	-1.2	CF(109): 1.6, RF(15): -0.1	2.3
2012	WNS	A+	21	510	77	28	5	22	90	45	144	18	3	.254/.325/.486	.287	.316	0.9	CF(110): 4.9, RF(6): -0.1	3.8
2012	BIR	AA	21	58	10	1	1	3	6	8	16	2	0	.280/.379/.520	.329	.355	-0.5	CF(13): -1.2, RF(1): -0.1	0.5
2012	CHR	AAA	21	20	1	2	0	0	0	2	6	1	0	.167/.250/.278	.184	.250	0.3	CF(4): 0.3, RF(1): -0.1	-0.1
2013	BIR	AA	22	590	78	23	5	15	73	60	139	25	8	.229/.321/.383	.274	.280	3.8	CF(67): -10.1, RF(62): 2.0	2.0
2014	CHA	MLB	23	250	27	9	1	8	29	18	78	4	1	.211/.274/.370	.236	.270	0.2	CF -1, RF 0	-0.1

If you squint at Thompson long enough you can almost see Mike Cameron: a tall, athletic center fielder with prodigious power, speed, a patient approach and plenty of swing-and-miss. Thompson has similarly loud tools and a high ceiling, but may not get the treasure he seeks on account of his obstacles. He's certainly not Cameron's match in center, with scouts continuing to whisper that a move to right field is inevitable. Thompson made the Faustian bargain last summer to trade some in-game power for better contact, but a small drop in his strikeout rate didn't make up for his 90-point drop in isolated power. If he can rediscover his boom stick next year while keeping his whiff rate manageable, he could have a breakout season—perhaps good enough that if you squint you might see Cameron's .300/.402/.600 smackdown during his second trip through the Southern League.

Dayan Viciedo   LF

Born: 3/10/1989 Age: 25
Bats: R Throws: R Height: 5' 11"
Weight: 230 Breakout: 2%
Improve: 52% Collapse: 1%
Attrition: 10% MLB: 97%

Comparables:
Adam Lind, Corey Hart, Lastings Milledge

YEAR	TEAM	LVL	AGE	PA	R	2B	3B	HR	RBI	BB	SO	SB	CS	AVG/OBP/SLG	TAv	BABIP	BRR	FRAA	WARP
2011	CHR	AAA	22	505	60	28	0	20	78	45	83	2	1	.296/.364/.491	.285	.324	2.7	RF(79): -7.3, 1B(10): -0.3	1.5
2011	CHA	MLB	22	113	11	3	0	1	6	9	23	1	0	.255/.327/.314	.236	.321	0.1	RF(21): -2.2, 1B(4): -0.1	-0.1
2012	CHA	MLB	23	543	64	18	1	25	78	28	120	0	2	.255/.300/.444	.259	.286	-1.6	LF(131): 2.9	1.2
2013	CHA	MLB	24	473	43	23	3	14	56	24	98	0	0	.265/.304/.426	.264	.308	-0.3	LF(109): -11.3	0.0
2014	CHA	MLB	25	461	50	19	1	17	61	24	96	1	0	.261/.305/.428	.268	.300	-0.9	LF -4, RF -1	0.8

It's been five years since the Sox signed Viciedo as a 20-year-old based on his massive power potential, and in that time the young outfielder has shown he can launch his pitch into orbit. Unfortunately, he's also shown that he considers every fastball on his hands, every slider away and every changeup in the dirt to be "his pitch." Pitchers have learned to let the free-swinging Cuban get himself out before giving him a chance to do some damage, causing Viciedo's power numbers to decline since a marginally productive 2012. On defense, Viciedo patrols left field with all the grace and confidence of a lost freshman searching for his homeroom, contributing to his current standing as a replacement-level player. Optimists can point to his .291/.327/.466 second-half line as proof of progress, but even those numbers are pedestrian at best for a likely future DH. If Viciedo can't improve his approach, his power will never produce much more than batting practice gasps.

Keenyn Walker   CF

Born: 8/12/1990 Age: 23
Bats: B Throws: R Height: 6' 3"
Weight: 190 Breakout: 0%
Improve: 0% Collapse: 1%
Attrition: 1% MLB: 1%

Comparables:
Drew Stubbs, Lorenzo Cain, Adron Chambers

YEAR	TEAM	LVL	AGE	PA	R	2B	3B	HR	RBI	BB	SO	SB	CS	AVG/OBP/SLG	TAv	BABIP	BRR	FRAA	WARP
2011	KAN	A	20	180	25	1	2	0	15	14	64	10	4	.228/.296/.259	.225	.374	1.5	RF(24): 0.4, CF(16): 1.5	0.0
2012	KAN	A	21	320	53	15	5	1	39	50	93	39	11	.282/.395/.387	.288	.425	8.5	CF(74): 1.5	2.6
2012	WNS	A+	21	168	31	7	1	3	16	24	50	17	4	.238/.345/.364	.264	.341	0	CF(23): 0.5, RF(8): 0.2	0.5
2013	BIR	AA	22	550	77	16	5	3	32	69	153	38	15	.201/.319/.277	.238	.294	4.5	RF(70): 1.5, CF(43): 9.9	1.9
2014	CHA	MLB	23	250	29	7	1	2	15	24	85	13	4	.198/.282/.271	.215	.300	1	CF 3, RF 0	0.0

Few prospects can match Walker's graceful athleticism, and fewer still can match his continuing struggles to make hard contact. Blessed with paint-peeling speed and acceleration, the former first-round pick plays an excellent center field, has a strong arm, takes the extra base and is a constant threat to steal. He drew enough walks in the low minors to fuel optimism that he could become a top-of-the-order threat, but the engine sputtered to a stop in Double-A. Walker has yet to develop any of the power his long, lean frame foretold, he struggles with pitch recognition and he strikes out at a rate that would make Russell Branyan blush. Already 23, Walker had best learn how to put bat to ball soon or he'll become an organizational afterthought.

PITCHERS

Dylan Axelrod

Born: 7/30/1985 Age: 28
Bats: R Throws: R Height: 6' 0" Weight: 185
Breakout: 30% Improve: 63% Collapse: 20%
Attrition: 48% MLB: 66%

Comparables:
Cha Seung Baek, Dustin Moseley, Justin Germano

YEAR	TEAM	LVL	AGE	W	L	SV	G	GS	IP	H	HR	BB	SO	BB9	SO9	GB%	BABIP	WHIP	ERA	FIP	FRA	WARP
2011	BIR	AA	25	3	2	0	11	9	59¹	52	1	14	57	2.1	8.6	37%	.333	1.11	3.34	2.46	3.05	0.8
2011	CHR	AAA	25	6	1	0	15	15	91¹	74	2	21	75	2.1	7.4	47%	.267	1.04	2.27	2.70	3.99	1.0
2011	CHA	MLB	25	1	0	0	4	3	18²	18	1	9	19	4.3	9.2	43%	.327	1.45	2.89	3.33	3.61	0.4
2012	CHR	AAA	26	7	5	0	16	16	97	81	8	31	92	2.9	8.5	38%	.283	1.15	2.88	3.35	4.44	0.6
2012	CHA	MLB	26	2	2	0	14	7	51	56	8	21	40	3.7	7.1	45%	.304	1.51	5.47	4.99	5.53	0.2
2013	CHA	MLB	27	4	11	0	30	20	128¹	170	24	43	73	3.0	5.1	42%	.330	1.66	5.68	5.47	5.66	-0.7
2014	CHA	MLB	28	6	7	0	25	18	119¹	127	15	37	82	2.8	6.2	43%	.300	1.38	4.49	4.64	4.88	0.1

When watching Axelrod pitch, it's natural for spectators to look askance at his junkball offerings and ask themselves how he can possibly get major-league hitters out. Midway through last season, major-league hitters had formulated their response: He can't, at least not with enough regularity to hold a spot in a big league rotation. Axelrod tries to protect his crushable upper-80s fastball through sequencing, guile and the liberal application of four off-speed pitches, but last season batters learned to wait him out, his strikeout rate sank and his home run rate was among the worst in the Junior Circuit. Without swing-and-miss stuff he doesn't profile well for a high-leverage bullpen spot, making him a swingman you'd rather not have to use.

Ronald Belisario

Born: 12/31/1982 Age: 31
Bats: R Throws: R Height: 6' 3" Weight: 240
Breakout: 28% Improve: 55% Collapse: 29%
Attrition: 16% MLB: 90%

Comparables:
Ramon Ramirez, Nick Masset, Pedro Feliciano

YEAR	TEAM	LVL	AGE	W	L	SV	G	GS	IP	H	HR	BB	SO	BB9	SO9	GB%	BABIP	WHIP	ERA	FIP	FRA	WARP
2012	LAN	MLB	29	8	1	1	68	0	71	47	3	29	69	3.7	8.7	65%	.243	1.07	2.54	3.14	4.02	0.3
2013	LAN	MLB	30	5	7	1	77	0	68	72	3	28	49	3.7	6.5	62%	.327	1.47	3.97	3.61	4.28	0.1
2014	CHA	MLB	31	3	1	1	65	0	61¹	55	6	24	50	3.5	7.4	56%	.284	1.29	3.64	4.29	3.96	0.6

On the surface, it appears that Belisario posted the same subpar walk rate two years running, but his 2013 mark was inflated by an astounding 10 intentional free passes. That led the majors, matched the team total of the World Series champions, equaled the career totals of Jon Lester and Max Scherzer *combined* and bumped Belisario's walk rate by 55 percent. His 95 mph sinker leads to copious grounders, which provides the impetus for a manager to have his catcher call four wide ones in pursuit of double plays and force outs. Not one of the 10 preceded a double play, mind you, while four of the intentional runners came around to score. Did we mention that part about the World Series champions?

Simon Castro

Born: 4/9/1988 Age: 26
Bats: R Throws: R Height: 6' 5" Weight: 230
Breakout: 49% Improve: 79% Collapse: 17%
Attrition: 75% MLB: 36%

Comparables:
Blake Hawksworth, Jeremy Hefner, Matt Shoemaker

YEAR	TEAM	LVL	AGE	W	L	SV	G	GS	IP	H	HR	BB	SO	BB9	SO9	GB%	BABIP	WHIP	ERA	FIP	FRA	WARP
2011	SAN	AA	23	5	6	0	16	16	89¹	95	9	16	73	1.6	7.4	41%	.302	1.24	4.33	3.79	4.58	1.4
2011	TUC	AAA	23	2	2	0	6	6	25²	37	5	18	21	6.3	7.4	32%	.364	2.14	10.17	6.78	7.43	0.1
2012	BIR	AA	24	6	4	0	15	15	90	89	4	21	72	2.1	7.2	50%	.304	1.22	3.70	2.92	4.12	0.7
2012	CHR	AAA	24	1	1	0	5	5	25	32	2	6	16	2.2	5.8	56%	.361	1.52	4.32	3.88	4.82	0.0
2013	CHR	AAA	25	3	7	0	27	12	92²	98	14	33	82	3.2	8.0	38%	.313	1.41	5.83	4.56	4.89	-0.3
2013	CHA	MLB	25	0	1	0	4	0	6²	5	1	3	6	4.1	8.1	23%	.250	1.20	2.70	5.03	3.86	0.1
2014	CHA	MLB	26	4	5	0	21	14	87²	94	13	30	62	3.1	6.3	43%	.297	1.42	4.87	5.04	5.29	-0.3

Castro was once the presumptive big prize from the Carlos Quentin deal two winters ago, a struggling former top prospect with an ideal starter's frame and a lively fastball/slider combination who would soon be eating innings in the White Sox' rotation. Flash forward two years, and Castro is still struggling and still has an ideal starter's frame, but is no longer a prospect or a starter. The organization moved him to the 'pen last summer, but working in short bursts just let Triple-A hitters light him up faster, as Castro allowed 10 home runs in 32 relief innings. He still generates his fair share of awkward swings and might someday find a role in middle relief if he improves his command, but time's a-wastin'.

Tyler Danish

Born: 9/12/1994 Age: 19
Bats: R Throws: R Height: 6' 2" Weight: 190
Breakout: 0% Improve: 0% Collapse: 0%
Attrition: 0% MLB: 0%

Comparables:
Brett Oberholtzer, Joe Ortiz, Zach McAllister

YEAR	TEAM	LVL	AGE	W	L	SV	G	GS	IP	H	HR	BB	SO	BB9	SO9	GB%	BABIP	WHIP	ERA	FIP	FRA	WARP
2014	CHA	MLB	19	1	0	1	16	0	32	38	5	19	17	5.5	4.8	50%	.306	1.79	6.22	6.28	6.76	-0.7

The Sox caused some head-scratching when they selected Danish, a short right-handed high schooler with a funky three-quarters delivery, in the second round of last year's draft. So far he looks to be worth the risk, as Danish was virtually unhittable last year in the Appy League. Armed with a heavy low-90s fastball and a potential plus slider, his stuff plays up and gets some extra wiggle from his deceptive delivery. If his changeup doesn't develop or his frame won't shoulder a starter's workload, Danish will still have the goods to work late innings. His full-season debut will be one to watch.

John Danks

Born: 4/15/1985 Age: 29
Bats: L Throws: L Height: 6' 1" Weight: 215
Breakout: 22% Improve: 46% Collapse: 27%
Attrition: 8% MLB: 97%

Comparables:
Dave Bush, Mark Mulder, Edwin Jackson

YEAR	TEAM	LVL	AGE	W	L	SV	G	GS	IP	H	HR	BB	SO	BB9	SO9	GB%	BABIP	WHIP	ERA	FIP	FRA	WARP
2011	CHA	MLB	26	8	12	0	27	27	170¹	182	19	46	135	2.4	7.1	46%	.313	1.34	4.33	3.86	4.21	2.5
2012	CHA	MLB	27	3	4	0	9	9	53²	57	7	23	30	3.9	5.0	46%	.284	1.49	5.70	4.97	5.46	0.0
2013	CHR	AAA	28	1	0	0	3	3	15²	13	1	12	14	6.9	8.0	49%	.286	1.60	3.45	4.93	6.18	-0.2
2013	CHA	MLB	28	4	14	0	22	22	138¹	151	28	27	89	1.8	5.8	42%	.283	1.29	4.75	5.09	5.55	-0.5
2014	CHA	MLB	29	7	7	0	20	20	124¹	122	15	37	91	2.7	6.6	44%	.287	1.28	3.97	4.43	4.31	0.9

Danks returned to the rotation last May after missing a full year recovering from shoulder surgery, and watching him take 22 turns without any further health issues was a heartwarming sight. However, Danks is being paid handsomely to get outs, not warm hearts, and on that front his season was undone by an acute case of the gopher ball. Nearly 17 percent of the fly balls he allowed last summer left the yard, among the highest rates in baseball and by far the worst of his career. If you're looking for signs that point to a bounceback 2014, consider this: Had Danks allowed home runs at an average rate last year, his FIP would have dropped from an awful 5.06 to a more respectable 4.08. His walk rate is among the lowest in baseball, compensating for his declining strikeout rate and velocity, and if he can hand out bleacher souvenirs at a more typical pace next year there's reason to think he can be a solid mid-rotation starter.

Deunte Heath

Born: 8/8/1985 Age: 28
Bats: R Throws: R Height: 6' 4" Weight: 240
Breakout: 33% Improve: 66% Collapse: 34%
Attrition: 56% MLB: 22%

Comparables:
Jon Meloan, Victor Garate, Pedro Viola

YEAR	TEAM	LVL	AGE	W	L	SV	G	GS	IP	H	HR	BB	SO	BB9	SO9	GB%	BABIP	WHIP	ERA	FIP	FRA	WARP
2011	CHR	AAA	25	4	7	1	30	16	102²	98	12	62	117	5.4	10.3	40%	.320	1.56	4.73	4.41	4.24	1.0
2012	CHR	AAA	26	4	3	3	36	4	67	47	4	20	74	2.7	9.9	34%	.253	1.00	1.48	2.80	3.58	1.2
2012	CHA	MLB	26	0	0	0	3	0	2	1	1	1	1	4.5	4.5	20%	.000	1.00	4.50	10.05	11.62	-0.1
2013	CHR	AAA	27	2	1	4	30	1	45	36	1	14	36	2.8	7.2	36%	.267	1.11	2.20	2.96	3.71	0.6
2013	CHA	MLB	27	0	0	0	5	0	7²	8	2	12	3	14.1	3.5	42%	.250	2.61	11.74	10.38	12.83	-0.6
2014	CHA	MLB	28	2	1	0	25	3	46¹	44	6	23	42	4.5	8.2	44%	.298	1.47	4.58	4.85	4.98	-0.0

Heath earned some positive attention from the White Sox organization after working hard to reduce what had once been a disastrously high walk rate, only to walk more than a batter per inning during three short stints with the big club last year. Back in Charlotte, he continued to work in the zone with his low-90s heater and iffy breaking stuff, but suffered a precipitous drop in his strikeout rate. Already 28, Heath won't earn any more big-league meal money until he finds that elusive sweet spot between wildness and hittability.

Erik Johnson

Born: 12/30/1989 Age: 24
Bats: R Throws: R Height: 6' 3" Weight: 235
Breakout: 37% Improve: 71% Collapse: 25%
Attrition: 39% MLB: 74%

Comparables:
Jason Windsor, Felipe Paulino, Wade Davis

YEAR	TEAM	LVL	AGE	W	L	SV	G	GS	IP	H	HR	BB	SO	BB9	SO9	GB%	BABIP	WHIP	ERA	FIP	FRA	WARP
2012	KAN	A	22	2	2	0	9	9	43	39	3	19	39	4.0	8.2	49%	.290	1.35	2.30	4.14	4.51	0.8
2012	WNS	A+	22	4	3	0	8	8	49¹	43	0	10	48	1.8	8.8	49%	.305	1.07	2.74	2.11	2.66	1.5
2013	BIR	AA	23	8	2	0	14	14	84²	57	6	21	74	2.2	7.9	50%	.228	0.92	2.23	2.90	4.40	0.7
2013	CHR	AAA	23	4	1	0	10	10	57¹	43	1	19	57	3.0	8.9	48%	.295	1.08	1.57	2.59	3.38	0.9
2013	CHA	MLB	23	3	2	0	5	5	27²	32	5	11	18	3.6	5.9	48%	.290	1.55	3.25	5.42	4.87	0.1
2014	CHA	MLB	24	7	8	0	22	22	124¹	120	14	45	97	3.2	7.0	46%	.288	1.32	4.00	4.42	4.34	0.9

Part of our mission here at *Baseball Prospectus* is to promote the use of advanced metrics and underscore the limitations of measuring pitchers by Wins and ERA, but there's no denying the resonance of numbers like 12-3 and 1.96. Johnson posted those while dominating at two stops in the high minors, before holding his own during a well-deserved September call-up. The Cal product shows excellent command of his low-90s fastball and can unleash a wipeout slider that helped him hold right-ies to a ridiculous .173/.220/.216 line across all levels last year. Lefties have given him significantly more trouble, however, so his ceiling may well depend on the development of his fringy changeup. Johnson has a solid frame designed to eat innings, and has a good chance to carve out a long career as a mid-rotation starter as soon as this spring.

Nathan Jones

Born: 1/28/1986 Age: 28
Bats: R Throws: R Height: 6' 5" Weight: 210
Breakout: 37% Improve: 53% Collapse: 27%
Attrition: 36% MLB: 62%

Comparables:
Merkin Valdez, Phil Coke, Sean Henn

YEAR	TEAM	LVL	AGE	W	L	SV	G	GS	IP	H	HR	BB	SO	BB9	SO9	GB%	BABIP	WHIP	ERA	FIP	FRA	WARP
2011	BIR	AA	25	2	3	12	42	0	63¹	58	3	27	67	3.8	9.5	52%	.333	1.34	3.27	3.18	3.74	0.7
2012	CHA	MLB	26	8	0	0	65	0	71²	67	4	32	65	4.0	8.2	48%	.317	1.38	2.39	3.34	4.39	0.8
2013	CHA	MLB	27	4	5	0	70	0	78	69	5	26	89	3.0	10.3	53%	.332	1.22	4.15	2.66	3.35	1.4
2014	CHA	MLB	28	3	1	1	53	0	62²	62	6	28	53	4.0	7.6	45%	.311	1.44	4.27	4.32	4.64	0.1

Jones struggled out of the gate last spring but soon righted the ship, working his way up the bullpen pecking order before settling into a set-up role. His upper-90s fastball can pop, sparkle and buzz electric, but it was the increased use and in-season improvement of his vicious slider that had hitters flailing at pitches out of the zone and muttering their way back to the dugout. Jones gets swinging strikes at a rate that rivals the game's most dominant closers, a fraternity he's now poised to join after the trade of Addison Reed.

Charles Leesman

Born: 3/10/1987 Age: 27
Bats: L Throws: L Height: 6' 4" Weight: 210
Breakout: 61% Improve: 71% Collapse: 29%
Attrition: 56% MLB: 19%

Comparables:
Josh Butler, Graham Godfrey, Eric Hacker

YEAR	TEAM	LVL	AGE	W	L	SV	G	GS	IP	H	HR	BB	SO	BB9	SO9	GB%	BABIP	WHIP	ERA	FIP	FRA	WARP
2011	BIR	AA	24	10	7	0	27	27	152	150	4	83	113	4.9	6.7	64%	.302	1.53	4.03	4.06	5.28	-0.4
2012	CHR	AAA	25	12	10	0	26	26	135	129	8	52	103	3.5	6.9	53%	.301	1.34	2.47	3.67	4.96	0.4
2013	CHR	AAA	26	4	3	0	16	16	88¹	90	11	41	78	4.2	7.9	56%	.304	1.48	3.87	4.59	5.94	-0.6
2013	CHA	MLB	26	0	0	0	8	1	15¹	16	2	16	13	9.4	7.6	57%	.311	2.09	7.04	6.40	6.38	-0.2
2014	CHA	MLB	27	5	7	0	17	17	94	103	12	48	56	4.6	5.4	54%	.300	1.60	5.32	5.56	5.78	-0.8

There's no questioning Leesman's determination, as the big lefty worked his way back from a brutal knee injury suffered in the 2012 Triple-A playoffs to anchor the Charlotte rotation and earn a September call-up. What can be questioned is whether his marginal stuff will play at the highest level. Leesman uses a heavy fastball that reaches the low 90s and a slurvy breaking ball to generate plenty of groundball outs, but continues to walk far too many batters for someone without a true swing-and-miss offering. A starter throughout his minor league career, it's hard to picture Leesman thriving at the back end of the rotation, though he might spend a few years as a LOOGY and designated bullpen double-play inducer.

Matt Lindstrom

Born: 2/11/1980 Age: 34
Bats: R Throws: R Height: 6' 3" Weight: 220
Breakout: 16% Improve: 36% Collapse: 37%
Attrition: 13% MLB: 86%

Comparables:
Matt Guerrier, Joe Beimel, Dennys Reyes

YEAR	TEAM	LVL	AGE	W	L	SV	G	GS	IP	H	HR	BB	SO	BB9	SO9	GB%	BABIP	WHIP	ERA	FIP	FRA	WARP
2011	COL	MLB	31	2	2	2	63	0	54	52	3	14	36	2.3	6.0	49%	.290	1.22	3.00	3.27	4.25	0.4
2012	BAL	MLB	32	1	0	0	34	0	36¹	35	2	12	30	3.0	7.4	51%	.308	1.29	2.72	3.43	4.42	0.4
2012	ARI	MLB	32	0	0	0	12	0	10²	10	0	2	10	1.7	8.4	52%	.290	1.12	2.53	2.10	3.02	0.1
2013	CHA	MLB	33	2	4	0	76	0	60²	64	2	23	46	3.4	6.8	57%	.326	1.43	3.12	3.17	3.39	0.9
2014	CHA	MLB	34	3	1	1	58	0	51	52	5	17	39	3.0	6.9	49%	.306	1.36	4.05	4.19	4.40	0.3

A vagabond product of Rexburg, Idaho, Lindstrom has never been able to parlay his upper-90s heater into any sustained ninth inning success, but continues to provide some marginal value in middle relief. Over the years he's stopped using his four-seamer as a crutch and relied more on a sinker-slider approach that last year made him one of the league's premier worm killers. He's never posted big strikeout numbers and often struggles against lefties, but he keeps the ball in the park—a particularly valuable trait when pitching in The Cell. The White Sox saw fit to exercise his $4 million option, so Lindstrom might actually pitch for the same team in consecutive seasons for the first time in six years.

Nestor Molina

Born: 1/9/1989 Age: 25
Bats: R Throws: R Height: 6' 1" Weight: 220
Breakout: 79% Improve: 85% Collapse: 7%
Attrition: 67% MLB: 16%

Comparables:
Tyler Cloyd, Darin Downs, Sandy Rosario

YEAR	TEAM	LVL	AGE	W	L	SV	G	GS	IP	H	HR	BB	SO	BB9	SO9	GB%	BABIP	WHIP	ERA	FIP	FRA	WARP
2011	DUN	A+	22	10	3	0	21	18	108¹	102	8	14	115	1.2	9.6	52%	.316	1.07	2.58	2.64	3.79	1.6
2011	NHP	AA	22	2	0	0	5	5	22	12	0	2	33	0.8	13.5	57%	.286	0.64	0.41	0.68	0.73	0.3
2012	BIR	AA	23	6	10	0	22	21	122²	156	7	26	84	1.9	6.2	46%	.361	1.48	4.26	3.20	3.89	1.4
2013	BIR	AA	24	1	1	1	17	4	36¹	44	2	11	29	2.7	7.2	47%	.353	1.51	4.71	3.11	3.11	0.6
2014	CHA	MLB	25	2	2	0	14	6	47¹	56	7	14	30	2.7	5.8	49%	.318	1.48	5.18	4.97	5.63	-0.3

Injuries and ineffectiveness have plagued Molina ever since he came to the White Sox in exchange for Sergio Santos two winters ago. Last season it was his shoulder that shelved him for two months, setting his development clock back further, and the organization finally bit the bullet and moved him into a relief role. Molina relies on solid command of his fringy stuff—a fastball that barely touches 90, a splitter and a changeup—and doesn't hurt himself with walks, but any 24-year-old who can't rack up strikeouts in a Double-A 'pen is a suspect, not a prospect.

Jake Petricka

Born: 6/5/1988 Age: 26
Bats: R Throws: R Height: 6' 5" Weight: 200
Breakout: 54% Improve: 80% Collapse: 20%
Attrition: 75% MLB: 29%

Comparables:
Sean Tracey, Chris Carpenter, Dennis Sarfate

YEAR	TEAM	LVL	AGE	W	L	SV	G	GS	IP	H	HR	BB	SO	BB9	SO9	GB%	BABIP	WHIP	ERA	FIP	FRA	WARP
2011	KAN	A	23	3	1	0	8	8	41²	39	0	13	48	2.8	10.4	53%	.361	1.25	2.81	2.16	3.35	1.1
2011	WNS	A+	23	4	7	0	13	13	67²	71	3	26	46	3.5	6.1	57%	.307	1.43	4.39	3.73	4.89	0.0
2012	WNS	A+	24	5	5	0	19	19	82²	93	2	46	84	5.0	9.1	63%	.374	1.68	5.33	3.45	4.84	0.7
2012	BIR	AA	24	3	3	0	10	10	57²	63	7	35	27	5.5	4.2	51%	.298	1.70	5.46	5.61	6.47	-0.9
2013	BIR	AA	25	3	0	0	21	1	39¹	36	1	18	41	4.1	9.4	57%	.350	1.37	2.06	2.61	3.25	0.8
2013	CHR	AAA	25	2	0	1	10	0	15¹	9	0	7	17	4.1	10.0	60%	.237	1.04	1.17	2.36	3.62	0.2
2013	CHA	MLB	25	1	1	0	16	0	19¹	20	0	10	10	4.7	4.7	64%	.312	1.55	3.26	3.75	4.57	0.1
2014	CHA	MLB	26	3	4	1	29	8	70²	77	8	39	48	4.9	6.1	54%	.311	1.64	5.34	5.23	5.80	-0.6

After washing out as a starter, Petricka has reinvented himself in the bullpen and seems poised to carve out a career as a multi-inning middle reliever. A sinker-slider specialist, the lanky righty routinely posts groundball rates above 60 percent and last year allowed only one home run in 74 innings, including 19 in the majors. Moving to the bullpen has allowed Petricka to adios his sketchy changeup and focus on improving command of his mid-90s heat, with mixed results. He continually struggles to repeat his delivery and at times is a walk waiting to happen, although his ground-pounding ways help him limit the damage. Still, the White Sox' development staff deserves kudos for turning Petricka into a potential bullpen contributor rather than a rotation bust.

Jose Quintana
Born: 1/24/1989 Age: 25
Bats: R Throws: L Height: 6' 1" Weight: 215
Breakout: 31% Improve: 61% Collapse: 17%
Attrition: 8% MLB: 98%

Comparables:
Jair Jurrjens, Jon Lester, John Danks

YEAR	TEAM	LVL	AGE	W	L	SV	G	GS	IP	H	HR	BB	SO	BB9	SO9	GB%	BABIP	WHIP	ERA	FIP	FRA	WARP
2011	TAM	A+	22	10	2	1	30	12	102	86	5	28	88	2.5	7.8	57%	.342	1.12	2.91	3.15	4.28	0.3
2012	BIR	AA	23	1	3	0	9	9	48²	43	1	14	41	2.6	7.6	55%	.300	1.17	2.77	2.59	3.23	1.0
2012	CHA	MLB	23	6	6	0	25	22	136¹	142	14	42	81	2.8	5.3	49%	.299	1.35	3.76	4.18	4.89	1.0
2013	CHA	MLB	24	9	7	0	33	33	200	188	23	56	164	2.5	7.4	44%	.282	1.22	3.51	3.85	3.93	2.7
2014	CHA	MLB	25	9	9	0	43	25	170¹	167	18	50	126	2.6	6.7	47%	.291	1.27	3.80	4.17	4.14	1.7

Common Wisdom held that big-league hitters had solved Quintana's tricks down the stretch in 2012 and they would soon launch him back into the celestial miasma from which he had so suddenly appeared. However, an unfazed Quintana spent last season quietly telling Common Wisdom to get stuffed, working 200 solid innings and ranking among the most valuable pitchers in the American League. Quintana's fastball clocked in a tick higher last year, his curveball had more bite and his changeup become a viable weapon against righties—all of which contributed to a much-improved strikeout rate. The young left-hander will never compete for Cy Young Awards, but as a viable third starter who won't reach free agency until 2019 Quintana is a certifiable building block.

Andre Rienzo
Born: 6/5/1988 Age: 26
Bats: R Throws: R Height: 6' 3" Weight: 190
Breakout: 31% Improve: 46% Collapse: 31%
Attrition: 66% MLB: 64%

Comparables:
Dustin Nippert, Kyle Weiland, Brad Mills

YEAR	TEAM	LVL	AGE	W	L	SV	G	GS	IP	H	HR	BB	SO	BB9	SO9	GB%	BABIP	WHIP	ERA	FIP	FRA	WARP
2011	WNS	A+	23	6	5	0	25	22	116	108	4	66	118	5.1	9.2	39%	.261	1.50	3.41	3.43	3.92	0.6
2012	WNS	A+	24	3	0	0	4	4	25	17	0	7	31	2.5	11.2	45%	.293	0.96	1.08	1.75	2.47	0.8
2012	BIR	AA	24	4	3	0	13	13	71²	56	2	33	72	4.1	9.0	44%	.271	1.24	3.27	2.92	2.92	1.7
2013	CHR	AAA	25	8	6	0	20	20	113	105	7	46	113	3.7	9.0	53%	.308	1.34	4.06	3.34	4.24	1.2
2013	CHA	MLB	25	2	3	0	10	10	56	55	11	28	38	4.5	6.1	50%	.257	1.48	4.82	5.88	6.18	-0.5
2014	CHA	MLB	26	7	9	0	25	25	134²	134	17	62	112	4.1	7.5	45%	.295	1.45	4.52	4.80	4.91	0.2

So how was your July? It probably wasn't better than Rienzo's, as the Sao Paulo native posted three wins, tossed a no-hitter in Charlotte and became the first Brazilian to pitch in the major leagues when he worked seven solid innings against the Indians. Things went downhill from there, as the Sox' bullpen blew the lead and cost him his first win, and Rienzo struggled to show any consistency over his next nine big-league starts. Rienzo's stuff—a low-90s fastball, cutter, curve and changeup—is more solid than spectacular, and his command remains shaky. His upside is that of a fifth starter, but he's more likely to wind up a seventh-inning guy.

Chris Sale
Born: 3/30/1989 Age: 25
Bats: L Throws: L Height: 6' 6" Weight: 180
Breakout: 17% Improve: 48% Collapse: 23%
Attrition: 10% MLB: 98%

Comparables:
Roger Clemens, Bert Blyleven, Stu Miller

YEAR	TEAM	LVL	AGE	W	L	SV	G	GS	IP	H	HR	BB	SO	BB9	SO9	GB%	BABIP	WHIP	ERA	FIP	FRA	WARP
2011	CHA	MLB	22	2	2	8	58	0	71	52	6	27	79	3.4	10.0	52%	.264	1.11	2.79	3.16	3.44	1.4
2012	CHA	MLB	23	17	8	0	30	29	192	167	19	51	192	2.4	9.0	46%	.294	1.14	3.05	3.22	3.70	3.7
2013	CHA	MLB	24	11	14	0	30	30	214¹	184	23	46	226	1.9	9.5	47%	.289	1.07	3.07	3.20	3.53	4.0
2014	CHA	MLB	25	11	7	8	73	18	184	153	18	46	198	2.2	9.7	46%	.290	1.08	2.70	3.26	2.93	4.4

Regardless of your baseball rooting interests, if you don't dig watching Sale pitch you're probably immune to joy. A rail-thin lefty scarecrow, Sale uses a flailing corkscrew delivery that he miraculously manages to repeat; hitters can't feel comfortable facing a mid-90s heater or darting slider delivered by a 6-foot-6 version of the Tasmanian Devil. Sale continues to confound those who expect his arm to fall off, reaching the 200-inning plateau for the first time last season and earning a non-inverted "W" in the All-Star Game. Pitching in the hitter-friendly Cell inflates his traditional numbers and masks some of his true value, but outstanding command of his dominating stuff makes Sale one of baseball's few true aces. At least until he breaks.

Scott Snodgress
Born: 9/20/1989 Age: 24
Bats: L Throws: L Height: 6' 6" Weight: 225
Breakout: 42% Improve: 42% Collapse: 16%
Attrition: 84% MLB: 22%

Comparables:
Ryan Cook, Rob Scahill, Doug Mathis

YEAR	TEAM	LVL	AGE	W	L	SV	G	GS	IP	H	HR	BB	SO	BB9	SO9	GB%	BABIP	WHIP	ERA	FIP	FRA	WARP
2012	KAN	A	22	3	3	0	19	19	99	86	4	49	84	4.5	7.6	40%	.286	1.36	3.64	4.10	4.59	1.4
2012	WNS	A+	22	4	0	0	8	8	42	26	2	15	44	3.2	9.4	54%	.233	0.98	1.50	3.05	3.45	0.9
2013	BIR	AA	23	11	11	0	26	26	143²	146	9	59	90	3.7	5.6	48%	.297	1.43	4.70	3.79	4.83	0.0
2014	CHA	MLB	24	6	10	0	25	25	119	130	16	57	71	4.3	5.4	45%	.296	1.57	5.28	5.49	5.74	-0.8

A former Stanford Cardinal standout, Snodgress is that rarest of birds: a lefty who can pump mid-90s gas for more than a few innings. Tall and long-levered, his low-three-quarters delivery adds deception but can be difficult to repeat, causing Snodgress to lose fastball command. His curve and changeup both have their moments but neither is a punchout pitch, helping to explain his underwhelming strikeout rate and surprising hittability in his first taste of the high minors. If he starts missing a few more bats or inducing a few more groundouts, Snodgress has the goods to eat innings as a solid fourth starter; if not, his fastball could play up in a relief role.

Eric Surkamp
Born: 7/16/1987 Age: 26
Bats: L Throws: L Height: 6' 5" Weight: 215
Breakout: 44% Improve: 61% Collapse: 28%
Attrition: 61% MLB: 66%
Comparables:
Jeff Niemann, Brad Mills, Kyle Weiland

YEAR	TEAM	LVL	AGE	W	L	SV	G	GS	IP	H	HR	BB	SO	BB9	SO9	GB%	BABIP	WHIP	ERA	FIP	FRA	WARP
2011	RIC	AA	23	10	4	0	23	22	142¹	110	5	44	165	2.8	10.4	45%	.287	1.08	2.02	2.58	3.11	2.4
2011	SFN	MLB	23	2	2	0	6	6	26²	32	1	17	13	5.7	4.4	33%	.349	1.84	5.74	4.64	4.61	-0.1
2013	SJO	A+	25	0	0	0	5	5	15¹	8	2	3	17	1.8	10.0	40%	.182	0.72	2.93	3.84	4.52	0.3
2013	FRE	AAA	25	7	1	0	11	11	71¹	56	4	20	54	2.5	6.8	41%	.256	1.07	2.78	3.71	4.03	1.2
2013	SFN	MLB	25	0	1	0	1	1	2²	9	2	0	0	0.0	0.0	21%	.500	3.38	23.62	15.02	13.73	-0.2
2014	CHA	MLB	26	3	3	0	10	10	56¹	55	6	23	47	3.6	7.5	43%	.298	1.38	4.16	4.38	4.52	0.3

Surkamp did everything he could to earn a spot in the Giants' whittled-down rotation, keeping a sub-3 ERA as a starter in the misanthropic Pacific Coast League. He then did everything he could to blow that spot as quickly as possible once he re-reached the majors, allowing nine runs in 2 ⅔ innings in his lone major-league start. Lefty junkballers can make it in The Show, of course, but they need at least one elite off-speed pitch. Scouts rate both his curve and his changeup as plus, but plus might not be enough playing off 87 mph heat. More likely org filler than a viable option for a big-league rotation.

Donnie Veal
Born: 9/18/1984 Age: 29
Bats: L Throws: L Height: 6' 4" Weight: 235
Breakout: 13% Improve: 25% Collapse: 62%
Attrition: 58% MLB: 32%
Comparables:
Matt Smith, Dennis Sarfate, Mark Malaska

YEAR	TEAM	LVL	AGE	W	L	SV	G	GS	IP	H	HR	BB	SO	BB9	SO9	GB%	BABIP	WHIP	ERA	FIP	FRA	WARP
2011	BRD	A+	26	0	1	0	7	4	19¹	17	1	6	18	2.8	8.4	22%	.167	1.19	2.79	3.60	5.27	0.0
2012	CHR	AAA	27	7	3	2	35	0	52	40	0	23	61	4.0	10.6	56%	.305	1.21	2.08	2.43	3.12	1.1
2012	CHA	MLB	27	0	0	1	24	0	13	5	0	4	19	2.8	13.2	39%	.192	0.69	1.38	1.05	1.29	0.4
2013	CHR	AAA	28	2	2	2	17	0	26²	23	1	14	30	4.7	10.1	48%	.338	1.39	2.70	3.24	4.70	0.1
2013	CHA	MLB	28	2	3	0	50	0	29¹	26	3	16	29	4.9	8.9	53%	.295	1.43	4.60	4.06	4.57	0.0
2014	CHA	MLB	29	3	1	0	51	0	48¹	42	5	27	47	5.1	8.7	46%	.290	1.44	4.16	4.61	4.52	0.2

Armed with a heavy fastball that can reach 95 and a solid power curve, Veal has the goods to retire big-league hitters but has never been able to stack them together. Last year, the big lefty broke camp with the White Sox but treated the strike zone like Chernobyl, walking more than a batter per inning in the early going. Finding his command in Charlotte, Veal returned to The Cell and delivered the first truly productive stretch of his big-league career. Veal held batters to a .208/.269/.306 line over 33 second-half appearances, dominating righties and lefties alike and fueling optimism that he's finally turned the corner and can be trusted to get big outs, something he'll be asked to do in 2014.

Daniel Webb
Born: 8/18/1989 Age: 24
Bats: R Throws: R Height: 6' 3" Weight: 210
Breakout: 54% Improve: 82% Collapse: 18%
Attrition: 44% MLB: 14%
Comparables:
Charlie Morton, Brian Omogrosso, Anthony Claggett

YEAR	TEAM	LVL	AGE	W	L	SV	G	GS	IP	H	HR	BB	SO	BB9	SO9	GB%	BABIP	WHIP	ERA	FIP	FRA	WARP
2011	LNS	A	21	4	5	2	18	12	66	80	7	24	51	3.3	7.0	62%	.313	1.58	5.59	4.56	5.56	-0.1
2012	KAN	A	22	1	8	3	31	4	62	73	2	27	50	3.9	7.3	51%	.346	1.61	5.81	3.84	4.62	0.8
2013	WNS	A+	23	1	0	2	8	0	15	10	0	5	19	3.0	11.4	56%	.278	1.00	0.00	1.82	2.16	0.6
2013	BIR	AA	23	0	0	4	13	0	20¹	11	0	5	21	2.2	9.3	39%	.216	0.79	1.77	1.73	3.06	0.4
2013	CHR	AAA	23	1	1	4	21	0	27¹	24	1	17	38	5.6	12.5	39%	.333	1.50	2.96	2.77	2.83	0.7
2013	CHA	MLB	23	0	0	0	9	0	11¹	9	0	4	10	3.2	7.9	56%	.281	1.15	3.18	2.37	2.59	0.3
2014	CHA	MLB	24	2	2	0	33	3	59¹	62	7	29	41	4.4	6.3	46%	.301	1.55	5.10	5.10	5.54	-0.4

When a young man spends his summer blowing away small crowds in Winston-Salem, Birmingham and Charlotte before finally earning a session in Chicago, he's either a newly signed Chess recording artist or a White Sox relief prospect. Webb used his mid-90s sinking fastball and power slider to leave hitters at three minor-league stops wailin' the blues and continued his bat-missing ways during a September call-up. His stuff has always borne the scent of late innings, but Webb had never managed to post an eye-popping strikeout rate before last season. He'll get a long look this spring, and if he continues his whiff-erific ways he could grow into an effective set-up man.

LINEOUTS

HITTERS

PLAYER	TEAM	LVL	AGE	PA	R	2B	3B	HR	RBI	BB	SO	SB-CS	AVG/OBP/SLG	TAv	BABIP	BRR	FRAA	WARP
C B. Anderson	CHR	AAA	26	235	26	14	1	7	26	24	60	2-0	.224/.302/.400	.241	.278	-2.1	C(61): 0.5	0.4
	CHA	MLB	26	19	1	1	0	0	2	1	5	0-0	.056/.105/.111	.082	.077	0	C(10): 0.1	-0.3
1B K. Barnum	KAN	A	20	223	22	13	1	5	26	19	65	0-0	.254/.315/.403	.267	.346	-1.6	1B(54): -0.8	0.1
2B J. DeMichele	WNS	A+	22	615	87	37	2	8	54	62	126	19-7	.246/.323/.366	.246	.304	3.3	2B(84): 0.6, SS(47): -4.4	0.9
C H. Gimenez	CHR	AAA	30	22	4	1	1	0	2	4	5	0-0	.294/.429/.471	.309	.417	1.2	C(5): 0.2	0.3
	CHA	MLB	30	80	8	4	0	2	10	7	22	0-0	.191/.275/.338	.254	.234	-0.1	C(23): 0.6	0.4
C M. Gonzalez	BIR	AA	22	132	12	5	1	2	16	10	25	3-1	.244/.318/.353	.231	.293	0.1	C(37): -0.7	0.2
	CHR	AAA	22	58	5	3	0	0	4	6	11	0-0	.280/.345/.340	.269	.341	0.9	C(16): 0.2	0.5
	CHA	MLB	22	9	0	0	0	0	0	0	3	0-0	.222/.222/.222	.248	.333	0	C(4): -0.0	0.0
2B M. Johnson	KAN	A	22	351	76	17	11	6	42	40	67	61-19	.342/.422/.530	.357	.422	5.5	2B(72): 8.2	6.0
	WNS	A+	22	228	28	7	4	1	15	10	27	22-7	.275/.309/.360	.234	.310	-1	2B(47): 6.6	0.4
	BIR	AA	22	22	2	0	0	0	1	0	4	1-0	.238/.227/.238	.175	.278	0.3	2B(5): 0.1	-0.1
3B A. Liddi	TAC	AAA	24	262	46	9	2	11	43	20	86	7-1	.262/.322/.454	.273	.364	0.8	3B(51): 2.0, 1B(7): -0.3	1.3
	NOR	AAA	24	198	20	11	3	4	22	11	58	4-1	.222/.269/.378	.221	.301	-1.8	1B(26): -1.5, 3B(22): -0.5	-1.0
	SEA	MLB	24	18	0	1	0	0	0	1	7	0-0	.059/.111/.118	.087	.100	0.1	1B(6): -0.5	-0.4
CF J. May	KAN	A	21	230	36	6	3	8	28	16	43	19-5	.286/.346/.461	.309	.325	1.6	CF(50): -5.1	1.7
1B M. McDade	CHR	AAA	24	390	36	18	0	10	46	28	96	1-0	.254/.313/.390	.243	.317	-2.4	1B(34): 0.1	-0.6
	COH	AAA	24	83	3	4	0	0	7	8	24	0-0	.230/.313/.284	.249	.340	-1.5	1B(21): -0.2	-0.2
C A. Nieto	POT	A+	23	452	68	29	1	11	53	53	82	4-2	.285/.373/.449	.280	.332	-0.4	C(86): 0.9	3.0
RF D. Phipps	LOU	AAA	27	482	48	27	2	9	49	48	99	14-3	.248/.331/.385	.262	.302	2.1	RF(91): -2.2, CF(24): 2.1	1.2
SS T. Saladino	BIR	AA	23	493	49	17	2	5	55	51	86	28-8	.229/.316/.314	.237	.271	0.7	SS(75): 1.6, 2B(43): 3.2	1.0
3B A. Sanchez	CHR	AAA	29	163	19	5	0	1	16	12	25	0-1	.189/.264/.243	.193	.221	0.2	3B(16): -1.6, SS(14): -1.9	-0.9
	CHA	MLB	29	2	0	0	0	0	0	0	0	0-0	.000/.000/.000	.012	.000	0	2B(1): 0.0	0.0
C K. Smith	WNS	A+	25	442	66	26	3	12	73	38	66	4-1	.286/.370/.464	.289	.317	2.2	C(92): -0.2	3.5
CF B. Tekotte	CHR	AAA	26	338	32	27	3	4	33	31	74	12-5	.236/.319/.389	.250	.300	1.5	CF(66): 1.2, RF(6): -0.4	0.9
	CHA	MLB	26	36	4	1	0	1	2	5	9	1-3	.226/.306/.355	.255	.273	-0.7	CF(16): -0.2, LF(1): -0.1	0.0
1B A. Wilkins	BIR	AA	24	285	37	16	0	10	49	38	58	3-0	.288/.386/.477	.312	.339	-3.5	1B(43): 2.2	1.7
	CHR	AAA	24	234	25	13	0	7	30	14	52	2-1	.265/.312/.423	.256	.314	0.7	1B(37): -1.6, 3B(2): -0.3	0.1
CF D. Wise	CHR	AAA	35	57	4	3	1	0	2	3	17	1-1	.170/.228/.264	.167	.250	0.2	CF(15): 0.2	-0.4
	CHA	MLB	35	66	6	3	0	1	3	2	14	1-1	.234/.258/.328	.211	.286	0.1	CF(22): 1.0, LF(4): 0.1	0.1

If being a backup-catcher-in-waiting is an actual thing, **Bryan Anderson** used to be one in St. Louis, but several years spent squatting in Triple-A and producing little noise with his once-promising lefty bat made him an organizational-backstop-in-perpetuity. ⊘ Former supplemental first-rounder **Keon Barnum** is built like a linebacker but makes far less contact, and won't tap into his massive raw power until he does. ⊘ **Joey DeMichele** showed some pop and drew a few walks but surprisingly struggled to make contact; with a fringy glove at both shortstop and second, he'll have to liven up his bat to grow into the grindy utilityman his name and tools can support. ⊘ Hats off to **Hector Gimenez**, who hit his first major-league home run last summer after surviving 900 minor-league games and 2,185 foul tips off his mask, cup or bruisable exposed flesh; his catch-and-throw skills will keep him employed as organizational depth as long as he's willing to eat the pain. ⊘ Venezuelan backstop **Miguel Gonzalez** isn't much of a hitter but gets solid marks for his work behind the dish; he might someday earn a card from the International Brotherhood of Backup Catchers. ⊘ Stealing 84 bases and posting a combined .312/.373/.451 line in the low minors certainly earned **Micah Johnson** some attention; if he can clean up his atrocious defense at the keystone and continue to reach base against more advanced pitching—and those are big ifs—he has a chance. ⊘ **Alex Liddi** has struck out in 39 percent of his major-league plate appearances and managed 31 percent at Triple-A in 2013, so if you're wondering how he's going to carve out a career, you're not the only one. ⊘ So far, so good for third-round pick **Jacob May**, as the fleet switch-hitter showed surprising pop and improving center-field defense in his Sally League debut. ⊘ Former Cleveland farmhand **Mike McDade** struggled to make contact in Triple-A and posted a slugging percentage only mothers and middle infielders could love; since he's a hulking, bat-only prospect limited to first base, that qualifies as a Very Bad Thing. ⃠ **Adrian Nieto** emerged in 2013, showing the ability to take a walk and flash pop. The White Sox nabbed him in the Rule 5 draft, shortening his path to big-league service time. ⃠ With some power, outfield utility and little else, **Denis Phipps** will spend his seasons stacking major-league coffee cups in his Triple-A locker. ⃠ **Tyler Saladino** got an even worse score on his second crack at the DBAT (Double-A Batting Aptitude Test), and won't grow into a big-league utilityman until his bat catches up with his legs and glove. ⃠ Thirty-something shortstop **Angel Sanchez** can still pick it and boasts a career .282/.347/.372 Triple-A line, but has never made his mark in parts of four big-league seasons and was released by the White Sox. ⃠ **Kevan Smith** put together a nice season at the plate in High-A, but his waxy catch-and-throw skills still need to be creamed and buffed with a fine chamois; chop chop, since he's already 25, and needs to show off his patience and power when facing pitchers his own age. ⃠ Minor-league center fielder **Blake Tekotte** plays solid defense and occasionally shows gap power, but several years of futility at the plate have made him an afterthought. ⃠ Putative slugger **Andy Wilkins** finally conquered Double-A and worked his way up to Charlotte, but the 25-year-old doesn't wield a big enough cudgel to profile as more than a stopgap first sacker. ⃠ Long-time fourth outfielder **DeWayne Wise** struggled last season and earned his release; at age 36 he may need to call it a career, but he still has his memories, his health and that groovy embroidered Crown Royal bag he got from Mark Buehrle.

PITCHERS

PLAYER	TEAM	LVL	AGE	W	L	SV	IP	H	HR	BB	SO	BB9	SO9	GB%	BABIP	WHIP	ERA	FIP	FRA	WARP
C. Beck	WNS	A+	22	11	8	0	118²	117	11	42	57	3.2	4.3	59%	.275	1.34	3.11	4.76	5.73	0.6
	BIR	AA	22	2	2	0	28	26	0	3	22	1.0	7.1	45%	.313	1.04	2.89	1.88	2.97	0.6
T. Bucciferro	KAN	A	23	3	5	1	72	80	2	5	71	0.6	8.9	55%	.351	1.18	2.50	2.12	3.16	1.6
F. De Los Santos	DUR	AAA	25	1	2	1	32	37	3	14	21	3.9	5.9	40%	.318	1.59	5.34	4.52	5.29	0.0
K. Hansen	KAN	A	22	6	9	1	96²	109	7	27	103	2.5	9.6	44%	.357	1.41	4.10	3.19	4.07	1.5
M. Jaye	KAN	A	21	4	1	0	41	36	2	17	37	3.7	8.1	55%	.301	1.29	2.20	3.70	4.50	0.4
	WNS	A+	21	9	6	0	118¹	122	8	44	89	3.3	6.8	51%	.312	1.40	4.11	4.02	5.39	0.7
F. Montas	GRN	A	20	2	9	0	85¹	94	10	32	96	3.4	10.1	39%	.349	1.48	5.70	3.98	4.70	0.7
	KAN	A	20	3	2	0	25²	20	1	18	31	6.3	10.9	47%	.302	1.48	4.56	3.68	4.04	0.3
B. Omogrosso	CHR	AAA	29	0	1	2	14²	20	2	4	14	2.5	8.6	43%	.383	1.64	4.91	3.89	4.28	0.1
	CHA	MLB	29	0	2	0	16¹	28	2	9	16	5.0	8.8	45%	.464	2.27	9.37	4.54	5.50	-0.1
B. Ortiz	KAN	A	21	0	4	3	62²	43	3	39	74	5.6	10.6	46%	.270	1.31	3.45	3.80	4.45	0.3
	WNS	A+	21	1	3	0	27¹	28	2	24	29	7.9	9.5	39%	.321	1.90	6.91	5.03	5.76	0.2
F. Paulino	OMA	AAA	29	0	3	0	19²	30	2	11	18	5.0	8.2	43%	.418	2.08	8.24	5.04	5.20	0.1
D. Purcey	CHR	AAA	31	0	2	3	38²	30	2	12	43	2.8	10.0	42%	.289	1.09	3.03	2.74	3.11	0.8
	CHA	MLB	31	1	1	0	25¹	19	2	17	23	6.0	8.2	42%	.246	1.42	2.13	4.54	4.16	0.1
Z. Putnam	IOW	AAA	25	1	1	4	19¹	20	0	6	22	2.8	10.2	73%	.364	1.34	3.26	2.22	3.00	0.6
	CHN	MLB	25	0	0	0	3¹	9	1	0	4	0.0	10.8	50%	.615	2.70	18.90	4.52	5.32	0.0
S. Rodriguez	BIR	AA	25	1	0	0	23	13	1	14	25	5.5	9.8	45%	.218	1.17	2.35	3.39	3.88	0.2
	CHR	AAA	25	1	0	0	24²	21	3	27	36	9.9	13.1	37%	.333	1.95	7.30	5.27	5.32	-0.1
R. Troncoso	CHR	AAA	30	1	1	8	24²	18	2	7	17	2.6	6.2	57%	.213	1.01	2.19	3.85	3.59	0.4
	CHA	MLB	30	1	4	0	30	30	4	16	18	4.8	5.4	53%	.265	1.53	4.50	5.31	5.11	-0.2
K. Vance	BIR	AA	22	2	6	7	69	55	4	36	84	4.7	11.0	38%	.293	1.32	3.91	2.84	3.29	1.2

Future innings-eater **Chris Beck** uses his heavy low-90s fastball and developing curve and changeup to induce plenty of groundballs but precious few strikeouts; so far he's kept runs off the board, but scouts question whether the same voodoo will work against more advanced hitters. ⃠ Joliet's own **Tony Bucciferro** doesn't light up radar guns, and college draftees are expected to dominate Low-A, but a 14:1 strikeout-to-walk ratio, bushels of groundballs and a 1.84 FIP certainly makes his developing sinker/slider combination worth keeping an eye on. ⃠ **Frank De Los Santos** suffered early from a tight forearm and on returning his numbers suffered from loose concentration. The Rays' LOOGY-rich system allowed them to add 40-man space by trading him to the White Sox during the regular season's final weekend. ⃠ Fellow 2012 draftee **Kyle Hansen** also generated plenty of whiffs and groundouts in Kannapolis by throwing his low-90s fastball on a steep downward plane, while his slider is sharp enough to envision a big league future in middle relief. ⃠ **Myles Jaye** has a fastball that can reach the mid-90s, a slider and changeup that still need work, a birth certificate that verifies he still has time to develop and a name that registers a sneaky

6 on the Honorary Mike Krzyzewski Copy Editor Frustration Scale. ⊘ A secondary piece in the Jake Peavy trade, **Francellis Montas** tests radar guns with his upper-90s fastball and managers with his walk totals and crooked-number innings; if he can develop some semblance of command and a reliable second pitch, he could become a late-inning weapon. ⊘ Honorary Rockette **Brian Omogrosso** tossed a few ineffective innings for the White Sox last summer before undergoing season-ending elbow surgery and earning his release; he can still pump mid-90s gas from a low three-quarter slot and may yet ROOGY his way onto someone's roster. ⊘ Stop us if you've heard this before, but **Braulio Ortiz** misses plenty of bats with his mid-90s fastball and developing slider but needs to avoid ball four and find better command; while his sturdy frame would support a starter's workload, his long-term home is the bullpen. ⊘ Oft-injured FIP darling **Felipe Paulino** didn't make good on his Internet-sleeper status while he was with the Royals, but the thing about Internet-sleeper status is how resilient it is. Now with the White Sox, he's a sleeper, according to the Internet. ⊘ Institutional-sized lefty **David Purcey** used his lively fastball to post an enviable ERA in the White Sox' bullpen, despite a walk rate that would choke a sabermetric horse; his stuff will continue to earn him chances, but his lack of control dooms him to low-leverage work. ⊘ Bone spurs resulting in August elbow surgery cut short **Zach Putnam**'s season, but his sinker/splitter combo generates enough strikeouts and groundballs to work in a bullpen. ⊘ Lefty **Santos Rodriguez** sports the traditional markings of a minor-league relief suspect: high strikeout rate, ridiculous walk rate, terrific velocity and a less-than-even chance of ever providing value in a big-league bullpen. ⊘ Sinker-slider specialist **Ramon Troncoso** spent a few ineffective months in the White Sox' bullpen and survived a frightening bout of pericarditis, but with his walk and strikeout rates in danger of crossing paths he's barely suited for mop-up duty. ⊘ Unlike so many lightning-armed relief suspects, **Kevin Vance** already knows how to get big outs, setting them up with solid fastball command and knocking them down with his big-breaking curve; don't be surprised if he carves out a long career in middle relief.

MANAGER: ROBIN VENTURA

YEAR	TEAM	W-L	Pythag +/-	Avg PC	100+ P	120+ P	QS	BQS	REL	REL w Zero R	IBB	PH	PH Avg	PH HR	SB2	CS2	SB3	CS3	SAC Att	SAC %	POS SAC	Squeeze	Swing	In Play
2012	CHA	85-77	1	98.8	91	6	86	4	466	381	29	63	.135	1	107	41	2	1	45	68.9%	29	0	317	88
2013	CHA	63-99	0	100.5	96	4	90	3	470	389	24	67	.125	1	102	41	2	1	27	70.4%	15	0	315	102

For all the talk about how Robin Ventura's personality distinguishes him from his predecessor, Ozzie Guillen, he also has some strategic differences. Whereas Guillen was generally willing to bunt, the 2013 White Sox had just 19 sacrifice hits, the lowest of any team in baseball and the third-fewest by any team this decade. Ventura also doesn't issue many intentional walks.

Fun fact: The White Sox haven't had a manager in his 50s since Bob Lemon, who ran the team from 1977 to 1978. (Well, fine, Don Cooper was older—but that was just two games as interim skipper after Ozzie Guillen resigned. That hardly counts.) For context, every other team has had at least once AARP member as manager since 2007. Twenty-three teams will have a manager 50 or older on Opening Day 2014. Yeah, the Sox like young managers. They haven't hired a retread manager since Jeff Torborg over 20 years ago. (For that matter, Sox owner Jerry Reinsdorf also like to hire first-time field generals with the other team he owns, the NBA's Chicago Bulls.)

Chicago Cubs

By Bruce Miles

In April 2012, the Chicago Sun-Times put new Cubs President Theo Epstein on the back cover. The photo captured Epstein, sharply dressed in a navy blue power suit, confidently mid-stride, Chicago's downtown skyline as a backdrop. Oh, yeah, there was one other thing: He was walking atop Lake Michigan.

"Hope and a prayer," the headline went, but six months later the same tabloid again featured Epstein, this time sunk to his neck in the same body of water. The natives, as the saying goes, are getting restless.

There is precedent for the sudden, subtle shifts in how Epstein and his crew (including General Manager Jed Hoyer) are viewed in Chicago, one of the only cities in America that still supports four daily newspapers (and all the scribes that come with them). Back in the fall of 1994, a man with similar intelligence and pedigree came to Chicago to turn around Cubs fortunes as team president: Andy MacPhail. After having won two world championships in Minnesota, just as Theo had done in Boston, MacPhail was seen as young, bright, successful and someone who would end the chaos that had been the hallmark of the Cubs organization in the early 1990s. He would build the organization "the right way."

By the end of MacPhail's third season in Chicago, he was booed during an on-field ceremony to honor the retiring Ryne Sandberg. If it's unrealistic to expect one man to end a century of misery, it's more unrealistic still to think he'll do it without losing Golden Boy status along the way. And so, just two years after taking over, and after arguably doing plenty to put the Cubs in position to win (eventually), the sentiment around the Cubs goes something like this: "We believe in Theo's plan, but ..."

A few things have fueled this nascent restlessness: the calcified impatience that comes with not having won a World Series since 1908, back-to-back losing seasons (totaling 197 losses) in Epstein's first two seasons, the regression of young hitters Starlin Castro and Anthony Rizzo and the firing of manager Dale Sveum after just two years on the job.

Sveum was never a beloved figure in Chicago, but Epstein managed to turn him into a sympathetic one by the end. After all, how could Epstein fire a manager after saddling him with two of the worst rosters in franchise history? On top of that, didn't Epstein and Hoyer thoroughly research their managerial candidates? Hadn't they boasted of putting them through "marathon sessions of questioning, brainstorming and game-playing" as part of the interview process?

"Either the hiring or the firing was a big mistake," *Daily-Herald* columnist Barry Rozner wrote, "but one way or the other, Epstein made a big mistake." After the Cubs whiffed in their pursuit of Joe Girardi to replace Sveum, the *Tribune* columnist David Haugh joined the alarm-sounding chorus: "For the first time since the baseball gods dropped Epstein out of the sky at Clark and Addison in 2011, he deserves healthy skepticism that he earned as much as the benefit of the doubt he brought to town." Haugh, like Rozner, used the word "mistake" to describe the Sveum situation, and that word kept coming in the news conference when Epstein announced Sveum's firing. At one point, an exasperated-sounding Epstein blurted out: "We know what we're doing!"

But the Sveum situation wasn't just about managerial X's and O's. It was about the biggest on-field disappointment of the Epstein years to date. Epstein referred to a lack of communication from Sveum toward Castro and Rizzo as a reason for making the managerial change. After a five-and-a-half week search for Sveum's replacement, Epstein and Hoyer settled on another baseball lifer, San Diego Padres bench coach Rick Renteria, as the next manager of the Cubs. To no one's surprise, Renteria talked of "communication" during his introductory news conference and said that he was fully

CUBS PROSPECTUS
2013 W-L: 66-96, 5th in NL Central

Pythag	.439	24th	DER	.717	3rd
RS/G	3.72	28th	B-Age	27.7	8th
RA/G	4.25	18th	P-Age	28.4	21st
TAv	.248	26th	Salary	$118.9	10th
BRR	-1.69	19th	M$/MW	$5.4	27th
TAv-P	.263	14th	DL Days	1093	21st
FIP	4.07	23rd	$ on DL	13%	9th

	Runs	HR/RH	HR/LH	Runs/RH	Runs/LH
Three-Year Park Factors	104	115	103	107	104

Top Hitter WARP	2.47 (Welington Castillo)
Top Pitcher WARP	2.38 (Jeff Samardzija)
Top Prospect	Javier Baez

familiar with "youth movements," having raised four children of his own.

There's no doubt that 2014 will be a crucial, perhaps pivotal season for many young Cubs, particularly Castro and Rizzo. Castro's situation is the more puzzling of the two. He came up in May 2010 and electrified the Cubs with a .300/.347/.408 line in 125 games. He was 20 years old. Given a full season in 2011, he led the National League in hits (207), put up a line of .307/.341/.432 and made the first of two successive All-Star teams.

But in the first year of Epstein's regime, Castro saw declines in his batting average and on-base percentage, with an overall line of .283/.323/.430. It was during the middle of that season that Castro made a shift in his approach, as the Cubs—in a collaborative effort involving Sveum, Epstein and Hoyer—wanted him to become more selective at the plate and draw more walks.

Castro did just that, drawing 24 walks after the All-Star break, compared to just 12 before the break. His OBP ticked up from .314 in the unofficial first half of the season to .332 in the second half. So far, so good.

But the bottom fell out in 2013. Castro's line dropped to .245/.284/.347; the team's putative star had turned into one of the worst-hitting shortstops in baseball. The patience from 2012 did not carry over, as his walk rate dropped to 4 percent and the strikeout rate went up to 18 percent, both career worsts. Castro's BABIP was a career low, as was his isolated power.

More than anything, though, Castro looked lost at the plate and in the field. During one unfortunate incident against the Cardinals, he caught a popup in short left field with the bases loaded and one out. He put his head down, and the baserunner scored from third base. It wasn't the first mental lapse for Castro—a camera once caught him with his back to the plate, kicking at the dirt, while a pitch was delivered—and his missteps in the field seem to draw a disproportionate amount of attention in Chicago. He said he learned from the latest gaffe.

As for Rizzo, he's a special project of the Epstein-Hoyer tandem, having played for one or both of them in three different organizations: Boston, San Diego and Chicago. After the Cubs traded for him in January of 2012, they handled him with kid gloves, allowing him to get 257 at-bats at Triple-A Iowa during the first three months of the 2012 season.

After Rizzo came up in late June of that year, he went .285/.342/.463 with 15 home runs after slugging 23 at Iowa. He won the starting first-base job to start the 2013 season, was a PECOTA darling, and slugged eight home runs in April. But it was a long struggle after that, as he hit .234/.325/.398 from May 1st on. His walk rate improved, but the damage he did on contact disappeared. And he hit just .189/.282/.342 against left-handers. The slump coincided with a seven-year, $41 million contract extension.

The drops in OBP for both Castro and Rizzo are emblematic of the problems facing the Cubs as an organization. The team's .300 OBP ranked 14th in the National League. Rizzo's modest .323 OBP led qualified Cubs batters (though the catching tandem of Welington Castillo (.349) and Dioner Navarro (.365) would have topped him with enough plate appearances).

The poor on-base results seemed to nettle Epstein. One of the many reasons Cubs fans hailed Epstein's arrival was that they had grown tired of the previous regime's seeming disregard for the things that led to high on-base percentages.

"Right now, we're nowhere close to where we want to be offensively," Epstein said in September. "Getting on base is going to be the hallmark of this organization, and we're not good at it yet. My choice of one type of hitter would be a guy who can really get on base and hit for power, who can really run and do all those things. We need to get on base more. That's something we need to change."

Both Castro and Rizzo will get a fresh opportunity to do that in 2014, and Castro in particular seemed ready for it as the season wound down. Asked what would make him successful, he replied: "Just be me." That seemed to signify a desire to buck the front office's prescriptions and go back to his aggressive approach, letting his hand-eye coordination generate hard contact and raise the OBP through hits again.

Otherwise, the Cubs' best chance of remaking the lineup will come out of a suddenly highly regarded farm system—and, especially, the elite quartet comprising shortstop Javier Baez, outfielder Jorge Soler, center fielder Albert Almora and third baseman Kris Bryant.

The most intriguing of these players at the moment is Bryant, whom the Cubs took with their first-round pick (second overall) in June. Bryant, a right-handed hitter, moved from short-season Boise to High-A Daytona and combined for a line of .336/.390/.688. A polished product of San Diego State, Bryant confidently proclaimed himself major-league ready upon being drafted.

Baez—the shortstop—went .282/.341/.578 with 37 home runs and 20 stolen bases split between Dayton and Double-A Tennessee. Almora, Epstein's first no. 1 draft pick, broke the hamate bone in his left hand but still hit .329/.376/.466 in A-ball. Soler, signed to a nine-year major-league contract in the summer of 2012, suffered a stress fracture of his left tibia early in the year and missed the summer, but slugged .688 in the Arizona Fall League. The four have such upside that the Cubs have been able to focus on adding young pitching in subsequent rounds of the draft, trades and last summer's international signings. Between the new manager, the disappointing turns Castro and Rizzo have taken and the Cubs' dependence on always-unpredictable prospects, Chicago's future is far from certain. But it's also far from hopeless.

And so, as the Cubs enter Year 3 of the the Epstein/Hoyer movement, and as they stare down the probability of yet another 90-loss season, they are reminded of the reason Epstein was so necessary: Sticking to a long-term vision can be *painful*. That Epstein was able to inspire so much confidence, and for so long, is perhaps more important than any of the actual team-building skills he had shown in Boston. If it took only two years for Cubs fans to start losing faith in Epstein, imagine another, less-inspiring boss trying to implement the fixes that the Cubs so desperately needed.

"We feel the same frustration [as Cubs fans]," Epstein said in December. "But I think I'd be really compromising the organization if we decided just because we were frustrated and people around us were frustrated that we would scrap the plan and try to add some things cosmetically to make it look better than it really is.

"There's a really high bar we're aiming for and we know we're going to get there and it's going to be sustainable."

Bruce Miles has been the Cubs beat writer for the Daily Herald *(Arlington Heights, Illinois) since 1998 and has covered major league baseball since 1989. Along with Cubs radio play-by-play announcer Pat Hughes, Miles co-authored the book* Harry Caray, Voice of the Fans *in 2007.*

HITTERS

Arismendy Alcantara SS
Born: 10/29/1991 Age: 22
Bats: B Throws: R Height: 5' 10''
Weight: 160 Breakout: 2%
Improve: 11% Collapse: 6%
Attrition: 13% MLB: 19%

Comparables:
Tony Abreu, Jordany Valdespin, Brad Harman

YEAR	TEAM	LVL	AGE	PA	R	2B	3B	HR	RBI	BB	SO	SB	CS	AVG/OBP/SLG	TAv	BABIP	BRR	FRAA	WARP
2011	PEO	A	19	390	45	14	5	2	37	16	76	8	8	.271/.303/.352	.253	.337	0.6	SS(36): 2.6, 2B(15): -2.0	0.8
2012	DAY	A+	20	359	47	13	7	7	51	19	61	25	4	.302/.339/.447	.278	.347	4.1	SS(71): -4.5, 3B(8): 0.6	2.2
2013	TEN	AA	21	571	69	36	4	15	69	62	125	31	6	.271/.352/.451	.287	.332	5.2	SS(66): 4.1, 2B(64): -0.1	4.2
2014	CHN	MLB	22	250	30	11	1	5	23	14	64	7	2	.242/.285/.373	.238	.300	0.7	SS 0, 2B -1	0.4

Who doesn't like a switch-hitting middle infielder with speed and power? Opposing managers, that's who. Alcantara rocketed up prospect charts last summer, opening eyes at the Futures Game and earning All-Star recognition as a 21-year-old in Double-A. The young Dominican generates easy bat speed and surprising pop from his compact frame, steals bases at a high success rate and even managed to cut down on his free-swinging ways against more advanced pitching. The organization has moved him to second base, a position that suits his offensive profile and eases his path to a big-league job. Other Cubs prospects may have louder tools, but don't sleep on Alcantara's broad-based skill set.

Albert Almora   CF
Born: 4/16/1994 Age: 20
Bats: R Throws: R Height: 6' 2''
Weight: 180 Breakout: 0%
Improve: 1% Collapse: 0%
Attrition: 1% MLB: 2%

Comparables:
Cedric Hunter, Engel Beltre, Abraham Almonte

YEAR	TEAM	LVL	AGE	PA	R	2B	3B	HR	RBI	BB	SO	SB	CS	AVG/OBP/SLG	TAv	BABIP	BRR	FRAA	WARP
2012	BOI	A-	18	65	9	7	0	1	6	0	5	0	1	.292/.292/.446	.232	.305	-3	CF(15): 1.9	0.0
2013	KNC	A	19	272	39	17	4	3	23	17	30	4	4	.329/.376/.466	.286	.362	-0.7	CF(59): 9.2	2.7
2014	CHN	MLB	20	250	23	12	1	3	21	8	51	0	0	.238/.266/.339	.220	.280	-0.4	CF 6	0.3

Almora overcame a series of nagging injuries during his first full season to display the wide-ranging tools, feel and makeup that place him among the game's brightest prospects. He's an outstanding center fielder, with an accurate arm and uncanny instincts that make up for average straight-line speed. At the plate, Almora waits for his pitch and attacks it, making consistent loud contact and showing the potential to hit for a high average with shipfuls of doubles and 20-plus home runs at his peak. If there are any concerns, they center on his health and an aggressive approach that might be exploited by more experienced pitchers, although few doubt he'll make needed adjustments as he climbs the organizational ladder. The kid's seemingly good at everything, so expect Almora to be the best pure hitter, fielder, baserunner, seed spitter, balky chainsaw starter and Mario Kart player on any team that's lucky enough to have him.

Javier Baez   SS
Born: 12/1/1992 Age: 21
Bats: R Throws: R Height: 6' 0''
Weight: 195 Breakout: 8%
Improve: 21% Collapse: 2%
Attrition: 10% MLB: 33%

Comparables:
Jay Bruce, Reid Brignac, Travis Snider

YEAR	TEAM	LVL	AGE	PA	R	2B	3B	HR	RBI	BB	SO	SB	CS	AVG/OBP/SLG	TAv	BABIP	BRR	FRAA	WARP
2012	PEO	A	19	235	41	10	5	12	33	9	48	20	3	.333/.383/.596	.348	.378	4.4	SS(52): 5.2	3.9
2012	DAY	A+	19	86	9	3	1	4	13	5	21	4	2	.188/.244/.400	.206	.200	-0.9	SS(23): -0.9	-0.4
2013	DAY	A+	20	337	59	19	4	17	57	21	78	12	2	.274/.338/.535	.299	.310	2.2	SS(73): 2.9	3.3
2013	TEN	AA	20	240	39	15	0	20	54	19	69	8	2	.294/.346/.638	.343	.333	1	SS(50): 1.5	3.4
2014	CHN	MLB	21	250	33	11	1	14	38	9	74	6	1	.243/.281/.475	.268	.290	0.6	SS 2	1.5

If you listen carefully when Baez swings from his heels and makes solid contact, you'll hear both a thunderclap and a choir of angels singing hosannas to the fastest bat in the minors. The young shortstop's raw power is unquestioned, and launching 20 bombs in a half-season taste of Double-A speaks volumes about his ability to hit advanced pitching. Baez has soft hands, a strong arm and enough range to stick at shortstop, but his top-peg intensity and aggressiveness can lead to rashes of errors in the field and whiffs at the plate. He made strides as the year wore on to slow the game down and work better counts, but there's still plenty of room for improvement, and if his glove remains unreliable he may need to slide down the defensive spectrum. Baez may never post high OBPs or win Gold Gloves, but the possibility of game-changing power at a premium position has Cubs fans hoping to see him in Wrigley this summer.

Darwin Barney   2B

Born: 11/8/1985 Age: 28
Bats: R Throws: R Height: 5' 10''
Weight: 185 Breakout: 0%
Improve: 28% Collapse: 11%
Attrition: 13% MLB: 85%

Comparables:
Brent Abernathy, Chris Getz, Placido Polanco

YEAR	TEAM	LVL	AGE	PA	R	2B	3B	HR	RBI	BB	SO	SB	CS	AVG/OBP/SLG	TAv	BABIP	BRR	FRAA	WARP
2011	CHN	MLB	25	570	66	23	6	2	43	22	67	9	2	.276/.313/.353	.241	.310	3.1	2B(135): 7.7, SS(5): 0.2	1.6
2012	CHN	MLB	26	588	73	26	4	7	44	33	58	6	1	.254/.299/.354	.239	.273	6.6	2B(155): 11.6, SS(3): 0.2	2.7
2013	CHN	MLB	27	555	49	25	1	7	41	36	64	4	2	.208/.266/.303	.202	.222	1.6	2B(141): -1.4	-1.8
2014	CHN	MLB	28	528	48	24	2	6	45	27	66	6	2	.250/.294/.344	.236	.280	0	2B 3, SS 0	0.8

Barney is a better ballplayer than last year's sub-replacement numbers indicate, but is by no means a building block. While our metrics weren't fond of his defense, others still show him to be a plus glove at the keystone, with sure hands, tremendous instincts and a strong arm making up for pedestrian range. At the plate he's a contact hitter with little power and a mediocre walk rate, making his value highly dependent on how many singles fall in. His batting average on balls in play fell to a league-low last summer, taking his batting average with it and making him the league's worst hitter as measured by TAv. With a more realistic BABIP his bat should rebound from abysmal to merely subpar, making Barney an ideal utility infielder but a lineup drag when he's penciled in every day.

Kristopher Bryant   3B

Born: 1/4/1992 Age: 22
Bats: R Throws: R Height: 6' 5''
Weight: 215 Breakout: 3%
Improve: 24% Collapse: 2%
Attrition: 22% MLB: 34%

Comparables:
Alex Liddi, Matt Davidson, Josh Bell

YEAR	TEAM	LVL	AGE	PA	R	2B	3B	HR	RBI	BB	SO	SB	CS	AVG/OBP/SLG	TAv	BABIP	BRR	FRAA	WARP
2013	BOI	A-	21	77	13	8	1	4	16	8	17	0	0	.354/.416/.692	.372	.404	-0.2	3B(16): 1.5	1.1
2013	DAY	A+	21	62	9	5	1	5	14	3	17	1	0	.333/.387/.719	.362	.400	-0.6	3B(13): 1.4	1.0
2014	CHN	MLB	22	250	26	10	1	10	32	13	71	1	0	.228/.274/.403	.243	.280	-0.3	3B 5	0.7

The second overall pick in last year's draft, Bryant wasted no time unleashing the power stroke that helped him hit more home runs than entire rival teams during his senior year at University of San Diego. Top college hitters are expected to tee off on short-season pitchers, and Bryant did, but he also managed a .333/.387/.719 line down the stretch with High-A Daytona to cement his place among the top hitting prospects in the game. He shows good actions at the hot corner but some scouts feel his future is in right field, where his strong arm and surprising athleticism will play nicely. Whatever comes of the organization's upcoming games of positional Plinko, Bryant's mature approach and middle-of-the-order thump may well land him in Wrigley before the summer is out.

Welington Castillo   C

Born: 4/24/1987 Age: 27
Bats: R Throws: R Height: 5' 10''
Weight: 210 Breakout: 6%
Improve: 43% Collapse: 7%
Attrition: 19% MLB: 85%

Comparables:
Geovany Soto, Travis Ishikawa, Ryan Garko

YEAR	TEAM	LVL	AGE	PA	R	2B	3B	HR	RBI	BB	SO	SB	CS	AVG/OBP/SLG	TAv	BABIP	BRR	FRAA	WARP
2011	DAY	A+	24	49	6	3	0	1	7	6	9	0	0	.238/.327/.381	.201	.273	-0.1	C(3): -0.0	-0.1
2011	IOW	AAA	24	251	38	9	0	15	35	20	57	0	0	.286/.351/.524	.322	.321	-1.1	C(40): -0.8	1.9
2011	CHN	MLB	24	13	0	0	0	0	0	0	4	0	0	.154/.154/.154	.128	.222	-0.2	C(4): -0.1	-0.1
2012	IOW	AAA	25	176	22	6	0	6	22	23	37	0	0	.260/.375/.425	.285	.305	-0.1	C(41): -0.8	1.1
2012	CHN	MLB	25	190	16	11	0	5	22	17	51	0	0	.265/.337/.418	.272	.348	-0.6	C(49): -1.5, 1B(1): -0.0	0.8
2013	CHN	MLB	26	428	41	23	0	8	32	34	97	2	0	.274/.349/.397	.266	.347	-1	C(111): -0.1	2.5
2014	CHN	MLB	27	378	41	18	0	12	47	31	94	1	0	.249/.322/.410	.267	.310	-0.8	C -1, 1B 0	1.9

With so much attention being paid to the struggles of young veterans Starlin Castro and Anthony Rizzo, it was easy to miss that Castillo spent last season establishing himself as a bona fide major-league catcher. Long known as a bat-first receiver with a strong arm but sketchy defensive instincts, Castillo took big steps forward behind the dish, especially in blocking pitches, and has become a solid backstop. At the plate, Castillo improved as the season wore on and did a better job of working himself into fastball counts, upping his patience and power and producing a .288/.388/.475 second-half line. He may yet tap into more of the power he showed in the minors, and if he can continue to lay off those sliders away, Castillo can be comfortably slotted into the second tier of big-league catchers.

Starlin Castro — SS

Born: 3/24/1990 Age: 24
Bats: R Throws: R Height: 5' 10"
Weight: 190 Breakout: 4%
Improve: 51% Collapse: 8%
Attrition: 14% MLB: 96%

Comparables:
Jose Reyes, Wil Cordero, Tom Tresh

YEAR	TEAM	LVL	AGE	PA	R	2B	3B	HR	RBI	BB	SO	SB	CS	AVG/OBP/SLG	TAv	BABIP	BRR	FRAA	WARP
2011	CHN	MLB	21	715	91	36	9	10	66	35	96	22	9	.307/.341/.432	.273	.344	0.3	SS(158): 2.8	4.4
2012	CHN	MLB	22	691	78	29	12	14	78	36	100	25	13	.283/.323/.430	.269	.315	1.1	SS(162): -0.7	4.0
2013	CHN	MLB	23	705	59	34	2	10	44	30	129	9	6	.245/.284/.347	.228	.290	0.1	SS(159): -4.0	0.0
2014	CHN	MLB	24	660	78	34	6	11	60	32	102	16	9	.279/.318/.405	.265	.320	-0.2	SS -1	3.1

Square peg, meet round hole. The Cubs spent much of last season trying to temper Castro's see-ball, hit-ball approach in favor of a more selective aggression, with disastrous results. The evidence is mixed on whether the organization's tinkering led to Castro's struggles at the plate—after all, his best stretch of the season was during a .292/.339/.442 July when he saw significantly more pitches per plate appearance (4.12) than at any point in his career—but that doesn't matter. Castro clearly *believed* it did, and seemed more at ease when he resumed his free-swinging ways down the stretch. Still only 24, a comfortable Castro is capable of batting .300 with adequate (if occasionally unfocused) shortstop defense, few walks and above-average power for the position. That's a tremendously valuable player, even if his low on-base percentage keeps him from being a table-setter. This season will go a long way toward determining if Castro becomes a long-term cog or a cautionary tale.

Brett Jackson — CF

Born: 8/2/1988 Age: 25
Bats: L Throws: R Height: 6' 2"
Weight: 220 Breakout: 5%
Improve: 13% Collapse: 4%
Attrition: 23% MLB: 31%

Comparables:
Joe Benson, Melky Mesa, Brent Clevlen

YEAR	TEAM	LVL	AGE	PA	R	2B	3B	HR	RBI	BB	SO	SB	CS	AVG/OBP/SLG	TAv	BABIP	BRR	FRAA	WARP
2011	TEN	AA	22	297	45	10	3	10	32	45	74	15	6	.256/.373/.443	.245	.323	1.9	CF(45): -2.5, RF(5): -0.6	0.1
2011	IOW	AAA	22	215	39	13	2	10	26	28	64	6	1	.297/.388/.551	.300	.402	2.3	CF(33): 0.7	1.6
2012	IOW	AAA	23	467	66	22	12	15	47	47	158	27	5	.256/.338/.479	.287	.372	0	CF(87): -6.1, RF(12): 0.2	2.1
2012	CHN	MLB	23	142	14	6	1	4	9	22	59	0	3	.175/.303/.342	.246	.298	-1.2	CF(39): 0.9	0.3
2013	TEN	AA	24	110	10	4	2	0	4	13	37	2	2	.200/.309/.284	.220	.328	-1.1	LF(15): 0.5, RF(8): -0.9	-0.5
2013	IOW	AAA	24	242	24	7	3	6	23	21	77	7	5	.223/.300/.367	.245	.316	-1	CF(36): -4.5, LF(15): -1.0	-0.6
2014	CHN	MLB	25	250	31	9	2	6	23	24	89	7	3	.205/.286/.352	.234	.300	0.6	CF -1, LF -1	-0.2

There's nothing wrong with being a Three True Outcomes player, especially if you can play center field, but Jackson no longer walks or launches enough bombs to be anything more than an animated version of the letter K. After striking out in over 40 percent of his plate appearances during his 2012 big-league cameo, Jackson retooled his swing to make more contact, but the resulting slight improvement in his whiff rate seemingly cost him the power and on-base skills that made him a prospect in the first place. Still athletic but no longer young, Jackson could still become a fourth outfielder if he regains his power stroke, but the odds are long.

George Kottaras — C

Born: 5/10/1983 Age: 31
Bats: L Throws: R Height: 6' 0"
Weight: 200 Breakout: 0%
Improve: 33% Collapse: 8%
Attrition: 12% MLB: 94%

Comparables:
Chris Snyder, Johnny Romano, Darren Daulton

YEAR	TEAM	LVL	AGE	PA	R	2B	3B	HR	RBI	BB	SO	SB	CS	AVG/OBP/SLG	TAv	BABIP	BRR	FRAA	WARP
2011	NAS	AAA	28	118	19	8	1	4	21	16	29	0	1	.343/.432/.559	.273	.449	-0.4	C(18): 0.3	0.4
2011	MIL	MLB	28	123	15	6	1	5	17	10	26	0	1	.252/.311/.459	.265	.284	0	C(36): 0.0	0.5
2012	OAK	MLB	29	93	10	2	1	6	19	8	24	0	0	.212/.280/.471	.274	.218	-0.5	C(27): 0.6	0.5
2012	MIL	MLB	29	116	10	4	0	3	12	29	24	0	0	.209/.409/.360	.276	.254	-0.2	C(27): -0.6, 1B(6): -0.1	0.5
2013	KCA	MLB	30	126	13	4	0	5	12	24	42	1	0	.180/.349/.370	.265	.245	-0.3	C(39): -0.6	0.5
2014	CHN	MLB	31	250	29	11	1	8	28	33	60	1	0	.220/.325/.386	.261	.260	-0.4	C -1, 1B -0	1.1

He can't hit a lick, but that's okay, as Kottaras can get on base via the walk. On a Royals team that is base on balls challenged, his 19 percent walk rate—even in the small sample size that comes with being a backup backstop—was notable. It was also the sole reason to keep him around, as his defense is below-average. Last year, though, he managed to gun down 26 percent of attempted stolen bases, right around average. Compare that to his career rate of 18 percent and you'd be wise to give credit to the Royals pitchers for keeping the runners close. The Cubs, who plucked him in December, could do worse when choosing a spare receiver and left-handed bat to come off the bench.

Junior Lake — SS

Born: 3/27/1990 Age: 24
Bats: R Throws: R Height: 6' 3"
Weight: 215 Breakout: 1%
Improve: 26% Collapse: 11%
Attrition: 18% MLB: 55%

Comparables:
Luke Hughes, Russell Mitchell, Joel Guzman

YEAR	TEAM	LVL	AGE	PA	R	2B	3B	HR	RBI	BB	SO	SB	CS	AVG/OBP/SLG	TAv	BABIP	BRR	FRAA	WARP
2011	DAY	A+	21	216	39	11	4	6	34	6	49	19	4	.315/.336/.498	.207	.384	0.6	SS(13): 1.3	0.2
2011	TEN	AA	21	262	41	10	2	6	17	13	60	19	2	.248/.300/.380	.217	.307	2.7	SS(50): 5.6, 3B(1): -0.0	0.9
2012	TEN	AA	22	448	56	26	3	10	50	35	105	21	12	.279/.341/.432	.281	.353	-0.4	SS(72): 0.8, 3B(29): 0.5	2.6
2013	IOW	AAA	23	170	30	10	2	4	18	10	33	14	5	.295/.341/.462	.287	.347	1.9	3B(36): 2.1, RF(6): -0.2	1.2
2013	CHN	MLB	23	254	26	16	0	6	16	13	68	4	4	.284/.332/.428	.280	.377	0.2	LF(32): 0.2, CF(27): -0.4	1.5
2014	CHN	MLB	24	267	30	13	1	6	27	12	72	11	4	.247/.288/.376	.245	.320	0.6	SS 1, LF 0	0.6

In the Cubs' fully stacked deck of hitting prospects, Lake is clearly the wild card. He's blessed with speed, raw power, a cannon arm and a penchant for errors and mental mistakes, and few players can look quite as good or quite as bad as Lake. Last year the good far outweighed the bad, as the former shortstop moved to the outfield and put his tools on full display during a half-season tour of the National League. The young Dominican can turn around fastballs with the best of them but struggles with breaking stuff, leading to plenty of strikeouts and a walk rate that will likely never support a high on-base percentage. His game needs polish both at the plate and in the field, and as pitchers learn to take advantage of his aggressive approach Lake will need to adjust. If everything breaks right, he could become a lunch-menu version of Alfonso Soriano; if not, his contact issues will make him a constant tease.

Donnie Murphy   3B
Born: 3/10/1983 Age: 31
Bats: R Throws: R Height: 5' 10"
Weight: 190 Breakout: 3%
Improve: 18% Collapse: 11%
Attrition: 29% MLB: 60%
Comparables:
Justin Ruggiano, Brooks Conrad, Laynce Nix

YEAR	TEAM	LVL	AGE	PA	R	2B	3B	HR	RBI	BB	SO	SB	CS	AVG/OBP/SLG	TAv	BABIP	BRR	FRAA	WARP
2011	JUP	A+	28	30	4	0	1	0	2	5	6	0	0	.130/.333/.217	.235	.176	0.4	3B(5): -0.4, SS(1): 0.0	0.0
2011	NWO	AAA	28	26	3	2	0	0	2	3	4	0	0	.087/.192/.174	.136	.105	0		0.0
2011	FLO	MLB	28	100	10	4	1	2	9	4	21	0	0	.185/.240/.315	.196	.214	0.6	SS(18): 0.1, 3B(15): 0.4	-0.2
2012	NWO	AAA	29	125	21	6	0	13	25	14	28	1	0	.302/.400/.726	.378	.288	-2.4	2B(19): -1.9, SS(11): 0.9	1.6
2012	MIA	MLB	29	129	13	6	2	3	12	9	35	1	1	.216/.281/.379	.243	.278	-0.9	3B(22): -2.9, 2B(13): -0.0	-0.4
2013	IOW	AAA	30	340	32	18	2	12	41	27	75	5	3	.265/.338/.457	.277	.312	-2.6	SS(73): -5.2, 2B(7): -0.2	0.9
2013	CHN	MLB	30	163	23	8	0	11	23	8	48	2	0	.255/.319/.530	.290	.300	0.5	3B(40): -2.0, SS(3): -0.3	0.9
2014	CHN	MLB	31	250	29	11	1	11	35	16	66	2	1	.236/.298/.442	.264	.280	-0.2	3B -3, SS -1	0.5

The first weeks of his Cubs career were worthy of a Tangerine Dream soundtrack, as Murphy blasted eight home runs and posted a .328/.381/.810 line during a magical 16-game stretch. It didn't last, of course, as the veteran utility infielder went off the tracks to the tune of .209/.280/.352 the rest of the way, showing why he's now in his seventh organization. With decent pop for a backup infielder, Murphy has his uses as a pinch-hitter and double-switch enabler, but is overexposed in a starting role. Look for him to ride the rails between Triple-A and The Show for a few more years.

Mike Olt   3B
Born: 8/27/1988 Age: 25
Bats: R Throws: R Height: 6' 2"
Weight: 210 Breakout: 8%
Improve: 19% Collapse: 11%
Attrition: 22% MLB: 48%
Comparables:
Mat Gamel, Zach Lutz, Brandon Wood

YEAR	TEAM	LVL	AGE	PA	R	2B	3B	HR	RBI	BB	SO	SB	CS	AVG/OBP/SLG	TAv	BABIP	BRR	FRAA	WARP
2011	MYR	A+	22	292	39	15	0	14	42	48	70	0	1	.267/.387/.504	.324	.314	-3.8	3B(56): 9.0	3.1
2012	FRI	AA	23	421	65	17	1	28	82	61	101	4	0	.288/.398/.579	.339	.327	1.7	3B(78): 0.9, 1B(13): -0.9	5.1
2012	TEX	MLB	23	40	2	1	0	0	5	5	13	1	1	.152/.250/.182	.205	.227	-1.3	1B(8): 0.8, 3B(5): 0.3	-0.2
2013	IOW	AAA	24	152	11	3	1	3	8	20	37	0	0	.168/.276/.275	.213	.207	-0.9	3B(38): 2.5	0.0
2013	ROU	AAA	24	268	37	15	0	11	32	35	89	0	0	.213/.317/.422	.268	.288	0.6	3B(63): 5.1	1.5
2014	CHN	MLB	25	250	30	10	0	11	34	29	75	0	0	.223/.314/.422	.269	.280	-0.5	3B 3, 1B 0	1.1

Olt was on the fast track to Arlington until his career took a tragic turn last summer, when persistent blurred vision, possibly related to a Winter League beaning, affected his game and drove him off the diamond. Numerous treatments followed, and Olt was eventually able to retake the field but his production continued to suffer, until the Rangers sent him packing in the Matt Garza deadline deal. When he's right, Olt is an excellent defender at the hot corner, draws walks and overcomes his high strikeout rate by launching moonshots.

Cody Ransom   3B
Born: 2/17/1976 Age: 38
Bats: R Throws: R Height: 6' 2"
Weight: 200 Breakout: 0%
Improve: 15% Collapse: 15%
Attrition: 24% MLB: 59%
Comparables:
Jose Hernandez, Sal Fasano, Ron Cey

YEAR	TEAM	LVL	AGE	PA	R	2B	3B	HR	RBI	BB	SO	SB	CS	AVG/OBP/SLG	TAv	BABIP	BRR	FRAA	WARP
2011	RNO	AAA	35	432	86	29	3	27	92	55	94	10	3	.317/.405/.629	.277	.358	0.7	SS(23): 0.9, 3B(13): -1.1	0.8
2011	ARI	MLB	35	37	3	2	0	1	4	3	9	1	0	.152/.243/.303	.189	.174	0.5	SS(8): 0.3, 3B(6): 0.3	-0.1
2012	RNO	AAA	36	40	5	2	0	2	9	6	14	0	0	.294/.400/.529	.304	.444	0.1	SS(9): -0.1, 3B(1): -0.1	0.4
2012	ARI	MLB	36	88	11	7	0	5	16	7	30	0	0	.269/.352/.551	.308	.372	-0.2	3B(18): -0.7, SS(7): -0.3	0.5
2012	MIL	MLB	36	194	18	7	0	6	26	23	79	0	1	.196/.293/.345	.225	.325	0.7	SS(41): 0.4, 3B(17): 1.1	0.3
2013	CHN	MLB	37	182	21	10	1	9	20	22	57	0	0	.203/.304/.449	.264	.250	1.4	3B(42): 2.3, 1B(4): -0.3	0.9
2013	SDN	MLB	37	11	0	0	0	0	0	0	5	0	0	.000/.000/.000	.011	.000	0	3B(4): 0.2	-0.2
2014	CHN	MLB	38	250	28	11	0	8	28	23	80	2	1	.207/.287/.372	.241	.280	-0.2	3B -2, SS -0	0.1

For the first time in a professional career spanning 16 seasons, Ransom didn't play a single game in the minors. Released by the Padres in April but claimed by the Cubs to help keep the hot corner warm for Mike Olt, or Christian Villanueva, or Kris Bryant, or Javier Baez, or Junior Lake, the veteran infielder was in at least one respect baseball's leading slugger last year: A whopping 63 percent of his hits went for extra bases, edging out Chris Davis, Khris Davis, and indeed Everyman Davis with as many plate appearances as him. The Cubs couldn't help but notice this was due more to a lack of singles than a surfeit of long hits, and released him in September. Fun times ahead, though: The Ransoms are going to Japan!

Anthony Rizzo 1B

Born: 8/8/1989 Age: 24
Bats: L Throws: L Height: 6' 3"
Weight: 240 Breakout: 4%
Improve: 61% Collapse: 3%
Attrition: 7% MLB: 99%

Comparables:
Ike Davis, Prince Fielder, Evan Longoria

YEAR	TEAM	LVL	AGE	PA	R	2B	3B	HR	RBI	BB	SO	SB	CS	AVG/OBP/SLG	TAv	BABIP	BRR	FRAA	WARP
2011	TUC	AAA	21	413	64	34	1	26	101	43	89	7	6	.331/.404/.652	.339	.369	2.6	1B(80): 10.0	5.4
2011	SDN	MLB	21	153	9	8	1	1	9	21	46	2	1	.141/.281/.242	.221	.210	-2.3	1B(45): -2.3	-1.0
2012	IOW	AAA	22	284	48	18	2	23	62	23	52	2	2	.342/.405/.696	.372	.357	-3.2	1B(66): 10.4	4.7
2012	CHN	MLB	22	368	44	15	0	15	48	27	62	3	2	.285/.342/.463	.289	.310	-0.7	1B(85): -0.8	1.6
2013	CHN	MLB	23	690	71	40	2	23	80	76	127	6	5	.233/.323/.419	.264	.258	-1.8	1B(159): 11.1	2.3
2014	CHN	MLB	24	618	78	34	1	27	88	56	129	5	4	.258/.332/.468	.289	.290	-1.4	1B 8	3.1

Rizzo was a revelation with the leather last season, posting the second-highest mark among first basemen in our Fielding Runs Above Average metric. Which is nice, but the Cubs are paying him to be a middle-of-the-order force, not the second coming of Doug Mientkiewicz. Rizzo led the team in home runs, but his .419 slugging percentage ranked 22nd among big-league first basemen, and he was helpless against same-side pitching. That last bit might just be a sample size fluke, as Rizzo never exhibited such ghastly platoon splits in the minors, but his .282 TAv against righties isn't exactly eye-popping, either. On the plus side, his walk rate is climbing and should eventually overcome his perpetually low batting average. With their plethora of minor-league bats overwhelmingly right-handed, the Cubs are counting on Rizzo to balance their future championship lineup, so he'll need to amp up the power posthaste.

Justin Ruggiano CF

Born: 4/12/1982 Age: 32
Bats: R Throws: R Height: 6' 1"
Weight: 210 Breakout: 2%
Improve: 31% Collapse: 2%
Attrition: 15% MLB: 93%

Comparables:
Rick Ankiel, Howard Johnson, Jim Edmonds

YEAR	TEAM	LVL	AGE	PA	R	2B	3B	HR	RBI	BB	SO	SB	CS	AVG/OBP/SLG	TAv	BABIP	BRR	FRAA	WARP
2011	DUR	AAA	29	190	29	13	1	7	34	20	42	12	2	.304/.378/.518	.258	.370	-0.3	LF(7): 0.6, RF(4): -0.1	0.1
2011	TBA	MLB	29	111	11	4	0	4	13	4	26	1	1	.248/.273/.400	.255	.289	-1.7	LF(27): 1.5, RF(6): 0.0	0.2
2012	OKL	AAA	30	138	21	13	1	5	29	18	24	5	3	.325/.409/.581	.325	.367	0.3	CF(21): -2.1, RF(7): 0.1	1.3
2012	MIA	MLB	30	320	38	23	1	13	36	29	84	14	8	.313/.374/.535	.323	.401	-0.1	CF(52): 2.3, LF(31): -1.1	2.9
2013	MIA	MLB	31	472	49	18	1	18	50	41	114	15	8	.222/.298/.396	.253	.260	1	CF(84): -2.7, LF(23): -0.4	0.7
2014	CHN	MLB	32	429	57	22	1	16	54	35	109	16	8	.250/.316/.434	.270	.300	0	CF -1, LF 1	1.6

Asking someone to repeat a .400 BABIP is like asking the Godfather for two favors on the day of his daughter's wedding. An exercise in the inflationary effects of luck, Ruggiano went from an OPS+ of 142 in 2012 to 90 in 2013 despite not doing anything differently. His walk rate, strikeout rate, home run rate, contact rate, swinging-strike rate all remained nearly identical to the previous season, but Ruggiano's magic beans didn't grow perennials. That said, he's a good player to have around until the Cubs' outfield of the future blossoms into full-time players, and his ability to play center field in a pinch makes him a useful reserve even without the magic beans.

Nate Schierholtz RF

Born: 2/15/1984 Age: 30
Bats: L Throws: R Height: 6' 2"
Weight: 215 Breakout: 0%
Improve: 47% Collapse: 7%
Attrition: 16% MLB: 99%

Comparables:
Moises Alou, Bubba Trammell, Kevin Bass

YEAR	TEAM	LVL	AGE	PA	R	2B	3B	HR	RBI	BB	SO	SB	CS	AVG/OBP/SLG	TAv	BABIP	BRR	FRAA	WARP
2011	SFN	MLB	27	362	42	22	1	9	41	21	61	7	4	.278/.326/.430	.288	.315	1.5	RF(96): -1.3, LF(8): 0.4	1.9
2012	PHI	MLB	28	73	5	4	0	1	5	5	10	0	0	.273/.319/.379	.257	.304	-0.1	RF(28): -0.6, CF(7): -0.2	0.1
2012	SFN	MLB	28	196	15	4	5	5	16	18	36	3	2	.251/.321/.417	.280	.287	-1.4	RF(52): -1.5	0.5
2013	CHN	MLB	29	503	56	32	3	21	68	29	94	6	3	.251/.301/.470	.274	.270	2.1	RF(126): 3.2	2.1
2014	CHN	MLB	30	428	46	23	2	12	51	27	77	6	3	.255/.307/.417	.262	.290	-0.4	RF 1, CF -0	1.0

If we were representing Schierholtz in an arbitration hearing, we'd be sure to point out that his 54 extra-base hits against righties last year tied Jay Bruce for the most among National League out-fielders. While his lefty stroke proved to be a terrific fit in Wrigley, such statistical cherry-picking hides the fact that Schierholtz doesn't hit for a high average, rarely walks, is stretched in center field and can't hit lefties. A 30-year-old platoon outfielder with decent speed and a serviceable glove, Schierholtz is a useful player, but as soon as those home runs start to die at the warning track, his salary will far outstrip his value.

Jorge Soler RF

Born: 2/25/1992 Age: 22
Bats: R Throws: R Height: 6' 4"
Weight: 215 Breakout: 1%
Improve: 14% Collapse: 2%
Attrition: 18% MLB: 27%

Comparables:
Shane Peterson, Domonic Brown, Aaron Cunningham

YEAR	TEAM	LVL	AGE	PA	R	2B	3B	HR	RBI	BB	SO	SB	CS	AVG/OBP/SLG	TAv	BABIP	BRR	FRAA	WARP
2012	PEO	A	20	88	14	5	0	3	15	6	6	4	1	.338/.398/.512	.333	.338	0.4	RF(19): 0.5	0.8
2013	DAY	A+	21	237	38	13	1	8	35	21	38	5	1	.281/.343/.467	.283	.304	1.8	RF(55): -0.9	1.1
2014	CHN	MLB	22	250	25	11	1	7	29	14	52	2	0	.239/.285/.384	.242	.280	-0.1	RF -1	0.0

Soler got off to a solid start in his first full season, drawing walks, showing a better hit tool than some had expected and beginning to tap into the raw power that his swing and large frame presage. His season was cut short by a stress fracture in his shin last June, keeping him out of game action until a rusty swing through the Arizona Fall League. More troubling to some, Soler was benched for not hustling and was suspended for five games after charging the opponent's dugout with a bat after a baserunning incident. The organization feels he's matured and isn't concerned about his makeup. The lost development time hurts, but Soler remains a top prospect with a prototypical right fielder's tool kit: speed, a laser arm and the potential for 30 knocks at his peak.

Ryan Sweeney   CF
Born: 2/20/1985 Age: 29
Bats: L Throws: L Height: 6' 4"
Weight: 225 Breakout: 1%
Improve: 45% Collapse: 2%
Attrition: 9% MLB: 98%

Comparables:
Jacoby Ellsbury, David DeJesus, Coco Crisp

YEAR	TEAM	LVL	AGE	PA	R	2B	3B	HR	RBI	BB	SO	SB	CS	AVG/OBP/SLG	TAv	BABIP	BRR	FRAA	WARP
2011	OAK	MLB	26	299	34	11	3	1	25	33	48	1	1	.265/.346/.341	.257	.319	-3.2	LF(41): -0.0, CF(34): 1.1	0.6
2012	BOS	MLB	27	219	22	19	2	0	16	12	43	0	0	.260/.303/.373	.234	.327	0.5	RF(49): 2.2, CF(19): -0.3	0.1
2013	IOW	AAA	28	91	12	2	2	6	16	8	15	1	0	.337/.396/.627	.337	.355	-0.6	RF(16): -0.8, LF(4): 0.1	0.6
2013	CHN	MLB	28	212	19	13	2	6	19	17	31	1	0	.266/.324/.448	.282	.288	-2	CF(45): 5.4, LF(10): 0.6	1.7
2014	CHN	MLB	29	250	24	14	2	4	26	20	39	1	0	.273/.333/.397	.268	.310	-0.3	CF 2, RF 1	1.1

A former top prospect with size and an attractive lefty swing, Sweeney's much-anticipated Power Bat Accessory Kit was finally delivered last summer—10 years late, and to the wrong Chicago address. Watching the former White Sox farmhand post something resembling a big boy slugging percentage while roaming Wrigley's center pasture must have rankled a few fans on the South Side, but let's not get carried away here: six home runs and 21 extra-base hits do not a Jim Edmonds make. Sweeney has a patient approach and showed the Cubs enough defensive versatility and offensive near-adequacy to earn a two-year, $3.5 million deal. He'll serve as a stopgap center fielder and fourth outfielder, a role Sweeney is perfectly capable of filling even if his power proves to be as fleeting as Brigadoon.

Matthew Szczur   CF
Born: 7/20/1989 Age: 24
Bats: R Throws: R Height: 6' 1"
Weight: 195 Breakout: 9%
Improve: 16% Collapse: 4%
Attrition: 17% MLB: 30%

Comparables:
Denard Span, Todd Cunningham, Darin Mastroianni

YEAR	TEAM	LVL	AGE	PA	R	2B	3B	HR	RBI	BB	SO	SB	CS	AVG/OBP/SLG	TAv	BABIP	BRR	FRAA	WARP
2011	PEO	A	21	298	55	15	1	5	27	21	28	17	5	.314/.366/.431	.301	.335	2	CF(39): 1.5, RF(8): -0.7	1.9
2011	DAY	A+	21	182	20	7	2	5	19	5	20	7	0	.260/.283/.410	.221	.268	0.8	CF(14): 0.8	0.0
2012	DAY	A+	22	352	68	19	4	2	34	47	50	38	12	.295/.394/.407	.283	.344	4.2	CF(50): 5.0, LF(7): 1.1	2.9
2012	TEN	AA	22	158	24	7	4	2	6	14	29	4	2	.210/.285/.357	.238	.250	2.7	CF(20): 0.1, RF(12): 1.4	0.4
2013	TEN	AA	23	574	78	27	4	3	44	50	75	22	12	.281/.350/.367	.264	.323	2.6	CF(92): -0.6, RF(23): -0.9	2.2
2014	CHN	MLB	24	250	28	11	1	3	18	16	46	9	3	.244/.297/.339	.234	.290	0.5	CF 2, RF -0	0.3

A former football wideout at Villanova, Szczur continues to use his blazing speed to run down gappers and flash a plus outfield glove, but the rest of his game is still a work in progress. He makes contact, uses his legs to reach base and isn't allergic to ball four, but his stolen base totals and success rate have declined and he'll never develop enough power to profile as a major-league regular. Still, his rare combination of speed, defense and consonant-rich surname could earn him a few years on a major-league bench.

Luis Valbuena   3B
Born: 11/30/1985 Age: 28
Bats: L Throws: R Height: 5' 10"
Weight: 170 Breakout: 4%
Improve: 46% Collapse: 8%
Attrition: 15% MLB: 88%

Comparables:
Casey McGehee, Jose Bautista, Danny Valencia

YEAR	TEAM	LVL	AGE	PA	R	2B	3B	HR	RBI	BB	SO	SB	CS	AVG/OBP/SLG	TAv	BABIP	BRR	FRAA	WARP
2011	COH	AAA	25	472	64	22	0	17	75	46	96	6	3	.302/.372/.476	.242	.355	-2.8	SS(32): -3.7, 2B(6): -0.3	-0.3
2011	CLE	MLB	25	44	4	0	0	1	1	1	9	1	0	.209/.227/.279	.183	.242	0.4	2B(11): -0.8, LF(2): -0.1	-0.3
2012	IOW	AAA	26	246	38	17	1	8	31	28	50	1	1	.303/.378/.507	.309	.352	0.8	SS(44): 1.8, 2B(9): 0.2	2.5
2012	CHN	MLB	26	303	26	20	0	4	28	36	55	0	2	.219/.310/.340	.237	.260	-0.5	3B(82): -0.6, 2B(5): -0.2	0.3
2013	CHN	MLB	27	391	34	15	1	12	37	53	63	1	4	.218/.331/.378	.260	.233	-0.2	3B(94): -1.8, 2B(6): -0.1	1.2
2014	CHN	MLB	28	381	39	19	1	9	42	39	76	2	2	.233/.315/.379	.254	.270	-0.9	3B -3, SS -0	0.4

Valbuena was a pleasant surprise on the North Side last summer, as the well-traveled infielder showed good pop and an uncharacteristically flashy glove while manning the hot corner. Always patient at the plate, Valbuena waits for his pitch and then swings from his heels, producing lots of fly balls, occasional home runs and a minuscule batting average. He draws enough walks to keep his OBP above sea level and hangs in well against lefties, but if he's your everyday third baseman, you're settling.

Christian Villanueva 3B

Born: 6/19/1991 Age: 23
Bats: R Throws: R Height: 5' 11"
Weight: 160 Breakout: 1%
Improve: 15% Collapse: 2%
Attrition: 9% MLB: 24%

Comparables:
Cody Asche, Jedd Gyorko, Brandon Laird

YEAR	TEAM	LVL	AGE	PA	R	2B	3B	HR	RBI	BB	SO	SB	CS	AVG/OBP/SLG	TAv	BABIP	BRR	FRAA	WARP
2011	HIC	A	20	529	78	30	3	17	84	37	86	32	6	.278/.338/.465	.288	.300	3.8	3B(112): 14.2, SS(2): 0.2	5.4
2012	MYR	A+	21	425	45	19	1	10	59	24	83	9	9	.285/.356/.421	.297	.338	-2.4	3B(90): -8.1, 2B(4): 0.5	2.4
2012	DAY	A+	21	95	14	5	0	4	9	10	24	5	2	.250/.337/.452	.264	.304	-0.1	3B(24): 4.5	1.0
2013	TEN	AA	22	542	60	41	2	19	72	34	117	5	7	.261/.317/.469	.275	.303	1.8	3B(124): -1.1	2.3
2014	CHN	MLB	23	250	26	13	0	8	29	10	61	3	2	.236/.278/.392	.241	.280	-0.3	3B 0, 2B 0	0.2

The Rodney Dangerfield of Cubs prospects, all Villanueva did last year in his first taste of the upper minors was hit more doubles and extra-base hits than anyone else in Double-A, launch 19 home runs and flash Gold Glove-quality defense at the hot corner. Yet there are those who dislike his hitchy swing, see little power projection in his slim frame and fret over the utility of his hit tool. Villanueva may not have the highest ceiling, but his mature approach, gap power, proven production and solid makeup give him a better chance to reach it than most 22-year-olds.

Josh Vitters   3B

Born: 8/27/1989 Age: 24
Bats: R Throws: R Height: 6' 2"
Weight: 200 Breakout: 1%
Improve: 17% Collapse: 17%
Attrition: 25% MLB: 47%

Comparables:
Ryan Wheeler, Brent Morel, Brandon Laird

YEAR	TEAM	LVL	AGE	PA	R	2B	3B	HR	RBI	BB	SO	SB	CS	AVG/OBP/SLG	TAv	BABIP	BRR	FRAA	WARP
2011	TEN	AA	21	488	56	28	2	14	81	22	54	4	10	.283/.322/.448	.252	.290	-2	3B(71): -6.0, 1B(24): -0.4	-0.2
2012	IOW	AAA	22	452	54	32	2	17	68	30	77	6	3	.304/.356/.513	.301	.337	0.1	3B(95): -2.2, 1B(9): -0.6	2.7
2012	CHN	MLB	22	109	7	2	0	2	5	7	33	2	0	.121/.193/.202	.153	.154	-0.7	3B(29): -1.1	-1.2
2013	IOW	AAA	23	100	14	4	0	5	12	11	19	1	0	.295/.380/.511	.305	.328	0	3B(18): -2.0, 1B(4): 0.1	0.6
2014	CHN	MLB	24	250	26	12	1	8	30	13	52	2	1	.240/.288/.397	.250	.280	-0.5	3B -4, 1B -0	-0.2

Vitters struggled to stay on the field last season, as a succession of minor injuries limited him to 28 Triple-A games and guaranteed yet another year of unfulfilled promise. When he did play, Vitters showed a more discriminating plate approach that led to a much-improved walk rate, while maintaining the batting average and power he showed in 2012. The former top prospect is now also a former third baseman, as the organization has shelved his TV-MA infielder's glove and is moving him to left field. Playing an outfield corner raises the offensive bar, and the acrid smoke from his MLB flameout two years ago still hangs in the air, but if Vitters can finally overcome his career-long struggle to differentiate the pitches he *can* hit from those he *should* hit, he might still carve out a career.

Dan Vogelbach   1B

Born: 12/17/1992 Age: 21
Bats: L Throws: R Height: 6' 0"
Weight: 250 Breakout: 2%
Improve: 11% Collapse: 1%
Attrition: 5% MLB: 22%

Comparables:
Anthony Rizzo, Chris Marrero, Thomas Neal

YEAR	TEAM	LVL	AGE	PA	R	2B	3B	HR	RBI	BB	SO	SB	CS	AVG/OBP/SLG	TAv	BABIP	BRR	FRAA	WARP
2012	BOI	A-	19	168	23	9	1	10	31	23	34	0	1	.322/.423/.608	.341	.364	-0.3	1B(29): -2.4	1.3
2013	KNC	A	20	502	55	21	0	17	71	57	76	4	4	.284/.364/.450	.288	.305	-5.6	1B(85): -0.7	1.4
2013	DAY	A+	20	66	13	2	0	2	5	16	13	1	0	.280/.455/.440	.322	.343	0.7	1B(7): -0.2	0.6
2014	CHN	MLB	21	250	26	10	0	9	31	21	60	0	0	.230/.297/.389	.249	.270	-0.5	1B -1	-0.1

He may look like every bar league's slo-pitch slugger with "Tiny" stenciled on his uniform, but once you see Vogelbach use his compact lefty stroke to launch shots from gap to gap or far beyond the right-field fence, you'll know why scouts take his future seriously. The former second-round pick is a liability with the glove but hits what he swings at, can work a walk and showed enough during his Low-A debut that the organization added his light-tower power to the Daytona roster for the August stretch run. As a DH-in-waiting he'll have to keep mashing to keep moving, but Vogelbach might just have the talent and makeup to leverage his bat into a big-league career.

Casper Wells   LF

Born: 11/23/1984 Age: 29
Bats: R Throws: R Height: 6' 2"
Weight: 220 Breakout: 5%
Improve: 35% Collapse: 3%
Attrition: 8% MLB: 76%

Comparables:
Fred Lewis, Marcus Thames, Ryan Raburn

YEAR	TEAM	LVL	AGE	PA	R	2B	3B	HR	RBI	BB	SO	SB	CS	AVG/OBP/SLG	TAv	BABIP	BRR	FRAA	WARP
2011	TOL	AAA	26	30	4	2	2	2	6	3	8	0	0	.370/.433/.815	.384	.471	-0.6	RF(3): 0.2	0.2
2011	DET	MLB	26	125	16	10	0	4	12	9	29	1	0	.257/.323/.451	.273	.312	-0.3	RF(52): 0.6, LF(6): 0.3	0.8
2011	SEA	MLB	26	116	14	1	0	7	15	9	42	2	2	.216/.310/.431	.288	.283	-0.4	LF(15): 1.4, RF(6): -0.2	0.7
2012	TAC	AAA	27	95	18	7	2	2	14	20	17	2	1	.239/.415/.479	.325	.283	0.8	RF(12): 0.6, LF(6): -0.4	1.0
2012	SEA	MLB	27	316	42	12	3	10	36	26	80	3	0	.228/.302/.396	.262	.282	-0.2	LF(52): 0.5, RF(25): -1.9	0.6
2013	PHI	MLB	28	26	2	1	0	0	0	2	8	0	0	.042/.115/.083	.122	.062	0.2	CF(3): 0.0, RF(2): 0.1	-0.3
2013	CHA	MLB	28	71	4	1	0	0	1	5	22	0	1	.167/.225/.182	.156	.250	-1.4	LF(14): 0.7, RF(9): -0.0	-0.7
2013	OAK	MLB	28	5	0	0	0	0	0	0	1	0	0	.000/.000/.000	.013	.000	0	LF(2): -0.1	-0.2
2014	CHN	MLB	29	250	29	11	2	9	30	21	67	2	2	.226/.302/.408	.260	.280	-0.3	LF 1, RF -1	0.5

Some day, Casper Wells' 2013 season will make for a fantastic trivia question. He wore the uniforms of five different teams, starting with the Mariners through March, going to the Jays between April 10-15, the Athletics from April 22-29, the White Sox from April 29-August 8, and the Phillies through the end of the season. Overall, he hit .126 on the season in 102 trips to the dish. His season ended in late August due to vision problems. He'll be on the comeback trail in 2014 and, if not for the .126 average, would be well on his way to setting the record for different uniforms worn during a career.

PITCHERS

Jake Arrieta

Born: 3/6/1986 Age: 28
Bats: R Throws: R Height: 6' 4" Weight: 225
Breakout: 17% Improve: 58% Collapse: 24%
Attrition: 38% MLB: 74%

Comparables:
Armando Galarraga, Brian Burres, Jeff Samardzija

YEAR	TEAM	LVL	AGE	W	L	SV	G	GS	IP	H	HR	BB	SO	BB9	SO9	GB%	BABIP	WHIP	ERA	FIP	FRA	WARP
2011	BAL	MLB	25	10	8	0	22	22	119¹	115	21	59	93	4.4	7.0	47%	.274	1.46	5.05	5.37	6.27	-0.6
2012	NOR	AAA	26	5	4	0	10	10	56	46	3	28	54	4.5	8.7	48%	.287	1.32	4.02	3.64	4.79	0.1
2012	BAL	MLB	26	3	9	0	24	18	114²	122	16	35	109	2.7	8.6	47%	.320	1.37	6.20	4.01	4.79	1.0
2013	NOR	AAA	27	5	3	0	9	8	49	45	4	14	38	2.6	7.0	52%	.285	1.20	4.41	3.63	4.80	0.2
2013	IOW	AAA	27	2	2	0	7	7	30¹	32	2	16	39	4.7	11.6	51%	.387	1.58	3.56	3.64	4.24	0.5
2013	CHN	MLB	27	4	2	0	9	9	51²	34	7	24	37	4.2	6.4	46%	.199	1.12	3.66	4.92	5.88	-0.4
2013	BAL	MLB	27	1	2	0	5	5	23²	25	2	17	23	6.5	8.7	33%	.343	1.77	7.23	4.64	4.87	0.1
2014	CHN	MLB	28	7	10	0	25	25	141	126	16	56	120	3.6	7.6	45%	.291	1.29	4.08	4.35	4.44	0.7

After a disastrous first half in Baltimore, Arrieta was traded to the Cubs at midseason and rebounded to post a mediocre ERA and "earn" a rotation shot going forward. The scare quotes are there due to Arrieta's continued dreadful peripherals, as the big righty suffered significant leakage in his strikeout and home run rates while still walking too many batters, leading to an alarming FIP in Chicago. Arrieta looks the part of an innings eater, with an ideal frame, a heavy sinker that can reach the mid-90s and two usable breaking pitches, yet still misses fewer bats than Kyle Lohse or Barry Zito. Worst of all, his results deteriorate as a game wears on, with hitters posting an .855 OPS the second time they face him, compared to .685 in their first at-bat. Running Arrieta out every fifth day is just setting him up to fail, and the Cubs would be wise to find out if his stuff will play up in the bullpen.

Scott Baker

Born: 9/19/1981 Age: 32
Bats: R Throws: R Height: 6' 4" Weight: 215
Breakout: 19% Improve: 47% Collapse: 29%
Attrition: 10% MLB: 84%

Comparables:
Ben Sheets, Aaron Harang, Freddy Garcia

YEAR	TEAM	LVL	AGE	W	L	SV	G	GS	IP	H	HR	BB	SO	BB9	SO9	GB%	BABIP	WHIP	ERA	FIP	FRA	WARP
2011	MIN	MLB	29	8	6	0	23	21	134²	126	15	32	123	2.1	8.2	36%	.293	1.17	3.14	3.48	4.16	1.9
2013	KNC	A	31	1	2	0	6	6	23¹	29	4	8	14	3.1	5.4	36%	.325	1.59	6.17	5.40	6.74	-0.1
2013	CHN	MLB	31	0	0	0	3	3	15	9	3	4	6	2.4	3.6	28%	.100	0.87	3.60	5.62	7.05	-0.2
2014	CHN	MLB	32	2	2	0	6	6	38²	35	5	9	33	2.2	7.7	36%	.292	1.16	3.64	3.95	3.95	0.4

The Cubs dropped $5.5 million on the pass line when they signed Baker prior to last season, hoping the former Twin would recover from Tommy John surgery quickly enough to be flippable for a choice prospect or two. The dice came up boxcars, however, as Baker didn't see a big-league mound until September and left his fastball velocity on the operating table. Baker was once stingy with ball four and sported a surprisingly robust strikeout rate, but has missed time in each of the past seven seasons and is on the wrong side of 30, clouding his future.

Daniel Bard

Born: 6/25/1985 Age: 29
Bats: R Throws: R Height: 6' 4" Weight: 215
Breakout: 35% Improve: 57% Collapse: 27%
Attrition: 14% MLB: 85%

Comparables:
David Aardsma, Neal Cotts, Jose Arredondo

YEAR	TEAM	LVL	AGE	W	L	SV	G	GS	IP	H	HR	BB	SO	BB9	SO9	GB%	BABIP	WHIP	ERA	FIP	FRA	WARP
2011	BOS	MLB	26	2	9	1	70	0	73	46	5	24	74	3.0	9.1	54%	.224	0.96	3.33	2.99	3.49	1.4
2012	PAW	AAA	27	3	2	0	31	1	32	31	2	29	32	8.2	9.0	56%	.322	1.88	7.03	5.63	6.85	-0.7
2012	BOS	MLB	27	5	6	0	17	10	59¹	60	9	43	38	6.5	5.8	44%	.288	1.74	6.22	6.32	6.93	-0.6
2013	PME	AA	28	0	1	0	13	0	12²	13	1	17	6	12.1	4.3	51%	.300	2.37	6.39	7.43	8.70	-0.4
2013	BOS	MLB	28	0	0	0	2	0	1	1	0	2	1	18.0	9.0	33%	.333	3.00	9.00	7.08	10.69	-0.1
2014	CHN	MLB	29	2	1	0	31	2	37²	29	4	18	38	4.3	9.1	49%	.279	1.25	3.55	4.18	3.86	0.4

Whenever there's a highway accident, it can take hours after the wreckage is removed for traffic patterns to return to normal. Bard has to hope that his recent struggles are merely the after-effects of his disastrous 2012, when an ill-advised conversion from dominant set-up man to impotent starter seemingly cost him his mechanics, velocity and control. After he struggled to pick up the pieces in the minors, Boston released him in September and he was scooped up by the Cubs, who promptly non-tendered him in December. When last seen, his velocity was still way down from its upper-90s peak, but if he can work out his mechanical kinks, build confidence and focus on regaining some feel for his once-devastating fastball/slider combo, Bard could still help out a big-league 'pen.

Michael Bowden

Born: 9/9/1986 Age: 27
Bats: R Throws: R Height: 6' 3" Weight: 215
Breakout: 45% Improve: 72% Collapse: 15%
Attrition: 31% MLB: 65%

Comparables:
Kazuhito Tadano, Francisco Rosario, Cory Wade

YEAR	TEAM	LVL	AGE	W	L	SV	G	GS	IP	H	HR	BB	SO	BB9	SO9	GB%	BABIP	WHIP	ERA	FIP	FRA	WARP
2011	PAW	AAA	24	3	3	16	41	0	52²	43	5	18	61	3.1	10.4	39%	.284	1.16	2.73	3.24	4.25	0.6
2011	BOS	MLB	24	0	0	0	14	0	20	19	3	11	17	4.9	7.7	29%	.271	1.50	4.05	4.96	3.95	0.4
2012	IOW	AAA	25	3	2	2	23	0	32²	19	2	17	35	4.7	9.6	46%	.208	1.10	2.76	3.88	4.63	0.4
2012	CHN	MLB	25	0	0	0	30	0	36²	30	4	16	29	3.9	7.1	38%	.263	1.25	2.95	4.36	4.63	0.2
2012	BOS	MLB	25	0	0	0	2	0	3	2	1	1	3	3.0	9.0	57%	.167	1.00	3.00	6.38	5.76	0.0
2013	IOW	AAA	26	0	0	2	13	0	18²	14	1	3	28	1.4	13.5	40%	.310	0.91	2.41	1.75	2.67	0.6
2013	CHN	MLB	26	1	3	0	34	0	37²	32	3	15	23	3.6	5.5	35%	.259	1.25	4.30	4.27	4.44	0.1
2014	CHN	MLB	27	2	2	0	31	3	51	45	6	18	41	3.3	7.3	36%	.283	1.25	3.85	4.26	4.18	0.4

The former Boston first-rounder couldn't keep a spot in one of the league's worst bullpens last summer, as the Cubs twice designated Bowden for assignment—the second time to make room for a 37-year-old Korean sidewinder on the rebuilding club's September roster. If that's not the definition of discouraging, it's at least a wordy synonym. Bowden has subpar velocity and forgettable secondary stuff, and doesn't miss bats or get groundouts, making him a likely fixture in Triple-A bullpens for the foreseeable future.

Alberto Cabrera

Born: 10/25/1988 Age: 25
Bats: R Throws: R Height: 6' 4" Weight: 210
Breakout: 42% Improve: 58% Collapse: 19%
Attrition: 72% MLB: 20%

Comparables:
Brayan Villarreal, Josh Zeid, Sandy Rosario

YEAR	TEAM	LVL	AGE	W	L	SV	G	GS	IP	H	HR	BB	SO	BB9	SO9	GB%	BABIP	WHIP	ERA	FIP	FRA	WARP
2011	TEN	AA	22	6	2	0	9	9	48²	60	4	21	34	3.9	6.3	41%	.318	1.66	5.36	4.40	5.90	0.2
2011	IOW	AAA	22	3	6	0	19	17	88²	118	11	53	67	5.4	6.8	48%	.379	1.93	6.60	5.78	6.57	0.1
2012	TEN	AA	23	2	1	5	23	0	35²	30	2	10	45	2.5	11.4	51%	.304	1.12	2.52	2.19	2.67	1.0
2012	IOW	AAA	23	2	0	0	13	0	19¹	29	4	4	29	1.9	13.5	50%	.481	1.71	4.19	4.29	4.29	0.5
2012	CHN	MLB	23	1	1	0	25	0	21²	16	1	18	27	7.5	11.2	43%	.288	1.57	5.40	3.87	4.01	0.1
2013	TEN	AA	24	9	3	0	18	18	112²	102	10	39	107	3.1	8.5	54%	.307	1.25	3.20	3.34	4.43	0.7
2013	IOW	AAA	24	1	3	0	15	0	20¹	26	4	12	19	5.3	8.4	40%	.361	1.87	7.08	6.03	5.85	-0.1
2013	CHN	MLB	24	0	0	0	7	0	6	7	0	5	4	7.5	6.0	37%	.368	2.00	4.50	4.69	4.58	0.0
2014	CHN	MLB	25	5	7	0	35	15	108²	113	14	49	88	4.1	7.3	46%	.319	1.49	5.11	4.77	5.56	-0.9

Your garden variety live-armed relief suspect, Cabrera can unleash a moving mid-90s fastball, a slider that gives righties fits, and a changeup that fools experienced lefty hitters approximately none of the time. The Cubs have finally given up on him as a starter and moved him to the 'pen, where he struggled down the stretch and in a brief September call-up. Given that he held righties to a .219/.301/.337 line last year—numbers consistent with his career—there's some hope they can teach him how to ROOGY.

C.J. Edwards

Born: 9/3/1991 Age: 22
Bats: R Throws: R Height: 6' 2" Weight: 155
Breakout: 41% Improve: 58% Collapse: 19%
Attrition: 29% MLB: 36%

Comparables:
Jake McGee, Danny Duffy, Tommy Hanson

YEAR	TEAM	LVL	AGE	W	L	SV	G	GS	IP	H	HR	BB	SO	BB9	SO9	GB%	BABIP	WHIP	ERA	FIP	FRA	WARP
2012	SPO	A-	20	2	3	0	10	10	47	26	0	19	60	3.6	11.5	50%	.250	0.96	2.11	2.11	2.81	1.5
2013	HIC	A	21	8	2	0	18	18	93¹	62	0	34	122	3.3	11.8	54%	.268	1.03	1.83	2.06	2.57	2.9
2013	DAY	A+	21	0	0	0	6	6	23	14	1	7	33	2.7	12.9	43%	.260	0.91	1.96	1.85	2.37	0.7
2014	CHN	MLB	22	4	5	0	19	14	89	75	9	41	88	4.1	8.9	47%	.299	1.30	3.87	4.03	4.21	0.7

Part of the package sent to Chicago in exchange for Matt Garza, Edwards put himself on the prospect map by rampaging through the low minors, striking out 155 batters in 116 innings while keeping his walks in check. Tall and willowy, Edwards can whip mid-90s fastballs and works in a curveball and changeup, both of which could become above-average offerings. His ceiling is that of a fourth starter, though scouts question whether his Tekulve-esque build will hold up to a starter's workload. If he moves to the 'pen, his fastball may play up and make him a weapon in the late innings.

Kyuji Fujikawa

Born: 7/21/1980 Age: 33
Bats: L Throws: R Height: 6' 0" Weight: 190
Breakout: 21% Improve: 46% Collapse: 31%
Attrition: 20% MLB: 87%

Comparables:
Joel Peralta, Tyler Walker, Justin Miller

YEAR	TEAM	LVL	AGE	W	L	SV	G	GS	IP	H	HR	BB	SO	BB9	SO9	GB%	BABIP	WHIP	ERA	FIP	FRA	WARP
2011	HNS	NPB	31	3	3	41	56	0	51	25	2	13	80	2.3	14.1	%	.263	0.75	1.24	0.00	0.00	0.0
2012	HNS	NPB	30	2	2	24	48	0	47²	34	1	15	58	2.8	10.9	%	.300	1.03	1.32	0.00	0.00	0.0
2013	CHN	MLB	32	1	1	2	12	0	12	11	1	2	14	1.5	10.5	50%	.323	1.08	5.25	2.77	3.69	0.1
2014	CHN	MLB	33	2	1	3	36	0	38²	33	4	11	37	2.6	8.7	45%	.298	1.15	3.41	3.63	3.70	0.5

Fujikawa's first season in North America was a lost one, as the veteran Japanese closer welcomed two unwanted visitors: forearm pain in April, and Dr. James Andrews in June. With recovery time from Tommy John surgery generally taking more than a year, there will be precious little time for the Cubs to get any return on their two-year, $9.5 million investment, or determine whether to exercise their $5.5 million option for 2015. When he did take the mound, Fujikawa suffered two disasterpiece outings but posted solid peripherals, using excellent command of his fastball/splitter combo to strike out more than a man per inning and avoid ball four. It will be deep into the summer before we learn whether Fujikawa still has the goods to work late innings.

Kevin Gregg

Born: 6/20/1978 Age: 36
Bats: R Throws: R Height: 6' 6" Weight: 245
Breakout: 21% Improve: 55% Collapse: 28%
Attrition: 10% MLB: 73%

Comparables:
Dae-Sung Koo, Barney Schultz, Billy Taylor

YEAR	TEAM	LVL	AGE	W	L	SV	G	GS	IP	H	HR	BB	SO	BB9	SO9	GB%	BABIP	WHIP	ERA	FIP	FRA	WARP
2011	BAL	MLB	33	0	3	22	63	0	59²	58	7	40	53	6.0	8.0	44%	.295	1.64	4.37	4.92	5.48	0.0
2012	BAL	MLB	34	3	2	0	40	0	43²	50	6	24	37	4.9	7.6	48%	.338	1.69	4.95	4.99	6.40	-0.4
2013	CHN	MLB	35	2	6	33	62	0	62	53	6	32	56	4.6	8.1	38%	.272	1.37	3.48	4.07	4.65	0.0
2014	CHN	MLB	36	3	1	12	56	0	54²	47	6	25	52	4.2	8.6	41%	.294	1.33	4.09	4.23	4.45	0.2

It sure felt like progress to us when the Cubs were unable to deal Gregg at last year's deadline. Wisely resurrected from the scrap heap as insurance against the inevitable Carlos Marmol meltdown and the unforeseen Kyuji Fujikawa injury, Gregg took over the ninth inning in late April and racked up 22 saves before the end of July. Not a single contender bit, however, as the league collectively looked past Gregg's intestinal fortitude, "proven closer" imprimatur and single glittering counting stat, and saw instead a mediocre reliever with an untenable walk rate and no true out pitch. You can't blame the Cubs for trying, though, and to his credit Gregg was better last year than in his disastrous Orioles days. It's just that he shouldn't ever work high-leverage innings for a team that wants to compete.

Justin Grimm

Born: 8/16/1988 Age: 25
Bats: R Throws: R Height: 6' 3" Weight: 200
Breakout: 31% Improve: 54% Collapse: 21%
Attrition: 34% MLB: 85%

Comparables:
Anthony Bass, Enrique Gonzalez, Travis Wood

YEAR	TEAM	LVL	AGE	W	L	SV	G	GS	IP	H	HR	BB	SO	BB9	SO9	GB%	BABIP	WHIP	ERA	FIP	FRA	WARP
2011	HIC	A	22	2	1	0	9	9	50¹	45	5	18	54	3.2	9.7	43%	.301	1.25	3.40	3.92	4.74	0.7
2011	MYR	A+	22	5	2	0	16	16	90¹	84	2	30	73	3.0	7.3	55%	.298	1.26	3.39	3.10	4.20	0.8
2012	FRI	AA	23	9	3	0	16	14	83²	70	3	14	73	1.5	7.9	50%	.288	1.00	1.72	2.54	3.46	1.7
2012	ROU	AAA	23	2	3	0	9	8	51	53	2	16	30	2.8	5.3	54%	.307	1.35	4.59	4.18	5.22	0.2
2012	TEX	MLB	23	1	1	0	5	2	14	22	1	3	13	1.9	8.4	45%	.438	1.79	9.00	2.76	3.81	0.3
2013	IOW	AAA	24	2	3	0	8	8	42¹	46	1	17	41	3.6	8.7	51%	.357	1.49	4.68	3.14	3.38	1.0
2013	TEX	MLB	24	7	7	0	17	17	89	116	15	31	68	3.1	6.9	45%	.347	1.65	6.37	4.82	5.35	0.1
2013	CHN	MLB	24	0	2	0	10	0	9	4	0	3	8	3.0	8.0	38%	.167	0.78	2.00	2.58	2.84	0.1
2014	CHN	MLB	25	7	10	0	26	26	137¹	137	14	42	103	2.8	6.7	48%	.309	1.30	4.21	4.04	4.57	0.5

Grimm spent the early part of last season toiling at the back of the Texas rotation, with little success. His big-breaking curveball is a big-league pitch, but as soon as hitters discovered his straight, low-90s fastball, plate appearances devolved into Tarantino revenge fantasies. Traded to the Cubs as part of the haul for Matt Garza, Grimm earned a September cup of coffee and turned in 10 successful relief outings. His fastball sat in the mid-90s when working out of the 'pen, and he broke out a slider that kept righties off balance. The Cubs still consider him a starter with mid-rotation potential, but if that doesn't pan out, his stuff might well play up in relief.

Matt Guerrier

Born: 8/2/1978 Age: 35
Bats: R Throws: R Height: 6' 3" Weight: 195
Breakout: 25% Improve: 50% Collapse: 29%
Attrition: 11% MLB: 81%

Comparables:
Dave Smith, Steve Kline, Joe Beimel

YEAR	TEAM	LVL	AGE	W	L	SV	G	GS	IP	H	HR	BB	SO	BB9	SO9	GB%	BABIP	WHIP	ERA	FIP	FRA	WARP
2011	LAN	MLB	32	4	3	1	70	0	66¹	59	4	25	50	3.4	6.8	42%	.267	1.27	4.07	3.40	4.31	0.1
2012	LAN	MLB	33	0	2	0	16	0	14	8	3	7	9	4.5	5.8	37%	.143	1.07	3.86	6.35	6.66	-0.3
2013	CHN	MLB	34	2	1	0	15	0	12²	11	0	5	9	3.6	6.4	43%	.297	1.26	2.13	2.78	3.03	0.2
2013	LAN	MLB	34	2	3	0	34	0	30	32	3	12	21	3.6	6.3	46%	.308	1.47	4.80	4.22	5.09	-0.2
2014	CHN	MLB	35	2	1	1	41	0	38¹	34	4	12	27	2.8	6.5	45%	.272	1.19	3.55	4.19	3.86	0.4

The Cubs and Dodgers each re-gifted an expensive disappointment when Guerrier came to Chicago in exchange for Carlos Marmol, and the veteran righty didn't help his new employers any more than his old ones. Guerrier provided 15 surprisingly solid innings in middle relief before the baling twine in his elbow began to unravel, leading to season-ending surgery. The Warrior was once a reliable set-up man, but injuries and Father Time have made off with his fastball's pop and his slider's snap. If he's healthy next year he might contribute 40 usable innings in middle relief, though you probably shouldn't bet on it.

Kyle Hendricks

Born: 12/7/1989 Age: 24
Bats: R Throws: R Height: 6' 3" Weight: 190
Breakout: 40% Improve: 59% Collapse: 33%
Attrition: 60% MLB: 48%

Comparables:
David Phelps, Carlos Rosa, Dillon Gee

YEAR	TEAM	LVL	AGE	W	L	SV	G	GS	IP	H	HR	BB	SO	BB9	SO9	GB%	BABIP	WHIP	ERA	FIP	FRA	WARP
2011	SPO	A-	21	2	2	3	20	0	32²	20	0	4	36	1.1	9.9	55%	.227	0.73	1.93	1.78	2.81	0.8
2012	DAY	A+	22	1	0	0	5	4	17	17	3	3	11	1.6	5.8	46%	.264	1.18	4.24	5.10	6.42	0.0
2012	MYR	A+	22	5	8	0	20	20	130²	123	8	15	112	1.0	7.7	54%	.304	1.06	2.82	2.95	3.88	1.5
2013	TEN	AA	23	10	3	0	21	21	126¹	107	3	26	101	1.9	7.2	58%	.281	1.05	1.85	2.36	3.81	1.8
2013	IOW	AAA	23	3	1	0	6	6	40	35	2	8	27	1.8	6.1	62%	.282	1.08	2.47	3.54	4.10	0.5
2014	CHN	MLB	24	7	8	1	33	20	139²	136	15	33	95	2.1	6.1	52%	.296	1.21	3.81	4.06	4.14	1.1

If broadcasters are right about the keys to pitching success—get ahead of hitters, change speeds, avoid walks—Hendricks is destined to be a booth favorite. The Dartmouth product doesn't have great stuff but he commands it well, varying his fastball from the mid-80s to the low 90s and mixing in a cutter, slider, curve and changeup. It's a combination that baffled hitters in the high minors last year, and earned Hendricks the organization's Pitcher of the Year award. The same approach currently earns millions for Kyle Lohse, though it's more likely Hendricks will settle into the back end of a big-league rotation or make his mark in middle relief.

Edwin Jackson

Born: 9/9/1983 Age: 30
Bats: R Throws: R Height: 6' 3" Weight: 210
Breakout: 16% Improve: 50% Collapse: 22%
Attrition: 9% MLB: 92%

Comparables:
Nate Robertson, Ervin Santana, Chris Capuano

YEAR	TEAM	LVL	AGE	W	L	SV	G	GS	IP	H	HR	BB	SO	BB9	SO9	GB%	BABIP	WHIP	ERA	FIP	FRA	WARP
2011	CHA	MLB	27	7	7	0	19	19	121²	134	8	39	97	2.9	7.2	49%	.334	1.42	3.92	3.28	3.78	2.2
2011	SLN	MLB	27	5	2	0	13	12	78	91	8	23	51	2.7	5.9	40%	.333	1.46	3.58	3.98	4.25	0.5
2012	WAS	MLB	28	10	11	0	31	31	189²	173	23	58	168	2.8	8.0	47%	.287	1.22	4.03	3.89	4.72	1.0
2013	CHN	MLB	29	8	18	0	31	31	175¹	197	16	59	135	3.0	6.9	52%	.333	1.46	4.98	3.76	4.69	0.6
2014	CHN	MLB	30	8	10	0	25	25	157¹	150	16	47	131	2.7	7.5	45%	.306	1.25	4.00	3.83	4.34	0.8

When a starting pitcher loses 18 games and posts a 4.98 ERA in the first year of a $52 million contract, it's natural for fans to climb out on a ledge. We're not here to say Jackson pitched well, but his numbers last year don't point toward a player who is suddenly awful so much as a mediocre innings eater having a randomly bad year. Jackson's peripherals were pretty normal for him, with a small uptick in walks and groundballs, a small drop in strikeouts and home runs and a FIP that ranked as the second-best of his career. The problem was his 63 percent strand rate—the lowest in the National League, and miles below his career average. While it's possible Jackson suddenly lost the guts to pitch out of jams, it's more likely that the hits and walks he allowed this year just happened to cluster together. Jackson is being paid for his durability and consistent mediocrity, and odds are that's exactly what he'll provide for three more years.

Chang-Yong Lim

Born: 6/4/1976 Age: 38
Bats: R Throws: R Height: 5' 11" Weight: 175
Breakout: 20% Improve: 49% Collapse: 24%
Attrition: 15% MLB: 57%

Comparables:
Vic Darensbourg, Brian Sweeney, Matt Whiteside

YEAR	TEAM	LVL	AGE	W	L	SV	G	GS	IP	H	HR	BB	SO	BB9	SO9	GB%	BABIP	WHIP	ERA	FIP	FRA	WARP
2011	YKL	NPB	35	4	2	32	65	0	62¹	40	2	22	69	3.2	10.0	%	.261	0.99	2.17	0.00	0.00	0.0
2013	IOW	AAA	37	0	0	0	11	0	11¹	5	0	4	12	3.2	9.5	64%	.200	0.79	0.79	2.51	3.50	0.2
2013	CHN	MLB	37	0	0	0	6	0	5	6	0	7	5	12.6	9.0	57%	.429	2.60	5.40	5.82	5.93	-0.1
2014	CHN	MLB	38	2	1	0	35	2	37	34	4	17	32	4.1	7.9	47%	.303	1.37	4.23	4.45	4.59	0.1

Although general managers are known to look for competent bullpen arms everywhere from the independent leagues to the waiver wire to their grandparents' couch cushions, it was still a bit surprising when the Cubs signed a 36-year-old former NPB closer rehabbing from his second Tommy John surgery. A former member of the Korean international team, Lim made his minor-league debut last June and promptly began carving up hitters with his low-90s fastball, slider and splitter, all delivered from a Nomo-esque windup and a sidearm slot. Lim had trouble finding the plate during a brief September call-up, but his stuff looks like it can miss bats and make righty hitters uncomfortable. He was non-tendered but deserves a long look this spring to be some team's solid situational righty.

Brett Marshall

Born: 3/22/1990 Age: 24
Bats: R Throws: R Height: 6' 1" Weight: 195
Breakout: 48% Improve: 85% Collapse: 7%
Attrition: 57% MLB: 15%

Comparables:
Jeff Locke, Travis Chick, Alex Wilson

YEAR	TEAM	LVL	AGE	W	L	SV	G	GS	IP	H	HR	BB	SO	BB9	SO9	GB%	BABIP	WHIP	ERA	FIP	FRA	WARP
2011	TAM	A+	21	9	7	0	27	26	140¹	142	6	48	114	3.1	7.3	57%	.343	1.35	3.78	3.43	3.42	0.6
2012	TRN	AA	22	13	7	0	27	27	158¹	151	15	53	120	3.0	6.8	51%	.292	1.29	3.52	4.09	5.11	0.6
2013	SWB	AAA	23	7	10	0	25	25	138²	144	17	68	120	4.4	7.8	47%	.312	1.53	5.13	4.63	5.82	-0.8
2013	NYA	MLB	23	0	0	0	3	0	12	13	3	7	7	5.2	5.2	51%	.278	1.67	4.50	7.16	6.81	-0.2
2014	CHN	MLB	24	6	11	0	25	25	139¹	142	20	60	96	3.9	6.2	47%	.299	1.45	4.97	5.18	5.41	-0.8

Marshall had three months to taste the bitterness of his ugly early-May major-league debut before cleaning his palate with two stronger outings in September. He spent those months in Scranton, where he walked too many batters, allowed too many long balls, and didn't induce enough grounders. The righty has a deep selection of off-speed stuff to go along with his sub-90 four-seamer and sinker, so he might offer opponents enough looks to get by in a long relief role. But it's not a great sign when a guy who survives by keeping the ball down in the zone can't keep the ball in the ballpark.

Blake Parker

Born: 6/19/1985 Age: 29
Bats: R Throws: R Height: 6' 3" Weight: 225
Breakout: 18% Improve: 31% Collapse: 62%
Attrition: 50% MLB: 41%

Comparables:
Mike Zagurski, Aaron Rakers, Jonah Bayliss

YEAR	TEAM	LVL	AGE	W	L	SV	G	GS	IP	H	HR	BB	SO	BB9	SO9	GB%	BABIP	WHIP	ERA	FIP	FRA	WARP
2011	TEN	AA	26	1	2	3	16	0	24	20	1	13	20	4.9	7.5	41%	.302	1.38	4.12	3.93	5.63	0.1
2011	IOW	AAA	26	3	3	4	37	0	51¹	37	5	27	60	4.7	10.5	39%	.244	1.25	2.81	4.41	3.33	1.1
2012	IOW	AAA	27	1	1	6	21	0	23²	16	3	6	22	2.3	8.4	42%	.213	0.93	3.42	4.21	4.62	0.2
2012	CHN	MLB	27	0	0	0	7	0	6	10	3	5	6	7.5	9.0	44%	.333	2.50	6.00	10.14	6.82	-0.2
2013	IOW	AAA	28	0	1	7	16	0	17²	8	1	10	26	5.1	13.2	28%	.200	1.02	2.04	3.23	2.63	0.6
2013	CHN	MLB	28	1	2	1	49	0	46¹	39	4	15	55	2.9	10.7	29%	.299	1.17	2.72	2.87	3.21	0.8
2014	CHN	MLB	29	2	1	0	44	0	52¹	42	6	22	56	3.8	9.5	44%	.288	1.23	3.56	3.93	3.87	0.5

Parker provided one of the few happy stories in the Chicago bullpen last year, as the former catcher and Triple-A closer bounced back from an injury-plagued 2012 to establish himself in the big-league bullpen. His fastball/curveball mix can generate plenty of awkward swings and strikeouts, but last year's breakthrough came when Parker finally stopped handing out walks like magazine subscription cards. Parker doesn't have an explosive fastball and likely won't maintain a top-shelf whiff rate, but there's every reason to think he can get by in a set-up role.

Brooks Raley

Born: 6/29/1988 Age: 26
Bats: L Throws: L Height: 6' 3" Weight: 200
Breakout: 60% Improve: 79% Collapse: 13%
Attrition: 80% MLB: 26%

Comparables:
Clayton Mortensen, Beltran Perez, Abe Alvarez

YEAR	TEAM	LVL	AGE	W	L	SV	G	GS	IP	H	HR	BB	SO	BB9	SO9	GB%	BABIP	WHIP	ERA	FIP	FRA	WARP
2011	TEN	AA	23	8	10	0	26	25	136¹	170	16	45	80	3.0	5.3	41%	.323	1.58	4.22	4.71	5.97	0.4
2012	TEN	AA	24	2	2	0	8	8	48²	47	2	12	29	2.2	5.4	47%	.296	1.21	3.51	3.47	4.38	0.4
2012	IOW	AAA	24	4	8	0	14	14	82	87	7	28	69	3.1	7.6	51%	.320	1.40	3.62	4.23	4.72	0.9
2012	CHN	MLB	24	1	2	0	5	5	24¹	33	7	11	16	4.1	5.9	41%	.321	1.81	8.14	6.92	7.64	-0.6
2013	IOW	AAA	25	8	10	1	27	25	141¹	142	13	45	95	2.9	6.0	47%	.287	1.32	4.46	4.50	5.03	0.8
2013	CHN	MLB	25	0	0	0	9	0	14	11	2	8	14	5.1	9.0	49%	.257	1.36	5.14	5.02	5.11	-0.1
2014	CHN	MLB	26	6	11	0	25	25	135¹	143	19	47	80	3.1	5.3	44%	.298	1.40	4.93	5.06	5.36	-0.7

Raley's sinker/slider routine works well enough to munch innings in Iowa, but doesn't have near enough velocity or wiggle to regularly put a kink in the plans of the world's best hitters. Lefty bullpen specialists don't spontaneously generate, so Raley might evolve into a career with more appearances than innings, but even that role might be beyond him.

Neil Ramirez

Born: 5/25/1989 Age: 25
Bats: R Throws: R Height: 6' 4" Weight: 190
Breakout: 46% Improve: 59% Collapse: 29%
Attrition: 77% MLB: 25%

Comparables:
Dustin Richardson, Corey Kluber, Chris Dwyer

YEAR	TEAM	LVL	AGE	W	L	SV	G	GS	IP	H	HR	BB	SO	BB9	SO9	GB%	BABIP	WHIP	ERA	FIP	FRA	WARP
2011	FRI	AA	22	1	0	0	6	6	19	13	1	8	24	3.8	11.4	22%	.412	1.11	1.89	2.96	2.40	0.5
2011	ROU	AAA	22	4	3	0	18	18	74¹	63	6	35	86	4.2	10.4	39%	.375	1.32	3.63	4.17	3.68	0.7
2012	FRI	AA	23	2	5	0	13	12	49¹	47	6	16	45	2.9	8.2	34%	.301	1.28	4.20	4.31	4.21	0.8
2012	ROU	AAA	23	6	8	0	15	15	74	78	12	31	63	3.8	7.7	30%	.301	1.47	7.66	5.57	5.95	0.0
2013	FRI	AA	24	9	3	0	21	21	103	77	8	42	127	3.7	11.1	44%	.295	1.16	3.84	2.97	3.56	2.1
2014	CHN	MLB	25	4	8	0	19	19	94²	88	12	42	86	4.0	8.2	35%	.303	1.38	4.65	4.59	5.05	-0.1

The player-to-be-named moving from Texas to Chicago in the Matt Garza trade, Ramirez has a greater chance to realize a big-league career than your standard-issue throw-in. A former supplemental first rounder, Ramirez has a big fastball that can sit in the mid-90s and a plus changeup, although he's yet to develop any consistency with his slider or curve. In fact, he's yet to develop any consistency at all, as he's prone to balky mechanics that affect his command, and recurring shoulder issues have slowed his development. When he's on he can dominate, and the Cubs will give him every chance to string together solid starts and realize his mid-rotation ceiling. If not, his fastball/changeup mix could be dominant in short bursts.

Hector Rondon

Born: 2/26/1988 Age: 26
Bats: R Throws: R Height: 6' 3" Weight: 180
Breakout: 31% Improve: 57% Collapse: 31%
Attrition: 42% MLB: 78%

Comparables:
Junichi Tazawa, Scott Mathieson, Ross Ohlendorf

YEAR	TEAM	LVL	AGE	W	L	SV	G	GS	IP	H	HR	BB	SO	BB9	SO9	GB%	BABIP	WHIP	ERA	FIP	FRA	WARP
2013	CHN	MLB	25	2	1	0	45	0	54²	52	6	25	44	4.1	7.2	45%	.283	1.41	4.77	4.37	5.11	-0.1
2014	CHN	MLB	26	2	1	0	34	0	42²	41	6	13	37	2.7	7.9	39%	.304	1.25	4.13	4.38	4.48	0.1

Rondon started last season as a Rule 5 pick who had lost most of the previous three seasons to elbow problems, but he finished it as a bullpen phoenix. He was certifiably awful for most of the season, but the rest of the Cubs' relief corps had built such an impenetrable Fortress of Suckitude around him that hardly anyone noticed, and Rondon kept getting chances until something clicked. A semblance of the excellent command he had shown in his Cleveland days reappeared, and he started putting up zeroes in September. His mid-90s fastball can work in the middle innings, and the long layoff means Rondon has more upside than most 26-year-olds.

Zachary Rosscup

Born: 6/9/1988 Age: 26
Bats: R Throws: L Height: 6' 2" Weight: 205
Breakout: 52% Improve: 67% Collapse: 22%
Attrition: 63% MLB: 37%

Comparables:
Dustin Richardson, Nick Hagadone, Ryan Verdugo

YEAR	TEAM	LVL	AGE	W	L	SV	G	GS	IP	H	HR	BB	SO	BB9	SO9	GB%	BABIP	WHIP	ERA	FIP	FRA	WARP
2011	DAY	A+	23	4	2	0	11	9	49²	43	4	19	50	3.4	9.1	23%	.263	1.25	2.54	3.69	4.47	-0.1
2012	TEN	AA	24	0	1	0	11	1	22¹	14	1	19	29	7.7	11.7	40%	.277	1.48	4.84	3.82	5.22	0.3
2013	TEN	AA	25	2	1	3	37	0	43¹	31	2	19	66	3.9	13.7	43%	.326	1.15	2.49	1.78	2.48	1.3
2013	CHN	MLB	25	0	0	0	10	0	6²	3	1	7	7	9.4	9.4	19%	.133	1.50	1.35	6.02	6.09	-0.1
2014	CHN	MLB	26	2	2	0	28	3	46²	40	5	24	49	4.6	9.4	41%	.305	1.37	4.06	4.19	4.42	0.2

It's not easy for a 25-year-old lefty reliever toiling away in Double-A to get the organization's attention, but striking out 44 percent of the lefties you face certainly helps. Last year Rosscup used his low-90s fastball and sweeping slider to turn same-side hitters into mincemeat, and the Cubs rewarded him with a spot on the 40-man roster and a September call-up. The former Rays farmhand isn't putty in the hands of righty hitters either, but he's often struggled with control and profiles best as a lefty specialist. Someone has to be the next Randy Choate, and Rosscup has as good a chance as any.

Chris Rusin

Born: 10/22/1986 Age: 27
Bats: L Throws: L Height: 6' 2" Weight: 195
Breakout: 42% Improve: 63% Collapse: 23%
Attrition: 57% MLB: 56%

Comparables:
Duane Below, Enrique Gonzalez, Ben Hendrickson

YEAR	TEAM	LVL	AGE	W	L	SV	G	GS	IP	H	HR	BB	SO	BB9	SO9	GB%	BABIP	WHIP	ERA	FIP	FRA	WARP
2011	TEN	AA	24	3	2	0	15	15	76	80	5	16	49	1.9	5.8	53%	.320	1.26	3.91	3.70	4.72	0.8
2011	IOW	AAA	24	5	2	0	11	9	62²	70	8	14	46	2.0	6.6	52%	.323	1.34	4.02	4.69	5.26	0.5
2012	IOW	AAA	25	8	9	0	25	25	140¹	146	17	53	94	3.4	6.0	52%	.299	1.42	4.55	5.20	6.02	0.0
2012	CHN	MLB	25	2	3	0	7	7	29²	38	4	11	21	3.3	6.4	45%	.360	1.65	6.37	4.89	4.85	0.3
2013	IOW	AAA	26	8	7	0	19	18	121	113	8	27	69	2.0	5.1	50%	.276	1.16	3.35	4.03	4.97	0.8
2013	CHN	MLB	26	2	6	0	13	13	66¹	66	8	24	36	3.3	4.9	48%	.288	1.36	3.93	4.72	5.51	-0.2
2014	CHN	MLB	27	8	12	0	29	29	157¹	158	20	46	97	2.6	5.6	51%	.292	1.30	4.46	4.69	4.85	0.1

There are ways to earn extended work in a big-league rotation without great stuff or a high strikeout rate. You can adhere to the Minnesota Meme and consider every walk a betrayal. You can follow the Duncan Directive and consider every pitch a potential groundball out. Or you can do what Rusin does, and be a mildly effective Triple-A sinkerballer when the big club ships out half its rotation at the trade deadline and needs someone, anyone, to fill a chair. Rusin gets the most he can out of his low-velo lefty assortment by inducing his share of two-hoppers and making hitters earn their way on, but you'll know the Cubs have graduated out of their rebuilding phase when Rusin is no longer mentioned as a rotation candidate.

James Russell

Born: 1/8/1986 Age: 28
Bats: L Throws: L Height: 6' 4" Weight: 200
Breakout: 34% Improve: 54% Collapse: 40%
Attrition: 29% MLB: 65%

Comparables:
Justin Lehr, Jeff Bennett, Jason Standridge

YEAR	TEAM	LVL	AGE	W	L	SV	G	GS	IP	H	HR	BB	SO	BB9	SO9	GB%	BABIP	WHIP	ERA	FIP	FRA	WARP
2011	CHN	MLB	25	1	6	0	64	5	67²	76	12	14	43	1.9	5.7	41%	.290	1.33	4.12	4.74	4.60	0.3
2012	CHN	MLB	26	7	1	2	77	0	69¹	67	5	23	55	3.0	7.1	40%	.298	1.30	3.25	3.53	3.08	1.2
2013	CHN	MLB	27	1	6	0	74	0	52²	46	7	18	37	3.1	6.3	34%	.258	1.22	3.59	4.43	5.79	-0.6
2014	CHN	MLB	28	3	1	2	58	0	49	49	7	13	37	2.4	6.7	38%	.294	1.25	4.34	4.50	4.72	-0.0

Dale Sveum summoned Russell from the 'pen a club-leading 74 times last summer, but the veteran lefty worked only 53 innings, highlighting his inexorable evolution from starter to reliever to LOOGY. Russell's slideriffic assortment has long been more effective against same-side hitters, but last year the chasm grew immense. Lefties posted a .207 TAv against Russell, compared to .351 for righties—roughly the difference between Brendan Ryan and Migual Cabrera—and the organization certainly noticed. Russell has his uses, but he needs to be spotted carefully or northpaws will eat him alive.

Jeff Samardzija

Born: 1/23/1985 Age: 29
Bats: R Throws: R Height: 6' 5" Weight: 225
Breakout: 35% Improve: 52% Collapse: 28%
Attrition: 25% MLB: 71%

Comparables:
Robinson Tejeda, Manny Parra, Boof Bonser

YEAR	TEAM	LVL	AGE	W	L	SV	G	GS	IP	H	HR	BB	SO	BB9	SO9	GB%	BABIP	WHIP	ERA	FIP	FRA	WARP
2011	CHN	MLB	26	8	4	0	75	0	88	64	5	50	87	5.1	8.9	43%	.253	1.30	2.97	3.63	3.87	0.9
2012	CHN	MLB	27	9	13	0	28	28	174²	157	20	56	180	2.9	9.3	45%	.302	1.22	3.81	3.59	4.11	2.2
2013	CHN	MLB	28	8	13	0	33	33	213²	210	25	78	214	3.3	9.0	50%	.320	1.35	4.34	3.75	4.10	2.4
2014	CHN	MLB	29	8	8	3	84	16	176²	158	21	69	164	3.5	8.4	44%	.298	1.28	3.99	4.18	4.33	1.0

Context is an interesting thing. Only several years removed from serving as a cautionary baseball punchline, Samardzija just completed his second quality season at the top of the Cubs' rotation, worked 200 innings, struck out 200 batters and ranked 13th among National League pitchers in WARP—yet many view his season as a disappointment, since he didn't turn into a "true ace." On the other hand, if you consider this a consolidation season for Samardzija, one in which he proved that his first season as a productive starter wasn't a fluke, and that his half-decade of flailing in the minors or in middle relief are irrevocably over, then it's hard to view this as anything but a triumph. Much like Edwin Jackson, Shark's inflated ERA isn't as bad as it looks and will likely go down this year. He's a solid second starter, and while that's not an ace, who would have thought it possible five years ago?

Pedro Strop

Born: 6/13/1985 Age: 29
Bats: R Throws: R Height: 6' 0" Weight: 215
Breakout: 27% Improve: 51% Collapse: 36%
Attrition: 32% MLB: 72%

Comparables:
Jose Veras, Doug Slaten, Evan Meek

YEAR	TEAM	LVL	AGE	W	L	SV	G	GS	IP	H	HR	BB	SO	BB9	SO9	GB%	BABIP	WHIP	ERA	FIP	FRA	WARP
2011	ROU	AAA	26	4	4	11	39	0	47²	53	2	24	55	4.5	10.4	53%	.371	1.62	3.59	3.59	4.40	0.2
2011	BAL	MLB	26	2	0	0	12	0	12¹	8	0	3	12	2.2	8.8	68%	.258	0.89	0.73	1.85	2.37	0.4
2011	TEX	MLB	26	0	1	0	11	0	9²	7	0	7	9	6.5	8.4	52%	.259	1.45	3.72	3.68	3.39	0.2
2012	BAL	MLB	27	5	2	3	70	0	66¹	52	2	37	58	5.0	7.9	64%	.275	1.34	2.44	3.54	3.95	0.9
2013	CHN	MLB	28	2	2	1	37	0	35	22	1	11	42	2.8	10.8	53%	.250	0.94	2.83	2.28	2.70	0.7
2013	BAL	MLB	28	0	3	0	29	0	22¹	23	4	15	24	6.0	9.7	52%	.292	1.70	7.25	5.54	6.71	-0.4
2014	CHN	MLB	29	3	1	2	59	0	55²	45	4	25	57	4.1	9.2	51%	.297	1.27	3.55	3.58	3.86	0.6

Armed with a heavy upper-90s fastball and a power slider, Cubs fans hope Strop is the late-inning gold into which Scott Feldman was spun—although his shaky control may well expose him as pyrite. Strop has never had problems lobbing thunderbolts and racking up strikeout victims, while the sinking action on his fastball provides the added benefit of numerous groundball outs. However, the estimable walk rate he posted during his brief Wrigley audition is a complete outlier, and it ain't a-gonna last. Strop may become Chicago's closer, but he'll be an Axford-class closer, swinging from dominance to combustibility depending on the state of his relationship with the strike zone.

Jose Veras

Born: 10/20/1980 Age: 33
Bats: R Throws: R Height: 6' 6" Weight: 240
Breakout: 24% Improve: 52% Collapse: 31%
Attrition: 15% MLB: 89%

Comparables:
Michael Wuertz, Will Ohman, Jason Frasor

YEAR	TEAM	LVL	AGE	W	L	SV	G	GS	IP	H	HR	BB	SO	BB9	SO9	GB%	BABIP	WHIP	ERA	FIP	FRA	WARP
2011	PIT	MLB	30	2	4	1	79	0	71	54	6	34	79	4.3	10.0	39%	.260	1.24	3.80	3.47	3.52	0.8
2012	MIL	MLB	31	5	4	1	72	0	67	61	5	40	79	5.4	10.6	46%	.322	1.51	3.63	3.63	3.74	1.0
2013	DET	MLB	32	0	1	2	25	0	19²	16	2	8	16	3.7	7.3	38%	.241	1.22	3.20	4.14	4.35	0.1
2013	HOU	MLB	32	0	4	19	42	0	43	29	4	14	44	2.9	9.2	46%	.240	1.00	2.93	3.42	4.17	0.4
2014	CHN	MLB	33	3	1	5	59	0	57	45	6	25	59	4.0	9.3	42%	.283	1.23	3.45	3.98	3.75	0.7

Veras ended up as a goat for the 2013 Tigers by relying on his best pitch—a filthy curveball—one time too many; Shane Victorino timed it, launched it, circled the bases and essentially ended Detroit's season. Reducing his season to that lone matchup diminishes how useful he was in 2013, first as trade bait—Houston could teach a weekend seminar on how to buy and flip unwanted junk for profit—and then as the Tigers' bridge to Benoit. Veras sacrificed a bit of his strikeout rate in exchange for a career-best walk rate. The improved command and control of his fastball should be sustainable, which means that despite Veras losing his sleeper status, the Cubs may still have found a bargain at $4 million.

Carlos Villanueva

Born: 11/28/1983 Age: 30
Bats: R Throws: R Height: 6' 2" Weight: 215
Breakout: 21% Improve: 53% Collapse: 17%
Attrition: 10% MLB: 94%

Comparables:
Sonny Siebert, Rick Aguilera, Jorge Sosa

YEAR	TEAM	LVL	AGE	W	L	SV	G	GS	IP	H	HR	BB	SO	BB9	SO9	GB%	BABIP	WHIP	ERA	FIP	FRA	WARP
2011	TOR	MLB	27	6	4	0	33	13	107	103	11	32	68	2.7	5.7	36%	.272	1.26	4.04	4.14	4.93	0.9
2012	TOR	MLB	28	7	7	0	38	16	125¹	113	23	46	122	3.3	8.8	38%	.275	1.27	4.16	4.66	4.77	1.2
2013	CHN	MLB	29	7	8	0	47	15	128²	117	14	40	103	2.8	7.2	42%	.289	1.22	4.06	3.84	4.64	0.3
2014	CHN	MLB	30	5	5	1	48	11	111	99	13	33	96	2.7	7.8	41%	.291	1.19	3.71	4.01	4.03	1.0

The rubber-armed Villanueva remains one of baseball's most reliable swingmen, gamely filling whatever role his employer desires. He's made double-digit starts each of the past three years with results that grade out around the mean, but the league has never trusted his five-pitch junkball assortment to work in the rotation over the long haul. He's therefore frequently moved back to long relief to make room for an inferior starter with perceived upside (we're looking at you, Jake Arrieta), and soaks up the middle innings while others audition for starring roles. Villanueva will never be a star, but every team in the league would be better if they had him.

Arodys Vizcaino

Born: 11/13/1990 Age: 23
Bats: R Throws: R Height: 6' 0" Weight: 190
Breakout: 38% Improve: 62% Collapse: 26%
Attrition: 59% MLB: 53%

Comparables:
Charlie Haeger, Casey Kelly, Nick Maronde

YEAR	TEAM	LVL	AGE	W	L	SV	G	GS	IP	H	HR	BB	SO	BB9	SO9	GB%	BABIP	WHIP	ERA	FIP	FRA	WARP
2011	LYN	A+	20	2	2	0	9	9	40¹	31	3	10	37	2.2	8.3	44%	.216	1.02	2.45	3.11	3.99	0.4
2011	MIS	AA	20	2	3	0	11	8	49²	44	3	18	55	3.3	10.0	54%	.349	1.25	3.81	3.15	2.66	0.5
2011	ATL	MLB	20	1	1	0	17	0	17¹	16	1	9	17	4.7	8.8	34%	.306	1.44	4.67	3.51	3.30	0.1
2014	CHN	MLB	23	2	2	0	15	5	37	36	4	14	29	3.3	7.0	41%	.301	1.33	4.25	4.28	4.61	0.1

Cubs fans can be excused if they have started to confuse Vizcaino with Keyser Soze, as it's been over two years since the young flamethrower has been seen on a professional mound. He needed another surgery last May to clean up his elbow, but the club is hopeful he'll be ready to climb back on the developmental horse this spring. Before his injury woes Vizcaino could unleash a moving mid-90s heater and a big-breaking curve, but suffered from occasional lack of command. Given his size and injury history his future likely lies in the bullpen, and if his stuff returns he might grow into the dominant closer Pedro Strop isn't.

Travis Wood
Born: 2/6/1987 Age: 27
Bats: R Throws: L Height: 5' 11" Weight: 175
Breakout: 20% Improve: 62% Collapse: 29%
Attrition: 15% MLB: 87%
Comparables:
Gavin Floyd, Wade Davis, Tom Gorzelanny

YEAR	TEAM	LVL	AGE	W	L	SV	G	GS	IP	H	HR	BB	SO	BB9	SO9	GB%	BABIP	WHIP	ERA	FIP	FRA	WARP
2011	LOU	AAA	24	2	3	0	10	10	52¹	64	6	17	47	2.9	8.1	43%	.370	1.55	5.33	4.02	4.15	0.4
2011	CIN	MLB	24	6	6	0	22	18	106	118	10	40	76	3.4	6.5	35%	.328	1.49	4.84	4.03	4.49	0.5
2012	IOW	AAA	25	3	3	0	7	7	41¹	48	5	11	39	2.4	8.5	39%	.359	1.43	4.57	4.22	4.75	0.6
2012	CHN	MLB	25	6	13	0	26	26	156	133	25	54	119	3.1	6.9	36%	.253	1.20	4.27	4.89	5.32	0.4
2013	CHN	MLB	26	9	12	0	32	32	200	163	18	66	144	3.0	6.5	34%	.245	1.14	3.11	3.86	4.43	1.1
2014	CHN	MLB	27	9	11	0	30	30	169²	147	18	50	133	2.6	7.1	38%	.281	1.16	3.50	4.03	3.81	2.1

Wood put in a breakthrough performance last year, working 200 innings, leading the staff in ERA and earning his first All-Star Game berth. The diminutive lefty doesn't have great velocity but everything he throws moves, and his baffling mix of cutters, sinkers, four-seamers, sliders and changeups keeps batters off balance and leads to plenty of awkward swings and weak contact. Wood is an extreme fly-ball pitcher yet kept most of them in the yard last year; that won't always be the case, but his low walk rate should help limit the damage when his home run rate spikes. If he can stay healthy, Wood looks set to be a low-priced mid-rotation stalwart for the next few years.

Wesley Wright
Born: 1/28/1985 Age: 29
Bats: R Throws: L Height: 5' 11" Weight: 185
Breakout: 45% Improve: 70% Collapse: 24%
Attrition: 22% MLB: 66%
Comparables:
Nick Masset, Jason Standridge, Scott Proctor

YEAR	TEAM	LVL	AGE	W	L	SV	G	GS	IP	H	HR	BB	SO	BB9	SO9	GB%	BABIP	WHIP	ERA	FIP	FRA	WARP
2011	OKL	AAA	26	3	1	2	39	3	65¹	49	4	23	52	3.2	7.2	30%	.258	1.10	2.07	4.18	7.37	-0.1
2011	HOU	MLB	26	0	0	0	21	0	12	6	1	5	11	3.8	8.2	58%	.200	0.92	1.50	3.49	4.05	0.1
2012	HOU	MLB	27	2	2	1	77	0	52¹	45	4	17	54	2.9	9.3	57%	.289	1.18	3.27	3.38	4.53	0.0
2013	HOU	MLB	28	0	4	0	54	0	41¹	45	5	16	40	3.5	8.7	50%	.333	1.48	3.92	4.09	5.04	-0.1
2013	TBA	MLB	28	0	0	0	16	0	12¹	9	2	3	15	2.2	10.9	63%	.250	0.97	2.92	3.48	4.38	0.0
2014	CHN	MLB	29	3	2	1	43	4	49²	45	6	19	44	3.4	7.9	47%	.299	1.29	4.12	4.36	4.48	0.2

Acquired by Tampa Bay from Houston in a mid-August waiver claim, the sub-six-foot Wright topped 70 appearances for the second year in a row. Pitching for the punchless Astros, the lefty was used as a traditional reliever more than a specialist, which negatively impacted his surface statistics. As a member of the more competitive Rays, his usage was limited to mostly left-handed batters, leading to much better results. Wright's fastball tops out near 90 mph, complemented by an assortment of secondary options. It is of note that his slider usage dropped by nearly half with the Rays in favor of more changeups and curveballs—at least, you hope the Cubs, who signed him in November, noted it.

LINEOUTS

HITTERS

PLAYER	TEAM	LVL	AGE	PA	R	2B	3B	HR	RBI	BB	SO	SB-CS	AVG/OBP/SLG	TAv	BABIP	BRR	FRAA	WARP
3B J. Candelario	KNC	A	19	572	71	35	1	11	57	68	88	1-0	.256/.346/.396	.257	.290	-0.6	3B(121): -4.8	1.2
LF D. McDonald	IOW	AAA	34	294	31	13	2	4	26	27	50	8-2	.236/.307/.346	.240	.275	1.8	LF(33): -2.3, RF(27): -0.3	0.0
	CHN	MLB	34	57	4	4	0	1	5	4	8	0-0	.302/.351/.434	.258	.341	0.1	RF(8): 0.2, LF(1): 1.1	0.1
RF T. Neal	SWB	AAA	25	297	36	17	0	2	29	23	53	2-1	.325/.391/.411	.284	.396	0.3	RF(40): 2.8, LF(21): 1.8	1.9
	CHN	MLB	25	4	0	0	0	0	0	0	0	0-0	.000/.000/.000	.022	.000	0.1	LF(1): 0.1	-0.1
	NYA	MLB	25	13	1	0	0	0	0	1	4	0-0	.182/.308/.182	.200	.286	0.1	RF(2): 0.0, LF(1): -0.1	-0.1
2B R. Roberts	DUR	AAA	32	148	12	5	0	1	13	21	30	3-1	.210/.320/.274	.224	.263	0.9	2B(19): 0.7, 3B(9): -0.3	0.0
	TBA	MLB	32	173	15	6	0	5	17	11	39	0-2	.247/.295/.377	.255	.297	-2.8	2B(48): -0.5, 3B(9): 0.3	0.2
1B R. Shoulders	KNC	A	21	503	61	27	0	18	74	66	143	0-0	.258/.352/.445	.274	.337	-1.3	1B(45): -1.2, LF(13): 0.2	1.1
SS C. Valaika	JUP	A+	27	43	3	1	0	1	4	2	6	0-1	.200/.256/.300	.205	.212	-0.3	SS(3): -0.2, 3B(3): 0.1	-0.1
	NWO	AAA	27	143	17	6	0	3	11	10	25	1-1	.246/.308/.362	.258	.282	-0.1	2B(23): 2.1, SS(6): 0.0	0.6
	MIA	MLB	27	70	4	5	0	1	9	3	16	0-0	.219/.261/.344	.220	.271	-0.3	2B(6): -0.2, SS(6): -0.3	-0.2
2B L. Watkins	IOW	AAA	23	472	51	18	7	8	26	52	98	10-9	.243/.333/.379	.263	.300	0.1	2B(90): -4.8, SS(13): -1.4	0.9
	CHN	MLB	23	42	2	1	0	0	0	3	14	0-0	.211/.268/.237	.195	.333	0.4	2B(9): -0.5	-0.2

Switch-hitting teenager **Jeimer Candelario** held his own in the Midwest League, displaying an advanced approach, an indifferent glove and a solid power stroke he should grow into; in a system positively filthy with talented third basemen, he'll go as far as his bat can carry him. ⊘ **Darnell McDonald** once again proved he's a tough out for lefties and can lurk inconspicuously in the corner outfield; he could still make a nice addition to a contender's bench. ⊘ **Thomas Neal** floated through the Indians, Yankees and Cubs' systems last year before separating his shoulder in August. He knows how to get on base but lacks a corner outfielder's thump or a fourth outfielder's defensive versatility. ⊘ **Ryan Roberts**, a curious (and disappointing) outlay of $3 million by the penny-pinching Rays, struggled so badly that he was eventually outrighted to Triple-A, where he also struggled, and spent time on the disabled list, too. Now he's a Cub. ⊘ Not to be confused with Brock Landers or Chest Rockwell, burly first sacker **Rock Shoulders** gained attention as 2012's Best Name in Minor League Baseball, and kept it by showing patience and thump; his bat is his only tool, so he'll need to put up pornographic power numbers to stay in the spotlight. ⊘ After seeing more playing time in the first five weeks of the 2013 season than in his previous two major-league campaigns combined, **Chris Valaika** had surgery in May to repair a broken left wrist and did not resurface in Miami even when healthy. ⊘ Versatile **Logan Watkins** can play the middle infield and center field, has good speed, a patient approach and little power; he might get some short-term play at second base, but will soon be steamrolled by the Cubs' plethora of top-end minor-league bats.

PITCHERS

PLAYER	TEAM	LVL	AGE	W	L	SV	IP	H	HR	BB	SO	BB9	SO9	GB%	BABIP	WHIP	ERA	FIP	FRA	WARP
R. Dolis	IOW	AAA	25	1	0	1	11²	11	1	7	13	5.4	10.0	62%	.323	1.54	5.40	4.26	4.81	0.1
	CHN	MLB	25	0	0	0	5	3	0	2	0	3.6	0.0	39%	.167	1.00	0.00	4.22	4.94	0.0
P. Johnson	KNC	A	22	5	5	0	69²	68	4	22	74	2.8	9.6	52%	.335	1.29	3.10	3.12	3.52	1.8
	DAY	A+	22	6	1	0	48²	41	1	21	50	3.9	9.2	43%	.333	1.27	2.22	2.99	4.23	0.6
D. Maples	KNC	A	21	0	2	1	34²	33	1	31	34	8.0	8.8	59%	.317	1.85	8.31	5.04	6.58	0.0
	BOI	A-	21	5	2	0	42	37	0	19	41	4.1	8.8	70%	.325	1.33	2.14	3.29	4.52	0.4
T. McNutt	TEN	AA	23	2	5	2	31¹	28	3	14	23	4.0	6.6	47%	.275	1.34	4.60	4.13	5.34	-0.1
H. Rodriguez	CHN	MLB	26	0	0	0	4	6	1	4	1	9.0	2.2	33%	.286	2.50	4.50	9.52	11.85	-0.3
	WAS	MLB	26	0	1	0	18	14	1	16	11	8.0	5.5	48%	.228	1.67	4.00	5.35	6.87	-0.4

Rafael Dolis continues to exert as much control over his mid-90s sinker as he does over the weather on Neptune, and lost three months last summer to forearm woes. If he can come back healthy and get to know the strike zone, he could still produce groundball outs in the seventh inning. ⊘ Former supplemental first-rounder **Pierce Johnson** put to rest injury concerns and used his low-90s fastball to strike out more than a batter per inning; if he can work the same voodoo against more advanced hitters this year, he just might grow into a mid-rotation workhorse. ⊘ Injury-plagued starter **Dillon Maples** can unleash a low-90s fastball and power curve, and his stuff misses bats and generates groundballs, but his full-season debut was marred by inconsistent mechanics and atrocious command. ⊘ A mid-90s fastball once made **Trey McNutt** a prospect, but injuries, ineffectiveness and a surprising lack of strikeouts have dogged him for years. Moved to the bullpen, he's still treading water in Double-A. ⊘ Armed with triple-digit heat and backstop-denting control, no one hands out free passes faster or more frequently than **Henry Rodriguez**; velocity's siren song will continue to earn him chances.

MANAGER: RICK RENTERIA

Dale Sveum's top job was making sure young players Starlin Castro and Anthony Rizzo developed under his watch. Both withered. The longer Sveum was in Chicago, the worse Castro hit. He regressed from a 21-year-old star to a 23-year-old disaster. Rizzo had a nice start in 2013, but batted .216 with a .691 OPS from May 12th onward.

Oddly enough, many other players did well under Sveum's watch. In fact, the 2013 Cubs had better offensive performances from their bench than their starters. So Sveum could get the most out of his scrubs—but his stars hit like scrubs. Maybe the double decline of Rizzo and Castro is just a sample size issue, but when each of the big names under your watch gets worse, you won't get a chance to prove it was a fluke.

The Cubs ranked dead last in sacrifice hits both seasons Sveum managed the Cubs —and by a good distance each time. Even if you adjust for opportunity (the offensively-challenged Cubs had fewer runners to move over via sacrifice than most teams), Sveum was the least bunt-happy manager in the NL each season. No wonder the sabermetrically friendly Cubs front office liked him. Random fact: the 2013 Cubs led the league in isolated power. Huh. Who knew?

Both seasons Dale Sveum helmed the Cubs, they issued the most walks by any team in the NL.

His replacement, Rick Renteria, is part of a trend. Of the six managers hired since the 2013 All-Star break, five have never managed before. If you think about it, that makes sense. So many longtime managers have left the game in recent years—LaRussa, Cox, Torre, Piniella, Leyland, Johnson, McKeon, Valentine, probably Charlie Manuel, and maybe Dusty Baker—that either you hire someone just starting out or you settle for someone second tier.

Cincinnati Reds

By Craig Fehrman

No one quite knows where the Big Red Machine came from. I speak here not of the team, which is still one of the four or five best in baseball history, but its name. One theory holds that Dave Bristol, the Reds' manager in the late '60s, started calling his squad "the machine" after it led the league in scoring in back-to-back seasons. Another suggests that Bob Hunter, a sportswriter, dubbed them the Big Red Machine after they beat the Phillies by a football-ish final score of 19–17. A third posits that Pete Rose invented it, though no one buys this one except maybe the Hit King himself.

Whatever the origin, I've always thought it telling that each of these theories centers on offense. Baseball's oldest franchise, after all, is also its most hitting-dependent. There's George Wright, the slugging, sideburned shortstop and star of the first professional team in 1869. There's Edd Roush, who used a 48-ounce Louisville Slugger to win batting titles in 1917 and 1919. There's Ted Kluszewski's cut-off sleeves, Frank Robinson's prodigious home runs (he hit them so far at Crosley Field they landed on I-75), Eric Davis and Barry Larkin's five-tool freakiness. And, yeah, there was the Big Red Machine.

Over the past four years, the Reds have gone on their best streak since the '70s, and it's tempting to see it as more of the run-scoring same. The team boasts Joey Votto and Jay Bruce. It plays its home games in a stadium that does to baseballs what the Hadron Collider does to particles. Yet the Reds' recent success has hinged as much on starting pitching—crucially, on homegrown starting pitching—as it has on hitting. In fact, the Reds can now claim one of the game's best collections of young moundsmen. This stands as a surreal development for a franchise that, during the draft era, has been baseball's single worst cultivator of starting pitching. But it's also scary—in part because those pitchers are getting

expensive, but, more importantly, because in developing them the Reds have depended on staggering amounts of luck.

Before we get to Cincinnati's current roster, it makes sense to look at some past ones. We're going to cover a lot of ground here, so let's stick to a simple statistical unit, something where it's easy to compare having two or four or a tragic zero—sort of like a Skyline Cheese Coney. This is our Coney: a pitcher who, over the course of any given season, starts in at least 60 percent of his appearances and manages a WAR of at least 2.0 (Baseball Reference version). In 1965 baseball had 20 franchises, and out of those 20—and from 1965 through 2013—the Reds rank dead last in the number of such seasons, with a paltry 92. In first place? The New York Yankees, with 141.

This survey starts in 1965 for two reasons. First, WAR is a counting stat, and it wasn't until Nixon's America that managers began paranoiacally dipping into their bullpens. This was actually a Reds innovation, which might seem exciting until you remember it's an innovation predicated on bad pitching. In 1975, Sparky Anderson called on so many relievers that the Reds' rotation finished next-to-last in innings per start. "The chief distinction of the Cincinnati bullpen," George Plimpton wrote that year, "is that it is always in use—the sweatshop of the major league ball parks."

The second reason is that 1965 marks the advent of baseball's draft. And it's only once we factor in player development—how many Coneys the Reds made from scratch—that things get truly bleak. A homegrown pitcher, of course, is one a team either drafts or signs internationally. (Jose Rijo doesn't count, for instance, since the Yankees signed him out of the Dominican.) From 1965 through 2013, the Reds had a homegrown starter earn two or more WAR only 43 times. Most of those seasons occurred early on, when guys like Gary

REDS PROSPECTUS
2013 W-L: 90-72, 3rd in NL Central

Pythag	.576	6th	DER	.723	2nd
RS/G	4.31	11th	B-Age	28.6	20th
RA/G	3.64	4th	P-Age	27.8	11th
TAv	.261	14th	Salary	$110.2	13th
BRR	6.09	7th	M$/MW	$2.34	11th
TAv-P	.253	6th	DL Days	823	12th
FIP	3.78	12th	$ on DL	16%	14th

	Runs	HR/RH	HR/LH	Runs/RH	Runs/LH
Three-Year Park Factors	103	110	116	100	104

Top Hitter WARP	6.68 (Joey Votto)
Top Pitcher WARP	3.35 (Mat Latos)
Top Prospect	Robert Stephenson

Nolan and Don Gullett were stringing together those good-but-hardly-great campaigns that sent Sparky to his 'pen. In the '80s, Cincinnati developed Mario Soto, who made three straight All-Star games, and Tom Browning, who served as a sturdy innings-muncher for the 1990 World Series champions. But then things got bleaker still: from 1991 through 2009, the Reds received exactly one two-WAR season from a homegrown starter—one.

This period happens to cover my own formative years as a Reds fan, and I know whom to blame. It started with the owner, Marge Schott. Regardless of her status as a human—maybe she was evil, maybe she was just insane—Marge had a limited baseball mind. "All scouts do is watch games," she once said, not incorrectly. So she hired the smallest staff in baseball. Under Marge, the Reds didn't even bother with Latin America.

There was also Jim Bowden, who became the team's general manager in 1992. Bowden talked a lot about developing young pitchers. Then again, Bowden talked a lot, period. He seemed far more concerned with signing worn-out veterans to patch up with Gullett, who was now the team's pitching coach. Bowden & Gullett: it sounds like dilapidated scrapyard, and for years the two tried (and sometimes briefly succeeded at) resurrecting Steve Parris, Mark Portugal, Paul Wilson, Pete Harnisch, Joey Hamilton and many, many more—each one the sporting equivalent of an old spider-webbed windshield.

Cincinnati didn't have the prospects to displace those guys. Sometimes, it's tough to tell whether a problem lies in the drafting or the developing. The Reds made it easy by being bad at both. At one point, they cycled through three pitching coordinators in three years. Their draft picks suffered gruesome injuries. (Bowden chose Chris Gruler, a high-schooler with 96 mph heat, third overall, only to watch him undergo three separate shoulder surgeries and then retire, having thrown 92 innings, none of them above Single-A.) During this period, Brett Tomko became the one home-grown starter to post a two-WAR season—and he did it only once, in 1997. Going to see him pitch at Riverfront was like going to the Cincinnati Zoo. Finally, after hearing so much about these exotic creatures, I got to see one in person.

By the end of his tenure, Bowden had turned desperate, even manic. From 1999 to 2003, he used four of his five first-rounders on pitching—during those drafts the Reds spent well over $10 million in signing bonuses for pitchers—but none of them came close to panning out. In that same span, Bowden traded for another 39 pitchers. And yet in 2003, the year the Reds moved into Great American Ball Park, their Opening Day roster featured only three homegrown hurlers, all of them in the bullpen. The team's Opening Day starter was 30-year-old Jimmy Haynes, who would finish the year with a record of 2-12 and a WAR of -1.5. Incredibly, these numbers *still* understate how awful the Reds were at cultivating pitchers. In 2003, the rest of baseball included 145 starters on their Opening Day rosters. Exactly one of those 145 slots belonged to a pitcher developed by the Reds—still Brett Tomko, who now toiled for the St. Louis Cardinals.

Marge had morphed into a new owner, Carl Lindner, and that summer he fired Bowden and rebooted the club's baseball operations. In 2004, the Reds hired a new scouting director, Terry Reynolds. Along with his successor Chris Buckley—and let's not forget Bob Castellini, the current owner, who has funneled tons of money into the farm—Reynolds and his scouts changed everything. That year, the team drafted Homer Bailey and signed Johnny Cueto. It took time for them to mature, and one reason the Reds drafted Mike Leake in 2009 was because they still needed a starter who could advance quickly. Nevertheless, the Reds now possess one of baseball's best rotations. In 2013, five of their starters posted a WAR of two or better—Bailey, Leake, Tony Cingrani, Bronson Arroyo and Mat Latos. (That doesn't include an oft-injured Cueto, who chipped in 1.4 WAR in 11 starts.) The only other team with five two-WAR starters was Detroit, and the Tigers and Reds finished first and second in innings per start.

The Reds' rotation looks even better when you combine it with 2012. In fact, it starts to look like one of the six best rotations in modern franchise history. If we total up the stats for all those two-WAR starters, we'll see that the team's rotation regulars produced 16.3 WAR in 2012 and 14.7 WAR in 2013. Since the advent of the draft, there's been only one comparable run: 1966 and 1967, when a youthful Gary Nolan led his fellow starters to amassing 31.6 WAR total. Even if we expand our scope back to 1900, when real men threw complete games and answered to names like Noodles Hahn, there are only a handful of rotations better than the Reds' current one: 1903 and 1904 (37.3 WAR), 1923 and 1924 (36.6 WAR), 1941 and 1942 (35.5 WAR), and 1962 and 1963 (35.1 WAR). I'll say it again, mostly because I still can't believe it myself: During the last two years, the Reds have marched out their sixth-best rotation in the modern era.

What's even more impressive, especially if you're a long-time Reds fan, is that this rotation is mostly homegrown. Cingrani, Bailey and Cueto all started out as Reds. So did Aroldis Chapman, who lurks as a potential starter. The team traded a clutch of prospects for Latos, as well, and each of these arms seems like an affirmation of Cincinnati's new focus on drafting and development. Where once there was Schottian chaos, now there are stable pros like Reynolds and Buckley and Mack Jenkins, who spent six years as the Reds' minor-league pitching coordinator and now works with his former protégés in the bigs.

But here's the thing about developing pitchers—even when you do everything right, and the Reds finally appear to be doing precisely that—you should still expect lots of failure. So much can go wrong with a fledgling pitcher: the shoulder, the elbow, the mechanics, the mind, any one of which can wreck your future ace. In a study for *Royals Review*, Scott McKinney demonstrated that young pitchers remain far more likely to flop than do young hitters. McKinney broke down the odds based on *Baseball America*'s Top 100 Prospects lists from 1990 to 2003, and by comparing his numbers to the Reds' starters and their peak rankings we can get a sense of how dicey it is to breed young pitching. *Baseball America* ranked Homer Bailey fifth on its list—but even prospects that high fizzle out 59 percent of the time. Aroldis Chapman made it to seventh, which still meant that, historically, there was also a 59 percent chance he'd be a bust. Cueto hit 34th—a 78 percent chance to bust. Leake peaked at 72nd, an 82 percent chance. Cingrani: 82nd, an 83 percent chance.

Each of those pitchers, of course, has ended up being the furthest thing from a flop. But the most astounding fact here isn't that the Reds have had so many successes—it's that they've had so few failures. Consider that on *Baseball America*'s latest lists, from 2005 to 2012, the Reds placed only one other pitcher in the Top 100: a college arm named Richie Gardner. In 2004, Gardner and his vile slider became the Reds' minor-league player of the year. The next year, *Baseball America* ranked him as the game's 93rd-best prospect. For once, the Reds prospect met his destiny (87 percent failure rate), tearing his labrum and never regaining his old stuff.

That's what happens with young pitchers—they fail. Yet Gardner was the Reds' only recent top-100 pitching prospect to self-destruct. Their other five prospects have turned into

terrific big league pitchers, and that represents lottery-winner luck.

This talent boom has rippled throughout the current roster. In previous Reds epochs, a pitcher like J.J. Hoover or Sam LeCure would be the team's great rotational hope—the new Brett Tomko. Today, they're simply cheap and devastating relievers. But the other problem with young pitchers is that once you do develop a few it isn't too long before they get expensive. Despite Castellini's savvy stewardship, the Reds remain a small-market team. In 2002, they actually played in the first game on YES Network—a preseason exhibition against the Yankees—but that's as close as Cincinnati will ever get to that kind of major-market clout. Bailey and Latos can hit the open market in the next two years, and it's easy to imagine them both receiving offers of $100 million or more.

So while Reds still have a chance to win the World Series with their current core, they probably have fewer chances than you might think. Reds fans will point to a new group of pitchers climbing the prospect ranks, notably Robert Stephenson and Daniel Corcino. But those fans should also realize that their favorite team has been on a run that, in many ways, is as improbable and unsustainable as their decades-long drought. Even if the Reds don't win that championship, their fans can still say they watched one of the best rotations in team history. But they—we—should also admit that this rotation was a total fluke. The only thing more impressive than having five prospects pan out is having five prospects pan out when you only have six to start with.

Craig Fehrman lives in Indiana and is writing a book about presidents and their books for Simon & Schuster.

HITTERS

Jason Bourgeois CF

Born: **1/4/1982** Age: **32**
Bats: **R** Throws: **R** Height: **5' 9"**
Weight: **190** Breakout: **4%**
Improve: **11%** Collapse: **9%**
Attrition: **20%** MLB: **38%**

Comparables:
Jason Tyner, Norris Hopper, Tike Redman

YEAR	TEAM	LVL	AGE	PA	R	2B	3B	HR	RBI	BB	SO	SB	CS	AVG/OBP/SLG	TAv	BABIP	BRR	FRAA	WARP
2011	HOU	MLB	29	252	30	8	2	1	16	10	24	31	6	.294/.323/.357	.246	.324	2.3	LF(34): 0.0, CF(34): -2.0	0.6
2012	OMA	AAA	30	247	41	7	1	3	8	21	24	7	5	.243/.314/.324	.231	.262	-0.2	RF(23): -0.8, LF(17): 0.5	0.0
2012	KCA	MLB	30	66	10	2	1	0	5	4	4	5	4	.258/.303/.323	.244	.276	0.7	CF(23): 0.4, LF(2): -0.1	0.2
2013	DUR	AAA	31	391	52	15	3	2	61	31	38	22	6	.290/.343/.368	.251	.315	3.8	LF(40): 1.5, CF(39): 1.0	1.4
2013	TBA	MLB	31	18	2	0	0	1	2	2	4	0	0	.188/.278/.375	.335	.182	0.5	LF(6): 0.1, RF(1): -0.0	0.2
2014	CIN	MLB	32	250	30	8	1	3	18	14	34	13	4	.258/.302/.340	.241	.290	1	CF -1, LF 0	0.2

Bourgeois was exactly what a general manager hopes for when he signs a minor-league free agent. Ranking no higher than third on the Rays' Triple-A outfield depth chart behind Brandon Guyer and Rich Thompson, he got a three-week call-up in late July when Desmond Jennings hit the disabled list—where Guyer and Thompson already were. Bourgeois' game-winning single on August 14th was enough all by itself to validate his temporary parking pass at the Trop, and this year he'll go to the Reds' Triple-A affiliate looking for a similar, perhaps longer chance to make a little big-league bank. It might take at least three injuries once again, though, and one of them would have to be to Billy Hamilton.

Jay Bruce — RF

Born: 4/3/1987 Age: 27
Bats: L Throws: L Height: 6' 3"
Weight: 215 Breakout: 2%
Improve: 63% Collapse: 5%
Attrition: 4% MLB: 100%

Comparables:
Roger Maris, Rocky Colavito, Vic Wertz

YEAR	TEAM	LVL	AGE	PA	R	2B	3B	HR	RBI	BB	SO	SB	CS	AVG/OBP/SLG	TAv	BABIP	BRR	FRAA	WARP
2011	CIN	MLB	24	664	84	27	2	32	97	71	158	8	7	.256/.341/.474	.281	.297	3.6	RF(155): -2.4	2.7
2012	CIN	MLB	25	633	89	35	5	34	99	62	155	9	3	.252/.327/.514	.295	.283	-4.2	RF(154): 8.8	3.8
2013	CIN	MLB	26	697	89	43	1	30	109	63	185	7	3	.262/.329/.478	.290	.322	1.9	RF(160): 9.2	5.1
2014	CIN	MLB	27	641	83	30	2	30	93	62	158	7	4	.251/.326/.468	.285	.290	-0.8	RF 8	3.6

Bruce has been Steady Reddy since he was the best prospect in baseball prior to the 2008 season. No, that consistency still hasn't produced star-level slash lines, even while plumped up by one of the league's most hitter-friendly ballparks. Bruce has never cracked a .300 TAv and on the eve of his age-27 season, he has increased his strikeout rate four consecutive years and is coming off a career-low 71 percent contact rate. But the Texas native is proof that a top prospect's value is not entirely wrapped up in star potential. Bruce is a defensive asset, especially with his arm. Over the past five seasons, he has 49 outfield assists (seventh-best in baseball), while committing one throwing error. That's not the achievement you had in mind when you saw him atop those lists six years ago, but stardom is often an entire package.

Zack Cozart — SS

Born: 8/12/1985 Age: 28
Bats: R Throws: R Height: 6' 0"
Weight: 195 Breakout: 3%
Improve: 46% Collapse: 6%
Attrition: 7% MLB: 94%

Comparables:
Ronny Cedeno, Angel Berroa, Brandon Phillips

YEAR	TEAM	LVL	AGE	PA	R	2B	3B	HR	RBI	BB	SO	SB	CS	AVG/OBP/SLG	TAv	BABIP	BRR	FRAA	WARP
2011	LOU	AAA	25	350	57	26	2	7	32	23	51	9	2	.310/.357/.467	.275	.348	2	SS(60): 0.7	1.9
2011	CIN	MLB	25	38	6	0	0	2	3	0	6	0	0	.324/.324/.486	.255	.345	-0.3	SS(11): 1.6	0.3
2012	CIN	MLB	26	600	72	33	4	15	35	31	113	4	0	.246/.288/.399	.248	.282	2	SS(138): 2.7	2.4
2013	CIN	MLB	27	618	74	30	3	12	63	26	102	0	0	.254/.284/.381	.242	.285	6.9	SS(150): -3.7	2.0
2014	CIN	MLB	28	577	64	29	2	14	58	28	105	3	1	.255/.292/.394	.248	.290	-0.4	SS 1	1.9

It's not Cozart's fault that Dusty Baker let him and his .284 on-base percentage appear in the no. 2 spot 291 times in 2013. The OBP itself is his fault, but, hey, every league needs an OBP underclass. The outs aren't a big deal when Cozart's playing quality defense at a tough position, but despite being generally regarded as above average, his FRAA dipped into negative waters for the first time last year. The Reds don't have anyone in a position to challenge him (especially now that Billy Hamilton has been moved to center field), so he's likely to maintain this job for the foreseeable future. He's a fine stopgap until someone better comes along, and if he can replicate his .282/.315/.400 second-half line he'll be a three-win player. A three-win player who should never bat higher than seventh.

Phillip Ervin — RF

Born: 7/17/1992 Age: 21
Bats: R Throws: R Height: 5' 11"
Weight: 190 Breakout: 0%
Improve: 2% Collapse: 0%
Attrition: 0% MLB: 2%

Comparables:
Moises Sierra, Lorenzo Cain, Ryan Kalish

YEAR	TEAM	LVL	AGE	PA	R	2B	3B	HR	RBI	BB	SO	SB	CS	AVG/OBP/SLG	TAv	BABIP	BRR	FRAA	WARP
2013	DYT	A	20	51	7	2	0	1	6	8	10	2	1	.349/.451/.465	.354	.438	-1.4	CF(8): -0.1, RF(4): -0.3	0.5
2014	CIN	MLB	21	250	24	8	0	6	26	17	71	3	0	.213/.271/.336	.225	.270	0	RF -2, CF -0	-0.6

Drafted 27th overall out of Samford University, Ervin signed for $1.8 million and was hitting .414 in the Pioneer League by the end of the week. His compact swing makes consistent and solid contact, and there's a hint of above-average power potential in his 5-foot-11 frame. Defensively, he has the arm for right field, though his speed gives him a chance to stick in center. A limited ceiling dropped him in the draft, but, barring setbacks, his advanced hit tool out of college will make him one of the first of the class to reach the majors.

Todd Frazier — 3B

Born: 2/12/1986 Age: 28
Bats: R Throws: R Height: 6' 3"
Weight: 220 Breakout: 4%
Improve: 43% Collapse: 7%
Attrition: 11% MLB: 94%

Comparables:
Chase Headley, Wilson Betemit, Ian Stewart

YEAR	TEAM	LVL	AGE	PA	R	2B	3B	HR	RBI	BB	SO	SB	CS	AVG/OBP/SLG	TAv	BABIP	BRR	FRAA	WARP
2011	LOU	AAA	25	359	47	18	1	15	46	34	82	17	4	.260/.340/.467	.296	.302	0.9	3B(28): 2.4, 1B(17): 0.6	2.3
2011	CIN	MLB	25	121	17	5	0	6	15	7	27	1	0	.232/.289/.438	.273	.253	1.3	3B(27): -0.9, LF(4): -0.0	0.7
2012	LOU	AAA	26	41	4	2	0	1	7	2	11	3	0	.231/.268/.359	.227	.296	0.2	3B(8): -0.0, LF(1): -0.1	0.0
2012	CIN	MLB	26	465	55	26	6	19	67	36	103	3	2	.273/.331/.498	.292	.316	0.1	3B(73): -1.5, 1B(39): -0.2	2.6
2013	CIN	MLB	27	600	63	29	3	19	73	50	125	6	5	.234/.314/.407	.260	.269	1.7	3B(147): -2.2, LF(2): -0.1	1.9
2014	CIN	MLB	28	542	65	26	2	20	71	43	124	9	4	.245/.315/.434	.274	.280	-0.2	3B -3, 1B 0	1.7

The pride of Toms River, New Jersey—where he first gained national attention by leading the charge toward a Little League World Series title—Frazier spent an entire season (save six innings in left field) at one position for the first time in his career. Unfortunately, he took a step back at the plate from his rookie season, dropping his OPS+ from 118 to 96 as clumps of line drives and fly balls turned into grounders. Like almost everyone else in the Cincinnati lineup, he took a turn in the no. 2 spot, but his .257 on-base percentage in 16 games there didn't earn him an extended look. Already 28 years old, with an average-at-best defensive profile, Frazier can still embrace the Michael Cuddyer career path if his bat can return to 2012 form.

Billy Hamilton CF

Born: 9/9/1990 Age: 23
Bats: B Throws: R Height: 6' 0''
Weight: 160 Breakout: 3%
Improve: 13% Collapse: 3%
Attrition: 7% MLB: 22%

Comparables:
Ezequiel Carrera, Peter Bourjos, Gorkys Hernandez

YEAR	TEAM	LVL	AGE	PA	R	2B	3B	HR	RBI	BB	SO	SB	CS	AVG/OBP/SLG	TAv	BABIP	BRR	FRAA	WARP
2011	DYT	A	20	610	99	18	9	3	50	52	133	103	20	.278/.340/.360	.230	.360	0.6	SS(24): -0.8	0.1
2012	BAK	A+	21	392	79	18	9	1	30	50	70	104	21	.323/.413/.439	.317	.404	13.1	SS(77): 9.0	6.2
2012	PEN	AA	21	213	33	4	5	1	15	36	43	51	16	.286/.406/.383	.296	.371	3.9	SS(48): 1.2	2.3
2013	LOU	AAA	22	547	75	18	4	6	41	38	102	75	15	.256/.308/.343	.232	.310	10.7	CF(118): 18.7, SS(1): 0.0	3.0
2013	CIN	MLB	22	22	9	2	0	0	1	2	4	13	1	.368/.429/.474	.358	.467	1.1	CF(7): 0.5	0.5
2014	CIN	MLB	23	250	40	8	2	3	15	19	58	38	8	.247/.305/.342	.240	.310	4.9	CF 4, SS 2	1.5

While you get carried away by Hamilton's game-changing speed, stay tethered with his black-hole offense: His negative 20.4 Batting Runs Above Average was the seventh worst in the International League. Even in Triple-A, that kind of production doesn't deserve 547 plate appearances unless the player is 1) blessed with 80 speed and 2) an impact defender in center field. Hamilton meets both criteria. As Dusty Baker's fancy pinch-runner in September, his efficiency on the basepaths was a Fun Fact spectacle. In just 13 games (three starts), he finished fourth in the NL in second-half stolen bases. He stole more bases than the team leader on two of the four LCS teams, and was just two steals behind a third. Excluding bunts, he hit seven grounders and scored four infield hits. He's going to challenge the historic landmarks of baseball thievery, as his 3.1-second times to second base are almost literally undefendable if he doesn't make any mistakes. Further, his baserunning impunity will give him every advantage at the plate; not just corner infielders but shortstop and second base have to pull in against him, opening up space for flairs and bouncers. And pitchers measuring the costs of a certain stolen base against his relatively punchless swing will no doubt feed him fastballs in the zone to avoid two- or three-base walks. He had those advantages in Triple-A, too, and still couldn't do better than a league-average BABIP, so nothing is automatic. But Hamilton has the quick wrists and athleticism to generate bat speed against velocity; his ability to consistently make solid contact and hit his way on base will determine whether he makes a run at Henderson.

Jack Hannahan 3B

Born: 3/4/1980 Age: 34
Bats: L Throws: R Height: 6' 2''
Weight: 210 Breakout: 4%
Improve: 41% Collapse: 8%
Attrition: 21% MLB: 80%

Comparables:
Daryl Spencer, Todd Zeile, Rico Petrocelli

YEAR	TEAM	LVL	AGE	PA	R	2B	3B	HR	RBI	BB	SO	SB	CS	AVG/OBP/SLG	TAv	BABIP	BRR	FRAA	WARP
2011	CLE	MLB	31	366	38	16	2	8	40	38	80	2	1	.250/.331/.388	.261	.308	-0.8	3B(104): 15.9, 1B(8): 0.2	2.9
2012	CLE	MLB	32	318	23	16	0	4	29	27	63	0	2	.244/.312/.341	.244	.299	-0.6	3B(96): 11.2, SS(7): 0.1	1.3
2013	CIN	MLB	33	162	12	5	1	1	14	19	38	0	0	.216/.317/.288	.217	.287	-1.3	3B(37): 0.5, 1B(10): -0.1	-0.3
2014	CIN	MLB	34	250	24	11	1	4	23	23	61	1	1	.226/.303/.336	.238	.290	-0.5	3B 7, 1B -0	0.8

Still owed a minimum of $3 million for Year 2 of his eminently regrettable contract, Hannahan continues to have a strong reputation in the field, but logged only 215 innings at the hot corner to show it off. That left him open to the quirks of small-sample defensive metrics, which helped put his total value below replacement level for the first time since 2006. On the bright side, he produced a .775 OPS in 45 plate appearances as a pinch hitter, but if this leads to him being used more in that role, it's not likely to be a good thing for the Reds.

Chris Heisey LF

Born: 12/14/1984 Age: 29
Bats: R Throws: R Height: 6' 1''
Weight: 210 Breakout: 4%
Improve: 48% Collapse: 1%
Attrition: 10% MLB: 96%

Comparables:
Al Martin, Cleon Jones, Larry Bigbie

YEAR	TEAM	LVL	AGE	PA	R	2B	3B	HR	RBI	BB	SO	SB	CS	AVG/OBP/SLG	TAv	BABIP	BRR	FRAA	WARP
2011	CIN	MLB	26	308	44	9	1	18	50	19	78	6	1	.254/.309/.487	.293	.283	0.5	LF(88): 0.4, CF(18): -0.3	1.7
2012	CIN	MLB	27	375	44	16	5	7	31	18	81	6	3	.265/.315/.401	.253	.328	-1.5	LF(63): 3.4, CF(36): -0.7	0.9
2013	LOU	AAA	28	22	1	1	0	0	1	1	6	0	0	.200/.227/.250	.172	.267	0.1	LF(4): 0.2	-0.2
2013	CIN	MLB	28	244	29	11	1	9	23	9	51	3	0	.237/.279/.415	.245	.265	-0.9	LF(69): 2.3, RF(6): 0.2	0.4
2014	CIN	MLB	29	259	33	10	1	9	29	15	63	4	1	.244/.299/.411	.258	.290	0.1	LF 3, CF -0	0.8

No one was in a better position to take advantage of Ryan Ludwick's Opening Day injury than Heisey, but the result was a bit of farce, a bit of tragedy and hard to watch, like Dane Cook adapting *Hamlet*. Heisey hit .173/.195/.293 in 79 April plate appearances before a strained hamstring cost him 52 games. Dusty Baker then small-sampled Heisey into the short side of a platoon (despite a substantial reverse split in his career) and his .796 OPS after the injury was spread over infrequent starts. He should get an opportunity to compete with Ludwick for the left field job this year, though he'll slot in as the underdog.

Cesar Izturis — SS

Born: 2/10/1980 Age: 34
Bats: B Throws: R Height: 5' 9"
Weight: 180 Breakout: 1%
Improve: 18% Collapse: 12%
Attrition: 25% MLB: 77%

Comparables:
Luis Aparicio, Bill Russell, Eddie Kasko

YEAR	TEAM	LVL	AGE	PA	R	2B	3B	HR	RBI	BB	SO	SB	CS	AVG/OBP/SLG	TAv	BABIP	BRR	FRAA	WARP
2011	BOW	AA	31	29	3	1	0	0	3	2	5	0	1	.240/.286/.280	.262	.286	-0.5	2B(2): -0.1, SS(2): -0.4	0.0
2011	BAL	MLB	31	33	4	0	0	0	1	2	10	0	0	.200/.250/.200	.168	.300	-0.5	SS(12): 1.6, 2B(3): -0.0	-0.1
2012	MIL	MLB	32	169	9	6	2	2	11	3	13	1	1	.235/.248/.333	.189	.245	-1.7	SS(45): 2.4, 3B(3): 0.2	-0.3
2012	WAS	MLB	32	4	4	1	0	0	0	0	0	0	0	.500/.500/.750	.408	.500	0.9	2B(1): -0.0, 3B(1): -0.0	0.2
2013	CIN	MLB	33	142	6	8	0	0	11	9	13	0	0	.209/.259/.271	.201	.231	-1	SS(29): 0.4, 2B(21): -0.0	-0.5
2014	CIN	MLB	34	250	21	9	1	2	18	12	32	3	2	.229/.271/.297	.211	.250	-0.2	SS 1, 2B -0	-0.2

Since 2005, Izturis is hitting .250 when it comes to finishing a season with a positive WARP. Better than his actual batting average over that time, but a sad state of affairs for both Izturis and his employer. On the bright side, by logging time in Cincinnati (and with the Astros' helpful move to the AL), he has become the only active player in all of baseball to play for every team in a single division. Now he can finally poke out the last piece of rotted candy from his NL Central advent calendar.

Ryan Ludwick — LF

Born: 7/13/1978 Age: 35
Bats: R Throws: L Height: 6' 2"
Weight: 215 Breakout: 3%
Improve: 26% Collapse: 18%
Attrition: 25% MLB: 82%

Comparables:
Wes Covington, Jim Rice, Raul Ibanez

YEAR	TEAM	LVL	AGE	PA	R	2B	3B	HR	RBI	BB	SO	SB	CS	AVG/OBP/SLG	TAv	BABIP	BRR	FRAA	WARP
2011	PIT	MLB	32	133	14	5	0	2	11	19	37	0	0	.232/.341/.330	.272	.324	-0.2	LF(22): -1.0, RF(13): 0.5	0.2
2011	SDN	MLB	32	420	42	18	0	11	64	32	87	1	1	.238/.301/.373	.252	.277	-2.2	LF(95): -6.4, RF(1): -0.1	-0.4
2012	CIN	MLB	33	472	53	28	1	26	80	42	97	0	1	.275/.346/.531	.299	.299	-0.1	LF(108): -2.8	2.6
2013	LOU	AAA	34	39	2	1	0	1	4	0	9	0	0	.132/.154/.237	.132	.143	-0.1	LF(10): -0.7	-0.6
2013	CIN	MLB	34	140	7	5	0	2	12	10	29	0	0	.240/.293/.326	.211	.293	-0.4	LF(32): -2.1	-0.8
2014	CIN	MLB	35	250	27	11	0	9	32	19	57	0	1	.244/.309/.411	.262	.280	-0.7	LF -3, RF 0	0.2

Nearly four and a half months into the season, Ludwick still had a pristine 1.000 on-base percentage. *The Kid Who Only Hit Homers*? Sadly, *The Kid Who Tore His Labrum Sliding On Day One*. He did return in August but was a shell of his 2012 self, finishing the year as the Reds' least valuable position player. Ludwick's role as he attempts to bounce back is uncertain, as is the central mystery of Ludwick's wild career swings: Which seasons are the outliers, and which are just him?

Donald Lutz — LF

Born: 2/6/1989 Age: 25
Bats: L Throws: R Height: 6' 3"
Weight: 250 Breakout: 5%
Improve: 11% Collapse: 5%
Attrition: 21% MLB: 26%

Comparables:
John Mayberry, Scott Van Slyke, Cole Garner

YEAR	TEAM	LVL	AGE	PA	R	2B	3B	HR	RBI	BB	SO	SB	CS	AVG/OBP/SLG	TAv	BABIP	BRR	FRAA	WARP
2011	DYT	A	22	506	85	23	3	20	75	34	125	5	4	.301/.358/.492	.298	.375	-0.9	1B(13): -0.2, LF(1): -0.1	0.3
2012	BAK	A+	23	277	42	18	3	17	51	19	71	7	2	.265/.325/.561	.300	.301	0.7	LF(28): -3.9, 1B(24): -1.2	1.3
2012	PEN	AA	23	165	17	5	1	5	15	13	32	1	3	.242/.315/.389	.260	.277	-2	LF(31): 2.3, 1B(14): 0.5	0.5
2013	PEN	AA	24	255	35	12	4	7	30	19	56	4	1	.245/.318/.424	.282	.293	1.4	LF(45): 2.4, 1B(8): -0.3	1.4
2013	CIN	MLB	24	59	5	1	0	1	8	1	14	2	0	.241/.254/.310	.196	.302	0.8	LF(17): 1.0, RF(1): 0.2	0.0
2014	CIN	MLB	25	250	26	10	1	8	30	12	67	2	1	.230/.274/.393	.244	.280	-0.1	LF 1, 1B -0	0.2

Lutz, the first German-raised player to debut in the majors, is armed with immense power and the supplementary Twitter handle "Braunerhulk." HULK SMASH SCREAMING LINE DRIVE FOR HULK'S FIRST HOMER, but HULK ALSO CHASE BREAKING BALLS, and pitchers quickly exploited his uncontrolled aggression. He'll need to tone it down and hit left-handed pitching to eclipse his apparent destiny as a platoon outfielder. Maybe he can learn from fellow lefty Jay Bruce Banner.

Devin Mesoraco — C

Born: 6/19/1988 Age: 26
Bats: R Throws: R Height: 6' 1"
Weight: 230 Breakout: 10%
Improve: 52% Collapse: 8%
Attrition: 17% MLB: 98%

Comparables:
Jonathan Lucroy, Ronny Paulino, Francisco Cervelli

YEAR	TEAM	LVL	AGE	PA	R	2B	3B	HR	RBI	BB	SO	SB	CS	AVG/OBP/SLG	TAv	BABIP	BRR	FRAA	WARP
2011	LOU	AAA	23	499	60	36	2	15	71	52	83	1	1	.289/.371/.484	.282	.325	0.2	C(81): 1.3	2.6
2011	CIN	MLB	23	53	5	3	0	2	6	3	10	0	0	.180/.226/.360	.210	.184	-0.4	C(16): -0.1	-0.1
2012	CIN	MLB	24	184	17	8	0	5	14	17	33	1	1	.212/.288/.352	.237	.234	-0.2	C(53): 0.9	0.5
2013	CIN	MLB	25	352	31	13	0	9	42	24	61	0	2	.238/.287/.362	.233	.264	-1.2	C(97): 1.0	0.8
2014	CIN	MLB	26	299	32	14	0	9	34	25	55	1	1	.241/.306/.395	.254	.270	-0.7	C 1	1.2

It was all too easy to blame Mesoraco's disappointing 2012 campaign on Dusty Baker's lineup obstinacy, but increased playing time in 2013 didn't win him sympathy in the Queen City. The biggest key to living up to his prospect hype at the plate will be hitting same-side pitching, as he's been held to a .584 career OPS against righties. On defense, he has improved from *Mess*oraco to M*esoso*raco. Further improvements on either front, along with a market correction on his by-all-appearances unlucky BABIP, can rekindle his promise. Having a new manager in town certainly won't hurt.

Xavier Paul   LF

Born: 2/25/1985 **Age:** 29
Bats: L **Throws:** R **Height:** 5' 9"
Weight: 205 **Breakout:** 2%
Improve: 30% **Collapse:** 7%
Attrition: 17% **MLB:** 76%

Comparables:
Fred Lewis, Michael Ryan, John Rodriguez

YEAR	TEAM	LVL	AGE	PA	R	2B	3B	HR	RBI	BB	SO	SB	CS	AVG/OBP/SLG	TAv	BABIP	BRR	FRAA	WARP
2011	LAN	MLB	26	11	0	0	0	0	0	0	5	0	0	.273/.273/.273	.190	.500	0.1	LF(5): 0.0, RF(1): -0.0	0.0
2011	PIT	MLB	26	251	30	6	5	2	20	13	57	16	6	.254/.293/.349	.248	.328	-0.5	RF(71): -1.8, LF(22): -0.9	0.0
2012	LOU	AAA	27	26	4	2	0	1	4	1	5	3	0	.480/.500/.680	.394	.579	0	RF(6): -0.8	0.3
2012	SYR	AAA	27	237	30	16	1	8	44	19	41	6	3	.315/.376/.512	.295	.360	-0.5	LF(28): 0.3, RF(17): -1.8	1.3
2012	CIN	MLB	27	96	8	5	1	2	7	9	18	4	2	.314/.379/.465	.290	.379	-1.3	LF(17): -1.1, RF(1): -0.1	0.3
2013	CIN	MLB	28	239	24	12	0	7	32	27	53	0	1	.244/.339/.402	.268	.295	-0.2	LF(59): -2.8	0.2
2014	CIN	MLB	29	250	28	12	1	6	28	18	56	6	3	.258/.316/.407	.264	.310	0.1	LF -2, RF -1	0.4

Coming into 2013, Paul had never finished a season with more major-league home runs than first names. But of all players on the Reds' roster to get at least 50 plate appearances, Paul's .741 OPS ranked fourth behind only Joey Votto, Shin-Soo Choo and Jay Bruce. His seven homers last season matched his total coming into the year, and they weren't cheapies—all of them were labeled as either "Plenty" or "No Doubt" by ESPN's Hit Tracker. Paul will need to keep hitting to justify a roster spot, as he's never posted a positive number in any of the major advanced fielding metrics. If he stays anywhere near his .273/.333/.576 line as a pinch-hitter, he'll get plenty of opportunities, although it likely won't be with the Reds, who non-tendered him in December.

Brayan Pena   C

Born: 1/7/1982 **Age:** 32
Bats: B **Throws:** R **Height:** 5' 9"
Weight: 230 **Breakout:** 3%
Improve: 35% **Collapse:** 14%
Attrition: 21% **MLB:** 91%

Comparables:
Bengie Molina, Johnny Estrada, Brian Harper

YEAR	TEAM	LVL	AGE	PA	R	2B	3B	HR	RBI	BB	SO	SB	CS	AVG/OBP/SLG	TAv	BABIP	BRR	FRAA	WARP
2011	KCA	MLB	29	240	17	11	0	3	24	12	24	0	0	.248/.288/.338	.221	.261	-1.8	C(69): -1.5	-0.1
2012	KCA	MLB	30	226	16	10	1	2	25	9	24	0	1	.236/.262/.321	.207	.253	-2	C(52): -0.7, 1B(3): -0.0	-0.7
2013	DET	MLB	31	243	19	11	0	4	22	6	26	0	2	.297/.315/.397	.260	.315	-2.9	C(64): -0.5, 1B(1): 0.0	0.5
2014	CIN	MLB	32	250	24	12	0	5	25	12	35	1	1	.250/.290/.368	.239	.270	-0.6	C -1, 1B -0	0.5

Pena was an adequate backup for the Tigers in 2013, turning in his best offensive work since 2009, but he wasn't a great fit—his best work comes against right-handed pitchers. That makes him a much better match for a team like, say, the Reds, who inked him days into the offseason. Pena's strengths fit the weaknesses of incumbent starter Devin Mesoraco, whose career OPS against righties is .581. Pena could see a career-high workload and emerge as something like a full-timer for the first time at age 32, even if his defense and receiving are nothing special.

Brandon Phillips   2B

Born: 6/28/1981 **Age:** 33
Bats: R **Throws:** R **Height:** 6' 0"
Weight: 200 **Breakout:** 1%
Improve: 36% **Collapse:** 5%
Attrition: 7% **MLB:** 95%

Comparables:
Orlando Hudson, Mark Ellis, Freddy Sanchez

YEAR	TEAM	LVL	AGE	PA	R	2B	3B	HR	RBI	BB	SO	SB	CS	AVG/OBP/SLG	TAv	BABIP	BRR	FRAA	WARP
2011	CIN	MLB	30	674	94	38	2	18	82	44	85	14	9	.300/.353/.457	.285	.322	6.4	2B(148): -6.7	3.5
2012	CIN	MLB	31	623	86	30	1	18	77	28	79	15	2	.281/.321/.429	.264	.298	1.7	2B(146): -5.0	1.3
2013	CIN	MLB	32	666	80	24	2	18	103	39	98	5	3	.261/.310/.396	.257	.281	-1.1	2B(151): 7.7	2.2
2014	CIN	MLB	33	617	68	28	2	16	70	36	89	11	5	.265/.314/.405	.263	.280	-0.4	2B -1	2.1

When he wasn't busy calling out beat writers, Phillips was having his worst offensive season since joining the Reds in 2006. In fact, each of the three numbers in his slash line was his lowest in that time frame. So naturally, Phillips set a career high in RBI with 103—hitting behind the National League's two best on-base men surely had noooothing to do with that. Phillips will turn 33 before the 2014 All-Star Game and second basemen don't tend to age gracefully. (To his credit, the last time he was placed on the disabled list, Lehman Brothers was still solvent.) He's owed $50 million over the next four seasons, but if his still-strong defense starts to go the way of his baserunning and bat, Phillips is a wrap.

Derrick Robinson   LF

Born: 9/28/1987 **Age:** 26
Bats: B **Throws:** L **Height:** 5' 11"
Weight: 190 **Breakout:** 3%
Improve: 6% **Collapse:** 5%
Attrition: 8% **MLB:** 13%

Comparables:
Elian Herrera, Brandon Fahey, Rene Tosoni

YEAR	TEAM	LVL	AGE	PA	R	2B	3B	HR	RBI	BB	SO	SB	CS	AVG/OBP/SLG	TAv	BABIP	BRR	FRAA	WARP
2011	NWA	AA	23	483	56	6	2	1	25	46	87	55	15	.251/.323/.282	.201	.311	4.3	CF(72): 3.6, LF(13): 1.4	-0.6
2012	OMA	AAA	24	488	73	12	3	2	28	50	84	23	9	.268/.344/.325	.243	.325	-1.7	LF(104): 2.7, CF(5): -0.3	0.6
2013	LOU	AAA	25	63	5	3	0	0	3	3	20	3	0	.220/.258/.271	.196	.333	0.6	LF(13): 1.0, CF(1): -0.1	-0.1
2013	CIN	MLB	25	216	21	7	3	0	8	18	44	4	5	.255/.322/.323	.252	.331	-0.1	LF(60): 4.5, CF(15): -0.6	0.6
2014	CIN	MLB	26	250	29	7	1	2	15	19	57	12	4	.227/.287/.295	.217	.280	0.9	LF 3, CF 0	0.0

The most surprising thing about Robinson's season was not that he accumulated more than 200 plate appearances, but that after years of preparation to be a speedy fifth outfielder he was only 4-for-9 in stolen base attempts. Despite this, the former Royals farmhand can still stick as a reserve based on his ability to play strong defense in center field. If it's in Cincinnati, Robinson will feel like Chris Kirkpatrick standing next to Justin Timberlake, as his skill set overlaps almost entirely (and entirely inferiorly) with that of Billy Hamilton.

Henry Rodriguez 3B

Born: 2/9/1990 Age: 24
Bats: B Throws: R Height: 5' 8"
Weight: 200 Breakout: 4%
Improve: 9% Collapse: 4%
Attrition: 15% MLB: 17%

Comparables:
William Bergolla, Donovan Solano, Eider Torres

YEAR	TEAM	LVL	AGE	PA	R	2B	3B	HR	RBI	BB	SO	SB	CS	AVG/OBP/SLG	TAv	BABIP	BRR	FRAA	WARP
2011	BAK	A+	21	254	37	17	0	8	44	14	35	12	7	.340/.378/.513	.301	.372	1.4	2B(41): -3.5, 3B(5): 0.3	1.4
2011	CAR	AA	21	312	39	19	1	5	37	25	43	18	3	.302/.367/.432	.239	.342	1	2B(17): 1.5, SS(3): -0.2	0.1
2012	PEN	AA	22	144	19	6	0	2	15	9	18	3	0	.348/.385/.439	.302	.386	-0.2	3B(29): 1.5, 2B(1): 0.0	1.2
2012	LOU	AAA	22	221	23	10	0	3	20	6	35	5	4	.244/.264/.333	.213	.278	-1.4	3B(28): 4.8, 2B(18): -0.6	-0.2
2012	CIN	MLB	22	16	0	1	0	0	2	2	2	0	0	.214/.312/.286	.207	.250	0	2B(2): -0.0	0.0
2013	LOU	AAA	23	514	45	17	0	4	41	28	69	6	5	.274/.319/.335	.226	.311	0.4	2B(63): -1.8, 3B(61): 1.7	-0.6
2013	CIN	MLB	23	10	0	0	0	0	0	1	4	0	0	.111/.200/.111	.131	.200	-0.4	2B(3): -0.1	-0.2
2014	CIN	MLB	24	250	23	10	0	4	24	9	45	4	2	.252/.281/.350	.231	.290	-0.2	3B 2, 2B -1	0.1

As a prospect, Rodriguez did a few things well. They haven't all kept up with his pace of promotion, leaving him now with just one thing: hitting for contact. The switch-hitter demonstrates good hand-eye coordination, which has kept his average up and strikeouts down. His short stature limits his power, and his isolated power was the fifth lowest in the International League. Rodriguez is average at third and lacks range at second, so consider him a bench talent who might be worthwhile in fantasy leagues that solely count singles.

Yorman Rodriguez RF

Born: 8/15/1992 Age: 21
Bats: R Throws: R Height: 6' 3"
Weight: 197 Breakout: 1%
Improve: 1% Collapse: 0%
Attrition: 1% MLB: 1%

Comparables:
Oswaldo Arcia, Marcell Ozuna, Moises Sierra

YEAR	TEAM	LVL	AGE	PA	R	2B	3B	HR	RBI	BB	SO	SB	CS	AVG/OBP/SLG	TAv	BABIP	BRR	FRAA	WARP
2011	DYT	A	18	310	38	10	4	7	40	25	84	20	8	.254/.318/.393	.182	.337	0.3	RF(10): -0.3, CF(7): -0.7	-0.4
2012	DYT	A	19	277	35	17	3	6	44	12	61	7	5	.271/.307/.430	.267	.332	1.4	RF(57): -4.3, CF(1): -0.1	0.2
2012	BAK	A+	19	94	7	4	0	0	7	3	39	4	0	.156/.181/.200	.149	.269	1	RF(19): -1.2, CF(4): 0.5	-0.9
2013	BAK	A+	20	278	41	20	4	9	35	22	77	6	3	.251/.319/.470	.265	.327	0.9	CF(55): -10.5, RF(1): -0.0	0.0
2013	PEN	AA	20	289	30	15	2	4	31	25	76	4	0	.267/.329/.385	.261	.359	-0.3	RF(66): -4.1	0.5
2014	CIN	MLB	21	250	21	11	1	5	24	11	81	3	1	.211/.247/.325	.210	.290	-0.1	RF -3, CF -2	-1.3

Rodriguez celebrated his five-year anniversary with the Reds organization, but the occasion merited sparks rather than fireworks. While he tantalizes with obvious power, speed and arm tools, he has shown no improvement in his disabled pitch recognition. Some of his power potential emerged and carried into a decent Arizona Fall League performance. Rodriguez is still extremely young with room to grow, a copy-and-paste statement for the past few years, though not for many more. He'll need to cut down his swing-and-miss to make good on the $2.5 million offered to him as a teenager.

Gabriel Rosa LF

Born: 7/2/1993 Age: 20
Bats: R Throws: R Height: 6' 4"
Weight: 185 Breakout: 0%
Improve: 0% Collapse: 0%
Attrition: 0% MLB: 0%

Comparables:
Jeremy Moore, Alfredo Marte, Trayvon Robinson

YEAR	TEAM	LVL	AGE	PA	R	2B	3B	HR	RBI	BB	SO	SB	CS	AVG/OBP/SLG	TAv	BABIP	BRR	FRAA	WARP
2013	–	–	–	–	–	–	–	–	–	–	–	–	–	–	–	–	–	–	–
2014	CIN	MLB	20	250	19	7	0	4	20	13	83	4	1	.170/.219/.251	.176	.240	0.1	LF 1, CF -1	-1.6

Rosa repeated the Pioneer League after missing most of 2012 with injuries, and the lousy line at least offers hints of improvement. His walk rate jumped from 4.5 percent to 11.8 percent, and when he escaped his pitcher-friendly home ballpark he hit .258/.378/.430. Rosa has a strong arm and an athletic body, both put to good use in all three outfield spots after a conversion from third base. The click didn't come last year, but one can't put eyes on Rosa without thinking it still might happen loudly.

Skip Schumaker 2B

Born: 2/3/1980 Age: 34
Bats: L Throws: R Height: 5' 10"
Weight: 195 Breakout: 1%
Improve: 27% Collapse: 11%
Attrition: 14% MLB: 91%

Comparables:
Mark Loretta, Bobby Avila, Tony Graffanino

YEAR	TEAM	LVL	AGE	PA	R	2B	3B	HR	RBI	BB	SO	SB	CS	AVG/OBP/SLG	TAv	BABIP	BRR	FRAA	WARP
2011	SLN	MLB	31	400	34	19	0	2	38	27	50	0	2	.283/.333/.351	.253	.321	-1.2	2B(95): 1.5, RF(31): 0.2	0.6
2012	MEM	AAA	32	25	5	2	0	0	0	4	3	1	0	.286/.400/.381	.313	.333	0.3	2B(4): -0.6, CF(2): -0.0	0.2
2012	SLN	MLB	32	304	37	14	4	1	28	27	50	1	1	.276/.339/.368	.256	.332	-0.3	2B(61): 0.4, CF(15): 0.0	0.8
2013	LAN	MLB	33	356	31	16	0	2	30	28	54	2	2	.263/.332/.332	.243	.312	-1.6	2B(44): -4.7, LF(35): -0.5	-0.8
2014	CIN	MLB	34	325	31	14	1	3	28	25	51	2	1	.263/.324/.352	.252	.300	-0.7	2B -2, CF -1	0.4

Schumaker is an interesting test case in the argument for positional flexibility. His light bat can be justified only if he's playing up the middle, and his glove is a liability regardless of position. He also struggles against southpaws, though Don Mattingly successfully shielded him from left-handers last year. It must have been particularly hard for a team paying $55 million (plus signing bonuses) for four other outfielders to see Schumaker grazing in the pasture during the postseason. The most interesting detail of Schumaker's utility is that he can take the mound in a blowout, as he did twice in 2013, averaging 88 mph with his fastball and mixing in some secondary pitches.

Neftali Soto   1B

Born: 2/28/1989 Age: 25
Bats: R Throws: R Height: 6' 1"
Weight: 215 Breakout: 8%
Improve: 14% Collapse: 9%
Attrition: 20% MLB: 28%

Comparables:
Danny Valencia, Joel Guzman, Matthew Brown

YEAR	TEAM	LVL	AGE	PA	R	2B	3B	HR	RBI	BB	SO	SB	CS	AVG/OBP/SLG	TAv	BABIP	BRR	FRAA	WARP
2011	CAR	AA	22	414	70	19	3	30	76	25	96	0	1	.272/.329/.575	.317	.286	-1.5	1B(27): -0.3	0.6
2012	LOU	AAA	23	512	55	30	0	14	59	41	116	2	1	.245/.312/.400	.234	.298	-5.6	1B(113): 12.6, 3B(1): 0.0	0.2
2013	LOU	AAA	24	495	54	21	0	15	61	26	103	3	1	.271/.313/.414	.247	.317	-2.8	3B(76): 0.3, 1B(47): 0.4	0.3
2013	CIN	MLB	24	13	0	0	0	0	0	0	6	0	0	.000/.077/.000	.022	.000	-0.6	1B(5): -0.1	-0.4
2014	CIN	MLB	25	250	26	11	0	9	32	12	65	0	0	.236/.279/.403	.247	.280	-0.5	1B 1, 3B -0	0.1

Egregious plate discipline has haunted Soto's career, whose sole offensive tool is power. Upon reaching the majors, he swung at 71 percent of pitches—the third-highest swing rate last year, minimum 35 pitches. The others in the top five? All pitchers. *One* of his plate appearances resulted in more than four pitches seen—four of which he swung at, one of which was a wild pitch and one of which, ironically, was taken for strike three down the middle. With little skill elsewhere, he will pinch-hit and see occasional first base duties, where his home run and walk totals will compete in a slow race to 10.

Joey Votto   1B

Born: 9/10/1983 Age: 30
Bats: L Throws: R Height: 6' 2"
Weight: 220 Breakout: 1%
Improve: 43% Collapse: 2%
Attrition: 4% MLB: 99%

Comparables:
Jeff Bagwell, Todd Helton, Lance Berkman

YEAR	TEAM	LVL	AGE	PA	R	2B	3B	HR	RBI	BB	SO	SB	CS	AVG/OBP/SLG	TAv	BABIP	BRR	FRAA	WARP
2011	CIN	MLB	27	719	101	40	3	29	103	110	129	8	6	.309/.416/.531	.328	.349	-3.9	1B(160): 14.2	7.5
2012	CIN	MLB	28	475	59	44	0	14	56	94	85	5	3	.337/.474/.567	.360	.404	-3.2	1B(109): 4.7	6.2
2013	CIN	MLB	29	726	101	30	3	24	73	135	138	6	3	.305/.435/.491	.329	.360	0.5	1B(161): 7.7	6.7
2014	CIN	MLB	30	634	90	35	1	25	92	99	126	7	3	.299/.413/.512	.332	.350	-1.2	1B 7	5.9

All Votto has done since winning his MVP award in 2010 is lead the National League in both walks and on-base percentage in each of the past three seasons. His plate apperances are a clinic in bat control, as he not only has the highest line-drive rate in baseball since 2010, but he's hit just three infield fly balls (at least by some definitions of the term) in those four seasons combined. For those who see the overflowing glass as somehow half empty, Votto did have the first season of his career with a slugging percentage below .500, driven by a career-low .187 isolated power. With all of the money the Reds owe him over the next 10 seasons ($225 million at a minimum), they're going to have to hope this isn't the start of a troubling trend for one of the game's best hitters.

Jesse Winker   LF

Born: 8/17/1993 Age: 20
Bats: L Throws: L Height: 6' 2"
Weight: 210 Breakout: 1%
Improve: 3% Collapse: 0%
Attrition: 4% MLB: 6%

Comparables:
Andrew Lambo, Matt Dominguez, Caleb Gindl

YEAR	TEAM	LVL	AGE	PA	R	2B	3B	HR	RBI	BB	SO	SB	CS	AVG/OBP/SLG	TAv	BABIP	BRR	FRAA	WARP
2013	DYT	A	19	486	73	18	5	16	76	63	75	6	1	.281/.379/.463	.290	.308	-1.6	LF(100): -6.1, RF(1): -0.0	2.1
2014	CIN	MLB	20	250	25	8	1	7	28	22	60	0	0	.223/.293/.361	.239	.270	-0.4	LF -2, RF -1	-0.3

Moving in with a significant other for the first time can be scary but full of promise. The months of dating might have been for show, or perhaps the relationship is on track to hit the next level. Fortunately for the Reds, Winker shined in his first full season at Low-A Dayton as the organization's new top hitting prospect. Just 20 years old, he possesses an advanced approach, bat control and emerging power, qualities that have only matured since draft day. He's a fringy runner and average defensively, but the Reds will tolerate those quirks if Winker can continue cooking with the bat.

PITCHERS

Bronson Arroyo

Born: 2/24/1977 Age: 37
Bats: R Throws: R Height: 6' 4" Weight: 195
Breakout: 6% Improve: 39% Collapse: 23%
Attrition: 19% MLB: 85%

Comparables:
Paul Byrd, Doyle Alexander, Mike Cuellar

YEAR	TEAM	LVL	AGE	W	L	SV	G	GS	IP	H	HR	BB	SO	BB9	SO9	GB%	BABIP	WHIP	ERA	FIP	FRA	WARP
2011	CIN	MLB	34	9	12	0	32	32	199	227	46	45	108	2.0	4.9	39%	.282	1.37	5.07	5.68	6.06	-1.5
2012	CIN	MLB	35	12	10	0	32	32	202	209	26	35	129	1.6	5.7	42%	.290	1.21	3.74	4.13	4.39	1.7
2013	CIN	MLB	36	14	12	0	32	32	202	199	32	34	124	1.5	5.5	46%	.275	1.15	3.79	4.46	5.10	-0.1
2014	CIN	MLB	37	9	10	0	27	27	170	166	26	38	103	2.0	5.4	43%	.277	1.20	4.07	4.81	4.43	0.6

It's plausible there is not a more underrated pitcher in baseball than the 37-year-old Arroyo. In three of the past four seasons, he has maintained an ERA below 4.00, kept his WHIP below 1.25 and thrown at least 200 innings in a hitter's ballpark. Sure, the strikeout rate is as unseemly as his cornrows were, but only two pitchers (Cliff Lee and Bartolo Colon) have had a lower walk rate than Arroyo's 4 percent over the past two seasons. He *has* allowed 40 more home runs than anybody in baseball since he landed in Cincinnati in 2006, so his free agency finally offered him a friendlier ballpark, and may spark another nature-or-nurture discussion about his results.

Homer Bailey

Born: 5/3/1986 Age: 28
Bats: R Throws: R Height: 6' 4" Weight: 230
Breakout: 20% Improve: 54% Collapse: 27%
Attrition: 13% MLB: 87%

Comparables:
Ian Kennedy, Clay Buchholz, Gavin Floyd

YEAR	TEAM	LVL	AGE	W	L	SV	G	GS	IP	H	HR	BB	SO	BB9	SO9	GB%	BABIP	WHIP	ERA	FIP	FRA	WARP
2011	LOU	AAA	25	2	1	0	6	6	30	34	1	6	22	1.8	6.6	38%	.333	1.33	3.00	2.80	4.10	0.3
2011	CIN	MLB	25	9	7	0	22	22	132	136	18	33	106	2.2	7.2	41%	.298	1.28	4.43	4.02	4.88	0.4
2012	CIN	MLB	26	13	10	0	33	33	208	206	26	52	168	2.2	7.3	45%	.291	1.24	3.68	4.01	4.05	2.3
2013	CIN	MLB	27	11	12	0	32	32	209	181	20	54	199	2.3	8.6	47%	.288	1.12	3.49	3.28	3.77	2.9
2014	CIN	MLB	28	10	10	0	30	30	175	159	20	47	153	2.4	7.9	44%	.295	1.17	3.55	3.87	3.86	2.0

Starting pitchers' fastballs are not supposed to jump 1.5 mph during middle age, but Bailey's did. Over the past two years, he has quietly gone from Phil Hughes and Joba Chamberlain's Disappointing Prospects club to pallin' around with Mat Latos and Johnny Cueto at the top of a division-best rotation. After posting career bests in ERA (3.49), FIP (3.28), strikeout rate (23 percent), whiff rate (10.7 percent) and strikeout-to-walk ratio (3.69) in 2013—while matching his career best in no-hitters (1!)—the big Texan will be out to prove, as in 2013, that he's not just coming off a career year, but blossoming into a consistently high-impact starter.

Jonathan Broxton

Born: 6/16/1984 Age: 30
Bats: R Throws: R Height: 6' 4" Weight: 310
Breakout: 30% Improve: 53% Collapse: 29%
Attrition: 10% MLB: 95%

Comparables:
J.J. Putz, Juan Rincon, Francisco Rodriguez

YEAR	TEAM	LVL	AGE	W	L	SV	G	GS	IP	H	HR	BB	SO	BB9	SO9	GB%	BABIP	WHIP	ERA	FIP	FRA	WARP
2011	LAN	MLB	27	1	2	7	14	0	12²	15	2	9	10	6.4	7.1	42%	.317	1.89	5.68	5.60	4.55	-0.1
2012	CIN	MLB	28	3	3	4	25	0	22¹	20	1	3	20	1.2	8.1	49%	.306	1.03	2.82	2.46	2.57	0.5
2012	KCA	MLB	28	1	2	23	35	0	35²	36	1	14	25	3.5	6.3	58%	.321	1.40	2.27	3.35	4.70	0.1
2013	CIN	MLB	29	2	2	0	34	0	30²	27	4	12	25	3.5	7.3	47%	.261	1.27	4.11	4.65	5.45	-0.1
2014	CIN	MLB	30	2	1	10	40	0	38¹	31	3	13	42	3.1	9.9	49%	.301	1.16	3.13	3.16	3.40	0.6

It was never likely that Broxton's newly minted three-year, $21 million contract would look good, but the Reds were certainly hoping for the first year to look better than this. After a very strong finish to the 2012 season in Cincinnati—driven, encouragingly, but an effective cutter he introduced in late August—he very nearly doubled his 2.42 FIP from that stretch. Then in August he underwent his second elbow surgery in three years to repair a torn flexor mass, putting him in doubt for spring training. The man who can famously fit two smaller relievers into his pants had the worst ERA, FIP, WHIP and strikeout-to-walk rate of any pitcher who threw at least 30 innings for the Reds this year. Despite that, he'll likely slot back into the eighth-inning role that his salary ordains.

Aroldis Chapman

Born: 2/28/1988 Age: 26
Bats: L Throws: L Height: 6' 4" Weight: 205
Breakout: 30% Improve: 59% Collapse: 22%
Attrition: 11% MLB: 91%

Comparables:
Sean Doolittle, Jonathan Broxton, David Robertson

YEAR	TEAM	LVL	AGE	W	L	SV	G	GS	IP	H	HR	BB	SO	BB9	SO9	GB%	BABIP	WHIP	ERA	FIP	FRA	WARP
2011	CIN	MLB	23	4	1	1	54	0	50	24	2	41	71	7.4	12.8	53%	.244	1.30	3.60	3.25	4.42	0.3
2012	CIN	MLB	24	5	5	38	68	0	71²	35	4	23	122	2.9	15.3	37%	.252	0.81	1.51	1.59	1.91	2.4
2013	CIN	MLB	25	4	5	38	68	0	63²	37	7	29	112	4.1	15.8	34%	.280	1.04	2.54	2.44	2.78	1.3
2014	CIN	MLB	26	4	2	23	44	4	59²	36	4	26	89	4.0	13.5	44%	.289	1.04	2.23	2.42	2.43	1.7

Death, taxes and hey maybe this is the year that the Reds put Chapman in the starting rotation. With new manager Bryan Price at the helm and new backup catcher (and fellow Cuban defector) Brayan Pena in place, there's just enough water power to restart the rumor mill. Regardless of role, the flame-throwing lefty saw his walk rate jump back up three percentage points from his career low of 8.3 in 2012. He also allowed more home runs in 2013 than in his first three seasons combined. That said, Chapman was closer to the vintage version from July on, averaging 100.0 mph on his fastball (versus 98.1 in the first three months) with 55 strikeouts and 12 walks in 29 innings. Keeping his walk rate in check will be the key to Chapman's success—whether that is remaining an elite closer or transitioning into the rotation.

Nick Christiani

Born: 7/17/1987 Age: 26
Bats: R Throws: R Height: 6' 0" Weight: 190
Breakout: 72% Improve: 72% Collapse: 16%
Attrition: 55% MLB: 7%

Comparables:
Dan Otero, Jean Machi, Colt Hynes

YEAR	TEAM	LVL	AGE	W	L	SV	G	GS	IP	H	HR	BB	SO	BB9	SO9	GB%	BABIP	WHIP	ERA	FIP	FRA	WARP
2011	CAR	AA	23	2	0	3	20	0	25²	16	0	5	22	1.8	7.7	56%	.259	0.82	1.75	2.18	1.73	0.4
2011	LOU	AAA	23	2	3	7	33	0	35²	46	2	15	19	3.8	4.8	55%	.305	1.71	5.30	4.33	5.49	-0.3
2012	LOU	AAA	24	2	5	1	54	0	72²	84	4	29	35	3.6	4.3	53%	.324	1.56	3.34	4.19	6.02	-0.7
2013	LOU	AAA	25	6	5	3	49	0	56	49	6	17	49	2.7	7.9	51%	.272	1.18	3.86	3.92	4.49	0.3
2013	CIN	MLB	25	0	0	0	3	0	4	2	1	2	1	4.5	2.2	42%	.091	1.00	2.25	8.02	8.26	-0.1
2014	CIN	MLB	26	2	1	1	43	0	55¹	57	7	18	35	3.0	5.7	50%	.296	1.35	4.63	4.72	5.03	-0.2

Drafted in the 13th round as a Vanderbilt senior, Christiani never looked like a big leaguer in the making. He was a reliever from day one, and even in that role he didn't dominate unripe minor leaguers the way advanced college pitchers are supposed to. Then the velocity spike came. He now throws 92 to 95, features a sinker/slider mix, and is quoted to be experimenting with a cutter and a changeup. He nearly doubled his strikeout rate in Louisville, made his debut in Cincinnati in the summer and now looks to have a role in middle relief.

Tony Cingrani

Born: 7/5/1989 Age: 24
Bats: L Throws: L Height: 6' 4" Weight: 215
Breakout: 27% Improve: 79% Collapse: 10%
Attrition: 13% MLB: 93%

Comparables:
Clay Buchholz, Matt Moore, Max Scherzer

YEAR	TEAM	LVL	AGE	W	L	SV	G	GS	IP	H	HR	BB	SO	BB9	SO9	GB%	BABIP	WHIP	ERA	FIP	FRA	WARP
2012	BAK	A+	22	5	1	0	10	10	56^2	39	2	13	71	2.1	11.3	45%	.276	0.92	1.11	2.46	2.41	2.3
2012	PEN	AA	22	5	3	0	16	15	89^1	59	7	39	101	3.9	10.2	42%	.268	1.10	2.12	3.24	3.70	1.5
2012	CIN	MLB	22	0	0	0	3	0	5	4	1	2	9	3.6	16.2	64%	.300	1.20	1.80	3.34	2.74	0.1
2013	LOU	AAA	23	3	0	0	6	6	31^1	14	1	11	49	3.2	14.1	50%	.236	0.80	1.15	1.64	2.42	1.0
2013	CIN	MLB	23	7	4	0	23	18	104^2	72	14	43	120	3.7	10.3	34%	.240	1.10	2.92	3.76	4.32	0.9
2014	CIN	MLB	24	7	6	0	21	21	116^1	87	13	43	133	3.3	10.3	41%	.280	1.12	3.03	3.54	3.30	2.2

Over the past 10 seasons, there have been seven pitchers who threw at least 100 innings while pumping in four-seam fastballs at at least an 80-plus percent clip. Collectively, that group has a 15 percent strikeout rate—and only two members whiffed better than 20 percent: Jaret Wright (20.4) in 2004 and Cingrani (28.6) in 2013. What Cingrani lacks in pure velocity, he makes up for in deceptiveness—this is the biggest key to his success, as he got more whiffs on his fastball than Matt Harvey, despite throwing 4 mph slower. Cingrani should start the season in the rotation, where he'll continue to try and prove to his doubters that he's not going to end up in the bullpen. History shows that somewhere along the line he's going to have to pick up a usable secondary pitch or this becomes a high-wire act.

Carlos Contreras

Born: 1/8/1991 Age: 23
Bats: R Throws: R Height: 5' 11" Weight: 205
Breakout: 89% Improve: 89% Collapse: 11%
Attrition: 76% MLB: 8%

Comparables:
Tanner Roark, Brayan Villarreal, Wily Peralta

YEAR	TEAM	LVL	AGE	W	L	SV	G	GS	IP	H	HR	BB	SO	BB9	SO9	GB%	BABIP	WHIP	ERA	FIP	FRA	WARP
2012	DYT	A	21	0	1	16	40	0	50^2	29	6	19	51	3.4	9.1	46%	.183	0.95	3.20	4.18	5.37	-0.1
2012	BAK	A+	21	1	0	4	9	0	10	9	1	5	12	4.5	10.8	67%	.276	1.40	2.70	4.21	4.17	0.2
2013	BAK	A+	22	5	7	0	18	18	90	70	9	41	96	4.1	9.6	43%	.269	1.23	3.80	4.44	5.20	1.1
2013	PEN	AA	22	3	2	0	8	8	42^1	36	2	21	26	4.5	5.5	47%	.270	1.35	2.76	4.07	4.70	0.0
2014	CIN	MLB	23	3	1	2	58	0	102^2	97	14	51	81	4.4	7.1	43%	.289	1.44	4.69	5.10	5.10	-0.5

Contreras is a sub-6-foot Dominican right-hander signed as an amateur by the Reds, but that's where the comparison to Johnny Cueto runs out. Contreras has had to be nurtured patiently, and he doesn't have the electric arsenal of a future star. But the Reds liked his low-to-mid-90s fastball and plus changeup enough to move him from relief to rotation last year, and he eluded enough bats to earn a place in the Futures Game. His ultimate role will hinge on the development of his inconsistent curveball, which showed progress, and if he's not destined to be Johnny Cueto he might at least be destined to share a clubhouse with Johnny Cueto.

Daniel Corcino

Born: 8/26/1990 Age: 23
Bats: R Throws: R Height: 5' 11" Weight: 205
Breakout: 81% Improve: 100% Collapse: 0%
Attrition: 78% MLB: 4%

Comparables:
Joel Carreno, Michael Kirkman, Alex Wilson

YEAR	TEAM	LVL	AGE	W	L	SV	G	GS	IP	H	HR	BB	SO	BB9	SO9	GB%	BABIP	WHIP	ERA	FIP	FRA	WARP
2011	DYT	A	20	11	7	0	26	26	139^1	128	10	34	156	2.2	10.1	39%	.329	1.16	3.42	2.96	4.95	0.1
2012	PEN	AA	21	8	8	0	26	26	143^1	111	9	65	126	4.1	7.9	40%	.267	1.23	3.01	3.69	4.59	1.4
2013	LOU	AAA	22	7	14	0	28	23	129	141	17	73	90	5.1	6.3	38%	.312	1.66	5.86	5.48	6.61	-1.7
2014	CIN	MLB	23	6	9	0	23	23	118^2	119	16	56	83	4.2	6.3	40%	.298	1.47	5.19	5.19	5.64	-1.0

After a promising 2012, Corcino collapsed in Louisville, as every statistic vaulted in the wrong direction. Most revealing is the 12 percent walk rate—a number that has risen annually due to command and control issues. Corcino throws across his body with high effort and he failed to find a consistent release point despite multiple attempted adjustments. The result: elevated, low-90s fastballs that met hard contact and an opponents' slugging percentage of .473. Standing just 5-foot-11, the lack of a downward plane is a depressant, but an above-average slider and sinking changeup perk him up. He'll have another year to work on his control; if he fails, relief duties might be in his future.

Johnny Cueto

Born: 2/15/1986 Age: 28
Bats: R Throws: R Height: 5' 11" Weight: 215
Breakout: 23% Improve: 57% Collapse: 23%
Attrition: 4% MLB: 96%

Comparables:
John Danks, Mark Mulder, Roy Halladay

YEAR	TEAM	LVL	AGE	W	L	SV	G	GS	IP	H	HR	BB	SO	BB9	SO9	GB%	BABIP	WHIP	ERA	FIP	FRA	WARP
2011	LOU	AAA	25	0	2	0	4	4	14^1	19	1	6	13	3.8	8.2	56%	.278	1.74	6.28	3.59	3.72	0.2
2011	CIN	MLB	25	9	5	0	24	24	156	123	8	47	104	2.7	6.0	55%	.256	1.09	2.31	3.42	4.09	1.3
2012	CIN	MLB	26	19	9	0	33	33	217	205	15	49	170	2.0	7.1	49%	.300	1.17	2.78	3.31	4.07	2.2
2013	CIN	MLB	27	5	2	0	11	11	60^2	46	7	18	51	2.7	7.6	52%	.237	1.05	2.82	3.78	4.46	0.3
2014	CIN	MLB	28	5	4	0	13	13	80^2	70	8	21	65	2.3	7.2	45%	.283	1.12	3.31	3.81	3.60	1.1

After throwing a career-high 217 innings in 2012, Cueto made up for gained time in 2013, requiring three separate stints on the disabled list for a strained shoulder. In the end, his 60-plus innings were of expected quality, though not without warning signs. While it might be lazy to look at his .236 BABIP and sound the regression alarm, the fact is that a BABIP that low is unsustainable when accompanied by a 25 percent line-drive rate. Opposing batters not only hit just .587 against Cueto on line drives (league average: .657), but were below .150 on both groundballs and fly balls. He did show a career-high strikeout rate and continued development of his cutter, which he threw 215 times while allowing just one extra-base hit. Alas, it's unlikely to make him healthier, which is most of the story for Cueto.

Zach Duke
Born: 4/19/1983 Age: 31
Bats: L Throws: L Height: 6' 2" Weight: 210
Breakout: 17% Improve: 48% Collapse: 20%
Attrition: 12% MLB: 52%

Comparables:
Jae Weong Seo, Pete Munro, Ryan Glynn

YEAR	TEAM	LVL	AGE	W	L	SV	G	GS	IP	H	HR	BB	SO	BB9	SO9	GB%	BABIP	WHIP	ERA	FIP	FRA	WARP
2011	ARI	MLB	28	3	4	1	21	9	76²	101	6	19	32	2.2	3.8	49%	.344	1.57	4.93	3.96	4.76	0.1
2012	SYR	AAA	29	15	5	0	26	26	164¹	178	16	39	91	2.1	5.0	53%	.302	1.32	3.51	4.05	5.86	-1.2
2012	WAS	MLB	29	1	0	0	8	0	13²	11	0	4	10	2.6	6.6	39%	.268	1.10	1.32	2.55	2.51	0.3
2013	LOU	AAA	30	2	0	2	26	0	27²	19	2	5	34	1.6	11.1	52%	.274	0.87	1.30	2.34	4.50	0.3
2013	CIN	MLB	30	0	1	0	14	0	10²	8	1	2	7	1.7	5.9	42%	.200	0.94	0.84	3.49	2.46	0.2
2013	WAS	MLB	30	1	1	0	12	1	20²	31	2	8	11	3.5	4.8	56%	.365	1.89	8.71	4.52	5.04	-0.1
2014	CIN	MLB	31	3	4	0	25	8	70²	76	9	17	43	2.2	5.4	50%	.306	1.32	4.60	4.48	5.00	-0.2

Among other things, 2013 will go down as the year Zach Duke, Starting Pitcher finally went the way of the dodo. After two abysmal months of low-leverage implosions in our nation's capital, Duke was picked up by Cincinnati and assigned to Triple-A Louisville as organizational depth. He thrived on the farm and, upon rejoining baseball's upper class in late August, he looked like a useful bullpen piece. The velocity uptick that never came in previous relief stints finally surfaced, as he sat in the low 90s in September. If he can hold that increase, Duke can remake himself into a serviceable reliever nine years after his rookie season fooled us all into expecting something more.

Amir Garrett
Born: 5/3/1992 Age: 22
Bats: L Throws: L Height: 6' 5" Weight: 210
Breakout: 0% Improve: 0% Collapse: 0%
Attrition: 0% MLB: 0%

Comparables:
Daniel Webb, Zac Rosscup, Pedro Figueroa

YEAR	TEAM	LVL	AGE	W	L	SV	G	GS	IP	H	HR	BB	SO	BB9	SO9	GB%	BABIP	WHIP	ERA	FIP	FRA	WARP
2013	DYT	A	21	1	3	0	8	8	34	40	4	16	15	4.2	4.0	40%	.305	1.65	6.88	5.57	6.87	-0.2
2014	CIN	MLB	22	1	2	0	18	5	44	52	7	25	18	5.0	3.6	49%	.306	1.75	6.50	6.43	7.06	-1.0

In the past year, Garrett has donned jerseys for the Billings Mustangs, Dayton Dragons, St. John's Red Storm and Cal State-Northridge Matadors, the latter two college basketball programs. Drafted late in 2011, Garrett received a $1 million signing bonus from the Reds, who, unconventionally, permitted him to play NCAA hoops. Nearly three years later, he hasn't decided on a sport. He's logged just 77 professional innings, so his delivery and pitchability are still unrefined. But scope his athletic 6-foot-5 frame, tack on a mid-90s fastball with movement, consider that he buys all his t-shirts from the Leftorium and you understand how scouts fell for him at first sight. As you know from your Nicholas Sparks romances, love comes easy, but commitment takes time.

Ismael Guillon
Born: 2/13/1992 Age: 22
Bats: L Throws: L Height: 6' 2" Weight: 218
Breakout: 59% Improve: 78% Collapse: 22%
Attrition: 100% MLB: 7%

Comparables:
Chris Dwyer, Tony Cingrani, Daniel Hudson

YEAR	TEAM	LVL	AGE	W	L	SV	G	GS	IP	H	HR	BB	SO	BB9	SO9	GB%	BABIP	WHIP	ERA	FIP	FRA	WARP
2012	DYT	A	20	2	0	0	4	4	24²	22	2	7	27	2.6	9.9	41%	.323	1.18	2.55	3.07	3.75	0.4
2013	DYT	A	21	7	8	0	27	26	121¹	95	14	95	134	7.0	9.9	29%	.275	1.57	4.75	5.00	5.47	1.0
2014	CIN	MLB	22	3	6	0	21	15	98¹	96	14	68	84	6.3	7.7	35%	.304	1.68	5.64	5.60	6.13	-1.3

Guillon battled significant control issues in his first full year at Low-A Dayton, walking 18 percent of batters and leading the Midwest League with 26 wild pitches. (Mark Buehrle has 25 career wild pitches.) He throws in the low 90s from the left side, wielding an advanced changeup as his strikeout weapon. There's mid-rotation potential here, and his final four starts provided a glimpse: 24 innings with a 1.11 ERA, 20 strikeouts and 16 baserunners. He's far from the majors, but a renegotiation of his original contract guarantees him a spot on the 40-man roster, so he will burn through option years as he progresses through the minors.

David Holmberg
Born: 7/19/1991 Age: 22
Bats: R Throws: L Height: 6' 3" Weight: 225
Breakout: 51% Improve: 75% Collapse: 10%
Attrition: 57% MLB: 43%

Comparables:
Liam Hendriks, Casey Kelly, Ian Krol

YEAR	TEAM	LVL	AGE	W	L	SV	G	GS	IP	H	HR	BB	SO	BB9	SO9	GB%	BABIP	WHIP	ERA	FIP	FRA	WARP
2011	SBN	A	19	8	3	0	14	14	83	65	3	13	81	1.4	8.8	52%	.253	0.94	2.39	2.60	2.71	0.8
2011	VIS	A+	19	4	6	0	13	13	71¹	73	5	35	76	4.4	9.6	42%	.363	1.51	4.67	4.33	3.98	1.7
2012	VIS	A+	20	6	3	0	12	12	78¹	62	6	14	86	1.6	9.9	44%	.281	0.97	2.99	3.15	3.98	1.9
2012	MOB	AA	20	5	5	0	15	15	95	104	8	23	67	2.2	6.3	46%	.320	1.34	3.60	3.62	4.27	1.1
2013	MOB	AA	21	5	8	0	26	26	157¹	138	12	50	116	2.9	6.6	41%	.269	1.19	2.75	3.52	4.60	0.4
2013	ARI	MLB	21	0	0	0	1	1	3²	6	0	3	0	7.4	0.0	29%	.353	2.45	7.36	5.48	7.27	-0.1
2014	CIN	MLB	22	7	9	0	23	23	136¹	138	18	46	95	3.1	6.3	44%	.299	1.35	4.54	4.67	4.93	-0.2

Pay no attention to his lone major-league appearance—that occurred way before scheduled for the 22-year-old. Holmberg was promoted straight from Double-A for a spot start in August, making him the fifth starting pitcher to debut for Arizona last year. Before that, Holmberg logged the third most innings in the Southern League while keeping an ERA on the good side of three. Had he not been called up, this section would consider his oeuvre of four decent pitches to be suited for a full season of Triple-A with a chance of a September call-up for his new team, and even with the major-league cameo this still seems like a good bet.

J.J. Hoover
Born: 8/13/1987 Age: 26
Bats: R Throws: R Height: 6' 3" Weight: 225
Breakout: 37% Improve: 65% Collapse: 22%
Attrition: 33% MLB: 88%

Comparables:
Andrew Bailey, Brayan Villarreal, Scott Mathieson

YEAR	TEAM	LVL	AGE	W	L	SV	G	GS	IP	H	HR	BB	SO	BB9	SO9	GB%	BABIP	WHIP	ERA	FIP	FRA	WARP
2011	MIS	AA	23	2	5	1	31	12	87	65	5	28	86	2.9	8.9	32%	.247	1.07	2.48	3.18	3.43	0.6
2011	GWN	AAA	23	1	1	1	12	2	18²	12	0	12	31	5.8	14.9	27%	.091	1.29	3.38	1.84	1.03	0.4
2012	LOU	AAA	24	4	0	13	30	0	37	15	1	12	55	2.9	13.4	33%	.203	0.73	1.22	1.59	2.68	1.0
2012	CIN	MLB	24	1	0	1	28	0	30²	17	2	13	31	3.8	9.1	26%	.197	0.98	2.05	3.23	3.32	0.5
2013	CIN	MLB	25	5	5	3	69	0	66	47	6	26	67	3.5	9.1	32%	.246	1.11	2.86	3.44	4.48	0.3
2014	CIN	MLB	26	3	2	1	46	2	58	49	6	22	57	3.4	8.8	37%	.289	1.22	3.64	3.82	3.96	0.5

It's now two seasons of data suggesting that Hoover, despite extreme fly-ball ways, can be successful in the Great American Bandbox. In fact, after a six-run meltdown in extra innings against the Cardinals on June 9th, Hoover was dominant for the remainder of the season—matching a sparkling 1.14 ERA and 0.89 WHIP with 40 strikeouts and only two home runs allowed in 39 innings. With Jonathan Broxton potentially sidelined for the start of the 2014 season, Hoover will look to reprise his set-up role. From the fun-stat department, he's yet to allow a run during his 21 career ninth-inning appearances—so if anything happens to Aroldis Chapman, he's got this.

Mat Latos
Born: 12/9/1987 Age: 26
Bats: R Throws: R Height: 6' 6" Weight: 245
Breakout: 20% Improve: 55% Collapse: 15%
Attrition: 9% MLB: 97%

Comparables:
Josh Johnson, Zack Greinke, Cole Hamels

YEAR	TEAM	LVL	AGE	W	L	SV	G	GS	IP	H	HR	BB	SO	BB9	SO9	GB%	BABIP	WHIP	ERA	FIP	FRA	WARP
2011	SDN	MLB	23	9	14	0	31	31	194¹	168	16	62	185	2.9	8.6	44%	.289	1.18	3.47	3.13	3.65	2.0
2012	CIN	MLB	24	14	4	0	33	33	209¹	179	25	64	185	2.8	8.0	47%	.272	1.16	3.48	3.90	4.51	1.6
2013	CIN	MLB	25	14	7	0	32	32	210²	197	14	58	187	2.5	8.0	47%	.305	1.21	3.16	3.08	3.50	3.3
2014	CIN	MLB	26	11	10	0	29	29	184¹	156	19	48	168	2.3	8.2	45%	.286	1.11	3.10	3.56	3.37	3.1

The nominal ace of the Reds' pitching staff, Latos logged the most innings on his team this year, but those innings looked a lot different in the two halves of the season—and did not match his performance. In the first half, he struck out more than a batter an inning and underperformed his 2.88 FIP (3.53 ERA). That strikeout rate dipped by more than a third in the second half (from 25 percent to 16), yet he outperformed his 3.40 FIP (2.68 ERA). There were whispers (including from Latos himself) of an abdominal injury that might have affected him as the season drew on. More disruptive were bone chips in his right elbow, which not only got him scratched from the Wild Card game, but sent him to the operating room in October. He's expected to back at full strength by spring training and will again look to take that step forward from nominal ace to ace.

Mike Leake
Born: 11/12/1987 Age: 26
Bats: R Throws: R Height: 5' 10" Weight: 185
Breakout: 11% Improve: 41% Collapse: 24%
Attrition: 14% MLB: 97%

Comparables:
Brad Radke, Oil Can Boyd, Larry Dierker

YEAR	TEAM	LVL	AGE	W	L	SV	G	GS	IP	H	HR	BB	SO	BB9	SO9	GB%	BABIP	WHIP	ERA	FIP	FRA	WARP
2011	CIN	MLB	23	12	9	0	29	26	167²	159	23	38	118	2.0	6.3	48%	.276	1.17	3.86	4.19	4.95	0.2
2012	CIN	MLB	24	8	9	0	30	30	179	201	26	41	116	2.1	5.8	49%	.312	1.35	4.58	4.47	5.01	0.4
2013	CIN	MLB	25	14	7	0	31	31	192¹	193	21	48	122	2.2	5.7	49%	.292	1.25	3.37	4.01	4.64	0.5
2014	CIN	MLB	26	9	10	0	26	26	164	162	21	38	115	2.1	6.3	48%	.297	1.21	4.04	4.27	4.39	0.7

Leake came into the season as the guy standing in the way of Aroldis Chapman starting, but ended it with a 113 ERA+ in nearly 200 innings. A 77.7 percent strand rate contributed, but he also had the lowest home run rate of his career—for the first time, he allowed less than one per nine. The biggest factor in his improvement was the growth of his curveball, which (by measures kept at FanGraphs) trailed only the curves of A.J. Burnett, Adam Wainwright, Stephen Strasburg and Clayton Kershaw in value added last year. He threw it nearly 15 percent of the time and got more whiffs (44) than in his first three seasons combined. With a substantial pay raise in his second year of arbitration eligibility, Leake's excess value continues to evaporate, but he remains a solid option in the back of the Reds' rotation.

Sam LeCure

Born: 5/4/1984 Age: 30
Bats: R Throws: R Height: 6' 0" Weight: 205
Breakout: 29% Improve: 46% Collapse: 42%
Attrition: 43% MLB: 49%

Comparables:
Dustin Nippert, Brian Stokes, Clay Hensley

YEAR	TEAM	LVL	AGE	W	L	SV	G	GS	IP	H	HR	BB	SO	BB9	SO9	GB%	BABIP	WHIP	ERA	FIP	FRA	WARP
2011	CIN	MLB	27	2	1	0	43	4	77²	57	10	21	73	2.4	8.5	46%	.245	1.00	3.71	3.75	4.20	0.6
2012	CIN	MLB	28	3	3	0	48	0	57¹	46	3	23	61	3.6	9.6	48%	.276	1.20	3.14	2.94	3.41	0.9
2013	CIN	MLB	29	2	1	1	63	0	61	50	4	24	66	3.5	9.7	44%	.297	1.21	2.66	2.94	3.07	0.9
2014	CIN	MLB	30	3	2	0	28	4	53²	47	6	18	49	3.0	8.2	44%	.292	1.21	3.62	3.95	3.94	0.5

If you had a pitch that generated a 44 percent whiff rate, a 46 percent groundball rate, a .116 batting average against and a .159 opponents' slugging percentage, you'd use it pretty often, right? Those are the career numbers for LeCure's curveball, and 2013 marked the second year in a row it saw a 10 percentage point rise in usage, to 27 percent. He's not a hard thrower by any means, and at some point game theory suggests he'll get diminishing returns from the curve, but the whiff rate actually ticked up in heavier usage last year. To top it off, through the wonders of small sample sorcery, LeCure even played the role of reverse specialist, as he held lefties to a minuscule .446 OPS.

Michael Lorenzen

Born: 1/4/1992 Age: 22
Bats: R Throws: R Height: 6' 3" Weight: 180
Breakout: 0% Improve: 0% Collapse: 0%
Attrition: 0% MLB: 0%

Comparables:
Danny Farquhar, Edgmer Escalona, Stephen Fife

YEAR	TEAM	LVL	AGE	W	L	SV	G	GS	IP	H	HR	BB	SO	BB9	SO9	GB%	BABIP	WHIP	ERA	FIP	FRA	WARP
—	—	—	—	—	—	—	—	—	—	—	—	—	—	—	—	—	—	—	—	—	—	—
2014	CIN	MLB	22	2	1	1	37	0	35²	36	5	17	25	4.4	6.4	46%	.303	1.51	5.15	5.30	5.60	-0.4

Prior to being drafted 38th overall, Lorenzen was serving Cal State Fullerton as both starting center fielder and closer. Despite his athletic five-tool profile, the Reds like the unrefined upper-90s arm even more. Finishing the college year with 19 saves, the Reds marched him through four levels in just two months. After he ended the minor-league season in Double-A, he was whisked to the Arizona Fall League, where he struggled badly in six starts (11.42 ERA). He gets an easy pass there, though, as his arm has never seen such a busy workload—that's six different teams he pitched for in 2013. One hopes the longer stay in Arizona gave him a chance to relax, see the sights and make some friends.

Sean Marshall

Born: 8/30/1982 Age: 31
Bats: L Throws: L Height: 6' 7" Weight: 225
Breakout: 21% Improve: 45% Collapse: 29%
Attrition: 11% MLB: 87%

Comparables:
Scot Shields, Ryan Madson, J.J. Putz

YEAR	TEAM	LVL	AGE	W	L	SV	G	GS	IP	H	HR	BB	SO	BB9	SO9	GB%	BABIP	WHIP	ERA	FIP	FRA	WARP
2011	CHN	MLB	28	6	6	5	78	0	75²	66	1	17	79	2.0	9.4	60%	.312	1.10	2.26	1.83	2.55	1.8
2012	CIN	MLB	29	5	5	9	73	0	61	55	3	16	74	2.4	10.9	56%	.325	1.16	2.51	2.28	2.67	1.5
2013	CIN	MLB	30	0	1	0	16	0	10¹	4	0	2	10	1.7	8.7	58%	.167	0.58	1.74	1.96	2.28	0.2
2014	CIN	MLB	31	2	1	3	44	0	39¹	32	3	10	42	2.3	9.7	51%	.299	1.07	2.66	2.84	2.89	0.9

Durability had been Marshall's calling card since he transitioned to the bullpen full time. Between 2010 and 2012, he led the majors with 231 appearances. His body finally caught up with his workload, and he missed four months with shoulder fatigue that turned into shoulder tendonitis that turned into a shoulder sprain. During his few moments on the mound, Marshall was extremely successful, but—feign surprise here—his velocity was significantly down. He averaged less than 90 mph with his four-seam fastball for the first time as a reliever. With two years and $12 million left on his contract, the Reds are paying Marshall like a set-up man but using him like a LOOGY. In a timely blip, he held right-handed batters hitless in 13 at-bats during 2013, which might be enough to convince new manager Bryan Price to be more aggressive with Marshall.

Logan Ondrusek

Born: 2/13/1985 Age: 29
Bats: R Throws: R Height: 6' 8" Weight: 230
Breakout: 49% Improve: 63% Collapse: 27%
Attrition: 19% MLB: 79%

Comparables:
Javier Lopez, Jeremy Accardo, Sean Burnett

YEAR	TEAM	LVL	AGE	W	L	SV	G	GS	IP	H	HR	BB	SO	BB9	SO9	GB%	BABIP	WHIP	ERA	FIP	FRA	WARP
2011	CIN	MLB	26	5	5	0	66	0	61¹	55	6	28	41	4.1	6.0	51%	.257	1.35	3.23	4.40	5.31	-0.3
2012	CIN	MLB	27	5	2	2	63	0	54²	51	8	31	39	5.1	6.4	44%	.269	1.50	3.46	5.48	5.59	-0.4
2013	CIN	MLB	28	3	1	0	52	0	55	53	8	16	53	2.6	8.7	47%	.298	1.25	4.09	3.91	4.46	0.2
2014	CIN	MLB	29	3	1	1	57	0	57	50	6	20	45	3.2	7.1	47%	.279	1.23	3.65	4.17	3.96	0.5

The big right-hander from Texas had been a consistently forgettable middle reliever in his major-league career, not good enough for high leverage nor bad enough to signal that it's time to leave the stadium and beat the traffic home. But something happened to Ondrusek in 2013, as the man who held a career 16 percent strikeout rate suddenly spiked up to 23 percent. His velocity in the second half of the season soared to new heights, averaging nearly 96 mph (94.2 mph was his previous season high) as he punched out 32 in 27 innings. If he can carry forward even a portion of that velocity jump—without his arm snapping under the strain—he becomes another intriguing option at the back of the Reds' bullpen.

Manny Parra

Born: 10/30/1982 Age: 31
Bats: L Throws: L Height: 6' 3" Weight: 205
Breakout: 26% Improve: 57% Collapse: 26%
Attrition: 28% MLB: 88%

Comparables:
Casey Fossum, Todd Wellemeyer, Scott Downs

YEAR	TEAM	LVL	AGE	W	L	SV	G	GS	IP	H	HR	BB	SO	BB9	SO9	GB%	BABIP	WHIP	ERA	FIP	FRA	WARP
2011	NAS	AAA	28	0	1	0	7	1	10¹	12	0	5	8	4.4	7.0	64%	.429	1.65	6.10	3.69	5.42	0.1
2012	MIL	MLB	29	2	3	0	62	0	58²	62	3	35	61	5.4	9.4	48%	.345	1.65	5.06	3.66	3.59	1.1
2013	CIN	MLB	30	2	3	0	57	0	46	40	5	15	56	2.9	11.0	45%	.318	1.20	3.33	3.04	3.74	0.5
2014	CIN	MLB	31	2	2	0	31	4	45²	44	5	19	42	3.8	8.4	49%	.318	1.39	4.36	4.11	4.74	0.0

Now more than three years removed from his last major-league start, Parra last year took a big step toward carving out a successful second act in the bullpen. After struggling out of the gate and missing more than a month with a strained pectoral muscle, he impressed with a 2.52 ERA, 0.94 WHIP, 49 strikeouts and 12 walks in 39 innings the rest of the way. A career-best walk rate was a big reason for his success (he'd never had a BB/9 below 4.0 in his career), but he'll have a job for a long time if he can continue to hold lefties to a .167/.237/.238 line. The Reds signed him to a two-year deal and hope he can do exactly that.

Curtis Partch

Born: 2/13/1987 Age: 27
Bats: R Throws: R Height: 6' 5" Weight: 240
Breakout: 74% Improve: 92% Collapse: 8%
Attrition: 61% MLB: 15%

Comparables:
Luke Putkonen, Joe Savery, Cesar Carrillo

YEAR	TEAM	LVL	AGE	W	L	SV	G	GS	IP	H	HR	BB	SO	BB9	SO9	GB%	BABIP	WHIP	ERA	FIP	FRA	WARP
2011	BAK	A+	24	6	11	0	21	21	121²	161	14	28	93	2.1	6.9	51%	.358	1.55	5.25	4.90	5.23	1.4
2011	CAR	AA	24	2	2	0	7	7	39	55	3	13	33	3.0	7.6	31%	.400	1.74	6.92	3.85	12.23	-0.2
2012	BAK	A+	25	0	0	2	7	0	12	7	1	3	15	2.2	11.2	71%	.222	0.83	1.50	3.15	3.43	0.3
2012	PEN	AA	25	7	4	6	45	4	70¹	75	7	33	64	4.2	8.2	48%	.337	1.54	4.73	4.20	7.02	-0.1
2013	LOU	AAA	26	1	2	2	24	0	28¹	27	2	12	31	3.8	9.8	35%	.325	1.38	4.13	3.42	3.28	0.6
2013	CIN	MLB	26	0	1	0	14	0	23¹	17	8	17	16	6.6	6.2	46%	.155	1.46	6.17	8.81	10.01	-0.9
2014	CIN	MLB	27	2	3	0	25	6	55²	62	9	24	36	3.9	5.8	47%	.310	1.54	5.66	5.56	6.16	-0.9

After seven seasons in the minors—insert "long dry spell" pun here—Partch made it to the majors as a mop-up man who made more messes. A tall converted starter, his fastball touches the upper 90s and is complemented by a bat-missing mid-80s slider. The repertoire sufficiently disposed of Triple-A hitters, but he'll need better command if he wants better assignments.

Greg Reynolds

Born: 7/3/1985 Age: 28
Bats: R Throws: R Height: 6' 7" Weight: 225
Breakout: 52% Improve: 71% Collapse: 29%
Attrition: 81% MLB: 24%

Comparables:
Bobby Livingston, Eddie Bonine, Josh Banks

YEAR	TEAM	LVL	AGE	W	L	SV	G	GS	IP	H	HR	BB	SO	BB9	SO9	GB%	BABIP	WHIP	ERA	FIP	FRA	WARP
2011	CSP	AAA	25	6	7	0	19	19	109²	160	10	32	65	2.6	5.3	46%	.389	1.75	6.81	4.71	5.31	2.4
2011	COL	MLB	25	3	0	0	13	3	32	40	6	10	18	2.8	5.1	41%	.317	1.56	6.19	5.34	6.71	-0.3
2012	ROU	AAA	26	11	9	0	27	27	163	208	22	46	69	2.5	3.8	50%	.322	1.56	5.30	5.57	6.26	-0.6
2013	LOU	AAA	27	12	3	0	23	21	156¹	139	6	26	97	1.5	5.6	55%	.274	1.06	2.42	2.98	4.13	2.0
2013	CIN	MLB	27	1	3	0	6	5	29¹	38	5	6	13	1.8	4.0	42%	.330	1.50	5.52	5.37	6.17	-0.3
2014	CIN	MLB	28	8	10	0	25	25	156²	168	21	35	87	2.0	5.0	48%	.299	1.30	4.56	4.64	4.96	-0.4

If Reynolds came into 2013 with the goal of further cementing himself as the worst second-overall pick in baseball history, then mission accomplished. What a strange mission! After knocking himself down another three-tenths of a win, his -1.4 career WARP remains second to none among second-to-ones—as long as you don't count Pete Broberg (yes, that's a real name and not the fake name Nick Swisher uses at hotels, probably), who was the second overall pick in 1968 but didn't sign. Even with a good Triple-A campaign prior to his call-up (2.42 ERA in 156 innings), Reynolds' major-league performance did nothing to guarantee him another chance to subtract to his historic career.

Alfredo Simon

Born: 5/8/1981 Age: 33
Bats: R Throws: R Height: 6' 6" Weight: 265
Breakout: 25% Improve: 53% Collapse: 27%
Attrition: 23% MLB: 82%

Comparables:
Brian Tallet, Scott Downs, Terry Adams

YEAR	TEAM	LVL	AGE	W	L	SV	G	GS	IP	H	HR	BB	SO	BB9	SO9	GB%	BABIP	WHIP	ERA	FIP	FRA	WARP
2011	BOW	AA	30	1	0	0	4	4	18	15	1	6	20	3.0	10.0	41%	.292	1.17	3.00	3.08	2.65	0.4
2011	BAL	MLB	30	4	9	0	23	16	115²	128	15	40	83	3.1	6.5	43%	.317	1.45	4.90	4.45	4.45	1.3
2012	CIN	MLB	31	3	2	1	36	0	61	65	2	22	52	3.2	7.7	55%	.339	1.43	2.66	3.23	3.45	1.1
2013	CIN	MLB	32	6	4	1	63	0	87²	68	8	26	63	2.7	6.5	46%	.229	1.07	2.87	3.93	4.78	0.0
2014	CIN	MLB	33	3	2	0	38	5	71²	67	9	23	58	2.9	7.3	45%	.292	1.26	4.15	4.38	4.51	0.2

It turns out that, among other things, Simon can eat innings. His innings total led the next busiest Reds reliever by more than 20, and they were surprisingly effective on the surface. For the second year in a row, Simon relied heavily on his two-seamer that sits in the mid-90s. Hitters found far fewer holes in 2013, as Simon's .232 BABIP on the pitch was 100 points lower than his career mark. In fact, this allowed Simon to net more innings pitched than hits allowed for the first time in his six-year tenure. He's done enough to earn himself a major-league role in 2014, but is behind many more talented arms in the Queen City.

Robert Stephenson

Born: 2/24/1993 Age: 21
Bats: R Throws: R Height: 6' 2" Weight: 190
Breakout: 38% Improve: 72% Collapse: 8%
Attrition: 45% MLB: 25%

Comparables:
Eric Hurley, Homer Bailey, Jarrod Parker

YEAR	TEAM	LVL	AGE	W	L	SV	G	GS	IP	H	HR	BB	SO	BB9	SO9	GB%	BABIP	WHIP	ERA	FIP	FRA	WARP
2012	DYT	A	19	2	4	0	8	8	34¹	32	4	15	35	3.9	9.2	40%	.301	1.37	4.19	4.40	5.55	0.0
2013	DYT	A	20	5	3	0	14	14	77	56	5	20	96	2.3	11.2	51%	.279	0.99	2.57	2.59	4.12	1.4
2013	BAK	A+	20	2	2	0	4	4	20²	19	3	2	22	0.9	9.6	39%	.286	1.02	3.05	3.82	3.97	0.5
2013	PEN	AA	20	0	2	0	4	4	16²	17	2	13	18	7.0	9.7	36%	.350	1.80	4.86	4.65	4.20	0.2
2014	CIN	MLB	21	5	7	0	19	19	90²	84	12	39	83	3.9	8.2	45%	.301	1.37	4.45	4.51	4.84	0.1

Stephenson obliterated Low-A in his final eight starts at Dayton: 49 innings, four earned runs, 61 strikeouts. He spent just four outings in High-A before graduating to Double-A, where he'll be honing his top-of-the-rotation arsenal this year. Stephenson throws an elite mid-90s fastball with movement, occasionally reaching back for the upper 90s late in games. His ascension on prospect lists can be attributed to an improving curve, a weapon that generates both called and swinging strikes. He needs to refine his overall command, but the rest—poise, athleticism, an easy delivery, a changeup that shows progress—point to a future rotation leader.

Nick Travieso

Born: 1/31/1994 Age: 20
Bats: R Throws: R Height: 6' 2" Weight: 215
Breakout: 0% Improve: 0% Collapse: 0%
Attrition: 0% MLB: 0%

Comparables:
Alex Burnett, Jose Alvarez, Dan Cortes

YEAR	TEAM	LVL	AGE	W	L	SV	G	GS	IP	H	HR	BB	SO	BB9	SO9	GB%	BABIP	WHIP	ERA	FIP	FRA	WARP
2013	DYT	A	19	7	4	0	17	17	81²	83	7	27	61	3.0	6.7	40%	.305	1.35	4.63	4.10	5.15	0.9
2014	CIN	MLB	20	2	2	1	21	3	60²	67	9	28	34	4.1	5.0	40%	.303	1.57	5.60	5.64	6.09	-0.9

Out of high school and in his first post-draft year, Travieso participated in extended spring training before joining Low-A Dayton in June. After an unsteady first month, he finished a nice developmental year. Travieso throws in the mid-90s with the ability to touch 98, though there is some effort in the delivery. His slider is a go-to secondary pitch, while his changeup requires conditioning to keep lefties honest. With due concern for his big, high-maintenance body, this 20-year-old has the potential to be a mid-rotation arm.

Pedro Villarreal

Born: 12/9/1987 Age: 26
Bats: R Throws: R Height: 6' 1" Weight: 230
Breakout: 33% Improve: 57% Collapse: 33%
Attrition: 89% MLB: 9%

Comparables:
Andrew Carpenter, Steve Garrison, Tobi Stoner

YEAR	TEAM	LVL	AGE	W	L	SV	G	GS	IP	H	HR	BB	SO	BB9	SO9	GB%	BABIP	WHIP	ERA	FIP	FRA	WARP
2011	BAK	A+	23	4	3	0	10	10	58	68	9	8	41	1.2	6.4	38%	.320	1.31	4.34	5.07	4.81	0.8
2011	CAR	AA	23	7	4	0	17	17	91²	92	11	20	68	2.0	6.7	33%	.302	1.22	4.42	4.27	4.90	0.3
2012	PEN	AA	24	1	2	0	6	6	35¹	31	2	6	26	1.5	6.6	41%	.280	1.05	3.57	3.00	4.14	0.5
2012	LOU	AAA	24	3	12	0	20	20	113¹	129	9	32	81	2.5	6.4	39%	.326	1.42	4.61	3.69	4.74	0.8
2012	CIN	MLB	24	0	0	0	1	0	1	0	0	0	1	0.0	9.0	%	.000	0.00	0.00	1.14	1.49	0.0
2013	LOU	AAA	25	4	9	2	33	18	109²	115	17	28	84	2.3	6.9	46%	.298	1.30	4.43	4.59	6.11	-0.5
2013	CIN	MLB	25	0	1	0	2	1	5²	13	4	3	4	4.8	6.4	23%	.444	2.82	12.71	12.37	11.79	-0.3
2014	CIN	MLB	26	5	7	0	27	18	106²	115	17	32	67	2.7	5.7	40%	.299	1.38	5.12	5.13	5.57	-0.9

Villarreal's seven trips between Triple-A Louisville and Cincinnati designated him "utility major leaguer." Among the players he substituted or made way for: Jonathan Broxton, Johnny Cueto, Billy Hamilton. True to his reputation of flex-man, he both started and came out of the bullpen at Louisville, more reliably as a reliever (3.22 ERA, 0.8 HR/9) than as a starter (5.08, 1.8). With a serviceable breaking ball and a low-90s fastball that's as unsinkable as Molly Brown, he projects to be the former.

LINEOUTS

HITTERS

PLAYER	TEAM	LVL	AGE	PA	R	2B	3B	HR	RBI	BB	SO	SB-CS	AVG/OBP/SLG	TAv	BABIP	BRR	FRAA	WARP
C T. Barnhart	PEN	AA	22	395	31	19	1	3	44	45	57	1-0	.260/.348/.348	.262	.300	-2.3	C(96): 1.9	2.2
DH S. Buckley	BAK	A+	23	23	1	0	0	0	2	1	9	0-0	.053/.174/.053	.119	.091	-1.1		-0.4
RF J. Duran	BAK	A+	21	456	55	15	3	20	66	45	134	5-6	.251/.323/.450	.274	.320	-2.2	RF(96): 2.3	1.3
CF R. LaMarre	PEN	AA	24	515	55	19	4	10	39	44	93	22-13	.246/.326/.373	.259	.288	2	CF(121): 14.3, RF(1): -0.0	4.0
1B S. Mejias-Brean	DYT	A	22	545	70	35	3	10	79	55	83	3-2	.305/.381/.453	.291	.350	-0.1	1B(79): -4.0, 3B(48): 7.7	3.4
C C. Miller	LOU	AAA	37	157	8	6	0	4	19	16	23	0-0	.200/.295/.333	.229	.209	-0.1	C(36): 0.3, 1B(4): -0.1	-0.2
	CIN	MLB	37	41	2	5	0	0	8	5	6	0-0	.257/.366/.400	.272	.310	0.3	C(16): 0.3	0.2
3B D. Vidal	BAK	A+	23	237	23	14	1	3	16	18	61	0-0	.225/.294/.343	.225	.300	2.7	3B(51): -0.4, P(1): -0.0	0.1
	PEN	AA	23	150	9	2	0	1	9	15	40	0-0	.206/.286/.244	.205	.286	-0.8	3B(41): -4.2	-0.9
2B R. Wright	BAK	A+	23	445	53	23	1	8	52	26	66	5-3	.265/.311/.384	.256	.296	3.9	2B(75): -3.3	0.9

What do you called a baserunner who tries to steal against strong-armed catcher **Tucker Barnhart**? Tuckered out. ⊘ **Sean Buckley** has power, but an arm injury cut his season short and he spent the rest of it tweeting about his adventures on Netflix. August 21st: "I gotta new found respect for Ryan Gosling." ⊘ **Juan Duran** posted diverging halves (.233/.298/.358 April-June, .275/.358/.581 July-September), though the story is the same in both: The power is there, the contact (29 percent strikeout rate in both halves) isn't. ⊘ **Ryan LaMarre**'s skill set and athleticism make him a bit like Billy Hamilton, but not *enough* like Billy Hamilton to suggest anything better than future fourth outfielder. ⊘ One could say **Seth Mejias-Brean**'s Midwest League performance was statistically similar to that of Carlos Correa, except Mejias-Brean is 1,266 days older than baseball's elite youngster. ⊘ **Corky Miller** might be best known for his 80-grade mustache, but he had the highest TAv of his career in (once again) limited playing time at 37 years of age. ⊘ **David Vidal**'s poor hitting dropped him back a level to High-A, where his struggles continued, making him a glove-only third baseman suddenly old for his level. ⊘ Speedy **Jonathan Reynoso** has multiple tools that project to be loud, but he'll need to develop the necessary baseball skills before the raw becomes a roar.. ⊘ **Ryan Wright**, like his first and last names, doesn't offer much flashiness, but he shows enough all-around ability to eventually make a name as a utilityman.

PITCHERS

PLAYER	TEAM	LVL	AGE	W	L	SV	IP	H	HR	BB	SO	BB9	SO9	GB%	BABIP	WHIP	ERA	FIP	FRA	WARP
A. Cisco	DYT	A	21	5	7	0	130²	148	11	16	99	1.1	6.8	47%	.332	1.26	3.86	3.33	4.32	2.1
J. Freeman	CIN	MLB	26	0	0	0	1	2	1	0	0	0.0	0.0	40%	.250	2.00	18.00	16.02	17.24	-0.1
S. Romano	DYT	A	19	7	11	0	120¹	134	10	57	89	4.3	6.7	52%	.334	1.59	4.86	4.61	6.45	-0.2
C. Wang	BUF	AAA	33	4	3	0	51²	46	3	12	30	2.1	5.2	60%	.262	1.12	3.48	3.55	5.24	-0.1
	SWB	AAA	33	4	4	0	58	57	2	10	25	1.6	3.9	59%	.269	1.16	2.33	3.36	4.96	-0.1
	TOR	MLB	33	1	2	0	27	40	5	9	14	3.0	4.7	59%	.368	1.81	7.67	5.45	6.16	-0.2

Control artist **Andrew Cisco** walked nobody in his final 21 innings, but his average repertoire is a bit too prone to contact. ⊘ A rash of pitcher injuries on the Reds' staff pushed **Justin Freeman** to a major-league mound for the first time in his career, and then the rash spread: A shoulder impingement disabled him, too. ⊘ **Dan Langfield**'s plus fastball and breaking ball have starter potential; his balky shoulder, which cost him the entire season, has go-back-and-complete-his-degree potential. ⊘ **Salvatore Romano** has a big, strong body and a low-90s sinker, good curve and change and the same name as *Mad Men's* most missed character. ⊘ **Chien-Ming Wang**, it's been said by his countrymen, could probably get elected to public office in Taiwan, where his future might lie after big-league hitters voted a resounding no on his bid to hang on to his seat in the rotation with deeply damaged stuff.

MANAGER: BRYAN PRICE

The problem for Dusty Baker isn't that sabermetric types have often been critical of him. Hey—what the hell do we really know? The problem for Baker is that twice his own team has opted to let him go after he led them to substantial success. He won a pennant with the 2002 Giants, and they let him walk in the 2002-03 offseason. Baker guided the Reds to their best four-year stretch since the Big Red Machine, and they fired him. The GMs letting him go—Brian Sabean and Walt Jocketty—are both well regarded honchos with plenty of success away from Baker. The only GM to ride Baker down to the second division was former Cubs boss Jim Hendry, who might never be a GM again.

The main criticism of Baker in his career was his handling of pitchers, but the Reds' starting staff has been especially healthy the last two years; historically so in 2012. How much credit does Baker deserve for that? I don't know—but Cincy just hired pitching coach Bryan Price as their new skipper.

Baker likes to bunt, always has. Despite an offense with plenty of power, the Reds ranked near the top of the league in bunts, not a rare occurrence under Baker.

His replacement, Bryan Price, is an interesting hire, if for no other reason than pitching coaches rarely become managers. Many successful pitching coaches become unsuccessful or even clueless managers (Phil Regan, Ray Miller, for example). Some have had success—Bud Black has survived in San Diego. John Farrell just had a nice year in Boston.

It's impossible to say too much about what Price will be like as a manager. He's praised for his dedication, smarts, accountability and, naturally, ability to work with pitchers.

Cleveland Indians

By Susan Petrone

The Cleveland Indians ended their first season under Terry Francona with 24 more wins than in 2012, 78 more runs scored, 183 fewer runs allowed and the first AL Wild Card spot. By any standard, that's a darn good season, and Francona deservedly won the Manager of the Year award. However, he is quick to say that "it's not a one-man show." He credits General Manager Chris Antonetti with fostering a working environment "that's fun to be part of," and the "tireless" efforts of his coaches. Ultimately, he says, "it all comes down to the players. They aren't always successful but they always try." This self-effacement is regulation MLB-speak, but it undersells his performance, as well as those of Antonetti and the team's coaches. On a roster with a decided dearth of superstars, the behind-the-scenes crew of Antonetti, Francona and pitching coach Mickey Callaway were key to the Indians' 2013 success and will be the architects of continued competitiveness.

INDIANS PROSPECTUS
2013 W-L: 92-70, 2nd in AL Central

Pythag	.555	8th	DER	.697	24th
RS/G	4.60	5th	B-Age	28.6	20th
RA/G	4.09	14th	P-Age	27.4	8th
TAv	.274	6th	Salary	$79	24th
BRR	3.37	11th	M$/MW	$1.51	4th
TAv-P	.265	15th	DL Days	964	16th
FIP	3.76	10th	$ on DL	15%	12th

	Runs	HR/RH	HR/LH	Runs/RH	Runs/LH
Three-Year Park Factors	97	88	94	99	100

Top Hitter WARP	4.85 (Jason Kipnis)
Top Pitcher WARP	2.55 (Scott Kazmir)
Top Prospect	Francisco Lindor

The 2012-13 offseason, though, brought Antonetti the unique convergence of an exceptional new manager (arguably the best hire Antonetti has made) and extra cash. The Dolan family, which owns the Indians, sold the Sports Time Ohio (STO) television network to Fox Sports in December 2012. The deal included the rights to broadcast Indians games for the next 10 years and should inject about $400 million into the franchise during that time. This estimated $40 million per year is respectable, putting the Tribe in the same company as the Tigers ($40 million per year), Twins ($29 million) and Blue Jays (around $36 million) and ahead of baseball's have-nots (Royals, A's, Pirates, Marlins, Brewers), though still far behind the have-mores (Angels, $140 million; Rangers, $80 million; Yankees, $90 million; and the behemoth Dodgers, $280 million). (These figures were helpfully compiled from a mass of public sources by Wendy Thurm at *FanGraphs*.)

The STO sale bumped the team's Opening Day payroll from approximately $67 million in 2012 to $78 million in 2013. It's estimated that the 2014 payroll will be around $80 million, keeping the Indians in the no. 18 to 22 range in MLB salary expenditures. In that sense, the TV windfall simply kept Cleveland competitive, as a number of teams made similar deals and have more to spend.

Antonetti's two splurges last offseason were Nick Swisher and Michael Bourn. A durable player with offensive consistency, Swisher also added a sorely needed big name to the roster. The qualifying offer attached to Bourn made many teams shy away from him, and as his price Antonetti took the gamble on a Gold Glove-winning, All-Star outfielder. Both players dealt with small but troublesome injuries and consequently underperformed in 2013, particularly in power production and stolen bases, respectively. Both, though, are under contract through at least 2016, and each is a reasonable bet to add more value in 2014 than he did in 2013.

SOME ASSEMBLY REQUIRED: CHRIS ANTONETTI

General managers typically don't get a lot of love from the average fan. When things are going well, their work is ignored. When the team is losing, fans scream for the guillotine. Chris Antonetti took over as GM at the end of the 2010 season, and his first two seasons resembled the Reign of Terror.

The Indians present particular challenges. They will never carry the biggest payroll or attract superstar players with a thriving media market. Cleveland has traditionally been the kind of place where players establish themselves before seeking more lucrative pastures (e.g. Manny Ramirez, Jim Thome, Albert Belle and, more recently, Scott Kazmir), or where players must be traded to maximize value before they are lost to free agency. Four and five years down the line, fans still bemoan the Cliff Lee and CC Sabathia deals.

Swisher and Bourn joined existing core players Jason Kipnis, Michael Brantley, Justin Masterson, Carlos Santana and Asdrubal Cabrera. The seemingly small trade of Esmil Rogers for Mike Aviles and Yan Gomes also paid dividends as Gomes established himself as the everyday catcher by the end of the season while Aviles filled well the role of infield utilityman. In all, Antonetti built a strong position-player core that remains under team control without mortgaging prospects or locking up all his payroll flexibility in one big hitter.

Antonetti also made a number of calculated risks of the type that small-market teams depend on to win, such as picking up Scott Kazmir, who hadn't played in a major-league game since the beginning of 2011, and Jason Giambi, for whom the term "grizzled veteran" was prophetically coined. Kazmir pitched well enough in 2013 to revive his career and get $22 million on his free-agent contract with the A's this offseason, while Giambi knocked a couple of walk-off home runs and provide veteran presence in the clubhouse. A one-year minor-league contract with an invitation to spring training for 2014 gives Giambi a chance to repeat that role. Of course, Antonetti isn't made of gold; for gambles that didn't turn out so well, see Mark Reynolds and Brett Myers.

Antonetti's 2014 buy-low bet is outfielder David Murphy, who had a horrendous season last year. The question going forward is whether the Tribe will see the .233 TAv hitter of 2013 or the lifetime .273 TAv player; the subquestion is whether the planned platoon will help him be the latter.

MANIPULATING THE DAY TO DAY: TERRY FRANCONA

For a franchise that approaches the playoffs like a recessive gene—skipping a generation between appearances—and for a city where championships are spoken of in the same hushed tones usually reserved for unicorns and Brigadoon, the arrival of Terry Francona in Cleveland was seen as a sign that the front office was genuinely serious about putting together a competitive team.

Francona says, "When you have less money to work with, you have less room for error. You have to go in and be better prepared. There are small market teams that are successful—Tampa, Oakland. They make good decisions and they make them consistently." Antonetti gave Francona an assemblage of players, a sprinkling of big names and All-Stars, some journeymen players, and a few "why not?" gambles. Francona earned his Manager of the Year award by consistently using those players to their best advantage.

The hallmark of the Francona era is already emerging: versatility. If you can't do more than one thing, you might not have a job. The team let long-time DH Travis Hafner move on in 2012, giving the Indians an extra glove on the roster. The DH role rotated among several players—11 had at least one at-bat as DH, most frequently Jason Giambi (DH, pinch-hitter, managerial proxy) and Carlos Santana (DH, 1B, C; he

then spent the offseason in the Dominican Republic learning third base).

Most of the starting nine bat lefty or, in the cases of Santana, Swisher and Cabrera, switch-hit. One of the most marked improvements under Francona was the result of using the platoon advantage more effectively, particularly against left-handed pitchers. The Indians hit a barrel-scraping .234/.312/.352 against left-handed pitching in 2012, but shot up to a top-of-the-table .271/.341/.425 line in 2013. The club had the highest percentage of platoon-advantage plate appearances in baseball.

With the addition of Murphy (essentially replacing Drew Stubbs), Francona now has a particularly potent one-two platoon punch in right field. The lefty-hitting David Murphy has a career .280/.347/.469 line against right-handed pitchers while returning utilityman Ryan Raburn has hit .263/.336/.492 against left-handers. "Our players are versatile," Francona said, "and we use it to our advantage. [Platooning] allows us to shift guys around while keeping their bats in the lineup."

With an outfield full of useful players and a relatively stable infield (only third baseman Lonnie Chisenhall has yet to solidify his position), the pitching staff is the team's major focus. Justin Masterson, Corey Kluber and Zach McAllister will return to the rotation in 2014, but Ubaldo Jimenez and Scott Kazmir pitched 340 innings for the Tribe in 2013. (As this book goes to press, Jimenez has not signed.) That's a lot of innings to replace. With the free-agent market inflating, in-house candidates for the rotation are the most affordable (and only realistic) option. Josh Tomlin had Tommy John surgery in late 2012 and pitched in rehab starts throughout the Indians' minor-league system during 2013, culminating in two scoreless innings of relief in September against the White Sox. He may be ready to return to starting. Carlos Carrasco has had his troubles over the past two seasons (Tommy John surgery and two suspensions for throwing at batters), but Francona also mentions him as a possibility. Danny Salazar, who started for the Indians in the Wild Card game, and Trevor Bauer, both of whom have enormous upside, are also in contention. "We have options and they might be really good ones," Francona says. "But you hate to go into a season with just five pitchers; you want seven or eight. We have pitchers. We just want more."

THE PITCHER WHISPERER: MICKEY CALLAWAY

One of the unsung heroes in the success of the 2013 season was pitching coach Mickey Callaway, who was in his first year coaching at the major-league level. While he successfully brought along Kluber and McAllister and acclimated Salazar to the majors, Callaway's biggest accomplishments were helping Jimenez finally become the pitcher the Indians traded for in 2011 and rebuilding Kazmir.

Indeed, of the 11 Cleveland pitchers who threw at least 50 innings in 2013, all but one topped PECOTA's weighted-mean forecast:

Pitcher	Projected 2013 ERA	Actual 2013 ERA	Difference
Justin Masterson	4.12	3.45	-0.67
Ubaldo Jimenez	3.73	3.30	-0.43
Scott Kazmir	4.85	4.04	-0.81
Corey Kluber	5.08	3.85	-1.23
Zach McAllister	4.52	3.75	-0.77
Bryan Shaw	4.74	3.24	-1.50
Cody Allen	3.63	2.43	-1.20
Joe Smith	3.65	2.29	-1.36
Matt Albers	4.38	3.14	-1.24
Chris Perez	3.52	4.33	0.81
Danny Salazar	6.01	3.12	-2.89

Of course, there's survivor bias at work—pitchers who did worse than projected, such as Trevor Bauer, aren't allowed to pitch 50 innings. But most of these pitchers were crucial parts of the Indians' plans coming out of spring training, and Callaway oversaw improvements staffwide.

You might want to call him the Pitcher Whisperer, but Callaway's key tool is his ears, not his mouth. "I think the best thing I did [last season] was listen. I made sure to listen to the guys," he says. "It wasn't a planned approach. I'll try to be open and listen even more [in 2014], maybe talking to them a bit more at times." Callaway's approach, cliched though it might be, allows players to figure things out for themselves and own the adjustments they make.

This is why he has faith in last season's two biggest disappointments on the pitching staff: Trevor Bauer and Vinnie Pestano.

The acquisition of Bauer in late 2012 had been seen as a coup. However, the long-tossing pitcher/would-be rapper survived only four starts. Still, Callaway thinks the 22-year-old has a good shot at eventually becoming part of the

starting rotation: "Obviously his stuff is always ready for that role. He's a guy that perseveres and he'll get over that little hump."

Pestano was placed on the 15-day DL early in the 2013 season with tendinitis. Callaway notes that Pestano "kind of taught himself the wrong way to throw when he was coming back from injury. That happens a lot. When you change your motion, then it affects your confidence. Once you lose it mentally, you're in a rough spot." Callaway was scheduled to work with Pestano in the offseason and predicts that taking time off will help the reliever "forget the bad habits and start throwing in a more natural way." Come spring training, he says "You'll see a different Vinnie. Or, rather, you'll see the Vinnie you knew."

Fixing Pestano is less of a worry than filling the holes in the bullpen left by the departures of set-up men Joe Smith and Matt Albers and erstwhile closer Chris Perez. A group of bullpen additions—ranging from fallen closer John Axford to nonroster invitees Mike Zagurski, Matt Capps and J.C. Ramirez to 40-man promotions Austin Adams and Brian Price—will give Callaway plenty of opportunity for listening, and probably some whispering, too.

***

The Indians had nowhere to go but up during Francona's first season. Expectations are guarded but high for 2014. As for Francona, he says: "I don't think my expectations have ever been low. You just don't know what's going to happen or what injuries are going to take place. We keep our expectations in the present." Francona did a lot of things right during his first season at Indians manager, but if you ask what he thinks he did right, he says simply: "If anything, I hope I got people to believe."

Believe, Indians fans. You have ample reason.

Susan Petrone is the co-owner of It's Pronounced Lajaway, *the Cleveland Indians blog of the ESPN SweetSpot network. She was formerly the Publicity & Member Services Manager for the Society for American Baseball Research.*

HITTERS

	YEAR	TEAM	LVL	AGE	PA	R	2B	3B	HR	RBI	BB	SO	SB	CS	AVG/OBP/SLG	TAv	BABIP	BRR	FRAA	WARP
David Adams 3B	2011	TAM	A+	24	57	6	3	0	0	4	4	8	0	2	.308/.368/.365	.225	.364	-0.4	2B(5): 0.2	-0.1
Born: 5/15/1987 Age: 27	2012	TRN	AA	25	383	44	23	0	8	48	38	53	3	1	.306/.385/.450	.299	.336	-0.8	2B(42): -0.5, 3B(23): 1.0	2.6
Bats: R Throws: R Height: 6' 1''	2013	SWB	AAA	26	255	28	11	2	5	21	29	43	0	0	.268/.366/.405	.278	.314	-2.4	3B(30): -0.0, 2B(28): -1.1	1.3
Weight: 205 Breakout: 2%	2013	NYA	MLB	26	152	10	5	1	2	13	9	43	0	0	.193/.252/.286	.197	.263	-0.8	3B(31): 1.1, 2B(9): 0.6	-0.3
Improve: 22% Collapse: 9%	2014	CLE	MLB	27	250	24	11	1	5	26	19	53	0	0	.245/.312/.365	.251	.300	-0.5	3B 1, 2B 1	0.7
Attrition: 14% MLB: 38%																				
Comparables: Adam Rosales, Brian Buscher, Travis Metcalf																				

With only a rehabbing Alex Rodriguez and a brittle Kevin Youkilis ahead of him on the Yankees' third base depth chart at the start of the season, Adams must have suspected that his arrival was imminent. A back injury cost him some of spring training, during which he was released and re-signed, but his opportunity arose, as expected, on May 15th, which was both his 26th birthday and the first day he was eligible for the 40-man. Adams had hit .316/.407/.490 in Triple-A to that point, but his bat was about to desert him. His TAv across four separate stints in the majors was the third-worst among hitters with at least 150 PA, and he managed only a .230/.333/.336 line over the rest of his reps in Scranton. Small samples, sure, but when players of his age and skill set flub their first chance, they don't always get another.

Mike Aviles SS
Born: 3/13/1981 Age: 33
Bats: R Throws: R Height: 5' 10"
Weight: 205 Breakout: 0%
Improve: 36% Collapse: 5%
Attrition: 12% MLB: 89%
Comparables:
Jack Wilson, Alex Gonzalez, Alvin Dark

YEAR	TEAM	LVL	AGE	PA	R	2B	3B	HR	RBI	BB	SO	SB	CS	AVG/OBP/SLG	TAv	BABIP	BRR	FRAA	WARP
2011	OMA	AAA	30	150	21	8	2	9	25	6	17	6	4	.307/.329/.586	.347	.291	-0.4	SS(22): 4.3	1.8
2011	KCA	MLB	30	202	14	11	3	5	31	9	27	10	2	.222/.261/.395	.224	.231	-1.7	3B(24): 1.0, 2B(20): -0.8	-0.3
2011	BOS	MLB	30	107	17	6	0	2	8	4	17	4	2	.317/.340/.436	.269	.361	-0.2	3B(22): 0.6, SS(8): 0.8	0.5
2012	BOS	MLB	31	546	57	28	0	13	60	23	77	14	6	.250/.282/.381	.243	.269	3.5	SS(128): -1.0, 2B(2): -0.0	1.4
2013	CLE	MLB	32	394	54	15	0	9	46	15	41	8	5	.252/.282/.368	.241	.257	1.4	3B(56): -2.2, SS(46): 1.1	0.5
2014	CLE	MLB	33	400	43	17	1	8	38	16	60	11	5	.249/.282/.365	.237	.270	0.1	SS 2, 3B -1	0.7

Aviles has posted a .282 on-base percentage the past two seasons, the lowest mark in baseball among players with 900 or more plate appearances. Despite this ignominious distinction, he can help a winning club *if* he's not soaking up so many plate appearances, as he's still an average (or nearly so) defensive shortstop who brings a solid glove to any other position he fills and contributes much more power than a typical reserve shortstop. Having such a versatile and competent backup effectively raises "replacement level" at multiple positions.

Michael Bourn CF
Born: 12/27/1982 Age: 31
Bats: L Throws: R Height: 5' 11"
Weight: 180 Breakout: 0%
Improve: 38% Collapse: 4%
Attrition: 11% MLB: 93%
Comparables:
Kenny Lofton, Jeff DaVanon, Ryan Freel

YEAR	TEAM	LVL	AGE	PA	R	2B	3B	HR	RBI	BB	SO	SB	CS	AVG/OBP/SLG	TAv	BABIP	BRR	FRAA	WARP
2011	ATL	MLB	28	249	30	8	3	1	18	15	50	22	7	.278/.321/.352	.255	.346	2.2	CF(53): -5.2	0.5
2011	HOU	MLB	28	473	64	26	7	1	32	38	90	39	7	.303/.363/.403	.273	.381	4.4	CF(103): -1.8	2.3
2012	ATL	MLB	29	703	96	26	10	9	57	70	155	42	13	.274/.348/.391	.272	.349	11.3	CF(153): 1.2	4.5
2013	CLE	MLB	30	575	75	21	6	6	50	40	132	23	12	.263/.316/.360	.251	.338	5.4	CF(128): -6.5	1.2
2014	CLE	MLB	31	567	72	23	6	4	39	47	121	36	11	.266/.330/.355	.254	.340	3.2	CF -2	1.5

Yet another Cleveland position player whose second half didn't live up to expectations, Bourn's first-half statistics didn't really live up to his substantial salary, either. Though nothing was mentioned about leg injuries, Bourn looked a step slow in every aspect of his game—ranging less rangily around center field, adding a slow step to second on stolen base attempts, reaching on a career-worst 26 percent of bunt attempts. Of course, Bourn down a step is still very fast, and his wheels will be getting serviced this offseason, so if anything was being hidden it should be cleared up by Opening Day. Bourn is well-liked and smart and is considered a good clubhouse presence, but leadership by example always works best, so getting back above the one-in-three on-base mark and swiping bases more frequently and efficiently will go a long way toward helping the team see the postseason again.

Michael Brantley LF
Born: 5/15/1987 Age: 27
Bats: L Throws: L Height: 6' 2"
Weight: 200 Breakout: 8%
Improve: 37% Collapse: 10%
Attrition: 23% MLB: 95%
Comparables:
Blake DeWitt, Jeremy Reed, Angel Pagan

YEAR	TEAM	LVL	AGE	PA	R	2B	3B	HR	RBI	BB	SO	SB	CS	AVG/OBP/SLG	TAv	BABIP	BRR	FRAA	WARP
2011	CLE	MLB	24	496	63	24	4	7	46	34	76	13	5	.266/.318/.384	.250	.303	0.5	LF(66): -2.8, CF(52): -1.5	0.4
2012	CLE	MLB	25	609	63	37	4	6	60	53	56	12	9	.288/.348/.402	.271	.310	2.7	CF(144): -11.5	1.5
2013	CLE	MLB	26	611	66	26	3	10	73	40	67	17	4	.284/.332/.396	.271	.304	2.4	LF(151): 0.5, CF(1): -0.0	2.5
2014	CLE	MLB	27	574	60	26	3	7	54	46	71	16	6	.272/.332/.373	.260	.300	0.6	LF -1, CF -2	1.2

On August 19th, Brantley broke Rocky Colavito's franchise record for most consecutive games without an error, a streak he pushed to 264 games by the end of the season. With 11 assists and the range of a recently converted center fielder, one might expect him to dominate left field defensive rankings. That he's barely above average according to FRAA (and worse in other advanced fielding metrics) paints a different picture, however. He was not included among the three left field finalists for Gold Glove voting in the American League and finished sixth in Fielding Bible voting. At the plate, the man who has "Dr. Smooth" on his baseball card does have an easy approach that has led to some very consistent stat lines, aided by great contact skills. Yet as in the field, the consistency—combined with some herculean clutch stats last year—tends to obscure the fact that he's not exactly Colavito when it comes to putting runs on the board.

Asdrubal Cabrera SS
Born: 11/13/1985 Age: 28
Bats: B Throws: R Height: 6' 0"
Weight: 205 Breakout: 0%
Improve: 58% Collapse: 1%
Attrition: 6% MLB: 99%
Comparables:
John Valentin, J.J. Hardy, Stephen Drew

YEAR	TEAM	LVL	AGE	PA	R	2B	3B	HR	RBI	BB	SO	SB	CS	AVG/OBP/SLG	TAv	BABIP	BRR	FRAA	WARP
2011	CLE	MLB	25	667	87	32	3	25	92	44	119	17	5	.273/.332/.460	.283	.302	2.4	SS(151): -19.0	2.4
2012	CLE	MLB	26	616	70	35	1	16	68	52	99	9	4	.270/.338/.423	.265	.303	3.3	SS(136): 2.7	2.9
2013	CLE	MLB	27	562	66	35	2	14	64	35	114	9	3	.242/.299/.402	.262	.283	-2.8	SS(129): -3.9	1.5
2014	CLE	MLB	28	539	59	29	2	12	60	38	95	10	4	.269/.328/.411	.271	.310	0	SS -6	2.2

It may be overly dramatic to say that his double play in the Wild Card game ended both the Indians' season and Cabrera's tenure with the team, but many a Wahoo certainly felt it did the former and wished for the latter. Truth be told, Cabrera was wearing out his welcome all season long, as memories of the 25 home runs from 2011 faded and even his recent defensive advances reversed. The problems arose from swinging at too many pitches outside the strike zone, leading to his increased strikeout percentage. An optimistic interpretation would mention that his walk rate was almost as high as in 2011, and that his isolated power was the second-highest of his career. With his contract expiring after this season, the stage is set for a strong rebound, though not even his home venue will be certain until the curtain rises on the new season.

Lonnie Chisenhall 3B
Born: 10/4/1988 Age: 25
Bats: L Throws: R Height: 6' 2''
Weight: 190 Breakout: 1%
Improve: 58% Collapse: 4%
Attrition: 13% MLB: 98%
Comparables:
Edwin Encarnacion, Alex Gordon, Kyle Seager

YEAR	TEAM	LVL	AGE	PA	R	2B	3B	HR	RBI	BB	SO	SB	CS	AVG/OBP/SLG	TAv	BABIP	BRR	FRAA	WARP
2011	COH	AAA	22	292	45	15	3	7	45	28	47	0	1	.267/.353/.431	.295	.300	-1.1	3B(23): -1.0	0.6
2011	CLE	MLB	22	223	27	13	0	7	22	8	49	1	0	.255/.284/.415	.251	.299	-0.3	3B(58): 4.0	0.9
2012	COH	AAA	23	126	16	12	0	4	17	4	22	0	0	.314/.341/.517	.271	.351	0.4	3B(27): 3.2	1.0
2012	CLE	MLB	23	151	16	6	1	5	16	8	27	2	1	.268/.311/.430	.267	.300	-1	3B(30): -0.3	0.4
2013	COH	AAA	24	125	21	8	2	6	26	12	24	2	0	.390/.456/.676	.388	.443	-1.3	3B(27): 0.6	2.2
2013	CLE	MLB	24	308	30	17	0	11	36	16	56	1	0	.225/.270/.398	.251	.243	0.6	3B(88): 0.2	0.7
2014	CLE	MLB	25	292	33	16	1	9	35	17	58	1	0	.262/.311/.431	.273	.300	-0.3	3B -0	1.1

Here's a can't-miss tip for the upcoming season: Chisenhall will have a significantly better season this year. Obviously, many factors can contribute to a low BABIP, but in the past decade there have been 753 player seasons of 500 or more plate appearances with a .173 or greater isolated power. Of those, 738 have topped Chisenhall's .243 BABIP. Toss in the natural anticipation that a young player will get better and the fact that Chisenhall battered Triple-A pitching when he was demoted and did quite well (.270/.325/.595) in his 40 plate appearances from September onward (followed by a 3-for-4 Wild Card game). Lest this be taken as a glowing endorsement, the pre-September part of the season was all but lost for the young third sacker, with reports—albeit unsupported by his defensive metrics—that he was taking his struggles at the plate to the field with him. The pressure to be a star should be reduced now, and expectations have to be lowered, but a breakout is still a possibility.

Clint Frazier CF
Born: 9/6/1994 Age: 19
Bats: R Throws: R Height: 6' 1''
Weight: 190 Breakout: 0%
Improve: 0% Collapse: 0%
Attrition: 0% MLB: 0%
Comparables:
Jay Bruce, Abraham Almonte, Joe Benson

YEAR	TEAM	LVL	AGE	PA	R	2B	3B	HR	RBI	BB	SO	SB	CS	AVG/OBP/SLG	TAv	BABIP	BRR	FRAA	WARP
2014	CLE	MLB	19	250	18	8	1	4	22	12	87	0	0	.184/.224/.273	.185	.270	-0.4	CF -1	-1.4

Since 2002, when Mark Shapiro first earned his turn in the general manager's chair, the Indians have only twice selected a prep player with a true first-round pick. Frazier, out of Loganville High School in Georgia, tantalized the Tribe with five-tool potential in center field—a package of outstanding pop, terrific speed, uncanny hitting ability and an 80-grade ginger mop—to nab a $3.5 million signing bonus. He made good on it immediately, with a home run in his first professional plate appearance, and should move steadily up the chain as he improves his plate discipline from stop to stop. Frazier has the makings of a star-level up-the-middle player, the type of center fielder who will help Indians fans forget what a healthy Grady Sizemore might have been.

Yan Gomes C
Born: 7/19/1987 Age: 26
Bats: R Throws: R Height: 6' 2''
Weight: 215 Breakout: 4%
Improve: 38% Collapse: 8%
Attrition: 11% MLB: 89%
Comparables:
Geovany Soto, J.P. Arencibia, Nick Hundley

YEAR	TEAM	LVL	AGE	PA	R	2B	3B	HR	RBI	BB	SO	SB	CS	AVG/OBP/SLG	TAv	BABIP	BRR	FRAA	WARP
2011	NHP	AA	23	309	34	18	1	13	51	25	75	0	0	.250/.317/.464	.346	.292	0.6	C(14): -0.2, 1B(8): -0.2	1.4
2012	LVG	AAA	24	335	44	29	1	13	59	25	72	4	0	.328/.380/.557	.309	.392	-3.7	C(35): 0.2, 3B(24): -1.4	2.6
2012	TOR	MLB	24	111	9	4	0	4	13	6	32	0	0	.204/.264/.367	.234	.246	-1	1B(20): 0.4, C(9): -0.1	-0.2
2013	COH	AAA	25	24	2	4	0	0	3	4	4	0	0	.300/.417/.500	.309	.375	-0.4	C(6): -0.1	0.1
2013	CLE	MLB	25	322	45	18	2	11	38	18	67	2	0	.294/.345/.481	.296	.342	0.1	C(85): 1.4, 1B(1): -0.0	3.1
2014	CLE	MLB	26	304	35	16	1	11	38	18	75	1	0	.263/.315/.438	.274	.320	-0.4	C 0, 1B 0	1.6

Gomes' career before 2013 could be used in a spy textbook on becoming anonymous. Avoid rookie attention? Sure, just spend too many days on the roster so you'll be ROY ineligible. (This is important so people don't go looking at your great Triple-A statistics.) Avoid attention for being an offensive contributor at a light-hitting position such as catcher? Check: Play several other positions as well, suggesting defensive liabilities. Avoid national attention? Try to get traded in November to a smaller-market team not expected to compete. For good measure, hitting .204 in a limited trial before the trade should complete the "stealth" outfitting. Make no mistake, "Yanimal" is for real, and a big part of the second-half surge by the Tribe. While he's unlikely to hit for such a high batting average again, and getting on base won't ever be a strong suit, he has enough catch-and-throw (and game calling) skills to start at catcher, and enough ISO to be welcome in any lineup.

Jason Kipnis 2B
Born: 4/3/1987 Age: 27
Bats: L Throws: R Height: 5' 11"
Weight: 190 Breakout: 2%
Improve: 53% Collapse: 6%
Attrition: 7% MLB: 98%
Comparables:
Ian Kinsler, Kelly Johnson, Chase Utley

YEAR	TEAM	LVL	AGE	PA	R	2B	3B	HR	RBI	BB	SO	SB	CS	AVG/OBP/SLG	TAv	BABIP	BRR	FRAA	WARP
2011	COH	AAA	24	400	65	16	9	12	55	44	72	12	1	.280/.362/.484	.287	.318	1.4	2B(32): 3.5	1.2
2011	CLE	MLB	24	150	24	9	1	7	19	11	34	5	0	.272/.333/.507	.291	.312	0	2B(36): -1.5	0.8
2012	CLE	MLB	25	672	86	22	4	14	76	67	109	31	7	.257/.335/.379	.262	.291	3	2B(146): -8.9	1.3
2013	CLE	MLB	26	658	86	36	4	17	84	76	143	30	7	.284/.366/.452	.309	.345	-0.8	2B(147): -2.5	4.9
2014	CLE	MLB	27	621	86	28	5	15	61	62	123	28	6	.266/.343/.414	.279	.310	2.9	2B -4	3.2

Kipnis has assumed his much anticipated position as one of the top offensive second basemen in the game, behind only Robinson Cano among American League keystoners in 2013. He even stole 30 bases again, leading a team with a trio of fleet outfielders. Kipnis has shown growth on the other side of the ball as well, making plays on far more balls and approaching average defense (despite the increase in errors). Considering his ability to get on base even when his power is M.I.A.—as it was in the second half, when his slugging percentage slid downward from a July 3rd high-water mark of .539—he's already one of the top young players in the game, and if his first-half bat sticks around for a full season and the Indians keep winning, he'll be in MVP discussions.

Francisco Lindor SS
Born: 11/14/1993 Age: 20
Bats: B Throws: R Height: 5' 11"
Weight: 175 Breakout: 1%
Improve: 14% Collapse: 0%
Attrition: 1% MLB: 14%
Comparables:
Ruben Tejada, Ehire Adrianza, Lonnie Chisenhall

YEAR	TEAM	LVL	AGE	PA	R	2B	3B	HR	RBI	BB	SO	SB	CS	AVG/OBP/SLG	TAv	BABIP	BRR	FRAA	WARP
2011	MHV	A-	17	20	4	0	0	0	2	1	5	1	0	.316/.350/.316	.290	.429	0	SS(2): -0.1	0.1
2012	LKC	A	18	568	83	24	3	6	42	61	78	27	12	.257/.352/.355	.260	.295	3.3	SS(120): 6.2	3.4
2013	CAR	A+	19	373	51	19	6	1	27	35	39	20	5	.306/.373/.410	.274	.341	-2.3	SS(82): 2.6	2.5
2013	AKR	AA	19	91	14	3	1	1	7	14	7	5	2	.289/.407/.395	.305	.309	-0.8	SS(21): -2.0	0.5
2014	CLE	MLB	20	250	26	10	1	2	18	19	47	5	2	.236/.298/.316	.231	.280	0.1	SS 0	0.4

The youngest participant in the 2012 Futures Game, Lindor was shut down in mid-August with a back strain. That hardly put a dent in his development, though, because the shortstop had already climbed all the way to Double-A, where he showed off his pitch recognition by walking twice as often as he struck out. Lindor's on-base percentage would have ranked fourth in the Eastern League if maintained over a full season, and it is just one of many testaments to the polish with which he dazzles scouts on both sides of the ball. Power may never be a part of Lindor's game, but with a Gold Glove skill set at shortstop, the hit tool and discipline to bat near the top of the order and the makeup and instincts to maximize his ability, there is one word to describe what lies in his near future: stardom.

Jake Lowery C
Born: 7/21/1990 Age: 23
Bats: L Throws: R Height: 6' 0"
Weight: 195 Breakout: 10%
Improve: 13% Collapse: 0%
Attrition: 7% MLB: 15%
Comparables:
Yasmani Grandal, Michael McKenry, Max Ramirez

YEAR	TEAM	LVL	AGE	PA	R	2B	3B	HR	RBI	BB	SO	SB	CS	AVG/OBP/SLG	TAv	BABIP	BRR	FRAA	WARP
2011	MHV	A-	20	310	43	23	1	6	43	54	56	3	2	.245/.377/.415	.263	.290	0.9	C(10): -0.2, 1B(3): 0.2	0.5
2012	LKC	A	21	165	25	10	2	7	28	24	39	1	0	.248/.358/.504	.303	.293	0.6	C(25): 0.4	1.4
2012	CAR	A+	21	233	20	15	0	2	25	28	71	0	1	.222/.315/.325	.217	.328	-2.1	C(49): 0.8	-0.2
2013	CAR	A+	22	50	4	2	1	1	5	9	12	0	0	.195/.340/.366	.250	.250	-0.6	C(7): -0.1, 1B(2): -0.0	-0.1
2013	AKR	AA	22	270	22	21	1	6	28	33	66	0	0	.275/.363/.449	.304	.358	-1.1	C(65): 0.7, 1B(3): -0.0	2.4
2014	CLE	MLB	23	250	24	11	0	5	24	24	76	0	0	.211/.288/.336	.232	.290	-0.5	C 0, 1B -0	0.3

If you look closely at the pitcher in the Perfect Game prospect batting practice videos, you will notice it is often the same man—he's Tim Lowery, a high school baseball coach whose sons are both catchers. The elder son, Jake, has a good arm and adequate receiving skills, to go with a swing honed by all the batting-practice fastballs he could ask for as a kid. A fourth-round pick out of James Madison in 2011, Lowery is not the sexiest prospect, but he is virtually assured of a big-league future as a solid backup who plays more often than most because he bats from the left side.

Francisco Mejia C
Born: 10/27/1995 Age: 18
Bats: B Throws: R Height: 5' 10"
Weight: 175 Breakout: 0%
Improve: 0% Collapse: 0%
Attrition: 0% MLB: 0%
Comparables:
Travis d'Arnaud, Miguel Gonzalez, Christian Bethancour

YEAR	TEAM	LVL	AGE	PA	R	2B	3B	HR	RBI	BB	SO	SB	CS	AVG/OBP/SLG	TAv	BABIP	BRR	FRAA	WARP
2014	CLE	MLB	18	250	19	8	0	4	23	9	73	1	0	.197/.229/.290	.192	.260	-0.4	C 0, LF 0	-0.7

Falling in love with a teenage backstop is like throwing your heart into a spring-break fling, but Mejia sure looks like a dime. A $350,000 signee in July 2012, he is a switch-hitter with impressive bat speed and a legitimate plus-plus arm behind the plate. Mejia's framing and blocking are works in progress, but the tools are there for him to blossom into an above-average defensive catcher. After handling the Arizona League with aplomb in his debut, he should warrant a full-season assignment at the age of 18. And if the rendezvous in Lake County goes well, then it might be time to think about a future together in Cleveland.

David Murphy LF

Born: 10/18/1981 Age: 32
Bats: L Throws: L Height: 6' 4"
Weight: 210 Breakout: 3%
Improve: 48% Collapse: 2%
Attrition: 25% MLB: 94%

Comparables:
Hideki Matsui, Don Baylor, Kevin McReynolds

YEAR	TEAM	LVL	AGE	PA	R	2B	3B	HR	RBI	BB	SO	SB	CS	AVG/OBP/SLG	TAv	BABIP	BRR	FRAA	WARP
2011	TEX	MLB	29	440	46	14	2	11	46	33	61	11	6	.275/.328/.401	.251	.299	-2	LF(78): 2.7, RF(32): -0.2	0.4
2012	TEX	MLB	30	521	65	29	3	15	61	54	74	10	5	.304/.380/.479	.306	.333	3.2	LF(120): -2.0, RF(17): -0.2	3.6
2013	TEX	MLB	31	476	51	26	1	13	45	37	59	1	4	.220/.282/.374	.235	.227	-0.9	LF(128): -4.6, P(1): -0.0	-0.5
2014	CLE	MLB	32	454	52	22	1	11	48	40	78	7	4	.261/.326/.399	.270	.300	-0.7	LF -1, RF -0	1.3

Fan and media favorite David Murphy followed up his career year in 2012 with a disastrous 2013 campaign, one that was particularly ill-timed given that it was a contract season. While one's sabermetric instinct is to write off his struggles as just BABIP bad luck—his isolated power and walk rate were about the same as in past years—Murphy was out of sync with his mechanics all year, and rolled over on pitches he'd been driving in previous seasons. He's better than he showed in 2013, though, and will give Cleveland some value for its $12 million investment.

Tyler Naquin CF

Born: 4/24/1991 Age: 23
Bats: L Throws: R Height: 6' 2"
Weight: 175 Breakout: 1%
Improve: 3% Collapse: 2%
Attrition: 3% MLB: 7%

Comparables:
Gorkys Hernandez, Alex Presley, Roger Bernadina

YEAR	TEAM	LVL	AGE	PA	R	2B	3B	HR	RBI	BB	SO	SB	CS	AVG/OBP/SLG	TAv	BABIP	BRR	FRAA	WARP
2012	MHV	A-	21	161	22	11	2	0	13	17	26	4	3	.270/.379/.380	.272	.333	-0.3	CF(34): 4.0	1.1
2013	CAR	A+	22	498	69	27	6	9	42	41	112	14	7	.277/.345/.424	.264	.351	0.9	CF(102): 1.6	2.8
2013	AKR	AA	22	85	9	3	0	1	6	5	22	1	3	.225/.271/.300	.237	.298	-1	CF(18): -1.0	-0.1
2014	CLE	MLB	23	250	25	10	1	4	20	13	70	2	1	.223/.269/.321	.221	.300	-0.3	CF 0	-0.3

The 15th overall choice in the 2012 draft drew lots of rants and few raves, but the outfielder muzzled skeptics by performing well in the pitcher-friendly Carolina League. The Texas A&M product lacks impact tools and is often pegged as a tweener, but the Indians believe his above-average speed, reliable reads and plus arm will play in center field, lessening the pressure on his bat. As an up-the-middle defender, Naquin could get by with gap power, though he must improve his walk rate and cut down on his strikeouts to hit at the top of the order. A move to either corner would render him a second-division player, one unworthy of selection ahead of Aggies teammate Michael Wacha, who went to the Cardinals four picks later.

Dorssys Paulino SS

Born: 11/21/1994 Age: 19
Bats: R Throws: R Height: 6' 0"
Weight: 175 Breakout: 0%
Improve: 0% Collapse: 0%
Attrition: 0% MLB: 0%

Comparables:
Hernan Perez, Jonathan Schoop, Chris Owings

YEAR	TEAM	LVL	AGE	PA	R	2B	3B	HR	RBI	BB	SO	SB	CS	AVG/OBP/SLG	TAv	BABIP	BRR	FRAA	WARP
2012	MHV	A-	17	62	5	5	0	1	8	3	14	2	1	.271/.306/.407	.251	.341	0.5	SS(15): -1.3	0.0
2013	LKC	A	18	523	56	28	3	5	46	30	91	12	7	.246/.297/.349	.229	.294	0	SS(116): -10.3	-0.8
2014	CLE	MLB	19	250	21	11	1	3	18	8	63	1	0	.214/.241/.296	.199	.270	-0.4	SS -4	-1.0

One of the Indians' most exciting prospects entering last season, Paulino went backward in two ways: His body got thicker, diminishing his chances of sticking at shortstop, and his bat stagnated, making it less likely he will hit enough to profile at a corner. Fortunately, Paulino is well ahead of the age curve, having played in the Midwest League as an 18-year-old, and he has plenty of time to showcase his plus-or-better hit tool. Paulino's power is more gap-to-gap, but he could hit 15 to 20 homers a year during his prime. That would make him a solid, bat-first second or third baseman—the type of player who is more valuable to his fantasy owners than his big-league club.

Ryan Raburn RF

Born: 4/17/1981 Age: 33
Bats: R Throws: R Height: 6' 0"
Weight: 185 Breakout: 0%
Improve: 23% Collapse: 6%
Attrition: 12% MLB: 90%

Comparables:
Matt Stairs, Jermaine Dye, Jeromy Burnitz

YEAR	TEAM	LVL	AGE	PA	R	2B	3B	HR	RBI	BB	SO	SB	CS	AVG/OBP/SLG	TAv	BABIP	BRR	FRAA	WARP
2011	DET	MLB	30	418	53	22	2	14	49	21	114	1	1	.256/.297/.432	.257	.324	-0.1	2B(56): -3.7, LF(52): 3.4	1.2
2012	TOL	AAA	31	66	8	2	0	4	12	5	15	1	0	.250/.318/.483	.250	.268	0.2	2B(11): -1.2, LF(6): 0.4	0.1
2012	DET	MLB	31	222	14	14	0	1	12	13	53	1	1	.171/.226/.254	.175	.224	-0.2	2B(32): -1.1, LF(30): -0.1	-1.8
2013	CLE	MLB	32	277	40	18	0	16	55	29	67	0	0	.272/.357/.543	.327	.311	0.7	RF(54): -1.1, LF(13): 0.0	2.4
2014	CLE	MLB	33	257	29	13	0	9	31	18	66	1	1	.245/.307/.419	.265	.300	-0.5	RF -1, 2B -2	0.5

Much like his new team, Raburn had a surprisingly good season last year. His OPS had declined for three straight seasons, cratering at a pathetic .480 in 2012. He made that a distant memory, and as late as September 17th was at more than twice that mark (.961). Inconsistencies are nothing new for the utilityman, and there's no indication that his 2013 heroics are any more likely to recur than his 2012 embarrassments. At 33, Raburn remains a useful spare part, capable of emergency keystone duties and almost-average corner outfield play while menacing southpaws and giving righties a mild spook. For a team starting three power-challenged lefty outfielders, he's a good fit.

Jose Ramirez 2B

Born: 9/17/1992 Age: 21
Bats: B Throws: R Height: 5' 9"
Weight: 165 Breakout: 3%
Improve: 9% Collapse: 1%
Attrition: 5% MLB: 12%

Comparables:
Alexi Amarista, Johnny Giavotella, Jose Altuve

YEAR	TEAM	LVL	AGE	PA	R	2B	3B	HR	RBI	BB	SO	SB	CS	AVG/OBP/SLG	TAv	BABIP	BRR	FRAA	WARP
2012	LKC	A	19	313	54	13	4	3	27	24	26	15	6	.354/.403/.462	.327	.378	-2.4	2B(62): 3.3, SS(2): 0.1	3.3
2013	AKR	AA	20	533	78	16	6	3	38	39	41	38	16	.272/.325/.349	.261	.290	3	2B(53): -0.6, SS(50): 3.0	3.0
2013	CLE	MLB	20	14	5	0	1	0	0	2	2	0	1	.333/.429/.500	.338	.400	0.5	2B(5): 0.3, SS(2): -0.0	0.3
2014	CLE	MLB	21	250	29	9	2	2	18	12	34	10	4	.260/.296/.344	.237	.290	0.4	2B 1, SS 1	0.6

Running speed and hitting for average are "young player skills." With an aptitude for contact and the potential to swipe 40 bags, Ramirez—the second-youngest qualifying player in the Eastern League last year—brings plenty of both. He doesn't have the natural size or strength to project into much of a power hitter, and while he doesn't really have a shortstop's arm, the organization has been doing everything possible to make him comfortable with the longer throws. He's already been exposed to the idea of playing multiple positions, and there are scouts who think his future is in a utility role. But if circumstances do conspire to give him a full-time opportunity, he could be a factor in fantasy leagues as soon as this season. More likely, he'll be helping someone's International League fantasy team.

Luigi Rodriguez CF

Born: 11/13/1992 Age: 21
Bats: B Throws: R Height: 5' 11"
Weight: 160 Breakout: 0%
Improve: 1% Collapse: 0%
Attrition: 0% MLB: 1%

Comparables:
Aaron Cunningham, Jeremy Moore, Tyler Colvin

YEAR	TEAM	LVL	AGE	PA	R	2B	3B	HR	RBI	BB	SO	SB	CS	AVG/OBP/SLG	TAv	BABIP	BRR	FRAA	WARP
2011	LKC	A	18	148	10	4	2	0	5	14	36	6	5	.250/.320/.311	.173	.340	-0.1	LF(2): 0.6	0.0
2012	LKC	A	19	521	75	21	5	11	48	50	133	24	9	.268/.338/.406	.275	.350	5.6	CF(98): -4.8, RF(5): 0.2	2.5
2013	LKC	A	20	88	14	2	0	1	9	10	25	5	3	.263/.345/.329	.266	.373	1.6	CF(20): -0.4, RF(2): -0.1	0.3
2013	CAR	A+	20	134	16	11	1	0	11	18	36	3	4	.283/.383/.398	.281	.410	0.4	LF(23): -2.2, RF(3): 0.3	0.5
2014	CLE	MLB	21	250	26	9	1	4	18	18	82	5	3	.212/.268/.305	.216	.310	-0.2	CF -2, LF -1	-0.7

No one with the first name "Luigi" has ever reached the majors (there have been nine Marios), but this speedy switch-hitter appears poised to change that if he can shake off the injuries that plagued him in 2013. A very good defensive center fielder, Rodriguez held his own in a brief tour of the Carolina League, and his approach in the box is coming along. That's important because his offensive value is likely to be maximized at the top of a lineup, where his patience and wheels can surmount fringy power. Rodriguez needs to stay on the field, improve his base-stealing instincts and continue to refine his strike zone judgment to emerge as a leadoff-hitting center fielder down the road.

Ronny Rodriguez SS

Born: 4/17/1992 Age: 22
Bats: R Throws: R Height: 6' 0"
Weight: 170 Breakout: 3%
Improve: 13% Collapse: 2%
Attrition: 12% MLB: 22%

Comparables:
Hector Gomez, Eduardo Escobar, Alcides Escobar

YEAR	TEAM	LVL	AGE	PA	R	2B	3B	HR	RBI	BB	SO	SB	CS	AVG/OBP/SLG	TAv	BABIP	BRR	FRAA	WARP
2011	LKC	A	19	394	41	28	7	11	42	13	83	10	7	.246/.274/.449	.295	.286	-0.2	SS(19): 2.9	0.9
2012	CAR	A+	20	483	67	20	4	19	66	19	88	7	7	.264/.300/.452	.271	.289	-3.1	SS(80): -0.4, 2B(45): 6.3	2.9
2013	AKR	AA	21	498	62	25	6	5	52	16	76	12	3	.265/.291/.376	.244	.304	2.9	SS(71): -3.8, 2B(44): -0.3	0.6
2014	CLE	MLB	22	250	23	10	1	6	24	4	54	3	1	.234/.249/.357	.221	.270	-0.1	SS -1, 2B 1	0.0

Rodriguez burst onto the scene with 19 homers in High-A during his second professional season, then took his lumps in Double-A last year, as many evaluators predicted. The Dominican infielder first signed with the Cubs in 2008, but that contract was voided when he attended high school in Boston, which forced him to wait until 2010 to join the Tribe. By that point, Rodriguez was behind on the development curve, and three years later the chinks in his armor came to light. There is four-tool potential here, though Rodriguez needs to shore up his plate approach for his power to play and improve his footwork to utilize his 70-grade arm at shortstop. Doing one of those in a repeat stint at Akron would revive his prospect stock; doing both could make Rodriguez a quality regular.

Carlos Santana 1B

Born: 4/8/1986 Age: 28
Bats: B Throws: R Height: 5' 11"
Weight: 210 Breakout: 0%
Improve: 46% Collapse: 0%
Attrition: 4% MLB: 98%

Comparables:
Brian McCann, Joe Ferguson, Ted Simmons

YEAR	TEAM	LVL	AGE	PA	R	2B	3B	HR	RBI	BB	SO	SB	CS	AVG/OBP/SLG	TAv	BABIP	BRR	FRAA	WARP
2011	CLE	MLB	25	658	84	35	2	27	79	97	133	5	3	.239/.351/.457	.284	.263	-1.8	C(95): -1.9, 1B(66): 1.5	3.3
2012	CLE	MLB	26	609	72	27	2	18	76	91	101	3	5	.252/.365/.420	.288	.278	-2.2	C(100): -0.7, 1B(21): 0.0	3.6
2013	CLE	MLB	27	642	75	39	1	20	74	93	110	3	1	.268/.377/.455	.312	.301	-2.6	C(84): -1.4, 1B(29): 0.7	4.8
2014	CLE	MLB	28	597	74	30	1	20	77	89	110	4	2	.254/.368/.439	.298	.290	-1.1	1B 1, 3B 0	3.3

Santana teased again by posting huge April stats before settling in as the best offensive "catcher" of the year. With Yan Gomes making such a strong showing, it was possible for the Tribe to limit Santana to only 81 games started behind the plate, where he was not what you would call the best defensive catcher of the year. To most observers, it seems to be a question of when—not if—the team will move him out from behind the dish permanently. His offensive profile is much more useful to a real lineup than a fantasy team, as he's very patient and his batting average suffers for his willingness to go deep into counts. Someday, the team will pop the question and he'll settle down at first base. Until then, he'll always be a bit of a tease.

Nick Swisher   RF
Born: 11/25/1980 Age: 33
Bats: B Throws: L Height: 6' 0''
Weight: 200 Breakout: 1%
Improve: 30% Collapse: 2%
Attrition: 9% MLB: 94%

Comparables:
Norm Cash, Paul Konerko, Ryan Klesko

YEAR	TEAM	LVL	AGE	PA	R	2B	3B	HR	RBI	BB	SO	SB	CS	AVG/OBP/SLG	TAv	BABIP	BRR	FRAA	WARP
2011	NYA	MLB	30	635	81	30	0	23	85	95	125	2	2	.260/.374/.449	.287	.295	-0.3	RF(141): 2.9, 1B(11): -0.2	3.4
2012	NYA	MLB	31	624	75	36	0	24	93	77	141	2	3	.272/.364/.473	.292	.324	0.3	RF(109): 8.0, 1B(41): 3.8	4.4
2013	CLE	MLB	32	634	74	27	2	22	63	77	138	1	0	.246/.341/.423	.283	.288	-1.6	1B(112): 5.6, RF(27): -0.1	3.2
2014	CLE	MLB	33	594	70	28	1	20	76	73	134	2	1	.252/.347/.429	.284	.300	-1.3	RF 3, 1B 4	2.9

As mediocre as the season was for the costliest Indian, Swisher's flurry at the end of the season—.294/.380/.588 from September 6th on—went a long way toward getting the Indians to October. Moving to the second slot in the lineup seemed to help turn around his slow start, as pitchers were less inclined to nibble and Swisher was able to translate some reduction in walks into much more power. He was also bothered by an early-season shoulder ailment that sapped power. All told, a healthy Swisher can be expected to produce stats closer to career norms than the 2013 edition—his offensive game remains the same as it ever was. Unfortunately for Tribe fans, his brief and hitless postseason performance underscored a career of subpar playoff showings, which now add up to a .165/.277/.297 line in 47 postseason games.

LeVon Washington   CF
Born: 7/26/1991 Age: 22
Bats: L Throws: R Height: 5' 11''
Weight: 170 Breakout: 0%
Improve: 2% Collapse: 2%
Attrition: 4% MLB: 5%

Comparables:
Aaron Hicks, Blake Tekotte, Matt Angle

YEAR	TEAM	LVL	AGE	PA	R	2B	3B	HR	RBI	BB	SO	SB	CS	AVG/OBP/SLG	TAv	BABIP	BRR	FRAA	WARP
2011	LKC	A	19	351	35	9	4	4	20	49	89	15	6	.218/.331/.315	.270	.296	0.3	CF(20): -1.6	0.2
2012	LKC	A	20	32	8	1	0	0	1	6	8	0	3	.440/.562/.480	.381	.647	-0.3	LF(4): -0.2, CF(2): -0.1	0.4
2013	LKC	A	21	229	33	19	4	1	19	32	46	14	4	.321/.425/.477	.307	.418	-0.5	CF(43): 0.4, LF(8): -1.4	1.5
2014	CLE	MLB	22	250	27	10	1	2	17	25	71	7	3	.214/.297/.296	.224	.300	0.1	CF -1, LF -2	-0.6

Injuries—most notably hip surgery that cost him a good deal of the 2012 season—and coachability questions have derailed Washington so far, but he enjoyed something of a coming-out party at Lake County last year, putting himself back on the map. Washington is a speed-oriented slap hitter with the athleticism to stick in center field, though he needs to brush up his reads to be an above-average defender. If he can do that and tweak his approach from passive to patient, Washington, who was twice selected in the top two rounds of the draft, will resurface as a top-10 player in the system.

Joseph Wendle   2B
Born: 4/26/1990 Age: 24
Bats: L Throws: R Height: 5' 11''
Weight: 190 Breakout: 2%
Improve: 18% Collapse: 8%
Attrition: 21% MLB: 35%

Comparables:
Jason Kipnis, Jesus Guzman, Ryan Adams

YEAR	TEAM	LVL	AGE	PA	R	2B	3B	HR	RBI	BB	SO	SB	CS	AVG/OBP/SLG	TAv	BABIP	BRR	FRAA	WARP
2012	MHV	A-	22	267	32	15	4	4	37	15	25	4	1	.327/.375/.469	.321	.349	-0.5	2B(32): -0.2, 3B(21): 3.0	2.8
2013	CAR	A+	23	474	73	32	5	16	64	44	79	10	2	.295/.372/.513	.298	.327	3.3	2B(101): 6.7	4.1
2014	CLE	MLB	24	250	24	11	1	7	29	14	55	0	0	.242/.292/.386	.249	.290	-0.3	2B 2, 3B 1	0.8

Wendle's career was nearly endangered in April when a throw skidded off the grass and broke the orbital bone around his eye, but he came back a month later no worse for the scare. He's a hitting machine, capable of squaring up velocity and spin alike, and a natural leader with plus-plus makeup that endears him to coaches and evaluators, leaving them confident he will make the most of his skills. Wendle's ceiling is more solid-average regular than star, but he is as likely to realize his potential as any prospect in the system.

Tony Wolters   C
Born: 6/9/1992 Age: 22
Bats: L Throws: R Height: 5' 10''
Weight: 177 Breakout: 6%
Improve: 7% Collapse: 5%
Attrition: 12% MLB: 13%

Comparables:
Lou Marson, J.R. Murphy, Michael McKenry

YEAR	TEAM	LVL	AGE	PA	R	2B	3B	HR	RBI	BB	SO	SB	CS	AVG/OBP/SLG	TAv	BABIP	BRR	FRAA	WARP
2011	MHV	A-	19	313	50	10	3	1	20	30	49	19	4	.292/.385/.363	.261	.353	-0.3	SS(22): -0.6	0.3
2012	CAR	A+	20	537	66	30	8	8	58	36	104	5	9	.260/.320/.404	.251	.314	-2.8	2B(63): 9.0, SS(61): 1.2	2.1
2013	CAR	A+	21	340	36	13	0	3	33	41	58	3	6	.277/.369/.353	.275	.333	-1.4	C(58): 0.3, 2B(1): -0.1	1.6
2014	CLE	MLB	22	250	24	9	1	3	19	15	60	2	1	.223/.275/.316	.222	.280	-0.4	C 0, SS 0	0.1

A middle infielder for the first two-plus seasons of his professional career, Wolters moved to catcher in 2013. By the time he went down to the desert for the Arizona Fall League, he looked the part. Wolters is a reliable receiver and compensates for middling arm strength by making accurate throws out of the squat. At the plate, he shows a line-drive stroke and good discipline, a combination that should result in adequate production for a regular, even without much pop. The 2010 third-rounder may not be taking the most direct route to The Show, but his plus personal drive should get him there by 2015.

PITCHERS

Cody Allen

Born: 11/20/1988 Age: 25
Bats: R Throws: R Height: 6' 1" Weight: 210
Breakout: 23% Improve: 46% Collapse: 29%
Attrition: 12% MLB: 90%

Comparables:
Fernando Cabrera, Bobby Jenks, Manny Delcarmen

YEAR	TEAM	LVL	AGE	W	L	SV	G	GS	IP	H	HR	BB	SO	BB9	SO9	GB%	BABIP	WHIP	ERA	FIP	FRA	WARP
2011	LKC	A	22	2	0	0	7	0	17	10	0	5	28	2.6	14.8	%	.000	0.88	0.00	0.95	1.41	0.1
2011	MHV	A-	22	3	1	0	14	0	33²	21	1	9	42	2.4	11.2	47%	.138	0.89	2.14	2.32	4.86	0.0
2012	COH	AAA	23	3	2	2	24	0	31²	22	3	9	35	2.6	9.9	42%	.244	0.98	2.27	3.03	3.64	0.6
2012	CLE	MLB	23	0	1	0	27	0	29	29	2	15	27	4.7	8.4	42%	.329	1.52	3.72	3.63	4.02	0.2
2013	CLE	MLB	24	6	1	2	77	0	70¹	62	7	26	88	3.3	11.3	33%	.309	1.25	2.43	3.02	2.91	1.3
2014	CLE	MLB	25	3	1	1	56	0	62²	53	6	21	70	3.1	10.1	39%	.297	1.19	3.11	3.34	3.38	1.0

It would be a surprise if Allen doesn't end up serving as a closer for at least a few years in his career, with his inauguration likely coming sometime this season. His fastball averages 96 and his curve 85, and he has the demeanor managers like in a high-pressure reliever. Nobody will confuse his control with Josh Tomlin's, and his fearless use of the entire zone leads to an uncomfortably high fly-ball percentage (and all the homers that naturally follow), but he's already good enough to close games, and any improvements in control or home run rate will just be icing on the cake.

Cody Anderson

Born: 9/14/1990 Age: 23
Bats: R Throws: R Height: 6' 4" Weight: 220
Breakout: 49% Improve: 65% Collapse: 25%
Attrition: 80% MLB: 20%

Comparables:
Steven Shell, Justin Grimm, Brett Marshall

YEAR	TEAM	LVL	AGE	W	L	SV	G	GS	IP	H	HR	BB	SO	BB9	SO9	GB%	BABIP	WHIP	ERA	FIP	FRA	WARP
2012	LKC	A	21	4	7	0	24	23	98¹	92	8	29	72	2.7	6.6	43%	.287	1.23	3.20	3.86	4.84	1.0
2013	CAR	A+	22	9	4	0	23	23	123¹	105	6	31	112	2.3	8.2	40%	.296	1.10	2.34	3.04	3.55	3.0
2013	AKR	AA	22	0	0	0	3	3	12²	16	2	9	10	6.4	7.1	24%	.359	1.97	5.68	5.93	5.67	0.0
2014	CLE	MLB	23	6	8	0	25	25	102¹	113	13	43	67	3.8	5.9	40%	.306	1.52	4.93	5.06	5.36	-0.3

With a sturdy frame and a four-pitch mix, Anderson has long had the toolset to start, but he was hidden as a closer at Feather River College until the Indians plucked him in the 14th round of the 2011 draft. The right-hander boasts a plus slider and a mid-90s fastball—the tandem he employed most often out of the bullpen—but he also spins a curveball and commands a changeup, which complement his best offerings and give him an adequate recipe to retire lefties. Anderson's arm has relatively low mileage because of his history in relief, though the downside is that he may need extra time to adjust to higher-level hitters. Once the command comes together, Anderson could settle in as a middle-of-the-rotation starter.

John Axford

Born: 4/1/1983 Age: 31
Bats: R Throws: R Height: 6' 5" Weight: 220
Breakout: 27% Improve: 49% Collapse: 30%
Attrition: 15% MLB: 81%

Comparables:
Jason Motte, Jose Veras, Michael Wuertz

YEAR	TEAM	LVL	AGE	W	L	SV	G	GS	IP	H	HR	BB	SO	BB9	SO9	GB%	BABIP	WHIP	ERA	FIP	FRA	WARP
2011	MIL	MLB	28	2	2	46	74	0	73²	59	4	25	86	3.1	10.5	50%	.289	1.14	1.95	2.38	2.96	1.6
2012	MIL	MLB	29	5	8	35	75	0	69¹	61	10	39	93	5.1	12.1	48%	.307	1.44	4.67	4.10	3.91	0.8
2013	MIL	MLB	30	6	7	0	62	0	54²	62	10	23	54	3.8	8.9	45%	.333	1.55	4.45	4.74	5.49	-0.3
2013	SLN	MLB	30	1	0	0	13	0	10¹	11	0	3	11	2.6	9.6	54%	.393	1.35	1.74	2.05	2.14	0.3
2014	CLE	MLB	31	3	1	12	61	0	59¹	50	5	25	70	3.8	10.6	46%	.305	1.26	3.24	3.33	3.52	0.9

Small sample, confirmation bias, whatever—no one was surprised to see Axford have success with the Cardinals. They had one of those Midas seasons where everything they touched turned to groundballs and strike throwers. Axford had already shown real talent with the Brewers, but he couldn't find the plate consistently and, when he did, missed location. So of course he has a 5 percent walk rate, doesn't allow a homer in his 13 appearances with St. Louis and gets a decent payday from Cleveland in December. He's got enough saves under his belt that he'll forever be talked about for an open ninth inning, but with his command he's strictly a second-tier closer.

Dylan Baker

Born: 4/6/1992 Age: 22
Bats: R Throws: R Height: 6' 2" Weight: 215
Breakout: 100% Improve: 100% Collapse: 0%
Attrition: 48% MLB: 2%

Comparables:
Evan Reed, Allen Webster, Jarred Cosart

YEAR	TEAM	LVL	AGE	W	L	SV	G	GS	IP	H	HR	BB	SO	BB9	SO9	GB%	BABIP	WHIP	ERA	FIP	FRA	WARP
2013	LKC	A	21	7	6	0	27	25	143²	124	3	62	117	3.9	7.3	55%	.285	1.29	3.63	3.36	4.47	1.9
2014	CLE	MLB	22	4	6	0	20	15	96²	110	12	53	57	5.0	5.3	50%	.306	1.69	5.60	5.60	6.09	-1.2

Baker has taken the road less traveled from birth to prospect land, starting his journey in Juneau, which has raised only one big leaguer, and attending Western Nevada College, which first fielded a baseball team in 2006. A fifth-round pick in 2012, the right-hander is now the Wildcats' finest graduate, firing mid-90s fastballs from a strong arm affixed to a sturdy frame. He has the body to start and the requisite pitch menu, too, though his fringy command and high-effort delivery might shoehorn him into a set-up role. If Baker can harness his stuff and improve his changeup to league average, he has an excellent chance to become the first Alaskan high schooler to earn a major-league win.

Trevor Bauer

Born: 1/17/1991 Age: 23
Bats: R Throws: R Height: 6' 1" Weight: 190
Breakout: 40% Improve: 56% Collapse: 15%
Attrition: 54% MLB: 51%

Comparables:
Gio Gonzalez, Juan Morillo, Andrew Oliver

YEAR	TEAM	LVL	AGE	W	L	SV	G	GS	IP	H	HR	BB	SO	BB9	SO9	GB%	BABIP	WHIP	ERA	FIP	FRA	WARP
2011	MOB	AA	20	1	1	0	4	4	16²	20	2	8	26	4.3	14.0	45%	.425	1.68	7.56	3.55	4.93	0.3
2012	MOB	AA	21	7	1	0	8	8	48¹	33	1	26	60	4.8	11.2	47%	.292	1.22	1.68	2.67	2.97	1.3
2012	RNO	AAA	21	5	1	0	14	14	82	74	8	35	97	3.8	10.6	44%	.327	1.33	2.85	3.85	4.04	2.1
2012	ARI	MLB	21	1	2	0	4	4	16¹	14	2	13	17	7.2	9.4	44%	.293	1.65	6.06	5.22	6.29	-0.1
2013	COH	AAA	22	6	7	0	22	22	121¹	119	14	73	106	5.4	7.9	43%	.307	1.58	4.15	5.08	5.78	-0.2
2013	CLE	MLB	22	1	2	0	4	4	17	15	3	16	11	8.5	5.8	36%	.240	1.82	5.29	7.08	8.39	-0.4
2014	CLE	MLB	23	7	8	0	23	23	121²	115	14	65	118	4.8	8.8	43%	.300	1.48	4.52	4.65	4.91	0.1

Nope. Can't fool us: That's not the real Trevor Bauer wearing no. 47 for the Indians. He's not touching 97, and his heralded command of 10 different pitches looks more like a "master of none" situation. He's still very young and has both a world of talent and all the intelligence one could hope for. Of course, everyone has a suggestion for him, from relaxing to changing his workout routine to thinking less to ceasing his biomechanics studies to working out of the stretch more to working out of the stretch less to hiring a psychic. If past results are any indication, he's in good hands with the Tribe coaching staff, and is a strong candidate to find himself this season or next, though there are never any guarantees in cases like his.

Sean Brady

Born: 6/9/1994 Age: 20
Bats: L Throws: L Height: 6' 0" Weight: 175
Breakout: 0% Improve: 0% Collapse: 0%
Attrition: 0% MLB: 0%

Comparables:
Jhoulys Chacin, Matt Magill, Brandon Maurer

YEAR	TEAM	LVL	AGE	W	L	SV	G	GS	IP	H	HR	BB	SO	BB9	SO9	GB%	BABIP	WHIP	ERA	FIP	FRA	WARP
—	—	—	—	—	—	—	—	—	—	—	—	—	—	—	—	—	—	—	—	—	—	—
2014	CLE	MLB	20	1	3	0	8	8	31	39	5	20	14	5.9	4.2	45%	.313	1.91	6.78	6.79	7.36	-0.7

At $800,000, Brady cashed by far the largest bonus check given to any 2013 fifth-rounder, but the Indians felt compelled to lure the southpaw away from his commitment to the University of Florida. Brady pairs excellent pitchability with a polished off-speed arsenal, featuring a changeup and curveball that could grade as plus pitches in time. What Brady lacks are present fastball velocity and the projection teams like to see in prep arms. He turns 20 midway through this season, and while he could move more quickly than most of the class of 2013, his ceiling is in the fourth-starter range. Brady should be ready for a full-season assignment and may not be tested until he reaches the upper minors because of his secondary stuff and IQ on the mound.

Mitch Brown

Born: 4/13/1994 Age: 20
Bats: R Throws: R Height: 6' 1" Weight: 195
Breakout: 0% Improve: 0% Collapse: 0%
Attrition: 0% MLB: 0%

Comparables:
Alex Torres, Allen Webster, Michael Kirkman

YEAR	TEAM	LVL	AGE	W	L	SV	G	GS	IP	H	HR	BB	SO	BB9	SO9	GB%	BABIP	WHIP	ERA	FIP	FRA	WARP
2013	LKC	A	19	1	1	0	5	5	15²	21	4	11	18	6.3	10.3	45%	.395	2.04	11.49	7.23	8.81	-0.3
2014	CLE	MLB	20	2	4	0	13	8	50²	61	8	33	29	6.0	5.1	44%	.314	1.87	6.68	6.49	7.26	-1.2

A Minnesota native, Brown grew up in a cold-weather climate with fewer opportunities to hone his command than other class of 2012 draft picks. He did not take the widely anticipated step forward last year, but still has a promising fastball, cutter and curveball, all of which could be above average in time. Brown's arm speed tends to wane on his secondary offerings, tipping off mature hitters, an issue he worked to resolve in instructs last fall. It may take several years, but Brown has mid-rotation upside if the stars align.

Carlos Carrasco

Born: 3/21/1987 Age: 27
Bats: R Throws: R Height: 6' 3" Weight: 210
Breakout: 44% Improve: 78% Collapse: 10%
Attrition: 35% MLB: 81%

Comparables:
Armando Galarraga, David Huff, Wade LeBlanc

YEAR	TEAM	LVL	AGE	W	L	SV	G	GS	IP	H	HR	BB	SO	BB9	SO9	GB%	BABIP	WHIP	ERA	FIP	FRA	WARP
2011	CLE	MLB	24	8	9	0	21	21	124²	130	15	40	85	2.9	6.1	51%	.294	1.36	4.62	4.32	5.03	0.4
2013	COH	AAA	26	3	1	1	16	14	71²	59	6	21	79	2.6	9.9	45%	.285	1.12	3.14	3.22	4.03	1.2
2013	CLE	MLB	26	1	4	0	15	7	46²	64	4	18	30	3.5	5.8	50%	.364	1.76	6.75	4.13	4.76	0.2
2014	CLE	MLB	27	4	5	0	21	15	84²	88	11	28	67	3.0	7.2	46%	.304	1.38	4.54	4.55	4.93	0.0

Carrasco took his foot off the brakes—successful Tommy John surgery pushed his velocity from 93 to 95 mph—and then hit the gas, moving to the bullpen and adding another mile after July. Injuries in Cleveland led to a spot start in August, which only reinforced the notion that's he's more effective and more valuable in relief. Including that outing, he allowed at least 10 hits in four of his seven starts; compare that to a .396 OPS as a reliever. The team still considers him a starting pitcher, and he has four quality pitches, but there will be talk of a permanent move to the bullpen until he re-establishes himself in the rotation.

Tyler Cloyd

Born: 5/16/1987 Age: 27
Bats: R Throws: R Height: 6' 3" Weight: 210
Breakout: 41% Improve: 66% Collapse: 28%
Attrition: 64% MLB: 41%

Comparables:
Ryan Feierabend, Clayton Mortensen, Jeremy Hefner

YEAR	TEAM	LVL	AGE	W	L	SV	G	GS	IP	H	HR	BB	SO	BB9	SO9	GB%	BABIP	WHIP	ERA	FIP	FRA	WARP
2011	CLR	A+	24	3	1	0	13	5	39¹	31	3	7	39	1.6	8.9	48%	.214	0.97	2.75	3.01	4.07	0.3
2011	REA	AA	24	6	3	0	18	17	106²	101	7	15	99	1.3	8.4	45%	.320	1.09	2.78	3.03	3.42	1.5
2012	REA	AA	25	3	0	0	4	4	25	22	1	3	20	1.1	7.2	40%	.304	1.00	1.80	2.60	3.75	0.4
2012	LEH	AAA	25	12	1	0	22	22	142	105	14	38	93	2.4	5.9	46%	.227	1.01	2.35	4.02	5.36	-0.6
2012	PHI	MLB	25	2	2	0	6	6	33	33	8	7	30	1.9	8.2	34%	.276	1.21	4.91	5.29	5.45	-0.1
2013	LEH	AAA	26	5	9	0	19	19	112²	125	21	26	93	2.1	7.4	43%	.307	1.34	4.71	4.70	5.77	-0.6
2013	PHI	MLB	26	2	7	0	13	11	60¹	83	7	25	41	3.7	6.1	42%	.377	1.79	6.56	4.46	4.74	0.3
2014	CLE	MLB	27	7	8	0	37	20	144	160	22	43	92	2.7	5.7	42%	.302	1.41	4.88	5.07	5.30	-0.7

Tyler Cloyd was useful in the sense that he was a warm-blooded mammal capable of hurling a small sphere in the vicinity of a pentagon placed on the surface of the Earth, with little value beyond that. Cloyd was recalled four separate times by the Phillies, and each time he confirmed that he was, indeed, a warm-blooded mammal capable of hurling a small sphere in the vicinity of a pentagon placed on the surface of the Earth (with little value beyond that). The Indians picked him up on waivers in early October, hoping they might be able to extract a bit more out of him than the Phillies did. You can imagine what they'll find.

Kyle Crockett

Born: 12/15/1991 Age: 22
Bats: L Throws: L Height: 6' 2" Weight: 170
Breakout: 49% Improve: 58% Collapse: 28%
Attrition: 28% MLB: 15%

Comparables:
Edward Mujica, Daniel Stange, Rich Thompson

YEAR	TEAM	LVL	AGE	W	L	SV	G	GS	IP	H	HR	BB	SO	BB9	SO9	GB%	BABIP	WHIP	ERA	FIP	FRA	WARP
2013	AKR	AA	21	1	0	0	9	0	10¹	7	0	2	9	1.7	7.8	67%	.259	0.87	0.00	2.16	2.75	0.2
2014	CLE	MLB	22	1	1	1	29	0	34¹	35	4	15	29	3.8	7.6	49%	.306	1.44	4.43	4.57	4.82	-0.0

A former teammate of Mariners' second-overall pick Danny Hultzen at the University of Virginia, Crockett—who was drafted in the fourth round two years later—now stands a once-unfathomable chance of beating Hultzen to the majors. While Hultzen suffered a serious shoulder injury Crockett breezed through the lower minors to reach Double-A in his first professional season. The Newport News native boasts outstanding command, which plays up his low-90s fastball and sweeping slider, both delivered from a low-three-quarters release. He is at least a lefty specialist with a chance to be a quality set-up man, and he might reach the majors before the year is out.

Preston Guilmet

Born: 7/27/1987 Age: 26
Bats: R Throws: R Height: 6' 2" Weight: 200
Breakout: 33% Improve: 64% Collapse: 26%
Attrition: 53% MLB: 39%

Comparables:
Robert Manuel, Nick Vincent, Matt Daley

YEAR	TEAM	LVL	AGE	W	L	SV	G	GS	IP	H	HR	BB	SO	BB9	SO9	GB%	BABIP	WHIP	ERA	FIP	FRA	WARP
2011	KIN	A+	23	1	1	35	52	0	58¹	43	4	11	60	1.7	9.3	41%	.248	0.93	2.16	2.63	3.75	0.5
2012	AKR	AA	24	2	2	24	50	0	52²	41	4	13	51	2.2	8.7	37%	.262	1.03	2.39	2.99	3.26	1.0
2013	COH	AAA	25	5	4	20	49	0	64¹	43	4	14	72	2.0	10.1	46%	.242	0.89	1.68	2.43	3.41	1.2
2013	CLE	MLB	25	0	0	0	4	0	5¹	8	0	3	1	5.1	1.7	33%	.333	2.06	10.12	4.39	4.43	0.0
2014	CLE	MLB	26	2	1	1	43	0	55¹	52	6	17	50	2.8	8.2	41%	.293	1.26	3.70	3.88	4.02	0.5

Guilmet (pronounced GIL-met) is a cagey fastball-splitter-slider pitcher who rarely reaches 90 mph with his slop. With an extreme over-the-top delivery, he offers a stark contrast to the bevy of Cleveland hurlers who drop down and deliver. His ticket to the majors—and to getting protected on the 40-man roster—is his outstanding control, as he has allowed fewer than two free passes per nine innings in his minor-league career. Already generating as much velocity as he can and already having great control, he doesn't have any obvious opportunities for big improvement, other than tightening up his breaking stuff and honing his command.

Nick Hagadone

Born: 1/1/1986 Age: 28
Bats: L Throws: L Height: 6' 5" Weight: 230
Breakout: 32% Improve: 50% Collapse: 29%
Attrition: 52% MLB: 53%

Comparables:
Mark McLemore, Dennis Sarfate, Dan Runzler

YEAR	TEAM	LVL	AGE	W	L	SV	G	GS	IP	H	HR	BB	SO	BB9	SO9	GB%	BABIP	WHIP	ERA	FIP	FRA	WARP
2011	AKR	AA	25	2	1	0	12	0	22²	14	0	7	24	2.8	9.5	39%	.255	0.93	1.59	2.22	2.69	0.4
2011	COH	AAA	25	4	3	4	34	0	48¹	42	5	15	53	2.8	9.9	38%	.345	1.18	3.35	3.32	4.68	0.1
2011	CLE	MLB	25	1	0	0	9	0	11	4	0	6	11	4.9	9.0	33%	.167	0.91	4.09	2.97	3.66	0.2
2012	CLE	MLB	26	1	0	1	27	0	25¹	26	4	15	26	5.3	9.2	37%	.310	1.62	6.39	4.82	5.22	0.0
2013	COH	AAA	27	2	3	7	27	0	32¹	24	1	17	46	4.7	12.8	41%	.315	1.27	2.51	2.34	2.30	1.1
2013	CLE	MLB	27	0	1	0	36	0	31¹	24	4	21	30	6.0	8.6	40%	.256	1.44	5.46	4.83	5.57	-0.4
2014	CLE	MLB	28	2	2	0	33	4	48²	44	5	28	48	5.1	9.0	45%	.298	1.47	4.15	4.49	4.52	0.2

At 28, Hagadone is still more of a thrower than a pitcher. His fastball still averages almost 95 mph, he uses his slider less than 20 percent of the time and he has no viable third pitch. All this could be true of a good pitcher, but Hagadone has never refined his control to trustworthiness. Even against left-handed batters, he issues too many walks to be a reliable LOOGY, despite a career .183 average by lefties. There are success stories that started similarly—Matt Thornton didn't even debut until his age-27 season—but a lot has to happen before managers are going to choose Hagadone in an important situation.

Rich Hill

Born: 3/11/1980 Age: 34
Bats: L Throws: L Height: 6' 5" Weight: 220
Breakout: 42% Improve: 50% Collapse: 35%
Attrition: 19% MLB: 37%

Comparables:
Stephen Randolph, Micah Bowie, Raul Valdes

YEAR	TEAM	LVL	AGE	W	L	SV	G	GS	IP	H	HR	BB	SO	BB9	SO9	GB%	BABIP	WHIP	ERA	FIP	FRA	WARP
2011	PAW	AAA	31	1	0	1	10	0	16	8	1	5	18	2.8	10.1	46%	.188	0.81	1.12	2.92	3.67	0.2
2011	BOS	MLB	31	0	0	0	9	0	8	3	0	3	12	3.4	13.5	36%	.214	0.75	0.00	1.56	2.50	0.2
2012	BOS	MLB	32	1	0	0	25	0	19²	17	0	11	21	5.0	9.6	43%	.333	1.42	1.83	2.59	3.48	0.3
2013	CLE	MLB	33	1	2	0	63	0	38²	38	3	29	51	6.8	11.9	44%	.361	1.73	6.28	3.85	3.77	0.2
2014	CLE	MLB	34	2	1	0	29	3	34¹	31	3	20	35	5.3	9.1	42%	.299	1.48	4.33	4.36	4.71	0.1

Hill accomplished something difficult in 2013: He stayed on a good team's roster all season while posting an ERA over 6 and tossing fewer than 40 innings. That he managed to survive an ERA spike to 8.44 on June 2nd makes the feat more amazing. His role was well defined, as he faced mostly lefty batters and recorded fewer than three outs in 45 of his 63 appearances. His repertoire is equally well defined, a homogenous mix of 90 mph fastballs and curves that occasionally still buckle knees. While no manager enjoys watching the extreme wildness that is now part of Hill's game, he did limit lefties to a .238 batting average and .321 slugging percentage last year, allowing for clever situational usage to provide a little value.

Ubaldo Jimenez

Born: 1/22/1984 Age: 30
Bats: R Throws: R Height: 6' 5" Weight: 210
Breakout: 16% Improve: 41% Collapse: 33%
Attrition: 18% MLB: 95%

Comparables:
Erik Bedard, Barry Zito, A.J. Burnett

YEAR	TEAM	LVL	AGE	W	L	SV	G	GS	IP	H	HR	BB	SO	BB9	SO9	GB%	BABIP	WHIP	ERA	FIP	FRA	WARP
2011	CLE	MLB	27	4	4	0	11	11	65¹	68	7	27	62	3.7	8.5	48%	.318	1.45	5.10	3.89	4.59	0.7
2011	COL	MLB	27	6	9	0	21	21	123	118	10	51	118	3.7	8.6	48%	.311	1.37	4.46	3.55	4.39	1.6
2012	CLE	MLB	28	9	17	0	31	31	176²	190	25	95	143	4.8	7.3	40%	.308	1.61	5.40	5.02	5.09	0.6
2013	CLE	MLB	29	13	9	0	32	32	182²	163	16	80	194	3.9	9.6	45%	.306	1.33	3.30	3.45	4.01	2.3
2014	CLE	MLB	30	10	9	0	27	27	158²	142	13	66	151	3.8	8.6	48%	.295	1.31	3.61	3.83	3.92	1.8

The morphing of Jimenez continues, and despite some superficial similarities to previous versions, the 2013 model was an entirely new being. He entered the season with a new delivery, much needed after everything went off the rails in 2012. Then—after a dreadfully bad trio of April games: 18 earned runs in 11 innings pitched—he mowed down the league for 28 starts, compiling a 2.61 ERA over the bulk of the season. Even during this masterful stretch, he was tinkering with his mechanics. One could assert that he's "learning how to pitch," posting his best strikeout rate despite velocity well below that of his earlier years. But his adjustments—such as increasing the percentage of sliders he throws—seem more like a walk-year ambush on unprepared hitters, and less like the subtle refinements of a repeatably effective repertoire. His 2014 team will be hoping that he's able to keep morphing one step ahead of batter adjustments.

Dace Kime

Born: 3/6/1992 Age: 22
Bats: R Throws: R Height: 6' 4" Weight: 200
Breakout: 0% Improve: 0% Collapse: 0%
Attrition: 0% MLB: 0%

Comparables:
Joe Savery, John Ely, Dan Jennings

YEAR	TEAM	LVL	AGE	W	L	SV	G	GS	IP	H	HR	BB	SO	BB9	SO9	GB%	BABIP	WHIP	ERA	FIP	FRA	WARP
2013	MHV	A-	21	0	2	0	9	9	24²	19	0	16	26	5.8	9.5	52%	.317	1.42	2.92	2.93	4.25	0.2
2014	CLE	MLB	22	2	3	0	9	9	32	37	4	19	19	5.4	5.4	45%	.313	1.78	6.07	5.72	6.60	-0.5

A town of fewer than 17,000, Defiance, Ohio, could soon boast three big-league pitchers if Kime follows in the footsteps of Chad Billingsley and Jonathon Niese. Kime was a reliever at the University of Louisville, but he moved into the rotation at Mahoning Valley and performed well in two-to-four-inning stints. The righty has a durable frame and repeats his delivery well, but while he shows feel for his breaking ball and cutter, the overall package needs refinement for him to become a mid-rotation starter at the highest level. His history in the bullpen gives him a fallback plan.

Corey Kluber

Born: 4/10/1986 Age: 28
Bats: R Throws: R Height: 6' 4" Weight: 215
Breakout: 35% Improve: 62% Collapse: 28%
Attrition: 61% MLB: 61%

Comparables:
Yusmeiro Petit, Cory Luebke, Brad Lincoln

YEAR	TEAM	LVL	AGE	W	L	SV	G	GS	IP	H	HR	BB	SO	BB9	SO9	GB%	BABIP	WHIP	ERA	FIP	FRA	WARP
2011	COH	AAA	25	7	11	0	27	27	150²	153	19	70	143	4.2	8.5	41%	.232	1.48	5.56	4.53	4.62	0.2
2011	CLE	MLB	25	0	0	0	3	0	4¹	6	0	3	5	6.2	10.4	40%	.400	2.08	8.31	4.22	3.26	0.1
2012	COH	AAA	26	11	7	0	21	21	125¹	121	9	49	128	3.5	9.2	48%	.316	1.36	3.59	3.34	4.58	1.5
2012	CLE	MLB	26	2	5	0	12	12	63	76	9	18	54	2.6	7.7	46%	.342	1.49	5.14	4.24	4.81	0.3
2013	COH	AAA	27	1	1	0	2	2	12¹	14	2	3	12	2.2	8.8	51%	.343	1.38	6.57	4.10	4.99	0.0
2013	CLE	MLB	27	11	5	0	26	24	147¹	153	15	33	136	2.0	8.3	48%	.330	1.26	3.85	3.33	3.97	2.0
2014	CLE	MLB	28	8	9	0	24	24	137²	144	15	50	123	3.3	8.0	43%	.319	1.41	4.49	4.18	4.88	0.0

Perhaps the most shocking thing about Kluber's electric breakout season is that it should have been even better. His ERA was higher than his FIP, and there's no reason to believe that his BABIP should be as abnormally high as it was. After failing to make the rotation out of spring training, he showed that pitchers can develop at any age: The sinker he'd begun preferring the year before was hitting its spots and generating groundballs aplenty. By the time he sprained his finger in August, he had 3.54 ERA and both his walk and strikeout rates were among the league leaders. It was ugly after his September return (fueled by a .395 BABIP), but his velocity, walks and strikeouts were all back, so expect next year to have a good beat that you can dance to.

C.C. Lee

Born: 10/21/1986 Age: 27
Bats: R Throws: R Height: 5' 11" Weight: 190
Breakout: 20% Improve: 48% Collapse: 36%
Attrition: 61% MLB: 47%

Comparables:
Brad Kilby, Josh Fields, Brad Salmon

YEAR	TEAM	LVL	AGE	W	L	SV	G	GS	IP	H	HR	BB	SO	BB9	SO9	GB%	BABIP	WHIP	ERA	FIP	FRA	WARP
2011	AKR	AA	24	2	1	0	23	0	39²	27	1	11	56	2.5	12.7	58%	.295	0.96	2.50	2.20	2.80	0.8
2011	COH	AAA	24	4	0	1	21	0	31²	26	2	12	43	3.4	12.2	44%	.222	1.20	2.27	2.57	2.64	0.3
2013	COH	AAA	26	1	0	0	19	0	19	14	1	5	24	2.4	11.4	47%	.310	1.00	2.37	2.31	3.23	0.4
2013	CLE	MLB	26	0	0	0	8	0	4¹	4	0	3	4	6.2	8.3	29%	.286	1.62	4.15	4.00	5.02	0.0
2014	CLE	MLB	27	1	1	0	25	0	35²	31	4	13	38	3.4	9.5	48%	.297	1.25	3.54	3.89	3.84	0.4

If the Indians were trying to corner the market on Tommy John returnees and low-slot sinker-slider pitchers, Lee helped with both goals. His velocity wasn't quite all the way back, but he continued to befuddle minor-league hitters, and has now posted double-digit K/9 rates in all eight of his minor-league stops. Atypically for his ilk, he's blown away left-handed batsmen at least as well as righties so far, and while major-league opponents won't be as confused by his unconventional delivery, being able to handle both sides will make him a late-inning candidate as long as he stays healthy.

Shaun Marcum

Born: 12/14/1981 Age: 32
Bats: R Throws: R Height: 6' 0" Weight: 195
Breakout: 16% Improve: 45% Collapse: 31%
Attrition: 10% MLB: 82%

Comparables:
Ben Sheets, John Lackey, Jake Peavy

YEAR	TEAM	LVL	AGE	W	L	SV	G	GS	IP	H	HR	BB	SO	BB9	SO9	GB%	BABIP	WHIP	ERA	FIP	FRA	WARP
2011	MIL	MLB	29	13	7	0	33	33	200²	175	22	57	158	2.6	7.1	39%	.267	1.16	3.54	3.70	4.39	1.7
2012	WIS	A	30	1	0	0	3	3	12²	9	1	3	10	2.1	7.1	41%	.222	0.95	2.84	3.51	4.22	0.2
2012	MIL	MLB	30	7	4	0	21	21	124	116	16	41	109	3.0	7.9	34%	.287	1.27	3.70	4.14	4.30	1.2
2013	NYN	MLB	31	1	10	0	14	12	78¹	85	7	21	60	2.4	6.9	37%	.332	1.35	5.29	3.61	3.86	0.6
2014	CLE	MLB	32	4	4	0	12	12	72²	70	8	19	58	2.4	7.2	40%	.290	1.23	3.63	4.02	3.94	0.8

Marcum appeared on a few "Offseason Bargains" lists when the Mets nabbed him for $4 million. Safe to say the investment failed, and yet there are signs Marcum wasn't as bad as traditional metrics indicate, and he might show up on a few "Offseason Bargains" lists again this spring after signing a minor-league deal with Cleveland. His 3.61 FIP is negligibly worse than what he put up in 2010 and 2011, and his .322 BABIP, while it doesn't jump off the page, is a career high. Empirically, it seems a fly-ball pitcher moving to a large ballpark means nothing if the outfielders can't catch anything. (By the time Juan Lagares took over center field in Queens, Marcum had been put out to pasture.) Marcum invented two new ways to get hurt—left (!) thumb soreness and thoracic outlet surgery—but at his present value, Cleveland will either be out a pittance or very pleasantly surprised.

Justin Masterson

Born: 3/22/1985 Age: 29
Bats: R Throws: R Height: 6' 6" Weight: 250
Breakout: 12% Improve: 49% Collapse: 23%
Attrition: 5% MLB: 95%

Comparables:
Dean Chance, Brandon Webb, Jose Rijo

YEAR	TEAM	LVL	AGE	W	L	SV	G	GS	IP	H	HR	BB	SO	BB9	SO9	GB%	BABIP	WHIP	ERA	FIP	FRA	WARP
2011	CLE	MLB	26	12	10	0	34	33	216	211	11	65	158	2.7	6.6	56%	.302	1.28	3.21	3.32	3.67	4.0
2012	CLE	MLB	27	11	15	0	34	34	206¹	212	18	88	159	3.8	6.9	57%	.309	1.45	4.93	4.11	5.31	0.1
2013	CLE	MLB	28	14	10	0	32	29	193	156	13	76	195	3.5	9.1	60%	.285	1.20	3.45	3.38	4.27	1.6
2014	CLE	MLB	29	10	9	0	26	26	165²	161	13	62	142	3.4	7.7	57%	.307	1.35	3.82	3.92	4.16	1.3

Not that anyone is considering moving the Indians' workhorse to the bullpen full-time anymore, but his time in relief to close out the season confirmed the expected—that he'd post amazing statistics if he only faced the Twins and White Sox. Seriously, it did show that he'd be a very effective reliever, with a more reliable platoon advantage. No pitcher who has faced 500 right-handed batters over the past three seasons has allowed a lower OPS (.537). Masterson's filthy mix of two fastballs and a slider remain less than nasty to left-handed hitters, especially those with the discipline to take. When one of those insolent lefties inevitably reaches, Masterson is severe toward potential basestealers, keeping most double play opportunities alive for the right-hander on deck.

Zach McAllister

Born: 12/8/1987 Age: 26
Bats: R Throws: R Height: 6' 6" Weight: 240
Breakout: 39% Improve: 67% Collapse: 14%
Attrition: 24% MLB: 85%

Comparables:
David Huff, Travis Wood, Ivan Nova

YEAR	TEAM	LVL	AGE	W	L	SV	G	GS	IP	H	HR	BB	SO	BB9	SO9	GB%	BABIP	WHIP	ERA	FIP	FRA	WARP
2011	COH	AAA	23	12	3	0	25	25	154²	155	11	31	128	1.8	7.4	42%	.311	1.20	3.32	3.22	3.47	1.0
2011	CLE	MLB	23	0	1	0	4	4	17²	26	1	7	14	3.6	7.1	43%	.403	1.87	6.11	3.40	4.33	0.2
2012	COH	AAA	24	5	2	0	11	11	63¹	59	5	19	52	2.7	7.4	40%	.300	1.23	2.98	3.54	4.51	0.8
2012	CLE	MLB	24	6	8	0	22	22	125¹	133	19	38	110	2.7	7.9	41%	.304	1.36	4.24	4.20	4.67	0.7
2013	CLE	MLB	25	9	9	0	24	24	134¹	134	13	49	101	3.3	6.8	39%	.296	1.36	3.75	4.06	4.31	1.1
2014	CLE	MLB	26	7	8	0	23	23	130	138	15	40	94	2.8	6.5	43%	.304	1.37	4.39	4.43	4.77	0.2

With all the miracles happening around him on the Tribe staff, McAllister's steady emergence as a solid major-league starter can go almost unnoticed. He doesn't throw hard, he doesn't follow the organization's blueprint for groundballing, doesn't keep the ball in the park, he doesn't even have pinpoint control. But he does have a nice four-seam fastball with some backup movement that is good enough for his show-me slider and changeup to stay in the background. While that should be enough to earn a spot in almost any rotation, he'll have to avoid injuries—such as the finger sprain of 2013—to improve his odds of staying in the Cleveland five. Or he could experience a pitching epiphany that adds his name to the Miracle List.

Brett Myers

Born: 8/17/1980 Age: 33
Bats: R Throws: R Height: 6' 4" Weight: 240
Breakout: 24% Improve: 51% Collapse: 26%
Attrition: 14% MLB: 83%

Comparables:
Jason Johnson, Rodrigo Lopez, Kyle Lohse

YEAR	TEAM	LVL	AGE	W	L	SV	G	GS	IP	H	HR	BB	SO	BB9	SO9	GB%	BABIP	WHIP	ERA	FIP	FRA	WARP
2011	HOU	MLB	30	7	14	0	34	33	216	226	31	57	160	2.4	6.7	48%	.297	1.31	4.46	4.23	5.12	-0.3
2012	CHA	MLB	31	3	4	0	35	0	34²	30	4	9	21	2.3	5.5	49%	.252	1.12	3.12	4.20	5.23	0.1
2012	HOU	MLB	31	0	4	19	35	0	30²	35	4	6	20	1.8	5.9	57%	.304	1.34	3.52	4.31	5.25	-0.1
2013	AKR	AA	32	1	2	0	6	3	10²	7	1	6	6	5.1	5.1	62%	.182	1.22	3.38	5.39	7.99	-0.1
2013	CLE	MLB	32	0	3	0	4	3	21¹	29	10	5	12	2.1	5.1	40%	.271	1.59	8.02	8.75	9.49	-0.7
2014	CLE	MLB	33	2	2	1	13	4	35¹	37	5	10	24	2.4	6.2	48%	.291	1.31	4.32	4.77	4.70	0.0

Myers didn't pitch much—UCL sprain—but he made up for it by allowing more home runs in 21 innings than Anibal Sanchez, Matt Harvey or Francisco Liriano did last year. Wait, is that how pitchers make up for not pitching much? Seems wrong. It's tempting (and probably prudent) to write him off based on his 88 mph heat, but that's about where he was as a starter in 2010 and 2011, and he made it work then. The Indians released him in August.

Josh Outman

Born: 9/14/1984 Age: 29
Bats: L Throws: L Height: 6' 1" Weight: 205
Breakout: 30% Improve: 57% Collapse: 26%
Attrition: 27% MLB: 78%

Comparables:
Jeff Niemann, Randy Wells, Robinson Tejeda

YEAR	TEAM	LVL	AGE	W	L	SV	G	GS	IP	H	HR	BB	SO	BB9	SO9	GB%	BABIP	WHIP	ERA	FIP	FRA	WARP
2011	SAC	AAA	26	8	3	0	17	17	78¹	77	7	47	72	5.4	8.3	47%	.308	1.58	3.91	4.98	4.72	0.8
2011	OAK	MLB	26	3	5	0	13	9	58¹	62	4	23	35	3.5	5.4	41%	.300	1.46	3.70	3.94	3.90	0.8
2012	TUL	AA	27	2	5	0	14	11	69¹	64	4	30	71	3.9	9.2	53%	.333	1.36	3.63	3.41	4.18	0.9
2012	COL	MLB	27	1	3	0	27	7	40²	47	7	20	40	4.4	8.9	47%	.355	1.65	8.19	4.88	5.50	0.2
2013	CSP	AAA	28	1	0	0	5	0	10²	8	1	4	14	3.4	11.8	69%	.280	1.12	0.84	3.29	3.68	0.3
2013	COL	MLB	28	3	0	0	61	0	54	56	3	23	53	3.8	8.8	52%	.342	1.46	4.33	3.22	4.00	0.5
2014	CLE	MLB	29	4	3	0	31	8	63	60	6	25	55	3.5	7.9	45%	.301	1.35	3.90	4.09	4.23	0.5

Outman's career ERA is 4.60 as a starter and 4.63 as a reliever, but make no mistake: The difference is huge, and the transition to full-time bullpen work will likely extend his career by a half decade. With a whiffworthy slider, two extra ticks on his sinker and an absurd platoon split, Outman the Reliever strikes out three more batters per nine, with half the home runs and a modestly improved walk rate. He ditched a curveball he never really had a handle on to throw more sliders in 2013, an obvious decision—his slider had baseball's third-best whiff/swing rate. Now that he has finally found the right cape, lefty evildoers should beware the Outman.

Vinnie Pestano
Born: 2/20/1985 Age: 29
Bats: R Throws: R Height: 6' 0" Weight: 200
Breakout: 27% Improve: 55% Collapse: 25%
Attrition: 21% MLB: 80%

Comparables:
Jose Veras, Henry Owens, Steve Delabar

YEAR	TEAM	LVL	AGE	W	L	SV	G	GS	IP	H	HR	BB	SO	BB9	SO9	GB%	BABIP	WHIP	ERA	FIP	FRA	WARP
2011	CLE	MLB	26	1	2	2	67	0	62	41	5	24	84	3.5	12.2	40%	.269	1.05	2.32	2.71	2.90	1.4
2012	CLE	MLB	27	3	3	2	70	0	70	53	7	24	76	3.1	9.8	41%	.263	1.10	2.57	3.38	3.41	1.0
2013	COH	AAA	28	0	0	0	14	0	13²	13	0	4	13	2.6	8.6	38%	.351	1.24	3.29	2.40	3.33	0.2
2013	CLE	MLB	28	1	2	6	37	0	35¹	37	6	21	37	5.3	9.4	36%	.330	1.64	4.08	5.06	4.79	0.0
2014	CLE	MLB	29	3	1	2	49	0	48	40	5	18	55	3.5	10.3	45%	.298	1.22	3.17	3.61	3.44	0.8

Oh, the fickleness of relief pitchers! Pestano burst onto the scene in 2011 after a change to his arm slot in 2010 led to far more strikeouts. The 2012 season confirmed he was the real deal, with the only question being whether he'd ever figure out left-handed batters. Last year he picked up where he left off, allowing just a 1.29 ERA in his first seven appearances, earning four holds in the process. But then came the elbow pain. And the loss of velocity. And the loss of control. And the demotion. Expectations are that there are no long-term effects, and that he'll regain the missing mph and resume the 3.3 BB/9 rate that he posted in 2011-12, but his September outings didn't allay any fears and the jury will be out until he strings together some good outings (and some good radar gun readings).

Marc Rzepczynski
Born: 8/29/1985 Age: 28
Bats: L Throws: L Height: 6' 1" Weight: 215
Breakout: 31% Improve: 59% Collapse: 24%
Attrition: 29% MLB: 74%

Comparables:
Bobby Parnell, Angel Guzman, Jeff Samardzija

YEAR	TEAM	LVL	AGE	W	L	SV	G	GS	IP	H	HR	BB	SO	BB9	SO9	GB%	BABIP	WHIP	ERA	FIP	FRA	WARP
2011	SLN	MLB	25	0	3	0	28	0	22²	22	1	11	28	4.4	11.1	64%	.368	1.46	3.97	2.69	3.90	0.1
2011	TOR	MLB	25	2	3	0	43	0	39¹	28	2	15	33	3.4	7.6	65%	.248	1.09	2.97	3.42	4.45	0.4
2012	SLN	MLB	26	1	3	0	70	0	46²	46	7	17	33	3.3	6.4	59%	.281	1.35	4.24	4.76	5.65	-0.5
2013	MEM	AAA	27	1	2	0	32	0	44	44	1	18	31	3.7	6.3	56%	.294	1.41	3.07	3.75	4.03	0.6
2013	CLE	MLB	27	0	0	0	27	0	20¹	11	1	6	20	2.7	8.9	58%	.204	0.84	0.89	3.08	3.76	0.1
2013	SLN	MLB	27	0	0	0	11	0	10¹	16	1	4	9	3.5	7.8	54%	.441	1.94	7.84	3.99	4.38	0.0
2014	CLE	MLB	28	3	2	1	44	5	60	58	6	25	54	3.7	8.1	57%	.305	1.37	4.17	4.23	4.53	0.2

Rzepczynski is a sinker-slider pitcher who generates copious groundballs and has limited left-handed batters to a meager .214/.288/.299 line for his career. He was at his worst last year, when he was roughed up early and demoted by St. Louis; he was also at his best last year, holding lefties to a .480 OPS after a July trade to Cleveland. Front office officials get paid healthy salaries to try to predict LOOGY streaks, hopelessly. Since Scrabble's debut as a starting pitcher, more than the life of a specialist has been expected of him, but no other role will fit if he never finds an adjustment against right-handed hitters, who collectively hit like Ben Zobrist against him. Even if no such breakthrough comes, he can look forward to a long career—probably continuing to bounce from team to team—giving lefties, and GMs, fits.

Danny Salazar
Born: 1/11/1990 Age: 24
Bats: L Throws: R Height: 6' 0" Weight: 190
Breakout: 42% Improve: 71% Collapse: 26%
Attrition: 34% MLB: 70%

Comparables:
Garrett Olson, Felipe Paulino, Dan Straily

YEAR	TEAM	LVL	AGE	W	L	SV	G	GS	IP	H	HR	BB	SO	BB9	SO9	GB%	BABIP	WHIP	ERA	FIP	FRA	WARP
2012	CAR	A+	22	1	2	0	16	16	53²	46	3	19	53	3.2	8.9	42%	.307	1.21	2.68	3.20	4.00	1.1
2012	AKR	AA	22	4	0	0	6	6	34	25	1	8	23	2.1	6.1	47%	.240	0.97	1.85	2.94	3.56	0.6
2013	AKR	AA	23	2	3	0	7	7	33²	27	1	10	51	2.7	13.6	33%	.366	1.10	2.67	1.57	2.39	1.2
2013	COH	AAA	23	4	2	1	14	13	59¹	44	4	14	78	2.1	11.8	42%	.303	0.98	2.73	2.26	3.44	1.3
2013	CLE	MLB	23	2	3	0	10	10	52	44	7	15	65	2.6	11.2	37%	.298	1.13	3.12	3.19	3.61	0.9
2014	CLE	MLB	24	6	7	0	23	23	108¹	106	13	40	98	3.3	8.1	39%	.301	1.35	4.09	4.27	4.44	0.8

Put that Wild Card game—especially the Delmon Young homer—out of mind. Salazar is a special talent. Another year removed from Tommy John surgery and another year of physical development led to routine 100 mph radar gun readings. With that hot rhythm playing most of the time, the monster split-finger hits like a dubstep drop that would make Skrillex proud. For truth in advertising, Salazar isn't *yet* among the elite starting pitchers in the game, despite having two filthy pitches. Skeptics still argue that his height—listed at six feet—and lack of a quality third pitch (though righties don't love his slider) will land him at the back of a bullpen someday. The optimist counters that his velocity belies his height, and if he is able to refine another pitch, the potential is out of sight.

Bryan Shaw
Born: 11/8/1987 Age: 26
Bats: B Throws: R Height: 6' 1" Weight: 210
Breakout: 42% Improve: 68% Collapse: 17%
Attrition: 21% MLB: 76%

Comparables:
Brandon League, Alberto Arias, Clay Hensley

YEAR	TEAM	LVL	AGE	W	L	SV	G	GS	IP	H	HR	BB	SO	BB9	SO9	GB%	BABIP	WHIP	ERA	FIP	FRA	WARP
2011	MOB	AA	23	3	1	7	15	0	20²	15	1	8	15	3.5	6.5	51%	.261	1.11	0.87	3.65	4.97	0.1
2011	RNO	AAA	23	1	0	9	16	0	17²	14	4	4	15	2.0	7.6	55%	.100	1.02	4.58	6.05	7.35	0.0
2011	ARI	MLB	23	1	0	0	33	0	28¹	30	2	8	24	2.5	7.6	60%	.333	1.34	2.54	3.49	3.62	0.2
2012	ARI	MLB	24	1	6	2	64	0	59¹	60	4	24	41	3.6	6.2	57%	.313	1.42	3.49	3.95	4.82	0.0
2013	CLE	MLB	25	7	3	1	70	0	75	60	4	28	73	3.4	8.8	46%	.271	1.17	3.24	3.10	3.22	1.3
2014	CLE	MLB	26	3	2	1	47	3	62	60	6	24	48	3.5	6.9	52%	.294	1.36	4.01	4.40	4.36	0.3

For now, Shaw is a very good reliever whose delivery and repertoire make him all but immune to right-handed opponents. Last year, he started finding the spots to retire left-handed batters more often, and squeezed their OPS against him down to a tidier .678. The news got even better as he held *all* batters to a stingy .454 OPS in the second half. He throws more than 70 percent cutters, and has improved as he has quit trying to get every out on the ground. While it would be insane to suggest he'll be the next Mariano Rivera, at least he's picked the right role model for his skills. How close he gets to Mo-dom will depend largely on how fine his command becomes as he matures.

LINEOUTS

HITTERS

PLAYER	TEAM	LVL	AGE	PA	R	2B	3B	HR	RBI	BB	SO	SB-CS	AVG/OBP/SLG	TAv	BABIP	BRR	FRAA	WARP
1B J. Aguilar	AKR	AA	23	567	66	28	0	16	105	56	107	0-1	.275/.349/.427	.284	.316	-5.1	1B(128): -0.6	1.6
CF E. Carrera	COH	AAA	26	464	57	16	5	5	31	38	87	43-12	.248/.312/.346	.245	.301	2.7	CF(41): 2.3, LF(38): 4.4	1.5
	PHI	MLB	26	16	2	0	0	0	0	1	4	0-0	.077/.250/.077	.146	.111	0	RF(5): 0.0, LF(1): 0.0	-0.1
	CLE	MLB	26	5	1	0	0	0	1	0	1	0-0	.500/.500/.500	.291	.667	0.6	RF(1): -0.1	0.1
RF M. Carson	COH	AAA	31	490	57	16	2	14	49	39	119	14-4	.252/.322/.394	.244	.315	0.9	RF(68): 9.8, CF(30): -0.5	1.9
	CLE	MLB	31	13	5	0	0	1	3	1	1	3-0	.636/.692/.909	.562	.667	0.1	RF(14): -0.0, LF(4): -0.0	0.5
DH J. Giambi	CLE	MLB	42	216	21	8	0	9	31	23	56	0-1	.183/.282/.371	.235	.202	-2.9		-0.6
1B M. LaPorta	COH	AAA	28	185	21	9	0	10	28	17	30	0-0	.238/.310/.476	.272	.230	-1	1B(24): -2.7	0.0
C A. Monsalve	AKR	AA	21	80	9	4	1	2	8	1	15	0-0	.295/.304/.449	.267	.344	0.2	C(20): 0.2	0.6
RF A. Santander	LKC	A	18	238	27	13	0	5	31	13	43	6-3	.242/.303/.370	.227	.281	-2	RF(61): 1.3	-0.6
C K. Shoppach	IND	AAA	33	27	0	1	0	0	2	1	9	0-0	.192/.222/.231	.152	.294	-0.5	C(7): 0.1	-0.4
	SYR	AAA	33	40	3	0	0	0	2	5	8	0-0	.219/.359/.219	.241	.292	0.1	C(10): -0.1	0.3
	SEA	MLB	33	125	11	7	0	3	9	12	45	0-0	.196/.293/.346	.252	.300	-1.3	C(35): -0.4	0.6
	CLE	MLB	33	2	0	0	0	0	0	0	1	0-0	.000/.000/.000	.003	.000	0	C(1): -0.0	0.0

Jesus Aguilar boasts above-average raw power and a good enough glove at first base, but he is stuck at that position and unlikely to hit enough to please a contender. ⊘ The Phillies swiped **Ezequiel Carrera** in an April waiver claim; the Indians swiped him back one month later. Fitting, considering his only skill is swiping bases. ⊘ If you search for "**Matt Carson**" on Google, a link to this minor-league journeyman outfielder's player page appears atop 37,899,999 other results, which puts some things in perspective. ⊘ Two seasons into his professional career, **D'vone McClure** still has not solved the Arizona League, but the Indians are encouraged by his work ethic and believe his upside remains high. ⊘ Rumors are unconfirmed that the Indians plan to bring **Jason Giambi** back for use only in walk-off home run situations, but if they do nobody could blame them. ⊘ **Matt LaPorta** will turn 29 in January and is trending toward complete irrelevance, though his pop and erstwhile prospect stock grant him a perennial opportunity to compete for a bench job. ⊘ **Alex Monsalve** missed most of the 2013 campaign while nursing an elbow injury, but held his own in Double-A and played in the Venezuelan League after the season; he hits left-handers well, is honing his receiving skills, and should at least develop into a bat-first backup. ⊘ A switch-hitting corner outfielder, **Anthony Santander** intrigued evaluators with strength and speed in 2012, but he fell flat in his first taste of full-season ball and is likely to repeat Lake County in 2014. ⊘ **Kelly Shoppach** still has a career slugging percentage over .500 against left-handed pitching and has thrown out 37 percent of would-be base thieves since 2011; there are, simply, many inferior backup catchers living in big houses.

PITCHERS

PLAYER	TEAM	LVL	AGE	W	L	SV	IP	H	HR	BB	SO	BB9	SO9	GB%	BABIP	WHIP	ERA	FIP	FRA	WARP
S. Armstrong	AKR	AA	22	2	3	0	33	32	2	21	43	5.7	11.7	36%	.353	1.61	4.09	3.60	3.53	0.7
S. Barnes	COH	AAA	25	3	3	0	27²	30	4	20	35	6.5	11.4	38%	.371	1.81	7.81	4.83	6.35	-0.3
	CLE	MLB	25	0	1	1	8²	8	3	3	10	3.1	10.4	43%	.250	1.27	7.27	7.00	8.36	-0.2
T. Haley	AKR	AA	23	1	4	7	44	37	0	39	46	8.0	9.4	53%	.333	1.73	4.70	4.44	5.21	0.0
T. House	AKR	AA	23	2	1	0	22¹	20	1	3	27	1.2	10.9	57%	.333	1.03	3.22	1.89	2.47	0.8
	COH	AAA	23	7	10	0	141²	163	11	54	110	3.4	7.0	56%	.338	1.53	4.32	3.89	5.01	0.6
C. Hynes	SAN	AA	28	1	0	0	12¹	10	0	0	16	0.0	11.7	57%	.357	0.81	0.73	0.46	1.60	0.4
	TUC	AAA	28	1	0	4	35	33	1	2	42	0.5	10.8	54%	.344	1.00	1.80	1.80	2.65	1.2
	SDN	MLB	28	0	0	0	17	25	3	9	13	4.8	6.9	47%	.379	2.00	9.00	5.55	5.45	-0.2
L. Lugo	LKC	A	19	0	1	0	14¹	14	1	5	14	3.1	8.8	26%	.317	1.33	3.77	3.34	4.46	0.2
	MHV	A-	19	1	4	0	50¹	39	1	11	30	2.0	5.4	41%	.259	0.99	1.97	3.12	4.02	0.4
J. Martinez	COH	AAA	30	3	7	0	130	163	19	27	90	1.9	6.2	51%	.332	1.46	5.26	4.44	5.53	-0.3
	CLE	MLB	30	1	0	0	5	4	0	0	3	0.0	5.4	19%	.250	0.80	1.80	1.88	2.62	0.1
B. Price	AKR	AA	26	1	0	2	16	6	0	4	17	2.2	9.6	54%	.162	0.62	0.56	1.95	2.26	0.5
	COH	AAA	26	1	3	2	59	51	5	12	75	1.8	11.4	45%	.317	1.07	2.44	2.58	2.73	1.7
J. Ramirez	LEH	AAA	24	4	2	3	42	42	2	23	36	4.9	7.7	42%	.310	1.55	4.71	3.75	4.35	0.3
	PHI	MLB	24	0	1	0	24	30	6	15	16	5.6	6.0	41%	.316	1.88	7.50	6.81	6.90	-0.6
J. Tomlin	COH	AAA	28	2	0	0	15	12	0	0	11	0.0	6.6	28%	.279	0.80	2.40	2.14	3.19	0.4
	CLE	MLB	28	0	0	0	2	2	0	0	0	0.0	0.0	38%	.250	1.00	0.00	3.08	3.80	0.0
B. Wood	COH	AAA	27	2	0	0	16²	11	0	10	23	5.4	12.4	51%	.297	1.26	2.16	2.42	2.98	0.4
	CLE	MLB	27	0	0	0	1¹	1	0	3	1	20.2	6.8	50%	.250	3.00	0.00	8.33	6.35	0.0
M. Zagurski	SWB	AAA	30	5	3	1	26¹	22	2	12	38	4.1	13.0	47%	.364	1.29	3.08	2.79	3.44	0.5
	IND	AAA	30	1	0	1	21	15	2	9	37	3.9	15.9	46%	.310	1.14	2.14	2.35	3.15	0.6
	PIT	MLB	30	0	0	0	6	10	1	8	5	12.0	7.5	57%	.450	3.00	15.00	8.02	9.10	-0.4
	NYA	MLB	30	0	0	0	0¹	1	0	0	0	0.0	0.0	%	.500	3.00	54.00	12.08	7.84	0.0

One of the better relief prospects in the organization, **Shawn Armstrong** can miss plenty of bats, but for now he also misses the zone far too often to be trusted in high-leverage situations. ⊘ With a slider and changeup that look above average on his good days, **Scott Barnes** is still considered a potential major-league reliever despite a pedestrian fastball and a forgettable season ended by a wrist sprain. ⊘ Barns in Nacogdoches, Texas had more to worry about from space shuttle debris than **Trey Haley**'s attempts to hit them with a pitch when he was growing up. He doesn't allow hits or power, so a slight improvement in navigation would go a long way. ⊘ Too old to be much of a prospect, **T.J. House** features a low-90s fastball and slider and gets lefties out better than righties, so his days as a starter are numbered. ⊘ After more than 300 minor-league appearances, **Colt Hynes** became the first 31st-round pick from 2007 to reach the big leagues; his freakish 29-to-1 K/BB rate at two levels last year got him to San Diego, where he was abused for 2 1/2 months as Joe Thatcher's replacement in the bullpen. ⊘ A 6-foot-5 hurler with three projectable pitches, **Luis Lugo** has the makings of a no. 4 starter. ⊘ **Joe Martinez** pitches to contact, which has allowed him to make contact with five employers in the past four years. ⊘ Acquired from the Red Sox in the Victor Martinez deal in 2009, former sandwich-rounder **Bryan Price** could earn a bullpen spot this spring if he wards off shoulder trouble and improves his fastball command. ⊘ **J.C. Ramirez** is just the latest of the three prospects acquired for Cliff Lee to officially disappoint, posting the NL's fifth-worst ERA. ⊘ **Josh Tomlin** is a strike-throwing savant who is all the way back from Tommy John surgery and would be welcome as a no. 4 in almost any rotation. That he may be a spare on the Indians is a sign of the club's pitching depth. ⊘ All of **Blake Wood**'s velocity and sinking action are back after Tommy John surgery, but his always-dicey control has totally crapped out. ⊘ Like a lot of walk-prone, non-specialist lefties who throw 93, **Mike Zagurski** keeps popping up in new places, but he's worth more on a Scrabble board (22 points!) than he is in a big-league bullpen.

MANAGER: TERRY FRANCONA

YEAR	TEAM	W-L	Pythag +/-	Avg PC	100+ P	120+ P	QS	BQS	REL	REL w Zero R	IBB	PH	PH Avg	PH HR	SB2	CS2	SB3	CS3	SAC Att	SAC %	POS SAC	Squeeze	Swing	In Play
2011	BOS	90-72	1	96.8	78	4	71	5	443	359	11	83	.176	2	93	40	9	1	33	66.7%	22	0	366	122
2013	CLE	92-70	1	94.9	68	0	73	5	540	454	26	58	.255	3	96	33	21	3	41	75.6%	30	0	332	85

Where does the manager start and the roster talent (or overall franchise philosophy) end? With the Red Sox, Terry Francona didn't bunt much. He was routinely one of the skippers most averse to giving up an out to move a runner over. That fit Boston's team philosophy. In Cleveland, Francona didn't bunt a huge amount, but he was league average, which is a notable difference from his Boston days.

Francona still has a quick hook with his relievers. His 2005 Red Sox were one of the first AL teams to ever average less than an inning per relief appearance, and last year the Indians had the fewest outs per relief appearance by any AL team.

Colorado Rockies

By Russell A. Carleton

This will about sum it all up for the Rockies in 2013: They scored the second-most runs in the National League, behind pennant winners St. Louis. They also gave up the most runs in the National League. If you like offense, at least 2013 was entertaining. The problem with the Rockies was that, once they got away from Coors Field, they scored the fourth-*fewest* runs in the league, but they still maintained their less-than-stellar record in giving up runs (third-worst in the NL). The hitting only seemed to work at home, and the pitching never worked. Stop me if you've heard this one in a Rockies recap before.

In fact, stop me if you've heard any of these other key Rockies storylines for 2013: Troy Tulowitzki is a fantastic shortstop who is good at hitting a baseball. But we kinda knew that already and he has the nine-digit contract to prove it.

ROCKIES PROSPECTUS
2013 W-L: 74-88, 5th in NL West

Pythag	.465	20th	DER	.681	30th
RS/G	4.36	10th	B-Age	27.6	5th
RA/G	4.69	28th	P-Age	28.1	17th
TAv	.253	21st	Salary	$80.7	23rd
BRR	11.13	3rd	M$/MW	$2.65	13th
TAv-P	.268	20th	DL Days	689	9th
FIP	3.93	20th	$ on DL	14%	11th

	Runs	HR/RH	HR/LH	Runs/RH	Runs/LH
Three-Year Park Factors	113	108	107	118	110

Top Hitter WARP	4.87 (Troy Tulowitzki)
Top Pitcher WARP	2.97 (Jhoulys Chacin)
Top Prospect	Jonathan Gray

Carlos Gonzalez and Dexter Fowler both proved that last season was not some weird fluke … for the fourth season in a row. (Strangely, Fowler's reward was a one-way ticket to Houston.) Todd Helton got the well-deserved, but underappreciated, send-off he deserved for a very underappreciated career. And no one can yet spell or pronounce the name Jhoulys.

In fairness, there were a couple of interesting things to note. I don't think anyone planned on uttering the words "batting title winner" and "Michael Cuddyer" in the same sentence, but … batting average. Nolan Arenado won a Gold Glove, but didn't really hit much. The Rockies also get extra credit points for ignoring the conventional wisdom and installing left-handed reliever Rex Brothers as their closer. Brothers joined the small fraternity of next-generation southpaw stoppers with Aroldis Chapman and Glen Perkins. So, yeah, it wasn't all 13-9 games in Denver last year.

Maybe the biggest news story of the Rockies' season was that it wasn't entirely clear who the general manager was. Long-time GM Dan O'Dowd was rumored to be losing influence to his right-hand man, Bill Geivett, although both men denied there was anything more than work-shifting going on. According to the Rockies' brass, Geivett still reported to O'Dowd, but O'Dowd was shifting his focus to player development, while Geivett was given more oversight for the "personnel aspect." I can't say that I'd blame O'Dowd if he wanted to get away from the personnel aspect. General Manager of the Rockies is an extra thankless job, because while the Rockies have had their share of excellent offensive players over the years, it always seems like it's the pitching that lets them down. In fact, in the 21 seasons that the Rockies have existed, their pitching staff has finished better than the league-average ERA exactly twice (2007 and 2009). Everyone knows the reason, that even with the now-legendary humidor Colorado is a place where ERAs go to die. Or at least to become inflated by a good run or so. It must be tough making that sales pitch to a decent free agent. Or even a 16-year-old kid from Venezuela.

The Rockies have tried a couple of pitching strategies over the years that seemed designed specifically to cope with the reality that they play 81 games per year at an altitude higher than a couple of college kids in Boulder on a Saturday night. Rockies pitchers are consistently among the league leaders in the percentage of groundballs that they give up. It's hard to hit a groundball home run. The problem is that most worm burner specialists rely on movement to trick the batter into swinging over the top of the ball so that he'll pound it into the ground. Even with the humidor, there's less air resistance at altitude, and a baseball moves because of the way that the seams of the ball interact with the air. Balls break less at altitude than they do at sea level. If your only trick is movement and you mess up the spin on the pitch, it's easier for a ball not to move where it's supposed to and just hang belt high. So it's not a perfect strategy, but at least it's clear what the Rockies have been trying to do.

While visitors to Coors Field know that they might be in for a bad weekend, they'll soon be back at sea level. The Rockies have no such escape. There's probably a Nobel Prize (or just a Neifi Perez) waiting for the person who solves the Coors Field quandary. Since, honestly, there's not a lot to review about 2013, perhaps we might look ahead to see what, if anything other than just learn to live with scores fit for the Broncos (and occasionally the Nuggets), the Rockies can do to find pitching that will work at altitude. Maybe it's a bit much to hope for Maddux, Glavine and Smoltz, but perhaps they might settle for beating the league ERA once in a while?

The narrative has always been that no matter what the Rockies and their pitchers try to do, there's no escaping the effects of Coors. Is that true?

WARNING! GORY MATHEMATICAL DETAILS AHEAD!

First off, let's talk about what a park effect really is by creating an absurd example. Let's pretend that at some park—we'll call it Doors Field in honor of Jim Morrison—there was an unnoticed magic force field machine out beyond the center field wall. When someone hit a fly ball, Morrison himself, who faked his own death in 1971 to focus on building his force field machine in Denver, would decide whether or not to flip a switch that would determine the trajectory of the ball. If he flipped the switch one way, it would be a home run. If not, it would be an ordinary fly ball. People wondered sometimes why a ball that was absolutely smoked suddenly stopped in mid-air so as not to fly over the fence and why some lazy pop ups seemed to be randomly sucked out over the fence, but then this is the same country that spent the summer of 2013 pondering various rhymes for "hug me." As long as Morrison is throwing (or not throwing) the switch randomly, whether a ball becomes a home run is strictly a function of the park (or at least Morrison's machine).

Now let's imagine that Morrison only hit the "home run" switch at a rate that was consistent with the league average. Even though the park was completely to blame (or credit, depending on your perspective) for the home run, it neither increased nor decreased the rate at which home runs were hit in the park, relative to the league average. So … there was no park effect? Of course there was a park effect! We've simply been defining "park effect" incorrectly. So far, we've only asked the question of how often an event—such as a home run in Coors—happens, relative to expectations. I'd argue that a second, and equally important, question is missing. In statistical terms, we need to figure out the composition of the variance. In layman's terms, we need to look closer at why the home run happened.

My data set was the years 2010 to 2012 (at press time, the 2013 data were not yet ready). To get some idea of what the Rockies were really like away from Coors Field, I calculated the home run rate (per PA) that each of the Rockies' hitters had, *ignoring all those in Denver*. I did similarly for all Rockies pitchers. And for all pitchers and hitters who came to visit Coors Field. We'll take these numbers as their real talent level away from Coors. Once you have an estimate of a pitcher's and a hitter's home run rates (or any percentage-based stat), there's a way to combine them into one probability that this particular pitcher-batter matchup will end in a home run. For the initiated, it's called the odds-ratio method. This will stand as our estimate of the probability of a home run based only on the talent in the batter's box and on the mound, stripped of any effect Coors might have on our estimates of that talent level. It's possible that Coors itself has comparatively little effect on home run rates, and that it's mostly about the talent on the field.

Next, I took the overall rate at which home runs were hit in Coors Field, again per PA. If the park is randomly assigning home runs, then this will be a strong predictor of whether an individual plate appearance ends in a home run, because Morrison's machine is random and doesn't care who's out there on the mound or in the batter's box. It's all the park's fault in that case.

I did similar calculations for 27 of the remaining 29 parks as well (Target Field and Marlins Park opened in the middle of my sampling frame) and the at-bats that happened there from 2010 to 2012. For each park, sequentially, I ran a binary logistic regression coding for whether each plate appearance ended in a home run and entered our estimate of the odds of a home run based on the batter-pitcher matchup (for the initiated, natural log transformed) and the odds based on the park average (again, natural log). The super-initiated will know that for binary logistic regression, there is no proper R-squared statistic. I am using the change in the proportional change in -2 log likelihood. If you don't know what any of that means, just know that a miracle happened, numbers appeared on the screen and I am a wizard.

The result was that among the 28 parks studied, Coors Field actually ranked third in the amount of variance that was picked up by the estimate of *talent*, behind Busch Stadium and AT&T Park. The park's average rate of home runs per PA was not significant in the regression, meaning that the idea of Coors Field randomly assigning home runs has very little support. The surprise conclusion is that talent at preventing (or giving up) home runs at sea level actually plays up more than average at Coors Field. Despite its reputation as a launching pad, the park does not seem to randomly award home runs because of the lack of air. Statistically, home runs were more likely to be given up by pitchers and hit by batters who did similarly at sea level, and the association was stronger at Coors than in most other parks. Yes, overall rates of home runs will be elevated because of the elevation, but in terms of how much can be attributed to the talent on the field and how much is "the ballpark made me do it," Coors is actually one of the places where talent shines through the brightest.

I also ran a series of analyses aimed at figuring out whether a certain type of pitcher (high strikeout rate? high fly-ball rate?) was more likely to give up a home run, again over and above what we might expect from him based on his performance (and those of his batting opponent) away from Coors. For the initiated, I again used binary logistic regression and controlled for talent level the same way as above, but this time I entered a series of additional "moderator" variables (e.g. pitcher's K rate), and the interaction between the moderator and the talent control. There was some (p < .10) evidence that pitchers who record more of their outs via the strikeout, rather than on balls in play, were less likely to give up home runs. If the batter swings and misses, it's hard to hit it over the fence.

The take-home message: If you're the sort of pitcher who's good at preventing home runs at sea level, Coors Field is a place where that will be rewarded. There's just one little problem. It still might not show up as a lower ERA relative to the league. To illustrate, let's again construct a silly example. Suppose there were a ballpark where 5 percent of plate appearances ended in home runs, on average. Within this ballpark, there was something that you could do to affect the chances of a home run that some people were good at and some people were bad at. Some pitchers could get that rate as low as 3 percent, while others had to suffer through a 7 percent rate. Contrast this to a park where 2 percent of all plate appearances ended in a home run, but no matter what a pitcher did, it would always be 2 percent. Rates of home runs will always be higher in the first ballpark, but talent matters much more there. The numbers are exaggerated, but that's Coors Field in a nutshell.

The hidden take-home message: The Rockies and their opponents both play in and breathe the same thin air 81 times per season. Within the context of a single game, which is being played in this park, the only things that matter are the strengths of the two teams relative to each other within this environment. And yes, the stat that does matter most is the number of times a team wins this game. In Colorado, the way to a championship is that you'll have to win a lot of 8-6

games, and even though those are wins, giving up six runs will not look nice in the final unadjusted stat sheet. However, the idea that the only solution is to throw up your hands because there is nothing to be done is wrong. Once you look at the problem from the perspective of what really matters (winning the game), you'll see that settling for table scraps in your pitching staff is not only throwing away an opportunity to improve, but also actively hurting the team's chances.

There's also a hopeful take-home message: Talent is talent, even at Coors Field. If the Rockies' general manager, whoever he may be at this particular moment, were able to find a few above-average starters and could construct a good sales pitch that would get them to come to Denver, the Rockies would benefit greatly from it—in fact, *more so* than most teams. But of course, in a world that can't be bothered to stop and adjust for context, who wants to come to Colorado when all it will do is make your raw stats look bad? There's the real Catch-22 of running the Rockies. The park drives away the good ones and the fact that only the bad ones are left is amplified by the park. It's hard to construct a sales pitch that says "Even though everyone else will think your stat line is ugly and won't pay you as much in your next free agent contract, you'll be contributing more to actual winning, because your talent will prevent more runs relative to what would have been scored here otherwise. Just take a look at this series of binary logistic regressions done by this nerd at *Baseball*…What's that? You're signing with San Diego?"

I'd love to say that 2014 will be Rosario-er (see what I did there?) for the Rockies, because that's a satisfying way to end any essay in this genre. The truth is that there's not a lot of pitching on the way in the minors, and right now that's what this team needs. In Colorado, the free agent pitchers aren't going to be knocking down your door, so you have to grow your own. The Rockies haven't developed much pitching, and that's going to hurt. No, it's not fair that their own home park is working against them, but that's reality, and you can only use that excuse for so long.

Russell A. Carleton has a Ph.D. in clinical psychology, but instead of using his superpowers to fight depression and anxiety, he writes for Baseball Prospectus.

HITTERS

Nolan Arenado   3B

Born: 4/16/1991 Age: 23
Bats: R Throws: R Height: 6' 1"
Weight: 205 Breakout: 3%
Improve: 36% Collapse: 3%
Attrition: 21% MLB: 57%

Comparables:
Blake DeWitt, Matt Dominguez, Willy Aybar

YEAR	TEAM	LVL	AGE	PA	R	2B	3B	HR	RBI	BB	SO	SB	CS	AVG/OBP/SLG	TAv	BABIP	BRR	FRAA	WARP
2011	MOD	A+	20	583	82	32	3	20	122	47	53	2	1	.298/.349/.487	.295	.293	1	3B(99): -8.5	2.6
2012	TUL	AA	21	573	55	36	1	12	56	39	58	0	2	.285/.337/.428	.277	.296	-4.1	3B(133): 27.4	6.3
2013	CSP	AAA	22	75	14	11	0	3	21	5	9	0	2	.364/.392/.667	.337	.368	-1.6	3B(17): 2.6	1.2
2013	COL	MLB	22	514	49	29	4	10	52	23	72	2	0	.267/.301/.405	.236	.296	1.1	3B(130): 14.8	2.4
2014	COL	MLB	23	460	44	26	2	11	53	23	63	1	1	.267/.305/.412	.250	.290	-0.8	3B 8	1.5

Arenado's .405 slugging percentage was his lowest professional mark since he was an 18-year-old in Rookie ball. His .301 OBP was the lowest by a third baseman in Rockies history, by

27 points. So how did he get Rookie of the Year votes? With one of the greatest defensive seasons by a third baseman ... ever? By Defensive Runs Saved, he upgraded the Rockies' hot corner defense by 52 runs over 2012; Chris Nelson had been that bad, and Arenado was that good. It got to the point that Arenado was repeatedly apologizing to Troy Tulowitzki for infringing on his turf at shortstop. If Arenado's bat reaches its full potential, the result could be one of the best all-around third basemen in the game.

Brandon Barnes — CF

Born: 5/15/1986 Age: 28
Bats: R Throws: R Height: 6' 2''
Weight: 205 Breakout: 3%
Improve: 29% Collapse: 14%
Attrition: 24% MLB: 64%

Comparables:
Brian Anderson, Luis Terrero, Roger Bernadina

YEAR	TEAM	LVL	AGE	PA	R	2B	3B	HR	RBI	BB	SO	SB	CS	AVG/OBP/SLG	TAv	BABIP	BRR	FRAA	WARP
2011	CCH	AA	25	224	25	13	0	7	27	14	42	6	3	.286/.335/.453	.231	.327	-0.5	LF(9): -0.0, CF(5): -0.1	-0.2
2011	OKL	AAA	25	263	34	13	5	8	27	29	69	5	1	.197/.294/.402	.286	.242	-0.5	CF(17): 1.3	0.5
2012	CCH	AA	26	183	30	20	0	7	31	14	42	7	2	.317/.377/.567	.326	.385	0.7	CF(37): 0.3, RF(4): 0.2	2.1
2012	OKL	AAA	26	263	51	19	1	5	38	23	49	14	4	.323/.383/.477	.295	.388	3.5	CF(57): 8.3, RF(3): 0.0	3.1
2012	HOU	MLB	26	105	8	3	0	1	7	5	29	1	1	.204/.250/.265	.195	.279	0.2	CF(32): 2.0, RF(5): -0.2	-0.1
2013	HOU	MLB	27	445	46	17	1	8	41	21	127	11	11	.240/.289/.346	.242	.327	0.5	CF(116): 11.7, RF(13): 0.1	1.7
2014	COL	MLB	28	404	51	21	1	8	37	24	102	13	6	.257/.308/.389	.246	.330	-0.2	CF 8, RF 0	1.4

After beginning the year as a corner outfielder, Barnes took over center in Houston when Justin Maxwell went down with a broken hand. He played occasionally spectacular defense and hit well enough that the Astros felt they could deal Maxwell to Kansas City. Barnes' WARP was almost entirely defense, but it was still enough for third among Astros hitters, behind Jason Castro and Matt Dominguez. Barnes was saved the ignominy of being forced to the bench by George Springer when he was traded to Colorado, not that he's likely to have a full-time role there, either.

Charlie Blackmon — CF

Born: 7/1/1986 Age: 27
Bats: L Throws: L Height: 6' 3''
Weight: 210 Breakout: 3%
Improve: 31% Collapse: 12%
Attrition: 22% MLB: 75%

Comparables:
Lorenzo Cain, Tony Gwynn, Trevor Crowe

YEAR	TEAM	LVL	AGE	PA	R	2B	3B	HR	RBI	BB	SO	SB	CS	AVG/OBP/SLG	TAv	BABIP	BRR	FRAA	WARP
2011	CSP	AAA	24	272	49	19	4	10	49	19	34	12	5	.337/.393/.572	.290	.356	1.7	RF(34): 1.3, LF(4): -0.3	1.4
2011	COL	MLB	24	102	9	1	0	1	8	3	8	5	1	.255/.277/.296	.192	.270	-0.5	LF(25): -1.2, CF(2): -0.0	-0.7
2012	TRI	A-	25	69	8	5	0	1	3	7	10	3	0	.237/.348/.373	.300	.271	-0.9	CF(9): -0.5, LF(1): 0.0	0.3
2012	CSP	AAA	25	264	55	18	4	5	34	29	42	10	0	.303/.385/.482	.290	.350	1.5	CF(55): -3.5, LF(3): -0.1	1.7
2012	COL	MLB	25	121	15	8	0	2	9	4	17	1	2	.283/.325/.407	.236	.319	0.9	RF(17): -0.1, LF(15): 1.5	0.4
2013	CSP	AAA	26	299	56	15	6	3	40	35	41	7	5	.288/.376/.428	.266	.329	2	CF(65): -4.9	0.9
2013	COL	MLB	26	258	35	17	2	6	22	7	49	7	0	.309/.336/.467	.273	.366	3	RF(34): -0.4, CF(25): -2.5	1.2
2014	COL	MLB	27	299	32	15	2	6	32	20	50	7	2	.267/.323/.400	.255	.310	0.4	CF -3, RF -0	0.3

The Rockies' glut of outfielders—especially left-handed outfielders—stuck Blackmon in Colorado Springs to begin 2013 despite a history of minor-league mashing. As injuries sidelined outfielder after outfielder, and the glut became a gulch, Blackmon earned a short call-up in May, nailed down a roster spot by July and became a starting outfielder with time at all three positions by September. Blackmon's got one of the highest swing rates in the league, and despite healthy walk rates in the minors has never topped 4 percent in a big league season. He showed enough power in 2013 to make pitchers think twice about challenging him, so he'll have to show he can lay off inside fastballs, outside changeups and breaking balls at his shoe-tops if he's to carry his success into 2014.

Michael Cuddyer — RF

Born: 3/27/1979 Age: 35
Bats: R Throws: R Height: 6' 2''
Weight: 220 Breakout: 3%
Improve: 25% Collapse: 7%
Attrition: 12% MLB: 93%

Comparables:
Dave Winfield, Moises Alou, Magglio Ordonez

YEAR	TEAM	LVL	AGE	PA	R	2B	3B	HR	RBI	BB	SO	SB	CS	AVG/OBP/SLG	TAv	BABIP	BRR	FRAA	WARP
2011	MIN	MLB	32	584	70	29	2	20	70	48	95	11	1	.284/.346/.459	.289	.312	0.1	RF(77): -6.1, 1B(46): 1.6	2.3
2012	COL	MLB	33	394	53	30	2	16	58	32	78	8	3	.260/.317/.489	.275	.287	1.3	RF(74): -2.1, 1B(26): -0.8	1.5
2013	COL	MLB	34	540	74	31	3	20	84	46	100	10	3	.331/.389/.530	.304	.382	1	RF(118): -12.5, 1B(15): 0.6	1.9
2014	COL	MLB	35	479	58	26	2	16	62	39	86	8	2	.278/.340/.458	.282	.310	0.2	RF -8, 1B -1	1.0

By the Black Ink measure, Cuddyer had his career year at age 34, winning the batting title and leading the league in an offensive category for the first time. By somewhat more sophisticated measures—more sophisticated than batting average, you say!?—it wasn't exactly a paradigm-shifting performance. His TAv was very good but not exceptional, his .382 BABIP was 70 points better than his career rate and he managed only four home runs in the second half. Tack on his defensive "contribution" and he was arguably a bit overpriced at $10.5 million, and will be even less of a bargain this year if he slides further down the defensive spectrum.

Charlie Culberson 2B
Born: 4/10/1989 Age: 25
Bats: R Throws: R Height: 6' 1"
Weight: 200 Breakout: 7%
Improve: 21% Collapse: 7%
Attrition: 28% MLB: 43%

Comparables:
Angel Chavez, Trevor Plouffe, Tyler Greene

YEAR	TEAM	LVL	AGE	PA	R	2B	3B	HR	RBI	BB	SO	SB	CS	AVG/OBP/SLG	TAv	BABIP	BRR	FRAA	WARP
2011	RIC	AA	22	587	69	34	2	10	56	22	129	14	4	.259/.293/.382	.259	.320	1.2	2B(121): -1.1	1.6
2012	FRE	AAA	23	380	53	14	6	10	53	20	76	8	2	.236/.283/.396	.240	.272	1.3	2B(88): -3.0	-0.1
2012	CSP	AAA	23	128	17	11	1	2	12	1	18	6	2	.336/.344/.488	.280	.377	1.1	2B(28): 1.3	0.9
2012	SFN	MLB	23	23	0	0	0	0	1	0	7	0	0	.136/.136/.136	.100	.200	0.5	2B(6): -0.4	-0.3
2013	CSP	AAA	24	419	63	27	8	14	64	17	74	13	9	.310/.338/.524	.275	.350	2.9	2B(46): 2.9, SS(46): 2.9	3.3
2013	COL	MLB	24	104	12	5	0	2	12	4	23	5	1	.293/.317/.404	.236	.360	0	LF(27): 0.6, 2B(4): -0.1	0.2
2014	COL	MLB	25	250	25	13	2	6	27	8	54	5	2	.254/.279/.393	.236	.300	0.2	2B -0, SS 0	0.3

Culberson had to shift from second base to left field to earn a major-league roster spot in Colorado. Considering Culberson was *Baseball America*'s best defensive second baseman in the 2012 PCL, this is not an exchange you'd like to see a team making, but utility provides its own sort of value. Culberson has major weaknesses—he doesn't take a walk and he has massive platoon splits—but between his defensive chops and an ability to hit for solid power against left-handers, Culberson is a useful bench player, but one who would struggle to hold down a starting job.

David Dahl CF
Born: 4/1/1994 Age: 20
Bats: L Throws: R Height: 6' 2"
Weight: 185 Breakout: 0%
Improve: 0% Collapse: 0%
Attrition: 0% MLB: 0%

Comparables:
Engel Beltre, Xavier Avery, Abraham Almonte

YEAR	TEAM	LVL	AGE	PA	R	2B	3B	HR	RBI	BB	SO	SB	CS	AVG/OBP/SLG	TAv	BABIP	BRR	FRAA	WARP
2013	ASH	A	19	42	9	4	1	0	7	2	8	2	0	.275/.310/.425	.259	.344	-0.1	CF(8): -1.1	0.0
2014	COL	MLB	20	250	23	10	2	3	20	10	62	1	1	.223/.253/.322	.201	.280	-0.1	CF -5, LF 0	-1.3

Dahl is an exciting talent, the kind of talent worth breaking old habits for. He was the first high school outfielder chosen by Colorado in the first round since Chris Nelson in 2004, and just the second high school position player. Of course, there's a reason such reluctance exists: Young prospects have growing pains. Dahl was disciplined early in the season for missing a flight and then missed all but 10 games of Low-A Asheville's season with a hamstring injury. He still has top-end upside and could turn into a premier center fielder, the sort of player Chris Nelson never dreamed of being.

Corey Dickerson LF
Born: 5/22/1989 Age: 25
Bats: L Throws: R Height: 6' 1"
Weight: 205 Breakout: 8%
Improve: 30% Collapse: 8%
Attrition: 25% MLB: 72%

Comparables:
Jerry Sands, Allen Craig, Eric Thames

YEAR	TEAM	LVL	AGE	PA	R	2B	3B	HR	RBI	BB	SO	SB	CS	AVG/OBP/SLG	TAv	BABIP	BRR	FRAA	WARP
2011	ASH	A	22	435	78	27	5	32	87	39	99	9	6	.282/.356/.629	.289	.296	0.4	LF(45): -3.3, RF(13): 0.5	1.4
2012	MOD	A+	23	270	43	24	4	9	43	25	42	9	5	.338/.396/.583	.353	.373	1.1	RF(30): -0.8, LF(18): 2.1	3.4
2012	TUL	AA	23	290	40	16	3	13	38	18	51	7	3	.274/.322/.504	.290	.293	2.4	LF(67): -7.6	0.8
2013	CSP	AAA	24	345	61	21	14	11	50	26	49	6	10	.371/.414/.632	.332	.409	-1.1	LF(63): -1.4, RF(5): -0.6	3.2
2013	COL	MLB	24	213	32	13	5	5	17	16	41	2	2	.263/.316/.459	.269	.307	0.3	LF(36): -0.2, CF(15): 0.8	0.9
2014	COL	MLB	25	276	33	14	4	10	38	17	55	3	3	.272/.318/.480	.273	.310	-0.2	LF -2, RF -0	0.8

It might be tempting to write Dickerson off as a player with a raw approach propped up by the Coors Field power boost. Not so fast. Dickerson has been a big power threat throughout his minor-league career and developed a better gap approach in 2012—a useful skill considering Colorado's expansive greenery. The bigger question surrounding Dickerson has been his defense, which was considered a "huge liability" by *Baseball America* in 2012. But the Rockies trusted him enough to give him 12 starts in center field, and even if that doesn't take he has enough bat to corner a corner. He'll have plenty of competition for a starting role, so a good spring is imperative if he is to begin 2014 in the majors.

Carlos Gonzalez CF
Born: 10/17/1985 Age: 28
Bats: L Throws: L Height: 6' 1"
Weight: 220 Breakout: 0%
Improve: 57% Collapse: 0%
Attrition: 3% MLB: 99%

Comparables:
Ryan Braun, Albert Belle, Kevin Mitchell

YEAR	TEAM	LVL	AGE	PA	R	2B	3B	HR	RBI	BB	SO	SB	CS	AVG/OBP/SLG	TAv	BABIP	BRR	FRAA	WARP
2011	COL	MLB	25	542	92	27	3	26	92	48	105	20	5	.295/.363/.526	.296	.326	0.5	LF(61): -2.2, RF(34): -0.7	3.2
2012	COL	MLB	26	579	89	31	5	22	85	56	115	20	5	.303/.371/.510	.279	.352	0.5	LF(131): -3.9	1.8
2013	COL	MLB	27	436	72	23	6	26	70	41	118	21	3	.302/.367/.591	.313	.368	1.9	LF(106): 0.4	3.6
2014	COL	MLB	28	439	64	22	4	20	65	37	94	17	4	.294/.356/.519	.300	.340	1.8	CF 1, LF -0	3.3

Gonzalez remains one of the best players in the major leagues when healthy. Alas, "when healthy" remains a significant caveat. This year, the ailment was a nagging finger sprain that stole 34 games across three months, joining a list of dents to his knee, wrist, hamstring and back over the past three years. When Gonzalez was on the field, he continued to hit the ball hard, and at 314 feet his average fly ball was baseball's longest. He hit even more balls in the air, for good measure, and his .289 isolated power marked a career high. None of this was a Rocky Mountain mirage, as CarGo actually posted higher marks in each slash stat when playing on the road. Gonzalez traded some contact for all that power, leading to a career-high strikeout percentage but, more importantly, a career-high TAv. Nice trade.

Todd Helton 1B

Born: 8/20/1973 Age: 40
Bats: L Throws: L Height: 6' 2"
Weight: 220 Breakout: 0%
Improve: 22% Collapse: 9%
Attrition: 14% MLB: 62%

Comparables:
Carl Yastrzemski, Al Kaline, Harold Baines

YEAR	TEAM	LVL	AGE	PA	R	2B	3B	HR	RBI	BB	SO	SB	CS	AVG/OBP/SLG	TAv	BABIP	BRR	FRAA	WARP
2011	COL	MLB	37	491	59	27	0	14	69	59	71	0	1	.302/.385/.466	.288	.328	-2.5	1B(119): 12.2	3.2
2012	COL	MLB	38	283	31	16	1	7	37	39	44	1	1	.238/.343/.400	.246	.260	-3.9	1B(67): -1.1	-0.9
2013	COL	MLB	39	442	41	22	1	15	61	40	87	0	0	.249/.314/.423	.258	.280	-3.4	1B(110): -2.8	-0.6
2014	COL	MLB	40	384	40	18	1	8	41	44	65	0	0	.258/.342/.384	.258	.300	-0.8	1B -0	0.2

Helton's retirement tour was at times tough to watch. His body was clearly run down and he struggled to catch up to elite velocity. Still, he managed to provide some special moments down the stretch: He notched his 2,500th hit late in the season, and slammed his 369th (and final) home run in his final game at Coors Field. His career line settles at .316/.414/.539, a remarkable feat even considering Coors Field and steroids-era offensive levels. A lengthy Hall of Fame debate awaits, but regardless of his Hall status, Helton's career was a special one, particularly for the fans in Colorado for whom he was the face of baseball for so long.

Rosell Herrera SS

Born: 10/16/1992 Age: 21
Bats: B Throws: R Height: 6' 3"
Weight: 180 Breakout: 1%
Improve: 11% Collapse: 0%
Attrition: 3% MLB: 11%

Comparables:
Trevor Plouffe, Asdrubal Cabrera, Tim Beckham

YEAR	TEAM	LVL	AGE	PA	R	2B	3B	HR	RBI	BB	SO	SB	CS	AVG/OBP/SLG	TAv	BABIP	BRR	FRAA	WARP
2012	ASH	A	19	237	22	8	2	1	26	21	49	6	3	.202/.271/.272	.207	.255	0.2	3B(29): -1.3, SS(29): 2.4	-0.3
2012	TRI	A-	19	211	30	6	2	1	30	14	34	7	3	.284/.332/.351	.270	.335	1.4	SS(44): 4.5	1.4
2013	ASH	A	20	546	83	33	0	16	76	61	96	21	8	.343/.419/.515	.316	.401	-0.8	SS(93): -4.1	4.9
2014	COL	MLB	21	250	22	9	1	4	24	17	59	1	1	.237/.289/.340	.223	.300	-0.3	SS -0, 3B -0	-0.1

In a second try at hitter's haven Asheville, Herrera took full advantage of his surroundings. The shortstop dominated the league, finishing in the top 10 in each slash stat and very nearly doubling his OPS from his first attempt. Scouts said Herrera hardly looked like the same player. He might get too big for shortstop—at 20, he's 6-foot-3 but only 180 pounds—but the power and contact ability he flashed were more than enough to suggest he could thrive at third or second base, especially as his body continues to mature.

DJ LeMahieu 2B

Born: 7/13/1988 Age: 25
Bats: R Throws: R Height: 6' 4"
Weight: 205 Breakout: 5%
Improve: 44% Collapse: 15%
Attrition: 35% MLB: 84%

Comparables:
Josh Harrison, Donovan Solano, Ruben Gotay

YEAR	TEAM	LVL	AGE	PA	R	2B	3B	HR	RBI	BB	SO	SB	CS	AVG/OBP/SLG	TAv	BABIP	BRR	FRAA	WARP
2011	TEN	AA	22	202	32	15	2	2	27	11	22	4	3	.358/.386/.492	.306	.389	0.2	3B(23): 0.8, 2B(19): 0.9	1.3
2011	IOW	AAA	22	247	23	7	1	3	23	14	27	5	5	.286/.328/.366	.276	.308	0.7	3B(26): 1.6, 2B(8): 1.1	1.2
2011	CHN	MLB	22	62	3	2	0	0	4	1	12	0	0	.250/.262/.283	.198	.312	-0.7	2B(15): -0.7, 3B(11): -0.0	-0.1
2012	CSP	AAA	23	280	33	14	2	1	31	23	29	13	6	.314/.368/.396	.266	.348	-1	2B(52): -1.4, 3B(7): 0.0	0.8
2012	COL	MLB	23	247	26	12	4	2	22	13	42	1	2	.297/.332/.410	.250	.353	2.6	2B(67): 7.4, 3B(9): -0.2	1.5
2013	CSP	AAA	24	158	34	8	5	1	22	10	19	8	2	.364/.405/.510	.292	.405	3.4	SS(30): 3.7, 2B(2): 0.0	2.2
2013	COL	MLB	24	434	39	21	3	2	28	19	67	18	7	.280/.311/.361	.228	.328	0.7	2B(90): 3.1, 3B(14): 0.5	0.2
2014	COL	MLB	25	427	48	20	3	3	33	22	66	12	5	.282/.318/.374	.244	.320	0.1	2B 3, 3B 1	1.2

LeMahieu hit for as empty a .280 as can be imagined at Coors Field, joining Willy Taveras, Aaron Miles, Juan Pierre and Walt Weiss as the only Rockies to produce an isolated power as low as .082 in a season at elevation. He managed to keep his starting spot through the end of the season thanks to excellent glovework, and as such is probably good enough to hold a roster spot as a utility infielder—he also has big-league experience at both infield corners and kept active at shortstop for Colorado Springs. His bat won't be good enough to stave off any major competition at second base, but it's been at least five years since the Rockies were able to produce any major competition at second base.

Justin Morneau 1B

Born: 5/15/1981 Age: 33
Bats: L Throws: R Height: 6' 4"
Weight: 215 Breakout: 0%
Improve: 24% Collapse: 3%
Attrition: 10% MLB: 95%

Comparables:
Mike Sweeney, Don Baylor, Lyle Overbay

YEAR	TEAM	LVL	AGE	PA	R	2B	3B	HR	RBI	BB	SO	SB	CS	AVG/OBP/SLG	TAv	BABIP	BRR	FRAA	WARP
2011	ROC	AAA	30	31	8	4	0	1	8	1	2	0	0	.367/.387/.600	.212	.370	0.1	1B(2): -0.1	-0.1
2011	MIN	MLB	30	288	19	16	0	4	30	19	44	0	0	.227/.285/.333	.218	.257	-1.7	1B(56): -5.2	-1.8
2012	MIN	MLB	31	570	63	26	2	19	77	49	102	1	0	.267/.333/.440	.269	.294	-4.2	1B(99): -4.6	0.4
2013	PIT	MLB	32	92	6	4	0	0	3	13	12	0	0	.260/.370/.312	.246	.303	-0.4	1B(25): -0.9	-0.2
2013	MIN	MLB	32	543	56	32	0	17	74	37	98	0	0	.259/.315/.426	.274	.288	-0.6	1B(112): -5.3	0.6
2014	COL	MLB	33	584	68	31	1	20	77	56	99	0	0	.270/.344/.447	.275	.300	-1	1B -5	0.8

That Morneau remained in Minnesota through the trade deadline must've irked him. He responded with an August tear during which he homered nine times after entering the month with just eight bombs. The Pirates took note and lassoed him from the Twins in exchange for two players. Yet Morneau stopped hitting home runs the moment he arrived, and went without a dinger for the remainder of the season. It's hard out there for a first baseman dependent on singles and walks for their offensive value, so Morneau will have to recapture some of his August magic if he wants to be a desired player at future deadlines. Signing a two-year deal to play in the Coors Field launching pad seems like a good first step.

Jordan Pacheco 1B
Born: 1/30/1986 Age: 28
Bats: R Throws: R Height: 6' 1"
Weight: 200 Breakout: 3%
Improve: 31% Collapse: 7%
Attrition: 13% MLB: 76%
Comparables:
Trevor Crowe, Broderick Perkins, Andres Blanco

YEAR	TEAM	LVL	AGE	PA	R	2B	3B	HR	RBI	BB	SO	SB	CS	AVG/OBP/SLG	TAv	BABIP	BRR	FRAA	WARP
2011	CSP	AAA	25	411	57	21	3	3	50	30	48	2	2	.278/.343/.377	.239	.308	4.3	C(68): 0.1, 3B(4): -0.1	0.9
2011	COL	MLB	25	88	5	1	0	2	14	3	9	0	0	.286/.318/.369	.238	.301	-0.6	1B(13): -0.2, 3B(7): -0.1	-0.2
2012	CSP	AAA	26	74	10	4	0	3	10	3	5	1	0	.433/.479/.627	.364	.441	0.4	3B(13): -1.2, C(4): -0.0	0.8
2012	COL	MLB	26	505	51	32	3	5	54	22	61	7	2	.309/.341/.421	.247	.344	0.5	3B(82): -4.4, 1B(43): -3.6	-0.5
2013	CSP	AAA	27	63	8	5	1	1	6	8	3	3	0	.315/.403/.500	.309	.320	0.4	C(9): -0.2, 1B(6): -0.6	0.5
2013	COL	MLB	27	262	23	15	0	1	22	10	38	0	0	.239/.276/.312	.207	.278	-0.7	1B(43): -1.8, C(15): -0.1	-1.2
2014	COL	MLB	28	313	28	16	1	3	30	16	42	2	1	.269/.312/.365	.239	.300	-0.3	1B -2, 3B -2	-0.4

Pacheco remains a relevant name in fantasy circles for one reason and one reason only: He started 11 games behind the plate for Colorado last season, and a catcher (or even a "catcher") playing in Colorado always has value somewhere. Pacheco, however, would need to learn to throw a slider and changeup to find a position his 2013 batting line could support. His power production disappeared and his line-drive stroke produced only a .278 BABIP. Even when he hit relatively well in 2012, he showed below-average power, and his defensive struggles across the diamond—not just at catcher but at the hot and cold corners—drastically lower his chances of receiving consistent playing time again.

Kyle Parker RF
Born: 9/30/1989 Age: 24
Bats: R Throws: R Height: 6' 0"
Weight: 200 Breakout: 0%
Improve: 34% Collapse: 6%
Attrition: 8% MLB: 47%
Comparables:
Eric Thames, Todd Frazier, Michael Taylor

YEAR	TEAM	LVL	AGE	PA	R	2B	3B	HR	RBI	BB	SO	SB	CS	AVG/OBP/SLG	TAv	BABIP	BRR	FRAA	WARP
2011	ASH	A	21	516	75	23	1	21	95	48	133	2	0	.285/.367/.483	.266	.355	-3.8	RF(79): -3.1	0.4
2012	MOD	A+	22	463	86	18	6	23	73	66	88	1	2	.308/.415/.562	.338	.346	-0.3	RF(77): -3.6	4.2
2013	TUL	AA	23	528	70	23	3	23	74	40	99	6	6	.288/.345/.492	.300	.318	-2	LF(77): -7.0, RF(20): -0.8	2.0
2014	COL	MLB	24	250	28	10	1	9	33	20	59	0	0	.258/.319/.434	.265	.310	-0.3	RF -1, LF -2	0.2

As expected, Parker didn't burn through the steamy Texas League like he did the dry desert air of the California League, but the former Clemson quarterback's athleticism continues to translate into good performances at the plate. His raw power is his best asset, and he matched the previous season's totals with 23 home runs and 49 extra-base hits—both numbers even more impressive coming in pitcher-friendly Tulsa. As would be expected of a former quarterback, he has the arm for right field and enough range to hack it despite mediocre speed. Corner outfield requires a big bat, especially with teams increasingly punting offense at premium positions, but Parker has the tools to be a great major-league hitter.

Wilin Rosario C
Born: 2/23/1989 Age: 25
Bats: R Throws: R Height: 5' 11"
Weight: 220 Breakout: 1%
Improve: 57% Collapse: 5%
Attrition: 11% MLB: 97%
Comparables:
Carlos Gonzalez, Ryan Doumit, Javy Lopez

YEAR	TEAM	LVL	AGE	PA	R	2B	3B	HR	RBI	BB	SO	SB	CS	AVG/OBP/SLG	TAv	BABIP	BRR	FRAA	WARP
2011	TUL	AA	22	426	52	15	3	21	48	19	91	1	2	.249/.284/.457	.245	.272	-0.6	C(76): -0.6, 1B(1): -0.0	1.0
2011	COL	MLB	22	57	6	3	1	3	8	2	20	0	0	.204/.228/.463	.228	.250	-1	C(14): -0.1	0.1
2012	COL	MLB	23	426	67	19	0	28	71	25	99	4	5	.270/.312/.530	.269	.289	-1.2	C(105): 0.6, 3B(3): -0.0	2.2
2013	COL	MLB	24	466	63	22	1	21	79	15	109	4	1	.292/.315/.486	.268	.344	3.1	C(106): -0.8, 1B(4): -0.1	2.5
2014	COL	MLB	25	430	53	19	1	22	65	20	104	3	2	.264/.298/.477	.267	.300	-0.7	C -1, 1B -0	2.2

Rosario still won't take a walk, but it's hard to blame him when he hits the ball so hard. His power dropped, but he eliminated some grounders in exchange for line drives and hit 27 more singles than he did in 2012. His .194 isolated power ranked behind just Jason Castro and Brian McCann among full-time catchers. His approach might not be ideal, but he has the bat speed and power to make it work. The bigger concern is his work behind the plate—Rosario allowed 12 fewer passed balls than in 2012 but still led the league again, and his career total in his first two-plus seasons is ... one fewer than Johnny Bench's at the same point. Huh.

Josh Rutledge SS
Born: 4/21/1989 Age: 25
Bats: R Throws: R Height: 6' 1"
Weight: 190 Breakout: 6%
Improve: 35% Collapse: 19%
Attrition: 37% MLB: 90%
Comparables:
Reid Brignac, Tony Abreu, Danny Richar

YEAR	TEAM	LVL	AGE	PA	R	2B	3B	HR	RBI	BB	SO	SB	CS	AVG/OBP/SLG	TAv	BABIP	BRR	FRAA	WARP
2011	MOD	A+	22	523	91	33	9	9	71	41	91	16	3	.348/.414/.517	.349	.417	0.2	SS(86): -7.8	4.6
2012	TUL	AA	23	379	57	27	3	13	35	14	69	14	4	.306/.338/.508	.311	.345	1.7	SS(67): -6.3, 2B(22): 0.0	2.8
2012	COL	MLB	23	291	37	20	5	8	37	9	54	7	0	.274/.306/.469	.252	.315	-0.3	SS(57): -3.5, 2B(7): -0.3	0.2
2013	CSP	AAA	24	162	24	17	1	4	24	12	21	1	2	.371/.444/.587	.336	.415	-0.4	SS(22): -0.4, 2B(16): 0.7	1.8
2013	COL	MLB	24	314	45	6	1	7	19	22	62	12	0	.235/.294/.337	.229	.276	4.2	2B(58): 1.4, SS(14): -0.4	0.7
2014	COL	MLB	25	360	44	19	3	9	37	17	71	7	1	.275/.317/.427	.260	.320	0.7	SS -4, 2B 0	1.1

Rutledge earned his shot as the Opening Day second baseman with a strong second-half debut filling in for Troy Tulowitzki in 2012. But while he showed good power for a rookie middle infielder, an alarming strikeout rate and limited plate discipline were red flags. He couldn't smooth out either flaw in 2013, and by the end of May he had just eight extra-base hits and was sent back to the minors. He hit well enough in September (.328/.381/.431 with four stolen bases) to keep his name fresh in management's mind, but he'll need to fight in spring training to earn a roster spot, much less another starting job.

Trevor Story SS
Born: 11/15/1992 Age: 21
Bats: R Throws: R Height: 6' 1"
Weight: 175 Breakout: 1%
Improve: 2% Collapse: 1%
Attrition: 3% MLB: 5%

Comparables:
Nick Franklin, Jonathan Villar, Yamaico Navarro

YEAR	TEAM	LVL	AGE	PA	R	2B	3B	HR	RBI	BB	SO	SB	CS	AVG/OBP/SLG	TAv	BABIP	BRR	FRAA	WARP
2012	ASH	A	19	548	96	43	6	18	63	60	121	15	3	.277/.367/.505	.289	.335	3.3	SS(85): 7.7, 3B(21): 1.8	4.8
2013	MOD	A+	20	554	71	34	5	12	65	45	183	23	1	.233/.305/.394	.270	.343	1.8	SS(125): -4.7, 3B(4): -0.1	3.0
2014	COL	MLB	21	250	27	11	1	6	23	17	78	3	0	.218/.273/.350	.220	.300	0.2	SS -0, 3B 0	0.0

Only teammate Harold Riggins notched more California League strikeouts than Story's 183, as the 20-year-old shortstop couldn't maintain the gaudy numbers he posted at Low-A the year prior. However, there were still plenty of positives to Story's season. He stuck at shortstop for another season after concerns he would need to move to third base. He finished fourth in the league in doubles and notched more than 50 extra-base hits for the second straight year. And perhaps most importantly, he did so in a league where only five other qualifying players were age 20 or younger. He'll have to work around the contact issues, but a shortstop with Story's pop is an exceedingly rare bird in today's game.

Drew Stubbs CF
Born: 10/4/1984 Age: 29
Bats: R Throws: R Height: 6' 4"
Weight: 205 Breakout: 6%
Improve: 49% Collapse: 5%
Attrition: 17% MLB: 88%

Comparables:
Chuck Hinton, Jeffrey Hammonds, Leo Burke

YEAR	TEAM	LVL	AGE	PA	R	2B	3B	HR	RBI	BB	SO	SB	CS	AVG/OBP/SLG	TAv	BABIP	BRR	FRAA	WARP
2011	CIN	MLB	26	681	92	22	3	15	44	63	205	40	10	.243/.321/.364	.252	.343	4.9	CF(157): -3.1	1.6
2012	CIN	MLB	27	544	75	13	2	14	40	42	166	30	7	.213/.277/.333	.227	.290	3.7	CF(135): -10.3	-0.8
2013	CLE	MLB	28	481	59	21	2	10	45	44	141	17	2	.233/.305/.360	.254	.319	2.4	RF(105): 2.5, CF(43): 2.2	2.0
2014	COL	MLB	29	466	63	17	3	11	42	43	129	24	5	.245/.318/.377	.249	.320	2.7	CF 0, RF 1	1.0

At first glance, it may appear that Stubbs belied his reputation as a Great American Ballpark-only hitter, as he more or less matched his career TAv despite playing home games in the unforgiving-for-righties Progressive Field. And the shift to right field helped him post improved defensive statistics much more in line with his reputation as a rangy outfielder. But he did feel the pain of the park shift, struggling to an awful .229/.298/.341 batting line at home. And good defense in right field is nice, but not as nice as good defense in center. That leaves only an excellent rate of successful stolen bases, not nearly enough to undo the drain of a career .226/.296/.356 batting line against right-handed pitching.

Yorvit Torrealba C
Born: 7/19/1978 Age: 35
Bats: R Throws: R Height: 5' 11"
Weight: 200 Breakout: 0%
Improve: 31% Collapse: 13%
Attrition: 28% MLB: 84%

Comparables:
Matt Treanor, Don Slaught, Phil Masi

YEAR	TEAM	LVL	AGE	PA	R	2B	3B	HR	RBI	BB	SO	SB	CS	AVG/OBP/SLG	TAv	BABIP	BRR	FRAA	WARP
2011	TEX	MLB	32	419	40	27	1	7	37	20	65	0	2	.273/.306/.399	.238	.310	-4.8	C(98): 0.1	0.4
2012	TOR	MLB	33	30	3	0	0	1	2	2	7	0	0	.214/.267/.321	.215	.250	0.3	C(9): 0.1, 1B(1): -0.0	0.0
2012	TEX	MLB	33	182	16	8	0	3	12	14	31	1	1	.236/.302/.342	.241	.271	-3.5	C(49): 0.3	0.1
2012	MIL	MLB	33	6	0	0	0	0	0	1	2	0	0	.000/.167/.000	.095	.000	0	C(2): -0.0	-0.1
2013	COL	MLB	34	196	10	8	0	0	16	13	24	0	0	.240/.295/.285	.198	.277	0.1	C(50): -0.9, 1B(3): -0.0	-0.5
2014	COL	MLB	35	250	24	12	0	3	22	17	42	2	1	.262/.315/.355	.238	.300	-0.6	C -0, 1B 0	0.5

Torrealba returned to Colorado and posted his worst season yet. He still makes consistent contact, but his power is completely gone—that his first season with a sub-.300 slugging percentage came at Coors Field is a No Through Road sign if we ever saw one. He still looked competent behind the plate, so he could find a job as a second or third catcher out of spring training, but his run as the league's 28th- or 29th-best starting catcher is over.

Troy Tulowitzki SS
Born: 10/10/1984 Age: 29
Bats: R Throws: R Height: 6' 3"
Weight: 215 Breakout: 6%
Improve: 50% Collapse: 0%
Attrition: 3% MLB: 98%

Comparables:
Robin Yount, Nomar Garciaparra, Hanley Ramirez

YEAR	TEAM	LVL	AGE	PA	R	2B	3B	HR	RBI	BB	SO	SB	CS	AVG/OBP/SLG	TAv	BABIP	BRR	FRAA	WARP
2011	COL	MLB	26	606	81	36	2	30	105	59	79	9	3	.302/.372/.544	.306	.305	-1.8	SS(140): -2.8	4.7
2012	COL	MLB	27	203	33	8	2	8	27	19	19	2	2	.287/.360/.486	.270	.284	1	SS(47): 0.6	1.3
2013	COL	MLB	28	512	72	27	0	25	82	57	85	1	0	.312/.391/.540	.306	.334	0.7	SS(121): 4.6	4.9
2014	COL	MLB	29	424	59	21	2	20	65	42	65	5	2	.296/.369/.521	.307	.310	-0.3	SS 0	3.9

Tulowitzki has now topped 150 games just once since 2008. In 2013, the cause of dearth was a rib fracture that held him out from mid-June through mid-July. Despite the slew of unrelated injuries

Tulowitzki has suffered over the years, there remains nobody in the league who can come close to topping him at the position. Since 2008, only on-again off-again shortstop Hanley Ramirez has a superior TAv. Tulowitzki is by far the superior defender, and there's a strong argument he's the best player in the National League when healthy. PECOTA says so, and who are we to say otherwise?

Ryan Wheeler 3B

Born: 7/10/1988 Age: 25
Bats: L Throws: R Height: 6' 3"
Weight: 235 Breakout: 10%
Improve: 22% Collapse: 18%
Attrition: 36% MLB: 51%

Comparables:
Brandon Laird, Joel Guzman, Josh Bell

YEAR	TEAM	LVL	AGE	PA	R	2B	3B	HR	RBI	BB	SO	SB	CS	AVG/OBP/SLG	TAv	BABIP	BRR	FRAA	WARP
2011	MOB	AA	22	531	69	30	2	16	89	45	102	3	4	.294/.358/.465	.275	.343	-5.7	3B(82): -3.3, 1B(14): -0.4	1.2
2012	RNO	AAA	23	399	56	27	4	15	90	26	67	3	1	.351/.388/.572	.306	.388	0.2	3B(49): 3.6, 1B(32): -2.2	2.9
2012	ARI	MLB	23	119	11	6	1	1	10	9	22	1	0	.239/.294/.339	.236	.287	-0.1	3B(23): -2.3, 1B(4): 0.2	-0.2
2013	CSP	AAA	24	480	74	29	2	12	89	31	91	4	1	.306/.351/.463	.271	.357	-3.4	3B(93): -5.0, 1B(13): -2.1	1.1
2013	COL	MLB	24	42	1	2	0	0	7	1	10	0	0	.220/.238/.268	.173	.290	-0.1	1B(7): -0.4, 3B(1): -0.1	-0.4
2014	COL	MLB	25	250	25	13	1	7	30	13	52	0	0	.271/.311/.423	.255	.320	-0.4	3B -2, 1B -1	0.0

Last year did nothing to dispel the notion of Wheeler as perennial "tweener:" He has the bat for third base and the glove for first. Although his season was a step down from a brilliant campaign in 2012, it's difficult to see what exactly Wheeler has left to learn in the minors. It can be tempting to leave this kind of player down in the minors and hope the other half of his game develops, but at 25 Wheeler might already have entered his brief window to be a productive reserve at the highest level. An awful 41-game stretch in the majors, however, may have punched yet another ticket back to Triple-A.

Tim Wheeler CF

Born: 1/21/1988 Age: 26
Bats: L Throws: R Height: 6' 4"
Weight: 205 Breakout: 0%
Improve: 2% Collapse: 3%
Attrition: 9% MLB: 9%

Comparables:
Steve Susdorf, Tommy Murphy, Daniel Nava

YEAR	TEAM	LVL	AGE	PA	R	2B	3B	HR	RBI	BB	SO	SB	CS	AVG/OBP/SLG	TAv	BABIP	BRR	FRAA	WARP
2011	TUL	AA	23	637	105	28	6	33	86	59	142	21	12	.287/.365/.535	.277	.329	-2.2	CF(109): -11.3	0.9
2012	CSP	AAA	24	415	67	27	4	2	37	29	69	7	7	.303/.357/.412	.262	.366	-1.7	RF(39): -3.2, LF(28): -2.0	0.4
2013	CSP	AAA	25	440	59	16	3	5	42	33	87	12	7	.262/.330/.355	.246	.324	-0.8	RF(46): -5.8, LF(31): 1.4	0.2
2014	COL	MLB	26	250	29	11	1	5	22	16	57	5	3	.248/.302/.371	.237	.300	-0.2	CF -1, RF -2	-0.3

Two years ago, Wheeler had huge power but a major problem with left-handed pitching. Oh, to recover even that flawed sparkle. His splits are no longer radical, but an effort to cut down on strikeouts has turned him into a slap hitter. It hardly takes any thump to match Wheeler's seven dingers in the past two years at Colorado Springs. It could work in center field, but Wheeler isn't considered anything more than a weak-armed left fielder. As such, unless he finds the power stroke again, a major-league career is unlikely.

PITCHERS

Brett Anderson

Born: 2/1/1988 Age: 26
Bats: L Throws: L Height: 6' 4" Weight: 235
Breakout: 17% Improve: 59% Collapse: 13%
Attrition: 17% MLB: 96%

Comparables:
Ricky Nolasco, Paul Maholm, Jaime Garcia

YEAR	TEAM	LVL	AGE	W	L	SV	G	GS	IP	H	HR	BB	SO	BB9	SO9	GB%	BABIP	WHIP	ERA	FIP	FRA	WARP
2011	OAK	MLB	23	3	6	0	13	13	83^1	86	8	25	61	2.7	6.6	59%	.307	1.33	4.00	4.00	5.15	0.1
2012	SAC	AAA	24	1	1	0	5	5	23^1	27	4	5	18	1.9	6.9	51%	.324	1.37	4.24	5.12	4.64	0.3
2012	OAK	MLB	24	4	2	0	6	6	35	29	1	7	25	1.8	6.4	61%	.272	1.03	2.57	2.68	3.31	0.6
2013	OAK	MLB	25	1	4	3	16	5	44^2	51	5	21	46	4.2	9.3	62%	.359	1.61	6.04	3.88	4.27	0.4
2014	COL	MLB	26	3	2	1	17	8	54^1	55	5	14	43	2.3	7.1	54%	.319	1.27	4.06	3.69	4.41	0.6

Anderson was slated to start Oakland's April 29th matchup with the Angels, but he was scratched due to a sprained ankle suffered 10 days prior. He was eventually called upon when the game went deep into the night and wound up throwing 79 pitches over five-plus frames in the 19-inning marathon. In another context, this would have been heroic, Willis Reedian stuff. This was April, though, so in retrospect the entire adventure seems reckless. Anderson's foundation was visibly compromised by the hobbled ankle on his landing leg and he exacerbated the injury so severely that he was sidelined for the next four months. Oakland picked up his $8 million option before trading him to Colorado for Drew Pomeranz and Chris Jensen; considering he has thrown just 163 innings total over the past three seasons, the tandem transactions give you a good sense of how tantalizing his stuff remains.

Tyler Anderson

Born: 12/30/1989 Age: 24
Bats: L Throws: L Height: 6' 4" Weight: 215
Breakout: 59% Improve: 64% Collapse: 10%
Attrition: 81% MLB: 20%

Comparables:
Alan Johnson, Mike Ekstrom, Chris Narveson

YEAR	TEAM	LVL	AGE	W	L	SV	G	GS	IP	H	HR	BB	SO	BB9	SO9	GB%	BABIP	WHIP	ERA	FIP	FRA	WARP
2012	ASH	A	22	12	3	0	20	20	120¹	102	5	28	81	2.1	6.1	54%	.270	1.08	2.47	3.55	4.63	1.9
2013	TRI	A-	23	1	1	0	3	3	15	9	0	3	13	1.8	7.8	66%	.205	0.80	0.60	2.18	3.30	0.3
2013	MOD	A+	23	3	2	0	13	13	74²	62	10	24	63	2.9	7.6	47%	.250	1.15	3.25	4.87	5.07	0.5
2014	COL	MLB	24	5	5	0	14	14	79²	88	11	32	42	3.6	4.8	48%	.304	1.51	5.32	5.30	5.78	-0.4

Anderson missed a significant portion of 2013 with a nagging shoulder issue, but when he was on the field he handled the leap to High-A Modesto well. Anderson has a reputation for being a finesse pitcher with trouble missing bats, a profile that often expires in the hitter-friendly California League. The 6-foot-4 right-hander held his own, though, as he used his downward plane to get groundballs and keep his home run rate at non-catastrophic levels. Anderson's upside is limited by a fastball that spends more time in the 80s than the 90s, but he owns a plus changeup and missed significantly more bats in 2013. He profiles as a bottom-of-the-rotation starter, but with enough control to eat some innings.

Matt Belisle

Born: 6/6/1980 Age: 34
Bats: R Throws: R Height: 6' 4" Weight: 225
Breakout: 24% Improve: 45% Collapse: 40%
Attrition: 11% MLB: 86%

Comparables:
Mike Adams, Steve Karsay, LaTroy Hawkins

YEAR	TEAM	LVL	AGE	W	L	SV	G	GS	IP	H	HR	BB	SO	BB9	SO9	GB%	BABIP	WHIP	ERA	FIP	FRA	WARP
2011	COL	MLB	31	10	4	0	74	0	72	77	5	14	58	1.8	7.2	54%	.335	1.26	3.25	3.04	4.24	0.7
2012	COL	MLB	32	3	8	3	80	0	80	91	5	18	69	2.0	7.8	51%	.341	1.36	3.71	3.01	3.83	1.4
2013	COL	MLB	33	5	7	0	72	0	73	76	6	15	62	1.8	7.6	50%	.321	1.25	4.32	3.01	3.83	1.1
2014	COL	MLB	34	3	1	2	66	0	69²	67	6	14	59	1.8	7.6	49%	.315	1.16	3.43	3.29	3.73	1.1

Quietly, Belisle has turned into one of the most dependable relievers in the league. Last year marked his fourth consecutive season with at least 70 appearances, at least 70 innings pitched, at least a 100 ERA+ and at least a 100 FRA+. Only Nationals reliever Tyler Clippard can claim the same. So why has Belisle's excellence been so quiet? Blame his modest arsenal—his fastball averages 90.6 mph and neither his slider or curveball stand out among relievers. Blame Coors Field for elevating his ERA in an era when multiple relievers in pitchers parks (see Atlanta) post marks under 2.00. Control relievers who toil in launching pads rarely get the spotlight, but Belisle deserves it.

Rafael Betancourt

Born: 4/29/1975 Age: 39
Bats: R Throws: R Height: 6' 2" Weight: 220
Breakout: 20% Improve: 41% Collapse: 33%
Attrition: 14% MLB: 75%

Comparables:
Trevor Hoffman, Billy Wagner, Tom Gordon

YEAR	TEAM	LVL	AGE	W	L	SV	G	GS	IP	H	HR	BB	SO	BB9	SO9	GB%	BABIP	WHIP	ERA	FIP	FRA	WARP
2011	COL	MLB	36	2	0	8	68	0	62¹	46	7	8	73	1.2	10.5	32%	.264	0.87	2.89	2.50	3.33	1.1
2012	COL	MLB	37	1	4	31	60	0	57²	53	6	12	57	1.9	8.9	36%	.292	1.13	2.81	3.14	3.33	1.3
2013	COL	MLB	38	2	5	16	32	0	28²	26	2	11	27	3.5	8.5	39%	.289	1.29	4.08	3.19	3.78	0.5
2014	COL	MLB	39	2	1	23	44	0	39²	32	4	9	44	2.0	10.0	34%	.298	1.04	2.65	2.93	2.88	1.0

The Rockies declined Betancourt's $4.25 million option after it became clear he was unlikely to pitch in 2014. Betancourt hoped to avoid Tommy John surgery with a rest-and-recovery program, but he has succumbed to the surgery and will have to place his hopes in 2015. The question is whether, at 39 and 40, he'll have the energy to rehab for a major-league job, or if this is the end for the one of the era's steadiest strike machines. Few ever made throwing fastballs on the outside corner look so easy.

Chad Bettis

Born: 4/26/1989 Age: 25
Bats: R Throws: R Height: 6' 1" Weight: 200
Breakout: 32% Improve: 60% Collapse: 18%
Attrition: 46% MLB: 77%

Comparables:
Christian Friedrich, Juan Nicasio, John Ely

YEAR	TEAM	LVL	AGE	W	L	SV	G	GS	IP	H	HR	BB	SO	BB9	SO9	GB%	BABIP	WHIP	ERA	FIP	FRA	WARP
2011	MOD	A+	22	12	5	0	27	27	169²	142	10	45	184	2.4	9.8	48%	.278	1.10	3.34	3.49	3.71	3.2
2013	TUL	AA	24	3	4	0	12	12	63	60	9	13	68	1.9	9.7	48%	.315	1.16	3.71	3.52	4.26	0.7
2013	COL	MLB	24	1	3	0	16	8	44²	55	6	20	30	4.0	6.0	47%	.329	1.68	5.64	4.90	5.04	0.4
2014	COL	MLB	25	5	5	0	15	15	77	78	9	27	60	3.2	7.1	47%	.310	1.37	4.57	4.31	4.97	0.3

Bettis missed all of 2012 with a rotator cuff injury, but he showed enough in his first 12 starts at Double-A Tulsa—mostly a magnificent 5.2 K/BB ratio—to make the jump straight to the majors for the season's final two months. Bettis had a couple of blowups—understandable for a rookie in Colorado—along with a couple of sharp outings against quality teams. He was mostly successful out of the bullpen besides one disastrous five-run, one-out appearance against Arizona in September. Bettis closed in college and could see a future home there in the majors. Roster makeup and spring training performances will determine his 2014 role.

Rex Brothers

Born: 12/18/1987 Age: 26
Bats: L Throws: L Height: 6' 0" Weight: 210
Breakout: 36% Improve: 61% Collapse: 21%
Attrition: 12% MLB: 83%

Comparables:
Manny Delcarmen, David Robertson, Clay Zavada

YEAR	TEAM	LVL	AGE	W	L	SV	G	GS	IP	H	HR	BB	SO	BB9	SO9	GB%	BABIP	WHIP	ERA	FIP	FRA	WARP
2011	CSP	AAA	23	3	2	0	25	0	28	29	2	15	45	4.8	14.5	57%	.400	1.57	2.89	3.10	3.38	0.9
2011	COL	MLB	23	1	2	1	48	0	40²	33	4	20	59	4.4	13.1	46%	.326	1.30	2.88	2.85	2.91	0.7
2012	COL	MLB	24	8	2	0	75	0	67²	63	5	37	83	4.9	11.0	48%	.347	1.48	3.86	3.33	3.66	1.3
2013	COL	MLB	25	2	1	19	72	0	67¹	51	5	36	76	4.8	10.2	50%	.280	1.29	1.74	3.33	3.61	1.0
2014	COL	MLB	26	4	2	5	66	0	63	48	5	30	77	4.3	11.0	49%	.307	1.24	3.24	3.24	3.52	1.2

Brothers didn't allow his second run of the season until June 28th, his 37th appearance. Over those first 36 appearances, he allowed 38 baserunners—22 hits and 16 walks—but just four extra-base hits, all doubles. His control is as shaky as a Paul Greengrass movie, but the fastball-slider combination is truly nasty. Hitters fouled off every other Brothers fastball they swung at last year, and flat-out missed half his sliders. The next step is proving he can consistently throw both pitches for strikes—they've been saying that since he was drafted—but Brothers is already good enough to be closer of the present.

Eddie Butler

Born: 3/13/1991 Age: 23
Bats: B Throws: R Height: 6' 2" Weight: 180
Breakout: 54% Improve: 71% Collapse: 16%
Attrition: 46% MLB: 31%

Comparables:
Travis Wood, Jarrod Parker, Kyle Gibson

YEAR	TEAM	LVL	AGE	W	L	SV	G	GS	IP	H	HR	BB	SO	BB9	SO9	GB%	BABIP	WHIP	ERA	FIP	FRA	WARP
2013	ASH	A	22	5	1	0	9	9	54¹	25	2	25	51	4.1	8.4	76%	.172	0.92	1.66	3.63	5.30	0.3
2013	MOD	A+	22	3	4	0	13	13	67²	58	7	21	67	2.8	8.9	49%	.280	1.17	2.39	4.16	4.67	0.9
2013	TUL	AA	22	1	0	0	6	6	27²	13	0	6	25	2.0	8.1	58%	.188	0.69	0.65	2.01	2.44	0.9
2014	COL	MLB	23	7	7	0	21	21	111²	112	13	49	75	4.0	6.1	55%	.298	1.44	4.72	4.82	5.13	0.2

Butler did wonders for his stock in 2013 as he tore through three leagues in his second professional season. Sampling Low-A, High-A and Double-A, Butler never posted an ERA above 2.50, struck out nearly a batter per inning at each level, and continued to roll up groundballs. His fastball is one of the best pitches in the Rockies' system, touching 99, and scouts suggest a future as a no. 2 starter. His curveball and changeup—the least of his three secondary pitches—will be key to his development, and both periodically looked like major-league offerings in 2013.

Jhoulys Chacin

Born: 1/7/1988 Age: 26
Bats: R Throws: R Height: 6' 3" Weight: 225
Breakout: 30% Improve: 66% Collapse: 14%
Attrition: 12% MLB: 95%

Comparables:
Jon Lester, David Price, Anibal Sanchez

YEAR	TEAM	LVL	AGE	W	L	SV	G	GS	IP	H	HR	BB	SO	BB9	SO9	GB%	BABIP	WHIP	ERA	FIP	FRA	WARP
2011	COL	MLB	23	11	14	0	31	31	194	168	20	87	150	4.0	7.0	55%	.264	1.31	3.62	4.20	5.01	1.3
2012	CSP	AAA	24	1	1	0	2	2	13²	10	1	5	5	3.3	3.3	62%	.220	1.10	2.63	4.98	6.96	0.0
2012	COL	MLB	24	3	5	0	14	14	69	80	10	32	45	4.2	5.9	39%	.324	1.62	4.43	5.19	5.47	0.6
2013	COL	MLB	25	14	10	0	31	31	197¹	188	11	61	126	2.8	5.7	47%	.296	1.26	3.47	3.44	3.95	3.0
2014	COL	MLB	26	10	7	0	26	26	150	133	13	58	117	3.5	7.0	52%	.288	1.27	3.84	4.02	4.18	1.9

Chacin's 3.47 ERA in 2013 has been bested just once in Rockies history by a pitcher making at least 20 starts. Ubaldo Jimenez, who posted a 3.47 ERA of his own in 2009, managed a 2.88 mark in 2010. Since Jimenez's exit in 2011, the Rockies have been desperately searching for any starter who could handle Coors Field with that kind of deftness. Chacin lacks Jimenez's flash, as he lives on the groundball, not the strikeout. (No active pitcher has allowed a lower career BABIP on grounders. No active pitcher is really even close.) He improved throughout the season in large part because he bought into his sinker, a pitch he used more than ever as he allowed only nine home runs over his final 20 starts. Chacin helped prove pitching success is still possible at Coors Field, surely a reassuring development following the debacle of 2012.

Tyler Chatwood

Born: 12/16/1989 Age: 24
Bats: R Throws: R Height: 6' 0" Weight: 185
Breakout: 26% Improve: 59% Collapse: 30%
Attrition: 40% MLB: 85%

Comparables:
John Lannan, Mike Pelfrey, Alex White

YEAR	TEAM	LVL	AGE	W	L	SV	G	GS	IP	H	HR	BB	SO	BB9	SO9	GB%	BABIP	WHIP	ERA	FIP	FRA	WARP
2011	SLC	AAA	21	1	2	0	4	4	16	21	2	11	11	6.2	6.2	47%	.358	2.00	5.06	6.47	6.06	0.2
2011	ANA	MLB	21	6	11	0	27	25	142	166	14	71	74	4.5	4.7	48%	.325	1.67	4.75	4.93	5.65	-0.9
2012	TUL	AA	22	1	1	0	4	4	24	17	2	7	22	2.6	8.2	67%	.242	1.00	3.00	3.41	4.20	0.3
2012	CSP	AAA	22	0	2	0	9	9	37¹	52	2	19	31	4.6	7.5	58%	.400	1.90	5.79	4.39	4.71	0.9
2012	COL	MLB	22	5	6	1	19	12	64²	74	9	33	41	4.6	5.7	56%	.305	1.65	5.43	5.21	5.78	0.0
2013	CSP	AAA	23	2	1	0	6	6	34	37	0	7	33	1.9	8.7	65%	.370	1.29	2.91	2.33	3.29	1.2
2013	COL	MLB	23	8	5	0	20	20	111¹	118	5	41	66	3.3	5.3	59%	.317	1.43	3.15	3.63	4.11	1.8
2014	COL	MLB	24	7	8	0	22	22	116²	126	12	53	73	4.1	5.7	52%	.318	1.53	5.06	4.78	5.50	-0.2

Chatwood was basically an afterthought heading into 2013 after a pair of brutal seasons to open his major-league career. After six brilliant Triple-A starts, he got a second crack at a Rockies rotation spot and seized it. He posted just the sixth season in Rockies history with a sub-3.50 ERA in at least 20 starts. Behind a powerful sinker and improved control, he allowed just five home runs. The resulting 0.4 HR/9 was the lowest mark in franchise history. The biggest problem facing the club of late has been a dearth of pitchers able to keep the ball in the park, and Chatwood's newfound ability to do so makes him a suddenly fascinating pitcher. Can he keep it up? His sky-high groundball rate may shout "Yes, Yes, Yes," but his unsustainably low rate of home runs per fly ball whispers "no, no, no."

Manuel Corpas

Born: 12/3/1982 Age: 31
Bats: R Throws: R Height: 6' 3" Weight: 210
Breakout: 33% Improve: 47% Collapse: 34%
Attrition: 31% MLB: 47%

Comparables:
Jack Cressend, Chris Ray, Julio Mateo

YEAR	TEAM	LVL	AGE	W	L	SV	G	GS	IP	H	HR	BB	SO	BB9	SO9	GB%	BABIP	WHIP	ERA	FIP	FRA	WARP
2012	IOW	AAA	29	0	2	0	19	0	33²	30	4	9	19	2.4	5.1	48%	.241	1.16	4.01	5.24	6.53	-0.3
2012	CHN	MLB	29	0	2	0	48	0	46²	50	7	16	28	3.1	5.4	46%	.281	1.41	5.01	5.24	5.09	-0.1
2013	CSP	AAA	30	3	3	1	21	0	41	45	5	15	35	3.3	7.7	49%	.328	1.46	5.49	4.62	5.50	0.4
2013	COL	MLB	30	1	2	0	31	0	41²	40	5	16	30	3.5	6.5	45%	.282	1.34	4.54	4.36	5.12	-0.1
2014	COL	MLB	31	3	1	0	58	0	74²	76	9	23	52	2.8	6.3	48%	.303	1.33	4.46	4.45	4.84	0.2

After a detour to Chicago's north side, Corpas returned to Colorado for another replacement-level run in the Rockies' bullpen. He was worse than the league average in all three components of FIP. Corpas manages a healthy number of groundballs with his sinker, so he made sense as a fallback option in Colorado's thin air. He didn't hold his spot on the 40-man roster, though, so he'll have to spend another spring training caring intensely about his performance.

Jorge De La Rosa

Born: 4/5/1981 Age: 33
Bats: L Throws: L Height: 6' 1" Weight: 220
Breakout: 14% Improve: 50% Collapse: 24%
Attrition: 19% MLB: 84%

Comparables:
Gil Meche, Vicente Padilla, Wandy Rodriguez

YEAR	TEAM	LVL	AGE	W	L	SV	G	GS	IP	H	HR	BB	SO	BB9	SO9	GB%	BABIP	WHIP	ERA	FIP	FRA	WARP
2011	COL	MLB	30	5	2	0	10	10	59	48	4	22	52	3.4	7.9	46%	.263	1.19	3.51	3.33	4.07	0.7
2012	COL	MLB	31	0	2	0	3	3	10²	17	5	2	6	1.7	5.1	33%	.324	1.78	9.28	8.67	8.14	-0.3
2013	COL	MLB	32	16	6	0	30	30	167²	170	11	62	112	3.3	6.0	48%	.313	1.38	3.49	3.74	4.36	1.9
2014	COL	MLB	33	8	7	0	23	23	121²	116	13	46	103	3.4	7.7	47%	.308	1.33	4.29	4.14	4.66	0.9

De La Rosa made just 13 starts between 2011 and 2012 due to Tommy John surgery, and he looked awful in his three 2012 appearances. Naturally, then, he rattled off one of the best seasons in Rockies history in 2013. De La Rosa made 30 starts with an ERA under 3.50, making him just the third pitcher to do so as a Rockie. Nothing about the peripherals suggests dramatic improvement, and he lost velocity, but Nolan Arenado and Troy Tulowitzki can do wonders for a left-handed groundball pitcher. De La Rosa picked up a $13 million player option last year, which gave the Rockies a $13 million club option for 2014—a no-brainer after his resurgent campaign.

Jeff Francis

Born: 1/8/1981 Age: 33
Bats: L Throws: L Height: 6' 5" Weight: 205
Breakout: 22% Improve: 52% Collapse: 25%
Attrition: 18% MLB: 70%

Comparables:
Claudio Vargas, Brian Lawrence, Dave Bush

YEAR	TEAM	LVL	AGE	W	L	SV	G	GS	IP	H	HR	BB	SO	BB9	SO9	GB%	BABIP	WHIP	ERA	FIP	FRA	WARP
2011	KCA	MLB	30	6	16	0	31	31	183	224	19	39	91	1.9	4.5	49%	.315	1.44	4.82	4.14	4.93	1.3
2012	LOU	AAA	31	3	6	0	12	12	77¹	84	6	18	65	2.1	7.6	53%	.345	1.32	3.72	3.22	4.78	0.4
2012	COL	MLB	31	6	7	0	24	24	113	145	15	22	76	1.8	6.1	50%	.353	1.48	5.58	4.31	4.78	1.6
2013	CSP	AAA	32	2	2	0	11	6	37¹	42	1	9	33	2.2	8.0	58%	.342	1.37	4.34	3.03	3.85	0.9
2013	COL	MLB	32	3	5	0	23	12	70¹	89	12	24	63	3.1	8.1	46%	.355	1.61	6.27	4.51	4.80	0.7
2014	COL	MLB	33	7	7	0	22	22	110²	126	13	25	73	2.0	5.9	48%	.326	1.37	4.73	4.19	5.14	0.3

Look, somebody has to pitch in Colorado, so why shouldn't it be Francis? Last year was the soft-tossing lefty's eighth pitching a mile high, and he was crushed once again, serving up a .306/.356/.512 line to 324 opposing hitters. The most similar hitters to that line are Adrian Beltre and Matt Carpenter—a pair of midballot MVP candidates. At least Francis ate innings, and at 33, if there are innings to eat again, one imagines he'll have the appetite.

Christian Friedrich

Born: 7/8/1987 Age: 26
Bats: R Throws: L Height: 6' 4" Weight: 215
Breakout: 37% Improve: 56% Collapse: 32%
Attrition: 49% MLB: 72%

Comparables:
John Ely, Jae Kuk Ryu, Charlie Furbush

YEAR	TEAM	LVL	AGE	W	L	SV	G	GS	IP	H	HR	BB	SO	BB9	SO9	GB%	BABIP	WHIP	ERA	FIP	FRA	WARP
2011	TUL	AA	23	6	10	0	25	25	133¹	156	20	43	103	2.9	7.0	45%	.298	1.49	4.99	4.82	5.72	1.1
2012	CSP	AAA	24	2	1	0	5	5	30	23	1	4	27	1.2	8.1	50%	.272	0.90	3.00	2.80	3.61	0.9
2012	COL	MLB	24	5	8	0	16	16	84²	102	14	30	74	3.2	7.9	44%	.343	1.56	6.17	4.67	5.44	0.7
2013	CSP	AAA	25	0	1	0	4	4	14²	13	1	8	8	4.9	4.9	54%	.244	1.43	4.30	5.00	6.33	0.1
2014	COL	MLB	26	2	2	0	7	7	36¹	38	5	14	29	3.4	7.1	45%	.315	1.42	4.77	4.67	5.19	0.1

Last year was a lost season for Friedrich. The 2008 first-rounder made just four starts for Triple-A Colorado Springs before a stress fracture in his back ended his campaign. Friedrich had a few promising starts and had decent peripherals in 2012, when he was part of Colorado's unorthodox and short-lived four-starter rotation plan, but his surface results were too poor to maintain a spot as pitchers like Jorge De La Rosa and Juan Nicasio returned from injury.

Jonathan Gray

Born: 11/5/1991 Age: 22
Bats: R Throws: R Height: 6' 4" Weight: 255
Breakout: 42% Improve: 61% Collapse: 16%
Attrition: 30% MLB: 37%

Comparables:
Jake McGee, Danny Duffy, Christian Friedrich

YEAR	TEAM	LVL	AGE	W	L	SV	G	GS	IP	H	HR	BB	SO	BB9	SO9	GB%	BABIP	WHIP	ERA	FIP	FRA	WARP
2013	MOD	A+	21	4	0	0	5	5	24	10	0	6	36	2.2	13.5	50%	.227	0.67	0.75	1.52	2.42	0.9
2014	COL	MLB	22	2	2	0	8	8	36²	35	4	16	35	3.9	8.4	44%	.316	1.38	4.30	4.11	4.67	0.3

Patience, they say, is a virtue. Gray took three cracks at the MLB Draft, and by 2013 he had worked his way up from a 13th-rounder (in 2010) to a 10th-rounder (in 2011) to the third-overall pick out of the University of Oklahoma. After a quick warm-up in Rookie ball, Gray brought the pain to the High-A California League. As a college pick, he is expected to move quickly through the minors. His fastball runs in the high 90s and he already has a nasty power slider, an arsenal that will only quicken his ascendance. Gray could reach Double-A to begin the season, which means a 2014 debut isn't out of the question.

LaTroy Hawkins

Born: 12/21/1972 Age: 41
Bats: R Throws: R Height: 6' 5" Weight: 220
Breakout: 17% Improve: 56% Collapse: 27%
Attrition: 19% MLB: 54%

Comparables:
Brian Shouse, Mike Timlin, Todd Jones

YEAR	TEAM	LVL	AGE	W	L	SV	G	GS	IP	H	HR	BB	SO	BB9	SO9	GB%	BABIP	WHIP	ERA	FIP	FRA	WARP
2011	MIL	MLB	38	3	1	0	52	0	48¹	50	1	10	28	1.9	5.2	63%	.297	1.24	2.42	2.73	3.93	0.5
2012	ANA	MLB	39	2	3	1	48	0	42	45	5	13	23	2.8	4.9	58%	.292	1.38	3.64	4.43	5.33	-0.2
2013	NYN	MLB	40	3	2	13	72	0	70²	71	6	10	55	1.3	7.0	51%	.304	1.15	2.93	3.03	3.24	0.9
2014	COL	MLB	41	3	1	4	62	0	58¹	61	6	14	39	2.2	6.0	52%	.308	1.29	4.07	3.98	4.43	0.5

And sometimes, pitchers just happen to stay healthy. At 40 years old, Hawkins had his best year since 2004, when he closed games for the Cubs. It was also his first year since 2008 that he didn't visit the DL. Somehow, despite age and all those injuries, Hawkins has lost only minimal velocity, but that says absolutely nothing about his future effectiveness, which seems entirely predicated on his health. And since Hawkins himself doesn't know what exotic malady might be next over the horizon, the paycheck he earns next year won't be much larger than the one before. That check will come from the Rockies, the first of Hawkins' nine previous employers to double dip.

Pedro Hernandez

Born: 4/12/1989 Age: 25
Bats: L Throws: L Height: 5' 10" Weight: 210
Breakout: 45% Improve: 67% Collapse: 27%
Attrition: 63% MLB: 42%

Comparables:
James Russell, Barry Enright, Carlos Monasterios

YEAR	TEAM	LVL	AGE	W	L	SV	G	GS	IP	H	HR	BB	SO	BB9	SO9	GB%	BABIP	WHIP	ERA	FIP	FRA	WARP
2011	LEL	A+	22	5	0	0	15	6	56²	52	3	6	44	1.0	7.0	36%	.455	1.02	2.70	3.40	0.04	0.3
2011	SAN	AA	22	3	2	0	9	8	41¹	39	4	10	43	2.2	9.4	44%	.204	1.19	3.48	3.28	4.45	0.4
2011	TUC	AAA	22	2	1	0	4	4	18	28	3	6	7	3.0	3.5	40%	.385	1.89	6.00	6.17	6.44	0.2
2012	BIR	AA	23	7	2	0	12	12	68²	68	6	18	37	2.4	4.8	45%	.278	1.25	2.75	3.99	4.18	0.5
2012	CHR	AAA	23	1	0	0	3	2	17	18	1	3	17	1.6	9.0	33%	.340	1.24	3.71	2.45	4.05	0.3
2012	ROC	AAA	23	0	2	0	4	4	17¹	25	1	1	11	0.5	5.7	40%	.387	1.50	5.19	2.81	3.84	0.2
2012	CHA	MLB	23	0	1	0	1	1	4	12	3	1	2	2.2	4.5	41%	.474	3.25	18.00	12.55	13.09	-0.3
2013	NBR	AA	24	1	0	0	2	2	11	9	0	3	6	2.5	4.9	49%	.243	1.09	0.82	3.05	3.52	0.2
2013	ROC	AAA	24	2	2	0	8	7	46	53	8	12	33	2.3	6.5	47%	.306	1.41	4.50	4.88	5.09	-0.1
2013	MIN	MLB	24	3	3	0	14	12	56²	80	10	23	29	3.7	4.6	41%	.348	1.82	6.83	5.56	6.41	-0.6
2014	COL	MLB	25	5	7	0	25	18	107	131	17	31	58	2.6	4.8	44%	.324	1.51	5.64	5.18	6.13	-0.9

Last year we described Hernandez as a "short command lefty … who could make it in short relief." After spending a full year in the Minnesota bullpen, we're happy to report that Hernandez remains both short and left-handed. He pitched somewhat better than his execrable 6.83 ERA, as evidenced by his well-nigh-but-not-quite-execrable 5.56 FIP. Hernandez has traditionally dominated same-side batters, but his numbers against righties have been so bad that the only way he'd survive as a LOOGY would be to fake a seizure whenever a pinch-hitter is announced. Released at season's end, Hernandez signed a minor league deal with the Rockies, where his extreme home run tendencies are likely to be a particularly bad fit.

Boone Logan

Born: 8/13/1984 Age: 29
Bats: R Throws: L Height: 6' 5" Weight: 215
Breakout: 35% Improve: 55% Collapse: 28%
Attrition: 17% MLB: 85%

Comparables:
Sergio Santos, Neal Cotts, Scott Dohmann

YEAR	TEAM	LVL	AGE	W	L	SV	G	GS	IP	H	HR	BB	SO	BB9	SO9	GB%	BABIP	WHIP	ERA	FIP	FRA	WARP
2011	NYA	MLB	26	5	3	0	64	0	41²	43	4	13	46	2.8	9.9	45%	.331	1.34	3.46	3.33	3.25	0.7
2012	NYA	MLB	27	7	2	1	80	0	55¹	48	6	28	68	4.6	11.1	40%	.311	1.37	3.74	3.62	3.52	0.8
2013	NYA	MLB	28	5	2	0	61	0	39	33	7	13	50	3.0	11.5	51%	.292	1.18	3.23	3.84	5.12	-0.3
2014	COL	MLB	29	3	1	1	51	0	37²	33	4	14	39	3.5	9.4	47%	.312	1.27	3.68	3.78	4.00	0.5

The Yankees don't have a strong recent record when it comes to developing pitchers, but they do hold the distinction of being the team that turned Logan into a reliable reliever after both the White Sox and Braves failed to do so. The southpaw experienced some elbow soreness in spring training—perhaps a result of his extreme slider usage and league-leading 80 appearances in 2012—and later developed a bone spur that cost him most of September and led to an offseason surgical cleanup. But between elbow ailments, Logan posted a career-high strikeout rate despite easing up on the breaking ball, with only an uncharacteristically high HR/FB rate spoiling what might otherwise have been his best year yet. Among pitchers who faced at least 75 lefties, Logan's 40 percent strikeout rate versus southpaws ranked third beyond Clayton Kershaw's and Koji Uehara's, which explains how he became Joe Girardi's highest-leverage reliever not named Rivera or Robertson. Nothing can explain the Rockies giving him a three-year deal for $16.5 million, though.

Wilton Lopez

Born: 7/19/1983 Age: 30
Bats: R Throws: R Height: 6' 0'' Weight: 205
Breakout: 28% Improve: 63% Collapse: 25%
Attrition: 19% MLB: 69%

Comparables:
Matt Belisle, Kameron Loe, Phil Coke

YEAR	TEAM	LVL	AGE	W	L	SV	G	GS	IP	H	HR	BB	SO	BB9	SO9	GB%	BABIP	WHIP	ERA	FIP	FRA	WARP
2011	HOU	MLB	27	2	6	0	73	0	71	72	6	18	56	2.3	7.1	57%	.311	1.27	2.79	3.40	3.71	0.7
2012	HOU	MLB	28	6	3	10	64	0	66¹	61	4	8	54	1.1	7.3	56%	.298	1.04	2.17	2.74	3.80	0.7
2013	COL	MLB	29	3	4	0	75	0	75¹	88	6	18	48	2.2	5.7	50%	.332	1.41	4.06	3.54	4.60	0.5
2014	COL	MLB	30	3	1	3	66	0	66²	72	7	13	46	1.7	6.1	54%	.322	1.27	4.14	3.82	4.50	0.5

Lopez saw his ERA inflate by nearly two runs in 2013 after the Astros shipped him up to Colorado, so things went just about as expected. His 4.06 ERA was still better than the league average after adjusting for altitude, and his ever-excellent control gave him good-looking peripherals even with a decline in strikeout rate. Still, as Lopez learned, consistent contact is a bad formula in Colorado, and he'll likely need to get more out of his slider (just 10 percent whiffs in 2013) if he is to turn back into the shutdown reliever he was for two years in Houston.

Jordan Lyles

Born: 10/19/1990 Age: 23
Bats: R Throws: R Height: 6' 4'' Weight: 215
Breakout: 40% Improve: 76% Collapse: 12%
Attrition: 33% MLB: 85%

Comparables:
Chris Volstad, Henderson Alvarez, John Danks

YEAR	TEAM	LVL	AGE	W	L	SV	G	GS	IP	H	HR	BB	SO	BB9	SO9	GB%	BABIP	WHIP	ERA	FIP	FRA	WARP
2011	OKL	AAA	20	3	3	0	12	10	62¹	64	4	17	42	2.5	6.1	36%	.326	1.30	3.61	4.33	5.52	0.1
2011	HOU	MLB	20	2	8	0	20	15	94	107	14	26	67	2.5	6.4	43%	.308	1.41	5.36	4.49	5.28	-0.1
2012	OKL	AAA	21	5	0	0	7	7	40²	41	2	8	33	1.8	7.3	60%	.339	1.20	3.54	3.71	5.02	0.4
2012	HOU	MLB	21	5	12	0	25	25	141¹	159	20	42	99	2.7	6.3	53%	.308	1.42	5.09	4.57	5.05	0.1
2013	OKL	AAA	22	2	2	0	6	5	23²	30	1	6	11	2.3	4.2	62%	.345	1.52	5.32	3.95	5.43	0.1
2013	HOU	MLB	22	7	9	1	27	25	141²	165	17	49	93	3.1	5.9	50%	.314	1.51	5.59	4.59	5.28	0.0
2014	COL	MLB	23	9	10	0	28	28	154¹	172	18	47	104	2.7	6.1	46%	.323	1.42	5.06	4.45	5.50	-0.3

When evaluating Lyles, the question is whether his age excuses his crummy performance. Despite not turning 23 until after the season ended, he's already got 65 big-league starts under his belt and his 2013 season was remarkably similar to his 2012. The problem is that they were similarly poor. Lyles was particularly lit up by same-side hitters, who feasted on his below-average slider. If you're looking for good news, Lyles' velocity has improved since his 2011 debut, pushing his average fastball up to 93 mph. Brought to Denver for Dexter Fowler, there's a chance he makes the hackneyed transition from thrower to pitcher under the Rockies' guidance. After all, he's only 23.

Tyler Matzek

Born: 10/19/1990 Age: 23
Bats: L Throws: L Height: 6' 3'' Weight: 210
Breakout: 67% Improve: 78% Collapse: 22%
Attrition: 61% MLB: 18%

Comparables:
Chris Archer, Cole Kimball, Jose Cisnero

YEAR	TEAM	LVL	AGE	W	L	SV	G	GS	IP	H	HR	BB	SO	BB9	SO9	GB%	BABIP	WHIP	ERA	FIP	FRA	WARP
2011	ASH	A	20	5	4	0	12	12	64	45	3	50	74	7.0	10.4	45%	.302	1.48	4.36	4.26	5.53	0.9
2011	MOD	A+	20	0	3	0	10	10	33	34	5	46	37	12.5	10.1	41%	.329	2.42	9.82	8.04	5.97	0.2
2012	MOD	A+	21	6	8	0	28	28	142¹	134	7	95	153	6.0	9.7	44%	.326	1.61	4.62	4.41	4.68	2.1
2013	TUL	AA	22	8	9	0	26	26	142¹	147	13	76	95	4.8	6.0	41%	.308	1.57	3.79	4.62	5.38	0.0
2014	COL	MLB	23	7	9	0	24	24	121	125	13	84	88	6.3	6.5	40%	.314	1.73	5.68	5.38	6.17	-1.0

After a pair of disastrous seasons in the low minors, Matzek finally found his way in the Texas League. He has always had plus stuff for a left-hander—a fastball capable of touching 95 and a curveball that has taken the jump to plus status. His wildness was the monster (yeah, that's a 12.5 BB/9 up there in 2011), and if he didn't vanquish it last year he at least stunned it. His walk rate was more than a point better than his career best; from July onward it was even lower, at 4.3, and in his final five starts it was 3.8. He has the stuff to be a second starter when he shows command—an excessive request, perhaps, but an arm like Matzek's is worth the patience.

Franklin Morales

Born: 1/24/1986 Age: 28
Bats: L Throws: L Height: 6' 1'' Weight: 210
Breakout: 38% Improve: 55% Collapse: 30%
Attrition: 22% MLB: 71%

Comparables:
Wesley Wright, David Aardsma, Santiago Casilla

YEAR	TEAM	LVL	AGE	W	L	SV	G	GS	IP	H	HR	BB	SO	BB9	SO9	GB%	BABIP	WHIP	ERA	FIP	FRA	WARP
2011	BOS	MLB	25	1	1	0	36	0	32¹	30	4	11	31	3.1	8.6	31%	.302	1.27	3.62	3.96	4.67	0.3
2011	COL	MLB	25	0	1	0	14	0	14	10	2	8	11	5.1	7.1	33%	.211	1.29	3.86	4.99	6.06	-0.1
2012	BOS	MLB	26	3	4	1	37	9	76¹	64	11	30	76	3.5	9.0	40%	.262	1.23	3.77	4.34	4.82	0.8
2013	PAW	AAA	27	0	1	0	5	2	11¹	5	3	3	12	2.4	9.5	35%	.087	0.71	4.76	5.32	9.44	-0.1
2013	BOS	MLB	27	2	2	0	20	1	25¹	24	2	15	21	5.3	7.5	40%	.310	1.54	4.62	4.58	5.31	0.0
2014	COL	MLB	28	3	1	0	36	3	46²	41	6	21	43	4.1	8.4	42%	.293	1.34	4.20	4.55	4.56	0.4

Morales' career looked like it was revived when he succeeded as a reliever and then as a part-time starter for the Sox, but 2013 brought back memories of his Colorado disappointment. A bulging disc in his lower back was followed by a strained pectoral, costing him 93 regular season games. Once he returned, his ability to pitch to righties vanished. More should be expected given his stuff and non-Rockies past—though a December trade sent him back to the scene of his crimes.

Juan Nicasio
Born: 8/31/1986 Age: 27
Bats: R Throws: R Height: 6' 3" Weight: 230
Breakout: 44% Improve: 80% Collapse: 11%
Attrition: 27% MLB: 84%

Comparables:
Dillon Gee, Armando Galarraga, David Huff

YEAR	TEAM	LVL	AGE	W	L	SV	G	GS	IP	H	HR	BB	SO	BB9	SO9	GB%	BABIP	WHIP	ERA	FIP	FRA	WARP
2011	TUL	AA	24	5	1	0	9	9	56²	48	3	10	63	1.6	10.0	42%	.323	1.02	2.22	2.37	2.71	1.9
2011	COL	MLB	24	4	4	0	13	13	71²	73	8	18	58	2.3	7.3	46%	.312	1.27	4.14	3.62	4.17	1.0
2012	COL	MLB	25	2	3	0	11	11	58	72	7	22	54	3.4	8.4	40%	.386	1.62	5.28	4.03	4.94	0.7
2013	CSP	AAA	26	1	0	0	2	2	11	8	0	1	8	0.8	6.5	62%	.250	0.82	0.82	2.39	3.16	0.4
2013	COL	MLB	26	9	9	0	31	31	157²	168	17	64	119	3.7	6.8	44%	.309	1.47	5.14	4.23	4.81	1.0
2014	COL	MLB	27	8	7	0	23	23	128²	134	14	41	100	2.9	7.0	44%	.319	1.36	4.47	4.10	4.86	0.6

Thankfully, Nicasio was finally able to avoid a major injury in 2013, as he made 31 starts as part of a much-improved Rockies staff. The bullpen was partially responsible for his lofty ERA, as 13 of 23 runners Nicasio bequeathed to relievers scored, well above the league's 30 percent rate. Nicasio kept the ball on the ground, and his 4.23 FIP was better than the park-adjusted league average. There were questions about whether he was too fragile for anything but relief work, but 2013 firmly establishes him as a starter.

Roy Oswalt
Born: 8/29/1977 Age: 36
Bats: R Throws: R Height: 6' 0" Weight: 190
Breakout: 19% Improve: 51% Collapse: 21%
Attrition: 13% MLB: 84%

Comparables:
Freddy Garcia, Bartolo Colon, Bruce Chen

YEAR	TEAM	LVL	AGE	W	L	SV	G	GS	IP	H	HR	BB	SO	BB9	SO9	GB%	BABIP	WHIP	ERA	FIP	FRA	WARP
2011	LEH	AAA	33	0	0	0	2	2	10	8	1	4	8	3.6	7.2	68%	.368	1.20	2.70	4.14	4.57	0.0
2011	PHI	MLB	33	9	10	0	23	23	139	153	10	33	93	2.1	6.0	45%	.327	1.34	3.69	3.41	3.71	1.3
2012	ROU	AAA	34	1	1	0	3	3	12	15	1	3	10	2.2	7.5	49%	.368	1.50	5.25	3.83	5.26	0.1
2012	TEX	MLB	34	4	3	0	17	9	59	79	11	11	59	1.7	9.0	46%	.378	1.53	5.80	4.18	4.42	0.8
2013	TUL	AA	35	3	2	0	5	5	33¹	24	5	7	25	1.9	6.8	52%	.226	0.93	2.16	4.14	4.83	0.1
2013	COL	MLB	35	0	6	0	9	6	32¹	49	3	9	34	2.5	9.5	40%	.447	1.79	8.63	3.05	4.01	0.7
2014	COL	MLB	36	4	3	0	11	11	63²	66	7	16	48	2.2	6.8	49%	.318	1.29	4.26	3.98	4.63	0.4

"The Astros righthander is five years into his career," Buster Olney wrote in 2005, "he's 28 and he's talking about the possibility of walking away from baseball at age 33." Instead, Oswalt spent his age-35 season riding Double-A buses in yet another comeback attempt. He again posted strong peripherals—that's his lowest FIP since 2002—but they didn't matter a lick. Hitters managed at least a .435 slugging percentage on all five of his pitches, and that .447 BABIP is the highest by any pitcher (min. 150 batters faced) in history. He'll get another chance in 2014 to walk away.

Adam Ottavino
Born: 11/22/1985 Age: 28
Bats: B Throws: R Height: 6' 5" Weight: 230
Breakout: 37% Improve: 54% Collapse: 27%
Attrition: 41% MLB: 66%

Comparables:
Juan Gutierrez, Dustin Nippert, Joel Hanrahan

YEAR	TEAM	LVL	AGE	W	L	SV	G	GS	IP	H	HR	BB	SO	BB9	SO9	GB%	BABIP	WHIP	ERA	FIP	FRA	WARP
2011	MEM	AAA	25	7	8	0	26	25	141	154	14	71	120	4.5	7.7	47%	.324	1.60	4.85	5.07	5.05	0.7
2012	CSP	AAA	26	0	0	0	13	0	19²	22	2	7	25	3.2	11.4	44%	.364	1.47	3.20	3.51	3.39	0.7
2012	COL	MLB	26	5	1	0	53	0	79	76	9	34	81	3.9	9.2	49%	.317	1.39	4.56	3.90	4.55	0.9
2013	COL	MLB	27	1	3	0	51	0	78¹	73	5	31	78	3.6	9.0	48%	.319	1.33	2.64	3.12	3.84	1.1
2014	COL	MLB	28	3	2	1	33	5	71¹	69	8	29	63	3.6	8.0	46%	.314	1.37	4.43	4.22	4.81	0.3

There's a reason guys like Ottavino don't exist much these days: As soon as they show they're as good as Ottavino is, they get bumped into a non-Ottavino role. For the second year, the Rockies leaned on him as a multiple-inning reliever who didn't stink, and for the second year he thrived. He recorded more than three outs 29 times, fewer than only the Diamondbacks' Josh Collmenter and the Twins' Anthony Swarzak, each of whom was used far more often when the game was already settled. The Rockies finally caved in August and moved him into a traditional set-up role. He was more interesting before but he's more valuable now, and he'll continue to be a nice weapon in any role.

Rob Scahill
Born: 2/15/1987 Age: 27
Bats: L Throws: R Height: 6' 2" Weight: 220
Breakout: 55% Improve: 70% Collapse: 19%
Attrition: 62% MLB: 45%

Comparables:
Marco Estrada, Philip Humber, Eric Stults

YEAR	TEAM	LVL	AGE	W	L	SV	G	GS	IP	H	HR	BB	SO	BB9	SO9	GB%	BABIP	WHIP	ERA	FIP	FRA	WARP
2011	TUL	AA	24	12	11	0	27	26	160²	164	12	60	104	3.4	5.8	51%	.293	1.39	3.92	4.27	4.92	2.0
2012	CSP	AAA	25	9	11	0	29	29	152	168	11	74	159	4.4	9.4	53%	.359	1.59	5.68	4.11	5.02	2.8
2012	COL	MLB	25	0	0	0	6	0	8²	7	0	3	4	3.1	4.2	50%	.269	1.15	1.04	3.25	4.02	0.1
2013	CSP	AAA	26	5	1	1	23	0	46	53	6	11	45	2.2	8.8	58%	.353	1.39	4.50	4.09	5.20	0.5
2013	COL	MLB	26	1	0	0	23	0	33¹	40	5	9	20	2.4	5.4	49%	.324	1.47	5.13	4.94	5.65	-0.1
2014	COL	MLB	27	4	4	0	23	11	83	87	9	35	61	3.7	6.7	50%	.319	1.47	4.87	4.56	5.29	-0.0

There's a movie trope you've seen a thousand times, where a hero throws a haymaker at a robot/monster/alien/big guy and connects, right in the face; the robot/monster/alien/big guy barely feels it, and our hero, mugging, knows it's time to run. Rob Scahill, meet your metaphor. The righty showed excellent control out of the bullpen, and had no problem getting two quick strikes on opponents. Without a putaway breaking pitch, though, he was pasted for a .298/.344/.596 line on two strikes. Time to mug and run—or, more likely keep working on the changeup and curveball that you've toyed with to back up your middling slider.

LINEOUTS

HITTERS

PLAYER	TEAM	LVL	AGE	PA	R	2B	3B	HR	RBI	BB	SO	SB-CS	AVG/OBP/SLG	TAv	BABIP	BRR	FRAA	WARP
SS C. Adames	TUL	AA	21	446	45	19	2	3	36	34	78	13-7	.267/.331/.350	.246	.326	0.3	SS(96): 2.4, 2B(7): -0.3	1.3
CF T. Colvin	CSP	AAA	27	272	47	8	6	9	32	36	62	6-3	.275/.377/.480	.279	.340	0.2	CF(28): -0.5, RF(23): -2.5	0.8
	COL	MLB	27	78	8	0	0	3	10	3	27	0-0	.160/.192/.280	.170	.200	0.6	CF(16): 0.2, LF(4): 0.1	-0.5
RF K. Matthes	TUL	AA	26	282	31	24	2	9	32	20	66	11-3	.270/.335/.484	.276	.331	-2.6	RF(59): -1.2, LF(2): -0.0	0.6
	CSP	AAA	26	188	25	6	1	11	31	10	40	6-1	.297/.333/.531	.288	.328	1	RF(45): -5.6	0.6
C T. Murphy	ASH	A	22	341	55	26	2	19	74	37	87	4-5	.288/.385/.590	.324	.346	-3.2	C(69): -0.7	3.5
	TUL	AA	22	74	9	5	0	3	9	4	16	0-0	.290/.338/.493	.294	.340	-1.9	C(14): -0.1	0.4
1B X. Nady	OMA	AAA	34	290	44	12	0	11	43	27	51	1-0	.309/.381/.484	.313	.347	-0.8	1B(34): -1.2, LF(17): 0.2	2.0
	CSP	AAA	34	206	25	14	0	4	22	14	40	3-0	.278/.332/.417	.255	.331	0.6	LF(29): -2.0, 1B(3): 0.4	0.2
1B H. Riggins	MOD	A+	23	482	77	25	1	22	65	57	192	4-3	.247/.353/.472	.303	.400	4.9	1B(96): 2.7	3.6
C W. Rodriguez	TRI	A-	19	167	15	5	0	1	19	18	25	2-4	.270/.355/.326	.290	.311	-1.4	C(19): -0.3	0.7
C W. Swanner	MOD	A+	21	407	52	25	1	13	51	44	129	7-4	.239/.324/.425	.273	.330	-3.9	C(83): 0.1	1.8
CF M. White	ASH	A	19	269	25	16	1	3	21	20	79	11-8	.226/.288/.337	.216	.319	-3.4	CF(68): 4.1	-0.3
RF J. Yan	ASH	A	21	210	22	12	1	5	20	14	64	12-9	.206/.279/.360	.218	.283	-2.6	RF(53): -5.4	-1.3
	TRI	A-	21	133	11	3	3	2	15	4	49	6-2	.213/.241/.331	.234	.325	0.8	RF(28): 5.1	0.5

Christhian Adames is expected to grow into at least middling home run power, but 2013 was not the year. ⌀ Can you say Quad-A? **Tyler Colvin** looked like a major-leaguer in the Pacific Coast League, which is not a major league. ⌀ **Kent Matthes** finally stayed healthy (mostly—stress fracture, lower back, June) and he continued to show the power and outfield arm to play a major-league right field. ⌀ **Ryan McMahon** turned down USC for slot money early in the second round last year, and his performance at Rookie ball made it look like a win for Colorado. ⌀ In his second pro season, **Tom Murphy** showed the power the Rockies drafted him for. More importantly, he was significantly better at stifling the running game, his major issue in 2012. ⌀ **Xavier Nady** barely hit at Colorado Springs, but considering he has undergone two Tommy John surgeries, just taking the field is an accomplishment. ⌀ Former Madison Mallards great **Harold Riggins** hit for power in a tough pitcher's park, but a long swing and high leg kick contributed to a massive strikeout rate. ⌀ **Wilfredo Rodriguez** was again among the younger catchers at his level in 2013, so his improved plate discipline seems like a more significant takeaway than his drop in power production. ⌀ After allowing 120 successful stolen bases in 133 attempts at Asheville, **Will Swanner** nearly tripled his caught stealing rate at High-A. ⌀ **Max White**—the ballplayer, not the toothpaste category—needs time to grow into his power and refine his approach to use it. He wasn't ready for full-season pitching at 19. ⌀ **Julian Yan** dominated the Pioneer League despite an overly complex swing. Full-season pitchers dismantled it, and he struck out every third plate appearance.

PITCHERS

PLAYER	TEAM	LVL	AGE	W	L	SV	IP	H	HR	BB	SO	BB9	SO9	GB%	BABIP	WHIP	ERA	FIP	FRA	WARP
J. Aquino	ASH	A	20	0	9	0	64	66	4	21	57	3.0	8.0	49%	.333	1.36	4.78	3.68	5.29	0.5
	TRI	A-	20	0	1	0	23	21	1	5	16	2.0	6.3	55%	.286	1.13	3.13	3.27	4.21	0.1
C. Bergman	TUL	AA	25	8	7	0	171	162	25	23	111	1.2	5.8	50%	.269	1.08	3.37	4.15	4.91	0.6
G. Burke	LVG	AAA	30	2	2	5	31²	33	3	10	34	2.8	9.7	42%	.341	1.36	4.55	3.79	4.15	0.7
	NYN	MLB	30	0	3	0	31²	43	3	15	28	4.3	8.0	54%	.370	1.83	5.68	3.90	4.35	0.1
E. Cabrera	COL	MLB	24	0	2	0	5²	9	3	7	5	11.1	7.9	45%	.353	2.82	11.12	11.96	10.36	-0.1
A. Galarraga	LOU	AAA	31	6	6	0	84²	84	8	34	62	3.6	6.6	50%	.302	1.39	2.98	4.32	5.64	-0.3
	CSP	AAA	31	0	2	0	36¹	36	4	12	21	3.0	5.2	42%	.268	1.32	5.20	4.92	6.62	0.1
C. Martin	PME	AA	27	2	0	3	21	9	0	6	27	2.6	11.6	46%	.220	0.71	0.00	1.61	1.71	0.8
	PAW	AAA	27	3	3	2	51	51	3	10	47	1.8	8.3	52%	.324	1.20	3.18	2.95	3.53	0.8

Jayson Aquino tailed off hard to end his season at Asheville—his command dominated in short-season ball, but after a promotion he paid for his lack of top-end velocity. ⊘ Double-A was **Christian Bergman**'s first test in an age-appropriate league, and he passed thanks to elite control. ⊘ Don't mistake **Greg Burke** for a righty specialist: He yielded a higher OPS to righties than he did to lefties (an awful .858 vs. an awful .854). He's relatively new to the whole submarining thing, so even at age 31 the right organization (for the moment, that's the Rockies, who signed him to a minor-league deal) might see some potential. ⊘ Somebody needs to tell **Edwar Cabrera** that "chicks dig the long ball" applies only to the dudes hitting them, not the dudes serving them up. ⊘ Another bad year for **Armando Galarraga**, who continues to plug along as baseball's version of Baby Jessica. ⊘ Come out upon my seas / Curse missed opportunities / Is **Chris Martin** part of the cure? / Or is he part of the disease?

MANAGER: WALT WEISS

YEAR	TEAM	W-L	Pythag +/-	Avg PC	100+ P	120+ P	QS	BQS	REL	REL w Zero R	IBB	PH	PH Avg	PH HR	SB2	CS2	SB3	CS3	SAC Att	SAC %	POS SAC	Squeeze	Swing	In Play
2013	COL	74-88	0	90.2	22	0	65	0	502	366	52	257	.282	6	97	28	15	4	100	65.0%	34	2	301	91

Walt Weiss is the sixth manager in franchise history, and so far all their other managers have had notable careers. Each of the first five managed more than 1,200 games. Four of them won a Manager of the Year Award, and the other one—Buddy Bell—came in second place once (in 1997). They haven't all had successful careers. In fact, Jim Leyland is the only one with a career winning record, and Bell is the only manager since Connie Mack to end his career more than 200 games under .500. But apparently the Rockies have the habit of hiring managers that are respected enough to land elsewhere.

As for Weiss himself, the team considerably improved at double plays on his watch—both in terms of fielding them and avoiding hitting into them. It isn't just that the raw numbers moved in the right direction—from 132 to 111 GIDP on offense, and from 138 to 162 twin killings turned on defense. It's even better when put into context. For example, the Rockies' fielders pulled off those extra 24 double plays despite allowing nearly 100 fewer singles and nearly 40 fewer walks (and even fewer hit batsmen) than in 2012. Double plays are a function of opportunities, and they had fewer opportunities but still made more double plays. It's less extreme on the hitters' side, but a general tendency is still there. In 2012, if you add together Rockies singles, walks, HBP and times reached on error, they hit into a double play once for every 11.8 opportunities. In 2013, it was once every 13.8 opportunity.

Double plays are a weird stat. Some managers have their teams consistently post surprisingly great numbers (Casey Stengel, Gene Mauch, Roger Craig) than you'd expect on a regular basis, or worse numbers (Tom Kelly). Maybe Weiss fits into that first category.

Detroit Tigers

By Paul Sporer

The Tigers broke camp as American League favorites. *Baseball Prospectus'* playoff odds gave them baseball's best chance of winning their division. In a preseason poll of BP authors, no Junior Circuit team got more votes to win the World Series. Vegas gave Detroit four times the likelihood of winning it all as the Red Sox had. The club didn't bring a flawless 25 from camp, but the foibles were easily covered by the blunt force of their star power: Saddled with a poor defense? Fine, just strike everyone out. Run the bases like the infield is underwater? Just smash the ball out of the park and jog home. Bullpen's a mess? Let a staff of ace starters pitch into the 10th if necessary. Alas, the best-laid schemes of mice and men often go awry—at least, in small samples and short series.

So the Tigers walked off the field in 2013 like 29 other teams—bummed—and entered the winter looking at a group that suddenly seemed problematic. The issues boiled down to one word: inflexibility. On the field, they had a lineup so skewed to the bottom of the defensive spectrum that it couldn't be tweaked without putting players out of position. Off the field, the star power that had carried them was getting more expensive. The bills on Detroit's MVP and Cy Young winners were coming due and threatened to strangle efforts to improve.

Enter the Texas Rangers.

In Arlington there was a fix for Detroit's inflexibility. Texas' front office had made eyes at Prince Fielder when he was a free agent two years earlier. In short order, GMs Jon Daniels and Dave Dombrowski consummated a blockbuster that nobody saw coming, but that made so much sense it seemed impossible we had missed the fit. Fielder and a bit of money went to Texas for Ian Kinsler, a straight-up deal. Despite their frustration with Fielder during the playoffs, Tigers fans were initially jarred; some were panicked. They calmed once they

remembered who had helmed the deal. When a trade goes down, you don't doubt Double D.

***

Dombrowski's reputation as one of the league's best GMs is generally unchallenged, but faith in his trades—even if they don't initially make sense—borders on absolute. It was that trust that assuaged the fears of Tigers fans who saw that Kinsler was coming off two career-worst (by OPS) offensive seasons, and who noticed how much he had leveraged his home ballpark into superstardom, with a career .710 road OPS that trails those of Maicer Izturis, Jeff Keppinger and Mike Fontenot. How, then, the assuaging?

Just look at the stars on the team that just ended up two wins away from a second consecutive World Series bid. The aforementioned award winners whose contracts need to be renewed soon were both acquired via lopsided trade. MVP Miguel Cabrera cost two blue-chip prospects, Cameron Maybin and Andrew Miller, plus the $29 million owed to Dontrelle Willis. The prospects haven't panned out—Cabrera came within a win in 2013 alone of matching Maybin and Miller's combined career totals—and the money spent on Willis hasn't hampered Detroit's ability to sign free agents. Cy Young winner Max Scherzer was acquired in a deal that sent Curtis Granderson—at the time, probably the most popular athlete in Detroit—to the Yankees of all teams, and yet the head-scratching move turned out to be a clear romp: Austin Jackson and Phil Coke also came over in the same deal.

Anibal Sanchez, who led the American League in ERA and FIP last year, was added in a trade in late July 2012. In the same move the Tigers got Omar Infante, who netted 3.2 WARP in 184 games, and who will now be replaced by Kinsler. The cost of that trade: Jacob Turner, another top prospect, and one who could still turn into something, but also a

TIGERS PROSPECTUS
2013 W-L: 93-69, 1st in AL Central

Pythag	.612	3rd	DER	.694	27th
RS/G	4.91	2nd	B-Age	30.1	28th
RA/G	3.85	7th	P-Age	28.1	17th
TAv	.284	2nd	Salary	$148.3	5th
BRR	-24.93	30th	M$/MW	$3.04	18th
TAv-P	.248	1st	DL Days	515	2nd
FIP	3.29	1st	$ on DL	6%	2nd

	Runs	HR/RH	HR/LH	Runs/RH	Runs/LH
Three-Year Park Factors	101	85	92	104	105

Top Hitter WARP	7.93 (Miguel Cabrera)
Top Pitcher WARP	4.60 (Anibal Sanchez)
Top Prospect	Nick Castellanos

pitcher whose stock is way down after a sub-replacement 2013 season that included a Triple-A knockaround.

Doug Fister was acquired late in 2011 for a youthful bundle highlighted by Francisco Martinez and Chance Ruffin. Fister looked at the time like a Safeco mirage, and many analysts immediately put the win in the Mariners' column. Then Fister went out and posted a 1.79 ERA and 0.84 WHIP in 70 post-trade innings, with an obscene 11.4 K/BB ratio. There was no way he could maintain that level over a full season, but he has continued to pitch better than anyone at the time expected. In 2013, though clearly hampered by bad infield defense, he had the AL's eighth-best FIP and third-highest groundball rate. Martinez, meanwhile, flamed out so hard with Seattle that they let him go altogether. He's now back with the Tigers.

Not every move brings back a superstar, but not every move needs to. When shortstop Jhonny Peralta was on the verge of being suspended for PEDs last summer, the Tigers turned to the trade market for 24-year-old defensive wizard Jose Iglesias. While he is nowhere near as threatening as Peralta at the dish, Iglesias' defensive prowess was arguably more valuable than Peralta's bat, given Detroit's league-high groundball rate. After taking over the position in Detroit, Iglesias recorded nearly one extra out every two days compared to Peralta's rate.

In addition to those mentioned, Dombrowski and his front office have pulled off deals to get Dmitri Young, Jeremy Bonderman, Carlos Pena, Carlos Guillen, Placido Polanco and Edgar Renteria. A total of 10 blockbusters, and the Renteria deal was the only dud of the bunch. The other nine—along with savvy extensions that followed in many cases—have all produced positive surplus WARP. The Dmitri Young move (in which Detroit lost Juan Encarnacion and a minor leaguer) is at the low end with a 2.4-WARP profit. The Cabrera deal, meanwhile, has produced a 28-WARP gain all by itself. In all, Dombrowski has added 100 extra wins via trade.

***

Just a week and a half after the Kinsler-Fielder swap, the transaction wire was electrified by another out-of-the-Tiger-blue trade. This time Dombrowski had dealt Fister. It had seemed a foregone conclusion after the Tigers' ALCS knockout that one of their starters would be moved to clear room for Drew Smyly in the rotation, and to clear payroll space for extension negotiations with Scherzer. After the vague initial report of the trade hit Twitter, news trickled out. Fister was going to Washington. Oh boy—if Dombrowski had been able to swindle Seattle when Fister was still an underrated asset, what sort of treasure would he get now that all of baseball knew Fister was one of the game's top arms?

Pitching prospect Robbie Ray was involved. Lefty reliever Ian Krol and utilityman Steve Lombardozzi, too. "Okay," the Tigers fan says to himself, "that's a good start. What's the final piece?" The Tigers' biggest remaining needs—a third baseman and a high-leverage reliever—both matched up with the Nationals' 40-man roster. Third base-capable Anthony Rendon was probably a pipe dream, though he would've made a worthwhile one-for-one exchange. One of Tyler Clippard, Rafael Soriano or Drew Storen would be a key bullpen addition ranging from "great" to "solid." Clippard was probably too much to hope for, considering the other names, but "too much" had never stopped Dombrowski before. If not him, maybe Storen would actually be better than Soriano as the fourth name—

But there was no fourth name.

Once the teams' official Twitter accounts confirmed the deal as-is, it was hard not to be underwhelmed by the return. This was Dombrowski. The Master. He couldn't possibly have just underrated his own asset, right? Fister gave the Tigers 7.5 WARP in less than two and a half years. He'd been even better in October, with a 2.98 ERA in 48 postseason innings, going at least six innings in all but one of his seven starts. Could he really net only a prospect (and a non-blue chipper at that), a lefty-killing reliever and a light-hitting Swiss Army Knife affectionately regarded as Don Kelly 2.0?

Maybe, some posited, the Tigers' brass knew something about Fister that would make him a lesser commodity. Maybe, many guessed, the Tigers' brass thought they alone saw something in Ray that made him a greater commodity. (Other teams said they didn't even know Fister was available, suggesting Dombrowski had zeroed in on his prize.) Either way, coming just as Dombrowski-as-Jedi talk was reaching a crescendo, and bucking as it did the conventional wisdom about the players involved, the trade created a fascinating dynamic for assessing the deal: Did his magic dwindle, or reach a new height?

The answer won't be known for quite some time. Ray is just 22, with 58 Double-A innings under his belt. Even an aggressive track—one often employed by the Tigers—would likely get him only a taste of the majors this year, and his ultimate value to Detroit won't even be guessable for at least two or three seasons after that. In the end Tigers fans and followers have to be open to the idea that Dombrowski might have just lost this one. No general manager has a 100 percent success rate with trades.

But, then again, only one has batted .900.

Paul Sporer's new pitching-focused website, PaintTheBlack. com, *is up and running; he can also be found on Twitter@ sporer.*

HITTERS

Craig Albernaz   C

Born: 10/30/1982 Age: 31
Bats: R Throws: R Height: 5' 8"
Weight: 185 Breakout: 1%
Improve: 10% Collapse: 12%
Attrition: 24% MLB: 27%

Comparables:
Cody Clark, J.C. Boscan, Ryan Budde

YEAR	TEAM	LVL	AGE	PA	R	2B	3B	HR	RBI	BB	SO	SB	CS	AVG/OBP/SLG	TAv	BABIP	BRR	FRAA	WARP
2011	MNT	AA	28	112	13	4	0	0	7	13	19	0	0	.220/.336/.264	.215	.270	-0.1	C(8): 0.0	0.1
2011	DUR	AAA	28	25	1	2	0	0	1	1	8	0	0	.167/.200/.250	.183	.250	-0.3	C(4): -0.0, P(1): -0.0	0.0
2012	DUR	AAA	29	72	2	3	0	0	3	5	23	1	0	.156/.229/.203	.161	.244	-0.9	C(22): 0.3, P(6): -0.1	-0.7
2013	DUR	AAA	30	115	11	5	0	1	11	7	22	3	0	.225/.279/.304	.213	.275	1.1	C(29): 0.6, P(3): 0.1	0.4
2014	DET	MLB	31	250	20	10	0	2	19	14	64	2	1	.213/.262/.288	.205	.280	-0.1	C 1	-0.2

Guys like Albernaz hold baseball together. Bald and compact as a human cannonball, he'll catch in Triple-A, Double-A; he'll wait on the temporary inactive or disabled list during roster musical chairs; and he's the guy in spring training behind the dish for countless prospects, suspects and even All-Stars—Albernaz went to big-league camp for the first time in 2013. Well-meaning comparisons to sports movie icon Rudy effectively belittle him and his value: Albernaz knows how to call a game and has a good arm. His lack of size and bat will keep him out of the bigs, but last year he hit his first Triple-A homer (in his fifth season there), a grand slam that hit the Bull and won him a goddamn steak.

Alex Avila   C

Born: 1/29/1987 Age: 27
Bats: L Throws: R Height: 5' 11"
Weight: 210 Breakout: 3%
Improve: 51% Collapse: 3%
Attrition: 6% MLB: 95%

Comparables:
Chris Iannetta, Ryan Doumit, Miguel Montero

YEAR	TEAM	LVL	AGE	PA	R	2B	3B	HR	RBI	BB	SO	SB	CS	AVG/OBP/SLG	TAv	BABIP	BRR	FRAA	WARP
2011	DET	MLB	24	551	63	33	4	19	82	73	131	3	1	.295/.389/.506	.309	.366	2.8	C(133): 1.3, 3B(1): -0.1	6.0
2012	DET	MLB	25	434	42	21	2	9	48	61	104	2	0	.243/.352/.384	.257	.312	-1	C(113): -2.8	1.7
2013	TOL	AAA	26	51	5	3	0	1	5	7	12	0	0	.250/.353/.386	.260	.323	0.4	C(6): 0.1	0.1
2013	DET	MLB	26	379	39	14	1	11	47	44	112	0	0	.227/.317/.376	.253	.305	-2.8	C(98): -0.1	0.9
2014	DET	MLB	27	376	43	17	1	10	42	46	94	1	0	.249/.342/.402	.271	.310	-0.5	C -1, 3B -0	2.0

Like soapbox cars, supermarket apples and Mickey Rourke, catchers spend most of their days banged up, bruised to hell or a little bit dazed. Avila takes more than his share of hits, tips and tumbles, and the constant nagging injuries have sapped his power and sent him to the DL three times in the past two years. Thus, he hasn't come close to repeating his breakout 2011. But he's among the game's best pitch framers, and his throwing numbers—skewed by his men on the mound—don't do him justice. His .905 OPS in 90 plate appearances after returning from a concussion in late August shows he's got some upside. Complain that he's too often injured, but if it weren't him playing at 80 percent capacity, it'd just be somebody else.

Miguel Cabrera   1B

Born: 4/18/1983 Age: 31
Bats: R Throws: R Height: 6' 4"
Weight: 240 Breakout: 2%
Improve: 43% Collapse: 2%
Attrition: 2% MLB: 99%

Comparables:
George Brett, Frank Robinson, Albert Pujols

YEAR	TEAM	LVL	AGE	PA	R	2B	3B	HR	RBI	BB	SO	SB	CS	AVG/OBP/SLG	TAv	BABIP	BRR	FRAA	WARP
2011	DET	MLB	28	688	111	48	0	30	105	108	89	2	1	.344/.448/.586	.346	.365	-2.7	1B(152): -11.8	5.9
2012	DET	MLB	29	697	109	40	0	44	139	66	98	4	1	.330/.393/.606	.325	.331	-5.6	3B(154): -2.4, 1B(2): -0.0	6.2
2013	DET	MLB	30	652	103	26	1	44	137	90	94	3	0	.348/.442/.636	.372	.356	-3	3B(145): -11.8	7.9
2014	DET	MLB	31	622	93	34	1	32	104	76	95	3	1	.322/.407/.566	.341	.340	-1	1B -6, 3B -1	5.0

While he technically missed only five games in September, you can essentially throw out the entire month, as it was played with perhaps 60 percent health at best. Cabrera hit one homer that month; he doubled once; his slugging percentage, at .333, was the lowest for any full month in his career, by 50 points. And so now consider that he still had the best season of his career, better than his Triple Crown campaign, good enough (by TAv) to be Hank Aaron's third-best season, to be Willie Mays' second-best season, to be Manny Ramirez's best season. In 45 fewer plate appearances, he matched his Triple Crown home run total, fell just two RBIs shy and added 18 points to his batting average. He hit .412/.412/.814 when he went the other way, the best line in baseball and the best line of his career. His plate coverage, strength and all-fields approach make him practically impossible to pitch to—he slugged .444 even on pitches outside the strike zone, and .447 even with two strikes. That he's gotten better as he passes 30 makes it difficult to see this elite production ending anytime soon, unless there are gremlins in his joints that cause more months like his last month. If so, we all mourn.

Ramon Cabrera   C

Born: 11/5/1989 Age: 24
Bats: B Throws: R Height: 5' 8"
Weight: 197 Breakout: 4%
Improve: 6% Collapse: 3%
Attrition: 11% MLB: 13%

Comparables:
Gaby Sanchez, Matt McBride, Matt Hague

YEAR	TEAM	LVL	AGE	PA	R	2B	3B	HR	RBI	BB	SO	SB	CS	AVG/OBP/SLG	TAv	BABIP	BRR	FRAA	WARP
2011	BRD	A+	21	379	46	25	4	3	53	38	29	5	1	.343/.410/.471	.249	.361	-1.2	C(26): -0.2	0.0
2012	ALT	AA	22	428	47	22	2	3	50	39	44	0	3	.276/.342/.367	.251	.305	-1.8	C(84): -0.6	0.8
2013	ERI	AA	23	362	44	22	2	0	54	44	34	4	0	.304/.392/.388	.294	.338	-4.3	C(31): -0.3	1.7
2013	TOL	AAA	23	165	13	9	1	1	15	14	21	0	1	.242/.311/.336	.248	.276	-1.5	C(19): -0.6	0.0
2014	DET	MLB	24	250	21	12	1	2	22	18	35	0	0	.257/.311/.343	.242	.290	-0.4	C -0	0.3

A quick start at Double-A led to an early-May promotion, but an unsuccessful two-month stay at Triple-A shoved him back to Double-A for the remainder of the season. Going backward isn't the same as being off the track, and, at just 24, he'll still be age-appropriate for another go this year. He showed marked improvements against lefties, a huge factor if he wants to back up Alex Avila.

Nick Castellanos LF
Born: 3/4/1992 Age: 22
Bats: R Throws: R Height: 6' 4"
Weight: 210 Breakout: 2%
Improve: 18% Collapse: 1%
Attrition: 25% MLB: 39%
Comparables: Joel Guzman, Andrew Lambo, Carlos Gonzalez

YEAR	TEAM	LVL	AGE	PA	R	2B	3B	HR	RBI	BB	SO	SB	CS	AVG/OBP/SLG	TAv	BABIP	BRR	FRAA	WARP
2011	WMI	A	19	562	65	36	3	7	76	45	130	3	2	.312/.367/.436	.312	.402	-5.9	3B(88): -13.5	1.8
2012	LAK	A+	20	243	37	17	3	3	32	22	42	3	2	.405/.461/.553	.341	.486	0.6	3B(51): -0.9	2.7
2012	ERI	AA	20	341	35	15	1	7	25	14	76	5	4	.264/.296/.382	.226	.322	-3.8	RF(51): -2.9, 3B(27): -0.8	-1.4
2013	TOL	AAA	21	595	81	37	1	18	76	54	100	4	1	.276/.343/.450	.282	.307	-0.6	LF(130): 2.6	3.1
2013	DET	MLB	21	18	1	0	0	0	0	0	1	0	0	.278/.278/.278	.206	.294	-0.1	LF(9): -0.3	-0.1
2014	DET	MLB	22	250	24	12	1	6	28	13	56	0	0	.265/.305/.397	.254	.320	-0.4	LF 0, 3B -2	0.2

The prize of the Detroit farm system, Castellanos' high minors work hasn't been overwhelming, but he had a career-best isolated power and set highs in doubles and home runs last year. He had the misfortune of coming up as a third baseman in an organization that's been pretty happy with its third baseman, thank you very much. His fortunes improved as he shifted to left field, as the Tigers haven't had a left fielder produce a .700 OPS in at least 500 plate appearances since Craig Monroe in 2006. His fortunes improved further when the Tigers traded Prince Fielder and moved Miguel Cabrera back to first, and all of a sudden the man without a position to play had two. Knowing the Tigers' nonchalant attitude toward defense, they just might let him cover both.

Harold Castro 2B
Born: 11/30/1993 Age: 20
Bats: L Throws: R Height: 6' 0"
Weight: 145 Breakout: 0%
Improve: 0% Collapse: 0%
Attrition: 0% MLB: 0%
Comparables: Corban Joseph, Cesar Hernandez, Marwin Gonzalez

YEAR	TEAM	LVL	AGE	PA	R	2B	3B	HR	RBI	BB	SO	SB	CS	AVG/OBP/SLG	TAv	BABIP	BRR	FRAA	WARP
2013	WMI	A	19	153	17	7	1	1	11	2	40	5	1	.231/.240/.313	.202	.308	-0.2	2B(40): 5.7	0.0
2013	LAK	A+	19	80	8	2	1	0	11	5	22	3	2	.274/.316/.329	.267	.385	-0.4	2B(21): -2.3	0.0
2014	DET	MLB	20	250	19	9	1	2	19	6	71	5	2	.212/.232/.285	.189	.280	0.3	2B 2	-0.7

One of the first things scouts and prospect mavens will tell you is to be wary of the numbers a prospect puts up, especially without other input. Castro's second season stateside saw subpar stats, yet he has found favor among those who watch him play. His bat-to-ball skills are noteworthy, particularly considering his age and aggressive April assignment at High-A. He was given only 80 plate appearances there before being bumped back to Low-A, but it was a useful experience. The numbers won't jump off the page—shoot, the numbers are lousy—but this is a prospect.

Rajai Davis LF
Born: 10/19/1980 Age: 33
Bats: R Throws: R Height: 5' 9"
Weight: 195 Breakout: 1%
Improve: 28% Collapse: 9%
Attrition: 14% MLB: 90%
Comparables: Jay Payton, Ralph Garr, Marvin Benard

YEAR	TEAM	LVL	AGE	PA	R	2B	3B	HR	RBI	BB	SO	SB	CS	AVG/OBP/SLG	TAv	BABIP	BRR	FRAA	WARP
2011	TOR	MLB	30	338	44	21	6	1	29	15	63	34	11	.238/.273/.350	.222	.292	5	CF(79): -2.8, RF(8): 0.6	-0.4
2012	TOR	MLB	31	487	64	24	3	8	43	29	102	46	13	.257/.309/.378	.240	.314	0.1	LF(114): 0.6, RF(24): 0.9	0.3
2013	TOR	MLB	32	360	49	16	2	6	24	21	67	45	6	.260/.312/.375	.251	.308	6.7	LF(57): 2.9, RF(35): -0.5	1.5
2014	DET	MLB	33	365	48	18	3	3	26	19	66	38	9	.265/.308/.360	.245	.320	4.4	LF 0, CF -0	0.9

Davis is still second in baseball in steals since 2009 (behind Michael Bourn), but his walk rate since then is 15th-lowest. That's worse than, um, Juan Pierre, as is Davis' cumulative five-year OBP. He figures to be valuable as an all-purpose fourth outfielder and pinch runner. If his new employers try him in a left-field platoon with Andy Dirks, though, they'll just have to keep their fingers crossed.

Andy Dirks LF
Born: 1/24/1986 Age: 28
Bats: L Throws: L Height: 6' 0"
Weight: 195 Breakout: 0%
Improve: 43% Collapse: 4%
Attrition: 17% MLB: 95%
Comparables: Kevin Mench, Wally Moon, Mark Carreon

YEAR	TEAM	LVL	AGE	PA	R	2B	3B	HR	RBI	BB	SO	SB	CS	AVG/OBP/SLG	TAv	BABIP	BRR	FRAA	WARP
2011	TOL	AAA	25	172	30	8	1	7	24	12	28	12	2	.325/.368/.522	.293	.355	0.6	CF(23): 2.3, RF(9): 1.3	1.5
2011	DET	MLB	25	235	34	13	0	7	28	11	36	5	2	.251/.296/.406	.239	.273	-0.4	LF(38): 2.7, RF(22): 0.6	0.1
2012	TOL	AAA	26	41	4	1	0	2	5	4	8	2	0	.216/.293/.405	.236	.222	0.2	RF(6): -0.8, CF(2): -0.1	0.1
2012	DET	MLB	26	344	56	18	5	8	35	23	53	1	1	.322/.370/.487	.296	.365	2	LF(59): -1.0, RF(24): -2.2	1.5
2013	DET	MLB	27	484	60	16	2	9	37	42	84	7	1	.256/.323/.363	.255	.298	-2.5	LF(116): 7.4, RF(15): 0.1	1.0
2014	DET	MLB	28	432	53	19	2	10	43	30	74	7	2	.272/.326/.408	.265	.310	0.4	LF 5, RF -1	1.7

A near-.400 BABIP against righties helped fuel a half-season surge in 2012, breeding outsize expectations for him in 2013. The righty's BABIP fell back to a more reasonable mark in 2013, and paired with his unshakable deficiencies against lefties added up to a fourth outfielder. Dirks has now logged over 1,000 PA with exactly a 100 OPS+, and as he plays his final pre-arbitration year you might consider this a contract push for him: a big season, 600 plate appearances and double-digit home runs and he'll set his family up for life; a marginal role and a .650 OPS and he'll fade away before his first big score.

Daniel Fields CF

Born: 1/23/1991 Age: 23
Bats: L Throws: R Height: 6' 2''
Weight: 215 Breakout: 1%
Improve: 2% Collapse: 3%
Attrition: 3% MLB: 9%

Comparables:
Bryan Petersen, Jai Miller, Jordan Danks

YEAR	TEAM	LVL	AGE	PA	R	2B	3B	HR	RBI	BB	SO	SB	CS	AVG/OBP/SLG	TAv	BABIP	BRR	FRAA	WARP
2011	LAK	A+	20	495	57	14	4	8	46	49	133	4	4	.220/.308/.326	.240	.297	-1.9	CF(91): -1.2	-0.3
2012	LAK	A+	21	267	31	11	4	1	26	19	55	14	7	.266/.318/.357	.243	.335	2.2	CF(59): -3.3, LF(1): -0.1	-0.1
2012	ERI	AA	21	122	13	4	0	2	7	13	21	9	1	.264/.352/.358	.260	.310	1.3	LF(23): 1.2, CF(5): 0.1	0.4
2013	ERI	AA	22	515	71	27	6	10	58	45	130	24	7	.284/.356/.435	.285	.374	2.7	CF(111): -10.3	1.7
2014	DET	MLB	23	250	24	10	2	4	23	16	69	6	2	.231/.284/.335	.228	.310	0.4	CF -3, LF 0	-0.4

Prior to 2013, Fields fit the profile of the rawly talented players who crowd the downballot portion of team prospect lists. Last year he finally put those skills toward production, as he matched or set career highs in nearly every category, and even every *type* of category: power, speed, rate stats; singles, doubles, triples, homers. He still needs to make more contact, or he'll see pitchers cut fastballs from his diet entirely. But even in that gloomy scenario, his defense and speed enhance his overall value and give him a legitimate fourth-outfielder future.

Bryan Holaday C

Born: 11/19/1987 Age: 26
Bats: R Throws: R Height: 6' 0''
Weight: 205 Breakout: 3%
Improve: 10% Collapse: 12%
Attrition: 18% MLB: 27%

Comparables:
Chris Stewart, Rob Johnson, Luis Exposito

YEAR	TEAM	LVL	AGE	PA	R	2B	3B	HR	RBI	BB	SO	SB	CS	AVG/OBP/SLG	TAv	BABIP	BRR	FRAA	WARP
2011	ERI	AA	23	371	35	18	0	7	42	27	76	6	1	.242/.304/.361	.207	.291	-0.6	C(39): 0.3	-0.2
2012	TOL	AAA	24	282	18	12	1	2	25	22	43	2	0	.240/.312/.320	.241	.280	-1.3	C(74): 0.3	0.6
2012	DET	MLB	24	13	3	1	0	0	0	0	2	0	0	.250/.250/.333	.200	.300	1.1	C(6): -0.0	0.1
2013	TOL	AAA	25	320	28	18	1	4	24	18	57	0	1	.260/.312/.372	.254	.309	-0.7	C(75): -1.8	1.0
2013	DET	MLB	25	33	8	1	0	1	2	2	3	0	0	.296/.367/.444	.341	.304	-0.9	C(14): 0.2	0.2
2014	DET	MLB	26	250	22	11	1	3	22	12	47	1	0	.242/.288/.339	.231	.280	-0.3	C -0	0.4

Like most people, Holaday is in the mix to replace Brayan Pena as the Tigers' backup catcher this year. He's the frontrunner, by virtue of already being on the 40-man roster and having tasted the coffee a couple times already. A capable defender, Holaday doesn't have any loud tools and his next .700 OPS will be his first, but he did set career-highs in average, OBP and slugging in a repeat spin through the International League. More importantly, he did his best work against lefties for the second straight year. With Alex Avila hitting a buck fifty against lefties over the past two years, Holaday suits the situation.

Torii Hunter RF

Born: 7/18/1975 Age: 38
Bats: R Throws: R Height: 6' 2''
Weight: 225 Breakout: 0%
Improve: 10% Collapse: 14%
Attrition: 20% MLB: 78%

Comparables:
Ken Griffey, Andre Dawson, Larry Walker

YEAR	TEAM	LVL	AGE	PA	R	2B	3B	HR	RBI	BB	SO	SB	CS	AVG/OBP/SLG	TAv	BABIP	BRR	FRAA	WARP
2011	ANA	MLB	35	649	80	24	2	23	82	62	125	5	7	.262/.336/.429	.277	.297	-1	RF(136): 0.4, CF(1): 0.1	2.4
2012	ANA	MLB	36	584	81	24	1	16	92	38	133	9	1	.313/.365/.451	.286	.389	5.5	RF(134): -1.8	3.4
2013	DET	MLB	37	652	90	37	5	17	84	26	113	3	2	.304/.334/.465	.292	.344	0.8	RF(143): -13.0	1.8
2014	DET	MLB	38	599	77	27	2	17	65	44	119	7	4	.278/.336/.428	.277	.320	-1	RF -4, CF 0	1.7

Hunter was unquestionably a plus player for the Tigers, but the distribution of his value—primarily as a singles and doubles hitter in the no. 2 spot—wasn't quite what they expected (or perhaps wanted). He was expected to boost a sagging defense, yet graded out as a severe negative both by advanced metrics and by the traditional rods-and-cones method of analysis. Poor routes, uninspired throws and uncharacteristic gaffes marred the 52-time Gold Glover's season in right field. It is hard to believe he lost that much going from 36 to 37 years old, but decline isn't always gradual or predictable in a player's late 30s. Encouragingly, he did maintain the batting average everyone said he couldn't, while also reversing a three-year downturn in isolated power.

Jose Iglesias SS

Born: 1/5/1990 Age: 24
Bats: R Throws: R Height: 5' 11''
Weight: 185 Breakout: 3%
Improve: 15% Collapse: 8%
Attrition: 17% MLB: 52%

Comparables:
Andres Blanco, Alcides Escobar, Emmanuel Burriss

YEAR	TEAM	LVL	AGE	PA	R	2B	3B	HR	RBI	BB	SO	SB	CS	AVG/OBP/SLG	TAv	BABIP	BRR	FRAA	WARP
2011	PAW	AAA	21	387	35	9	0	1	31	21	58	12	4	.235/.285/.269	.208	.279	-0.4	SS(83): 9.9	0.5
2011	BOS	MLB	21	6	3	0	0	0	0	0	2	0	0	.333/.333/.333	.229	.500	-0.6	SS(8): -0.2	0.0
2012	PAW	AAA	22	396	46	9	1	1	23	27	46	12	3	.266/.318/.306	.232	.299	0.3	SS(88): 11.4	1.6
2012	BOS	MLB	22	77	5	2	0	1	2	4	16	1	0	.118/.200/.191	.151	.137	0.9	SS(24): 0.8	-0.3
2013	PAW	AAA	23	133	17	2	0	4	15	9	18	5	3	.202/.262/.319	.203	.204	1.2	SS(32): 2.5, 3B(1): -0.1	0.0
2013	DET	MLB	23	148	12	6	0	2	10	4	30	2	1	.259/.306/.348	.236	.320	-0.4	SS(42): 1.0, 3B(3): 0.2	0.5
2013	BOS	MLB	23	234	27	10	2	1	19	11	30	3	1	.330/.376/.409	.285	.376	0.1	3B(34): -0.9, SS(29): -0.1	1.5
2014	DET	MLB	24	366	35	12	1	3	30	17	57	7	3	.257/.300/.331	.235	.290	0.1	SS 3, 3B -1	0.8

Never let a good crisis go to waste, Winston Churchill might or might not have said, and the Tigers didn't. When shortstop Jhonny Peralta accepted a 50-game PED suspension in the middle of August, it left a gaping hole at shortstop. More gaping, even, than the hole when Peralta is playing. They scooped up the defensively dazzling Iglesias and found him to be a perfect fit for a team with the league's highest groundball rate and the league's least leftwardly mobile third baseman. As Winston Churchill famously said, "his glove alone will make him a net positive, even with the more realistic slash line he produced after the trade."

Austin Jackson CF
Born: 2/1/1987 Age: 27
Bats: R Throws: R Height: 6' 1"
Weight: 185 Breakout: 2%
Improve: 51% Collapse: 4%
Attrition: 6% MLB: 97%
Comparables:
Tony Gonzalez, Tom Tresh, B.J. Upton

YEAR	TEAM	LVL	AGE	PA	R	2B	3B	HR	RBI	BB	SO	SB	CS	AVG/OBP/SLG	TAv	BABIP	BRR	FRAA	WARP
2011	DET	MLB	24	668	90	22	11	10	45	56	181	22	5	.249/.317/.374	.244	.340	0.7	CF(152): 5.6	1.6
2012	DET	MLB	25	617	103	29	10	16	66	67	134	12	9	.300/.377/.479	.301	.371	2.9	CF(137): 8.0	5.7
2013	DET	MLB	26	614	99	30	7	12	49	52	129	8	4	.272/.337/.417	.277	.333	4.4	CF(129): -6.0	2.8
2014	DET	MLB	27	581	71	26	7	9	52	50	141	13	5	.271/.337/.400	.270	.350	0.6	CF 0	2.4

Injuries hobbled Jackson for a second straight season, though this time there was no career year in the making for them to interrupt. Jackson's power regressed in 2013, his BABIP followed the rules for once, his defense was savaged by advanced metrics, and he lost a quarter of his walks from the year before. That all said, he cut his strikeout rate, still reaches base more often than the average leadoff man, impresses all who see him chase fly balls, and continues to add incrementally to his offensive game. He's underrated, entering his physical prime and poised for big things.

Ian Kinsler 2B
Born: 6/22/1982 Age: 32
Bats: R Throws: R Height: 6' 0"
Weight: 200 Breakout: 1%
Improve: 46% Collapse: 2%
Attrition: 9% MLB: 94%
Comparables:
Jose Vidro, Brian Roberts, Jackie Robinson

YEAR	TEAM	LVL	AGE	PA	R	2B	3B	HR	RBI	BB	SO	SB	CS	AVG/OBP/SLG	TAv	BABIP	BRR	FRAA	WARP
2011	TEX	MLB	29	723	121	34	4	32	77	89	71	30	4	.255/.355/.477	.282	.243	11.6	2B(144): 8.6	6.1
2012	TEX	MLB	30	731	105	42	5	19	72	60	90	21	9	.256/.326/.423	.259	.270	7	2B(144): -3.8, 3B(1): -0.0	2.0
2013	TEX	MLB	31	614	85	31	2	13	72	51	59	15	11	.277/.344/.413	.291	.288	3.5	2B(124): 13.3	5.4
2014	DET	MLB	32	601	82	29	3	16	62	57	74	19	7	.258/.336/.415	.276	.270	0.5	2B 7	3.7

It's a cold, cold business sometimes. Eighteen months after the Rangers signed Ian Kinsler to a contract extension and proclaimed him part of their core, he was shipped off to Detroit to make room for the new hotness, Jurickson Profar. The combination of keystoners' tendency to age poorly and Kinsler's problems staying healthy had the organization considering a position switch, but the chance to snag Prince Fielder was too good an opportunity to let pass. Kinsler made many Ranger fans crazy—he was an elite baserunner who nevertheless got caught napping on the basepaths too much, a quality defender who seemed prone to the routine error, a guy with power who fans felt tried to hit everything out of the park too often—but at the end of the day, Kinsler was an All-Star-caliber second baseman over his Ranger career, one of the best players in franchise history and a critical part of the best Rangers teams of all time.

Steve Lombardozzi 2B
Born: 9/20/1988 Age: 25
Bats: B Throws: R Height: 6' 0"
Weight: 200 Breakout: 4%
Improve: 51% Collapse: 11%
Attrition: 22% MLB: 94%
Comparables:
Blake DeWitt, Josh Harrison, Ruben Gotay

YEAR	TEAM	LVL	AGE	PA	R	2B	3B	HR	RBI	BB	SO	SB	CS	AVG/OBP/SLG	TAv	BABIP	BRR	FRAA	WARP
2011	HAR	AA	22	291	40	12	7	4	23	18	38	16	3	.309/.366/.454	.320	.348	3.8	2B(53): -4.6, SS(3): -0.4	2.0
2011	SYR	AAA	22	325	46	13	2	4	29	21	40	14	5	.310/.354/.408	.246	.344	0.3	2B(48): 1.7, SS(8): 0.7	0.6
2011	WAS	MLB	22	32	3	1	0	0	1	1	4	0	0	.194/.219/.226	.169	.222	-0.7	3B(3): 0.3, 2B(3): -0.0	-0.3
2012	WAS	MLB	23	416	40	16	3	3	27	19	46	5	3	.273/.317/.354	.248	.304	-2.5	2B(51): 5.7, LF(41): -0.5	0.8
2013	WAS	MLB	24	307	25	15	1	2	22	8	34	4	3	.259/.278/.338	.226	.284	1.7	2B(48): 3.2, LF(23): 0.2	0.3
2014	DET	MLB	25	310	35	13	2	4	25	14	39	7	3	.272/.310/.371	.246	.300	0.2	2B 0, LF -0	0.6

For a free swinger with a tiny 15 percent three-true-outcomes rate, a 20-point BABIP drop is crushing. For a bench as empty as Washington's, so too is a replacement-level turn from a piece as important as Lombardozzi. The superutility guy failed to get on base or hit for any power; he has decent speed, but rarely got the chance to show it off; and he plays a variety of positions, but doesn't excel at any of them. Lombardozzi will take on the same role for Detroit in 2014, and given his offensive profile there's close to a win riding on the fickle nature of batted balls.

Dixon Machado SS
Born: 2/22/1992 Age: 22
Bats: R Throws: R Height: 6' 1"
Weight: 170 Breakout: 0%
Improve: 1% Collapse: 0%
Attrition: 1% MLB: 1%
Comparables:
Ryan Jackson, Pedro Lopez, Ehire Adrianza

YEAR	TEAM	LVL	AGE	PA	R	2B	3B	HR	RBI	BB	SO	SB	CS	AVG/OBP/SLG	TAv	BABIP	BRR	FRAA	WARP
2011	WMI	A	19	491	47	1	2	0	28	46	77	25	5	.235/.314/.247	.236	.285	4.6	SS(84): 5.3	1.0
2012	LAK	A+	20	490	59	16	1	2	37	51	61	23	5	.195/.283/.252	.202	.223	0.5	SS(118): -7.4	-1.7
2013	LAK	A+	21	163	19	5	2	1	12	10	19	1	0	.215/.264/.295	.194	.240	0.4	SS(36): 0.3	-0.5
2014	DET	MLB	22	250	23	7	1	2	15	15	49	5	1	.202/.252/.264	.192	.240	0.4	SS -1	-0.7

Talk to anyone about Machado and you are guaranteed to hear about his elite defense, slight build and inability to hit. That's been the chorus since he joined the organization five years ago, and while he's still relatively young, the outlook on the last note is getting bleaker. He has a contact rate that allows him to put his one offensive skill—speed—into play, but lacks even enough muscle to pound grounders past infielders. Machado is blessed to have missed the power boom of the previous decade, as the league's renewed interested in infield defense instead of infielders' forearms gives him a fighting chance.

Francisco Martinez 3B
Born: 9/1/1990 Age: 23
Bats: R Throws: R Height: 6' 2"
Weight: 210 Breakout: 0%
Improve: 2% Collapse: 0%
Attrition: 2% MLB: 2%

Comparables:
Jeff Baisley, Chris Johnson, Josh Fields

YEAR	TEAM	LVL	AGE	PA	R	2B	3B	HR	RBI	BB	SO	SB	CS	AVG/OBP/SLG	TAv	BABIP	BRR	FRAA	WARP
2011	ERI	AA	20	372	63	14	4	7	46	19	80	7	8	.282/.319/.405	.238	.346	1.7	3B(39): 5.0	0.9
2011	WTN	AA	20	137	20	7	3	3	23	4	24	3	2	.310/.326/.481	.269	.356	0.6	3B(15): 0.2	0.3
2012	WTN	AA	21	402	55	16	1	2	23	43	85	27	7	.227/.315/.295	.233	.294	4.8	3B(78): 1.5, CF(11): -0.2	0.5
2013	LAK	A+	22	314	38	13	1	3	28	21	55	11	3	.295/.347/.378	.260	.353	1.3	3B(66): 6.8, SS(7): 0.9	1.7
2013	WTN	AA	22	136	8	6	0	0	5	6	43	7	0	.206/.242/.254	.193	.313	-0.3	CF(28): 0.3	-0.6
2014	DET	MLB	23	250	22	9	1	3	20	13	62	7	2	.228/.270/.308	.215	.290	0.5	3B 3, CF -0	-0.1

Once a top 10 prospect with the Tigers, then a key part going to the Mariners in the Doug Fister deal, then a Double-A flop for Seattle, Martinez finally made his way home to Detroit—or at least Lakeland—after being DFA'd. His performance surged upon rejoining the organization, but it happened in High-A, a level he last saw in 2010. Despite the stalled progress, he is still just 23 years old, with good speed, batting practice power and at least a tinge of promise. The Mariners had started a transition to center field, but the Tigers returned him to the infield.

Victor Martinez 1B
Born: 12/23/1978 Age: 35
Bats: B Throws: R Height: 6' 2"
Weight: 210 Breakout: 1%
Improve: 33% Collapse: 4%
Attrition: 18% MLB: 91%

Comparables:
Rusty Staub, Hideki Matsui, Mark Grace

YEAR	TEAM	LVL	AGE	PA	R	2B	3B	HR	RBI	BB	SO	SB	CS	AVG/OBP/SLG	TAv	BABIP	BRR	FRAA	WARP
2011	DET	MLB	32	595	76	40	0	12	103	46	51	1	0	.330/.380/.470	.291	.343	-3.5	C(26): -0.4, 1B(6): 0.3	2.6
2013	DET	MLB	34	668	68	36	0	14	83	54	62	0	2	.301/.355/.430	.280	.313	-6.2	1B(11): 0.8, C(3): 0.1	1.6
2014	DET	MLB	35	494	53	25	1	11	58	40	55	1	1	.294/.351/.426	.282	.310	-1	1B 0, C -0	1.9

There were some concerns about how a mid-30s DH would rebound from an ACL injury and a year of inactivity. Those fears were exacerbated by Martinez's first two months, as he clearly didn't have his legs beneath him and mustered a meager .578 OPS. His second half was his best since 2005, though, with a .361/.413/.500 line that makes you wonder whether the unthinkably slow 35-year-old might actually have a future batting title in him. He looked sharp at first base in a tiny 11-game sample, so the team should perhaps consider using him to occasionally spell Miguel Cabrera if it helps keep both players healthy, engaged and in the lineup.

James McCann C
Born: 6/13/1990 Age: 24
Bats: R Throws: R Height: 6' 2"
Weight: 210 Breakout: 4%
Improve: 4% Collapse: 2%
Attrition: 10% MLB: 10%

Comparables:
Brett Hayes, Carlos Corporan, Konrad Schmidt

YEAR	TEAM	LVL	AGE	PA	R	2B	3B	HR	RBI	BB	SO	SB	CS	AVG/OBP/SLG	TAv	BABIP	BRR	FRAA	WARP
2011	WMI	A	21	38	0	1	0	0	1	2	12	0	0	.059/.132/.088	.085	.087	-0.2	C(5): -0.1	-0.4
2012	LAK	A+	22	177	24	10	0	0	20	10	29	3	0	.288/.345/.350	.260	.346	-0.3	C(45): 0.1	1.0
2012	ERI	AA	22	230	15	12	0	2	19	8	44	2	2	.200/.227/.282	.177	.240	-2.2	C(64): -0.3	-1.3
2013	ERI	AA	23	486	50	30	1	8	54	30	85	3	3	.277/.328/.404	.266	.321	-0.5	C(100): -0.3	2.0
2014	DET	MLB	24	250	19	12	0	3	23	8	54	0	0	.233/.262/.324	.215	.280	-0.5	C -0	-0.1

Say hello to Eligible Backup Catcher Number Three. McCann squeezed a bit of everything into 2013: an empty high batting average in the early going, then a summer swoon that nearly sank his season in July, followed by unprecedented power in a five-homer August. A year ago in this space we sketched out a future for McCann as a defense-first catcher capable of giving Alex Avila a blow against lefties, and if his rollercoaster season did anything it reinforced that notion. It might be McCann's time to (very modestly) shine.

Steven Moya RF
Born: 9/8/1991 Age: 22
Bats: L Throws: R Height: 6' 6"
Weight: 230 Breakout: 2%
Improve: 3% Collapse: 0%
Attrition: 1% MLB: 3%

Comparables:
Carlos Peguero, Cole Garner, Jeremy Moore

YEAR	TEAM	LVL	AGE	PA	R	2B	3B	HR	RBI	BB	SO	SB	CS	AVG/OBP/SLG	TAv	BABIP	BRR	FRAA	WARP
2011	WMI	A	19	337	38	10	1	13	39	12	127	1	1	.204/.234/.362	.229	.288	1.3	RF(53): -1.2	-0.6
2012	WMI	A	20	258	28	14	3	9	47	11	59	5	3	.288/.319/.481	.297	.345	-2.5	RF(57): -1.5	1.0
2013	LAK	A+	21	388	52	19	5	12	55	18	106	6	0	.255/.296/.433	.254	.327	1.3	RF(78): -4.0	-0.1
2014	DET	MLB	22	250	21	9	1	7	28	6	87	0	0	.214/.232/.352	.211	.300	-0.2	RF -2	-1.0

This hulking mess of human mass carries heavy expectations in the Tigers' thin system, where he's pushed up the rankings more than his skills might otherwise merit. The power is there now, and the rest is very much not. Both Moya and opposing pitchers know he needs to sell out for his power, so a .178 isolated power is mitigated by a 27 percent strikeout rate and the lowest walk rate a 6-foot-6 slugger can realistically produce in A-ball. Still, baseball's power shortage will save a seat for such a high-power/high-strikeout hitter, particularly if he can avoid clogging up the DH spot. The Tigers are short on sure things, but they have a bundle of intriguing raw specimens like Moya. They won't all hit, but the ones who do will be fun.

Hernan Perez 2B

Born: 3/26/1991 Age: 23
Bats: R Throws: R Height: 6' 1"
Weight: 185 Breakout: 3%
Improve: 7% Collapse: 2%
Attrition: 4% MLB: 10%

Comparables:
William Bergolla, Eider Torres, Jordany Valdespin

YEAR	TEAM	LVL	AGE	PA	R	2B	3B	HR	RBI	BB	SO	SB	CS	AVG/OBP/SLG	TAv	BABIP	BRR	FRAA	WARP
2011	WMI	A	20	566	69	23	3	8	42	38	87	23	6	.258/.314/.364	.270	.293	5	2B(77): -3.4, SS(12): 0.0	1.9
2012	LAK	A+	21	479	50	11	4	5	44	24	70	27	4	.261/.298/.338	.228	.296	-1	2B(111): 6.3, SS(15): -0.8	0.0
2012	DET	MLB	21	2	1	0	0	0	0	0	0	0	0	.500/.500/.500	.325	.500	0	2B(1): -0.0	0.0
2013	ERI	AA	22	384	45	28	2	4	35	12	48	24	7	.301/.325/.423	.269	.335	4.3	2B(59): -1.9, SS(28): -1.4	1.8
2013	TOL	AAA	22	74	3	3	0	0	4	5	7	4	0	.299/.356/.343	.257	.333	-1.1	2B(16): 0.4	0.1
2013	DET	MLB	22	71	13	0	1	0	5	2	15	1	0	.197/.217/.227	.187	.250	0.1	2B(25): -0.5, SS(2): -0.0	-0.5
2014	DET	MLB	23	250	27	10	1	3	19	7	45	8	2	.245/.266/.334	.217	.280	0.9	2B -0, SS 0	-0.1

Perez's first turn around the high minors yielded his best offensive results to date and added some hope to his ceiling. He still profiles as a defense-first utilityman, with second base his best fit, but he can hang at shortstop and even has the arm to pass at third. Perez was clearly overmatched at the dish in his short big league stint, but the utility and speed earned him a spot on the postseason roster over more heralded young players. If he can continue to build on his gap power without losing speed he could become a useful bench player for several years to come.

Ramon Santiago 2B

Born: 8/31/1979 Age: 34
Bats: B Throws: R Height: 5' 11"
Weight: 175 Breakout: 1%
Improve: 22% Collapse: 11%
Attrition: 22% MLB: 87%

Comparables:
Tom Herr, Bobby Avila, Nick Punto

YEAR	TEAM	LVL	AGE	PA	R	2B	3B	HR	RBI	BB	SO	SB	CS	AVG/OBP/SLG	TAv	BABIP	BRR	FRAA	WARP
2011	DET	MLB	31	294	29	11	3	5	30	17	38	0	0	.260/.311/.384	.242	.283	1.3	2B(75): -2.4, SS(27): 3.4	0.9
2012	DET	MLB	32	259	19	7	1	2	17	20	39	1	0	.206/.283/.272	.198	.239	1.1	2B(71): 2.4, SS(20): -1.1	-0.9
2013	DET	MLB	33	234	27	8	1	1	14	21	32	0	1	.224/.298/.288	.230	.260	-0.7	2B(33): 0.3, 3B(27): 0.6	0.2
2014	DET	MLB	34	250	23	8	1	3	21	18	42	1	1	.241/.306/.322	.231	.280	-0.3	2B -0, SS 1	0.2

Santiago's early 30s have seen a significant drop from a very low perch. It's telling, really, that his best season came in just 156 plate appearances back in 2008, and he has managed to exceed that playing time allotment every season since. Solid defense keeps him employed—has netted him $9 million in career earnings, no less—but his reputation as a gloveman will have to really take off if he expects to stay employed with his current slash lines.

Eugenio Suarez SS

Born: 7/18/1991 Age: 22
Bats: R Throws: R Height: 5' 11"
Weight: 180 Breakout: 3%
Improve: 19% Collapse: 5%
Attrition: 20% MLB: 25%

Comparables:
Marcus Semien, Yamaico Navarro, Brandon Hicks

YEAR	TEAM	LVL	AGE	PA	R	2B	3B	HR	RBI	BB	SO	SB	CS	AVG/OBP/SLG	TAv	BABIP	BRR	FRAA	WARP
2011	ONE	A-	19	229	37	11	5	5	24	18	43	9	5	.250/.323/.426	.236	.295	0.2	SS(18): 1.3	0.3
2012	WMI	A	20	604	82	34	5	6	67	65	116	21	9	.288/.380/.409	.303	.356	-4.4	SS(119): -1.1, 2B(15): 0.5	4.9
2013	LAK	A+	21	122	17	6	2	1	12	14	25	2	3	.311/.410/.437	.305	.397	-0.3	SS(24): 1.1, 2B(1): 0.1	1.4
2013	ERI	AA	21	496	53	24	4	9	45	46	98	9	11	.253/.332/.387	.268	.307	-0.3	SS(111): 4.3	3.2
2014	DET	MLB	22	250	27	10	1	4	20	18	61	3	2	.236/.297/.340	.236	.300	-0.4	SS 1, 2B 0	0.5

Suarez needs to be a plus defender at shortstop to keep his prospect shine, so it's bad news that his defense faltered last year. Well, okay, to be fair, some observers say he didn't falter at all; he just wasn't all that great to begin with. A big April earned him a promotion to Double-A, where he held his own but exposed some flaws at the plate. Suarez can draw a walk, but some of that comes from a lack of aggression. He makes regular contact, but it's soft. He can be an average hitter if he adds strength and adjusts his plan against advanced pitching.

Devon Travis 2B

Born: 2/21/1991 Age: 23
Bats: R Throws: R Height: 5' 9"
Weight: 183 Breakout: 1%
Improve: 18% Collapse: 2%
Attrition: 15% MLB: 36%

Comparables:
Matt Antonelli, Brad Emaus, Jemile Weeks

YEAR	TEAM	LVL	AGE	PA	R	2B	3B	HR	RBI	BB	SO	SB	CS	AVG/OBP/SLG	TAv	BABIP	BRR	FRAA	WARP
2012	ONE	A-	21	107	17	2	2	3	11	8	10	3	1	.280/.352/.441	.320	.284	0.1	2B(23): 0.7	0.9
2013	WMI	A	22	339	55	17	2	6	42	35	32	14	3	.352/.430/.486	.341	.375	3.3	2B(68): 8.4	5.2
2013	LAK	A+	22	237	38	11	2	10	34	18	32	8	1	.350/.401/.561	.340	.371	2.4	2B(53): -5.9	2.5
2014	DET	MLB	23	250	26	10	1	7	30	15	46	1	0	.271/.319/.411	.264	.310	-0.2	2B 0	1.0

Reports on Travis range from "don't trust the raw numbers" to "sleeper on the rise," but it's hard not to get at least somewhat excited by what the 22-year-old did across two levels in 2013. The Tigers paid the 13th-rounder double-slot money because he can flat hit, and he promptly earned the system's minor-league player of the year award in his first full season. Travis doesn't have much speed, so his success rate stealing 22 bags might actually be the most impressive, or at least surprising, contribution. His size and lack of raw tools will breed skeptics, but all he's got to do to silence them is hit .351/.418/.518 every year forever.

PITCHERS

Al Alburquerque
Born: 6/10/1986 Age: 28
Bats: R Throws: R Height: 6' 0" Weight: 195
Breakout: 36% Improve: 45% Collapse: 43%
Attrition: 32% MLB: 71%
Comparables:
Vinnie Pestano, Jose Veras, Allan Simpson

YEAR	TEAM	LVL	AGE	W	L	SV	G	GS	IP	H	HR	BB	SO	BB9	SO9	GB%	BABIP	WHIP	ERA	FIP	FRA	WARP
2011	DET	MLB	25	6	1	0	41	0	43¹	21	0	29	67	6.0	13.9	58%	.250	1.15	1.87	2.12	2.10	1.4
2012	TOL	AAA	26	1	0	0	9	0	10²	9	1	4	18	3.4	15.2	43%	.364	1.22	1.69	2.41	3.06	0.2
2012	DET	MLB	26	0	0	0	8	0	13¹	6	0	8	18	5.4	12.1	67%	.222	1.05	0.68	2.15	2.54	0.4
2013	TOL	AAA	27	0	1	1	10	0	14¹	9	2	13	27	8.2	17.0	17%	.318	1.53	3.14	3.97	4.44	0.1
2013	DET	MLB	27	4	3	0	53	0	49	39	5	34	70	6.2	12.9	40%	.312	1.49	4.59	3.75	4.18	0.4
2014	DET	MLB	28	2	1	0	46	0	51²	40	4	29	67	5.1	11.8	47%	.305	1.33	3.35	3.50	3.64	0.8

Alburquerque spent his first two seasons walking the crooked and narrow: astronomical walk rate, minuscule hit rate, margins so slim that any stumble could quickly turn disastrous. Then he stumbled. He lost nearly a third of his groundballs in 2013, and almost every one of those missing grounders showed up as a line drive. Meanwhile, he allowed the first regular-season home run of his major-league career in mid-July, and within the next 20 innings had already surrendered five. He still amassed 60 of his 70 strikeouts with a devastating slider, but he couldn't get enough out of his mid-90s fastball to set it up. He has closer potential if he can harness the command of his heater, but Alburquerque's already at an age where this type of repertoire often stops working, rather than starts.

Jose Alvarez
Born: 5/6/1989 Age: 25
Bats: L Throws: L Height: 5' 11" Weight: 180
Breakout: 36% Improve: 57% Collapse: 18%
Attrition: 56% MLB: 49%
Comparables:
Bryan Augenstein, Kyle McPherson, Chris Schwinden

YEAR	TEAM	LVL	AGE	W	L	SV	G	GS	IP	H	HR	BB	SO	BB9	SO9	GB%	BABIP	WHIP	ERA	FIP	FRA	WARP
2011	JUP	A+	22	6	5	0	15	14	82	79	2	19	73	2.1	8.0	49%	.352	1.20	2.96	2.66	3.09	1.4
2011	JAX	AA	22	2	6	0	12	12	65²	80	9	22	45	3.0	6.2	36%	.341	1.55	5.35	4.77	5.94	-0.1
2012	JAX	AA	23	6	9	0	25	24	136¹	141	8	26	70	1.7	4.6	44%	.295	1.22	4.22	3.58	4.64	1.1
2013	TOL	AAA	24	8	6	1	21	20	128²	114	11	25	115	1.7	8.0	47%	.283	1.08	2.80	3.18	4.34	0.8
2013	DET	MLB	24	1	5	0	14	6	38²	42	7	16	31	3.7	7.2	42%	.304	1.50	5.82	5.22	5.60	-0.1
2014	DET	MLB	25	7	8	0	27	20	131²	152	18	38	80	2.6	5.4	43%	.310	1.44	4.90	4.88	5.32	-0.4

Alvarez is a lefty control artist acquired via minor-league free agency. His career year in Triple-A earned him frequent-flyer miles, but until September's roster expansion he had spent only 26 days on the big-league roster in four separate call-ups. He's more control than command at this point, and his size won't do him any favors. Alvarez showed enough to stay on the radar, but so do migrating birds and runaway mylar balloons.

Endrys Briceno
Born: 2/7/1992 Age: 22
Bats: R Throws: R Height: 6' 5" Weight: 171
Breakout: 0% Improve: 0% Collapse: 0%
Attrition: 0% MLB: 0%
Comparables:
Daniel Webb, Zac Rosscup, Enerio Del Rosario

YEAR	TEAM	LVL	AGE	W	L	SV	G	GS	IP	H	HR	BB	SO	BB9	SO9	GB%	BABIP	WHIP	ERA	FIP	FRA	WARP
2012	ONE	A-	20	4	3	0	12	12	57²	60	3	22	30	3.4	4.7	50%	.298	1.42	5.15	4.48	5.58	-0.6
2013	WMI	A	21	7	9	0	25	25	116²	124	5	51	65	3.9	5.0	53%	.305	1.50	4.47	4.25	5.65	-0.1
2014	DET	MLB	22	2	2	1	23	5	84	112	12	48	26	5.1	2.7	46%	.317	1.90	6.99	6.59	7.60	-2.2

Don't scout the statline—this lean righty is one of the more intriguing arms in the system, with easy velocity that steams up scouts' glasses. As he fills out his rail-thin frame, he could add another tick or two of velocity and will certainly improve his stamina. His changeup is impressive for a 21-year-old who just finished his first full-season assignment. And here's one from the "intangibles" file: After two brutal mid-August starts, he was a few bad innings away from heading into the offseason in a very dark place. He rallied with six shutout innings in his final start of the season and got to fly home to Venezuela feeling pretty, pretty, pretty good.

Joba Chamberlain

Born: 9/23/1985 Age: 28
Bats: R Throws: R Height: 6' 2'' Weight: 250
Breakout: 25% Improve: 50% Collapse: 29%
Attrition: 11% MLB: 97%

Comparables:
Carlos Villanueva, Chad Gaudin, Gaylord Perry

YEAR	TEAM	LVL	AGE	W	L	SV	G	GS	IP	H	HR	BB	SO	BB9	SO9	GB%	BABIP	WHIP	ERA	FIP	FRA	WARP
2011	NYA	MLB	25	2	0	0	27	0	28²	23	3	7	24	2.2	7.5	60%	.267	1.05	2.83	3.58	4.58	0.2
2012	NYA	MLB	26	1	0	0	22	0	20²	26	3	6	22	2.6	9.6	46%	.371	1.55	4.35	3.97	3.80	0.4
2013	NYA	MLB	27	2	1	1	45	0	42	47	8	26	38	5.6	8.1	43%	.315	1.74	4.93	5.67	5.97	-0.5
2014	DET	MLB	28	2	1	0	39	0	37²	38	4	14	34	3.4	8.2	48%	.313	1.39	4.26	4.18	4.63	0.1

In retrospect, the Yankees might have been better off if Joe Girardi had not only taken the ball at the end of Chamberlain's two-walk, three-run Opening Day outing, but told him not to bother coming back. The large and rarely in charge right-hander missed most of May with an oblique strain and was a mess the rest of the way. His walk rate rose and his strikeout rate fell, thanks to his lowest chase rate as a reliever, and he gave up homers at a higher clip than Phil Hughes, which is saying something. After the break, he was one of the lowest-leverage relievers in the game. We'll never know how to distribute the blame for Chamberlain's disappointing first six years of service time between the various factors that could have contributed—injuries, makeup and the Yankees' indecision about his role—but it will take more than a move to the Motor City to bring back the wicked slider and high-90s heat he had in 2007.

Phil Coke

Born: 7/19/1982 Age: 31
Bats: L Throws: L Height: 6' 1'' Weight: 210
Breakout: 25% Improve: 61% Collapse: 22%
Attrition: 9% MLB: 89%

Comparables:
Jeff Fassero, Jeremy Affeldt, Dennys Reyes

YEAR	TEAM	LVL	AGE	W	L	SV	G	GS	IP	H	HR	BB	SO	BB9	SO9	GB%	BABIP	WHIP	ERA	FIP	FRA	WARP
2011	DET	MLB	28	3	9	1	48	14	108²	118	5	40	69	3.3	5.7	45%	.315	1.45	4.47	3.60	4.30	1.5
2012	DET	MLB	29	2	3	1	66	0	54	71	5	18	51	3.0	8.5	50%	.388	1.65	4.00	3.42	3.52	1.0
2013	DET	MLB	30	0	5	1	49	0	38¹	43	3	21	30	4.9	7.0	48%	.325	1.67	5.40	4.17	5.21	-0.1
2014	DET	MLB	31	2	1	1	38	2	42¹	44	4	15	33	3.3	7.1	46%	.314	1.39	4.18	4.12	4.54	0.2

An impressive 2012 postseason put Coke on the table for Detroit's open closer's job, despite right-handers' tendency to smoke anything he throws while drawing copious free bases. Given first shot, Coke cracked, blowing his first two save chances and never sniffing another one. From there, he hit rock bottom, as even lefties had a high OPS against him. If he can get back to dealing against lefties he'll have some use as a lower-leverage LOOGY, but by this point his manager should be wary of overdosing.

Jonathon Crawford

Born: 11/1/1991 Age: 22
Bats: R Throws: R Height: 6' 2'' Weight: 205
Breakout: 100% Improve: 100% Collapse: 0%
Attrition: 0% MLB: 1%

Comparables:
Joe Savery, Brett Marshall, Dan Jennings

YEAR	TEAM	LVL	AGE	W	L	SV	G	GS	IP	H	HR	BB	SO	BB9	SO9	GB%	BABIP	WHIP	ERA	FIP	FRA	WARP
2013	ONE	A-	21	0	2	0	8	8	19	15	0	9	21	4.3	9.9	60%	.288	1.26	1.89	2.46	3.22	0.4
2014	DET	MLB	22	2	3	0	9	9	32	39	4	18	18	5.2	5.0	47%	.316	1.79	6.20	5.69	6.74	-0.4

You may need to sit down for this news: Yes, the Tigers *did* take a power arm with their top pick in the 2013 draft. We jest, but the joke isn't *on* the Tigers by any stretch. Stocking power arms works, and the Tigers have taken a big arm with eight of their last 11 top picks. For every Verlander (2004) there's a Ryan Perry (2008), to be sure, but even the power arms that flop (Andrew Miller, 2005) or lose some power (Jacob Turner, 2009) bring back All-Star trade returns. Some see Crawford's future in the bullpen, but that's a long way off—he'll get every chance to refine his command and changeup as a starter. Even as a reliever his ceiling would be high, as his fastball and slider each grade out as plus.

Casey Crosby

Born: 9/17/1988 Age: 25
Bats: R Throws: L Height: 6' 5'' Weight: 225
Breakout: 41% Improve: 62% Collapse: 23%
Attrition: 70% MLB: 37%

Comparables:
David Purcey, Donnie Veal, Chris Dwyer

YEAR	TEAM	LVL	AGE	W	L	SV	G	GS	IP	H	HR	BB	SO	BB9	SO9	GB%	BABIP	WHIP	ERA	FIP	FRA	WARP
2011	ERI	AA	22	9	7	0	25	25	131²	122	11	77	121	5.3	8.3	52%	.297	1.51	4.10	4.53	4.79	0.1
2012	TOL	AAA	23	7	9	0	22	22	125²	112	12	65	112	4.7	8.0	50%	.286	1.41	4.01	4.17	5.19	0.0
2012	DET	MLB	23	1	1	0	3	3	12¹	15	2	11	9	8.0	6.6	51%	.351	2.11	9.49	6.37	10.12	-0.4
2013	TOL	AAA	24	2	5	0	13	13	57²	55	3	40	61	6.2	9.5	56%	.342	1.65	4.84	3.90	4.93	0.3
2014	DET	MLB	25	3	5	0	12	12	61¹	63	7	35	51	5.1	7.4	50%	.307	1.60	5.07	4.95	5.51	-0.3

A former top prospect, the 25-year-old lefty has seen his ceiling come down considerably. Crosby has struggled in the high minors, particularly with control—he walked at least four batters in more than half his outings last year. Without a reliable changeup he is helpless against righties, and subsequently an unlikely starter. Lost among his ugly composite line is real success against lefties, who managed just a .573 OPS while fanning every fourth plate appearance against him. He has the stuff to become an important lefty in the big-league bullpen once he curbs the free passes.

Octavio Dotel

Born: 11/25/1973 Age: 40
Bats: R Throws: R Height: 6' 0" Weight: 230
Breakout: 22% Improve: 38% Collapse: 28%
Attrition: 7% MLB: 64%

Comparables:
Rudy Seanez, Mike Remlinger, Dan Plesac

YEAR	TEAM	LVL	AGE	W	L	SV	G	GS	IP	H	HR	BB	SO	BB9	SO9	GB%	BABIP	WHIP	ERA	FIP	FRA	WARP
2011	TOR	MLB	37	2	1	1	36	0	29^1	20	5	12	30	3.7	9.2	29%	.205	1.09	3.68	4.66	5.36	-0.1
2011	SLN	MLB	37	3	3	2	29	0	24^2	16	1	5	32	1.8	11.7	37%	.259	0.85	3.28	1.53	2.71	0.4
2012	DET	MLB	38	5	3	1	57	0	58	50	3	12	62	1.9	9.6	43%	.301	1.07	3.57	2.25	2.66	1.5
2013	DET	MLB	39	0	0	0	6	0	4^2	10	0	4	4	7.7	7.7	40%	.500	3.00	13.50	3.93	3.95	0.0
2014	DET	MLB	40	2	1	1	39	0	35^1	31	3	14	39	3.6	9.9	38%	.300	1.29	3.59	3.46	3.90	0.4

Right elbow issues that struck in April cost Dotel virtually the entire season and cost Detroit one of its most reliable relievers. Dotel was determined to avoid surgery, but his rehabilitation was continually halted by forearm stiffness, and a final attempt to return in September didn't go well. That is tough to deal with for any pitcher, but it could be conclusive for a 40-year-old who has been through the injury wringer throughout a 15-year career. He says he'd like to return—perhaps with an MLB record 14th team—for another shot this year, but as we go to press, he's a free man still.

Ian Krol

Born: 5/9/1991 Age: 23
Bats: L Throws: L Height: 6' 1" Weight: 210
Breakout: 49% Improve: 67% Collapse: 26%
Attrition: 53% MLB: 47%

Comparables:
Bryan Augenstein, Nick Maronde, Alex Burnett

YEAR	TEAM	LVL	AGE	W	L	SV	G	GS	IP	H	HR	BB	SO	BB9	SO9	GB%	BABIP	WHIP	ERA	FIP	FRA	WARP
2012	STO	A+	21	1	7	0	21	15	86^1	95	13	24	79	2.5	8.2	46%	.315	1.38	5.21	4.88	5.06	1.2
2012	MID	AA	21	1	2	0	8	0	10^2	11	0	2	10	1.7	8.4	62%	.379	1.22	5.06	1.97	3.09	0.3
2013	HAR	AA	22	0	0	1	21	0	26	14	1	7	29	2.4	10.0	48%	.197	0.81	0.69	2.63	2.55	0.7
2013	WAS	MLB	22	2	1	0	32	0	27^1	28	5	8	22	2.6	7.2	40%	.284	1.32	3.95	4.67	4.83	-0.1
2014	DET	MLB	23	3	3	0	21	8	52^2	56	7	18	36	3.2	6.1	45%	.299	1.42	4.66	4.86	5.06	0.0

Krol's flaws as a starter—the lack of a third pitch and poor command—haven't bothered him since his transition to relief: A bump in velocity has allowed him to get away with some poor placement, while his lack of a changeup won't mean a thing once he settles in as a lefty specialist. Washington tried to use him as more than that, but right-handers teed off for a .304/.350/.607 line, more than 350 points of OPS higher than lefties managed. The obligatorily thrown-in relief pitcher in the Doug Fister trade, he'll see more success in Detroit as he's used more judiciously.

Melvin Mercedes

Born: 11/2/1990 Age: 23
Bats: R Throws: R Height: 6' 3" Weight: 250
Breakout: 0% Improve: 0% Collapse: 0%
Attrition: 0% MLB: 0%

Comparables:
Bobby Cassevah, Luis Garcia, Dan Otero

YEAR	TEAM	LVL	AGE	W	L	SV	G	GS	IP	H	HR	BB	SO	BB9	SO9	GB%	BABIP	WHIP	ERA	FIP	FRA	WARP
2011	ONE	A-	20	3	1	3	21	0	33^2	32	0	16	21	4.3	5.6	73%	.192	1.43	2.67	3.63	4.68	0.0
2012	WMI	A	21	0	3	9	37	0	64^1	54	3	23	43	3.2	6.0	57%	.268	1.20	2.80	3.79	4.87	0.1
2013	LAK	A+	22	3	1	11	24	0	28	23	1	5	17	1.6	5.5	54%	.256	1.00	0.96	3.13	3.77	0.3
2013	ERI	AA	22	2	1	12	26	0	25	23	3	9	19	3.2	6.8	40%	.256	1.28	1.44	4.68	5.01	0.1
2014	DET	MLB	23	1	0	1	33	0	43	50	6	24	21	4.9	4.4	50%	.301	1.70	5.86	6.08	6.37	-0.7

Mercedes is tremendous, physically, leading to Bruce Rondon comps, but he lacks a strikeout pitch anywhere near that of his portly colleague. His mid-90s heat can push even higher at times, but Mercedes doesn't miss enough bats to be more than intriguing right now. Still, after a slow burn through the minors, he posted elite ERAs at two levels last year.

Joe Nathan

Born: 11/22/1974 Age: 39
Bats: R Throws: R Height: 6' 4" Weight: 230
Breakout: 19% Improve: 40% Collapse: 37%
Attrition: 16% MLB: 76%

Comparables:
Tom Gordon, Trevor Hoffman, Billy Wagner

YEAR	TEAM	LVL	AGE	W	L	SV	G	GS	IP	H	HR	BB	SO	BB9	SO9	GB%	BABIP	WHIP	ERA	FIP	FRA	WARP
2011	MIN	MLB	36	2	1	14	48	0	44^2	38	7	14	43	2.8	8.7	37%	.250	1.16	4.84	4.32	4.58	0.4
2012	TEX	MLB	37	3	5	37	66	0	64^1	55	7	13	78	1.8	10.9	46%	.306	1.06	2.80	2.74	3.32	1.4
2013	TEX	MLB	38	6	2	43	67	0	64^2	36	2	22	73	3.1	10.2	34%	.224	0.90	1.39	2.29	2.43	1.7
2014	DET	MLB	39	3	1	33	56	0	54	44	5	16	61	2.7	10.1	42%	.286	1.11	2.78	3.21	3.03	1.2

And Nathan just keeps on rolling. The guy drafted 19 years ago as a shortstop is now 10th all-time in saves. In the live ball era only two pitchers 38 or older have had an ERA better than Nathan's 1.39 in 50 or more innings: 44-year-old Hoyt Wilhelm in 1967, and Nathan's 2012 teammate Koji Uehara for Boston last year. Nathan's ERA is misleading, as his .224 BABIP and 3 percent rate of home runs per fly ball aren't sustainable, his stuff was down from 2012 and his fastball and slider velocity were both down a few ticks. That may help explain why Texas made no effort to keep him from signing with Detroit.

Rick Porcello

Born: 12/27/1988 Age: 25
Bats: R Throws: R Height: 6' 5" Weight: 200
Breakout: 14% Improve: 49% Collapse: 18%
Attrition: 5% MLB: 99%

Comparables:
Mike Leake, Mike Mussina, Rick Reuschel

YEAR	TEAM	LVL	AGE	W	L	SV	G	GS	IP	H	HR	BB	SO	BB9	SO9	GB%	BABIP	WHIP	ERA	FIP	FRA	WARP
2011	DET	MLB	22	14	9	0	31	31	182	210	18	46	104	2.3	5.1	54%	.316	1.41	4.75	4.09	4.60	1.8
2012	DET	MLB	23	10	12	0	31	31	176¹	226	16	44	107	2.2	5.5	55%	.344	1.53	4.59	3.86	4.76	1.5
2013	DET	MLB	24	13	8	0	32	29	177	185	18	42	142	2.1	7.2	56%	.315	1.28	4.32	3.56	4.76	1.1
2014	DET	MLB	25	9	9	0	26	26	153	168	15	37	97	2.2	5.7	54%	.312	1.34	4.14	4.15	4.50	0.9

The "if you don't count …" statistics game is a cheating way to tell a happy story, and yet the game has some merit with Porcello. If he hadn't faced the Angels last year, he would have had a 3.61 ERA in 172 innings. The improvements in his game would have been far more obvious and much more widely noticed—nobody's impressed by a quarter-run improvement in ERA, but a full run turns some heads. He cut his WHIP dramatically, recorded a career-best 19 percent strikeout rate and even topped his previous best groundball rate. He also allowed 17 runs in five innings to the Angels, including a nine-run, -inning massacre in late April. Is there any reason not to count starts against the Angels? Of course not. But at least it puts in perspective the relatively small margin between a breakout we notice and a breakout we might miss. With five full seasons of work—each with minor improvements from the last—before his 25th birthday, Porcello looks like he might still be a future star.

Luke Putkonen

Born: 5/10/1986 Age: 28
Bats: R Throws: R Height: 6' 6" Weight: 215
Breakout: 52% Improve: 73% Collapse: 22%
Attrition: 49% MLB: 23%

Comparables:
Lance Broadway, Pedro Liriano, Cesar Ramos

YEAR	TEAM	LVL	AGE	W	L	SV	G	GS	IP	H	HR	BB	SO	BB9	SO9	GB%	BABIP	WHIP	ERA	FIP	FRA	WARP
2011	LAK	A+	25	2	6	0	18	8	65	77	10	18	52	2.5	7.2	49%	.360	1.46	5.54	4.76	6.63	-0.5
2011	ERI	AA	25	1	7	0	11	11	52¹	68	8	22	23	3.8	4.0	51%	.330	1.72	7.57	5.89	7.03	-0.6
2012	TOL	AAA	26	3	3	0	24	2	56²	68	3	20	46	3.2	7.3	48%	.365	1.55	4.92	3.33	4.65	0.3
2012	DET	MLB	26	0	2	1	12	0	16	19	0	8	10	4.5	5.6	54%	.352	1.69	3.94	3.30	4.34	0.1
2013	TOL	AAA	27	2	0	1	20	1	37²	25	0	13	38	3.1	9.1	53%	.258	1.01	1.91	2.22	3.14	0.8
2013	DET	MLB	27	1	3	0	30	0	29²	30	4	9	28	2.7	8.5	60%	.306	1.31	3.03	3.85	4.86	0.1
2014	DET	MLB	28	2	3	0	20	6	54²	65	7	23	30	3.7	5.0	50%	.317	1.61	5.52	5.27	6.00	-0.6

Putkonen is certainly not the first, but at least the latest, to show that "fast" alone doesn't make for a good fastball. His sits in the mid-90s yet got smacked around for an .839 OPS last season, leaving his secondary stuff—a plus curve and solid splitter—to do the heavy lifting. His command gets wobbly at times, and the 6-foot-6 frame can be hard to rein in, but the raw stuff is there for a late-inning reliever of some consequence.

Robbie Ray

Born: 10/1/1991 Age: 22
Bats: L Throws: L Height: 6' 2" Weight: 170
Breakout: 51% Improve: 88% Collapse: 12%
Attrition: 82% MLB: 16%

Comparables:
Adam Ottavino, Dan Straily, Jeurys Familia

YEAR	TEAM	LVL	AGE	W	L	SV	G	GS	IP	H	HR	BB	SO	BB9	SO9	GB%	BABIP	WHIP	ERA	FIP	FRA	WARP
2011	HAG	A	19	2	3	0	20	20	89	71	3	38	95	3.8	9.6	42%	.293	1.22	3.13	3.52	3.29	2.4
2012	POT	A+	20	4	12	0	22	21	105²	122	14	49	86	4.2	7.3	35%	.332	1.62	6.56	5.18	5.90	0.0
2013	POT	A+	21	6	3	0	16	16	84	60	9	41	100	4.4	10.7	45%	.273	1.20	3.11	3.97	4.77	1.2
2013	HAR	AA	21	5	2	0	11	11	58	56	4	21	60	3.3	9.3	44%	.317	1.33	3.72	3.55	3.59	1.2
2014	DET	MLB	22	6	9	0	23	23	108²	117	14	56	85	4.6	7.0	41%	.308	1.59	5.33	5.23	5.79	-0.7

Ray revived his hype status after a brutal 2012 season; Tigers GM Dave Dombrowski goosed it further by requesting Ray as the centerpiece of the Doug Fister trade. The culprit during Ray's struggles was a decline in velocity, as his low-90s fastball dropped into the high 80s. He returned to the scene of the crime (High-A) to begin 2013 and brought his velocity back with him, touching 96 mph. After a promotion to Double-A, he continued to generate groundballs with a powerful sinker and miss bats with a sharpened breaking ball.

Evan Reed

Born: 12/31/1985 Age: 28
Bats: R Throws: R Height: 6' 4" Weight: 255
Breakout: 44% Improve: 56% Collapse: 29%
Attrition: 77% MLB: 25%

Comparables:
Jailen Peguero, Jeff Ridgway, Connor Robertson

YEAR	TEAM	LVL	AGE	W	L	SV	G	GS	IP	H	HR	BB	SO	BB9	SO9	GB%	BABIP	WHIP	ERA	FIP	FRA	WARP
2011	JUP	A+	25	0	1	0	11	0	15²	9	0	10	13	5.7	7.5	48%	.296	1.21	4.02	3.84	3.09	0.1
2012	JAX	AA	26	3	1	12	27	0	34²	24	1	11	43	2.9	11.2	43%	.280	1.01	2.34	1.99	2.62	0.9
2012	NWO	AAA	26	2	3	1	23	0	32²	43	2	16	27	4.4	7.4	49%	.373	1.81	7.16	4.28	5.05	0.1
2013	TOL	AAA	27	1	4	1	32	0	49²	38	1	20	49	3.6	8.9	47%	.296	1.17	2.54	2.70	3.51	0.7
2013	DET	MLB	27	0	1	0	16	0	23¹	28	2	8	17	3.1	6.6	53%	.338	1.54	4.24	3.89	4.83	0.0
2014	DET	MLB	28	2	1	0	42	0	59²	61	5	25	50	3.8	7.5	44%	.316	1.45	4.28	4.04	4.66	0.2

Reed can run it up to 98 mph but can't fool anybody. For a team whose biggest flaw in the playoffs has been the bullpen, Reed stands in as a significant organizational test. They should be able to cultivate something useful out of the raw talent in his arm, as well as those of Putkonen and Alburquerque. If they don't, they're stuck playing Reliever Roulette on the free agent market, a game that has destroyed many a big-budget team and cost Detroit in consecutive Octobers.

Bruce Rondon

Born: 12/9/1990 Age: 23
Bats: R Throws: R Height: 6' 3" Weight: 275
Breakout: 34% Improve: 40% Collapse: 47%
Attrition: 48% MLB: 32%

Comparables:
Eduardo Sanchez, Jon Meloan, Stephen Pryor

YEAR	TEAM	LVL	AGE	W	L	SV	G	GS	IP	H	HR	BB	SO	BB9	SO9	GB%	BABIP	WHIP	ERA	FIP	FRA	WARP
2011	WMI	A	20	2	2	19	41	0	40	22	0	34	61	7.7	13.7	53%	.314	1.40	2.03	3.23	3.16	0.7
2012	LAK	A+	21	1	0	15	22	0	23¹	12	1	10	34	3.9	13.1	57%	.239	0.94	1.93	2.45	3.71	0.4
2012	ERI	AA	21	0	1	12	21	0	21²	15	1	9	23	3.7	9.6	52%	.264	1.11	0.83	3.48	3.74	0.4
2013	TOL	AAA	22	1	1	14	30	0	29²	14	1	13	40	3.9	12.1	51%	.210	0.91	1.52	2.46	3.67	0.4
2013	DET	MLB	22	1	2	1	30	0	28²	28	2	11	30	3.5	9.4	47%	.329	1.36	3.45	3.04	3.29	0.5
2014	DET	MLB	23	2	1	1	46	0	47²	41	5	25	51	4.7	9.6	49%	.300	1.39	3.88	4.25	4.22	0.4

Don't get hung up on what Rondon is right now; at some point in his career, he'll be everything. Right now he's going through his Jordan Walden phase—a fastball that averages 100 mph and touches 103, but no weapon to retire lefties. Next will be the Addison Reed phase, baserunners and saves and trying to figure out how this thing works. He'll have a couple vintage Jose Mesa seasons when he develops his command, and a few months—maybe even a year or two—when you'll think he's moved into the Chapman/Kimbrel class of reliable relievers. Then he'll start to lose his velocity but make up for it with sterling walk rates, before losing even more velocity and having to rely ever more on his slider. Through it all he'll be striking batters out, but by the slider phase he'll be back up to five walks per nine and eventually end up on the surgeon's table. He'll return with just 91 or 92 on his fastball, but he'll have developed a nasty cutter, and he'll be the closer that bad teams sign to trade to good teams in July. Finally, it'll just be a new city each winter, chasing different set-up roles. He'll be the famous former closer with just enough fire in his arm to keep the actual closer wary of usurpation. He'll do all those things and more, in time, but for now he's just 23 years old, learning on the job with just 60 innings in the high minors on his resume, and one absolute heck of an arm.

Anibal Sanchez

Born: 2/27/1984 Age: 30
Bats: R Throws: R Height: 6' 0" Weight: 205
Breakout: 10% Improve: 39% Collapse: 28%
Attrition: 13% MLB: 93%

Comparables:
John Lackey, Adam Wainwright, Gavin Floyd

YEAR	TEAM	LVL	AGE	W	L	SV	G	GS	IP	H	HR	BB	SO	BB9	SO9	GB%	BABIP	WHIP	ERA	FIP	FRA	WARP
2011	FLO	MLB	27	8	9	0	32	32	196¹	187	20	64	202	2.9	9.3	45%	.313	1.28	3.67	3.31	3.82	2.2
2012	DET	MLB	28	4	6	0	12	12	74²	81	8	15	57	1.8	6.9	47%	.313	1.29	3.74	3.64	4.23	1.1
2012	MIA	MLB	28	5	7	0	19	19	121	119	12	33	110	2.5	8.2	50%	.311	1.26	3.94	3.47	3.83	1.3
2013	DET	MLB	29	14	8	0	29	29	182	156	9	54	202	2.7	10.0	48%	.308	1.15	2.57	2.42	2.98	4.6
2014	DET	MLB	30	10	8	0	25	25	156¹	152	14	47	138	2.7	8.0	46%	.306	1.28	3.63	3.67	3.95	1.9

It speaks to the major-league scouting of GM Dave Dombrowski and his team that they continue to acquire players who immediately show improvement upon arrival. Doug Fister and Sanchez were quality arms with Seattle and Miami, respectively, but the reviews were mixed when the trades were made. Yet each took his game to a new level with Detroit. Sanchez added a mile per hour to his fastball, which led to whiff-rate spikes for each of his four pitches. He led the league in ERA and FIP, and had he not missed four starts with a shoulder strain might have been the only credible threat to Max Scherzer's Cy Young campaign. He still hasn't thrown 200 innings in a season, but he's far more durable than he once was. Benchmark or not, he's an ace.

Max Scherzer

Born: 7/27/1984 Age: 29
Bats: R Throws: R Height: 6' 3" Weight: 220
Breakout: 16% Improve: 42% Collapse: 30%
Attrition: 3% MLB: 97%

Comparables:
Jake Peavy, Josh Beckett, Tim Lincecum

YEAR	TEAM	LVL	AGE	W	L	SV	G	GS	IP	H	HR	BB	SO	BB9	SO9	GB%	BABIP	WHIP	ERA	FIP	FRA	WARP
2011	DET	MLB	26	15	9	0	33	33	195	207	29	56	174	2.6	8.0	42%	.315	1.35	4.43	4.18	4.74	2.1
2012	DET	MLB	27	16	7	0	32	32	187²	179	23	60	231	2.9	11.1	38%	.334	1.27	3.74	3.22	3.50	4.4
2013	DET	MLB	28	21	3	0	32	32	214¹	152	18	56	240	2.4	10.1	38%	.259	0.97	2.90	2.77	3.23	4.6
2014	DET	MLB	29	11	9	0	28	28	173¹	157	19	52	182	2.7	9.4	42%	.302	1.20	3.41	3.62	3.71	2.6

Even on his worst days it is obvious how talented Scherzer is, but prior to 2013 he managed only short bursts of his best days. In 2010, he was demoted after eight starts, then returned to post a 2.46 ERA for four months. In 2011, he turned in six starts of six or more earned runs. In 2012, he ended April with a 7.77 ERA. In each case, he was undone by lefties. Scherzer finally pocketed the slider in favor of a devastating curveball against southpaws—they produced just a .539 OPS against the pitch—and repeatedly credited the change with his turnaround in 2013. Notably, he improved by just as much against righties, who hit just .165/.219/.275 against him, suggesting his breakout goes deeper than he allows. If the Tigers haven't locked him up by the time you read this, then it'll be his walk year.

Drew Smyly

Born: 6/13/1989 Age: 25
Bats: L Throws: L Height: 6' 3" Weight: 190
Breakout: 26% Improve: 56% Collapse: 23%
Attrition: 15% MLB: 97%

Comparables:
Carlos Villanueva, James Shields, Brandon McCarthy

YEAR	TEAM	LVL	AGE	W	L	SV	G	GS	IP	H	HR	BB	SO	BB9	SO9	GB%	BABIP	WHIP	ERA	FIP	FRA	WARP
2011	LAK	A+	22	7	3	0	14	14	80¹	71	1	21	77	2.4	8.6	47%	.353	1.15	2.58	2.53	3.26	1.3
2011	ERI	AA	22	4	3	0	8	7	45²	32	1	15	53	3.0	10.4	60%	.257	1.03	1.18	2.42	2.96	0.3
2012	TOL	AAA	23	0	2	0	7	7	17²	22	3	8	25	4.1	12.7	35%	.413	1.70	6.11	4.06	4.70	0.2
2012	DET	MLB	23	4	3	0	23	18	99¹	93	12	33	94	3.0	8.5	42%	.296	1.27	3.99	3.78	4.23	1.6
2013	DET	MLB	24	6	0	2	63	0	76	62	4	17	81	2.0	9.6	43%	.291	1.04	2.37	2.34	2.95	1.6
2014	DET	MLB	25	4	3	1	30	9	71	66	7	21	70	2.6	8.9	43%	.305	1.22	3.46	3.57	3.76	1.1

Smyly is too good for a reliever's workload, and certainly too good for the limited LOOGY work he got in October, when the rest of the Detroit bullpen crumbled around him. Ironically, the better Smyly pitched the smaller his role, as he went from full-inning work early in the season to one-out appearances in August, September and October. While Smyly is, indeed, better against lefties, he was effective against righties, too—more effective, for instance, than Al Alburquerque or Luke Putkonen. With the trade of Doug Fister, Smyly will likely move back into the rotation, a role in which he flourished in 2012. However, if he doesn't earn a starting gig, at his current trajectory he'll be throwing one pitch per outing by the All-Star break. At least it'll be a great pitch.

Jake Thompson
Born: 1/31/1994 Age: 20
Bats: R Throws: R Height: 6' 4" Weight: 235
Breakout: 53% Improve: 86% Collapse: 14%
Attrition: 56% MLB: 6%
Comparables:
Jarrod Parker, Carlos Carrasco, Mat Latos

YEAR	TEAM	LVL	AGE	W	L	SV	G	GS	IP	H	HR	BB	SO	BB9	SO9	GB%	BABIP	WHIP	ERA	FIP	FRA	WARP
2013	WMI	A	19	3	3	0	17	16	83¹	79	4	32	91	3.5	9.8	45%	.325	1.33	3.13	3.33	3.91	1.6
2014	DET	MLB	20	3	5	0	13	13	61	67	8	32	46	4.7	6.7	45%	.313	1.62	5.39	5.30	5.86	-0.4

Not one word of Thompson's story changed with his introduction to full-season ball: future quality mid-rotation starter in, future quality mid-rotation starter out. The 20-year-old's slider is his best pitch, and makes it easy for him to rack up strikeouts despite work needed on his fastball command, changeup and nascent curveball. Thompson projects as more of a groundball machine, eventually. Early returns on the 2012 second-rounder are appealing, and while the upside doesn't wow, he's headed for a future as, well, a quality major-league starter.

Jose Valverde
Born: 3/24/1978 Age: 36
Bats: R Throws: R Height: 6' 4" Weight: 255
Breakout: 30% Improve: 51% Collapse: 37%
Attrition: 12% MLB: 74%
Comparables:
Damaso Marte, Jason Isringhausen, Brian Fuentes

YEAR	TEAM	LVL	AGE	W	L	SV	G	GS	IP	H	HR	BB	SO	BB9	SO9	GB%	BABIP	WHIP	ERA	FIP	FRA	WARP
2011	DET	MLB	33	2	4	49	75	0	72¹	52	5	34	69	4.2	8.6	44%	.247	1.19	2.24	3.59	3.74	1.2
2012	DET	MLB	34	3	4	35	71	0	69	59	3	27	48	3.5	6.3	36%	.264	1.25	3.78	3.57	3.97	0.9
2013	TOL	AAA	35	0	0	7	11	0	11	14	1	6	10	4.9	8.2	36%	.406	1.82	4.09	4.48	4.97	0.0
2013	DET	MLB	35	0	1	9	20	0	19¹	18	6	6	19	2.8	8.8	40%	.235	1.24	5.59	6.39	6.90	-0.3
2014	DET	MLB	36	2	1	16	36	0	35¹	31	3	15	33	3.9	8.4	42%	.283	1.30	3.65	4.00	3.96	0.4

The short-lived Valverde experiment actually made *some* sense for the Tigers, given the $7 million paycut he took and the sorry state of Detroit's bullpen after the 2012 postseason. Of course, he was a major cause of that sorriness, but plenty of incumbents have been reelected to clean up their own messes. He didn't last two months but he did manage to allow his most home runs in a season since 2008. Valverde is down three miles per hour from his fastball peak, and he rarely throws his once-unhittable splitter anymore, but he's got enough of a track record to merit a few minor-league deals.

Justin Verlander
Born: 2/20/1983 Age: 31
Bats: R Throws: R Height: 6' 5" Weight: 225
Breakout: 13% Improve: 49% Collapse: 24%
Attrition: 7% MLB: 88%
Comparables:
Johan Santana, Erik Bedard, Roger Clemens

YEAR	TEAM	LVL	AGE	W	L	SV	G	GS	IP	H	HR	BB	SO	BB9	SO9	GB%	BABIP	WHIP	ERA	FIP	FRA	WARP
2011	DET	MLB	28	24	5	0	34	34	251	174	24	57	250	2.0	9.0	42%	.236	0.92	2.40	3.03	3.53	5.1
2012	DET	MLB	29	17	8	0	33	33	238¹	192	19	60	239	2.3	9.0	43%	.273	1.06	2.64	2.90	3.12	5.7
2013	DET	MLB	30	13	12	0	34	34	218¹	212	19	75	217	3.1	8.9	40%	.317	1.31	3.46	3.30	3.39	4.5
2014	DET	MLB	31	13	9	0	29	29	198²	170	16	54	203	2.5	9.2	41%	.291	1.13	2.81	3.15	3.05	4.6

Consider the bookends: Verlander had a 1.83 ERA in April and a 2.27 in September. Try to ignore the books: a 4.26 ERA and 1.41 WHIP in the middle four months. His fastball velocity was down a mile from 2012, but the struggles had more to do with his command and control. A "down" season from Verlander still yielded four WARP, and after he punctuated it with a postseason for the ages—23 innings, a single run allowed as his velocity was all the way back—you'd have to consider him once again the Cy Young favorite entering this season. Sorry, Scherzer. Sorry, Sanchez. He's still the ace.

Kevin Ziomek
Born: 3/21/1992 Age: 22
Bats: R Throws: L Height: 6' 3" Weight: 190
Breakout: 0% Improve: 0% Collapse: 0%
Attrition: 0% MLB: 0%
Comparables:
David Phelps, Garrett Richards, Ryan Cook

YEAR	TEAM	LVL	AGE	W	L	SV	G	GS	IP	H	HR	BB	SO	BB9	SO9	GB%	BABIP	WHIP	ERA	FIP	FRA	WARP
2014	DET	MLB	22	1	3	0	8	8	31¹	40	5	18	13	5.3	3.7	46%	.316	1.87	6.70	6.51	7.28	-0.6

Tabbed a potential first-rounder by some analysts, Ziomek fell to the Tigers in the second round of the 2013 draft after a breakout season for Vanderbilt. Wonky command, down velocity and unspectacular secondary stuff marred his sophomore season, but all three rebounded in the Cape Cod League before his junior year. With low-90s heat and an advanced changeup, Ziomek carried Vanderbilt to the SEC's best record last year. He'll need to improve his breaking stuff, but he's already a polished prospect with a mid-rotation future.

LINEOUTS

HITTERS

PLAYER	TEAM	LVL	AGE	PA	R	2B	3B	HR	RBI	BB	SO	SB-CS	AVG/OBP/SLG	TAv	BABIP	BRR	FRAA	WARP
LF T. Collins	ERI	AA	23	530	67	29	0	21	79	51	122	4-5	.240/.323/.438	.282	.277	0.9	LF(88): 1.3, RF(18): 1.0	2.0
1B M. Hessman	LOU	AAA	35	482	60	32	0	25	56	53	134	0-2	.240/.328/.495	.287	.286	-0.3	1B(103): 0.4, 3B(5): -0.1	1.8
LF D. Kelly	DET	MLB	33	251	33	6	1	6	23	27	28	2-0	.222/.309/.343	.252	.226	0.9	LF(38): -1.5, CF(25): -1.5	0.2
CF A. Schotts	WMI	A	19	213	22	6	1	1	17	14	75	9-5	.192/.248/.249	.195	.303	1.3	CF(58): 2.1, RF(1): -0.0	-0.7
	ONE	A-	19	246	25	7	3	1	13	20	71	22-3	.229/.305/.303	.246	.333	2.9	CF(60): 9.0	1.5
2B D. Worth	TOL	AAA	27	345	33	19	2	1	22	35	91	9-5	.223/.305/.308	.235	.315	0.9	2B(29): -0.1, 3B(28): -1.0	0.3
	DET	MLB	27	2	0	0	0	0	0	0	1	0-0	.000/.000/.000	.174	.000	0	3B(2): 0.1	-0.1

As **Tyler Collins**' power emerged, his ability to make consistent contact eroded. He tripled his home run rate, doubled his strikeout rate and traded 40 points of OBP for nine of slugging.   ⊘ **Mike Hessman** is what materialized when baseball scientists asked, "What if it's possible to achieve higher than 80 power by giving the specimen 20s everywhere else?"   ⊘ The retirement of Jim Leyland was the worst news of **Don Kelly**'s career, as it definitely marks the end of him batting third in a big-league lineup. ⊘ **Austin Schotts**' overly aggressive approach bred skeptics even during his promising debut, and he delivered on their doubts: a 32 percent strikeout rate tanked his followup. He's young enough to rebound. ⊘ **Danny Worth** will try to become Brad Ausmus' Don Kelly.

PITCHERS

PLAYER	TEAM	LVL	AGE	W	L	SV	IP	H	HR	BB	SO	BB9	SO9	GB%	BABIP	WHIP	ERA	FIP	FRA	WARP
D. Below	NWO	AAA	27	5	5	0	74	77	3	21	53	2.6	6.4	41%	.316	1.32	2.55	3.56	3.74	1.1
	TOL	AAA	27	1	2	0	25²	15	1	4	15	1.4	5.3	40%	.184	0.74	2.10	3.01	4.25	0.2
	MIA	MLB	27	0	1	0	2²	6	0	2	2	6.8	6.8	30%	.600	3.00	10.12	3.77	3.02	0.0
J. Bonderman	TAC	AAA	30	2	4	0	63²	77	7	18	33	2.5	4.7	46%	.323	1.49	4.52	4.86	5.19	0.2
	SEA	MLB	30	1	3	0	38¹	40	4	17	16	4.0	3.8	45%	.271	1.49	4.93	5.08	5.31	-0.1
	DET	MLB	30	1	1	0	16²	18	3	10	16	5.4	8.6	40%	.319	1.68	6.48	5.30	5.40	0.0
W. Clinard	LAK	A+	23	1	2	2	28¹	21	1	5	23	1.6	7.3	58%	.260	0.92	1.59	2.92	4.58	0.1
	ERI	AA	23	2	3	1	34¹	37	6	20	26	5.2	6.8	42%	.307	1.66	5.50	6.00	6.15	-0.3
K. Faulk	TOL	AAA	26	0	3	1	44¹	26	3	31	52	6.3	10.6	38%	.221	1.29	3.65	3.84	4.85	0.1
J. Jurrjens	NOR	AAA	27	6	6	0	94²	102	5	24	52	2.3	4.9	39%	.304	1.33	4.18	3.65	4.46	0.9
	TOL	AAA	27	1	4	0	39¹	45	3	14	24	3.2	5.5	44%	.326	1.50	5.49	4.12	4.67	0.2
	BAL	MLB	27	0	0	0	7¹	9	1	1	6	1.2	7.4	25%	.348	1.36	4.91	3.62	5.07	0.0
C. Knebel	WMI	A	21	2	1	15	31	14	0	10	41	2.9	11.9	56%	.212	0.77	0.87	1.66	2.69	0.8
K. Lobstein	ERI	AA	23	7	4	0	95¹	92	6	27	83	2.5	7.8	50%	.322	1.25	3.12	3.25	3.67	1.7
	TOL	AAA	23	6	3	0	72¹	73	2	25	65	3.1	8.1	47%	.330	1.35	3.48	2.97	4.14	0.7
J. Marinez	CHR	AAA	24	2	4	2	28	26	7	16	26	5.1	8.4	36%	.250	1.50	6.11	6.53	6.52	-0.4
L. Marte	DET	MLB	25	1	0	0	22¹	19	4	9	19	3.6	7.7	31%	.250	1.25	2.82	5.02	5.22	0.1
J. Ortega	TOL	AAA	24	4	3	4	48¹	28	2	33	56	6.1	10.4	50%	.234	1.26	1.86	3.54	4.29	0.3
	DET	MLB	24	0	2	0	11²	10	2	6	10	4.6	7.7	51%	.242	1.37	3.86	5.39	6.11	-0.1
J. Thompson	WMI	A	21	2	2	1	45	41	3	19	42	3.8	8.4	51%	.297	1.33	3.80	3.74	4.28	0.5
D. VerHagen	LAK	A+	22	5	3	0	67¹	49	1	27	35	3.6	4.7	58%	.231	1.13	2.81	3.82	5.24	-0.1
	ERI	AA	22	2	5	0	60	53	3	17	40	2.5	6.0	60%	.272	1.17	3.00	3.69	4.54	0.5

After being released by the Marlins in August, **Duane Below** latched on with the KIA Tigers in Korea, then signed with the *Detroit* Tigers in December. Based on our experience watching late-'90s Bill Murray comedies, we're guessing Korea was just the zany result of a clerical error. ⊘ Returning to the majors for 55 innings is a big win for **Jeremy Bonderman**. They weren't special innings, but weren't they, really? ⊘ **William Clinard** lost his aim after a promotion to Double-A, though one eight-run outing in mid-June sabotaged his bottom line. ⊘ Lefties went 3-for-48 against **Kenny Faulk** in Triple-A; 14 free passes boosted their OBP to .270, but Faulk has a LOOGY future, and maybe more. ⊘ There was a time when the **Jair Jurrjens** trade was seriously lamented by Tigers fans, and yet his return to the team's minor-league system likely went unnoticed by most of those folks. ⊘ **Corey Knebel**, a 2013 supplemental pick, wowed in his pro debut and even earned a special exemption to play in the Arizona Fall League. If left as a reliever, he could follow a fast-track path similar to that of Addison Reed. ⊘ Former second-rounder **Kyle Lobstein** rebounded from a down 2012 to have his best full season as a pro. He's not much of a prospect, but he'll soon start wearing a path between Toledo and Detroit. ⊘ **Jhan Marinez** struggled through another Triple-A season plagued by injury, ineffectiveness, gopher balls and the same lack of command that keeps him from leveraging his upper-90s heat and wipeout slider into a major-league bullpen gig; if he ever learns how to pitch, look out. ⊘ Injuries plagued **Luis Marte** throughout 2013, but the 26-year-old is useful as a 26th man, ready on a day's notice for some relief innings. ⊘ "You have to choose! It's either her or me," **Jose Ortega**'s 1.86 ERA demanded when she saw that he's still in touch with his 16 percent walk rate. ⊘ **Brenny Paulino** went another year without throwing. Time is still on the 21-year-old's side, figuratively, but a bad shoulder is still on his side, literally. ⊘ **Jeff Thompson** would fit in nicely with the Tigers' big-league bullpen: he's massive, fights walks and has a mid-90s fastball that goes too straight to qualify as plus. ⊘ **Drew VerHagen** had gaudy results, but his secondary pitches lag. At least one needs to take a leap if he's to avoid ending up in a bullpen.

MANAGER: BRAD AUSMUS

Jim Leyland heads out into the sunset a borderline Hall of Famer. He won a ton of games, but he also finished barely over .500. He was always a prominent manager, but also overshadowed by the trinity of Tony LaRussa, Bobby Cox and Joe Torre. Only two men have ever won pennants with three teams and both are in Cooperstown: Bill McKechnie and Dick Williams. Leyland nearly became the third, as he went to the Fall Classic with the Marlins and Tigers and came a pinch-hit single from advancing with the Pirates. Just think—Francisco Cabrera might be what keeps Leyland out of Cooperstown.

Incoming manager Brad Ausmus hasn't managed a single game yet, so it's hard to say much about him. We do have some idea who he learned from, though. In 18 seasons, he played in 1,971 games for nine skippers, and it breaks down as follows:

- 585 games for Phil Garner
- 343 games for Jimy Williams
- 286 games for Larry Dierker
- 153 games for Bruce Bochy
- 150 games for Jim Riggleman
- 127 games for Larry Parrish
- 95 games for Cecil Cooper
- 75 games for Buddy Bell
- 57 games for Joe Torre

Make of that what you will.

Houston Astros

February 2014
Zachary Levine
Baseball Prospectus
1 Swinganda Drive
New York, NY 10001

Jeff Luhnow
Houston Astros
501 Crawford Street
Houston, TX 77002

Dear Mr. Luhnow,

If you are detecting a sense of inevitability in opening this letter, let me assure you that I share the feeling. Maybe it's not inevitability in a predestination sense—let's not get too deep here—but more of a rite of passage. Like so many who have come before me here at Baseball Prospectus, with this letter, I submit my application to work in baseball operations for the Houston Astros.

Before you read about my qualifications on the attached resume, let me assure you that people will laugh if you hire me. They laughed when you hired pro scouting coordinator Kevin Goldstein as your second BP alum. I had personnel from other front offices call me unsolicited in my media role and ask if I knew what the hell you were doing. And if you knew what the hell you were doing. A business school guy out to "disrupt" the industry and "leverage" the talent out there and everything else they teach you in business school that would clearly never work in baseball.

When you hired Colin Wyers as a mathematical modeler, your third BP alum, it was more just a feeling of "yeah, of course." That was the refrain from those who think you're turning baseball into something it's not. But don't let that dissuade you. In fact, in applying, I encourage you to think back to business school when you learned about relative advantages and core competencies. You were there that day, right? The race for analysts is the only race you're winning

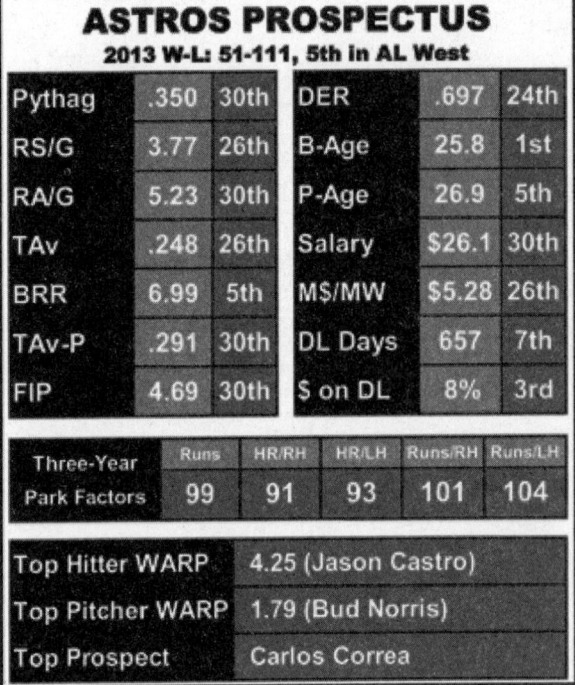

ASTROS PROSPECTUS
2013 W-L: 51-111, 5th in AL West

Pythag	.350	30th	DER	.697	24th
RS/G	3.77	26th	B-Age	25.8	1st
RA/G	5.23	30th	P-Age	26.9	5th
TAv	.248	26th	Salary	$26.1	30th
BRR	6.99	5th	M$/MW	$5.28	26th
TAv-P	.291	30th	DL Days	657	7th
FIP	4.69	30th	$ on DL	8%	3rd

	Runs	HR/RH	HR/LH	Runs/RH	Runs/LH
Three-Year Park Factors	99	91	93	101	104

Top Hitter WARP	4.25 (Jason Castro)
Top Pitcher WARP	1.79 (Bud Norris)
Top Prospect	Carlos Correa

because it's the only way you can win. Your team, if this won't disqualify me from consideration, stinks. Your front office outside baseball operations has been a nightmare. But when you brought over Sig Mejdal from the Cardinals as grand poobah of decision sciences and paired him with BP's own Mike Fast, you were finding your niche, and while there is something to be said for diminishing marginal returns (remember microeconomics?) there is also something to be said for increasing your edge on the competition and getting to each landmark first.

I'll warn you, though, they're going to keep laughing as long as you keep losing 100 games. I'm sure I don't have to tell you, nor will it score me any points in the interview to say it, but only the expansion Mets have lost more games over a three-year period than you have since 2011. As you thaw out of Houston's deep freeze of the high 50s, you're doing so on a 15-game losing streak.

I'm here to help turn that around, because while I'm pretty sure you'll tell me you have passed the inflection point and *are* turning things around, that's a story I've heard before. The Astros bottomed out in 2011 when your predecessors traded Hunter Pence and Michael Bourn. But actually, you bottomed out in 2012 when you traded Carlos Lee and Wandy Rodriguez and Brett Myers, because that had to be it. There was nobody else who made any money. But then you started trading the guys who didn't, and that was the bottom. It wasn't 106 losses. It wasn't 107. It was 111 that was the bottom.

Well, that probably was the bottom.

I remember reading your vision of the Astros in *Baseball Prospectus 2013*, when you talked about how all the changes in your front office were in good shape and now it was time to start remaking the baseball club. "Now we've got to figure out where we add strategically to improve results in 2013" were the exact words.

Obviously that didn't happen, and I'm totally on board with that. If I had been your employee at the time, I probably would have advocated doing the same thing. Why spend? It's been the question the last few years as the effort has begun to move this team in the right direction.

Really, it's just been wandering, though.

Look at where you've been at shortstop. Unless Jonathan Villar gets the majority of the action at shortstop this year, and I have no indication that this is anything resembling a certainty, y'all are about to use your sixth starting shortstop in six seasons. Miguel Tejada, Tommy Manzella, Clint Barmes, Jed Lowrie, Villar and whoever serves as the latest placeholder for Carlos Correa, whom I would love to see get a shot at being a 19-year-old in Double-A at some point this year.

Not that you care, but that would put you only one short of the record. Only nine teams have ever used a different primary shortstop six years in a row, including the Twins, who have leafed through Jason Bartlett, Nick Punto, Orlando Cabrera, J.J. Hardy, Tsuyoshi Nishioka, Brian Dozier and Pedro Florimon over the last seven years. But hey, there's a reason I'm not applying to the Twins.

Anyway, since the dismantling began with the trades of Lance Berkman and Roy Oswalt in 2010, nobody until this year has entered three consecutive seasons as the starter at his position.

Year	C	1B	2B	3B	SS	LF	CF	RF	DH
2010	Towles	Berkman	Matsui	Feliz	Manzella	Lee	Bourn	Pence	
2011	Quintero	Wallace	Hall	Johnson	Barmes	Lee	Bourn	Pence	
2012	Castro	Lee	Altuve	Johnson	Lowrie	Martinez	Schafer	Bogusevic	
2013	Castro	Wallace	Altuve	Dominguez	Cedeno	Carter	Maxwell	Ankiel	Pena

Catcher Jason Castro is the man in Houston this year, the only player who was even arbitration-eligible at the tender deadline, which would have had me assuming you were trading him in past years. You can certainly trade Jose Altuve's contract, though moving Delino DeShields Jr. back to outfield makes me doubt you'll do it, and that's a little progress too.

It's certainly not how I envisioned this going down when your predecessor Ed Wade started this teardown and addition of prospects, some of whom were very close to the majors when they were acquired nearly four years ago. I figured in 2012 we'd start to see the young core, 2013 would look like a decent preview with young players making good contributions and 2014 would be when this thing really turns on. But I recognize now that more patience will be needed.

Pretty much all the progress that's been made has been in the minor leagues. Sure there is Jarred Cosart, who disappointed in the peripherals but wowed in the overall performance as a rookie. Brett Oberholtzer was a nice surprise too, and Altuve's still extremely young. But this isn't at all the wave that four years of trades would be expected to produce.

In part, this feeling of wandering comes from the emphasis on quantity in the trades, which haven't produced anything resembling a top talent. Of the trio from the Oswalt trade, neither J.A. Happ nor Brett Wallace became anything better than league average, and Villar is all that's left to salvage there. Berkman turned into a long trade tree, from Mark Melancon to Jed Lowrie to now Chris Carter—an ace reliever turned into an above-average shortstop turned into a 27-year-old DH who *might* be worth one win above replacement annually. Unless Oberholtzer keeps contributing, the most disappointing return came for Michael Bourn, who netted a pile of Oberholtzer, Juan Abreu, Paul Clemens and Jordan Schafer, none of whom has made an impact. It's been evident that you've prioritized bulk instead of high-end talent, and while you'll continue not to bust completely, you run the risk of continuing the wandering. After all, as you know from the Capital Asset Pricing Model, reducing your exposure to risk also lowers your expected return.

While you were a young team last year, you didn't seem like a team that was getting anything out of young players. Even the kids, in a lot of cases, were placeholders. Only four teams got fewer wins out of players 25 and under, which is the number that we here tend to use as a cutoff to evaluate young talent. To be fair, the number gets better when isolating only the 23-and-unders.

- Players 23 and under: 3.9 WARP (11th)
- Players 24 and under: 3.0 WARP (19th)
- Players 25 and under: 2.4 WARP (26th)
- Players 26 and under: 7.0 WARP (22nd)

As for selling a better hope, I recognize that one of the main jobs of anyone who takes on a role in your office will be to win back the fans, so I understand why you said what you did about spending in 2013. Now your owner is on board—at least by word—in 2014, and I get that, too, and am ready to do whatever I have to do to get that message across.

Houston is a baseball town even though nobody says it is, and that's what excites me the most about the opportunity. It's not a baseball town the way Boston or St. Louis is, but Boston and St. Louis don't have baseball the way Houston does. They don't have the one Little League team that produced Carl Crawford and Michael Bourn. They don't have Bellaire High School or The Woodlands or Rice University or the Baseball USA complex. They don't have the new no. 1 place to revive careers with the independent Sugar Land Skeeters. Houston is where baseball people want to be and where baseball is still a big game no matter how the Astros have been.

But a boost is definitely needed, with the average attendance down 45 percent from 2007 despite the draws of your first American League season. Houston is the type of town that will come back, though. I know I can't call it a fair-weather town if I work there, but between us, it's a fair-weather town. They'll come back.

If I've been too honest in this, please recognize that I know how much of the current predicament is not your fault. There's little that you (or maybe soon we) as a team can do without the resolution of this cable situation that's been a mixture of heartbreaking, scintillating, juicy and downright pathetic to follow.

The sports network that you co-own launched in the last week of your 2012 season and still hasn't gained any carriage with cable companies. In the long run, there's a business school case study here for you to take back to your Kellogg friends. Did you expand your business in the middle of the cable television industry bubble? Or was it just a matter of having no leverage trying to sell a 111-loss team at YES Network-like prices to the cable companies? Probably the latter, and it's somewhat surprising. The network you share with Comcast also has the Houston Rockets as an investor and you still couldn't sell distribution to cable companies beyond the parent company. Not even Jeremy Lin and Dwight Howard could get this network carriage and get you past the 40 percent of Houston that could watch your games last year?

Your organization claims to be losing millions from the lack of carriage, and while it's really, really, really, really, really hard to cry poor in baseball given the centralized revenue streams, I do believe you. Securing proper carriage across the region is paramount to building a good team given the obligations to the ownership partners and the amount of debt that was taken on in the purchase.

To me, the real low point of this Astros chapter wasn't any of the 111 losses or any of the trades of players who were barely arbitration eligible. I understood those were means to somewhat of an end. The low point was in mid-November when your team was in court against your old owner, accusing him of selling "an asset they knew at the time to be overpriced and broken." The sadder part might have been that this took place less than a mile from your ballpark, an MLB owner suing an ex-MLB owner for fraud, and it got no coverage except in the local paper and a few other Houston outlets. Nobody cared. Even your scandals aren't part of the news cycle. It's time to make your bad news news too.

It's all up Tal's Hill from here. Or down Tal's Hill, which seems much more fun.

You have clearly established an outstanding group of employees ready to lead you into prominence. With Mike Fast, Kevin Goldstein, Colin Wyers and maybe a few smart guys that we at BP for one reason or another failed to hire first, the organization is trending the right way. I have worked at BP for 15 months now and consider it not only a privilege but a right to come in for an interview. I'm free on Thursdays.

Sincerely,

Zachary Levine

Baseball Prospectus

Zachary Levine covered the Astros for the Houston Chronicle *from 2009 to 2012 and has been with BP since November 2012.*

HITTERS

Jose Altuve   2B

Born: 5/6/1990 Age: 24
Bats: R Throws: R Height: 5' 5''
Weight: 175 Breakout: 1%
Improve: 45% Collapse: 13%
Attrition: 17% MLB: 96%

Comparables:
Jose Lopez, Jose Lind, Paul Molitor

YEAR	TEAM	LVL	AGE	PA	R	2B	3B	HR	RBI	BB	SO	SB	CS	AVG/OBP/SLG	TAv	BABIP	BRR	FRAA	WARP
2011	LNC	A+	21	238	38	13	7	5	34	19	26	19	9	.408/.451/.606	.378	.443	-0.8	2B(26): 0.5	1.9
2011	CCH	AA	21	153	21	9	3	5	25	7	14	5	5	.361/.388/.569	.276	.373	-0.6	3B(5): 0.1, 2B(4): -0.0	0.1
2011	HOU	MLB	21	234	26	10	1	2	12	5	29	7	3	.276/.297/.357	.237	.309	-2.2	2B(55): -0.3	-0.2
2012	HOU	MLB	22	630	80	34	4	7	37	40	74	33	11	.290/.340/.399	.272	.321	3.6	2B(147): 6.1	3.9
2013	HOU	MLB	23	672	64	31	2	5	52	32	85	35	13	.283/.316/.363	.243	.316	0.9	2B(145): -6.9	-0.1
2014	HOU	MLB	24	623	79	30	3	7	49	31	79	33	13	.285/.324/.384	.260	.310	1.3	2B -1, 3B -0	2.2

Altuve hit well in April and September, but cratered in the months in between, including a dismal August in which he hit .200/.226/.264. Despite sustaining a number of injuries, included dislocating his jaw in a collision with teammate Jimmy Paredes, he never landed on the DL, and he tied for the team lead in games played. In July, Houston bought out the arbitration years of its diminutive second baseman, signing him through 2017 with two team options. Keep in mind that 2014 will be his age-24 season and it's reasonable to expect Altuve to bounce back and even improve over the life of his contract. Even if he doesn't, at just over $3.3 million average annual value, it should work out for Houston (assuming anything ever works out for Houston).

Chris Carter   1B

Born: 12/18/1986 Age: 27
Bats: R Throws: R Height: 6' 4''
Weight: 245 Breakout: 7%
Improve: 39% Collapse: 6%
Attrition: 12% MLB: 79%

Comparables:
Chris Davis, Victor Diaz, Brad Eldred

YEAR	TEAM	LVL	AGE	PA	R	2B	3B	HR	RBI	BB	SO	SB	CS	AVG/OBP/SLG	TAv	BABIP	BRR	FRAA	WARP
2011	STO	A+	24	28	3	0	0	3	7	4	8	0	0	.333/.429/.708	.400	.385	-0.2	1B(5): -0.2	0.5
2011	SAC	AAA	24	344	55	18	2	18	72	42	85	5	1	.274/.366/.530	.284	.321	-0.6	1B(30): -1.9, LF(1): -0.0	0.3
2011	OAK	MLB	24	46	2	0	0	0	0	2	20	0	0	.136/.174/.136	.117	.250	-0.1	1B(11): -0.3	-0.7
2012	SAC	AAA	25	324	48	19	1	12	53	38	74	5	1	.279/.367/.486	.293	.332	0.3	1B(47): -4.5	1.1
2012	OAK	MLB	25	260	38	12	0	16	39	39	83	0	0	.239/.350/.514	.315	.295	-1.4	1B(55): 0.3	1.6
2013	HOU	MLB	26	585	64	24	2	29	82	70	212	2	0	.223/.320/.451	.281	.311	-2	1B(61): -3.4, LF(49): -4.6	0.8
2014	HOU	MLB	27	524	66	21	1	25	75	60	165	2	1	.226/.319/.440	.275	.290	-0.5	1B -4, LF -2	0.8

Carter played an alarming 335 innings in left field just to keep his bat in the lineup, but he's a substantial liability in the pasture. At the plate, Carter is one of the more confounding players in baseball. Acquired by Houston last February as part of the Jed Lowrie trade, he combines effortless power and discerning strike zone judgment with a swiss cheese swing. He also struggled mightily at Minute Maid Park last season despite its friendliness to right-handed power hitters. Perhaps those Crawford Boxes are just too tempting *not* to shoot for. More likely it's just a fluke.

Not a fluke? The strikeouts. Oh boy the strikeouts. Herewith, some facts: in 2013, Carter struck out the third-most times in MLB history; the wind from Carter's swings powered three hot dog stands in Houston; the only players with a higher career strikeout rate than Carter (500 PA min., 1910 to present) are Melvin Nieves, Taylor Teagarden and 53 pitchers; Carter's concentration at the plate has been known to lapse due to serious internal debate about whether the Russell-Einstein Manifesto applies to his bat; Carter has a higher career strikeout rate than *423* pitchers (same parameters); and Carter's career *minor-league* strikeout rate would have ranked 20th among qualified major-league hitters in 2013. (Some of these facts are truer than others.)

Jason Castro   C

Born: 6/18/1987 Age: 27
Bats: L Throws: R Height: 6' 3"
Weight: 215 Breakout: 2%
Improve: 46% Collapse: 5%
Attrition: 8% MLB: 95%

Comparables:
Miguel Montero, Ryan Doumit, Matt Wieters

YEAR	TEAM	LVL	AGE	PA	R	2B	3B	HR	RBI	BB	SO	SB	CS	AVG/OBP/SLG	TAv	BABIP	BRR	FRAA	WARP
2012	HOU	MLB	25	295	29	15	2	6	29	31	61	0	0	.257/.334/.401	.265	.309	-0.1	C(79): -1.7	0.9
2013	HOU	MLB	26	491	63	35	1	18	56	50	130	2	1	.276/.350/.485	.305	.351	2.1	C(98): -0.2	4.3
2014	HOU	MLB	27	425	44	21	1	10	48	44	95	1	0	.249/.330/.393	.265	.300	-0.7	C -1	2.0

The All-Star catcher was having a fantastic year until knee issues ended his season in September. Despite missing the final month, he was the best player on the Astros by a huge margin—his WARP total was nearly as much as the next *two* position players (Matt Dominguez and Brandon Barnes) combined. Castro continues to improve behind the plate as well: He made strides in both his receiving and throwing, nabbing 25 percent of would-be basestealers, compared to 19 percent in 2012. A note of caution: Castro did slug 117 points better at Minute Maid Park than on the road despite the team as a whole showing little split. Chalk it up to home cooking.

Carlos Corporan   C

Born: 1/7/1984 Age: 30
Bats: B Throws: R Height: 6' 2"
Weight: 230 Breakout: 3%
Improve: 15% Collapse: 11%
Attrition: 26% MLB: 54%

Comparables:
Kevin Cash, Humberto Quintero, Rob Johnson

YEAR	TEAM	LVL	AGE	PA	R	2B	3B	HR	RBI	BB	SO	SB	CS	AVG/OBP/SLG	TAv	BABIP	BRR	FRAA	WARP
2011	OKL	AAA	27	92	9	4	0	3	12	8	16	0	1	.250/.330/.412	.208	.274	0	C(3): -0.0	0.0
2011	HOU	MLB	27	173	9	8	1	0	11	10	49	0	0	.188/.253/.253	.179	.271	-1.4	C(50): 0.1	-0.9
2012	OKL	AAA	28	229	35	15	0	6	31	15	46	2	0	.286/.349/.447	.284	.340	0.3	C(67): -0.1	2.0
2012	HOU	MLB	28	85	5	2	0	4	13	4	19	0	1	.269/.310/.449	.258	.304	-0.2	C(24): 0.6	0.4
2013	HOU	MLB	29	210	16	5	0	7	20	10	60	0	0	.225/.287/.361	.242	.288	-1.8	C(57): -1.1, 1B(1): -0.0	0.4
2014	HOU	MLB	30	250	23	10	1	5	24	13	66	0	0	.219/.275/.334	.224	.280	-0.4	C -0, 1B -0	0.2

Catching is a bad business. Catchers get hurt pretty much continually. Sometimes they go down catastrophically, like Buster Posey in 2011, and sometimes they accumulate dings and nicks. Corporan illustrates a third type of injury of which we are becoming more aware: the foul-tip concussion. Corporan's caused him to miss 20 games, and when he returned from the DL, he posted a ghastly .380 OPS through the end of the season. Ultimately, though, he handled the staff well, was a solid receiver and threw out would-be basestealers at around the league average, making him a perfectly reasonable backup backstop at the minimum salary.

Carlos Correa   SS

Born: 9/22/1994 Age: 19
Bats: R Throws: R Height: 6' 4"
Weight: 205 Breakout: 0%
Improve: 10% Collapse: 0%
Attrition: 4% MLB: 14%

Comparables:
Manny Machado, Jurickson Profar, Elvis Andrus

YEAR	TEAM	LVL	AGE	PA	R	2B	3B	HR	RBI	BB	SO	SB	CS	AVG/OBP/SLG	TAv	BABIP	BRR	FRAA	WARP
2013	QUD	A	18	519	73	33	3	9	86	58	83	10	10	.320/.405/.467	.314	.375	-2.3	SS(115): -6.8	4.7
2014	HOU	MLB	19	250	26	11	1	4	22	17	59	0	0	.242/.299/.353	.242	.300	-0.4	SS -3	0.2

If Correa's exceptional makeup could be quantified, bottled and sold, the Astros would own a premium designer line in their franchise shortstop. Despite being the fourth-youngest hitter in the Midwest League, he flashed maturity, instincts and smarts beyond anyone else on the field, so it wasn't a surprise to see Correa's dazzling tools already manifesting in his season batting line. He led his championship-winning River Bandits in each of the slash stats even though his power has yet to reach its full potential. His bat, elite arm and good glove make an All-Star package, and he's a leader in the clubhouse as well as on the stat sheet. When the doubles turn into homers—High-A Lancaster's inflated park factors will surely help—watch out.

Delino DeShields 2B

Born: 8/16/1992 Age: 21
Bats: R Throws: R Height: 5' 9"
Weight: 205 Breakout: 1%
Improve: 5% Collapse: 0%
Attrition: 2% MLB: 5%

Comparables:
L.J. Hoes, Steve Lombardozzi, Adrian Cardenas

YEAR	TEAM	LVL	AGE	PA	R	2B	3B	HR	RBI	BB	SO	SB	CS	AVG/OBP/SLG	TAv	BABIP	BRR	FRAA	WARP
2011	LEX	A	18	541	73	17	2	9	48	52	118	30	11	.220/.305/.322	.234	.271	4.4	2B(98): -5.5	-0.2
2012	LEX	A	19	523	96	22	5	10	52	70	108	83	14	.298/.401/.439	.295	.373	7.3	2B(108): -8.5	3.3
2012	LNC	A+	19	114	17	2	3	2	9	13	23	18	5	.237/.336/.381	.244	.288	2	2B(24): -2.8	0.0
2013	LNC	A+	20	534	100	25	14	5	54	57	91	51	18	.317/.405/.468	.296	.387	7.1	2B(107): -9.5	3.4
2014	HOU	MLB	21	250	31	8	2	3	16	20	64	16	5	.221/.291/.307	.222	.290	1.7	2B -5	-0.4

DeShields is the opposite of Carlos Correa in many ways. Correa is quite tall; DeShields is Nick Punto's height. Correa has all-time makeup; DeShields is suspect, especially on the field. Correa has a plus glove and cannon arm; DeShields' own rate as below average. As a result of the glove and arm differences, the two play at opposite sides of the middle infield. (For now, anyway. With Jose Altuve's contract extension, DeShields began his training for center field in the Arizona Fall League. The team hopes his 80 run will, uh, speed up the learning curve.) Correa has massive power potential; DeShields may intermittently reach double-digit homers at the highest level. In the end, DeShields only has two legitimate tools (hit, run) while Correa flashes sixes and sevens all around his scouting reports. Naturally, their slash lines last year were nearly identical.

Matt Dominguez 3B

Born: 8/28/1989 Age: 24
Bats: R Throws: R Height: 6' 1"
Weight: 215 Breakout: 5%
Improve: 44% Collapse: 7%
Attrition: 15% MLB: 84%

Comparables:
Mike Moustakas, Willy Aybar, Gerardo Parra

YEAR	TEAM	LVL	AGE	PA	R	2B	3B	HR	RBI	BB	SO	SB	CS	AVG/OBP/SLG	TAv	BABIP	BRR	FRAA	WARP
2011	JUP	A+	21	20	0	0	0	0	2	1	3	0	0	.167/.250/.167	.170	.200	-0.3	3B(4): 0.3	-0.1
2011	NWO	AAA	21	356	47	18	1	12	55	24	50	0	1	.258/.312/.431	.291	.270	-0.8	3B(27): 1.8	0.9
2011	FLO	MLB	21	48	2	4	0	0	2	2	8	0	0	.244/.292/.333	.208	.297	-1.6	3B(16): -0.4	-0.3
2012	NWO	AAA	22	315	27	14	0	7	46	23	31	0	1	.234/.291/.357	.239	.239	-3.2	3B(78): -3.1	-0.3
2012	OKL	AAA	22	177	21	10	0	2	23	11	21	0	0	.298/.347/.398	.274	.329	0.6	3B(45): -0.8	0.8
2012	HOU	MLB	22	113	14	2	2	5	16	4	17	0	0	.284/.310/.477	.269	.299	-2.6	3B(31): 0.1	0.3
2013	HOU	MLB	23	589	56	25	0	21	77	30	96	0	1	.241/.286/.403	.249	.254	-0.3	3B(149): 11.9	2.8
2014	HOU	MLB	24	517	51	22	1	16	62	27	83	0	0	.247/.291/.398	.252	.260	-1	3B 3	1.1

The 2013 campaign was Dominguez's first full season in the majors, and he emerged as a legitimate big leaguer. He was a defense-first (defense-only?) prospect, and he can still pick it at third, but the not-too-horrible offense was a nice surprise. Dominguez hit right-handed pitching at about a league-average rate because of very good power production. He favors the inside pitch, and can turn on pitches off the plate, but lefties seem to give him trouble when they work him away. He did fare well against southpaws in the minors and true reverse-split hitters are exceedingly rare, so we can expect him to make an adjustment to the superior control and off-speed stuff he's seeing in the Show. Dominguez is one of the few 2013 Astros likely to be a part of the next winning Houston team.

Dexter Fowler CF

Born: 3/22/1986 Age: 28
Bats: B Throws: R Height: 6' 4"
Weight: 190 Breakout: 0%
Improve: 42% Collapse: 1%
Attrition: 7% MLB: 96%

Comparables:
Nate McLouth, Milton Bradley, Carlos Beltran

YEAR	TEAM	LVL	AGE	PA	R	2B	3B	HR	RBI	BB	SO	SB	CS	AVG/OBP/SLG	TAv	BABIP	BRR	FRAA	WARP
2011	CSP	AAA	25	114	17	6	1	2	9	15	24	2	1	.237/.345/.381	.226	.296	0.4	CF(23): 0.0	-0.2
2011	COL	MLB	25	563	84	35	15	5	45	68	130	12	9	.266/.363/.432	.280	.354	7.1	CF(122): 9.9	4.9
2012	COL	MLB	26	530	72	18	11	13	53	68	128	12	5	.300/.389/.474	.279	.390	1.6	CF(131): -9.1	1.8
2013	COL	MLB	27	492	71	18	3	12	42	65	105	19	9	.263/.369/.407	.265	.323	3.9	CF(110): -7.4	1.1
2014	HOU	MLB	28	471	59	20	6	7	40	58	115	13	6	.248/.346/.381	.267	.320	0.5	CF -3	1.5

Fowler is one of baseball's most consistent hitters. For the fifth straight season, he posted a walk rate between 11 percent and 14 percent, a strikeout rate between 20 and 25 percent, and an isolated power between .140 and .175. His contact is softer than what is generally expected from a slugging outfielder, but his excellent plate discipline and speed more than make up for it. Age 27 didn't provide any great leaps forward, and anybody waiting for Fowler's star turn is likely to be disappointed—especially if he remains a groundball hitter. But if his consistency to date is any indication, he'll be above average for Houston in 2014.

Marwin Gonzalez SS

Born: 3/14/1989 Age: 25
Bats: B Throws: R Height: 6' 1"
Weight: 210 Breakout: 5%
Improve: 40% Collapse: 7%
Attrition: 35% MLB: 68%

Comparables:
Alcides Escobar, Omar Quintanilla, Dee Gordon

YEAR	TEAM	LVL	AGE	PA	R	2B	3B	HR	RBI	BB	SO	SB	CS	AVG/OBP/SLG	TAv	BABIP	BRR	FRAA	WARP
2011	TEN	AA	22	239	29	18	1	2	20	17	27	4	2	.301/.359/.421	.247	.335	-1.5	SS(32): -1.2, 2B(13): -0.0	0.2
2011	IOW	AAA	22	226	24	12	1	2	19	16	21	3	1	.274/.326/.376	.235	.292	-1.7	SS(39): 3.9, 2B(1): -0.0	0.5
2012	OKL	AAA	23	43	2	4	0	1	10	3	7	0	0	.333/.395/.513	.335	.387	-1.3	SS(10): -2.3	0.2
2012	HOU	MLB	23	219	21	13	0	2	12	13	29	3	3	.234/.280/.327	.215	.264	-3	SS(47): -0.2, 3B(14): 0.4	-0.4
2013	OKL	AAA	24	183	16	10	1	1	15	8	23	4	1	.262/.293/.349	.234	.295	-0.5	SS(29): -3.5, 2B(13): 1.6	-0.1
2013	HOU	MLB	24	222	22	8	0	4	14	9	37	6	2	.221/.252/.319	.222	.250	1.1	SS(53): -4.3, 2B(10): 1.7	0.1
2014	HOU	MLB	25	250	23	12	1	3	21	12	40	4	2	.241/.281/.339	.229	.270	-0.1	SS -2, 2B 1	0.2

The 2013 season was Gonzalez's eighth pro campaign, but he's still just 24, and it shows. He can show flashes of the elite defender and baserunner he may someday be, but other times, well, he can look like a kid who's played less than a season's worth of big-league games. He showed substantial improvement against lefties and made strides with the glove and on the basepaths, but with Carlos Correa knocking on the door, Gonzalez may soon be a man without a position. In the meantime, though, there are less fun things to do with your life than be Jose Altuve's double-play partner.

Robbie Grossman CF

Born: 9/16/1989 Age: 24
Bats: B Throws: L Height: 6' 0"
Weight: 205 Breakout: 2%
Improve: 22% Collapse: 14%
Attrition: 19% MLB: 53%

Comparables:
Shin-Soo Choo, Chad Huffman, Jeff Fiorentino

YEAR	TEAM	LVL	AGE	PA	R	2B	3B	HR	RBI	BB	SO	SB	CS	AVG/OBP/SLG	TAv	BABIP	BRR	FRAA	WARP
2011	BRD	A+	21	616	127	34	2	13	56	104	111	24	10	.294/.418/.451	.336	.351	1.2	RF(33): -3.5, CF(4): 0.5	1.6
2012	ALT	AA	22	417	59	20	4	7	36	59	78	9	10	.266/.378/.406	.285	.325	0.4	CF(94): -12.1	1.4
2012	CCH	AA	22	160	22	8	2	3	11	18	43	4	1	.267/.371/.422	.283	.367	1.2	CF(27): -1.3, LF(6): 0.6	0.9
2013	OKL	AAA	23	310	42	11	2	2	20	48	66	15	8	.281/.396/.364	.277	.371	-0.2	CF(33): -2.4, LF(32): -2.9	0.9
2013	HOU	MLB	23	288	29	14	0	4	21	23	70	6	7	.268/.332/.370	.259	.353	2	LF(45): -1.7, CF(29): -2.6	0.2
2014	HOU	MLB	24	328	41	13	2	5	27	35	81	9	6	.246/.333/.362	.255	.310	-0.5	CF -5, LF -1	-0.1

Grossman's debut was not a *success* per se, but he didn't bomb out, either. The read on him coming up was that he would not stay in center and might not bring enough pop and/or speed to maximize his discerning eye at the plate (14 percent minor-league walk rate), especially given the high offensive standards in an outfield corner. The book wasn't exactly wrong, as Grossman's slugging, caught-stealing and fielding numbers show, but there are enough positives in his play to see a major-league role, even if as a reserve. Is it what you dream of as a general manager? No. Will you take it for $500,000 and put the savings elsewhere on the roster? Yes.

Jesus Guzman 1B

Born: 6/14/1984 Age: 30
Bats: R Throws: R Height: 6' 1"
Weight: 200 Breakout: 0%
Improve: 29% Collapse: 3%
Attrition: 9% MLB: 64%

Comparables:
Lance Niekro, Garrett Jones, Andy Phillips

YEAR	TEAM	LVL	AGE	PA	R	2B	3B	HR	RBI	BB	SO	SB	CS	AVG/OBP/SLG	TAv	BABIP	BRR	FRAA	WARP
2011	TUC	AAA	27	286	40	22	1	8	57	34	42	4	4	.332/.423/.529	.298	.374	-2.9	3B(41): -1.4, LF(6): -0.6	1.2
2011	SDN	MLB	27	271	33	22	2	5	44	22	43	9	2	.312/.369/.478	.319	.360	2.2	1B(53): 1.3, LF(6): 0.4	2.3
2012	SDN	MLB	28	321	32	18	2	9	48	29	71	3	3	.247/.319/.418	.275	.297	0.9	LF(52): 1.1, 1B(19): 1.0	1.5
2013	SDN	MLB	29	318	33	17	0	9	35	27	79	3	0	.226/.297/.378	.240	.280	-2.5	1B(38): -1.3, LF(35): 0.1	-0.1
2014	HOU	MLB	30	299	33	16	1	8	34	25	65	4	2	.258/.327/.409	.268	.310	-0.3	1B 0, LF 0	0.8

Fans in San Diego demanded more Blanks and less Guzman last year, despite their similar numbers. Unlike in seasons past, Guzman was useless at home: his .457 OPS at Petco Park was second-lowest in that venue's history (minimum 100 plate appearances). He also stopped dominating southpaws, which is problematic for a platoon player who fields all four corner spots with equal hilarity. Clutch hitting may not be a repeatable skill, but his career .894 OPS in high-leverage situations is impressive, as is his bat-flipping ability. Guzman isn't a horrible guy for Houston to have on its bench, although his 2013 struggles against lefties and rising strikeout rates are yellow flags.

L.J. Hoes RF

Born: 3/5/1990 Age: 24
Bats: R Throws: R Height: 6' 0"
Weight: 190 Breakout: 3%
Improve: 23% Collapse: 13%
Attrition: 24% MLB: 53%

Comparables:
Chris Snelling, Brian Horwitz, Desmond Jennings

YEAR	TEAM	LVL	AGE	PA	R	2B	3B	HR	RBI	BB	SO	SB	CS	AVG/OBP/SLG	TAv	BABIP	BRR	FRAA	WARP
2011	FRU	A+	21	173	23	7	0	3	17	10	25	4	2	.241/.297/.342	.235	.267	-0.1	2B(21): -1.7, LF(15): -0.9	-0.3
2011	BOW	AA	21	393	47	17	1	6	54	43	56	16	7	.305/.379/.413	.307	.347	0.7	LF(61): -1.0, RF(9): -1.8	2.6
2012	BOW	AA	22	229	25	9	3	2	16	31	33	12	5	.265/.368/.372	.273	.311	-0.6	CF(47): -0.6, LF(2): -0.1	0.7
2012	NOR	AAA	22	357	54	14	4	3	38	34	43	8	7	.300/.374/.397	.270	.338	2.9	LF(46): 7.3, RF(24): 0.7	2.3
2012	BAL	MLB	22	1	0	0	0	0	0	0	0	0	0	.000/.000/.000	.012	.000	0	LF(1): -0.0	0.0
2013	NOR	AAA	23	430	62	25	1	3	40	58	56	7	7	.304/.406/.403	.297	.352	-0.1	RF(68): -2.1, LF(23): 0.7	2.2
2013	BAL	MLB	23	3	0	0	0	0	0	0	1	0	0	.000/.000/.000	.001	.000	0	LF(1): 0.1	-0.1
2013	HOU	MLB	23	181	24	7	2	1	10	12	34	7	1	.287/.337/.371	.261	.353	3.2	RF(44): -0.9, CF(2): -0.0	0.4
2014	HOU	MLB	24	270	28	11	2	3	26	25	46	5	3	.270/.342/.373	.267	.320	-0.2	RF -2, LF 1	0.7

Hoes was acquired by Houston in the Bud Norris deal. He appeared in 46 games with the Astros, bolstering Houston's outfield ranks, which had been decimated by poor performance (RIP Rick Ankiel) and injury (J.D. Martinez, Trevor Crowe). Hoes is young, athletic and cost-controlled, which makes a good fit in Houston. If he can maintain this level of production—essentially league-average at the plate—he could compete for a job alongside the forthcoming waves of Astros prospects.

Marc Krauss — LF

Born: 10/5/1987 Age: 26
Bats: L Throws: R Height: 6' 2"
Weight: 235 Breakout: 4%
Improve: 17% Collapse: 10%
Attrition: 27% MLB: 49%

Comparables: Brandon Jones, Justin Huber, Danny Putnam

YEAR	TEAM	LVL	AGE	PA	R	2B	3B	HR	RBI	BB	SO	SB	CS	AVG/OBP/SLG	TAv	BABIP	BRR	FRAA	WARP
2011	MOB	AA	23	504	69	25	6	16	65	64	123	3	3	.242/.340/.439	.267	.299	1.7	RF(46): 0.8, LF(36): -1.0	1.1
2012	CCH	AA	24	35	11	2	0	5	16	6	5	1	0	.414/.514/1.000	.493	.368	0.6	LF(7): 0.1	1.0
2012	MOB	AA	24	434	75	29	2	15	61	73	91	6	4	.283/.416/.509	.321	.339	-2.2	LF(52): 1.1, 1B(30): 0.1	3.2
2012	OKL	AAA	24	66	3	0	0	0	2	6	20	1	1	.123/.203/.123	.137	.184	-0.2	RF(13): -0.5, LF(4): 0.5	-0.8
2013	OKL	AAA	25	314	38	16	2	10	39	53	52	3	3	.281/.401/.478	.307	.310	0	LF(27): -0.6, 1B(17): -0.4	1.6
2013	HOU	MLB	25	146	11	9	0	4	13	10	45	2	0	.209/.267/.366	.228	.279	0.6	LF(18): -0.8, RF(9): 0.2	-0.3
2014	HOU	MLB	26	250	28	11	1	8	31	29	65	1	1	.227/.321/.398	.262	.280	-0.4	LF -1, RF -1	0.3

The former Diamondbacks farmhand got the call in late June when Trevor Crowe hit the disabled list. Krauss struggled in his first go-round, hitting just .169 over 82 plate appearances, but he performed far better in a September stint. If pinch-hitters still existed, he could be a lefty threat off the bench. The Astros believe in the patience and power potential, so if you squint, you can picture Krauss as a platoon guy, but he'll really need to rake to overcome the fact that he's subtracting value everywhere else on the field. Limited players like Krauss would be well served learning magic or volunteering to make the clubhouse iTunes mix—baseball skills alone can carry the stars, but the mere mortals need any edge they can get.

J.D. Martinez — LF

Born: 8/21/1987 Age: 26
Bats: R Throws: R Height: 6' 3"
Weight: 220 Breakout: 7%
Improve: 58% Collapse: 6%
Attrition: 14% MLB: 93%

Comparables: Jason Kubel, Lastings Milledge, Luis Gonzalez

YEAR	TEAM	LVL	AGE	PA	R	2B	3B	HR	RBI	BB	SO	SB	CS	AVG/OBP/SLG	TAv	BABIP	BRR	FRAA	WARP
2011	CCH	AA	23	370	50	25	1	13	72	42	55	1	0	.338/.414/.546	.317	.367	-1.2	LF(24): -0.2	1.0
2011	HOU	MLB	23	226	29	13	0	6	35	13	48	0	1	.274/.319/.423	.258	.325	-2.4	LF(51): -0.3, RF(1): -0.0	0.2
2012	OKL	AAA	24	95	6	6	0	0	4	4	17	0	1	.233/.263/.300	.191	.284	-1.7	LF(19): -2.7	-0.8
2012	HOU	MLB	24	439	34	14	3	11	55	40	96	0	2	.241/.311/.375	.238	.290	-4	LF(100): -10.4	-1.7
2013	CCH	AA	25	20	1	2	0	1	5	0	1	0	0	.300/.300/.550	.287	.278	0	RF(2): -0.3, LF(2): -0.3	0.0
2013	HOU	MLB	25	310	24	17	0	7	36	10	82	2	0	.250/.272/.378	.244	.319	-2.3	LF(50): -5.5, RF(25): -2.0	-1.1
2014	HOU	MLB	26	330	32	15	1	8	37	22	75	1	1	.249/.302/.386	.253	.300	-0.6	LF -5, RF -1	-0.2

Knee and wrist injuries sidelined Martinez for two months, further dimming his major-league outlook in a season in which he was below average in every aspect of the game. (He was two-for-two stealing bases, at least?) That Martinez finished seventh on the Astros in plate appearances despite his ugly, ugly season is either an indictment of the team or a sign that the plan (no. 1 overall draft pick secured! Again!) is working. Martinez hit the absolute snot out of the ball in the minors, but the swing mechanics haven't translated to big-league success, so, with an invasion of sexy prospects twirling their way into the Astros' outfield, mediocrity, rather than injuries, will be what sends Martinez to pasture for good.

Domingo Santana — RF

Born: 8/5/1992 Age: 21
Bats: R Throws: R Height: 6' 5"
Weight: 230 Breakout: 5%
Improve: 16% Collapse: 1%
Attrition: 7% MLB: 26%

Comparables: Jay Bruce, Travis Snider, Greg Halman

YEAR	TEAM	LVL	AGE	PA	R	2B	3B	HR	RBI	BB	SO	SB	CS	AVG/OBP/SLG	TAv	BABIP	BRR	FRAA	WARP
2011	LWD	A	18	391	45	29	4	7	32	26	120	4	1	.269/.345/.434	.303	.390	-1.9	RF(40): -3.1	1.6
2011	LEX	A	18	76	13	4	0	5	21	6	15	1	0	.382/.447/.662	.357	.438	-1.1	RF(16): -1.9	0.7
2012	LNC	A+	19	525	87	26	6	23	97	55	148	7	1	.302/.385/.536	.310	.397	-1.1	RF(114): -7.6	2.9
2013	CCH	AA	20	476	72	23	2	25	64	46	139	12	5	.252/.345/.498	.296	.316	0.2	RF(100): -3.9, CF(8): 0.0	2.9
2014	HOU	MLB	21	250	27	10	1	9	32	18	84	1	0	.230/.297/.404	.259	.320	-0.2	RF -3, CF -0	0.2

Santana's 50 extra-base hits in Corpus Christi proved his power output wasn't a fluke of the absurd run environment in Lancaster. His isolated slugging ranked third in Double-A, an impressive feat for a 20-year-old. Like fellow prospect George Springer, Santana will miss pitches in the zone with a long swing, a danger that has yet to drastically deter his progress. At his age—he was one of just three age-20 minor leaguers with 400 plate appearances at Double-A last year—he'll have time to trim his 29 percent strikeout rate and continue lofting fly balls. If the power fills out to fit his stature, his bat and plus arm will be a natural fit in right field.

Jonathan Singleton — 1B

Born: 9/18/1991 Age: 22
Bats: L Throws: L Height: 6' 2"
Weight: 235 Breakout: 1%
Improve: 21% Collapse: 0%
Attrition: 11% MLB: 32%

Comparables: Chris Parmelee, Kyle Blanks, Anthony Rizzo

YEAR	TEAM	LVL	AGE	PA	R	2B	3B	HR	RBI	BB	SO	SB	CS	AVG/OBP/SLG	TAv	BABIP	BRR	FRAA	WARP
2011	CLR	A+	19	382	48	14	0	9	47	56	83	3	3	.284/.387/.412	.276	.352	-2	1B(35): -0.0, LF(23): -0.3	0.8
2011	LNC	A+	19	148	20	9	1	4	16	14	40	0	0	.333/.405/.512	.310	.448	0.3	1B(27): 0.3, RF(1): -0.0	0.8
2012	CCH	AA	20	555	94	27	4	21	79	88	131	7	2	.284/.396/.497	.313	.350	1	1B(113): 5.5, LF(19): -1.6	4.0
2013	QUD	A	21	25	6	2	0	3	5	4	5	0	0	.286/.400/.810	.420	.231	0.5	1B(5): 0.3	0.6
2013	CCH	AA	21	48	5	2	1	2	8	9	16	0	0	.263/.396/.526	.351	.381	-0.7	1B(10): -0.5	0.4
2013	OKL	AAA	21	294	31	13	0	6	31	46	89	1	0	.220/.340/.347	.247	.314	-1.4	1B(68): -5.0	-1.1
2014	HOU	MLB	22	250	27	10	1	7	29	32	75	0	0	.227/.325/.377	.261	.310	-0.3	1B 1, LF -0	0.3

Singleton was one of the major pieces in the huge Hunter Pence haul. Astros fans expected him to join the big club at some point in 2013, but a second "drug of abuse" (marijuana, in this case) infraction earned him a 50-game suspension, which kept him off the field until the end of May. When he returned, Singleton made brief stops in Low-A and Double-A, but spent the bulk of the season in Oklahoma City. To say that he struggled there would be an understatement: the much-lauded hit tool and power were nowhere to be found. Fitness was certainly a factor, and Singleton finished the year strong as he worked himself back into playing shape. He's still on track to make his debut in 2014 and the upside is still tremendous, but expectations aren't quite as sky-high as they once were.

George Springer CF
Born: 9/19/1989 Age: 24
Bats: R Throws: R Height: 6' 3"
Weight: 200 Breakout: 3%
Improve: 24% Collapse: 16%
Attrition: 18% MLB: 56%
Comparables: Mike Olt, Joe Benson, Nolan Reimold

YEAR	TEAM	LVL	AGE	PA	R	2B	3B	HR	RBI	BB	SO	SB	CS	AVG/OBP/SLG	TAv	BABIP	BRR	FRAA	WARP
2011	TCV	A-	21	33	8	3	0	1	3	2	2	4	0	.179/.303/.393	.157	.160	0.5	CF(6): -0.0	-0.1
2012	LNC	A+	22	500	101	18	10	22	82	56	131	28	6	.316/.398/.557	.327	.404	8.9	CF(103): -1.6	5.9
2012	CCH	AA	22	81	8	3	0	2	5	6	25	4	2	.219/.288/.342	.232	.304	1.4	CF(13): 0.3, RF(7): -0.3	0.1
2013	CCH	AA	23	323	56	20	0	19	55	42	96	23	5	.297/.399/.579	.350	.390	4.9	CF(70): -2.8, LF(3): -0.0	4.4
2013	OKL	AAA	23	267	50	7	4	18	53	41	65	22	3	.311/.425/.626	.373	.362	1.6	CF(47): -0.7, RF(11): -0.4	4.1
2014	HOU	MLB	24	250	35	8	2	11	35	26	79	10	2	.247/.331/.455	.289	.320	1.2	CF -1, RF -0	1.4

After conquering Triple-A in the second half of 2013, Springer's major-league debut is imminent. Fans will drool over his power/speed combo, but they should be cognizant of his swing-and-miss propensity, a weakness that could keep him from reaching his very high ceiling. With a career 12 percent walk rate, the plate discipline isn't the concern; he simply swings hard and fails to make contact on pitches in the zone. Regardless, one can't overlook the historic 37-homer, 45-steal minor-league season. That fleetness of foot aids his range in center field, where a plus arm and improved glove complete the toolset. With the Astros mum on his official start date, Springer will have all eyes on him in spring training.

Max Stassi C
Born: 3/15/1991 Age: 23
Bats: R Throws: R Height: 5' 10"
Weight: 205 Breakout: 3%
Improve: 12% Collapse: 2%
Attrition: 15% MLB: 26%
Comparables: Devin Mesoraco, Josh Donaldson, Michael McKenry

YEAR	TEAM	LVL	AGE	PA	R	2B	3B	HR	RBI	BB	SO	SB	CS	AVG/OBP/SLG	TAv	BABIP	BRR	FRAA	WARP
2011	STO	A+	20	139	22	6	0	2	19	16	22	1	1	.231/.331/.331	.283	.268	0.6		0.4
2012	STO	A+	21	360	48	18	0	15	45	27	83	3	1	.268/.331/.468	.289	.304	-1.5	C(66): -0.3	2.1
2013	CCH	AA	22	323	40	20	1	17	60	19	68	1	1	.277/.333/.529	.299	.301	-3.4	C(50): 0.3	2.2
2013	HOU	MLB	22	8	0	0	0	0	1	0	2	0	0	.286/.375/.286	.210	.400	-0.4	C(1): -0.0	-0.1
2014	HOU	MLB	23	250	26	10	0	9	31	14	65	0	0	.231/.285/.394	.247	.280	-0.4	C -0	0.6

Stassi, whose first major-league RBI came via a bases-loaded hit-by-pitch—in the face—celebrated another improved offensive season with additional power and hitting to all fields. He's touted for his makeup and catcher defense, as he calls a solid game and throws out 37 percent of basestealers. That's up from his 24 percent mark in High-A, albeit in a smaller sample. His durability and contact rate are question marks, restricting him to a backup profile for now.

Danry Vasquez LF
Born: 1/8/1994 Age: 20
Bats: L Throws: R Height: 6' 3"
Weight: 177 Breakout: 0%
Improve: 0% Collapse: 0%
Attrition: 0% MLB: 0%
Comparables: Alfredo Marte, Christian Yelich, Engel Beltre

YEAR	TEAM	LVL	AGE	PA	R	2B	3B	HR	RBI	BB	SO	SB	CS	AVG/OBP/SLG	TAv	BABIP	BRR	FRAA	WARP
2012	WMI	A	18	112	5	3	0	1	7	7	20	0	0	.162/.218/.222	.173	.185	1.3	LF(28): -0.8	-0.8
2012	ONE	A-	18	311	36	16	2	2	35	13	45	6	4	.311/.341/.401	.302	.361	-2.1	LF(62): -0.2, RF(9): 1.1	2.1
2013	QUD	A	19	128	12	2	1	3	20	6	15	2	0	.288/.323/.398	.285	.304	-1.1	LF(32): 1.3	0.5
2013	WMI	A	19	423	47	16	5	6	40	31	56	9	8	.283/.334/.400	.279	.313	-0.7	LF(96): 0.2	1.3
2014	HOU	MLB	20	250	18	8	1	4	23	9	56	0	0	.220/.248/.313	.205	.270	-0.3	LF 0, RF -0	-0.9

A prize piece in the Jose Veras trade, Vasquez rebounded from a poor 2012, showcasing excellent contact skills with his natural hitting ability. His tall and lanky frame projects some power to go with his plus hit tool. It'll likely come as doubles rather than homers, but he has a sweet all-fields swing nonetheless. Defensively, he's probably stuck in left field with an average arm and fringy speed.

Jonathan Villar SS
Born: 5/2/1991 Age: 23
Bats: B Throws: R Height: 6' 1"
Weight: 195 Breakout: 8%
Improve: 25% Collapse: 1%
Attrition: 15% MLB: 34%
Comparables: Junior Lake, Jason Donald, Sean Rodriguez

YEAR	TEAM	LVL	AGE	PA	R	2B	3B	HR	RBI	BB	SO	SB	CS	AVG/OBP/SLG	TAv	BABIP	BRR	FRAA	WARP
2011	LNC	A+	20	207	26	7	4	4	26	25	56	20	6	.259/.353/.414	.274	.350	1.1	SS(25): -1.5	0.5
2011	CCH	AA	20	367	52	16	2	10	26	29	100	14	6	.231/.301/.386	.248	.301	1.1	SS(25): -1.0	0.4
2012	CCH	AA	21	377	54	7	2	11	50	35	87	39	8	.261/.336/.396	.266	.319	3.9	SS(85): 7.2	2.9
2013	OKL	AAA	22	386	47	16	8	8	41	32	93	31	7	.277/.341/.442	.272	.358	1.2	SS(88): 9.3	3.5
2013	HOU	MLB	22	241	26	9	2	1	8	24	71	18	8	.243/.321/.319	.237	.362	3.4	SS(58): -6.2	0.0
2014	HOU	MLB	23	281	39	10	2	5	22	21	80	21	6	.234/.297/.354	.237	.310	2.4	SS -1	0.8

Villar spent about a third of the season with the major-league club, where he provided a spark at the top of Bo Porter's order, though he was thrown out stealing far too often (eight times in 26 attempts). It's reasonable to assume that the youngster's thievery will improve with experience; the tools are there. One could say the same about his defense, as his physical gifts were often mitigated by poor decision making. Villar's youth and minimum salary make him a good option until Carlos Correa arrives.

	Brett Wallace 1B		YEAR	TEAM	LVL	AGE	PA	R	2B	3B	HR	RBI	BB	SO	SB	CS	AVG/OBP/SLG	TAv	BABIP	BRR	FRAA	WARP
Born: 8/26/1986 **Age:** 27			2011	OKL	AAA	24	126	16	10	0	1	24	15	28	1	0	.356/.437/.481	.308	.456	0.5	1B(10): -0.4	0.4
Bats: L **Throws:** R **Height:** 6' 2''			2011	HOU	MLB	24	378	37	22	0	5	29	36	91	1	1	.259/.334/.369	.246	.339	-3.9	1B(96): 7.7	0.1
Weight: 235 **Breakout:** 7%			2012	OKL	AAA	25	351	54	16	0	16	57	27	87	0	1	.300/.379/.506	.295	.370	-3.9	3B(47): 5.7, 1B(29): -2.6	2.1
Improve: 27% **Collapse:** 12%			2012	HOU	MLB	25	254	24	10	1	9	24	18	73	0	0	.253/.323/.424	.266	.331	-1.3	1B(58): -0.4, 3B(8): -0.4	0.3
Attrition: 20% **MLB:** 64%			2013	OKL	AAA	26	261	36	16	2	11	37	24	69	1	0	.326/.398/.554	.324	.425	1	1B(41): -2.0, 3B(10): 0.2	2.1
Comparables:			2013	HOU	MLB	26	285	35	14	1	13	36	18	104	1	1	.221/.284/.431	.253	.310	-1	1B(61): -0.5, 3B(9): -0.6	-0.2
Travis Ishikawa, Ryan Garko, Ryan Shealy			2014	HOU	MLB	27	342	36	15	1	11	42	24	99	1	0	.243/.312/.401	.259	.320	-0.6	1B 1, 3B -0	0.4

After more than 300 big-league games and 1,000 plate appearances, we have a sense of what Brett Wallace is: a replacement-level player. He's proven that he can't handle third base, meaning he's limited to first base or DH, but even the worst team in baseball can't justify a sub-.260 True Average in those spots. The footsteps Wallace is hearing belong to one Jonathan Singleton, who should put Wallace out of work in 2014.

PITCHERS

	Matt Albers		YEAR	TEAM	LVL	AGE	W	L	SV	G	GS	IP	H	HR	BB	SO	BB9	SO9	GB%	BABIP	WHIP	ERA	FIP	FRA	WARP
Born: 1/20/1983 **Age:** 31			2011	BOS	MLB	28	4	4	0	56	0	64²	62	7	31	68	4.3	9.5	48%	.309	1.44	4.73	4.04	4.72	0.6
Bats: L **Throws:** R **Height:** 6' 1'' **Weight:** 225			2012	ARI	MLB	29	1	1	0	23	0	21	16	3	7	19	3.0	8.1	60%	.241	1.10	2.57	4.33	5.19	-0.1
Breakout: 37% **Improve:** 64% **Collapse:** 20%			2012	BOS	MLB	29	2	0	0	40	0	39¹	30	6	15	25	3.4	5.7	56%	.218	1.14	2.29	4.98	5.95	-0.3
Attrition: 11% **MLB:** 93%			2013	CLE	MLB	30	3	1	0	56	0	63	57	2	23	35	3.3	5.0	66%	.274	1.27	3.14	3.52	4.52	0.1
Comparables: Joe Beimel, John Franco, Dan Kolb			2014	HOU	MLB	31	2	1	1	46	0	51¹	50	5	23	40	4.0	7.0	53%	.295	1.42	4.24	4.50	4.61	0.1

Albers picked up last year where he left off the previous season, churning out a constant stream of groundballs with a sinking fastball that regularly brushes 94. He's refined his delivery enough now that his wildness is a distant memory, and he's no longer trying to strike everyone out. The result was another season of useful anonymity, as he was used in multiple non-glory roles—coming in two dozen times with runners on base, pitching multiple innings 20 times, and rarely seeing the end of a game. He ended with the third-highest groundball percentage in the majors among pitchers with 60 or more innings, after finishing 24th in that category the year before.

	Hector Ambriz		YEAR	TEAM	LVL	AGE	W	L	SV	G	GS	IP	H	HR	BB	SO	BB9	SO9	GB%	BABIP	WHIP	ERA	FIP	FRA	WARP
Born: 5/24/1984 **Age:** 30			2012	COH	AAA	28	0	1	1	20	1	33	29	3	17	25	4.6	6.8	54%	.274	1.39	3.55	4.37	5.69	0.1
Bats: L **Throws:** R **Height:** 6' 2'' **Weight:** 235			2012	OKL	AAA	28	1	1	2	18	0	24¹	28	1	11	18	4.1	6.7	52%	.355	1.60	3.33	4.20	4.52	0.3
Breakout: 31% **Improve:** 54% **Collapse:** 27%			2012	HOU	MLB	28	1	1	0	18	0	19¹	14	0	11	22	5.1	10.2	52%	.292	1.29	4.19	2.88	2.96	0.4
Attrition: 57% **MLB:** 27%			2013	OKL	AAA	29	1	2	3	14	0	16²	23	3	3	12	1.6	6.5	40%	.333	1.56	5.40	5.01	4.91	0.1
Comparables: Jon Leicester, Chris Bootcheck, Fu-Te Ni			2013	HOU	MLB	29	2	4	2	43	0	36¹	50	8	14	27	3.5	6.7	48%	.347	1.76	5.70	5.69	6.08	-0.4
			2014	HOU	MLB	30	2	1	1	44	0	52	58	7	19	42	3.3	7.2	43%	.321	1.48	4.94	4.69	5.37	-0.3

Ambriz was one of nine players to pitch for the Astros in both 2012 and 2013, one of eight who recorded a save for them in 2013, one of dozens whose fastball can't touch 97 mph, and one of five relievers whose FIP exceeded 5.50. He was also the only reliever in baseball to strike out Mike Trout, Miguel Cabrera and Josh Donaldson. Everybody has something!

Mark Appel

Born: **7/15/1991** Age: **22**
Bats: **R** Throws: **R** Height: **6' 5''** Weight: **190**
Breakout: **100%** Improve: **100%** Collapse: **0%**
Attrition: **0%** MLB: **2%**

Comparables:
Chad Bettis, Kyle Kendrick, Brett Marshall

YEAR	TEAM	LVL	AGE	W	L	SV	G	GS	IP	H	HR	BB	SO	BB9	SO9	GB%	BABIP	WHIP	ERA	FIP	FRA	WARP
2013	QUD	A	21	3	1	0	8	8	33	30	2	9	27	2.5	7.4	54%	.277	1.18	3.82	3.40	4.58	0.4
2014	HOU	MLB	22	1	3	0	8	8	32²	38	5	16	18	4.5	5.0	47%	.308	1.68	5.81	5.87	6.31	-0.4

It's been over a year since the Astros surprised everyone in the 2012 draft, crowning Carlos Correa as the first overall pick. Appel wound up with the Pirates in the eighth slot, but opted not to sign. Returning to Stanford worked out for his development. The management science and engineering degrees might not see use, but the refined changeup, increased aggression and consistency were positive signs that led to Houston adding this potential ace. His four-seam fastball sits in the mid-90s, delivered on a steep plane from his six-foot-five frame, and more movement can be found in a low-90s two-seamer. A slider with two-plane break is his strikeout weapon, and the repertoire is packaged in highly praised, clean mechanics. If it sounds like Appel checks off every box, that's because he does.

Anthony Bass

Born: **11/1/1987** Age: **26**
Bats: **R** Throws: **R** Height: **6' 2''** Weight: **195**
Breakout: **36%** Improve: **66%** Collapse: **21%**
Attrition: **27%** MLB: **74%**

Comparables:
Dillon Gee, Hector Noesi, Dustin Moseley

YEAR	TEAM	LVL	AGE	W	L	SV	G	GS	IP	H	HR	BB	SO	BB9	SO9	GB%	BABIP	WHIP	ERA	FIP	FRA	WARP
2011	SAN	AA	23	6	4	0	13	13	69²	62	6	21	62	2.7	8.0	46%	.292	1.19	3.75	3.62	4.15	1.2
2011	SDN	MLB	23	2	0	0	27	3	48¹	41	3	21	24	3.9	4.5	47%	.252	1.28	1.68	4.17	4.97	-0.2
2012	SDN	MLB	24	2	8	1	24	15	97	89	10	39	80	3.6	7.4	49%	.278	1.32	4.73	4.06	5.19	-0.2
2013	TUC	AAA	25	4	6	0	15	15	79¹	108	11	17	60	1.9	6.8	40%	.374	1.58	5.45	4.54	4.69	1.1
2013	SDN	MLB	25	0	0	0	24	0	42	51	4	20	31	4.3	6.6	46%	.343	1.69	5.36	4.21	5.43	-0.4
2014	HOU	MLB	26	4	7	0	27	16	98¹	106	12	35	66	3.2	6.1	46%	.302	1.43	4.69	4.76	5.09	-0.1

The once-promising Bass continued to backslide, splitting time between the Tucson rotation and the big-league bullpen, where he was used in low-leverage situations. He got hammered in both places and struggled to throw strikes in San Diego. Away from Petco, batters hit .345/.419/.545 against him, and his career OPS against on the road is 180 points higher than at home—a trick that'll be tougher to pull now that his home is hitter-friendly Minute Maid Park. Bass works with a low-90s fastball and mid-80s slider and changeup, but only the slider misses bats. Lefties, who have always fared better against him than righties, torched him for a .974 OPS between two levels last year. His inconsistent command will keep him swinging between the rotation and bullpen and the majors and minors,

Erik Bedard

Born: **3/5/1979** Age: **35**
Bats: **L** Throws: **L** Height: **6' 1'** Weight: **200**
Breakout: **21%** Improve: **43%** Collapse: **24%**
Attrition: **10%** MLB: **92%**

Comparables:
A.J. Burnett, Vicente Padilla, Ryan Dempster

YEAR	TEAM	LVL	AGE	W	L	SV	G	GS	IP	H	HR	BB	SO	BB9	SO9	GB%	BABIP	WHIP	ERA	FIP	FRA	WARP
2011	BOS	MLB	32	1	2	0	8	8	38	41	3	18	38	4.3	9.0	43%	.349	1.55	4.03	3.51	4.65	0.5
2011	SEA	MLB	32	4	7	0	16	16	91¹	77	11	30	87	3.0	8.6	42%	.270	1.17	3.45	3.74	4.14	0.9
2012	PIT	MLB	33	7	14	0	24	24	125²	129	14	56	118	4.0	8.5	45%	.321	1.47	5.01	4.11	4.58	0.9
2013	HOU	MLB	34	4	12	1	32	26	151	149	18	75	138	4.5	8.2	39%	.308	1.48	4.59	4.41	4.29	1.8
2014	HOU	MLB	35	6	9	1	26	22	126¹	122	15	56	118	4.0	8.4	44%	.302	1.41	4.32	4.44	4.70	0.5

Bedard was an effective starting pitcher in 2013, except when he wasn't. Unfortunately, that was often: He failed to make it through five innings in eight of his 26 starts. One particular start against Oakland badly skewed his stats, as he allowed six earned runs and recorded just a single out. So while he pitched better than his record, the ravages of age have taken their toll on his stuff. This showed in the component numbers: His walks were up and his strikeouts were down over the previous season—you know, the year he got released by the Pirates?—but at least Bedard can hang his hat on his first 150-inning season since his 2007 heyday.

Jose Cisnero

Born: **4/11/1989** Age: **25**
Bats: **R** Throws: **R** Height: **6' 3''** Weight: **230**
Breakout: **42%** Improve: **69%** Collapse: **21%**
Attrition: **52%** MLB: **53%**

Comparables:
Andrew Oliver, Donnie Veal, Brayan Villarreal

YEAR	TEAM	LVL	AGE	W	L	SV	G	GS	IP	H	HR	BB	SO	BB9	SO9	GB%	BABIP	WHIP	ERA	FIP	FRA	WARP
2011	LNC	A+	22	8	11	0	27	27	123¹	115	13	75	152	5.5	11.1	39%	.303	1.54	6.06	4.88	5.29	2.1
2012	CCH	AA	23	9	6	0	20	20	108²	93	7	46	116	3.8	9.6	34%	.297	1.28	3.40	3.34	3.14	3.0
2012	OKL	AAA	23	4	1	0	8	8	39²	52	1	18	32	4.1	7.3	38%	.398	1.76	4.54	3.97	4.33	0.6
2013	OKL	AAA	24	1	1	0	12	1	17²	25	2	13	24	6.6	12.2	31%	.469	2.15	8.66	4.87	7.86	0.1
2013	HOU	MLB	24	2	2	0	28	0	43²	49	5	22	41	4.5	8.5	40%	.341	1.63	4.12	4.27	4.10	0.5
2014	HOU	MLB	25	2	2	1	35	5	67	67	8	38	60	5.1	8.1	40%	.304	1.56	4.95	5.01	5.38	-0.3

Shortly after his 24th birthday, Cisnero debuted in Houston as a multi-inning mop-up man. Such is employment as a rookie: starting at the bottom, cleaning up messes. Like most corporate settings though, performance is rewarded with greater opportunity, and Cisnero's janitorial efforts did not go unnoticed. He quickly climbed the ladder to higher-leverage situations, entering one-run games in the seventh and eighth innings. He collected four holds in June while other Astros relievers shuffled around, cut or injured. With a Jose Veras trade imminent, his dream promotion was close—ninth-inning duties in just his first year! Alas, this story doesn't have a happy ending. Cisnero faltered in July (8.22 ERA), losing his confidence and command of his fastball. After Veras was dealt, Cisnero was demoted to Triple-A, watching sadly as four other rookies each collected their first career save with Houston. Next year, Jose.

Jarred Cosart

Born: 5/25/1990 Age: 24
Bats: R Throws: R Height: 6' 3" Weight: 180
Breakout: 38% Improve: 67% Collapse: 27%
Attrition: 47% MLB: 64%

Comparables:
Charlie Haeger, Juan Gutierrez, Robbie Ross

YEAR	TEAM	LVL	AGE	W	L	SV	G	GS	IP	H	HR	BB	SO	BB9	SO9	GB%	BABIP	WHIP	ERA	FIP	FRA	WARP
2011	CLR	A+	21	9	8	0	20	19	108	98	7	43	79	3.6	6.6	52%	.277	1.31	3.92	4.18	5.38	0.0
2011	CCH	AA	21	1	2	0	7	7	36¹	33	4	13	22	3.2	5.4	48%	.240	1.27	4.71	4.67	9.89	-0.1
2012	CCH	AA	22	5	5	0	15	15	87	83	3	38	68	3.9	7.0	62%	.307	1.39	3.52	3.72	4.36	1.1
2012	OKL	AAA	22	1	2	0	6	5	27²	26	0	13	24	4.2	7.8	58%	.325	1.41	2.60	3.45	3.99	0.6
2013	OKL	AAA	23	7	4	0	18	17	93	74	5	50	93	4.8	9.0	60%	.276	1.33	3.29	3.98	4.80	1.0
2013	HOU	MLB	23	1	1	0	10	10	60	46	3	35	33	5.2	4.9	55%	.246	1.35	1.95	4.38	4.91	0.1
2014	HOU	MLB	24	6	9	0	22	22	122²	117	12	62	90	4.5	6.6	54%	.287	1.46	4.41	4.82	4.80	0.3

The good: Cosart's mid-90s fastball is a legitimate weapon. The bad: Cosart's K/BB in the bigs last year was under one. We're talking about just 60 innings, and bear in mind that Cosart was a young 23, but the control, or lack thereof, is a legitimate concern. His mechanics are noisy and the failure to develop a killer secondary pitch is troubling. Cosart's curve could be a knockout, but it's still inconsistent. If that pitch and the changeup continue to develop, Cosart can be a legitimate mid-rotation hurler; if not, he can still be an effective late-inning reliever.

Jorge De Leon

Born: 8/15/1987 Age: 26
Bats: R Throws: R Height: 6' 0" Weight: 185
Breakout: 58% Improve: 71% Collapse: 10%
Attrition: 74% MLB: 14%

Comparables:
Anthony Claggett, Marcos Mateo, Trystan Magnuson

YEAR	TEAM	LVL	AGE	W	L	SV	G	GS	IP	H	HR	BB	SO	BB9	SO9	GB%	BABIP	WHIP	ERA	FIP	FRA	WARP
2011	LEX	A	23	6	4	16	43	0	55¹	48	5	13	51	2.1	8.3	46%	.268	1.10	3.42	3.62	4.27	0.8
2012	LNC	A+	24	2	9	6	40	14	87²	116	11	44	60	4.5	6.2	38%	.351	1.83	7.70	5.72	6.57	0.5
2013	CCH	AA	25	0	3	6	29	3	52²	42	7	15	36	2.6	6.2	42%	.240	1.08	4.27	4.39	6.03	-0.1
2013	OKL	AAA	25	0	0	6	12	0	15	8	0	2	12	1.2	7.2	58%	.195	0.67	0.60	2.37	2.99	0.4
2013	HOU	MLB	25	0	1	0	11	0	10	12	1	7	6	6.3	5.4	36%	.314	1.90	5.40	5.58	4.56	0.0
2014	HOU	MLB	26	2	2	1	40	4	63²	70	9	29	38	4.1	5.3	41%	.297	1.56	5.31	5.55	5.77	-0.6

De Leon, an infielder until 2010, lost his 40-man spot after an abysmal 2012 in High-A, but the Astros' desperate need for pitching and De Leon's relative success as a closer in the high minors led to a late-season call-up. The fastball is live—he sits 95 and can touch 97—and the slider can neutralize righties, but he's helpless against left-handed hitters. De Leon's control took a big step forward, but the improvement wasn't sufficient to warrant a spot on the 40-man roster, so he was outrighted again in October.

Scott Feldman

Born: 2/7/1983 Age: 31
Bats: L Throws: R Height: 6' 7" Weight: 230
Breakout: 7% Improve: 37% Collapse: 25%
Attrition: 16% MLB: 89%

Comparables:
Brad Penny, Carl Pavano, Kyle Lohse

YEAR	TEAM	LVL	AGE	W	L	SV	G	GS	IP	H	HR	BB	SO	BB9	SO9	GB%	BABIP	WHIP	ERA	FIP	FRA	WARP
2011	ROU	AAA	28	2	1	0	8	8	40²	48	5	9	24	2.0	5.3	60%	.000	1.40	4.43	4.94	3.28	0.1
2011	TEX	MLB	28	2	1	0	11	2	32	25	3	10	22	2.8	6.2	63%	.239	1.09	3.94	4.03	4.81	0.3
2012	TEX	MLB	29	6	11	0	29	21	123²	139	14	32	96	2.3	7.0	43%	.317	1.38	5.09	3.77	4.55	1.6
2013	BAL	MLB	30	5	6	0	15	15	90²	80	9	31	65	3.1	6.5	51%	.262	1.22	4.27	4.16	4.62	0.4
2013	CHN	MLB	30	7	6	0	15	15	91	79	10	25	67	2.5	6.6	50%	.264	1.14	3.46	3.90	4.53	0.5
2014	HOU	MLB	31	6	9	0	32	22	142	143	15	45	100	2.8	6.3	47%	.292	1.32	4.08	4.38	4.43	0.9

Feldman has established a firm base of skills over the past three seasons, with adequate 17 percent strikeout and 7.5 percent walk rates, though the results have vacillated in that span due in large part to batted-ball variance. His upside is still a league-average (or slightly above) innings eater—this is not pejorative. Feldman can pitch well into his 30s with that profile, especially if he sprinkles in a 2009 or 2013 every couple of years. He works best with a nimble infield defense behind him, as he's always been well above average in groundball rate. This also means that Houston's homer-happiness won't affect him as much as other pitchers.

Michael Feliz

Born: 9/28/1993 Age: 20
Bats: R Throws: R Height: 6' 4" Weight: 210
Breakout: 0% Improve: 0% Collapse: 0%
Attrition: 0% MLB: 0%

Comparables:
Dan Cortes, Mason Tobin, Jarred Cosart

YEAR	TEAM	LVL	AGE	W	L	SV	G	GS	IP	H	HR	BB	SO	BB9	SO9	GB%	BABIP	WHIP	ERA	FIP	FRA	WARP
2013	TCV	A-	19	4	2	1	14	10	69	53	2	13	78	1.7	10.2	53%	.288	0.96	1.96	1.91	2.96	1.7
2014	HOU	MLB	20	1	3	0	11	7	50	58	7	31	31	5.5	5.6	47%	.311	1.76	6.08	5.98	6.61	-0.8

Feliz originally signed with the Athletics as a 16-year-old, but a positive test for stanozolol voided his $800,000 deal, and the Astros swooped in for a half-price discount. Three years later, it's looking to be a wise investment. His 6-foot-4 frame and easy mid-90s velocity are dreamy for a still-teenage prospect, as are his 2013 results: walk and strikeout rates of 5 and 29 percent, respectively. His secondary offerings include a low-80s slider, potentially plus, and a little-used changeup, which will have to come into play at higher levels. With a long, perilous journey ahead, Feliz's projection range is large, from reliever to middle-rotation starter, but guarded optimism is entirely appropriate.

Josh Fields
Born: 8/19/1985 Age: 28
Bats: R Throws: R Height: 6' 0" Weight: 180
Breakout: 35% Improve: 51% Collapse: 36%
Attrition: 65% MLB: 49%

Comparables:
Jorge Vasquez, Josh Roenicke, Jeff Bajenaru

YEAR	TEAM	LVL	AGE	W	L	SV	G	GS	IP	H	HR	BB	SO	BB9	SO9	GB%	BABIP	WHIP	ERA	FIP	FRA	WARP
2011	WTN	AA	25	1	2	3	20	0	26	17	0	19	26	6.6	9.0	—	.258	1.38	2.77	3.96	4.30	0.0
2011	PME	AA	25	3	0	1	9	0	17¹	10	2	10	25	5.2	13.0	46%	.385	1.15	3.12	3.93	1.37	0.3
2011	TAC	AAA	25	0	0	0	9	0	13	11	2	13	13	9.0	9.0	38%	.257	1.85	6.23	6.78	6.45	0.1
2012	PME	AA	26	3	3	8	32	0	44²	30	4	16	59	3.2	11.9	46%	.255	1.03	2.62	2.87	3.20	1.1
2012	PAW	AAA	26	1	0	4	10	0	13²	8	0	2	19	1.3	12.5	36%	.286	0.73	0.00	0.82	0.74	0.6
2013	HOU	MLB	27	1	3	5	41	0	38	31	8	18	40	4.3	9.5	38%	.245	1.29	4.97	5.13	4.79	-0.1
2014	HOU	MLB	28	2	1	2	33	0	41	36	5	21	43	4.5	9.5	43%	.293	1.38	4.01	4.43	4.36	0.2

It took longer than he hoped, and he's doing it for a different organization, but Josh Fields is finally a big-league closer. Houston claimed Fields, a former first-rounder, from Boston in the 2012 Rule 5 draft. He pitched adequately, averaging a strikeout per inning but a walk every two, and took over the ninth-inning role in September. He's got the velocity for the role, but his mid-90s fastball is poker-straight, and repeating his delivery and command of his arsenal can be issues. The 2014 Astros can afford to let him work it out at the big-league level, though they might consider one of their imported relievers (Chad Qualls, Matt Albers) easier to plump up into Proven Closer trade bait.

Mike Foltynewicz
Born: 10/7/1991 Age: 22
Bats: R Throws: R Height: 6' 4" Weight: 200
Breakout: 100% Improve: 100% Collapse: 0%
Attrition: 100% MLB: 1%

Comparables:
Anthony Ortega, J.C. Ramirez, Brian Flynn

YEAR	TEAM	LVL	AGE	W	L	SV	G	GS	IP	H	HR	BB	SO	BB9	SO9	GB%	BABIP	WHIP	ERA	FIP	FRA	WARP
2011	LEX	A	19	5	11	0	26	26	134	149	10	51	88	3.4	5.9	46%	.329	1.49	4.97	4.48	5.56	0.9
2012	LEX	A	20	14	4	0	27	27	152	145	11	62	125	3.7	7.4	49%	.298	1.36	3.14	4.20	4.65	2.3
2013	LNC	A+	21	1	0	0	7	5	26	31	4	14	29	4.8	10.0	46%	.360	1.73	3.81	5.16	4.63	0.9
2013	CCH	AA	21	5	3	3	23	16	103¹	75	8	52	95	4.5	8.3	55%	.254	1.23	2.87	3.88	4.71	1.0
2014	HOU	MLB	22	4	8	0	24	18	107¹	117	14	61	68	5.1	5.7	47%	.302	1.66	5.57	5.65	6.05	-1.1

Like Lance McCullers Jr., Foltynewicz demonstrated the potency of pure arm strength during the Astros' piggyback rotation experiment. High-90s velocity in four-inning bursts is a cheat code for pitching and Foltynewicz brandished the heat during the first half of his Double-A stint (1.86 ERA, 26 percent strikeout rate). Houston will gladly take that from the pre-Luhnow first-rounder who repeated Low-A in 2012. He cooled when the organization transitioned to a six-man rotation (3.63 ERA, 20 percent strikeout rate) but continued to regularly touch triple digits on the gun. Elite velocity by itself won't sustain those statistics in the majors, and his middling secondary stuff—a potentially plus curve and ordinary change, neither an out pitch yet—may limit him to no. 3 starter. A workhorse with over 415 professional innings before his 22nd birthday, Foltynewicz will take it one step at a time; his stock is up, and he still has plenty of room to improve.

Lucas Harrell
Born: 6/3/1985 Age: 29
Bats: B Throws: R Height: 6' 2" Weight: 210
Breakout: 32% Improve: 68% Collapse: 17%
Attrition: 18% MLB: 51%

Comparables:
Dana Eveland, Yunesky Maya, Mitch Talbot

YEAR	TEAM	LVL	AGE	W	L	SV	G	GS	IP	H	HR	BB	SO	BB9	SO9	GB%	BABIP	WHIP	ERA	FIP	FRA	WARP
2011	CHR	AAA	26	7	3	0	13	12	74¹	67	6	26	56	3.1	6.8	54%	.290	1.25	3.27	3.87	4.44	0.5
2011	OKL	AAA	26	5	2	0	9	9	52¹	42	0	24	38	4.1	6.5	50%	.283	1.26	1.72	3.82	4.23	0.4
2011	CHA	MLB	26	0	0	0	3	0	5	11	0	1	5	1.8	9.0	60%	.550	2.40	7.20	1.66	1.71	0.2
2011	HOU	MLB	26	0	2	0	6	2	13	12	0	7	10	4.8	6.9	54%	.282	1.46	3.46	3.30	4.38	0.1
2012	HOU	MLB	27	11	11	0	32	32	193²	185	13	78	140	3.6	6.5	57%	.297	1.36	3.76	3.79	5.09	-0.1
2013	HOU	MLB	28	6	17	0	36	22	153²	174	20	88	89	5.2	5.2	53%	.307	1.70	5.86	5.44	6.38	-1.5
2014	HOU	MLB	29	6	10	0	31	22	140	149	14	67	88	4.3	5.6	54%	.303	1.54	4.79	4.93	5.21	-0.3

If teams suddenly turned full Mean Girl and handed out Least Valuable Player awards, Harrell would be the Astros' winner. He racked up the most negative WARP on a bad Houston club; no excuses, either, as he earned every ounce of it. A 1:1 strikeout-to-walk ratio, more than one home run and 10 hits per nine innings: these are flat-out bad numbers. He was demoted from the rotation to middle relief about halfway through the season and didn't handle it well, at least initially, pitching poorly out of the 'pen and in a couple of spot starts. The Astros reportedly tried, and failed, to move him before the trade deadline. He'll have to battle just to stick around the majors.

Dallas Keuchel
Born: 1/1/1988 Age: 26
Bats: L Throws: L Height: 6' 3" Weight: 200
Breakout: 48% Improve: 77% Collapse: 13%
Attrition: 18% MLB: 76%
Comparables:
Jeff Karstens, Wade Miley, Justin Germano

YEAR	TEAM	LVL	AGE	W	L	SV	G	GS	IP	H	HR	BB	SO	BB9	SO9	GB%	BABIP	WHIP	ERA	FIP	FRA	WARP
2011	CCH	AA	23	9	7	0	20	20	127²	116	9	27	76	1.9	5.4	58%	.279	1.12	3.17	3.83	5.54	0.3
2011	OKL	AAA	23	1	1	0	7	7	36	52	5	12	15	3.0	3.8	50%	.500	1.78	7.50	5.76	8.05	-0.1
2012	OKL	AAA	24	6	4	0	16	16	92¹	92	5	20	50	1.9	4.9	59%	.289	1.21	3.90	3.94	5.16	0.8
2012	HOU	MLB	24	3	8	0	16	16	85¹	93	14	39	38	4.1	4.0	53%	.280	1.55	5.27	5.78	6.91	-1.1
2013	HOU	MLB	25	6	10	0	31	22	153²	184	20	52	123	3.0	7.2	58%	.340	1.54	5.15	4.28	4.47	1.0
2014	HOU	MLB	26	6	10	0	23	23	140	157	18	46	82	2.9	5.3	55%	.305	1.45	4.81	4.94	5.23	-0.5

Keuchel began the year in the bullpen as a swingman, but was pressed into a starting role by mid-May. Despite not beginning the year in the rotation, he finished the season with more than 150 innings pitched and gave Houston something it needed badly: a starter who could eat innings. None of Keuchel's offerings is overpowering; he gets by on command and the ability to induce groundballs with his high-80s sinker. If things go well for Houston next year, they won't need Keuchel in the rotation and he can return to the swingman role, for which he is better suited.

Chia-Jen Lo
Born: 4/7/1986 Age: 28
Bats: R Throws: R Height: 5' 11" Weight: 190
Breakout: 45% Improve: 53% Collapse: 31%
Attrition: 71% MLB: 37%
Comparables:
Jailen Peguero, Roy Corcoran, Andy Cavazos

YEAR	TEAM	LVL	AGE	W	L	SV	G	GS	IP	H	HR	BB	SO	BB9	SO9	GB%	BABIP	WHIP	ERA	FIP	FRA	WARP
2012	LNC	A+	26	0	0	0	11	0	19	14	1	4	20	1.9	9.5	49%	.310	0.95	1.42	3.18	3.94	0.4
2013	HOU	MLB	27	0	3	2	19	0	19¹	14	2	13	16	6.1	7.4	42%	.226	1.40	4.19	4.78	6.76	-0.3
2014	HOU	MLB	28	1	1	3	27	0	34¹	31	4	18	32	4.8	8.4	44%	.292	1.44	4.24	4.75	4.61	0.1

Lo missed the first 10 weeks of the season with shoulder troubles, but sped through three minor-league levels before landing with the big club (skipping entirely over Triple-A) at the end of July. He had a brief audition as closer but ended the year in middle relief. Lo features an explosive fastball that averages 94 mph, but his breaking ball needs refinement and walking six hitters per nine simply will not do. A stern talking-to may be in order.

David Martinez
Born: 8/4/1987 Age: 26
Bats: R Throws: R Height: 6' 2" Weight: 180
Breakout: 60% Improve: 75% Collapse: 25%
Attrition: 49% MLB: 17%
Comparables:
Levale Speigner, Tim Dillard, Jamie Vermilyea

YEAR	TEAM	LVL	AGE	W	L	SV	G	GS	IP	H	HR	BB	SO	BB9	SO9	GB%	BABIP	WHIP	ERA	FIP	FRA	WARP
2011	LEX	A	23	5	7	2	37	5	66²	77	7	17	44	2.3	5.9	47%	.316	1.41	4.18	4.47	4.64	0.7
2012	LNC	A+	24	9	5	0	27	26	160¹	181	19	33	114	1.9	6.4	52%	.321	1.33	4.38	4.64	5.75	1.4
2013	CCH	AA	25	14	2	1	26	18	129¹	109	10	20	86	1.4	6.0	53%	.259	1.00	2.02	3.27	4.08	1.8
2013	OKL	AAA	25	0	2	0	3	3	11	15	1	11	10	9.0	8.2	45%	.378	2.36	9.00	5.93	6.52	0.0
2013	HOU	MLB	25	1	0	0	4	0	11¹	16	1	3	6	2.4	4.8	49%	.357	1.68	7.15	3.96	4.40	0.1
2014	HOU	MLB	26	5	8	1	31	17	122¹	140	16	43	63	3.2	4.6	48%	.300	1.50	5.09	5.20	5.53	-0.8

The 2013 season was one long coming-out party for Martinez. He'd toiled in relative obscurity for years in the lower levels of the Astros' system before dominating hitters in both Double- and Triple-A, earning a September call-up. It remains to be seen what his role will be: He's started, relieved, and been a long man, and done all three with varying levels of success. He can dial the fastball up into the mid-90s in short bursts, which is an argument for late-inning relief, but his four-pitch arsenal, especially his power sinker, could make him an effective starter.

Lance McCullers
Born: 10/2/1993 Age: 20
Bats: L Throws: R Height: 6' 2" Weight: 205
Breakout: 63% Improve: 100% Collapse: 0%
Attrition: 44% MLB: 4%
Comparables:
Mat Latos, Chris Tillman, Jon Niese

YEAR	TEAM	LVL	AGE	W	L	SV	G	GS	IP	H	HR	BB	SO	BB9	SO9	GB%	BABIP	WHIP	ERA	FIP	FRA	WARP
2013	QUD	A	19	6	5	0	25	19	104²	92	3	49	117	4.2	10.1	57%	.327	1.35	3.18	3.05	3.99	1.9
2014	HOU	MLB	20	3	6	0	18	13	73	77	9	43	59	5.3	7.3	50%	.311	1.64	5.30	5.30	5.76	-0.5

McCullers, born the year of his father's retirement from relief pitching, easily outpitched Lance Sr.'s age-19 season when the père was coming up with Low-A Spartanburg (4.03 ERA in 1983). While it's not the fairest comparison, baseball bloodlines give birth to lots of Fun Facts. Junior's mid-90s fastball and big curve rang up 26 percent of the batters he faced and the former pitch, which McCullers can dial up to the high 90s when needed, also generated a healthy number of groundballs. Like most Astros minor-league starters, McCullers shined during Jeff Luhnow's "piggyback rotation" phase (1.89 ERA early in the season, but 5.22 after the piggyback was scuttled). The effort in his delivery is a real obstacle and McCullers needs further development on his changeup to push past his floor projection as a high-leverage reliever.

Collin McHugh

Born: 6/19/1987 Age: 27
Bats: R Throws: R Height: 6' 2'' Weight: 195
Breakout: 54% Improve: 70% Collapse: 17%
Attrition: 46% MLB: 54%

Comparables:
Sam LeCure, Philip Humber, Marco Estrada

YEAR	TEAM	LVL	AGE	W	L	SV	G	GS	IP	H	HR	BB	SO	BB9	SO9	GB%	BABIP	WHIP	ERA	FIP	FRA	WARP
2011	SLU	A+	24	1	2	1	9	6	35²	47	3	14	39	3.5	9.8	58%	.300	1.71	6.31	3.56	4.64	0.3
2011	BIN	AA	24	8	2	2	18	16	93¹	78	2	32	100	3.1	9.6	44%	.320	1.18	2.89	2.83	2.94	1.8
2012	BIN	AA	25	5	5	0	12	12	74²	63	4	17	65	2.0	7.8	47%	.280	1.07	2.41	3.04	3.65	1.3
2012	BUF	AAA	25	2	4	0	13	13	73²	60	8	29	70	3.5	8.6	49%	.261	1.21	3.42	3.93	4.88	0.4
2012	NYN	MLB	25	0	4	0	8	4	21¹	27	5	8	17	3.4	7.2	36%	.355	1.64	7.59	6.00	6.23	-0.1
2013	TUL	AA	26	1	1	0	2	2	13	9	1	0	12	0.0	8.3	47%	.258	0.69	1.38	2.21	3.02	0.3
2013	CSP	AAA	26	2	2	0	9	9	46²	52	5	14	47	2.7	9.1	43%	.366	1.41	4.63	3.21	4.02	1.1
2013	LVG	AAA	26	3	2	0	9	9	53¹	57	3	13	41	2.2	6.9	46%	.325	1.31	2.87	3.72	4.01	1.3
2013	COL	MLB	26	0	3	0	4	4	19	33	4	2	8	0.9	3.8	38%	.397	1.84	9.95	5.23	6.83	-0.2
2013	NYN	MLB	26	0	1	0	3	1	7	12	2	3	3	3.9	3.9	50%	.375	2.14	10.29	7.16	6.61	-0.2
2014	HOU	MLB	27	5	9	0	22	22	119¹	125	14	43	93	3.2	7.1	47%	.307	1.41	4.62	4.57	5.03	-0.0

After another disastrous season—this one split between the Mets and Rockies, preceding an offseason waiver claim by the Astros—it's time to ask what McHugh really offers a major-league team. The only pitches he routinely throws for strikes—his fastball and slider—were hammered for slugging percentages over .550 (as was his sinker, at .952). His only asset appears to be his changeup, a groundball machine. But nothing about that arsenal suggests McHugh would succeed out of the bullpen, either—his fastball is just too hittable, and none of his breaking pitches have shown swing-and-miss movement. On second thought, maybe it's not time to ask the question, but rather to answer it.

Brett Oberholtzer

Born: 7/1/1989 Age: 24
Bats: L Throws: L Height: 6' 1'' Weight: 235
Breakout: 40% Improve: 75% Collapse: 20%
Attrition: 52% MLB: 53%

Comparables:
Justin Germano, Jae Kuk Ryu, Anthony Swarzak

YEAR	TEAM	LVL	AGE	W	L	SV	G	GS	IP	H	HR	BB	SO	BB9	SO9	GB%	BABIP	WHIP	ERA	FIP	FRA	WARP
2011	MIS	AA	21	9	9	0	21	21	127²	119	6	42	93	3.0	6.6	52%	.327	1.26	3.74	3.47	4.94	0.1
2011	CCH	AA	21	2	3	0	6	6	27¹	28	3	10	28	3.3	9.2	39%	.417	1.39	5.27	3.96	7.57	-0.1
2012	CCH	AA	22	5	3	0	13	13	77	81	11	21	68	2.5	7.9	54%	.308	1.32	4.21	4.23	4.60	1.0
2012	OKL	AAA	22	5	7	0	15	15	89²	105	13	19	69	1.9	6.9	39%	.332	1.38	4.52	4.71	5.01	1.0
2013	OKL	AAA	23	6	6	0	16	16	80¹	77	9	25	72	2.8	8.1	51%	.296	1.27	4.37	4.24	5.50	0.5
2013	HOU	MLB	23	4	5	0	13	10	71²	66	7	13	45	1.6	5.7	36%	.260	1.10	2.76	3.68	3.92	0.8
2014	HOU	MLB	24	6	10	0	23	23	128²	140	18	39	91	2.7	6.4	45%	.302	1.39	4.75	4.76	5.17	-0.3

Oberholtzer was a pleasant surprise in a year with precious few. He yo-yo'd back and forth between Oklahoma City and Houston before eventually ending up in the Astros' rotation, where he performed respectably. He doesn't light up the radar gun (his fastball tops out at 92 and he typically works at 90) and his breaking ball (curve or slider, depending on the grip and velocity) remains a work in progress, but the changeup is a plus pitch that can baffle righties when it's on. Oberholtzer also features excellent command and control, and fills up the zone with quality strikes.

Brad Peacock

Born: 2/2/1988 Age: 26
Bats: R Throws: R Height: 6' 1'' Weight: 175
Breakout: 35% Improve: 52% Collapse: 31%
Attrition: 64% MLB: 62%

Comparables:
Virgil Vasquez, Dustin Nippert, Charlie Furbush

YEAR	TEAM	LVL	AGE	W	L	SV	G	GS	IP	H	HR	BB	SO	BB9	SO9	GB%	BABIP	WHIP	ERA	FIP	FRA	WARP
2011	HAR	AA	23	10	2	0	16	14	98²	62	4	23	129	2.1	11.8	39%	.279	0.86	2.01	2.08	2.90	1.9
2011	SYR	AAA	23	5	1	0	9	9	48	36	5	24	48	4.5	9.0	34%	.223	1.25	3.19	4.22	4.82	0.2
2011	WAS	MLB	23	2	0	0	3	2	12	7	0	6	4	4.5	3.0	32%	.189	1.08	0.75	3.83	3.98	0.1
2012	SAC	AAA	24	12	9	0	28	25	134²	147	16	66	139	4.4	9.3	35%	.340	1.58	6.01	4.73	4.55	1.9
2013	OKL	AAA	25	6	2	0	14	13	79	65	9	22	76	2.5	8.7	39%	.273	1.10	2.73	4.00	4.14	1.0
2013	HOU	MLB	25	5	6	0	18	14	83¹	78	15	37	77	4.0	8.3	39%	.270	1.38	5.18	5.01	4.95	0.2
2014	HOU	MLB	26	6	10	0	24	24	133¹	130	18	56	117	3.8	7.9	41%	.294	1.40	4.51	4.73	4.90	0.1

Peacock began 2013 as the Astros' fourth starter, but before April was out he was remanded to the bullpen, where he was equally ineffective. That led to a demotion to Oklahoma City, where he spent about half the year. Eventually he was recalled to Houston for good in August, where he again worked as a starter and finished strong. Ultimately Peacock is a fastball-heavy pitcher with a below-average fastball—never a recipe for great success—and it seems unlikely that he will dramatically overhaul his pitch mix coming into his age-26 season. For now, however, he's a cheap if not terribly effective bridge to the Appels and Foltynewiczes of the world, though he might note nervously that PECOTA comp Dustin Nippert has pitched the last three years in Korea.

Chad Qualls

Born: 8/17/1978 Age: 35
Bats: R Throws: R Height: 6' 4" Weight: 240
Breakout: 20% Improve: 45% Collapse: 39%
Attrition: 14% MLB: 78%

Comparables:
Masa Kobayashi, Lindy McDaniel, Carl Willis

YEAR	TEAM	LVL	AGE	W	L	SV	G	GS	IP	H	HR	BB	SO	BB9	SO9	GB%	BABIP	WHIP	ERA	FIP	FRA	WARP
2011	SDN	MLB	32	6	8	0	77	0	74¹	73	7	20	43	2.4	5.2	59%	.281	1.25	3.51	3.87	5.02	-0.5
2012	NYA	MLB	33	1	0	0	8	0	7¹	10	0	3	2	3.7	2.5	54%	.357	1.77	6.14	3.73	4.74	0.0
2012	PHI	MLB	33	1	1	0	35	0	31¹	39	7	9	19	2.6	5.5	56%	.308	1.53	4.60	5.69	6.52	-0.5
2012	PIT	MLB	33	0	0	0	17	0	13²	14	0	2	6	1.3	4.0	60%	.280	1.17	6.59	2.70	3.30	0.2
2013	MIA	MLB	34	5	2	0	66	0	62	57	4	19	49	2.8	7.1	65%	.298	1.23	2.61	3.29	3.82	0.4
2014	HOU	MLB	35	3	1	1	56	0	50²	54	6	14	37	2.5	6.6	57%	.307	1.34	4.23	4.36	4.60	0.1

Last year's Annual proclaimed that "until Qualls adjusts his arsenal or tweaks his slider, he's unlikely to profile as anything more than a below-average middle reliever." And yet Qualls posted his best season since the late '90s. He didn't add a pitch and his slider didn't move more than it had in seasons past. How'd he increase his strikeout rate and maintain the highest ground-ball rate of his career? It's time for the Randomness of Relief Pitching quiz! Is the answer A) Health; B) Luck; C) Goat Sacrifice; D) All of the Above; or E) Just C? The answer will be revealed this year; Houston's clubhouse has a no-goat-sacrifice policy.

Vincent Velasquez

Born: 6/7/1992 Age: 22
Bats: B Throws: R Height: 6' 3" Weight: 203
Breakout: 42% Improve: 88% Collapse: 12%
Attrition: 86% MLB: 16%

Comparables:
Charlie Furbush, Duane Below, Jake Odorizzi

YEAR	TEAM	LVL	AGE	W	L	SV	G	GS	IP	H	HR	BB	SO	BB9	SO9	GB%	BABIP	WHIP	ERA	FIP	FRA	WARP
2012	TCV	A-	20	4	1	0	9	9	45²	37	2	17	51	3.4	10.1	44%	.299	1.18	3.35	2.98	3.84	0.6
2013	QUD	A	21	9	4	0	25	16	110	90	7	33	123	2.7	10.1	52%	.292	1.12	3.19	2.99	4.24	1.8
2013	LNC	A+	21	0	2	0	3	3	14²	14	2	8	19	4.9	11.7	33%	.353	1.50	6.14	5.00	5.75	0.1
2014	HOU	MLB	22	3	6	0	21	14	88²	92	12	45	72	4.6	7.3	44%	.306	1.55	5.10	5.17	5.54	-0.5

If he makes the majors, Vincent Velasquez would be the fourth player with "V" as alliterating initials, joining Virgil Vasquez, Vince Ventura and Vito Valentinetti. "Velasquez," a 70-grade Scrabble surname, pairs perfectly with his potential 70 change. (The alliterations and segues are out of control in this comment, huh?) Velasquez's fastball sits in the mid-90s and sets up the changeup at 79 to 83. Solid velocity separation and similar arm speed make it a vicious pitch that contributed to 123 strikeout victims (second in the Midwest League). It was Velasquez's first full season, and he showed no ill effects from Tommy John surgery in September 2010; according to him, it added velocity. A developing curveball completes his arsenal, one he commands effectively to merit a vault toward the upper reaches of Astros prospect lists.

Asher Wojciechowski

Born: 12/21/1988 Age: 25
Bats: R Throws: R Height: 6' 4" Weight: 235
Breakout: 42% Improve: 56% Collapse: 24%
Attrition: 64% MLB: 39%

Comparables:
J.D. Martin, David Phelps, Daniel McCutchen

YEAR	TEAM	LVL	AGE	W	L	SV	G	GS	IP	H	HR	BB	SO	BB9	SO9	GB%	BABIP	WHIP	ERA	FIP	FRA	WARP
2011	DUN	A+	22	11	9	0	25	22	130¹	156	15	31	96	2.1	6.6	43%	.340	1.43	4.70	4.22	5.53	0.7
2012	DUN	A+	23	7	3	0	18	18	93¹	91	3	22	76	2.1	7.3	46%	.320	1.21	3.57	3.05	3.78	1.9
2012	CCH	AA	23	2	2	0	8	8	43²	30	0	14	34	2.9	7.0	43%	.242	1.01	2.06	3.03	3.75	0.7
2013	CCH	AA	24	2	1	1	6	3	26	17	1	7	27	2.4	9.3	52%	.254	0.92	2.08	2.29	2.90	0.6
2013	OKL	AAA	24	9	7	0	22	21	134	116	10	44	104	3.0	7.0	35%	.268	1.19	3.56	4.00	4.52	1.5
2014	HOU	MLB	25	6	8	0	23	20	129	130	14	45	90	3.1	6.3	41%	.291	1.35	4.16	4.49	4.52	0.6

Wojciechowski's repertoire features a fastball, cutter, and slider, all average to above-average offerings, which translated into average to above-average results. Splitting time between Corpus Christi and Oklahoma City, he led the Astros organization in innings pitched, earning props for being a hard worker. His ceiling isn't high, but he'll certainly have utility at the major-league level in 2014, either as a back-end starter or middle reliever.

Josh Zeid

Born: 3/24/1987 Age: 27
Bats: R Throws: R Height: 6' 4" Weight: 220
Breakout: 46% Improve: 74% Collapse: 10%
Attrition: 64% MLB: 33%

Comparables:
B.J. Rosenberg, Jeremy Horst, Brent Leach

YEAR	TEAM	LVL	AGE	W	L	SV	G	GS	IP	H	HR	BB	SO	BB9	SO9	GB%	BABIP	WHIP	ERA	FIP	FRA	WARP
2011	REA	AA	24	2	3	2	21	11	63²	63	9	27	56	3.8	7.9	35%	.275	1.41	5.65	4.90	7.09	-0.2
2011	CCH	AA	24	0	1	0	14	1	16	23	5	6	15	3.4	8.4	41%	.360	1.81	10.12	6.88	7.46	-0.1
2012	CCH	AA	25	2	0	1	47	0	56¹	57	6	20	66	3.2	10.5	40%	.338	1.37	5.59	3.60	5.34	0.2
2013	OKL	AAA	26	4	1	13	43	0	43²	36	3	27	53	5.6	10.9	39%	.311	1.44	3.50	3.89	4.38	0.6
2013	HOU	MLB	26	0	1	1	25	0	27²	26	3	12	24	3.9	7.8	52%	.295	1.37	3.90	4.16	4.87	-0.1
2014	HOU	MLB	27	2	2	1	36	4	57²	59	8	28	51	4.3	8.0	42%	.305	1.49	4.72	4.96	5.13	-0.1

Yet another guy with a big arm and control issues. Sound familiar? Zeid started the season in Triple-A, eventually being promoted to closer. He earned a call-up to the big club for the last two months of the season despite a walk rate that would look terrible in the majors, much less Triple-A. The Astros weren't fooled about what Zeid was, though, as they used him in middle relief. Zeid's slider still grades out as plus, but "one good pitch, can't throw strikes" is closer to an epitaph than a commendation.

LINEOUTS

HITTERS

PLAYER	TEAM	LVL	AGE	PA	R	2B	3B	HR	RBI	BB	SO	SB-CS	AVG/OBP/SLG	TAv	BABIP	BRR	FRAA	WARP
1B J. Amador	OKL	AAA	26	43	2	0	0	0	2	0	8	0-0	.302/.302/.302	.196	.371	-0.1	1B(3): -0.0	-0.3
C C. Clark	OKL	AAA	31	158	16	5	0	1	12	7	32	0-0	.217/.258/.273	.198	.273	0.9	C(38): -0.2	-0.5
	HOU	MLB	31	40	1	1	0	0	0	1	15	0-0	.105/.128/.132	.105	.174	-0.6	C(16): -0.1	-0.3
LF T. Crowe	OKL	AAA	29	264	40	7	2	3	23	22	34	16-7	.304/.364/.388	.267	.343	-0.5	LF(40): 1.9, CF(3): -0.3	0.8
	HOU	MLB	29	181	18	7	1	1	13	16	39	6-1	.218/.287/.291	.225	.280	0.7	RF(25): 0.2, LF(24): -0.6	0.0
SS N. Fontana	LNC	A+	22	499	88	18	6	8	60	102	100	16-5	.259/.415/.399	.283	.327	3.9	SS(95): -7.6	2.8
LF L. Heras	CCH	AA	23	48	7	2	1	1	5	8	11	1-0	.205/.354/.385	.297	.259	0.4	LF(8): 0.1, CF(3): -0.1	0.3
CF T. Hernandez	QUD	A	20	565	97	25	9	13	55	41	135	24-11	.271/.328/.435	.280	.344	6.4	CF(108): -11.0, RF(15): -0.2	2.8
2B A. Kemp	QUD	A	21	120	21	1	1	1	9	19	18	4-2	.255/.387/.316	.269	.304	0.9	2B(17): 1.1, CF(3): -0.2	0.7
	TCV	A-	21	204	25	7	2	1	13	21	29	17-9	.282/.355/.362	.278	.325	-1.1	2B(47): 1.2, LF(3): 0.1	0.9
SS J. Mier	CCH	AA	22	416	44	10	0	5	28	46	97	9-8	.194/.293/.265	.214	.252	1.9	SS(101): -2.5, 3B(1): 0.0	-0.2
1B T. Nash	LNC	A+	22	269	43	10	0	16	48	37	93	1-0	.246/.357/.500	.285	.333	-5.9	1B(51): -1.3, RF(1): -0.0	0.3
C C. Perez	CCH	AA	22	60	6	4	0	1	5	4	11	0-0	.283/.356/.415	.259	.341	0	C(12): -0.2	0.3
	OKL	AAA	22	296	29	14	0	2	32	25	39	1-1	.269/.328/.345	.254	.304	-1	C(71): 0.7	1.5
3B R. Ruiz	QUD	A	19	472	46	33	1	12	63	50	92	12-3	.260/.335/.430	.275	.303	-3.6	3B(111): -8.0	1.3

Japhet Amador hit .368/.419/.693 in Mexico and mashed in the Arizona Fall League. No-position hitters carrying at least 315 pounds could be the new market inefficiency if they're able to drop about 100 of those pounds. ⌀ **Cody Clark**, an 11-year minor-league veteran, finally made his debut but it was a late-season fluke. The 32-year-old backstop was kicked off the 40-man roster after the season. ⌀ **Trevor Crowe**'s career batting line in the majors (.240/.294/.322) proves that it *can* rain all the time. ⌀ **Nolan Fontana**'s outstanding pitch recognition and baseball intelligence give him top grades in fundamentals despite a lack of tools. He's a safe bet to carve out a major-league career as a utility infielder. ⌀ From the Mexican League, where aging former major-leaguers Luis Terrero and Juan Miranda are OPS leaders, the Astros plucked relative youngster **Leo Heras** (.310/.398/.519). They hope his contact ability will provide a good return on their innovation dollars. ⌀ With excellent speed, a developing bat and the chops for center field, **Teoscar Hernandez** won't stay buried under the plethora of Astros top prospects for much longer. ⌀ Like Jose Altuve, diminutive fifth-rounder **Anthony Kemp** plays second base, exhibits high effort and is speedy on the basepaths. In other words, he's Jose Altuve. ⌀ Touted for his arm and range at shortstop, 2009 first-round selection **Jiovanni Mier** lost the illusions of hitter-friendly Lancaster when he moved to Double-A and displayed gap power at best. ⌀ In his second year at High-A Lancaster, **Telvin Nash** lowered his strikeout rate from 44 percent to 35 percent. Along with his increased walk rate, it's somewhat encouraging for him and his plus raw power. ⌀ Average defense and a passable bat at catcher spells second-division starter for **Carlos Perez**, but that opportunity won't come soon with the Astros' influx of talent at the position. ⌀ **Rio Ruiz** hit .297/.354/.521 in the second half, which began a month after his 19th birthday. The list of lefty-swinging third basemen with such precocious numbers and a plus arm is exceedingly short.

PITCHERS

PLAYER	TEAM	LVL	AGE	W	L	SV	IP	H	HR	BB	SO	BB9	SO9	GB%	BABIP	WHIP	ERA	FIP	FRA	WARP
J. Buchanan	CCH	AA	23	7	2	1	82	67	4	9	44	1.0	4.8	57%	.250	0.93	2.09	3.02	4.52	0.8
	OKL	AAA	23	5	5	0	76¹	85	6	13	55	1.5	6.5	58%	.326	1.28	3.89	3.66	4.40	0.8
K. Chapman	OKL	AAA	25	1	2	2	50²	42	2	36	61	6.4	10.8	55%	.310	1.54	3.20	3.87	3.67	1.0
	HOU	MLB	25	1	1	1	20¹	13	1	13	15	5.8	6.6	45%	.211	1.28	1.77	4.30	3.88	0.1
P. Clemens	OKL	AAA	25	3	2	0	30	27	1	11	16	3.3	4.8	49%	.257	1.27	4.50	4.24	5.69	0.1
	HOU	MLB	25	4	7	0	73¹	82	16	26	49	3.2	6.0	37%	.287	1.47	5.40	5.72	5.62	-0.5
L. Cruz	LNC	A+	22	8	6	2	113¹	111	10	40	129	3.2	10.2	46%	.331	1.33	5.16	3.94	3.70	3.3
	CCH	AA	22	2	0	0	17	5	0	4	21	2.1	11.1	48%	.152	0.53	0.53	1.29	2.49	0.5
R. Cruz	OKL	AAA	26	1	2	2	41²	34	6	32	38	6.9	8.2	45%	.257	1.58	4.75	6.14	6.67	-0.4
	HOU	MLB	26	0	2	0	21¹	25	2	11	10	4.6	4.2	32%	.319	1.69	3.38	5.18	4.98	0.0
D. Downs	TOL	AAA	28	0	1	0	15²	9	0	6	12	3.4	6.9	43%	.205	0.96	2.30	2.82	4.42	0.0
	DET	MLB	28	0	2	0	35¹	36	4	11	37	2.8	9.4	48%	.330	1.33	4.84	3.56	4.24	0.3
E. Gonzalez	BUF	AAA	30	1	0	0	19²	26	2	2	15	0.9	6.9	43%	.369	1.42	5.49	3.61	4.58	0.2
	HOU	MLB	30	0	1	0	10	17	4	3	8	2.7	7.2	24%	.382	2.00	7.20	7.58	6.90	-0.2
	TOR	MLB	30	0	0	0	8	9	2	5	3	5.6	3.4	34%	.259	1.75	7.88	7.83	7.70	-0.2
J. Hader	QUD	A	19	2	0	0	22¹	14	0	12	16	4.8	6.4	56%	.230	1.16	3.22	4.05	6.40	-0.1
	DEL	A	19	3	6	0	85	67	4	42	79	4.4	8.4	47%	.266	1.28	2.65	3.93	4.79	0.3
A. Houser	TCV	A-	20	0	4	0	50	57	1	10	39	1.8	7.0	54%	.348	1.34	3.42	2.70	3.77	0.6
P. Moylan	ABQ	AAA	34	4	1	4	46	38	1	20	45	3.9	8.8	53%	.294	1.26	2.74	3.33	4.11	0.9
	LAN	MLB	34	1	0	0	15¹	23	3	7	6	4.1	3.5	29%	.358	1.96	6.46	6.15	7.02	-0.4
R. Owens	OKL	AAA	25	0	3	0	17	20	0	9	13	4.8	6.9	58%	.364	1.71	3.71	3.63	5.48	0.2
D. Rollins	LNC	A+	23	8	5	3	97¹	81	9	32	96	3.0	8.9	43%	.274	1.16	3.98	4.11	5.70	2.1
	CCH	AA	23	0	3	0	33	38	4	10	33	2.7	9.0	37%	.362	1.45	4.36	3.63	3.91	0.6
K. Smith	WIL	A+	20	5	4	0	104¹	93	9	29	96	2.5	8.3	47%	.287	1.17	2.85	3.61	4.42	1.2
	LNC	A+	20	1	1	0	23¹	26	4	9	21	3.5	8.1	31%	.328	1.50	7.33	5.74	7.22	0.3
A. Thurman	TCV	A-	21	4	2	1	39²	43	5	11	43	2.5	9.8	35%	.349	1.36	3.86	3.63	4.24	0.3
N. Tropeano	CCH	AA	22	7	10	5	133²	140	15	39	130	2.6	8.8	45%	.333	1.34	4.11	3.51	4.22	2.3
R. Valdes	LEH	AAA	35	4	5	0	78²	67	5	22	66	2.5	7.6	35%	.273	1.13	2.86	3.27	3.77	1.5
	PHI	MLB	35	1	1	0	35	42	7	8	37	2.1	9.5	28%	.344	1.43	7.46	4.36	4.84	0.0
A. White	COL	MLB	23	2	9	0	98	114	13	51	64	4.7	5.9	55%	.322	1.68	5.51	5.27	6.42	-0.4

Jake Buchanan keeps his high-80s fastball down, batters from reaching ball four and balls from leaving the yard. His divergent stat lines in Corpus Christi and Oklahoma reflected a tale of two BABIPs. ⊘ **Kevin Chapman** might have been effectively wild in 2013, but was more likely just lucky; either way, he could be a viable specialist with reasonable heat from the port side. ⊘ **Paul Clemens** spent the majority of the season with the major-league team, but he doesn't have the arsenal to make him a viable starter; his future is likely in middle relief, where the fastball plays up enough to make him useful. ⊘ **Luis Cruz** was pitching well in the organization's tandem-starters experiment; his ERA jumped by three runs in six High-A starts after going back to a regular schedule. Still, Houston put him on the 40-man roster after the season. ⊘ **Rhiner Cruz**'s lack of effective secondary offerings limits his ceiling, but his fastball, which can touch 98 and averages 95, is a legitimate weapon. ⊘ **Darin Downs'** improved strikeout and walk rates were cancelled out by a regression to a league-average HR/FB rate, which boosted his ERA by more than a run. ⊘ It took 13 ⅓ innings for **Christian Garcia** to succumb to yet another injury (partial flexor tear). He has good stuff, but the injury goblins have even better stuff. ⊘ **Edgar Gonzalez** took a six-week hiatus with the Blue Jays before returning to the Astros in May, but he did not magically acquire an arsenal of major-league pitches while on his Canadian walkabout. ⊘ Acquired in the Bud Norris trade with Baltimore, **Josh Hader** throws a lively low-90s fastball from a low three-quarters arm slot. At 19, his repertoire, which also includes a curve and change, is a work in progress. ⊘ Tall starters seem to exist at every level of Houston's system, and **Adrian Houser** is another 6-foot-4 prospect with an athletic body. He made strides with his command in short-season ball at Tri-City. ⊘ **Peter Moylan** logged more innings in 2013 than in the two previous years combined, but three-fourths of those frames were pitched in the minors, and four-fourths of those innings lacked Moylan's previously excellent groundball utility. ⊘ **Rudy Owens** was primed to bring his strike-throwing ways to the majors before a stress fracture in his left foot ended his season in April. ⊘ Trivia time! **David Rollins** was one of three minor-leaguers to make starts in High-A, Double-A and Triple-A without having played at those levels prior to 2013. The other two were fellow Astros Brady Rodgers and Kyle Hallock. ⊘ **Kyle Smith**, armed with a curveball he throws for strikes, dominated in High-A Wilmington before Houston acquired him for Justin Maxwell and assigned him to Lancaster, where his home run rate doubled. ⊘ Drafted out of UC Irvine in the second round, **Andrew Thurman** is a polished four-pitch right-hander who majored in political science and fastball command, the latter with honors. ⊘ Another six-foot-four Astros starter, **Nick Tropeano**'s Double-A peripherals were essentially identical to 2012's in High-A Lancaster. He relies on command and a sinking changeup, daring hitters to play his game of deception. ⊘ **Raul Valdes** was an unsung hero in the Phillies' bullpen in 2012, but—despite nice defense-independent numbers—one of their least reliable arms in 2013. Such is the way of the bullpen. ⊘ **Alex White**'s unique repertoire features a fastball, splitter and slider, but it wasn't put to use as he missed the year recovering from Tommy John surgery.

MANAGER: BO PORTER

YEAR	TEAM	W-L	Pythag +/-	Avg PC	100+ P	120+ P	QS	BQS	REL	REL w Zero R	IBB	PH	PH Avg	PH HR	SB2	CS2	SB3	CS3	SAC Att	SAC %	POS SAC	Squeeze	Swing	In Play
2013	HOU	51-111	0	95.5	50	1	75	4	447	319	32	85	.213	2	87	52	22	7	70	65.7%	43	5	330	82

Last time a rookie manager took over a team that had led the league in losses the year before: Alan Trammell with the 2003 Tigers. So Bo Porter took over under the worst circumstances of any newbie manager since then. Yeah, that sounds right.

In 2013, the Astros led the league in sacrifice hits, which is especially impressive because they had the lowest on-base percentage in the AL (and thus had the fewest opportunities for sacrifice hits). He also had his players run fairly often on the bases—too much, actually. The Astros had one of the worst success rates when trying to swipe a base.

The 2013 Astros batters struck out 1,535 times while their pitches fanned 1,084 batters. That's a strikeout differential of -451, the second worst ever, behind the 2010 Diamondbacks (-459).

Kansas City Royals

By Craig Brown

"Pitching is the currency of the game."

> — *Dayton Moore,*
> *shortly after taking over as the*
> *Royals general manager, June 2006.*

In the autumn of 2012, Royals General Manager Dayton Moore moved like a Black Friday shopper. Three days after the World Series ended, he traded for Ervin Santana, a $12 million small-market gamble that Santana could rebound from a career-worst season. By Thanksgiving Moore had re-signed free agent Jeremy Guthrie, whom he had traded for the previous year (in a small-market gamble that Guthrie could rebound from a career-worst season). Finally, Moore pulled off what became known to Royals fans as simply The Trade: uber-prospect Wil Myers and assorted minor-league parts to Tampa in exchange for James Shields and Wade Davis. In three moves—for just a shade over $31 million—Moore had assembled four-fifths of his 2013 starting rotation.

The results were fantastic. The quartet combined to throw 785 innings, paced by Shields' 229, the second most by a Royal in 15 years. Kansas City starters as a group shaved more than a run off their ERA from 2012, and the revamped front four had cascading effects on the rest of the staff: Royals pitchers overall went from surrendering a below-league-average 4.6 runs per game in 2012 to a league-best 3.7 runs per game in 2013.

While the Royals' pitching staff was stellar, they also benefited from having one of the game's top defenses behind them. Moore has stressed the importance of defense and made several moves over the years to assemble a team consisting of solid glovemen, especially up the middle. Center fielder Lorenzo Cain and shortstop Alcides Escobar came over from Milwaukee in the Zack Greinke trade; each was a Gold Glove finalist at a premium position. Catcher Salvador

Perez was signed as an international free agent and developed into one of the best defensive backstops in the game. With a solid defensive backbone, the Royals' fielding has gone from a liability to an asset. The club's park-adjusted defensive efficiency was a solid 0.93, good for third best in the AL, behind playoff teams Oakland and Tampa. They fielded three Gold Glove winners for the first time in franchise history with Perez, Alex Gordon and Eric Hosmer.

Pitching and defense win championships. That's how the cliche goes. Yet among the seven American League clubs that finished better than league average in run prevention only the Royals failed to advance past game 162. They inhabited the same leaderboard real estate as the postseason teams, but alone fell short. Moore went "all in" with his pitching and his team still finished third in the AL Central, five games out of the Wild Card.

Oh, yeah. Hitting still matters.

***

"It's an eight- to 10-year process (to build a winning team). Knowing how these jobs are, especially in today's climate, it's tough to get that much time. It takes three to five years to get guys to the major-league level, and then two to four years playing at the major-league level." — Dayton Moore, February 2, 2012

For the second consecutive season, the Royals' offense got worse. The scapegoat following the 2012 season was hitting coach Kevin Seitzer. He was replaced by new hitting co-coach Jack Maloof, who claimed—less than two months on the job, with the offense again dragging—that there was no reward for the Royals to try to hit home runs. Credit to the Royals in showing Maloof and co-coach Andre David the door shortly after those comments. In their stead, the Royals hired legend George Brett on an interim basis to work in tandem with Pedro Grifol. So many hitting coaches, so little productivity. The offense never really improved, and Brett

ROYALS PROSPECTUS
2013 W-L: 86-76, 3rd in AL Central

Pythag	.534	12th	DER	.710	5th
RS/G	4.00	18th	B-Age	26.9	3rd
RA/G	3.71	6th	P-Age	29.6	27th
TAv	.254	18th	Salary	$81.2	22nd
BRR	3.22	12th	M$/MW	$1.81	6th
TAv-P	.258	10th	DL Days	414	1st
FIP	3.85	14th	$ on DL	3%	1st

	Runs	HR/RH	HR/LH	Runs/RH	Runs/LH
Three-Year Park Factors	100	79	87	97	103

Top Hitter WARP	4.12 (Alex Gordon)
Top Pitcher WARP	2.77 (James Shields)
Top Prospect	Yordano Ventura

stepped down two months later to return to his role in the front office.

The Royals' fan base has been well attuned to The Process described by Moore in the previous quote. The Process contains a few shades of grey, but can be neatly broken down into three steps: 1) Rebuild the farm system, 2) Restock the major-league roster, and 3) Contention. Lather, rinse, repeat.

The first step in The Process was achieved early, when through savvy drafts and aggressive moves on the international market the Royals assembled one of the top farm systems in baseball—arguably in baseball history. ("The best, it's not close/Moose, Hosmer, tons of lefties/Tim Collins is small," Kevin Goldstein haiku'd at the time.) Populated with both highly rated prospects and depth, this was the first brick in what was to be a solid organizational foundation.

The stumbling block came with the second step. While the Royals' minor-league hitters have consistently been ahead of the pitchers on the developmental curve, as a collective they have all struggled when reaching the majors. Hosmer had a fine rookie campaign, but followed that with a horrific sophomore season. He stumbled out of the gate in 2013 before finally turning it around after Brett arrived. There's a real reason to be optimistic about his future. The other homegrown hitters? Not so much. Fellow first-rounder Mike Moustakas is a streaky bat, but has looked lost at the plate for the majority of his career, which has now spanned nearly 1,500 plate appearances. Johnny Giavotella is a spare part, and Christian Colon might not be even that. There are still hitting prospects in the minors, most notably Raul Mondesi Jr. and Jorge Bonifacio, but they are still off in the distance, making it far too early to declare victory. They are meant to be Phase Two of The Process, filling in the gaps behind what were to be the premium bats of Hosmer, Moustakas and Myers.

And, remember: the young hitters have been *ahead* of the pitchers in development. Only Danny Duffy has emerged as a homegrown starter, producing just 1.6 WARP over his career and missing parts of the past two seasons after undergoing Tommy John surgery. Former top prospects John Lamb, Mike Montgomery, Chris Dwyer and Tim Melville either hit their ceilings before they reached the majors or were derailed by injury. While the Royals' deep farm system has had little difficulty finding the arms to stock what has become one of the best bullpens in the game, the club hasn't been able to fill out a rotation. And so Moore had to trade Myers, arguably the best hitter the system produced, for pitching, cannibalizing from one weak spot to fill another.

The offensive difficulties have been an ongoing issue for the Royals since Moore's arrival, suggesting he's part of the problem, failing to fill in the gaps with quality bats. Only once in Moore's tenure (2011) have the Royals finished in the top half of the AL in TAv. Last summer, the Royals' team TAv of .249 was their lowest since 2007. Impatient to a fault,

they haven't finished above the league average in walks since Moore became the Royals' GM. In 2012 they were last, and in 2013 avoided that distinction by just 11 free passes. They don't hit with power—their .119 ISO was dead last in the AL. Moustakas was supposed to be the prospect with the highest power potential, but is more likely to foul out to third than drive a ball with authority. Offensive stalwarts Butler and Gordon aren't going to hit for power, and both saw their ISO and slugging percentages nosedive.

No on-base threats, no thunder in the middle—add it all up and it's not surprising they scored just four runs per game in 2013, well below the league average of 4.3 and their worst showing of the Dayton Moore era.

***

"When I look at our roster, I believe all of our players who are signed long-term, that are under control, they are all going to get better. That's a comforting feeling. Is it just going to happen? No. They're going to have to continue to work hard. They're going to have to continue to apply instruction, to make adjustments. They're going to have to continue to commit to being great players. We feel like they will." — Dayton Moore, October 1, 2013

While the GM struggles to assemble a coherent 25-man roster and his staff has difficulty with player development, Moore does excel at salesmanship. The above comment was made at 2013's post-mortem press conference. Yes, the Royals did win 86 games last season, their highest total since 1989. Yes, the win total was propelled by the pitching moves Moore made the previous winter and an improved defense. Yes, the Royals were on the periphery of the pennant race until September. A good season for a franchise that hasn't seen success in nearly three decades, one that some will see as a building block to future success. That is the big question heading into 2014: Can the Royals ride the momentum of 2013 and finally return to October?

Moore fielded a tremendously young starting offensive nine last year. The average Royals hitter was 27; only Houston and Atlanta were younger. This core group is either still in their pre-arbitration years or signed to team-friendly long-term contracts. It would all be going according to The Process, if these had shown they could actually produce.

Can everyone improve, as Moore believes? Is that a reasonable expectation? It's possible Butler or Gordon—who both had their lowest TAvs since 2010—can rebound from down years. Hosmer paced the Royals' offense in 2013; the signs are there that he can continue to build upon his breakout final four months. Perez saw his power dip, but just finished his first full season, has shown positive flashes with the bat and is young enough that we can expect improvement. And at least Moore knows he needs to add to the offense: The December acquisition of Norichika Aoki gives the Royals a legitimate on-base threat at the top of their order and Omar

Infante fixes the Royals' second base problem, which has seen KC keystoners since 2010 produce the second-lowest WARP of any position on any team. But the Royals continue to need a lot of players to take a step forward at the same time, a highly doubtful, highly optimistic expectation. While the Royals are a young team, they don't necessarily lack major-league experience, or major-league baggage.

And if the offense is a work in progress, the rotation has some work to do to replicate its 2013 success. Free agent Jason Vargas gives the Royals a solid starter—but one who lacks the upside of the departed Santana. The rest of the rotation behind Shields remains similarly questionable. There are some young arms in the system who might be ready to step forward, but they can't be counted upon when projecting the 2014 season, especially with the Royals' track record of developing starting pitching.

***

"And there's an emotion and there's an expectation and there's an excitement around this group of players, and in a small way, I feel like we've won the World Series. Because we have captured a fan base that is excited." — Dayton Moore, October 1, 2013

Moore has always been about managing expectations, even when those expectations are mediocre in nature. His timetable for success seems to slide on a regular basis, adding another year or two every season without said success.

He has attempted to explain away the bumps on the road of player development. Coming off an 86-win season after decades of futility in Kansas City, the upcoming season truly feels like a watershed moment in Moore's tenure.

In October, manager Ned Yost signed a two-year contract that will keep him in the dugout through the 2015 season. In November, Moore signed a contract extension that will keep him in his position as the Royals' general manager through 2016 (or, at least, paid by the Royals until then). It's both a reward for the Royals' 2013 season and an acknowledgement from ownership they feel the team is on the right path.

The Royals enter 2014 with expectations higher than anytime since the first George Bush was in the White House. But as the Royals will soon learn, contention treads a fine line. The margin for error is minimal. With Shields in the final year of his contract and the players in the first wave of The Process in their physical primes, the Royals are geared for a season of playoffs or bust. If it's the latter, it's anybody's guess when the Royals, and every Royals fan born since October 1985, will get another chance.

The pressure is firmly on Moore. It might feel like the Royals won a World Series to him, but a fan base well versed in futility should be a little more demanding.

Craig Brown is co-founder of Royals Authority *and the managing editor of* Royals Review.

HITTERS

Norichika Aoki   RF

Born: 1/5/1982 Age: 32
Bats: L Throws: R Height: 5' 9"
Weight: 175 Breakout: 1%
Improve: 39% Collapse: 0%
Attrition: 10% MLB: 94%

Comparables:
Juan Pierre, Floyd Robinson, Ichiro Suzuki

YEAR	TEAM	LVL	AGE	PA	R	2B	3B	HR	RBI	BB	SO	SB	CS	AVG/OBP/SLG	TAv	BABIP	BRR	FRAA	WARP
2012	MIL	MLB	30	588	81	37	4	10	50	43	55	30	8	.288/.355/.433	.281	.304	1.5	RF(107): 2.8, CF(19): -2.4	2.9
2013	MIL	MLB	31	674	80	20	3	8	37	55	40	20	12	.286/.356/.370	.269	.295	-4.2	RF(149): -0.9, CF(2): -0.1	1.6
2014	KCA	MLB	32	616	75	28	3	5	48	44	48	23	9	.281/.343/.370	.269	.290	0.2	RF 0, CF -1	1.7

Teams haven't yet cracked the mystery of which skills best carry over from Japan to the States. Aoki arrived at Ellis Island with no fanfare, only a very few (million) dollars to his name and no apparent role on his new club. So, naturally, he's a hit: His total value ranks third all-time among Japanese-born players in their first two years stateside. Aoki has elite contact skills that have translated: He swung and missed just 82 times at 2,490 total pitches in 2013. The 3.3 percent whiff rate trailed just Marco Scutaro (1.5) and Martin Prado (3.2), two players who swung less often than Aoki. His power dipped in 2013, and he was less effective stealing bases, but Aoki's discipline and ability to put the ball in the play make him an on-base threat and an effective option in right field. Traded to the Royals, Aoki will be doubly valuable providing a speedy table setter at the top of the Kansas City order and evicting the gaggle of speedy table emptiers who squatted there last year.

Emilio Bonifacio   2B

Born: 4/23/1985 Age: 29
Bats: B Throws: R Height: 5' 11"
Weight: 205 Breakout: 3%
Improve: 41% Collapse: 5%
Attrition: 15% MLB: 98%

Comparables:
Ray Durham, Steve Sax, Don Buford

YEAR	TEAM	LVL	AGE	PA	R	2B	3B	HR	RBI	BB	SO	SB	CS	AVG/OBP/SLG	TAv	BABIP	BRR	FRAA	WARP
2011	FLO	MLB	26	641	78	26	7	5	36	59	129	40	11	.296/.360/.393	.279	.372	7.9	SS(67): -5.9, 3B(36): 0.4	3.7
2012	JUP	A+	27	36	6	1	0	0	4	6	9	3	1	.167/.306/.200	.207	.238	0.9	CF(9): -0.2	0.0
2012	MIA	MLB	27	274	30	3	4	1	11	25	52	30	3	.258/.330/.316	.246	.325	1.3	CF(51): -3.7, 2B(15): 0.7	0.0
2013	KCA	MLB	28	179	21	6	2	0	11	17	37	16	2	.285/.352/.348	.258	.369	3.7	2B(31): -1.3, 3B(6): -0.1	0.7
2013	TOR	MLB	28	282	33	16	1	3	20	13	66	12	6	.218/.258/.321	.217	.277	2.6	2B(59): 0.8, LF(20): 0.9	0.0
2014	KCA	MLB	29	400	49	13	4	2	26	30	77	26	6	.261/.318/.335	.241	.320	3	2B -0, CF -2	0.5

When looking for a position player, the Royals under Dayton Moore covet two tools: speed and versatility. That makes it a given that Bonifacio should don the Royal blue at some point. That he had an 89 percent stolen base success rate while fielding three positions means his mid-season acquisition from Toronto was an unqualified success, at least in the eyes of management. What he truly did was to temporarily fill the offensive void that occurs when you employ the troika of Chris Getz, Eliot Johnson and Miguel Tejada at second base. His previous employer was still complaining of his defense after his departure, but his glove plays solid at second, with good lateral range. With a final year of arbitration eligibility ahead of him, the Royals will give him an opportunity to claim the second base job to open the year.

Billy Butler 1B

Born: 4/18/1986 Age: 28
Bats: R Throws: R Height: 6' 1''
Weight: 240 Breakout: 0%
Improve: 49% Collapse: 2%
Attrition: 5% MLB: 97%

Comparables:
Justin Morneau, Todd Helton, Kent Hrbek

YEAR	TEAM	LVL	AGE	PA	R	2B	3B	HR	RBI	BB	SO	SB	CS	AVG/OBP/SLG	TAv	BABIP	BRR	FRAA	WARP
2011	KCA	MLB	25	673	74	44	0	19	95	66	95	2	1	.291/.361/.461	.279	.316	-4.1	1B(11): -0.9	1.6
2012	KCA	MLB	26	679	72	32	1	29	107	54	111	2	1	.313/.373/.510	.301	.341	-4.7	1B(20): -0.2	3.1
2013	KCA	MLB	27	668	62	27	0	15	82	79	102	0	0	.289/.374/.412	.283	.326	-6.3	1B(7): 0.2	1.6
2014	KCA	MLB	28	630	73	34	1	18	79	59	93	1	0	.295/.364/.452	.295	.320	-1.2	1B -0	3.1

Where oh where did the power go? A year after posting a career-best ISO Butler gave nearly 80 points back and tied a career low. The answer may be underground. Or more accurately, on the ground. Butler hit more groundballs than ever in 2013, with over 53 percent of all balls hugging grass—a recipe for lots of singles and a solid batting average, but few moonshots. Perhaps the lack of power has to do with how he was pitched, as the opposition threw more pitches outside the strike zone and he finished with the highest walk rate of his career. The upside was his OBP was firm, but the Royals were counting on something more in the power department. He's a candidate to rebound, but only if he stops slaughtering so many worms.

Lorenzo Cain CF

Born: 4/13/1986 Age: 28
Bats: R Throws: R Height: 6' 2''
Weight: 205 Breakout: 3%
Improve: 43% Collapse: 12%
Attrition: 20% MLB: 72%

Comparables:
Roger Bernadina, Brian Anderson, Charles Thomas

YEAR	TEAM	LVL	AGE	PA	R	2B	3B	HR	RBI	BB	SO	SB	CS	AVG/OBP/SLG	TAv	BABIP	BRR	FRAA	WARP
2011	OMA	AAA	25	549	84	28	7	16	81	40	102	16	6	.312/.380/.497	.301	.366	-0.1	CF(69): 0.7, RF(26): -4.5	2.7
2011	KCA	MLB	25	23	4	1	0	0	1	1	4	0	0	.273/.304/.318	.215	.333	0.3	RF(4): -0.3, CF(2): -0.2	0.0
2012	NWA	AA	26	24	4	1	0	1	1	0	6	0	0	.208/.208/.375	.228	.235	0.2	CF(5): 0.3	0.0
2012	OMA	AAA	26	31	4	3	0	1	6	2	4	0	0	.321/.355/.536	.304	.333	-0.5	CF(5): -0.2	0.1
2012	KCA	MLB	26	244	27	9	2	7	31	15	56	10	0	.266/.316/.419	.264	.319	0.6	CF(50): 2.0, RF(9): 0.6	1.3
2013	KCA	MLB	27	442	54	21	3	4	46	33	90	14	6	.251/.310/.348	.245	.309	-1.3	CF(92): 6.6, RF(32): 1.3	1.4
2014	KCA	MLB	28	382	40	16	3	5	37	26	76	13	3	.264/.320/.375	.257	.320	1.3	CF 4, RF -0	1.4

The oft-injured Cain managed to stay in the lineup for four months before he missed time due to injury. That was progress. He doesn't walk or reach base enough to be a leadoff hitter and doesn't hit with enough power to bat in the heart of the order. The swing can get long and he will fish outside the zone for the fastball. Cain's value lies in the leather, and various metrics had him as the AL's best defensive center fielder. He tracks the ball well, gets great jumps and has the speed to make up for his rare mistakes. For some reason, the Royals had him in right field down the stretch. Typical.

Jamey Carroll 2B

Born: 2/18/1974 Age: 40
Bats: R Throws: R Height: 5' 11''
Weight: 175 Breakout: 0%
Improve: 13% Collapse: 10%
Attrition: 20% MLB: 57%

Comparables:
Tony Fernandez, Wade Boggs, Melvin Mora

YEAR	TEAM	LVL	AGE	PA	R	2B	3B	HR	RBI	BB	SO	SB	CS	AVG/OBP/SLG	TAv	BABIP	BRR	FRAA	WARP
2011	LAN	MLB	37	510	52	14	6	0	17	47	58	10	0	.290/.359/.347	.271	.332	1.6	2B(81): 4.3, SS(66): -6.7	2.5
2012	MIN	MLB	38	537	65	18	1	1	40	52	65	9	5	.268/.343/.317	.244	.306	-0.1	2B(66): 0.8, 3B(44): 0.1	1.4
2013	KCA	MLB	39	43	5	3	0	0	2	4	4	0	1	.111/.190/.194	.172	.118	-0.3	3B(14): -0.6, 2B(1): -0.1	-0.3
2013	MIN	MLB	39	206	21	6	0	0	9	13	35	2	0	.230/.283/.262	.210	.282	0.8	3B(33): -0.2, 2B(17): -2.3	-0.6
2014	KCA	MLB	40	291	30	9	1	0	18	25	42	5	2	.260/.327/.307	.238	.300	0.1	2B 0, 3B -1	0.3

As the Royals found themselves on the periphery of the race post-All Star break, they looked under every rock they could to find a competent second baseman. They even called the Twins, which was where they found Carroll. He provides what you would expect from a light-hitting middle infielder approaching his fourth decade: a lot of light hitting with limited and decreasing range, and clubhouse tales of the time he saw Nirvana at an all-ages show in Evansville. The Royals removed him from their 40-man roster in October and he became a free agent when he declined an assignment to the minors. This appears to be the end, though his beginning appeared to be the end, so who knows.

Pedro Ciriaco SS

Born: 9/27/1985 Age: 28
Bats: R Throws: R Height: 6' 0''
Weight: 180 Breakout: 1%
Improve: 11% Collapse: 6%
Attrition: 9% MLB: 25%

Comparables:
Joaquin Arias, Ed Rogers, Anderson Hernandez

YEAR	TEAM	LVL	AGE	PA	R	2B	3B	HR	RBI	BB	SO	SB	CS	AVG/OBP/SLG	TAv	BABIP	BRR	FRAA	WARP
2011	IND	AAA	25	289	31	7	3	2	24	5	49	13	7	.231/.243/.300	.208	.272	1.8	SS(37): -3.6, 2B(17): -3.6	-1.1
2011	PIT	MLB	25	34	4	2	1	0	6	1	6	2	1	.303/.324/.424	.277	.370	-1.1	SS(7): 0.7, 3B(2): 0.0	0.2
2012	PAW	AAA	26	289	41	13	2	4	21	6	49	14	8	.301/.318/.406	.252	.351	-1.1	SS(37): 4.2, 2B(23): -1.0	1.0
2012	BOS	MLB	26	272	33	15	2	2	19	8	47	16	3	.293/.315/.390	.249	.352	0.7	3B(35): 3.0, 2B(16): 0.0	1.4
2013	OMA	AAA	27	171	19	8	1	1	15	6	22	4	1	.281/.310/.362	.250	.319	2.7	SS(30): -2.1, 3B(7): 0.7	0.6
2013	BOS	MLB	27	58	4	2	1	1	4	6	12	2	1	.216/.293/.353	.258	.256	-0.8	3B(10): -0.2, SS(8): -1.6	-0.2
2013	KCA	MLB	27	11	0	1	0	0	0	0	1	1	0	.182/.182/.273	.229	.200	0.5	SS(3): -0.1	0.1
2013	SDN	MLB	27	68	5	1	1	1	4	3	10	6	0	.238/.284/.333	.221	.269	-0.4	SS(18): -1.6, 2B(2): 0.1	-0.1
2014	KCA	MLB	28	250	27	10	2	2	18	5	43	10	3	.260/.277/.344	.228	.300	0.9	SS -1, 3B 1	0.1

Some years, it just doesn't pay to unpack. Ciriaco was waived—and claimed—three times before the Royals were able to smuggle him to Triple-A. A look at the offensive numbers above gives you a clue as to why he was on the move so often. While the glove is versatile and rates as above average, you just can't keep employment if you hit like you're allergic to maple. For some reason the Royals added him back to their 40-man roster in a September call-up, but don't be surprised if he's on the move again—and again—in 2014.

Christian Colon SS

Born: 5/14/1989 Age: 25
Bats: R Throws: R Height: 5' 10''
Weight: 185 Breakout: 0%
Improve: 1% Collapse: 5%
Attrition: 9% MLB: 11%

Comparables:
Callix Crabbe, William Bergolla, Brian Dinkelman

YEAR	TEAM	LVL	AGE	PA	R	2B	3B	HR	RBI	BB	SO	SB	CS	AVG/OBP/SLG	TAv	BABIP	BRR	FRAA	WARP
2011	NWA	AA	22	568	69	14	2	8	61	46	51	17	7	.257/.325/.342	.226	.271	-2.3	SS(79): 4.4, 2B(14): 0.8	0.6
2012	NWA	AA	23	315	33	9	2	5	27	31	27	12	6	.289/.364/.392	.269	.305	-2.6	SS(54): 2.3, 2B(17): 0.1	1.3
2012	OMA	AAA	23	21	4	1	0	1	5	2	1	0	0	.412/.429/.647	.380	.353	-0.3	SS(4): -0.8, 2B(1): -0.0	0.2
2013	OMA	AAA	24	577	72	12	3	12	58	41	57	15	4	.273/.335/.379	.256	.288	2.1	2B(75): 2.4, SS(54): -5.4	1.9
2014	KCA	MLB	25	250	27	8	1	3	20	15	29	4	2	.252/.302/.338	.235	.270	0.1	SS -0, 2B 1	0.4

After a difficult year in Triple-A, the prospect shine has dulled for Colon. The attributes the Royals loved—his superior pitch recognition and contact rates—were still solid, but his line-drive rate dipped to 10 percent and his BABIP suffered a corresponding drop. He was drafted as a shortstop, but scouts long have felt his more natural position was second base. The Royals finally had him taking more reps at the keystone, but even with their struggles at the major-league level he couldn't buy an appearance in the bigs. Destined to be the answer to the trivia question: Who was picked after Bryce Harper, Jamison Taillon and Manny Machado were off the board in the 2010 draft?

Hunter Dozier 3B

Born: 8/22/1991 Age: 22
Bats: R Throws: R Height: 6' 4''
Weight: 220 Breakout: 0%
Improve: 0% Collapse: 0%
Attrition: 0% MLB: 0%

Comparables:
Chase Headley, Jedd Gyorko, Luke Hughes

YEAR	TEAM	LVL	AGE	PA	R	2B	3B	HR	RBI	BB	SO	SB	CS	AVG/OBP/SLG	TAv	BABIP	BRR	FRAA	WARP
2013	LEX	A	21	59	6	6	0	0	9	3	5	0	0	.327/.373/.436	.322	.360	-0.5	3B(13): 0.1	0.6
2014	KCA	MLB	22	250	19	10	0	3	21	15	55	0	0	.215/.264/.295	.208	.270	-0.4	3B -1, SS -0	-0.8

The Royals shocked the draft gurus when they selected Dozier as the eighth overall pick in 2013. Seen as a reach, it was part of a larger draft strategy that allowed the Royals to move around the cash in their bonus pool. One of the top college bats in the draft, Dozier lived up to expectations in his first pro taste. Possessing a solid understanding of the strike zone, his hit tool projects as slightly above average with some power potential. He's solid defender at short but his long-term home looks to be third. He cruised through the Pioneer League and will likely open 2014 in High-A.

Jarrod Dyson CF

Born: 8/15/1984 Age: 29
Bats: L Throws: R Height: 5' 9''
Weight: 160 Breakout: 2%
Improve: 34% Collapse: 13%
Attrition: 23% MLB: 71%

Comparables:
Chris Duffy, Trevor Crowe, Craig Gentry

YEAR	TEAM	LVL	AGE	PA	R	2B	3B	HR	RBI	BB	SO	SB	CS	AVG/OBP/SLG	TAv	BABIP	BRR	FRAA	WARP
2011	OMA	AAA	26	369	69	10	3	3	26	35	47	38	2	.279/.356/.357	.276	.320	5.7	CF(29): 1.1, RF(16): -0.8	2.3
2011	KCA	MLB	26	53	8	1	0	0	3	7	14	11	1	.205/.308/.227	.190	.290	2.4	CF(17): 0.4	0.1
2012	OMA	AAA	27	71	12	3	3	0	5	4	5	7	1	.333/.373/.476	.260	.362	2.6	CF(14): 0.8	0.7
2012	KCA	MLB	27	330	52	8	5	0	9	30	56	30	5	.260/.328/.322	.239	.318	6	CF(88): 8.8	2.0
2013	OMA	AAA	28	58	8	2	0	0	1	3	12	5	0	.154/.228/.192	.185	.200	0.6	CF(14): 0.1	-0.2
2013	KCA	MLB	28	239	30	9	4	2	17	21	45	34	6	.258/.326/.366	.246	.317	3.2	CF(73): 0.6	0.9
2014	KCA	MLB	29	260	35	10	3	1	15	21	47	27	4	.247/.311/.325	.236	.300	4	CF 5, RF -0	1.0

With a static TAv, Dyson drew fewer walks but hit for more power in 2013. We didn't think that was possible. The man who coined the phrase "That's what speed do," doesn't "do" much other than run. In the 92 times he was on first or second with the next base open, he attempted to swipe that base 40 times. Defensively, he continues to struggle getting quick reads and will take some questionable routes from time to time. He's not anywhere in the same class as fellow center fielder Lorenzo Cain, but the plus speed has the Royals thinking this is the case. A one-dimensional player who happens to own the one dimension Dayton Moore most covets, he's a useful set of legs off the bench.

	YEAR	TEAM	LVL	AGE	PA	R	2B	3B	HR	RBI	BB	SO	SB	CS	AVG/OBP/SLG	TAv	BABIP	BRR	FRAA	WARP
Alcides Escobar SS	2011	KCA	MLB	24	598	69	21	8	4	46	25	73	26	9	.254/.290/.343	.235	.285	0.7	SS(158): 0.9	0.8
Born: 12/16/1986 Age: 27	2012	KCA	MLB	25	648	68	30	7	5	52	27	100	35	5	.293/.331/.390	.251	.344	1.6	SS(155): -11.5	1.4
Bats: R Throws: R Height: 6' 1''	2013	KCA	MLB	26	642	57	20	4	4	52	19	84	22	0	.234/.259/.300	.205	.264	2.2	SS(158): -0.3	-0.7
Weight: 195 Breakout: 4%	2014	KCA	MLB	27	604	61	22	6	4	47	26	81	25	5	.260/.297/.344	.236	.290	3.6	SS -4	1.2
Improve: 39% Collapse: 15%																				
Attrition: 15% MLB: 97%																				
Comparables: Erick Aybar, Tsuyoshi Nishioka, Yuniesky Betancourt																				

Following a stellar 2012, Escobar gave back those gains and then some at the dish. His TAv was the worst among AL regulars. Even his defense couldn't save him from WARP oblivion. Lacking options at short, the Royals stuck with him through the season. Lacking common sense, the Royals hit him second more than any player on their roster. Lacking common strike zone discipline, he struggled with all types of pitches but was particularly useless against sliders and cut fastballs. A good—not great—defender, Escobar excels moving to the hole between short and third, where he can plant his back foot and show off a plus arm. One nifty move can't compensate for one nothing bat.

	YEAR	TEAM	LVL	AGE	PA	R	2B	3B	HR	RBI	BB	SO	SB	CS	AVG/OBP/SLG	TAv	BABIP	BRR	FRAA	WARP
Marten Gasparini SS	2014	–	–	–	–	–	–	–	–	–	–	–	–	–	–	–	–	–	–	–
Born: 5/24/1997 Age: 16																				
Bats: B Throws: R Height: 6'0''																				
Weight: 175																				

The Royals shelled out $1.3 million for the 16-year-old Italian shortstop, a record bonus paid to a European player. While the tools are obviously raw, his bat speed and line-drive stroke draw raves. Some believe his ability to make consistent contact and his developing gap power make him an ideal candidate to hit at the top of the order. Defensively, the Royals will keep him at short, but if he struggles on the infield, his speed will play well in center. Gasparini began his professional odyssey in September in the instructional league.

	YEAR	TEAM	LVL	AGE	PA	R	2B	3B	HR	RBI	BB	SO	SB	CS	AVG/OBP/SLG	TAv	BABIP	BRR	FRAA	WARP
Chris Getz 2B	2011	KCA	MLB	27	429	50	6	3	0	26	30	45	21	7	.255/.313/.287	.226	.288	1.1	2B(110): 4.0, SS(4): 0.2	0.1
Born: 8/30/1983 Age: 30	2012	OMA	AAA	28	47	7	2	1	0	8	4	4	1	0	.279/.340/.372	.258	.308	0	2B(9): 0.4	0.1
Bats: L Throws: R Height: 5' 11''	2012	KCA	MLB	28	210	22	10	3	0	17	11	17	9	3	.275/.312/.360	.238	.299	2.6	2B(61): -3.6	0.1
Weight: 185 Breakout: 1%	2013	OMA	AAA	29	88	7	5	1	1	10	1	5	3	1	.310/.318/.429	.280	.312	-1	2B(11): -0.1, SS(7): 0.4	0.4
Improve: 37% Collapse: 3%	2013	KCA	MLB	29	237	29	6	1	1	18	20	24	16	3	.220/.288/.273	.198	.245	1.2	2B(68): 2.6	-0.2
Attrition: 10% MLB: 93%	2014	KCA	MLB	30	250	26	9	2	1	17	17	28	13	3	.254/.310/.315	.234	.280	1.3	2B -0, SS 0	0.3
Comparables: Fernando Vina, Dave Cash, Billy Goodman																				

The Royals have inexplicably handed Getz over 1,100 plate appearances in the last four seasons; slap-hitting middle infielders with limited defensive skills shouldn't get so much opportunity. Management might think Getz is "mistake free" but they could no longer ignore the cumulative -0.8 WARP he's provided over the last four seasons and went looking for alternatives. Ideally he could fill a utility role, but he's limited to only playing second, so he lacks a certain level of versatility. And offensively? Ugh. There isn't a Mendoza Line for TAv. May we propose the Getz Line?

	YEAR	TEAM	LVL	AGE	PA	R	2B	3B	HR	RBI	BB	SO	SB	CS	AVG/OBP/SLG	TAv	BABIP	BRR	FRAA	WARP
Johnny Giavotella 2B	2011	OMA	AAA	23	503	67	34	2	9	72	40	57	9	5	.338/.390/.481	.316	.367	0.3	2B(70): 1.5, LF(2): -0.3	3.1
Born: 7/10/1987 Age: 26	2011	KCA	MLB	23	187	20	9	4	2	21	6	32	5	2	.247/.273/.376	.226	.288	-0.6	2B(46): -0.0	-0.1
Bats: R Throws: R Height: 5' 8''	2012	OMA	AAA	24	418	67	20	2	10	71	46	40	7	1	.323/.404/.472	.306	.339	0.1	2B(79): -1.7, 3B(4): 0.2	3.3
Weight: 180 Breakout: 7%	2012	KCA	MLB	24	189	21	7	1	1	15	8	35	3	0	.238/.270/.304	.210	.290	0.3	2B(45): -5.1	-1.0
Improve: 42% Collapse: 10%	2013	OMA	AAA	25	426	48	24	0	7	46	51	59	8	4	.286/.369/.408	.286	.320	0.2	2B(46): -0.8, 3B(29): 0.7	2.4
Attrition: 30% MLB: 70%	2013	KCA	MLB	25	48	4	3	0	0	4	5	4	0	0	.220/.333/.293	.253	.243	-0.6	2B(13): -0.0	0.0
Comparables: Chris Getz, Danny Richar, Kevin Frandsen	2014	KCA	MLB	26	250	24	12	1	4	25	19	37	3	1	.267/.325/.378	.260	.300	-0.1	2B -2, 3B 0	0.6

For the third consecutive season, Giavotella put up impressive Triple-A numbers. For the third consecutive season, he earned a call to The Show. And for the third consecutive season, he failed to capitalize on his opportunity. Sensing a trend? The bat speed that works in Omaha is exploited in Kansas City. Giovatella was more selective this time around, which helped his walk rate, but the rest of his offensive game didn't realize similar gains. With his limited range in the field the Royals continue to eye his defense with suspicion. It's possible he can get a look with the big club once again, but this feels more and more like a marriage that's not going to work. It's probably best for both parties to move on with their lives.

Alex Gordon — LF

Born: 2/10/1984 Age: 30
Bats: L Throws: R Height: 6' 1"
Weight: 220 Breakout: 3%
Improve: 53% Collapse: 3%
Attrition: 9% MLB: 100%

Comparables:
Seth Smith, Jonny Gomes, Milton Bradley

YEAR	TEAM	LVL	AGE	PA	R	2B	3B	HR	RBI	BB	SO	SB	CS	AVG/OBP/SLG	TAv	BABIP	BRR	FRAA	WARP
2011	KCA	MLB	27	688	101	45	4	23	87	67	139	17	8	.303/.376/.502	.303	.358	3	LF(148): 9.8, 1B(7): 0.1	6.5
2012	KCA	MLB	28	721	93	51	5	14	72	73	140	10	5	.294/.368/.455	.285	.356	0.5	LF(160): 8.4	4.8
2013	KCA	MLB	29	700	90	27	6	20	81	52	141	11	3	.265/.327/.422	.277	.310	4.2	LF(155): 3.4	4.1
2014	KCA	MLB	30	662	87	33	3	17	70	66	140	11	5	.268/.348/.425	.281	.320	-0.4	LF 7, 1B 0	3.7

Gordon continues to regress at the plate since his 2011 breakout, as his TAv, batting average, OBP and slugging percentage have now declined in each of the past two seasons. Pitchers continue to work him away, but last year he barreled fewer pitches on the outer half. The result was a drop in his line-drive rate and a related uptick in fly balls, leading to a few more home runs but a noticeable doubles brown-out. Gordon made his first All-Star team but struggled in the second half, hitting .244/.291/.428 over his final 67 games. His FRAA declined, but his defense in left remains elite—given the number of outfield assists he continues to rack up, we have to wonder if anyone pays attention to defensive scouting reports. If Gordon can rediscover his line-drive stroke, he'll remain one of the more valuable outfielders around.

Brett Hayes — C

Born: 2/13/1984 Age: 30
Bats: R Throws: R Height: 6' 0"
Weight: 200 Breakout: 3%
Improve: 12% Collapse: 9%
Attrition: 21% MLB: 33%

Comparables:
Eliezer Alfonzo, Dee Brown, Koyie Hill

YEAR	TEAM	LVL	AGE	PA	R	2B	3B	HR	RBI	BB	SO	SB	CS	AVG/OBP/SLG	TAv	BABIP	BRR	FRAA	WARP
2011	FLO	MLB	27	144	19	9	0	5	16	11	39	0	0	.231/.291/.415	.262	.291	-0.5	C(50): 0.8, RF(1): -0.0	0.8
2012	NWO	AAA	28	63	9	4	0	3	8	3	13	0	0	.356/.397/.576	.319	.419	0	C(15): 0.0	0.6
2012	MIA	MLB	28	118	7	6	0	0	3	4	49	1	0	.202/.229/.254	.169	.354	0	C(33): 1.4	-0.4
2013	OMA	AAA	29	298	39	15	1	17	44	17	64	2	0	.233/.279/.480	.273	.239	-1.1	C(75): 0.3, 3B(1): -0.0	1.5
2013	KCA	MLB	29	18	2	3	0	1	2	0	3	0	0	.278/.278/.611	.313	.286	0.1	C(5): -0.0	0.2
2014	KCA	MLB	30	250	24	12	0	7	27	12	63	0	0	.228/.268/.368	.231	.280	-0.4	C 1, 1B -0	0.5

Looking at his offensive numbers, it's not difficult to ascertain that Hayes has stuck around as a backstop for his defense. He gets down in the dirt enough to please his battery mates and has a slightly above-average catch and release. His solid, if unspectacular, defense isn't enough to make up for his abysmal bat, and it's unlikely anybody will ever make the mistake of assuming it is.

Eric Hosmer — 1B

Born: 10/24/1989 Age: 24
Bats: L Throws: L Height: 6' 4"
Weight: 220 Breakout: 3%
Improve: 59% Collapse: 7%
Attrition: 2% MLB: 98%

Comparables:
Randy Ready, Carlos May, Ron Blomberg

YEAR	TEAM	LVL	AGE	PA	R	2B	3B	HR	RBI	BB	SO	SB	CS	AVG/OBP/SLG	TAv	BABIP	BRR	FRAA	WARP
2011	OMA	AAA	21	118	21	5	0	3	15	19	16	3	0	.439/.525/.582	.445	.500	0.1	1B(12): -0.4	1.4
2011	KCA	MLB	21	563	66	27	3	19	78	34	82	11	5	.293/.334/.465	.274	.314	1	1B(127): -7.0	1.0
2012	KCA	MLB	22	598	65	22	2	14	60	56	95	16	1	.232/.304/.359	.241	.255	1.7	1B(148): 5.8, RF(3): -0.2	0.3
2013	KCA	MLB	23	680	86	34	3	17	79	51	100	11	4	.302/.353/.448	.291	.335	-0.4	1B(158): 8.1, RF(1): -0.1	3.7
2014	KCA	MLB	24	623	72	28	2	16	73	48	93	13	3	.281/.336/.424	.277	.310	0.5	1B 3, RF -0	2.0

A season like a Dickens novel, on May 29th Hosmer was hitting .262/.323/.331 with just nine extra-base hits. He had pulled a total of 10 balls in the air. Coming off his lackluster sophomore season, this wasn't your garden-variety slump—it called for drastic action. The Royals dumped their hitting coaches and brought in George Brett in an interim role. From the date of that hire to the end of the season, Hosmer rallied, hitting .317/.365/.492. With 45 extra-base hits, he was back to pulling the ball and hitting it with authority. Defensive metrics haven't always been kind, but he made strides in 2013, flashing wider range and improved footwork around the bag on his way to winning his first Gold Glove. Moving forward, great expectations.

Omar Infante — 2B

Born: 12/26/1981 Age: 32
Bats: R Throws: R Height: 5' 11"
Weight: 195 Breakout: 0%
Improve: 46% Collapse: 4%
Attrition: 6% MLB: 93%

Comparables:
Freddy Sanchez, Brandon Phillips, Bobby Avila

YEAR	TEAM	LVL	AGE	PA	R	2B	3B	HR	RBI	BB	SO	SB	CS	AVG/OBP/SLG	TAv	BABIP	BRR	FRAA	WARP
2011	FLO	MLB	29	640	55	24	8	7	49	34	67	4	2	.276/.315/.382	.266	.298	-1.7	2B(146): 21.6	4.5
2012	DET	MLB	30	241	27	7	5	4	20	9	23	7	2	.257/.283/.385	.237	.269	0.3	2B(61): 0.7, 3B(6): -0.3	0.0
2012	MIA	MLB	30	347	42	23	2	8	33	12	42	10	1	.287/.312/.442	.268	.307	5	2B(83): 4.6	2.5
2013	TOL	AAA	31	21	1	0	0	0	1	2	2	0	0	.211/.286/.211	.160	.235	0.3	2B(4): -0.4	-0.2
2013	DET	MLB	31	476	54	24	3	10	51	20	44	5	2	.318/.345/.450	.285	.333	-0.2	2B(118): 4.8	3.1
2014	KCA	MLB	32	474	54	19	3	7	42	22	51	7	2	.288/.322/.394	.262	.310	0.2	2B 7, 3B 0	2.5

Infante played only 118 games, a four-year low, but he quietly produced the best season of his career. After an uneven start to his career, Infante has developed into one of the league's surest bets. His contact-oriented approach is a great fit for the latter third of a batting order, while the reemergence of his early-career power makes him passable in the no. 2 spot. A serious ankle injury in July, caused by a Colby Rasmus takeout slide, reminded everybody not named Dayton Moore why second basemen don't generally age well, even when they do.

Justin Maxwell CF

Born: 11/6/1983 Age: 30
Bats: R Throws: R Height: 6' 5''
Weight: 220 Breakout: 4%
Improve: 29% Collapse: 5%
Attrition: 11% MLB: 68%

Comparables:
Ryan Ludwick, Joe Borchard, Nelson Cruz

YEAR	TEAM	LVL	AGE	PA	R	2B	3B	HR	RBI	BB	SO	SB	CS	AVG/OBP/SLG	TAv	BABIP	BRR	FRAA	WARP
2011	SWB	AAA	27	204	36	8	1	16	35	26	72	11	2	.260/.358/.588	.313	.337	2.1	LF(18): 2.9, CF(17): 1.5	2.4
2012	HOU	MLB	28	352	46	13	3	18	53	32	114	9	4	.229/.304/.460	.273	.292	0.9	CF(59): 3.2, LF(38): 1.2	2.1
2013	CCH	AA	29	23	1	0	0	0	2	1	8	1	0	.048/.087/.048	.110	.071	0	CF(3): 0.0, RF(2): -0.1	-0.3
2013	OKL	AAA	29	32	5	0	0	1	3	3	6	0	0	.179/.250/.286	.180	.182	-0.1	RF(6): 0.3, CF(2): -0.1	-0.2
2013	HOU	MLB	29	151	21	10	2	2	8	12	43	4	1	.241/.311/.387	.257	.337	2.2	CF(25): 3.4, RF(17): -0.5	0.8
2013	KCA	MLB	29	111	14	6	1	5	17	11	35	2	1	.268/.351/.505	.305	.362	0.4	RF(30): -0.2, CF(2): -0.2	0.7
2014	KCA	MLB	30	275	34	10	2	9	32	28	86	10	3	.229/.315/.398	.261	.310	0.7	CF 2, RF -0	1.0

On a quest for right-handed power, the Royals acquired Maxwell from Houston at the trade deadline. He's been dogged by injuries his entire career and last season was no different, as he missed time with a broken hand and suffered a concussion while with the Astros. Injury-free in KC, he had a scorching August (.311/.391/.590), but stumbled to the finish line in September (.194/.286/.361). As always, the truth lies somewhere in between. When he's healthy he can do a bit of everything. He plays a solid right field (and can hang in center), has a strong arm, can swipe a bag. However, he's turning 30 and will have to finally stay healthy or be haunted by the dreaded "P" word—potential.

Adalberto Mondesi SS

Born: 7/27/1995 Age: 18
Bats: B Throws: R Height: 6' 1''
Weight: 165 Breakout: 0%
Improve: 0% Collapse: 0%
Attrition: 0% MLB: 0%

Comparables:
Hernan Perez, Juan Lagares, Adrian Cardenas

YEAR	TEAM	LVL	AGE	PA	R	2B	3B	HR	RBI	BB	SO	SB	CS	AVG/OBP/SLG	TAv	BABIP	BRR	FRAA	WARP
2013	LEX	A	17	536	61	13	7	7	47	34	118	24	10	.261/.311/.361	.257	.331	1.1	SS(108): 2.3	2.0
2014	KCA	MLB	18	250	22	7	2	2	17	9	65	3	1	.222/.249/.292	.197	.290	0.2	SS 1	-0.4

What were you doing when you turned 18? Mondesi, son of Raul, was clubbing extra-base hits and swiping bags as the youngest player in the Sally League. It wasn't always easy (in his sixth game of the year, he went 0-for-6 at the plate with six whiffs, and he had a .582 OPS in June) but he always found a way to bounce back—he had seven extra-base hits and an .806 OPS in July. With his compact, clean stroke, scouts salivate over his hit tool, and his glove carries enough upside that he won't have to move off shortstop. With plus instincts and feel for the game, he's one of the top prospects in the Royals organization.

Adam Moore C

Born: 5/8/1984 Age: 30
Bats: R Throws: R Height: 6' 3''
Weight: 215 Breakout: 3%
Improve: 8% Collapse: 7%
Attrition: 16% MLB: 26%

Comparables:
Koyie Hill, Brad Davis, Eli Whiteside

YEAR	TEAM	LVL	AGE	PA	R	2B	3B	HR	RBI	BB	SO	SB	CS	AVG/OBP/SLG	TAv	BABIP	BRR	FRAA	WARP
2011	SEA	MLB	27	6	0	1	0	0	0	0	2	0	0	.167/.167/.333	.151	.250	0	C(2): -0.0	-0.1
2012	OMA	AAA	28	135	18	8	0	3	22	14	24	2	0	.296/.381/.443	.285	.344	-0.9	C(35): -0.5	0.8
2012	TAC	AAA	28	94	10	5	0	3	11	5	14	0	0	.209/.247/.372	.234	.211	0.5	C(22): -0.4	0.4
2012	KCA	MLB	28	12	1	1	0	1	2	1	3	0	0	.182/.250/.545	.274	.143	0	C(3): -0.0	0.0
2013	OMA	AAA	29	148	20	4	0	8	23	17	52	0	0	.191/.284/.405	.232	.239	-1	C(40): 1.1, 1B(1): -0.0	0.1
2013	KCA	MLB	29	11	1	1	0	0	0	1	2	1	0	.300/.364/.400	.282	.375	0	C(5): 0.1	0.1
2014	KCA	MLB	30	250	24	10	0	6	25	15	58	1	0	.237/.288/.358	.237	.290	-0.4	C -0	0.5

A one-time catching prospect, Moore is now classified as organizational filler. He once had power potential, but hasn't slugged double-digit home runs in a season since 2009. He has missed his fair share of time with an assortment of ailments, and a torn groin short-circuited Moore's Triple-A season. He was removed from the 40-man roster last summer, but was then signed by the Royals to a contract that runs through 2014. New paper aside, it would be surprising to see him for an extended period of time in the big leagues.

Mike Moustakas 3B

Born: 9/11/1988 Age: 25
Bats: L Throws: R Height: 6' 0''
Weight: 210 Breakout: 5%
Improve: 60% Collapse: 5%
Attrition: 12% MLB: 97%

Comparables:
Jeff Cirillo, Ty Wigginton, Randy Ready

YEAR	TEAM	LVL	AGE	PA	R	2B	3B	HR	RBI	BB	SO	SB	CS	AVG/OBP/SLG	TAv	BABIP	BRR	FRAA	WARP
2011	OMA	AAA	22	250	38	15	1	10	44	19	44	1	1	.287/.347/.498	.315	.314	-2.6	3B(35): 3.9	2.0
2011	KCA	MLB	22	365	26	18	1	5	30	22	51	2	0	.263/.309/.367	.246	.296	-1	3B(89): 1.3	0.8
2012	KCA	MLB	23	614	69	34	1	20	73	39	124	5	2	.242/.296/.412	.252	.274	-2.4	3B(149): 17.9	3.4
2013	KCA	MLB	24	514	42	26	0	12	42	32	83	2	4	.233/.287/.364	.234	.257	-3	3B(134): 3.8	0.5
2014	KCA	MLB	25	503	51	25	1	13	57	31	87	3	2	.250/.301/.392	.252	.280	-0.9	3B 5	1.3

While the Royals were assembling the "Best Farm System in Baseball," the prospect with the most power potential was Moustakas. Yet two and a half years into his major-league career he has realized none of that potential, with a .141 ISO that's good enough to match Zack Cozart's in the same time. The 2013 season was a tremendous step in the wrong direction, as Moustakas managed to drive in just 9 percent of runners on base, the worst rate in the majors among hitters with more than 450 plate appearances. That stat carries zero weight going forward, but it was a good indication of the depth of his struggles. He seemed to carry his offensive struggles to the field with him, displaying a slower first step and diminished range. To say 2014 is a pivotal year for his future would be an understatement. The clock is ticking, and has been for some time.

Carlos Pena 1B
Born: 5/17/1978 Age: 36
Bats: L Throws: L Height: 6' 2"
Weight: 225 Breakout: 0%
Improve: 13% Collapse: 12%
Attrition: 12% MLB: 72%

Comparables:
Mickey Tettleton, Greg Vaughn, John Jaha

YEAR	TEAM	LVL	AGE	PA	R	2B	3B	HR	RBI	BB	SO	SB	CS	AVG/OBP/SLG	TAv	BABIP	BRR	FRAA	WARP
2011	CHN	MLB	33	606	72	27	3	28	80	101	161	2	2	.225/.357/.462	.294	.267	0.1	1B(153): -0.2	2.5
2012	TBA	MLB	34	600	72	17	2	19	61	87	182	2	3	.197/.330/.354	.263	.264	-4.2	1B(153): -2.6	0.1
2013	OMA	AAA	35	22	5	0	1	2	6	4	3	0	0	.333/.455/.778	.428	.308	0	1B(5): -0.1	0.4
2013	HOU	MLB	35	325	38	13	1	8	25	43	89	1	3	.209/.324/.350	.257	.278	-1.8	1B(44): 1.4	0.2
2013	KCA	MLB	35	3	0	0	0	0	0	0	3	0	0	.000/.000/.000	.020	—	0	1B(2): -0.1	-0.1
2014	KCA	MLB	36	366	44	13	1	15	47	51	102	2	2	.212/.331/.402	.270	.260	-0.7	1B -2	0.5

Big-swinging power hitters seldom age gracefully, and Pena's TAv has declined nearly every season since he turned 30. The Royals picked him up from the Astros after he was designated for assignment, hoping he could provide some left-handed pop down the stretch. Instead, Pena's season was cut short by an appendectomy. He now provides only two of the Three Outcomes, eschewing—cue sad trombone—home runs. A free agent, he will get a look from some team in spring training, but it would take some doing to wrangle steady major-league work at this point.

Salvador Perez C
Born: 5/10/1990 Age: 24
Bats: R Throws: R Height: 6' 3"
Weight: 245 Breakout: 1%
Improve: 60% Collapse: 7%
Attrition: 10% MLB: 100%

Comparables:
Ted Simmons, Billy Butler, Brian McCann

YEAR	TEAM	LVL	AGE	PA	R	2B	3B	HR	RBI	BB	SO	SB	CS	AVG/OBP/SLG	TAv	BABIP	BRR	FRAA	WARP
2011	NWA	AA	21	309	35	14	0	9	43	16	30	0	1	.283/.329/.427	.245	.290	-1	C(64): -1.1	0.5
2011	OMA	AAA	21	49	5	5	0	1	10	0	6	0	0	.333/.347/.500	.320	.366	0.9	C(8): -0.1	0.5
2011	KCA	MLB	21	158	20	8	2	3	21	7	20	0	0	.331/.361/.473	.296	.362	-1.5	C(39): -0.4	1.1
2012	OMA	AAA	22	53	11	2	0	0	7	2	5	0	0	.340/.365/.380	.251	.378	-0.7	C(8): 0.0	0.0
2012	KCA	MLB	22	305	38	16	0	11	39	12	27	0	0	.301/.328/.471	.270	.299	-1.8	C(74): -1.7	1.8
2013	KCA	MLB	23	526	48	25	3	13	79	21	63	0	0	.292/.323/.433	.277	.311	-2.3	C(137): -1.6, 1B(1): -0.0	3.4
2014	KCA	MLB	24	456	46	23	2	11	55	18	51	0	0	.294/.325/.432	.275	.310	-0.7	C -1, 1B -0	2.6

In just his first full season, Perez solidified his position as the top young defensive catcher in the American League. He gunned down a league-best 35 percent of all would be base stealers and earned kudos for handling the Kansas City staff. Offensively, he was a bit of a mixed bag. A free swinger with a high contact rate, he can be prone to streakiness. Nine of his 13 home runs were clubbed after August 16th. Still, the Royals will live with even a league-average OBP and power potential if Perez continues to shine defensively. Signed to an extremely club-friendly deal that controls him for the next six seasons at just $20 million, he's the catcher of the Royals' future, and the future is now.

Bubba Starling CF
Born: 8/3/1992 Age: 21
Bats: R Throws: R Height: 6' 4"
Weight: 180 Breakout: 1%
Improve: 4% Collapse: 0%
Attrition: 1% MLB: 4%

Comparables:
Michael Saunders, Brett Jackson, Austin Jackson

YEAR	TEAM	LVL	AGE	PA	R	2B	3B	HR	RBI	BB	SO	SB	CS	AVG/OBP/SLG	TAv	BABIP	BRR	FRAA	WARP
2013	LEX	A	20	498	51	21	4	13	63	53	128	22	3	.241/.329/.398	.287	.309	1	CF(117): 2.2	3.3
2014	KCA	MLB	21	250	23	8	1	6	26	17	74	2	0	.214/.270/.336	.222	.280	0.1	CF 2	-0.1

Bonus baby or bonus bust? A former local high school star, Starling struggled mightily in his first exposure to full-season baseball. He was hitting .213/.286/.354 when he left Lexington for Lasik eye surgery in mid-May. He finally put together a solid stretch when he hit .333/.404/.595 in 94 plate appearances in August, but the usual small sample size disclaimer applies. Overall, he whiffed in 26 percent of his plate appearances and struggled with pitch recognition all summer. Some scouts remain convinced the tools will develop, but after his performance, there's plenty of space available on the Bubba Bandwagon. No one denies the tools or the athleticism. It's the bat that remains the question mark.

Miguel Tejada 3B
Born: 5/25/1974 Age: 40
Bats: R Throws: R Height: 5' 9"
Weight: 220 Breakout: 0%
Improve: 15% Collapse: 10%
Attrition: 26% MLB: 61%

Comparables:
Mark Grudzielanek, Craig Biggio, Melvin Mora

YEAR	TEAM	LVL	AGE	PA	R	2B	3B	HR	RBI	BB	SO	SB	CS	AVG/OBP/SLG	TAv	BABIP	BRR	FRAA	WARP
2011	SFN	MLB	37	343	28	16	0	4	26	12	35	4	4	.239/.270/.326	.231	.254	-0.4	3B(44): 5.7, SS(42): 1.1	1.1
2012	NOR	AAA	38	151	10	5	0	0	18	11	16	1	0	.259/.325/.296	.236	.289	-0.9	3B(30): -0.2, SS(3): -0.4	-0.1
2013	KCA	MLB	39	167	15	5	0	3	20	6	25	1	0	.288/.317/.378	.256	.326	-0.1	2B(26): -1.1, 3B(22): -0.4	0.1
2014	KCA	MLB	40	250	23	11	0	3	22	7	25	1	1	.265/.293/.352	.239	.280	-0.4	3B 1, 2B -1	0.3

Plucked from the baseball scrap heap, Tejada somehow was handed $1.1 million and 167 plate appearances by the Royals. That was before the inevitable injury. Oh, and the seemingly inevitable suspension for amphetamines. Scolded with the second-longest ban in baseball history—105 games—this is certainly the end of the road for the former MVP.

Danny Valencia 3B
Born: 9/19/1984 Age: 29
Bats: R Throws: R Height: 6' 2''
Weight: 220 Breakout: 1%
Improve: 42% Collapse: 12%
Attrition: 18% MLB: 84%

Comparables:
Casey McGehee, Greg Dobbs, Jayson Nix

YEAR	TEAM	LVL	AGE	PA	R	2B	3B	HR	RBI	BB	SO	SB	CS	AVG/OBP/SLG	TAv	BABIP	BRR	FRAA	WARP
2011	MIN	MLB	26	608	63	28	2	15	72	40	102	2	6	.246/.294/.383	.243	.275	-1.4	3B(147): -6.3	-0.1
2012	ROC	AAA	27	284	30	17	1	7	37	15	40	1	2	.250/.289/.399	.247	.270	0.9	3B(56): 0.1	0.3
2012	PAW	AAA	27	53	3	3	0	1	8	3	12	0	2	.306/.358/.429	.276	.389	-0.9	3B(12): 0.7	0.2
2012	BOS	MLB	27	29	1	0	0	1	4	0	6	0	0	.143/.138/.250	.163	.136	0	3B(10): -0.3	-0.3
2012	MIN	MLB	27	132	13	6	1	2	17	3	32	0	1	.198/.212/.310	.180	.242	0.1	3B(34): 0.5	-0.8
2013	NOR	AAA	28	282	40	20	1	14	51	17	48	1	1	.286/.326/.531	.306	.300	1.6	3B(48): -2.5, 1B(6): -0.4	2.1
2013	BAL	MLB	28	170	20	14	1	8	23	8	33	0	2	.304/.335/.553	.307	.339	-0.4	3B(6): -0.4	1.0
2014	KCA	MLB	29	250	24	13	1	6	29	13	44	1	1	.262/.301/.403	.258	.300	-0.7	3B -1, 1B -0	0.3

After an impressive rookie showing, Valencia suffered from overexposure in 2011, particularly against righties, and never got anything going in 2012 before eventually being demoted. He has always displayed prowess against lefties, so the Orioles did what his previous teams wouldn't or couldn't, deploying him as a platoon hitter. The end result (albeit likely coupled with some luck) was Valencia's best offensive season. The Royals liked the platoon idea so much they traded for Valencia to serve as buffer between Mike Moustakas and left-handed pitchers.

PITCHERS

Jason Adam
Born: 8/4/1991 Age: 22
Bats: R Throws: R Height: 6' 4'' Weight: 219
Breakout: 52% Improve: 84% Collapse: 8%
Attrition: 62% MLB: 25%

Comparables:
Ricky Romero, Felix Doubront, Will Smith

YEAR	TEAM	LVL	AGE	W	L	SV	G	GS	IP	H	HR	BB	SO	BB9	SO9	GB%	BABIP	WHIP	ERA	FIP	FRA	WARP
2011	KNC	A	19	6	9	0	21	21	104[1]	94	9	25	76	2.2	6.6	42%	.306	1.14	4.23	3.92	5.38	-0.1
2012	WIL	A+	20	7	12	0	27	27	158	148	18	36	123	2.1	7.0	46%	.284	1.16	3.53	4.24	4.70	0.4
2013	NWA	AA	21	8	11	0	26	26	144	153	12	54	126	3.4	7.9	42%	.328	1.44	5.19	3.83	4.72	1.2
2014	KCA	MLB	22	8	8	0	22	22	123	143	16	47	73	3.4	5.3	43%	.310	1.55	5.40	5.22	5.87	-1.1

Adam found the transition to Double-A Northwest Arkansas difficult, as he struggled to command his pitches against hitters of a more patient variety. While his strikeout rate has increased at every stop, so too has his batting average against. Texas League hitters touched him for a .277/.353/.409 line, including the league's fourth-highest OBP among pitchers who logged at least 120 innings. He features a fastball that lives in the low 90s, complemented by a mundane power curve. He has made strides with his change, but that too projects as an average pitch. If Adam ever makes it to the bigs, he profiles as a back-of-the-rotation type, which isn't a lot but is the sort of thing Dayton Moore has spent a fair amount of talent and treasure on lately.

Miguel Almonte
Born: 4/4/1993 Age: 21
Bats: R Throws: R Height: 6' 2'' Weight: 180
Breakout: 58% Improve: 85% Collapse: 15%
Attrition: 42% MLB: 5%

Comparables:
Zach McAllister, Jake Odorizzi, Brett Oberholtzer

YEAR	TEAM	LVL	AGE	W	L	SV	G	GS	IP	H	HR	BB	SO	BB9	SO9	GB%	BABIP	WHIP	ERA	FIP	FRA	WARP
2013	LEX	A	20	6	9	0	25	25	130[2]	115	6	36	132	2.5	9.1	47%	.297	1.16	3.10	3.04	3.98	1.4
2014	KCA	MLB	21	2	1	1	19	2	92[1]	106	11	40	53	3.9	5.2	47%	.310	1.58	5.29	5.21	5.75	-0.8

Almonte, tabbed in these pages last year as a prospect to watch, indeed made positive strides in his development and made the jump to depth chart-worthy prospect. The right-hander carries an impressive mix of stuff and poise that is rare for someone of his age and experience, and he made a seamless transition from the Dominican Summer League to Low-A Lexington. He features a clean, repeatable delivery and a fastball that lives in the mid-90s with great life. The pitch scouts rave about, however, is his changeup, which he will feature to both left and right-handed batters and has already developed into a killer out pitch. Almonte has top-of-the-rotation potential, which *is* a lot and is the sort of thing Dayton Moore has spent loads of talent and treasure on lately.

Noel Arguelles

Born: 1/12/1990 Age: 24
Bats: L Throws: L Height: 6' 3" Weight: 225
Breakout: 100% Improve: 100% Collapse: 0%
Attrition: 49% MLB: 2%

Comparables:
Tom Layne, Trystan Magnuson, Zac Rosscup

YEAR	TEAM	LVL	AGE	W	L	SV	G	GS	IP	H	HR	BB	SO	BB9	SO9	GB%	BABIP	WHIP	ERA	FIP	FRA	WARP
2011	WIL	A+	21	4	5	0	21	21	104	93	6	24	64	2.1	5.5	38%	.269	1.12	3.20	3.59	4.67	0.2
2012	NWA	AA	22	4	14	0	25	25	119¹	146	12	66	59	5.0	4.4	44%	.324	1.78	6.41	5.31	6.56	-0.9
2013	NWA	AA	23	1	8	0	25	11	71¹	73	6	53	44	6.7	5.6	46%	.291	1.77	5.93	5.23	6.84	-0.6
2014	KCA	MLB	24	4	5	0	24	13	72¹	89	9	41	27	5.1	3.3	41%	.306	1.80	6.39	6.08	6.94	-1.3

Four years into the Royals' $7 million international outlay, Arguelles has given the club a grand total of 190 innings above A-ball. The former Cuban star battled shoulder injury, command issues and a decline in velocity. Bonus aside, no pitcher can overcome that trifecta. Last summer, his opponents' OBP of .384 was the highest in the Texas League and he walked one more per nine than his closest competition. The Royals cut his season short by moving him to the 60-day DL with shoulder fatigue. In the final season of his five-year deal, Arguelles' time in the organization is rapidly approaching the end.

Francisley Bueno

Born: 3/5/1981 Age: 33
Bats: L Throws: L Height: 5' 10" Weight: 215
Breakout: 54% Improve: 67% Collapse: 27%
Attrition: 48% MLB: 18%

Comparables:
Bobby Korecky, Brandon Villafuerte, Mike Koplove

YEAR	TEAM	LVL	AGE	W	L	SV	G	GS	IP	H	HR	BB	SO	BB9	SO9	GB%	BABIP	WHIP	ERA	FIP	FRA	WARP
2012	OMA	AAA	31	1	4	6	35	0	55²	43	5	15	54	2.4	8.7	50%	.253	1.04	2.75	3.86	5.17	0.4
2012	KCA	MLB	31	1	1	0	18	0	17¹	16	0	2	7	1.0	3.6	59%	.271	1.04	1.56	2.76	3.85	0.2
2013	OMA	AAA	32	3	3	1	36	1	67²	64	5	24	56	3.2	7.4	47%	.296	1.30	2.66	3.98	4.54	0.6
2013	KCA	MLB	32	1	0	0	7	0	8¹	4	0	2	5	2.2	5.4	58%	.167	0.72	0.00	2.60	3.98	0.1
2014	KCA	MLB	33	2	1	0	42	0	64¹	64	6	21	42	2.9	5.9	44%	.290	1.31	3.96	4.36	4.30	0.4

An organizational grinder, Bueno has made brief appearances in the Royals' bullpen over the past few seasons. He features a two-seam fastball with heavy sink to keep the ball on the ground, scrapped his slider in favor of a curve that can be effective against left-handed bats, and continues to go with a changeup against righties. For all that variety, he lacks a put-away pitch, finds too many bats and has a reverse platoon split that will limit him to sub-LOOGY status.

Bruce Chen

Born: 6/19/1977 Age: 37
Bats: L Throws: L Height: 6' 2" Weight: 215
Breakout: 9% Improve: 40% Collapse: 23%
Attrition: 21% MLB: 72%

Comparables:
Esteban Loaiza, Kevin Millwood, Bartolo Colon

YEAR	TEAM	LVL	AGE	W	L	SV	G	GS	IP	H	HR	BB	SO	BB9	SO9	GB%	BABIP	WHIP	ERA	FIP	FRA	WARP
2011	KCA	MLB	34	12	8	0	25	25	155	152	18	50	97	2.9	5.6	37%	.278	1.30	3.77	4.42	4.88	1.4
2012	KCA	MLB	35	11	14	0	34	34	191²	215	33	47	140	2.2	6.6	34%	.304	1.37	5.07	4.68	4.65	2.3
2013	KCA	MLB	36	9	4	0	34	15	121	107	13	36	78	2.7	5.8	29%	.255	1.18	3.27	4.15	4.20	1.2
2014	KCA	MLB	37	7	5	1	27	17	112¹	116	15	35	76	2.8	6.1	35%	.289	1.35	4.38	4.78	4.76	0.3

Chen has returned from the dead so often, even zombies are jealous. Exiled to the bullpen to open 2013, he was just another high-priced arm toiling under an ill-advised Dayton Moore contract. But after posting a 2.41 ERA in 33 relief innings (while striking out a very unChen-like 24 batters) he earned another crack at the rotation. In 15 starts from July 12th to the end of the year, he limited opponents to a slash line of .222/.274/.369 and a 3.61 ERA. Add it together and that's how you get a 1.2 WARP performance. We say this every season, but the peripherals indicate a correction is around the corner. But would you bet against him providing value again? Zombie Chen just laughs at your peripherals.

Maikel Cleto

Born: 5/1/1989 Age: 25
Bats: R Throws: R Height: 6' 3" Weight: 250
Breakout: 52% Improve: 65% Collapse: 17%
Attrition: 61% MLB: 26%

Comparables:
Brayan Villarreal, Donnie Veal, Sergio Escalona

YEAR	TEAM	LVL	AGE	W	L	SV	G	GS	IP	H	HR	BB	SO	BB9	SO9	GB%	BABIP	WHIP	ERA	FIP	FRA	WARP
2011	PMB	A+	22	1	1	0	5	5	29	20	2	10	33	3.1	10.2	31%	.250	1.03	2.48	3.25	5.72	-0.1
2011	SFD	AA	22	2	2	0	7	6	34¹	40	2	12	36	3.1	9.4	53%	.368	1.51	3.93	3.52	4.11	0.3
2011	MEM	AAA	22	5	3	0	13	13	71¹	57	6	43	66	5.4	8.3	40%	.233	1.40	4.29	4.96	4.59	0.4
2011	SLN	MLB	22	0	0	0	3	0	4¹	7	2	4	6	8.3	12.5	47%	.385	2.54	12.46	8.99	10.46	-0.3
2012	MEM	AAA	23	3	2	2	45	0	53²	51	4	22	66	3.7	11.1	48%	.348	1.36	5.37	3.63	4.28	0.8
2012	SLN	MLB	23	0	0	0	9	0	9	13	4	2	15	2.0	15.0	30%	.474	1.67	7.00	6.58	6.45	-0.2
2013	MEM	AAA	24	2	3	0	16	9	53¹	49	4	53	53	8.9	8.9	40%	.310	1.91	6.92	5.71	5.62	-0.2
2013	OMA	AAA	24	1	2	1	19	1	38	35	1	21	36	5.0	8.5	49%	.315	1.47	3.55	3.75	5.31	0.5
2013	SLN	MLB	24	0	0	0	1	0	2¹	5	1	1	5	3.9	19.3	14%	.667	2.57	19.29	8.16	11.81	-0.2
2014	KCA	MLB	25	4	3	1	30	10	77	83	9	40	63	4.7	7.3	46%	.317	1.60	5.23	4.96	5.68	-0.5

Nabbed off the waiver wire from the Cardinals, Cleto brings the heat but lacks the ability to locate. He was walking more than 20 percent of all batters in Triple-A Memphis when St. Louis showed him the door. But when you work in the upper 90s and have a slider with some bite, there's always another organization who thinks it can teach you command. He settled down a bit in Omaha, walking just over 12 percent of all batters. With two good pitches, he will always be in the mix for a back-of-the-bullpen job, but until he can gain a better semblance of command, he's simply the reliever who gives managers ulcers.

Louis Coleman
Born: 4/4/1986 Age: 28
Bats: R Throws: R Height: 6' 4" Weight: 205
Breakout: 38% Improve: 48% Collapse: 43%
Attrition: 25% MLB: 75%

Comparables:
Vinnie Pestano, Sergio Romo, Jose Veras

YEAR	TEAM	LVL	AGE	W	L	SV	G	GS	IP	H	HR	BB	SO	BB9	SO9	GB%	BABIP	WHIP	ERA	FIP	FRA	WARP
2011	KCA	MLB	25	1	4	1	48	0	59²	44	9	26	64	3.9	9.7	33%	.246	1.17	2.87	4.34	4.03	0.8
2012	OMA	AAA	26	0	2	3	11	1	19²	13	1	8	26	3.7	11.9	28%	.267	1.07	3.20	2.90	3.48	0.6
2012	KCA	MLB	26	0	0	0	42	0	51	41	10	26	65	4.6	11.5	22%	.270	1.31	3.71	4.63	5.07	-0.1
2013	OMA	AAA	27	3	2	6	24	0	44²	36	1	17	52	3.4	10.5	37%	.304	1.19	1.61	2.67	2.74	1.4
2013	KCA	MLB	27	3	0	0	27	0	29²	19	1	6	32	1.8	9.7	42%	.257	0.84	0.61	2.06	2.29	0.7
2014	KCA	MLB	28	2	1	0	42	0	63²	52	6	23	71	3.2	10.0	35%	.284	1.16	3.03	3.46	3.29	1.2

A wiry right-hander with a whipsaw arm action and three-quarters delivery, Coleman is murder against same-side batters. Last summer, he posted a slash of .162/.219/.221 against right-handers, while also stomping lefties to the upbeat tune of .235/.278/.324. His fastball is in the low 90s, but his bread and butter is a devastating slider that he throws to right-handed hitters with a particular cold-heartedness. His command has always been a question mark, but he cut down on the walks and was particularly lethal with men on, stranding 97 percent of all baserunners.

Tim Collins
Born: 8/21/1989 Age: 24
Bats: L Throws: L Height: 5' 7" Weight: 165
Breakout: 38% Improve: 53% Collapse: 23%
Attrition: 23% MLB: 91%

Comparables:
Chris Perez, Joe Smith, Chris Ray

YEAR	TEAM	LVL	AGE	W	L	SV	G	GS	IP	H	HR	BB	SO	BB9	SO9	GB%	BABIP	WHIP	ERA	FIP	FRA	WARP
2011	KCA	MLB	21	4	4	0	68	0	67	52	5	48	60	6.4	8.1	41%	.264	1.49	3.63	4.48	4.66	0.5
2012	KCA	MLB	22	5	4	0	72	0	69²	55	8	34	93	4.4	12.0	43%	.297	1.28	3.36	3.42	3.71	1.0
2013	KCA	MLB	23	3	6	0	66	0	53¹	49	3	28	52	4.7	8.8	40%	.307	1.44	3.54	3.43	4.18	0.4
2014	KCA	MLB	24	3	1	1	50	0	50	41	4	25	58	4.5	10.4	41%	.298	1.32	3.42	3.57	3.72	0.7

For three seasons now, the Royals have tried to convince themselves that Collins is a true lefty specialist, even though there seemed to be evidence he could be effective against hitters from both sides of the plate. Even last summer, when he had his first real platoon split, the difference was primarily in BABIP. He relied more on his change than ever before—throwing it over 20 percent of the time—and used it to his advantage against left-handed batters. But he missed fewer bats, threw fewer first pitch strikes and allowed more hits on contact than at any time during his career. His ineffectiveness apparently got him assigned to some sort of super-secret mission in September, as he went 10 consecutive games without an appearance.

Aaron Crow
Born: 11/10/1986 Age: 27
Bats: R Throws: R Height: 6' 3" Weight: 195
Breakout: 43% Improve: 77% Collapse: 14%
Attrition: 22% MLB: 79%

Comparables:
Fernando Nieve, Jon Leicester, Tyler Clippard

YEAR	TEAM	LVL	AGE	W	L	SV	G	GS	IP	H	HR	BB	SO	BB9	SO9	GB%	BABIP	WHIP	ERA	FIP	FRA	WARP
2011	KCA	MLB	24	4	4	0	57	0	62	55	8	31	65	4.5	9.4	53%	.290	1.39	2.76	4.14	4.10	0.9
2012	KCA	MLB	25	3	1	2	73	0	64²	54	4	22	65	3.1	9.0	53%	.298	1.18	3.48	2.91	3.95	0.7
2013	KCA	MLB	26	7	5	1	57	0	48	49	6	22	44	4.1	8.2	51%	.316	1.48	3.38	4.37	4.44	0.0
2014	KCA	MLB	27	2	1	1	47	0	44	44	5	18	38	3.7	7.9	53%	.307	1.42	4.27	4.38	4.64	0.1

A declining strikeout rate and increasing walk and home run rates represented a triple crown of disappointment for Crow. His Tick Licker is a two-seam fastball with heavy sink, but he uncharacteristically left it up in the zone with alarming frequency last year; opponents took advantage, posting a .280 TAv. Nevertheless, he had the second-highest leverage index among Royal relievers and appeared in more tie games than any member of the relief corps. Then, he seemed to lose the faith of his manager in September, making just four appearances in the season's final month. Maybe with good reason.

Wade Davis
Born: 9/7/1985 Age: 28
Bats: R Throws: R Height: 6' 5" Weight: 225
Breakout: 17% Improve: 53% Collapse: 22%
Attrition: 24% MLB: 73%

Comparables:
Manny Parra, Gavin Floyd, Jesse Litsch

YEAR	TEAM	LVL	AGE	W	L	SV	G	GS	IP	H	HR	BB	SO	BB9	SO9	GB%	BABIP	WHIP	ERA	FIP	FRA	WARP
2011	TBA	MLB	25	11	10	0	29	29	184	190	23	63	105	3.1	5.1	38%	.280	1.38	4.45	4.70	4.46	1.2
2012	TBA	MLB	26	3	0	0	54	0	70¹	48	5	29	87	3.7	11.1	40%	.264	1.09	2.43	2.73	2.82	1.5
2013	KCA	MLB	27	8	11	0	31	24	135¹	169	15	58	114	3.9	7.6	42%	.361	1.68	5.32	4.21	4.92	0.7
2014	KCA	MLB	28	7	5	0	41	14	111²	116	12	41	83	3.3	6.7	42%	.302	1.41	4.38	4.46	4.76	0.3

When the Royals traded for Davis in December 2012, they banked on lessons he had learned in the bullpen translating back to the rotation. Alas, after 24 starts where hitters hooked him for a .320/.386/.465 line and a 5.67 ERA, he was exiled back to the 'pen. Once there, he reduced his number of sinkers and completely eliminated his change. With just a fastball, cutter and curve, he limited opponents to a slash line of .090/.194/.156. Therein is the issue: He lacks the variety in his arsenal to be an effective starter and can be a very useful asset in short exposures, but he's becoming expensive ($4.8 million this year) for a bullpen arm. The Royals will likely ignore evidence to the contrary and try him once again in the rotation this year.

Danny Duffy
Born: **12/21/1988** Age: **25**
Bats: **L** Throws: **L** Height: **6' 3"** Weight: **200**
Breakout: **43%** Improve: **68%** Collapse: **16%**
Attrition: **25%** MLB: **91%**

Comparables:
Jordan Zimmermann, Felix Doubront, Angel Guzman

YEAR	TEAM	LVL	AGE	W	L	SV	G	GS	IP	H	HR	BB	SO	BB9	SO9	GB%	BABIP	WHIP	ERA	FIP	FRA	WARP
2011	OMA	AAA	22	3	1	0	8	8	42	37	5	10	48	2.1	10.3	43%	.279	1.12	3.43	3.97	3.01	0.8
2011	KCA	MLB	22	4	8	0	20	20	105¹	119	15	51	87	4.4	7.4	39%	.330	1.61	5.64	4.86	4.77	1.1
2012	KCA	MLB	23	2	2	0	6	6	27²	26	2	18	28	5.9	9.1	33%	.329	1.59	3.90	3.91	4.22	0.4
2013	NWA	AA	24	0	2	0	4	4	16	16	3	5	28	2.8	15.8	38%	.448	1.31	3.94	3.49	4.01	0.3
2013	OMA	AAA	24	3	0	0	12	10	53	50	4	25	59	4.2	10.0	38%	.329	1.42	4.08	3.85	4.04	0.8
2013	KCA	MLB	24	2	0	0	5	5	24¹	19	0	14	22	5.2	8.1	31%	.284	1.36	1.85	3.12	3.41	0.5
2014	KCA	MLB	25	5	4	0	16	16	70	70	7	30	64	3.8	8.3	40%	.315	1.43	4.36	4.21	4.74	0.4

Almost 14 months after undergoing Tommy John surgery, Duffy made his return to the big-league mound. Like many who take their first steps following elbow ligament replacement, his velocity was there but his command was not—although his history of inflated walk rates makes it difficult to tell if that's a hangover from his injury or just Duffy being Duffy. He still has a frustrating tendency to jump ahead of hitters and then get too fine and lose the battle. With a mid-90s fastball and a curve with bite, the stuff can be electric, but his inability to locate his off-speed pitches and put hitters away can be frustrating. There's still upside here.

Chris Dwyer
Born: **4/10/1988** Age: **26**
Bats: **R** Throws: **L** Height: **6' 3"** Weight: **210**
Breakout: **39%** Improve: **82%** Collapse: **12%**
Attrition: **68%** MLB: **22%**

Comparables:
James Houser, Lance Pendleton, Tom Koehler

YEAR	TEAM	LVL	AGE	W	L	SV	G	GS	IP	H	HR	BB	SO	BB9	SO9	GB%	BABIP	WHIP	ERA	FIP	FRA	WARP
2011	NWA	AA	23	8	10	0	27	27	141¹	124	14	78	126	5.0	8.0	42%	.299	1.43	5.60	4.67	5.78	1.1
2012	NWA	AA	24	5	8	0	17	16	85²	79	13	44	71	4.6	7.5	40%	.269	1.44	5.25	5.28	6.73	-0.4
2012	OMA	AAA	24	3	4	0	9	9	50¹	73	10	24	33	4.3	5.9	45%	.366	1.93	6.97	6.43	6.70	-0.2
2013	OMA	AAA	25	10	11	0	29	28	159²	140	15	72	112	4.1	6.3	39%	.262	1.33	3.55	4.80	5.24	0.5
2013	KCA	MLB	25	0	0	0	2	0	3	2	0	1	2	3.0	6.0	50%	.250	1.00	0.00	2.74	0.16	0.1
2014	KCA	MLB	26	9	8	0	24	24	131²	139	17	65	89	4.4	6.1	40%	.296	1.55	5.09	5.28	5.53	-0.7

Dwyer was part of the Royals' bumper crop of pitching prospects that elevated the Kansas City farm system to "Best in Baseball" a couple seasons ago. As he lacks a plus pitch and carries below-average command, success has eluded him in the upper minors. The good news: His walk rate has declined since his promotion to Double-A in 2010. The bad news: It's yet to drop below four per nine innings. While he's started throughout his minor-league career, if he's ever going to make it in The Show it will likely be out of the bullpen as a long-relief option. He earned a late season call-up in 2013 and could contribute as a bullpen piece in some manner in 2014.

Jeremy Guthrie
Born: **4/8/1979** Age: **35**
Bats: **R** Throws: **R** Height: **6' 1"** Weight: **205**
Breakout: **31%** Improve: **57%** Collapse: **15%**
Attrition: **8%** MLB: **85%**

Comparables:
Bronson Arroyo, Cory Lidle, Jarrod Washburn

YEAR	TEAM	LVL	AGE	W	L	SV	G	GS	IP	H	HR	BB	SO	BB9	SO9	GB%	BABIP	WHIP	ERA	FIP	FRA	WARP
2011	BAL	MLB	32	9	17	0	34	32	208	213	26	66	130	2.9	5.6	41%	.285	1.34	4.33	4.52	5.09	0.8
2012	KCA	MLB	33	5	3	0	14	14	91	84	9	19	56	1.9	5.5	41%	.268	1.13	3.16	3.79	4.50	0.9
2012	COL	MLB	33	3	9	0	19	15	90²	122	21	31	45	3.1	4.5	43%	.329	1.69	6.35	6.41	6.89	-0.6
2013	KCA	MLB	34	15	12	0	33	33	211²	236	30	59	111	2.5	4.7	45%	.295	1.39	4.04	4.82	5.18	0.2
2014	KCA	MLB	35	12	9	0	29	29	177	192	23	50	96	2.5	4.9	42%	.289	1.36	4.59	4.97	4.99	-0.0

We all know someone who lives beyond his means, mortgaged to the hilt, underwater on his refrigerator. Guthrie was that starting pitcher last year. With a microscopic strikeout rate and a contact rate almost 10 percentage points above league average, his peripherals pointed to a pitcher who had no business posting an ERA in the neighborhood of the low fours. With a sinker-slider combo and occasional change, he keeps the ball in the zone and pitches to contact. It worked last year because the Royals fielded an excellent defense behind him. He made $5 million in 2013, but in 2014, his contract more than doubles to $11 million. The Royals co-signed on everything he bought, so they'll find out what it's like when the repo man comes knocking.

Kelvin Herrera

Born: 12/31/1989 Age: 24
Bats: R Throws: R Height: 5' 10" Weight: 200
Breakout: 31% Improve: 51% Collapse: 22%
Attrition: 23% MLB: 96%

Comparables:
Manny Corpas, Addison Reed, Joe Smith

YEAR	TEAM	LVL	AGE	W	L	SV	G	GS	IP	H	HR	BB	SO	BB9	SO9	GB%	BABIP	WHIP	ERA	FIP	FRA	WARP
2011	WIL	A+	21	2	1	1	8	0	14²	8	1	2	12	1.2	7.4	56%	.156	0.68	0.61	2.89	2.85	0.2
2011	NWA	AA	21	4	0	7	23	0	36	22	4	6	40	1.5	10.0	66%	.214	0.78	1.75	3.18	4.46	0.6
2011	OMA	AAA	21	1	0	6	14	0	17	12	1	7	18	3.7	9.5	57%	.235	1.12	2.12	3.67	2.79	0.5
2011	KCA	MLB	21	0	1	0	2	0	2	2	1	0	0	0.0	0.0	38%	.143	1.00	13.50	11.06	15.99	-0.2
2012	KCA	MLB	22	4	3	3	76	0	84¹	79	4	21	77	2.2	8.2	57%	.312	1.19	2.35	2.66	3.24	1.6
2013	OMA	AAA	23	0	1	2	10	3	16	6	1	6	22	3.4	12.4	47%	.161	0.75	1.12	3.13	4.12	0.4
2013	KCA	MLB	23	5	7	2	59	0	58¹	48	9	21	74	3.2	11.4	49%	.281	1.18	3.86	3.73	3.37	1.0
2014	KCA	MLB	24	3	1	1	58	0	67	59	6	20	66	2.7	8.9	51%	.292	1.18	3.27	3.51	3.55	1.1

Armed with a fastball with an average velocity of 98 mph, Herrera throws pure heat. Mix in a filthy change and it's a two-pitch combo that is as lethal as you can find in the game. Yet his arsenal was as effective as wet gunpowder through his first 19 appearances. In those 20 innings, he surrendered eight home runs, including three in an inning against the Braves in mid-April, earning him a trip to Triple-A. He was up and down one more time before returning for good to the Royals' bullpen in July. Over his final 30 innings, he allowed just a single home run and was one of the club's more effective relievers down the stretch.

Luke Hochevar

Born: 9/15/1983 Age: 30
Bats: R Throws: R Height: 6' 5" Weight: 215
Breakout: 21% Improve: 52% Collapse: 19%
Attrition: 14% MLB: 86%

Comparables:
Brett Myers, Jorge De La Rosa, Dave Bush

YEAR	TEAM	LVL	AGE	W	L	SV	G	GS	IP	H	HR	BB	SO	BB9	SO9	GB%	BABIP	WHIP	ERA	FIP	FRA	WARP
2011	KCA	MLB	27	11	11	0	31	31	198	192	23	62	128	2.8	5.8	51%	.275	1.28	4.68	4.32	5.01	1.3
2012	KCA	MLB	28	8	16	0	32	32	185¹	202	27	61	144	3.0	7.0	44%	.316	1.42	5.73	4.58	5.33	0.7
2013	KCA	MLB	29	5	2	2	58	0	70¹	41	8	17	82	2.2	10.5	36%	.214	0.82	1.92	2.99	3.22	1.1
2014	KCA	MLB	30	4	3	0	30	8	74	74	9	22	56	2.7	6.8	47%	.297	1.30	4.24	4.42	4.61	0.3

Strange what a change of role can do for a pitcher. A former 1:1 draft pick turned below-average starter, Hochevar moved to the bullpen and may have salvaged his career. The stuff that was inconsistent in the rotation did extremely well in small doses. Velocity on his fastball was up three miles, his swinging strike rate nearly doubled and his command improved with all pitches. At the end of 2012, Royals pitching coach Dave Eiland said his pupil threw too many different pitches. Coming out of the 'pen, he ditched his slider and his change and went fastball, curve and cutter. Can't argue with the results. The Royals might be tempted to shift him back to the rotation. Those who don't learn from history are doomed to finish in third place.

Greg Holland

Born: 11/20/1985 Age: 28
Bats: R Throws: R Height: 5' 10" Weight: 200
Breakout: 37% Improve: 49% Collapse: 38%
Attrition: 22% MLB: 83%

Comparables:
Joey Devine, Edwar Ramirez, Pat Neshek

YEAR	TEAM	LVL	AGE	W	L	SV	G	GS	IP	H	HR	BB	SO	BB9	SO9	GB%	BABIP	WHIP	ERA	FIP	FRA	WARP
2011	OMA	AAA	25	2	0	2	13	0	21²	13	1	11	27	4.6	11.2	43%	.190	1.11	2.08	3.41	1.46	0.6
2011	KCA	MLB	25	5	1	4	46	0	60	37	3	19	74	2.8	11.1	45%	.250	0.93	1.80	2.24	2.85	1.6
2012	KCA	MLB	26	7	4	16	67	0	67	58	2	34	91	4.6	12.2	47%	.346	1.37	2.96	2.24	2.03	2.3
2013	KCA	MLB	27	2	1	47	68	0	67	40	3	18	103	2.4	13.8	40%	.282	0.87	1.21	1.39	1.49	2.2
2014	KCA	MLB	28	3	1	19	47	0	55²	44	4	21	68	3.4	11.0	44%	.302	1.17	2.70	2.93	2.94	1.3

What can you say? It gets filthy in the Dirty South. Holland's moniker is appropriate, as his improved command and further refinement of a wicked slider turned him into one of the true lock-down closers in the game. His slider had the league's second-highest whiff rate, and when he was ahead in the count batters hit .101 and slugged .131 against him. He never made an appearance over an inning and started the frame in 67 of his 68 appearances, joining Dan Quisenberry, Jeff Montgomery and Joakim Soria in the Royal Pantheon of Closers with more than 40 saves in a season. The shelf life of closers is short, but in a sense the shelf life for all of us is short.

Donnie Joseph

Born: 11/1/1987 Age: 26
Bats: L Throws: L Height: 6' 3" Weight: 190
Breakout: 26% Improve: 50% Collapse: 42%
Attrition: 58% MLB: 41%

Comparables:
Anthony Slama, A.J. Ramos, John Gaub

YEAR	TEAM	LVL	AGE	W	L	SV	G	GS	IP	H	HR	BB	SO	BB9	SO9	GB%	BABIP	WHIP	ERA	FIP	FRA	WARP
2011	CAR	AA	23	1	3	8	57	0	58¹	67	8	30	66	4.6	10.2	42%	.364	1.66	6.94	4.63	3.88	0.5
2012	PEN	AA	24	4	2	13	26	0	30¹	13	1	8	46	2.4	13.6	65%	.214	0.69	0.89	1.43	2.10	0.9
2012	OMA	AAA	24	1	0	2	11	0	17¹	21	1	13	19	6.8	9.9	56%	.377	1.96	4.15	4.47	3.94	0.5
2012	LOU	AAA	24	4	1	5	18	0	22	22	0	9	22	3.7	9.0	52%	.333	1.41	2.86	2.39	3.58	0.4
2013	OMA	AAA	25	4	3	6	47	0	54²	39	5	40	84	6.6	13.8	47%	.312	1.45	3.95	4.05	3.81	1.0
2013	KCA	MLB	25	0	0	0	6	0	5²	4	0	4	7	6.4	11.1	36%	.286	1.41	0.00	2.72	3.12	0.1
2014	KCA	MLB	26	2	1	1	47	0	55	47	5	27	65	4.4	10.6	49%	.308	1.34	3.62	3.70	3.93	0.6

Acquired from Cincinnati for Jonathan Broxton, the left-handed Joseph spins a fastball-slider combination. With consistent arm action, the slider has good velocity separation from his fastball and serves to keep hitters off balance. As he's moved up the minor-league food chain, opposing hitters with a more selective eye have been laying off his pitches out of the zone. Joseph has also struggled with repeating his delivery and can struggle with command. Over his minor-league career, his extreme platoon split has pointed toward a future as a LOOGY, but the swing-and-miss stuff—especially to left-handed batters—will earn him a look in any bullpen.

Sean Manaea
Born: 2/1/1992 Age: 22
Bats: L Throws: L Height: 6' 5" Weight: 235

YEAR	TEAM	LVL	AGE	W	L	SV	G	GS	IP	H	HR	BB	SO	BB9	SO9	GB%	BABIP	WHIP	ERA	FIP	FRA	WARP
2014	–	–	–	–	–	–	–	–	–	–	–	–	–	–	–	–	–	–	–	–	–	–

Manaea was one of the top left-handed pitching prospects in the 2013 draft before he injured his hip pitching for Indiana State in March. The injury knocked him out of the first round but the Royals gave him a $3.55 million signing bonus—a record for a supplemental pick. He had surgery for a labrum tear in his hip shortly after he signed and will make his professional debut in 2014. Manaea throws from a three-quarters angle, which gives his fastball late life. His slider has plus-pitch potential and he also works in a change. Despite his injury, he finished third in NCAA Division I with 11.4 strikeouts per nine.

Luis Mendoza
Born: 10/31/1983 Age: 30
Bats: R Throws: R Height: 6' 3" Weight: 245
Breakout: 25% Improve: 52% Collapse: 40%
Attrition: 53% MLB: 38%

Comparables:
John Rheinecker, Lenny DiNardo, Cha Seung Baek

YEAR	TEAM	LVL	AGE	W	L	SV	G	GS	IP	H	HR	BB	SO	BB9	SO9	GB%	BABIP	WHIP	ERA	FIP	FRA	WARP
2011	OMA	AAA	27	12	5	2	33	18	144¹	126	5	54	81	3.4	5.1	47%	.320	1.25	2.18	4.38	4.02	1.9
2011	KCA	MLB	27	2	0	0	2	2	14²	11	0	5	7	3.1	4.3	46%	.239	1.09	1.23	3.54	4.08	0.2
2012	KCA	MLB	28	8	10	0	30	25	166	176	15	59	104	3.2	5.6	54%	.310	1.42	4.23	4.23	4.94	0.8
2013	KCA	MLB	29	2	6	0	22	15	94	106	10	43	54	4.1	5.2	50%	.313	1.59	5.36	4.78	5.38	-0.2
2014	KCA	MLB	30	6	5	0	19	14	92²	104	9	33	49	3.2	4.8	49%	.307	1.48	4.80	4.79	5.22	-0.2

Mendoza opened 2013 as the Royals' fifth starter, shifted to the bullpen for the second half and proved to be uninspiring in either role. His modus operandi is to start hitters with a sinker and follow up with a curve when he can get ahead. Mendoza struggled with his command, which the Royals said was understandable—he rarely got regular work as a fifth starter and his sinker is a "feel" pitch. The lack of routine can't excuse his lack of deception and subsequent bat-missing inabilities. While his sinker nets a groundball in close to half of all balls put in play, Mendoza allows too much hard contact to be reliable in any role.

Ervin Santana
Born: 12/12/1982 Age: 31
Bats: R Throws: R Height: 6' 2" Weight: 185
Breakout: 13% Improve: 46% Collapse: 26%
Attrition: 24% MLB: 92%

Comparables:
Vicente Padilla, Gil Meche, Rodrigo Lopez

YEAR	TEAM	LVL	AGE	W	L	SV	G	GS	IP	H	HR	BB	SO	BB9	SO9	GB%	BABIP	WHIP	ERA	FIP	FRA	WARP
2011	ANA	MLB	28	11	12	0	33	33	228²	207	26	72	178	2.8	7.0	45%	.272	1.22	3.38	4.03	4.68	1.1
2012	ANA	MLB	29	9	13	0	30	30	178	165	39	61	133	3.1	6.7	45%	.240	1.27	5.16	5.58	6.18	-1.4
2013	KCA	MLB	30	9	10	0	32	32	211	190	26	51	161	2.2	6.9	47%	.265	1.14	3.24	3.96	4.62	1.1
2014	KCA	MLB	31	12	8	0	26	26	172¹	172	24	52	126	2.7	6.6	42%	.286	1.30	4.25	4.73	4.62	0.6

The Royals traded for Santana with the idea that he'd be a stop-gap starter. A one-year rental. Then, something strange happened: He had his best season since 2008. Relying more on his slider than in the recent past, he also leaned on a two-seam fastball for the first time and accelerated his trajectory toward becoming a groundball pitcher. As always with Santana, though, it was his slider that was especially lethal. Just 15 percent of all sliders thrown were put in play and opponents hit just .180 against the pitch. The Royals wisely made a qualifying offer. Santana wisely turned them down. The relationship was a win-win all around, but given how hard it is to find good starters the Royals might have wished he had been just a little bit worse in 2013.

James Shields
Born: 12/20/1981 Age: 32
Bats: R Throws: R Height: 6' 4" Weight: 215
Breakout: 15% Improve: 46% Collapse: 33%
Attrition: 9% MLB: 89%

Comparables:
Aaron Harang, Mike Mussina, Dan Haren

YEAR	TEAM	LVL	AGE	W	L	SV	G	GS	IP	H	HR	BB	SO	BB9	SO9	GB%	BABIP	WHIP	ERA	FIP	FRA	WARP
2011	TBA	MLB	29	16	12	0	33	33	249¹	195	26	65	225	2.3	8.1	47%	.258	1.04	2.82	3.45	3.96	3.1
2012	TBA	MLB	30	15	10	0	33	33	227²	208	25	58	223	2.3	8.8	53%	.293	1.17	3.52	3.42	4.19	2.0
2013	KCA	MLB	31	13	9	0	34	34	228²	215	20	68	196	2.7	7.7	43%	.299	1.24	3.15	3.50	4.02	2.8
2014	KCA	MLB	32	14	9	0	31	31	197¹	198	22	48	164	2.2	7.5	46%	.306	1.25	3.81	3.90	4.14	1.9

The Royals acquired Shields with the idea that he would be their ace, an Opening Day starter who would save the bullpen by pitching deep into games. He fit the bill, pacing the club in WARP and VORP and topping 200 innings for the seventh consecutive season. Shields threw his cut fastball more often last season, and paired it with his natural, devastating changeup to work over left-handed batters. Against same-side hitters, he still went to his changeup, though not with the same frequency, often sticking to fastballs while ahead in the count. Either way, his change remains one of the most effective pitches in the game, thrown in any count to any batter. He's in the final year of his contract, and the constantly inflating market for starting pitchers means Kansas City will be unwilling (or unable) to bring him back once he's a free agent. If the Royals are on the outside of the Wild Card race at the trading deadline, the Internet may not be large enough to house all the trade rumors.

Everett Teaford
Born: 5/15/1984 Age: 30
Bats: L Throws: L Height: 6' 0" Weight: 165
Breakout: 46% Improve: 63% Collapse: 18%
Attrition: 42% MLB: 22%
Comparables:
Bryan Bullington, Kurt Birkins, Eric Stults

YEAR	TEAM	LVL	AGE	W	L	SV	G	GS	IP	H	HR	BB	SO	BB9	SO9	GB%	BABIP	WHIP	ERA	FIP	FRA	WARP
2011	OMA	AAA	27	3	2	0	16	3	35	23	5	11	33	2.8	8.5	39%	.217	0.97	3.34	4.78	3.82	0.4
2011	KCA	MLB	27	2	1	1	26	3	44	36	8	14	28	2.9	5.7	46%	.226	1.14	3.27	5.18	5.77	0.0
2012	OMA	AAA	28	4	0	0	7	6	33	24	2	8	25	2.2	6.8	42%	.247	0.97	1.09	3.76	4.17	0.6
2012	KCA	MLB	28	1	4	0	18	5	61¹	68	11	21	35	3.1	5.1	45%	.294	1.45	4.99	5.36	6.00	-0.4
2013	OMA	AAA	29	4	6	0	31	14	95¹	92	7	39	99	3.7	9.3	40%	.320	1.37	3.49	3.83	3.65	1.8
2013	KCA	MLB	29	0	0	0	1	0	0²	1	0	0	0	0.0	0.0	%	.333	1.50	0.00	3.08	3.60	0.0
2014	KCA	MLB	30	5	3	0	27	10	83²	86	11	29	58	3.1	6.2	40%	.293	1.38	4.43	4.83	4.82	0.2

When you have a bullpen as deep as the Royals, mediocrity is no way to get noticed. Teaford had sipped a couple of nondescript cups of coffee in the majors, accumulating -0.6 WARP. Then in 2013, his cup was so small it wouldn't even qualify as a sample. He profiles as an average Triple-A player, and his walk, strikeout and contact rates are all in line with the PCL average. That's nice, but we know what happens to "average" Triple-A pitchers when their stuff doesn't translate to the next level. In previous seasons, he did well against same-side batters, but last year saw his platoon split reverse, a curiosity to us but an annoyance to a manager. He needs to correct that if he's to make his way back to the big leagues for more than a sip.

Jason Vargas
Born: 2/2/1983 Age: 31
Bats: L Throws: L Height: 6' 0" Weight: 215
Breakout: 7% Improve: 42% Collapse: 28%
Attrition: 20% MLB: 80%
Comparables:
Brian Bannister, Jeff Francis, Kyle Lohse

YEAR	TEAM	LVL	AGE	W	L	SV	G	GS	IP	H	HR	BB	SO	BB9	SO9	GB%	BABIP	WHIP	ERA	FIP	FRA	WARP
2011	SEA	MLB	28	10	13	0	32	32	201	205	22	59	131	2.6	5.9	39%	.285	1.31	4.25	4.12	3.96	2.3
2012	SEA	MLB	29	14	11	0	33	33	217¹	201	35	55	141	2.3	5.8	42%	.255	1.18	3.85	4.64	5.27	-0.6
2013	ANA	MLB	30	9	8	0	24	24	150	162	17	46	109	2.8	6.5	42%	.310	1.39	4.02	4.12	4.38	0.9
2014	KCA	MLB	31	10	7	0	23	23	143²	154	18	39	86	2.5	5.4	39%	.292	1.35	4.39	4.65	4.77	0.3

Good golly, could it be? A decent idea gone right. Vargas was the third and most successful starter Angels GM Jerry Dipoto added to shore up his rotation. Although his game doesn't have centerfold appeal, Vargas is a steady arm who succeeds with deception. Be it the Felix Hernandez-like twist in his delivery or his willingness to throw his changeup whenever, the command-and-control southpaw gets the job done. He shouldn't be one of the three best starters on a team, but he deserves a rotation spot in the majors until he's too old to throw strikes.

Yordano Ventura
Born: 6/3/1991 Age: 23
Bats: R Throws: R Height: 5' 11" Weight: 180
Breakout: 44% Improve: 64% Collapse: 19%
Attrition: 52% MLB: 55%
Comparables:
Daniel Hudson, Juan Morillo, Jaime Garcia

YEAR	TEAM	LVL	AGE	W	L	SV	G	GS	IP	H	HR	BB	SO	BB9	SO9	GB%	BABIP	WHIP	ERA	FIP	FRA	WARP
2011	KNC	A	20	4	6	0	19	19	84¹	82	8	24	88	2.6	9.4	61%	.464	1.26	4.27	3.54	5.65	-0.1
2012	WIL	A+	21	3	5	0	16	16	76¹	66	7	28	98	3.3	11.6	43%	.314	1.23	3.30	3.31	3.50	1.5
2012	NWA	AA	21	1	2	0	6	6	29¹	23	1	13	25	4.0	7.7	52%	.275	1.23	4.60	3.76	4.29	0.4
2013	NWA	AA	22	3	2	0	11	11	57²	39	3	20	74	3.1	11.5	43%	.279	1.02	2.34	2.41	2.91	1.6
2013	OMA	AAA	22	5	4	0	15	14	77	80	4	33	81	3.9	9.5	42%	.357	1.47	3.74	3.54	3.53	1.7
2013	KCA	MLB	22	0	1	0	3	3	15¹	13	3	6	11	3.5	6.5	51%	.227	1.24	3.52	5.36	5.17	0.0
2014	KCA	MLB	23	7	6	0	26	21	119²	118	12	50	108	3.8	8.2	44%	.310	1.40	4.23	4.20	4.59	0.7

In the PITCHf/x era, Justin Verlander has thrown the second, third, fourth, fifth, sixth, seventh, eighth, ninth and 10th fastest fastballs by a starter. But the no. 1 spot belongs to Ventura, who hit 101.9 with a pitch against Cleveland in his big-league debut in September, just a year removed from High-A. He complements that with a hammer curve that snaps from 12 to 6. The knock against Ventura-as-a-starter has always been his size and potential durability, but more likely the final say will be his command and his continued development of a changeup. Of all the Royals' arms, he has the best chance to develop into a front-line impact starter. If, that is, they can remain convinced he can hang in the rotation.

Kyle Zimmer

Born: 9/13/1991 Age: 22
Bats: R Throws: R Height: 6' 3" Weight: 215
Breakout: 43% Improve: 68% Collapse: 13%
Attrition: 31% MLB: 40%

Comparables:
Clay Buchholz, Danny Duffy, Gio Gonzalez

YEAR	TEAM	LVL	AGE	W	L	SV	G	GS	IP	H	HR	BB	SO	BB9	SO9	GB%	BABIP	WHIP	ERA	FIP	FRA	WARP
2012	KNC	A	20	2	3	0	6	6	29²	34	1	8	29	2.4	8.8	57%	.367	1.42	2.43	3.05	4.30	0.4
2013	WIL	A+	21	4	8	0	18	18	89²	80	9	31	113	3.1	11.3	55%	.318	1.24	4.82	3.27	4.37	1.3
2013	NWA	AA	21	2	1	0	4	4	18²	11	2	5	27	2.4	13.0	56%	.231	0.86	1.93	2.68	3.21	0.5
2014	KCA	MLB	22	5	4	0	18	13	80¹	81	9	31	73	3.5	8.2	52%	.312	1.40	4.38	4.27	4.76	0.3

The fifth pick in the 2012 draft, Zimmer has put up elite pitching numbers in his brief professional career, justifying his draft position. His fastball lives in the upper 90s, so it grades as a potential plus pitch, but lacks deception and hitters are able to track it. It's his curve that has scouts and coaches drooling. The hook has a wicked break and he already has an excellent feel for its command. Zimmer made it to Double-A and it won't be a surprise if the Royals keep him on the fast track, as long as he stays healthy. He was shut down last August with right shoulder stiffness, the second time in as many professional seasons he made an early exit due to injury.

LINEOUTS

HITTERS

PLAYER	TEAM	LVL	AGE	PA	R	2B	3B	HR	RBI	BB	SO	SB-CS	AVG/OBP/SLG	TAv	BABIP	BRR	FRAA	WARP
RF J. Bonifacio	WIL	A+	20	234	32	11	3	2	29	23	40	0-2	.296/.368/.408	.289	.353	-1.7	RF(50): 0.9	1.1
	NWA	AA	20	105	15	7	0	2	19	11	23	2-1	.301/.371/.441	.302	.377	0.8	RF(23): -1.8	0.8
SS O. Calixte	NWA	AA	21	536	59	25	4	8	36	42	131	14-11	.250/.312/.368	.243	.325	1	SS(101): -5.6, 3B(11): -0.7	0.5
3B C. Cuthbert	WIL	A+	20	254	32	21	2	2	31	27	37	1-2	.280/.354/.418	.283	.324	-2.2	3B(57): -2.0	1.0
	NWA	AA	20	264	25	16	0	6	28	20	51	5-2	.215/.279/.359	.218	.246	-2.9	3B(59): 4.4	-0.3
CF B. Eibner	NWA	AA	24	504	74	17	9	19	41	53	149	7-3	.243/.330/.451	.273	.319	0.3	CF(106): -9.8	1.4
LF B. Fletcher	NWA	AA	24	221	37	9	1	12	37	13	41	6-2	.314/.353/.541	.298	.342	2.8	LF(32): -1.6	1.3
	OMA	AAA	24	115	14	5	0	5	17	5	33	1-0	.250/.287/.435	.247	.310	-0.1	LF(19): 2.4	0.3
C C. Gallagher	LEX	A	20	256	19	15	0	2	18	24	28	0-0	.212/.302/.306	.246	.231	-0.3	C(57): 0.5	0.4
3B B. Laird	OKL	AAA	25	513	75	33	0	16	79	29	87	1-0	.277/.324/.449	.286	.305	2.5	3B(85): 5.5, 1B(19): 0.5	3.4
	HOU	MLB	25	76	7	3	0	5	11	3	26	0-0	.169/.224/.423	.219	.175	-0.6	1B(13): -0.5, 3B(4): 0.4	-0.3
CF M. Mesa	SWB	AAA	26	332	40	15	3	13	39	11	112	13-2	.261/.295/.452	.266	.361	0.2	CF(71): 2.2, RF(9): -0.7	1.4
	NYA	MLB	26	14	2	2	0	0	1	1	2	0-1	.385/.429/.538	.349	.455	0.1	LF(3): 0.2, CF(1): 0.0	0.3

The younger of the Royals' Good Face Brothers, **Jorge Bonifacio** missed a month and a half with a hand injury and never found the power in his short, compact swing. ⦸ A solid defensive shortstop with a strong arm, **Orlando Calixte** struggled with off-speed pitches and suffered from an unrefined approach at the plate. ⦸ After solving High-A, **Cheslor Cuthbert** found Double-A to be more of a challenge. The upside is in his strong contact skills, developing power and his youth relative to the rest of the league. ⦸ A hitter in the "grip it and rip it" tradition, **Brett Eibner** further refined his power stroke but his 70 percent contact rate was the fifth lowest in the Texas League. ⦸ A two-way player at Georgia Tech, fourth-round pick **Zane Evans** moved from the mound to behind the dish, and abused all those pitchers he left behind. ⦸ **Brian Fletcher** only periodically shows enough power to think he'll make it to the majors despite lacking a defensive position. Last season was one of the good ones. ⦸ In his first exposure to A-ball, **Cameron Gallagher** struggled both at and behind the plate. The Royals' second-round pick in the 2011 draft hit just .193/.254/.228 against left-handed pitching. ⦸ **Brandon Laird**, the younger brother of Gerald, spent his third full season at Triple-A and could stand to take a pitch now and again. ⦸ After **Melky Mesa**'s second season at Triple-A yielded a 10-to-1 strikeout-to-walk ratio, the Yankees decided one decade in the organization was enough and released him.

PITCHERS

PLAYER	TEAM	LVL	AGE	W	L	SV	IP	H	HR	BB	SO	BB9	SO9	GB%	BABIP	WHIP	ERA	FIP	FRA	WARP
C. Binford	LEX	A	20	8	7	0	135	129	7	25	130	1.7	8.7	56%	.319	1.14	2.67	2.94	3.68	1.9
B. Brickhouse	LEX	A	21	4	4	0	60	54	3	21	49	3.2	7.3	62%	.288	1.25	2.25	3.70	4.81	0.0
A. Brooks	WIL	A+	23	2	3	0	56¹	60	4	11	43	1.8	6.9	51%	.320	1.26	4.47	3.33	4.61	0.6
	NWA	AA	23	7	7	0	103²	113	13	11	67	1.0	5.8	51%	.301	1.20	4.17	3.80	4.84	0.3
J. Lamb	WIL	A+	22	4	12	0	92²	109	13	19	76	1.8	7.4	38%	.334	1.38	5.63	4.28	4.73	1.0
	OMA	AAA	22	1	2	0	16	15	1	7	10	3.9	5.6	41%	.269	1.38	6.75	4.82	5.35	0.0
C. Mortensen	PAW	AAA	28	3	0	0	43²	34	4	20	39	4.1	8.0	44%	.265	1.24	2.47	4.12	4.40	-0.1
	BOS	MLB	28	1	2	0	30¹	32	3	16	21	4.7	6.2	47%	.296	1.58	5.34	4.86	5.48	-0.2
S. Selman	WIL	A+	22	11	9	0	125¹	88	3	85	128	6.1	9.2	47%	.262	1.38	3.38	3.99	4.88	1.1
P. Walters	ROC	AAA	28	7	5	0	103¹	110	5	46	82	4.0	7.1	49%	.332	1.51	4.18	3.81	4.73	0.9
	MIN	MLB	28	2	5	0	39¹	51	5	18	22	4.1	5.0	42%	.336	1.75	5.95	5.06	6.18	-0.2

Lexington's Pitcher of the Year, lanky **Christian Binford** has shown positive command and healthy groundball rates in his brief minor-league career. ⊘ **Bryan Brickhouse** was stacked and that's a fact, until Tommy John surgery grounded his prospect-on-the-rise status in early July. ⊘ Right-handed batters managed only a .248/.272/.373 line against starter **Aaron Brooks** in his stops at High-A and Double-A. ⊘ **John Lamb**, a former top 20 prospect, returned from Tommy John surgery to make some point about the sad futility of ambition. ⊘ **Clayton Mortensen** was acquired by the Royals from the Red Sox at the end of August for Quintin Berry. With the Royals' bullpen depth, he's only organizational filler. ⊘ While his fastball is above average and his slider is projectable, lack of command of all pitches will conspire to keep **Sam Selman** in the bullpen if he ever does make the majors. ⊘ After spending years scouting journeyman **P.J. Walters** and his collection of off-speed junk up and down the Four-A rollercoaster, we're ready to update his entry to "mostly harmless."

MANAGER: NED YOST

YEAR	TEAM	W-L	Pythag +/-	Avg PC	100+ P	120+ P	QS	BQS	REL	REL w Zero R	IBB	PH	PH Avg	PH HR	SB2	CS2	SB3	CS3	SAC Att	SAC %	POS SAC	Squeeze	Swing	In Play
2011	KCA	71-91	0	96.9	74	0	75	5	420	339	42	36	.152	1	130	48	23	8	75	73.3%	51	2	399	113
2012	KCA	72-90	0	90.5	55	0	69	4	500	411	44	55	.208	3	109	34	22	4	42	61.9%	25	1	334	97
2013	KCA	86-76	1	98.5	78	2	95	4	424	371	21	74	.210	1	133	29	18	2	56	66.1%	36	1	366	98

Ned Yost prefers a stable lineup. My God, does he ever. He's had the fewest or second-fewest lineups in the AL each of the four seasons he's been in KC. Overall, the Royals have had 313 lineups under Royals watch. Every other big-league team has had at least 332 in that period.

Yost doesn't make many mid-game substitutions. In 10 years on the job as a club's primary manager, his clubs have had the most position-player complete games six times. They've been in the top three another trio of times, including 2013. (His 2007 Brewers ranked just sixth. Something must have been off that year.)

The biggest knock on Yost from his days in Milwaukee was his inability to handle the bullpen. The 2013 Royals relievers posted a 2.55 ERA, the lowest mark by an AL bullpen since the 1990 A's. Did Yost learn or was he just lucky? We'll see this year.

Los Angeles Angels of Anaheim

By Matt Welch

When word leaked out before the July trading deadline that the Angels were open to moving Howie Kendrick, it was more than mere admission that Arte Moreno's once-model franchise was writing off yet another win-now season. By considering a salary dump for one of the game's half-dozen best second basemen even though he's owed only $18.85 million from ages 30-31, General Manager Jerry Dipoto was signaling that his team is desperate for even an inch of wiggle room under its massive, backloaded free agent burden. The message to Mike Scioscia in his 14th and most tenuous year as manager was that the last vestiges of the ballyhooed first generation of Scioscia/Bill Stoneman homegrowns had been reduced to rebuilding bait instead of pennant-waving advertisements for the Angel Way. And the Kendrick trial balloon, which kept floating into the offseason, heralded a shocking if long-rising reality: This franchise has utterly squandered what was once one of the sport's largest surpluses of talent. It's a cautionary tale for any team that's grown accustomed to winning: This too shall pass, maybe more quickly than you ever thought possible. Failure in Anaheim, to invert a cliche, has had many fathers, most of whom are still in senior management positions. To right this foundering ship they're going to need a clear-eyed look at what went so horribly wrong.

It's kind of hard to remember now, but for a good while there it almost felt like the Angels had beaten baseball's business cycle. From 2002 to 2009, the Halos averaged 94 wins a year and made the playoffs six times. The only team to top those numbers during that period was the Yankees, and they spent almost twice the money. The Angels of Anaheim, unlike the Empire of Evil, managed these feats while also cultivating one of baseball's best farm systems: From 2003 to 2007, the organization never placed lower than fifth in *Baseball America's* annual minor-league rankings; the Yanks during

that stretch only once finished higher than 17th. New waves of cheap talent allowed older favorites to seek their golden parachutes elsewhere, often bringing back valuable draft picks in return. Darin Erstad would yield to Casey Kotchman, who could be flipped for a great half-season of Mark Teixeira because Kendrys Morales was coming right behind; the compensation pick for a departing Teixeira was a kid named Mike Trout. From 2004 to 2010, while the average major-league team raised payroll by one-third, the Angels increased theirs by a rounding error of $4 million. In 2009, when they won 97 games and yet another AL West crown, the team picked five of the first 48 players in the June draft, then conducted their offseason such that the next year they would control five of the first 40. Moreno's juggernaut seemed on the verge of self-perpetuation, yet it's been all pratfalls ever since. As Fred Willard once put it, wha' happen?

It's too easy to blame it all on Dipoto's predecessor Tony Reagins (2008-2011) and his deservedly infamous January 2011 trade of Mike Napoli and Juan Rivera for the right to owe Vernon Wells $84 million. While that foul swap exposed three of Mike Scioscia's most glaring tics—fetishization of catcher defense, intolerance of clubhouse partiers and stubborn deference to veterans long past their sell-by dates—it also reflected a panicky organizational short-sightedness that had set in long before, and remains in evidence to this day.

Like most real-world decline narratives, there is no one magic self-inflicted bullet responsible for puncturing the Angels' success. The international scouting system has been a mess for a decade. Can't-miss third basemen Dallas McPherson and Brandon Wood failed to materialize. Top pitching prospect Nick Adenhart died in a 2009 car crash. Kendrys Morales broke his leg in a freak 2010 accident at home plate. The Scioscia style of play, or "program," as many

ANGELS PROSPECTUS
2013 W-L: 78-84, 3rd in AL West

Pythag	.497	15th	DER	.699	21st
RS/G	4.52	7th	B-Age	27.8	11th
RA/G	4.55	24th	P-Age	29.4	26th
TAv	.276	5th	Salary	$141	6th
BRR	-2.34	21st	M$/MW	$4.34	22nd
TAv-P	.275	27th	DL Days	1032	17th
FIP	4.11	25th	$ on DL	19%	20th

	Runs	HR/RH	HR/LH	Runs/RH	Runs/LH
Three-Year Park Factors	97	84	83	103	96

Top Hitter WARP	10.43 (Mike Trout)
Top Pitcher WARP	2.78 (C.J. Wilson)
Top Prospect	Taylor Lindsey

players used to call it, leaked out of the big-league club bit by bit, suggesting a defense-and-baserunning manager philosophically unmoored from an increasingly station-to-station roster. Perhaps the best explanation is simply that success blinded the organization to its underlying flaws, whose impact have grown more malign over time.

You can trace the Angels' 21st century arc through the rise and fall of its bullpens. Last year, for the fourth time in five seasons, Halo relievers were just brutal, blowing 17 saves, walking nearly four batters per nine innings, compiling an ERA of 4.12 in a pitchers' park and allowing one-third of inherited runners to score. The only ERA+s above 104 in the 'pen among those who pitched 10 innings or more belonged to Scott Downs (who was flipped to Atlanta before the trading deadline) and 30-year-old rookie Dane De La Rosa. Though such giant sucking sounds have become depressingly familiar in Orange County, it was not ever thus.

From 2002 to 2004, Angels bullpens led the American League in ERA each year, with a mostly dirt-cheap mix of homegrown talent (Scot Shields, Frankie Rodriguez) and diamonds-in-the-dump reclamation projects (Ben Weber, Brendan Donnelly), topped by the lone high salary of Troy Percival. In 2005, after Percival walked (bringing the team back two draft picks), the Angels' bullpen still had just the seventh-lowest ERA in the major leagues while costing less than $4 million. Of the many reasons other teams were busy trying to hire away Scioscia/Stoneman coaches and scouts, bullpen management ranked right up there. Yet the regime was already entering a cycle of careless stewardship and reckless ring chasing that by 2007-2010 would produce consistently poor relief results for more than five times the 2005 price.

Beginning after the 2004 season, the Angels started giving away talented young arms for nothing and importing expensive mediocrites on multi-year deals. Derrick Turnbow was the first to go, claimed off waivers by Milwaukee, for whom he saved 39 games with a 1.74 ERA in 2005. Then the Angels signed Esteban Yan and his career 90 ERA+ to a two-year, $2.25 million contract, during which he (surprise!) put up an ERA+ of 89. To make way for Yan, the Angels dropped three-time *Baseball America* top-100 prospect Bobby Jenks, who went on to record the final out of the next World Series. Jenks was a five-cent head and Turnbow a former drug-test failure, but the same couldn't be said for the similarly unprotected Joel Peralta and Jake Woods after their decent 2005 rookie seasons, nor for Kevin Gregg and Brendan Donnelly after 2006, when the two were traded for guys who combined to pitch just 4 ⅓ more innings of major-league ball.

Meanwhile, joining Yan on the multi-year gravy train were disappointments Hector Carrasco (two years/$5.6 million), Justin Speier (four/$18 million), Brian Fuentes (two/$17.5 million, plus the no. 32 draft pick), Fernando Rodney (two/$11 million) and Hisanori Takahashi (two/$8 million). The six would combine to produce 3.3 WARP in Angels uniforms, barely topping even the 2013 value of two squandered former Angels: Baltimore's Darren O'Day, who was Rule 5'd after being unprotected in 2008; and Tampa's Alex Torres, who (along with Sean Rodriguez and a minor-league scrub) was part of the midseason 2009 package that allowed Anaheim to pay Scott Kazmir more than $20 million for 188 innings of 5.31-ERA baseball.

So lopsided was this exchange of cheap meat for expensive "Spam" that the Angels started trying to address it with yet another surplus: an unparalleled collection of infield talent. So 21-year-old shortstop Alexi Casilla, on the verge of launching a big-league career that's still active eight years later, was exchanged before his 2006 debut for a single 6.70-ERA season of reliever J.C. Romero. The 23-year-old second baseman Alberto Callaspo, then stuck in the graduation line behind Howie Kendrick, was traded for wild Triple-A strikeout artist Jason Bulger, who would produce exactly one helpful season in six forgettable years in Anaheim; near the end of which the Angels belatedly realized that Callaspo could fill their perennial hole at third base, a head-slapping moment that cost them top left-handed pitching prospect Will Smith. The once-magic coaching touch that seemed to convert every random Al Levine or Lou Pote into a solidly above-average reliever seemed to depart the team altogether with the poaching of pitching coach Bud Black after the 2006 season. A bullpen that never finished lower than seventh in major-league ERA under Black from 2000-2006 has only twice finished higher than 19th under Black's embattled successor, Mike Butcher.

It's notable that the Angels' most immediate moves this offseason came at the coaching level: former Rockies manager and Angel hero Don Baylor hired as hitting coach, former Pawtucket manager and Angel favorite Gary DiSarcina as third base coach, former Nationals hitting coach and brother-of-Angel-favorite Rick Eckstein as a hybrid coach; plus former Diamondbacks Double-A manager Rico Brogna as a minor-league instructor and special assistant to Dipoto. While gossip outside of the team interpreted this infusion of decidedly managerial talent as a not-so-veiled threat to Scioscia's job security, it might also represent a long-overdue recognition that instructional and motivational levels have sagged on the big club since the brain drains of Black, Joe Maddon and Ron Roenicke. The Angels of the past few years, quite unlike the Maddon/Black/Roenicke days, have been sluggish in the field and stupid on the basepaths—converting a woeful 68.3 percent of batted balls into outs (same as lead-footed Detroit), leading the majors in baserunning outs and outs at third base, even while swiping a Scioscia-era low of 83 bags. Some of this is attributable to changing personnel, as the team has gone from a 1980s Cardinals-style construction of talented rabbits clustered around a lone thumper to a sluggers-and-starters model that better resembles the 1978-79 Angels. But, coupled with several recent slow-out-of-the-gate starts, such disheveled performance suggests a team no longer responding to its collegiate-style manager.

But coaching alone can't make an empty cupboard look full, and for that Scioscia's organizational rival in the general manager's box deserves his share of blame, too. Dipoto fans in the analytics community tend to pin the mammoth and so-far disappointing Albert Pujols and Josh Hamilton contracts on Arte Moreno instead of his young GM, but even within those friendly parameters Dipoto's performance has been mixed at best. Yes, the Angels are no longer blowing $20 million per year on a bullpen filled with multi-year contracts, but the results of Dipoto's dumpster diving still stink: Sean Burnett, Ryan Madson, Latroy Hawkins, Jason Isringhausen and Mark Lowe have yet to produce even one pleasant surprise.

Dipoto's golden straightjacket, which requires penny-pinching in every other category even while payroll balloons to accommodate the Big Four contracts of Pujols, Hamilton, Jered Weaver and C.J. Wilson (whose combined haul grows from $61 million in 2013 to $73 million this year, $86 million in '15 and $98 million the year after), has led to such highly questionable long-term decisions as nickel-and-diming Mike Trout's salary increases instead of locking up the game's best player to a forever extension, and jettisoning Ervin Santana and Dan Haren (as well as former All-Star fireballing reliever Jordan Walden) in the extremely unlikely hope that career meatballer Joe Blanton and shoulder be-hamburgered Tommy Hanson could reproduce even the deeply disappointing 2012 performances of Santana and Haren. When they couldn't—and they really couldn't, going a combined 6-17 with a 5.82 ERA in 206 innings, compared to their predecessors' 21-26, 4.75 in 355 innings—the 2013 season was toast, regardless of Pujols' bum heel and Hamilton's shaky nerves. That's because Dipoto had finished off the squandering of a third surplus: an entire generation of hot young pitching prospects whose achievements will likely be haunting Anaheim for the next decade.

This is where the Kendrick trade rumors (and those involving his keystone partner Erick Aybar) really come back home to bite. The Angels announced to the world that they were ready to consider trading their reasonably priced, prime-age, up-the-middle talent for cost-controlled, MLB-ready rotation help—even though Dipoto had traded the last of the organization's middle-infield depth and rotation prospects in panicky in-season 2012 moves for closer Ernesto Frieri and a half season of compensation-less Zack Greinke. So not only does the team get to watch Jean Segura make All-Star teams in Milwaukee, it does so knowing that no. 2 on the shortstop depth chart in Anaheim is a guy (Andrew Romine) four years older, whose career minor-league OPS is .721;

and that Kendrick's putative 2014 replacement, 26-year-old Grant Green, both looks and measures horribly at the pivot. And that's not the worst of it.

Those well-stocked 2009-2010 drafts, in addition to producing Mike Trout, brought forth a stable of young pitching studs—Tyler Skaggs, Patrick Corbin, Garrett Richards, Donn Roach. The draft before turned up Tyler Chatwood, Will Smith and Johnny Hellweg. Appallingly, only Richards from that generation has remained in the organization since being drafted. In 2013 already, Corbin (who left in the block-buster mid-2010 Dan Haren trade engineered by then-interim Arizona GM Jerry Dipoto) and Chatwood combined to pitch about as well as Angel aces Weaver and Wilson: 22-13, 3.32 ERA, 122 ERA+ and 5.3 WARP in 320 innings for the C&C boys, for less than 4 percent of the salary of W&W's 28-15, 3.34 ERA, 113 ERA+ and 3.6 WARP in 367 innings.

Will Smith, a 6-foot-5 left-hander, struck out 43 and walked just seven in 33 innings of 128-ERA+ relief for the Royals in his age-23 year, after ripping up the Pacific Coast League as a swingman. Hellweg (Greinke trade), a 6-foot-9 right-hander with control issues, pitched well at Triple-A in his age-24 season (though bombed in seven starts in Milwaukee). Roach (Frieri trade) had a good year in Double-A at age 23, as did Ariel Pena in the Brewers system at 24. All these departed pitchers are younger than Garrett Richards or any of the Angels' Triple-A starters still in the organization. Perhaps in belated recognition of this giveaway, the squandered Tyler Skaggs (Haren trade), another 6-foot-5 left-hander who went from no. 83 to no. 13 to no. 12 in *Baseball America*'s preseason prospect rankings the previous three seasons, was reacquired in a December trade (along with promising 26-year-old White Sox lefty swingman Hector Santiago) for home run leader Mark Trumbo and Triple-A blah-prospect A.J. Schugel. Still, all the Angels have in return for their lost generation of cost-controlled starters are Ernesto Frieri (he of the career 4.4 BB/9 rate, in addition to the outta-sight 12.3 K/9 rate), the fallen if intriguing infield prospect Grant Green and bat-oriented backstop Chris Iannetta.

So is all hope lost? Not on a team with Mike Trout and Jered Weaver, and not in an American League where Boston can go from worst to first with a canny mixture of contract shedding, free agent-shopping and strategic coaching turnover. While the Angels' rotation remained dangerously thin even after acquiring Skaggs and Santiago, the bullpen could conceivably improve with the signing of free agent Joe Smith, the acquisition of strikeout artist Brian Moran via trade, and the return of the injured Burnett. And it's possible that the win-now trade of center field defensive phenom Peter Bourjos for the older and more grizzled third baseman David Freese might fill a hole with surplus for a year or two. Josh Hamilton's face-plant in 2013 thankfully did not come with any serious injury, and his strong second-half—.285/.345/.486 over his last 76 games, .329/.392/.518 his last 45—pointed to a reversion much closer to his core comp group of guys like Andre Dawson, Carlos Beltran and Jim Edmonds. And if Albert Pujols can indeed run faster to first base than eight seconds flat, he's a solid bet to hit more like his last year in St. Louis than his first two in Anaheim. Getting 9-10 WARP out of those two instead of 4-5 would certainly go a long way.

But like Walter White in the final episode of *Breaking Bad*, the Angels are going to need nearly everything to go their way to get back on top. While this would provide a temporary reprieve for Dipoto and Scioscia (the latter of whom especially looks vulnerable should the team get off to another

lousy start), the quick hit of a return playoff engagement still won't fix the organization's long-term trajectory. For that they'll need to restock a depleted farm system, rebuild a broken international scouting system and figure out a way to not lose Mickey Mantle 2.0 as he enters his prime. Winning now might sound fun, but Arte Moreno & Co. need to start remembering how to win next year, too.

Matt Welch is Editor in Chief of Reason *magazine, co-host of* The Independents *on Fox Business Network, co-author of* The Declaration of Independents: How Libertarian Politics Can Fix What's Wrong With America *and a regular contributor to* Halos Heaven.

HITTERS

Erick Aybar   SS
Born: 1/14/1984 Age: 30
Bats: B Throws: R Height: 5' 10"
Weight: 180 Breakout: 7%
Improve: 48% Collapse: 4%
Attrition: 14% MLB: 100%

Comparables:
Rafael Furcal, Alexei Ramirez, Jack Wilson

YEAR	TEAM	LVL	AGE	PA	R	2B	3B	HR	RBI	BB	SO	SB	CS	AVG/OBP/SLG	TAv	BABIP	BRR	FRAA	WARP
2011	ANA	MLB	27	605	71	33	8	10	59	31	68	30	6	.279/.322/.421	.271	.301	4.4	SS(142): 3.3	3.9
2012	ANA	MLB	28	554	67	31	5	8	45	22	61	20	4	.290/.324/.416	.277	.316	1.4	SS(139): -5.4	2.8
2013	ANA	MLB	29	589	68	33	5	6	54	23	59	12	7	.271/.301/.382	.250	.292	4	SS(138): -10.5	1.1
2014	ANA	MLB	30	547	64	26	5	6	44	29	65	19	6	.275/.319/.381	.258	.300	1.4	SS -6	1.9

Most people reading this know to approach defensive metrics with skepticism. That's important to note with Aybar because his defensive evaluation is the difference between saying he's an okay player and a good player. Most who watch Aybar daily swear he's average at worst—and likely considerably better—which is a different picture than FRAA paints. With two seasons remaining on an affordable contract, expect to see his name pop up in trade rumors if the Angels continue to underachieve—especially if teams believe in the glove.

Kole Calhoun   RF
Born: 10/14/1987 Age: 26
Bats: L Throws: L Height: 5' 10"
Weight: 190 Breakout: 6%
Improve: 34% Collapse: 11%
Attrition: 22% MLB: 73%

Comparables:
John Bowker, Joe Mather, Steve Pearce

YEAR	TEAM	LVL	AGE	PA	R	2B	3B	HR	RBI	BB	SO	SB	CS	AVG/OBP/SLG	TAv	BABIP	BRR	FRAA	WARP
2011	SBR	A+	23	594	94	36	6	22	99	73	96	20	10	.324/.410/.547	.343	.362	1.1	RF(12): -0.1, 1B(8): -0.0	1.7
2012	SLC	AAA	24	463	79	30	7	14	73	44	88	12	3	.298/.369/.507	.290	.346	5.3	CF(52): 2.5, RF(41): -2.7	3.3
2012	ANA	MLB	24	25	2	1	0	0	1	2	6	1	0	.174/.240/.217	.182	.235	0.6	RF(14): 0.2, LF(4): -0.0	-0.1
2013	SLC	AAA	25	274	48	15	6	12	49	32	32	10	2	.354/.431/.617	.332	.371	-0.4	CF(31): -1.1, RF(17): -1.5	2.4
2013	ANA	MLB	25	222	29	7	2	8	32	21	41	2	2	.282/.347/.462	.294	.311	1.5	RF(54): 4.3, 1B(6): 0.5	1.8
2014	ANA	MLB	26	265	32	12	2	8	32	25	53	7	2	.262/.333/.427	.279	.300	0.4	RF 0, CF 0	1.2

No matter the level, Calhoun continues to hit professional pitching. In his first extended look in the majors, he was comfortable at the plate, showing a good eye, solid contact skills and more power than his frame might suggest. He uses a stutter-step slash toe-tap for timing, with most of his power coming to to his pull side. That said, he shows good plate coverage and can poke the ball the opposite way. He bullies pitches that move vertically, but struggles a bit when there is some horizontal tilt. In a continued trend, he was able to hold his own against left-handed pitchers, albeit in a limited selection. He has experience at three positions in the outfield and can fill in at first base if needed. Because of his bat, versatility and contract status, Calhoun should be a valuable role player going forward, with the capability for more with some additional seasoning.

Hank Conger   C
Born: 1/29/1988 Age: 26
Bats: B Throws: R Height: 6' 1"
Weight: 220 Breakout: 8%
Improve: 39% Collapse: 13%
Attrition: 18% MLB: 79%

Comparables:
Lou Marson, Jeff Mathis, Nick Hundley

YEAR	TEAM	LVL	AGE	PA	R	2B	3B	HR	RBI	BB	SO	SB	CS	AVG/OBP/SLG	TAv	BABIP	BRR	FRAA	WARP
2011	SLC	AAA	23	114	14	4	0	5	26	12	18	0	0	.300/.375/.490	.274	.325	-1.2	C(16): 0.1	0.4
2011	ANA	MLB	23	197	14	8	0	6	19	17	37	0	0	.209/.282/.356	.241	.231	0.3	C(56): -0.5	0.3
2012	SLC	AAA	24	288	48	17	0	10	42	19	49	2	0	.295/.347/.473	.272	.329	1.4	C(59): 0.1	1.7
2012	ANA	MLB	24	22	0	0	0	0	1	1	0	0	0	.167/.238/.167	.162	.158	-0.2	C(7): 0.1	-0.1
2013	ANA	MLB	25	255	23	13	1	7	21	17	61	0	1	.249/.310/.403	.259	.307	-0.2	C(71): -0.2	0.9
2014	ANA	MLB	26	250	26	11	1	6	27	20	49	0	0	.245/.311/.380	.256	.280	-0.5	C -1	0.9

For the first time in his big-league career, Conger showed he belonged—not just to us, but to baseball's version of Anna Wintour. The famously demanding Mike Scioscia praised Conger's improved pitch receiving, and simple framing metrics dig him too. He overcame a case of the near-yips in spring training and had perhaps his best season of throwing. As for his offense—always the B storyline for catchers in Anaheim—that OPS is better than league average when adjusted for ballpark, and his isolated power edges that of a typical catcher. The Angels protect him from lefties—including the minors, the switch-hitter has a bigger platoon split than most pure lefties—but don't be surprised if he sets another career high for playing time.

Kaleb Cowart   3B

Born: 6/2/1992 Age: 22
Bats: B Throws: R Height: 6' 3"
Weight: 195 Breakout: 1%
Improve: 1% Collapse: 0%
Attrition: 3% MLB: 3%

Comparables:
Jesus Guzman, Jedd Gyorko, Brent Morel

YEAR	TEAM	LVL	AGE	PA	R	2B	3B	HR	RBI	BB	SO	SB	CS	AVG/OBP/SLG	TAv	BABIP	BRR	FRAA	WARP
2012	CDR	A	20	290	42	16	3	9	54	22	44	9	4	.293/.348/.479	.284	.319	2.2	3B(63): 7.5	2.7
2012	SBR	A+	20	316	48	15	4	7	49	45	67	5	3	.259/.366/.426	.306	.316	-1.3	3B(62): 4.0	3.0
2013	ARK	AA	21	546	48	20	1	6	42	38	124	14	5	.221/.279/.301	.216	.280	3.1	3B(131): -10.8	-1.5
2014	ANA	MLB	22	250	21	9	1	3	22	16	64	2	1	.216/.269/.306	.218	.280	-0.2	3B -1, 1B 0	-0.6

Another season like 2013, and the pundits will go back to touting Cowart's promise on the mound over his skill with the bat. The 21-year-old switch-hitter failed to deliver the thump necessary to offset a 23 percent K rate, managing only an .080 isolated power mark. That was discouraging enough to prompt Angels GM Jerry Dipoto to use one of his few precious trade assets to patch the Halos' hole at third base (with David Freese) even before addressing gaping holes in the rotation. Cowart's potential for doubles, walks and standout defense keep him among the top five prospects in a dilapidated system, but he's off the fast track now, so he will return to Arkansas looking for his lost power stroke.

Collin Cowgill   CF

Born: 5/22/1986 Age: 28
Bats: R Throws: L Height: 5' 9"
Weight: 185 Breakout: 5%
Improve: 29% Collapse: 14%
Attrition: 23% MLB: 58%

Comparables:
Rajai Davis, Choo Freeman, Charles Thomas

YEAR	TEAM	LVL	AGE	PA	R	2B	3B	HR	RBI	BB	SO	SB	CS	AVG/OBP/SLG	TAv	BABIP	BRR	FRAA	WARP
2011	RNO	AAA	25	456	95	24	8	13	70	51	63	30	3	.354/.430/.554	.278	.397	1.8	CF(35): 3.3, RF(2): 0.0	1.5
2011	ARI	MLB	25	100	8	3	0	1	9	8	28	4	2	.239/.300/.304	.234	.333	-1.3	LF(18): 2.3, CF(10): -0.3	0.1
2012	SAC	AAA	26	285	33	17	1	4	37	20	50	8	2	.254/.312/.373	.261	.298	-0.4	CF(30): 0.9, LF(18): 0.2	1.0
2012	OAK	MLB	26	116	10	2	0	1	9	11	27	3	4	.269/.336/.317	.238	.351	-1	LF(16): 0.9, CF(15): -0.5	0.2
2013	LVG	AAA	27	145	22	6	0	5	12	17	25	4	0	.268/.366/.439	.267	.301	2.8	LF(18): 2.9, CF(14): -0.4	1.1
2013	ANA	MLB	27	99	11	3	2	2	8	5	27	1	0	.231/.271/.374	.256	.306	0.4	LF(26): -1.0, RF(17): 1.0	0.1
2013	NYN	MLB	27	63	7	2	0	2	8	2	15	0	0	.180/.206/.311	.209	.205	-0.4	CF(17): -1.5, LF(6): -0.2	-0.4
2014	ANA	MLB	28	250	30	10	1	4	20	18	56	9	2	.240/.299/.345	.246	.300	0.7	CF 0, LF 2	0.6

Cowgill escaped from Oakland, where he was lost behind more talented outfielders. After a brief stay in New York, he found himself trapped again—this time in Los Angeles traffic, vying for playing time in a congested group of Angels in the outfield. Cowgill can play all three outfield positions, but his production at the plate is most worthy of a role on the bench. He generates strikeout rates of a slugger without actually slugging. He can chase fly balls and take the extra base, which might be enough to keep him sporadically useful.

C.J. Cron   1B

Born: 1/5/1990 Age: 24
Bats: R Throws: R Height: 6' 4"
Weight: 235 Breakout: 1%
Improve: 4% Collapse: 5%
Attrition: 14% MLB: 15%

Comparables:
Mark Trumbo, Wes Bankston, Clint Robinson

YEAR	TEAM	LVL	AGE	PA	R	2B	3B	HR	RBI	BB	SO	SB	CS	AVG/OBP/SLG	TAv	BABIP	BRR	FRAA	WARP
2012	SBR	A+	22	557	73	32	2	27	123	17	72	3	4	.293/.327/.516	.301	.295	-5.2	1B(95): -0.2	2.7
2013	ARK	AA	23	565	56	36	1	14	83	23	83	8	4	.274/.319/.428	.278	.298	-1.5	1B(124): 2.2	1.6
2014	ANA	MLB	24	250	23	12	0	7	29	5	46	0	0	.248/.274/.392	.246	.280	-0.5	1B 0	-0.1

Cron has benefitted mightily from the launching-pad parks he's hit in since his amateur days. When he's had friendly environments—in the Pioneer League, the Arizona Fall League and on the road in the California League—he has slashed a cumulative .327/.371/.635. Good times. On the flip side, while playing in more difficult home parks at Inland Empire and Arkansas, he has managed to hit only .275/.314/.418 in 526 at-bats. Not what you'd like to see from a first-round investment who will have to earn his keep hitting into Anaheim's marine layer night after night. Cron also had issues with same-side pitching in 2013, resulting in a paltry .258/.297/.400 line against a pretty good cohort of Texas League righties. He's got that rep for elite power to all fields—earned with batting practice displays and the occasional in-game bomb—but how many home runs will he have to hit in Salt Lake to make himself relevant to Anaheim?

David Freese 3B

Born: 4/28/1983 Age: 31
Bats: R Throws: R Height: 6' 2"
Weight: 225 Breakout: 0%
Improve: 35% Collapse: 10%
Attrition: 11% MLB: 93%

Comparables:
Ty Wigginton, Eric Chavez, Joe Torre

YEAR	TEAM	LVL	AGE	PA	R	2B	3B	HR	RBI	BB	SO	SB	CS	AVG/OBP/SLG	TAv	BABIP	BRR	FRAA	WARP
2011	SLN	MLB	28	363	41	16	1	10	55	24	75	1	0	.297/.350/.441	.279	.356	-3.3	3B(88): 0.3, 1B(5): -0.1	1.6
2012	SLN	MLB	29	567	70	25	1	20	79	57	122	3	3	.293/.372/.467	.290	.352	-3.5	3B(134): 2.3	3.2
2013	SLN	MLB	30	521	53	26	1	9	60	47	106	1	2	.262/.340/.381	.252	.320	-1.6	3B(132): -14.6	-0.4
2014	ANA	MLB	31	501	54	22	1	13	58	43	112	2	1	.270/.340/.407	.277	.330	-1.1	3B -6, 1B -0	1.4

Freese's modest production caused some to suggest he was living off his 2011 postseason glory and a change was necessary. That overlooks the fact that he was quite good in 2012. No, the problem in 2013 was the same one that caused his late bloom in the first place: shoddy health. A lower back issue grounded him to start the season and seemed to linger, sapping his power. Freese remains one of baseball's most fly ball-averse batsmen, and some regression from his 20 percent homer-per-fly ratio in 2012 was all but guaranteed. Still, a meager .119 isolated power is an overcorrection. The Angels acquired him to fill the hole left by the Alberto Callaspo trade, and if he regains his health he'll fit nicely for two years before hitting free agency at 33. Retaining him beyond that point would probably suck.

Grant Green 2B

Born: 9/27/1987 Age: 26
Bats: R Throws: R Height: 6' 3"
Weight: 180 Breakout: 12%
Improve: 37% Collapse: 9%
Attrition: 33% MLB: 61%

Comparables:
Eric Patterson, Ryan Adams, Danny Richar

YEAR	TEAM	LVL	AGE	PA	R	2B	3B	HR	RBI	BB	SO	SB	CS	AVG/OBP/SLG	TAv	BABIP	BRR	FRAA	WARP
2011	MID	AA	23	587	76	33	1	9	62	39	119	6	8	.291/.343/.408	.233	.355	-0.1	SS(29): -2.6, CF(15): -0.5	-0.2
2012	SAC	AAA	24	562	73	28	6	15	75	33	75	13	9	.296/.338/.458	.276	.320	1.7	LF(49): -2.1, CF(30): -0.8	2.6
2013	SAC	AAA	25	415	66	27	3	11	50	27	70	4	1	.325/.379/.500	.313	.376	-0.6	2B(73): -11.4, 1B(1): -0.1	2.3
2013	SLC	AAA	25	28	2	1	0	0	3	3	7	0	1	.333/.393/.375	.285	.444	0	3B(4): 0.3, 2B(2): 0.0	0.2
2013	ANA	MLB	25	137	16	8	1	1	16	10	38	0	0	.280/.336/.384	.260	.391	-0.9	2B(40): -3.1	-0.2
2013	OAK	MLB	25	16	0	0	0	0	0	1	0	6	0	0	.000/.000/.000	.027	.000	0	2B(5): -0.4	-0.5
2014	ANA	MLB	26	250	28	11	1	5	23	12	51	2	2	.263/.303/.384	.258	.310	-0.4	2B -3, LF -0	0.2

As it now stands, Dipoto's 2013 position player trades sum up to Alberto Callaspo, Peter Bourjos and Randal Grichuk for David Freese and Green. Seems obvious that the Halos lose that swap on paper, and most of the baseball world agrees. Green will have to play extremely well over the next five seasons to reverse that perception, and he hit enough with the Angels to make a good start of things. But a .391 BABIP masked contact issues that hint at collapse with more exposure to major-league pitching. His defense at second base was uninspiring, so his glove won't help him stick on the big-league roster. He'll duke it out with the more polished Andrew Romine for a bench spot, making a year in Salt Lake likely. He could use it.

Josh Hamilton RF

Born: 5/21/1981 Age: 33
Bats: L Throws: L Height: 6' 4"
Weight: 225 Breakout: 1%
Improve: 29% Collapse: 1%
Attrition: 8% MLB: 96%

Comparables:
Dave Winfield, Jayson Werth, Dale Murphy

YEAR	TEAM	LVL	AGE	PA	R	2B	3B	HR	RBI	BB	SO	SB	CS	AVG/OBP/SLG	TAv	BABIP	BRR	FRAA	WARP
2011	TEX	MLB	30	538	80	31	5	25	94	39	93	8	1	.298/.346/.536	.300	.317	-2	LF(85): 2.8, CF(35): 0.6	3.8
2012	TEX	MLB	31	636	103	31	2	43	128	60	162	7	4	.285/.354/.577	.310	.320	1.7	CF(95): -3.6, LF(84): -0.2	4.5
2013	ANA	MLB	32	636	73	32	5	21	79	47	158	4	0	.250/.307/.432	.269	.303	3.3	RF(83): 2.5, LF(19): 3.1	2.6
2014	ANA	MLB	33	598	74	30	3	24	83	45	136	7	2	.273/.330/.470	.289	.320	0	RF 1, LF 2	3.3

One of the many concerns about signing a 30-something veteran to a multi-year deal is durability. Add in various past ailments and unknown damage to his body due to previous substance abuse, and you can see why Angels fans were uneasy about Hamilton's signing last winter. The good news is Hamilton's body held up. He appeared in 150-plus games for the second time in his career, the first since 2008. The bad news is Hamilton hit like a middle infielder while cashing middle-of-the-order checks. He can still turn on a fastball, but sliders ... oh sliders are a problem. Nearly a third of his 158 strikeouts came on sliders, while almost half of his swings against the pitch turned up empty. Though his best days are behind him, Hamilton still has enough skill—most notably power—to be a productive member of the lineup. At least for the second year of his five-year pact, that is.

Chris Iannetta C

Born: 4/8/1983 Age: 31
Bats: R Throws: R Height: 6' 0"
Weight: 230 Breakout: 0%
Improve: 33% Collapse: 6%
Attrition: 9% MLB: 94%

Comparables:
Chris Snyder, Johnny Romano, Joe Ferguson

YEAR	TEAM	LVL	AGE	PA	R	2B	3B	HR	RBI	BB	SO	SB	CS	AVG/OBP/SLG	TAv	BABIP	BRR	FRAA	WARP
2011	COL	MLB	28	426	51	17	1	14	55	70	89	6	3	.238/.370/.414	.271	.276	-1	C(105): -0.1, 1B(2): -0.0	2.5
2012	SLC	AAA	29	25	3	2	0	0	2	3	7	0	0	.273/.360/.364	.260	.400	-0.2	C(4): -0.0	0.1
2012	ANA	MLB	29	253	27	6	1	9	26	29	60	1	3	.240/.332/.398	.267	.288	0.1	C(78): -0.5	1.5
2013	ANA	MLB	30	399	40	15	0	11	39	68	100	0	1	.225/.358/.372	.275	.284	-3.1	C(113): -0.9	1.4
2014	ANA	MLB	31	349	42	12	1	11	39	48	82	2	1	.222/.339/.379	.269	.270	-0.8	C 0, 3B -0	1.9

Iannetta's second season with the Angels went much better than his first, not because his numbers were markedly better—they weren't—but because he stayed healthy. When right, Iannetta combines a healthy walk rate with a decent amount of pop. Add it together and it's enough to make up for brutal batting averages. Given Conger's emergence and the team-friendly extension Iannetta signed after the 2012 season, the veteran's value to the Angels heading forward could extend beyond the playing field and into trade negotiations.

Raul Ibanez   LF

Born: 6/2/1972 Age: 42
Bats: L Throws: R Height: 6' 2''
Weight: 225 Breakout: 0%
Improve: 13% Collapse: 25%
Attrition: 36% MLB: 69%

Comparables:
Hank Sauer, Matt Stairs, Dave Winfield

YEAR	TEAM	LVL	AGE	PA	R	2B	3B	HR	RBI	BB	SO	SB	CS	AVG/OBP/SLG	TAv	BABIP	BRR	FRAA	WARP
2011	PHI	MLB	39	575	65	31	1	20	84	33	106	2	0	.245/.289/.419	.264	.268	-0.6	LF(134): -4.2	0.8
2012	NYA	MLB	40	425	50	19	3	19	62	35	67	3	0	.240/.308/.453	.264	.243	0.7	LF(80): 0.2, RF(13): -1.1	0.8
2013	SEA	MLB	41	496	54	20	2	29	65	42	128	0	0	.242/.306/.487	.288	.273	-1.9	LF(99): -4.1, RF(1): -0.1	1.3
2014	ANA	MLB	42	452	48	20	2	15	56	35	93	2	0	.240/.300/.408	.262	.270	-0.4	LF -1, RF -1	0.7

Death, taxes and Ibanez's power stroke. Ibanez is one of just five players to take at least 300 PA and record an isolated power of at least .150 every year since the turn of the millennium, along with Albert Pujols, Alfonso Soriano, Aramis Ramirez and David Ortiz. Ibanez posted his highest slugging percentage and home run total in four years in a move to Seattle that was initially seen as a victory lap for a solid career. His limitations are severe: The strikeout rate jumped to a career-high 26 percent, he is a statue in the outfield and he can't post the on-base percentage necessary to justify the lack of positional value. But he can still put a hurt on the ball, and the Angels signed him cheap to replace Mark Trumbo's high-slug/low-OBP slash line at DH.

Luis Jimenez   3B

Born: 1/18/1988 Age: 26
Bats: R Throws: R Height: 6' 1''
Weight: 205 Breakout: 3%
Improve: 9% Collapse: 9%
Attrition: 17% MLB: 23%

Comparables:
Russell Mitchell, Angel Chavez, Jeff Baisley

YEAR	TEAM	LVL	AGE	PA	R	2B	3B	HR	RBI	BB	SO	SB	CS	AVG/OBP/SLG	TAv	BABIP	BRR	FRAA	WARP
2011	ARK	AA	23	541	62	40	1	18	94	27	72	15	6	.290/.335/.486	.262	.303	0.8	3B(81): 1.6	2.1
2012	SLC	AAA	24	517	78	38	2	16	85	19	70	17	7	.309/.334/.495	.272	.331	-0.3	3B(118): 16.9	4.8
2013	SLC	AAA	25	218	28	9	2	4	42	12	26	11	3	.284/.326/.411	.260	.301	1.6	3B(36): 3.4, SS(6): 0.0	1.5
2013	ANA	MLB	25	110	15	6	0	0	5	2	28	0	2	.260/.291/.317	.240	.351	-1.3	3B(29): 3.6, 1B(2): -0.0	0.6
2014	ANA	MLB	26	250	25	13	0	5	25	9	46	6	2	.250/.281/.367	.241	.290	0	3B 5, SS -0	0.6

Jimenez received his first cup of coffee last season and spat it out. Forever known as a bat-only prospect, his affinity for singles and doubles didn't translate to the majors. His undisciplined approach, meanwhile, is more of a universally understood frown. Not only did he strike out 14 times as often as he walked, but he also looked helpless against soft or spinning. Though the Angels left him at third base for most of his minor-league career, they finally experimented with him at other positions in Salt Lake. Indications have always been that his defense is just average, but the Angels even tried him at shortstop—delusional, perhaps; desperate, maybe; but a telling indication of what they see in him.

Howard Kendrick   2B

Born: 7/12/1983 Age: 30
Bats: R Throws: R Height: 5' 10''
Weight: 205 Breakout: 0%
Improve: 46% Collapse: 5%
Attrition: 7% MLB: 93%

Comparables:
Ryne Sandberg, Brandon Phillips, Kelly Johnson

YEAR	TEAM	LVL	AGE	PA	R	2B	3B	HR	RBI	BB	SO	SB	CS	AVG/OBP/SLG	TAv	BABIP	BRR	FRAA	WARP
2011	ANA	MLB	27	583	86	30	6	18	63	33	119	14	6	.285/.338/.464	.280	.338	0.9	2B(108): 0.4, LF(23): -2.5	2.5
2012	ANA	MLB	28	594	57	32	3	8	67	29	115	14	6	.287/.325/.400	.262	.347	3.8	2B(143): 9.6, LF(2): 0.0	3.4
2013	ANA	MLB	29	513	55	21	4	13	54	23	89	6	3	.297/.335/.439	.290	.340	-6.6	2B(118): -1.2, LF(1): 0.0	2.0
2014	ANA	MLB	30	498	53	25	3	10	54	26	91	10	4	.281/.325/.412	.275	.330	0.1	2B 0, LF -0	2.4

Kendrick missed a month with a knee sprain late in the season, but once again flirted with a .300 average while showing good pop from the keystone position. Though he maintains a solid average, he is not a contact-driven hitter; he will expand his zone, strike out a bit and walk once a week. He makes it up with the ability to spoil good pitches, quick hands—especially on the inner half—and bat control that allows him to hit to all fields. Defensively, he is more substance than style as he rates average to slightly above-average at second base. Though he may never get that projected batting title, Kendrick remains good hitter, m.A.A.d city.

Taylor Lindsey   2B

Born: 12/2/1991 Age: 22
Bats: L Throws: R Height: 6' 0''
Weight: 195 Breakout: 4%
Improve: 17% Collapse: 10%
Attrition: 24% MLB: 31%

Comparables:
Luis Valbuena, Adrian Cardenas, Travis Denker

YEAR	TEAM	LVL	AGE	PA	R	2B	3B	HR	RBI	BB	SO	SB	CS	AVG/OBP/SLG	TAv	BABIP	BRR	FRAA	WARP
2012	SBR	A+	20	589	79	26	6	9	58	29	66	8	6	.289/.328/.408	.273	.313	-4.3	2B(123): 8.0	2.6
2013	ARK	AA	21	567	68	22	6	17	56	48	91	4	4	.274/.339/.441	.288	.303	0	2B(134): -6.2	2.3
2014	ANA	MLB	22	250	25	10	1	4	22	12	46	1	0	.246/.284/.357	.239	.280	-0.3	2B -0	0.2

Lindsey did his usual line-drives-to-all-fields thing in 2013, surprising no one. Say what you will about his unconventional setup, but he gets the bat into the zone quickly and can sting the baseball. What did surprise folks were the 17 bombs, and that pull power catapulted him to the top of Angels prospect lists. There were other positives too, including a 200-point jump in OPS against lefties and general competence at the keystone, something that his critics have acknowledged only begrudgingly. Overall, his bat projects as more solid than spectacular, but if Lindsey's power continues to grow even a little, he could surpass that. His contact rate and approach give him a high floor, so he should be ready to replace Howie Kendrick as a consistent two-plus win player by the time the latter's contract is up after 2015. That's assuming Lindsey's emergence and gaps in the Angels' rotation don't force a Kendrick trade first.

Efren Navarro 1B

Born: 5/14/1986 Age: 28
Bats: L Throws: L Height: 6' 0"
Weight: 200 Breakout: 3%
Improve: 4% Collapse: 2%
Attrition: 9% MLB: 9%

Comparables:
Blake Lalli, Micah Hoffpauir, Josh Kroeger

YEAR	TEAM	LVL	AGE	PA	R	2B	3B	HR	RBI	BB	SO	SB	CS	AVG/OBP/SLG	TAv	BABIP	BRR	FRAA	WARP
2011	SLC	AAA	25	547	76	36	6	12	73	42	78	5	5	.317/.368/.488	.275	.352	1.9	1B(101): -1.1, RF(1): 0.0	1.2
2011	ANA	MLB	25	12	1	1	0	0	0	1	1	0	0	.200/.273/.300	.181	.222	0	1B(8): -0.0	-0.1
2012	SLC	AAA	26	577	79	35	1	7	74	36	70	3	2	.294/.336/.403	.258	.321	1.1	1B(140): 1.7	1.4
2013	SLC	AAA	27	586	83	39	3	7	81	68	99	8	5	.326/.404/.454	.288	.390	1.7	1B(130): 2.8	3.2
2013	ANA	MLB	27	6	0	0	0	0	1	2	1	1	0	.250/.500/.250	.326	.333	0.1	1B(2): 0.1	0.1
2014	ANA	MLB	28	250	21	12	1	2	23	18	46	1	1	.254/.307/.342	.244	.300	-0.5	1B 0, RF -0	-0.2

Navarro might have been the world's best defensive first baseman in 2011 and 2012, but sadly, that's not enough to earn a big-league job when you hit like a middle infielder. He hit a little better than that last year, so the Halos added him to the 40-man roster rather than lose him to minor-league free agency, but it's unclear where he'll see playing time, either in Anaheim or Salt Lake.

Albert Pujols 1B

Born: 1/16/1980 Age: 34
Bats: R Throws: R Height: 6' 3"
Weight: 230 Breakout: 1%
Improve: 32% Collapse: 3%
Attrition: 5% MLB: 98%

Comparables:
Todd Helton, Lance Berkman, Ted Kluszewski

YEAR	TEAM	LVL	AGE	PA	R	2B	3B	HR	RBI	BB	SO	SB	CS	AVG/OBP/SLG	TAv	BABIP	BRR	FRAA	WARP
2011	SLN	MLB	31	651	105	29	0	37	99	61	58	9	1	.299/.366/.541	.317	.277	-0.9	1B(146): 13.3, 3B(7): 0.4	6.3
2012	ANA	MLB	32	670	85	50	0	30	105	52	76	8	1	.285/.343/.516	.302	.282	-2.8	1B(120): 7.1, 3B(3): -0.0	3.9
2013	ANA	MLB	33	443	49	19	0	17	64	40	55	1	1	.258/.330/.437	.285	.258	1.7	1B(34): 2.1	2.2
2014	ANA	MLB	34	461	65	24	0	23	72	51	54	6	1	.286/.368/.516	.317	.280	-0.2	1B 7, 3B 0	4.0

Think back to the 2009 season, just after Pujols won his third MVP award. He was 29 years old and the reigning NL leader in home runs, on-base percentage and slugging percentage. He was two years from free agency and a living legend in St. Louis. Think back to that time and imagine being told that Pujols would not be considered the best player in baseball once the 2014 season began. How about that Pujols would lose the crown to his 21-year-old teammate? Ridiculous, right? If that weren't enough, Pujols' last three seasons have been the worst three of his career, and he missed the final two months of the year due to injury.

None of this sounds like a positive development for the Angels, who have Pujols signed through the 2021 season, but there is good news to be found. The aging slugger had been hobbled with plantar fasciitis for almost a decade before he tore his plantar fascia last season. While that sounds bad, the torn fascia has the same effect as the operation that fixes the plantar fasciitis. As a result, Pujols' days of nagging foot pain should be over. Obviously, that doesn't mean Pujols is going to return to his Best Player In The World status, yet he should regain some mobility, overall speed (remember, he used to be a very good baserunner) and the lower-body leverage that was missing from his swing last year. Here's one last beacon of hope: Even at his worst, Pujols has still been a pretty good hitter. He might be overpaid going forward, but that doesn't mean he's a bad player.

Jose Rondon SS

Born: 3/3/1994 Age: 20
Bats: R Throws: R Height: 6' 1"
Weight: 160 Breakout: 0%
Improve: 0% Collapse: 0%
Attrition: 0% MLB: 0%

Comparables:
Didi Gregorius, Juan Diaz, Argenis Diaz

YEAR	TEAM	LVL	AGE	PA	R	2B	3B	HR	RBI	BB	SO	SB	CS	AVG/OBP/SLG	TAv	BABIP	BRR	FRAA	WARP
2014	ANA	MLB	20	250	19	8	0	1	14	11	62	1	1	.189/.226/.239	.178	.250	-0.4	SS 0	-1.1

In a system as thin as the Angels', the young-with-upside will attract attention, whatever their shortcomings. Rondon had something of a breakout year: He was a teenage shortstop who hit the snot out of the ball for two months, flashing bat speed, a polished batting eye and enough arm and athleticism to stick on the left side of the infield. But the million-dollar question with Rondon is whether he'll develop enough pop to be more than a utility player, and he didn't provide much fuel for optimism there. True, a wrist injury gives him a mulligan for the meager .106 isolated power that he posted in the hitter-happy Pioneer League, but he's managed only two home runs over three professional seasons. He's interesting, but remains a long way from claiming the "Angels' shortstop of the future" mantle.

J.B. Shuck LF
Born: 6/18/1987 Age: 27
Bats: L Throws: L Height: 5' 11"
Weight: 195 Breakout: 7%
Improve: 38% Collapse: 9%
Attrition: 22% MLB: 88%
Comparables: Jeremy Reed, Reggie Willits, Blake DeWitt

YEAR	TEAM	LVL	AGE	PA	R	2B	3B	HR	RBI	BB	SO	SB	CS	AVG/OBP/SLG	TAv	BABIP	BRR	FRAA	WARP
2011	OKL	AAA	24	419	60	11	7	0	30	56	30	20	11	.297/.398/.367	.299	.323	-1.6	LF(14): 0.2, CF(2): -0.1	0.4
2011	HOU	MLB	24	92	9	2	1	0	3	11	7	2	0	.272/.359/.321	.244	.297	-0.2	RF(16): -0.0, CF(9): 0.7	0.1
2012	OKL	AAA	25	358	49	11	3	0	33	39	20	12	8	.298/.374/.352	.279	.316	3.3	LF(50): -0.1, RF(27): -0.6	1.7
2013	ANA	MLB	26	478	60	20	3	2	39	27	54	8	4	.293/.331/.366	.262	.325	0.6	LF(97): -3.4, RF(9): -0.1	0.7
2014	ANA	MLB	27	396	45	15	2	2	27	31	43	12	6	.275/.333/.343	.256	.300	-0.3	LF -3, RF -0	0.3

Shuck's season was a good litmus test for the Angels' season. Had he performed the same in half the plate appearances, people would've praised Dipoto's acquisition as prudent, the kind of move that separates the okay general managers from the good ones. Instead, Shuck led AL rookies in plate appearances; his presence as more than an extra outfielder is the kind of demand that separates the okay general managers from the good ones. He's a better ballplayer than his inability to make the Astros suggests, but Angels ain't Astros.

Mike Trout CF
Born: 8/7/1991 Age: 22
Bats: R Throws: R Height: 6' 2"
Weight: 230 Breakout: 2%
Improve: 56% Collapse: 1%
Attrition: 2% MLB: 93%
Comparables: Justin Upton, Jason Heyward, Giancarlo Stanton

YEAR	TEAM	LVL	AGE	PA	R	2B	3B	HR	RBI	BB	SO	SB	CS	AVG/OBP/SLG	TAv	BABIP	BRR	FRAA	WARP
2011	ARK	AA	19	412	82	18	13	11	38	45	76	33	10	.326/.414/.544	.316	.390	7.2	CF(73): -2.3, LF(1): -0.0	3.8
2011	ANA	MLB	19	135	20	6	0	5	16	9	30	4	0	.220/.281/.390	.260	.247	0.8	CF(13): 0.9, RF(13): -0.3	0.4
2012	SLC	AAA	20	93	21	4	5	1	13	11	16	6	1	.403/.467/.623	.360	.476	-0.4	CF(8): -0.9, LF(5): 0.2	1.1
2012	ANA	MLB	20	639	129	27	8	30	83	67	139	49	5	.326/.399/.564	.350	.383	7.9	CF(110): 3.9, LF(67): 2.2	8.9
2013	ANA	MLB	21	716	109	39	9	27	97	110	136	33	7	.323/.432/.557	.367	.376	1.7	CF(111): 0.1, LF(47): 2.2	10.4
2014	ANA	MLB	22	668	109	30	9	24	83	79	138	38	7	.305/.394/.512	.330	.360	4.8	CF -1, LF 3	7.3

What do you do to follow a rookie season in which you reach base nearly 40 percent of the time and smash 65 extra-base hits in 559 at-bats? You reach base *43* percent of the time and tally *10 more* extra-base knocks. A lightning-quick bat and tremendous strength give Trout ownership of the inner half of the plate, while a great eye, stick control and reach give him lease to the outer half as well. There is not a pitch he can't muscle to the replica of Pride Rock beyond the Angel Stadium fence. Trout's 10 Batter WARP season was higher than the output of several franchises. If he does not win an MVP award soon, Kanye West might need to jump on a stage to get the job done.

Alex Yarbrough 2B
Born: 8/3/1991 Age: 22
Bats: B Throws: R Height: 5' 11"
Weight: 180 Breakout: 2%
Improve: 7% Collapse: 3%
Attrition: 17% MLB: 22%
Comparables: Henry Rodriguez, Scooter Gennett, Jeff Bianchi

YEAR	TEAM	LVL	AGE	PA	R	2B	3B	HR	RBI	BB	SO	SB	CS	AVG/OBP/SLG	TAv	BABIP	BRR	FRAA	WARP
2012	CDR	A	20	257	35	12	9	0	27	10	20	9	2	.287/.320/.410	.254	.312	0.6	2B(58): -1.2	0.5
2013	SBR	A+	21	615	77	32	10	11	80	27	106	14	4	.313/.341/.459	.302	.364	0.5	2B(126): -19.9	2.4
2014	ANA	MLB	22	250	18	10	2	2	22	6	50	1	0	.245/.262/.331	.223	.300	-0.1	2B -6	-0.7

There wasn't much great pitching in the Cal League in 2013, so facing Giants' flamethrower Kyle Crick was perhaps the sternest test for the High-A 66ers last year. Yarbrough passed with the highest marks, turning around mid-90s heat with ease. Bad luck robbed him of two hits, but he stung the baseball and affirmed projections that his hit tool will play against the best competition. It will need to, because otherwise he's just a fringe guy with little defensive utility and below-average secondary skills. Despite leading the minors in hits, Yarbrough eked out only a .800 OPS in a hitters league. Think Alexi Amarista, but without the knack for spectacular playmaking.

PITCHERS

R.J. Alvarez
Born: 6/8/1991 Age: 23
Bats: R Throws: R Height: 6' 1" Weight: 180
Breakout: 46% Improve: 50% Collapse: 22%
Attrition: 47% MLB: 12%
Comparables: Steven Geltz, Donnie Joseph, Sammy Gervacio

YEAR	TEAM	LVL	AGE	W	L	SV	G	GS	IP	H	HR	BB	SO	BB9	SO9	GB%	BABIP	WHIP	ERA	FIP	FRA	WARP
2012	CDR	A	21	3	2	0	23	0	27^1	22	2	11	38	3.6	12.5	46%	.303	1.21	3.29	3.28	4.65	0.4
2013	SBR	A+	22	4	2	4	37	2	48^2	34	2	27	79	5.0	14.6	38%	.327	1.25	2.96	2.85	2.56	1.6
2014	ANA	MLB	23	2	1	1	32	0	38^2	34	4	20	44	4.6	10.3	42%	.309	1.39	3.92	4.09	4.26	0.2

Since Mike Trout graduated from the farm, the common refrain has been that the Angels have little immediate help on the way. That rang false in 2013, when the Angels graduated a group that together ranked toward the top of the league in rookie contributions. Guys like Kole Calhoun and Dane de la Rosa might be role players, but they played their roles well. Alvarez is the best bet to claim a role in

2014. His fastball is flat-out nasty in a Frieri sort of way, with plus-plus movement to go with big velocity. He's still experimenting with the right shape and velocity for his breaking ball, which is a big bender running from the high 70s to low 80s. It can look like a monster pitch—straight out of a video game—but the professionals think it'll need to tighten up to fool big leaguers regularly. Barring injury or collapse, Alvarez should get a big-league look before 2014 is out.

Cam Bedrosian
Born: **10/2/1991** Age: **22**
Bats: **R** Throws: **R** Height: **6' 0"** Weight: **205**
Breakout: **0%** Improve: **0%** Collapse: **0%**
Attrition: **0%** MLB: **0%**

Comparables:
Charles Brewer, Garrett Olson, Alberto Cabrera

YEAR	TEAM	LVL	AGE	W	L	SV	G	GS	IP	H	HR	BB	SO	BB9	SO9	GB%	BABIP	WHIP	ERA	FIP	FRA	WARP
2012	CDR	A	20	3	11	0	21	21	82²	91	5	52	48	5.7	5.2	47%	.316	1.73	6.31	5.15	6.47	-0.2
2013	BUR	A	21	1	5	7	37	2	54¹	55	4	22	69	3.6	11.4	57%	.362	1.42	5.30	3.25	6.04	0.8
2014	ANA	MLB	22	2	2	1	34	5	54²	63	7	35	33	5.7	5.4	47%	.314	1.79	6.07	5.96	6.60	-1.1

After succumbing to Tommy John surgery in 2010, Bedrosian took the long road back to relevance. He's throwing hard again, and sat at 91-94 mph while touching 96 mph in the Arizona Fall League. He lives and dies by the four-seamer: At its best, the fastball shows explosive life, especially in the upper slice of the strike zone. At its worst, the heater is predictable and lifeless, tending to drift up thigh-high when he misses the low target. He made an attempt to diversify last year by adding a cutter, and his command of the pitch led to promising early returns. The 13:2 K/BB ratio he posted in the AFL was a career best. Toss in a decent breaking ball that flashes plus, and Bedrosian has the makings of a quality high-leverage reliever. That is, if he can just tame that fastball.

Jeremy Berg
Born: **7/17/1986** Age: **27**
Bats: **R** Throws: **R** Height: **6' 0"** Weight: **180**
Breakout: **22%** Improve: **56%** Collapse: **30%**
Attrition: **53%** MLB: **34%**

Comparables:
Rob Wooten, Jesse Carlson, Leo Rosales

YEAR	TEAM	LVL	AGE	W	L	SV	G	GS	IP	H	HR	BB	SO	BB9	SO9	GB%	BABIP	WHIP	ERA	FIP	FRA	WARP
2011	ARK	AA	24	2	1	0	9	0	12¹	13	2	3	10	2.2	7.3	59%	.276	1.30	3.65	5.32	3.17	0.2
2011	SLC	AAA	24	1	1	3	43	0	61¹	64	1	24	47	3.5	6.9	54%	.366	1.43	4.70	3.83	4.40	1.2
2012	SLC	AAA	25	2	2	0	46	1	70¹	70	8	19	68	2.4	8.7	46%	.312	1.27	3.97	4.23	4.43	1.2
2013	SLC	AAA	26	5	0	1	52	0	76¹	69	6	17	69	2.0	8.1	39%	.292	1.13	2.71	3.65	3.71	1.8
2014	ANA	MLB	27	2	1	2	45	0	66¹	63	6	20	56	2.7	7.6	46%	.297	1.25	3.52	3.88	3.82	0.7

Over 208 Pacific Coast League innings, Berg has posted a 3.72 ERA while striking out 184 batters and yielding just six home runs. He might not be closer material, but given the Halos' years of bullpen woes, it's bonkers that the sidearmer has yet to get a shot at big leaguers. Now buried behind the similar but superior Joe Smith, he'll likely get that shot only with a new club.

Joe Blanton
Born: **12/11/1980** Age: **33**
Bats: **R** Throws: **R** Height: **6' 2"** Weight: **220**
Breakout: **26%** Improve: **57%** Collapse: **22%**
Attrition: **9%** MLB: **85%**

Comparables:
Harvey Haddix, Jon Lieber, Shane Reynolds

YEAR	TEAM	LVL	AGE	W	L	SV	G	GS	IP	H	HR	BB	SO	BB9	SO9	GB%	BABIP	WHIP	ERA	FIP	FRA	WARP
2011	PHI	MLB	30	1	2	0	11	8	41¹	52	5	9	35	2.0	7.6	58%	.360	1.48	5.01	3.60	4.19	0.1
2012	LAN	MLB	31	2	4	0	10	10	57²	66	7	16	51	2.5	8.0	48%	.352	1.42	4.99	3.78	4.65	0.3
2012	PHI	MLB	31	8	9	0	21	20	133¹	141	22	18	115	1.2	7.8	43%	.304	1.19	4.59	4.03	4.25	1.1
2013	ANA	MLB	32	2	14	0	28	20	132²	180	29	34	108	2.3	7.3	45%	.345	1.61	6.04	5.15	5.58	-0.9
2014	ANA	MLB	33	7	8	0	22	22	126²	145	20	30	97	2.2	6.9	45%	.317	1.38	4.84	4.65	5.26	-0.6

A decent idea gone wrong, part one. When the Angels signed Blanton, it looked like a match. Dipoto wanted an innings eater near the back of his rotation, someone with limited flaws who the club could count on every fifth day. Blanton was coming from Philadelphia, where his skill set didn't match the grounds; Anaheim's big outfield and fleet outfielders should have cured his ills. Instead, he continued to allow too many home runs. It's now more than 800 flies since his HR/FB rate vaulted way over the league's average; regression is not only not coming, it's running in the other direction. On the bright side: The deal's half over.

Buddy Boshers
Born: **5/9/1988** Age: **26**
Bats: **L** Throws: **L** Height: **6' 3"** Weight: **205**
Breakout: **68%** Improve: **79%** Collapse: **7%**
Attrition: **45%** MLB: **26%**

Comparables:
Sergio Escalona, Jeremy Horst, Miguel Socolovich

YEAR	TEAM	LVL	AGE	W	L	SV	G	GS	IP	H	HR	BB	SO	BB9	SO9	GB%	BABIP	WHIP	ERA	FIP	FRA	WARP
2011	SBR	A+	23	2	5	1	43	4	75¹	88	7	41	61	4.9	7.3	41%	.306	1.71	4.30	5.21	7.73	-0.2
2012	SBR	A+	24	4	2	1	26	0	39¹	30	4	16	48	3.7	11.0	55%	.263	1.17	2.52	3.92	4.74	0.4
2012	ARK	AA	24	1	0	0	19	0	24	28	3	5	27	1.9	10.1	56%	.357	1.38	3.75	3.41	3.63	0.4
2013	ARK	AA	25	3	2	1	28	0	28²	20	1	13	35	4.1	11.0	51%	.279	1.15	3.14	2.43	2.72	0.7
2013	SLC	AAA	25	1	0	1	16	0	19²	18	1	12	26	5.5	11.9	56%	.347	1.53	3.66	3.42	3.97	0.5
2013	ANA	MLB	25	0	0	0	25	0	15¹	13	0	8	13	4.7	7.6	44%	.317	1.37	4.70	3.14	2.90	0.2
2014	ANA	MLB	26	2	1	0	38	2	52²	55	6	24	43	4.1	7.2	48%	.309	1.50	4.77	4.68	5.19	-0.3

Before 2012, Boshers appeared headed for a short career as A-ball bullpen filler. Then the lefty's stuff took a big step forward, precipitating a rapid rise through the system that culminated in a 2013 big-league debut. He impressed with the Angels, touching the mid-90s with his fastball and spinning a curveball with nice depth. The lefty specialist job looks like his to lose going into spring training, but he'll have to cut down on the walks to make the gig permanent.

Sean Burnett

Born: 9/17/1982 Age: 31
Bats: L Throws: L Height: 6' 1" Weight: 180
Breakout: 23% Improve: 52% Collapse: 29%
Attrition: 12% MLB: 89%

Comparables:
Peter Moylan, Chad Qualls, Greg McMichael

YEAR	TEAM	LVL	AGE	W	L	SV	G	GS	IP	H	HR	BB	SO	BB9	SO9	GB%	BABIP	WHIP	ERA	FIP	FRA	WARP
2011	WAS	MLB	28	5	5	4	69	0	56²	54	6	21	33	3.3	5.2	56%	.268	1.32	3.81	4.48	5.14	-0.4
2012	WAS	MLB	29	1	2	2	70	0	56²	58	4	12	57	1.9	9.1	60%	.331	1.24	2.38	2.84	3.15	0.9
2013	ANA	MLB	30	0	0	0	13	0	9²	9	1	4	7	3.7	6.5	66%	.286	1.34	0.93	4.21	4.58	0.0
2014	ANA	MLB	31	2	1	1	43	0	36	33	3	12	31	3.0	7.7	52%	.287	1.24	3.33	3.74	3.62	0.5

Signed to a two-year deal in the winter, Burnett had been one of the league's best left-handed specialists but never got the chance to prove it to Angels fans. He hit the disabled list a few appearances in with forearm inflammation, and returned for a beat before heading back to the DL with elbow discomfort. Burnett's season ended there, as he underwent surgery for a torn flexor tendon in his throwing arm. The good news is he should be right as rain by the time you read this. Whether he is a few weeks from now is anybody's guess.

Dane De La Rosa

Born: 2/1/1983 Age: 31
Bats: R Throws: R Height: 6' 7" Weight: 245
Breakout: 34% Improve: 61% Collapse: 28%
Attrition: 26% MLB: 28%

Comparables:
Josh Kinney, Tim Hamulack, Chris Schroder

YEAR	TEAM	LVL	AGE	W	L	SV	G	GS	IP	H	HR	BB	SO	BB9	SO9	GB%	BABIP	WHIP	ERA	FIP	FRA	WARP
2011	DUR	AAA	28	6	5	6	52	0	70¹	63	8	26	83	3.3	10.6	56%	.300	1.27	3.20	3.63	3.78	0.4
2011	TBA	MLB	28	0	0	0	7	0	7¹	10	1	3	8	3.7	9.8	52%	.409	1.77	9.82	3.88	3.71	0.1
2012	DUR	AAA	29	0	4	20	54	0	67²	36	2	42	87	5.6	11.6	41%	.239	1.15	2.79	3.01	4.17	0.8
2012	TBA	MLB	29	0	0	0	5	0	5	7	2	2	5	3.6	9.0	53%	.385	1.80	12.60	7.45	10.34	-0.2
2013	ANA	MLB	30	6	1	2	75	0	72¹	56	3	28	65	3.5	8.1	53%	.275	1.16	2.86	3.02	3.61	0.7
2014	ANA	MLB	31	3	1	1	51	0	62	55	5	26	61	3.8	8.8	49%	.298	1.30	3.36	3.73	3.66	0.8

After struggling to find regular work in Tampa Bay, the "Dude" returned to his home state and quickly gained Mike Scioscia's trust; had he not spent the first week of the season in Triple-A he might have set a new franchise record for appearances. Equipped with a big frame, he relied heavily on a mid-90s fastball that served as judge, jury and executioner on most nights. A pair of 80-something secondary pitches serve as character witnesses to the heater. Improved control lowered his walk rate while producing a decent amount of strikeouts and groundballs. With a sense of belonging and the stuff to miss bats, he might be able to work his laid-back style into a high-stress role.

Ernesto Frieri

Born: 7/19/1985 Age: 28
Bats: R Throws: R Height: 6' 2" Weight: 205
Breakout: 41% Improve: 55% Collapse: 34%
Attrition: 23% MLB: 69%

Comparables:
Tyler Clippard, Matt Riley, Fernando Cabrera

YEAR	TEAM	LVL	AGE	W	L	SV	G	GS	IP	H	HR	BB	SO	BB9	SO9	GB%	BABIP	WHIP	ERA	FIP	FRA	WARP
2011	SDN	MLB	25	1	2	0	59	0	63	51	3	34	76	4.9	10.9	24%	.314	1.35	2.71	3.25	2.77	1.0
2012	SDN	MLB	26	1	0	0	11	0	11²	9	2	4	18	3.1	13.9	27%	.292	1.11	2.31	3.82	4.04	0.0
2012	ANA	MLB	26	4	2	23	56	0	54¹	26	7	26	80	4.3	13.3	27%	.188	0.96	2.32	3.49	3.48	0.9
2013	ANA	MLB	27	2	4	37	67	0	68²	55	11	30	98	3.9	12.8	26%	.293	1.24	3.80	3.75	3.12	1.1
2014	ANA	MLB	28	3	1	21	58	0	59	47	6	27	69	4.1	10.5	30%	.284	1.25	3.42	3.81	3.72	0.7

Frieri had his worst season as a big leaguer, posting an ERA above 3.00 for the first time. The fly-ball pitcher allowed 11 home runs despite playing his home games in a park that plays big—especially by the time Frieri enters, when the night air is damp and heavy. His game plan is simple: blow fastballs past his opponents. He uses a funky delivery that includes crossing his front leg over his back leg and a herky-jerk move with his hand. The ball explodes on the hitter with mid-90s heat, and he backs it up with a mid-80s slider and occasional off-speed pitch. Even in a frustrating season, he maintained an elite level of strikeouts. Whether he is a closer or not, he is a late-inning weapon on the right side of 30 and a few years from free agency.

Hunter Green

Born: 7/12/1995 Age: 18
Bats: L Throws: L Height: 6' 4" Weight: 175
Breakout: 0% Improve: 0% Collapse: 0%
Attrition: 0% MLB: 0%

Comparables:
Aneury Rodriguez, Julio Teheran, Martin Perez

YEAR	TEAM	LVL	AGE	W	L	SV	G	GS	IP	H	HR	BB	SO	BB9	SO9	GB%	BABIP	WHIP	ERA	FIP	FRA	WARP
2014	ANA	MLB	18	2	4	0	12	12	30²	39	4	21	11	6.2	3.1	43%	.311	1.97	7.01	6.68	7.62	-0.7

As the Angels' top pick (albeit a second-rounder) in a year when their farm was universally hailed as hitting rock bottom, Green and his arm hold a lot of symbolic value. Sadly for the Angels, the early returns were disappointing: The 18-year-old lefty coughed up 16 walks in 16-plus complex innings while striking out just 11. His delivery and subsequent control were a mess. After draft-day reports had touted plus velocity, his fastball frequently dipped to the mid-

80s. He may have all of the makings of a big-league starter, with athleticism, arm speed and feel for a changeup, but he and the Angels have a very long way to go before he becomes poster boy for a resurgent system.

	YEAR	TEAM	LVL	AGE	W	L	SV	G	GS	IP	H	HR	BB	SO	BB9	SO9	GB%	BABIP	WHIP	ERA	FIP	FRA	WARP
Juan Gutierrez Born: 7/14/1983 Age: 30 Bats: R Throws: R Height: 6' 3'' Weight: 245 Breakout: 34% Improve: 69% Collapse: 23% Attrition: 12% MLB: 75% **Comparables:** Chris Ray, Nick Masset, Scott Stewart	2011	ARI	MLB	27	0	0	0	20	0	18¹	22	3	9	23	4.4	11.3	46%	.358	1.69	5.40	4.25	4.24	0.1
	2012	OMA	AAA	28	0	1	0	10	0	11	13	2	3	7	2.5	5.7	23%	.297	1.45	8.18	5.57	6.03	0.0
	2013	ANA	MLB	29	1	4	0	28	0	26	26	3	12	28	4.2	9.7	42%	.315	1.46	5.19	3.81	4.28	0.1
	2013	KCA	MLB	29	0	1	0	25	0	29¹	30	2	8	17	2.5	5.2	41%	.304	1.30	3.38	3.72	4.07	0.3
	2014	ANA	MLB	30	2	1	0	42	0	42²	42	5	16	36	3.3	7.7	44%	.301	1.36	4.03	4.44	4.38	0.2

Gutierrez resurfaced in the majors after missing the 2012 season due to Tommy John surgery. (In addition to the ulnar collateral, doctors replaced his first name with initials—Juan now goes by J.C.) The arm was healthy enough to fire mid-90s fastball after mid-90s fastball at batters, but there's something not quite right about the pudgy right-hander. He's one of those classic relievers with better stuff than results, mostly due to below-average command. E.g. with the Angels: He struck out about 10 batters per nine innings, yet allowed far too many hits and home runs to be effective with his walk rate. Gutierrez is likely to keep getting chances because he has a big arm and a few saves to his names, and he's likely to squander most of them.

	YEAR	TEAM	LVL	AGE	W	L	SV	G	GS	IP	H	HR	BB	SO	BB9	SO9	GB%	BABIP	WHIP	ERA	FIP	FRA	WARP
Tommy Hanson Born: 8/28/1986 Age: 27 Bats: R Throws: R Height: 6' 6'' Weight: 220 Breakout: 21% Improve: 58% Collapse: 25% Attrition: 12% MLB: 94% **Comparables:** Ervin Santana, Ian Snell, Phil Hughes	2011	ATL	MLB	24	11	7	0	22	22	130	106	17	46	142	3.2	9.8	41%	.270	1.17	3.60	3.64	4.16	1.1
	2012	ATL	MLB	25	13	10	0	31	31	174²	183	27	71	161	3.7	8.3	41%	.323	1.45	4.48	4.61	4.90	0.4
	2013	SLC	AAA	26	0	2	0	4	4	19²	23	5	6	15	2.7	6.9	41%	.281	1.47	5.49	6.42	6.50	0.0
	2013	ANA	MLB	26	4	3	0	15	13	73	83	10	30	56	3.7	6.9	33%	.320	1.55	5.42	4.68	4.33	0.6
	2014	ANA	MLB	27	6	6	0	19	19	99²	94	11	33	90	3.0	8.1	40%	.293	1.27	3.79	4.06	4.12	1.0

A decent idea gone wrong, part two. Dipoto tried patching his rotation by trading Jordan Walden to the Braves for Hanson. It was buying low all the way: The once-promising Hanson had fallen from favor in Atlanta due to injuries and spotty performance. Unfortunately, there was good reason for his stock's decline. Hanson's health issues had robbed his stuff of its former quality. His delivery, which relies on bow-and-arrow arm action and a high degree of shoulder abduction, portends future issues as well. Not long ago Hanson was a chic choice to become a front-of-the-rotation starter. Consider it a win if he's in a big-league rotation a year from now.

	YEAR	TEAM	LVL	AGE	W	L	SV	G	GS	IP	H	HR	BB	SO	BB9	SO9	GB%	BABIP	WHIP	ERA	FIP	FRA	WARP
Kevin Jepsen Born: 7/26/1984 Age: 29 Bats: R Throws: R Height: 6' 3'' Weight: 235 Breakout: 48% Improve: 61% Collapse: 25% Attrition: 19% MLB: 72% **Comparables:** Santiago Casilla, Yhency Brazoban, Chad Cordero	2011	SLC	AAA	26	1	3	7	24	0	28¹	32	4	8	20	2.5	6.4	49%	.316	1.41	4.45	5.05	5.67	0.3
	2011	ANA	MLB	26	1	2	0	16	0	13	21	2	9	6	6.2	4.2	56%	.380	2.31	7.62	6.45	5.94	-0.1
	2012	SLC	AAA	27	2	2	2	23	0	25	18	1	9	35	3.2	12.6	39%	.321	1.08	3.24	2.47	3.35	0.7
	2012	ANA	MLB	27	3	2	2	49	0	44²	39	3	12	38	2.4	7.7	37%	.293	1.14	3.02	3.16	3.74	0.6
	2013	ANA	MLB	28	1	3	0	45	0	36	41	3	14	36	3.5	9.0	42%	.345	1.53	4.50	3.41	4.17	0.3
	2014	ANA	MLB	29	2	1	1	44	0	39²	39	3	16	36	3.7	8.2	50%	.317	1.39	3.91	3.75	4.25	0.2

Mo' money, mo' problems. Commanding seven figures for the first time in his career, Jepsen spent half the season dealing with injuries. A shoulder sprain in early April and an appendectomy in late August disabled him for nearly 90 days. In between, he allowed more than a baserunner and a half per inning. Jepsen curtailed the use of his cutter for the traditional heater—a mid-90s pitch that is nonetheless hittable—while tossing a handful of curveballs and changeups to keep up appearances. The breaking ball flashes as an out pitch and could be a weapon against batters on either side of the plate. Perhaps in an attempt to find more consistency, Jepsen has stretched his arm action and flip-flopped spots on the rubber. One of these days he's going to figure it all out and leave opposing batters in a trail of tumbleweeds.

	YEAR	TEAM	LVL	AGE	W	L	SV	G	GS	IP	H	HR	BB	SO	BB9	SO9	GB%	BABIP	WHIP	ERA	FIP	FRA	WARP
Michael Kohn Born: 6/26/1986 Age: 28 Bats: R Throws: R Height: 6' 2'' Weight: 200 Breakout: 36% Improve: 51% Collapse: 38% Attrition: 39% MLB: 64% **Comparables:** Jason Motte, Jack Taschner, Rich Thompson	2011	SLC	AAA	25	1	3	12	46	0	48¹	47	5	20	64	3.7	11.9	45%	.375	1.39	4.10	3.91	4.54	1.0
	2011	ANA	MLB	25	0	1	1	14	0	12¹	14	6	9	9	6.6	6.6	24%	.229	1.86	7.30	10.36	10.21	-0.6
	2013	ANA	MLB	27	1	4	0	63	0	53	42	7	28	52	4.8	8.8	24%	.248	1.32	3.74	4.58	3.20	0.5
	2014	ANA	MLB	28	2	1	1	42	0	40¹	34	4	21	44	4.6	9.9	37%	.292	1.36	3.79	4.13	4.12	0.3

Kohn made a successful return to the mound after Tommy John surgery wiped out his 2012 season. A former position player in college, Kohn is still finding himself as a pitcher. He no longer short arms the ball to the plate, and is throwing from a higher release point, likely in an effort to find the control that has eluded him as a professional. He hides the ball well versus right-handers before exploding through the zone with a mid-90s fastball with arm-side run. One would think lefties would have a better look, but they too have struggled to hit his heater. Fastball aside, he mixes in a hard slider that is average and experiments with a changeup at times. If you squint you can see the makings of a high-leverage reliever, but blink and you might come up with a replacement-level hurler.

Michael Morin

Born: 5/3/1991 Age: 23
Bats: R Throws: R Height: 6' 4" Weight: 218
Breakout: 8% Improve: 12% Collapse: 88%
Attrition: 92% MLB: 19%

Comparables:
Fernando Hernandez, Osiris Matos, Daniel Stange

YEAR	TEAM	LVL	AGE	W	L	SV	G	GS	IP	H	HR	BB	SO	BB9	SO9	GB%	BABIP	WHIP	ERA	FIP	FRA	WARP
2013	SBR	A+	22	3	1	13	30	0	39	30	2	5	43	1.2	9.9	42%	.297	0.90	1.85	2.69	3.33	0.9
2013	ARK	AA	22	0	2	10	26	0	31	26	2	5	33	1.5	9.6	51%	.296	1.00	2.03	2.44	2.76	0.7
2014	ANA	MLB	23	2	1	2	38	0	49^1	50	5	18	41	3.3	7.4	45%	.307	1.38	4.14	4.20	4.51	0.1

Morin followed a ridiculously good season split between High-A and Double-A with a solid showing in the Arizona Fall League. He put up a combined WHIP of 0.89 while fanning 28 percent of all the batters he faced in 2013. His fastball rarely tops 92 mph, but he can pull the string down to the low 70s with a dynamite changeup, and he keeps hitters further off balance by varying the shape and velocity of a breaking ball that runs up to 80. He's a good bet to see big-league time in 2014, and might just carve out a role as a bullpen mainstay for the next half-decade.

Mark Mulder

Born: 8/5/1977 Age: 36
Bats: L Throws: L Height: 6' 6" Weight: 200

YEAR	TEAM	LVL	AGE	W	L	SV	G	GS	IP	H	HR	BB	SO	BB9	SO9	GB%	BABIP	WHIP	ERA	FIP	FRA	WARP
2014	–	–	–	–	–	–	–	–	–	–	–	–	–	–	–	–	–	–	–	–	–	–

As we neared our print date, Mulder was said to be closing in on a deal with the Angels, more than five years after he threw his final pitch in the majors. That pitch was ball four; it knocked him out of his final start in the first inning; it boosted his ERA to 10.80 in his final season and to 7.73 in his final three seasons. We don't know if he signed that minor-league contract, we don't know whether he'll pitch, and if he does we don't know how he'll do. But we know one thing: Oh, wait, no, actually we don't know one thing. We don't know anything about anything. About baseball, or phsyics, or aging, or the human condition. Mark Mulder. Mark Mulder!

Cory Rasmus

Born: 11/6/1987 Age: 26
Bats: R Throws: R Height: 6' 0" Weight: 200
Breakout: 74% Improve: 92% Collapse: 4%
Attrition: 48% MLB: 27%

Comparables:
Mike Dunn, Jake Diekman, Anthony Varvaro

YEAR	TEAM	LVL	AGE	W	L	SV	G	GS	IP	H	HR	BB	SO	BB9	SO9	GB%	BABIP	WHIP	ERA	FIP	FRA	WARP
2011	LYN	A+	23	1	5	0	7	7	26^2	28	5	12	40	4.1	13.5	39%	.354	1.50	7.09	4.47	5.51	-0.1
2012	MIS	AA	24	3	5	7	50	0	58^2	45	3	32	62	4.9	9.5	36%	.281	1.31	3.68	3.43	3.66	0.6
2013	GWN	AAA	25	3	1	14	37	0	36^2	20	2	22	48	5.4	11.8	42%	.240	1.15	1.72	3.18	3.50	0.7
2013	ATL	MLB	25	0	0	0	3	0	6^2	8	4	3	6	4.1	8.1	27%	.222	1.65	8.10	10.37	9.88	-0.3
2013	ANA	MLB	25	1	1	0	16	0	15	16	2	10	14	6.0	8.4	33%	.304	1.73	4.20	4.94	5.15	0.0
2014	ANA	MLB	26	3	2	0	29	5	54^2	54	7	31	46	5.1	7.5	39%	.297	1.55	4.93	5.17	5.36	-0.3

He touches 95 mph and has a three-pitch off-speed arsenal. He's raw and his command is mediocre—traits that PECOTA emphasizes in Rasmus' below-replacement-level projection—but if something clicks, the stuff is there for him to become a back-of-the-bullpen force. At some point, Dipoto has to catch a lucky break with his wheeling and dealing, and Rasmus' 2014 just might be it.

Garrett Richards

Born: 5/27/1988 Age: 26
Bats: R Throws: R Height: 6' 3" Weight: 215
Breakout: 46% Improve: 73% Collapse: 17%
Attrition: 18% MLB: 83%

Comparables:
Clayton Richard, Roberto Hernandez, Wade Miley

YEAR	TEAM	LVL	AGE	W	L	SV	G	GS	IP	H	HR	BB	SO	BB9	SO9	GB%	BABIP	WHIP	ERA	FIP	FRA	WARP
2011	ARK	AA	23	12	2	0	22	21	143	123	10	40	103	2.5	6.5	52%	.278	1.14	3.15	3.85	4.08	2.1
2011	ANA	MLB	23	0	2	0	7	3	14	16	4	7	9	4.5	5.8	43%	.286	1.64	5.79	6.99	6.99	-0.2
2012	SLC	AAA	24	7	3	0	14	14	77	87	5	35	65	4.1	7.6	52%	.346	1.58	4.21	4.42	4.41	1.6
2012	ANA	MLB	24	4	3	1	30	9	71	77	7	34	47	4.3	6.0	47%	.308	1.56	4.69	4.57	5.06	0.0
2013	ANA	MLB	25	7	8	1	47	17	145	151	12	44	101	2.7	6.3	59%	.302	1.34	4.16	3.69	4.62	0.3
2014	ANA	MLB	26	7	6	0	34	18	125^2	131	12	47	87	3.4	6.2	52%	.304	1.42	4.33	4.41	4.71	0.1

Richards entered the season as one of the club's best young pitchers—now there's faint praise—and exited no worse for the wear. The Angels used him out of the bullpen at the onset of the year, but an injury to Jered Weaver opened the door for him to make a few starts in late April. He returned to the bullpen until late July, when he rejoined the rotation for a 13-start trial run.

The results were good enough that Richards—who does his work with a mid-90s fastball and slider—should be in line to take a back-end rotation spot from the get-go in 2014.

Michael Roth

Born: 2/15/1990 Age: 24
Bats: L Throws: L Height: 6' 1" Weight: 210
Breakout: 44% Improve: 61% Collapse: 23%
Attrition: 53% MLB: 57%

Comparables:
Kyle Drabek, Shairon Martis, Ryan Tucker

YEAR	TEAM	LVL	AGE	W	L	SV	G	GS	IP	H	HR	BB	SO	BB9	SO9	GB%	BABIP	WHIP	ERA	FIP	FRA	WARP
2013	ARK	AA	23	6	3	0	17	15	79¹	77	8	36	51	4.1	5.8	50%	.290	1.42	4.20	4.78	5.60	-0.5
2013	ANA	MLB	23	1	1	0	15	1	20	24	0	6	17	2.7	7.7	42%	.375	1.50	7.20	2.43	3.24	0.4
2014	ANA	MLB	24	4	5	0	25	14	71²	79	8	33	44	4.1	5.5	47%	.307	1.56	5.06	5.15	5.50	-0.4

It's likely that no coach has ever told Roth to just throw strikes and trust his stuff ... because he's got no stuff. He has command, and he has guile, but he must live on the corners to avoid hard contact. That said, the 2012 draftee received little credit when he arrived in spring training firing 90-91 mph bullets after every offseason scouting report had pegged his fastball as mid-80s. The velocity didn't hold through the summer, but the springtime bump, combined with his smarts and the Angels' desperation, earned him 20 innings of big-league time. Roth undoubtedly needs more reps in the minors to master the crafty lefty craft, but the Angels' continued desperation might just mean more shots to be bullpen cannon fodder.

Fernando Salas

Born: 5/30/1985 Age: 29
Bats: R Throws: R Height: 6' 2" Weight: 210
Breakout: 31% Improve: 53% Collapse: 25%
Attrition: 18% MLB: 82%

Comparables:
George Sherrill, Darren O'Day, Jerry Blevins

YEAR	TEAM	LVL	AGE	W	L	SV	G	GS	IP	H	HR	BB	SO	BB9	SO9	GB%	BABIP	WHIP	ERA	FIP	FRA	WARP
2011	SLN	MLB	26	5	6	24	68	0	75	50	7	21	75	2.5	9.0	36%	.228	0.95	2.28	3.13	3.73	0.8
2012	SLN	MLB	27	1	4	0	65	0	58²	56	5	27	60	4.1	9.2	40%	.315	1.41	4.30	3.63	3.48	0.6
2013	MEM	AAA	28	1	2	12	22	0	23²	15	1	5	21	1.9	8.0	36%	.222	0.85	1.90	3.10	3.55	0.4
2013	SLN	MLB	28	0	3	0	27	0	28	27	3	6	22	1.9	7.1	34%	.282	1.18	4.50	3.59	4.08	0.2
2014	ANA	MLB	29	2	1	1	44	0	46	40	4	15	45	2.9	8.7	37%	.286	1.19	3.17	3.50	3.45	0.7

Remember when Salas was a closer? He was excellent in the role two years ago, but has since been relegated to low leverage with mixed success. His superfluousness in St. Louis got him included in the David Freese / Peter Bourjos trade, with Randal Grichuk heading to the Cardinals as well. He's still probably a middle reliever in Anaheim, but he's a middle reliever with a skosh more job security than he had with the Cardinals. Team context! It matters.

Hector Santiago

Born: 12/16/1987 Age: 26
Bats: R Throws: L Height: 6' 0" Weight: 210
Breakout: 37% Improve: 68% Collapse: 14%
Attrition: 23% MLB: 89%

Comparables:
Ryan Rowland-Smith, Denny Bautista, Fernando Nieve

YEAR	TEAM	LVL	AGE	W	L	SV	G	GS	IP	H	HR	BB	SO	BB9	SO9	GB%	BABIP	WHIP	ERA	FIP	FRA	WARP
2011	WNS	A+	23	2	3	0	8	8	44	38	7	14	43	2.9	8.8	42%	.360	1.18	3.68	4.50	3.00	0.2
2011	BIR	AA	23	7	5	0	15	15	83¹	71	4	39	74	4.2	8.0	50%	.295	1.32	3.56	3.70	4.87	0.3
2011	CHA	MLB	23	0	0	0	2	0	5¹	1	0	1	2	1.7	3.4	60%	.067	0.38	0.00	2.87	3.06	0.1
2012	CHR	AAA	24	1	0	0	3	3	14²	9	0	6	13	3.7	8.0	51%	.257	1.02	0.00	2.61	3.39	0.3
2012	CHA	MLB	24	4	1	4	42	4	70¹	54	10	40	79	5.1	10.1	39%	.259	1.34	3.33	4.65	4.97	0.4
2013	CHA	MLB	25	4	9	0	34	23	149	137	17	72	137	4.3	8.3	39%	.289	1.40	3.56	4.47	4.24	1.4
2014	ANA	MLB	26	6	5	1	43	14	119²	111	12	55	108	4.2	8.1	41%	.296	1.39	4.07	4.41	4.42	0.6

Santiago's stock in trade is versatility, as the young lefty has variously started, closed, set up and worked in long relief over the past two seasons. He seems to take it as a personal challenge to check every box in the PITCHf/x chart during a single inning, leavening his effective low-90s fastball and bread-and-butter changeup with the occasional cutter, curveball, sinker or scroogie. Santiago moved into the rotation last June and posted workmanlike peripherals, with a few more walks and home runs than you'd like to see, and with his FIP coming in almost a full run higher than his ERA some regression is in order. Still, there are far less talented and effective hurlers than Santiago filling out the back end of major-league rotations, which is where he profiles after the Angels acquired him in the Mark Trumbo trade.

Mark Sappington

Born: 11/17/1990 Age: 23
Bats: R Throws: R Height: 6' 5" Weight: 209
Breakout: 78% Improve: 82% Collapse: 18%
Attrition: 57% MLB: 19%

Comparables:
Glen Perkins, Billy Buckner, Kyle Weiland

YEAR	TEAM	LVL	AGE	W	L	SV	G	GS	IP	H	HR	BB	SO	BB9	SO9	GB%	BABIP	WHIP	ERA	FIP	FRA	WARP
2013	SBR	A+	22	11	4	0	22	22	130²	103	10	62	110	4.3	7.6	47%	.262	1.26	3.38	4.62	4.97	0.9
2013	ARK	AA	22	1	1	0	5	5	25²	23	1	20	26	7.0	9.1	52%	.306	1.68	3.86	4.11	4.30	0.2
2014	ANA	MLB	23	6	9	0	37	30	108²	114	13	64	72	5.3	6.0	48%	.297	1.64	5.19	5.50	5.64	-0.5

No pitcher in the Halos' system improved his stock more than Sappington, who thrived in an aggressive assignment to the California League before earning a July promotion to Double-A.

His walk rate spiked in the Texas League, where better hitters challenged his command, but his K rate climbed in proportion. Sappington has an excellent fastball that regularly hits the mid-90s, with both good plane and riding action. His slider also projects as above average, but opinions about his changeup vary. He leaned on it increasingly as the year progressed, and some in the organization now view it as a big-league weapon. Despite above-average athleticism, Sappington's delivery features some rigidity and extra effort, making him prone to losing his mechanics in games. If he can master his delivery—a big if—he has the ceiling of a no. 2 starter. He could see time as spot-starter in 2014 where success, paradoxically, could land him a role in the big-league bullpen for the remainder of the season.

Matt Shoemaker
Born: 9/27/1986 Age: 27
Bats: R Throws: R Height: 6' 2" Weight: 225
Breakout: 43% Improve: 57% Collapse: 34%
Attrition: 69% MLB: 23%
Comparables:
Todd Redmond, Virgil Vasquez, Thad Weber

YEAR	TEAM	LVL	AGE	W	L	SV	G	GS	IP	H	HR	BB	SO	BB9	SO9	GB%	BABIP	WHIP	ERA	FIP	FRA	WARP
2011	ARK	AA	24	12	5	0	23	23	156¹	132	17	35	129	2.0	7.4	41%	.265	1.07	2.48	3.97	4.24	1.9
2011	SLC	AAA	24	0	2	0	4	4	21	28	3	12	12	5.1	5.1	45%	.347	1.90	8.14	6.35	6.80	0.1
2012	SLC	AAA	25	11	10	0	29	29	176²	229	25	45	124	2.3	6.3	42%	.350	1.55	5.65	4.95	5.52	1.8
2013	SLC	AAA	26	11	13	0	29	29	184¹	212	27	29	160	1.4	7.8	44%	.332	1.31	4.64	4.34	5.04	2.5
2013	ANA	MLB	26	0	0	0	1	1	5	2	0	2	5	3.6	9.0	42%	.167	0.80	0.00	2.28	3.22	0.1
2014	ANA	MLB	27	9	10	0	26	26	159²	176	22	47	112	2.6	6.3	42%	.306	1.40	4.70	4.74	5.11	-0.5

Shoemaker's 2012 campaign was a remarkable exercise of physical and emotional endurance: He somehow led the minor leagues in innings pitched while yielding a cumulative .318/.358/.526 slash line to PCL hitters. Shoemaker added a curveball to his repertoire over the offseason, and then continued to pound the strike zone in 2013. He again paced the minors in innings pitched, but this time with an ERA a full run lower. The former undrafted free agent also made his major-league debut in spectacular fashion, going five scoreless innings with five strikeouts, including three in the first to kick off his MLB career. He should spend the next three years on the margins of the Halos' depth chart and just might surprise people, especially if moved to the bullpen, where his splitter could play up.

Tyler Skaggs
Born: 7/13/1991 Age: 22
Bats: L Throws: L Height: 6' 5" Weight: 215
Breakout: 45% Improve: 63% Collapse: 15%
Attrition: 39% MLB: 53%
Comparables:
Chris Tillman, Jaime Garcia, Franklin Morales

YEAR	TEAM	LVL	AGE	W	L	SV	G	GS	IP	H	HR	BB	SO	BB9	SO9	GB%	BABIP	WHIP	ERA	FIP	FRA	WARP
2011	VIS	A+	19	5	5	0	17	17	100²	81	6	34	125	3.0	11.2	51%	.303	1.14	3.22	3.40	3.57	2.4
2011	MOB	AA	19	4	1	0	10	10	57²	45	4	15	73	2.3	11.4	42%	.284	1.04	2.50	2.56	2.91	1.3
2012	MOB	AA	20	5	4	0	13	13	69²	63	8	21	71	2.7	9.2	44%	.306	1.21	2.84	3.55	4.23	1.1
2012	RNO	AAA	20	4	2	0	9	9	52²	49	4	16	45	2.7	7.7	46%	.308	1.23	2.91	3.91	4.75	1.1
2012	ARI	MLB	20	1	3	0	6	6	29¹	30	6	13	21	4.0	6.4	38%	.273	1.47	5.83	5.90	7.01	-0.6
2013	RNO	AAA	21	6	10	0	19	17	104	114	5	39	107	3.4	9.3	44%	.353	1.47	4.59	3.44	4.10	2.3
2013	ARI	MLB	21	2	3	0	7	7	38²	38	7	15	36	3.5	8.4	43%	.288	1.37	5.12	4.83	4.95	0.1
2014	ANA	MLB	22	8	7	0	24	24	126²	124	14	45	110	3.2	7.8	45%	.301	1.33	3.94	4.21	4.29	1.0

Quick, everybody man their knee-jerk reaction stations and try to figure out what's wrong with a 22-year-old pitcher! Jose Fernandez might have spoiled us for young studs with worlds of promise, which Skaggs is. But as he bounced between Triple-A and the big leagues, Skaggs' fastball pumped the brakes a little, dipping from the low 90s to high 80s. Rather than calling every pitching coach in the phone book to tinker and fix his mechanics or approach, the Diamondbacks simply chose to omit him during September call-ups, giving him a chance to clear his young mind. Expectations might be tempered after this herky-jerky year, but he'll get every chance to fit in Anaheim's rotation this year.

Joe Smith
Born: 3/22/1984 Age: 30
Bats: R Throws: R Height: 6' 2" Weight: 205
Breakout: 29% Improve: 52% Collapse: 26%
Attrition: 17% MLB: 86%
Comparables:
Brandon League, Ramon Ramirez, Sean Burnett

YEAR	TEAM	LVL	AGE	W	L	SV	G	GS	IP	H	HR	BB	SO	BB9	SO9	GB%	BABIP	WHIP	ERA	FIP	FRA	WARP
2011	CLE	MLB	27	3	3	0	71	0	67	52	1	21	45	2.8	6.0	58%	.258	1.09	2.01	2.94	3.67	1.0
2012	CLE	MLB	28	7	4	0	72	0	67	53	4	25	53	3.4	7.1	60%	.253	1.16	2.96	3.45	4.38	0.4
2013	CLE	MLB	29	6	2	3	70	0	63	54	5	23	54	3.3	7.7	52%	.282	1.22	2.29	3.63	3.63	0.7
2014	ANA	MLB	30	3	1	1	60	0	54²	48	4	21	44	3.5	7.2	56%	.283	1.27	3.37	3.91	3.67	0.7

Consistency, thy name is Joe Smith. Eighteen relievers have pitched for the same team each of the past five seasons; Smith has the steady group's seventh-best ERA. Always unpleasant for right-handed batters with his sidearm delivery and sinker-slider combo, Smith's learned ability to retire lefties with four-seamers has promoted him to a full-inning threat. Nothing short of a trip to court will change his nondescript name, but attention—and dollars—came his way when the Angels inked him to a three-year deal last November. Smith's patented blend of middle-innings competence should be a boon to the Halos' woeful bullpen.

Jered Weaver
Born: 10/4/1982 Age: 31
Bats: R Throws: R Height: 6' 7" Weight: 210
Breakout: 12% Improve: 44% Collapse: 24%
Attrition: 8% MLB: 94%

Comparables:
Roy Oswalt, Adam Wainwright, Johan Santana

YEAR	TEAM	LVL	AGE	W	L	SV	G	GS	IP	H	HR	BB	SO	BB9	SO9	GB%	BABIP	WHIP	ERA	FIP	FRA	WARP
2011	ANA	MLB	28	18	8	0	33	33	235²	182	20	56	198	2.1	7.6	34%	.250	1.01	2.41	3.24	3.31	4.6
2012	ANA	MLB	29	20	5	0	30	30	188²	147	20	45	142	2.1	6.8	37%	.241	1.02	2.81	3.70	4.37	1.5
2013	ANA	MLB	30	11	8	0	24	24	154¹	139	17	37	117	2.2	6.8	32%	.270	1.14	3.27	3.85	4.52	1.0
2014	ANA	MLB	31	9	6	0	21	21	139	121	14	37	118	2.4	7.7	35%	.275	1.14	3.03	3.77	3.29	2.5

Weaver posted nearly identical peripheral statistics last season as he did in 2012, but saw his win total drop by nine. The plunge had more to do with a poor team effort and a fractured left elbow that cost him nearly 10 starts, though there are some small signs of decline starting to creep in. Weaver can hit 90 mph on a good day, but generally lives to the mid-upper-80s. What he lacks in velocity he makes up with a fantastic curveball that flirts with 70 mph, an upper-70s changeup and a slider that has lost some of its bite over the last few seasons—most notably versus right-handed batters. Jeff's baby brother is one of the extreme fly-ball pitchers in the league, which makes him a perfect match for the ballpark and (at least before Peter Bourjos was shipped out) the outfielders behind him. His team-friendly contract is still a coup even if he's just a middle-of-the-rotation type instead of a staff anchor.

Jerome Williams
Born: 12/4/1981 Age: 32
Bats: R Throws: R Height: 6' 3" Weight: 240
Breakout: 29% Improve: 57% Collapse: 34%
Attrition: 30% MLB: 43%

Comparables:
R.A. Dickey, Calvin Maduro, Josh Towers

YEAR	TEAM	LVL	AGE	W	L	SV	G	GS	IP	H	HR	BB	SO	BB9	SO9	GB%	BABIP	WHIP	ERA	FIP	FRA	WARP
2011	SLC	AAA	29	7	2	0	11	10	73²	78	10	15	60	1.8	7.3	52%	.295	1.26	3.91	4.69	4.39	1.2
2011	ANA	MLB	29	4	0	0	10	6	44	45	6	15	28	3.1	5.7	51%	.291	1.36	3.68	4.65	5.70	-0.3
2012	SBR	A+	30	1	0	0	2	2	11	11	1	1	9	0.8	7.4	69%	.294	1.09	3.27	3.90	3.92	0.2
2012	ANA	MLB	30	6	8	1	32	15	137²	139	17	35	98	2.3	6.4	54%	.294	1.26	4.58	4.10	4.95	0.0
2013	ANA	MLB	31	9	10	0	37	25	169¹	181	23	55	107	2.9	5.7	48%	.294	1.39	4.57	4.62	5.28	-0.5
2014	ANA	MLB	32	7	7	0	31	20	144²	154	18	44	93	2.8	5.8	49%	.298	1.37	4.53	4.69	4.93	-0.2

Williams continued the second phase of his career as a swingman, making 25 starts and 12 relief appearances last season. That said, he has no business starting for a contender beyond the rare case of food poisoning or paternity leave in the rotation. He threw a harder fastball—low 90s—only to see it hit hard in return. Poorly located heaters to left-handed batters accounted for nine of the 23 home runs he allowed. His ideal role would be as a situational reliever specializing in right-handed batters, against whom his breaking ball flourishes. The fact that Williams made his major-league debut in 2003 and is still arbitration-eligible a decade later about sums up where his career has gone.

C.J. Wilson
Born: 11/18/1980 Age: 33
Bats: L Throws: L Height: 6' 1" Weight: 210
Breakout: 11% Improve: 48% Collapse: 23%
Attrition: 19% MLB: 92%

Comparables:
David Cone, A.J. Burnett, Doug Davis

YEAR	TEAM	LVL	AGE	W	L	SV	G	GS	IP	H	HR	BB	SO	BB9	SO9	GB%	BABIP	WHIP	ERA	FIP	FRA	WARP
2011	TEX	MLB	30	16	7	0	34	34	223¹	191	16	74	206	3.0	8.3	51%	.288	1.19	2.94	3.28	4.08	3.6
2012	ANA	MLB	31	13	10	0	34	34	202¹	181	19	91	173	4.0	7.7	50%	.282	1.34	3.83	4.00	4.27	1.7
2013	ANA	MLB	32	17	7	0	33	33	212¹	200	15	85	188	3.6	8.0	46%	.302	1.34	3.39	3.54	3.77	2.8
2014	ANA	MLB	33	12	9	0	30	30	186²	164	12	74	165	3.6	7.9	49%	.293	1.28	3.47	3.68	3.77	2.3

It was not quite head & shoulders above his 2012 output, but Wilson did improve in his second season with the Angels. The former starter turned closer turned starter topped 200 innings for the fourth consecutive year since returning to the rotation. Wilson saw his strikeouts increase slightly while dropping his walks by a decent amount. The straight-edged racer still throws in the low 90s with a variety of secondary offerings. He showed a renewed faith in his slider and was rewarded with empty swings in return. He fancies an upper-80s cutter, but the pitch bleeds over the plate versus right-handed batters, which causes some extreme splits. The low mileage from his relief days makes him a viable middle-of-the-rotation piece even as he approaches his mid-30s.

LINEOUTS

HITTERS

PLAYER	TEAM	LVL	AGE	PA	R	2B	3B	HR	RBI	BB	SO	SB-CS	AVG/OBP/SLG	TAv	BABIP	BRR	FRAA	WARP
LF Z. Borenstein	SBR	A+	22	465	76	22	7	28	95	43	88	5-5	.337/.403/.631	.368	.366	-4.5	LF(79): -3.0, RF(1): -0.0	5.7
SS T. Field	SLC	AAA	26	372	56	20	2	11	49	44	68	6-2	.303/.391/.484	.301	.350	0.3	SS(46): -5.2, 2B(30): -0.1	2.4
	ANA	MLB	26	27	4	0	0	0	0	1	7	0-0	.154/.185/.154	.117	.211	-0.2	2B(9): -0.9, SS(5): -0.4	-0.5
RF B. Hawpe	SLC	AAA	34	153	21	8	0	6	28	21	40	1-1	.305/.405/.504	.314	.400	-1.2	RF(9): -0.7, 1B(5): 0.8	0.9
	ANA	MLB	34	32	2	0	0	0	2	5	14	0-0	.185/.312/.185	.204	.385	-0.8	1B(7): -0.0, RF(5): -0.2	-0.3
C J. Hester	SLC	AAA	29	284	40	13	1	8	29	27	75	3-1	.237/.307/.391	.242	.301	0.6	C(67): -1.0	0.5
	ANA	MLB	29	1	1	0	0	0	0	1	0	0-0		.624	—	0	C(1): -0.0	0.0
3B C. Nelson	SLC	AAA	27	144	20	11	0	6	24	8	23	4-0	.328/.361/.545	.296	.355	-0.1	3B(14): 1.9, SS(10): 0.0	1.2
	COL	MLB	27	71	6	1	2	0	4	4	19	0-0	.242/.282/.318	.212	.333	0.2	3B(19): 0.1	-0.1
	ANA	MLB	27	119	10	1	2	3	18	8	36	2-1	.220/.277/.349	.229	.296	-1	3B(28): -1.8, 2B(2): 0.0	-0.3
	NYA	MLB	27	37	3	2	0	0	2	1	11	0-0	.222/.243/.278	.150	.320	0.2	3B(10): -0.4	-0.3
SS A. Romine	SLC	AAA	27	416	61	16	5	4	39	43	68	15-6	.287/.367/.391	.259	.341	1.8	SS(59): 1.7, 2B(20): -1.1	2.0
	ANA	MLB	27	123	9	3	0	0	10	7	24	1-0	.259/.308/.287	.226	.329	2.2	3B(24): -0.3, SS(17): -0.3	0.1
SS E. Stamets	SBR	A+	21	571	80	28	4	4	53	34	66	16-4	.281/.335/.375	.276	.315	3.6	SS(125): 14.0	5.4

Zach Borenstein arrived in the Arizona Fall League riding the momentum of an epic .337/.403/.631 California League campaign. He then went 3 for his first 28 in the Arizona sun, after which his opportunities dwindled, so he'll head to Double-A looking to get things moving again. ⌀ As the equivalent of a rising high school senior, **Natanael Delgado** showed a knack for hard contact and ranked sixth in the Arizona Summer League in total bases. The secondary skills and defense were far less impressive, but he could put up spectacular numbers in the Pioneer League before turning 19. ⌀ Acquired off waivers before the season began, **Tommy Field** has the potential to become a utility infielder and the franchise's scrappiest player since David Eckstein. ⌀ The good news is that **Brad Hawpe** robbed Kole Calhoun and J.B. Shuck of only 34 plate appearances in 2013. There's room on the Angels' Double-A and Triple-A affiliates for a lefty-swinging DH, but Hawpe will do best in organizations where he hasn't been so conspicuously lapped on the depth chart. ⌀ **John Hester** once mashed Triple-A pitching, believe it or not. That was way back in 2010. Since then, his best offensive contribution has been slugging .400 or so in the upper minors while serving as fourth catcher on the depth charts. ⌀ Once a prized prospect, **Chris Nelson** is now collecting jerseys as he bounces around the league looking for work as a reserve infielder who is below average on both sides of the ball. ⌀ **Andrew Romine** continues to be a glove-first utility infielder who would not hit a fly, mostly because he can't hit anything. ⌀ **Erick Salcedo** fits the mold of scrappy Angels organizational soldier, and might just make it as a utility guy down the road. ⌀ **Eric Stamets** already has the reputation for packing an MLB-caliber glove, so he'll see plenty of time on the margins of big-league depth charts even if the bat has a long way to go.

PITCHERS

PLAYER	TEAM	LVL	AGE	W	L	SV	IP	H	HR	BB	SO	BB9	SO9	GB%	BABIP	WHIP	ERA	FIP	FRA	WARP
R. Brasier	SLC	AAA	25	5	2	10	56²	69	6	16	57	2.5	9.1	45%	.364	1.50	4.13	3.78	3.80	1.4
	ANA	MLB	25	0	0	0	9	7	1	4	7	4.0	7.0	38%	.261	1.22	2.00	4.30	5.26	-0.1
R. Carson	LVG	AAA	24	3	3	11	44¹	48	3	19	36	3.9	7.3	50%	.326	1.51	4.06	4.11	4.72	0.8
	NYN	MLB	24	0	0	0	19²	21	9	7	8	3.2	3.7	36%	.167	1.42	8.24	9.38	10.02	-1.0
R. Coello	SLC	AAA	28	1	0	4	18²	15	1	11	29	5.3	14.0	45%	.341	1.39	4.82	3.09	3.37	0.6
	ANA	MLB	28	2	2	1	17	14	1	8	23	4.2	12.2	31%	.317	1.29	3.71	2.55	2.16	0.5
C. Cordero	SLC	AAA	31	2	3	2	49²	64	5	11	39	2.0	7.1	34%	.362	1.51	5.44	4.21	4.61	0.7
W. LeBlanc	OKL	AAA	28	3	1	1	49²	55	5	16	47	2.9	8.5	49%	.340	1.43	4.71	3.95	4.57	0.7
	MIA	MLB	28	1	5	0	48²	63	6	15	31	2.8	5.7	43%	.356	1.60	5.18	4.40	4.65	-0.1
	HOU	MLB	28	0	0	0	6¹	9	1	5	2	7.1	2.8	38%	.286	2.21	7.11	7.34	7.88	-0.2
N. Maronde	ARK	AA	23	2	4	0	56¹	41	4	37	63	5.9	10.1	46%	.266	1.38	3.51	3.82	4.51	0.3
	ANA	MLB	23	0	0	0	5¹	4	1	8	5	13.5	8.4	53%	.214	2.25	6.75	8.14	8.33	-0.2
B. Moran	TAC	AAA	24	2	5	4	62²	70	4	20	85	2.9	12.2	35%	.410	1.44	3.45	2.79	2.72	2.0
C. Rapada	COH	AAA	32	0	0	1	24	18	1	9	20	3.4	7.5	50%	.262	1.12	1.12	3.20	3.87	0.3
	CLE	MLB	32	0	0	0	2	1	0	2	0	9.0	0.0	29%	.143	1.50	0.00	6.08	8.66	-0.1
R. Scoggins	BUR	A	22	1	4	0	65	53	1	35	76	4.8	10.5	57%	.317	1.35	3.46	2.95	3.72	1.5
B. Sisk	OMA	AAA	26	3	2	8	67¹	59	8	32	73	4.3	9.8	37%	.297	1.35	2.54	4.51	4.01	1.4
A. Taylor	ANA	MLB	25	0	0	0	2¹	3	0	4	0	15.4	0.0	30%	.300	3.00	11.57	8.19	6.78	-0.1
C. Volstad	CSP	AAA	26	7	6	0	127²	156	12	44	57	3.1	4.0	57%	.329	1.57	4.58	4.98	6.64	-0.4
	COL	MLB	26	0	0	0	8¹	19	1	1	3	1.1	3.2	41%	.421	2.40	10.80	4.94	5.28	0.0
J. Wall	ABQ	AAA	26	1	2	3	27¹	27	3	16	25	5.3	8.2	40%	.311	1.57	5.60	4.92	5.83	0.0
	NWO	AAA	26	1	1	1	22	23	0	8	21	3.3	8.6	52%	.333	1.41	3.27	2.89	2.39	0.7
	LAN	MLB	26	0	1	0	7	17	2	6	7	7.7	9.0	45%	.517	3.29	18.00	7.31	8.50	-0.4
A. Wood	SBR	A+	22	0	3	0	21²	25	1	12	18	5.0	7.5	51%	.348	1.71	4.15	4.37	4.86	0.3

Reports out of the 2012 Instructional League had **Victor Alcantara** working in the upper 90s. Exciting stuff, right? June rolled around, and the Owlz didn't see any of that velo, so when he touched 94 a couple of times in August, it was cause for celebration. On the plus side, his changeup has developed rapidly. ⊘ **Ryan Brasier**'s resume boasts a mid-90s fastball and a minor-league no-hitter that he threw as a starter back in 2010. He hasn't kept many hits off the board since, yielding a 24 percent line-drive rate and .366 BABIP in two seasons at Salt Lake. ⊘ **Robert Carson** misses as often with his fastball as with any of his other "pitches," but when the fastball misses, it's within the strike zone. As you can imagine, that's becoming a problem. ⊘ **Robert Coello**'s WTF pitch caused a stir, and his numbers weren't bad, but no team showed interest when the Angels outrighted him from the 40-man roster after the season. ⊘ It was a nice story: **Chad Cordero** came all the way back from surgery and personal tragedy to land in the Angels' big-league camp in February, but things slid downhill from there, and he spent a futile year traveling from Inland Empire to Salt Lake. ⊘ The only real surprise about soft-tossing lefty **Wade LeBlanc**'s career is that he didn't reach the "can't even stick on the 40-man roster" phase more quickly. ⊘ **Eduar Lopez** and his swing-and-miss hammer led the Dominican Summer League in K rate for the second year, racking up 83 punchouts while yielding just 27 hits in 62 innings. ⊘ After hitting 95 in a promising 2012 debut, **Nick Maronde** had a much tougher time maintaining velocity or command in 2013. The organization won't use the "I" word, but clearly something broke a little. ⊘ Draft day reports of mid-90s velocity and a wipeout slider keyed up expectations for **Keynan Middleton**, but he struggled to command a lifeless fastball that was more 89 than 95. The slider really was legit, however, so with his athleticism and a half-decade of pro development he could go from project to mid-rotation. ⊘ **Brian Moran** has maintained brilliant peripherals at all levels. His fastball averages just 87 mph, but his sustained success will get him a shot in the majors. So too will the requirements of the Rule 5 draft, which obligate the Angels to keep him rostered all season. ⊘ **Clay Rapada**, an effective LOOGY (if the world's *least* qualified ROOGY) was released by the Yankees to make room on the 40-man roster for Lyle Overbay. After the Indians picked him up he allowed three earned runs in 26 innings, mostly at Triple-A. Overbay hit .240/.295/.393. ⊘ **Reid Scoggins** looked like one of the few bright lights on the farm over the summer, taming a stiff delivery and reaping a nice Midwestern League harvest in K's. Then he blew out his arm. The Halos' farm in 2013 had all the lucky breaks of a Cormac McCarthy homestead. ⊘ Before the 2013 season, the Angels swapped one year of Ervin Santana for six years of **Brandon Sisk**. Two months later, Sisk went under the knife. After using the savings of that trade to commit $15 million to Joe Blanton, do ya think the Halos would take it all back? ⊘ Former sleeper **Andrew Taylor**'s misguided flirtation with starting, and a decline in velocity, culminated in a labrum tear that kept him on the bench in 2013. Maybe he comes back firing bullets in 2014, but don't hold your breath. ⊘ Now 26, **Chris Volstad**'s first-round pedigree will keep him around for a few more years, but nothing he did in 2013 suggested he can hack it as anything more than a hack. ⊘ A full-time reliever since 2011, **Josh Wall** went east in the Nolasco trade after accidentally changing the difficulty settings from Rookie to All-Madden in seven innings with Los Angeles. ⊘ With his booming mid-90s fastball, **Austin Wood** was a guy the Halos hoped would help return the farm to respectability. It didn't happen. Wood will miss the 2014 season with Tommy John surgery.

MANAGER: MIKE SCIOSCIA

YEAR	TEAM	W-L	Pythag +/-	Avg PC	100+ P	120+ P	QS	BQS	REL	REL w Zero R	IBB	PH	PH Avg	PH HR	SB2	CS2	SB3	CS3	SAC Att	SAC %	POS SAC	Squeeze	Swing	In Play
2011	ANA	86-76	1	101.0	98	11	98	8	386	313	34	75	.154	2	116	47	18	4	78	64.1%	46	1	417	144
2012	ANA	89-73	1	97.4	87	4	91	3	444	365	20	68	.203	2	121	27	12	4	72	65.3%	43	3	419	132
2013	ANA	78-84	0	97.7	77	6	87	5	492	396	36	83	.214	3	70	32	10	1	54	70.4%	35	0	346	110

In 2013, the Angels ranked eighth in walk rate. That's their best rank since 2000, Mike Scioscia's rookie season. Scioscia has always had very clear tendencies as a manager. From 2000-2013, only the Pirates, Orioles, and Royals have drawn fewer walks than Scioscia's Angels. Yet those three teams have generally been pitiful while Scioscia's teams have been frequent contenders. They've been great at contact hitting, ranking fifth in hits under him, while having the fewest offensive Ks by any team in baseball over the past 14 years. They're also second in steals, behind only Tampa Bay. (However, the Angels have the most caught steals in the 21st century).

On the pitching side: They've allowed the fourth fewest hits by any AL team, and fifth fewest walks. These tendencies have all generally moderated in recent years, but that's the sort of ball Scioscia seems to prefer.

Los Angeles Dodgers

By Wendy Thurm

The 2013 Los Angeles Dodgers kicked off spring training with high expectations and the highest payroll in the majors. The $216 million in player commitments exclaimed to anyone who would listen that new owners Guggenheim Investments and Magic Johnson would do whatever it took to bring the World Series trophy to Chavez Ravine. Just a few months earlier, Ned Colletti, backed by the new ownership's Mariana-deep pockets, had pulled off a stunning trade with the Red Sox to acquire Adrian Gonzalez, Carl Crawford, Josh Beckett and Nick Punto and their $100 million per year in combined salaries. Those players joined Hanley Ramirez, also obtained in a 2012 trade, and the $31.5 million remaining on his contract. Zack Greinke joined the party in the 2012-13 offseason, after the Dodgers agreed to pay him $147 million over six years.

Gonzalez, Crawford, Ramirez and Greinke are star-level players. Ramirez, Beckett and Greinke play premium positions. Fat-cat teams are supposed to used their built-in advantages to pay for star-level players who play premium positions. By the quasi-ortho-doxy that outlets like *Baseball Prospectus* have (regrettably?) helped to develop, nobody, fat-cat or not, is supposed to pay money for relief pitching, especially when that money is doled out in multiyear deals for players with "proven closer" stitched on their jersey in strangely invisible thread.

Colletti's best bullpen move fit the orthodoxy well, as he added lefty J.P. Howell on a one-year deal worth just under $3 million. Howell spent six seasons with the Rays, but his solid overall stat line obscured his up-and-down career in Tampa Bay: He was lights-out in 2008 and 2009, missed all of 2010 after surgery to repair his labrum, and struggled to regain his form in 2011. He showed some signs of life in 2012, but he also gave up an alarming number of homers and didn't see his strikeout rate bounce back to his peak form. The sabermetric baseball gods rewarded the Dodgers for taking a buy-low shot on Howell in the form of 62 innings of a 2.86 FIP fueled largely by his allowing just two dingers all year.

On the other hand, Colletti also doled out a three-year, $22.5 million contract to former Mariner Brandon League after acquiring him at the 2012 trade deadline to replace Josh Lindblom, gone to the Phillies in exchange for Shane Victorino. The Dodgers apparently liked what they saw from League in August and September, particularly after he made mechanical adjustments under the tutelage of pitching coach Rick Honeycutt and bullpen coach Ken Howell. Even so, League's overall performance for the Dodgers was good, not great: 27 strikeouts, 14 walks, 17 hits and seven runs in 27 innings, which comes out to a 2.81 FIP that, were it his full-season line, would have ranked 35th in baseball among pitchers with at least 20 innings. That kind of partial-season performance doesn't justify a three-year commitment for $22.5 million.

League, though, was also an expensive insurance policy on the health of Kenley Jansen, the 24-year-old flamethrower who had replaced Javy Guerra as the Dodgers' closer in 2012 before being sidelined with a heart arrhythmia. Jansen had been magnificent, posting a 39 percent strikeout rate in 65 innings. After the season, doctors removed the heart tissue causing the problem, but the Dodgers were wary of the risk of a recurrence leaving them without late-innings depth.

The problem is that the deal almost cost the team more than money. When the front office hands a manager a "proven closer" with a $7 million contract, the manager doesn't have the wiggle room to say, "Well that's nice, but I'm going to use Kenley Jansen instead." It's one of the dangers of managing a big-spending team: There's a real reluctance

DODGERS PROSPECTUS

2013 W-L: 92-70, 1st in NL West

Pythag	.549	9th	DER	.706	11th
RS/G	4.01	16th	B-Age	30.7	29th
RA/G	3.59	3rd	P-Age	28.1	17th
TAv	.267	9th	Salary	$223.1	2nd
BRR	-4.27	22nd	M$/MW	$4.83	25th
TAv-P	.253	6th	DL Days	1312	25th
FIP	3.41	5th	$ on DL	29%	28th

	Runs	HR/RH	HR/LH	Runs/RH	Runs/LH
Three-Year Park Factors	99	102	105	101	104

Top Hitter WARP	4.81 (Hanley Ramirez)
Top Pitcher WARP	5.06 (Clayton Kershaw)
Top Prospect	Julio Urias

to bench expensive underperformers even when there is a better option available.

To start the season, Don Mattingly tabbed Ronald Belisario for the seventh inning, Jansen for the eighth and League as the closer. By June 22nd, the Dodgers found themselves in last place and facing a long shot to win the division. League had made 28 appearances, recording 14 saves against four blown saves and three losses. He'd struck out only 13 while allowing 43 baserunners and 20 runs. The expensive closer was quite clearly costing the team games.

The next day, League threw to one batter in the eighth inning with the score tied. When Adrian Gonzalez and Hanley Ramirez hit back-to-back home runs in the top of the ninth, Mattingly turned to Jansen for the save. Narrative neatness would call for this to be the end of League's line, but Mattingly gave him another chance on June 25th, handing him a three-run lead against the Giants only to watch him allow a single, double and single in three batters. *Then* came the neatness: Paco Rodriguez came on in relief and shut the door; League never saw another ninth-inning save situation.

As you would expect, League was hardly the only Dodgers reliever to struggle in the first half. Notably, Belisario, who had been dominant as Mattingly's eighth-inning stopper in 2012, was much less so in 2013. His strikeout rate dropped from 24 to 19 percent through the All-Star break and batted balls that found gloves in 2012 (.243 BABIP) found unoccupied grass last year (.388 BABIP). Collectively, Dodgers relievers accounted for 12 blown saves and were charged with 17 of the team's 47 losses. Only the Mets, Marlins and Padres had more bullpen losses in the first half.

Unless you're Rip Van Winkle, you know what happened next. Between June 23rd and the All-Star break, the bullpen recorded just one more loss and no blown saves, then took it to another level in the second half. Among National League bullpens, they posted the second-best strikeout rate (24.2 percent) and the fifth-best FIP (3.45). The results showed in the box scores: The bullpen was responsible for only seven Dodgers losses after the All-Star break, the fewest among NL teams.

Moving Jansen into the closer role and limiting League's innings to lower-leverage situations were important first steps, but it was the addition of three new arms that steered the Dodgers' bullpen in the right direction, with each of the three representing a different model of bullpen-building.

Build from within: Chris Withrow is big, strong righthander with a 96 mph fastball, stellar slider and usable curve. The Dodgers drafted Withrow out of high school in 2007 and he threw 471 innings in the minors before making his major-league debut at Dodger Stadium on June 12th. Withrow took the mound in the top of the seventh, with the Dodgers clinging to a 4-3 lead. He retired the first two batters, but gave up three consecutive singles—and the tying run—and then a walk, before Mattingly pulled him. That was

the least effective two-thirds of an inning he pitched all season. In total, he threw 34 innings with 43 strikeouts against 13 walks. He allowed just 10 runs.

Build from the scrap-heap: The Dodgers picked up Carlos Marmol from the Cubs in July in exchange for Matt Guerrier. Marmol's electricity, both good and bad, is visible from his statistical record, even if you've never seen him pitch—his career strikeout rate is just shy of 30 percent, but he has managed a K/BB ratio of worse than 2. In 2010 he struck out more than *40 percent* of the batters he faced. In 2009 he walked almost 20 percent. What sort of expectations can a team have for a pitcher like that? How about: 18 innings in August and September with an 0.96 ERA and an OPS allowed of .473.

Build from financial muscle and Dodgers mystique: And then there's Brian Wilson. The Giants' former closer had Tommy John surgery in April 2012 and continued to rehab his elbow and regain his pitching strength well into 2013. When he was ready to return to the majors, he signed on with his former rivals for $1 million. As little as a million dollars is to a baseball team, it is likely that not every team has a spare one sitting around in August that they can spend on a rehabbing reliever. It's also impossible not to wonder whether the Dodgers benefited from Wilson's frustration that the Giants had non-tendered him after 2012. In any event, the bet paid off: Wilson posted an 0.66 ERA in 18 appearances and maintained his performance as he was utilized in higher leverage situations as the season wound down.

As good bullpen pitchers do, Withrow, Marmol and Wilson had a chain effect, revitalizing a worn-out Dodgers relief corps, as their effectiveness gave Mattingly a bevy of good options, allowing him to ease off Rodriguez and Belisario, who both struggled down the stretch. Jansen and Howell also carried a lighter load as the Dodgers geared up for the postseason.

Add Withrow, Marmol and Wilson to Kenley Jansen (**Build by converting failed catcher prospects**) and Paco Rodriguez (**Build by drafting college closers and bringing them to the majors with fewer than 20 innings of minor-league experience**) and you get a bullpen built by myriad methods, which is to say that you get a bullpen built by the only method there is: however you can, using whatever tools you have at the moment.

Ned Colletti isn't alone among general managers who have overpaid for experienced relievers only to watch them burn up more than money. And making a $22 million mistake—like the Dodgers did with Brandon League—isn't as significant when your yearly payroll is over $200 million, at least not to the bottom line. But money isn't all there is, and Colletti did well using other resources to retool his bullpen midway through the season.

Wendy Thurm writes about baseball for FanGraphs, Bay Area Sports Guy, Sports on Earth *and other places. She's a recovering lawyer. You can follow her on Twitter@ hangingsliders.*

HITTERS

Mike Baxter   RF
Born: 12/7/1984 Age: 29
Bats: L Throws: R Height: 6' 0"
Weight: 195 Breakout: 0%
Improve: 14% Collapse: 5%
Attrition: 14% MLB: 42%

Comparables:
Jorge Piedra, Travis Buck, Jesus Guzman

YEAR	TEAM	LVL	AGE	PA	R	2B	3B	HR	RBI	BB	SO	SB	CS	AVG/OBP/SLG	TAv	BABIP	BRR	FRAA	WARP
2011	LEL	A+	26	46	5	1	0	0	2	9	8	0	1	.278/.413/.306	.278	.345	0		0.0
2011	BUF	AAA	26	71	4	0	2	1	7	5	19	1	0	.188/.257/.297	.171	.250	0.1	RF(7): -0.7, LF(5): -0.5	-0.7
2011	NYN	MLB	26	40	6	2	1	1	4	5	9	0	0	.235/.350/.441	.283	.292	-0.3	RF(10): -1.0, LF(3): 0.1	0.2
2012	BUF	AAA	27	27	2	1	0	0	3	2	7	0	0	.375/.444/.417	.312	.529	-0.4	LF(3): -0.3, RF(2): -0.1	0.2
2012	NYN	MLB	27	211	26	14	2	3	17	25	45	5	3	.263/.365/.413	.287	.331	3	RF(45): -1.4, LF(18): -0.2	1.0
2013	LVG	AAA	28	216	38	12	5	7	22	24	27	4	5	.289/.380/.519	.282	.305	0.2	LF(25): -2.9, RF(19): -2.3	0.3
2013	NYN	MLB	28	155	14	6	1	0	4	17	28	5	2	.189/.303/.250	.227	.238	-0.9	RF(30): 1.7, LF(17): 2.0	0.0
2014	LAN	MLB	29	250	31	12	2	5	23	23	48	5	3	.245/.326/.383	.264	.290	-0.2	RF -1, LF -0	0.6

If ever there was a year for Baxter to be a major-league regular, it was 2013. Instead, Marlon Byrd turned a minor-league deal into a career year, and Baxter never got out of the blocks. Recreating his pinch-hitting form of 2012 would have been nearly impossible; Baxter didn't, and spent time at Triple-A as a result. Opportunites like The Amazin' 2013 Mets Outfield come along maybe once every 500 years, so for Baxter not to capitalize means the Quad-A tag is probably permanent. The hit tool is real, though, and that should keep him kicking for a few years yet.

Carl Crawford   LF
Born: 8/5/1981 Age: 32
Bats: L Throws: L Height: 6' 2"
Weight: 215 Breakout: 2%
Improve: 36% Collapse: 3%
Attrition: 16% MLB: 93%

Comparables:
Eric Byrnes, Kevin McReynolds, Jose Cruz

YEAR	TEAM	LVL	AGE	PA	R	2B	3B	HR	RBI	BB	SO	SB	CS	AVG/OBP/SLG	TAv	BABIP	BRR	FRAA	WARP
2011	BOS	MLB	29	538	65	29	7	11	56	23	104	18	6	.255/.289/.405	.244	.299	3	LF(127): 2.6	1.0
2012	BOS	MLB	30	125	23	10	2	3	19	3	22	5	0	.282/.306/.479	.266	.319	0.8	LF(30): -1.9	0.1
2013	LAN	MLB	31	469	62	30	3	6	31	28	66	15	4	.283/.329/.407	.273	.321	1.9	LF(107): 6.9	2.6
2014	LAN	MLB	32	379	49	18	3	7	34	23	64	17	4	.274/.321/.406	.270	.320	1.8	LF 4	1.9

Crawford possesses a multifaceted skill set, but make no mistake—his 30s have turned him into a gunslinger without a gun. Leaving the Tropicana turf was expected to save his legs, but the player who averaged 50 stolen bases and more than 12 triples per full season with the Rays has vanished. After producing a .905 OPS out of the leadoff spot in April, his hamstrings flared up and sent him to the disabled list. The Dodgers would say he earned his 2013 paycheck with a four-homer playoff run, but there's little chance that a 32-year-old with problematic platoon splits and declining speed will justify a $20 million annual price tag for the next four seasons.

A.J. Ellis   C
Born: 4/9/1981 Age: 33
Bats: R Throws: R Height: 6' 3"
Weight: 220 Breakout: 2%
Improve: 31% Collapse: 4%
Attrition: 10% MLB: 81%

Comparables:
Josh Bard, Sherm Lollar, Miguel Ojeda

YEAR	TEAM	LVL	AGE	PA	R	2B	3B	HR	RBI	BB	SO	SB	CS	AVG/OBP/SLG	TAv	BABIP	BRR	FRAA	WARP
2011	ABQ	AAA	30	248	36	15	0	2	28	50	23	0	1	.304/.467/.418	.302	.338	0.5	C(15): 0.2	0.6
2011	LAN	MLB	30	103	8	1	1	2	11	14	16	0	1	.271/.392/.376	.290	.313	-1	C(29): -0.2	0.6
2012	LAN	MLB	31	505	44	20	1	13	52	65	107	0	0	.270/.373/.414	.289	.329	-2.9	C(131): -0.0	3.8
2013	LAN	MLB	32	448	43	17	1	10	52	45	78	0	2	.238/.318/.364	.265	.269	-0.6	C(113): -1.3	2.3
2014	LAN	MLB	33	433	45	16	1	7	40	53	81	1	1	.247/.345/.349	.265	.290	-1	C 0	2.2

The modern catcher is employed primarily to manage a pitching staff and hang tough behind the dish, so any offense is icing. The fact that Ellis carries a potent walking stick buffers his value when the results on contact are compromised, as was the case in 2013. He further made up for lost offense by nailing 44 percent of runners attempting to steal, the highest rate in baseball among regular catchers, though he received an assist from a pitching staff skilled at keeping baserunners close. At his advanced age, Ellis could suffer from a rapid decline at almost any moment, but given his late bloom it's *all* icing.

Andre Ethier   RF
Born: 4/10/1982 Age: 32
Bats: L Throws: L Height: 6' 2"
Weight: 205 Breakout: 0%
Improve: 46% Collapse: 2%
Attrition: 6% MLB: 99%

Comparables:
Carlos Beltran, Bernie Williams, Al Kaline

YEAR	TEAM	LVL	AGE	PA	R	2B	3B	HR	RBI	BB	SO	SB	CS	AVG/OBP/SLG	TAv	BABIP	BRR	FRAA	WARP
2011	LAN	MLB	29	551	67	30	0	11	62	58	103	0	1	.292/.368/.421	.296	.348	-2.2	RF(126): 1.3	2.7
2012	LAN	MLB	30	618	79	36	1	20	89	50	124	2	2	.284/.351/.460	.307	.333	-0.6	RF(146): -8.2, CF(1): 0.1	3.2
2013	LAN	MLB	31	553	54	33	2	12	52	61	95	4	3	.272/.360/.423	.284	.315	-2	CF(74): -8.3, RF(54): 1.9	1.8
2014	LAN	MLB	32	533	62	29	0	17	68	51	98	2	2	.274/.349/.441	.291	.310	-1.3	RF -3, CF -4	2.0

Ethier's 2013 season was eerily similar to his 2011, and his OPS has been perched at 20 percent above the league average for the past three seasons (despite a toxic reaction to lefties). L.A.'s outfield was overcrowded with expensive contracts to flawed players, but his ability to stay in the lineup does have significant value on a club that employs Carl Crawford and Matt Kemp. But his career is following a stereotypical arc, and the Dodgers are on the hook for at least $70 million to find out how he progresses through his thirties. He was miscast in center field during the playoffs, and his role on a championship-caliber club could be limited to that of a six-inning hitter neutralized by the first LOOGY out of the bullpen.

Tim Federowicz   C

Born: 8/5/1987 Age: 26
Bats: R Throws: R Height: 5' 10"
Weight: 215 Breakout: 1%
Improve: 17% Collapse: 13%
Attrition: 17% MLB: 55%

Comparables:
Welington Castillo, Martin Maldonado, Max Ramirez

YEAR	TEAM	LVL	AGE	PA	R	2B	3B	HR	RBI	BB	SO	SB	CS	AVG/OBP/SLG	TAv	BABIP	BRR	FRAA	WARP
2011	PME	AA	23	382	46	20	0	8	52	32	63	1	0	.277/.338/.407	.291	.312	-0.1	C(18): 0.4	0.8
2011	ABQ	AAA	23	102	17	7	0	6	17	15	20	0	0	.325/.431/.627	.470	.356	-0.5	C(2): -0.0	0.2
2011	LAN	MLB	23	16	0	0	0	0	1	2	4	0	0	.154/.312/.154	.209	.222	-0.1	C(7): 0.1	0.0
2012	ABQ	AAA	24	475	71	34	1	11	76	52	91	0	1	.294/.371/.461	.264	.347	-3.2	C(108): 4.3	2.8
2012	LAN	MLB	24	4	0	0	0	0	0	1	2	0	0	.333/.500/.333	.355	.000	0	C(2): -0.0	0.1
2013	ABQ	AAA	25	98	20	8	1	8	25	14	26	0	0	.418/.500/.848	.421	.532	-1	C(19): -0.4	2.1
2013	LAN	MLB	25	173	12	8	0	4	16	10	56	0	0	.231/.275/.356	.218	.327	-1.5	C(45): 0.5, 1B(2): -0.0	0.1
2014	LAN	MLB	26	250	25	12	0	6	28	21	64	0	0	.244/.308/.384	.255	.310	-0.6	C 1, 1B -0	1.0

"FedEx" was shipped back and forth between Albuquerque and Los Angeles absolutely, positively anytime during the first two months of the season. He made the 800-mile trek on six different occasions before the end of May, but was installed as the permanent backup catcher after Ramon Hernandez was sidelined in June. Federowicz presents a different value proposition than the man he replaced, despite the mirage created by his laying waste to the PCL in hitter-friendly stomping grounds. He's renowned more for his work with leather, not lumber.

Adrian Gonzalez   1B

Born: 5/8/1982 Age: 32
Bats: L Throws: L Height: 6' 2"
Weight: 225 Breakout: 0%
Improve: 21% Collapse: 2%
Attrition: 13% MLB: 96%

Comparables:
Ted Kluszewski, Mark Teixeira, Todd Helton

YEAR	TEAM	LVL	AGE	PA	R	2B	3B	HR	RBI	BB	SO	SB	CS	AVG/OBP/SLG	TAv	BABIP	BRR	FRAA	WARP
2011	BOS	MLB	29	715	108	45	3	27	117	74	119	1	0	.338/.410/.548	.314	.380	-8.1	1B(156): 8.9, RF(2): -0.2	4.8
2012	BOS	MLB	30	527	63	37	0	15	86	31	81	0	0	.300/.343/.469	.286	.329	-0.4	1B(115): 12.4, RF(18): -1.2	3.1
2012	LAN	MLB	30	157	12	10	1	3	22	11	29	2	0	.297/.344/.441	.288	.351	-2.7	1B(36): 1.6	0.6
2013	LAN	MLB	31	641	69	32	0	22	100	47	98	1	0	.293/.342/.461	.293	.315	-3.8	1B(151): -2.4	2.1
2014	LAN	MLB	32	611	77	30	0	23	85	61	101	1	0	.291/.363/.476	.304	.320	-1.1	1B 7, RF -1	4.0

Gonzalez was once the rare player whose prodigious power could defeat San Diego's dense marine layer, but his homer total hasn't matched his age since leaving his hometown for friendlier ballparks. His isolated power exceeded .210 in each of his last four seasons with the Padres, and Gonzo hit the .210 mark on the nose in his first season in Boston, but his ISO has been planted below .170 for the past two seasons. The trend took a disturbing turn in 2013 with the disappearance of his opposite-field power—the batter who had previously knocked homers all over the yard has cleared the left-field wall just once since donning a Dodger uniform. Perhaps a change of approach resulted in a single-year blip on the spray chart, but the sheer magnitude of change is a concern for a player who is owed $106 million over the next five years.

Dee Gordon   SS

Born: 4/22/1988 Age: 26
Bats: L Throws: R Height: 5' 11"
Weight: 160 Breakout: 4%
Improve: 45% Collapse: 13%
Attrition: 24% MLB: 94%

Comparables:
Emmanuel Burriss, Jason Bartlett, Alcides Escobar

YEAR	TEAM	LVL	AGE	PA	R	2B	3B	HR	RBI	BB	SO	SB	CS	AVG/OBP/SLG	TAv	BABIP	BRR	FRAA	WARP
2011	ABQ	AAA	23	313	51	10	6	0	24	18	40	30	4	.333/.373/.410	.255	.382	-2.6	SS(19): -1.5	-0.1
2011	LAN	MLB	23	233	34	9	2	0	11	7	27	24	7	.304/.325/.362	.255	.345	3	SS(54): -2.4	1.0
2012	ABQ	AAA	24	32	3	0	1	0	1	2	3	2	1	.267/.312/.333	.200	.296	0.6	SS(8): -0.4	-0.1
2012	LAN	MLB	24	330	38	9	2	1	17	20	62	32	10	.228/.280/.281	.222	.281	1.6	SS(79): -4.1	-0.3
2013	ABQ	AAA	25	433	65	17	9	0	33	51	70	49	11	.297/.385/.390	.277	.364	7.2	SS(73): 9.8, 2B(20): -0.5	4.3
2013	LAN	MLB	25	106	9	1	1	1	6	10	21	10	2	.234/.314/.298	.234	.292	1.4	SS(27): 1.3, 2B(3): 0.1	0.5
2014	LAN	MLB	26	250	33	9	2	1	15	17	42	24	6	.256/.309/.329	.242	.300	2.6	SS -2, 2B -0	0.7

Gordon carries only one tool in his toolbox; any more and the wisp wouldn't be able to pick it up. The raw speed is elite but his stolen-base skills carry minimal value if he can't get on base. To his credit, he has increased his walk rate by three percentage points in each of the past two seasons, and another similar jump would represent a boon to his value on offense. Beyond the wheels, his greatest asset is positional value in the field, and word around the campfire is that the Dodgers will try to maximize this utility by training Gordon in center field. If the experiment works, Gordon could pay dividends by covering for the oft-injured Dodgers stars who are irregularly penciled in up the middle.

Alexander Guerrero   2B

Born: 12/20/1986 Age: 27
Bats: R Throws: R Height: 5'10"
Weight: 197

YEAR	TEAM	LVL	AGE	PA	R	2B	3B	HR	RBI	BB	SO	SB	CS	AVG/OBP/SLG	TAv	BABIP	BRR	FRAA	WARP
2014	–		–	–	–	–	–	–	–	–	–	–		–	–	–		–	–

The Dodgers continued to throw their weight around in one of the few amateur arenas where they can still flex their financial muscles: the Cuban market. Guerrero might not have the defensive chops to stick at short as he transitions to the majors, but his value will be sustainable so long as he can handle the keystone. The power is legit—Guerrero has been one of the best hitters in Cuban baseball for the past four seasons—and for $28 million the Dodgers will get to enjoy the next four years of his theoretical prime. He doesn't need to lead the army for L.A. to conquer the National League, but the squad's odds will be greatly enhanced if he can just be Alexander at the plate.

Matt Kemp CF

Born: **9/23/1984** Age: **29**
Bats: **R** Throws: **R** Height: **6' 4"**
Weight: **215** Breakout: **3%**
Improve: **57%** Collapse: **2%**
Attrition: **1%** MLB: **96%**

Comparables:
Ken Griffey, Duke Snider, Dale Murphy

YEAR	TEAM	LVL	AGE	PA	R	2B	3B	HR	RBI	BB	SO	SB	CS	AVG/OBP/SLG	TAv	BABIP	BRR	FRAA	WARP
2011	LAN	MLB	26	689	115	33	4	39	126	74	159	40	11	.324/.399/.586	.357	.380	4.6	CF(159): -8.3	9.5
2012	LAN	MLB	27	449	74	22	2	23	69	40	103	9	4	.303/.367/.538	.325	.354	0.9	CF(105): -7.0	4.0
2013	LAN	MLB	28	290	35	15	0	6	33	22	76	9	0	.270/.328/.395	.252	.353	3.6	CF(70): -5.2	0.8
2014	LAN	MLB	29	313	44	14	1	14	45	26	73	11	4	.282/.344/.486	.302	.330	0.6	CF -3	2.0

Injuries didn't strike Kemp *immediately* after he signed his eight-year, $160 million deal following the 2011 season, but it was close enough for a primitive culture to conclude that all those zeroes infuriated some god somewhere. His early-2012 MVP pace was disrupted by a thigh strain, then a shoulder injury sapped his power in September. Offseason shoulder surgery was supposed to put all the oomph back in his swing for 2013, but he didn't hit his third home run until July. There was inflammation in that shoulder that put him on the DL in June, after a hamstring strain put him on the DL in May, but before a severe ankle strain put him on the DL in September and (contradicting initial optimism) knocked him out of the playoffs. He underwent surgery for both the shoulder and the ankle early in the offseason, but if that's enough to make you optimistic you've simply lost count: both hamstrings, an ankle, two shoulder surgeries, and at least two recoveries that took longer than expected. At full health, Kemp is a dynamic player with 40/40 skills at a premium position, a nine-win player as recently as 24 months ago, and under 30 to boot. His shoulder strength will determine the power ceiling, while his ankle stability dictates mobility in the field and on the bases. No other Dodger has a wider range of potential outcomes, and perhaps no other player in baseball will have a greater impact on his team's fortunes this season. Godspeed.

Joc Pederson CF

Born: **4/21/1992** Age: **22**
Bats: **L** Throws: **L** Height: **6' 1"**
Weight: **185** Breakout: **1%**
Improve: **19%** Collapse: **1%**
Attrition: **11%** MLB: **60%**

Comparables:
Colby Rasmus, Brett Jackson, Wil Myers

YEAR	TEAM	LVL	AGE	PA	R	2B	3B	HR	RBI	BB	SO	SB	CS	AVG/OBP/SLG	TAv	BABIP	BRR	FRAA	WARP
2011	GRL	A	19	60	4	0	0	0	1	7	9	2	0	.160/.288/.160	.162	.195	0.8	LF(2): 0.1, CF(1): 0.2	0.1
2012	RCU	A+	20	499	96	26	4	18	70	51	81	26	14	.313/.396/.516	.329	.350	5.7	CF(76): -6.0, LF(33): 1.4	5.4
2013	CHT	AA	21	519	81	24	3	22	58	70	114	31	8	.278/.381/.497	.313	.327	3.9	CF(106): -0.3, LF(6): 0.5	5.3
2014	LAN	MLB	22	250	34	10	0	8	27	22	59	8	3	.247/.317/.406	.266	.300	0.3	CF -1, LF 1	0.8

In May, the Dodgers held internal discussions about which promising Double-A outfielder with prospect cred and big numbers to call up to the big club. Ultimately, they went not with Pederson but with Puig, and an L.A. Story was written. Pederson's story will come soon enough: A big-bonus 11th-round pick in the 2010 draft, Pederson has exceeded expectations throughout his pro career. He's got a groovy five-tool blend, though there's a little bit of a flaw in every plan for him: The raw speed is a little light for center field, the pure arm strength doesn't quite stand up to right field and the offensive demands on left fielders create a perpetual barrier for entry. But Pederson's power is developing into a weapon, and his bat will force the issue soon—though it might be in a trade rather than a promotion to Chavez Ravine. Pederson's scouting reports are stamped with the word "grinder" at the top of every page, with implications of a high baseball IQ and the effort to succeed beyond his tools.

Yasiel Puig RF

Born: **12/7/1990** Age: **23**
Bats: **R** Throws: **R** Height: **6' 3"**
Weight: **245** Breakout: **3%**
Improve: **60%** Collapse: **2%**
Attrition: **5%** MLB: **98%**

Comparables:
Justin Upton, Jay Bruce, Matt Kemp

YEAR	TEAM	LVL	AGE	PA	R	2B	3B	HR	RBI	BB	SO	SB	CS	AVG/OBP/SLG	TAv	BABIP	BRR	FRAA	WARP
2012	RCU	A+	21	59	10	2	0	1	4	6	8	7	4	.327/.407/.423	.335	.372	-0.1	RF(8): -0.4	0.5
2013	CHT	AA	22	167	26	12	3	8	37	15	29	13	5	.313/.383/.599	.348	.339	1	RF(31): 0.9, CF(4): -0.2	2.1
2013	LAN	MLB	22	432	66	21	2	19	42	36	97	11	8	.319/.391/.534	.329	.383	0.6	RF(93): -4.2, CF(10): -0.5	4.0
2014	LAN	MLB	23	356	55	16	1	15	45	27	79	12	6	.289/.354/.488	.307	.340	-0.2	RF -3, CF -0	2.0

Puig announced his presence immediately upon his June 3rd call-up, ending his first game with an outfield assist and hitting a pair of homers in his second. One month later his slash line stood at a ridiculous .443/.473/.745. You can see the missing walks in that line, but Puig's feast of NL pitchers provided little incentive to turn down the dials of aggression. (He did finish the season with 29 walks in his final 62 games.) The dynamics of his debut taught us a lot about learning curves in the Hot Takes era. Dubbed "the wild horse" by legend-maker Vin Scully, Puig is the type of player whose enthusiasm and swagger are loved by teammates, tsked at by opponents and greedily slurped down by opportunistic sportswriters who couldn't always keep their stories straight. His post-clinching foray into the Chase Field swimming pool might be the only event from last season you still remember 50 years from now. If his first week announced his presence, that cannonball announced his dominion.

Hanley Ramirez   SS

Born: 12/23/1983 Age: 30
Bats: R Throws: R Height: 6' 2"
Weight: 225 Breakout: 2%
Improve: 51% Collapse: 1%
Attrition: 7% MLB: 100%

Comparables:
Nomar Garciaparra, Chase Utley, David Wright

YEAR	TEAM	LVL	AGE	PA	R	2B	3B	HR	RBI	BB	SO	SB	CS	AVG/OBP/SLG	TAv	BABIP	BRR	FRAA	WARP
2011	JUP	A+	27	22	6	1	1	0	4	1	2	1	0	.476/.500/.619	.369	.526	0.9	SS(3): -0.1	0.4
2011	FLO	MLB	27	385	55	16	0	10	45	44	66	20	10	.243/.333/.379	.258	.275	1.2	SS(86): -8.7	0.7
2012	MIA	MLB	28	395	49	18	2	14	48	37	72	14	4	.246/.322/.428	.275	.271	3.1	3B(90): -12.6	0.8
2012	LAN	MLB	28	272	30	11	2	10	44	17	60	7	3	.271/.324/.450	.281	.319	1.8	SS(57): -3.3, 3B(8): 0.1	1.7
2013	LAN	MLB	29	336	62	25	2	20	57	27	52	10	2	.345/.402/.638	.360	.363	-1.6	SS(76): 0.3	4.8
2014	LAN	MLB	30	384	53	19	0	14	51	34	64	15	5	.285/.352/.467	.299	.310	0.5	SS -5, 3B -4	2.2

For Ramirez, last season was a tale of heroism and seduction, bookended by injuries. He tore a ligament in his thumb during the World Baseball Classic and missed the first 24 games of the regular season, and was back in action for just five days before a strained hamstring sent him back to the disabled list. He finally returned on June 4th, one day after Yasiel Puig made his debut, and the pair of sluggers proceeded to ignite something special. Ramirez was a monster, accumulating more offensive VORP than any shortstop in baseball despite appearing in just 86 games, posting a TAv that trailed only Mike Trout and Miguel Cabrera and flashing a surprisingly nimble glove for the first time in years. Alas, he was pelted by a Joe Kelly two-seamer in the first game of the NLCS, fracturing a rib that compromised his play at the plate and in the field. This is his walk year, the final season in a six-year deal that looked like a bargain, then a burden, and now a crazy steal once more. He's been hurt in two of the past three seasons, and mediocre in two of the past three seasons, and it's not a stretch to say that he'll double his next contract by being neither in 2014.

Corey Seager   SS

Born: 4/27/1994 Age: 20
Bats: L Throws: R Height: 6' 4"
Weight: 215 Breakout: 3%
Improve: 7% Collapse: 0%
Attrition: 5% MLB: 9%

Comparables:
Nick Franklin, Jeff Bianchi, Xander Bogaerts

YEAR	TEAM	LVL	AGE	PA	R	2B	3B	HR	RBI	BB	SO	SB	CS	AVG/OBP/SLG	TAv	BABIP	BRR	FRAA	WARP
2013	GRL	A	19	312	45	18	3	12	57	34	58	9	4	.309/.389/.529	.330	.353	-0.5	SS(74): -5.5	3.2
2013	RCU	A+	19	114	10	2	1	4	15	12	31	1	0	.160/.246/.320	.221	.179	0.2	SS(25): -4.1, 3B(1): -0.0	-0.6
2014	LAN	MLB	20	250	24	9	1	8	29	17	65	0	0	.221/.273/.362	.235	.270	-0.4	SS -8, 3B -0	-0.4

Corey has older brother Kyle's skill set, swinging heavy lumber and flashing both the leather and the cannon to stay on the left side. Seager has been young for his levels as he has climbed the minor-league ladder, and after posting nearly identical slash lines in Rookie ball and Single-A, he finally faced adversity with his initial taste of High-A. Undeterred, the Dodgers assigned Seager to the Arizona Fall League, where he was the youngest player in the circuit. He was overmatched, to be sure, but at this age the achievement is often in the matching. He'll hit and field enough for either short or third, depending on which All-Stars the Dodgers are already paying eight figures to when his time comes. Plenty of scouts will tell you Corey will be the superior Seager when it's all said and done.

Darnell Sweeney   SS

Born: 2/1/1991 Age: 23
Bats: B Throws: R Height: 6' 1"
Weight: 150 Breakout: 5%
Improve: 10% Collapse: 1%
Attrition: 12% MLB: 12%

Comparables:
Brock Holt, Diory Hernandez, Pete Kozma

YEAR	TEAM	LVL	AGE	PA	R	2B	3B	HR	RBI	BB	SO	SB	CS	AVG/OBP/SLG	TAv	BABIP	BRR	FRAA	WARP
2012	GRL	A	21	229	34	8	4	5	23	24	41	17	4	.291/.372/.447	.291	.344	4.9	SS(49): -5.6	1.7
2013	RCU	A+	22	613	79	34	16	11	77	43	151	48	20	.275/.329/.455	.276	.355	4.7	SS(107): -10.9, 2B(29): 2.7	3.2
2014	LAN	MLB	23	250	29	9	2	3	17	13	67	12	4	.221/.263/.319	.216	.290	1	SS -5, 2B 1	-0.4

Sweeney has already surpassed the expectations of a 13th-round pick, but the enthusiasm triggered by his stat line should be tempered. Speed is the only plus tool, and his instincts on the bases need work. He's full of swing-and-miss, and an inflated slugging percentage was a combination of Cal League ballparks and leg triples. Double-A will give a more realistic idea of his eventual role.

Juan Uribe   3B

Born: 3/22/1979 Age: 35
Bats: R Throws: R Height: 6' 0"
Weight: 235 Breakout: 0%
Improve: 28% Collapse: 9%
Attrition: 16% MLB: 91%

Comparables:
Eric Chavez, Al Smith, Don Money

YEAR	TEAM	LVL	AGE	PA	R	2B	3B	HR	RBI	BB	SO	SB	CS	AVG/OBP/SLG	TAv	BABIP	BRR	FRAA	WARP
2011	LAN	MLB	32	295	21	12	0	4	28	17	60	2	0	.204/.264/.293	.206	.245	0.5	3B(59): 0.6, 2B(18): -1.4	-0.9
2012	LAN	MLB	33	179	15	9	0	2	17	13	37	0	1	.191/.258/.284	.200	.234	1.8	3B(46): 2.5, SS(1): -0.1	-0.1
2013	LAN	MLB	34	426	47	22	2	12	50	30	81	5	0	.278/.331/.438	.279	.322	1.9	3B(123): 9.3, 1B(4): 0.1	3.9
2014	LAN	MLB	35	352	36	16	1	10	41	22	68	2	1	.243/.295/.390	.254	.280	-0.3	3B 5, 2B 0	1.2

Uribe's first two seasons in Dodger blue were an unmitigated disaster, as he flirted with the Mendoza line and showed little in the way of secondary skills. He picked an opportune time to mend and clear fences, finishing with a pair of homers in the NL Division Series. Uribe has earned more than $40 million playing baseball, which isn't half bad for a guy whose career on-base percentage sits under .300. His 2013 OBP was, at .331, the highest single-season rate of Uribe's career, and enough to give his GM amnesia. Colletti re-upped him for two years.

Jesmuel Valentin 2B

Born: 5/12/1994 Age: 20
Bats: B Throws: R Height: 5' 9"
Weight: 180 Breakout: 0%
Improve: 0% Collapse: 0%
Attrition: 0% MLB: 0%

Comparables:
Jose Altuve, Logan Watkins, Everth Cabrera

YEAR	TEAM	LVL	AGE	PA	R	2B	3B	HR	RBI	BB	SO	SB	CS	AVG/OBP/SLG	TAv	BABIP	BRR	FRAA	WARP
2013	GRL	A	19	122	12	6	1	0	5	16	28	4	3	.212/.325/.293	.248	.292	-0.2	SS(17): -2.6, 2B(16): -0.3	-0.1
2014	LAN	MLB	20	250	21	8	0	1	15	20	65	1	0	.186/.253/.243	.192	.250	-0.4	2B -1, SS -2	-1.2

Switch-hitters who can play in the middle of the diamond get a long leash; prospects with big-league bloodlines are especially revered in the Dodger organization. The son of Jose Valentin has inherited much of pop's skill set, from positional flexibility to a patient approach at the plate. Valentin is still an apprentice in the craft of pitch recognition and identifying those that he can drive, but he sees enough pitches per game to augment his education. Valentin has his work cut out for him in the years ahead, but he also possesses the defensive chops to hold down the keystone if his bat continues to develop.

Scott Van Slyke 1B

Born: 7/24/1986 Age: 27
Bats: R Throws: R Height: 6' 5"
Weight: 250 Breakout: 4%
Improve: 22% Collapse: 12%
Attrition: 21% MLB: 55%

Comparables:
Jake Fox, Jeff Larish, Mark Hamilton

YEAR	TEAM	LVL	AGE	PA	R	2B	3B	HR	RBI	BB	SO	SB	CS	AVG/OBP/SLG	TAv	BABIP	BRR	FRAA	WARP
2011	CHT	AA	24	529	81	45	4	20	92	65	100	6	5	.348/.427/.595	.333	.406	-1.2	LF(24): 0.4, 1B(14): 0.0	1.5
2012	ABQ	AAA	25	411	68	34	1	18	67	46	64	5	3	.327/.404/.578	.311	.354	-1.2	RF(43): -1.7, 1B(39): -1.4	2.2
2012	LAN	MLB	25	57	4	2	0	2	7	2	14	1	0	.167/.196/.315	.188	.184	0.9	RF(12): 0.5, LF(11): 0.1	-0.2
2013	ABQ	AAA	26	263	55	17	2	12	48	50	61	8	2	.348/.479/.627	.338	.437	1	1B(51): 2.2, 1B(8): 0.1	3.1
2013	LAN	MLB	26	152	13	8	0	7	19	20	37	1	1	.240/.342/.465	.285	.276	-1	LF(30): 0.4, RF(13): 0.3	0.6
2014	LAN	MLB	27	250	32	12	0	10	34	27	58	3	1	.259/.342/.450	.291	.300	-0.4	1B 0, LF 1	1.3

Speaking of bloodlines, the son of Andy Van Slyke was a good source of power in the desperate days pre-Puig and sans Han-Ram. Van Slyke was called up to the majors in early May and most of his damage was concentrated in his first 19 games, as he hit six bombs and five doubles in his first 60 plate appearances. Pitchers began burying their offerings under the zone once they had the book on him and Van Slyke failed to adjust, with walks being his only safety valve en route to a .230/.359/.311 line the rest of the way.

Michael Young 3B

Born: 10/19/1976 Age: 37
Bats: R Throws: R Height: 6' 1"
Weight: 200 Breakout: 0%
Improve: 17% Collapse: 16%
Attrition: 15% MLB: 75%

Comparables:
Melvin Mora, Miguel Tejada, Joe Randa

YEAR	TEAM	LVL	AGE	PA	R	2B	3B	HR	RBI	BB	SO	SB	CS	AVG/OBP/SLG	TAv	BABIP	BRR	FRAA	WARP
2011	TEX	MLB	34	689	88	41	6	11	106	47	78	6	2	.338/.380/.474	.289	.367	0.7	3B(40): -0.4, 1B(36): -3.6	2.8
2012	TEX	MLB	35	651	79	27	3	8	67	33	70	2	2	.277/.312/.370	.240	.299	-1.2	1B(41): 0.3, 3B(25): -1.2	-0.7
2013	LAN	MLB	36	53	3	2	1	0	4	1	5	0	0	.314/.321/.392	.239	.340	-1.2	3B(8): -0.4, 1B(8): -0.1	-0.2
2013	PHI	MLB	36	512	49	24	4	8	42	42	78	1	0	.276/.336/.395	.250	.316	-0.8	3B(99): -9.1, 1B(26): -0.8	-0.7
2014	LAN	MLB	37	548	52	26	2	8	56	34	83	3	1	.278/.323/.385	.265	.320	-0.8	3B -6, 1B -2	0.4

Young takes a lot of flak for playing past his expiration date, but he remains a line-drive machine whose consistent contact keeps his batting average floor high enough to be useful. He can still hit the fastball, and his tendency to inside-out pitches to the opposite field allows him to cover for the expected drop in bat speed. Meanwhile, his positional flexibility increases his utility, even if his inability to play any position well crushes his value stats. Young spent his entire career in a Rangers uniform before last year, but he is at a stage of his career in which loyalty goes out the window in pursuit of playing time or a ring.

PITCHERS

Chris Anderson

Born: 7/29/1992 Age: 21
Bats: R Throws: R Height: 6' 4" Weight: 215
Breakout: 53% Improve: 73% Collapse: 8%
Attrition: 62% MLB: 15%

Comparables:
Casey Crosby, Christian Friedrich, Gio Gonzalez

YEAR	TEAM	LVL	AGE	W	L	SV	G	GS	IP	H	HR	BB	SO	BB9	SO9	GB%	BABIP	WHIP	ERA	FIP	FRA	WARP
2013	GRL	A	20	3	0	0	12	12	46	32	0	24	50	4.7	9.8	41%	.288	1.22	1.96	2.79	3.15	1.2
2014	LAN	MLB	21	2	3	0	9	9	36¹	35	4	18	29	4.5	7.2	42%	.306	1.46	4.58	4.65	4.98	-0.0

Anderson was a rapid riser leading up to the 2013 draft, and the Dodgers nabbed the Jacksonville University product with the 18th pick and slot bonus. He has an advanced repertoire, including a 91-94 mph fastball that scrapes 97. The fastball features sinking action that Anderson locates well on the lower shelf of the strike zone. His best pitch is a knockout slider with sharp bite, and scouts were impressed with the development of his changeup during the spring. His pitching mechanics offer an excellent blend of power and stability, with strong momentum and heavy torque supported by a balanced frame throughout the delivery. The 6-foot-4 right-hander coasted through his Single-A orientation, and he could progress quickly in an organization that is not afraid to promote players aggressively.

Josh Beckett

Born: 5/15/1980 Age: 34
Bats: R Throws: R Height: 6' 5" Weight: 225
Breakout: 19% Improve: 50% Collapse: 14%
Attrition: 12% MLB: 88%

Comparables:
Kevin Millwood, Johan Santana, Wandy Rodriguez

YEAR	TEAM	LVL	AGE	W	L	SV	G	GS	IP	H	HR	BB	SO	BB9	SO9	GB%	BABIP	WHIP	ERA	FIP	FRA	WARP
2011	BOS	MLB	31	13	7	0	30	30	193	146	21	52	175	2.4	8.2	42%	.245	1.03	2.89	3.61	4.13	2.9
2012	BOS	MLB	32	5	11	0	21	21	127¹	131	16	38	94	2.7	6.6	42%	.293	1.33	5.23	4.22	5.38	0.5
2012	LAN	MLB	32	2	3	0	7	7	43	43	5	14	38	2.9	8.0	49%	.306	1.33	2.93	3.86	3.72	0.6
2013	LAN	MLB	33	0	5	0	8	8	43¹	50	8	15	41	3.1	8.5	41%	.347	1.50	5.19	4.64	4.82	0.1
2014	LAN	MLB	34	4	4	0	10	10	62²	55	7	16	55	2.3	7.9	45%	.289	1.15	3.39	3.75	3.68	0.7

After a five-year run of declining velocity, Beckett was enjoying a slight uptick in the first six weeks of the 2013 season. Pitchers generally heat up further as the season progresses, but Beckett's momentum was halted by injuries in mid-May. The trouble started with a groin strain, followed by numbness in his fingers while he recuperated. Doctors found nerve irritation in his neck, and Beckett eventually underwent surgery for Thoracic Outlet Syndrome to repair the damage. He is expected to be ready for spring training, but Chris Carpenter never really returned from the same procedure.

Chad Billingsley

Born: 7/29/1984 Age: 29
Bats: R Throws: R Height: 6' 1" Weight: 240
Breakout: 16% Improve: 40% Collapse: 29%
Attrition: 11% MLB: 97%

Comparables:
Jason Jennings, Vicente Padilla, Gil Meche

YEAR	TEAM	LVL	AGE	W	L	SV	G	GS	IP	H	HR	BB	SO	BB9	SO9	GB%	BABIP	WHIP	ERA	FIP	FRA	WARP
2011	LAN	MLB	26	11	11	0	32	32	188	189	14	84	152	4.0	7.3	46%	.314	1.45	4.21	3.80	4.24	1.0
2012	LAN	MLB	27	10	9	0	25	25	149²	148	11	45	128	2.7	7.7	46%	.309	1.29	3.55	3.38	3.80	1.8
2013	LAN	MLB	28	1	0	0	2	2	12	12	1	5	6	3.8	4.5	45%	.297	1.42	3.00	4.35	5.94	-0.2
2014	LAN	MLB	29	2	2	0	6	6	37²	35	3	13	31	3.1	7.3	47%	.305	1.27	3.81	3.70	4.14	0.2

The Dodgers entered the spring with a perceived overabundance of starting pitchers, and nearly every sportswriter with a keyboard ordered the team to deal from this excess to fill weaknesses elsewhere. Then the staff proceeded to demonstrate why teams can never have too much pitching, or too few sportswriters. Billingsley was the first hurler to fall to a major injury. Anointed the no. 5 out of camp, Bills made it through two starts for one Tommy John surgery, which knocked him out for the season and put his 2014 status in question. Elbow injuries typically sap command, an element that could be a major issue for a pitcher who had only recently overcome wild tendencies.

Chris Capuano

Born: 8/19/1978 Age: 35
Bats: L Throws: L Height: 6' 3" Weight: 215
Breakout: 19% Improve: 49% Collapse: 16%
Attrition: 12% MLB: 83%

Comparables:
Freddy Garcia, Rick Helling, Darrell May

YEAR	TEAM	LVL	AGE	W	L	SV	G	GS	IP	H	HR	BB	SO	BB9	SO9	GB%	BABIP	WHIP	ERA	FIP	FRA	WARP
2011	NYN	MLB	32	11	12	0	33	31	186	198	27	53	168	2.6	8.1	43%	.326	1.35	4.55	4.01	4.36	1.3
2012	LAN	MLB	33	12	12	0	33	33	198¹	188	25	54	162	2.5	7.4	41%	.296	1.22	3.72	3.99	4.29	1.3
2013	LAN	MLB	34	4	7	0	24	20	105²	125	11	24	81	2.0	6.9	47%	.335	1.41	4.26	3.52	4.37	0.7
2014	LAN	MLB	35	6	7	0	21	21	113¹	112	14	28	89	2.2	7.1	43%	.304	1.23	4.00	4.04	4.35	0.4

Capuano began the 2013 season in the bullpen, replaced Zack Greinke in the rotation after Greinke was hurt fighting Carlos Quentin and then lasted all of two innings before he joined his teammate on the disabled list. Calf, shoulder and groin strains marred his campaign, and though he returned in time for the playoffs he was left off the NLCS roster despite a St. Louis opponent that was soft against lefties. He carries extreme platoon splits that are easily exploitable by opposing managers: 74 percent of the hitters Capuano faced stood on the right (which is to say, wrong) side last season, and those batters enjoyed a 300-point advantage in OPS, including all 11 homers he surrendered.

Jose Dominguez

Born: 8/7/1990 Age: 23
Bats: R Throws: R Height: 6' 0" Weight: 160
Breakout: 56% Improve: 67% Collapse: 29%
Attrition: 53% MLB: 18%

Comparables:
Waldis Joaquin, Jeff Beliveau, Luis Avilan

YEAR	TEAM	LVL	AGE	W	L	SV	G	GS	IP	H	HR	BB	SO	BB9	SO9	GB%	BABIP	WHIP	ERA	FIP	FRA	WARP
2012	GRL	A	21	4	3	4	33	5	72	77	4	47	78	5.9	9.8	46%	.349	1.72	5.25	4.07	5.24	0.4
2013	CHT	AA	22	1	0	5	14	0	17¹	8	0	8	28	4.2	14.5	52%	.258	0.92	2.60	1.24	1.84	0.6
2013	LAN	MLB	22	0	0	0	9	0	8¹	11	0	3	4	3.2	4.3	39%	.355	1.68	2.16	3.50	4.20	0.1
2014	LAN	MLB	23	1	1	0	21	1	37²	34	4	19	34	4.5	8.1	44%	.307	1.42	4.33	4.48	4.71	-0.1

When Dominguez made his big-league debut on June 30th, topping 100 mph with the second, fourth, 10th, 13th and 14th pitches he threw, it was immediately clear what had fueled his rapid rise through the minors. He leverages tremendous torque into an average fastball velocity of 99.23 mph, trailing only the Tigers' Bruce Rondon among big leaguers. That gas made him virtually unhittable across two upper-minors stops, where hitters literally had better odds when leaving the bat on the shoulder than actually swinging. Dominguez suffered a quad strain on July 22nd and was very slow to recover, eventually landing on the 60-day disabled list and prematurely ending his electric tease.

Stephen Fife

Born: 10/4/1986 Age: 27
Bats: R Throws: R Height: 6' 3" Weight: 220
Breakout: 43% Improve: 59% Collapse: 27%
Attrition: 61% MLB: 58%

Comparables:
Duane Below, Anthony Lerew, Doug Mathis

YEAR	TEAM	LVL	AGE	W	L	SV	G	GS	IP	H	HR	BB	SO	BB9	SO9	GB%	BABIP	WHIP	ERA	FIP	FRA	WARP
2011	CHT	AA	24	3	0	0	6	6	33²	36	2	15	25	4.0	6.7	60%	.255	1.51	4.01	4.02	3.76	0.4
2011	PME	AA	24	11	4	0	19	18	103¹	107	7	37	70	3.2	6.1	51%	.313	1.39	3.66	4.18	3.55	0.5
2012	ABQ	AAA	25	11	7	0	25	24	135¹	157	13	44	93	2.9	6.2	49%	.334	1.49	4.66	4.74	5.75	1.7
2012	LAN	MLB	25	0	2	0	5	5	26²	25	2	12	20	4.1	6.8	43%	.311	1.39	2.70	4.19	3.98	0.2
2013	ABQ	AAA	26	2	4	0	10	8	37¹	46	3	21	33	5.1	8.0	54%	.378	1.79	6.03	4.86	6.86	0.2
2013	LAN	MLB	26	4	4	0	12	10	58¹	69	7	20	45	3.1	6.9	53%	.345	1.53	3.86	4.32	4.88	0.0
2014	LAN	MLB	27	5	7	0	19	19	99	102	11	33	66	3.0	6.0	50%	.305	1.36	4.46	4.46	4.85	-0.2

Fife was the company yo-yo last season, spinning up and down from the majors to the bush leagues. He made four separate trips to Los Angeles, including a pair of single-game spot starts over the summer, and was then used out of the bullpen when rosters expanded in September. Such is the life of a swingman on the 40-man roster who has options remaining. The modest stuff and sketchy peripheral stats are indicators that the Dodgers will continue to limit Fife's exposure, keeping him confined to low-impact scenarios and emergency situations.

Onelki Garcia

Born: 8/2/1989 Age: 24
Bats: L Throws: L Height: 6' 3" Weight: 220
Breakout: 51% Improve: 79% Collapse: 13%
Attrition: 46% MLB: 29%

Comparables:
Jon Meloan, Juan Morillo, Jeff Stevens

YEAR	TEAM	LVL	AGE	W	L	SV	G	GS	IP	H	HR	BB	SO	BB9	SO9	GB%	BABIP	WHIP	ERA	FIP	FRA	WARP
2013	CHT	AA	23	2	3	1	25	6	52¹	41	3	32	53	5.5	9.1	60%	.284	1.39	2.75	3.58	5.81	0.3
2013	LAN	MLB	23	0	0	0	3	0	1¹	1	1	4	1	27.0	6.8	67%	.000	3.75	13.50	20.27	25.75	-0.3
2014	LAN	MLB	24	2	2	1	28	4	47¹	41	5	22	45	4.1	8.5	52%	.298	1.32	3.85	4.14	4.19	0.3

Garcia joined the cadre of Cuban baseballers to be plucked by the Dodgers, and he climbed to Chavez Ravine in short order. The hard-throwing southpaw displayed strong balance in his brief major-league stint, but his timing was erratic and he struggled to hit targets. Garcia had offseason surgery to clean up his left elbow, but he should be ready for the 2014 season.

Zack Greinke

Born: 10/21/1983 Age: 30
Bats: R Throws: R Height: 6' 2" Weight: 195
Breakout: 7% Improve: 40% Collapse: 30%
Attrition: 11% MLB: 94%

Comparables:
Jered Weaver, Josh Beckett, Jake Peavy

YEAR	TEAM	LVL	AGE	W	L	SV	G	GS	IP	H	HR	BB	SO	BB9	SO9	GB%	BABIP	WHIP	ERA	FIP	FRA	WARP
2011	MIL	MLB	27	16	6	0	28	28	171²	161	19	45	201	2.4	10.5	48%	.322	1.20	3.83	2.95	3.90	2.9
2012	MIL	MLB	28	9	3	0	21	21	123	120	7	28	122	2.0	8.9	55%	.320	1.20	3.44	2.58	3.17	3.3
2012	ANA	MLB	28	6	2	0	13	13	89¹	80	11	26	78	2.6	7.9	45%	.279	1.19	3.53	3.84	4.42	0.7
2013	LAN	MLB	29	15	4	0	28	28	177²	152	13	46	148	2.3	7.5	47%	.285	1.11	2.63	3.20	3.81	2.3
2014	LAN	MLB	30	10	8	0	26	26	163¹	140	13	37	154	2.0	8.5	45%	.299	1.08	2.94	3.06	3.20	2.9

Greinke's season caught a bad break when Carlos Quentin charged his mound in April; Greinke lost the battle on impact. He returned from a broken left clavicle a month later and—as he actually predicted to reporters—struggled to find consistency upon his return. It finally reclicked: He had a 1.85 ERA in the second half, and shined in three postseason starts, giving the Dodgers a strong return in the first year of their seven-year lease. Greinke's velocity is trending slightly downward, following the typical aging curve, but his outstanding command of a cornucopia of pitches—a pair of fastballs, a cutter, a slider, a slow curve and a changeup—effectively shields him from a lot of velo-related decline. Still, Greinke always seems to find a way to not quiiiite pitch like an ace.

Javy Guerra

Born: 10/31/1985 Age: 28
Bats: R Throws: R Height: 6' 1" Weight: 190
Breakout: 33% Improve: 56% Collapse: 32%
Attrition: 40% MLB: 57%

Comparables:
Royce Ring, Francis Beltran, Matt Hensley

YEAR	TEAM	LVL	AGE	W	L	SV	G	GS	IP	H	HR	BB	SO	BB9	SO9	GB%	BABIP	WHIP	ERA	FIP	FRA	WARP
2011	CHT	AA	25	1	0	3	14	0	17	8	1	5	15	2.6	7.9	1.%	.500	0.76	1.06	3.19	-0.93	0.2
2011	LAN	MLB	25	2	2	21	47	0	46²	37	2	18	38	3.5	7.3	44%	.261	1.18	2.31	3.27	4.33	0.2
2012	LAN	MLB	26	2	3	8	45	0	45	44	1	23	37	4.6	7.4	50%	.321	1.49	2.60	3.38	3.69	0.5
2013	ABQ	AAA	27	0	4	12	27	4	39¹	46	6	14	36	3.2	8.2	49%	.345	1.53	3.66	4.94	5.08	0.4
2013	LAN	MLB	27	0	0	0	9	0	10²	15	1	6	12	5.1	10.1	39%	.400	1.97	6.75	3.96	4.18	0.0
2014	LAN	MLB	28	3	1	4	45	2	50	46	4	21	42	3.7	7.6	44%	.304	1.33	3.94	3.94	4.28	0.2

A year after opening the 2012 season as the Dodgers' closer, Guerra opened the 2013 season as an Isotopes starter, pitching first innings for the first time since 2008. The ABQ is a terrible place to break bad habits or learn good ones, and his attempts at finding footing were further shaken up by changing roles (the starting pitcher experiment ended after April), travel (he was recalled but quickly optioned back down after allowing a 38 percent line-drive rate in May) and visits to the disabled list. On the bright side, who knows what amazing surprises the next year might hold for him. Don't answer that, PECOTA.

Dan Haren

Born: 9/17/1980 Age: 33
Bats: R Throws: R Height: 6' 5" Weight: 215
Breakout: 17% Improve: 47% Collapse: 28%
Attrition: 14% MLB: 89%

Comparables:
Aaron Harang, Johan Santana, Fergie Jenkins

YEAR	TEAM	LVL	AGE	W	L	SV	G	GS	IP	H	HR	BB	SO	BB9	SO9	GB%	BABIP	WHIP	ERA	FIP	FRA	WARP
2011	ANA	MLB	30	16	10	0	35	34	238¹	211	20	33	192	1.2	7.3	45%	.272	1.02	3.17	3.02	3.75	3.3
2012	ANA	MLB	31	12	13	0	30	30	176²	190	28	38	142	1.9	7.2	41%	.303	1.29	4.33	4.20	4.42	1.3
2013	WAS	MLB	32	10	14	1	31	30	169²	179	28	31	151	1.6	8.0	38%	.305	1.24	4.67	4.06	4.47	1.5
2014	LAN	MLB	33	9	8	0	25	25	154²	143	19	27	133	1.6	7.7	43%	.292	1.10	3.37	3.65	3.66	1.8

A second consecutive season of a 4+ ERA (and FIP) won't make anyone think Haren is back to his old self, because he's not. At 33 years old, Haren is his *old* self, as he failed to crack 180 innings again after surpassing 200 every year from 2005-2011. He can still miss bats (21 percent strikeout rate) and can still pound the zone (4 percent walk rate). But perhaps he's in the zone too much, with a HR/FB rate well above the league's average that risks undoing an otherwise very good pitcher. Haren was far more effective after returning from a mid-season DL stint, with opponents posting a .636 OPS against him in the second half, and earned himself a potential two-year deal with the Dodgers. If Haren can continue to keep fly balls in the yard at his more representative late-summer rate, he could be a bargain.

J.P. Howell

Born: 4/25/1983 Age: 31
Bats: L Throws: L Height: 6' 0" Weight: 185
Breakout: 26% Improve: 55% Collapse: 28%
Attrition: 15% MLB: 96%

Comparables:
John Grabow, Pedro Feliciano, Jeff Montgomery

YEAR	TEAM	LVL	AGE	W	L	SV	G	GS	IP	H	HR	BB	SO	BB9	SO9	GB%	BABIP	WHIP	ERA	FIP	FRA	WARP
2011	TBA	MLB	28	2	3	1	46	0	30²	30	5	18	26	5.3	7.6	54%	.287	1.57	6.16	5.44	5.88	-0.3
2012	TBA	MLB	29	1	0	0	55	0	50¹	39	7	22	42	3.9	7.5	53%	.250	1.21	3.04	4.74	5.13	-0.1
2013	LAN	MLB	30	4	1	0	67	0	62²	42	2	23	54	3.3	7.8	58%	.233	1.05	2.03	2.86	2.76	1.1
2014	LAN	MLB	31	3	1	0	59	0	51	40	5	20	49	3.6	8.7	52%	.281	1.19	3.30	3.85	3.58	0.6

Shoulder injuries take time to mend fully, and some pitchers never recover their peak function. Howell's a happy reminder that some do. He enjoyed his best season since 2010 labrum surgery, as his average velocity gained 1.5 mph and reached a career best. Opposing hitters were unable to elevate his sinker, and Howell induced his highest rate of grounders while surrendering his fewest extra-base hits. He was the Dodgers' lefty of choice in critical situations in the fall, where he proved effective versus batters from both sides of the plate. His primary flaw—and it's a weird one—is a tendency to completely lose his balance, requiring him to brace himself by planting his glove hand on the ground after throwing. Otherwise, he'd fall on his face during follow-through. It's a bizarre trait that seems to occur only in critical situations.

Kenley Jansen

Born: 9/30/1987 Age: 26
Bats: B Throws: R Height: 6' 5" Weight: 260
Breakout: 28% Improve: 56% Collapse: 26%
Attrition: 8% MLB: 93%

Comparables:
Jonathan Broxton, Sean Doolittle, Francisco Rodriguez

YEAR	TEAM	LVL	AGE	W	L	SV	G	GS	IP	H	HR	BB	SO	BB9	SO9	GB%	BABIP	WHIP	ERA	FIP	FRA	WARP
2011	LAN	MLB	23	2	1	5	51	0	53²	30	3	26	96	4.4	16.1	28%	.300	1.04	2.85	1.71	1.41	1.5
2012	LAN	MLB	24	5	3	25	65	0	65	33	6	22	99	3.0	13.7	32%	.223	0.85	2.35	2.44	2.78	1.3
2013	LAN	MLB	25	4	3	28	75	0	76²	48	6	18	111	2.1	13.0	39%	.273	0.86	1.88	1.96	2.46	1.9
2014	LAN	MLB	26	4	2	21	62	0	67	40	5	23	99	3.1	13.4	36%	.288	0.94	1.71	2.25	1.86	2.3

Jansen continued to develop in his fourth year of education at the Mariano Rivera school for elite relievers, using his 93 mph cutter 89 percent of the time. The firehose approach gives his secondary pitches extra ambush power, so both his slider and sinker subsequently play as swing-and-miss pitches—his sinker, in fact, had baseball's highest whiff rate. Jansen has progressively honed his pitch command each year, and last year's career-low walk rate shows he has erased his only real weakness. He has no platoon disadvantage, and became hysterical in high leverage, holding batters to a .136/.176/.192 line. But perhaps the most gratifying aspect of his 2013 season was a successful recovery from offseason surgery to remedy the cardiac arrhythmia that had frighteningly disrupted his previous two seasons.

Clayton Kershaw

Born: 3/19/1988 Age: 26
Bats: L Throws: L Height: 6' 3" Weight: 220
Breakout: 21% Improve: 54% Collapse: 19%
Attrition: 4% MLB: 96%

Comparables:
Rich Harden, Felix Hernandez, Carlos Zambrano

YEAR	TEAM	LVL	AGE	W	L	SV	G	GS	IP	H	HR	BB	SO	BB9	SO9	GB%	BABIP	WHIP	ERA	FIP	FRA	WARP
2011	LAN	MLB	23	21	5	0	33	33	233¹	174	15	54	248	2.1	9.6	44%	.276	0.98	2.28	2.44	2.83	4.9
2012	LAN	MLB	24	14	9	0	33	33	227²	170	16	63	229	2.5	9.1	48%	.266	1.02	2.53	2.93	3.41	3.1
2013	LAN	MLB	25	16	9	0	33	33	236	164	11	52	232	2.0	8.8	48%	.253	0.92	1.83	2.36	2.90	5.1
2014	LAN	MLB	26	13	9	0	29	29	195²	145	14	53	196	2.4	9.0	45%	.275	1.01	2.35	2.94	2.55	5.1

A year ago you could have found a debate over the best pitcher in baseball, but not any more. Kershaw won his third consecutive ERA title (and second ERA+ title), and became the first starter to drop under the hard deck of 2.00 since Clemens in 2005, which suggests the terrifying possibility that he's only getting better. Even scarier: He spent much of the year without a functioning changeup, throwing only a dozen over a two-month stretch after the All-Star break. Instead, his cliff-diving curveball took a more prominent role, holding batters to a .095 average with no extra-base hits in more than 400 pitches. It's not hard to imagine yet another leap forward from Kershaw should he ever really master the changeup; he enters spring training just 25 years old, after all.

Brandon League
Born: 3/16/1983 Age: 31
Bats: R Throws: R Height: 6' 2" Weight: 215
Breakout: 35% Improve: 61% Collapse: 23%
Attrition: 8% MLB: 94%

Comparables:
Matt Guerrier, Braden Looper, Lindy McDaniel

YEAR	TEAM	LVL	AGE	W	L	SV	G	GS	IP	H	HR	BB	SO	BB9	SO9	GB%	BABIP	WHIP	ERA	FIP	FRA	WARP
2011	SEA	MLB	28	1	5	37	65	0	61¹	56	3	10	45	1.5	6.6	58%	.279	1.08	2.79	2.82	3.77	0.7
2012	LAN	MLB	29	2	1	6	28	0	27¹	17	0	14	27	4.6	8.9	58%	.258	1.13	2.30	2.81	2.86	0.4
2012	SEA	MLB	29	0	5	9	46	0	44²	48	1	19	27	3.8	5.4	48%	.322	1.50	3.63	3.40	3.63	0.4
2013	LAN	MLB	30	6	4	14	58	0	54¹	69	8	15	28	2.5	4.6	60%	.314	1.55	5.30	4.90	5.23	-0.4
2014	LAN	MLB	31	3	1	9	57	0	57	52	5	16	43	2.5	6.8	57%	.296	1.20	3.60	3.77	3.91	0.4

The three-year, $22.5 million contract the Dodgers gave League was overindulgent nuttiness, the most compelling evidence that the Dodgers with money might somehow be worse than the Dodgers without money. But even the most hyperbolic of critics wouldn't have predicted such a steep downfall. League's strikeout rate cratered, and each of his pitch types was less effective than in years past. His hallmark splitter lost an inch and a half of vertical drop from 2012, and almost four inches from 2011, resulting in a glut of splits that found the bottom of the strike zone instead of tumbling beneath it. League missed fewer bats with both the splitter and his high-speed sinker, as a lack of command had his pitches catching fat patches of home plate. His stat-sheet might have benefited in the walks department, but the results on contact were a disaster that cost him the closer job in early summer. It's money flushed, but the Dodgers will barely notice as League fades harmlessly into the background.

Zach Lee
Born: 9/13/1991 Age: 22
Bats: R Throws: R Height: 6' 3" Weight: 190
Breakout: 45% Improve: 86% Collapse: 7%
Attrition: 59% MLB: 32%

Comparables:
Hector Rondon, Patrick Corbin, Daryl Thompson

YEAR	TEAM	LVL	AGE	W	L	SV	G	GS	IP	H	HR	BB	SO	BB9	SO9	GB%	BABIP	WHIP	ERA	FIP	FRA	WARP
2011	GRL	A	19	9	6	0	24	24	109	101	9	32	91	2.6	7.5	52%	.276	1.22	3.47	3.84	4.83	0.3
2012	RCU	A+	20	2	3	0	12	12	55¹	60	9	10	52	1.6	8.5	48%	.315	1.27	4.55	4.65	4.58	1.2
2012	CHT	AA	20	4	3	0	13	13	65²	69	6	22	51	3.0	7.0	47%	.318	1.39	4.25	3.83	4.72	0.4
2013	CHT	AA	21	10	10	0	28	25	142²	132	13	35	131	2.2	8.3	48%	.310	1.17	3.22	3.08	4.02	1.6
2014	LAN	MLB	22	6	8	0	22	22	117²	120	15	33	82	2.6	6.3	46%	.304	1.30	4.47	4.41	4.86	-0.2

The 2013 season was Lee's most successful as a professional. He spent the entire season at Double-A, posting a career-best ERA and K/BB ratio. Lee has command of a four-pitch mix, and though only his slider grades out as a plus offering, the depth of his repertoire could play in the back half of a big-league rotation. His mechanics are marked by the lengthy extension of his arms as he completes the stride phase of his delivery, before the rotational elements kick into gear, and he finishes with an over-the-top arm slot that encourages downhill plane. Lee's 2013 performance earned him minor-league pitcher of the year honors in the Dodger system. His next assignment will be to survive the Pacific Coast League, and the bounce house that the Albuquerque Isotopes call home.

Ted Lilly
Born: 1/4/1976 Age: 38
Bats: L Throws: L Height: 6' 0" Weight: 195
Breakout: 13% Improve: 35% Collapse: 29%
Attrition: 12% MLB: 74%

Comparables:
Kevin Millwood, Pedro Martinez, Don Sutton

YEAR	TEAM	LVL	AGE	W	L	SV	G	GS	IP	H	HR	BB	SO	BB9	SO9	GB%	BABIP	WHIP	ERA	FIP	FRA	WARP
2011	LAN	MLB	35	12	14	0	33	33	192²	172	28	51	158	2.4	7.4	34%	.270	1.16	3.97	4.18	4.14	1.3
2012	RCU	A+	36	0	1	0	4	4	11	10	3	2	7	1.6	5.7	37%	.219	1.09	5.73	6.63	8.50	-0.1
2012	LAN	MLB	36	5	1	0	8	8	48²	36	3	19	31	3.5	5.7	45%	.232	1.13	3.14	3.96	4.41	0.2
2013	RCU	A+	37	1	4	0	5	5	24¹	35	5	7	24	2.6	8.9	37%	.390	1.73	8.14	5.70	5.11	0.3
2013	LAN	MLB	37	0	2	0	5	5	23	27	4	10	18	3.9	7.0	37%	.293	1.61	5.09	5.15	4.62	0.1
2014	LAN	MLB	38	3	3	0	9	9	54¹	48	7	13	42	2.2	7.0	36%	.273	1.13	3.55	4.11	3.86	0.5

Lilly's season was once again decimated by injury, an element which defines his Dodger tenure. He got a late start after labrum surgery, then his return was delayed by a strained rib cage. After five forgettable starts in Los Angeles, a neck injury put him on the shelf for 45 days. Lilly was released upon his return, finishing his three-year pact with a total of 264 innings of 3.91-ERA baseball to show for the Dodgers' $33 million. The diminutive lefty retired in November, bringing an end to his 15-year seminar on overcoming mundane velocity through sequencing, strike-throwing and the occasional jam-ball on the hands. We'll always have his epic 2007 NLDS glove-slam.

Carlos Marmol

Born: 10/14/1982 Age: 31
Bats: R Throws: R Height: 6' 2" Weight: 215
Breakout: 25% Improve: 38% Collapse: 36%
Attrition: 20% MLB: 92%

Comparables:
Ryne Duren, Jim Kern, Brian Fuentes

YEAR	TEAM	LVL	AGE	W	L	SV	G	GS	IP	H	HR	BB	SO	BB9	SO9	GB%	BABIP	WHIP	ERA	FIP	FRA	WARP
2011	CHN	MLB	28	2	6	34	75	0	74	54	5	48	99	5.8	12.0	41%	.295	1.38	4.01	3.51	4.06	0.8
2012	CHN	MLB	29	3	3	20	61	0	55¹	40	4	45	72	7.3	11.7	41%	.290	1.54	3.42	4.02	4.12	0.4
2013	CHN	MLB	30	2	4	2	31	0	27²	26	6	21	32	6.8	10.4	42%	.303	1.70	5.86	6.13	6.85	-0.5
2013	LAN	MLB	30	0	0	0	21	0	21¹	14	1	19	27	8.0	11.4	44%	.277	1.55	2.53	3.91	4.08	0.2
2014	LAN	MLB	31	3	1	7	54	0	52²	34	4	33	72	5.6	12.3	38%	.289	1.27	3.07	3.54	3.34	0.8

The Cubs finally admitted they had a problem, trading Marmol and a bag of cash for Matt Guerrier in June. The human walk machine had been particularly homer-prone during his final three months in Chicago—say what you will about him, but he's always been tough to hit. On June 16th, he entered a 3-0 game, gave up a solo home run to Marlon Byrd, and then the walk-off dinger to Kirk Nieuwenhuis, who entered the game slugging .138 and being Kirk Nieuwenhuis. That punched Marmol's ticket out of town. The Dodgers let Marmol stretch his wings in the minors for a few weeks before inviting him to Chavez Ravine, where he reverted to his usual walk-wielding, homer-suppressing ways. Other than acquiring punchline status, Marmol is basically the same pitcher he has always been, with a 94 mph fastball, a wayward slider that he uses with near-equal frequency and 20-grade balance that produces unpredictable pitch locations.

Chris Perez

Born: 7/1/1985 Age: 28
Bats: R Throws: R Height: 6' 4" Weight: 230
Breakout: 20% Improve: 50% Collapse: 29%
Attrition: 7% MLB: 96%

Comparables:
Jeff Reardon, Jorge Julio, Frank Dipino

YEAR	TEAM	LVL	AGE	W	L	SV	G	GS	IP	H	HR	BB	SO	BB9	SO9	GB%	BABIP	WHIP	ERA	FIP	FRA	WARP
2011	CLE	MLB	25	4	7	36	64	0	59²	46	5	26	39	3.9	5.9	31%	.234	1.21	3.32	4.30	5.48	-0.2
2012	CLE	MLB	26	0	4	39	61	0	57²	49	6	16	59	2.5	9.2	41%	.270	1.13	3.59	3.29	3.52	0.9
2013	CLE	MLB	27	5	3	25	54	0	54	56	11	21	54	3.5	9.0	45%	.294	1.43	4.33	5.11	5.10	-0.1
2014	LAN	MLB	28	3	1	32	58	0	56¹	45	6	20	55	3.2	8.8	39%	.277	1.15	3.37	3.86	3.66	0.6

Two dates when it all unraveled: On May 13th, Perez reported shoulder soreness. His velocity vanished, and his walk rate returned to pre-2012 levels. Then, a month later, on June 5th, Perez was arrested for possession of marijuana. The righty narrowly held on to his closer role for a while, but without pinpoint control or peak velocity he eventually pitched his way into a committee position by year's end. On the positive side, his fastball and slider velocities were creeping back to earlier levels by season's end, and there are not expected to be any long-ranging effects from his shoulder troubles. Further, the drug charges didn't result in jail time or an MLB suspension, so if he's able to stay in control in his personal life, the troubles will be behind him after his one-year probation ends. Cleveland didn't wait to see, non-tendering him just after the World Series ended, and Perez signed with Los Angeles, where he'll be third (at best) in line for saves.

Chris Reed

Born: 5/20/1990 Age: 24
Bats: L Throws: L Height: 6' 4" Weight: 195
Breakout: 46% Improve: 59% Collapse: 29%
Attrition: 63% MLB: 21%

Comparables:
D.J. Mitchell, Clayton Mortensen, Josh Collmenter

YEAR	TEAM	LVL	AGE	W	L	SV	G	GS	IP	H	HR	BB	SO	BB9	SO9	GB%	BABIP	WHIP	ERA	FIP	FRA	WARP
2012	RCU	A+	22	1	4	0	7	6	35	25	1	14	38	3.6	9.8	60%	.279	1.11	3.09	3.30	4.38	0.7
2012	CHT	AA	22	0	4	0	12	11	35¹	31	2	20	29	5.1	7.4	60%	.299	1.44	4.84	4.28	4.89	0.3
2013	CHT	AA	23	4	11	0	29	25	137²	128	9	63	106	4.1	6.9	61%	.297	1.39	3.86	3.73	5.60	-0.6
2014	LAN	MLB	24	6	8	0	24	24	109	106	12	47	74	3.9	6.1	55%	.301	1.40	4.47	4.73	4.86	-0.1

The great debate is whether Reed can refine his command and develop his changeup enough to hold down a starting gig, or if his stuff profiles better in the bullpen. The former Stanford reliever has a mid-90s fastball and an effective slider to finish at-bats; both pitches can be valuable assets provided the southpaw can locate. Reed has poor balance in his delivery, an element which leads to inconsistent release points and wreaks devastation on pitch command. That will dog Reed in any role. His ability to maintain balance and find a repeatable delivery will likely determine whether he is eventually limited to lefty specialism.

Paco Rodriguez

Born: 4/16/1991 Age: 23
Bats: L Throws: L Height: 6' 3" Weight: 220
Breakout: 29% Improve: 51% Collapse: 29%
Attrition: 15% MLB: 91%

Comparables:
Joel Zumaya, Chris Sale, Jonathan Broxton

YEAR	TEAM	LVL	AGE	W	L	SV	G	GS	IP	H	HR	BB	SO	BB9	SO9	GB%	BABIP	WHIP	ERA	FIP	FRA	WARP
2012	CHT	AA	21	1	0	3	15	0	13²	7	0	6	22	4.0	14.5	46%	.269	0.95	1.32	1.46	1.82	0.5
2012	LAN	MLB	21	0	1	0	11	0	6²	3	0	4	6	5.4	8.1	44%	.188	1.05	1.35	3.14	2.19	0.1
2013	LAN	MLB	22	3	4	2	76	0	54¹	30	5	19	63	3.1	10.4	50%	.210	0.90	2.32	3.06	3.26	0.5
2014	LAN	MLB	23	3	2	2	58	0	42²	30	4	14	51	2.9	10.7	47%	.284	1.03	2.38	3.04	2.58	1.0

The southpaw second-rounder from the 2012 draft uses a unique technique in his delivery—holding the ball high as if to coax hitters into changing their eye level—to fire countless fastball variations that sink, cut and dodge through and around the strike zone. Rodriguez pairs it with a slider that accounted for 49 of his 63 strike threes and limited batters to a .103 batting average, and .115 slugging percentage, on the pitch through

August. And then, abruptly, the magic wore off. He gave up as many home runs in September as he had all season prior, and the Dodgers saw enough in his stuff to trust the numbers: Rodriguez was left off the NLCS roster entirely. That won't happen again—there aren't a half-dozen relievers in the game tougher against lefties than he is.

Hyun-jin Ryu
Born: 3/25/1987 Age: 27
Bats: R Throws: L Height: 6' 2" Weight: 255
Breakout: 22% Improve: 51% Collapse: 25%
Attrition: 12% MLB: 97%

Comparables:
Joe Blanton, Johnny Cueto, John Danks

YEAR	TEAM	LVL	AGE	W	L	SV	G	GS	IP	H	HR	BB	SO	BB9	SO9	GB%	BABIP	WHIP	ERA	FIP	FRA	WARP
2013	LAN	MLB	26	14	8	0	30	30	192	182	15	49	154	2.3	7.2	52%	.295	1.20	3.00	3.21	3.84	1.8
2014	LAN	MLB	27	8	7	0	22	22	135¹	124	12	33	106	2.2	7.0	49%	.296	1.16	3.27	3.54	3.55	1.7

Ryu had an inspired introduction to the majors, impressing his new hosts with the sleek walk rate that he brought from the KBO. The southpaw kept the ball on the ground en route to 26 double plays, third-most in the NL, largely due to an 80 mph "hadouken" changeup. The off-speed pitch silenced right-handed bats, and he finished with a reverse platoon split of more than 100 points of OPS. His atypical tendency to throw the changeup when behind in the count coaxed mistimed swings from overzealous hitters sitting on heat. He might not fit the traditional mold of a championship-caliber starter, but the results speak for themselves.

Julio Urias
Born: 8/12/1996 Age: 17
Bats: L Throws: L Height: 5' 11" Weight: 160

YEAR	TEAM	LVL	AGE	W	L	SV	G	GS	IP	H	HR	BB	SO	BB9	SO9	GB%	BABIP	WHIP	ERA	FIP	FRA	WARP
2014	—	—	—	—	—	—	—	—	—	—	—	—	—	—	—	—	—	—	—	—	—	—

When some of us were 16 years old, we were sneaking out to drive dad's car, trying to crash a college party. Julio Urias was striking out college-aged hitters and making enough money to buy his dad a car. An international free agent out of Mexico, Urias was given an unthinkable assignment to the Midwest League; he's younger than most high school juniors. More unthinkable: he thrived. The southpaw showed considerable growth throughout the year, raising the bar of his listed height and adding fuel to his fastball. Urias entered the season with velocity reports in the upper 80s, was sitting 91-93 and touching 95 by summer, and spiked to 97 in his final game of the season. The remarkable story of Julio Urias might just earn him the label of the most interesting man in the sport, though if he's ever caught drinking a Dos Equis he's so grounded.

Brian Wilson
Born: 3/16/1982 Age: 32
Bats: R Throws: R Height: 6' 2" Weight: 205
Breakout: 22% Improve: 48% Collapse: 29%
Attrition: 7% MLB: 98%

Comparables:
J.J. Putz, Francisco Cordero, Scot Shields

YEAR	TEAM	LVL	AGE	W	L	SV	G	GS	IP	H	HR	BB	SO	BB9	SO9	GB%	BABIP	WHIP	ERA	FIP	FRA	WARP
2011	SFN	MLB	29	6	4	36	57	0	55	50	2	31	54	5.1	8.8	54%	.307	1.47	3.11	3.30	3.48	0.5
2012	SFN	MLB	30	0	0	1	2	0	2	4	0	2	2	9.0	9.0	25%	.500	3.00	9.00	4.14	6.53	0.0
2013	LAN	MLB	31	2	1	0	18	0	13²	8	0	4	13	2.6	8.6	56%	.250	0.88	0.66	2.00	2.10	0.3
2014	LAN	MLB	32	2	1	1	39	0	39	31	3	13	42	3.1	9.6	50%	.299	1.13	2.75	3.09	2.99	0.7

After 16 months spent recovering from Tommy John surgery, Blackbeard returned to pillage the villages of the NL West. The casualties from Wilson's fall siege at Chavez Ravine were reminiscent of his glory days, and earned him a pivotal role at the back of the Dodger bullpen in the postseason—indeed, it seemed by the end that he was the only pitcher Don Mattingly trusted between his starters and Kenley Jansen. The velocity returned to 2011 levels, if not his peak form of 2009-10, but the anecdotal evidence suggests a different type of pitcher came out of surgery. He stuck to the cutter on almost 70 percent of his deliveries, and nearly every pitch that he threw was forced away from opposing batters, either glove-side to right-handed hitters or arm-side to lefties. He'll have to dig deeper to succeed over a full season, but the Dodgers had enough faith in the old dog's new tricks to sign him to a $10 million deal.

Thomas Windle
Born: 3/10/1992 Age: 22
Bats: L Throws: L Height: 6' 4" Weight: 215
Breakout: 80% Improve: 100% Collapse: 0%
Attrition: 66% MLB: 5%

Comparables:
Blake Wood, Brian Flynn, Ricky Romero

YEAR	TEAM	LVL	AGE	W	L	SV	G	GS	IP	H	HR	BB	SO	BB9	SO9	GB%	BABIP	WHIP	ERA	FIP	FRA	WARP
2013	GRL	A	21	5	1	0	13	12	53²	50	2	20	51	3.4	8.6	44%	.308	1.30	2.68	3.15	3.71	1.2
2014	LAN	MLB	22	2	3	0	9	9	39	41	5	18	26	4.1	6.0	43%	.308	1.50	4.96	5.06	5.39	-0.2

Windle and fellow 2013 draftee Chris Anderson are both Minnesota natives, but Windle stayed home for college while Anderson left the land of lakes for the Florida sun. Mr. Windle had a relatively smooth introduction to the pros, with low-90s velocity that plays up from the left side, but there are some mechanical issues that will need to be ironed out. He has an aggressive motion that lacks stability, with major disruptions to his balance throughout the delivery. These elements will conspire against Windle's pitch command until he is able to right the ship. The Dodgers have already begun to work with him to make the necessary adjustments.

Chris Withrow

Born: 4/1/1989 Age: 25
Bats: R Throws: R Height: 6' 4" Weight: 215
Breakout: 51% Improve: 71% Collapse: 20%
Attrition: 49% MLB: 57%

Comparables:
Brayan Villarreal, Donnie Veal, Francisco Cruceta

YEAR	TEAM	LVL	AGE	W	L	SV	G	GS	IP	H	HR	BB	SO	BB9	SO9	GB%	BABIP	WHIP	ERA	FIP	FRA	WARP
2011	CHT	AA	22	6	6	0	25	25	128²	111	8	75	130	5.2	9.1	48%	.242	1.45	4.20	3.96	5.26	0.3
2012	CHT	AA	23	3	3	2	22	7	60	52	3	36	64	5.4	9.6	53%	.303	1.47	4.65	3.56	5.28	0.2
2013	ABQ	AAA	24	4	0	0	25	0	26¹	25	0	13	33	4.4	11.3	56%	.353	1.44	1.71	2.54	2.50	1.1
2013	LAN	MLB	24	3	0	1	26	0	34²	20	5	13	43	3.4	11.2	38%	.208	0.95	2.60	3.54	4.06	0.2
2014	LAN	MLB	25	2	2	1	30	4	51²	47	6	25	47	4.4	8.2	42%	.302	1.40	4.31	4.49	4.69	-0.1

After four years of near-5 ERAs as a starter in Double-A, Withrow was re-imagined as a reliever and thrived. With a prototypical pitcher's build and a ferocious fastball that averaged 97, the former first-rounder has the makings of a shutdown reliever who could fit near the back of the bullpen. He mixes in a solid set of secondary pitches, including a tight slider with vertical break and a curveball that he uses when ahead in the count. He still has some work to do with fastball command, but Withrow's simple delivery should allow for a repeatable release point in the future. Notable, if you're some kind of weirdo: He's the only active pitcher with "throw" in his name.

Jamey Wright

Born: 12/24/1974 Age: 39
Bats: R Throws: R Height: 6' 6" Weight: 235
Breakout: 26% Improve: 61% Collapse: 18%
Attrition: 17% MLB: 64%

Comparables:
Doug Brocail, John Franco, Rheal Cormier

YEAR	TEAM	LVL	AGE	W	L	SV	G	GS	IP	H	HR	BB	SO	BB9	SO9	GB%	BABIP	WHIP	ERA	FIP	FRA	WARP
2011	SEA	MLB	36	2	3	1	60	0	68¹	61	6	30	48	4.0	6.3	58%	.279	1.33	3.16	4.33	5.43	-0.4
2012	LAN	MLB	37	5	3	0	66	0	67²	72	2	30	54	4.0	7.2	69%	.329	1.51	3.72	3.43	4.61	0.0
2013	TBA	MLB	38	2	2	0	66	1	70	61	4	23	65	3.0	8.4	52%	.300	1.20	3.09	3.16	4.30	0.3
2014	LAN	MLB	39	3	1	0	55	0	61¹	57	5	25	46	3.7	6.8	58%	.300	1.34	4.03	4.14	4.38	0.1

It took 18 years and almost as many major-league uniforms for Wright to take his first sip of postseason champagne. A true journeyman, the veteran right-hander showed up to Rays camp without a guaranteed contract, marking the sixth straight season he cracked an Opening Day roster as an NRI. Make no mistake, Wright is not a charity case or someone clinging on for the sake of not letting go. As he prepares to complete his fourth decade on the planet, he is still one of the more durable relief arms in the game. He uses an upper-80s sinker to generate groundball rates that border on extreme, a cutter of similar velocity and a big loopy curveball in the upper 70s that buckles knees. The cutter has given him a new lease on life, and the Sooner State native shows no signs of slowing down.

LINEOUTS

HITTERS

PLAYER	TEAM	LVL	AGE	PA	R	2B	3B	HR	RBI	BB	SO	SB-CS	AVG/OBP/SLG	TAv	BABIP	BRR	FRAA	WARP
C J. Boscan	IOW	AAA	33	258	17	9	0	0	18	21	44	1-1	.232/.297/.270	.209	.284	-1.2	C(71): -0.1	-0.6
	CHN	MLB	33	10	1	1	0	0	0	0	2	0-0	.222/.300/.333	.232	.286	-0.2	C(4): -0.0	0.0
RF N. Buss	ABQ	AAA	26	518	84	29	11	17	100	41	90	21-2	.303/.363/.525	.293	.339	2.6	RF(53): 2.8, LF(50): 2.6	4.3
	LAN	MLB	26	20	0	0	0	0	0	1	1	0-0	.105/.150/.105	.113	.111	-0.1	RF(3): -0.1, LF(3): 0.0	-0.3
C D. Butera	ROC	AAA	29	94	8	2	0	2	10	2	15	0-0	.218/.247/.310	.209	.236	0.2	C(22): -0.5	-0.2
	ABQ	AAA	29	57	3	3	1	0	3	4	14	0-0	.135/.196/.231	.151	.184	0.4	C(16): 0.1	-0.1
	MIN	MLB	29	3	0	0	0	0	0	0	1	0-0	.000/.000/.000	.016	.000	0	C(2): -0.0	-0.1
	LAN	MLB	29	7	0	0	0	0	0	0	4	0-0	.143/.143/.143	.052	.333	-0.3	C(2): -0.0, 1B(2): -0.1	-0.2
3B J. Hairston	LAN	MLB	37	226	17	7	0	2	22	14	22	0-0	.211/.265/.275	.208	.224	-0.6	3B(28): -0.4, LF(23): 0.8	-0.9
SS B. Harris	ROU	AAA	32	49	7	0	0	2	5	7	7	0-0	.244/.367/.390	.260	.250	-0.3	SS(12): -0.0	0.3
	SWB	AAA	32	87	9	3	0	1	4	13	12	0-0	.233/.356/.315	.269	.267	0.4	SS(10): -1.0, 2B(7): 0.1	0.3
	ANA	MLB	32	117	14	4	0	4	9	6	29	0-1	.206/.252/.355	.243	.240	-0.3	SS(21): -2.3, 3B(7): 0.0	0.0
RF S. Schebler	RCU	A+	22	534	95	29	13	27	91	35	140	16-5	.296/.360/.581	.321	.364	2.3	RF(76): -5.7, LF(50): -3.2	3.5
SS J. Sellers	ABQ	AAA	27	366	39	26	4	6	65	25	54	4-0	.270/.326/.429	.258	.301	2.9	SS(59): 1.0, 2B(19): -0.6	1.7
	LAN	MLB	27	77	6	1	0	1	2	5	20	0-0	.188/.263/.246	.191	.250	0.2	SS(22): -1.8	-0.5
3B I. Stewart	IOW	AAA	28	133	19	6	1	5	20	17	45	0-0	.168/.286/.372	.236	.219	-1.3	3B(23): -1.2, 1B(9): 0.0	-0.6
	ABQ	AAA	28	105	13	6	0	2	6	17	36	0-0	.174/.324/.314	.238	.271	0.4	3B(26): 1.4, 1B(1): -0.0	0.3

Veteran no-hit backstop **J.C. Boscan** has a solid defensive reputation and worked six games for the Cubs last September, which means his count of big-league games played (17) has finally caught up to his count of seasons in the minors. ⏀ **Nick Buss** found a cure-all in Albuquerque, where all of his previously demonstrated skills showed up in one place. The performance spike coincided with his adopting "Chili"—his baseball-inspired middle name—as a regular moniker, but he's more mild than hot. ⏀ One organization lost its patience with **Drew Butera** last year and another lost a PTBNL. ⏀ **Jerry Hairston** personifies utility, having played every position on the diamond aside from pitcher and catcher over the past three years. When he's standing it's usually at third or left, but more frequently he waits for his turn to pinch-hit. ⏀ Old infielders never die, they just lose their utility. **Brendan Harris** was in three organizations in 2013, and the Dodgers signed him as a Triple-A insurance policy for this year. ⏀ Former second-round pick **Alex Santana** enjoyed an offensive spike with improved bat-to-ball skills during his second tour of Ogden. His power has yet to materialize in games, but he has the physical profile to project significant gains. ⏀ Former 26th-rounder **Scott Schebler** parlayed a changed approach at the plate into a breakout season in High-A, earning the Branch Rickey Award for the organization's position player of the year. ⏀ **Justin Sellers** took over shortstop during Hanley Ramirez's April absence and cranked as many extra-base hits over 20 starts as Ramirez managed in just his second game back. Even after Ramirez's quick return to the DL, Sellers was not invited to reprise. ⏀ The once-promising power bat of **Ian Stewart** is now a punchless weapon that neither high altitude nor Triple-A pitching could punch up; his future is taking the Wile E. Coyote route down.

PITCHERS

PLAYER	TEAM	LVL	AGE	W	L	SV	IP	H	HR	BB	SO	BB9	SO9	GB%	BABIP	WHIP	ERA	FIP	FRA	WARP
Z. Bird	GRL	A	18	2	5	0	60	56	5	45	50	6.8	7.5	48%	.290	1.68	5.10	5.11	5.94	0.1
S. Elbert	LAN	MLB	26	1	1	0	32²	27	3	13	29	3.6	8.0	36%	.279	1.22	2.20	3.84	4.42	0.0
Y. Garcia	CHT	AA	22	4	6	19	60¹	35	9	14	85	2.1	12.7	31%	.217	0.81	2.54	2.83	3.36	1.1
G. Gould	RCU	A+	21	2	7	0	76²	89	10	31	59	3.6	6.9	42%	.326	1.57	7.04	5.22	6.12	0.0
	CHT	AA	21	3	5	0	41¹	42	5	15	45	3.3	9.8	52%	.315	1.38	5.88	3.40	5.29	0.2
M. Magill	ABQ	AAA	23	6	2	0	85²	72	7	50	101	5.3	10.6	43%	.330	1.42	3.47	4.06	4.06	2.0
	LAN	MLB	23	0	2	0	27²	27	6	28	26	9.1	8.5	43%	.275	1.99	6.51	7.10	7.58	-0.4
J. Ravin	PEN	AA	25	1	3	0	40¹	44	4	27	39	6.0	8.7	44%	.351	1.76	5.58	4.50	5.97	-0.4
	LOU	AAA	25	0	0	0	10²	12	1	11	9	9.3	7.6	42%	.344	2.16	6.75	5.83	6.56	-0.1
S. Rosin	REA	AA	24	9	6	0	126²	120	13	35	96	2.5	6.8	39%	.282	1.22	4.33	4.04	4.65	1.3
J. Sanchez	ABQ	AAA	30	7	3	0	66²	72	12	42	79	5.7	10.7	34%	.356	1.71	5.13	5.56	6.09	0.4
	PIT	MLB	30	0	3	0	13²	25	7	8	15	5.3	9.9	41%	.429	2.41	11.85	9.68	7.29	-0.2
R. Stripling	RCU	A+	23	2	0	0	33²	24	1	11	34	2.9	9.1	57%	.261	1.04	2.94	3.12	3.13	1.0
	CHT	AA	23	6	4	1	94	91	4	19	83	1.8	7.9	54%	.312	1.17	2.78	2.31	3.87	1.2

Zachary Bird started 2013 in the Midwest League, was sent to the bullpen after an eight-walk outing and was demoted to Ogden by the end of June. Back on track by season's end, he's got enough raw stuff to keep our interest. ⏀ **Scott Elbert's** left elbow has been his Achilles heel, which is an odd place for an Achilles heel to be, or an elbow to be. He had Tommy John surgery in June, and his 2014 is in jeopardy. ⏀ **Yimi Garcia** owns a devastating slider that invokes swings and misses by the truckload, and the significant improvements he showed with command could have him in the Dodgers' bullpen quickly. ⏀ Knocked around for three months, **Garrett Gould** was finally released from the California League penitentiary and promoted to Double-A, where the only thing that changed was he lost his excuse. He throws strikes, but they're bad strikes. ⏀ Pitchers who struggle with command in the minors typically experience exponential decay at the highest level, and **Matt Magill** was no exception. His plus changeup fuels an impressive strikeout rate, but when he walks he's on a short leash. ⏀ **Josh Ravin** is another reminder that, as with Wall Street traders and men in strip clubs and renegade cops on basic cable dramas, lack of control can be a fatal flaw for triple-digit strong arms. ⏀ **Seth Rosin**, acquired by the Phillies in the Hunter Pence deal, then acquired by the Mets in the Rule 5 draft, then acquired by the Dodgers in the Cash Considerations deal, had a penchant for missing bats at the lower levels but it disappeared in his first year at Double-A. ⏀ The Dodgers picked up **Jonathan Sanchez** after the lefty allowed seven homers in 13-plus innings with Pittsburgh, then sent him to get knocked around the PCL. ⏀ **Ross Stripling** breezed through the California League gantlet and continued to utilize his deft pitch command and budding velocity to silence bats after a promotion to the Southern League, thereby upping the price on his prospect ceiling.

MANAGER: DON MATTINGLY

YEAR	TEAM	W-L	Pythag +/–	Avg PC	100+ P	120+ P	QS	BQS	REL	REL w Zero R	IBB	PH	PH Avg	PH HR	SB2	CS2	SB3	CS3	SAC Att	SAC %	POS SAC	Squeeze	Swing	In Play
2011	LAN	82-79	1	97.8	66	3	94	4	461	369	48	229	.199	4	108	31	17	9	101	70.3%	38	2	360	118
2012	LAN	86-76	1	96.2	66	0	93	5	506	426	62	241	.281	2	93	39	10	2	122	67.2%	33	2	329	97
2013	LAN	92-70	1	95.1	69	2	93	2	504	424	44	208	.209	4	74	22	4	5	113	62.8%	32	0	283	93

It's tough to analyze managers. Sometimes the best decision a manager makes is the one he doesn't make. On June 21st, things looked terrible for Don Mattingly. The high-payroll Dodgers stood at 30-42, and rumors abounded of Mattingly's imminent departure. Rather than making a move just to make a move, Mattingly stayed the course. Was he ever rewarded, as the Dodgers went on the best 50-game run since the Tinker-Evers-Chance Cubs over 100 years earlier. Many skippers would made maneuvers out of desperation under that pressure, but Mattingly didn't.

That said, Mattingly is far from a passive manager. He is rather active, in fact. He likes to bunt. In 2012, he led the league in sacrifice hits, and in 2013 was near the top—despite having maybe the best offense in the game. He also had the most batting orders by any NL managers in 2013. He ranked second in 2011. Mattingly has always used his bench a lot. Granted he has had injuries to deal with, but 2013 was the first time he ever had his main eight position players account for over 60 percent of the team's PA (and barely that, at 61.3 percent). Usually there are just five NL teams a year under 60 percent.

Miami Marlins

By David Roth

The fate of the Miami Marlins, in 2014 and years to come, will not in any meaningful way depend upon Chris Valaika. This is also true of every other major-league team. It's true because Chris Valaika is Chris Valaika, a fringy owns-a-bunch-of-gloves infield type who has done some striking out and some playing-of-various-positions and not much else over small parts of three big league seasons, the most recent of which came in Miami in 2013.

But the statement above is also true, in a more immediate sense, because Chris Valaika will not be with the Marlins in 2014—he signed a minor league deal with the Cubs a couple weeks before Thanksgiving after earning a career-high 70 plate appearances with the second-worst team in baseball. But, for all the mostly negligible impact that Valaika made with the Marlins—16 strikeouts and a homer, a fifth of a negative win per WARP—his brief time in Miami says something about this team's immediate future, uneasy present and cynical, cyclical, prototypically Floridian past.

Which sounds sweeping, but mostly means this: The Marlins are too messed-up a place to work for this particular minor league journeyman. Valaika is a special case, maybe. He was one of several Marlins players who went to ownership with complaints that first-time hitting coach Tino Martinez was sort of extremely forceful and sort of just a jerk to some of the young players in his charge early in the season, laying hands and dropping f-bombs on Valaika and Derek Dietrich after they were reluctant to pick up balls during soft toss sessions. This eventually led to Martinez resigning, and further led to Valaika and Dietrich—who figured to have a bigger role with the Marlins in the future than Valaika—being punished with demotions, and later having subsequent promotions personally vetoed by owner Jeffrey Loria himself. For short, baseball fans refer to this sort of thing as Some Real Marlins Shit.

This would seem to be no way to think or talk about a team that has won two World Series in the last 16 years, but the Marlins are a unique organization, and the 2014 Marlins, for all the talent and promise on their roster—yes, even without Chris Valaika—are screwed in a uniquely Marlins way, and for some thoroughly Marlins reasons. The Marlins have one of the better farm systems in baseball, and several of its best players—2013 Rookie of the Year and precocious swaggy super-ace Jose Fernandez and outfielders Christian Yelich, Marcell Ozuna and Jake Marisnick—have already shown varying degrees of promise in the bigs. There is reason, in that sense, for hope, and even reason to think the Marlins might be an interesting team to watch. But, finally and fundamentally, the Marlins are the Marlins—a team that has won and could win again, but which nevertheless exudes a specific type of willful, wanton hopelessness that no other big-league team can match.

When Valaika signed his minor league deal with the Cubs, his agent served up what seemed like a bit of transactional boilerplate—his client was, apparently, "excited to be with a first-class organization." The *Miami Herald* puzzled over whether this remark was a subtle dig at the Marlins; this was worth the parsing because Valaika's agent also represents Giancarlo Stanton, the best hitter in the Marlins organization and arguably the National League East, and a player the team would do well not to alienate.

But leave aside the hot-stove overparsing and pseudo-psychoanalytic Stantonian soothsaying for a moment—not to mention the reasonable question of why and whether Stanton, the one really good position player on Miami's roster, would want to play for this team any longer than he absolutely must—and look at what this resolutely minor Valaika transaction coldly and damningly is. The Miami Marlins are a big league franchise in a major American city, a place in

MARLINS PROSPECTUS
2013 W-L: 62-100, 5th in NL East

Pythag	.400	28th	DER	.703	18th
RS/G	3.17	30th	B-Age	27.6	5th
RA/G	3.99	12th	P-Age	25.8	1st
TAv	.235	30th	Salary	$38	29th
BRR	-0.45	16th	M$/MW	$1.83	7th
TAv-P	.268	20th	DL Days	1559	30th
FIP	3.66	7th	$ on DL	14%	11th

	Runs	HR/RH	HR/LH	Runs/RH	Runs/LH
Three-Year Park Factors	96	86	82	97	98

Top Hitter WARP	3.78 (Giancarlo Stanton)
Top Pitcher WARP	2.81 (Jose Fernandez)
Top Prospect	Andrew Heaney

which it is alarmingly easy to have more or less unconscionable amounts of fun; they're a team with a splashy new facility; and they're lousy enough to offer opportunities galore for big-league playing time.

All inarguably true, and yet, all things considered, Chris Valaika decided he'd rather spend much of the next year of his life in Iowa City, waiting for Darwin Barney to strain an oblique. That's the Marlins, and that's the problem.

***

The 1998 Marlins lost 108 games; they're the only team in franchise history to post a worse record than 2013's 100-loss team. That '98 team was a strange one, mostly because it entered the season as a defending World Series champion and then consciously and very quickly turned itself into an expansion team. There was a poignantly brief Mike Piazza cameo, and a little bit of end-stage Donn Pall and a weirdly large amount of Todd Dunwoody, and 74 innings and 14 starts given over to Andy Larkin, who allowed 156 baserunners and 87 runs in that stretch.

Some bad teams are stranger than others, but all bad teams are weird in something like this way—lifers collect their last weary big-league passport stamps, randos and goofs seize their last best shots or GIDP their way towards a pension, and young players are sprung, too early and terrified, into actual counts-in-the-standings action. Your Andy Larkins are allowed to give up a home run every 20 or so batters over the course of a season because your Andy Larkins are honestly the best pitchers available at the moment.

This is why they're bad teams, and most every organization has this sort of season—a weird summer of bleary recess in which senior citizens and hobos and toddlers tear-ass ineffectually around the same shabby lot. For the 1998 Marlins, Jim Leyland was the lunch lady barking Winston-scented warnings against horseplay and waiting for management to get on the stick. When the Marlins won it all in 2003, just a handful of players remained from that '98 team, let alone 1997's champion. One of those alumni was backup catcher Mike Redmond, now entering his second year as Miami's manager.

Through the dim magic of post hoc ergo propter hoc, we can say—and maybe even be correct—that this sort of failure can lead to a certain kind of success. Bonds are forged and chops are established and learning is done on the job. We are mostly imagining this, but we could someday imagine it about the 2013 Marlins, which was very definitively that type of bad team.

If every franchise goes through some version of this rock-bottom rebuilding, it's worth noting that the Marlins, first under founding owner Wayne Huizenga and then under current owner Jeffrey Loria, seem to go through it more readily and ruthlessly than others. Miami's bad teams have gotten worse, and follow more closely on the good ones. In the decade since the team's last World Series, the bad teams have mostly just followed each other, with the team slipping off the old cycle of triumphant boom and resounding bust and settling into an enervating sort of intentional and vexingly profitable betwixt-and-between mediocrity.

The old brutal tear-downs have stopped giving way to significant build-outs, and the false dawn of 2012—when the team rather haphazardly spent six figures to append a passel of free agents to the team's young core—quickly fed another clammy, frantic cashing-out. The star-studded Marlins that very briefly existed—Jose Reyes and Mark Buehrle and (um) Heath Bell, all with the team for only slightly longer than ur-punchline Piazza—didn't win, and didn't draw fans to the splashy new taxpayer-funded, human-unfriendly stadium that Loria built through frank and brazen white-collar criminality.

And so the general manager who built that team—the same GM who built the team's 2003 World Series winners—rapidly tore it down at his owner's behest, before that flawed roster was given a chance to reach anything like its level. And then, after the season, the owner fired the GM, whose name is Larry Beinfest and who had been in the organization for almost 12 years. Beinfest restocked the farm system in deals that sent the roster's erstwhile stars to Los Angeles and Toronto and Detroit, but the nauseous year that preceded his departure made it difficult to think much of the team's future, and to believe that the seasick present really does have a horizon. It is tough, in short, to believe that the Marlins will somehow stop doing Marlins things.

There could be another good team stirring under this newest coat of ash, but The Marlins Thing is not just an abstract problem. The baseball questions have prosaic baseball answers—the young players will develop or they won't; Greg Dobbs will play a lot, and play a lot like Greg Dobbs; new veterans will check into the Miami Marlins Hospice and ride out the last portion of their careers' shoulder in relative peace and quiet. The bigger question—how today's queasiness could give way to a happier future, and whether the Marlins can be more than what they've been under Loria and his doof-junta—is a tougher one.

How many times can a team do this particular thing in this particular way, to itself and its employees and the people expected to care about it, and for how long, before it becomes unsustainable and toxic? It is possible, scanning the farm system and the degraded National League East, to imagine the Marlins as a competitive enough baseball team. But it is also difficult not to see them as a bigger and sadder and more emblematic thing, and precisely the sort of towering crude pop art that wouldn't be out of place in Jeffrey Loria's esteemed personal collection—a garish crystallization of all the shameless, ravenously predatory pastel brutality at work in the Miamis of Charles Willeford and Elmore Leonard and Michael Mann and Rick Ross; a bleak example of the dissolving social compact between teams and their communities; proof of the friction between longstanding community-oriented loyalties and the corrosive effects of impunity and vast profit.

None of which conflicts are, it should be noted, unique to this particular messed-up franchise. But the Marlins also really are unique. As they presently exist, the Marlins are baseball's most robustly haunted ghost-yacht, bobbing away far from land with the caviar still cool in the fridge, but the crew spookily absent and various creaks and silences alternating exactly as they ought not—a big glossy chunk of luxurious jetsam, with various leaks slowly weeping the whole gilded thing down to the bottom.

***

"We want to get out there and get going," Marlins President David Samson told Fox Sports Florida early in the offseason. "We're getting ready for another season, and we're going to win more. I promise you this: We're not going to lose 100 games next year. Not close."

Samson, Loria's stepson and a man who bragged in a speech to local swells about ripping off Miami's taxpayers on the $600 million funding for the team's stadium, is not an easy person to agree with. But he is probably not wrong. It is difficult to lose 100 games two seasons in a row, even for a team that's only faintly trying not to lose 100 games.

The young players already with the team will develop; Yelich, in particular, could be an All-Star. Others who have not yet arrived could do so during 2014, including lefty starters Andrew Heaney, Adam Conley and Justin Nicolino and ace defensive backstop J.T. Realmuto. Marisnick and Ozuna, despite their big league auditions in '13, may need more time in the minors, although possibly not much more. If there's a plan to speak of in Miami, this is it: graduate a class of prospects onto the big-league roster and let them grow up together into what could be a very good team if some

percentage reach their potential. Most of those prospects don't quite project as stars—Heaney is the only top-of-the-rotation big league arm in the farm system by most rankings and Marisnick and Realmuto, for all their considerable tools and defensive chops, have not yet hit especially well, even in the minors. They will all, however, be exactly as cheap and exactly as controllable—and exactly as unpredictable and contingent on circumstance and likely to bust—as any other rookies.

Which brings us back to the haunted yacht. The Marlins' roster, as it stands, is mostly holes—the team got production below replacement level from every infield position besides third base in 2013, with shortstop Adeiny Hechevarria, another piece acquired in the Great Toronto Ship-Off, standing out as a Yuniesky Betancourtian disaster. By spring, the Marlins will find players to fill those positions, one way or another—either with the young players they develop or with the kind of castoffs the Marlins usually wind up rescuing. The team that results will do its best to win games under these circumstances. It happens every year.

But that's just it. If it is possible to look at the Miami Marlins and imagine an intriguing future and promising present, there is also the crucial, crippling contextual counterweight of The Marlins Thing. The team's goal is to have its young players grow up healthy and strong and productive, which is as reasonable a plan as any. Winning teams are built that way. But the environment in which those kids will grow up—subject to the weird whims of a meddlesome, bullying owner; playing in the pastel tomb of a stadium he built; working in an atmosphere of cheesy, chiseling disregard and towering uncommitment—is not a happy or nurturing or safe or healthy one. We might as well wish the kids well.

David Roth is a co-founder of and editor at The Classical, *and a writer for* SB Nation.

HITTERS

Brian Bogusevic RF	YEAR	TEAM	LVL	AGE	PA	R	2B	3B	HR	RBI	BB	SO	SB	CS	AVG/OBP/SLG	TAv	BABIP	BRR	FRAA	WARP
Born: 2/18/1984 Age: 30	2011	OKL	AAA	27	254	27	11	5	3	35	30	49	20	3	.261/.362/.399	.231	.323	-1.4	RF(11): 0.1, LF(2): -0.1	-0.3
Bats: L Throws: L Height: 6' 3''	2011	HOU	MLB	27	182	22	14	1	4	15	15	40	4	2	.287/.348/.457	.263	.355	-0.5	RF(40): 0.7, LF(13): 0.4	0.6
Weight: 220 Breakout: 3%	2012	HOU	MLB	28	404	39	9	2	7	28	41	96	15	4	.203/.297/.299	.233	.257	0.9	RF(104): 1.4, CF(20): -0.4	0.0
Improve: 19% Collapse: 4%	2013	IOW	AAA	29	310	50	14	3	10	32	41	58	16	2	.317/.416/.506	.335	.376	0.7	RF(41): 5.1, CF(28): 2.9	4.3
Attrition: 15% MLB: 48%	2013	CHN	MLB	29	155	18	7	1	6	16	10	35	2	0	.273/.323/.462	.277	.320	-0.1	LF(29): 1.5, CF(10): 0.7	1.0
Comparables: Eric Valent, Abraham Nunez, Delwyn Young	2014	MIA	MLB	30	250	27	10	1	4	24	24	57	8	1	.238/.317/.347	.257	.300	0.9	RF 2, LF 1	0.8

In some alternate universe the Astros immediately stuck Bogusevic in the outfield after making him their top pick in 2005, and he's likely enjoying Nick Markakis' career. In our world, however, Bogusevic lost four years of precious development time toiling fruitlessly on minor league mounds before moving to the outfield, and was eventually released. Signed by the Cubs, Bogusevic earned steady playing time after the midseason trades of David DeJesus and Alfonso Soriano, and showed enough down the stretch to prove his value as a bench bat and occasional platoon mate. He's nobody's idea of an everyday starter, as Bogusevic is helpless against lefties, struggles with breaking stuff, is stretched in center field, and doesn't swing enough lumber to be an asset in a corner. That said, he posted a solid .295 TAv against righties last season, which should earn him part-time employment in various cities until all those great prospects you're always reading about come up.

Rob Brantly C	YEAR	TEAM	LVL	AGE	PA	R	2B	3B	HR	RBI	BB	SO	SB	CS	AVG/OBP/SLG	TAv	BABIP	BRR	FRAA	WARP
Born: **7/14/1989** Age: **24**	2011	WMI	A	21	317	42	16	1	7	44	24	39	2	2	.303/.366/.440	.300	.331	-1.2	C(51): -0.4	1.9
Bats: **L** Throws: **R** Height: **6' 1"**	2011	LAK	A+	21	155	16	6	0	3	18	5	17	0	0	.219/.239/.322	.195	.223	-0.9	C(22): 0.0	-0.4
Weight: **195** Breakout: **5%**	2012	ERI	AA	22	195	16	16	1	3	24	12	17	0	3	.311/.359/.461	.281	.329	0.5	C(36): -0.7	1.1
Improve: **17%** Collapse: **5%**	2012	TOL	AAA	22	139	11	4	0	0	6	7	25	0	0	.254/.295/.285	.198	.311	1.3	C(30): -0.7	-0.5
Attrition: **15%** MLB: **33%**	2012	NWO	AAA	22	54	7	4	0	2	11	1	9	0	0	.365/.389/.558	.327	.415	-0.3	C(13): 0.5	0.7
	2012	MIA	MLB	22	113	14	8	0	3	8	13	16	1	1	.290/.372/.460	.303	.321	0.6	C(28): 0.0	1.1
Comparables:	2013	NWO	AAA	23	74	9	3	0	1	3	3	8	0	0	.186/.219/.271	.217	.197	1.1	C(19): -0.0	0.1
Francisco Cervelli, Jason Castro, Shane Costa	2013	MIA	MLB	23	243	11	9	0	1	18	15	53	0	0	.211/.263/.265	.191	.267	0.1	C(65): 1.6	-0.5
	2014	MIA	MLB	24	260	21	12	1	3	24	14	46	0	0	.239/.284/.330	.234	.280	-0.5	C 0	0.5

Another feather in the cap of the "never trust September stats" crowd: Momentum of Brantly's 2012 season, during which he came over from Detroit in the Anibal Sanchez trade and hit .324/.410/.500 for his new team in September, came to a crashing halt. Brantly had the worst TAv of any player in the majors with 200 plate appearances. His plate discipline cratered, as his walk-to-strikeout rate took a palindromic turn: 0.82 in 2012 to 0.28 in 2013. His above-average catch-and-throw skills were canceled out by below-average framing. The UC-Riverside product will be crowded out of playing time by Jarrod Saltalamacchia for the next three years.

Chris Coghlan CF	YEAR	TEAM	LVL	AGE	PA	R	2B	3B	HR	RBI	BB	SO	SB	CS	AVG/OBP/SLG	TAv	BABIP	BRR	FRAA	WARP
Born: **6/18/1985** Age: **29**	2011	JUP	A+	26	41	4	1	0	0	2	5	5	1	1	.343/.415/.371	.321	.387	0.2	CF(8): -0.8	0.3
Bats: **L** Throws: **R** Height: **6' 0"**	2011	JAX	AA	26	23	3	1	0	0	0	4	1	0	0	.211/.348/.263	.255	.222	0.5	CF(4): -0.6	0.0
Weight: **195** Breakout: **5%**	2011	NWO	AAA	26	68	11	4	0	1	7	8	5	3	1	.245/.358/.377	.266	.240	0		0.0
Improve: **38%** Collapse: **8%**	2011	FLO	MLB	26	298	33	20	1	5	22	22	49	7	6	.230/.296/.368	.247	.263	-2.3	CF(65): 3.0	0.5
Attrition: **19%** MLB: **93%**	2012	NWO	AAA	27	368	42	21	3	7	31	46	44	10	2	.284/.375/.435	.299	.309	0.2	RF(41): 3.5, LF(36): 1.3	2.8
	2012	MIA	MLB	27	105	10	1	0	1	10	9	12	0	2	.140/.212/.183	.156	.146	0.7	LF(21): 0.8, CF(13): -0.7	-0.9
Comparables:	2013	JUP	A+	28	28	1	0	1	0	2	1	6	0	0	.185/.214/.259	.165	.238	0.4	3B(6): -0.9	-0.3
Jeremy Reed, David Murphy, Ben Francisco	2013	MIA	MLB	28	214	10	10	3	1	10	17	43	2	0	.256/.318/.354	.263	.322	-0.1	LF(18): 2.0, CF(17): 0.8	0.7
	2014	MIA	MLB	29	250	28	12	2	3	20	22	40	4	2	.257/.326/.365	.263	.300	-0.1	CF -0, LF 0	0.7

A motley group of 11 received Rookie of the Year votes in 2009, and none has produced fewer WARP since the ceremony than Coghlan. A back injury limited him to just 70 games last season, and it's a shame, really—with one home run and a .354 slugging percentage, it was Coghlan's best season in some time. He did start eight games at third base, his first action there, but even if he masters the hot corner, he doesn't hit for average or power, get on base or run well. Otherwise, though.

Matt Diaz LF	YEAR	TEAM	LVL	AGE	PA	R	2B	3B	HR	RBI	BB	SO	SB	CS	AVG/OBP/SLG	TAv	BABIP	BRR	FRAA	WARP
Born: **3/3/1978** Age: **36**	2011	ATL	MLB	33	37	2	1	0	0	1	1	8	1	0	.286/.297/.314	.208	.357	-0.3	RF(9): 0.3, LF(3): -0.2	-0.2
Bats: **R** Throws: **R** Height: **6' 0"**	2011	PIT	MLB	33	231	14	12	1	0	19	11	44	4	2	.259/.303/.324	.231	.324	-0.8	RF(45): -4.0, LF(15): -0.5	-0.9
Weight: **215** Breakout: **0%**	2012	ATL	MLB	34	118	10	6	0	2	13	9	21	0	0	.222/.280/.333	.225	.256	-1.6	LF(19): 0.6, RF(6): 0.3	-0.2
Improve: **31%** Collapse: **10%**	2013	NWO	AAA	35	91	8	4	0	2	10	6	7	6	0	.341/.385/.459	.277	.355	-2.4	LF(13): -0.4, 1B(3): 0.2	0.2
Attrition: **17%** MLB: **76%**	2013	MIA	MLB	35	19	1	1	0	0	1	1	3	0	0	.167/.211/.222	.157	.200	0	LF(4): -0.2	-0.2
Comparables: Brian Jordan, Jose Cruz, Mark DeRosa	2014	MIA	MLB	36	250	24	11	1	3	24	16	50	5	1	.253/.309/.358	.255	.310	0.3	LF 0, RF -2	0.3

Formerly a respectable option on the short side of a platoon, Diaz has struggled to reclaim his former glory over the past few seasons. After being released by the Yankees toward the end of spring training, he latched on with the Marlins and got a call in early May, put up a miserable small-sample slash line, then proceeded to miss the final four months of the season with a left knee contusion. As a sort of permanent wanderer now, Diaz will be looking to find an organization willing to build a time machine to take him back to 2010, when he was last a major league-caliber player. And you thought Boras clients were demanding.

Derek Dietrich 2B

Born: 7/18/1989 Age: 24
Bats: L Throws: R Height: 6' 0"
Weight: 200 Breakout: 2%
Improve: 26% Collapse: 15%
Attrition: 33% MLB: 68%

Comparables:
Sean Rodriguez, Josh Bell, Fernando Martinez

YEAR	TEAM	LVL	AGE	PA	R	2B	3B	HR	RBI	BB	SO	SB	CS	AVG/OBP/SLG	TAv	BABIP	BRR	FRAA	WARP
2011	BGR	A	21	538	73	34	4	22	81	38	128	5	7	.277/.346/.502	.317	.331	-2.2	SS(68): -5.8	2.2
2012	PCH	A+	22	417	49	21	9	10	58	25	78	4	2	.282/.343/.468	.281	.329	3.2	SS(75): -7.0, 2B(17): -2.8	1.9
2012	MNT	AA	22	146	22	7	1	4	17	7	36	0	1	.271/.324/.429	.254	.340	0.2	2B(34): 1.1	0.6
2013	JAX	AA	23	257	35	13	3	11	38	29	60	3	0	.271/.381/.509	.316	.327	0.2	2B(50): -3.7, 3B(8): -0.5	1.9
2013	MIA	MLB	23	233	32	10	2	9	23	11	56	1	0	.214/.275/.405	.260	.247	0.7	2B(57): -2.6	0.3
2014	MIA	MLB	24	277	28	12	2	9	34	14	70	1	0	.234/.287/.400	.256	.280	-0.2	2B -3, SS -2	0.3

A .247 BABIP happens, but when it's accompanied by a very strong 25 percent line-drive rate it's quite rare indeed. Dietrich's low-walk, high-strikeout approach will always inhibit his average and on-base percentage, but not likely to this extent. His defense is passable at second base, but he's a better fit at the hot corner in the long run. Given the Marlins' lack of infield depth, he's likely to get a chance to prove himself at both spots—his long-term upside trumps those of both Donovan Solano and Ed Lucas.

Greg Dobbs 1B

Born: 7/2/1978 Age: 35
Bats: L Throws: R Height: 6' 1"
Weight: 210 Breakout: 0%
Improve: 19% Collapse: 10%
Attrition: 24% MLB: 69%

Comparables:
Vance Wilson, Ted Simmons, Freddy Sanchez

YEAR	TEAM	LVL	AGE	PA	R	2B	3B	HR	RBI	BB	SO	SB	CS	AVG/OBP/SLG	TAv	BABIP	BRR	FRAA	WARP
2011	FLO	MLB	32	439	38	23	0	8	49	22	83	0	0	.275/.311/.389	.254	.325	-1.9	3B(100): -4.6, 1B(4): 0.3	0.2
2012	MIA	MLB	33	342	26	13	2	5	39	14	53	4	2	.285/.313/.386	.259	.321	-2.3	3B(36): -4.6, LF(21): -1.0	-0.3
2013	MIA	MLB	34	267	21	11	0	2	22	22	40	1	1	.228/.303/.300	.237	.263	-0.6	1B(51): 1.5, RF(1): 0.0	-0.3
2014	MIA	MLB	35	266	23	11	1	4	25	15	49	2	1	.242/.288/.335	.237	.280	-0.4	1B 1, 3B -2	-0.3

Through the age of 31, Dobbs had never started a game in the cleanup spot; in three years since, he has started 34 games there, all while hitting .267/.310/.366 overall. In an era of 12- and 13-man bullpens, Dobbs is probably not good enough to merit a spot on most teams' bench, but he's big thunder in Miami's lineup. So Jeffrey Loria re-signed him, reportedly without informing his now-departed team president Larry Beinfest first. The owner's keen scouting eye must have seen something in Dobbs, but since A) it's Loria and B) it's Dobbs, we can't tell you what it is.

Rafael Furcal 2B

Born: 10/24/1977 Age: 36
Bats: B Throws: R Height: 5' 8"
Weight: 195 Breakout: 0%
Improve: 30% Collapse: 9%
Attrition: 19% MLB: 72%

Comparables:
Mark Ellis, Tony Graffanino, Roberto Alomar

YEAR	TEAM	LVL	AGE	PA	R	2B	3B	HR	RBI	BB	SO	SB	CS	AVG/OBP/SLG	TAv	BABIP	BRR	FRAA	WARP
2011	RCU	A+	33	25	10	0	0	0	1	3	3	1	0	.318/.400/.318	.274	.368	0		0.0
2011	LAN	MLB	33	152	15	4	0	1	12	11	21	5	3	.197/.272/.248	.220	.226	0.4	SS(36): 0.6	0.0
2011	SLN	MLB	33	217	29	11	0	7	16	17	18	4	2	.255/.316/.418	.269	.250	2	SS(49): 2.6	1.7
2012	SLN	MLB	34	531	69	18	3	5	49	44	57	12	4	.264/.325/.346	.246	.289	4.3	SS(120): 0.5	2.3
2014	MIA	MLB	36	250	28	10	2	2	19	21	32	7	2	.254/.319/.346	.258	.280	0.3	2B 0, SS 0	0.8

Furcal's flash of youth after moving to St. Louis in the summer of 2011 was short-lived, as he struggled in his first full season with the club and missed the second entirely after having Tommy John surgery. The injury bug has always bothered Furcal in a 14-year career, but at this point, and after so much time away, it will be hard to tell whether he's hurt or just old when he's scuffling along in June. The Marlins signed him for a small guaranteed salary to play second base, and he'll get a chance to chase 2,000 hits in a clean, well-lit and mostly empty environment.

Adeiny Hechavarria SS

Born: 4/15/1989 Age: 25
Bats: R Throws: R Height: 6' 0"
Weight: 185 Breakout: 6%
Improve: 52% Collapse: 9%
Attrition: 33% MLB: 82%

Comparables:
Brandon Phillips, Alcides Escobar, Ronny Cedeno

YEAR	TEAM	LVL	AGE	PA	R	2B	3B	HR	RBI	BB	SO	SB	CS	AVG/OBP/SLG	TAv	BABIP	BRR	FRAA	WARP
2011	NHP	AA	22	502	58	22	6	6	46	25	78	19	13	.235/.275/.347	.248	.267	-0.2	SS(37): -2.3	0.0
2011	LVG	AAA	22	116	16	6	2	2	11	8	21	1	2	.389/.431/.537	.298	.471	1.2	SS(17): -3.4	0.6
2012	LVG	AAA	23	490	78	20	6	6	63	38	86	8	2	.312/.363/.424	.258	.371	1.6	SS(95): 4.4, 2B(8): 1.9	2.6
2012	TOR	MLB	23	137	10	8	0	2	15	4	32	0	0	.254/.280/.365	.227	.323	0.2	3B(18): 0.8, SS(17): -0.8	0.0
2013	MIA	MLB	24	578	30	14	8	3	42	30	96	11	10	.227/.267/.298	.204	.270	-5.5	SS(148): -5.2	-2.3
2014	MIA	MLB	25	515	52	18	5	3	35	28	100	11	7	.242/.284/.320	.231	.290	0	SS -2, 3B 0	0.5

Calling someone defense-oriented is usually a nice way of saying he can't hit. In Hechavarria's case, that's ... fair. It's also usually a nice way of saying he *can* field, but in Hechavarria's case the jury is out. Scouts praise his range, strong arm and athleticism in the field, but so far the advanced metrics don't back that up; besides FRAA's scold, Defensive Runs Saved gives him a negative rating and UZR dismisses his range. Best case, Hechavarria is Andrelton Simmons without the power or Jose Iglesias without the luck, but even if he turns out to be a truly terrific defender, he'll have to orient himself toward a few hits if he wants to hold a starting job.

Garrett Jones   1B

Born: 6/21/1981 Age: 33
Bats: L Throws: L Height: 6' 4"
Weight: 230 Breakout: 2%
Improve: 32% Collapse: 3%
Attrition: 11% MLB: 89%

Comparables:
Erubiel Durazo, Ernie Banks, Orlando Cepeda

YEAR	TEAM	LVL	AGE	PA	R	2B	3B	HR	RBI	BB	SO	SB	CS	AVG/OBP/SLG	TAv	BABIP	BRR	FRAA	WARP
2011	PIT	MLB	30	477	51	30	1	16	58	48	104	6	3	.243/.321/.433	.274	.283	-0.5	RF(90): 1.0, 1B(34): -1.6	1.4
2012	PIT	MLB	31	515	68	28	3	27	86	33	103	2	0	.274/.317/.516	.307	.293	-3.2	1B(72): -1.2, RF(66): -1.3	2.4
2013	PIT	MLB	32	440	41	26	2	15	51	31	101	2	0	.233/.289/.419	.260	.271	-3.7	1B(83): 0.4, RF(32): -1.4	0.0
2014	MIA	MLB	33	428	48	22	1	15	54	35	93	4	1	.246/.307/.420	.271	.280	-0.2	1B -0, RF -1	1.0

There are platoons and then there are *platoons*. Jones faced right-handed pitching in 85 percent of his plate appearances in his first two seasons under Pirates manager Clint Hurdle. That rate increased to 95 percent in 2013, yet Jones experienced his worst offensive season with the crimson-faced skipper. Is there such a thing as too much of a good platoon, or is the former minor-league vet on the downside of his career? South Floridians will know the answer this time next year.

Ed Lucas   3B

Born: 5/21/1982 Age: 32
Bats: R Throws: R Height: 6' 3"
Weight: 210 Breakout: 2%
Improve: 5% Collapse: 6%
Attrition: 19% MLB: 32%

Comparables:
Nick Green, Norihiro Nakamura, Brendan Harris

YEAR	TEAM	LVL	AGE	PA	R	2B	3B	HR	RBI	BB	SO	SB	CS	AVG/OBP/SLG	TAv	BABIP	BRR	FRAA	WARP
2011	MIS	AA	29	181	32	6	0	7	26	15	38	0	0	.270/.344/.440	.293	.310	0.6	SS(9): -0.7	0.2
2011	GWN	AAA	29	295	25	14	1	3	29	28	74	4	0	.218/.294/.313	.194	.289	0.7	2B(18): 1.5, SS(4): -0.2	-0.5
2012	SLC	AAA	30	453	61	20	2	12	52	28	82	5	4	.262/.316/.408	.242	.299	-0.2	SS(77): 7.9, 2B(25): 0.7	1.2
2013	NWO	AAA	31	196	26	12	0	5	14	12	37	2	1	.304/.354/.453	.304	.360	-0.5	2B(22): 1.1, SS(17): 0.3	1.9
2013	MIA	MLB	31	384	43	14	1	4	28	26	78	1	1	.256/.311/.336	.243	.319	0	3B(61): 1.9, 1B(25): 0.6	0.6
2014	MIA	MLB	32	368	32	14	1	5	31	22	82	2	1	.230/.282/.319	.232	.290	-0.5	3B 1, SS 1	0.2

As far as baseball stories go, a 10-year minor-league veteran who gets his first taste of the big leagues at 31 and manages to stick is very strong. The first Dartmouth graduate to play in the major leagues since Mike Remlinger retired in 2006, Lucas started 52 games in the second spot in the Marlins' lineup—more a reflection of the state of the organization than of his talent level. He was a real weapon against left-handed pitchers, however, hitting .330/.374/.509 in 116 plate appearances. Despite being the old square on a team of kids, Lucas has the inside track for a utility role in Miami this year.

Jake Marisnick   CF

Born: 3/30/1991 Age: 23
Bats: R Throws: R Height: 6' 3"
Weight: 225 Breakout: 1%
Improve: 21% Collapse: 4%
Attrition: 13% MLB: 40%

Comparables:
Felix Pie, Aaron Cunningham, Ryan Kalish

YEAR	TEAM	LVL	AGE	PA	R	2B	3B	HR	RBI	BB	SO	SB	CS	AVG/OBP/SLG	TAv	BABIP	BRR	FRAA	WARP
2011	LNS	A	20	523	68	27	6	14	77	43	91	37	8	.320/.392/.496	.408	.371	0.7	CF(19): 0.3	2.1
2012	DUN	A+	21	306	41	18	7	6	35	26	55	10	5	.263/.349/.451	.272	.309	-1.2	CF(63): 2.1	1.8
2012	NHP	AA	21	247	25	11	3	2	15	11	45	14	4	.233/.286/.336	.239	.278	2.5	CF(55): 3.3	1.0
2013	JAX	AA	22	298	43	13	3	12	46	17	68	11	6	.294/.358/.502	.311	.351	1.9	CF(54): 3.4, LF(11): 0.3	3.3
2013	MIA	MLB	22	118	6	2	1	1	5	6	27	3	1	.183/.231/.248	.193	.232	0.4	CF(32): 0.8	-0.1
2014	MIA	MLB	23	250	30	9	2	5	21	12	59	10	3	.232/.283/.358	.244	.280	0.9	CF 3, LF 0	0.8

As part of the package the Marlins got for regifting their 2012 free agent haul to Toronto, Marisnick saw his stock drop, then rise with a swing adjustment, then stagnate after a late-July promotion. The toolsy center fielder never found a groove in Miami, despite consistent playing time. He's got a long swing that didn't adapt well to advanced breaking pitches: Against 144 sliders or curves, he slugged just .171. Marisnick's advantage is his wealth of above-average skills, as opposed to one or two truly elite tools, and his ability to stick in center will help his offense play up. He had a knee scope in October to repair a torn meniscus, but will be ready to compete for the starting job in the spring.

Jeff Mathis   C

Born: 3/31/1983 Age: 31
Bats: R Throws: R Height: 6' 0"
Weight: 205 Breakout: 2%
Improve: 25% Collapse: 16%
Attrition: 20% MLB: 81%

Comparables:
Andy Etchebarren, Chad Kreuter, Juan Espino

YEAR	TEAM	LVL	AGE	PA	R	2B	3B	HR	RBI	BB	SO	SB	CS	AVG/OBP/SLG	TAv	BABIP	BRR	FRAA	WARP
2011	ANA	MLB	28	281	18	12	0	3	22	15	75	1	2	.174/.225/.259	.188	.233	-0.8	C(91): 0.2	-0.9
2012	TOR	MLB	29	227	25	13	0	8	27	9	68	1	0	.218/.249/.393	.216	.279	-1.7	C(66): -1.2, P(2): -0.0	-0.1
2013	MIA	MLB	30	256	14	7	1	5	29	21	76	0	0	.181/.251/.284	.204	.243	1	C(73): -0.9	0.0
2014	MIA	MLB	31	250	21	9	1	4	21	16	72	1	1	.197/.253/.297	.209	.260	-0.3	C 0	-0.1

Another year of Jeff Mathis doing all the things that make fans grind their teeth—his 48 OPS+ was the fifth-worst in Marlins franchise history, though only the third-worst of his career. But also another year that his ex-catcher manager was probably quite happy with. Mathis distinguished himself by returning from injury in May to become Jose Fernandez's personal backstop, and it's Fernandez's numbers—1.56 ERA throwing to Mathis, 3.27 to everybody else—that Mathis would no doubt prefer on the back of his baseball card.

Colin Moran — 3B

Born: 10/1/1992 Age: 21
Bats: L Throws: R Height: 6' 4"
Weight: 190 Breakout: 0%
Improve: 1% Collapse: 0%
Attrition: 3% MLB: 3%

Comparables:
Taylor Green, Jermaine Curtis, Tony Cruz

YEAR	TEAM	LVL	AGE	PA	R	2B	3B	HR	RBI	BB	SO	SB	CS	AVG/OBP/SLG	TAv	BABIP	BRR	FRAA	WARP
2013	GRB	A	20	175	19	8	1	4	23	15	25	1	0	.299/.354/.442	.300	.323	-1	3B(33): -0.5	1.0
2014	MIA	MLB	21	250	20	9	1	3	22	16	54	1	0	.223/.273/.307	.223	.280	-0.3	3B -2	-0.5

Moran was, according to the mock-draft set, in the running to be the top overall pick in June. Instead, the Marlins landed him with the sixth pick—franchise-crippling 93-loss seasons being, in Marlinsland, the gifts that keep on giving. The University of North Carolina third baseman has an advanced feel for hitting, with line-drive power and control of the strike zone, easing at least some of the suspicion of his quirky left-handed swing. His A-ball debut was encouraging—he homered in his first pro at-bat, and nearly led his team in OBP—and even a rough (and small) Arizona Fall League sample carried some good news, as he walked 12 times and struck out just 18 in a hundred trips. Don't like this guy? Get a brain! Morans.

Marcell Ozuna — RF

Born: 11/12/1990 Age: 23
Bats: R Throws: R Height: 6' 1"
Weight: 220 Breakout: 1%
Improve: 29% Collapse: 3%
Attrition: 13% MLB: 51%

Comparables:
Fernando Martinez, Dayan Viciedo, Carlos Gonzalez

YEAR	TEAM	LVL	AGE	PA	R	2B	3B	HR	RBI	BB	SO	SB	CS	AVG/OBP/SLG	TAv	BABIP	BRR	FRAA	WARP
2011	GRB	A	20	552	87	28	5	23	71	46	121	17	2	.266/.330/.482	.282	.308	2.1	RF(57): 4.0, CF(1): -0.0	2.0
2012	JUP	A+	21	539	89	27	2	24	95	44	116	8	3	.266/.328/.476	.282	.301	1.1	RF(107): 17.3, CF(14): -0.4	4.3
2013	JAX	AA	22	47	6	3	1	5	15	3	9	1	0	.333/.383/.810	.414	.310	0.4	RF(10): -0.6	0.9
2013	MIA	MLB	22	291	31	17	4	3	32	13	57	5	1	.265/.303/.389	.258	.326	1.4	RF(36): 1.9, CF(33): -2.3	1.0
2014	MIA	MLB	23	289	30	13	2	8	34	15	69	3	1	.243/.285/.400	.256	.290	0.2	RF 4, CF -1	0.8

The second example of a player the Marlins had no qualms about promoting despite little to no experience in the upper minors, Ozuna had a whole 47 plate appearances at Double-A before getting the call to take Giancarlo Stanton's roster spot on April 30th. They certainly caught lightning in a bottle during May, when he hit .330/.372/.462 in 106 at-bats. But after falling back down to Earth, Ozuna still finds himself needing a Stanton trade to have a clear path to playing time, as he's behind both Christian Yelich and Jake Marisnick on the outfield depth chart. His contact rate's step forward in 2013 bodes well for his future, as his power remains his offensive carrying tool. In the field, he showed off his other big-time weapon, racking up eight outfield assists in fewer than 70 games.

Noah Perio — 2B

Born: 11/14/1991 Age: 22
Bats: L Throws: R Height: 6' 0"
Weight: 170 Breakout: 0%
Improve: 1% Collapse: 0%
Attrition: 3% MLB: 3%

Comparables:
Hernan Perez, Nick Noonan, Eric Sogard

YEAR	TEAM	LVL	AGE	PA	R	2B	3B	HR	RBI	BB	SO	SB	CS	AVG/OBP/SLG	TAv	BABIP	BRR	FRAA	WARP
2011	GRB	A	19	519	76	30	3	6	52	19	64	15	6	.295/.323/.406	.236	.327	1.9	2B(49): -4.0, SS(2): -0.2	-0.2
2012	JUP	A+	20	502	50	22	2	1	40	27	68	6	4	.248/.293/.311	.214	.286	-0.6	2B(112): 1.0	-1.3
2013	JUP	A+	21	178	17	4	0	0	16	10	12	6	2	.241/.282/.265	.207	.257	0.5	2B(41): -0.4	-0.5
2013	JAX	AA	21	196	20	7	0	1	14	16	27	2	0	.232/.297/.288	.237	.267	0.7	2B(53): 2.8, 1B(1): -0.1	0.3
2014	MIA	MLB	22	250	21	10	1	1	15	10	45	2	1	.218/.249/.274	.204	.260	-0.3	2B 0, 1B -0	-0.6

Perio dropped to the 39th round four years ago because he was expected to concentrate on football, but the Marlins redirected him with $150,000. Since then, he has played pretty much like a 39th-rounder. Perio is athletic, he can handle a glove and he finally figured out the strike zone last year, but he simply doesn't hit the ball hard. It's the classic football player lotto ticket: If it clicks, it's a buck well spent, but discarded lotto tickets cover liquor store parking lots for a reason.

Juan Pierre — LF

Born: 8/14/1977 Age: 36
Bats: L Throws: L Height: 5' 10"
Weight: 180 Breakout: 0%
Improve: 26% Collapse: 10%
Attrition: 25% MLB: 71%

Comparables:
Manny Mota, Harvey Kuenn, Matty Alou

YEAR	TEAM	LVL	AGE	PA	R	2B	3B	HR	RBI	BB	SO	SB	CS	AVG/OBP/SLG	TAv	BABIP	BRR	FRAA	WARP
2011	CHA	MLB	33	711	80	17	4	2	50	43	41	27	17	.279/.329/.327	.240	.294	10	LF(155): -10.3	-0.3
2012	PHI	MLB	34	439	59	10	6	1	25	23	27	37	7	.307/.351/.371	.269	.327	2.9	LF(107): 2.8	2.1
2013	MIA	MLB	35	330	36	11	2	1	8	13	27	23	6	.247/.284/.305	.217	.268	3.4	LF(64): 5.8	-0.1
2014	MIA	MLB	36	332	40	9	3	0	19	18	26	22	7	.271/.322/.321	.240	.280	1.9	LF 1	0.4

Any chance Pierre's 2012 signaled a career rebirth was buried by an avalanche of suck, or, put another way, Pierre's $100,000 bonus for winning league MVP didn't vest. The sad part for Pierre is his batted ball numbers last season were pretty similar to his career numbers, with two exceptions: He hit far more infield pop-ups and he had far fewer infield hits. Simply put, Pierre hit as bad as ever and couldn't take advantage of his signature skill to sneak hits. It's a bad sign, though not the only sign, that time has stolen all that was left to steal.

Placido Polanco   3B

Born: 10/10/1975 Age: 38
Bats: R Throws: R Height: 5' 9"
Weight: 190 Breakout: 0%
Improve: 22% Collapse: 13%
Attrition: 21% MLB: 66%

Comparables:
Mark Loretta, Wade Boggs, Craig Counsell

YEAR	TEAM	LVL	AGE	PA	R	2B	3B	HR	RBI	BB	SO	SB	CS	AVG/OBP/SLG	TAv	BABIP	BRR	FRAA	WARP
2011	PHI	MLB	35	523	46	14	0	5	50	42	44	3	0	.277/.335/.339	.257	.292	-2	3B(118): 12.7, 2B(1): -0.0	2.6
2012	PHI	MLB	36	328	28	15	0	2	19	18	25	0	0	.257/.302/.327	.236	.274	-1.6	3B(80): 5.1	0.5
2013	MIA	MLB	37	416	33	13	0	1	23	23	31	2	0	.260/.315/.302	.233	.278	-0.5	3B(109): -5.5	-0.7
2014	MIA	MLB	38	375	35	14	1	0	24	21	32	2	0	.260/.308/.311	.243	.280	-0.3	3B 3, 2B 0	0.6

Last year in this space we wrote that "the Marlins signed [Polanco] to a cheap one-year deal in the hope that there's something left in the tank." We know the ending to that plot: there wasn't. Polanco contributed next to nothing, slugging .264 in 300 tries against right-handers while serving as the Marlins' putative middle-of-the-order muscle. The fact that Miami kept running him out there captures well the mess that was. Polanco has had a long and productive career (28.1 WARP in 16 seasons is nothing to snarf at) and has hinted at calling it quits. PECOTA is already shopping for retirement gifts.

Jacob Realmuto   C

Born: 3/18/1991 Age: 23
Bats: R Throws: R Height: 6' 1"
Weight: 205 Breakout: 4%
Improve: 10% Collapse: 0%
Attrition: 11% MLB: 14%

Comparables:
Jeff Clement, Bryan Anderson, Matt McBride

YEAR	TEAM	LVL	AGE	PA	R	2B	3B	HR	RBI	BB	SO	SB	CS	AVG/OBP/SLG	TAv	BABIP	BRR	FRAA	WARP
2011	GRB	A	20	381	46	16	3	12	49	26	78	13	6	.287/.347/.454	.299	.341	0.7	C(38): 0.1	1.7
2012	JUP	A+	21	499	63	16	0	8	46	37	64	13	5	.256/.319/.345	.241	.279	-0.9	C(95): 1.1, 1B(1): -0.0	0.9
2013	JAX	AA	22	416	41	21	3	5	39	36	68	9	1	.239/.310/.353	.253	.275	-1.6	C(99): -1.2	1.5
2014	MIA	MLB	23	250	21	10	1	3	22	15	50	3	1	.225/.276/.318	.229	.270	-0.1	C -0, 1B -0	0.3

Contrary to popular belief, "Realmuto" is not Spanish for "Real Muto" but ancient Sumerian for "catcher of the future." By all accounts, Realmuto improved both his defense and the accoutrements of catching in his long stay in Jacksonville. Some power is present, but his bat still needs work. Scouts are optimistic that his athleticism will help him reach the majors, even if it's as a backup, defense-first, good-in-the-clubhouse, knows-how-to-call-a-game guy.

Avery Romero   2B

Born: 5/11/1993 Age: 21
Bats: R Throws: R Height: 5' 11"
Weight: 195 Breakout: 1%
Improve: 2% Collapse: 0%
Attrition: 1% MLB: 2%

Comparables:
Steve Clevenger, Jordany Valdespin, Luis Valbuena

YEAR	TEAM	LVL	AGE	PA	R	2B	3B	HR	RBI	BB	SO	SB	CS	AVG/OBP/SLG	TAv	BABIP	BRR	FRAA	WARP
2012	JAM	A-	19	25	3	0	0	0	4	3	0	1	0	.381/.458/.381	.299	.381	-0.6	3B(5): -0.1, 2B(3): -0.2	0.1
2013	GRB	A	20	40	5	1	0	1	5	4	5	0	0	.147/.237/.265	.204	.143	-0.1	2B(9): -0.8	-0.2
2013	BAT	A-	20	235	27	18	0	2	30	15	34	3	4	.297/.357/.411	.289	.339	-1.2	2B(53): 6.6	2.0
2014	MIA	MLB	21	250	18	9	1	3	21	13	57	0	0	.206/.254/.284	.207	.260	-0.5	2B 1, 3B -0	-0.4

After splitting time between second and third in his first taste of professional ball, Romero focused exclusively on the keystone in 2013 with encouraging results. The big question with Romero is whether he can be an average defender there, since his bat may have a tough time profiling at the hot corner. His approach at the plate is advanced for his level right now, but he's going to need to turn his power potential into power production if he wants to play an everyday role on the Marlins' next winning team. The 2012 third-round draft pick should return to Low-A Greensboro to start the season, but could move quickly.

Jarrod Saltalamacchia C

Born: 5/2/1985 Age: 29
Bats: B Throws: R Height: 6' 4"
Weight: 235 Breakout: 5%
Improve: 47% Collapse: 13%
Attrition: 17% MLB: 94%

Comparables:
Hector Villanueva, Todd Hundley, Mickey Tettleton

YEAR	TEAM	LVL	AGE	PA	R	2B	3B	HR	RBI	BB	SO	SB	CS	AVG/OBP/SLG	TAv	BABIP	BRR	FRAA	WARP
2011	BOS	MLB	26	386	52	23	3	16	56	24	119	1	0	.235/.288/.450	.249	.304	-1.2	C(101): -2.0	0.7
2012	BOS	MLB	27	448	55	17	1	25	59	38	139	0	1	.222/.288/.454	.265	.265	-0.4	C(104): 0.5, 1B(1): -0.0	2.1
2013	BOS	MLB	28	470	68	40	0	14	65	43	139	4	1	.273/.338/.466	.288	.372	0.8	C(119): -0.2	3.4
2014	MIA	MLB	29	437	48	21	1	14	51	36	129	2	1	.228/.294/.395	.256	.300	-0.6	C -1	1.7

You could point to Saltalamacchia's .372 BABIP and assume he'll fall back to pre-2013 levels, and there may be some truth to that, but Magic BABIP Wand-waving is lazy and unfair. Salty was known to sell out for power prior to last summer, but he showed better pitch recognition in 2013, especially in the second half. The result was less power than usual, but his average and doubles climbed, inflating his on-base percentage. He still struck out constantly, but cut it from one-third of the time in the season's first half to 24 percent in the second. If he can hold on to some of those gains, he should survive whatever BABIP drop may be in the offing. If not, the Marlins signed him cheaply enough that it barely matters.

Donovan Solano 2B
Born: 12/17/1987 Age: 26
Bats: R Throws: R Height: 5' 9"
Weight: 195 Breakout: 5%
Improve: 43% Collapse: 15%
Attrition: 25% MLB: 93%
Comparables:
Jemile Weeks, Ronny Cedeno, Brandon Phillips

YEAR	TEAM	LVL	AGE	PA	R	2B	3B	HR	RBI	BB	SO	SB	CS	AVG/OBP/SLG	TAv	BABIP	BRR	FRAA	WARP
2011	SFD	AA	23	104	5	7	0	2	10	3	16	0	0	.228/.250/.356	.163	.253	-0.7	2B(12): -0.0, SS(1): -0.0	-0.5
2011	MEM	AAA	23	258	22	21	1	1	23	19	35	2	0	.284/.336/.397	.227	.325	-1.4	SS(8): 0.4, 2B(8): 0.3	-0.1
2012	NWO	AAA	24	160	14	7	1	0	14	10	27	4	0	.262/.327/.326	.236	.322	-0.4	2B(18): 2.3, SS(17): -1.2	0.2
2012	MIA	MLB	24	316	29	11	3	2	28	21	58	7	0	.295/.342/.375	.266	.357	2.1	2B(58): 4.6, LF(10): -0.3	1.8
2013	NWO	AAA	25	73	8	3	1	2	9	4	11	0	0	.379/.411/.545	.366	.418	0	2B(9): 0.2, 3B(4): -0.0	1.2
2013	MIA	MLB	25	395	33	13	1	3	34	23	57	3	1	.249/.305/.316	.230	.287	-1.8	2B(93): 8.1, 3B(2): -0.0	0.5
2014	MIA	MLB	26	387	40	16	2	3	29	23	67	4	1	.255/.306/.340	.246	.300	0.3	2B 7, SS -0	1.5

There's only so much value that a player with no power, no speed and a fringy hit tool can bring to the table—and when said player can't play shortstop (even in a pinch), it can be tough for him to warrant even a roster spot. Fortunately for Solano, he's on the Marlins, where that package of skills was strong enough to make him the everyday second baseman. With Rafael Furcal now ahead of him on the depth chart, Solano would be lucky to get more than 140 or 150 starts this year.

Giancarlo Stanton RF
Born: 11/8/1989 Age: 24
Bats: R Throws: R Height: 6' 6"
Weight: 240 Breakout: 4%
Improve: 60% Collapse: 8%
Attrition: 8% MLB: 99%
Comparables:
Reggie Jackson, Darryl Strawberry, Mark McGwire

YEAR	TEAM	LVL	AGE	PA	R	2B	3B	HR	RBI	BB	SO	SB	CS	AVG/OBP/SLG	TAv	BABIP	BRR	FRAA	WARP
2011	FLO	MLB	21	601	79	30	5	34	87	70	166	5	5	.262/.356/.537	.318	.314	-2.5	RF(142): 11.3, CF(1): 0.0	5.8
2012	MIA	MLB	22	501	75	30	1	37	86	46	143	6	2	.290/.361/.608	.342	.344	0.1	RF(117): 6.0	6.2
2013	MIA	MLB	23	504	62	26	0	24	62	74	140	1	0	.249/.365/.480	.316	.313	0.2	RF(116): 0.4	3.8
2014	MIA	MLB	24	477	68	23	2	28	79	53	131	4	2	.261/.349/.523	.315	.310	-0.5	RF 6, CF 0	4.2

Viewed against his teammates, Stanton was Ruthian, one of only two Marlins position players to produce more than one WARP. Otherwise, his season was a step back, as he set career lows in batting average, isolated power and HR/FB rate. With virtually no incentive to pitch to him—the Marlins were at or near the bottom of the NL in OPS from the first, second, fourth and fifth spots in the lineup—the league did little to tempt him, and Stanton often seemed uncertain of whether to expand the zone or just jog down to first to ponder the nature of loneliness. It's always seemed certain that, barring injuries, he'll be on a stage in Cooperstown in 20 or 25 years, but the clearer threat right now is that another couple years with the Marlins will ruin him.

Jordany Valdespin 2B
Born: 12/23/1987 Age: 26
Bats: L Throws: R Height: 6' 0"
Weight: 190 Breakout: 10%
Improve: 46% Collapse: 6%
Attrition: 27% MLB: 80%
Comparables:
Chris Nelson, Danny Richar, Jason Donald

YEAR	TEAM	LVL	AGE	PA	R	2B	3B	HR	RBI	BB	SO	SB	CS	AVG/OBP/SLG	TAv	BABIP	BRR	FRAA	WARP
2011	BIN	AA	23	441	62	24	3	15	51	21	68	33	14	.297/.341/.483	.296	.325	-0.8	SS(61): -2.2, 2B(14): -1.7	1.9
2011	BUF	AAA	23	113	7	8	0	2	9	4	25	4	4	.280/.304/.411	.224	.346	-1.5	SS(16): -0.4, 2B(5): 0.7	-0.1
2012	BUF	AAA	24	163	22	2	1	5	23	10	22	10	8	.285/.331/.411	.250	.304	1	2B(22): -1.0, CF(15): 0.0	0.4
2012	NYN	MLB	24	206	28	9	1	8	26	10	44	10	3	.241/.286/.424	.266	.273	0.3	LF(21): -0.6, 2B(16): -0.2	0.7
2013	LVG	AAA	25	67	14	4	2	3	24	8	7	2	3	.466/.537/.759	.399	.500	0.9	2B(14): 1.1, RF(2): -0.1	1.4
2013	NYN	MLB	25	144	16	3	1	4	16	8	28	4	3	.188/.250/.316	.224	.208	0.7	CF(16): -0.2, 2B(12): -0.0	-0.3
2014	MIA	MLB	26	250	35	10	1	7	24	13	47	12	7	.251/.296/.396	.260	.280	0.2	2B -0, CF 0	0.7

The most amusing, mind-boggling subplot of the 2013 Mets centered on Valdespin, who found himself in controversy upon controversy, sparking a local media freakout over whether the firebrand was worth the fire. Thus far, he hasn't done anything to earn the right to cause any controversy at all. As in 2012, some late-game heroism obfuscated a lack of production, and after he was finally sent to the minors in July he missed the remainder of the year on a PED suspension. The Mets gave him free agency and the Marlins signed him, but it's unclear what his best position is, so the only extended shot his new employer can give him is probably in Triple-A.

Christian Yelich LF
Born: 12/5/1991 Age: 22
Bats: L Throws: R Height: 6' 4"
Weight: 195 Breakout: 1%
Improve: 39% Collapse: 0%
Attrition: 14% MLB: 62%
Comparables:
Travis Snider, Adam Jones, Joel Guzman

YEAR	TEAM	LVL	AGE	PA	R	2B	3B	HR	RBI	BB	SO	SB	CS	AVG/OBP/SLG	TAv	BABIP	BRR	FRAA	WARP
2011	GRB	A	19	521	73	32	1	15	77	55	102	32	5	.312/.388/.484	.272	.373	-0.3	LF(37): 1.4, CF(13): -0.2	0.7
2012	JUP	A+	20	447	76	29	5	12	48	49	85	20	6	.330/.404/.519	.324	.397	2.4	CF(96): -0.1, LF(7): -0.3	4.6
2013	JUP	A+	21	30	3	0	0	2	4	4	8	0	0	.231/.333/.462	.271	.250	0.2	CF(6): -1.3	0.1
2013	JAX	AA	21	222	33	13	6	7	29	26	52	5	5	.280/.365/.518	.322	.346	-1	CF(27): -0.9, LF(22): -1.0	1.9
2013	MIA	MLB	21	273	34	12	1	4	16	31	66	10	0	.288/.370/.396	.295	.380	3.3	LF(59): -0.4, CF(5): 0.1	1.7
2014	MIA	MLB	22	296	33	13	1	6	32	26	75	9	2	.259/.325/.395	.272	.330	0.7	LF -1, CF -1	1.0

After taking it one step per year with Yelich, the Marlins finally figured to heck with it and jumped him from Double-A to the big leagues midway through July, after just 49 games in the high minors. He'd certainly shown that slow-and-steady was no challenge for him, as he produced something close to the classically beautiful .300/.400/.500 line at every stop. "Yelich is the top bat for me in the minors; even better than Taveras," a front-office executive told BP just before the call-up. His swing is the physical equivalent of that .300/.400/.500 line, pure and powerful and geared (for now) toward doubles. There's no shame in being just shy of home run oomph at this stage of his career, and in his final 30 games he hit .330/.431/.468.

PITCHERS

Arquimedes Caminero

Born: 6/16/1987 Age: 27
Bats: R Throws: R Height: 6' 4" Weight: 255
Breakout: 14% Improve: 39% Collapse: 48%
Attrition: 63% MLB: 33%

Comparables:
Jim Miller, Josh Judy, Scott Maine

YEAR	TEAM	LVL	AGE	W	L	SV	G	GS	IP	H	HR	BB	SO	BB9	SO9	GB%	BABIP	WHIP	ERA	FIP	FRA	WARP
2012	JUP	A+	25	1	0	1	19	0	20²	12	0	9	27	3.9	11.8	42%	.250	1.02	0.44	2.52	2.61	0.6
2012	JAX	AA	25	0	0	2	12	0	17²	16	0	10	17	5.1	8.7	48%	.333	1.47	3.06	2.92	3.13	0.4
2013	JAX	AA	26	5	2	5	42	0	52¹	34	4	21	68	3.6	11.7	35%	.257	1.05	3.61	2.68	3.24	0.8
2013	MIA	MLB	26	0	0	0	13	0	13	10	2	3	12	2.1	8.3	25%	.235	1.00	2.77	4.10	3.68	0.1
2014	MIA	MLB	27	2	1	1	39	0	52²	44	5	25	54	4.3	9.2	41%	.298	1.31	3.76	3.99	4.09	0.2

The first Caminero and the first Arquimedes in major-league history, this stringy right-hander has a four-seam fastball that sits on 96 with late life. As with most rookies who throw that hard, the command is the problem. Caminero made strides last year, cutting his walk rate in a repeat of Double-A and cutting further still upon arrival in Miami. It's still not ideal, but if he can stick around 3.5 walks per nine he'll be no wilder than Jordan Walden, Vinnie Pestano, John Axford and a slew of other viable relievers have been.

Carter Capps

Born: 8/7/1990 Age: 23
Bats: R Throws: R Height: 6' 5" Weight: 220
Breakout: 39% Improve: 53% Collapse: 30%
Attrition: 21% MLB: 68%

Comparables:
Drew Storen, Ryan Perry, Joey Devine

YEAR	TEAM	LVL	AGE	W	L	SV	G	GS	IP	H	HR	BB	SO	BB9	SO9	GB%	BABIP	WHIP	ERA	FIP	FRA	WARP
2011	CLN	A	20	1	1	0	4	4	18	19	1	10	21	5.0	10.5	67%	.417	1.61	6.00	3.75	3.59	0.1
2012	WTN	AA	21	2	3	19	38	0	50	40	2	12	72	2.2	13.0	44%	.328	1.04	1.26	1.56	1.66	2.2
2012	SEA	MLB	21	0	0	0	18	0	25	25	0	11	28	4.0	10.1	41%	.357	1.44	3.96	2.13	2.35	0.7
2013	TAC	AAA	22	0	0	0	7	0	11	6	0	4	9	3.3	7.4	54%	.214	0.91	1.64	3.84	3.78	0.1
2013	SEA	MLB	22	3	3	0	53	0	59	73	12	23	66	3.5	10.1	41%	.365	1.63	5.49	4.75	4.39	0.1
2014	MIA	MLB	23	3	1	0	56	0	69¹	60	6	22	75	2.9	9.7	43%	.312	1.18	3.20	3.16	3.47	0.8

Stuff? [X] Capps' fastball averaged 95 mph, and his slider drew whiffs at close to a 20 percent rate. Control and command? [_] Capps struggled to throw strikes with any of his off-speed pitches (primarily a slider, but also a curveball and a changeup), but at 23 years old and working with what already ranks as one of the nastiest arsenals around, he'll get plenty of time to work out his issues. He flew kitty-corner across the country after being traded to the Marlins for Logan Morrison.

Steve Cishek

Born: 6/18/1986 Age: 28
Bats: R Throws: R Height: 6' 6" Weight: 215
Breakout: 35% Improve: 51% Collapse: 28%
Attrition: 24% MLB: 76%

Comparables:
Luke Gregerson, Kevin Jepsen, Brandon Medders

YEAR	TEAM	LVL	AGE	W	L	SV	G	GS	IP	H	HR	BB	SO	BB9	SO9	GB%	BABIP	WHIP	ERA	FIP	FRA	WARP
2011	NWO	AAA	25	1	1	0	15	0	23	18	1	12	19	4.7	7.4	53%	.222	1.30	2.35	4.52	3.79	0.2
2011	FLO	MLB	25	2	1	3	45	0	54²	45	1	19	55	3.1	9.1	55%	.295	1.17	2.63	2.43	2.93	0.9
2012	MIA	MLB	26	5	2	15	68	0	63²	54	3	29	68	4.1	9.6	54%	.302	1.30	2.69	3.26	3.15	0.8
2013	MIA	MLB	27	4	6	34	69	0	69²	53	3	22	74	2.8	9.6	55%	.274	1.08	2.33	2.49	2.95	1.1
2014	MIA	MLB	28	3	1	14	55	0	62¹	49	4	22	60	3.1	8.7	49%	.288	1.13	2.93	3.33	3.19	0.9

Picking up where he left off in 2012, the tall New Englander set out to show the world he could vault himself into Proven Closer territory—and he now has the club's smoking jacket as bona fides for future employers. Over the past three seasons, Cishek has been fifth in the majors in OPS allowed to right-handed batters, behind possibly the most predictable top four: Craig Kimbrel, Kenley Jansen, Sergio Romo and Brad Ziegler. He must have had some wicked Memorial Day cookout, as from that point on, he registered a 1.28 ERA and 0.91 WHIP, while saving 29 of 30 games. That streak coincided with an even heavier reliance on his wipeout slider (up to 46 percent in September), which, like adding more bacon to any meal, is never a bad thing in the short term. As a Super Two player, he was in line for a big pay raise through arbitration but is set to resume ninth inning duties for the Marlins in 2014.

Adam Conley

Born: 5/24/1990 Age: 24
Bats: L Throws: L Height: 6' 3" Weight: 185
Breakout: 32% Improve: 59% Collapse: 32%
Attrition: 65% MLB: 43%

Comparables:
Kyle Gibson, Chad Bettis, Lance Lynn

YEAR	TEAM	LVL	AGE	W	L	SV	G	GS	IP	H	HR	BB	SO	BB9	SO9	GB%	BABIP	WHIP	ERA	FIP	FRA	WARP
2012	GRB	A	22	7	3	0	14	14	74¹	58	4	24	84	2.9	10.2	57%	.289	1.10	2.78	3.07	4.24	1.5
2012	JUP	A+	22	4	2	0	12	12	52²	59	0	19	51	3.2	8.7	56%	.364	1.48	4.44	2.60	3.16	1.5
2013	JAX	AA	23	11	7	0	26	25	138²	125	7	37	129	2.4	8.4	47%	.299	1.17	3.25	2.66	3.48	2.1
2014	MIA	MLB	24	6	8	0	22	22	117	112	10	40	93	3.1	7.2	48%	.307	1.30	3.91	3.85	4.25	0.4

After a strong season in Double-A, the 2011 second-round pick out of Washington State continues to make a beeline toward the back half of the Marlins' rotation of the future. With a strong fastball-change combination and a slider that projects to be usable, Conley will challenge Andrew Heaney to be the first prospect called up when Mike Redmond pleads for something with upside. In 2013, Conley struggled slightly out of the gate as he adjusted to life in the upper minors, but from the start of June to the end of the season he had a 2.45 ERA and allowed only two home runs in 92 innings. He'll likely start 2014 in the Triple-A rotation.

Grant Dayton

Born: 11/25/1987 Age: 26
Bats: L Throws: L Height: 6' 2" Weight: 205
Breakout: 43% Improve: 54% Collapse: 36%
Attrition: 55% MLB: 25%

Comparables:
Brandon Gomes, Josh Lueke, Jon Link

YEAR	TEAM	LVL	AGE	W	L	SV	G	GS	IP	H	HR	BB	SO	BB9	SO9	GB%	BABIP	WHIP	ERA	FIP	FRA	WARP
2011	GRB	A	23	7	1	5	49	0	71²	59	5	24	99	3.0	12.4	51%	.314	1.16	2.89	2.89	2.31	1.2
2012	JUP	A+	24	2	5	2	31	6	60	48	1	18	71	2.7	10.6	38%	.307	1.10	2.10	2.24	3.32	1.6
2012	JAX	AA	24	2	1	0	7	0	13	12	2	4	19	2.8	13.2	47%	.333	1.23	4.15	3.14	4.49	0.2
2013	JAX	AA	25	4	4	1	30	0	38	33	4	12	56	2.8	13.3	46%	.337	1.18	2.37	2.36	2.55	1.0
2014	MIA	MLB	26	2	1	1	25	1	40	34	3	16	42	3.6	9.5	43%	.308	1.25	3.48	3.32	3.78	0.3

The 11th-round draft pick from 2010 was supposed to have his breakthrough season in 2013, but a stress fracture in his pitching elbow, and subsequent surgery, delayed his first pitch until May 20th. Armed with a plus fastball and sharp slider, Dayton carried forward his very strong strikeout rate for a third straight year. After being added to the 40-man roster in the winter, he should be close to his major-league debut and could hold a prominent role in the Marlins' bullpen in relatively short order.

Anthony DeSclafani

Born: 4/18/1990 Age: 24
Bats: R Throws: R Height: 6' 2" Weight: 195
Breakout: 53% Improve: 94% Collapse: 0%
Attrition: 61% MLB: 27%

Comparables:
Randy Wells, Scott Diamond, Nick Tepesch

YEAR	TEAM	LVL	AGE	W	L	SV	G	GS	IP	H	HR	BB	SO	BB9	SO9	GB%	BABIP	WHIP	ERA	FIP	FRA	WARP
2012	LNS	A	22	11	3	0	28	21	123	145	3	25	92	1.8	6.7	58%	.367	1.38	3.37	2.85	4.58	1.7
2013	JUP	A+	23	4	2	0	12	12	54	48	3	9	53	1.5	8.8	54%	.304	1.06	1.67	2.56	3.94	0.6
2013	JAX	AA	23	5	4	0	13	13	75	74	7	14	62	1.7	7.4	48%	.319	1.17	3.36	3.19	4.69	0.2
2014	MIA	MLB	24	5	7	0	24	19	107²	113	11	34	71	2.8	6.0	50%	.316	1.37	4.39	4.26	4.77	-0.2

After spending a whole offseason as "that other guy from the Blue Jays" in the big, bad Marlins dump trade, the New Jersey native set out to prove that he's more than just a difficult player to Google. DeSclafani spent the first half of the season stealing some of Andrew Heaney's spotlight in the Florida State League before moving to the more age-appropriate Southern League and holding his own. With a major-league fastball and secondary pitches that need work, it's still more likely that he ends up a bullpen arm—though he has a better chance of sticking in a rotation than he did at this time last year. His advanced control could lead to major-league action this year in either role.

Michael Dunn

Born: 5/23/1985 Age: 29
Bats: L Throws: L Height: 6' 0" Weight: 205
Breakout: 26% Improve: 58% Collapse: 25%
Attrition: 22% MLB: 72%

Comparables:
Jose Veras, Steve Delabar, Henry Owens

YEAR	TEAM	LVL	AGE	W	L	SV	G	GS	IP	H	HR	BB	SO	BB9	SO9	GB%	BABIP	WHIP	ERA	FIP	FRA	WARP
2011	FLO	MLB	26	5	6	0	72	0	63	51	9	31	68	4.4	9.7	40%	.271	1.30	3.43	4.26	4.62	-0.3
2012	NWO	AAA	27	1	1	0	12	0	17²	19	0	7	24	3.6	12.2	49%	.404	1.47	4.58	2.14	2.31	0.7
2012	MIA	MLB	27	0	3	1	60	0	44	49	3	29	47	5.9	9.6	36%	.357	1.77	4.91	3.86	3.64	0.5
2013	MIA	MLB	28	3	4	2	75	0	67²	53	5	28	72	3.7	9.6	42%	.273	1.20	2.66	3.09	3.86	0.5
2014	MIA	MLB	29	4	1	2	66	0	61¹	48	5	30	68	4.4	10.0	39%	.300	1.27	3.36	3.54	3.65	0.6

The top left-handed option in a surprisingly effective Marlins bullpen, Dunn continued making strides with his walk rate, bringing it below 10 percent for the first time in his career. And while Dunn is better against left-handed hitters, his .655 OPS allowed to righties showed an improved approach while facing the platoon advantage head on. In fact, in a combination of improved skill and ephemera, Dunn had the exact same number of strikeouts (36) and walks (14) against both righties and lefties during 2013. However, his strongest asset remains a lefty-neutralizing slider that he threw 238 times to same-siders without allowing an extra-base hit.

Nathan Eovaldi

Born: **2/13/1990** Age: **24**
Bats: **R** Throws: **R** Height: **6' 2"** Weight: **210**
Breakout: **32%** Improve: **64%** Collapse: **26%**
Attrition: **36%** MLB: **87%**

Comparables:
John Lannan, Mike Pelfrey, Alex White

YEAR	TEAM	LVL	AGE	W	L	SV	G	GS	IP	H	HR	BB	SO	BB9	SO9	GB%	BABIP	WHIP	ERA	FIP	FRA	WARP
2011	CHT	AA	21	6	5	0	20	19	103	76	3	46	99	4.0	8.7	45%	.217	1.18	2.62	3.16	5.21	0.1
2011	LAN	MLB	21	1	2	0	10	6	34²	28	2	20	23	5.2	6.0	43%	.253	1.38	3.63	4.32	5.11	-0.1
2012	CHT	AA	22	2	2	0	9	8	35	30	2	13	30	3.3	7.7	56%	.318	1.23	3.09	3.46	4.95	0.3
2012	LAN	MLB	22	1	6	0	10	10	56¹	63	5	20	34	3.2	5.4	47%	.329	1.47	4.15	4.15	4.82	0.0
2012	MIA	MLB	22	3	7	0	12	12	63	70	5	27	44	3.9	6.3	44%	.327	1.54	4.43	4.20	4.97	0.1
2013	JAX	AA	23	1	0	0	3	3	11²	13	0	4	9	3.1	6.9	47%	.361	1.46	5.40	2.40	3.73	0.2
2013	MIA	MLB	23	4	6	0	18	18	106¹	100	7	40	78	3.4	6.6	45%	.293	1.32	3.39	3.57	4.01	0.8
2014	MIA	MLB	24	6	8	0	21	21	110²	110	9	45	73	3.7	6.0	46%	.304	1.40	4.27	4.26	4.65	-0.1

It's one thing to have a powerful fastball, and it's another to know what to do with it. In 2013, Eovaldi's average fastball velocity of 97 mph was the best in baseball among starters (barely edging out Gerrit Cole), but his strikeout rate of 17.3 percent was more than 2.5 percentage points below league average. That comes partly from not inducing enough swings outside the strike zone—his 25 percent swing rate on such pitches was fourth-worst in baseball by a starter. On the bright side, he has increased the whiff rate on his slider each year he's been in the majors, reaching 33 percent in 2013. He might be an average major-league starter even without a grade jump in command, but the potential of his raw stuff has yet to be fulfilled.

Jose Fernandez

Born: **7/31/1992** Age: **21**
Bats: **R** Throws: **R** Height: **6' 2"** Weight: **240**
Breakout: **30%** Improve: **62%** Collapse: **11%**
Attrition: **17%** MLB: **62%**

Comparables:
Felix Hernandez, Clayton Kershaw, Fernando Valenzuela

YEAR	TEAM	LVL	AGE	W	L	SV	G	GS	IP	H	HR	BB	SO	BB9	SO9	GB%	BABIP	WHIP	ERA	FIP	FRA	WARP
2012	GRB	A	19	7	0	0	14	14	79	51	2	18	99	2.1	11.3	47%	.282	0.87	1.59	2.16	2.85	2.5
2012	JUP	A+	19	7	1	0	11	11	55	38	0	17	59	2.8	9.7	47%	.273	1.00	1.96	2.34	3.30	1.3
2013	MIA	MLB	20	12	6	0	28	28	172²	111	10	58	187	3.0	9.7	46%	.247	0.98	2.19	2.70	3.31	2.8
2014	MIA	MLB	21	9	7	0	25	25	141	102	9	45	152	2.9	9.7	45%	.281	1.05	2.38	2.87	2.59	3.6

As Sam Miller wrote on *Baseball Prospectus* this year, "a team that won 31 percent of its games with any other starter won 64 percent of its games when Fernandez started. When he was on the mound, a 110-loss team became a 100-win team." Brought up to the majors after not throwing a pitch above Single-A (and few even at that level), Fernandez arrived packing a 99 mph four-seamer and two plus off-speed offerings. He showed the ability to absolutely dominate—in consecutive starts around the trade deadline, he struck out a total of 27 and walked one, with 40 swinging strikes—and the ability to avoid big innings, allowing more than three runs in just three starts. He had a 1.50 ERA in his final 18 starts, and the second-best ERA+ in history by a starter younger than 21. That sick anxiety you have about him getting injured because every pitcher does? We all have it.

Brian Flynn

Born: **4/19/1990** Age: **24**
Bats: **L** Throws: **L** Height: **6' 7"** Weight: **240**
Breakout: **32%** Improve: **66%** Collapse: **19%**
Attrition: **47%** MLB: **50%**

Comparables:
Garrett Richards, Zach McAllister, John Gast

YEAR	TEAM	LVL	AGE	W	L	SV	G	GS	IP	H	HR	BB	SO	BB9	SO9	GB%	BABIP	WHIP	ERA	FIP	FRA	WARP
2011	WMI	A	21	7	2	0	13	13	67²	58	3	23	57	3.1	7.6	47%	.301	1.20	3.46	3.45	5.39	0.0
2012	LAK	A+	22	8	4	0	18	18	102	113	5	32	84	2.8	7.4	46%	.341	1.42	3.71	3.41	4.53	1.3
2012	JAX	AA	22	3	0	0	8	8	45	48	3	13	32	2.6	6.4	46%	.314	1.36	3.80	3.72	4.89	0.2
2013	JAX	AA	23	1	1	0	4	4	23	18	2	3	25	1.2	9.8	47%	.311	0.91	1.57	2.39	2.41	0.5
2013	NWO	AAA	23	6	11	0	23	23	138	127	7	40	122	2.6	8.0	55%	.305	1.21	2.80	3.42	3.79	2.2
2013	MIA	MLB	23	0	2	0	4	4	18	27	4	13	15	6.5	7.5	38%	.442	2.22	8.50	6.41	7.12	-0.3
2014	MIA	MLB	24	7	10	0	26	26	146	148	13	50	104	3.1	6.4	47%	.311	1.35	4.17	4.06	4.54	-0.1

After another strong season, this time mostly at Triple-A, Flynn reached the major-league level in September. Unfortunately, his four rough starts were a setback as much as a breakthrough. The big lefty still struggles to find a consistent release point, and has more control than command at this point. The fastball that routinely touched the mid-90s in previous seasons only cleared 94 mph three times in Miami. For an organization that prioritizes thrift, Flynn is valuable as a back-end rotation option who can eat a lot of innings, provided you don't mind a bit of mess.

Brad Hand

Born: 3/20/1990 Age: 24
Bats: L Throws: L Height: 6' 3" Weight: 215
Breakout: 38% Improve: 60% Collapse: 27%
Attrition: 60% MLB: 45%

Comparables:
Tyler Clippard, Aneury Rodriguez, Andrew Oliver

YEAR	TEAM	LVL	AGE	W	L	SV	G	GS	IP	H	HR	BB	SO	BB9	SO9	GB%	BABIP	WHIP	ERA	FIP	FRA	WARP
2011	JAX	AA	21	11	4	0	19	18	108²	90	11	50	71	4.1	5.9	38%	.256	1.29	3.40	4.72	4.46	0.8
2011	FLO	MLB	21	1	8	0	12	12	60	53	10	35	38	5.2	5.7	27%	.249	1.47	4.20	5.69	6.54	-0.9
2012	NWO	AAA	22	11	7	0	27	27	148¹	129	15	75	141	4.6	8.6	43%	.293	1.38	4.00	4.60	4.87	1.5
2012	MIA	MLB	22	0	1	0	1	1	3²	6	1	6	3	14.7	7.4	54%	.417	3.27	17.18	9.95	8.88	-0.1
2013	NWO	AAA	23	3	5	0	15	15	81²	69	7	45	81	5.0	8.9	49%	.289	1.40	3.42	4.43	4.71	0.7
2013	MIA	MLB	23	1	1	0	7	2	20²	13	2	8	15	3.5	6.5	40%	.200	1.02	3.05	3.99	4.70	0.0
2014	MIA	MLB	24	5	7	0	18	18	98	92	10	51	72	4.7	6.7	46%	.291	1.45	4.52	4.73	4.91	-0.4

Maybe it only seems like the Marlins have more swingmen than the entire NBA. One of the many, Hand is a former second-round draft pick from 2008 who doesn't have the control to profile as a long-term starting pitcher. Even as he posted a walk rate below 10 percent in 2013 (an above-average showing based on his minor-league track record), he still got into the hole often, throwing first-pitch strikes only 52 percent of the time (nearly eight percentage points below league average). Meanwhile, his velocity saw a tick upward, as he averaged 94 mph on his fastball in his two September starts with Miami. He had never averaged even 92 in any of 13 starts with the Marlins prior to 2013.

Andrew Heaney

Born: 6/5/1991 Age: 23
Bats: L Throws: L Height: 6' 2" Weight: 190
Breakout: 35% Improve: 62% Collapse: 13%
Attrition: 52% MLB: 29%

Comparables:
Adam Warren, Enrique Gonzalez, Blake Wood

YEAR	TEAM	LVL	AGE	W	L	SV	G	GS	IP	H	HR	BB	SO	BB9	SO9	GB%	BABIP	WHIP	ERA	FIP	FRA	WARP
2012	GRB	A	21	1	2	0	4	4	20	25	0	4	21	1.8	9.4	54%	.373	1.45	4.95	2.23	3.15	0.7
2013	JUP	A+	22	5	2	0	13	12	61²	45	2	17	66	2.5	9.6	49%	.257	1.01	0.88	2.64	3.00	1.4
2013	JAX	AA	22	4	1	0	6	6	33²	31	2	9	23	2.4	6.1	40%	.280	1.19	2.94	3.12	3.13	0.6
2014	MIA	MLB	23	4	5	0	14	14	72¹	69	6	27	55	3.3	6.8	45%	.300	1.33	4.07	4.01	4.42	0.1

The left-hander who led the NCAA in strikeouts during his junior season was not considered one of the "Big Three" college starters available in the 2012 draft—those were Mark Appel, Kevin Gausman and Kyle Zimmer. While not keeping that company isn't a sin, Heaney is not your run-of-the-mill southpaw with pitchability. The Oklahoma State product made a mockery of Florida State League hitters for two-plus months before getting more of a challenge at Double-A, and he capped off his first professional season by shining in the Arizona Fall League. With a plus fastball, plus slider and a changeup that flashes similar potential, Heaney might reach the majors before the 2014 Futures Game and could eventually slide into that no. 2 role behind staff demigod Jose Fernandez.

Dan Jennings

Born: 4/17/1987 Age: 27
Bats: L Throws: L Height: 6' 3" Weight: 210
Breakout: 35% Improve: 44% Collapse: 44%
Attrition: 58% MLB: 54%

Comparables:
Ehren Wassermann, Cody Eppley, Marcus McBeth

YEAR	TEAM	LVL	AGE	W	L	SV	G	GS	IP	H	HR	BB	SO	BB9	SO9	GB%	BABIP	WHIP	ERA	FIP	FRA	WARP
2011	JAX	AA	24	4	1	2	21	0	25²	26	1	11	29	3.9	10.2	63%	.340	1.44	3.16	2.84	2.75	0.6
2011	NWO	AAA	24	1	3	2	24	0	30²	34	3	17	27	5.0	7.9	63%	.529	1.66	7.04	4.96	5.97	0.0
2012	NWO	AAA	25	1	3	2	42	0	51²	48	2	16	48	2.8	8.4	60%	.319	1.24	3.14	3.24	3.55	1.0
2012	MIA	MLB	25	1	0	0	22	0	19	18	2	11	8	5.2	3.8	44%	.254	1.53	1.89	5.72	6.63	-0.4
2013	NWO	AAA	26	4	2	1	18	0	25	19	1	11	25	4.0	9.0	68%	.265	1.20	1.80	3.41	3.98	0.3
2013	MIA	MLB	26	2	4	0	47	0	40²	39	1	16	38	3.5	8.4	49%	.325	1.35	3.76	2.65	2.80	0.7
2014	MIA	MLB	27	3	1	0	51	0	58²	54	4	25	48	3.8	7.3	54%	.307	1.34	3.79	3.77	4.12	0.2

In 2013, there were two Marlins pitchers to post lower FIPs than staff stud Jose Fernandez: Steve Cishek and Jennings. Armed with a nearly 93 mph fastball from the left side and a slider for a chase pitch, Jennings had the exact opposite splits you would expect from his repertoire. His TAv against lefties was around 20 points higher than against righties—odder, it was so for the second year in a row. The former eighth-round draft pick, who already has one 50-game PED suspension under his belt, will slot back in as the second lefty in the Marlins' bullpen behind Michael Dunn, without much room for advancement. That little tickle in your mind is because "Dan Jennings" is also the name of the Marlins' general manager. You're forgiven if you didn't know that—no team has a baseball operations staff more overshadowed by ownership than Miami.

Tom Koehler
Born: 6/29/1986 Age: 28
Bats: R Throws: R Height: 6' 3" Weight: 235
Breakout: 46% Improve: 75% Collapse: 20%
Attrition: 62% MLB: 49%

Comparables:
Billy Buckner, Clayton Mortensen, Enrique Gonzalez

YEAR	TEAM	LVL	AGE	W	L	SV	G	GS	IP	H	HR	BB	SO	BB9	SO9	GB%	BABIP	WHIP	ERA	FIP	FRA	WARP
2011	NWO	AAA	25	12	7	0	28	28	150¹	144	18	79	116	4.7	6.9	44%	.248	1.48	4.97	5.47	5.57	0.4
2012	NWO	AAA	26	12	11	0	28	27	151	154	15	61	138	3.6	8.2	47%	.323	1.42	4.17	4.46	4.97	1.2
2012	MIA	MLB	26	0	1	0	8	1	13¹	15	4	2	13	1.4	8.8	24%	.294	1.27	5.40	5.54	6.54	-0.2
2013	NWO	AAA	27	0	2	0	4	4	23	16	2	12	18	4.7	7.0	48%	.224	1.22	2.74	4.70	5.19	-0.1
2013	MIA	MLB	27	5	10	0	29	23	143	140	14	54	92	3.4	5.8	49%	.294	1.36	4.41	4.24	4.95	-0.3
2014	MIA	MLB	28	7	10	0	25	25	139	132	14	52	99	3.4	6.4	44%	.293	1.32	4.17	4.35	4.54	-0.1

Every team needs a pitcher who is durable and can both start and relieve in a pinch—someone like Koehler. For most organizations, this player would get 30-50 innings and shuffle back and forth between the major-league roster and Triple-A, but the Marlins aren't most organizations. In Miami, this player gets to throw 140-plus innings, no matter the damage. With a nothing-special fastball, Koehler needed something to keep hitters somewhat off balance, and he did that with his curve, which was incredibly effective against both lefties and righties. In fact, he allowed only four extra-base hits (all doubles) on the 608 curveballs he threw. Ideally, someone will beat him out for a rotation spot in the spring, but on a team with enough fires he'd have value as an extinguisher.

John Maine
Born: 5/8/1981 Age: 33
Bats: R Throws: R Height: 6' 4" Weight: 220
Breakout: 21% Improve: 62% Collapse: 28%
Attrition: 33% MLB: 33%

Comparables:
Brandon Duckworth, R.A. Dickey, Tim Redding

YEAR	TEAM	LVL	AGE	W	L	SV	G	GS	IP	H	HR	BB	SO	BB9	SO9	GB%	BABIP	WHIP	ERA	FIP	FRA	WARP
2011	CSP	AAA	30	1	3	0	11	11	46	58	6	37	35	7.2	6.8	50%	.352	2.07	7.43	6.57	7.74	0.4
2012	SWB	AAA	31	8	5	0	16	15	79²	76	7	31	66	3.5	7.5	49%	.287	1.34	4.97	3.96	5.34	-0.1
2013	MIA	MLB	32	0	0	0	4	0	7¹	15	2	5	7	6.1	8.6	46%	.542	2.73	12.27	6.70	8.23	-0.3
2014	MIA	MLB	33	2	2	0	8	6	36¹	34	4	17	28	4.1	6.9	42%	.294	1.41	4.47	4.62	4.86	-0.1

The list of players with states for surnames is short. Besides the common Washington, there were a couple minor leaguers named Colorado, Jim Missouri (four years in the Negro National League) and David Nebraska (28 games in the Appalachian League). This means John Maine might just be the most famous non-Washington-surnamed baseball player ever. He's a Triple-A innings sponge now, but he'll always be John Maine from Virginia. Don't forget him.

Alejandro Ramos
Born: 9/20/1986 Age: 27
Bats: R Throws: R Height: 5' 10" Weight: 210
Breakout: 40% Improve: 47% Collapse: 28%
Attrition: 29% MLB: 71%

Comparables:
Al Alburquerque, Vinnie Pestano, Alex Hinshaw

YEAR	TEAM	LVL	AGE	W	L	SV	G	GS	IP	H	HR	BB	SO	BB9	SO9	GB%	BABIP	WHIP	ERA	FIP	FRA	WARP
2011	JUP	A+	24	1	4	25	49	0	50²	37	2	19	71	3.4	12.6	47%	.321	1.11	1.78	2.52	2.41	1.1
2012	JAX	AA	25	3	3	21	55	0	68²	36	3	21	89	2.8	11.7	48%	.223	0.83	1.44	2.04	3.11	1.4
2012	MIA	MLB	25	0	0	0	11	0	9¹	8	2	4	13	3.9	12.5	33%	.316	1.29	3.86	4.74	5.24	0.0
2013	MIA	MLB	26	3	4	0	68	0	80	58	4	43	86	4.8	9.7	40%	.267	1.26	3.15	3.21	3.95	0.6
2014	MIA	MLB	27	3	2	2	62	0	72¹	54	5	32	82	4.0	10.2	44%	.289	1.18	2.90	3.20	3.16	1.1

Ramos entered 2013 as a sleeper to take over the closer role in Miami, but with Steve Cishek holding that down just fine, he had to settle for being one of the most reliable middle relievers on the roster. Despite allowing more than a walk every other inning, Ramos was able to take a step forward by keeping the ball in the park and dominating right-handed hitters—they hit just .185 and slugged .223 against the diminutive Texan. With Cishek always one Jeffrey Loria bender away from the trade block, Ramos will once again find himself close to the closer role, but there's some reason for concern: He was worked hard in 2013 (his 80 innings were a professional high), and he suffered a velocity drop of more than a mile and a half in September.

Angel Sanchez
Born: 11/28/1989 Age: 24
Bats: R Throws: R Height: 6' 3" Weight: 180
Breakout: 44% Improve: 55% Collapse: 10%
Attrition: 78% MLB: 9%

Comparables:
Armando Galarraga, Cory Luebke, Gonzalez Germen

YEAR	TEAM	LVL	AGE	W	L	SV	G	GS	IP	H	HR	BB	SO	BB9	SO9	GB%	BABIP	WHIP	ERA	FIP	FRA	WARP
2011	GRL	A	21	8	4	0	20	16	99	72	5	39	84	3.5	7.6	39%	.322	1.12	2.82	3.62	5.72	0.0
2012	RCU	A+	22	6	12	0	27	23	130	157	26	51	103	3.5	7.1	46%	.326	1.60	6.58	6.12	6.23	0.3
2013	GRL	A	23	2	7	0	14	14	72	80	6	28	70	3.5	8.8	48%	.332	1.50	4.88	3.73	4.26	1.0
2013	JUP	A+	23	4	3	0	10	10	50¹	45	5	21	42	3.8	7.5	42%	.274	1.31	3.22	4.17	4.72	0.1
2014	MIA	MLB	24	5	10	0	23	23	119	128	16	53	75	4.0	5.7	43%	.307	1.52	5.28	5.17	5.74	-1.5

After getting his Rancho Cucamonga handed to him in the California League during 2012, Sanchez recovered a bit in 2013—though it took a return to Low-A, and even at that wasn't much for a reprise. In July, he was included in the Ricky Nolasco trade and had a strong run to close the season in Jupiter. Sanchez relies on the strength of his fastball/slider combination, and it's that combination that is likely to land him in the bullpen in the end. His changeup just hasn't made the strides necessary to hold down a rotation spot.

Kevin Slowey

Born: **5/4/1984** Age: **30**
Bats: **R** Throws: **R** Height: **6' 2"** Weight: **200**
Breakout: **18%** Improve: **49%** Collapse: **15%**
Attrition: **12%** MLB: **79%**

Comparables:
Jeff Karstens, Josh Towers, Jose Acevedo

YEAR	TEAM	LVL	AGE	W	L	SV	G	GS	IP	H	HR	BB	SO	BB9	SO9	GB%	BABIP	WHIP	ERA	FIP	FRA	WARP
2011	FTM	A+	27	0	1	0	4	4	12	9	1	1	9	0.8	6.8	47%	.214	0.83	3.75	3.22	7.34	0.0
2011	ROC	AAA	27	1	2	0	7	7	38	44	3	5	29	1.2	6.9	31%	.328	1.29	3.55	3.53	4.26	0.5
2011	MIN	MLB	27	0	8	0	14	8	59^1	78	10	5	34	0.8	5.2	33%	.330	1.40	6.67	4.51	4.68	0.5
2012	COH	AAA	28	3	3	0	8	8	49	52	7	13	34	2.4	6.2	39%	.288	1.33	5.14	4.48	5.32	0.3
2013	MIA	MLB	29	3	6	0	20	14	92	106	12	18	76	1.8	7.4	31%	.333	1.35	4.11	3.78	3.96	1.0
2014	MIA	MLB	30	4	5	0	14	14	73	75	8	13	55	1.6	6.8	36%	.311	1.22	4.05	3.77	4.40	0.1

As one of more extreme fly-ball pitchers in baseball, Slowey will always have trouble with the long ball (and 2013 was no exception), but pitching in a more forgiving ballpark in the easier league led to the best FIP of his career. After spending a healthy portion of his 2012 feeding meatballs to hungry hitters in Columbus, he came out of the gate very strong for Miami—a 1.81 ERA, 0.94 WHIP and 36 strikeouts in 44 innings during his first seven starts. However, a 6.42 ERA the rest of the way and a forearm strain that cost him the last two months of the season put a damper on his comeback. Slowey will compete once again for a back-end rotation spot in Miami, which continues to be a great fit for his skill set.

Jacob Turner

Born: **5/21/1991** Age: **23**
Bats: **R** Throws: **R** Height: **6' 5"** Weight: **215**
Breakout: **42%** Improve: **77%** Collapse: **12%**
Attrition: **31%** MLB: **81%**

Comparables:
Jesse Litsch, Greg Reynolds, Tommy Hunter

YEAR	TEAM	LVL	AGE	W	L	SV	G	GS	IP	H	HR	BB	SO	BB9	SO9	GB%	BABIP	WHIP	ERA	FIP	FRA	WARP
2011	ERI	AA	20	3	5	0	17	17	113^2	102	9	32	90	2.5	7.1	54%	.268	1.18	3.48	3.89	4.52	0.1
2011	TOL	AAA	20	1	0	0	3	3	17^1	15	1	3	20	1.6	10.4	46%	.311	1.04	3.12	2.20	3.90	0.2
2011	DET	MLB	20	0	1	0	3	3	12^2	17	3	4	8	2.8	5.7	43%	.318	1.66	8.53	6.06	6.63	0.0
2012	LAK	A+	21	1	2	0	4	4	21^2	17	1	7	17	2.9	7.1	53%	.267	1.11	1.66	3.53	3.91	0.4
2012	NWO	AAA	21	2	0	0	5	5	27^1	27	2	12	16	4.0	5.3	42%	.286	1.43	1.98	4.76	4.26	0.3
2012	TOL	AAA	21	4	2	0	10	10	62^2	52	2	24	40	3.4	5.7	56%	.265	1.21	3.16	3.54	4.84	0.1
2012	DET	MLB	21	1	1	0	3	3	12^1	17	4	7	7	5.1	5.1	53%	.302	1.95	8.03	7.83	8.94	-0.3
2012	MIA	MLB	21	1	4	0	7	7	42^2	33	5	9	29	1.9	6.1	42%	.231	0.98	3.38	3.93	4.54	0.1
2013	NWO	AAA	22	3	4	0	10	10	56^1	59	7	14	35	2.2	5.6	54%	.289	1.30	4.47	4.85	5.43	-0.2
2013	MIA	MLB	22	3	8	0	20	20	118	116	11	54	77	4.1	5.9	48%	.299	1.44	3.74	4.40	4.84	-0.1
2014	MIA	MLB	23	8	11	0	31	31	151^1	143	15	52	101	3.1	6.0	47%	.287	1.29	3.97	4.31	4.32	0.5

Tell me if you've heard this story before: The Tigers draft a highly touted pitching prospect in the first round, rush him to the majors, then deal him to the Marlins. He's expected to become the ace of a developing rotation, but it turns out he's not actually all that good. "Hi, I'm Jacob Turner. You may know me from such movies as *Tiger Days* and *Unfulfilled Expectations*." Last season we identified the warning sign as his strikeout rate, which has never been particularly good throughout his pro career. That hasn't changed and, until it does, neither will his projection as a back-of-the-rotation starter or middle reliever. Yes, he's still young. But if in four seasons Turner ends up in Boston alongside Andrew Miller as a middle reliever, don't say we didn't warn you.

LINEOUTS

HITTERS

PLAYER	TEAM	LVL	AGE	PA	R	2B	3B	HR	RBI	BB	SO	SB-CS	AVG/OBP/SLG	TAv	BABIP	BRR	FRAA	WARP
1B J. Brown	NWO	AAA	29	324	31	22	0	2	28	24	34	0-2	.289/.346/.385	.271	.318	0.3	1B(52): -4.3, LF(20): -0.2	0.5
	MIA	MLB	29	17	0	1	0	0	5	1	1	0-0	.200/.235/.267	.204	.200	0		-0.1
3B Z. Cox	JAX	AA	24	325	32	15	2	3	29	38	68	2-0	.269/.357/.367	.268	.341	-1.2	3B(66): -8.8, 1B(3): 0.1	0.4
SS N. Green	NWO	AAA	34	343	39	11	1	12	34	18	82	1-2	.214/.264/.368	.229	.249	-1.2	SS(43): 1.4, 2B(25): -1.7	0.0
	MIA	MLB	34	65	4	2	0	1	6	3	14	0-0	.236/.302/.327	.242	.286	-0.4	SS(8): -0.2, 1B(6): -0.3	-0.1
C K. Hill	NWO	AAA	34	206	18	14	0	1	14	15	38	0-0	.237/.291/.326	.220	.289	-2	C(57): 1.5	0.0
	MIA	MLB	34	61	3	2	0	0	0	2	18	0-0	.155/.183/.190	.138	.225	-0.3	C(18): -0.1	-0.6
RF K. Jensen	JAX	AA	25	291	43	16	0	16	42	33	73	5-3	.237/.354/.498	.305	.268	0.1	RF(53): -4.5, LF(11): -0.2	1.4
	NWO	AAA	25	226	31	15	0	12	36	17	71	1-0	.233/.293/.485	.296	.285	1.8	LF(29): 0.8, RF(21): 0.3	1.8
RF A. Kearns	MIA	MLB	33	31	3	0	0	0	0	4	8	0-0	.185/.290/.185	.186	.263	-0.3	RF(3): 0.3, LF(1): 0.1	-0.2
1B C. Kotchman	JUP	A+	30	69	7	4	0	0	8	7	7	0-0	.295/.377/.361	.269	.333	-0.2	1B(10): -0.2	0.1
	MIA	MLB	30	21	0	0	0	0	1	1	1	0-0	.000/.048/.000	.020	.000	0	1B(6): -0.0	-0.6
1B J. Mahoney	JUP	A+	26	34	4	1	0	2	2	1	9	0-0	.303/.324/.515	.300	.364	0	1B(8): 0.6	0.2
	NWO	AAA	26	200	9	8	0	2	16	3	66	1-0	.190/.200/.262	.172	.271	-0.9	1B(48): -2.1	-1.9
	MIA	MLB	26	29	2	1	0	1	4	0	4	0-0	.276/.276/.414	.273	.292	-0.2	1B(7): -0.2	0.0
1B C. McGehee	PIT	MLB	29	293	27	13	1	8	35	24	60	1-1	.230/.297/.377	.252	.266	-1.5	1B(77): 2.6, 3B(9): 0.1	0.3
RF J. Paredes	OKL	AAA	24	358	50	21	6	8	37	28	67	16-7	.287/.345/.462	.284	.340	6.2	RF(35): -0.3, SS(20): 1.8	2.7
	HOU	MLB	24	135	8	4	0	1	10	6	44	4-4	.192/.231/.248	.189	.280	-0.3	RF(39): -2.0, 2B(3): 0.1	-1.2
C K. Skipworth	NWO	AAA	23	257	22	13	2	11	30	12	82	0-0	.188/.241/.397	.235	.231	-0.8	C(68): 2.5	0.7
	MIA	MLB	23	4	0	0	0	0	0	1	1	0-0	.000/.250/.000	.060	.000	0	C(1): -0.0	-0.1
RF J. Solorzano	GRB	A	22	523	72	29	3	15	66	24	111	33-4	.285/.325/.450	.284	.339	3.7	RF(78): 4.8, CF(45): 2.0	3.6

Jordan Brown, now on the wrong side of 30, has cycled through three of the shallowest organizations in baseball over the past three seasons without acquiring much more than a sniff of service time. ⊘ A former first-round pick of the Cardinals, **Zack Cox** has seen his stock tumble over the past two seasons as he's been unable to hit for either average or power—not that those things are important at alllll at the hot corner. ⊘ With a .546 OPS in 99 big-league at-bats over his past four seasons, **Nick Green** couldn't capitalize on the most wide open opportunity for playing time he's had in years, and it seems likely that he's seen his last days in a major-league uniform. ⊘ He's the organization's backup Jeff Mathis, but **Koyie Hill** has now been worth -2.1 WARP for his career and doesn't have anywhere near the defensive acumen to forgive a sub-.400 OPS the past two seasons. ⊘ **Kyle Jensen** fits the mold of a Quad-A slugger, as he's right-handed and the only thing more prodigious than his power is his ability to swing and miss. ⊘ The bad news: Hospitalized with an irregular heartbeat in mid-April, **Austin Kearns** missed most of the Marlins' season. The good news: Hospitalized with an irregular heartbeat in mid-April, Kearns missed most of the Marlins' season. ⊘ Before **Casey Kotchman**, 10 non-pitchers in history had at least 20 at-bats in a hitless season; one of them was David Ortiz, so you're saying there's a chance. ⊘ Shortly after hitting his first major-league homer, **Joe Mahoney** fell off the roster by straining his hamstring and stayed off it by putting together a 66-to-3 strikeout-to-walk rate at Triple-A. ⊘ When **Casey McGehee** boarded his flight to Japan after the 2012 season, the Marlins were a terrible team that had a bunch of pretty good players. Now they're a terrible team that has a bunch of pretty bad players, of which he is one. ⊘ **Jimmy Paredes** earned five call-ups to Houston in 2013 because he's a switch-hitter who can play multiple positions, but even the worst team in baseball can't permanently carry a guy with his lack of stick. What that says about the Marlins, who claimed him in November, is up to you. ⊘ Former sixth overall pick **Kyle Skipworth** is officially a bust, but at least he got to make his major-league debut in April, before those ghastly Triple-A numbers gave him away. ⊘ **Jesus Solorzano**'s got big tools—he's fast, strong and makes a lot of hard contact—but an unrefined approach has kept him about a year behind where you'd like him to be.

PITCHERS

PLAYER	TEAM	LVL	AGE	W	L	SV	IP	H	HR	BB	SO	BB9	SO9	GB%	BABIP	WHIP	ERA	FIP	FRA	WARP
S. Ames	ABQ	AAA	25	2	2	8	34¹	45	4	13	29	3.4	7.6	53%	.369	1.69	3.67	4.62	5.79	0.2
	NWO	AAA	25	1	0	0	12	14	2	4	5	3.0	3.8	45%	.316	1.50	3.75	5.90	6.79	-0.2
	MIA	MLB	25	0	1	0	4	6	0	2	4	4.5	9.0	61%	.462	2.00	4.50	2.52	2.52	0.1
S. Dyson	JAX	AA	25	3	7	0	75¹	72	0	23	41	2.7	4.9	64%	.291	1.26	2.63	3.14	4.73	0.1
	NWO	AAA	25	1	3	0	31	23	1	12	16	3.5	4.6	62%	.231	1.13	2.61	4.21	4.49	0.3
	MIA	MLB	25	0	2	0	11	16	2	5	5	4.1	4.1	67%	.351	1.91	9.00	6.11	7.75	-0.3
C. Hatcher	NWO	AAA	28	4	3	33	67¹	69	8	28	65	3.7	8.7	46%	.314	1.44	3.61	4.48	3.93	1.0
	MIA	MLB	28	0	1	0	8²	13	1	4	7	4.2	7.3	39%	.367	1.96	12.46	4.29	4.71	0.0
M. Hope	GRB	A	21	6	6	1	98¹	100	12	53	73	4.9	6.7	45%	.291	1.56	4.94	5.38	7.24	-1.4
C. James	GRB	A	22	2	6	0	53¹	57	6	28	57	4.7	9.6	40%	.357	1.59	5.74	4.83	5.28	0.3
E. Olmos	JAX	AA	23	4	2	1	50¹	47	1	27	41	4.8	7.3	44%	.307	1.47	2.50	3.21	3.46	0.6
	MIA	MLB	23	0	1	0	5	7	2	3	2	5.4	3.6	50%	.250	2.00	7.20	9.22	13.23	-0.4
Z. Phillips	NWO	AAA	26	4	2	1	59	49	3	24	74	3.7	11.3	54%	.322	1.24	2.44	2.99	2.91	1.4
	MIA	MLB	26	0	1	0	1²	3	0	3	1	16.2	5.4	67%	.500	3.60	5.40	7.22	7.91	-0.1
J. Sanchez	NAS	AAA	25	4	3	7	70	69	5	18	50	2.3	6.4	38%	.291	1.24	2.83	3.88	4.03	0.9
J. Urena	JUP	A+	21	10	7	0	149²	148	8	29	107	1.7	6.4	50%	.299	1.18	3.73	3.21	4.45	0.3

Another arm without much upside sent away in the Ricky Nolasco trade, **Steve Ames** has seen his once meteoric minor-league strikeout rates come down to the level of his perfectly average stuff. ⊘ It's tough to overcome strikeout rates as low as **Sam Dyson** puts up, though a 60 percent groundball rate and four homers allowed in 185 career minor-league innings boost his odds of a major-league future. ⊘ A low-profile conversion project back in 2011, **Chris Hatcher** flashed a plus-plus fastball in short bursts for the Marlins, but needs to develop a secondary pitch that misses bats at the highest level if he wants to stick in a bullpen role. ⊘ Currently best known as a former high school teammate of Archie Bradley, **Mason Hope** had a rough go in his first taste of full-season ball, though he still holds the ceiling of a mid-rotation starter if he can harness his fastball-curve combination. ⊘ Formerly one of the more promising arms in the Marlins' system, **Chad James** has taken two consecutive steps backward and ended the year getting knocked around at Low-A Greensboro—the same place he started his career four seasons ago. ⊘ A hard-throwing portsider, **Edgar Olmos** continues to have a lot of trouble figuring out where it's going and he ended the season getting lit up in the Arizona Fall League; he'll continue to get opportunities to figure it out in the bullpen. ⊘ **Zach Phillips** was called up in September and allowed four of the five left-handed batters he faced to reach base, which (for a southpaw reliever) is like an applicant for a copy editing position submitting a resume that's four pages long and filled with spelling errors. ⊘ A converted catcher in just his second season as a full-time reliever, **Jesus Sanchez** has taken well to the transition. ⊘ **Jose Urena** has a mid-90s fastball and plenty of room in his frame to add mass. With improvement to his changeup he'll stick as a starter; without, he should add even more velocity when he's converted to relief.

MANAGER: MIKE REDMOND

YEAR	TEAM	W-L	Pythag +/−	Avg PC	100+ P	120+ P	QS	BQS	REL	REL w Zero R	IBB	PH	PH Avg	PH HR	SB2	CS2	SB3	CS3	SAC Att	SAC %	POS SAC	Squeeze	Swing	In Play
2013	MIA	62-100	0	91.4	41	0	82	1	471	368	58	237	.235	1	64	24	14	5	90	63.3%	27	0	291	85

The Marlins issued the second most intentional walks of any team in baseball in 2013, trailing just the Giants. Much of that came early in the year. In Mike Redmond's first 54 games, he had 27 intentional walks. The rest of the way he ordered just 31.

On the other hand, Redmond likes to juggle his lineup. He set a new Marlins franchise record with 132 different batting orders, and tied another franchise record with 100 different defensive lineups. True, Redmond's willingness to mix it up was partially caused by the lack of talent on hand, but this is hardly the first year the Marlins have fielded a rotten roster. Their 108-loss club in 1998 had just 105 batting orders, for instance.

Milwaukee Brewers

By Jack Moore

Some franchises have history. Some have parks festooned with pennants and statues marking the championships and conquests of players past.

The Milwaukee Brewers have a retractable roof, a big plastic slide and a sausage race.

This is why, even with the disappointments of the 2012 and 2013 seasons, Mark Attanasio's nine-year ownership tenure has been one of the most successful periods in Brewers history. The club has averaged 82 wins per season under Attanasio, a mark not achieved since the franchise's golden era of the late 1970s and 1980s, and made the playoffs twice since 2008 after coming up empty in their 25 prior attempts. This is not wholly unprecedented success for Milwaukee baseball, but the season not being over before it starts is a new feeling for multiple generations of Brewers fans.

But the cost of the successful 2008 and 2011 squads, was huge—the Brewers gave up big prospect hauls to acquire CC Sabathia, Shaun Marcum and Zack Greinke. Additionally, the club opted not to trade pending free agent Prince Fielder in the summer of 2011, choosing (wisely) their first NL Central championship over a bunch of prospect ping pong balls.

BREWERS PROSPECTUS
2013 W-L: 74-88, 4th in NL Central

Pythag	.468	19th	DER	.709	6th
RS/G	3.95	19th	B-Age	27.8	11th
RA/G	4.24	17th	P-Age	28.5	22nd
TAv	.248	26th	Salary	$88.8	19th
BRR	0.14	15th	M$/MW	$2.97	17th
TAv-P	.261	13th	DL Days	1102	22nd
FIP	4.1	24th	$ on DL	27%	27th

	Runs	HR/RH	HR/LH	Runs/RH	Runs/LH
Three-Year Park Factors	106	109	113	106	108

Top Hitter WARP	6.04 (Carlos Gomez)
Top Pitcher WARP	1.36 (Kyle Lohse)
Top Prospect	Tyrone Taylor

Player	WARP (2010–12)
Michael Fiers	3.2
Mark Rogers	1.2
Mike McClendon	0.5
Zach Braddock	0.4
Logan Schafer	0.2
Tyler Thornburg	0.0
Eric Farris	-0.1
Taylor Green	-0.4

Predictably, the farm system has suffered. After graduating Jonathan Lucroy in 2010, the Brewers went through an extraordinary dry spell of minor-league promotions. Over the next three seasons, just eight players who were drafted and developed by the team graduated to the majors, and collectively those eight produced only 5.0 WARP. More than half of that total came in a 10-week stretch by Michael Fiers in 2012. (See the table.)

After the failures of 2012 and 2013—magnified by the stain of Ryan Braun's steroid suspension—the idea of blowing it all up and entering a full-on rebuilding phase can be tempting. Tempting, but, in the Brewers' case, wrong.

Throughout sports—not just baseball—the idea of creation anew through the nuclear option has become popular. Trade off the best players for minor-league value, lose for a few seasons, stockpile talented draft picks and win with a wave of talent down the road. This is clearly the plan for Jeff Luhnow's Astros. With nothing resembling a star player on the roster and a dearth of even average players in the organization, Houston cleaned house of all but the very few assets that might have value three or more years down the road. As a result, the Astros entered this offseason with just over $14 million in player salary committed to 2014 and beyond. With 25 players at the $500,000 minimum salary, the lowest possible MLB team salary is $12.5 million. As such, the Astros have nearly total payroll flexibility to add outside talent as the organization's development—supplemented by three first-overall picks from 2012 through 2014—deems necessary.

Moving across sports, the NBA's Oklahoma City Thunder represent the most successful tankers, and they are the team we likely have to thank for tanking's *en vogue* status. In 2007, when they were still the Seattle SuperSonics (RIP), the club finished 31-51, in last place, and picked up the second-overall pick in the draft lottery (and landed Kevin Durant, now one of the league's best offensive players). Seattle then traded an aging former star (Ray Allen) for another lottery pick, and let a star forward (Rashard Lewis—a good player, but not good enough to be the best player on a championship team) walk in free agency.

The resulting 2008 Sonics team finished a franchise-worst 20-62 and the first Thunder team in 2009 finished 23-59. Over the next two drafts, Seattle/Oklahoma City drafted early and often, picking up guards Russell Westbrook and James Harden and forward Serge Ibaka, three star-caliber players. These days, the Thunder are a powerhouse, with four straight seasons of a .600-plus winning percentage and an NBA Finals appearance.

In baseball, the closest analogue to the Oklahoma City/Seattle tank is the Tampa Bay Rays. Whether intentional or not, the Devil Rays' consistent losses in the 2000s supplied the team with consistent early draft picks. Although the Rays had their misses with high picks—Josh Hamilton, Dewon Brazelton, Jeff Niemann and Wade Townsend were all top-10 picks who produced less than four WARP in Tampa Bay—the club picked up franchise keys Evan Longoria and David Price as well as Rocco Baldelli, B.J. Upton and Delmon Young (another sub-4.0 WARP player, but the key piece in the Matt Garza trade). Clearly, the Rays can point to their time in the cellar as a major reason that they managed to acquire the talent necessary for four playoff appearances in the past six seasons.

The common link between these three teams prior to their tank strategy is key: None had the star core to compete. The free agent and trade markets could only offer them role players or lesser stars. As such, attempts to improve without bottoming out would result in something much like Drayton McLane's final Astros teams: aging former greats stubbornly spending a long summer lurching toward mediocrity.

But the problem with the Milwaukee Brewers in the Attanasio years has never been an absence of top-end talent. Consider the stars to play in Milwaukee since the 2008 playoff season: Prince Fielder, Ryan Braun, Ben Sheets, Zack Greinke, Corey Hart, Carlos Gomez, J.J. Hardy, Rickie Weeks and Jean Segura have all made All-Star appearances, and CC Sabathia's 2008 run through the National League was the stuff of legends.

The winning clubs in 2008 and 2011 were great because they managed to surround their stars with solid role players. Veterans Mike Cameron, Russell Branyan and Gabe Kapler supplemented the budding trio of Prince Fielder, Ryan Braun and J.J. Hardy in 2008. Up-and-comers Carlos Gomez, Yovani Gallardo and Jonathan Lucroy and role players Nyjer Morgan and Jerry Hairston Jr. supported Braun, Fielder, Marcum and Greinke in 2011.

But after both seasons, the departures of star players (Sabathia and Sheets in 2009, Fielder and Greinke in 2012) doomed Milwaukee primarily because the organization's lackluster drafts in the latter half of the Aughts left them

without depth. There were still stars in Milwaukee; there just weren't enough qualified major-leaguers to fill a competent lineup and pitching staff around them.

The worst of it has been on the pitching side. Fiers was a fluke discovery: He was a 22nd-round pick in 2009 and didn't reach Double-A until age 25. Wily Peralta was signed out of the Dominican Republic. Thornburg is the only starting pitcher to graduate from the Brewers' farm from 2010 to 2012 who was also a high draft pick (third round, 2010).

Brewers pitchers drafted in the first three rounds since 2006 have failed in droves. Eric Arnett (first round, 2009) has yet to reach Double-A at age 25. Kyle Heckathorn (first/supplemental, 2009) was left off the 40-man roster following a shift to relief in 2013. Seth Lintz (second, 2008) spent 2013 playing independent-league ball. Cody Adams (second, 2008) last appeared in organized baseball in 2009. Jeremy Jeffress (first, 2006) struggled through multiple drug suspensions and wound up as a throw-in for Greinke. The only success has been Jake Odorizzi (first/supplemental, 2008), who Kansas City acquired in the Greinke trade and then flipped to Tampa Bay.

In 2012, Milwaukee had a used Izturis playing shortstop and received next to nothing from the bullpen and back end of the starting rotation. In 2013, Brewers first basemen (primarily Alex Gonzalez (!), Juan Francisco, Yuniesky Betancourt (!!) and Sean Halton) combined for -1.5 WARP, worst in the league by nearly a full win, and suffered from injuries in the rotation until Thornburg's arrival and Peralta's rebirth in the second half. Only two teams gave more innings to sub-replacement pitchers than Milwaukee last year, and only five teams got more negative-WARP production out of sub-replacement hitters.

Finally, in late 2013, came the arrival of reinforcements that give the Brewers hope. Remarkably, the Brewers went 33-32 in the 65 games following Braun's suspension. Teams win meaningless games in September all the time, but Milwaukee's success was notable because of who powered it.

With Braun suspended and Aramis Ramirez and Rickie Weeks dealing with injuries, the Brewers had room to give minor-league players extended playing time. At second base, Scooter Gennett was a revelation in his 69 games, hitting .324/.356/.479 and showing far more punch than anybody expected out of his 5-foot-10, 180 pound frame. Khris Davis gave reason to believe in his excellent minor-league statistics, as he hit 11 home runs in just 153 plate appearances en route to an astounding .279/.353/.596 line. Caleb Gindl, a 5-foot-7 bowling ball of a left fielder, notched 14 extra-base hits in 155 plate appearances and looked like an ideal left-handed platoon option.

On the mound, Thornburg earned his first extended starting opportunity and was fantastic: 1.47 ERA and 34 strikeouts in 43 innings in the rotation. Jimmy Nelson threw 10 strong innings in September and put himself in consideration for a rotation spot if he can impress in the spring. And Peralta turned around his season with a sharp finish, posting a 3.05 ERA with 84 strikeouts over 103 innings in his final 17 starts.

These six players posted a collective 4.6 WARP, just shy of what Milwaukee's non-Lucroy graduated players contributed in the three previous years combined. They were the major reason the Brewers performed respectably during Braun's suspension and in the absence of other key players.

In the short term, competing in a rejuvenated National League Central bolstered by Pittsburgh's rise seems like a tough task for a team coming off consecutive poor seasons. But in the world of the second Wild Card, a third-place finish could be enough for a playoff berth, as it was for Cincinnati in 2013. Additionally, the divisional landscape can change in an instant, and the Brewers have every core player under control through at least the end of the 2015 season.

It must be noted as well that much of the Brewers' success since 2008 can be attributed to a galvanized fanbase. Despite playing in the smallest media market in MLB, Milwaukee has routinely finished in the top half in attendance. Only last year, as the club limped out to a 22-37 start, did their attendance dip into the bottom half of the National League. If the team wants to retain the talent graduated at the end of last season, it will need to maintain fan interest, and to do so will require competitive squads over the next few seasons.

When you don't have history, there isn't a way to keep the fans coming back when the teams are losing. This is hardly a reason to cling to mediocrity. But in Milwaukee, the core talent appears to be in place. Ryan Braun's 2011 and Carlos Gomez's 2013 were two of the best player seasons in Brewers history. Young players like Jonathan Lucroy and Jean Segura have All-Star potential. The problem is filling roster spots 16 through 25. The farm system finally showed some life in 2013, and those performances were even partially real, the top-tier players on the Brewers may have the kind of supporting cast that has lifted them to glory twice before.

Jack Moore is a freelance sports writer based in Minneapolis whose work can currently be seen at Sports on Earth, The Score *and* Beacon Reader.

HITTERS

Yuniesky Betancourt   3B

Born: **1/31/1982** Age: **32**
Bats: **R** Throws: **R** Height: **5' 10"**
Weight: **205** Breakout: **2%**
Improve: **33%** Collapse: **11%**
Attrition: **15%** MLB: **85%**

Comparables:
Frank Malzone, B.J. Surhoff, Ray Knight

YEAR	TEAM	LVL	AGE	PA	R	2B	3B	HR	RBI	BB	SO	SB	CS	AVG/OBP/SLG	TAv	BABIP	BRR	FRAA	WARP
2011	MIL	MLB	29	584	51	27	3	13	68	16	63	4	4	.252/.271/.381	.230	.259	1.2	SS(149): 4.0	1.4
2012	KCA	MLB	30	228	21	14	1	7	36	9	25	0	1	.228/.256/.400	.230	.226	-1.6	2B(46): -6.6, 3B(8): -0.2	-1.1
2013	MIL	MLB	31	409	35	15	1	13	46	14	71	0	0	.212/.240/.355	.209	.226	0	1B(68): -2.4, 3B(59): -0.8	-1.4
2014	*MIL*	*MLB*	*32*	*351*	*33*	*15*	*2*	*9*	*37*	*13*	*46*	*1*	*1*	*.237/.268/.370*	*.228*	*.250*	*-0.6*	*3B -1, SS -0*	*-0.6*

Betancourt's major-league career is unkillable. That is the only answer after the Cuban Rasputin yet again remained on a roster for the entire season. It was once again the Brewers dragging him through the dog days of 2013, as Betancourt posted his fifth negative WARP in the past seven years. After a torrid April that saw him homer eight times, Betancourt still managed to post the worst offensive season of his career, while playing primarily first base. With the Brewers out of the race early in the season, Betancourt at least offered a flexible option capable of soaking up plate appearances as infielder after infielder headed toward the disabled list, especially early in the season. The next mystery: How will Betancourt inevitably find his way onto a roster in 2014?

Jeff Bianchi   SS

Born: **10/5/1986** Age: **27**
Bats: **R** Throws: **R** Height: **5' 11"**
Weight: **180** Breakout: **3%**
Improve: **13%** Collapse: **6%**
Attrition: **19%** MLB: **33%**

Comparables:
German Duran, Joaquin Arias, Tim Olson

YEAR	TEAM	LVL	AGE	PA	R	2B	3B	HR	RBI	BB	SO	SB	CS	AVG/OBP/SLG	TAv	BABIP	BRR	FRAA	WARP
2011	NWA	AA	24	499	63	23	2	2	48	39	85	20	5	.259/.320/.333	.234	.313	0.6	2B(49): 2.9, SS(30): 2.2	0.8
2012	HUN	AA	25	85	11	4	0	0	6	6	11	3	1	.351/.398/.403	.295	.409	-2	SS(18): 0.5	0.6
2012	NAS	AAA	25	278	33	13	1	5	19	22	48	11	5	.317/.374/.438	.284	.376	1.2	SS(69): 6.8	3.0
2012	MIL	MLB	25	76	8	2	0	3	9	4	13	0	0	.188/.230/.348	.224	.185	0.7	SS(14): 0.5, 3B(6): -0.1	0.1
2013	NAS	AAA	26	43	6	1	1	1	6	2	8	0	0	.244/.279/.390	.220	.281	0.1	3B(3): -0.1, SS(3): -0.4	-0.2
2013	MIL	MLB	26	252	22	8	1	1	25	11	46	4	4	.237/.272/.292	.203	.288	2.5	3B(42): 6.9, SS(20): 1.0	0.6
2014	*MIL*	*MLB*	*27*	*254*	*24*	*10*	*1*	*3*	*23*	*13*	*49*	*6*	*2*	*.248/.289/.340*	*.227*	*.290*	*0*	*SS 2, 3B 3*	*0.6*

Bianchi was exposed at the plate as the Brewers' constant injuries forced the utility infielder into semi-regular duty. He entirely lacks power and didn't hit his first home run until September, and he does nothing else well enough to make him a productive hitter. Still, his skill set appears to have some value—he can play all non-first base infield positions well, and that versatility could end up saving a team a roster spot for a bat instead of another backup infielder. More was expected of Bianchi's career when he was younger, but as a Tommy John survivor, simply proving he has a niche in the majors counts as a victory.

Ryan Braun — RF

Born: 11/17/1983 Age: 30
Bats: R Throws: R Height: 6' 2"
Weight: 205 Breakout: 0%
Improve: 53% Collapse: 1%
Attrition: 7% MLB: 100%

Comparables:
Matt Holliday, Pedro Guerrero, Jason Bay

YEAR	TEAM	LVL	AGE	PA	R	2B	3B	HR	RBI	BB	SO	SB	CS	AVG/OBP/SLG	TAv	BABIP	BRR	FRAA	WARP
2011	MIL	MLB	27	629	109	38	6	33	111	58	93	33	6	.332/.397/.597	.345	.350	0.2	LF(147): 2.2	6.8
2012	MIL	MLB	28	677	108	36	3	41	112	63	128	30	7	.319/.391/.595	.327	.346	0.5	LF(151): 0.1	6.2
2013	MIL	MLB	29	253	30	14	2	9	38	27	56	4	5	.298/.372/.498	.300	.360	1.8	LF(59): 2.3	2.2
2014	MIL	MLB	30	322	47	17	2	14	48	28	56	11	3	.303/.371/.522	.318	.330	0.6	RF 0, LF 0	2.6

The big story with Braun was of course his 65-game suspension after the Biogenesis fallout, but things were looking down for Braun even before the scandal. Entering the season, Braun said his goal was to walk more often than he struck out. He set a career high in walk rate at 11 percent, but his strikeout rate skyrocketed to 22 percent, his worst since his rookie year. The rise in strikeouts effectively canceled out all the gains from the improved discipline. Given the PED bust, more focus will be on his power dip—his nine home runs in 253 plate appearances had him on pace for just his second sub-30 home run season—but power is fickle in small samples. More concern should be paid to his health, as Braun lost 31 games to injury before the suspension, more than he had missed in the previous six seasons combined. He'll need to spend more time on the field, especially trotting slowly around the bases, to win back his disillusioned fans.

Clint Coulter — C

Born: 7/30/1993 Age: 20
Bats: R Throws: R Height: 6' 3"
Weight: 210 Breakout: 0%
Improve: 0% Collapse: 0%
Attrition: 0% MLB: 0%

Comparables:
Wilin Rosario, J.R. Murphy, Travis d'Arnaud

YEAR	TEAM	LVL	AGE	PA	R	2B	3B	HR	RBI	BB	SO	SB	CS	AVG/OBP/SLG	TAv	BABIP	BRR	FRAA	WARP
2013	WIS	A	19	135	18	5	1	3	13	11	31	1	0	.207/.299/.345	.252	.250	0.8	C(28): -0.1	0.6
2014	MIL	MLB	20	250	21	7	1	5	24	16	72	0	0	.198/.260/.305	.208	.260	-0.3	C 0	-0.4

Learning to hit professionally as a 20-year-old is hard enough, Trouts and Harpers notwithstanding. Applying those lessons while learning the catcher position, too? As (silver screen) Ron Washington would say, it's incredibly hard. Coulter was shuffled between Low-A and Rookie ball multiple times as he failed to find a groove. His catching chops remain raw, so it might be best for his development as a hitter if he changes positions sooner rather than later.

Khris Davis — LF

Born: 12/21/1987 Age: 26
Bats: R Throws: R Height: 5' 11"
Weight: 200 Breakout: 2%
Improve: 21% Collapse: 19%
Attrition: 29% MLB: 71%

Comparables:
Mike Carp, Allen Craig, Joe Mather

YEAR	TEAM	LVL	AGE	PA	R	2B	3B	HR	RBI	BB	SO	SB	CS	AVG/OBP/SLG	TAv	BABIP	BRR	FRAA	WARP
2011	BRV	A+	23	371	50	21	1	15	68	51	70	10	5	.309/.415/.533	.293	.350	-0.3	LF(22): -0.3	0.5
2011	HUN	AA	23	136	10	7	1	2	16	10	23	0	0	.210/.272/.331	.201	.240	0.6	LF(17): -0.4	-0.2
2012	HUN	AA	24	154	23	9	0	8	23	20	33	2	2	.383/.484/.641	.380	.471	-1.1	LF(28): 4.5	2.6
2012	NAS	AAA	24	140	23	12	0	4	24	20	27	1	0	.310/.414/.522	.324	.360	0	LF(27): -3.1, RF(2): -0.1	1.1
2013	NAS	AAA	25	281	35	12	1	13	37	31	59	6	4	.255/.349/.473	.295	.283	-1.3	LF(55): 4.0, RF(10): -0.1	1.9
2013	MIL	MLB	25	153	27	10	0	11	27	11	34	3	0	.279/.353/.596	.322	.293	1.2	LF(34): -1.7	1.2
2014	MIL	MLB	26	250	33	11	1	11	36	23	58	3	2	.256/.338/.465	.288	.290	-0.3	LF 2, RF -0	1.4

Davis's minor-league numbers mirrored Prince Fielder's at the same age through the same system, but his game—both at the plate and in the field—is somewhat awkward and doesn't appear athletic. Still, he just kept hitting in 2013. After a brief stint on the big-league bench to begin the season, Davis mashed for a second consecutive campaign at Triple-A Nashville and eventually moved into regular outfield duty following Ryan Braun's suspension. His biggest asset is gigantic pop, as he has maintained an isolated power above .200 at every level and hit 29 percent of his fly balls for home runs as a Brewer. With five years of destroying the ball as a professional under his belt and an impressive 56-game showing with the Brewers, he'll have a real shot at a starting spot entering spring training.

Nick Delmonico — 3B

Born: 7/12/1992 Age: 21
Bats: L Throws: R Height: 6' 2"
Weight: 200 Breakout: 2%
Improve: 3% Collapse: 0%
Attrition: 10% MLB: 12%

Comparables:
Matt Dominguez, Alex Liddi, Lonnie Chisenhall

YEAR	TEAM	LVL	AGE	PA	R	2B	3B	HR	RBI	BB	SO	SB	CS	AVG/OBP/SLG	TAv	BABIP	BRR	FRAA	WARP
2012	DEL	A	19	393	49	22	0	11	54	47	73	8	1	.249/.351/.411	.282	.286	-1.8	1B(57): -2.5, 2B(31): 2.4	1.6
2013	BRV	A+	20	87	8	4	1	0	9	12	21	2	1	.194/.333/.278	.261	.275	0	3B(15): -0.8	0.2
2013	FRD	A+	20	263	33	12	0	13	30	36	59	5	1	.243/.350/.469	.285	.273	-0.2	3B(42): -3.7, 1B(6): -0.0	0.5
2014	MIL	MLB	21	250	25	9	0	8	29	22	65	0	0	.217/.292/.364	.241	.270	-0.4	3B -2, 1B -1	-0.3

The Brewers took a chance in April and re-signed Francisco Rodriguez to a minor-league contract; three months later, they flipped him for Delmonico. A nifty trick, though it should come as no surprise that Delmonico is a flawed prospect. His positional home is up in the air and will more likely be first base than third. He doesn't run well. But he hits, and he hits for power. He has 24 home runs and 38 doubles as a 21-year-old professional player with just 743 plate appearances under his belt, and that's a fine return for a reliever plucked off the free agent list in April.

Juan Francisco 1B

Born: 6/24/1987 Age: 27
Bats: L Throws: R Height: 6' 2"
Weight: 240 Breakout: 8%
Improve: 23% Collapse: 10%
Attrition: 19% MLB: 58%

Comparables:
Victor Diaz, Brad Eldred, Chris Davis

YEAR	TEAM	LVL	AGE	PA	R	2B	3B	HR	RBI	BB	SO	SB	CS	AVG/OBP/SLG	TAv	BABIP	BRR	FRAA	WARP
2011	LOU	AAA	24	314	46	23	1	15	50	10	65	0	0	.307/.334/.540	.287	.348	-1.1	3B(52): 0.7, RF(1): -0.1	1.6
2011	CIN	MLB	24	97	10	7	1	3	15	4	24	1	0	.258/.289/.452	.254	.318	0.8	3B(24): -1.8	0.2
2012	ATL	MLB	25	205	17	11	0	9	32	11	70	1	1	.234/.278/.432	.241	.316	-1.9	3B(49): -1.5	0.0
2013	MIL	MLB	26	270	26	10	1	13	32	25	95	0	1	.221/.300/.433	.256	.299	0.8	1B(67): -2.3, 3B(4): -0.2	0.1
2013	ATL	MLB	26	115	10	2	0	5	16	7	43	0	1	.241/.287/.398	.244	.350	-1	3B(30): 2.4	0.3
2014	MIL	MLB	27	326	38	14	1	15	47	17	95	1	1	.253/.296/.456	.264	.320	-0.5	1B -3, 3B -0	0.1

Somewhere, somehow, Francisco just struck out again. With the Brewers' first base situation annihilated by the injury to Corey Hart and the insult of Yuniesky Betancourt, Francisco had every chance to grab hold of the position after he came over from Atlanta. His power, raw as ever, was intriguing enough to catch the Brewers' attention. Even with the contact issues, his bat could play at third if the glove was up to it, but at first base the strikeouts keep his productive at-bats too few and far between. He took the golden sombrero (four strikeouts in a game) a league-leading four times in Milwaukee alone, a feat that seems destined to relegate him to a bench role in 2014.

Mat Gamel 1B

Born: 7/26/1985 Age: 28
Bats: L Throws: R Height: 6' 0"
Weight: 215 Breakout: 2%
Improve: 15% Collapse: 18%
Attrition: 33% MLB: 52%

Comparables:
Jeff Clement, Steve Pearce, Max Ramirez

YEAR	TEAM	LVL	AGE	PA	R	2B	3B	HR	RBI	BB	SO	SB	CS	AVG/OBP/SLG	TAv	BABIP	BRR	FRAA	WARP
2011	NAS	AAA	25	545	90	29	0	28	96	46	84	2	0	.310/.372/.540	.362	.326	0.6	1B(72): 2.5, 3B(16): -0.6	5.1
2011	MIL	MLB	25	27	1	1	0	0	2	1	4	0	0	.115/.148/.154	.097	.136	0	3B(3): -0.1, LF(2): 0.0	-0.4
2012	MIL	MLB	26	75	10	2	1	1	6	4	15	3	0	.246/.293/.348	.226	.296	1.4	1B(20): -1.8, 3B(1): -0.0	-0.2
2014	MIL	MLB	28	250	29	11	1	9	32	23	61	1	0	.258/.333/.429	.274	.320	-0.3	1B -1, 3B -1	0.5

If timing is everything, Gamel has nothing. With first base vacated by Prince Fielder's free agent departure in 2012 and then by Corey Hart's knee injury in 2013, Gamel had his first real chances at extended major-league playing time in his career. But Gamel lasted less than a month before tearing his ACL in 2012. Last year provided a second chance, but just days after it appeared he had locked up an Opening Day job, Gamel tore his ACL again during the Brewers' first full-squad workout of 2013. Once a major prospect in the Brewers' system, he's now buried deep on Atlanta's depth chart as a 28-year-old hobbled first baseman who never proved he can hit in the majors. Timing is everything.

Scooter Gennett 2B

Born: 5/1/1990 Age: 24
Bats: L Throws: R Height: 5' 10"
Weight: 180 Breakout: 2%
Improve: 20% Collapse: 8%
Attrition: 18% MLB: 51%

Comparables:
Joaquin Arias, DJ LeMahieu, Jimmy Paredes

YEAR	TEAM	LVL	AGE	PA	R	2B	3B	HR	RBI	BB	SO	SB	CS	AVG/OBP/SLG	TAv	BABIP	BRR	FRAA	WARP
2011	BRV	A+	21	601	74	20	6	9	51	27	69	11	10	.300/.334/.406	.274	.326	3.8	2B(40): -3.7	0.8
2012	HUN	AA	22	573	66	30	2	5	44	28	71	11	5	.293/.330/.385	.249	.328	-2.6	2B(127): 4.2	0.9
2013	NAS	AAA	23	350	44	10	5	3	22	21	59	10	5	.280/.327/.371	.264	.333	-1.4	2B(77): 8.5	2.0
2013	MIL	MLB	23	230	29	11	2	6	21	10	42	2	1	.324/.356/.479	.308	.380	2.2	2B(59): -2.8	1.8
2014	MIL	MLB	24	291	28	12	2	5	30	11	50	4	2	.273/.303/.384	.247	.310	-0.2	2B 0	0.6

A short, slight second baseman with a fun nickname, it's easy to compare Ryan "Scooter" Gennett to 1980s Brewers second base standby Jim "Gumby" Gantner. Like Gumby, Scooter makes consistent solid contact and doesn't care to take a walk. Gennett's six home runs, however, already matched Gumby's best single-season total. Good thing, too, because if Gennett is going to be an impact second baseman, it will have to be on the strength of his bat. Where Gumby was a defensive whiz, Gennett will have to put in his work just to be average at the position.

Caleb Gindl RF

Born: 8/31/1988 Age: 25
Bats: L Throws: L Height: 5' 7"
Weight: 205 Breakout: 11%
Improve: 22% Collapse: 8%
Attrition: 26% MLB: 47%

Comparables:
Shin-Soo Choo, Chris Pettit, Justin Huber

YEAR	TEAM	LVL	AGE	PA	R	2B	3B	HR	RBI	BB	SO	SB	CS	AVG/OBP/SLG	TAv	BABIP	BRR	FRAA	WARP
2011	NAS	AAA	22	538	84	23	5	15	60	63	93	6	5	.307/.390/.472	.281	.357	-1.1	RF(58): 3.2, CF(26): -3.5	1.3
2012	NAS	AAA	23	498	54	27	5	12	50	37	98	4	1	.261/.317/.423	.261	.306	2	RF(78): 1.9, CF(28): -1.0	1.5
2013	NAS	AAA	24	347	33	21	3	11	51	30	72	1	2	.295/.358/.487	.294	.351	-2.5	CF(36): -5.9, RF(33): -0.3	1.7
2013	MIL	MLB	24	155	17	7	2	5	14	20	25	2	1	.242/.340/.439	.278	.262	0.8	LF(30): -2.2, RF(5): -0.3	0.5
2014	MIL	MLB	25	250	25	11	2	6	29	20	54	1	1	.249/.311/.394	.253	.300	-0.2	RF -1, LF -1	0.1

At 5-foot-7 and 205, Gindl packs a punch in a dense package. Still, he mashed a pair of triples as part of his 14 extra-base hits in just a quarter of a season. The profile doesn't suggest he can hold down a position all by himself—all but 16 of his plate appearances came against right-handed pitching. His glove won't keep him on the field, as his shape doesn't help his range at all. Still, between healthy discipline and power, Gindl has enough to make it as a platoon outfielder with pretty slash lines.

Carlos Gomez — CF

Born: 12/4/1985 Age: 28
Bats: R Throws: R Height: 6' 3"
Weight: 215 Breakout: 2%
Improve: 38% Collapse: 2%
Attrition: 3% MLB: 97%

Comparables: Aaron Rowand, Corey Patterson, Ellis Burks

YEAR	TEAM	LVL	AGE	PA	R	2B	3B	HR	RBI	BB	SO	SB	CS	AVG/OBP/SLG	TAv	BABIP	BRR	FRAA	WARP
2011	MIL	MLB	25	258	37	11	3	8	24	15	64	16	2	.225/.276/.403	.246	.273	0	CF(87): 7.1	1.4
2012	MIL	MLB	26	452	72	19	4	19	51	20	98	37	6	.260/.305/.463	.265	.296	4	CF(128): 0.8	2.2
2013	MIL	MLB	27	590	80	27	10	24	73	37	146	40	7	.284/.338/.506	.293	.344	2.1	CF(145): 14.1	6.0
2014	MIL	MLB	28	528	70	21	5	16	59	31	122	35	7	.251/.305/.413	.256	.300	5.1	CF 6	2.5

Carlos Gomez is the post-hype sleeper, awakened. He is why former first-round picks stay employed, why the prospect at the top of the lists from eight years ago keeps getting paid. The signs were there in late 2012, and in 2013 everything clicked for the former Mets top prospect. He continued to hit the ball in the air and take advantage of his huge raw power. He became the first Brewer in franchise history to hit 20 home runs and steal 40 bases. And, to boot, he was the best defensive center fielder in the major leagues. Even in the likely scenario in which 2013 is Gomez's career year, he should be a star in center field for the foreseeable future.

Mitch Haniger — RF

Born: 12/23/1990 Age: 23
Bats: R Throws: R Height: 6' 2"
Weight: 180 Breakout: 2%
Improve: 2% Collapse: 0%
Attrition: 0% MLB: 4%

Comparables: Andrew Lambo, Moises Sierra, Matt Joyce

YEAR	TEAM	LVL	AGE	PA	R	2B	3B	HR	RBI	BB	SO	SB	CS	AVG/OBP/SLG	TAv	BABIP	BRR	FRAA	WARP
2012	WIS	A	21	58	9	4	0	1	8	7	13	1	0	.286/.379/.429	.299	.361	0.9	CF(12): -0.7	0.5
2013	WIS	A	22	178	24	12	2	5	25	25	24	7	0	.297/.399/.510	.327	.314	1.8	RF(23): 0.9, CF(12): -0.7	2.0
2013	BRV	A+	22	365	52	24	3	6	43	32	68	2	2	.250/.323/.396	.266	.298	1.7	RF(45): -3.1, CF(42): 6.1	1.7
2014	MIL	MLB	23	250	23	11	1	5	26	19	59	0	0	.225/.287/.351	.231	.280	-0.3	RF -1, CF 1	-0.2

Haniger slipped to the first supplemental round in 2012 largely due to a brutal knee injury suffered in his final amateur season. The Brewers saw exactly what they hoped for in his first couple months at Low-A Wisconsin, as Haniger mashed in a league that tilts decidedly toward pitching (the league hit .252/.318/.370). Haniger slipped back near the league average when he moved up to High-A Brevard County but still managed 33 extra-base hits in 88 games. He split his time between center field and right, but is expected to settle in the corner thanks to a great arm and fringy speed.

Corey Hart — RF

Born: 3/24/1982 Age: 32
Bats: R Throws: R Height: 6' 6"
Weight: 235 Breakout: 0%
Improve: 26% Collapse: 6%
Attrition: 13% MLB: 95%

Comparables: Glenn Davis, Ernie Banks, Roger Freed

YEAR	TEAM	LVL	AGE	PA	R	2B	3B	HR	RBI	BB	SO	SB	CS	AVG/OBP/SLG	TAv	BABIP	BRR	FRAA	WARP
2011	MIL	MLB	29	551	80	25	4	26	63	51	114	7	6	.285/.356/.510	.300	.323	-1.4	RF(126): 1.5	2.9
2012	MIL	MLB	30	622	91	35	4	30	83	44	151	5	0	.270/.334/.507	.279	.318	-0.9	1B(103): 0.9, RF(53): -3.4	1.6
2014	MIL	MLB	32	250	31	11	1	10	34	19	56	3	1	.263/.328/.459	.283	.300	-0.2	RF -2, 1B 0	0.8

Hart was supposed to be back in late April, then late May, and then by the All-Star break, and then reality set in. The nightmare contract-year scenario played out, as Hart missed the entirety of the 2013 season thanks to his second knee surgery in the past two years. Hart has been slowing down for years now, and after this latest procedure, his days in the outfield might be over for good. Still, if he returns to form at the plate, he has more than enough power to play first base or DH for Seattle: He was one of just eight players to record a .500-plus slugging percentage each season from 2010 through 2012.

Jonathan Lucroy — C

Born: 6/13/1986 Age: 28
Bats: R Throws: R Height: 6' 0"
Weight: 195 Breakout: 1%
Improve: 41% Collapse: 2%
Attrition: 11% MLB: 97%

Comparables: Kurt Suzuki, Ken Retzer, Thurman Munson

YEAR	TEAM	LVL	AGE	PA	R	2B	3B	HR	RBI	BB	SO	SB	CS	AVG/OBP/SLG	TAv	BABIP	BRR	FRAA	WARP
2011	MIL	MLB	25	468	45	16	1	12	59	29	99	2	1	.265/.312/.391	.247	.317	2.2	C(132): -2.1	1.6
2012	MIL	MLB	26	346	46	17	4	12	58	22	44	4	1	.320/.368/.513	.300	.338	-2.3	C(88): -2.4	2.3
2013	MIL	MLB	27	580	59	25	6	18	82	46	69	9	1	.280/.340/.455	.274	.290	-7.6	C(126): -1.4, 1B(14): -0.3	2.2
2014	MIL	MLB	28	501	55	20	2	13	58	34	77	6	1	.272/.325/.410	.265	.300	0.2	C -1, 1B -0	2.4

Given Lucroy's early-career offensive struggles and his highly regarded receiving skills, it can be easy to forget the Brewers drafted him for his bat. His defense was considered a work in progress by many scouts throughout his minor-league career, while his strike zone recognition and line-drive stroke repeatedly earned spots on top-prospect lists. Now, most of Lucroy's national cred comes from his pitch-framing abilities, but his bat has caught up over the past two years. His .827 OPS since 2012 ranks fifth among catchers with at least 600 plate appearances, trailing just Buster Posey, Joe Mauer, Yadier Molina and Mike Napoli. With his receiving prowess, he clearly belongs in the elite tier of catchers. To boot, his contract pays just $14 million over the next four years, making him one of the biggest assets for any team around the league.

Martin Maldonado — C

Born: 8/16/1986 Age: 27
Bats: R Throws: R Height: 6' 0''
Weight: 235 Breakout: 8%
Improve: 34% Collapse: 10%
Attrition: 26% MLB: 78%

Comparables:
Jeff Mathis, Rob Bowen, Guillermo Quiroz

YEAR	TEAM	LVL	AGE	PA	R	2B	3B	HR	RBI	BB	SO	SB	CS	AVG/OBP/SLG	TAv	BABIP	BRR	FRAA	WARP
2011	HUN	AA	24	241	24	13	0	3	34	19	56	2	1	.264/.349/.370	.294	.344	-1	C(41): 0.2	1.3
2011	NAS	AAA	24	160	23	5	0	8	25	16	21	0	0	.321/.410/.537	.330	.330	-1.8	C(30): -0.3	1.4
2011	MIL	MLB	24	1	0	0	0	0	0	0	1	0	0	.000/.000/.000	.009	—	0	C(3): -0.0	0.0
2012	NAS	AAA	25	138	10	6	0	4	13	9	37	0	2	.198/.270/.347	.218	.241	0.2	C(34): 0.1	0.1
2012	MIL	MLB	25	256	22	9	0	8	30	17	56	1	1	.266/.321/.408	.251	.320	1.8	C(69): 0.9, 1B(4): -0.0	1.1
2013	MIL	MLB	26	202	13	7	1	4	22	13	53	0	0	.169/.236/.284	.197	.214	0.3	C(47): 1.3, 1B(10): -0.2	-0.5
2014	MIL	MLB	27	250	26	9	0	7	27	17	60	1	0	.235/.298/.372	.241	.280	-0.5	C 1, 1B -0	0.6

Maldonado has the glove to enjoy a fruitful career as a backup catcher, but 2013 renewed doubts that his bat can play even in that limited role. He remains susceptible to the strikeout, limiting his chances to profit from his strong raw power. The problem isn't so much his ability to make contact—his 76 percent contact rate was in line with the league average—as his eagerness to swing at anything. Still, he continues to impress defensively and he built a strong rapport with rookie Wily Peralta, which can only help him in his quest to hold on to a roster spot as a backup.

Hunter Morris — 1B

Born: 10/7/1988 Age: 25
Bats: L Throws: R Height: 6' 2''
Weight: 226 Breakout: 4%
Improve: 29% Collapse: 3%
Attrition: 13% MLB: 39%

Comparables:
Mark Trumbo, Tyler Moore, Jake Fox

YEAR	TEAM	LVL	AGE	PA	R	2B	3B	HR	RBI	BB	SO	SB	CS	AVG/OBP/SLG	TAv	BABIP	BRR	FRAA	WARP
2011	BRV	A+	22	531	75	28	5	19	67	18	84	7	3	.271/.299/.461	.242	.289	0.1	1B(33): -1.8, 3B(2): -0.3	-0.3
2012	HUN	AA	23	571	77	40	6	28	113	40	117	2	1	.303/.357/.563	.313	.342	0.9	1B(136): -11.2	3.1
2013	NAS	AAA	24	546	61	26	3	24	73	43	122	3	1	.247/.310/.457	.272	.280	-3.1	1B(123): -8.3	0.2
2014	MIL	MLB	25	250	28	12	1	11	36	13	60	1	0	.246/.289/.450	.261	.280	-0.3	1B -4, 3B -0	-0.2

With a strong spring training, Morris might have been able to parlay his 2012 Southern League MVP season into a starting gig with the 2013 Brewers, especially after injuries turned first base into a wasteland. Morris scuffled all spring, though, and his Triple-A performance exposed him as a one-tool hitter. Morris hit for power, and he'll do it again and again as long as he's playing, but without an improvement in either discipline or contact he'll never put together the full profile for a first-base slugger. He's not, incidentally, the same Hunter Morris from *The Rookie*, though that kid's about the same age right now.

Aramis Ramirez — 3B

Born: 6/25/1978 Age: 36
Bats: R Throws: R Height: 6' 1''
Weight: 210 Breakout: 0%
Improve: 27% Collapse: 6%
Attrition: 8% MLB: 88%

Comparables:
Scott Rolen, Mike Lowell, Casey Blake

YEAR	TEAM	LVL	AGE	PA	R	2B	3B	HR	RBI	BB	SO	SB	CS	AVG/OBP/SLG	TAv	BABIP	BRR	FRAA	WARP
2011	CHN	MLB	33	626	80	35	1	26	93	43	69	1	1	.306/.361/.510	.307	.308	-5.3	3B(145): -14.5	3.0
2012	MIL	MLB	34	630	92	50	3	27	105	44	82	9	2	.300/.360/.540	.304	.310	-2.5	3B(143): -4.0	4.2
2013	MIL	MLB	35	351	43	18	0	12	49	36	55	0	1	.283/.370/.461	.288	.308	-2.8	3B(80): -11.2	0.4
2014	MIL	MLB	36	385	46	19	1	15	53	28	58	2	1	.271/.334/.458	.283	.290	-0.6	3B -8	0.9

The risk when the Brewers signed Ramirez to a three-year, $36 million contract prior to the 2012 season wasn't that he'd stop hitting. Ramirez hasn't, as his .282 TAv marked his ninth season with at least a .280 mark in the past 10 years. But there was the question of when Ramirez's body, already notably slower and stiffer, would really begin to break down. It did in 2013, as Ramirez played fewer than 100 games for just the second time since 2000. Ramirez's contract is heavily backloaded, with $16 million due in 2014 (and beyond, thanks to options and deferred payments), and with his defense swiftly degrading, he'll have to hit *and* stay healthy to be worth that kind of scratch.

Victor Roache — LF

Born: 9/17/1991 Age: 22
Bats: R Throws: R Height: 6' 1''
Weight: 225 Breakout: 0%
Improve: 1% Collapse: 0%
Attrition: 1% MLB: 3%

Comparables:
Jeremy Moore, Brandon Barnes, Cole Garner

YEAR	TEAM	LVL	AGE	PA	R	2B	3B	HR	RBI	BB	SO	SB	CS	AVG/OBP/SLG	TAv	BABIP	BRR	FRAA	WARP
2013	WIS	A	21	519	62	14	4	22	74	46	137	6	2	.248/.322/.440	.274	.302	-1	LF(86): 1.7	1.7
2014	MIL	MLB	22	250	24	7	1	9	30	15	81	0	0	.207/.258/.361	.223	.270	-0.3	LF 1	-0.4

The Brewers' decision to select Roache in the first round in 2012 was, in a sense, playing it safe—Roache had a broken wrist and was a lock to sign under slot as a result. But Milwaukee thought Roache was worth it on talent, too, and he showed it in 2013, particularly in the second half. From July onward, Roache hit .278/.342/.530 with 15 of his 22 home runs. Nobody in the system can match his pop, and that pop could earn him work as Milwaukee's starting right fielder in two or three years.

Logan Schafer — CF

Born: 9/8/1986 Age: 27
Bats: L Throws: L Height: 6' 1"
Weight: 180 Breakout: 5%
Improve: 23% Collapse: 9%
Attrition: 29% MLB: 56%

Comparables:
Bryan Petersen, Alejandro De Aza, Shane Costa

YEAR	TEAM	LVL	AGE	PA	R	2B	3B	HR	RBI	BB	SO	SB	CS	AVG/OBP/SLG	TAv	BABIP	BRR	FRAA	WARP
2011	BRV	A+	24	41	4	0	0	0	1	5	4	1	1	.306/.390/.306	.283	.344	0.6	CF(3): -0.7	0.1
2011	HUN	AA	24	211	31	9	4	0	19	17	25	10	5	.302/.368/.392	.302	.348	1.1	CF(30): 2.4	1.2
2011	NAS	AAA	24	194	31	13	2	5	23	17	18	5	3	.331/.401/.521	.323	.345	1.2	CF(32): 0.3	2.0
2011	MIL	MLB	24	5	1	0	0	0	0	1	1	0	0	.333/.500/.333	.291	.500	0	RF(1): -0.0, CF(1): -0.0	0.0
2012	NAS	AAA	25	513	72	23	9	11	40	29	72	16	7	.278/.332/.438	.268	.307	2.5	CF(118): 6.0, LF(2): 0.0	2.7
2012	MIL	MLB	25	25	3	1	2	0	5	1	3	0	1	.304/.320/.522	.299	.333	0	CF(5): 0.3, LF(2): 0.1	0.2
2013	MIL	MLB	26	337	29	15	3	4	33	25	60	7	1	.211/.279/.322	.219	.252	1.9	LF(56): 4.6, CF(28): 0.5	0.2
2014	MIL	MLB	27	316	37	13	3	6	28	19	54	8	3	.249/.305/.375	.242	.280	0.4	CF 2, LF 3	0.8

Forced into regular action by Ryan Braun's suspension, Schafer showed that his excellent defensive reputation in the minors was deserved. Sure, he failed to begin a triple play on a ball caught off his head, as he did at Triple-A Nasvhille in 2011, but Schafer added four outfield assists (and many more held runners) and excellent range in the outfield. He was overmatched at the plate and doesn't have the power for a starting outfield spot, but his glove makes him worthy of a fourth or fifth out-fielder role.

Jean Segura — SS

Born: 3/17/1990 Age: 24
Bats: R Throws: R Height: 5' 10"
Weight: 200 Breakout: 6%
Improve: 52% Collapse: 2%
Attrition: 9% MLB: 95%

Comparables:
Josh Barfield, Howie Kendrick, Alcides Escobar

YEAR	TEAM	LVL	AGE	PA	R	2B	3B	HR	RBI	BB	SO	SB	CS	AVG/OBP/SLG	TAv	BABIP	BRR	FRAA	WARP
2011	SBR	A+	21	202	26	9	4	3	21	15	26	18	6	.281/.337/.422	.337	.312	0.6	SS(6): 0.5	0.4
2012	HUN	AA	22	37	7	3	0	0	4	4	4	4	0	.433/.500/.533	.346	.481	-0.8	SS(8): 0.6	0.4
2012	ARK	AA	22	414	50	10	5	7	40	23	57	33	13	.294/.346/.404	.286	.329	2.6	SS(80): 6.6, 2B(2): -0.0	3.6
2012	MIL	MLB	22	163	19	4	3	0	14	13	21	7	1	.264/.321/.331	.237	.305	1	SS(43): -2.7	0.1
2012	ANA	MLB	22	3	0	0	0	0	0	0	2	0	0	.000/.000/.000	.247	.000	-0.1	SS(1): 0.1	0.0
2013	MIL	MLB	23	623	74	20	10	12	49	25	84	44	13	.294/.329/.423	.265	.326	2.6	SS(144): 23.5	5.6
2014	MIL	MLB	24	548	75	19	6	10	48	27	81	35	11	.282/.323/.403	.263	.320	3.5	SS 12, 2B 0	4.2

Segura's season tailed off heavily at the end, but his 2013 still checks in as a rousing success. His defense improved—though FRAA is about a 20-run outlier, compared to the other leading defensive metrics—and his arm particularly looked to be a huge asset. He added weight to his lower half and hit for far more power, particularly in the first half. In the second half, he managed just a .610 OPS as the power disappeared. Still, he continued to make consistent contact even as his numbers tumbled, and chances are the power will just be more spread out over subsequent seasons. In a league bereft of hitting shortstops, Segura looks like a major bargain for years to come.

Rickie Weeks — 2B

Born: 9/13/1982 Age: 31
Bats: R Throws: R Height: 5' 10"
Weight: 215 Breakout: 0%
Improve: 45% Collapse: 6%
Attrition: 6% MLB: 97%

Comparables:
Dan Uggla, Bobby Grich, Kelly Johnson

YEAR	TEAM	LVL	AGE	PA	R	2B	3B	HR	RBI	BB	SO	SB	CS	AVG/OBP/SLG	TAv	BABIP	BRR	FRAA	WARP
2011	MIL	MLB	28	515	77	26	2	20	49	50	107	9	2	.269/.350/.468	.287	.310	2.6	2B(115): 0.3	3.2
2012	MIL	MLB	29	677	85	29	4	21	63	74	169	16	3	.230/.328/.400	.262	.285	-0.9	2B(152): -14.2	0.4
2013	MIL	MLB	30	399	40	20	1	10	24	40	105	7	3	.209/.306/.357	.235	.268	0.6	2B(95): -5.0	-0.7
2014	MIL	MLB	31	430	58	17	2	14	47	42	105	8	2	.240/.330/.406	.271	.290	0.2	2B -5	1.5

Weeks' season was once again cut off by a horrendous leg injury, this time a blown hamstring suffered running to first in August. Weeks was terrible prior to the injury, as his poor contact skills poisoned everything and diminished power and discipline could no longer make up the balance. He hasn't looked himself since he suffered an awful ankle injury that cost him much of 2011's second half. Weeks has hit just .222/.320/.384 since, after he hit .269/.357/.472 from 2009 through 2011.

PITCHERS

Michael Blazek

Born: 3/16/1989 Age: 25
Bats: R Throws: R Height: 6' 0" Weight: 200
Breakout: 58% Improve: 73% Collapse: 19%
Attrition: 62% MLB: 19%

Comparables:
Merkin Valdez, Sergio Escalona, Brayan Villarreal

YEAR	TEAM	LVL	AGE	W	L	SV	G	GS	IP	H	HR	BB	SO	BB9	SO9	GB%	BABIP	WHIP	ERA	FIP	FRA	WARP
2011	SFD	AA	22	11	6	0	24	24	133²	148	25	64	128	4.3	8.6	48%	.346	1.59	5.45	5.53	7.15	-0.1
2011	MEM	AAA	22	2	0	0	2	2	12	8	1	9	6	6.8	4.5	—	.194	1.42	3.75	6.12	6.65	0.0
2012	SFD	AA	23	5	8	0	40	7	80	61	11	34	83	3.8	9.3	44%	.254	1.19	4.16	4.38	6.22	-0.3
2013	SFD	AA	24	0	0	7	17	0	19²	11	0	10	25	4.6	11.4	56%	.244	1.07	0.92	2.04	2.59	0.5
2013	MEM	AAA	24	1	2	2	19	0	26	17	1	16	27	5.5	9.3	35%	.250	1.27	2.77	3.84	4.64	0.2
2013	SLN	MLB	24	0	0	0	11	0	10¹	10	2	10	10	8.7	8.7	47%	.286	1.94	6.97	6.79	6.37	-0.2
2013	MIL	MLB	24	0	1	0	7	0	7	6	1	3	4	3.9	5.1	40%	.208	1.29	3.86	5.02	7.20	-0.2
2014	MIL	MLB	25	2	2	0	29	5	58	56	8	29	47	4.5	7.3	43%	.298	1.47	4.90	5.04	5.33	-0.3

In many ways, Blazek resembles John Axford, the man Milwaukee traded for him in August. Blazek makes his living with a fastball averaging 96 mph and the ability to tap 99. As with many fireballing relievers, Blazek showed poor control of two off-speed pitches—mostly a slider and curveball, both of which went for balls 40 percent of the time. The slider, however, is vicious when controlled, and in his limited time in the majors more than half of batters' swings at the pitch have come up empty. The fastball-slider pair is the archetypal late-inning reliever's arsenal, and Blazek will use it to attempt to follow Axford into the same role.

Hiram Burgos

Born: 8/4/1987 Age: 26
Bats: R Throws: R Height: 5' 11" Weight: 210
Breakout: 55% Improve: 64% Collapse: 32%
Attrition: 79% MLB: 47%

Comparables:
Philip Humber, Shane Komine, Chris Schwinden

YEAR	TEAM	LVL	AGE	W	L	SV	G	GS	IP	H	HR	BB	SO	BB9	SO9	GB%	BABIP	WHIP	ERA	FIP	FRA	WARP
2011	BRV	A+	23	6	8	0	24	22	119²	142	13	35	80	2.6	6.0	38%	.347	1.48	4.89	4.52	5.42	0.1
2012	BRV	A+	24	2	1	0	7	6	41¹	21	1	6	41	1.3	8.9	47%	.198	0.65	0.87	2.23	3.02	0.9
2012	HUN	AA	24	6	1	0	13	13	83¹	68	3	28	77	3.0	8.3	47%	.312	1.15	1.94	2.88	3.62	1.6
2012	NAS	AAA	24	2	2	0	8	8	46¹	39	4	15	35	2.9	6.8	41%	.261	1.17	2.91	4.31	4.54	0.7
2013	NAS	AAA	25	1	4	0	7	7	30²	25	6	12	24	3.5	7.0	39%	.237	1.21	3.82	5.82	7.27	-0.5
2013	MIL	MLB	25	1	2	0	6	6	29¹	38	5	11	18	3.4	5.5	40%	.326	1.67	6.44	5.34	5.48	-0.2
2014	MIL	MLB	26	3	5	0	12	12	71²	73	10	26	51	3.2	6.4	44%	.302	1.38	4.71	4.86	5.12	-0.2

After an impressive World Baseball Classic campaign for Puerto Rico, Burgos earned Milwaukee's first few available spot starts in April. The control and command he showcased in the Classic were apparent in his first few starts, but the league rapidly figured him out. Burgos didn't break 90 mph in two of his starts, and his fastball typically sat in the 85-88 range. Major-league hitters can hit that speed even when perfectly placed, and they did so repeatedly against Burgos. He served up eight extra-base hits on 36 fastballs in play (.333 ISO on contact) and was dispatched to the minor leagues for the rest of the year after just six starts.

Marco Estrada

Born: 7/5/1983 Age: 30
Bats: R Throws: R Height: 5' 11" Weight: 200
Breakout: 25% Improve: 52% Collapse: 24%
Attrition: 24% MLB: 71%

Comparables:
Buddy Carlyle, Jeremy Guthrie, Rich Hill

YEAR	TEAM	LVL	AGE	W	L	SV	G	GS	IP	H	HR	BB	SO	BB9	SO9	GB%	BABIP	WHIP	ERA	FIP	FRA	WARP
2011	MIL	MLB	27	4	8	0	43	7	92²	83	11	29	88	2.8	8.5	42%	.290	1.21	4.08	3.64	4.51	0.5
2012	MIL	MLB	28	5	7	0	29	23	138¹	129	18	29	143	1.9	9.3	36%	.295	1.14	3.64	3.39	4.02	2.3
2013	MIL	MLB	29	7	4	0	21	21	128	109	19	29	118	2.0	8.3	39%	.271	1.08	3.87	3.83	4.51	0.8
2014	MIL	MLB	30	6	6	0	35	16	117	106	15	30	102	2.3	7.9	41%	.292	1.16	3.57	3.95	3.88	1.5

The defining question for Estrada appears to be this: Can he throw his breaking pitches for strikes? He couldn't in the first half—his curveball, in particular, was a ball more than 50 percent of the time. The result was a lot of fastballs, specifically in hitters counts. Estrada served up 14 home runs in the first half, eight of which came on traditional fastball counts. The second half, and a return from a hamstring injury, turned the tides. He dialed both his curveball and changeup in for regular strikes, struck out 5.1 batters per walk, held opponents to a .467 OPS and had baseball's eighth-best ERA among starters after the break. This is the precision that earned Estrada his first chance in the rotation, and maintaining it will be key to his success in 2014.

Mike Fiers

Born: 6/15/1985 Age: 29
Bats: R Throws: R Height: 6' 2" Weight: 195
Breakout: 28% Improve: 69% Collapse: 14%
Attrition: 30% MLB: 54%

Comparables:
Sam LeCure, Guillermo Moscoso, David Purcey

YEAR	TEAM	LVL	AGE	W	L	SV	G	GS	IP	H	HR	BB	SO	BB9	SO9	GB%	BABIP	WHIP	ERA	FIP	FRA	WARP
2011	HUN	AA	26	5	3	5	22	8	61¹	42	7	14	63	2.1	9.2	52%	.242	0.91	2.64	3.52	2.49	1.1
2011	NAS	AAA	26	8	0	0	12	10	64²	41	4	22	69	3.1	9.6	41%	.221	0.97	1.11	3.61	4.29	1.0
2011	MIL	MLB	26	0	0	0	2	0	2	2	0	3	2	13.5	9.0	25%	.500	2.50	0.00	5.49	1.17	0.0
2012	NAS	AAA	27	1	3	0	10	10	55	49	6	18	49	2.9	8.0	42%	.291	1.22	4.42	4.45	4.85	0.7
2012	MIL	MLB	27	9	10	0	23	22	127²	125	12	36	135	2.5	9.5	33%	.328	1.26	3.74	3.14	3.32	3.4
2013	NAS	AAA	28	1	2	0	5	5	28²	24	3	12	30	3.8	9.4	45%	.300	1.26	2.20	4.09	4.24	0.4
2013	MIL	MLB	28	1	4	0	11	3	22¹	28	8	6	15	2.4	6.0	37%	.282	1.52	7.25	7.14	6.74	-0.3
2014	MIL	MLB	29	4	4	0	16	11	70²	62	9	22	66	2.8	8.4	40%	.291	1.19	3.70	4.06	4.02	0.8

Fiers' season in Milwaukee's rotation was basically over as soon as it started. He served up nine hits, including two home runs, in the club's fifth game of the year and was immediately buried in the bullpen (with the exception of a pair of spot starts). Fiers was able to sneak his fastball by just enough hitters to succeed in 2012, but his control deserted him in 2013. The result was far too many hitters counts for a pitcher who threw just 12 of his 243 fastballs above 90 mph, and hitters tagged the fastball alone for six home runs in his limited action. He threw his last pitch in the majors on June 2nd, broke his arm on a Kevin Kouzmanoff line drive in Triple-A two weeks later and now faces an uphill battle to reach the show again.

Alfredo Figaro

Born: 7/7/1984 Age: 29
Bats: R Throws: R Height: 6' 0" Weight: 175
Breakout: 33% Improve: 73% Collapse: 18%
Attrition: 24% MLB: 46%

Comparables:
Chad Durbin, Garrett Mock, Dave Borkowski

YEAR	TEAM	LVL	AGE	W	L	SV	G	GS	IP	H	HR	BB	SO	BB9	SO9	GB%	BABIP	WHIP	ERA	FIP	FRA	WARP
2013	NAS	AAA	28	1	0	0	3	3	13	14	0	9	8	6.2	5.5	57%	.325	1.77	2.77	4.42	5.61	0.1
2013	MIL	MLB	28	3	3	1	33	5	74	77	15	15	54	1.8	6.6	49%	.282	1.24	4.14	4.84	5.91	-0.5
2014	MIL	MLB	29	3	4	0	18	9	62²	64	8	20	45	2.9	6.5	47%	.305	1.36	4.71	4.51	5.12	-0.1

The Brewers became enamored with Figaro thanks to a strong showing in the Dominican Summer League, and a competent spring training earned him his first major-league roster spot—and his first American roster spot at any level—since 2010. Figaro showed big-league velocity with a fastball that touched 98 and regularly sat above 95, but it had little life, leading to home run issues. Still, he could control it, and a big fastball with control is usually enough to survive in the majors. Will Figaro thrive? Without improvement, he seems destined for long relief, but considering their small investment the Brewers should be satisfied with their marriage to Figaro.

Yovani Gallardo

Born: 2/27/1986 Age: 28
Bats: R Throws: R Height: 6' 2" Weight: 215
Breakout: 30% Improve: 65% Collapse: 19%
Attrition: 8% MLB: 96%

Comparables:
Josh Beckett, Chris Young, John Lackey

YEAR	TEAM	LVL	AGE	W	L	SV	G	GS	IP	H	HR	BB	SO	BB9	SO9	GB%	BABIP	WHIP	ERA	FIP	FRA	WARP
2011	MIL	MLB	25	17	10	0	33	33	207¹	193	27	59	207	2.6	9.0	47%	.295	1.22	3.52	3.56	4.27	2.1
2012	MIL	MLB	26	16	9	0	33	33	204	185	26	81	204	3.6	9.0	48%	.293	1.30	3.66	3.98	4.44	2.4
2013	MIL	MLB	27	12	10	0	31	31	180²	180	18	66	144	3.3	7.2	51%	.303	1.36	4.18	3.87	4.49	1.0
2014	MIL	MLB	28	9	10	0	27	27	161	140	16	54	154	3.0	8.6	46%	.298	1.21	3.52	3.63	3.83	2.1

When Gallardo went down with a hamstring injury on July 30th, his season was a disaster. He owned a 4.91 ERA. His K/9 was 7.1, nearly two punchouts lower than his *worst* rate from the past four years. His average fastball velocity dipped to a career-low 91 mph. Then, after his return, Gallardo made eight brilliant starts with a 2.41 ERA. His velocity was still down, and his strikeout rate was still lower than normal, but he exhibited far better control (2.6 walks per nine). Gallardo has been a nibbler for much of his career, willing to walk a batter because he could always reach back for a strikeout if needed. The Brewers hope his second half shows he has the adaptability to handle the velocity drop.

Michael Gonzalez

Born: 5/23/1978 Age: 36
Bats: R Throws: L Height: 6' 2" Weight: 200
Breakout: 26% Improve: 49% Collapse: 32%
Attrition: 7% MLB: 72%

Comparables:
Brad Lidge, Octavio Dotel, Ron Mahay

YEAR	TEAM	LVL	AGE	W	L	SV	G	GS	IP	H	HR	BB	SO	BB9	SO9	GB%	BABIP	WHIP	ERA	FIP	FRA	WARP
2011	BAL	MLB	33	2	2	1	49	0	46¹	46	7	18	46	3.5	8.9	41%	.302	1.38	4.27	4.33	4.34	0.4
2011	TEX	MLB	33	0	0	0	7	0	7	5	0	3	5	3.9	6.4	50%	.250	1.14	5.14	2.92	3.64	0.1
2012	WAS	MLB	34	0	0	0	47	0	35²	31	2	16	39	4.0	9.8	43%	.309	1.32	3.03	3.02	2.69	0.8
2013	MIL	MLB	35	0	3	0	75	0	50	58	10	25	60	4.5	10.8	36%	.353	1.66	4.68	4.84	4.74	-0.1
2014	MIL	MLB	36	3	1	1	59	0	47¹	39	5	19	53	3.6	10.1	40%	.302	1.23	3.65	3.66	3.96	0.5

Gonzalez reinforced the wisdom of keeping him a couple hundred feet away from right-handed hitters. He served up a .284/.378/.484 line to 76 righties in 2012 and followed it with a .290/.393/.535 line against 117 right-handers in 2013. The twist: Gonzalez, for the first extended stretch of his career, wasn't even effective against left-handers in 2013. He tied a career high with four home runs allowed against southpaws. In 2012, his slider was devastating to lefties—he didn't allow an extra-base hit off it. But hitters knocked two out of the park in 2013 and connected on four more doubles. The movement, velocity and location of those sliders was in line with previous successful seasons, so this might be a blip, but if the pitch doesn't fool lefties Gonzalez won't cut it in a major-league bullpen.

Tom Gorzelanny
Born: **7/12/1982** Age: **31**
Bats: **R** Throws: **L** Height: **6' 2"** Weight: **210**
Breakout: **22%** Improve: **54%** Collapse: **31%**
Attrition: **28%** MLB: **77%**

Comparables:
Scott Downs, Luke Hudson, John Maine

YEAR	TEAM	LVL	AGE	W	L	SV	G	GS	IP	H	HR	BB	SO	BB9	SO9	GB%	BABIP	WHIP	ERA	FIP	FRA	WARP
2011	WAS	MLB	28	4	6	0	30	15	105	102	15	33	95	2.8	8.1	37%	.293	1.29	4.03	4.16	4.27	0.8
2012	WAS	MLB	29	4	2	1	45	1	72	65	7	30	62	3.8	7.8	43%	.282	1.32	2.88	4.01	4.18	0.5
2013	MIL	MLB	30	3	6	0	43	10	85¹	77	11	31	83	3.3	8.8	45%	.283	1.27	3.90	3.91	4.48	0.7
2014	MIL	MLB	31	3	4	0	26	9	71¹	64	8	26	63	3.3	7.9	42%	.294	1.26	3.92	4.12	4.26	0.6

Gorzelanny's flexibility was a big reason Milwaukee was willing to pony up nearly $6 million guaranteed last year. Left-handed relief was a big hole for the Brewers in 2012, and the club's starting pitching depth projected as less than adequate in 2013 even before injuries ravaged the staff by midseason. As expected, Gorzo was competent as a reliever—2.70 ERA in 36 innings with six extra-base hits allowed—and around replacement level as a starter—4.81 ERA in 49 innings, with 18 extra-base hits allowed. Gorzelanny's ability to start is a nice safety valve, but he's at his best in relief and shouldn't be counted on to start for long stretches if it can be avoided.

Donovan Hand
Born: **4/20/1986** Age: **28**
Bats: **R** Throws: **R** Height: **6' 3"** Weight: **210**
Breakout: **54%** Improve: **64%** Collapse: **26%**
Attrition: **56%** MLB: **26%**

Comparables:
Greg Burke, Steven Jackson, Levale Speigner

YEAR	TEAM	LVL	AGE	W	L	SV	G	GS	IP	H	HR	BB	SO	BB9	SO9	GB%	BABIP	WHIP	ERA	FIP	FRA	WARP
2011	HUN	AA	25	0	0	1	9	0	11¹	16	0	1	12	0.8	9.5	47%	.412	1.50	2.38	1.45	2.17	0.2
2011	NAS	AAA	25	2	6	1	39	0	55	66	6	21	32	3.4	5.2	56%	.351	1.58	3.60	5.18	5.60	0.2
2012	NAS	AAA	26	3	3	0	44	3	79²	90	7	18	54	2.0	6.1	48%	.329	1.36	3.84	4.17	4.49	1.1
2013	NAS	AAA	27	3	1	0	20	0	35²	34	4	11	38	2.8	9.6	53%	.306	1.26	3.28	3.82	3.92	0.5
2013	MIL	MLB	27	1	5	0	31	7	68¹	71	10	21	37	2.8	4.9	48%	.291	1.35	3.69	4.98	5.22	-0.1
2014	MIL	MLB	28	3	2	1	50	3	86¹	92	12	24	53	2.5	5.5	49%	.303	1.34	4.63	4.77	5.04	-0.2

Hand spent parts of four years routinely retiring Pacific Coast League hitters, but a sub-90s fastball and lack of an eye-popping secondary pitch kept Hand in the bullpen down in Nashville. A raft of injuries to starters and relievers in Milwaukee, however, eventually earned Hand a chance at both jobs. He was overmatched as a starter, allowing nine home runs and five doubles in just seven starts. In relief, though, he kept the ball on the ground and allowed just two extra-base hits over 31 innings of work. He was able to rely more on his secondary pitches and less on his milquetoast fastball. Hand's leg up on the larger sect of generic right-handed relievers is his ability to go multiple innings—he recorded at least four outs in 11 of his 24 relief outings.

Johnny Hellweg
Born: **10/29/1988** Age: **25**
Bats: **R** Throws: **R** Height: **6' 9"** Weight: **205**
Breakout: **73%** Improve: **77%** Collapse: **7%**
Attrition: **77%** MLB: **32%**

Comparables:
Elvin Ramirez, Rafael Dolis, Aaron Poreda

YEAR	TEAM	LVL	AGE	W	L	SV	G	GS	IP	H	HR	BB	SO	BB9	SO9	GB%	BABIP	WHIP	ERA	FIP	FRA	WARP
2011	SBR	A+	22	6	4	0	28	14	89¹	75	2	59	113	5.9	11.4	65%	.294	1.50	3.73	4.20	4.11	0.7
2012	HUN	AA	23	2	1	0	7	2	20	16	0	15	17	6.8	7.7	72%	.302	1.55	2.70	3.84	5.11	0.2
2012	ARK	AA	23	5	10	0	21	21	119²	105	8	60	88	4.5	6.6	56%	.286	1.38	3.38	4.51	5.43	-0.4
2013	NAS	AAA	24	12	5	0	23	23	125²	103	6	81	89	5.8	6.4	58%	.274	1.46	3.15	5.04	5.41	0.1
2013	MIL	MLB	24	1	4	0	8	7	30²	40	3	26	9	7.6	2.6	56%	.318	2.15	6.75	7.03	7.45	-0.7
2014	MIL	MLB	25	6	10	1	41	22	135²	128	14	85	94	5.6	6.2	52%	.291	1.57	5.15	5.38	5.60	-0.9

Hellweg won Pitcher of the Year in the Pacific Coast League despite striking out just eight more batters than he walked. Of course, this is not the whole story—the 6-foot-9 Hellweg used his height to induce groundball after groundball, which allowed him to keep his ERA low in a league that allowed 4.8 runs per game. Hellweg struggled just as much to throw strikes in his Milwaukee stint, however, and major-league hitters didn't let him off the hook by chasing. His sinker is too powerful and his curveball is too tight to dismiss him, but right now, the calculus is simple: Either learn how to repeat your delivery and start throwing strikes soon or get ready for a career in the bullpen.

Jim Henderson
Born: **10/21/1982** Age: **31**
Bats: **L** Throws: **R** Height: **6' 5"** Weight: **220**
Breakout: **34%** Improve: **64%** Collapse: **27%**
Attrition: **27%** MLB: **22%**

Comparables:
Josh Kinney, Tim Hamulack, Chris Schroder

YEAR	TEAM	LVL	AGE	W	L	SV	G	GS	IP	H	HR	BB	SO	BB9	SO9	GB%	BABIP	WHIP	ERA	FIP	FRA	WARP
2011	HUN	AA	28	4	1	5	22	0	30²	22	4	8	39	2.3	11.4	47%	.250	0.98	2.64	3.53	4.13	0.3
2011	NAS	AAA	28	3	1	0	20	0	30¹	24	4	23	30	6.8	8.9	23%	.235	1.55	5.93	5.89	3.53	0.5
2012	NAS	AAA	29	4	3	15	35	0	48	36	2	22	56	4.1	10.5	35%	.301	1.21	1.69	3.37	3.13	1.3
2012	MIL	MLB	29	1	3	3	36	0	30²	26	1	13	45	3.8	13.2	45%	.357	1.27	3.52	1.99	2.84	0.8
2013	MIL	MLB	30	5	5	28	61	0	60	44	8	24	75	3.6	11.2	29%	.261	1.13	2.70	3.55	3.14	1.0
2014	MIL	MLB	31	3	1	12	49	0	57²	47	6	25	61	3.9	9.6	39%	.289	1.24	3.54	3.84	3.85	0.7

Henderson's fastball (96 mph average velocity) can get him a swinging strike in any count. More importantly, unlike the two-pitch closers Milwaukee has had in the past (think John Axford and Derrick Turnbow), Henderson can throw his slider for a strike almost at will. His 66 percent strike rate was well above the league average. The ability to change speeds in some form is key for a two-pitch reliever, as both Turnbow and Axford discovered when control of their breaking balls (both shaky to begin with) disappeared in their second years as closer. Henderson has that ability, and it should keep him working high-leverage innings for the foreseeable future.

Taylor Jungmann
Born: 12/18/1989 Age: 24
Bats: R Throws: R Height: 6' 6" Weight: 210
Breakout: 43% Improve: 63% Collapse: 23%
Attrition: 81% MLB: 20%

Comparables:
Charlie Leesman, Clayton Richard, Robert Mosebach

YEAR	TEAM	LVL	AGE	W	L	SV	G	GS	IP	H	HR	BB	SO	BB9	SO9	GB%	BABIP	WHIP	ERA	FIP	FRA	WARP
2012	BRV	A+	22	11	6	0	26	26	153	159	7	46	99	2.7	5.8	56%	.308	1.34	3.53	3.81	4.89	0.4
2013	HUN	AA	23	10	10	0	26	26	139¹	117	11	73	82	4.7	5.3	58%	.254	1.36	4.33	4.55	6.48	-1.8
2014	MIL	MLB	24	5	10	0	22	22	120¹	128	16	53	63	4.0	4.7	53%	.298	1.51	5.22	5.44	5.68	-0.9

Jungmann, the club's top pick in 2011, was supposed to be a low-ceiling, high-floor pitcher who could move quickly to bolster Milwaukee's rotation following the exits of Zack Greinke and Shaun Marcum. Instead Double-A stumped him. Jungmann is not and does not ever project to be a strikeout pitcher, as his arsenal—low-90s fastball, curveball, changeup—has groundball ambitions. But his walk rate doubled, and high HBP and wild pitch totals verify he lacks the control to thread fine needles. The Brewers made a clear choice for polish over ceiling with Jungmann, and it backfired. He'll get another chance to solve Double-A in 2014.

Brandon Kintzler
Born: 8/1/1984 Age: 29
Bats: R Throws: R Height: 5' 10" Weight: 185
Breakout: 23% Improve: 45% Collapse: 41%
Attrition: 30% MLB: 75%

Comparables:
Cory Wade, Craig Breslow, Ryan Mattheus

YEAR	TEAM	LVL	AGE	W	L	SV	G	GS	IP	H	HR	BB	SO	BB9	SO9	GB%	BABIP	WHIP	ERA	FIP	FRA	WARP
2011	MIL	MLB	26	1	1	0	9	0	14²	14	3	3	15	1.8	9.2	59%	.250	1.16	3.68	4.22	5.10	-0.1
2012	HUN	AA	27	0	2	9	31	0	35²	35	1	12	20	3.0	5.0	63%	.306	1.32	3.28	3.56	4.96	0.1
2012	NAS	AAA	27	0	1	0	8	0	11²	8	0	2	11	1.5	8.5	70%	.267	0.86	1.54	2.29	3.05	0.3
2012	MIL	MLB	27	3	0	0	14	0	16²	18	1	7	14	3.8	7.6	49%	.354	1.50	3.78	3.50	3.82	0.2
2013	MIL	MLB	28	3	3	0	71	0	77	66	2	16	58	1.9	6.8	59%	.283	1.06	2.69	2.51	3.48	1.1
2014	MIL	MLB	29	3	1	1	58	0	66²	60	6	18	54	2.4	7.3	55%	.297	1.17	3.43	3.64	3.73	0.9

Kintzler is all of the following: former 40th-round pick, elbow surgery survivor, former independent league player and, most importantly, successful relief pitcher. After a bullpen disaster in 2012, the Brewers decided to see if his mid-90s sinker (along with changeup and slider) could play, and lo, it did. The sinker kept the ball in the yard and racked up the strikes while his changeup was one of the best pitches in the majors—it induced 26 percent whiffs (nearly matching Koji Uehara's splitter) and a mere .278 slugging percentage on contact. He took a circuitous route, but the 29-year-old might have shown enough to earn a high-leverage role in 2014.

Kyle Lohse
Born: 10/4/1978 Age: 35
Bats: R Throws: R Height: 6' 2" Weight: 210
Breakout: 21% Improve: 48% Collapse: 19%
Attrition: 11% MLB: 86%

Comparables:
Carl Pavano, Roy Oswalt, Brad Radke

YEAR	TEAM	LVL	AGE	W	L	SV	G	GS	IP	H	HR	BB	SO	BB9	SO9	GB%	BABIP	WHIP	ERA	FIP	FRA	WARP
2011	SLN	MLB	32	14	8	0	30	30	188¹	178	16	42	111	2.0	5.3	42%	.278	1.17	3.39	3.64	4.45	0.6
2012	SLN	MLB	33	16	3	0	33	33	211	192	19	38	143	1.6	6.1	42%	.269	1.09	2.86	3.55	3.98	2.1
2013	MIL	MLB	34	11	10	0	32	32	198²	196	26	36	125	1.6	5.7	41%	.284	1.17	3.35	4.05	4.30	1.4
2014	MIL	MLB	35	8	11	0	28	28	166	166	21	38	107	2.0	5.8	43%	.292	1.23	4.12	4.35	4.48	0.8

There were plenty of reasons Lohse didn't fetch the $45 million-plus contract he was looking for last offseason: his age; his less-than-impressive peripheral statistics; the poor performance of most pitchers who leave St. Louis as free agents. Lost in all that, though, is the fact that Lohse had been one of the best pitchers in baseball the previous two years, and even with some decline he would be worth an eight-figure deal. He was easily that in Milwaukee, as his ability to get hitters out on pitches outside the zone continued to make him an above-average pitcher by ERA. Lohse now ranks 15th among all starters in ERA+ over the past three years, and any warning signs over him are fading.

Santo Manzanillo
Born: 12/20/1988 Age: 25
Bats: R Throws: R Height: 6' 2" Weight: 225
Breakout: 0% Improve: 0% Collapse: 0%
Attrition: 0% MLB: 0%

Comparables:
Marcus McBeth, Frank Mata, Anderson Garcia

YEAR	TEAM	LVL	AGE	W	L	SV	G	GS	IP	H	HR	BB	SO	BB9	SO9	GB%	BABIP	WHIP	ERA	FIP	FRA	WARP
2011	BRV	A+	22	1	0	10	28	0	41¹	31	2	14	43	3.0	9.4	48%	.207	1.09	1.52	3.03	3.26	0.2
2011	HUN	AA	22	0	1	7	20	0	20¹	13	2	12	19	5.3	8.4	37%	.206	1.23	2.21	4.63	4.81	0.1
2012	HUN	AA	23	0	4	1	12	0	13¹	13	2	10	10	6.8	6.8	42%	.289	1.73	6.07	5.84	7.19	-0.3
2013	BRV	A+	24	0	5	2	20	0	29²	32	3	18	16	5.5	4.9	45%	.290	1.69	4.25	5.50	6.98	-0.7
2013	HUN	AA	24	1	3	1	26	0	29	39	3	21	19	6.5	5.9	41%	.372	2.07	7.45	5.33	6.22	-0.5
2014	MIL	MLB	25	1	0	1	33	0	48	54	7	28	27	5.2	5.0	43%	.308	1.70	5.99	5.96	6.51	-0.9

A car crash in November 2011 appears to be the calamitous turning point in Manzanillo's career. The 25-year-old was a tantalizing relief prospect with a fastball capable of touching triple digits. He dominated High-A and Double-A that season and was well on track for a job in Milwaukee's bullpen. Since the crash, however, he simply hasn't been able to find the strike zone. Repeating his delivery was enough of a problem before he was working with a restructured shoulder, and the past two years have been so much of a struggle he has found his way off the 40-man roster.

Chris Narveson
Born: 12/20/1981 Age: 32
Bats: L Throws: L Height: 6' 3" Weight: 205
Breakout: 28% Improve: 56% Collapse: 29%
Attrition: 26% MLB: 56%
Comparables:
Casey Fossum, Tony Armas, Josh Towers

YEAR	TEAM	LVL	AGE	W	L	SV	G	GS	IP	H	HR	BB	SO	BB9	SO9	GB%	BABIP	WHIP	ERA	FIP	FRA	WARP
2011	MIL	MLB	29	11	8	0	30	28	161²	160	17	65	126	3.6	7.0	43%	.297	1.39	4.45	4.03	4.93	0.6
2012	MIL	MLB	30	1	1	0	2	2	9	10	2	4	5	4.0	5.0	42%	.276	1.56	7.00	6.25	7.08	-0.1
2013	NAS	AAA	31	4	7	0	15	15	77	85	9	24	59	2.8	6.9	40%	.314	1.42	5.14	4.57	5.17	0.3
2013	MIL	MLB	31	0	0	0	2	0	2	1	0	1	0	4.5	0.0	57%	.143	1.00	0.00	4.52	4.52	0.0
2014	MIL	MLB	32	3	4	0	11	11	58¹	57	7	20	43	3.0	6.6	41%	.295	1.31	4.32	4.45	4.69	0.2

Twelve pitchers got a shot to join the Brewers' depleted rotation, but fate gave Chris Narveson the middle finger (sprain). He missed 74 games with the injury, then was hammered in 15 Triple-A starts. His soft-tossing arsenal was barely clinging to major-league credibility as it was, and it's unlikely the 31-year-old will find a better chance at a consistent gig than he had, and blew, in 2013.

Jimmy Nelson
Born: 6/5/1989 Age: 25
Bats: R Throws: R Height: 6' 5" Weight: 245
Breakout: 47% Improve: 66% Collapse: 17%
Attrition: 63% MLB: 45%
Comparables:
Chris Carpenter, Justin Wilson, J.D. Durbin

YEAR	TEAM	LVL	AGE	W	L	SV	G	GS	IP	H	HR	BB	SO	BB9	SO9	GB%	BABIP	WHIP	ERA	FIP	FRA	WARP
2011	WIS	A	22	8	9	0	26	25	146	146	9	65	120	4.0	7.4	56%	.305	1.45	4.38	3.98	5.21	-0.3
2012	BRV	A+	23	4	4	0	13	13	81¹	63	3	25	77	2.8	8.5	61%	.273	1.08	2.21	3.09	3.88	1.2
2012	HUN	AA	23	2	4	0	10	10	46	34	2	37	42	7.2	8.2	57%	.258	1.54	3.91	4.49	4.94	0.3
2013	HUN	AA	24	5	4	0	12	12	69	63	5	15	72	2.0	9.4	52%	.324	1.13	2.74	2.81	3.96	0.9
2013	NAS	AAA	24	5	6	0	15	15	83¹	74	2	50	91	5.4	9.8	62%	.333	1.49	3.67	3.64	3.94	1.5
2013	MIL	MLB	24	0	0	0	4	1	10	2	0	5	8	4.5	7.2	42%	.083	0.70	0.90	2.92	3.47	0.1
2014	MIL	MLB	25	6	8	0	28	19	128²	123	14	62	102	4.3	7.1	54%	.301	1.44	4.57	4.68	4.97	-0.1

The highest-profile pitchers from Milwaukee's recent drafts have disappointed, but Nelson was impressive enough in just his third full professional season to breeze through Double-A and Triple-A and earn a cup of coffee in September. Nelson's stuff—four-seam and two-seam fastballs in the mid-90s, a slider and a changeup—ranks (for some scouts) as the best in the Brewers' system. At 6-foot-6, he gets healthy sink on his two-seamer and has the ever-important projectable frame. Nelson is still working on his changeup, a pitch that will be key if he is to succeed against left-handed batters at the major-league level, but his arsenal is promising and could see him to a major-league rotation as soon as 2014.

Michael Olmsted
Born: 5/2/1987 Age: 27
Bats: R Throws: R Height: 6' 6" Weight: 245
Breakout: 8% Improve: 42% Collapse: 35%
Attrition: 46% MLB: 43%
Comparables:
Josh Fields, Brad Salmon, Blake Parker

YEAR	TEAM	LVL	AGE	W	L	SV	G	GS	IP	H	HR	BB	SO	BB9	SO9	GB%	BABIP	WHIP	ERA	FIP	FRA	WARP
2011	GRN	A	24	1	0	4	18	0	28¹	17	0	9	44	2.9	14.0	50%	.375	0.92	1.59	1.59	1.40	0.4
2012	SLM	A+	25	0	2	16	33	0	39¹	25	1	8	61	1.8	14.0	33%	.289	0.84	2.29	1.38	2.03	1.4
2012	PME	AA	25	1	2	3	14	0	20	11	0	7	31	3.2	13.9	39%	.268	0.90	0.00	1.30	2.12	0.7
2013	NAS	AAA	26	1	1	0	49	0	52¹	54	6	40	52	6.9	8.9	44%	.320	1.80	6.71	5.65	4.96	0.2
2014	MIL	MLB	27	2	1	2	49	0	57²	48	6	26	61	4.1	9.6	41%	.300	1.30	3.88	3.95	4.22	0.4

Olmsted was Milwaukee's rehabilitation project in 2013. Despite never throwing a pitch in the major leagues, the Brewers gave him a major-league contract in hopes Olmsted's 6-foot-6, 270-pound frame and mid-90s fastball could turn him into a major league reliever. Instead, he was one of Milwaukee's final cuts off the spring roster and he proceeded to struggle through his worst professional season at Triple-A. His walk rate was double his previous career worst. Brewers manager Ron Roenicke said he was impressed with Olmsted's stuff and deception in spring training, but none of that will be worth anything unless he can reacquaint himself with the strike zone. Time is running out, as Olmsted turns 27 in May.

Wily Peralta
Born: 5/8/1989 Age: 25
Bats: R Throws: R Height: 6' 1" Weight: 245
Breakout: 40% Improve: 66% Collapse: 20%
Attrition: 34% MLB: 85%
Comparables:
Dustin Nippert, John Maine, Derek Thompson

YEAR	TEAM	LVL	AGE	W	L	SV	G	GS	IP	H	HR	BB	SO	BB9	SO9	GB%	BABIP	WHIP	ERA	FIP	FRA	WARP
2011	HUN	AA	22	9	7	0	21	21	119²	106	9	48	117	3.6	8.8	52%	.274	1.29	3.46	3.63	4.13	1.3
2011	NAS	AAA	22	2	0	0	5	5	31	21	0	11	40	3.2	11.6	52%	.290	1.03	2.03	2.36	2.46	1.2
2012	NAS	AAA	23	7	11	0	28	28	146²	154	9	78	143	4.8	8.8	52%	.361	1.58	4.66	4.29	4.62	2.2
2012	MIL	MLB	23	2	1	0	6	5	29	24	0	11	23	3.4	7.1	54%	.324	1.21	2.48	2.69	2.98	0.7
2013	MIL	MLB	24	11	15	0	32	32	183¹	187	19	73	129	3.6	6.3	51%	.302	1.42	4.37	4.27	5.14	0.0
2014	MIL	MLB	25	8	11	0	29	29	156²	149	16	69	126	4.0	7.3	49%	.305	1.39	4.43	4.39	4.82	0.3

The Brewers did not immediately commit a 2013 rotation spot to Peralta, and considering his early-season growing pains, it's easy to see why. The finer points of pitching evaded Peralta in April and May, as he limped to a 6.35 ERA in his first 11 starts. His fastball was electric as ever—consistently 95 or higher, trailing only STephen Strasburg, Jose Fernandez and Matt Harvey among starters—but he lacked trust in his slider, and major leaguers can hit any fastball when they know it's coming. Then, on June 1st, Peralta threw 41 sliders in a seven-inning, two-run start against Philadephia. From then on, Peralta relied more on his slider, a pitch with a sharp 16 percent whiff rate and the one responsible for 73 of his 129 third strikes on the season. Peralta posted a 3.48 ERA and allowed a .683 OPS from June onward, and if he continues to rely on that power slider he will live up to his top-of-the-rotation billing.

Will Smith

Born: 7/10/1989 Age: 24
Bats: R Throws: L Height: 6' 5" Weight: 250
Breakout: 32% Improve: 65% Collapse: 22%
Attrition: 48% MLB: 69%

Comparables:
Hayden Penn, Billy Buckner, Jeanmar Gomez

YEAR	TEAM	LVL	AGE	W	L	SV	G	GS	IP	H	HR	BB	SO	BB9	SO9	GB%	BABIP	WHIP	ERA	FIP	FRA	WARP
2011	NWA	AA	21	13	9	0	27	27	161¹	171	13	45	108	2.5	6.0	44%	.314	1.34	3.85	4.03	4.93	2.2
2012	OMA	AAA	22	4	4	0	15	15	89²	104	8	22	74	2.2	7.4	45%	.340	1.41	3.61	3.98	4.52	1.5
2012	KCA	MLB	22	6	9	0	16	16	89²	111	12	33	59	3.3	5.9	43%	.340	1.61	5.32	4.61	4.95	0.5
2013	OMA	AAA	23	6	4	4	28	10	89	81	7	24	100	2.4	10.1	47%	.325	1.18	3.03	3.26	3.53	1.9
2013	KCA	MLB	23	2	1	0	19	1	33¹	24	6	7	43	1.9	11.6	44%	.243	0.93	3.24	3.56	4.61	0.1
2014	MIL	MLB	24	5	6	2	40	13	117¹	120	16	36	92	2.7	7.0	44%	.310	1.33	4.49	4.43	4.88	0.0

A starter for most of his career until the Royals moved him to the bullpen last summer, Smith took to his new role with aplomb. With a low-90s fastball and last year's most swing-and-missable slider, he struck out 27 of 54 left-handed batters he faced. While that may scream LOOGY, his starter pedigree gives him more utility on a pitching staff. The Royals had him in a multi-inning relief role initially, but as it became apparent that his stuff played up in bursts he was shifted to the final third of games. Kansas City seems to have a knack for finding quality relievers, freeing them to trade Smith in December for Nori Aoki.

Tyler Thornburg

Born: 9/29/1988 Age: 25
Bats: R Throws: R Height: 5' 11" Weight: 190
Breakout: 37% Improve: 66% Collapse: 16%
Attrition: 27% MLB: 89%

Comparables:
James McDonald, Jake Arrieta, Tyson Ross

YEAR	TEAM	LVL	AGE	W	L	SV	G	GS	IP	H	HR	BB	SO	BB9	SO9	GB%	BABIP	WHIP	ERA	FIP	FRA	WARP
2011	WIS	A	22	7	0	0	12	12	68²	49	3	25	76	3.3	10.0	40%	.271	1.08	1.57	2.98	3.83	0.5
2011	BRV	A+	22	3	6	0	12	12	68	45	5	33	84	4.4	11.1	35%	.167	1.15	3.57	3.51	3.47	0.4
2012	HUN	AA	23	8	1	0	13	13	75	57	6	24	71	2.9	8.5	39%	.260	1.08	3.00	3.33	4.37	0.9
2012	NAS	AAA	23	2	3	0	8	8	37²	38	1	13	42	3.1	10.0	53%	.353	1.35	3.58	2.98	3.58	1.0
2012	MIL	MLB	23	0	0	0	8	3	22	24	8	7	20	2.9	8.2	44%	.291	1.41	4.50	7.14	6.43	-0.1
2013	NAS	AAA	24	0	9	0	15	15	74²	90	11	29	87	3.5	10.5	36%	.382	1.59	5.79	4.48	3.92	1.5
2013	MIL	MLB	24	3	1	0	18	7	66²	53	1	26	48	3.5	6.5	36%	.279	1.18	2.03	3.08	3.29	1.3
2014	MIL	MLB	25	6	8	0	30	22	124	112	15	45	114	3.3	8.3	40%	.298	1.27	3.95	4.19	4.29	1.1

Thornburg pitched 23 innings out of the bullpen out of necessity for Milwaukee, but 2013 was more about establishing himself as a contender for a 2014 rotation spot. He took seven turns for Milwaukee and recorded a quality start in each, while allowing just one home run all season despite Milwaukee's homer-friendly fences. Consensus early in Thornburg's career was that his short stature and max-effort delivery would limit him to the bullpen, but after this taste of success, he's shown too much promise to concede a career in relief.

Devin Williams

Born: 9/21/1994 Age: 19
Bats: R Throws: R Height: 6' 3" Weight: 165
Breakout: 0% Improve: 0% Collapse: 0%
Attrition: 0% MLB: 0%

Comparables:
Joe Wieland, Michael Kirkman, Matt Magill

YEAR	TEAM	LVL	AGE	W	L	SV	G	GS	IP	H	HR	BB	SO	BB9	SO9	GB%	BABIP	WHIP	ERA	FIP	FRA	WARP
2014	MIL	MLB	19	1	2	0	12	5	33²	37	5	22	20	5.9	5.3	48%	.312	1.77	6.29	6.21	6.84	-0.6

Williams, the 54th overall pick and (thanks to the Kyle Lohse signing) the Brewers' top choice, signed quickly and pitched in the Arizona League, where he made a quick impression on scouts. He flashed a fastball ranging from 92 to 96 mph and a changeup in the low 80s. He's working on a slider but doesn't have a clear breaking pitch yet. Williams turned 19 within weeks of the season's conclusion, so he'll have plenty of time to develop it, and his 6-foot-3 frame suggests he can add even more bite to his arsenal as he bulks up.

	YEAR	TEAM	LVL	AGE	W	L	SV	G	GS	IP	H	HR	BB	SO	BB9	SO9	GB%	BABIP	WHIP	ERA	FIP	FRA	WARP
Rob Wooten	2011	BRV	A+	25	2	0	1	12	0	21¹	15	0	3	18	1.3	7.6	25%	.167	0.84	2.53	2.12	3.29	0.1
Born: **7/21/1985** Age: **28**	2011	HUN	AA	25	3	3	7	36	0	42²	41	3	15	41	3.2	8.6	38%	.304	1.31	3.38	3.71	4.02	0.4
Bats: **R** Throws: **R** Height: **6' 1"** Weight: **210**	2012	HUN	AA	26	3	0	8	17	0	20²	18	1	7	21	3.0	9.1	46%	.293	1.21	1.74	2.90	2.81	0.5
Breakout: **35%** Improve: **50%** Collapse: **33%**	2012	NAS	AAA	26	0	2	7	40	0	52²	49	4	16	49	2.7	8.4	45%	.304	1.23	3.93	3.82	4.53	0.7
Attrition: **68%** MLB: **31%**	2013	NAS	AAA	27	0	1	20	40	0	52	40	4	12	45	2.1	7.8	45%	.248	1.00	2.94	3.65	3.90	0.7
Comparables:	2013	MIL	MLB	27	3	1	0	27	0	27²	27	1	8	18	2.6	5.9	44%	.299	1.27	3.90	3.17	3.49	0.3
Santiago Ramirez, Carlos Guevara, Carlos Muniz	2014	MIL	MLB	28	3	1	1	57	0	69²	63	8	21	60	2.7	7.8	44%	.294	1.21	3.74	4.02	4.06	0.6

Wooten's 2009 season looked like it would be the one to elevate the former 13th-round pick into "real prospect" status. He allowed a 2.67 ERA with 12 K/9 between High-A and Double-A as a 23-year-old, his second consecutive year with eye-popping strikeout numbers. Tommy John surgery to begin the 2010 season halted Wooten's ascension up the organizational ladder, but he has consistently pitched well since his return and finally earned his first crack at the majors with an excellent season at Triple-A Nashville. Wooten doesn't do anything exceptionally well, but he was at least average in every peripheral statistic in his time with Milwaukee. It's a performance that should give him a good shot at a bullpen job in 2014.

LINEOUTS

HITTERS

PLAYER	TEAM	LVL	AGE	PA	R	2B	3B	HR	RBI	BB	SO	SB-CS	AVG/OBP/SLG	TAv	BABIP	BRR	FRAA	WARP
SS O. Arcia	WIS	A	18	486	67	14	5	4	39	35	40	20-9	.251/.314/.333	.241	.268	1.8	SS(120): 7.3	2.4
C C. Garfield	BRV	A+	22	440	40	20	5	8	48	14	99	1-2	.250/.280/.379	.241	.308	-0.9	C(93): 0.2	0.7
SS H. Gomez	HUN	AA	25	406	23	12	2	2	25	18	77	6-9	.196/.238/.255	.192	.241	-2.9	SS(110): 13.3, 2B(1): -0.0	0.0
1B A. Gonzalez	MIL	MLB	36	118	14	3	0	1	8	3	26	0-0	.177/.203/.230	.158	.218	0.4	1B(22): -0.3, 3B(11): -0.1	-1.0
1B T. Green	MIL	MLB	25	117	8	7	0	3	14	10	24	0-0	.184/.265/.340	.220	.205	-0.8	1B(18): 0.4, 3B(13): -0.1	-0.4
RF S. Halton	NAS	AAA	26	399	51	29	2	11	51	35	92	6-2	.273/.348/.460	.293	.336	0.2	RF(48): 2.4, LF(27): 0.4	2.8
	MIL	MLB	26	111	9	4	0	4	17	5	31	0-0	.238/.291/.396	.233	.299	-1.1	1B(25): 0.1, LF(3): -0.0	-0.3
2B E. Herrera	ABQ	AAA	28	476	69	13	1	7	43	48	76	16-3	.282/.367/.370	.254	.330	2.7	2B(76): 2.4, 3B(20): 0.0	1.6
	LAN	MLB	28	8	0	0	0	0	0	0	2	0-0	.250/.250/.250	.132	.333	-0.1	LF(2): -0.2	-0.1
LF M. Owings	HUN	AA	30	45	3	0	0	1	3	3	17	0-0	.195/.250/.268	.233	.304	0.1	LF(7): 0.3, P(6): 0.1	0.2
	SYR	AAA	30	213	28	13	3	8	31	10	71	2-0	.265/.305/.480	.287	.369	0.5	LF(29): -2.1, RF(2): -0.1	0.6
C M. Pagnozzi	GWN	AAA	30	321	31	10	1	6	31	21	64	0-0	.210/.274/.314	.212	.249	-0.5	C(86): -1.7	-0.2
	HOU	MLB	30	22	1	0	0	0	0	1	3	0-0	.143/.182/.143	.134	.167	-0.3	C(7): -0.1	-0.2
CF J. Prince	NAS	AAA	25	490	68	18	2	11	53	60	105	25-8	.237/.338/.368	.262	.289	2.6	CF(56): -2.5, SS(31): 4.0	2.1
	MIL	MLB	25	9	3	1	0	0	0	1	1	0-0	.125/.222/.250	.135	.143	0.5	LF(2): -0.0, 3B(1): -0.0	0.5
SS Y. Rivera	BRV	A+	21	524	51	16	2	5	37	32	80	13-8	.241/.300/.314	.242	.279	1.4	SS(129): 20.2	3.6
1B J. Rogers	HUN	AA	25	549	69	25	2	22	87	59	86	7-2	.270/.346/.468	.297	.283	-2.4	1B(129): 3.8, LF(2): -0.2	3.1
CF T. Taylor	WIS	A	19	549	69	33	2	8	57	35	63	19-8	.274/.338/.400	.266	.299	2.4	CF(108): 12.2, LF(4): 0.0	3.5
2B E. Velez	NAS	AAA	31	175	23	10	3	2	21	19	25	9-3	.377/.437/.523	.333	.430	0.5	2B(35): -2.9, CF(2): -0.0	1.6
	BUF	AAA	31	259	31	10	3	7	24	35	38	21-5	.270/.372/.437	.280	.299	1.4	LF(39): 0.1, 2B(13): -0.9	0.8

Orlando Arcia continued to show solid discipline and good contact skills after returning from a broken ankle. His glove at shortstop is excellent, so he'll need to develop only moderate power to build a major-league skill set. ⊘ **Cameron Garfield** was finally able to stay on the field, but failed to showcase an upper-level bat. His thoughts on Mondays are unknown. ⊘ In the two years since **Hector Gomez** made it to the show with Colorado, he has a combined .957 OPS. Combined as in summed. ⊘ Nobody knows what caused the **Alex Gonzalez**ae to go extinct after so many years roaming the infield, but scientists trace the final surviving member of the species to June 2013. ⊘ A hip injury cost **Taylor Green** the entire season and a chance to start at first base, but he's still got one or two shots at platoon corner infielder ahead of him. ⊘ Brewers season in a nutshell: Their first basemen, as a group, hit like **Sean Halton**, who was so bad he might never get another shot in the big leagues. ⊘ The speed and defensive versatility of **Elian Herrera** support his candidacy for big-league utilityman, but it's damning that he amassed just eight appearances for a Dodger club that endured as many injuries as a utilityman could possibly voodoo up. ⊘ **Tucker Neuhaus** had to overcome tremendous adversity—injuries and family tragedy—in his final two years of high school, so the Brewers were willing to look past the poor performance that caused him to drop into the second round. ⊘ **Micah Owings** showed big power in his first professional season as a full-time hitter, but the strikeout and walk rates suggest that hitting—like a foreign language or the Internet—is just too hard to learn after 30. ⊘ **Matt Pagnozzi**'s last three years saw him play in the minors for Colorado, Cleveland and Atlanta and the majors for Colorado, Pittsburgh and Houston. This would be an amusing tidbit except for his deadly serious .609 career minor-league OPS. ⊘ Unlike a former Milwaukee Prince, **Josh Prince**'s one tool is speed. His conversion from shortstop to centerfield was inconveniently timed to coincide with Carlos Gomez's breakout and contract extension. ⊘ **Yadiel Rivera** can't hit, but his glove at short ranks as the best in the Brewers' system, and one of the best in the low minors. ⊘ **Jason Rogers** made his Double-A debut as a 25-year-old and won the organization's Player of the Year honors, more because the system is woebegone than because he's got a future. ⊘ Scouts buzz about **Tyrone Taylor**'s tools; now he just needs to bulk up and turn some of those 33 doubles into home runs. ⊘ In 2011, **Eugenio Velez** went 0-for-37, the longest hitless season by a non-pitcher in history. In 2013, he led the PCL in batting. What do you think about that, smart guy?

PITCHERS

PLAYER	TEAM	LVL	AGE	W	L	SV	IP	H	HR	BB	SO	BB9	SO9	GB%	BABIP	WHIP	ERA	FIP	FRA	WARP
N. Bucci	BRV	A+	21	2	2	0	31²	25	3	15	37	4.3	10.5	32%	.278	1.26	1.99	3.99	3.48	0.7
M. De Los Santos	FRI	AA	23	3	2	0	58²	54	8	34	70	5.2	10.7	33%	.311	1.50	5.22	4.41	3.77	0.8
D. Gagnon	BRV	A+	23	3	4	0	45¹	46	2	15	50	3.0	9.9	38%	.346	1.35	5.16	2.73	3.85	0.6
	HUN	AA	23	4	9	0	84	94	12	42	58	4.5	6.2	42%	.325	1.62	5.57	5.14	5.77	-0.5
A. Laffey	NAS	AAA	28	2	5	0	49²	68	5	19	26	3.4	4.7	56%	.346	1.75	7.25	5.40	6.79	-0.5
	ABQ	AAA	28	4	3	0	61	72	12	22	29	3.2	4.3	53%	.289	1.54	5.61	6.41	7.34	-0.3
	TOR	MLB	28	0	0	0	2²	2	0	5	0	16.9	0.0	67%	.222	2.62	6.75	8.70	12.24	-0.1
	NYN	MLB	28	0	0	0	10	16	1	5	9	4.5	8.1	38%	.484	2.10	7.20	4.62	5.14	0.0
A. Pena	HUN	AA	24	8	9	0	142¹	115	17	79	131	5.0	8.3	41%	.263	1.36	3.73	4.33	4.76	0.7
M. Rogers	BRV	A+	27	0	2	0	15	17	0	7	12	4.2	7.2	41%	.347	1.60	3.60	3.04	4.41	0.2
C. Scarpetta	BRV	A+	24	0	5	0	34	37	2	36	25	9.5	6.6	39%	.330	2.15	7.15	5.89	6.47	-0.5

Nicholas Bucci was starting to get exciting before shoulder injuries crept in. Now, he's mostly exciting to Dr. James Andrews, who has spent enough billable hours with Bucci to pay for a new lake house (or a house on the body of water of his choice). ⊘ **Miguel De Los Santos** missed the entire season with visa issues, as Dominican officials haven't been able to verify his identity. He has a big, wild arm with absurd strikeout potential, whoever he is. ⊘ A classic minor-league story: **Drew Gagnon**'s lack of a plus pitch finally caught up to him against Double-A hitters, and his premium walk rate turned pedestrian. ⊘ **Aaron Laffey** puts the "emergency" in emergency starter. ⊘ **Ariel Pena**'s emergence as a prospect turned out to be a blip rather than a breakout, and the final third of the Zack Greinke trade remains stuck in Double-A with control problems. ⊘ **Mark Rogers** spent yet another season hurt and ineffective. The former fifth-overall pick got plenty of chances during his decade in the Brewers' system, but he was finally removed from the 40-man roster in September. ⊘ Poor results aside, **Cody Scarpetta** returning to the mound after Tommy John surgery was a win for both player and system. The real test will come next year.

MANAGER: RON ROENICKE

YEAR	TEAM	W-L	Pythag +/–	Avg PC	100+ P	120+ P	QS	BQS	REL	REL w Zero R	IBB	PH	PH Avg	PH HR	SB2	CS2	SB3	CS3	SAC Att	SAC %	POS SAC	Squeeze	Swing	In Play
2011	MIL	96-66	1	99.3	85	2	98	7	434	342	16	257	.222	5	82	23	12	5	117	72.6%	45	5	297	109
2012	MIL	83-79	1	97.1	84	0	85	3	512	370	20	315	.223	4	134	32	24	5	129	58.9%	45	8	356	90
2013	MIL	74-88	0	91.6	45	0	82	3	501	399	29	265	.210	4	120	40	21	4	106	72.6%	35	10	352	101

Ron Roenicke is the most pro-small-ball manager in the game these days. He loves to move runners over. In his rookie season in 2011, his Brewers finished second in the NL in sacrifice bunts. They also finished runner-up in 2012 and again in 2013. No team has more bunts from 2011 to 2013 than Milwaukee's 238. In that same span, the Brewers rank fourth in stolen base attempts, with 514, behind only the Padres, Royals and Rangers. His teams have always had a nice success rate on the bases, never ranking worse than sixth in the league. Mind you, he's done this despite helming a roster that's more suited to the big inning. In 2011 and 2012 the Brewers posted the highest slugging percentage in the NL, and they were among the highest in 2013. Roenicke isn't always an active manager, though. Twice his Brewers have been in the bottom of the league in issuing intentional walks.

Under Roenicke, the Brewers have surged in the second half like no other team. After stumbling to 127-144 (.469) start before the All-Star game the past three years, Roenicke's teams are 126-89 (.586) after the break. Last year was typical: 38-56 early and 36-32 late.

Minnesota Twins

By Aaron Gleeman

Prospect lists are considered pornography in the state of Minnesota.

Have been for a while now, ever since the Twins' big-league roster finally fell apart following an impressive run of six American League Central titles in nine seasons and the farm system started adding high-upside talent in bunches via top-five draft picks, veteran-for-prospect trades and shrewd, uncharacteristically bold international spending.

Sure, the Twins lost 99, 96 and 96 games during the past three seasons while playing some of the most hideous, unwatchable baseball you'll ever see. And sure, attendance at gorgeous Target Field has already plummeted from nonstop sellouts to Metrodome levels after just four seasons, leading to slashed payrolls. But did you see that Miguel Sano centerfold? Have you read that erotica about Byron Buxton getting down the first base line in 3.9 seconds? Do you realize Alex Meyer's strikeout rate isn't even airbrushed?

Baseball Prospectus' own Jason Parks rates Buxton as the best prospect in the world at age 19—just two years after being drafted no. 2 overall out of a Georgia high school—and calls the Twins' overall farm system the best in baseball. Parks even said—and be warned, this gets disgustingly not-safe-for-work—the Twins have so much depth beyond studs Buxton, Sano, Meyer and 2013 first-round pick Kohl Stewart that if you removed their top 10 prospects they'd *still* have a better all-around farm system than the Angels. Parks' articles are wrapped in black plastic sleeves and distributed only in backrooms here in the Land of 10,000 Lakes.

And luckily for the prospect-list connoisseur there is no shortage of options on those back shelves. Jim Callis and Jonathan Mayo of MLB.com—a filth-mongering duo if ever there was one—rate Buxton and Sano as the no. 1 and no. 3 prospects in baseball, with only Oscar Taveras of the Cardinals in between. They also rank Meyer at 31, Stewart at

61, Eddie Rosario at 63 and 2012 supplemental first-rounder Jose Berrios at 77.

Baseball America also has Buxton ranked as baseball's best prospect and Sano joins him in their top five, which is extremely rare. In fact, only seven times in the past 25 years of *Baseball America* rankings has a team placed two prospects in the top five:

2009: Braves had Tommy Hanson at 4 and Jason Heyward at 5.

2006: Diamondbacks had Justin Upton at 4 and Stephen Drew at 5.

2004: Devil Rays had B.J. Upton at 2 and Delmon Young at 3.

1999: Cardinals had J.D. Drew at 1 and Rick Ankiel at 2.

1998: Dodgers had Paul Konerko at 2 and Adrian Beltre at 3.

1995: Yankees had Ruben Rivera at 2 and Derek Jeter at 4.

1994: Blue Jays had Alex Gonzalez at 4 and Carlos Delgado at 5.

But wait, because here's where my buzzkilling skills come into play: Of those seven pairs of top-five prospect teammates only the Dodgers' duo of Konerko and Beltre both went on to have lengthy, star-caliber careers. Drew and Ankiel for the 1999 Cardinals were both headed to sustained stardom before Ankiel's pitching career imploded suddenly and the 2009 Braves' pair of Hanson and Heyward were briefly both stars before injuries wrecked Hanson.

In general, having two top-five prospects has usually meant ending up with just one star. And in general that's the danger of pinning your hopes and dreams to prospects: Usually they don't work out, or at least they don't work out anywhere near the extent you've been fantasizing. Heck, just go back to 2011 when the Royals' farm system was universally regarded as the best in baseball, and frequently mentioned among the elite farm systems ever. An all-time record of nine Kansas City prospects cracked the top 100

TWINS PROSPECTUS
2013 W-L: 66-96, 4th in AL Central

Pythag	.386	29th	DER	.690	28th
RS/G	3.79	25th	B-Age	28.3	16th
RA/G	4.86	29th	P-Age	28.0	13th
TAv	.257	16th	Salary	$82	21st
BRR	-1.43	18th	M$/MW	$3.94	21st
TAv-P	.280	29th	DL Days	656	6th
FIP	4.26	27th	$ on DL	12%	8th

	Runs	HR/RH	HR/LH	Runs/RH	Runs/LH
Three-Year Park Factors	100	81	87	102	102

Top Hitter WARP	4.62 (Joe Mauer)
Top Pitcher WARP	1.97 (Mike Pelfrey)
Top Prospect	Byron Buxton

that year—including Eric Hosmer, Mike Moustakas and Wil Myers in the top 10—and five Royals prospects were given the maximum five-star rating by then-*Baseball Prospectus* prospect analyst Kevin Goldstein. It was an embarrassment of prospect riches. And yet four years later the Royals are hardly a dominant force in the division, winning 86 games last year after posting losing records in 2011 and 2012. Only one of those many top prospects still looks likely to become a star—and it'll be for the Rays.

Circling back to that silly porn analogy I've foisted upon the otherwise upstanding editors of this book, prospects can be a whole lot of fun to look at and dream on, but they still can't compare to the real thing that is productive big leaguers. And what happens to the Twins' long-term fortunes if, say, only half of their stud prospects turn into actual stud major leaguers? What happens if Buxton proves to be something less than a Willie Mays/Mike Trout hybrid and Sano develops into "only" a really strong power hitter who struggles to post good batting averages or add anything defensively?

Well, then the Twins need to find a way to supplement their young talent with veteran acquisitions and that's where things could get dicey. It'll be awfully tough for the Twins not to build a strong lineup around the Buxton/Sano combo, onbase machine Joe Mauer and last year's top-100 prospect list graduate Oswaldo Arcia, but unfortunately that same type of potential doesn't appear to be there with the pitching staff. Meyer is the only pitching prospect above Single-A who looks even remotely capable of being a top-of-the-rotation starter. Meanwhile, for all the lip service paid to adding hardthrowers the Twins' rotation had MLB's lowest fastball velocity and fewest strikeouts—by a wide margin—in each of the past two seasons.

From 2011 to 2013 the Twins' rotation managed 1,635 strikeouts. Not only was that the lowest total in baseball, no other team had fewer than 1,800, the only other team with fewer than 1,980 played half its games at Coors Field, and six teams had more than 2,500. Not coincidentally, the Twins were also the only team with a rotation ERA above 5.00 in that span. Last season eight pitchers started at least 10 games for the Twins and none of them averaged more than six strikeouts per nine innings. Two seasons ago nine pitchers started at least 10 games for the Twins and only one of them—Francisco Liriano, he of the "pitch to contact" kerfuffle in Minnesota and Comeback Player of the Year award in Pittsburgh—averaged more than six strikeouts per nine.

That's not just a recent trend. Here's a complete list of every Twins pitcher in the past 20 years to start 10 or more games in a season with a strikeout rate of 8.25 or higher per nine innings: Johan Santana, Liriano. That's it. That's the whole list, at a time when strikeouts and velocity are rising to historic levels. At this point there are serious long-term questions about the Twins' capacity to identify, willingness

to invest in and ability to develop hard-throwing starters with strikeout-generating raw stuff; those questions stretch from manager Ron Gardenhire and his longtime pitching coach Rick Anderson to General Manager Terry Ryan and the front office.

To Ryan's credit, he finally made the rotation a priority this offseason after merely dipping his toes into the free agency waters for Kevin Correia and Mike Pelfrey last time around. The Twins finally spent some money, signing Ricky Nolasco and Phil Hughes for a combined $73 million. Within the grand scheme of baseball salaries those are hardly eyepopping numbers, but from 1961 to 2013 the most the Twins spent on an outside free agent was $21 million for three years of Josh Willingham. Similarly, while Hughes and Nolasco have great strikeout rates relative to the Twins' recent starters, among the 79 pitchers who threw at least 400 innings as starters from 2011 to 2013 they ranked just 42nd and 57th in strikeout rate, and 32nd and 56th in average fastball velocity.

Baby steps are still steps.

While they were winning all those division titles the Twins were viewed as a small-payroll marvel doing things "the right way." Scouting and development, promoting from within, consistency on and off the field, pitching and defense. That all started to fall apart when Ryan voluntarily stepped down in October 2007, at a time when the team was facing a ton of key personnel decisions. Little-known assistant Bill Smith replaced him as GM in a prime example of mispromoting from within and was fired four years later, as much for oftcited poor communication skills and botched trades as for the 99 losses produced by a roster decimated by injuries.

Minnesota had gotten so used to winning that hopping right back on track after a one-year blip seemed like a very real possibility. Instead they lost 96 games in 2012 and 96 games in 2013—slicing about $20 million off the payroll each year to fall back into the bottom third of MLB spending—and 2014 doesn't figure to be much prettier. It's easy to blame everything on Smith, who was portrayed as supremely overmatched, and the Twins turned back to the man he replaced to clean up the mess Winston Wolfe-style after Ryan's selfimposed four-year absence.

Smith botched the Johan Santana trade and the Matt Garza-for-Delmon Young trade and the J.J. Hardy trade and the Wilson Ramos-for-Matt Capps trade and any number of other key moves that dug a deeper and deeper hole without the Twins realizing just how far underground they were. However, they also suffered an incredible number of significant injuries to key big leaguers and top prospects alike, which—along with some empty draft classes—caused the once-constant stream of cheap, young talent to dry up completely.

Without a steady influx of high-upside youth the organization's longstanding refusal to spend competitively in free agency left a roster full of replacement-level talent. Ryan was supposed to come in, right the ship and get the machine humming again, but the turnaround has become a much bigger, messier project than initially expected and now the Twins have essentially forced themselves (and their fans) to hold their nose and wait for the cavalry to arrive in waves from the farm system.

It's been seven years and counting since Ryan was at the helm of a winning team. Like the clichè about relationships in which what was once cute or quirky in a partner eventually becomes annoying, the Twins' old-school approach now seems like more of a weakness than a strength. Rightly or wrongly there's a growing sense that they've been left behind the rest of MLB, analytically and monetarily, although this offseason's signings and some recent additions to the team's stathead crew are encouraging.

Ryan frequently insists that he's not worried about the amount of money he has to spend—even leaving about $20 million in approved payroll unused in 2013—and cites the success of low-payroll teams like the A's and Rays. Of course, Oakland and Tampa Bay are at the forefront of analytics and also do things at the margins of team-building like frequent platooning of hitters and defensive shifts that Ryan has somewhat oddly scoffed at as "band-aid" fixes. Low-payroll teams don't win because they have low payrolls, they win in spite of having low payrolls. And in most cases they're able to do that winning because they excel at other keys areas.

When asked recently about his thoughts on platooning hitters, Gardenhire told Mike Berardino of the *St. Paul Pioneer Press*: "I don't recall ever having a platoon. I'm not against it. I'll tell you that. I wouldn't have a problem having a platoon if it fits. If it makes sense numbers-wise and it works, then you go with it." In reality Gardenhire has literally never utilized a righty/lefty platoon for any significant length of time during his 12 seasons at the helm, instead forcing obviously flawed hitters like Jacque Jones, Jason Kubel and Trevor Plouffe into full-time roles in which they flail away against same-sided pitchers. His actions speak much louder than his words.

And for his part, Ryan told Berardino that he's fine with the manager's lack of platooning, saying: "I don't think he likes to platoon players at all. I don't either. Put guys out there that are everyday players, then you don't have to platoon. You're always looking for players that can play 162 games, right? That's what I'm looking for. I don't go out looking for platoon players." Meanwhile, over the past three seasons the Twins have scored the fewest runs in the league while other AL teams like the A's, Rays and Orioles have had a ton of success employing multiple platoons. (Going back even further, some guy named Earl Weaver did okay with it too.)

Not platooning might seem like a small thing, and when viewed individually so might not utilizing modern defensive data for shifts, not spending competitively in free agency, not building a robust analytics department and not focusing on hard-throwing, high-strikeout pitchers. But collectively the Twins' lack of evolution on those issues and more has been frustrating. It's not clear that they're especially interested in many of those areas, let alone capable of excelling at them, and so it's natural to question where exactly their competitive advantages would come from.

The easy answer is scouting and development, just like the old days, and the upcoming wave of potential high-end, impact players means there's finally some reason for hope on the horizon. Aside from Mauer, Arcia, Nolasco, Hughes, Glen Perkins and maybe Aaron Hicks and Brian Dozier, none of the regulars on the 2013 roster can (or at least should) be counted on for 2015 and beyond, which shows just how much of the future is tied to the farm system. But it won't be as easy as just letting all the prospects show up.

Barring some incredibly bad luck with prospects this team is a couple years away from being pretty good again, but whether they have the decision-makers in place to supplement that long-awaited influx of young talent with the proper veteran help and all-around organizational approach remains to be seen. Can the Twins rebuild what they once had, with the same manager and GM, and can they do it using the same methods they did the first time despite the wide-reaching changes that have occurred across baseball since then?

In choosing to bring back Ryan as Smith's replacement and retaining Gardenhire with a multi-year contract following 291 losses in three seasons the Twins have essentially decided to hit "reset" with the same people in place, and relying on the same things that once made them successful. The degree of difficulty across baseball has changed since then and the money being spent is higher than ever, and whether the Twins as currently constructed can offset those differences is a question that supersedes "can Miguel Sano hit a ball so far that even Byron Buxton can't catch it?"

Aaron Gleeman has been blogging about the Twins since 2002 at AaronGleeman.com *and writes about the other 29 teams at* HardballTalk *on* NBCSports.com.

HITTERS

Oswaldo Arcia — RF

Born: 5/9/1991 Age: 23
Bats: L Throws: R Height: 6' 0"
Weight: 220 Breakout: 0%
Improve: 31% Collapse: 2%
Attrition: 13% MLB: 65%

Comparables:
Travis Snider, Anthony Rizzo, Jay Bruce

YEAR	TEAM	LVL	AGE	PA	R	2B	3B	HR	RBI	BB	SO	SB	CS	AVG/OBP/SLG	TAv	BABIP	BRR	FRAA	WARP
2011	BLT	A	20	81	18	8	1	5	18	9	16	2	2	.352/.420/.704	.159	.392	0		-0.1
2011	FTM	A+	20	227	27	14	2	8	32	9	53	1	1	.263/.300/.460	.266	.312	0.6	RF(41): -2.4	0.2
2012	FTM	A+	21	235	22	16	3	7	31	23	45	1	3	.309/.376/.517	.299	.361	0.5	RF(51): -0.1	1.7
2012	NBR	AA	21	299	54	20	5	10	67	28	62	3	2	.328/.398/.557	.344	.392	1.3	RF(55): 1.3, CF(4): -0.1	3.7
2013	ROC	AAA	22	155	25	6	0	10	30	22	37	2	1	.312/.426/.594	.338	.366	-0.7	RF(17): -0.8, LF(2): 0.2	1.4
2013	MIN	MLB	22	378	34	17	2	14	43	23	117	1	2	.251/.304/.430	.267	.336	-1.6	LF(56): 1.9, RF(29): -1.1	0.9
2014	MIN	MLB	23	367	41	17	2	13	48	24	101	1	1	.256/.313/.439	.271	.320	-0.5	RF -1, LF 1	1.1

Arcia spent last season dealing with hand and wrist issues and alternately raking in Triple-A and struggling in Minnesota. They throw ungodly breaking stuff in The Show and the young Venezuelan had difficulty identifying it, continually chasing pitches and whiffing in 31 percent of his big-league plate appearances, compared to his 22 percent career rate in the high minors. He's never been one to draw walks and plays an indifferent corner outfield, but when Arcia connects he can sting the ball to all fields, with the potential for 25 home runs and plenty of doubles at his peak. Only 22 on Opening Day, there's plenty of time for Arcia to improve his pitch recognition, make a bit more contact and grow into a middle-of-the-order force.

Byron Buxton — CF

Born: 12/18/1993 Age: 20
Bats: R Throws: R Height: 6' 2"
Weight: 189 Breakout: 10%
Improve: 18% Collapse: 0%
Attrition: 8% MLB: 22%

Comparables:
Mike Trout, Fernando Martinez, Andrew McCutchen

YEAR	TEAM	LVL	AGE	PA	R	2B	3B	HR	RBI	BB	SO	SB	CS	AVG/OBP/SLG	TAv	BABIP	BRR	FRAA	WARP
2013	CDR	A	19	321	68	15	10	8	55	44	56	32	11	.341/.431/.559	.349	.402	4.6	CF(66): 3.5	5.0
2013	FTM	A+	19	253	41	4	8	4	22	32	49	23	8	.326/.415/.472	.320	.404	5	CF(55): 5.1	3.6
2014	MIN	MLB	20	250	32	8	3	5	21	22	62	11	4	.250/.319/.374	.257	.320	0.9	CF 4, LF 0	1.1

Remember that scene in *Excalibur* where King Arthur, having drunk from the Holy Grail, rides out into battle and the long-dormant and decaying land flowers into Technicolor life behind him? Exchange Buxton for Arthur and Target Field for the British countryside and you've captured the future that reverent scouts have presaged for the young Twins center fielder. The consensus top prospect in the land, Buxton has every tool imaginable—speed, raw power potential, a cannon arm, a plus hit tool and tremendous defensive instincts—and both the surprisingly advanced plate approach and solid makeup to turn them into tremendous production. Buxton dominated the low minors as a 19-year-old in his first full professional season and will take aim at Double-A this year. If he continues to rake against more advanced pitching, he might see big-league action before the season is out. Get your tickets early.

Chris Colabello — 1B

Born: 10/24/1983 Age: 30
Bats: R Throws: R Height: 6' 4"
Weight: 220 Breakout: 2%
Improve: 10% Collapse: 7%
Attrition: 17% MLB: 32%

Comparables:
Jeff Larish, Jason Dubois, Jason Botts

YEAR	TEAM	LVL	AGE	PA	R	2B	3B	HR	RBI	BB	SO	SB	CS	AVG/OBP/SLG	TAv	BABIP	BRR	FRAA	WARP
2012	NBR	AA	28	562	78	37	1	19	98	47	94	0	0	.284/.358/.478	.292	.314	-1	1B(124): 5.7	3.0
2013	ROC	AAA	29	391	58	25	0	24	76	43	89	2	1	.352/.427/.639	.350	.413	-2	1B(67): -1.9, RF(14): -0.5	3.9
2013	MIN	MLB	29	181	14	3	0	7	17	20	58	0	1	.194/.287/.344	.240	.253	-0.9	1B(26): 1.0, RF(11): -0.5	-0.3
2014	MIN	MLB	30	259	30	12	0	10	35	21	64	0	0	.257/.324/.443	.278	.310	-0.5	1B 1, RF -0	0.8

Colabello is a tremendous underdog story. He slogged his way through seven years in the Canadian-American Association while living with his parents and making ends meet as a substitute teacher before signing a minor league contract in 2012, winning the International League MVP award last summer and making his big league debut. Unfortunately, we know how this story ends. Prior to Colabello, the last seven I.L. MVPs (Mauro Gomez, Russ Canzler, Dan Johnson, Shelley Duncan, Jeff Bailey, Mike Hessman and Kevin Witt) were similarly slugging corner-men nearing their thirties, and in the years since they have produced a grand total of 1.5 WARP—almost all of it by Duncan. Dennis Quaid may someday play him in a movie, and he may make the roster as a bench bat, but Colabello is unlikely to provide much help to the retooling Twins.

Brian Dozier — 2B

Born: 5/15/1987 Age: 27
Bats: R Throws: R Height: 5' 11"
Weight: 190 Breakout: 3%
Improve: 45% Collapse: 7%
Attrition: 18% MLB: 83%

Comparables:
Russ Adams, Josh Barfield, Chris Getz

YEAR	TEAM	LVL	AGE	PA	R	2B	3B	HR	RBI	BB	SO	SB	CS	AVG/OBP/SLG	TAv	BABIP	BRR	FRAA	WARP
2011	FTM	A+	24	218	32	11	5	2	22	27	20	13	4	.322/.423/.472	.316	.350	0.8	SS(22): 2.9, 2B(8): 0.5	1.8
2011	NBR	AA	24	351	60	22	7	7	34	28	46	11	7	.318/.384/.502	.303	.357	2.7	SS(45): -6.3, 2B(12): -1.3	1.7
2012	ROC	AAA	25	200	15	11	1	2	17	14	34	3	2	.232/.286/.337	.229	.270	0.2	SS(42): -1.5, 2B(4): -0.8	-0.1
2012	MIN	MLB	25	340	33	11	1	6	33	16	58	9	2	.234/.271/.332	.223	.267	-2	SS(83): 4.2	0.4
2013	MIN	MLB	26	623	72	33	4	18	66	51	120	14	7	.244/.312/.414	.263	.278	3.9	2B(146): 6.4	3.8
2014	MIN	MLB	27	552	66	26	3	11	50	37	101	14	6	.246/.301/.380	.251	.280	0.3	2B 0, SS -1	1.6

After a disastrous turn at shortstop in 2012, Dozier moved to the other side of the infield last year and flourished. He proved to be slick and reliable with the leather, smacked 18 home runs—a club record for second basemen—and gave the Twins their first three-win season from the keystone since Chuck Knoblauch left for the Bronx. Dozier scrapped the hacktastic approach he showed in his rookie campaign and worked deeper counts, upping his walk rate and tattooing his pitch when he finally saw it. Not everything is gravy, however, as he continues to do most of his damage against southpaws—his .232 TAv against same-side pitchers was among the worst in baseball. Still, this was progress, and Dozier may have played his way into Minnesota's long-range plans.

Eduardo Escobar SS

Born: 1/5/1989 Age: 25
Bats: B Throws: R Height: 5' 10"
Weight: 175 Breakout: 4%
Improve: 28% Collapse: 10%
Attrition: 35% MLB: 64%

Comparables:
Omar Quintanilla, Eduardo Nunez, Donovan Solano

YEAR	TEAM	LVL	AGE	PA	R	2B	3B	HR	RBI	BB	SO	SB	CS	AVG/OBP/SLG	TAv	BABIP	BRR	FRAA	WARP
2011	CHR	AAA	22	536	55	23	4	4	49	27	104	13	8	.266/.303/.354	.226	.327	-3.4	SS(84): 1.1, 2B(26): 0.5	-0.2
2011	CHA	MLB	22	7	0	0	0	0	0	0	1	0	0	.286/.286/.286	.195	.333	0	SS(3): 0.1, 2B(2): -0.0	0.0
2012	ROC	AAA	23	151	19	3	3	1	9	8	26	3	1	.217/.259/.304	.206	.259	0.7	3B(17): -3.5, SS(10): -1.0	-0.8
2012	CHA	MLB	23	97	14	4	1	0	3	9	23	2	0	.207/.281/.276	.207	.281	0.6	3B(22): 0.4, 2B(6): -0.4	-0.2
2012	MIN	MLB	23	49	4	0	0	0	6	2	8	1	0	.227/.271/.227	.190	.270	0.1	2B(8): 0.6, SS(6): 0.4	-0.1
2013	ROC	AAA	24	188	22	16	2	4	27	17	37	6	2	.307/.380/.500	.290	.373	0.1	SS(29): -0.2, 3B(6): 0.4	1.7
2013	MIN	MLB	24	179	23	5	2	3	10	11	34	0	2	.236/.282/.345	.241	.279	-2	SS(38): -0.8, 3B(23): -2.1	-0.3
2014	MIN	MLB	25	250	23	11	2	2	21	13	49	4	2	.244/.286/.340	.230	.290	0	SS 1, 3B -2	-0.1

Making solid contact against professional pitching requires incredible skill, and the number of people on earth capable of doing so better than Escobar is a statistical insignificance. He should be proud of that. Unfortunately, when you place Escobar in the context of men competing for jobs in a major league infield, his .280 career on-base percentage paints him as a liability. His defensive chops will still find him work as a futility infielder, but the more familiar a club grows with his bat, the less special his glove seems.

Pedro Florimon Jr. SS

Born: 12/10/1986 Age: 27
Bats: B Throws: R Height: 6' 2"
Weight: 180 Breakout: 18%
Improve: 31% Collapse: 11%
Attrition: 27% MLB: 64%

Comparables:
Brent Lillibridge, Reid Brignac, Jason Donald

YEAR	TEAM	LVL	AGE	PA	R	2B	3B	HR	RBI	BB	SO	SB	CS	AVG/OBP/SLG	TAv	BABIP	BRR	FRAA	WARP
2011	BOW	AA	24	520	53	27	4	8	60	51	114	15	12	.267/.344/.396	.292	.336	-2.2	SS(114): 8.7, CF(1): 0.0	4.4
2011	BAL	MLB	24	10	1	1	0	0	2	1	6	0	0	.125/.222/.250	.228	.500	0.1	SS(4): 0.1	0.1
2012	NBR	AA	25	127	11	4	0	2	8	11	28	7	1	.283/.347/.372	.256	.361	0.7	SS(30): 3.7	1.0
2012	ROC	AAA	25	345	38	16	2	3	27	23	89	6	7	.251/.308/.344	.229	.341	3.6	SS(83): 7.9	1.3
2012	MIN	MLB	25	150	16	5	2	1	10	10	30	3	1	.219/.272/.307	.215	.274	1.7	SS(43): 0.7	0.1
2013	MIN	MLB	26	446	44	17	0	9	44	33	115	15	6	.221/.281/.330	.227	.284	2.7	SS(133): 7.0	1.3
2014	MIN	MLB	27	416	43	17	2	6	35	29	104	10	5	.234/.291/.337	.229	.300	-0.1	SS 4, 2B -0	1.0

If you were to take Eduardo Escobar, stretch him out a few inches, inject some home run juice into his bat and insert an extra ring or two under his bark, you'd wind up with Florimon. Of course, only a twisted Bond-villain archetype would actually order such a bizarre and painful transformation, and even if said Bond-villain archetype owned your favorite team (we're looking at you, South Florida), it wouldn't get them much closer to a championship. Florimon is smooth and rangy with a little pop, but unless he starts channeling Alex Gonzalez and launching 15 to 20 home runs annually, he makes far too many outs to be a viable starting shortstop for a team that wants to compete.

Chris Herrmann C

Born: 11/24/1987 Age: 26
Bats: L Throws: R Height: 6' 0"
Weight: 200 Breakout: 0%
Improve: 6% Collapse: 15%
Attrition: 15% MLB: 28%

Comparables:
Curtis Thigpen, Guillermo Quiroz, Eric Fryer

YEAR	TEAM	LVL	AGE	PA	R	2B	3B	HR	RBI	BB	SO	SB	CS	AVG/OBP/SLG	TAv	BABIP	BRR	FRAA	WARP
2011	FTM	A+	23	106	14	5	1	1	16	15	6	1	0	.310/.404/.425	.342	.317	-1.3	LF(8): -1.0, C(3): -0.1	0.6
2011	NBR	AA	23	406	53	14	5	7	46	64	68	9	3	.258/.380/.392	.291	.305	0.2	C(45): -0.4, LF(17): 0.4	2.0
2012	NBR	AA	24	558	91	25	1	10	61	58	89	2	1	.276/.350/.392	.272	.315	2.1	C(83): 0.4, LF(27): -1.0	2.9
2012	MIN	MLB	24	19	0	0	0	0	1	1	5	0	0	.056/.105/.056	.073	.077	0	C(3): -0.0, LF(2): -0.1	-0.4
2013	ROC	AAA	25	275	31	9	3	2	22	24	61	3	2	.227/.297/.312	.225	.292	1.2	C(40): 1.9, LF(18): -1.1	0.1
2013	MIN	MLB	25	178	16	7	0	4	18	18	49	0	1	.204/.286/.325	.218	.269	1.3	C(27): 0.2, RF(21): -2.0	-0.2
2014	MIN	MLB	26	250	26	9	1	4	20	23	54	1	0	.230/.301/.332	.237	.280	-0.2	C 0, LF -0	0.2

The versatile Herrmann spent his first extended time in the big leagues last summer, yet struggled through the least productive season of his career. He's never been a top prospect, but his discerning eye, lefty gap power and ability to catch as well as play an outfield corner gave him the luster of an intriguing utility option. Solid behind the plate, Herrmann uses his strong arm and quick release to gun down runners at a high rate, but last year he mysteriously stopped making contact or drawing walks and saw his on-base percentage plummet. The Twins are looking for someone to caddy for Josmil Pinto, and if Herrmann can rediscover the patience of his youth, he could be less of an automatic out than your typical backup backstop.

Aaron Hicks　CF

Born: 10/2/1989 Age: 24
Bats: B Throws: R Height: 6' 2"
Weight: 190 Breakout: 7%
Improve: 28% Collapse: 7%
Attrition: 17% MLB: 44%

Comparables:
Jordan Schafer, Franklin Gutierrez, Felix Pie

YEAR	TEAM	LVL	AGE	PA	R	2B	3B	HR	RBI	BB	SO	SB	CS	AVG/OBP/SLG	TAv	BABIP	BRR	FRAA	WARP
2011	FTM	A+	21	528	79	31	5	5	38	78	110	17	9	.242/.354/.368	.243	.308	5.1	CF(86): 9.4	2.6
2012	NBR	AA	22	563	100	21	11	13	61	79	116	32	11	.286/.384/.460	.301	.348	8.7	CF(114): 3.3, LF(3): 0.2	5.3
2013	ROC	AAA	23	82	7	4	2	0	5	10	21	1	0	.222/.317/.333	.242	.314	0.2	CF(19): 0.3	0.1
2013	MIN	MLB	23	313	37	11	3	8	27	24	84	9	3	.192/.259/.338	.237	.241	1.1	CF(81): 2.3	0.6
2014	MIN	MLB	24	311	37	11	3	6	26	31	78	9	3	.222/.301/.349	.240	.280	0.8	CF 2, LF 0	0.6

Spring training statistics tend to possess all the predictive powers of a blindfold and a dartboard, yet last March the Twins saw fit to anoint the rookie Hicks, who'd never played above Double-A, their starting center fielder and leadoff hitter based on a few good weeks in Florida. Oops. The former top pick got off to a nightmarish 2-for-56 start and never heard his wake-up call, struggling through injuries, demotions and continuing impotence at the plate during his Triple-A stays. It's tempting to write off last year as a one-off, the unfortunate byproduct of an unready prospect wilting under the bright lights, and buy low on Hicks as a post-hype sleeper. However, Hicks has always been longer on tools than production—his power has never developed and his strikeout rate will always keep his batting average low. A stellar defensive outfielder with speed, a cannon arm and on-base ability might be a valuable player, but with each passing year Hicks looks more and more like a sidekick, not a star.

Max Kepler　CF

Born: 2/10/1993 Age: 21
Bats: L Throws: L Height: 6' 4"
Weight: 180 Breakout: 0%
Improve: 0% Collapse: 0%
Attrition: 0% MLB: 0%

Comparables:
Josmil Pinto, Nick Evans, Thomas Neal

YEAR	TEAM	LVL	AGE	PA	R	2B	3B	HR	RBI	BB	SO	SB	CS	AVG/OBP/SLG	TAv	BABIP	BRR	FRAA	WARP
2013	CDR	A	20	263	35	11	3	9	40	24	43	2	0	.237/.312/.424	.268	.254	-1.4	1B(24): -1.4, LF(15): 2.2	0.8
2014	MIN	MLB	21	250	22	9	1	6	26	15	58	0	0	.216/.265/.339	.224	.260	-0.2	CF 0, LF 1	-0.3

The German-born Kepler missed half a season recovering from elbow surgery; the after-effects showed up in his lackluster numbers during his first taste of Low-A. Signed as a 16-year-old with the highest bonus ever paid to a European player, Kepler has grown into a slugger's frame and has raw power potential, a surprisingly mature approach, good contact skills and plus makeup. He's not a gifted defender, as his arm limits him to left field or first base, so the offensive bar Kepler will need to clear is high. Still only 20, the Twins think enough of his future to stash him on the 40-man roster. Ask again later.

Jason Kubel　LF

Born: 5/25/1982 Age: 32
Bats: L Throws: R Height: 6' 0"
Weight: 220 Breakout: 2%
Improve: 28% Collapse: 3%
Attrition: 14% MLB: 94%

Comparables:
Roy Sievers, Cliff Floyd, Charlie Maxwell

YEAR	TEAM	LVL	AGE	PA	R	2B	3B	HR	RBI	BB	SO	SB	CS	AVG/OBP/SLG	TAv	BABIP	BRR	FRAA	WARP
2011	ROC	AAA	29	21	3	1	0	1	2	3	4	0	0	.333/.429/.556	.306	.385	0	RF(3): 0.0	0.2
2011	MIN	MLB	29	401	37	21	1	12	58	32	86	1	1	.273/.332/.434	.270	.326	-2	RF(50): -1.8, LF(9): -0.3	0.7
2012	ARI	MLB	30	571	75	30	4	30	90	57	151	1	1	.253/.327/.506	.287	.296	-5.4	LF(124): -11.7, RF(2): -0.0	1.2
2013	CLE	MLB	31	23	0	1	0	0	0	5	10	0	0	.167/.348/.222	.212	.375	-0.1	RF(3): 0.1, LF(3): 0.0	-0.1
2013	ARI	MLB	31	267	21	8	1	5	32	24	82	0	1	.220/.288/.324	.226	.308	-3	LF(53): -3.9, RF(5): -0.4	-1.5
2014	MIN	MLB	32	328	37	15	1	12	43	30	77	1	1	.253/.322/.430	.271	.300	-0.6	LF -4, RF -0	0.6

Kubel's value can more or less be summarized by, and in relation to, his career .483 slugging against right-handed pitching. That this number plummeted to .338 last year explains why he was designated for assignment by the Diamondbacks and his former team picked up much of the tab when he was sent to Cleveland in late August. His career has been marred by injuries, and while he refused to blame his struggles last year on numerous aches (back, quad) and pains (knee, quad again), it was obvious they weren't helping him as the season wore on and his stroke broke down. It's always a crapshoot to invest in injury-prone players, but Kubel is only one year removed from a 30-homer season, so the Twins took the chance that their doctors can work miracles.

Darin Mastroianni　LF

Born: 8/26/1985 Age: 28
Bats: R Throws: R Height: 5' 11"
Weight: 190 Breakout: 14%
Improve: 31% Collapse: 10%
Attrition: 27% MLB: 48%

Comparables:
Quintin Berry, Choo Freeman, Jerry Owens

YEAR	TEAM	LVL	AGE	PA	R	2B	3B	HR	RBI	BB	SO	SB	CS	AVG/OBP/SLG	TAv	BABIP	BRR	FRAA	WARP
2011	NHP	AA	25	198	29	8	3	1	13	22	24	14	3	.254/.342/.355	.223	.286	0.8	LF(14): 0.9	0.1
2011	LVG	AAA	25	364	63	18	6	2	23	40	54	20	7	.276/.358/.389	.264	.327	0.8	CF(52): -0.0, LF(7): 0.0	1.3
2011	TOR	MLB	25	3	0	0	0	0	0	0	1	0	0	.000/.000/.000	.103	.000	0	CF(1): -0.0	0.0
2012	NBR	AA	26	40	6	1	0	0	0	4	11	4	1	.143/.231/.171	.176	.208	-0.1	LF(8): -0.2, CF(1): 0.0	-0.3
2012	ROC	AAA	26	85	10	2	2	0	11	5	14	10	1	.346/.393/.423	.305	.422	1.8	LF(15): -0.3, 2B(5): 0.4	0.9
2012	MIN	MLB	26	186	22	3	2	3	17	18	45	21	3	.252/.328/.350	.251	.328	0.9	RF(34): 1.2, LF(25): -0.0	0.5
2013	ROC	AAA	27	63	9	1	0	0	5	10	11	4	0	.240/.397/.260	.282	.308	1.3	CF(11): -0.7, LF(3): -0.3	0.3
2013	MIN	MLB	27	73	5	2	0	0	5	3	23	2	1	.185/.229/.215	.178	.279	-0.1	LF(19): 0.1, RF(9): 0.2	-0.6
2014	MIN	MLB	28	250	31	9	2	1	15	21	55	18	4	.235/.306/.308	.235	.300	2.2	LF -0, RF 1	0.2

A slappy fourth outfielder type, Mastroianni lost most of last season to a stress fracture in his ankle but should be healthy in time for spring training. His numbers last year were also fractured, but when he's right Mastroianni grinds through every at-bat, makes contact, draws walks and is a threat on the basepaths. In the field he's everything Oswaldo Arcia and Josh Willingham aren't, so look for him to finish a lot more games than he starts, assuming he gets back to the majors at all after being outrighted off the 40-man in December.

Joe Mauer   1B

Born: 4/19/1983 Age: **31**
Bats: **L** Throws: **R** Height: **6' 5"**
Weight: **230** Breakout: **0%**
Improve: **40%** Collapse: **1%**
Attrition: **3%** MLB: **98%**

Comparables:
Ted Simmons, Victor Martinez, Kent Hrbek

YEAR	TEAM	LVL	AGE	PA	R	2B	3B	HR	RBI	BB	SO	SB	CS	AVG/OBP/SLG	TAv	BABIP	BRR	FRAA	WARP
2011	FTM	A+	28	27	3	2	0	1	6	3	1	0	0	.261/.370/.478	.289	.238	0.2	C(6): 0.2	0.3
2011	MIN	MLB	28	333	38	15	0	3	30	32	38	0	0	.287/.360/.368	.263	.319	-1.4	C(52): -0.3, 1B(18): 2.5	1.4
2012	MIN	MLB	29	641	81	31	4	10	85	90	88	8	4	.319/.416/.446	.296	.364	-2.1	C(74): -1.7, 1B(30): -2.2	3.1
2013	MIN	MLB	30	508	62	35	0	11	47	61	89	0	1	.324/.404/.476	.315	.383	-0.5	C(75): -0.2, 1B(8): 0.0	4.6
2014	MIN	MLB	31	504	59	28	1	10	59	58	67	3	2	.312/.393/.448	.306	.350	-1.1	1B 2, C -0	3.0

Much like Brian Wilson's *Smile* or Axl Rose's *Chinese Democracy*, fans have been expecting the release of Joe Mauer's *Pickin' Machine!* for a long time, and started discussing its merits long before it officially dropped. Moving Mauer to first base theoretically costs the Twins some short-term value, as his bat is historically potent for a backstop but merely very, very good for a first sacker, in exchange for better health, greater longevity and a higher total return on the five years and $115 million remaining on his contract. Then again, if Josmil Pinto is ready right now and if the Twins let him start over Kurt Suzuki, the short-term cost might not be that high.

If moving him out from behind the dish means Mauer will stay in the lineup, get more at-bats and produce at his current level deeper into his career, this should work out—though it must be noted that Minnesota's last star first baseman had his career derailed by concussion, so health is never guaranteed. Mauer remains one of the best pure hitters of his generation, with a career on-base percentage over .400 and a .324 batting average that leads current players and is a rounding error away from Joe DiMaggio's career mark. The longer we get to watch him play, the better.

Chris Parmelee   1B

Born: 2/24/1988 Age: **26**
Bats: **L** Throws: **L** Height: **6' 1"**
Weight: **220** Breakout: **5%**
Improve: **42%** Collapse: **10%**
Attrition: **17%** MLB: **80%**

Comparables:
Shin-Soo Choo, Lucas Duda, John Bowker

YEAR	TEAM	LVL	AGE	PA	R	2B	3B	HR	RBI	BB	SO	SB	CS	AVG/OBP/SLG	TAv	BABIP	BRR	FRAA	WARP
2011	NBR	AA	23	610	76	30	5	13	83	68	94	0	1	.287/.366/.436	.318	.322	-0.6	1B(84): 2.5, RF(18): -0.4	3.7
2011	MIN	MLB	23	88	8	6	0	4	14	12	13	0	0	.355/.443/.592	.354	.390	-0.3	1B(20): 1.6	1.0
2012	ROC	AAA	24	282	45	17	1	17	49	51	52	1	1	.338/.457/.645	.382	.373	-2.7	1B(62): 7.3	4.7
2012	MIN	MLB	24	210	18	10	2	5	19	13	52	0	0	.229/.290/.380	.232	.287	-0.7	1B(38): 0.1, RF(18): -0.6	-0.4
2013	ROC	AAA	25	198	23	13	1	3	22	22	32	1	0	.231/.318/.370	.253	.264	-1.5	1B(28): 1.5, RF(18): -0.1	0.0
2013	MIN	MLB	25	333	21	13	0	8	24	33	81	1	1	.228/.309/.354	.244	.284	-5.4	RF(68): -6.9, 1B(23): -1.3	-1.1
2014	MIN	MLB	26	352	38	17	2	10	42	34	74	0	0	.259/.334/.415	.273	.310	-0.5	1B 2, RF -2	1.0

Parmelee's sub-replacement WARP was the lowest of any Twins player last year, and now that he's reached his mid-twenties and crossed the 500 at-bat plateau, it's fair to wonder whether he's destined to be a 4-A slugger. The former first-round pick has posted a .292/.400/.526 line during two seasons in Rochester, but big-league hurlers have treated his bat like Swiss cheese, striking him out in nearly a quarter of his plate appearances. Now that The Franchise has moved to first base, Parmelee's best shot at playing time is in an outfield corner, but his glacial footspeed makes him a liability. Given Minnesota's top-shelf talent in the lower minors, Parmelee's window for carving out a role is in danger of slamming shut.

Josmil Pinto   C

Born: 3/31/1989 Age: **25**
Bats: **R** Throws: **R** Height: **5' 11"**
Weight: **210** Breakout: **4%**
Improve: **30%** Collapse: **7%**
Attrition: **31%** MLB: **58%**

Comparables:
Geovany Soto, Josh Donaldson, Ryan Lavarnway

YEAR	TEAM	LVL	AGE	PA	R	2B	3B	HR	RBI	BB	SO	SB	CS	AVG/OBP/SLG	TAv	BABIP	BRR	FRAA	WARP
2011	BLT	A	22	36	4	3	0	1	9	2	10	0	0	.250/.278/.438	.007	.304	0	C(1): -0.0	-0.1
2011	FTM	A+	22	236	21	11	1	5	32	12	36	1	0	.262/.305/.389	.240	.293	-1.6	C(31): -0.6	-0.1
2012	FTM	A+	23	393	45	22	2	12	51	39	63	0	0	.295/.361/.473	.285	.326	-2.5	C(56): 0.1	2.4
2012	NBR	AA	23	52	8	4	1	2	9	4	10	0	0	.298/.365/.553	.321	.343	0.2	C(2): -0.0	0.4
2013	NBR	AA	24	453	59	23	1	14	68	64	71	0	2	.308/.411/.482	.320	.349	-1.5	C(60): 0.0	3.9
2013	ROC	AAA	24	75	6	9	0	1	6	2	12	0	0	.314/.333/.486	.248	.356	-1.3	C(14): -0.3	0.1
2013	MIN	MLB	24	83	10	5	0	4	12	6	22	0	0	.342/.398/.566	.337	.440	-0.4	C(20): -0.2	1.1
2014	MIN	MLB	25	250	26	12	1	7	30	20	51	0	0	.264/.324/.417	.269	.310	-0.5	C -0	1.0

Pinto blazed from Double-A to the majors with a bullet last season, and now that Joe Mauer is moving to first base, Pinto looks set to take over behind the dish. A bat-first receiver with a good approach who consistently hits for high averages and shows developing power, Pinto walked almost as much as he whiffed during his breakout Double-A season and wasn't intimidated in his brief Twin Cities cameo. Pinto has a strong arm and may look like a Molina behind the plate compared to Ryan Doumit, but his defense is still a work in progress. He'll never match Mauer's virtuosity, but if Pinto can get better at smothering 58-foot curveballs and learn to call a better game, he'll be adequate. He's no Johnny Bench, but a catcher capable of hitting .280 with a solid OBP and 15-20 bombs is quite an asset.

Trevor Plouffe 3B

Born: 6/15/1986 Age: 28
Bats: R Throws: R Height: 6' 2"
Weight: 205 Breakout: 4%
Improve: 44% Collapse: 15%
Attrition: 19% MLB: 90%

Comparables:
Jayson Nix, Casey McGehee, Chris Johnson

YEAR	TEAM	LVL	AGE	PA	R	2B	3B	HR	RBI	BB	SO	SB	CS	AVG/OBP/SLG	TAv	BABIP	BRR	FRAA	WARP
2011	ROC	AAA	25	220	33	11	3	15	33	21	39	3	1	.312/.384/.635	.327	.319	-1.8	SS(26): 5.6, 2B(9): -1.1	2.7
2011	MIN	MLB	25	320	47	18	1	8	31	25	71	3	3	.238/.305/.392	.256	.286	-0.7	SS(45): -5.9, 2B(17): -1.3	0.3
2012	MIN	MLB	26	465	56	19	1	24	55	37	92	1	3	.235/.301/.455	.260	.244	-2.6	3B(95): -2.7, RF(15): -0.7	0.4
2013	MIN	MLB	27	522	44	22	1	14	52	34	112	2	1	.254/.309/.392	.261	.301	-0.4	3B(120): -13.7, 1B(2): -0.0	0.1
2014	MIN	MLB	28	483	53	21	2	17	61	33	104	3	2	.242/.301/.414	.260	.280	-0.9	3B -7, SS -0	0.3

Plouffe has spent most of the last two years as Minnesota's primary third baseman, but with the Twins' farm system about to serve up a cornucopia of top-shelf talent, he'd best not get used to seeing his name in the lineup every day. The former first round pick can launch the occasional bomb, but outside of one productive month in 2012, Plouffe has essentially been a replacement-level player. His high strikeout rate keeps his batting average low, he rarely walks and he can barely keep his glove above Miguel Cabrera level. While Plouffe generally picks on lefties, he's posted a wince-inducing .227/.284/.382 line against same-side pitching in his career. Drafted as a shortstop, Plouffe's defensive versatility may allow him to stick as a utility bat after Sano settles in at the hot corner, but nothing more.

Alex Presley LF

Born: 7/25/1985 Age: 28
Bats: L Throws: L Height: 5' 10"
Weight: 190 Breakout: 5%
Improve: 39% Collapse: 16%
Attrition: 29% MLB: 75%

Comparables:
Ryan Spilborghs, Chris Denorfia, Alejandro De Aza

YEAR	TEAM	LVL	AGE	PA	R	2B	3B	HR	RBI	BB	SO	SB	CS	AVG/OBP/SLG	TAv	BABIP	BRR	FRAA	WARP
2011	IND	AAA	25	376	58	18	5	8	41	28	54	22	8	.333/.388/.485	.296	.376	1.4	LF(57): 3.6, CF(18): 0.9	2.9
2011	PIT	MLB	25	231	27	12	6	4	20	13	40	9	3	.298/.339/.465	.283	.349	0.8	LF(48): -3.7, CF(5): -0.3	0.7
2012	IND	AAA	26	179	24	3	4	5	22	24	26	7	2	.307/.399/.477	.299	.341	0.1	CF(22): 0.0, LF(16): -0.1	1.3
2012	PIT	MLB	26	370	46	14	7	10	25	18	72	9	7	.237/.279/.405	.246	.273	3.1	LF(81): 2.6, RF(8): -0.5	0.7
2013	IND	AAA	27	391	57	17	6	5	27	40	56	17	6	.298/.376/.427	.281	.343	3.1	CF(80): -6.9, LF(2): 0.4	1.7
2013	MIN	MLB	27	122	9	4	1	1	11	8	21	1	3	.283/.336/.363	.266	.341	1.1	CF(28): 0.5	0.6
2013	PIT	MLB	27	73	8	1	1	2	4	1	18	0	1	.264/.274/.389	.246	.327	-0.7	LF(12): 0.6, RF(12): -0.3	0.0
2014	MIN	MLB	28	298	37	12	4	6	28	18	53	8	4	.278/.326/.416	.270	.320	0.4	LF 0, CF -1	1.0

Presley came to Minnesota in the Justin Morneau trade and provided an immediate upgrade in center field, which tells you all you need to know about the struggling Aaron Hicks and the fungible Clete Thomas. A lefty grinder with marginal range for center and marginal power for a corner, Presley boasts a career .309/.377/.460 Triple-A line, but when he travels to the bigs he leaves his bat at home lest the TSA confiscate it. Sometimes players like this turn into Jon Jay, but more likely Presley serves as a marginally competent short-term bridge to Byron Buxton.

Eddie Rosario 2B

Born: 9/28/1991 Age: 22
Bats: L Throws: R Height: 6' 0"
Weight: 170 Breakout: 3%
Improve: 16% Collapse: 8%
Attrition: 21% MLB: 30%

Comparables:
Travis Denker, Corban Joseph, Luis Valbuena

YEAR	TEAM	LVL	AGE	PA	R	2B	3B	HR	RBI	BB	SO	SB	CS	AVG/OBP/SLG	TAv	BABIP	BRR	FRAA	WARP
2012	BLT	A	20	429	60	32	4	12	70	31	69	11	11	.296/.345/.490	.296	.329	0.2	2B(67): -0.3, CF(19): -0.2	3.2
2013	FTM	A+	21	231	40	13	5	6	35	17	29	3	6	.329/.377/.527	.317	.350	-2.5	2B(50): 8.9	2.9
2013	NBR	AA	21	313	40	19	3	4	38	21	67	7	4	.284/.330/.412	.269	.355	-1	2B(65): -5.8	0.6
2014	MIN	MLB	22	250	24	12	2	5	26	11	56	3	2	.251/.286/.382	.242	.300	-0.4	2B -0, CF 0	0.3

Anyone who pays attention to the Twins knows that Rosario can hit. After all, this is the kid who out-slugged *Miguel Freakin' Sano* when they were Appy League teammates. Rosario spent last summer lashing gappers all over the Florida State League and worked his way up to Double-A, once again looking for all the world like a future top-of-the-order fixture. The big question is where he'll play defensively. He's made some progress at the keystone, but opinions are mixed on whether he can play there in the bigs, and the 50-game drug of abuse suspension he'll serve to begin the season will eat into his precious game-day reps. If Rosario has to drop down the defensive spectrum, his offensive profile will drop with it, from "special" to "ordinary-plus."

Miguel Sano 3B

Born: 5/11/1993 Age: 21
Bats: R Throws: R Height: 6' 3"
Weight: 195 Breakout: 7%
Improve: 23% Collapse: 1%
Attrition: 8% MLB: 34%

Comparables:
Giancarlo Stanton, Jay Bruce, Colby Rasmus

YEAR	TEAM	LVL	AGE	PA	R	2B	3B	HR	RBI	BB	SO	SB	CS	AVG/OBP/SLG	TAv	BABIP	BRR	FRAA	WARP
2012	BLT	A	19	553	75	28	4	28	100	80	144	8	3	.258/.373/.521	.305	.307	1.9	3B(125): -2.9, 1B(1): -0.1	4.4
2013	FTM	A+	20	243	51	15	2	16	48	29	61	9	2	.330/.424/.655	.366	.397	2.8	3B(56): -1.4	3.6
2013	NBR	AA	20	276	35	15	3	19	55	36	81	2	1	.236/.344/.571	.312	.265	-0.9	3B(64): 2.8	2.4
2014	MIN	MLB	21	250	32	10	1	13	38	25	79	1	0	.229/.312/.461	.274	.290	-0.2	3B -1, SS -0	0.9

Minor league pitchers were lobbying last year to have Sano's bat X-rayed, not because they expected to find cork or Super Balls, but a miniaturized Arc Reactor. Sano spent the second half of last season as a 20-year-old in Double-A and managed to launch 19 of his 35 bombs there, proving once again he is the most exciting power prospect in the game. Advanced pitchers did manage to find a few holes in his swing, as his already-high strikeout rate climbed to near 30 percent and his batting average dropped below .240. Contact will likely always be an issue for him, but Sano's willingness to take a walk when pitchers nibble outside the zone should keep his on-base percentage high. He's no Gold Glover, but he's improved in the field and most scouts expect he'll be adequate at the hot corner for at least a few years. If Sano can continue to adapt as he moves up the ladder, the Twins can eventually expect .250/.340/.550 lines out of their clean-up spot, with the potential for even more.

Daniel Santana SS

Born: 11/7/1990 Age: 23
Bats: B Throws: R Height: 5' 11"
Weight: 173 Breakout: 8%
Improve: 33% Collapse: 6%
Attrition: 28% MLB: 44%

Comparables:
Eduardo Nunez, Adeiny Hechavarria, Hector Gomez

YEAR	TEAM	LVL	AGE	PA	R	2B	3B	HR	RBI	BB	SO	SB	CS	AVG/OBP/SLG	TAv	BABIP	BRR	FRAA	WARP
2011	BLT	A	20	409	55	15	5	7	41	25	98	24	15	.247/.298/.373	.234	.313	0	SS(15): -1.7, CF(6): 0.2	0.0
2012	FTM	A+	21	547	70	21	9	8	60	29	77	17	11	.286/.329/.410	.267	.322	-0.4	SS(85): -8.6, 2B(32): -1.9	1.0
2013	NBR	AA	22	588	66	22	10	2	45	24	94	30	13	.297/.333/.386	.268	.353	1.5	SS(125): 0.7, 2B(3): -0.1	3.0
2014	MIN	MLB	23	250	26	9	3	2	18	6	49	7	4	.254/.278/.344	.228	.300	0.3	SS -3, 2B 0	0.0

Speed and contact are Santana's calling cards, as the willowy young shortstop swiped 30 bags last year, legged out 10 triples and hit for a decent average in his Double-A debut. He's overly aggressive in every phase of the game, treating walks like a badge of cowardice, running into outs and amassing high error totals to undermine his strong arm and excellent range in the field. If Santana can smooth out the rough edges he can be a solid utility option, and with only the punchless law firm of Escobar and Florimon ahead of him on the depth chart, he might actually be an upgrade in the starting lineup.

Kurt Suzuki C

Born: 10/4/1983 Age: 30
Bats: R Throws: R Height: 5' 11"
Weight: 205 Breakout: 0%
Improve: 38% Collapse: 8%
Attrition: 9% MLB: 98%

Comparables:
Brian Harper, Paul Lo Duca, A.J. Pierzynski

YEAR	TEAM	LVL	AGE	PA	R	2B	3B	HR	RBI	BB	SO	SB	CS	AVG/OBP/SLG	TAv	BABIP	BRR	FRAA	WARP
2011	OAK	MLB	27	515	54	26	0	14	44	38	64	2	2	.237/.301/.385	.255	.244	-1.6	C(129): -1.7	1.5
2012	WAS	MLB	28	164	17	5	0	5	25	11	20	1	0	.267/.321/.404	.268	.274	-0.4	C(42): 0.5	0.8
2012	OAK	MLB	28	278	19	15	0	1	18	9	53	1	0	.218/.250/.286	.198	.267	-1.6	C(75): -1.1	-0.3
2013	OAK	MLB	29	35	6	2	0	2	7	2	3	0	0	.303/.343/.545	.343	.286	-1.1	C(15): 0.4	0.5
2013	WAS	MLB	29	281	19	11	1	3	25	20	32	2	0	.222/.283/.310	.227	.240	1	C(78): -0.1	0.0
2014	MIN	MLB	30	322	33	16	1	7	33	18	38	2	1	.251/.303/.379	.252	.270	-0.4	C -0	1.2

With John Jaso already out, a Derek Norris toe injury forced the A's to look to a familiar face and reacquire Suzuki from the Nationals in late August. (The A's had picked up a substantial portion of his salary in a swap the previous year; Washington picked up a substantial portion of his salary this time. The A's accountants have accountants.) His bat has only intermittently been an asset the past four years, but he did enjoy his 15-game cameo in Oakland. Suzuki is particularly athletic for a catcher, frequently making goalie-like saves on balls in the dirt, but his overall defensive game still grades out around average. With his perilous offensive decline (despite *just* turning 30), Suzuki was not exactly weighing nine-figure offers. Still, the Proven Catcher label could buy him another five years of riding big-league benches even if the skills of his youth never resurface.

Josh Willingham LF

Born: 2/17/1979 Age: 35
Bats: R Throws: R Height: 6' 2"
Weight: 230 Breakout: 3%
Improve: 20% Collapse: 13%
Attrition: 19% MLB: 94%

Comparables:
Pat Burrell, David Justice, Jimmy Wynn

YEAR	TEAM	LVL	AGE	PA	R	2B	3B	HR	RBI	BB	SO	SB	CS	AVG/OBP/SLG	TAv	BABIP	BRR	FRAA	WARP
2011	OAK	MLB	32	563	69	26	0	29	98	56	150	4	1	.246/.332/.477	.302	.287	-0.3	LF(96): -3.0	3.2
2012	MIN	MLB	33	615	85	30	1	35	110	76	141	3	2	.260/.366/.524	.304	.287	0.9	LF(119): 5.8	4.6
2013	MIN	MLB	34	471	42	20	0	14	48	66	128	1	0	.208/.342/.368	.273	.269	-0.6	LF(72): -2.6	1.1
2014	MIN	MLB	35	473	59	21	1	19	64	55	115	3	1	.241/.344/.436	.285	.290	-0.6	LF -2	2.0

No one expected Willingham to duplicate his 2012 career year, but few thought his power would dry up faster than a Death Valley downpour. Injury may have played a part, as Willingham aggravated his oft-tender knee during an awkward slide in late April and soldiered on for two months before finally going under the knife. His batting eye and walk rate remain solid, but he struggled to make solid contact and balls that had once been bleacher souvenirs started dying at the track. Whether this was due to age or injury is an open question, but Willingham has been beating the odds his entire career, so we're betting his bat bounces back. However, his defense in left remains spottier and covers less ground than a Twister mat, so he'll have to rake to make himself worthy of a prospect or two at the deadline.

PITCHERS

Andrew Albers

Born: 10/6/1985 Age: 28
Bats: R Throws: L Height: 6' 1" Weight: 195
Breakout: 43% Improve: 73% Collapse: 20%
Attrition: 59% MLB: 52%

Comparables:
Daniel McCutchen, Rick VandenHurk, Josh Banks

YEAR	TEAM	LVL	AGE	W	L	SV	G	GS	IP	H	HR	BB	SO	BB9	SO9	GB%	BABIP	WHIP	ERA	FIP	FRA	WARP
2011	FTM	A+	25	4	1	4	22	2	52¹	48	2	7	46	1.2	7.9	58%	.337	1.05	1.55	2.59	4.83	0.6
2011	NBR	AA	25	4	1	0	13	5	43¹	44	0	7	34	1.5	7.1	45%	.344	1.18	2.91	2.67	3.49	0.5
2012	NBR	AA	26	4	3	0	19	17	98¹	111	7	12	73	1.1	6.7	49%	.346	1.25	3.75	3.07	3.83	1.6
2013	ROC	AAA	27	11	5	0	22	22	132¹	124	14	32	116	2.2	7.9	41%	.297	1.18	2.86	3.55	4.36	1.4
2013	MIN	MLB	27	2	5	0	10	10	60	64	6	7	25	1.0	3.8	46%	.278	1.18	4.05	3.99	4.63	0.3
2014	MIN	MLB	28	7	9	1	38	22	147²	162	17	32	95	2.0	5.8	45%	.307	1.31	4.23	4.27	4.60	0.7

A low-velo, pitch-to-contact type rescued by Minnesota after Tommy John surgery and a stint in the independent leagues, Albers typifies the old-school view of Twins starters. No American League hurler was stingier with ball four last year than Albers, whose 2.8 percent walk rate made Koji Uehara look like Mitch Williams. In fact, only six times this century has an American League pitcher worked 60-plus innings and allowed a higher percentage of batted balls than Albers did last season, and three of those seasons belong to infamous Twins archetype Carlos Silva. Albers was called up in August, made 10 starts, and worked 17 innings before allowing a run, finishing the year with a credible FIP. His mid-80s fastball and off-speed lefty junk look like an accident waiting to happen, but Albers commands it well and keeps hitters off balance—at least for now. The margin of error for hurlers like Albers is razor thin, and if the Twins see fit to stick him in the rotation they might want to stencil "Caution: Flammable" on the back of his hat, just in case.

Jose Berrios

Born: 5/27/1994 Age: 20
Bats: R Throws: R Height: 6' 0" Weight: 187
Breakout: 53% Improve: 83% Collapse: 17%
Attrition: 61% MLB: 7%

Comparables:
Jarrod Parker, Carlos Carrasco, Mat Latos

YEAR	TEAM	LVL	AGE	W	L	SV	G	GS	IP	H	HR	BB	SO	BB9	SO9	GB%	BABIP	WHIP	ERA	FIP	FRA	WARP
2013	CDR	A	19	7	7	0	19	19	103²	105	6	40	100	3.5	8.7	45%	.330	1.40	3.99	3.58	4.69	1.5
2014	MIN	MLB	20	3	5	0	24	11	75	83	9	37	53	4.5	6.4	43%	.314	1.61	5.35	5.16	5.81	-0.6

Welcome to the new normal for Minnesota pitching prospects. In an organization long thought to value control and groundballs over velocity and strikeouts, Berrios is the poster child for a new wave of bat-missing fireballers on their way to Target Field. As a teenager in his full-season debut, Berrios oozed confidence and held his own against Low-A hitters, striking out nearly a batter per inning and showing surprisingly advanced feel. His low-90s fastball has late movement, his curve already flashes plus, and his changeup is more than a show-me offering. His lack of height is a red flag for some, but Berrios has already shown an ability to maintain velocity and has a good chance at staying in the rotation. It would be nice if he could cut down on the walks, if only for old time's sake, but even if he doesn't Berrios has every chance of becoming a mid-rotation starter on the next great Twins team.

Jared Burton

Born: 6/2/1981 Age: 33
Bats: R Throws: R Height: 6' 5" Weight: 225
Breakout: 27% Improve: 49% Collapse: 32%
Attrition: 29% MLB: 70%

Comparables:
Justin Miller, Jesus Colome, Mike MacDougal

YEAR	TEAM	LVL	AGE	W	L	SV	G	GS	IP	H	HR	BB	SO	BB9	SO9	GB%	BABIP	WHIP	ERA	FIP	FRA	WARP
2011	LOU	AAA	30	2	0	0	11	0	13	12	1	5	11	3.5	7.6	49%	.324	1.31	4.15	4.39	4.84	0.0
2011	CIN	MLB	30	0	0	0	6	0	4²	6	1	3	3	5.8	5.8	38%	.333	1.93	3.86	6.42	5.74	-0.1
2012	MIN	MLB	31	3	2	5	64	0	62	41	5	16	55	2.3	8.0	48%	.220	0.92	2.18	3.34	3.88	0.9
2013	MIN	MLB	32	2	9	2	71	0	66	61	6	22	61	3.0	8.3	45%	.294	1.26	3.82	3.64	3.89	0.7
2014	MIN	MLB	33	3	1	2	57	0	56	52	5	19	46	3.0	7.4	46%	.287	1.27	3.77	4.01	4.10	0.5

Over the last seven years Burton has posted five solid seasons and lost the other two to shoulder woes—consistent production that's surprisingly rare for a middle reliever. Armed with a low-90s fastball, a big-league changeup and solid guitar chops, Burton's plus-plus sense of humor produced one of the brighter moments of an otherwise gray season when he conspired with Brian Duensing to play-act a sucker punch when a home run ball landed near them in the bullpen. Signed for $3.25 million this year with a reasonable $3.6 million club option for 2015, if Burton puts up a randomly dominant three-month stretch he might find some suitors at the deadline.

Kevin Correia
Born: 8/24/1980 Age: 33
Bats: R Throws: R Height: 6' 3" Weight: 200
Breakout: 25% Improve: 51% Collapse: 27%
Attrition: 17% MLB: 83%

Comparables:
John Burkett, Bryn Smith, Ron Reed

YEAR	TEAM	LVL	AGE	W	L	SV	G	GS	IP	H	HR	BB	SO	BB9	SO9	GB%	BABIP	WHIP	ERA	FIP	FRA	WARP
2011	PIT	MLB	30	12	11	0	27	26	154	175	24	39	77	2.3	4.5	45%	.297	1.39	4.79	4.82	5.75	-0.9
2012	PIT	MLB	31	12	11	0	32	28	171	176	20	46	89	2.4	4.7	52%	.286	1.30	4.21	4.48	5.17	-0.5
2013	MIN	MLB	32	9	13	0	31	31	185¹	218	24	45	101	2.2	4.9	45%	.313	1.42	4.18	4.43	4.82	0.5
2014	MIN	MLB	33	7	12	0	27	27	154	177	21	43	86	2.5	5.0	46%	.306	1.42	4.76	4.94	5.18	-0.3

Last year analysts were uniformly dismissive when Minnesota signed Correia to bring his patented mix of ... hey, *wait* a minute. Correia doesn't own the patent on soft-tossing junkballers with microscopic walk and strikeout rates, the Twins do! Perhaps the organization thought it would be cheaper to buy out the veteran righty than hire attorneys to sue him, which would at least provide some semblance of logic to the otherwise questionable decision for a rebuilding team to shell out $10 million over two years for a replacement-level starter. Correia was Correia last season, if not more so, and is just one randomly low BABIP away from earning another multiyear deal.

Samuel Deduno
Born: 7/2/1983 Age: 30
Bats: R Throws: R Height: 6' 3" Weight: 190
Breakout: 31% Improve: 53% Collapse: 35%
Attrition: 51% MLB: 35%

Comparables:
David Purcey, Jason Stanford, Jimmy Serrano

YEAR	TEAM	LVL	AGE	W	L	SV	G	GS	IP	H	HR	BB	SO	BB9	SO9	GB%	BABIP	WHIP	ERA	FIP	FRA	WARP
2011	TUC	AAA	27	4	6	0	40	12	105¹	101	2	58	85	5.0	7.3	53%	.322	1.51	3.93	4.27	4.60	2.0
2011	SDN	MLB	27	0	0	0	2	0	3	5	0	3	4	9.0	12.0	89%	.556	2.67	3.00	3.33	1.55	0.1
2012	ROC	AAA	28	1	2	0	9	9	42	27	2	22	46	4.7	9.9	65%	.250	1.17	2.14	3.44	4.91	0.1
2012	MIN	MLB	28	6	5	0	15	15	79	69	10	53	57	6.0	6.5	59%	.266	1.54	4.44	5.45	6.55	-0.6
2013	ROC	AAA	29	0	0	0	3	3	16²	14	1	10	17	5.4	9.2	50%	.317	1.44	2.70	3.74	4.10	0.2
2013	MIN	MLB	29	8	8	0	18	18	108	105	7	41	67	3.4	5.6	61%	.293	1.35	3.83	4.07	5.01	0.0
2014	MIN	MLB	30	5	6	1	34	15	103²	98	8	54	79	4.7	6.9	57%	.291	1.46	4.26	4.59	4.63	0.5

Another former Padre helping to prop up the creaky Twins rotation, Deduno built on his successful WBC stint and was in the midst of his first marginally successful big league run when the injury bug bit him in the shoulder, resulting in season-ending surgery. Long known for his big curveball and a jitterbug fastball that flouts authority, Deduno cut his walk rate in half last year by aiming his four-seamer over the plate and letting its sharp natural movement shy away from bats. His heater often acts like a cutter, boring in on lefty batters and helping Deduno hold them to a .204/.288/.296 line during his brief big league career. He should be healthy enough to compete for a rotation spot this spring, but if last year's unexpected command turns out to be fleeting, his Wiffle ball action might work in the late innings.

Cole DeVries
Born: 2/12/1985 Age: 29
Bats: R Throws: R Height: 6' 1" Weight: 180
Breakout: 36% Improve: 60% Collapse: 16%
Attrition: 46% MLB: 21%

Comparables:
Josh Banks, Josh Geer, Hector Ambriz

YEAR	TEAM	LVL	AGE	W	L	SV	G	GS	IP	H	HR	BB	SO	BB9	SO9	GB%	BABIP	WHIP	ERA	FIP	FRA	WARP
2011	NBR	AA	26	0	0	9	15	0	27²	17	3	5	33	1.6	10.7	44%	.222	0.80	2.28	2.98	4.84	0.0
2011	ROC	AAA	26	4	2	0	30	2	62¹	74	4	18	42	2.6	6.1	38%	.347	1.48	3.90	3.59	4.98	0.2
2012	ROC	AAA	27	3	5	0	12	12	70	75	7	10	50	1.3	6.4	37%	.306	1.21	4.37	3.50	4.04	0.6
2012	MIN	MLB	27	5	5	0	17	16	87²	88	16	18	58	1.8	6.0	33%	.258	1.21	4.11	4.85	5.30	0.5
2013	NBR	AA	28	0	2	0	3	3	16	12	3	2	11	1.1	6.2	39%	.196	0.88	1.69	4.95	6.14	-0.1
2013	ROC	AAA	28	3	4	0	10	10	50	77	6	13	24	2.3	4.3	38%	.368	1.80	7.02	4.64	5.90	-0.1
2013	MIN	MLB	28	0	2	0	4	2	15	22	6	9	12	5.4	7.2	26%	.327	2.07	10.80	8.48	9.16	-0.6
2014	MIN	MLB	29	3	5	0	30	11	90²	110	14	28	53	2.7	5.3	40%	.313	1.51	5.52	5.24	6.00	-1.0

An undrafted University of Minnesota product, DeVries lived the dream in 2012 when he made 16 starts for his hometown Twins before cracking his ribs, and injuries again dogged him last year. Elbow soreness kept him in and out of various minor league rotations all summer, and when he finally worked his way back to Target Field in September, big-league hitters treated him like a piñata. Released in October, DeVries' upper-80s fastball and indifferent secondary stuff didn't exactly have teams chasing him like Matt Garza, but he's already come much farther than your typical Mankato Moondog.

Scott Diamond
Born: 7/30/1986 Age: 27
Bats: L Throws: L Height: 6' 3" Weight: 220
Breakout: 42% Improve: 79% Collapse: 12%
Attrition: 37% MLB: 75%

Comparables:
Billy Traber, Anthony Swarzak, Ross Detwiler

YEAR	TEAM	LVL	AGE	W	L	SV	G	GS	IP	H	HR	BB	SO	BB9	SO9	GB%	BABIP	WHIP	ERA	FIP	FRA	WARP
2011	ROC	AAA	24	4	14	0	23	23	123	158	11	36	90	2.6	6.6	54%	.353	1.58	5.56	3.84	4.80	0.7
2011	MIN	MLB	24	1	5	0	7	7	39	51	3	17	19	3.9	4.4	48%	.338	1.74	5.08	4.39	4.35	0.5
2012	ROC	AAA	25	4	1	0	6	6	34²	35	1	7	26	1.8	6.8	49%	.321	1.21	2.60	2.73	3.80	0.5
2012	MIN	MLB	25	12	9	0	27	27	173	184	17	31	90	1.6	4.7	54%	.293	1.24	3.54	3.89	4.95	0.9
2013	ROC	AAA	26	4	0	0	6	6	41	33	4	9	19	2.0	4.2	48%	.223	1.02	2.41	4.20	5.38	0.1
2013	MIN	MLB	26	6	13	0	24	24	131	163	21	36	52	2.5	3.6	47%	.305	1.52	5.43	5.21	6.12	-1.0
2014	MIN	MLB	27	7	12	0	26	26	154	182	16	43	83	2.5	4.8	51%	.316	1.46	4.93	4.50	5.36	-0.6

Well, that didn't last long, not that anyone really expected it to. After posting numbers resembling a solid mid-rotation starter in his rookie season, Diamond imploded last year and saw his ERA swell nearly two runs. As is often the case, Diamond's true talent lies somewhere between his 2012 dream and 2013 nightmare. His minuscule walk and strikeout rates once again bore that familiar Minnesota piney scent but they each moved in the wrong direction. Diamond also allowed more baserunners, induced far fewer potential double-play grounders, surrendered more gappers and posted a strand rate that was among the worst in the league. All those small changes added up to big trouble. Diamond is clearly hittable, but that doesn't mean he can't be effective, and if he can induce a few more two-hoppers he can still hold a spot at the back of the rotation.

Brian Duensing

Born: 2/22/1983 Age: 31
Bats: L Throws: L Height: 6' 0'' Weight: 205
Breakout: 14% Improve: 46% Collapse: 27%
Attrition: 20% MLB: 79%

Comparables:
Jorge Sosa, Scott Downs, Tim Stauffer

YEAR	TEAM	LVL	AGE	W	L	SV	G	GS	IP	H	HR	BB	SO	BB9	SO9	GB%	BABIP	WHIP	ERA	FIP	FRA	WARP
2011	MIN	MLB	28	9	14	0	32	28	161²	193	21	52	115	2.9	6.4	46%	.330	1.52	5.23	4.31	4.85	1.1
2012	MIN	MLB	29	4	12	0	55	11	109	126	10	27	69	2.2	5.7	48%	.319	1.40	5.12	3.77	4.49	1.2
2013	MIN	MLB	30	6	2	1	73	0	61	68	4	22	56	3.2	8.3	43%	.348	1.48	3.98	3.27	3.13	1.1
2014	MIN	MLB	31	3	3	0	29	7	62	68	6	18	40	2.6	5.9	47%	.311	1.38	4.31	4.26	4.68	0.2

Duensing is a veteran lefty swingman whose fastball works in the low 90s and last year struck out nearly a batter per inning, which in the local lexicon makes him a "fireballer." His peripherals were once indistinguishable from the rest of Lake Wobegon's staff, where all the pitchers are good-looking and all contact rates are above average, but last year the home nine used him entirely in relief. The bump in Duensing's strikeout rate came partially from his stuff playing up in shorter bursts, but mostly from avoiding the righty bats that have long tortured him. Spotted carefully, Duensing can be a reliable lefty bullpen arm, but his days in the rotation should be over.

Ryan Eades

Born: 12/15/1991 Age: 22
Bats: R Throws: R Height: 6' 2'' Weight: 178
Breakout: 0% Improve: 0% Collapse: 0%
Attrition: 0% MLB: 0%

Comparables:
Mark Hamburger, David Hale, Chuckie Fick

YEAR	TEAM	LVL	AGE	W	L	SV	G	GS	IP	H	HR	BB	SO	BB9	SO9	GB%	BABIP	WHIP	ERA	FIP	FRA	WARP
2014	MIN	MLB	22	1	0	0	1	19	30¹	40	4	21	12	6.2	3.6	45%	.319	2.00	7.18	6.65	7.81	-1.0

What happens in Elizabethton stays in Elizabethton—or so the Twins hope. Minnesota's second-round pick last summer, Eades didn't exactly set Rookie ball on fire, as the former LSU star had trouble finding the strike zone and walked nearly as many men as he whiffed. Don't get too worked up over ten Appalachian League appearances, however, since Eades still has a fastball that can reach the mid-90s, a sharp curve, a developing change and every chance to grow into a mid-rotation starter. If he walks seven men per nine innings over a full season, *then* it's time to start breathing into a paper bag.

Casey Fien

Born: 10/21/1983 Age: 30
Bats: R Throws: R Height: 6' 2'' Weight: 205
Breakout: 29% Improve: 56% Collapse: 22%
Attrition: 42% MLB: 44%

Comparables:
Jesse Carlson, Doug Slaten, Greg Jones

YEAR	TEAM	LVL	AGE	W	L	SV	G	GS	IP	H	HR	BB	SO	BB9	SO9	GB%	BABIP	WHIP	ERA	FIP	FRA	WARP
2011	OKL	AAA	27	2	2	3	21	0	24¹	28	7	8	24	3.0	8.9	33%	.333	1.48	4.81	6.54	-0.96	0.3
2012	ROC	AAA	28	2	5	9	33	0	46	39	5	14	42	2.7	8.2	32%	.268	1.15	4.30	3.66	4.64	0.1
2012	MIN	MLB	28	2	1	0	35	0	35	25	3	9	32	2.3	8.2	26%	.229	0.97	2.06	3.19	3.76	0.4
2013	MIN	MLB	29	5	2	0	73	0	62	51	9	12	73	1.7	10.6	40%	.280	1.02	3.92	3.19	3.65	0.8
2014	MIN	MLB	30	3	1	0	50	0	54²	51	7	14	49	2.4	8.1	37%	.290	1.20	3.56	4.01	3.87	0.7

A Tigers castoff, Fien has quietly emerged in the Minnesota 'pen as one of baseball's better seventh-inning options. Relying heavily on his low-90s cutter, Fien surprisingly posted one of baseball's highest swinging-strike rates last year, struck out more than a batter per inning and posted the Junior Circuit's second best strikeout-to-walk ratio. That's a lot of juicy peripheral goodness, although Fien remains a fly-ball pitcher who can be (and occasionally was) undone by the homer. His solid work last year showed he's not a fluke, and it wouldn't be surprising to see Fien pitching later and later in games as the season wears on.

Kyle Gibson

Born: 10/23/1987 Age: 26
Bats: R Throws: R Height: 6' 6'' Weight: 210
Breakout: 33% Improve: 57% Collapse: 27%
Attrition: 54% MLB: 68%

Comparables:
David Phelps, Brad Lincoln, Dustin Nippert

YEAR	TEAM	LVL	AGE	W	L	SV	G	GS	IP	H	HR	BB	SO	BB9	SO9	GB%	BABIP	WHIP	ERA	FIP	FRA	WARP
2011	ROC	AAA	23	3	8	0	18	18	95¹	109	11	27	91	2.5	8.6	59%	.349	1.43	4.81	3.71	4.53	0.9
2013	ROC	AAA	25	7	5	0	17	17	101²	85	5	33	87	2.9	7.7	57%	.279	1.16	2.92	3.11	4.08	1.4
2013	MIN	MLB	25	2	4	0	10	10	51	69	7	20	29	3.5	5.1	51%	.350	1.75	6.53	5.19	5.48	-0.2
2014	MIN	MLB	26	6	10	0	32	32	111¹	120	12	35	77	2.8	6.2	54%	.310	1.39	4.44	4.41	4.82	0.7

Gibson returned to full-time duty after missing most of 2012 recovering from Tommy John surgery, and the former top pick looked like his old self while carving up the International League. He was shellacked during a midseason stint with the big club, however, showing that he still has some work to do. Blessed with great height and a classic starter's frame, Gibson can deliver his low-90s fastball on a steep downward plane, generating plenty of ground balls and his fair share of strikeouts. Lack of fastball command is what doomed him in the bigs last summer, but if he can fine-tune his pitches and better mix in his slider and change, he could slot into the back end of the Twins' rotation as soon as this summer.

Sean Gilmartin
Born: 5/8/1990 Age: 24
Bats: L Throws: L Height: 6' 2" Weight: 190
Breakout: 51% Improve: 85% Collapse: 12%
Attrition: 64% MLB: 28%
Comparables:
Todd Redmond, Steven Wright, Josh Banks

YEAR	TEAM	LVL	AGE	W	L	SV	G	GS	IP	H	HR	BB	SO	BB9	SO9	GB%	BABIP	WHIP	ERA	FIP	FRA	WARP
2011	ROM	A	21	2	1	0	5	5	21¹	18	3	2	30	0.8	12.7	29%	.341	0.94	2.53	2.82	3.53	0.5
2012	MIS	AA	22	5	8	0	20	20	119¹	111	9	26	86	2.0	6.5	46%	.291	1.15	3.54	3.44	4.50	0.1
2012	GWN	AAA	22	1	2	0	7	7	37²	41	6	13	25	3.1	6.0	33%	.289	1.43	4.78	4.94	5.49	-0.1
2013	GWN	AAA	23	3	8	0	17	17	91	112	12	33	65	3.3	6.4	39%	.333	1.59	5.74	4.61	5.30	0.3
2014	MIN	MLB	24	4	8	0	19	19	96	112	14	28	58	2.6	5.4	41%	.307	1.46	5.05	4.99	5.49	-0.4

Hockey coach John Tortorella used to hang a sign in the locker room that read, "Safe is death." There's no need to get fatalistic about Gilmartin yet, but the so-called safe prospect is in trouble, and has been since reaching Triple-A. Missing time with shoulder tendinitis does not convince anyone otherwise. When healthy, the Florida State product throws three average or better pitches, and relies on location and gimmickry. Naturally, then, the Twins asked for him in the Ryan Doumit trade. Gilmartin gets a third crack at Triple-A in 2014; if he has yet another poor showing it will be time to check his prospect pulse.

Phil Hughes
Born: 6/24/1986 Age: 28
Bats: R Throws: R Height: 6' 5" Weight: 240
Breakout: 22% Improve: 58% Collapse: 22%
Attrition: 7% MLB: 93%
Comparables:
Ervin Santana, Jeff Francis, Javier Vazquez

YEAR	TEAM	LVL	AGE	W	L	SV	G	GS	IP	H	HR	BB	SO	BB9	SO9	GB%	BABIP	WHIP	ERA	FIP	FRA	WARP
2011	NYA	MLB	25	5	5	0	17	14	74²	84	9	27	47	3.3	5.7	34%	.304	1.49	5.79	4.61	4.68	0.8
2012	NYA	MLB	26	16	13	0	32	32	191¹	196	35	46	165	2.2	7.8	33%	.286	1.26	4.23	4.52	4.45	2.1
2013	NYA	MLB	27	4	14	0	30	29	145²	170	24	42	121	2.6	7.5	32%	.321	1.46	5.19	4.52	4.78	0.9
2014	MIN	MLB	28	7	10	0	25	25	137²	140	17	36	114	2.4	7.5	36%	.301	1.28	3.98	4.14	4.33	1.2

Fish out of water aren't as ill-suited to their environment as Hughes was to Yankee Stadium. Among pitchers who threw at least 100 innings, only Bruce Chen had a lower groundball rate, but Hughes didn't have the luxury of pitching in a favorable park for fly balls. On the road, Hughes was an above-average starter; at home, he gave up two homers per nine innings and posted a 6.32 ERA. And just in case the Yankees weren't decided about bringing him back, he averaged seven outs in his first September starts. At this point, Hughes is about as likely to start getting grounders as a gasping fish is to grow lungs, so he needs rangy defenders and deep outfield fences behind him to avoid being flushed down the drain. A three-year deal with Minnesota guarantees at least the latter half.

Kris Johnson
Born: 10/14/1984 Age: 29
Bats: L Throws: L Height: 6' 4" Weight: 195
Breakout: 14% Improve: 72% Collapse: 28%
Attrition: 100% MLB: 7%
Comparables:
Eric Hacker, Heath Phillips, Ty Taubenheim

YEAR	TEAM	LVL	AGE	W	L	SV	G	GS	IP	H	HR	BB	SO	BB9	SO9	GB%	BABIP	WHIP	ERA	FIP	FRA	WARP
2011	PAW	AAA	26	2	2	0	8	3	20²	41	7	6	12	2.6	5.2	30%	.414	2.27	12.63	7.49	8.53	-0.4
2012	ALT	AA	27	3	2	1	15	9	56	50	3	24	42	3.9	6.8	54%	.281	1.32	2.09	3.84	4.16	0.8
2012	IND	AAA	27	5	2	0	20	4	45²	42	7	18	33	3.5	6.5	47%	.261	1.31	4.53	4.95	4.55	-0.2
2013	IND	AAA	28	10	4	2	26	21	135²	116	6	43	94	2.9	6.2	55%	.278	1.17	2.39	3.43	4.66	0.7
2013	PIT	MLB	28	0	2	0	4	1	10¹	12	0	4	9	3.5	7.8	47%	.375	1.55	6.10	2.73	3.48	0.1
2014	MIN	MLB	29	4	8	0	26	17	106	127	13	42	58	3.5	4.9	47%	.313	1.59	5.58	5.18	6.06	-1.1

Johnson, originally a supplemental first-round pick by the Red Sox, signed with the Pirates before the 2012 season as a minor-league free-agent. Nobody anticipated him reaching the majors, but that's what he did last August. A big southpaw, Johnson throws a low-90s sinker, slider and changeup. Could he fake it as a back-of-the-rotation starter? Probably, and his offseason trade to the pitching-starved Twins might give him his shot, though a career in the bullpen seems more likely and more fruitful.

Trevor May
Born: 9/23/1989 Age: 24
Bats: R Throws: R Height: 6' 5" Weight: 215
Breakout: 34% Improve: 56% Collapse: 33%
Attrition: 65% MLB: 33%
Comparables:
Radhames Liz, David Hernandez, Thomas Diamond

YEAR	TEAM	LVL	AGE	W	L	SV	G	GS	IP	H	HR	BB	SO	BB9	SO9	GB%	BABIP	WHIP	ERA	FIP	FRA	WARP
2011	CLR	A+	21	10	8	0	27	27	151¹	121	8	67	208	4.0	12.4	37%	.356	1.24	3.63	2.75	3.40	2.5
2012	REA	AA	22	10	13	0	28	28	149²	139	22	78	151	4.7	9.1	42%	.295	1.45	4.87	4.88	5.31	0.7
2013	NBR	AA	23	9	9	0	27	27	151²	149	14	67	159	4.0	9.4	40%	.328	1.42	4.51	3.91	4.09	2.3
2014	MIN	MLB	24	6	10	0	24	24	125²	128	16	71	119	5.1	8.5	39%	.313	1.58	5.05	4.94	5.49	-0.5

Part of Minnesota's return in the Ben Revere trade, May has all the attributes of a top pitching prospect: an ideal starter's build, a fastball that can reach the mid-90s, two off-speed pitches that he can throw for strikes and more than a whiff per inning during his minor league career. Yet dodgy command continues to be a problem, and instead of delivering his fastball on a steep plane that produces groundball outs, his drop-and-drive delivery undercuts his height and causes his fastball to flatten out. May looks for all the world like a future innings-eater, which isn't a bad thing, yet that seems a little disappointing when his size and stuff have the potential to produce so much more.

Alex Meyer
Born: 1/3/1990 Age: 24
Bats: R Throws: R Height: 6' 9" Weight: 220
Breakout: 37% Improve: 78% Collapse: 19%
Attrition: 52% MLB: 57%

Comparables:
Jake Arrieta, James Paxton, Matt Maloney

YEAR	TEAM	LVL	AGE	W	L	SV	G	GS	IP	H	HR	BB	SO	BB9	SO9	GB%	BABIP	WHIP	ERA	FIP	FRA	WARP
2012	HAG	A	22	7	4	0	18	18	90	68	4	34	107	3.4	10.7	54%	.292	1.13	3.10	3.01	3.57	2.4
2012	POT	A+	22	3	2	0	7	7	39	29	2	11	32	2.5	7.4	53%	.252	1.03	2.31	3.41	4.00	0.7
2013	NBR	AA	23	4	3	0	13	13	70	60	3	29	84	3.7	10.8	61%	.317	1.27	3.21	2.85	3.79	1.4
2014	MIN	MLB	24	4	5	0	15	15	73^1	72	7	32	66	3.9	8.1	51%	.306	1.41	4.21	4.20	4.58	0.5

The top pitching prospect in the Minnesota system, when Meyer unwinds his towering frame he can unleash fastballs that flirt with triple digits, along with a solid power breaker and a changeup that could develop into an actual weapon. Stuff has never been the question with him, but his ceiling and eventual role depends primarily on how well he can repeat his delivery. There's a lot of Meyer to get moving in a coordinated way, and when his mechanics get out of whack he loses command, hands out free passes and stops dominating. Minor shoulder issues limited his time on the mound last season, but he had a clean bill of health by fall and wowed scouts, broadcasters, concessionaires and random passersby during a strong Arizona Fall League campaign. If Meyer can maintain command of his plus offerings, he's got the goods to front the Twins' rotation for years to come; if not, he'll become a late-innings beast.

Ricky Nolasco
Born: 12/13/1982 Age: 31
Bats: R Throws: R Height: 6' 2" Weight: 235
Breakout: 11% Improve: 50% Collapse: 21%
Attrition: 14% MLB: 91%

Comparables:
Joe Blanton, James Shields, Odalis Perez

YEAR	TEAM	LVL	AGE	W	L	SV	G	GS	IP	H	HR	BB	SO	BB9	SO9	GB%	BABIP	WHIP	ERA	FIP	FRA	WARP
2011	FLO	MLB	28	10	12	0	33	33	206	244	20	44	148	1.9	6.5	47%	.333	1.40	4.67	3.50	4.18	1.2
2012	MIA	MLB	29	12	13	0	31	31	191	214	18	47	125	2.2	5.9	48%	.315	1.37	4.48	3.92	4.26	1.2
2013	MIA	MLB	30	5	8	0	18	18	112^1	112	11	25	90	2.0	7.2	42%	.301	1.22	3.85	3.47	4.12	0.6
2013	LAN	MLB	30	8	3	0	16	15	87	83	6	21	75	2.2	7.8	44%	.309	1.20	3.52	3.12	3.72	1.3
2014	MIN	MLB	31	8	11	0	27	27	160	174	19	32	120	1.8	6.7	43%	.313	1.29	4.24	4.05	4.61	0.7

Nolasco personifies the distinction between command and control. His strike-throwing abilities are unquestioned, but Nolasco often struggles to command his pitches within the strike zone and batters take advantage when his offerings catch too much of the plate. His propensity for high rates of hits and homers conflict with his otherwise clean rates of true outcomes, a factor which underlies the continual discrepancy between his ERA and his FIP. Nolasco had a sweet introduction to L.A., including a dominant string of eight starts from August to early September with a 1.59 ERA, but he lost the glass slipper and was rocked in his final three starts of the regular season. The downfall set the stage for the Dodgers skipping him in favor of an unrested Clayton Kershaw in the NLDS. One might posit that decision led to the Dodger ace's poor performance later on, in the NLCS. One also might not.

Mike Pelfrey
Born: 1/14/1984 Age: 30
Bats: R Throws: R Height: 6' 7" Weight: 250
Breakout: 18% Improve: 56% Collapse: 19%
Attrition: 12% MLB: 92%

Comparables:
Jason Marquis, Brian Lawrence, Paul Maholm

YEAR	TEAM	LVL	AGE	W	L	SV	G	GS	IP	H	HR	BB	SO	BB9	SO9	GB%	BABIP	WHIP	ERA	FIP	FRA	WARP
2011	NYN	MLB	27	7	13	0	34	33	193^2	220	21	65	105	3.0	4.9	47%	.298	1.47	4.74	4.43	5.13	-0.8
2012	NYN	MLB	28	0	0	0	3	3	19^2	24	0	4	13	1.8	5.9	51%	.365	1.42	2.29	2.42	2.42	0.6
2013	MIN	MLB	29	5	13	0	29	29	152^2	184	13	53	101	3.1	6.0	45%	.337	1.55	5.19	4.02	4.13	2.0
2014	MIN	MLB	30	5	9	0	19	19	116	134	11	37	63	2.9	4.9	49%	.315	1.48	4.79	4.55	5.21	-0.3

The Twins signed Pelfrey to a make-good contract coming off Tommy John surgery, and the veteran innings-muncher proved he was a quick healer, making 29 starts and showing he's still a perfectly cromulent starting pitcher. His ERA sat above 5.00 most of the year, which was unfortunate since it dampened any chance of a prospect-bringing deadline trade that might have allowed Pelfrey's signing to make at least one small contribution to a potential Twins championship. His peripherals were better than the runs-allowed, but mostly in an Arby's-is-better-than-Long-John-Silver's sort of way, and the 30-year-old Pelfrey profiles as little more than rotation filler going forward.

Glen Perkins
Born: 3/2/1983 Age: 31
Bats: L Throws: L Height: 6' 0" Weight: 205
Breakout: 32% Improve: 56% Collapse: 28%
Attrition: 31% MLB: 61%

Comparables:
Matt Belisle, Buddy Carlyle, Adam Bernero

YEAR	TEAM	LVL	AGE	W	L	SV	G	GS	IP	H	HR	BB	SO	BB9	SO9	GB%	BABIP	WHIP	ERA	FIP	FRA	WARP
2011	MIN	MLB	28	4	4	2	65	0	61^2	55	2	21	65	3.1	9.5	52%	.323	1.23	2.48	2.45	2.40	1.7
2012	MIN	MLB	29	3	1	16	70	0	70^1	57	8	16	78	2.0	10.0	44%	.278	1.04	2.56	3.12	3.55	1.2
2013	MIN	MLB	30	2	0	36	61	0	62^2	43	5	15	77	2.2	11.1	37%	.271	0.93	2.30	2.52	3.21	1.2
2014	MIN	MLB	31	3	2	9	34	4	51	53	5	13	41	2.4	7.3	44%	.312	1.30	3.99	3.86	4.34	0.4

There's a school of thought that says a top-notch closer is a depreciating luxury item that rebuilding small-market teams can't afford to keep, but the decision not to move Perkins at last year's deadline might well have been the right one. He is signed through 2015 at a club-friendly price and has an affordable 2016 option, a fact that makes the dominant power lefty extremely attractive to a contender. Of course, if the Twins were a contender, they'd find Perkins extremely attractive as well, and with a wealth of minor-league talent nearing fruition, contention may find them sooner than you think. It's certainly possible Perkins is at his peak value right now, and by keeping him the Twins are risking an injury or ineffectiveness that reduces him from an asset to a liability. However, whatever players the Twins would get for him in trade carry the exact same risk—if you don't believe us, ask Kenny Williams about the Sergio Santos trade—and with Perkins potentially in the fold for three more seasons, there's a case to be made for biding time and watching how things play out.

Ryan Pressly
Born: 12/15/1988 Age: 25
Bats: R Throws: R Height: 6' 3" Weight: 205
Breakout: 49% Improve: 63% Collapse: 22%
Attrition: 68% MLB: 50%

Comparables:
Beltran Perez, Jeff Samardzija, Ryan Tucker

YEAR	TEAM	LVL	AGE	W	L	SV	G	GS	IP	H	HR	BB	SO	BB9	SO9	GB%	BABIP	WHIP	ERA	FIP	FRA	WARP
2011	SLM	A+	22	6	11	0	26	26	130	125	9	53	72	3.7	5.0	57%	.273	1.37	4.50	4.55	6.15	-0.6
2012	SLM	A+	23	5	3	0	20	12	76	86	9	26	61	3.1	7.2	50%	.329	1.47	6.28	4.50	5.78	-0.2
2012	PME	AA	23	2	2	0	14	0	27²	23	2	10	21	3.3	6.8	46%	.266	1.19	2.93	3.71	4.24	0.3
2013	MIN	MLB	24	3	3	0	49	0	76²	71	5	27	49	3.2	5.8	46%	.284	1.28	3.87	3.70	4.63	0.2
2014	MIN	MLB	25	2	4	0	24	8	65	73	8	30	36	4.1	5.0	47%	.302	1.58	5.20	5.36	5.65	-0.4

A Rule 5 draftee prior to last season, Pressly came to Minnesota from the Red Sox and proved to be a reasonably effective multi-inning reliever until tiring down the stretch. A former starter whose fastball can reach the mid-90s in relief, Pressly doesn't miss a lot of bats but manages to keep the ball in the park and doesn't hurt himself with too many walks. If that doesn't sound sexy, well, it isn't, but someone's going to get paid to get five outs when the home team is down by three in the middle innings, and Pressly is as good a choice as any to act as a wobbly rope bridge to the set-up men.

Josh Roenicke
Born: 8/4/1982 Age: 31
Bats: R Throws: R Height: 6' 3" Weight: 200
Breakout: 40% Improve: 52% Collapse: 31%
Attrition: 41% MLB: 42%

Comparables:
Brandon Medders, Pat Neshek, Randy Choate

YEAR	TEAM	LVL	AGE	W	L	SV	G	GS	IP	H	HR	BB	SO	BB9	SO9	GB%	BABIP	WHIP	ERA	FIP	FRA	WARP
2011	CSP	AAA	28	0	1	0	23	0	30²	30	3	7	22	2.1	6.5	54%	.287	1.21	3.52	4.40	4.81	0.6
2011	LVG	AAA	28	1	3	0	16	0	22¹	25	3	15	20	6.0	8.1	49%	.318	1.79	6.04	6.02	8.10	-0.1
2011	COL	MLB	28	0	0	0	19	0	16²	14	1	7	12	3.8	6.5	46%	.277	1.26	3.78	3.77	3.89	0.2
2012	COL	MLB	29	4	2	1	63	0	88²	85	9	43	54	4.4	5.5	50%	.285	1.44	3.25	4.76	5.92	-0.2
2013	MIN	MLB	30	3	1	1	63	0	62	63	6	36	45	5.2	6.5	43%	.295	1.60	4.35	4.67	4.44	0.3
2014	MIN	MLB	31	2	1	1	47	0	58²	59	5	26	44	4.0	6.7	47%	.296	1.44	4.33	4.38	4.71	0.1

If the Twins looked at Ryan Pressly last year and saw a shaky but passable span to the late innings, they likely envisioned Roenicke as the Tacoma Narrows Bridge. Not because his results or stuff were significantly worse than the mediocre Pressly's—they weren't—but due to the harmonic resonance produced by his high walk rate, an engineering flaw the organization was sure would eventually lead to disaster. Released at season's end, Roenicke could theoretically provide a randomly solid 50 innings, but we doubt it.

Kohl Stewart
Born: 10/7/1994 Age: 19
Bats: R Throws: R Height: 6' 3" Weight: 195
Breakout: 0% Improve: 0% Collapse: 0%
Attrition: 0% MLB: 0%

Comparables:
Joe Wieland, Alex Torres, Michael Kirkman

YEAR	TEAM	LVL	AGE	W	L	SV	G	GS	IP	H	HR	BB	SO	BB9	SO9	GB%	BABIP	WHIP	ERA	FIP	FRA	WARP
2014	MIN	MLB	19	1	3	0	10	6	31	39	4	20	15	5.8	4.4	45%	.316	1.89	6.65	6.27	7.23	-0.6

The Twins drafted Stewart with the fourth overall pick in last summer's draft and sent him to the Gulf Coast League to cut his professional teeth—only to watch the Gulf Coast cut his newly professional feet, as a laceration suffered during a barefoot beach stroll shelved him for 18 days. When the young Texan was able to lace up his spikes, he flashed the power stuff that has the organization expecting him to sprint through the minors. His mid-90s fastball dominated Rookie ball hitters, his slider and changeup both flashed as potential plus pitches and his ideal frame will continue to fill out as he matures. If Stewart can add a pair of flip-flops to his otherwise complete toolset, the Twins may have found their future ace.

Anthony Swarzak
Born: 9/10/1985 Age: 28
Bats: R Throws: R Height: 6' 4" Weight: 210
Breakout: 27% Improve: 52% Collapse: 26%
Attrition: 39% MLB: 76%

Comparables:
Jeff Karstens, Edgar Gonzalez, Ryan Rowland-Smith

YEAR	TEAM	LVL	AGE	W	L	SV	G	GS	IP	H	HR	BB	SO	BB9	SO9	GB%	BABIP	WHIP	ERA	FIP	FRA	WARP
2011	ROC	AAA	25	2	1	0	6	6	32¹	35	3	7	25	1.9	7.0	36%	.308	1.30	3.90	3.55	3.86	0.6
2011	MIN	MLB	25	4	7	0	27	11	102	111	9	26	55	2.3	4.9	40%	.296	1.34	4.32	4.07	4.52	1.0
2012	MIN	MLB	26	3	6	0	44	5	96²	106	15	31	62	2.9	5.8	44%	.300	1.42	5.03	4.74	5.57	-0.1
2013	MIN	MLB	27	3	2	0	48	0	96	89	7	22	69	2.1	6.5	46%	.286	1.16	2.91	3.30	4.27	0.8
2014	MIN	MLB	28	3	3	0	30	5	78²	87	9	22	46	2.5	5.3	39%	.304	1.39	4.50	4.58	4.89	0.0

Like Brian Duensing, the Twins used Swarzak entirely in relief for the first time last year, and like Duensing, his strikeout rate perked up like a recently watered begonia. Not that Swarzak suddenly morphed into Bob Gibson, mind you, but when you mix even a middling whiff percentage with Swarzak's microscopic walk rate, some fleeting effectiveness is bound to appear. Given their opposite handedness and backgrounds in the rotation it would be fun to see what Duensing and Swarzak could do in a tandem starter arrangement, but that's not about to happen, so Twins fans will have to content themselves with knowing Swarzak has finally found a role that suits him.

Caleb Thielbar

Born: 1/31/1987 Age: 27
Bats: R Throws: L Height: 6' 0" Weight: 195
Breakout: 43% Improve: 53% Collapse: 36%
Attrition: 67% MLB: 38%

Comparables:
Carlos Martinez, Josh Newman, Marino Salas

YEAR	TEAM	LVL	AGE	W	L	SV	G	GS	IP	H	HR	BB	SO	BB9	SO9	GB%	BABIP	WHIP	ERA	FIP	FRA	WARP
2012	FTM	A+	25	1	1	1	7	0	12¹	4	0	2	16	1.5	11.7	36%	.160	0.49	0.00	1.77	2.29	0.4
2012	NBR	AA	25	2	0	4	16	0	25	18	1	3	26	1.1	9.4	52%	.262	0.84	1.80	2.00	2.70	0.7
2012	ROC	AAA	25	3	1	1	25	1	40¹	42	5	16	32	3.6	7.1	44%	.298	1.44	3.57	4.45	5.97	-0.1
2013	ROC	AAA	26	1	1	1	17	0	26¹	27	1	8	34	2.7	11.6	44%	.371	1.33	3.76	2.14	2.58	0.9
2013	MIN	MLB	26	3	2	0	49	0	46	24	4	14	39	2.7	7.6	27%	.175	0.83	1.76	3.42	3.95	0.3
2014	MIN	MLB	27	2	1	0	42	0	59	60	7	20	44	3.0	6.7	42%	.298	1.35	4.33	4.51	4.70	0.1

Thielbar materialized in the Twins' bullpen last May and promptly held batters to an otherworldly .083/.176/.117 batting line during the 19 2/3 inning scoreless streak that started his career. That couldn't last, of course, and the young lefty plummeted all the way from ridiculous to really quite good, allowing a .198/.252/.427 line the rest of the way. A Minnesota native and veteran of the St. Paul Saints, Thielbar lives off a fastball that sits around 90 mph and doesn't have a lot of wiggle, but somehow exerts a powerful magnetic force that repulses bats and leads to plenty of strikeouts and weak contact. Thielbar's .175 batting average on balls in play was the American League's lowest last year, and the seventh lowest in a century, which means he's overdue for a visit from the Regression Fairy. Still, his deceptive delivery gives him enough swing-and-miss stuff to work as a competent set-up man, and if that doesn't work out, he can always find employment as a LOOGY.

Michael Tonkin

Born: 11/19/1989 Age: 24
Bats: R Throws: R Height: 6' 7" Weight: 220
Breakout: 64% Improve: 79% Collapse: 21%
Attrition: 62% MLB: 20%

Comparables:
Justin De Fratus, Ryan Rowland-Smith, Jason Miller

YEAR	TEAM	LVL	AGE	W	L	SV	G	GS	IP	H	HR	BB	SO	BB9	SO9	GB%	BABIP	WHIP	ERA	FIP	FRA	WARP
2011	BLT	A	21	4	3	2	48	3	76²	82	3	24	69	2.8	8.1	73%	.378	1.38	3.87	3.32	3.98	0.1
2012	BLT	A	22	3	0	6	22	0	39	29	1	9	53	2.1	12.2	55%	.311	0.97	1.38	1.74	2.71	1.1
2012	FTM	A+	22	1	1	6	22	0	30¹	24	2	11	44	3.3	13.1	37%	.324	1.15	2.97	2.64	2.94	0.8
2013	NBR	AA	23	1	2	7	22	0	24¹	21	0	8	30	3.0	11.1	60%	.313	1.19	2.22	2.21	2.00	1.0
2013	ROC	AAA	23	1	2	14	30	0	32²	33	3	8	36	2.2	9.9	49%	.330	1.26	4.41	3.02	3.79	0.6
2013	MIN	MLB	23	0	0	0	9	0	11¹	9	0	3	10	2.4	7.9	44%	.265	1.06	0.79	2.10	2.10	0.3
2014	MIN	MLB	24	2	2	0	32	3	57¹	63	6	22	42	3.4	6.7	47%	.315	1.48	4.94	4.55	5.37	-0.3

A towering right-hander with mid-90s heat, Tonkin stacked up strikeout victims in the high minors before impressing the brass during a brief September java stop. A former late-round pick, The Gulf has struck out more than a batter per inning while touring the bus leagues, generates plenty of ground balls and maintains a low walk rate that should satisfy the strict Target Field zoning requirements. The organization is high on his future, and his stuff should start making late-inning batters groan as soon as this summer.

Vance Worley

Born: 9/25/1987 Age: 26
Bats: R Throws: R Height: 6' 2" Weight: 230
Breakout: 43% Improve: 70% Collapse: 13%
Attrition: 22% MLB: 81%

Comparables:
Ivan Nova, David Huff, Wade Davis

YEAR	TEAM	LVL	AGE	W	L	SV	G	GS	IP	H	HR	BB	SO	BB9	SO9	GB%	BABIP	WHIP	ERA	FIP	FRA	WARP
2011	LEH	AAA	23	5	2	0	9	9	50²	41	5	12	50	2.1	8.9	47%	.258	1.05	2.31	3.37	5.33	0.1
2011	PHI	MLB	23	11	3	0	25	21	131²	116	10	46	119	3.1	8.1	41%	.291	1.23	3.01	3.29	3.83	1.0
2012	PHI	MLB	24	6	9	0	23	23	133	154	12	47	107	3.2	7.2	46%	.351	1.51	4.20	3.90	4.18	1.6
2013	ROC	AAA	25	6	3	0	9	9	58	65	3	17	34	2.6	5.3	42%	.316	1.41	3.88	3.64	4.84	0.2
2013	MIN	MLB	25	1	5	0	10	10	48²	82	9	15	25	2.8	4.6	48%	.406	1.99	7.21	5.56	5.78	-0.1
2014	MIN	MLB	26	4	7	0	17	17	97²	112	11	32	63	2.9	5.8	45%	.318	1.47	4.94	4.60	5.37	-0.4

Worley's first season in Minnesota featured a rapid and panicky descent reminiscent of the airplane scene in *Almost Famous*, as the former Phillie plummeted from Opening Day starter to struggling Triple-A hurler to enigmatic injury casualty in the space of three months. The Vanimal has never had overpowering stuff but commanded it well, generating a higher strikeout rate and less hard contact than you'd think his upper-80s fastball could produce. But his ten starts in Minnesota were disastrous, highlighted by a .401 BABIP that was due more to laser shows than luck. Shipped down to Rochester, Worley was marginally better but shoulder woes soon set in that kept him off the mound all summer. It may be that the league his finally caught on to his low-velocity tricks, and with his health and headspace an open question, nobody knows what the Twins can expect going forward.

LINEOUTS

HITTERS

PLAYER	TEAM	LVL	AGE	PA	R	2B	3B	HR	RBI	BB	SO	SB-CS	AVG/OBP/SLG	TAv	BABIP	BRR	FRAA	WARP
SS D. Bernier	ROC	AAA	33	353	47	15	5	3	41	31	74	4-2	.295/.370/.407	.272	.377	-3	SS(91): 3.7	2.1
	MIN	MLB	33	64	9	3	0	0	5	8	15	2-1	.226/.339/.283	.232	.316	1	SS(20): 2.0, 3B(7): -0.0	0.3
C E. Fryer	ROC	AAA	27	243	32	11	2	5	31	35	47	8-0	.215/.339/.365	.251	.252	-0.9	C(61): -0.0	0.8
	MIN	MLB	27	16	2	1	0	1	4	3	3	0-0	.385/.500/.692	.400	.444	0.1	C(5): -0.1	0.3
SS N. Goodrum	CDR	A	21	455	62	22	4	4	45	60	105	20-4	.260/.364/.369	.263	.345	-2.9	SS(81): 11.8, 3B(6): 0.6	2.8
3B T. Harrison	CDR	A	20	537	66	28	6	15	59	68	125	2-4	.253/.366/.416	.282	.316	1.2	3B(112): -3.0, LF(1): -0.1	2.1
1B D. Hicks	CDR	A	23	400	50	31	0	13	82	34	85	0-1	.297/.355/.494	.293	.350	-2.6	1B(85): -2.2	1.3
	FTM	A+	23	176	18	8	0	4	28	22	38	0-1	.270/.364/.405	.284	.327	-2.2	1B(34): -1.4	0.3
C M. Koch	FTM	A+	24	393	38	20	1	7	40	35	75	1-1	.278/.346/.401	.270	.333	-3.8	C(81): -0.2, 1B(3): -0.0	1.3
SS A. Mejia	FTM	A+	21	328	41	10	1	0	28	26	30	14-10	.308/.359/.349	.269	.337	1.3	SS(50): -0.1, 2B(13): -1.4	1.4
2B J. Polanco	CDR	A	19	523	76	32	10	5	78	42	59	4-4	.308/.362/.452	.297	.336	-0.4	2B(57): -0.2, SS(49): -4.5	2.9
RF W. Ramirez	NBR	AA	27	31	3	1	0	0	0	2	6	1-0	.172/.226/.207	.187	.217	-0.2	RF(1): 0.0, LF(1): -0.0	-0.2
	MIN	MLB	27	87	5	6	1	0	6	3	23	0-0	.272/.302/.370	.243	.373	-1.1	CF(9): 0.4, RF(9): 0.7	0.0
LF N. Roberts	BLT	A	23	352	60	18	3	4	33	44	37	27-8	.299/.433/.427	.308	.332	2.6	LF(36): 3.5, RF(34): 2.6	3.3
1B K. Vargas	FTM	A+	22	520	68	33	1	19	93	50	105	0-0	.267/.344/.468	.284	.304	-0.9	1B(81): -3.9	1.5
RF A. Walker	CDR	A	21	553	83	31	7	27	109	31	115	10-0	.278/.319/.526	.287	.304	0.2	RF(122): -6.8	2.0
LF J. Williams	CDR	A	22	324	65	12	6	8	42	47	67	15-7	.281/.391/.461	.296	.342	2.2	LF(72): 2.7, CF(2): 0.1	2.9
	FTM	A+	22	162	17	5	0	1	16	19	38	11-6	.236/.333/.293	.242	.314	0.1	LF(40): -1.9	-0.1

Huzzahs for minor league veteran **Doug Bernier**, who leveraged his first decent season since 2008 into two punchless months in the Minnesota infield before elbow woes set in; he can draw a few walks and make some weak contact, but isn't even a good bet for a utility infield job going forward. ⊘ Minor-league backstop **Eric Fryer** spent a few weeks in Minnesota keeping pitched balls from hitting the umpire, and can now tell his grandkids that he once posted a higher WARP than Justin Morneau; he could be in the backup catcher mix, but his career .208/.312/.313 Triple-A line speaks volumes about his bat. ⊘ Athletic switch-hitter **Niko Goodrum** has speed, a mature approach and some juice in his bat, but continues to miss too many hittable pitches; he likely won't stick at shortstop, but could become a nice utility option. ⊘ The Twins snagged **Travis Harrison** as a supplemental first-rounder in 2011 and have been rewarded with some serious thumpage; opinions are mixed on whether he'll stick at the hot corner, and advanced pitchers may take advantage of his aggressive approach, but he's definitely one to watch. ⊘ Man-mountain **D.J. Hicks** mashed in Low-A but lost some of his power in the Florida State League; already 24 and at the bottom of the defensive spectrum, he'll need to keep putting up eye-popping numbers to move up the prospect charts. ⊘ Strong-armed backstop **Matthew Koch** was a little old for High-A last summer, but any time a catcher gives off the slightest whiff of competency with the bat, it should get the organization's attention. ⊘ **Aderlin Mejia** has good speed, a quick bat, contact ability and no power; his glove at shortstop is more steady than flashy, so the Twins have moved him all over the diamond to help enable his future as a switch-hitting utility man. ⊘ Switch-hitting infielder **Jorge Polanco** impressed as a 20-year-old in the Midwest League, waiting for his pitch and spraying line drives all over the yard; he may be stretched at shortstop but flashes a plus glove at the keystone, and with solid all-around tools and developing gap power he has a future. ⊘ Toolsy former Tigers farmhand **Wilkin Ramirez** spent some forgettable time on the Minnesota roster before a foul ball fractured his tibia; his agent is working on an endorsement deal for an aptly-named upscale cologne called "Unfulfilled." ⊘ On-base machine **Nate Roberts** can hit, steals bases and shows a remarkable determination to take one for the team; injuries cost him yet another season, but he could be an asset at the top of the order if he can ever stay in the lineup. ⊘ Man-mountain **Kennys Vargas** improved his approach last season and launched plenty of fireworks in the pitcher-friendly Florida State League; he's a below-average defender at first base, so he'll go as far as his power bat carries him. ⊘ **Adam Walker** led the Midwest League in home runs and flashes a strong arm and average range for right field; his aggressive approach may lead to contact issues as he moves into the upper minors, but the power is real and could eventually earn him big-league meal money. ⊘ **J.D. Williams** improved his approach, shortened his swing, and made more contact during a successful trip through the Midwest League; limited to left field, he'll likely need to find a little more thunder in his bat to have a career.

PITCHERS

PLAYER	TEAM	LVL	AGE	W	L	SV	IP	H	HR	BB	SO	BB9	SO9	GB%	BABIP	WHIP	ERA	FIP	FRA	WARP
D. Baxendale	FTM	A+	22	7	0	0	57[1]	34	2	11	48	1.7	7.5	35%	.213	0.78	1.10	2.70	3.81	0.7
	NBR	AA	22	5	7	0	92[2]	110	13	22	64	2.1	6.2	36%	.317	1.42	5.63	4.54	4.78	0.6
L. Darnell	NBR	AA	24	6	6	0	96[2]	96	4	23	77	2.1	7.2	54%	.321	1.23	2.61	3.23	3.80	1.6
	ROC	AAA	24	4	4	0	57	63	5	22	43	3.5	6.8	49%	.339	1.49	4.26	4.20	5.18	0.2
P. Dean	NBR	AA	24	6	11	0	125	151	12	17	61	1.2	4.4	44%	.310	1.34	4.68	4.05	4.61	1.2
	ROC	AAA	24	3	2	0	40	38	0	5	22	1.1	4.9	48%	.288	1.08	2.03	2.55	3.91	0.6
M. Hoffman	TOL	AAA	24	4	3	0	35	32	2	16	35	4.1	9.0	46%	.323	1.37	2.06	3.40	4.87	0.0
Z. Jones	FTM	A+	22	4	3	14	48[2]	28	2	28	70	5.2	12.9	44%	.277	1.15	1.85	2.75	3.04	1.1
S. Martis	ROC	AAA	26	2	4	11	80[1]	68	8	31	65	3.5	7.3	34%	.258	1.23	4.26	4.04	5.46	-0.1
	MIN	MLB	26	0	1	0	9[2]	6	3	4	7	3.7	6.5	39%	.120	1.03	5.59	6.90	7.87	-0.3
M. Melotakis	CDR	A	22	11	4	1	111	106	6	39	84	3.2	6.8	51%	.293	1.31	3.16	3.72	4.48	1.7
T. Rogers	CDR	A	22	0	1	0	10	14	1	4	10	3.6	9.0	64%	.371	1.80	7.20	3.84	5.02	0.1
	FTM	A+	22	11	6	0	130[2]	119	5	32	83	2.2	5.7	56%	.286	1.16	2.55	3.41	5.23	-0.2

A supplemental first-rounder in 2012, former Georgia Tech closer **Luke Bard** lost most of his first pro season to shoulder woes; now healthy, the Twins may take another look at him as a starter, but his mid-90s heat and darting slider will likely work best in relief. ⊘ A typical Twin with an atypical name, **D.J. Baxendale** used his upper-80s fastball and excellent command to minimize walks and dominate in High-A, but struggled in the second half against more advanced hitters; pitchers with such low strikeout rates walk a fine line, but if everything breaks right he could grow into a major league swingman. ⊘ **Logan Darnell** earned a spot on the 40-man roster after posting indifferent peripherals and a solid ERA in the high minors; while his low-90s fastball and mundane secondary stuff don't scream "big league starter," his .220/.289/.306 line against lefties whispers "LOOGY." ⊘ A stereotypical Twin with a typical name, **Pat Dean** fills the strike zone with lefty junk, finds bats and lets his defense do the work; he looks like rotation filler at best, but the Twins have a rotation that needs filling, so you never know. ⊘ Minnesota looked past his marijuana-related high school suspension and inconsistent production and took **Stephen Gonsalves** in the fourth round of last summer's draft; the young lefty rewarded their faith with a dominant debut in rookie ball, and, with good lefty velocity and a starter's frame, he could become a mid-rotation workhorse if his secondary stuff and command develop. ⊘ A couple of late-season DL stints came at a bad time for **Matt Hoffman**, as the Tigers' lack of second lefty would have otherwise meant his major-league debut. He signed with the Twins in December, giving him a new depth chart to watch anxiously. ⊘ **Zach Jones** has the complete closer-in-waiting accessory kit—mid-90s heat, developing slider, plenty of missed bats, a fondness for Dethklok—and if he lowers his walk rate could become a bullpen beast. ⊘ After romping through the Appy League as a teenager, **Felix Jorge** will tote his electric mid-90s fastball and developing slider and changeup into his first full season this summer; if he grows into his frame and improves his command, he could find work in the middle of a big-league rotation, and if not the late innings beckon. ⊘ **Shairon Martis** moved to the 'pen last year and earned a September call-up to Minnesota but didn't make much of an impression; while his background in Curaçao differentiates him from most minor league relievers, his low-velo assortment is all too familiar. ⊘ Lightning-armed lefty **Mason Melotakis** doesn't miss as many bats as his mid-90s heat, solid slider and developing changeup would predict; his strikeout rate went up in a few late-season relief outings, a fact the Twins may chew on as food for thought. ⊘ Lefty **Taylor Rogers** is a Twin City throwback, having found success in his full-season debut with average stuff, plus command, few walks and a typically low strikeout rate; if he can work the same magic as he moves into the high minors, he could eventually fill a fifth-starter/swingman role. ⊘ There's plenty to like about towering lefty **Aaron Slegers**: a fastball that hits the low 90s and generates groundballs, a surprisingly repeatable delivery, developing off-speed stuff that could keep him in the rotation and excellent control that led to nine strikeouts for each walk in his brief Appy league stay; his full-season debut will be closely watched. ⊘ It's a long way from the complex leagues to Target Field, but Aussie tyro **Lewis Thorpe** looks like he owns a jetpack and a map after posting an 11:1 strikeout-to-walk ratio as a 17-year-old. With surprisingly advanced command of a lively low-90s fastball, if his secondary stuff develops and he bulks up as he matures, he could grow into a second starter.

MANAGER: RON GARDENHIRE

YEAR	TEAM	W-L	Pythag +/−	Avg PC	100+ P	120+ P	QS	BQS	REL	REL w Zero R	IBB	PH	PH Avg	PH HR	SB2	CS2	SB3	CS3	SAC Att	SAC %	POS SAC	Squeeze	Swing	In Play
2011	MIN	63-99	0	95.2	66	2	80	9	457	340	37	87	.175	0	86	33	6	4	52	59.6%	31	1	361	135
2012	MIN	66-96	0	88.0	29	0	62	3	499	390	43	59	.260	0	111	33	24	3	52	63.5%	32	1	384	108
2013	MIN	66-96	0	91.1	44	0	62	6	511	415	31	97	.163	1	50	31	1	2	40	72.5%	26	0	292	93

The Twins are the same type of team now that they were in their early 21st century glory run under Ron Gardenhire—it's just that now they suck. Back when the Twins claimed six division titles in nine years, their strongest points were their pitcher control, especially in the bullpen. In eight straight seasons, the Twins under Gardy and longtime pitching coach Rick Anderson finished first or second in the majors in fewest walks issued. (They finished a lousy fourth best of all clubs in 2002.) Since then, they've still been good, but not insanely good. This year they finished seventh of the 30 teams in walks allowed. In those same glory years, the Twins consistently had one of the best bullpens around. Their bullpen is still a strength—but now the team has flipped. Instead of being defined by its strengths, the Twins are defined by their weaknesses. They always liked control pitchers instead of strikeout artists—think Brad Radke—but now they are comically inept at fanning people. The Twins have followed the same formula down a dead end.

Gardenhire has lost 291 games in the last three years, but is slated to be back for 2014. He'll be just the fourth manager since 1950 to come back after losing that many games in three years with one club. The other three have two things in common: 1) they all managed expansion teams in their first three seasons, and 2) they all lost the job during the fourth year—Casey Stengel with the Mets, Preston Gomez with San Diego and Darrell Johnson with Seattle. Folks, Gardenhire better start looking to update his resume.

New York Mets

By Emma Span

"I was thinking, if the world had ended on Saturday, we wouldn't have to deal with these things." —Mets General Manager Sandy Alderson, discussing the team's budget, May 2011

"Outfield? What outfield? We're probably gonna have to bring the fences in another 150 feet!" —Sandy Alderson, November 2012

"I was upstairs stacking our money … Don't get excited. They were all fives." —Sandy Alderson, November 2013

This offseason has been hyped for years as the one when the Mets could finally spend again. So now that it has come and (mostly) gone: Was it? Can they?

Well …

There is a tendency, whenever things go wrong with the Mets, to just chalk it up to their inherent Metsness. Mets gonna Mets! LOLMets. However, the Mets' current issues are not their usual issues—or any team's usual issues. The Mets are not especially, at the moment, Metsing. They are still trying to claw their way back to a position from which they can Mets.

It wasn't so long ago that the Mets had a tendency to spend lots of money, sometimes unwisely (see, for example, $153,550,596 in 2009, per Cot's Baseball Contracts—second only to the Yankees' payroll—in exchange for 70 wins). This could be frustrating. But for the past few offseasons, they've had virtually no money at all to spend. That's frustrating in its own way.

But this offseason? Going into the winter, it was hard to know for sure how much money the Mets actually had to spend, because these days it's not entirely up to them: It depends in part on JPMorgan Chase, to whom they have a loan of around $250 million coming due this summer. And that's just the most immediate debt. Overall, as the reporting of Howard Megdal at *Capital New York* has made clear, the Wilpons, through their various holdings, owe more than

a billion dollars. More than $600 million of that, borrowed against television network SNY, comes due in 2015, which means the team and its fans will very possibly have to go through all of this again next offseason.

Can the Mets refinance? Can they come up with the money? How much will their creditors allow them to give to capable and pricey players, in the interests of the team's long-term health, before their debt is paid? That last question has been partially answered this winter, and the answer appears to be: Some, but not enough.

Going into the offseason, the Mets' needs on the field were much clearer than their situation off it: At least one reliable innings-eater on staff to bolster their promising young pitching; a shortstop who can hit his way out of a damp paper bag; at least one but preferably two good bullpen arms; at least one but preferably two outfield bats; and ideally, a veteran catcher to back up and mentor top catching prospect Travis d'Arnaud.

With the team's signing of outfielder Curtis Granderson (four years, $60 million) and starting pitcher Bartolo Colon (two years, $20 million), they filled several holes. Granderson will be 33 in 2014 and Colon will turn an eye-popping 41 in May—reason for caution, especially combined with Colon's 2012 suspension for synthetic testosterone. Still, Colon was excellent last season, giving the A's 190 innings with a 2.65 ERA, striking out 117 and walking just 29, good for an ERA+ of 141. While he can't replace injured ace Matt Harvey, who will spend 2014 recovering from Tommy John surgery—no one can—he should help. The Mets also signed outfielder Chris Young to a one-year, $7.25 million deal. Young's defense should be a significant plus, but he's unlikely to be much better than league average at the plate—though league average is still a significant improvement for a team whose outfield in 2013 only qualified as such on a technicality.

METS PROSPECTUS
2013 W-L: 74-88, 3rd in NL East

Pythag	.455	22nd	DER	.700	20th
RS/G	3.82	23rd	B-Age	28.1	14th
RA/G	4.22	16th	P-Age	28.3	19th
TAv	.252	22nd	Salary	$93.7	15th
BRR	20.18	1st	M$/MW	$3.16	19th
TAv-P	.272	24th	DL Days	1318	26th
FIP	3.76	10th	$ on DL	42%	30th

	Runs	HR/RH	HR/LH	Runs/RH	Runs/LH
Three-Year Park Factors	97	107	97	101	93

Top Hitter WARP	5.84 (David Wright)
Top Pitcher WARP	4.23 (Matt Harvey)
Top Prospect	Noah Syndergaard

However, the Mets were not in on most of the bigger free agents. Shin-Soo Choo, Robinson Cano and Jacoby Ellsbury were all clearly too pricey; the Mets were reluctant to even meet with Cano's representatives, and did so only while protesting that they were really just being polite. That leaves a lot of areas of need still needy. General Manager Sandy Alderson told reporters that the Mets might just have to "live with certain weaknesses."

It isn't Alderson's fault. This gig was supposed to represent a chance for him (and for Paul DePodesta and J.P. Ricciardi, who came on board with him) to see what he could do with resources behind him, finally: "Moneyball with money." Instead, the Mets' payroll had fallen, per the Cot's figures, to $94 million in 2013, and that only because of contracts signed before Alderson arrived, including those of Jason Bay ($18 million) and Johan Santana ($25 million), neither of whom played for the team last year. Relieved of those two burdens, the Mets were able spend more this winter than the jaw-droppingly low $5 million they put into the market last offseason. But Alderson is still not working with anywhere near the resources he was once expected to have. The Mets' 2014 payroll is shaping up to be somewhere around their 2013 level—these days, quite low for a team in the biggest market in the country.

While Alderson could probably have done a better job of managing expectations and communicating realistically with fans, he didn't get the Mets into this mess, and he has been diligently trying to dig them out of it since his arrival. He's done a solid job of getting some building blocks into place via the trades of Carlos Beltran and R.A. Dickey, which, if the team is able to actually build on them, could provide a foundation for success.

Given this winter's relatively weak, top-heavy free agent class, it would have been a long shot for the Mets to leap from 74 wins in 2013 to contention in 2014 under the best of monetary circumstances. Even *with* Harvey it would have been tough, though Harvey makes all things seem possible. Almost every free agent decision would need to be a smart one, and prospects would have to develop at just the right pace. But it certainly wouldn't be a stretch for them to take some significant strides in the right direction—and at this point, a .500 season would be real progress.

Baseball Prospectus ranked the Mets as the 10th-best farm system in baseball going into last season. Regardless of where precisely they end up ranked going into 2014, they're developing players who can help the team—but they're still not the Cardinals. To be more than an afterthought in the National League, the Mets are going to have to spend.

What the Mets do have, though, is no small thing: organizational pitching depth. Harvey was (and is, or will be upon his expected 2015 return) obviously the star, and it's too much to expect even the best prospects to be as incredibly good immediately upon arrival as he was. But the Mets also have the serviceable Jonathon Niese and Dillon Gee in their rotation, as well as top-level prospect Zack Wheeler, acquired in the trade of Beltran to the Giants; he already got his feet wet in the big leagues last season. Noah Syndegaard, who came over in the Dickey trade, is, along with Rafael Montero, the standout among the Mets' minor-league prospects. The system also includes less-striking but still intriguing young pitchers like Jeurys Familia and Jacob DeGrom. The hope is that one or both of Syndegaard and Montero could help this season, but neither has performed in the majors yet, hence the need for an established horse like Colon to anchor the rotation.

When it comes to the other half of the game, things are a lot less encouraging.

In 2013, the Mets had the second-worst OPS in the National League (and the fourth-worst OPS+). They had the second-worst batting average, the third-worst on base percentage and the fourth-fewest home runs. They had a run differential of -65, and their Pythagorean record was identical to their actual record, 74-88.

Give manager Terry Collins some credit for keeping the team from completely imploding, despite injuries and the obviousness of the fact that no one expected anything from this group. The Mets were never going to be good with that roster, but they did not give up on games, and the losing season, their fifth in a row, did not spiral out of control. (Some fans will wonder forever if Harvey's injury could have been mitigated by shutting him down at the very first sign of discomfort or tenderness; pitcher elbows are mysterious and fragile things, and we'll probably never know for certain.)

David Wright is still awesome, of course, but he is the only player who hit for the Mets last year who could be described as such. Their second-best hitter was Marlon Byrd, who was unexpectedly excellent, and so was shipped off to the Pirates in August for a 19-year-old second baseman and a reliever. From Wright and Byrd it was a steep drop-off to ... Daniel Murphy, a moderately above-average second baseman? Part-timers Josh Satin (and his eyebrows) and Lucas Duda? The latter, if there is a merciful god, will never be forced to play the outfield again. It was like watching an eager but uncoordinated puppy trying to play catch with a Frisbee sized for a St. Bernard.

While the system has a number of tantalizing pitchers for fans to dream on, it won't help them score. With the exception of d'Arnaud and maybe third baseman Wilmer Flores (blocked by Wright unless he can master second base), their best positional prospects are a ways off. Meanwhile they need several more solid bats before their lineup causes opposing pitchers to lose sleep, even with Granderson on board. Can they afford to acquire those bats? Not this year, it seems. And what will have changed by next year?

It's tempting to wonder who, exactly, is making these decisions at JPMorgan Chase. A group of people? The intraoffice fantasy league winner? Who's in charge? Is he or she a baseball fan? Presumably, they would want the Mets to do well, if only so that the team can be profitable and repay its debts more quickly. But do they understand what the team needs? Do they watch the games? Do they pay attention to advanced statistics? Do they follow the prospect rankings? Probably they care about attendance as an indicator of financial health, but do they understand why fans have been staying away these last few years? Do they care? Do they have an opinion on Travis d'Arnaud's plate discipline? Do bankers dream of electric corner outfield bats?

Media relations personnel at JPMorgan Chase, unsurprisingly, did not respond to request for comment.

For years, the Mets have been asking their fans to be patient. Time is running out on that front. Attendance has fallen in each of the past five seasons, from 4.0 million in 2008, Shea Stadium's last year, to 3.2 million in (smaller) Citi

Field's first year, down to 2.1 million in 2013, the league's third worst total. Fans will be back when the team earns them back—but if that's going to happen, if the team is going to succeed in the next several years, what they'll really need is the patience of its creditors.

It's long been an overrated truism that you can't rebuild in New York, that fans won't stand for it. In fact, fans can grasp perfectly well the need to occasionally blow things up and start again—as long as there seems to be a clear, intelligent plan behind it. The killer for Mets fans is not the waiting for success, but the uncertainty that it will ever arrive under the current ownership. Right now, it's hard not to feel that the goalposts are simply being moved back every year.

Emma Span is a Senior Editor at Sports on Earth *and the author of the book* 90% of the Game is Half Mental: And Other Tales from the Edge of Baseball Fandom.

HITTERS

Andrew Brown RF
Born: 9/10/1984 Age: 29
Bats: R Throws: R Height: 6' 0''
Weight: 185 Breakout: 4%
Improve: 27% Collapse: 3%
Attrition: 10% MLB: 59%

Comparables:
Nelson Cruz, Todd Linden, Michael Restovich

YEAR	TEAM	LVL	AGE	PA	R	2B	3B	HR	RBI	BB	SO	SB	CS	AVG/OBP/SLG	TAv	BABIP	BRR	FRAA	WARP
2011	MEM	AAA	26	428	67	12	3	20	73	56	105	4	4	.284/.382/.501	.392	.340	0.3	RF(10): -0.2, LF(9): -1.1	1.4
2011	SLN	MLB	26	22	1	1	0	0	3	0	8	0	0	.182/.182/.227	.139	.286	0.4	RF(7): -0.0	-0.2
2012	CSP	AAA	27	438	81	33	4	24	98	37	100	3	1	.308/.364/.597	.324	.350	-2.9	LF(60): 1.4, RF(41): -0.8	3.8
2012	COL	MLB	27	126	14	7	0	5	11	12	34	2	2	.232/.302/.429	.243	.280	-1.1	RF(24): 1.0, LF(12): 0.2	0.4
2013	LVG	AAA	28	185	39	15	6	7	41	23	34	0	0	.346/.432/.660	.355	.393	-0.4	RF(33): 0.2, 1B(4): -0.1	2.3
2013	NYN	MLB	28	165	16	5	0	7	24	13	44	1	0	.227/.288/.400	.258	.273	0.3	RF(25): 0.6, LF(14): -0.8	0.4
2014	NYN	MLB	29	250	30	11	1	11	35	21	69	1	1	.244/.311/.445	.281	.300	-0.3	RF 0, LF -1	1.0

Brown weighs about 185 pounds and plays the game like he's pushing three bills. He swings out of his shoes in case he makes contact, generating incredible torque from his legs to turn around anything up in the zone. Sure, he whiffed every fourth plate appearance, but he showed enough pop to keep up with the cast of thousands vying for three hots and a cot from the 2014 Mets. As for playing the outfield, let's just say he's a cruiserweight with super heavyweight speed.

Gavin Cecchini SS
Born: 12/22/1993 Age: 20
Bats: R Throws: R Height: 6' 1''
Weight: 180 Breakout: 0%
Improve: 0% Collapse: 0%
Attrition: 0% MLB: 0%

Comparables:
Pete Kozma, Eduardo Escobar, Juan Lagares

YEAR	TEAM	LVL	AGE	PA	R	2B	3B	HR	RBI	BB	SO	SB	CS	AVG/OBP/SLG	TAv	BABIP	BRR	FRAA	WARP
2013	BRO	A-	19	212	18	8	0	0	14	14	30	2	3	.273/.319/.314	.277	.319	0.1	SS(50): 5.7	1.9
2014	NYN	MLB	20	250	19	8	0	1	15	12	69	0	0	.191/.233/.247	.188	.260	-0.5	SS 2	-0.7

He's only just turned 20, but you know what you're getting with Cecchini: a steady, low-mistake shortstop with decent plate discipline. Basically, he won't screw anything up. But the former 12th overall pick isn't setting the world on fire, either, and did nothing to assuage concerns about his power, with just eight extra-base hits in 212 plate appearances. The consensus is he'll make a fine defensive shortstop one day, but "fine" doesn't make an impact; he's yet to even reach High-A, but the past two years have aggravated speculation over how much these tools can develop—or, in the case of his power, whether it exists at all.

Travis d'Arnaud C
Born: 2/10/1989 Age: 25
Bats: R Throws: R Height: 6' 2''
Weight: 195 Breakout: 4%
Improve: 34% Collapse: 5%
Attrition: 29% MLB: 74%

Comparables:
Ryan Lavarnway, Devin Mesoraco, Jeff Clement

YEAR	TEAM	LVL	AGE	PA	R	2B	3B	HR	RBI	BB	SO	SB	CS	AVG/OBP/SLG	TAv	BABIP	BRR	FRAA	WARP
2011	NHP	AA	22	466	72	33	1	21	78	33	100	4	2	.311/.371/.542	.342	.365	0.5	C(31): -0.5	1.8
2012	LVG	AAA	23	303	45	21	2	16	52	19	59	1	1	.333/.380/.595	.303	.374	0.1	C(55): 0.4, 1B(2): -0.1	2.8
2013	BIN	AA	24	30	2	2	1	3	3	9	0	0	.222/.300/.481	.266	.294	-0.8	C(7): 0.3	0.2
2013	LVG	AAA	24	78	19	8	0	2	12	21	12	0	0	.304/.487/.554	.355	.349	-1.2	C(18): 0.6	1.1
2013	NYN	MLB	24	112	4	3	0	1	5	12	21	0	0	.202/.286/.263	.205	.244	-0.5	C(30): -0.3	-0.2
2014	NYN	MLB	25	250	27	11	1	8	31	21	56	1	0	.252/.318/.416	.273	.300	-0.4	C -0, 1B -0	1.4

A foul ball broke d'Arnaud's foot in April and delayed his big-league arrival, adding to what's become a troubling record of injuries for the young catcher. Worse, though, the injury doesn't explain why d'Arnaud showed none of the power potential he'd shown while in Blue Jays system. The Mets' coaching staff blames d'Arnaud's swing, particularly his tendency to wrap the bat when he tries to add oomph. If the bat speed doesn't improve, we may be looking at the French Paul Lo Duca; he'll still almost certainly be the best Mets catcher since Mike Piazza, but in Queens they know what faint praise that is.

Ike Davis 1B

Born: 3/22/1987 Age: 27
Bats: L Throws: L Height: 6' 4"
Weight: 230 Breakout: 5%
Improve: 60% Collapse: 5%
Attrition: 7% MLB: 96%

Comparables:
Don Mincher, Mark Teixeira, Jason Thompson

YEAR	TEAM	LVL	AGE	PA	R	2B	3B	HR	RBI	BB	SO	SB	CS	AVG/OBP/SLG	TAv	BABIP	BRR	FRAA	WARP
2011	NYN	MLB	24	149	20	8	1	7	25	17	31	0	0	.302/.383/.543	.329	.344	1.7	1B(36): 1.0	1.7
2012	NYN	MLB	25	584	66	26	0	32	90	61	141	0	2	.227/.308/.462	.272	.246	-2.5	1B(148): 2.6	1.6
2013	LVG	AAA	26	92	21	7	0	7	13	17	18	0	0	.293/.424/.667	.344	.300	-1.5	1B(19): 0.7	0.9
2013	NYN	MLB	26	377	37	14	0	9	33	57	101	4	0	.205/.326/.334	.249	.268	-0.6	1B(96): -2.6	-0.5
2014	NYN	MLB	27	409	50	18	0	17	55	49	100	2	1	.238/.332/.429	.283	.280	-0.8	1B 2	1.5

What do you make of a career .927 OPS in September ... and .584 in May? What do you make of a dead-pull hitter spending months standing miles back from home plate ... and never adjusting when pitchers predictably started pitching him outside? What do you make of a guy who was sent to Triple-A hitting .161 ... and ended up third in the majors in second-half OBP? As in 2012, Davis authored a late-season surge, but the sequel was crazier than the original. Most players would kill for a 131 OPS+, but that was *the spread* between Davis' first- and second-half marks. The flesh is willing, but the spirit is often weak—going forward, maturity, age and coaching (or, alternately, a profligate trade partner) are the Mets' best hopes for Davis.

Matt Den Dekker CF

Born: 8/10/1987 Age: 26
Bats: L Throws: L Height: 6' 1"
Weight: 205 Breakout: 7%
Improve: 18% Collapse: 8%
Attrition: 25% MLB: 36%

Comparables:
Blake Tekotte, Scott Cousins, Brandon Barnes

YEAR	TEAM	LVL	AGE	PA	R	2B	3B	HR	RBI	BB	SO	SB	CS	AVG/OBP/SLG	TAv	BABIP	BRR	FRAA	WARP
2011	SLU	A+	23	302	54	19	8	6	36	24	65	12	5	.296/.362/.494	.294	.369	4.9	CF(41): -2.5	1.8
2011	BIN	AA	23	314	49	13	3	11	32	27	91	12	5	.235/.312/.426	.276	.305	1.8	CF(55): -3.6	1.1
2012	BIN	AA	24	268	47	21	4	8	29	20	64	10	7	.340/.397/.563	.331	.429	1.9	CF(56): -1.5, RF(1): -0.1	2.8
2012	BUF	AAA	24	317	37	10	4	9	47	14	90	11	2	.220/.256/.373	.217	.279	4	CF(76): -1.3	-0.1
2013	SLU	A+	25	62	8	2	0	0	4	3	6	1	0	.276/.306/.310	.238	.302	-0.2	CF(14): -1.2	-0.2
2013	LVG	AAA	25	202	34	8	4	6	38	20	46	8	1	.296/.366/.486	.282	.364	2.6	CF(49): -0.0, LF(2): 0.1	1.6
2013	NYN	MLB	25	63	7	1	0	1	6	4	23	4	1	.207/.270/.276	.211	.324	1.8	CF(16): -1.0, RF(7): 0.1	-0.1
2014	NYN	MLB	26	250	30	9	2	6	23	15	75	7	2	.224/.276/.364	.239	.300	0.6	CF -3, RF -0	0.0

Den Dekker is something of an outlier in the Mets' system: The bat is a question mark, but—are you sitting down?—he has a position, and he can field it. Better still, despite a broken wrist cutting his season in half, he made strides offensively, cutting his strikeout rate by more than a fifth. Following his major-league promotion in late August, den Dekker whiffed on a phenomenal 22 percent of fastballs, and generally did his best to undercut the first part of this comment. But if he can acclimatize himself to big-league pitching and curb his aggressiveness even slightly, the power is already there—and so too might be an everyday center fielder.

Lucas Duda LF

Born: 2/3/1986 Age: 28
Bats: L Throws: R Height: 6' 4"
Weight: 255 Breakout: 3%
Improve: 49% Collapse: 8%
Attrition: 15% MLB: 88%

Comparables:
Seth Smith, David Murphy, Alex Gordon

YEAR	TEAM	LVL	AGE	PA	R	2B	3B	HR	RBI	BB	SO	SB	CS	AVG/OBP/SLG	TAv	BABIP	BRR	FRAA	WARP
2011	BUF	AAA	25	157	22	8	0	10	24	23	27	0	0	.302/.414/.597	.326	.309	-0.6	RF(14): -1.1, LF(12): -1.8	1.0
2011	NYN	MLB	25	347	38	21	3	10	50	33	57	1	0	.292/.370/.482	.314	.326	-3.8	1B(43): 1.2, RF(42): -2.3	1.9
2012	BUF	AAA	26	107	12	4	0	3	8	10	21	0	0	.260/.327/.396	.264	.301	-1.1	LF(18): -0.7, RF(4): 0.1	0.2
2012	NYN	MLB	26	459	43	15	0	15	57	51	120	1	0	.239/.329/.389	.261	.301	-4.7	RF(81): -7.8, LF(24): -0.7	-0.9
2013	SLU	A+	27	30	4	2	0	1	5	2	7	0	0	.250/.300/.429	.235	.300	-0.7	LF(5): 0.2	-0.1
2013	LVG	AAA	27	78	13	3	0	0	8	14	15	1	0	.306/.423/.355	.272	.388	-0.9	1B(12): 0.2, LF(3): 0.1	0.2
2013	NYN	MLB	27	384	42	16	0	15	33	55	102	0	3	.223/.352/.415	.286	.276	0.6	LF(58): -3.8, 1B(34): -0.4	1.1
2014	NYN	MLB	28	407	47	18	1	14	52	45	96	1	0	.241/.335/.415	.279	.290	-0.8	LF -2, RF -3	1.0

Unfortunately for Duda, there's a strong argument that his past two seasons are what we can expect going forward—that the league really has "figured him out." Unlike most hulking left-handed sluggers, Duda is downright vulnerable to the low-and-inside pitch; his inability to turn on the ball hampers his power production, and he hasn't made himself a threat to the opposite field. He crushes mistakes up in the zone, but that's about it. The plate discipline and walks are a real weapon, but until further notice, Duda's greatest skill is the *idea* that he might hit the ball.

Allan Dykstra 1B

Born: 5/21/1987 Age: 27
Bats: L Throws: R Height: 6' 5"
Weight: 215 Breakout: 1%
Improve: 6% Collapse: 9%
Attrition: 19% MLB: 34%

Comparables:
Josh Whitesell, Mark Hamilton, Jeff Larish

YEAR	TEAM	LVL	AGE	PA	R	2B	3B	HR	RBI	BB	SO	SB	CS	AVG/OBP/SLG	TAv	BABIP	BRR	FRAA	WARP
2011	BIN	AA	24	475	57	22	1	19	77	69	131	1	1	.267/.389/.474	.309	.348	-3.8	1B(65): -4.3	1.3
2012	SLU	A+	25	40	3	3	0	0	2	8	11	1	0	.258/.400/.355	.246	.381	-0.1	1B(6): 0.5	0.0
2012	BIN	AA	25	248	35	9	0	7	25	51	65	1	0	.262/.423/.419	.304	.355	-0.9	1B(41): 1.5	1.5
2013	BIN	AA	26	489	56	22	0	21	82	102	123	0	0	.274/.436/.503	.345	.346	-7.5	1B(58): -2.0	4.0
2014	NYN	MLB	27	250	30	8	0	8	31	38	74	0	0	.225/.353/.389	.280	.300	-0.5	1B -1	0.7

We have a rule around here: Anyone who gets nominated for MiLB Offensive Player of the Year gets a comment, even if, like Allan Dykstra, his prospect status remains very much in question. Dykstra had a phenomenal season at Double-A, featuring that perfectly time-consuming combination of a discerning eye and a swing too long to get to the pitches he likes. The biggest problem, though, is he's entering his age-27 season, and was drafted the same year as Ike Davis. Then again, given their respective 2013s, how far apart are they really?

Wilmer Flores 3B

Born: 8/6/1991 Age: 22
Bats: R Throws: R Height: 6' 3"
Weight: 190 Breakout: 4%
Improve: 23% Collapse: 11%
Attrition: 28% MLB: 43%

Comparables:
Adrian Cardenas, Tony Abreu, Luis Valbuena

YEAR	TEAM	LVL	AGE	PA	R	2B	3B	HR	RBI	BB	SO	SB	CS	AVG/OBP/SLG	TAv	BABIP	BRR	FRAA	WARP
2011	SLU	A+	19	559	52	26	2	9	81	27	68	2	2	.269/.309/.380	.265	.291	-1.9	SS(92): 8.2	2.4
2012	SLU	A+	20	272	31	12	0	10	42	18	30	3	2	.289/.336/.463	.272	.286	-2.9	3B(61): -3.1, 2B(3): 0.2	0.6
2012	BIN	AA	20	275	37	18	2	8	33	20	30	0	0	.311/.361/.494	.291	.326	-1.4	3B(26): -2.0, 2B(24): 0.9	1.3
2013	LVG	AAA	21	463	69	36	4	15	86	25	63	1	3	.321/.357/.531	.300	.342	-1.2	2B(79): -4.8, 1B(11): 0.7	2.7
2013	NYN	MLB	21	101	8	5	0	1	13	5	23	0	0	.211/.248/.295	.200	.264	-0.3	3B(26): 1.8, 2B(2): -0.1	-0.2
2014	NYN	MLB	22	250	23	12	1	6	28	11	46	0	0	.247/.281/.384	.249	.280	-0.5	3B -1, 2B -1	0.3

Flores' hit tool is further along than most of the other 2013 Mets debutants, but the questions about his defense are right there with the rest of them. With David Wright, the Mets have exactly one position locked down for the foreseeable future, and that's the only position at which Flores might approach average. He is the prototypical B athlete, and his unnatural throwing motion will cost him wherever he plays. Flores has a wealth of minor-league experience for a 22-year-old, and the bat showed flashes at the major-league level, so the lack of production is not of much concern. But if he's to stay a Met, a Daniel Murphy-esque positional hunt—perhaps including left field—could be in order.

Curtis Granderson LF

Born: 3/16/1981 Age: 33
Bats: L Throws: R Height: 6' 1"
Weight: 195 Breakout: 1%
Improve: 29% Collapse: 3%
Attrition: 9% MLB: 94%

Comparables:
Ken Griffey, Jim Edmonds, Ellis Burks

YEAR	TEAM	LVL	AGE	PA	R	2B	3B	HR	RBI	BB	SO	SB	CS	AVG/OBP/SLG	TAv	BABIP	BRR	FRAA	WARP
2011	NYA	MLB	30	691	136	26	10	41	119	85	169	25	10	.262/.364/.552	.308	.295	4.8	CF(155): -12.9	5.0
2012	NYA	MLB	31	684	102	18	4	43	106	75	195	10	3	.232/.319/.492	.287	.260	2.3	CF(157): -11.7	3.1
2013	SWB	AAA	32	21	2	0	0	1	3	1	4	0	0	.400/.429/.550	.339	.467	0.4	LF(2): 0.0, RF(2): -0.1	0.2
2013	NYA	MLB	32	245	31	13	2	7	15	27	69	8	2	.229/.317/.407	.264	.302	0.6	CF(25): 1.1, RF(14): 0.7	0.9
2014	NYN	MLB	33	324	47	10	3	14	40	35	85	8	2	.231/.318/.434	.277	.270	0.8	LF -3, RF 0	1.1

Well, *that* went well. No sooner had Granderson made a mid-May return from the fractured forearm he suffered in his first spring training at-bat than he was hit by another bone-breaking pitch that kept him out until August. When he did get back for good, he'd been displaced in center by Brett Gardner, which probably would have happened even if he hadn't been hurt. Perhaps as a result of the injuries, he didn't hit for his typical power, and he batted just .177 in September, striking out in close to 40 percent of his at-bats. If there's a silver lining, it's that he held his own against southpaws for the third straight season. The Mets signed the salmon-loving Granderson to a four-year deal in December and are hoping his bones will prove less brittle going forward, though he's now at an age when the body begins to break down in more subtle ways that only get worse with time.

Juan Lagares CF

Born: 3/17/1989 Age: 25
Bats: R Throws: R Height: 6' 1"
Weight: 175 Breakout: 6%
Improve: 40% Collapse: 6%
Attrition: 36% MLB: 69%

Comparables:
Angel Pagan, Julio Borbon, Lorenzo Cain

YEAR	TEAM	LVL	AGE	PA	R	2B	3B	HR	RBI	BB	SO	SB	CS	AVG/OBP/SLG	TAv	BABIP	BRR	FRAA	WARP
2011	SLU	A+	22	335	51	15	6	7	49	21	47	5	6	.338/.380/.494	.277	.379	-0.4	LF(30): 1.8, CF(6): 1.3	1.3
2011	BIN	AA	22	170	21	11	3	2	22	5	29	10	2	.370/.391/.512	.357	.439	0.9	RF(18): 2.1, LF(13): 1.6	2.2
2012	BIN	AA	23	548	69	29	6	4	48	37	93	21	10	.283/.334/.389	.265	.337	2.8	CF(70): 13.2, RF(47): 7.0	4.8
2013	LVG	AAA	24	82	13	3	2	3	9	4	14	2	3	.346/.378/.551	.320	.393	0.4	CF(17): 1.0	1.0
2013	NYN	MLB	24	421	35	21	5	4	34	20	96	6	3	.242/.281/.352	.232	.310	0.3	CF(108): 7.6, RF(14): 0.5	2.0
2014	NYN	MLB	25	389	41	17	3	5	31	19	86	8	4	.251/.289/.356	.245	.310	0.1	CF 8, RF 2	1.6

No one knows what body snatchers or gremlins were afoot on Lagares' mystical plane ride from Triple-A Las Vegas, but after the Mets didn't consider him a minor-league center fielder until 2012, Lagares was a defensive superstar the moment he arrived in Flushing. Conversely, his Triple-A offensive numbers went almost completely out the window: He never walked much to begin with, but his lack of on-base was less a "free-swinging" thing and more an "I'm completely overmatched" thing. If he keeps up the defense, his bat won't need to improve all that much.

Zach Lutz 3B
Born: 6/3/1986 Age: 28
Bats: R Throws: R Height: 6' 1"
Weight: 220 Breakout: 0%
Improve: 9% Collapse: 6%
Attrition: 13% MLB: 22%
Comparables:
Mike Hollimon, Jack Hannahan, Matthew Brown

YEAR	TEAM	LVL	AGE	PA	R	2B	3B	HR	RBI	BB	SO	SB	CS	AVG/OBP/SLG	TAv	BABIP	BRR	FRAA	WARP
2011	BUF	AAA	25	250	38	12	0	11	31	27	70	0	0	.295/.380/.500	.297	.388	0	3B(31): 0.2, 1B(13): -0.3	1.4
2012	SLU	A+	26	26	2	2	0	1	8	4	5	0	0	.250/.346/.500	.284	.250	-1.4	3B(5): -0.1	0.0
2012	BUF	AAA	26	294	34	16	1	10	35	42	75	0	0	.299/.410/.496	.305	.391	-2.3	3B(56): -3.1, 1B(10): -1.0	1.4
2012	NYN	MLB	26	11	1	0	0	0	0	0	5	0	0	.091/.091/.091	.034	.167	0.1	1B(1): -0.0	-0.3
2013	LVG	AAA	27	466	62	27	4	13	80	54	102	0	2	.293/.377/.479	.283	.357	-2.7	3B(69): -5.0, 1B(28): 1.2	1.6
2013	NYN	MLB	27	26	2	2	0	0	2	6	6	0	0	.300/.462/.400	.319	.429	-0.4	3B(3): -0.0, 1B(1): -0.0	0.1
2014	NYN	MLB	28	250	26	11	1	7	29	26	70	0	0	.239/.326/.385	.268	.320	-0.5	3B -3, 1B -0	0.4

If every Mets prospect is right-handed, and every Mets offensive prospect shows some power but has no true position, and Zach Lutz is a Mets offensive prospect … you get the idea. Lutz has shown remarkable offensive consistency as he's risen through the system, so if anything he underachieved with yet another rock-solid campaign in homer-happy Las Vegas. Unfortunately, he's also been consistent about having no place to play; the Mets tried him at every corner infield and outfield position, but ultimately, as with Wilmer Flores, David Wright plays the only position he can handle. Unlike Flores, it's all likely moot, because Lutz is a bench bat.

Daniel Murphy 2B
Born: 4/1/1985 Age: 29
Bats: L Throws: R Height: 6' 2"
Weight: 205 Breakout: 4%
Improve: 51% Collapse: 3%
Attrition: 7% MLB: 99%
Comparables:
Aaron Hill, Jose Vidro, Orlando Hudson

YEAR	TEAM	LVL	AGE	PA	R	2B	3B	HR	RBI	BB	SO	SB	CS	AVG/OBP/SLG	TAv	BABIP	BRR	FRAA	WARP
2011	NYN	MLB	26	423	49	28	2	6	49	24	42	5	5	.320/.362/.448	.284	.345	-3.3	1B(52): 0.1, 3B(28): -0.5	1.8
2012	NYN	MLB	27	612	62	40	3	6	65	36	82	10	2	.291/.332/.403	.268	.329	4	2B(138): -2.6, 1B(12): -0.3	2.3
2013	NYN	MLB	28	697	92	38	4	13	78	32	95	23	3	.286/.319/.415	.265	.315	7.6	2B(150): -7.9, 1B(7): 0.4	2.2
2014	NYN	MLB	29	638	75	37	2	11	59	37	89	14	3	.275/.318/.400	.269	.300	0.6	2B -5, 1B 0	2.2

Murphy is the sort of player the Mets seem to be developing in abundance: He hits for a decent average, but paucities of on-base and slugging force his questionable defense into more demanding positions than he can play. The -7.5 FRAA don't tell the whole story: When Ike Davis is repeatedly caught off first base because he needs to pursue everything to his right, that's rarified air. Three years ago, the Mets thought they had a big-league hitter on their hands, and searched desperately for a place to play him. But the hitting leveled off and the search has failed. He may hit at this rate through the end of the decade, but he won't be a viable starter nearly as long.

Brandon Nimmo CF
Born: 3/27/1993 Age: 21
Bats: L Throws: R Height: 6' 3"
Weight: 185 Breakout: 0%
Improve: 0% Collapse: 0%
Attrition: 0% MLB: 0%
Comparables:
Aaron Hicks, Michael Saunders, Joe Benson

YEAR	TEAM	LVL	AGE	PA	R	2B	3B	HR	RBI	BB	SO	SB	CS	AVG/OBP/SLG	TAv	BABIP	BRR	FRAA	WARP
2012	BRO	A-	19	321	41	20	2	6	40	46	78	1	5	.248/.372/.406	.308	.328	0.6	CF(69): 5.1	3.3
2013	SAV	A	20	480	62	16	6	2	40	71	131	10	7	.273/.397/.359	.301	.402	2	CF(106): -1.2	4.0
2014	NYN	MLB	21	250	24	7	1	3	18	27	82	0	0	.197/.291/.278	.222	.300	-0.3	CF 0	-0.3

Expectations for hitters are always tempered in the pitcher-friendly South Atlantic League, but few moreso than those for Nimmo. His unusual background—Nimmo's native Wyoming is one of three states that does not offer high school baseball—and underwhelming offense at Low-A Brooklyn raised serious questions for his full-season debut. Shouldn't have worried. Nimmo shows an above-average eye and mature approach, all the more remarkable considering a still-hitchy swing that has negated his power potential. Overall, he may not have a 7 tool in his bag, but the full package looks much better than it did a year ago.

Kevin Plawecki C
Born: 2/26/1991 Age: 23
Bats: R Throws: R Height: 6' 2"
Weight: 205 Breakout: 3%
Improve: 21% Collapse: 1%
Attrition: 11% MLB: 31%
Comparables:
Russell Martin, Jason Castro, Josh Thole

YEAR	TEAM	LVL	AGE	PA	R	2B	3B	HR	RBI	BB	SO	SB	CS	AVG/OBP/SLG	TAv	BABIP	BRR	FRAA	WARP
2012	BRO	A-	21	252	26	8	0	7	27	25	24	0	0	.250/.345/.384	.283	.250	-0.1	C(36): -0.4, 1B(1): -0.0	1.5
2013	SAV	A	22	282	35	24	1	6	43	23	32	1	0	.314/.390/.494	.355	.336	-3.7	C(46): 0.6	3.7
2013	SLU	A+	22	239	25	14	0	2	37	19	21	0	0	.294/.391/.392	.295	.319	-1.9	C(42): -1.0, 1B(17): 1.5	1.5
2014	NYN	MLB	23	250	23	11	0	5	25	16	46	0	0	.236/.303/.348	.248	.270	-0.5	C -0, 1B 0	0.6

A mini-slump to end his first full professional season was just a blip on the radar for Plawecki, who should be a fast riser from here on in. Yet a key question has cropped up: Is he a first baseman or a catcher? The Mets gave him an extended run at first base, but all indications are he's an asset behind the dish despite an average arm. As with Plawecki's fandom of both Tim Tebow and Ke$ha, the Mets really need to pick one and move forward. Plawecki makes great contact with a superb eye, so a major-league regular will find himself under pressure soon—whether that's Travis d'Arnaud or the Mets' first baseman du jour remains to be seen.

Anthony Recker　C

Born: 8/29/1983 Age: 30
Bats: R Throws: R Height: 6' 2"
Weight: 240 Breakout: 6%
Improve: 17% Collapse: 10%
Attrition: 20% MLB: 34%

Comparables:
Chris Gimenez, Pete Laforest, Ryan Shealy

YEAR	TEAM	LVL	AGE	PA	R	2B	3B	HR	RBI	BB	SO	SB	CS	AVG/OBP/SLG	TAv	BABIP	BRR	FRAA	WARP
2011	SAC	AAA	27	412	61	24	1	16	48	56	81	7	5	.287/.388/.501	.283	.328	-0.3	C(23): 0.7, 1B(5): 0.1	1.0
2011	OAK	MLB	27	21	3	1	0	0		4	7	0	0	.176/.333/.235	.239	.300	-0.3	C(5): 0.1	0.0
2012	SAC	AAA	28	229	29	7	0	9	29	28	56	3	1	.265/.358/.435	.280	.326	-1.7	C(44): -0.5, LF(3): 0.1	1.4
2012	CHN	MLB	28	21	1	1	0	1	4	2	2	0	0	.167/.286/.389	.245	.133	-0.1	C(5): 0.1, 1B(1): -0.0	0.1
2012	OAK	MLB	28	37	3	1	0	0	0	4	13	0	0	.129/.250/.161	.180	.222	0.4	C(12): -0.2	0.0
2013	NYN	MLB	29	151	17	7	0	6	19	13	49	0	1	.215/.280/.400	.264	.280	-1.2	C(38): -0.3, P(1): -0.0	0.4
2014	*NYN*	*MLB*	*30*	*250*	*29*	*9*	*1*	*8*	*28*	*27*	*72*	*3*	*1*	*.216/.304/.370*	*.254*	*.280*	*-0.4*	*C 0, 1B 0*	*0.9*

Recker's time in the big leagues is going to be brief: He looks overmatched at the plate, and neither his throwing nor his receiving grants him much leeway. He earns a full comment here because he is, without a doubt, the best looking player in the league. You may commence Googling now. His surname's outstanding nickname potential might be wasted on a career backup, but "Home-Recker" has some legs. Yeah, we're pretty clever around here.

Josh Satin　1B

Born: 12/23/1984 Age: 29
Bats: R Throws: R Height: 6' 2"
Weight: 200 Breakout: 2%
Improve: 10% Collapse: 6%
Attrition: 16% MLB: 34%

Comparables:
Josh Whitesell, Juan Miranda, Shelley Duncan

YEAR	TEAM	LVL	AGE	PA	R	2B	3B	HR	RBI	BB	SO	SB	CS	AVG/OBP/SLG	TAv	BABIP	BRR	FRAA	WARP
2011	BIN	AA	26	404	60	35	2	11	60	57	91	2	2	.325/.423/.538	.352	.411	1.7	3B(30): -3.5, 2B(24): -3.8	2.9
2011	BUF	AAA	26	160	17	8	0	1	16	14	33	1	2	.317/.381/.393	.271	.405	-1.4	3B(17): -0.7, 1B(9): 0.2	0.3
2011	NYN	MLB	26	27	3	1	0	0	2	1	11	0	0	.200/.259/.240	.173	.357	-0.1	1B(8): 0.2, 3B(1): -0.0	-0.2
2012	BUF	AAA	27	527	72	25	1	14	60	77	109	3	4	.286/.391/.442	.292	.346	-0.6	1B(79): 0.1, 2B(36): 0.6	2.8
2012	NYN	MLB	27	1	0	0	0	0	0	0	1	0	0	.000/.000/.000	.017	—	0		0.0
2013	LVG	AAA	28	264	46	14	0	9	32	43	45	0	2	.305/.420/.491	.312	.349	-0.9	1B(47): 2.6, LF(1): -0.0	1.9
2013	NYN	MLB	28	221	23	15	0	3	17	30	56	1	1	.279/.376/.405	.283	.379	-1.8	1B(33): 2.0, 3B(17): -0.6	0.9
2014	*NYN*	*MLB*	*29*	*266*	*28*	*13*	*0*	*6*	*30*	*32*	*67*	*0*	*0*	*.254/.347/.391*	*.280*	*.330*	*-0.7*	*1B 1, 3B -1*	*0.8*

Satin reignited possibly the most common phrase in the Mets' clubhouse: "Ahhh, we'll stick him at first." (Close second: "Hey, anyone here throw left-handed?") Satin is being squeezed out of an opportunity by other, similar players, but in the right organization he's a valuable bat; he's short to the ball, but not at the expense of power. Some will unfairly judge him for being a 28-year-old rookie, ignoring that Satin has hit wherever he's been and was held down due to positional ambiguity and not quite enough power. The team willing to play him full time at first base probably won't be very good, but hey, it only takes one.

Dominic Smith　1B

Born: 6/15/1995 Age: 19
Bats: L Throws: L Height: 6' 0"
Weight: 185 Breakout: 0%
Improve: 0% Collapse: 0%
Attrition: 0% MLB: 0%

Comparables:
Logan Morrison, Derek Norris, Cedric Hunter

YEAR	TEAM	LVL	AGE	PA	R	2B	3B	HR	RBI	BB	SO	SB	CS	AVG/OBP/SLG	TAv	BABIP	BRR	FRAA	WARP
2014	*NYN*	*MLB*	*19*	*250*	*18*	*8*	*0*	*3*	*21*	*15*	*76*	*0*	*0*	*.187/.239/.265*	*.193*	*.260*	*-0.5*	*1B 1*	*-1.4*

The last time the Mets used a first-round pick on a power-hitting, plus-armed first baseman with nominal outfielding abilities, they got Ike Davis. That's where the comparison ends, because these are two very different hitters: Smith has a relatively compact swing, with only a slight uppercut, and he relies on his natural strength. If there is a swing flaw, it's that he's a natural front-foot hitter, and he'll need to compensate for that as he rises through the system. While it might be too soon to accurately judge plate discipline and pitch recognition, Smith raised no red flags in dominating the Gulf Coast League. Of note: he has played first base exclusively so far as a professional.

Ruben Tejada　SS

Born: 10/27/1989 Age: 24
Bats: R Throws: R Height: 5' 11"
Weight: 185 Breakout: 3%
Improve: 46% Collapse: 7%
Attrition: 14% MLB: 93%

Comparables:
Aaron Hill, Omar Quintanilla, Yuniesky Betancourt

YEAR	TEAM	LVL	AGE	PA	R	2B	3B	HR	RBI	BB	SO	SB	CS	AVG/OBP/SLG	TAv	BABIP	BRR	FRAA	WARP
2011	BUF	AAA	21	231	26	7	3	3	21	19	30	4	2	.246/.314/.353	.243	.274	2.2	SS(47): -2.4, 2B(1): 0.1	0.3
2011	NYN	MLB	21	376	31	15	1	0	36	35	50	5	1	.284/.360/.335	.273	.331	1.8	2B(55): 1.0, SS(41): -0.7	2.2
2012	BUF	AAA	22	21	3	1	0	0	2	1	3	0	0	.200/.238/.250	.152	.235	0.8	SS(6): -0.2	-0.1
2012	NYN	MLB	22	501	53	26	0	1	25	27	73	4	4	.289/.333/.351	.262	.339	2.4	SS(112): -5.4	2.0
2013	LVG	AAA	23	269	38	14	1	2	24	14	30	1	1	.288/.337/.379	.252	.316	2.7	SS(58): -2.1, 2B(1): -0.0	1.1
2013	NYN	MLB	23	227	20	12	0	0	10	15	24	2	1	.202/.259/.260	.203	.228	1.8	SS(55): 3.1	0.1
2014	*NYN*	*MLB*	*24*	*313*	*31*	*14*	*0*	*2*	*22*	*20*	*47*	*2*	*1*	*.249/.307/.321*	*.244*	*.290*	*-0.7*	*SS -2, 2B 0*	*0.5*

Tejada's was a lost season if ever there was one. He didn't just regress in every conceivable category, he had his work ethic called into question from the beginning of spring training. When Tejada and Ike Davis were sent down following terrible starts, the organization wasn't subtle about which player it wanted to succeed, and which was persona non grata. Tejada's minor-league numbers in 2013 mirrored his major-league contributions a year earlier, yet he earned only a September cameo despite Omar Quintanilla's uninspiring three-month stewardship of shortstop.

Justin Turner 2B
Born: 11/23/1984 Age: 29
Bats: R Throws: R Height: 6' 0"
Weight: 210 Breakout: 5%
Improve: 27% Collapse: 13%
Attrition: 20% MLB: 79%
Comparables:
Angel Sanchez, Jeff Keppinger, Luis Rivas

YEAR	TEAM	LVL	AGE	PA	R	2B	3B	HR	RBI	BB	SO	SB	CS	AVG/OBP/SLG	TAv	BABIP	BRR	FRAA	WARP
2011	BUF	AAA	26	44	6	3	2	0	2	2	6	0	0	.300/.364/.475	.290	.353	0.8	2B(8): 0.9, 3B(2): -0.2	0.4
2011	NYN	MLB	26	487	49	30	0	4	51	39	59	7	2	.260/.334/.356	.256	.292	0.9	2B(78): 2.4, 3B(36): -2.7	1.2
2012	NYN	MLB	27	185	20	13	1	2	19	9	24	1	1	.269/.319/.392	.274	.301	0.7	2B(14): -0.4, 3B(11): -0.4	0.6
2013	NYN	MLB	28	214	12	13	1	2	16	11	34	0	1	.280/.319/.385	.262	.327	0.3	3B(23): -1.1, SS(18): -0.8	0.4
2014	NYN	MLB	29	250	27	14	0	3	21	18	37	2	1	.259/.322/.365	.264	.290	-0.4	2B 0, 3B -2	0.5

If Justin Turner didn't already feel like God is watching over him, then witnessing the Mets' sheer number of poor-fielding infield prospects would have converted him by now. They kept booting it around the infield, and Turner ended up as comfortable in his role as any utilityman in the league. Lo and behold, Turner has established enough of an offensive track record that he's never a total disaster when a starter pulls a hammy. He'll never, ever—not ever—be more than what he is now, but his defensive versatility retains a bit of value. He even made a one-inning cameo in left field, which felt like something his agent thought he should have on his resumé heading into free agency.

David Wright 3B
Born: 12/20/1982 Age: 31
Bats: R Throws: R Height: 6' 0"
Weight: 210 Breakout: 1%
Improve: 38% Collapse: 3%
Attrition: 3% MLB: 98%
Comparables:
Ron Santo, Morgan Ensberg, Scott Rolen

YEAR	TEAM	LVL	AGE	PA	R	2B	3B	HR	RBI	BB	SO	SB	CS	AVG/OBP/SLG	TAv	BABIP	BRR	FRAA	WARP
2011	SLU	A+	28	27	9	3	0	0	2	6	3	1	0	.476/.593/.619	.433	.556	1.1	3B(4): -0.0	0.7
2011	NYN	MLB	28	447	60	23	1	14	61	52	97	13	2	.254/.345/.427	.289	.302	-2.1	3B(101): -10.9, SS(1): -0.0	1.3
2012	NYN	MLB	29	670	91	41	2	21	93	81	112	15	10	.306/.391/.492	.315	.347	1.6	3B(155): -0.0, SS(1): -0.0	6.6
2013	NYN	MLB	30	492	63	23	6	18	58	55	79	17	3	.307/.390/.514	.326	.340	3.9	3B(111): 5.4	5.8
2014	NYN	MLB	31	498	64	25	2	15	62	55	108	14	5	.274/.358/.445	.298	.330	0.2	3B -4, SS -0	2.8

Whether the Mets contend this decade or not, Wright showed why they extended him instead of Jose Reyes to be their franchise cornerstone. In 2009, Reyes was supposed to miss a month with a calf injury, but missed the rest of the year amid concerns he wasn't too concerned about rehabilitation. Wright has now twice played the counterpoint: He came back from a concussion at the end of 2009, and came back from a hamstring strain homering to give meaning to the otherwise meaningless final 10 days of 2013. The Mets need to engender trust somewhere, and with Wright cynical fans know there's at least one professional in the organization. And he's the best third baseman in the league to boot.

Chris Young RF
Born: 9/5/1983 Age: 30
Bats: R Throws: R Height: 6' 2"
Weight: 190 Breakout: 5%
Improve: 49% Collapse: 5%
Attrition: 8% MLB: 100%
Comparables:
Curtis Granderson, Amos Otis, Jason Michaels

YEAR	TEAM	LVL	AGE	PA	R	2B	3B	HR	RBI	BB	SO	SB	CS	AVG/OBP/SLG	TAv	BABIP	BRR	FRAA	WARP
2011	ARI	MLB	27	659	89	38	3	20	71	80	139	22	9	.236/.331/.420	.277	.275	5.3	CF(155): -5.9	2.9
2012	ARI	MLB	28	363	36	24	0	14	41	36	79	8	3	.231/.311/.434	.261	.263	-0.3	CF(87): 0.7	1.4
2013	OAK	MLB	29	375	46	18	3	12	40	36	93	10	3	.200/.280/.379	.247	.237	1	CF(54): 2.8, RF(26): 2.9	1.1
2014	NYN	MLB	30	352	43	16	1	11	41	39	85	11	4	.221/.310/.390	.263	.260	0.5	RF 8, CF -0	1.8

Young looked primed for a rebound after an injury-marred 2012: He had shown off shiny tools in the past, though he would have to hit in order to justify the $8.5 million commitment (plus $1.5 million buyout of his 2014 option) that was the highest on Oakland's 2013 roster. Contact has always been the gap in Young's game, and the problem grew to canyon dimensions last season. The offensive sinkhole was all-encompassing, including his worst walk and strikeout rates since 2008 and 2009, respectively, and the lowest power numbers since he was a rookie. Young's season was a lemon no matter how you slice it—versus lefties or righties, home or away, in the first half or the second. Young could rebuild his value with the Mets, or this could be the first of a series of short deals leading to the inevitable "minor-league contract or retirement?" phase.

Eric Young   LF

Born: 5/25/1985 Age: 29
Bats: B Throws: R Height: 5' 10''
Weight: 180 Breakout: 1%
Improve: 33% Collapse: 12%
Attrition: 21% MLB: 82%

Comparables:
Nyjer Morgan, Tony Gwynn, Gregor Blanco

YEAR	TEAM	LVL	AGE	PA	R	2B	3B	HR	RBI	BB	SO	SB	CS	AVG/OBP/SLG	TAv	BABIP	BRR	FRAA	WARP
2011	CSP	AAA	26	275	61	18	9	2	28	39	36	17	1	.363/.454/.552	.306	.416	4	CF(23): -1.5, 2B(15): -0.4	1.7
2011	COL	MLB	26	229	34	4	3	0	10	26	38	27	4	.247/.342/.298	.228	.304	4	LF(35): -1.6, 2B(7): -0.6	-0.1
2012	COL	MLB	27	196	36	7	2	4	15	13	31	14	2	.316/.377/.448	.274	.367	5	CF(15): 1.9, RF(11): -0.7	1.4
2013	COL	MLB	28	180	22	9	3	1	6	11	33	8	4	.242/.290/.352	.225	.298	-2.7	RF(20): -2.5, CF(10): 0.6	-0.9
2013	NYN	MLB	28	418	48	18	4	1	26	35	67	38	7	.251/.318/.329	.239	.303	7.4	LF(88): 5.9, CF(8): -0.7	1.4
2014	NYN	MLB	29	482	62	17	4	3	30	43	96	37	8	.237/.312/.318	.244	.290	4.5	LF 1, CF 0	0.8

How do you steal 46 bases without ever getting on base? You'd have to ask Eric Young, who might be the best baserunner in the league—he isn't much for getting to first, but once he does he isn't one for staying. It isn't just the absurd stolen-base efficiency (he was caught only three times); it's nights like August 6th, when he tagged and advanced to second on a fly out, and then scored from second on an infield hit. Young personified the Mets' teamwide dedication to baserunning—the Mets blitzed the competition in team Baserunning Runs—and though he's ultimately a fourth outfielder, he has earned the "lunch pail" reputation that could keep him in the league well past his use-by date.

PITCHERS

David Aardsma

Born: 12/27/1981 Age: 32
Bats: R Throws: R Height: 6' 3'' Weight: 205
Breakout: 26% Improve: 55% Collapse: 21%
Attrition: 15% MLB: 78%

Comparables:
Tyler Walker, Jose Veras, Bobby Seay

YEAR	TEAM	LVL	AGE	W	L	SV	G	GS	IP	H	HR	BB	SO	BB9	SO9	GB%	BABIP	WHIP	ERA	FIP	FRA	WARP
2012	NYA	MLB	30	0	0	0	1	0	1	1	1	1	1	9.0	9.0	67%	.000	2.00	9.00	17.05	14.68	-0.1
2013	NWO	AAA	31	1	0	0	10	0	14	9	2	8	12	5.1	7.7	32%	.200	1.21	2.57	5.43	4.67	0.1
2013	NYN	MLB	31	2	2	0	43	0	39²	39	7	19	36	4.3	8.2	35%	.299	1.46	4.31	5.24	5.03	-0.5
2014	NYN	MLB	32	3	1	1	49	0	47²	38	5	22	49	4.2	9.3	38%	.282	1.27	3.54	4.03	3.85	0.3

Aardsma landed with the Mets in mid-May and, despite no longer throwing in the mid-90s, somehow still left you wanting more. So what's new? Well, the slider has improved substantially; he threw it twice as often in 2013 *and* doubled his whiff rate with it. Unfortunately, his fastball isn't any more accurate at 92 than it was at 95—he misses as much within the zone as he does outside it, and the power numbers against him reflect that. The slider's development is great news, but ultimately fastball command will dictate whether he has a few more years left.

Victor Black

Born: 5/23/1988 Age: 26
Bats: R Throws: R Height: 6' 4'' Weight: 215
Breakout: 37% Improve: 59% Collapse: 33%
Attrition: 46% MLB: 55%

Comparables:
Sammy Gervacio, Pedro Strop, Kam Mickolio

YEAR	TEAM	LVL	AGE	W	L	SV	G	GS	IP	H	HR	BB	SO	BB9	SO9	GB%	BABIP	WHIP	ERA	FIP	FRA	WARP
2011	WVA	A	23	2	1	1	22	0	29	30	0	16	23	5.0	7.1	53%	.338	1.59	5.28	3.80	5.42	0.0
2012	ALT	AA	24	2	3	13	51	0	60	40	2	29	85	4.3	12.8	55%	.297	1.15	1.65	2.45	3.07	1.4
2013	IND	AAA	25	5	3	17	38	0	46²	28	2	21	63	4.1	12.1	44%	.252	1.05	2.51	2.48	2.85	1.1
2013	NYN	MLB	25	3	0	1	15	0	13	11	1	4	12	2.8	8.3	24%	.270	1.15	3.46	3.33	4.03	0.1
2013	PIT	MLB	25	0	0	0	3	0	4	6	0	2	3	4.5	6.8	47%	.400	2.00	4.50	3.77	2.77	0.1
2014	NYN	MLB	26	3	1	2	49	0	57¹	44	5	26	65	4.0	10.2	46%	.294	1.22	3.28	3.57	3.56	0.6

Black was the player to be named in the deal that sent Marlon Byrd and John Buck to Pittsburgh. He immediately endeared himself by asking for "any number they will give me," taking the 7 train to Citi Field and showing an upper-90s fastball with a devastating, 12-to-6 power curve. Black was so impressive that one or two "Closer of the Future" stories popped up; he's battled control problems his entire career, but when the ball is down, he's close to unhittable. One negative: A guy named "Vic Black" should have to pitch in a dark suit and sunglasses, and take his glove out of an attaché case. The real Vic Black looks like he'd make you a mixtape in his free time.

Andrew Church

Born: 10/7/1994 Age: 19
Bats: R Throws: R Height: 6' 2'' Weight: 190
Breakout: 0% Improve: 0% Collapse: 0%
Attrition: 0% MLB: 0%

Comparables:
Jose Alvarez, Josh Wall, Alex Burnett

YEAR	TEAM	LVL	AGE	W	L	SV	G	GS	IP	H	HR	BB	SO	BB9	SO9	GB%	BABIP	WHIP	ERA	FIP	FRA	WARP
2014	NYN	MLB	19	1	3	0	8	6	32²	40	5	21	11	5.6	3.1	45%	.309	1.85	6.80	6.79	7.39	-0.9

Church was a curious pick in the 2013 second round, a right-handed high schooler without apparent top-end potential. Of his secondary pitches, the curveball projects the best, but between mechanical issues and a turbulent high school career that left him pitching side sessions for scouts, the whole package has a long way to go.

Bartolo Colon
Born: 5/24/1973 Age: 41
Bats: R Throws: R Height: 5' 11" Weight: 265
Breakout: 11% Improve: 51% Collapse: 27%
Attrition: 9% MLB: 72%

Comparables:
Greg Maddux, Gaylord Perry, Andy Pettitte

YEAR	TEAM	LVL	AGE	W	L	SV	G	GS	IP	H	HR	BB	SO	BB9	SO9	GB%	BABIP	WHIP	ERA	FIP	FRA	WARP
2011	NYA	MLB	38	8	10	0	29	26	164¹	172	21	40	135	2.2	7.4	45%	.306	1.29	4.00	3.86	4.45	2.0
2012	OAK	MLB	39	10	9	0	24	24	152¹	161	17	23	91	1.4	5.4	47%	.286	1.21	3.43	3.78	3.90	1.7
2013	OAK	MLB	40	18	6	0	30	30	190¹	193	14	29	117	1.4	5.5	43%	.295	1.17	2.65	3.26	3.63	2.7
2014	NYN	MLB	41	9	10	0	28	28	165¹	160	18	33	117	1.8	6.4	45%	.294	1.17	3.57	3.86	3.88	1.3

The rotund righty continues to defy skeptics, riding an 88-92 mph fastball at an 85 percent frequency to post the lowest ERA of his lengthy career. The 40-year-old stood out in an Oakland rotation that was otherwise full of young guns, and his contact-heavy approach minimized his Three True Outcomes for the second straight season. Colon relies on excellent command and subtle manipulations of his four-seam and two-seam fastballs to generate weak contact, and his catchers have said that they just call for the number one and let him decide on the movement. Colon's flamethrower days are long gone, but every once in a while, he'll sell out his mechanics for velocity and pump one in around 96. Watching this happen, you can't escape the feeling he's doing it because it's just so much damn fun to throw a baseball real hard.

Jacob DeGrom
Born: 6/19/1988 Age: 26
Bats: L Throws: R Height: 6' 4" Weight: 185
Breakout: 40% Improve: 76% Collapse: 22%
Attrition: 73% MLB: 28%

Comparables:
Joe Martinez, Hector Ambriz, Chaz Roe

YEAR	TEAM	LVL	AGE	W	L	SV	G	GS	IP	H	HR	BB	SO	BB9	SO9	GB%	BABIP	WHIP	ERA	FIP	FRA	WARP
2012	SAV	A	24	6	3	0	15	15	89²	77	3	14	78	1.4	7.8	52%	.277	1.01	2.51	2.78	3.14	2.3
2012	SLU	A+	24	3	0	0	4	4	21²	14	1	6	18	2.5	7.5	39%	.213	0.92	2.08	3.30	4.17	0.4
2013	SLU	A+	25	1	0	0	2	2	12	12	1	2	13	1.5	9.8	47%	.333	1.17	3.00	2.91	3.80	0.1
2013	BIN	AA	25	2	5	0	10	10	60	69	4	20	44	3.0	6.6	45%	.348	1.48	4.80	3.82	4.06	0.9
2013	LVG	AAA	25	4	2	0	14	14	75²	87	6	24	63	2.9	7.5	47%	.342	1.47	4.52	3.93	4.50	1.5
2014	NYN	MLB	26	6	9	0	23	23	125	126	14	41	90	2.9	6.5	46%	.302	1.33	4.35	4.32	4.72	-0.2

It didn't look good for deGrom as a ninth-round pick who almost immediately underwent Tommy John surgery, but his consistency over just two minor-league seasons since his recovery makes him a contender for the fifth starter's spot in 2014. The power righty's strikeout numbers took a hit with his graduation to the high minors; that can be expected with such a rapid rise, but further acclimation might be useful before the big jump. One added plus: His power arsenal—a mid-90s fastball with sink and a hard slider—would translate well to the bullpen if need be.

Josh Edgin
Born: 12/17/1986 Age: 27
Bats: L Throws: L Height: 6' 1" Weight: 225
Breakout: 41% Improve: 50% Collapse: 33%
Attrition: 46% MLB: 60%

Comparables:
Sam Demel, Marcus McBeth, Jason Bulger

YEAR	TEAM	LVL	AGE	W	L	SV	G	GS	IP	H	HR	BB	SO	BB9	SO9	GB%	BABIP	WHIP	ERA	FIP	FRA	WARP
2011	SAV	A	24	1	0	16	24	0	31	14	0	10	41	2.9	11.9	61%	.215	0.77	0.87	1.85	0.81	1.5
2011	SLU	A+	24	2	1	11	25	0	35	30	2	13	35	3.3	9.0	57%	.312	1.23	2.06	3.33	4.57	0.3
2012	BUF	AAA	25	3	2	1	35	0	37	34	0	18	40	4.4	9.7	43%	.324	1.41	3.89	2.54	3.24	0.8
2012	NYN	MLB	25	1	2	0	34	0	25²	19	5	10	30	3.5	10.5	41%	.233	1.13	4.56	4.73	5.58	-0.2
2013	LVG	AAA	26	2	0	0	11	0	10²	14	1	2	12	1.7	10.1	41%	.419	1.50	5.91	3.38	4.43	0.2
2013	NYN	MLB	26	1	1	1	34	0	28²	26	2	12	20	3.8	6.3	44%	.282	1.33	3.77	4.00	5.24	-0.2
2014	NYN	MLB	27	2	1	1	42	0	47²	41	5	19	46	3.6	8.7	48%	.294	1.26	3.72	3.96	4.04	0.2

Edgin is the most talented of the gaggle of left-handed relievers on the Mets' 40-man roster. He brings a mid-90s fastball from an angle that doesn't normally produce mid-90s fastballs. Though his slider doesn't really play against righties, you can keep him in to face one if there's another lefty on deck—he becomes a one-pitch pitcher against righties, to be sure, but consider this a testament to how good his fastball can be. Edgin has profiled as a LOOGY to date, but if he returns healthy from a season-ending stress fracture in his ribs, he has the potential for more than one-out cameos.

Jeurys Familia
Born: 10/10/1989 Age: 24
Bats: R Throws: R Height: 6' 4" Weight: 230
Breakout: 46% Improve: 70% Collapse: 15%
Attrition: 58% MLB: 28%

Comparables:
Casey Crosby, Merkin Valdez, Drake Britton

YEAR	TEAM	LVL	AGE	W	L	SV	G	GS	IP	H	HR	BB	SO	BB9	SO9	GB%	BABIP	WHIP	ERA	FIP	FRA	WARP
2011	SLU	A+	21	1	1	0	6	6	36¹	21	1	8	36	2.0	8.9	53%	.208	0.80	1.49	2.51	3.36	0.7
2011	BIN	AA	21	4	4	0	17	17	87²	85	10	35	96	3.6	9.9	36%	.351	1.37	3.49	4.17	4.43	0.9
2012	BUF	AAA	22	9	9	0	28	28	137	145	8	73	128	4.8	8.4	54%	.335	1.59	4.73	3.73	4.67	1.2
2012	NYN	MLB	22	0	0	0	8	1	12¹	10	0	9	10	6.6	7.3	50%	.312	1.54	5.84	3.70	4.17	0.1
2013	NYN	MLB	23	0	0	1	9	0	10²	12	2	9	8	7.6	6.8	53%	.312	1.97	4.22	6.49	5.35	-0.2
2014	NYN	MLB	24	2	3	0	12	7	39¹	37	4	21	34	4.7	7.7	48%	.304	1.47	4.70	4.59	5.11	-0.2

Two years ago, Familia seemed a future fixture in a rotation, or perhaps the end of a bullpen. Well, a lackluster 2012, elbow surgery in 2013 and wildness in the Arizona Fall League have at least answered that question: he's a reliever. Still, he's likely to be a very good one. The post-surgery velocity still approaches triple digits, and the slider still buckles knees. Familia may need more time than most due to some maturity concerns, but when he finally gains a measure of control, opposing hitters won't be any less afraid.

Frank Francisco
Born: 9/11/1979 Age: 34
Bats: R Throws: R Height: 6' 2" Weight: 250
Breakout: 22% Improve: 41% Collapse: 34%
Attrition: 11% MLB: 84%

Comparables:
Michael Gonzalez, Will Ohman, Jay Witasick

YEAR	TEAM	LVL	AGE	W	L	SV	G	GS	IP	H	HR	BB	SO	BB9	SO9	GB%	BABIP	WHIP	ERA	FIP	FRA	WARP
2011	TOR	MLB	31	1	4	17	54	0	50²	49	7	18	53	3.2	9.4	40%	.300	1.32	3.55	3.83	3.33	1.0
2012	NYN	MLB	32	1	3	23	48	0	42¹	47	5	21	47	4.5	10.0	33%	.339	1.61	5.53	3.94	3.70	0.5
2013	NYN	MLB	33	1	0	1	8	0	6¹	4	0	3	6	4.3	8.5	44%	.250	1.11	4.26	3.02	2.76	0.1
2014	NYN	MLB	34	2	1	15	42	0	38¹	32	4	13	42	3.1	9.8	37%	.297	1.17	3.27	3.44	3.56	0.4

And when the Mets do dip some money into the free agent pitcher game, this is what they get. Francisco had offseason surgery before 2013 to remove bone spurs from his elbow, and three separate rehab setbacks delayed his season debut until September. The velocity was there upon his return, which of course led to speculation about how motivated he was to come back in the first place. We won't speculate on that, but ultimately his biggest crime was timing his return too late for the Mets to trade what remained of his $6 million contract for a prospect.

Dillon Gee
Born: 4/28/1986 Age: 28
Bats: R Throws: R Height: 6' 1" Weight: 205
Breakout: 15% Improve: 49% Collapse: 24%
Attrition: 31% MLB: 82%

Comparables:
Luke Hochevar, Brian Bannister, Tom Gorzelanny

YEAR	TEAM	LVL	AGE	W	L	SV	G	GS	IP	H	HR	BB	SO	BB9	SO9	GB%	BABIP	WHIP	ERA	FIP	FRA	WARP
2011	BUF	AAA	25	1	1	0	2	2	11²	7	1	5	8	3.9	6.2	41%	.194	1.03	4.63	4.52	6.49	-0.2
2011	NYN	MLB	25	13	6	0	30	27	160²	150	18	71	114	4.0	6.4	48%	.285	1.38	4.43	4.62	5.21	-0.6
2012	NYN	MLB	26	6	7	0	17	17	109²	108	12	29	97	2.4	8.0	51%	.303	1.25	4.10	3.75	4.07	1.1
2013	NYN	MLB	27	12	11	0	32	32	199	208	24	47	142	2.1	6.4	43%	.301	1.28	3.62	3.98	4.12	1.5
2014	NYN	MLB	28	8	10	0	27	27	156¹	143	18	47	132	2.7	7.6	44%	.292	1.22	3.84	4.09	4.18	0.6

Gee didn't overpower anybody to begin with, so when he revealed in June that he was battling elbow tendonitis, one might've thought he couldn't afford to lose any more velocity. Though the strikeouts took a nosedive and he surrendered more hits than ever, Gee could still accomplish the best year of his career because his success was never predicated on velocity in the first place. If the elbow cooperates in 2014 and Gee gets consistently back to the low 90s, he could have a nice run as a third starter. He's an established regular either way, even if he'll always captain the "How the hell does this guy get anyone out?" All-Stars.

Aaron Harang
Born: 5/9/1978 Age: 36
Bats: R Throws: R Height: 6' 7" Weight: 260
Breakout: 26% Improve: 58% Collapse: 17%
Attrition: 17% MLB: 80%

Comparables:
Jack Morris, Earl Wilson, Kevin Millwood

YEAR	TEAM	LVL	AGE	W	L	SV	G	GS	IP	H	HR	BB	SO	BB9	SO9	GB%	BABIP	WHIP	ERA	FIP	FRA	WARP
2011	SDN	MLB	33	14	7	0	28	28	170²	175	20	58	124	3.1	6.5	42%	.307	1.37	3.64	4.14	4.47	0.2
2012	LAN	MLB	34	10	10	0	31	31	179²	167	14	85	131	4.3	6.6	39%	.284	1.40	3.61	4.18	4.56	0.7
2013	SEA	MLB	35	5	11	0	22	22	120¹	133	21	28	87	2.1	6.5	38%	.292	1.34	5.76	4.72	5.24	-0.1
2013	NYN	MLB	35	0	1	0	4	4	23	20	5	12	26	4.7	10.2	30%	.255	1.39	3.52	5.28	5.42	-0.2
2014	NYN	MLB	36	7	10	0	25	25	138	140	18	46	108	3.0	7.1	39%	.305	1.34	4.49	4.45	4.88	-0.5

Exiled from the Dodgers' eight-man spring rotation, traded by the Rockies without so much as an appearance, cut from a Mariners team that let Joe Saunders throw a beanbag underhand for 32 starts—and finally, the indignity of four not-half-bad outings for the 2013 Mets. Harang became more sinker/slider-dominant in 2013 than in previous years, likely just going with whatever keeps him competent enough to stay employed. And he'll likely stay employed, somewhere; he hasn't lost a tick of velocity in two years, even if he's gained a few ticks on the scale. Wherever he is, he may want to keep his bags packed.

Matt Harvey
Born: 3/27/1989 Age: 25
Bats: R Throws: R Height: 6' 4" Weight: 225
Breakout: 28% Improve: 58% Collapse: 26%
Attrition: 15% MLB: 98%

Comparables:
Francisco Liriano, Tommy Hanson, Daniel Hudson

YEAR	TEAM	LVL	AGE	W	L	SV	G	GS	IP	H	HR	BB	SO	BB9	SO9	GB%	BABIP	WHIP	ERA	FIP	FRA	WARP
2011	SLU	A+	22	8	2	0	14	14	76	67	5	24	92	2.8	10.9	50%	.355	1.20	2.37	2.85	4.10	1.2
2011	BIN	AA	22	5	3	0	12	12	59²	58	4	23	64	3.5	9.7	54%	.331	1.36	4.53	3.44	4.91	0.2
2012	BUF	AAA	23	7	5	0	20	20	110	97	9	48	112	3.9	9.2	46%	.297	1.32	3.68	3.66	4.65	0.8
2012	NYN	MLB	23	3	5	0	10	10	59¹	42	5	26	70	3.9	10.6	39%	.272	1.15	2.73	3.34	3.88	0.7
2013	NYN	MLB	24	9	5	0	26	26	178¹	135	7	31	191	1.6	9.6	49%	.285	0.93	2.27	1.98	2.66	4.2
2014	NYN	MLB	25	9	8	0	25	25	147²	117	12	43	153	2.6	9.3	46%	.291	1.08	2.82	3.12	3.06	2.8

Is there a villain in Harvey's season, somebody who should have steered him off his elbow surgery trajectory? When disaster strikes, the blame game begins, but it was difficult to see the warning signs when April and May's Best Pitcher in the World became July and August's Merely Top 5 Pitcher in the World. Harvey hadn't quite been the leviathan he was early in the season, sure, but this is a man who struck out Miguel Cabrera on three pitches with a partially torn UCL. After a dalliance with rehab and a throwing program, Harvey opted for Tommy John surgery, which has a success rate of around 85 percent; for Harvey, "success" means a return to pitching perfection.

Jeremy Hefner
Born: 3/11/1986 Age: 28
Bats: R Throws: R Height: 6' 4" Weight: 215
Breakout: 39% Improve: 67% Collapse: 21%
Attrition: 57% MLB: 52%

Comparables:
Andrew Good, Tim Stauffer, Craig Stammen

YEAR	TEAM	LVL	AGE	W	L	SV	G	GS	IP	H	HR	BB	SO	BB9	SO9	GB%	BABIP	WHIP	ERA	FIP	FRA	WARP
2011	TUC	AAA	25	9	7	0	28	28	157¹	178	21	61	120	3.5	6.9	43%	.326	1.52	4.98	5.21	6.29	1.0
2012	BUF	AAA	26	5	2	0	10	9	61²	55	4	10	37	1.5	5.4	48%	.270	1.05	2.77	3.29	4.65	0.4
2012	NYN	MLB	26	4	7	0	26	13	93²	110	9	18	62	1.7	6.0	45%	.328	1.37	5.09	3.70	4.19	0.7
2013	NYN	MLB	27	4	8	0	24	23	130²	132	20	37	99	2.5	6.8	44%	.296	1.29	4.34	4.46	4.75	0.3
2014	NYN	MLB	28	6	8	0	20	20	114	115	14	33	81	2.6	6.4	42%	.298	1.29	4.28	4.38	4.65	-0.2

One Mets pitcher allowed two earned runs or fewer in eight consecutive starts, and it wasn't Matt Harvey. That feat belongs to Hefner, who out of nowhere became baseball's best pitcher in June and early July. It's hard to explain exactly what Hefner did differently—the empirical evidence always tended to scream "Quadruple-A," anyway—and a slight uptick in velocity and decrease in BABIP aren't telling the whole story. Unfortunately, it may all be moot: He underwent Tommy John surgery on August 28th, and it's as difficult to imagine him reaching those heights again as it was in the first place.

Daisuke Matsuzaka
Born: 9/13/1980 Age: 33
Bats: R Throws: R Height: 6' 0" Weight: 185
Breakout: 17% Improve: 50% Collapse: 24%
Attrition: 19% MLB: 53%

Comparables:
Wade Miller, Victor Zambrano, Casey Fossum

YEAR	TEAM	LVL	AGE	W	L	SV	G	GS	IP	H	HR	BB	SO	BB9	SO9	GB%	BABIP	WHIP	ERA	FIP	FRA	WARP
2011	BOS	MLB	30	3	3	0	8	7	37¹	32	4	23	26	5.5	6.3	32%	.248	1.47	5.30	4.99	5.91	0.0
2012	PAW	AAA	31	1	3	0	11	11	51	42	6	17	41	3.0	7.2	38%	.247	1.16	3.18	4.37	5.26	0.0
2012	BOS	MLB	31	1	7	0	11	11	45²	58	11	20	41	3.9	8.1	42%	.326	1.71	8.28	5.89	6.76	-0.4
2013	COH	AAA	32	5	8	0	19	19	103¹	93	11	39	95	3.4	8.3	36%	.290	1.28	3.92	3.97	4.96	0.4
2013	NYN	MLB	32	3	3	0	7	7	38²	32	4	16	33	3.7	7.7	29%	.277	1.24	4.42	4.29	4.78	0.0
2014	NYN	MLB	33	6	8	0	23	23	119²	107	14	49	106	3.7	7.9	38%	.289	1.30	4.03	4.36	4.38	0.3

If there's one way to further aggravate a disgruntled fan base, it's making them sit through Daisuke Matsuzaka. But after the Indians cut him loose from Triple-A Columbus, Daisuke signed with the Mets and allowed just four earned runs over his final 27 innings. Daisuke gets a bad rap because he's infuriating to watch, but now that he's no longer among the most overpaid players in baseball he's officially undervalued and worth a flyer. On second thought … are stadium employees paid by the hour?

Steven Matz
Born: 5/29/1991 Age: 23
Bats: R Throws: L Height: 6' 2" Weight: 195
Breakout: 54% Improve: 62% Collapse: 29%
Attrition: 66% MLB: 21%

Comparables:
Bud Norris, Casey Crosby, Matt Magill

YEAR	TEAM	LVL	AGE	W	L	SV	G	GS	IP	H	HR	BB	SO	BB9	SO9	GB%	BABIP	WHIP	ERA	FIP	FRA	WARP
2013	SAV	A	22	5	6	0	21	21	106¹	86	4	38	121	3.2	10.2	55%	.315	1.17	2.62	2.91	3.42	1.8
2014	NYN	MLB	23	4	6	0	16	16	78	72	9	39	69	4.5	7.9	48%	.305	1.42	4.44	4.59	4.82	-0.2

Historically hesitant to go over slot, the Mets doubled the recommended value after drafting Matz in the first round in 2009. Tommy John surgery pushed his pro debut all the way back to 2012, but he's been healthy and lighting it up ever since. He still works mostly off the fastball, but there's plenty of time for the curve and change to come along. More worrisome is his funky, high-effort delivery, which—though it hides the ball well—may suit him best in the bullpen. His trajectory is difficult to predict given all the question marks, but on the list of great Long Islanders in Mets history, we suspect he'll land closer to Frank Viola than Frank Catalanotto. Make no mistake: Like a spotted owl in Panama, the Mets have themselves an actual left-handed pitching prospect.

Jenrry Mejia
Born: 10/11/1989 Age: 24
Bats: R Throws: R Height: 6' 0" Weight: 205
Breakout: 30% Improve: 66% Collapse: 21%
Attrition: 42% MLB: 82%

Comparables:
Zach Britton, Ross Detwiler, Tom Gorzelanny

YEAR	TEAM	LVL	AGE	W	L	SV	G	GS	IP	H	HR	BB	SO	BB9	SO9	GB%	BABIP	WHIP	ERA	FIP	FRA	WARP
2011	BUF	AAA	21	1	2	0	5	5	28¹	16	1	14	21	4.4	6.7	41%	.203	1.06	2.86	3.91	5.56	-0.1
2012	SLU	A+	22	1	0	0	2	2	11	7	1	2	8	1.6	6.5	55%	.200	0.82	2.45	3.67	4.99	0.1
2012	BUF	AAA	22	3	4	0	26	10	73²	75	4	24	39	2.9	4.8	56%	.287	1.34	3.54	3.82	5.42	-0.3
2012	NYN	MLB	22	1	2	0	5	3	16	20	2	9	8	5.1	4.5	69%	.346	1.81	5.62	5.45	5.48	0.0
2013	BIN	AA	23	2	0	0	2	2	11	6	1	4	9	3.3	7.4	41%	.192	0.91	0.82	3.96	4.44	0.1
2013	NYN	MLB	23	1	2	0	5	5	27¹	28	2	4	27	1.3	8.9	59%	.315	1.17	2.30	2.44	2.97	0.6
2014	NYN	MLB	24	3	3	0	22	8	54¹	50	5	21	42	3.5	7.0	57%	.293	1.31	3.92	4.13	4.27	0.2

You have to feel for Mejia. First he inexplicably made the Mets as a reliever out of 2010 spring training, botching his burgeoning development as a starter. Once he'd cleared that hurdle, he underwent Tommy John surgery in mid-2011. After recovering from that, he reported to Triple-A Buffalo in 2012, where the Mets once again couldn't decide if he should start or relieve. And finally, after all that, Mejia made five solid major-league starts in 2013, with 27 strikeouts against four walks in 27 innings … and on August 28th, he underwent season-ending surgery to remove bone chips from his elbow. There's a great pitcher in here, we swear—try as the Mets and Mother Nature might to keep him down.

Rafael Montero
Born: 10/17/1990 Age: 23
Bats: R Throws: R Height: 6' 0" Weight: 170
Breakout: 39% Improve: 62% Collapse: 20%
Attrition: 47% MLB: 45%

Comparables:
Kevin Slowey, Wade LeBlanc, J.D. Martin

YEAR	TEAM	LVL	AGE	W	L	SV	G	GS	IP	H	HR	BB	SO	BB9	SO9	GB%	BABIP	WHIP	ERA	FIP	FRA	WARP
2012	SAV	A	21	6	3	0	12	12	71¹	61	4	8	54	1.0	6.8	37%	.260	0.97	2.52	3.17	3.45	1.4
2012	SLU	A+	21	5	2	0	8	8	50²	35	2	11	56	2.0	9.9	41%	.270	0.91	2.13	2.47	2.99	1.5
2013	BIN	AA	22	7	3	0	11	11	66²	51	2	10	72	1.4	9.7	40%	.278	0.92	2.43	2.00	2.57	2.2
2013	LVG	AAA	22	5	4	0	16	16	88²	85	4	25	78	2.5	7.9	38%	.319	1.24	3.05	3.24	3.59	2.6
2014	NYN	MLB	23	6	6	0	28	18	129¹	114	12	35	110	2.4	7.6	39%	.289	1.15	3.20	3.57	3.48	1.7

Montero quickly showed he was too good for Double-A, and a couple of early hiccups obscured what was really a seamless transition to Triple-A Las Vegas. Scouts had been reluctant to commit to Montero for a few reasons: He's an undersized right-hander without a truly plus pitch, which makes his tendency toward fly balls a little more of a red flag. But Montero's pinpoint control and command of three pitches—he won't go above 92, but the late movement is a killer—has outclassed minor leaguers at every level. At a certain point, we ignore the dimensions and remember that great pitchers don't all come in the same package; Montero is long past that point.

Jon Niese
Born: 10/27/1986 Age: 27
Bats: L Throws: L Height: 6' 4" Weight: 215
Breakout: 20% Improve: 56% Collapse: 21%
Attrition: 19% MLB: 91%

Comparables:
Paul Maholm, Matt Harrison, Kyle Davies

YEAR	TEAM	LVL	AGE	W	L	SV	G	GS	IP	H	HR	BB	SO	BB9	SO9	GB%	BABIP	WHIP	ERA	FIP	FRA	WARP
2011	NYN	MLB	24	11	11	0	27	26	157¹	178	14	44	138	2.5	7.9	53%	.345	1.41	4.40	3.33	3.72	2.6
2012	NYN	MLB	25	13	9	0	30	30	190¹	174	22	49	155	2.3	7.3	48%	.275	1.17	3.40	3.85	4.16	1.7
2013	NYN	MLB	26	8	8	0	24	24	143	158	10	48	105	3.0	6.6	52%	.339	1.44	3.71	3.55	3.91	1.3
2014	NYN	MLB	27	7	9	0	23	23	138²	134	14	39	117	2.5	7.6	50%	.309	1.25	3.89	3.77	4.23	0.4

After signing a four-year, $24.2 million extension before the season, Niese started Opening Day and on some nights looked like a bargain frontline starter. Although his ERA doesn't initially stand up to scrutiny—the strikeouts went down, the walks went up and Niese missed eight weeks with a shoulder strain—it's encouraging that he was much better after returning from the DL. His velocity ticked up a tad, which made his changeup that much more effective against right-handers: Batters put the change in play over 20 percent of the time before the injury, and just 7 percent after. So the next time someone tells you the Mets can't properly rehab an injury, you can point to Niese … and probably no one else. But still!

Bobby Parnell
Born: 9/8/1984 Age: 29
Bats: R Throws: R Height: 6' 4" Weight: 200
Breakout: 42% Improve: 63% Collapse: 23%
Attrition: 19% MLB: 90%

Comparables:
Jared Burton, Kevin Gregg, C.J. Wilson

YEAR	TEAM	LVL	AGE	W	L	SV	G	GS	IP	H	HR	BB	SO	BB9	SO9	GB%	BABIP	WHIP	ERA	FIP	FRA	WARP
2011	NYN	MLB	26	4	6	6	60	0	59¹	60	4	27	64	4.1	9.7	55%	.329	1.47	3.64	3.18	3.25	1.0
2012	NYN	MLB	27	5	4	7	74	0	68²	65	4	20	61	2.6	8.0	62%	.303	1.24	2.49	3.03	3.18	1.2
2013	NYN	MLB	28	5	5	22	49	0	50	38	1	12	44	2.2	7.9	53%	.264	1.00	2.16	2.30	3.27	0.7
2014	NYN	MLB	29	2	1	7	46	0	47	41	3	15	45	2.9	8.6	52%	.302	1.19	3.21	3.10	3.49	0.5

Oh, and it was all going so well, too. Parnell was following up his breakout 2012 with an even better 2013 until August, when a herniated disc in his neck required season-ending surgery. By now, though, we know what he is—the fastball doesn't miss quite as many bats as the velocity might indicate, but that doesn't matter because the contact is always on the ground. One possible monkey wrench: Parnell allegedly dropped 30 pounds following surgery. Going by his listed weight, that puts him at 170 pounds, which might not be enough to drop and drive.

Scott Rice
Born: 9/21/1981 Age: 32
Bats: L Throws: L Height: 6' 6" Weight: 225
Breakout: 49% Improve: 63% Collapse: 23%
Attrition: 67% MLB: 32%

Comparables:
Josh Kinney, Francisley Bueno, Scott Strickland

YEAR	TEAM	LVL	AGE	W	L	SV	G	GS	IP	H	HR	BB	SO	BB9	SO9	GB%	BABIP	WHIP	ERA	FIP	FRA	WARP
2011	CHT	AA	29	4	4	1	34	0	50²	42	3	17	42	3.0	7.5	73%	.288	1.16	1.95	3.48	3.59	0.5
2012	ABQ	AAA	30	2	3	9	54	0	59¹	58	3	22	47	3.3	7.1	66%	.301	1.35	4.40	4.05	5.45	0.8
2013	NYN	MLB	31	4	5	0	73	0	51	42	1	27	41	4.8	7.2	64%	.284	1.35	3.71	3.37	3.93	0.1
2014	NYN	MLB	32	2	1	1	48	0	47	41	4	21	37	4.1	7.0	61%	.284	1.32	3.77	4.22	4.10	0.2

The only thing more puzzling than Mets announcer Gary Cohen's quixotic attempt to establish "Every Minute Rice" as a nickname was Rice's name being on Cohen's lips at all. A 1999 first-round pick of the Orioles, Rice's career went from bad to worse to injured to independent ball; before making the 2013 Mets out of spring training, he had been only marginally effective at Triple-A. Amazin', then, that Rice held opposing left-handers to an OBP under .250 over 73 appearances as the Mets' go-to LOOGY. He is batting practice against righties (.507 OBP!), but his low-effort sinker-slider arsenal is a weapon. Seriously, though, no righties.

Johan Santana

Born: 3/13/1979 Age: 35
Bats: L Throws: L Height: 6' 0" Weight: 210
Breakout: 24% Improve: 47% Collapse: 22%
Attrition: 14% MLB: 91%

Comparables:
Koji Uehara, Roy Oswalt, Kevin Millwood

YEAR	TEAM	LVL	AGE	W	L	SV	G	GS	IP	H	HR	BB	SO	BB9	SO9	GB%	BABIP	WHIP	ERA	FIP	FRA	WARP
2012	NYN	MLB	33	6	9	0	21	21	117	117	17	39	111	3.0	8.5	34%	.303	1.33	4.85	4.13	4.16	1.4
2014	NYN	MLB	35	2	2	0	6	6	38²	35	4	10	33	2.4	7.6	40%	.288	1.16	3.40	3.68	3.70	0.4

Santana, so recently on a Hall of Fame pace, has been adamant that he intends to pitch again following shoulder surgery, and it's difficult to imagine a healthy Santana, however weakened, being anything less than a league-average starter. No pitcher repeats his motion better than Santana, so the changeup figures to remain effective, and because he can work fastball-to-changeup and changeup-to-fastball against both righties and lefties, his backers can expect at worst a late-career Tom Glavine. That is, again, presuming a healthy Santana (however weakened). His body might not function, but he's too smart to fail completely.

Noah Syndergaard

Born: 8/29/1992 Age: 21
Bats: L Throws: R Height: 6' 6" Weight: 240
Breakout: 37% Improve: 77% Collapse: 10%
Attrition: 41% MLB: 34%

Comparables:
Shelby Miller, Brett Anderson, Chad Billingsley

YEAR	TEAM	LVL	AGE	W	L	SV	G	GS	IP	H	HR	BB	SO	BB9	SO9	GB%	BABIP	WHIP	ERA	FIP	FRA	WARP
2011	VAN	A-	18	1	2	0	4	4	18	15	0	5	22	2.5	11.0	52%	.326	1.11	2.00	2.00	2.79	0.6
2012	LNS	A	19	8	5	1	27	19	103²	81	3	31	122	2.7	10.6	58%	.299	1.08	2.60	2.36	3.51	2.3
2013	SLU	A+	20	3	3	0	12	12	63²	61	3	16	64	2.3	9.0	53%	.333	1.21	3.11	2.64	3.90	0.9
2013	BIN	AA	20	6	1	0	11	11	54	46	8	12	69	2.0	11.5	43%	.301	1.07	3.00	3.36	3.97	1.2
2014	NYN	MLB	21	5	6	0	25	18	100	88	11	36	97	3.2	8.8	49%	.300	1.24	3.69	3.86	4.01	0.8

Syndergaard translated his ungodly K/BB numbers to Double-A Binghamton thanks to a plus-plus fastball that he can throw to a teacup. While there has been chatter about ditching the curve in favor of a power slider—which is still a project at this point—Syndergaard is likely better off sticking with the curve, which would help clear his lone blemish from 2013: a lack of success against lefties. He could probably do a decent Matt Harvey impression at the major-league level right now, with the way he works off the fastball—the curve and change are nearly ready, and so is he. Terry Collins called the idea of Syndergaard starting 2014 in the Mets' rotation "conceivable."

Carlos Torres

Born: 10/22/1982 Age: 31
Bats: R Throws: R Height: 6' 1" Weight: 185
Breakout: 31% Improve: 58% Collapse: 13%
Attrition: 49% MLB: 36%

Comparables:
Jason Stanford, David Purcey, Jeff Fulchino

YEAR	TEAM	LVL	AGE	W	L	SV	G	GS	IP	H	HR	BB	SO	BB9	SO9	GB%	BABIP	WHIP	ERA	FIP	FRA	WARP
2012	CSP	AAA	29	5	4	0	14	13	61	62	6	25	59	3.7	8.7	47%	.344	1.43	3.98	4.29	4.97	1.2
2012	COL	MLB	29	5	3	0	31	0	53	49	2	26	42	4.4	7.1	44%	.315	1.42	5.26	3.74	4.56	0.6
2013	LVG	AAA	30	6	3	0	12	12	71²	71	7	19	67	2.4	8.4	51%	.314	1.26	3.89	3.85	4.41	1.4
2013	NYN	MLB	30	4	6	0	33	9	86¹	79	15	17	75	1.8	7.8	44%	.270	1.11	3.44	4.27	4.89	0.0
2014	NYN	MLB	31	6	7	0	35	17	128²	111	13	50	116	3.5	8.1	46%	.287	1.25	3.61	4.01	3.93	0.9

Torres' lack of a reliable second pitch kept him nibbling at corners in previous big league cameos, but in 2013 his walk rate plummeted, and those balls in play turned into outs. The BABIP will likely right itself next year, but the real adjustment needs to be made by the organization: For goodness sakes, this man is a reliever! Torres' rubber arm allows him to float between spot starting and long relief, but that doesn't mean he should be going through an order more than once. He pitched to a 0.87 WHIP in relief, and threw more than 80 percent fastballs overall. Mariano Rivera he isn't, but at least Rivera's organization knew how to use him.

Jeffrey Walters

Born: 11/6/1987 Age: 26
Bats: R Throws: R Height: 6' 3" Weight: 170
Breakout: 60% Improve: 69% Collapse: 15%
Attrition: 74% MLB: 19%

Comparables:
Andrew Albers, Ryan Sadowski, Greg Burke

YEAR	TEAM	LVL	AGE	W	L	SV	G	GS	IP	H	HR	BB	SO	BB9	SO9	GB%	BABIP	WHIP	ERA	FIP	FRA	WARP
2011	BRO	A-	23	4	6	0	14	14	65	62	3	24	48	3.3	6.6	53%	.282	1.32	3.32	3.78	4.41	0.4
2012	SAV	A	24	3	2	4	17	0	28¹	20	0	4	30	1.3	9.5	51%	.267	0.85	0.95	1.99	2.53	0.8
2012	SLU	A+	24	1	3	0	19	0	26¹	27	1	8	19	2.7	6.5	36%	.306	1.33	3.76	3.58	4.35	0.4
2013	BIN	AA	25	4	3	38	53	0	56	46	2	16	60	2.6	9.6	39%	.306	1.11	2.09	2.56	2.91	1.5
2014	NYN	MLB	26	2	1	1	35	1	47	45	5	18	37	3.5	7.1	43%	.300	1.35	4.14	4.31	4.50	-0.0

A fringy-at-best prospect until 2012, Walters saved 38 games last year at Double-A Binghamton, the second-highest total in Eastern League history. He's yet another hard-throwing righty in a Mets organization full of them, but his low-90s sinker has better control and command. There's a lot to like about Walters: His delivery is compact and he hides the ball well, making him as difficult against lefties as righties. On the negative side, he's a bit of a short-armer with a high-effort delivery, though it's no more worrisome than many short relievers' high-effort deliveries. Most importantly, his mullet is major-league ready, and he flashes plus-plus mutton chops.

	YEAR	TEAM	LVL	AGE	W	L	SV	G	GS	IP	H	HR	BB	SO	BB9	SO9	GB%	BABIP	WHIP	ERA	FIP	FRA	WARP
Zack Wheeler	2011	SJO	A+	21	7	5	0	16	16	88	74	7	47	98	4.8	10.0	51%	.339	1.38	3.99	4.50	5.33	0.5
Born: 5/30/1990 Age: 24	2011	SLU	A+	21	2	2	0	6	6	27	26	0	5	31	1.7	10.3	49%	.358	1.15	2.00	1.87	3.64	0.5
Bats: L Throws: R Height: 6' 4'' Weight: 185	2012	BIN	AA	22	10	6	0	19	19	116	92	2	43	117	3.3	9.1	48%	.303	1.16	3.26	2.80	3.66	2.0
Breakout: 45% Improve: 75% Collapse: 18%	2012	BUF	AAA	22	2	2	0	6	6	33	23	2	16	31	4.4	8.5	46%	.256	1.18	3.27	3.61	4.52	0.3
Attrition: 32% MLB: 86%	2013	LVG	AAA	23	4	2	0	13	13	68²	61	9	27	73	3.5	9.6	42%	.282	1.28	3.93	4.41	4.68	1.2
Comparables:	2013	NYN	MLB	23	7	5	0	17	17	100	90	10	46	84	4.1	7.6	45%	.279	1.36	3.42	4.14	3.91	1.0
Ubaldo Jimenez, Franklin Morales, Marc Rzepczynski	2014	NYN	MLB	24	8	10	1	43	30	143¹	121	14	63	133	4.0	8.4	47%	.288	1.28	3.71	4.09	4.03	1.2

Wheeler's numbers would look even better were it not for a pitch-tipping issue that marred his first few starts. (If you're wondering how the Mets could not know their most recent call-up had been tipping pitches, you'll find no answers here.) Tipping pitches, of course, is a problem exacerbated by throwing four-seamers or sinkers on nearly 75 percent of pitches, which is what Wheeler did over his first nine starts. Once he was able to locate the fastball and get ahead in counts, though, he was phenomenal: He threw 50 percent more breaking balls over his final eight starts, and although fatigue might have affected him late in the year, the foundation is laid for a potential Harvey-esque breakout in 2014.

LINEOUTS

HITTERS

PLAYER	TEAM	LVL	AGE	PA	R	2B	3B	HR	RBI	BB	SO	SB-CS	AVG/OBP/SLG	TAv	BABIP	BRR	FRAA	WARP
RF R. Ankiel	HOU	MLB	33	65	6	3	0	5	11	3	35	0-0	.194/.231/.484	.255	.318	0.2	RF(22): 1.5	0.3
	NYN	MLB	33	71	7	4	1	2	7	5	25	0-1	.182/.239/.364	.223	.256	0.1	CF(17): -1.0, RF(4): -0.1	-0.1
C J. Centeno	BIN	AA	23	24	4	1	1	0	3	0	5	0-0	.261/.261/.391	.224	.333	-0.8	C(6): -0.1	0.1
	LVG	AAA	23	237	25	10	2	0	28	12	24	1-1	.305/.346/.371	.234	.339	0.2	C(62): -1.5	0.9
	NYN	MLB	23	10	0	0	0	0	1	0	1	0-0	.300/.300/.300	.228	.333	0	C(4): -0.0	0.0
2B D. Herrera	SAV	A	19	24	6	0	0	0	4	3	6	3-0	.316/.417/.316	.350	.429	0.2	2B(6): -0.4	0.3
	WVA	A	19	479	69	27	3	11	56	37	110	11-6	.265/.330/.421	.294	.328	-0.1	2B(103): 5.5	3.6
CF K. Nieuwenhuis	LVG	AAA	25	330	60	15	2	14	37	40	78	6-2	.248/.345/.465	.264	.293	4.2	CF(42): 0.1, RF(29): 2.9	1.9
	NYN	MLB	25	108	10	3	1	3	14	12	32	2-0	.189/.278/.337	.233	.246	-0.8	CF(25): -1.3, LF(9): -0.3	-0.1
RF C. Puello	BIN	AA	22	377	63	21	2	16	73	28	82	24-7	.326/.403/.547	.350	.391	3.7	RF(85): 10.1, CF(4): -0.1	6.0
SS O. Quintanilla	LVG	AAA	31	148	26	9	2	2	18	20	25	1-1	.333/.419/.484	.303	.396	0.4	SS(43): -0.2	1.3
	NYN	MLB	31	359	28	9	2	2	21	38	70	2-0	.222/.306/.283	.218	.278	2.3	SS(92): -3.8, 3B(1): -0.0	-0.4
RF A. Seratelli	OMA	AAA	30	487	61	17	3	11	41	77	81	24-1	.272/.395/.412	.296	.318	1.3	RF(84): 4.9, 3B(17): 0.5	4.0
SS W. Tovar	BIN	AA	21	486	70	14	4	4	36	33	49	12-7	.263/.323/.340	.255	.287	2.3	SS(127): -6.4, 2B(4): -0.1	1.6
	NYN	MLB	21	19	1	0	0	0	2	1	3	1-0	.200/.294/.200	.150	.250	-0.7	SS(7): 0.0	-0.3

Rick Ankiel was released by the Astros, signed with the Mets four days later and rushed to Busch Stadium to hit leadoff and play center field, even though his bats and glove were still in Houston. The Mets have outfield problems. ⊘ **Juan Centeno** caught Billy Hamilton stealing as a September call-up. If he does it again, it'll probably be at Triple-A. ⊘ **Dilson Herrera** is a decent value for the Pirates' rental of John Buck and Marlon Byrd. He's a converted third baseman offering good speed and surprising power despite a slight frame. The hit tool is real, as are the strikeout rates. ⊘ If he weren't so devastatingly handsome, more people would realize that **Kirk Nieuwenhuis** is a C- in every category. As it is, he projects best in a supporting role … in a strikingly realistic, yet-to-be-filmed baseball movie to be named later. ⊘ Hey, the Mets might really have something in **Cesar Puello**! The raw power was always there, but he finally put it all together in—oh, he was suspended for PED use. Well, there goes that. ⊘ Through injury, indigence and whatever happened to Ruben Tejada, **Omar Quintanilla** racked up another 95 big-league games. His poor defense makes the next 95 an uphill battle. ⊘ Gavin Cecchini is further along, but scouts agree the upside is in **Amed Rosario**, who held his own as a 17-year-old in the Appalachian League. He's a big, rangy shortstop with the frame to add power. ⌀ Versatile **Anthony Seratelli** finished sixth in the PCL in OBP despite an almost impossible 8 percent line-drive rate. ⌀ Not many teams have the luxury of bringing a plus shortstop off the bench, and **Wilfredo Tovar**'s bat probably won't make him anything more than that. He'll likely get his first taste of Triple-A in 2014.

PITCHERS

PLAYER	TEAM	LVL	AGE	W	L	SV	IP	H	HR	BB	SO	BB9	SO9	GB%	BABIP	WHIP	ERA	FIP	FRA	WARP
S. Atchison	NYN	MLB	37	3	3	0	45¹	45	4	12	28	2.4	5.6	50%	.275	1.26	4.37	3.73	4.51	-0.1
T. Byrdak	SLU	A+	39	1	1	3	12¹	6	0	7	13	5.1	9.5	31%	.207	1.05	2.19	2.84	3.98	0.1
	NYN	MLB	39	0	0	0	4²	5	2	2	3	3.9	5.8	29%	.250	1.50	7.71	8.59	12.25	-0.3
P. Feliciano	BIN	AA	36	0	0	0	14¹	9	0	2	14	1.3	8.8	64%	.250	0.77	1.26	2.00	1.52	0.6
	NYN	MLB	36	0	2	0	11¹	11	1	6	9	4.8	7.1	49%	.294	1.50	3.97	4.43	3.54	0.0
M. Fulmer	SLU	A+	20	2	2	0	34	24	1	18	29	4.8	7.7	38%	.245	1.24	3.44	3.86	4.56	0.2
G. Germen	LVG	AAA	25	3	3	4	44	47	7	11	51	2.2	10.4	48%	.330	1.32	5.52	4.07	4.27	1.0
	NYN	MLB	25	1	2	1	34¹	32	1	16	33	4.2	8.7	37%	.312	1.40	3.93	2.87	3.32	0.5
E. Goeddel	BIN	AA	24	9	7	0	134	135	14	58	125	3.9	8.4	40%	.320	1.44	4.37	4.27	4.19	2.1
L. Mateo	BRO	A-	22	4	5	0	73¹	57	2	9	85	1.1	10.4	49%	.296	0.90	2.45	1.98	2.81	1.7
C. Mazzoni	BIN	AA	23	5	3	0	66	70	4	19	74	2.6	10.1	41%	.363	1.35	4.36	2.82	3.70	1.3
R. Reid	IND	AAA	28	7	2	2	59¹	49	4	22	56	3.3	8.5	69%	.278	1.20	2.73	3.36	4.88	0.1
	PIT	MLB	28	0	0	1	11	9	1	3	7	2.5	5.7	56%	.242	1.09	1.64	4.29	5.64	-0.2
H. Robles	SLU	A+	22	5	4	0	84²	83	8	29	66	3.1	7.0	39%	.296	1.32	3.72	4.15	4.62	0.3
D. Tapia	SLU	A+	21	3	9	0	101¹	87	3	63	89	5.6	7.9	59%	.291	1.48	4.62	3.88	5.39	-0.3

If this is the end for **Scott Atchison**, let his epitaph read: He gutted out 50 appearances for a lousy team with a partially torn UCL, and he pitched pretty well, considering everyone thought he was 63 years old the entire time. ⌀ That **Tim Byrdak** pitched at all in 2013 at age 39 was remarkable, given the severity of his shoulder injury. More remarkable, though, is that it was no more remarkable than any number of other unremarkable stops in his remarkable career. Remarkable. ⌀ **Pedro Feliciano**? Again?! ⌀ **Michael Fulmer**'s season was derailed by a torn meniscus, and he could've used the time to develop his changeup. That pitch will determine whether he's a starter or a reliever. ⌀ **Gonzalez Germen** has a lively fastball that sits around 94, but to be a trusted reliever, he's going to have to develop a second pitch and learn to repeat his motion. His arm drags behind the rest of his body. ⌀ **Erik Goeddel** was added to the 40-man roster after another sturdy season as a starter. His future role is probably in the bullpen, where Goeddel can be an interesting short man. *Wink.* ⌀ **Luis Mateo** always had a live arm, but by the time he recovers from last June's Tommy John surgery he'll be at least two seasons behind where he should be. ⌀ **Cory Mazzoni**'s K/9 jumped to 10.4—thanks to a heater that sits 93-94 with movement—and he could make his big league debut in 2014. He's always been a starter, but for an undersized right-hander who will impact the rotation, see Montero, Rafael. ⌀ **Ryan Reid** became the second big leaguer from Maine's Deering High School, joining Ryan Flaherty. Many think Flaherty's brother, Regan, is the next Ram to reach the majors, but things are supposed to come in threes, so we're on the look-out for another Ryan. ⌀ **Hansel Robles** just keeps getting outs despite a lack of size and stuff, but he's been old for every level at which he's played. Sometime in 2014 he'll crack Double-A, where we'll find out if it's all a parlor trick. ⌀ **Domingo Tapia**'s control completely left him in 2013; he was a walk away from doubling his 2012 total in fewer innings. But don't count him out, as he still has the best fastball in the organization—so good, in fact, that his two-seamer suffices as an off-speed pitch.

MANAGER: TERRY COLLINS

YEAR	TEAM	W-L	Pythag +/-	Avg PC	100+ P	120+ P	QS	BQS	REL	REL w Zero R	IBB	PH	PH Avg	PH HR	SB2	CS2	SB3	CS3	SAC Att	SAC %	POS SAC	Squeeze	Swing	In Play
2011	NYN	77-85	0	95.7	63	6	84	7	514	398	48	306	.203	8	113	32	16	4	102	63.7%	26	2	347	114
2012	NYN	74-88	0	95.5	69	2	101	1	505	380	29	322	.240	10	66	35	13	3	82	78.0%	19	4	321	108
2013	NYN	74-88	0	95.7	69	2	94	3	534	417	38	262	.207	4	99	31	15	4	82	64.6%	26	0	310	87

On Opening Day, Terry Collins will be the oldest manager in baseball. He was fourth-oldest a year ago, but Davey Johnson, Charlie Manuel and Jim Leyland are now all gone (as is Dusty Baker, who was the fifth-oldest skipper last year). Until Collins turns 65 on May 27th, baseball will be without a senior citizen manager. Last time that happened: the 1992 season, when a 64-year-old Tommy Lasorda was the eldest skipper.

His teams have typically been bad at turning double plays. With the Mets, his defenses have been bad in general. From 2011 to 2013, they are third-worst in baseball by Defensive Runs Saved. Collins' teams have typically been built around bats. In his nine years, 69 percent of the teams' Baseball-Reference WAR has come from offense, the highest percentage for any currently employed manager with more than one year of experience.

Last year was just the third time a Collins-led team played better in the second half. He's 402-369 (.521) before the All-Star break and 286-336 (.460) after it. That is the worst second-half drop of any current skipper.

New York Yankees

By Andy McCullough

The commissioner of Major League Baseball considers him an inveterate cheater. His own general manager believes him untrustworthy and refuses to say more than "hello" or "goodbye" to him. Various, often unsubstantiated accounts have painted him as a slumlord, a scoundrel, a deviant, a blight on baseball's history. But after one season covering Alex Rodriguez, the worst thing I can say about him is he caused me indigestion one time—and that's only because I like to eat lunch around 11 a.m.

The day in question, July 24, 2013, began like any other for me as Yankees beat writer for the *Star-Ledger*. I awoke in a Courtyard by Marriott in Arlington, a 1,400-yard walk across the hot coals of north Texas summer from Rangers Ballpark. Around 11 a.m. central time, I stumbled from my darkened room, ventured through a parking lot and gorged on shrimp, red beans and rice at Pappadeaux.

This figured to be a normal afternoon, or as normal as possible, considering the shadow Rodriguez cast over the team from afar. A few weeks prior, Rodriguez had pledged to rejoin the Yankees for this series. But he tweaked his quadriceps during a rehab assignment for his surgically repaired left hip. The Yankees tabled his return for another two weeks, a decision Rodriguez protested but lacked the recourse to combat. On July 22nd, Ryan Braun accepted a 65-game suspension for his role in the Biogenesis scandal, a concrete sign that baseball's pincers of justice would soon crunch Rodriguez as well.

After sufficiently stuffing myself at lunch, I returned to my room to transcribe an interview with Adam Warren, the team's seldom-used long reliever. (My life is not riveting.) But at 12:15 eastern, Jimmy Traina, then of SI.com, noticed a curious interview occurring on WFAN. Soon after, someone retweeted Traina into my feed: "Wow. Mike Francesca inter-

viewing doctor who examined ARod. Dr says ARod does NOT have a quad injury & he's fine."

To my credit, I did not vomit. But my body did undergo some sort of seismic shudder.

***

It is worthwhile here to pause. There is a reason you, faithful consumer, are reading about my dietary habits in an essay about the Yankees. The media—that hodgepodge of reporters, analysts, radio hosts and television personalities—played a critical role in this entire process. Most of the machinations involved heavy hitters: Major League Baseball apparently enlisted Today Show host Matt Lauer to spring a public trap on one of Rodriguez's lawyers; Rodriguez utilized Mike Francesca's massive WFAN audience as his bully pulpit on the fateful November day he walked out of his arbitration hearing.

But even the lower-level foot soldiers, the beat writers like myself, played a role in the drama. Each day could create a new bit of slapstick: I skipped the All-Star Game to hang out in Reading, Pennsylvania, with a former WWE superstar and other members of Rodriguez's security detail on a rehab assignment. You learned to embrace the chaos; there was no other option. Rodriguez operated as an incredible centrifugal force and you were forced to ride the wave.

***

A month prior to Dr. Gross' radio appearance, a similar scenario had unfolded. The Yankees said Rodriguez was not cleared for rehab games. Soon after, Rodriguez wrote on Twitter that he had been cleared. "Well, that's funny," I thought to myself, then went back to watching that night's game. Andrew Marchand, a sharp reporter for ESPN New York with a keen sense of these flashpoints, was far more astute. He relayed Rodriguez's tweet to General Manager Brian

YANKEES PROSPECTUS
2013 W-L: 85-77, 3rd in AL East

Pythag	.485	17th	DER	.698	22nd
RS/G	4.01	16th	B-Age	31.9	30th
RA/G	4.14	15th	P-Age	31.5	30th
TAv	.251	23rd	Salary	$228.1	1st
BRR	4.81	9th	M$/MW	$5.9	28th
TAv-P	.266	17th	DL Days	1396	28th
FIP	3.92	19th	$ on DL	36%	29th

	Runs	HR/RH	HR/LH	Runs/RH	Runs/LH
Three-Year Park Factors	100	96	90	102	104

Top Hitter WARP	6.26 (Robinson Cano)
Top Pitcher WARP	2.78 (Hiroki Kuroda)
Top Prospect	Gary Sanchez

Cashman, who responded with the immortal line, "Alex should just shut the **** up."

Think about that. Even for the organization's storied history of infighting, that was incredible. Billy Martin found himself ousted after calling Reggie Jackson a liar and making reference to George Steinbrenner's illegal contributions to Richard Nixon's reelection campaign. Cashman told Rodriguez to "*shut the *** up*," yet that was far from the most outrageous occurrence of the summer.

In 2013, Rodriguez lived out a campaign that was both historic and preposterous. His covert battles with his employer spilled out into a public war. He charged team officials with trying to ruin his career by forcing him to play injured during the 2012 playoffs. He sued the team doctor for withholding information about the October 2012 torn labrum that cost him half of the next season. He accused Bud Selig of conducting a "witch hunt" in the Biogenesis investigation. He received the largest suspension ever for violating the league's performance-enhancing drug policy—*and he played his first game of the season on the same day the suspension was levied.*

But when I think back on 2013, my mind always drifts to that July afternoon in Arlington, when I came to embrace the absurdity of this assignment. I did the first thing that came to mind: I called the doctor. I spoke with the soon-to-be infamous orthopedic surgeon, a man who either bit off more than he could chew or could not comprehend how rancid what he bit into would become.

What compelled you to call in to the radio station? I asked.

"That's irrelevant," he said, though a few hours later—before his own hospital moved to distance itself from his words and before his recent reprimand for improper distribution of steroids and human growth hormone to patients became public knowledge, but after he learned of the budding controversy—he admitted to another reporter that he thought this moment would be his "five minutes of fame."

At some point, I attended a baseball game, and perhaps even wrote about it. But my day unfolded in a pattern that became familiar over the coming weeks: calls to Yankees officials, calls to Rodriguez's representatives, calls to anyone in baseball who could help suss just what the hell was going on.

There were worthwhile questions. How did Rodriguez get here? How did the Yankees allow this to occur? How did their relationship deteriorate to such an extent? These were the critical issues of 2013, the plotlines that subsumed an otherwise ho-hum 85-win campaign. Conspiracy theories littered the landscape: The Yankees would try to void Rodriguez's contract; Rodriguez would fake an injury as insurance fraud to recoup his money. During this time, I did not particularly distinguish myself in the reportage: I wrote enough to stay afloat, but produced only incremental crumbs of news. In the process, though, a window opened into the organization's bruising culture, their lingering resentment toward Rodriguez and the escalating stakes of their feud.

No player exists in a vacuum; each creates a cascading effect through its organization's subsequent decisions. But with Rodriguez, those ripples are profound. His arbitration hearing handcuffed the Yankees from splashing cash at the outset of the winter. His albatross contract colored their negotiations with free agent Robinson Cano, prompted ownership to forbid any subsequent 10-year deals and precipitated Cano's departure for Seattle. He is an emblem of their past and an obstruction to their future. Even in exile, he is the axis around which their world revolves. To borrow his own garbled phraseology, he is "the pink elephant in the room."

***

Here's a fun game: Pick Alex Rodriguez's best season.

According to WARP and Baseball-Reference WAR, it was 2000 for Seattle: 41 HR, 132 RBI, 34 doubles, a 1.026 OPS.

According to FanGraphs WAR, it was 2002 for Texas: 57 HR, 142 RBI, 27 doubles, 1.105 OPS.

Rodriguez says it was his rookie season with the Mariners in 1996: 36 HR, 123 RBI, 54 doubles, 1.045 OPS.

Think about how preposterous those numbers are. Then understand they are not even his best offensive seasons. Those occurred with the Yankees: His highest TAv was in 2005; his highest wRC+ was in 2007. He was—and still can be, at the plate, on occasion—incredible.

At the GM Meetings last year, one executive told me he set up a Google alert with Rodriguez's name. He couldn't help himself. A-Rod gossip was his guilty pleasure. The stories diverted him from the agita of his own job. But it is worth remembering Rodriguez's greatness on the diamond. Otherwise, all of these conversations wouldn't be worth our time.

***

Yet as his performance wanes, his personality holds sway. In the days before his suspension on August 5th, one associate painted Rodriguez as a man adrift in a swirl of chaos, surrounded by an ever-changing cadre of crisis managers, lawyers and publicists kowtowing to his demands. Rodriguez churns through support staff at an alarming rate. His attempts at public relations appear bumbling. Rodriguez looks awkward in interviews, prone to a blend of cryptic statements and malapropisms.

In the spring of 2009, Rodriguez held a press conference to discuss his admission of past steroid use as a Texas Ranger. During his opening statement, he paused after mentioning his teammates. He had already delivered a series of apologies when he began to speak about the men assembled there to support him. In a 37-second sequence of silence, Rodriguez smirked, slumped in his chair, stared at the ground, snared a water bottle off the table, smothered a grimace, sipped from the bottle and then shifted his weight forward.

"Thank you," was all he said to the group, a head-scratching opening to a 30-minute public pillorying. That same afternoon, Cashman referred to Rodriguez as Humpty-Dumpty: "We've got to put him back together again." Observers described his tone as dejected. His remarks displayed the fissure created by Rodriguez's admission, how it tarnished the organization's plans for him.

"We've invested in him as an asset," Cashman said that day. "And because of that, this is an asset that is going through a crisis. So we'll do everything we can to protect that asset and support that asset and try to salvage that asset."

***

Five seasons later, the time for dejection had passed. Now anger reigned, a calm and measured form of anger, but anger nonetheless in the voice of team president Randy Levine. It was August 17th, another afternoon like that one in Arlington. Earlier on, Rodriguez's attorney had cast Levine as a sinister figure in this saga, accusing him of telling the surgeon who operated on Rodriguez's hip the previous winter to make sure Rodriguez never played again.

It was an audacious charge, one Levine called "completely fictitious, false and specious." When I called Levine that afternoon, shortly after reading a story in the *New York Times* about Rodriguez's latest charges, he was stewing with indignation. He presented two options for Rodriguez: Either release his medical records to the public or file a grievance against the team.

"Put up or shut up," Levine said, and insisted that the only real issue here was "Did Alex Rodriguez use performance-enhancing drugs or not?"

It was one of the few times the organization publicly acknowledged the charges against Rodriguez in a specific manner. In years past, Levine said, he often emailed Rodriguez offering encouragement and motivation. Now, it appeared, he just wanted him to go away. So much had changed from the spring of 2009 to 2013 for Rodriguez, the Yankees and Major League Baseball, all of which made Rodriguez's presence on the roster more cumbersome.

When Rodriguez opted out of his contract after the 2007 season, the Yankees went back on their previously issued threats and negotiated a new contract with him, a 10-year, $275 million pact, with $30 million in bonuses. His dalliances with performance-enhancing drugs poisoned the team's plans to market his chase of Barry Bonds' home run record. But they did not alter his contract. If Rodriguez hits six more homers, he'll have 660 for his career, and receive a $6 million bonus. Similar bonuses await him at No. 714, No. 755, No. 762 and No. 763. Upon considering these bonuses last summer, a few folks in the pressbox laughed.

"I want to be a fly on the wall in the room when they have to cut that check," one wag said.

"It'll probably be direct deposit," another cracked.

Yet the financial sting will be real, even for a team like the Yankees. In the last five seasons, Rodriguez led the team to one World Series title, helped them contend for three others, then staged a sideshow as the team tumbled in 2013. All around him, though, the realities of the game shifted.

A new collective bargaining agreement leveled the fiscal playing field for spending in the draft or in Latin America. A raft of new television contracts infused cash around the game, so teams could afford to lock up their young stars before they reached free agency. The Yankees could no longer outspend other teams in acquiring amateur talent, nor could they poach players from smaller markets.

Rare now is the superstar who reaches free agency—and the competition for those players has grown ever fiercer. The last portion is critical. Out west, a new ownership group transformed the Dodgers into a financial behemoth. At the GM Meetings in 2013, both executives and reporters spoke of the Dodgers as operating without limits, willing to throw gobs of money without consequence, glad to seize the free-spending throne from their former rivals in The Bronx.

In the past, perhaps, the Yankees held that mantle, but managing general partner Hal Steinbrenner has ushered in a new era of fiscal restraint. The team entered last winter hell-bent on reducing payroll beneath the $189 million luxury-tax threshold, a mark the Yankees had soared past in every season but one since 2005. If the team can meet the goal, it'll save up to $100 million over the subsequent two years, the *New York Post*'s Joel Sherman has reported. Steinbrenner has grown tired of losing that money through taxes distributed to other teams.

So Rodriguez's salary is no longer just a drag on a money-making machine. It is a $33.5 million (the average annual value of his contract plus the likely bonuses) credit against the luxury-tax figure. And when they scoffed at Cano's original $300 million asking price, they did so fully aware of how Rodriguez's deal has hamstrung them.

"Things are in the saddle, / And ride mankind," Ralph Waldo Emerson once wrote, which is an eloquent summary of chaos theory (I think). When the Yankees granted Rodriguez that historic extension, could they have foreseen the game's landscape? Doubtful. And they can't predict his actions to come.

As a reporter, this is what makes Rodriguez so maddening and so fascinating. The rabbit hole never ends. In November, when Rodriguez stormed out of his hearing, his lawyers threatened to take his case to federal court—a dubious outcome, but I wouldn't bet against them making it interesting. Meanwhile, Joel Sherman has written that the Yankees can't ban Rodriguez from spring training, even if he's suspended. I can't wait for that sideshow. No, there is not much negative I can say about Alex Rodriguez. The pink elephant may never leave the room, and for that I thank him.

Andy McCullough covers the Yankees for the Newark Star-Ledger, *and you can follow him on Twitter at @McCulloughSL.*

HITTERS

Zoilo Almonte — LF

Born: 6/10/1989 Age: 25
Bats: B Throws: R Height: 6' 0"
Weight: 205 Breakout: 10%
Improve: 27% Collapse: 7%
Attrition: 31% MLB: 58%

Comparables:
Todd Frazier, Justin Huber, Allen Craig

YEAR	TEAM	LVL	AGE	PA	R	2B	3B	HR	RBI	BB	SO	SB	CS	AVG/OBP/SLG	TAv	BABIP	BRR	FRAA	WARP
2011	TAM	A+	22	296	38	15	3	12	54	31	60	14	4	.293/.368/.514	.357	.335	-1	LF(24): 2.0	1.6
2011	TRN	AA	22	191	23	11	1	3	23	14	45	4	1	.251/.309/.377	.237	.320	0.3	RF(14): 0.2, LF(2): 0.1	-0.1
2012	TRN	AA	23	451	64	23	1	21	70	25	103	15	4	.277/.322/.487	.286	.319	2.4	RF(88): 11.5, CF(7): -0.4	3.3
2013	SWB	AAA	24	293	30	12	1	6	36	30	47	4	1	.297/.369/.421	.282	.340	-1	LF(53): -1.7, CF(14): -1.8	0.9
2013	NYA	MLB	24	113	9	4	0	1	9	6	19	3	1	.236/.274/.302	.223	.276	-1.8	LF(25): 0.4, RF(3): 0.0	-0.4
2014	NYA	MLB	25	250	29	10	0	9	32	16	56	5	1	.253/.301/.419	.263	.290	0.2	LF 0, RF 2	0.8

Prior to 2013, some Yankees scouts saw Almonte as a future average everyday right fielder, but the 24-year-old did little last season to make that projection seem prescient. Most of the switch-hitter's Trenton power from 2012 didn't translate to Triple-A, and even less made it to the majors. He made frequent contact, but much of it came outside the strike zone, which took away walks and led to weak batted balls; the Mark of Zoilo was a grounder to the pull side. Almonte sprained his ankle running through the first-base bag in late July, and his rehab was delayed by a wisdom teeth extraction, so he didn't have much time to acclimate to the league. With age and adjustments—particularly at the plate versus southpaws, whom he hasn't hit lately—he should become a useable bench bat.

Carlos Beltran — RF

Born: 4/24/1977 Age: 37
Bats: B Throws: R Height: 6' 1"
Weight: 210 Breakout: 0%
Improve: 27% Collapse: 12%
Attrition: 14% MLB: 88%

Comparables:
Magglio Ordonez, Sid Gordon, Torii Hunter

YEAR	TEAM	LVL	AGE	PA	R	2B	3B	HR	RBI	BB	SO	SB	CS	AVG/OBP/SLG	TAv	BABIP	BRR	FRAA	WARP
2011	NYN	MLB	34	419	61	30	2	15	66	60	61	3	0	.289/.391/.513	.328	.310	-0.4	RF(91): -8.3	2.8
2011	SFN	MLB	34	179	17	9	4	7	18	11	27	1	2	.323/.369/.551	.327	.353	-0.1	RF(43): 0.1	1.5
2012	SLN	MLB	35	619	83	26	1	32	97	65	124	13	6	.269/.346/.495	.297	.291	0.1	RF(132): -6.5, CF(9): -0.1	2.8
2013	SLN	MLB	36	600	79	30	3	24	84	38	90	2	1	.296/.339/.491	.289	.314	2	RF(137): 1.3	3.1
2014	NYA	MLB	37	567	71	27	2	21	77	55	99	6	3	.271/.344/.459	.290	.300	-0.5	RF -6, CF -0	2.2

It has *never* been about talent with Beltran. He has always reigned among baseball's best outfielders. The only reason Cooperstown hasn't already made a down payment on Beltran's plaque is his health: He's played 150 games in fewer than half of his 15 seasons and three times has not even cracked 100. Beltran has actually been reasonably durable in his mid-30s, all things considered, falling just two 2011 plate appearances shy of three straight seasons of 600-plus trips. The only real flaws in his game are a five-year decline against lefties and the inevitable erosion of his outfield range. Inked by the Yankees to a three-year, $45 million deal, Beltran will soon be penning odes to the short porch in right, and his health and longevity should benefit from occasional rotation through the DH spot.

Francisco Cervelli — C

Born: 3/6/1986 Age: 28
Bats: R Throws: R Height: 6' 1"
Weight: 205 Breakout: 4%
Improve: 29% Collapse: 14%
Attrition: 29% MLB: 78%

Comparables:
J.R. Towles, Rob Johnson, Brayan Pena

YEAR	TEAM	LVL	AGE	PA	R	2B	3B	HR	RBI	BB	SO	SB	CS	AVG/OBP/SLG	TAv	BABIP	BRR	FRAA	WARP
2011	NYA	MLB	25	137	17	4	0	4	22	9	29	4	1	.266/.324/.395	.258	.315	0.2	C(41): -0.0, 3B(2): -0.0	0.6
2012	SWB	AAA	26	417	43	15	2	2	39	39	82	6	0	.246/.341/.316	.237	.308	-2.7	C(96): 0.6	0.7
2012	NYA	MLB	26	2	1	0	0	0	0	1	0	0	0	.000/.500/.000	.277	.000	0.1	C(3): -0.0	0.0
2013	NYA	MLB	27	61	12	3	0	3	8	8	9	0	0	.269/.377/.500	.321	.275	-0.3	C(16): 0.5, 2B(1): -0.0	0.8
2014	NYA	MLB	28	250	25	9	1	4	23	20	47	2	1	.249/.323/.350	.252	.290	-0.2	C 1, 2B 0	1.0

Cervelli has made himself into a strong defensive catcher, but no one expected the offensive outburst with which he started the season. Given his past offensive performance, it likely wouldn't have lasted, but Cervelli didn't get the chance to prove that it wasn't a fluke. A foul tip fractured his hand in late April, shortly after he'd seized a starting role, and a subsequent stress reaction in his elbow complicated his recovery and jeopardized his season, making early August the perfect time for him to be hit with a Biogenesis suspension. Cervelli accepted the 50-game punishment and served it while on the DL, so he'll start next season with a clean slate and, hopefully, a healthy hand and elbow.

Jacoby Ellsbury — CF

Born: 9/11/1983 Age: 30
Bats: L Throws: L Height: 6' 1"
Weight: 195 Breakout: 1%
Improve: 50% Collapse: 6%
Attrition: 7% MLB: 100%

Comparables:
Shane Victorino, Vernon Wells, Coco Crisp

YEAR	TEAM	LVL	AGE	PA	R	2B	3B	HR	RBI	BB	SO	SB	CS	AVG/OBP/SLG	TAv	BABIP	BRR	FRAA	WARP
2011	BOS	MLB	27	729	119	46	5	32	105	52	98	39	15	.321/.376/.552	.315	.336	3.2	CF(154): 11.3	7.8
2012	BOS	MLB	28	323	43	18	0	4	26	19	43	14	3	.271/.313/.370	.243	.304	3.3	CF(73): -2.2	0.3
2013	BOS	MLB	29	636	92	31	8	9	53	47	92	52	4	.298/.355/.426	.277	.341	5.3	CF(134): 6.9	4.4
2014	NYA	MLB	30	536	77	24	3	12	51	38	73	35	6	.285/.341/.421	.276	.310	4.2	CF 2	3.1

When healthy, Ellsbury is one of the game's more dynamic players. He's a machine on the basepaths, especially as his running from first-to-third and second-to-home has improved, and his routes and first steps in center look better with time, a depressing notion for offenses used to Ellsbury relying entirely on his speed to make a play. While his bat is unlikely to approach 2011 levels again, he is plenty productive thanks to his ability to make consistent, solid contact and draw a walk when he needs to. He's also healthier more often than many think: Ellsbury has had his share of nagging injuries, but he's only missed significant time on two occasions. Adrian Beltre broke his ribs in 2010, and misdiagnoses caused him to miss additional time. Reid Brignac was the culprit in another collision in 2012, this one causing a shoulder dislocation. So long as no one crashes into Ellsbury going forward, the Yankees will enjoy their $153 million investment.

Brett Gardner LF

Born: 8/24/1983 Age: 30
Bats: L Throws: L Height: 5' 10"
Weight: 185 Breakout: 1%
Improve: 48% Collapse: 4%
Attrition: 7% MLB: 100%

Comparables:
Kenny Lofton, Shane Victorino, Michael Bourn

YEAR	TEAM	LVL	AGE	PA	R	2B	3B	HR	RBI	BB	SO	SB	CS	AVG/OBP/SLG	TAv	BABIP	BRR	FRAA	WARP
2011	NYA	MLB	27	588	87	19	8	7	36	60	93	49	13	.259/.345/.369	.254	.303	7.7	LF(149): 13.0, CF(18): 0.8	3.3
2012	NYA	MLB	28	37	7	2	0	0	3	5	7	2	2	.323/.417/.387	.294	.417	0.5	LF(15): -0.2	0.2
2013	NYA	MLB	29	609	81	33	10	8	52	52	127	24	8	.273/.344/.416	.279	.342	3.4	CF(138): -6.4	2.7
2014	NYA	MLB	30	459	61	17	6	5	34	48	85	28	8	.261/.347/.368	.263	.310	2.8	LF 7, CF -0	2.3

Gardner revamped his offensive approach in 2013, adopting hitting coach Kevin Long's advice to be more aggressive inside the strike zone. Whereas the old Gardner averaged one swing for every two pitches in the center of the strike zone, the new-look model offered at three out of five, bumping his overall swing rate from third-lowest among hitters who saw at least 1,000 pitches in 2011 to 44th-lowest last year. The result: fewer walks and more strikeouts, but also an increase in extra-base hits. The difference didn't amount to much; for all the tinkering, the semi-selective Gardner was no more or less productive at the plate than the ultra-selective edition. But that same old offensive value, combined with solid defense in center, some baserunning value and good health that lasted until a mid-September oblique strain, was enough to make the lineup's only under-30 mainstay the most valuable Yankees position player not named Cano. Gardner is now the team's sixth most famous outfielder, but on talent alone deserves to be the everyday left fielder (absent a trade, rumors of which dogged him after the Yankees signed Carlos Beltran and Jacoby Ellsbury).

Travis Hafner DH

Born: 6/3/1977 Age: 37
Bats: L Throws: R Height: 6' 3"
Weight: 240 Breakout: 0%
Improve: 22% Collapse: 9%
Attrition: 15% MLB: 70%

Comparables:
Cliff Floyd, Kevin Mitchell, Eduardo Perez

YEAR	TEAM	LVL	AGE	PA	R	2B	3B	HR	RBI	BB	SO	SB	CS	AVG/OBP/SLG	TAv	BABIP	BRR	FRAA	WARP
2011	CLE	MLB	34	368	41	16	0	13	57	36	78	0	0	.280/.361/.449	.289	.332	-1.2		1.4
2012	CLE	MLB	35	263	23	6	2	12	34	32	47	0	0	.228/.346/.438	.287	.233	-1.7		0.8
2013	NYA	MLB	36	299	31	8	1	12	37	32	79	2	0	.202/.301/.378	.251	.240	0		0.1
2014	NYA	MLB	37	275	33	11	0	9	33	29	60	1	0	.245/.337/.410	.273	.290	-0.4		0.8

For the first month of the season, Hafner looked like the baseball equivalent of a priceless document found in the frame of a painting purchased for 50 cents at a yard sale. Signed to a classic incentive-laden contract after earning roughly $11 million per win over his final five seasons in Cleveland, the left-hander hit .318/.438/.667 in the heart of New York's depleted April lineup, production that wouldn't have looked out of place in his late 20s. But just when Yankees fans began to believe that the sight of the Stadium's short porch had miraculously healed him, his body broke down. Playing through shoulder pain, Hafner hit .167/.249/.286 from May through late July before succumbing to a rotator cuff strain that kept him on the disabled list for the rest of the season. If the Yankees had cut bait at the first hint of trouble, he would have been well worth what they paid him, which should serve as a lesson to his future employers: Give up on the hurt Hafner before he undoes any good that the healthy Hafner did.

Slade Heathcott CF

Born: 9/28/1990 Age: 23
Bats: L Throws: L Height: 6' 0"
Weight: 195 Breakout: 1%
Improve: 12% Collapse: 4%
Attrition: 10% MLB: 28%

Comparables:
Trayvon Robinson, Kirk Nieuwenhuis, Austin Jackson

YEAR	TEAM	LVL	AGE	PA	R	2B	3B	HR	RBI	BB	SO	SB	CS	AVG/OBP/SLG	TAv	BABIP	BRR	FRAA	WARP
2011	CSC	A	20	237	36	11	4	4	16	19	57	6	7	.271/.342/.419	.357	.353	-2.4	CF(17): 1.4	1.3
2012	TAM	A+	21	243	38	16	2	5	27	20	66	17	4	.307/.378/.470	.288	.421	1.1	CF(16): 1.0, LF(3): 0.3	1.4
2013	TRN	AA	22	444	59	22	7	8	49	36	107	15	8	.261/.327/.411	.274	.336	1.7	CF(90): -5.8	1.6
2014	NYA	MLB	23	250	30	11	1	6	23	15	70	7	3	.237/.288/.370	.239	.310	0.2	CF -2, LF 0	-0.1

Most scouts will say that Heathcott is one of the most physically talented players in the minors. But the physical talent that he doesn't have—durability—might make his other abilities moot. In his fourth professional season, Heathcott got into a career-high 103 games, but he still found time for an injury; this time, patella tendonitis in his right knee, which could be a consequence of his intense style of play. The ailment ended his season on August 10th, which was a shame, since Heathcott had turned his season around—coincidentally or not—after making a mechanical change to smooth out his pre-pitch movement, hitting .307/.367/.518 in 150 post-June plate appearances after a .237/.306/.355 start. A fast runner with good power, he still has a chance to be an asset in center if his health cooperates.

Eric Jagielo   3B

Born: 5/17/1992 Age: 22
Bats: L Throws: R Height: 6' 2"
Weight: 195 Breakout: 0%
Improve: 0% Collapse: 0%
Attrition: 1% MLB: 1%

Comparables:
Mike Olt, Jedd Gyorko, Chase Headley

YEAR	TEAM	LVL	AGE	PA	R	2B	3B	HR	RBI	BB	SO	SB	CS	AVG/OBP/SLG	TAv	BABIP	BRR	FRAA	WARP
2013	STA	A-	21	218	19	14	1	6	27	26	54	0	0	.266/.376/.451	.315	.344	-1.9	3B(42): -1.3	1.6
2014	NYA	MLB	22	250	21	8	0	5	24	18	74	0	0	.197/.262/.304	.209	.260	-0.4	3B -2	-1.0

In Jagielo, their top pick in 2013 and the 26th overall selection, the Yankees went safe without sacrificing ceiling. The third baseman, whose lefty bat should be a good fit for Yankee Stadium, signed an exactly-slot bonus and got into games before the end of June, showing a good eye and plus power in the New York-Penn League. Nothing about his offensive approach raises red flags, and he has a good arm and hands at third, where he should be able to play all the way up the ladder. The junior out of Notre Dame represents a change in draft direction for the organization, which has been burned under scouting director Damon Oppenheimer by high school hitters Carl Henry, Cito Culver and Dante Bichette Jr. Jagielo is the first college position player the Yankees have signed with their top pick since John-Ford Griffin in 2001, and all indications are that this one will work out better than the last one did.

Derek Jeter   SS

Born: 6/26/1974 Age: 40
Bats: R Throws: R Height: 6' 3"
Weight: 195 Breakout: 0%
Improve: 18% Collapse: 9%
Attrition: 21% MLB: 66%

Comparables:
Tony Fernandez, Paul Molitor, Kenny Lofton

YEAR	TEAM	LVL	AGE	PA	R	2B	3B	HR	RBI	BB	SO	SB	CS	AVG/OBP/SLG	TAv	BABIP	BRR	FRAA	WARP
2011	NYA	MLB	37	607	84	24	4	6	61	46	81	16	6	.297/.355/.388	.268	.336	-2.7	SS(122): -10.1	1.5
2012	NYA	MLB	38	740	99	32	0	15	58	45	90	9	4	.316/.362/.429	.273	.347	-1.2	SS(135): -7.8	3.0
2013	SWB	AAA	39	23	4	1	0	0	1	5	3	0	0	.222/.391/.278	.285	.267	-0.1	SS(6): 0.0	0.1
2013	NYA	MLB	39	73	8	1	0	1	7	8	10	0	0	.190/.288/.254	.201	.208	0.9	SS(13): -1.9	-0.3
2014	NYA	MLB	40	250	29	10	1	3	20	19	37	5	2	.277/.336/.358	.258	.320	0	SS -5	0.4

Prior to Jeter joining the group in 2012, only a select ensemble of six Hall of Famers (plus Rafael Palmeiro, if you give him credit for a strike year) had posted streaks of at least 17 consecutive seasons with 500-plus plate appearances. Given all that good fortune, the Yankees can't curse the gods that the days Jeter didn't miss as a younger man seemed to hit him all at once in 2013, but his struggles were still tough to watch. The ankle fracture that he vowed to be back from by Opening Day delayed his debut until just before the All-Star break, and it continued to bother him as he was struck by a series of cascade injuries caused by age and lower-body weakness. It's possible that he'll look like the old Jeter, as opposed to an old Jeter, after an offseason of rest; the last time he was healthy, he hit. It's equally likely that he'll stumble off the stage instead of taking a Rivera-esque curtain call. If Jeter is healthy, he'll make history one way or another: Either he'll join Honus Wagner, Luke Appling and Omar Vizquel on over-40-shortstop Mount Rushmore, or we'll finally see him play another position, something sabermetricians have been clamoring for since he was still in his 20s.

Kelly Johnson   2B

Born: 2/22/1982 Age: 32
Bats: L Throws: R Height: 6' 1"
Weight: 200 Breakout: 6%
Improve: 30% Collapse: 10%
Attrition: 24% MLB: 90%

Comparables:
Dusty Baker, Gary Matthews, Charlie Maxwell

YEAR	TEAM	LVL	AGE	PA	R	2B	3B	HR	RBI	BB	SO	SB	CS	AVG/OBP/SLG	TAv	BABIP	BRR	FRAA	WARP
2011	TOR	MLB	29	132	16	4	2	3	9	16	31	3	3	.270/.364/.417	.283	.346	-0.9	2B(33): -1.4	0.6
2011	ARI	MLB	29	481	59	23	5	18	49	44	132	13	3	.209/.287/.412	.245	.257	1.1	2B(108): -11.5	-0.7
2012	TOR	MLB	30	581	61	19	2	16	55	62	159	14	2	.225/.313/.365	.245	.292	1.1	2B(136): -6.1	0.3
2013	TBA	MLB	31	407	41	12	2	16	52	35	99	7	4	.235/.305/.410	.268	.276	1.5	LF(53): -2.3, 2B(22): 0.6	1.6
2014	NYA	MLB	32	417	55	17	2	13	44	41	101	9	3	.234/.314/.398	.259	.280	0.3	2B -3, LF -1	0.8

For six seasons, Johnson made a living as an offensive-minded second baseman for three different organizations. Naturally, he signed with the Rays and started at four different positions, including two he had never played in a major-league game (first and third base) and one he had not played since 2005 (left field). He began the season as a regular in the Rays' lineup but lost playing time as the club improved the roster around him. He profiles as a semi-regular player with good pop and newfound defensive versatility, though the Yankees, who lost Robinson Cano shortly after signing Johnson, might have to stretch him past that role.

Gosuke Katoh   2B

Born: 10/8/1994 Age: 19
Bats: L Throws: R Height: 6' 2"
Weight: 180 Breakout: 0%
Improve: 0% Collapse: 0%
Attrition: 0% MLB: 0%

Comparables:
Starlin Castro, Logan Watkins, Alex Liddi

YEAR	TEAM	LVL	AGE	PA	R	2B	3B	HR	RBI	BB	SO	SB	CS	AVG/OBP/SLG	TAv	BABIP	BRR	FRAA	WARP
2014	NYA	MLB	19	250	20	8	1	5	24	16	76	0	0	.196/.250/.303	.203	.260	-0.4	2B -7	-1.5

It's rare for a high school second baseman to be viewed as a prospect; if you can't cut it at a premium position at that level, the thinking goes, there's little hope for you in the big leagues. Katoh, the Yankees' second-round selection last season, is an exception: Although his arm would be stretched at shortstop, the plus runner would have the range for the left side of the infield, which makes him a real asset at the keystone. At the plate, his Ichiro-esque line-drive swing produces surprising power; Katoh led the GCL with six homers after signing for slot value, also hitting for average with walks. Katoh's thin build makes him look even younger than he is, but his game produces the opposite impression.

Brian McCann   C

Born: 2/20/1984 Age: 30
Bats: L Throws: R Height: 6' 3"
Weight: 230 Breakout: 3%
Improve: 54% Collapse: 7%
Attrition: 8% MLB: 96%

Comparables:
Victor Martinez, Gary Carter, Bill Freehan

YEAR	TEAM	LVL	AGE	PA	R	2B	3B	HR	RBI	BB	SO	SB	CS	AVG/OBP/SLG	TAv	BABIP	BRR	FRAA	WARP
2011	ATL	MLB	27	527	51	19	0	24	71	57	89	3	2	.270/.351/.466	.291	.287	-2.6	C(126): 3.3	3.9
2012	ATL	MLB	28	487	44	14	0	20	67	44	76	3	0	.230/.300/.399	.245	.234	-0.6	C(114): 2.9	1.5
2013	ATL	MLB	29	402	43	13	0	20	57	39	66	0	1	.256/.336/.461	.288	.261	-1.7	C(92): -0.0	2.7
2014	NYA	MLB	30	398	50	16	0	17	56	40	67	2	1	.256/.336/.449	.283	.270	-0.8	C 2	2.9

McCann's final season in Atlanta didn't pass without fireworks. The backstop drew the Internet's ire for confronting two opposing players who, he believed, disrespected the Braves. While McCann was painted as a joyless hothead on the outside, the reality is that kind of take-charge attitude is what teams want from their catchers. We'll never know for sure, but it's possible that McCann earned a few extra dollars as a free agent when he blocked home plate during the last leg of Carlos Gomez's slow home run trot. Complain about baseball's macho code if you want, but this might be the most literal opportunity to drop a "don't hate the player, hate the game."

JR Murphy   C

Born: 5/13/1991 Age: 23
Bats: R Throws: R Height: 5' 11"
Weight: 195 Breakout: 3%
Improve: 15% Collapse: 1%
Attrition: 12% MLB: 28%

Comparables:
Bryan Anderson, Josh Donaldson, Jonathan Lucroy

YEAR	TEAM	LVL	AGE	PA	R	2B	3B	HR	RBI	BB	SO	SB	CS	AVG/OBP/SLG	TAv	BABIP	BRR	FRAA	WARP
2011	CSC	A	20	277	31	23	0	6	32	19	38	2	0	.297/.343/.457	.265	.327	-1.6	C(13): 0.2, 3B(3): -0.1	0.2
2011	TAM	A+	20	89	8	6	0	1	14	2	9	0	0	.259/.270/.365	.386	.273	0.2	C(2): -0.0, 3B(1): -0.1	0.2
2012	TAM	A+	21	294	39	14	1	5	28	26	41	4	3	.257/.322/.374	.239	.286	1.8	C(59): 0.6, 3B(1): -0.0	0.6
2012	TRN	AA	21	170	23	12	1	4	16	16	32	0	0	.231/.306/.408	.272	.259	1.1	C(38): 0.8	1.3
2013	TRN	AA	22	211	34	10	0	6	25	24	32	1	0	.268/.352/.421	.307	.293	1.4	C(49): 0.1	2.6
2013	SWB	AAA	22	257	26	19	0	6	21	23	41	0	1	.270/.342/.430	.264	.304	0.6	C(56): -0.8	1.5
2013	NYA	MLB	22	27	3	1	0	0	1	1	9	0	0	.154/.185/.192	.146	.235	0	C(15): 0.1	-0.1
2014	NYA	MLB	23	250	24	13	0	7	28	17	50	0	0	.236/.291/.379	.246	.270	-0.5	C 0, 3B -0	0.7

In a down year for the Yankees' system, Murphy put himself on the prospect map, leapfrogging some of the bigger names who'd placed ahead of him on the preseason rankings. In his first season spent exclusively behind the plate, he provided correct answers to both questions on the catch-and-throw quiz: His framing skills saved an estimated 18 runs between Double- and Triple-A—fifth-most in the upper minors—and he erased over 37 percent of attempted basestealers. Most encouraging of all, he had his best season with the bat, matching his Trenton OPS after a June promotion to Scranton. Murphy's offense suffered in a September cup of coffee, but his success over the first five months of the season raised his ceiling above "backup." He'll be 28 when Brian McCann's contract expires, though.

Jayson Nix   3B

Born: 8/26/1982 Age: 31
Bats: R Throws: R Height: 5' 11"
Weight: 195 Breakout: 1%
Improve: 38% Collapse: 9%
Attrition: 11% MLB: 77%

Comparables:
Tom Tresh, Brian Giles, Jose Valentin

YEAR	TEAM	LVL	AGE	PA	R	2B	3B	HR	RBI	BB	SO	SB	CS	AVG/OBP/SLG	TAv	BABIP	BRR	FRAA	WARP
2011	LVG	AAA	28	182	30	12	2	8	29	14	38	3	0	.270/.341/.515	.273	.305	0.6	3B(13): 2.8, SS(8): -0.2	1.3
2011	TOR	MLB	28	151	15	5	1	4	16	12	42	4	1	.169/.245/.309	.203	.209	1.6	3B(41): 3.4, 2B(4): 0.1	0.3
2012	SWB	AAA	29	35	5	4	0	0	4	3	9	0	0	.233/.314/.367	.228	.318	-0.3	2B(5): -0.2, 3B(2): 0.2	0.0
2012	NYA	MLB	29	202	24	13	0	4	18	14	53	6	3	.243/.306/.384	.239	.325	-1	3B(29): 1.3, SS(18): -0.9	0.2
2013	NYA	MLB	30	303	32	9	1	3	24	24	80	13	1	.236/.308/.311	.237	.321	2.7	SS(48): 5.7, 3B(41): 1.1	1.5
2014	NYA	MLB	31	271	31	11	1	7	28	20	69	7	2	.222/.290/.360	.238	.270	0.5	3B 2, SS 1	0.7

A decent defender who can play every infield position and the occasional outfield corner, Nix was a capable replacement in 2012, when he started fewer than 60 games, completed just over 30 and made most of his plate appearances against lefties. He's not suited to be a starter, but he was pressed into regular service as the Yankees' other options on the left side of the infield dwindled. Nix wasn't immune to the injury epidemic: A hamstring strain cost him most of July, and an R.A. Dickey knuckleball fractured his hand and ended his season on August 21st. Despite missing more than two months, he still made 300 plate appearances, and righties ate him alive (.220/.278/.301) in an everyday role. Joe Girardi compounded the problem by batting Nix second more than 20 times, but the real damage was done when the Yankees lost their infield alternatives.

Eduardo Nunez — SS

Born: 6/15/1987 Age: 27
Bats: R Throws: R Height: 6' 0''
Weight: 185 Breakout: 7%
Improve: 38% Collapse: 9%
Attrition: 24% MLB: 83%

Comparables:
Jason Bartlett, Brendan Ryan, Ben Zobrist

YEAR	TEAM	LVL	AGE	PA	R	2B	3B	HR	RBI	BB	SO	SB	CS	AVG/OBP/SLG	TAv	BABIP	BRR	FRAA	WARP
2011	NYA	MLB	24	338	38	18	2	5	30	22	37	22	6	.265/.313/.385	.245	.287	0.5	SS(50): -4.2, 3B(40): -1.1	0.4
2012	SWB	AAA	25	172	18	4	0	2	16	7	28	16	3	.227/.256/.288	.190	.259	2.1	SS(35): 1.8	-0.1
2012	NYA	MLB	25	100	14	4	1	1	11	6	12	11	2	.292/.330/.393	.275	.312	0.8	SS(16): -0.3, 3B(9): 0.1	0.5
2013	NYA	MLB	26	336	38	17	4	3	28	20	51	10	3	.260/.307/.372	.255	.298	-0.2	SS(75): -10.6, 3B(14): -0.7	-0.1
2014	NYA	MLB	27	294	33	13	1	3	24	18	41	16	3	.259/.307/.357	.244	.290	1.7	SS -5, 3B -1	0.2

Nunez won last season's Warm Body Award, earning regular playing time more through the unavailability of others than any tools he brought to the table. In the field, he wasn't much more mobile than Jeter, and he didn't have a fractured ankle or advanced age as an excuse. Nor is he dependable on balls hit right at him, with an arm so erratic that reporters clustered in foul territory are sometimes forced to scatter when he throws on the side during batting practice. This is the point in the profile of many defensively limited players where we'd write "But boy, can he hit," but Nunez doesn't do that either. Had the Yankees had anyone better to turn to than rejects from the other 29 teams, the strained ribcage that cost Nunez two months might have been a blessing.

Lyle Overbay — 1B

Born: 1/28/1977 Age: 37
Bats: L Throws: L Height: 6' 2''
Weight: 235 Breakout: 1%
Improve: 25% Collapse: 12%
Attrition: 16% MLB: 62%

Comparables:
Fred McGriff, Don Baylor, Andre Thornton

YEAR	TEAM	LVL	AGE	PA	R	2B	3B	HR	RBI	BB	SO	SB	CS	AVG/OBP/SLG	TAv	BABIP	BRR	FRAA	WARP
2011	ARI	MLB	34	49	3	4	0	1	10	6	11	1	0	.286/.388/.452	.295	.367	0.1	1B(11): 0.8	0.3
2011	PIT	MLB	34	391	40	17	1	8	37	36	77	1	1	.227/.300/.349	.235	.269	-1.5	1B(98): -2.9	-0.8
2012	GWN	AAA	35	28	3	3	0	0	3	6	6	0	0	.273/.429/.409	.288	.375	-0.2	1B(6): -0.2	0.1
2012	ARI	MLB	35	110	11	9	0	2	10	12	26	0	0	.292/.367/.448	.278	.377	-3.5	1B(21): 0.2	0.0
2012	ATL	MLB	35	21	1	1	0	0	0	1	8	0	0	.100/.143/.150	.106	.167	0.2	1B(2): -0.0	-0.3
2013	NYA	MLB	36	485	43	24	1	14	59	36	111	2	0	.240/.295/.393	.248	.287	-0.7	1B(130): -0.2, RF(4): -0.1	-0.3
2014	NYA	MLB	37	389	39	20	1	9	43	40	88	1	0	.233/.313/.374	.253	.280	-0.6	1B 0, RF -0	0.1

On March 17th, Mark Teixeira admitted that he might miss all of May. Nine days later, the desperate-for-depth Yankees snapped up Overbay immediately after the Red Sox released him. The platoon candidate provided some pop early in the season, but he was exposed by too much playing time as Teixeira's injury lingered. Overbay's glove isn't what it once was, he's bad on the bases and his splits were unsightly: He was useless against lefties, awful on the road and atrocious overall in the second half. In his last three seasons combined, Overbay has been two wins below replacement level; at age 37, he's not even fit for the box labeled "break glass in case of broken first baseman."

Mark Reynolds — 1B

Born: 8/3/1983 Age: 30
Bats: R Throws: R Height: 6' 2''
Weight: 220 Breakout: 1%
Improve: 50% Collapse: 10%
Attrition: 16% MLB: 97%

Comparables:
Craig Wilson, Ken Phelps, Cecil Fielder

YEAR	TEAM	LVL	AGE	PA	R	2B	3B	HR	RBI	BB	SO	SB	CS	AVG/OBP/SLG	TAv	BABIP	BRR	FRAA	WARP
2011	BAL	MLB	27	620	84	27	1	37	86	75	196	6	4	.221/.323/.483	.280	.266	-2.3	3B(114): -14.7, 1B(44): 0.2	1.2
2012	BAL	MLB	28	538	65	26	0	23	69	73	159	1	3	.221/.335/.429	.265	.282	-1.2	1B(108): -14.0, 3B(15): -1.4	-0.7
2013	CLE	MLB	29	384	40	8	0	15	48	43	123	3	0	.215/.307/.373	.255	.285	0	1B(41): 0.5, 3B(40): -3.1	0.2
2013	NYA	MLB	29	120	15	6	0	6	19	8	31	0	1	.236/.300/.455	.271	.274	-0.2	1B(24): -1.1, 3B(14): 0.3	0.2
2014	NYA	MLB	30	481	65	17	0	24	67	58	156	4	3	.219/.321/.436	.275	.280	-1	1B -5, 3B -2	0.7

If Franklin Pierce Adams had lived to see last August's Rodriguez to Reynolds to Overbay double play, he might have revised his stance on the saddest of possible words. Reynolds' start at the keystone last season was one of many signs of the apocalypse in the Bronx, and it was also indicative of the lack of depth a team has to have to make room for him on its roster. He's less of a liability in the field at first base than he was at the other infield corner, but his bat can't clear the higher bar. Reynolds is the only player to go deep 40 times over the past two seasons and still be below replacement level, a feat that only 23 players have pulled off in any consecutive seasons since 1950. Even when he was walking more often and hitting 30-plus bombs, Reynolds' extreme contact issues and disastrous defense made him barely adequate as a starter. Now that he's no longer hitting a homer every 15 at-bats, he's barely adequate on the bench.

Alex Rodriguez — 3B

Born: 7/27/1975 Age: 38
Bats: R Throws: R Height: 6' 3''
Weight: 225 Breakout: 0%
Improve: 14% Collapse: 10%
Attrition: 15% MLB: 75%

Comparables:
Ken Caminiti, Sid Gordon, Casey Blake

YEAR	TEAM	LVL	AGE	PA	R	2B	3B	HR	RBI	BB	SO	SB	CS	AVG/OBP/SLG	TAv	BABIP	BRR	FRAA	WARP
2011	NYA	MLB	35	428	67	21	0	16	62	47	80	4	1	.276/.362/.461	.284	.311	2	3B(89): 5.0	3.1
2012	NYA	MLB	36	529	74	17	1	18	57	51	116	13	1	.272/.353/.430	.281	.323	-1.6	3B(81): -4.8	1.7
2013	TAM	A+	37	20	2	1	0	0	3	1	5	0	0	.176/.300/.235	.193	.250	-0.6	3B(3): 0.0	-0.2
2013	NYA	MLB	37	181	21	7	0	7	19	23	43	4	2	.244/.348/.423	.273	.292	-1	3B(27): -0.3	0.7
2014	NYA	MLB	38	250	31	9	0	9	33	27	52	4	1	.254/.342/.429	.280	.290	0	3B 0	1.1

At the beginning of August, Time Warner blacked out CBS in several major markets, depriving New York soap fans of their fixes of The Bold and the Beautiful and The Young and the Restless.

Sensing an opportunity to corner the market on daily drama, Rodriguez returned from injury a few days later, appealing an unprecedented 211-day PED suspension to play on. Some of the he-said, he-said storylines that dogged Rodriguez both before and after the comeback would have fit right in on daytime TV, and amidst all the furor what he did on the field felt like an afterthought. After a productive August, he slumped during a 28-percent-strikeout-rate September, dooming his TAv to a seventh straight decline, though it's tough to untangle Rodriguez's performance from the fact that he spent the season as the player with the media's (and maybe America's) lowest approval rating. If it's any consolation to viewers who've had enough of this arc, Rodriguez should lack the talent to inspire the same vitriol the next time he takes the field.

Austin Romine   C

Born: 11/22/1988 Age: 25
Bats: R Throws: R Height: 6' 0"
Weight: 215 Breakout: 9%
Improve: 19% Collapse: 13%
Attrition: 29% MLB: 45%

Comparables:
Guillermo Quiroz, Jeff Mathis, Rene Rivera

YEAR	TEAM	LVL	AGE	PA	R	2B	3B	HR	RBI	BB	SO	SB	CS	AVG/OBP/SLG	TAv	BABIP	BRR	FRAA	WARP
2011	TRN	AA	22	373	43	13	0	6	47	32	60	2	2	.286/.351/.378	.238	.331	-0.4	C(18): 0.3	0.1
2011	NYA	MLB	22	20	2	0	0	0	0	1	5	0	0	.158/.200/.158	.130	.214	-0.2	C(8): -0.1	-0.2
2012	SWB	AAA	23	71	6	2	0	3	9	8	10	0	0	.213/.296/.393	.260	.200	-0.4	C(13): -0.1	0.3
2013	SWB	AAA	24	46	5	0	0	1	4	4	12	0	0	.333/.391/.405	.282	.448	-0.2	C(14): -0.2	0.3
2013	NYA	MLB	24	148	15	9	0	1	10	8	37	1	0	.207/.255/.296	.189	.276	1.4	C(59): 0.2	-0.2
2014	NYA	MLB	25	250	23	10	0	5	25	16	57	1	1	.227/.280/.340	.228	.280	-0.4	C -0	0.2

Pressed into service when injuries and a Biogenesis suspension torpedoed Francisco Cervelli's season, Romine spent much of the year at the major-league level, spelling starter Chris Stewart. Like most of the Yankees' post-Posada catchers, Romine can make borderline balls look like strikes; his receiving saved seven runs in limited playing time. That's the end of the good news. Romine threw out only eight of 38 basestealers, his TAv was tied for last among AL batters with at least 140 plate appearances and a concussion kept him out for most of September. It's easy to come up with excuses for Romine's offensive struggles, aside from "small sample size"—he missed most of 2012, he had little Triple-A seasoning and his starts were sporadic—but the younger J.R. Murphy might have passed him in the pecking order.

Brendan Ryan   SS

Born: 3/26/1982 Age: 32
Bats: R Throws: R Height: 6' 2"
Weight: 195 Breakout: 0%
Improve: 33% Collapse: 8%
Attrition: 13% MLB: 93%

Comparables:
Tony Fernandez, Nick Punto, Tony Graffanino

YEAR	TEAM	LVL	AGE	PA	R	2B	3B	HR	RBI	BB	SO	SB	CS	AVG/OBP/SLG	TAv	BABIP	BRR	FRAA	WARP
2011	SEA	MLB	29	494	51	19	3	3	39	34	87	13	3	.248/.313/.326	.248	.299	2.5	SS(123): 13.3	3.5
2012	SEA	MLB	30	470	42	19	3	3	31	44	98	11	5	.194/.277/.278	.227	.244	-1	SS(138): 12.0	1.9
2013	NYA	MLB	31	62	7	2	0	1	1	2	13	0	0	.220/.258/.305	.209	.267	0.7	SS(17): 2.9	0.2
2013	SEA	MLB	31	287	23	10	0	3	21	21	60	4	2	.192/.254/.265	.201	.237	-2.1	SS(84): 4.9	0.1
2014	NYA	MLB	32	352	34	14	2	4	28	25	63	8	3	.231/.294/.324	.229	.270	0.2	SS 10	1.5

Ryan has always had a "good field, no hit" reputation, but he took it to an extreme last season, as his contact rate continued to drop. Among American Leaguers with at least 300 plate appearances, only Alcides Escobar turned in a lower TAv. Whether or not Ryan's formerly elite glove slipped slightly, as the defensive metrics suggested, he wasn't worth starting at that level of offensive inadequacy, a conclusion the Mariners came to in late June, when they promoted Brad Miller. After a September trade, Ryan resurfaced in New York, where he gave Yankees fans their first real glimpse of a plus defensive shortstop since Alvaro Espinoza. As he enters his age-32 season, Ryan's days as a surprisingly productive starter are likely behind him, but in a bench role, his career could have a long, John McDonald-like denouement. With Brian Roberts and Derek Jeter also in the middle infield, Ryan might see more playing time than anybody would deem healthy.

Gary Sanchez   C

Born: 12/2/1992 Age: 21
Bats: R Throws: R Height: 6' 2"
Weight: 220 Breakout: 4%
Improve: 8% Collapse: 1%
Attrition: 6% MLB: 15%

Comparables:
Wilson Ramos, Austin Romine, Chris Marrero

YEAR	TEAM	LVL	AGE	PA	R	2B	3B	HR	RBI	BB	SO	SB	CS	AVG/OBP/SLG	TAv	BABIP	BRR	FRAA	WARP
2011	CSC	A	18	343	49	16	1	17	52	36	93	2	1	.256/.335/.485	.272	.308	-0.1	C(25): -0.0	0.7
2012	CSC	A	19	289	44	19	0	13	56	22	65	11	4	.297/.353/.517	.296	.348	-1.5	C(53): -1.0	2.1
2012	TAM	A+	19	185	21	10	1	5	29	10	41	4	0	.279/.330/.436	.267	.341	-0.5	C(38): -0.8	0.7
2013	TAM	A+	20	399	38	21	0	13	61	28	71	3	1	.254/.313/.420	.259	.280	-0.3	C(76): -1.8, 1B(1): -0.0	1.8
2013	TRN	AA	20	110	12	6	0	2	10	13	16	0	0	.250/.364/.380	.285	.280	-0.5	C(20): 0.2	0.8
2014	NYA	MLB	21	250	26	10	0	9	32	13	64	1	0	.231/.277/.395	.244	.270	-0.4	C -1	0.5

Sanchez remains a promising prospect, but his season left a sour taste in scouts' mouths. Reviews of his defense continue to sound like they were lifted from a report on Jesus Montero, leaving his positional future in doubt; on occasion, Sanchez had trouble catching pitches right over the plate. He has big power and a quick swing, but the setup is busy, he's often off balance and his offensive performance failed to improve in his second exposure to Tampa. Nonetheless, he earned an August promotion to Trenton, where he was among the Eastern League's youngest players. He's a high-ceiling, high-risk type you'd feel better about if he had a reputation for maximizing his talent. Instead, mixed reports on his makeup lower the probability that he'll reach his rosier forecasts.

Alfonso Soriano   LF

Born: 1/7/1976 Age: 38
Bats: R Throws: R Height: 6' 1"
Weight: 195 Breakout: 0%
Improve: 11% Collapse: 16%
Attrition: 23% MLB: 75%

Comparables:
Reggie Sanders, Fred Lynn, John Lowenstein

YEAR	TEAM	LVL	AGE	PA	R	2B	3B	HR	RBI	BB	SO	SB	CS	AVG/OBP/SLG	TAv	BABIP	BRR	FRAA	WARP
2011	CHN	MLB	35	508	50	27	1	26	88	27	113	2	1	.244/.289/.469	.261	.266	0.8	LF(128): -8.0	0.6
2012	CHN	MLB	36	615	68	33	2	32	108	44	153	6	2	.262/.322/.499	.282	.303	-3	LF(145): 7.7	3.2
2013	CHN	MLB	37	383	47	24	1	17	51	15	89	10	5	.254/.287/.467	.268	.290	0.6	LF(86): 3.5	1.2
2013	NYA	MLB	37	243	37	8	0	17	50	21	67	8	4	.256/.325/.525	.300	.287	-1.4	LF(48): 4.2	2.0
2014	NYA	MLB	38	586	71	28	1	26	80	36	147	9	4	.236/.288/.434	.260	.270	-0.4	LF 0	1.0

When the Yankees traded for Soriano, they hadn't hit a homer from the right side in over a month. Soriano had hit 10 in that time. The acquisition addressed their primary weakness not only on paper, but in practice: Soriano kept slugging after the swap, going deep as many times in 58 games with the Yankees as he had in 93 with the Cubs. Not only is there still some thump in his bat, but he's made himself into an adequate defensive outfielder and earned acclaim for mentoring youngers (not that he'll meet many in his current clubhouse). Give the 38-year-old credit for changing the negative narrative after acquiring an albatross rep—he's amassed more WARP in each of the past two seasons than he did in the three before that combined.

Ichiro Suzuki   RF

Born: 10/22/1973 Age: 40
Bats: L Throws: R Height: 5' 11"
Weight: 170 Breakout: 0%
Improve: 19% Collapse: 9%
Attrition: 26% MLB: 67%

Comparables:
Lou Piniella, Bob Boyd, Kenny Lofton

YEAR	TEAM	LVL	AGE	PA	R	2B	3B	HR	RBI	BB	SO	SB	CS	AVG/OBP/SLG	TAv	BABIP	BRR	FRAA	WARP
2011	SEA	MLB	37	721	80	22	3	5	47	39	69	40	7	.272/.310/.335	.242	.295	8.9	RF(151): -18.0	-0.7
2012	NYA	MLB	38	240	28	13	1	5	27	5	21	14	5	.322/.340/.454	.279	.337	-1.3	RF(39): -2.1, LF(35): 0.1	0.5
2012	SEA	MLB	38	423	49	15	5	4	28	17	40	15	2	.261/.288/.353	.234	.279	1.8	RF(93): 6.8	0.9
2013	NYA	MLB	39	555	57	15	3	7	35	26	63	20	4	.262/.297/.342	.240	.285	4.1	RF(128): -5.3, CF(13): -0.2	0.0
2014	NYA	MLB	40	543	64	20	3	5	41	24	64	24	5	.281/.315/.362	.247	.310	2.4	RF -4, LF 0	0.2

In his first full season in New York, Ichiro stayed off the DL, which is more than most of his teammates could say. Even at an advanced age, he was an asset in the field (FRAA was critical but the outlier metric), and he excelled on the basepaths when he managed to work his way on. But the late-career renaissance that followed his 2012 trade proved short lived, as Suzuki's offensive stats fell further than they had during his dark days in Seattle. Although his batted-ball stats were in line with career rates, the longtime high-BABIP hitter didn't have his usual success when he put pitches in play. He hit .227/.252/.295 away from his lefty-friendly home park, and his bat disappeared down the stretch. Suzuki spent his 20s and 30s doing things no other player could do; at 40, *he* can't do those things either. With the pile-up of outfielders on the roster, look for him to set a new career low in playing time.

Mark Teixeira   1B

Born: 4/11/1980 Age: 34
Bats: B Throws: R Height: 6' 3"
Weight: 215 Breakout: 0%
Improve: 37% Collapse: 3%
Attrition: 6% MLB: 94%

Comparables:
Paul Konerko, Norm Cash, Ted Kluszewski

YEAR	TEAM	LVL	AGE	PA	R	2B	3B	HR	RBI	BB	SO	SB	CS	AVG/OBP/SLG	TAv	BABIP	BRR	FRAA	WARP
2011	NYA	MLB	31	684	90	26	1	39	111	76	110	4	1	.248/.341/.494	.293	.239	-3.3	1B(147): -1.3	2.1
2012	NYA	MLB	32	524	66	27	1	24	84	54	83	2	1	.251/.332/.475	.297	.250	-3.5	1B(119): 7.6	2.9
2013	NYA	MLB	33	63	5	1	0	3	12	8	19	0	0	.151/.270/.340	.231	.156	0.1	1B(14): 0.1	-0.1
2014	NYA	MLB	34	250	32	11	0	11	36	28	45	1	0	.248/.342/.459	.290	.260	-0.4	1B 1	1.1

Teixeira spent most of last season on the disabled list, making Lyle Overbay and assorted insurance executives sweat. The switch-hitter injured the tendon sheath in his right wrist while hitting off a tee before the World Baseball Classic, delaying his season debut until May 31st. It took only 15 games for him to aggravate the injury, and after a cortisone shot failed to alleviate his discomfort and a quartet of doctors advised surgery, he went under the knife on July 1st. The saving grace for the Steinbrenners was that the WBC and their own insurers combined to pick up most of his paycheck. Teixeira is expected to be at full strength in time for spring training, and while we don't have a large sample of previous tendon sheath repairs, the two most prominent players to have similar surgeries—Rickie Weeks and Jose Bautista—showed no obvious ill effects the following season. Teixeira has cost the Yankees $8 million per win over what was supposed to be the affordable portion of his eight-year contract; only three easy payments of $22.5 million to go.

Vernon Wells LF

Born: 12/8/1978 Age: 35
Bats: R Throws: R Height: 6' 1"
Weight: 230 Breakout: 0%
Improve: 24% Collapse: 16%
Attrition: 22% MLB: 77%

Comparables:
Eric Byrnes, Jay Payton, Ken Griffey

YEAR	TEAM	LVL	AGE	PA	R	2B	3B	HR	RBI	BB	SO	SB	CS	AVG/OBP/SLG	TAv	BABIP	BRR	FRAA	WARP
2011	ANA	MLB	32	529	60	15	4	25	66	20	86	9	4	.218/.248/.412	.244	.214	-1.4	LF(111): 8.1, CF(12): 0.0	0.9
2012	SLC	AAA	33	28	2	1	0	2	3	0	6	3	0	.308/.357/.577	.286	.333	-0.6	LF(4): 0.0, RF(1): 0.0	0.0
2012	ANA	MLB	33	262	36	9	0	11	29	16	35	3	1	.230/.279/.403	.252	.226	3.2	LF(69): 3.6, CF(6): -0.4	0.8
2013	NYA	MLB	34	458	45	16	0	11	50	30	73	7	3	.233/.282/.349	.238	.256	2.7	LF(73): 3.1, RF(23): 0.4	0.8
2014	NYA	MLB	35	395	43	17	1	13	47	25	61	7	2	.240/.290/.398	.253	.260	0	LF 5, RF 0	1.1

Wells' April was one of last season's most misleading months. Until the calendar turned to May, he hit like he did during his best years with the Blue Jays; thereafter, he hit .216/.258/.296, which was like his Angels seasons on the opposite of steroids. (Performance Eradicating Drugs?) The only players who have hit worse than Wells in as much playing time as he's had over the past three years are plus defenders at premium positions, and Yuniesky Betancourt. His presence in a big-league lineup isn't quite as baffling as Betancourt's, but at this point the only things that can keep Wells in uniform are injuries to superior players and the Angels' obligation to pay 90 percent of his salary.

Mason Williams CF

Born: 8/21/1991 Age: 22
Bats: L Throws: R Height: 6' 1"
Weight: 180 Breakout: 0%
Improve: 3% Collapse: 1%
Attrition: 2% MLB: 4%

Comparables:
A.J. Pollock, Cedric Hunter, Rafael Ortega

YEAR	TEAM	LVL	AGE	PA	R	2B	3B	HR	RBI	BB	SO	SB	CS	AVG/OBP/SLG	TAv	BABIP	BRR	FRAA	WARP
2011	STA	A-	19	298	42	11	6	3	31	20	41	28	12	.349/.395/.468	.325	.399	1.8	CF(51): 2.8	3.1
2012	CSC	A	20	311	55	19	4	8	28	21	33	19	9	.304/.359/.489	.298	.319	0.3	CF(66): 0.8	2.6
2012	TAM	A+	20	86	13	3	0	3	7	3	14	1	4	.277/.302/.422	.251	.303	0.3	CF(22): 0.5	0.3
2013	TAM	A+	21	461	56	21	3	3	24	39	61	15	9	.261/.327/.350	.245	.299	3.3	CF(98): 6.6	1.7
2013	TRN	AA	21	76	7	3	1	1	4	1	18	0	0	.153/.164/.264	.146	.189	-0.5	CF(15): 0.3	-0.7
2014	NYA	MLB	22	250	28	10	1	5	21	11	51	6	3	.231/.267/.346	.218	.260	-0.1	CF 2	-0.1

Williams entered 2013 second to Sanchez among Yankees prospects, and like Sanchez he earned a promotion to Trenton despite seeing his stock fall. An April DUI charge set the tone for his season. After starting slow, he hit for average in June and August, but the hits were almost all singles, and he looked overmatched in the Eastern League. He's a slap-and-run hitter, so while he doesn't strike out much, he shows little pull power and probably won't develop much without a change in approach. Although he has speed, he needs to develop better baserunning instincts or stop trying to steal; after a 15-for-24 season, his career tally stands at 64-for-100. Williams' defense in center might be major-league ready right now, but it's not clear that the other aspects of his game can catch up.

Kevin Youkilis 3B

Born: 3/15/1979 Age: 35
Bats: R Throws: R Height: 6' 1"
Weight: 220 Breakout: 1%
Improve: 28% Collapse: 6%
Attrition: 8% MLB: 97%

Comparables:
Chipper Jones, Ron Cey, Eddie Mathews

YEAR	TEAM	LVL	AGE	PA	R	2B	3B	HR	RBI	BB	SO	SB	CS	AVG/OBP/SLG	TAv	BABIP	BRR	FRAA	WARP
2011	BOS	MLB	32	517	68	32	2	17	80	68	100	3	0	.258/.373/.459	.288	.296	0.5	3B(112): -1.7, 1B(6): 0.4	2.6
2012	BOS	MLB	33	165	25	7	1	4	14	14	39	0	0	.233/.315/.377	.247	.288	0	3B(33): -0.8, 1B(13): -0.1	-0.1
2012	CHA	MLB	33	344	47	8	1	15	46	37	69	0	0	.236/.346/.425	.263	.257	1.9	3B(78): -1.6, 1B(13): -0.4	1.2
2013	NYA	MLB	34	118	12	7	0	2	8	8	31	0	0	.219/.305/.343	.237	.292	-0.5	3B(22): -2.6, 1B(6): -0.2	-0.3
2014	NYA	MLB	35	250	31	11	1	9	32	29	53	1	0	.254/.358/.434	.291	.300	-0.3	3B -2, 1B -0	1.1

Signed to fill in for the injured Alex Rodriguez, Youkilis instead spent most of the season alongside him on the 60-day DL. The 34-year-old made it through most of April before being sidelined with a recurrence of the back problems that have plagued him for the past several years, then made it back at the end of May only to succumb again in mid-June. Surgery to repair a herniated disc ended his season later that month. When he was on the field, he posted an unYouk-like 3.9 strikeout-to-walk ratio with little power, so either he was playing through pain or the injuries have severely sapped his skills. Now a Rakuten Golden Eagle (that's in Japan), it's a shame that a guy who got started late is exiting MLB this early, but Youkilis was more likely to extend his five-season DL streak than to be durable or productive at age 35.

PITCHERS

Dellin Betances
Born: 3/23/1988 Age: 26
Bats: R Throws: R Height: 6' 8" Weight: 260
Breakout: 50% Improve: 71% Collapse: 20%
Attrition: 62% MLB: 48%

Comparables:
Thomas Diamond, Dustin Richardson, Christian Garcia

YEAR	TEAM	LVL	AGE	W	L	SV	G	GS	IP	H	HR	BB	SO	BB9	SO9	GB%	BABIP	WHIP	ERA	FIP	FRA	WARP
2011	TRN	AA	23	4	6	0	21	21	105[1]	86	7	55	115	4.7	9.8	50%	.264	1.34	3.42	3.91	4.16	0.3
2011	SWB	AAA	23	0	3	0	4	4	21	16	2	15	27	6.4	11.6	33%	.286	1.48	5.14	4.19	4.39	0.0
2011	NYA	MLB	23	0	0	0	2	1	2[2]	1	0	6	2	20.2	6.8	14%	.143	2.62	6.75	9.44	11.29	-0.1
2012	TRN	AA	24	3	4	0	11	10	56[2]	73	4	30	53	4.8	8.4	41%	.392	1.82	6.51	4.15	5.18	0.2
2012	SWB	AAA	24	3	5	0	16	16	74[2]	71	9	69	71	8.3	8.6	43%	.298	1.88	6.39	5.84	7.01	-1.0
2013	SWB	AAA	25	6	4	5	38	6	84	52	2	42	108	4.5	11.6	45%	.269	1.12	2.68	2.69	3.84	1.7
2013	NYA	MLB	25	0	0	0	6	0	5	9	1	2	10	3.6	18.0	36%	.615	2.20	10.80	2.88	5.36	0.0
2014	NYA	MLB	26	5	4	0	25	12	81	76	10	48	81	5.3	9.0	42%	.301	1.52	4.75	4.93	5.16	-0.0

After six starts for Scranton, Betances had a 6.00 ERA and 16 walks in 24 innings, despite some spring training mechanical tweaks. Those struggles, along with the giant righty's dwindling supply of minor-league options, convinced the Yankees that the perennial bullpen conversion candidate should finally make the move to short bursts. In 60 innings as a reliever over 35 subsequent Triple-A appearances, Betances posted a 1.35 ERA, allowing only one home run, striking out 83 and walking 26 (which was efficient for him). That successful transition earned him a couple call-ups to New York, where his heater topped out at 99.8 and his fastball/curveball combo helped him whiff almost 40 percent of the batters he faced. Running out of options was the best thing that could have happened to Betances; it forced the Yankees to confront the fact that his options were limited all along.

Jose Campos
Born: 7/27/1992 Age: 21
Bats: R Throws: R Height: 6' 4" Weight: 195
Breakout: 75% Improve: 82% Collapse: 4%
Attrition: 25% MLB: 19%

Comparables:
Jair Jurrjens, Vance Worley, Joe Wieland

YEAR	TEAM	LVL	AGE	W	L	SV	G	GS	IP	H	HR	BB	SO	BB9	SO9	GB%	BABIP	WHIP	ERA	FIP	FRA	WARP
2011	EVE	A-	18	5	5	0	14	14	81[1]	66	4	13	85	1.4	9.4	53%	.271	0.97	2.32	2.79	4.16	1.4
2012	CSC	A	19	3	0	0	5	5	24[2]	20	2	8	26	2.9	9.5	43%	.269	1.14	4.01	3.62	4.26	0.4
2013	CSC	A	20	4	2	2	26	19	87	82	5	16	77	1.7	8.0	50%	.301	1.13	3.41	3.11	4.06	1.0
2014	NYA	MLB	21	2	2	0	16	8	60	69	9	25	35	3.8	5.3	45%	.304	1.56	5.39	5.58	5.85	-0.5

After missing much of 2012 with an elbow injury, Campos started slow but got stronger as the season went on, pitching to a 2.88 ERA after his first outing in May. The right-hander's workload was limited all year, and he pitched out of the bullpen down the stretch in a further attempt to protect his arm. His future, however, lies in the rotation, and if his health holds up his command of three viable pitches (fastball, changeup, slider) should make multiple trips through the lineup possible. The next test will be Tampa; if he passes that, he'll have a good shot at being the best thing to come out of either end of the Montero-Pineda trade.

Preston Claiborne
Born: 1/21/1988 Age: 26
Bats: R Throws: R Height: 6' 2" Weight: 225
Breakout: 36% Improve: 49% Collapse: 36%
Attrition: 38% MLB: 63%

Comparables:
Warner Madrigal, Sam Demel, Craig Breslow

YEAR	TEAM	LVL	AGE	W	L	SV	G	GS	IP	H	HR	BB	SO	BB9	SO9	GB%	BABIP	WHIP	ERA	FIP	FRA	WARP
2011	TAM	A+	23	3	7	5	38	0	81	73	8	30	75	3.3	8.3	48%	.235	1.27	3.11	4.19	3.71	0.5
2012	TRN	AA	24	2	2	5	30	0	48[2]	33	1	24	49	4.4	9.1	49%	.258	1.17	2.22	3.00	4.25	0.5
2012	SWB	AAA	24	4	0	1	20	0	33[1]	31	2	12	29	3.2	7.8	47%	.305	1.29	4.05	3.28	4.87	0.1
2013	SWB	AAA	25	0	0	3	8	0	10[1]	14	0	1	10	0.9	8.7	67%	.375	1.45	3.48	1.56	2.10	0.3
2013	NYA	MLB	25	0	2	0	44	0	50[1]	51	7	14	42	2.5	7.5	46%	.295	1.29	4.11	4.17	4.62	0.1
2014	NYA	MLB	26	2	1	0	37	0	54	53	6	20	45	3.4	7.6	45%	.295	1.35	4.04	4.33	4.39	0.3

When Joba Chamberlain suffered an oblique strain in late April, Claiborne came up and did a decent impression of Chamberlain's 2007 debut, posting a 0.55 ERA through his first month of work. Working off a 94 mph four-seamer and mixing in a sinker, slider and change, Claiborne remained effective for most of the season, gradually pushing Chamberlain out of the late-inning picture. Just as he gained acceptance into Joe Girardi's high-leverage inner circle, he imploded, allowing home runs in four straight September appearances and spoiling his full-season stats. It's just as well that Claiborne pulled an Icarus at the end of the year, since the 26-year-old doesn't miss enough bats or retire enough lefties to be anything more than a middle-inning commoner with an aristocratic name.

Ian Clarkin
Born: 2/14/1995 Age: 19
Bats: L Throws: L Height: 6' 2" Weight: 186
Breakout: 0% Improve: 0% Collapse: 0%
Attrition: 0% MLB: 0%

Comparables:
Brandon Maurer, Xavier Cedeno, Trevor Bell

YEAR	TEAM	LVL	AGE	W	L	SV	G	GS	IP	H	HR	BB	SO	BB9	SO9	GB%	BABIP	WHIP	ERA	FIP	FRA	WARP
2014	NYA	MLB	19	2	3	0	7	7	30[2]	39	5	21	13	6.3	3.7	45%	.310	1.97	7.12	7.00	7.74	-0.7

"I cannot stand the Yankees," Clarkin declared in a pre-draft video aired on MLB Network, but he grew much more fond of them after they took him with the no. 33 pick and offered him full slot value to sign. The prep lefty has good command and an advanced feel for pitching, and he doesn't lack for stuff, packing a low-90s fastball that can touch higher and a curve with plus potential. Like many teenaged arms, he'll have to refine his changeup to survive multiple looks from opposing lineups. A twisted ankle prevented Clarkin from making his professional debut until the end of August, and he'll be brought along slowly, but a cost-effective mid-rotation starter would be worth the wait.

Rafael De Paula
Born: 3/24/1991 Age: 23
Bats: R Throws: R Height: 6' 2" Weight: 212
Breakout: 52% Improve: 66% Collapse: 14%
Attrition: 76% MLB: 15%

Comparables:
Brad Boxberger, Christian Garcia, Preston Guilmet

YEAR	TEAM	LVL	AGE	W	L	SV	G	GS	IP	H	HR	BB	SO	BB9	SO9	GB%	BABIP	WHIP	ERA	FIP	FRA	WARP
2013	CSC	A	22	6	2	0	13	13	64¹	43	3	23	96	3.2	13.4	37%	.305	1.03	2.94	2.32	2.50	1.9
2013	TAM	A+	22	1	3	0	11	10	49	54	5	30	50	5.5	9.2	29%	.345	1.71	6.06	4.67	4.85	0.2
2014	NYA	MLB	23	4	4	0	19	12	85²	84	11	47	84	4.9	8.8	38%	.309	1.53	4.81	4.85	5.23	-0.1

In a season that saw almost every prominent Yankees prospect stagnate or regress, De Paula was one of the few minor-league success stories. A virtual unknown prior to 2013 due to visa issues that had limited him to the Dominican Summer League, De Paula came stateside last season and solved much of the mystery with a lofty strikeout rate in the Sally League. His stats took a tumble after a mid-season promotion to Tampa, but the stuff is legit: a fastball that touches the high-90s and a hard curve and changeup that show the potential to be plus pitches. The Yankees' lone representative in the Futures Game—where he struck out consensus top prospect in baseball Byron Buxton—De Paula is now at the top of the team's pitching prospect pyramid, and could move quickly.

David Huff
Born: 8/22/1984 Age: 29
Bats: B Throws: L Height: 6' 2" Weight: 215
Breakout: 36% Improve: 73% Collapse: 19%
Attrition: 19% MLB: 49%

Comparables:
Dustin Moseley, Jason Berken, Matt Chico

YEAR	TEAM	LVL	AGE	W	L	SV	G	GS	IP	H	HR	BB	SO	BB9	SO9	GB%	BABIP	WHIP	ERA	FIP	FRA	WARP
2011	COH	AAA	26	9	3	0	18	18	107	111	10	30	66	2.5	5.6	34%	.282	1.32	3.87	4.12	5.23	-0.2
2011	CLE	MLB	26	2	6	0	11	10	50²	55	6	17	36	3.0	6.4	35%	.292	1.42	4.09	4.19	4.32	1.0
2012	COH	AAA	27	7	6	0	24	22	134	155	27	34	79	2.3	5.3	38%	.293	1.41	4.97	5.40	6.13	-0.2
2012	CLE	MLB	27	3	1	0	6	4	26²	30	5	5	19	1.7	6.4	40%	.298	1.31	3.38	4.73	5.38	0.1
2013	COH	AAA	28	3	1	0	9	2	24¹	21	4	9	28	3.3	10.4	33%	.274	1.23	4.07	4.15	4.41	0.2
2013	SWB	AAA	28	1	6	1	13	12	68	76	4	13	64	1.7	8.5	35%	.346	1.31	3.84	2.79	3.45	1.4
2013	CLE	MLB	28	0	0	0	3	0	3	7	0	1	5	3.0	15.0	67%	.778	2.67	15.00	0.74	1.17	0.2
2013	NYA	MLB	28	3	1	0	11	2	34²	26	7	8	26	2.1	6.8	40%	.202	0.98	4.67	4.98	5.96	-0.2
2014	NYA	MLB	29	7	6	0	25	18	114²	128	18	35	71	2.7	5.6	40%	.298	1.42	5.01	5.17	5.45	-0.5

Huff couldn't crack Cleveland's rocky rotation, but after the waiver-wire pickup delivered three excellent long-relief outings in late August and early September Yankees fans started to wonder, despite themselves, what would happen if the lefty took the ball from the first inning on. On September 7th, they got their answer: The 29-year-old started in Phil Hughes' stead against the Red Sox and lasted 3 ⅓ innings, allowing eight hits, two homers and nine runs. Like reaching into electrical sockets and touching hot stoves, giving Huff starts never seems to go out of style, but the results—a career 5.57 ERA and 12.2 percent strikeout rate in the rotation—are equally predictable, and painful.

Shawn Kelley
Born: 4/26/1984 Age: 30
Bats: R Throws: R Height: 6' 2" Weight: 220
Breakout: 33% Improve: 59% Collapse: 28%
Attrition: 14% MLB: 85%

Comparables:
Scott Proctor, Frank Francisco, Michael Wuertz

YEAR	TEAM	LVL	AGE	W	L	SV	G	GS	IP	H	HR	BB	SO	BB9	SO9	GB%	BABIP	WHIP	ERA	FIP	FRA	WARP
2011	TAC	AAA	27	1	0	0	12	0	14²	11	3	6	15	3.7	9.2	14%	.286	1.16	1.84	5.62	2.02	0.4
2011	SEA	MLB	27	0	0	0	10	0	12²	7	0	3	10	2.1	7.1	38%	.206	0.79	0.00	2.19	2.33	0.3
2012	TAC	AAA	28	2	0	6	14	0	20	9	0	4	25	1.8	11.2	43%	.214	0.65	0.90	1.77	1.50	0.8
2012	SEA	MLB	28	2	4	0	47	0	44¹	43	5	15	45	3.0	9.1	31%	.304	1.31	3.25	3.50	3.26	0.7
2013	NYA	MLB	29	4	2	0	57	0	53¹	47	8	23	71	3.9	12.0	34%	.312	1.31	4.39	3.66	3.82	0.5
2014	NYA	MLB	30	2	1	0	47	0	48²	43	6	16	52	3.0	9.6	38%	.294	1.22	3.47	3.82	3.77	0.6

Everything about Kelley is average, and therefore forgettable: his height, his career ERA, his fastball velocity, his mix of pitches (strictly fastball-slider). But for a fraction of last season, he looked like something more memorable than a generic right-handed reliever. Through May, he'd struck out more than 15 batters per nine, relying on the strength of a slider that was suddenly missing bats on close to 50 percent of swings. After that, the breaking ball gradually lost horizontal movement, the whiff rate fell and he missed some time with a triceps strain, no surprise for a guy with an inverted W and more elbow surgeries than 50-inning seasons. For someone who figured to be Triple-A filler, Kelley was a success, but going forward he's likely to be what he was before the small-sample excitement: a fragile middle-inning arm who'll deliver a strikeout an inning with too many walks and homers for high-leverage work.

Hiroki Kuroda

Born: 2/10/1975 Age: 39
Bats: R Throws: R Height: 6' 1" Weight: 205
Breakout: 7% Improve: 51% Collapse: 21%
Attrition: 3% MLB: 75%

Comparables:
Mike Mussina, Greg Maddux, Andy Pettitte

YEAR	TEAM	LVL	AGE	W	L	SV	G	GS	IP	H	HR	BB	SO	BB9	SO9	GB%	BABIP	WHIP	ERA	FIP	FRA	WARP
2011	LAN	MLB	36	13	16	0	32	32	202	196	24	49	161	2.2	7.2	45%	.288	1.21	3.07	3.75	3.99	1.3
2012	NYA	MLB	37	16	11	0	33	33	219²	205	25	51	167	2.1	6.8	53%	.282	1.17	3.32	3.81	4.49	2.0
2013	NYA	MLB	38	11	13	0	32	32	201¹	191	20	43	150	1.9	6.7	47%	.283	1.16	3.31	3.59	4.00	2.8
2014	NYA	MLB	39	12	7	0	26	26	173	173	20	43	124	2.2	6.4	50%	.290	1.25	3.85	4.23	4.19	1.5

Unfazed by advancing age and changes in country, coast, league and ballpark, Kuroda keeps delivering value; despite a $5 million raise, he was worth every penny, even after struggling over his final eight starts. The righty has never walked fewer than 5 or more than 6 percent of opposing batters, and since his rookie season, his K/BB has been on cruise control between 3.3 and 3.6. In fact, he's so consistent that his sameness extends to factors supposedly outside his control: even his BABIPs have barely budged. If Kuroda had made it to the States a little sooner, he'd be known as Japan's best pitching export; a couple more carbon-copy seasons, and he still might, at least until Yu Darvish takes over the title.

Mark Montgomery

Born: 8/30/1990 Age: 23
Bats: R Throws: R Height: 5' 11" Weight: 205
Breakout: 39% Improve: 42% Collapse: 32%
Attrition: 41% MLB: 20%

Comparables:
Donnie Joseph, David Robertson, Tony Sipp

YEAR	TEAM	LVL	AGE	W	L	SV	G	GS	IP	H	HR	BB	SO	BB9	SO9	GB%	BABIP	WHIP	ERA	FIP	FRA	WARP
2011	CSC	A	20	0	0	14	22	0	24¹	17	0	11	41	4.1	15.2	50%	.318	1.15	1.85	1.64	0.88	0.7
2012	TAM	A+	21	4	1	14	31	0	40¹	23	0	16	61	3.6	13.6	56%	.287	0.97	1.34	1.78	2.00	1.5
2012	TRN	AA	21	3	1	1	15	0	24	12	1	6	38	2.2	14.2	34%	.239	0.75	1.88	1.33	2.43	0.7
2013	SWB	AAA	22	2	3	0	25	0	40	36	4	25	49	5.6	11.0	31%	.333	1.52	3.38	4.00	3.98	0.5
2014	NYA	MLB	23	2	1	1	30	0	42¹	35	4	20	53	4.2	11.2	41%	.301	1.28	3.38	3.57	3.67	0.6

Recycled relievers like Chris Bootcheck, Jim Miller, Matt Daley and Mike Zagurski appeared in pinstripes last season, but Montgomery—who was expected to be an important part of the team's bullpen picture—never made it to New York. The compact righty showed up to spring training out of shape, according to the team, and his velocity was down a few ticks early on, sitting near 89-90. He was effective out of the gate, recording a 1.72 ERA and a 12.6 K/9 rate through May 9th, but he pitched through pain and fell apart after a 3 ⅓-inning, 58-pitch appearance on May 12th, posting a 5.06 ERA the rest of the way with six walks per nine. A month after that marathon outing he hit the disabled list with shoulder fatigue, then returned to the DL with shoulder problems twice more before the end of the season. If healthy, the fastball-slider guy could be to David Robertson what Robertson was to Rivera, but there's now a real risk that he could end up on the sizable pile of failed Yankees pitching prospects.

Ivan Nova

Born: 1/12/1987 Age: 27
Bats: R Throws: R Height: 6' 4" Weight: 225
Breakout: 20% Improve: 64% Collapse: 28%
Attrition: 17% MLB: 83%

Comparables:
Gavin Floyd, Wade Davis, Tom Gorzelanny

YEAR	TEAM	LVL	AGE	W	L	SV	G	GS	IP	H	HR	BB	SO	BB9	SO9	GB%	BABIP	WHIP	ERA	FIP	FRA	WARP
2011	SWB	AAA	24	1	2	0	3	3	16	16	3	2	18	1.1	10.1	46%	.282	1.12	3.38	3.80	4.67	-0.1
2011	NYA	MLB	24	16	4	0	28	27	165¹	163	13	57	98	3.1	5.3	54%	.284	1.33	3.70	4.04	4.78	1.2
2012	NYA	MLB	25	12	8	0	28	28	170¹	194	28	56	153	3.0	8.1	46%	.331	1.47	5.02	4.55	4.82	1.0
2013	SWB	AAA	26	2	0	0	3	3	17²	15	1	4	17	2.0	8.7	56%	.298	1.08	2.04	2.70	3.26	0.3
2013	NYA	MLB	26	9	6	0	23	20	139¹	135	9	44	116	2.8	7.5	54%	.313	1.28	3.10	3.50	4.22	1.4
2014	NYA	MLB	27	9	6	0	22	22	136	140	14	47	99	3.1	6.6	50%	.304	1.37	4.25	4.39	4.62	0.6

Remember that scene at the end of *Children of Men*, when the sight of a newborn baby causes a ceasefire and gives hope to a world that had none? Nova's appearances didn't stop play, but his strong starts for a team almost devoid of mid-20s talent had a similarly inspiring effect. After a DL stint for triceps inflammation, a detour to the bullpen and a demotion due to roster crunch, the righty rejoined the rotation in late June and recorded a 2.70 ERA in 17 games and 16 starts the rest of the way. Nova's new sinker yielded the desired uptick in groundball rate, and his decision to increase his curveball usage at the expense of his slider worked out as well; only Yu Darvish had a higher whiff rate with his curve. By himself, Nova's not a youth movement, but at least he's a helpful reminder of what one would look like.

Vidal Nuno

Born: 7/26/1987 Age: 26
Bats: L Throws: L Height: 5' 11" Weight: 195
Breakout: 42% Improve: 64% Collapse: 28%
Attrition: 75% MLB: 53%

Comparables:
Bryan Augenstein, Chris Schwinden, Shane Komine

YEAR	TEAM	LVL	AGE	W	L	SV	G	GS	IP	H	HR	BB	SO	BB9	SO9	GB%	BABIP	WHIP	ERA	FIP	FRA	WARP
2011	CSC	A	23	2	1	0	7	7	40	37	4	2	37	0.4	8.3	47%	.244	0.98	1.80	3.13	3.50	0.4
2011	STA	A-	23	5	0	1	8	5	25	14	0	3	29	1.1	10.4	47%	.245	0.68	0.72	1.40	2.24	0.7
2012	TAM	A+	24	1	1	0	11	1	24¹	22	2	6	26	2.2	9.6	43%	.299	1.15	2.96	3.19	3.99	0.5
2012	TRN	AA	24	9	5	0	20	20	114	109	10	27	100	2.1	7.9	38%	.304	1.19	2.45	3.35	3.94	1.8
2013	SWB	AAA	25	2	0	0	5	5	25	14	2	2	30	0.7	10.8	44%	.211	0.64	1.44	2.08	2.85	0.6
2013	NYA	MLB	25	1	2	0	5	3	20	16	2	6	9	2.7	4.1	36%	.219	1.10	2.25	4.53	4.75	0.1
2014	NYA	MLB	26	3	2	0	11	8	49²	52	7	15	37	2.8	6.7	38%	.298	1.36	4.50	4.73	4.90	0.1

Drafted by the Indians in the 48th round in 2009, Nuno was released by Cleveland two years later and signed by the Yankees after a stint in the Frontier League. Since then, he's made them look smart, recording a 2.10 ERA in 248 innings across every level from Low-A to the majors. Called up to the big club in late April when Ivan Nova went down, Nuno BABIPed his way to success over three starts and two relief appearances, but after being sent down to Scranton, he injured his groin and missed the rest of the season. A classic crafty lefty with a high-80s heater and plenty of supporting stuff—including a sinker, a slider, a curve and a changeup that's become a reliable out pitch—Nuno isn't overpowering but hits his spots. He won't miss as many bats in the big leagues as he has at lower levels, so he might be more of a long man than a long-term starter, but even that would be a win considering where he came from.

Andy Pettitte

Born: 6/15/1972 Age: 42
Bats: L Throws: L Height: 6' 5'' Weight: 225
Breakout: 15% Improve: 30% Collapse: 25%
Attrition: 15% MLB: 65%

Comparables:
Kevin Brown, John Smoltz, Tim Wakefield

YEAR	TEAM	LVL	AGE	W	L	SV	G	GS	IP	H	HR	BB	SO	BB9	SO9	GB%	BABIP	WHIP	ERA	FIP	FRA	WARP
2012	NYA	MLB	40	5	4	0	12	12	75¹	65	8	21	69	2.5	8.2	56%	.274	1.14	2.87	3.43	3.99	1.2
2013	NYA	MLB	41	11	11	0	30	30	185¹	198	17	48	128	2.3	6.2	48%	.308	1.33	3.74	3.73	4.16	1.9
2014	NYA	MLB	42	10	7	0	24	24	145¹	146	15	46	106	2.9	6.5	48%	.298	1.33	3.90	4.22	4.24	1.3

If not for the ageless Mariano Rivera's presence on the same staff, Pettitte would have been the one celebrated for being so well preserved. Although his cutter wasn't quite as acclaimed as his longtime teammate's, he showed the same career-long consistency—in both his first and last nine seasons, Pettitte posted a 117 ERA+. Despite the lefty's status last season as the oldest starter in baseball, the most serious ailments he suffered were back spasms and a trapezius strain, and his peripherals wouldn't have looked out of place at any point in his career. Between his regular-season success and his large sample of nearly identical postseason stats, he's close enough to Cooperstown that taking 2011 off could have cost him a plaque. Appropriately, Pettitte closed the book on his career with a complete-game victory; if you want to make that final start sound even more storybook, don't mention that he made it in Houston.

David Phelps

Born: 10/9/1986 Age: 27
Bats: R Throws: R Height: 6' 2'' Weight: 200
Breakout: 47% Improve: 74% Collapse: 14%
Attrition: 30% MLB: 82%

Comparables:
Josh Collmenter, J.A. Happ, John Stephens

YEAR	TEAM	LVL	AGE	W	L	SV	G	GS	IP	H	HR	BB	SO	BB9	SO9	GB%	BABIP	WHIP	ERA	FIP	FRA	WARP
2011	SWB	AAA	24	6	6	0	18	18	107¹	115	11	26	90	2.2	7.5	36%	.340	1.31	3.19	3.73	4.13	0.4
2012	NYA	MLB	25	4	4	0	33	11	99²	81	14	38	96	3.4	8.7	45%	.258	1.19	3.34	4.27	4.73	0.8
2013	NYA	MLB	26	6	5	0	22	12	86²	88	8	35	79	3.6	8.2	44%	.323	1.42	4.98	3.84	4.74	0.5
2014	NYA	MLB	27	5	4	0	19	13	85	86	10	30	69	3.2	7.3	46%	.302	1.37	4.18	4.41	4.55	0.5

Like Adam Warren, Phelps is difficult to classify. He's floated between the bullpen and rotation in each of his first two seasons, and it's hard to say what his out pitch is. His fastball sits at 91, and with two strikes on righties, he uses four offerings (four-seamer, sinker, slider, curve) over 20 percent of the time each. He's probably a bit below average as a starter and slightly above average in short bursts, which means he'll keep ping-ponging based on team needs. The big ERA increase last season was the result of a BABIP overcorrection that masked mostly similar peripherals. The real concern was the more than two months he missed with multiple forearm strains, though he made it back in mid-September.

Michael Pineda

Born: 1/18/1989 Age: 25
Bats: R Throws: R Height: 6' 7'' Weight: 260
Breakout: 33% Improve: 62% Collapse: 24%
Attrition: 19% MLB: 98%

Comparables:
Clay Buchholz, Daniel Hudson, Francisco Liriano

YEAR	TEAM	LVL	AGE	W	L	SV	G	GS	IP	H	HR	BB	SO	BB9	SO9	GB%	BABIP	WHIP	ERA	FIP	FRA	WARP
2011	SEA	MLB	22	9	10	0	28	28	171	133	18	55	173	2.9	9.1	39%	.258	1.10	3.74	3.46	3.77	2.5
2013	SWB	AAA	24	1	1	0	6	6	23¹	18	2	6	26	2.3	10.0	52%	.267	1.03	3.86	3.12	5.15	0.2
2014	NYA	MLB	25	3	2	0	7	7	36¹	32	4	11	35	2.8	8.7	43%	.282	1.18	3.35	3.88	3.64	0.6

Pineda played professional baseball in 2013, which made his second season as a Yankee an improvement over the first. He didn't make it back to the mound until June and was shut down with shoulder stiffness/fatigue in early August, but he pitched well in what innings he had, striking out a batter per inning across three-minor league levels. He relied on his slider to miss bats and didn't show the same stuff he had before shoulder surgery, but the organization insists that he finished the year healthy and will compete for a rotation spot this spring. The bad news is that injuries have already eaten most of Pineda's pre-arb period, when players provide much of their surplus value. The good news is that the 40-man roster spot the Yankees freed up in the trade they made to get him has thus far been the best acquisition on either side of the swap.

Jose A. Ramirez
Born: 1/21/1990 Age: 24
Bats: R Throws: R Height: 6' 3" Weight: 190
Breakout: 57% Improve: 66% Collapse: 13%
Attrition: 91% MLB: 8%

Comparables:
Steve Johnson, Thad Weber, Corey Kluber

YEAR	TEAM	LVL	AGE	W	L	SV	G	GS	IP	H	HR	BB	SO	BB9	SO9	GB%	BABIP	WHIP	ERA	FIP	FRA	WARP
2011	CSC	A	21	5	7	0	15	15	79	84	9	32	74	3.6	8.4	43%	.274	1.47	4.90	4.50	4.33	0.3
2011	TAM	A+	21	0	5	0	6	6	24¹	35	3	11	25	4.1	9.2	44%	.425	1.89	8.14	4.42	5.16	0.1
2012	TAM	A+	22	7	6	0	21	18	98²	92	7	30	94	2.7	8.6	45%	.295	1.24	3.19	3.47	4.06	1.8
2013	TRN	AA	23	1	3	1	9	8	42¹	28	7	15	50	3.2	10.6	44%	.233	1.02	2.76	4.39	5.40	0.1
2013	SWB	AAA	23	1	3	0	8	8	31¹	29	3	21	28	6.0	8.0	46%	.321	1.60	4.88	5.06	6.34	-0.3
2014	NYA	MLB	24	4	4	0	13	13	62²	66	10	31	45	4.4	6.5	44%	.297	1.55	5.40	5.72	5.87	-0.5

The title of "Top Yankees pitching prospect" has been closer to a curse than a blessing in recent seasons, but whether he likes it or not Ramirez holds it today. The righty started the season on the DL due to fatigue but had no trouble with Trenton after his late-April activation, earning a mid-June ticket to Triple-A, where an oblique injury ended his season early. He has the best stuff in the system, showing off a plus-plus fastball and changeup and a solid-average slider. That's a devastating repertoire in the hands of a pitcher who can command all three pitches and remain on the mound; in the hands of the occasionally inconsistent, high-effort and often-injured Ramirez, who hasn't pitched 100 innings since 2011 or ever topped 115, it's of more promise—and a possible bullpen profile—than practical use.

Mariano Rivera
Born: 11/29/1969 Age: 44
Bats: R Throws: R Height: 6' 2" Weight: 195
Breakout: 42% Improve: 49% Collapse: 24%
Attrition: 17% MLB: 60%

Comparables:
Hoyt Wilhelm, Doug Jones, Mike Timlin

YEAR	TEAM	LVL	AGE	W	L	SV	G	GS	IP	H	HR	BB	SO	BB9	SO9	GB%	BABIP	WHIP	ERA	FIP	FRA	WARP
2011	NYA	MLB	41	1	2	44	64	0	61¹	47	3	8	60	1.2	8.8	48%	.275	0.90	1.91	2.23	2.95	1.6
2012	NYA	MLB	42	1	1	5	9	0	8¹	6	0	2	8	2.2	8.6	46%	.273	0.96	2.16	1.85	2.20	0.2
2013	NYA	MLB	43	6	2	44	64	0	64	58	6	9	54	1.3	7.6	47%	.280	1.05	2.11	3.08	3.33	1.1
2014	NYA	MLB	44	3	1	39	48	0	46²	41	4	9	42	1.8	8.0	50%	.285	1.07	2.68	3.30	2.91	1.1

Rivera's consistency made him a comforting, fascinating freak, a player so unreproachable that his approaching retirement made even unsentimental fans lapse into Mitch Albom-like language. The older he got, the more we marveled at his continued dominance, and the more we worried that his career would come to an ugly end. As we wrote in *Baseball Prospectus 2012*, "The only thing worse than not having him would be seeing him fail." In retrospect, the worrying was a waste of our time. Save for a homer-happy August and a slightly lower innings total—which had as much to do with league-wide workload trends as it did with his age—Rivera at 43 was as effective as he'd been a decade (or more) before. For all the gifts Rivera received on his 2013 farewell tour, the greatest gift was the one he gave us: the chance to watch him pitch. Dammit—there we go, Alboming again.

David Robertson
Born: 4/9/1985 Age: 29
Bats: R Throws: R Height: 5' 11" Weight: 195
Breakout: 24% Improve: 54% Collapse: 35%
Attrition: 13% MLB: 96%

Comparables:
Michael Gonzalez, Jose Valverde, Francisco Rodriguez

YEAR	TEAM	LVL	AGE	W	L	SV	G	GS	IP	H	HR	BB	SO	BB9	SO9	GB%	BABIP	WHIP	ERA	FIP	FRA	WARP
2011	NYA	MLB	26	4	0	1	70	0	66²	40	1	35	100	4.7	13.5	48%	.289	1.12	1.08	1.88	0.90	2.5
2012	NYA	MLB	27	2	7	2	65	0	60²	52	5	19	81	2.8	12.0	45%	.331	1.17	2.67	2.44	2.89	1.5
2013	NYA	MLB	28	5	1	3	70	0	66¹	51	5	18	77	2.4	10.4	52%	.287	1.04	2.04	2.64	3.32	1.0
2014	NYA	MLB	29	3	1	1	58	0	55¹	43	4	22	72	3.6	11.7	48%	.304	1.17	2.66	2.89	2.89	1.3

In 2011, Robertson's teammates took to calling him "Houdini" because of his tendency to get into trouble with walks, only to escape via the strikeout. The nickname no longer applies. Somewhere around the 2012 All-Star break, Robertson decided that the easiest way to get out of jams was to avoid them entirely. In 91 innings from 2011 through the first half of 2012, he struck out 13.8 batters per nine innings and walked 4.6. In 102 innings since then, he's fanned 10.4 and walked 2.2, trading some speed for increased command. He's not necessarily a more effective pitcher now, but he is much more likely to get the ninth-inning nod. After three straight seasons of set-up dominance, there isn't much more he could do to deserve it.

CC Sabathia
Born: 7/21/1980 Age: 33
Bats: L Throws: L Height: 6' 7" Weight: 290
Breakout: 11% Improve: 47% Collapse: 26%
Attrition: 21% MLB: 91%

Comparables:
Josh Beckett, Chris Carpenter, Johan Santana

YEAR	TEAM	LVL	AGE	W	L	SV	G	GS	IP	H	HR	BB	SO	BB9	SO9	GB%	BABIP	WHIP	ERA	FIP	FRA	WARP
2011	NYA	MLB	30	19	8	0	33	33	237¹	230	17	61	230	2.3	8.7	49%	.319	1.23	3.00	2.91	3.60	4.9
2012	NYA	MLB	31	15	6	0	28	28	200	184	22	44	197	2.0	8.9	50%	.288	1.14	3.38	3.29	3.71	3.4
2013	NYA	MLB	32	14	13	0	32	32	211	224	28	65	175	2.8	7.5	47%	.309	1.37	4.78	4.12	4.95	0.2
2014	NYA	MLB	33	14	7	0	27	27	188	175	17	50	165	2.4	7.9	48%	.296	1.20	3.41	3.61	3.71	2.6

Sabathia's recent trajectory is the latest reminder that it takes only a season or two for a starter to go from Cooperstown-bound ace to below-average liability. The lefty pitched well in 2012 despite showing some signs of fragility in the second half and undergoing offseason bone spur surgery, but while he avoided the DL in 2013 until a late-September hamstring strain and extended his 200-inning streak to five, he rarely flashed his old effectiveness. After losing over 1.5 miles per hour on his four-seamer in 2012, he surrendered another mile per hour last season, although his velo did trend upward throughout the season until dipping somewhat in September. And while the separation between his fastball and changeup has stayed the same, the lower max speed of the former has robbed the latter of some of its impact. In the second half, Sabathia posted an ERA over 6.00 with a walk rate well over 4.0 per nine, and at times, the southpaw sounded downcast and defeated. Declining velo, a lower arm slot, a body more prone to breaking down: all dismaying signs, but none of them surprising for a 33-year-old starter with as much mileage as Sabathia has on his arm.

Nik Turley
Born: 9/11/1989 Age: 24
Bats: L Throws: L Height: 6' 4" Weight: 195
Breakout: 68% Improve: 74% Collapse: 17%
Attrition: 66% MLB: 23%

Comparables:
Drake Britton, Aaron Crow, Bruce Billings

YEAR	TEAM	LVL	AGE	W	L	SV	G	GS	IP	H	HR	BB	SO	BB9	SO9	GB%	BABIP	WHIP	ERA	FIP	FRA	WARP
2011	CSC	A	21	4	6	0	15	15	82¹	70	8	21	82	2.3	9.0	42%	.283	1.11	2.51	3.86	3.69	0.8
2012	TAM	A+	22	9	5	0	23	21	112	97	7	44	116	3.5	9.3	49%	.308	1.26	2.89	3.55	3.97	1.9
2013	TRN	AA	23	11	8	0	27	26	139	119	11	73	137	4.7	8.9	44%	.290	1.38	3.88	4.30	4.68	1.1
2014	NYA	MLB	24	8	7	0	23	23	117	122	16	59	88	4.5	6.8	43%	.299	1.55	5.17	5.38	5.62	-0.6

The former 50th-rounder is going to get to the big leagues. Just as he did in 2012, Turley spent almost a whole season at a single level, save for one start the next rung up on the minor-league ladder. But this time, that single level was Double-A, putting him in the mix for the back of the Bronx rotation in 2014. Turley's fastball has arm-side life and sits low 90s, spiking higher, and his height and over-the-top delivery add deception and downhill plane. He has a plus curve to go with the heater and a useable changeup. Best of all, he's left-handed, which makes the five preceding sentences sound so much sweeter.

Adam Warren
Born: 8/25/1987 Age: 26
Bats: R Throws: R Height: 6' 1" Weight: 200
Breakout: 38% Improve: 63% Collapse: 27%
Attrition: 55% MLB: 63%

Comparables:
Pat Misch, Jeff Manship, Doug Fister

YEAR	TEAM	LVL	AGE	W	L	SV	G	GS	IP	H	HR	BB	SO	BB9	SO9	GB%	BABIP	WHIP	ERA	FIP	FRA	WARP
2011	SWB	AAA	23	6	8	0	27	27	152¹	145	13	53	111	3.1	6.6	38%	.291	1.30	3.60	4.09	4.79	0.0
2012	SWB	AAA	24	7	8	0	26	26	152²	167	11	46	107	2.7	6.3	49%	.319	1.40	3.71	3.68	4.98	0.6
2012	NYA	MLB	24	0	0	0	1	1	2¹	8	2	2	1	7.7	3.9	29%	.500	4.29	23.14	15.90	9.38	-0.1
2013	NYA	MLB	25	3	2	1	34	2	77	80	10	30	64	3.5	7.5	47%	.312	1.43	3.39	4.35	4.60	0.4
2014	NYA	MLB	26	4	3	0	21	10	78	84	10	28	53	3.2	6.1	48%	.302	1.43	4.60	4.86	5.00	0.0

After two nearly identical seasons as a starter in Scranton, Warren pitched his way to the parent club in spring training and brought similar stats to the big-league bullpen. The righty wasn't bothered by any uncertainty about his assignments; alternating between long-relief outings, late-inning assignments and even spot starts, he made as many as eight outings in a month and as few as three, facing anywhere from one to 23 batters in an outing. Lefties hit him hard (.301/.370/.526); that wasn't a problem in Triple-A, so it might've been a blip. Regardless of his role, Warren relied on a starter's five-pitch repertoire, working off a near-94 mph fastball. He has enough stuff to stick at the end of a rotation, but in a situational world dominated by strictly defined relief roles he might be of more use as a middle-inning multi-tool.

LINEOUTS

HITTERS

PLAYER	TEAM	LVL	AGE	PA	R	2B	3B	HR	RBI	BB	SO	SB-CS	AVG/OBP/SLG	TAv	BABIP	BRR	FRAA	WARP
RF T. Austin	TRN	AA	21	366	43	17	1	6	40	41	79	4-0	.257/.344/.373	.260	.321	-0.4	RF(69): -4.6	0.6
SS A. Avelino	STA	A-	18	76	10	2	0	0	6	4	6	2-0	.243/.303/.271	.265	.266	1.4	SS(17): -1.2	0.3
1B G. Bird	CSC	A	20	573	84	36	3	20	84	107	132	1-1	.288/.428/.511	.347	.364	-0.5	1B(90): -7.9	5.4
RF B. Boesch	SWB	AAA	28	37	6	2	0	0	2	7	8	0-0	.200/.351/.267	.283	.273	0.6	RF(7): -0.3	0.2
	NYA	MLB	28	53	6	2	1	3	8	2	9	0-0	.275/.302/.529	.273	.282	-1.2	RF(15): 0.6	0.1
3B R. Canzler	IND	AAA	27	148	9	1	1	1	13	15	25	0-0	.194/.277/.240	.199	.226	-1.1	3B(10): 1.0, 1B(9): -0.3	-0.8
	NOR	AAA	27	375	46	15	1	11	49	47	76	1-1	.276/.369/.430	.272	.328	-3.6	1B(34): -2.3, LF(13): -0.5	0.3
3B L. Cruz	LAN	MLB	29	128	12	2	0	1	6	5	20	0-0	.127/.175/.169	.138	.143	0.6	3B(28): 0.9, SS(15): 2.2	-0.6
	NYA	MLB	29	59	6	1	0	0	5	1	13	1-0	.182/.224/.200	.150	.238	0.5	3B(13): 1.8, SS(5): 0.5	-0.1
LF R. Flores	TRN	AA	21	620	79	25	6	6	55	77	98	7-6	.260/.353/.363	.281	.306	-1.1	LF(104): -4.7, CF(23): -2.1	2.3
RF F. Martinez	SWB	AAA	24	94	9	7	0	4	18	6	12	1-0	.325/.394/.554	.336	.338	-0.6	RF(21): 0.4	0.8
	OKL	AAA	24	117	12	5	1	3	21	11	31	0-0	.219/.291/.371	.232	.278	0.2	RF(12): 0.3, LF(3): 0.1	-0.2
	HOU	MLB	24	35	1	0	0	1	3	1	12	0-0	.182/.229/.273	.186	.250	0.1	LF(8): -0.3, RF(2): -0.1	-0.3
SS Y. Navarro	NOR	AAA	25	452	59	21	1	12	53	53	73	9-2	.267/.354/.418	.273	.296	2.5	SS(84): 7.7, 2B(15): 0.0	3.6
	BAL	MLB	25	31	3	0	1	0	2	2	8	0-0	.286/.333/.357	.235	.400	0.1	2B(8): -0.3	0.0
C P. O'Brien	CSC	A	22	226	47	22	1	11	41	22	58	0-0	.325/.394/.619	.396	.397	0.9	C(53): -0.2	4.6
	TAM	A+	22	280	31	17	3	11	55	19	76	0-1	.265/.314/.486	.280	.326	0.1	3B(38): -3.9, C(12): -0.1	1.0
SS G. Velazquez	NWO	AAA	33	307	30	8	0	0	24	43	53	3-5	.277/.376/.309	.265	.343	-1.7	SS(50): -1.8, 2B(22): 0.5	1.1
	SWB	AAA	33	85	4	0	0	0	2	8	11	0-1	.173/.253/.173	.166	.203	0	SS(25): 2.4, 2B(2): -0.0	-0.2
	MIA	MLB	33	1	0	0	0	0	0	0	0	0-0	.000/.000/.000	.012	.000	0	3B(1): -0.0	0.0

After entering last season as one of the team's top five prospects, **Tyler Austin** suffered wrist soreness that slowed his bat in the first half and made him miss most of the second. That wasn't what the Yankees wanted to see from a player whom some scouts already feared wouldn't hit for enough power to support a right-field profile. ⊘ A fine defensive shortstop with a contact-oriented, line-drive swing that has produced little power, **Abiatal Avelino** might have the future the Yankees once foresaw for first-rounder Cito Culver. ⊘ Lefty slugger **Gregory Bird** had one of the 10 best offensive seasons in the minors. As a first baseman with below-average range, he can't afford to lose much offensively, but the raw is real. ⊘ Time may heal the shoulder problems that ended **Brennan Boesch**'s season, but it won't relieve the pain of being released from rosters to make room for Andy Dirks and Brent Lillibridge. ⊘ Minor-league journeyman **Russ Canzler** continued his tour of the International League but lost his 40-man roster spot after struggling in Indianapolis. ⊘ Future generations will look back and wonder why **Luis Cruz** started at short for 2013's two top-payroll teams. History won't hold any answers. ⊘ **Ramon Flores**' .110 ISO doesn't cut it in a corner, and his defense isn't fit for center. Scouts have a word for players with his profile; it rhymes with wiener, and it's just as derogatory as wiener was in third grade. ⊘ For the fifth straight season, **Fernando Martinez** made the majors, more than most failed prospects can say. But the Astros traded Martinez to the Yankees in June for a 37th-round reliever, and he sat out most of the second half with a Biogenesis suspension. ⊘ **Yamaico Navarro** has already been with four organizations, but the 26-year-old has played everywhere but catcher at least once in the minors and can hit a bit, so he has at least four more chances coming. ⊘ A catcher in college and his first pro season, 2012 second-rounder and bat-only power prospect **Pete O'Brien**'s future is at first base. He spent most of his time in Tampa at DH and third base, where he committed 18 errors in 38 games. ⊘ On the bright side, **Gil Velazquez** has now gone four of his five major-league stints without being set down on strikes, but his career .637 OPS in 16 minor-league seasons is slightly more telling.

PITCHERS

PLAYER	TEAM	LVL	AGE	W	L	SV	IP	H	HR	BB	SO	BB9	SO9	GB%	BABIP	WHIP	ERA	FIP	FRA	WARP
M. Banuelos	SWB	AAA	21	0	2	0	24	29	2	10	22	3.8	8.2	43%	.360	1.62	4.50	3.78	5.15	0.1
D. Burawa	TRN	AA	24	6	3	4	66	47	1	42	66	5.7	9.0	54%	.271	1.35	2.59	3.43	4.37	0.4
C. Cabral	TRN	AA	24	1	0	0	19^2	22	2	9	22	4.1	10.1	52%	.370	1.58	5.49	4.09	3.19	0.4
	SWB	AAA	24	0	1	0	10	12	0	5	16	4.5	14.4	48%	.480	1.70	7.20	1.80	2.55	0.3
	NYA	MLB	24	0	0	0	3^2	3	0	1	6	2.5	14.7	29%	.429	1.09	2.45	1.44	2.24	0.1
M. Daley	SWB	AAA	31	2	3	1	39	28	3	6	53	1.4	12.2	29%	.278	0.87	2.54	2.10	2.63	1.0
	NYA	MLB	31	1	0	0	6	2	0	0	8	0.0	12.0	58%	.167	0.33	0.00	0.91	2.29	0.2
R. Davis	CSC	A	20	0	0	0	10	9	0	0	8	0.0	7.2	43%	.300	0.90	0.00	2.48	3.01	0.2
	STA	A-	20	2	4	0	42	46	1	13	39	2.8	8.4	50%	.336	1.40	2.36	2.62	3.84	0.6
S. Greene	TAM	A+	24	4	6	0	75	83	4	10	69	1.2	8.3	49%	.348	1.24	3.60	2.61	3.94	0.9
	TRN	AA	24	8	4	0	79^1	92	6	20	68	2.3	7.7	51%	.347	1.41	3.18	3.61	4.00	1.0
B. Mitchell	TAM	A+	22	4	11	0	126^2	144	5	53	104	3.8	7.4	49%	.346	1.56	5.12	3.51	4.54	0.5
	TRN	AA	22	0	0	0	18^2	14	0	5	16	2.4	7.7	44%	.269	1.02	1.93	2.57	3.09	0.4
L. Severino	CSC	A	19	1	1	0	17^2	21	1	4	21	2.0	10.7	46%	.392	1.42	4.08	2.52	2.58	0.5

Former top prospect **Manny Banuelos** hasn't seen the mound since May 2012, save for simulated games. He and his new UCL will have had 18 months to bond by Opening Day, when he'll still be only 23. ⊘ After missing 2012 with multiple injuries, St. John's grad **Danny Burawa** had a healthy, successful season in Trenton. A low home run rate obscured control problems, but his high-90s heater and sharp-breaking slider fit a seventh- or eighth-inning role. ⊘ After a May return from the fractured elbow that cost him most of 2012, **Cesar Cabral** took time to get reacquainted with the strike zone, but settled in and made a case for situational work by fanning 40 percent of the lefties he faced across four levels. ⊘ Hang around as long as soft-tossing journeyman **Matt Daley**, and you too could become the answer to a trivia question as destined to baffle future fans as "Who finished Mariano Rivera's final game?" ⊘ Meaty, thick-thighed **Rookie Davis**, a right-hander signed over slot in 2011, earned a late-season promotion to Charleston after 11 strong starts for Staten Island. His fastball tops out at 95, with a changeup and decent curve thrown almost exclusively to righties. ⊘ Righty **Shane Greene**, a recent addition to the 40-man, reduced his walk rate dramatically and made it to Trenton as a starter, but his fastball-slider arsenal spells bullpen. ⊘ **Ty Hensley**, the Yankees' top 2012 pick, entered 2013 as the team's no. 2 pitching prospect. April hip surgery cost him the whole season, so while he has mid-rotation potential, we're years from knowing whether his promising curve and changeup will develop alongside a plus fastball. ⊘ Pay attention to **Bryan Mitchell**'s 3.51 FIP in the Florida State League, not his five-plus ERA. His smooth delivery produces high-90s heat to go with a 91-93 mph cutter, a future average changeup and the best curveball on the farm. ⊘ **Luis Severino**, a Dominican righty whom a Yankees source said had the "best stuff in our system," earned a mid-season promotion to Charleston after looking like one of the Gulf Coast League's most polished pitchers. He commands a low-mid-90s fastball and plus slider, so he'll be a bullpen weapon if his frame can't stand up to starting.

MANAGER: JOE GIRARDI

YEAR	TEAM	W-L	Pythag +/−	Avg PC	100+ P	120+ P	QS	BQS	REL	REL w Zero R	IBB	PH	PH Avg	PH HR	SB2	CS2	SB3	CS3	SAC Att	SAC %	POS SAC	Squeeze	Swing	In Play
2011	NYA	97-65	1	95.7	69	2	84	6	465	404	43	54	.196	0	125	42	21	3	54	66.7%	29	0	357	94
2012	NYA	95-67	1	97.9	84	3	82	7	485	409	32	129	.148	4	77	24	16	3	50	62.0%	28	0	321	88
2013	NYA	85-77	0	95.7	82	1	84	11	428	356	34	99	.242	1	96	27	18	4	53	67.9%	35	0	302	94

Joe Girardi prefers a set lineup, but last year he had to scramble. In all previous seasons, his clubs ranked in the top three in percentage of plate appearances going to the main starters. (Sure, the Yankees have a lineup full of big names, but even the 2006 Marlins ranked third in the NL in this.) But in 2013, the Yankees ranked 13th, ahead of only the Mariners and Astros.

Trying to evaluate Girardi is a little tricky. His teams get on base a lot, have power and are older than most. But then again, that would be the case for the Yankees regardless of who their manager is. It's worth noting that many predicted the Yankees would have a flat rotten year due to injuries this year, but they made it over .500 despite playing in baseball's toughest division. He's also the guy that had an impressive crop of rookie performances with the 2006 Marlins. He gets the most out of his teams.

Oakland Athletics

By Ken Arneson

I am an Oakland A's fan. That's an unusual thing to say in a *Baseball Prospectus* team essay. But there's a small change this year: a byline. When the author is anonymous, it is difficult to write in anything other than a detached, formal, objective, third-person voice. But this time, my name is above this essay. What does this rule change mean?

On the one hand, I can write a more intimate, personal and subjective story than was possible before. I don't have to follow the linear path of a rational argument. I can be lyrical or impressionistic, mysterious or romantic. How can you not be romantic about baseball?

On the other hand, readers have traditionally purchased this publication for its objective analysis, not its poetry. History establishes precedents, creates expectations. Human beings fear loss more than they enjoy gains. Change will be resisted.

* * *

After the 2011 season, the A's traded Gio Gonzalez, Trevor Cahill, Craig Breslow and Andrew Bailey. These players were all about halfway to free agency. In return, the A's received players with almost the full six years of team control left.

In hindsight, the trades were successful. The A's got younger and more talented. Two consecutive division titles followed.

At the time, however, Oakland A's fans like me looked at these trades and thought, "Oh, no, not again."

* * *

Historically, the Athletics franchise has been more sensitive to change than other teams. Perhaps this sensitivity is a result of their birth. They were founded not by a rich businessman, but by a coach and former player, Connie Mack. His business partner, Ben Shibe, became wealthy primarily by manufacturing baseballs. They were both entirely

creatures of the baseball industry itself, so if the business of baseball caught a cold, the Athletics sneezed.

* * *

It must have been the evening of Sunday, July 11, 1976. I'm not 100 percent sure about this, but that's the date that makes the most sense. I was 10 years old. That was the day I first learned what it meant to be an A's fan.

* * *

You know what I love most about baseball? Every pitch is related to every other pitch in the history of baseball. The past affects the present.

For four games in the 2013 Division Series, the Oakland A's pounded Miguel Cabrera with fastballs in. They figured that because of a hip injury, Cabrera was having trouble getting around on that pitch. For four games, the strategy worked. Maybe it worked because of his injury, but maybe it also worked because teams don't usually pitch him that way. But by game five, Cabrera had a good idea how the A's were pitching him. He guessed fastball in, got it and deposited Sonny Gray's pitch over the fence for a two-run homer. It was all the runs Justin Verlander would need to eliminate the A's from the playoffs for the second year in a row.

On second thought, maybe that's not what I love most about baseball.

* * *

Connie Mack twice had to dismantle dynasties because of external changes. In 1914, after four pennants in five years, the A's faced massive inflation in player salaries caused by the upstart Federal League. After three straight pennants from 1929 to 1931, the Great Depression hit the A's finances hard.

But the A's also suffered a self-inflicted blow. Mack failed to act on one of the biggest baseball innovations of the era: the farm system. Partly because of financial limitations and partly because Mack was resistant to the change (he derided

ATHLETICS PROSPECTUS 2013 W-L: 96-66, 1st in AL West					
Pythag	.594	5th	DER	.724	1st
RS/G	4.73	4th	B-Age	28.3	16th
RA/G	3.86	9th	P-Age	28.0	13th
TAv	.281	3rd	Salary	$62	27th
BRR	-0.61	17th	M$/MW	$1.02	1st
TAv-P	.261	13th	DL Days	747	11th
FIP	3.86	15th	$ on DL	17%	16th

Three-Year Park Factors	Runs	HR/RH	HR/LH	Runs/RH	Runs/LH
	94	89	78	100	94

Top Hitter WARP	6.22 (Josh Donaldson)
Top Pitcher WARP	2.68 (Bartolo Colon)
Top Prospect	Addison Russell

farm systems as "chain store baseball"), the A's ended up with a deficient system for finding and developing talent. After that 1931 pennant, it would be four decades before the A's made the postseason again.

* * *

In contrast, the A's were early to act on the innovations in statistical analysis. This is well chronicled in *Moneyball*.

Scene from the film: Billy Beane says to Eric Chavez, "You get on base, we win. You don't, we lose. And I *hate* losing, Chavvy. I *hate* it. I hate losing even more than I want to win."

* * *

Studies on loss aversion show that humans feel a loss about twice as intensely as a victory. In general, we will risk losing $100 only if we have a chance of winning roughly $200.

It makes you wonder why people love baseball at all. Baseball is a zero-sum game. On average, baseball fans are going to lose exactly as often as they win. Whatever it is that makes us love baseball, the benefit has to be at least twice as good as the joy of winning; otherwise it wouldn't overcome the loss aversion deficit built into human nature.

* * *

"There is something wrong here," A's owner Lew Wolff told *USA TODAY Sports* in an interview on September 18, 2013. "It's depressing. I really expected the crowds to be huge this week."

At a 2:1 loss-aversion ratio, a baseball team needs to win 108 games to be a psychologically attractive product on winning alone. The 2013 Oakland A's only won 96.

* * *

You know what I like least about baseball analytics? It's that it can't yet explain how every pitch is related to every other pitch in the history of baseball.

How did Bartolo Colon end up with a 2.65 ERA last year while throwing 85 percent fastballs? I'd hypothesize that it's in the way he sequences the location and movement of those fastballs, that it's significant that few other pitchers sequence fastballs the way he does. It's about how Colon and every other pitcher create expectations in batters' minds, and how he uses his unique personal toolbox of pitches to defy those expectations.

Perhaps the A's have internal analytics that allow them to explain how Colon does this. But our public methods today, which depend in large part on cheap and ubiquitous relational database technology, lack good tools for this kind of analysis.

Relational databases have provided us great insights, but they have their limitations, too. They are great at manipulating sets of data, but poor at manipulating sequences of data.

This type of sequential analysis can be done, but it requires expertise and effort, which is expensive. So public baseball analytics are done the way we can afford to do them: as if the game of baseball is structured like a relational database, as if each pitch and each batted ball is not an event in a long sequence of interrelated events but an entirely independent event in a randomized soup of other entirely independent events.

* * *

Human beings long to feel connected to something greater than themselves. If you can bottle this longing and sell it, if you can make people feel they are a part of history, connected both to the distant past and a hopeful future, you can probably make a lot of money.

That's what the innovation at Camden Yards did for baseball. It reinvented grandma's homemade chicken noodle soup. It tasted delicious, and was good for the soul.

After a bowl of that, who wants to buy an ugly thermos full of randomized independent event soup? And yet, three years after Camden Yards opened, the A's completely whiffed on bottling the retro ballpark innovation and let the architectural disaster that is Mount Davis happen.

* * *

The A's never recovered from their late start on the farm system innovation of the 1930s until another change in the rules in 1965 gave the A's a second chance: the amateur draft. The A's under Charlie Finley were quick to recognize what the change meant. In the year before the draft went into effect, the A's signed 80 amateur free agents for a then-record $650,000 before these players could be subject to the draft. Among these players were Catfish Hunter, Joe Rudi, Blue Moon Odom and Rollie Fingers. Then, in the first three years of the draft, the A's acquired Rick Monday, Sal Bando, Gene Tenace, Vida Blue and Reggie Jackson.

The A's built their 1970s dynasty upon taking advantage of that rule change. A different rule change caused it to fall apart.

* * *

I was at the Oakland Airport with my mom to pick up my dad from a business trip. We were waiting at baggage claim. I told my parents I had to go to the bathroom, and wandered off to find one.

On my way back to the baggage claim area, I found myself walking side by side with a larger gentleman. I looked up, and I recognized him.

"Oh my God," I thought as I gazed up at my favorite baseball player in the world. "That's REGGIE JACKSON!"

* * *

After the 1975 season, an arbitration ruling effectively ended the Reserve Clause. A contract could only be renewed once, and then the player would be a free agent.

Like he did in 1964, Finley saw the change coming and sought to act early. He knew he was going to lose a bunch of players to free agency after the 1976 season and wanted to get value for his assets. He traded Reggie Jackson and Ken Holtzman to Baltimore in spring training. At the trade deadline, he tried to sell Rollie Fingers, Joe Rudi and Vida Blue for cash, only to have Commissioner Bowie Kuhn void the deals.

A year later, a new collective bargaining agreement established a six-year window before a player reached free agency. Had Finley known this would happen, he could have maximized the value of his assets by trying to trade for minor leaguers instead of cash. Alas, he did not, and the A's 1970s dynasty quickly fell apart.

* * *

Just as Charlie Finley rescued the A's franchise from a previous owner's self-inflicted disaster of missing out on the farm system revolution, current A's owner Lew Wolff hopes that a move to San Jose can rescue the A's from the mistakes his predecessors made in missing out on the retro ballpark revolution.

Unfortunately for Wolff, the San Francisco Giants hold the territorial rights to Santa Clara County. In 2009, Commissioner Bud Selig formed a blue-ribbon committee to look into Wolff's request. Four years later, no decision had been made. The ballpark issue remained unresolved. Wolff was left waiting for a change in the rules, a change other owners resisted.

* * *

Reggie Jackson's Baltimore Orioles played in Anaheim earlier that day, the last game before the 1976 All-Star break. Because he had held out for a month after his trade, he failed to make the All-Star Game. He was probably heading back to his home in Oakland for the break.

I wanted to say something, anything, to him, but I was so stunned to be walking right beside him in the flesh, I couldn't think of a word to say.

* * *

In November 2011, a new CBA was signed. It created a new process for free agency and placed fixed caps on amateur spending. It was a change designed to give teams more incentive to invest their discretionary funds in major-league players. No longer was it possible to do as Finley did in 1964 and make a strategic decision to invest heavily in amateurs.

For a low-revenue team like the A's who can't expect to win free agent bidding wars, these changes meant that manipulating the six-year window before free agency was more important than ever.

As a result, the A's stopped pursuing players one year from free agency like Matt Holliday, Josh Willingham and David DeJesus. They signed Yoenis Cespedes, an amateur not subject to the spending caps. They made those "Oh no, not again" trades.

* * *

Scene from *Moneyball*: Billy Beane asks Peter Brand, "Would you rather get one shot in the head, or five in the chest and bleed to death?"

Brand replies, "Are those my only two options?"

* * *

If you project out this 2014 team with so many key players with one or two years of service time, Billy Beane will have an interesting dilemma. He can ride this group the full six years and risk having to do a full rebuild later. Or he can try to sustain a consistent level of quality over a longer time by being more ruthless than ever in flipping good players piece by piece as they reach their peak trade values.

Unless, that is, some rule suddenly changes and the A's find themselves moving into a new ballpark.

* * *

In a 2011 MLB.com Town Hall chat, Bud Selig said about the A's move to San Jose, "I know there are some people who think it's taken too long and I understand that. I'm willing to accept that. But you make decisions like this; I've always said, you'd better be careful. Better to get it done right than to get it done fast."

I'll have five bullets to the chest and a side order of bleed to death slowly, please.

* * *

The Oakland A's are likely to have a good baseball team in 2014. The A's commitment to objective analysis is the source of that.

But merely fielding a winning team in 2014 is not enough for a franchise as a whole to be healthy in 2014. The product that baseball sells is not just about winning. The product is an emotional connection.

Every time a good player leaves prematurely, a little piece of the past and a little piece of the future gets disconnected from the present. And every new day that the ballpark situation goes unresolved, the fear grows in Bay Area A's fans that they will be left without their team just like Kansas City and Philadelphia A's fans before them. It makes the fans a little bit more reluctant to commit emotionally, to buy that season ticket, to carve out the extra time in their lives to watch that game on TV.

For the Athletics franchise to provide maximum value to its customers, the 2014 team needs to be connected in a straight line to both the 1974 team and the 2054 team. Otherwise, all they can sell is today's game for its own sake alone, an independent event.

* * *

Reggie's holdout was a signal to this 10-year-old A's fan that he was as upset about the trade as I was. He was an A's fan at heart, just like me.

I kept walking, silently, side-by-side with Reggie all the way to the baggage carousel. Reggie walked over to a piece of luggage and picked it up.

In an instant, I understood how naïve I was about how baseball worked. I was stunned. Shocked. Dismayed. My innocence was over.

Reggie Jackson's luggage had Baltimore Orioles decals plastered all over it.

* * *

Scene from *Moneyball*: Peter Brand shows Billy Beane a video.

"It's a metaphor," says Brand.

"I know it's a metaphor," says Beane.

Ken Arneson founded the Baseball Toaster blog network in 2005 and operated it for four years. There he wrote about the Oakland A's for his blog, Catfish Stew.

HITTERS

Daric Barton　1B

Born: 8/16/1985 Age: 28
Bats: L Throws: R Height: 6' 0"
Weight: 205 Breakout: 3%
Improve: 40% Collapse: 9%
Attrition: 13% MLB: 87%

Comparables:
Gaby Sanchez, Ryan Garko, Dan Johnson

YEAR	TEAM	LVL	AGE	PA	R	2B	3B	HR	RBI	BB	SO	SB	CS	AVG/OBP/SLG	TAv	BABIP	BRR	FRAA	WARP
2011	SAC	AAA	25	75	10	2	0	0	4	14	16	0	0	.197/.347/.230	.212	.267	0	1B(7): 0.7	0.0
2011	OAK	MLB	25	280	27	13	0	0	21	39	47	2	1	.212/.325/.267	.234	.260	1.6	1B(65): 2.2	-0.1
2012	SAC	AAA	26	336	49	14	3	8	35	66	53	7	1	.255/.411/.425	.302	.286	0.9	1B(57): -1.4, 3B(1): -0.0	1.6
2012	OAK	MLB	26	136	8	7	0	1	6	22	32	1	0	.204/.338/.292	.246	.275	0.2	1B(43): -1.0	-0.1
2013	SAC	AAA	27	488	77	29	1	7	69	87	57	1	2	.297/.423/.430	.310	.327	-0.2	1B(80): 12.0, 3B(29): -1.3	4.4
2013	OAK	MLB	27	120	15	2	0	3	16	13	18	0	0	.269/.350/.375	.296	.294	0.9	1B(36): 3.3	1.1
2014	OAK	MLB	28	250	30	12	1	4	22	38	41	1	0	.241/.361/.359	.275	.280	-0.4	1B 3, 3B -0	0.9

Barton's misfit skill set muddles his utility. Over the past seven years, he has logged more than 2,000 plate appearances with frequent trips up and down Interstate 80, though recently he's spent the bulk of his time in Triple-A. He has maintained an exceptional walk rate and strong defense throughout his professional tenure, but his power has not developed to the level expected of a first baseman. Barton took a more aggressive approach into his late-season call-up last season, resulting in marginal benefits, and the 28-year-old's big-league future likely hinges on his ability to morph his game into something more befitting his position on the diamond.

Alberto Callaspo　3B

Born: 4/19/1983 Age: 31
Bats: B Throws: R Height: 5' 9"
Weight: 225 Breakout: 0%
Improve: 32% Collapse: 5%
Attrition: 12% MLB: 97%

Comparables:
Edgardo Alfonzo, Bill Madlock, George Kell

YEAR	TEAM	LVL	AGE	PA	R	2B	3B	HR	RBI	BB	SO	SB	CS	AVG/OBP/SLG	TAv	BABIP	BRR	FRAA	WARP
2011	ANA	MLB	28	536	54	23	0	6	46	58	48	8	1	.288/.366/.375	.269	.310	-1	3B(129): 14.1	3.8
2012	ANA	MLB	29	520	55	20	0	10	53	56	59	4	3	.252/.331/.361	.266	.268	1.8	3B(131): 3.2	2.8
2013	ANA	MLB	30	336	32	13	0	5	36	34	22	0	2	.252/.324/.347	.253	.254	-1.9	3B(84): 0.3	0.5
2013	OAK	MLB	30	180	20	7	0	5	22	19	25	0	0	.270/.350/.409	.286	.292	1.2	2B(32): -3.7, 3B(9): 0.1	0.6
2014	OAK	MLB	31	487	47	22	1	7	48	45	47	3	2	.261/.328/.367	.266	.280	-0.8	3B 3, 2B -1	1.7

Callaspo was the American League's toughest man to strike out last season, whiffing in just 9 percent of his plate appearances. Acquired by the A's at the trade deadline in exchange for former first-rounder Grant Green, the switch-hitting Callaspo was a great fit for an Oakland club that values versatility in the lineup. Two-thirds of his plate appearances came from the left side, and while his on-base percentage was identical from either side of the plate, he slugged 91 points higher when batting right-handed. Primarily a fastball hitter, Callaspo hit nine of his 10 home runs on heat.

Yoenis Cespedes　LF

Born: 10/18/1985 Age: 28
Bats: R Throws: R Height: 5' 10"
Weight: 210 Breakout: 1%
Improve: 54% Collapse: 1%
Attrition: 3% MLB: 98%

Comparables:
Josh Willingham, Matt Holliday, Wes Covington

YEAR	TEAM	LVL	AGE	PA	R	2B	3B	HR	RBI	BB	SO	SB	CS	AVG/OBP/SLG	TAv	BABIP	BRR	FRAA	WARP
2011	GRA	CNS	25	415	89	17	1	33	99	49	40	11	3	.333/.424/.667	.362	.299	—	—	—
2012	OAK	MLB	26	540	70	25	5	23	82	43	102	16	4	.292/.356/.505	.319	.326	0	LF(56): -1.4, CF(48): -0.8	4.7
2013	OAK	MLB	27	574	74	21	4	26	80	37	137	7	7	.240/.294/.442	.279	.274	-0.1	LF(94): -0.1, CF(18): -0.7	2.2
2014	OAK	MLB	28	535	68	22	3	22	73	39	115	11	5	.262/.323/.456	.288	.300	0.1	LF -2, CF -0	2.5

The concept of a sophomore slump is predicated on the idea that teams will learn to exploit a batter's weaknesses after a season's worth of exposure. The onus is then on the player to make adjustments in response to a variant approach. Cespedes was an exceptional test case given the lack of minor-league experience from which to draw information. His most glaring weakness from 2012 was right-handed curveballs, although he was adept at hitting the hammer when ahead in the count. Opposing right-handers adjusted last season by saving their benders until the count was in their favor, helping to fuel a platoon split that was 200 points of OPS lower versus same-side pitchers (after Cespedes posted neutral splits in 2012). His strikeouts went up, his walks went down, his batted-ball profile changed in ways that likely affected his BABIP negatively and his slash line suffered the consequences. It is worth noting the possibility that some part of the 52-point BABIP decline was simply random variance, though it's an untestable point—if Cespedes bounces back in 2014, was it regression or did he change his approach?

Coco Crisp — CF

Born: 11/1/1979 Age: 34
Bats: B Throws: R Height: 5' 10''
Weight: 185 Breakout: 1%
Improve: 22% Collapse: 14%
Attrition: 19% MLB: 93%

Comparables:
Frank Catalanotto, Tommy Holmes, Shannon Stewart

YEAR	TEAM	LVL	AGE	PA	R	2B	3B	HR	RBI	BB	SO	SB	CS	AVG/OBP/SLG	TAv	BABIP	BRR	FRAA	WARP
2011	OAK	MLB	31	583	69	27	5	8	54	41	65	49	9	.264/.314/.379	.261	.284	4.3	CF(133): 6.9	2.8
2012	OAK	MLB	32	508	68	25	7	11	46	45	64	39	4	.259/.325/.418	.271	.280	3.1	CF(97): 2.0, LF(16): -0.8	2.3
2013	OAK	MLB	33	584	93	22	3	22	66	61	65	21	5	.261/.335/.444	.295	.258	4.1	CF(110): 5.3	4.3
2014	OAK	MLB	34	534	73	23	5	11	47	48	70	33	6	.255/.321/.392	.268	.270	4.6	CF 4, LF -0	2.8

Crisp is a force of nature. The leadoff hitter is a spark plug for the offense and a magnet for fans. Whether he's rocking an Afro, leading the Bernie lean or managing the pie cart in a post-game victory celebration, Coco stirs the milk in Oakland's cereal. He was electric to kick off the 2013 season, including a torrid stretch in which he hit four homers and four doubles in four games. His bat went into hibernation over the summer, but Crisp woke up in late August with another power surge that would make the Bash Brothers proud, hitting eight homers in a stretch of 14 games and padding his best slugging percentage since he was 25. He has single-handedly inspired more themed T-shirts than any A's player since Rickey Henderson; picking up his $7.5 million option for 2014 was no decision at all.

Josh Donaldson — 3B

Born: 12/8/1985 Age: 28
Bats: R Throws: R Height: 6' 0''
Weight: 220 Breakout: 2%
Improve: 43% Collapse: 8%
Attrition: 17% MLB: 89%

Comparables:
Scott Sizemore, Chase Headley, Seth Smith

YEAR	TEAM	LVL	AGE	PA	R	2B	3B	HR	RBI	BB	SO	SB	CS	AVG/OBP/SLG	TAv	BABIP	BRR	FRAA	WARP
2011	SAC	AAA	25	503	79	28	0	17	70	51	100	13	4	.261/.344/.439	.287	.301	0.2	C(28): -0.2, 3B(10): 1.2	1.8
2012	SAC	AAA	26	234	38	12	2	13	45	23	34	5	2	.335/.402/.598	.342	.350	-0.2	3B(26): -1.8, C(22): -0.0	2.8
2012	OAK	MLB	26	294	34	16	0	9	33	14	61	4	1	.241/.289/.398	.257	.278	0.5	3B(71): 5.5, C(3): -0.0	1.7
2013	OAK	MLB	27	668	89	37	3	24	93	76	110	5	2	.301/.384/.499	.326	.333	-2.9	3B(155): 1.2, SS(1): 0.0	6.2
2014	OAK	MLB	28	581	70	28	1	21	76	54	114	7	2	.258/.332/.440	.288	.290	-0.4	3B 2, C 0	3.4

The hot bat Donaldson swung in second half of the 2012 season carried over and the converted catcher experienced an across-the-board breakout that placed him among the American League leaders in WARP, on-base percentage, slugging percentage and walks. Pitchers quickly learned their lesson when they tried to beat him with heat early in the count, as Donaldson's quick bat punished fastballs on the inner half, resulting in a heavier diet of breaking pitches as the season progressed. Donaldson inflicted most of his damage with runners on base, posting a slash line of .364/.454/.572 when opposing pitchers were forced into the stretch, a trait that further increased the value of Oakland's 2013 team MVP. So too does the Beane-tickling fact that he won't make more than the league minimum until he's nearly 30.

Nathan Freiman — 1B

Born: 12/31/1986 Age: 27
Bats: R Throws: R Height: 6' 8''
Weight: 250 Breakout: 4%
Improve: 24% Collapse: 8%
Attrition: 19% MLB: 43%

Comparables:
Steve Pearce, Nick Evans, Jeff Clement

YEAR	TEAM	LVL	AGE	PA	R	2B	3B	HR	RBI	BB	SO	SB	CS	AVG/OBP/SLG	TAv	BABIP	BRR	FRAA	WARP
2011	LEL	A+	24	618	81	35	4	22	111	50	93	6	1	.288/.354/.487	.259	.308	-1.5	1B(29): 3.1	0.2
2012	SAN	AA	25	581	80	31	1	24	105	49	95	0	2	.298/.370/.502	.315	.324	-7.9	1B(129): -4.3	2.7
2013	OAK	MLB	26	208	10	8	1	4	24	14	31	0	0	.274/.327/.389	.262	.306	-2.2	1B(59): 0.9	0.1
2014	OAK	MLB	27	250	27	11	1	8	31	17	46	1	0	.254/.311/.412	.269	.280	-0.4	1B 0	0.5

Freiman made the jump from Double-A (as a Rule 5 pick of the Astros, later claimed by the A's at the end of spring) and spent the entirety of his rookie season at the major-league level serving as the right-handed complement to Brandon Moss at first base. Freiman crushed southpaws in the minors and posted a solid .304/.352/.453 line versus major-league lefties last season, but he hit like a farsighted pitcher when he was on the wrong side of the platoon, slashing .167/.239/.167, though Bob Melvin wisely limited Freiman to just 46 such plate appearances. Standing 6-foot-8, Freiman is one of the game's all-time tallest position players, and he had to duck his way through the outstretched arms of his teammates as he barged through the A's "home run tunnel" after each of his four dingers.

Craig Gentry — CF

Born: 11/29/1983 Age: 30
Bats: R Throws: R Height: 6' 2''
Weight: 190 Breakout: 3%
Improve: 27% Collapse: 8%
Attrition: 18% MLB: 62%

Comparables:
Chris Duffy, Chris Denorfia, Jason Tyner

YEAR	TEAM	LVL	AGE	PA	R	2B	3B	HR	RBI	BB	SO	SB	CS	AVG/OBP/SLG	TAv	BABIP	BRR	FRAA	WARP
2011	ROU	AAA	27	123	21	5	1	1	10	11	17	5	1	.245/.325/.336	.231	.283	0.2	LF(3): 0.1, CF(1): -0.0	0.0
2011	TEX	MLB	27	153	26	5	1	1	13	10	27	18	0	.271/.347/.346	.239	.330	2.5	CF(55): 4.7, RF(7): -0.3	0.9
2012	TEX	MLB	28	269	31	12	3	1	26	14	41	13	7	.304/.367/.392	.275	.364	-1.2	CF(114): 5.5, RF(3): 0.0	1.9
2013	TEX	MLB	29	287	39	12	4	2	22	29	46	24	3	.280/.373/.386	.293	.337	4.6	CF(71): 5.9, LF(34): 0.0	3.2
2014	OAK	MLB	30	268	30	10	2	2	20	20	48	16	3	.254/.327/.335	.256	.300	1.9	CF 3, LF 0	1.2

A fan favorite, Craig Gentry was christened "Kittenface" (just check out a picture of him), and ended up displacing former first-round pick Julio Borbon as the team's "speed and defense" outfielder since 2011. Most defensive metrics love Gentry's glove in both left and center, and his slash line suggests he would be a quality starting center fielder, but concerns about his durability and ability to handle right-handers—particularly those that throw hard—have relegated him to a bench role. Billy Beane, always keen to an underused asset, acquired him in a December trade, and he'll fit in nicely with Oakland's platoon fetish.

Chris Gimenez   C

Born: 12/27/1982 Age: 31
Bats: R Throws: R Height: 6' 2"
Weight: 220 Breakout: 0%
Improve: 12% Collapse: 15%
Attrition: 31% MLB: 45%

Comparables:
Luke Carlin, Steve Holm, Guillermo Rodriguez

YEAR	TEAM	LVL	AGE	PA	R	2B	3B	HR	RBI	BB	SO	SB	CS	AVG/OBP/SLG	TAv	BABIP	BRR	FRAA	WARP
2011	TAC	AAA	28	56	8	1	0	1	4	7	13	0	1	.265/.357/.347	.212	.343	-0.5	C(8): 0.1, 1B(2): 0.0	-0.2
2011	SEA	MLB	28	70	6	1	0	1	6	10	13	0	1	.203/.314/.271	.234	.239	0.3	C(20): -0.4, LF(3): -0.1	0.1
2012	DUR	AAA	29	301	39	15	0	10	49	33	57	0	3	.310/.389/.483	.287	.359	0.6	C(47): -0.1, RF(11): 0.6	2.2
2012	TBA	MLB	29	109	10	4	0	1	9	8	24	0	0	.260/.315/.330	.226	.333	-1.4	C(39): 0.2, 3B(1): -0.0	0.0
2013	DUR	AAA	30	375	43	16	0	3	22	57	63	1	1	.224/.350/.305	.237	.270	-1.6	C(56): 1.3, RF(19): 0.2	0.1
2013	TBA	MLB	30	4	0	1	0	0	0	1	1	0	0	.333/.500/.667	.334	.500	-0.8	3B(1): -0.0, 1B(1): -0.0	0.0
2014	OAK	MLB	31	250	23	9	0	4	24	27	57	0	0	.220/.307/.326	.242	.270	-0.6	C 0, RF -0	0.4

An injured ligament sheath in his hand sent him to the disabled list for a month, weakened his swing when he returned and ruined his offensive production, but the affable, steady Gimenez handled the Rays' young Triple-A pitching prospects very well. His teammates in Durham called him "coach," hinting at his second career to come. Gimenez was healthy enough by September 1st to earn an expanded-roster call-up as Tampa Bay's third backstop. He's just what you want in a Triple-A catcher on the 40-man, and his plate discipline is decent enough to keep from embarrassing you if you have to give him more than a few big-league at-bats. You can also stick him at first base, third base and, in a pinch, corner outfield.

John Jaso   C

Born: 9/19/1983 Age: 30
Bats: L Throws: R Height: 6' 2"
Weight: 205 Breakout: 1%
Improve: 41% Collapse: 4%
Attrition: 1% MLB: 97%

Comparables:
Russell Martin, Bill Freehan, Yadier Molina

YEAR	TEAM	LVL	AGE	PA	R	2B	3B	HR	RBI	BB	SO	SB	CS	AVG/OBP/SLG	TAv	BABIP	BRR	FRAA	WARP
2011	DUR	AAA	27	22	2	2	0	0	4	2	3	0	0	.300/.364/.400	.280	.353	0	C(2): -0.0	0.0
2011	TBA	MLB	27	273	26	15	1	5	27	25	36	1	2	.224/.298/.354	.229	.244	0.7	C(82): -0.9	0.0
2012	SEA	MLB	28	361	41	19	2	10	50	56	51	5	0	.276/.394/.456	.337	.298	0.1	C(43): -0.4	3.7
2013	OAK	MLB	29	249	31	12	0	3	21	38	45	2	1	.271/.387/.372	.291	.331	-0.7	C(48): -0.0, 1B(1): -0.0	1.4
2014	OAK	MLB	30	256	29	12	1	4	25	34	35	2	1	.256/.359/.379	.282	.290	-0.2	C -0	1.5

In yet another example of Bob Melvin's strategic use of platoon pairings, Jaso formed the left-handed portion of the A's catching tandem for the first half of the season (and became the lefty DH when a Coco Crisp injury forced defensive shuffling in May). Just 29 of Jaso's plate appearances came versus left-handed pitching, and though his offense regressed from his 2012 breakout, the net result was an OBP that ranked second in baseball among catchers with at least 200 plate appearances (behind Joe Mauer). Jaso's season was cut short by a concussion that resulted from taking foul tips off his mask in consecutive games, causing vertigo and tinnitus that lasted for weeks. Concussions are the most unpredictable of injuries, and it is anyone's guess whether there will be any long-term side effects that carry over into this season. Jaso's defense does not, shall we say, inspire plaudits. Assuming health, 2014 may see him semipermanently installed at DH.

Jed Lowrie   SS

Born: 4/17/1984 Age: 30
Bats: B Throws: R Height: 6' 0"
Weight: 190 Breakout: 3%
Improve: 43% Collapse: 3%
Attrition: 6% MLB: 92%

Comparables:
Stephen Drew, Alan Trammell, John Valentin

YEAR	TEAM	LVL	AGE	PA	R	2B	3B	HR	RBI	BB	SO	SB	CS	AVG/OBP/SLG	TAv	BABIP	BRR	FRAA	WARP
2011	BOS	MLB	27	341	40	14	4	6	36	23	60	1	1	.252/.303/.382	.247	.289	1.9	SS(49): -1.4, 3B(33): 2.9	0.9
2012	HOU	MLB	28	387	43	18	0	16	42	43	65	2	0	.244/.331/.438	.284	.257	0.6	SS(93): 5.0	3.3
2013	OAK	MLB	29	662	80	45	2	15	75	50	91	1	0	.290/.344/.446	.291	.319	-0.1	SS(119): -6.7, 2B(24): -3.3	3.7
2014	OAK	MLB	30	568	59	29	2	14	66	50	91	2	1	.254/.323/.403	.272	.280	-0.8	SS -4, 2B -1	2.5

The oft-injured Lowrie logged more playing time than anyone predicted, besting his previous high by 57 games and marking his first season-long avoidance of the disabled list since 2008. His defense at shortstop was suspect, but Lowrie more than made up for those deficiencies with his handiwork at the plate, registering more VORP with his bat than any other shortstop in the American League. Lowrie's line-drive rate was excellent (though exactly how high and where it ranked depends on your data source), and his 45 doubles were the second-best total in the circuit. His bat will play anywhere on the infield, and his positional flexibility plays right into the hands of manager Bob Melvin and his penchant for mixing and matching his roster on a daily basis.

Billy McKinney · CF
Born: 8/23/1994 Age: 19
Bats: L Throws: L Height: 6' 1"
Weight: 195 Breakout: 0%
Improve: 0% Collapse: 0%
Attrition: 0% MLB: 0%

Comparables:
Che-Hsuan Lin, Joe Benson, Abraham Almonte

YEAR	TEAM	LVL	AGE	PA	R	2B	3B	HR	RBI	BB	SO	SB	CS	AVG/OBP/SLG	TAv	BABIP	BRR	FRAA	WARP
2013	VER	A-	18	37	5	2	1	1	6	3	4	1	1	.353/.405/.559	.371	.379	-0.5	CF(9): 0.6	0.6
2014	OAK	MLB	19	250	21	8	1	2	17	11	64	1	0	.200/.239/.271	.197	.260	-0.3	CF -1	-1.1

With the 24th-overall pick in the 2013 draft, the A's continued their recent infatuation with high school position players—a little late, considering they nearly talked themselves into picking Mike Trout once upon a time. McKinney's selection followed a 2012 draft that saw Oakland pop high school bats with their first three selections. McKinney was one of the top prep hitters in the nation, with a compact swing from the left side that produces excellent bat speed. Nobody doubts the hit tool—his bat-to-ball skills were evident during his pro debut—but questions remain regarding McKinney's power ceiling. His other tools grade out as merely average; the stick will be the weapon that carves his career path as he transitions to an outfield corner.

Brandon Moss · 1B
Born: 9/16/1983 Age: 30
Bats: L Throws: R Height: 6' 0"
Weight: 210 Breakout: 0%
Improve: 20% Collapse: 8%
Attrition: 18% MLB: 79%

Comparables:
Michael Morse, Josh Phelps, Ryan Ludwick

YEAR	TEAM	LVL	AGE	PA	R	2B	3B	HR	RBI	BB	SO	SB	CS	AVG/OBP/SLG	TAv	BABIP	BRR	FRAA	WARP
2011	LEH	AAA	27	506	66	31	1	23	80	62	127	4	6	.275/.368/.509	.269	.334	1.7	LF(25): -1.0, RF(22): -0.3	1.0
2011	PHI	MLB	27	6	0	0	0	0	0	0	2	0	0	.000/.000/.000	.060	.000	0	RF(1): 0.1	-0.2
2012	SAC	AAA	28	224	32	11	1	15	33	22	40	4	0	.286/.371/.582	.322	.289	-0.6	LF(14): -0.2, 1B(13): -0.6	1.9
2012	OAK	MLB	28	296	48	18	0	21	52	26	90	1	1	.291/.358/.596	.334	.359	-0.3	1B(55): -3.4, RF(13): 0.1	2.3
2013	OAK	MLB	29	505	73	23	3	30	87	50	140	4	2	.256/.337/.522	.328	.301	-1.9	1B(111): -5.4, RF(27): 0.3	3.5
2014	OAK	MLB	30	460	55	20	2	19	62	41	118	4	3	.238/.312/.435	.276	.280	-0.7	1B -5, RF -1	0.8

Moss played in 145 games and provided the immense power that distinguished his 2012 season (as well as his minor-league career), fueling the perception that he had grown into a full-time player. But only 115 of those games were starts and 83 percent of his plate appearances came against right-handed pitchers, as Bob Melvin expertly leveraged Moss' skills to reap the most possible value from his potent bat. Moss led the A's in the power categories, including the first 30-homer season of his career, and he improved his rates of both walks and strikeouts. Perhaps no player better represents the A's ability to spin someone else's straw into Green and Gold, as Moss cost a mere $1.6 million in 2013 after putting up a .682 major-league OPS through 2011.

Hiroyuki Nakajima · 3B
Born: 7/31/1982 Age: 31
Bats: R Throws: R Height: 5' 11"
Weight: 200 Breakout: 2%
Improve: 6% Collapse: 5%
Attrition: 10% MLB: 12%

Comparables:
Juan Melo, Brian Barden, Ramon Nivar

YEAR	TEAM	LVL	AGE	PA	R	2B	3B	HR	RBI	BB	SO	SB	CS	AVG/OBP/SLG	TAv	BABIP	BRR	FRAA	WARP
2011	SEI	NPB	28	633	82	27	1	16	100	44	93	21	2	.297/.354/.433	.275	.328	—	—	—
2012	SEI	NPB	29	567	69	29	1	13	74	52	76	7	6	.311/.382/.451	.294	.343	—	—	—
2013	SAC	AAA	30	384	40	17	0	4	34	23	83	3	1	.283/.331/.367	.266	.351	-1.5	3B(37): -2.2, SS(28): -0.6	0.7
2014	OAK	MLB	31	250	21	10	0	3	20	12	60	0	0	.232/.276/.311	.228	.300	-0.5	3B -2, SS -0	-0.4

Prior to last season, the Athletics paid Nakajima $6.5 million to help solve their infield conundrum, but his big-league career never got off the ground. He had a poor spring that punched a ticket to Sacramento, followed by a strained hamstring that kept him out of action until late May. The power that was so instrumental to Nakajima's value in the other pacific coast league failed to appear in this Pacific Coast League, further dampening the odds of his sticking at the highest level. He spent significant time at second and third base in addition to shortstop while with the River Cats, in the hopes that positional flexibility might allow the A's to recoup some value on their investment before his contract expires at the end of 2014.

Derek Norris · C
Born: 2/14/1989 Age: 25
Bats: R Throws: R Height: 6' 0"
Weight: 210 Breakout: 1%
Improve: 45% Collapse: 2%
Attrition: 17% MLB: 88%

Comparables:
Chris Iannetta, Mike Napoli, Matt Wieters

YEAR	TEAM	LVL	AGE	PA	R	2B	3B	HR	RBI	BB	SO	SB	CS	AVG/OBP/SLG	TAv	BABIP	BRR	FRAA	WARP
2011	HAR	AA	22	423	75	17	1	20	46	77	117	13	4	.210/.367/.446	.314	.251	2	C(82): 0.3	4.5
2012	SAC	AAA	23	246	39	14	2	9	38	21	41	5	1	.271/.329/.477	.278	.287	-0.6	C(58): -0.4	1.6
2012	OAK	MLB	23	232	19	8	1	7	34	21	66	5	1	.201/.276/.349	.231	.255	-0.3	C(58): 0.0	0.1
2013	OAK	MLB	24	308	41	16	0	9	30	37	71	5	0	.246/.345/.409	.289	.301	0.3	C(91): 0.3, 1B(1): 0.0	2.4
2014	OAK	MLB	25	306	36	12	1	10	37	34	77	5	1	.226/.318/.394	.270	.270	0.2	C 0, 1B 0	1.8

Norris—a catcher who, in the right situation, can hit like a cornerman—presents an extreme example of roster utility. After showing no platoon split at all in 2012, Norris had a 2013 OPS split of nearly 550 points—.149/.261/.184 against righties but .320/.410/.580 with the platoon advantage—which helps explain why 56 percent of his plate appearances came versus southpaws. (Lefties accounted for 40 percent of the typical right-handed batter's opponents.) The number might have been higher but for John Jaso's concussion issues and the fact that even a healthy Jaso is a poor defensive catcher. The physical demands at the catcher position encourage the use of job-sharing arrangements, especially for an American League club with a roster full of flexible fielders, so expect the A's to keep finding a round hole for this particular peg.

Renato Nunez 3B

Born: 4/4/1994 Age: 20
Bats: R Throws: R Height: 6' 1"
Weight: 185 Breakout: 0%
Improve: 0% Collapse: 0%
Attrition: 0% MLB: 0%

Comparables:
Brandon Laird, Alex Liddi, Neftali Soto

YEAR	TEAM	LVL	AGE	PA	R	2B	3B	HR	RBI	BB	SO	SB	CS	AVG/OBP/SLG	TAv	BABIP	BRR	FRAA	WARP
2013	BLT	A	19	546	69	27	0	19	85	28	136	2	2	.258/.301/.423	.248	.315	-1.6	3B(114): 3.9	1.2
2014	OAK	MLB	20	250	20	9	0	6	26	7	76	0	0	.205/.231/.326	.208	.270	-0.5	3B 1	-0.6

Nunez has plus power potential, but his ability to tap into that power depends on making adjustments to his approach at the plate. An aggressive hitter, Nunez plays into a pitcher's strengths by falling behind early in the count, limiting his opportunities to sit dead-red and wait for his pitch. A third baseman with pop can be a tremendous asset, as the A's experienced last season with Donaldson manning the hot corner, but the whispers are getting louder that Nunez will be forced to move across the diamond to first base, where there will be more pressure on his bat to carry value.

Matthew Olson 1B

Born: 3/29/1994 Age: 20
Bats: L Throws: R Height: 6' 4"
Weight: 236 Breakout: 2%
Improve: 2% Collapse: 0%
Attrition: 3% MLB: 3%

Comparables:
Chris Marrero, Chris Carter, Logan Morrison

YEAR	TEAM	LVL	AGE	PA	R	2B	3B	HR	RBI	BB	SO	SB	CS	AVG/OBP/SLG	TAv	BABIP	BRR	FRAA	WARP
2013	BLT	A	19	558	69	32	0	23	93	72	148	4	3	.225/.326/.435	.266	.272	0.1	1B(127): 6.5	1.9
2014	OAK	MLB	20	250	23	9	0	8	28	20	80	0	0	.191/.258/.339	.224	.250	-0.5	1B 2	-0.4

Olson endured an up-and-down season in which he tinkered with his swing in an effort to channel more of his raw power. The result was an approach full of holes and a 27 percent strikeout rate. Though he earned plenty of walks by working deep counts, Olson struggled to consistently make hard contact. The power potential is substantial, and he did hit 10 home runs over the last month of the season to save his overall batting line, but his athleticism has received poor reviews and he has already shown vulnerability against same-side pitchers, so he will need to make continued adjustments in order to advance.

Nick Punto 2B

Born: 11/8/1977 Age: 36
Bats: B Throws: R Height: 5' 9"
Weight: 195 Breakout: 0%
Improve: 23% Collapse: 10%
Attrition: 25% MLB: 75%

Comparables:
Craig Counsell, Phil Rizzuto, John Valentin

YEAR	TEAM	LVL	AGE	PA	R	2B	3B	HR	RBI	BB	SO	SB	CS	AVG/OBP/SLG	TAv	BABIP	BRR	FRAA	WARP
2011	SFD	AA	33	26	3	1	0	0	2	2	3	1	0	.333/.385/.375	.279	.381	0		0.0
2011	SLN	MLB	33	166	21	8	4	1	20	25	21	1	1	.278/.388/.421	.294	.319	1.8	2B(45): 2.2, SS(8): -0.3	1.7
2012	LAN	MLB	34	43	6	1	0	0	0	6	9	1	0	.286/.390/.314	.274	.385	0.6	2B(11): 0.8, 3B(5): -0.0	0.4
2012	BOS	MLB	34	148	14	6	0	1	10	19	33	5	0	.200/.301/.272	.206	.258	-0.2	3B(26): 2.0, 2B(15): -0.8	-0.2
2013	LAN	MLB	35	335	34	15	0	2	21	33	67	3	3	.255/.328/.327	.236	.322	-0.5	SS(49): -1.2, 3B(35): 0.8	0.0
2014	OAK	MLB	36	286	27	11	1	1	19	33	54	5	2	.225/.317/.287	.233	.270	0	2B -1, SS -1	0.3

Punto is a plug-n-play option whose switch-hitting ability and positional flexibility on the infield provide a manager with multiple options when filling out the lineup card. Such utility comes in handy when a team suffers critical injuries to the starting squad, as was the case with the Dodgers last year, resulting in Punto collecting his most playing time since the 2009 season. He filled in most often on days when Hanley Ramirez was unavailable; the substitution cost the lineup approximately 400 points of OPS, but the 36-year-old Punto earned some extra credit for his chemistry bonds in the clubhouse.

Josh Reddick RF

Born: 2/19/1987 Age: 27
Bats: L Throws: R Height: 6' 2"
Weight: 180 Breakout: 1%
Improve: 46% Collapse: 13%
Attrition: 19% MLB: 93%

Comparables:
Jorge Piedra, Shin-Soo Choo, David Murphy

YEAR	TEAM	LVL	AGE	PA	R	2B	3B	HR	RBI	BB	SO	SB	CS	AVG/OBP/SLG	TAv	BABIP	BRR	FRAA	WARP
2011	PAW	AAA	24	231	37	9	1	14	36	33	39	4	1	.230/.333/.508	.285	.207	-0.6	CF(26): -3.2, RF(15): 1.0	0.8
2011	BOS	MLB	24	278	41	18	3	7	28	19	50	1	2	.280/.327/.457	.281	.318	0.6	RF(56): 4.9, LF(21): 1.4	1.9
2012	OAK	MLB	25	673	85	29	5	32	85	55	151	11	1	.242/.305/.463	.275	.269	1.9	RF(136): 2.4, CF(14): 0.4	3.0
2013	OAK	MLB	26	441	54	19	2	12	56	46	86	9	2	.226/.307/.379	.263	.255	2.8	RF(113): 4.2	1.9
2014	OAK	MLB	27	463	52	21	3	15	57	37	94	7	2	.238/.300/.412	.266	.270	0.2	RF 4, CF -0	1.6

Reddick showed up in spring training looking like he had spent the winter holed up in a log cabin in Walla Walla, sporting a beard that would make Bigfoot jealous. The ferocious facial fur had tons of entertainment value, but it did him no favors at the plate. PECOTA predicted some regression following a three-year run of improved performance, but Reddick skated past the expected decline and stumbled right into the performance gutter.

His season was hampered by recurring issues with his right wrist, which was sprained in April, sent him to the disabled list in May, flared up again in August, and required another DL stint in September. The wrist injury compromised Reddick's performance, particularly denting his ability to turn on fastballs, though his pie-throwing skills remained intact. On the bright side, the former inveterate hacker continued his four-year run of increased pitches per plate appearance. A healthy Reddick might just rediscover his upward trajectory of performance in 2014 and, if nothing else, he's a lock to laser three to five of the season's most entertaining throws from right field.

Daniel Robertson SS

Born: **3/22/1994** Age: **20**
Bats: **R** Throws: **R** Height: **6' 0"**
Weight: **190** Breakout: **0%**
Improve: **4%** Collapse: **0%**
Attrition: **0%** MLB: **4%**

Comparables:
Yamaico Navarro, Lonnie Chisenhall, Charlie Culberson

YEAR	TEAM	LVL	AGE	PA	R	2B	3B	HR	RBI	BB	SO	SB	CS	AVG/OBP/SLG	TAv	BABIP	BRR	FRAA	WARP
2012	VER	A-	18	104	9	2	0	1	8	7	31	1	1	.181/.238/.234	.185	.258	0.4	SS(18): 1.5, 3B(9): -0.5	-0.3
2013	BLT	A	19	451	59	21	1	9	46	41	79	1	7	.277/.353/.401	.272	.324	-0.6	SS(99): -8.9	1.6
2014	OAK	MLB	20	250	23	9	0	4	20	15	62	0	0	.212/.263/.305	.218	.270	-0.5	SS -3, 3B 0	-0.4

The A's supplemental pick in their prep-driven draft of 2012, Robertson joined his draftmates in the Beloit infield last season. He anchored shortstop, though many evaluators see him sliding to third base in the long term. Robertson has the strong arm to play at either spot on the left side of the diamond. The bat is also an asset, though his power development will be a critical element of his projection. His impending move to the California League should produce better raw numbers, but also the tricky task of teasing out environment from development. Robertson's future gets murky if his glove demands a shift to the hot corner and his power fails to evolve, leaving him in the classic tweener role, but he's a good bet to provide some type of value at the highest level.

Addison Russell SS

Born: **1/23/1994** Age: **20**
Bats: **R** Throws: **R** Height: **6' 0"**
Weight: **195** Breakout: **6%**
Improve: **13%** Collapse: **0%**
Attrition: **7%** MLB: **15%**

Comparables:
Jeff Bianchi, Xander Bogaerts, Nick Franklin

YEAR	TEAM	LVL	AGE	PA	R	2B	3B	HR	RBI	BB	SO	SB	CS	AVG/OBP/SLG	TAv	BABIP	BRR	FRAA	WARP
2012	BUR	A	18	66	8	4	2	0	9	5	12	5	1	.310/.369/.448	.299	.383	1.5	SS(15): -0.2	0.9
2012	VER	A-	18	57	9	2	2	1	7	4	13	2	0	.340/.386/.509	.347	.436	0.2	SS(12): 0.5	0.8
2013	STO	A+	19	504	85	29	10	17	60	61	116	21	3	.275/.377/.508	.321	.338	1	SS(105): -4.6	5.3
2014	OAK	MLB	20	250	28	10	2	5	22	20	67	3	1	.225/.293/.348	.246	.290	0.4	SS -3	0.4

Russell is a beast who is moving quickly in pursuit of the Oakland lineup. The A's challenged him with an aggressive assignment to High-A as a 19-year-old, and though Russell sputtered out of the gate, he quickly made adjustments at the plate and was raking the California League in time for summer (.319/.421/.578 from June 1st on). He made tremendous strides on defense, quieting the notion that he would not be able to stick at shortstop, and his rapid development both in the field and at the plate has accelerated his timetable. The A's rewarded Russell with a three-day vacation in Sacramento at the end of the season before sending him off for more work in the Arizona Fall League, and though he'll likely detour through Double-A before he returns to the Golden State, he could arrive in Oakland in late 2014.

Eric Sogard 2B

Born: **5/22/1986** Age: **28**
Bats: **L** Throws: **R** Height: **5' 10"**
Weight: **190** Breakout: **4%**
Improve: **31%** Collapse: **10%**
Attrition: **19%** MLB: **69%**

Comparables:
Justin Turner, Matt Tolbert, Kevin Frandsen

YEAR	TEAM	LVL	AGE	PA	R	2B	3B	HR	RBI	BB	SO	SB	CS	AVG/OBP/SLG	TAv	BABIP	BRR	FRAA	WARP
2011	SAC	AAA	25	366	55	16	2	5	37	40	34	13	3	.298/.381/.410	.302	.319	-0.2	SS(22): 0.7	1.1
2011	OAK	MLB	25	74	7	3	0	2	4	4	13	0	0	.200/.243/.329	.196	.218	-0.9	SS(14): 0.0, 3B(10): -0.2	-0.3
2012	SAC	AAA	26	180	29	5	2	5	22	23	17	11	3	.331/.417/.484	.321	.348	0.6	2B(30): 6.1, SS(5): 0.1	2.5
2012	OAK	MLB	26	108	8	3	1	2	7	5	17	2	0	.167/.206/.275	.185	.181	0.2	SS(15): 1.1, 3B(14): 0.2	-0.2
2013	OAK	MLB	27	410	45	24	3	2	35	27	51	10	5	.266/.322/.364	.266	.301	-1.5	2B(113): 0.4, SS(15): 0.6	1.3
2014	OAK	MLB	28	346	37	15	2	4	29	30	48	10	4	.256/.324/.355	.260	.290	0.3	2B 1, SS 1	1.5

The bespectacled infielder was accepted into the fraternity of the A's clubhouse, as teammates and fans alike embraced the "Nerd Power" meme during the 2013 season. Sogard fits the mold of the modern Oakland Athletics with his ability to slide around the diamond on defense, and his up-the-middle glove helps to cover for a lack of secondary skills at the plate. His minor-league track record suggests that there could be more walks in Sogard's future, and though his theoretical prime is now, the window is open for the A's to reap value as he develops his game. A certain portion of our audience will be delighted to notice that Sogard is a dead ringer for Michael Shanks of *Stargate SG-1* fame.

Michael Taylor   RF

Born: 12/19/1985 Age: 28
Bats: R Throws: R Height: 6' 5"
Weight: 255 Breakout: 1%
Improve: 9% Collapse: 10%
Attrition: 19% MLB: 28%

Comparables:
Bronson Sardinha, Cole Gillespie, Joe Mather

YEAR	TEAM	LVL	AGE	PA	R	2B	3B	HR	RBI	BB	SO	SB	CS	AVG/OBP/SLG	TAv	BABIP	BRR	FRAA	WARP
2011	SAC	AAA	25	400	51	16	0	16	64	46	80	14	5	.272/.360/.456	.328	.310	1.8	LF(25): 0.7, RF(20): 2.3	2.3
2011	OAK	MLB	25	35	4	0	0	1	1	5	11	0	0	.200/.314/.300	.266	.278	0.1	RF(8): 0.6, LF(3): -0.1	0.1
2012	SAC	AAA	26	543	81	31	1	12	67	86	105	18	3	.287/.405/.441	.307	.349	3.6	RF(107): -8.4, LF(1): 0.0	3.1
2012	OAK	MLB	26	21	2	1	0	0	0	0	10	0	0	.143/.143/.190	.105	.273	0.4	RF(4): 0.3, LF(2): -0.0	-0.2
2013	SAC	AAA	27	481	54	25	1	18	85	50	88	5	2	.281/.360/.474	.301	.312	-0.2	RF(81): 6.5, LF(16): -1.0	3.3
2013	OAK	MLB	27	25	0	0	0	0	0	2	5	0	0	.043/.120/.043	.058	.056	0	RF(6): -0.3, LF(5): 0.2	-0.5
2014	OAK	MLB	28	250	28	10	0	7	29	26	56	4	1	.243/.325/.390	.270	.290	-0.1	RF -0, LF -0	0.7

There might not be a greater hard-luck story in the system than that of Taylor. Once a prized prospect who was part of the domino rally of trades involving Carlos Gonzalez, Matt Holliday and Brett Wallace, among others, Taylor has stalled in Triple-A for the last four years (and actually first reached that level all the way back in 2009). Taylor has lost himself like a bunny rabbit on 8 Mile in the few opportunities that he has been granted at the highest level, despite developing something approaching a multi-skill toolset in Sacramento. The now-28-year-old has completely lost his prospect status and has to hope for an opportunity to ride the bench in order to finally earn a consistent big-league paycheck.

Stephen Vogt   C

Born: 11/1/1984 Age: 29
Bats: L Throws: R Height: 6' 0"
Weight: 215 Breakout: 4%
Improve: 15% Collapse: 7%
Attrition: 24% MLB: 37%

Comparables:
Rene Rivera, Jose Morales, Chris Carter

YEAR	TEAM	LVL	AGE	PA	R	2B	3B	HR	RBI	BB	SO	SB	CS	AVG/OBP/SLG	TAv	BABIP	BRR	FRAA	WARP
2011	MNT	AA	26	427	52	21	6	13	85	30	51	4	2	.301/.344/.487	.309	.310	1.2	C(14): -0.1, LF(14): -0.5	1.4
2011	DUR	AAA	26	131	15	14	1	4	20	4	29	0	0	.290/.305/.516	.290	.340	-0.1	C(3): -0.0, RF(2): 0.0	0.3
2012	DUR	AAA	27	396	48	18	4	9	43	42	61	1	0	.272/.350/.424	.260	.306	-2.4	C(37): -0.5, LF(23): -1.5	0.7
2012	TBA	MLB	27	27	0	0	0	0	0	2	2	0	0	.000/.074/.000	.042	.000	0	C(7): -0.0, LF(2): 0.0	-0.5
2013	SAC	AAA	28	338	55	21	3	13	58	38	45	0	1	.324/.398/.547	.325	.344	-0.2	C(65): 0.2	4.3
2013	OAK	MLB	28	148	18	6	1	4	16	9	28	0	1	.252/.295/.400	.255	.286	-0.4	C(44): -0.5	0.5
2014	OAK	MLB	29	250	25	11	2	6	29	19	44	1	0	.248/.306/.395	.261	.280	-0.3	C -0, LF -0	0.9

Vogt was hitless in his 2012 cup of coffee with Tampa Bay, but he got off the schneid last season with a solo home run against the Cardinals on June 28th. It was his third game in an Oakland uniform after being called upon to cover for John Jaso, who was dealing with a hand injury. Vogt took over the A's lefty-hitting catcher job for good when Jaso went down with a concussion in late July. He earned the gig with a career-best line for the River Cats over the first three months of the season and personified many of Oakland's team strengths last season, from the strategic deployment of platoon bats (88 percent of his plate appearances came against right-handers) to the system's positional depth. He also flashed a 1.75 second pop time in October, exceptional for anybody, let alone a guy who caught full-time for the first time last year.

PITCHERS

Raul Alcantara

Born: 12/4/1992 Age: 21
Bats: R Throws: R Height: 6' 3" Weight: 180
Breakout: 69% Improve: 69% Collapse: 18%
Attrition: 31% MLB: 5%

Comparables:
Alex Burnett, Collin Balester, Trevor Bell

YEAR	TEAM	LVL	AGE	W	L	SV	G	GS	IP	H	HR	BB	SO	BB9	SO9	GB%	BABIP	WHIP	ERA	FIP	FRA	WARP
2011	LOW	A-	18	0	3	0	4	4	17^1	25	0	6	14	3.1	7.3	41%	.469	1.79	6.23	2.96	5.00	0.1
2012	BUR	A	19	6	11	0	27	17	102^2	119	12	38	57	3.3	5.0	53%	.327	1.53	5.08	5.07	6.59	-0.5
2013	BLT	A	20	7	1	0	13	13	77^1	84	3	7	58	0.8	6.8	47%	.324	1.18	2.44	2.77	3.79	1.7
2013	STO	A+	20	5	5	0	14	14	79	73	8	17	66	1.9	7.5	41%	.280	1.14	3.76	4.21	4.57	1.1
2014	OAK	MLB	21	4	5	1	28	13	118^2	139	15	47	49	3.6	3.7	45%	.300	1.57	5.39	5.53	5.86	-1.5

Alcantara made noticeable improvements in his second year in the A's organization. He rediscovered his control of the strike zone and his fastball command took a step forward. Alcantara spotted his low-to-mid-90s heater on both sides of the plate and, when at his best, kept the ball down in the zone. He fits the mold of A's pitching prospects, with plus balance and strong posture from first movement through release. The strategy supports a low arm slot, and with it comes a greater range of lateral variation on his pitches, which underscores the importance of a consistent release point. His changeup and slider earn average grades, and, as is true of many pitchers his age, Alcantara's future role will ultimately be determined by the development of his secondary pitches.

Grant Balfour
Born: 12/30/1977 Age: 36
Bats: R Throws: R Height: 6' 2" Weight: 200
Breakout: 32% Improve: 47% Collapse: 42%
Attrition: 11% MLB: 80%

Comparables:
Jason Isringhausen, Brian Fuentes, J.J. Putz

YEAR	TEAM	LVL	AGE	W	L	SV	G	GS	IP	H	HR	BB	SO	BB9	SO9	GB%	BABIP	WHIP	ERA	FIP	FRA	WARP
2011	OAK	MLB	33	5	2	2	62	0	62	44	8	20	59	2.9	8.6	39%	.232	1.03	2.47	3.80	4.31	0.3
2012	OAK	MLB	34	3	2	24	75	0	74²	41	4	28	72	3.4	8.7	36%	.201	0.92	2.53	2.98	3.88	0.7
2013	OAK	MLB	35	1	3	38	65	0	62²	48	7	27	72	3.9	10.3	40%	.263	1.20	2.59	3.52	4.07	0.4
2014	OAK	MLB	36	3	1	20	57	0	56¹	45	5	22	56	3.5	9.0	38%	.274	1.19	2.97	3.69	3.23	0.9

Balfour converted his first 26 save opportunities and carried a sub-2.00 ERA into late August before a four-run blow-up at the hands of Torii Hunter and the Tigers bloated his ERA by more than half a run. Balfour was aggressive with his slider early in the count against right-handed batters and he carried an inverted platoon split in 2013 despite a fastball-heavy approach against lefties. (His career split is essentially neutral.) "Aggressive" describes everything about Balfour on the mound, who always challenges hitters, sometimes literally, as we saw in an ALDS dust-up with Victor Martinez. The right-field bleacher denizens in Oakland lived for Balfour's appearances, creating an exhaustingly spastic quasi-dance to herald his coming that is better Googled than described.

Jesse Chavez
Born: 8/21/1983 Age: 30
Bats: R Throws: R Height: 6' 2" Weight: 160
Breakout: 28% Improve: 52% Collapse: 36%
Attrition: 34% MLB: 55%

Comparables:
Chad Cordero, Brian Tallet, Wil Ledezma

YEAR	TEAM	LVL	AGE	W	L	SV	G	GS	IP	H	HR	BB	SO	BB9	SO9	GB%	BABIP	WHIP	ERA	FIP	FRA	WARP
2011	OMA	AAA	27	2	4	16	45	0	57²	63	6	16	54	2.5	8.4	49%	.327	1.37	3.75	4.10	3.39	1.0
2011	KCA	MLB	27	0	0	0	4	0	7²	12	3	5	8	5.9	9.4	58%	.391	2.22	10.57	8.02	10.73	-0.3
2012	LVG	AAA	28	8	5	1	19	17	95	90	10	20	86	1.9	8.1	48%	.294	1.16	3.98	3.89	4.49	2.0
2012	SAC	AAA	28	0	0	1	2	1	10	8	0	2	9	1.8	8.1	45%	.276	1.00	1.80	2.47	2.56	0.3
2012	TOR	MLB	28	1	1	0	9	2	21¹	25	6	10	27	4.2	11.4	37%	.321	1.64	8.44	5.86	7.07	-0.3
2012	OAK	MLB	28	0	0	0	4	0	3¹	9	1	1	3	2.7	8.1	44%	.533	3.00	18.90	6.95	7.98	-0.1
2013	SAC	AAA	29	2	2	0	5	5	30	35	1	5	26	1.5	7.8	41%	.351	1.33	2.70	2.87	3.10	0.8
2013	OAK	MLB	29	2	4	1	35	0	57¹	50	3	20	55	3.1	8.6	47%	.283	1.22	3.92	3.04	2.71	1.2
2014	OAK	MLB	30	4	3	1	42	6	84	82	10	25	69	2.7	7.4	42%	.290	1.28	3.82	4.20	4.15	0.5

Chavez is the rare pitcher whose performance and fastball velocity show an inverse correlation. Once a flamethrower who routinely pumped gas at 95-plus mph, Chavez has expanded his arsenal as the pitch has lost a couple of ticks. He has ramped up the use of his slow curve from a bit role in 2010 to a major portion of his arsenal while essentially eliminating the hard slider of old, but the most dramatic change is the addition of a 90 mph cutter that Chavez went to 42 percent of the time in 2013. The most glaring statistical impact of his altered approach has been realized on contact, as the pitcher who served up 34 homers in 177 innings entering 2013 allowed just three last season. There is a lot of lean in the right-hander's delivery, which is the only thing standing between him and a sidearm slot.

Ryan Cook
Born: 6/30/1987 Age: 27
Bats: R Throws: R Height: 6' 2" Weight: 215
Breakout: 43% Improve: 71% Collapse: 18%
Attrition: 28% MLB: 84%

Comparables:
Jonny Venters, Josh Outman, Andrew Bailey

YEAR	TEAM	LVL	AGE	W	L	SV	G	GS	IP	H	HR	BB	SO	BB9	SO9	GB%	BABIP	WHIP	ERA	FIP	FRA	WARP
2011	MOB	AA	24	1	4	13	34	0	44	28	2	14	50	2.9	10.2	59%	.277	0.95	2.25	2.72	3.74	0.7
2011	RNO	AAA	24	0	1	6	14	0	17	13	0	8	12	4.2	6.4	50%	.000	1.24	2.12	3.96	3.61	0.0
2011	ARI	MLB	24	0	1	0	12	0	7²	11	0	8	7	9.4	8.2	46%	.423	2.48	7.04	4.30	4.92	0.0
2012	OAK	MLB	25	6	2	14	71	0	73¹	42	4	27	80	3.3	9.8	48%	.220	0.94	2.09	2.84	2.97	1.2
2013	OAK	MLB	26	6	4	2	71	0	67¹	62	2	25	67	3.3	9.0	46%	.306	1.29	2.54	2.76	3.14	1.1
2014	OAK	MLB	27	3	2	3	38	5	59¹	55	5	25	48	3.8	7.3	49%	.289	1.35	3.79	4.22	4.12	0.4

Cook characterized the Oakland bullpen of 2013, as he fell back a smidge from 2012 yet maintained his status as a top-shelf reliever. Batters continued to be mystified by Cook's slider, though his fastball no longer caught anyone by surprise. While he was once again the hardest thrower on the team, the results on contact left much to be desired. Compounding the issue was the fact that Cook actually leaned on heat a bit more in 2013 at the expense of his sinker. Fast is fast, but this is the major leagues.

Sean Doolittle
Born: 9/26/1986 Age: 27
Bats: L Throws: L Height: 6' 3" Weight: 210
Breakout: 22% Improve: 47% Collapse: 30%
Attrition: 12% MLB: 96%

Comparables:
Bobby Jenks, Chris Ray, Jonathan Papelbon

YEAR	TEAM	LVL	AGE	W	L	SV	G	GS	IP	H	HR	BB	SO	BB9	SO9	GB%	BABIP	WHIP	ERA	FIP	FRA	WARP
2012	STO	A+	25	0	0	0	6	0	10¹	5	0	2	21	1.7	18.3	50%	.357	0.68	0.87	0.91	-0.10	0.7
2012	MID	AA	25	0	0	1	8	0	11	2	0	4	19	3.3	15.5	47%	.118	0.55	0.82	1.19	3.08	0.3
2012	OAK	MLB	25	2	1	1	44	0	47¹	40	3	11	60	2.1	11.4	37%	.316	1.08	3.04	2.03	1.96	1.4
2013	OAK	MLB	26	5	5	2	70	0	69	53	4	13	60	1.7	7.8	35%	.262	0.96	3.13	2.74	2.52	1.5
2014	OAK	MLB	27	3	1	2	54	0	58²	47	4	14	65	2.2	10.0	40%	.289	1.04	2.37	2.73	2.58	1.5

The fastball-philic Doolittle upped his frequency of heaters in 2013, going to the pitch eight out of every nine times. He also bucked the common trend by turning up the dials compared to 2012, nudging his average velocity up to more than 95 mph. His component ratios went south, though that includes both good and bad: His walks, strikeouts, hits and homers all fell. For the second consecutive year, the recent convert to pitching shut down right-handers, and 2013 saw a reversal of the weirdly bad results against lefties (.516 OPS allowed in 2013 after a .794 mark in 2012). With Grant Balfour entering free agency, the stage appeared to be set for Doolittle's audition as the Athletics closer of the future. That was before Billy Beane added Jim Johnson and Luke Gregerson to the roster, though, so Doolittle will have to wait a while longer for his ninth-inning shot.

Sonny Gray

Born: 11/7/1989 Age: 24
Bats: R Throws: R Height: 5' 11" Weight: 200
Breakout: 34% Improve: 77% Collapse: 17%
Attrition: 30% MLB: 83%

Comparables:
Travis Wood, Tom Gorzelanny, Felipe Paulino

YEAR	TEAM	LVL	AGE	W	L	SV	G	GS	IP	H	HR	BB	SO	BB9	SO9	GB%	BABIP	WHIP	ERA	FIP	FRA	WARP
2011	MID	AA	21	1	0	0	5	5	20	15	0	6	18	2.7	8.1	64%	.222	1.05	0.45	2.48	4.69	0.2
2012	MID	AA	22	6	9	0	26	26	148	148	8	57	97	3.5	5.9	57%	.302	1.39	4.14	3.91	4.95	0.8
2013	SAC	AAA	23	10	7	0	20	20	118¹	117	5	39	118	3.0	9.0	52%	.337	1.32	3.42	3.11	3.62	2.7
2013	OAK	MLB	23	5	3	0	12	10	64	51	4	20	67	2.8	9.4	52%	.276	1.11	2.67	2.73	3.30	1.2
2014	OAK	MLB	24	9	9	0	26	26	151²	145	13	54	116	3.2	6.9	52%	.294	1.31	3.65	4.01	3.97	1.3

Gray's first taste of the majors was a resounding success. He rode his 93-to-95-mph fastball and overhand curve to leaguewide acclaim in a season that culminated in a pair of intense ALDS duels with Justin Verlander. Gray's dominant performance in Game Two was his most impressive outing of the season, as he notched nine strikeouts across eight shutout innings. The starting pitchers on the Athletics staff tend to share certain mechanical similarities, but Gray's delivery stands out due to his plus momentum and exaggerated spine tilt, the latter of which contributes to his downhill plane and the vertical action on his curve but also creates obstacles at release point. Pun-makers everywhere should be rooting for Gray's success. Bleacher fans would do well to start making their Sonny Gray Real Estate signs now.

Luke Gregerson

Born: 5/14/1984 Age: 30
Bats: L Throws: R Height: 6' 3" Weight: 200
Breakout: 27% Improve: 47% Collapse: 28%
Attrition: 12% MLB: 94%

Comparables:
Bobby Jenks, Justin Duchscherer, Scott Linebrink

YEAR	TEAM	LVL	AGE	W	L	SV	G	GS	IP	H	HR	BB	SO	BB9	SO9	GB%	BABIP	WHIP	ERA	FIP	FRA	WARP
2011	SDN	MLB	27	3	3	0	61	0	55²	57	2	19	34	3.1	5.5	51%	.298	1.37	2.75	3.37	4.12	0.0
2012	SDN	MLB	28	2	0	9	77	0	71²	57	7	21	72	2.6	9.0	52%	.265	1.09	2.39	3.40	3.36	0.8
2013	SDN	MLB	29	6	8	4	73	0	66¹	49	3	18	64	2.4	8.7	47%	.258	1.01	2.71	2.67	2.99	1.1
2014	OAK	MLB	30	3	2	4	62	0	58¹	48	5	16	56	2.5	8.7	50%	.279	1.10	2.69	3.40	2.93	1.2

Gregerson worked 60-plus games yet again, one of six pitchers to do so in each of the last five years. The fact that his velocity is down 2 or 3 mph from his 2009 debut hasn't diminished his effectiveness. His slider whiff rate remains above 20 percent, although he relied less on it last year (56 percent, down from 66 in 2012), particularly over the final two months. His platoon splits are minimal, with his changeup giving lefties more trouble than in the past. Gregerson started strong and finished strong, weathering a brief rough patch in June. He was less dominant in high-leverage situations last season, but that is likely noise. He continues to be a reliable set-up man who could close if needed—after a trade to Oakland for Seth Smith, he's one of about four guys in the bullpen with that profile.

A.J. Griffin

Born: 1/28/1988 Age: 26
Bats: R Throws: R Height: 6' 5" Weight: 230
Breakout: 38% Improve: 67% Collapse: 17%
Attrition: 19% MLB: 95%

Comparables:
Scott Baker, Jordan Zimmermann, Kevin Slowey

YEAR	TEAM	LVL	AGE	W	L	SV	G	GS	IP	H	HR	BB	SO	BB9	SO9	GB%	BABIP	WHIP	ERA	FIP	FRA	WARP
2011	BUR	A	23	4	0	0	8	8	52	36	2	5	46	0.9	8.0	40%	.211	0.79	1.56	2.49	3.35	0.4
2011	STO	A+	23	5	3	0	12	12	70²	64	8	14	82	1.8	10.4	42%	.298	1.10	3.57	3.78	2.68	2.1
2011	MID	AA	23	2	2	0	6	6	32	39	6	11	20	3.1	5.6	43%	.310	1.56	6.47	5.78	5.89	0.0
2012	MID	AA	24	3	1	0	7	7	43¹	31	4	7	44	1.5	9.1	44%	.250	0.88	2.49	3.00	3.95	0.6
2012	SAC	AAA	24	4	2	0	10	10	58²	48	3	11	47	1.7	7.2	41%	.260	1.01	3.07	3.50	3.82	1.2
2012	OAK	MLB	24	7	1	0	15	15	82¹	74	10	19	64	2.1	7.0	38%	.264	1.13	3.06	3.80	4.11	0.9
2013	OAK	MLB	25	14	10	0	32	32	200	171	36	54	171	2.4	7.7	33%	.242	1.12	3.83	4.58	5.06	-0.4
2014	OAK	MLB	26	10	7	3	84	16	171	152	21	42	139	2.2	7.3	38%	.267	1.14	3.23	4.11	3.51	2.4

Griffin followed up his impressive rookie campaign by leading the team in innings, hitting 200 frames on the nose, while continuing to limit the free passes and upping his modest strikeout rate. The downside of throwing so many strikes is that opposing hitters will occasionally win the battle, as reflected in Griffin's MLB-leading 36 home runs allowed. One shudders to imagine the escalation of that number in a less friendly ballpark. With his height and very high arm slot, Griffin struggles to generate grounders—indeed, he induced a lower percentage of them than any other qualified starter. Even in Oakland's park and with Oakland's defense, giving up so much contact in the air is a recipe for trouble, illustrated by Griffin's high rate of homers per fly. That could be bad luck or a sign that any slippage in his already mediocre stuff will lead to being pounded right out of the league, and if you can consistently distinguish between those two possibilities, please submit your resume to Billy Beane, O.co Coliseum, Oakland, California.

Jim Johnson

Born: 6/27/1983 Age: 31
Bats: R Throws: R Height: 6' 6" Weight: 240
Breakout: 27% Improve: 54% Collapse: 32%
Attrition: 13% MLB: 88%

Comparables:
Brandon Lyon, Chad Bradford, Matt Guerrier

YEAR	TEAM	LVL	AGE	W	L	SV	G	GS	IP	H	HR	BB	SO	BB9	SO9	GB%	BABIP	WHIP	ERA	FIP	FRA	WARP
2011	BAL	MLB	28	6	5	9	69	0	91	80	5	21	58	2.1	5.7	63%	.269	1.11	2.67	3.26	4.34	0.9
2012	BAL	MLB	29	2	1	51	71	0	68²	55	3	15	41	2.0	5.4	64%	.251	1.02	2.49	3.21	4.16	0.7
2013	BAL	MLB	30	3	8	50	74	0	70¹	72	5	18	56	2.3	7.2	59%	.327	1.28	2.94	3.47	4.01	0.6
2014	OAK	MLB	31	3	1	46	57	0	60²	57	4	16	42	2.4	6.2	54%	.289	1.21	3.21	3.71	3.49	0.8

Those betting on sharp regression for Johnson were ready to cash in their tickets by Memorial Day as he was toting an ERA that started with "5" and fending off rumors of a role change. From May 29th on, however, he was as good as ever, posting a 1.75 ERA fully supported by his strikeout, walk and groundball numbers. Especially the groundball numbers. Johnson isn't the conventional fireballing closer that populates many bullpens across the league, but he now has three years of excellent work under his belt, not to mention the coveted Billy Beane Stamp of Approval, as the A's decided they were willing to pay Johnson's salary after acquiring him in a trade even though he was fourth-year arbitration-eligible and saves are very expensive.

Scott Kazmir

Born: 1/24/1984 Age: 30
Bats: L Throws: L Height: 6' 0" Weight: 185
Breakout: 29% Improve: 58% Collapse: 17%
Attrition: 17% MLB: 84%

Comparables:
Wandy Rodriguez, Casey Fossum, Manny Parra

YEAR	TEAM	LVL	AGE	W	L	SV	G	GS	IP	H	HR	BB	SO	BB9	SO9	GB%	BABIP	WHIP	ERA	FIP	FRA	WARP
2011	SLC	AAA	27	0	5	0	5	5	15¹	22	0	20	14	11.7	8.2	55%	.500	2.74	17.02	7.04	10.12	-0.2
2011	ANA	MLB	27	0	0	0	1	1	1²	5	1	2	0	10.8	0.0	30%	.444	4.20	27.00	18.06	12.21	-0.1
2013	CLE	MLB	29	10	9	0	29	29	158	162	19	47	162	2.7	9.2	42%	.325	1.32	4.04	3.54	3.83	2.5
2014	OAK	MLB	30	6	8	0	22	22	111²	112	13	45	88	3.7	7.1	39%	.298	1.41	4.51	4.63	4.90	-0.1

Kazmir utilized an unconventional offseason training regimen to restore at least two of the mph he'd lost from his once-nuclear heater. Perhaps more importantly, he found confidence in the new delivery and exhibited control and command beyond anybody's wildest hopes for his old delivery. He looks completely healthy now, and—despite his rather pedestrian 4.04 ERA last year—almost every indicator suggests he's likely to be among the top pitchers in baseball this year if he can stay that way. Obviously, whenever a reclamation project works out well there's a desire to understand what was different about this time; we've been burned before, after all. Beyond the obvious medical repairs leading to restored confidence (which can take years), it takes a combination of good direction and intensely hard work by the athlete. If Kazmir indeed returns to his former glory, much credit likely will be given (rightfully) to the offseason training program and the Indians' coaches. But there are no magic bullets, and nothing that can promise a 35 percent drop in walk rate. The dedication and hard work required to make that sort of improvement bode extremely well for Kazmir's future in Oakland. PECOTA—which ignores offseason training, confidence, new mechanics, medical repairs, good direction, intensely hard work, Indians coaches and dedication—says "nope."

Josh Lindblom

Born: 6/15/1987 Age: 27
Bats: R Throws: R Height: 6' 4" Weight: 240
Breakout: 47% Improve: 72% Collapse: 16%
Attrition: 32% MLB: 74%

Comparables:
Junichi Tazawa, Kazuhito Tadano, Sean Henn

YEAR	TEAM	LVL	AGE	W	L	SV	G	GS	IP	H	HR	BB	SO	BB9	SO9	GB%	BABIP	WHIP	ERA	FIP	FRA	WARP
2011	CHT	AA	24	1	3	17	34	0	42¹	30	3	14	54	3.0	11.5	44%	.333	1.04	2.13	2.95	1.78	0.3
2011	LAN	MLB	24	1	0	0	27	0	29²	21	0	10	28	3.0	8.5	33%	.288	1.04	2.73	2.32	2.48	0.6
2012	PHI	MLB	25	1	3	1	26	0	23¹	19	4	17	27	6.6	10.4	31%	.263	1.54	4.63	5.36	5.70	-0.2
2012	LAN	MLB	25	2	2	0	48	0	47²	42	9	18	43	3.4	8.1	40%	.268	1.26	3.02	5.11	4.87	-0.1
2013	ROU	AAA	26	8	4	0	20	18	108	86	12	31	79	2.6	6.6	45%	.237	1.08	3.08	4.61	5.09	0.3
2013	TEX	MLB	26	1	3	0	8	5	31¹	35	4	11	21	3.2	6.0	35%	.307	1.47	5.46	4.45	5.23	0.1
2014	OAK	MLB	27	6	5	1	53	11	107²	103	12	38	84	3.1	7.0	41%	.285	1.30	3.94	4.42	4.28	0.5

Sent to Texas when the Rangers foisted Michael Young on the Phillies, Lindblom was deployed to Triple-A to work on converting from relief work to the rotation. Injuries in Texas pressed Lindblom into swingman duty on multiple occasions, so while he showed progress at Round Rock it was a season of starts, stops and other irregularities. Sent to California in the Craig Gentry deal, he'll fight for a job in a crowded (and talented) Oakland 'pen; given that he'll be on his last option, he could find himself traded once more by the time final spring training cuts are made.

Tommy Milone

Born: 2/16/1987 Age: 27
Bats: L Throws: L Height: 6' 0" Weight: 205
Breakout: 39% Improve: 79% Collapse: 15%
Attrition: 29% MLB: 87%

Comparables:
Dillon Gee, Edgar Gonzalez, Jason Vargas

YEAR	TEAM	LVL	AGE	W	L	SV	G	GS	IP	H	HR	BB	SO	BB9	SO9	GB%	BABIP	WHIP	ERA	FIP	FRA	WARP
2011	SYR	AAA	24	12	6	0	24	24	148¹	137	9	16	155	1.0	9.4	40%	.331	1.03	3.22	2.28	3.63	2.1
2011	WAS	MLB	24	1	0	0	5	5	26	28	2	4	15	1.4	5.2	34%	.312	1.23	3.81	3.53	3.70	0.3
2012	OAK	MLB	25	13	10	0	31	31	190	207	24	36	137	1.7	6.5	39%	.310	1.28	3.74	3.88	4.18	2.2
2013	SAC	AAA	26	0	0	0	2	2	10¹	16	0	1	15	0.9	13.1	52%	.516	1.65	1.74	0.96	2.10	0.5
2013	OAK	MLB	26	12	9	0	28	26	156¹	160	25	39	126	2.2	7.3	36%	.283	1.27	4.14	4.33	4.28	1.1
2014	OAK	MLB	27	9	9	0	26	26	149²	157	17	33	113	2.0	6.8	40%	.304	1.27	3.98	4.00	4.32	0.7

Your prototypical back-end starter, Milone was bumped from the rotation when Sonny Gray began to emerge late in the season. The southpaw might have been over his head a bit in 2012, and his high rate of unearned runs over the past two seasons suggests that, even aside from Oakland's helpful pitching environment, his ERA might not be a good representation of his ability. Still, durable lefties with solid command of the strike zone can carve out long careers in the majors. Milone is an insurance policy at this point, in case the more heralded arms of the Oakland system fail to pan out, but a team could do much worse than having a command-wielding lefty as the "break glass in case of emergency" option.

Pat Neshek

Born: 9/4/1980 Age: 33
Bats: B Throws: R Height: 6' 3" Weight: 210
Breakout: 46% Improve: 55% Collapse: 41%
Attrition: 56% MLB: 35%

Comparables:
Doug Slaten, Vinnie Chulk, Ken Ray

YEAR	TEAM	LVL	AGE	W	L	SV	G	GS	IP	H	HR	BB	SO	BB9	SO9	GB%	BABIP	WHIP	ERA	FIP	FRA	WARP
2011	TUC	AAA	30	1	2	3	24	0	26¹	29	5	10	13	3.4	4.4	46%	.275	1.48	4.10	6.40	6.74	0.0
2011	SDN	MLB	30	1	1	0	25	0	24²	19	4	22	20	8.0	7.3	27%	.242	1.66	4.01	6.28	6.72	-0.7
2012	NOR	AAA	31	3	2	11	35	0	44	42	1	7	49	1.4	10.0	42%	.345	1.11	2.66	1.77	2.86	1.0
2012	OAK	MLB	31	2	1	0	24	0	19²	10	3	6	16	2.7	7.3	35%	.137	0.81	1.37	4.47	4.71	0.1
2013	OAK	MLB	32	2	1	0	45	0	40¹	40	6	15	29	3.3	6.5	34%	.262	1.36	3.35	4.69	4.36	0.1
2014	OAK	MLB	33	2	1	1	38	0	39²	38	5	16	29	3.6	6.6	39%	.280	1.37	4.20	4.82	4.56	0.0

After three years spent trying to regain his pre-surgery form, a period which involved a lot of patience in the minors, the side-winding Neshek re-established himself with a full season of big-league baseball in Oakland. He has become increasingly reliant on his slider, topping 70 percent of his pitches overall, and opposing right-handed batters were treated with a slider-strict diet that reached an incredible 96 percent. The strategy has as much to do with the pitch's effectiveness as it does the lack of success with the rest of his arsenal, though left-handed hitters teed off on Neshek's fastball and changeup. Neshek's fly-ball tendencies despite extreme, Chad Bradfordian pitching mechanics are less a subject for sabermetric analysis and more for resolution through the Hegelian dialectic.

Danny Otero

Born: 2/19/1985 Age: 29
Bats: R Throws: R Height: 6' 3" Weight: 215
Breakout: 24% Improve: 48% Collapse: 50%
Attrition: 55% MLB: 36%

Comparables:
Ehren Wassermann, Steve Schmoll, Chris Leroux

YEAR	TEAM	LVL	AGE	W	L	SV	G	GS	IP	H	HR	BB	SO	BB9	SO9	GB%	BABIP	WHIP	ERA	FIP	FRA	WARP
2011	RIC	AA	26	2	1	1	23	0	38	34	0	4	40	0.9	9.5	61%	.320	1.00	1.42	1.78	2.72	0.8
2011	FRE	AAA	26	2	3	12	33	0	36	38	4	7	36	1.8	9.0	43%	.312	1.25	3.25	3.81	3.60	0.8
2012	FRE	AAA	27	5	5	0	48	0	62	70	4	8	45	1.2	6.5	56%	.333	1.26	2.90	3.58	4.27	1.1
2012	SFN	MLB	27	0	0	0	12	0	12¹	19	0	2	8	1.5	5.8	64%	.452	1.70	5.84	2.81	3.04	0.2
2013	SAC	AAA	28	1	0	15	23	0	27¹	14	0	1	22	0.3	7.2	63%	.187	0.55	0.99	2.18	2.93	0.6
2013	OAK	MLB	28	2	0	0	33	0	39	42	0	6	27	1.4	6.2	57%	.328	1.23	1.38	2.15	2.73	0.9
2014	OAK	MLB	29	2	1	1	45	0	56	56	4	11	39	1.8	6.3	54%	.299	1.21	3.43	3.52	3.73	0.6

The sinkerballing sidearmer was allergic to true outcomes in 2013. This includes striking out few batters, but his penchant for worm-burners kept the damage to a minimum. The 29-year-old with impeccable command steadily earned trust from Bob Melvin as the year went on, culminating in four appearances in the ALDS. (True to form, he struck out just two of 21 batters while inducing 12 grounders. No runs, allowed, natch.) Had Billy Beane simply let Grant Balfour move on to greener ($$$) pastures and bumped everyone in the remaining bullpen up a notch, Otero might have found himself with a nice seventh-inning role on Opening Day 2014. Instead, Beane did Beane Things and acquired Jim Johnson and Luke Gregerson, so Otero will have to scrap for high-leverage work once again.

Dillon Overton

Born: 8/17/1991 Age: 22
Bats: L Throws: L Height: 6' 2" Weight: 172

YEAR	TEAM	LVL	AGE	W	L	SV	G	GS	IP	H	HR	BB	SO	BB9	SO9	GB%	BABIP	WHIP	ERA	FIP	FRA	WARP
2014	–	–	–	–	–	–	–	–	–	–	–	–	–	–	–	–	–	–	–	–	–	–

The A's selected Overton in the second round of the 2013 draft despite a questionable medical profile. Oakland leveraged those concerns into a deal that was well below slot, paying him just a $400,000 bonus and scheduling him for Tommy John surgery within weeks of signing. The lanky lefty was the Saturday starter for an Oklahoma rotation that was fronted by third-overall pick Jonathan Gray. Prior to surgery, Overton had been armed with a low-90s fastball and a potential plus slider. The evolution of a solid changeup will be a necessary piece of his development plan once the southpaw regains his functional strength.

Jarrod Parker

Born: 11/24/1988 Age: 25
Bats: R Throws: R Height: 6' 1" Weight: 195
Breakout: 27% Improve: 60% Collapse: 21%
Attrition: 14% MLB: 97%

Comparables:
Matt Garza, Tom Gorzelanny, Jon Lester

YEAR	TEAM	LVL	AGE	W	L	SV	G	GS	IP	H	HR	BB	SO	BB9	SO9	GB%	BABIP	WHIP	ERA	FIP	FRA	WARP
2011	MOB	AA	22	11	8	0	26	26	130²	112	7	55	112	3.8	7.7	53%	.273	1.28	3.79	3.80	4.96	1.0
2011	ARI	MLB	22	0	0	0	1	1	5²	4	0	1	1	1.6	1.6	44%	.222	0.88	0.00	3.17	3.75	0.1
2012	SAC	AAA	23	1	0	0	4	4	20²	22	2	6	21	2.6	9.1	55%	.345	1.35	2.18	3.76	4.03	0.5
2012	OAK	MLB	23	13	8	0	29	29	181¹	166	11	63	140	3.1	6.9	45%	.293	1.26	3.47	3.38	3.70	2.7
2013	OAK	MLB	24	12	8	0	32	32	197	178	25	63	134	2.9	6.1	42%	.260	1.22	3.97	4.43	4.81	0.0
2014	OAK	MLB	25	10	10	0	29	29	169²	160	16	58	125	3.1	6.7	46%	.285	1.29	3.63	4.21	3.95	1.5

If you ignore the first and last months of the season, Parker's 2013 can be viewed as a big step forward. The right-hander posted a 2.81 ERA from May through August, but the bookend months added nearly a full run to the overall slate. His mechanical timing was out of whack to start the year and it took a few weeks to right the ship; Parker was then a stable force in the rotation before tiring down the stretch. His changeup was once again one of the best in the game, generating a 49 percent rate of whiffs-per-swing that was the highest mark in all of baseball for el cambio (min. 50 changeups). Parker was notable in 2012 for building velocity throughout the season, but he demonstrated the opposite trend in 2013, peaking in April and dropping as the year progressed. Depending on which part of the elephant you touch, you might see 2014 regression or potential for improvement. It's a confounding mix for prognosticators, but the key likely boils down to physical consistency.

Drew Pomeranz
Born: 11/22/1988 Age: 25
Bats: R Throws: L Height: 6' 5" Weight: 240
Breakout: 40% Improve: 69% Collapse: 17%
Attrition: 22% MLB: 92%

Comparables:
Jordan Zimmermann, Felix Doubront, Angel Guzman

YEAR	TEAM	LVL	AGE	W	L	SV	G	GS	IP	H	HR	BB	SO	BB9	SO9	GB%	BABIP	WHIP	ERA	FIP	FRA	WARP
2011	KIN	A+	22	3	2	0	15	15	77	56	2	32	95	3.7	11.1	50%	.297	1.14	1.87	2.39	2.78	1.7
2011	AKR	AA	22	0	1	0	3	3	14	10	1	6	17	3.9	10.9	29%	.273	1.14	2.57	3.20	3.50	0.2
2011	TUL	AA	22	1	0	0	2	2	10	2	0	0	7	0.0	6.3	24%	.080	0.20	0.00	1.98	3.02	0.3
2011	COL	MLB	22	2	1	0	4	4	18¹	19	0	5	13	2.5	6.4	46%	.333	1.31	5.40	2.56	3.14	0.5
2012	CSP	AAA	23	4	4	0	9	9	46²	52	2	20	46	3.9	8.9	55%	.341	1.54	2.51	3.54	4.25	1.3
2012	COL	MLB	23	2	9	0	22	22	96²	97	14	46	83	4.3	7.7	44%	.307	1.48	4.93	4.85	5.25	1.0
2013	CSP	AAA	24	8	1	0	15	15	85²	83	6	33	96	3.5	10.1	47%	.342	1.35	4.20	3.50	4.04	2.3
2013	COL	MLB	24	0	4	0	8	4	21²	25	4	19	19	7.9	7.9	53%	.345	2.03	6.23	6.44	6.58	-0.2
2014	OAK	MLB	25	6	6	0	19	19	101²	93	10	44	92	3.9	8.1	46%	.293	1.35	3.87	4.18	4.20	0.7

Can we start over at hello? If Pomeranz had never been promoted last year, his impending Oakland debut would soon be must-see TV for us all. A sturdy lefty with a uniquely lethal curveball, coming off a season with 10 Ks per nine and tolerable walk rates in a Triple-A hitter's haven? By all means! Instead, Pomeranz killed the mystique in Colorado last year with a string of awful major-league performances, and a three-week stretch in 2013 doomed his entire season to lost-year status. In four starts, he walked five more than he struck out and failed to complete the fifth inning, before hitting the disabled list for a month with biceps tendonitis. Traded in December for Brett Anderson, Pomeranz will try to finally make good on his stuff and first-round pedigree in the East Bay.

Nolan Sanburn
Born: 7/21/1991 Age: 22
Bats: R Throws: R Height: 6' 0" Weight: 175
Breakout: 100% Improve: 100% Collapse: 0%
Attrition: 0% MLB: 2%

Comparables:
Cesar Cabral, Trevor Rosenthal, Michael Blazek

YEAR	TEAM	LVL	AGE	W	L	SV	G	GS	IP	H	HR	BB	SO	BB9	SO9	GB%	BABIP	WHIP	ERA	FIP	FRA	WARP
2012	VER	A-	20	0	1	0	7	7	18²	23	2	6	19	2.9	9.2	53%	.375	1.55	3.86	3.65	3.70	0.3
2013	BLT	A	21	1	3	0	14	1	26	17	1	9	20	3.1	6.9	47%	.225	1.00	1.38	3.34	4.47	0.3
2014	OAK	MLB	22	1	1	1	17	2	32²	37	4	17	18	4.8	5.1	46%	.302	1.66	5.49	5.54	5.97	-0.5

Sanburn's 2013 debut was delayed by a shoulder injury suffered in spring training. He didn't make his first appearance until the end of June. The A's were cautious upon his return, limiting him to exactly two innings in 13 of his 14 games. The one exception was a ninth-inning appearance on July 18th in which he entered with the bases loaded and promptly gave up a grand slam to lose the ballgame 7-6. Sanburn performed well in the short stints, and though the long-term plan is still to develop a rotation anchor, the short-term focus was on building arm strength as he recovered from injury. His fastball registered in the low 90s during the short stints, which is an encouraging sign given that velocity is often the last thing to return following a shoulder injury.

Evan Scribner
Born: 7/19/1985 Age: 28
Bats: R Throws: R Height: 6' 3" Weight: 190
Breakout: 37% Improve: 57% Collapse: 30%
Attrition: 45% MLB: 57%

Comparables:
Chris Hatcher, Matt Daley, Jesse Carlson

YEAR	TEAM	LVL	AGE	W	L	SV	G	GS	IP	H	HR	BB	SO	BB9	SO9	GB%	BABIP	WHIP	ERA	FIP	FRA	WARP
2011	TUC	AAA	25	2	3	10	28	0	28²	27	2	12	27	3.8	8.5	29%	.321	1.36	4.71	4.06	4.80	0.6
2011	SDN	MLB	25	0	0	0	10	0	14	18	1	4	10	2.6	6.4	42%	.362	1.57	7.07	3.35	5.56	-0.2
2012	SAC	AAA	26	3	0	8	26	0	35²	26	4	10	38	2.5	9.6	39%	.250	1.01	3.03	3.83	4.61	0.4
2012	OAK	MLB	26	2	0	1	30	0	35¹	30	2	12	30	3.1	7.6	40%	.269	1.19	2.55	3.10	3.68	0.5
2013	SAC	AAA	27	3	1	1	31	0	44²	32	2	9	58	1.8	11.7	35%	.278	0.92	2.22	2.16	1.95	1.8
2013	OAK	MLB	27	0	0	0	18	0	26²	26	3	7	19	2.4	6.4	35%	.271	1.24	4.39	3.90	4.00	0.2
2014	OAK	MLB	28	3	1	0	48	0	61¹	54	6	18	58	2.7	8.5	38%	.286	1.19	3.27	3.61	3.55	0.8

"Quadruple-A player" usually calls to mind an immobile slugger bashing 35 homers in Triple-A but unable to find a home in the majors because of awful defense or an inability to hit Uncle Charlie. Scribner is the pitching equivalent, with dynamite minor-league stats across the board that have not translated well to the highest level. His two-pitch repertoire includes a steep curve and a running fastball that sits on the border of 90 mph, a tenuous velocity against the best hitters in the world. Scribner exhibits solid command of both pitches, but the heater gets punished when it straightens out and catches too much of the plate. The 2014 season will be pivotal in determining whether he has a future in the major leagues or just near the majors.

Dan Straily

Born: 12/1/1988 Age: 25
Bats: R Throws: R Height: 6' 2'' Weight: 215
Breakout: 35% Improve: 67% Collapse: 17%
Attrition: 25% MLB: 93%

Comparables:
Boof Bonser, Jason Hirsh, Jeremy Hellickson

YEAR	TEAM	LVL	AGE	W	L	SV	G	GS	IP	H	HR	BB	SO	BB9	SO9	GB%	BABIP	WHIP	ERA	FIP	FRA	WARP
2011	STO	A+	22	11	9	0	28	26	160²	160	10	40	154	2.2	8.6	48%	.310	1.24	3.87	3.85	4.21	2.8
2012	MID	AA	23	3	4	0	14	14	85¹	70	6	23	108	2.4	11.4	44%	.312	1.09	3.38	2.65	3.59	2.1
2012	SAC	AAA	23	6	3	0	11	11	66²	40	3	19	82	2.6	11.1	41%	.247	0.88	2.03	2.69	2.91	2.1
2012	OAK	MLB	23	2	1	0	7	7	39¹	36	11	16	32	3.7	7.3	31%	.225	1.32	3.89	6.43	5.60	0.0
2013	SAC	AAA	24	3	1	0	5	5	31²	24	1	9	33	2.6	9.4	46%	.264	1.04	1.14	2.75	3.27	0.8
2013	OAK	MLB	24	10	8	0	27	27	152¹	132	16	57	124	3.4	7.3	39%	.267	1.24	3.96	4.07	4.07	1.7
2014	OAK	MLB	25	9	9	0	27	27	158¹	143	17	58	135	3.3	7.7	41%	.280	1.27	3.70	4.23	4.02	1.3

Straily was able to calm the fear-inducing rate of homers from 2012, partially through taking his fly-ball frequency down a peg. However, he lost a tick off his fastball velocity, averaging 91 mph, and he is left vulnerable when his command of the heat wavers. The slider is the butter on his bread, accounting for the majority of his strikeouts and producing the best results on contact, but his 27 percent usage rate could raise long-term health concerns. [Ed.: Did you catch that? How butter is a metaphor for the slider, and overuse of the slider can cause health problems? Just like how you shouldn't overuse butter? Stand back, now, professionals operating here.]

Robert Wahl

Born: 3/21/1992 Age: 22
Bats: R Throws: R Height: 6' 2'' Weight: 210
Breakout: 100% Improve: 100% Collapse: 0%
Attrition: 20% MLB: 3%

Comparables:
Michael Blazek, Trevor Rosenthal, Vic Black

YEAR	TEAM	LVL	AGE	W	L	SV	G	GS	IP	H	HR	BB	SO	BB9	SO9	GB%	BABIP	WHIP	ERA	FIP	FRA	WARP
2013	VER	A-	21	0	0	2	9	4	20²	20	3	6	27	2.6	11.8	32%	.321	1.26	3.92	3.24	4.17	0.2
2014	OAK	MLB	22	1	2	0	14	6	32²	36	4	19	20	5.1	5.6	41%	.306	1.69	5.63	5.60	6.12	-0.4

Wahl entered the college season with first-round aspirations, but he battled blisters that hampered his command. There were questions about his signability when the right-hander slipped to the fifth round of the draft, but the A's gave him a $500,000 deal that was well above slot and convinced Ole Miss's Friday-night starter to turn pro. Wahl has a powerful delivery that involves a King Felix-like twist as he charges toward the plate and a mid-90s fastball and two-plane breaker that will play at the highest level. He could progress quickly if he refines his command, though (you've heard this before) development of the changeup will determine his ultimate role—without that reliable third pitch, he'll likely hit a developmental wall [Ed.: See? Professionals] and wind up in the bullpen.

LINEOUTS

HITTERS

PLAYER	TEAM	LVL	AGE	PA	R	2B	3B	HR	RBI	BB	SO	SB-CS	AVG/OBP/SLG	TAv	BABIP	BRR	FRAA	WARP
LF B. Boyd	VER	A-	19	300	39	13	2	8	32	35	66	8-6	.285/.375/.442	.325	.353	-0.5	LF(56): 1.3, CF(11): -0.1	2.9
CF C. Brown	SYR	AAA	27	438	57	26	1	19	56	40	132	12-4	.254/.326/.473	.278	.332	1.1	CF(61): -1.2, RF(22): -0.7	2.5
	WAS	MLB	27	15	2	1	0	1	1	3	4	1-0	.167/.333/.500	.255	.143	-0.1	LF(5): -0.1, RF(3): 0.0	0.0
LF B. Burns	POT	A+	23	402	70	8	9	0	29	52	37	54-5	.312/.422/.391	.295	.349	0.1	LF(73): 3.5, CF(18): -2.2	2.7
	HAR	AA	23	138	26	4	0	0	8	20	17	20-2	.325/.434/.360	.305	.381	3.5	CF(17): 1.7, LF(13): -0.5	1.7
3B M. Head	MID	AA	22	163	13	4	0	2	8	12	42	0-1	.196/.264/.264	.184	.257	-1.5	3B(19): -4.3, 1B(3): -0.2	-1.7
C B. Maxwell	BLT	A	22	228	25	14	0	2	28	24	29	0-0	.286/.360/.387	.279	.324	-2.2	C(38): -0.2	0.8
	STO	A+	22	197	19	8	0	5	21	19	34	0-0	.263/.335/.394	.275	.297	0.9	C(45): -0.7	1.0
1B M. Muncy	STO	A+	22	428	67	13	1	21	76	64	68	1-1	.285/.400/.507	.330	.295	0.6	1B(85): -2.4	3.6
	MID	AA	22	197	22	12	2	4	24	24	34	0-1	.250/.340/.413	.257	.289	-1	1B(43): 1.4	0.3
SS A. Parrino	SAC	AAA	27	420	43	16	3	4	36	43	102	3-1	.210/.300/.302	.227	.278	-1.2	SS(85): 2.7, 3B(18): -0.8	0.1
	OAK	MLB	27	36	2	2	0	0	1	2	12	0-0	.118/.167/.176	.112	.182	0	SS(7): 0.3, 2B(5): -0.4	-0.5
CF S. Peterson	SAC	AAA	25	553	70	25	1	12	79	77	127	17-2	.251/.358/.387	.284	.315	-1.5	CF(63): -1.3, LF(33): -3.0	2.1
	OAK	MLB	25	8	1	0	0	0	1	1	3	0-0	.143/.250/.143	.167	.250	0	1B(2): 0.0	0.0
SS C. Pinder	VER	A-	21	161	14	4	0	3	8	12	41	1-0	.200/.286/.293	.262	.253	-0.9	SS(33): -3.2, 3B(2): -0.0	0.1
2B S. Sizemore	OAK	MLB	28	6	0	1	0	0	0	0	2	0-0	.167/.167/.333	.168	.250	0	2B(2): -0.2	-0.1

B.J. Boyd has an intriguing combination of strength and speed but a glove that is destined for left field. With his uncommon physical profile, there is a wide range of opinions as to how his skills will coalesce into a big-league future. ⊘ While regular playing time would expose **Corey Brown**'s contact woes, the 27-year-old could be a solid power bat off the bench, with ability to play all three outfield positions in a pinch. ⊘ The Nationals' minor-league player of the year, **Billy Burns** is an OBP machine who can flat-out fly—good thing, considering that's the most efficient way to travel from Washington to Oakland, which traded Jerry Blevins for him. ⊘ Still plagued by a shoulder injury suffered in the 2012 Arizona Fall League, **Miles Head** hit the wall at Double-A last season, swimming beneath the Mendoza line for six weeks before the shoulder took him back out of the lineup. ⊘ Take the hitting numbers with big grains of salt: **Bruce Maxwell**'s focus was on his development on defense in the hopes that his plus power can stick behind the plate. ⊘ The power projection for **Max Muncy** has skyrocketed since he was selected in the fifth round in 2012 thanks to a revamped approach that focuses on pulling pitches on the inner half of the plate. ⊘ He may not have the bat to carry a starting gig, but **Andy Parrino** owns a legitimate shortstop's glove and can take a pitch. ⊘ On a team with less depth, **Shane Peterson** would have no problem carving out a seat on the bench—his ability to work the count and efficient thievery on the bases complement his positional flexibility. ⊘ The Athletics' second-round pick out of Virginia Tech, **Chad Pinder** brings a solid glove and a strong arm to the left side of the infield. As he's likely a third baseman down the road, his future paycheck hinges on his development at the plate. ⊘ The ACL injury that sidelined **Scott Sizemore** for all of 2012 came back with a vengeance, knocking him out for another year. He did sneak into a pair of April contests before re-encountering the scalpel, but The Sizemore Curse has now limited Scott and his not-brother Grady to a grand total of six professional plate appearances over the last two seasons.

PITCHERS

PLAYER	TEAM	LVL	AGE	W	L	SV	IP	H	HR	BB	SO	BB9	SO9	GB%	BABIP	WHIP	ERA	FIP	FRA	WARP
F. Abad	SYR	AAA	27	1	0	0	17	17	0	2	12	1.1	6.4	52%	.296	1.12	1.06	2.15	2.86	0.4
	WAS	MLB	27	0	3	0	37²	42	3	10	32	2.4	7.6	40%	.322	1.38	3.35	3.23	3.19	0.6
A. Carignan	OAK	MLB	25	1	1	0	9²	8	0	10	8	9.3	7.4	46%	.308	1.86	4.66	4.49	6.07	-0.1
P. Figueroa	SAC	AAA	27	3	4	2	59¹	57	9	33	49	5.0	7.4	44%	.282	1.52	4.10	5.66	5.85	-0.1
	OAK	MLB	27	0	0	0	3	6	2	3	3	9.0	9.0	50%	.400	3.00	12.00	12.74	13.41	-0.3
D. Granier	STO	A+	24	6	3	0	83	71	5	40	97	4.3	10.5	44%	.310	1.34	3.25	3.88	3.32	2.4
	MID	AA	24	3	6	0	72¹	82	9	42	56	5.2	7.0	45%	.322	1.71	5.23	4.95	6.02	-0.1
D. Hooker	SFD	AA	24	1	4	8	47	38	4	10	61	1.9	11.7	49%	.309	1.02	3.64	2.33	3.57	0.9
	MEM	AAA	24	0	0	0	20²	20	2	8	14	3.5	6.1	49%	.277	1.35	5.23	4.63	6.18	-0.1
P. Humber	OKL	AAA	30	2	4	0	50	57	7	18	38	3.2	6.8	39%	.318	1.50	4.68	5.67	6.16	-0.2
	HOU	MLB	30	0	8	0	54²	75	9	20	36	3.3	5.9	47%	.342	1.74	7.90	5.05	5.76	-0.4
A. Leon	MID	AA	24	4	5	0	72²	87	9	11	48	1.4	5.9	49%	.324	1.35	3.84	3.96	5.06	0.7
	SAC	AAA	24	5	3	0	71¹	81	4	13	49	1.6	6.2	48%	.333	1.32	4.42	3.60	3.93	1.3
H. Okajima	SAC	AAA	37	1	3	1	42²	40	5	9	45	1.9	9.5	43%	.299	1.15	4.22	3.62	3.95	0.7
	OAK	MLB	37	0	0	0	4	7	1	2	1	4.5	2.2	50%	.353	2.25	2.25	7.33	6.08	-0.1
T. Peters	STO	A+	22	12	8	0	165²	167	24	27	159	1.5	8.6	41%	.304	1.17	4.07	4.22	4.64	2.3
C. Resop	SAC	AAA	30	1	2	0	35²	48	5	13	29	3.3	7.3	46%	.371	1.71	6.81	5.03	7.14	0.0
	OAK	MLB	30	1	1	0	18	22	3	10	13	5.0	6.5	42%	.322	1.78	6.00	5.80	5.79	-0.3
F. Rodriguez	HOU	MLB	28	2	10	0	70¹	68	10	34	78	4.4	10.0	38%	.314	1.45	5.37	4.26	3.48	1.0
A. Werner	SAC	AAA	26	12	14	0	165	202	20	38	111	2.1	6.1	45%	.336	1.45	5.78	4.65	5.19	0.4
M. Ynoa	BLT	A	21	2	1	0	54²	45	3	18	48	3.0	7.9	51%	.275	1.15	2.14	3.67	4.50	1.1
	STO	A+	21	1	2	1	21	23	2	17	20	7.3	8.6	37%	.333	1.90	7.71	5.82	6.80	-0.1

Despite better peripherals against left-handed hitters, **Fernando Abad** displayed his first reverse platoon split; LOOGY or not, it was a solid season. ⊘ **Jeremy Barfield** accumulated nearly 1,200 plate appearances at Double-A Midland before he earned a promotion, but his bat came up empty in his first go-around in the PCL. With his career at a crossroads, Barfield will take advantage of his genetically gifted left arm and follow the Sean Doolittle path to the mound. ⊘ **Andrew Carignan** was unable to get into a game last season after he suffered a setback in his rehab from Tommy John surgery, but he is determined to come back in the spring with the new ligament in his elbow and a chip on his shoulder. ⊘ **Pedro Figueroa** was used mostly as a lefty specialist in his September call-up, but all of the damage that he absorbed came at the hands of right-handed Angels hitters.

His minor-league walk rate does not augur well for the majors, but lefties who throw 96 mph don't gueroa'n trees. ⊘ **Drew Granier** sat near the top of the Cal League in strikeouts for two months and earned a promotion to Double-A, but his lack of command caught up to him there. He's a notoriously hard worker, though, and is in great hands to structure his development. ⊘ **Deryk Hooker** garnered some success as a full-time reliever with a low-90s heater and solid curveball, but he will need to catch a break to stick in the majors given the depth of excellent arms throughout the organization. ⊘ **Philip Humber** has spent the last two years allowing a homer every five innings and bombed out of the Astros' rotation after seven starts, but perfect games fly forever. ⊘ **Arnold Leon** is a control artist with a low-90s fastball and functional slider that might not play multiple times through a big-league order, but a reliever's workload should fit his stuff just fine. ⊘ **Hideki Okajima** returned to the U.S. after a successful season in Japan, and though he pitched well in Triple-A, the 37-year-old southpaw stood behind a long line of superior relievers in the Oakland pecking order and was designated for assignment in September. ⊘ **Tanner Peters** is accustomed to climbing uphill against the gravity of doubt as a six-foot-none, 155-pound low-round pick with a 90-mph fastball, but he is also a testament to the success that can be attained in the low minors with plus command. ⊘ In terms of strikeout rate, **Chris Resop** is half the man he used to be, and he played the role of punching bag across two levels last season. With a dissipating fastball and vacating pitch command, his big-league opportunities could be numbered. ⊘ Pitch command has long been at the top of **Fernando Rodriguez**'s bucket list; after missing the entire 2013 season recovering from Tommy John surgery, he could be a long way from crossing off that particular item. ⊘ **Andrew Werner** lives at the mercy of balls in play, and he lacks the velocity differential in his secondaries to allow his 88 mph fastball to function at an above-average level. Pitch command is his only hope, but Werner walks the tightrope between throwing strikes and getting hammered. ⊘ The clock is ticking on former phenom **Michael Ynoa**, whose service time requires a place on the 40-man roster despite the fact that he has pitched all of 115 innings since signing with Oakland in 2008 and has yet to clear the hurdle of High-A.

MANAGER: BOB MELVIN

YEAR	TEAM	W-L	Pythag +/-	Avg PC	100+ P	120+ P	QS	BQS	REL	REL w Zero R	IBB	PH	PH Avg	PH HR	SB2	CS2	SB3	CS3	SAC Att	SAC %	POS SAC	Squeeze	Swing	In Play
2011	OAK	47-52	0	100.4	51	1	55	3	282	220	9	30	.276	2	56	26	19	2	38	57.9%	20	0	229	63
2012	OAK	93-67	1	92.7	52	0	88	4	456	381	34	93	.231	3	87	24	33	5	42	64.3%	26	0	297	74
2013	OAK	96-66	1	94.8	56	0	92	2	447	370	23	130	.135	5	58	24	17	3	37	56.8%	21	2	253	87

Each season Melvin has managed the A's, Oakland has had the league's most improved offense in the second half of the season. From 2011-2013, the A's have scored 3.89 runs per game in the first half of the year, before exploding to 4.99 runs per contest after the break. Across the AL as a whole, run scoring per game actually goes down a tick in the second half.

The 2013 A's drew 145 more walks than they surrendered. That makes Oakland the third franchise to post a walk differential better than +100 under Melvin. The 2003 Mariners and 2008 Diamondbacks also did it. The only other skippers to do that since World War II are Leo Durocher, Steve O'Neill and Gene Mauch. Typically, his batters are better with walks than his pitchers. His teams have never led the league in walks drawn or come in second place, but in five of his eight full seasons as manager his clubs have finished in the top four in walks drawn.

Philadelphia Phillies

By Tommy Bennett

Here's the argument: Philadelphia Phillies General Manager Ruben Amaro Jr. is as good a reason for reviving the strong version of the Sapir-Whorf hypothesis as I have heard. Sapir-Whorf—a linguistic theory mostly discredited in the 1960s—contends that the language you speak determines the concepts you know. The strong version says that concepts from other languages are *inaccessible* to non-speakers. A common example of this claim is that some languages have names for colors that other languages do not. In those languages where the color has no name, the argument goes, speakers are much more likely to describe an object of that color as being some other color. If your language had no word for blue, you might say the sky was light green or light purple, basically.

Put slightly differently: Amaro and the rest of the Phillies' front office don't get it, and they never will, because they're speaking an entirely different language. So poorly is this team managed that any attempt to describe what might happen next must be informed by an evaluation of the enormity of the front office's blunders to date. So let's step back for a moment to consider the consequences of this front office's missteps.

To accurately describe how most Phillies fans feel about their team's vertiginous plunge in fortune might run me afoul of BP's standards-and-practices department. Put it this way: When Amaro appeared at Phillies Alumni Day in August—to celebrate his contribution to the 1993 club, as a *player*, mind you—he was roundly booed. Between the Phillies' first championship in a generation, in 2008, and the 2011 season, they averaged 96 wins. In 2012, they were a .500 team. In 2013, the Phillies fielded their worst squad since 1997.

That '97 team, you hopefully do not recall, featured Rico Brogna and his .724 OPS at first base. But it was a switch-hitting fourth outfielder, a feel-good throwback to the team's 1993 glory days, that best exemplified how miserable things had gotten down Broad Street. Amaro got exactly 200 plate appearances and hit just .234/.320/.314, a line that barely bested Rex Hudler's .221/.264/.377 and Kevin Sefcik's .269/.298/.345. All of which is to say that Amaro has finally been given the chance to remake the Phillies in his own image.

The old-look Phillies—call 'em Delmon Young and the Gang!—had the third-worst unadjusted offense in the league, ahead of only the Cubs and Marlins. (That might not sound so bad until you realize that at 3.17 runs per game the 2013 Marlins scored fewer runs than any National League team since the 1971 Padres.) In scoring just 3.77 runs per game, Kevin Frandsen and the Pips recorded the team's worst offensive season since 1988. It's almost as if, in a seeming effort to litter Phillies media guides with worse seasons than his own 1997, Amaro went about collecting lousy hitters with an abandon typically seen on a 3 a.m. rerun of *Hoarders*. Instead of major-league outfielders, the 2013 Phillies had Ben Revere (.338 OBP and .352 SLG), Young (.302 OBP and .397 SLG), John Mayberry (.286 OBP and .391 SLG), Cesar Hernandez (.344 OBP and .331 SLG), Roger Bernadina (.256 OBP and .347 SLG) and the ghostly Casper Wells (one hit and eight strikeouts in 26 PA). And while the Phillies signed prodigal 2003 Rookie of the Year candidate Marlon Byrd this offseason (two years, $16 million, with a vesting option for the third year), he is a career .272 TAv hitter who is already 36 years old. (Congratulations on your second World Series ring, Mr. Victorino.)

All of this wouldn't be such a mystery if it weren't for the fact that the Phillies' pitching was *even worse* last year. This is a team that, two years ago, had commentators breathlessly wondering if they had assembled the greatest starting rotation in baseball history; the three best of those pitchers—Roy Halladay, Cliff Lee, Cole Hamels—remained on

PHILLIES PROSPECTUS
2013 W-L: 73-89, 4th in NL East

Pythag	.407	27th	DER	.687	29th
RS/G	3.77	26th	B-Age	30.1	28th
RA/G	4.62	25th	P-Age	28.9	24th
TAv	.248	26th	Salary	$159.6	3rd
BRR	6.54	6th	M$/MW	$5.99	29th
TAv-P	.273	25th	DL Days	950	15th
FIP	3.91	18th	$ on DL	22%	23rd

	Runs	HR/RH	HR/LH	Runs/RH	Runs/LH
Three-Year Park Factors	105	117	108	108	109

Top Hitter WARP	3.40 (Chase Utley)
Top Pitcher WARP	3.66 (Cliff Lee)
Top Prospect	Maikel Franco

the 2013 roster. But it is simultaneously a team that allowed 4.62 runs per game, beating only the Rockies (a team that, oddly enough, employed the 2011 Phillies' fourth horseman, Roy Oswalt, to the tune of an 8.63 ERA in 32 innings). Yes, Halladay's departure and retirement is mitigated by the addition of Cuban signee Miguel Gonzalez (three years, $12 million). But the new third starter is a *signo de interrogación* if ever there was one: He enters spring training having pitched precisely zero professional innings in the United States.

"Speed-Dial" Amaro's failure to pick up the phone and rid the team of its unaffordable luxury item, Jonathan Papelbon, means that the closer will likely return during the ninth—and *only* the ninth—in 2014. Papelbon's remaining presence on the team is attributable at least in part to his comparatively poor performance in the second half of 2013: His 3.91 ERA helped push the team's bullpen ERA up to 4.19 (the league-wide number was 3.50). While Papelbon would have been by far the best closer available in June, he was obscured in the offseason trade market by the availability of free agents Joe Nathan, Grant Balfour and Joaquin Benoit.

What explains the rapid decline of what was, just two seasons ago, a 102-win juggernaut? Until last season, you might have chalked it up to Amaro's desire to win in the short term—to forestall his eventual ouster. This is the J.P. Ricciardi theory: GMs on short leashes compound the problem by focusing on the near future because they're unlikely to see the next round of bonus babies get their first cup of coffee. You might think that if you were trying to maximize short-term success, you'd acquire players who can hit, field or pitch. Ruben Amaro Jr. would disagree.

Since the trade deadline in 2012, the Phillies have traded or said farewell to Hunter Pence, Shane Victorino, Roy Halladay and Vance Worley. Each of those players had demonstrated the capacity to record a three-win season. But rather than signing flashy free agents to three-year deals in order to replace them, Amaro has acquired lousy players and paid too much for the privilege. Since the end of the 2012, the Phillies have added (in chronological order): Humberto Quintero, Ben Revere, Michael Young, Mauricio Robles, John Lannan, Mike Adams, Delmon Young, Yuniesky Betancourt, Chad Durbin, Luis Garcia, Ezequiel Carrera, John McDonald, Roger Bernardina, Miguel A. Gonzalez, Marlon Byrd, Brad Lincoln and Wil Nieves. Consider: the second-best player on that list (after Byrd) is almost certainly Gonzalez, and he's never thrown a pitch in front of a paying audience in America.

Wait a minute. Isn't this what we *want* GMs of declining, aging teams to do? *Not* buy old free agents who can barely forestall the inevitable? Well, maybe. At least, it's good to save money. But some of the players cost young talent (Revere, acquired for Worley and top-100 prospect Trevor May; Young, who cost the Phillies their best relief prospect in Lisalverto Bonilla, along with Josh Lindblom). And others cost serious,

as opposed to lottery-ticket, money: The Phillies agreed to pay Young more than $7 million, guaranteed Mike Adams $12 million (over two years), paid Chad Durbin $1.1 million, paid John Lannan $2.5 million and agreed to pay Delmon Young three quarters of a million dollars. Those signings were so pennywise but pound-foolish you can practically hear your grandmother decrying them.

So how'd they do, this cadre of castoffs acquired without the benefit of any discount? Michael Young cost the Phillies 0.5 WARP; Durbin cost the team 0.3 WARP; Adams cost the team 0.2 WARP; and Delmon Young cost the team 0.1 WARP. But hey, at least John Lannan was worth 0.3 WARP. Altogether, the Phillies agreed to pay those players more than $15 million in 2013 (they actually paid less after trading some away midseason), but got a total of negative 0.8 WARP on the deals. If this was a bid by Amaro to save his job, it was a truly terrible one. It's the general managing equivalent of a Delmon Young GIDP: as bad an outcome as you can imagine made worse by the realization that just about everyone saw it coming.

Perhaps Amaro is just a traditionalist. He doesn't buy into sabermetrics, doesn't hire analytics people,* and doesn't care for your acronyms. As assistant GM Scott Proefrock told the *Inquirer*'s Bob Brookover in 2012, "I honestly can't tell you the last time WAR or VORP or any of those things were brought up in a conversation. We're aware of them, and we understand what they are. It's just not something we find relevant." Maybe the Phillies' front office was pursuing a different measure of value based on traditional stats. Could this explain the violence with which they assaulted both the balance sheet and the win-loss record?

Maybe, but Michael Young hit .277 with eight home runs and 67 RBI the year before he joined the Phillies, and that was in *Texas*. Delmon Young, for his part, was a .267/18/74 guy in 2012, but he also struck out 112 times. Adams was coming off his worst ERA season in a decade. And Lannan spent most of 2012 in the minor leagues. So even if you asked the Topps Corporation, the *best* The Five Stairsteps were going to do was stanch the bleeding, not return the Phillies to glory.

And we see more of the same this offseason. You can wish on Gonzalez as much as you want, but he's unlikely to be more than a no. 3 starter. And a league-average season from Byrd (that is, something just north of his .276/.324/.395 line from 2011) would be considered a *good* outcome. Meanwhile, as we go to print, the team is shopping Domonic Brown and Jonathan Papelbon in search of another mid-rotation starter, perhaps because of the questions surrounding Gonzalez or because the Phillies apparently want to have zero above-average outfielders.

The point here isn't just that the Phillies have signed bad players to replace the good ones who have departed. It isn't that the Phillies, as a team, posted a .306 OBP in 2013 or that they explicitly disclaim reliance on numerical analysis. It isn't even that the team's recent signings turned out, in retrospect, to be unwise.

No, the point is this: There is no rational method that could have led to the decisions the Phillies have made in the past 16 months.

Imagine building an artificial intelligence that would mimic the decisions that Amaro has made. We'd need an algorithm to describe his decision-making procedure. In a nod to PECOTA, we'd call it JELTZ. We'd run regressions on the kinds of factors a team *should* consider: you know, expected performance. We'd even throw in variables representing the kinds of things misguided teams consider: GWRBI and hot-foot skills.

We could never build JELTZ. The best we could do would be a random-number generator. There's no pattern here, at least not one that is consistent with a desire to win baseball games or keep one's own gainful employment. This is the dartboard of your nightmares: Throwing blindfolded, you accidentally end up not on triple 20s but on triple "Dear God, Roger Bernadina is up to bat *again*?!" In order to create an accurate JELTZ system, we'd need to build a machine we could tell to go to the store for milk and have it come home with Delmon Young.

So let's come back to the argument you were promised at the outset of this essay: that Amaro represents the strongest point in favor of the strong-form Sapir-Whorf hypothesis.

Now, we know Amaro, Proefrock, et al. don't bring VORP up in conversation. But what if they meant that they *literally* don't speak the language of analytics? That would certainly impoverish them of sophisticated tools like TAv and advance fielding metrics. But the language of analytics isn't about specific statistics so much as it is about an approach to problem-solving under conditions of uncertainty. So the Phillies front office's unfamiliarity with that language might also rob them of critical grammatical concepts like *maximization subject to constraints* and *evaluation of relevant alternatives*, and perhaps even the concept of *cardinal, as opposed to ordinal, value*. Like the other 99 Inuit words for snow are to us, such concepts would be foreign to a non-speaker of the language of analytics. If you gave these guys, in a double-blind study, the choice between $20 in beer money and signing Ryan Howard to a five-year extension a year early, they'd pick Howard—but only if they could give him the $20, too.

This explains Amaro's most puzzling decision: the one he made to be neither a buyer nor a seller at the 2013 trade deadline. To us, it looks like the kind of indecision at a critical moment that leaves a middling team unequipped to compete and unable to rebuild. But to the Phillies' front office, perhaps this is the kind of advance move that transcends strategy. Maybe letting Papelbon rot on the vine was the ultimate in post-decisive management philosophy. Without being able to speak their language, we'll never know.

In the end, Charlie Manuel got the axe for Amaro's mistakes. The 2013 Phillies were a 73-win team because their players were not very good at baseball, at least not compared to the major-league average. And the numbers guys can snark at Amaro until they're red in the face. But they will only look at you and see green.

Ah, well. Look on the bright side. There's always whichever year comes after Amaro's last as GM.

* In November, the Phillies announced that they had hired an analytics expert to assist their front-office operations. Shock! Horror! But then the full story came out: The Commissioner's office contacted the Phillies and suggested they hire someone who knew the difference between a fraction and a sum. Assistant GM Proefrock calls the arrangement an "externship." This is the only analytics guy in the entire organization. I swear I'm not making this up.

Tommy Bennett clerks for a federal judge in Manhattan, where he waits patiently for a case or controversy providing an appropriate vehicle to consider the ongoing vitality of Federal Baseball Club of Baltimore, Inc. v. National League of Professional Baseball Clubs, *259 U.S. 200 (1922).*

HITTERS

	YEAR	TEAM	LVL	AGE	PA	R	2B	3B	HR	RBI	BB	SO	SB	CS	AVG/OBP/SLG	TAv	BABIP	BRR	FRAA	WARP
Cody Asche 3B Born: 6/30/1990 Age: 24 Bats: L Throws: R Height: 6' 1" Weight: 180 Breakout: 1% Improve: 22% Collapse: 18% Attrition: 31% MLB: 59% **Comparables:** Josh Bell, Ryan Wheeler, Brandon Laird	2011	WPT	A-	21	268	14	11	0	2	19	24	50	0	3	.192/.273/.264	.219	.234	-1.9	2B(51): 3.1	-0.2
	2012	CLR	A+	22	270	31	13	3	2	25	12	37	10	2	.349/.378/.447	.277	.399	-0.6	3B(61): -3.0	0.6
	2012	REA	AA	22	289	42	20	3	10	47	22	56	1	1	.300/.360/.513	.306	.348	-1	3B(67): -1.3	2.2
	2013	LEH	AAA	23	446	52	24	4	15	68	35	95	11	3	.295/.352/.485	.285	.349	0.5	3B(103): 4.9	2.8
	2013	PHI	MLB	23	179	18	8	1	5	22	15	43	1	0	.235/.302/.389	.250	.287	0.9	3B(44): -0.7	0.6
	2014	PHI	MLB	24	266	28	13	2	8	32	15	63	2	1	.257/.301/.413	.256	.310	-0.1	3B -1, 2B 0	0.5

With fellow third base prospect Maikel Franco grabbing all of the Phillies-related scouthound headlines, Cody Asche flew under the radar. But the former fourth-round pick led his Triple-A team in slugging and, with a head start on Franco, gets first crack at the position in the majors. Asche's defense has progressed slowly over his minor-league career, but he looked comfortable in Philadelphia. He is still a below-average defender but is a hard worker who has overcome weaknesses before. He's the favorite to win the starting job, though he'll surely be keeping an eye on those Franco headlines.

Roger Bernadina CF

Born: 6/12/1984 Age: 30
Bats: L Throws: L Height: 6' 2"
Weight: 200 Breakout: 1%
Improve: 43% Collapse: 6%
Attrition: 13% MLB: 88%

Comparables:
Larry Bigbie, Joel Youngblood, Jeff DaVanon

YEAR	TEAM	LVL	AGE	PA	R	2B	3B	HR	RBI	BB	SO	SB	CS	AVG/OBP/SLG	TAv	BABIP	BRR	FRAA	WARP
2011	SYR	AAA	27	188	26	9	0	6	14	18	47	14	5	.250/.339/.415	.289	.315	0.4	CF(25): -4.5, LF(9): -0.0	0.6
2011	WAS	MLB	27	337	40	12	2	7	27	27	63	17	3	.243/.301/.362	.245	.285	1.4	CF(56): -6.0, LF(36): 1.2	0.0
2012	WAS	MLB	28	261	25	11	0	5	25	28	53	15	3	.291/.372/.405	.284	.359	-1.3	LF(57): 0.1, CF(37): 0.2	1.6
2013	WAS	MLB	29	167	18	6	1	2	6	12	44	3	0	.178/.247/.270	.187	.236	1.2	LF(29): -0.6, RF(28): -0.9	-0.9
2013	PHI	MLB	29	83	8	4	1	2	5	4	21	1	0	.187/.256/.347	.215	.231	0.8	RF(12): -0.2, CF(12): 0.2	-0.1
2014	PHI	MLB	30	250	33	10	1	6	23	20	56	11	4	.239/.308/.371	.248	.290	1.1	CF -3, LF -0	0.1

When Ben Revere went down in July, the Phillies plugged center field with a series of implausible solutions, primarily 6-foot-6 John Mayberry, whom UZR rates as 19 runs below average per 150 games in center. They finally claimed Bernadina off waivers in mid-August, but the offensive struggles that got him waived traveled with him. His cumulative line was fourth-worst in baseball, minimum 250 plate appearances, a filter he's unlikely to clear again this season.

Domonic Brown LF

Born: 9/3/1987 Age: 26
Bats: L Throws: L Height: 6' 5"
Weight: 205 Breakout: 3%
Improve: 47% Collapse: 8%
Attrition: 14% MLB: 96%

Comparables:
Chase Headley, Desmond Jennings, Chris Coghlan

YEAR	TEAM	LVL	AGE	PA	R	2B	3B	HR	RBI	BB	SO	SB	CS	AVG/OBP/SLG	TAv	BABIP	BRR	FRAA	WARP
2011	CLR	A+	23	21	4	1	0	2	4	2	3	0	0	.368/.429/.737	.364	.357	0.1	RF(5): -0.9	0.2
2011	LEH	AAA	23	174	22	6	0	3	15	28	33	12	4	.261/.391/.370	.307	.311	-0.6	LF(14): -0.5, RF(5): 0.1	0.5
2011	PHI	MLB	23	210	28	10	1	5	19	25	35	3	1	.245/.333/.391	.283	.276	2.8	RF(52): -4.3	0.5
2012	LEH	AAA	24	239	33	13	2	5	28	17	42	4	6	.286/.335/.432	.268	.331	-2.2	LF(43): -0.1, CF(11): -0.9	0.5
2012	PHI	MLB	24	212	21	11	2	5	26	21	34	0	0	.235/.316/.396	.252	.260	-3.5	RF(38): -0.8, LF(29): 1.1	0.0
2013	PHI	MLB	25	540	65	21	4	27	83	39	97	8	3	.272/.324/.494	.292	.287	2.7	LF(132): -13.6, RF(2): 0.1	2.0
2014	PHI	MLB	26	474	59	22	2	18	63	39	93	9	4	.265/.327/.453	.282	.300	-0.2	LF -5, RF -1	1.4

Despite being the team's best prospect back in 2009-10, Brown was always made to perform to earn a job at the major-league level. Injuries, inconsistent playing time and frequent shuttles between Triple-A and the majors nearly erased his status as a prospect within the organization. In 2013, he hit 12 home runs in May alone, earning his first All-Star nomination and finishing as one of only a handful of Phillies to provide above-average value. He has, at long last, cemented his spot on the Phillies' roster. Now, for an encore.

Marlon Byrd RF

Born: 8/30/1977 Age: 36
Bats: R Throws: R Height: 6' 0"
Weight: 245 Breakout: 0%
Improve: 22% Collapse: 10%
Attrition: 11% MLB: 76%

Comparables:
Kirby Puckett, Dave Winfield, Hank Bauer

YEAR	TEAM	LVL	AGE	PA	R	2B	3B	HR	RBI	BB	SO	SB	CS	AVG/OBP/SLG	TAv	BABIP	BRR	FRAA	WARP
2011	CHN	MLB	33	482	51	22	2	9	35	25	78	3	2	.276/.324/.395	.262	.316	-1.6	CF(118): 0.6	1.6
2012	CHN	MLB	34	47	1	0	0	0	2	3	10	0	1	.070/.149/.070	.136	.091	-0.4	CF(13): 0.9	-0.4
2012	BOS	MLB	34	106	9	2	0	1	7	2	21	0	2	.270/.286/.320	.232	.325	-0.5	CF(33): 0.7, RF(2): -0.0	0.1
2013	PIT	MLB	35	115	14	9	0	3	17	6	20	0	0	.318/.357/.486	.291	.365	-0.6	RF(27): -1.7, LF(2): -0.1	0.4
2013	NYN	MLB	35	464	61	26	5	21	71	25	124	2	4	.285/.330/.518	.311	.350	0.1	RF(111): -5.6, CF(2): -0.3	2.7
2014	PHI	MLB	36	459	47	25	1	12	53	21	94	3	3	.264/.310/.411	.265	.310	-1.1	RF -4, CF -0	0.7

A strong effort in winter ball earned Byrd a spring look with the Mets. That he broke camp with the team was no surprise, but his subsequent performance turned heads. Byrd was a good player before he was struck in the face with a pitch in 2011 and fell apart entirely in 2012, but posted career-bests across the board in 2013 when accounting for the run environment. He continued to hit after being sent to Pittsburgh, and finished with an eventful postseason. It's impossible to bank on an old player sustaining career-best production, but there's a chance Byrd is back to being a legitimate starter. Ruben Amaro is betting that he is.

J.P. Crawford SS

Born: 1/11/1995 Age: 19
Bats: L Throws: R Height: 6' 2"
Weight: 180 Breakout: 0%
Improve: 0% Collapse: 0%
Attrition: 0% MLB: 0%

Comparables:
Jonathan Schoop, Ruben Tejada, Elvis Andrus

YEAR	TEAM	LVL	AGE	PA	R	2B	3B	HR	RBI	BB	SO	SB	CS	AVG/OBP/SLG	TAv	BABIP	BRR	FRAA	WARP
2013	LWD	A	18	60	10	1	0	0	2	7	10	2	1	.208/.300/.226	.220	.256	-0.3	SS(14): 0.1	0.1
2014	PHI	MLB	19	250	25	9	1	3	18	18	65	3	1	.209/.268/.291	.208	.270	-0.1	SS 0	-0.3

The Phillies selected Crawford 16th overall in June, their reward for falling well short of expectations the year prior. Crawford handled the Rookie league and Low-A just fine in his first taste of professional baseball, posting a .405 on-base percentage and producing nearly as many walks as strikeouts. He likely won't ever hit for power, but if his current tools progress as expected, the club will be able to live with it. The Phillies have traditionally brought players along slowly, so it will be interesting to see whether they rush Crawford to be ready to succeed Jimmy Rollins when his contract expires, likely after 2015.

Maikel Franco 3B

Born: 8/26/1992 Age: 21
Bats: R Throws: R Height: 6' 1"
Weight: 180 Breakout: 7%
Improve: 15% Collapse: 1%
Attrition: 16% MLB: 26%

Comparables:
Lonnie Chisenhall, Dayan Viciedo, Josh Vitters

YEAR	TEAM	LVL	AGE	PA	R	2B	3B	HR	RBI	BB	SO	SB	CS	AVG/OBP/SLG	TAv	BABIP	BRR	FRAA	WARP
2011	LWD	A	18	67	6	2	0	1	6	1	15	0	0	.123/.149/.200	.143	.143	0	3B(14): -0.9	-0.7
2011	WPT	A-	18	229	19	17	1	2	38	25	30	0	0	.287/.367/.411	.294	.327	-3.4	3B(27): 0.2	0.8
2012	LWD	A	19	554	70	32	3	14	84	38	80	3	1	.280/.336/.439	.273	.306	-0.2	3B(122): -13.1	1.1
2013	CLR	A+	20	289	42	23	1	16	52	20	39	0	0	.299/.349/.576	.315	.297	-0.5	3B(64): -6.1	2.2
2013	REA	AA	20	292	47	13	2	15	51	10	31	1	2	.339/.363/.563	.336	.338	0.9	3B(59): 3.4, 1B(8): -0.3	3.7
2014	PHI	MLB	21	250	26	12	1	9	33	8	49	0	0	.257/.284/.432	.256	.280	-0.4	3B -3, 1B -0	0.1

Franco will enter 2014 as the no. 1 prospect in the Phillies' system. Admittedly, it's a weak system, but that doesn't diminish Franco's luster. He got his first taste of life above A-ball in mid-June and, at just 20, he circled his competition. The Phillies haven't had a homegrown third baseman since Scott Rolen, plodding through the years since with Placido Polanco, David Bell, Pedro Feliz, Polanco again and Michael Young. Cody Asche put a claim on the starting job with a strong second-half debut, but the position ultimately is Franco's to lose in 2015 and beyond. He'll start the 2014 season with Triple-A Lehigh Valley.

Kevin Frandsen 2B

Born: 5/24/1982 Age: 32
Bats: R Throws: R Height: 6' 0"
Weight: 185 Breakout: 3%
Improve: 15% Collapse: 7%
Attrition: 21% MLB: 48%

Comparables:
Sean Burroughs, Jason Tyner, Jim Rushford

YEAR	TEAM	LVL	AGE	PA	R	2B	3B	HR	RBI	BB	SO	SB	CS	AVG/OBP/SLG	TAv	BABIP	BRR	FRAA	WARP
2011	LEH	AAA	29	322	32	13	3	4	40	11	31	10	3	.303/.356/.412	.286	.322	0.5	3B(13): -1.1, 2B(9): -0.8	0.8
2012	LEH	AAA	30	418	38	34	0	1	33	14	21	2	4	.302/.337/.396	.251	.323	0.5	2B(81): -0.1, 1B(10): -0.8	0.7
2012	PHI	MLB	30	210	24	10	3	2	14	9	18	0	1	.338/.383/.451	.294	.366	-1.7	3B(52): -3.0	0.8
2013	PHI	MLB	31	278	27	10	1	5	26	12	29	1	0	.234/.296/.341	.233	.245	-1.6	1B(40): -0.1, 2B(20): -0.6	-0.5
2014	PHI	MLB	32	298	32	14	1	4	25	12	35	2	1	.258/.308/.363	.246	.280	-0.5	2B -0, 3B -1	0.1

Well, yeah, the guy's great when he has a .366 BABIP, and he's terrible when he has a .245 BABIP, and there's Kevin Frandsen's entire bio with the Phillies. The question is whether those BABIPs just *happen* or whether he's an agent of change, and the answer suggests the good ones just happen and the bad ones are his signature. Frandsen is one of the worm-killingest hitters in the league, and of the dozen players with higher groundball rates in 2013 all but two or three could be considered speedsters. Frandsen's not, and his career BABIP is just .275. He turns 32 in May and doesn't provide much in the way of power, speed or defense, but does offer enough utility to fit onto a roster.

Freddy Galvis SS

Born: 11/14/1989 Age: 24
Bats: B Throws: R Height: 5' 10"
Weight: 170 Breakout: 2%
Improve: 19% Collapse: 7%
Attrition: 22% MLB: 50%

Comparables:
Yuniesky Betancourt, Alcides Escobar, Andres Blanco

YEAR	TEAM	LVL	AGE	PA	R	2B	3B	HR	RBI	BB	SO	SB	CS	AVG/OBP/SLG	TAv	BABIP	BRR	FRAA	WARP
2011	REA	AA	21	464	63	22	4	8	35	28	68	19	11	.273/.326/.400	.267	.308	1.9	SS(75): 10.3	2.6
2011	LEH	AAA	21	126	15	6	1	0	8	3	18	4	2	.298/.315/.364	.196	.350	1.2	SS(17): -0.2	0.0
2012	PHI	MLB	22	200	14	15	1	3	24	7	29	0	0	.226/.254/.363	.211	.253	0.7	2B(55): 3.3, SS(5): 0.7	-0.2
2013	LEH	AAA	23	266	26	14	2	3	25	11	51	3	1	.245/.274/.357	.221	.290	0.4	SS(56): -5.7, 2B(3): -0.3	-0.3
2013	PHI	MLB	23	222	13	5	4	6	19	13	45	1	0	.234/.283/.385	.238	.273	1	2B(23): 0.1, 3B(16): 0.6	0.4
2014	PHI	MLB	24	250	27	12	2	5	22	10	47	4	2	.240/.275/.366	.227	.270	0.1	SS 0, 2B 1	0.3

Galvis does one thing very well—pick it—and one thing very poorly—hit it—but, roster inflexibility being what it is in Philadelphia, he spent part of 2013 in left field, neither picking nor hitting. The bat is just punchy enough to support a strong defensive shortstop (which Galvis is), but not a corner outfielder. So, while the experience in left adds a wrinkle to his resume, it doesn't do much for his long-term value.

Cesar Hernandez 2B

Born: 5/23/1990 Age: 24
Bats: B Throws: R Height: 5' 10"
Weight: 175 Breakout: 2%
Improve: 18% Collapse: 7%
Attrition: 17% MLB: 43%

Comparables:
Emilio Bonifacio, Jonathan Herrera, Hernan Iribarren

YEAR	TEAM	LVL	AGE	PA	R	2B	3B	HR	RBI	BB	SO	SB	CS	AVG/OBP/SLG	TAv	BABIP	BRR	FRAA	WARP
2011	CLR	A+	21	452	47	7	4	4	37	23	80	23	10	.268/.306/.333	.248	.322	1.3	2B(88): 1.8	0.7
2012	REA	AA	22	450	50	26	11	2	51	27	67	16	12	.304/.345/.436	.280	.358	0.7	2B(102): -1.4	1.9
2012	LEH	AAA	22	129	13	4	1	0	6	4	11	5	3	.248/.270/.298	.229	.270	0.7	2B(30): 0.1	0.0
2013	LEH	AAA	23	440	59	12	9	2	34	41	81	32	8	.309/.375/.402	.281	.384	3.8	2B(79): -2.5, CF(19): -0.0	2.4
2013	PHI	MLB	23	131	17	5	0	0	10	9	26	0	3	.289/.344/.331	.237	.368	-1.2	CF(22): -1.0, 2B(10): -0.0	-0.2
2014	PHI	MLB	24	250	28	9	3	2	19	13	49	9	4	.268/.307/.364	.246	.320	0.5	2B -1, CF -0	0.4

The Phillies brought Hernandez through the system as a second baseman, but decided to test him in center field midway through the International League season. This proved prescient—or, if you're an unhinged conspiracy theorist able to fit any evidence into your fantastical worldview, very suspicious—when, two weeks later, Ben Revere broke his foot. He got a

September call-up and, to the Phillies' delight, played well. His newfound versatility should open up some doors for him in 2014, assuming the Illuminati make sure somebody on the Phillies gets conveniently disabled.

Ryan Howard 1B
Born: 11/19/1979 Age: 34
Bats: L Throws: L Height: 6' 4"
Weight: 240 Breakout: 0%
Improve: 22% Collapse: 7%
Attrition: 17% MLB: 91%
Comparables:
Carlos Pena, Jose Canseco, Richie Sexson

YEAR	TEAM	LVL	AGE	PA	R	2B	3B	HR	RBI	BB	SO	SB	CS	AVG/OBP/SLG	TAv	BABIP	BRR	FRAA	WARP
2011	PHI	MLB	31	644	81	30	1	33	116	75	172	1	0	.253/.346/.488	.310	.303	-9.4	1B(149): 0.2	2.5
2012	PHI	MLB	32	292	28	11	0	14	56	25	99	0	0	.219/.295/.423	.247	.287	-4.1	1B(67): -3.8	-0.9
2013	PHI	MLB	33	317	34	20	2	11	43	23	95	0	0	.266/.319/.465	.278	.349	-1.6	1B(76): -1.9	0.6
2014	PHI	MLB	34	296	38	13	1	15	44	28	85	1	0	.251/.328/.472	.285	.310	-0.4	1B -0	1.0

We told you so.

Tommy Joseph C
Born: 7/16/1991 Age: 22
Bats: R Throws: R Height: 6' 1"
Weight: 215 Breakout: 1%
Improve: 5% Collapse: 6%
Attrition: 16% MLB: 17%
Comparables:
Josh Phegley, Luis Exposito, Austin Romine

YEAR	TEAM	LVL	AGE	PA	R	2B	3B	HR	RBI	BB	SO	SB	CS	AVG/OBP/SLG	TAv	BABIP	BRR	FRAA	WARP
2011	SJO	A+	19	560	80	33	2	22	95	29	102	1	0	.270/.317/.471	.290	.295	-1.9	C(33): 0.4, 1B(7): 0.6	1.8
2012	REA	AA	20	114	12	8	0	3	10	9	32	0	1	.250/.327/.420	.256	.333	-0.4	C(24): -0.6, 1B(2): -0.1	0.3
2012	RIC	AA	20	335	32	16	0	8	38	25	64	0	3	.260/.313/.391	.261	.300	-2.2	C(50): -0.2, 1B(14): -0.6	1.0
2013	CLR	A+	21	42	0	2	0	0	1	0	13	0	0	.095/.095/.143	.095	.138	-0.5	C(8): -0.1	-0.6
2013	LEH	AAA	21	72	6	1	0	3	14	4	15	0	1	.209/.264/.358	.209	.224	-1.2	C(21): -0.6	-0.3
2014	PHI	MLB	22	250	22	11	0	7	28	12	66	0	0	.226/.267/.366	.229	.280	-0.6	C -1, 1B -0	0.1

Joseph was the prize acquired from the Giants in the Hunter Pence trade. The 22-year-old was expected to be the eventual successor to Carlos Ruiz, but a concussion in May fractured his season and might ultimately force a move to first base. In 72 games spent mostly between Single-A and Double-A, Joseph posted an aggregate .514 OPS, with his power almost completely sapped. Combined with the progression of Cameron Rupp, Joseph might not get a shot until September 2014, if he gets one at all.

John Mayberry CF
Born: 12/21/1983 Age: 30
Bats: R Throws: R Height: 6' 6"
Weight: 225 Breakout: 1%
Improve: 27% Collapse: 5%
Attrition: 13% MLB: 74%
Comparables:
Will Venable, Joe Borchard, Eric Valent

YEAR	TEAM	LVL	AGE	PA	R	2B	3B	HR	RBI	BB	SO	SB	CS	AVG/OBP/SLG	TAv	BABIP	BRR	FRAA	WARP
2011	LEH	AAA	27	122	16	8	0	4	15	5	23	2	0	.265/.287/.442	.170	.289	0.6	RF(5): -0.3, CF(4): -0.1	-0.4
2011	PHI	MLB	27	296	37	17	1	15	49	26	55	8	3	.273/.341/.513	.310	.293	-0.4	CF(32): -0.1, LF(21): 0.2	2.3
2012	PHI	MLB	28	479	53	24	0	14	46	34	111	1	0	.245/.301/.395	.257	.296	-2.4	LF(70): 4.1, CF(58): 0.5	1.3
2013	PHI	MLB	29	384	47	23	1	11	39	27	90	5	3	.227/.286/.391	.252	.273	-0.6	RF(79): -2.9, CF(46): 1.2	0.2
2014	PHI	MLB	30	380	43	18	1	13	48	27	92	5	2	.241/.301/.413	.263	.290	-0.2	CF 0, RF -1	1.1

Mayberry is the kind of player a team like the Athletics would creatively utilize. With the Phillies since 2009, however, he has been comically miscast. He has faced right-handed pitching in more than three-fifths of his career plate appearances despite posting a .668 OPS against them (think Elvis Andrus). He also possesses poor instincts and scant range defensively, but that didn't stop the Phillies from putting him in center when Ben Revere was hurt just before the All-Star break. Mayberry is a mediocre player who can be quite useful when in capable hands. The Phillies don't have anyone on payroll with such hands.

Wil Nieves C
Born: 9/25/1977 Age: 36
Bats: R Throws: R Height: 5' 11"
Weight: 190 Breakout: 2%
Improve: 19% Collapse: 10%
Attrition: 24% MLB: 60%
Comparables:
Henry Blanco, Buddy Rosar, Bo Diaz

YEAR	TEAM	LVL	AGE	PA	R	2B	3B	HR	RBI	BB	SO	SB	CS	AVG/OBP/SLG	TAv	BABIP	BRR	FRAA	WARP
2011	GWN	AAA	33	79	8	2	0	1	6	6	11	1	0	.282/.333/.352	.205	.317	-0.2	C(10): -0.2	-0.2
2011	NAS	AAA	33	95	3	2	0	1	6	4	11	0	0	.170/.213/.227	.146	.182	-0.6	C(15): -0.1	-0.6
2011	MIL	MLB	33	54	2	2	0	0	0	3	12	0	0	.140/.189/.180	.119	.184	0.3	C(17): 0.7	-0.4
2012	CSP	AAA	34	123	15	4	0	3	16	6	20	1	1	.306/.336/.423	.252	.344	0.2	C(31): -0.1	0.5
2012	COL	MLB	34	51	3	2	0	1	5	3	9	0	0	.298/.333/.404	.229	.342	-2.7	C(12): 0.1, 1B(2): -0.0	-0.3
2012	ARI	MLB	34	38	4	1	0	1	3	1	8	0	1	.306/.324/.417	.249	.370	0.2	C(12): 0.0	0.1
2013	ARI	MLB	35	206	16	11	0	1	22	8	32	0	0	.297/.320/.369	.246	.345	-2.2	C(47): 0.3	0.5
2014	PHI	MLB	36	250	21	10	0	3	21	12	50	1	0	.235/.275/.320	.215	.280	-0.5	C 1, 1B -0	0.1

Look up "sexy" in the dictionary and you might read "36-year-old free agent backup catcher," provided you're reading that gag dictionary you got for the holidays. But Nieves did what Arizona asked of him: He showed up every fifth day, filled in when the starting catcher was hurt for a month and held his own at the plate. Everything about him is okay, except for his age. Despite the sudden revival of his batting average the past two years, it'll suggest something has gone wrong for his team if he steps to plate 200 times again this year.

Laynce Nix — LF

Born: 10/30/1980 Age: 33
Bats: L Throws: L Height: 6' 1''
Weight: 220 Breakout: 2%
Improve: 24% Collapse: 7%
Attrition: 15% MLB: 85%

Comparables:
Preston Wilson, Joe Carter, Casey Blake

YEAR	TEAM	LVL	AGE	PA	R	2B	3B	HR	RBI	BB	SO	SB	CS	AVG/OBP/SLG	TAv	BABIP	BRR	FRAA	WARP
2011	WAS	MLB	30	351	38	15	1	16	44	23	82	2	2	.250/.299/.451	.281	.284	-1.6	LF(73): -2.6, RF(12): -0.3	1.1
2012	CLR	A+	31	20	1	2	0	1	4	4	2	0	0	.250/.400/.562	.303	.231	0	1B(3): 0.1	0.1
2012	PHI	MLB	31	127	13	10	0	3	16	12	42	0	0	.246/.315/.412	.267	.357	-1.4	LF(18): 0.1, RF(10): 0.0	0.3
2013	PHI	MLB	32	136	11	4	0	2	7	8	44	1	0	.180/.228/.258	.182	.256	0.6	RF(25): 0.8, 1B(8): -0.0	-0.6
2014	PHI	MLB	33	250	26	13	1	8	31	17	67	1	1	.236/.291/.404	.251	.290	-0.4	LF -1, RF 0	0.2

To paraphrase Jay Sherman from *The Critic*, "he stinks." Nix, signed by the Phillies before the 2012 season to be an effective bat off the bench, hit .180 with a .486 OPS before being released in early August. He struck out at a Ryan Howard clip (32 percent), drew very few walks (6 percent) and had almost no power (.078 ISO). Cliff Lee and Cole Hamels nearly out-hit him. Though GM Ruben Amaro had signed him to an ill-advised two-year deal, it meant relatively little in the big picture, so the Phillies will simply dust themselves off and go back to the drawing board when they look for a new left-handed bat off the bench.

Roman Quinn — SS

Born: 5/14/1993 Age: 21
Bats: B Throws: R Height: 5' 10''
Weight: 170 Breakout: 0%
Improve: 5% Collapse: 0%
Attrition: 2% MLB: 5%

Comparables:
Tim Beckham, Trevor Plouffe, Jeff Bianchi

YEAR	TEAM	LVL	AGE	PA	R	2B	3B	HR	RBI	BB	SO	SB	CS	AVG/OBP/SLG	TAv	BABIP	BRR	FRAA	WARP
2012	WPT	A-	19	309	56	9	11	1	23	28	61	30	6	.281/.370/.408	.300	.357	7.1	SS(66): -9.3	2.1
2013	LWD	A	20	298	37	7	3	5	21	27	64	32	9	.238/.323/.346	.263	.297	0.1	SS(65): -14.3	-0.6
2014	PHI	MLB	21	250	31	7	2	4	18	15	68	13	4	.210/.269/.314	.215	.270	1.4	SS -11	-1.1

Measured purely by excitement, Quinn might very well have been the most thrilling prospect in the Phillies' system. This says nothing about his quality as a player or his likelihood of making the majors, but he's been fun to watch—just look up his 14-second trip around the bases on an April inside-the-parker. His speed has drawn legit comparisons to that of Billy Hamilton, and he might reach triple-digits stolen base totals if given enough playing time. The Phillies drafted him out of high school in the second round in 2011, and he has handled the low minors well, stealing 30-plus bases in each of two half seasons. Then he went and ruptured his Achilles tendon in an offseason workout, which will cost him at least the first half of 2014. If Plan B involves developing power, Quinn is in trouble.

Ben Revere — CF

Born: 5/3/1988 Age: 26
Bats: L Throws: R Height: 5' 9''
Weight: 170 Breakout: 1%
Improve: 53% Collapse: 11%
Attrition: 19% MLB: 92%

Comparables:
Julio Borbon, Jacoby Ellsbury, Michael Bourn

YEAR	TEAM	LVL	AGE	PA	R	2B	3B	HR	RBI	BB	SO	SB	CS	AVG/OBP/SLG	TAv	BABIP	BRR	FRAA	WARP
2011	ROC	AAA	23	141	15	3	1	1	9	6	11	8	2	.303/.338/.364	.235	.325	0.1	CF(24): 2.5, LF(3): -0.3	0.2
2011	MIN	MLB	23	481	56	9	5	0	30	26	41	34	9	.267/.310/.309	.228	.293	8	CF(89): -2.7, LF(13): 0.7	0.0
2012	ROC	AAA	24	101	9	1	0	0	6	4	6	6	2	.330/.360/.340	.257	.348	1.6	CF(12): 0.6, LF(6): 0.4	0.5
2012	MIN	MLB	24	553	70	13	6	0	32	29	54	40	9	.294/.333/.342	.242	.325	9.6	RF(84): 2.7, CF(39): -1.0	1.5
2013	PHI	MLB	25	336	37	9	3	0	17	16	36	22	8	.305/.338/.352	.250	.344	1.5	CF(87): 6.5	1.5
2014	PHI	MLB	26	371	46	10	3	2	25	20	43	23	7	.279/.321/.348	.248	.310	2.2	CF 2, RF 0	1.0

Fast dude, slow start: Revere had a .456 OPS when the Phillies bumped him down in the lineup midway through April. But over the next two months the Phillies got the player they had traded for, an above-average defensive center fielder with a high batting average and speed on the bases. He hit .347 with 17 stolen bases from May 1st until July 13th, when he fouled a ball off his right foot and ended his season. It's not the sort of injury that should linger.

Jimmy Rollins — SS

Born: 11/27/1978 Age: 35
Bats: B Throws: R Height: 5' 8''
Weight: 180 Breakout: 0%
Improve: 32% Collapse: 4%
Attrition: 14% MLB: 85%

Comparables:
Marco Scutaro, Orlando Cabrera, Alan Trammell

YEAR	TEAM	LVL	AGE	PA	R	2B	3B	HR	RBI	BB	SO	SB	CS	AVG/OBP/SLG	TAv	BABIP	BRR	FRAA	WARP
2011	PHI	MLB	32	631	87	22	2	16	63	58	59	30	8	.268/.338/.399	.283	.275	-0.1	SS(138): 1.1	4.4
2012	PHI	MLB	33	699	102	33	5	23	68	62	96	30	5	.250/.316/.427	.269	.262	5.4	SS(156): -9.2	3.3
2013	PHI	MLB	34	666	65	36	2	6	39	59	93	22	6	.252/.318/.348	.241	.288	1.9	SS(153): -4.0	1.2
2014	PHI	MLB	35	632	81	29	3	15	59	50	81	24	5	.247/.308/.382	.251	.260	2.3	SS -8	1.6

Rollins had a terrible 2013 season, posting a career low .667 OPS with his highest strikeout rate since 2003. While his average and on-base percentage were similar to those put up in 2012, his power went dead. That sub-.100 ISO put him in the company of Michael Bourn and Darwin Barney—a far cry from the shortstop who slugged 30 home runs in 2007, or even the one with 61 extra-base hits a year earlier. Rollins has also lost range at shortstop and speed on the bases. He need look only a few feet to his left to find an example of a mid-30s infielder reversing a career decline, but he need only look a few feet to his right to see his replacement, Freddy Galvis, waiting greedily.

Darin Ruf   1B

Born: **7/28/1986** Age: **27**
Bats: **R** Throws: **R** Height: **6' 3"**
Weight: **220** Breakout: **5%**
Improve: **24%** Collapse: **11%**
Attrition: **22%** MLB: **59%**

Comparables:
Brandon Allen, Allen Craig, Jason Botts

YEAR	TEAM	LVL	AGE	PA	R	2B	3B	HR	RBI	BB	SO	SB	CS	AVG/OBP/SLG	TAv	BABIP	BRR	FRAA	WARP
2011	CLR	A+	24	554	72	43	1	17	82	56	95	0	1	.308/.388/.506	.320	.351	-2.3	1B(51): 2.4, LF(5): -0.4	3.0
2012	REA	AA	25	584	93	32	1	38	104	65	102	2	0	.317/.408/.620	.348	.325	-2.2	1B(107): -3.5, LF(29): -1.5	5.9
2012	PHI	MLB	25	37	4	2	1	3	10	2	12	0	0	.333/.351/.727	.369	.400	-0.2	LF(6): -0.4, 1B(3): 0.1	0.4
2013	LEH	AAA	26	350	44	22	0	7	46	36	88	1	2	.266/.343/.407	.264	.343	-0.5	LF(60): -2.1, 1B(19): -0.3	0.7
2013	PHI	MLB	26	293	36	11	0	14	30	33	91	0	0	.247/.348/.458	.279	.324	0.7	1B(36): 0.9, RF(29): -1.7	0.8
2014	PHI	MLB	27	346	42	17	0	15	50	31	90	0	0	.255/.333/.463	.285	.310	-0.7	1B -0, LF -1	1.1

Many expected Ruf to be overmatched by a longer exposure to major-league pitching. He not only held his own, but more or less matched the breakout season of hype machine Domonic Brown. Righties didn't bother him, and he drew walks in a lineup that otherwise doesn't. Curiously, it was lefties who gave him the most trouble, holding him to a .656 OPS in 81 plate appearances, but Ruf crushed lefties in the mnors so consider that more likely fluke than trend. Doubters, though, remain, and the swing-and-miss in his game will make 2014 a year of adjustments. Like Ryan Howard, Ruf has exploitable tendencies; unlike Howard, he doesn't have 80 power.

Carlos Ruiz   C

Born: **1/22/1979** Age: **35**
Bats: **R** Throws: **R** Height: **5' 10"**
Weight: **205** Breakout: **0%**
Improve: **32%** Collapse: **6%**
Attrition: **15%** MLB: **89%**

Comparables:
Smoky Burgess, Yogi Berra, Mike Lieberthal

YEAR	TEAM	LVL	AGE	PA	R	2B	3B	HR	RBI	BB	SO	SB	CS	AVG/OBP/SLG	TAv	BABIP	BRR	FRAA	WARP
2011	PHI	MLB	32	472	49	23	0	6	40	48	48	1	0	.283/.371/.383	.291	.308	-1.7	C(128): 0.7, 3B(1): -0.0	3.7
2012	PHI	MLB	33	421	56	32	0	16	68	29	50	4	0	.325/.394/.540	.325	.339	-1.9	C(106): 2.6	5.1
2013	PHI	MLB	34	341	30	16	0	5	37	18	39	1	0	.268/.320/.368	.246	.291	4	C(86): 0.7	1.6
2014	PHI	MLB	35	340	39	19	0	7	37	30	44	1	0	.275/.354/.413	.277	.300	-0.5	C 1	2.3

Exhibit A in the case against the Walk Year Effect. A 25-game sentence for amphetamines delayed Ruiz's season by 25 games; a slow start and a strained right hamstring kept him from producing anything of value until late June. He finally got going, but he wasn't the same player who was one of the game's best catchers over the previous three seasons: his walk rate was half of what it was in 2011, his isolated power took a 115-point freefall and he let about twice as many balls past him for wild pitches. Ruiz has enough intangibles to be a poor man's Yadier Molina, handling a pitching staff well and calling a good game. Those intangibles are just going to cost his team a lot less than he might have expected a year ago.

Cameron Rupp   C

Born: **9/28/1988** Age: **25**
Bats: **R** Throws: **R** Height: **6' 1"**
Weight: **240** Breakout: **3%**
Improve: **8%** Collapse: **6%**
Attrition: **15%** MLB: **20%**

Comparables:
Alvin Colina, Luke Montz, Anthony Recker

YEAR	TEAM	LVL	AGE	PA	R	2B	3B	HR	RBI	BB	SO	SB	CS	AVG/OBP/SLG	TAv	BABIP	BRR	FRAA	WARP
2011	LWD	A	22	368	33	19	1	4	44	31	96	0	0	.272/.346/.373	.284	.368	-2.2	C(83): -1.4	1.8
2012	CLR	A+	23	390	32	22	1	10	49	40	77	0	0	.267/.345/.424	.273	.317	-1.8	C(104): -0.2	2.5
2013	REA	AA	24	161	18	6	0	8	21	14	36	0	0	.245/.329/.455	.257	.273	-0.3	C(32): 0.1	0.4
2013	LEH	AAA	24	194	18	10	0	6	24	10	55	1	1	.269/.309/.423	.250	.352	-2.2	C(52): 1.8	0.8
2013	PHI	MLB	24	14	1	1	0	0	2	1	4	0	0	.308/.357/.385	.265	.444	-0.2	C(3): -0.0	0.0
2014	PHI	MLB	25	250	25	10	0	7	27	15	71	0	0	.232/.284/.373	.239	.300	-0.5	C 0	0.6

The Phillies have had trouble bringing catchers through their system. The career arcs of Jason Jaramillo, Lou Marson, Sebastian Valle and Tommy Joseph haven't gone as expected, and they traded away the one catcher, Travis d'Arnaud, who still looks promising. They now hope Cameron Rupp can succeed Carlos Ruiz where others have failed. Rupp started 2013 at Double-A and worked his way up to a brief cup of coffee in September. He'll provide a low average with moderate power, and he plays adequate defense to boot. Rupp will start 2014 at Triple-A, but he will be the big club's first line of defense in the event of an injury.

Clete Thomas   CF

Born: **11/14/1983** Age: **30**
Bats: **L** Throws: **R** Height: **5' 11"**
Weight: **195** Breakout: **5%**
Improve: **15%** Collapse: **5%**
Attrition: **16%** MLB: **37%**

Comparables:
Joe Mather, Chris Dickerson, George Lombard

YEAR	TEAM	LVL	AGE	PA	R	2B	3B	HR	RBI	BB	SO	SB	CS	AVG/OBP/SLG	TAv	BABIP	BRR	FRAA	WARP
2011	TOL	AAA	27	406	37	15	2	12	53	32	130	20	3	.251/.314/.401	.235	.352	0.4	RF(45): 4.2, CF(45): 4.7	1.1
2012	ROC	AAA	28	426	47	22	5	12	47	27	109	15	4	.232/.281/.405	.242	.288	-0.3	CF(98): -12.7, RF(4): 1.3	-0.9
2012	MIN	MLB	28	29	2	1	0	1	4	0	16	0	0	.143/.172/.286	.153	.273	0	RF(9): 0.1, LF(1): -0.0	-0.2
2013	ROC	AAA	29	143	17	8	0	9	25	18	35	6	4	.296/.385/.576	.308	.346	0.3	CF(32): -0.3, LF(1): -0.1	1.1
2013	MIN	MLB	29	322	39	15	0	4	13	30	92	1	3	.214/.290/.307	.228	.299	1.1	CF(50): 0.8, LF(26): 3.2	0.6
2014	PHI	MLB	30	316	36	14	2	8	31	26	94	8	3	.221/.291/.363	.240	.300	0.4	CF -1, LF 1	0.3

Long known for his incurable whiffitis, Thomas saw more time in the Twins' outfield last summer than any other player. One way Minnesotans can rid themselves of that painful memory is by sharing it with a White Sox fan right before pointing out that the Twins still managed to be three games better than the Pale Hose. A better way is to close your eyes and picture Byron Buxton in a Twins uniform. A fifth outfielder with a steady glove and an impotent lefty bat, Thomas signed with the Phillies and will likely continue to haunt the periphery of major-league rosters for the foreseeable future.

	YEAR	TEAM	LVL	AGE	PA	R	2B	3B	HR	RBI	BB	SO	SB	CS	AVG/OBP/SLG	TAv	BABIP	BRR	FRAA	WARP
Chase Utley 2B	2011	CLR	A+	32	36	4	2	0	1	4	3	6	1	0	.281/.361/.438	.329	.320	0	2B(5): -0.8	0.2
Born: 12/17/1978 Age: 35	2011	PHI	MLB	32	454	54	21	6	11	44	39	47	14	0	.259/.344/.425	.291	.269	0.9	2B(100): 8.5	3.5
Bats: L Throws: R Height: 6' 1"	2012	CLR	A+	33	38	3	0	0	1	5	3	5	1	0	.156/.263/.250	.228	.148	0.1	2B(4): 0.3	0.0
Weight: 200 Breakout: 1%	2012	PHI	MLB	33	362	48	15	2	11	45	43	43	11	1	.256/.365/.429	.286	.261	2.9	2B(81): 4.1	2.8
Improve: 26% Collapse: 8%	2013	PHI	MLB	34	531	73	25	6	18	69	45	79	8	3	.284/.348/.475	.292	.305	1.6	2B(125): 2.6	3.4
Attrition: 11% MLB: 94%	2014	PHI	MLB	35	472	60	19	3	15	59	48	71	11	2	.260/.353/.435	.285	.280	1.2	2B 5	3.5

Comparables: Carlos Guillen, Ray Durham, Barry Larkin

The Phillies have nowhere to go but younger, but they made an exception for Utley when they signed him in August to a two-year extension with three vesting options. Utley, at 34, was no MVP candidate, but he was the team's best position player, reaching 500 plate appearances for the first time since 2010 while producing the second-best OPS+ among NL second basemen. The .191 isolated power was his highest mark since 2009, and the above-average defense was just another reminder that Utley does everything well. Aging is his next challenge.

PITCHERS

	YEAR	TEAM	LVL	AGE	W	L	SV	G	GS	IP	H	HR	BB	SO	BB9	SO9	GB%	BABIP	WHIP	ERA	FIP	FRA	WARP
Mike Adams	2011	SDN	MLB	32	3	1	1	48	0	48	26	2	9	49	1.7	9.2	46%	.202	0.73	1.12	2.06	2.70	0.8
Born: 7/29/1978 Age: 35	2011	TEX	MLB	32	2	3	1	27	0	25²	18	3	5	25	1.8	8.8	46%	.231	0.90	2.10	3.22	4.25	0.3
Bats: R Throws: R Height: 6' 5" Weight: 195	2012	TEX	MLB	33	5	3	1	61	0	52¹	56	4	17	45	2.9	7.7	48%	.327	1.39	3.27	3.47	3.40	1.0
Breakout: 22% Improve: 47% Collapse: 30%	2013	PHI	MLB	34	1	4	0	28	0	25	23	5	11	23	4.0	8.3	54%	.269	1.36	3.96	5.22	5.45	-0.2
Attrition: 17% MLB: 91%	2014	PHI	MLB	35	2	1	0	42	0	39²	31	4	10	40	2.3	9.2	46%	.282	1.05	2.76	3.30	3.00	0.8

Comparables: J.J. Putz, Rafael Betancourt, Heath Bell

The Phillies signed Adams to a two-year deal even though the right-hander was coming off surgery to alleviate his thoracic outlet syndrome. (Unlike you, they probably knew what thoracic outlet syndrome was. Mayo Clinic says: "A group of disorders that occur when the blood vessels or nerves in the space between your collarbone and your first rib become compressed. This can cause pain in your shoulders and neck and numbness in your fingers.") Adams had been one of the best relievers in the game going back to 2008, but in his first year with the Phillies, something clearly wasn't right. His control was uncharacteristically spotty and he allowed more home runs in 25 innings than he did in twice the innings the year before. Following a June 19th appearance, the Phillies discovered two labrum tears and a torn rotator cuff. He said after surgery in August that he'll be ready by spring training, and that his doctor told him he'll feel better than he has in years.

	YEAR	TEAM	LVL	AGE	W	L	SV	G	GS	IP	H	HR	BB	SO	BB9	SO9	GB%	BABIP	WHIP	ERA	FIP	FRA	WARP
Phillippe Aumont	2011	REA	AA	22	1	5	4	25	0	31	23	2	11	41	3.2	11.9	55%	.266	1.10	2.32	2.76	2.94	0.5
Born: 1/7/1989 Age: 25	2011	LEH	AAA	22	1	0	3	18	0	22²	21	0	14	37	5.6	14.7	44%	.469	1.54	3.18	2.09	3.23	0.3
Bats: L Throws: R Height: 6' 7" Weight: 260	2012	LEH	AAA	23	3	1	15	41	0	44¹	34	3	34	59	6.9	12.0	57%	.304	1.53	4.26	4.01	4.97	0.0
Breakout: 52% Improve: 57% Collapse: 38%	2012	PHI	MLB	23	0	1	2	18	0	14²	10	0	9	14	5.5	8.6	76%	.244	1.30	3.68	3.27	3.02	0.2
Attrition: 68% MLB: 24%	2013	LEH	AAA	24	0	2	2	32	0	35²	29	0	38	42	9.6	10.6	47%	.326	1.88	4.04	4.55	5.36	-0.1
	2013	PHI	MLB	24	1	3	0	22	0	19¹	24	0	13	19	6.1	8.8	50%	.400	1.91	4.19	3.54	3.48	0.3
	2014	PHI	MLB	25	3	2	1	33	4	54²	49	5	33	55	5.4	9.0	49%	.313	1.50	4.76	4.44	5.18	-0.2

Comparables: Emiliano Fruto, Jeremy Jeffress, Jose Ceda

In a handful of late-2012 appearances, it looked like the Phillies would be able to salvage at least something out of the trade that sent Cliff Lee to the Mariners. Fans salivated over Aumont's biting slider, which made many a hitter—including Dan Uggla of .gif infamy—look foolish. His control, though; his control. He started the 2013 season in the Phillies' bullpen, but walked a batter in each of his first five appearances and was eventually demoted to Triple-A. He accused the organization of sending him mixed messages, which now makes him seem like an obvious "change of scenery" candidate.

Antonio Bastardo

Born: 9/21/1985 Age: 28
Bats: R Throws: L Height: 5' 11" Weight: 200
Breakout: 40% Improve: 54% Collapse: 33%
Attrition: 17% MLB: 89%

Comparables:
Hong-Chih Kuo, Tyler Clippard, Sergio Santos

YEAR	TEAM	LVL	AGE	W	L	SV	G	GS	IP	H	HR	BB	SO	BB9	SO9	GB%	BABIP	WHIP	ERA	FIP	FRA	WARP
2011	PHI	MLB	25	6	1	8	64	0	58	28	6	26	70	4.0	10.9	27%	.179	0.93	2.64	3.27	3.26	0.7
2012	PHI	MLB	26	2	5	1	65	0	52	40	7	26	81	4.5	14.0	30%	.306	1.27	4.33	3.39	3.65	0.8
2013	PHI	MLB	27	3	2	2	48	0	42²	33	2	21	47	4.4	9.9	35%	.287	1.27	2.32	2.97	2.64	1.0
2014	PHI	MLB	28	3	1	1	49	0	42	31	4	16	51	3.4	10.9	34%	.291	1.12	2.99	3.27	3.25	0.8

Bastardo accepted and served a 50-game suspension at the end of the season for his involvement in the Biogenesis scandal, ending what was superficially a decent year. He had a 2.32 ERA and was one of the few reliable bullpen arms the Phillies found among a gaggle of impostors. The ERA, however, hid declining velocity and a plummeting strikeout rate. Bastardo's ability to generate whiffs is his lone calling card, as he owns a high walk rate and ranks among the most fly-liable relievers. Bastardo might now trail fellow lefty Jake Diekman on the club's high-leverage hierarchy, due to Diekman's strong showing and lack of drug-related offenses.

Jesse Biddle

Born: 10/22/1991 Age: 22
Bats: L Throws: L Height: 6' 4" Weight: 225
Breakout: 58% Improve: 68% Collapse: 23%
Attrition: 69% MLB: 17%

Comparables:
Dan Cortes, Carlos Carrasco, Jordan Walden

YEAR	TEAM	LVL	AGE	W	L	SV	G	GS	IP	H	HR	BB	SO	BB9	SO9	GB%	BABIP	WHIP	ERA	FIP	FRA	WARP
2011	LWD	A	19	7	8	0	25	24	133	104	5	66	124	4.5	8.4	44%	.290	1.28	2.98	3.71	3.90	1.4
2012	CLR	A+	20	10	6	0	26	26	142²	129	10	54	151	3.4	9.5	41%	.308	1.28	3.22	3.43	4.22	2.4
2013	REA	AA	21	5	14	0	27	27	138¹	104	10	82	154	5.3	10.0	44%	.285	1.34	3.64	3.88	4.28	2.2
2014	PHI	MLB	22	6	9	0	23	23	119²	111	14	65	105	4.9	7.9	42%	.302	1.47	4.63	4.75	5.04	-0.1

Biddle will grab the title of top Phillies pitching prospect, but that's like being the youngest guy at a Rolling Stones concert. Biddle wouldn't necessarily be even a top 10 prospect in some systems because of his alarming control issues. The lefty walked a staggering 14 percent of batters in 2013, his first year at Double-A. Some of it could be blamed on his plantar fasciitis, but the control problems have been a persistent issue throughout his career. If Biddle can start spotting his secondary pitches consistently, he might earn a September call-up, but otherwise don't expect him until 2015 at the earliest.

Justin De Fratus

Born: 10/21/1987 Age: 26
Bats: B Throws: R Height: 6' 4" Weight: 220
Breakout: 38% Improve: 54% Collapse: 29%
Attrition: 36% MLB: 69%

Comparables:
Randor Bierd, Jonathan Albaladejo, Tom Mastny

YEAR	TEAM	LVL	AGE	W	L	SV	G	GS	IP	H	HR	BB	SO	BB9	SO9	GB%	BABIP	WHIP	ERA	FIP	FRA	WARP
2011	REA	AA	23	4	0	8	23	0	34¹	28	1	14	43	3.7	11.3	68%	.297	1.22	2.10	2.77	2.59	0.7
2011	LEH	AAA	23	2	3	7	28	0	41	35	3	11	56	2.4	12.3	52%	.373	1.12	3.73	2.48	2.75	0.6
2011	PHI	MLB	23	1	0	0	5	0	4	1	0	3	3	6.8	6.8	56%	.111	1.00	2.25	4.49	5.24	0.0
2012	LEH	AAA	24	0	1	3	17	0	21²	15	2	3	22	1.2	9.1	54%	.241	0.83	2.49	2.74	4.00	0.2
2012	PHI	MLB	24	0	0	0	13	0	10²	7	0	5	8	4.2	6.8	52%	.226	1.12	3.38	3.04	3.61	0.1
2013	LEH	AAA	25	3	0	0	13	0	19	18	0	6	17	2.8	8.1	62%	.327	1.26	1.89	2.68	3.72	0.3
2013	PHI	MLB	25	3	3	0	58	0	46²	45	3	25	42	4.8	8.1	46%	.318	1.50	3.86	3.98	4.24	0.2
2014	PHI	MLB	26	2	1	0	49	0	55²	51	6	20	49	3.3	8.0	50%	.303	1.29	4.00	4.09	4.35	0.3

De Fratus is part of a long line of young arms that haven't lived up to expectations for the Phillies. The right-hander throws hard, with a four-seamer that lives in the mid-90s, but a flexor pronator injury in his right elbow limited his playing time and his effectiveness. Still, his 3.86 ERA adjusted for Phillieness is not bad. The team unloaded an armored truck full of cash on Jonathan Papelbon's lawn, and as a direct result will rely on an otherwise young and unproven bullpen this year. In that context, the 26-year-old De Fratus could be a stalwart with a solid effort.

Jake Diekman

Born: 1/21/1987 Age: 27
Bats: L Throws: L Height: 6' 4" Weight: 200
Breakout: 39% Improve: 48% Collapse: 41%
Attrition: 52% MLB: 52%

Comparables:
Dewon Day, Dan Runzler, Jason Bulger

YEAR	TEAM	LVL	AGE	W	L	SV	G	GS	IP	H	HR	BB	SO	BB9	SO9	GB%	BABIP	WHIP	ERA	FIP	FRA	WARP
2011	REA	AA	24	0	1	3	53	0	65	47	3	44	83	6.1	11.5	58%	.284	1.40	3.05	3.72	4.32	0.2
2012	LEH	AAA	25	1	1	7	25	0	26²	19	0	13	37	4.4	12.5	56%	.306	1.20	1.69	2.07	2.71	0.7
2012	PHI	MLB	25	1	1	0	32	0	27¹	25	1	20	35	6.6	11.5	55%	.343	1.65	3.95	3.58	3.55	0.4
2013	LEH	AAA	26	1	0	11	30	0	30	31	1	24	37	7.2	11.1	62%	.380	1.83	5.70	3.67	4.88	0.1
2013	PHI	MLB	26	1	4	0	45	0	38¹	34	1	16	41	3.8	9.6	53%	.311	1.30	2.58	2.47	2.85	0.7
2014	PHI	MLB	27	3	1	0	58	0	61	52	5	34	64	5.0	9.4	48%	.306	1.41	4.25	4.00	4.62	0.1

Diekman used a mid-90s fastball and mid-80s slider to strike out one in four batters he faced, qualifying him as one of the few bright spots on the Phillies' staff. He also induced groundballs at a better than 50 percent clip, and finished the season with a 2.58 ERA, incredible considering he was at 4.29 on August 10th. From that point on, he struck out 24, walked four and allowed one run in 17 innings. That'll earn him consideration for a high-leverage role.

Chad Durbin

Born: 12/3/1977 Age: 36
Bats: R Throws: R Height: 6' 2" Weight: 225
Breakout: 23% Improve: 57% Collapse: 25%
Attrition: 6% MLB: 75%

Comparables:
Aurelio Lopez, Barney Schultz, Ricky Bottalico

YEAR	TEAM	LVL	AGE	W	L	SV	G	GS	IP	H	HR	BB	SO	BB9	SO9	GB%	BABIP	WHIP	ERA	FIP	FRA	WARP
2011	CLE	MLB	33	2	2	0	56	0	68¹	86	12	26	59	3.4	7.8	41%	.339	1.64	5.53	4.89	4.59	0.5
2012	ATL	MLB	34	4	1	1	76	0	61	52	9	28	49	4.1	7.2	48%	.251	1.31	3.10	4.82	5.24	-0.3
2013	PHI	MLB	35	1	0	0	16	0	16	25	4	9	16	5.1	9.0	47%	.412	2.12	9.00	5.96	6.88	-0.3
2014	PHI	MLB	36	2	1	0	36	0	36²	34	5	15	33	3.8	8.2	45%	.300	1.36	4.46	4.61	4.84	-0.0

Stop me if you've heard this one before: The Phillies signed an aged reliever and it didn't work out. In 2010 and '11, it was Danys Baez; in 2012, it was Chad Qualls; and in 2013, it was Chad Durbin. Durbin made it through May before he got the boot, posting a flat 9.00 ERA in 16 innings. In such a short amount of time, he walked nine and allowed four home runs, the culprits for his downfall. He retired in November.

Miguel Gonzalez

Born: 5/27/1984 Age: 29
Bats: R Throws: R Height: 6' 1" Weight: 170

YEAR	TEAM	LVL	AGE	W	L	SV	G	GS	IP	H	HR	BB	SO	BB9	SO9	GB%	BABIP	WHIP	ERA	FIP	FRA	WARP
2014	—	—	—	—	—	—	—	—	—	—	—	—	—	—	—	—	—	—	—	—	—	—

Gonzalez marks the Phillies' first recent, significant venture into the foreign free agent market. He was originally signed to a six-year, $48 million deal, but after a physical, the Phillies renegotiated a three-year, $12 million deal. Gonzalez will initially compete for a job in the starting rotation, but many see a future as a reliever. He throws a vast array of pitches including a mid-90s fastball, a splitter and a slider. Under new manager Ryne Sandberg, Gonzalez will work with a new cast of coaches after long time pitching coach Rich Dubee was given the pink slip. Their ability to mold Gonzalez and hone his arsenal will play a big role in his success or failure with the Phillies.

Roy Halladay

Born: 5/14/1977 Age: 37
Bats: R Throws: R Height: 6' 6" Weight: 225
Breakout: 5% Improve: 37% Collapse: 26%
Attrition: 19% MLB: 89%

Comparables:
Chris Carpenter, Andy Pettitte, Hiroki Kuroda

YEAR	TEAM	LVL	AGE	W	L	SV	G	GS	IP	H	HR	BB	SO	BB9	SO9	GB%	BABIP	WHIP	ERA	FIP	FRA	WARP
2011	PHI	MLB	34	19	6	0	32	32	233²	208	10	35	220	1.3	8.5	53%	.303	1.04	2.35	2.17	2.72	5.4
2012	PHI	MLB	35	11	8	0	25	25	156¹	155	18	36	132	2.1	7.6	44%	.308	1.22	4.49	3.73	4.34	1.2
2013	PHI	MLB	36	4	5	0	13	13	62	55	12	36	51	5.2	7.4	43%	.261	1.47	6.82	6.12	6.93	-0.9
2014	PHI	MLB	37	5	4	0	12	12	83¹	76	9	15	74	1.7	8.0	51%	.302	1.10	3.23	3.46	3.51	1.3

Halladay in 2013 was a lot like Henry Rowengartner at the end of *Rookie of the Year*: He had no confidence and he had nothing on his fastball. Frankly, he should have tried throwing the ball underhand. The two-time Cy Young Award winner struggled through his first seven starts, posting an 8.65 ERA before undergoing shoulder surgery. He returned at the end of August but still couldn't get anything on his fastball; a three-batter disaster in his final September start saw him top out at 83 mph. Few had Halladay's work ethic, so when he called it quits in December—citing persistent back pain—you could appreciate just what a struggle a comeback would have been. Halladay bridged the gap between Roger Clemens and Clayton Kershaw as baseball's best pitcher, and had he put up his numbers in another era he'd likely be a no-doubt Hall of Famer. Alas, the modern BBWAA's None Shall Pass standards make enshrinement far less certain. Considering that similarly qualified Kevin Brown couldn't muster the 5 percent necessary to stay on the ballot, that Curt Schilling couldn't top 40 percent in his first try, and that Mike Mussina appears to have a long wait ahead of him, Halladay might consider the next five years best spent working on a dazzling marketing campaign. A fun fact for the road: From 2003 to 2012, Halladay threw more complete games than all but six teams.

Cole Hamels

Born: 12/27/1983 Age: 30
Bats: L Throws: L Height: 6' 3" Weight: 195
Breakout: 8% Improve: 48% Collapse: 22%
Attrition: 8% MLB: 95%

Comparables:
James Shields, Dan Haren, Josh Beckett

YEAR	TEAM	LVL	AGE	W	L	SV	G	GS	IP	H	HR	BB	SO	BB9	SO9	GB%	BABIP	WHIP	ERA	FIP	FRA	WARP
2011	PHI	MLB	27	14	9	0	32	31	216	169	19	44	194	1.8	8.1	54%	.260	0.99	2.79	3.02	3.67	1.8
2012	PHI	MLB	28	17	6	0	31	31	215¹	190	24	52	216	2.2	9.0	44%	.303	1.12	3.05	3.35	3.66	3.2
2013	PHI	MLB	29	8	14	0	33	33	220	205	21	50	202	2.0	8.3	43%	.303	1.16	3.60	3.23	3.69	3.4
2014	PHI	MLB	30	11	9	0	27	27	187¹	166	22	41	175	2.0	8.4	45%	.295	1.10	3.37	3.59	3.66	2.5

It's hard to unlearn what our dads taught us, so it's hard to not at least notice Hamels' 8-14 record, or his 3.60 ERA. But a legitimately bad first half (bad changeup command; cascading effects on his fastball's effectiveness) gave way to a strong second one, and the combined result was another block in a fine career. Hamels' Fair Run Averages over the past four seasons: 3.80, 3.67, 3.62, 3.69. He will be 30 on Opening Day and is only two WARP behind Justin Verlander's mark at the same age.

Roberto Hernandez

Born: 8/30/1980 Age: 33
Bats: R Throws: R Height: 6' 4" Weight: 230
Breakout: 18% Improve: 39% Collapse: 26%
Attrition: 24% MLB: 73%

Comparables:
Nate Robertson, Josh Fogg, Carl Pavano

YEAR	TEAM	LVL	AGE	W	L	SV	G	GS	IP	H	HR	BB	SO	BB9	SO9	GB%	BABIP	WHIP	ERA	FIP	FRA	WARP
2011	CLE	MLB	30	7	15	0	32	32	188²	205	22	60	109	2.9	5.2	56%	.292	1.40	5.25	4.60	5.65	-0.7
2012	LKC	A	31	1	1	0	2	2	12¹	12	5	1	13	0.7	9.5	54%	.233	1.05	3.65	6.76	7.74	-0.3
2012	COH	AAA	31	1	0	0	2	2	12	13	0	3	7	2.2	5.2	56%	.317	1.33	4.50	2.74	4.21	0.2
2012	CLE	MLB	31	0	3	0	3	3	14¹	17	4	3	2	1.9	1.3	50%	.250	1.40	7.53	7.23	7.04	-0.3
2013	TBA	MLB	32	6	13	1	32	24	151	164	24	38	113	2.3	6.7	56%	.309	1.34	4.89	4.66	5.34	-1.0
2014	PHI	MLB	33	6	8	0	20	20	117²	120	15	36	80	2.8	6.1	57%	.300	1.33	4.60	4.64	5.00	-0.2

Hernandez debuted a new name in 2012 and a new uniform last year. A surprise signing by the Rays, the former Fausto Carmona was unable to find the Tampa Bay magic others have used to score bigger paydays. Despite the poor surface numbers, he boasted a strikeout-to-walk ratio of nearly 3:1 while continuing to gather groundballs in bunches. The copious homers seem anomalous: Hernandez had baseball's highest home-run-per-fly-ball rate among pitchers with 140 innings, far above his career average. He proved durable after missing most of the 2012 season with legal and physical issues. Hernandez has size and stuff (low-90s sinker, mid-80s slider, good changeup) that can't be taught, but he's also never missed bats, not even in his peak 2007 season. He's a fifth starter, and at 33, he's probably not even that for much longer. He is in that sense a nice fit on a one-year deal for the Phillies.

Jeremy Horst

Born: 10/1/1985 Age: 28
Bats: L Throws: L Height: 6' 3" Weight: 215
Breakout: 45% Improve: 69% Collapse: 22%
Attrition: 48% MLB: 45%

Comparables:
Casey Daigle, A.J. Murray, Steven Jackson

YEAR	TEAM	LVL	AGE	W	L	SV	G	GS	IP	H	HR	BB	SO	BB9	SO9	GB%	BABIP	WHIP	ERA	FIP	FRA	WARP
2011	LOU	AAA	25	1	4	0	36	0	51¹	41	2	14	42	2.5	7.4	45%	.286	1.07	2.81	3.04	3.94	0.5
2011	CIN	MLB	25	0	0	0	12	0	15¹	18	2	6	9	3.5	5.3	39%	.308	1.57	2.93	4.69	4.93	0.0
2012	LEH	AAA	26	2	1	2	26	0	38¹	43	3	18	32	4.2	7.5	44%	.342	1.59	2.11	4.07	3.89	0.4
2012	PHI	MLB	26	2	0	0	32	0	31¹	21	1	14	40	4.0	11.5	46%	.290	1.12	1.15	2.43	2.93	0.6
2013	PHI	MLB	27	0	2	0	28	0	26	35	4	12	21	4.2	7.3	39%	.369	1.81	6.23	5.02	4.92	0.0
2014	PHI	MLB	28	1	1	0	29	0	36²	37	5	14	30	3.4	7.3	43%	.310	1.38	4.67	4.69	5.07	-0.1

Acquired from the Reds for Wilson Valdez, Horst had a wonderful 2012 for the Phillies, posting a 1.15 ERA while striking out 32 percent of batters he faced. He figured to be a good bullpen piece again, even considering expected regression, but his elbow regressed more than expected. Before soreness ended his season in mid-June, he had seen his fastball velocity drop by a mile and a half and his strikeout rate nearly halved. He hasn't had surgery—yet—and the Phillies, with a surfeit of young bullpen arms, can afford to let him slowly ease back to health.

Kyle Kendrick

Born: 8/26/1984 Age: 29
Bats: R Throws: R Height: 6' 3" Weight: 210
Breakout: 38% Improve: 52% Collapse: 16%
Attrition: 19% MLB: 79%

Comparables:
Shawn Hill, Clayton Richard, Jae Weong Seo

YEAR	TEAM	LVL	AGE	W	L	SV	G	GS	IP	H	HR	BB	SO	BB9	SO9	GB%	BABIP	WHIP	ERA	FIP	FRA	WARP
2011	PHI	MLB	26	8	6	0	34	15	114²	110	14	30	59	2.4	4.6	44%	.259	1.22	3.22	4.52	5.47	-0.9
2012	PHI	MLB	27	11	12	0	37	25	159¹	154	20	49	116	2.8	6.6	46%	.283	1.27	3.90	4.37	4.81	0.7
2013	PHI	MLB	28	10	13	0	30	30	182	207	18	47	110	2.3	5.4	49%	.321	1.40	4.70	3.99	4.35	2.2
2014	PHI	MLB	29	8	9	0	35	24	155²	157	20	40	94	2.3	5.4	47%	.291	1.27	4.40	4.59	4.78	0.2

At the advice of both his father and former pitching coach Rich Dubee, Kendrick downgraded his cutter and polished up his changeup, and something seemed to click. He ended the 2012 season on a nearly elite run, then carried a 3.56 ERA through June 2013. Cue dark, discordant music. From the start of July on, he posted a 6.49 ERA. Blood, guts, gore, sobbing, pleading, slashing, screaming. After his final start, in mid-September, he went on the DL with shoulder inflammation. Turns out we were watching that kind of movie all along.

John Lannan

Born: 9/27/1984 Age: 29
Bats: L Throws: L Height: 6' 4" Weight: 235
Breakout: 39% Improve: 68% Collapse: 13%
Attrition: 16% MLB: 73%

Comparables:
Charlie Morton, Ricardo Rodriguez, Sergio Mitre

YEAR	TEAM	LVL	AGE	W	L	SV	G	GS	IP	H	HR	BB	SO	BB9	SO9	GB%	BABIP	WHIP	ERA	FIP	FRA	WARP
2011	WAS	MLB	26	10	13	0	33	33	184²	194	15	76	106	3.7	5.2	56%	.306	1.46	3.70	4.25	5.25	-1.0
2012	SYR	AAA	27	9	11	0	24	24	148²	164	16	50	86	3.0	5.2	57%	.303	1.44	4.30	4.43	6.19	-1.4
2012	WAS	MLB	27	4	1	0	6	6	32²	33	0	14	17	3.9	4.7	55%	.323	1.44	4.13	3.75	3.68	0.5
2013	PHI	MLB	28	3	6	0	14	14	74¹	86	6	27	38	3.3	4.6	55%	.321	1.52	5.33	4.34	4.68	0.3
2014	PHI	MLB	29	5	6	0	16	16	90¹	95	10	30	53	3.0	5.2	54%	.305	1.38	4.73	4.64	5.14	-0.2

Lannan was one of many small-scale signings the Phillies made that couldn't have gone worse. The lefty finished with the worst ERA of his career and needed two stints on the disabled list (strained left quad, patellar tendinitis in his left knee). The silver lining is that it gave the team a great opportunity to test Jonathan Pettibone at the major-league level, but the roster spot was infected; Pettibone eventually caught the injury bug, too. Lannan's control and groundball skills aren't all that notable, so he is even more reliant on his defense than most low-strikeout hurlers.

Cliff Lee

Born: 8/30/1978 Age: 35
Bats: L Throws: L Height: 6' 3" Weight: 205
Breakout: 17% Improve: 45% Collapse: 30%
Attrition: 9% MLB: 90%

Comparables:
Roy Halladay, Mike Mussina, Curt Schilling

YEAR	TEAM	LVL	AGE	W	L	SV	G	GS	IP	H	HR	BB	SO	BB9	SO9	GB%	BABIP	WHIP	ERA	FIP	FRA	WARP
2011	PHI	MLB	32	17	8	0	32	32	232²	197	18	42	238	1.6	9.2	47%	.296	1.03	2.40	2.57	3.05	4.0
2012	PHI	MLB	33	6	9	0	30	30	211	207	26	28	207	1.2	8.8	44%	.318	1.11	3.16	3.17	3.52	3.4
2013	PHI	MLB	34	14	8	0	31	31	222²	193	22	32	222	1.3	9.0	46%	.296	1.01	2.87	2.80	3.51	3.7
2014	PHI	MLB	35	12	9	0	26	26	189¹	171	19	26	176	1.3	8.3	44%	.305	1.04	3.02	3.08	3.28	3.4

Lee's strike rate is always around 71 percent, as it was last year; his swinging strike rate is always around 14 percent, as it was last year; his FIP is always around 2.80, as it was last year. But for all that consistency, Lee will occasionally rip off a few weeks that stand out. In September, he struck out 54 and walked *one* in 39 innings, spanning five starts. Overall in 2013, he went at least eight innings in 13 of 31 starts, topping Clayton Kershaw's 12 and Adam Wainwright's 10 for most in baseball. Lee, who has two years remaining on his five-year deal with the Phillies, told local media in September that he'll retire at the end of that contract. That will make it even harder for the Phillies to acknowledge that he might have the most value to them as trade bait.

Jeff Manship

Born: 1/16/1985 Age: 29
Bats: R Throws: R Height: 6' 2" Weight: 210
Breakout: 35% Improve: 61% Collapse: 26%
Attrition: 44% MLB: 34%

Comparables:
Cesar Ramos, J.D. Martin, Eric Stults

YEAR	TEAM	LVL	AGE	W	L	SV	G	GS	IP	H	HR	BB	SO	BB9	SO9	GB%	BABIP	WHIP	ERA	FIP	FRA	WARP
2011	ROC	AAA	26	1	2	0	11	3	25	24	4	4	21	1.4	7.6	53%	.274	1.12	4.32	4.12	4.25	0.1
2011	MIN	MLB	26	0	0	0	5	0	3¹	5	0	4	2	10.8	5.4	23%	.385	2.70	8.10	5.46	5.34	0.0
2012	ROC	AAA	27	6	3	0	22	11	80¹	79	5	35	52	3.9	5.8	55%	.303	1.42	2.91	4.02	5.00	-0.3
2012	MIN	MLB	27	0	0	0	12	0	21²	29	4	7	12	2.9	5.0	50%	.338	1.66	7.89	5.45	6.74	-0.3
2013	CSP	AAA	28	6	8	0	24	17	104	114	8	32	71	2.8	6.1	52%	.321	1.40	4.85	4.16	5.29	1.3
2013	COL	MLB	28	0	5	0	11	4	30²	37	6	12	18	3.5	5.3	45%	.303	1.60	7.04	5.56	6.81	-0.5
2014	PHI	MLB	29	5	6	0	33	16	113	122	15	36	76	2.9	6.1	50%	.312	1.39	4.83	4.66	5.25	-0.4

As a Rockie in 2013, Manship took the ball as a starter for the first time since 2010, and it was immediately obvious why he hadn't faced a leadoff hitter in years. In four starts, he posted a 6.86 ERA, allowed the equivalent of Jay Bruce's slash line, lost all four games, altogether sucked, the whole deal. His fortunes were even worse out of the bullpen, as he allowed a *.976 OPS* and nine runs in 9 ⅔ innings. Coors Field is one heck of an excuse, but Colorado still has to fill the same 1,500 or so innings as every other team, and seasons like Manship's are the inevitable result.

Ethan Martin

Born: 6/6/1989 Age: 25
Bats: R Throws: R Height: 6' 2" Weight: 195
Breakout: 44% Improve: 54% Collapse: 38%
Attrition: 71% MLB: 31%

Comparables:
Andrew Oliver, Steve Johnson, Donnie Veal

YEAR	TEAM	LVL	AGE	W	L	SV	G	GS	IP	H	HR	BB	SO	BB9	SO9	GB%	BABIP	WHIP	ERA	FIP	FRA	WARP
2011	RCU	A+	22	4	4	0	16	9	55	65	8	37	61	6.1	10.0	58%	.292	1.85	7.36	5.91	3.68	0.6
2011	CHT	AA	22	5	3	2	21	3	40¹	31	3	29	43	6.5	9.6	41%	.321	1.49	4.02	4.30	5.16	0.1
2012	CHT	AA	23	8	6	0	20	20	118	89	5	61	112	4.7	8.5	42%	.274	1.27	3.58	3.42	4.36	1.2
2012	REA	AA	23	5	0	0	7	7	39²	29	3	18	35	4.1	7.9	44%	.248	1.18	3.18	3.78	4.42	0.5
2013	LEH	AAA	24	11	5	0	21	21	115²	94	11	67	107	5.2	8.3	41%	.281	1.39	4.12	4.54	5.93	-0.5
2013	PHI	MLB	24	2	5	0	15	8	40	42	9	26	47	5.8	10.6	30%	.320	1.70	6.07	5.62	5.49	-0.1
2014	PHI	MLB	25	7	10	0	27	27	133²	122	17	77	120	5.2	8.1	40%	.296	1.49	4.85	4.98	5.27	-0.4

Martin has a legitimate mid-90s fastball, a loopy curve and a biting slider, enough to give big leaguers trouble. The problem was, he just didn't have the stamina to get through the lineup more than once. From the first through the fifth innings, his fastball averaged 95, 94, 93.5, 93 and 93 mph. His curve and slider also lost about 2 mph as the game progressed. The Phillies noticed, too, and moved him to the bullpen after seven starts. He could serve as a swingman, starting every so often as necessary, but he'll thrive with regular one-inning stints.

Zach Miner

Born: 3/12/1982 Age: 32
Bats: R Throws: R Height: 6' 4" Weight: 225
Breakout: 61% Improve: 76% Collapse: 0%
Attrition: 26% MLB: 25%

Comparables:
Clay Condrey, Tim Corcoran, Jose Santiago

YEAR	TEAM	LVL	AGE	W	L	SV	G	GS	IP	H	HR	BB	SO	BB9	SO9	GB%	BABIP	WHIP	ERA	FIP	FRA	WARP
2011	NWA	AA	29	1	6	0	11	11	44	55	8	18	24	3.7	4.9	49%	.311	1.66	7.16	5.95	6.45	0.3
2011	OMA	AAA	29	2	1	1	12	0	22²	16	1	10	20	4.0	7.9	40%	.213	1.15	1.59	3.92	3.30	0.4
2012	TOL	AAA	30	2	0	2	23	0	36	23	3	20	16	5.0	4.0	46%	.182	1.19	2.50	5.10	5.78	-0.4
2013	LEH	AAA	31	5	6	2	27	12	85¹	90	5	28	54	3.0	5.7	55%	.310	1.38	3.90	3.83	5.60	-0.3
2013	PHI	MLB	31	0	2	0	16	3	28²	33	4	17	20	5.3	6.3	50%	.314	1.74	4.40	5.43	5.17	0.0
2014	PHI	MLB	32	4	4	1	37	12	89¹	92	12	37	55	3.7	5.6	49%	.298	1.44	4.96	5.13	5.39	-0.4

Miner hadn't thrown a pitch in the majors since October 2009, but that didn't stop the Phillies from calling him up in August to contribute as a reliever. His ERA was nice; his defense-independent stats screamed "hadn't thrown a pitch in the majors since

October 2009." Out of necessity, the Phillies gave him three spot starts at the end of September, but he never made it into the fifth inning. His days as a regular starter are long gone, but he's good enough to be organizational fodder for some time more.

Adam Morgan

Born: 2/27/1990 Age: 24
Bats: L Throws: L Height: 6' 1" Weight: 195
Breakout: 34% Improve: 78% Collapse: 16%
Attrition: 61% MLB: 36%

Comparables:
Brandon Workman, John Ely, John Gast

YEAR	TEAM	LVL	AGE	W	L	SV	G	GS	IP	H	HR	BB	SO	BB9	SO9	GB%	BABIP	WHIP	ERA	FIP	FRA	WARP
2011	WPT	A-	21	3	3	0	11	11	53²	42	2	14	43	2.3	7.2	49%	.207	1.04	2.01	3.14	4.46	0.2
2012	CLR	A+	22	4	10	0	21	20	123	103	7	28	140	2.0	10.2	45%	.307	1.07	3.29	2.59	3.52	2.8
2012	REA	AA	22	4	1	0	6	6	35²	34	2	11	29	2.8	7.3	38%	.317	1.26	3.53	3.23	3.81	0.6
2013	LEH	AAA	23	2	7	0	16	16	71¹	84	10	26	49	3.3	6.2	37%	.329	1.54	4.04	4.96	5.12	0.4
2014	PHI	MLB	24	5	5	0	14	14	83	83	11	28	66	3.0	7.2	41%	.306	1.34	4.49	4.49	4.88	0.0

Morgan started the 2013 season rated as one of the Phillies' best prospects, having enjoyed success against hitters in Double-A in just his second year of professional ball. His debut at Triple-A started off a bit bumpy, as hitters were squaring him up like he was throwing beach balls. In his eighth start on May 15th, he allowed 10 runs, chasing his ERA up to 4.93. Doctors later found he had a small tear in his rotator cuff. He opted not to have surgery, returned on July 22nd, and posted a 2.67 ERA in eight successful starts through the end of the season. The Phillies, bereft of pitching depth, are hopeful Morgan can continue to make strides, stay healthy and join the back of a rotation.

Jonathan Papelbon

Born: 11/23/1980 Age: 33
Bats: R Throws: R Height: 6' 4" Weight: 225
Breakout: 15% Improve: 48% Collapse: 35%
Attrition: 9% MLB: 95%

Comparables:
J.J. Putz, Scot Shields, Rafael Betancourt

YEAR	TEAM	LVL	AGE	W	L	SV	G	GS	IP	H	HR	BB	SO	BB9	SO9	GB%	BABIP	WHIP	ERA	FIP	FRA	WARP
2011	BOS	MLB	30	4	1	31	63	0	64¹	50	3	10	87	1.4	12.2	38%	.309	0.93	2.94	1.57	1.87	2.4
2012	PHI	MLB	31	5	6	38	70	0	70	56	8	18	92	2.3	11.8	44%	.296	1.06	2.44	2.94	3.23	1.3
2013	PHI	MLB	32	5	1	29	61	0	61²	59	6	11	57	1.6	8.3	42%	.296	1.14	2.92	3.02	3.61	0.8
2014	PHI	MLB	33	3	1	29	58	0	58²	46	5	15	69	2.2	10.5	40%	.296	1.04	2.62	2.77	2.85	1.4

Papelbon's 2013 season felt much worse than his ERA. In the month leading into the All-Star break, Papelbon blew five of 12 save opportunities. Overall, his strikeout rate dropped by 10 percentage points, and he lost about 2 mph from his fastball. He leaned on his slider as an alternative, but that lost more than 3 mph. Two years (and $26 million) remain on his deal, and a third year will vest if he holds onto the closer job, so a big decline might actually help the Phillies more than a little one.

Jonathan Pettibone

Born: 7/19/1990 Age: 23
Bats: L Throws: R Height: 6' 6" Weight: 225
Breakout: 40% Improve: 63% Collapse: 18%
Attrition: 47% MLB: 63%

Comparables:
Alex Sanabia, Casey Coleman, Jenrry Mejia

YEAR	TEAM	LVL	AGE	W	L	SV	G	GS	IP	H	HR	BB	SO	BB9	SO9	GB%	BABIP	WHIP	ERA	FIP	FRA	WARP
2011	CLR	A+	20	10	11	0	27	27	161	149	5	34	115	1.9	6.4	46%	.279	1.14	2.96	3.11	3.89	1.9
2012	REA	AA	21	9	7	0	19	19	117¹	115	9	27	81	2.1	6.2	52%	.293	1.21	3.30	3.64	3.98	1.7
2012	LEH	AAA	21	4	1	0	7	7	42¹	31	0	22	32	4.7	6.8	52%	.263	1.25	2.55	3.20	4.34	0.3
2013	LEH	AAA	22	0	2	0	4	4	17¹	26	1	5	10	2.6	5.2	42%	.397	1.79	6.75	4.01	5.29	0.0
2013	PHI	MLB	22	5	4	0	18	18	100¹	109	9	38	66	3.4	5.9	51%	.326	1.47	4.04	4.16	4.38	0.8
2014	PHI	MLB	23	6	8	0	20	20	110	114	12	39	68	3.2	5.6	48%	.300	1.39	4.61	4.62	5.01	-0.1

Pettibone was never a major prospect but he did have good results in 2012, pushing him up the depth chart. That got him the call when John Lannan went on the disabled list in April. Pettibone's arsenal is a lot like that of Kyle Kendrick. It's not intimidating, but he controls it well and skates by with a quality start more often than not. He joined Lannan on the DL in July, with a strained rotator cuff, so the Phillies can add "starting pitching depth" to their list of needs.

B.J. Rosenberg

Born: 9/17/1985 Age: 28
Bats: R Throws: R Height: 6' 3" Weight: 220
Breakout: 39% Improve: 64% Collapse: 27%
Attrition: 40% MLB: 32%

Comparables:
Marcos Mateo, Dewon Day, Dirk Hayhurst

YEAR	TEAM	LVL	AGE	W	L	SV	G	GS	IP	H	HR	BB	SO	BB9	SO9	GB%	BABIP	WHIP	ERA	FIP	FRA	WARP
2011	REA	AA	25	5	7	2	39	14	109¹	114	11	38	103	3.1	8.5	49%	.332	1.39	4.28	4.10	5.03	0.5
2012	LEH	AAA	26	4	2	0	20	6	54	49	4	16	63	2.7	10.5	51%	.336	1.20	2.00	2.84	4.02	1.0
2012	PHI	MLB	26	1	2	0	22	1	25	18	4	14	24	5.0	8.6	37%	.241	1.28	6.12	5.22	5.89	-0.2
2013	LEH	AAA	27	3	6	2	28	10	75²	80	5	34	59	4.0	7.0	46%	.322	1.51	4.52	4.09	5.79	0.2
2013	PHI	MLB	27	2	0	1	22	0	19²	20	0	9	19	4.1	8.7	39%	.351	1.47	4.58	2.46	2.68	0.5
2014	PHI	MLB	28	4	3	0	42	8	85²	83	10	32	75	3.4	7.9	45%	.310	1.34	4.43	4.25	4.81	0.1

Honestly, B.J. Rosenberg isn't interesting. He's a 28-year-old Quad-A type reliever, utilizing a mid-90s fastball and not much else. You can see his Triple-A stats above; they're boring. He walks too many batters and doesn't miss bats often enough to be anything but low-leverage help. As part of a bullpen already teeming with young, high-ceiling arms, there just isn't enough room for Rosenberg. You might see him during the season, as injuries take their toll as usual. More likely, you've already forgotten about him.

Joe Savery
Born: 11/4/1985 Age: 28
Bats: L Throws: L Height: 6' 3" Weight: 235
Breakout: 54% Improve: 78% Collapse: 15%
Attrition: 34% MLB: 28%
Comparables:
Cesar Ramos, Troy Cate, Ryan Mattheus

YEAR	TEAM	LVL	AGE	W	L	SV	G	GS	IP	H	HR	BB	SO	BB9	SO9	GB%	BABIP	WHIP	ERA	FIP	FRA	WARP
2011	LEH	AAA	25	4	0	2	18	0	25	23	0	6	26	2.2	9.4	59%	.385	1.16	1.80	1.88	2.92	0.3
2011	PHI	MLB	25	0	0	0	4	0	2²	1	0	0	2	0.0	6.8	57%	.143	0.38	0.00	1.49	2.35	0.1
2012	LEH	AAA	26	1	1	2	20	0	23¹	27	3	9	26	3.5	10.0	45%	.353	1.54	4.24	3.89	5.00	0.1
2012	PHI	MLB	26	1	2	0	19	0	25	26	4	8	16	2.9	5.8	46%	.286	1.36	5.40	5.02	5.08	-0.1
2013	LEH	AAA	27	3	1	2	20	0	23²	18	2	9	29	3.4	11.0	66%	.281	1.14	3.80	2.99	4.66	0.2
2013	PHI	MLB	27	2	0	0	18	0	20	15	1	11	14	4.9	6.3	56%	.241	1.30	3.15	3.92	5.27	0.0
2014	PHI	MLB	28	2	2	0	19	3	38²	41	5	16	25	3.8	5.8	48%	.306	1.49	5.09	4.97	5.54	-0.3

Savery was the Phillies' 2007 first-round pick out of Rice University. He struggled early in his professional career and converted from pitcher to hitter; that didn't work, either, so Savery became a pitcher again. He's popped up in the big-league 'pen occasionally over the past two seasons, but he doesn't have much use to a club whose relief corps is teeming with power arms. Savery, comparatively, has a fastball that barely registers 90, and his secondary stuff—a slider and a changeup—are both below average. Savery is just one of many draft choices made in the late 2000s that simply haven't panned out for the Phillies, though in Savery's case it's certainly not for lack of imagination.

Michael Stutes
Born: 9/4/1986 Age: 27
Bats: R Throws: R Height: 6' 1" Weight: 185
Breakout: 54% Improve: 72% Collapse: 15%
Attrition: 43% MLB: 51%
Comparables:
Troy Cate, Casey Daigle, A.J. Murray

YEAR	TEAM	LVL	AGE	W	L	SV	G	GS	IP	H	HR	BB	SO	BB9	SO9	GB%	BABIP	WHIP	ERA	FIP	FRA	WARP
2011	LEH	AAA	24	2	1	1	7	0	10	9	0	4	14	3.6	12.6	25%	.500	1.30	1.80	1.64	2.67	0.2
2011	PHI	MLB	24	6	2	0	57	0	62	49	7	28	58	4.1	8.4	35%	.256	1.24	3.63	4.04	3.96	0.3
2012	PHI	MLB	25	0	0	0	6	0	5²	7	0	4	5	6.4	7.9	20%	.350	1.94	6.35	3.49	3.40	0.1
2013	LEH	AAA	26	1	2	2	20	0	27	21	1	11	25	3.7	8.3	47%	.256	1.19	3.33	3.28	3.72	0.4
2013	PHI	MLB	26	3	1	0	16	0	17²	14	1	8	9	4.1	4.6	40%	.241	1.25	4.58	4.27	5.88	-0.1
2014	PHI	MLB	27	1	1	0	29	0	36¹	34	4	16	30	4.0	7.4	41%	.292	1.38	4.58	4.50	4.98	-0.1

The once-promising career of Michael Stutes was put on hold by a shoulder injury in April 2012. He had surgery that June and didn't return until nearly a year later, then managed only 14 appearances before thudding back on the DL for 77 more games with biceps tendinitis. Back when he was healthy in 2011, Stutes looked like he would be a crucial bullpen piece if he could only harness his control. The to-do list is now twice as long, as he'll have to show he can stay healthy, too.

LINEOUTS

HITTERS

PLAYER	TEAM	LVL	AGE	PA	R	2B	3B	HR	RBI	BB	SO	SB-CS	AVG/OBP/SLG	TAv	BABIP	BRR	FRAA	WARP
3B R. Brignac	CSP	AAA	27	194	25	8	0	2	11	20	33	2-1	.230/.325/.315	.230	.273	-0.3	3B(19): 0.5, SS(17): -1.9	-0.3
	NYA	MLB	27	45	1	1	0	0	0	1	17	0-0	.114/.133/.136	.079	.185	-0.9	SS(17): -2.2	-1.0
	COL	MLB	27	53	4	3	0	1	6	3	13	0-0	.250/.294/.375	.206	.324	0	3B(8): -0.2, 2B(3): -0.1	-0.1
RF L. Castro	LEH	AAA	24	458	48	23	1	8	55	15	77	20-7	.256/.280/.368	.228	.294	2.3	RF(57): 2.9, LF(42): 0.5	0.3
CF Z. Collier	REA	AA	22	513	57	14	9	8	36	47	129	17-6	.222/.310/.348	.241	.293	0.1	CF(88): -0.2, LF(23): 0.3	0.1
RF K. Dugan	CLR	A+	22	248	37	12	3	10	36	24	60	1-3	.318/.401/.539	.334	.401	-0.8	RF(50): 5.6	3.1
	REA	AA	22	226	25	12	1	10	23	5	54	0-1	.264/.299/.472	.273	.309	-0.8	RF(28): 0.7, LF(24): 3.7	1.2
CF T. Gillies	REA	AA	24	191	24	8	4	7	21	12	39	4-3	.267/.312/.477	.277	.305	-0.7	CF(29): -1.5, LF(12): 0.7	0.7
	LEH	AAA	24	237	31	7	2	3	8	19	55	13-2	.220/.286/.313	.219	.282	1.2	CF(45): -3.1, LF(12): 1.1	-0.3
LF L. Greene	LWD	A	20	457	45	22	1	4	28	55	163	8-8	.212/.306/.302	.251	.345	-2.6	LF(111): -8.5	-0.8
CF T. Gwynn	ABQ	AAA	30	391	53	12	5	2	27	49	52	12-9	.300/.393/.384	.274	.349	-1.2	CF(48): 2.1, LF(37): -1.9	1.2
C L. Marson	COH	AAA	27	23	0	0	0	0	1	3	8	0-0	.100/.217/.100	.144	.167	-0.2	C(7): -0.1	-0.3
	CLE	MLB	27	5	0	0	0	0	0	0	2	0-0	.000/.400/.000	.260	.000	0	C(3): -0.0	0.0
2B P. Orr	LEH	AAA	34	352	40	17	6	4	31	17	61	9-7	.258/.300/.385	.240	.305	1.6	2B(45): 4.3, SS(28): -1.5	0.9
	PHI	MLB	34	22	1	0	0	0	0	2	8	0-0	.200/.273/.200	.192	.333	0	LF(2): 0.1, 3B(2): 0.0	-0.1
LF D. Sappelt	IOW	AAA	26	355	39	15	3	5	45	27	38	4-7	.252/.305/.364	.264	.268	0	LF(36): 1.6, RF(25): 2.6	1.4
	CHN	MLB	26	78	6	3	0	0	4	3	14	3-1	.240/.269/.280	.199	.295	-1.6	CF(13): -1.0, RF(7): -0.2	-0.6
RF S. Susdorf	LEH	AAA	27	359	43	20	1	2	36	37	52	11-7	.313/.390/.403	.292	.363	-2.6	RF(54): -5.6, LF(9): -0.3	1.1
	PHI	MLB	27	7	1	1	0	0	0	0	1	0-0	.143/.143/.286	.103	.167	0.1	LF(2): -0.0	-0.1
CF C. Tocci	LWD	A	17	459	40	17	0	0	26	22	77	6-7	.209/.261/.249	.206	.253	-0.3	CF(116): 16.4	0.5
C S. Valle	REA	AA	22	379	38	15	2	12	41	19	88	1-1	.203/.245/.359	.228	.234	-0.1	C(90): 1.9, LF(1): 0.0	0.2

Reid Brignac has a pulse and can play a passable major-league shortstop, so expect him to cling to major-league rosters like a barnacle on a passing ship. ⊘ **Leandro Castro** has played center field off and on in recent years, which is significant: His moderate speed and power could make him a useful bench player, but it won't play in a corner. ⊘ If **Zach Collier** hit for a higher average, he would be useful. He doesn't. ⊘ **Kelly Dugan** struck out 54 times and drew just five walks in his first taste of Double-A pitching. He also hit 10 home runs in 226 trips to the plate, so he is not to be overlooked. ⊘ **Tyson Gillies**—part of the Roy Halladay/Cliff Lee/Tyson Gillies trade—is a speedy outfielder on his last legs after posting a .599 OPS in his seventh year of pro ball. Too many strikeouts, not enough walks and an inefficient basestealer to boot. ⊘ The Phillies took **Larry Greene** one spot ahead of Jackie Bradley Jr. in the first round of the 2011 draft. Oops. Greene is stuck in the mud at the lower levels of the Phillies' system after a disappointing 2013. ⊘ The 2013 season was an indictment of **Tony Gwynn**'s present-day value, as he failed to record a major-league at bat for the first time since 2005 despite a Dodgers outfield gutted by injuries. ⊘ **Lou Marson** won't be sending Desmond Jennings any Christmas cards, after an early April home-plate collision wiped out his season. Probably wasn't sending him one, anyway. ⊘ **Pete Orr** has done yeoman's work for the Phillies in three years at Triple-A Lehigh Valley, but he just doesn't offer a major-league roster much beyond experience. ⊘ Compact outfielder **Dave Sappelt** slumped badly at the plate but plays a solid center field, runs well and can touch up the occasional lefty; in the disco era he would have found steady work on a National League bench, but today he'll likely spend his prime years as a Triple-A insurance policy. ⊘ If the Phillies think **Steve Susdorf** can maintain his high Triple-A average, they would be wise to see what the 28-year-old can offer off the bench. ⊘ **Carlos Tocci** is just 18 years old and already has two years of professional baseball under his belt. His offensive skill set has tons of potential, but is highly dependent on further physical development. ⊘ **Sebastian Valle** was once thought to be Carlos Ruiz's successor, until he put up some of pro ball's worst K/BB ratios. He's been stuck in neutral at Double-A while Cameron Rupp has passed him on Philadelphia's organizational depth chart.

PITCHERS

PLAYER	TEAM	LVL	AGE	W	L	SV	IP	H	HR	BB	SO	BB9	SO9	GB%	BABIP	WHIP	ERA	FIP	FRA	WARP
S. Camp	RNO	AAA	37	0	0	0	22¹	22	2	5	19	2.0	7.7	39%	.308	1.21	2.42	3.70	4.96	0.3
	CHN	MLB	37	1	1	0	23	34	7	9	13	3.5	5.1	51%	.333	1.87	7.04	7.02	7.22	-0.6
B. Colvin	REA	AA	22	3	2	0	77¹	79	9	54	36	6.3	4.2	38%	.276	1.72	6.40	6.31	6.50	-0.7
L. Garcia	CLR	A+	26	0	1	7	19²	15	2	5	20	2.3	9.2	58%	.260	1.02	1.37	3.44	3.75	0.2
	REA	AA	26	2	1	1	11	10	1	3	13	2.5	10.6	50%	.360	1.18	2.45	2.96	3.30	0.3
	LEH	AAA	26	0	0	3	11	5	0	4	8	3.3	6.5	60%	.167	0.82	0.82	2.84	2.94	0.2
	PHI	MLB	26	1	1	0	31¹	27	3	23	23	6.6	6.6	58%	.282	1.60	3.73	5.09	6.79	-0.5
P. Garner	CLR	A+	24	6	6	0	121¹	130	6	62	95	4.6	7.0	53%	.334	1.58	4.30	4.05	5.36	-0.3
K. Giles	CLR	A+	22	2	2	6	25²	23	4	19	34	6.7	11.9	32%	.306	1.64	6.31	4.96	5.87	-0.3
S. Gonzalez	LWD	A	20	3	0	0	21¹	10	1	3	31	1.3	13.1	47%	.214	0.61	1.69	1.75	2.91	0.5
	CLR	A+	20	3	5	0	75²	66	4	19	82	2.3	9.8	32%	.318	1.12	2.02	2.59	2.97	1.9
C. Jimenez	LEH	AAA	28	4	2	3	66¹	61	3	26	64	3.5	8.7	41%	.317	1.31	3.12	3.04	3.84	1.4
	PHI	MLB	28	1	1	0	17	14	1	10	11	5.3	5.8	40%	.250	1.41	3.71	4.43	4.51	0.0
B. Lincoln	BUF	AAA	28	3	2	5	26¹	22	2	8	29	2.7	9.9	48%	.312	1.14	2.05	3.13	4.88	0.1
	TOR	MLB	28	1	2	0	31²	28	4	22	25	6.3	7.1	41%	.261	1.58	3.98	5.51	6.61	-0.6
K. Munson	MOB	AA	24	2	2	13	31²	17	5	15	39	4.3	11.1	42%	.179	1.01	3.41	4.30	5.28	-0.1
	RNO	AAA	24	0	2	1	23	25	1	7	27	2.7	10.6	52%	.358	1.39	5.09	2.83	4.25	0.5
S. O'Sullivan	TUC	AAA	25	8	5	0	115	130	7	31	99	2.4	7.7	50%	.350	1.40	3.83	3.58	4.43	2.0
	SDN	MLB	25	0	2	0	25	31	0	14	12	5.0	4.3	45%	.345	1.80	3.96	3.86	4.59	0.0
M. Robles	REA	AA	24	3	1	2	26	19	1	13	37	4.5	12.8	35%	.321	1.23	2.77	2.48	2.90	0.7
	LEH	AAA	24	2	2	7	38	16	0	31	26	7.3	6.2	53%	.165	1.24	1.42	4.36	5.73	-0.3
	PHI	MLB	24	0	0	0	4²	7	0	3	6	5.8	11.6	50%	.438	2.14	1.93	2.38	2.37	0.2
S. Watson	LWD	A	19	4	6	0	72	63	12	28	53	3.5	6.6	53%	.229	1.26	4.75	5.47	6.58	-0.7
C. Zambrano	CLR	A+	32	1	0	0	10¹	7	0	4	5	3.5	4.4	55%	.212	1.06	0.00	3.43	4.07	0.1
	LEH	AAA	32	1	0	0	19	19	0	10	18	4.7	8.5	49%	.333	1.53	3.32	3.05	4.13	0.2

Career set-up man **Shawn Camp** is nearing the end of his set-up man career. After an abrupt release from the Cubs he finished out the year in Reno and continued to throw hittable strikes. ⊘ **Brody Colvin** has the stuff to compete at the big-league level, but he walked 54 and struck out 36 with Double-A Reading. ⊘ The Phillies will find room for **Luis Garcia** in the bullpen if he can bring his walk rate way, way down. ⊘ Injuries and inconsistency have slowed **Perci Garner**'s progress. His fastball is live but he lacks command, and his secondary stuff doesn't match up. ⊘ **Kenneth Giles** impressed in the Arizona Fall League, flashing a fastball that pushed 100 mph but that he often had no control over. If he ever tames it, he will be a very useful reliever. ⊘ For every $500,000 international signee who does nothing, there's a $14,000 **Severino Gonzalez** who adds five ticks to his fastball, dominates in his stateside debut and earns himself a big dot on the prospect map. ⊘ **Cesar Jimenez** has a career minor-league walk rate of 9 percent, and he just kept walking at the major-league level. Like the rest of the Phillies' bullpen, he'd have the chance to stand out if he could just learn to throw strikes. ⊘ **Brad Lincoln** split yet another year between the majors and Triple-A, but neither organizational nor role change (full-time relief) made a difference—except for the worst, as Lincoln's control completely deserted him in the big leagues. ⊘ Command issues have nagged **Kevin Munson** throughout his career, so his K/BB ratio in Triple-A comes as terrific news. ⊘ **Sean O'Sullivan** performed admirably in his now-familiar role of lovable rogue who waits for something bad to happen at headquarters so he can hop on a plane and arrive in time to photobomb the team picture. ⊘ **Mauricio Robles** was another in the cadre of young arms the Phillies used who had great stuff but absolutely no control over it. Control+C, Control+V. ⊘ **Shane Watson** is among the better arms in the Phillies' system, but it says more about the organization's lack of depth than anything else. Decent fastball and a nice curve but not much else. ⊘ **Carlos Zambrano** was released after seven minor-league starts, so this might be farewell to a pitcher who could roll out of bed and hit .238.

MANAGER: RYNE SANDBERG

YEAR	TEAM	W-L	+/-	Pythag PC	Avg P	100+ P	120+	QS	BQS	REL	REL w Zero R	IBB	PH	PH Avg	PH HR	SB2	CS2	SB3	CS3	SAC Att	SAC %	POS SAC	Squeeze	Swing	In Play
2013	PHI	20-22	0	89.7	15	1		22	0	135	104	10	64	.203	0	6	5	3	0	19	63.2%	3	1	57	21

What can you say about Ryne Sandberg after just 42 games? He has a good pedigree. He won a minor league Manager of the Year Award while in the Cubs' organization, and also served on Charlie Manuel's major-league staff. So on paper he has potential. The Phillies did improve under Sandberg's watch, but one shouldn't make too much of that. Half of the 42 games he managed were decided by one run, and Philadelphia was 14-7 in them. They were 6-15 in the others. Thus did a team outscored 154-197 play nearly .500 ball.

Charlie Manuel's firing last year, right after his 1,000th career win, will likely end his career for good. He's in his 70s now, and very few managers get hired at that age.

Pittsburgh Pirates

By Michael Clair

Neal Huntington is a witch. Or a warlock, I've never really been certain of the nomenclature. Regardless of the title, the general manager of the Pittsburgh Pirates is a man who consorts with the four winds.

Not that you could blame him. Coming into the year, the Pirates were on a 20-year losing streak, the worst in major American sports. Since taking over the team in 2007, Huntington has watched the Pirates' farm system, once bereft of talent, burst forth with both depth and high-end players. He gutted a major-league roster that was once a halfway house for the aged (Jeromy Burnitz, Matt Morris), streamlining it with an eye not for 75-win mediocrity but World Series contention.

In 2011 and '12, it nearly worked. Sure, all the necessary pieces hadn't yet arrived, but the Pirates found themselves playing competitive baseball deep into the summer. Both times, the luck ran out early, the team posting records of 18-38 and 20-39 from August on. Pirates fans, well accustomed to losing, now had to deal with the pangs of dashed dreams.

And so, while looking for that additional edge in 2013, The Extra 2% that stats or scouts can't come up with, Neal Huntington turned to sportcery. In the dead of night during the Winter Meetings, Huntington, team president Frank Coonelly and assorted members of the Pirates' front office went into the woods, stripped to the waist and offered a blood sacrifice to the New Moon.

Baseball teams turning to the occult is not a new idea. In 1975, a Kenyan witch doctor named John Agunga was called upon to put a curse on the Red Sox. Ron Cey was known to wear a magical cologne. The Angels briefly had the help of a witch named Louise Huebner in 1977. Wade Boggs drank beer by the case to ward off demons. But as far as recorded information goes, no general manager had ever been the one behind the cauldron. Until now.

Before the Pirates' Game Five loss against the Cardinals in the Division Series, everything that could go right did, their season less like a marathon and more like a six-month tantric sex session. That's not baseball, that's magic.

CONSIDER: THE ELEMENTS OF NATURE

Witches honor the elemental forces: earth, water, fire, wind and spirit. Basically, they're Planeteers without the cool rings. The Pirates' pitching staff had a 54 percent groundball rate, the highest since 2002 (**Earth**); after installing an actual shark tank in the clubhouse, the 'Shark Tank' bullpen morphed into one of the best in baseball despite containing a number of castoffs and nobodies (**Water**); their closer, or (**Fire**) man, is named Jason **Grill**i; at this point I'm amazed that BuzzFeed hasn't created an article titled "20 Industrial Box Fans that Create Less of a Breeze than Pedro Alvarez" (**Wind**); and, considering Clint Hurdle's purple-hued face, are we sure he's not actually a vengeful ghost (**Spirit**)?

ANDREW MCCUTCHEN: MVP

I'm certainly not claiming that Andrew McCutchen's absurd 2013 (.317/.404/.508) was solely due to Neal Hungtinton's impression of Fairuza Balk in *The Craft*. But can you really deny that it contributed? McCutchen, already a superstar with his face gracing the cover of *MLB 13: The Show*, cut down on his strikeouts, upped his walks and improved his defense. (FRAA still doesn't like him, pegging him at -8, but his DRS was a career best +7.) Even more miraculous than his MVP victory, McCutchen will be teaming with David Ortiz as an executive producer on an MTV2 show geared towards attracting new baseball fans. That's right, a player from Pittsburgh will be used to lure in the younger demographic. I don't remember Jack Wilson ever doing that.

PIRATES PROSPECTUS
2013 W-L: 94-68, 2nd in NL Central

Pythag	.542	10th	DER	.709	6th
RS/G	3.91	20th	B-Age	27.8	11th
RA/G	3.56	2nd	P-Age	28.4	21st
TAv	.262	12th	Salary	$66.8	26th
BRR	-5.33	23rd	M$/MW	$1.18	3rd
TAv-P	.252	4th	DL Days	1070	20th
FIP	3.39	3rd	$ on DL	24%	24th

	Runs	HR/RH	HR/LH	Runs/RH	Runs/LH
Three-Year Park Factors	98	88	97	98	99

Top Hitter WARP	6.13 (Andrew McCutchen)
Top Pitcher WARP	2.69 (A.J. Burnett)
Top Prospect	Jameson Taillon

FRANCISCO LIRIANO'S BROKEN ARM

In 2011-12, the former top prospect posted a 5.23 ERA in 291 innings with a mind-numbing five walks per nine. After breaking his arm while trying to scare his children on Christmas, the Pirates were able to land him for the bargain price of $1 million plus incentives before watching him go 16-8 with a 3.02 ERA, cut his walk rate to 3.5 and earn his second Comeback Player of the Year Award. Sure, the Pirates claim that Liriano's success was a fortunate result of the injury, allowing him to work with pitching guru Jim Benedict in extended spring training, fine-tuning his delivery and building up his arm strength. But come on. We know the truth. Something nefarious was afoot.

THE ROOKIE HURLERS

While the Pirates leaned heavily on Liriano and A.J. Burnett, they needed plenty of help along the way. Injuries decimated the rest of the rotation, forcing Wandy Rodriguez and Charlie Morton to miss extended time. Jeff Karstens' majestic pitchface never did see game action. Fortunately there were two young arms, aided by devilry, ready to help.

Jeff Locke, the stand-in for *Dexter*'s Ice Truck Killer, somehow parlayed his mediocre left-handed offerings and poor command into a 2.15 first half ERA and All-Star appearance, sure signs of enchantment at work. But when he fell apart in the second half, batters no longer fooled by his 90 mph fastball or Huntington's dark mutterings from the bowels of the stadium, there was *Baseball Prospectus'* top pitching prospect, Gerrit Cole, ready to take his place.

Called up in June, the fireballing starter worried some fans with underwhelming strikeout numbers in Triple-A, a warning sign that bore out when he struck out only 25 batters during his first 41 innings. Cole was still getting decent results thanks to his upper-90s heat, but this wasn't the dream Pirates fans had of the first-overall selection. So Neal Huntington did something about it. On the eve of Cole's July 23rd start against the Nationals on July 23rd—a night that just happened to be a full moon and witches esbat—Huntington called him into his hotel suite. The two remained there for six hours; hotel staff claimed sulfur and the screams of tortured souls emanated from the room.

Whatever the two conjured in there, it worked. Cole pitched seven innings of one-run ball the next day, and, after utilizing his slider more often, struck out 71 batters over his final 68 innings. Cole then garnered big-game experience by outdueling Yu Darvish in a narrative-friendly September start after the Pirates had been swept by the Cardinals. He went on to make two starts in the Division Series, including getting the nod over Burnett in the fifth game, where a David Freese two-run homer was his only mistake.

WITCHY DATES

According to the website *Witch Way*, there are four sabbats, extremely powerful and meaningful dates to Wiccans, that fall during the baseball season: May 1st, June 21st, August 1st and September 21st. The Pirates went 3-1 on those dates, losing only to the Cardinals, the team that, as it turned out, was seemingly immune to Huntington's thaumaturgy.

Coincidence?

MARLON BYRDEMIC 2: THE RESURRECTION

Huntington reserved his most daring spell for the end of the season, though. After years of missing on bats (Andy LaRoche, early Brandon Moss, Ryan Ludwick, Travis Snider) and with the Pirates hanging on in the NL Central, Huntington knew he had to do something, even as previous deadline acquisitions had failed to stem the tide of losing.

Calling upon the spirits of Honus Wagner, Roberto Clemente and Willie Stargell, Huntington extracted Marlon Byrd, then hitting .285/.330/.518 with a career-high 21 home runs, and John Buck from the Mets in exchange for reliever Vic Black and second base prospect Dilson Herrera. But there was a third team in on this trade too, one that went unreported in the daily trades. It was the Devil, with Neal Huntington offering up his soul should the Pirates fail to reach the playoffs.

With a gaping wound in right field (the Pirates had received a .232/.297/.369 cumulative line from the position at the time of the trade), Huntington knew he had to act, but there was plenty of risk surrounding Byrd, his PED suspension and disappointing 2011 and '12 seasons still fresh in the mind. How often do 35-year-olds truly have breakout seasons? Those are concerns for mortals, however. Huntington had little reason to worry: He had the power of the dead on his side.

Thanks to the dark and dangerous magicks, Byrd didn't regress, instead hitting .318/.357/.486 in 30 games with the Pirates, supplying an additional eight hits and a home run during the truncated playoff run. Byrd then parlayed the performance into a two-year, $16 million deal with the Phillies. Huntington escaped with his earthly soul (and his budget) intact.

EVERYTHING ELSE

Then there was the rest:
- Starling Marte broke out (41 steals and good defense).
- The Clint Barmes/Jordy Mercer timeshare worked in perfect harmony.
- Gaby Sanchez (.333/.448/.539 against lefties) provided protection for Garrett Jones.
- Charlie Morton returned from Tommy John surgery to lead all starters (100 innings min.) in groundball rate.

- After signing the largest contract in Pirates free agent history (two years, $17 million), Russell Martin hit 15 homers and, using Max Marchi's model, saved 33 runs through his pitch handling, second only to Yadier Molina.
- Clint Hurdle left his old-school ways in the past and embraced defensive shifts, the team thereby more than quadrupling their total number of shifts in 2012 and devouring damn near every groundball.

A few of those happening would be normal baseball variance, a handful a bout of good luck, but all of them taken together? That's *Fantasia*-level magic, all culminating in the biggest game Pirates fans have seen since Sid Bream's slide: the Wild Card play-in game against the Reds.

Held in PNC Park, the home base of Huntington's coven, Pirates fans flocked to the stadium decked in black, confirming that this was a team whose powers came from the shadows and unseen worlds. Like a soccer crowd or demonic cult (same difference), chants rose and fell all game, perhaps causing Johnny Cueto to lose his concentration and possibly even guiding Marlon Byrd and Russell Martin's home runs over the outfield wall. Francisco Liriano picked up a base hit, the surest sign of magic at work given Liriano's laissez faire attitude toward swinging the bat.

Of course, the Pirates ran out of steam against the Cardinals, though they pushed St. Louis to the brink of elimination before nearly being no-hit by Michael Wacha and then stymied by Adam Wainwright in the clincher. It became clear that Huntington's brand of hoodoo isn't strong enough when going up against the collective energy of The Best Fans in Baseball.

By now, word of the GM's charms will have spread through the league, the other general managers adding grimoires to their libraries and magicians to their payrolls. There are rumors that Jed Hoyer has turned to Kabbalah and that Jerry Dipoto is using the power of positive thinking. Magic is the new inefficiency and the Pirates will not be able to expect this kind of spell-aided good fortune again.

As always, money will continue to be an issue. Even after a string of sold-out dates and the extra revenue from the playoffs, the club could not afford to make a $14.1 million qualifying offer to Burnett, hoping instead that Edinson Volquez can be remolded into something terrible and powerful in Jim Benedict's laboratory.

While it did not shake out this way, it was possible at the start of the offseason that, thanks to those qualifying offers, the Yankees could draft five players in 2014 before the Pirates got to select their second. Add in the spending caps on amateur signings and it's as if the collective bargaining agreement is directly aimed at Pittsburgh—Neal Huntington's teams are routinely among the leaders in draft spending. (Though even with these restrictions, the Pirates had an extremely strong 2013 draft class, selecting possible stars in catcher Reese McGuire and outfielder Austin Meadows in the first round.)

Fortunately, while there are a few holes on the roster, the minor league larder is stocked, ranking among the best in baseball. The team can hope for Jameson Taillon to pull a Gerrit Cole Part 2 when he's called up midseason. Beyond Taillon, the future is bright with pitchers Nick Kingham, Tyler Glasnow and Luis Heredia mowing through batters in the lower minors.

Jose Tabata's hot streak over the last two months (.312/.357/.490) gives hope that he could once again be the answer in right field, possibly finding himself in a platoon with the 25-year-old Andrew Lambo (32 homers between Double- and Triple-A, though he struck out in 25 percent of his plate appearances along the way) or freshly acquired walk machine Jaff Decker. If not, there's the toolsy outfielder Gregory Polanco quickly absorbing skills like a baseball robot with advanced AI, and shortstop Alen Hanson could find himself called upon should the Barmes/Mercer combo fail to repeat its success.

Add in the established players like McCutchen and Alvarez and future ace Cole and, for the first time in a generation, the Pirates are in a good position to win. There's quality depth at almost every position, the minor-league system is humming, and the coaching staff, stats people, scouting department and spellmasters are all working in lockstep. Neal Huntington deserves plenty of credit for assembling this group out of the smoldering pit that was left for him when he took over, especially after nearly losing his job following the 2012 collapse.

Even with all those strengths, this is a team that can't afford many mistakes. With the Cardinals, Reds and quickly improving Cubs offering plenty of competition next season, should the Pirates regress—whether it's the bullpen or rotation taking a step backward, McCutchen not having an MVP campaign or Alvarez swinging and missing a few more times—the team could be in for a difficult year.

But that's true of nearly every team: Winning 90-plus games and traveling to the playoffs is the result of good planning, a deep roster ... and a lot of luck. While the Pirates may have been the heartwarming underdogs in 2013, they now have the talent to compete every year. That's magic in and of itself.

Michael Clair writes Old Time Family Baseball *and contributes to* The Platoon Advantage *and* MLB Daily Dish. *His work sometimes shows up at* Sports on Earth, Baseball Prospectus, *and other Internet addresses.*

HITTERS

Pedro Alvarez 3B

Born: 2/6/1987 Age: 27
Bats: L Throws: R Height: 6' 3"
Weight: 235 Breakout: 5%
Improve: 56% Collapse: 1%
Attrition: 4% MLB: 96%

Comparables:
Mark Reynolds, Troy Glaus, Chris Duncan

YEAR	TEAM	LVL	AGE	PA	R	2B	3B	HR	RBI	BB	SO	SB	CS	AVG/OBP/SLG	TAv	BABIP	BRR	FRAA	WARP
2011	BRD	A+	24	21	2	0	0	1	2	3	5	0	0	.188/.381/.375	.277	.200	0		0.0
2011	IND	AAA	24	148	16	5	1	5	19	22	42	0	1	.256/.365/.432	.272	.342	-1	3B(26): 3.2	0.9
2011	PIT	MLB	24	262	18	9	1	4	19	24	80	1	0	.191/.272/.289	.198	.272	-2	3B(66): 5.0	-0.5
2012	PIT	MLB	25	586	64	25	1	30	85	57	180	1	0	.244/.317/.467	.283	.308	0.5	3B(145): -5.1	2.5
2013	PIT	MLB	26	614	70	22	2	36	100	48	186	2	0	.233/.296/.473	.274	.276	0	3B(150): 11.9	4.5
2014	PIT	MLB	27	571	67	22	1	25	79	52	173	2	1	.234/.306/.428	.271	.300	-0.8	3B 4	2.5

Alvarez isn't the superstar he was expected to become, but he's a solid player, a Three True Outcomes slugger who makes up for not having a gaudy walk rate by playing third base. The rest of Alvarez's game conforms to type: He strikes out about 30 percent of the time and hits for a ton of power. He remains a liability against left-handed pitching, and it's unclear whether he'll stick at third base for the long haul (though defensive metrics liked him in 2013). Still, Alvarez does enough right to start most days and to merit All-Star Game consideration most summers. PECOTA sees regression in Alvarez's power and defense, with the former perhaps reflecting the difficulty of any player maintaining a .240 isolated power rather than a particular judgment on Alvarez himself.

Clint Barmes SS

Born: 3/6/1979 Age: 35
Bats: R Throws: R Height: 6' 1"
Weight: 200 Breakout: 1%
Improve: 33% Collapse: 12%
Attrition: 25% MLB: 77%

Comparables:
Alex Gonzalez, Dave Concepcion, Juan Castro

YEAR	TEAM	LVL	AGE	PA	R	2B	3B	HR	RBI	BB	SO	SB	CS	AVG/OBP/SLG	TAv	BABIP	BRR	FRAA	WARP
2011	HOU	MLB	32	495	47	27	0	12	39	38	88	3	1	.244/.312/.386	.250	.279	-2	SS(122): 5.5	2.0
2012	PIT	MLB	33	493	34	16	1	8	45	20	106	0	2	.229/.272/.321	.222	.280	2.1	SS(142): 8.9, 1B(1): -0.0	0.9
2013	PIT	MLB	34	330	22	15	0	5	23	14	70	0	0	.211/.249/.309	.211	.257	0.7	SS(106): 3.2	-0.1
2014	PIT	MLB	35	343	31	14	0	7	32	18	70	2	1	.222/.272/.330	.228	.260	-0.8	SS 5, 1B -0	0.9

Though never an offensive force, Barmes has had two of his worst seasons at the plate during his time in Pittsburgh. The man can still field the position, though, so the Pirates kept him around, even with Jordy Mercer in the fold. Barmes' glove should keep him employable for the next season or two, even if his bat is bankrupt.

Josh Bell RF

Born: 8/14/1992 Age: 21
Bats: B Throws: R Height: 6' 3"
Weight: 213 Breakout: 3%
Improve: 8% Collapse: 0%
Attrition: 6% MLB: 11%

Comparables:
Moises Sierra, Josh Reddick, Oswaldo Arcia

YEAR	TEAM	LVL	AGE	PA	R	2B	3B	HR	RBI	BB	SO	SB	CS	AVG/OBP/SLG	TAv	BABIP	BRR	FRAA	WARP
2012	WVA	A	19	66	6	5	0	1	11	2	21	1	0	.274/.288/.403	.228	.381	-0.1	RF(14): -1.3	-0.3
2013	WVA	A	20	519	75	37	2	13	76	52	90	1	2	.279/.353/.453	.318	.319	-1.1	RF(83): 2.9	4.1
2014	PIT	MLB	21	250	22	11	0	5	26	13	58	0	0	.232/.274/.350	.237	.280	-0.5	RF -0	-0.2

Bell, whose first pro season ended with a knee injury, opened the season with a slow bat caused by rust. He improved as the year burned on, and by season's end his numbers were respectable given his age and level. Still, Bell has work to do: His right-handed hitting mechanics are panned by scouts, and he'll need to continue to develop offensively. Bell is a below-average runner with a subpar arm, meaning his power development will determine whether he's a first-division starter. The Pirates paid Bell $5 million in 2012 to lure him from his Texas commitment, so we know where they stand.

John Buck C

Born: 7/7/1980 Age: 33
Bats: R Throws: R Height: 6' 3"
Weight: 245 Breakout: 0%
Improve: 26% Collapse: 15%
Attrition: 21% MLB: 91%

Comparables:
Gene Oliver, Carlton Fisk, Ramon Castro

YEAR	TEAM	LVL	AGE	PA	R	2B	3B	HR	RBI	BB	SO	SB	CS	AVG/OBP/SLG	TAv	BABIP	BRR	FRAA	WARP
2011	FLO	MLB	30	530	41	15	1	16	57	54	115	0	1	.227/.316/.367	.250	.268	-0.3	C(135): -2.0	1.4
2012	MIA	MLB	31	398	29	15	1	12	41	49	103	0	0	.192/.297/.347	.238	.235	-0.7	C(105): 3.4	1.2
2013	NYN	MLB	32	407	38	11	0	15	60	29	99	2	1	.215/.285/.367	.245	.250	1.1	C(97): -0.5	1.2
2013	PIT	MLB	32	24	1	0	0	0	2	0	5	0	0	.333/.333/.333	.236	.421	0	C(7): -0.0	0.0
2014	PIT	MLB	33	398	43	14	1	13	45	29	99	1	0	.226/.291/.376	.251	.270	-0.7	C -0	1.5

Buck started the season as the Mets' everyday catcher and homered nine times in April. From that point forward, he went deep just six more times before the Mets traded him to the Pirates as part of the Marlon Byrd deal. Buck's power production has declined since his big 2010 season, and he no longer merits starting consideration. The thing is, he's not a particularly good defender, either, which is often a prerequisite to serve as a backup. That leaves Buck as an offensive-minded reserve whose best days are behind him.

Jaff Decker CF

Born: 2/23/1990 Age: 24
Bats: L Throws: L Height: 5' 10"
Weight: 190 Breakout: 5%
Improve: 13% Collapse: 9%
Attrition: 18% MLB: 35%

Comparables:
Desmond Jennings, Chad Huffman, Ryan Kalish

YEAR	TEAM	LVL	AGE	PA	R	2B	3B	HR	RBI	BB	SO	SB	CS	AVG/OBP/SLG	TAv	BABIP	BRR	FRAA	WARP
2011	SAN	AA	21	613	90	29	2	19	92	103	145	15	5	.236/.373/.417	.274	.291	-0.9	LF(88): 2.0, CF(4): 0.6	1.7
2012	SAN	AA	22	190	30	3	2	3	9	40	37	6	2	.184/.365/.293	.273	.224	-1.4	RF(36): 0.3, CF(7): -0.5	0.6
2013	TUC	AAA	23	415	63	23	1	10	40	55	94	4	6	.286/.381/.443	.284	.361	2.5	CF(66): -2.8, RF(39): -2.9	2.2
2013	SDN	MLB	23	31	3	0	0	1	2	3	4	0	1	.154/.233/.269	.196	.136	-0.5	LF(8): 0.3	-0.3
2014	PIT	MLB	24	250	30	10	1	5	23	32	61	3	1	.223/.326/.350	.259	.280	-0.4	CF -1, RF -1	0.4

Prior to being designated for assignment and traded to Pittsburgh this winter, Decker was one of the last vestiges of Grady Fuson's tenure as the Padres' draft honcho. He finally got his cup of coffee in 2013, but aside from launching a home run in a blowout loss at Coors Field, he didn't do much with it. Decker's hyper-patient approach at the plate represents an organizational philosophy of previous regimes. He doesn't walk as much as he once did, doesn't hit as many homers and still strikes out at a rate not justified by his lack of power. Despite being a better defensive outfielder than he often gets credit for, Decker doesn't hit enough to start. He could stick as a left-handed bat off the bench, but so could a lot of guys.

Alen Hanson SS

Born: 10/22/1992 Age: 21
Bats: B Throws: R Height: 5' 11"
Weight: 170 Breakout: 7%
Improve: 19% Collapse: 2%
Attrition: 13% MLB: 24%

Comparables:
Asdrubal Cabrera, Yamaico Navarro, Trevor Plouffe

YEAR	TEAM	LVL	AGE	PA	R	2B	3B	HR	RBI	BB	SO	SB	CS	AVG/OBP/SLG	TAv	BABIP	BRR	FRAA	WARP
2012	WVA	A	19	558	99	33	13	16	62	55	105	35	19	.309/.381/.528	.314	.364	6.3	SS(103): -14.0	4.2
2013	BRD	A+	20	409	51	23	8	7	48	33	70	24	14	.281/.339/.444	.283	.325	2	SS(92): 2.4	3.4
2013	ALT	AA	20	150	13	4	5	1	10	8	26	6	2	.255/.299/.380	.273	.306	-0.9	SS(34): -1.6	0.6
2014	PIT	MLB	21	250	29	10	3	4	20	14	59	9	4	.236/.281/.356	.238	.290	0.5	SS -4, 2B -0	0.1

Hanson started the season in Bradenton and earned a promotion in June after a few hot weeks. Although the Pirates continue to play him at shortstop, many scouts think he lacks the requisite physical tools to stick at the position, as his arm and glove currently receive average-at-best projections. If and when Hanson moves to second base, he should fit right in. His bat is fast and looks quicker thanks to a direct-to-the-ball swing. Hanson is unlikely to hit a ton of home runs, but he should rack up doubles due to his plus speed and line-drive sensibilities. Provided he figures out Double-A pitching, Hanson isn't far off from the majors.

Josh Harrison 2B

Born: 7/8/1987 Age: 26
Bats: R Throws: R Height: 5' 8"
Weight: 200 Breakout: 6%
Improve: 51% Collapse: 11%
Attrition: 28% MLB: 94%

Comparables:
Alexi Casilla, Daniel Descalso, Jason Kipnis

YEAR	TEAM	LVL	AGE	PA	R	2B	3B	HR	RBI	BB	SO	SB	CS	AVG/OBP/SLG	TAv	BABIP	BRR	FRAA	WARP
2011	IND	AAA	23	254	35	15	2	5	23	15	28	13	5	.310/.365/.460	.287	.333	-2	3B(32): -1.4, 2B(17): 2.7	1.1
2011	PIT	MLB	23	204	21	13	2	1	16	3	24	4	1	.272/.281/.374	.235	.304	-0.7	3B(50): 3.9, 2B(6): 0.1	0.5
2012	PIT	MLB	24	276	34	9	5	3	16	10	37	7	3	.233/.279/.345	.238	.259	0.3	2B(28): -0.3, SS(25): -2.0	0.1
2013	IND	AAA	25	296	50	29	5	4	34	20	39	19	7	.317/.373/.507	.297	.360	1	2B(33): 4.6, SS(29): 3.3	3.0
2013	PIT	MLB	25	95	10	1	2	3	14	2	10	2	0	.250/.290/.409	.239	.253	0.7	RF(14): -0.8, 2B(11): 0.9	0.1
2014	PIT	MLB	26	250	30	13	2	3	21	9	35	10	3	.266/.305/.387	.258	.290	0.7	2B 2, SS -0	1.0

Pittsburgh's odd loyalty to Harrison ceased last season, as he spent most of the year in the minors. When he did dress for the big-league club, he produced better than expected thanks to an unanticipated power surge. Realistically, it's hard to see the pipsqueak-sized Harrison hitting for much pop heading forward, and that leaves his ability to produce offensively in doubt. His plate discipline is putrid and, while he can put the bat on the ball, it's often poor contact. To Harrison's credit, he can play all over the place; he just doesn't own a position well enough to overcome his shortcomings.

Andrew Lambo RF

Born: 8/11/1988 Age: 25
Bats: L Throws: L Height: 6' 3"
Weight: 225 Breakout: 6%
Improve: 18% Collapse: 6%
Attrition: 22% MLB: 36%

Comparables:
Marc Krauss, Justin Maxwell, Justin Huber

YEAR	TEAM	LVL	AGE	PA	R	2B	3B	HR	RBI	BB	SO	SB	CS	AVG/OBP/SLG	TAv	BABIP	BRR	FRAA	WARP
2011	ALT	AA	22	286	35	17	0	8	41	26	59	4	3	.274/.345/.437	.283	.324	0.6	RF(54): -2.0, LF(1): -0.0	1.1
2011	IND	AAA	22	207	19	11	0	3	17	17	48	1	0	.184/.257/.292	.190	.228	-0.5	RF(38): 2.6, LF(1): 0.0	-1.0
2012	ALT	AA	23	108	13	3	1	4	16	14	19	0	1	.250/.346/.435	.285	.271	-0.9	RF(26): 4.1	1.0
2013	ALT	AA	24	247	35	9	4	14	46	20	60	6	1	.291/.351/.559	.319	.336	-0.3	LF(38): 3.5, 1B(18): -0.3	2.3
2013	IND	AAA	24	254	32	15	1	18	53	24	67	1	0	.272/.344/.589	.306	.303	0.7	RF(32): 0.5, LF(22): 0.2	1.9
2013	PIT	MLB	24	33	4	2	0	1	2	3	11	0	1	.233/.303/.400	.253	.333	0.4	RF(6): -0.8, LF(2): 0.1	0.0
2014	PIT	MLB	25	250	27	11	1	9	32	18	66	1	0	.231/.289/.406	.255	.280	-0.3	RF 1, LF 0	0.5

Lambo wasn't in last year's book. Years after being a top prospect with the Dodgers, his stock plummeted to the point where a big-league future seemed unlikely. But he's rebounded since, and reached the majors in 2013. In fact, for a while he served as a cause céèbre among Pirates fans. Lambo didn't get a long look, nor did he do much to move the needle; expect him to get more big-league exposure in 2014, with the chance to carve out a niche as a platoon outfielder if all goes well.

Starling Marte LF

Born: 10/9/1988 Age: 25
Bats: R Throws: R Height: 6' 1"
Weight: 185 Breakout: 3%
Improve: 39% Collapse: 2%
Attrition: 20% MLB: 88%

Comparables:
Cameron Maybin, Travis Snider, Peter Bourjos

YEAR	TEAM	LVL	AGE	PA	R	2B	3B	HR	RBI	BB	SO	SB	CS	AVG/OBP/SLG	TAv	BABIP	BRR	FRAA	WARP
2011	ALT	AA	22	572	91	38	8	12	50	22	100	24	12	.332/.370/.500	.316	.390	6.1	CF(110): 3.1	5.9
2012	IND	AAA	23	431	64	21	13	12	62	28	91	21	12	.286/.347/.500	.284	.344	-2.2	CF(76): 2.1, LF(16): 2.3	2.8
2012	PIT	MLB	23	182	18	3	6	5	17	8	50	12	5	.257/.300/.437	.271	.333	-1.1	LF(43): -2.0, CF(4): -0.0	0.3
2013	PIT	MLB	24	566	83	26	10	12	35	25	138	41	15	.280/.343/.441	.286	.363	3.1	LF(124): -2.1, CF(13): -0.0	2.9
2014	PIT	MLB	25	507	70	22	7	12	48	21	120	27	11	.271/.318/.424	.273	.340	1.8	LF -1, CF -0	2.0

Entering the season, the concern was that Marte's undisciplined approach would limit his offensive ability. So much for that. Marte showed off his special blend of power and speed, and in effect gave the Pirates two center fielders when he was on the field next to Andrew McCutchen. The talented young outfielder must still refine his approach—his on-base percentage was buoyed by 24 hit-by-pitches—and his efficiency on stolen-base attempts. Still, he's an electric talent who should hang around for a while.

Russell Martin C

Born: 2/15/1983 Age: 31
Bats: R Throws: R Height: 5' 10"
Weight: 215 Breakout: 0%
Improve: 27% Collapse: 10%
Attrition: 10% MLB: 94%

Comparables:
Earl Battey, Smoky Burgess, Bill Freehan

YEAR	TEAM	LVL	AGE	PA	R	2B	3B	HR	RBI	BB	SO	SB	CS	AVG/OBP/SLG	TAv	BABIP	BRR	FRAA	WARP
2011	NYA	MLB	28	476	57	17	0	18	65	50	81	8	2	.237/.324/.408	.251	.252	-0.7	C(125): -0.5, 3B(3): -0.0	1.8
2012	NYA	MLB	29	485	50	18	0	21	53	53	95	6	1	.211/.311/.403	.254	.222	1.2	C(128): -0.6	1.9
2013	PIT	MLB	30	506	51	21	0	15	55	58	108	9	5	.226/.327/.377	.260	.266	0.4	C(120): 1.5, 3B(3): -0.1	2.8
2014	PIT	MLB	31	471	54	17	0	11	47	51	84	8	3	.231/.324/.353	.261	.260	-0.5	C -0, 3B -0	2.2

The marquee acquisition of the Huntington era, Martin's two-year deal worth $17 million looked like a bargain in year one. Martin continued his consistency at the plate by finishing with a True Average between .250 and .259 for the fifth year in a row. Defensively, he was an appreciable upgrade over Rod Barajas, not just in throwing runners out but in receiving the ball as well. Martin also tallied 500 plate appearances for the first time since leaving Los Angeles, easing concerns about his durability. It wasn't a slam-dunk signing at the time, but Martin has the chance to make it one in retrospect with another strong season.

Michael Martinez SS

Born: 9/16/1982 Age: 31
Bats: B Throws: R Height: 5' 9"
Weight: 175 Breakout: 1%
Improve: 14% Collapse: 13%
Attrition: 19% MLB: 51%

Comparables:
Angel Berroa, Matt Tolbert, Omar Quintanilla

YEAR	TEAM	LVL	AGE	PA	R	2B	3B	HR	RBI	BB	SO	SB	CS	AVG/OBP/SLG	TAv	BABIP	BRR	FRAA	WARP
2011	PHI	MLB	28	234	25	5	2	3	24	18	35	3	0	.196/.258/.282	.226	.220	1.7	3B(26): -1.0, 2B(19): 0.7	-0.1
2012	LEH	AAA	29	122	12	4	2	2	15	10	12	3	1	.271/.331/.402	.260	.281	-0.9	SS(13): -0.5, CF(7): -0.6	0.2
2012	PHI	MLB	29	122	10	3	0	2	7	5	21	0	0	.174/.208/.252	.169	.196	0.4	2B(16): -2.1, 3B(10): 0.7	-0.6
2013	LEH	AAA	30	266	35	11	3	3	28	18	37	6	5	.300/.352/.407	.260	.343	0	SS(46): 1.7, 2B(12): 0.5	1.4
2013	PHI	MLB	30	40	5	0	0	0	3	0	12	1	0	.175/.175/.175	.118	.250	0.9	CF(13): 0.1, SS(3): -0.2	-0.4
2014	PIT	MLB	31	250	22	8	1	3	21	14	41	3	1	.230/.275/.318	.227	.260	0	SS 1, 2B -0	0.0

When the Phillies took Martinez from the Nationals in the Rule 5 draft, they committed to keeping him on the big-league roster throughout the 2011 season. So that's the excuse for the first year; the years since are all on the front office and manager. Martinez has hit .187/.234/.261 as a Phillie, and never finished above the Mendoza line in any single season. He's utile, capable of playing any position behind the pitcher, but he's subpar at each, according to most metrics. Yet the Phillies have always found a way to get him playing time. They finally threw the hand away in October.

Wyatt Mathisen C

Born: 12/30/1993 Age: 20
Bats: R Throws: R Height: 6' 1"
Weight: 210 Breakout: 0%
Improve: 0% Collapse: 0%
Attrition: 0% MLB: 0%

Comparables:
Hector Sanchez, Miguel Gonzalez, Devin Mesoraco

YEAR	TEAM	LVL	AGE	PA	R	2B	3B	HR	RBI	BB	SO	SB	CS	AVG/OBP/SLG	TAv	BABIP	BRR	FRAA	WARP
2013	WVA	A	19	138	13	3	0	0	9	9	22	1	0	.185/.256/.210	.226	.222	0.5	C(32): -0.9	0.0
2013	JAM	A-	19	33	4	0	0	0	3	5	7	1	0	.269/.394/.269	.285	.350	0.3	C(5): -0.1	0.3
2014	PIT	MLB	20	250	18	8	0	1	18	13	57	2	1	.203/.254/.256	.203	.260	-0.4	C -1	-0.6

The Pirates challenged Mathisen in his first full season with an aggressive Opening Day assignment to West Virginia. He struggled before tearing his labrum—an injury that cost him two months—and reported to a lower level when he returned. Regardless of performance, there's a lot to like here. Mathisen has impressive tools at and behind the plate, including plus raw power and arm strength. Scouts praise his makeup and work ethic—which materialized in altered hitting mechanics—and believe he can develop into a solid-average regular.

Andrew McCutchen CF

Born: **10/10/1986** Age: **27**
Bats: **R** Throws: **R** Height: **5' 10"**
Weight: **190** Breakout: **3%**
Improve: **54%** Collapse: **10%**
Attrition: **10%** MLB: **100%**

Comparables:
Grady Sizemore, Chet Lemon, Rickey Henderson

YEAR	TEAM	LVL	AGE	PA	R	2B	3B	HR	RBI	BB	SO	SB	CS	AVG/OBP/SLG	TAv	BABIP	BRR	FRAA	WARP
2011	PIT	MLB	24	678	87	34	5	23	89	89	126	23	10	.259/.364/.456	.303	.291	-2.8	CF(155): 9.4	5.6
2012	PIT	MLB	25	673	107	29	6	31	96	70	132	20	12	.327/.400/.553	.339	.375	-0.5	CF(156): -9.9	6.4
2013	PIT	MLB	26	674	97	38	5	21	84	78	101	27	10	.317/.404/.508	.330	.353	1	CF(155): -8.9	6.1
2014	PIT	MLB	27	633	85	30	5	20	80	68	110	23	9	.286/.369/.465	.308	.320	0.7	CF -7	4.3

The NL's Most Valuable Player, McCutchen had almost exactly the same season that he did in 2012. But since his team reached the postseason, his candidacy earned extra consideration. This is not to quibble with McCutchen's victory: In addition to being one of the best players in baseball, he projects the image every team wants from their franchise cornerstone. It's hard to find anything negative to write about McCutchen but, if there is one thing, it's whether he'll eventually slide to a corner spot to accommodate a better center-field defender.

Reese McGuire C

Born: **3/2/1995** Age: **19**
Bats: **L** Throws: **R** Height: **6' 0"**
Weight: **181** Breakout: **0%**
Improve: **0%** Collapse: **0%**
Attrition: **0%** MLB: **0%**

Comparables:
Wilson Ramos, Travis d'Arnaud, Salvador Perez

YEAR	TEAM	LVL	AGE	PA	R	2B	3B	HR	RBI	BB	SO	SB	CS	AVG/OBP/SLG	TAv	BABIP	BRR	FRAA	WARP
2014	PIT	MLB	19	250	16	8	0	1	19	10	63	0	0	.202/.237/.258	.191	.260	-0.4	C 1	-0.9

Once an organization void of catching talent, Pittsburgh is now squatting in it. The 14th pick in the draft is a cinch to remain behind the plate, which is always a question with prep backstops. McGuire looks the part and has the necessary physical and mental attributes to become a defensive asset: His arm flashes plus-plus, his feet are quick and he's already an on-the-field leader. Things are less certain offensively, though there's promise in the stick. McGuire has leveled his swing and shortened his stride in an effort to improve his contact abilities; those changes sacrificed some power, but there is still a belief he can tally a dozen-plus home runs. This all adds up to all-star potential, in a general sense, anyway—the focus on offense for the actual All-Star Game might leave McGuire underappreciated even if he does reach his ceiling.

Michael McKenry C

Born: **3/4/1985** Age: **29**
Bats: **R** Throws: **R** Height: **5' 10"**
Weight: **210** Breakout: **3%**
Improve: **19%** Collapse: **15%**
Attrition: **34%** MLB: **69%**

Comparables:
John Baker, Eliezer Alfonzo, Mike Rabelo

YEAR	TEAM	LVL	AGE	PA	R	2B	3B	HR	RBI	BB	SO	SB	CS	AVG/OBP/SLG	TAv	BABIP	BRR	FRAA	WARP
2011	PAW	AAA	26	111	10	5	0	3	12	14	24	1	0	.274/.369/.421	.283	.333	-1.7	C(24): -0.2	0.4
2011	PIT	MLB	26	201	17	12	0	2	11	14	49	0	1	.222/.276/.322	.227	.290	-0.2	C(58): -0.4, 3B(1): -0.0	0.0
2012	PIT	MLB	27	275	25	14	0	12	39	29	73	0	0	.233/.320/.442	.284	.278	-0.4	C(80): 1.4	2.1
2013	PIT	MLB	28	122	9	6	0	3	14	5	24	0	0	.217/.262/.348	.223	.250	-0.8	C(31): 0.7	-0.2
2014	PIT	MLB	29	250	25	11	0	6	26	19	61	0	0	.226/.291/.356	.245	.280	-0.5	C 0, 3B -0	0.8

Oh how things change. McKenry was the most popular catcher on the roster in 2012, but was an afterthought last season. He suffered a torn meniscus in July that ended his campaign and the Pirates were in good hands with Russell Martin, Tony Sanchez and John Buck. McKenry didn't hit before the injury anyway, and that's a problem; he can pass as a backup when he's walking and flashing power, but otherwise profiles as a third catcher. It's a bad sign if your fans are begging for McKenry, so consider Pittsburgh's indifference (expressed through non-tender) a step forward.

Austin Meadows CF

Born: **5/3/1995** Age: **19**
Bats: **L** Throws: **L** Height: **6' 3"**
Weight: **200** Breakout: **0%**
Improve: **0%** Collapse: **0%**
Attrition: **0%** MLB: **0%**

Comparables:
Greg Halman, Jay Bruce, Aaron Hicks

YEAR	TEAM	LVL	AGE	PA	R	2B	3B	HR	RBI	BB	SO	SB	CS	AVG/OBP/SLG	TAv	BABIP	BRR	FRAA	WARP
2013	JAM	A-	18	22	8	0	0	2	2	5	4	0	0	.529/.636/.882	.506	.636	0.5	CF(5): 0.5	0.8
2014	PIT	MLB	19	250	21	7	1	5	24	16	77	0	0	.197/.253/.303	.212	.270	-0.4	CF 1	-0.5

Pittsburgh drafted Meadows with the compensatory pick it received for failing to sign Mark Appel in 2012, leading to the debate: Meadows or Appel? The Georgia native is no stranger to draft-related spats: Scouts spent the spring weighing his merits against those of fellow draftee Clint Frazier. The disagreements extend to Meadows' projection—though there's no doubting his polarize tool has elite potential. True believers see a good center fielder with the bat to hit third or fourth in a championship lineup; others see a future left fielder with an average arm and a flat swing. Depending on how things work out, the Pirates might argue he's the steal of the draft.

Jordy Mercer SS

Born: 8/27/1986 Age: 27
Bats: R Throws: R Height: 6' 3"
Weight: 205 Breakout: 8%
Improve: 37% Collapse: 14%
Attrition: 28% MLB: 83%

Comparables:
Zack Cozart, Jayson Nix, Ben Francisco

YEAR	TEAM	LVL	AGE	PA	R	2B	3B	HR	RBI	BB	SO	SB	CS	AVG/OBP/SLG	TAv	BABIP	BRR	FRAA	WARP
2011	ALT	AA	24	301	40	17	1	13	48	23	35	6	3	.268/.329/.487	.321	.260	-2	SS(63): 4.6	3.2
2011	IND	AAA	24	250	39	13	1	6	21	13	43	3	3	.239/.304/.385	.234	.271	1.7	2B(29): -1.7, SS(19): 1.7	0.3
2012	IND	AAA	25	236	28	14	1	4	27	20	45	3	5	.287/.357/.421	.282	.346	1.8	SS(33): 2.5, 2B(11): 1.5	2.0
2012	PIT	MLB	25	68	7	5	1	1	5	4	14	0	1	.210/.265/.371	.232	.250	0.1	SS(28): 0.4, 2B(7): 0.7	0.1
2013	IND	AAA	26	109	11	6	1	1	19	12	17	3	1	.333/.404/.448	.293	.392	-0.3	SS(23): 3.4, 2B(2): 0.2	1.2
2013	PIT	MLB	26	365	33	22	2	8	27	22	62	3	2	.285/.336/.435	.274	.330	-4	SS(78): -0.9, 2B(26): 2.9	1.6
2014	PIT	MLB	27	328	34	17	1	8	37	20	61	3	2	.257/.310/.397	.265	.290	-0.7	SS 1, 2B 3	1.9

Last year, we wondered if Mercer would ever get the opportunity to show his stuff with Pittsburgh. For a while there in 2013, it looked like the answer was no. The Pirates started him in Triple-A in favor of Brandon Inge and John McDonald, and later sent him down after a brief but solid cameo. Injuries forced the club's hand, and by the end of the season Hurdle was using Mercer in concert with Barmes at shortstop. With Barmes hitting the open market, it seems like the shortstop job is Mercer's for the taking. He'll need to improve his defense and performance against same-handed pitchers, but this is the best shot he'll have at becoming a big-league regular.

Gregory Polanco CF

Born: 9/14/1991 Age: 22
Bats: L Throws: L Height: 6' 4"
Weight: 220 Breakout: 1%
Improve: 23% Collapse: 5%
Attrition: 21% MLB: 45%

Comparables:
Andrew McCutchen, Ryan Kalish, Austin Jackson

YEAR	TEAM	LVL	AGE	PA	R	2B	3B	HR	RBI	BB	SO	SB	CS	AVG/OBP/SLG	TAv	BABIP	BRR	FRAA	WARP
2012	WVA	A	20	485	84	26	6	16	85	44	64	40	15	.325/.388/.522	.320	.352	5.7	CF(98): -2.5	4.8
2013	BRD	A+	21	241	29	17	0	6	30	16	37	24	4	.312/.364/.472	.311	.350	1.3	CF(56): -0.0	2.3
2013	ALT	AA	21	286	36	13	2	6	41	36	36	13	7	.263/.354/.407	.286	.282	1.7	CF(58): 6.3, RF(6): -0.3	2.6
2014	PIT	MLB	22	250	28	10	1	5	25	17	49	10	3	.245/.298/.366	.252	.280	0.8	CF 2, RF 0	0.8

Polanco is the meatball in the Pirates' position-player spaghetti; he has a chance to be a five-tool player, albeit of the cheapened five-average-or-better-tools variety. At the plate Polanco has quick hands and easy power projection; defensively his motions are fluid and he should stick in center. There are some nuance aspects he must continue to improve upon—namely his outfield routes, covering the inner-third of the plate, and hitting breaking balls—but he has the chance to be a special, all-star-quality player. Don't be surprised if by the time you read this, he's a consensus top-10 prospect league-wide.

Gaby Sanchez 1B

Born: 9/2/1983 Age: 30
Bats: R Throws: R Height: 6' 1"
Weight: 235 Breakout: 1%
Improve: 37% Collapse: 6%
Attrition: 7% MLB: 87%

Comparables:
Ryan Garko, Mike Sweeney, Wally Joyner

YEAR	TEAM	LVL	AGE	PA	R	2B	3B	HR	RBI	BB	SO	SB	CS	AVG/OBP/SLG	TAv	BABIP	BRR	FRAA	WARP
2011	FLO	MLB	27	661	72	35	0	19	78	74	97	3	1	.266/.352/.427	.289	.287	-2.8	1B(153): 3.9	2.8
2012	NWO	AAA	28	144	20	7	0	5	18	22	23	2	2	.302/.431/.491	.328	.337	0.7	1B(31): -0.4	1.4
2012	MIA	MLB	28	196	12	10	0	3	17	12	36	1	0	.202/.250/.306	.201	.234	-0.1	1B(54): 5.8	-0.6
2012	PIT	MLB	28	130	18	6	0	4	13	13	20	0	0	.241/.323/.397	.245	.261	0.5	1B(41): 0.7	0.3
2013	PIT	MLB	29	320	29	18	0	7	36	44	51	1	0	.254/.361/.402	.290	.282	1.8	1B(113): -1.2, 3B(1): -0.0	1.1
2014	PIT	MLB	30	318	35	15	0	9	37	31	50	1	0	.251/.331/.399	.274	.270	-0.5	1B 0, 3B -0	0.8

Once an All-Star, Sanchez is the rare example of a bench player whose lone position is first base. Few teams bother with those anymore, but the Pirates like Sanchez's ability to punish left-handed pitching. True to form the ex-Hurricane posted a .206 isolated power and got on base nearly 45 percent of the time against southpaws. So long as Sanchez keeps it up, he's likely to find work as a bench man for a National League team.

Tony Sanchez C

Born: 5/20/1988 Age: 26
Bats: R Throws: R Height: 5' 11"
Weight: 225 Breakout: 0%
Improve: 6% Collapse: 17%
Attrition: 19% MLB: 32%

Comparables:
Jose Lobaton, Luke Montz, Michael McKenry

YEAR	TEAM	LVL	AGE	PA	R	2B	3B	HR	RBI	BB	SO	SB	CS	AVG/OBP/SLG	TAv	BABIP	BRR	FRAA	WARP
2011	ALT	AA	23	469	46	14	1	5	44	47	76	5	5	.241/.340/.318	.254	.285	1.7	C(88): 0.6	1.1
2012	ALT	AA	24	162	22	14	1	0	17	18	33	1	1	.277/.370/.390	.286	.361	-2.7	C(37): 0.4	0.8
2012	IND	AAA	24	236	21	12	0	8	26	23	46	0	0	.233/.316/.408	.248	.260	-1.7	C(59): -0.7	0.4
2013	IND	AAA	25	296	35	26	0	10	42	28	60	0	0	.288/.368/.504	.285	.339	-0.8	C(72): -0.6	1.7
2013	PIT	MLB	25	66	9	4	0	2	5	3	14	0	0	.233/.288/.400	.271	.267	0.2	C(16): -0.2	0.3
2014	PIT	MLB	26	250	23	12	0	5	26	18	54	0	0	.232/.299/.354	.248	.280	-0.6	C -0	0.8

Okay, so Sanchez is never going to live up to his draft slot; that doesn't mean he can't be a useful piece on good Pittsburgh teams. The Boston College product made his big-league debut in 2013, after Michael McKenry was hurt and before John Buck was added, and displayed some pop and defensive chops—he appeared to be a skilled receiver. Add in that Sanchez showed more offensive life than usual in the minors, and there's a chance he ascends beyond career backup status.

Travis Snider   RF

Born: 2/2/1988 Age: 26
Bats: L Throws: L Height: 6' 0"
Weight: 235 Breakout: 6%
Improve: 55% Collapse: 14%
Attrition: 19% MLB: 94%

Comparables:
Travis Buck, Cody Ross, Brandon Moss

YEAR	TEAM	LVL	AGE	PA	R	2B	3B	HR	RBI	BB	SO	SB	CS	AVG/OBP/SLG	TAv	BABIP	BRR	FRAA	WARP
2011	LVG	AAA	23	277	47	22	2	4	42	25	44	12	1	.327/.394/.480	.289	.383	-0.8	LF(28): 1.7, RF(7): -1.1	1.1
2011	TOR	MLB	23	202	23	14	0	3	30	11	56	9	3	.225/.269/.348	.215	.300	1.5	LF(44): -0.4, CF(6): -0.0	-0.3
2012	DUN	A+	24	23	3	1	0	0	1	1	5	2	0	.227/.261/.273	.185	.294	0.4	LF(3): 0.0, CF(1): -0.0	-0.1
2012	LVG	AAA	24	246	49	16	0	13	56	34	42	2	4	.335/.423/.598	.320	.363	0.2	LF(34): -0.7, RF(10): -0.5	2.0
2012	PIT	MLB	24	145	17	5	1	1	9	14	34	2	0	.250/.324/.328	.250	.326	0.5	RF(33): 0.6, LF(5): 0.1	0.3
2012	TOR	MLB	24	40	6	2	0	3	8	3	14	0	0	.250/.300/.556	.302	.300	0	LF(10): 0.6	0.3
2013	IND	AAA	25	38	4	1	0	0	5	5	8	1	1	.344/.421/.375	.318	.440	0.2	RF(5): -0.6	0.3
2013	PIT	MLB	25	285	28	12	2	5	25	24	75	2	3	.215/.281/.333	.230	.282	-3.3	RF(79): 3.7, LF(5): -0.0	-0.4
2014	PIT	MLB	26	286	32	14	1	8	33	23	71	5	2	.248/.312/.396	.264	.310	-0.3	RF -0, LF -1	0.6

It's time to call a bust a bust. Snider has changed teams, managers and perspectives and none of it inspired him to be anything better than below-average. He's failed to improve with age, and it's not clear how he fits on a major league roster. Snider's pedigree has afforded him this many opportunities, but at some point that's no longer enough. He's still youngish, so someone will gamble on him. Just don't be surprised if he fails to bloom.

Chris Stewart   C

Born: 2/19/1982 Age: 32
Bats: R Throws: R Height: 6' 4"
Weight: 210 Breakout: 4%
Improve: 30% Collapse: 14%
Attrition: 31% MLB: 92%

Comparables:
Jim Essian, Mike Redmond, Dave Engle

YEAR	TEAM	LVL	AGE	PA	R	2B	3B	HR	RBI	BB	SO	SB	CS	AVG/OBP/SLG	TAv	BABIP	BRR	FRAA	WARP
2011	FRE	AAA	29	112	9	5	0	0	10	11	16	3	1	.221/.312/.274	.200	.262	-0.3	C(28): 1.0, 1B(1): -0.0	-0.1
2011	SFN	MLB	29	183	20	8	0	3	10	16	18	0	1	.204/.283/.309	.228	.213	0.2	C(63): 1.0, 1B(3): 0.0	0.7
2012	NYA	MLB	30	157	15	8	0	1	13	10	21	2	0	.241/.292/.319	.237	.273	0.4	C(54): -0.5	0.4
2013	NYA	MLB	31	340	28	6	0	4	25	30	49	4	0	.211/.293/.272	.219	.237	-2.7	C(108): 0.6, 1B(2): -0.0	-0.1
2014	PIT	MLB	32	283	25	10	0	2	21	21	40	3	1	.221/.289/.292	.227	.250	-0.1	C 1, 1B -0	0.5

The Yankees acquired Stewart because of his strong receiving skills, and he was as good as advertised at turning borderline balls into strikes, finishing in the top 10 among catchers in framing runs saved. He also threw out runners at an above-average rate, which helped offset the damage done by his 12 passed balls. However, the Yankees needed every stolen strike to make up for the downside of starting Stewart: he can't hit. Among catchers with at least 300 plate appearances, his TAv ranked second worst, ahead of only J.P. Arencibia (who was also the only one to let more passed balls through). The problem wasn't playing Stewart, but starting him. Future employers probably won't make the same mistake, and the Pirates wisely acquired him to be Russell Martin's understudy, a role he knows well.

Jose Tabata   RF

Born: 8/12/1988 Age: 25
Bats: R Throws: R Height: 5' 11"
Weight: 210 Breakout: 1%
Improve: 53% Collapse: 5%
Attrition: 11% MLB: 97%

Comparables:
Terry Puhl, Ryan Sweeney, Steve Hovley

YEAR	TEAM	LVL	AGE	PA	R	2B	3B	HR	RBI	BB	SO	SB	CS	AVG/OBP/SLG	TAv	BABIP	BRR	FRAA	WARP
2011	IND	AAA	22	38	6	6	0	0	2	5	4	0	2	.333/.421/.515	.279	.379	-0.5	RF(4): 0.2, LF(2): -0.0	0.0
2011	PIT	MLB	22	382	53	18	1	4	21	40	61	16	7	.266/.349/.362	.254	.312	3	LF(76): 1.7, RF(15): -1.9	0.7
2012	IND	AAA	23	173	21	9	0	0	15	10	20	5	2	.297/.353/.354	.249	.338	0.5	CF(25): -0.1, RF(15): 1.4	0.7
2012	PIT	MLB	23	374	43	20	3	3	16	29	58	8	12	.243/.315/.348	.246	.287	-0.2	RF(77): -0.5, LF(32): 2.3	0.3
2013	IND	AAA	24	32	1	1	0	0	0	3	7	1	0	.179/.281/.214	.180	.238	0.2	RF(8): -0.0	-0.2
2013	PIT	MLB	24	341	35	17	5	6	33	23	45	3	1	.282/.342/.429	.279	.315	0.9	RF(50): -4.4, LF(40): 1.4	1.1
2014	PIT	MLB	25	352	42	16	2	4	28	26	54	10	6	.269/.331/.368	.264	.310	-0.3	RF -2, LF 2	0.9

Pay attention, folks: Tabata just showed us what a bounce back season looks like. Despite seeing his role reduced due to Starling Marte (and later Marlon Byrd), the Venezuela native performed well when he was called upon. Forever known as a tweener, Tabata posted a career-high isolated power while showing little to no interest in stealing bases. The contract extension he signed in late 2011 no longer looks like it has bargain potential, but it does ensure that he'll remain affordable for the next few seasons. Whether Tabata sticks with Pittsburgh or finds a new home elsewhere, he's a useful piece to have around.

Neil Walker   2B

Born: 9/10/1985 Age: 28
Bats: B Throws: R Height: 6' 3"
Weight: 210 Breakout: 1%
Improve: 47% Collapse: 4%
Attrition: 12% MLB: 96%

Comparables:
Daniel Murphy, Brandon Phillips, Kelly Johnson

YEAR	TEAM	LVL	AGE	PA	R	2B	3B	HR	RBI	BB	SO	SB	CS	AVG/OBP/SLG	TAv	BABIP	BRR	FRAA	WARP
2011	PIT	MLB	25	662	76	36	4	12	83	54	112	9	6	.273/.334/.408	.266	.315	1	2B(159): -5.9	1.8
2012	PIT	MLB	26	530	62	27	0	14	69	47	104	7	5	.280/.342/.426	.284	.326	-1.1	2B(125): -0.9	2.4
2013	PIT	MLB	27	551	62	24	4	16	53	50	85	1	2	.251/.339/.418	.278	.274	0.8	2B(132): 3.6	2.9
2014	PIT	MLB	28	517	56	27	2	13	59	41	95	5	3	.262/.327/.408	.274	.300	-0.9	2B -5	1.9

Walker is the rare player who is underrated nationally and overrated locally. His consistency at the plate and improvements defensively make him an above-average second baseman. Yet that he's a local kid makes him into something he's not: a face of the franchise. Walker is a good player, and one the Pirates should value having around, but he's not fit to be the second- or third-best player on a good team. Pittsburgh learned that the hard way before 2013.

PITCHERS

A.J. Burnett

Born: 1/3/1977 Age: 37
Bats: R Throws: R Height: 6' 4" Weight: 225
Breakout: 6% Improve: 37% Collapse: 28%
Attrition: 14% MLB: 79%

Comparables:
Chuck Finley, Jerry Koosman, Jim Bunning

YEAR	TEAM	LVL	AGE	W	L	SV	G	GS	IP	H	HR	BB	SO	BB9	SO9	GB%	BABIP	WHIP	ERA	FIP	FRA	WARP
2011	NYA	MLB	34	11	11	0	33	32	190¹	190	31	83	173	3.9	8.2	51%	.294	1.43	5.15	4.81	5.50	0.1
2012	PIT	MLB	35	16	10	0	31	31	202¹	189	18	62	180	2.8	8.0	57%	.299	1.24	3.51	3.57	3.70	2.8
2013	PIT	MLB	36	10	11	0	30	30	191	165	11	67	209	3.2	9.8	58%	.314	1.21	3.30	2.77	3.54	2.7
2014	PIT	MLB	37	9	10	0	28	28	165	149	16	58	151	3.2	8.2	51%	.305	1.26	3.85	3.85	4.19	0.7

Burnett proved his first season with the Pirates was no fluke, and along the way set a new career-high in strikeouts per nine. Which raises the question: Why is this guy talking about retiring? He's still got the stuff to be an effective big-league pitcher, and he's treading close to beloved status in the Steel City. At this writing, Burnett is set to pick between returning for another season with the Pirates or riding off into the sunset. Here's hoping he takes one more shot at delivering a World Series title to Pittsburgh.

Gerrit Cole

Born: 9/8/1990 Age: 23
Bats: R Throws: R Height: 6' 4" Weight: 240
Breakout: 29% Improve: 77% Collapse: 12%
Attrition: 29% MLB: 85%

Comparables:
Michael Pineda, Brian Matusz, Matt Garza

YEAR	TEAM	LVL	AGE	W	L	SV	G	GS	IP	H	HR	BB	SO	BB9	SO9	GB%	BABIP	WHIP	ERA	FIP	FRA	WARP
2012	BRD	A+	21	5	1	0	13	13	67	53	5	21	69	2.8	9.3	51%	.276	1.10	2.55	3.38	4.18	1.2
2012	ALT	AA	21	3	6	0	12	12	59	54	2	23	60	3.5	9.2	50%	.313	1.31	2.90	2.88	3.81	1.1
2013	IND	AAA	22	5	3	0	12	12	68	44	4	28	47	3.7	6.2	49%	.221	1.06	2.91	4.00	4.48	0.5
2013	PIT	MLB	22	10	7	0	19	19	117¹	109	7	28	100	2.1	7.7	50%	.320	1.17	3.22	2.88	3.53	1.4
2014	PIT	MLB	23	9	9	0	27	27	151	131	13	45	128	2.7	7.6	48%	.295	1.16	3.24	3.61	3.52	2.0

So *that's* why the Pirates took Cole first overall a few years back. Although his performance looks flat compared to, say, Jose Fernandez, the former UCLA star was an above-average starter out of the gates. Cole did not pitch deep into either of his two postseason starts, yet he showed the poise and maturity that he was often accused of missing. Cole will need to prove he can handle a big-league workload, but that shouldn't be a problem. The only concerns now are how good he'll become and how long it'll take him to get there.

Brandon Cumpton

Born: 11/16/1988 Age: 25
Bats: R Throws: R Height: 6' 2" Weight: 220
Breakout: 52% Improve: 73% Collapse: 11%
Attrition: 66% MLB: 52%

Comparables:
Jeff Manship, Kevin Mulvey, Juan Gutierrez

YEAR	TEAM	LVL	AGE	W	L	SV	G	GS	IP	H	HR	BB	SO	BB9	SO9	GB%	BABIP	WHIP	ERA	FIP	FRA	WARP
2011	WVA	A	22	7	4	0	13	12	67	60	6	18	48	2.4	6.4	55%	.271	1.16	4.30	4.47	5.27	0.5
2011	BRD	A+	22	3	3	0	13	12	66¹	73	6	12	42	1.6	5.7	49%	.318	1.28	3.66	4.11	4.79	0.4
2012	ALT	AA	23	12	11	0	27	27	152¹	149	9	46	88	2.7	5.2	60%	.292	1.28	3.84	4.02	5.09	0.4
2013	IND	AAA	24	6	7	0	21	19	122	115	6	44	90	3.2	6.6	62%	.299	1.30	3.32	3.65	5.03	0.0
2013	PIT	MLB	24	2	1	0	6	5	30²	26	1	5	22	1.5	6.5	53%	.267	1.01	2.05	2.60	3.17	0.5
2014	PIT	MLB	25	8	9	0	26	26	140²	141	14	42	81	2.7	5.2	54%	.295	1.30	4.21	4.46	4.58	0.0

Cumpton reached the majors and appeared in six games with good results. Don't be thrown, though: He's not Gerrit Cole 2.0 or anything close. Rather, Cumpton is a back-of-the-rotation type, equipped with a low-90s sinker and two workable secondary pitches. He must keep the ball on the ground to succeed, and he did just that throughout 2013. Cumpton could probably make another team's rotation, yet if he stays in Pittsburgh he's likely to serve as an extra starter for the time being.

Tyler Glasnow

Born: 8/23/1993 Age: 20
Bats: L Throws: R Height: 6' 7" Weight: 195
Breakout: 88% Improve: 95% Collapse: 5%
Attrition: 15% MLB: 20%

Comparables:
Clayton Kershaw, Danny Duffy, Shelby Miller

YEAR	TEAM	LVL	AGE	W	L	SV	G	GS	IP	H	HR	BB	SO	BB9	SO9	GB%	BABIP	WHIP	ERA	FIP	FRA	WARP
2013	WVA	A	19	9	3	0	24	24	111¹	54	9	61	164	4.9	13.3	49%	.215	1.03	2.18	3.47	3.99	1.6
2014	PIT	MLB	20	5	7	0	24	24	84²	69	9	47	89	5.0	9.4	46%	.295	1.37	4.02	4.31	4.37	0.5

No Pirate increased his stock like Glasnow, who entered the season with 12 career starts and exited as a legitimate top-50 prospect. The spindly right-hander has two plus pitches, a mid-90s fastball and a big breaking ball that he delivers on a steep downward plane. Glasnow's delivery features some deception; his sinewy limbs are obscured by his body, and he kicks his leg high before coming to the plate. He needs to add strength and further refine the two Cs of starting—command and changeup—but he could develop into a good number three starter.

Jeanmar Gomez

Born: 2/10/1988 Age: 26
Bats: R Throws: R Height: 6' 3" Weight: 220
Breakout: 48% Improve: 75% Collapse: 12%
Attrition: 19% MLB: 83%

Comparables:
Vin Mazzaro, Jeff Karstens, Ivan Nova

YEAR	TEAM	LVL	AGE	W	L	SV	G	GS	IP	H	HR	BB	SO	BB9	SO9	GB%	BABIP	WHIP	ERA	FIP	FRA	WARP
2011	COH	AAA	23	10	7	0	21	21	137²	123	8	49	107	3.2	7.0	48%	.301	1.25	2.55	3.61	4.19	0.3
2011	CLE	MLB	23	5	3	0	11	10	58¹	73	6	15	31	2.3	4.8	53%	.325	1.51	4.47	4.16	4.68	0.5
2012	COH	AAA	24	6	5	0	11	11	69¹	75	6	17	54	2.2	7.0	55%	.319	1.33	4.41	3.50	5.43	0.2
2012	CLE	MLB	24	5	8	0	20	17	90²	95	15	34	47	3.4	4.7	49%	.271	1.42	5.96	5.42	6.20	-0.6
2013	PIT	MLB	25	3	0	0	34	8	80²	65	6	28	53	3.1	5.9	56%	.250	1.15	3.35	3.83	4.45	0.1
2014	PIT	MLB	26	5	5	0	21	14	88²	87	9	26	58	2.7	5.9	48%	.295	1.27	4.05	4.22	4.40	0.2

Last January, the Pirates traded a minor-league outfielder for Gomez in a yawn-inspiring move. Nobody would've predicted then that Gomez would throw four innings in Game One of the NLDS. Although he split the season between the rotation and the bullpen, the impetus to eat innings remained the same regardless of the role. Gomez ate well and, despite ugly peripherals, provided more value to the Pirates than anyone expected. He should reprise a rubber-arm role in 2014.

Jason Grilli

Born: 11/11/1976 Age: 37
Bats: R Throws: R Height: 6' 4" Weight: 235
Breakout: 20% Improve: 47% Collapse: 28%
Attrition: 7% MLB: 84%

Comparables:
Octavio Dotel, Al Reyes, Rudy Seanez

YEAR	TEAM	LVL	AGE	W	L	SV	G	GS	IP	H	HR	BB	SO	BB9	SO9	GB%	BABIP	WHIP	ERA	FIP	FRA	WARP
2011	LEH	AAA	34	4	1	3	28	0	32²	26	2	12	43	3.3	11.8	43%	.231	1.16	1.93	2.59	4.02	0.2
2011	PIT	MLB	34	2	1	1	28	0	32²	24	2	15	37	4.1	10.2	49%	.256	1.19	2.48	3.27	3.04	0.5
2012	PIT	MLB	35	1	6	2	64	0	58²	45	7	22	90	3.4	13.8	32%	.309	1.14	2.91	2.85	2.46	1.4
2013	PIT	MLB	36	0	2	33	54	0	50	40	4	13	74	2.3	13.3	36%	.327	1.06	2.70	1.94	2.38	1.3
2014	PIT	MLB	37	3	1	10	49	0	48¹	36	4	17	61	3.1	11.5	41%	.303	1.09	2.68	2.88	2.92	0.9

The Giants no doubt envisioned Grilli one day gracing *Sports Illustrated* covers when they chose him fourth-overall in the 1997 draft. Alas, that feels like a lifetime ago. (Which it is if you're currently in college.) Grilli, who didn't pitch in the majors in 2010, returned to The Show with the Pirates in 2011 and has since become a shutdown reliever. He made his first career All-Star Game at age 36 and, by notching 33 of his 38 career saves, proved once again that closers are made, not born. There isn't much reason to think he won't do it all again in 2014.

Luis Heredia

Born: 8/10/1994 Age: 19
Bats: R Throws: R Height: 6' 6" Weight: 205
Breakout: 0% Improve: 0% Collapse: 0%
Attrition: 0% MLB: 0%

Comparables:
Felix Doubront, Liam Hendriks, Julio Teheran

YEAR	TEAM	LVL	AGE	W	L	SV	G	GS	IP	H	HR	BB	SO	BB9	SO9	GB%	BABIP	WHIP	ERA	FIP	FRA	WARP
2012	SCO	A-	17	4	2	0	14	14	66¹	53	2	20	40	2.7	5.4	55%	.252	1.10	2.71	3.47	4.82	0.1
2013	WVA	A	18	7	3	0	14	13	65	52	5	37	55	5.1	7.6	39%	.272	1.37	3.05	4.77	4.70	0.1
2014	PIT	MLB	19	3	5	0	14	14	54²	59	7	31	28	5.1	4.6	42%	.299	1.63	5.60	5.81	6.09	-0.8

When did Heredia get this old—and when did his doubters get this loud? The prodigy turned 19 late in the season, but few celebrated. He arrived to camp with poor conditioning, leading the Pirates to shelve his debut until late June. Everyone knew Heredia's body—complete with long limbs and embonpoint—could halt his ascent to the majors; few accepted the threat's immediacy. Heredia's fastball didn't have its previous zip and his control remained poor. The 2014 season is his last as a teenager, yet he's already going through a mid-hype crisis. With a strong season Heredia will reaffirm his top-100 prospect status. With a poor season he might find himself off prospect lists entirely.

Jared Hughes

Born: 7/4/1985 Age: 28
Bats: R Throws: R Height: 6' 7" Weight: 245
Breakout: 49% Improve: 73% Collapse: 19%
Attrition: 43% MLB: 60%

Comparables:
Tom Wilhelmsen, Justin Hampson, Pat Misch

YEAR	TEAM	LVL	AGE	W	L	SV	G	GS	IP	H	HR	BB	SO	BB9	SO9	GB%	BABIP	WHIP	ERA	FIP	FRA	WARP
2011	ALT	AA	25	3	4	0	13	11	61²	62	2	18	33	2.6	4.8	53%	.289	1.30	4.09	4.03	5.41	-0.5
2011	IND	AAA	25	3	1	0	35	0	42²	35	1	18	45	3.8	9.5	73%	.323	1.24	2.11	2.91	3.19	0.7
2011	PIT	MLB	25	0	1	0	12	0	11	9	1	4	10	3.3	8.2	67%	.276	1.18	4.09	3.45	3.71	0.1
2012	PIT	MLB	26	2	2	2	66	0	75²	65	7	22	50	2.6	5.9	59%	.256	1.15	2.85	4.09	5.15	-0.4
2013	IND	AAA	27	1	0	2	18	1	21	17	0	7	18	3.0	7.7	67%	.293	1.14	0.43	2.63	3.96	0.4
2013	PIT	MLB	27	2	3	0	29	0	32	37	2	16	23	4.5	6.5	58%	.333	1.66	4.78	4.08	4.41	0.0
2014	PIT	MLB	28	2	2	0	27	5	53²	52	5	17	36	2.9	6.1	55%	.299	1.30	4.23	4.21	4.60	-0.1

Not as bad as his 2013 nor as good as his 2012. Hughes is a large human with a heavy sinker and groundball tendencies. That combination has led to Kameron Loe comparisons, and though not overly flattering, they do paint an accurate picture. Under the right supervision, Hughes could be a useful reliever for a long time. If, that is, the shoulder inflammation he suffered through last season doesn't turn into a bigger problem.

Nick Kingham

Born: 11/8/1991 Age: 22
Bats: R Throws: R Height: 6' 5" Weight: 220
Breakout: 52% Improve: 78% Collapse: 11%
Attrition: 63% MLB: 27%

Comparables:
Anthony Swarzak, Josh Lindblom, Jarrod Parker

YEAR	TEAM	LVL	AGE	W	L	SV	G	GS	IP	H	HR	BB	SO	BB9	SO9	GB%	BABIP	WHIP	ERA	FIP	FRA	WARP
2011	SCO	A-	19	6	2	0	15	15	71	63	5	15	47	1.9	6.0	44%	.292	1.10	2.15	3.67	5.72	0.0
2012	WVA	A	20	6	8	0	27	27	127	115	15	36	117	2.6	8.3	50%	.286	1.19	4.39	4.34	4.98	1.7
2013	BRD	A+	21	6	3	0	13	13	70	55	6	14	75	1.8	9.6	46%	.274	0.99	3.09	3.20	4.27	0.7
2013	ALT	AA	21	3	3	0	14	12	73¹	70	1	30	69	3.7	8.5	45%	.330	1.36	2.70	2.97	3.18	1.5
2014	PIT	MLB	22	6	7	0	24	21	119	115	13	43	94	3.3	7.1	45%	.301	1.33	4.25	4.30	4.62	-0.0

Overshadowed by elite talent for years, Kingham is a solid prospect in his own right. The physical Nevada native has a solid three-pitch mix, headed by a plus fastball that sits in the low 90s. He commands the pitch well and complements it with two improving secondary offerings, a potentially plus curveball and an above-average changeup. The stuff and body are good, but there's more to his game: Kingham has a good feel for the craft and pitches on a steep downward plane. A middle-of-the-rotation projection won't give him the most upside in the system, though his high floor makes him a near-lock to pitch in the majors.

Francisco Liriano

Born: 10/26/1983 Age: 30
Bats: L Throws: L Height: 6' 2" Weight: 215
Breakout: 19% Improve: 41% Collapse: 30%
Attrition: 20% MLB: 91%

Comparables:
Jonathan Sanchez, Erik Bedard, John Lackey

YEAR	TEAM	LVL	AGE	W	L	SV	G	GS	IP	H	HR	BB	SO	BB9	SO9	GB%	BABIP	WHIP	ERA	FIP	FRA	WARP
2011	MIN	MLB	27	9	10	0	26	24	134¹	125	14	75	112	5.0	7.5	49%	.288	1.49	5.09	4.58	5.33	0.2
2012	CHA	MLB	28	3	2	0	12	11	56²	54	7	32	58	5.1	9.2	42%	.307	1.52	5.40	4.46	5.15	0.4
2012	MIN	MLB	28	3	10	0	22	17	100	89	12	55	109	4.9	9.8	47%	.297	1.44	5.31	4.20	5.26	0.5
2013	IND	AAA	29	2	0	0	3	3	16	15	1	1	23	0.6	12.9	55%	.333	1.00	3.38	1.52	2.96	0.5
2013	PIT	MLB	29	16	8	0	26	26	161	134	9	63	163	3.5	9.1	52%	.299	1.22	3.02	2.90	3.61	2.2
2014	PIT	MLB	30	9	9	0	28	28	154²	131	13	59	155	3.4	9.0	47%	.304	1.23	3.41	3.53	3.71	1.7

Liriano's Pirates career got off to a bad start. The enigmatic southpaw broke his arm after agreeing to a two-year contract, leading the club to rework the deal. The sides agreed to a one-year, $1 million guarantee with a vesting/club option for 2014. Under pitching coach Ray Searage's guidance, Liriano added a windup to his delivery. The design was to improve his rhythm and his control, which seemed to work. The Pirates trusted Liriano enough to give him the nod in the Wild Card Game, and he rewarded their faith. They'll hope he does the same this year, now that he's making (by Pirates standards) real money again.

Jeff Locke

Born: 11/20/1987 Age: 26
Bats: L Throws: L Height: 6' 0" Weight: 185
Breakout: 39% Improve: 66% Collapse: 24%
Attrition: 26% MLB: 76%

Comparables:
Sean West, Ross Detwiler, Jason Berken

YEAR	TEAM	LVL	AGE	W	L	SV	G	GS	IP	H	HR	BB	SO	BB9	SO9	GB%	BABIP	WHIP	ERA	FIP	FRA	WARP
2011	ALT	AA	23	7	8	0	23	22	125	118	9	46	114	3.3	8.2	46%	.308	1.31	4.03	3.82	5.00	-0.2
2011	IND	AAA	23	1	2	0	5	5	28¹	25	1	9	25	2.9	7.9	46%	.307	1.20	2.22	2.88	4.06	0.3
2011	PIT	MLB	23	0	3	0	4	4	16²	21	3	10	5	5.4	2.7	36%	.321	1.86	6.48	6.71	7.43	-0.4
2012	IND	AAA	24	10	5	0	24	24	141²	126	9	43	131	2.7	8.3	46%	.300	1.19	2.48	3.19	4.00	1.9
2012	PIT	MLB	24	1	3	0	8	6	34¹	36	6	11	34	2.9	8.9	49%	.315	1.37	5.50	4.48	5.33	-0.2
2013	PIT	MLB	25	10	7	0	30	30	166¹	146	11	84	125	4.5	6.8	54%	.285	1.38	3.52	4.00	4.24	1.0
2014	PIT	MLB	26	6	8	0	26	20	141¹	136	14	55	109	3.5	6.9	47%	.302	1.35	4.24	4.26	4.61	-0.1

Taken as a whole, it's hard to understand the fuss over Locke's season. Look deeper, however, and it becomes clear. Locke finished the first half with an All-Star berth on the strength of a 2.15 ERA; he appeared en route to a career year and perhaps a playoff assignment. But then the second half started, and so did Locke's problems. Conditions worsened to the point where the Pirates demoted him to the minors late in the season and left him off the postseason roster altogether. The expectations for Locke have been of the back-end variety, and Pittsburgh would probably take his overall numbers again—if they come without the extremes.

Vin Mazzaro

Born: 9/27/1986 Age: 27
Bats: R Throws: R Height: 6' 2" Weight: 220
Breakout: 25% Improve: 65% Collapse: 26%
Attrition: 22% MLB: 78%

Comparables:
Wade Davis, Glen Perkins, Kason Gabbard

YEAR	TEAM	LVL	AGE	W	L	SV	G	GS	IP	H	HR	BB	SO	BB9	SO9	GB%	BABIP	WHIP	ERA	FIP	FRA	WARP
2011	OMA	AAA	24	7	2	0	22	22	123²	140	9	60	107	4.4	7.8	52%	.360	1.62	4.29	4.65	4.40	1.4
2011	KCA	MLB	24	1	1	0	7	4	28¹	39	4	15	10	4.8	3.2	47%	.347	1.91	8.26	5.88	7.15	-0.5
2012	OMA	AAA	25	2	2	5	22	8	67	69	4	20	62	2.7	8.3	55%	.349	1.33	3.63	3.62	4.99	0.9
2012	KCA	MLB	25	4	3	0	18	6	44	55	3	19	26	3.9	5.3	48%	.354	1.68	5.73	4.25	4.95	0.2
2013	PIT	MLB	26	8	2	1	57	0	73²	68	3	21	46	2.6	5.6	52%	.281	1.21	2.81	3.28	3.49	0.8
2014	PIT	MLB	27	4	4	0	25	9	74²	73	7	25	55	3.0	6.6	49%	.306	1.31	3.98	4.08	4.33	0.2

Who knew? We wrote Mazzaro off last year because the Royals had traded him; perhaps we should have considered who traded for him. Pittsburgh has a knack for finding useful relievers on the cheap, and Mazzaro was no different. He's never going to be a late-inning threat, but he makes sense as a middle reliever with a rubber arm.

James McDonald

Born: 10/19/1984 Age: 29
Bats: L Throws: R Height: 6' 4" Weight: 205
Breakout: 32% Improve: 51% Collapse: 23%
Attrition: 22% MLB: 74%

Comparables:
Kyle Davies, Tom Gorzelanny, Manny Parra

YEAR	TEAM	LVL	AGE	W	L	SV	G	GS	IP	H	HR	BB	SO	BB9	SO9	GB%	BABIP	WHIP	ERA	FIP	FRA	WARP
2011	PIT	MLB	26	9	9	0	31	31	171	176	24	78	142	4.1	7.5	39%	.307	1.49	4.21	4.65	5.15	-0.3
2012	PIT	MLB	27	12	8	0	30	29	171	147	21	69	151	3.6	7.9	41%	.273	1.26	4.21	4.25	4.58	1.0
2013	IND	AAA	28	1	3	0	4	4	20²	26	2	9	12	3.9	5.2	39%	.348	1.69	6.53	4.90	5.77	-0.1
2013	PIT	MLB	28	2	2	0	6	6	29²	29	1	20	25	6.1	7.6	39%	.305	1.65	5.76	4.10	4.42	0.2
2014	PIT	MLB	29	4	5	0	14	14	74²	66	8	29	66	3.5	7.9	38%	.295	1.28	3.88	4.12	4.21	0.4

When the Pirates acquired McDonald and Andrew Lambo for Octavio Dotel in July 2010, everyone screamed robbery. More than three years later, the trade doesn't seem so criminal. McDonald had shown signs of becoming a no. 4 starter the previous two seasons, though inconsistency remained a problem. He adopted a new curveball-heavy strategy in 2013 and perhaps it would've worked if not for those meddl—er, a shoulder strain that sidelined him for four months. The Pirates designated McDonald for assignment once he returned and he elected free agency instead of an outright assignment.

Mark Melancon

Born: 3/28/1985 Age: 29
Bats: R Throws: R Height: 6' 2" Weight: 215
Breakout: 31% Improve: 55% Collapse: 31%
Attrition: 20% MLB: 83%

Comparables:
Matt Lindstrom, Jerry Blevins, Darren O'Day

YEAR	TEAM	LVL	AGE	W	L	SV	G	GS	IP	H	HR	BB	SO	BB9	SO9	GB%	BABIP	WHIP	ERA	FIP	FRA	WARP
2011	HOU	MLB	26	8	4	20	71	0	74¹	65	5	26	66	3.1	8.0	59%	.288	1.22	2.78	3.22	4.54	0.2
2012	PAW	AAA	27	0	0	11	21	0	21²	15	0	3	27	1.2	11.2	63%	.278	0.83	0.83	1.36	2.55	0.6
2012	BOS	MLB	27	0	2	1	41	0	45	45	8	12	41	2.4	8.2	51%	.285	1.27	6.20	4.54	6.40	-0.3
2013	PIT	MLB	28	3	2	16	72	0	71	60	1	8	70	1.0	8.9	62%	.296	0.96	1.39	1.61	2.61	1.5
2014	PIT	MLB	29	3	1	5	58	0	63¹	53	5	17	59	2.4	8.4	55%	.294	1.10	2.95	3.28	3.21	1.0

Can Melancon handle the pressure or not? After a much-maligned stint in Boston, he was traded to the Pirates as part of a package for Joel Hanrahan. In Pittsburgh, Melancon flourished as a set-up man and posted video game numbers across the board. Then the postseason came and Melancon yielded two home runs in four appearances—or one more than he had during the entire regular season. Those performances could have reignited the argument about whether he has the stomach for late-inning work, but, save for his time in Boston, Melancon's regular-season work suggests he's more than capable.

Bryan Morris

Born: 3/28/1987 Age: 27
Bats: L Throws: R Height: 6' 3" Weight: 225
Breakout: 49% Improve: 64% Collapse: 13%
Attrition: 59% MLB: 48%

Comparables:
Juan Mateo, Adam Russell, Carlos Fisher

YEAR	TEAM	LVL	AGE	W	L	SV	G	GS	IP	H	HR	BB	SO	BB9	SO9	GB%	BABIP	WHIP	ERA	FIP	FRA	WARP
2011	ALT	AA	24	3	4	3	35	6	78	72	2	33	64	3.8	7.4	61%	.312	1.35	3.35	3.41	5.58	-0.1
2012	IND	AAA	25	2	2	5	46	0	81	76	8	17	79	1.9	8.8	58%	.293	1.15	2.67	3.12	4.32	0.7
2012	PIT	MLB	25	0	0	0	5	0	5	2	0	2	6	3.6	10.8	73%	.182	0.80	1.80	2.54	3.02	0.1
2013	PIT	MLB	26	5	7	0	55	0	65	57	8	28	37	3.9	5.1	58%	.255	1.31	3.46	4.87	6.17	-1.1
2014	PIT	MLB	27	2	2	0	30	4	64²	62	7	23	46	3.2	6.4	54%	.297	1.33	4.16	4.38	4.53	-0.0

The last remaining piece of the Jason Bay trade, Morris had a shiny ERA and dull peripherals in the first half—guess which side won in the second half. One of those rare pitchers who throws a secondary pitch (a slider) more often than his fastball, Morris can sling it in there and missed more bats than his strikeout rate indicates. To his credit, he kept the ball low and generated a nice rate of groundballs. Still, his home-run rate was too high for comfort and his reliance upon the defense doesn't help matters. For now he should remain in middle relief.

Charlie Morton

Born: 11/12/1983 Age: 30
Bats: R Throws: R Height: 6' 5" Weight: 235
Breakout: 23% Improve: 45% Collapse: 36%
Attrition: 37% MLB: 63%

Comparables:
Runelvys Hernandez, Randy Wells, Dontrelle Willis

YEAR	TEAM	LVL	AGE	W	L	SV	G	GS	IP	H	HR	BB	SO	BB9	SO9	GB%	BABIP	WHIP	ERA	FIP	FRA	WARP
2011	PIT	MLB	27	10	10	0	29	29	171²	186	6	77	110	4.0	5.8	60%	.328	1.53	3.83	3.74	4.67	0.2
2012	PIT	MLB	28	2	6	0	9	9	50¹	62	5	11	25	2.0	4.5	57%	.318	1.45	4.65	4.21	5.04	-0.2
2013	ALT	AA	29	1	1	0	4	4	18²	10	2	6	11	2.9	5.3	59%	.154	0.86	2.41	4.50	4.79	0.1
2013	IND	AAA	29	0	1	0	4	4	19	16	1	10	12	4.7	5.7	61%	.250	1.37	3.79	4.36	5.91	-0.1
2013	PIT	MLB	29	7	4	0	20	20	116	113	6	36	85	2.8	6.6	64%	.317	1.28	3.26	3.57	4.56	0.1
2014	PIT	MLB	30	6	8	0	21	21	118	118	10	39	80	2.9	6.1	54%	.309	1.33	4.25	4.15	4.62	-0.0

Not long ago, Morton was known as the guy trying to capture Roy Halladay's brilliance by mimicking his mechanics. Nowadays, Halladay would be well-served to study Morton. The well-built sinkerballer has become the key piece in the Nate McLouth trade, and had his best season to date in 2013 after returning from Tommy John surgery in June. Morton's walk rate is a bit deceiving because it doesn't include his 16 hit batsmen, but he's made progress and earned a three-year extension to stay in the middle of Pittsburgh's rotation.

Stolmy Pimentel

Born: 2/1/1990 Age: 24
Bats: R Throws: R Height: 6' 3" Weight: 230
Breakout: 45% Improve: 56% Collapse: 19%
Attrition: 71% MLB: 21%

Comparables:
Tobi Stoner, Nick Tepesch, Doug Mathis

YEAR	TEAM	LVL	AGE	W	L	SV	G	GS	IP	H	HR	BB	SO	BB9	SO9	GB%	BABIP	WHIP	ERA	FIP	FRA	WARP
2011	SLM	A+	21	6	4	0	11	10	51²	50	8	16	35	2.8	6.1	48%	.222	1.28	4.53	5.28	7.75	-0.5
2011	PME	AA	21	0	9	0	15	15	50¹	75	8	23	30	4.1	5.4	30%	.343	1.95	9.12	6.13	7.24	-0.2
2012	PME	AA	22	6	7	0	22	22	115²	115	9	42	86	3.3	6.7	52%	.298	1.36	4.59	3.87	5.06	0.7
2013	ALT	AA	23	4	3	0	13	13	77¹	74	8	35	61	4.1	7.1	44%	.287	1.41	3.61	4.64	5.18	0.1
2013	IND	AAA	23	2	6	0	14	14	92	76	6	21	62	2.1	6.1	50%	.253	1.05	3.13	3.45	4.89	0.2
2013	PIT	MLB	23	0	0	0	5	0	9¹	6	0	2	9	1.9	8.7	44%	.222	0.86	1.93	1.73	1.99	0.3
2014	PIT	MLB	24	7	10	0	25	25	144	145	17	52	90	3.2	5.6	44%	.292	1.36	4.56	4.75	4.95	-0.7

Acquired as part of the Joel Hanrahan trade, Pimentel elicited a comparison to an Italian sports car in last year's book because, while he looks amazing, he "never works right." Fair enough. Pimentel's fastball is a plus offering and his best pitch. His changeup is solid-average, but he lacks a third offering and has been slow to take to a breaking pitch. Pimentel enters the season out of options and will try to stick as a reliever. This is exactly the type of profile that leads to a trade as spring training winds down, but we can't be waiting around on Pimentel to get this book into your eager mitts.

Wandy Rodriguez

Born: 1/18/1979 Age: 35
Bats: B Throws: L Height: 5' 10" Weight: 195
Breakout: 22% Improve: 45% Collapse: 19%
Attrition: 10% MLB: 90%

Comparables:
Kevin Millwood, Esteban Loaiza, Koji Uehara

YEAR	TEAM	LVL	AGE	W	L	SV	G	GS	IP	H	HR	BB	SO	BB9	SO9	GB%	BABIP	WHIP	ERA	FIP	FRA	WARP
2011	HOU	MLB	32	11	11	0	30	30	191	182	25	69	166	3.3	7.8	45%	.289	1.31	3.49	4.12	4.47	1.2
2012	HOU	MLB	33	7	9	0	21	21	130²	134	13	32	89	2.2	6.1	51%	.296	1.27	3.79	3.85	4.38	1.2
2012	PIT	MLB	33	5	4	0	13	12	75	71	8	24	50	2.9	6.0	46%	.266	1.27	3.72	4.19	4.48	0.3
2013	PIT	MLB	34	6	4	0	12	12	62²	58	10	12	46	1.7	6.6	43%	.255	1.12	3.59	4.39	4.48	0.4
2014	PIT	MLB	35	5	5	0	13	13	80	74	8	22	61	2.4	6.8	46%	.292	1.19	3.69	3.92	4.01	0.5

In Rodriguez's first full season with the Pirates, he made fewer starts than he did the year before, when he was acquired at the deadline to shore up the rotation. Rodriguez spent the entire second half on the disabled list due to forearm tightness. A late-season comeback attempt failed, and the Pirates opted to shut him down. Given the injury, it was hard to envision Rodriguez not exercising his $13 million player option.

Jameson Taillon

Born: 11/18/1991 Age: 22
Bats: R Throws: R Height: 6' 6" Weight: 235
Breakout: 48% Improve: 73% Collapse: 15%
Attrition: 55% MLB: 33%

Comparables:
Anthony Swarzak, Josh Lindblom, Cesar Carrillo

YEAR	TEAM	LVL	AGE	W	L	SV	G	GS	IP	H	HR	BB	SO	BB9	SO9	GB%	BABIP	WHIP	ERA	FIP	FRA	WARP
2011	WVA	A	19	2	3	0	23	23	92²	89	9	22	97	2.1	9.4	47%	.323	1.20	3.98	3.70	4.41	1.4
2012	BRD	A+	20	6	8	0	23	23	125	109	10	37	98	2.7	7.1	47%	.267	1.17	3.82	3.90	4.66	1.7
2012	ALT	AA	20	3	0	0	3	3	17	11	0	1	18	0.5	9.5	38%	.262	0.71	1.59	1.26	2.33	0.6
2013	ALT	AA	21	4	7	0	20	19	110¹	112	8	36	106	2.9	8.6	51%	.332	1.34	3.67	3.46	3.95	1.5
2013	IND	AAA	21	1	3	0	6	6	37	31	1	16	37	3.9	9.0	36%	.297	1.27	3.89	3.18	3.58	0.6
2014	PIT	MLB	22	7	9	0	23	23	130²	127	13	44	100	3.0	6.9	45%	.301	1.30	4.15	4.15	4.51	0.1

There's a point in every prospect's career where fatigue sets in. Taillon might be at that point. He's been talked about as an elite prospect since the Pirates selected him second in the 2010 draft. Yet, while bookend selections Bryce Harper and Manny Machado have experienced playoff baseball, Taillon has not pitched in the majors; that context can leave people wondering what the Canadian's problem is. In truth, there are two problems: Taillon has spotty fastball command and a subpar changeup. Because he's one of the few minor-league pitchers who have two legitimate plus-plus pitches—his fastball and curveball—he's still a potential number two starter. But how the command and changeup develop will determine if Taillon reaches his upside, and whether all this hype was worth it.

Edinson Volquez

Born: 7/3/1983 Age: 30
Bats: R Throws: R Height: 6' 0" Weight: 220
Breakout: 29% Improve: 55% Collapse: 22%
Attrition: 25% MLB: 73%

Comparables:
Oliver Perez, Ian Snell, Tom Gorzelanny

YEAR	TEAM	LVL	AGE	W	L	SV	G	GS	IP	H	HR	BB	SO	BB9	SO9	GB%	BABIP	WHIP	ERA	FIP	FRA	WARP
2011	LOU	AAA	27	4	2	0	13	13	87¹	72	5	29	83	3.0	8.6	52%	.275	1.16	2.37	3.21	3.95	1.0
2011	CIN	MLB	27	5	7	0	20	20	108²	106	19	65	104	5.4	8.6	52%	.304	1.57	5.71	5.26	5.77	-0.8
2012	SDN	MLB	28	11	11	0	32	32	182²	160	14	105	174	5.2	8.6	51%	.299	1.45	4.14	4.10	4.74	0.5
2013	LAN	MLB	29	0	2	0	6	5	28	25	5	8	26	2.6	8.4	45%	.274	1.18	4.18	4.34	4.93	-0.1
2013	SDN	MLB	29	9	10	0	27	27	142¹	168	14	69	116	4.4	7.3	48%	.341	1.67	6.01	4.19	4.39	0.8
2014	PIT	MLB	30	8	10	0	29	29	153²	137	15	68	138	4.0	8.1	48%	.298	1.34	4.12	4.15	4.47	0.3

After joining the Dodgers, the Walkman posted a better-than-average free-pass rate for the first time in his career. Such was the trend for L.A.'s starting pitchers, as every pitcher with more than 80 frames walked fewer than 2.4 batters per nine innings. In Volquez's case, however, the low total of freebies was more the residue of sample size than the magic touch of Rick Honeycutt—spy the five wild pitches that Volquez uncorked in his five starts, for instance. His 16 wild ones on the season were the second most in the National League, and he finished with the highest total of earned runs in the circuit. The Pirates signed him cheap, perhaps imagining a Liriano-like resurgence. But the Walkman has been out of style for several years now, to the point that functional use is questionable.

Tony Watson
Born: 5/30/1985 Age: 29
Bats: L Throws: L Height: 6' 4" Weight: 225
Breakout: 21% Improve: 48% Collapse: 32%
Attrition: 29% MLB: 74%

Comparables:
Chris Resop, Tom Wilhelmsen, Juan Gutierrez

YEAR	TEAM	LVL	AGE	W	L	SV	G	GS	IP	H	HR	BB	SO	BB9	SO9	GB%	BABIP	WHIP	ERA	FIP	FRA	WARP
2011	IND	AAA	26	3	3	0	26	1	34¹	24	2	11	35	2.9	9.2	40%	.263	1.02	2.36	3.09	4.29	0.2
2011	PIT	MLB	26	2	2	0	43	0	41	34	6	20	37	4.4	8.1	35%	.269	1.32	3.95	4.63	4.67	-0.1
2012	PIT	MLB	27	5	2	0	68	0	53¹	37	5	23	53	3.9	8.9	42%	.241	1.12	3.38	3.72	3.81	0.3
2013	PIT	MLB	28	3	1	2	67	0	71²	51	5	12	54	1.5	6.8	46%	.227	0.88	2.39	3.17	3.73	0.6
2014	PIT	MLB	29	3	2	1	43	2	59²	49	6	18	53	2.8	8.0	37%	.275	1.13	3.18	3.78	3.46	0.8

It's tempting to call every southpaw with a low release point a LOOGY, but Watson is proof that it's inaccurate. He faced more right-handed batters last season than lefties again, yet he continued to pitch well against batters of either hand. Watson throws three pitches—a mid-90s fastball, changeup and slider—and did well to avoid walks. Sprinkle some wits over that package and you have a good set-up man with the ability to retire lefties and righties alike.

Duke Welker
Born: 2/10/1986 Age: 28
Bats: L Throws: R Height: 6' 7" Weight: 240
Breakout: 78% Improve: 78% Collapse: 22%
Attrition: 25% MLB: 9%

Comparables:
Adalberto Mendez, Jean Machi, Steve Delabar

YEAR	TEAM	LVL	AGE	W	L	SV	G	GS	IP	H	HR	BB	SO	BB9	SO9	GB%	BABIP	WHIP	ERA	FIP	FRA	WARP
2011	BRD	A+	25	3	5	6	36	0	52	33	2	25	41	4.3	7.1	68%	.211	1.12	2.25	3.87	3.06	0.2
2011	ALT	AA	25	1	0	0	8	0	10	11	0	1	9	0.9	8.1	58%	.333	1.20	5.40	2.21	2.51	0.3
2012	ALT	AA	26	2	1	5	15	0	23¹	19	0	7	19	2.7	7.3	64%	.271	1.11	2.31	2.47	3.47	0.4
2012	IND	AAA	26	0	1	0	26	0	31²	24	1	18	30	5.1	8.5	54%	.284	1.33	2.27	3.47	4.46	0.2
2013	IND	AAA	27	3	4	9	48	0	63	53	3	31	65	4.4	9.3	52%	.303	1.33	3.57	3.33	3.89	0.8
2013	PIT	MLB	27	0	0	0	2	0	1¹	0	0	0	1	0.0	6.8	33%	.000	0.00	0.00	1.52	2.50	0.0
2014	PIT	MLB	28	2	1	1	43	0	54²	51	5	29	41	4.8	6.8	53%	.297	1.46	4.57	4.63	4.96	-0.4

Shipped to Minnesota as part of the Justin Morneau trade and then reacquired in November for Kris Johnson, Welker has no fewer than three things working for him. First, his size: he's listed at 6-foot-7 and looks the part. Then there's the hot fastball that can touch the upper 90s with ease. Lastly there's the name. Add it together and the question is why the Pirates would ever have traded this guy in the first place? The answer comes down to control. Scouts argue about whether strike-throwing can be taught or not, but with Welker the arrow points toward not. Now 28, he's unlikely to reduce his walk rate too much heading forward. The Pirates are left to hope for a marginal improvement, which could be enough to make him a worthwhile middle reliever.

Justin Wilson
Born: 8/18/1987 Age: 26
Bats: L Throws: L Height: 6' 2" Weight: 205
Breakout: 34% Improve: 56% Collapse: 28%
Attrition: 54% MLB: 66%

Comparables:
Dustin Nippert, Michael Kirkman, Kevin Hart

YEAR	TEAM	LVL	AGE	W	L	SV	G	GS	IP	H	HR	BB	SO	BB9	SO9	GB%	BABIP	WHIP	ERA	FIP	FRA	WARP
2011	IND	AAA	23	10	8	3	30	21	124¹	121	12	67	94	4.8	6.8	48%	.299	1.51	4.13	4.69	5.72	-0.3
2012	IND	AAA	24	9	6	0	29	25	135²	91	12	66	138	4.4	9.2	37%	.234	1.16	3.78	3.89	5.08	0.3
2012	PIT	MLB	24	0	0	0	8	0	4²	10	0	3	7	5.8	13.5	20%	.667	2.79	1.93	2.06	2.83	0.1
2013	PIT	MLB	25	6	1	0	58	0	73²	50	4	28	59	3.4	7.2	55%	.226	1.06	2.08	3.39	3.84	0.5
2014	PIT	MLB	26	4	4	0	23	11	73	63	7	32	59	4.0	7.2	47%	.282	1.31	3.93	4.29	4.27	0.3

Formerly a starting pitcher prospect with back-of-the-rotation aspirations, Wilson shifted to the bullpen and won a job with the big-league club. The move helped Wilson's peripherals: His walk rate improved along with his groundball rate, and his strikeouts remained solid. He averaged more than an inning per appearance and shut down batters (especially lefties) with his high release point, upper-90s fastball and low-90s cutter. Expect to see him work near the end of ballgames in 2014.

LINEOUTS

HITTERS

PLAYER	TEAM	LVL	AGE	PA	R	2B	3B	HR	RBI	BB	SO	SB-CS	AVG/OBP/SLG	TAv	BABIP	BRR	FRAA	WARP
1B S. Allie	WVA	A	22	285	42	16	1	17	61	36	79	6-1	.324/.414/.607	.369	.413	-4	1B(41): 0.2	3.1
	BRD	A+	22	284	28	18	0	4	25	41	82	2-3	.229/.342/.356	.264	.323	-1.7	1B(49): 0.7	0.1
2B R. Andino	TAC	AAA	29	167	17	5	1	3	12	12	38	2-1	.229/.281/.333	.213	.281	-0.1	2B(19): -0.7, SS(18): -2.0	-0.5
	IND	AAA	29	105	7	8	0	0	9	5	20	0-1	.302/.330/.385	.259	.372	-0.1	SS(24): 3.3, 2B(1): -0.0	0.8
	SEA	MLB	29	85	5	4	0	0	4	7	27	0-0	.184/.253/.237	.186	.286	0.1	SS(18): -1.0, 2B(8): 0.3	-0.6
CF B. Barnes	WVA	A	21	206	26	9	0	5	24	17	48	10-3	.268/.338/.399	.291	.336	1.5	CF(45): -0.2	1.2
SS C. d'Arnaud	IND	AAA	26	262	33	8	4	4	20	18	43	17-5	.233/.288/.350	.223	.268	2.1	SS(39): 1.1, 2B(16): 0.5	0.5
RF E. Escobar	JAM	A-	18	199	25	8	2	1	23	9	47	9-4	.268/.293/.350	.273	.340	0.3	RF(42): -2.5, LF(5): 0.5	0.7
C J. Jhang	JAM	A-	20	211	22	8	1	5	34	17	24	0-1	.277/.338/.413	.280	.289	0.7	C(44): 0.9	2.0
SS G. Ngoepe	BRD	A+	23	123	17	7	3	0	6	21	35	7-1	.292/.424/.427	.304	.459	2.2	SS(28): 3.1	1.6
	ALT	AA	23	259	29	10	2	3	16	28	82	10-3	.177/.278/.282	.235	.261	0.5	SS(72): -1.5	0.3
CF F. Pie	IND	AAA	28	396	53	17	4	8	40	37	83	38-9	.251/.325/.390	.253	.307	2.4	CF(43): -4.5, LF(43): 3.0	1.0
	PIT	MLB	28	31	5	1	0	0	2	2	13	1-2	.138/.194/.172	.167	.250	-0.3	LF(13): -0.3, CF(5): -0.0	-0.3
CF H. Ramirez	JAM	A-	18	310	42	11	4	5	40	23	52	23-11	.285/.354/.409	.293	.332	1.6	CF(31): -3.6, RF(22): 0.9	2.2

Pitcher-turned-hitter **Stetson Allie** was having a fairy-tale season until the Pirates promoted him to the Florida State League. The big-bodied Ohio native has legit raw power, but the odds of a big-league career are against him. ⊘ **Robert Andino's** middle name is Lazaro, which is almost ironic since his poor play gave Brendan Ryan second life in Seattle. ⊘ Scouts like **Barrett Barnes'** speed and power, but do not like his chances of sticking in center nor the likelihood that he makes enough contact to take advantage of those gifts. ⊘ Speedster **Chase d'Arnaud**, who missed time recovering from thumb surgery, can now list outfield on his defensive resume. ⊘ Tiny Venezuelan outfielder **Elvis Escobar** is a line-drive hitter with an average arm, average speed, and years yet until he can legally drink. ⊘ Taiwanese catcher **Jin-De Jhang** has a solid bat and better-than-expected athleticism, giving him a chance to be a solid prospect. ⊘ **Gift Ngoepe** has a good glove, a better background story and the best name; now if only he could hit. ⊘ After he reached the majors following a career-worst stretch in Triple-A, **Felix Pie** confused correlation with causation and tried keeping his big-league job with another career-worst performance. ⊘ Colombian outfielder **Harold Ramirez** has plus-plus speed and plus-size pants. He does not have the arm for right field, so if his thick lower half saps his wheels, he'll have to move to left.

PITCHERS

PLAYER	TEAM	LVL	AGE	W	L	SV	IP	H	HR	BB	SO	BB9	SO9	GB%	BABIP	WHIP	ERA	FIP	FRA	WARP
O. Castro	WVA	A	21	7	4	0	74²	65	5	6	63	0.7	7.6	51%	.266	0.95	1.93	3.07	3.98	0.8
	BRD	A+	21	2	3	1	33¹	39	3	11	21	3.0	5.7	40%	.330	1.50	4.32	4.14	5.45	0.1
K. Farnsworth	TBA	MLB	37	2	0	0	29²	37	4	7	19	2.1	5.8	49%	.337	1.48	5.76	4.36	4.72	0.0
	PIT	MLB	37	1	1	2	8²	6	1	3	9	3.1	9.3	48%	.250	1.04	1.04	3.48	3.68	0.1
C. Holmes	WVA	A	20	5	6	0	119	106	7	69	90	5.2	6.8	57%	.283	1.47	4.08	4.78	5.85	-0.9
P. Irwin	IND	AAA	26	1	0	0	10	5	0	3	8	2.7	7.2	46%	.154	0.80	0.90	3.10	3.68	0.2
	PIT	MLB	26	0	0	0	4²	6	0	4	4	7.7	7.7	61%	.462	2.14	7.71	3.88	5.55	-0.1
J. Karstens	PIT	MLB	29	5	4	0	90²	89	8	15	66	1.5	6.6	38%	.297	1.15	3.97	3.36	3.97	1.0
K. McPherson	PIT	MLB	24	0	2	0	26¹	24	3	7	21	2.4	7.2	46%	.282	1.18	2.73	4.05	4.02	0.2
M. Mikolas	TUC	AAA	24	4	2	26	61	62	6	17	40	2.5	5.9	51%	.287	1.30	3.25	4.37	4.88	0.6
	SDN	MLB	24	0	0	0	1²	0	0	1	1	5.4	5.4	%	.000	0.60	0.00	5.42	5.40	0.0
A. Oliver	IND	AAA	25	5	4	0	124¹	99	6	112	138	8.1	10.0	49%	.292	1.70	4.05	4.44	5.07	0.6
A. Sampson	BRD	A+	21	5	8	0	140	177	18	22	85	1.4	5.5	47%	.332	1.42	5.14	4.32	5.60	-0.7

Orlando Castro is a small, finesse southpaw whose parents have a bumper sticker that reads, "Our son is a second lefty." ⊘ If this is the end for **Kyle Farnsworth**, then he lasted longer and finished stronger than anyone expected. If it's not, well, we'll probably just repeat this comment next year. ⊘ **Clay Holmes**, Pittsburgh's ninth-round pick in 2011, is a work in progress. He has a huge frame and two good pitches—a fastball and curveball—but everything else needs polish for him to become a middle-of-the-rotation workhorse. ⚾ High point: Command-and-control righty **Phil Irwin** made his big-league debut. Low point: He missed most of the rest of the season following ulnar nerve transposition surgery. ⚾ Veteran starter **Jeff Karstens**, non-tendered then re-signed by the Pirates, missed most of the season due to a bum shoulder, which really isn't very River Wizard-y when you think about it. ⚾ Potential middle-of-the-rotation starter **Kyle McPherson** underwent Tommy John surgery in July, leaving him unavailable for at least the first half of 2014. ⚾ After pitching reasonably well in a 2012 audition, **Miles Mikolas** spent last season collecting saves at Triple-A Tucson and fishing with Brad Boxberger and catcher Eddy Rodriguez on off-days; the sinker/curveball artist will get another look this year, but it'll be in Pittsburgh. ⚾ Former second-round pick **Andrew Oliver** has a big-league body and fastball, but he'd walk a batting tee on five pitches. ⚾ An under-the-radar JuCo draftee, **Adrian Sampson** struggled after an aggressive assignment to Bradenton. He could develop three average or better pitches. Or he could not. Search for the answer in the stars.

MANAGER: CLINT HURDLE

YEAR	TEAM	W-L	Pythag +/–	Avg PC	100+ P	120+ P	QS	BQS	REL	REL w Zero R	IBB	PH	PH Avg	PH HR	SB2	CS2	SB3	CS3	SAC Att	SAC %	POS SAC	Squeeze	Swing	In Play
2011	PIT	72-90	0	89.5	26	0	78	2	549	452	65	275	.201	1	95	47	13	3	110	68.2%	37	1	384	114
2012	PIT	79-83	0	90.4	42	0	83	2	483	398	30	266	.173	2	66	45	7	3	93	66.7%	30	2	271	94
2013	PIT	94-68	1	89.7	41	0	83	2	465	395	26	285	.207	7	83	36	10	6	93	66.7%	35	1	347	100

In 10 seasons as a manager (well, 10 seasons in which he managed over 50 games in the season), Clint Hurdle has piloted teams to winning records just twice—but both of those teams made the postseason. Hurdle didn't push his starting pitchers very hard this year. Pirates starting pitchers, despite finishing fourth in the NL with a 3.50 ERA, ranked 13th in innings pitched. In fact, in three years in Pittsburgh, only twice has someone topped 175 innings for Hurdle. Both times it's been A.J. Burnett.

Every year he's run a team, his batters' strikeouts have been greater than his pitchers' strikeouts. Hurdle's teams have the second worst career strikeout differential by any manager ever, behind just Sparky Anderson.

San Diego Padres

By Geoff Young

TREADING WATER

Can the Padres ever consistently contend? After moving into Petco Park in 2004, they enjoyed four straight winning seasons for the first time in franchise history, including two playoff appearances and a painful near-miss in 2007, but they have since endured five losing seasons in six. The lone outlier came in 2010, when they led the NL West for much of the year before falling on the season's final day to the eventual world champion Giants.

The Padres finished 76-86 in both 2012 and 2013. Despite the identical records, they made progress. Second baseman Jedd Gyorko graduated from the minors, shortstop Everth Cabrera began to emerge before a season-ending PED suspension and young right-handers Andrew Cashner and Tyson Ross justified General Manager Josh Byrnes' decision to acquire them.

The Padres, using a blueprint familiar to small- and mid-market teams everywhere, are striving to build a sustainably competitive ballclub by procuring and retaining good, cheap talent. They have done this via the amateur draft (Gyorko, Chase Headley, Nick Hundley, Will Venable), trade (Yonder Alonso, Cashner, Robbie Erlin, Yasmani Grandal, Cameron Maybin, Ross) and even the Rule 5 draft (Cabrera).

Conspicuously absent are the pricey free agents of larger-market teams. San Diego, which Nielsen ranks as the 28th-largest television market in the country (behind Baltimore, ahead of Nashville), can't afford to carry the bloated contract of some first baseman who was good five years ago. With a payroll that typically lies between $40 and $60 million a season, the Padres can't outspend their mistakes.

The acquire-develop-retain model is viable. The A's and Rays have perfected it. Books have been written trumpeting their ability to exploit market inefficiencies and beat baseball's Goliaths despite having less money. Last year the

PADRES PROSPECTUS					
2013 W-L: 76-86, 3rd in NL West					
Pythag	.443	23rd	DER	.704	17th
RS/G	3.81	24th	B-Age	28.0	13th
RA/G	4.32	21st	P-Age	28.8	23rd
TAv	.254	18th	Salary	$68.3	25th
BRR	-2.12	20th	M$/MW	$2	8th
TAv-P	.271	22nd	DL Days	1271	24th
FIP	3.97	21st	$ on DL	25%	25th

	Runs	HR/RH	HR/LH	Runs/RH	Runs/LH
Three-Year Park Factors	98	98	109	97	103

Top Hitter WARP	3.11 (Everth Cabrera)
Top Pitcher WARP	2.17 (Eric Stults)
Top Prospect	Austin Hedges

Indians and Pirates joined them as small-market winners. For many reasons–some their fault, some not–the Padres have been less successful. Three ownership groups in five years hasn't helped, nor has the resulting front-office carousel.

For the first half of 2012, the Padres essentially had no owner and therefore had even less money than usual. Three years after Jeff Moorad reached an agreement to buy the club in February 2009, he was given the boot by Bud Selig and his minions. Before Moorad left, he let GM Jed Hoyer and Assistant GM Jason McLeod go to the Cubs, installing Byrnes–who had been GM of the Diamondbacks under Moorad–as Hoyer's successor. One of Byrnes' first moves was to trade Mat Latos to the Reds for four players, including Alonso. A few weeks later, he shipped presumed first baseman of the future Anthony Rizzo–whom Hoyer had drafted while with the Red Sox and traded for while with the Padres–to Hoyer's new team for Cashner.

This series of moves was poorly received by fans. Under Hoyer, the Padres had appeared to be building around Latos and Rizzo. Less than three months into Byrnes' tenure, those two were gone, replaced by unfamiliar names the new regime would have to sell to locals, a group not inclined to buy in light of ongoing organizational turmoil, as foundations of the future.

Between not knowing who owned the team and one GM seemingly undoing the good work of his predecessor, the situation was as tense as a half-inch of rain on the I-5. Fans were angry and confused, and more importantly, the on-field product didn't improve. Slapping at the water is not the same as swimming.

CONTROLLING THE KIDS

Although the Padres have struggled with the acquire and develop portions of this model (more on that in a moment), they have retained their young talent. In March 2012, the Padres extended Hundley, Cory Luebke and Maybin. All three got hurt. (See Table 1.) This was sound process torpedoed by external factors.

All were coming off career years, but all were young enough to sustain or improve their performance. They have since spent a combined 563 days on the disabled list.

Hundley and Maybin also played hurt, depressing their numbers when not on the shelf. Foreseeable risk? Luebke and Maybin had never sustained serious injuries, but down they went. The Padres' recent struggles to keep players healthy might indicate a larger problem, but it also could be terrible luck. Without closer scrutiny than publicly available information permits, it's impossible to know.

Player	Before Extension			Since Extension			Contract
	PA or IP	WARP	DL Days	PA or IP	WARP	DL Days	
Nick Hundley	1120	5.8	126	633	0.4	49	Three years, $9 million
Cory Luebke	157	2.7	0	31	0.4	351	Four years, $12 million with club options at $7.5 and $10 million
Cameron Maybin	1178	5.9	16	618	1.2	163	Five years, $25 million with club option at $9 million

TRYING AGAIN

Misfortune should not push the Padres into abandoning a prudent strategy. Although their earlier extensions backfired, they should explore similar long-term deals with Cabrera, Cashner and Gyorko. (You could also make a case for Ross.) Each comes with risk:

- Adam Wainwright, who signed a five-year, $97.5 million extension that kicks in this year. Wainwright finished second in the Cy Young voting last year.
- Were Cabrera's gains real? He only played 95 games last year and slumped before his suspension, but showed improved on-base and defensive skills. Also, he is a Scott Boras client.
- Can Cashner stay healthy? He pitched well in his first go-round as a regular rotation member, especially down the stretch, but the injury history cannot be ignored.
- Will Gyorko control the strike zone and stay at second base? The power is nice; the OBP hovering around .300 isn't. Also, his body is not that of a typical middle infielder.

Despite these valid concerns, there is ample upside to such deals. The most striking example is the Rays buying out Evan Longoria's arbitration years in April 2008 with a guaranteed six-year, $17.5 million deal, which turned into nine years and $44.5 million thanks to club options that erased his first three free-agent seasons. He is a unique talent, but the same principle applies to lesser players.

The Padres have also done this in the past with Adrián González. When they inked him to a four-year, $9.5 million extension in March 2007, his career line of .285/.340/.475 resembled Paul Konerko's at the same age. Two months before his 25th birthday and coming off his best season, González continued to improve, making the contract a steal. After getting González's most productive years, the Padres flipped

the soon-to-be-expensive first baseman to Boston for Casey Kelly, Rizzo and Reymond Fuentes. Converting a veteran name-brand falling star into two mid-rotation starters (assuming Kelly finds health and Cashner keeps it) and a fourth outfielder is exactly what a team like the Padres must do.

But name brands draw fans, which brings us back to extending familiar players. Cabrera, Cashner and Gyorko aren't stars, but they help win games and are among the more–if you'll indulge the oxymoron–well-known Padres. No strategy is flawless, but extending young players for less money than equivalent talent on the open market is one way the Padres can narrow the gap between themselves and their richer competitors. They are wise to exploit it.

Player	PA or IP	WARP	DL Days	Age
Everth Cabrera	1572	8.2	127	27
Andrew Cashner	286	3.2	211	27
Jedd Gyorko	525	1.4	32	25

SWEATING THE DETAILS

What kinds of deals should be made? The number of variables is overwhelming, so we'll focus on general concepts, giving details for illustrative purposes only and with an armada of disclaimers.

For Cabrera, the Padres could use recent extensions of Stephen Drew in January 2011 (2 years, $15.75 million plus a mutual option) and Asdrubal Cabrera in April 2012 (2 years, $16.5 million) as models. Cabrera is less accomplished than they were, but this gives us a starting point. He still has three years of arbitration eligibility; if the Padres could buy those and–Boras permitting–his first year of free agency for a mutually agreeable amount, it would help them at a position they have historically had trouble filling. For Cabrera, it would provide security, a factor Longoria cited in signing his deal. Drew, incidentally, is a Boras client. So is Elvis Andrus, who signed a February 2012 extension that eliminated his arbitration years. The agent's presence may be a complicating factor, but history shows that it isn't a deal-breaker.

As for Cashner, Tim Dierkes at MLB Trade Rumors suggests "five years and less than $30 million," which would be like extensions signed by Jon Niese and Derek Holland in 2012, or Trevor Cahill a year earlier. Cashner is older and less experienced than they were; that and the injury risk make five years a tad aggressive. Buying out his arbitration and first free-agent seasons, as the Reds did with Johnny Cueto in January 2011 (four years, $27 million, $10 million club option) or the Blue Jays did with Brandon Morrow in January 2012 (three years, $21 million, $10 million club option), seems more realistic. The downside is illustrated by Cueto and Morrow missing significant time since signing. If the Padres want to mitigate the risk inherent in pitchers, they could try to compromise with a two-year deal similar to those signed by Jhoulys Chacin and Latos before the 2013 season.

The team doesn't have to negotiate with Gyorko, who is pre-arbitration, but a deal could save the Padres money now and foster player loyalty in the future. Two young second basemen to sign extensions in recent years are Ian Kinsler in February 2008 (five years, $22 million, $9.5 million club option) and José Altuve in July 2013 (four years, $12.5 million, two club options totaling another $12.5 million). Maybe Gyorko and the Padres can reach a similar agreement. Potential extensions for all three Padres are set out in Table 3.

The strategy carries risk. Fortunately for the Padres, Byrnes is well aware of the benefits. In a June radio interview, he called signing young players to long-term deals a "win-win contract model," acknowledging that the Padres won't outbid other teams for free agents and reminding listeners that he and the Indians followed a similar path in the mid-'90s. The key difference is that 20 years ago, he worked for a team that drafted Albert Belle, Jim Thome and Manny Ramirez, which brings us to an important point.

BLOWING THE DRAFT

The Padres must constantly replenish their system by drafting and developing better players. Questionable choices have undermined recent efforts. The debacle of 2004, when the Padres targeted polished collegians Stephen Drew, Jeff Niemann and Jered Weaver for several months before abruptly picking local high-school product Matt Bush in an ill-advised attempt to save money, is well-documented. That was a one-time process failure. The larger issue is that they haven't popped any franchise-type players in a long time.

Their last decent first-round pick was Tim Stauffer in 2003. Khalil Greene, taken a year earlier, enjoyed a few good seasons. Before that? Sean Burroughs in 1998. Ben Davis in 1995, another disappointment. Dustin Hermanson, 1994? He landed the Padres Quilvio Veras. Derrek Lee, 1993? He fetched Kevin Brown in trade.

Veras and Brown played for the 1998 World Series team that helped convince voters to approve a new downtown ballpark, but it's been two decades since the Padres drafted an impact player in the first round and longer since one succeeded in San Diego: Joey Hamilton, 1991; Andy Benes, 1988.

We can't yet judge 2011 to 2013, but the last 10 years (Table 4) are ugly. A team that relies on developing its own cost-controlled talent cannot burn draft picks like matchsticks. Some of this is bad luck, but some is bad process.

		Everth Cabrera			Andrew Cashner			Jedd Gyorko	
Year	Age	Status	Salary	Age	Status	Salary	Age	Status	Salary
2014	27	arb2	$2.5M	27	arb1	$2.5M	25	pre-arb	$1.0M
2015	28	arb3	$4.5M	28	arb2	$4.5M	26	pre-arb	$2.0M
2016	29	arb4	$7.0M	29	arb3	$7.0M	27	arb1	$3.0M
2017	30	FA	$10M (opt)	30	FA	$9.0M	28	arb2	$4.0M
2018	31	FA	n/a	31	FA	$10M (opt)	29	arb3	$5.0M
2019	32	FA	n/a	32	FA	n/a	30	FA	$8.0M (opt)

Year	Pick	Name	WARP	Notes
2004	1	Matt Bush	N/A	Traded by Padres in February 2009; currently in Florida state prison, due to be released in 2016
2005	18	Cesar Carrillo	-0.5	Released by Padres in September 2010; suspended 100 games for violating minor-league drug policy in March 2013
2006	17	Matt Antonelli	-0.2	Released by Padres in December 2010; currently a student assistant coach at Wake Forest
2007	23	Nick Schmidt	N/A	Missed 2008 due to Tommy John surgery; traded to Rockies for Huston Street in December 2011
2008	23	Allan Dykstra	N/A	Traded to Mets for Eddie Kunz in March 2011; spent last three seasons at Double-A
2009	3	Donavan Tate	N/A	Injuries and drug suspensions have limited him to 194 professional games, none above High-A
2010	9	Karsten Whitson	N/A	Did not sign
2011	10	Cory Spangenberg	N/A	.292/.346/.407 between High-A and Double-A in 2013
2011	25	Joe Ross	N/A	3.75 ERA at Low-A in 2013
2012	7	Max Fried	N/A	3.49 ERA at Low-A in 2013
2013	13	Hunter Renfroe	N/A	.271/.308/.459 between short-season ball and Low-A in 2013

Carrillo looked like a front-end rotation type before blowing out his elbow. Antonelli, Schmidt and Dykstra incurred injuries as well, although none had the upside of Carrillo even when healthy. All were classic Grady Fuson picks–polished college players expected to contribute soon. Tate, the rare toolsy high school player, likewise saw injuries impede his progress. He had the added "benefit" of off-field issues. As for Whitson, the Padres thought they had a predraft deal with him. The player thought otherwise and attended the University of Florida, where he hurt his shoulder.

Before Tate and Whitson, the typical Padres first-round pick was a low-ceiling guy who ended up hurt. Those two had higher ceilings but also ended up hurt, suspended and/or unsigned, negating any potential upside.

Fortunately, the Padres have had some success outside of their top picks. The aforementioned Luebke and Gyorko were a 2007 supplemental and 2010 second-rounder, respectively. Headley (second), Hundley (second) and Venable (seventh) were drafted in 2005. David Freese (ninth) and Latos (11th) came a year later, though Freese was discarded for the charred remains of Jim Edmonds' career, and even the Latos trade looks questionable now, given Yasmani Grandal's suspension and injury, but the motivation–turn one talented young player into two–was defensible.

Other useful players include Tommy Medica (2010, 14th), who could be a bat off the bench, Burch Smith (2011, 14th), who stumbled in a brief audition last year but has big-league stuff, Matt Stites (2011, 17th), part of the package for Ian Kennedy, and Austin Hedges (2011, second) and Matt Wisler (2011, seventh), who rank among baseball's top prospects.

All of this doesn't undo a decade of damage, but it's a start.

PULLING IT ALL TOGETHER

Last September the Padres signed Will Venable to a two-year, $8.5 million deal. He isn't young (he'll play those seasons at ages 31 and 32) but has spent his entire career with the franchise and is known by fans. Venable provides value on the field as well as continuity, stability and identity to a team deficient in those areas. González did the same before transforming from cheap star to expensive above-average player. Headley could follow González's path, forcing the Padres to make a difficult decision. Despite his subpar 2013, he may have priced himself out of the San Diego market.

Do the Padres pay top dollar to keep one of their own at the risk of limiting future payroll flexibility and, consequently, their ability to compete? Do they cash him in for prospects who might fail? Do they let him walk as a free agent, further alienating fans who are weary of seeing familiar players leave for more opulent pastures? These are difficult questions that depend on many complicated variables, most of which involve a staggering amount of money. Teams with smaller budgets will have different answers than ones in major media markets.

The Padres can't play the free-agent game, so they must win the draft game. If they find good players, keep them in San Diego, and start contending, they might preserve or even grow their fan base.

Acquire, develop, retain. It's a simple formula that is difficult to execute. It also guarantees nothing. Still, it gives the Padres a fighting chance, which is more than they've had in a while.

Geoff Young, founder of the first Padres blog Ducksnorts, *writes for* PadresPublic.com; *his work has also appeared at* Baseball Prospectus, The Hardball Times, ESPN *and other online outlets, as well as in several books.*

HITTERS

Yonder Alonso   **1B**

Born: 4/8/1987 Age: 27
Bats: L Throws: R Height: 6' 2''
Weight: 250 Breakout: 2%
Improve: 47% Collapse: 7%
Attrition: 17% MLB: 88%

Comparables:
Willy Aybar, Ryan Garko, Daniel Murphy

YEAR	TEAM	LVL	AGE	PA	R	2B	3B	HR	RBI	BB	SO	SB	CS	AVG/OBP/SLG	TAv	BABIP	BRR	FRAA	WARP
2011	LOU	AAA	24	409	46	24	4	12	56	46	60	6	5	.296/.374/.486	.275	.324	-0.6	LF(48): -7.9, 1B(17): 2.0	0.7
2011	CIN	MLB	24	98	9	4	0	5	15	10	21	0	0	.330/.398/.545	.316	.387	0.9	LF(16): -0.5, 1B(3): 0.1	0.7
2012	SDN	MLB	25	619	47	39	0	9	62	62	101	3	0	.273/.348/.393	.274	.318	-5.3	1B(149): 5.9	1.9
2013	SDN	MLB	26	375	34	11	0	6	45	32	47	6	0	.281/.341/.368	.262	.306	-3	1B(92): 2.8, LF(1): -0.0	0.6
2014	SDN	MLB	27	403	43	19	1	8	44	37	68	4	1	.268/.336/.396	.271	.310	-0.3	1B 4, LF -1	1.2

The line drive-hitting Alonso spent 2013 battling right wrist and hand injuries that sapped his already limited power. He knocked as many extra-base hits all year as Will Venable did in August. His uncanny Bruce Bochte impression made our previous comparisons to Lyle Overbay look overly ambitious. Positives? Alonso has good on-base skills and has hit better at Petco (.287/.363/.407) than away (.266/.329/.362) in two seasons with the Padres. He is perfect in nine career stolen base attempts, which says less about his speed and more about the challenges of throwing while doubled over laughing. This year is critical for Alonso, whose career .395 SLG is acceptable for a shortstop but won't let him start at first base much longer.

Alexi Amarista 2B

Born: 4/6/1989 Age: 25
Bats: L Throws: R Height: 5' 8"
Weight: 150 Breakout: 1%
Improve: 58% Collapse: 7%
Attrition: 17% MLB: 94%

Comparables:
Nate McLouth, Jordan Schafer, Erick Aybar

YEAR	TEAM	LVL	AGE	PA	R	2B	3B	HR	RBI	BB	SO	SB	CS	AVG/OBP/SLG	TAv	BABIP	BRR	FRAA	WARP
2011	SLC	AAA	22	396	49	24	5	4	50	22	56	15	8	.292/.337/.419	.263	.333	-2	2B(44): 7.0, CF(16): -0.7	1.4
2011	ANA	MLB	22	56	2	3	1	0	5	2	8	0	0	.154/.182/.250	.167	.178	-1.2	2B(14): -1.0, LF(8): 0.0	-0.7
2012	SLC	AAA	23	83	11	6	2	0	12	3	6	1	0	.273/.289/.403	.231	.284	0.7	2B(8): -0.3, 3B(6): 0.8	0.1
2012	TUC	AAA	23	51	6	1	0	1	6	1	6	3	0	.286/.300/.367	.276	.310	0.2	2B(5): -0.4, SS(3): 0.2	0.2
2012	SDN	MLB	23	300	35	15	5	5	32	17	42	8	4	.240/.282/.385	.243	.265	2.6	2B(52): -3.3, LF(27): 0.7	0.3
2013	SDN	MLB	24	396	35	14	4	5	32	22	57	4	2	.236/.282/.337	.226	.267	2.2	CF(87): 1.6, 2B(23): 0.7	0.4
2014	SDN	MLB	25	369	39	16	3	5	29	18	58	7	3	.237/.277/.347	.233	.260	0.3	2B 1, CF -0	0.4

When a punchless backup middle infielder inhabits center field and finishes second on the team in games played, you might have a problem. Amarista hits like Aurelio Rodríguez and often engages evasive maneuver pattern delta five when chasing fly balls. The Little Ninja runs well but is not a basestealing threat. Already hard to see at 5-foot-8, he disappeared in the second half, hitting just .218/.276/.259. Amarista is best suited to second base and, the occasional spectacular diving catch to rob Juan Uribe of extra bases notwithstanding, shouldn't be given much time in the outfield. He and his career .275 OBP also shouldn't be given 140 plate appearances in the two hole again.

Kyle Blanks 1B

Born: 9/11/1986 Age: 27
Bats: R Throws: R Height: 6' 6"
Weight: 265 Breakout: 7%
Improve: 47% Collapse: 6%
Attrition: 15% MLB: 89%

Comparables:
Nelson Cruz, Shin-Soo Choo, Todd Linden

YEAR	TEAM	LVL	AGE	PA	R	2B	3B	HR	RBI	BB	SO	SB	CS	AVG/OBP/SLG	TAv	BABIP	BRR	FRAA	WARP
2011	SAN	AA	24	201	33	16	3	4	27	17	41	3	0	.282/.353/.475	.282	.341	0.2	1B(22): 1.4, LF(1): 0.2	0.6
2011	TUC	AAA	24	152	36	12	2	11	35	16	37	0	1	.351/.421/.716	.315	.414	0	1B(18): -0.9, LF(7): -0.1	0.7
2011	SDN	MLB	24	190	21	7	1	7	26	16	51	2	0	.229/.300/.406	.273	.281	0.5	LF(37): -0.3, 1B(13): 0.0	0.8
2012	SDN	MLB	25	6	0	0	0	0	0	1	2	0	0	.200/.333/.200	.228	.333	-0.2	1B(1): -0.0, LF(1): -0.0	0.0
2013	TUC	AAA	26	46	8	3	0	1	4	6	10	0	0	.237/.370/.395	.271	.296	-0.5	1B(7): 0.0, LF(5): 0.2	0.2
2013	SDN	MLB	26	308	31	14	0	8	35	21	85	1	1	.243/.305/.379	.256	.317	1.5	RF(37): 2.2, LF(35): -1.2	0.7
2014	SDN	MLB	27	250	28	10	1	8	31	23	72	1	0	.232/.315/.401	.270	.300	-0.3	1B 1, LF -1	0.6

On June 16th, Blanks pounded his eighth homer of the season, against Arizona's David Hernandez. At the end of that game, his line stood at .281/.365/.511. He went homerless the rest of the way, hitting .207/.243/.255 while striking out more than a third of the time. The fact that right-handers turned Blanks into Humberto Quintero reduces his future utility. So does an assortment of injuries—right foot, right elbow, left shoulder, or last year's left Achilles tendon—that have caused him to miss an average of 77 games per year since 2009. He's a guy at the right (a/k/a wrong) end of the defensive spectrum who kills lefties when healthy, which is never.

Everth Cabrera SS

Born: 11/17/1986 Age: 27
Bats: B Throws: R Height: 5' 10"
Weight: 190 Breakout: 3%
Improve: 52% Collapse: 8%
Attrition: 10% MLB: 97%

Comparables:
Erick Aybar, Jason Bartlett, Ronny Cedeno

YEAR	TEAM	LVL	AGE	PA	R	2B	3B	HR	RBI	BB	SO	SB	CS	AVG/OBP/SLG	TAv	BABIP	BRR	FRAA	WARP
2011	TUC	AAA	24	278	52	12	4	2	15	29	40	29	8	.297/.370/.402	.265	.346	2.5	SS(48): 3.7	1.7
2011	SDN	MLB	24	9	1	0	0	0	0	1	3	2	0	.125/.222/.125	.324	.200	0.2	SS(2): 0.0	0.1
2012	TUC	AAA	25	159	27	9	1	0	15	12	28	15	0	.333/.389/.410	.300	.414	2.7	SS(17): -2.6, 3B(10): -0.5	1.4
2012	SDN	MLB	25	449	49	19	3	2	24	43	110	44	4	.246/.324/.324	.247	.336	5.8	SS(111): 7.0, 2B(6): -0.1	2.9
2013	SDN	MLB	26	435	54	15	5	4	31	41	69	37	12	.283/.355/.381	.280	.337	2.2	SS(95): 0.7	3.1
2014	SDN	MLB	27	432	57	16	4	3	29	39	91	34	8	.252/.324/.341	.253	.310	4	SS 2, 2B -0	2.2

While speeding toward an apparent second straight NL stolen base title, Cabrera drew a season-ending suspension in August as part of the Biogenesis scandal. His success rate declined, especially after a left hamstring strain derailed him following his debut as the Padres' annual "Sir Not Appearing in This All-Star Game" contest winner. His post-injury .568 OPS didn't impress either. The switch-hitter, whose game centers on reaching base and running wild, made better contact in 2013 and raised his OPS against left-handers by more than 400 points. Cabrera is a capable shortstop, occasionally making spectacular plays and last year improving his reliability. If he stays clean—and the tears at his unscripted press conference moved more than one jaded reporter—he'll be a valuable contributor again.

Chris Denorfia RF

Born: 7/15/1980 Age: 33
Bats: R Throws: R Height: 6' 0"
Weight: 195 Breakout: 1%
Improve: 32% Collapse: 6%
Attrition: 7% MLB: 86%

Comparables:
Jody Gerut, Kevin Mench, Joe Inglett

YEAR	TEAM	LVL	AGE	PA	R	2B	3B	HR	RBI	BB	SO	SB	CS	AVG/OBP/SLG	TAv	BABIP	BRR	FRAA	WARP
2011	TUC	AAA	30	20	0	1	0	0	0	3	4	0	0	.118/.250/.176	.243	.154	0.2	CF(1): -0.0, RF(1): -0.0	0.0
2011	SDN	MLB	30	340	38	13	2	5	19	28	49	11	6	.277/.337/.381	.263	.314	0.7	RF(62): 0.8, LF(33): 0.3	1.0
2012	SDN	MLB	31	382	56	19	6	8	36	27	52	13	5	.293/.345/.451	.284	.323	2.5	RF(79): -4.3, LF(53): 0.8	1.9
2013	SDN	MLB	32	520	67	21	2	10	47	42	84	11	0	.279/.337/.395	.273	.319	3.9	RF(97): 1.3, LF(58): -0.1	2.7
2014	SDN	MLB	33	461	56	19	3	9	42	33	74	12	3	.265/.318/.386	.266	.300	0.8	RF 0, CF 0	1.5

For the fourth straight season, Denorfia set a new career-high in plate appearances. Injuries to other Padres outfielders forced him to face more righties (he hits them like Yorvit Torrealba, while he hits southpaws like Victor Martinez) than the year before, dragging his numbers down a bit. Still, when everything falls apart, it's good to have duct tape. Denorfia pops the occasional homer, runs well, plays solid defense on the corners and is serviceable in center if he doesn't stay there too long. His all-out style ("gritty" is not always a euphemism for "useless") has endeared him to fans in San Diego, leaving them with more important arguments, like whether his nickname should be Deno or Norf.

Logan Forsythe 2B	YEAR	TEAM	LVL	AGE	PA	R	2B	3B	HR	RBI	BB	SO	SB	CS	AVG/OBP/SLG	TAv	BABIP	BRR	FRAA	WARP
Born: 1/14/1987 Age: 27	2011	TUC	AAA	24	218	41	12	0	8	34	33	50	8	4	.326/.445/.528	.321	.413	1.8	2B(23): -1.3, 3B(14): -0.3	1.8
Bats: R Throws: R Height: 6' 1''	2011	SDN	MLB	24	169	12	9	1	0	12	12	33	3	1	.213/.281/.287	.221	.269	0.7	3B(26): 1.4, 2B(23): -2.2	-0.2
Weight: 195 Breakout: 1%	2012	TUC	AAA	25	74	12	2	3	1	9	13	18	3	0	.259/.419/.448	.308	.359	-0.5	3B(7): 0.8, SS(5): 0.5	0.8
Improve: 56% Collapse: 6%	2012	SDN	MLB	25	350	45	13	3	6	26	28	57	8	2	.273/.343/.390	.270	.316	0	2B(81): -3.0, SS(5): 0.1	1.0
Attrition: 12% MLB: 94%	2013	TUC	AAA	26	33	6	2	2	2	5	8	7	0	0	.360/.515/.840	.378	.438	0.6	SS(4): -0.3, 2B(3): -0.1	0.6
Comparables:	2013	SDN	MLB	26	243	22	6	1	6	19	19	54	6	1	.214/.281/.332	.234	.255	1.5	2B(34): 0.9, 3B(11): 0.2	0.2
Neil Walker, Jed Lowrie, Brandon Phillips	2014	SDN	MLB	27	263	33	10	2	6	24	24	55	6	2	.243/.323/.374	.265	.290	0.4	2B -2, 3B 0	0.9

Forsythe's minor-league on-base skills haven't materialized at the highest level. Injuries are part of the problem. He didn't make his debut until June 10th thanks to plantar fasciitis in his right foot, after surgery on his *left* foot cost him a good chunk of the previous season. Forsythe hit .300/.351/.471 in his first 18 games back, then .173/.248/.267 the rest of the way. He is a solid third baseman, an adequate second baseman and stretched at shortstop or in the outfield. If he stays healthy (he was still having trouble with the foot in September) and pushes his OBP up near 2012 levels, he has value, but he's got work to do before anyone crowns him the new Vance Law.

Reymond Fuentes CF	YEAR	TEAM	LVL	AGE	PA	R	2B	3B	HR	RBI	BB	SO	SB	CS	AVG/OBP/SLG	TAv	BABIP	BRR	FRAA	WARP
Born: 2/12/1991 Age: 23	2011	LEL	A+	20	573	84	15	9	5	45	44	117	41	14	.275/.342/.369	.267	.347	1.2	CF(24): -3.6	0.2
Bats: L Throws: L Height: 6' 0''	2012	SAN	AA	21	541	53	20	4	4	34	52	133	35	9	.218/.301/.302	.236	.292	3.3	CF(134): 7.8	1.4
Weight: 160 Breakout: 1%	2013	SAN	AA	22	403	56	21	2	6	35	41	71	29	10	.316/.396/.441	.324	.381	1.2	RF(41): -5.2, LF(26): 2.0	3.2
Improve: 6% Collapse: 2%	2013	TUC	AAA	22	67	17	4	0	0	8	10	10	6	1	.418/.515/.491	.357	.511	1.4	CF(14): 1.9	1.2
Attrition: 2% MLB: 13%	2013	SDN	MLB	22	36	4	0	0	0	1	3	16	3	0	.152/.222/.152	.145	.294	0.8	CF(15): 0.2, LF(2): 0.1	-0.2
Comparables:	2014	SDN	MLB	23	250	30	9	1	3	17	20	64	14	4	.231/.297/.321	.234	.300	1.3	CF 1, RF -1	0.1
Franklin Gutierrez, Xavier Avery, Trevor Crowe																				

Coming off a miserable Double-A campaign in 2012, Fuentes focused on improving his two-strike approach and keeping the ball on the ground to exploit his speed. It worked. He made better contact and became a top-of-the-order threat. Despite repeating the level, he was still young for the Texas League. Although his plate discipline took a break in July after he missed 17 games with a hamstring injury and again in a late-season cameo with the big club, overall it was better than in the past. Fuentes cited confidence and mental toughness as keys to his newfound success. The lack of punch suggests a future spare outfielder, but his improvement at such a young age hints at the possibility of something more.

Yasmani Grandal C	YEAR	TEAM	LVL	AGE	PA	R	2B	3B	HR	RBI	BB	SO	SB	CS	AVG/OBP/SLG	TAv	BABIP	BRR	FRAA	WARP
Born: 11/8/1988 Age: 25	2011	BAK	A+	22	251	47	14	0	10	40	41	57	0	0	.296/.410/.510	.305	.359	-0.2	C(38): -0.1	2.2
Bats: B Throws: R Height: 6' 2''	2011	CAR	AA	22	172	20	15	0	4	26	13	39	0	1	.301/.360/.474	.225	.377	-1.4	C(13): -0.3	0.1
Weight: 215 Breakout: 3%	2012	TUC	AAA	23	235	40	18	0	6	35	37	35	0	0	.335/.443/.521	.317	.381	0.5	C(45): -1.3	2.3
Improve: 40% Collapse: 3%	2012	SDN	MLB	23	226	28	7	1	8	36	31	39	0	0	.297/.394/.469	.317	.333	-3.2	C(55): 0.3	2.0
Attrition: 18% MLB: 83%	2013	TUC	AAA	24	38	3	3	0	0	2	2	8	0	0	.306/.342/.389	.262	.393	-1.5	C(5): 0.2	-0.1
Comparables:	2013	SDN	MLB	24	108	13	8	0	1	9	18	18	0	0	.216/.352/.341	.260	.257	0.9	C(26): 0.8, 1B(1): -0.0	0.6
Chris Iannetta, Buster Posey, Jeff Clement	2014	SDN	MLB	25	250	27	11	0	6	29	32	53	0	0	.252/.350/.396	.279	.300	-0.5	C 0, 1B -0	1.6

Grandal's season started with a 50-game PED suspension and ended with a torn right ACL that required reconstructive surgery in August. Two inflamed tendons in his left middle finger kept Grandal from swinging a bat until just before spring training, which contributed to a slow start after the suspension. He postd a .505 OPS in his first 13 games and an .883 OPS in his last 15. Those are tiny samples, but his bat appeared to be coming around before the knee injury. Grandal blends power and patience from both sides of the plate, but is still a bit rough behind it. Assuming his rehab goes well, he should be ready in April.

Jedd Gyorko 2B

Born: 9/23/1988 Age: 25
Bats: R Throws: R Height: 5' 10''
Weight: 210 Breakout: 3%
Improve: 39% Collapse: 11%
Attrition: 22% MLB: 88%

Comparables:
Danny Espinosa, Neil Walker, Wladimir Balentien

YEAR	TEAM	LVL	AGE	PA	R	2B	3B	HR	RBI	BB	SO	SB	CS	AVG/OBP/SLG	TAv	BABIP	BRR	FRAA	WARP
2011	LEL	A+	22	382	78	35	2	18	74	38	64	11	3	.365/.429/.638	.340	.408	0.9	3B(7): -0.4	0.8
2011	SAN	AA	22	265	41	12	0	7	40	26	50	1	0	.288/.358/.428	.274	.337	0.5	3B(40): 2.3	1.5
2012	SAN	AA	23	149	18	4	0	6	17	17	27	1	1	.262/.356/.431	.272	.289	1.2	3B(17): 0.3, 2B(17): 0.3	0.8
2012	TUC	AAA	23	408	62	24	0	24	83	34	68	4	3	.328/.380/.588	.321	.344	-1	3B(56): -0.4, 2B(30): 4.1	4.4
2013	SDN	MLB	24	525	62	26	0	23	63	33	123	1	1	.249/.301/.444	.264	.287	0.2	2B(117): -5.6, 3B(13): 0.6	1.3
2014	SDN	MLB	25	456	54	20	1	20	64	31	104	3	1	.256/.309/.449	.279	.290	-0.7	2B -1, 3B 0	2.2

Gyorko led the Padres and all rookies in homers despite hitting none in April and missing 37 games, mostly due to a right groin strain incurred in June. Among rookie second basemen in baseball history, only Joe Gordon (1938) and Dan Uggla (2006) hit more home runs. Although defensive metrics don't love the garden gnome-shaped former third baseman, his soft hands and improving footwork should keep him at second for now. He showed passable plate discipline in the minors, but his hacktastic approach in San Diego produced a vintage Khalil Greene season. In his first 53 games back from injury, Gyorko fanned 60 times against four walks. Recognizing the need to adjust, he walked nine times in his final 12 games, restoring hope for the future.

Chase Headley 3B

Born: 5/9/1984 Age: 30
Bats: B Throws: R Height: 6' 2''
Weight: 220 Breakout: 1%
Improve: 33% Collapse: 2%
Attrition: 22% MLB: 97%

Comparables:
Eric Chavez, Morgan Ensberg, Ron Cey

YEAR	TEAM	LVL	AGE	PA	R	2B	3B	HR	RBI	BB	SO	SB	CS	AVG/OBP/SLG	TAv	BABIP	BRR	FRAA	WARP
2011	SDN	MLB	27	439	43	28	1	4	44	52	92	13	2	.289/.374/.399	.291	.368	0.3	3B(107): -9.0	1.9
2012	SDN	MLB	28	699	95	31	2	31	115	86	157	17	6	.286/.376/.498	.319	.337	-2	3B(159): -6.3, 1B(1): -0.0	5.8
2013	SDN	MLB	29	600	59	35	2	13	50	67	142	8	4	.250/.347/.400	.278	.319	-4.1	3B(140): -8.1	1.6
2014	SDN	MLB	30	585	68	28	1	14	66	60	130	12	4	.262/.342/.405	.280	.320	0	3B -9, 1B -0	1.8

Headley missed the season's first two weeks with a fractured left thumb sustained in spring training, then played all year with a torn meniscus in his left knee that required surgery in October. He said the knee "wasn't a huge issue," but damage to that joint can make it difficult to pivot, which is a necessary element of hitting. Injuries can also cause people to compensate in ways they aren't aware of until later, which may help explain his late-August lower back stiffness. Despite his physical problems, Headley posted decent numbers. Last year we claimed that "20-25 homers is a more reasonable baseline than the previously established 10-15," and he responded with 13. Assuming he is healthy, expect that number to rise in 2014.

Austin Hedges C

Born: 8/18/1992 Age: 21
Bats: R Throws: R Height: 6' 1''
Weight: 190 Breakout: 1%
Improve: 6% Collapse: 0%
Attrition: 4% MLB: 6%

Comparables:
J.R. Murphy, Bryan Anderson, Hector Sanchez

YEAR	TEAM	LVL	AGE	PA	R	2B	3B	HR	RBI	BB	SO	SB	CS	AVG/OBP/SLG	TAv	BABIP	BRR	FRAA	WARP
2012	FTW	A	19	373	44	28	0	10	56	23	62	14	9	.279/.334/.451	.286	.312	-1	C(94): 0.3	3.2
2013	LEL	A+	20	266	34	22	1	4	30	22	45	5	4	.270/.343/.425	.279	.314	0.7	C(61): 0.9	2.2
2013	SAN	AA	20	75	4	3	0	0	8	6	9	3	1	.224/.297/.269	.225	.259	0.4	C(18): 0.0	0.1
2014	SDN	MLB	21	250	22	11	0	4	23	13	55	3	2	.222/.270/.328	.226	.270	-0.4	C 0	0.3

No qualifiers needed: Hedges is the best defensive catcher in the minors. His strong arm, quick release, ability to frame and block pitches, and game-calling prowess have some observers saying he could catch in the big leagues right now. On offense, Hedges held his own last year but showed less power than in his 2012 full-season debut. Missing a month in May after getting hit in the hand with a fastball may be to blame. He has worked extensively with three-time Gold Glove catcher Brad Ausmus and shown a swoon-worthy desire to improve, saying after his August promotion to Double-A, "I'm not happy with any part of my game. I want every part of my game to get better."

Nick Hundley C

Born: 9/8/1983 Age: 30
Bats: R Throws: R Height: 6' 1''
Weight: 195 Breakout: 0%
Improve: 39% Collapse: 6%
Attrition: 15% MLB: 94%

Comparables:
Mike Macfarlane, Ozzie Virgil, Dave Nilsson

YEAR	TEAM	LVL	AGE	PA	R	2B	3B	HR	RBI	BB	SO	SB	CS	AVG/OBP/SLG	TAv	BABIP	BRR	FRAA	WARP
2011	SAN	AA	27	29	1	0	0	0	1	6	10	0	0	.174/.345/.174	.259	.308	-0.2	C(4): -0.0	0.0
2011	SDN	MLB	27	308	34	16	5	9	29	22	74	1	1	.288/.347/.477	.309	.362	-0.1	C(76): -0.1	3.3
2012	TUC	AAA	28	47	4	1	1	0	7	4	9	0	1	.190/.255/.262	.178	.235	-0.3	C(13): -0.1	-0.2
2012	SDN	MLB	28	225	14	7	1	3	22	15	56	0	3	.157/.219/.245	.173	.196	0.4	C(56): 1.8	-0.5
2013	SDN	MLB	29	408	35	19	0	13	44	26	98	1	0	.233/.290/.389	.251	.279	-1.9	C(112): 0.5	0.9
2014	SDN	MLB	30	352	36	16	2	9	38	26	86	1	2	.230/.292/.377	.250	.280	-0.8	C 1	1.3

Recovered from August 2012 right knee surgery, Hundley resumed being Jason LaRue without the defense. He set a career high in homers (Petco Park's new dimensions made no difference; he is tied for fifth all-time in home runs there) while exhibiting his trademark awful plate discipline. Behind the dish, he has become a good field general but is average at throwing out would-be thieves and poor at framing pitches, according to Max Marchi's model. Hundley's competitiveness may delay his inevitable transition to backup catcher, but unless he somehow rediscovers 2011's magic, that time is drawing near.

Ryan Jackson   SS

Born: 5/10/1988 Age: 26
Bats: R Throws: R Height: 6' 3"
Weight: 180 Breakout: 2%
Improve: 13% Collapse: 6%
Attrition: 10% MLB: 25%

Comparables:
Angel Sanchez, Oswaldo Navarro, Sean Kazmar

YEAR	TEAM	LVL	AGE	PA	R	2B	3B	HR	RBI	BB	SO	SB	CS	AVG/OBP/SLG	TAv	BABIP	BRR	FRAA	WARP
2011	SFD	AA	23	599	65	34	3	11	73	44	91	2	0	.278/.334/.415	.248	.314	-0.7	SS(56): -3.1	0.2
2012	MEM	AAA	24	503	60	23	1	10	47	43	75	2	0	.272/.334/.396	.261	.306	1.6	SS(102): -6.5, 2B(13): -1.4	1.2
2012	SLN	MLB	24	18	2	0	0	0	0	1	3	0	0	.118/.167/.118	.073	.143	0.4	2B(8): 0.3	-0.3
2013	MEM	AAA	25	510	49	19	1	3	34	52	91	9	0	.278/.352/.346	.265	.338	-0.4	SS(72): 2.5, 3B(32): -3.3	2.0
2013	SLN	MLB	25	7	0	0	0	0	0	0	2	0	0	.000/.000/.000	.012	.000	0	3B(3): -0.1, 2B(2): 0.0	-0.2
2014	SDN	MLB	26	250	25	9	1	3	20	19	49	1	0	.236/.295/.324	.235	.280	-0.2	SS -1, 3B -1	0.1

Ryan Jackson is Pete Kozma without the publicist, which means that, when the problem is Pete Kozma, the answer sure as heck isn't Ryan Jackson. The Cardinals let him loose on waivers in November, and after a connecting flight in Houston he ended up traded to San Diego. His best bet as a Padre is to muscle in on Logan Forsythe's utility turf, and the easiest way to do that is to hit. Easy being, of course, relative.

Travis Jankowski   CF

Born: 6/15/1991 Age: 23
Bats: L Throws: R Height: 6' 2"
Weight: 190 Breakout: 1%
Improve: 2% Collapse: 1%
Attrition: 2% MLB: 4%

Comparables:
Derrick Robinson, Kevin Kiermaier, Darin Mastroianni

YEAR	TEAM	LVL	AGE	PA	R	2B	3B	HR	RBI	BB	SO	SB	CS	AVG/OBP/SLG	TAv	BABIP	BRR	FRAA	WARP
2012	FTW	A	21	256	32	10	4	1	23	13	44	17	7	.282/.318/.370	.244	.337	3.1	CF(58): 3.5	1.0
2013	LEL	A+	22	556	89	19	6	1	38	54	96	71	14	.286/.356/.355	.281	.350	10.4	CF(117): 16.0	5.3
2014	SDN	MLB	23	250	28	8	1	1	14	15	56	16	4	.225/.272/.283	.214	.290	1.8	CF 5	0.3

Jankowski spent his full-season debut leading the California League in stolen bases by 20. Sure, he didn't have the Billy Hamilton Show to compete with, but Jankowski's speed is legitimate, as are his aggressiveness on the bases (last spring he startled spectators and the other team by scoring from second on a routine grounder to first in a back-field game) and ability to play center field. Unfortunately, though his OBP teetered on the edge of respectability, he has Jason Tyner's power game. Jankowski's season ended a couple of weeks early thanks to a sprained ankle that wasn't considered serious. If the bat improves enough to keep defenses honest, he could be a Dave Roberts-type table-setter. Otherwise, he's a fourth outfielder.

Rymer Liriano   RF

Born: 6/20/1991 Age: 23
Bats: R Throws: R Height: 6' 0"
Weight: 225 Breakout: 2%
Improve: 4% Collapse: 0%
Attrition: 1% MLB: 6%

Comparables:
Scott Van Slyke, Andrew Lambo, Matt Joyce

YEAR	TEAM	LVL	AGE	PA	R	2B	3B	HR	RBI	BB	SO	SB	CS	AVG/OBP/SLG	TAv	BABIP	BRR	FRAA	WARP
2011	FTW	A	20	519	81	30	8	12	62	47	95	65	20	.319/.383/.499	.325	.373	-0.6	RF(65): -4.3, CF(11): 1.9	2.9
2011	LEL	A+	20	61	8	1	1	0	6	6	13	1	1	.127/.213/.182	.149	.167	0		0.0
2012	LEL	A+	21	314	41	22	2	5	41	21	69	22	7	.298/.360/.443	.288	.374	-2.1	RF(66): -2.7, CF(3): 0.0	1.0
2012	SAN	AA	21	206	24	10	2	3	20	20	50	10	1	.251/.335/.377	.251	.331	1.9	RF(49): 0.7, CF(9): -0.6	0.5
2014	SDN	MLB	23	250	29	10	1	5	23	15	66	15	5	.230/.282/.347	.236	.300	1.5	RF -2, CF 0	-0.1

Liriano was supposed to fine-tune his game in the high minors last year and compete for a big-league job this spring. Unfortunately, after an impressive Arizona Fall League showing, he blew out his elbow in December 2012 and spent the summer recovering from Tommy John surgery. A stocky kid who figures to have more power and less speed as he gets older, Liriano also features a strong arm (or at least he did before the injury), with his overall game eliciting comparisons to Raul Mondesi. He could arrive in the second half of 2014, although initial struggles are to be expected. If the elbow is healthy and he keeps his weight in check, Liriano will be an impact player soon.

Cameron Maybin   CF

Born: 4/4/1987 Age: 27
Bats: R Throws: R Height: 6' 3"
Weight: 205 Breakout: 7%
Improve: 53% Collapse: 3%
Attrition: 8% MLB: 93%

Comparables:
Dexter Fowler, Franklin Gutierrez, Drew Stubbs

YEAR	TEAM	LVL	AGE	PA	R	2B	3B	HR	RBI	BB	SO	SB	CS	AVG/OBP/SLG	TAv	BABIP	BRR	FRAA	WARP
2011	SDN	MLB	24	568	82	24	8	9	40	44	125	40	8	.264/.323/.393	.270	.331	7.2	CF(136): 7.5	3.6
2012	SDN	MLB	25	561	67	20	5	8	45	44	110	26	7	.243/.306/.349	.248	.293	2.7	CF(145): 4.5	1.5
2013	TUC	AAA	26	56	7	1	0	4	5	10	9	1	1	.261/.393/.543	.338	.242	-0.1	CF(13): 0.5	0.7
2013	SDN	MLB	26	57	7	1	0	1	5	4	9	4	1	.157/.232/.235	.158	.171	0.8	CF(14): -0.2	-0.4
2014	SDN	MLB	27	250	28	9	2	5	25	20	55	11	3	.249/.314/.375	.261	.300	1.2	CF 3	1.2

After hitting .091/.167/.121 through 10 games, Maybin landed on the disabled list with a right wrist impingement and stayed there for seven weeks. He then played a four-game series at Coors Field in June before returning to the DL with a season-ending torn posterior cruciate ligament in his left knee. The knee didn't require surgery, but the wrist—which had been bothering him for a couple of years—did. He'll be ready for spring training, albeit with considerable rust. Still, he's young and athletic enough to build on the dreams of 2011. The Padres have to hope he does: they owe him at least $21 million over the next three years.

Jace Peterson   SS

Born: 5/9/1990 Age: 24
Bats: L Throws: R Height: 6' 0''
Weight: 205 Breakout: 0%
Improve: 2% Collapse: 6%
Attrition: 14% MLB: 17%

Comparables:
Paul Janish, Alberto Gonzalez, Oswaldo Navarro

YEAR	TEAM	LVL	AGE	PA	R	2B	3B	HR	RBI	BB	SO	SB	CS	AVG/OBP/SLG	TAv	BABIP	BRR	FRAA	WARP
2011	EUG	A-	21	333	48	9	5	2	27	50	53	39	10	.243/.360/.333	.283	.290	3	SS(65): -2.9	2.1
2012	FTW	A	22	521	78	23	9	2	48	62	63	51	13	.286/.378/.392	.286	.328	5.8	SS(107): -4.4	3.5
2013	LEL	A+	23	496	78	17	13	7	66	54	58	42	10	.303/.382/.454	.314	.332	4.7	SS(106): -4.4	4.8
2014	SDN	MLB	24	250	29	8	2	2	16	22	46	13	4	.228/.299/.308	.232	.270	1.5	SS -3	0.2

Some see in Peterson a future utility infielder beating up on younger pitching in a hitter-friendly league. Others, such as Shawn Wooten, his manager at Lake Elsinore, see a legitimate shortstop with top-of-the-order skills. Peterson had no trouble against left-handed pitching last year, clearing a .900 OPS in more than 100 plate appearances. He also finished strong, hitting .332/.424/.526 from June to season's end. A former college defensive back, Peterson draws praise for his strike-zone judgment, intensity (growing up in Louisiana, he idolized Craig Biggio) and baserunning instincts. He may not be a star, but he will play in the big leagues.

Carlos Quentin   LF

Born: 8/28/1982 Age: 31
Bats: R Throws: R Height: 6' 2''
Weight: 240 Breakout: 0%
Improve: 42% Collapse: 1%
Attrition: 3% MLB: 96%

Comparables:
Brian Giles, Rico Carty, Billy Williams

YEAR	TEAM	LVL	AGE	PA	R	2B	3B	HR	RBI	BB	SO	SB	CS	AVG/OBP/SLG	TAv	BABIP	BRR	FRAA	WARP
2011	CHA	MLB	28	483	53	31	0	24	77	34	84	1	1	.254/.340/.499	.297	.261	-0.7	RF(102): -4.4	1.8
2012	SDN	MLB	29	340	44	21	0	16	46	36	41	0	1	.261/.374/.504	.317	.252	-1.3	LF(69): -3.3, RF(3): -0.4	2.0
2013	SDN	MLB	30	320	42	21	0	13	44	31	55	0	0	.275/.362/.493	.315	.297	-0.8	LF(69): -3.0	1.8
2014	SDN	MLB	31	308	38	15	1	13	44	27	51	1	0	.246/.337/.454	.294	.260	-0.6	LF -2, RF -1	1.3

Quentin is baseball's Wile E. Coyote, forever pursuing that elusive healthy season, only to be distracted by mysterious packages: "Buy Two Right Knee Surgeries, Get the Third Free"; "Acme Explosive Tennis Balls"; "Zack Greinke Ahead." Since joining his hometown Padres, Quentin has hit .268/.368/.498 with 29 homers in 660 plate appearances despite playing half his games at Petco Park. Unfortunately, it has taken him two seasons to get there, as the only thing he hurts more frequently than baseballs is himself. He has little speed and is a liability in left field. If the National League adopts the designated hitter rule and he avoids anvils, he'll be fine—until he runs off a cliff and looks down.

Hunter Renfroe   RF

Born: 1/28/1992 Age: 22
Bats: R Throws: R Height: 6' 1''
Weight: 200 Breakout: 0%
Improve: 0% Collapse: 0%
Attrition: 0% MLB: 0%

Comparables:
John Mayberry, Zoilo Almonte, Bryan Petersen

YEAR	TEAM	LVL	AGE	PA	R	2B	3B	HR	RBI	BB	SO	SB	CS	AVG/OBP/SLG	TAv	BABIP	BRR	FRAA	WARP
2013	FTW	A	21	72	6	5	0	2	7	4	23	0	0	.212/.268/.379	.230	.293	-1	RF(16): -1.2	-0.4
2013	EUG	A-	21	111	20	9	0	4	18	5	26	2	0	.308/.333/.510	.335	.368	1.1	RF(25): 1.2	1.4
2014	SDN	MLB	22	250	20	8	1	6	24	11	80	1	0	.196/.234/.307	.202	.260	-0.3	RF -2	-1.3

Renfroe was a first-team All-American at Mississippi State before being taken 13th overall in the 2013 draft. The former catcher also featured a mid- to upper-90s fastball as a reliever. He has been compared to Tom Brunansky, Nelson Cruz, Raul Mondesi and Tim Salmon. All of his tools rate above average, with power being the best. The one weakness in his pro debut was poor plate discipline, which could be exploited at higher levels unless he makes adjustments, but Renfroe's ability to hit tape-measure homers cannot be ignored. Neither can his hitting philosophy, as told to David Laurila: "I just try to hit the ball right in the face."

Seth Smith   RF

Born: 9/30/1982 Age: 31
Bats: L Throws: L Height: 6' 3''
Weight: 210 Breakout: 0%
Improve: 41% Collapse: 6%
Attrition: 9% MLB: 90%

Comparables:
Ryan Klesko, Benny Ayala, Will Clark

YEAR	TEAM	LVL	AGE	PA	R	2B	3B	HR	RBI	BB	SO	SB	CS	AVG/OBP/SLG	TAv	BABIP	BRR	FRAA	WARP
2011	COL	MLB	28	533	67	32	9	15	59	46	93	10	2	.284/.347/.483	.281	.320	2	RF(107): 0.3, LF(25): -0.5	1.8
2012	OAK	MLB	29	441	55	23	2	14	52	50	98	2	2	.240/.333/.420	.280	.285	1.6	LF(57): 2.0, RF(13): -0.6	2.0
2013	OAK	MLB	30	410	49	27	0	8	40	39	94	0	0	.253/.329/.391	.265	.320	1.1	LF(50): 2.3, RF(9): -0.6	1.2
2014	SDN	MLB	31	392	43	19	3	11	47	38	82	3	1	.247/.324/.411	.272	.290	-0.2	RF -1, LF 2	1.3

Bob Melvin continued to maximize Smith's opportunities by minimizing his exposure to lefties, but the Coors hangover persisted in his second season away from the thin air; a December trade to San Diego and Petco Park won't help. Smith was never considered a fast player, but the speed indicators were a bit worrisome, as he was the only Athletic with more than 400 plate appearances who failed to hit a triple or steal a base. His bat hit a valley over the summer, at which point Smith underwent a "touch-up" LASIK surgery to correct an astigmatism (he first had the procedure done in 2006), and the small-sample results upon his return were encouraging. He re-entered the lineup on

August 23rd, and from that point until the end of the regular season he hit .341/.431/.568 (albeit in just 51 plate appearances), casting a brighter light as Smith heads deeper into his 30s.

Cory Spangenberg 2B

Born: 3/16/1991 Age: 23
Bats: L Throws: R Height: 6' 0"
Weight: 195 Breakout: 2%
Improve: 11% Collapse: 1%
Attrition: 4% MLB: 16%

Comparables:
Eric Young, Emilio Bonifacio, Cesar Hernandez

YEAR	TEAM	LVL	AGE	PA	R	2B	3B	HR	RBI	BB	SO	SB	CS	AVG/OBP/SLG	TAv	BABIP	BRR	FRAA	WARP
2011	FTW	A	20	209	35	7	1	2	24	14	42	15	4	.286/.345/.365	.265	.359	1.7	2B(36): 1.8	1.0
2011	EUG	A-	20	121	20	10	0	1	20	31	15	10	4	.384/.545/.535	.393	.444	-1	2B(21): -0.8	1.6
2012	LEL	A+	21	426	53	12	8	1	40	26	72	27	9	.271/.324/.352	.254	.327	4.5	2B(96): 1.9	1.7
2013	LEL	A+	22	253	33	13	6	4	31	23	51	17	3	.296/.364/.460	.299	.368	1.5	2B(52): -7.2	1.3
2013	SAN	AA	22	319	35	10	3	2	20	17	61	19	11	.289/.331/.366	.270	.358	0.9	2B(75): 2.2, LF(1): -0.0	1.7
2014	SDN	MLB	23	250	27	8	2	2	16	13	58	9	3	.233/.276/.308	.222	.290	0.8	2B -1, LF -0	-0.1

After his 2012 campaign was derailed by a concussion, Spangenberg worked with former Phillies infielder Greg Legg during the offseason. It paid off, as he was named to the California League All-Star team (he missed the game thanks to a promotion to Double-A). At the plate, Spangenberg focused on "not swinging hard" and "not falling off-balance." He has soft hands at second base and runs well enough to be a table-setter, but his plate discipline could be better. He hung in against lefties and hit .349/.366/.465 over the final five weeks, finishing his season with a 15-game hitting streak. Another year in the minors should have him ready to compete for a big-league job in 2015.

Will Venable RF

Born: 10/29/1982 Age: 31
Bats: L Throws: L Height: 6' 2"
Weight: 210 Breakout: 1%
Improve: 42% Collapse: 9%
Attrition: 7% MLB: 94%

Comparables:
Ryan Church, Ryan Ludwick, Raul Mondesi

YEAR	TEAM	LVL	AGE	PA	R	2B	3B	HR	RBI	BB	SO	SB	CS	AVG/OBP/SLG	TAv	BABIP	BRR	FRAA	WARP
2011	TUC	AAA	28	64	14	3	2	3	11	5	13	3	0	.276/.328/.552	.270	.302	1	RF(14): -0.3	0.2
2011	SDN	MLB	28	411	49	14	7	9	44	31	92	26	3	.246/.310/.395	.277	.300	3.3	RF(91): 0.8, CF(14): -0.4	2.0
2012	SDN	MLB	29	470	62	26	8	9	45	41	94	24	6	.264/.335/.429	.278	.320	3.8	RF(114): 4.9, CF(21): -1.3	2.4
2013	SDN	MLB	30	515	64	22	8	22	53	29	118	22	6	.268/.312/.484	.281	.313	2.1	RF(97): 1.3, CF(80): -0.6	2.2
2014	SDN	MLB	31	475	67	19	5	15	50	36	116	23	5	.247/.309/.419	.266	.300	3.1	RF 2, CF -1	1.9

It's easy to conclude from Venable's 2013 numbers that he is a late bloomer who had a breakout season. He established career highs in many categories and raised his OPS against southpaws by 150 points. Most of Venable's damage came in July and August, when he hit .345/.380/.616. The other four months were less kind: .224/.273/.408. Whereas Venable usually gets hot for two weeks, last year he got hot for two months. If Chase Headley taught us anything a season earlier, it's that the difference between a breakout and a hot streak isn't always obvious. This may well be a new Venable, but let him do it for more than two months before betting the farm.

PITCHERS

Joaquin Benoit

Born: 7/26/1977 Age: 36
Bats: R Throws: R Height: 6' 3" Weight: 220
Breakout: 32% Improve: 49% Collapse: 39%
Attrition: 6% MLB: 80%

Comparables:
J.J. Putz, Rafael Betancourt, Tom Henke

YEAR	TEAM	LVL	AGE	W	L	SV	G	GS	IP	H	HR	BB	SO	BB9	SO9	GB%	BABIP	WHIP	ERA	FIP	FRA	WARP
2011	DET	MLB	33	4	3	2	66	0	61	47	5	17	63	2.5	9.3	40%	.268	1.05	2.95	3.00	3.78	1.0
2012	DET	MLB	34	5	3	2	73	0	71	59	14	22	84	2.8	10.6	38%	.269	1.14	3.68	4.22	4.20	0.8
2013	DET	MLB	35	4	1	24	66	0	67	47	5	22	73	3.0	9.8	44%	.256	1.03	2.01	2.90	3.09	1.3
2014	SDN	MLB	36	4	2	7	64	0	62²	45	6	18	73	2.6	10.5	39%	.276	1.00	2.34	2.98	2.54	1.5

In November 2010, after Benoit signed a three-year, $16.5 million deal, the spelling-challenged reporter Jon Heyman tweeted: "this is real players' market. exces are complaining buck & benoit were overpaid. in a month, they will look like steals." It took more than a month, but there's no doubt now that the Benoit signing was a bargain. He stayed healthy, showed no decline with age, and even settled into the closer role by the middle of 2013, saving 24 games in 26 attempts. Benoit can get strikeouts with all three of his pitches, and unlike many power closers doesn't show the wild or fly-ball tendencies that make ninth innings scary. In San Diego, he's an expensive set-up man, but with Huston Street hitting the disabled list in each of the last four years, odds are very good he'll get his chances in the ninth.

Brad Boxberger

Born: 5/27/1988 Age: 26
Bats: R Throws: R Height: 6' 2" Weight: 220
Breakout: 40% Improve: 54% Collapse: 34%
Attrition: 38% MLB: 61%

Comparables:
Al Alburquerque, Michael Kohn, Rich Thompson

YEAR	TEAM	LVL	AGE	W	L	SV	G	GS	IP	H	HR	BB	SO	BB9	SO9	GB%	BABIP	WHIP	ERA	FIP	FRA	WARP
2011	CAR	AA	23	1	2	4	30	0	34¹	16	2	13	57	3.4	14.9	58%	.360	0.84	1.31	1.88	2.32	0.4
2011	LOU	AAA	23	1	2	7	25	0	27²	16	2	15	36	4.9	11.7	51%	.204	1.12	2.93	3.20	4.27	0.2
2012	TUC	AAA	24	2	2	5	37	0	43¹	37	0	19	62	3.9	12.9	50%	.370	1.29	2.70	2.26	2.11	1.9
2012	SDN	MLB	24	0	0	0	24	0	27²	22	3	18	33	5.9	10.7	41%	.306	1.45	2.60	4.33	4.53	-0.1
2013	TUC	AAA	25	2	4	5	42	0	57¹	50	3	19	89	3.0	14.0	35%	.376	1.20	3.61	2.14	2.74	2.0
2013	SDN	MLB	25	0	1	1	18	0	22	19	3	13	24	5.3	9.8	48%	.302	1.45	2.86	4.38	4.77	-0.1
2014	SDN	MLB	26	3	2	1	47	3	70	54	6	31	84	3.9	10.8	45%	.305	1.21	3.32	3.30	3.61	0.8

Boxberger spent another year collecting Southwest frequent flier miles, being recalled to the big club once in every month except July. He misses bats but also the plate with a low-90s fastball and changeup around 80 mph, making him intriguing yet unreliable, like Scout in *To Kill a Mockingbird*. Manager Bud Black calls it a "swing-and-a-miss change" (which might help explain his extreme reverse platoon splits last year) but notes that sequencing has been a challenge. Then again, when you alternate between a month in the minors and a week in the majors, everything is a challenge. Boxberger has good bloodlines: father Rod, also a pitcher, was named College World Series Most Outstanding Player in 1978 for USC.

Andrew Cashner

Born: 9/11/1986 Age: 27
Bats: R Throws: R Height: 6' 6" Weight: 220
Breakout: 17% Improve: 59% Collapse: 29%
Attrition: 15% MLB: 87%

Comparables:
Clay Buchholz, Wade Davis, Ian Kennedy

YEAR	TEAM	LVL	AGE	W	L	SV	G	GS	IP	H	HR	BB	SO	BB9	SO9	GB%	BABIP	WHIP	ERA	FIP	FRA	WARP
2011	CHN	MLB	24	0	0	0	7	1	10²	3	1	4	8	3.4	6.8	60%	.083	0.66	1.69	3.84	4.29	0.1
2012	SAN	AA	25	2	0	0	3	3	14¹	10	0	3	22	1.9	13.8	50%	.357	0.91	1.88	1.26	1.51	0.7
2012	SDN	MLB	25	3	4	0	33	5	46¹	42	5	19	52	3.7	10.1	55%	.316	1.32	4.27	3.59	4.07	0.4
2013	SDN	MLB	26	10	9	0	31	26	175	151	12	47	128	2.4	6.6	53%	.279	1.13	3.09	3.32	4.18	1.8
2014	SDN	MLB	27	8	6	1	51	18	132	111	11	43	113	3.0	7.7	50%	.283	1.16	3.19	3.63	3.47	1.9

The questions entering 2013 were whether Cashner could handle a starter's workload and how effective he would be in that role. A right thumb injured while hunting required December 2012 surgery and forced him to the bullpen for the first three weeks. Once in the rotation, he proved durable, finishing second on the Padres in innings. His velocity and strikeouts dropped, both by design so he could work deeper into games. He lost his hard, biting slider for a while but found it in time to log at least seven innings in each of his last seven starts and turn opponents into Brendan Ryan over the final two months. Health is never a given with Cashner, but he looks like a second or third starter.

Zach Eflin

Born: 4/8/1994 Age: 20
Bats: R Throws: R Height: 6' 4" Weight: 200
Breakout: 100% Improve: 100% Collapse: 0%
Attrition: 0% MLB: 2%

Comparables:
Henderson Alvarez, Sean O'Sullivan, Rick Porcello

YEAR	TEAM	LVL	AGE	W	L	SV	G	GS	IP	H	HR	BB	SO	BB9	SO9	GB%	BABIP	WHIP	ERA	FIP	FRA	WARP
2013	FTW	A	19	7	6	0	22	22	118²	110	7	31	86	2.4	6.5	42%	.275	1.19	2.73	3.54	4.14	2.1
2014	SDN	MLB	20	3	4	1	30	9	85²	91	11	37	48	3.9	5.0	40%	.297	1.49	5.04	5.22	5.48	-0.9

After battling triceps tendinitis and mononucleosis in 2012, Eflin enjoyed a strong full-season debut as one of the Midwest League's youngest pitchers. His fastball and changeup are ahead of his breaking ball, with the latter's development determining his future role. Despite his fly-ball tendencies, Eflin didn't allow more than two homers in any single month. He was especially tough with runners on, lopping more than 60 points off his batting average against and 120 off his slugging. His below-average strikeout rate bears watching, although Fort Wayne manager José Valentín didn't seem concerned, saying after an Eflin playoff win, "He's not overpowering anybody, but he knows how to pitch."

Robbie Erlin

Born: 10/8/1990 Age: 23
Bats: R Throws: L Height: 5' 11" Weight: 190
Breakout: 32% Improve: 50% Collapse: 21%
Attrition: 56% MLB: 51%

Comparables:
Eric Hurley, Liam Hendriks, Joe Wieland

YEAR	TEAM	LVL	AGE	W	L	SV	G	GS	IP	H	HR	BB	SO	BB9	SO9	GB%	BABIP	WHIP	ERA	FIP	FRA	WARP
2011	MYR	A+	20	3	2	0	9	9	54²	25	7	5	62	0.8	10.2	33%	.177	0.55	2.14	3.07	3.75	0.6
2011	FRI	AA	20	5	2	0	11	10	66²	73	9	7	61	0.9	8.2	41%	.317	1.20	4.32	3.71	3.59	1.4
2011	SAN	AA	20	1	0	0	6	6	26	26	2	4	31	1.4	10.7	34%	.340	1.15	1.38	2.45	2.86	0.8
2012	SAN	AA	21	3	1	0	11	11	52¹	53	6	14	72	2.4	12.4	39%	.359	1.28	2.92	2.99	2.86	1.6
2013	TUC	AAA	22	8	3	0	20	20	99¹	125	11	34	84	3.1	7.6	37%	.353	1.60	5.07	4.38	4.51	1.8
2013	SDN	MLB	22	3	3	0	11	9	54²	53	6	15	40	2.5	6.6	39%	.290	1.24	4.12	3.81	4.47	0.3
2014	SDN	MLB	23	7	8	0	24	24	125²	120	15	35	106	2.5	7.6	38%	.301	1.23	3.89	3.95	4.23	0.7

Believers in short southpaws cite Mike Hampton, while skeptics choose Matt Chico. The truth with Erlin, whose stuff matches his stature, lies between those extremes. The fly-ball pitcher fared well at Petco Park as a rookie but got torched away from it in admittedly small samples. When his command isn't sharp, he will implode, as in his June 16th start against Reno when he allowed 11 runs in two innings. Remove that and his ERA at Triple-A drops from 5.07 to 4.17. But you can't remove that; it happened and you just accept such outings as part of his game. Erlin figures to be at the back of a big-league rotation in 2014 and should stay there awhile.

Max Fried
Born: 1/18/1994 Age: 20
Bats: L Throws: L Height: 6' 4" Weight: 185
Breakout: 0% Improve: 0% Collapse: 0%
Attrition: 0% MLB: 0%
Comparables:
J.C. Ramirez, Brad Hand, Jordan Walden

YEAR	TEAM	LVL	AGE	W	L	SV	G	GS	IP	H	HR	BB	SO	BB9	SO9	GB%	BABIP	WHIP	ERA	FIP	FRA	WARP
2013	FTW	A	19	6	7	0	23	23	118²	107	7	56	100	4.2	7.6	59%	.304	1.37	3.49	4.04	5.46	0.6
2014	SDN	MLB	20	3	3	1	37	6	86	86	10	47	59	4.9	6.2	52%	.301	1.55	5.14	5.16	5.58	-1.0

The first left-hander taken in the 2012 draft, Fried works with a low-90s fastball and powerful but inconsistent curve that works at a variety of speeds. His changeup is a little behind (e.g. 90 percent of extra-base hits he allowed last year were to right-handed hitters), but he is a good athlete with clean mechanics, and there is time to develop it. Although he didn't dominate the Midwest League, he more than held his own as one of the circuit's younger pitchers. Fried needs to get more reps at higher levels and tighten his command. If he does that and improves his ability to change speeds, he'll be a no. 2 or 3 starter.

Josh Johnson
Born: 1/31/1984 Age: 30
Bats: L Throws: R Height: 6' 7" Weight: 250
Breakout: 7% Improve: 38% Collapse: 30%
Attrition: 12% MLB: 94%
Comparables:
Adam Wainwright, John Lackey, Gavin Floyd

YEAR	TEAM	LVL	AGE	W	L	SV	G	GS	IP	H	HR	BB	SO	BB9	SO9	GB%	BABIP	WHIP	ERA	FIP	FRA	WARP
2011	FLO	MLB	27	3	1	0	9	9	60¹	39	2	20	56	3.0	8.4	50%	.247	0.98	1.64	2.61	3.38	0.8
2012	MIA	MLB	28	8	14	0	31	31	191¹	180	14	65	165	3.1	7.8	46%	.313	1.28	3.81	3.44	3.83	2.1
2013	TOR	MLB	29	2	8	0	16	16	81¹	105	15	30	83	3.3	9.2	48%	.359	1.66	6.20	4.65	4.92	0.4
2014	SDN	MLB	30	7	6	0	18	18	109¹	95	9	31	100	2.5	8.3	48%	.298	1.15	3.10	3.35	3.36	1.7

Here we go round the injury bush. Johnson lost half the year to arm trouble and knee tendinitis, and when he was healthy enough to pitch, the results were ugly: his hit, line-drive and homer rates were the highest he's ever had, the latter nearly triple his career clip due to an absurd 18.5 percent home-run-to-flyball rate (fourth highest among pitchers who threw 80 innings). Whether the solid-contact problem owes to Johnson's velocity drop or to sheer command problems from injury rust, his ineffectiveness removed the ace from his hand and his vestiges of hope for a big free-agent payday. He went to take the cure at Petco, where the Padres secured a cheap second-year option in case Johnson loses the first to major surgery.

Casey Kelly
Born: 10/4/1989 Age: 24
Bats: R Throws: R Height: 6' 3" Weight: 210
Breakout: 33% Improve: 77% Collapse: 14%
Attrition: 37% MLB: 46%
Comparables:
Alex Cobb, Chris Seddon, Justin Germano

YEAR	TEAM	LVL	AGE	W	L	SV	G	GS	IP	H	HR	BB	SO	BB9	SO9	GB%	BABIP	WHIP	ERA	FIP	FRA	WARP
2011	SAN	AA	21	11	6	0	27	27	142¹	153	8	46	105	2.9	6.6	55%	.289	1.40	3.98	3.77	4.96	1.3
2012	SAN	AA	22	0	1	0	3	3	16²	11	1	3	18	1.6	9.7	45%	.256	0.84	3.78	2.62	3.93	0.2
2012	TUC	AAA	22	0	0	0	2	2	12	12	0	0	14	0.0	10.5	52%	.387	1.00	2.25	1.58	2.31	0.5
2012	SDN	MLB	22	2	3	0	6	6	29	39	5	10	26	3.1	8.1	55%	.391	1.69	6.21	4.83	5.25	0.1
2014	SDN	MLB	24	2	3	0	7	7	37	37	4	13	26	3.1	6.4	48%	.303	1.35	4.40	4.37	4.79	-0.0

One of the Padres' most promising young arms, Kelly has worked fewer than 70 innings over the last two years thanks to elbow issues, missing all of 2013 while recovering from April Tommy John surgery. He doesn't overpower, but is athletic (he played shortstop in the low minors) and has good bloodlines (father Pat is a former minor-league catcher who had a cup of coffee with the Blue Jays in 1980). Kelly was playing catch by season's end and should see action in 2014. Assuming he picks up where he left off before surgery, his three-pitch arsenal makes him a potential mid-rotation candidate now and into the future.

Ian Kennedy
Born: 12/19/1984 Age: 29
Bats: R Throws: R Height: 6' 0" Weight: 190
Breakout: 19% Improve: 42% Collapse: 28%
Attrition: 7% MLB: 97%
Comparables:
John Patterson, Adam Eaton, Gil Meche

YEAR	TEAM	LVL	AGE	W	L	SV	G	GS	IP	H	HR	BB	SO	BB9	SO9	GB%	BABIP	WHIP	ERA	FIP	FRA	WARP
2011	ARI	MLB	26	21	4	0	33	33	222	186	19	55	198	2.2	8.0	38%	.273	1.09	2.88	3.19	3.68	2.9
2012	ARI	MLB	27	15	12	0	33	33	208¹	216	28	55	187	2.4	8.1	39%	.310	1.30	4.02	4.08	4.45	1.9
2013	ARI	MLB	28	3	8	0	21	21	124	128	18	48	108	3.5	7.8	38%	.301	1.42	5.23	4.57	4.84	0.0
2013	SDN	MLB	28	4	2	0	10	10	57¹	52	9	25	55	3.9	8.6	42%	.284	1.34	4.24	4.56	4.93	0.1
2014	SDN	MLB	29	10	9	0	27	27	166²	143	19	50	151	2.7	8.1	39%	.283	1.16	3.52	3.90	3.83	1.5

With a fastball that barely pushes into the 90s, Kennedy must be precise. His strikeout-to-walk ratio has slipped from 3.6 to 3.4 to 2.2 since 2011, reducing an already small margin for error. The fly-ball pitcher continued to see more of his offerings leave the yard (a career-high 9.6 percent of his flies went for homers). He struggled with runners on and was useless after 75 pitches, which hadn't been problems in the past. Kennedy owns a career 2.41 ERA in 71 innings at Petco Park, where even with the shorter fences he won't be punished as severely as elsewhere. If the command returns, he'll eat innings at the back of a rotation a la Jon Garland or Jason Marquis.

Cory Luebke
Born: 3/4/1985 Age: 29
Bats: R Throws: L Height: 6' 4" Weight: 205
Breakout: 19% Improve: 72% Collapse: 16%
Attrition: 17% MLB: 70%

Comparables:
Miguel Gonzalez, Marco Estrada, Dustin Nippert

YEAR	TEAM	LVL	AGE	W	L	SV	G	GS	IP	H	HR	BB	SO	BB9	SO9	GB%	BABIP	WHIP	ERA	FIP	FRA	WARP
2011	SDN	MLB	26	6	10	0	46	17	139²	105	12	44	154	2.8	9.9	39%	.277	1.07	3.29	2.89	3.39	1.8
2012	SDN	MLB	27	3	1	0	5	5	31	28	1	8	23	2.3	6.7	48%	.283	1.16	2.61	2.85	3.74	0.4
2014	SDN	MLB	29	2	2	0	10	5	38²	33	4	11	33	2.7	7.7	45%	.282	1.16	3.39	3.76	3.69	0.4

As a reminder that Tommy John surgery isn't the magic bullet some imagine it to be, Luebke missed the entire season while recovering from his May 2012 procedure. He suffered numerous setbacks along the way and had his left elbow re-examined in September, changing plans to have him pitch in winter ball. Last year's optimism about his future has been replaced by uncertainty. Although $10 million over the next two years (with reasonable options for 2016 and 2017) is a bargain for a pitcher of Luebke's caliber, this becomes less true if he can't actually throw a baseball.

Jason Marquis
Born: 8/21/1978 Age: 35
Bats: L Throws: R Height: 6' 1" Weight: 220
Breakout: 21% Improve: 52% Collapse: 20%
Attrition: 9% MLB: 83%

Comparables:
Shawn Estes, Brad Penny, Barry Zito

YEAR	TEAM	LVL	AGE	W	L	SV	G	GS	IP	H	HR	BB	SO	BB9	SO9	GB%	BABIP	WHIP	ERA	FIP	FRA	WARP
2011	ARI	MLB	32	0	1	0	3	3	11¹	22	3	4	5	3.2	4.0	59%	.413	2.29	9.53	6.88	6.36	-0.2
2011	WAS	MLB	32	8	5	0	20	20	120²	132	8	39	71	2.9	5.3	54%	.312	1.42	3.95	3.75	4.11	0.3
2012	NBR	AA	33	1	0	0	2	2	14	12	1	0	11	0.0	7.1	61%	.289	0.86	1.93	2.56	3.84	0.2
2012	MIN	MLB	33	2	4	0	7	7	34	52	9	14	12	3.7	3.2	55%	.352	1.94	8.47	7.28	7.74	-0.7
2012	SDN	MLB	33	6	7	0	15	15	93²	94	14	28	79	2.7	7.6	52%	.295	1.30	4.04	4.32	5.21	-0.3
2013	SDN	MLB	34	9	5	0	20	20	117²	111	18	68	72	5.2	5.5	53%	.262	1.52	4.05	5.62	6.48	-1.8
2014	SDN	MLB	35	6	7	0	19	19	107²	108	13	40	67	3.3	5.6	53%	.296	1.37	4.55	4.80	4.95	-0.4

Despite undergoing season-ending Tommy John surgery in July, Marquis tied for the team lead in home runs allowed. His ERA with the Padres didn't change from 2012 to 2013, but last year he did it while flinging baseballs all over the place (he had more strikeouts than walks in just seven of 20 starts). Marquis relies on hitters getting themselves out by chasing his tantalizing high-80s sinker and low-80s slider. He used to eat innings, but now he eats ... well, he doesn't eat innings anymore. Although he has expressed a desire to pitch again, his age, stuff and command point to a future as promising as a *Battlefield Earth* sequel.

Adys Portillo
Born: 12/20/1991 Age: 22
Bats: R Throws: R Height: 6' 2" Weight: 235
Breakout: 100% Improve: 100% Collapse: 0%
Attrition: 100% MLB: 1%

Comparables:
Bryan Morris, Chris Dwyer, John Ely

YEAR	TEAM	LVL	AGE	W	L	SV	G	GS	IP	H	HR	BB	SO	BB9	SO9	GB%	BABIP	WHIP	ERA	FIP	FRA	WARP
2011	FTW	A	19	3	11	0	23	20	82¹	89	10	55	97	6.0	10.6	40%	.359	1.75	7.11	4.70	5.51	0.0
2012	FTW	A	20	6	6	0	18	18	91²	54	3	45	81	4.4	8.0	43%	.212	1.08	1.87	3.58	4.34	1.2
2012	SAN	AA	20	2	5	0	8	8	35	34	4	25	26	6.4	6.7	45%	.286	1.69	7.20	5.85	7.01	-0.6
2014	SDN	MLB	22	2	3	0	8	8	34¹	34	4	22	25	5.8	6.4	43%	.299	1.65	5.50	5.35	5.98	-0.4

Hoping to build on a 2012 campaign that finally saw his results catch up to his stuff, Portillo instead spent most of the year on the disabled list. He hurt his right triceps in spring training and reaggravated the injury during a third rehab start that ended his season. His fastball runs in the mid-90s, but his command and secondary offerings need more work than the 45 batters he faced last summer gave him. Portillo did throw in the Arizona Fall League, but strikes remained an endangered species. If he stays healthy enough to improve his command, he could reach the big leagues, most likely as a reliever.

Kevin Quackenbush
Born: 11/28/1988 Age: 25
Bats: R Throws: R Height: 6' 3" Weight: 220
Breakout: 36% Improve: 57% Collapse: 31%
Attrition: 74% MLB: 44%

Comparables:
Donnie Joseph, C.C. Lee, Michael Schwimer

YEAR	TEAM	LVL	AGE	W	L	SV	G	GS	IP	H	HR	BB	SO	BB9	SO9	GB%	BABIP	WHIP	ERA	FIP	FRA	WARP
2011	FTW	A	22	1	1	9	18	0	21¹	12	0	6	38	2.5	16.0	47%	.375	0.84	0.84	0.64	1.28	0.7
2011	EUG	A-	22	1	0	9	17	0	20²	13	0	6	33	2.6	14.4	61%	.364	0.92	0.44	1.29	0.74	0.9
2012	LEL	A+	23	3	2	27	52	0	57²	42	1	22	70	3.4	10.9	50%	.301	1.11	0.94	2.76	2.91	1.6
2013	SAN	AA	24	2	0	13	29	0	31	16	1	10	46	2.9	13.4	53%	.246	0.84	0.29	1.77	2.14	0.9
2013	TUC	AAA	24	8	2	4	28	0	34	33	0	19	38	5.0	10.1	49%	.359	1.53	2.91	3.19	3.33	0.9
2014	SDN	MLB	25	3	1	2	51	0	58	46	5	25	65	3.9	10.0	48%	.300	1.22	3.14	3.46	3.41	0.8

Ignoring for now the duck in the room, while others were cracking wise, Quackenbush was busy abusing Double-A hitters before a mid-June promotion to Triple-A. Although he didn't fare as well at Tucson, he finished on a high note, with 10 straight scoreless outings. His fastball runs in the low 90s, but a deceptive delivery makes it appear faster (or, as some have said, "invisible"). Although he will continue to have doubters thanks to pedestrian velocity and underwhelming secondaries, he could see time in the big leagues this year. At some point, dismissing a career 1.15 ERA makes you look silly. Like a goose.

Clayton Richard
Born: 9/12/1983 Age: 30
Bats: L Throws: L Height: 6' 5'' Weight: 245
Breakout: 17% Improve: 51% Collapse: 16%
Attrition: 13% MLB: 89%
Comparables:
Mike Maroth, John Burkett, Tomo Ohka

YEAR	TEAM	LVL	AGE	W	L	SV	G	GS	IP	H	HR	BB	SO	BB9	SO9	GB%	BABIP	WHIP	ERA	FIP	FRA	WARP
2011	SDN	MLB	27	5	9	0	18	18	99²	104	8	38	53	3.4	4.8	50%	.308	1.42	3.88	4.18	4.64	0.0
2012	SDN	MLB	28	14	14	0	33	33	218²	228	31	42	107	1.7	4.4	54%	.276	1.23	3.99	4.66	5.74	-1.6
2013	TUC	AAA	29	0	1	0	2	2	12	10	0	0	12	0.0	9.0	72%	.312	0.83	2.25	1.82	2.21	0.4
2013	SDN	MLB	29	2	5	0	12	11	52²	65	13	21	24	3.6	4.1	54%	.290	1.63	7.01	6.51	7.45	-1.2
2014	SDN	MLB	30	4	5	0	15	15	81¹	81	10	25	48	2.7	5.3	51%	.293	1.31	4.34	4.66	4.72	-0.1

Concerns about Richard's ability to survive in a smaller Petco Park proved to be well founded, as his mild gopheritis exploded into a virulent strain of Ken Dixon Syndrome. He only ranked fourth among Padres pitchers in home runs allowed. Then again, his season ended in mid-June thanks to a shoulder that required surgery—his second in three years—a month later. The good news is that where his 2011 procedure repaired the labrum and rotator cuff, the most recent one involved shaving the clavicle to prevent future problems with the AC joint on top of his shoulder, and he should pitch this year. The bad news is that doctors can't shave points off his ERA.

Donn Roach
Born: 12/14/1989 Age: 24
Bats: R Throws: R Height: 6' 1'' Weight: 200
Breakout: 53% Improve: 63% Collapse: 26%
Attrition: 72% MLB: 26%
Comparables:
T.J. McFarland, Brandon Cumpton, Jon Huber

YEAR	TEAM	LVL	AGE	W	L	SV	G	GS	IP	H	HR	BB	SO	BB9	SO9	GB%	BABIP	WHIP	ERA	FIP	FRA	WARP
2011	CDR	A	21	5	5	2	45	0	70¹	73	1	20	68	2.6	8.7	57%	.286	1.32	3.45	2.59	3.45	0.2
2012	LEL	A+	22	5	1	0	8	7	46²	41	1	11	44	2.1	8.5	71%	.303	1.11	1.74	3.17	3.69	0.9
2012	SBR	A+	22	5	0	0	6	6	41²	36	1	3	29	0.6	6.3	79%	.271	0.94	2.16	3.02	4.41	0.5
2012	SAN	AA	22	1	1	0	4	3	17	9	0	8	5	4.2	2.6	70%	.167	1.00	1.59	4.28	6.11	-0.2
2013	SAN	AA	23	8	12	0	28	28	142²	138	7	40	77	2.5	4.9	65%	.281	1.25	3.53	3.56	4.93	0.3
2014	SDN	MLB	24	6	7	0	29	19	120	120	12	43	65	3.2	4.9	61%	.290	1.36	4.38	4.63	4.76	-0.2

Roach is a groundball machine whose low-90s two-seam fastball is backed by a curve and changeup. He pounds the bottom of the strike zone and resolves at-bats quickly, something he learned in the Angels organization. Former Padres hurler Randy Jones compared Roach to himself. His low strikeout rate and an ERA away from cavernous Wolff Stadium more than twice what it was at home are caution signs. Roach's lack of overpowering stuff relegates him to the back of the rotation at best, but after a blistering second half of 2013, he should compete for a big-league job this spring. If he doesn't win one then, he will be up during the season.

Joe Ross
Born: 5/21/1993 Age: 21
Bats: R Throws: R Height: 6' 3'' Weight: 185
Breakout: 0% Improve: 0% Collapse: 0%
Attrition: 100% MLB: 1%
Comparables:
Alex Cobb, Pedro Beato, Brett Marshall

YEAR	TEAM	LVL	AGE	W	L	SV	G	GS	IP	H	HR	BB	SO	BB9	SO9	GB%	BABIP	WHIP	ERA	FIP	FRA	WARP
2012	FTW	A	19	0	2	0	6	6	27¹	33	2	11	27	3.6	8.9	48%	.365	1.61	6.26	3.53	4.74	0.3
2012	EUG	A-	19	0	2	0	8	8	26²	16	1	9	28	3.0	9.4	62%	.238	0.94	2.03	2.84	4.25	0.4
2013	FTW	A	20	5	8	0	23	23	122¹	124	7	40	79	2.9	5.8	52%	.298	1.34	3.75	3.89	5.19	0.8
2014	SDN	MLB	21	5	9	0	24	24	95²	104	12	45	54	4.3	5.0	48%	.302	1.55	5.27	5.29	5.73	-0.9

Ross features a low- to mid-90s fastball, and while his slider and changeup are improving, his command of those pitches still wavers. Fort Wayne pitching coach Burt Hooton emphasized keeping the ball down in the zone and maintaining focus throughout the course of a start. Ross threw strikes in the first half and gave hitters trouble (.244 average against, 2.9 K/BB through June), but was less consistent from July to season's end (.296, 1.1). He is still learning his mechanics and how to make in-game adjustments. He cites older brother Tyson as a positive influence, particularly in the areas of workout and nutrition regimen. Ross projects as a mid-rotation starter, but it won't happen soon.

Tyson Ross
Born: 4/22/1987 Age: 27
Bats: R Throws: R Height: 6' 6'' Weight: 230
Breakout: 35% Improve: 75% Collapse: 15%
Attrition: 20% MLB: 87%
Comparables:
Jake Arrieta, Marc Rzepczynski, Jeff Niemann

YEAR	TEAM	LVL	AGE	W	L	SV	G	GS	IP	H	HR	BB	SO	BB9	SO9	GB%	BABIP	WHIP	ERA	FIP	FRA	WARP
2011	SAC	AAA	24	3	2	0	9	9	36²	52	5	22	34	5.4	8.3	47%	.382	2.02	7.61	5.50	6.18	0.1
2011	OAK	MLB	24	3	3	0	9	6	36	33	1	13	24	3.2	6.0	49%	.299	1.28	2.75	3.17	3.69	0.4
2012	SAC	AAA	25	6	2	0	15	13	78¹	69	4	29	64	3.3	7.4	61%	.283	1.25	2.99	3.92	4.47	1.0
2012	OAK	MLB	25	2	11	0	18	13	73¹	96	7	37	46	4.5	5.6	52%	.360	1.81	6.50	4.75	5.18	-0.1
2013	TUC	AAA	26	1	1	0	4	2	11²	12	0	6	9	4.6	6.9	60%	.343	1.54	4.63	3.57	4.08	0.3
2013	SDN	MLB	26	3	8	0	35	16	125	100	8	44	119	3.2	8.6	56%	.285	1.15	3.17	3.17	4.18	0.8
2014	SDN	MLB	27	6	6	0	35	18	118²	106	10	46	99	3.5	7.5	54%	.297	1.28	3.76	3.89	4.08	0.8

Ross' nickname should be "Slider" after the pitch that transformed him from abusable swingman in Oakland to abusive starter in San Diego. With a long, lean body and a 95 mph fastball, he looks like a pitcher. Thanks to pitching coach Darren Balsley, who helped him improve coordination of his upper and lower body last spring, in 2013 he started acting like one. Ross mixed his pitches more, although he is still learning to change speeds. After he hurt his left (non-throwing) shoulder while batting in April, the Padres retooled his swing to make it less violent. The shoulder required October surgery, but no lingering effects are anticipated. Ross looks like a solid mid-rotation option into the future.

Keyvius Sampson
Born: 1/6/1991 Age: 23
Bats: R Throws: R Height: 6' 0" Weight: 185
Breakout: 50% Improve: 66% Collapse: 22%
Attrition: 56% MLB: 28%

Comparables:
Jake Arrieta, Matt Harvey, Scott Barnes

YEAR	TEAM	LVL	AGE	W	L	SV	G	GS	IP	H	HR	BB	SO	BB9	SO9	GB%	BABIP	WHIP	ERA	FIP	FRA	WARP
2011	FTW	A	20	12	3	0	24	24	118	81	8	49	143	3.7	10.9	37%	.232	1.10	2.90	3.22	4.36	1.1
2012	SAN	AA	21	8	11	0	26	25	122¹	108	11	57	122	4.2	9.0	44%	.287	1.35	5.00	3.95	4.91	0.7
2013	SAN	AA	22	10	4	0	19	18	103¹	74	9	33	110	2.9	9.6	44%	.252	1.04	2.26	3.10	3.73	1.5
2013	TUC	AAA	22	2	3	0	9	9	38	44	5	29	25	6.9	5.9	36%	.328	1.92	7.11	6.33	6.88	-0.1
2014	SDN	MLB	23	7	8	0	24	24	119²	104	14	58	107	4.4	8.1	41%	.285	1.36	4.11	4.49	4.46	0.3

Sampson scuffled at Double-A in 2012, then started slowly again at Triple-A last year before returning to the Texas League a few weeks later. He worked with pitching coach Jimmy Jones to add a slider and improve his fastball command, both of which helped lead to better results, including three double-digit-strikeout games in less than a month. As Sampson told the *San Antonio Express-News* after fanning a career-high 12 batters against Tulsa, "My slider is picking up, and I am locating my fastball better. I'm attacking the zone more and not messing around." If he keeps doing that, he will find himself in the middle of a big-league rotation soon, perhaps as early as this season.

Burch Smith
Born: 4/12/1990 Age: 24
Bats: R Throws: R Height: 6' 4" Weight: 215
Breakout: 44% Improve: 72% Collapse: 22%
Attrition: 39% MLB: 73%

Comparables:
Tyler Thornburg, Garrett Olson, Jason Windsor

YEAR	TEAM	LVL	AGE	W	L	SV	G	GS	IP	H	HR	BB	SO	BB9	SO9	GB%	BABIP	WHIP	ERA	FIP	FRA	WARP
2012	LEL	A+	22	9	6	0	26	26	128²	127	11	27	137	1.9	9.6	43%	.330	1.20	3.85	3.59	3.80	3.0
2013	SAN	AA	23	1	2	0	6	6	31¹	17	1	6	37	1.7	10.6	53%	.217	0.73	1.15	1.88	3.08	0.7
2013	TUC	AAA	23	5	1	0	12	12	61	56	4	17	65	2.5	9.6	38%	.329	1.20	3.39	3.18	3.36	1.8
2013	SDN	MLB	23	1	3	0	10	7	36¹	39	9	21	46	5.2	11.4	25%	.333	1.65	6.44	5.44	5.37	-0.2
2014	SDN	MLB	24	7	7	0	23	23	112	99	13	37	111	2.9	8.9	40%	.299	1.21	3.67	3.80	3.99	1.0

Smith got the call after six Double-A starts, becoming the first big-leaguer ever named Burch. His initial frame was perfect, but then he got knocked off his perch by hitters less bothered by straight hard fastballs than those in the minors. There is no lurch in his motion, although he does hide the ball well. His good name has not been besmirched by a few rough outings at the highest level. His stuff may play better in short bursts out of the bullpen, but for now he'll continue to search for ways to make it through a lineup more than once or twice a game.

Tim Stauffer
Born: 6/2/1982 Age: 32
Bats: R Throws: R Height: 6' 1" Weight: 215
Breakout: 22% Improve: 51% Collapse: 26%
Attrition: 19% MLB: 68%

Comparables:
Jorge Sosa, Casey Fossum, Matt Belisle

YEAR	TEAM	LVL	AGE	W	L	SV	G	GS	IP	H	HR	BB	SO	BB9	SO9	GB%	BABIP	WHIP	ERA	FIP	FRA	WARP
2011	SDN	MLB	29	9	12	0	31	31	185²	180	20	53	128	2.6	6.2	53%	.292	1.25	3.73	4.00	4.87	0.2
2012	LEL	A+	30	0	1	0	4	4	13¹	15	0	2	11	1.4	7.4	50%	.357	1.27	3.38	2.61	2.78	0.4
2012	SDN	MLB	30	0	0	0	1	1	5	7	1	3	5	5.4	9.0	53%	.429	2.00	5.40	5.54	5.42	0.0
2013	TUC	AAA	31	2	2	0	8	8	42²	50	1	15	38	3.2	8.0	50%	.383	1.52	3.16	3.22	4.24	0.9
2013	SDN	MLB	31	3	1	0	43	0	69²	59	7	20	64	2.6	8.3	52%	.282	1.13	3.75	3.52	4.23	0.3
2014	SDN	MLB	32	4	4	0	34	10	85²	81	9	24	63	2.5	6.6	49%	.295	1.22	3.73	4.05	4.05	0.6

A study in perseverance, Stauffer has pitched in numerous roles when not sidelined by a cascade of injuries that have plagued his career. After starting in 2011 and missing almost all of 2012 with elbow issues that required surgery, he returned to the bullpen last year, working the sixth and seventh innings. Stauffer conquered lefties with an improved changeup and held batters to a .188/.265/.299 line after the All-Star break. His fastball had a tad more velocity than in previous years and his curve had more bite, generating more swings and misses by right-handed batters. Although his career hasn't gone as planned since being picked fourth overall in 2003, he will remain marginally useful as long as his right arm allows.

Huston Street

Born: **8/2/1983** Age: **30**
Bats: **R** Throws: **R** Height: **6' 0"** Weight: **195**
Breakout: **32%** Improve: **50%** Collapse: **27%**
Attrition: **13%** MLB: **94%**

Comparables:
Rollie Fingers, Justin Duchscherer, Dan Wheeler

YEAR	TEAM	LVL	AGE	W	L	SV	G	GS	IP	H	HR	BB	SO	BB9	SO9	GB%	BABIP	WHIP	ERA	FIP	FRA	WARP
2011	COL	MLB	27	1	4	29	62	0	58¹	62	10	9	55	1.4	8.5	38%	.317	1.22	3.86	3.85	4.32	0.6
2012	SDN	MLB	28	2	1	23	40	0	39	17	2	11	47	2.5	10.8	43%	.179	0.72	1.85	2.24	2.80	0.7
2013	SDN	MLB	29	2	5	33	58	0	56²	44	12	14	46	2.2	7.3	32%	.213	1.02	2.70	4.89	5.14	-0.4
2014	SDN	MLB	30	3	1	26	50	0	49²	38	6	10	51	1.9	9.2	40%	.272	0.97	2.47	3.35	2.68	1.1

Street threw the final pitch of baseball's 2013 regular season, a walk-off single to the Giants' Hunter Pence. Before that outing, Street had been untouchable for three months, allowing one run (on a solo homer) in his previous 30 appearances and holding opponents to a .137/.170/.206 line. This was in direct contrast to the start of his season, when he allowed 10 home runs in his first 26 ⅓ innings. Conventional wisdom holds that a "proven closer" is a luxury item wasted on rebuilding teams, but the Padres' young pitchers surely appreciate having Street—who has turned batters into Yovani Gallardo since coming to San Diego—protect their leads. Plus he has two French Bulldogs. How cute is that?

Eric Stults

Born: **12/9/1979** Age: **34**
Bats: **L** Throws: **L** Height: **6' 0"** Weight: **230**
Breakout: **21%** Improve: **48%** Collapse: **27%**
Attrition: **23%** MLB: **62%**

Comparables:
Tomo Ohka, Tim Redding, Claudio Vargas

YEAR	TEAM	LVL	AGE	W	L	SV	G	GS	IP	H	HR	BB	SO	BB9	SO9	GB%	BABIP	WHIP	ERA	FIP	FRA	WARP
2011	CSP	AAA	31	4	4	1	52	0	68	76	11	16	69	2.1	9.1	38%	.346	1.35	4.63	4.56	4.58	1.7
2011	COL	MLB	31	0	0	0	6	0	12	11	4	4	7	3.0	5.2	29%	.176	1.25	6.00	7.41	9.01	-0.4
2012	CHR	AAA	32	1	1	0	5	5	28²	25	0	10	26	3.1	8.2	42%	.316	1.22	2.20	2.39	2.80	0.8
2012	SDN	MLB	32	8	3	0	18	14	92¹	86	7	23	51	2.2	5.0	39%	.269	1.18	2.92	3.80	4.06	0.9
2012	CHA	MLB	32	0	0	0	2	1	6²	6	0	4	4	5.4	5.4	57%	.286	1.50	2.70	4.10	4.13	0.1
2013	SDN	MLB	33	11	13	0	33	33	203²	219	18	40	131	1.8	5.8	41%	.310	1.27	3.93	3.50	3.88	2.2
2014	SDN	MLB	34	8	8	1	57	19	162	162	16	44	107	2.4	5.9	41%	.298	1.27	4.01	4.05	4.36	0.4

You know the cliché: Lefty out of Indiana gets drafted in the 15th round, spends a decade in the minors, pitches in Japan for a year, lands in San Diego after a few more stops and finally stays in the big leagues for an entire season, leading the Padres in starts, innings and strikeouts at age 33 despite working with a high-80s fastball. So overdone. Stults throws strikes (he walked more than two batters in just three of his 33 starts) but seldom puts the ball past hitters (his career-high 12 strikeouts came against a Mariners lineup not known for making contact). He was hit hard away from Petco, had severe platoon splits and faded badly in the second half.

Dale Thayer

Born: **12/17/1980** Age: **33**
Bats: **R** Throws: **R** Height: **6' 0"** Weight: **215**
Breakout: **43%** Improve: **53%** Collapse: **40%**
Attrition: **53%** MLB: **37%**

Comparables:
Vinnie Chulk, Willie Eyre, Scott Atchison

YEAR	TEAM	LVL	AGE	W	L	SV	G	GS	IP	H	HR	BB	SO	BB9	SO9	GB%	BABIP	WHIP	ERA	FIP	FRA	WARP
2011	BUF	AAA	30	4	3	21	54	0	71	54	8	15	66	1.9	8.4	51%	.235	0.97	2.66	3.52	4.26	0.5
2011	NYN	MLB	30	0	3	0	11	0	10¹	12	0	0	5	0.0	4.4	44%	.306	1.16	3.48	2.03	2.87	0.2
2012	SDN	MLB	31	2	2	7	64	0	57²	53	4	12	47	1.9	7.3	43%	.288	1.13	3.43	3.08	3.85	0.5
2013	SDN	MLB	32	3	5	1	69	0	65	59	8	22	64	3.0	8.9	42%	.293	1.25	3.32	3.76	3.74	0.3
2014	SDN	MLB	33	3	1	2	54	0	59	53	6	16	47	2.4	7.3	45%	.290	1.18	3.38	3.85	3.68	0.6

Thayer's chief weapons out of the bullpen are control, durability and an almost fanatical devotion to the Pope. In 2013 he had the unfortunate distinction of seeing his OPS allowed rise every month. His velocity was down a tick, but he still got whiffs often enough to keep hitters from getting too comfortable. A useful set-up man, his greatest distinction lies in being indistinguishable from most other set-up men. Captain Kirk wouldn't hesitate to beam him down to a planet, knowing full well a replacement was standing by. Thayer probably isn't closer material, but as many have demonstrated, saveworthiness is in the eye of the manager.

Nick Vincent

Born: **7/12/1986** Age: **27**
Bats: **R** Throws: **R** Height: **6' 0"** Weight: **185**
Breakout: **37%** Improve: **46%** Collapse: **34%**
Attrition: **47%** MLB: **60%**

Comparables:
Cesar Jimenez, Cody Eppley, Warner Madrigal

YEAR	TEAM	LVL	AGE	W	L	SV	G	GS	IP	H	HR	BB	SO	BB9	SO9	GB%	BABIP	WHIP	ERA	FIP	FRA	WARP
2011	SAN	AA	24	8	2	3	66	0	79¹	54	6	20	89	2.3	10.1	42%	.265	0.93	2.27	2.99	4.08	1.2
2012	TUC	AAA	25	1	1	2	23	0	21²	27	2	11	19	4.6	7.9	43%	.368	1.75	5.82	4.91	5.05	0.3
2012	SDN	MLB	25	2	0	0	27	0	26¹	19	2	7	28	2.4	9.6	39%	.250	0.99	1.71	2.91	3.89	0.2
2013	TUC	AAA	26	4	3	0	24	0	25¹	26	4	12	24	4.3	8.5	35%	.301	1.50	3.55	5.27	4.67	0.4
2013	SDN	MLB	26	6	3	1	45	0	46¹	33	1	11	49	2.1	9.5	46%	.270	0.95	2.14	2.03	2.44	1.0
2014	SDN	MLB	27	3	1	0	52	0	61¹	52	6	20	58	3.0	8.6	43%	.288	1.17	3.31	3.65	3.59	0.7

Recalled at the end of May after missing much of spring training with an inflamed tendon in his right forearm, Vincent didn't allow a run until his 12th appearance and finished the season as one of the Padres' most reliable set-up men. Righties hit .122/.168/.144 against him, striking out more than 30 percent of the time. His stuff isn't overpowering, but he is aggressive in throwing strikes and hides the ball well, making his high-80s late-breaking cutter seem faster. Bud Black praises Vincent's approach and the fact that "he doesn't scare off." His career ERA won't remain under 2.00, but he'll survive in the bigs for a while despite pedestrian velocity.

Joe Wieland
Born: **1/21/1990** Age: **24**
Bats: **R** Throws: **R** Height: **6' 3"** Weight: **205**
Breakout: **40%** Improve: **75%** Collapse: **18%**
Attrition: **44%** MLB: **45%**

Comparables:
Daryl Thompson, Chris Seddon, Eric Hurley

YEAR	TEAM	LVL	AGE	W	L	SV	G	GS	IP	H	HR	BB	SO	BB9	SO9	GB%	BABIP	WHIP	ERA	FIP	FRA	WARP
2011	MYR	A+	21	6	3	0	14	13	85^2	78	7	4	96	0.4	10.1	46%	.317	0.96	2.10	2.26	3.11	1.7
2011	FRI	AA	21	4	0	0	7	7	44	35	2	11	36	2.2	7.4	47%	.196	1.05	1.23	3.08	3.79	0.8
2011	SAN	AA	21	3	1	0	5	5	26	23	0	6	18	2.1	6.2	38%	.279	1.12	2.77	2.92	3.77	0.6
2012	SDN	MLB	22	0	4	0	5	5	27^2	26	5	9	24	2.9	7.8	43%	.260	1.27	4.55	4.83	5.57	-0.1
2014	SDN	MLB	24	2	2	0	6	6	37^1	37	4	12	27	2.9	6.5	43%	.300	1.31	4.24	4.21	4.61	-0.0

Wieland had a disappointing aborted recovery from July 2012 Tommy John surgery. (If you think you've read the words "Tommy" and "John" a lot in this chapter, that's because you have. The Padres either have a top-notch elbow-wrecking training program or, more likely, they've run into a real rash of bad luck with pitcher injuries the last few years.) He threw a 100-pitch bullpen in April and felt "close to 100 percent," saying that "I've really turned a corner and gotten to the point where I'm not feeling any pain at all." A month later, he said, "I'm very confident in how my elbow feels." Then a stress reaction in the elbow shelved plans for a summer rehab assignment. By September, he hoped to pitch "10 or 15 innings" of winter ball, saying, "I don't want to go to spring training in the dark wondering if it's going to happen again." The no. 4 starter's calling card is command, which is hard to establish without pitching in games.

Matt Wisler
Born: **9/12/1992** Age: **21**
Bats: **R** Throws: **R** Height: **6' 3"** Weight: **195**
Breakout: **32%** Improve: **78%** Collapse: **9%**
Attrition: **46%** MLB: **39%**

Comparables:
Chad Billingsley, Michael Bowden, Carlos Martinez

YEAR	TEAM	LVL	AGE	W	L	SV	G	GS	IP	H	HR	BB	SO	BB9	SO9	GB%	BABIP	WHIP	ERA	FIP	FRA	WARP
2012	FTW	A	19	5	4	0	24	23	114	95	1	28	113	2.2	8.9	45%	.299	1.08	2.53	2.35	3.53	2.8
2013	LEL	A+	20	2	1	0	6	6	31	22	1	6	28	1.7	8.1	43%	.253	0.90	2.03	3.06	3.46	0.7
2013	SAN	AA	20	8	5	0	20	20	105	85	7	27	103	2.3	8.8	39%	.282	1.07	3.00	2.79	3.42	1.8
2014	SDN	MLB	21	7	7	0	23	23	113^2	103	11	40	95	3.2	7.5	41%	.295	1.26	3.72	3.92	4.04	0.9

Wisler, the Texas League's youngest pitcher last year, throws four pitches with a funky three-quarters delivery. A low- to mid-90s fastball and late-breaking slider are his best offerings, while a changeup and loose mid-70s curve lag behind. Righties hit .184/.212/.271 against him in 2013, with a Saberhagenesque 11.8 strikeouts for every walk; lefties hit .254/.327/.421, with a Marquis-like 1.5 K/BB. Greater separation between the fastball and changeup might help him against southpaws. Good command and a "bulldog" attitude on the mound (he allowed one run in 16 playoff innings for the Missions) work in Wisler's favor. If his secondaries improve, he'll be a mid-rotation starter. Otherwise, late-inning relief is an option. Either way, there is no hurry.

LINEOUTS

HITTERS

PLAYER	TEAM	LVL	AGE	PA	R	2B	3B	HR	RBI	BB	SO	SB-CS	AVG/OBP/SLG	TAv	BABIP	BRR	FRAA	WARP
RF Y. Asencio	LEL	A+	23	257	34	20	2	5	44	10	29	1-1	.296/.319/.457	.280	.315	1.6	RF(48): -7.6	0.4
	SAN	AA	23	309	25	15	3	2	32	13	29	3-2	.261/.298/.354	.248	.282	-0.3	RF(73): 4.4, CF(1): 0.0	0.9
SS R. Cedeno	SDN	MLB	30	133	12	2	2	2	9	8	31	3-3	.268/.318/.366	.252	.344	0.9	SS(35): -0.9, 3B(1): -0.0	0.5
	HOU	MLB	30	155	12	6	1	1	12	6	42	2-1	.220/.260/.298	.208	.303	1.3	SS(41): -0.5, 1B(1): 0.0	-0.2
C R. Daal	FTW	A	19	299	30	13	2	8	39	14	58	6-4	.271/.317/.424	.261	.317	-0.5	C(79): 0.9, 3B(1): -0.0	1.2
RF A. Dickerson	ALT	AA	23	491	61	36	3	17	68	27	89	10-7	.288/.337/.494	.304	.325	-1.8	RF(114): -6.3, LF(6): -0.2	2.2
2B J. Galvez	TUC	AAA	22	455	66	24	1	6	51	34	104	22-7	.278/.342/.385	.253	.358	-0.4	2B(74): 2.0, LF(22): 0.0	0.8
LF M. Kotsay	SDN	MLB	37	171	8	2	0	1	12	13	25	0-2	.194/.253/.226	.192	.221	-1.2	LF(19): -1.5, RF(6): -0.5	-1.2
1B T. Medica	SAN	AA	25	320	48	20	3	18	57	28	67	4-2	.296/.372/.582	.334	.327	-1.4	1B(51): 2.4, LF(1): -0.0	3.1
	SDN	MLB	25	79	9	2	0	3	10	10	23	0-0	.290/.380/.449	.312	.395	0.2	1B(19): 0.5	0.4
C R. Rivera	TUC	AAA	29	276	36	18	0	5	38	17	42	0-2	.343/.382/.474	.289	.388	-1.9	C(68): 0.3, 1B(3): 0.1	2.5
	SDN	MLB	29	71	4	3	1	0	7	2	16	0-0	.254/.268/.328	.224	.321	-1.4	C(21): -0.1	0.2

Formerly known as Yoan Alcantara, outfielder **Yeison Asencio** is less exciting than he was before his name changed and he aged over two years; he is very aggressive at the plate and has some power, although it seldom appears in games. ⊘ Signed to a minor-league contract as insurance a few days before Everth Cabrera's suspension, **Ronny Cedeño** played a solid short-stop and provided some key hits in meaningless games, earning him a look or three from the Brotherhood of Utility Guys (BUG). ⊘ **Rodney Daal** showed good power in his full-season debut and drew praise for his handling of pitchers (the ability to speak five languages helps) as one of the youngest regulars in the Midwest League, but defense remains a work in progress. ⊘ **Alex Dickerson** returned to the outfield and showed more power last season, yet scouts remain unmoved by his glove and doubt he hits enough to start at first base. ⊘ Despite playing in a cozy home park, **Jonathan Galvez** saw his numbers fall again at a higher level; he is young and can hit a little but keeps drifting rightward on the defensive spectrum, where his bat may not be good enough. ⊘ **Mark Kotsay**, who retires ranking among the top 30 Padres in numerous offensive categories, was heavily involved in charity throughout his 17th season—both giving to his community and receiving from his employer. ⊘ Despite missing most of May and June with a left oblique strain, **Tommy Medica** tied Jedd Gyorko for the organizational lead with 23 homers at three levels. The catcher-turned-first baseman isn't young but has destroyed minor-league pitching (.295/.388/.538), especially lefties, and could maybe turn into Ron Coomer or even John Jaha. ⊘ **Rene Rivera** nailed nine of 16 potential basestealers last year, hit his first big-league triple (against Zack Wheeler), knocked a personal-best seven RBI and raised his career TAv to a frosty .200.

PITCHERS

PLAYER	TEAM	LVL	AGE	W	L	SV	IP	H	HR	BB	SO	BB9	SO9	GB%	BABIP	WHIP	ERA	FIP	FRA	WARP
M. Andriese	SAN	AA	23	8	2	0	76	71	3	17	63	2.0	7.5	61%	.296	1.16	2.37	2.70	3.55	1.3
	TUC	AAA	23	3	5	0	58²	64	2	12	42	1.8	6.4	56%	.343	1.30	4.45	3.30	5.00	0.6
J. Barbato	LEL	A+	20	3	6	14	88	90	8	33	89	3.4	9.1	40%	.339	1.40	5.01	4.26	5.63	1.0
L. Campos	FTW	A	25	2	1	5	36¹	19	2	22	63	5.4	15.6	48%	.274	1.13	2.23	2.49	2.00	1.5
	SAN	AA	25	1	0	2	30²	14	0	16	43	4.7	12.6	50%	.233	0.98	0.88	1.82	1.75	1.1
J. De Paula	SAN	AA	25	4	6	0	74²	84	3	11	57	1.3	6.9	50%	.342	1.27	3.86	2.57	3.36	1.6
J. Hancock	FTW	A	22	5	1	0	67²	54	0	20	44	2.7	5.9	43%	.265	1.09	1.73	3.01	3.96	1.3
	LEL	A+	22	3	7	0	63	81	5	36	39	5.1	5.6	48%	.339	1.86	5.14	5.52	5.64	0.4
D. Jones	BOW	AA	22	4	7	0	123¹	146	17	48	108	3.5	7.9	46%	.349	1.57	5.84	4.65	5.39	0.4
J. Lane	TUC	AAA	36	2	2	0	46¹	55	7	6	33	1.2	6.4	41%	.320	1.32	5.24	4.50	5.24	0.5
J. Oramas	SAN	AA	23	3	2	0	55²	52	4	16	64	2.6	10.3	32%	.340	1.22	3.07	2.72	3.18	1.3
W. Weickel	FTW	A	19	3	6	0	110²	125	8	43	82	3.5	6.7	51%	.326	1.52	5.04	4.18	5.40	0.8

Employing a sinking fastball, curve, cutter and changeup, **Matt Andriese** throws strikes, generates groundballs and projects as a back-end starter; his improvement against left-handed batters last year could help him advance quickly. ⊘ Drawing comparisons to Addison Reed before the season, **Johnny Barbato** began the year in the bullpen and ended it in the rotation, pitching well in spurts but being undermined by too many big innings against A-ball hitters. ⊘ **Leonel Campos**, who backs mid-90s heat with a hard slider, allowed half his runs last year in his first four appearances after missing 2012 thanks to Tommy John surgery; he held right-handers to a sub-.400 OPS and saw his numbers improve after leapfrogging over High-A in June. ⊘ After visa issues caused him to miss 2012, **Jose De Paula** walked more than one batter in just three of 14 starts before being shut down in mid-June with tightness in his left rotator cuff. ⊘ **Justin Hancock**, a 2011 ninth-round pick, was leading the Midwest League in ERA before being promoted in June; don't be fooled by Hancock's struggles at Lake Elsinore and lackluster strikeout rates at both levels, which say more about his approach than his stuff. ⊘ **Devin Jones** continued his transition into the rotation with uninspiring results. The groundball specialist lost all feel for his command as a full-time starter and may soon return to the bullpen. ⊘ Perhaps inspired by Jeff Suppan and Kip Wells, who pitched for the Padres in 2012 without even being left-handed, former big-league outfielder **Jason Lane** logged a few innings at Tucson after averaging 4.5 K/9 in the independent Atlantic League at age 36, but the great arm-destroying pandemic foretold by Franciscus Jobicus during the reign of Bartholomew the Bewildered proved to be nothing more than a misreading of faded parchment by well-intentioned yet grossly incompetent post-doctoral fellows at a since-discredited institution. ⊘ A little over a year after June 2012 Tommy John surgery, changeup specialist **Juan Oramas**—who also features a low-90s fastball and a curveball that is effective against lefties—returned to action and saw his command improve as the season progressed; he could advance quickly. ⊘ Built like an Ent, **Walker Weickel** works with a fastball in the low 90s and improving secondaries; his full-season debut wasn't pretty, but how many 19-year-olds say things like, "Being able to welcome failure and being able to understand it makes it that much easier to overcome"?

MANAGER: BUD BLACK

YEAR	TEAM	W-L	Pythag +/-	Avg PC	100+ P	120+ P	QS	BQS	REL	REL w Zero R	IBB	PH	PH Avg	PH HR	SB2	CS2	SB3	CS3	SAC Att	SAC %	POS SAC	Squeeze	Swing	In Play
2011	SDN	71-91	0	96.7	65	1	91	4	489	416	56	283	.160	2	147	42	21	2	86	64.0%	23	4	391	88
2012	SDN	76-86	0	92.2	49	1	75	5	529	449	48	278	.248	6	129	42	25	2	107	58.9%	30	1	396	88
2013	SDN	76-86	0	93.9	59	2	87	2	488	402	31	266	.206	8	105	31	13	3	92	56.5%	23	1	284	75

Last year, Bud Black's Padres finished 12th in the league in batting average. That ties the highest rank they've ever had in his seven years on the job. I don't know if that tells you anything about Black given the talent on hand and the park, but that's impressive. San Diego has hit .246 from 2007 to 2013.

Black juggles his batting order. He consistently ranks among the league leaders in most orders, and in 2013 set a new personal high with 145. Black's Padres have had 917 batting orders, second only to Arizona in the NL during his career. His 729 lineups is second only to San Francisco in that span. As a result, he leans on his main starters less than most skippers. His main eight players accounted for just 58.4 percent of all plate appearances for the 2013 Padres, which ranks 14th in the NL. That's typical for Black. He has ranked in the bottom three for starter PA four times in his seven campaigns.

San Francisco Giants

By Dave Flemming

A game at San Francisco's AT&T Park has become a singular baseball experience. It's not just that Giants fans have the longest sellout streak in the sport—now at 246 consecutive regular season games—or that they get to enjoy breathtaking views of the bay. Big crowds and passion for baseball exist on a similar scale in other markets, after all, and there are other historic and beautiful ballparks.

No, it's the combination of baseball and carnival—of ballgame and costume party—that turned San Francisco into a baseball town unlike any other. Scan the crowd on any night of the season—a Friday night against the Dodgers or a Tuesday against the Marlins—and you see panda hats and orange boas, partying twenty-somethings and dancing grandmothers. AT&T Park is a college frat party blended with a Sand Hill Road cocktail hour, mixed with the annual Bay to Breakers race across the city.

That atmosphere has mirrored the experience of being a fan of the actual baseball team these past few seasons. The Giants won two World Series in three years. They have thrown no-hitters and a perfect game; won MVPs and led All-Star heroics; won postseason sweeps and postseason miracles. Heck, Barry Zito got a World Series hit against Justin Verlander while outpitching the Tigers' ace. That's a lot to savor for what had been a long-tortured fan base.

But San Franciscans know parties and parades often come to an inglorious end. Sometimes the campus cops show up, and the lights come on, and kids are scrambling to get out the back door. Bay to Breakers ends every year with thousands of exhausted, sobered-up "runners" trying to hail a cab in their underwear in 55 degree San Francisco fog.

That's sort of what happened in 2013 for the Giants. On May 13th the Giants led the NL West by 2 1/2 games, and were eight games over .500. The next day in Toronto began a 17-35 stretch that sent the Giants out of the division race and

their playoff hopes into oblivion. It was a crash landing that Giants fans did not see coming. The best three years in San Francisco Giants history were wistful memories, and the season ended with a 16-game chasm between these Giants and the suddenly unstoppable, eternally unlikeable Dodgers.

What, exactly, went wrong? This was, after all, a team that brought back nearly every player from the Detroit dogpile. More importantly, how can the Giants get the good times rolling again—not just in the stands, but on the field?

There was plenty of consternation about an offense that was at times anemic. The Giants finished 10th in the league in runs, and only the Marlins hit fewer home runs. They managed all of nine homers as a team in July, the same number the Rangers' Adrian Beltre hit. Angel Pagan and Marco Scutaro were supposed to give the Giants a high-OBP table-setting tandem, but Pagan missed 82 games with a hamstring strain requiring surgery, forcing the Giants to ask too much of Gregor Blanco and Andres Torres. Scutaro battled a painful back and hip for much of the year and his production dipped after a hot start. World Series MVP Pablo Sandoval continued to tease, with a solid season that was nevertheless below expectations. And 2012 MVP Buster Posey was a contender for the award again until the All-Star break, after which he hit just .244 with nine-extra base hits—the quietest stretch of his career. Posey selflessly played through a broken finger in September, but he was not himself.

And yet, through all of that, the Giants offense was by most measures not the problem. The team's final TAv of .260 ranked third-best in the NL, and the Giants scored the fifth-most road runs in the NL. With Brandon Belt's emergence and Hunter Pence's rebound they had the extended middle of the order they lacked even on the World Series teams. It's not easy to see because of AT&T Park—arguably the toughest

GIANTS PROSPECTUS
2013 W-L: 76-86, 3rd in NL West

Pythag	.457	21st	DER	.702	19th
RS/G	3.88	21st	B-Age	28.6	20th
RA/G	4.27	19th	P-Age	29.3	25th
TAv	.256	17th	Salary	$136.9	7th
BRR	-5.72	24th	M$/MW	$4.51	24th
TAv-P	.266	17th	DL Days	674	8th
FIP	3.77	11th	$ on DL	12%	8th

	Runs	HR/RH	HR/LH	Runs/RH	Runs/LH
Three-Year Park Factors	100	97	88	103	100

Top Hitter WARP	5.14 (Hunter Pence)
Top Pitcher WARP	2.76 (Madison Bumgarner)
Top Prospect	Kyle Crick

place to hit in the big leagues, suppressing power for both left- and right-handed hitters—but the Giants have put together enough offense to win a championship.

But the same ballpark fog that hides their offensive competence also covers for what really went wrong for the Giants in 2013. The Giants had built two world champions on that old classic: pitching and defense. They had strong starting staffs, flexible bullpens and range in an extreme pitchers park. But that pitching strength began to erode in the second championship season and collapsed in 2013. Despite the advantages of AT&T Park, the Giants' team ERA was the third-worst in the league. Only the Cubs walked more batters. The staff's vaunted ability to allow all the fly balls with none of the home runs vanished, as the Giants allowed a league-average home run rate for the first time since 2001.

The defense did not help—the Giants had long stretches of sloppy play and finished with the NL's third-worst defensive efficiency. Yet defense doesn't fully explain what happened to the starting rotation, where Madison Bumgarner—whose age-23 season pushed him into the game's top tier of lefties—was the only pitcher to approach a top-level performance. Staff ace Matt Cain slogged through a horrendous first half, with home run problems and some of the worst outings of his career. (He allowed a total of 15 earned runs in two separate innings against the Cardinals).

But Cain's second half was much better (5.06 ERA pre-break; 2.36 after) and the Giants believe his rough stretch was an aberration. The real disasters came at the bottom of the rotation. Ryan Vogelsong, one of the Giants' great successes since 2011, missed almost three months with a broken finger, and posted an ERA of 5.73 in 19 starts. Barry Zito, after banking World Series heroics in his San Francisco legacy fund, finished his Giants career with his worst season. The pair combined to pitch 236 innings, and allowed a whopping 399 baserunners; adjusted for ballpark, the two tied for the worst ERA in baseball.

Only a little higher on that ignominious leaderboard was Tim Lincecum, a franchise icon. His own disastrous 2012 gave way to an improved but still spotty 2013. He pitched his first career no-hitter on July 13th in San Diego, and finished 11th in the NL in strikeouts per nine while allowing fewer hits than innings. But walks remained a major problem for the two-time Cy Young winner, and he finished with a 4.37 ERA.

The Giants believed that fatigue was a problem for the entire staff. Two long playoff runs in three years added extra innings for many, especially staff ace Cain. Management was not thrilled with Ryan Vogelsong's participation in the World Baseball Classic, and believed his aggressive spring training in preparation for the tournament was costly once the regular season began.

A theme emerged in these pitchers' struggles, and in the injuries that sent the offense careening for entire months.

The Giants have an enviable collection of high-end talent, but are sorely lacking the organizational depth (at least major league-ready depth) to withstand injury and unexpected dips. In contrast, playoff teams like the Cardinals, Dodgers and Pirates summoned Michael Wacha, Yasiel Puig, Gerrit Cole and others to the rescue as they dealt with their own crises. The Giants just didn't have those options.

They tried the young lefties Mike Kickham (10.23 ERA in 28 innings) and Eric Surkamp (seven earned runs in one ineffective start). Veteran journeymen Chad Gaudin and Yusmeiro Petit had some nice moments, but a franchise that has developed pitching as well as any in the game ran out of options at the upper levels of the system.

Similarly, when Pagan went down the Giants were forced to stick with Blanco and Torres in the outfield, despite their limitations, because call-ups Roger Kieschnick, Juan Perez and Brett Pill failed to produce at the plate.

So what happened in the minor leagues to create this void? In the previous decade the Giants had a string of astoundingly successful first-round picks who formed the core of their championship teams. Cain, Lincecum, Bumgarner, Posey—all Giants homegrown first-rounders, three of them plucked in consecutive drafts. Yet the top of the last three drafts (albeit much lower in the first round, a result of the Giants' success) have produced outfielder Gary Brown, infielder Joe Panik and righty Chris Stratton. All three still have time to develop, but none was ready to provide a jolt to a struggling team last year, and it seems likely the Giants won't get impact major-league performance from those picks. Right-hander Zack Wheeler was a highly successful San Francisco first-round pick, but Wheeler is emerging as a star for the Mets, not the Giants, thanks to the Carlos Beltran trade in 2011. The trade was defensible at the time, but Wheeler would be a big part of the future were he still in the fold.

There is enough pitching depth in the lower minors for the Giants to believe they will start getting some significant major-league value from young players in 2015 and beyond. Right-hander Kyle Crick has a chance to be elite, with dominant power stuff, and there's an inventory of promising arms alongside him. The odds seem good that in a year or two the Giants will have at least a couple productive major-league pitchers from that group.

But the Giants know that the depth of talent in the organization has to be stronger. The amateur draft must start producing again, and the 2013 draft class might be a start, but it's not unreasonable to think the Giants could adjust their draft philosophy and target some higher-ceiling, higher-risk talents. Those upside talents are currently in short supply in the Giants' system. The club has openly expressed an increasing willingness to spend in the international market. It seems inevitable that at some point San Francisco—with its status as a cultural center on the Pacific Rim—will welcome an impact talent from Japan to the Giants.

But in the short term, the Giants are going to need a lot to go right to compete with the emerging powerhouse in Los Angeles. Pence returns to San Francisco with a big new contract after a career year. He's been a good fit with the Giants, but will have to age well under a big contract. Sandoval figures to be highly motivated in the season leading into his free agency. The decision to keep Sandoval will be a difficult one, considering his problems with health and conditioning, but the Giants would love for Sandoval to force their hand with a big season. Posey is committed to being a catcher, and is one of the most valuable players in baseball at that position, but it's fair to say the Giants have to make sure he stays fresh and productive through a long season. Posey promised an offseason dedicated to conditioning and strengthening his lower body, and the Giants are determined to pace him more judiciously, which likely means fewer "off-days" at first base and more true days of rest.

Brandon Belt took a long awaited leap forward in 2013 and led the Giants with an .841 OPS. A significant mechanical change—Belt altered his hold on the bat to a more conventional grip, and moved back in the batter's box—triggered his offensive emergence in the second half of the year. A major question for the future of the Giants is how permanent that emergence is—it seems possible that there's room still for Belt to become one of the better hitters in the NL.

The Giants entered the offseason determined to add more pitching depth. They re-signed Lincecum and Javier Lopez and replaced Zito with Tim Hudson on a two-year deal. Hudson is recovering from a major ankle injury, but assuming he's healthy, it's likely he will represent a three- or four-win upgrade from Zito. Vogelsong comes back, but will face competition in Petit and the emerging young starters if he falters again.

Over the longer term, the Giants are committed to a very solid core. Posey, Bumgarner, Cain, Pence and Belt are a good base for any roster. All are signed or under team control through at least 2018, and only Pence (at 30) is older than 29.

Through the ballpark, a strong social media presence and a powerful broadcast reach (do the announcers get any credit for that?) Giants fans are heavily invested in their team. Ownership values and has provided stability in long-tenured General Manager Brian Sabean and manager Bruce Bochy. There's a Posey jersey on seemingly every corner of San Francisco, and the region's Little League overpopulation has reached near-crisis levels. Baseball is booming in the Bay Area.

The Dodgers are intent on building a monster team, and the Giants have their work cut out to keep up. The landscape in the NL West has changed, and it might not be the Giants' party anymore. But they, more than any team in the division, are equipped to crash it.

Dave Flemming enters his 11th season as a radio and television broadcaster for the Giants and is also a play-by-play voice for ESPN.

HITTERS

Joaquin Arias   3B

Born: 9/21/1984 Age: 29
Bats: R Throws: R Height: 6' 1"
Weight: 160 Breakout: 4%
Improve: 20% Collapse: 18%
Attrition: 29% MLB: 59%

Comparables:
Hector Luna, Michael Martinez, Matt Tolbert

YEAR	TEAM	LVL	AGE	PA	R	2B	3B	HR	RBI	BB	SO	SB	CS	AVG/OBP/SLG	TAv	BABIP	BRR	FRAA	WARP
2011	OMA	AAA	26	259	37	12	4	3	25	14	28	7	1	.232/.272/.353	.206	.250	1.8	3B(38): -0.2, 1B(9): 0.0	-0.8
2012	FRE	AAA	27	74	14	5	0	2	17	3	11	0	1	.400/.432/.557	.339	.456	0.1	SS(16): -0.2	0.8
2012	SFN	MLB	27	344	30	13	5	5	34	13	44	5	1	.270/.304/.389	.250	.295	2	3B(74): 1.7, SS(50): -1.6	1.1
2013	SFN	MLB	28	236	17	9	2	1	19	4	33	1	0	.271/.284/.342	.230	.311	-0.2	3B(55): 1.3, SS(24): -0.6	-0.1
2014	SFN	MLB	29	253	22	10	2	3	21	9	36	3	1	.250/.280/.341	.234	.280	0.3	3B 1, SS -1	0.1

That Arias is able to play on the far side of the infield with what amounts to a barely functioning right arm shows pure #want. That arm was once considered elite, but a 2008 shoulder injury nearly cost him his baseball career. When making throws across the diamond, his mechanics must be impeccable; his whole body follows the ball toward his target. Even with a .237 TAv, he proved his utility spelling Pablo Sandoval and Marco Scutaro for prolonged periods. Appendicitis required a 15-day absence, but he's qualified to return in 2014 as the Giants' superutility infielder.

Christian Arroyo   SS

Born: 5/30/1995 Age: 19
Bats: R Throws: R Height: 6' 1"
Weight: 180 Breakout: 0%
Improve: 0% Collapse: 0%
Attrition: 0% MLB: 0%

Comparables:
Adrian Cardenas, Hernan Perez, Marwin Gonzalez

YEAR	TEAM	LVL	AGE	PA	R	2B	3B	HR	RBI	BB	SO	SB	CS	AVG/OBP/SLG	TAv	BABIP	BRR	FRAA	WARP
2014	SFN	MLB	19	250	20	9	1	2	17	13	68	0	0	.198/.239/.271	.193	.260	-0.4	SS 7	0.1

The Giants tend to favor pitchers with their early-round draft picks, but broke habit to take the big shortstop from the Tampa area 25th overall. Evaluators don't think he'll stick at the position as a big leaguer, as he features a shortstop's arm but not a shortstop's quickness. That leaves him as a player without a fit: The power isn't likely to play at third base, and his lack of quickness might make even second base a stretch. The Giants will stick with him at short for the time being and if he ultimately hits they'll find a place for him. Early returns from his Arizona League debut were promising, but there are at least three or four years of obstacles and opportunities between Arroyo and The Show.

Brandon Belt   1B

Born: 4/20/1988 Age: 26
Bats: L Throws: L Height: 6' 5''
Weight: 220 Breakout: 3%
Improve: 47% Collapse: 1%
Attrition: 5% MLB: 99%

Comparables:
Ike Davis, Mark Teixeira, Robert Fick

YEAR	TEAM	LVL	AGE	PA	R	2B	3B	HR	RBI	BB	SO	SB	CS	AVG/OBP/SLG	TAv	BABIP	BRR	FRAA	WARP
2011	FRE	AAA	23	212	32	12	0	8	32	42	47	4	4	.309/.448/.527	.298	.381	0.9	LF(22): -0.7, RF(10): 1.2	1.1
2011	SFN	MLB	23	209	21	6	1	9	18	20	57	3	2	.225/.306/.412	.267	.273	0.1	1B(31): -0.5, LF(31): 0.6	0.5
2012	SFN	MLB	24	472	47	27	6	7	56	54	106	12	2	.275/.360/.421	.302	.351	-0.7	1B(139): -2.6, LF(4): -0.1	2.6
2013	SFN	MLB	25	571	76	39	4	17	67	52	125	5	2	.289/.360/.481	.310	.351	2.5	1B(143): 6.1	4.4
2014	SFN	MLB	26	517	60	27	3	14	62	54	118	8	3	.265/.346/.430	.286	.330	-0.1	1B 2, LF -0	2.1

The season was something of a beautillion ball for Brandon Belt. Evaluators had long lauded his plate discipline and hit tool but felt his power wasn't where it should be. Belt's batting average and on-base percentage both ticked up in 2013, but his slugging sprung: from .421 in 2012 to .481, in a park that typically suffocates left-handed power. Whether you credit the mechanical adjustments he made or the maturation of his body and approach isn't important; the results speak for themselves. Coupled with his plus defense at first, you can pencil Belt in as San Francisco's starting first baseman for at least the next four seasons.

Gregor Blanco   CF

Born: 12/24/1983 Age: 30
Bats: L Throws: L Height: 5' 11''
Weight: 185 Breakout: 3%
Improve: 33% Collapse: 10%
Attrition: 19% MLB: 83%

Comparables:
Chris Duffy, Tony Gwynn, Nyjer Morgan

YEAR	TEAM	LVL	AGE	PA	R	2B	3B	HR	RBI	BB	SO	SB	CS	AVG/OBP/SLG	TAv	BABIP	BRR	FRAA	WARP
2011	SYR	AAA	27	178	28	7	2	3	10	27	35	15	1	.203/.335/.343	.246	.245	2.5	LF(27): 4.4, CF(16): 0.7	0.9
2011	OMA	AAA	27	74	13	5	0	0	4	17	15	9	1	.196/.384/.286	.387	.268	0.6	LF(9): 0.6	0.7
2012	SFN	MLB	28	453	56	14	5	5	34	51	104	26	6	.244/.333/.344	.265	.318	5.1	RF(54): -2.4, LF(53): -2.8	1.5
2013	SFN	MLB	29	511	50	17	6	3	41	52	95	14	9	.265/.341/.350	.259	.328	0.2	CF(76): -3.2, LF(72): -1.6	0.9
2014	SFN	MLB	30	469	56	16	3	4	32	54	97	20	6	.239/.328/.322	.248	.300	1.6	CF -3, LF -1	0.2

Given the rate at which Giants outfield prospects have flamed out in recent years, Blanco has been a nice, reliable insurance policy. FRAA is the pessimistic outlier on his outfield defense, which rates above average elsewhere; he draws walks and hits enough to stay in the lineup. He's certainly nobody's aspirational idea of a corner outfielder, but things inevitably go wrong, and Blanco's the best-case worst-case outcome.

Gary Brown   CF

Born: 9/28/1988 Age: 25
Bats: R Throws: R Height: 6' 1''
Weight: 190 Breakout: 4%
Improve: 10% Collapse: 6%
Attrition: 17% MLB: 21%

Comparables:
Clay Timpner, Alex Presley, Josh Prince

YEAR	TEAM	LVL	AGE	PA	R	2B	3B	HR	RBI	BB	SO	SB	CS	AVG/OBP/SLG	TAv	BABIP	BRR	FRAA	WARP
2011	SJO	A+	22	638	115	34	13	14	80	46	77	53	19	.336/.407/.519	.335	.369	-2	CF(47): 3.6	3.1
2012	RIC	AA	23	610	73	32	2	7	42	40	87	33	18	.279/.347/.385	.279	.318	3.7	CF(127): -2.0, LF(6): -0.1	3.8
2013	FRE	AAA	24	608	79	29	6	13	50	33	135	17	11	.231/.286/.375	.228	.282	0.4	CF(133): -0.6, LF(3): -0.2	0.2
2014	SFN	MLB	25	250	30	11	1	4	19	12	52	11	5	.231/.281/.339	.231	.280	0.4	CF -0, LF -0	0.0

Prospecters were high on the Giants' 2010 first-rounder, salivating over how well Brown's elite speed would play on both sides of the ball. But after a torrid 2011 season in San Jose, Brown's offense has steadily gone down with each step up the organizational ladder, and he hasn't even earned a September call-up to let him know he's still alive. Triple-A pitchers exposed previously dormant swing-and-miss in his game, and advanced pitcher-catcher tandems shut down his speed on the basepaths. He's now 25, so the 2014 season will be make or break—assuming, perhaps generously, that 2013 didn't break him already.

Brandon Crawford   SS

Born: 1/21/1987 Age: 27
Bats: L Throws: R Height: 6' 2''
Weight: 215 Breakout: 0%
Improve: 45% Collapse: 11%
Attrition: 8% MLB: 98%

Comparables:
Toby Harrah, Edgar Renteria, Jimmy Rollins

YEAR	TEAM	LVL	AGE	PA	R	2B	3B	HR	RBI	BB	SO	SB	CS	AVG/OBP/SLG	TAv	BABIP	BRR	FRAA	WARP
2011	SJO	A+	24	69	14	5	1	3	15	9	13	0	0	.322/.412/.593	.349	.372	-0.2	SS(6): -0.1	0.5
2011	FRE	AAA	24	118	13	5	1	1	9	9	20	5	2	.234/.291/.327	.223	.276	0	SS(25): 1.4	0.2
2011	SFN	MLB	24	220	22	5	2	3	21	23	31	1	3	.204/.288/.296	.213	.228	0.4	SS(65): 0.4	0.0
2012	SFN	MLB	25	476	44	26	3	4	45	33	95	1	4	.248/.304/.349	.246	.307	0.8	SS(139): 12.7	2.9
2013	SFN	MLB	26	550	52	24	3	9	43	42	96	1	2	.248/.311/.363	.247	.290	2.1	SS(147): -1.1	1.6
2014	SFN	MLB	27	502	48	23	2	8	46	39	91	3	3	.241/.303/.353	.245	.280	-1.2	SS 5	1.9

Crawford slugged .499 in three years at UCLA, so he wasn't always seen as a defense-only shortstop. After hitting dreadfully in his rookie season and showing signs of life in 2012, his TAv climbed into the middle of the pack for MLB shortstops last year. He's defense-first, to be sure, but not defense-only, making the Giants' dearth of shortstop prospects less concerning than it would otherwise be.

Adam Duvall 3B

Born: 9/4/1988 Age: 25
Bats: R Throws: R Height: 6' 1"
Weight: 205 Breakout: 15%
Improve: 23% Collapse: 16%
Attrition: 37% MLB: 46%

Comparables:
Luke Hughes, Danny Valencia, Russ Canzler

YEAR	TEAM	LVL	AGE	PA	R	2B	3B	HR	RBI	BB	SO	SB	CS	AVG/OBP/SLG	TAv	BABIP	BRR	FRAA	WARP
2011	AUG	A	22	510	69	30	4	22	87	59	98	4	4	.285/.385/.527	.328	.320	0.6	3B(83): -2.5	4.0
2012	SJO	A+	23	598	101	24	4	30	100	47	116	8	2	.258/.327/.487	.302	.274	2.4	3B(117): 3.3, 1B(1): -0.0	5.2
2013	RIC	AA	24	430	61	23	4	17	58	35	72	2	1	.252/.320/.465	.288	.268	0.2	3B(90): 6.1, 1B(7): -0.2	3.3
2014	SFN	MLB	25	250	26	10	1	9	32	16	55	0	0	.229/.285/.406	.253	.260	-0.3	3B 1, 1B -0	0.5

Third basemen who can hit with power are worth their weight in gold (offer void if you weigh as much as Pablo Sandoval). That was the scouting report on Duvall coming out of the University of Louisville, but he's yet to prove he can handle the first two words of that equation: Duvall's .931 fielding percentage in 2013 was the *best* he's had in a pro season, and plenty of skeptics doubt he'll stick at the hot corner. If he needs to move to first or left, it'll demand too much from his all-or-nothing bat. If his ceiling is a first-division third baseman, his floor is a third-division first baseman.

Jeff Francoeur RF

Born: 1/8/1984 Age: 30
Bats: R Throws: R Height: 6' 4"
Weight: 210 Breakout: 0%
Improve: 40% Collapse: 7%
Attrition: 22% MLB: 97%

Comparables:
Juan Encarnacion, Mark Carreon, Ruben Sierra

YEAR	TEAM	LVL	AGE	PA	R	2B	3B	HR	RBI	BB	SO	SB	CS	AVG/OBP/SLG	TAv	BABIP	BRR	FRAA	WARP
2011	KCA	MLB	27	656	77	47	4	20	87	37	123	22	10	.285/.329/.476	.274	.323	-2.7	RF(153): 6.8	3.6
2012	KCA	MLB	28	603	58	26	3	16	49	34	119	4	7	.235/.287/.378	.229	.272	-1.9	RF(145): -18.6, CF(3): -0.4	-2.5
2013	KCA	MLB	29	193	19	8	2	3	13	8	49	2	0	.208/.249/.322	.198	.267	-0.3	RF(54): -0.6	-1.0
2013	SFN	MLB	29	63	1	2	0	0	4	1	12	1	0	.194/.206/.226	.167	.240	-0.3	LF(16): -0.6, CF(2): -0.2	-0.4
2014	SFN	MLB	30	312	31	15	1	7	33	17	59	5	3	.245/.291/.378	.247	.280	-0.3	RF -3, LF -1	-0.2

BP's forecasting tools don't have a percentile low enough to describe Frenchy's 2013 season. His -12.1 VORP was baseball's fourth-worst, and he accrued that in just 81 games. Imagine what he could have done in a full season! (Or just multiply by two.) His benefactor, Dayton Moore, finally decided he had seen enough and declared the $3 million he owed Francoeur officially sunk. The Giants, desperate for right-handed power, took a flyer, but Francoeur is all right-handed and no power these days. Deciding that the illness couldn't be worse than the 'coeur, San Francisco quickly gave him his second pink slip of the season.

Ryder Jones 3B

Born: 6/7/1994 Age: 20
Bats: L Throws: R Height: 6' 2"
Weight: 200 Breakout: 0%
Improve: 0% Collapse: 0%
Attrition: 0% MLB: 0%

Comparables:
Will Middlebrooks, Juan Francisco, Mat Gamel

YEAR	TEAM	LVL	AGE	PA	R	2B	3B	HR	RBI	BB	SO	SB	CS	AVG/OBP/SLG	TAv	BABIP	BRR	FRAA	WARP
2014	SFN	MLB	20	250	16	8	0	2	18	12	76	0	0	.184/.228/.245	.181	.260	-0.4	3B 1	-1.4

Jones was considered by many to be a second-round reach, but he is nonetheless intriguing: a lefty-hitting third baseman with plenty of arm to stick at the hot corner. He's built lean, with room to add easy muscle. The power didn't show in his complex-league debut, but a low strikeout rate and high on-base percentage did. Some scouts are skeptical about the bat speed, but his short, simple swing allows him to let the ball get deep and spray it to all fields. The next couple of years will be rough, but don't be surprised if Jones opens up shop at third down the line.

Mike Morse RF

Born: 3/22/1982 Age: 32
Bats: R Throws: R Height: 6' 5"
Weight: 245 Breakout: 1%
Improve: 31% Collapse: 2%
Attrition: 9% MLB: 90%

Comparables:
Nelson Cruz, Ryan Ludwick, Dave Parker

YEAR	TEAM	LVL	AGE	PA	R	2B	3B	HR	RBI	BB	SO	SB	CS	AVG/OBP/SLG	TAv	BABIP	BRR	FRAA	WARP
2011	WAS	MLB	29	575	73	36	0	31	95	36	126	2	3	.303/.360/.550	.322	.344	1.3	1B(85): -0.0, LF(55): -1.9	4.2
2012	WAS	MLB	30	430	53	17	1	18	62	16	97	0	1	.291/.321/.470	.273	.339	-4.3	LF(67): -3.6, RF(36): 1.6	0.5
2013	TAC	AAA	31	26	3	1	0	1	2	2	6	0	0	.250/.308/.417	.240	.294	0.2	RF(3): 0.1	0.0
2013	SEA	MLB	31	307	31	13	0	13	27	20	80	0	0	.226/.283/.410	.259	.267	-1.5	RF(53): -2.9, LF(11): 0.1	-0.1
2013	BAL	MLB	31	30	3	0	0	0	0	1	7	0	0	.103/.133/.103	.092	.136	-0.2	LF(8): 0.4, RF(2): -0.1	-0.5
2014	SFN	MLB	32	342	39	16	1	13	46	22	79	1	1	.264/.320/.446	.281	.310	-0.7	RF -0, LF -1	1.1

Morse's 2013 is a great case study of the notion that just because someone is playing, they're not necessarily healthy. The nagging injuries came early and often for Morse, putting him on the disabled list for most of July and costing him several other multi-game spans. He was a shell of himself with Seattle and a complete non-entity with Baltimore. The power is still an obviously loud tool and the extinction of his 2011 skills isn't a foregone conclusion, but his walk year was a terrible time for Morse's body to fail him. The Giants inked him to a one-year deal, hoping his bat can rediscover enough juice to overcome his sketchy outfield glove.

Nick Noonan SS

Born: 5/4/1989 Age: 25
Bats: L Throws: R Height: 6' 1"
Weight: 170 Breakout: 1%
Improve: 4% Collapse: 5%
Attrition: 11% MLB: 22%

Comparables:
Pete Kozma, Ivan De Jesus, Matt Tolbert

YEAR	TEAM	LVL	AGE	PA	R	2B	3B	HR	RBI	BB	SO	SB	CS	AVG/OBP/SLG	TAv	BABIP	BRR	FRAA	WARP
2011	SJO	A+	22	135	14	6	1	1	16	12	18	1	2	.246/.311/.336	.222	.279	-0.1	3B(5): 0.5, 2B(1): -0.1	0.0
2011	RIC	AA	22	299	28	11	0	3	25	33	60	2	2	.212/.303/.288	.232	.261	-1	SS(65): 3.1	0.5
2011	FRE	AAA	22	41	6	0	0	1	4	4	2	1	0	.297/.366/.378	.268	.294	-0.4	SS(9): -1.5	0.0
2012	FRE	AAA	23	541	65	26	3	9	62	40	84	7	3	.296/.347/.416	.268	.338	-2.7	SS(97): -1.1, 3B(13): 1.6	2.2
2013	FRE	AAA	24	188	20	13	1	0	20	17	44	1	2	.255/.323/.345	.238	.339	1.9	2B(36): 2.5, 3B(9): -0.3	0.8
2013	SFN	MLB	24	111	12	2	0	0	5	6	24	0	0	.219/.261/.238	.181	.284	0.9	2B(22): -1.3, 3B(15): 0.5	-0.5
2014	SFN	MLB	25	250	20	10	1	2	21	19	53	1	1	.230/.288/.312	.225	.290	-0.4	SS -0, 2B -0	0.0

The Giants had high hopes for Noonan when they selected him 32nd overall in 2007. Comped (hysterically, one might say) to Chase Utley—athletic second baseman who would someday hit with power—he never approached that ceiling, and he's still looking for his first double-digit home run season at any level. He broke camp with the big club last April, ostensibly as a superutility man and insurance policy for Marco Scutaro, but he couldn't hit enough to hold on to that modest role, and instead got another chance to underwhelm in Triple-A. It's tough to give up on a guy who is just 24, but it's easy enough to just quit paying attention to him until he sets off at least one motion detector.

Angel Pagan CF

Born: 7/2/1981 Age: 32
Bats: B Throws: R Height: 6' 2"
Weight: 200 Breakout: 2%
Improve: 44% Collapse: 3%
Attrition: 11% MLB: 96%

Comparables:
Vernon Wells, Coco Crisp, Cesar Cedeno

YEAR	TEAM	LVL	AGE	PA	R	2B	3B	HR	RBI	BB	SO	SB	CS	AVG/OBP/SLG	TAv	BABIP	BRR	FRAA	WARP
2011	SLU	A+	29	36	6	1	1	1	2	4	5	0	2	.226/.333/.419	.262	.240	0		0.0
2011	NYN	MLB	29	532	68	24	4	7	56	44	62	32	7	.262/.322/.372	.263	.285	4	CF(121): 1.2	2.3
2012	SFN	MLB	30	659	95	38	15	8	56	48	97	29	7	.288/.338/.440	.289	.329	1.4	CF(151): 5.5	4.7
2013	FRE	AAA	31	22	1	0	0	0	3	2	2	0	0	.278/.364/.278	.237	.294	0.2	CF(5): -0.2	0.0
2013	SFN	MLB	31	305	44	16	3	5	30	23	36	9	4	.282/.334/.414	.277	.307	2.6	CF(71): -4.5	1.2
2014	SFN	MLB	32	363	45	18	4	5	31	27	52	16	4	.273/.326/.399	.269	.310	1.6	CF -0	1.6

Alas, the repeat—by Pagan, or by the Giants—was not to be, as the center fielder missed 84 games with a left hamstring strain and the Giants went 32-52 in his absence. When healthy, he has performed at All-Star levels, playing plus defense in center and flashing gap power for a team that craves muscle in any form. Brian Sabean's decision to re-sign Pagan to a four-year extension last offseason was otherwise prescient, anticipating both the struggles of prospect flop Gary Brown and the market bubble for outfield talent. Even if Brown or another upstart were to force the issue between now and 2016, Pagan could slide into a corner and easily justify his annual $10 million salary.

Joe Panik SS

Born: 10/30/1990 Age: 23
Bats: L Throws: R Height: 6' 1"
Weight: 190 Breakout: 1%
Improve: 12% Collapse: 0%
Attrition: 7% MLB: 16%

Comparables:
Callix Crabbe, Jermaine Curtis, Scott Sizemore

YEAR	TEAM	LVL	AGE	PA	R	2B	3B	HR	RBI	BB	SO	SB	CS	AVG/OBP/SLG	TAv	BABIP	BRR	FRAA	WARP
2011	SLO	A-	20	304	49	10	3	6	54	28	25	13	5	.341/.401/.467	.322	.354	-0.2	SS(33): 1.0	1.6
2012	SJO	A+	21	605	93	27	4	7	76	58	54	10	4	.297/.368/.402	.301	.317	4.2	SS(122): 9.8	6.1
2013	RIC	AA	22	599	64	27	4	4	57	58	68	10	5	.257/.333/.347	.260	.285	-0.8	2B(117): -5.8, SS(20): 0.2	1.0
2014	SFN	MLB	23	250	24	11	1	2	18	18	35	1	1	.241/.297/.317	.234	.270	-0.3	SS 1, 2B -1	0.3

Everybody sees and everybody says the same thing about Panik: There's no one tool that really stands out, but he's a solid all-around ballplayer. Good athlete, fields his position well, good makeup, maybe a little pop down the road. That last bit hasn't come yet, and even the consistent hit tool is looking suspect: All aspects of his slash line have dropped substantially each year since the Giants picked him 29th overall, and his exceptional contact skills no longer lead to exceptional contact. Still, the climb has been steady and should ultimately lead to at least a bench role. No truth to the rumor that the Giants have set aside a room off the clubhouse solely for his use.

Hunter Pence RF

Born: 4/13/1983 Age: 31
Bats: R Throws: R Height: 6' 4"
Weight: 220 Breakout: 0%
Improve: 45% Collapse: 4%
Attrition: 2% MLB: 95%

Comparables:
Michael Cuddyer, Roberto Clemente, George Hendrick

YEAR	TEAM	LVL	AGE	PA	R	2B	3B	HR	RBI	BB	SO	SB	CS	AVG/OBP/SLG	TAv	BABIP	BRR	FRAA	WARP
2011	HOU	MLB	28	432	49	26	3	11	62	30	86	7	1	.308/.356/.471	.300	.368	1.4	RF(100): -1.0	2.8
2011	PHI	MLB	28	236	35	12	2	11	35	26	38	1	1	.324/.394/.560	.348	.348	0.2	RF(53): -3.4	2.6
2012	PHI	MLB	29	440	59	15	2	17	59	37	85	4	2	.271/.336/.447	.278	.305	0	RF(101): -8.4	0.7
2012	SFN	MLB	29	248	28	11	2	7	45	19	60	1	0	.219/.287/.384	.258	.261	-0.2	RF(58): -1.2	0.1
2013	SFN	MLB	30	687	91	35	5	27	99	52	115	22	3	.283/.339/.483	.294	.308	-0.4	RF(162): 14.8	5.1
2014	SFN	MLB	31	646	77	29	3	21	82	51	117	13	4	.271/.329/.440	.284	.300	0.5	RF 2	3.0

Once Pence's jumble of misbegotten limbs gets going, it somehow makes for an excellent baseballer, and the 2013 season might have been his best yet. He led the Giants in slugging, home runs and extra-base hits while effectively patrolling one of the toughest right fields in the game. Pence was a beloved member of the organization even when he was scuffling through the worst stretch of his career, in 2012; no surprise, then, that when things turned around Pence made lots of noises about wanting to remain in San Francisco. He and The City consummated just before the season ended, with a $90 million pact covering the next five years. Pence is unlikely to be this good in five years, but $18 million is unlikely to seem so expensive in five years.

Juan Perez   RF

Born: 11/13/1986 Age: 27
Bats: R Throws: R Height: 5' 11"
Weight: 185 Breakout: 1%
Improve: 11% Collapse: 6%
Attrition: 16% MLB: 23%

Comparables:
Scott Cousins, Greg Golson, Nick Stavinoha

YEAR	TEAM	LVL	AGE	PA	R	2B	3B	HR	RBI	BB	SO	SB	CS	AVG/OBP/SLG	TAv	BABIP	BRR	FRAA	WARP
2011	RIC	AA	24	497	58	25	10	4	40	28	95	22	6	.256/.303/.381	.260	.313	1.3	CF(102): 19.7, LF(8): 1.0	3.7
2012	RIC	AA	25	513	65	26	4	11	53	22	85	18	15	.302/.341/.441	.292	.349	3.4	RF(94): 3.2, CF(16): 0.4	4.2
2013	FRE	AAA	26	409	52	27	5	10	50	15	75	18	6	.291/.323/.466	.282	.337	2.6	RF(50): 9.0, 3B(34): -0.4	3.1
2013	SFN	MLB	26	97	8	5	0	1	8	6	21	2	0	.258/.302/.348	.232	.324	-0.3	CF(20): 2.0, LF(11): 0.4	0.6
2014	SFN	MLB	27	250	24	12	2	4	24	9	54	7	3	.251/.282/.368	.244	.300	0.3	RF 1, CF 3	0.7

You never saw Perez's name on top prospect lists, and the few optimistic comments one did see always conceded his advanced age relative to level. But while perennial prospect Gray Brown continued to struggle and languish in Triple-A, Perez was the one earning multiple call-ups. He can cover all three outfield positions well: The metrics loved the limited data he provided, and he had a knack for getting on highlight shows. He has hit right-handed pitchers better than lefties throughout his career, so if you squint you could forecast some slight offensive improvement as he finds his form against southpaws. More likely, his OBP tops out around .300 and he serves as a fourth or fifth outfielder.

Brett Pill   1B

Born: 9/9/1984 Age: 29
Bats: R Throws: R Height: 6' 4"
Weight: 225 Breakout: 3%
Improve: 8% Collapse: 8%
Attrition: 19% MLB: 32%

Comparables:
Chris Carter, Scott Thorman, Michael Aubrey

YEAR	TEAM	LVL	AGE	PA	R	2B	3B	HR	RBI	BB	SO	SB	CS	AVG/OBP/SLG	TAv	BABIP	BRR	FRAA	WARP
2011	FRE	AAA	26	576	82	36	3	25	107	25	54	6	6	.312/.341/.530	.280	.305	-2.6	1B(71): -1.9, 2B(49): -4.4	1.1
2011	SFN	MLB	26	53	7	3	2	2	9	2	8	0	1	.300/.321/.560	.315	.317	-0.3	1B(14): 1.0	0.4
2012	FRE	AAA	27	268	35	18	1	11	45	13	36	0	0	.285/.336/.500	.287	.294	-2.4	1B(54): -2.0, LF(2): 0.2	0.6
2012	SFN	MLB	27	114	10	3	0	4	11	6	19	1	0	.210/.265/.352	.220	.220	-1.2	1B(24): 2.5, LF(7): -0.1	-0.1
2013	FRE	AAA	28	298	48	21	2	18	79	15	40	1	0	.344/.379/.630	.345	.347	-1	1B(65): -0.0, 3B(3): -0.0	3.2
2013	SFN	MLB	28	92	11	4	0	3	12	5	17	0	0	.224/.272/.376	.237	.242	0.1	1B(13): -0.1, LF(8): 0.1	0.1
2014	SFN	MLB	29	250	26	13	1	9	32	10	40	1	1	.256/.291/.430	.265	.270	-0.4	1B 0, LF 0	0.4

Pill is a tweener who slugs against Triple-A pitching but has struggled in sporadic big-league experience, while aging out of the key demographic. He's a hitter without a natural position, and experiments all over the diamond (1B, 2B, 3B, LF) haven't turned up any sweet deals. Having joined the KIA Tigers in Korea, Pill's place in this book is a monument to that awkward time a significant number of concerned citizens convinced themselves he was better than Brandon Belt.

Buster Posey   C

Born: 3/27/1987 Age: 27
Bats: R Throws: R Height: 6' 1"
Weight: 220 Breakout: 2%
Improve: 62% Collapse: 6%
Attrition: 9% MLB: 100%

Comparables:
Carlos Santana, Brian McCann, Carlos Quentin

YEAR	TEAM	LVL	AGE	PA	R	2B	3B	HR	RBI	BB	SO	SB	CS	AVG/OBP/SLG	TAv	BABIP	BRR	FRAA	WARP
2011	SFN	MLB	24	185	17	5	0	4	21	18	30	3	0	.284/.368/.389	.274	.326	-1	C(41): -0.2, 1B(2): 0.0	1.1
2012	SFN	MLB	25	610	78	39	1	24	103	69	96	1	1	.336/.408/.549	.347	.368	-3.6	C(114): -0.6, 1B(29): -2.1	7.6
2013	SFN	MLB	26	595	61	34	1	15	72	60	70	2	1	.294/.371/.450	.296	.312	-4.5	C(121): 0.3, 1B(21): -0.6	4.1
2014	SFN	MLB	27	562	68	30	1	18	74	56	80	2	1	.296/.372/.468	.308	.320	-1	C 0, 1B -1	4.9

By Buster Posey standards, 2013 was a down year: His TAv and WARP both represent substantial drops from the previous year's MVP-level production. He still managed to lead NL catchers in both categories, so, you know, everything is relative. He has an excuse (not that he'll claim it), as those numbers were dragged down by a sub-.600 OPS after he fractured a finger in early September. That'll always be the risk with the Giants putting their best player behind the plate 120 times a year. Brandon Belt's emergence at first base seals off one exit strategy, so the latest chatter puts Posey's long-term future at the hot corner. The bat and the arm will play there, and any hit in his value might be offset by a gain in durability and better Septembers to come.

Brian Ragira   1B

Born: 1/22/1992 Age: 22
Bats: R Throws: R Height: 6' 2"
Weight: 185 Breakout: 0%
Improve: 0% Collapse: 0%
Attrition: 0% MLB: 0%

Comparables:
Yan Gomes, Russ Canzler, Ike Davis

YEAR	TEAM	LVL	AGE	PA	R	2B	3B	HR	RBI	BB	SO	SB	CS	AVG/OBP/SLG	TAv	BABIP	BRR	FRAA	WARP
2013	SLO	A-	21	213	29	12	1	3	36	26	54	1	1	.263/.371/.391	.296	.355	0.8	1B(18): -1.9, RF(18): -0.7	0.9
2014	SFN	MLB	22	250	18	8	1	2	20	17	76	0	0	.191/.250/.265	.197	.270	-0.4	1B -2, RF -1	-1.6

From a distance, the fourth-rounder Ragira looks similar to Austin Wilson, his former Stanford teammate and a second-round pick in June by Seattle. As you get closer, the differences become apparent. Unlike the athletic, broad-shouldered Wilson, Ragira has a thick lower half and is a below-average runner. He hit for power in college, but there are doubts about how his swing will play with wood bats. If his numbers in short-season ball are any indication, it's going to be a struggle. Given his defensive profile—strictly first base or an outfield corner—he's going to need to do a lot more than draw walks to crack a big-league lineup.

Hector Sanchez C

Born: 11/17/1989 Age: 24
Bats: B Throws: R Height: 6' 0"
Weight: 235 Breakout: 10%
Improve: 41% Collapse: 11%
Attrition: 24% MLB: 77%

Comparables:
Wilson Ramos, Guillermo Quiroz, Kurt Suzuki

YEAR	TEAM	LVL	AGE	PA	R	2B	3B	HR	RBI	BB	SO	SB	CS	AVG/OBP/SLG	TAv	BABIP	BRR	FRAA	WARP
2011	SJO	A+	21	228	31	14	1	11	58	11	49	0	1	.302/.338/.533	.334	.342	-0.5	C(15): -0.3	1.0
2011	FRE	AAA	21	168	15	9	0	1	26	13	22	0	1	.261/.315/.340	.225	.295	0.5	C(37): 0.7	0.2
2011	SFN	MLB	21	34	0	2	0	0	1	3	6	0	0	.258/.324/.323	.228	.320	0.1	C(11): -0.0	0.0
2012	SFN	MLB	22	227	22	15	0	3	34	5	52	0	0	.280/.295/.390	.246	.349	-1.8	C(56): -1.1	0.2
2013	FRE	AAA	23	99	10	4	0	3	11	12	15	0	0	.271/.364/.424	.275	.294	-0.3	C(18): -0.3	0.6
2013	SFN	MLB	23	140	8	4	0	3	19	7	29	0	0	.248/.300/.349	.241	.296	-0.9	C(33): 0.0	0.1
2014	SFN	MLB	24	250	22	12	0	5	26	13	51	0	0	.248/.292/.365	.244	.290	-0.5	C -0	0.6

Sanchez has played most of two big-league seasons and didn't turn 24 until after the 2013 campaign concluded. His offense has improved each year, and his on-base average and his walk and strikeout rates all headed in the right direction last year. He can easily clear the low offensive bar for catchers; the issue is his defense, which doesn't show any trajectory of note. His big body, questionable athleticism and noisy pitch receiving will likely prevent him from being an everyday catcher. If the bat continues to improve, the Giants will find a spot that even his body can fit, or at least another team that will.

Pablo Sandoval 3B

Born: 8/11/1986 Age: 27
Bats: B Throws: R Height: 5' 11"
Weight: 240 Breakout: 12%
Improve: 55% Collapse: 6%
Attrition: 9% MLB: 100%

Comparables:
George Brett, Ryan Zimmerman, Chipper Jones

YEAR	TEAM	LVL	AGE	PA	R	2B	3B	HR	RBI	BB	SO	SB	CS	AVG/OBP/SLG	TAv	BABIP	BRR	FRAA	WARP
2011	FRE	AAA	24	22	4	0	0	2	7	2	0	0	0	.278/.318/.611	.316	.167	0	3B(4): -0.7, 1B(1): -0.1	0.2
2011	SFN	MLB	24	466	55	26	3	23	70	32	63	2	4	.315/.357/.552	.329	.320	-1.7	3B(106): 7.9, 1B(6): 0.1	5.8
2012	SJO	A+	25	23	1	2	0	1	1	1	5	0	0	.273/.304/.500	.273	.312	0	3B(4): -0.7	0.0
2012	SFN	MLB	25	442	59	25	2	12	63	38	59	1	1	.283/.342/.447	.293	.301	-0.2	3B(102): 8.1, 1B(3): 0.1	3.6
2013	SFN	MLB	26	584	52	27	2	14	79	47	79	0	0	.278/.341/.417	.275	.301	-4.8	3B(137): -14.9	0.4
2014	SFN	MLB	27	525	61	29	2	17	70	41	68	2	1	.290/.346/.468	.298	.300	-1.1	3B -4, 1B -0	2.9

It's easy to hate Pablo Sandoval. Here's a fall-out-of-bed hitter and, quite often, an astoundingly good defender given his ... physical limitations, yet he's on the verge of eating himself out of baseball. He's a chubby-cheeked poster child for squandered potential, an affront to everyone who ever loved playing baseball but had no aptitude. But it's even easier to *love* Pablo Sandoval, because he's a jolly fat guy who lives to swing, an inspiration to everyone who ever loved playing baseball but couldn't stick to a diet. His offensive numbers slipped for the second consecutive season, but his production was still enough to finish in the top third of big-league third basemen. The main concern is his health; while he hit the DL just once, he added 10 other entries to his table in the BP Injury History database. Conventional wisdom said he'd end up a DH, but unless he can maintain his health—all manners of it—even that outcome is in jeopardy.

Marco Scutaro 2B

Born: 10/30/1975 Age: 38
Bats: R Throws: R Height: 5' 10"
Weight: 185 Breakout: 0%
Improve: 29% Collapse: 11%
Attrition: 23% MLB: 71%

Comparables:
Jamey Carroll, Chris Gomez, Mark Loretta

YEAR	TEAM	LVL	AGE	PA	R	2B	3B	HR	RBI	BB	SO	SB	CS	AVG/OBP/SLG	TAv	BABIP	BRR	FRAA	WARP
2011	BOS	MLB	35	445	59	26	1	7	54	38	36	4	2	.299/.358/.423	.267	.312	2	SS(109): -0.7, 2B(2): 0.0	2.2
2012	COL	MLB	36	415	47	16	3	4	30	27	35	7	3	.271/.324/.361	.236	.287	1.2	2B(72): 5.5, SS(27): 3.1	1.2
2012	SFN	MLB	36	268	40	16	1	3	44	13	14	2	1	.362/.385/.473	.311	.366	0.5	2B(46): -4.0, 3B(15): 1.7	1.9
2013	SFN	MLB	37	547	57	23	3	2	31	45	34	2	0	.297/.357/.369	.271	.314	1.2	2B(121): -0.9	2.0
2014	SFN	MLB	38	541	57	25	1	3	40	45	54	5	2	.268/.330/.345	.255	.290	-0.7	2B -0, SS -0	1.6

Scutaro didn't get a shot as an everyday guy until he was already 28 years old, past the conventional sweet spot. He turned 37 in 2013, meaning he now has a full decade as a regular and, finally, an All-Star appearance. He couldn't touch the numbers he put up down the stretch in 2012, but still managed a TAv better than his career mark, putting him squarely in the middle of the pack for qualified second basemen. He led the league in contact rate, and had the third-lowest swing rate on pitches out of the zone, so even as age erodes his power he refuses to relinquish that shot that he had to work so long to earn.

Andrew Susac   C

Born: 3/22/1990 Age: 24
Bats: R Throws: R Height: 6' 2"
Weight: 210 Breakout: 0%
Improve: 6% Collapse: 7%
Attrition: 10% MLB: 21%

Comparables:
Josh Donaldson, George Kottaras, Michael McKenry

YEAR	TEAM	LVL	AGE	PA	R	2B	3B	HR	RBI	BB	SO	SB	CS	AVG/OBP/SLG	TAv	BABIP	BRR	FRAA	WARP
2012	SJO	A+	22	426	58	16	3	9	52	55	100	1	1	.244/.351/.380	.279	.311	-0.7	C(97): 0.3	3.1
2013	RIC	AA	23	310	32	17	0	12	46	42	68	1	0	.256/.362/.458	.310	.299	-0.6	C(71): -0.5, 1B(9): -0.7	3.0
2014	SFN	MLB	24	250	25	10	1	6	27	26	65	0	0	.220/.305/.354	.247	.280	-0.4	C -0, 1B -0	0.7

Susac has lived up to his pre-draft reputation as a defense-first catcher with a potentially average bat. He put down 40 percent of baserunners last year (after throwing out Billy Hamilton five times in 2012) while learning to handle a more advanced breed of pro pitchers. Many Giants farmhands find it difficult to make the adjustment from the highly charged California League to the oppressive Double-A Eastern League, but Susac actually boosted his slash line with a promotion. He's probably only a year away from qualifying to serve as Buster Posey's backup, so the real question for his future is whether Posey plans to stay in a squat forever.

Andres Torres   CF

Born: 1/26/1978 Age: 36
Bats: B Throws: R Height: 5' 10"
Weight: 195 Breakout: 1%
Improve: 26% Collapse: 14%
Attrition: 22% MLB: 71%

Comparables:
Greg Norton, David Dellucci, Charlie Maxwell

YEAR	TEAM	LVL	AGE	PA	R	2B	3B	HR	RBI	BB	SO	SB	CS	AVG/OBP/SLG	TAv	BABIP	BRR	FRAA	WARP
2011	FRE	AAA	33	62	10	2	2	4	11	6	13	1	0	.273/.355/.600	.301	.289	1	CF(11): 0.9	0.6
2011	SFN	MLB	33	398	50	24	1	4	19	42	95	19	6	.221/.312/.330	.251	.293	5.5	CF(106): 0.5, RF(4): 0.3	1.7
2012	NYN	MLB	34	434	47	17	7	3	35	52	90	13	5	.230/.327/.337	.254	.293	1.1	CF(124): 0.5	1.4
2013	SFN	MLB	35	300	33	17	1	2	21	22	61	4	3	.250/.302/.342	.239	.310	0.6	LF(56): 3.9, CF(30): 1.5	0.5
2014	SFN	MLB	36	311	37	16	3	4	25	30	72	10	3	.236/.312/.362	.252	.300	0.7	CF 2, LF 3	1.2

There's always been something confounding about Torres. He's clearly a gifted athlete, with an excess of natural speed and strength, but he only briefly put it all together in an outlier 2010 season. A natural righty who picked up switch-hitting late, Torres has always struggled from the left side, but in 2013 he was downright dismal against right-handers—he got on base against them less than 26 percent of the time and struck out *more* than 26 percent of the time. His league-average-ish production against lefties buoyed his overall line, but that unremarkable final slash is unlikely to lure a manager into promising him full-time play. Torres' season ended in late August, when he hit the 60-day DL to have surgery on his Achilles tendon, putting him one year further from 2010.

Angel Villalona   1B

Born: 8/13/1990 Age: 23
Bats: R Throws: R Height: 6' 3"
Weight: 257 Breakout: 0%
Improve: 1% Collapse: 0%
Attrition: 2% MLB: 2%

Comparables:
Mauro Gomez, Russell Mitchell, Neftali Soto

YEAR	TEAM	LVL	AGE	PA	R	2B	3B	HR	RBI	BB	SO	SB	CS	AVG/OBP/SLG	TAv	BABIP	BRR	FRAA	WARP
2013	SJO	A+	22	309	37	16	0	14	42	15	76	0	0	.229/.278/.433	.266	.258	-0.3	1B(70): -0.5	0.4
2013	RIC	AA	22	209	23	11	0	8	28	8	60	0	0	.235/.273/.413	.248	.292	-2.1	1B(44): -0.8	-0.5
2014	SFN	MLB	23	250	23	10	0	8	29	9	73	0	0	.212/.246/.361	.222	.260	-0.5	1B 0	-0.6

With dismissed murder charges and related visa issues finally behind him, Villalona returned stateside in 2013 at the ripe old age of 22. He struggled mightily between High-A and Double-A, as he was clearly out of shape and an immature approach smothered the remnants of his once-elite power. The 2014 season may be a better indication of his progress; his conditioning should be improved, and, as you've deduced, he'll still be just 23. (And in case you didn't deduce that, we've also helpfully printed his 2014 age above. At your service.)

Mac Williamson   RF

Born: 7/15/1990 Age: 23
Bats: R Throws: R Height: 6' 5"
Weight: 240 Breakout: 1%
Improve: 17% Collapse: 7%
Attrition: 12% MLB: 35%

Comparables:
Wladimir Balentien, Domonic Brown, Nate Schierholtz

YEAR	TEAM	LVL	AGE	PA	R	2B	3B	HR	RBI	BB	SO	SB	CS	AVG/OBP/SLG	TAv	BABIP	BRR	FRAA	WARP
2012	SLO	A-	21	126	22	8	0	7	25	6	19	0	0	.342/.392/.596	.326	.360	0	RF(23): -0.4	1.0
2013	SJO	A+	22	599	94	31	2	25	89	51	132	10	1	.292/.375/.504	.332	.345	2.8	RF(115): 1.4	6.1
2014	SFN	MLB	23	250	26	10	0	8	30	15	63	0	0	.242/.301/.394	.258	.300	-0.4	RF 0	0.4

At 6-foot-5 and 240 pounds, Mac Williamson provides a lot of Mac Williamson to like. After making some adjustments at the plate early in the summer, he added some bulk to his stats, too: He hit .332/.408/.574 after July 1st, a line that includes stirring improvements in his strikeout and walk rates. Double-A will be a tougher test, particularly as he'll be in a hitting environment that more closely resembles his ultimate destination.

PITCHERS

Jeremy Affeldt

Born: 6/6/1979 Age: 35
Bats: L Throws: L Height: 6' 4" Weight: 225
Breakout: 30% Improve: 53% Collapse: 28%
Attrition: 16% MLB: 86%

Comparables:
Scott Downs, Roberto Hernandez, Scott Eyre

YEAR	TEAM	LVL	AGE	W	L	SV	G	GS	IP	H	HR	BB	SO	BB9	SO9	GB%	BABIP	WHIP	ERA	FIP	FRA	WARP
2011	SFN	MLB	32	3	2	3	67	0	61²	47	5	24	54	3.5	7.9	63%	.249	1.15	2.63	3.66	4.26	0.0
2012	SFN	MLB	33	1	2	3	67	0	63¹	57	1	23	57	3.3	8.1	62%	.306	1.26	2.70	2.77	3.96	0.5
2013	SFN	MLB	34	1	5	0	39	0	33²	27	2	17	21	4.5	5.6	57%	.245	1.31	3.74	4.42	5.47	-0.3
2014	SFN	MLB	35	2	1	1	41	0	38	32	3	15	32	3.5	7.6	57%	.290	1.23	3.42	3.89	3.72	0.4

You may remember Jeremy Affeldt from such DL stints as "Laceration from Attempted Separation of Ground Beef Patty" or "Gravity-Induced Collision With Dugout Steps in Avoidance of Foul Ball." This year he starred in "Sneezing Fit With Near Tragic Consequences for Oblique," and "Injured Left Groin II," a sequel to his 2005 vehicle. When he was on the field, he looked much like the Affeldt of old, holding lefties to just two extra-base hits (both doubles) while putting up a credible fight against righties. But then there's the strikeout rate, the walk rate, the Fair Run Average—the scary indications that Affeldt's 2013 was the stealth transition from pretty good to pretty unreliable. Relievers are flaky by nature, so you put up with a guy who's sometimes bad; you put up with a guy who's sometimes injured. Marry the two and you start to worry about the last two years on that contract.

Bryce Bandilla

Born: 1/17/1990 Age: 24
Bats: L Throws: L Height: 6' 4" Weight: 235
Breakout: 50% Improve: 71% Collapse: 24%
Attrition: 40% MLB: 15%

Comparables:
Brad Boxberger, Victor Garate, Jeff Beliveau

YEAR	TEAM	LVL	AGE	W	L	SV	G	GS	IP	H	HR	BB	SO	BB9	SO9	GB%	BABIP	WHIP	ERA	FIP	FRA	WARP
2012	AUG	A	22	2	4	0	11	9	44¹	44	1	28	48	5.7	9.7	44%	.341	1.62	3.05	3.60	3.51	1.0
2013	SJO	A+	23	1	4	5	38	0	44¹	26	5	25	72	5.1	14.6	35%	.262	1.15	3.65	3.75	3.44	0.9
2014	SFN	MLB	24	2	1	1	22	3	41	36	4	22	41	4.9	9.0	43%	.307	1.43	4.27	4.17	4.65	-0.0

Bryce Bandilla's strikeout rate as San Jose's set-up man was crazy, like Kanye West or Joaquin Phoenix. His walk rate was crazy, like a bunch of people you haven't heard of because they never accomplished a darned thing. That's probably a bit too much crazy for success, even for a left-hander who can crank it up to 97. A move from the Cal League to the more pitcher-friendly Eastern League should encourage Bandilla to challenge hitters with his fastball and plus changeup, and with that arsenal and fewer free passes it would be easy to project him as somebody worth watching.

Ty Blach

Born: 10/20/1990 Age: 23
Bats: R Throws: L Height: 6' 1" Weight: 200
Breakout: 50% Improve: 59% Collapse: 21%
Attrition: 54% MLB: 25%

Comparables:
Dillon Gee, Dallas Keuchel, Jeremy Sowers

YEAR	TEAM	LVL	AGE	W	L	SV	G	GS	IP	H	HR	BB	SO	BB9	SO9	GB%	BABIP	WHIP	ERA	FIP	FRA	WARP
2013	SJO	A+	22	12	4	0	22	20	130¹	124	8	18	117	1.2	8.1	48%	.304	1.09	2.90	3.23	3.70	2.5
2014	SFN	MLB	23	6	5	0	15	15	92²	95	9	28	59	2.7	5.7	46%	.303	1.32	4.17	4.18	4.54	0.1

Blach didn't command a lot of hype entering his first pro campaign, and it's easy to understand why: Only hitters get excited about finesse lefties who profile as back-end starters. But Blach opened eyes in San Jose, finishing fourth in the league in ERA and second in K/BB ratio while dodging the Cal League's every-fan-gets-a-home-run-ball policy. His fastball velocity is average—touching 93—and he depends on pinpoint command and a changeup with excellent arm action to bamboozle righties. Both breaking balls (curve and slider) can flash plus but are inconsistent; if Blach can smooth that particular flaw, he *should* wind up in the rotation for the big club. He'll begin 2014 with Double-A Richmond.

Clayton Blackburn

Born: 1/6/1993 Age: 21
Bats: L Throws: R Height: 6' 3" Weight: 220
Breakout: 45% Improve: 80% Collapse: 12%
Attrition: 61% MLB: 39%

Comparables:
Michael Bowden, Brett Anderson, David Holmberg

YEAR	TEAM	LVL	AGE	W	L	SV	G	GS	IP	H	HR	BB	SO	BB9	SO9	GB%	BABIP	WHIP	ERA	FIP	FRA	WARP
2012	AUG	A	19	8	4	0	22	22	131¹	116	3	18	143	1.2	9.8	60%	.315	1.02	2.54	2.29	3.08	2.9
2013	SJO	A+	20	7	5	0	23	23	133	111	12	35	138	2.4	9.3	49%	.280	1.10	3.65	3.86	4.25	2.0
2014	SFN	MLB	21	7	7	1	33	21	117¹	113	12	40	89	3.1	6.8	51%	.300	1.30	4.07	4.15	4.43	0.4

Like his San Jose rotationmate Kyle Crick, Blackburn is a big righty who bats left-handed. Blackburn's build is thicker and softer, though, and he depends on above-average off-speed pitches and advanced (for a 20-year-old) pitchability. Blackburn's K/BB dominance of the Sally League slipped a bit in the volatile Cal League, but he was the league's second-youngest starter and he finished especially strong, with a 2.08 ERA in his final nine starts.

Madison Bumgarner

Born: 8/1/1989 Age: 24
Bats: R Throws: L Height: 6' 5" Weight: 235
Breakout: 27% Improve: 55% Collapse: 14%
Attrition: 12% MLB: 100%

Comparables:
Brian Matusz, Clayton Kershaw, Mat Latos

YEAR	TEAM	LVL	AGE	W	L	SV	G	GS	IP	H	HR	BB	SO	BB9	SO9	GB%	BABIP	WHIP	ERA	FIP	FRA	WARP
2011	SFN	MLB	21	13	13	0	33	33	204²	202	12	46	191	2.0	8.4	47%	.329	1.21	3.21	2.64	3.14	3.2
2012	SFN	MLB	22	16	11	0	32	32	208¹	183	23	49	191	2.1	8.3	49%	.275	1.11	3.37	3.54	4.11	1.7
2013	SFN	MLB	23	13	9	0	31	31	201¹	146	15	62	199	2.8	8.9	48%	.257	1.03	2.77	3.03	3.58	2.8
2014	SFN	MLB	24	11	8	0	27	27	170	146	15	42	145	2.2	7.7	45%	.287	1.11	3.07	3.45	3.34	2.7

Bumgarner has 115 major-league starts and two World Series rings; there are guys on top-prospect lists that are older than he is. (James Paxton is older than he is!) His demeanor on and off the mound reinforces the impression that he's been around forever: He's unflappable, impassive and freakishly consistent, with the National League's seventh-best FIP in 2013. While the traditional trajectory for an ace is to start with unhittable gas and adjust as time levies its tax, Bumgarner is unlike his peers—he's already an off-speed-majority pitcher, and made his changeup and curveball even bigger parts of his repertoire in 2013. So if he's already got the late-career junkballer routine down pat, does that make him relatively age-proof? The Giants hope so: He signed an extension in April that, with club options, could keep him in orange and black through 2019.

Matt Cain

Born: 10/1/1984 Age: 29
Bats: R Throws: R Height: 6' 3" Weight: 230
Breakout: 13% Improve: 42% Collapse: 20%
Attrition: 4% MLB: 98%

Comparables:
Roy Oswalt, Freddy Garcia, Jered Weaver

YEAR	TEAM	LVL	AGE	W	L	SV	G	GS	IP	H	HR	BB	SO	BB9	SO9	GB%	BABIP	WHIP	ERA	FIP	FRA	WARP
2011	SFN	MLB	26	12	11	0	33	33	221²	177	9	63	179	2.6	7.3	43%	.265	1.08	2.88	2.88	3.47	2.1
2012	SFN	MLB	27	16	5	0	32	32	219¹	177	21	51	193	2.1	7.9	40%	.261	1.04	2.79	3.44	3.66	2.5
2013	SFN	MLB	28	8	10	0	30	30	184¹	158	23	55	158	2.7	7.7	38%	.262	1.16	4.00	3.90	4.47	1.0
2014	SFN	MLB	29	11	7	0	25	25	163	135	15	44	130	2.5	7.2	39%	.270	1.10	3.04	3.68	3.30	2.6

Cain already has *eight* full seasons of service in the big leagues—and he's still just 29 years old. It's hard to think of another pitcher who has been as consistently effective as Cain over that long a stretch—until this year, his worst by any metric you care to mention. His stathead-confounding homer-per-fly rate topped 10 percent for the first time in his career. His pitch mix changed dramatically as well: 2013 was the first year in which he threw less than half fastballs or depended so heavily on the slider, which he threw 28 percent of the time after never before topping 20 percent. The fastball is still Cain's best pitch, the velocity is still there and the data suggest he would do well to return to his old country hardball ways.

Santiago Casilla

Born: 7/25/1980 Age: 33
Bats: R Throws: R Height: 6' 0" Weight: 210
Breakout: 24% Improve: 45% Collapse: 34%
Attrition: 14% MLB: 90%

Comparables:
Matt Lindstrom, Will Ohman, Felix Rodriguez

YEAR	TEAM	LVL	AGE	W	L	SV	G	GS	IP	H	HR	BB	SO	BB9	SO9	GB%	BABIP	WHIP	ERA	FIP	FRA	WARP
2011	SFN	MLB	30	2	2	6	49	0	51²	33	1	25	45	4.4	7.8	54%	.235	1.12	1.74	3.07	3.39	0.5
2012	SFN	MLB	31	7	6	25	73	0	63¹	55	8	22	55	3.1	7.8	55%	.254	1.22	2.84	4.18	4.84	-0.4
2013	SFN	MLB	32	7	2	2	57	0	50	39	2	25	38	4.5	6.8	55%	.262	1.28	2.16	3.64	3.77	0.3
2014	SFN	MLB	33	3	1	8	55	0	52¹	44	4	22	44	3.7	7.6	48%	.285	1.26	3.54	3.89	3.85	0.4

In the four years since the Giants plucked Casilla from the scrap heap, he has the fifth-best ERA in baseball (min. 200 innings), behind relief aces Craig Kimbrel, Koji Uehara, Sergio Romo and Kenley Jansen. That he's done it with lackluster peripherals is still concerning; it's only 200 innings, after all, and we'd be plenty skeptical of a starter who had one great BABIP-driven season. Those peripherals plummeted this year, though it seems fair to blame part of it on a bum knee. After missing two months for surgery, Casilla came back throwing his fastball and slider 2 mph harder, helping repair his walk rate.

Kyle Crick

Born: 11/30/1992 Age: 21
Bats: L Throws: R Height: 6' 4" Weight: 220
Breakout: 42% Improve: 85% Collapse: 8%
Attrition: 28% MLB: 25%

Comparables:
Chris Tillman, Trevor Cahill, Scott Elbert

YEAR	TEAM	LVL	AGE	W	L	SV	G	GS	IP	H	HR	BB	SO	BB9	SO9	GB%	BABIP	WHIP	ERA	FIP	FRA	WARP
2012	AUG	A	19	7	6	0	23	22	111¹	75	1	67	128	5.4	10.3	48%	.279	1.28	2.51	3.53	3.36	2.5
2013	SJO	A+	20	3	1	0	14	14	68²	48	1	39	95	5.1	12.5	45%	.324	1.27	1.57	2.94	2.96	2.2
2014	SFN	MLB	21	4	4	0	13	13	66	56	5	40	65	5.5	8.8	45%	.304	1.46	4.14	4.19	4.50	0.2

Crick may not make Giants fans forget Zack Wheeler, but he'll at least soften the blow of having lost a potential ace. Crick fits the classic power-pitcher profile at 6-foot-4 and 220, a body that can maintain mid-90s velocity deep into games. He gets good downhill plane with the fastball and pairs it with a plus slider, along with a changeup that shows plus potential. Like Wheeler at the same age, he's unhittable by Single-A bats, but too wild to call a finished product. He missed two months with an oblique injury but won his league's ERA title, and it wouldn't be a surprise to see him start his age-21 season in Double-A Richmond.

Jake Dunning
Born: 8/12/1988 Age: 25
Bats: R Throws: R Height: 6' 4" Weight: 190
Breakout: 58% Improve: 75% Collapse: 25%
Attrition: 51% MLB: 24%

Comparables:
Aaron Loup, Romulo Sanchez, Billy Petrick

YEAR	TEAM	LVL	AGE	W	L	SV	G	GS	IP	H	HR	BB	SO	BB9	SO9	GB%	BABIP	WHIP	ERA	FIP	FRA	WARP
2011	SJO	A+	22	6	3	10	41	7	76	86	7	24	71	2.8	8.4	46%	.402	1.45	4.74	4.46	6.36	0.4
2012	RIC	AA	23	5	2	0	44	0	68	74	2	22	53	2.9	7.0	53%	.338	1.41	4.10	3.17	4.14	0.6
2013	FRE	AAA	24	2	2	1	34	0	48¹	47	3	14	44	2.6	8.2	47%	.326	1.26	1.49	3.74	4.13	0.8
2013	SFN	MLB	24	0	2	0	29	0	25¹	20	2	11	16	3.9	5.7	55%	.250	1.22	2.84	4.44	6.54	-0.4
2014	SFN	MLB	25	2	1	0	45	0	63²	63	6	22	45	3.2	6.4	48%	.306	1.34	4.25	4.21	4.62	-0.1

It's easy to get excited about guys who throw sinkers whose radar gun readings start with a 9, especially when those same guys allow a home run only every six weeks in the homer-happy PCL. Dunning's audition with the big club was nothing special, but he induced double plays at better than twice the league average, and he avoided any immediate pastings by left-handed hitters. He's especially young for his age, having moved from shortstop to the mound in 2010. There's room on his long, lanky physique to add mass and plenty of time for him to learn the peculiarities of pitching, if necessary.

Chad Gaudin
Born: 3/24/1983 Age: 31
Bats: R Throws: R Height: 5' 10" Weight: 185
Breakout: 25% Improve: 54% Collapse: 36%
Attrition: 23% MLB: 86%

Comparables:
Jorge Sosa, Todd Wellemeyer, Gary Glover

YEAR	TEAM	LVL	AGE	W	L	SV	G	GS	IP	H	HR	BB	SO	BB9	SO9	GB%	BABIP	WHIP	ERA	FIP	FRA	WARP
2011	SYR	AAA	28	0	2	0	6	2	12¹	17	0	3	14	2.2	10.2	60%	.467	1.62	4.38	1.94	2.54	0.4
2011	LVG	AAA	28	2	3	0	6	6	29¹	37	2	9	13	2.8	4.0	51%	.333	1.57	6.14	5.11	6.16	0.3
2011	WAS	MLB	28	1	1	0	10	0	8¹	12	1	8	10	8.6	10.8	33%	.423	2.40	6.48	5.03	4.75	0.0
2012	MIA	MLB	29	4	2	0	46	0	69¹	72	6	26	57	3.4	7.4	43%	.317	1.41	4.54	3.87	4.18	0.4
2013	SFN	MLB	30	5	2	0	30	12	97	81	6	40	88	3.7	8.2	40%	.275	1.25	3.06	3.31	3.97	0.9
2014	SFN	MLB	31	3	2	0	39	6	77²	72	7	31	67	3.6	7.7	45%	.303	1.33	4.08	3.96	4.43	0.2

Gaudin was a pleasant surprise in a year when the Giants had precious few. Pressed into a starter role when the rotation was hit with injuries and ineffectiveness, Gaudin made 12 starts and ended up with the Giants' second-best ERA as a starter. That helped him hit free agency with a little bit of gloss, but only a little bit: His success is quickly tracked back to his home ballpark, where he didn't allow a single home run. On the road, he was the 4.41-ERA Gaudin you'd expect. Carpal Tunnel Syndrome ended his season in August, so whichever team signs him this winter should invest in an ergonomic chair.

Joan Gregorio
Born: 1/12/1992 Age: 22
Bats: R Throws: R Height: 6' 7" Weight: 180
Breakout: 48% Improve: 88% Collapse: 12%
Attrition: 87% MLB: 11%

Comparables:
James Houser, Dan Straily, Bruce Billings

YEAR	TEAM	LVL	AGE	W	L	SV	G	GS	IP	H	HR	BB	SO	BB9	SO9	GB%	BABIP	WHIP	ERA	FIP	FRA	WARP
2012	SLO	A-	20	7	7	0	16	16	76¹	85	9	23	69	2.7	8.1	43%	.321	1.41	5.54	4.07	4.65	1.4
2013	AUG	A	21	6	3	0	14	13	69²	65	3	17	84	2.2	10.9	35%	.341	1.18	4.00	2.45	2.94	1.8
2014	SFN	MLB	22	2	2	0	12	6	61¹	64	7	29	44	4.2	6.4	38%	.312	1.51	4.98	4.82	5.41	-0.5

"Long levered" doesn't begin to describe Gregorio. He uses every inch of his 6-foot-7 frame to launch a mid-90s fastball, most often up in the zone and generally with enough sproing to get swinging strikes. His secondaries—a slurvy curve with two-plane break and a developing changeup—can flash plus, but are inconsistent; getting all those arms and legs to sync up can be a challenge for the young right-hander. Injuries limited his time on the field in 2013, but if he's able to stay healthy and add some mass to his frame, you can start to project something pretty special. He's in a race with Pittsburgh's Joan Montero to be the first Joan in major-league history. (Milwaukee has an 18-year-old Joan De La Cruz, but he hasn't even pitched in the U.S. yet.)

Heath Hembree
Born: 1/13/1989 Age: 25
Bats: R Throws: R Height: 6' 4" Weight: 210
Breakout: 32% Improve: 46% Collapse: 42%
Attrition: 74% MLB: 49%

Comparables:
Sammy Gervacio, Billy Sadler, R.J. Swindle

YEAR	TEAM	LVL	AGE	W	L	SV	G	GS	IP	H	HR	BB	SO	BB9	SO9	GB%	BABIP	WHIP	ERA	FIP	FRA	WARP
2011	SJO	A+	22	0	0	21	26	0	24²	16	1	12	44	4.4	16.1	47%	.316	1.14	0.73	2.49	2.15	0.5
2011	RIC	AA	22	1	1	17	28	0	28²	20	1	13	34	4.1	10.7	33%	.288	1.15	2.83	2.85	2.98	0.6
2012	FRE	AAA	23	1	1	15	39	0	38	29	2	20	36	4.7	8.5	40%	.257	1.29	4.74	4.35	4.39	0.6
2013	FRE	AAA	24	1	4	31	54	0	55¹	54	7	16	63	2.6	10.2	36%	.318	1.27	4.07	3.86	3.91	1.2
2013	SFN	MLB	24	0	0	0	9	0	7²	4	0	2	12	2.3	14.1	53%	.267	0.78	0.00	0.67	2.24	0.2
2014	SFN	MLB	25	3	1	1	55	0	55	44	5	21	58	3.5	9.5	41%	.292	1.19	3.23	3.51	3.51	0.7

Hembree has a big body and big stuff: He can work in the mid-90s with his four-seamer and cut the fastball grip as well, and the slider can be devastating when it's on. Control, or rather lack thereof, has been a knock on Hembree for years now, but he dramatically curtailed his walks in Triple-A, more than doubling his K/BB ratio over 2012. Hembree set the single-season saves record in Fresno and did well in a September audition in San Francisco, appearing in nine games without allowing a run. The relief ace most saw as Brian Wilson's heir apparent has returned, now rebranded as Sergio Romo's heir apparent. (Brian Wilson's hair apparent is another story.)

Tim Hudson

Born: 7/14/1975 Age: 38
Bats: R Throws: R Height: 6' 1" Weight: 175
Breakout: 19% Improve: 44% Collapse: 21%
Attrition: 12% MLB: 77%

Comparables:
Derek Lowe, Jose Contreras, Chris Carpenter

YEAR	TEAM	LVL	AGE	W	L	SV	G	GS	IP	H	HR	BB	SO	BB9	SO9	GB%	BABIP	WHIP	ERA	FIP	FRA	WARP
2011	ATL	MLB	35	16	10	0	33	33	215	189	14	56	158	2.3	6.6	57%	.275	1.14	3.22	3.36	4.41	1.0
2012	GWN	AAA	36	2	0	0	2	2	10²	8	0	5	8	4.2	6.8	62%	.235	1.22	0.84	3.06	4.47	0.1
2012	ATL	MLB	36	16	7	0	28	28	179	168	12	48	102	2.4	5.1	55%	.281	1.21	3.62	3.82	5.09	-0.2
2013	ATL	MLB	37	8	7	0	21	21	131¹	120	10	36	95	2.5	6.5	55%	.281	1.19	3.97	3.43	4.07	1.3
2014	SFN	MLB	38	8	6	0	19	19	123¹	111	9	35	79	2.6	5.7	59%	.282	1.18	3.33	3.84	3.62	1.5

Hudson's season ended in late July when he fractured his ankle in an ugly bang-bang play at first base. The play seemed at the time to be an unfair ending to an otherwise outstanding career, but that fear appears to have been premature as Hudson signed a two-year deal with San Francisco. Long known for his clubhouse leadership and ability to prevent runs well above the level of his mundane peripherals, there's no reason to think Hudson won't continue to thrive in his new surroundings. At some point Father Time will have his say, but Hudson's age may well reach the big four-oh before his ERA does.

Stephen Johnson

Born: 2/21/1991 Age: 23
Bats: R Throws: R Height: 6' 4" Weight: 205
Breakout: 100% Improve: 100% Collapse: 0%
Attrition: 100% MLB: 2%

Comparables:
A.J. Ramos, Michael Schwimer, B.J. Rosenberg

YEAR	TEAM	LVL	AGE	W	L	SV	G	GS	IP	H	HR	BB	SO	BB9	SO9	GB%	BABIP	WHIP	ERA	FIP	FRA	WARP
2012	SLO	A-	21	0	2	2	17	0	19¹	19	2	12	19	5.6	8.8	47%	.309	1.60	4.66	4.57	5.37	0.1
2013	AUG	A	22	5	1	8	45	0	52¹	41	2	30	71	5.2	12.2	51%	.320	1.36	3.61	3.16	3.56	0.6
2014	SFN	MLB	23	2	1	1	36	0	42	40	4	24	37	5.1	7.9	46%	.310	1.52	4.74	4.49	5.15	-0.3

Johnson was having an unremarkable college career as a starter for Division II St. Edwards in Austin, Texas, but a move to closer in his junior year put him on just about everybody's radar. The new role allowed him to dial the fastball up to 100 and pile up 74 strikeouts in 43 innings. He had been projected to go as high as the second round, but fell to the Giants in the sixth. His messy delivery might have been one reason he sank: Lots of moving parts led to questionable control and too many walks. Small gains in command will make him a late-game weapon soon.

George Kontos

Born: 6/12/1985 Age: 29
Bats: R Throws: R Height: 6' 3" Weight: 215
Breakout: 11% Improve: 38% Collapse: 51%
Attrition: 56% MLB: 32%

Comparables:
Fu-Te Ni, Matt Daley, Carlos Fisher

YEAR	TEAM	LVL	AGE	W	L	SV	G	GS	IP	H	HR	BB	SO	BB9	SO9	GB%	BABIP	WHIP	ERA	FIP	FRA	WARP
2011	SWB	AAA	26	4	4	2	40	4	89¹	72	12	26	91	2.6	9.2	36%	.251	1.10	2.62	3.89	4.34	0.1
2011	NYA	MLB	26	0	0	0	7	0	6	4	1	3	6	4.5	9.0	20%	.214	1.17	3.00	4.73	4.41	0.0
2012	FRE	AAA	27	2	0	1	23	0	31²	24	1	7	26	2.0	7.4	54%	.250	0.98	1.71	3.19	3.35	0.8
2012	SFN	MLB	27	2	1	0	44	0	43²	34	3	12	44	2.5	9.1	49%	.261	1.05	2.47	2.84	3.67	0.4
2013	FRE	AAA	28	3	2	4	18	0	23²	19	3	3	26	1.1	9.9	45%	.250	0.93	4.18	3.40	3.91	0.5
2013	SFN	MLB	28	2	2	0	52	0	55¹	60	7	18	47	2.9	7.6	39%	.323	1.41	4.39	4.05	4.40	0.2
2014	SFN	MLB	29	3	1	1	53	0	69	61	7	23	59	3.1	7.7	41%	.288	1.22	3.74	3.90	4.06	0.4

Kontos probably shouldn't be in the big leagues at all. Senior sign, elbow injuries, a Rule 5 claimee who was returned to his original club—these are not typically markers of the players who populate major-league rosters. The Giants got one season and postseason of serviceable relief from him, then watched his luck and stuff go south last year: walks, hits and homers were up and strikeouts were down. Both fastballs—the four-seamer and the two-seamer—were below-average pitches that allowed above-average hit rates. The slider remains a legitimate swing-and-miss offering, but really only against righties; consequently, lefties hit .339/.411/.613 against him. It would be reasonable to expect a little bounce back from Kontos in 2014, but if his no-frills backstory is no longer a concern his vulnerability to lefties is.

Tim Lincecum

Born: 6/15/1984 Age: 30
Bats: L Throws: R Height: 5' 11" Weight: 170
Breakout: 17% Improve: 42% Collapse: 28%
Attrition: 14% MLB: 94%

Comparables:
Erik Bedard, Josh Beckett, John Lackey

YEAR	TEAM	LVL	AGE	W	L	SV	G	GS	IP	H	HR	BB	SO	BB9	SO9	GB%	BABIP	WHIP	ERA	FIP	FRA	WARP
2011	SFN	MLB	27	13	14	0	33	33	217	176	15	86	220	3.6	9.1	48%	.287	1.21	2.74	3.14	3.89	1.4
2012	SFN	MLB	28	10	15	0	33	33	186	183	23	90	190	4.4	9.2	45%	.313	1.47	5.18	4.22	4.77	0.1
2013	SFN	MLB	29	10	14	0	32	32	197²	184	21	76	193	3.5	8.8	46%	.308	1.32	4.37	3.71	3.96	1.7
2014	SFN	MLB	30	11	8	0	28	28	170¹	144	15	61	174	3.2	9.2	47%	.301	1.21	3.33	3.43	3.62	2.1

"What happened to Tim Lincecum?" is the great mystery of our time, and no one knows the answer—not even Big-Time Timmy Jim himself. After dominating the baseball world for four seasons, Lincecum lost it entirely and ended up in the bullpen by the end of 2012. That made 2013, his free-agent walk year, the anticipated conclusion to the series—but, instead, it left most of the mystery unanswered. He improved his FRA and regained the devastating fade on his split-change. But he also lost another small tick off his fastball (and more than that off his slider) and had the National League's third-worst ERA+ among qualifiers (after finishing last in the same category in 2012). If his name were anything else, he'd be seeking a non-roster invite instead of re-signing for $35 million, but tis far better to have rocked and lost it than never to have rocked at all.

Javier Lopez
Born: 7/11/1977 Age: 36
Bats: L Throws: L Height: 6' 5" Weight: 220
Breakout: 31% Improve: 55% Collapse: 35%
Attrition: 12% MLB: 69%
Comparables:
Hideki Okajima, Steve Kline, D.J. Carrasco

YEAR	TEAM	LVL	AGE	W	L	SV	G	GS	IP	H	HR	BB	SO	BB9	SO9	GB%	BABIP	WHIP	ERA	FIP	FRA	WARP
2011	SFN	MLB	33	5	2	1	70	0	53	42	0	26	40	4.4	6.8	64%	.276	1.28	2.72	3.13	4.46	-0.3
2012	SFN	MLB	34	3	0	7	70	0	36	37	1	14	28	3.5	7.0	60%	.318	1.42	2.50	3.11	2.94	0.4
2013	SFN	MLB	35	4	2	1	69	0	39¹	30	1	12	37	2.7	8.5	65%	.261	1.07	1.83	2.38	2.02	0.7
2014	SFN	MLB	36	3	1	2	58	0	37²	34	2	14	29	3.4	6.8	58%	.295	1.27	3.58	3.53	3.89	0.3

Lopez was an integral part of the Giants' bullpen in their 2010 run, but appeared more human over the next two seasons, prompting many to presume that he was on the downside of a pretty good career. Instead, he had a pretty good career year: His paltry 2.02 FRA included holding batters to a .146/.250/.188 line in high-leverage situations. He's always been good against lefties, of course—his big, sweeping slider is all but unhittable by those standing in the wrong batter's box—but 2013 saw him hold them to a career-best .152/.208/.222 line. His performance against righties improved slightly over the previous year as well, as his BABIP regressed toward career average from an inexplicable .476 in 2012. Signed for three more years, Lopez has proven that he's among the game's best lefty specialists, if not the best.

Jean Machi
Born: 2/1/1982 Age: 32
Bats: R Throws: R Height: 6' 0" Weight: 260
Breakout: 35% Improve: 59% Collapse: 22%
Attrition: 62% MLB: 33%
Comparables:
Dale Thayer, Scott Strickland, Royce Ring

YEAR	TEAM	LVL	AGE	W	L	SV	G	GS	IP	H	HR	BB	SO	BB9	SO9	GB%	BABIP	WHIP	ERA	FIP	FRA	WARP
2012	FRE	AAA	30	2	1	15	53	0	56²	67	7	17	44	2.7	7.0	52%	.323	1.48	3.97	4.78	6.31	0.1
2012	SFN	MLB	30	0	0	0	8	0	6²	7	2	1	4	1.4	5.4	39%	.238	1.20	6.75	6.29	6.54	-0.1
2013	FRE	AAA	31	3	1	2	16	0	18¹	13	0	3	19	1.5	9.3	47%	.289	0.87	0.98	2.15	2.94	0.4
2013	SFN	MLB	31	3	1	0	51	0	53	46	2	12	51	2.0	8.7	54%	.297	1.09	2.38	2.27	3.10	0.9
2014	SFN	MLB	32	3	1	1	58	0	61¹	55	6	21	50	3.0	7.4	50%	.293	1.23	3.60	3.92	3.91	0.5

Machi sports a mid-90s fastball, a forkball that's a weapon against lefties and righties and very fine component numbers. He has also reliably melted down in high-leverage situations, a maddening bit of minutiae that sometimes feels like the whole darned thing. In 32 low-leverage innings this year, Machi held opposing hitters to a .486 OPS, with 34 strikeouts and three walks; in 9 ⅓ high-leverage innings, it's .774, 10 and seven. Surely some of this is just dumb luck and sample-size vagaries, and maybe all of it is just dumb luck and sample-size vagaries, but even if there's no mental component to it, you'll never convince the rest of the world of that. The bad news for him is that 31-year-old rookies don't get very long to correct the record.

Adalberto Mejia
Born: 6/20/1993 Age: 21
Bats: L Throws: L Height: 6' 3" Weight: 195
Breakout: 55% Improve: 76% Collapse: 10%
Attrition: 40% MLB: 13%
Comparables:
Joe Wieland, Jair Jurrjens, James Parr

YEAR	TEAM	LVL	AGE	W	L	SV	G	GS	IP	H	HR	BB	SO	BB9	SO9	GB%	BABIP	WHIP	ERA	FIP	FRA	WARP
2012	AUG	A	19	10	7	0	30	14	106²	122	4	21	79	1.8	6.7	44%	.332	1.34	3.97	3.29	4.18	1.2
2013	SJO	A+	20	7	4	0	16	16	87	75	11	23	89	2.4	9.2	38%	.277	1.13	3.31	4.20	4.50	1.2
2014	SFN	MLB	21	4	4	0	22	11	82	87	10	30	49	3.3	5.4	40%	.303	1.44	4.83	4.81	5.25	-0.6

Mejia began 2013 as the youngest pitcher in the Cal League and was up to the challenge. The 20-year-old works off a heavy two-seamer and keeps hitters off balance with a good slider and a changeup that has a chance to be a legitimate third pitch. He walked more hitters than in 2012, but he also ratcheted up the strikeouts to keep his K/BB steady. The only thing that slowed him down was an early six-week stint on the disabled list, but he was able to make up that lost development time by playing in the 2013 Arizona Fall League. A promotion to Double-A will let him continue to experience the pleasure of being one of the youngest people in the room.

Keury Mella
Born: 8/2/1993 Age: 20
Bats: R Throws: R Height: 6' 2" Weight: 200
Breakout: 0% Improve: 0% Collapse: 0%
Attrition: 0% MLB: 0%
Comparables:
Yordano Ventura, Kevin Siegrist, Rafael Dolis

YEAR	TEAM	LVL	AGE	W	L	SV	G	GS	IP	H	HR	BB	SO	BB9	SO9	GB%	BABIP	WHIP	ERA	FIP	FRA	WARP
2014	SFN	MLB	20	1	1	0	8	3	34¹	37	4	21	22	5.5	5.7	51%	.313	1.70	5.71	5.44	6.21	-0.6

The 20-year-old righty generated plenty of buzz based on his Dominican Summer League debut in 2012, and his performance in the complex league last year suggests the hype was warranted. Mella is a big, well-proportioned right-hander who throws a heavy fastball in the low-to-mid-90s, with control that's notable for a man of his birthdate. Given his age and projectable body, it's only a little bit greedy to count on even more velocity. As you might expect, at this stage the secondary offerings are works in progress: His curve can flash plus, and scouts say his changeup has the potential to play at the highest level.

Jose Mijares

Born: 10/29/1984 Age: 29
Bats: L Throws: L Height: 5' 11" Weight: 265
Breakout: 26% Improve: 51% Collapse: 25%
Attrition: 11% MLB: 90%

Comparables:
Fernando Rodney, Mark Lowe, Juan Oviedo

YEAR	TEAM	LVL	AGE	W	L	SV	G	GS	IP	H	HR	BB	SO	BB9	SO9	GB%	BABIP	WHIP	ERA	FIP	FRA	WARP
2011	MIN	MLB	26	0	2	0	58	0	49	53	4	30	30	5.5	5.5	33%	.304	1.69	4.59	4.92	5.08	-0.1
2012	SFN	MLB	27	1	0	0	27	0	17²	14	0	8	20	4.1	10.2	39%	.304	1.25	2.55	2.23	1.92	0.4
2012	KCA	MLB	27	2	2	0	51	0	38²	36	3	13	37	3.0	8.6	34%	.297	1.27	2.56	3.46	3.70	0.5
2013	SFN	MLB	28	0	3	0	60	0	49	67	3	20	54	3.7	9.9	38%	.411	1.78	4.22	3.02	2.74	0.8
2014	SFN	MLB	29	3	1	1	64	0	49	45	4	19	45	3.4	8.2	39%	.306	1.29	3.82	3.70	4.15	0.2

Lefties who can throw strikes will always be able to find work; lefties who can't throw strikes do okay, too, as Mijares shows. The walks don't hurt as much when he's not getting stung by bad luck, but his BABIP in 2013 was more than 100 points higher than in any of his other big-league seasons. That mark was the worst in the league (min. 40 innings), and was accompanied by one of the league's dozen worst line-drive rates. The fastball velocity is still there, the slider can still be a weapon and he keeps establishing new career-best strikeout rates, so Mijares is as good a bet as any reliever to shave a run or two off his ERA this year.

Yusmeiro Petit

Born: 11/22/1984 Age: 29
Bats: R Throws: R Height: 6' 1" Weight: 255
Breakout: 26% Improve: 65% Collapse: 18%
Attrition: 35% MLB: 45%

Comparables:
Guillermo Moscoso, Kei Igawa, Philip Humber

YEAR	TEAM	LVL	AGE	W	L	SV	G	GS	IP	H	HR	BB	SO	BB9	SO9	GB%	BABIP	WHIP	ERA	FIP	FRA	WARP
2012	FRE	AAA	27	7	7	0	28	28	166²	178	14	36	153	1.9	8.3	31%	.328	1.28	3.46	3.59	3.71	4.6
2012	SFN	MLB	27	0	0	0	1	1	4²	7	0	4	1	7.7	1.9	33%	.467	2.36	3.86	5.28	4.42	0.0
2013	FRE	AAA	28	5	6	0	15	15	87²	92	16	13	91	1.3	9.3	38%	.309	1.20	4.52	4.31	4.72	1.0
2013	SFN	MLB	28	4	1	0	8	7	48	46	4	11	47	2.1	8.8	32%	.318	1.19	3.56	2.83	3.04	1.1
2014	SFN	MLB	29	7	6	0	29	19	127	120	16	33	109	2.4	7.7	33%	.299	1.21	3.81	3.93	4.14	0.8

On September 6th, this journeyman right-hander came within one batter of making history; unfortunately for him, Eric Chavez ended his perfect-game bid with a single. Not bad for a guy who twice cleared waivers during the 2013 season. Coaches and evaluators have long lauded Petit's control, but his upper-80s fastball gives him a very narrow margin of error. Now with his fifth organization, Petit has been around forever but only in small doses, so the Giants control his rights for the next three seasons. His approach is more effective in a spacious park like AT&T, and his occasional early exits are more tolerable to a team with holes in the back of its rotation, so that second-half run makes him a viable option at starter.

Sergio Romo

Born: 3/4/1983 Age: 31
Bats: R Throws: R Height: 5' 10" Weight: 185
Breakout: 22% Improve: 44% Collapse: 25%
Attrition: 11% MLB: 91%

Comparables:
Rafael Soriano, Jonathan Papelbon, Robb Nen

YEAR	TEAM	LVL	AGE	W	L	SV	G	GS	IP	H	HR	BB	SO	BB9	SO9	GB%	BABIP	WHIP	ERA	FIP	FRA	WARP
2011	SFN	MLB	28	3	1	1	65	0	48	29	2	5	70	0.9	13.1	36%	.276	0.71	1.50	0.93	1.81	1.2
2012	SFN	MLB	29	4	2	14	69	0	55¹	37	5	10	63	1.6	10.2	50%	.239	0.85	1.79	2.74	2.85	0.8
2013	SFN	MLB	30	5	8	38	65	0	60¹	53	5	12	58	1.8	8.7	42%	.276	1.08	2.54	2.82	3.31	0.8
2014	SFN	MLB	31	4	2	20	67	0	56²	42	4	11	64	1.8	10.1	38%	.284	0.95	2.22	2.47	2.41	1.5

Unlike most sliders, Romo's lacks the "red dot" that most hitters use to identify the pitch, making it lethal against right-handers (one in four induces a swinging strike) and unusually effective against lefties, who have hit just .175 against the pitch in Romo's career. The slider makes his upper-80s fastball play up, so while he doesn't resemble the typical closer on a scouting report, he does from the batter's box. Romo has made a career out of proving the doubters wrong, from his emergence out of the Division II college ranks (he was a 28th-round pick) to his shedding of the ROOGY label at the highest level. He now heads into his walk year with multiple seasons of dominance under his belt, and the years of hard work put him on the doorstep of a very big payday.

Sandy Rosario

Born: 8/22/1985 Age: 28
Bats: R Throws: R Height: 6' 1" Weight: 210
Breakout: 36% Improve: 54% Collapse: 35%
Attrition: 67% MLB: 40%

Comparables:
Steven Jackson, Greg Burke, A.J. Murray

YEAR	TEAM	LVL	AGE	W	L	SV	G	GS	IP	H	HR	BB	SO	BB9	SO9	GB%	BABIP	WHIP	ERA	FIP	FRA	WARP
2011	JAX	AA	25	3	2	23	46	0	47²	52	4	17	46	3.2	8.7	45%	.310	1.45	4.15	3.54	3.94	0.5
2011	FLO	MLB	25	0	0	0	4	0	3²	5	0	2	2	4.9	4.9	57%	.357	1.91	2.45	3.54	3.92	0.0
2012	NWO	AAA	26	0	2	16	25	0	26	20	0	2	24	0.7	8.3	44%	.271	0.85	1.04	2.17	2.72	0.7
2012	MIA	MLB	26	0	0	0	4	0	3	8	0	0	2	0.0	6.0	57%	.500	2.67	18.00	1.80	3.08	0.1
2013	FRE	AAA	27	1	1	4	21	0	32¹	30	1	10	35	2.8	9.7	37%	.329	1.24	2.78	2.73	3.10	0.9
2013	SFN	MLB	27	3	2	0	43	0	41²	38	1	20	24	4.3	5.2	45%	.274	1.39	3.02	3.62	4.01	0.2
2014	SFN	MLB	28	2	1	0	44	0	59	60	6	21	46	3.2	7.0	44%	.314	1.36	4.19	4.09	4.56	-0.0

In a 30-day period last winter, Rosario was traded to the A's from the Red Sox, then waived and claimed three different times. Just before Christmas he finally settled with the Giants, where he turned out to be just the stocking stuffer the Giants needed.

Rosario came up as a closer, featuring a mid-90s fastball with some natural arm-side run and a potent slider. While he's unlikely to close in the majors, credit the Giants' front office staff for another successful no-risk/moderate-return reliever. Credit the Red Sox, A's, Red Sox again and Cubs merely with making life hell for his mail carrier.

Chris Stratton
Born: 8/22/1990 Age: 23
Bats: R Throws: R Height: 6' 3" Weight: 186
Breakout: 100% Improve: 100% Collapse: 0%
Attrition: 74% MLB: 3%
Comparables:
Josh Collmenter, Joel Carreno, Alex Wilson

YEAR	TEAM	LVL	AGE	W	L	SV	G	GS	IP	H	HR	BB	SO	BB9	SO9	GB%	BABIP	WHIP	ERA	FIP	FRA	WARP
2012	SLO	A-	21	0	1	0	8	5	16¹	14	1	10	16	5.5	8.8	50%	.302	1.47	2.76	4.37	5.35	0.2
2013	AUG	A	22	9	3	0	22	22	132	128	5	47	123	3.2	8.4	49%	.327	1.33	3.27	3.25	4.05	1.0
2014	SFN	MLB	23	5	8	0	34	23	94²	101	11	47	60	4.5	5.7	45%	.312	1.56	5.14	5.10	5.59	-0.7

Stratton had a rough start to his pro career: Two months after he was drafted, he suffered a concussion while shagging balls in short-season Salem-Keizer. He returned in 2013 and survived the long season, averaging six innings per start and challenging for the league lead in innings pitched. Stratton's delivery is clean and repeatable, and as the season progressed he leaned more and more on a low-90s two-seamer to break bats and get quick outs. The slider is advanced, and he'll show a curve and changeup. The Giants see him as a starting pitcher.

Ryan Vogelsong
Born: 7/22/1977 Age: 36
Bats: R Throws: R Height: 6' 4" Weight: 215
Breakout: 31% Improve: 57% Collapse: 22%
Attrition: 18% MLB: 74%
Comparables:
Chan Ho Park, Shawn Estes, Bruce Chen

YEAR	TEAM	LVL	AGE	W	L	SV	G	GS	IP	H	HR	BB	SO	BB9	SO9	GB%	BABIP	WHIP	ERA	FIP	FRA	WARP
2011	FRE	AAA	33	2	0	0	2	2	11¹	8	1	5	17	4.0	13.5	44%	.292	1.15	1.59	3.25	3.24	0.4
2011	SFN	MLB	33	13	7	0	30	28	179²	164	15	61	139	3.1	7.0	47%	.284	1.25	2.71	3.63	4.05	1.0
2012	FRE	AAA	34	1	0	0	2	2	10	9	0	4	12	3.6	10.8	46%	.375	1.30	1.80	2.47	2.48	0.4
2012	SFN	MLB	34	14	9	0	31	31	189²	171	17	62	158	2.9	7.5	43%	.288	1.23	3.37	3.74	3.84	1.8
2013	RIC	AA	35	2	0	0	2	2	11	10	1	2	8	1.6	6.5	38%	.290	1.09	0.82	3.60	3.52	0.2
2013	SFN	MLB	35	4	6	0	19	19	103²	124	15	38	67	3.3	5.8	40%	.331	1.56	5.73	4.88	5.26	-0.4
2014	SFN	MLB	36	7	6	0	26	18	115²	112	12	43	90	3.4	7.0	43%	.303	1.34	4.25	4.23	4.62	0.0

Vogelsong's storybook 2011 and 2012 seasons offended the sensibilities of the baseball gods, who took revenge in the form of a Craig Stammen pitch that fractured the pinky on his pitching hand. Vogelsong missed nearly half the 2013 season and was mediocre in the 19 starts he did make. But the 36-year-old hurler was already in decline before the broken hand. He faded down the stretch in 2012 and dealt with a strained lower back, which might explain the loss of velocity he saw in 2013. His fastball and slider each saw a 1.5 mph drop from the previous year, while the curve and change each dropped by a half tick. That led to fewer whiffs across the board and big jumps in line-drive and HR/FB rates. The Giants turned down Vogelsong's option but then negotiated an incentives-based deal that could actually give him a raise. Barring glowing and credible health reports this spring, pencil in a continuing drop in velocity and a corresponding drop in effectiveness.

Luis Ysla
Born: 4/27/1992 Age: 22
Bats: L Throws: L Height: 6' 1" Weight: 185
Breakout: 0% Improve: 0% Collapse: 0%
Attrition: 0% MLB: 0%
Comparables:
Garrett Richards, Buddy Boshers, Josh Wall

YEAR	TEAM	LVL	AGE	W	L	SV	G	GS	IP	H	HR	BB	SO	BB9	SO9	GB%	BABIP	WHIP	ERA	FIP	FRA	WARP
2014	SFN	MLB	22	2	3	0	8	8	33²	38	4	21	19	5.5	5.0	47%	.312	1.73	5.96	5.68	6.47	-0.6

Ysla came out of nowhere (okay, Venezuela, if you want to get technical) and put up great numbers in his pro debut in the complex league. He's 21, so the usual age-for-level concerns apply, but his performance was good enough to get him on the AZL All-League Team. Ysla doesn't have much to dream on: average size, a low-90s fastball, plus control. But he throws a sweeping breaking ball that neutralizes lefties, which suggests a future LOOGY role (even if he was equally good against righties last year). Call him a high-floor, low-ceiling proposition: Lefties with some aim will always get paid, even in this economy.

Barry Zito
Born: 5/13/1978 Age: 36
Bats: L Throws: L Height: 6' 2" Weight: 205
Breakout: 22% Improve: 56% Collapse: 19%
Attrition: 16% MLB: 80%
Comparables:
Todd Stottlemyre, Bob Feller, Jeff Suppan

YEAR	TEAM	LVL	AGE	W	L	SV	G	GS	IP	H	HR	BB	SO	BB9	SO9	GB%	BABIP	WHIP	ERA	FIP	FRA	WARP
2011	SJO	A+	33	2	1	0	3	3	21¹	15	2	5	19	2.1	8.0	47%	.226	0.94	2.53	4.37	4.66	0.2
2011	FRE	AAA	33	2	0	0	3	3	17²	10	1	5	17	2.5	8.7	47%	.214	0.85	2.55	3.44	4.18	0.4
2011	SFN	MLB	33	3	4	0	13	9	53²	51	10	24	32	4.0	5.4	41%	.268	1.40	5.87	5.57	6.97	-1.0
2012	SFN	MLB	34	15	8	0	32	32	184¹	186	20	70	114	3.4	5.6	41%	.289	1.39	4.15	4.53	4.59	0.4
2013	SFN	MLB	35	5	11	0	30	25	133¹	173	19	54	86	3.6	5.8	37%	.349	1.70	5.74	4.89	5.03	0.1
2014	SFN	MLB	36	7	8	0	22	22	126¹	125	15	50	84	3.6	6.0	40%	.297	1.38	4.53	4.75	4.92	-0.4

The Barry Zito Era ended not with a whimper, but with a long, long series of whimpers, seven seasons of whimpers. For $126 million, Zito delivered the Giants about 2 WARP, total, and he saved his worst for last. And yet: "As crazy as this sounds, if I had to do it over again, I would have done what we did to sign Barry Zito," Brian Sabean said in October. Zito did stay healthy—2011 was the anomaly—and his benefactors did win two World Series during his contract. The Giants are still paying Zito a $7 million buyout on his 2014 option, which can buy quite a few ... well, quite a few of anything Barry might want, except for another chance.

LINEOUTS

HITTERS

PLAYER	TEAM	LVL	AGE	PA	R	2B	3B	HR	RBI	BB	SO	SB-CS	AVG/OBP/SLG	TAv	BABIP	BRR	FRAA	WARP
2B T. Abreu	FRE	AAA	28	71	9	9	0	1	9	1	15	1-1	.338/.366/.523	.310	.412	-0.9	2B(16): -0.3, 3B(1): -0.1	0.4
	SFN	MLB	28	147	21	12	3	2	14	6	33	0-2	.268/.301/.442	.254	.337	0.2	2B(30): -1.4, SS(3): 0.0	0.1
SS E. Adrianza	RIC	AA	23	291	31	12	0	2	23	31	45	11-6	.240/.331/.312	.251	.283	1.5	SS(72): 2.7	1.4
	FRE	AAA	23	177	23	7	6	0	12	23	31	6-2	.310/.409/.441	.293	.391	0.8	SS(44): 2.8	1.8
	SFN	MLB	23	20	3	1	0	1	3	1	5	0-0	.222/.263/.444	.237	.250	0.3	SS(6): -0.1	0.1
3B C. Dominguez	FRE	AAA	26	497	60	24	5	15	65	23	112	4-5	.294/.334/.464	.268	.358	1.2	3B(96): -0.2, 1B(23): 2.5	2.1
SS M. Duffy	AUG	A	22	339	48	14	3	4	43	45	41	22-6	.307/.405/.418	.321	.346	5.8	SS(74): 11.3	5.6
	SJO	A+	22	115	17	6	1	5	14	7	16	3-1	.292/.342/.509	.302	.306	0	SS(25): 0.9	1.1
RF R. Kieschnick	FRE	AAA	26	422	50	27	9	13	56	40	102	4-1	.273/.339/.497	.285	.335	-0.6	RF(62): -0.9, LF(34): -0.6	1.7
	SFN	MLB	26	95	6	0	1	0	5	11	29	0-0	.202/.295/.226	.196	.309	-0.3	LF(25): 0.2	-0.2
1B R. Oropesa	SJO	A+	23	253	30	16	0	8	38	24	55	0-0	.295/.368/.477	.320	.352	-1.2	1B(55): 4.9	2.2
	RIC	AA	23	259	19	6	0	6	23	15	74	0-0	.207/.255/.307	.209	.270	-2.9	1B(59): 1.6	-1.4
RF J. Parker	RIC	AA	24	524	72	18	5	18	57	60	161	13-11	.245/.355/.430	.293	.343	1.2	RF(110): 7.9, CF(17): -0.2	4.0
C G. Quiroz	FRE	AAA	31	42	2	2	0	0	8	6	7	0-0	.294/.405/.353	.286	.357	-0.1	C(10): 0.3	0.4
	SFN	MLB	31	95	5	7	0	1	6	5	21	0-0	.186/.237/.302	.190	.231	-0.8	C(35): -0.0	-0.2

Tony Abreu's switch-hitting ability made him Bruce Bochy's go-to bench bat, and Abreu rewarded him with an extra-base hit every nine trips to the plate. ⊘ **Ehire Adrianza** took steps to shaking the "all-glove/no-hit" tag this season, adding 200 points to his OPS after a mechanical adjustment and promotion to the PCL. ⊘ **Chris Dominguez** disappeared from top-prospect lists years ago, but he continues to improve incrementally. It's not likely he'll break through at 27, but stranger things have happened. ⊘ Late-rounder **Matthew Duffy** led Augusta in OBP and continued to hit after a promotion to High-A San Jose. Oh yeah! Duffman is thrusting in the direction of the majors. ⊘ An impressive season in Triple-A gave the Giants hope that **Roger Kieschnick**'s bat was coming around, but a mouthful of sand in 2013 showed it to be a mirage. ⊘ **Ricky Oropesa**'s bat came alive after a mid-year demotion to San Jose, but doubt remains about his ability to hit breaking stuff, which in turn raises doubt about his ability to hit outside the California League. ⊘ **Jarrett Parker**'s stock was sunk after a so-so repeat of High-A in 2012, but he held his own in the Eastern League last year. He mostly abandoned center field, though, and the bat won't hold a corner. ⊘ Journeyman catcher **Guillermo Quiroz** stepped in as Buster Posey's backup when Hector Sanchez hit the DL; he was adequate, and then he was DFA'd.

PITCHERS

PLAYER	TEAM	LVL	AGE	W	L	SV	IP	H	HR	BB	SO	BB9	SO9	GB%	BABIP	WHIP	ERA	FIP	FRA	WARP
M. Agosta	AUG	A	22	9	3	0	91²	57	4	43	109	4.2	10.7	37%	.254	1.09	2.06	3.31	4.17	0.6
B. Bochy	FRE	AAA	25	1	1	2	56¹	51	2	16	57	2.6	9.1	30%	.308	1.19	3.99	3.02	3.16	1.5
E. Cordier	IND	AAA	27	4	2	4	53	51	3	28	65	4.8	11.0	48%	.351	1.49	4.58	3.19	4.18	0.5
E. Escobar	SJO	A+	21	3	4	0	74²	68	3	17	92	2.0	11.1	41%	.323	1.14	2.89	2.55	2.93	2.2
	RIC	AA	21	5	4	0	54	44	2	13	54	2.2	9.0	43%	.290	1.06	2.67	2.64	3.31	1.4
K. Flores	AUG	A	21	10	6	0	141²	113	11	17	137	1.1	8.7	39%	.267	0.92	2.73	3.00	3.74	1.6
C. Hall	SJO	A+	25	2	0	2	33²	15	2	7	48	1.9	12.8	46%	.194	0.65	1.34	2.41	2.50	1.1
	RIC	AA	25	2	2	8	26¹	17	4	8	27	2.7	9.2	38%	.203	0.95	2.39	4.39	5.32	0.1
C. Heston	FRE	AAA	25	7	6	0	108²	129	14	46	97	3.8	8.0	48%	.350	1.61	5.80	4.98	5.55	0.5
C. Johnson	SLO	A-	21	3	2	0	41	36	3	12	37	2.6	8.1	55%	.289	1.17	4.17	3.64	5.01	0.4
M. Kickham	FRE	AAA	24	7	7	0	110²	105	9	49	90	4.0	7.3	50%	.299	1.39	4.31	4.33	5.70	0.4
	SFN	MLB	24	0	3	0	28¹	46	8	10	29	3.2	9.2	44%	.402	1.98	10.16	5.70	6.55	-0.7
D. Law	AUG	A	22	0	3	3	35	27	1	10	48	2.6	12.3	42%	.310	1.06	2.31	2.05	2.23	1.0
	SJO	A+	22	4	0	11	25²	20	1	1	45	0.4	15.8	51%	.380	0.82	2.10	1.01	0.66	1.5
M. Lively	FRE	AAA	27	7	5	0	124	111	15	55	99	4.0	7.2	37%	.268	1.34	4.72	4.90	4.95	1.5
G. Moscoso	IOW	AAA	29	7	5	0	94	75	14	47	94	4.5	9.0	42%	.252	1.30	3.93	5.07	5.60	0.3
	SFN	MLB	29	2	2	0	30	20	5	21	31	6.3	9.3	16%	.234	1.37	5.10	5.52	6.50	-0.5
D. Runzler	FRE	AAA	28	3	7	1	52¹	58	5	37	50	6.4	8.6	58%	.331	1.82	5.68	5.31	5.71	0.1

Martin Agosta put together a dominant full-season debut and made the Giants look smart for popping him in the second round; expect them to hammer home the point by promoting him aggressively. ⊘ The 20th-round nepotism pick **Brett Bochy** just keeps generating excellent peripherals; if he were called up now it wouldn't look suspect at all. ⊘ **Erik Cordier** doesn't command his straight fastball, but he lights up radar guns so he gets a comment. ⊘ Lefty **Edwin Escobar**, with more than 400 pro innings under his belt, just keeps improving; the Giants haven't found the promotion yet that doesn't make his numbers better. ⊘ The Dominican righty **Kendry Flores** put himself firmly on the prospect radar on August 21st, when he fanned 15 in eight innings. In truth, his breakout had been showing all season. ⊘ **Cody Hall** is darned old for his levels, but the standard concerns about that are mitigated by his limited pitching experience and instruction. He has dominated younger hitters and some projectability remains. ⊘ It took former 12th-rounder **Chris Heston** just one year to undo all the goodwill he had built up with a sparkling 2012 season, and he was released in the summer to free up a spot on the 40-man roster. ⊘ A reliever at Cal Poly, third-rounder **Chase Johnson** worked as a starter for short-season Salem-Keizer in his pro debut. He faltered down the stretch, suggesting a possible return to the 'pen. ⊘ **Michael Kickham** is a big lefty with a slider that flashes plus, but he'll need to keep righties from slugging .679 against him if he hopes to crack another big-league rotation. Otherwise a LOOGY. ⊘ **Derek Law** struck out 45 and walked one—really!—while allowing just one home run as the Little Giants' closer; his violent, max-effort delivery cements his path to big-league relief work. ⊘ A reliever his entire pro career, **Mitch Lively** tried his hand at starting in his second turn at Triple-A. That the Giants didn't call him up despite a bullet-riddled rotation speaks volumes about his future. ⊘ Acquired from the Cubs in late July to bolster a beleaguered pitching staff, **Guillermo Moscoco** was an adequate near-replica of Guillermo Mota. Even got the name about right. ⊘ In the five years since LOOGY **Dan Runzler** debuted, he has a league-average ERA in the majors but just 72 innings of work, as he quietly implodes in the far-flung outposts of the Pacific Coast League.

MANAGER: BRUCE BOCHY

YEAR	TEAM	W-L	Pythag +/-	Avg PC	100+ P	120+ P	QS	BQS	REL	REL w Zero R	IBB	PH	PH Avg	PH HR	SB2	CS2	SB3	CS3	SAC Att	SAC %	POS SAC	Squeeze	Swing	In Play
2011	SFN	86-76	0	99.8	90	7	103	3	480	411	46	244	.212	4	76	42	7	6	86	72.1%	29	2	395	118
2012	SFN	94-68	1	100.0	91	3	93	6	526	440	42	214	.217	3	111	35	6	2	100	69.0%	27	0	382	123
2013	SFN	76-86	0	96.1	79	2	80	2	524	429	64	258	.213	4	64	24	3	1	86	76.7%	25	2	329	119

In his 12 years in San Diego, Bruce Bochy's Padres drew 654 more walks than they issued. In seven years with the Giants, even though they are a much better team, it's been very different: 713 more walks issued than drawn.

With strikeouts, Bochy has been far more consistent. His teams almost always issue more Ks than they receive. In 19 seasons, it's added up to 1,664 more strikeouts handed out than given. That's the second-best strikeout differential by any manager, behind only Walter Alston.

He makes plenty of in-game substitutions for his position players. The Giants ranked fifth in fewest complete games by position players in 2013, and that was by far their highest showing under Bochy in a while. They had the fewest position player complete games in 2010 and second fewest in 2011, 2009 and 2008. They were third fewest in 2007.

Seattle Mariners

By Mike Curto

In Round Rock, Texas on August 14th, there was a rain delay in the sixth inning. The Tacoma Rainiers—the Seattle Mariners' Triple-A affiliate—were trailing the Express, 6-3. Enough baseball had been played for it to be an official game. If the rain didn't let up, it was going to be a very costly loss for Tacoma, who had entered play in second place, six games behind first-place Salt Lake. With just 20 games remaining the team's playoff hopes hinged on a late-season rush.

"We were sitting in the locker room during the delay, and the crew chief and general manager walked in to go meet with our manager," said a veteran player the next day. "As they walked through the player's area, a bunch of guys start yelling 'bang it—let's go home.'"

The former major leaguer who has played for several teams paused for dramatic effect.

"That, in a nut shell, is why the Mariners organization is never going to win."

Never mind the fact that the rain did stop, the game did resume, and Tacoma did come back and win it. The question remains: Is there anything the Mariners can do to change a culture of losing?

***

The 2013 Seattle Mariners went 71-91, winning four fewer games than the 2012 club and producing a run differential that suggested the true talent of a 67-win team. It was the eighth time in the past 10 seasons that Seattle had posted a losing record, with six of those teams losing 90-plus games.

By the end of the year every bit of Mariners news was greeted with public indifference. When club officials removed General Manager Jack Zduriencik from the hot seat—announcing his contract had been extended by an unknown number of years—fans barely registered a reaction. When manager Eric Wedge walked away from his job (citing the timeless rock and roll cliché; of philosophical differences),

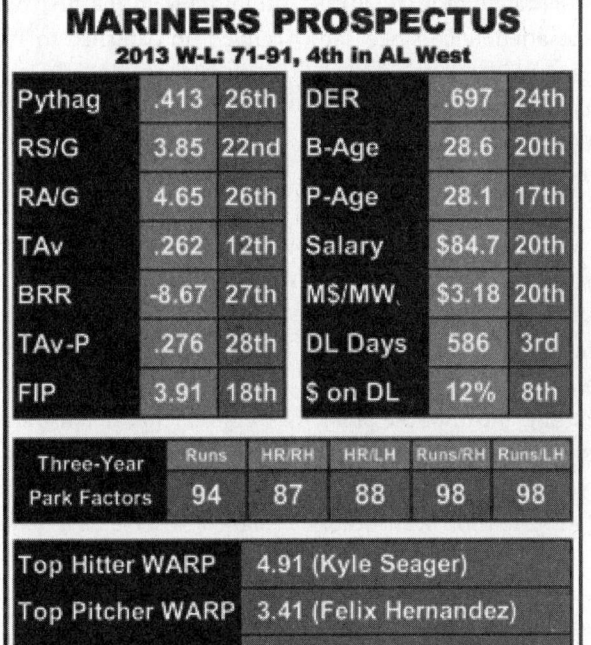

MARINERS PROSPECTUS
2013 W-L: 71-91, 4th in AL West

Pythag	.413	26th	DER	.697	24th
RS/G	3.85	22nd	B-Age	28.6	20th
RA/G	4.65	26th	P-Age	28.1	17th
TAv	.262	12th	Salary	$84.7	20th
BRR	-8.67	27th	M$/MW	$3.18	20th
TAv-P	.276	28th	DL Days	586	3rd
FIP	3.91	18th	$ on DL	12%	8th

Three-Year	Runs	HR/RH	HR/LH	Runs/RH	Runs/LH
Park Factors	94	87	88	98	98

Top Hitter WARP	4.91 (Kyle Seager)
Top Pitcher WARP	3.41 (Felix Hernandez)
Top Prospect	Taijuan Walker

Puget Sound sports fans barely looked up from their Seattle Seahawks depth charts to wonder why a major-league manager would quit and tell the newspaper "if they'd offered me a five-year contract, I wouldn't have come back here."

You would think the hiring of Lloyd McClendon to replace Wedge would cause a reaction, due either to the fact that he's highly respected throughout the industry or that in five seasons managing he never fared better than 12 games under .500.

Nothing.

The Mariners were living in a vacuum, totally neglected by all but the die-hard fans. The perennial losing caused attendance to plummet 50 percent since a franchise record of 3,540,482 was set in 2002; the 1,761,546 final 2013 attendance figure marked the third straight sub-2 million season at the gate.

When you did hear the general public talk about the Mariners, it was usually people complaining about the team's upper management—particularly CEO Howard Lincoln and President Chuck Armstrong, the common threads in the hiring of six managers (plus two interims) and two GMs in 10 disappointing seasons.

Fans rooting for Lincoln and Armstrong to go out for coffee and never come back got one wish granted, as Armstrong's retirement was set to go into effect in January. But by then the Mariners' front office drama seemed to be spreading. In a scathing December 8th *Seattle Times* exposé, Wedge and former front office employees went on the record to call the organization dysfunctional, disruptive, intrusive and out of touch with modern trends and baseball culture. (Typical example: "Lincoln and Armstrong wanted Felix Hernandez ... to throw live batting practice between starts so position players could work on bunting.") The ex-officials argued that the Mariners have lost some of their best minds, as intraoffice squabbles have led to finger-pointing firings and done-with-it desertions. The blame, they said, went through the GMs office, through the president's office, to the CEO's office.

However, Mariners ownership has stood behind the leadership duo for very good reasons. The team is controlled by Nintendo Corporation of America, and Lincoln and Armstrong have a fiduciary responsibility to turn an annual profit—something they have been able to do despite the losing records and sinking attendance figures.

As a part of the lease agreement with Safeco Field, the team is required to submit financial statements to the Public Facilities District board. The team has reported a profit in all but two seasons since moving into Safeco midway through the 1999 season. This included a $5.8 million profit in 2012, when the team reported its lowest attendance since the move. Revenues will presumably rise with the acquisition of regional sports network Root Sports last April, and it appears that the Mariners are now ready to spend some serious coin.

But Zduriencik has found that his checkbook is often no good when he's chasing stars. Two winters ago, it was former Zduriencik draftee Prince Fielder who turned down a huge offer from the Mariners. An aggressive offer to Josh Hamilton was (fortuitously) turned down last winter. Later last offseason, Zduriencik worked out a trade for Justin Upton only to have the young star invoke his no-trade clause. And, this offseason—though maybe we're getting ahead of the story here—David Price went out of his way to announce that if the Mariners traded for him he wouldn't consider signing an extension. Would he consider an extension with other teams? Oh, sure. But not Seattle.

The Mariners finally landed a big fish this year, inking Robinson Cano to a reported 10-year, $240 million contract, swiping the Yankees' best player by doing something previously considered impossible: They blew away New York's best financial offer. By some accounts, Seattle offered Cano $65 million more than his next-highest offer. The mix of Cano's age (31) and the financial commitment speeds up the Mariners' calendar. The team is now pressured to win in the next few years, before Cano's skills severely decline.

***

Within a week of the Cano signing, Zduriencik acquired Corey Hart and Logan Morrison, effectively giving the team three DH/first basemen. (Incumbent first-sacker Justin Smoak is the only one of the trio who is not recovering from surgery to both knees.) The additions of Hart and Morrison are reminiscent of the previous winter, when the Mariners went big for home runs. They moved in the fences, traded for Kendrys Morales and Michael Morse and signed Raul Ibanez and Jason Bay. This lineup of sluggers resulted in a team that finished second in the majors with 188 home runs, and 26th in Defensive Efficiency.

Adding high-profile trade acquisition Jesus Montero (January 2012) to our tally, it's fair to say the Mariners in the past two years have added *seven* players who are most qualified to play DH, a position many teams ignore altogether. And while Zduriencik has been focused on the low end of the defensive spectrum, other stations in the production line have fallen behind, particularly when it comes to preventing runs.

After two straight seasons with the 12th-best bullpen ERA in the majors, the Mariners slipped to 29th in 2013. They lost 27 games in their opponents' final at-bat. A high-velocity relief unit fell victim to injuries (Stephen Pryor) and command woes (Carter Capps) and clocks striking midnight (Tom Wilhelmsen, the bartender-turned-closer who was unhittable in the first two months, lost it completely and ended up banished to Triple-A). By the end of the season, high-leverage bullpen innings were going to rookies Yoervis Medina and Danny Farquhar. Closer-of-the-future Capps was shipped off to Miami for Morrison; nobody knows what to expect from closer-of-the-past Wilhelmsen.

The other half of the battery has been another murky area. The team used a franchise-record seven catchers in 2013, eventually settling on 2012 first-round draft pick Mike Zunino. A prospect of some intrigue, Zunino was rushed to the big leagues while many rival scouts thought he belonged in Double-A. As a group, the Seattle Seven produced the worst catcher defense in baseball, according to Defensive Runs Saved. The Mariners appear committed to Zunino moving forward, even bringing in the venerable Henry Blanco to serve as a player/mentor during the second half of the 2013 season.

Then there's the rotation, where Felix Hernandez and Hisashi Iwakuma thrived despite sketchy defense, finishing eighth and third in Cy Young balloting and giving the Mariners a one-two punch that might have been unstoppable in a postseason series. There was, of course, no postseason series. It's best not to think about how a team with two Cy Young candidates managed to finish 20 games under .500, but the rest of the rotation gets pretty close to the answer. Five other pitchers started at least five games for Seattle. Their ERAs: 4.93, 4.98, 5.26, 5.76, 6.30. While Seattle has been hoarding DHs like Bitcoins, the bottom of the rotation has fallen into wait-for-the-prospects mode.

The good news is that Felix and Kuma are locked up for years to come—Hernandez signed a seven-year, $175 million extension that will take him through the 2019 season, and Iwakuma is inked to a club-friendly $6.5 million deal for 2014, with a $7 million team option for 2015. Unless Seattle manages to consummate one of the trades for starting pitching it had been pursuing through December, the rest of the rotation will be filled by rookies or unproven second-year players. In the case of no. 1 prospect Taijuan Walker, that's exciting. In the case of burly lefty James Paxton, whose erratic Triple-A campaign gave way to three dominant September outings in Seattle, it's intriguing but uncertain. In the case of the fifth spot in the rotation, pray for rain. Wait—the Mariners play under a roof.

***

All that said, the rebuilding movement has produced some grand successes, and a veteran core of Felix, Cano and Iwakuma will be backed by one of the league's best—and youngest, and least expensive—left sides of the infield. Even more than the addition of Cano, it is here that the dour Mariners fan can find hope that the culture might turn around.

The team has developed a bona fide winning player at third base, where the extraordinarily underrated Kyle Seager posted 4.9 WARP in 2013. That ranked seventh among all major-league third basemen—ahead of Pedro Alvarez and Ryan Zimmerman, just a smidge behind Adrian Beltre.

To Seager's left stands shortstop Brad Miller, who began the season in Double-A and was the Mariners' everyday shortstop by the end of June. Miller showed some pop at the plate, slugging .418 with 25 extra-base hits in 76 major-league games. With improved consistency on defense, Miller could hold the shortstop position in Seattle for years to come.

But Miller's not just a good player. He has the makeup and personality to become a team leader once he establishes himself in the majors. He's the sort of player who wouldn't be calling out "Bang it!" in the middle of a pennant race rain delay. From the moment he walks into the clubhouse in the afternoon to the end of the game, Miller is upbeat, outspoken and brimming with energy in a non-annoying way. He is part of a core of Southeastern players the Mariners have developed—a group that includes Zunino (Cape Coral, Florida) and fellow Orlando-area product Nick Franklin, who played with Miller on youth baseball all-star teams. As Seattle's front office press clippings have made clear, if there's going to be a winning culture in the Pacific Northwest it'll start with the players, and particularly with the Southeastern contingent.

It is still unclear exactly how many quality major leaguers will emerge from the Mariners' draft-and-develop rebuilding plan, yet the impact is already clear: Going young and cheap in 2012 and 2013 opened up a massive chunk of payroll space, and the team is now spending it. If they spend it wisely, and if Miller and Seager lead the youth movement, maybe they'll stop losing—which, in Seattle, is both the end and the means.

Mike Curto is the broadcaster for the Tacoma Rainiers.

HITTERS

Dustin Ackley CF
Born: 2/26/1988 Age: 26
Bats: L Throws: R Height: 6' 1"
Weight: 195 Breakout: 3%
Improve: 53% Collapse: 8%
Attrition: 15% MLB: 99%

Comparables:
Aaron Hill, Ian Kinsler, Gordon Beckham

YEAR	TEAM	LVL	AGE	PA	R	2B	3B	HR	RBI	BB	SO	SB	CS	AVG/OBP/SLG	TAv	BABIP	BRR	FRAA	WARP
2011	TAC	AAA	23	331	57	17	3	9	35	55	38	7	3	.303/.421/.487	.319	.324	-1	2B(47): -2.3	1.8
2011	SEA	MLB	23	376	39	16	7	6	36	40	79	6	0	.273/.348/.417	.296	.339	-0.5	2B(86): -1.7, 1B(1): -0.0	2.5
2012	SEA	MLB	24	668	84	22	2	12	50	59	124	13	3	.226/.294/.328	.242	.265	3.2	2B(142): -1.9, 1B(11): -0.2	0.3
2013	TAC	AAA	25	126	21	8	0	2	14	19	14	0	0	.365/.472/.500	.339	.409	0.5	2B(12): -1.0, CF(9): -0.7	1.4
2013	SEA	MLB	25	427	40	18	2	4	31	37	72	2	3	.253/.319/.341	.251	.301	1.8	2B(53): 3.5, CF(50): -1.8	1.2
2014	SEA	MLB	26	468	54	20	3	8	42	45	84	6	2	.255/.329/.374	.267	.300	0	CF -6, LF 0	1.1

Ackley's struggles got him bounced back to the minor leagues for a month mid-season, and manager Eric Wedge placed some of the blame on "sabermetrics." That's absurd—sabermetrics might be to blame for making many of us unpopular, a drag to talk to at cocktail parties and "not exactly husband material," but worse hitters? Not likely. Wedge's point—that Ackley has a tendency to take too many pitches, focusing on walks instead of letting them flow as a byproduct of his overall approach—is a legitimate concern, part of the difficult balance every smart hitter must find, but no indictment of the spreadsheet crowd. Consider this passage that we once wrote for a promising hitter: "He learned the critical distinction between working counts to try to get his pitch and kill it, versus working counts for a walk as an end unto itself. A walk isn't a bad result, but they teach their hitters that it isn't the ideal one. The optimal choice is to learn pitch identification, and know what to do with your pitch when you get it." That's from the 2005 Annual, and it's about the A's efforts with Nick Swisher. Saberfreakingmetrics.
Whatever takes the blame among Seattle's finger-pointing leadership, the good news is that Ackley flashed more reason for hope after the demotion. The former no. 2 overall pick hit a sharp .285/.354/.404 in 68 games following his return to the majors. It's a line more befitting the outfield, which appears to be his new home, presuming that Ackley/Cano doesn't turn into the bruising spring training battle that bored beat writers might wish for.

Abraham Almonte CF

Born: 6/27/1989 Age: 25
Bats: B Throws: R Height: 5' 9"
Weight: 205 Breakout: 11%
Improve: 36% Collapse: 8%
Attrition: 38% MLB: 64%

Comparables:
Chris Denorfia, David Murphy, Chris Heisey

YEAR	TEAM	LVL	AGE	PA	R	2B	3B	HR	RBI	BB	SO	SB	CS	AVG/OBP/SLG	TAv	BABIP	BRR	FRAA	WARP
2011	TAM	A+	22	598	92	27	11	4	52	52	100	30	11	.268/.333/.382	.262	.320	-0.3	CF(37): 0.4	0.6
2012	TRN	AA	23	359	47	17	4	4	25	37	59	30	5	.276/.350/.392	.261	.327	5	CF(30): -2.7, RF(27): 5.6	2.5
2013	WTN	AA	24	120	18	6	1	4	18	18	28	6	1	.255/.367/.451	.281	.314	-2.4	CF(11): -0.4, RF(8): 0.1	0.3
2013	TAC	AAA	24	396	63	17	5	11	50	49	66	20	7	.314/.403/.491	.325	.363	1.6	CF(83): -0.6, LF(5): 0.3	4.5
2013	SEA	MLB	24	82	10	4	0	2	9	6	21	1	0	.264/.312/.403	.262	.333	1.5	CF(15): -2.0, RF(7): 0.3	0.2
2014	SEA	MLB	25	250	33	10	2	5	21	22	55	12	3	.249/.318/.370	.257	.300	1.2	CF -3, RF 1	0.6

Almonte was all but off the prospect radar for the past five years. He struggled with an alcohol addiction that only intensified after he required labrum surgery on his shoulder in 2010, but once he broke through the addiction in 2011 he began to play the best baseball of his career. Seattle grabbed him in a trade of Shawn Kelley, and in 2013 he made his way from Double-A all the way to the majors. He showed excellent speed and a well-rounded batting profile at three levels. A brief 25-game debut as a major-league center fielder last season went well enough, and he'll go into spring training with an outside shot at a starting job.

Brandon Bantz C

Born: 1/7/1987 Age: 27
Bats: R Throws: R Height: 6' 1"
Weight: 205 Breakout: 10%
Improve: 12% Collapse: 9%
Attrition: 19% MLB: 22%

Comparables:
Matt Pagnozzi, Omir Santos, Mike Nickeas

YEAR	TEAM	LVL	AGE	PA	R	2B	3B	HR	RBI	BB	SO	SB	CS	AVG/OBP/SLG	TAv	BABIP	BRR	FRAA	WARP
2011	WTN	AA	24	289	27	9	0	1	20	32	55	0	1	.216/.321/.267	.196	.276	-0.1	C(17): -0.1	-0.2
2012	TAC	AAA	25	123	11	7	0	2	14	5	28	1	1	.229/.261/.349	.228	.277	0.5	C(34): 0.3	0.3
2013	WTN	AA	26	74	5	2	0	1	4	4	21	1	0	.159/.205/.232	.156	.213	-1.1	C(22): 0.2	-0.4
2013	TAC	AAA	26	137	8	2	2	2	11	11	27	0	3	.252/.324/.350	.233	.309	-0.7	C(37): 0.4	0.5
2013	SEA	MLB	26	2	0	0	0	0	0	0	1	0	0	.000/.000/.000	.017	.000	0	C(1): -0.0	-0.1
2014	SEA	MLB	27	250	20	9	1	3	20	15	62	1	1	.206/.259/.293	.209	.260	-0.5	C 0	-0.1

Bantz stuck on Seattle's 40-man roster through the end of 2013 solely for his catching ability. The 30th-round pick hasn't hit since his age-22 season back in Low-A—where he was old for the league—and now owns a .638 OPS in five minor-league seasons. He has a strong arm and could fill a role as an emergency defensive replacement, but his .437 OPS in 22 games at Double-A Jackson as a 26-year-old scream loud and clear that his bat won't play in the major leagues. There's certainly a chance that 2013's two plate appearances will be his only ones; at -0.1 career WARP, that would leave him either first or last among all players taken in his draft round, depending on how you feel about Null.

Steven Baron C

Born: 12/7/1990 Age: 23
Bats: R Throws: R Height: 6' 0"
Weight: 205 Breakout: 0%
Improve: 0% Collapse: 0%
Attrition: 0% MLB: 0%

Comparables:
Eddy Rodriguez, Chris Robinson, Jordan Pacheco

YEAR	TEAM	LVL	AGE	PA	R	2B	3B	HR	RBI	BB	SO	SB	CS	AVG/OBP/SLG	TAv	BABIP	BRR	FRAA	WARP
2011	CLN	A	20	219	17	13	0	4	20	17	49	6	3	.197/.266/.323	.246	.240	-0.9	C(13): -0.4	0.1
2012	CLN	A	21	271	29	18	2	4	30	13	49	10	1	.241/.280/.378	.247	.280	1.6	C(53): -0.2	1.0
2013	HDS	A+	22	353	31	18	5	5	47	18	93	7	0	.208/.247/.338	.200	.271	-0.3	C(86): -0.3	-0.4
2014	SEA	MLB	23	250	18	10	1	2	18	8	72	2	1	.186/.214/.263	.183	.250	0.1	C -1	-0.9

Baron's bat has always trailed his glove—the driving factor behind his supplemental first round selection in 2009—but after five seasons below Double-A, it's losing time to catch up. The hitter's paradise at High Desert is often a cure for offensive ails, but instead Baron posted a sub-.600 OPS for the fourth time in five tries. As tempting as his receiving skills might be, Baron's inability to make contact or hit for power has his career careening toward bust territory.

Jason Bay LF

Born: 9/20/1978 Age: 35
Bats: R Throws: R Height: 6' 2"
Weight: 210 Breakout: 5%
Improve: 28% Collapse: 13%
Attrition: 22% MLB: 91%

Comparables:
Andruw Jones, Kirk Gibson, David Justice

YEAR	TEAM	LVL	AGE	PA	R	2B	3B	HR	RBI	BB	SO	SB	CS	AVG/OBP/SLG	TAv	BABIP	BRR	FRAA	WARP
2011	NYN	MLB	32	509	59	19	1	12	57	56	109	11	1	.245/.329/.374	.263	.295	0.6	LF(122): -1.6	1.2
2012	SLU	A+	33	20	0	0	0	0	1	4	6	1	0	.133/.300/.133	.178	.200	-0.4	LF(2): -0.0	-0.2
2012	NYN	MLB	33	215	21	2	0	8	20	19	58	5	1	.165/.237/.299	.209	.185	0.4	LF(65): 4.8	-0.2
2013	SEA	MLB	34	236	30	6	0	11	20	26	62	3	1	.204/.298/.393	.261	.231	0.3	LF(38): -1.3, RF(25): 0.9	0.3
2014	SEA	MLB	35	250	29	9	1	8	29	28	64	5	1	.227/.319/.382	.268	.280	0.4	LF 0, RF 0	0.9

Bay finally rediscovered his power stroke in 2013, and with it he saved any shot at continuing his career. Bay's .186 ISO was his highest in the past four years by more 40 points. Unfortunately, his contact abilities keep eroding and his .208 BABIP over the past two seasons is the worst among all hitters with at least 300 plate appearances. "BABIP, that's the luck one, right?" asks your uncle hopefully when you tell him this, but no, it's a skill stat that's merely spiked with luck: The rest of the names at the bottom of that particular leaderboard go Shelley Duncan, Casey Kotchman, Rod Barajas, Don Kelly, Yuniesky Betancourt ...

Willie Bloomquist   SS

Born: **11/27/1977** Age: **36**
Bats: **R** Throws: **R** Height: **5' 11"**
Weight: **190** Breakout: **0%**
Improve: **32%** Collapse: **8%**
Attrition: **17%** MLB: **78%**

Comparables:
Mark Grudzielanek, John McDonald, Mark Ellis

YEAR	TEAM	LVL	AGE	PA	R	2B	3B	HR	RBI	BB	SO	SB	CS	AVG/OBP/SLG	TAv	BABIP	BRR	FRAA	WARP
2011	ARI	MLB	33	381	44	10	2	4	26	23	51	20	10	.266/.317/.340	.236	.300	0.3	SS(59): -2.8, LF(25): -0.3	0.1
2012	ARI	MLB	34	338	47	21	5	0	23	12	55	7	10	.302/.325/.398	.262	.362	0.3	SS(64): -8.8, 3B(11): 0.3	0.6
2013	RNO	AAA	35	23	5	0	1	0	9	2	2	0	0	.429/.478/.524	.310	.474	0.7	2B(5): -0.1, SS(1): 0.1	0.3
2013	ARI	MLB	35	150	16	5	1	0	14	8	11	0	2	.317/.360/.367	.262	.341	2.2	2B(15): -0.9, SS(9): -0.3	0.5
2014	SEA	MLB	36	250	27	9	2	1	17	12	41	7	5	.258/.297/.330	.239	.300	-0.4	SS -4, 2B -1	0.0

Look at that. Eleven seasons in, the often-hecklable Bloomquist managed back-to-back above-average hitting lines! This calls for a celebration of plucky utility infielders. Besides missing three months in separate trips to the DL, Bloomquist completed his two-year, $3.8 million contract as a sound fill-in, having now played every position in his career except pitcher and catcher. Nagging injuries remain a concern, and don't expect him to post another .260-plus TAv, but everybody needs a superutility guy, and Willie's super enough to keep getting looks in that role.

Robinson Cano   2B

Born: **10/22/1982** Age: **31**
Bats: **L** Throws: **R** Height: **6' 0"**
Weight: **210** Breakout: **0%**
Improve: **42%** Collapse: **1%**
Attrition: **1%** MLB: **99%**

Comparables:
Chase Utley, Aramis Ramirez, Vladimir Guerrero

YEAR	TEAM	LVL	AGE	PA	R	2B	3B	HR	RBI	BB	SO	SB	CS	AVG/OBP/SLG	TAv	BABIP	BRR	FRAA	WARP
2011	NYA	MLB	28	681	104	46	7	28	118	38	96	8	2	.302/.349/.533	.306	.316	2.8	2B(157): 6.0	6.0
2012	NYA	MLB	29	697	105	48	1	33	94	61	96	3	2	.313/.379/.550	.319	.326	-1.6	2B(154): 6.3	6.9
2013	NYA	MLB	30	681	81	41	0	27	107	65	85	7	1	.314/.383/.516	.324	.327	-0.9	2B(153): -1.8, SS(1): -0.0	6.3
2014	SEA	MLB	31	643	77	40	2	21	87	45	88	5	2	.297/.352/.482	.307	.320	-0.7	2B 2, SS -0	5.4

On an aging roster that required constant triage, Cano was the one player who didn't give Joe Girardi gray hairs. The second baseman accounted for 68 percent of the Yankees' BWARP, the highest percentage accrued by any player on a non-last-place team. All Cano had to do to cash in on his contract year was replicate his production from the previous season, and he couldn't have come closer to achieving that goal, matching his career-high TAv from 2012 and extending his streak of seasons of at least 159 games to seven. With the caveat that age 31 is close to when players begin to crater, especially at second base, a player who's averaged six wins over the past four seasons, shown no signs of decline, and missed one game due to injury since 2006 isn't one of the worst bets in the wonderful world of long-term, guaranteed contracts. The last few years of his new 10-year deal are certain to be an overpay, but if signing Cano can help pump up Seattle's deflated fan base, it will be worth it.

Endy Chavez   RF

Born: **2/7/1978** Age: **36**
Bats: **L** Throws: **L** Height: **5' 11"**
Weight: **170** Breakout: **0%**
Improve: **26%** Collapse: **4%**
Attrition: **19%** MLB: **76%**

Comparables:
Quinton McCracken, Jim Eisenreich, So Taguchi

YEAR	TEAM	LVL	AGE	PA	R	2B	3B	HR	RBI	BB	SO	SB	CS	AVG/OBP/SLG	TAv	BABIP	BRR	FRAA	WARP
2011	ROU	AAA	33	142	16	8	2	2	17	10	6	6	0	.305/.353/.445	.325	.306	-0.2	CF(5): -1.4	0.1
2011	TEX	MLB	33	274	37	11	3	5	27	10	30	10	5	.301/.323/.426	.268	.321	1.6	CF(66): -3.0, LF(12): -0.4	0.8
2012	NOR	AAA	34	53	2	3	0	0	4	2	6	0	0	.149/.192/.213	.163	.163	-0.8	RF(10): 0.3, LF(4): -0.1	-0.5
2012	BAL	MLB	34	169	15	6	0	2	12	6	24	3	2	.203/.236/.278	.195	.227	-1.2	LF(35): -1.0, RF(21): 0.9	-0.9
2013	TAC	AAA	35	31	8	1	0	0	1	3	3	0	2	.429/.484/.464	.389	.480	-0.1	CF(5): -0.2, LF(1): -0.0	0.5
2013	SEA	MLB	35	279	22	10	0	2	14	9	31	1	3	.267/.290/.327	.232	.295	0.8	RF(50): 2.5, CF(24): 0.5	0.2
2014	SEA	MLB	36	254	26	9	1	2	18	12	35	5	3	.250/.286/.325	.233	.280	-0.3	RF 1, CF -1	-0.1

Chavez didn't have the bat for a corner outfield spot at his best, and that certainly didn't change at age 35. Seattle's outfield, though, had a most unfortunate combination of injuries and incompetence, so 97 games (including, alarmingly, 59 starts) opened up for Chavez. His resilience is impressive and his glove can still play, but either his speed has been disappeared or he's trying to make a very self-destructive point: Chavez stole just one base in 78 times on base in 2013 and was caught three times, and he failed to hit a triple for the second consecutive season. Without fleetness of foot, Endy's end is near.

Nick Franklin　2B

Born: 3/2/1991 Age: 23
Bats: B Throws: R Height: 6' 1"
Weight: 195 Breakout: 0%
Improve: 32% Collapse: 1%
Attrition: 15% MLB: 54%

Comparables:
Asdrubal Cabrera, Andy Marte, Colby Rasmus

YEAR	TEAM	LVL	AGE	PA	R	2B	3B	HR	RBI	BB	SO	SB	CS	AVG/OBP/SLG	TAv	BABIP	BRR	FRAA	WARP
2011	HDS	A+	20	297	50	10	5	5	20	31	56	13	1	.275/.356/.411	.167	.333	-0.8	SS(10): -0.7, 2B(2): -0.6	-0.6
2011	WTN	AA	20	92	13	3	2	2	6	6	18	5	3	.325/.371/.482	.256	.397	0	2B(5): -0.3, SS(5): -0.5	0.0
2012	WTN	AA	21	239	25	17	4	4	26	24	38	9	2	.322/.394/.502	.304	.378	-0.3	SS(39): -4.3, 2B(14): 2.0	1.7
2012	TAC	AAA	21	296	39	15	5	7	29	24	68	3	2	.243/.310/.416	.247	.301	-0.1	2B(34): -2.9, SS(30): 0.4	0.3
2013	TAC	AAA	22	177	28	9	0	4	20	30	20	7	0	.324/.440/.472	.339	.350	0.9	2B(23): 1.0, SS(15): 0.2	2.2
2013	SEA	MLB	22	412	38	20	1	12	45	42	113	6	1	.225/.303/.382	.260	.290	-1.3	2B(96): 14.8, SS(3): 0.1	2.5
2014	SEA	MLB	23	395	47	18	2	9	37	35	95	8	2	.238/.308/.377	.254	.300	0.6	2B 6, SS -2	1.7

Strikeout issues persisted through Franklin's early career, but strong discipline and a surprising amount of power from a middle infielder boosted his stock. When Franklin dominated Triple-A to begin 2013, he earned a shot at replacing the failing Dustin Ackley. The discipline and power played just as well in the majors—Franklin's 34 extra-base hits represented his best total since his year at notorious High Desert in 2010. As such, Franklin's bat was MLB-quality, despite the second-highest strikeout rate by a middle infielder last year. Even a marginal uptick in bat-to-ball matchmaking would make him above average at the keystone, though Jay-Z and Robinson Cano made sure that such an uptick will like occur elsewhere.

Gabriel Guerrero　RF

Born: 12/11/1993 Age: 20
Bats: R Throws: R Height: 6' 3"
Weight: 190 Breakout: 0%
Improve: 0% Collapse: 0%
Attrition: 0% MLB: 0%

Comparables:
Moises Sierra, Lorenzo Cain, Avisail Garcia

YEAR	TEAM	LVL	AGE	PA	R	2B	3B	HR	RBI	BB	SO	SB	CS	AVG/OBP/SLG	TAv	BABIP	BRR	FRAA	WARP
2013	CLN	A	19	499	60	23	3	4	50	21	113	12	3	.271/.303/.358	.251	.344	1.8	RF(121): 10.0	1.3
2014	SEA	MLB	20	250	18	9	1	3	21	5	72	0	0	.217/.234/.304	.205	.290	-0.4	RF 2	-0.7

Yes, Gabriel—he prefers "Gabby"—is one of those Guerreros. Vladimir's nephew dominated the Dominican Summer League and Arizona Rookie League as an 18-year-old, so the Mariners decided to test him. Guerrero was vaulted straight to Low-A Clinton as a 19-year-old, where 485 of his 499 plate appearances were taken against older pitchers. The elders turned out to be Guerrero's betters, taking advantage of his free-swinging ways, particularly early in the season. He limped to a .226/.251/.316 line with a 24 percent strikeout rate through May. They weren't all going to be as easy as the Dominican Summer League. Guerrero rebounded, however, and hit .298/.333/.384 from June on and .303/.331/.437—including all four of his home runs—in his final 30 games. His ability to adjust and grow over the course of a difficult year can be nothing but encouraging.

Franklin Gutierrez　CF

Born: 2/21/1983 Age: 31
Bats: R Throws: R Height: 6' 2"
Weight: 195 Breakout: 1%
Improve: 45% Collapse: 14%
Attrition: 14% MLB: 88%

Comparables:
Lee Lacy, Juan Encarnacion, Joel Youngblood

YEAR	TEAM	LVL	AGE	PA	R	2B	3B	HR	RBI	BB	SO	SB	CS	AVG/OBP/SLG	TAv	BABIP	BRR	FRAA	WARP
2011	TAC	AAA	28	47	7	2	2	0	6	6	7	0	0	.275/.362/.425	.218	.324	0	CF(2): -0.1	-0.1
2011	SEA	MLB	28	344	26	13	0	1	19	16	56	13	2	.224/.261/.273	.199	.266	0.9	CF(92): 4.7	-0.3
2012	TAC	AAA	29	72	11	5	0	2	8	8	13	0	1	.258/.333/.435	.297	.286	-0.2	CF(10): 1.2	0.6
2012	SEA	MLB	29	163	18	10	1	4	17	9	31	3	1	.260/.309/.420	.271	.302	-0.5	CF(38): 1.0	0.5
2013	TAC	AAA	30	213	27	16	0	3	25	15	60	4	2	.211/.272/.340	.217	.286	1.1	RF(25): -0.8, CF(2): -0.2	-0.8
2013	SEA	MLB	30	151	18	7	0	10	24	5	43	3	1	.248/.273/.503	.289	.283	-0.5	RF(21): -0.4, CF(17): 0.5	0.7
2014	SEA	MLB	31	250	30	11	1	5	23	16	55	6	2	.242/.294/.366	.249	.290	0.4	CF 1, RF -1	0.5

What was it this year, you ask? Left groin tightness (three days), right hamstring strain (60 days) and right hamstring again (63 days). Once again, Gutierrez looked like more than a capable center fielder when he was healthy. More importantly, though, Gutierrez is a 31-year-old who has played just 173 games over the past three seasons, and just 81 over the past two. His durability issues might make him a candidate to be a nifty short-side platoon option in center field—Gutierrez's career OPS is 172 points higher against lefties, and the consistent rest could help stave off more injuries.

Brad Miller　SS

Born: 10/18/1989 Age: 24
Bats: L Throws: R Height: 6' 2"
Weight: 185 Breakout: 3%
Improve: 31% Collapse: 15%
Attrition: 22% MLB: 85%

Comparables:
Stephen Drew, Dustin Ackley, Josh Rutledge

YEAR	TEAM	LVL	AGE	PA	R	2B	3B	HR	RBI	BB	SO	SB	CS	AVG/OBP/SLG	TAv	BABIP	BRR	FRAA	WARP
2011	CLN	A	21	59	9	4	1	0	7	4	9	1	0	.415/.458/.528	.349	.489	0		0.0
2012	HDS	A+	22	473	89	33	5	11	56	52	79	19	6	.339/.412/.524	.300	.394	1.8	SS(97): 6.4	5.1
2012	WTN	AA	22	170	21	7	2	4	12	22	26	4	1	.320/.406/.476	.308	.364	-0.3	SS(37): -2.2	1.3
2013	WTN	AA	23	175	27	7	1	6	25	20	30	4	3	.294/.379/.471	.313	.333	-0.4	SS(29): 0.9, 2B(6): -0.4	1.3
2013	TAC	AAA	23	122	26	5	1	6	28	15	18	2	1	.356/.426/.596	.369	.373	1.8	SS(22): 1.8, 2B(3): 0.0	2.5
2013	SEA	MLB	23	335	41	11	6	8	36	24	52	5	3	.265/.318/.418	.279	.294	2.3	SS(68): -3.8, 2B(13): -0.7	1.6
2014	SEA	MLB	24	369	45	15	3	8	37	30	70	5	2	.265/.325/.403	.270	.310	0	SS -1, 2B -1	1.8

Miller earned comparisons to Kyle Seager throughout his minor-league career, so it's only fitting that he joined Seager as an overachiever on the 2013 Mariners. Miller charged through the high minors with good power and better contact skills, particularly for a middle infielder. Pitchers challenged him with fastballs once he reached the majors, but he made them pay, as six of his eight home runs came on hard pitches. He doesn't grade out as a great fielder, but his bat is well above the short-stop standard and appears to be worth taking a minor defensive hit.

Jesus Montero 1B
Born: 11/28/1989 Age: 24
Bats: R Throws: R Height: 6' 3"
Weight: 230 Breakout: 6%
Improve: 54% Collapse: 6%
Attrition: 15% MLB: 100%
Comparables: Miguel Montero, Wilson Ramos, Jesus Flores

YEAR	TEAM	LVL	AGE	PA	R	2B	3B	HR	RBI	BB	SO	SB	CS	AVG/OBP/SLG	TAv	BABIP	BRR	FRAA	WARP
2011	SWB	AAA	21	463	52	19	1	18	67	36	98	0	0	.288/.348/.467	.283	.336	-2	C(75): -1.5	2.1
2011	NYA	MLB	21	69	9	4	0	4	12	7	17	0	0	.328/.406/.590	.332	.400	-2.1	C(3): -0.0	0.4
2012	SEA	MLB	22	553	46	20	0	15	62	29	99	0	2	.260/.298/.386	.253	.292	-6.6	C(56): -0.6	0.0
2013	TAC	AAA	23	82	12	6	2	1	9	8	24	0	0	.247/.317/.425	.256	.347	-0.3	1B(16): -1.3, C(1): -0.0	0.0
2013	SEA	MLB	23	110	6	1	1	3	9	8	21	0	1	.208/.264/.327	.227	.231	-0.4	C(26): -0.1	-0.1
2014	SEA	MLB	24	250	26	11	1	8	31	16	51	0	0	.260/.309/.414	.270	.300	-0.5	1B -3	0.1

The Montero acquisition remains a disaster for Seattle. His career as a catcher was all but ended in May, when the Mariners optioned him back to Tacoma to end the ill-fated experiment and teach him first base. Montero was limited by a knee injury and didn't hit much in 19 games for Tacoma, but that turned out to be the least of the Mariners' problems, as he wound up one of the 14 players suspended in the wake of the Biogenesis case and missed August and September as a result. Any leeway purchased with his top-prospect status has officially been suspended, too.

Kendrys Morales 1B
Born: 6/20/1983 Age: 31
Bats: B Throws: R Height: 6' 1"
Weight: 225 Breakout: 1%
Improve: 36% Collapse: 5%
Attrition: 6% MLB: 94%
Comparables: Glenn Davis, Orlando Cepeda, Rafael Palmeiro

YEAR	TEAM	LVL	AGE	PA	R	2B	3B	HR	RBI	BB	SO	SB	CS	AVG/OBP/SLG	TAv	BABIP	BRR	FRAA	WARP
2012	ANA	MLB	29	522	61	26	1	22	73	31	116	0	1	.273/.320/.467	.293	.315	-2.5	1B(28): 0.5	2.1
2013	SEA	MLB	30	657	64	34	0	23	80	49	114	0	1	.277/.336/.449	.290	.309	-4.5	1B(31): -1.3	2.0
2014	SEA	MLB	31	590	69	30	1	23	82	42	117	1	1	.273/.329/.463	.293	.310	-1.5	1B -0	2.7

Perhaps the most remarkable part of Morales' recovery from a broken leg is that he had to rehabilitate not one but two swings. Morales might have been a good defender once, but the injury hindered him in the field, so it was important for him to show he could handle DHing from both sides of the plate. Where the Angels generally held him out against left-handed pitching in 2012, Seattle unleashed him against righties in 2013, and Morales managed at least a .780 OPS from each side of the plate, above the positional average for DH. Sexy, sexy Mariners History tidbit: Morales' excellent season would have been, by OPS+, just the 13th-best of Edgar Martinez's career.

Julio Morban RF
Born: 2/13/1992 Age: 22
Bats: L Throws: L Height: 6' 1"
Weight: 205 Breakout: 1%
Improve: 11% Collapse: 0%
Attrition: 9% MLB: 21%
Comparables: Marcell Ozuna, Carlos Gonzalez, Oswaldo Arcia

YEAR	TEAM	LVL	AGE	PA	R	2B	3B	HR	RBI	BB	SO	SB	CS	AVG/OBP/SLG	TAv	BABIP	BRR	FRAA	WARP
2011	CLN	A	19	336	44	12	7	4	28	26	99	10	5	.256/.315/.382	.234	.365	-0.7	LF(9): 0.2, CF(6): -0.2	-0.2
2012	HDS	A+	20	330	56	16	2	17	52	21	67	5	1	.313/.361/.550	.307	.352	0.3	CF(25): -1.6, LF(23): -1.2	2.4
2013	WTN	AA	21	326	46	20	5	7	44	28	95	7	2	.295/.362/.468	.289	.415	0.5	RF(47): -3.1, CF(4): -0.0	1.2
2014	SEA	MLB	22	250	24	10	1	6	27	12	76	2	1	.234/.274/.364	.237	.320	-0.1	RF -2, CF -1	-0.4

It took Morban a few years to find his footing stateside, as injuries kept the million-dollar bonus recipient in the low minors until 2013. In his first try at pitcher-friendly Jackson (the Double-A Southern League hit just .241/.314/.358 overall), Morban was an offensive force. If his power grows as expected, he could be a 20-homer threat as a right fielder. Unfortunately, Morban suffered another injury just before the end of the season—a broken leg—providing another challenge heading into 2014. Playing baseball is hard enough when you're healthy.

Logan Morrison 1B
Born: 8/25/1987 Age: 26
Bats: L Throws: L Height: 6' 3"
Weight: 245 Breakout: 3%
Improve: 46% Collapse: 1%
Attrition: 7% MLB: 99%
Comparables: Conor Jackson, Billy Butler, Justin Smoak

YEAR	TEAM	LVL	AGE	PA	R	2B	3B	HR	RBI	BB	SO	SB	CS	AVG/OBP/SLG	TAv	BABIP	BRR	FRAA	WARP
2011	NWO	AAA	23	27	3	2	0	1	5	2	4	0	0	.167/.222/.375	.195	.150	0		0.0
2011	FLO	MLB	23	525	54	25	4	23	72	54	99	2	1	.247/.330/.468	.294	.265	-2.4	LF(119): -2.9, 1B(1): -0.1	2.4
2012	MIA	MLB	24	334	30	15	1	11	36	31	58	1	0	.230/.308/.399	.253	.248	-0.7	LF(59): -4.1, 1B(21): 2.6	0.1
2013	JUP	A+	25	27	0	0	0	0	3	4	0	0	1	.174/.296/.174	.218	.174	-1.4	1B(3): 0.4	-0.2
2013	JAX	AA	25	35	5	0	0	2	7	2	4	0	0	.182/.229/.364	.212	.148	0.1	1B(7): 0.0	-0.2
2013	MIA	MLB	25	333	32	13	4	6	36	38	56	0	0	.242/.333/.375	.262	.281	-0.1	1B(79): -1.6	0.4
2014	SEA	MLB	26	322	35	15	2	9	39	35	58	1	0	.247/.335/.415	.281	.280	-0.3	1B 1, LF -1	1.2

Morrison's injury history over the past three seasons shows 11 different knee-related items, including the surgery on his right patellar tendon that cost him 123 games between 2012 and 2013. Hence, he remains more Twitter notable than baseball notable. His approach, which was always a big part of his prospect status, turned more aggressive in 2013. His swing rate of 45 percent was a career high by more than five percentage points and led to weaker contact—his isolated power and slugging percentages were both career worsts. The Mariners bought low, but if his terrible defense gets worse with age they might end up selling even lower someday.

Miguel Olivo C

Born: 7/15/1978 Age: 35
Bats: R Throws: R Height: 6' 0''
Weight: 230 Breakout: 0%
Improve: 22% Collapse: 20%
Attrition: 22% MLB: 85%

Comparables:
Mark Parent, Adam Melhuse, Del Wilber

YEAR	TEAM	LVL	AGE	PA	R	2B	3B	HR	RBI	BB	SO	SB	CS	AVG/OBP/SLG	TAv	BABIP	BRR	FRAA	WARP
2011	SEA	MLB	32	507	54	19	1	19	62	20	140	6	5	.224/.253/.388	.241	.270	-0.3	C(127): 1.6	1.1
2012	SEA	MLB	33	323	27	14	0	12	29	7	85	3	6	.222/.239/.381	.243	.266	0.8	C(73): 2.0	1.5
2013	MIA	MLB	34	80	5	2	0	4	9	5	23	0	0	.203/.250/.392	.231	.229	-0.9	C(21): 0.2, 1B(1): -0.0	-0.1
2014	SEA	MLB	35	250	26	9	1	9	30	11	73	3	2	.226/.261/.387	.241	.280	-0.4	C 0, 1B -0	0.6

Oftentimes, players have a hard time seeing that the end has come. Judging by his fallout with the Marlins, Olivo saw it and, most appropriately, took an ugly hack as it dove away from the strike zone. After Olivo was released at the end of spring training by the Reds, Miami jumped at the opportunity to bring him in as Rob Brantly's backup. Sadly, America's favorite free swinger was none too pleased with his playing time and walked out on his team after three unsuccessful attempts to gain his release, landing him on the restricted list. Yes, Olivo's major-league baseball career may have ended by way of the world's saddest microcosm.

Carlos Peguero RF

Born: 2/22/1987 Age: 27
Bats: L Throws: L Height: 6' 5''
Weight: 260 Breakout: 7%
Improve: 17% Collapse: 6%
Attrition: 21% MLB: 42%

Comparables:
Casper Wells, Justin Ruggiano, Cory Aldridge

YEAR	TEAM	LVL	AGE	PA	R	2B	3B	HR	RBI	BB	SO	SB	CS	AVG/OBP/SLG	TAv	BABIP	BRR	FRAA	WARP
2011	TAC	AAA	24	258	44	15	2	13	47	15	82	8	0	.317/.364/.558	.299	.434	1.9	LF(18): -1.1, RF(13): -1.3	1.2
2011	SEA	MLB	24	155	14	3	2	6	19	8	54	0	1	.196/.252/.371	.230	.262	-0.4	LF(40): 2.1, RF(3): 0.1	0.2
2012	TAC	AAA	25	322	47	13	1	21	54	29	103	2	2	.285/.366/.562	.333	.369	-1.4	RF(51): 3.3, LF(23): -3.5	3.0
2012	SEA	MLB	25	57	2	2	1	2	7	1	28	0	0	.179/.193/.357	.210	.308	-0.1	RF(11): 0.8, LF(2): 0.1	0.0
2013	TAC	AAA	26	505	60	28	3	19	83	42	156	11	8	.260/.321/.460	.275	.346	1.6	RF(80): -4.4, LF(11): -0.5	1.7
2013	SEA	MLB	26	7	1	0	0	1	1	1	2	1	0	.333/.429/.833	.441	.333	0	RF(2): -0.0	0.1
2014	SEA	MLB	27	250	29	10	1	10	33	16	88	3	2	.226/.282/.411	.255	.310	-0.1	RF 2, LF -0	0.5

At 26, Peguero has reached the point where he is the perfect emergency call-up. He's good enough to fake it as a major-league outfielder for 50 or so plate appearances, and chances are he doesn't have anything left to learn at Triple-A, but he is too free a swinger to truly succeed in the majors. It always feels too early to write off someone with Peguero's physical talent, but at some point the "if only he didn't swing so much" comments cease to be legitimate possibilities for the future and instead take on a tinge of melancholy for what could have been. We can't put pictures in the book, so let these six words be your thousand: 30 percent strikeout rate in Tacoma.

Douglas Peterson 3B

Born: 12/31/1991 Age: 22
Bats: R Throws: R Height: 6' 1''
Weight: 190 Breakout: 4%
Improve: 21% Collapse: 1%
Attrition: 20% MLB: 30%

Comparables:
Alex Liddi, Brandon Laird, Josh Bell

YEAR	TEAM	LVL	AGE	PA	R	2B	3B	HR	RBI	BB	SO	SB	CS	AVG/OBP/SLG	TAv	BABIP	BRR	FRAA	WARP
2013	CLN	A	21	107	16	5	1	7	20	7	24	1	0	.293/.346/.576	.321	.324	-0.1	3B(21): -0.6	0.9
2013	EVE	A-	21	123	20	6	0	6	27	13	18	0	1	.312/.382/.532	.331	.326	-0.6	3B(24): -2.9, 1B(1): -0.0	0.9
2014	SEA	MLB	22	250	25	9	1	9	31	13	67	0	0	.224/.265/.383	.240	.270	-0.4	3B -4, 1B -0	-0.4

Peterson was drafted for his power, and he showed it in 55 games after signing with Seattle as the 12th overall pick. Even at Low-A Everett, a tough hitter's park, Peterson managed a strong .220 isolated power, which should help alleviate concerns that his amateur pop was a result of playing at high elevations in New Mexico. Peterson isn't considered to be a defensive asset—he'll be tried at third base, but the consensus is he'll end up as a bat-first left fielder or first baseman.

Humberto Quintero C

Born: 8/2/1979 Age: 34
Bats: R Throws: R Height: 5' 9''
Weight: 215 Breakout: 2%
Improve: 25% Collapse: 21%
Attrition: 27% MLB: 82%

Comparables:
Brook Fordyce, Jose Molina, Matt Batts

YEAR	TEAM	LVL	AGE	PA	R	2B	3B	HR	RBI	BB	SO	SB	CS	AVG/OBP/SLG	TAv	BABIP	BRR	FRAA	WARP
2011	HOU	MLB	31	272	22	12	1	2	25	6	53	1	0	.240/.258/.317	.206	.292	0.1	C(77): 0.1	-0.5
2012	NAS	AAA	32	100	9	8	0	1	12	1	21	0	0	.263/.283/.379	.215	.324	-0.3	C(25): -0.4	0.1
2012	KCA	MLB	32	144	7	12	0	1	19	4	28	0	1	.232/.257/.341	.213	.282	-2.6	C(43): 0.4	-0.1
2013	LEH	AAA	33	32	7	1	0	2	4	4	5	0	0	.292/.419/.583	.361	.278	-0.3	C(8): -0.2	0.5
2013	PHI	MLB	33	68	3	4	0	2	9	3	15	0	0	.250/.294/.406	.219	.298	-0.4	C(21): 0.2	-0.1
2013	SEA	MLB	33	72	5	1	0	2	4	3	15	0	0	.224/.257/.328	.203	.260	0	C(21): 0.1	-0.1
2014	SEA	MLB	34	250	20	11	0	3	21	8	57	0	0	.223/.256/.311	.215	.280	-0.5	C 0	0.0

The good news: Quintero tied a career high in home runs in 2013. The bad news: His career high in home runs is still four. Still, teams can always use a catcher with a strong arm, and Quintero was able to demonstrate his wing still has some spring, catching 12 of 33 basestealers. He has now caught at least 35 percent of would-be thieves in five of the past six seasons. Now count to 60 and see if you can tell us one thing you remember about Humberto Quintero.

Stefen Romero 2B

Born: 10/17/1988 Age: 25
Bats: R Throws: R Height: 6' 2"
Weight: 220 Breakout: 5%
Improve: 20% Collapse: 9%
Attrition: 32% MLB: 44%

Comparables:
Todd Frazier, Scott Van Slyke, John Mayberry

YEAR	TEAM	LVL	AGE	PA	R	2B	3B	HR	RBI	BB	SO	SB	CS	AVG/OBP/SLG	TAv	BABIP	BRR	FRAA	WARP
2011	CLN	A	22	478	62	22	4	16	65	32	69	16	9	.280/.342/.462	.323	.298	-1	2B(12): 0.3, 3B(9): 0.1	1.1
2012	HDS	A+	23	276	47	19	3	11	51	13	35	6	2	.357/.391/.581	.308	.379	-1.2	2B(53): -2.0	1.8
2012	WTN	AA	23	240	38	15	4	12	50	14	37	6	2	.347/.392/.620	.343	.366	0.1	2B(54): -0.1	2.7
2013	HDS	A+	24	21	1	1	0	0	2	2	1	0	0	.278/.381/.333	.229	.294	-0.1	3B(4): -0.0	0.0
2013	TAC	AAA	24	411	51	23	4	11	74	28	87	8	4	.277/.331/.448	.273	.331	0.6	LF(73): 2.3, 2B(2): -0.2	1.4
2014	SEA	MLB	25	250	27	12	1	7	30	10	53	4	2	.257/.293/.411	.261	.300	-0.1	2B -1, LF 1	0.7

After dominating Single- and Double-A in his first two minor-league seasons, Romero finally hit a bit of a roadblock at Tacoma. He dealt with injuries early in the season and was learning a new position after his lack of speed and the emergence of other middle infield prospects pushed him off second base. Still, even in his worst minor-league season by the raw stat line, Romero was a league-average hitter and continued to show plus power despite facing mostly older, more experienced pitchers. He'll likely get a second crack at the level, this time with a little more familiarity and, if all goes well, a lot more contempt.

Michael Saunders CF

Born: 11/19/1986 Age: 27
Bats: L Throws: R Height: 6' 4"
Weight: 225 Breakout: 3%
Improve: 58% Collapse: 4%
Attrition: 7% MLB: 94%

Comparables:
Dexter Fowler, Franklin Gutierrez, Chris Young

YEAR	TEAM	LVL	AGE	PA	R	2B	3B	HR	RBI	BB	SO	SB	CS	AVG/OBP/SLG	TAv	BABIP	BRR	FRAA	WARP
2011	TAC	AAA	24	291	51	11	3	7	38	50	71	10	3	.288/.415/.449	.300	.384	2.1	CF(44): 7.0, LF(12): 1.1	2.8
2011	SEA	MLB	24	179	16	5	0	2	8	12	56	6	2	.149/.207/.217	.163	.212	0.8	CF(46): 2.6, LF(12): 0.7	-0.9
2012	SEA	MLB	25	553	71	31	3	19	57	43	132	21	4	.247/.306/.432	.280	.297	1.7	CF(113): -3.3, LF(22): 0.6	2.5
2013	SEA	MLB	26	468	59	23	3	12	46	54	118	13	5	.236/.323/.397	.281	.298	2.1	CF(78): -2.1, RF(34): 0.8	2.2
2014	SEA	MLB	27	459	54	19	3	12	47	45	117	13	4	.229/.306/.376	.257	.290	1	CF 0, LF 1	1.4

Saunders rescued his seasonal line with eight extra-base hits and a .289/.386/.632 line over his final 12 games. He had carried a .689 OPS up to that point and lost time in center field to the suddenly surging Abraham Almonte when rosters expanded. Saunders continues to show poor contact skills, but even in a generally down season, he flashed above-average discipline and power, especially considering Safeco Field played as a pitchers park even after the fences were moved in. The Saunders the Mariners have seen for the past two seasons is a quality player, but not of such quality that he's been able to lock down a starting spot. He'll have to do so soon if he's ever going to: 2014 marks his first arbitration season, and the scrutiny will only get heavier from here.

Kyle Seager 3B

Born: 11/3/1987 Age: 26
Bats: L Throws: R Height: 6' 0"
Weight: 215 Breakout: 1%
Improve: 53% Collapse: 3%
Attrition: 5% MLB: 98%

Comparables:
Edwin Encarnacion, Puddin Head Jones, Richie Hebner

YEAR	TEAM	LVL	AGE	PA	R	2B	3B	HR	RBI	BB	SO	SB	CS	AVG/OBP/SLG	TAv	BABIP	BRR	FRAA	WARP
2011	WTN	AA	23	299	33	25	1	4	37	26	38	8	5	.312/.381/.459	.222	.350	0.8	2B(13): -0.4, SS(3): -0.2	-0.1
2011	TAC	AAA	23	117	24	8	2	3	17	11	12	3	1	.387/.444/.585	.330	.418	0.5	3B(11): -0.3, 2B(10): -0.0	1.5
2011	SEA	MLB	23	201	22	13	0	3	13	13	36	3	1	.258/.312/.379	.264	.303	-1.1	3B(42): 2.6, SS(10): -0.9	0.7
2012	SEA	MLB	24	651	62	35	1	20	86	46	110	13	5	.259/.316/.423	.273	.286	0.5	3B(138): -2.8, 2B(18): 1.6	2.9
2013	SEA	MLB	25	695	79	32	2	22	69	68	122	9	3	.260/.338/.426	.290	.290	0.9	3B(160): 2.0	4.9
2014	SEA	MLB	26	644	73	33	1	17	75	51	112	12	5	.264/.327/.415	.277	.300	-0.3	3B -1, 2B -0	2.7

Seager has played alongside a number of premium-pedigree prospects, but 2013 established the third-round pick as the gem of Seattle's recent minor-league graduates. He notched his second consecutive 20-home run season and is one of just five third basemen to homer 20 times in both 2012 and 2013. Seager has done it in the toughest pitching park of the group, to boot. He exhibited better plate discipline in 2013 as he adjusted to being the main weapon in the lineup. He won't be the best hitter on a playoff team, but that's the worst you can say.

Justin Smoak   1B

Born: 12/5/1986 Age: 27
Bats: B Throws: L Height: 6' 4"
Weight: 220 Breakout: 3%
Improve: 49% Collapse: 5%
Attrition: 9% MLB: 96%

Comparables:
Dan Johnson, Jason Kubel, Matt LaPorta

YEAR	TEAM	LVL	AGE	PA	R	2B	3B	HR	RBI	BB	SO	SB	CS	AVG/OBP/SLG	TAv	BABIP	BRR	FRAA	WARP
2011	SEA	MLB	24	489	38	24	0	15	55	55	105	0	0	.234/.323/.396	.273	.273	-3.1	1B(108): -6.1	0.3
2012	TAC	AAA	25	82	10	6	1	0	4	16	16	1	0	.242/.390/.364	.265	.320	0.4	1B(19): -0.2	0.1
2012	SEA	MLB	25	535	49	14	0	19	51	49	111	1	0	.217/.290/.364	.238	.242	-2.5	1B(131): -9.4	-2.1
2013	TAC	AAA	26	22	2	2	0	0	1	0	5	0	0	.238/.273/.333	.266	.312	0.3	1B(3): -0.2	0.0
2013	SEA	MLB	26	521	53	19	0	20	50	64	119	0	0	.238/.334/.412	.281	.278	-5.1	1B(125): -8.1	0.2
2014	SEA	MLB	27	505	56	20	0	16	61	58	112	0	0	.233/.323/.389	.268	.270	-1	1B -5	0.3

Smoak took a step toward saving his career after returning from a disabled list stint in mid-June. In 85 games following the injury, he clubbed 17 homers and hit .237/.326/.447. Unimpressive for a first baseman, sure, but it represented 15 more points of on-base percentage and 74 more points of slugging than his career marks to that point. Unfortunately, only half of Smoak's swing looks fixed, as he posted a brutal .548 OPS as a right-hander. Smoak was arbitration-eligible for the first time this winter, so if he doesn't start *really* hitting soon, he's likely to be on the open market sooner rather than later.

Carlos Triunfel   SS

Born: 2/27/1990 Age: 24
Bats: R Throws: R Height: 5' 11"
Weight: 205 Breakout: 0%
Improve: 6% Collapse: 6%
Attrition: 23% MLB: 34%

Comparables:
Angel Chavez, Adeiny Hechavarria, Diory Hernandez

YEAR	TEAM	LVL	AGE	PA	R	2B	3B	HR	RBI	BB	SO	SB	CS	AVG/OBP/SLG	TAv	BABIP	BRR	FRAA	WARP
2011	WTN	AA	21	433	45	22	2	6	35	25	71	5	7	.281/.340/.392	.275	.330	-0.5	SS(19): 1.2	0.4
2011	TAC	AAA	21	117	7	6	1	0	10	2	17	1	0	.279/.302/.351	.227	.326	-1.4	SS(20): 1.8, 2B(1): 0.0	0.1
2012	TAC	AAA	22	543	74	31	2	10	62	23	89	3	2	.260/.308/.391	.256	.297	1.2	SS(108): -0.4, 2B(22): -2.3	1.4
2012	SEA	MLB	22	24	2	2	0	0	3	1	4	0	0	.227/.261/.318	.217	.278	0.2	SS(7): -0.1, 2B(2): 0.2	0.0
2013	TAC	AAA	23	413	55	22	3	5	31	17	76	6	4	.282/.328/.394	.272	.340	1	SS(84): -7.3, 2B(13): 0.3	1.3
2013	SEA	MLB	23	47	1	1	0	0	2	0	11	0	0	.136/.152/.159	.118	.176	-0.2	SS(10): -0.9, 2B(4): -0.5	-0.7
2014	SEA	MLB	24	250	21	12	1	3	21	7	51	2	1	.238/.273/.335	.233	.290	-0.5	SS -3, 2B -1	-0.1

The Mariners, apparently tired of seeing Triunfel flail in Tacoma, decided to watch him flail in the majors. After 17 games and more flailing, Triunfel returned to Triple-A. His end results there showed a marginal but definite improvement, which is never a bad thing for a 23-year-old, but Triunfel has been banging his head against the high minors for four years. The Mariners should certainly be asking how much more they can expect him to learn there.

Mike Zunino   C

Born: 3/25/1991 Age: 23
Bats: R Throws: R Height: 6' 2"
Weight: 220 Breakout: 1%
Improve: 32% Collapse: 4%
Attrition: 18% MLB: 68%

Comparables:
Devin Mesoraco, Anthony Rizzo, Jesus Montero

YEAR	TEAM	LVL	AGE	PA	R	2B	3B	HR	RBI	BB	SO	SB	CS	AVG/OBP/SLG	TAv	BABIP	BRR	FRAA	WARP
2012	EVE	A-	21	133	29	10	0	10	35	18	26	1	0	.373/.474/.736	.386	.413	-0.6	C(19): 0.4	2.4
2012	WTN	AA	21	57	6	4	0	3	8	5	7	0	0	.333/.386/.588	.322	.333	0.1	C(12): 0.1	0.6
2013	TAC	AAA	22	229	38	12	3	11	43	17	66	0	0	.227/.297/.478	.285	.269	2.1	C(50): 0.2	1.9
2013	SEA	MLB	22	193	22	5	0	5	14	16	49	1	0	.214/.290/.329	.247	.267	-0.8	C(50): 0.0	0.4
2014	SEA	MLB	23	250	27	10	1	9	32	18	66	0	0	.231/.295/.401	.262	.280	-0.3	C 0	1.2

A left wrist fracture cost Zunino 34 games from late July through early September, and his bat was unimpressive when he was healthy, as he showed major contact issues, striking out over 25 percent of the time at both Triple-A Tacoma and Seattle. (He did clobber the ball when he made contact in Tacoma, though.) Zunino's swing rate was one of the highest in the majors and the result was a number of quick, unproductive at-bats. He struggled defensively as well, throwing out just six of 34 basestealers with Seattle. It's worth wondering whether Zunino, even as a big-time prospect coming out of a big-time college program, was rushed and what exactly the point was supposed to be. On a losing team, was it truly that important to avoid giving Brandon Bantz at-bats? Even with the issues, however, Zunino's bat is already good enough to stick in the majors at catcher; if he can work out the kinks over the next couple of years, he should turn into at least a solid regular.

PITCHERS

Blake Beavan

Born: 1/17/1989 Age: 25
Bats: R Throws: R Height: 6' 7" Weight: 255
Breakout: 28% Improve: 49% Collapse: 30%
Attrition: 45% MLB: 75%

Comparables:
Tim Stauffer, Jeff Karstens, Jeanmar Gomez

YEAR	TEAM	LVL	AGE	W	L	SV	G	GS	IP	H	HR	BB	SO	BB9	SO9	GB%	BABIP	WHIP	ERA	FIP	FRA	WARP
2011	TAC	AAA	22	5	3	0	16	16	93	118	10	20	64	1.9	6.2	44%	.340	1.48	4.45	4.48	4.22	1.7
2011	SEA	MLB	22	5	6	0	15	15	97	106	13	15	42	1.4	3.9	39%	.280	1.25	4.27	4.49	5.09	-0.2
2012	TAC	AAA	23	4	0	0	6	6	38	39	3	9	15	2.1	3.6	42%	.277	1.26	2.61	4.77	4.56	0.3
2012	SEA	MLB	23	11	11	0	26	26	152¹	168	23	24	67	1.4	4.0	39%	.281	1.26	4.43	4.80	4.96	0.0
2013	TAC	AAA	24	6	6	0	16	16	94	120	15	23	47	2.2	4.5	45%	.327	1.52	5.55	5.54	5.79	0.0
2013	SEA	MLB	24	0	2	0	12	2	39²	46	8	8	27	1.8	6.1	40%	.292	1.36	6.13	5.02	5.59	-0.4
2014	SEA	MLB	25	6	7	0	25	18	126²	147	17	23	60	1.7	4.3	43%	.298	1.34	4.67	4.82	5.07	-0.6

Just 24 last year, Beavan was young enough and working with enough tools to push for a spot in the rotation even given distressing results the two prior seasons. Unfortunately, 2013 was Beavan's worst year yet: He earned only two starts, his ERA ballooned despite the easier task of pitching out of the bullpen and his homer rate was awful—six bombs in 59 road batters faced is remarkable. He's a former first-rounder and was part of Seattle's haul for Cliff Lee once upon a time, but the low-90s fastball and lack of a swing-and-miss secondary pitch promise generic Triple-A right-hander.

Danny Farquhar

Born: 2/17/1987 Age: 27
Bats: R Throws: R Height: 5' 9" Weight: 180
Breakout: 35% Improve: 47% Collapse: 34%
Attrition: 49% MLB: 65%

Comparables:
Josh Roenicke, Cory Gearrin, Pedro Strop

YEAR	TEAM	LVL	AGE	W	L	SV	G	GS	IP	H	HR	BB	SO	BB9	SO9	GB%	BABIP	WHIP	ERA	FIP	FRA	WARP
2011	LVG	AAA	24	4	5	14	50	0	51²	63	4	18	43	3.1	7.5	53%	.333	1.57	4.70	4.40	4.57	1.1
2011	TOR	MLB	24	0	0	0	3	0	2	4	0	2	1	9.0	4.5	25%	.500	3.00	13.50	5.06	8.10	-0.1
2012	NHP	AA	25	0	1	1	20	0	30¹	28	2	10	33	3.0	9.8	42%	.306	1.25	2.97	3.17	3.65	0.5
2012	TRN	AA	25	1	0	4	6	0	11	2	0	0	14	0.0	11.5	48%	.095	0.18	0.00	0.66	2.06	0.3
2012	TAC	AAA	25	1	0	4	12	0	16²	9	0	5	16	2.7	8.6	48%	.214	0.84	0.54	2.83	2.61	0.5
2013	TAC	AAA	26	0	1	6	15	0	20	17	1	4	30	1.8	13.5	50%	.340	1.05	2.25	1.82	2.35	0.7
2013	SEA	MLB	26	0	3	16	46	0	55²	44	2	22	79	3.6	12.8	43%	.336	1.19	4.20	1.89	2.42	1.4
2014	SEA	MLB	27	3	1	13	48	0	63¹	52	5	27	66	3.9	9.4	48%	.290	1.25	3.29	3.66	3.58	0.8

Farquhar had the classic live-but-raw arm (albeit in a small package) when he was acquired from the Yankees for Ichiro and the raw was on stark display to begin 2013. Hitters mashed line drive after line drive as they hung a 7.61 ERA on Farquhar over his first 17 appearances. The signs of success remained nonetheless: Farquhar struck out 35 batters in those games behind his high-90s fastball. Despite the ugly results, this electricity earned him a shot at the closer's role following Tom Wilhemsen's collapse, and he ran with it, posting a 2.38 ERA and 33 percent strikeout rate over the season's final two months. Chalk up another one for closers being made, not born.

Charlie Furbush

Born: 4/11/1986 Age: 28
Bats: L Throws: L Height: 6' 5" Weight: 215
Breakout: 33% Improve: 52% Collapse: 27%
Attrition: 47% MLB: 66%

Comparables:
Dustin Nippert, Ezequiel Astacio, D.J. Houlton

YEAR	TEAM	LVL	AGE	W	L	SV	G	GS	IP	H	HR	BB	SO	BB9	SO9	GB%	BABIP	WHIP	ERA	FIP	FRA	WARP
2011	TOL	AAA	25	5	3	0	10	9	54	35	7	16	61	2.7	10.2	39%	.220	0.94	3.17	3.61	4.97	0.2
2011	DET	MLB	25	1	3	0	17	2	32¹	36	5	14	26	3.9	7.2	45%	.341	1.55	3.62	5.04	5.73	0.0
2011	SEA	MLB	25	3	7	0	11	10	53	61	11	16	41	2.7	7.0	43%	.309	1.45	6.62	5.29	5.60	-0.3
2012	TAC	AAA	26	1	0	0	7	0	10	7	1	3	13	2.7	11.7	33%	.261	1.00	3.60	3.27	4.16	0.1
2012	SEA	MLB	26	5	2	0	48	0	46¹	28	3	16	53	3.1	10.3	45%	.231	0.95	2.72	2.77	3.41	0.6
2013	SEA	MLB	27	2	6	0	71	0	65	48	5	29	80	4.0	11.1	42%	.264	1.18	3.74	3.09	3.40	0.7
2014	SEA	MLB	28	3	2	1	34	4	54²	52	7	20	53	3.2	8.6	42%	.295	1.31	4.01	4.26	4.36	0.2

The Pride of Maine, Furbush was the only Downeaster to spend the whole season on a major-league roster in 2013. After two seasons and 119 appearances without a start, it seems safe to say the lefty has established himself as a reliever. He's excellent against his fellow port-siders, allowing just a .502 OPS, but his .688 mark against righties gave him the ability to go multiple batters, or even innings, if needed. Perhaps "adaptable bullpen piece" is not the most glamorous title, but Furbush was not drafted out of high school and initially played college ball at the decidedly non-powerhouse Division III Saint Joseph's of Maine, so it's nice just to have a niche.

Felix Hernandez
Born: 4/8/1986 Age: 28
Bats: R Throws: R Height: 6' 3" Weight: 230
Breakout: 22% Improve: 53% Collapse: 19%
Attrition: 5% MLB: 98%
Comparables:
CC Sabathia, Brandon Webb, Josh Beckett

YEAR	TEAM	LVL	AGE	W	L	SV	G	GS	IP	H	HR	BB	SO	BB9	SO9	GB%	BABIP	WHIP	ERA	FIP	FRA	WARP
2011	SEA	MLB	25	14	14	0	33	33	233²	218	19	67	222	2.6	8.6	52%	.308	1.22	3.47	3.17	3.77	2.8
2012	SEA	MLB	26	13	9	0	33	33	232	209	14	56	223	2.2	8.7	50%	.308	1.14	3.06	2.79	3.29	3.8
2013	SEA	MLB	27	12	10	0	31	31	204¹	185	15	46	216	2.0	9.5	53%	.314	1.13	3.04	2.63	3.41	3.4
2014	SEA	MLB	28	12	8	0	26	26	180²	158	13	46	175	2.3	8.7	53%	.298	1.13	2.86	3.13	3.11	3.4

Hernandez's season was cut short a couple starts earlier than usual due to a minor back injury. Before he went out, he compiled a year that ranks up with anything we've seen from the Mariners' ace, setting career bests in strikeout and walk rate to go with his best ERA in three years. Hernandez's changeup remains one of the most devastating pitches in baseball. It is the fastest one in the league, averaging 89.5 mph, just under three miles slower than the fastball, but it drew swings almost 60 percent of the time and fewer than 30 percent of those swings resulted in fair contact. Only Kris Medlen and Cole Hamels (min. 200 changeups thrown) had a higher percentage of their changeups get whiffs. That pitch assures he'll be in the Cy Young conversation for years to come; whether he's ever in the playoffs is up to Jack Zduriencik.

Danny Hultzen
Born: 11/28/1989 Age: 24
Bats: L Throws: L Height: 6' 3" Weight: 200
Breakout: 40% Improve: 74% Collapse: 22%
Attrition: 55% MLB: 59%
Comparables:
James Paxton, Jake McGee, Jake Arrieta

YEAR	TEAM	LVL	AGE	W	L	SV	G	GS	IP	H	HR	BB	SO	BB9	SO9	GB%	BABIP	WHIP	ERA	FIP	FRA	WARP
2012	WTN	AA	22	8	3	0	13	13	75¹	38	2	32	79	3.8	9.4	50%	.207	0.93	1.19	2.79	3.59	1.5
2012	TAC	AAA	22	1	4	0	12	12	48²	49	2	43	57	8.0	10.5	37%	.351	1.89	5.92	4.75	5.32	0.4
2013	TAC	AAA	23	4	1	0	6	6	30²	19	1	7	34	2.1	10.0	44%	.225	0.85	2.05	2.56	2.78	0.9
2014	SEA	MLB	24	3	3	0	9	9	43¹	36	4	21	44	4.3	9.2	44%	.286	1.31	3.53	4.08	3.84	0.5

For Hultzen, September 2013 was supposed to be about a cup of coffee and preparation for a 2014 in the starting rotation. Instead, it ended on the surgical table of Dr. James Andrews, as Hultzen needed his shoulder fixed after a season bouncing on and off the disabled list. The second overall pick in 2011 could miss all of 2014, and when he does return it's not all Segways and moon colonies in his future: Shoulder surgeries don't carry nearly the survival rate that elbow surgeries do. At least Hultzen was lights out when he could pitch after a disastrous first run through Triple-A in 2012.

Hisashi Iwakuma
Born: 4/12/1981 Age: 33
Bats: R Throws: R Height: 6' 3" Weight: 210
Breakout: 14% Improve: 43% Collapse: 30%
Attrition: 17% MLB: 90%
Comparables:
Johan Santana, Kevin Millwood, John Smoltz

YEAR	TEAM	LVL	AGE	W	L	SV	G	GS	IP	H	HR	BB	SO	BB9	SO9	GB%	BABIP	WHIP	ERA	FIP	FRA	WARP
2012	SEA	MLB	31	9	5	2	30	16	125¹	117	17	43	101	3.1	7.3	54%	.282	1.28	3.16	4.30	4.87	-0.2
2013	SEA	MLB	32	14	6	0	33	33	219²	179	25	42	185	1.7	7.6	50%	.252	1.01	2.66	3.47	4.03	2.1
2014	SEA	MLB	33	10	8	1	35	23	171²	157	20	42	140	2.2	7.3	50%	.280	1.16	3.38	4.00	3.67	2.1

Two years later, Seattle's decision to throw Iwakuma out of the bullpen to begin 2012 seems downright silly. In 49 starts, Iwakuma owns a 2.66 ERA over 314 innings and has struck out nearly four times as many batters as he has walked. Iwakuma's splitter in particular has become one of the nastiest pitches in baseball. It's his out pitch and, at 86 mph, it comes in just a few ticks slower than the four-seamer and the sinker, but it falls off the table like a bowl of SpaghettiO's. Hitters came up empty on 32 percent of their swings and pounded it into the ground 72 percent of the time on contact. Iwakuma is not a one-trick pony—he commands and controls his fastball, sinker and slider as well—but it's the splitter that has established him as a legitimate rotation force.

Lucas Luetge
Born: 3/24/1987 Age: 27
Bats: L Throws: L Height: 6' 4" Weight: 205
Breakout: 48% Improve: 62% Collapse: 26%
Attrition: 50% MLB: 43%
Comparables:
David Carpenter, Fernando Abad, Marcus McBeth

YEAR	TEAM	LVL	AGE	W	L	SV	G	GS	IP	H	HR	BB	SO	BB9	SO9	GB%	BABIP	WHIP	ERA	FIP	FRA	WARP
2011	HUN	AA	24	1	3	3	46	1	69	63	3	23	69	3.0	9.0	55%	.250	1.25	3.13	2.92	3.27	1.2
2012	SEA	MLB	25	2	2	2	63	0	40²	37	3	24	38	5.3	8.4	49%	.304	1.50	3.98	3.98	3.79	0.2
2013	TAC	AAA	26	0	0	1	22	0	31	28	4	16	45	4.6	13.1	50%	.353	1.42	4.35	3.89	3.99	0.5
2013	SEA	MLB	26	1	3	0	35	0	37	42	2	16	27	3.9	6.6	52%	.339	1.57	4.86	3.78	4.73	-0.1
2014	SEA	MLB	27	2	1	1	45	0	54²	56	6	24	45	4.0	7.3	46%	.307	1.46	4.51	4.55	4.90	-0.2

Luetge the LOOGY? Luetge's struggles saw him bounce between Tacoma and Seattle. Despite the poor overall numbers both places, Luetge still looked the part of a major leaguer against lefties. He allowed just two extra-base hits to 61 left-handed batters while walking only three. Righties, however, have touched him up for a .468 slugging percentage over his two seasons. He won't be able to consistently face righties and succeed, and he certainly won't succeed if he faces them at the 63 percent rate Eric Wedge sent him out for last season.

Brandon Maurer

Born: 7/3/1990 Age: 23
Bats: R Throws: R Height: 6' 5" Weight: 215
Breakout: 36% Improve: 67% Collapse: 11%
Attrition: 55% MLB: 71%

Comparables:
Alex White, Justin Germano, Tyler Clippard

YEAR	TEAM	LVL	AGE	W	L	SV	G	GS	IP	H	HR	BB	SO	BB9	SO9	GB%	BABIP	WHIP	ERA	FIP	FRA	WARP
2011	CLN	A	20	1	3	0	7	6	37	28	2	14	44	3.4	10.7	—	.292	1.14	3.41	2.98	3.24	0.0
2011	HDS	A+	20	2	4	0	9	7	42¹	47	8	11	37	2.3	7.9	45%	.346	1.37	6.38	5.65	11.41	-0.2
2012	WTN	AA	21	9	2	0	24	24	137²	133	4	48	117	3.1	7.6	48%	.322	1.31	3.20	3.00	3.81	2.3
2013	TAC	AAA	22	3	4	0	10	10	46²	48	2	26	47	5.0	9.1	39%	.341	1.59	5.21	4.11	3.83	0.8
2013	SEA	MLB	22	5	8	0	22	14	90	114	16	27	70	2.7	7.0	45%	.346	1.57	6.30	4.93	5.19	-0.3
2014	SEA	MLB	23	6	8	0	32	22	121¹	131	14	45	90	3.3	6.7	45%	.314	1.45	4.68	4.62	5.08	-0.3

Maurer's spring training was impressive enough to earn the former 23rd-round pick the fifth starter role at just 22. The rest of his season was significantly less impressive. Although Maurer had no troubles hitting the strike zone, his ventures within it were less than successful. Maurer ranked in the 10th percentile among starters (min. 50 IP) in both homer and hit rate. His slider looked like an excellent pitch, as he was able to locate it (68 percent strikes) and miss bats (18 percent whiffs). The four-seamer, however, was just too hittable, inducing whiplash to the tune of a .621 slugging percentage on contact. Maurer's sinker, despite being 2 mph slower, was tougher to hit, though he still allowed a .488 slugging percentage on that pitch *and* he could not throw it for strikes consistently. The physical ability appears to be there for Maurer; now it's a matter of refining and learning how to keep his fastballs off opposing barrels.

Yoervis Medina

Born: 7/27/1988 Age: 25
Bats: R Throws: R Height: 6' 3" Weight: 245
Breakout: 53% Improve: 75% Collapse: 14%
Attrition: 22% MLB: 79%

Comparables:
Tyler Clippard, Hector Santiago, Jordan Walden

YEAR	TEAM	LVL	AGE	W	L	SV	G	GS	IP	H	HR	BB	SO	BB9	SO9	GB%	BABIP	WHIP	ERA	FIP	FRA	WARP
2011	HDS	A+	22	1	13	0	20	19	101	139	19	38	73	3.4	6.5	60%	.273	1.75	6.50	6.23	4.35	0.4
2011	WTN	AA	22	0	1	0	4	4	25	23	5	9	17	3.2	6.1	51%	.306	1.28	4.68	5.87	4.70	0.1
2012	WTN	AA	23	5	5	5	46	1	69¹	63	5	35	77	4.5	10.0	55%	.320	1.41	3.25	3.59	4.65	1.2
2013	SEA	MLB	24	4	6	1	63	0	68	49	5	40	71	5.3	9.4	55%	.257	1.31	2.91	3.88	4.34	0.1
2014	SEA	MLB	25	3	1	1	44	2	62¹	57	6	30	57	4.4	8.2	48%	.293	1.40	4.07	4.35	4.42	0.1

Medina has prospered since moving to the bullpen at Double-A in 2012. His curveball and sinker ranked among the best pitches in the league when he could control them—hitters whiffed at nearly half the curveballs they offered at, and his sinker induced a grounder on 60 percent of balls in play. But the qualifier is key, as Medina's walk rate was the worst in baseball among relievers with at least 50 innings pitched. If he can rein that in, the raw stuff can play in a set-up role.

Hector Noesi

Born: 1/26/1987 Age: 27
Bats: R Throws: R Height: 6' 3" Weight: 205
Breakout: 43% Improve: 68% Collapse: 23%
Attrition: 47% MLB: 67%

Comparables:
Dustin Moseley, Rick VandenHurk, John Stephens

YEAR	TEAM	LVL	AGE	W	L	SV	G	GS	IP	H	HR	BB	SO	BB9	SO9	GB%	BABIP	WHIP	ERA	FIP	FRA	WARP
2011	SWB	AAA	24	1	1	0	6	5	24²	28	0	9	17	3.3	6.2	40%	.333	1.50	3.28	3.20	4.32	0.2
2011	NYA	MLB	24	2	2	0	30	2	56¹	63	6	22	45	3.5	7.2	43%	.331	1.51	4.47	4.13	4.19	0.9
2012	TAC	AAA	25	2	6	0	11	11	64¹	80	7	22	55	3.1	7.7	40%	.349	1.59	5.74	4.49	5.29	0.5
2012	SEA	MLB	25	2	12	0	22	18	106²	107	21	39	68	3.3	5.7	38%	.266	1.37	5.82	5.48	6.13	-1.1
2013	WTN	AA	26	1	0	0	2	2	11	5	0	3	12	2.5	9.8	52%	.200	0.73	0.00	1.82	3.03	0.2
2013	TAC	AAA	26	2	3	0	15	11	66¹	80	12	14	49	1.9	6.6	41%	.313	1.42	5.83	5.12	5.32	0.6
2013	SEA	MLB	26	0	1	0	12	1	27¹	42	3	12	21	4.0	6.9	36%	.402	1.98	6.59	4.39	4.58	0.2
2014	SEA	MLB	27	5	6	0	25	15	103²	114	14	32	76	2.8	6.6	39%	.308	1.41	4.66	4.65	5.07	-0.4

Noesi served up line shot after line shot in yet another disastrous campaign. His fastball was consistently ripped (eight extra-base hits in just 54 at-bats) and he failed to locate his secondary pitches (the changeup, slider and curveball all resulted in at least 39 percent balls). More distressing, Noesi hasn't even offered a glimmer of hope in his pair of stints and 22 starts with Tacoma. Not even the minor pieces can avoid the full-on carnage the Jesus Montero trade wound up becoming.

James Paxton

Born: 11/6/1988 Age: 25
Bats: L Throws: L Height: 6' 4" Weight: 220
Breakout: 39% Improve: 69% Collapse: 17%
Attrition: 44% MLB: 71%

Comparables:
Lance Lynn, Eric Surkamp, Jason Windsor

YEAR	TEAM	LVL	AGE	W	L	SV	G	GS	IP	H	HR	BB	SO	BB9	SO9	GB%	BABIP	WHIP	ERA	FIP	FRA	WARP
2011	CLN	A	22	3	3	0	10	10	56	45	1	30	80	4.8	12.9	36%	.273	1.34	2.73	2.40	2.26	0.2
2011	WTN	AA	22	3	0	0	7	7	39	28	2	13	51	3.0	11.8	64%	.182	1.05	1.85	2.43	1.92	0.2
2012	WTN	AA	23	9	4	0	21	21	106¹	96	5	54	110	4.6	9.3	49%	.322	1.41	3.05	3.24	3.75	2.4
2013	TAC	AAA	24	8	11	0	28	26	145²	158	10	58	131	3.6	8.1	51%	.338	1.48	4.45	3.92	4.07	2.3
2013	SEA	MLB	24	3	0	0	4	4	24	15	2	7	21	2.6	7.9	58%	.190	0.92	1.50	3.28	4.40	0.2
2014	SEA	MLB	25	8	8	0	25	25	139	134	13	55	120	3.5	7.8	49%	.302	1.36	3.88	4.06	4.22	0.9

If anything can give Mariners fans hope, it's the young front-line pitching in the organization. Paxton spent his minor-league season at Tacoma inducing grounder after grounder in front of a putrid infield defense, leading to a mediocre ERA but fine peripherals. Any concern over that ERA should be dashed by his excellent major-league showing. Over 24 innings, he commanded a mid-to-high-90s fastball and continued to showcase a plus curve. The changeup is a work in progress—it was a ball nearly 50 percent of the time—and will end up deciding whether he can be an ace or merely a mid-rotation pitcher.

Oliver Perez
Born: 8/15/1981 Age: 32
Bats: L Throws: L Height: 6' 3" Weight: 220
Breakout: 41% Improve: 65% Collapse: 7%
Attrition: 14% MLB: 51%
Comparables:
Gary Knotts, Seth McClung, Rich Hill

YEAR	TEAM	LVL	AGE	W	L	SV	G	GS	IP	H	HR	BB	SO	BB9	SO9	GB%	BABIP	WHIP	ERA	FIP	FRA	WARP
2011	HAR	AA	29	3	5	0	16	15	75²	78	10	27	58	3.2	6.9	36%	.310	1.39	3.09	4.82	5.53	-0.3
2012	TAC	AAA	30	2	2	1	22	0	31	33	4	19	42	5.5	12.2	41%	.382	1.68	4.65	4.47	4.26	0.7
2012	SEA	MLB	30	1	3	0	33	0	29²	27	1	10	24	3.0	7.3	35%	.295	1.25	2.12	2.88	2.92	0.5
2013	SEA	MLB	31	3	3	2	61	0	53	50	6	26	74	4.4	12.6	31%	.361	1.43	3.74	3.28	3.44	0.7
2014	SEA	MLB	32	2	2	0	28	4	45	46	6	27	42	5.4	8.4	36%	.309	1.61	5.19	5.18	5.64	-0.5

Sandy Koufax he ain't, but Perez might just have carved out a career as a left-handed specialist with his last two seasons in Seattle. His overall numbers declined from his excellent 2012, but that drop can be largely attributed to right-handers figuring him out—they hit .256/.323/.463 against him and accounted for 59 percent of his batters faced. Perez held lefties to a .238/.358/.288 line and allowed just two extra-base hits in 80 at-bats. The lack of control is less than ideal for a player charged with getting one out at a time, however, and as such his margin for error in other facets of the game will be slim.

Tyler Pike
Born: 1/26/1994 Age: 20
Bats: L Throws: L Height: 6' 0" Weight: 180
Breakout: 0% Improve: 0% Collapse: 0%
Attrition: 0% MLB: 0%
Comparables:
Phillippe Aumont, Wilmer Font, Mauricio Robles

YEAR	TEAM	LVL	AGE	W	L	SV	G	GS	IP	H	HR	BB	SO	BB9	SO9	GB%	BABIP	WHIP	ERA	FIP	FRA	WARP
2013	CLN	A	19	7	4	0	22	22	110¹	73	5	57	90	4.6	7.3	41%	.233	1.18	2.37	3.87	4.73	0.9
2014	SEA	MLB	20	1	1	1	16	2	76¹	79	9	47	50	5.5	5.9	42%	.295	1.65	5.31	5.58	5.77	-1.0

Pike, Seattle's third-rounder in 2012, put up excellent numbers once again as a 19-year-old. Although he lacked control, Pike still ranked 11th in his league in ERA, fifth among full-time starters. Right now, however, Pike is mainly getting by on his advanced feel for pitching. He was left off most postseason prospect lists due to a lack of stuff. He'll have to keep putting up numbers against more advanced bats before he gains converts.

Stephen Pryor
Born: 7/23/1989 Age: 24
Bats: R Throws: R Height: 6' 4" Weight: 250
Breakout: 24% Improve: 44% Collapse: 24%
Attrition: 27% MLB: 56%
Comparables:
Josh Spence, Hong-Chih Kuo, Rex Brothers

YEAR	TEAM	LVL	AGE	W	L	SV	G	GS	IP	H	HR	BB	SO	BB9	SO9	GB%	BABIP	WHIP	ERA	FIP	FRA	WARP
2011	HDS	A+	21	1	0	4	22	0	27	28	2	26	34	8.7	11.3	26%	.421	2.00	7.67	5.51	3.65	0.2
2011	WTN	AA	21	2	1	6	17	0	22²	9	0	7	27	2.8	10.7	54%	.231	0.71	1.19	1.98	0.99	0.3
2012	WTN	AA	22	1	0	7	11	0	16	7	0	5	24	2.8	13.5	41%	.219	0.75	1.12	1.08	1.33	0.7
2012	TAC	AAA	22	0	0	3	16	0	20	11	0	11	20	4.9	9.0	37%	.224	1.10	0.00	3.32	2.84	0.5
2012	SEA	MLB	22	3	1	0	26	0	23	22	5	13	27	5.1	10.6	39%	.288	1.52	3.91	5.22	5.82	-0.3
2013	SEA	MLB	23	0	0	0	7	0	7¹	3	0	1	7	1.2	8.6	39%	.167	0.55	0.00	1.58	2.28	0.2
2014	SEA	MLB	24	2	1	0	30	0	35²	30	3	16	38	4.0	9.5	42%	.293	1.30	3.51	3.69	3.81	0.3

Pryor, yet another big, projectable right-hander with a blazing fastball out of the Mariners' bullpen, opened the season with 7 ⅓ promising innings. He threw his nasty slider for strikes, a scary development for the rest of the league. Unfortunately, his season was prematurely terminated by a torn latissimus dorsi below his throwing shoulder. The injury required surgery and forced Pryor to keep his arm in a sling until late September. He dropped 10 pounds as a result. "I lost a bunch of muscle," he said, and physical therapy will be a major part of his offseason. Pryor relied heavily on a 96 mph fastball, so keep an eye on his velocity in spring training.

Erasmo Ramirez
Born: 5/2/1990 Age: 24
Bats: R Throws: R Height: 5' 11" Weight: 200
Breakout: 22% Improve: 62% Collapse: 24%
Attrition: 31% MLB: 85%
Comparables:
Scott Baker, Vance Worley, Liam Hendriks

YEAR	TEAM	LVL	AGE	W	L	SV	G	GS	IP	H	HR	BB	SO	BB9	SO9	GB%	BABIP	WHIP	ERA	FIP	FRA	WARP
2011	WTN	AA	21	7	6	0	19	19	110¹	127	10	19	81	1.5	6.6	39%	.511	1.32	4.73	3.75	5.10	0.2
2011	TAC	AAA	21	3	2	0	7	7	42¹	51	4	13	35	2.8	7.4	38%	.337	1.51	5.10	4.42	4.51	0.7
2012	TAC	AAA	22	6	3	0	15	15	77¹	81	5	18	58	2.1	6.8	48%	.299	1.28	3.72	3.86	4.56	1.1
2012	SEA	MLB	22	1	3	0	16	8	59	47	6	12	48	1.8	7.3	41%	.244	1.00	3.36	3.50	3.58	0.8
2013	TAC	AAA	23	3	3	0	7	7	43²	43	4	14	42	2.9	8.7	45%	.315	1.31	3.09	3.87	3.75	0.9
2013	SEA	MLB	23	5	3	0	14	13	72¹	79	12	26	57	3.2	7.1	44%	.303	1.45	4.98	4.86	5.18	-0.3
2014	SEA	MLB	24	7	7	0	20	20	113¹	116	13	30	82	2.4	6.5	46%	.295	1.29	4.02	4.30	4.37	0.5

Ramirez succeeded in a brief stint with the Mariners in 2012 on the strength of a brilliant changeup. Hitters managed just five hits (one for extra-bases) off 178 changeups while swinging and missing at more than a quarter of them. Not so much in 2013. Ramirez made 13 starts for Seattle and saw his change get hammered: On 199 offerings, hitters smacked three homers and a double and their whiff rate dropped by a third. He doesn't have the breaking pitches to succeed without an elite change-of-pace, which means the 24-year-old will struggle to find a rotation spot if he can't rediscover that old 2012 magic.

Chance Ruffin
Born: 9/8/1988 Age: 25
Bats: R Throws: R Height: 6' 0" Weight: 195
Breakout: 48% Improve: 65% Collapse: 16%
Attrition: 54% MLB: 33%

Comparables:
Arnie Munoz, Billy Petrick, Rafael Rodriguez

YEAR	TEAM	LVL	AGE	W	L	SV	G	GS	IP	H	HR	BB	SO	BB9	SO9	GB%	BABIP	WHIP	ERA	FIP	FRA	WARP
2011	ERI	AA	22	3	3	10	31	0	34	23	2	16	43	4.2	11.4	33%	.256	1.15	2.12	3.15	4.67	0.0
2011	TOL	AAA	22	0	0	9	13	0	14²	14	1	6	17	3.7	10.4	42%	.273	1.36	1.84	3.03	2.84	0.3
2011	DET	MLB	22	0	0	0	2	0	3²	5	2	0	3	0.0	7.4	23%	.273	1.36	4.91	8.52	6.93	0.0
2011	SEA	MLB	22	1	0	0	13	0	14	13	2	9	15	5.8	9.6	37%	.306	1.57	3.86	4.70	5.91	-0.1
2012	TAC	AAA	23	0	5	1	50	0	70²	75	8	35	54	4.5	6.9	38%	.300	1.56	5.99	5.22	5.19	0.3
2013	WTN	AA	24	4	4	0	16	16	83	82	11	23	57	2.5	6.2	37%	.274	1.27	3.90	4.35	4.72	0.3
2013	TAC	AAA	24	1	2	0	15	2	29²	28	3	6	25	1.8	7.6	44%	.291	1.15	3.94	4.11	4.52	0.4
2013	SEA	MLB	24	0	2	0	9	0	9²	14	3	5	15	4.7	14.0	33%	.458	1.97	8.38	6.18	5.79	-0.1
2014	SEA	MLB	25	4	4	1	52	8	97²	100	13	37	75	3.4	6.9	39%	.295	1.40	4.70	4.84	5.10	-0.5

Ruffin had just one clean outing in his nine September appearances with Seattle. He saw his four-seam fastball, his primary pitch, blistered for a .790 slugging percentage thanks to three home runs on just 89 pitches. On the bright side, his minor-league campaign was his best in years—he had moderate success as a starter at Double-A but was swiftly returned to the bullpen at the Triple-A level, where he thrived on excellent control. Unless he can do something to get hitters off his 93 mph fastball, though, that control isn't going to matter.

Joe Saunders
Born: 6/16/1981 Age: 33
Bats: L Throws: L Height: 6' 3" Weight: 215
Breakout: 24% Improve: 47% Collapse: 22%
Attrition: 16% MLB: 83%

Comparables:
Charles Nagy, John Burkett, Jamie Moyer

YEAR	TEAM	LVL	AGE	W	L	SV	G	GS	IP	H	HR	BB	SO	BB9	SO9	GB%	BABIP	WHIP	ERA	FIP	FRA	WARP
2011	ARI	MLB	30	12	13	0	33	33	212	210	29	67	108	2.8	4.6	46%	.278	1.31	3.69	4.74	5.39	-1.3
2012	ARI	MLB	31	6	10	0	21	21	130	146	17	31	89	2.1	6.2	43%	.314	1.36	4.22	4.23	4.35	1.1
2012	BAL	MLB	31	3	3	0	7	7	44²	49	4	8	23	1.6	4.6	42%	.302	1.28	3.63	3.72	4.15	0.5
2013	SEA	MLB	32	11	16	0	32	32	183	232	25	61	107	3.0	5.3	54%	.333	1.60	5.26	4.75	5.06	0.3
2014	SEA	MLB	33	9	11	0	26	26	162¹	181	21	50	89	2.8	4.9	47%	.301	1.42	4.81	4.93	5.22	-1.0

Saunders ate 183 innings in 2013, and that's the extent of the praise he deserves for his performance. Only his league-average control allows him to tread water at replacement level, as he doesn't miss bats and saw 11 of his sinkers leave the yard in a homer-laden season. Still, every team needs to fill around 1,500 innings over the course of 162 games, and as such Saunders should be able to find work if he wants it, though at this point the only thing he offers over the typical freely available talent is familiarity and a pair of left-handed scissors.

Taijuan Walker
Born: 8/13/1992 Age: 21
Bats: R Throws: R Height: 6' 4" Weight: 210
Breakout: 32% Improve: 70% Collapse: 9%
Attrition: 47% MLB: 34%

Comparables:
Danny Duffy, Shelby Miller, Eric Hurley

YEAR	TEAM	LVL	AGE	W	L	SV	G	GS	IP	H	HR	BB	SO	BB9	SO9	GB%	BABIP	WHIP	ERA	FIP	FRA	WARP
2011	CLN	A	18	6	5	0	18	18	96²	69	4	39	113	3.6	10.5	52%	.333	1.12	2.89	2.86	4.93	0.0
2012	WTN	AA	19	7	10	0	25	25	126²	124	12	50	118	3.6	8.4	43%	.313	1.37	4.69	3.98	4.82	0.9
2013	WTN	AA	20	4	7	0	14	14	84	58	6	30	96	3.2	10.3	47%	.259	1.05	2.46	2.84	3.66	1.2
2013	TAC	AAA	20	5	3	0	11	11	57¹	54	5	27	64	4.2	10.0	49%	.331	1.41	3.61	3.99	3.87	1.2
2013	SEA	MLB	20	1	0	0	3	3	15	11	0	4	12	2.4	7.2	39%	.250	1.00	3.60	2.28	2.72	0.4
2014	SEA	MLB	21	7	6	1	36	18	128	120	14	49	116	3.4	8.2	44%	.297	1.32	4.00	4.22	4.35	0.6

Walker debuted with a trio of five-inning starts in September and was as advertised. His fastball touched 99, sitting in the high 90s, and he showed excellent control of a quality changeup. Given Walker's success in Tacoma, a tough park for pitchers, as well as in his brief major-league stint, there's reason to believe he could be a fine major-league pitcher right away in 2014. He does need to figure out a couple of things yet to hit his ceiling—he struggled to control his curveball, a pitch he's still developing, and he's still feeling out a cutter, too. But hey: When those are the only obstacles left to clear at age 21, the retractable roof is the limit.

Tom Wilhelmsen

Born: **12/16/1983** Age: **30**
Bats: **R** Throws: **R** Height: **6' 6"** Weight: **220**
Breakout: **22%** Improve: **51%** Collapse: **34%**
Attrition: **33%** MLB: **61%**
Comparables:
Wil Ledezma, Angel Guzman, Brian Tallet

YEAR	TEAM	LVL	AGE	W	L	SV	G	GS	IP	H	HR	BB	SO	BB9	SO9	GB%	BABIP	WHIP	ERA	FIP	FRA	WARP
2011	WTN	AA	27	4	5	0	14	12	60²	66	8	26	40	3.9	5.9	55%	.216	1.52	5.49	5.33	5.83	0.1
2011	SEA	MLB	27	2	0	0	25	0	32²	25	2	13	30	3.6	8.3	35%	.258	1.16	3.31	3.40	4.19	0.1
2012	SEA	MLB	28	4	3	29	73	0	79¹	59	5	29	87	3.3	9.9	48%	.266	1.11	2.50	2.84	2.93	1.3
2013	TAC	AAA	29	0	1	0	8	2	12	19	3	5	15	3.8	11.2	42%	.485	2.00	10.50	6.07	7.49	0.0
2013	SEA	MLB	29	0	3	24	59	0	59	45	2	33	45	5.0	6.9	44%	.253	1.32	4.12	3.72	4.26	0.2
2014	SEA	MLB	30	3	2	12	40	5	63¹	57	6	27	55	3.9	7.8	44%	.286	1.33	3.75	4.19	4.08	0.5

An abysmal 10.97 ERA and three blown saves over 12 appearances in June and a dramatic blowup to begin August—four runs allowed without recording an out—meant the Bartender would no longer be presiding over closing time. The main culprit after a brilliant first two months was a loss of control. Wilhelmsen walked 18 batters in 23 innings from June 1st through August 1st as hitters stopped biting at the curveball—from 39 percent swings in the first two months down to 29 percent afterward—leaving his fastball as the only offering he was consistently able to locate. Even with a 97 mph fireball like Wilhelmsen's, one pitch is rarely enough to thrive in the major leagues. Wilhelmsen's first job in 2014 will be to prove he can throw strikes again.

LINEOUTS

HITTERS

PLAYER	TEAM	LVL	AGE	PA	R	2B	3B	HR	RBI	BB	SO	SB-CS	AVG/OBP/SLG	TAv	BABIP	BRR	FRAA	WARP
LF J. Blash	HDS	A+	23	332	42	16	3	16	53	40	85	14-8	.258/.358/.505	.297	.308	-0.4	LF(36): -3.0, RF(22): -0.1	1.6
	WTN	AA	23	120	13	3	0	9	21	20	28	1-1	.309/.442/.619	.381	.350	0	RF(23): 1.3, LF(2): 0.2	2.0
3B P. Kivlehan	CLN	A	23	247	26	12	1	3	31	17	42	5-3	.283/.344/.386	.271	.333	-2.1	3B(49): -2.5	0.8
	HDS	A+	23	302	48	13	2	13	59	26	65	10-3	.320/.384/.530	.314	.373	-3	3B(66): 3.9	2.9
2B T. Lopes	CLN	A	19	365	40	15	3	1	36	20	46	10-7	.272/.315/.344	.245	.310	-1.1	2B(77): 2.4, SS(7): 0.1	0.8
2B J. Marder	WTN	AA	23	315	32	10	2	4	22	24	59	8-4	.218/.298/.313	.237	.262	1.4	2B(58): -4.1, LF(18): 1.7	-0.3
SS K. Marte	CLN	A	19	406	61	15	5	0	29	15	39	16-8	.304/.330/.370	.263	.336	-1.3	SS(70): 3.1, 2B(24): -1.4	1.7
	HDS	A+	19	92	18	0	2	1	8	4	11	4-3	.256/.289/.337	.244	.284	1.6	SS(15): -0.0, 2B(2): 0.2	0.3
LF G. Pimentel	CLN	A	20	224	24	10	2	6	30	20	68	4-3	.257/.330/.416	.270	.359	-3.3	LF(23): 0.7, CF(14): -0.7	0.4
	HDS	A+	20	67	10	3	1	4	14	2	18	0-0	.333/.358/.603	.298	.405	0.4	RF(6): -0.7, LF(3): -0.4	0.3
1B S. Proscia	HDS	A+	23	97	15	8	1	4	18	4	15	5-1	.306/.371/.565	.303	.324	1	1B(21): -0.4	0.6
	WTN	AA	23	339	37	9	1	10	28	20	92	11-4	.201/.249/.331	.215	.248	1.1	1B(66): 1.7, 3B(7): -0.0	-1.1
C J. Sucre	TAC	AAA	25	95	10	3	0	0	8	7	10	1-1	.299/.351/.333	.277	.338	1.5	C(23): -0.3	0.8
	SEA	MLB	25	29	1	0	0	0	3	2	1	0-0	.192/.241/.192	.162	.192	0.3	C(8): 0.3	-0.1
RF A. Wilson	EVE	A-	21	226	22	11	3	6	27	17	42	2-4	.241/.319/.414	.297	.277	-0.3	RF(45): -1.9, CF(3): 0.1	1.2

Jabari Blash mashed in Double-A and chiseled away at his giant strikeout rate, the main obstacle between the 6-foot-5 toolshed and the major leagues. ⊘ **Joseph DeCarlo**, 2012's second-round pick, remains in short-season ball, missed most of the final two months in 2013, and is likely to be moved off shortstop sooner rather than later. Identical .368 OBPs in his first two professional seasons are pretty neat, though. ⊘ **Patrick Kivlehan**'s success in 2013 must be seen through a High Desert launching pad lens, but slashed strikeout rates signal real growth. ⊘ **Timothy Lopes** profiles as the slappiest of slap hitters. He's just 19, but he isn't expected to develop a home run stroke. ⊘ Another High Desert mirage: **Jack Marder**'s OPS dropped by 398 points and he hit 22 fewer extra-base hits upon a promotion away from the hitter's paradise. ⊘ **Ketel Marte** was one of just 16 regular players under age 20 in the Midwest League, so it seems prudent to focus on his excellent season there as opposed to his poor 19 games in the California League. ⊘ The son of a bodybuilder, **Tyler O'Neill** is a chip off the old block. The power wasn't evident in his first pro season, but he has a reputation for mashing fastballs. ⊘ **Guillermo Pimentel** rebounded well after a disastrous 2012, reaching High-A at just 20 years old. Once one of the best prospects in the rookie-level Arizona League, it's too early to give up on him. ⊘ **Steven Proscia**'s aggressive approach (4 percent walk rate) worked wonders at High Desert, but—surprise!—the first baseman collapsed upon a move to Double-A and a pitcher's park. ⊘ **Jesus Sucre** makes contact with almost everything but can't do anything with it. He could see regular September action as a third catcher, but probably not much else. ⊘ The gigantic **Austin Wilson**'s pitch-recognition issues were apparent in short-season ball, but between power, speed and arm he has all the tools to play right field at the highest level.

PITCHERS

PLAYER	TEAM	LVL	AGE	W	L	SV	IP	H	HR	BB	SO	BB9	SO9	GB%	BABIP	WHIP	ERA	FIP	FRA	WARP
A. Fernandez	WTN	AA	23	9	8	0	120	117	13	40	74	3.0	5.6	41%	.278	1.31	4.43	4.14	5.52	-0.5
B. LaFromboise	TAC	AAA	27	6	0	5	61	66	5	18	63	2.7	9.3	39%	.349	1.38	3.39	3.50	4.21	1.1
	SEA	MLB	27	0	1	0	10^2	12	0	4	11	3.4	9.3	38%	.375	1.50	5.91	2.14	2.58	0.2
J. Ogando	CLN	A	20	1	3	3	59^2	53	1	32	56	4.8	8.4	48%	.311	1.42	3.32	3.59	3.98	0.8
V. Sanchez	CLN	A	18	6	6	0	113^1	106	4	18	79	1.4	6.3	46%	.282	1.09	2.78	3.01	4.02	1.8
C. Smith	WTN	AA	23	1	3	15	50	33	1	17	71	3.1	12.8	72%	.294	1.00	1.80	1.65	2.23	1.5

What do you do with **Anthony Fernandez**, a four-pitch lefty with prototypical size but stuff that couldn't even overpower Double-A hitters? Ritual sacrifice to your preferred deity might work. ⊘ **Ryan Horstman**, a draft-eligible freshman from St. John's, was late to sign and got nearly 20 percent above slot value in the fourth round. His 13.5 strikeouts per nine looks awesome until you realize it came in two innings. ⊘ **Bobby LaFromboise** earned a crack at the majors with excellent numbers in the high minors over the last three years, but his high-80s fastball was knocked around in his brief Seattle stint despite a strikeout per inning. ⊘ **Jochi Ogando** is still transitioning from basketball player to baseball player, making his first full-season performance, including 56 strikeouts and just one homer allowed in 60 innings pitched, even more impressive. ⊘ **Victor Sanchez** was the only 18-year-old to pitch in the High-A Midwest League and he more than held his own, particularly regarding his utter disdain for handing out free passes. Try not to think too hard about the 1995 birthdate. ⊘ Yet another addition to the Mariners' stable of hard-throwing relievers, **Carson Smith** touches 97 with the fastball and is moving toward a future as a set-up man.

MANAGER: LLOYD MCCLENDON

Incredible but true: Of all the men who worked as managers in 2013, only three were younger than Eric Wedge. Not bad for a guy with 1,620 games under his belt.

Eric Wedge's team differentials (this works out pretty easily, because he's managed 10 full seasons and no partial seasons):

- +556 in walks
- +186 in double plays*
- +98 in HBP
- +14 in home runs
- -18 in intentional walks
- -222 in stolen bases
- -421 in hits
- -1,260 in strikeouts

That strikeout differential is the third worst ever, behind just Sparky Anderson and Clint Hurdle. But it's the ninth-best double play differential ever. He's had positive DP differentials in nine of his 10 seasons. The Indians had a negative DP differential nine straight years before he arrived and in two of the three seasons after he left. But they were +99 in his seven seasons there. Until he showed up in Seattle, their best three-year DP differential was +75 (in 1980-82). They were +87 under Wedge from 2011-2013.

Lloyd McClendon replaces Wedge. The Pirates kept losing during McClendon's tenure in Pittsburgh, but then again they had no talent. Actually, they avoided 90 losses three straight seasons for him from 2002-2004, which is the only time they've done that since strike. OK, they lost 89, 87, and 89 games in those years, but it's still several games better than they typically did in that 20-year death spot in franchise history.

*(The double play differential is imperfect, as defensive totals include all double plays, offensive double plays are just those grounded into. I do make an adjustment, his big double play differential is real).

St. Louis Cardinals

By Will Leitch

Every Cardinals fan is tired of talking about Albert Pujols, so I hope they will forgive me for briefly talking about Albert Pujols. Because the reason the Cardinals have the best organization in baseball right now is Albert Pujols.

On February 8, 2006, *Baseball America* released its organizational talent rankings, stacking the farm systems of all 30 teams against each other. No. 30 on the list: the St. Louis Cardinals. They put one player on *BA's* top 100, Anthony Reyes. On February 5, 2013, minor-league expert John Sickels put together his farm system rankings. No. 1 on the list: the St. Louis Cardinals. Money quote: "Strengths: Everything. They have pitching, hitting, high upside, and depth." In between those two sets of rankings, in which the Cardinals went from having the worst farm system in baseball to having the best, the team also won two World Series. It is an excellent time to be a Cardinals fan. And this all happened thanks to Albert Pujols.

Before the 2006 season, Cardinals owner Bill DeWitt, seeing the escalating nature of baseball salaries, decided that he would have to make some changes to keep Pujols a Cardinal forever. (It is worth remembering that this was once a foregone conclusion: It wasn't just Cardinals fans saying they couldn't imagine Pujols in another uniform.) Pujols had just signed a seven-year, team-friendly extension before the 2004 season, and two years in he had established himself as the next Lou Gehrig. With Alex Rodriguez signing $250 million contracts, DeWitt knew that the way the Cardinals were doing business under General Manager Walt Jocketty—leveraging the farm system in trades for players like Larry Walker, Scott Rolen and Mark Mulder—was unsustainable. The Cardinals could not pay for veterans every year; that year's roster, which featured Chris Duncan as the second best hitter behind Pujols, was proof of how top-heavy the team had become. The only way the Cardinals would be able to hold on to Pujols forever

would be to surround him with young, cheap talent. They would have to remake the whole farm system. They had five years to do it.

Jocketty, already unhappy with the appointment of Jeff Luhnow as the head of amateur scouting, wasn't on board for a rebuild, so he left for Cincinnati. After a failed attempt to pry loose Cleveland's Chris Antonetti, St. Louis promoted John Mozeliak to the top job. He and Luhnow went about revamping the farm system not only to improve the team, of course, but also to make sure they could come up with the money Pujols would want. Suffice it to say that Luhnow was successful: As Derrick Goold of the *St. Louis Post-Dispatch* pointed out, you could put together a quality major-league roster solely of players acquired by Luhnow during his six years atop the Cardinals' amateur scouting program.

CARDINALS PROSPECTUS
2013 W-L: 97-65, 1st in NL Central

Pythag	.624	1st	DER	.698	22nd
RS/G	4.83	3rd	B-Age	28.9	21st
RA/G	3.68	5th	P-Age	26.8	3rd
TAv	.258	15th	Salary	$116.5	12th
BRR	13.37	2nd	M$/MW	$2.13	9th
TAv-P	.252	4th	DL Days	930	14th
FIP	3.36	2nd	$ on DL	20%	21st

	Runs	HR/RH	HR/LH	Runs/RH	Runs/LH
Three-Year Park Factors	102	94	96	97	106

Top Hitter WARP	7.25 (Matt Carpenter)
Top Pitcher WARP	4.61 (Adam Wainwright)
Top Prospect	Oscar Taveras

C	Tony Cruz
1B	Matt Adams
2B	Kolten Wong
SS	Pete Kozma
3B	Matt Carpenter
OF	Jon Jay
OF	Colby Rasmus
OF	Allen Craig
OF	Oscar Taveras
SP	Shelby Miller
SP	Carlos Martinez
SP	Jaime Garcia
SP	Lance Lynn
SP	Joe Kelly
RP	Trevor Rosenthal
RP	Chris Perez
RP	Kevin Siegrist

After the Cardinals pulled off their amazing, reality-defying, pants-wetting 2011 World Championship, it was obvious the plan had worked. With free-agent money coming off the books and cheap, team-controlled talent flooding the system, the Cardinals would be able to give Albert what he wanted and still compete. Except: Albert wanted more. Or, more to the point, Arte Moreno offered more than the Cardinals' budget, in the team's estimation, could hold. Mozeliak was reportedly devastated by Pujols' exit, saying the process was "exhausting, frustrating and very emotional" and admitting he needed several hours to collect himself after Pujols chose the Angels. There has been some talk in the past two years that somehow the Cardinals were "smart" for not bringing back Pujols, but there was never any question that Mozeliak and company wanted to re-sign Pujols. That had been the plan all along.

Two years later: It's now clear the situation couldn't have worked out better for Mozeliak and the Cardinals, who ended up cleaning their financial plate and eating all the food on it too. Even ignoring Pujols' injury issues and regression since arriving in Anaheim—and considering there are still eight years to go on that contract, that might not be so easy to do—the Cardinals were able to use the money they would have spent on Pujols and give it to:

- Adam Wainwright, who signed a five-year, $97.5 million extension that kicks in this year. Wainwright finished second in the Cy Young voting last year.
- Yadier Molina, who signed a five-year, $75 million deal starting in 2013. Molina finished third in the MVP voting last year.
- Carlos Beltran, who signed a two-year, $26 million deal and hit .282/.343/.493 in 296 regular-season games and .306/.410/.571 in 29 postseason games.
- Jhonny Peralta, who signed a four-year, $53 million deal, filling a hole the Cardinals have had at shortstop since, essentially, Edgar Renteria. (If you'll forgive the David Eckstein snub.)

The Cardinals were able to add and/or hold onto those players almost entirely because they weren't paying $24 million a year to Pujols. And because they had *planned* on paying near that amount for him, those players are mere supplements to the real meat of the team, the cheap young superstars like Shelby Miller, Michael Wacha, Matt Carpenter, Trevor Rosenthal, Oscar Taveras (soon), et al. The plan was to win by building around Albert. When he left, he made the plan even better. The only time you hear Pujols' name come up that much anymore, *vis a vis* the Cardinals, is when people point out that a draft pick they received in compensation for his signing with the Angels turned out to be Wacha. (The second one they received was used to select outfielder Stephen Piscotty, currently a well-regarded prospect in his own right.) But the story with Pujols and this roster doesn't end there. Pujols' stamp is all over this team. Pujols is the reason it exists.

The Cardinals ruined a ton of Hot Stove fun this offseason—while making it easier for chroniclers in certain baseball annuals to turn in their essays on time—by moving before Thanksgiving to correct the failings exposed during their World Series loss to Boston. In that Sox series, spots one through five in the Cardinals' lineup—Matt Carpenter, Beltran, Matt Holliday, Allen Craig and Molina—all had an OPS over .600: not great, but not a short-series disaster. (As a matter of comparison, the Sox had one hitter with an OPS over .600, David Ortiz, who checked in at a terrifying-to-even-look-at 1.948.) But here's the OPS of the sixth through eighth spots: David Freese, .438; Jon Jay, .452; Daniel Descalso, .350.

The total lack of production from the bottom of the order murdered the Cardinals in the series, and it didn't help that none of those three played particularly solid defense at third base, center field and shortstop, respectively. So Mozeliak went about fixing all three spots.

His first move took care of two of them: He traded civic hero Freese to Anaheim, along with forgotten reliever Fernando Salas, for center field wizard Peter Bourjos and prospect Randal Grichuk. Sending out Freese allows Carpenter to play his natural position of third base while promoting top prospect Kolten Wong to play second, upgrading two positions through the extraction of a player who was about to get expensive. (And the Angels threw in one of their top prospects!) Bourjos fixes a major issue of the 2013 Cardinals: outfield defense. Holliday is aging in left (and wasn't that great in the first place), and right field will be manned by Craig, who not only has injury issues but also is a first baseman. (And at that, only barely.) Bourjos might be the best defensive center fielder in the game and the Cardinals are buying on the upside of his offense as well. There has been talk that the team will platoon Bourjos and Jay, but considering the gulf between them defensively, and the similarity offensively, that ultimately seems doubtful. And having Bourjos around also allows the Cardinals to ease in Taveras, who, oh by the way, is one of the best hitting prospects in baseball.

And Mozeliak's second move was to sign Peralta, which, while probably an overpay, still solves the shortstop issue for at least a couple of years and assures that a World Series-contending NL team isn't trotting out an eighth-place hitter who is only slightly better than its ninth.

Mozeliak did all this while still using his Pujols strategy: horde prospects and draft picks. The Cardinals arguably have eight options for their rotation this year: Wainwright, Miller, Jaime Garcia, Wacha, Lance Lynn, Joe Kelly, Carlos Martinez and Tyler Lyons. Mozeliak hung onto all of them. The Cardinals have five men for the four corner spots: Holliday, Craig, Jay, Taveras, Matt Adams. Mozeliak hung onto all of them too. He'll need them. Teams always do. Mozeliak and the Cardinals aren't just amassing talent; they're stashing it.

The Cardinals will likely never have a player like Albert Pujols again: He was once-in-a-generation. You cannot count on someone like that coming around often ... or, for that matter, producing at that level forever. Albert Pujols gave the Cardinals 11 years of All-World production. Because of their preparation for his free agency, the Cardinals might have set themselves up for Pujols to give them 11 more. Even in Anaheim, he's still a Cardinals MVP. St. Louis is going to compete for a World Series this year, and next year, and the year after that. That's the thing about running a baseball franchise rather than wedding yourself to one human player: You can keep getting older, but your players, man, they stay the same age.

Will Leitch is a senior writer at Sports On Earth *and a contributing editor at* New York *magazine. He is the founder of* Deadspin *and the author of four books, most recently* Are We Winning? Fathers, Sons and the New Golden Age of Baseball.

HITTERS

Matt Adams   1B

Born: 8/31/1988 Age: 25
Bats: L Throws: R Height: 6' 3"
Weight: 260 Breakout: 0%
Improve: 45% Collapse: 5%
Attrition: 11% MLB: 86%

Comparables:
Chris Davis, Paul Goldschmidt, Mike Jacobs

YEAR	TEAM	LVL	AGE	PA	R	2B	3B	HR	RBI	BB	SO	SB	CS	AVG/OBP/SLG	TAv	BABIP	BRR	FRAA	WARP
2011	SFD	AA	22	513	80	23	2	32	101	40	90	0	1	.300/.357/.566	.267	.308	0.1	1B(45): -0.6	0.2
2012	MEM	AAA	23	276	41	22	0	18	50	15	57	3	1	.329/.362/.624	.338	.360	0.5	1B(59): 2.7	3.0
2012	SLN	MLB	23	91	8	6	0	2	13	5	24	0	0	.244/.286/.384	.229	.317	-1.6	1B(24): 0.6	-0.3
2013	SLN	MLB	24	319	46	14	0	17	51	23	80	0	1	.284/.335/.503	.289	.337	-1.6	1B(74): -0.2	1.1
2014	SLN	MLB	25	289	36	14	0	15	44	16	69	1	0	.267/.310/.483	.283	.300	-0.6	1B 1	1.1

Adams is another one of the organization's amazing success stories: A portly 23rd-round pick, he has done nothing but hit at every level, and turned out to be essential when Allen Craig was injured late in the season. Because this is the Cardinals we're talking about, Adams happened to get hot at just that moment, with an eight-homer September, with four of those bombs coming in the ninth inning or later. St. Louis has six good players for four spots, so Adams will likely be underutilized and loads of fun once again.

Peter Bourjos   CF

Born: 3/31/1987 Age: 27
Bats: R Throws: R Height: 6' 1"
Weight: 185 Breakout: 7%
Improve: 52% Collapse: 4%
Attrition: 8% MLB: 92%

Comparables:
Franklin Gutierrez, Luis Terrero, Drew Stubbs

YEAR	TEAM	LVL	AGE	PA	R	2B	3B	HR	RBI	BB	SO	SB	CS	AVG/OBP/SLG	TAv	BABIP	BRR	FRAA	WARP
2011	ANA	MLB	24	552	72	26	11	12	43	32	124	22	9	.271/.327/.438	.278	.338	5.6	CF(147): -7.1	2.7
2012	SLC	AAA	25	32	4	1	3	0	3	3	6	0	0	.310/.375/.552	.289	.391	1.5	CF(4): -0.2	0.3
2012	ANA	MLB	25	195	27	7	0	3	19	15	44	3	1	.220/.291/.315	.230	.274	1.5	CF(90): 7.2	1.2
2013	SLC	AAA	26	55	13	4	0	2	7	4	19	0	0	.208/.291/.417	.248	.286	0.9	CF(7): 0.5	0.2
2013	ANA	MLB	26	196	26	3	3	3	12	10	43	6	0	.274/.333/.377	.259	.346	1.9	CF(53): -0.4	0.6
2014	SLN	MLB	27	250	29	9	4	5	25	13	54	8	2	.255/.308/.397	.258	.310	1.1	CF 1	0.9

The saga continues. Bourjos has alternated between good and bad in each of his four big-league seasons—last year qualifies for "good" considering his ballpark and role. It was abbreviated by poor health, though, as he missed time due to a strained hamstring and a fractured wrist. The Angels traded Kendrys Morales partly to make room for him, yet he finished with fewer than 200 plate appearances for the second year in a row. He remains a brilliant defender with great speed, but it's unclear whether he'll ever outrun the extra-outfielder label, especially after being traded onto a crowded Cardinals roster.

Joey Butler   RF

Born: 3/12/1986 Age: 28
Bats: R Throws: R Height: 6' 2"
Weight: 220 Breakout: 1%
Improve: 9% Collapse: 15%
Attrition: 26% MLB: 35%

Comparables:
Mike Wilson, Nick Gorneault, Brent Clevlen

YEAR	TEAM	LVL	AGE	PA	R	2B	3B	HR	RBI	BB	SO	SB	CS	AVG/OBP/SLG	TAv	BABIP	BRR	FRAA	WARP
2011	FRI	AA	25	55	11	1	0	2	4	7	16	2	1	.227/.382/.386	.251	.308	0.1	RF(9): 0.1	-0.1
2011	ROU	AAA	25	474	73	27	5	12	57	43	138	13	4	.322/.388/.493	.350	.451	0.4	RF(20): -1.8, CF(7): 0.2	1.3
2012	ROU	AAA	26	584	93	28	1	20	78	79	128	6	4	.290/.392/.473	.315	.351	-1.6	RF(125): -11.9, CF(9): 0.3	3.5
2013	ROU	AAA	27	505	71	26	0	12	51	69	119	1	2	.291/.395/.437	.306	.376	-3.9	RF(53): 0.3, LF(47): -1.7	2.8
2013	TEX	MLB	27	15	3	2	0	0	1	3	6	0	0	.333/.467/.500	.348	.667	0.3	LF(3): -0.1, RF(2): 0.0	0.2
2014	SLN	MLB	28	250	28	11	0	6	29	28	65	2	1	.255/.346/.397	.278	.330	-0.5	RF -2, LF -1	0.7

Butler appeared to get his big break when Nelson Cruz's Biogenesis suspension opened a spot for a right-hand-hitting corner outfield/DH type. Unfortunately for the 27-year-old, the Rangers acquired Alex Rios just a few days later, and Butler was thus returned to Round Rock to finish out his third straight season with the Express. While Butler has put up solid offensive numbers in Triple-A, he is considered a sub-par defender in right field, and there are questions about whether he has the bat speed to handle major-league velocity. The Cardinals claimed him on waivers in October, so he will no doubt start hitting .300 with 20 homers in the bigs after they sprinkle him with their magic Cardinal farm system dust.

Matt Carpenter 3B

Born: 11/26/1985 Age: 28
Bats: L Throws: R Height: 6' 3"
Weight: 215 Breakout: 0%
Improve: 49% Collapse: 1%
Attrition: 8% MLB: 98%

Comparables:
Ian Kinsler, Kelly Johnson, Chase Utley

YEAR	TEAM	LVL	AGE	PA	R	2B	3B	HR	RBI	BB	SO	SB	CS	AVG/OBP/SLG	TAv	BABIP	BRR	FRAA	WARP
2011	MEM	AAA	25	535	61	29	3	12	70	84	68	5	4	.300/.417/.463	.358	.328	-0.5	3B(32): 1.8	1.9
2011	SLN	MLB	25	19	0	1	0	0	0	4	4	0	0	.067/.263/.133	.156	.091	-0.2	3B(5): 0.2	-0.2
2012	SLN	MLB	26	340	44	22	5	6	46	34	63	1	1	.294/.365/.463	.293	.346	-0.7	1B(44): -1.2, 3B(33): -0.9	1.3
2013	SLN	MLB	27	717	126	55	7	11	78	72	98	3	3	.318/.392/.481	.312	.359	8.4	2B(132): 1.8, 3B(42): 0.4	7.3
2014	SLN	MLB	28	601	74	37	4	11	60	63	95	4	3	.291/.370/.439	.294	.330	-1.1	3B 8, 2B 0	4.3

Even the romantics, the optimists, the delusional and the Carpenters failed to forecast anything like this breakout, which saw across-the-board improvement, league bests in hits, doubles and runs scored, and a fourth-place MVP finish. He was a perfect low-speed leadoff hitter, drawing enough walks to be a catalyst and hitting with enough power to make pitchers tread carefully. Carpenter proved to be a quick study at second base, but with the trade of David Freese he should slide back to the hot corner; his newfound defensive versatility allows the Cardinals to plug him in wherever he's most needed. Nothing in the former 13th-round pick's skill set stands out as an egregious outlier, making it difficult to see him falling *too* far from this lofty perch. Even if he's more of a true talent .290 hitter, he will still be among the game's best leadoff men, and perhaps former scouting director Jeff Luhnow's most impressive find.

Allen Craig RF

Born: 7/18/1984 Age: 29
Bats: R Throws: R Height: 6' 2"
Weight: 215 Breakout: 9%
Improve: 57% Collapse: 1%
Attrition: 7% MLB: 91%

Comparables:
Adam Lind, Glenn Davis, Bob Horner

YEAR	TEAM	LVL	AGE	PA	R	2B	3B	HR	RBI	BB	SO	SB	CS	AVG/OBP/SLG	TAv	BABIP	BRR	FRAA	WARP
2011	MEM	AAA	26	39	9	2	1	1	5	3	3	0	0	.286/.359/.486	.426	.290	0.4	LF(1): -0.1	0.2
2011	SLN	MLB	26	219	33	15	0	11	40	15	40	5	0	.315/.362/.555	.324	.344	1.6	LF(26): -0.5, RF(18): 0.5	2.3
2012	SLN	MLB	27	514	76	35	0	22	92	37	89	2	1	.307/.354/.522	.307	.334	-3.6	1B(91): -7.5, RF(23): -0.3	1.7
2013	SLN	MLB	28	563	71	29	2	13	97	40	100	2	0	.315/.373/.457	.297	.368	-2.5	1B(95): 1.5, LF(25): -0.6	2.3
2014	SLN	MLB	29	523	62	29	1	18	70	37	97	2	1	.290/.345/.468	.294	.330	-0.7	RF -7, 1B -1	1.9

While Craig technically avoided the disabled list for the first time in his career, it was only because the inevitable injury struck after rosters expanded in September, rendering the 15-day DL moot. He still logged a career high in playing time and continued to rake, but the full season remains elusive, even dating back to his minor-league days. Craig's obscene work with runners in scoring position masks the very noticeable and worrisome power decline he suffered in 2013, however. While the nine-homer decline does not leap off the page, the 73-point dip in isolated power does. Part of the problem appears to be an ever-increasing ground-to-fly ratio. If he shifts to the outfield, that level of production is far more acceptable than if he were to stay at first base, although it would expose his postage-stamp range and indifferent glove. The .454 average with runners in scoring position is bound to come down, so if the power drop is more than just a stark outlier, his production will suffer in 2014.

Tony Cruz C

Born: 8/18/1986 Age: 27
Bats: R Throws: R Height: 5' 11"
Weight: 215 Breakout: 6%
Improve: 36% Collapse: 8%
Attrition: 28% MLB: 91%

Comparables:
Mike Lieberthal, Joe Azcue, Mark Salas

YEAR	TEAM	LVL	AGE	PA	R	2B	3B	HR	RBI	BB	SO	SB	CS	AVG/OBP/SLG	TAv	BABIP	BRR	FRAA	WARP
2011	MEM	AAA	24	164	13	5	1	4	25	11	31	0	1	.262/.315/.389	.118	.304	0.1	C(10): 0.1	-0.5
2011	SLN	MLB	24	72	8	5	0	0	6	6	13	0	1	.262/.333/.338	.255	.327	0	C(20): 0.0, 3B(3): 0.0	0.2
2012	SLN	MLB	25	131	11	9	1	1	11	3	19	0	1	.254/.267/.365	.224	.287	-0.8	C(47): 0.4, 1B(2): 0.0	0.1
2013	SLN	MLB	26	129	13	6	1	1	13	4	25	0	0	.203/.240/.293	.178	.247	0.7	C(44): -0.5, 3B(3): -0.0	-0.5
2014	SLN	MLB	27	250	22	12	1	3	22	13	44	1	1	.237/.281/.340	.230	.280	-0.5	C 0, 3B -0	0.4

Backing up Yadier Molina has to be one of the most boring jobs in baseball: The starter never takes a day off, never gets hurt, and never needs a pinch-hitter. But Molina did finally hit the disabled list in 2013, and Cruz—perhaps having forgotten what they taught him at orientation—made little of the opportunity, hitting to a .557 OPS in his 13 games as man of the house. The durability of Molina aside, the Cards should consider strengthening their backup catcher—Cruz hasn't ever shown much, is getting worse, and is one of the few spots where the Cardinals aren't practically perfect.

Daniel Descalso   2B

Born: 10/19/1986 Age: 27
Bats: L Throws: R Height: 5' 10"
Weight: 190 Breakout: 5%
Improve: 47% Collapse: 5%
Attrition: 15% MLB: 91%

Comparables:
Jason Bartlett, Cliff Pennington, Russ Adams

YEAR	TEAM	LVL	AGE	PA	R	2B	3B	HR	RBI	BB	SO	SB	CS	AVG/OBP/SLG	TAv	BABIP	BRR	FRAA	WARP
2011	SLN	MLB	24	375	35	20	3	1	28	33	65	2	2	.264/.334/.353	.266	.323	-0.3	3B(117): -8.9, 2B(18): 0.5	0.6
2012	SLN	MLB	25	426	41	10	7	4	26	37	83	6	3	.227/.303/.324	.240	.279	5	2B(96): 4.8, SS(26): 1.8	1.2
2013	SLN	MLB	26	358	43	25	1	5	43	22	56	6	3	.238/.290/.366	.243	.271	3.9	SS(55): 0.8, 2B(39): 1.5	1.5
2014	SLN	MLB	27	350	33	17	2	3	30	26	58	4	2	.245/.309/.346	.246	.280	-0.2	2B 1, SS 1	0.8

Descalso's raison d'être is his glove and his ability to take it all over the infield. However, the advanced metrics—as well as the eye test—suggest that it's no longer the carrying tool that it once was, making it difficult to justify dispensing 350 plate appearances to him again. A great ending to this comment would go something like: "It's clear that Descalso and Pete Kozma aren't the answer at shortstop, and there's nobody waiting in the wings. Jhonny Peralta's free agency presents a real opportunity to match supply with demand and benefit all parties. Well, except Descalso." The Peralta signing came down long before this volume went to press, though, and we're honest folk, so instead: "R.I.P. Descalso's chance at a starting job."

Mark Ellis   2B

Born: 6/6/1977 Age: 37
Bats: R Throws: R Height: 5' 10"
Weight: 190 Breakout: 1%
Improve: 25% Collapse: 13%
Attrition: 13% MLB: 72%

Comparables:
Roberto Alomar, Orlando Cabrera, Jerry Hairston

YEAR	TEAM	LVL	AGE	PA	R	2B	3B	HR	RBI	BB	SO	SB	CS	AVG/OBP/SLG	TAv	BABIP	BRR	FRAA	WARP
2011	OAK	MLB	34	233	21	11	1	1	16	8	32	7	2	.217/.253/.290	.212	.249	0.7	2B(59): 4.8, 1B(2): 0.1	0.1
2011	COL	MLB	34	286	34	13	0	6	25	14	43	7	3	.274/.317/.392	.240	.307	2.4	2B(64): -0.3	0.1
2012	LAN	MLB	35	464	62	21	1	7	31	40	70	5	0	.258/.333/.364	.263	.296	-1.2	2B(110): 1.2	1.4
2013	LAN	MLB	36	480	46	13	2	6	48	26	74	4	1	.270/.323/.351	.260	.310	3.1	2B(119): 3.3, 3B(1): -0.0	2.1
2014	SLN	MLB	37	450	48	19	1	5	36	26	67	6	2	.254/.307/.343	.243	.290	-0.3	2B 3, 1B 0	1.1

Ellis fits the traditional prototype of a no. 2 hitter, with the contact skills to hit the ball to the right side and move a runner over; it's 2014, though, and not all traditions are as timeless as Vin Scully and Farmer John's Dodger Dogs. Ellis can't hit enough to front a modern-day lineup, but that didn't stop Mattingly from penciling him into one of the top two spots 63 times. His real worth comes not from grounding into sacrificial 4-3 putouts, but from his glove—even at 36 he was a Gold Glove finalist and the second runner-up for a Fielding Bible award. What offense does come is usually thanks to a walk rate that comes and goes, ebbing with the calendar in an inverted-Saberhagen pattern; 2014 is due to be one of the good years, ye eternal optimists.

Randal Grichuk   RF

Born: 8/13/1991 Age: 22
Bats: R Throws: R Height: 6' 1"
Weight: 195 Breakout: 1%
Improve: 13% Collapse: 2%
Attrition: 21% MLB: 38%

Comparables:
Carlos Gonzalez, Josh Reddick, Shane Peterson

YEAR	TEAM	LVL	AGE	PA	R	2B	3B	HR	RBI	BB	SO	SB	CS	AVG/OBP/SLG	TAv	BABIP	BRR	FRAA	WARP
2011	CDR	A	19	131	12	7	4	2	13	6	29	0	1	.230/.267/.402	.165	.280	0.3	RF(10): 1.0	-0.2
2011	SBR	A+	19	57	13	4	2	1	6	0	13	0	0	.283/.316/.491	.215	.350	0.5	RF(4): -0.4	0.1
2012	SBR	A+	20	575	79	30	9	18	71	23	92	16	6	.298/.335/.488	.299	.329	3.2	RF(88): 0.8, CF(38): 1.9	4.6
2013	ARK	AA	21	542	85	27	8	22	64	28	92	9	5	.256/.306/.474	.285	.272	3	RF(95): 13.0, CF(23): -0.8	4.3
2014	SLN	MLB	22	250	24	11	2	7	29	7	51	2	1	.244/.271/.398	.245	.280	0	RF 3, CF 0	0.4

Dear Baseball Writers of America: I am sick of being introduced as the guy selected one pick before the best player of our generation. Please do some homework, find another hook and let that comparison die. Here's another possible intro: The Rawlings Gold Glove committee tabbed me the world's best minor-league right fielder in 2013, and Baseball Prospectus' Fielding Runs Above Average agreed, attributing 13 runs saved to my glove. And stop slandering me with contact issues! Did anyone notice that I struck out less than 17 percent of the time, and that my (uncharacteristically) low batting average was due to a 55-point BABIP drop from my career average? I nevertheless posted a .218 isolated power in quite possibly the worst hitters park in the minors. I was going to make one hell of a platoon partner and defensive replacement for Josh Hamilton, once the Angels finally conceded his need to sit against lefties. Now, I'm a very nice fourth outfield option with starter upside for the Cards. Really, they might have gotten a bargain here. Sincerely, and with all due respect, Randal Grichuk.

Matt Holliday   LF

Born: 1/15/1980 Age: 34
Bats: R Throws: R Height: 6' 4"
Weight: 250 Breakout: 1%
Improve: 39% Collapse: 3%
Attrition: 7% MLB: 96%

Comparables:
Sid Gordon, Josh Willingham, Larry Walker

YEAR	TEAM	LVL	AGE	PA	R	2B	3B	HR	RBI	BB	SO	SB	CS	AVG/OBP/SLG	TAv	BABIP	BRR	FRAA	WARP
2011	SLN	MLB	31	516	83	36	0	22	75	60	93	2	1	.296/.388/.525	.319	.330	0	LF(115): -8.1	3.2
2012	SLN	MLB	32	688	95	36	2	27	102	75	132	4	4	.295/.379/.497	.310	.337	0.7	LF(152): -9.6	4.1
2013	SLN	MLB	33	602	103	31	1	22	94	69	86	6	1	.300/.389/.490	.300	.322	3	LF(136): -4.6	3.4
2014	SLN	MLB	34	583	75	32	1	21	80	60	98	5	2	.289/.371/.476	.307	.320	-1	LF -6	3.4

Remember when Holliday was said to be a product of Coors Field? Whoops. He has been every bit as good as a Cardinal and possesses a skill set that should age gracefully—especially if he continues to improve his strikeout and walk rates. The 2013 season was his first on the wrong side of a .200 isolated power since 2005, but it didn't stop him from having the highest OPS+ of any left fielder. Holliday has more than earned the front end of his seven-year contract, creating a surplus that affords some wiggle room for his mid-30s; his current path suggests he won't need it.

Jon Jay CF

Born: 3/15/1985 Age: 29
Bats: L Throws: L Height: 5' 11"
Weight: 195 Breakout: 1%
Improve: 42% Collapse: 3%
Attrition: 8% MLB: 98%

Comparables:
Jacoby Ellsbury, Denard Span, Angel Pagan

YEAR	TEAM	LVL	AGE	PA	R	2B	3B	HR	RBI	BB	SO	SB	CS	AVG/OBP/SLG	TAv	BABIP	BRR	FRAA	WARP
2011	SLN	MLB	26	503	56	24	2	10	37	28	81	6	7	.297/.344/.424	.275	.340	0.3	CF(75): 1.8, RF(56): 2.8	2.2
2012	SLN	MLB	27	502	70	22	4	4	40	34	71	19	7	.305/.373/.400	.284	.355	-0.5	CF(116): 12.1	3.9
2013	SLN	MLB	28	628	75	27	2	7	67	52	103	10	5	.276/.351/.370	.263	.325	3.6	CF(152): -3.0	1.9
2014	SLN	MLB	29	566	68	27	2	8	49	39	90	12	6	.281/.344/.389	.269	.320	-0.4	CF 4, RF -0	2.5

Jay had established a level of offensive production comfortably above league average during his first three years in the majors, but year-over-year declines against lefties shortened his margin for error against righties. It all came to a head in 2013. He had his biggest decline against lefties yet, while also slipping against righties, and all of a sudden he was treading just above average. He was awful in the postseason on both sides of the ball, and the Cardinals saw it as enough of a problem that they acquired Peter Bourjos in the offseason. At best, Jay's going to have competition; at worst, he's got to have a lot more free time.

Carson Kelly 3B

Born: 7/14/1994 Age: 19
Bats: R Throws: R Height: 6' 2"
Weight: 200 Breakout: 0%
Improve: 0% Collapse: 0%
Attrition: 0% MLB: 0%

Comparables:
Josh Vitters, Matt Davidson, Nolan Arenado

YEAR	TEAM	LVL	AGE	PA	R	2B	3B	HR	RBI	BB	SO	SB	CS	AVG/OBP/SLG	TAv	BABIP	BRR	FRAA	WARP
2013	PEO	A	18	168	18	6	0	2	13	13	25	0	0	.219/.288/.301	.242	.248	0.2	3B(31): -4.9	-0.3
2013	SCO	A-	18	299	35	16	1	4	32	20	31	1	0	.277/.340/.387	.260	.301	-0.9	3B(64): -7.2	-0.1
2014	SLN	MLB	19	250	19	9	0	4	23	10	55	0	0	.211/.246/.300	.204	.250	-0.5	3B -9	-1.8

Kelly didn't blow away scouts and analysts in his first full pro season, but at 18 years old, it was hardly a disaster. His raw power impresses when it's on display and his glove grades very well at third base—given the positional value of an infielder versus a corner outfielder, sticking there will go a long way toward getting Kelly to the majors. A move back to the New York-Penn League helped get his season back on track and he ended on a high note, putting up his highest OPS in August. Patience: There's plenty of time for Kelly to blossom.

Pete Kozma SS

Born: 4/11/1988 Age: 26
Bats: R Throws: R Height: 6' 0"
Weight: 190 Breakout: 3%
Improve: 35% Collapse: 17%
Attrition: 34% MLB: 78%

Comparables:
Ramiro Pena, Ray Olmedo, Reid Brignac

YEAR	TEAM	LVL	AGE	PA	R	2B	3B	HR	RBI	BB	SO	SB	CS	AVG/OBP/SLG	TAv	BABIP	BRR	FRAA	WARP
2011	MEM	AAA	23	448	48	17	2	3	47	36	91	2	2	.214/.280/.289	.127	.265	-0.1	2B(11): 0.5, SS(7): 0.5	-0.7
2011	SLN	MLB	23	22	2	1	0	0	1	4	4	0	0	.176/.333/.235	.215	.231	-0.4	2B(10): 0.0, SS(3): -0.3	-0.1
2012	MEM	AAA	24	500	61	16	3	11	63	41	74	7	4	.232/.292/.355	.238	.251	4	2B(84): 8.0, SS(45): -4.8	1.5
2012	SLN	MLB	24	82	11	5	3	2	14	7	19	2	0	.333/.383/.569	.325	.415	1.1	SS(25): 0.5, 2B(1): -0.0	1.3
2013	SLN	MLB	25	448	44	20	0	1	35	34	91	3	1	.217/.275/.273	.203	.274	3.2	SS(139): 16.8, LF(1): 0.0	1.6
2014	SLN	MLB	26	408	36	16	2	5	34	29	82	4	2	.221/.277/.316	.221	.260	-0.3	SS 6, 2B 1	0.9

Saying David Freese is living off his postseason magic is wrong, but hanging that tag on Kozma is probably the most correct thing ever. And it wasn't even a whole postseason! It was a .955 OPS in 22 plate appearances against Washington in the NLDS. That effort along with Rafael Furcal's Tommy John surgery and a lack of obviously better options in St. Louis earned Kozma a full season of playing time, during which he was baseball's third-worst hitter by OPS+. St. Louis raised some eyebrows by signing Jhonny Peralta for four years early in the offseason; they might have raised Branch Rickey from the dead if they'd given Kozma another 448 plate appearances.

Yadier Molina C

Born: 7/13/1982 Age: 31
Bats: R Throws: R Height: 5' 11"
Weight: 220 Breakout: 0%
Improve: 33% Collapse: 4%
Attrition: 6% MLB: 97%

Comparables:
Victor Martinez, Smoky Burgess, Josh Bard

YEAR	TEAM	LVL	AGE	PA	R	2B	3B	HR	RBI	BB	SO	SB	CS	AVG/OBP/SLG	TAv	BABIP	BRR	FRAA	WARP
2011	SLN	MLB	28	518	55	32	1	14	65	33	44	4	5	.305/.349/.465	.286	.311	-4.8	C(137): -0.0, 1B(2): -0.0	3.1
2012	SLN	MLB	29	563	65	28	0	22	76	45	55	12	3	.315/.373/.501	.316	.316	-4.3	C(136): 2.3, 1B(3): 0.1	6.6
2013	SLN	MLB	30	541	68	44	0	12	80	30	55	3	2	.319/.359/.477	.297	.338	-5.6	C(131): -0.7, 1B(5): -0.2	4.2
2014	SLN	MLB	31	513	57	27	0	11	59	36	51	6	3	.291/.346/.423	.281	.300	-0.9	C 1, 1B -0	3.5

What does premium catcher defense and game-calling earn you in the big leagues? The opportunity to hit for an 82 OPS+ in 2,979 plate appearances with nary a tsk of disapproval from those around you. Enough time to finally emerge as a hitter and turn into a perennial All-Star and two-time MVP candidate. That sort of slow build could never happen at first base or in the outfield regardless of how good the defense was, but at a defense-first position you can "hide" for six-plus seasons, learning how to hit big league pitching. Few do like Molina did, of course. If there was any flaw in his game in 2013 it was the marginal drop in power, as Molina traded 10 homers for 16 doubles, though it's fair to conclude that 2012 was simply an outlier, ready for regression. Yadi may never again launch 20 bombs, but his peerless work behind the dish and steady bat will keep him among the league's most valuable assets.

Jhonny Peralta SS

Born: 5/28/1982 Age: 32
Bats: R Throws: R Height: 6' 2"
Weight: 215 Breakout: 1%
Improve: 42% Collapse: 4%
Attrition: 9% MLB: 95%

Comparables:
Vern Stephens, Juan Uribe, Michael Young

YEAR	TEAM	LVL	AGE	PA	R	2B	3B	HR	RBI	BB	SO	SB	CS	AVG/OBP/SLG	TAv	BABIP	BRR	FRAA	WARP
2011	DET	MLB	29	576	68	25	3	21	86	40	95	0	2	.299/.345/.478	.280	.325	-1.9	SS(145): 2.0, 1B(1): -0.0	3.5
2012	DET	MLB	30	585	58	32	3	13	63	49	105	1	2	.239/.305/.384	.239	.275	-0.8	SS(149): -6.0	0.6
2013	DET	MLB	31	448	50	30	0	11	55	35	98	3	3	.303/.358/.457	.293	.374	-2.8	SS(106): 8.6, LF(3): -0.0	4.0
2014	SLN	MLB	32	448	46	22	1	10	46	34	87	2	1	.257/.316/.387	.260	.300	-1	SS 1, LF -0	1.9

A PED suspension derailed what could have been a career year for Peralta, who made the All-Star team and nearly matched a career-best TAv. Instead, he got a long summer vacation. Back just in time for the playoffs, Peralta earned the forgiveness of teammates and fans with an .898 postseason OPS, and an anything-for-the-team willingness to move to left field. He signed with the Cardinals, who, being both sensible and in need of a shortstop, won't want to revisit the outfield experiment.

Stephen Piscotty RF

Born: 1/14/1991 Age: 23
Bats: R Throws: R Height: 6' 3"
Weight: 210 Breakout: 2%
Improve: 21% Collapse: 2%
Attrition: 10% MLB: 34%

Comparables:
Caleb Gindl, Nate Schierholtz, Adam Eaton

YEAR	TEAM	LVL	AGE	PA	R	2B	3B	HR	RBI	BB	SO	SB	CS	AVG/OBP/SLG	TAv	BABIP	BRR	FRAA	WARP
2012	QUD	A	21	237	29	18	1	4	27	18	25	3	0	.295/.376/.448	.295	.320	0.3	3B(36): -0.4	1.4
2013	PMB	A+	22	264	30	14	2	9	35	18	27	4	5	.292/.348/.477	.296	.300	1.1	RF(59): -1.7	1.4
2013	SFD	AA	22	207	17	9	0	6	24	19	19	7	3	.299/.364/.446	.292	.304	-4.3	RF(48): 0.6	0.6
2014	SLN	MLB	23	250	25	11	1	6	28	14	38	2	1	.260/.308/.393	.259	.280	-0.4	RF -1, 3B -0	0.3

Sometimes it seems like every Cardinals college prospect will hit to high heaven. The only thing that distinguishes Piscotty from the others like him is that he wasn't drafted in the billionth round: Allen Craig (eighth round), Matt Carpenter (13th) and Matt Adams (23rd) were diamonds in the rough, but Piscotty was a supplemental first-round scoop in 2012. Like his future teammates, though, he has made mincemeat of the minors. Piscotty has a high-contact approach with emerging power and he walks almost as much as he strikes out. Look for him to get a smidge more seasoning at Double-A to start 2014 before moving to Triple-A Memphis. This organization is a frighteningly well-oiled machine.

Oscar Taveras CF

Born: 6/19/1992 Age: 22
Bats: L Throws: L Height: 6' 2"
Weight: 200 Breakout: 2%
Improve: 33% Collapse: 2%
Attrition: 23% MLB: 62%

Comparables:
Colby Rasmus, Wil Myers, Ryan Kalish

YEAR	TEAM	LVL	AGE	PA	R	2B	3B	HR	RBI	BB	SO	SB	CS	AVG/OBP/SLG	TAv	BABIP	BRR	FRAA	WARP
2011	QUD	A	19	347	52	27	5	8	62	32	52	1	4	.386/.444/.584	.337	.440	-0.7	RF(10): -0.0, CF(5): -0.4	0.8
2012	SFD	AA	20	531	83	37	7	23	94	42	56	10	1	.321/.380/.572	.335	.323	-2	CF(93): -1.6, RF(15): -0.3	5.3
2013	MEM	AAA	21	186	25	12	0	5	32	9	22	5	1	.306/.341/.462	.288	.324	-1	CF(34): -1.4, RF(6): -0.5	0.8
2014	SLN	MLB	22	250	28	14	1	8	32	12	35	2	1	.284/.323/.454	.282	.300	-0.1	CF -1, RF -0	1.0

Taveras began 2013 ready to ascend to the Best Prospect throne, if not finish off his prospect status altogether with a major-league stint. Instead, he managed just 47 games as leg injuries cut his season far too short. The Memphis Redbirds' ticket sales office might never recover from his absence, but Taveras will; nothing has changed the overall outlook, and he'll be six months clear of the injuries by spring training. The superstar ceiling remains well within reach and it won't be a surprise if he hits immediately upon arrival. The only tool that isn't clearly plus right now is his fielding, but he can hang in center and has the arm for right.

Charlie Tilson CF

Born: 12/2/1992 Age: 21
Bats: L Throws: L Height: 5' 11"
Weight: 175 Breakout: 1%
Improve: 5% Collapse: 0%
Attrition: 1% MLB: 5%

Comparables:
Eury Perez, Gorkys Hernandez, Carlos Gomez

YEAR	TEAM	LVL	AGE	PA	R	2B	3B	HR	RBI	BB	SO	SB	CS	AVG/OBP/SLG	TAv	BABIP	BRR	FRAA	WARP
2013	PEO	A	20	411	49	8	6	4	30	25	58	15	6	.303/.349/.388	.269	.349	2.5	CF(71): -4.1, LF(17): -0.1	1.7
2013	PMB	A+	20	39	1	1	1	0	0	5	6	0	0	.294/.385/.382	.290	.357	-0.9	CF(9): -0.4	0.2
2014	SLN	MLB	21	250	23	8	2	2	18	10	53	1	1	.241/.274/.316	.219	.290	0	CF -3, LF 0	-0.6

The 2011 second-round pick had to spend last year making up for lost time after missing all of 2012 with a shoulder injury. He did just that with a strong effort in a full-season assignment. The power lagged, though the simple fact is that he lacks significant pop—we can't blame this on the shoulder. His slugging will be generated by gap shots and speed allowing him to nab extra bases, as illustrated by his six triples, tied for the team high despite 151 fewer plate appearances than co-leader Breyvic Valera. Delayed though it may have been, 2013 represented a solid first step toward Tilson justifying his healthy signing bonus and high draft position.

Patrick Wisdom   3B

Born: 8/27/1991 Age: 22
Bats: R Throws: R Height: 6' 2"
Weight: 210 Breakout: 2%
Improve: 5% Collapse: 0%
Attrition: 6% MLB: 6%

Comparables:
Will Middlebrooks, Mike Olt, Josh Bell

YEAR	TEAM	LVL	AGE	PA	R	2B	3B	HR	RBI	BB	SO	SB	CS	AVG/OBP/SLG	TAv	BABIP	BRR	FRAA	WARP
2012	BAT	A-	20	279	40	16	5	6	32	31	58	2	1	.282/.373/.465	.316	.346	1.8	3B(58): -0.5	2.9
2013	PEO	A	21	423	54	20	4	13	62	42	114	4	1	.231/.312/.411	.271	.294	2.9	3B(63): -0.6, 1B(28): -1.5	2.2
2013	PMB	A+	21	102	8	4	0	2	11	9	23	1	0	.250/.317/.359	.260	.313	-0.7	3B(24): -2.6	-0.1
2014	SLN	MLB	22	250	22	9	1	6	26	17	77	0	0	.207/.264/.329	.221	.280	-0.3	3B -3, 1B -0	-0.8

The opinions on Wisdom were already wide-ranging before a rough season that saw his long swing exposed to the tune of a 26 percent strikeout rate. The strikeouts are made more tolerable by Wisdom's virtues: He displays strike-zone discernment, has pop and provides legitimate defensive value at the hot corner. In fact, his glove was part of the reason Stephen Piscotty shifted to the outfield. The Cardinals are flush with third base talent, but Wisdom is the furthest along. If he can shave down the strikeouts in 2014, he'll finish in Triple-A.

Kolten Wong   2B

Born: 10/10/1990 Age: 23
Bats: L Throws: R Height: 5' 9"
Weight: 185 Breakout: 0%
Improve: 29% Collapse: 2%
Attrition: 12% MLB: 41%

Comparables:
Steve Lombardozzi, Luis Valbuena, Adrian Cardenas

YEAR	TEAM	LVL	AGE	PA	R	2B	3B	HR	RBI	BB	SO	SB	CS	AVG/OBP/SLG	TAv	BABIP	BRR	FRAA	WARP
2011	QUD	A	20	222	39	15	2	5	25	21	24	9	5	.335/.401/.510	.143	.355	1	2B(7): 0.6	-0.3
2012	SFD	AA	21	579	79	23	6	9	52	44	74	21	11	.287/.348/.405	.277	.318	4.1	2B(123): 2.6	3.2
2013	MEM	AAA	22	463	68	21	8	10	45	41	60	20	1	.303/.369/.466	.307	.332	0.7	2B(102): 12.9	4.9
2013	SLN	MLB	22	62	6	1	0	0	0	3	12	3	0	.153/.194/.169	.143	.191	0.6	2B(18): 1.3	-0.4
2014	SLN	MLB	23	250	29	10	2	4	21	15	39	7	2	.260/.308/.369	.252	.300	0.6	2B 4	1.1

Wong appeared ready after an excellent effort in Triple-A, so the Cardinals called him up in mid-August with the intention of shifting Matt Carpenter to third and David Freese to the bench. That plan was ditched faster than a tag-along baby brother when it became apparent Wong wasn't quite ready for full-time duty. His 3 OPS+ was baseball's second-worst among non-pitchers. The Cardinals, who didn't get to where they are by being dummies, thought he was ready for another shot; they cleared his path by trading David Freese early in the winter. If they could tolerate 400 plate appearances by Pete Kozma in the infield last year, surely they'll survive whatever Wong's worst case is.

PITCHERS

Mitchell Boggs

Born: 2/15/1984 Age: 30
Bats: R Throws: R Height: 6' 4" Weight: 235
Breakout: 32% Improve: 57% Collapse: 33%
Attrition: 35% MLB: 57%

Comparables:
Zach Miner, Brandon Villafuerte, Wil Ledezma

YEAR	TEAM	LVL	AGE	W	L	SV	G	GS	IP	H	HR	BB	SO	BB9	SO9	GB%	BABIP	WHIP	ERA	FIP	FRA	WARP
2011	MEM	AAA	27	0	2	0	4	4	14²	12	1	5	14	3.1	8.6	40%	.400	1.16	2.45	4.19	4.63	0.1
2011	SLN	MLB	27	2	3	4	51	0	60²	62	4	21	48	3.1	7.1	53%	.322	1.37	3.56	3.41	3.89	0.3
2012	SLN	MLB	28	4	1	0	78	0	73¹	56	5	21	58	2.6	7.1	55%	.246	1.05	2.21	3.46	3.91	0.7
2013	CSP	AAA	29	1	4	0	12	0	16¹	33	1	11	7	6.1	3.9	59%	.416	2.69	8.27	5.71	5.93	-0.1
2013	MEM	AAA	29	0	2	0	18	3	23²	30	2	11	14	4.2	5.3	40%	.329	1.73	5.70	5.39	6.07	-0.3
2013	COL	MLB	29	0	0	0	9	0	8²	7	2	5	5	5.2	5.2	63%	.200	1.38	3.12	6.94	6.61	-0.1
2013	SLN	MLB	29	0	3	2	18	0	14²	21	3	15	11	9.2	6.8	52%	.353	2.45	11.05	7.66	8.03	-0.6
2014	SLN	MLB	30	3	1	1	67	0	71²	71	7	28	52	3.5	6.6	50%	.309	1.38	4.53	4.39	4.93	-0.3

How far can a reliever fall in two months? Boggs may have set the bar in 2013, when he plummeted from Cardinals closer, to being sold for the proverbial bag of balls, to getting shelled on the regular at Triple-A Colorado Springs. The Sky Sox play in a notoriously springy ballpark, but no park on God's earth or moon could justify two hits per inning. Things improved with a September call-up, but the peripherals fail to inspire confidence. On the bright side: How far can a reliever rise in two months? Boggs may have set the bar in 2012, when he ...

Chris Carpenter

Born: 4/27/1975 Age: 39
Bats: R Throws: R Height: 6' 6" Weight: 230
Breakout: 7% Improve: 48% Collapse: 21%
Attrition: 5% MLB: 73%

Comparables:
Andy Pettitte, Kevin Brown, Mike Mussina

YEAR	TEAM	LVL	AGE	W	L	SV	G	GS	IP	H	HR	BB	SO	BB9	SO9	GB%	BABIP	WHIP	ERA	FIP	FRA	WARP
2011	SLN	MLB	36	11	9	0	34	34	237¹	243	16	55	191	2.1	7.2	47%	.320	1.26	3.45	3.03	3.67	2.7
2012	SLN	MLB	37	0	2	0	3	3	17	16	2	3	12	1.6	6.4	46%	.280	1.12	3.71	4.14	4.16	0.2
2014	SLN	MLB	39	2	2	0	6	6	39	36	3	8	30	1.9	6.9	51%	.302	1.14	3.30	3.40	3.59	0.5

Carpenter called it a career after his injuries simply became too much for the 39-year-old to overcome. Honestly, the fact that he accomplished as much as he did was a major upset given that he hit the disabled list 11 times with a bevy of injuries that would have sent a lesser man packing. And don't forget that he was a bit of a bust prior to arriving in St. Louis. A three-time top-100 prospect on *Baseball America*'s annual list, Carpenter managed just a 4.38 ERA and a 1.9 strikeout-to-walk ratio with Toronto before turning it all around with the Cardinals, dodging multiple would-be career-ending injuries en route to a 3.07 ERA and 3.7 K/BB ratio in 1,349 innings with St. Louis.

Carpenter's certainly not a Hall of Famer, but his handful of brilliant seasons, his Cy Young Award (and two other top-three finishes), his solid record of "Black Ink" (in important categories—no league-leading balks totals for Carpenter) and the ever-present sense that he would have been immortal had things just gone a *little* differently with his shoulder and elbow add up to easy membership in the Hall of Very Good. He is, and we mean no insult by faint praise, probably the best New Hampshire-born player in baseball history.

Randy Choate
Born: 9/5/1975 Age: 38
Bats: L Throws: L Height: 6' 1" Weight: 210
Breakout: 25% Improve: 47% Collapse: 26%
Attrition: 10% MLB: 81%

Comparables:
Ron Mahay, Brendan Donnelly, Salomon Torres

YEAR	TEAM	LVL	AGE	W	L	SV	G	GS	IP	H	HR	BB	SO	BB9	SO9	GB%	BABIP	WHIP	ERA	FIP	FRA	WARP
2011	FLO	MLB	35	1	1	0	54	0	24²	13	3	13	31	4.7	11.3	62%	.189	1.05	1.82	3.89	4.36	-0.2
2012	LAN	MLB	36	0	0	0	36	0	13¹	13	1	9	11	6.1	7.4	69%	.293	1.65	4.05	4.94	5.06	-0.2
2012	MIA	MLB	36	0	0	1	44	0	25¹	16	0	9	27	3.2	9.6	61%	.246	0.99	2.49	2.43	2.75	0.4
2013	SLN	MLB	37	2	1	0	64	0	35¹	26	0	11	28	2.8	7.1	68%	.260	1.05	2.29	2.54	3.72	0.2
2014	SLN	MLB	38	4	2	1	76	0	38²	32	3	14	34	3.2	7.9	59%	.289	1.18	3.25	3.68	3.53	0.5

It's no exaggeration to say that, if he threw right-handed, Randy Choate would be selling chili pepper seeds by mail order out of a garage in Brownsville. (Or something.) Since reinventing himself as a LOOGY in 2009, Choate has logged 180 innings in 344 appearances while earning $5.1 million; he's got at least $3 million more coming on his current contract. Only Aroldis Chapman and Craig Kimbrel have been tougher against lefties in that time, by OPS, so if the Cardinals find he's superfluous in a lefty-packed bullpen they'll find plenty of takers around the league.

Tim Cooney
Born: 12/19/1990 Age: 23
Bats: L Throws: L Height: 6' 3" Weight: 195
Breakout: 35% Improve: 56% Collapse: 24%
Attrition: 53% MLB: 27%

Comparables:
Burch Smith, Jeremy Sowers, Adam Warren

YEAR	TEAM	LVL	AGE	W	L	SV	G	GS	IP	H	HR	BB	SO	BB9	SO9	GB%	BABIP	WHIP	ERA	FIP	FRA	WARP
2012	BAT	A-	21	3	3	0	13	11	55²	56	4	8	43	1.3	7.0	57%	.319	1.15	3.40	3.26	4.85	0.2
2013	PMB	A+	22	3	3	0	6	6	36	38	1	4	23	1.0	5.8	43%	.316	1.17	2.75	2.74	4.16	0.2
2013	SFD	AA	22	7	10	0	20	20	118¹	132	8	18	125	1.4	9.5	49%	.366	1.27	3.80	2.43	3.29	3.0
2014	SLN	MLB	23	6	7	0	26	23	118²	126	12	30	88	2.3	6.7	47%	.321	1.31	4.23	3.92	4.60	0.4

Late-round college hitters who turn into studs are currently the organization's chief export, but polished lefties who zoom through the system are an industry on the rise. Cooney is paving the way. The Wake Forest alumnus spent the bulk of his first full-season assignment in Double-A and acquitted himself brilliantly, boasting a 6.9 K/BB ratio that helped him rank second in all of the minors (min. 100 innings). The control is spot-on, but success at the next level will be dependent on improved command that allows him to push hitters off balance and soften contact. Cooney allowed too many hits in 2013 to confidently predict success in this endeavor.

Samuel Freeman
Born: 6/24/1987 Age: 27
Bats: R Throws: L Height: 5' 11" Weight: 165
Breakout: 37% Improve: 47% Collapse: 38%
Attrition: 60% MLB: 40%

Comparables:
Joe Paterson, Josh Newman, Robbie Weinhardt

YEAR	TEAM	LVL	AGE	W	L	SV	G	GS	IP	H	HR	BB	SO	BB9	SO9	GB%	BABIP	WHIP	ERA	FIP	FRA	WARP
2011	SFD	AA	24	2	2	3	52	0	59¹	53	5	28	52	4.2	7.9	43%	.290	1.37	3.03	4.24	4.41	0.4
2012	SFD	AA	25	1	3	1	15	0	17¹	12	1	4	12	2.1	6.2	48%	.216	0.92	1.56	3.51	4.09	0.2
2012	MEM	AAA	25	2	2	0	27	0	30¹	25	3	12	27	3.6	8.0	42%	.272	1.22	2.08	4.36	4.58	0.3
2012	SLN	MLB	25	0	2	0	24	0	20	17	2	10	18	4.5	8.1	46%	.278	1.35	5.40	4.29	4.40	0.1
2013	MEM	AAA	26	7	2	2	49	0	69²	57	4	27	66	3.5	8.5	48%	.273	1.21	2.97	3.71	3.73	1.1
2013	SLN	MLB	26	1	0	0	13	0	12¹	8	0	5	8	3.6	5.8	39%	.222	1.05	2.19	2.94	3.19	0.2
2014	SLN	MLB	27	3	1	1	61	0	71	64	7	28	56	3.5	7.0	45%	.287	1.29	3.88	4.19	4.22	0.3

Why the whole league hatches evil plots against the St. Louis Cardinals, Exhibit A: This 27-year-old, 32nd-round college pick has thrown 268 minor-league innings with a 2.75 ERA and 249 strikeouts while sitting at 94-96 from the left side. In a short 2013 sample at the big-league level he didn't allow a single hit on his changeup or slider. While he's good enough to pitch in a big-league bullpen in 2014, the Cardinals could easily shop him to one of the many teams that don't already have more lefties than they currently need—a situation known as Why the whole league hatches evil plots against the St. Louis Cardinals, Exhibit B.

Jaime Garcia

Born: 7/8/1986 Age: 27
Bats: L Throws: L Height: 6' 2" Weight: 215
Breakout: 21% Improve: 56% Collapse: 23%
Attrition: 13% MLB: 94%

Comparables:
Paul Maholm, Ricky Nolasco, Matt Harrison

YEAR	TEAM	LVL	AGE	W	L	SV	G	GS	IP	H	HR	BB	SO	BB9	SO9	GB%	BABIP	WHIP	ERA	FIP	FRA	WARP
2011	SLN	MLB	24	13	7	0	32	32	194²	207	15	50	156	2.3	7.2	53%	.323	1.32	3.56	3.19	4.37	1.0
2012	SFD	AA	25	1	0	0	2	2	10¹	8	2	0	11	0.0	9.6	48%	.261	0.77	5.23	3.67	5.05	0.0
2012	SLN	MLB	25	7	7	0	20	20	121²	136	7	30	98	2.2	7.2	55%	.353	1.36	3.92	3.01	3.94	1.6
2013	SLN	MLB	26	5	2	0	9	9	55¹	57	6	15	43	2.4	7.0	63%	.316	1.30	3.58	3.69	4.82	0.2
2014	SLN	MLB	27	4	3	0	10	10	61²	58	5	15	50	2.3	7.3	55%	.310	1.20	3.52	3.38	3.83	0.7

It speaks to the depth of the Cardinals organization that they could lose their number two starter after just 55 innings and still make the World Series. Garcia has battled injuries throughout his career and, despite never seeming to be at 100 percent in 2013, still posted a league-average ERA and quality underlying skills before succumbing to shoulder surgery. Garcia is on track for spring training, but if yet another arm injury drags him down, well, that's why you develop organizational depth.

John Gast

Born: 2/16/1989 Age: 25
Bats: L Throws: L Height: 6' 1" Weight: 195
Breakout: 40% Improve: 60% Collapse: 20%
Attrition: 66% MLB: 54%

Comparables:
Kevin Hart, Kevin Mulvey, Dustin Moseley

YEAR	TEAM	LVL	AGE	W	L	SV	G	GS	IP	H	HR	BB	SO	BB9	SO9	GB%	BABIP	WHIP	ERA	FIP	FRA	WARP
2011	PMB	A+	22	5	4	0	13	12	82	85	7	28	59	3.1	6.5	49%	.294	1.38	3.95	4.38	7.14	-0.4
2011	SFD	AA	22	4	4	0	13	13	79¹	80	9	33	54	3.7	6.1	47%	.304	1.42	4.08	4.89	6.21	0.1
2012	SFD	AA	23	4	2	0	8	8	51¹	38	5	13	41	2.3	7.2	47%	.244	0.99	1.93	3.77	4.54	0.4
2012	MEM	AAA	23	9	5	0	20	20	109¹	124	10	42	86	3.5	7.1	47%	.339	1.52	5.10	4.49	5.20	1.1
2013	MEM	AAA	24	3	1	0	7	7	38²	28	0	13	35	3.0	8.1	54%	.289	1.06	1.16	3.00	2.92	0.9
2013	SLN	MLB	24	2	0	0	3	3	12¹	11	1	5	8	3.6	5.8	54%	.263	1.30	5.11	3.99	4.83	0.0
2014	SLN	MLB	25	3	4	0	11	11	59	59	6	21	41	3.3	6.2	47%	.301	1.36	4.38	4.32	4.76	0.0

Gast has never been a major prospect for the Cardinals—a reflection of their organizational depth as much as a mark against him—but he gets better every year and appears headed for a serviceable career as a back-of-the-rotation innings eater (surname be darned). The young lefty struggled with his first exposures to both Double- and Triple-A, but in his second tour of each posted a sub-2 ERA. Gast keeps the ball down, doesn't walk too many batters and misses some bats. None of his three pitches stands out, but the sum of his parts says major-league starter, perhaps as soon as 2014.

Marco Gonzales

Born: 2/16/1992 Age: 22
Bats: L Throws: L Height: 6' 0" Weight: 185
Breakout: 54% Improve: 83% Collapse: 17%
Attrition: 71% MLB: 6%

Comparables:
Zach Phillips, Ubaldo Jimenez, Kyle Weiland

YEAR	TEAM	LVL	AGE	W	L	SV	G	GS	IP	H	HR	BB	SO	BB9	SO9	GB%	BABIP	WHIP	ERA	FIP	FRA	WARP
2013	PMB	A+	21	0	0	0	4	4	16²	10	1	5	13	2.7	7.0	33%	.214	0.90	1.62	3.36	4.48	0.1
2014	SLN	MLB	22	2	3	0	12	9	36	37	4	16	24	4.0	6.1	44%	.308	1.48	4.87	4.78	5.30	-0.1

Gonzales pulled first-round status with polish and quality secondary stuff, including an excellent changeup. St. Louis is exactly the organization that can target this kind of high floor/low upside pick in the first round given the amount of impact talent flooding their system elsewhere. Don't take that as any sort of pejorative against Gonzales, though. He could follow the path of Michael Wacha and find himself in the majors as quickly as mid-2014. He would make for an interesting change-of-pace arm as a finesse lefty in a rotation of power righties.

Tyrell Jenkins

Born: 7/20/1992 Age: 21
Bats: R Throws: R Height: 6' 4" Weight: 204
Breakout: 0% Improve: 0% Collapse: 0%
Attrition: 0% MLB: 0%

Comparables:
Joel Carreno, Pedro Beato, Brett Marshall

YEAR	TEAM	LVL	AGE	W	L	SV	G	GS	IP	H	HR	BB	SO	BB9	SO9	GB%	BABIP	WHIP	ERA	FIP	FRA	WARP
2012	QUD	A	19	4	4	0	19	19	82¹	84	5	36	80	3.9	8.7	56%	.336	1.46	5.14	3.62	4.73	0.7
2013	PEO	A	20	4	4	0	10	10	49¹	51	4	24	34	4.4	6.2	58%	.303	1.52	4.74	4.53	5.12	0.2
2013	PMB	A+	20	0	0	0	3	3	10	13	0	1	6	0.9	5.4	58%	.361	1.40	4.50	2.34	3.71	0.2
2014	SLN	MLB	21	3	5	0	12	12	56¹	63	7	28	32	4.4	5.1	51%	.315	1.61	5.61	5.36	6.10	-0.7

An injury shut Jenkins down in July and a few weeks later he was in for shoulder surgery that put his target return somewhere around spring training. Armed with an electric mid-90s heater that he struggles to command, Jenkins is one of the golden roses of the St. Louis farm, but he has been coming along at a deliberate pace. The injury slowed that pace even further, but the Cardinals are one of the few organizations that can afford to deal with the gradual emergence of a high-potential arm. Jenkins was always seen as a risky prospect, and this setback both illustrates and heightens that risk. A future in the bullpen is a legitimate possibility. While he could still grow strong, temper your expectations for 2014.

Rob Kaminsky
Born: 9/2/1994 Age: 19
Bats: R Throws: L Height: 5' 11" Weight: 191
Breakout: 0% Improve: 0% Collapse: 0%
Attrition: 0% MLB: 0%

Comparables:
Alex Torres, Zach Braddock, Jon Niese

YEAR	TEAM	LVL	AGE	W	L	SV	G	GS	IP	H	HR	BB	SO	BB9	SO9	GB%	BABIP	WHIP	ERA	FIP	FRA	WARP
2014	SLN	MLB	19	1	3	0	12	7	34	38	4	21	19	5.5	5.0	46%	.315	1.73	6.04	5.74	6.57	-0.6

With Marco Gonzales—a nearly completed product—in their back pocket from the first round, the Cardinals were able to absorb some extra risk in the supplemental round and select Kaminsky in the hopes of convincing him to eschew his North Carolina commitment. The undersized lefty typically pumps his heater in at 89 to 92 mph, but has been clocked at 95. His meal ticket is an excellent curve with plus-plus potential, but he also shows real promise with the changeup, a major plus and a relatively rarity for a high school pick. Projections vary on Kaminsky's ultimate ceiling, but the consensus is a future in the rotation.

Joe Kelly
Born: 6/9/1988 Age: 26
Bats: R Throws: R Height: 6' 1" Weight: 175
Breakout: 44% Improve: 73% Collapse: 14%
Attrition: 22% MLB: 84%

Comparables:
Aaron Laffey, Ivan Nova, Wade Davis

YEAR	TEAM	LVL	AGE	W	L	SV	G	GS	IP	H	HR	BB	SO	BB9	SO9	GB%	BABIP	WHIP	ERA	FIP	FRA	WARP
2011	PMB	A+	23	5	2	0	12	11	72²	56	1	34	62	4.2	7.7	52%	.258	1.24	2.60	3.59	4.91	0.1
2011	SFD	AA	23	6	4	0	11	11	59¹	70	7	25	51	3.8	7.7	59%	.297	1.60	5.01	4.71	5.16	0.3
2012	MEM	AAA	24	2	5	0	12	12	72¹	75	2	21	45	2.6	5.6	56%	.329	1.33	2.86	3.82	4.34	1.0
2012	SLN	MLB	24	5	7	0	24	16	107	112	10	36	75	3.0	6.3	52%	.320	1.38	3.53	4.04	4.99	0.2
2013	SLN	MLB	25	10	5	0	37	15	124	124	10	44	79	3.2	5.7	51%	.294	1.35	2.69	3.98	4.25	0.7
2014	SLN	MLB	26	6	6	0	28	17	114²	115	10	40	75	3.1	5.9	53%	.306	1.36	4.26	4.23	4.63	0.2

Box-score scouting will lead you astray in your analysis of Kelly—it's easy to conclude from his stat line that he's a soft-tossing groundballer capable of eating innings but unable to dominate a lineup with raw stuff. Yet the bespectacled righty sits around 95 to 97 mph with his sinker and has devastating movement on all of his offerings. So what's with the meager strikeout rates? Commanding the aforementioned movement has been part of the problem (which explains his elevated walk rate as well). Kelly also doesn't earn enough whiffs with his heater. He used his fastball in 53 percent of two-strike counts, but netted a strikeout just 33 percent of time. This was below the league average, with the highest rates in the league checking in over 50 percent. Kelly isn't a finished product, but the foundation laid thus far is encouraging. He is already the best Joe Kelly to ever play the game (by bWAR), though he's got a *long* way to go to catch Hall of Famer Joe Kelley.

Lance Lynn
Born: 5/12/1987 Age: 27
Bats: R Throws: R Height: 6' 5" Weight: 240
Breakout: 25% Improve: 69% Collapse: 20%
Attrition: 16% MLB: 88%

Comparables:
Bud Norris, Edinson Volquez, Jake Arrieta

YEAR	TEAM	LVL	AGE	W	L	SV	G	GS	IP	H	HR	BB	SO	BB9	SO9	GB%	BABIP	WHIP	ERA	FIP	FRA	WARP
2011	MEM	AAA	24	7	3	0	12	12	75	79	2	25	64	3.0	7.7	38%	.347	1.39	3.84	3.50	3.53	0.7
2011	SLN	MLB	24	1	1	1	18	2	34²	25	3	11	40	2.9	10.4	59%	.269	1.04	3.12	2.85	3.66	0.3
2012	SLN	MLB	25	18	7	0	35	29	176	168	16	64	180	3.3	9.2	45%	.328	1.32	3.78	3.53	3.71	3.0
2013	SLN	MLB	26	15	10	0	33	33	201²	189	14	76	198	3.4	8.8	44%	.319	1.31	3.97	3.25	3.48	3.5
2014	SLN	MLB	27	10	9	0	40	26	170¹	154	15	59	157	3.1	8.3	45%	.309	1.25	3.69	3.67	4.02	1.4

Lynn's got the strangest case of Seasonal Affective Disorder: After showing up from the winter in chipper spirits and plowing through April and May, he gets all sorts of down in the summer months—a 2.73 ERA in the season's first two months for his career, 4.83 in the hot ones. Every player's got a weird split or two on his page, and this would ordinarily be chalked up to random chance but for concerns about Lynn's stamina. He lost 40 pounds before the 2013 season in an effort to get into better shape—"it's a lifestyle change," he said—but the problems continued. There are as many critics who will blame struggles on weight lost as on weight gained, but Lynn can quiet pundits of all types with a solid, consistent summer.

Tyler Lyons
Born: 2/21/1988 Age: 26
Bats: B Throws: L Height: 6' 4" Weight: 200
Breakout: 26% Improve: 53% Collapse: 29%
Attrition: 54% MLB: 72%

Comparables:
David Phelps, Josh Tomlin, Virgil Vasquez

YEAR	TEAM	LVL	AGE	W	L	SV	G	GS	IP	H	HR	BB	SO	BB9	SO9	GB%	BABIP	WHIP	ERA	FIP	FRA	WARP
2011	PMB	A+	23	9	4	1	33	12	94	93	8	29	79	2.8	7.6	42%	.344	1.30	4.50	3.87	6.38	-0.2
2012	SFD	AA	24	5	4	0	12	12	64¹	70	6	19	54	2.7	7.6	57%	.332	1.38	3.92	3.75	4.47	0.7
2012	MEM	AAA	24	4	9	0	15	15	88¹	87	9	18	89	1.8	9.1	39%	.318	1.19	4.28	3.65	3.48	2.3
2013	MEM	AAA	25	7	2	0	17	16	100¹	85	6	19	86	1.7	7.7	51%	.286	1.04	3.32	3.38	4.22	1.2
2013	SLN	MLB	25	2	4	0	12	8	53	49	5	16	43	2.7	7.3	51%	.291	1.23	4.75	3.70	4.37	0.2
2014	SLN	MLB	26	7	7	0	27	21	132¹	127	14	30	103	2.0	7.0	46%	.304	1.18	3.75	3.81	4.08	1.0

You've heard this one before: Lyons is a big league-ready lefty, and almost unusable at this point because of the Cardinals' surplus of pitchers. Of course, tell the 2013 Dodgers about having too much pitching. It's a myth: No team can ever have too much, and while Lyons will struggle to crack the Opening Day rotation the chances will come. His biggest issue in 53 major-league innings has been finding an effective out pitch for righties, as they beat both his fastball and changeup around the yard. His slider was more effective, but that's no long-term strategy for a left-handed starter.

Seth Maness
Born: 10/14/1988 Age: 25
Bats: R Throws: R Height: 6' 0" Weight: 190
Breakout: 34% Improve: 53% Collapse: 21%
Attrition: 44% MLB: 67%

Comparables:
Trevor Bell, Zach McAllister, Daniel Barone

YEAR	TEAM	LVL	AGE	W	L	SV	G	GS	IP	H	HR	BB	SO	BB9	SO9	GB%	BABIP	WHIP	ERA	FIP	FRA	WARP
2011	BAT	A-	22	0	1	0	10	7	39²	27	0	3	31	0.7	7.0	73%	.244	0.76	0.91	2.10	3.25	0.6
2012	PMB	A+	23	3	1	0	7	7	46	45	5	1	29	0.2	5.7	58%	.282	1.00	2.15	3.61	5.20	0.0
2012	SFD	AA	23	11	3	0	20	20	123²	122	13	9	83	0.7	6.0	54%	.282	1.06	3.27	3.67	4.80	0.8
2013	MEM	AAA	24	2	2	0	4	4	25	34	2	3	18	1.1	6.5	40%	.376	1.48	4.32	3.65	4.39	0.2
2013	SLN	MLB	24	5	2	1	66	0	62	65	4	13	35	1.9	5.1	70%	.314	1.26	2.32	3.41	4.10	0.4
2014	SLN	MLB	25	5	3	1	57	7	89²	94	10	16	50	1.6	5.0	54%	.302	1.22	4.04	4.19	4.39	0.3

It takes a 95 mph fastball to unlock the bullpen gate at Busch Stadium, but Maness—who throws "only" 91 to 93—apparently applied for an exemption. What he lacks in heat he makes up for with sink. Only Brad Ziegler recorded a higher groundball rate, and only Jim Johnson recorded more double plays in relief. Put it this way: Adam Wainwright led baseball in double plays induced, but Maness recorded twice as many on a per-inning basis. In the three years since he was drafted, he has walked a total of 24 batters unintentionally, so there's definitely cult-favorite potential here.

Carlos Martinez
Born: 9/21/1991 Age: 22
Bats: R Throws: R Height: 6' 0" Weight: 185
Breakout: 41% Improve: 60% Collapse: 12%
Attrition: 39% MLB: 54%

Comparables:
Chris Tillman, Sean Gallagher, Jenrry Mejia

YEAR	TEAM	LVL	AGE	W	L	SV	G	GS	IP	H	HR	BB	SO	BB9	SO9	GB%	BABIP	WHIP	ERA	FIP	FRA	WARP
2011	QUD	A	19	3	2	0	8	8	38²	27	1	14	50	3.3	11.6	57%	.148	1.06	2.33	2.51	4.79	0.1
2011	PMB	A+	19	3	3	0	10	10	46	49	2	30	48	5.9	9.4	39%	.352	1.72	5.28	4.21	5.39	0.0
2012	PMB	A+	20	2	2	0	7	7	33	29	0	10	34	2.7	9.3	51%	.319	1.18	3.00	2.79	3.55	0.6
2012	SFD	AA	20	4	3	0	15	14	71¹	62	6	22	58	2.8	7.3	62%	.278	1.18	2.90	3.92	4.46	0.8
2013	SFD	AA	21	1	0	0	3	3	11²	11	1	1	9	0.8	6.9	57%	.278	1.03	2.31	3.14	3.52	0.3
2013	MEM	AAA	21	5	3	0	13	13	68	54	3	27	63	3.6	8.3	56%	.267	1.19	2.51	3.75	4.03	0.9
2013	SLN	MLB	21	2	1	1	21	1	28¹	31	1	9	24	2.9	7.6	55%	.357	1.41	5.08	3.06	4.11	0.2
2014	SLN	MLB	22	4	4	0	25	13	94²	87	8	33	75	3.1	7.1	52%	.299	1.27	3.92	3.99	4.26	0.6

Of all the rookie arms for the Cardinals in 2013, Martinez may well end up the best of the bunch. Yes, that group includes Shelby Miller, Trevor Rosenthal and Michael Wacha and yes, Martinez did possess the fourth-worst ERA of the dozen Cardinals rookie hurlers, but the 22-year-old has overwhelming raw stuff. The biggest hurdle right now is one that plagues many young arms: a reliable third pitch. He and Miller both used their changeup just 6 percent of the time in 2013, but Martinez's version was dominant in the scant sample and, as a full-time reliever, the need for the pitch was lower. (It is worth noting that Miller made it through 173 excellent innings as a starter without a reliable change.) His stature and ferocious delivery still breed skeptics about his eventual role, but the Cardinals will give Martinez every shot to succeed as a starter given his immense ceiling.

Shelby Miller
Born: 10/10/1990 Age: 23
Bats: R Throws: R Height: 6' 3" Weight: 215
Breakout: 31% Improve: 74% Collapse: 13%
Attrition: 32% MLB: 81%

Comparables:
Johnny Cueto, Matt Garza, Brian Matusz

YEAR	TEAM	LVL	AGE	W	L	SV	G	GS	IP	H	HR	BB	SO	BB9	SO9	GB%	BABIP	WHIP	ERA	FIP	FRA	WARP
2011	PMB	A+	20	2	3	0	9	9	53	40	2	20	81	3.4	13.8	34%	.286	1.13	2.89	2.01	3.39	0.3
2011	SFD	AA	20	9	3	0	16	16	86²	72	2	33	89	3.4	9.2	43%	.283	1.21	2.70	2.90	3.06	1.3
2012	MEM	AAA	21	11	10	0	27	27	136²	138	24	50	160	3.3	10.5	34%	.323	1.38	4.74	4.95	4.72	2.0
2012	SLN	MLB	21	1	0	0	6	1	13²	9	0	4	16	2.6	10.5	41%	.281	0.95	1.32	1.89	2.41	0.4
2013	SLN	MLB	22	15	9	0	31	31	173¹	152	20	57	169	3.0	8.8	39%	.288	1.21	3.06	3.64	3.88	2.1
2014	SLN	MLB	23	9	9	0	28	28	144¹	129	17	45	141	2.8	8.8	39%	.301	1.20	3.63	3.84	3.95	1.6

Whether it was a conscious effort to protect his arm or the rigors of a full major-league season setting in, Miller saw the seventh inning in just three starts after June 1st, spanning 20 outings in all. He still managed a perfectly capable 3.89 ERA in those 104 innings, but it was a far cry from the 1.89 ERA through his first 69 innings. His biggest action item remains a reliable way to counter lefties. After holding them to a .600 OPS in those first 11 starts, he was pummeled for an .862 mark in the final 20. His changeup actually progressed some as the season wore on, but his fastball and curveball degraded against southpaws and the change wasn't reliable enough to use as an out pitch, leaving him without a paddle and up some sort of foul creek. While most teams would be figuring out ways to sign him to a pre-arb deal, the Cardinals have the luxury of listening to offers—though trading him isn't a priority.

Jason Motte

Born: 6/22/1982 Age: 32
Bats: R Throws: R Height: 6' 0" Weight: 205
Breakout: 29% Improve: 48% Collapse: 31%
Attrition: 4% MLB: 96%

Comparables:
Rafael Betancourt, J.J. Putz, Roberto Hernandez

YEAR	TEAM	LVL	AGE	W	L	SV	G	GS	IP	H	HR	BB	SO	BB9	SO9	GB%	BABIP	WHIP	ERA	FIP	FRA	WARP
2011	SLN	MLB	29	5	2	9	78	0	68	49	2	16	63	2.1	8.3	45%	.260	0.96	2.25	2.45	3.13	0.9
2012	SLN	MLB	30	4	5	42	67	0	72	49	9	17	86	2.1	10.8	41%	.242	0.92	2.75	3.16	3.74	0.7
2014	SLN	MLB	32	2	1	28	41	0	39²	32	4	10	41	2.4	9.3	41%	.287	1.06	2.86	3.25	3.10	0.7

Early indications are that Motte should be ready no later than May, though it seems unlikely that he will return to the closer's role he left when surrendering to Tommy John surgery early last year. He does have the requisite high-90s fastball, so the Cardinal Bullpen Council of Elders has agreed to let him come back to the team. Baseball does have a way of turning set-up men into closers at the drop of a hat, especially when those set-up men are former closers. As a former catcher who got a late start on his big-league career, Motte has to use 2014 to impress somebody enough to give him a multi-year deal starting in 2015. He's probably too old to get multiple bites at that apple.

Zachary Petrick

Born: 7/29/1989 Age: 24
Bats: R Throws: R Height: 6' 3" Weight: 195
Breakout: 48% Improve: 65% Collapse: 21%
Attrition: 59% MLB: 47%

Comparables:
Zach Stewart, Josh Lindblom, A.J. Griffin

YEAR	TEAM	LVL	AGE	W	L	SV	G	GS	IP	H	HR	BB	SO	BB9	SO9	GB%	BABIP	WHIP	ERA	FIP	FRA	WARP
2013	PEO	A	23	1	0	7	16	0	32²	24	1	8	46	2.2	12.7	57%	.307	0.98	0.83	1.84	2.36	1.2
2013	PMB	A+	23	3	0	1	9	4	33¹	21	0	4	32	1.1	8.6	52%	.241	0.75	0.27	1.68	2.71	0.7
2013	SFD	AA	23	3	3	0	9	9	47¹	44	3	15	44	2.9	8.4	44%	.306	1.25	3.99	3.10	4.35	0.7
2014	SLN	MLB	24	4	4	1	26	11	87¹	82	8	31	71	3.2	7.4	47%	.304	1.29	3.92	3.94	4.27	0.5

Of *course* St. Louis has an undrafted free agent who pitched to a sub-2.00 ERA while striking out more than a batter per inning. That's so Cardinals. Perhaps Petrick can join 21st-rounder Trevor Rosenthal and 41st-rounder—a round that no longer exists—Kevin Siegrist to form the most undervalued bullpen ever. The stumbling block is that due to the addition of a couple ticks on his fastball (to the 92 mph range) and refinement of his changeup, he may surpass Rosenthal and Siegrist and wind up in the rotation. Petrick's final 13 appearances of 2013 came as a starter; in that role, he posted a 2.80 ERA with a 3.6 K/BB ratio in 71 innings split between High-A and Double-A. Draft shmaft.

Trevor Rosenthal

Born: 5/29/1990 Age: 24
Bats: R Throws: R Height: 6' 2" Weight: 220
Breakout: 34% Improve: 67% Collapse: 13%
Attrition: 20% MLB: 85%

Comparables:
Kris Medlen, Neftali Feliz, Dana Eveland

YEAR	TEAM	LVL	AGE	W	L	SV	G	GS	IP	H	HR	BB	SO	BB9	SO9	GB%	BABIP	WHIP	ERA	FIP	FRA	WARP
2011	QUD	A	21	7	7	0	22	22	120¹	111	7	39	133	2.9	9.9	57%	.318	1.25	4.11	3.20	5.51	-0.2
2012	SFD	AA	22	8	6	0	17	17	94	67	6	37	83	3.5	7.9	46%	.244	1.11	2.78	3.59	4.53	0.9
2012	MEM	AAA	22	0	0	0	3	3	15	11	1	5	21	3.0	12.6	59%	.323	1.07	4.20	3.13	3.27	0.5
2012	SLN	MLB	22	0	2	0	19	0	22²	14	2	7	25	2.8	9.9	55%	.222	0.93	2.78	3.14	2.96	0.4
2013	SLN	MLB	23	2	4	3	74	0	75¹	63	4	20	108	2.4	12.9	46%	.341	1.10	2.63	1.88	1.80	2.4
2014	SLN	MLB	24	4	3	1	42	8	77²	63	6	26	81	3.1	9.4	49%	.298	1.15	3.15	3.25	3.42	1.3

An injury to Jason Motte started a chain reaction that led to the failed Mitchell Boggs experiment, a host of trade rumors for a proven closer and eventually the Edward Mujica success story. But it was Rosenthal who ultimately claimed the ninth in October, and watching St. Louis shorten ballgames against playoff opponents you'd have never guessed there was any uncertainty. Many clamored for Rosenthal to get a shot back in April, but he got comfortable as an elite set-up man, striking out 30 and walking just two in one 20-inning scoreless stretch before the All-Star break. Now comes the inevitable controversy that follows an elite prospect making his name in relief: Motte is coming back, so Rosenthal could be closing games, starting games or pitching somewhere in between by this time next year. The key for St. Louis will be decisiveness, lest they end up with a pitcher who is hurt (like Neftali Feliz), horrible (Joba Chamberlain) or unhappy (as Aroldis Chapman nearly was).

Kevin Siegrist

Born: 7/20/1989 Age: 24
Bats: L Throws: L Height: 6' 5" Weight: 215
Breakout: 45% Improve: 74% Collapse: 23%
Attrition: 46% MLB: 69%

Comparables:
Jordan Walden, Scott Elbert, Tyson Ross

YEAR	TEAM	LVL	AGE	W	L	SV	G	GS	IP	H	HR	BB	SO	BB9	SO9	GB%	BABIP	WHIP	ERA	FIP	FRA	WARP
2011	QUD	A	21	8	1	0	9	8	54²	38	1	15	34	2.5	5.6	53%	.236	0.97	1.15	3.18	3.80	0.2
2011	PMB	A+	21	0	3	0	11	11	52²	44	3	30	45	5.1	7.7	20%	.440	1.41	3.42	4.24	4.31	0.1
2012	PMB	A+	22	6	0	0	10	10	55¹	33	3	22	41	3.6	6.7	41%	.200	0.99	2.28	4.13	4.96	0.2
2012	SFD	AA	22	1	2	0	8	5	32¹	26	4	9	27	2.5	7.5	54%	.241	1.08	3.62	4.52	5.82	-0.1
2013	SFD	AA	23	1	1	1	13	0	20	8	2	7	35	3.2	15.8	42%	.207	0.75	2.25	2.06	2.77	0.5
2013	SLN	MLB	23	3	1	0	45	0	39²	17	1	18	50	4.1	11.3	41%	.195	0.88	0.45	2.26	2.24	0.9
2014	SLN	MLB	24	3	3	0	26	7	59¹	50	6	25	53	3.8	8.1	43%	.285	1.26	3.69	4.17	4.01	0.5

It's almost unfair, we tell you. Siegrist is a 41st-round community college pick from 2008, of whom it was said last year that developing into a LOOGY would be an upset. So, as a rookie, he puts up the best ERA+ since the Deadball Era and holds opponents to a .171 TAv, lowest in the National League. Perhaps most impressive is that he did it with essentially one pitch—a blistering 96 mph fastball that he threw 84 percent of the time. Pitching is easy.

Michael Wacha

Born: **7/1/1991** Age: **22**
Bats: **R** Throws: **R** Height: **6' 6"** Weight: **210**
Breakout: **45%** Improve: **69%** Collapse: **15%**
Attrition: **22%** MLB: **74%**

Comparables:
Brandon McCarthy, Brett Anderson, Chad Billingsley

YEAR	TEAM	LVL	AGE	W	L	SV	G	GS	IP	H	HR	BB	SO	BB9	SO9	GB%	BABIP	WHIP	ERA	FIP	FRA	WARP
2013	MEM	AAA	21	5	3	0	15	15	85	65	9	19	73	2.0	7.7	37%	.246	0.99	2.65	3.90	3.69	1.5
2013	SLN	MLB	21	4	1	0	15	9	64²	52	5	19	65	2.6	9.0	45%	.272	1.10	2.78	2.90	3.55	1.0
2014	SLN	MLB	22	6	5	1	25	17	107²	90	10	27	101	2.3	8.5	43%	.287	1.09	2.94	3.31	3.19	2.1

Wacha was a luxury pick for the Cardinals in 2012, one of two compensation picks for losing Albert Pujols. They chose the high floor to ensure they got something back for the departed superstar, and his quick ascendence wasn't all that surprising: His polish and command were evident at Texas A&M, as well as in his 21 innings across three levels the summer after he was drafted. That he dominated for 65 innings in the regular season last year and became a playoff ace 15 months after he was popped—well, that you could call a surprise. The bucket of cold water is that it's still just 95 innings against big leaguers, he lacks a dependable third pitch and a second trip through the league might take more tricks than he's currently got. His leg up is that it's the breaking ball that's missing, and his advanced (and dominant) changeup will prevent platoon abuse.

Adam Wainwright

Born: **8/30/1981** Age: **32**
Bats: **R** Throws: **R** Height: **6' 7"** Weight: **235**
Breakout: **13%** Improve: **37%** Collapse: **41%**
Attrition: **13%** MLB: **89%**

Comparables:
Chris Carpenter, CC Sabathia, Josh Beckett

YEAR	TEAM	LVL	AGE	W	L	SV	G	GS	IP	H	HR	BB	SO	BB9	SO9	GB%	BABIP	WHIP	ERA	FIP	FRA	WARP
2012	SLN	MLB	30	14	13	0	32	32	198²	196	15	52	184	2.4	8.3	51%	.315	1.25	3.94	3.14	3.96	2.5
2013	SLN	MLB	31	19	9	0	34	34	241²	223	15	35	219	1.3	8.2	49%	.310	1.07	2.94	2.52	3.30	4.6
2014	SLN	MLB	32	13	9	0	30	30	201¹	176	15	41	180	1.8	8.1	50%	.302	1.08	2.94	3.02	3.19	3.7

So much for ramping up slowly in the aftermath of Tommy John surgery. Wainwright endured a full load in 2012, his first year after the procedure, and was pushed to another level in 2013 with career highs (and MLB bests) in innings and starts. He is actually improving with age, too. Wainwright's control was unreal last year, beginning with walking just six batters through his first 11 starts. Tim Lincecum walked seven batters in his first five innings of the season. Wainwright is probably the best bet among the 30-plus set to win a Cy Young Award. He's been the bridesmaid plenty, with three top-three showings in the last five years.

Jake Westbrook

Born: **9/29/1977** Age: **36**
Bats: **R** Throws: **R** Height: **6' 3"** Weight: **210**
Breakout: **10%** Improve: **44%** Collapse: **31%**
Attrition: **13%** MLB: **77%**

Comparables:
Jeff Suppan, Steve Rogers, Tommy John

YEAR	TEAM	LVL	AGE	W	L	SV	G	GS	IP	H	HR	BB	SO	BB9	SO9	GB%	BABIP	WHIP	ERA	FIP	FRA	WARP
2011	SLN	MLB	33	12	9	0	33	33	183¹	208	16	73	104	3.6	5.1	59%	.322	1.53	4.66	4.22	4.51	1.0
2012	SLN	MLB	34	13	11	0	28	28	174²	191	12	52	106	2.7	5.5	58%	.316	1.39	3.97	3.85	5.02	-0.1
2013	SLN	MLB	35	7	8	0	21	19	116²	132	7	50	44	3.9	3.4	57%	.315	1.56	4.63	4.59	5.54	-0.9
2014	SLN	MLB	36	7	8	0	20	20	119	126	11	38	68	2.9	5.1	56%	.311	1.38	4.57	4.38	4.97	-0.3

The sun is rapidly setting on Westbrook's career. While he posted a 1.78 ERA through his first eight starts of 2013, that figure was the miragest mirage that ever miraged, coming complete as it did with more walks than strikeouts in that span. It's nearly impossible to thrive without a K/BB ratio over two; when you've got more walks than strikeouts, you start asking about survival. Thriving is out of the question. Thus, things came crashing down predictably and quickly for Westbrook as he posted a 6.85 ERA over the rest of the season. Humans have a surprising capacity to reinvent themselves, but unless Westbrook learns the knuckleball or becomes a submariner (or Namor the Sub-Mariner, better yet), his days of being a decent, cheap-ish asset are over.

LINEOUTS

HITTERS

PLAYER	TEAM	LVL	AGE	PA	R	2B	3B	HR	RBI	BB	SO	SB-CS	AVG/OBP/SLG	TAv	BABIP	BRR	FRAA	WARP
RF A. Chambers	MEM	AAA	26	393	51	13	4	8	43	39	75	16-2	.252/.338/.387	.283	.297	-0.6	RF(58): 5.7, CF(38): 4.1	3.0
	SLN	MLB	26	29	5	1	0	0	1	3	11	0-1	.154/.241/.192	.185	.267	0.9	LF(11): -0.2, RF(6): -0.0	-0.1
3B J. Curtis	MEM	AAA	25	436	45	17	1	5	49	52	53	10-2	.257/.355/.349	.272	.284	-0.4	3B(104): -5.2, 2B(2): 0.3	1.6
	SLN	MLB	25	5	0	0	0	0	0	1	1	0-0	.000/.400/.000	.233	.000	-0.1	LF(1): -0.0	0.0
LF A. Garcia	PMB	A+	21	386	37	16	1	13	45	26	95	6-2	.217/.286/.383	.238	.257	0.1	LF(81): 10.4	1.0
SS G. Garcia	MEM	AAA	23	424	50	23	4	3	35	49	70	14-2	.271/.377/.384	.290	.331	2.4	SS(73): -6.7, 2B(21): -1.9	2.5
C R. Johnson	MEM	AAA	30	221	27	8	1	7	32	24	42	0-2	.236/.317/.395	.277	.264	-2.4	C(57): 0.1	1.2
	SLN	MLB	30	38	2	1	1	0	2	3	6	0-0	.171/.237/.257	.209	.207	-0.5	C(15): 0.0	-0.1
LF M. O'Neill	SFD	AA	25	434	66	13	2	2	35	71	26	18-4	.320/.431/.384	.291	.339	2.1	LF(87): -2.5	2.5
	MEM	AAA	25	133	16	3	0	0	3	20	11	1-0	.295/.402/.321	.271	.327	0.2	LF(26): 0.1, CF(6): -0.9	0.3
C A. Perez	SFD	AA	24	222	16	12	0	6	26	3	39	0-1	.209/.234/.349	.188	.229	-1.3	C(56): -0.2	-0.7
	MEM	AAA	24	93	7	3	0	0	7	2	10	0-0	.211/.228/.244	.172	.238	0.5	C(25): 0.3	-0.4
	SLN	MLB	24	1	0	0	0	0	0	0	1	0-0	.000/.000/.000	.001	—	0	C(1): -0.0	0.0
CF T. Pham	SFD	AA	25	188	27	6	6	6	28	20	42	6-3	.301/.388/.521	.303	.371	0	CF(36): 2.8, RF(1): -0.0	1.8
	MEM	AAA	25	113	6	6	1	1	13	7	25	2-1	.264/.310/.368	.261	.338	0.3	CF(28): 2.8, LF(2): 0.0	0.5
CF J. Ramsey	PMB	A+	23	77	17	5	2	1	7	12	12	1-0	.361/.481/.557	.396	.429	0.4	CF(18): 0.7	1.5
	SFD	AA	23	416	61	11	2	15	44	53	108	8-4	.251/.356/.424	.273	.316	3	CF(76): -4.3, RF(12): -0.9	1.6
RF S. Robinson	SLN	MLB	28	171	22	2	1	2	16	23	17	5-1	.250/.345/.319	.260	.264	0.3	RF(34): 2.6, CF(27): 1.2	0.6
CF S. Rodriguez	PMB	A+	23	150	19	9	0	1	14	13	21	3-1	.293/.360/.383	.301	.336	0.3	CF(32): -2.7	0.8
	SFD	AA	23	275	25	12	2	6	36	14	62	8-2	.254/.309/.391	.257	.311	0	2B(42): -0.2, LF(23): 3.2	0.5
2B B. Valera	PEO	A	20	562	71	18	6	0	48	40	30	13-7	.309/.358/.367	.269	.326	-0.7	2B(46): 0.9, LF(41): -2.0	2.2
1B T. Wigginton	SLN	MLB	35	63	9	2	0	0	3	5	19	0-1	.158/.238/.193	.156	.237	-0.3	1B(7): -0.4, LF(6): -0.1	-0.6
2B J. Wilson	PEO	A	22	409	63	24	1	15	72	40	54	6-5	.264/.350/.468	.303	.268	-2.2	2B(65): 0.1, LF(1): -0.0	2.6
	PMB	A+	22	137	12	4	0	3	10	17	20	0-1	.179/.294/.291	.224	.191	1.2	2B(31): 4.6	0.7

Adron Chambers' left-handedness, exceptional defense and impressive speed have earned him cups of coffee the last three years. He could be eyeing a fourth if the Cardinals don't remedy their bench issues. ⊘ While **Jermaine Curtis** has seen his power evaporate over the last three years, his approach and contact ability have led to just 20 more strikeouts than walks over 2,000-plus professional plate appearances. ⊘ **Anthony Garcia**'s June efforts (seven homers, 1.225 OPS) saved him from a completely disastrous season. The power is evident, but little else has developed thus far. ⊘ **Greg Garcia** has the makings of a utility infielder with a good approach against righties that includes a nearly even strikeout-to-walk ratio in 985 plate appearances against them. ⊘ **Rob Johnson** can't hit, but he can catch, so hiccups in the world economy don't concern him. ⊘ **Mike O'Neill**, a 31st rounder in 2010, has been an excellent table-setter throughout his professional career (.435 on-base percentage) but he lacks anything close to the desired power for a left fielder. ⊘ **Audry Perez** has the profile of a 35-year-old backup catcher after a .551 OPS across two levels in 2013, though being a decade younger means there is at least some hope for improvement. ⊘ A series of fits and starts has left **Thomas Pham** with just 595 games played in eight seasons, but he's done his best work at the upper levels with an .886 OPS in 135 games at Double-A. With health, he could be a late-bloomer. ⊘ The best tool in **James Ramsey**'s kit is his 80-grade makeup, which helps explain why the 2012 first-rounder does not crack many top 10 lists (though the insanely deep system Cardinals system also contributes). ⊘ **Shane Robinson** is a useful 25th man, running around catching things and sliding places and chewing gum. ⊘ **Starlin Rodriguez** is hardly devoid of talent, but he's progressing slowly and doesn't have the loud tools that make him worth the wait. ⊘ In a thinner system, someone like **Breyvic Valera** would land in the back end of a top 20 list because of his solid hit tool and positional flexibility, but in the deep waters of St. Louis, he's overlooked and might end up an appealing second piece of a trade. ⊘ **Ty Wigginton** was so bad in 2013 that he couldn't secure a spot on the Cardinals' bench, easily the worst unit of their otherwise excellent team. He now has five straight years of below average production and with no discernible defensive value to carry his weakened bat, the end is nigh for the 36-year-old. ⊘ **Jacob Wilson** could be the latest mid-to-late-round college pick to blossom from organizational depth to legitimate major leaguer. He struggled with a late-season promotion to High-A, but the 1.2 strikeout-to-walk ratio there shows that he was not completely overmatched.

PITCHERS

PLAYER	TEAM	LVL	AGE	W	L	SV	IP	H	HR	BB	SO	BB9	SO9	GB%	BABIP	WHIP	ERA	FIP	FRA	WARP
S. Blair	SFD	AA	24	3	9	0	129²	149	18	48	117	3.3	8.1	40%	.347	1.52	5.07	4.38	4.59	1.3
K. Butler	SFD	AA	24	0	0	7	13²	8	1	2	21	1.3	13.8	54%	.259	0.73	0.66	1.37	2.19	0.5
	MEM	AAA	24	3	2	2	27¹	21	3	9	28	3.0	9.2	38%	.257	1.10	3.62	3.94	3.95	0.3
	SLN	MLB	24	0	0	0	20	13	0	11	16	4.9	7.2	27%	.232	1.20	4.05	3.22	3.64	0.2
E. Fornataro	MEM	AAA	25	1	4	1	55¹	65	5	23	39	3.7	6.3	59%	.339	1.59	6.02	5.02	4.99	-0.3
V. Marte	MEM	AAA	32	2	3	11	54²	62	2	27	55	4.4	9.1	48%	.358	1.63	4.94	3.62	3.66	0.9
	SLN	MLB	32	0	1	0	3	4	0	3	2	9.0	6.0	73%	.364	2.33	6.00	5.69	4.78	0.0
J. Rondon	MEM	AAA	25	3	5	1	67²	72	6	37	42	4.9	5.6	54%	.300	1.61	3.06	5.21	5.37	-0.2
S. Tuivailala	PEO	A	20	0	3	1	35¹	31	0	20	50	5.1	12.7	58%	.365	1.44	5.35	2.55	3.23	0.8
B. Whiting	SFD	AA	23	3	2	0	30²	28	2	7	34	2.1	10.0	45%	.309	1.14	2.93	2.67	3.35	0.7
	MEM	AAA	23	5	5	0	105²	107	11	40	99	3.4	8.4	32%	.322	1.39	4.09	4.21	3.78	2.0

A tumor in his middle finger washed out 2012 for **Seth Blair**, but he managed a full season in 2013 and fared relatively well considering the circumstances. His control rebounded, but now he needs to regain the command that made him a first round pick in 2010. ⊘ **Keith Butler** had a quality season across three levels, but he only throws 92 mph. Unless he's willing to reach into Seth Maness' sternum and rip out his still-beating heart as an act of aggression and conquest, the under-95 spot is already taken. ⊘ The shift to the bullpen has given **Eric Fornataro** a tinge of prospect status with the emergence of some mid-90s heat, but he struggled to command anything in 2013 and got passed by about 819 other flame-throwing relievers. ⊘ The emergence of so many young arms in the Cardinals' bullpen rendered **Victor Marte** somewhat redundant despite his mid-90s heat and memories of the 1980s. Unlike his youthful teammates, he is unable to effectively command his velocity. ⊘ If **Jorge Rondon** could command his stuff at all then he would likely have been among the throng of rookies to debut in 2013; alas, he had just five more strikeouts than walks. ⊘ **Samuel Tuivailala** began his transition to the mound in 2012 and so far has shown a penchant for missing bats but little else, though he has just 48 innings under his belt. ⊘ **Boone Whiting** gets buried in this bountiful system and could become trade bait with a command and control profile that has yielded low-profile quality results throughout his career.

MANAGER: MIKE MATHENY

YEAR	TEAM	W-L	Pythag +/-	Avg PC	100+ P	120+ P	QS	BQS	REL	REL w Zero R	IBB	PH	PH Avg	PH HR	SB2	CS2	SB3	CS3	SAC Att	SAC %	POS SAC	Squeeze	Swing	In Play
2012	SLN	88-74	1	94.2	49	1	99	4	506	400	28	279	.190	1	72	27	18	5	104	66.3%	34	0	287	100
2013	SLN	97-65	1	96.0	67	5	88	3	483	411	26	234	.202	3	33	20	11	2	94	59.6%	17	0	242	87

Mike Matheny became the youngest manager to win the pennant since Ozzie Guillen in 2005, and is still just the third-youngest skipper in baseball. If things work out, Matheny could be around a long time. That would be part of a pattern in St. Louis. No team has had a longer streak of prominent managers. Aside from a half-season of Mike Jorgensen and a few weeks of interim duty from franchise stalwart Red Schoendienst, the last 30-plus years have been Whitey Herzog, Joe Torre, Tony LaRussa and now Matheny.

In each of his seasons, his squads have been among the least likely to issue intentional walks.

He's willing to use young players, as he showed by going to a rookie closer late in the year and Michael Wacha late in the season and in October.

The 2013 Cardinals were the best team in recent years at turning double plays. They were second overall to Minnesota in double plays (178 to 177) but the Twins put on more baserunners. Using a rough measure of double-play chances (1B+BB+HBP-SH) the Cardinals turned a double play in 12.5 percent of their opportunities to do so, the best by any team since 2005.

Matheny leaned heavily on his starters. His main eight position players tallied three-fourths of the St. Louis plate appearances, the most by any NL team in the 2010s so far.

Tampa Bay Rays

By R.J. Anderson

There are three clocks overseeing all business in Andrew Friedman's office, ticking in different directions and in different dimensions. One counts up, keeping track of David Price's service time; each tick makes him more expensive. Another counts down from Price's free agent eligibility; every second makes him less valuable to a potential trade partner. And the final clock—complete with a blurry display, wonky wiring and uncertain rhythm—predicts when league-wide trends and rules changes will conspire to steal every conceivable advantage that the Rays hold over big-market teams.

The last clock's display got more ominous when the new Collective Bargaining Agreement was agreed upon in November 2011. Understandably, there was outcry over new spending restrictions on the amateur draft and international free-agent market. Teams could still technically spend as much as they wanted, but if they did they would have to pay taxes and sacrifice certain privileges. Overspenders might forfeit a first-round pick or lose the right to sign an international player for more than $250,000 the next season. These changes, aimed (per the MLB company line) at promoting competitive balance, capped the earning power of non-veteran players and tilted the amateur market away from savvy teams.

For years, teams unable to buy wins on the free-agent market (like the Rays) and unwilling to sell future wins for instant gratification on the trade market (like the Rays) turned to good foreign scouting to enhance their futures. The payoffs were often slow, if existent, which kept the big, rich dogs away from the bowl. With the CBA shakeup, teams were mostly on equal footing. Sure, the worst teams got more spending money than the best, but now the diehards weren't allowed to spend much more than the apathetic teams, thereby eliminating free will. As one general manager

told Kevin Goldstein at the time, the relative freedom teams had enjoyed before was "about giving teams options and letting us make our own decisions. If we're not capable of making these decisions then we shouldn't be sitting in the seat. These new rules make it look like we're afraid of ourselves, and frankly it's a little embarrassing."

While many executives voiced displeasure anonymously or privately, the Rays were the first team to take action. In its first year, the CBA limited teams to a $2.9 million spending cap on international free-agents, according to *Baseball America's* Ben Badler. The Rays blew past that number, signing players for a sum roughly 30 percent greater than the cap. There were legitimate baseball reasons behind the overspending—the Rays secured a number of talented youngsters (notably left-handed pitcher Jose Castillo, righty Jose Mujica, catcher David Rodriguez and shortstop Cristian Toribio) who could be on top-prospect lists soon—but the suspicion that they did so in protest couldn't be shaken. Nor would that suspicion go away after team president Matthew Silverman described the competitive balance lottery draft picks—a contrived new development in which the league's teams with the lowest revenue take part in a raffle, with the prize being another selection—as "trifling."

That third clock didn't jolt to attention because of the international restrictions alone. The league changed the free-agent compensation system in a way that put the screws to the Rays and other small-budget teams. It used to be that a team could offer arbitration to any player who qualified as a Type A or B free agent, and if the player declined the offer and signed elsewhere the team received a draft pick. Under the new CBA, teams can theoretically net a draft pick for any player, but first they must extend to the player a one-year deal worth the average amount of the sport's 125

RAYS PROSPECTUS
2013 W-L: 91-71, 2nd in AL East

Pythag	.535	11th	DER	.715	4th
RS/G	4.29	12th	B-Age	29.4	24th
RA/G	3.98	11th	P-Age	28.2	18th
TAv	.277	4th	Salary	$61.9	28th
BRR	-6.3	25th	M$/MW	$1.13	2nd
TAv-P	.255	8th	DL Days	610	4th
FIP	3.74	8th	$ on DL	12%	8th

	Runs	HR/RH	HR/LH	Runs/RH	Runs/LH
Three-Year Park Factors	95	82	96	96	100

Top Hitter WARP	6.24 (Evan Longoria)
Top Pitcher WARP	3.13 (David Price)
Top Prospect	Enny Romero

richest contracts. (This offseason, that amounted to a $14 million bid. The Rays have never paid a player $14 million in a season.)

As if that weren't enough, the league ticked off small-market teams by making two other tweaks: Teams would now receive one pick, instead of two, and that pick would come at the end of the first round, instead of wherever the departing free agent's new team had been scheduled to pick. It's enough to make small-market executives, like Friedman, pine for the good old days.

Back then, the Rays could game the system. They infamously earned 10 compensatory picks in the 2011 draft—some for legitimate losses (Carl Crawford, Rafael Soriano, Grant Balfour, Joaquin Benoit and Randy Choate) and others for in-season acquisitions who had no chance at a good free-agent contract (Chad Qualls and Brad Hawpe) but went along for the ride anyway. Under the new rules, Tampa Bay might have received one or two draft picks that winter, and those picks wouldn't have been high enough for the Rays to snatch Taylor Guerrieri or Mikie Mahtook—their top two selections from that year.

The new system also hurts small-budget teams by removing the shroud of ambiguity. Players and agents used to weigh their optimism against the uncertainty of arbitration. Now they choose between the open market and a guaranteed $14 million. Behavioral science research suggests humans shy away from possibilities with small likelihoods of failure, even if the sure-thing alternative results in a lesser payout; ergo, agents who might have recommended free agency instead of a risky arbitration hearing are now more likely to advise the $14 million certainty instead of a risky free agency.

For a big market team, that's fine. They can pay a good-not-elite player $14 million. The Rays cannot. Consider last winter, when the Red Sox extended the qualifying offer to Stephen Drew, a solid everyday shortstop. Had it been the Rays and their solid everyday shortstop, Yunel Escobar, the odds are Andrew Friedman would not have been able to take the same risk. His budget would have been busted if Escobar said yes—remember, Tampa Bay has only twice in its history paid players more than $10 million in a season. Compare Escobar and Drew's numbers over the past three seasons (.266/.333/.374 and 8.0 WARP for Escobar, .245/.322/.403 and 3.9 WARP for Drew) and you come away with one thought: the Rays aren't just punished by being poor. They are punished for being poor.

And yet, for all the CBA's violence against the Rays, it might have also widened a new inefficiency for them to exploit—one that only the Rays seem willing to take advantage of and one that keeps that third clock beating at a glacial pace. It goes like this: With less freedom to spend money away from the big-league payroll and less incentive to let players walk via free agency, teams are now locking up their talented players before they hit the open market. That means there are fewer and fewer quality players available for rich teams to add to the mix, thereby increasing the demand for impact-level talents who become available on the trade market.

This plays right into Friedman's hands. Few winning teams have traded as much big-league talent over the past few years as the Rays. At one point last season, four-fifths of Tampa Bay's 2008 rotation started on the same day—and none took the mound in St. Petersburg. The pace of turnover will only accelerate in coming years. The Rays are no longer assured a draft pick when a player hits free agency, and they can rarely afford to keep good players deep into the earning process, so trades are now the only way to get value out of the soon-to-be departed.

The challenges for Friedman become maintaining leverage when other teams know he's working against the clocks and keeping enough good players to remain competitive amid the brisk pace. As Billy Beane told the *San Jose Mercury News* in 2012, "[You] used to be able to trade a five-plus [years of service time] player and get a good return. Now, very few people want to give up young players for that. Then it was four-plus, now it keeps shrinking and shrinking. The key for us is to make sure we get some return." That just so happens to be the same key for the similarly built and run Rays. It's no surprise, then, that the story of the Rays' offseason was the possibility of trading David Price.

Price entered the offseason two years away from free agency. The ace's achievements include winning the Cy Young Award, finishing second another year, starting an All-Star Game and posting shiny regular-season numbers. In short, Price is going to get paid when he hits the open market just after his 30th birthday. Until then he's going to earn a pretty penny through the arbitration process, which limits but does not eliminate a player's earning potential. He's exactly the kind of player every team would love to have, and exactly the kind of player the Rays cannot afford to keep. Friedman knew this, so he planted the seeds for a Price trade in 2012, a year before he was ready to make a deal. This is how the Rays have to operate: With one eye on the future and one on the present; one eye on the first clock and one on the second.

This is how Friedman must operate, and how he'll proceed should his other young, talented players—the Wil Myerses, Chris Archers and Alex Torreses of the world—develop as planned. Perhaps one signs a team-friendly extension that changes his clocks, like Matt Moore did. Most will take Price's route, where they go year to year until the Rays can no longer justify letting the first clock win the zero-sum game it plays with the second.

The concept of a franchise player has never been taken more literally than in Tampa Bay, where the only high-salaried talent likely to hang on for a while is Evan Longoria.

For the rest, Friedman will trade them and start the process over again—remember, Myers, Archer and Torres were each acquired in trades for previous club stalwarts: James Shields, Matt Garza and Scott Kazmir. This is the current state of the Rays: wheeling and dealing and trying to outrun the inescapable darkness that haunts poor teams.

But their future could be different for reasons beyond Friedman's negotiating prowess. For years, the Rays have tried to coerce locals into financing a new stadium, even if it requires an in-state move across the bridge linking St. Petersburg to Tampa. There's a renewed sense of local optimism since the election of pro-stadium St. Petersburg mayor

Rick Kriseman, but it's too soon to know whether his election promises—"Rather than simply ignoring the concerns of the Rays, I will initiate conversations about the future of the team in St. Pete"—are legitimate or just part of the game. The vacant threats of relocation or—gasp!—contraction aside, a new stadium wouldn't turn the Rays into the Yankees. It would allow Friedman to keep players for a little longer than he otherwise could—an important, if underestimated development.

Until there is stadium resolution—if ever—Friedman, the Rays, and their clocks will continue ticking away.

R.J. Anderson is an author at Baseball Prospectus.

HITTERS

Tim Beckham — SS

Born: 1/27/1990 Age: 24
Bats: R Throws: R Height: 6' 0"
Weight: 190 Breakout: 0%
Improve: 6% Collapse: 6%
Attrition: 26% MLB: 36%

Comparables:
Chris Nelson, Zack Cozart, Trevor Plouffe

YEAR	TEAM	LVL	AGE	PA	R	2B	3B	HR	RBI	BB	SO	SB	CS	AVG/OBP/SLG	TAv	BABIP	BRR	FRAA	WARP
2011	MNT	AA	21	468	82	25	2	7	57	39	91	15	4	.275/.339/.395	.262	.334	1.6	SS(30): -5.1	0.2
2011	DUR	AAA	21	111	12	3	2	5	13	3	29	2	1	.255/.282/.462	.232	.306	-0.9	SS(15): 0.9	0.1
2012	DUR	AAA	22	323	40	10	1	6	28	29	71	6	0	.256/.325/.361	.234	.316	1.9	SS(48): -1.9, 2B(25): -3.4	-0.1
2013	DUR	AAA	23	522	71	25	7	4	51	44	108	17	7	.276/.342/.387	.250	.348	2.4	SS(106): 0.4, 2B(15): 0.9	1.6
2013	TBA	MLB	23	8	1	0	0	0	1	0	0	0	0	.429/.375/.429	.349	.375	0.1	2B(3): 0.1, SS(1): -0.0	0.1
2014	TBA	MLB	24	250	28	9	2	4	20	16	60	6	2	.236/.290/.345	.239	.300	0.5	SS -4, 2B -1	0.1

The salient problem with Beckham's numbers is that Beckham produced them. Ordinarily, a 23-year-old showing decently in his first full Triple-A season would encourage optimism, but Beckham's no. 1 draft pick history fastens an unjust, scarlet-number shame to his jersey. True, the power hasn't come and he won't play shortstop full-time, but he could refashion himself as a serviceable part-time middle infielder, especially if he can master stealing bases. That's the role the Rays might have been envisioning for Beckham when they gave him his first big-league call-up late last season. For now, they'll have to keep dreaming: Beckham tore his ACL in December and is out until at least midsummer.

Vincent Belnome — 1B

Born: 3/11/1988 Age: 26
Bats: L Throws: R Height: 5' 11"
Weight: 205 Breakout: 6%
Improve: 16% Collapse: 7%
Attrition: 23% MLB: 35%

Comparables:
Juan Miranda, Gaby Sanchez, Josh Whitesell

YEAR	TEAM	LVL	AGE	PA	R	2B	3B	HR	RBI	BB	SO	SB	CS	AVG/OBP/SLG	TAv	BABIP	BRR	FRAA	WARP
2011	SAN	AA	23	318	56	19	1	17	62	47	59	0	5	.333/.432/.603	.302	.373	-2.7	2B(40): 3.8, 1B(17): -0.6	1.9
2012	TUC	AAA	24	303	28	11	1	5	33	43	72	5	1	.275/.380/.384	.260	.363	-2.1	1B(25): -4.1, 2B(24): 0.6	0.1
2013	DUR	AAA	25	533	77	35	3	8	67	84	109	0	2	.300/.408/.446	.293	.378	-0.6	1B(63): 1.9, 3B(32): -0.6	2.6
2014	TBA	MLB	26	250	26	11	1	5	27	32	61	0	0	.249/.346/.383	.274	.320	-0.4	1B -1, 2B -0	0.6

The selective Belnome "led [his] Little League team in walks." He was hitting .342/.447/.518 two days after playing in the Triple-A All-Star game, sparkling like yet another Rays minor-league jewel heist. (Belnome was acquired from San Diego for a 41st-round A-ball reliever.) But his major-injury history (shoulder, mostly) caught up with him: In his first fully healthy season since 2010, Belnome wore down badly after the break, mentally as well as physically, and nearly lost his precious .300 batting average. His selection to the postseason International League All-Star team as "Utility Player" was by process of elimination, not commendation: he has no natural position despite playing first, second and third last year, and his gap-hitting tendencies don't fit at DH. But his eye alone will keep him in baseball, perhaps even get him to the majors.

Ryan Brett — 2B

Born: 10/9/1991 Age: 22
Bats: R Throws: R Height: 5' 9"
Weight: 180 Breakout: 3%
Improve: 15% Collapse: 7%
Attrition: 15% MLB: 26%

Comparables:
Tony Abreu, Adrian Cardenas, Jordany Valdespin

YEAR	TEAM	LVL	AGE	PA	R	2B	3B	HR	RBI	BB	SO	SB	CS	AVG/OBP/SLG	TAv	BABIP	BRR	FRAA	WARP
2012	BGR	A	20	456	77	20	3	6	35	37	73	48	8	.285/.348/.393	.273	.332	4.5	2B(88): -11.3	1.0
2013	PCH	A+	21	225	38	11	4	4	22	15	27	22	7	.340/.396/.490	.307	.377	1	2B(47): -2.0	1.5
2013	MNT	AA	21	114	19	6	1	3	16	8	14	4	0	.238/.289/.400	.257	.247	1.8	2B(25): 1.1	0.5
2014	TBA	MLB	22	250	30	9	1	4	19	13	53	12	3	.235/.277/.335	.232	.290	1.4	2B -3	0.0

Previously overshadowed—both in size and draft round—by his friend Josh Sale, Brett now dwarfs his fellow Washingtonian in prospect status. Unlike Sale, Brett made a successful return from a 2012 drug suspension to reach Double-A last season. The compact infielder is a line-drive hitter who attacks the ball with tenacity. His size limits his power ceiling but has not hampered his ability to hit to the gaps. He is a good athlete with above-average speed, though his arm is suited for the right side of the infield. He has made great strides on defense, showing better quickness, range and an improved pivot. He still has room to grow on defense and he'll need better pitch recognition and selection as he climbs the organizational ladder.

Nick Ciuffo — C

Born: 3/7/1995 Age: 19
Bats: L Throws: R Height: 6' 1"
Weight: 205 Breakout: 0%
Improve: 0% Collapse: 0%
Attrition: 0% MLB: 0%

Comparables:
Wilin Rosario, Travis d'Arnaud, Kyle Skipworth

YEAR	TEAM	LVL	AGE	PA	R	2B	3B	HR	RBI	BB	SO	SB	CS	AVG/OBP/SLG	TAv	BABIP	BRR	FRAA	WARP
2014	TBA	MLB	19	250	15	8	1	2	18	10	80	0	0	.178/.212/.237	.171	.250	-0.3	C 0	-1.4

Ciuffo was one of the top prep catchers in last year's draft, and the backstop-thin Rays took him 21st overall. From the left side, his swing is concise with good bat speed. His power is currently relegated to the gaps, but some have seen it play up much more. Behind the plate, he brings passion and legitimate tools for the trade. He has an above-average arm with a fluid motion, although he could stand to tighten his release. He earns high praise as a receiver and blocks the ball well. Ciuffo could become an everyday catcher in the mold of A.J. Pierzynski.

David DeJesus — CF

Born: 12/20/1979 Age: 34
Bats: L Throws: L Height: 5' 11"
Weight: 190 Breakout: 0%
Improve: 31% Collapse: 15%
Attrition: 19% MLB: 92%

Comparables:
Jason Michaels, Brady Anderson, Jeff DaVanon

YEAR	TEAM	LVL	AGE	PA	R	2B	3B	HR	RBI	BB	SO	SB	CS	AVG/OBP/SLG	TAv	BABIP	BRR	FRAA	WARP
2011	OAK	MLB	31	506	60	20	5	10	46	45	86	4	3	.240/.323/.376	.261	.274	1.5	RF(116): 7.3, CF(8): -1.0	1.8
2012	CHN	MLB	32	582	76	28	8	9	50	61	89	7	8	.263/.350/.403	.278	.301	2.8	RF(100): -2.8, CF(50): -0.8	2.0
2013	CHN	MLB	33	318	39	19	3	6	27	29	55	3	0	.250/.330/.401	.268	.291	3	CF(73): 5.8, LF(3): 0.2	2.1
2013	WAS	MLB	33	4	0	0	0	0	0	0	1	0	0	.000/.000/.000	.079	.000	0	RF(2): -0.1, CF(1): -0.0	-0.1
2013	TBA	MLB	33	117	13	10	0	2	11	10	23	2	3	.260/.328/.413	.279	.312	-0.8	LF(27): -0.6, CF(7): -0.2	0.4
2014	TBA	MLB	34	443	51	20	4	7	39	39	76	5	4	.251/.327/.375	.265	.290	-0.7	CF 1, RF 0	1.4

DeJesus started the season in Chicago but landed in Tampa Bay after a brief stay in D.C. Relying on contact skills and a firm understanding of the strike zone, DeJesus remains a slightly above-average hitter as he creeps into his mid-30s. More athletic than fast, he is a good defender with the ability to cover all three outfield positions. He is a below-average basestealer (bad jumps) but a good baserunner. DeJesus fit well in the Rays' clubhouse, and in early November they locked him up for three years of strong-side platoon duty.

Yunel Escobar — SS

Born: 11/2/1982 Age: 31
Bats: R Throws: R Height: 6' 2"
Weight: 210 Breakout: 0%
Improve: 30% Collapse: 9%
Attrition: 13% MLB: 99%

Comparables:
Barry Larkin, Alex Cora, David Eckstein

YEAR	TEAM	LVL	AGE	PA	R	2B	3B	HR	RBI	BB	SO	SB	CS	AVG/OBP/SLG	TAv	BABIP	BRR	FRAA	WARP
2011	TOR	MLB	28	590	77	24	3	11	48	61	70	3	3	.290/.369/.413	.279	.316	0.3	SS(132): -3.9	3.2
2012	TOR	MLB	29	608	58	22	1	9	51	35	70	5	1	.253/.300/.344	.230	.273	1.4	SS(143): 5.9	1.5
2013	TBA	MLB	30	578	61	27	1	9	56	57	73	4	4	.256/.332/.366	.264	.281	1	SS(153): -2.2	2.8
2014	TBA	MLB	31	549	61	21	1	7	46	49	69	4	2	.258/.330/.352	.259	.280	-0.9	SS 2	2.5

The Rays gladly took Escobar off the Marlins' hands after he landed in Miami as part of the block- buster trade with the Blue Jays. With a style of play that was described as "beyond arrogant" by a rival major league executive, it should come as no surprise that Escobar thrived under the guidance of Joe Maddon. Defensively, the Cuban solidified a Rays middle infield that was in flux in 2012. His strong arm, wide range and quick reactions should keep him at shortstop into his mid-30s. Offensively, he rebounded from a poor start to produce numbers relatively close to career averages, relying on solid contact skills and a disciplined approach.

Sam Fuld — LF

Born: 11/20/1981 Age: 32
Bats: L Throws: L Height: 5' 10"
Weight: 175 Breakout: 4%
Improve: 29% Collapse: 8%
Attrition: 26% MLB: 72%

Comparables:
Oscar Robles, Luis Rodriguez, Tike Redman

YEAR	TEAM	LVL	AGE	PA	R	2B	3B	HR	RBI	BB	SO	SB	CS	AVG/OBP/SLG	TAv	BABIP	BRR	FRAA	WARP
2011	TBA	MLB	29	346	41	18	5	3	27	32	49	20	8	.240/.313/.360	.254	.276	0.5	LF(75): 7.3, RF(9): 0.5	1.8
2012	DUR	AAA	30	21	0	1	0	0	0	3	3	0	1	.167/.286/.222	.173	.200	-1.2	RF(2): 0.4, CF(1): -0.0	-0.2
2012	TBA	MLB	30	107	14	3	2	0	5	8	14	7	2	.255/.318/.327	.237	.298	-0.6	RF(15): 0.1, LF(14): 0.3	0.0
2013	TBA	MLB	31	200	25	0	3	2	17	17	28	8	2	.199/.270/.267	.202	.223	1.7	LF(55): 0.3, CF(29): 0.7	-0.4
2014	TBA	MLB	32	250	27	9	3	1	18	26	34	11	4	.234/.316/.322	.245	.270	0.9	LF 3, CF 1	0.9

Everybody's favorite substitute, Fuld appeared in 119 games, mostly as a defensive replace- ment and pinch-runner, though he did not run as often as expected. Despite hitting below the Mendoza line, he walked at a decent rate considering opposing pitchers have little reason not to throw him strikes. Do not be surprised if he lands in a front office after his tires go flat, and expect his Wikipedia page to crack 20,000 words before then.

Brandon Guyer RF
Born: 1/28/1986 Age: 28
Bats: R Throws: R Height: 6' 2"
Weight: 210 Breakout: 3%
Improve: 10% Collapse: 14%
Attrition: 26% MLB: 35%
Comparables:
Jorge Padilla, Cole Gillespie, Prentice Redman

YEAR	TEAM	LVL	AGE	PA	R	2B	3B	HR	RBI	BB	SO	SB	CS	AVG/OBP/SLG	TAv	BABIP	BRR	FRAA	WARP
2011	DUR	AAA	25	443	78	29	5	14	61	35	79	16	6	.312/.384/.521	.345	.360	-0.5	RF(16): 0.8, CF(14): 1.4	1.9
2011	TBA	MLB	25	43	7	1	0	2	3	1	9	0	0	.195/.214/.366	.220	.200	0.4	RF(11): -0.2, LF(3): 0.2	0.0
2012	DUR	AAA	26	97	9	3	1	3	13	7	15	2	0	.294/.365/.459	.296	.324	1	RF(12): 1.3, CF(6): -0.1	0.7
2012	TBA	MLB	26	7	2	0	0	1	1	0	1	0	0	.143/.143/.571	.329	.000	0	LF(3): -0.0	0.1
2013	DUR	AAA	27	405	73	23	6	7	41	29	62	22	3	.301/.374/.458	.285	.346	0.7	RF(41): 1.3, CF(29): 2.8	2.7
2014	TBA	MLB	28	250	30	10	2	6	28	15	45	10	2	.267/.328/.414	.276	.300	1.1	RF 0, LF 2	1.4

There's a skill to staying healthy and Guyer doesn't have it: The toolsy outfielder has a knack not only for getting hurt, but at the worst times, too. Last season, good Triple-A numbers recommended him for a promotion when Desmond Jennings was injured, but Guyer was already out with a broken finger, hit by a pitch while bunting. That was emblematic—although Guyer doesn't crowd the plate, he's been top-two in the International League in HBPs in his past two full seasons. Hurt finds him. Considered a key piece in the 2010 Matt Garza deal, Guyer now finds his prospecthood aging and frayed, if not completely torn.

Ryan Hanigan C
Born: 8/16/1980 Age: 33
Bats: R Throws: R Height: 6' 0"
Weight: 210 Breakout: 1%
Improve: 28% Collapse: 10%
Attrition: 14% MLB: 90%
Comparables:
Jason Kendall, Carlos Ruiz, Mark Grace

YEAR	TEAM	LVL	AGE	PA	R	2B	3B	HR	RBI	BB	SO	SB	CS	AVG/OBP/SLG	TAv	BABIP	BRR	FRAA	WARP
2011	CIN	MLB	30	304	27	6	0	6	31	35	32	0	0	.267/.356/.357	.272	.285	0.9	C(89): -1.9	1.7
2012	CIN	MLB	31	371	25	14	0	2	24	44	37	0	0	.274/.365/.338	.258	.302	0.8	C(110): -0.2	2.3
2013	CIN	MLB	32	260	17	8	0	2	21	29	27	0	1	.198/.306/.261	.219	.216	-1.1	C(72): 0.9	0.2
2014	TBA	MLB	33	268	26	9	0	2	22	31	31	0	0	.248/.342/.323	.258	.270	-0.5	C -0	1.2

There were only two players in the majors to post a slugging percentage lower than Hanigan's .267 in more than 200 plate appearances: Ruben Tejada and Jamey Carroll. Hanigan's mark was depressed by a .222 BABIP, despite no significant change to his batted ball profile; once a BABIP gets this low, it becomes hard to distinguish between bad luck and bad hitting, each of which probably played some part. Cincinnati assumed it was the latter and shipped him to the Rays, who promptly signed him to an inexpensive multi-year deal. Hanigan may lack punch but remains a fine defensive backstop who controls the running game, frames pitches, draws walks and makes contact—he's the only player in the majors to have more walks than strikeouts in each of the past six seasons. If his new employers focus on what Hanigan can do, rather than what he can't, they'll be happy with their investment.

Desmond Jennings CF
Born: 10/30/1986 Age: 27
Bats: R Throws: R Height: 6' 2"
Weight: 200 Breakout: 6%
Improve: 51% Collapse: 5%
Attrition: 13% MLB: 93%
Comparables:
Dexter Fowler, Nate McLouth, Ryan Sweeney

YEAR	TEAM	LVL	AGE	PA	R	2B	3B	HR	RBI	BB	SO	SB	CS	AVG/OBP/SLG	TAv	BABIP	BRR	FRAA	WARP
2011	DUR	AAA	24	397	68	19	3	12	39	45	78	17	1	.275/.374/.456	.257	.325	2.1	CF(20): 1.2, RF(3): 0.4	0.6
2011	TBA	MLB	24	287	44	9	4	10	25	31	59	20	6	.259/.356/.449	.292	.303	1.4	LF(53): -0.8, CF(8): -0.2	1.5
2012	TBA	MLB	25	563	85	19	7	13	47	46	120	31	2	.246/.314/.388	.261	.298	5.6	LF(111): 0.2, CF(21): -0.1	2.4
2013	TBA	MLB	26	602	82	31	6	14	54	64	115	20	8	.252/.334/.414	.287	.295	5.7	CF(136): 1.7	4.3
2014	TBA	MLB	27	560	75	24	6	11	50	54	111	29	6	.248/.327/.387	.268	.290	3.7	CF 3, LF 0	2.7

When the Rays lost Carl Crawford to free agency, they inserted Jennings in left field. When B.J. Upton followed Crawford out the door, they simply shifted Jennings 100 feet to his left. The 27-year-old has not been the offensive dynamo some had hoped for, but the Trop's tough hitting environment masks that he's actually been above average with the bat overall. Add that to excellent speed and fine defensive work and you get a very fine player just entering the prime of his career. Once thought of as a leadoff man, he has found some success lower in the lineup where his aggressive approach against fastballs comes in handy with runners on base.

Matt Joyce RF
Born: 8/3/1984 Age: 29
Bats: L Throws: R Height: 6' 2"
Weight: 205 Breakout: 6%
Improve: 42% Collapse: 1%
Attrition: 2% MLB: 94%
Comparables:
Seth Smith, Shin-Soo Choo, Carlos Quentin

YEAR	TEAM	LVL	AGE	PA	R	2B	3B	HR	RBI	BB	SO	SB	CS	AVG/OBP/SLG	TAv	BABIP	BRR	FRAA	WARP
2011	TBA	MLB	26	522	69	32	2	19	75	49	106	13	1	.277/.347/.478	.300	.317	-0.3	RF(126): -4.1, LF(15): 0.2	2.7
2012	TBA	MLB	27	462	55	18	3	17	59	55	102	4	3	.241/.341/.429	.277	.281	2.3	RF(89): -2.2, LF(33): -0.8	1.4
2013	TBA	MLB	28	481	61	22	0	18	47	59	87	7	3	.235/.328/.419	.285	.251	-1.2	RF(58): -2.7, LF(58): 2.8	1.8
2014	TBA	MLB	29	450	55	22	2	15	57	55	95	7	3	.246/.343/.431	.285	.280	-0.3	RF -1, LF 1	2.1

Once again it was feast or famine for Joyce, who as usual did most of his feasting prior to the All-Star break. He knocked 27 extra-base hits in his first 85 games but managed just 13 in the last 55. The lack of production led to sporadic playing time down the stretch and in October. His left-handed bat is still productive against right-handed pitchers, but developing into an everyday player is unlikely. Because he is largely average as a corner outfielder and on the bases, hitting will keep him employed; however, he will need to do more of it in order to justify his increasing salary.

Kevin Kiermaier   CF

Born: 4/22/1990 Age: 24
Bats: L Throws: R Height: 6' 1"
Weight: 200 Breakout: 11%
Improve: 18% Collapse: 2%
Attrition: 17% MLB: 33%

Comparables:
Brandon Guyer, Charlie Blackmon, Shane Peterson

YEAR	TEAM	LVL	AGE	PA	R	2B	3B	HR	RBI	BB	SO	SB	CS	AVG/OBP/SLG	TAv	BABIP	BRR	FRAA	WARP
2011	BGR	A	21	459	54	11	8	4	39	37	99	27	10	.241/.316/.338	.260	.308	-0.2	CF(66): 8.3, RF(2): 0.0	2.4
2012	PCH	A+	22	212	16	7	6	0	12	26	38	10	4	.260/.361/.367	.261	.331	-2.8	CF(53): 5.1, RF(4): 0.0	0.9
2013	MNT	AA	23	417	65	14	9	5	28	31	61	14	11	.307/.370/.434	.302	.354	2.5	CF(89): 10.5	5.1
2013	DUR	AAA	23	154	24	7	6	1	13	14	26	7	1	.263/.338/.423	.258	.315	3.6	CF(38): 7.6	1.7
2014	TBA	MLB	24	250	27	8	4	2	18	16	53	7	3	.242/.298/.341	.239	.300	0.6	CF 8, RF 0	1.1

Kiermaier made his major-league debut in the ninth inning of Game 163, then reappeared late in the Wild Card game two days later. In neither game was he involved in a play, giving him a Moonlight Graham appeal, but the kid should have staying power. He is a 70-grade runner, gobbles up everything in center field and can hit the catcher on the fly from the warning track. His Double-A team's MVP, the 2010 31st-rounder moved up to Triple-A in July and showed off not only his elite defense but good plate discipline and a bit of pop, and he hits lefties as well as righties. Kiermaier might be the Rays' starting center fielder by 2015, and he stands a good chance of landing the fourth outfielder job this season. He's also handsome.

Jose Lobaton   C

Born: 10/21/1984 Age: 29
Bats: B Throws: R Height: 6' 0"
Weight: 210 Breakout: 1%
Improve: 23% Collapse: 12%
Attrition: 31% MLB: 76%

Comparables:
John Baker, George Kottaras, Mike Rabelo

YEAR	TEAM	LVL	AGE	PA	R	2B	3B	HR	RBI	BB	SO	SB	CS	AVG/OBP/SLG	TAv	BABIP	BRR	FRAA	WARP
2011	PCH	A+	26	20	0	4	0	0	2	2	5	0	0	.444/.500/.667	.461	.615	-0.7		0.0
2011	DUR	AAA	26	224	24	10	1	8	31	37	50	0	0	.293/.410/.489	.347	.362	-1.7	C(11): 0.1	1.0
2011	TBA	MLB	26	39	2	1	0	0	0	4	8	0	0	.118/.231/.147	.138	.154	0	C(14): 0.0	-0.3
2012	TBA	MLB	27	197	16	10	0	2	20	24	46	0	1	.222/.323/.317	.238	.289	-1.5	C(66): 0.6	0.2
2013	TBA	MLB	28	311	38	15	2	7	32	30	65	0	1	.249/.320/.394	.280	.300	-3.2	C(96): -0.0	1.5
2014	TBA	MLB	29	274	27	12	1	5	26	28	62	1	0	.231/.313/.348	.250	.280	-0.5	C -0	0.9

Rewarded with ice cream after hitting home runs and walk-offs, Lobaton had his share of brain freezes last season. His most memorable moment came in Game Three of the ALDS when his solo blast off Koji Uehara temporarily saved the Rays from elimination. The younger Jose in Tampa Bay's catching platoon, he set career-highs in nearly every offensive category. The switch-hitting Venezuelan does not do any one thing particularly well at the plate, but his production is acceptable for the position. Defensively, he is active behind the dish and has improved as a game-caller; however, he has not controlled runners well. Several people in and around the organization credit his productive season with increased comfort at the highest level, as well as soaking up knowledge from the veterans around him.

James Loney   1B

Born: 5/7/1984 Age: 30
Bats: L Throws: L Height: 6' 3"
Weight: 220 Breakout: 1%
Improve: 34% Collapse: 10%
Attrition: 11% MLB: 91%

Comparables:
Casey Kotchman, Conor Jackson, Pete O'Brien

YEAR	TEAM	LVL	AGE	PA	R	2B	3B	HR	RBI	BB	SO	SB	CS	AVG/OBP/SLG	TAv	BABIP	BRR	FRAA	WARP
2011	LAN	MLB	27	582	56	30	1	12	65	42	67	4	0	.288/.339/.416	.276	.309	-1.4	1B(150): 3.3	2.1
2012	BOS	MLB	28	106	5	2	0	2	8	5	12	0	0	.230/.264/.310	.211	.241	-0.3	1B(28): 2.6	-0.2
2012	LAN	MLB	28	359	32	18	0	4	33	23	39	0	3	.254/.302/.344	.224	.277	-2.2	1B(105): 1.4	-1.0
2013	TBA	MLB	29	598	54	33	0	13	75	44	77	3	1	.299/.348/.430	.282	.326	-2.7	1B(154): -3.0	1.5
2014	TBA	MLB	30	535	54	26	1	10	57	42	68	3	2	.268/.327/.389	.267	.290	-0.9	1B -0	0.8

Loney was left looking for short-term work after splitting a disastrous season between Los Angeles and Boston. Like many wayward baseball souls before him, he sought and found salvation in Tampa Bay. Loney rewarded his new organization with a torrid first half, but cooled off considerably after the break. Still, the net result was a better-than-average offensive season with well-regarded defense at first. Obvious comparisons to Casey Kotchman's run with the Rays will be made, but Loney's rebound was sparked by mechanical adjustments that produced numbers similar to his career marks, which means 2012 may have the outlier. The Rays are certainly betting that way, agreeing to a three-year extension in December.

Evan Longoria   3B

Born: 10/7/1985 Age: 28
Bats: R Throws: R Height: 6' 2"
Weight: 210 Breakout: 0%
Improve: 49% Collapse: 0%
Attrition: 3% MLB: 100%

Comparables:
David Wright, Ron Santo, Eddie Mathews

YEAR	TEAM	LVL	AGE	PA	R	2B	3B	HR	RBI	BB	SO	SB	CS	AVG/OBP/SLG	TAv	BABIP	BRR	FRAA	WARP
2011	TBA	MLB	25	574	78	26	1	31	99	80	93	3	2	.244/.355/.495	.311	.239	-2.1	3B(130): 9.1	6.1
2012	DUR	AAA	26	39	0	0	0	0	3	7	9	0	0	.200/.359/.200	.239	.273	-0.1		-0.1
2012	TBA	MLB	26	312	39	14	0	17	55	33	61	2	3	.289/.369/.527	.321	.313	-1.2	3B(50): -1.5	2.5
2013	TBA	MLB	27	693	91	39	3	32	88	70	162	1	0	.269/.343/.498	.309	.312	-0.8	3B(147): 7.9	6.2
2014	TBA	MLB	28	580	75	31	2	25	84	65	119	4	2	.266/.353/.482	.305	.300	-0.8	3B 6	4.6

Longoria became the first $100 million player in Rays history prior to last season, a risky move for a club that operates on a strict budget. The deal was a bit more of a gamble considering he missed more than half the year in 2012 with a hamstring injury and underwent surgery after the season. Longoria did his best to ease fears by setting a career high in games played, belting 30-plus homers for the third time and playing fantastic defense. He did encounter a month-long slump during the summer, which coincided with a battle with plantar fasciitis. Throughout the struggle, he maintained that the two were unrelated. Though not much of a baserunner anymore, he is a two-way, franchise player with his best seasons potentially still ahead of him.

Jose Molina C

Born: 6/3/1975 Age: 39
Bats: R Throws: R Height: 6' 2"
Weight: 250 Breakout: 4%
Improve: 16% Collapse: 17%
Attrition: 29% MLB: 56%

Comparables:
Henry Blanco, Elston Howard, Clyde McCullough

YEAR	TEAM	LVL	AGE	PA	R	2B	3B	HR	RBI	BB	SO	SB	CS	AVG/OBP/SLG	TAv	BABIP	BRR	FRAA	WARP
2011	TOR	MLB	36	191	19	12	1	3	15	15	44	2	1	.281/.342/.415	.273	.363	-1	C(48): -1.3	0.9
2012	TBA	MLB	37	274	27	9	0	8	32	20	60	3	1	.223/.286/.355	.244	.262	-3	C(102): -1.9	0.4
2013	TBA	MLB	38	313	26	14	0	2	18	22	63	2	1	.233/.290/.304	.222	.290	-0.4	C(96): -1.6	-0.2
2014	TBA	MLB	39	286	26	11	1	4	24	20	64	2	1	.224/.285/.315	.229	.280	-0.3	C -1	0.3

Arguably the best carpenter in the business because of his noted framework (*rimshot* *crickets*), Molina continued to handle a steady workload for Tampa Bay as he creeps toward his 40th birthday. The middle Molina receives a lot of praise for his work behind the plate, but his best attributes might be imaginary. He has been the stabilizing force for a pitching staff that perennially infuses youth as well as a role model for the organization's young backstops. These traits are likely to keep him around the game long after he has stolen his last strike. For now, the framing alone is enough—the Rays inked Molina to a new two-year deal last November.

Wil Myers RF

Born: 12/10/1990 Age: 23
Bats: R Throws: R Height: 6' 3"
Weight: 205 Breakout: 0%
Improve: 34% Collapse: 5%
Attrition: 18% MLB: 78%

Comparables:
Jay Bruce, Travis Snider, Matt Kemp

YEAR	TEAM	LVL	AGE	PA	R	2B	3B	HR	RBI	BB	SO	SB	CS	AVG/OBP/SLG	TAv	BABIP	BRR	FRAA	WARP
2011	NWA	AA	20	416	50	23	1	8	49	52	87	9	2	.254/.353/.393	.250	.312	2	RF(66): 4.0, CF(11): -0.3	1.0
2012	NWA	AA	21	152	32	11	1	13	30	16	42	4	1	.343/.414/.731	.386	.412	-0.3	CF(20): 3.6, RF(13): 0.1	2.9
2012	OMA	AAA	21	439	66	15	5	24	79	45	98	2	2	.304/.378/.554	.311	.349	-1.6	CF(67): -7.8, 3B(13): -0.9	2.7
2013	DUR	AAA	22	289	44	13	2	14	57	29	71	7	1	.286/.356/.520	.290	.335	0.3	RF(56): 8.1	2.2
2013	TBA	MLB	22	373	50	23	0	13	53	33	91	5	2	.293/.354/.478	.303	.362	0.3	RF(72): -2.3, CF(8): 0.9	2.0
2014	TBA	MLB	23	390	47	18	2	15	53	34	102	3	1	.259/.326/.451	.286	.320	-0.2	RF 2, CF -0	2.1

Myers took two months to master his new Triple-A league before earning a mid-June promotion to the majors—where he made a beeline for the Rookie of the Year Award. Myers also won the league's Rookie of the Month in September (.308/.362/.542), carrying much of the weight in dragging the Rays into the playoffs. The strikeouts were to be expected of a young power hitter, but the rate was consistent with his upper-minors history, and the walk rate was passable. Myers can run and field better than expected, too. James Shields had a good year in Kansas City, but year one post-trade suggests (as most pundits predicted) that the Rays ate the Royals' lunch.

Sean Rodriguez SS

Born: 4/26/1985 Age: 29
Bats: R Throws: R Height: 6' 0"
Weight: 200 Breakout: 3%
Improve: 40% Collapse: 2%
Attrition: 6% MLB: 83%

Comparables:
Ben Francisco, Jose Bautista, John Rodriguez

YEAR	TEAM	LVL	AGE	PA	R	2B	3B	HR	RBI	BB	SO	SB	CS	AVG/OBP/SLG	TAv	BABIP	BRR	FRAA	WARP
2011	TBA	MLB	26	436	45	20	3	8	36	38	87	11	7	.223/.323/.357	.251	.268	1.6	SS(60): -2.9, 2B(48): 1.5	1.2
2012	TBA	MLB	27	342	36	14	1	6	32	27	75	5	0	.213/.281/.326	.225	.260	0.9	3B(49): 4.0, SS(47): 4.2	0.8
2013	TBA	MLB	28	222	21	10	1	5	23	17	59	1	3	.246/.320/.385	.272	.323	-0.3	LF(47): 0.4, 1B(23): 0.4	0.9
2014	TBA	MLB	29	250	29	10	1	7	27	21	63	4	2	.230/.313/.383	.260	.280	-0.1	SS -0, LF 0	1.1

Rodriguez, a coach's son, transformed himself from middle infielder to outfielder/first baseman in the span of a season. The Rays' opening day shortstop in 2012 made just a handful of appearances up the middle while serving as the short-side of a platoon in left field and at first. This is not a knock on Rodriguez but a testament to the athleticism and versatility that allowed the Rays to upgrade their core while using him to augment other areas of need. Though his strikeout rate climbed, he was actually more disciplined in regards to chasing bad pitches. The ability to play up to seven positions at a relatively low cost while popping a few southpaws makes him a useful piece at the bottom of the roster.

Joshua Sale   LF

Born: 7/5/1991 Age: 22
Bats: L Throws: R Height: 6' 0"
Weight: 215 Breakout: 1%
Improve: 2% Collapse: 1%
Attrition: 3% MLB: 5%

Comparables:
Brandon Barnes, Andrew Lambo, L.J. Hoes

YEAR	TEAM	LVL	AGE	PA	R	2B	3B	HR	RBI	BB	SO	SB	CS	AVG/OBP/SLG	TAv	BABIP	BRR	FRAA	WARP
2012	BGR	A	20	297	35	10	4	10	44	51	62	7	6	.264/.391/.464	.319	.308	-4.2	LF(66): -0.4, RF(4): -0.3	2.1
2014	TBA	MLB	22	250	24	7	1	6	24	26	69	1	0	.201/.284/.322	.229	.260	-0.2	LF 1, RF -0	-0.2

This club can't even handle Josh Sale right now. Don't be fooled by the former first-rounder's blank 2013 stat line; he wasn't hurt. Just after returning in the spring from 2012's 50-game suspension for meth/Adderall (he denied using it but didn't appeal), Sale earned a second, season-long vacation for throwing coins at a stripper, getting kicked out of the nightclub, and then stupidly bragging about it (and slurring her) on Facebook. Sale wouldn't appear here at all except that he exemplifies the Rays' peculiarly erratic, often self-sabotaging judgment when it comes to evaluating players' characters: A persistent misprision is bound up in their genius for finding undervalued gems. During the 2013 suspension Sale did "everything we asked of him," according to a Rays official. But do we trust them to have made the right requests?

Jerry Sands   RF

Born: 9/28/1987 Age: 26
Bats: R Throws: R Height: 6' 4"
Weight: 225 Breakout: 4%
Improve: 22% Collapse: 6%
Attrition: 18% MLB: 43%

Comparables:
Wladimir Balentien, Brandon Jones, Clete Thomas

YEAR	TEAM	LVL	AGE	PA	R	2B	3B	HR	RBI	BB	SO	SB	CS	AVG/OBP/SLG	TAv	BABIP	BRR	FRAA	WARP
2011	ABQ	AAA	23	418	78	21	3	29	88	38	86	3	1	.278/.344/.586	.220	.282	0.1	LF(8): -0.8, RF(7): 1.2	-0.1
2011	LAN	MLB	23	227	20	15	0	4	26	25	51	3	3	.253/.338/.389	.268	.319	1.5	LF(41): 0.9, RF(22): -0.7	0.9
2012	ABQ	AAA	24	522	84	17	4	26	107	59	106	1	0	.296/.375/.524	.286	.329	4.4	LF(60): 4.8, 1B(44): 1.1	3.4
2012	LAN	MLB	24	24	2	2	0	0	1	1	9	0	0	.174/.208/.261	.159	.286	0	LF(6): -0.1, 1B(1): 0.0	-0.2
2013	IND	AAA	25	397	37	17	2	7	34	50	105	0	1	.207/.311/.329	.229	.276	0	RF(73): 2.8, LF(15): -0.3	0.2
2014	TBA	MLB	26	250	26	10	1	7	29	25	65	1	0	.220/.300/.372	.251	.270	-0.3	RF 0, LF 1	0.4

After being ignored by the Dodgers and Red Sox, Sands entered spring with a new team and a fresh start. So much for that. Last year we wrote Sands "doesn't serve a purpose on the Pirates' roster" and, sure enough, he spent the season in Indianapolis, buried behind superior players. He doesn't hit well enough to make a roster as a first baseman or left fielder and doesn't field well enough to play elsewhere. The Rays claimed him just before Christmas, but if Sands is on the 40-man roster as you read this then consider it a surprise; like his namesake on a beach, Quad-A hitters are everywhere.

Luke Scott   LF

Born: 6/25/1978 Age: 36
Bats: L Throws: R Height: 6' 0"
Weight: 220 Breakout: 0%
Improve: 21% Collapse: 14%
Attrition: 10% MLB: 81%

Comparables:
Travis Hafner, Derrek Lee, Cliff Floyd

YEAR	TEAM	LVL	AGE	PA	R	2B	3B	HR	RBI	BB	SO	SB	CS	AVG/OBP/SLG	TAv	BABIP	BRR	FRAA	WARP
2011	BAL	MLB	33	236	24	11	0	9	22	24	54	1	1	.220/.301/.402	.252	.250	-1.1	LF(45): 1.2, 1B(12): -0.5	0.2
2012	PCH	A+	34	32	6	1	0	2	6	6	7	0	0	.308/.438/.577	.313	.353	-0.3	1B(2): 0.1	0.2
2012	TBA	MLB	34	344	35	22	1	14	55	21	80	5	0	.229/.285/.439	.258	.259	-0.3	1B(6): 0.0	0.3
2013	TBA	MLB	35	291	27	13	2	9	40	30	63	1	1	.241/.326/.415	.281	.281	-1.1	LF(6): 0.0, 1B(5): -0.0	0.8
2014	TBA	MLB	36	294	34	13	1	11	39	29	67	2	1	.237/.316/.424	.273	.270	-0.3	LF 0, 1B -0	0.9

Scott's second year in Tampa Bay resembled the first in many ways. He landed on the disabled list twice (back and calf) and was prone to prolonged slumps when active. Despite the left-handed bat, he is playable against southpaws, although a platoon partner would not hurt. He was limited defensively even before the injuries, making it unlikely he will ever return to regular field duty. Scott still has good power for a graybeard, but the expanding medical records make it hard to rely on him as a regular producer. He signed to play the 2014 season in Korea, presumably because of Obamacare.

Richie Shaffer   3B

Born: 3/15/1991 Age: 23
Bats: R Throws: R Height: 6' 3"
Weight: 218 Breakout: 0%
Improve: 4% Collapse: 0%
Attrition: 3% MLB: 4%

Comparables:
Josh Fields, Ryan Wheeler, Mike Costanzo

YEAR	TEAM	LVL	AGE	PA	R	2B	3B	HR	RBI	BB	SO	SB	CS	AVG/OBP/SLG	TAv	BABIP	BRR	FRAA	WARP
2012	HUD	A-	21	138	25	5	2	4	26	16	31	0	0	.308/.406/.487	.347	.386	0.3	3B(24): -1.0	1.5
2013	PCH	A+	22	519	55	33	1	11	73	35	106	6	0	.254/.308/.399	.258	.299	-2.5	3B(107): 0.0	1.4
2014	TBA	MLB	23	250	21	10	1	6	26	13	70	0	0	.211/.258/.331	.220	.270	-0.4	3B -1	-0.6

Shaffer failed to produce as expected during his first full season in the minors, perhaps partly a result of skipping a level of A-ball. At times, he played "big" and looked to overpower the ball. Like a lot of power prospects, he tends to lean to his pull side, but he has shown power to all fields. His bat speed rates above average and his approach progressed with the calendar—maybe a sign of him relaxing and using his hands more. A solid athlete, Shaffer continued to play third base last year but is likely to move around a bit to increase his overall stock.

Andrew Toles CF	YEAR	TEAM	LVL	AGE	PA	R	2B	3B	HR	RBI	BB	SO	SB	CS	AVG/OBP/SLG	TAv	BABIP	BRR	FRAA	WARP

YEAR	TEAM	LVL	AGE	PA	R	2B	3B	HR	RBI	BB	SO	SB	CS	AVG/OBP/SLG	TAv	BABIP	BRR	FRAA	WARP
2013	BGR	A	21	552	79	35	16	2	57	22	105	62	17	.326/.359/.466	.295	.402	7.1	CF(110): 1.6, RF(6): 0.1	4.6
2014	TBA	MLB	22	250	27	10	2	2	16	5	67	12	4	.229/.249/.315	.211	.310	1.4	CF 1, RF 0	-0.3

Andrew Toles CF
Born: 5/24/1992 Age: 22
Bats: L Throws: R Height: 5' 10"
Weight: 185 Breakout: 0%
Improve: 2% Collapse: 0%
Attrition: 2% MLB: 2%

Comparables:
Juan Lagares, A.J. Pollock, Alfredo Marte

A third-round pick in 2010, Toles' tools exploded last year. The Rays' 2013 minor-league player of the year led the Midwest League in hitting while swiping 62 bases. His speed has helped him overcome his size to this point, but at advanced levels and as he slows with age, the lack of physicality might become an issue. He will also need to improve his overall plate discipline, especially with two strikes. He has enough natural ability to be an average hitter or better. Defensively, Toles tracks down balls in center field with ease and should continue to play the position.

YEAR	TEAM	LVL	AGE	PA	R	2B	3B	HR	RBI	BB	SO	SB	CS	AVG/OBP/SLG	TAv	BABIP	BRR	FRAA	WARP
2012	BGR	A	20	562	80	24	5	15	69	51	117	20	11	.275/.340/.432	.285	.328	-1.9	RF(117): -2.0, CF(12): -1.2	3.4
2013	PCH	A+	21	516	50	29	6	4	62	40	78	5	7	.274/.331/.388	.257	.318	-5.4	RF(118): -6.1, CF(1): -0.1	-0.3
2014	TBA	MLB	22	250	22	9	1	4	24	15	64	2	1	.220/.267/.325	.224	.280	-0.2	RF -2, CF -0	-0.7

Drew Vettleson RF
Born: 7/19/1991 Age: 22
Bats: L Throws: R Height: 6' 1"
Weight: 185 Breakout: 0%
Improve: 1% Collapse: 0%
Attrition: 1% MLB: 1%

Comparables:
Moises Sierra, Matt Joyce, Abraham Almonte

Vettleson possesses a balanced skill set with the ceiling of a regular corner outfielder. His 2012 power evaporated in 2013, but some see that as a product of the hitting environment—he impressed big-league executives in the spring and during batting practice. Defensively, he is solid overall but made 14 errors in right field. The adjustment from the Florida State League—with its big ballparks and heavy air conspiring to crush the hopes of hitters—to the more balanced Southern League will be an important one for the former supplemental-round pick.

YEAR	TEAM	LVL	AGE	PA	R	2B	3B	HR	RBI	BB	SO	SB	CS	AVG/OBP/SLG	TAv	BABIP	BRR	FRAA	WARP
2011	ROC	AAA	25	32	5	3	0	2	5	1	5	0	0	.290/.312/.581	.315	.292	-0.1	LF(4): -0.1	0.2
2011	MIN	MLB	25	325	26	16	0	4	32	18	55	1	0	.266/.305/.357	.234	.310	-0.9	LF(75): -2.8	-0.5
2011	DET	MLB	25	178	28	5	1	8	32	5	30	0	0	.274/.298/.458	.267	.286	1.1	LF(40): -2.8	0.4
2012	DET	MLB	26	608	54	27	1	18	74	20	112	0	2	.267/.296/.411	.249	.299	-3.4	LF(31): -1.1	-0.5
2013	MNT	AA	27	31	4	0	0	1	3	1	7	0	0	.233/.258/.333	.211	.273	-0.1		-0.1
2013	TBA	MLB	27	70	8	3	0	3	7	6	9	0	0	.258/.329/.452	.301	.255	-0.9	RF(1): -0.0	0.3
2013	PHI	MLB	27	291	22	13	0	8	31	14	69	0	0	.261/.302/.397	.253	.320	-2.8	RF(64): -1.3	-0.1
2014	TBA	MLB	28	398	40	19	1	11	48	18	77	1	1	.261/.300/.407	.263	.300	-0.9	RF -1, LF -2	0.5

Delmon Young RF
Born: 9/14/1985 Age: 28
Bats: R Throws: R Height: 6' 3"
Weight: 240 Breakout: 1%
Improve: 57% Collapse: 0%
Attrition: 10% MLB: 96%

Comparables:
Ruben Sierra, Felipe Alou, Xavier Nady

The prodigal son returned to Tampa Bay after five-plus seasons with three different organizations. After the Phillies released Young midseason, the Rays, moved with compassion, ran toward him, kissed him, and let him start at DH even against right-handers in the ALDS. Even at his worst Young always had the ability to hit left-handed pitchers, and seemed to benefit from working on his hitting mechanics in Arizona during his two weeks between teams. If his mechanical adjustments are more of a fix than a band-aid, he is a cheap, durable asset for a team looking to cut corners on a role that does not require a glove.

YEAR	TEAM	LVL	AGE	PA	R	2B	3B	HR	RBI	BB	SO	SB	CS	AVG/OBP/SLG	TAv	BABIP	BRR	FRAA	WARP
2011	TBA	MLB	30	674	99	46	6	20	91	77	128	19	6	.269/.353/.469	.300	.310	5	2B(131): -5.7, RF(38): 0.1	4.0
2012	TBA	MLB	31	668	88	39	7	20	74	97	103	14	9	.270/.377/.471	.311	.296	-5.2	RF(71): 1.7, 2B(58): -7.4	4.7
2013	TBA	MLB	32	698	77	36	3	12	71	72	91	11	3	.275/.354/.402	.283	.303	-0.9	2B(125): 0.4, RF(39): 0.4	3.4
2014	TBA	MLB	33	650	77	32	4	15	73	82	112	15	5	.258/.354/.413	.286	.290	0.4	2B -3, RF 1	3.8

Ben Zobrist 2B
Born: 5/26/1981 Age: 33
Bats: B Throws: R Height: 6' 3"
Weight: 210 Breakout: 0%
Improve: 22% Collapse: 6%
Attrition: 9% MLB: 97%

Comparables:
Chase Utley, Craig Biggio, Jackie Robinson

The Robin to Longoria's Batman, Zobrist continues to fly under the national radar as one of the pillars of the Rays organization. The addition of Yunel Escobar allowed him to return to second base while maintaining cameo appearances in the corner outfield. The slash player maintained a stellar average and reached base often, but saw a steep drop in power. No concrete reason for the outage has been put forward publicly, but it is fair to wonder if age and mileage are catching up to him. There is also a chance it is just random variance as he still smacked doubles around the yard. Zobrist still does so many other things well that even a legitimate loss of power will not make him a below-average player. (See, for instance, his PECOTA line above.)

PITCHERS

Chris Archer
Born: 9/26/1988 Age: 25
Bats: R Throws: R Height: 6' 3" Weight: 200
Breakout: 33% Improve: 64% Collapse: 14%
Attrition: 24% MLB: 92%

Comparables:
Jake Arrieta, Jason Hirsh, Ian Kennedy

YEAR	TEAM	LVL	AGE	W	L	SV	G	GS	IP	H	HR	BB	SO	BB9	SO9	GB%	BABIP	WHIP	ERA	FIP	FRA	WARP
2011	MNT	AA	22	8	7	0	25	25	134¹	136	11	80	118	5.4	7.9	47%	.308	1.61	4.42	4.62	4.48	0.4
2011	DUR	AAA	22	1	0	0	2	2	13	11	0	6	12	4.2	8.3	50%	.364	1.31	0.69	2.78	1.38	0.3
2012	DUR	AAA	23	7	9	0	25	25	128	99	6	62	139	4.4	9.8	49%	.293	1.26	3.66	3.21	4.19	1.8
2012	TBA	MLB	23	1	3	0	6	4	29¹	23	3	13	36	4.0	11.0	44%	.299	1.23	4.60	3.35	4.70	0.2
2013	DUR	AAA	24	5	3	0	10	10	50	50	6	23	52	4.1	9.4	57%	.312	1.46	3.96	4.18	5.03	0.5
2013	TBA	MLB	24	9	7	0	23	23	128²	107	15	38	101	2.7	7.1	47%	.253	1.13	3.22	4.09	4.42	0.7
2014	TBA	MLB	25	10	9	0	29	29	149¹	131	15	68	134	4.1	8.1	48%	.284	1.33	3.78	4.35	4.11	1.3

In honor of Archer's self-styled literariness, some Steinbeck: "A boy becomes a man when a man is needed." Archer seemed bored and callow in Triple-A, his work there inconsistent. Then David Price got hurt. Archer was thrust into the big-league rotation and promptly had one of the best Julys in the history of rookie pitchers. The slider-loving righty needed The Show to show him, finally, that fastball command is the key to manly pitching. That enlightenment resulted in the lowest walk rate of Archer's career at any level. Along with that came the lowest strikeout rate (and an elevated homer rate), but the overall results bear out the lessons of command. All he needs this year, when expectations will be high, is to continue refining (to quote Steinbeck again) his "sureness of touch."

Heath Bell
Born: 9/29/1977 Age: 36
Bats: R Throws: R Height: 6' 3" Weight: 250
Breakout: 22% Improve: 39% Collapse: 48%
Attrition: 13% MLB: 80%

Comparables:
Eddie Guardado, Rich Gossage, Rollie Fingers

YEAR	TEAM	LVL	AGE	W	L	SV	G	GS	IP	H	HR	BB	SO	BB9	SO9	GB%	BABIP	WHIP	ERA	FIP	FRA	WARP
2011	SDN	MLB	33	3	4	43	64	0	62²	51	4	21	51	3.0	7.3	45%	.261	1.15	2.44	3.20	3.06	0.7
2012	MIA	MLB	34	4	5	19	73	0	63²	70	5	29	59	4.1	8.3	48%	.344	1.55	5.09	3.76	4.35	0.2
2013	ARI	MLB	35	5	2	15	69	0	65²	74	12	16	72	2.2	9.9	44%	.337	1.37	4.11	4.07	3.63	0.7
2014	TBA	MLB	36	3	1	12	62	0	59²	54	6	20	61	3.0	9.1	48%	.303	1.24	3.37	3.66	3.66	0.7

What happens when an ineffective closer is traded to a ballpark with less favorable conditions? Must-see TV, that's what happens. Arizona knew all this, yet Bell was given another shot to close when J.J. Putz was on the mend, and the results were rather variable, depending on the month. To some degree, the season marked a return to form, as he recovered his strikeout, walk, and batted ball rates. But a total inability to keep the ball in the park at home (where batters slugged .609 against him) eventually got him relegated to the seventh and eighth innings. That's more his bailiwick, and now two former employers will be paying him in absentia to pitch for Tampa Bay.

Alex Cobb
Born: 10/7/1987 Age: 26
Bats: R Throws: R Height: 6' 3" Weight: 190
Breakout: 40% Improve: 66% Collapse: 20%
Attrition: 21% MLB: 94%

Comparables:
Daniel Hudson, Jeremy Hellickson, Jordan Zimmermann

YEAR	TEAM	LVL	AGE	W	L	SV	G	GS	IP	H	HR	BB	SO	BB9	SO9	GB%	BABIP	WHIP	ERA	FIP	FRA	WARP
2011	DUR	AAA	23	5	1	0	12	12	67¹	61	4	16	70	2.1	9.4	50%	.320	1.14	1.87	2.73	6.23	-0.1
2011	TBA	MLB	23	3	2	0	9	9	52²	49	3	21	37	3.6	6.3	55%	.284	1.33	3.42	3.65	3.97	0.6
2012	DUR	AAA	24	1	4	0	8	8	41¹	44	1	18	44	3.9	9.6	57%	.355	1.50	4.14	2.79	3.38	1.0
2012	TBA	MLB	24	11	9	0	23	23	136¹	130	11	40	106	2.6	7.0	60%	.295	1.25	4.03	3.62	4.34	0.9
2013	TBA	MLB	25	11	3	0	22	22	143¹	120	13	45	134	2.8	8.4	57%	.279	1.15	2.76	3.39	4.03	1.1
2014	TBA	MLB	26	8	7	0	24	24	132	125	12	44	112	3.0	7.6	53%	.299	1.29	3.70	3.90	4.02	1.3

In an organization filled with top-shelf arms, it would be easy for Cobb—one with lesser natural ability—to get lost. Instead, he stands out as the most consistent performer in a talented rotation. Save for a line drive off the head that cost him most of the summer, Cobb was the Rays' best right-handed starter last season. Using a heavy low-90s sinker, he continued to post an above-average groundball rate while using one of the best changeups in the league and a plus curveball to strike out nearly a quarter of the batters he faced. On top of the impressive secondary offerings, he also has advanced control and command stemming from an extremely balanced delivery. Few young starters can change speed, shift eye levels and game-plan like Cobb. The combination makes him an ideal candidate for long-term investment.

Alex Colome
Born: 12/31/1988 Age: 25
Bats: R Throws: R Height: 6' 2" Weight: 185
Breakout: 27% Improve: 58% Collapse: 28%
Attrition: 69% MLB: 53%

Comparables:
Brad Mills, Philip Humber, P.J. Walters

YEAR	TEAM	LVL	AGE	W	L	SV	G	GS	IP	H	HR	BB	SO	BB9	SO9	GB%	BABIP	WHIP	ERA	FIP	FRA	WARP
2011	PCH	A+	22	9	5	0	19	19	105²	78	8	44	92	3.7	7.8	41%	.299	1.15	3.66	4.05	5.45	0.0
2011	MNT	AA	22	3	4	0	9	9	52	41	5	28	31	4.8	5.4	38%	.176	1.33	4.15	5.33	4.22	0.1
2012	MNT	AA	23	8	3	0	14	14	75	69	2	34	75	4.1	9.0	47%	.332	1.37	3.48	2.85	3.91	1.2
2012	DUR	AAA	23	0	1	0	3	3	16²	12	1	9	15	4.9	8.1	44%	.262	1.26	3.24	3.94	4.62	0.2
2013	DUR	AAA	24	4	6	0	14	14	70¹	63	5	29	72	3.7	9.2	42%	.301	1.31	3.07	3.49	4.01	1.2
2013	TBA	MLB	24	1	1	0	3	3	16	14	2	9	12	5.1	6.8	46%	.239	1.44	2.25	5.08	5.64	-0.1
2014	TBA	MLB	25	4	5	0	15	15	74¹	71	9	36	61	4.3	7.4	44%	.291	1.44	4.43	4.86	4.81	0.1

He looked promising in his three-game big-league debut, but a frayed elbow ligament, while not rising to the level of Dr. James Andrews project, shelved Colome after the first half. He has a violent release, more so since he scrapped his old, traditional windup for a near-stretch simplification—the arm has to generate almost all of the power. Colome's elbow problem was by no means his first injury, and the increasing signs of wear on a pitcher his age point to a potential move to the bullpen, where his mid-90s heater, ruthless new cutter and serviceable change and curve could make him an effective platoon complement to another converted starter, Alex Torres.

Jesse Crain
Born: 7/5/1981 Age: 32
Bats: R Throws: R Height: 6' 1" Weight: 215
Breakout: 22% Improve: 46% Collapse: 23%
Attrition: 7% MLB: 95%

Comparables:
Jason Frasor, Fernando Rodney, Will Ohman

YEAR	TEAM	LVL	AGE	W	L	SV	G	GS	IP	H	HR	BB	SO	BB9	SO9	GB%	BABIP	WHIP	ERA	FIP	FRA	WARP
2011	CHA	MLB	29	8	3	1	67	0	65¹	50	7	31	70	4.3	9.6	36%	.269	1.24	2.62	3.73	3.43	1.1
2012	CHA	MLB	30	2	3	0	51	0	48	29	5	23	60	4.3	11.2	39%	.229	1.08	2.44	3.40	2.94	0.9
2013	CHA	MLB	31	2	3	0	38	0	36²	31	0	11	46	2.7	11.3	38%	.330	1.15	0.74	1.55	1.10	1.4
2014	TBA	MLB	32	2	1	1	37	0	36	29	3	15	39	3.8	9.6	41%	.283	1.23	3.10	3.54	3.37	0.6

Crain posted one of the best half-seasons ever for a middle reliever before a right shoulder injury ended his campaign prematurely in July. Despite the ailment, the White Sox traded him at the deadline to the Rays; however, he never threw a pitch for Tampa Bay. Crain's fastball hovers around 94 mph, but it is a pair of breaking balls and a splitter that have led to a recent spike in strikeouts. The mid-80s slider is a plague on right-handed batters while the splitter and curve have helped him combat the platoon split versus lefties. Shoulder injuries have a way of making outside prognostications look foolish. Crain's 2014 could go any number of directions, from terrific to terrible to completely absent.

Brandon Gomes
Born: 7/15/1984 Age: 29
Bats: R Throws: R Height: 5' 11" Weight: 185
Breakout: 20% Improve: 35% Collapse: 49%
Attrition: 53% MLB: 46%

Comparables:
Josh Kinney, Aaron Rakers, Mike Zagurski

YEAR	TEAM	LVL	AGE	W	L	SV	G	GS	IP	H	HR	BB	SO	BB9	SO9	GB%	BABIP	WHIP	ERA	FIP	FRA	WARP
2011	DUR	AAA	26	0	1	7	20	0	25¹	17	1	7	40	2.5	14.2	31%	.692	0.95	1.07	1.54	0.09	0.5
2011	TBA	MLB	26	2	1	0	40	0	37	34	3	16	32	3.9	7.8	33%	.290	1.35	2.92	3.76	3.78	0.5
2012	DUR	AAA	27	5	4	9	40	0	55¹	44	5	14	73	2.3	11.9	29%	.307	1.05	3.09	2.62	3.34	1.3
2012	TBA	MLB	27	2	2	0	15	0	17²	16	2	12	15	6.1	7.6	37%	.269	1.58	5.09	5.20	5.31	-0.1
2013	DUR	AAA	28	0	0	0	9	0	10¹	7	1	1	14	0.9	12.2	33%	.261	0.77	2.61	2.33	3.86	0.2
2013	TBA	MLB	28	3	1	0	26	0	19¹	18	4	7	29	3.3	13.5	26%	.326	1.29	6.52	3.85	3.84	0.1
2014	TBA	MLB	29	2	1	1	32	0	37²	32	4	14	43	3.4	10.3	39%	.299	1.23	3.30	3.58	3.59	0.5

Another dreadful season against lefties recommends Gomes for strict platoon usage going forward. In 2013, he faced 38 percent lefties, and they torched him for an 1.137 OPS after a 1.047 in approximately the same usage in 2012. In other words, Gomes' splitter has never quite come around and his fastball (often slowed by injuries) isn't zippy enough to get by swinging bats. Gomes missed time early in 2012 recovering from back surgery, and lost more than half of 2013 to a latissimus dorsi strain. Gomes' sidearm delivery has ball-hiding advantages, but for now he's a guy to put on the Triple-A taxi squad and use sparingly.

Jeremy Hellickson
Born: 4/8/1987 Age: 27
Bats: R Throws: R Height: 6' 1" Weight: 190
Breakout: 25% Improve: 62% Collapse: 26%
Attrition: 19% MLB: 87%

Comparables:
Homer Bailey, Jordan Zimmermann, Micah Owings

YEAR	TEAM	LVL	AGE	W	L	SV	G	GS	IP	H	HR	BB	SO	BB9	SO9	GB%	BABIP	WHIP	ERA	FIP	FRA	WARP
2011	TBA	MLB	24	13	10	0	29	29	189	146	21	72	117	3.4	5.6	36%	.223	1.15	2.95	4.47	4.93	0.5
2012	TBA	MLB	25	10	11	0	31	31	177	163	25	59	124	3.0	6.3	43%	.262	1.25	3.10	4.55	4.59	1.0
2013	TBA	MLB	26	12	10	0	32	31	174	185	24	50	135	2.6	7.0	41%	.307	1.35	5.17	4.25	4.60	0.8
2014	TBA	MLB	27	10	8	0	27	27	155	138	18	48	123	2.8	7.2	40%	.272	1.20	3.46	4.27	3.77	1.9

Hellickson became the poster boy for regression following two years in which his runs-allowed stats outperformed his core components. Those rates were much better last season but the runs piled up in bunches. Many were comfortable writing off 2013 as haunted by luck dragons and the strand man, but two tangible demons were actually behind the perceived bad fortune: selection and location. Hellickson's fastball is average, but also the most important piece of his arsenal. A well-commanded heater allows his plus changeup and solid curveball to play up even more. Far too often last season he left pitches out over the plate and used his arsenal out of sequence. These flaws are correctable and do not require lucky charms.

Josh Lueke

Born: **12/5/1984** Age: **29**
Bats: **R** Throws: **R** Height: **6' 5"** Weight: **220**
Breakout: **21%** Improve: **38%** Collapse: **53%**
Attrition: **55%** MLB: **40%**

Comparables:
Aaron Rakers, Josh Roenicke, Chris Leroux

YEAR	TEAM	LVL	AGE	W	L	SV	G	GS	IP	H	HR	BB	SO	BB9	SO9	GB%	BABIP	WHIP	ERA	FIP	FRA	WARP
2011	TAC	AAA	26	2	4	11	30	0	42¹	34	1	12	35	2.6	7.4	51%	.255	1.09	2.76	3.64	3.10	1.0
2011	SEA	MLB	26	1	1	0	25	0	32²	34	2	13	29	3.6	8.0	44%	.327	1.44	6.06	3.28	3.96	0.3
2012	DUR	AAA	27	2	6	2	42	0	67²	85	6	17	71	2.3	9.4	40%	.389	1.51	5.59	2.97	4.16	0.9
2012	TBA	MLB	27	0	0	0	3	0	3¹	9	0	3	2	8.1	5.4	19%	.562	3.60	18.90	4.55	5.66	0.0
2013	DUR	AAA	28	3	1	17	40	0	57¹	41	1	15	81	2.4	12.7	46%	.310	0.98	0.63	1.50	1.79	2.3
2013	TBA	MLB	28	0	2	0	19	0	21¹	23	3	12	25	5.1	10.5	33%	.345	1.64	5.06	4.39	4.00	0.0
2014	TBA	MLB	29	3	1	0	49	0	67	62	6	22	68	2.9	9.2	44%	.310	1.25	3.51	3.50	3.81	0.7

Lueke's velocity increased, mostly thanks to better conditioning via offseason workouts with fellow fastball-slider-splitter buddy Brandon Gomes. But even at 95 to 97 mph, which is fast enough to dominate Triple-A, Lueke's flat fastball doesn't move off the middle of the plate enough to miss major-league bats. He threw too many of them right down the middle to right-handers, and resisted challenging lefties inside. His toothless secondary pitches didn't tempt hitters, who waited them out for hittable heat. There's enough velocity in Lueke's arm to keep him in a major-league bullpen, but his approach with or command of it needs work.

Jake McGee

Born: **8/6/1986** Age: **27**
Bats: **L** Throws: **L** Height: **6' 3"** Weight: **230**
Breakout: **42%** Improve: **67%** Collapse: **19%**
Attrition: **19%** MLB: **84%**

Comparables:
Antonio Bastardo, Tyler Clippard, Rafael Perez

YEAR	TEAM	LVL	AGE	W	L	SV	G	GS	IP	H	HR	BB	SO	BB9	SO9	GB%	BABIP	WHIP	ERA	FIP	FRA	WARP
2011	DUR	AAA	24	4	2	9	24	0	33¹	30	4	8	38	2.2	10.3	41%	.318	1.14	2.70	3.33	3.45	0.1
2011	TBA	MLB	24	5	2	0	37	0	28	30	5	12	27	3.9	8.7	33%	.312	1.50	4.50	4.74	4.20	0.0
2012	TBA	MLB	25	5	2	0	69	0	55¹	33	3	11	73	1.8	11.9	44%	.244	0.80	1.95	1.76	1.51	1.6
2013	TBA	MLB	26	5	3	1	71	0	62²	52	8	22	75	3.2	10.8	43%	.286	1.18	4.02	3.44	3.80	0.6
2014	TBA	MLB	27	3	2	1	43	4	53	44	5	18	59	3.1	10.1	42%	.294	1.18	3.04	3.35	3.30	0.9

McGee is blessed with a golden left arm that routinely fires fastballs in the upper 90s. A rough start to the season led to an inflated ERA, but a strong rebound soon after brought his overall numbers closer to respectability. Despite using one pitch more than 90 percent of the time, McGee excels against batters on both sides of the plate because of his command of that pitch. With the ability to hit several different spots in the zone, the single fastball plays like multiple offerings. Because of his high strikeout rate and velocity, some peg him as a future closer, but the Rays have been reluctant to give him save opportunities, perhaps as a way to keep his cost down through arbitration.

Mike Montgomery

Born: **7/1/1989** Age: **24**
Bats: **L** Throws: **L** Height: **6' 4"** Weight: **200**
Breakout: **25%** Improve: **54%** Collapse: **43%**
Attrition: **69%** MLB: **29%**

Comparables:
Cesar Carrillo, Josh Collmenter, Clayton Mortensen

YEAR	TEAM	LVL	AGE	W	L	SV	G	GS	IP	H	HR	BB	SO	BB9	SO9	GB%	BABIP	WHIP	ERA	FIP	FRA	WARP
2011	OMA	AAA	21	5	11	0	28	27	150²	157	15	69	129	4.1	7.7	49%	.299	1.50	5.32	4.88	4.64	1.7
2012	NWA	AA	22	2	6	0	10	10	58	69	12	21	44	3.3	6.8	49%	.318	1.55	6.67	5.69	7.11	-0.8
2012	OMA	AAA	22	3	6	0	17	17	91²	110	12	43	67	4.2	6.6	49%	.323	1.67	5.69	5.41	6.13	0.1
2013	DUR	AAA	23	7	8	0	20	19	108²	111	9	48	77	4.0	6.4	50%	.305	1.46	4.72	4.36	5.75	0.1
2014	TBA	MLB	24	6	7	0	20	20	107²	108	13	47	77	3.9	6.4	48%	.289	1.44	4.57	4.95	4.97	-0.2

Maybe the worst thing to befall Montgomery was being named the Royals' top prospect before the 2012 season, when he was just 22. Still green in his development, he wasn't ready for that mantle; two seasons later he's no readier, not even after a change of organizations and a year under the Rays' esteemed pitching tutelage. He's mechanically inconsistent, mentally fragile and prone to the big inning. He's also been unsuccessful so far at mastering a cutter to complicate his fastball-change-curve arsenal. The Rays dispatched Montgomery to the AFL to keep working out his many kinks. The well-armed club is in no rush for his big-league payoff, so they'll send him back to Triple-A and hope for incremental rather than quantum-leap improvement.

Matt Moore

Born: 6/18/1989 Age: 25
Bats: L Throws: L Height: 6' 3" Weight: 210
Breakout: 32% Improve: 65% Collapse: 22%
Attrition: 22% MLB: 97%

Comparables:
Edinson Volquez, Ubaldo Jimenez, Tommy Hanson

YEAR	TEAM	LVL	AGE	W	L	SV	G	GS	IP	H	HR	BB	SO	BB9	SO9	GB%	BABIP	WHIP	ERA	FIP	FRA	WARP
2011	MNT	AA	22	8	3	0	18	18	102¹	68	8	28	131	2.5	11.5	51%	.290	0.94	2.20	2.73	3.17	0.9
2011	DUR	AAA	22	4	0	0	9	9	52²	33	3	18	79	3.1	13.5	43%	.265	0.97	1.37	2.06	2.03	0.8
2011	TBA	MLB	22	1	0	0	3	1	9¹	9	1	3	15	2.9	14.5	46%	.381	1.29	2.89	2.20	3.41	0.3
2012	TBA	MLB	23	11	11	0	31	31	177¹	158	18	81	175	4.1	8.9	39%	.294	1.35	3.81	3.88	3.75	2.5
2013	TBA	MLB	24	17	4	0	27	27	150¹	119	14	76	143	4.5	8.6	41%	.260	1.30	3.29	3.98	4.33	1.1
2014	TBA	MLB	25	9	7	0	24	24	138²	117	13	66	148	4.3	9.6	42%	.291	1.32	3.56	3.93	3.87	1.5

There was opportunity last season for Moore to seize control of the Rays' rotation, but poor control led to an exorbitant walk rate, which in turn led to several early exits, traits not befitting an alpha pitcher. He also spent time on the disabled list with elbow inflammation and lost several ticks on his fastball. Still, there is plenty to like about the 24-year-old lefty, including his team-friendly contract. His breaking ball and changeup—both thrown in the low 80s—are legitimate weapons against right-handed batters, which is important since he sees one nearly 70 percent of the time. He also experimented with same-side changeups versus lefties prior to the injury. Moore's won-lost record and ERA look like that of a young ace, but the coronation should probably be delayed for at least one more year.

Jake Odorizzi

Born: 3/27/1990 Age: 24
Bats: R Throws: R Height: 6' 2" Weight: 185
Breakout: 39% Improve: 70% Collapse: 25%
Attrition: 46% MLB: 67%

Comparables:
Eric Hurley, Dan Straily, Wade LeBlanc

YEAR	TEAM	LVL	AGE	W	L	SV	G	GS	IP	H	HR	BB	SO	BB9	SO9	GB%	BABIP	WHIP	ERA	FIP	FRA	WARP
2011	WIL	A+	21	5	4	0	15	15	78¹	68	4	22	103	2.5	11.8	42%	.353	1.15	2.87	2.18	2.54	2.0
2011	NWA	AA	21	5	3	0	12	12	68²	66	13	22	54	2.9	7.1	28%	.286	1.28	4.72	5.27	5.94	0.5
2012	NWA	AA	22	4	2	0	7	7	38	27	2	10	47	2.4	11.1	36%	.269	0.97	3.32	2.28	3.28	1.1
2012	OMA	AAA	22	11	3	0	19	18	107¹	105	12	40	88	3.4	7.4	30%	.292	1.35	2.93	4.65	4.46	2.1
2012	KCA	MLB	22	0	1	0	2	2	7¹	8	1	4	4	4.9	4.9	39%	.280	1.64	4.91	5.36	5.90	0.0
2013	DUR	AAA	23	9	6	0	22	22	124¹	101	12	40	124	2.9	9.0	37%	.282	1.13	3.33	3.45	4.54	1.6
2013	TBA	MLB	23	0	1	1	7	4	29²	28	3	8	22	2.4	6.7	34%	.287	1.21	3.94	3.92	3.61	0.4
2014	TBA	MLB	24	8	7	0	23	23	128	120	15	46	107	3.2	7.5	37%	.285	1.29	3.84	4.36	4.17	1.0

Odorizzi is advanced for his age. None of his four pitches is a dazzler, but he commands them all and he works astutely and rationally on the mound. He's next in line behind Hellickson and Cobb in the Rays' march of smart, even-tempered righty hurlers who get the most out of good-not-great raw stuff. Odorizzi's fastball will touch 94 but sits lower, and he ran into some trouble with excessive foul balls in limited major-league action; he doesn't yet have a reliable put-away pitch. Sharper sequencing may solve that problem. He has a good shot at the Opening Day starting rotation, but if he isn't in it, he'll be the first guy up from Triple-A, and he's likely to spend more time in Tampa Bay than Durham.

Joel Peralta

Born: 3/23/1976 Age: 38
Bats: R Throws: R Height: 5' 11" Weight: 205
Breakout: 27% Improve: 48% Collapse: 24%
Attrition: 8% MLB: 80%

Comparables:
Al Reyes, Trevor Hoffman, Troy Percival

YEAR	TEAM	LVL	AGE	W	L	SV	G	GS	IP	H	HR	BB	SO	BB9	SO9	GB%	BABIP	WHIP	ERA	FIP	FRA	WARP
2011	TBA	MLB	35	3	4	6	71	0	67²	44	7	18	61	2.4	8.1	28%	.218	0.92	2.93	3.40	3.82	0.8
2012	TBA	MLB	36	2	6	2	76	0	67	49	9	17	84	2.3	11.3	32%	.261	0.99	3.63	3.09	3.52	0.9
2013	TBA	MLB	37	3	8	1	80	0	71¹	47	7	34	74	4.3	9.3	27%	.227	1.14	3.41	3.71	3.38	0.8
2014	TBA	MLB	38	3	2	1	62	0	61²	49	6	20	62	3.0	9.1	34%	.267	1.12	2.89	3.62	3.14	1.1

Peralta accepted less money to return to Tampa Bay, even tacking on three club options to his deal with no buyout to ensure his stay with the club. Advanced age has not slowed down the Dominican native, who led the league in relief appearances last season. His rubber arm propels a fastball that barely tops out at 90 mph, a loopy curve that often fails to hit 80 on the gun and a devastating splitter. It is the effectiveness of the splitter that has made him one of the best relievers against left-handed batters even though he throws with his right hand. The high-leverage ace does not rack up saves. He just collects outs with the game on the line.

David Price

Born: 8/26/1985 Age: 28
Bats: L Throws: L Height: 6' 6" Weight: 220
Breakout: 24% Improve: 55% Collapse: 23%
Attrition: 7% MLB: 96%

Comparables:
Josh Johnson, CC Sabathia, John Danks

YEAR	TEAM	LVL	AGE	W	L	SV	G	GS	IP	H	HR	BB	SO	BB9	SO9	GB%	BABIP	WHIP	ERA	FIP	FRA	WARP
2011	TBA	MLB	25	12	13	0	34	34	224¹	192	22	63	218	2.5	8.7	45%	.281	1.14	3.49	3.36	3.70	3.7
2012	TBA	MLB	26	20	5	0	31	31	211	173	16	59	205	2.5	8.7	53%	.286	1.10	2.56	3.00	3.75	3.1
2013	TBA	MLB	27	10	8	0	27	27	186²	178	16	27	151	1.3	7.3	47%	.299	1.10	3.33	3.05	3.53	3.1
2014	TBA	MLB	28	11	7	0	25	25	166²	144	15	48	153	2.6	8.2	47%	.284	1.15	3.02	3.57	3.28	2.9

The uncontested king of the Rays' jungle, Price struggled in the early going before a triceps injury landed him on the disabled list for the first time. You could argue the case that he improved on his 2012 Cy Young performance when he returned healthy in early July. His strikeout rate dropped a bit, but his command and control have never been better. Price lost some velocity off his fastball, but he had room for a decline, as he still clocked in with an average of 94 mph. Following that heat with a low-80s changeup and curveball along with a cutter in the upper 80s that he commands to his arm side ... well, it's easy to see why he's one of the best pitchers in the game. And he won't turn 30 until late in 2015.

Cesar Ramos

Born: 6/22/1984 Age: 30
Bats: L Throws: L Height: 6' 2" Weight: 205
Breakout: 27% Improve: 42% Collapse: 44%
Attrition: 63% MLB: 37%

Comparables:
Scott Randall, Jason Davis, Edgar Gonzalez

YEAR	TEAM	LVL	AGE	W	L	SV	G	GS	IP	H	HR	BB	SO	BB9	SO9	GB%	BABIP	WHIP	ERA	FIP	FRA	WARP
2011	TBA	MLB	27	0	1	0	59	0	43²	36	4	25	31	5.2	6.4	50%	.248	1.40	3.92	4.76	5.03	0.0
2012	DUR	AAA	28	5	5	1	25	7	62	58	10	16	46	2.3	6.7	43%	.262	1.19	3.77	4.54	5.59	0.1
2012	TBA	MLB	28	1	0	0	17	1	30	19	2	10	29	3.0	8.7	53%	.221	0.97	2.10	3.18	3.14	0.6
2013	TBA	MLB	29	2	2	1	48	0	67¹	66	6	22	53	2.9	7.1	42%	.293	1.31	4.14	3.73	4.20	0.4
2014	TBA	MLB	30	3	2	0	38	5	61	62	7	24	42	3.5	6.2	46%	.293	1.41	4.33	4.75	4.71	0.0

The Rays have shifted from a specialized to a free-form bullpen in recent seasons, leaving a flexible arm like Ramos filling several different roles. At times, he has been used as a one-out lefty, but he has also served as the de facto long man and even made a spot start along the way. The former starter continues to use a four-pitch mix, including a low-90s fastball, a mid-80s changeup and a pair of breaking balls that have more than 10 mph of separation. Arbitration-eligible for the first time, Ramos is still a bargain considering his versatility and quality arsenal.

C.J. Riefenhauser

Born: 1/30/1990 Age: 24
Bats: L Throws: L Height: 6' 0" Weight: 180
Breakout: 71% Improve: 71% Collapse: 21%
Attrition: 58% MLB: 22%

Comparables:
Jason Miller, Justin De Fratus, Ryan Rowland-Smith

YEAR	TEAM	LVL	AGE	W	L	SV	G	GS	IP	H	HR	BB	SO	BB9	SO9	GB%	BABIP	WHIP	ERA	FIP	FRA	WARP
2011	BGR	A	21	6	5	0	18	18	101¹	77	7	25	99	2.2	8.8	51%	.271	1.01	2.31	3.10	3.86	0.8
2011	PCH	A+	21	1	3	0	8	7	37	35	3	11	24	2.7	5.8	40%	.276	1.24	4.14	4.12	6.69	-0.1
2012	PCH	A+	22	7	8	1	23	14	96¹	98	11	32	103	3.0	9.6	36%	.331	1.35	4.76	3.92	5.49	1.0
2012	MNT	AA	22	1	1	0	9	1	18¹	15	4	8	15	3.9	7.4	28%	.220	1.25	3.44	6.14	6.27	-0.3
2013	MNT	AA	23	4	0	11	34	0	53	28	3	11	48	1.9	8.2	53%	.187	0.74	0.51	2.52	2.70	1.2
2013	DUR	AAA	23	2	1	0	17	0	20²	14	2	8	22	3.5	9.6	36%	.240	1.06	3.05	3.50	4.27	0.2
2014	TBA	MLB	24	3	2	1	27	5	64¹	62	9	26	51	3.6	7.2	41%	.287	1.37	4.35	4.91	4.73	-0.0

The top-heavy, chest-and-shoulders lefty, whose promise got him a gig in the Futures Game, was plain mean to same-siders in 2013 (.122 average against across Double- and Triple-A). At his best, he commands a low-90s fastball and nasty slider down in the zone, and he has a changeup to annoy righties, too, although LOOGY life might await him in the majors. The Rays traded his fellow Triple-A bullpen lefty, Frank De Los Santos, to Chicago last September, then added Riefenhauser to the 40-man in November, formalizing his position in the pecking order. You're likely to see his super-long name straining the shoulders of a Rays jersey this season.

Fernando Rodney

Born: 3/18/1977 Age: 37
Bats: R Throws: R Height: 5' 11" Weight: 220
Breakout: 24% Improve: 55% Collapse: 31%
Attrition: 7% MLB: 78%

Comparables:
Joey Eischen, Francisco Cordero, Brian Fuentes

YEAR	TEAM	LVL	AGE	W	L	SV	G	GS	IP	H	HR	BB	SO	BB9	SO9	GB%	BABIP	WHIP	ERA	FIP	FRA	WARP
2011	ANA	MLB	34	3	5	3	39	0	32	26	1	28	26	7.9	7.3	59%	.272	1.69	4.50	4.75	5.72	-0.3
2012	TBA	MLB	35	2	2	48	76	0	74²	43	2	15	76	1.8	9.2	59%	.220	0.78	0.60	2.08	2.42	1.8
2013	TBA	MLB	36	5	4	37	68	0	66²	53	3	36	82	4.9	11.1	50%	.298	1.34	3.38	2.87	2.83	1.3
2014	TBA	MLB	37	3	1	36	61	0	58¹	51	4	28	55	4.4	8.5	51%	.289	1.35	3.64	3.91	3.96	0.5

Following the greatest relief season in history (by ERA), Rodney was merely better than the average relief pitcher last season. The Rays reformed his mechanics in 2012, but he proved old habits die hard as he struggled to find a consistent delivery last year. This led to a familiar battle with control, though he did strike out more batters than ever before. Rodney keeps the ball on the ground and has allowed just six home runs in the past three seasons. His fastball reaches triple digits and his changeup is of the utmost quality. The free passes mean that it's probably safer if he is the second-best pitcher in a bullpen, but he has no issue handling the ninth-inning spotlight.

Enny Romero

Born: 1/24/1991 Age: 23
Bats: L Throws: L Height: 6' 3" Weight: 165
Breakout: 66% Improve: 84% Collapse: 16%
Attrition: 50% MLB: 38%

Comparables:
Justin Wilson, Chris Archer, Jarred Cosart

YEAR	TEAM	LVL	AGE	W	L	SV	G	GS	IP	H	HR	BB	SO	BB9	SO9	GB%	BABIP	WHIP	ERA	FIP	FRA	WARP
2011	BGR	A	20	5	5	0	26	26	114	104	9	68	140	5.4	11.1	57%	.285	1.51	4.26	3.82	4.00	1.0
2012	PCH	A+	21	5	7	0	25	23	126	89	5	76	107	5.4	7.6	47%	.244	1.31	3.93	4.19	5.68	0.1
2013	MNT	AA	22	11	7	0	27	27	140¹	110	9	73	110	4.7	7.1	44%	.252	1.30	2.76	3.78	4.49	0.8
2013	TBA	MLB	22	0	0	0	1	1	4²	1	0	4	0	7.7	0.0	64%	.071	1.07	0.00	5.65	5.26	0.0
2014	TBA	MLB	23	7	8	0	24	24	119¹	115	13	76	82	5.7	6.2	47%	.280	1.59	4.87	5.44	5.29	-0.5

"I could come pitch tomorrow": So Romero tweeted from his Dominican home four days after the Triple-A season ended, and one day before the Rays had no fresh arms to start a game in the hot-and-heavy final week of the regular season. So the Rays took him up on it—he started on September 22nd, showing exactly what he offers: a fastball that touches 97 mph, thrown from a big frame and complemented by a change and curve, and persistent control trouble somewhat mitigated by the difficulty of hitting him. Romero will start the season in Triple-A, where he probably needs at least a full season to ready himself not just to "come pitch tomorrow" but for many big-league years beyond. There's a good chance his walk rate forces him to the bullpen in the long term, though.

Ryne Stanek
Born: 7/26/1991 Age: 22
Bats: R Throws: R Height: 6' 4" Weight: 180

YEAR	TEAM	LVL	AGE	W	L	SV	G	GS	IP	H	HR	BB	SO	BB9	SO9	GB%	BABIP	WHIP	ERA	FIP	FRA	WARP
2014	—	—	—	—	—	—	—	—	—	—	—	—	—	—	—	—	—	—	—	—	—	—

Once a potential top 10 pick in the draft, Stanek nearly fell out of the first round altogether before the Rays selected him 29th overall. The concerns on the Arkansas right-hander range from health to control, and his future role hangs in the balance. He will be groomed as a starter, but his mid-90s fastball and plus breaking ball have some thinking late-inning reliever in the Daniel Bard ilk. Kiley McDaniel of Scout.com reported in December that many teams had concerns about the state of Stanek's pitching elbow and that elbow may have been the reason he did not debut in 2013; a winter surgery on the labrum in his right hip will delay him even further, reportedly until mid-summer.

Alex Torres
Born: 12/8/1987 Age: 26
Bats: L Throws: L Height: 5' 10" Weight: 175
Breakout: 33% Improve: 56% Collapse: 31%
Attrition: 52% MLB: 68%

Comparables:
Michael Kirkman, Brian Slocum, Frankie
De La Cruz

YEAR	TEAM	LVL	AGE	W	L	SV	G	GS	IP	H	HR	BB	SO	BB9	SO9	GB%	BABIP	WHIP	ERA	FIP	FRA	WARP
2011	DUR	AAA	23	9	7	0	27	27	146¹	134	7	83	156	5.1	9.6	45%	.319	1.48	3.08	3.55	3.58	1.0
2011	TBA	MLB	23	1	1	0	4	0	8	8	0	7	9	7.9	10.1	59%	.364	1.88	3.38	3.81	5.00	0.0
2012	DUR	AAA	24	3	7	0	26	14	69	70	6	63	91	8.2	11.9	47%	.368	1.93	7.30	4.52	6.01	0.5
2013	DUR	AAA	25	2	2	0	9	9	46	34	2	21	61	4.1	11.9	50%	.288	1.20	3.52	2.62	3.90	1.0
2013	TBA	MLB	25	4	2	0	39	0	58	32	1	20	62	3.1	9.6	46%	.221	0.90	1.71	2.35	2.42	1.2
2014	TBA	MLB	26	4	4	0	31	12	82	72	7	45	82	5.0	9.0	51%	.298	1.44	4.02	4.19	4.37	0.5

"... or thrive in the bullpen," we concluded at the end of last year's comment about the nearly ruined starting prospect. Thrive indeed. The Rays, bedeviled by early-season relief woes, called Torres up from the Triple-A starting rotation in May for two games, then again for good in early June. They watched him get all the way to August before he allowed his second run of the season. Relieving allowed the tightly wound Torres to attack hitters with more immediate purpose and urgency. Like Chris Archer, another plus arm with suspect minor-league control, Torres posted the lowest walk rate of his professional career in his first substantial major-league action. So that's what pitching coaches do.

Kirby Yates
Born: 3/25/1987 Age: 27
Bats: L Throws: R Height: 5' 10" Weight: 170
Breakout: 16% Improve: 43% Collapse: 39%
Attrition: 63% MLB: 40%

Comparables:
Robert Coello, Kevin Whelan, Josh Fields

YEAR	TEAM	LVL	AGE	W	L	SV	G	GS	IP	H	HR	BB	SO	BB9	SO9	GB%	BABIP	WHIP	ERA	FIP	FRA	WARP
2011	PCH	A+	24	2	0	2	16	0	33¹	14	0	22	45	5.9	12.1	35%	.300	1.08	1.62	3.12	4.28	0.1
2012	MNT	AA	25	4	2	16	50	0	68	48	4	39	94	5.2	12.4	43%	.299	1.28	2.65	2.91	2.94	1.8
2013	DUR	AAA	26	3	2	20	51	0	61²	38	2	23	93	3.4	13.6	41%	.286	0.99	1.90	1.97	2.43	1.9
2014	TBA	MLB	27	2	2	1	29	4	52	43	5	26	59	4.5	10.3	41%	.297	1.33	3.65	3.96	3.96	0.5

Yates lacks the size of older brother Tyler, the former Braves/Pirates reliever. The younger's gaudy strikeout rates in the upper minors come instead from his funky, ass-before-elbows, earflip delivery, which hides the ball from hitters and puts some late English on his 93 to 94 mph fastball. Yates complements the heater with a good slider and a not-ready-for-prime-time changeup. Competitive and dogged on the mound, with late-inning composure, Yates will get a long look in spring training and has a good shot to make the big-league club.

LINEOUTS

HITTERS

PLAYER	TEAM	LVL	AGE	PA	R	2B	3B	HR	RBI	BB	SO	SB-CS	AVG/OBP/SLG	TAv	BABIP	BRR	FRAA	WARP
1B L. Anderson	DUR	AAA	31	494	52	28	1	14	74	50	58	2-3	.292/.372/.459	.283	.308	-3.2	1B(44): 0.4, LF(41): -0.6	1.9
1B S. Duncan	DUR	AAA	33	376	36	21	1	11	54	33	82	0-0	.215/.287/.382	.225	.247	-2.3	1B(35): -1.2, LF(10): -0.4	-1.5
	TBA	MLB	33	64	6	1	0	2	6	9	14	0-0	.182/.297/.309	.215	.205	-1.3	1B(4): -0.0	-0.4
3B C. Figueroa	DUR	AAA	26	533	65	20	4	3	62	54	30	10-2	.286/.361/.367	.256	.296	0.1	3B(94): -11.5, 2B(20): -2.5	0.3
2B M. Fontenot	DUR	AAA	33	472	53	32	2	4	42	37	87	6-1	.264/.335/.379	.240	.322	-1.2	2B(82): -2.2, SS(15): -0.8	0.1
C O. Hernandez	HUD	A-	19	181	22	6	0	6	33	11	24	9-1	.228/.282/.371	.251	.232	-0.6	C(38): 1.3	0.8
SS H. Lee	DUR	AAA	22	57	13	3	1	1	7	11	9	6-2	.422/.536/.600	.387	.514	2.7	SS(15): -0.7	1.2
RF M. Mahtook	MNT	AA	23	568	71	30	8	7	68	43	102	25-8	.254/.322/.386	.261	.303	-0.1	RF(85): 0.9, CF(43): 0.4	1.7
1B A. Segovia	PCH	A+	23	436	48	22	1	14	51	44	66	0-1	.281/.376/.457	.298	.306	-2.2	1B(41): 0.8, 3B(1): 0.0	2.2

Leslie Anderson steadily improved through all four years of his minor-league tenure with the Rays; that they never called him up despite a $1.725 million investment (and Michael Lewis' fulsome early praise) sums up his big-league value. ⊘ **Shelley Duncan** was inadvertently left out of the 2013 Annual, and after his miserable season he probably wishes we'd left him out of this one, too; sorry, Shelley. ⊘ Undersized, underpowered and underspeeded, **Cole Figueroa** overperforms his physical attributes by a mile, but this economy coupe will have to do more than repeat his Triple-A specs to earn a big-league job. ⊘ **Mike Fontenot** just wants to celebrate and live his life. ⊘ In his first—and only—American inning of baseball since 2009, September add-on Fast **Freddy Guzman** flew in from Mexico, pinch-ran and scored a crucial 11th-inning run in the Rays' playoff sprint. TOTALLY WORTH IT. ⊘ **Oscar Hernandez** made noise at the plate as a teenager in Venezuela with good bat speed, advanced feel for the zone and raw power; since then, his work with the glove has impressed stateside. ⊘ **Hak-Ju Lee** lost 2013 to a gruesome knee ligament injury, pushing his big-league arrival date back to at least 2015. ⊘ **Mikie Mahtook**'s first full year at Double-A (in just his second pro season) saw Kevin Kiermaier bump him to right field. Regression accompanied extended exposure to the rigors of the level, but the Rays expect Mahtook to reach Triple-A in 2014. ⊘ **Alejandro Segovia** stopped catching last season but continued to hit, hit, hit, making him an under-the-radar, offense-first prospect. ⊘ **Riley Unroe**'s athleticism and tools convinced the Rays to lure him away from Southern Cal for $1 million in last year's second round. The son of former big-leaguer Tim, the Team USA grad started as a shortstop but could switch to center field, like another former Tampa Bay prospect whose five-letter last name starts with U. ⊘ **Kean Wong**, younger brother of stud Cardinals prospect Kolten, went to the Rays in the fourth round last year and quickly whipped out his impressive hit tool in Rookie ball, including an advanced ability to go to the opposite field.

PITCHERS

PLAYER	TEAM	LVL	AGE	W	L	SV	IP	H	HR	BB	SO	BB9	SO9	GB%	BABIP	WHIP	ERA	FIP	FRA	WARP
J. Ames	BGR	A	22	9	4	0	114²	87	10	38	83	3.0	6.5	34%	.237	1.09	2.98	4.15	5.15	0.8
J. Beliveau	DUR	AAA	26	2	3	1	44²	41	1	22	76	4.4	15.3	37%	.404	1.41	2.62	1.64	1.98	1.9
	TBA	MLB	26	0	0	0	0²	1	0	1	0	13.5	0.0	33%	.333	3.00	0.00	7.58	6.65	0.0
D. Floro	BGR	A	22	9	2	0	109¹	103	4	19	85	1.6	7.0	67%	.305	1.12	1.81	2.81	4.30	1.6
	PCH	A+	22	2	0	0	28	20	0	2	14	0.6	4.5	56%	.235	0.79	1.61	2.56	3.96	0.2
S. Geltz	DUR	AAA	25	5	3	3	67	35	8	24	80	3.2	10.7	33%	.189	0.88	2.82	3.49	5.08	0.4
T. Guerrieri	BGR	A	20	6	2	0	67	54	5	12	51	1.6	6.9	67%	.266	0.99	2.01	3.77	5.03	0.6
J. Hahn	PCH	A+	23	2	1	0	67	55	1	18	63	2.4	8.5	63%	.284	1.09	2.15	2.49	3.53	1.4
M. Kelly	MNT	AA	24	5	6	0	73²	54	3	31	41	3.8	5.0	43%	.231	1.15	4.15	3.71	4.71	0.1
	DUR	AAA	24	8	4	0	84²	74	4	34	70	3.6	7.4	41%	.281	1.28	3.19	3.48	4.93	0.6
J. Martin	DUR	AAA	30	16	4	0	160¹	168	15	26	116	1.5	6.5	45%	.303	1.21	2.75	3.63	4.50	1.6
J. Niemann	TBA	MLB	29	2	3	0	38	30	2	12	34	2.8	8.1	53%	.264	1.11	3.08	3.05	3.98	0.6
F. Rivero	PCH	A+	21	9	7	0	127	122	7	52	91	3.7	6.4	47%	.299	1.37	3.40	3.92	5.24	-0.1
B. Snell	BGR	A	20	4	9	0	99	90	8	73	106	6.6	9.6	57%	.318	1.65	4.27	4.52	5.28	0.7

Jeff Ames is a big right-hander with a mid-90s fastball and a good slider that may play up in relief if starting passes him by. ⊘ **Jeff Beliveau**, an early-season waiver claim from the Rangers, was called up four different times in 2013 and finally got to pitch two-thirds of an inning in a September 27th blowout, consummating a season's worth of dry humps. ⊘ Plenty of teenagers with big fastballs draw notice way down the pipeline, but it was **Jose Castillo**'s heater that had a Rays official drooling in September. ⊘ A two-time draft pick of the Rays, **Dylan Floro** was named Tampa Bay's minor-league pitcher of the year after dominating the Midwest League with a low-90s sinker and a mid-80s slider. ⊘ **Steve Geltz** and his impressive minor-league strikeout rates live by the high fastball; major-league power hitters live on high fastballs, too. ⊘ **Taylor Guerrieri**, Tampa Bay's top pick in the 2011 draft, followed up his mid-season Tommy John surgery by taking the Tim Beckham approach to Rays first-rounderhood: he got busted for smoking pot. The suspension and rehab time will run concurrently, however, so he should not actually miss any games. ⊘ Post-draft Tommy John surgery in 2010 delayed **Jesse Hahn**'s climb up the prospect ladder, but the big righty, a high school teammate of Matt Harvey's, skipped a level of A-ball in 2013, suffocated the Florida State League with a heavy mid-90s fastball, and was added to the 40-man. ⊘ **Merrill Kelly**, a finesse changeup specialist out of Arizona State, blipped onto the radar with a surprisingly strong, heady showing in half a season at Triple-A, so the Rays packed him and his wavering control off to the AFL hoping to be further convinced. Eighteen hits in 11 innings there didn't do him any favors. ⊘ **J.D. Martin**, an intelligent, poised soft-tosser, harnessed his cutter and had a glorious 2013, posting the International League's lowest walk rate and winning its Most Valuable Pitcher award, which he parlayed into millions—of Korean won, from the Samsung Lions. ⊘ **Jeff Niemann**, never known for his durability, has a cloudy future after a shoulder injury ended his 2013 season before it started. ⊘ **Felipe Rivero** touches 95 with his heater and has what one Rays official called "wiry strength," although the Ron Guidry comparison seemed a little much. ⊘ One Rays official thinks finesse lefty **Blake Snell** had "the best changeup in the Midwest League" last year, and Snell's formerly snail velocity inched up, too, with the occasional heater touching 94. ⊘ With a name this manly, Arkansan **Hunter Wood** just *has* to be a prospect, but his 94 mph fastball doesn't hurt, and the Rays think they might have a find with this 2013 29th-round pick.

MANAGER: JOE MADDON

YEAR	TEAM	W-L	Pythag +/-	Avg PC	100+ P	120+ P	QS	BQS	REL	REL w Zero R	IBB	PH	PH Avg	PH HR	SB2	CS2	SB3	CS3	SAC Att	SAC %	POS SAC	Squeeze	Swing	In Play
2011	TBA	91-71	1	102.1	98	5	99	10	438	355	38	129	.252	1	134	54	20	8	63	58.7%	35	5	441	138
2012	TBA	90-72	1	99.9	91	7	90	2	471	415	35	135	.178	3	122	38	11	5	62	54.8%	32	3	354	105
2013	TBA	91-71	1	94.7	64	2	79	2	485	399	38	168	.230	1	61	34	11	3	39	61.5%	24	0	292	93

Joe Maddon is probably the most universally well regarded manager in the big leagues these days. In his eight years on the job, Tampa has the most stolen base attempts of any team (1,537). They have one of the best success rates, too: 73.8 percent of all attempts have succeeded, the ninth-best rate in all baseball. Using the old Pete Palmer valuation of a stolen base being worth 0.3 runs and a caught stealing costing twice that, Tampa has gained 99 runs stealing bases under Maddon, third behind Philadelphia and the Mets in that time.

2013 was the first time that Maddon's Rays fanned fewer times than league average.

Maddon has a quick hook with his relievers. In fact, the 2011 Rays have the all-time AL record for fewest innings per relief appearance. Runner up is the 2009 Rays. The 2010 and 2012 Rays are also in the top five. (Ozzie Guillen and the 2007 White Sox prevent a clean sweep for Maddon). Obviously, there is an era bias, but even still—Maddon has easily the quickest hook among modern AL managers.

Texas Rangers

By Lana Berry

'm rocking back and forth. My hands are clasped so tightly I can see the whites of my knuckles. I'm not religious but I'm praying to something. I feel delirious, drunk on baseball, drunk on Yu Darvish's slider. There are two outs in the ninth inning. I was lucky enough to be in attendance at Kenny Rogers' perfect game, but I was just a kid then. I knew the meaning of it, but it felt nothing like this. This feels worse. I am a nervous wreck. I can barely enjoy the magnificence I'm watching. Even in the early innings, it's as if the music starts the second the baseball departs Darvish's fingertips. The ball moves to the music, it glides and flutters around. And then it teases you. It appears in front of you. You think it's yours for the taking. You swing and before you know it the ball has curled around past you. I can't help but giggle in delight at the sight of it. Darvish keeps giving me slider after slider, strikeout after strikeout. I wipe drool from the corner of my mouth. Try to keep myself composed. Is it hot in here? It feels like love. I'm giddy. It's only the second game of the season. How did I get so lucky? But as the innings go on, I feel the weight of the situation. What all this means. A.J. Pierzynski caught Philip Humber's perfect game only a year ago. They are now on opposing teams and exchange glances. This is it. I'm excited but also nervous. Is this really happening? I remind myself to breathe.

Inhale. Exhale.

Darvish has struck out 14. There's one batter left. Marwin Gonzalez. What kind of name is Marwin? Darvish is rushing it. He's rushed the entire inning. He wants it to be over. He's tired. Now I've picked my deity: I'm praying to Baseball Jesus. I close my eyes before Darvish even throws the pitch. I hear the crack of the bat. My eyes open. It's a sharp grounder right between Darvish's legs. It's impossible to field. It's a hit. I think I'm going to cry. All I feel is disappointment. Followed hard by anger at myself for being disappointed.

I just watched something amazing and I'm upset about it. To come so close and fall short at the last second. The last out. The last strike. That's something I'm all too familiar with as a Rangers fan.

Inhale. Exhale.

Expectations are a funny thing. When your team has been terrible for years, and I mean a lot of years, your expectations stay low. It's a protective measure to save yourself the heartache every October. I've adapted so much to the "low expectations" model that actually having heightened hopes for my team is uncomfortable, a little tight in the fit. It makes sense, though. The Rangers went to the World Series twice, and even though they lost both times, those were two more World Series than they'd ever attended before. But two 90-plus-win seasons later, without another playoff run (no, losing the 2012 Wild Card game does not count as a playoff run), and suddenly Rangers fans are running out of fingers to point. Blog comments, the Rangers' Facebook page, a quick Twitter search—it doesn't take long to find a mess of people calling for the firing of Jon Daniels. Or complaining about Darvish not knowing how to win. Or wanting to trade whoever is currently slumping. Some aren't as severe as others, but what is with all the complaining? The team is the best it's ever been. Get over it. You can't go to the World Series every year. I know the higher expectations make it sting, but, seriously, it's going to be okay. The Rangers have remained competitive through injuries and slumps, and this is what they get in response from the fans? This is why we can't have nice things.

Inhale. Exhale.

Dallas is not a baseball town, but that's fine because the Rangers play in Arlington. When I was growing up, the only things in Arlington were Six Flags, the water park across the street from Six Flags, and Rangers baseball, first in Arlington

RANGERS PROSPECTUS					
2013 W-L: 91-71, 2nd in AL West					
Pythag	.565	7th	DER	.707	10th
RS/G	4.49	8th	B-Age	29.6	25th
RA/G	3.90	10th	P-Age	27.0	6th
TAv	.270	8th	Salary	$125.3	9th
BRR	5.17	8th	M$/MW	$2.66	14th
TAv-P	.258	10th	DL Days	1104	23rd
FIP	3.8	13th	$ on DL	16%	14th

	Runs	HR/RH	HR/LH	Runs/RH	Runs/LH
Three-Year Park Factors	101	84	90	100	102

Top Hitter WARP	5.67 (Adrian Beltre)
Top Pitcher WARP	3.28 (Yu Darvish)
Top Prospect	Rougned Odor

Stadium and later in the Ballpark in Arlington. Sure, the Cowboys have recently moved their stadium into town (right next to the Ballpark, so rude), but Arlington will always remain a "baseball town" (I hate this phrase, for the record) in the eyes of Rangers fans. Being located in Arlington gives the Rangers a small-market feel. Except they're not a small-market team. At all. They're not a big-market team either. In a world that loves nothing more than to label everything, this team has remained unlabeled, not just in market type, but in philosophy and identity too. The lack of identity keeps them under the radar of the "haters." The Rangers have consistently proven themselves to be a team to beat, which could certainly inspire some sort of grudge, rivalry, resentment, but mostly they're just ... good. And it's the nongrating way they go about being so good, not buying up all the good players on the free-agent market, not being the overachieving darlings who inspire a bestselling book by buying fat players and guys who throw funny. Instead, the core of the organization is a farm system that is consistently replenished with a crop of fresh talent. That talent produces major leaguers directly, but also allows the team to fill holes through trade. Jon Daniels hoarded middle infielders for a while, so now Ian Kinsler can be traded away for Prince Fielder and Jurickson Profar steps in to play every day. This approach has prevented the Rangers from being forced to overspend on free agents every year to stay competitive. Yet with all this in the background, I still see people asking why the Rangers "refuse to spend money."

Inhale. Exhale.

They just don't *need* to overspend. That's not to say they won't shell out when it's necessary. Adrian Beltre has proved to be more than worth his contract, and that one guy Yu Darvish has turned out pretty okay. But the heart of the team is homegrown. If Colby Lewis and Matt Harrison manage to return from the dead and to the rotation this year, four of the Rangers' starting pitchers will have come through the Rangers' minor-league system. Neftali Feliz, too. The Rangers have a strong knack for spotting talent and nurturing that talent. Ian Kinsler was a 17th-round draft pick who became one of the best second basemen in the league. Derek Holland was a 25th-round pick who has developed into a solid middle-of-the-rotation pitcher. The bullpen, built from dudes named things like "Tanner" and "Chaz," has not only been strong, it's been so strong that the team basically told Joe Nathan, who earned 80 saves over the last two seasons, "Look, it's been fun and you're really great but we've got like three other guys who can do your job and we don't have to pay them out the ass for it, so enjoy free agency." Between the front office being one of the best in the league and the team just being so damn fun to watch (seriously, keep an iso camera on Beltre and Elvis the whole game, we'll all watch it), the Rangers are really

going out of their way to make you not dislike them. Even Ron Washington provides an old school "bunting" vibe if that's what you're into. Something for everybody! Some people will surely keep complaining and nitpicking, but they're really just missing all the fun.

Inhale. Exhale.

"I want the world. I want the whole world. I want to lock it all up in my pocket. It's my bar of chocolate. Give it to me now!" That's Veruca Salt, the greedy little girl in *Willy Wonka & the Chocolate Factory* who constantly wants more than she is given. She's repulsive, and she represents most people in this world. She certainly represents most baseball fans. Except instead of a bar of chocolate it's wins or runs or beer, and oh hell, sometimes it's chocolate. There is never a point of satisfaction. You desire more. What you have isn't enough. Something else out there is better. So caught up in greed and desire that you completely lose any sense of reality. Wanting more of a good thing is a normal human reaction. The problem arises when you get so caught up in wanting more that you don't appreciate what you have. You might think you will stop wanting more once your team wins a World Series, except I have seen people freak out the year after their team won the trophy. They want more. You'll want more. You want a World Series. And then you want two. Never enough. You want the world. You want the whole world. And you want it now. But you must know, the grass isn't greener in a different ballpark; they're all pretty much the same shade.

Inhale. Exhale.

Yu Darvish ended 2013 with 277 strikeouts. (That's 11.9 strikeouts per nine innings, if you're keeping track.) No one else came close to that number. Clearly no one came very close to hitting his pitches either. It's not just that he has a stacked arsenal, including some pitches we've probably never heard of; it's that they're all so effective. He doesn't have one out-pitch; he has 12. Hitters never know what they're going to get, but they do know they're going to have a hard time with it. For all that, though, Yu Darvish has yet to pitch a complete game in the majors. The unhittability of his pitches means the ball isn't being put into play for early outs. Which means a higher pitch count. This seems logical. But the problem with raised expectations is it brings out the illogical side. Fans want more. They want it now. I was told many times over the course of the 2013 season that Darvish isn't an ace because he can't close out games and he just doesn't win. The facts: Darvish pitched 12 games in which he struck out at least 10 batters. In four of those, he struck out 14. In one he struck out 15. The Rangers won only half of them. In five of the six losses, they provided two runs or fewer in support. Darvish had a stunningly spectacular season, one that will sadly be viewed by many as a disappointment. But isn't that fitting? The Rangers had 91 wins despite an injury-riddled season, but there was no playoff run, so it's all a disappointment. You want the whole world.

Inhale. Exhale.

Lana Berry is a professional party crasher, sometimes writer and Internet inhabitant.

HITTERS

Jim Adduci   RF

Born: 5/15/1985 Age: 29
Bats: L Throws: L Height: 6' 2"
Weight: 210 Breakout: 0%
Improve: 1% Collapse: 5%
Attrition: 8% MLB: 10%

Comparables:
Darnell McDonald, Mike Vento, T.J. Bohn

YEAR	TEAM	LVL	AGE	PA	R	2B	3B	HR	RBI	BB	SO	SB	CS	AVG/OBP/SLG	TAv	BABIP	BRR	FRAA	WARP
2011	TEN	AA	26	267	44	13	2	4	20	26	33	21	4	.308/.379/.430	.267	.345	2.1	LF(28): -0.3, RF(18): -1.8	0.7
2012	TEN	AA	27	293	40	12	1	5	27	31	47	11	3	.294/.367/.409	.282	.340	2	LF(33): -1.0, CF(29): 5.8	2.6
2012	IOW	AAA	27	170	27	9	2	2	17	17	40	7	4	.306/.377/.435	.292	.402	1.5	RF(27): 0.1, LF(14): -0.5	1.1
2013	ROU	AAA	28	551	75	24	3	16	65	65	107	32	9	.298/.381/.463	.306	.351	-0.9	RF(59): -5.8, CF(34): 0.4	3.5
2013	TEX	MLB	28	34	2	1	0	0	0	3	9	2	0	.258/.324/.290	.254	.364	0.4	LF(8): -0.0, 1B(4): -0.1	0.1
2014	TEX	MLB	29	250	28	10	1	5	25	21	55	10	3	.257/.322/.371	.253	.310	0.8	RF -1, CF 0	0.4

It was a breakout year for Adduci, despite what his major-league numbers might indicate. The former 42nd-round draft pick of the Florida Marlins came to spring training with the Rangers as an afterthought, a minor-league free agent expected to simply provide depth in Triple-A, but he almost immediately generated positive buzz among camp watchers. Solid play for Round Rock earned Adduci a promotion to the majors (and corresponding spot on the 40-man roster), and while he didn't hit during his September cup of coffee, he is expected to go to camp in 2014 battling with Engel Beltre for a backup outfielder job. Not bad for a 28-year-old viewed as a minor-league lifer before the season.

Jorge Alfaro   C

Born: 6/11/1993 Age: 21
Bats: R Throws: R Height: 6' 2"
Weight: 185 Breakout: 0%
Improve: 0% Collapse: 0%
Attrition: 0% MLB: 0%

Comparables:
Welington Castillo, Kyle Skipworth, Wilson Ramos

YEAR	TEAM	LVL	AGE	PA	R	2B	3B	HR	RBI	BB	SO	SB	CS	AVG/OBP/SLG	TAv	BABIP	BRR	FRAA	WARP
2011	SPO	A-	18	171	18	9	1	6	23	4	54	1	0	.300/.345/.481	.280	.420	-1	C(34): 0.6	0.6
2012	HIC	A	19	300	40	21	5	5	34	16	84	7	3	.261/.320/.430	.263	.355	1.2	C(29): -0.2, 1B(17): -0.1	0.7
2013	HIC	A	20	420	63	22	1	16	53	28	111	16	3	.258/.338/.452	.280	.324	-0.4	C(82): 1.4, 1B(17): -1.2	2.8
2014	TEX	MLB	21	250	22	9	1	6	26	10	81	1	0	.211/.258/.335	.218	.290	-0.2	C 0, 1B -0	-0.2

Rangers fans lamenting the team's failure to bring Brian McCann into the fold are hoping that the team's decision to pass on the chief of the Unwritten Rules Police is motivated by its belief that Jorge Alfaro—#TheLegend—will soon be ready for The Show. Signed out of Colombia in 2010 to a then-record $1.3 million bonus, Alfaro has big-time power and a big-time arm, but the rest of his game is still a work in progress and his aggressiveness at the plate will be exploited as he climbs the ladder. The positive is that observers felt he took strides behind the plate in 2013, and 2014 could see leaps. If Alfaro continues to improve his catching skills, he's got a very good chance of having a major-league career, but the maturity of his bat will determine whether that future is more Lance Parrish or Miguel Olivo.

Elvis Andrus   SS

Born: 8/26/1988 Age: 25
Bats: R Throws: R Height: 6' 0"
Weight: 200 Breakout: 2%
Improve: 47% Collapse: 9%
Attrition: 3% MLB: 96%

Comparables:
Russ Adams, Alex Cintron, Barry Larkin

YEAR	TEAM	LVL	AGE	PA	R	2B	3B	HR	RBI	BB	SO	SB	CS	AVG/OBP/SLG	TAv	BABIP	BRR	FRAA	WARP
2011	TEX	MLB	22	665	96	27	3	5	60	56	74	37	12	.279/.347/.361	.256	.312	7.1	SS(147): 2.6	3.3
2012	TEX	MLB	23	711	85	31	9	3	62	57	96	21	10	.286/.349/.378	.257	.332	5.7	SS(153): 3.0	3.6
2013	TEX	MLB	24	698	91	17	4	4	67	52	97	42	8	.271/.328/.331	.251	.312	6.8	SS(146): -5.2	2.4
2014	TEX	MLB	25	658	81	23	5	4	47	55	91	32	10	.274/.341/.351	.256	.310	2.4	SS -1	2.7

On March 31st, Ken Rosenthal tweeted that the Rangers and Elvis Andrus were close on a long-term contract extension, and it appeared to be an early April Fools' joke. Jurickson Profar was knocking on the door, Ian Kinsler was locked up. Besides, Andrus is a Scott Boras client, and Boras clients always test free agency, right? But sure enough, the Rangers and Andrus announced an eight-year, $120 million extension running from 2015 to 2022, with Andrus having the right to opt out after 2018 or 2019. While the Twitterati were quick to rip the Rangers for overpaying and not properly utilizing their resources, Jon Daniels was just as quick to point out that Andrus was a 24-year-old star at a premium position, explaining that, "in a lot of ways, he is everything we're all about." The Rangers locked up a terrific defender and baserunner who is at least league average with the bat relative to his position and entering his physical prime. After a poor first half, Elvis hit .313/.369/.405 in the second half, and if he can continue that sort of performance going forward, the contract extension will look like a bargain.

J.P. Arencibia — C

Born: 1/5/1986 Age: 28
Bats: R Throws: R Height: 6' 0"
Weight: 200 Breakout: 4%
Improve: 42% Collapse: 14%
Attrition: 17% MLB: 92%

Comparables:
Jarrod Saltalamacchia, Nick Hundley, Eliezer Alfonzo

YEAR	TEAM	LVL	AGE	PA	R	2B	3B	HR	RBI	BB	SO	SB	CS	AVG/OBP/SLG	TAv	BABIP	BRR	FRAA	WARP
2011	TOR	MLB	25	486	47	20	4	23	78	36	133	1	1	.219/.282/.438	.254	.255	-2.3	C(122): 1.3	1.8
2012	TOR	MLB	26	372	45	16	0	18	56	18	108	1	0	.233/.275/.435	.250	.281	0.1	C(94): 1.0	1.5
2013	TOR	MLB	27	497	45	18	0	21	55	18	148	0	2	.194/.227/.365	.217	.231	-1.9	C(131): 0.4	-0.5
2014	TEX	MLB	28	443	50	18	1	20	58	26	120	1	1	.224/.274/.417	.251	.260	-0.8	C -0	1.6

Last year, Arencibia was the worst everyday catcher in baseball—and that's despite having improved his previously worst-in-baseball pitch framing by working with Sal Fasano. There are many stats to shield your eyes from, but here's the one unlikely to improve: In his three seasons as a starter, Arencibia has the worst walk-to-strikeout ratio among players with 1,000 plate appearances. His isolated power, which had compensated a little for the lack of discipline, sank to a career-low .171. Arencibia didn't help his cause by getting into a public spat with Blue Jays analysts (including Dirk Hayhurst) who had the temerity to say he wasn't good. The Jays nontendered him; he'll try to get his mojo back in Arlington.

Jeff Baker — 1B

Born: 6/21/1981 Age: 33
Bats: R Throws: R Height: 6' 2"
Weight: 210 Breakout: 1%
Improve: 27% Collapse: 12%
Attrition: 20% MLB: 87%

Comparables:
Xavier Nady, Eric Karros, Roger Freed

YEAR	TEAM	LVL	AGE	PA	R	2B	3B	HR	RBI	BB	SO	SB	CS	AVG/OBP/SLG	TAv	BABIP	BRR	FRAA	WARP
2011	CHN	MLB	30	212	20	12	1	3	23	10	46	0	0	.269/.302/.383	.248	.333	2.5	1B(19): -0.7, 2B(18): -0.2	0.1
2012	CHN	MLB	31	144	16	10	1	4	20	8	28	4	1	.269/.306/.448	.264	.308	-0.3	1B(20): -2.4, RF(14): 0.1	0.0
2012	DET	MLB	31	37	1	2	0	0	4	2	10	0	0	.200/.243/.257	.201	.280	-0.1	RF(11): -0.2, 3B(4): 0.0	-0.2
2012	ATL	MLB	31	20	1	0	0	0	1	1	10	0	0	.105/.150/.105	.102	.222	0	LF(3): -0.1, 2B(1): 0.0	-0.3
2013	TEX	MLB	32	175	21	8	0	11	21	18	48	1	0	.279/.360/.545	.318	.333	-1.8	LF(21): -0.3, 1B(21): -1.2	0.9
2014	TEX	MLB	33	250	25	12	1	6	27	17	60	2	0	.253/.307/.387	.257	.320	-0.1	1B -3, LF -1	0.1

Baker had a .317/.391/.695 line through his first 92 plate appearances while getting starts against most lefties. Then an overly aggressive high five (administered by a player whose identity is as closely guarded a secret as the special ingredient in Nolan Ryan's beef) sprained Baker's thumb and put him on the disabled list. Baker wasn't the same after his return, putting up a .236/.325/.375 slash in 83 plate appearances the rest of the way. Given that his 2011 and 2012 campaigns were disappointing, there has to be at least some concern that his pre-injury 2013 performance was his last hurrah, and that his days as a quality right-handed platoon partner/bench bat are behind him.

Adrian Beltre — 3B

Born: 4/7/1979 Age: 35
Bats: R Throws: R Height: 5' 11"
Weight: 220 Breakout: 1%
Improve: 23% Collapse: 5%
Attrition: 11% MLB: 97%

Comparables:
Aramis Ramirez, Mike Lowell, Mark DeRosa

YEAR	TEAM	LVL	AGE	PA	R	2B	3B	HR	RBI	BB	SO	SB	CS	AVG/OBP/SLG	TAv	BABIP	BRR	FRAA	WARP
2011	TEX	MLB	32	525	82	33	0	32	105	25	53	1	1	.296/.331/.561	.305	.273	1	3B(112): 2.9	4.6
2012	TEX	MLB	33	654	95	33	2	36	102	36	82	1	0	.321/.359/.561	.321	.319	0	3B(129): -6.2	5.7
2013	TEX	MLB	34	690	88	32	0	30	92	50	78	1	0	.315/.371/.509	.312	.322	-1.7	3B(146): -5.2	5.7
2014	TEX	MLB	35	641	77	33	1	25	91	36	87	2	1	.293/.338/.479	.294	.310	-1	3B 1	3.9

Is this the Golden Age of third basemen? Adrian Beltre, Scott Rolen and Chipper Jones all debuted in the 90s, and all slot pretty comfortably in the top 10 third basemen of all time. David Wright and Evan Longoria, meanwhile, look like solid bets to join those three, meaning five out of the top dozen third basemen ever would have entered the majors in a span of 15 seasons, including five years where they all overlapped. That's not even counting Miguel Cabrera, who has been a Dick Allen/Pete Rose-type Player Without a Permanent Position in his career. Beltre as a Hall of Famer has been gaining momentum among saber-types the past couple of seasons, and he has a certain mystique (team leader, run producer) that suggests he will garner significant support from the more traditional voters. While he seems to be slowing defensively, no one does the charge-and-throw-to-first on a bunt or slow roller better than Beltre.

Engel Beltre — CF

Born: 11/1/1989 Age: 24
Bats: L Throws: L Height: 6' 2"
Weight: 180 Breakout: 5%
Improve: 18% Collapse: 0%
Attrition: 10% MLB: 25%

Comparables:
Angel Pagan, Juan Lagares, Gorkys Hernandez

YEAR	TEAM	LVL	AGE	PA	R	2B	3B	HR	RBI	BB	SO	SB	CS	AVG/OBP/SLG	TAv	BABIP	BRR	FRAA	WARP
2011	FRI	AA	21	482	64	15	6	1	28	28	103	16	6	.231/.285/.300	.202	.299	1.5	CF(76): 3.4, RF(9): 0.4	-0.5
2012	FRI	AA	22	614	80	17	17	13	55	26	118	36	10	.261/.307/.420	.259	.307	2.3	CF(119): 12.8, RF(2): 0.2	3.7
2012	ESP	INT	22	21	4	0	1	0	3	4	1	3	0	.375/.524/.500	.377	.400	0		0.0
2013	ROU	AAA	23	439	58	19	1	7	34	28	84	15	12	.292/.340/.398	.277	.351	-3.9	CF(94): 1.7	2.2
2013	TEX	MLB	23	42	7	1	0	0	2	0	5	1	2	.250/.268/.275	.227	.286	0.5	RF(6): 0.0, CF(5): 0.4	0.1
2014	TEX	MLB	24	250	28	9	2	3	19	10	57	8	4	.239/.275/.341	.226	.290	0.6	CF 3, LF 0	0.3

Enigmatic Engel, a guy who has been around forever, it seems, without ever really taking a step forward. Acquired by the Rangers in 2007 for Eric Gagne—who has been out of baseball so long he was eligible for the Hall of Fame this offseason— Beltre has seemingly had the same scouting report since the day he was signed: lots of tools, little in the way of skills, awful approach at the plate, could be terrific if it ever clicks. At 24 and out of options, Beltre's ceiling is no longer sky-high, but he gives you elite defense in the outfield, so if nothing else he has the opportunity to carve out a career as a reserve outfielder who can pinch-run and come in for defense.

Lance Berkman   RF

Born: 2/10/1976 Age: 38
Bats: B Throws: L Height: 6' 1"
Weight: 220 Breakout: 0%
Improve: 12% Collapse: 11%
Attrition: 15% MLB: 81%

Comparables:
Rafael Palmeiro, Billy Williams, Stan Musial

YEAR	TEAM	LVL	AGE	PA	R	2B	3B	HR	RBI	BB	SO	SB	CS	AVG/OBP/SLG	TAv	BABIP	BRR	FRAA	WARP
2011	SLN	MLB	35	587	90	23	2	31	94	92	93	2	6	.301/.412/.547	.346	.315	-1.7	RF(110): -10.0, 1B(21): 0.5	4.9
2012	MEM	AAA	36	20	1	1	0	0	1	3	3	0	0	.235/.350/.294	.236	.286	0.1	1B(5): 0.0	0.0
2012	SLN	MLB	36	97	12	7	1	2	7	14	19	2	0	.259/.381/.444	.300	.317	0	1B(23): -1.1	0.5
2013	TEX	MLB	37	294	27	10	1	6	34	38	52	0	0	.242/.340/.359	.251	.283	-2.6	1B(4): 0.3	-0.2
2014	TEX	MLB	38	250	31	10	1	8	32	37	47	1	1	.256/.367/.430	.290	.290	-0.6	RF -2, 1B 0	1.0

After failing in their efforts to sign or trade for a big bat, the Rangers went with Lance Berkman as Plan F. And "F" is a pretty fair grade for Berkman's 2013 season—after putting up decent numbers in April, he was awful the rest of the season, battling physical problems that landed him on the disabled list for two months. Berkman didn't have a hit after July 3rd or a walk after July 6th, and his uselessness resulted in the Rangers effectively having to use a 20-year-old shortstop as their DH in the second half. Berkman has never been one of those you thought would try to play until they tore the uniform off him, and after two straight bad, injured-plagued years, this would be a predictable end to a Hall of Very Good career.

Chris Bostick   2B

Born: 3/24/1993 Age: 21
Bats: R Throws: R Height: 5' 11"
Weight: 185 Breakout: 1%
Improve: 3% Collapse: 0%
Attrition: 2% MLB: 4%

Comparables:
Brett Lawrie, Nick Noonan, Jonathan Schoop

YEAR	TEAM	LVL	AGE	PA	R	2B	3B	HR	RBI	BB	SO	SB	CS	AVG/OBP/SLG	TAv	BABIP	BRR	FRAA	WARP
2012	VER	A-	19	316	41	16	4	3	29	27	66	12	5	.251/.325/.369	.278	.318	2.1	2B(53): 1.0, SS(10): -1.0	1.9
2013	BLT	A	20	555	75	25	8	14	89	51	122	25	8	.282/.354/.452	.280	.346	4.7	2B(125): -10.3	2.0
2014	TEX	MLB	21	250	26	9	1	5	21	15	71	3	1	.219/.268/.333	.219	.290	0.1	2B -3, SS -0	-0.6

When a team is drafting in the 44th round, it is mostly looking to fill the organizational depth chart as opposed to penciling in future starters. Bostick, then, was a savvy find out of upstate New York by Oakland. He is a strong athlete who plays a solid second base, and he outhit his more heralded teammates on a prospect-laden Beloit club, displaying surprising skills in nearly every phase of the game. The bat has made a believer out of many scouts—including, presumably, those of the Rangers, who acquired him as part of the Craig Gentry trade. Bostick is a quick study and continued development of his tool kit will further solidify his position on the prospect map.

Robinson Chirinos   C

Born: 6/5/1984 Age: 30
Bats: R Throws: R Height: 6' 1"
Weight: 205 Breakout: 4%
Improve: 13% Collapse: 5%
Attrition: 17% MLB: 27%

Comparables:
Steve Holm, Mike Nickeas, JD Closser

YEAR	TEAM	LVL	AGE	PA	R	2B	3B	HR	RBI	BB	SO	SB	CS	AVG/OBP/SLG	TAv	BABIP	BRR	FRAA	WARP
2011	DUR	AAA	27	319	24	13	1	6	24	29	69	1	1	.259/.343/.376	.171	.324	-1.1	C(21): 0.1	-0.8
2011	TBA	MLB	27	60	4	2	0	1	7	5	13	0	0	.218/.283/.309	.243	.268	-1	C(19): -0.1, 1B(1): 0.0	-0.1
2013	ROU	AAA	29	311	35	10	2	8	40	38	55	2	0	.257/.356/.400	.287	.294	1.7	C(51): -0.3, 3B(10): -0.6	2.2
2013	TEX	MLB	29	30	3	3	0	0	0	2	6	0	0	.179/.233/.286	.183	.227	-0.4	1B(4): 0.0, C(3): -0.0	-0.2
2014	TEX	MLB	30	250	24	9	1	4	23	23	53	0	0	.226/.303/.332	.238	.270	-0.3	C 0, 3B -0	0.4

The Rangers are persistent when it comes to getting their guy. According to Peter Gammons, they tried to acquire Robinson Chirinos from the Cubs in the 2010-11 offseason, planning to then package him with Derek Holland, Engel Beltre and Frank Francisco to the Rays for Matt Garza. That deal fell through, but the Rangers snagged Chirinos prior to the 2013 season, and stashed him in Triple-A as their third catcher. A.J. Pierzynski's injured stint and an overall lack of bench bats resulted in Chirinos spending more time in the majors than the team would have preferred, though his actual playing time was limited. Chirinos offers versatility by playing the corner infield spots as well as catching, and will likely be squirreled away in Round Rock in 2014 as insurance, though he has a shot at sticking as the last guy on the bench if the coaching staff likes his bat in spring training.

Michael Choice   CF

Born: 11/10/1989 Age: 24
Bats: R Throws: R Height: 6' 0''
Weight: 215 Breakout: 0%
Improve: 18% Collapse: 9%
Attrition: 12% MLB: 36%

Comparables:
Eric Thames, Todd Frazier, Michael Taylor

YEAR	TEAM	LVL	AGE	PA	R	2B	3B	HR	RBI	BB	SO	SB	CS	AVG/OBP/SLG	TAv	BABIP	BRR	FRAA	WARP
2011	STO	A+	21	542	79	28	1	30	82	61	134	9	5	.285/.376/.542	.329	.336	1	CF(76): -0.9	3.8
2012	MID	AA	22	402	59	15	2	10	58	33	88	5	1	.287/.356/.423	.279	.352	1.7	CF(85): -7.9	1.1
2013	SAC	AAA	23	600	90	29	1	14	89	69	115	1	2	.302/.390/.445	.303	.358	-4.9	LF(55): -4.5, CF(52): -2.5	3.0
2013	OAK	MLB	23	19	2	1	0	0	0	1	6	0	0	.278/.316/.333	.294	.417	0	RF(4): 0.1, LF(2): -0.0	0.1
2014	TEX	MLB	24	250	27	10	0	8	30	21	61	0	0	.253/.324/.403	.265	.310	-0.4	CF -2, LF -1	0.4

Choice revamped his swing prior to 2013, simplifying his leg kick and quieting the load, adjustments that allowed him to be quicker to the ball and react to inside fastballs. The results of his altered approach are reflected in a shrunken strikeout rate and better results on contact, though the prodigious power that previously propelled his prospect position was possibly poisoned. Choice was homerless in his final 143 plate appearances of the year, but the overall results speak to his ability to respond to instruction and make adjustments, factors that bode well for his development path. Swapped for Craig Gentry, he'll begin the difficult process of turning Texas pro-Choice.

Shin-Soo Choo   LF

Born: 7/13/1982 Age: 31
Bats: L Throws: L Height: 5' 11''
Weight: 205 Breakout: 1%
Improve: 45% Collapse: 3%
Attrition: 4% MLB: 98%

Comparables:
Carlos Beltran, Fred Lynn, Bernie Williams

YEAR	TEAM	LVL	AGE	PA	R	2B	3B	HR	RBI	BB	SO	SB	CS	AVG/OBP/SLG	TAv	BABIP	BRR	FRAA	WARP
2011	CLE	MLB	28	358	37	11	3	8	36	36	78	12	5	.259/.344/.390	.268	.317	1.2	RF(85): 3.6	1.4
2012	CLE	MLB	29	686	88	43	2	16	67	73	150	21	7	.283/.373/.441	.293	.353	-0.2	RF(154): 0.2	3.7
2013	CIN	MLB	30	712	107	34	2	21	54	112	133	20	11	.285/.423/.462	.318	.338	1.1	CF(150): -4.5, LF(3): -0.1	6.3
2014	TEX	MLB	31	664	96	31	3	17	70	82	140	20	8	.277/.382/.435	.298	.340	0.1	LF -5, CF -0	3.5

When Choo landed in Cincinnati in the winter of 2012, the biggest debate was whether his defense in center field would be atrocious or unbearable. Not only was it merely below average, but he brought along the best offensive season of his career. In fact, Choo would have been nearly unstoppable if it were illegal for pitchers to throw with their left hands. His .612 OPS against southpaws in 2013 was bad even by his standards, and he's going to need a recovery in that department to avoid being platooned in the near future—although it will be tough to justify, optics-wise, under his new $130 million contract.

Nelson Cruz   RF

Born: 7/1/1980 Age: 33
Bats: R Throws: R Height: 6' 2''
Weight: 230 Breakout: 1%
Improve: 26% Collapse: 4%
Attrition: 10% MLB: 97%

Comparables:
Juan Gonzalez, Steve Souchock, Dave Winfield

YEAR	TEAM	LVL	AGE	PA	R	2B	3B	HR	RBI	BB	SO	SB	CS	AVG/OBP/SLG	TAv	BABIP	BRR	FRAA	WARP
2011	TEX	MLB	30	513	64	28	1	29	87	33	116	9	5	.263/.312/.509	.275	.288	-2.4	RF(109): 8.2, LF(18): 0.7	2.2
2012	TEX	MLB	31	642	86	45	0	24	90	48	140	8	4	.260/.319/.460	.278	.301	-0.7	RF(151): 5.6, LF(6): -0.2	3.0
2013	TEX	MLB	32	456	49	18	0	27	76	35	109	5	1	.266/.327/.506	.294	.295	-0.9	RF(102): -2.5	1.9
2014	TEX	MLB	33	465	60	23	1	21	66	37	108	8	3	.258/.320/.465	.282	.300	-0.1	RF 7, LF 0	2.7

Cruz didn't stick in the majors until 2009, so fans forget how old he is—older than Hank Blalock and Chris Snelling and Sean Burroughs, older than Shane Victorino (who was dismissed as washed up two years ago), older than CC Sabathia, who seems ancient. Hell, he's older than Mark Prior, who threw his final pitch 10 days after Nelson Cruz's first home run. Cruz is largely known for his defensive gaffe in Game Six of the 2011 World Series and for his involvement with Biogenesis, which is unfortunate; he's a great lesson in perseverance, he's well liked and respected in the clubhouse, and his career 1.018 OPS in 137 postseason plate appearances is a big part of the reason the Rangers advanced to back-to-back World Series. His speed and defense are almost gone, but his power stroke is still there, and when he gets all of a pitch, few hitters hit it farther.

Prince Fielder   1B

Born: 5/9/1984 Age: 30
Bats: L Throws: R Height: 5' 11''
Weight: 275 Breakout: 2%
Improve: 45% Collapse: 4%
Attrition: 4% MLB: 99%

Comparables:
Todd Helton, Lance Berkman, Nick Johnson

YEAR	TEAM	LVL	AGE	PA	R	2B	3B	HR	RBI	BB	SO	SB	CS	AVG/OBP/SLG	TAv	BABIP	BRR	FRAA	WARP
2011	MIL	MLB	27	692	95	36	1	38	120	107	106	1	1	.299/.415/.566	.329	.306	-3.3	1B(159): -0.7	5.4
2012	DET	MLB	28	690	83	33	1	30	108	85	84	1	0	.313/.412/.528	.320	.321	-8	1B(159): 0.8	4.3
2013	DET	MLB	29	712	82	36	0	25	106	75	117	1	1	.279/.362/.457	.297	.307	-5.5	1B(151): -6.4	2.4
2014	TEX	MLB	30	665	92	29	1	29	99	90	112	1	1	.281/.390/.493	.316	.300	-1.4	1B -3	4.0

Here is the good thing about Fielder's 2013 effort: His worst year since his rookie season still produced a 120 OPS+ in 162 games played. Further, he looked downright Fielderian in both April (1.009 OPS) and September (.933). And the bad thing about Fielder's 2013 effort: the rest, at a cost of $23 million. He sank near these depths once before, in 2010—saved only by an MLB-high 114 walks, propping up his OBP—and rebounded with a massive 2011, so there's no reason to believe this is the start of an early demise to a wonderful career. It would have been more worrisome if his impeccable record of durability had faltered, but he still played every game even as he dealt with personal issues off the field.

Joey Gallo   3B

Born: 11/19/1993 Age: 20
Bats: L Throws: R Height: 6' 5"
Weight: 205 Breakout: 6%
Improve: 17% Collapse: 1%
Attrition: 8% MLB: 21%

Comparables:
Giancarlo Stanton, Xander Bogaerts, Travis Snider

YEAR	TEAM	LVL	AGE	PA	R	2B	3B	HR	RBI	BB	SO	SB	CS	AVG/OBP/SLG	TAv	BABIP	BRR	FRAA	WARP
2012	SPO	A-	18	67	9	2	0	4	9	11	26	0	0	.214/.343/.464	.293	.308	-0.9	3B(16): 1.6	0.5
2013	HIC	A	19	446	82	19	5	38	78	48	165	14	1	.245/.334/.610	.316	.305	3.1	3B(100): -3.6	3.7
2014	TEX	MLB	20	250	33	7	1	16	41	21	98	1	0	.209/.278/.464	.262	.270	0	3B -2	0.5

Prior to the 2005 draft, a publication described Georgia Tech pitcher Jason Neighborgall—he of the 80 fastball, 80 curveball and 20 command—as having the highest ceiling and lowest chance of reaching it of any pitcher in the draft. Gallo brings that anecdote to mind: He has as much raw power as anyone in professional baseball, a big arm that could potentially play on the mound if this whole hitting thing doesn't work out and enormous problems making enough contact for his power to be utilizable. An incredible 56 percent of his plate appearances for Hickory ended in one of the Three True Outcomes, including 165 strikeouts in 446 plate appearances. Gallo is a fascinating, polarizing prospect, someone whose dream ceiling is a dominant middle-of-the-order hitter in the majors, but who is much more likely to end up as another Russ Branyan or Dean Palmer, and might be more likely to make the All-Star Game down the road as a reliever than as a position player.

Leonys Martin   CF

Born: 3/6/1988 Age: 26
Bats: L Throws: R Height: 6' 2"
Weight: 190 Breakout: 4%
Improve: 63% Collapse: 8%
Attrition: 14% MLB: 91%

Comparables:
Shane Victorino, Nate McLouth, Cameron Maybin

YEAR	TEAM	LVL	AGE	PA	R	2B	3B	HR	RBI	BB	SO	SB	CS	AVG/OBP/SLG	TAv	BABIP	BRR	FRAA	WARP
2011	FRI	AA	23	135	24	9	2	4	24	15	8	10	8	.348/.435/.571	.325	.347	1.6	CF(22): -1.3, LF(3): 0.1	1.3
2011	ROU	AAA	23	192	27	7	1	0	17	11	24	9	2	.263/.316/.314	.159	.303	0	CF(9): 0.7	-0.3
2011	TEX	MLB	23	8	2	1	0	0	0	0	1	0	0	.375/.375/.500	.346	.429	-0.1	CF(8): 0.2	0.1
2012	ROU	AAA	24	260	48	18	2	12	42	24	39	10	9	.359/.422/.610	.352	.392	2.1	CF(46): 2.9, LF(8): -0.6	3.9
2012	TEX	MLB	24	52	6	5	2	0	6	4	12	3	0	.174/.235/.370	.191	.229	-0.2	CF(14): 0.4, LF(4): 0.3	-0.2
2013	TEX	MLB	25	508	66	21	6	8	49	28	104	36	9	.260/.312/.385	.256	.319	4.1	CF(127): 4.2, RF(21): -0.4	2.5
2014	TEX	MLB	26	417	59	20	4	9	38	27	78	24	9	.266/.322/.410	.262	.300	1.6	CF 3, RF -0	1.7

When the Rangers signed Martin in 2011, the book on the Cuban defector was that he was a quality defender and baserunner, but there were questions about his bat. After spending most of 2011 and 2012 in the minors, he got an opportunity to play every day in the majors in 2013. So what's the report on him now? He's a quality defender and baserunner, but there are questions about his bat. The Rangers gave Martin a guaranteed $15.5 million because they thought he could be an offensive catalyst at the top of the order, but at the major-league level he hasn't catalyzed squat. A .422 Triple-A OBP in 2012 suggests better, and the plan is for Martin to bat leadoff in 2014.

Mitch Moreland   1B

Born: 9/6/1985 Age: 28
Bats: L Throws: L Height: 6' 2"
Weight: 240 Breakout: 1%
Improve: 37% Collapse: 6%
Attrition: 13% MLB: 90%

Comparables:
Adam Lind, Lance Niekro, Ryan Garko

YEAR	TEAM	LVL	AGE	PA	R	2B	3B	HR	RBI	BB	SO	SB	CS	AVG/OBP/SLG	TAv	BABIP	BRR	FRAA	WARP
2011	TEX	MLB	25	512	60	22	1	16	51	39	92	2	2	.259/.320/.414	.255	.290	0.2	1B(99): -2.8, RF(34): 0.9	0.3
2012	TEX	MLB	26	357	41	18	0	15	50	23	71	1	1	.275/.321/.468	.271	.306	-1.9	1B(95): 7.1, RF(3): 0.1	1.6
2013	TEX	MLB	27	518	60	24	1	23	60	45	117	0	0	.232/.299/.437	.269	.255	-2.1	1B(146): 3.4, RF(1): -0.0	1.2
2014	TEX	MLB	28	459	53	21	1	16	56	40	94	1	1	.251/.321/.421	.267	.290	-0.9	1B 1, RF -0	0.9

Not many teams have even one 17th-round draft pick starting for them, but the Rangers had a pair doing so from 2011 to 2013, with Moreland at first base and Ian Kinsler 15 paces to his right. The Rangers passed on bringing Mike Napoli back in 2013 because they felt Moreland was ready to take a step forward and establish himself as a quality first baseman. Instead, he regressed, setting career lows in average, OBP and slugging. Moreland's pattern has been to start the season hot before getting hurt and then struggling to the finish. The Rangers still like his power potential, but with Prince Fielder coming to town, Moreland is looking at a bench role, a platoon or a new zip code.

Rougned Odor   2B

Born: 2/3/1994 Age: 20
Bats: L Throws: R Height: 5' 11"
Weight: 170 Breakout: 5%
Improve: 8% Collapse: 0%
Attrition: 5% MLB: 9%

Comparables:
Jonathan Schoop, Jose Ramirez, Adrian Cardenas

YEAR	TEAM	LVL	AGE	PA	R	2B	3B	HR	RBI	BB	SO	SB	CS	AVG/OBP/SLG	TAv	BABIP	BRR	FRAA	WARP
2011	SPO	A-	17	258	33	9	3	2	29	13	37	10	4	.262/.323/.352	.249	.301	-0.9	2B(51): -0.6	0.1
2012	HIC	A	18	471	60	23	4	10	47	25	65	19	10	.259/.313/.400	.261	.284	0.8	2B(85): 0.6, SS(15): -0.7	1.5
2013	MYR	A+	19	425	65	33	4	5	59	26	67	27	8	.305/.369/.454	.293	.355	1.4	2B(84): 4.3	3.6
2013	FRI	AA	19	144	20	8	2	6	19	9	24	5	2	.306/.354/.530	.314	.337	-0.4	2B(30): 2.5	1.6
2014	TEX	MLB	20	250	28	11	1	5	21	8	52	6	2	.240/.274/.355	.232	.290	0.2	2B 2, SS -0	0.3

Odor had just turned 19 when the 2013 season started, and was the youngest player in the Carolina League on Opening Day, so it would have been understandable if he had been overmatched in High-A. But Odor continued to impress with his hit tool, his solid glove at second base and his hard-nosed attitude. One of the phrases you hear about Odor is that he plays "with a chip on his shoulder," and if he makes it to the majors, he will no doubt be one of those players who fans love and opposing fans absolutely despise. Like his double play partner Luis Sardinas, his path to the majors is currently blocked, but there will be teams lining up to acquire him if Texas makes him available.

Jurickson Profar SS

Born: 2/20/1993 Age: 21
Bats: B Throws: R Height: 6' 0"
Weight: 165 Breakout: 4%
Improve: 21% Collapse: 2%
Attrition: 8% MLB: 28%

Comparables:
Starlin Castro, Elvis Andrus, Ruben Tejada

YEAR	TEAM	LVL	AGE	PA	R	2B	3B	HR	RBI	BB	SO	SB	CS	AVG/OBP/SLG	TAv	BABIP	BRR	FRAA	WARP
2011	HIC	A	18	516	86	37	8	12	65	65	63	23	9	.286/.390/.493	.321	.309	4.3	SS(103): -3.6	5.2
2012	FRI	AA	19	562	76	26	7	14	62	66	79	16	4	.281/.368/.452	.296	.306	-0.8	SS(97): -8.9, 2B(25): -1.8	3.1
2012	TEX	MLB	19	17	2	2	0	1	2	0	4	0	0	.176/.176/.471	.202	.167	-0.4	2B(5): -0.2, SS(3): -0.1	-0.2
2013	ROU	AAA	20	166	27	7	2	4	19	21	24	6	1	.278/.370/.438	.289	.310	1.5	SS(30): 0.6, 2B(7): -0.6	1.3
2013	TEX	MLB	20	324	30	11	0	6	26	26	63	2	4	.234/.308/.336	.248	.280	-0.8	2B(32): -2.2, SS(18): 0.1	0.2
2014	TEX	MLB	21	335	40	15	2	7	32	30	59	5	2	.249/.321/.387	.260	.280	0	SS -2, 2B -2	0.8

Profar, a 20-year-old shortstop, was pressed into duty at the major-league level as a utility player in the middle of a pennant race, was asked to play a variety of positions, and managed to perform respectably despite irregular playing time. The fact that so many fans and media members saw that as a failure suggests that Bryce Harper and Mike Trout have warped all of our views about what 20-year-old prospects ought to be able to do. Profar isn't likely to be a superstar, but he should be a very, very good player who has a long major-league career. The trade of Ian Kinsler means that Profar will be the Rangers' starting second baseman in 2014, a role he appears ready to handle.

Alex Rios RF

Born: 2/18/1981 Age: 33
Bats: R Throws: R Height: 6' 5"
Weight: 210 Breakout: 0%
Improve: 38% Collapse: 7%
Attrition: 8% MLB: 96%

Comparables:
Randy Winn, Brian Jordan, Lee Maye

YEAR	TEAM	LVL	AGE	PA	R	2B	3B	HR	RBI	BB	SO	SB	CS	AVG/OBP/SLG	TAv	BABIP	BRR	FRAA	WARP
2011	CHA	MLB	30	570	64	22	2	13	44	27	68	11	6	.227/.265/.348	.215	.237	2.1	CF(143): -1.2	-0.7
2012	CHA	MLB	31	640	93	37	8	25	91	26	92	23	6	.304/.334/.516	.291	.323	5.8	RF(156): 14.3	5.2
2013	CHA	MLB	32	465	57	22	2	12	55	32	78	26	6	.277/.328/.421	.267	.314	3	RF(108): 3.2	2.1
2013	TEX	MLB	32	197	26	11	2	6	26	9	30	16	1	.280/.315/.457	.276	.305	2.1	RF(47): 2.2, CF(1): -0.0	1.2
2014	TEX	MLB	33	617	73	29	3	15	67	33	99	28	7	.262/.305/.402	.257	.290	2.6	RF 7, CF 0	2.0

The Rangers' lineup was already a bat or two light when Nelson Cruz was popped with a 50-game suspension, making the acquisition of Alex Rios (for infielder Leury Garcia) less luxury than necessity. Rios' year-to-year performance has been as stable as Tila Tequila, but in his good years he's a grade-6 player who doesn't have any real weaknesses. Texas has a $13.5 million option on Rios for 2015 with a $1 million buyout, and given how the free agent market is blowing up, it seems more likely than not that the Rangers will pick that option up.

Adam Rosales SS

Born: 5/20/1983 Age: 31
Bats: R Throws: R Height: 6' 1"
Weight: 195 Breakout: 0%
Improve: 19% Collapse: 11%
Attrition: 15% MLB: 66%

Comparables:
Brendan Harris, Omar Quintanilla, Ramon Santiago

YEAR	TEAM	LVL	AGE	PA	R	2B	3B	HR	RBI	BB	SO	SB	CS	AVG/OBP/SLG	TAv	BABIP	BRR	FRAA	WARP
2011	SAC	AAA	28	164	23	5	1	3	22	13	32	1	1	.265/.323/.374	.218	.313	0.1	SS(14): 0.5, 3B(2): -0.0	0.1
2011	OAK	MLB	28	68	5	0	0	2	8	4	13	0	0	.098/.162/.197	.152	.083	0.2	SS(7): -0.3, 3B(6): -0.6	-0.7
2012	SAC	AAA	29	310	46	21	1	8	47	26	57	4	2	.280/.340/.451	.286	.319	0.9	SS(57): -2.1, 2B(13): 3.0	2.7
2012	OAK	MLB	29	111	12	5	0	2	8	11	24	0	0	.222/.297/.333	.234	.270	-0.9	2B(21): -2.0, SS(11): 0.0	-0.2
2013	SAC	AAA	30	42	4	2	0	0	6	3	7	1	1	.211/.262/.263	.218	.250	-0.3	SS(7): -0.3, 2B(1): 0.1	0.0
2013	OAK	MLB	30	154	11	5	0	4	8	10	31	0	0	.191/.267/.316	.223	.218	0	SS(36): 5.0, 2B(13): 0.6	0.5
2013	TEX	MLB	30	12	4	0	0	1	4	0	3	0	0	.182/.167/.455	.311	.125	0.5	1B(4): 0.1, SS(3): 0.0	0.1
2014	TEX	MLB	31	250	25	10	1	6	25	19	53	2	1	.234/.298/.360	.244	.280	-0.4	SS 2, 2B 0	0.7

Rosales is pretty much the definition of the modern utility infielder, if your dictionary of choice is descriptive rather than prescriptive. Rosales hustles, he's enthusiastic, he plays multiple positions adequately and he doesn't hit, the traits that seem to define an American League UTIL in the 21st century. Rosales became the answer to a trivia question last summer when he was DFA'd three times in 11 days, bouncing from Oakland to Texas, back to Oakland, and back to Texas once again. He will be the Rangers' utility-man in 2014, and given how little Ron Washington rests his starting infielders he'll likely get fewer than 200 ups in that role.

Luis Sardinas SS

Born: 5/16/1993 Age: 21
Bats: B Throws: R Height: 6' 1"
Weight: 150 Breakout: 4%
Improve: 7% Collapse: 1%
Attrition: 7% MLB: 8%

Comparables:
Carlos Triunfel, Alcides Escobar, Leury Garcia

YEAR	TEAM	LVL	AGE	PA	R	2B	3B	HR	RBI	BB	SO	SB	CS	AVG/OBP/SLG	TAv	BABIP	BRR	FRAA	WARP
2012	HIC	A	19	412	65	14	2	2	30	29	52	32	9	.291/.346/.356	.258	.331	3.7	SS(76): 2.5, 2B(14): -0.4	2.0
2013	MYR	A+	20	432	69	15	3	1	31	32	54	27	8	.298/.358/.360	.261	.339	3.9	SS(92): -3.6, 2B(1): -0.1	2.0
2013	FRI	AA	20	141	12	4	0	1	15	4	21	5	2	.259/.286/.311	.225	.301	-1.7	SS(29): 0.9	0.0
2014	TEX	MLB	21	250	25	8	1	1	16	10	47	7	2	.244/.276/.303	.216	.290	0.4	SS -0, 2B -0	-0.1

Sardinas was signed in the same 2009 J-2 class as Jurickson Profar, and was considered by many at the time to be the more promising of the two. While Profar rocketed forward in the fast lane, however, Sardinas seemed stalled in the pits, with injuries and questions about his desire to improve clouding his status. Sardinas turned a corner in 2012 with a solid Low-A campaign, and followed that up with a nice 2013 season that saw him hold his own in High-A Myrtle Beach (as the fifth-youngest player in the Carolina League on Opening Day) and earn a late-season promotion to Double-A. Sardinas is an old school throwback shortstop, a terrific defender with a lot of speed who is never going to hit for power. With Elvis Andrus locked up for nearly a decade, Sardinas' path to becoming a major-league shortstop necessarily leads out of town.

Geovany Soto	**C**			
Born: 1/20/1983 Age: 31				
Bats: R Throws: R Height: 6' 1"				
Weight: 235 Breakout: 0%				
Improve: 31% Collapse: 12%				
Attrition: 13% MLB: 95%				
Comparables:				
Chris Snyder, Johnny Romano,				
Matthew Lecroy				

YEAR	TEAM	LVL	AGE	PA	R	2B	3B	HR	RBI	BB	SO	SB	CS	AVG/OBP/SLG	TAv	BABIP	BRR	FRAA	WARP
2011	CHN	MLB	28	474	46	26	0	17	54	45	124	0	0	.228/.310/.411	.254	.280	-2.3	C(122): 3.2	2.0
2012	TEX	MLB	29	164	19	6	0	5	25	11	41	1	0	.196/.253/.338	.228	.231	0.3	C(44): -0.1	0.1
2012	CHN	MLB	29	197	26	6	1	6	14	19	35	0	0	.199/.284/.347	.229	.215	1.2	C(52): -0.7	0.2
2013	TEX	MLB	30	184	20	9	0	9	22	20	60	1	2	.245/.328/.466	.289	.330	-3.3	C(53): 0.9, 3B(1): -0.0	1.2
2014	TEX	MLB	31	250	29	11	0	8	29	28	61	1	0	.226/.317/.393	.262	.270	-0.5	C 0, 3B -0	1.2

What a mystifying career Geovany Soto has had. At this point, it'd be no shock if Soto posts a .600 OPS in 2014, and it'd be no shock if Soto posts a .900 OPS in 2014. After a disastrous 2012, Soto had a solid bounce-back season as A.J. Pierzynski's part-time backup, crediting new hitting coach Dave Magadan with getting him back on track. The Rangers' brass was impressed enough to re-up him early in the offseason for one year at $3.05 million, announcing that they planned on Soto being the starting catcher in 2014. He has a good reputation for his game calling, and Yu Darvish has seemingly expressed a preference for pitching to him, which certainly couldn't hurt Soto's job security.

PITCHERS

Cory Burns	
Born: 10/9/1987 Age: 26	
Bats: R Throws: R Height: 6' 0" Weight: 205	
Breakout: 38% Improve: 60% Collapse: 29%	
Attrition: 37% MLB: 61%	
Comparables:	
Cory Doyne, R.J. Swindle, Kam Mickolio	

YEAR	TEAM	LVL	AGE	W	L	SV	G	GS	IP	H	HR	BB	SO	BB9	SO9	GB%	BABIP	WHIP	ERA	FIP	FRA	WARP
2011	AKR	AA	23	2	5	35	54	0	59²	47	3	15	70	2.3	10.6	48%	.317	1.04	2.11	2.47	2.16	1.6
2012	TUC	AAA	24	1	2	3	54	0	66	49	1	17	78	2.3	10.6	56%	.300	1.00	3.14	2.45	3.04	2.1
2012	SDN	MLB	24	0	1	0	17	0	18	26	1	10	18	5.0	9.0	58%	.410	2.00	5.50	3.69	3.34	0.3
2013	ROU	AAA	25	0	2	20	38	0	37²	39	0	15	48	3.6	11.5	62%	.382	1.43	2.15	2.30	1.91	1.6
2013	TEX	MLB	25	1	0	0	10	0	11¹	12	1	7	5	5.6	4.0	34%	.275	1.68	3.18	5.46	4.84	0.0
2014	TEX	MLB	26	2	1	0	46	0	50	46	4	18	52	3.3	9.3	52%	.311	1.29	3.55	3.45	3.86	0.6

Acquired from San Diego in November 2012, Burns was one of several Rangers pitchers who shuttled back and forth between Arlington and Round Rock when injuries or exigencies necessitated fresh arms. Burns is unusual in that he throws a changeup the majority of the time, with his fastball as a secondary pitch alongside an occasional breaking ball. His most likely 2014 fate is a return to Round Rock, with instructions to keep a bag packed for when he has to catch a flight with three hours' notice to wherever the big club is playing.

Travis Blackley	
Born: 11/4/1982 Age: 31	
Bats: L Throws: L Height: 6' 3" Weight: 205	
Breakout: 30% Improve: 54% Collapse: 17%	
Attrition: 40% MLB: 37%	
Comparables:	
Kyle Snyder, Jerome Williams, Jeff Harris	

YEAR	TEAM	LVL	AGE	W	L	SV	G	GS	IP	H	HR	BB	SO	BB9	SO9	GB%	BABIP	WHIP	ERA	FIP	FRA	WARP
2012	FRE	AAA	29	3	0	1	4	3	23¹	13	1	3	19	1.2	7.3	54%	.214	0.69	0.39	2.98	3.51	0.6
2012	SFN	MLB	29	0	0	0	4	0	5	7	0	2	2	3.6	3.6	55%	.350	1.80	9.00	3.54	5.59	-0.1
2012	OAK	MLB	29	6	4	0	24	15	102²	91	10	30	69	2.6	6.0	48%	.263	1.18	3.86	3.93	4.35	1.0
2013	TEX	MLB	30	1	1	0	4	3	15¹	16	2	2	11	1.2	6.5	50%	.318	1.17	4.70	3.73	4.51	0.1
2013	HOU	MLB	30	1	1	0	42	0	35	30	10	20	29	5.1	7.5	44%	.217	1.43	4.89	6.93	7.19	-0.8
2014	OAK	MLB	31	3	3	0	26	7	57	55	6	21	42	3.4	6.7	44%	.285	1.34	4.07	4.44	4.42	0.2

Mamas, don't let your children grow up to throw right-handed. One of the legion Mariners pitching prospects in the early 21st century whose careers were derailed due to injury, Blackley missed all of 2005 with shoulder problems and never was the same afterward. After pitching in his native Australia and in Korea in 2010 and 2011, Blackley has somehow logged 153 major-league innings over the past two seasons. Don't be surprised if he's in the 2024 edition of this book.

Neal Cotts

Born: 3/25/1980 Age: 34
Bats: L Throws: L Height: 6' 1" Weight: 200
Breakout: 23% Improve: 40% Collapse: 44%
Attrition: 13% MLB: 67%

Comparables:
Jason Bulger, Ryota Igarashi, Joe Nelson

YEAR	TEAM	LVL	AGE	W	L	SV	G	GS	IP	H	HR	BB	SO	BB9	SO9	GB%	BABIP	WHIP	ERA	FIP	FRA	WARP
2012	ROU	AAA	32	2	1	3	25	0	31²	32	2	15	41	4.3	11.7	40%	.361	1.48	4.55	3.41	1.82	1.6
2013	ROU	AAA	33	3	1	2	15	0	23	13	1	5	42	2.0	16.4	54%	.353	0.78	0.78	1.13	1.37	1.0
2013	TEX	MLB	33	8	3	1	58	0	57	36	2	18	65	2.8	10.3	46%	.246	0.95	1.11	2.20	2.50	1.4
2014	TEX	MLB	34	3	1	1	51	0	57²	48	5	23	66	3.5	10.3	45%	.297	1.22	3.15	3.41	3.42	1.0

The latest example of why you don't want to spend big dollars on "proven" relievers. Cotts, a second-round pick by Oakland in that pre-*Moneyball* draft where Billy Beane threw the chair, missed all of 2010 and 2011 due to injuries that had teams refusing to sign him because of worker's comp concerns. After not embarrassing himself in Round Rock in 2012, Cotts earned another minor-league deal for 2013. The Rangers' reward on that small investment was seeing Cotts morph into SuperReliever, mowing down Triple-A hitters for six weeks before a mid-May promotion to the majors, where he continued to dominate. His 1.11 ERA is the 17th-best since World War II for any pitcher with at least 50 innings, and Cotts was actually more effective against righties (.436 OPS allowed) than lefties (.565 OPS allowed), so he isn't relegated to a LOOGY role. Despite his age, his service time is so low that the Rangers have one year of club control remaining before he hits free agency next winter.

Yu Darvish

Born: 8/16/1986 Age: 27
Bats: R Throws: R Height: 6' 5" Weight: 225
Breakout: 25% Improve: 58% Collapse: 18%
Attrition: 5% MLB: 99%

Comparables:
Hideo Nomo, Rich Harden, Tim Lincecum

YEAR	TEAM	LVL	AGE	W	L	SV	G	GS	IP	H	HR	BB	SO	BB9	SO9	GB%	BABIP	WHIP	ERA	FIP	FRA	WARP
2012	TEX	MLB	25	16	9	0	29	29	191¹	156	14	89	221	4.2	10.4	47%	.294	1.28	3.90	3.24	3.77	3.3
2013	TEX	MLB	26	13	9	0	32	32	209²	145	26	80	277	3.4	11.9	42%	.264	1.07	2.83	3.30	3.78	3.3
2014	TEX	MLB	27	13	6	0	24	24	177¹	135	16	71	218	3.6	11.0	44%	.289	1.16	2.92	3.31	3.17	3.7

What must it be like to have so much ability that, no matter how well you perform, there are those who think you should have done better? Yu Darvish has such an array of pitches, throws so hard, has breaking balls with such bite, that you don't just marvel at his skills but wonder how he ever allows a hit. Leading the AL in strikeouts and finishing fourth in ERA despite a bandbox home park deserves praise, but as the 2013 season progressed, Yu was a whipping boy for the local media and the team's broadcasters. They complained that he didn't execute enough shutdown innings, didn't raise his performance in close games, simply didn't know how to win, with four 1-0 losses—an MLB record—fueling an asinine controversy. Yu's lone weakness is inconsistent command—if that improves, he will rival Clayton Kershaw as the best pitcher in baseball.

Neftali Feliz

Born: 5/2/1988 Age: 26
Bats: R Throws: R Height: 6' 3" Weight: 225
Breakout: 40% Improve: 65% Collapse: 18%
Attrition: 13% MLB: 88%

Comparables:
Jonathan Papelbon, Ramon Ramirez, Renyel Pinto

YEAR	TEAM	LVL	AGE	W	L	SV	G	GS	IP	H	HR	BB	SO	BB9	SO9	GB%	BABIP	WHIP	ERA	FIP	FRA	WARP
2011	TEX	MLB	23	2	3	32	64	0	62¹	42	4	30	54	4.3	7.8	38%	.232	1.16	2.74	3.61	4.72	0.6
2012	TEX	MLB	24	3	1	0	8	7	42²	28	5	23	37	4.9	7.8	38%	.213	1.20	3.16	4.59	5.78	0.1
2013	TEX	MLB	25	0	0	0	6	0	4²	5	0	2	4	3.9	7.7	29%	.357	1.50	0.00	3.29	4.30	0.0
2014	TEX	MLB	26	2	1	0	30	2	36²	29	3	14	37	3.6	9.1	42%	.275	1.18	2.95	3.65	3.20	0.8

It's been two lost seasons for Feliz, who was moved to the rotation and got a handful of starts under his belt in 2012 before being shelved for Tommy John surgery; the recovery cost him most of last year as well. There's reason to believe that Feliz's ligament problems predated 2012, as he didn't flash the same stuff and command in 2011 that wowed onlookers his first two years in the league. The Rangers are resettling Feliz in the bullpen in 2014, and with Joe Nathan departing he will vie (against stiff competition) for the closer's job. As is, the Rangers have burned four years of his service time on 210 innings.

Jason Frasor

Born: 8/9/1977 Age: 36
Bats: R Throws: R Height: 5' 9" Weight: 180
Breakout: 29% Improve: 46% Collapse: 42%
Attrition: 11% MLB: 79%

Comparables:
Trevor Miller, Joe Borowski, Rich Gossage

YEAR	TEAM	LVL	AGE	W	L	SV	G	GS	IP	H	HR	BB	SO	BB9	SO9	GB%	BABIP	WHIP	ERA	FIP	FRA	WARP
2011	CHA	MLB	33	1	2	0	20	0	17²	20	3	11	20	5.6	10.2	35%	.354	1.75	5.09	5.04	4.15	0.2
2011	TOR	MLB	33	2	1	0	44	0	42¹	38	4	15	37	3.2	7.9	41%	.283	1.25	2.98	3.75	4.36	0.5
2012	TOR	MLB	34	1	1	0	50	0	43²	42	6	22	53	4.5	10.9	42%	.333	1.47	4.12	4.05	5.23	0.2
2013	TEX	MLB	35	4	3	0	61	0	49	36	4	20	48	3.7	8.8	47%	.250	1.14	2.57	3.40	3.70	0.5
2014	TEX	MLB	36	2	1	1	46	0	41	37	4	17	41	3.6	9.0	43%	.300	1.31	3.66	3.96	3.98	0.4

Early in the 2013 season, it looked like Frasor might be in danger of losing his roster spot once Joakim Soria returned from the disabled list; a couple of rough outings had him in Ron Washington's doghouse. After that bad beginning, however, Frasor righted the ship and quietly put together a very solid season in middle relief, working his way back into Wash's Circle of Trust. Frasor apparently liked it in Texas, as he re-upped with the Rangers for $1.75 million without even testing the free agent waters. He will once again be called on to pitch in the sixth and seventh innings.

Matt Garza

Born: 11/26/1983 Age: 30
Bats: R Throws: R Height: 6' 4'' Weight: 215
Breakout: 10% Improve: 38% Collapse: 26%
Attrition: 12% MLB: 95%

Comparables:
John Lackey, Gavin Floyd, Adam Wainwright

YEAR	TEAM	LVL	AGE	W	L	SV	G	GS	IP	H	HR	BB	SO	BB9	SO9	GB%	BABIP	WHIP	ERA	FIP	FRA	WARP
2011	CHN	MLB	27	10	10	0	31	31	198	186	14	63	197	2.9	9.0	47%	.307	1.26	3.32	2.92	3.36	3.9
2012	CHN	MLB	28	5	7	0	18	18	103²	90	15	32	96	2.8	8.3	51%	.274	1.18	3.91	4.21	5.42	0.1
2013	CHN	MLB	29	6	1	0	11	11	71	61	8	20	62	2.5	7.9	42%	.264	1.14	3.17	3.75	4.15	0.7
2013	TEX	MLB	29	4	5	0	13	13	84¹	89	12	22	74	2.3	7.9	41%	.308	1.32	4.38	3.99	4.22	0.7
2014	TEX	MLB	30	9	6	0	21	21	133	124	15	43	115	2.9	7.8	43%	.289	1.25	3.76	4.14	4.09	1.4

For the second year in a row, the Rangers traded prospects to the Cubs for a free-agent-to-be starting pitcher, and for the second year in a row, the rental from the Cubbies let them down. The Rangers shipped four prospects to the North Side for Garza, who had opened the season on the disabled list but seemed to have found his groove at the time of the trade. Alas, after looking great in his first two starts as a Ranger, Garza allowed four runs or more in eight of his final 11 games, and got into an embarrassing Twitter fight with Eric Sogard's wife. Though Garza had been on Jon Daniels' wish list for some time, his 13 starts were apparently enough for the front office to get over its Garza jones.

Alex Gonzalez

Born: 1/15/1992 Age: 22
Bats: R Throws: R Height: 6' 2'' Weight: 195
Breakout: 100% Improve: 100% Collapse: 0%
Attrition: 0% MLB: 1%

Comparables:
Chad Bettis, Brett Marshall, Adam Warren

YEAR	TEAM	LVL	AGE	W	L	SV	G	GS	IP	H	HR	BB	SO	BB9	SO9	GB%	BABIP	WHIP	ERA	FIP	FRA	WARP
2013	SPO	A-	21	0	4	0	9	9	23²	30	1	7	20	2.7	7.6	69%	.382	1.56	4.56	3.19	3.77	0.5
2013	MYR	A+	21	0	0	0	5	5	19	15	1	9	15	4.3	7.1	59%	.264	1.26	2.84	3.88	5.59	0.1
2014	TEX	MLB	22	2	3	0	9	9	32¹	39	4	17	18	4.7	4.9	50%	.311	1.72	5.90	5.56	6.42	-0.3

And lo, just three suns after the final shortstopping Alex Gonzalez disappeared from baseball, a new hope for the species emerged with only slight mutations: As a pitcher, and known as Chi Chi. The Rangers were expected to go with a prep player with their first 2013 pick, but when the Oral Roberts righthander slid to them at no. 23 they snatched him up and went above slot to sign him. Gonzalez sports a low- to mid-90s fastball with cutting action that is his primary pitch, along with a quality slider and changeup. Although he was roughed up a bit initially in Spokane, Gonzalez settled in and pitched well in the Carolina League at the end of the minor-league season, then got rave reviews in the Instructional League. ♪Nants ingonyama bagithi Baba, Sithi uhm ingonyama♪

Matt Harrison

Born: 9/16/1985 Age: 28
Bats: L Throws: L Height: 6' 4'' Weight: 250
Breakout: 18% Improve: 60% Collapse: 21%
Attrition: 5% MLB: 92%

Comparables:
Mark Mulder, Joe Blanton, Justin Masterson

YEAR	TEAM	LVL	AGE	W	L	SV	G	GS	IP	H	HR	BB	SO	BB9	SO9	GB%	BABIP	WHIP	ERA	FIP	FRA	WARP
2011	TEX	MLB	25	14	9	0	31	30	185²	180	13	57	126	2.8	6.1	50%	.292	1.28	3.39	3.55	4.22	3.0
2012	TEX	MLB	26	18	11	0	32	32	213¹	210	22	59	133	2.5	5.6	50%	.284	1.26	3.29	3.98	4.63	1.5
2013	TEX	MLB	27	0	2	0	2	2	10²	14	2	7	12	5.9	10.1	47%	.400	1.97	8.44	5.23	5.71	0.0
2014	TEX	MLB	28	3	2	0	13	6	47²	48	5	16	32	3.0	6.1	48%	.298	1.34	4.05	4.43	4.40	0.3

It was a lost season for Harrison, who had as many back surgeries—two—as big-league starts. Harrison then topped off his Season From Hell by undergoing his second surgery for thoracic outlet syndrome, an ailment that seems to be unusually common among Ranger players (Hank Blalock, Kenny Rogers, Jarrod Saltalamacchia and Mike Adams having also been stricken). Harrison had established himself the prior two years as a ground-ball machine, making up for his low strikeout rates by inducing hitters to pound the ball harmlessly into the dirt, and Texas will be looking for Harrison to return to health and resume his duties as an innings-eating third starter.

Derek Holland

Born: 10/9/1986 Age: 27
Bats: B Throws: L Height: 6' 2'' Weight: 210
Breakout: 21% Improve: 52% Collapse: 24%
Attrition: 12% MLB: 93%

Comparables:
Ricky Nolasco, Jeremy Bonderman, Ervin Santana

YEAR	TEAM	LVL	AGE	W	L	SV	G	GS	IP	H	HR	BB	SO	BB9	SO9	GB%	BABIP	WHIP	ERA	FIP	FRA	WARP
2011	TEX	MLB	24	16	5	0	32	32	198	201	22	67	162	3.0	7.4	48%	.305	1.35	3.95	3.98	4.65	2.3
2012	TEX	MLB	25	12	7	0	29	27	175¹	162	32	52	145	2.7	7.4	44%	.262	1.22	4.67	4.71	5.50	0.0
2013	TEX	MLB	26	10	9	0	33	33	213	210	20	64	189	2.7	8.0	43%	.308	1.29	3.42	3.46	3.99	2.8
2014	TEX	MLB	27	12	9	0	31	31	178	174	22	57	153	2.9	7.7	44%	.297	1.30	4.04	4.26	4.39	1.3

After taking a step back with a disappointing 2012 campaign, Holland took two steps forward in 2013, combining with Yu Darvish to give the Rangers a potent one-two combo at the top of the rotation. When Holland is on, he has the stuff to be unhittable—he has more career shutouts than Justin Verlander, Andy Pettitte, Jake Peavy, and on and on—but his command issues result in inconsistency and make him prone to leaving balls out over the plate where they can be mashed. Holland's inconsistency, combined with his irreverence and willingness to act goofy in public, frustrate the "get off my lawn" crowd, who think if he'd just buckle down and stop spending so much time doing Harry Caray imitations he could be a legitimate top-of-the-rotation starter. Holland may be doomed to be one of those players who is very good, but not ever good enough to satisfy his critics.

Luke Jackson

Born: 8/24/1991 Age: 22
Bats: R Throws: R Height: 6' 2" Weight: 185
Breakout: 69% Improve: 88% Collapse: 12%
Attrition: 81% MLB: 12%

Comparables:
Casey Crosby, Dellin Betances, Nick Hagadone

YEAR	TEAM	LVL	AGE	W	L	SV	G	GS	IP	H	HR	BB	SO	BB9	SO9	GB%	BABIP	WHIP	ERA	FIP	FRA	WARP
2011	HIC	A	19	5	6	0	19	19	75	83	9	48	78	5.8	9.4	41%	.338	1.75	5.64	5.09	5.57	0.6
2012	HIC	A	20	5	5	0	13	13	64	63	4	33	72	4.6	10.1	48%	.347	1.50	4.92	3.92	4.54	1.3
2012	MYR	A+	20	5	2	0	13	13	65²	67	2	32	74	4.4	10.1	42%	.376	1.51	4.39	3.17	3.96	0.9
2013	MYR	A+	21	9	4	0	19	19	101	79	6	47	104	4.2	9.3	48%	.284	1.25	2.41	3.55	4.22	1.6
2013	FRI	AA	21	2	0	0	6	4	27	13	0	12	30	4.0	10.0	47%	.213	0.93	0.67	2.17	2.58	0.7
2014	TEX	MLB	22	6	6	0	19	19	100	105	12	60	84	5.4	7.6	43%	.312	1.65	5.29	5.18	5.75	-0.7

A supplemental first-round pick in 2010, Jackson took a big step forward in 2013, doing a better job of harnessing a fastball that can touch the upper 90s to put away minor-league hitters. The Rangers chose to part with fellow minor-league righties Neil Ramirez and C.J. Edwards in the Matt Garza trade rather than give up Jackson, who appears slated to start the 2014 season in Double-A Frisco. Jackson is still battling command issues, and how much he improves his command will dictate whether his future is in the bullpen or the rotation, though he has the stuff for high leverage if he does end up in the 'pen. He and 2013 first-rounder Chi Chi Gonzalez give the Rangers a pair of quality upper-minors arms with mid-rotation ceilings.

Colby Lewis

Born: 8/2/1979 Age: 34
Bats: R Throws: R Height: 6' 4" Weight: 240
Breakout: 17% Improve: 48% Collapse: 14%
Attrition: 8% MLB: 87%

Comparables:
Javier Vazquez, Ted Lilly, Ben Sheets

YEAR	TEAM	LVL	AGE	W	L	SV	G	GS	IP	H	HR	BB	SO	BB9	SO9	GB%	BABIP	WHIP	ERA	FIP	FRA	WARP
2011	TEX	MLB	31	14	10	0	32	32	200¹	187	35	56	169	2.5	7.6	35%	.267	1.21	4.40	4.57	5.21	1.1
2012	TEX	MLB	32	6	6	0	16	16	105	99	16	14	93	1.2	8.0	34%	.279	1.08	3.43	3.83	3.82	1.9
2013	FRI	AA	33	0	1	0	5	5	18	23	4	4	15	2.0	7.5	37%	.328	1.50	7.00	4.95	5.29	0.0
2014	TEX	MLB	34	3	2	0	6	6	36	34	5	10	32	2.5	8.1	39%	.288	1.23	3.82	4.27	4.16	0.3

One of the heroes of the Rangers' two World Series teams, Colby Lewis didn't pitch in the majors in 2013 while trying to come back from tendon flexor surgery. He also had surgery to remove bone spurs from his hip, a problem that plagued him through much of 2011 and 2012. The Rangers have signed Lewis to a minor-league deal in the hopes that he will be healthy and able enough for fifth-startering. When well, he is an innings-eater who throws strikes and allows homers.

Alexi Ogando

Born: 10/5/1983 Age: 30
Bats: R Throws: R Height: 6' 4" Weight: 200
Breakout: 12% Improve: 41% Collapse: 30%
Attrition: 17% MLB: 89%

Comparables:
Dustin McGowan, Jose Rijo, Curt Schilling

YEAR	TEAM	LVL	AGE	W	L	SV	G	GS	IP	H	HR	BB	SO	BB9	SO9	GB%	BABIP	WHIP	ERA	FIP	FRA	WARP
2011	TEX	MLB	27	13	8	0	31	29	169	149	16	43	126	2.3	6.7	38%	.267	1.14	3.51	3.69	4.28	3.1
2012	TEX	MLB	28	2	0	3	58	1	66	49	9	17	66	2.3	9.0	39%	.237	1.00	3.27	3.68	4.22	0.7
2013	ROU	AAA	29	0	1	0	3	3	13	12	4	4	4	2.8	2.8	38%	.186	1.23	6.23	7.88	9.47	-0.4
2013	TEX	MLB	29	7	4	0	23	18	104¹	87	11	41	72	3.5	6.2	43%	.254	1.23	3.11	4.39	4.60	0.7
2014	TEX	MLB	30	7	4	1	41	13	98	85	10	31	81	2.8	7.4	41%	.274	1.18	3.22	4.03	3.50	1.8

It was a frustrating year for Ogando, who returned to the rotation after spending 2012 in the bullpen only to endure three different stints on the disabled list with arm issues. He relied more heavily on his changeup in 2013, but he is primarily a fastball/slider pitcher, which some believe makes him better suited for the bullpen. Repeated DL trips (biceps once, shoulder twice) gave ammunition to those who believe he lacks the durability to start. The Rangers' preference appears to be preparing him to start once again, but if Colby Lewis or Nick Tepesch or Bachelor No. 3 steps up and wins the fifth starter job, Ogando will go back to the bullpen.

Joseph Ortiz

Born: 8/13/1990 Age: 23
Bats: L Throws: L Height: 5' 7" Weight: 175
Breakout: 26% Improve: 30% Collapse: 70%
Attrition: 74% MLB: 26%

Comparables:
Jose Ascanio, Edward Mujica, Fernando Hernandez

YEAR	TEAM	LVL	AGE	W	L	SV	G	GS	IP	H	HR	BB	SO	BB9	SO9	GB%	BABIP	WHIP	ERA	FIP	FRA	WARP
2011	MYR	A+	20	5	5	5	40	0	67	54	4	14	55	1.9	7.4	60%	.240	1.01	2.15	2.99	4.26	0.4
2012	FRI	AA	21	1	2	4	27	0	30²	26	2	6	29	1.8	8.5	49%	.279	1.04	2.35	2.82	2.96	0.7
2012	ROU	AAA	21	1	1	2	24	0	32	31	6	3	23	0.8	6.5	54%	.266	1.06	1.97	4.95	5.45	0.1
2013	ROU	AAA	22	2	1	2	19	0	26¹	24	2	8	29	2.7	9.9	56%	.319	1.22	3.08	3.27	4.49	0.3
2013	TEX	MLB	22	2	2	0	32	0	44²	46	5	10	27	2.0	5.4	43%	.283	1.25	4.23	3.99	4.35	0.3
2014	TEX	MLB	23	2	1	0	41	0	59	60	7	17	44	2.7	6.8	50%	.295	1.31	4.11	4.29	4.46	0.3

The short, thick lefty made enough of an impression in spring training that he earned a spot in the Rangers' bullpen coming out of camp. Ron Washington rode him hard early in the season, which seemed to take a toll, as his stuff wasn't as sharp thereafter. Folks within the Rangers organization have compared Ortiz to Eddie Guardado, and when his slider is biting he can be a weapon out of the bullpen. With fellow lefties Neal Cotts and Robbie Ross seeming locks for the major-league 'pen, Ortiz will likely start the 2014 season back in Round Rock.

Martin Perez

Born: 4/4/1991 Age: **23**
Bats: **L** Throws: **L** Height: **6' 0"** Weight: **190**
Breakout: **32%** Improve: **70%** Collapse: **13%**
Attrition: **40%** MLB: **79%**

Comparables:
Alex White, Matt Harrison, Homer Bailey

YEAR	TEAM	LVL	AGE	W	L	SV	G	GS	IP	H	HR	BB	SO	BB9	SO9	GB%	BABIP	WHIP	ERA	FIP	FRA	WARP
2011	FRI	AA	20	4	2	0	17	16	88¹	80	6	36	83	3.7	8.5	46%	.294	1.31	3.16	3.64	3.85	1.5
2011	ROU	AAA	20	4	4	0	10	10	49	72	4	20	37	3.7	6.8	56%	.327	1.88	6.43	4.56	4.97	0.2
2012	ROU	AAA	21	7	6	0	22	21	127	122	10	56	69	4.0	4.9	52%	.277	1.40	4.25	5.02	5.45	0.4
2012	TEX	MLB	21	1	4	0	12	6	38	47	3	15	25	3.6	5.9	50%	.333	1.63	5.45	4.10	4.23	0.4
2013	ROU	AAA	22	5	1	0	6	6	36	29	1	8	28	2.0	7.0	59%	.280	1.03	1.75	3.21	3.26	0.8
2013	TEX	MLB	22	10	6	0	20	20	124¹	129	15	37	84	2.7	6.1	49%	.292	1.34	3.62	4.26	4.54	0.7
2014	TEX	MLB	23	9	8	0	28	28	139	149	16	56	97	3.7	6.3	49%	.305	1.48	4.73	4.73	5.14	0.0

A broken arm suffered in spring training on a hard hit ball up the middle kept Perez out of the Rangers' opening week rotation, but he battled back from that setback and ended up spending the bulk of the season taking the ball every fifth day in the big leagues. Perez had a reputation in the minors for not responding well to adversity, letting his emotions get the most of him, but he showed remarkable poise during a tight pennant race. He throws hard, with a fastball that hits 92-94 mph, but his out pitch is a changeup that has invoked comparisons to that of Johan Santana. Texas saw enough from him to sign him to a team-friendly extension that guarantees him $12.5 million over four years, and which could keep him under team control through 2020.

Chaz Roe

Born: 10/9/1986 Age: **27**
Bats: **R** Throws: **R** Height: **6' 5"** Weight: **190**
Breakout: **46%** Improve: **70%** Collapse: **18%**
Attrition: **58%** MLB: **39%**

Comparables:
Cesar Valdez, Marco Estrada, Shane Komine

YEAR	TEAM	LVL	AGE	W	L	SV	G	GS	IP	H	HR	BB	SO	BB9	SO9	GB%	BABIP	WHIP	ERA	FIP	FRA	WARP
2011	TAC	AAA	24	0	7	2	33	10	99²	133	16	38	83	3.4	7.5	43%	.345	1.72	6.59	5.47	5.68	1.1
2013	RNO	AAA	26	0	0	7	22	0	22	15	0	4	20	1.6	8.2	55%	.250	0.86	1.23	2.71	2.59	0.7
2013	ARI	MLB	26	1	0	0	21	0	22¹	18	3	13	24	5.2	9.7	57%	.283	1.39	4.03	4.36	4.29	0.0
2014	TEX	MLB	27	2	1	1	19	2	34¹	37	4	13	24	3.3	6.3	45%	.308	1.46	4.70	4.69	5.11	-0.1

After the former first-rounder fizzled in the Rockies organization, Roe was flipped in a dump trade to Seattle in 2011, spent 2012 on the indie league circuit as a reliever then caught a minor-league bone thrown by the Diamondbacks. Reliable middle innings in Triple-A, coupled with malevolent injury gremlins to Arizona relievers, resulted in his promotion; they also got him claimed by the Rangers just after the World Series. A sinker/slider specialist better at retiring righties than lefties, Roe likely won't break camp in the majors but if he keeps the ball inside the fences and on the ground, he'll earn more cameos down the road, a much better fate than his outlook two years ago, which was something non-baseball-related.

Robbie Ross

Born: 6/24/1989 Age: **25**
Bats: **L** Throws: **L** Height: **5' 11"** Weight: **215**
Breakout: **36%** Improve: **63%** Collapse: **18%**
Attrition: **30%** MLB: **86%**

Comparables:
Joe Kelly, Enrique Gonzalez, Anthony Bass

YEAR	TEAM	LVL	AGE	W	L	SV	G	GS	IP	H	HR	BB	SO	BB9	SO9	GB%	BABIP	WHIP	ERA	FIP	FRA	WARP
2011	MYR	A+	22	9	4	0	21	20	123¹	102	1	28	98	2.0	7.2	58%	.290	1.05	2.26	2.57	3.97	0.9
2011	FRI	AA	22	1	1	0	6	6	38	33	5	5	36	1.2	8.5	48%	.239	1.00	2.61	3.59	4.08	0.5
2012	TEX	MLB	23	6	0	0	58	0	65	55	3	23	47	3.2	6.5	63%	.274	1.20	2.22	3.35	4.11	0.7
2013	TEX	MLB	24	4	2	0	65	0	62¹	63	4	19	58	2.7	8.4	45%	.326	1.32	3.03	3.20	3.57	0.9
2014	TEX	MLB	25	3	2	0	36	3	53²	56	5	19	37	3.2	6.1	55%	.301	1.40	4.33	4.40	4.71	0.1

Ross has done a Jekyll and Hyde act in each of the past two seasons—outstanding early in the year, resulting in Ron Washington riding him hard in April and May, followed by struggles. His peripherals were acceptable in the second half of 2013, but his .354 BABIP was no fluke, as he left too many mistakes out over the plate and saw grounders turn into line drives. Historically, Ross has been an extreme groundball pitcher who doesn't strike out a lot of batters, but he moved toward average in both measures last year. One of several undersized lefties the Rangers have spent high picks on under the Jon Daniels regime, Ross will get a look as a starter in spring training.

Tanner Scheppers

Born: 1/17/1987 Age: **27**
Bats: **R** Throws: **R** Height: **6' 4"** Weight: **200**
Breakout: **41%** Improve: **59%** Collapse: **28%**
Attrition: **28%** MLB: **72%**

Comparables:
Fu-Te Ni, Shawn Kelley, Jesse Chavez

YEAR	TEAM	LVL	AGE	W	L	SV	G	GS	IP	H	HR	BB	SO	BB9	SO9	GB%	BABIP	WHIP	ERA	FIP	FRA	WARP
2011	FRI	AA	24	2	1	0	17	0	23	18	1	9	24	3.5	9.4	41%	.302	1.17	3.13	3.16	4.51	0.2
2011	ROU	AAA	24	2	0	2	11	1	20²	23	0	12	20	5.2	8.7	60%	.000	1.69	4.35	3.88	2.50	0.1
2012	ROU	AAA	25	1	2	11	27	0	31	30	2	4	31	1.2	9.0	39%	.322	1.10	3.48	3.18	3.72	0.6
2012	TEX	MLB	25	1	1	1	39	0	32¹	47	6	9	30	2.5	8.4	44%	.390	1.73	4.45	4.62	4.47	0.3
2013	TEX	MLB	26	6	2	1	76	0	76²	58	6	24	59	2.8	6.9	51%	.252	1.07	1.88	3.77	3.86	0.8
2014	TEX	MLB	27	3	1	0	49	2	61¹	58	6	20	55	3.0	8.1	44%	.303	1.29	3.80	3.96	4.13	0.6

Such a strange year for Scheppers. He was lampooned for being one of five relievers on the final ballot for the All-Star Game (with critics saying players less anonymous should have been listed), and then made headlines when he was involved in a bar fight in Cleveland. On the field, meanwhile, Scheppers put up a terrific ERA despite having peripherals that would suggest his performance was mediocre, at best. Scheppers has swing-and-miss stuff with a mid- to upper-90s fastball and sharp breaking ball, so it's reasonable to believe his strikeout rate will improve. Scheppers is one of the candidates to replace the departed Joe Nathan as the Rangers' closer, which would likely put him in All-Star consideration without snickers.

Joakim Soria

Born: 5/18/1984 Age: 30
Bats: R Throws: R Height: 6' 3" Weight: 200
Breakout: 28% Improve: 48% Collapse: 30%
Attrition: 10% MLB: 96%

Comparables:
Bruce Sutter, Juan Rincon, Francisco Rodriguez

YEAR	TEAM	LVL	AGE	W	L	SV	G	GS	IP	H	HR	BB	SO	BB9	SO9	GB%	BABIP	WHIP	ERA	FIP	FRA	WARP
2011	KCA	MLB	27	5	5	28	60	0	60¹	60	7	17	60	2.5	9.0	43%	.312	1.28	4.03	3.53	4.12	0.8
2013	TEX	MLB	29	1	0	0	26	0	23²	18	2	14	28	5.3	10.6	53%	.286	1.35	3.80	3.71	4.33	0.2
2014	TEX	MLB	30	2	1	1	37	0	36²	31	3	12	40	2.8	10.0	44%	.295	1.16	3.10	3.21	3.37	0.7

The Rangers knew when they signed Soria that, coming off of Tommy John surgery, he wasn't going to be ready at the start of the 2013 season. His return was further delayed by a strained pectoral muscle suffered while rehabbing. Once Soria was added to the 25-man roster in July, he showed flashes of the guy who was one of the best relievers in baseball pre-surgery, but overall he was clearly still a return in progress. Texas has Soria through 2015 (if it picks up a club option), so the team's hope is that last year merely gave him a chance to throw off the rust.

Nick Tepesch

Born: 10/12/1988 Age: 25
Bats: R Throws: R Height: 6' 4" Weight: 225
Breakout: 35% Improve: 55% Collapse: 22%
Attrition: 51% MLB: 76%

Comparables:
Junichi Tazawa, Zach McAllister, John Koronka

YEAR	TEAM	LVL	AGE	W	L	SV	G	GS	IP	H	HR	BB	SO	BB9	SO9	GB%	BABIP	WHIP	ERA	FIP	FRA	WARP
2011	HIC	A	22	7	5	0	29	23	138¹	147	14	33	118	2.1	7.7	47%	.329	1.30	4.03	4.13	5.36	1.3
2012	MYR	A+	23	5	3	0	12	12	71²	68	3	18	59	2.3	7.4	61%	.307	1.20	2.89	3.33	4.21	0.6
2012	FRI	AA	23	6	3	0	16	14	90¹	97	10	26	68	2.6	6.8	52%	.316	1.36	4.28	4.18	4.94	0.4
2013	TEX	MLB	24	4	6	0	19	17	93	100	12	27	76	2.6	7.4	47%	.309	1.37	4.84	4.22	4.68	0.5
2014	TEX	MLB	25	6	6	0	18	18	97¹	109	12	33	65	3.0	6.0	49%	.309	1.45	4.86	4.79	5.28	-0.2

Tepesch, a Matthew Modine lookalike signed to an above-slot deal as a 14th-round pick in 2010, was pressed into duty as the Rangers' fifth starter out of spring training because of injuries to his colleagues, and he did better than one would expect from a guy with just 14 starts above A-ball. Tepesch is a strike thrower who gets raves for maintaining his poise and calm demeanor on the mound, no matter what the situation, but his limited repertoire made him vulnerable as the lineup turned over—he allowed a .472 OPS to batters in their first plate appearance of the game, but an 1.198 OPS in their third trip. Tepesch will be in the mix for the fifth starter job in 2014, but more likely will start the season back in Triple-A for some necessary grooming.

Ross Wolf

Born: 10/18/1982 Age: 31
Bats: R Throws: R Height: 6' 0" Weight: 180
Breakout: 29% Improve: 78% Collapse: 14%
Attrition: 14% MLB: 13%

Comparables:
Oscar Villarreal, Sean Henn, Nick Regilio

YEAR	TEAM	LVL	AGE	W	L	SV	G	GS	IP	H	HR	BB	SO	BB9	SO9	GB%	BABIP	WHIP	ERA	FIP	FRA	WARP
2011	OKL	AAA	28	4	3	3	56	0	73²	83	4	27	55	3.3	6.7	54%	.263	1.49	4.76	4.18	4.50	0.4
2012	FRI	AA	29	3	1	9	36	0	43	36	1	8	44	1.7	9.2	58%	.312	1.02	2.09	2.16	3.25	0.8
2012	ROU	AAA	29	0	0	0	7	0	11¹	12	2	5	7	4.0	5.6	68%	.256	1.50	4.76	6.05	6.63	-0.1
2013	ROU	AAA	30	1	1	0	7	6	35²	27	1	10	26	2.5	6.6	52%	.255	1.04	1.77	3.40	3.83	0.5
2013	TEX	MLB	30	1	3	0	22	3	47²	58	5	15	21	2.8	4.0	50%	.321	1.53	4.15	4.56	4.78	0.1
2014	TEX	MLB	31	3	2	0	41	3	67¹	70	7	26	45	3.5	6.1	54%	.297	1.43	4.49	4.61	4.88	0.1

An 18th-round pick of the Marlins in 2002, with just a handful of major-league innings in a journeyman career, Wolf was called up for a spot start on May 22nd to cover for a blister in the rotation. The feel-good story threw five solid innings and picked up the win, and with the Rangers' pitching staff decimated by injuries, he stuck around on the major-league staff, generally acquitting himself acceptably as a long man. Wolf signed a 2014 minor-league deal with the Rangers, then exercised an opt-out clause to pitch in Korea. Root for a post-retirement career on Wall Street.

LINEOUTS

HITTERS

PLAYER	TEAM	LVL	AGE	PA	R	2B	3B	HR	RBI	BB	SO	SB-CS	AVG/OBP/SLG	TAv	BABIP	BRR	FRAA	WARP
CF L. Brinson	HIC	A	19	503	64	18	2	21	52	48	191	24-7	.237/.322/.427	.268	.362	-0.1	CF(119): 4.0	2.5
RF A. Castellanos	ABQ	AAA	26	441	75	14	5	19	61	41	112	19-5	.257/.347/.468	.272	.315	0.3	RF(66): -2.8, LF(16): -0.0	1.2
	LAN	MLB	26	18	2	1	0	1	1	0	5	0-0	.167/.167/.389	.193	.167	-0.3	RF(6): -0.4, LF(2): -0.1	-0.2
1B R. Guzman	HIC	A	18	191	17	8	0	4	26	11	27	0-0	.272/.325/.387	.264	.297	-0.8	1B(45): -0.3	0.0
RF N. Mazara	HIC	A	18	506	48	23	2	13	62	44	131	1-2	.236/.310/.382	.254	.301	-2.5	RF(114): -4.7	0.4
1B C. McGuiness	ROU	AAA	25	436	52	29	1	11	63	68	86	1-0	.246/.369/.423	.286	.292	-0.8	1B(90): 5.0, LF(5): 0.2	2.1
	TEX	MLB	25	34	0	1	0	0	1	0	13	0-0	.176/.176/.206	.135	.286	-0.3	1B(10): 0.3	-0.4
CF R. Ortega	TUL	AA	22	178	22	4	2	1	10	19	26	9-4	.228/.315/.297	.234	.267	-1.8	CF(39): 3.5	0.3
DH M. Ramirez	ROU	AAA	41	119	7	3	0	3	13	10	14	0-0	.259/.328/.370	.251	.275	-1.6		-0.2
3B D. Robinson	MYR	A+	21	523	62	26	7	8	70	72	124	10-2	.257/.369/.404	.275	.339	-1.7	3B(115): -1.0	2.3
2B R. Rua	HIC	A	23	430	70	24	1	29	82	49	91	13-2	.251/.356/.559	.332	.253	0.3	2B(87): 3.3, 3B(8): -0.8	4.9
	FRI	AA	23	95	19	2	1	3	9	7	24	1-0	.233/.305/.384	.244	.288	0.8	3B(23): -2.2	-0.1
2B K. Tanaka	FRE	AAA	32	400	54	14	3	1	32	42	36	22-10	.329/.400/.397	.293	.358	1.8	2B(55): -2.6, LF(30): 0.6	2.5
	SFN	MLB	32	34	4	0	0	0	2	4	3	2-0	.267/.353/.267	.245	.296	0.1	LF(9): -0.5	0.0
LF N. Williams	HIC	A	19	404	70	19	12	17	60	15	110	8-5	.293/.337/.543	.303	.371	-0.4	LF(73): -3.7, CF(8): -1.8	2.3
2B J. Wilson	RNO	AAA	32	206	17	8	0	4	20	13	44	1-3	.219/.268/.323	.212	.264	0	2B(32): -1.4, SS(20): -1.7	-0.9
	ARI	MLB	32	65	9	1	1	1	4	5	17	0-0	.200/.262/.300	.192	.262	0.5	2B(17): 0.3, 3B(4): 0.0	-0.2

A broken hamate bone and a half-season suspension for allegedly lying about his birthdate limited slugging outfield prospect **Jairo Beras** to just 17 Rookie-ball games in his debut summer. ⊘ Despite whiffing at a 38 percent rate as a 19-year-old in Low-A last season, **Lewis Brinson** posted a 20-20 campaign while flashing a potential plus-plus glove in center. ⊘ After toying around with a return to the infield in 2012, **Alex Castellanos** went back to full-time outfield duty last year. After toying around with offensive excellence in 2011 and 2012, he went back to full-time mediocrity last year. ⊘ Infielder **Travis Demeritte** is searching for a home defensively, but his quick bat and developing approach could warrant a full-season assignment in 2014. ⊘ One of the Rangers' 2011 international bonus babies, **Ronald Guzman** is big and gets praise for an advanced hit tool. Limited to first base, his bat will have to carry him. ⊘ Famous for his record $5 million bonus in 2011, **Nomar Mazara** has impressive power potential, but needs a lot of development if he's going to display that power in the bigs. ⊘ Selected in the Rule 5 draft by Cleveland, but then sent back to Texas, **Chris McGuiness** was overmatched when pressed into a major-league fill-in role. ⊘ **Rafael Ortega**'s plate discipline—likely the deciding factor for his major-league future—appeared to have improved, but between injuries and ineffectiveness 2013 was largely a lost season. ⊘ Unfortunately for legendary batsman **Manny Ramirez**, "Manny being Manny" these days means a month-long stint in Triple-A with a mid-.300s slugging percentage. ⊘ A versatile lefty with good on-base skills, **Drew Robinson** appears bound for Double-A, and if he survives the jump he has a chance for a career in the Todd Walker/Mark Bellhorn mold. ⊘ **Ryan Rua** transformed himself from organizational player into prospect by blasting 32 home runs in an age-23 season split between Low-A and Double-A, though his hit tool and glove remain in question. ⊘ "We signed Tanaka!!!" would have been the most misleading letter to season ticket holders ever, as it was Triple-A superutility type **Kensuke Tanaka** that Texas inked in December. ⊘ A potential 2012 first-rounder who slipped after a bad senior season, **Nick Williams** has an advanced hit tool but lacks refinement in the rest of his game. ⊘ Platinum frequent flyer status utilityman **Josh Wilson** surprisingly made the Opening Day roster for Arizona, then was given a top secret task in mid-June: "Find a good Polish restaurant in Reno."

PITCHERS

PLAYER	TEAM	LVL	AGE	W	L	SV	IP	H	HR	BB	SO	BB9	SO9	GB%	BABIP	WHIP	ERA	FIP	FRA	WARP
L. Bonilla	FRI	AA	23	2	0	6	30¹	16	0	9	50	2.7	14.8	55%	.286	0.82	0.30	0.85	1.44	1.3
	ROU	AAA	23	5	5	0	43	52	8	24	56	5.0	11.7	54%	.376	1.77	7.95	5.13	4.77	0.4
C. Buckel	FRI	AA	20	5	5	0	69	56	7	23	68	3.0	8.9	41%	.280	1.14	3.78	3.85	4.56	0.4
W. Font	FRI	AA	23	1	2	10	32	14	2	24	45	6.8	12.7	48%	.197	1.19	1.41	3.49	4.14	0.3
	ROU	AAA	23	1	0	4	20	8	0	10	26	4.5	11.7	29%	.195	0.90	0.45	2.77	2.66	0.5
	TEX	MLB	23	0	0	0	1¹	1	0	2	0	13.5	0.0	20%	.200	2.25	0.00	7.58	6.14	0.0
J. Germano	BUF	AAA	30	8	9	0	151	184	12	27	103	1.6	6.1	52%	.342	1.40	4.47	3.55	4.84	0.7
	TOR	MLB	30	0	0	0	2	6	1	0	1	0.0	4.5	46%	.500	3.00	9.00	8.58	6.50	0.0
R. Henry	FRI	AA	23	2	0	1	50²	32	1	7	40	1.2	7.1	56%	.220	0.77	1.07	2.21	2.89	1.2
M. Kirkman	ROU	AAA	26	2	3	0	29²	31	3	19	23	5.8	7.0	50%	.322	1.69	6.98	5.36	6.79	-0.2
	TEX	MLB	26	0	2	1	22	36	2	15	25	6.1	10.2	37%	.466	2.32	8.18	4.03	3.62	0.3
K. Lotzkar	BAK	A+	23	1	2	1	29²	31	1	26	33	7.9	10.0	38%	.358	1.92	6.98	5.32	6.13	0.0
K. McClellan	FRI	AA	29	2	0	0	27	29	2	6	27	2.0	9.0	46%	.355	1.30	3.33	2.80	2.68	0.8
	TEX	MLB	29	0	1	0	9¹	7	2	5	3	4.8	2.9	32%	.172	1.29	7.71	7.15	10.26	-0.4
R. Mendez	FRI	AA	22	2	0	2	24²	12	1	11	24	4.0	8.8	31%	.180	0.93	1.82	3.22	4.63	0.1
B. Rowen	FRI	AA	24	3	0	10	33²	23	1	11	28	2.9	7.5	67%	.253	1.01	0.53	2.76	4.15	0.4
	ROU	AAA	24	3	1	3	32	18	0	6	30	1.7	8.4	78%	.212	0.75	0.84	2.26	3.25	0.6
S. Tolleson	LAN	MLB	25	0	0	0	0	0	0	2	0	0.0	0.0	—	—	0.00	0.00	0.00	4572.53	-0.2
M. West	MYR	A+	23	0	3	0	20¹	18	1	16	14	7.1	6.2	52%	.279	1.67	6.64	5.30	6.31	-0.4

Armed with a low-mid-90s fastball and knockout changeup, righty reliever **Lisalverto Bonilla** posted a disastrous 7.95 ERA in 43 Triple-A innings before surrendering just one run in 30 Double-A frames. ⊘ Righty **Akeem Bostick**, Texas' second-round pick in 2013, already shows a promising fastball-curveball combo with room for projection in his athletic 6-foot-4 frame. ⊘ After entering last season as one of the organization's top pitching prospects, 21-year-old righty **Cody Buckel** developed a case of the yips and walked 35 batters over 10 ⅔ innings before being shut down. ⊘ Hulking right-hander **Wilmer Font** has a dominant fastball that touches triple digits, but his suspect command and lack of a reliable off-speed pitch have kept him from making an impact in Arlington. ⊘ **Justin Germano** has had an honorable career as a Triple-A demimondaine, including pitching a perfect game in 2011 as a Columbus Clipper, but the Blue Jays never gave him a big-league start last year despite constant rotation trouble, a fact which should sufficiently elaborate his abilities. ⊘ With a lively arsenal and outstanding command, cutter specialist **Randy Henry** is ticketed for Triple-A and could provide middle relief depth this summer. ⊘ **Michael Kirkman** was one of the most impressive pitchers in camp last spring, but was thwarted by command problems and sidelined by a cancer recurrence. A good arm who is a "change of scenery" candidate. ⊘ **Kyle Lotzkar**'s recurring injuries finally relegated him to a bullpen role, where his seventh pro season spiraled out of control because of lack of control. ⊘ Veteran swingman **Kyle McClellan** scuffled in his return from shoulder surgery last season, logging only seven big-league relief appearances before being sent to Double-A. ⊘ **Roman Mendez** had his season cut short by a stress fracture in his elbow, which has required surgery twice in less than a year. ⊘ Although submariner **Ben Rowen** rarely tops 82 mph on the radar gun, his mixture of deception and movement yielded an elite groundball rate and a 0.69 ERA between Double-A and Triple-A last season. ⊘ **Shawn Tolleson** spent a week in Albuquerque, returned to L.A to face two batters—walking both—and then went under the knife to repair a herniated disc in his lower back. A hip injury put a bummer into his rehab and ended a frustrating season. ⊘ Fireballing reliever **Matt West** will look to rediscover his mid-upper-90s heat as he returns from Tommy John surgery in 2014.

MANAGER: RON WASHINGTON

YEAR	TEAM	W-L	Pythag +/-	Avg PC	100+ P	120+ P	QS	BQS	REL	REL w Zero R	IBB	PH	PH Avg	PH HR	SB2	CS2	SB3	CS3	SAC Att	SAC %	POS SAC	Squeeze	Swing	In Play
2011	TEX	96-66	1	99.2	103	3	99	5	417	335	21	59	.204	1	123	39	18	4	63	61.9%	38	3	374	117
2012	TEX	93-69	1	98.7	87	4	86	3	428	366	15	86	.187	4	81	40	10	3	57	63.2%	33	2	338	96
2013	TEX	91-71	1	95.8	67	4	77	7	470	409	34	118	.274	2	130	40	17	5	64	70.3%	44	4	385	127

Ron Washington has never been considered an in-game tactical genius. (That's a nice way of putting it.) He's always been seen more as a motivator and a manager of people rather than of the game. In that regard, Texas' back-to-back fades at the end of the season in 2012 and 2013 especially hurt his reputation.

That said, Washington has had his successes with his players over the year. He's the only guy to get a great season from the troubled Milton Bradley. He also oversaw an MVP performance and five All-Star seasons from Josh Hamilton.

Despite helming teams with plenty of power and offense overall, Washington likes to play small ball. In fact, since taking the reins in Texas in 2007, the Rangers have laid more sacrifice bunts than any other team: 307. Second place are the Angels, way back at 283.

Toronto Blue Jays

By Shi Davidi

These are judgment days for Alex Anthopoulos, his winter of dreams in 2012 leading to a season of nightmares in 2013, Toronto's 20th consecutive playoff-free autumn only further fueling the pessimistic fatalism growing within the Blue Jays fan base.

Yes, last year really hurt, a 74-88 mess that drained the franchise not only of its electric energy, but also of the carefully gathered assets that had for so long promised a brighter future. Where visions of Jose Reyes, R.A. Dickey, Josh Johnson and Mark Buehrle popping champagne had once negated worries about the farm-system's sudden depletion, lament for the surrendered prospects is now at full volume on radio call-in shows, social media and even some of the more reasoned fan blogs. *Oh Noah Syndergaard, Travis d'Arnaud, Justin Nicolino, Jake Marisnick and Adeiny Hechavarria, if only we hadn't let you go*, goes a typical cry, the expectation that all will blossom into stars, obviously.

That's the environment in which Anthopoulos set out to rebuild his wunderkind rep and patch the roster flaws exposed by a brutal April that the Blue Jays never recovered from. An apt slogan for the times: In AA, We Still Sort Of Trust. There is very much a put up or shut up feel in the air.

Still, largely ignored by the public, and perhaps more important than any other concern, is the overarching issue of what exactly Blue Jays as an organization are about approaching their fifth year under Anthopoulos' stewardship. Gone are the days of building through youth, prospects now seemingly viewed more as chips than cornerstones. Here in their place are the times of servicing and supporting the big-league roster's substantial payroll commitments. The abrupt shift in mode from asset-gathering to win-now buried the implications in the closet, but it's worth noting that to this point the vision isn't yet clear.

BLUE JAYS PROSPECTUS
2013 W-L: 74-88, 5th in AL East

Pythag	.472	18th	DER	.706	11th
RS/G	4.40	9th	B-Age	29.0	22nd
RA/G	4.67	27th	P-Age	31.3	29th
TAv	.265	10th	Salary	$127.8	8th
BRR	7.84	4th	M$/MW	$4.5	23rd
TAv-P	.274	26th	DL Days	1449	29th
FIP	4.32	28th	$ on DL	27%	27th

	Runs	HR/RH	HR/LH	Runs/RH	Runs/LH
Three-Year Park Factors	102	97	99	104	106

Top Hitter WARP	4.42 (Edwin Encarnacion)
Top Pitcher WARP	2.42 (Mark Buehrle)
Top Prospect	Marcus Stroman

"Everyone talks about a certain style, people talk about the Minnesota Twins play a certain way, or Anaheim plays a certain way—we're still developing, and part of that is because there's been such turnover to the roster, (2013) was the fourth year, and because we've brought in players from all over the place," says Anthopoulos. "Most teams want the same things, playing a certain way, doing things a certain way, but it changes pretty quickly. If I asked you what the Red Sox way was a year ago compared to currently it would be totally different.

"In a perfect world you have power arms in the rotation, you have a deep 'pen, great defensive team, two-way players and obviously you have guys who profile from a position player standpoint."

Since no one in baseball is fielding this uber-team outside of the All-Star game, Anthopoulos can be forgiven for not having a squad to fit the ideal in place. But how close has he come? And what kind of identity have the Blue Jays created under his watch?

The Blue Jays finished the 2013 season with a deep bullpen under affordable contractual control, a handful of two-way players in a largely one-dimensional lineup, some significant defensive holes and, most crucially, a rotation distinctly lacking in power arms. The health concerns of Brandon Morrow and Johnson contributed in large measure to that, but of note is that the club's two most effective and reliable starters were Dickey, a knuckleballer, and Buehrle, the finessiest lefty of them all, both way out on the opposite end of the spectrum.

There's nothing wrong with that—Buehrle pitched to a 2.4 WARP and Dickey to 1.6 in a down year—but it underlines one key spot where the blueprint has yet to come to life. The power arms Anthopoulos so dearly covets are typically obtained in the draft, yet despite four drafts since taking over, the Blue Jays have gotten exactly one start from any of their picks—Sean Nolin's messy 1 ⅓-inning debut last May.

While Nolin remains a prospect and the Blue Jays do have some young arms coming—Marcus Stroman is very likely to debut in 2014, while Aaron Sanchez should break through by early 2015—they have yet to churn out the type of impact arms that have carried the Tampa Bay Rays. And in the American League East, an unsteady rotation is the equivalent of building on quicksand.

"I can tell you we're going to try to get to that point where we have a deep rotation and hopefully young rotation, but it takes time to do that, especially if you're going to draft a bunch of high school guys, knowing the injury rate," says Anthopoulos. "Some guys might come from the college ranks, some guys might come from high school ranks, but if they come from the high school ranks—you look at a guy like Chris Archer, he's a high school draft pick, he's 25 years old now and he's finally settling in, but he's drafted as a 17-year-old. He's seven years down the road.

"That's ultimately where we would get to in time."

The perils of that strategy are evidenced in the lack of pitching depth the Blue Jays have had the past four seasons. Combined with the lack of success from some of the J.P. Ricciardi drafts and an inability to find a quick mover like Chris Sale or Michael Wacha, Toronto has been left to rely on dodgy stopgaps to fill holes in the big-league rotation. Consider that Dana Eveland made nine starts in 2010, Jo-Jo Reyes made 20 starts in 2011, Aaron Laffey made 16 starts in 2012 and Todd Redmond made 14 starts in 2013—not good.

Factor in the Blue Jays' problems acquiring starters from outside the organization—"There's an emotional bias against playing outside the United States, so for Alex to be trying to draw from an equal talent pool is very, very challenging," says one agent—and building a strong rotation has been Anthopoulos' biggest and most significant failing thus far.

"In the American League East, it's going to be hard to recruit free agents," says Anthopoulos. "We've had our challenges getting free agent starters to come here, whether it's the ballpark, the division, the dollars you have to commit. If you're ultimately going to go the route of trying to build that homegrown rotation, you're going to take quite a while to do it."

To be fair, the Blue Jays have had some very poor fortune on that front, too. Ricky Romero went from All-Star and ace in 2011 to non-roster afterthought, a fall from grace that includes two claim-free trips through waivers and a $7.75 million price tag for each of the next two seasons. Brett Cecil fell apart as a starter following a solid 1.7-WARP season in 2010, finally reinventing himself as an All-Star set-up man last year. In June 2012, Kyle Drabek—having shown brilliant flashes while posting a 4.67 ERA in 13 outings—and rookie Drew Hutchison blew out their elbows two days apart. Any team would have a tough time absorbing those losses.

Regardless, Anthopoulos decided to take his shot with the Marlins and Mets deals, betting that a six-man combination of Dickey, Morrow, Buehrle, Johnson, Romero and J.A. Happ would be good enough to overcome the lack of organizational depth. It was a costly miscalculation that kept the Blue Jays' rotation from providing the backbone the GM envisioned.

While the starters continued to search for an identity, the lineup that finished 2013 was also a ways from the club's goal of a versatile, pitch-eating lineup with both quick-strike capability and the tools to manufacture offense when needed.

Instead, Blue Jays batters were another iteration of the grip-it-and-rip-it bands Anthopoulos has cobbled together the past four years, finishing fourth in the American League with 185 home runs. That sounds great, but a .318 OBP meant 110 of them were solo shots. Even at that, homers accounted for 283, or 42 percent, of their 669 RBIs, underlining how they remain the same one-dimensional outfit Anthopoulos inherited from Ricciardi. Hitting coach Chad Mottola was let go after the season and replaced with Kevin Seitzer, who preaches a middle-of-the-field approach and going the other way with two strikes. Sensible stuff, sure, but only to hitters who are receptive to such a mindset.

"You have to bring in those types of players," says Anthopoulos. "You can talk about the players or the coaching staff having to get guys to walk more, be on-base guys—I think that can be slightly improved—but you have to draft those types of players, or get guys who are predisposed to do some of those things. The same way if you want to have a young rotation with power arms, you're not going to bring a guy in and teach him velocity, so we have to get those guys in trades, or get those guys in the draft. But ultimately it takes time."

Yes it does, but there's no time to wait any longer for the Blue Jays, not after the failed 2013 and the millions upon millions invested.

Off the field there is more of an established Blue Jays way, with a robust professional and amateur scouting staff scouring North America and filing a steady stream of reports, a front office that works relentlessly and an analytics department that's a key part of the organization's player evaluations.

Last January the club launched The BEST (pronounced Beest, after club president Paul Beeston), a database designed to house scouting reports, proprietary analytics data, medical reports and contractual data in a single spot. The project was in development for two and a half years under recently departed assistant GM Jay Sartori and baseball information analyst Joe Sheehan before finally going live. While Anthopoulos was looking to replace Sartori, he also wanted to expand the analytics department.

Criticized privately in some corners for being too stats-oriented, Anthopoulos says the numbers are only part of the Blue Jays' player-evaluation process.

"There are so many components to it," he says. "You're evaluating contractual status, age, medical information, makeup, tools, the analytics, the stats—the further away from the major-leagues how much can you rely on those, how much can you trust those, how many of those things match, how many of them pair, how much of what the analytics or statistics are telling you are the scouts confirming, can you put it all together?

"There's no magic bullet, there's no one single thing you look at. You're putting it all together and you're trying to come up with a determination."

The determinations from a year ago certainly didn't go to plan for Anthopoulos, and Blue Jays fans are hoping he and his staff were better in their judgments this past offseason. A year-over-year attendance increase at Rogers Centre of more than 20 percent—up 436,899 to 2.5 million—was the largest in baseball in 2013 and demonstrated how eager the club's supporters are to embrace a winner. Providing one for them won't be easy, especially now that the organization's internal clock has been sped up and there's no slowing it back down. As for creating an organizational identity, fans only care to see the Blue Jays become the one thing they haven't been in a long, long time—a winner.

Shi Davidi is the baseball columnist for Sportsnet *in Toronto. He's also co-author of* Great Expectations: The Lost Toronto Blue Jays Season.

HITTERS

Franklin Barreto   SS
Born: 2/27/1996 Age: 18
Bats: R Throws: R Height: 5' 9"
Weight: 174 Breakout: 0%
Improve: 0% Collapse: 0%
Attrition: 0% MLB: 0%

Comparables:
Adrian Cardenas, Jonathan Villar, Hernan Perez

YEAR	TEAM	LVL	AGE	PA	R	2B	3B	HR	RBI	BB	SO	SB	CS	AVG/OBP/SLG	TAv	BABIP	BRR	FRAA	WARP
2014	TOR	MLB	18	250	23	9	1	4	18	9	79	3	2	.189/.227/.286	.186	.260	-0.1	SS -2	-1.1

Probably the top international prospect on the market last summer, the Venezuelan Barreto has been wowing onlookers since before his voice broke. He has two Pan-American tournament MVP awards under his belt, among other honors. Barreto has a legit, advanced bat, and good speed that some think will ease his transition off shortstop (where he doesn't project, ultimately) and out to center field. The Jays lavished a $1.45 million bonus on Barreto, making him their prized prospect in the lower minors.

Jose Bautista   RF
Born: 10/19/1980 Age: 33
Bats: R Throws: R Height: 6' 0"
Weight: 190 Breakout: 2%
Improve: 25% Collapse: 4%
Attrition: 8% MLB: 97%

Comparables:
J.D. Drew, Frank Robinson, Stan Musial

YEAR	TEAM	LVL	AGE	PA	R	2B	3B	HR	RBI	BB	SO	SB	CS	AVG/OBP/SLG	TAv	BABIP	BRR	FRAA	WARP
2011	TOR	MLB	30	655	105	24	2	43	103	132	111	9	5	.302/.447/.608	.358	.309	1.4	RF(116): 6.0, 3B(25): 4.1	9.4
2012	TOR	MLB	31	399	64	14	0	27	65	59	63	5	2	.241/.358/.527	.307	.215	3.8	RF(90): 1.1, 1B(4): 0.1	3.5
2013	TOR	MLB	32	528	82	24	0	28	73	69	84	7	2	.259/.358/.498	.307	.259	-1.5	RF(109): -8.5, 3B(3): -0.3	3.1
2014	TOR	MLB	33	471	71	19	1	27	77	71	86	6	2	.256/.375/.516	.318	.260	-0.4	RF -4, 3B 0	3.2

A hip bruise, sustained when he pulled up abruptly rather than slide into home, ended Bautista's season about six weeks early, yet another casualty of the Jays' injury-bitten 2013. Bautista showed small signs of slippage across the rate-stat board, but he seems to have come down from two years of shocking superstardom and settled into late-career reliability. His excellent plate discipline should help offset any power erosion, unless the growing injury trend worsens. Bautista's owed $28 million over the two guaranteed years remaining on his contract. That's reasonable at his current production level, but further decline or lost time will make the money seem like a retrospective overpay, offsetting the outrageous value of his world-devouring 2010 and 2011.

Melky Cabrera   LF
Born: 8/11/1984 Age: 29
Bats: B Throws: L Height: 6' 0"
Weight: 200 Breakout: 2%
Improve: 37% Collapse: 3%
Attrition: 10% MLB: 98%

Comparables:
Martin Prado, Shannon Stewart, Carl Crawford

YEAR	TEAM	LVL	AGE	PA	R	2B	3B	HR	RBI	BB	SO	SB	CS	AVG/OBP/SLG	TAv	BABIP	BRR	FRAA	WARP
2011	KCA	MLB	26	706	102	44	5	18	87	35	94	20	10	.305/.339/.470	.280	.332	4.2	CF(144): -17.6, LF(12): 0.2	2.3
2012	SFN	MLB	27	501	84	25	10	11	60	36	63	13	5	.346/.390/.516	.331	.379	0.6	LF(106): 2.0, RF(11): -1.0	5.2
2013	TOR	MLB	28	372	39	15	2	3	30	23	47	2	2	.279/.322/.360	.252	.313	-0.2	LF(77): -3.2	-0.1
2014	TOR	MLB	29	379	47	21	2	8	38	26	52	7	3	.282/.332/.424	.273	.310	-0.1	LF -1, CF -1	1.1

It seemed like a reasonable gamble to sign the reputation-damaged Cabrera to a two-year, $16 million deal, but those on the PED witch hunt wound up with a useful whipping boy. Plagued by left knee problems all season (he spent 83 games on the disabled list), Cabrera was shut down for good in early August; he was later discovered to have a benign tumor on his spine, perhaps the source of the leg problems. The tumor was removed in September, but the uncertainty about Cabrera's future remains. He's still young enough to stabilize an erratic career, but is he smart enough? The fake website, even his failure to mask elevated testosterone levels—which is apparently easy enough to do—don't suggest a canny guy taking the long view.

Mark DeRosa 3B

Born: 2/26/1975 Age: 39
Bats: R Throws: R Height: 6' 1"
Weight: 215 Breakout: 1%
Improve: 15% Collapse: 13%
Attrition: 21% MLB: 58%

Comparables:
Melvin Mora, Graig Nettles, Geoff Blum

YEAR	TEAM	LVL	AGE	PA	R	2B	3B	HR	RBI	BB	SO	SB	CS	AVG/OBP/SLG	TAv	BABIP	BRR	FRAA	WARP
2011	FRE	AAA	36	43	6	1	0	0	3	0	8	0	0	.310/.310/.333	.213	.382	0.1	3B(5): 0.2, 2B(3): 0.9	0.1
2011	SFN	MLB	36	97	9	2	0	0	12	8	18	1	1	.279/.351/.302	.267	.348	1.6	3B(16): -1.0, 1B(10): -0.1	0.5
2012	WAS	MLB	37	101	13	5	0	0	6	14	18	1	0	.188/.300/.247	.204	.235	-1.1	3B(11): -0.0, LF(9): -0.4	-0.5
2013	TOR	MLB	38	236	23	12	1	7	36	24	49	0	0	.235/.326/.407	.268	.272	0.9	2B(29): 0.1, 3B(25): -0.6	0.8
2014	TOR	MLB	39	250	25	10	0	6	27	22	54	1	1	.228/.303/.363	.245	.270	-0.5	3B -2, 2B 0	0.0

In a year when practically every Blue Jay got hurt, who would have guessed that the increasingly fragile (and pretty old) DeRosa would have stayed healthy? All the injuries made his utility and steady clubhouse presence a welcome tonic in a year rashy with rancor and losing (but shame on Gibbons for giving him 14 games at DH, where DeRosa posted a positional-split-low .558 OPS). And it wasn't all "intangibles": DeRosa still hit lefties fine (.267/.368/.443). The Blue Jays picked up DeRosa's $750,000 option, presumably because they liked his influence on Brett Lawrie and because he looked so handsome doing postseason TV commentary. Apparently, however, DeRosa got hooked on the talking-head gig; he retired to join fellow Penn alum Doug Glanville on the MLB Network.

Edwin Encarnacion 1B

Born: 1/7/1983 Age: 31
Bats: R Throws: R Height: 6' 2"
Weight: 230 Breakout: 1%
Improve: 35% Collapse: 1%
Attrition: 4% MLB: 96%

Comparables:
Justin Morneau, Kent Hrbek, Rafael Palmeiro

YEAR	TEAM	LVL	AGE	PA	R	2B	3B	HR	RBI	BB	SO	SB	CS	AVG/OBP/SLG	TAv	BABIP	BRR	FRAA	WARP
2011	TOR	MLB	28	530	70	36	0	17	55	43	77	8	2	.272/.334/.453	.271	.292	-3.6	3B(36): -2.1, 1B(25): -2.4	0.7
2012	TOR	MLB	29	644	93	24	0	42	110	84	94	13	3	.280/.384/.557	.324	.266	-3.9	1B(68): -6.3, LF(3): -0.0	3.8
2013	TOR	MLB	30	621	90	29	1	36	104	82	62	7	1	.272/.370/.534	.319	.247	1.8	1B(79): -5.5, 3B(10): 1.1	4.4
2014	TOR	MLB	31	588	80	27	1	28	88	64	89	8	2	.259/.346/.479	.295	.260	-0.2	1B -6, 3B -1	2.2

Only Miguel Cabrera and Chris Davis have hit more home runs than Encarnacion over the past two seasons. Add Giancarlo Stanton and you have the only three players with higher isolated power in that span. Unlike Davis and Stanton—and just about every other power hitter in today's game—Encarnacion walks a lot and doesn't strike out much. He's a superstar in all but image. If he lucks into an unusually high BABIP (his has been among the 20 lowest in baseball over the past five seasons), he could win an MVP award and secure his celebrity. It will need to happen before he's relegated to full-time DH, where MVPs are basically banned.

Ryan Goins SS

Born: 2/13/1988 Age: 26
Bats: L Throws: R Height: 5' 10"
Weight: 170 Breakout: 3%
Improve: 19% Collapse: 6%
Attrition: 14% MLB: 35%

Comparables:
Jeff Bianchi, Anderson Hernandez, J.J. Furmaniak

YEAR	TEAM	LVL	AGE	PA	R	2B	3B	HR	RBI	BB	SO	SB	CS	AVG/OBP/SLG	TAv	BABIP	BRR	FRAA	WARP
2011	DUN	A+	23	398	50	24	5	3	52	32	67	2	2	.286/.343/.408	.249	.343	1.7	SS(71): 2.6	1.2
2012	NHP	AA	24	618	66	33	4	7	61	47	78	15	9	.289/.342/.403	.269	.323	-0.7	SS(114): 0.2, 2B(23): 1.8	3.7
2013	BUF	AAA	25	418	42	22	1	6	46	29	85	3	5	.257/.311/.369	.242	.316	0.6	SS(101): 6.5, 2B(9): -1.0	1.3
2013	TOR	MLB	25	121	11	5	0	2	8	2	28	0	0	.252/.264/.345	.231	.315	-1.4	2B(32): 1.0, SS(2): 0.0	-0.1
2014	TOR	MLB	26	250	25	12	1	4	21	14	51	2	1	.244/.286/.354	.229	.290	-0.5	SS 1, 2B 0	0.3

When Maicer Izturis went down for the year with a sprained ankle in late August, the Blue Jays called up their Buffalo shortstop and made him a big-league starter at second base. Why not? The position was a sinkhole (team-worst .556 OPS) and the Jays had gone into a late-season youth movement. Goins, a former fourth-rounder, doesn't have the bat to project as a regular, but his glove and range are legit, and he could develop into a useful utility player.

Anthony Gose CF

Born: 8/10/1990 Age: 23
Bats: L Throws: L Height: 6' 1"
Weight: 195 Breakout: 0%
Improve: 13% Collapse: 4%
Attrition: 8% MLB: 27%

Comparables:
Felix Pie, Trayvon Robinson, Xavier Avery

YEAR	TEAM	LVL	AGE	PA	R	2B	3B	HR	RBI	BB	SO	SB	CS	AVG/OBP/SLG	TAv	BABIP	BRR	FRAA	WARP
2011	NHP	AA	20	587	87	20	7	16	59	62	154	70	15	.253/.349/.415	.248	.332	5.4	CF(42): -0.2	1.0
2012	LVG	AAA	21	482	87	21	10	5	43	49	101	34	12	.286/.366/.419	.272	.365	7.4	CF(98): -6.8, LF(3): -0.4	2.2
2012	TOR	MLB	21	189	25	7	3	1	11	17	59	15	3	.223/.303/.319	.225	.340	1.8	RF(24): -0.3, CF(22): 1.5	0.1
2013	BUF	AAA	22	448	64	17	6	3	27	38	121	22	13	.239/.316/.336	.233	.336	4	CF(85): -6.9, RF(14): 1.1	-0.3
2013	TOR	MLB	22	153	15	6	5	2	12	5	37	4	3	.259/.283/.408	.233	.333	0	CF(34): -2.3, LF(15): -0.3	-0.2
2014	TOR	MLB	23	274	35	10	3	4	20	21	76	16	5	.229/.295/.341	.233	.310	1.7	CF -1, RF 0	0.0

It's easy to worry about Gose after he repeated much of 2012's big-league line in roughly the same number of games. Nonetheless, this is probably the year the Jays give the still young, still very gifted Gose a starting job or something close to it. It would be nice if he could use his speed to actually steal bases: His minor-league success rate has nearly always been poor. The strikeouts probably aren't coming down, either. But if he gets closer to his solid upper-minors walk rates, he'll contribute this year and could certainly still reach his All-Star ceiling down the road. And it'll be a bonus if he and Goins both stick, giving the Jays a duo of bizarro-world conjugations of "go."

Maicer Izturis 2B

Born: 9/12/1980 Age: 33
Bats: B Throws: R Height: 5' 8"
Weight: 170 Breakout: 1%
Improve: 22% Collapse: 6%
Attrition: 7% MLB: 93%

Comparables:
Mark Loretta, Red Schoendienst, Ryan Theriot

YEAR	TEAM	LVL	AGE	PA	R	2B	3B	HR	RBI	BB	SO	SB	CS	AVG/OBP/SLG	TAv	BABIP	BRR	FRAA	WARP
2011	ANA	MLB	30	494	51	35	0	5	38	33	65	9	6	.276/.334/.388	.262	.311	1.2	2B(49): -0.3, 3B(37): 0.3	2.2
2012	ANA	MLB	31	319	35	11	0	2	20	25	38	17	2	.256/.320/.315	.229	.289	0	3B(30): -1.7, 2B(29): -0.1	-0.4
2013	TOR	MLB	32	399	33	12	0	5	32	27	38	1	5	.236/.288/.310	.224	.249	2.3	2B(59): -2.2, 3B(36): -2.9	-0.6
2014	TOR	MLB	33	359	42	19	1	5	30	28	45	8	4	.258/.321/.365	.251	.280	-0.4	2B -1, 3B -2	0.4

Izturis had the ninth-lowest isolated power in baseball last year among players with 400 plate appearances (okay, 399). That would be fine for a little kisser who can flirt his way to first base with some regularity, but his OBP caved as well: he finished in the bottom 20. All in all, he was one of the poorest hitters in the game. He also sported the worst FRAA of his career. Izturis presents a textbook case of aging, where all the skills crash at once. His season-ending ankle injury in August was almost a relief. On the bright (?) side, the Jays can buy out his $1 million option. Oh—in 2016. Never mind.

A.J. Jimenez C

Born: 5/1/1990 Age: 24
Bats: R Throws: R Height: 6' 0"
Weight: 210 Breakout: 4%
Improve: 7% Collapse: 2%
Attrition: 15% MLB: 17%

Comparables:
Manny Pina, Bobby Wilson, Brett Hayes

YEAR	TEAM	LVL	AGE	PA	R	2B	3B	HR	RBI	BB	SO	SB	CS	AVG/OBP/SLG	TAv	BABIP	BRR	FRAA	WARP
2011	DUN	A+	21	422	49	29	1	4	52	28	60	11	2	.303/.353/.417	.285	.348	1.4	C(66): 0.2	2.6
2012	NHP	AA	22	113	14	4	1	2	10	5	14	2	3	.257/.295/.371	.241	.278	-1.2	C(27): 0.2	0.3
2013	DUN	A+	23	29	5	3	0	1	9	1	3	0	0	.429/.448/.643	.391	.458	-2.4	C(7): -0.1	0.3
2013	NHP	AA	23	223	28	15	0	3	29	16	37	1	2	.276/.327/.394	.271	.319	-0.7	C(40): 1.9	1.3
2013	BUF	AAA	23	31	0	1	0	0	0	1	2	0	1	.233/.258/.267	.189	.250	-0.5	C(7): -0.0	-0.1
2014	TOR	MLB	24	250	22	13	0	4	24	12	47	2	1	.246/.283/.353	.230	.290	-0.5	C 0	0.3

Jimenez is the top catching prospect, both in level and ranking, in a farm system boasting a few. He fell slightly off the radar because of Tommy John surgery, from which he returned in June. He worked mostly in Double-A before a mid-August taste of Triple-A, but was shut down a few days before season's end with nerve irritation in the repaired elbow. If that was nothing serious, Jimenez will be the regular catcher in Triple-A in 2014, with a chance to reach the majors and a decent shot at the big-league starting job in 2015. He draws raves for his work behind the plate and with pitchers, and for his overall makeup. The bat, which is line-drive rather than long-ball oriented, needs another year to develop.

Munenori Kawasaki SS

Born: 6/3/1981 Age: 33
Bats: L Throws: R Height: 5' 10"
Weight: 165 Breakout: 1%
Improve: 25% Collapse: 9%
Attrition: 15% MLB: 90%

Comparables:
Spike Owen, Johnny Pesky, Omar Vizquel

YEAR	TEAM	LVL	AGE	PA	R	2B	3B	HR	RBI	BB	SO	SB	CS	AVG/OBP/SLG	TAv	BABIP	BRR	FRAA	WARP
2012	SEA	MLB	31	115	13	1	0	0	7	8	18	2	2	.192/.257/.202	.185	.233	-0.7	SS(38): -1.9, 2B(10): 0.4	-0.7
2013	BUF	AAA	32	81	9	0	0	0	3	14	12	3	0	.250/.400/.250	.234	.312	-0.9	SS(12): -0.1, 2B(11): -0.1	-0.1
2013	TOR	MLB	32	289	27	6	5	1	24	32	41	7	1	.229/.326/.308	.245	.269	0.9	SS(60): -3.1, 2B(18): 1.5	0.5
2014	TOR	MLB	33	250	25	8	2	2	19	25	41	5	1	.233/.319/.314	.233	.270	0.5	SS -3, 2B 1	0.1

What does a dreadfully disappointing team need? A distraction. Kawasaki replaced the injured Jose Reyes early in the season and made everybody happy (well, less sad) with his irrepressible antics. He even went from being "unspeakably bad," as we called him last year, to merely mediocre, his hugely improved True Average (tied with the great Nick Punto's) good for 26th among 38 shortstops with 280+ plate appearances. The improvement owed to a simple change, one that was also Puntoesque: Kawasaki stopped swinging the damn bat so much. His swing rate was fifth-lowest in baseball, a dramatic plunge from its previous mid-pack rank. Pitchers will wise up this year and pound the zone; the Blue Jays didn't, and after declining his option re-signed him to a minor-league deal. Heck, guess every team can use some comic relief.

Erik Kratz C

Born: 6/15/1980 Age: 34
Bats: R Throws: R Height: 6' 4"
Weight: 255 Breakout: 0%
Improve: 17% Collapse: 6%
Attrition: 18% MLB: 65%

Comparables:
Corky Miller, Mike Rivera, Oscar Salazar

YEAR	TEAM	LVL	AGE	PA	R	2B	3B	HR	RBI	BB	SO	SB	CS	AVG/OBP/SLG	TAv	BABIP	BRR	FRAA	WARP
2011	LEH	AAA	31	409	56	19	0	15	53	38	72	2	0	.288/.372/.466	.312	.322	1.1	C(45): -0.2	2.0
2011	PHI	MLB	31	6	0	1	0	0	0	0	1	0	0	.333/.333/.500	.299	.400	-0.1	C(1): 0.0	0.1
2012	LEH	AAA	32	141	17	10	0	8	30	10	20	0	0	.266/.326/.540	.279	.250	-1.1	C(31): -0.6	0.8
2012	PHI	MLB	32	157	14	9	0	9	26	11	34	0	0	.248/.306/.504	.286	.257	-1.4	C(41): 0.8	1.4
2013	PHI	MLB	33	218	21	7	0	9	26	18	45	0	0	.213/.280/.386	.223	.228	1.1	C(60): -0.5	0.1
2014	TOR	MLB	34	250	29	12	0	10	32	20	54	0	0	.231/.303/.418	.257	.260	-0.5	C 1	1.1

Erik Kratz was a great story in 2012. He was a 32-year-old rookie, hitting a game-tying home run off Craig Kimbrel, contributing to a contender attempting to win the NL East for the sixth straight year. This all earned him the nickname "Turkey Bacon," inspired by his appearance in a local TV ad featuring a talking cartoon fowl. The success was short. He started the 2013 season as the everyday catcher while Carlos Ruiz served a 25-game suspension, but he never got rolling, finishing with exactly as many HR and RBI as he had in 2012, but in 61 more plate appearances. He was exposed as a full-timer and sent to Toronto for Brad Lincoln, but as far as backup catchers go, you could do worse.

Brett Lawrie   3B
Born: 1/18/1990 Age: 24
Bats: R Throws: R Height: 6' 0"
Weight: 225 Breakout: 1%
Improve: 61% Collapse: 3%
Attrition: 3% MLB: 99%

Comparables:
Pablo Sandoval, Edwin Encarnacion, Ryan Zimmerman

YEAR	TEAM	LVL	AGE	PA	R	2B	3B	HR	RBI	BB	SO	SB	CS	AVG/OBP/SLG	TAv	BABIP	BRR	FRAA	WARP
2011	LVG	AAA	21	329	64	24	6	18	61	26	53	13	2	.353/.415/.661	.319	.383	-0.9	3B(60): 3.3	3.0
2011	TOR	MLB	21	171	26	8	4	9	25	16	31	7	1	.293/.373/.580	.327	.318	0.2	3B(43): 9.3	3.0
2012	TOR	MLB	22	536	73	26	3	11	48	33	86	13	8	.273/.324/.405	.258	.311	2.4	3B(123): 20.6, SS(1): -0.0	4.0
2013	TOR	MLB	23	442	41	18	3	11	46	30	68	9	5	.254/.315/.397	.263	.280	0.3	3B(103): 3.6, 2B(6): -0.7	1.7
2014	TOR	MLB	24	441	52	21	3	13	54	30	75	11	4	.269/.327/.435	.276	.300	0.3	3B 12, 2B 0	3.2

When Lawrie's healthy, his extreme-sports demeanor ("I'm out there going 100 miles an hour"), grade-A glove, and increasing all-fields hitting have scouts declaring him an imminent superstar. Absorb the superlatives in that sentence, but re-read the first three words. The youngster's screaming intensity, not fragility, sends him to the disabled list every year—the ankle sprain that cost him a month and a half occurred on an awkward over-slide into second. The influence of vet Mark DeRosa, who lockered next to him in spring training last year, took a while to rub off—Lawrie publicly chastised fellow Canuck Russell Martin for skipping the World Baseball Classic—but in June, after Lawrie shot an angry tweet at critical fans, he deleted it (so mature!). If Lawrie falls short of his sky-high ceiling, it will be because of character, not talent.

Adam Lind   1B
Born: 7/17/1983 Age: 30
Bats: L Throws: L Height: 6' 2"
Weight: 220 Breakout: 2%
Improve: 44% Collapse: 4%
Attrition: 16% MLB: 93%

Comparables:
Benny Ayala, Ryan Klesko, Adam LaRoche

YEAR	TEAM	LVL	AGE	PA	R	2B	3B	HR	RBI	BB	SO	SB	CS	AVG/OBP/SLG	TAv	BABIP	BRR	FRAA	WARP
2011	TOR	MLB	27	542	56	16	0	26	87	32	107	1	1	.251/.295/.439	.260	.265	2	1B(109): -4.6	0.1
2012	LVG	AAA	28	143	24	10	0	8	29	15	26	1	0	.392/.448/.664	.355	.436	-3.7	1B(25): -1.4	1.1
2012	TOR	MLB	28	353	28	14	2	11	45	29	61	0	0	.255/.314/.414	.256	.282	-0.1	1B(61): -4.0	-0.3
2013	TOR	MLB	29	521	67	26	1	23	67	51	103	1	0	.288/.357/.497	.301	.324	-3.2	1B(76): -1.3	2.3
2014	TOR	MLB	30	475	56	23	1	19	67	38	97	1	0	.264/.324/.457	.279	.300	-0.8	1B -3	1.1

Lind might say it was offseason yoga (although his back nonetheless seized up on him midseason) or "swinging 90 percent," as he described his new-age approach. His manager, however, might take credit for physical discipline of his own, and of a very different type: He had Lind assume an extreme platoon split, allowing him to face a lefty in a career-low 19 percent of his plate appearances. The result? Lind had his best year since the breakout 2009 that made him look like a future star. He may never be one, but he made his $7 million option easy to exercise, and as a year-to-year club-option player at reasonable rates through 2016 ($7.5 million and $8 million, with smallish buyouts), he's a useful asset as long as he skips games started by southpaws and goes to yoga class instead.

Brent Morel   3B
Born: 4/21/1987 Age: 27
Bats: R Throws: R Height: 6' 2"
Weight: 225 Breakout: 4%
Improve: 21% Collapse: 9%
Attrition: 22% MLB: 52%

Comparables:
Casey McGehee, Chris Nelson, Tim Olson

YEAR	TEAM	LVL	AGE	PA	R	2B	3B	HR	RBI	BB	SO	SB	CS	AVG/OBP/SLG	TAv	BABIP	BRR	FRAA	WARP
2011	CHA	MLB	24	444	44	18	1	10	41	22	57	5	4	.245/.287/.366	.243	.262	-0.9	3B(125): -1.3	0.4
2012	WNS	A+	25	24	2	4	0	0	2	2	4	0	0	.227/.292/.409	.205	.278	-0.1	3B(5): -0.5	-0.1
2012	CHR	AAA	25	132	12	4	0	1	10	8	28	0	0	.194/.242/.250	.184	.242	0.4	3B(26): 4.4	-0.4
2012	CHA	MLB	25	125	14	2	0	0	5	7	39	4	1	.177/.225/.195	.174	.270	0	3B(33): -0.2	-0.8
2013	CHR	AAA	26	452	55	30	3	6	54	48	104	14	3	.266/.349/.403	.265	.344	0.8	3B(86): 2.6, 1B(4): 0.2	1.8
2013	CHA	MLB	26	30	3	0	0	0	1	5	7	1	1	.200/.333/.200	.202	.278	-0.3	3B(9): 0.3, 1B(3): 0.0	0.0
2014	TOR	MLB	27	250	26	13	1	5	24	16	51	4	1	.248/.298/.372	.246	.300	-0.1	3B 0, 1B 0	0.3

First, the good stuff: Morel finally seems recovered from the back issues that had recently plagued him, remains a solid defender, has developed more patience at the plate and lit up lefties to the tune of .317/.409/.468 at Triple-A last year. Unfortunately, none of that is likely to overcome his continuing struggles against same-side pitching in general and major-league pitching in particular, and there isn't much of a market for players who can make up the short side of a third base platoon. Look for Morel to become an achingly familiar site on the Triple-A-to-MLB shuttle.

Dioner Navarro   C

Born: 2/9/1984 Age: 30
Bats: B Throws: R Height: 5' 9"
Weight: 205 Breakout: 0%
Improve: 36% Collapse: 10%
Attrition: 13% MLB: 86%

Comparables:
Carlos Ruiz, Brayan Pena, Jason Phillips

YEAR	TEAM	LVL	AGE	PA	R	2B	3B	HR	RBI	BB	SO	SB	CS	AVG/OBP/SLG	TAv	BABIP	BRR	FRAA	WARP
2011	LAN	MLB	27	202	13	6	1	5	17	20	35	0	0	.193/.276/.324	.231	.210	-1.5	C(54): 0.1	0.1
2012	LOU	AAA	28	240	24	12	0	5	32	23	24	0	0	.319/.382/.449	.282	.332	-3.8	C(49): -0.5	1.3
2012	CIN	MLB	28	73	6	3	1	2	12	2	12	0	0	.290/.306/.449	.260	.321	0.9	C(21): -0.2	0.5
2013	CHN	MLB	29	266	31	7	0	13	34	23	36	0	1	.300/.365/.492	.301	.307	-5.3	C(55): 0.2	1.6
2014	TOR	MLB	30	250	27	10	0	7	27	20	38	1	0	.247/.312/.386	.252	.260	-0.5	C -0	0.8

Navarro signed on last season to mentor Welington Castillo, and the veteran backstop went on to enjoy his first productive season since the Bush administration. A switch-hitter whose palate bends toward lefty pitching, Navarro made a meal out of southpaws last season, held his own against righties, and was acceptable behind the dish. He also launched a career-best 13 bombs, but that's not likely to last—his rate of home runs per fly ball nearly doubled his previous career best, and looks rather suspicious lurking with downcast eyes between the rates of Mike Napoli and Joey Votto. Now the best of a handful of imperfect options in Toronto, Navarro is likely to disappoint when given a full-time workload, but can still provide value in a platoon role.

Kevin Pillar   LF

Born: 1/4/1989 Age: 25
Bats: R Throws: R Height: 6' 0"
Weight: 200 Breakout: 10%
Improve: 30% Collapse: 7%
Attrition: 32% MLB: 50%

Comparables:
Dave Sappelt, Alex Presley, A.J. Pollock

YEAR	TEAM	LVL	AGE	PA	R	2B	3B	HR	RBI	BB	SO	SB	CS	AVG/OBP/SLG	TAv	BABIP	BRR	FRAA	WARP
2012	LNS	A	23	375	49	20	4	5	57	35	53	35	6	.322/.390/.451	.291	.371	0.1	LF(49): 4.0, RF(15): 2.7	2.9
2012	DUN	A+	23	178	16	8	2	1	34	5	17	16	3	.323/.339/.415	.285	.342	1.6	RF(18): -0.7, CF(16): -0.5	1.1
2013	NHP	AA	24	327	44	20	2	5	30	19	31	15	8	.312/.361/.441	.284	.336	1.3	CF(53): 2.2, LF(20): -1.3	2.4
2013	BUF	AAA	24	218	30	19	4	4	27	12	39	8	5	.299/.341/.493	.294	.350	1.9	LF(21): 2.5, CF(20): -0.7	1.9
2013	TOR	MLB	24	110	11	4	0	3	13	4	29	0	1	.206/.250/.333	.219	.257	-1.7	LF(33): 1.2, RF(1): -0.0	-0.2
2014	TOR	MLB	25	250	26	13	1	5	26	11	47	7	3	.258/.295/.387	.246	.300	0.4	LF 2, CF 0	0.6

Of salt or wisdom? In other words, just a pinch, or does he provide all the answers? Pillar *might* hold up the lower ceiling of a fourth outfielder. It's iffy not because of a platoon problem—he hits righties—but because none of his tools grades out (right now, anyway) as a starter's. He's a gap hitter who doesn't walk much; he has good fielding instincts, but only average speed, pushing him mostly to the corners, where his power is insufficient. But he's also a gamer with great makeup and drive, and he won't undershoot his potential. He'll be a good guy to have around while Gose learns on the job, and he could wind up starting—in Toronto or elsewhere—if he finds a general manager who isn't looking over his shoulder.

Colby Rasmus   CF

Born: 8/11/1986 Age: 27
Bats: L Throws: L Height: 6' 2"
Weight: 190 Breakout: 0%
Improve: 50% Collapse: 4%
Attrition: 5% MLB: 98%

Comparables:
Andruw Jones, Ron Gant, Mitch Webster

YEAR	TEAM	LVL	AGE	PA	R	2B	3B	HR	RBI	BB	SO	SB	CS	AVG/OBP/SLG	TAv	BABIP	BRR	FRAA	WARP
2011	TOR	MLB	24	140	14	10	0	3	13	5	39	0	0	.173/.201/.316	.188	.217	-0.3	CF(35): -0.6	-0.8
2011	SLN	MLB	24	386	61	14	6	11	40	45	77	5	2	.246/.332/.420	.269	.286	0.4	CF(92): -3.0	1.3
2012	TOR	MLB	25	625	75	21	5	23	75	47	149	4	3	.223/.289/.400	.240	.259	0.6	CF(145): -9.1	0.1
2013	TOR	MLB	26	458	57	26	1	22	66	37	135	0	1	.276/.338/.501	.297	.356	1	CF(114): 7.6	4.1
2014	TOR	MLB	27	464	61	22	2	18	56	40	114	4	2	.245/.314/.436	.267	.290	-0.6	CF -4	1.2

Rasmus had the eighth-highest WARP and fifth-highest FRAA among major-league center fielders despite missing nearly a quarter of the season (most of that due to a strained oblique). Career-high isolated power offset a career-worst walk-to-strikeout ratio, driven less by a complete aversion to the free base (8.1 percent walk rate) than by the 10th-highest strikeout rate in baseball (and highest of his career). The BABIP is well out of line with his career norm, but it's in line with research suggesting that players who swing very hard miss a lot (high strikeout rate) and hit the ball hard when they do make contact (high isolated power, high BABIP). That power and his good outfielding give him value even with unsightly peripherals—but for which team? It seemed like foreshadowing when Gose, his upcoming rival, sent the third-year arbitration-eligible Rasmus back to the disabled list by hitting him in the face with an errant warmup toss just before the end of the season.

Jose Reyes   SS

Born: 6/11/1983 Age: 31
Bats: B Throws: R Height: 6' 1"
Weight: 195 Breakout: 0%
Improve: 36% Collapse: 1%
Attrition: 3% MLB: 98%

Comparables:
Nomar Garciaparra, Jimmy Rollins, Alan Trammell

YEAR	TEAM	LVL	AGE	PA	R	2B	3B	HR	RBI	BB	SO	SB	CS	AVG/OBP/SLG	TAv	BABIP	BRR	FRAA	WARP
2011	NYN	MLB	28	586	101	31	16	7	44	43	41	39	7	.337/.384/.493	.317	.353	4.6	SS(124): -1.3	6.3
2012	MIA	MLB	29	716	86	37	12	11	57	63	56	40	11	.287/.347/.433	.293	.298	4.3	SS(160): -15.0	4.2
2013	TOR	MLB	30	419	58	20	0	10	37	34	47	15	6	.296/.353/.427	.283	.315	2.2	SS(92): 1.4	3.3
2014	TOR	MLB	31	457	63	23	5	9	45	34	47	22	6	.289/.342/.439	.281	.300	2.2	SS -6	2.6

And back to the disabled list he goes. On April 12th, Reyes messed up his trailing ankle on a weird slide while stealing second base, scotching him until late June. That he then managed to be the

10th-best shortstop in baseball by WARP (with the seventh-highest True Average) is a tribute to his indomitable talent and his almost unvarying essential rate stats. His joyful peacocking is also tremendously fun to watch. The question is about the sheer quantity of talent and fun he's able to provide going forward: With Derek Jeter's GDP-sized contract expired, Reyes is the highest-paid shortstop in baseball, and he'll only get costlier from 2015-17 ($22 million per year). Anything less than, say, 150 games a year from him will devalue even elite production.

Moises Sierra RF
Born: 9/24/1988 Age: 25
Bats: R Throws: R Height: 6' 0"
Weight: 230 Breakout: 5%
Improve: 20% Collapse: 9%
Attrition: 25% MLB: 49%
Comparables:
Franklin Gutierrez, Cody Ross, Tyler Colvin

YEAR	TEAM	LVL	AGE	PA	R	2B	3B	HR	RBI	BB	SO	SB	CS	AVG/OBP/SLG	TAv	BABIP	BRR	FRAA	WARP
2011	NHP	AA	22	551	81	19	3	18	67	39	93	16	14	.277/.342/.436	.268	.307	1.3	RF(40): -2.2	0.5
2012	LVG	AAA	23	422	62	16	1	17	63	39	86	7	6	.289/.360/.472	.272	.333	-2.3	RF(87): -0.5, LF(7): 0.9	1.7
2012	TOR	MLB	23	157	14	4	0	6	15	8	44	1	0	.224/.274/.374	.222	.278	-0.6	RF(39): -0.1	-0.4
2013	BUF	AAA	24	412	57	18	5	11	51	16	106	12	4	.261/.309/.422	.250	.331	3.1	RF(75): 1.6, CF(17): 0.6	1.4
2013	TOR	MLB	24	122	11	13	1	1	13	14	29	1	0	.290/.369/.458	.308	.385	-1.1	RF(29): 0.4, LF(2): 0.3	0.7
2014	TOR	MLB	25	250	28	11	1	8	29	16	63	5	3	.241/.299/.395	.252	.300	-0.2	RF -1, CF 0	0.2

Phrases like "lack of focus" and "half the acumen" and "forget[s] the number of outs when running the bases" are all code for something. (Not sure what? How about "dumb as a stump" and "dumb as a rock," both of which have turned up on Blue Jays message boards.) Sierra's going to hit, no question. Is he going to hit enough to offset running through stop signs and in zigzags in the outfield? Given the number of good and/or promising outfielders in Toronto, will he even get the chance? Endless injuries got him playing time last year; he'll probably have to do more to earn it this season.

Josh Thole C
Born: 10/28/1986 Age: 27
Bats: L Throws: R Height: 6' 0"
Weight: 215 Breakout: 8%
Improve: 30% Collapse: 8%
Attrition: 24% MLB: 88%
Comparables:
Lou Marson, Dioner Navarro, Francisco Cervelli

YEAR	TEAM	LVL	AGE	PA	R	2B	3B	HR	RBI	BB	SO	SB	CS	AVG/OBP/SLG	TAv	BABIP	BRR	FRAA	WARP
2011	NYN	MLB	24	386	22	17	0	3	40	38	47	0	2	.268/.345/.344	.256	.300	-3	C(102): 1.8	1.2
2012	NYN	MLB	25	354	24	15	0	1	21	27	50	0	0	.234/.294/.290	.208	.273	1.3	C(100): 0.6	-0.1
2013	BUF	AAA	26	167	18	5	1	7	31	14	25	0	1	.322/.383/.510	.293	.345	-2.2	C(37): 0.1, 1B(1): 0.1	1.1
2013	TOR	MLB	26	135	11	3	1	1	8	12	25	0	0	.175/.256/.242	.190	.213	0.4	C(39): -0.6, 1B(2): -0.1	-0.6
2014	TOR	MLB	27	250	25	12	1	4	24	22	35	0	0	.257/.327/.366	.251	.290	-0.5	C 0, 1B -0	0.9

Thole is evidence of the secondary perils of knuckleballers. Acquired with R.A. Dickey from the Mets, Thole caught every Dickey start beginning June 9th, after the release of ancient placeholder Henry Blanco, who was also signed because he'd caught Dickey before. Thole managed to place fifth in the majors in passed balls despite starting just 35 games (the dreadful J.P. Arencibia was tops with 13, so Thole was actually a vast improvement), but the bigger problem was carrying his bat, which helped give Thole the second-worst WARP (-0.7) among all catchers in baseball. Arencibia was third worst. Know who was worst of all? Henry Blanco. Thanks, R.A.!

PITCHERS

Mark Buehrle
Born: 3/23/1979 Age: 35
Bats: L Throws: L Height: 6' 2" Weight: 245
Breakout: 23% Improve: 49% Collapse: 23%
Attrition: 9% MLB: 84%
Comparables:
Brad Radke, Jimmy Key, Paul Byrd

YEAR	TEAM	LVL	AGE	W	L	SV	G	GS	IP	H	HR	BB	SO	BB9	SO9	GB%	BABIP	WHIP	ERA	FIP	FRA	WARP
2011	CHA	MLB	32	13	9	0	31	31	205¹	221	21	45	109	2.0	4.8	46%	.295	1.30	3.59	4.02	4.46	2.0
2012	MIA	MLB	33	13	13	0	31	31	202¹	197	26	40	125	1.8	5.6	41%	.283	1.17	3.74	4.22	4.88	-0.1
2013	TOR	MLB	34	12	10	0	33	33	203²	223	24	51	139	2.3	6.1	48%	.306	1.35	4.15	4.13	4.34	2.4
2014	TOR	MLB	35	10	11	0	27	27	175²	192	22	39	101	2.0	5.2	46%	.297	1.31	4.29	4.58	4.66	0.7

Publicly hating on the trade from Miami, particularly Ontario's pit bull ban (his family and pooch stayed behind in Missouri), Buehrle started his Toronto career like a dog himself. Through nine starts, his ERA was 6.33; was the jig finally up? Nope. By early September it was under 4.00 (a subsequent eight-run shellacking pushed it back up), and he finished with his 13th straight 200-inning season. Only one other pitcher has matched that run since 1980: Greg Maddux. A closer comp might be Livan Hernandez, of course, minus Livan's bat, but sheer quantity does count for something. With Andy Pettitte's retirement, Buehrle is now the active career innings-pitched leader. He's likely to give Toronto two more league-average years despite a fastball that's now officially under 85 mph. He matched the highest strikeout rate of his career with it, natch. Oh—how many perfect games have *you* thrown?

Brett Cecil
Born: 7/2/1986 Age: 27
Bats: R Throws: L Height: 6' 1" Weight: 215
Breakout: 25% Improve: 68% Collapse: 22%
Attrition: 19% MLB: 84%

Comparables:
Jason Hammel, Homer Bailey, Micah Owings

YEAR	TEAM	LVL	AGE	W	L	SV	G	GS	IP	H	HR	BB	SO	BB9	SO9	GB%	BABIP	WHIP	ERA	FIP	FRA	WARP
2011	LVG	AAA	24	8	2	0	12	12	78²	89	15	24	63	2.7	7.2	42%	.303	1.44	5.26	5.58	6.29	0.9
2011	TOR	MLB	24	4	11	0	20	20	123²	122	22	42	87	3.1	6.3	40%	.267	1.33	4.73	5.13	5.65	0.0
2012	NHP	AA	25	3	2	0	9	9	42²	44	2	14	34	3.0	7.2	45%	.318	1.36	3.38	3.34	3.49	0.9
2012	LVG	AAA	25	1	2	0	6	6	39²	36	1	7	33	1.6	7.5	50%	.312	1.08	2.50	2.93	3.27	1.2
2012	TOR	MLB	25	2	4	0	21	9	61¹	70	11	23	51	3.4	7.5	40%	.326	1.52	5.72	4.99	5.05	0.3
2013	TOR	MLB	26	5	1	1	60	0	60²	44	4	23	70	3.4	10.4	53%	.267	1.10	2.82	2.91	3.18	1.1
2014	*TOR*	*MLB*	*27*	*3*	*3*	*0*	*29*	*8*	*64²*	*64*	*8*	*21*	*50*	*2.9*	*7.0*	*47%*	*.293*	*1.32*	*4.24*	*4.47*	*4.61*	*0.3*

A move to the bullpen revived Cecil's jeopardized spot on the 25-man roster. His velocity increased, he leaned harder on a new pet cutter (shades of Mark Melancon), and his groundball rate rose while his home runs plunged. He was ridiculous against lefties (.186/.223/.235) but reasonable against righties, too (.212/.341/.394), and he finished third on the team in pitcher WARP, behind only Mark Buehrle and Steve Delabar. The only downside, potentially a steep one, was arm inflammation that shut Cecil down in mid-September. If he's healthy, he could secure an integral, higher-leverage role in the Toronto bullpen. If not, Ronald Belisario will be happy to buy his glasses from him.

Steve Delabar
Born: 7/17/1983 Age: 30
Bats: R Throws: R Height: 6' 4" Weight: 230
Breakout: 33% Improve: 52% Collapse: 31%
Attrition: 16% MLB: 89%

Comparables:
Michael Wuertz, Grant Balfour, Bill Bray

YEAR	TEAM	LVL	AGE	W	L	SV	G	GS	IP	H	HR	BB	SO	BB9	SO9	GB%	BABIP	WHIP	ERA	FIP	FRA	WARP
2011	HDS	A+	27	1	1	3	7	0	12¹	12	0	8	20	5.8	14.6	47%	.467	1.62	4.38	3.14	2.14	0.3
2011	WTN	AA	27	1	3	12	23	0	30²	23	0	26	30	7.6	8.8	38%	.276	1.60	2.05	3.99	3.42	0.3
2011	TAC	AAA	27	1	1	0	10	0	13	11	0	6	18	4.2	12.5	50%	.500	1.31	0.69	2.86	0.13	0.6
2011	SEA	MLB	27	1	1	0	6	0	7	5	1	4	7	5.1	9.0	31%	.267	1.29	2.57	5.06	5.54	0.0
2012	TAC	AAA	28	0	1	1	9	0	12	11	0	12	12	9.0	9.0	46%	.314	1.92	3.75	4.92	4.82	0.1
2012	TOR	MLB	28	2	2	0	27	0	29¹	23	3	15	46	4.6	14.1	41%	.323	1.30	3.38	2.77	2.65	0.8
2012	SEA	MLB	28	2	1	0	34	0	36²	23	9	11	46	2.7	11.3	48%	.182	0.93	4.17	5.04	6.25	-0.5
2013	TOR	MLB	29	5	5	1	55	0	58²	50	4	29	82	4.4	12.6	32%	.338	1.35	3.22	2.75	2.68	1.4
2014	*TOR*	*MLB*	*30*	*3*	*1*	*1*	*49*	*0*	*56¹*	*45*	*6*	*24*	*72*	*3.9*	*11.5*	*40%*	*.297*	*1.23*	*3.38*	*3.55*	*3.67*	*0.9*

More four-seamer, less splitter and voilà, the feel-good story is complete: Steve Delabar, All-Star. (He's also a walking advertisement for svengali Tom House's weighted-ball training.) Like pretty much every Blue Jay, Delabar dealt with an injury, but he must have been quietly glad it was shoulder inflammation and nothing to do with his erector-set elbow. The lost month kept Delabar's innings down, yet only two pitchers in baseball racked up a higher VORP in fewer innings. He also had the eighth-highest strikeout rate in baseball. The guy Seattle got when they traded Delabar, Eric Thames, was designated for assignment in June.

R.A. Dickey
Born: 10/29/1974 Age: 39
Bats: R Throws: R Height: 6' 2" Weight: 215
Breakout: 9% Improve: 51% Collapse: 22%
Attrition: 5% MLB: 72%

Comparables:
Kevin Brown, Mike Mussina, Jose Contreras

YEAR	TEAM	LVL	AGE	W	L	SV	G	GS	IP	H	HR	BB	SO	BB9	SO9	GB%	BABIP	WHIP	ERA	FIP	FRA	WARP
2011	NYN	MLB	36	8	13	0	33	32	208²	202	18	54	134	2.3	5.8	51%	.289	1.23	3.28	3.74	4.38	0.6
2012	NYN	MLB	37	20	6	0	34	33	233²	192	24	54	230	2.1	8.9	47%	.282	1.05	2.73	3.31	3.71	3.0
2013	TOR	MLB	38	14	13	0	34	34	224²	207	35	71	177	2.8	7.1	42%	.265	1.24	4.21	4.61	4.81	0.9
2014	*TOR*	*MLB*	*39*	*11*	*11*	*0*	*28*	*28*	*192¹*	*186*	*24*	*56*	*142*	*2.6*	*6.6*	*48%*	*.283*	*1.25*	*3.91*	*4.50*	*4.24*	*1.6*

Win Cy Young Award, climb Kilimanjaro, write best-selling memoir, *New Yorker* profile: quite a bucket list Dickey's been working on. In 2013 he crossed off another item: disappointing star. It wasn't really his fault—how many knuckleballers have ever been staff aces? Like Mark Buehrle, Dickey got off to a poor start, improving when he found the missing miles per hour on his knuckler, which he threw more than ever last year (as though trying to get a grip on it). For the $25 million he's still owed, Dickey seems a dubious investment, but (again like Buehrle) he's likely to eat innings, and he'll play amicable ambassador to fans (he thanked them in September for bearing the Jays' "agonizing season ... you deserve better"). If he can master his pet pitch again, maybe he'll cross Comeback Player of the Year off his list before his contract expires.

Kyle Drabek

Born: 12/8/1987 Age: 26
Bats: R Throws: R Height: 6' 1" Weight: 230
Breakout: 41% Improve: 73% Collapse: 18%
Attrition: 22% MLB: 77%

Comparables:
Dillon Gee, Tyson Ross, Dustin Moseley

YEAR	TEAM	LVL	AGE	W	L	SV	G	GS	IP	H	HR	BB	SO	BB9	SO9	GB%	BABIP	WHIP	ERA	FIP	FRA	WARP
2011	LVG	AAA	23	5	4	0	15	15	75	111	12	41	45	4.9	5.4	50%	.358	2.03	7.44	6.38	5.96	1.0
2011	TOR	MLB	23	4	5	0	18	14	78²	87	10	55	51	6.3	5.8	45%	.310	1.81	6.06	5.55	6.60	-0.7
2012	TOR	MLB	24	4	7	0	13	13	71¹	67	10	47	47	5.9	5.9	55%	.267	1.60	4.67	5.57	6.47	-0.4
2013	DUN	A+	25	0	1	0	8	6	20²	14	2	3	20	1.3	8.7	61%	.231	0.82	2.61	3.14	3.98	0.2
2013	BUF	AAA	25	1	2	0	4	3	14¹	14	1	2	12	1.3	7.5	52%	.302	1.12	3.77	2.86	4.44	0.2
2013	TOR	MLB	25	0	0	0	3	0	2¹	4	1	2	3	7.7	11.6	50%	.429	2.57	7.71	9.93	8.79	-0.1
2014	*TOR*	*MLB*	*26*	*2*	*3*	*0*	*8*	*8*	*40¹*	*41*	*5*	*19*	*28*	*4.3*	*6.2*	*48%*	*.289*	*1.49*	*4.84*	*5.09*	*5.26*	*0.0*

Brian Wilson had two Tommy John surgeries, too, so there's hope for Drabek. He resumed pitching ahead of schedule in late June, a year after his operation. After quickly scaling the minor-league ladder via truncated starts, he got three September relief appearances in Toronto. They didn't go well, but it wasn't clear whether the Jays just wanted to ease him back into action or if they have plans for him as a reliever. Given the haze of their starting rotation, they'd do well to try him as a starter again before moving him to a bullpen that is currently their only full-strength asset.

J.A. Happ

Born: 10/19/1982 Age: 31
Bats: L Throws: L Height: 6' 6" Weight: 195
Breakout: 15% Improve: 45% Collapse: 32%
Attrition: 30% MLB: 78%

Comparables:
John Maine, Brandon Backe, Wade Miller

YEAR	TEAM	LVL	AGE	W	L	SV	G	GS	IP	H	HR	BB	SO	BB9	SO9	GB%	BABIP	WHIP	ERA	FIP	FRA	WARP
2011	OKL	AAA	28	1	0	0	3	3	18	11	0	9	16	4.5	8.0	34%	.172	1.11	1.50	3.51	4.36	0.3
2011	HOU	MLB	28	6	15	0	28	28	156¹	157	21	83	134	4.8	7.7	34%	.302	1.54	5.35	4.66	4.85	0.1
2012	TOR	MLB	29	3	2	0	10	6	40¹	35	2	17	46	3.8	10.3	38%	.317	1.29	4.69	2.75	2.61	1.4
2012	HOU	MLB	29	7	9	0	18	18	104¹	112	17	39	98	3.4	8.5	47%	.316	1.45	4.83	4.53	4.78	0.4
2013	BUF	AAA	30	0	2	0	3	3	13¹	17	2	8	13	5.4	8.8	44%	.385	1.88	6.75	5.00	5.62	0.0
2013	TOR	MLB	30	5	7	0	18	18	92²	91	10	45	77	4.4	7.5	38%	.288	1.47	4.56	4.34	4.45	0.9
2014	*TOR*	*MLB*	*31*	*5*	*7*	*0*	*19*	*19*	*104*	*104*	*14*	*47*	*83*	*4.1*	*7.2*	*39%*	*.293*	*1.45*	*4.69*	*4.96*	*5.10*	*0.1*

His season will be remembered for Desmond Jennings' line drive that fractured Happ's skull in Tampa Bay on May 7th. Remarkably, Happ returned to the big leagues three months later, actually lowered his ERA after coming back, and even beat the Rays in his final start of the season. Assuming he's healthy, Happ will probably make the starting rotation. Under the freak-injury circumstances, it does seem a bit churlish to suggest that that might not be a good thing. He hasn't been a very valuable pitcher since his starry rookie year, and even before 2013's near-catastrophe there were injury problems. But he's owed over $5 million this season, so the Jays will try to get their money's worth.

Casey Janssen

Born: 9/17/1981 Age: 32
Bats: R Throws: R Height: 6' 3" Weight: 225
Breakout: 27% Improve: 53% Collapse: 28%
Attrition: 9% MLB: 93%

Comparables:
Heath Bell, Kevin Gregg, Todd Coffey

YEAR	TEAM	LVL	AGE	W	L	SV	G	GS	IP	H	HR	BB	SO	BB9	SO9	GB%	BABIP	WHIP	ERA	FIP	FRA	WARP
2011	TOR	MLB	29	6	0	2	55	0	55²	47	2	14	53	2.3	8.6	49%	.296	1.10	2.26	2.49	3.31	1.2
2012	TOR	MLB	30	1	1	22	62	0	63²	44	7	11	67	1.6	9.5	44%	.240	0.86	2.54	3.03	3.51	1.2
2013	TOR	MLB	31	4	1	34	56	0	52²	39	3	13	50	2.2	8.5	49%	.254	0.99	2.56	2.77	3.40	0.8
2014	*TOR*	*MLB*	*32*	*2*	*1*	*16*	*43*	*0*	*45*	*42*	*4*	*12*	*40*	*2.5*	*8.0*	*48%*	*.294*	*1.20*	*3.44*	*3.61*	*3.74*	*0.6*

Kenley Jansen? No, but the confusingly similar names are a salubrious reminder that closers are nearly indistinguishable at the bottom line: They pretty much all convert seven of every eight save chances. Janssen's outlandish 2012 strikeout-to-walk ratio fell to human levels in 2013 (though it was still excellent), but his home run rate dropped in compensation. Janssen's elite hit rate stayed stable, though, below seven per nine innings for the second straight year. How does he do it? His line-drive and infield-fly rates aren't especially out of step with the league. Instead, Janssen works the edges of the zone effectively and he's a heady pitcher who studies charts and video heavily. His brains should keep helping his modest stuff play up. The Jays gladly exercised their $4 million team option.

Jeremy Jeffress

Born: 9/21/1987 Age: 26
Bats: R Throws: R Height: 6' 0" Weight: 195
Breakout: 43% Improve: 60% Collapse: 30%
Attrition: 37% MLB: 64%

Comparables:
Tom Mastny, Randor Bierd, Jordan Norberto

YEAR	TEAM	LVL	AGE	W	L	SV	G	GS	IP	H	HR	BB	SO	BB9	SO9	GB%	BABIP	WHIP	ERA	FIP	FRA	WARP
2011	NWA	AA	23	1	3	0	9	8	31²	32	2	22	20	6.3	5.7	58%	.299	1.71	4.26	5.21	5.06	0.3
2011	OMA	AAA	23	2	3	3	16	3	24	27	5	18	24	6.8	9.0	55%	.400	1.88	7.12	6.87	4.94	0.0
2011	KCA	MLB	23	1	1	1	14	0	15¹	12	1	11	13	6.5	7.6	58%	.262	1.50	4.70	4.37	5.90	0.0
2012	OMA	AAA	24	5	4	2	37	0	58	52	4	25	61	3.9	9.5	50%	.318	1.33	4.97	3.75	4.49	0.8
2012	KCA	MLB	24	0	0	0	13	0	13¹	19	0	13	13	8.8	8.8	49%	.404	2.40	6.75	4.02	4.88	0.0
2013	BUF	AAA	25	1	0	7	25	0	27¹	22	0	13	28	4.3	9.2	56%	.324	1.28	1.65	2.58	2.95	0.7
2013	TOR	MLB	25	1	0	0	10	0	10¹	8	1	5	12	4.4	10.5	69%	.280	1.26	0.87	3.46	3.87	0.2
2014	*TOR*	*MLB*	*26*	*2*	*1*	*0*	*28*	*1*	*38²*	*35*	*4*	*23*	*37*	*5.2*	*8.7*	*50%*	*.298*	*1.50*	*4.47*	*4.64*	*4.86*	*0.1*

Turns out his marijuana use was medical, more or less. Jeffress had been quietly suffering from juvenile epilepsy for years, and his incorrectly prescribed medication wasn't effective. Anxiety over unpredictable seizures led to his dubious (okay, fine, "doobieous") self-treatment. Nor could it have helped that he gave up a homer to the very first batter he faced last year (the only dinger he allowed at any level) and was immediately optioned to Triple-A. After a proper diagnosis and an adjusted prescription in June, plus a change in his mechanics—dropping to a three-quarters arm slot, which essentially made him a sinkerballer—Jeffress showed improved control in Triple-A and in a brief late-season return to the majors. With his elite velocity, regularly 97 mph, he's a candidate to be a bullpen mainstay this year.

Chad Jenkins

Born: **12/22/1987** Age: **26**
Bats: **R** Throws: **R** Height: **6' 3"** Weight: **225**
Breakout: **58%** Improve: **85%** Collapse: **7%**
Attrition: **46%** MLB: **16%**

Comparables:
Bob Keppel, Luis Atilano, Jordan Smith

YEAR	TEAM	LVL	AGE	W	L	SV	G	GS	IP	H	HR	BB	SO	BB9	SO9	GB%	BABIP	WHIP	ERA	FIP	FRA	WARP
2011	DUN	A+	23	4	5	0	11	11	67¹	71	3	14	44	1.9	5.9	59%	.309	1.26	3.07	3.28	5.09	0.3
2011	NHP	AA	23	5	7	0	16	16	100¹	93	8	27	74	2.4	6.6	44%	.218	1.20	4.13	3.84	5.59	-0.2
2012	NHP	AA	24	5	9	0	20	20	114¹	145	17	31	57	2.4	4.5	49%	.322	1.54	4.96	5.08	5.96	-0.8
2012	TOR	MLB	24	1	3	0	13	3	32	32	5	11	16	3.1	4.5	43%	.262	1.34	4.50	5.20	5.40	0.0
2013	NHP	AA	25	0	0	0	4	3	15	11	0	2	9	1.2	5.4	65%	.224	0.87	1.20	2.52	3.23	0.4
2013	BUF	AAA	25	0	3	0	5	5	21²	33	6	4	8	1.7	3.3	55%	.329	1.71	7.48	6.62	8.40	-0.7
2013	TOR	MLB	25	1	0	0	10	3	33¹	31	3	6	15	1.6	4.1	47%	.262	1.11	2.70	3.98	4.37	0.2
2014	TOR	MLB	26	3	5	0	17	12	71¹	85	12	23	30	2.9	3.8	49%	.296	1.51	5.53	5.80	6.01	-0.6

Shoulder inflammation delayed the beginning of Jenkins' season. After three so-so May starts in Toronto, he was optioned to Buffalo, and when he wasn't quickly recalled his confidence sank, followed by his effectiveness. In late June, his shoulder started hurting again, and the layoff actually helped: It got Jenkins off the mound and out of his head; and when he returned to action, first in Rookie ball and then Double-A, the results were much improved. Recalled in late August and moved to the bullpen, Jenkins pitched well and set himself up for 2014 as a long man/spot-starter type (a role he declared himself amenable to), or as Triple-A insurance in a system positively lousy with promising young arms.

Aaron Loup

Born: **12/19/1987** Age: **26**
Bats: **L** Throws: **L** Height: **6' 0"** Weight: **210**
Breakout: **39%** Improve: **56%** Collapse: **25%**
Attrition: **38%** MLB: **60%**

Comparables:
Daniel Herrera, Darren O'Day, Carlos Martinez

YEAR	TEAM	LVL	AGE	W	L	SV	G	GS	IP	H	HR	BB	SO	BB9	SO9	GB%	BABIP	WHIP	ERA	FIP	FRA	WARP
2011	DUN	A+	23	4	3	5	48	0	65²	67	6	27	56	3.7	7.7	46%	.346	1.43	4.66	4.38	5.85	-0.1
2012	NHP	AA	24	0	3	3	37	0	45¹	46	4	14	43	2.8	8.5	51%	.318	1.32	2.78	3.71	3.73	0.8
2012	TOR	MLB	24	0	2	0	33	0	30²	26	0	2	21	0.6	6.2	57%	.277	0.91	2.64	1.87	2.69	0.8
2013	TOR	MLB	25	4	6	2	64	0	69¹	66	5	13	53	1.7	6.9	61%	.299	1.14	2.47	3.35	4.38	0.4
2014	TOR	MLB	26	2	1	1	48	0	58	60	7	18	43	2.8	6.7	49%	.303	1.35	4.40	4.57	4.79	0.1

Probably best reserved for LOOGY duty (.203/.263/.228 career versus lefties), Loup wasn't afforded that luxury, especially with southpaw Luis Perez recovering from Tommy John surgery. On the contrary, he led the team in appearances and relief innings pitched. To be fair, Perez wasn't all that before he went under the knife, the other left-handed Perez (Juan) also shredded his UCL, fellow southpaw Brett Cecil ended the year on the disabled list, and the durable Loup has posted consecutive ERAs well under 3.00 despite a worrisome 2013 decline in his previously excellent peripherals. He's cheap, too, and durable. All of that means he's not likely to play LOOGY any time soon. He could even lead the Jays in relief innings again.

Dustin McGowan

Born: **3/24/1982** Age: **32**
Bats: **R** Throws: **R** Height: **6' 3"** Weight: **230**
Breakout: **44%** Improve: **64%** Collapse: **17%**
Attrition: **32%** MLB: **51%**

Comparables:
John Parrish, Chad Durbin, Jason Grilli

YEAR	TEAM	LVL	AGE	W	L	SV	G	GS	IP	H	HR	BB	SO	BB9	SO9	GB%	BABIP	WHIP	ERA	FIP	FRA	WARP
2011	DUN	A+	29	0	2	0	7	7	15²	13	0	7	17	4.0	9.8	48%	.310	1.28	2.87	2.56	3.98	0.3
2011	NHP	AA	29	0	2	0	5	5	19²	18	2	7	18	3.2	8.2	40%	.310	1.27	2.75	3.97	5.89	0.0
2011	TOR	MLB	29	0	2	0	5	4	21	20	4	13	20	5.6	8.6	48%	.276	1.57	6.43	5.63	6.70	-0.2
2013	TOR	MLB	31	0	0	0	25	0	25²	19	2	12	26	4.2	9.1	47%	.236	1.21	2.45	3.70	3.89	0.3
2014	TOR	MLB	32	2	2	0	22	4	34	33	4	16	31	4.2	8.1	48%	.291	1.43	4.53	4.55	4.93	0.1

In 2005 and 2006, the Blue Jays tried the always-injured McGowan in the bullpen, and in hindsight they should have kept him there. McGowan pitched in just five big-league games from 2009-12, with multiple major shoulder surgeries and plantar fasciitis costing him his prime years. He was reasonably effective in relief last year (he chalked up the elevated walk rate to years of rust), but managed to get hurt yet again, straining his oblique while throwing a pitch on July 29th. He returned after a month, but there's no reason to think he can stay healthy enough to give Toronto a full season out of the bullpen. If he can, his mid-90s stuff still plays.

Brandon Morrow

Born: 7/26/1984 Age: 29
Bats: R Throws: R Height: 6' 3" Weight: 200
Breakout: 26% Improve: 45% Collapse: 27%
Attrition: 8% MLB: 87%

Comparables:
Francisco Liriano, Felipe Paulino, Shaun Marcum

YEAR	TEAM	LVL	AGE	W	L	SV	G	GS	IP	H	HR	BB	SO	BB9	SO9	GB%	BABIP	WHIP	ERA	FIP	FRA	WARP
2011	TOR	MLB	26	11	11	0	30	30	179¹	162	21	69	203	3.5	10.2	36%	.300	1.29	4.72	3.67	4.03	3.3
2012	NHP	AA	27	1	0	0	3	3	14¹	10	2	3	12	1.9	7.5	39%	.216	0.91	2.51	3.97	4.52	0.2
2012	TOR	MLB	27	10	7	0	21	21	124²	98	12	41	108	3.0	7.8	42%	.252	1.11	2.96	3.60	4.14	2.2
2013	TOR	MLB	28	2	3	0	10	10	54¹	63	12	18	42	3.0	7.0	39%	.302	1.49	5.63	5.45	5.48	0.1
2014	TOR	MLB	29	4	4	0	11	11	63²	58	7	26	64	3.6	9.1	39%	.296	1.31	3.95	4.05	4.29	0.6

It means "tomorrow," and apparently it will never come. The Jays now have picks no. 4 (Brad Lincoln) and no. 5 (Morrow) from the 2006 draft, and each has failed in different ways. Lincoln has simply been ineffective, but search "Brandon Morrow" online and the text helpfully auto-completes by offering "hockey" first and "injury" second. An entrapped radial nerve was the culprit this time, and it shut Morrow down at the end of May. Andrew Miller was the sixth pick in 2006, so expect to see him disappointing Jays fans soon.

Sean Nolin

Born: 12/26/1989 Age: 24
Bats: L Throws: L Height: 6' 5" Weight: 235
Breakout: 35% Improve: 68% Collapse: 24%
Attrition: 59% MLB: 53%

Comparables:
Matt Maloney, Lance Lynn, Boof Bonser

YEAR	TEAM	LVL	AGE	W	L	SV	G	GS	IP	H	HR	BB	SO	BB9	SO9	GB%	BABIP	WHIP	ERA	FIP	FRA	WARP
2011	LNS	A	21	4	4	1	25	21	108¹	102	9	31	113	2.6	9.4	44%	.333	1.23	3.49	3.32	6.08	0.0
2012	DUN	A+	22	9	0	0	17	15	86¹	72	7	21	90	2.2	9.4	45%	.293	1.08	2.19	3.23	3.91	1.6
2012	NHP	AA	22	1	0	0	3	3	15	9	0	6	18	3.6	10.8	43%	.257	1.00	1.20	2.20	3.34	0.3
2013	NHP	AA	23	8	3	0	17	17	92²	89	6	25	103	2.4	10.0	36%	.333	1.23	3.01	2.82	2.84	3.0
2013	BUF	AAA	23	1	1	0	3	3	17²	13	1	10	13	5.1	6.6	39%	.267	1.30	1.53	4.34	4.97	0.0
2013	TOR	MLB	23	0	1	0	1	1	1¹	7	1	1	0	6.8	0.0	30%	.667	6.00	40.50	15.08	12.58	-0.1
2014	TOR	MLB	24	5	6	0	18	18	91²	92	12	35	80	3.5	7.8	40%	.304	1.39	4.34	4.55	4.72	0.5

Nolin was rushed to the majors for one start last May, which owed more to the tatters of the Jays' rotation than to Nolin's readiness—he had barely pitched above A-ball through 2012. Nonetheless, the big lefty's confident, well-commanded four-pitch mix makes him one of the top starting prospects in the system. Walks are a concern, but the strikeouts have offset them so far despite Nolin's merely average velocity; there's pitchability there. Wanting to give him more innings after last season, the Jays sent Nolin not to the too-brief Arizona Fall League but instead to winter ball, where longer and tougher competition accelerated his seasoning. He projects as a fourth starter and should be on the big-league mound every fifth day this year.

Darren Oliver

Born: 10/6/1970 Age: 43
Bats: R Throws: L Height: 6' 3" Weight: 250
Breakout: 31% Improve: 48% Collapse: 26%
Attrition: 27% MLB: 48%

Comparables:
Trevor Hoffman, Hoyt Wilhelm, Takashi Saito

YEAR	TEAM	LVL	AGE	W	L	SV	G	GS	IP	H	HR	BB	SO	BB9	SO9	GB%	BABIP	WHIP	ERA	FIP	FRA	WARP
2011	TEX	MLB	40	5	5	2	61	0	51	47	3	11	44	1.9	7.8	43%	.282	1.14	2.29	2.81	2.89	1.4
2012	TOR	MLB	41	3	4	2	62	0	56²	43	3	15	52	2.4	8.3	46%	.272	1.02	2.06	2.91	3.52	1.0
2013	TOR	MLB	42	3	4	0	50	0	49	47	6	15	40	2.8	7.3	52%	.291	1.27	3.86	4.08	4.60	0.2
2014	TOR	MLB	43	3	1	1	48	0	44²	41	4	13	41	2.6	8.2	47%	.293	1.20	3.36	3.63	3.66	0.7

The amazingly ageless Oliver finally started to show signs of decline last season. He went to the disabled list for the first time since 2009, missing three weeks with a shoulder strain, while logging his fewest appearances and innings since he became a full-time reliever in 2006. He also recorded his highest ERA, FRA and FIP, falling to near replacement level after five years as a one-win lock. But the velocity was still mostly there, and he had the same season overall as George Kontos, more or less. That wasn't good enough for him, apparently. Oliver, ageful after all, retired just before his 43rd birthday. Farewell!

Ramon Ortiz

Born: 5/23/1973 Age: 41
Bats: R Throws: R Height: 6' 0" Weight: 175
Breakout: 15% Improve: 48% Collapse: 25%
Attrition: 15% MLB: 60%

Comparables:
Ken Takahashi, David Wells, Sal Maglie

YEAR	TEAM	LVL	AGE	W	L	SV	G	GS	IP	H	HR	BB	SO	BB9	SO9	GB%	BABIP	WHIP	ERA	FIP	FRA	WARP
2011	IOW	AAA	38	6	3	0	16	16	99¹	115	12	20	81	1.8	7.3	52%	.364	1.36	4.26	4.42	4.35	1.3
2011	CHN	MLB	38	1	2	0	22	2	33¹	31	6	11	25	3.0	6.8	43%	.250	1.26	4.86	4.82	5.79	-0.3
2012	SWB	AAA	39	13	6	0	27	27	169¹	167	18	37	104	2.0	5.5	47%	.281	1.20	3.45	4.06	5.46	-0.3
2013	BUF	AAA	40	2	0	0	4	3	20²	15	4	7	13	3.0	5.7	43%	.193	1.06	2.18	6.06	6.69	-0.3
2013	TOR	MLB	40	1	2	0	7	4	25¹	34	7	11	8	3.9	2.8	44%	.300	1.78	6.04	7.46	7.50	-0.5
2014	TOR	MLB	41	3	3	0	17	8	58	64	9	18	34	2.8	5.2	46%	.292	1.42	4.97	5.27	5.40	-0.2

"The athlete's brain, like his body, is as strong as that of a bull," said Diogenes. His partial namesake, Ramon Diogenes Ortiz, showed last June what can happen to the brain when the body finally gives out: After hurting his arm throwing a pitch, Ortiz fell to a distraught crouch and started crying in baseball. It was one of the year's saddest moments, sadder still if it was the last pitch the 40-year-old ever throws.

Roberto Osuna

Born: 2/7/1995 Age: 19
Bats: R Throws: R Height: 6' 2" Weight: 230
Breakout: 100% Improve: 100% Collapse: 0%
Attrition: 100% MLB: 1%

Comparables:
Jordan Lyles, Tyler Skaggs, Martin Perez

YEAR	TEAM	LVL	AGE	W	L	SV	G	GS	IP	H	HR	BB	SO	BB9	SO9	GB%	BABIP	WHIP	ERA	FIP	FRA	WARP
2012	VAN	A-	17	1	0	0	5	5	19²	14	1	9	25	4.1	11.4	44%	.265	1.17	3.20	2.97	4.19	0.4
2013	LNS	A	18	3	5	0	10	10	42¹	39	6	11	51	2.3	10.8	51%	.311	1.18	5.53	3.69	5.17	0.5
2014	TOR	MLB	19	1	2	0	10	7	34¹	36	5	17	28	4.6	7.3	45%	.302	1.55	5.21	5.21	5.67	-0.1

Though he's still just 19, Osuna has been on the prospect radar for three years, drawing eyewitness raves from BP's Jason Parks back in 2011. He has a big arm, generating heat up to 97 mph, but he has also long occasioned doubts about his "body" and "conditioning," which are nice ways of worrying that he's gonna be fat. (Did no one read *Moneyball* after all?) But his waistline isn't the immediate worry: Osuna had Tommy John surgery in August, and he probably won't return to the active radar until 2015. How the Big O handles his extended recovery time, especially at the level of sheer conditioning, will go a long way toward determining his post-surgery prospects.

Juan Perez

Born: 9/3/1978 Age: 35
Bats: R Throws: L Height: 6' 0" Weight: 170
Breakout: 37% Improve: 53% Collapse: 35%
Attrition: 38% MLB: 50%

Comparables:
Winston Abreu, Alberto Castillo, Randy Williams

YEAR	TEAM	LVL	AGE	W	L	SV	G	GS	IP	H	HR	BB	SO	BB9	SO9	GB%	BABIP	WHIP	ERA	FIP	FRA	WARP
2011	LEH	AAA	32	0	5	4	36	0	36¹	37	5	25	53	6.2	13.1	39%	.395	1.71	5.70	4.17	4.61	0.0
2011	PHI	MLB	32	1	0	0	8	0	5	1	0	5	8	9.0	14.4	38%	.125	1.20	3.60	2.79	3.80	0.0
2012	NAS	AAA	33	4	2	0	38	0	40	32	3	20	54	4.5	12.1	61%	.315	1.30	3.60	3.52	4.14	0.7
2012	MIL	MLB	33	0	1	0	10	0	7	6	2	8	10	10.3	12.9	44%	.286	2.00	5.14	7.85	8.35	-0.2
2013	BUF	AAA	34	2	1	3	17	0	21	12	0	11	25	4.7	10.7	57%	.245	1.10	0.86	2.40	3.00	0.5
2013	TOR	MLB	34	1	2	0	19	0	31²	23	3	15	33	4.3	9.4	60%	.253	1.20	3.69	3.74	4.35	0.3
2014	TOR	MLB	35	2	1	1	39	0	43	36	5	24	47	5.0	9.8	47%	.286	1.39	3.97	4.48	4.32	0.3

The longtime up-and-down lefty was recalled from Buffalo in late May and proceeded to post a perfect ERA through 14 mostly low-leverage relief appearances (albeit with four unearned runs). Then he sprung a major leak, allowing 13 runs, all earned, in his next 9 ⅔ innings over five appearances. Unsurprisingly, it was discovered in August that he was injured: Perez had a badly frayed UCL and was done for season. He opted for rehab rather than Tommy John, so his prospects rest on the success of his offseason recovery, and whether his weathered arm can hold up on the other side of it.

Luis Perez

Born: 1/20/1985 Age: 29
Bats: L Throws: L Height: 6' 0" Weight: 210
Breakout: 39% Improve: 55% Collapse: 26%
Attrition: 36% MLB: 32%

Comparables:
Shane Youman, David Pauley, Dan Meyer

YEAR	TEAM	LVL	AGE	W	L	SV	G	GS	IP	H	HR	BB	SO	BB9	SO9	GB%	BABIP	WHIP	ERA	FIP	FRA	WARP
2011	LVG	AAA	26	2	2	0	8	8	45	37	5	23	43	4.6	8.6	64%	.271	1.33	4.60	5.05	6.33	0.5
2011	TOR	MLB	26	3	3	0	37	4	65	74	9	27	54	3.7	7.5	61%	.327	1.55	5.12	4.68	5.63	0.0
2012	TOR	MLB	27	2	2	0	35	0	42	38	3	16	39	3.4	8.4	50%	.307	1.29	3.43	3.48	4.43	0.4
2013	TOR	MLB	28	0	1	0	6	0	5	4	0	2	6	3.6	10.8	54%	.308	1.20	5.40	1.88	2.43	0.2
2014	TOR	MLB	29	2	2	0	12	4	34	34	4	16	23	4.3	6.1	56%	.291	1.48	4.93	5.14	5.36	-0.1

Perez missed almost the entire season recovering from Tommy John surgery. He returned to the minors on rehab in August (after a premature outing in June, resulting in two more months on the shelf). Half a dozen appearances in the majors in September gave cause for neither concern nor excitement. That's probably about what one should expect in 2014, as well. Think of him not as a LOOGY (although he does fare significantly better against lefties) but as an ELLLY: Everyday Low-Leverage LeftY.

Todd Redmond

Born: 5/17/1985 Age: 29
Bats: R Throws: R Height: 6' 3" Weight: 235
Breakout: 27% Improve: 54% Collapse: 15%
Attrition: 48% MLB: 23%

Comparables:
Scott Richmond, Corey Thurman, Virgil Vasquez

YEAR	TEAM	LVL	AGE	W	L	SV	G	GS	IP	H	HR	BB	SO	BB9	SO9	GB%	BABIP	WHIP	ERA	FIP	FRA	WARP
2011	GWN	AAA	26	10	8	0	28	27	169²	152	18	47	142	2.5	7.5	33%	.287	1.17	2.92	3.91	3.74	1.0
2012	LOU	AAA	27	2	5	0	8	7	43	43	7	11	40	2.3	8.4	34%	.296	1.26	3.77	4.25	6.05	-0.1
2012	GWN	AAA	27	6	6	0	18	18	105²	107	11	28	96	2.4	8.2	33%	.311	1.28	3.58	3.55	4.43	1.3
2012	CIN	MLB	27	0	1	0	1	1	3¹	7	1	5	2	13.5	5.4	31%	.417	3.60	10.80	10.34	7.21	-0.1
2013	BUF	AAA	28	3	1	0	6	5	26²	29	2	5	29	1.7	9.8	39%	.370	1.27	5.06	2.57	3.96	0.4
2013	TOR	MLB	28	4	3	0	17	14	77	70	13	23	76	2.7	8.9	31%	.279	1.21	4.32	4.43	4.60	0.6
2014	TOR	MLB	29	5	7	0	17	17	94	98	15	31	76	3.0	7.3	35%	.295	1.36	4.77	4.91	5.19	-0.0

From 2009 to 2013, Redmond threw 583 innings for the Gwinnett Braves, plus 70 more in Louisville and Buffalo, cellaring his non-vintage stuff in Triple-A while waiting for a thirsty team. He finally found one when the Jays' rotation self-destructed. Called up in July, Redmond made 14 perfectly fifth-starter starts, here shutting down the Orioles, there imploding against the Astros. (The St. Petersburg native also had a chance to keep his hometown team out of the playoffs on the final day of the season, but the Rays knocked him out of the box in the first inning.) His scary fly-ball rate was the lowest it's been in a career of low fly-ball rates, and homers are a given, but if your team needs a fifth starter for a while, you can definitely do worse.

Esmil Rogers

Born: 8/14/1985 Age: 28
Bats: R Throws: R Height: 6' 1" Weight: 190
Breakout: 23% Improve: 46% Collapse: 33%
Attrition: 44% MLB: 71%

Comparables:
Ross Ohlendorf, Anthony Reyes, Boof Bonser

YEAR	TEAM	LVL	AGE	W	L	SV	G	GS	IP	H	HR	BB	SO	BB9	SO9	GB%	BABIP	WHIP	ERA	FIP	FRA	WARP
2011	CSP	AAA	25	1	2	0	5	5	23	36	3	5	15	2.0	5.9	47%	.419	1.78	6.26	5.09	4.87	0.7
2011	COL	MLB	25	6	6	0	18	13	83	110	14	47	63	5.1	6.8	42%	.364	1.89	7.05	5.58	5.80	-0.3
2012	COL	MLB	26	0	2	0	23	0	25²	36	2	18	29	6.3	10.2	48%	.416	2.10	8.06	4.23	4.04	0.5
2012	CLE	MLB	26	3	1	0	44	0	53	47	5	12	54	2.0	9.2	48%	.294	1.11	3.06	3.08	3.57	0.7
2013	TOR	MLB	27	5	9	0	44	20	137²	152	21	44	96	2.9	6.3	48%	.305	1.42	4.77	4.75	5.05	0.8
2014	TOR	MLB	28	5	6	0	41	14	108²	117	14	40	87	3.3	7.2	45%	.314	1.44	4.85	4.69	5.27	-0.2

The return, via Mike Aviles, for skipper John Farrell, Rogers was transferred from the bullpen to the rotation, just like every Blue Jay whose arm wasn't mush and had ever started a big-league game, as Rogers had last done in 2011 with Colorado. The so-so overall numbers are really the result of five disastrous starts rather than thoroughgoing mediocrity. Rogers pitched very well in stretches, showing off a remastered sinker (often preferring it to his four-seamer), and kept his rotation spot for virtually all of the remainder of the season. A cheerful clubhouse presence in a glum year—not for nothing is "Esmil" an anagram for "smile"—Rogers' sheer likeability should recommend him for at least a shot at the rotation again. You're on your own with "miles," "limes" and "slime." Bonus Blue Jays starter anagram: "Y Dice-K?"

Ricky Romero

Born: 11/6/1984 Age: 29
Bats: R Throws: L Height: 6' 0" Weight: 225
Breakout: 35% Improve: 57% Collapse: 19%
Attrition: 16% MLB: 83%

Comparables:
Runelvys Hernandez, Tom Gorzelanny, Kyle Davies

YEAR	TEAM	LVL	AGE	W	L	SV	G	GS	IP	H	HR	BB	SO	BB9	SO9	GB%	BABIP	WHIP	ERA	FIP	FRA	WARP
2011	TOR	MLB	26	15	11	0	32	32	225	176	26	80	178	3.2	7.1	56%	.243	1.14	2.92	4.23	5.12	1.0
2012	TOR	MLB	27	9	14	0	32	32	181	198	21	105	124	5.2	6.2	54%	.312	1.67	5.77	5.09	6.03	-0.9
2013	BUF	AAA	28	5	8	0	22	22	113²	136	11	63	81	5.0	6.4	48%	.341	1.75	5.78	4.81	6.34	-1.0
2013	TOR	MLB	28	0	2	0	4	2	7¹	11	2	8	5	9.8	6.1	46%	.375	2.59	11.05	8.94	10.31	-0.4
2014	TOR	MLB	29	7	9	0	24	24	127¹	125	14	56	98	4.0	6.9	53%	.297	1.42	4.49	4.70	4.88	0.4

The bottom finally fell out—as in, the major-league floor—and Romero crashed all the way to the basement: he was sent to A-ball after spring training. The Jays' early-season rotation collapse quickly had him back in the bigs, but two starts in Toronto, one rocky, one disastrous, were enough to outright him to Triple-A, where he continued to struggle. Romero had two September relief outings in the majors, but those didn't go well either, and he was outrighted again in October. Will the Blue Jays continue their bullpen experiment with Romero? Who knows, maybe they can deploy his bizarre reverse-split tendencies in a cognitively dissonant R/LOOGY role and revive his dying career? They've got two more years and $15 million of him to tinker with.

Aaron Sanchez

Born: 7/1/1992 Age: 21
Bats: R Throws: R Height: 6' 4" Weight: 190
Breakout: 58% Improve: 71% Collapse: 14%
Attrition: 50% MLB: 13%

Comparables:
Zack Wheeler, Casey Crosby, Scott Elbert

YEAR	TEAM	LVL	AGE	W	L	SV	G	GS	IP	H	HR	BB	SO	BB9	SO9	GB%	BABIP	WHIP	ERA	FIP	FRA	WARP
2011	VAN	A-	18	0	1	0	3	3	11²	8	0	8	13	6.2	10.0	50%	.182	1.37	4.63	3.70	3.75	0.2
2012	LNS	A	19	8	5	0	25	18	90¹	64	3	51	97	5.1	9.7	62%	.279	1.27	2.49	3.56	4.73	1.1
2013	DUN	A+	20	4	5	0	22	20	86¹	63	4	40	75	4.2	7.8	61%	.250	1.19	3.34	3.67	5.19	0.2
2014	TOR	MLB	21	3	5	0	18	14	69¹	69	9	43	55	5.6	7.1	53%	.295	1.62	5.19	5.53	5.65	-0.2

Four years in the book, and now four comments noting that Sanchez has superb raw stuff—among the best in the minors—and work to do with his command. In two seasons of full-season ball he has allowed 70 percent as many walks as hits; among all major leaguers in history, Nolan Ryan made that work, followed in career WARP by ... Armando Benitez, Mitch Williams, Rob Dibble and a whole bunch of frustrating relievers. He's got inconsistencies in his delivery, a growing injury sheet, an uninspiring approach on the mound—and yet still has knowledgeable backers who insist he's the best prospect in a deep farm system. So that's how superb the raw stuff is.

Sergio Santos

Born: 7/4/1983 Age: 30
Bats: R Throws: R Height: 6' 3" Weight: 240
Breakout: 34% Improve: 58% Collapse: 24%
Attrition: 17% MLB: 85%

Comparables:
Michael Wuertz, Bill Bray, George Sherrill

YEAR	TEAM	LVL	AGE	W	L	SV	G	GS	IP	H	HR	BB	SO	BB9	SO9	GB%	BABIP	WHIP	ERA	FIP	FRA	WARP
2011	CHA	MLB	27	4	5	30	63	0	63¹	41	6	29	92	4.1	13.1	43%	.269	1.11	3.55	2.90	3.05	1.5
2012	TOR	MLB	28	0	1	2	6	0	5	6	1	4	4	7.2	7.2	50%	.333	2.00	9.00	6.45	4.84	0.0
2013	TOR	MLB	29	1	1	1	29	0	25²	11	1	4	28	1.4	9.8	50%	.175	0.58	1.75	1.87	1.69	0.7
2014	TOR	MLB	30	2	1	3	38	0	35²	30	3	15	41	3.9	10.3	43%	.299	1.27	3.40	3.51	3.70	0.5

Another injury-plagued season kept Santos out of the closer role the Jays must have envisioned when they took on his $8.25 million dollar contract before 2012. He missed more than three months with a triceps strain, but the good news is that when he returned in August, he was less pleasant to face than ever, perhaps the result of a career-high usage of a wipe-out slider so beloved that fans make GIFs of it when they should be working instead. In an ideal world, Santos would take his job back from Casey Janssen, whose $4 million dollar club option was even costlier than the guaranteed $3.75 million owed to Santos. But the Jays picked up Janssen's option, pushing Santos into the second-banana role again.

Matt Smoral
Born: 3/18/1994 Age: 20
Bats: L Throws: L Height: 6' 8" Weight: 220
Breakout: 0% Improve: 0% Collapse: 0%
Attrition: 0% MLB: 0%

Comparables:
Gregory Infante, Wily Peralta, Michael Kirkman

YEAR	TEAM	LVL	AGE	W	L	SV	G	GS	IP	H	HR	BB	SO	BB9	SO9	GB%	BABIP	WHIP	ERA	FIP	FRA	WARP
2014	TOR	MLB	20	1	2	0	17	5	30²	37	5	23	16	6.7	4.7	47%	.310	1.96	7.06	7.00	7.67	-0.8

Smoral is a year behind in his development, having lost his putative 2012 debut to a stress fracture in his foot. That dropped him to 50th in the draft, where the (overly?) optimistic Blue Jays paid him $2 million not to go to North Carolina. Smoral's sheer height and left-handedness make his low-90s fastball play up, and he has a plus slider to go with it. It remains to be seen whether he's Randy Johnson or Andrew Miller (who once took the UNC scholarship Smoral declined), but for now he's a messy-mechanical pencil whose working parts need serious refinement. If he manages that, he's likely to move through the system quickly.

Mickey Storey
Born: 3/16/1986 Age: 28
Bats: R Throws: R Height: 6' 1" Weight: 185
Breakout: 35% Improve: 49% Collapse: 29%
Attrition: 69% MLB: 33%

Comparables:
Brad Kilby, R.J. Swindle, Will Harris

YEAR	TEAM	LVL	AGE	W	L	SV	G	GS	IP	H	HR	BB	SO	BB9	SO9	GB%	BABIP	WHIP	ERA	FIP	FRA	WARP
2011	MID	AA	25	3	3	4	27	0	38	41	3	13	31	3.1	7.3	33%	.405	1.42	4.03	4.04	1.43	0.7
2011	OKL	AAA	25	1	0	2	23	0	29¹	35	3	12	28	3.7	8.6	43%	.391	1.60	3.99	4.43	4.23	0.2
2012	OKL	AAA	26	7	4	2	38	2	65	62	8	14	72	1.9	10.0	42%	.312	1.17	3.05	3.83	3.99	1.5
2012	HOU	MLB	26	0	1	0	26	0	30¹	27	2	10	34	3.0	10.1	39%	.312	1.22	3.86	2.84	3.08	0.5
2013	BUF	AAA	27	0	2	2	36	0	59²	43	5	16	70	2.4	10.6	37%	.266	0.99	2.56	2.85	3.86	1.0
2013	TOR	MLB	27	0	0	0	3	0	4	6	0	1	6	2.2	13.5	25%	.500	1.75	6.75	0.83	0.79	0.2
2014	TOR	MLB	28	2	1	0	38	0	58	53	7	18	57	2.8	8.9	42%	.292	1.23	3.73	3.94	4.05	0.6

The book on Storey is pretty simple: he doesn't throw fastballs. His slider and curve are nice pitches, and he gets whiffs on them, but he only offers his 89 mph "heater" about 35 percent of the time. You can surprise unsuspecting hitters with a bender-vender in short, sporadic appearances, but in multiple printings Storey gives hitters too much time to guess the ending. The Blue Jays' deep bullpen—even in a year of widespread pitcher meltdown—required his services for only three games. He's a natural fit for a team of market-misfits like the A's, but oops—the A's drafted him in 2008 and dealt him to the Astros three years later. He's not likely to stick in Toronto for long, either.

Marcus Stroman
Born: 5/1/1991 Age: 23
Bats: R Throws: R Height: 5' 9" Weight: 185
Breakout: 55% Improve: 72% Collapse: 16%
Attrition: 71% MLB: 51%

Comparables:
Jeremy Hellickson, James McDonald, Wade LeBlanc

YEAR	TEAM	LVL	AGE	W	L	SV	G	GS	IP	H	HR	BB	SO	BB9	SO9	GB%	BABIP	WHIP	ERA	FIP	FRA	WARP
2012	VAN	A-	21	1	0	0	7	0	11¹	8	0	3	15	2.4	11.9	48%	.296	0.97	3.18	1.47	3.11	0.3
2013	NHP	AA	22	9	5	0	20	20	111²	99	13	27	129	2.2	10.4	46%	.301	1.13	3.30	3.33	4.11	2.1
2014	TOR	MLB	23	4	2	2	46	5	79²	76	11	28	78	3.1	8.8	45%	.298	1.30	3.96	4.33	4.31	0.7

Stroman put his close-knit-family money where his mouth was, drawing *awwws* for buying out his mom's mortgage with part of his $1.8 million signing bonus. He drew *awwws* of a different inflection from Eastern League hitters, whom he dominated in his second pro season out of Duke, skipping two levels to Double-A without skipping a beat. Until proven otherwise, his size remains a non-issue (ditto his 2012 PED suspension, an apparent anomaly from a good, earnest kid). His great arm speed generates easy cheese up to 95 mph, and comes equipped with a sharp slider and an advanced changeup that virtually drugged AFL hitters. Sanchez or Stroman? Stroman or Sanchez? The top pitching prospect battle goes major-league this season.

Neil Wagner
Born: 1/1/1984 Age: 30
Bats: R Throws: R Height: 6' 0" Weight: 215
Breakout: 39% Improve: 47% Collapse: 48%
Attrition: 52% MLB: 24%

Comparables:
Agustin Montero, Jose Valdez, Clay Rapada

YEAR	TEAM	LVL	AGE	W	L	SV	G	GS	IP	H	HR	BB	SO	BB9	SO9	GB%	BABIP	WHIP	ERA	FIP	FRA	WARP
2011	MID	AA	27	1	3	4	28	0	37¹	31	0	13	53	3.1	12.8	61%	.226	1.18	3.38	1.66	2.09	0.5
2011	SAC	AAA	27	2	1	2	22	0	29	27	2	10	34	3.1	10.6	29%	.300	1.28	3.10	3.37	4.30	0.3
2011	OAK	MLB	27	0	0	0	6	0	5	6	1	3	4	5.4	7.2	50%	.333	1.80	7.20	6.46	7.15	-0.1
2012	SAC	AAA	28	1	1	1	15	0	19²	20	1	6	24	2.7	11.0	38%	.365	1.32	5.49	3.11	4.83	0.3
2012	TUC	AAA	28	3	1	0	31	0	43	57	2	17	32	3.6	6.7	47%	.379	1.72	5.44	3.97	4.58	0.8
2013	BUF	AAA	29	1	0	16	23	0	23²	13	0	9	38	3.4	14.5	41%	.317	0.93	0.76	1.39	1.85	0.9
2013	TOR	MLB	29	2	4	0	36	0	38	39	5	13	33	3.1	7.8	47%	.312	1.37	3.79	4.15	4.41	0.2
2014	TOR	MLB	30	2	1	0	42	0	51¹	50	6	22	49	3.9	8.6	47%	.308	1.40	4.27	4.35	4.64	0.2

"I scrapped the big, loopy curveball I had last year and started throwing more of a slider," Wagner said in June, and presto—he finally became a big leaguer in his eighth season of toting his upper-90s fastball all around the minors with four different organizations. He was probably glad to hang out in Toronto with fellow bookish type R.A. Dickey; Wagner is an avowed poetry lover, with Dickinson and Frost particular favorites. We'll give you the pleasure of composing your own road-less-traveled quip.

Thad Weber
Born: 9/28/1984 Age: 29
Bats: R Throws: R Height: 6' 2" Weight: 205
Breakout: 38% Improve: 59% Collapse: 27%
Attrition: 60% MLB: 14%

Comparables:
Andy Van Hekken, Matt Childers, Heath Phillips

YEAR	TEAM	LVL	AGE	W	L	SV	G	GS	IP	H	HR	BB	SO	BB9	SO9	GB%	BABIP	WHIP	ERA	FIP	FRA	WARP
2011	TOL	AAA	26	5	11	0	27	27	151¹	176	28	49	111	2.9	6.6	47%	.310	1.49	5.65	5.25	6.19	-1.5
2012	TUC	AAA	27	1	0	0	3	3	18¹	22	1	3	14	1.5	6.9	59%	.362	1.36	4.42	3.50	5.08	0.3
2012	TOL	AAA	27	7	11	0	22	21	128²	123	16	31	97	2.2	6.8	51%	.278	1.20	4.20	4.13	5.48	-0.5
2012	DET	MLB	27	0	1	0	2	0	4	10	0	2	1	4.5	2.2	81%	.476	3.00	9.00	4.05	4.17	0.1
2013	BUF	AAA	28	8	5	0	18	15	100	91	5	21	88	1.9	7.9	46%	.301	1.12	2.61	2.72	3.87	1.4
2013	TUC	AAA	28	4	1	0	6	6	34¹	38	0	4	26	1.0	6.8	52%	.349	1.22	3.93	2.49	3.16	1.2
2013	SDN	MLB	28	0	0	0	3	0	9	5	1	5	6	5.0	6.0	56%	.182	1.11	2.00	4.80	5.42	-0.1
2013	TOR	MLB	28	0	1	0	5	0	6	7	1	3	4	4.5	6.0	53%	.333	1.67	3.00	5.41	4.59	0.0
2014	TOR	MLB	29	6	8	0	19	19	122	133	19	35	74	2.6	5.5	47%	.294	1.38	4.83	5.15	5.25	-0.3

The Blue Jays claimed Weber off waivers from the Padres during last season's Mayday decimation panic. He was then called up four different times from Buffalo, where he had been a starter, and used as a reliever in five big-league appearances (which tells you how he was regarded him as a starter, even by a desperate team). Twice, Weber relieved in a single game for Toronto, was optioned the very next day, and went right back to starting in Triple-A. Enough of that: after the season, Weber optioned himself to Korea.

LINEOUTS

HITTERS

PLAYER	TEAM	LVL	AGE	PA	R	2B	3B	HR	RBI	BB	SO	SB-CS	AVG/OBP/SLG	TAv	BABIP	BRR	FRAA	WARP
CF D. Davis	VAN	A-	17	23	3	0	0	0	0	5	6	1-1	.167/.348/.167	.210	.250	0.3	CF(5): 1.2	0.1
1B L. Jimenez	BUF	AAA	31	402	57	16	2	18	73	39	65	3-1	.285/.351/.494	.288	.297	-2.3	1B(39): -1.7	1.2
1B D. Johnson	SWB	AAA	33	560	57	26	0	21	69	93	82	1-0	.253/.379/.447	.294	.264	-5.1	1B(113): 3.7, 3B(5): -0.1	2.5
	BAL	MLB	33	5	0	0	0	0	0	0	1	0-0	.000/.000/.000	.027	.000	0	1B(1): -0.0	-0.1
3B A. LaRoche	BUF	AAA	29	413	45	21	1	12	51	37	55	4-4	.271/.339/.433	.269	.285	-5.1	3B(89): -1.8, 2B(7): 0.4	1.2
	TOR	MLB	29	4	0	0	0	0	0	0	1	0-0	.000/.000/.000	.021	.000	0	3B(1): 0.1	-0.1
CF A. Loewen	NHP	AA	29	491	60	22	3	15	60	57	125	10-5	.269/.358/.439	.278	.347	-0.9	CF(35): -0.6, LF(27): -0.3	1.8
C S. Nessy	LNS	A	20	242	23	15	0	5	23	13	59	0-0	.241/.293/.375	.232	.304	-0.9	C(54): -0.0	0.2
C M. Nickeas	BUF	AAA	30	200	16	12	0	1	11	17	40	0-0	.166/.255/.251	.186	.209	-2.3	C(57): -0.2	-1.1

D.J. Davis should have shown improved stolen-base success with his elite speed, especially in a repeat of Rookie ball, but while we're waiting for him to find his inner Billy Hamilton we can admire his developing pop (.178 isolated power last year) and start hoping for Tim Raines instead. ⊘ **Matt Dean** repeated Rookie ball but led the Appalachian League in batting average and wRC+, encouraging us to overlook the .436 BABIP and 4:1 strikeout-to-walk ratio. ⊘ This **Luis Jimenez** does not appear among the five answering to that description on BP's site; you have to search for the full "Luis Antonio Jimenez" because he's just that big—although he does beat it down the line kinda fast for his size. ⊘ **Dan Johnson** has logged 3,550 plate appearances in Triple-A, or about as many as Evan Longoria has in the majors, but he hasn't slugged over .500 at the level since 2010. ⊘ **Andy LaRoche** will log his 1,500th Triple-A plate appearance with his sixth Triple-A team in 2014. ⊘ **Adam Loewen** was healthy last year and kept his converted-pitcher story alive at Double-A New Hampshire, but we could have said the same thing in the 2011 Annual, when he put up suspiciously similar numbers for the exact same team. He's 30 this season. ⊘ **Santiago Nessy** missed about two months with undisclosed injuries, which hampered his progress at the plate, but his leadership abilities and power potential retain believers; you'd be one, too, if your starting big-league catcher was

J.P. Arencibia. ⊘ **Mike Nickeas** was thrown into the R.A. Dickey trade to catch Dickey's knuckleballs in case Josh Thole got hurt; no luck, so Nickeas played home games in newly affiliated Buffalo for a fourth straight season and caught Buddy Carlyle instead.

PITCHERS

PLAYER	TEAM	LVL	AGE	W	L	SV	IP	H	HR	BB	SO	BB9	SO9	GB%	BABIP	WHIP	ERA	FIP	FRA	WARP
D. Hutchison	BUF	AAA	22	0	3	0	19	28	2	6	20	2.8	9.5	27%	.433	1.79	6.63	4.05	5.80	0.0
I. Kadish	LNS	A	24	5	4	0	67	63	6	15	79	2.0	10.6	43%	.318	1.16	3.36	2.86	3.44	1.6
D. McGuire	NHP	AA	24	9	10	0	157¹	148	12	59	143	3.4	8.2	35%	.299	1.32	4.86	3.70	4.63	1.8
D. Norris	LNS	A	20	1	7	0	85²	84	6	44	99	4.6	10.4	51%	.342	1.49	4.20	3.62	4.08	2.0
J. Stilson	BUF	AAA	22	6	2	4	47¹	36	3	15	47	2.9	8.9	53%	.268	1.08	2.09	3.06	3.65	0.8

Drew Hutchison finished his Tommy John rehab and made 10 starts before heading to the Arizona Fall League; he's likely to work in Triple-A this year and has a shot at the rotation if it all breaks his way. ⊘ **Chase DeJong**'s solid-average profile on draft day in 2012 gained appeal because of his advanced control and head for the game; his dominance in Rookie ball suggests a mid-rotation ceiling. ⊘ **Ian Kadish** and **Arik Sikula** both went to Marshall, are both live-armed righty relievers, and some mysterious force posits that one of them will wind up making a big-league difference; send in your guesses now, while lamenting the demise of Kadish's blog and @bearjew36 Twitter handle. ⊘ **Deck McGuire**'s cumulative ERA above five over two straight years and 300 innings at Double-A isn't what the Blue Jays were hoping for when they made him their top draft pick in 2010, but his peripherals improved (especially halving his home run rate) in round two at New Hampshire, leaving reasons for optimism. ⊘ It's often said that big-bonus-baby **Daniel Norris** has a long way to go, but his rate stats last year compared favorably to the more highly regarded Aaron Sanchez's, at the same age and level. He's one to watch. ⊘ **John Stilson** throws hard and with heart (he's highly animated on the mound), and in another team's weaker bullpen might have thrown some big-league innings last year; look for him to get them this season. ⊘ **Alberto Tirado** has some of the more impressive potential among the Blue Jays' strong crop of arms in the lower minors, with occasionally electric stuff that belies his smallish frame.

MANAGER: JOHN GIBBONS

YEAR	TEAM	W-L	Pythag +/-	Avg PC	100+ P	120+ P	QS	BQS	REL	REL w Zero R	IBB	PH	PH Avg	PH HR	SB2	CS2	SB3	CS3	SAC Att	SAC %	POS SAC	Squeeze	Swing	In Play
2013	TOR	74-88	0	92.3	56	1	67	6	487	391	33	102	.220	3	87	38	25	3	44	65.9%	26	0	353	99

Over his career, John Gibbons has been a fairly anti-smallball manager, but in 2013 that really wasn't the case. In 2005-2006, his Blue Jays issued 37 sacrifice hits, whereas an average AL team would've laid down 67 in that time. In his more recent full seasons, 2007 and 2013, he issued 62 sacrifice hits, a tad below the AL average of 65 in that time. Similarly, in Gibbons' first turn with Toronto, his club didn't steal very much. In 2013, however, Toronto had 112 steals in 153 attempts, both higher than AL averages (95 steals in 129 attempts).

Washington Nationals

By Jorge Arangure Jr.

The offseason minor-league transaction page can often be full of recognizable names, once-coveted prospects who have floundered and begun to bounce from team to team, mostly unwanted, as their skills never reached their predicted levels. Rarely do phenoms turn out to be superstars. Baseball is cruel that way.

In the winter of 2013, a name that would be unfamiliar to most popped up on the list of Washington Nationals minor-league free agents. Carlos Daniel Alvarez Lugo was a 27-year-old who earned just seven plate appearances for the Gulf Coast League Nationals in 2013. In his seven-year minor-league career in the Washington system, Lugo played in 297 games, hit .291 and posted an .824 OPS, but he never climbed higher than A-ball. He was as marginal a minor-league player as you can get.

Yet the reason most fans wouldn't recognize Lugo's name isn't his unspectacular career. His anonymity comes mostly from his name, because, you see, when fans first became aware of him in 2006 after he signed a lucrative $1.4 million contract, his name was not Lugo at all. At that time, he was known as Esmailyn "Smiley" Gonzalez, the 16-year-old prized Dominican prospect whose signing was supposed to turn the Nationals into major players in the Latin American amateur player market.

Gonzalez was the face of Washington's attempt by new owner Mark Lerner to show baseball that the Nationals would be a powerful franchise open to signing any player in the world for whatever money it took. The Nationals would not be content to be national, but instead aimed to be international.

"Ownership had the right idea to make a statement, but it was unfortunate that their first effort came back to bite them," former Nationals president Stan Kasten said. "That was the saddest part for me."

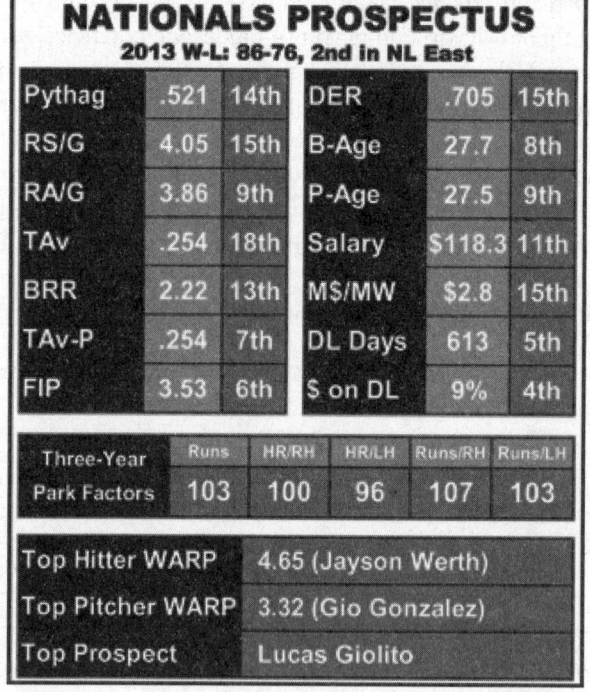

The problem was that the face of the expected face of the franchise did not match the face of the person on the submitted birth certificate. A lengthy and complicated investigation by Major League Baseball conducted between 2008 and 2009 determined that Smiley had lied about his age and identity. He was discovered to actually be Carlos Daniel Alvarez Lugo and he was four years older than he had claimed to be. Suddenly, the face of the franchise became the face of corruption in the signing of Latin American players.

In the wake of the revelations, the Nationals underwent a dramatic makeover. Special assistant Jose Rijo was fired after being implicated in the fraud. General Manager Jim Bowden was pushed to resign because of his close association with Rijo, although Bowden has never been tied to any criminal wrongdoing.

Mike Rizzo, then the assistant general manager, was tasked with leading the team through the controversy, and partly as a result of his handling of the situation was eventually given the full-time GM job. One can trace every subsequent Rizzo move back to the Gonzalez case. Without the fraud, Rizzo might have never been given the job, and perhaps the Nationals would not have been turned into contenders.

"It was a great proving ground for Mike Rizzo," Kasten said. "He went in there like General [Douglas] MacArthur and got it done beautifully."

Also as a result of the Gonzalez case, MLB drastically reformed its Dominican Republic operations. A new investigative system was put into place. Players were now required to be registered with MLB prior to their signing. Baseball became heavily involved in the process after years of mostly neglect.

When news of Gonzalez's situation broke publicly, nobody quite knew just how baseball would be affected, and many didn't think much of the news at all. Yet five years later, the Smiley situation has turned out to be a landmark case in baseball history.

"I think that baseball feels that a new system has been put in place that vastly improves the protection of both the players and clubs in a mutually beneficial manner to protect against fraud, theft and corruption as well as to protect the integrity of the game, its players and the clubs," Bowden said.

***

At the time of Daniel Halem's hiring in 2007 as baseball's senior vice president and general counsel, bonuses for players in the Dominican Republic were skyrocketing. While the Dominican was once considered a place to find cheap talent, in the early to mid-2000s 16-year-old boys began to routinely get bonuses comparable to some American amateur players. Million-dollar bonuses, once reserved for only the most special players, were now handed out to the most raw talents. But teams found that paying millions of dollars for teenagers who had proven to be just as good as their American counterparts was still a good investment compared to the amateur draft.

While many teams in 2006 had thought that Esmailyn Gonzalez was a talented player, nobody could quite say he was a sure thing. Yet the Nationals gave him $1.4 million, claiming at that time that he was a combination of Ozzie Smith and Miguel Tejada—though, even then, most teams considered that an overstatement. The next highest bid for Gonzalez, according to *Sports Illustrated*, was $700,000 from the Texas Rangers.

But signing players in the Dominican has always carried a risk. The government's antiquated and poor system of identifying its own citizens could lead to age and identity fraud. In the Dominican, parents are required to register their children with the government soon after birth, but there's no penalty for failing to do so and there is no official birth certificate handed out. In many cases, in poor and rural areas, many children aren't born in a hospital or they are born in facilities that can hardly accommodate any official documentation. Children often aren't registered until they are older, and some children are never registered at all.

Many found this to be the perfect environment for falsity. For example, a 19-year-old player who was attracting very little attention from scouts could easily enhance his value by changing his age to say he was three years younger. Suddenly a 16-year-old player with a 19-year-old body and advanced skills was regarded as a phenom and could pocket a million-dollar payday.

It was commonly known throughout the game that some of the biggest Dominican players in the majors had once lied about their age. But since they were signed for a minimal bonus, nobody gave it much thought.

But soon after taking the job with MLB, Halem started to hear concerns from the U.S. government.

"As bonuses got higher, the U.S. Consulate began to take a closer look at all the players vying for visas in the Dominican Republic," Halem said. "The issue became more on the forefront. Clubs were making significant investments on players not knowing if he was who he said he was."

But Halem soon realized that the issue of identity was a complex one in the Dominican Republic. There were cultural and economic complications that made it unwise for baseball to demand that the Dominican government make significant changes to its citizen registration system. These were issues larger than baseball, and any pressure from MLB to make changes might have been perceived as imperialistic.

MLB needed a case to help push their reform agenda. They soon found it.

***

Almost from the moment that Gonzalez signed his record deal, Kasten began to hear whispers about possible fraud. While rumors of age and identity falsification follow almost every top player signed in the country, the rumors about Gonzalez never went away. But the Nationals had no reliable evidence.

It took an anonymous phone call to MLB's Dominican office to break the case wide open. MLB, not content with the work of its contracted investigators—several of whom were later found to have accepted bribes in order to deliver passing investigations for several prospects—sent in a group of former police officers and detectives from an investigative unit that had just been created in the wake of the Mitchell Report.

After months of detective work, investigators uncovered an elaborate plot in which Gonzalez/Alvarez had taken the identity of another person, and had gone so far as to live with that person's family for several months in order for neighbors to get accustomed to seeing him in the area. It was one of the more extreme fraud cases many had ever seen.

Investigators visited Washington to reveal their findings to the Nationals' front office. Kasten was appalled at what he heard. Although the $1.4 million was likely lost forever—the team would get nowhere trying to sue the player, who had likely already spent the money—Kasten was certain that something had to be done.

"We were not going to allow this to be swept under the rug," Kasten said. "We felt it wasn't right and it had to end."

While Kasten, a longtime baseball man, had once been part of the establishment that felt age fraud in the Dominican was "just the cost of doing business," he now believed that major reform was needed due to the brazen nature of Gonzalez's lie and the money that had been lost.

Armed with its signature case, and with the backing of the U.S. Consulate, MLB pressured the Dominican government to cooperate in catching age and identity fraud. Longtime Bud Selig ally Sandy Alderson was named a liaison between baseball and the Dominican Republic. Alderson, who as part of the commissioner's office had helped open MLB's Dominican office in 2000, immediately threatened local trainers that continued fraud in amateur signings could result in a worldwide draft, a development that would cost prospects and trainers hundreds of thousands of dollars.

Major League Baseball was so pleased with the work of its investigative department's work in the Gonzalez case that it set up a permanent presence for the unit in the Dominican, headed by former New Jersey police officer Nelson Tejada. The unit's investigations are as thorough as they have ever been, and age fraud is much more rare now.

"It was imperative that the Consulate had the confidence that MLB would do thorough investigations," Halem said.

Subsequently, baseball began a registration program that aimed to identify players as soon as they made initial contact with a team. This would help MLB get a head start in the investigating process. Finally, MLB made bonus payments contingent on a player being issued a visa. The wild, wild west—as the Dominican amateur market was often called by scouts and executives—was suddenly getting tamer.

"We've made tremendous progress in all areas," Halem said. "The sense among clubs, trainers and government officials is that the prevalence of age and identity fraud has been reduced. And it has been reduced because there are more safeguards. And all of these efforts started at the time of Smiley Gonzalez."

Despite MLB's successes in reducing fraud, the push for a worldwide draft remains, and can be traced directly back to the Gonzalez case.

The Nationals continue to be embroiled in the Gonzalez case even five years after the initial findings were revealed publicly. Although Kasten left the organization in 2010, the team still won't allow the case to be swept under the rug. This summer the team sued an insurance company to recoup $1 million of the bonuses given to Gonzalez.

Of course, nobody was more affected than Lugo. Although he was not forced to give the money back, his standing within the organization would never be the same. Aside from the obvious mistrust the team now had in him, the more important part of the situation was that the four years he aged meant his ceiling was no longer that of Miguel Tejada and Ozzie Smith. Instead, he would become just another player in the Nationals' minor-league system. As a result of the fraud, Lugo was unable to get a visa to play in the United States until 2011, when he was 25 years old. His seven years in the organization produced 11 home runs.

Now that he's a free agent, it's likely that his playing career is over, although his legacy will continue to live on. His name, or rather his pretended name, will always be associated with one of the landmark cases in baseball history.

Jorge Arangure Jr. is a contributing writer for the New York Times *and* Sports on Earth *and has previously been a staff writer at* ESPN *and the* Washington Post.

HITTERS

Ian Desmond SS

Born: 9/20/1985 Age: 28
Bats: R Throws: R Height: 6' 3"
Weight: 210 Breakout: 3%
Improve: 49% Collapse: 9%
Attrition: 10% MLB: 99%

Comparables:
Craig Wilson, Stephen Drew, Dan Uggla

YEAR	TEAM	LVL	AGE	PA	R	2B	3B	HR	RBI	BB	SO	SB	CS	AVG/OBP/SLG	TAv	BABIP	BRR	FRAA	WARP
2011	WAS	MLB	25	639	65	27	5	8	49	35	139	25	10	.253/.298/.358	.247	.317	4.8	SS(152): -3.6	1.9
2012	WAS	MLB	26	547	72	33	2	25	73	30	113	21	6	.292/.335/.511	.287	.332	0.8	SS(128): -15.0	1.8
2013	WAS	MLB	27	655	77	38	3	20	80	43	145	21	6	.280/.331/.453	.273	.336	0.2	SS(158): 5.0	3.8
2014	WAS	MLB	28	594	70	30	2	15	67	35	125	21	6	.271/.319/.418	.267	.320	1.2	SS -7	2.4

Desmond's breakout came in 2012—All-Star, MVP votes, franchise record for home runs by a shortstop—but 2013 was arguably a bigger deal for anybody handicapping his future. He made marginal gains in his baserunning, defense and walk rate, which crept up to a career-high 6.6 percent. And while he didn't match 2012 home run for home run, he did top the 20-dinger mark again, establishing himself as the National League's second- or third-best power threat at the six position. A repeat is sometimes more telling than a breakout, and Desmond's consolidation season puts him comfortably among the game's most complete shortstops. Wisely, he hasn't shown any inclination to sign a discounted extension with the Nationals.

Danny Espinosa 2B

Born: 4/25/1987 Age: 27
Bats: B Throws: R Height: 6' 0"
Weight: 205 Breakout: 4%
Improve: 49% Collapse: 10%
Attrition: 16% MLB: 90%

Comparables:
Freddie Bynum, Jed Lowrie, Luke Hughes

YEAR	TEAM	LVL	AGE	PA	R	2B	3B	HR	RBI	BB	SO	SB	CS	AVG/OBP/SLG	TAv	BABIP	BRR	FRAA	WARP
2011	WAS	MLB	24	658	72	29	5	21	66	57	166	17	6	.236/.323/.414	.266	.292	2.7	2B(158): 11.6	3.6
2012	WAS	MLB	25	658	82	37	2	17	56	46	189	20	6	.247/.315/.402	.255	.333	-0.3	2B(126): 2.7, SS(36): 3.1	2.1
2013	SYR	AAA	26	313	32	12	1	2	22	19	101	6	1	.216/.280/.286	.210	.324	1.3	2B(41): -3.0, SS(35): -0.6	-0.8
2013	WAS	MLB	26	167	11	9	0	3	12	4	47	1	0	.158/.193/.272	.178	.202	-0.3	2B(43): 0.7, SS(1): -0.1	-1.0
2014	WAS	MLB	27	301	33	13	1	8	33	21	83	7	2	.228/.295/.374	.244	.290	0.3	2B 2, SS 0	0.8

It turns out playing with a broken wrist negatively affects one's play. Small sample size warnings apply, of course, but it *does* stand to reason. Espinosa was never an offensive dynamo, registering

TAvs right around league average in the two seasons prior to 2013; his defense was generous enough to pick up the slack. Last season saw the complete erosion of value on both sides of the ball: His walk rate dropped below the Yuniesky Line, he underslugged a frat boy's BAC and FRAA downgraded his defensive credit rating from AA to B. Espinosa had been replaced by Anthony Rendon by season's end, but a return to health should result in a utility role much needed on the Nationals' bench.

Brian Goodwin — CF

Born: 11/2/1990 Age: 23
Bats: L Throws: R Height: 6' 1"
Weight: 195 Breakout: 0%
Improve: 15% Collapse: 3%
Attrition: 9% MLB: 35%

Comparables:
Trayvon Robinson, Jordan Danks, Dexter Fowler

YEAR	TEAM	LVL	AGE	PA	R	2B	3B	HR	RBI	BB	SO	SB	CS	AVG/OBP/SLG	TAv	BABIP	BRR	FRAA	WARP
2012	HAG	A	21	266	47	18	1	9	38	43	39	15	4	.324/.438/.542	.340	.357	0.4	CF(55): 2.6	3.4
2012	HAR	AA	21	186	17	8	1	5	14	18	50	3	3	.223/.306/.373	.246	.288	0	CF(42): -5.3	0.0
2013	HAR	AA	22	533	82	19	11	10	40	66	121	19	11	.252/.355/.407	.286	.321	2	CF(116): -0.7	3.4
2014	WAS	MLB	23	250	30	9	2	5	22	24	63	5	2	.232/.309/.356	.247	.300	0	CF -2	0.2

Last year, Goodwin's top comp was Willie Mays. This year, it's … well, it's not Willie Mays. It's not even Willie Harris, or Joe Mays, though at least it's mercifully not Chet Haze. Goodwin's struggles in 2012 were predictable—he'd skipped from Low-A to Double-A—but most observers expected more than he showed in a full season at Harrisburg in 2013. That's not altogether fair to the system's best position prospect, though. He *did* reward scouts' faith by improving his walk rate (up three percentage points) and he *did* cut down his strikeout rate, by four percentage points. The five-tool talent still has the ability to be an impact performer, and if he's no threat to challenge Willie Mays for the title of "greatest ballplayer who ever lived," he will challenge Tom for the title of "greatest Goodwin who ever lived."

Scott Hairston — RF

Born: 5/25/1980 Age: 34
Bats: R Throws: R Height: 6' 0"
Weight: 205 Breakout: 1%
Improve: 23% Collapse: 11%
Attrition: 21% MLB: 91%

Comparables:
Jose Guillen, Andre Dawson, Matt Diaz

YEAR	TEAM	LVL	AGE	PA	R	2B	3B	HR	RBI	BB	SO	SB	CS	AVG/OBP/SLG	TAv	BABIP	BRR	FRAA	WARP
2011	NYN	MLB	31	145	20	8	1	7	24	11	34	1	1	.235/.303/.470	.277	.264	-0.5	RF(15): -0.5, LF(10): 0.1	0.5
2012	NYN	MLB	32	398	52	25	3	20	57	19	83	8	2	.263/.299/.504	.289	.287	0.3	LF(59): -4.9, RF(48): 2.1	1.9
2013	CHN	MLB	33	112	13	2	0	8	19	7	25	2	0	.172/.232/.434	.245	.129	-0.1	RF(29): -2.9, LF(1): 0.0	-0.3
2013	WAS	MLB	33	62	5	3	0	2	7	2	19	0	0	.224/.246/.379	.223	.289	-0.6	LF(15): -0.1, RF(2): -0.2	-0.3
2014	WAS	MLB	34	250	29	11	1	10	32	14	52	4	1	.244/.294/.423	.262	.270	0.1	RF -2, LF -0	0.5

Signed by the Cubs to a two-year, $5 million base contract in January, Hairston was forcibly relocated to Washington less than six months later. The Nationals picked up his salary; the Cubs agreed not to send over the *.129* BABIP Hairston was carrying at the time of the trade. (Hairston's BABIP regressed immediately to career norms; unfortunately for the Nats, his overall production still lagged.) There aren't any obvious platoon candidates in the Washington outfield, but Hairston does give new manager Matt Williams a lefty-masher off the bench, and a competent outfielder who could stand in should somebody (↓↓↓) face-mash a wall.

Bryce Harper — LF

Born: 10/16/1992 Age: 21
Bats: L Throws: R Height: 6' 2"
Weight: 230 Breakout: 6%
Improve: 43% Collapse: 7%
Attrition: 11% MLB: 75%

Comparables:
Justin Upton, Jason Heyward, Frank Robinson

YEAR	TEAM	LVL	AGE	PA	R	2B	3B	HR	RBI	BB	SO	SB	CS	AVG/OBP/SLG	TAv	BABIP	BRR	FRAA	WARP
2011	HAG	A	18	305	49	17	1	14	46	44	61	19	5	.318/.423/.554	.328	.372	1.2	RF(47): -0.1, CF(17): -1.9	3.0
2011	HAR	AA	18	147	14	7	1	3	12	15	26	7	2	.256/.329/.395	.261	.294	2	LF(34): -2.2	0.4
2012	SYR	AAA	19	84	8	4	1	1	3	9	14	1	1	.243/.325/.365	.258	.288	-0.3	CF(13): -1.1, RF(6): -0.2	0.1
2012	WAS	MLB	19	597	98	26	9	22	59	56	120	18	6	.270/.340/.477	.288	.310	5.6	CF(92): 2.2, RF(65): 2.8	5.2
2013	WAS	MLB	20	497	71	24	3	20	58	61	94	11	4	.274/.368/.486	.303	.306	-0.6	LF(97): -1.2, RF(16): 1.1	3.4
2014	WAS	MLB	21	499	65	22	3	18	65	51	102	13	4	.266/.344/.453	.288	.300	0.7	LF -1, CF -1	2.7

Not since John Wayne Gacy has one man done so much damage to the reputation of clowns. Harper followed up his debut season with across-the-board improvements, hitting for a higher average, raising his walk rate, lowering his strikeout rate and hitting for more power. Not bad for an encore. These improvements were partially overshadowed by the five weeks Harper missed after injuring himself (face-mashing a wall), and by accusations of lollygagging in late August. Once decried for hustling too much, Harper now received criticism for not running out a groundball. Some might scoff at the notion that *Bryce Friggin Harper* is underhyped, but he just notched a .302 TAv as a 20-year old and still gets more attention for what he doesn't do.

Adam LaRoche 1B

Born: 11/6/1979 Age: 34
Bats: L Throws: L Height: 6' 2"
Weight: 200 Breakout: 0%
Improve: 25% Collapse: 8%
Attrition: 18% MLB: 89%

Comparables:
Fred McGriff, Vic Wertz, Chili Davis

YEAR	TEAM	LVL	AGE	PA	R	2B	3B	HR	RBI	BB	SO	SB	CS	AVG/OBP/SLG	TAv	BABIP	BRR	FRAA	WARP
2011	WAS	MLB	31	177	15	4	0	3	15	25	37	1	0	.172/.288/.258	.210	.205	1.7	1B(43): 3.0	-0.4
2012	WAS	MLB	32	647	76	35	1	33	100	67	138	1	1	.271/.343/.510	.302	.298	-2.9	1B(153): 11.1	4.3
2013	WAS	MLB	33	590	70	19	3	20	62	72	131	4	1	.237/.332/.403	.265	.277	-0.6	1B(149): 1.3	0.8
2014	WAS	MLB	34	566	65	25	1	21	73	57	136	2	1	.246/.322/.420	.268	.290	-1	1B 7	1.7

LaRoche's regression from a four-win player to a half-win player explains a big chunk of the Nationals' slide. But what explains LaRoche's slide? Against right-handers he was as good as ever, and overall his batted ball profile held mostly steady. But his HR/FB rate dropped by 25 percent as his power stroke disappeared against lefties. He tumbled from his best season against southpaws in 2012 (.825 OPS, .506 slugging) to one of his worst (.566 OPS, .313 slugging). Always streaky, LaRoche matched a brutal April with a white-hot May but couldn't recover from an ugly July, and by mid-August he was benched against most left-handed starters. He's locked into one more year at $12 million, with a mutual option for 2015.

Nate McLouth LF

Born: 10/28/1981 Age: 32
Bats: L Throws: R Height: 5' 11"
Weight: 180 Breakout: 8%
Improve: 36% Collapse: 2%
Attrition: 18% MLB: 86%

Comparables:
Bobby Higginson, Luis Gonzalez, Frank Catalanotto

YEAR	TEAM	LVL	AGE	PA	R	2B	3B	HR	RBI	BB	SO	SB	CS	AVG/OBP/SLG	TAv	BABIP	BRR	FRAA	WARP
2011	ATL	MLB	29	321	35	12	2	4	16	44	52	4	2	.228/.344/.333	.256	.270	2.6	CF(55): -0.5, LF(26): -1.0	0.7
2012	NOR	AAA	30	209	29	5	2	10	33	18	26	5	0	.244/.325/.461	.278	.231	2.6	CF(28): -0.7, RF(12): -1.6	1.0
2012	BAL	MLB	30	236	35	12	1	7	18	22	43	12	1	.268/.342/.435	.273	.306	4	LF(55): 0.2, CF(6): -0.0	1.1
2012	PIT	MLB	30	62	4	2	0	0	2	5	18	0	0	.140/.210/.175	.151	.205	0.5	LF(9): -0.5, CF(4): 0.2	-0.6
2013	BAL	MLB	31	593	76	31	4	12	36	53	86	30	7	.258/.329/.399	.269	.288	4	LF(136): 1.9, CF(3): 0.0	2.5
2014	WAS	MLB	32	523	68	21	2	12	48	52	90	19	4	.239/.323/.371	.254	.270	1.7	LF -1, CF -0	1.0

An EKG doesn't bounce around as much as McLouth's reputation has throughout his nine-year career. His last two years have reestablished him as someone with enough talent to be on a 25-man roster, but he should be limited to the heavy side of a platoon, facing as many righties as possible and not showing up to the stadium until the seventh inning when a lefty is on the mound. His career-best 30 stolen bases in 2013 were a pleasant surprise for the fantasy-inclined, but the peculiar distribution puts their repeatability in serious doubt, as he stole 24 in the first three months before grinding to a halt. He's a nice fit for a Nationals team with three clear starting-caliber outfielders and the right-handed Scott Hairston on the bench.

Tyler Moore 1B

Born: 1/30/1987 Age: 27
Bats: R Throws: R Height: 6' 2"
Weight: 220 Breakout: 9%
Improve: 28% Collapse: 8%
Attrition: 21% MLB: 65%

Comparables:
Allen Craig, Scott Hairston, Brandon Allen

YEAR	TEAM	LVL	AGE	PA	R	2B	3B	HR	RBI	BB	SO	SB	CS	AVG/OBP/SLG	TAv	BABIP	BRR	FRAA	WARP
2011	HAR	AA	24	561	70	35	4	31	90	30	139	2	0	.270/.314/.532	.313	.307	-0.9	1B(108): 5.0	3.9
2012	SYR	AAA	25	115	15	6	1	9	26	12	26	1	0	.307/.374/.653	.339	.324	-1.9	1B(24): 1.9, LF(3): -0.3	1.2
2012	WAS	MLB	25	171	20	9	0	10	29	14	46	3	0	.263/.327/.513	.273	.310	-2.2	LF(40): -3.7, 1B(14): -0.4	-0.1
2013	SYR	AAA	26	200	26	14	1	10	46	23	39	1	0	.318/.395/.584	.336	.354	-1.3	LF(21): -0.2, 1B(19): 0.2	1.9
2013	WAS	MLB	26	178	16	9	0	4	21	8	58	0	0	.222/.260/.347	.238	.311	-0.2	LF(29): -3.1, 1B(14): -0.2	-0.9
2014	WAS	MLB	27	250	30	12	0	12	37	16	67	1	0	.254/.305/.461	.275	.300	-0.4	1B 1, LF -4	0.5

After looking like a potential second-division regular in his debut season, Moore backslid in a major way in his sophomore campaign. His walk rate dropped almost 4 full percentage points. He struck out in a third of his at-bats—it took Adam Dunn 10 seasons and 354 home runs to reach such strikeout profligacy. He led the team in slugging in 2012; he was outslugged by pitcher Tanner Roark last year. Barring a trade, Moore will likely be strictly limited to backing up first base and pinch-hitting, as the answer to "why did they trade for Scott Hairston?" is suddenly so very clear.

Eury Perez CF

Born: 5/30/1990 Age: 24
Bats: R Throws: R Height: 6' 0"
Weight: 180 Breakout: 4%
Improve: 14% Collapse: 2%
Attrition: 10% MLB: 25%

Comparables:
Clay Timpner, Juan Lagares, Tony Campana

YEAR	TEAM	LVL	AGE	PA	R	2B	3B	HR	RBI	BB	SO	SB	CS	AVG/OBP/SLG	TAv	BABIP	BRR	FRAA	WARP
2011	POT	A+	21	465	54	9	2	1	41	22	63	45	15	.283/.319/.321	.244	.326	2.8	CF(101): 3.1, LF(6): 0.4	1.1
2012	HAR	AA	22	373	34	11	2	0	30	7	53	26	10	.299/.325/.342	.249	.351	1.8	CF(82): 8.0, RF(2): -0.0	2.2
2012	SYR	AAA	22	173	21	7	1	0	10	8	26	20	5	.333/.373/.390	.263	.398	2.1	CF(25): 2.0, LF(12): 0.3	1.2
2012	WAS	MLB	22	5	3	0	0	0	0	0	0	3	0	.200/.200/.200	.163	.200	-0.6	CF(4): -0.1, LF(3): -0.0	-0.1
2013	SYR	AAA	23	433	55	18	5	7	28	13	64	23	8	.300/.336/.422	.263	.343	2.2	CF(68): -5.6, LF(15): 0.6	1.2
2013	WAS	MLB	23	8	1	0	0	0	0	0	3	1	0	.125/.125/.125	.082	.200	0.1	CF(4): 0.1, LF(3): 0.1	-0.1
2014	WAS	MLB	24	250	30	8	1	2	17	5	44	14	4	.273/.296/.343	.234	.320	1.2	CF 1, LF 0	0.3

Perez has spent the last year and a half at Triple-A, receiving only 13 major-league plate appearances in that time; sounds like "Quad-A veteran," except that 2014 will be only his age-24 season. He has proved throughout his minor-league career that he can hit for average, but a lack of secondary skills destines him to be a fourth or fifth outfielder. The last time he posted a walk rate above 5 percent was in 2009, when he was in rookie ball, and while he makes solid contact it comes with little to no pop. His elite speed will keep him employed, but as no more than pinch-runner/defensive replacement/eventual Quad-A veteran.

Wilson Ramos   C

Born: 8/10/1987 Age: 26
Bats: R Throws: R Height: 6' 0"
Weight: 220 Breakout: 5%
Improve: 49% Collapse: 4%
Attrition: 11% MLB: 100%

Comparables:
Miguel Montero, Matt Wieters, Ronny Paulino

YEAR	TEAM	LVL	AGE	PA	R	2B	3B	HR	RBI	BB	SO	SB	CS	AVG/OBP/SLG	TAv	BABIP	BRR	FRAA	WARP
2011	WAS	MLB	23	435	48	22	1	15	52	38	76	0	2	.267/.334/.445	.271	.297	0.7	C(108): -1.4	2.6
2012	WAS	MLB	24	96	11	2	0	3	10	12	19	0	0	.265/.354/.398	.284	.306	0.6	C(24): 0.3	0.6
2013	WAS	MLB	25	303	29	9	0	16	59	15	42	0	1	.272/.307/.470	.268	.270	-1.1	C(77): -0.3	1.8
2014	WAS	MLB	26	250	28	11	0	8	30	16	42	0	0	.265/.315/.420	.267	.290	-0.6	C -0	1.3

Ramos, a deft receiver with a powerful arm, returned strong from the ACL injury that stubbed out his 2012. He had shown impressive plate discipline prior to the injury, but was a different player last year, sacrificing patience for pop. His .777 OPS might not jump off the page, but it ranked 13th among catchers with at least 200 plate appearances. He was eased back into catching, but after the August trade of Kurt Suzuki, Ramos started 33 of the Nationals' last 36 games. He socked eight home runs to ace his final exam.

Anthony Rendon   2B

Born: 6/6/1990 Age: 24
Bats: R Throws: R Height: 6' 0"
Weight: 195 Breakout: 4%
Improve: 46% Collapse: 6%
Attrition: 12% MLB: 93%

Comparables:
Dustin Ackley, Gordon Beckham, Asdrubal Cabrera

YEAR	TEAM	LVL	AGE	PA	R	2B	3B	HR	RBI	BB	SO	SB	CS	AVG/OBP/SLG	TAv	BABIP	BRR	FRAA	WARP
2012	AUB	A-	22	32	7	2	0	1	3	4	6	0	0	.259/.375/.444	.290	.300	0.4	3B(5): 0.3	0.2
2012	POT	A+	22	32	5	2	3	0	0	5	4	0	0	.333/.438/.630	.416	.391	-0.1	3B(6): 0.3	0.6
2012	HAR	AA	22	82	14	3	1	3	3	11	16	0	0	.162/.305/.368	.249	.163	1.6	3B(18): 1.5	0.5
2013	HAR	AA	23	152	17	11	2	6	24	30	25	1	0	.319/.461/.603	.376	.352	-0.5	3B(24): 3.5, 2B(5): -0.5	2.8
2013	WAS	MLB	23	394	40	23	1	7	35	31	69	1	1	.265/.329/.396	.261	.307	1.3	2B(82): 0.9, 3B(15): 0.5	1.3
2014	WAS	MLB	24	336	35	17	1	8	38	33	63	1	0	.256/.337/.402	.270	.300	-0.4	2B -0, 3B 3	1.6

A bright spot in a stagnant Washington summer, Rendon earned an unexpected promotion (skipping Triple-A entirely) to replace the injured and ineffective Danny Espinosa in late April. His stay was brief and strugglesome, but upon returning for good in June he did a pretty good impression (.267/.326/.405) of the league's average second baseman (.261/.320/.391). The big concern going forward will be his ability to stay healthy. He has suffered three ankle injuries dating back to his college days, and is now tasked with playing the joint-endangering keystone.

Steven Souza   RF

Born: 4/24/1989 Age: 25
Bats: R Throws: R Height: 6' 3"
Weight: 220 Breakout: 8%
Improve: 21% Collapse: 4%
Attrition: 27% MLB: 48%

Comparables:
Jai Miller, Nelson Cruz, Nolan Reimold

YEAR	TEAM	LVL	AGE	PA	R	2B	3B	HR	RBI	BB	SO	SB	CS	AVG/OBP/SLG	TAv	BABIP	BRR	FRAA	WARP
2011	POT	A+	22	478	58	17	2	11	56	75	131	25	9	.228/.360/.367	.267	.308	1.4	1B(99): 4.8, SS(1): -0.0	1.0
2012	HAG	A	23	293	48	20	2	17	72	22	49	7	7	.290/.346/.576	.319	.294	2.9	RF(44): 2.4	2.8
2012	POT	A+	23	107	16	2	1	6	13	13	25	7	1	.319/.421/.560	.336	.383	0.2	CF(16): -0.3, RF(9): -0.6	1.0
2013	HAR	AA	24	323	54	23	1	15	44	41	76	20	6	.300/.396/.557	.348	.360	0.5	RF(72): -2.0, CF(5): -0.1	3.8
2014	WAS	MLB	25	250	31	10	0	9	31	24	68	7	3	.239/.318/.409	.267	.300	0.1	RF -1, 1B 0	0.6

The Nationals are deep in prospects who are either interesting but aged or light years away from the majors, and Souza fits in with the former. Drafted in 2007 as a toolsy third-round gamble, Souza languished in the low minors before something clicked late in 2011, with the results bearing fruit in 2012. At 25, he finally got his first crack at Double-A and produced the league's second-best OPS. He might be old for the level but he has legitimate throw, run and power tools. A converted third baseman, his outfield defense still requires work, but there's a major-league future here.

Denard Span   CF

Born: 2/27/1984 Age: 30
Bats: L Throws: L Height: 6' 0"
Weight: 210 Breakout: 1%
Improve: 50% Collapse: 4%
Attrition: 10% MLB: 98%

Comparables:
Johnny Damon, Shane Victorino, Curt Flood

YEAR	TEAM	LVL	AGE	PA	R	2B	3B	HR	RBI	BB	SO	SB	CS	AVG/OBP/SLG	TAv	BABIP	BRR	FRAA	WARP
2011	ROC	AAA	27	40	4	1	0	0	2	0	5	3	0	.205/.205/.231	.160	.235	-0.1	CF(10): 0.2	-0.3
2011	MIN	MLB	27	311	37	11	5	2	16	27	36	6	1	.264/.328/.359	.253	.297	2.2	CF(67): 7.6	1.5
2012	MIN	MLB	28	568	71	38	4	4	41	47	62	17	6	.283/.342/.395	.261	.315	-1	CF(125): 8.3	2.5
2013	WAS	MLB	29	662	75	28	11	4	47	42	77	20	6	.279/.327/.380	.251	.313	0.3	CF(153): 8.8	2.7
2014	WAS	MLB	30	603	70	24	6	4	46	50	75	19	5	.275/.338/.366	.261	.310	1.7	CF 7	2.8

When the Nationals sent Alex Meyer to Minnesota for Span, they thought the final piece of the puzzle was snapping snugly into place. Finally, after years of pursuit, they had found a top-of-the-order hitter and a center fielder to build an outfield defense around. Then, naturally, he struggled, as the Nationals fell out of contention early. The second half was better for all involved, as Span hit a more characteristic .302/.337/.413. Speed is a major part of his game, so it's worth noting that his bunting success plummeted, from 57 percent in 2012 to 11 percent in 2013. A sign Span lost a step? His 20 stolen bases and league-leading 11 triples say no, but it's something to keep an eye on.

Michael Taylor CF

Born: 3/26/1991 Age: 23
Bats: R Throws: R Height: 6' 4"
Weight: 205 Breakout: 2%
Improve: 2% Collapse: 1%
Attrition: 2% MLB: 3%

Comparables:
Roger Bernadina, Drew Stubbs, Justin Maxwell

YEAR	TEAM	LVL	AGE	PA	R	2B	3B	HR	RBI	BB	SO	SB	CS	AVG/OBP/SLG	TAv	BABIP	BRR	FRAA	WARP
2011	HAG	A	20	488	64	26	7	13	68	32	120	23	12	.253/.310/.432	.244	.316	-0.6	CF(86): -5.5, RF(20): -0.2	0.0
2012	POT	A+	21	431	51	33	2	3	37	40	113	19	9	.242/.318/.362	.246	.335	0.7	CF(108): 12.9, RF(1): -0.1	2.7
2013	POT	A+	22	581	79	41	6	10	87	55	131	51	7	.263/.340/.426	.265	.331	7.5	CF(117): 14.3, RF(4): 0.1	5.0
2014	WAS	MLB	23	250	24	11	1	3	21	14	73	9	3	.211/.259/.310	.211	.290	0.9	CF 3, RF -0	-0.1

Repeating High-A as a 22-year-old puts a stop sign on a player's prospect status, but plenty of observers still hold out hope for Taylor, a rangy center fielder with game-changing speed and enough raw power to produce dreams of a fantasy-stud future. Contact has always been the concern, and the strides he made in 2013 were only modestly encouraging given the league repeat. He'll get a new league in which to prove it's real this year.

Zach Walters SS

Born: 9/5/1989 Age: 24
Bats: B Throws: R Height: 6' 2"
Weight: 220 Breakout: 1%
Improve: 11% Collapse: 12%
Attrition: 21% MLB: 30%

Comparables:
Brandon Hicks, Danny Valencia, Brandon Wood

YEAR	TEAM	LVL	AGE	PA	R	2B	3B	HR	RBI	BB	SO	SB	CS	AVG/OBP/SLG	TAv	BABIP	BRR	FRAA	WARP
2011	SBN	A	21	412	69	27	6	9	56	42	96	12	10	.302/.377/.485	.273	.386	-0.3	SS(9): 1.7, 3B(6): 0.4	0.6
2011	POT	A+	21	126	15	7	1	0	11	8	33	7	1	.293/.336/.371	.260	.405	1.8	SS(24): -1.1	0.4
2012	POT	A+	22	207	24	8	1	5	24	10	43	6	3	.269/.304/.399	.252	.318	0.6	SS(33): -0.2, 3B(9): -0.9	0.5
2012	HAR	AA	22	172	23	11	4	6	19	8	38	1	0	.293/.326/.518	.289	.350	0.1	SS(43): 1.4	1.4
2012	SYR	AAA	22	105	9	4	0	1	6	6	28	0	0	.214/.260/.286	.210	.290	-0.3	SS(29): 3.8	0.2
2013	SYR	AAA	23	521	69	32	5	29	77	20	134	4	3	.253/.286/.517	.276	.285	-0.7	SS(102): -0.7, 3B(27): 1.5	2.8
2013	WAS	MLB	23	9	2	0	1	0	1	1	0	0	0	.375/.444/.625	.332	.375	-0.2	SS(2): 0.1, 3B(2): 0.0	0.1
2014	WAS	MLB	24	250	27	11	1	9	31	9	67	3	2	.241/.272/.412	.246	.290	-0.1	SS 2, 3B 0	0.8

Even Michael Jordan had a higher minor-league OBP than Walters produced last year in Triple-A, but considering context, it's not hard to see Walters having an impact in the big leagues. An impressive athlete, he plays an up-the-middle position and slugged .517 in Triple-A. It's always fair to question Triple-A numbers, but he did his damage in the International League, not the pinball alley known as the PCL. While the Nationals have their shortstop of the present and future in Ian Desmond, Walters has the athleticism to play multiple positions and punch up the Nationals' punchless bench.

Drew Ward 3B

Born: 11/25/1994 Age: 19
Bats: L Throws: R Height: 6' 4"
Weight: 210 Breakout: 0%
Improve: 0% Collapse: 0%
Attrition: 0% MLB: 0%

Comparables:
Matt Davidson, Josh Vitters, Chris Carter

YEAR	TEAM	LVL	AGE	PA	R	2B	3B	HR	RBI	BB	SO	SB	CS	AVG/OBP/SLG	TAv	BABIP	BRR	FRAA	WARP
2014	WAS	MLB	19	250	17	8	0	2	19	15	77	0	0	.189/.242/.249	.185	.270	-0.5	3B -1	-1.5

Like Bryce Harper, Ward graduated high school a year early so he could enter the draft as soon as possible; like Bryce Harper, he's a lefty with big raw strength. That's where the comparisons end, but, hey, how many players can even put one "like Bryce Harper" on a resume? The third-rounder was old for his high school class, so the early exit just brought him back to where he should have been. He has a big body and the Nationals immediately shifted him to third base, but the third-rounder has power and a clue at the plate, so he'll be one to watch.

Jayson Werth RF

Born: 5/20/1979 Age: 35
Bats: R Throws: R Height: 6' 5"
Weight: 225 Breakout: 3%
Improve: 28% Collapse: 7%
Attrition: 8% MLB: 97%

Comparables:
Dwight Evans, J.D. Drew, Larry Walker

YEAR	TEAM	LVL	AGE	PA	R	2B	3B	HR	RBI	BB	SO	SB	CS	AVG/OBP/SLG	TAv	BABIP	BRR	FRAA	WARP
2011	WAS	MLB	32	649	69	26	1	20	58	74	160	19	3	.232/.330/.389	.264	.286	2.1	RF(134): 3.0, CF(19): 2.0	2.7
2012	SYR	AAA	33	27	4	2	0	0	4	6	5	0	0	.238/.407/.333	.248	.312	-0.2	RF(5): -0.2, CF(2): -0.1	0.0
2012	WAS	MLB	33	344	42	21	3	5	31	42	57	8	2	.300/.387/.440	.300	.356	-1	RF(76): 5.8, CF(11): -1.0	2.3
2013	POT	A+	34	20	6	1	0	2	8	2	0	0	0	.556/.600/.944	.464	.500	-0.8	RF(6): 0.5	0.5
2013	WAS	MLB	34	532	84	24	0	25	82	60	101	10	1	.318/.398/.532	.325	.358	3.2	RF(126): -0.9	4.7
2014	WAS	MLB	35	470	61	21	1	16	61	55	106	10	2	.267/.358/.442	.292	.320	0.4	RF 3, CF 0	2.8

"Why's it always gotta be about some money?" the Harlem rapper Ma$e once asked in a rhyme, a question that might strike no one so close to home as Werth. While he took a circuitous and painful route to stardom and the money that goes with it, his performance since arriving in the District has been overlooked. His TAv last year set a new a career high and would have merited MVP votes if not for injury absences and decreasing defensive contributions. For now, topics of talk around Werth tend to go like this: 1. Beard 2. Contract 3. Performance. That's exactly the wrong order.

Ryan Zimmerman 3B
Born: 9/28/1984 Age: 29
Bats: R Throws: R Height: 6' 3"
Weight: 230 Breakout: 9%
Improve: 55% Collapse: 1%
Attrition: 4% MLB: 98%

Comparables:
David Wright, Hanley Ramirez, Eric Chavez

YEAR	TEAM	LVL	AGE	PA	R	2B	3B	HR	RBI	BB	SO	SB	CS	AVG/OBP/SLG	TAv	BABIP	BRR	FRAA	WARP
2011	WAS	MLB	26	440	52	21	2	12	49	41	73	3	1	.289/.355/.443	.284	.326	-0.7	3B(97): -1.7	2.8
2012	WAS	MLB	27	641	93	36	1	25	95	57	116	5	2	.282/.346/.478	.287	.313	-0.2	3B(145): 5.6	4.7
2013	WAS	MLB	28	633	84	26	2	26	79	60	133	6	0	.275/.344/.465	.284	.316	0.9	3B(141): 1.2	3.9
2014	WAS	MLB	29	597	75	28	1	23	82	58	111	4	1	.280/.351/.464	.295	.310	-0.6	3B -2	3.5

For one of the best defenders in baseball, the $100 million contract extension the Nationals handed Zimmerman in February 2012 seemed reasonable, if premature. The timing was odd, as Zimmerman was coming off an injury-shortened 2011, but given the strength of his 2009-10 work, it wasn't an atrocity. While Zimmerman has returned to full-time play, he hasn't been nearly the same. Following surgery on his right shoulder, Zimmerman's defense is badly damaged. Not only does he feature diminished range, but his ability to throw has up and left, tragironically mirroring the location of his tosses. While Zimmerman's bat is still above average, his defense is playing Frederick Sykes to the Nationals' Richard Kimble. Oh, and that contract extension? It starts in 2014.

PITCHERS

Jerry Blevins
Born: 9/6/1983 Age: 30
Bats: L Throws: L Height: 6' 6" Weight: 175
Breakout: 30% Improve: 70% Collapse: 18%
Attrition: 22% MLB: 75%

Comparables:
Santiago Casilla, John Foster, Manny Acosta

YEAR	TEAM	LVL	AGE	W	L	SV	G	GS	IP	H	HR	BB	SO	BB9	SO9	GB%	BABIP	WHIP	ERA	FIP	FRA	WARP
2011	SAC	AAA	27	2	0	0	27	0	29²	25	3	7	35	2.1	10.6	35%	.278	1.08	4.85	3.55	2.67	0.6
2011	OAK	MLB	27	0	0	0	26	0	28¹	24	2	14	26	4.4	8.3	41%	.282	1.34	2.86	3.73	3.96	0.2
2012	OAK	MLB	28	5	1	1	63	0	65¹	45	7	25	54	3.4	7.4	39%	.224	1.07	2.48	4.16	4.27	0.3
2013	OAK	MLB	29	5	0	0	67	0	60	47	7	17	52	2.5	7.8	33%	.242	1.07	3.15	3.91	4.43	0.0
2014	WAS	MLB	30	3	1	1	59	0	54²	48	6	17	51	2.8	8.4	41%	.295	1.18	3.51	3.81	3.81	0.6

Blevins often enters the ballgame to face tough left-handed batters in critical situations, but it would be wrong to characterize him as a specialist, as he is typically deployed for longer stretches: He stayed in the game for four or more batters in nearly half his appearances last season. As a result, Blevins wound up facing more righties than lefties, which worked out fine because he posted a reverse platoon split. His four-pitch mix is effective against all types of hitters, and improving command could put him in the swing-man seat, though he's at an age when physical degradation could start to set in. The A's sent him to Washington for younger, cheaper parts after the season. Even though he's not a LOOGY now, his wide-left release could help him stick in the majors in that role long after his all-around game expires.

Tyler Clippard
Born: 2/14/1985 Age: 29
Bats: R Throws: R Height: 6' 3" Weight: 200
Breakout: 19% Improve: 56% Collapse: 31%
Attrition: 10% MLB: 95%

Comparables:
Jose Valverde, Rafael Soriano, Frank Francisco

YEAR	TEAM	LVL	AGE	W	L	SV	G	GS	IP	H	HR	BB	SO	BB9	SO9	GB%	BABIP	WHIP	ERA	FIP	FRA	WARP
2011	WAS	MLB	26	3	0	0	72	0	88¹	48	11	26	104	2.6	10.6	24%	.197	0.84	1.83	3.14	3.12	1.4
2012	WAS	MLB	27	2	6	32	74	0	72²	55	7	29	84	3.6	10.4	32%	.259	1.16	3.72	3.36	3.49	1.1
2013	WAS	MLB	28	6	3	0	72	0	71	37	9	24	73	3.0	9.3	29%	.170	0.86	2.41	3.80	4.51	0.2
2014	WAS	MLB	29	3	2	8	59	0	64¹	44	6	23	75	3.2	10.5	33%	.264	1.04	2.51	3.16	2.73	1.6

It was more of the same in 2013 for Clippard: Another solid season of set-up duties, with the occasional save mixed in. Another season of outperforming his peripherals, a feat he has accomplished every year of his career but one. More high fastballs, more changeups disappearing under antsy swings. Same old fly-ball pitcher, as only three qualified relievers induced fewer groundballs. Same old Clippard ... mostly. He mixed things up in September when he introduced a splitter, a few ticks harder than his changeup and with more drop instead of fade. He threw only nine, but it's a pitch he had worked on in bullpens and that he hopes will generate grounders. It's unlikely to change his approach dramatically, so expect to see more splitters next year, but otherwise more of the same.

A.J. Cole
Born: 1/5/1992 Age: 22
Bats: R Throws: R Height: 6' 4'' Weight: 180
Breakout: 35% Improve: 79% Collapse: 11%
Attrition: 48% MLB: 32%

Comparables:
Jeremy Hellickson, Hector Rondon, John Danks

YEAR	TEAM	LVL	AGE	W	L	SV	G	GS	IP	H	HR	BB	SO	BB9	SO9	GB%	BABIP	WHIP	ERA	FIP	FRA	WARP
2011	HAG	A	19	4	7	0	20	18	89	87	6	24	108	2.4	10.9	39%	.342	1.25	4.04	2.85	2.87	3.3
2012	BUR	A	20	6	3	0	19	19	95²	78	7	19	102	1.8	9.6	47%	.291	1.01	2.07	2.89	3.88	1.9
2012	STO	A+	20	0	7	0	8	8	38	60	7	10	31	2.4	7.3	37%	.405	1.84	7.82	5.60	5.38	0.2
2013	POT	A+	21	6	3	0	18	18	97¹	96	12	23	102	2.1	9.4	38%	.317	1.22	4.25	3.69	4.44	1.8
2013	HAR	AA	21	4	2	0	7	7	45¹	31	3	10	49	2.0	9.7	40%	.252	0.90	2.18	2.68	2.84	1.2
2014	WAS	MLB	22	7	9	0	26	26	122	124	15	39	101	2.9	7.4	40%	.314	1.34	4.39	4.20	4.77	0.3

Cole hasn't wandered far from the Gio Gonzalez Career Path, a trail designed for adventurous climbers only. He has the occasional brilliance, followed by underwhelming performances. He has the "getting traded from and to the same team within a calendar year" part down. He has a similar profile, of a no. 2 starter if it all comes together, but risk in proportion. Cole was just mediocre in his second go at High-A, but he flourished upon a promotion to Double-A, nearly equaling his career bests in strikeout rate (28 percent) and walk rate (6 percent). If Cole can tighten his breaking ball to go with his lively fastball and solid change, he'll be within shouting distance of the majors by 2015.

Ross Detwiler
Born: 3/6/1986 Age: 28
Bats: R Throws: L Height: 6' 5'' Weight: 200
Breakout: 15% Improve: 50% Collapse: 24%
Attrition: 37% MLB: 80%

Comparables:
Clayton Richard, Charlie Morton, Clay Hensley

YEAR	TEAM	LVL	AGE	W	L	SV	G	GS	IP	H	HR	BB	SO	BB9	SO9	GB%	BABIP	WHIP	ERA	FIP	FRA	WARP
2011	SYR	AAA	25	6	6	0	16	16	87¹	98	4	32	63	3.3	6.5	54%	.354	1.49	4.53	3.52	4.53	0.6
2011	WAS	MLB	25	4	5	0	15	10	66	63	7	20	41	2.7	5.6	46%	.272	1.26	3.00	4.18	4.51	0.3
2012	WAS	MLB	26	10	8	0	33	27	164¹	149	15	52	105	2.8	5.8	51%	.272	1.22	3.40	4.09	4.82	0.8
2013	WAS	MLB	27	2	7	0	13	13	71¹	92	5	14	39	1.8	4.9	48%	.340	1.49	4.04	3.64	3.79	1.0
2014	WAS	MLB	28	4	5	0	15	15	78¹	82	7	24	50	2.8	5.8	49%	.312	1.36	4.43	4.13	4.81	0.1

Detwiler has done well to turn himself into a fifth starter at the major-league level after a torn hip labrum sucked away his velocity. He mixes his pitches well and has managed to keep his arm healthy. The rest of his body is less accommodating: Besides that old hip surgery, he dealt with an oblique strain last May and a herniated disc in his back. Injuries heal, but Detwiler might have been Pipp'd by rookies Taylor Jordan and Tanner Roark. While nothing is set in stone with the back end of the Nationals rotation, a shift to the bullpen (and possible bump in velocity) might help Detwiler miss more bats and beef up a middling strikeout rate.

Doug Fister
Born: 2/4/1984 Age: 30
Bats: L Throws: R Height: 6' 8'' Weight: 210
Breakout: 14% Improve: 43% Collapse: 24%
Attrition: 12% MLB: 87%

Comparables:
Mark Buehrle, Cliff Lee, Jason Vargas

YEAR	TEAM	LVL	AGE	W	L	SV	G	GS	IP	H	HR	BB	SO	BB9	SO9	GB%	BABIP	WHIP	ERA	FIP	FRA	WARP
2011	DET	MLB	27	8	1	0	11	10	70¹	54	4	5	57	0.6	7.3	51%	.245	0.84	1.79	2.52	3.17	1.7
2011	SEA	MLB	27	3	12	0	21	21	146	139	7	32	89	2.0	5.5	47%	.285	1.17	3.33	3.31	4.08	1.0
2012	DET	MLB	28	10	10	0	26	26	161²	156	15	37	137	2.1	7.6	53%	.296	1.19	3.45	3.37	4.17	2.4
2013	DET	MLB	29	14	9	0	33	32	208²	229	14	44	159	1.9	6.9	56%	.331	1.31	3.67	3.29	3.63	3.5
2014	WAS	MLB	30	11	10	0	28	28	188¹	184	15	34	134	1.6	6.4	48%	.307	1.16	3.48	3.46	3.78	2.1

At his best Fister is one of the more underrated arms in the game, a command-and-control wizard who induces tons of groundballs while missing more bats than the scouts or stats ever projected. He's been on the wrong team, is all. The Tigers' infield had just one plus defender behind him—and for only the final two months of last season at that. He allowed eight hits or more in a MLB-high 16 starts, and his .332 BABIP was the second-highest among qualified starters. On grounders, his BABIP was 47 points higher than league average, a difference of 17 hits against expectations. Washington's infield defense should be a step up from the Sleestaks who wandered the diamond in Comerica last summer, so Fister could be in line for some kind of season.

Lucas Giolito
Born: 7/14/1994 Age: 19
Bats: R Throws: R Height: 6' 6'' Weight: 225
Breakout: 0% Improve: 0% Collapse: 0%
Attrition: 0% MLB: 0%

Comparables:
Jeurys Familia, Jenrry Mejia, Alberto Cabrera

YEAR	TEAM	LVL	AGE	W	L	SV	G	GS	IP	H	HR	BB	SO	BB9	SO9	GB%	BABIP	WHIP	ERA	FIP	FRA	WARP
2013	AUB	A-	18	1	0	0	3	3	14	9	1	4	14	2.6	9.0	67%	.250	0.93	0.64	3.31	3.56	0.3
2014	WAS	MLB	19	2	3	0	9	9	34¹	38	4	20	20	5.2	5.4	48%	.316	1.69	5.84	5.48	6.34	-0.4

Perhaps the top overall talent in the 2012 draft, Giolito had a realistic chance of becoming the first right-handed high school pitcher ever selected first overall. Those chances dimmed when he sprained his UCL and missed much of his senior season, and the Nationals subsequently found him hanging around for them at no. 16. He had Tommy John surgery after just two pro innings, but returned in 2013 again showing a big fastball and hammer curve, even flashing a plus changeup. He also built a ping pong table with high school teammate Max Fried, but that's ... well, that's probably not relevant. With mound presence and positive makeup to complete the package, Giolito is the rare prospect who deserves a "potential ace" label.

Gio Gonzalez

Born: 9/19/1985 Age: 28
Bats: R Throws: L Height: 6' 0" Weight: 200
Breakout: 25% Improve: 49% Collapse: 34%
Attrition: 12% MLB: 95%

Comparables:
Jon Lester, Erik Bedard, Ubaldo Jimenez

YEAR	TEAM	LVL	AGE	W	L	SV	G	GS	IP	H	HR	BB	SO	BB9	SO9	GB%	BABIP	WHIP	ERA	FIP	FRA	WARP
2011	OAK	MLB	25	16	12	0	32	32	202	175	17	91	197	4.1	8.8	48%	.286	1.32	3.12	3.68	3.94	2.5
2012	WAS	MLB	26	21	8	0	32	32	199¹	149	9	76	207	3.4	9.3	49%	.271	1.13	2.89	2.87	3.36	4.1
2013	WAS	MLB	27	11	8	0	32	32	195²	169	17	76	192	3.5	8.8	43%	.294	1.25	3.36	3.38	3.50	3.3
2014	WAS	MLB	28	10	9	0	27	27	167¹	140	14	66	162	3.5	8.7	47%	.296	1.23	3.42	3.59	3.72	2.2

Considering questions about his makeup that popped up when he was a prospect, one might have worried that Gonzalez's season could have been derailed by allegations (found later to be unsubstantiated) that he was involved with the Biogenesis scandal. Instead, he pitched near All-Star levels for the fourth year in a row. Ten fewer wins will have some saying he wasn't the same pitcher as in 2012, but the only real backsliding Gonzalez saw was in his HR/FB percentage, which returned to career norms. The overall package should be enough to keep the southpaw in Washington, no small feat considering he's been traded four times in his young career. The list of PECOTA comps, meanwhile, should be enough to give his pitching coach night sweats.

Jacob Johansen

Born: 1/23/1991 Age: 23
Bats: R Throws: R Height: 6' 6" Weight: 235
Breakout: 0% Improve: 100% Collapse: 0%
Attrition: 100% MLB: 1%

Comparables:
Josh Zeid, Rob Scahill, Luis Perez

YEAR	TEAM	LVL	AGE	W	L	SV	G	GS	IP	H	HR	BB	SO	BB9	SO9	GB%	BABIP	WHIP	ERA	FIP	FRA	WARP
2013	AUB	A-	22	1	1	0	10	10	42¹	22	1	18	44	3.8	9.4	71%	.200	0.94	1.06	2.67	3.84	0.7
2014	WAS	MLB	23	2	3	0	8	8	35	39	4	19	21	4.8	5.5	52%	.313	1.64	5.59	5.28	6.08	-0.4

Drafted in the second round, Johansen was the Nationals' top pick in 2013 and signed for slot money. At 6-foot-6 with a fastball that runs up to 99, he's an imposing figure on the mound, but the stuff often underwhelms. There's little movement to the heater, and his college ERA in three seasons at Dallas Baptist was just over 6. He lists James 1:2-4 as his favorite Bible passage: "Consider it pure joy whenever you face trials, because the testing produces perseverance." He'll be tested.

Taylor Jordan

Born: 1/17/1989 Age: 25
Bats: R Throws: R Height: 6' 3" Weight: 190
Breakout: 56% Improve: 78% Collapse: 11%
Attrition: 55% MLB: 64%

Comparables:
Clayton Richard, Mitchell Boggs, Zach Jackson

YEAR	TEAM	LVL	AGE	W	L	SV	G	GS	IP	H	HR	BB	SO	BB9	SO9	GB%	BABIP	WHIP	ERA	FIP	FRA	WARP
2011	HAG	A	22	9	4	0	18	17	94¹	90	1	23	63	2.2	6.0	57%	.292	1.20	2.48	3.25	4.24	1.5
2012	HAG	A	23	3	4	0	9	9	40	52	2	9	28	2.0	6.3	59%	.376	1.52	4.05	3.95	4.71	0.8
2012	AUB	A-	23	0	0	0	6	6	14¹	19	0	2	17	1.3	10.7	68%	.404	1.47	8.16	2.22	3.96	0.3
2013	POT	A+	24	2	1	0	6	6	36¹	31	1	6	29	1.5	7.2	56%	.280	1.02	1.24	2.61	3.23	1.1
2013	HAR	AA	24	7	0	0	9	8	54	37	0	9	43	1.5	7.2	55%	.248	0.85	0.83	2.51	3.14	1.2
2013	WAS	MLB	24	1	3	0	9	9	51²	59	3	11	29	1.9	5.1	57%	.331	1.35	3.66	3.47	4.37	0.3
2014	WAS	MLB	25	6	7	0	19	19	104²	112	10	32	56	2.7	4.8	52%	.309	1.38	4.59	4.47	4.99	-0.1

It's difficult to call Jordan a fast mover, given his two stops at short-season ball and three at Low-A. He finally accelerated, from High-A to the majors in the span of one season, with good marks at each level. He made 14 starts between High-A and Double-A and bullied his younger opponents, posting a 1.00 ERA in 90 innings. He was 24, so the dominant stretch didn't so much put him on the prospect map as keep him from falling off of it. Called up to make two or three starts as a rotation fill-in, he ended up earning a permanent pass, his 3.66 ERA in the bigs belying an even better FIP. The only blemish is his low strikeout rate, but he gets grounders, avoids walks and excels at little things like holding runners on.

Nate Karns

Born: 11/25/1987 Age: 26
Bats: R Throws: R Height: 6' 3" Weight: 230
Breakout: 40% Improve: 56% Collapse: 27%
Attrition: 68% MLB: 60%

Comparables:
Francisco Cruceta, J.A. Happ, Ramon A. Ramirez

YEAR	TEAM	LVL	AGE	W	L	SV	G	GS	IP	H	HR	BB	SO	BB9	SO9	GB%	BABIP	WHIP	ERA	FIP	FRA	WARP
2011	AUB	A-	23	3	2	0	8	8	36²	27	1	27	33	6.6	8.1	44%	.293	1.47	3.44	4.46	4.70	0.1
2012	HAG	A	24	3	2	0	11	5	44¹	23	1	21	61	4.3	12.4	50%	.237	0.99	2.03	2.74	3.83	1.1
2012	POT	A+	24	8	4	0	13	13	71²	47	1	26	87	3.3	10.9	53%	.287	1.02	2.26	2.39	2.90	2.0
2013	HAR	AA	25	10	6	0	23	23	132²	109	14	48	155	3.3	10.5	46%	.294	1.18	3.26	3.60	3.87	2.2
2013	WAS	MLB	25	0	1	0	3	3	12	17	5	6	11	4.5	8.2	37%	.333	1.92	7.50	8.35	7.62	-0.3
2014	WAS	MLB	26	6	7	0	25	20	122¹	108	14	50	120	3.7	8.8	46%	.303	1.29	3.90	4.09	4.24	0.9

It was nearly two years between Karns' signing—for an over-slot $225,000 as a 12th-rounder—and his pro debut, as shoulder surgery wiped out a season and put him way behind his draft peers' pace. Despite excellent performances at each level since, he was still in Double-A at 25, until the Nationals plucked him for emergency-starter duties in May. Karns has a heavy mid-90s fastball and a swing-and-miss curve, and his lone bugaboo—walks—seems to be behind him. Still, after three starts (and five home runs), the Nationals sent him back down; perhaps tellingly, they went with other old-for-his-level options when they needed emergency starters later in the season.

Ryan Mattheus
Born: 11/10/1983 Age: 30
Bats: R Throws: R Height: 6' 3" Weight: 215
Breakout: 18% Improve: 63% Collapse: 26%
Attrition: 29% MLB: 66%

Comparables:
Willie Eyre, Gary Majewski, Orber Moreno

YEAR	TEAM	LVL	AGE	W	L	SV	G	GS	IP	H	HR	BB	SO	BB9	SO9	GB%	BABIP	WHIP	ERA	FIP	FRA	WARP
2011	HAR	AA	27	2	1	4	13	0	14²	9	1	5	18	3.1	11.0	50%	.259	0.95	2.45	3.07	3.45	0.2
2011	SYR	AAA	27	0	0	2	9	0	10	3	0	3	10	2.7	9.0	59%	.136	0.60	0.00	2.14	2.98	0.2
2011	WAS	MLB	27	2	2	0	35	0	32	26	1	15	12	4.2	3.4	52%	.240	1.28	2.81	4.24	4.79	-0.1
2012	WAS	MLB	28	5	3	0	66	0	66¹	57	8	19	41	2.6	5.6	48%	.255	1.15	2.85	4.46	5.13	-0.1
2013	WAS	MLB	29	0	2	0	37	0	35¹	52	1	15	22	3.8	5.6	58%	.405	1.90	6.37	3.42	4.17	0.2
2014	WAS	MLB	30	3	1	0	49	0	49²	47	5	17	35	3.1	6.4	52%	.298	1.31	3.97	4.27	4.31	0.2

Some catastrophes (hurricanes, earthquakes) are simple; others (financial crises, Amanda Bynes) are complicated—culminations of so many factors that it's hard to know what to blame. So it was with Mattheus in 2013. His 2.85 ERA from 2012 was clearly unsustainable based on his peripherals, and regression hit as expected. He broke his pitching hand after punching a locker in May, and his stuff was notably worse after that. His BABIP moved into freak-show territory. His sinker lost a mile per hour. He increasingly turned to a splitter that he has almost no control of. His strand rate was one of the league's worst. There's no easy patch here, though many a beleaguered region has found hope in prayer.

Ross Ohlendorf
Born: 8/8/1982 Age: 31
Bats: R Throws: R Height: 6' 4" Weight: 240
Breakout: 38% Improve: 68% Collapse: 20%
Attrition: 35% MLB: 48%

Comparables:
Ryan Jensen, Jae Weong Seo, Chris Narveson

YEAR	TEAM	LVL	AGE	W	L	SV	G	GS	IP	H	HR	BB	SO	BB9	SO9	GB%	BABIP	WHIP	ERA	FIP	FRA	WARP
2011	IND	AAA	28	1	1	0	4	4	24¹	22	2	8	12	3.0	4.4	44%	.260	1.23	3.33	4.43	4.92	0.0
2011	PIT	MLB	28	1	3	0	9	9	38²	60	9	15	27	3.5	6.3	39%	.397	1.94	8.15	6.25	6.53	-0.6
2012	PAW	AAA	29	4	3	0	10	10	52²	57	5	15	37	2.6	6.3	39%	.310	1.37	4.61	4.30	5.11	0.1
2012	TUC	AAA	29	1	1	0	3	0	17	19	2	3	17	1.6	9.0	39%	.362	1.29	4.24	3.90	5.11	0.2
2012	SDN	MLB	29	4	4	0	13	9	48²	62	7	24	39	4.4	7.2	30%	.349	1.77	7.77	4.94	4.56	0.3
2013	SYR	AAA	30	4	6	0	14	13	74²	65	5	30	71	3.6	8.6	41%	.286	1.27	4.22	3.50	4.17	0.9
2013	WAS	MLB	30	4	1	0	16	7	60¹	56	8	14	45	2.1	6.7	39%	.273	1.16	3.28	4.00	4.18	0.7
2014	WAS	MLB	31	6	7	0	26	19	118	120	15	38	87	2.9	6.6	41%	.303	1.34	4.57	4.54	4.97	-0.1

Last season was, for Ohlendorf, all about reaching back. Not only did he reach back for a little extra velocity on his fastball—which sat at 93 for the first time since 2008—but he reached back in time, with a new rocking delivery reminiscent of windups from the '50s and '60s. The new motion wasn't the only thing that changed for Ohlendorf: he abandoned his sinker, a pitch he had used frequently since his debut in 2007, and relied much more heavily on his four-seam fastball. He posted his best-ever ERA and FIP and likely saved his career.

Matt Purke
Born: 7/17/1990 Age: 23
Bats: L Throws: L Height: 6' 4" Weight: 205
Breakout: 66% Improve: 86% Collapse: 7%
Attrition: 73% MLB: 13%

Comparables:
Bruce Billings, Brett Marshall, Yoervis Medina

YEAR	TEAM	LVL	AGE	W	L	SV	G	GS	IP	H	HR	BB	SO	BB9	SO9	GB%	BABIP	WHIP	ERA	FIP	FRA	WARP
2012	HAG	A	21	0	2	0	3	3	15¹	15	1	12	14	7.0	8.2	49%	.318	1.76	5.87	5.14	5.90	0.1
2013	HAG	A	22	1	1	0	6	6	29	25	3	7	41	2.2	12.7	46%	.333	1.10	2.48	2.83	3.61	0.7
2013	POT	A+	22	5	3	0	12	12	61	67	3	18	41	2.7	6.0	51%	.325	1.39	4.43	3.73	5.19	0.6
2014	WAS	MLB	23	3	5	0	13	13	66²	72	8	28	45	3.8	6.1	46%	.315	1.50	5.03	4.81	5.47	-0.4

Signing a $4 million major-league contract out of the draft will draw some attention. Sign it as a third-round pick, and now everyone's interest is piqued. But since Purke signed that deal in 2011, he hasn't produced like a top pick and he hasn't moved through the system like a top pick, struggling with injuries and command and flopping in his first exposure to each level. He has wobbly command borne from a crossfire delivery, and neither his fastball nor changeup is better than fringe-average at present—a recipe for a backend starter at best. He'll begin his age-23 season at Double-A; if patterns hold, he'll struggle.

Tanner Roark
Born: 10/5/1986 Age: 27
Bats: R Throws: R Height: 6' 2" Weight: 220
Breakout: 45% Improve: 67% Collapse: 19%
Attrition: 51% MLB: 43%

Comparables:
Esmailin Caridad, Daniel McCutchen, Marco Estrada

YEAR	TEAM	LVL	AGE	W	L	SV	G	GS	IP	H	HR	BB	SO	BB9	SO9	GB%	BABIP	WHIP	ERA	FIP	FRA	WARP
2011	HAR	AA	24	9	9	0	21	21	117	125	10	39	92	3.0	7.1	50%	.344	1.40	4.69	4.05	5.17	-0.4
2012	SYR	AAA	25	6	17	0	28	26	147²	161	14	47	130	2.9	7.9	44%	.341	1.41	4.39	3.81	5.04	0.5
2013	SYR	AAA	26	9	3	2	33	11	105²	85	6	20	84	1.7	7.2	46%	.259	0.99	3.15	3.01	4.28	1.5
2013	WAS	MLB	26	7	1	0	14	5	53²	38	1	11	40	1.8	6.7	51%	.245	0.91	1.51	2.39	3.04	1.0
2014	WAS	MLB	27	6	7	1	30	19	127²	130	15	40	93	2.8	6.5	44%	.307	1.33	4.33	4.33	4.71	0.2

While Roark has shown a history of improving in his second attempt at a level, it's going to be hard for him to do so next year—his 1.51 ERA leaves little room for improvement. While regression is certain—particularly to his home run rate—there's a bit of Kyle Lohse here: a very stingy attitude toward walks, paired with credible strikeout and groundball rates and a good idea of how to manage a four-pitch mix. He should be a solid back-of-the-rotation option going forward.

Sammy Solis
Born: 8/10/1988 Age: 25
Bats: R Throws: L Height: 6' 5" Weight: 230
Breakout: 39% Improve: 69% Collapse: 27%
Attrition: 81% MLB: 19%
Comparables:
Blake Hawksworth, Mike Parisi, Tommy Hottovy

YEAR	TEAM	LVL	AGE	W	L	SV	G	GS	IP	H	HR	BB	SO	BB9	SO9	GB%	BABIP	WHIP	ERA	FIP	FRA	WARP
2011	HAG	A	22	2	1	0	7	7	40¹	39	3	12	40	2.7	8.9	54%	.322	1.26	4.02	3.55	4.77	0.4
2011	POT	A+	22	6	2	0	10	10	56¹	61	5	11	53	1.8	8.5	54%	.323	1.28	2.72	3.20	3.64	0.8
2013	POT	A+	24	2	1	0	13	12	57²	58	3	19	40	3.0	6.2	48%	.314	1.34	3.43	3.63	5.02	0.8
2014	WAS	MLB	25	2	3	0	10	10	41²	44	5	16	27	3.4	5.9	48%	.314	1.45	4.76	4.74	5.17	-0.1

A former top-100 prospect, Solis is way behind the development curve after missing all of 2012 for Tommy John surgery. He finally returned to action in late May, but an assessment of his performance—decent outcomes, poor peripherals—is skewed in one direction by his age and in another by a post-recovery grace period. He looked great in the Arizona Fall League, and he can still become a fourth starter, but first he needs to get to Double-A, and time is running out.

Rafael Soriano
Born: 12/19/1979 Age: 34
Bats: R Throws: R Height: 6' 1" Weight: 210
Breakout: 12% Improve: 35% Collapse: 50%
Attrition: 8% MLB: 91%
Comparables:
Rafael Betancourt, Bob Howry, Hideki Okajima

YEAR	TEAM	LVL	AGE	W	L	SV	G	GS	IP	H	HR	BB	SO	BB9	SO9	GB%	BABIP	WHIP	ERA	FIP	FRA	WARP
2011	NYA	MLB	31	2	3	2	42	0	39¹	33	4	18	36	4.1	8.2	36%	.276	1.30	4.12	4.00	4.90	0.3
2012	NYA	MLB	32	2	1	42	69	0	67²	55	6	24	69	3.2	9.2	38%	.274	1.17	2.26	3.27	3.17	1.4
2013	WAS	MLB	33	3	3	43	68	0	66²	65	7	17	51	2.3	6.9	35%	.287	1.23	3.11	3.62	4.44	0.3
2014	WAS	MLB	34	4	2	43	65	0	62²	51	5	18	62	2.6	8.9	36%	.287	1.09	2.87	3.13	3.12	1.2

Soriano's debut season with the Nationals was both more of the same and quite a departure. He notched 43 saves and kept runs off the board, but also saw a worrisome drop in his strikeout rate. Perhaps this is due to his transition from a slider-dominant pitcher to a fastball-first guy, and he was able to reduce his walk rate by two percentage points. If it's not, then he would be approximately the millionth closer to see his peripherals disappear a season before the saves did. And, given Soriano's injury history, we might wonder whether his change in approach is more about maintaining and managing his health than outfoxing hitters.

Craig Stammen
Born: 3/9/1984 Age: 30
Bats: R Throws: R Height: 6' 3" Weight: 215
Breakout: 30% Improve: 49% Collapse: 34%
Attrition: 31% MLB: 65%
Comparables:
Glen Perkins, Brian Duensing, Matt Belisle

YEAR	TEAM	LVL	AGE	W	L	SV	G	GS	IP	H	HR	BB	SO	BB9	SO9	GB%	BABIP	WHIP	ERA	FIP	FRA	WARP
2011	SYR	AAA	27	10	7	0	25	24	142	163	18	40	127	2.5	8.0	55%	.336	1.43	4.75	3.96	5.05	0.0
2011	WAS	MLB	27	1	1	0	7	0	10¹	3	0	4	12	3.5	10.5	50%	.136	0.68	0.87	1.83	1.40	0.3
2012	WAS	MLB	28	6	1	1	59	0	88¹	70	7	36	87	3.7	8.9	47%	.263	1.20	2.34	3.49	3.72	1.2
2013	WAS	MLB	29	7	6	0	55	0	81²	78	4	27	79	3.0	8.7	61%	.333	1.29	2.76	2.79	3.27	1.3
2014	WAS	MLB	30	3	3	0	29	7	71²	70	7	21	52	2.6	6.5	52%	.301	1.27	4.00	3.94	4.34	0.4

Dayton's all-time strikeouts leader has been bounced from starting to relieving dating back to his college days. He's finally found a home (or, one might say, his limit) as a multi-inning reliever in the majors, with nearly half of his outings extending past three outs. In that role, Stammen turned in his best peripheral stats, resulting in an impressive sub-3 FIP. The 12th-round pick attacks hitters with a sinker-slider repertoire, a combo just short of starter standards but enough (thanks to a velocity bump) to turn him into one of the game's best long relievers.

Drew Storen
Born: 8/11/1987 Age: 26
Bats: B Throws: R Height: 6' 1" Weight: 225
Breakout: 29% Improve: 54% Collapse: 28%
Attrition: 12% MLB: 87%
Comparables:
Joe Smith, Jeremy Accardo, Chris Ray

YEAR	TEAM	LVL	AGE	W	L	SV	G	GS	IP	H	HR	BB	SO	BB9	SO9	GB%	BABIP	WHIP	ERA	FIP	FRA	WARP
2011	WAS	MLB	23	6	3	43	73	0	75¹	57	8	20	74	2.4	8.8	48%	.246	1.02	2.75	3.29	3.73	0.7
2012	WAS	MLB	24	3	1	4	37	0	30¹	22	0	8	24	2.4	7.1	52%	.265	0.99	2.37	2.44	2.59	0.7
2013	WAS	MLB	25	4	2	3	68	0	61²	65	7	19	58	2.8	8.5	44%	.319	1.36	4.52	3.59	3.99	0.6
2014	WAS	MLB	26	3	1	3	62	0	60²	50	5	17	59	2.5	8.8	44%	.293	1.10	2.96	3.24	3.22	1.1

On July 24th, with game one of a doubleheader out of hand, Storen was called upon to save the rest of the bullpen's bullets. Single, double, home run, 11-0 final score, and next thing you know Storen was in the minors.

This didn't go over well. The pitcher had required an IV earlier in the game, and Storen's father tweeted, "102 degree temperature, sicker than a dog...Let's make him wear it!" Teammate Tyler Clippard sounded off on the demotion and criticized the club's decision to strip Storen of the closing job the previous offseason. "He's only human. It's going to get to anybody," Clippard said after the nightcap. And here is, in a nutshell, the paradox of the modern closer: Having a closer is supposed to make everybody more comfortable. Managers like to have defined roles, predictable patterns, a man for the seventh, a man for the eighth and a man for the ninth, because the players themselves say they are better when they know their roles and can anticipate the call. But putting somebody in a role that, decades of save-counting have shown us, typically has a very short tenure ensures this sort of drama: perceived insults, disrespect and, ultimately, *un*comfortable team dynamics. Consider it the Closing Time problem: Every new beginning comes from some other beginning's end.

Whether the Nationals erred by letting Storen "wear it" that day, the pitcher's performance all season justified the demotion. Storen moved away from his sinker last year—from 40 percent usage to 27 percent, while relying on his changeup more often—and suffered for it. He had the worst groundball rate of his career, and predictably allowed the most home runs, too, plumping up his ERA and FIP to further career worsts. When he returned from Triple-A three weeks later, he had a bit of a leg kick and an aggressive four-seam/slider approach. He didn't allow a homer in 19 innings the rest of the way.

Stephen Strasburg

Born: **7/20/1988** Age: **25**
Bats: **R** Throws: **R** Height: **6' 4"** Weight: **200**
Breakout: **24%** Improve: **60%** Collapse: **19%**
Attrition: **10%** MLB: **99%**

Comparables:
Yovani Gallardo, Tim Lincecum, Clayton Kershaw

YEAR	TEAM	LVL	AGE	W	L	SV	G	GS	IP	H	HR	BB	SO	BB9	SO9	GB%	BABIP	WHIP	ERA	FIP	FRA	WARP
2011	WAS	MLB	22	1	1	0	5	5	24	15	0	2	24	0.8	9.0	43%	.250	0.71	1.50	1.24	2.55	0.7
2012	WAS	MLB	23	15	6	0	28	28	159¹	136	15	48	197	2.7	11.1	43%	.325	1.15	3.16	2.87	3.17	3.9
2013	WAS	MLB	24	8	9	0	30	30	183	136	16	56	191	2.8	9.4	51%	.260	1.05	3.00	3.18	4.12	1.7
2014	WAS	MLB	25	10	7	0	28	28	155¹	117	13	41	175	2.3	10.2	49%	.293	1.02	2.54	2.88	2.76	4.2

The remnant gloom of 2012's shutdown combined with a losing record in 2013 left many fans discouraged with Strasburg's season. That's not nearly fair to Strasburg, as he continued his return from Tommy John surgery by throwing 24 more innings while allowing the same number of hits. His strikeouts remained in elite territory and his walks better than league average. He upped his groundball percentage by pounding the lower third of the zone, even as he relied on pitches other than his sinker to get outs. The next step on Strasburg's road to acedom is 200 innings pitched. It's a benchmark he should reach easily in 2014, our ability to jinx things in these pages being notably weak.

Austin Voth

Born: **6/26/1992** Age: **22**
Bats: **R** Throws: **R** Height: **6' 1"** Weight: **190**
Breakout: **48%** Improve: **90%** Collapse: **10%**
Attrition: **72%** MLB: **12%**

Comparables:
Bruce Billings, Justin Wilson, Zach Phillips

YEAR	TEAM	LVL	AGE	W	L	SV	G	GS	IP	H	HR	BB	SO	BB9	SO9	GB%	BABIP	WHIP	ERA	FIP	FRA	WARP
2013	HAG	A	21	1	0	0	2	2	10²	8	0	2	9	1.7	7.6	41%	.250	0.94	3.38	2.36	3.58	0.1
2013	AUB	A-	21	2	0	0	7	7	30²	21	0	4	42	1.2	12.3	46%	.313	0.82	1.47	0.85	2.22	1.1
2014	WAS	MLB	22	2	3	0	8	8	35²	37	4	16	26	4.2	6.5	44%	.315	1.51	4.99	4.67	5.42	-0.2

Pegged as a reliever by many, the stout Voth performed well out of the chute, compiling a 1.75 ERA across three levels and 46 innings in his pro debut. The fifth-round pick attacks hitters with a fastball and ... well, *other* fastballs. He throws both a two- and four-seam fastball that play up due to his ability to command to all parts of the zone. He mixes in the occasional slider or changeup, but they lag behind the rest of his game. There are pitchers—really good ones—who thrive in the majors with little more than a fastball, but Voth's best bet is to develop at least one secondary pitch.

Jordan Zimmermann

Born: **5/23/1986** Age: **28**
Bats: **R** Throws: **R** Height: **6' 2"** Weight: **220**
Breakout: **20%** Improve: **57%** Collapse: **24%**
Attrition: **3%** MLB: **93%**

Comparables:
James Shields, Dave Bush, Jeremy Bonderman

YEAR	TEAM	LVL	AGE	W	L	SV	G	GS	IP	H	HR	BB	SO	BB9	SO9	GB%	BABIP	WHIP	ERA	FIP	FRA	WARP
2011	WAS	MLB	25	8	11	0	26	26	161¹	154	12	31	124	1.7	6.9	40%	.296	1.15	3.18	3.13	3.81	1.8
2012	WAS	MLB	26	12	8	0	32	32	195²	186	18	43	153	2.0	7.0	43%	.292	1.17	2.94	3.55	3.83	3.1
2013	WAS	MLB	27	19	9	0	32	32	213¹	192	19	40	161	1.7	6.8	48%	.281	1.09	3.25	3.33	3.98	2.5
2014	WAS	MLB	28	11	10	0	30	30	179¹	165	18	37	144	1.9	7.2	44%	.295	1.13	3.44	3.63	3.74	2.3

Zimmermann's most recent step toward completion was to go deeper into games, as he added 18 innings to his total while making the same number of starts. Further, he faced 60 more batters while throwing six *fewer* pitches. While he'll never rank among the elite when it comes to strikeouts, Zimmermann's strikeout-to-walk ratio was healthy thanks to his phenomenal control. With his 19 wins leading the National League, it's unlikely that Zimmermann continues to fly below other fantasy owners' radars, but he might still be undervalued—his minor-league numbers suggest there could be more strikeouts in that arm, if Zimmermann desires them.

LINEOUTS

HITTERS

PLAYER	TEAM	LVL	AGE	PA	R	2B	3B	HR	RBI	BB	SO	SB-CS	AVG/OBP/SLG	TAv	BABIP	BRR	FRAA	WARP
1B M. Gomez	BUF	AAA	28	453	58	21	1	29	73	43	131	2-2	.249/.322/.521	.281	.290	-3.1	1B(60): -1.6, 3B(10): 0.1	0.9
LF J. Kobernus	SYR	AAA	25	412	59	19	2	1	36	28	59	42-9	.318/.366/.388	.283	.373	3.7	LF(49): -2.4, 2B(15): 2.8	2.3
	WAS	MLB	25	36	8	0	0	1	1	5	6	3-2	.167/.306/.267	.216	.174	0.5	LF(6): 0.0, CF(3): -0.0	0.0
C S. Leon	HAR	AA	24	361	35	12	1	3	26	47	57	0-0	.177/.291/.252	.216	.207	1.4	C(93): -1.0	0.2
	WAS	MLB	24	1	0	0	0	0	0	0	1	0-0	.000/.000/.000	.006	—	0	C(1): -0.0	0.0
LF E. Martinez	HAG	A	21	410	57	22	1	4	48	36	74	20-4	.253/.324/.352	.264	.303	1.4	LF(47): -0.5, 1B(33): -0.5	0.8
RF B. Miller	HAG	A	23	442	62	26	2	18	72	34	135	3-1	.243/.308/.456	.286	.313	1.2	RF(99): -1.3, LF(2): -0.2	2.3
	POT	A+	23	120	11	6	3	2	16	7	29	3-1	.300/.350/.464	.278	.388	-2.1	LF(16): -0.2, RF(10): 1.1	0.4
1B B. Peterson	MEM	AAA	29	508	69	30	1	25	86	44	114	1-1	.296/.364/.531	.317	.345	-0.6	1B(118): -3.1	3.4
	SLN	MLB	29	28	0	0	0	0	2	2	11	0-0	.077/.143/.077	.166	.133	0.1	LF(5): -0.1, 1B(4): 0.0	-0.2
2B T. Renda	HAG	A	22	606	99	43	3	3	51	68	65	30-6	.294/.380/.405	.309	.328	8.5	2B(117): 11.4	7.0
3B M. Skole	POT	A+	22	76	11	10	1	0	12	5	17	1-0	.314/.355/.486	.298	.407	0.6	3B(12): -0.0	0.6
C J. Solano	SYR	AAA	27	148	9	7	1	0	10	5	17	0-0	.214/.245/.279	.185	.242	-1.3	C(37): 0.3	-0.5
	WAS	MLB	27	50	2	2	0	0	2	2	7	0-1	.146/.180/.188	.114	.171	0	C(19): -0.3	-0.7
3B C. Tracy	WAS	MLB	33	136	6	4	0	4	11	7	25	0-2	.202/.243/.326	.209	.220	-1.9	3B(14): -0.3, 1B(10): -0.1	-0.5

Another graduate of their Dominican program, **Rafael Bautista** doesn't pack much of a punch but has the makings of a classic tablesetter. ⊘ **Mauro Gomez**'s swing-and-miss certainly qualifies him as a flawed player but his 29 home runs represent an increasingly rare asset: power off the bench. ⊘ While gamer, grinder and baseball rat can all describe **Jeff Kobernus**, the second-generation major leaguer does have a legitimate plus tool in his speed. It's unclear whether the tangible or the intangible will do more to help him reach his utilityman ceiling. ⊘ Defensive specialist **Sandy Leon**'s offensive line is putrid enough to become a filthy euphemism. You've probably even performed a Sandy Leon on a passed-out friend before, you knave. ⊘ **Estarlin Martinez** spent three years in Rookie ball and his stat line didn't sparkle in his first year at Low-A, but he has the athleticism and power to earn his keep moving up. ⊘ Age is working against **Brandon Miller** but the corner outfielder boasts impressive power and intriguing athleticism. ⊘ **Brock Peterson** earned a chance to be a key bench bat after a huge season with Memphis, but he sputtered in 28 sporadic plate appearances. He has hit throughout his minor-league career so he should and will get another shot. ⊘ While old for his level, **Tony Renda** has more in his toolbag than just the heart, grit and hustle that earned him the Nationals' inaugural Bob Boone Award for hearty, hustly grit. ⊘ It's not often a first baseman suffers a torn UCL, but when an errant throw led **Matt Skole** into a runner that's exactly what happened. The 24-year old will return to Double-A in 2014. ⊘ In 24 games, **Jhonatan Solano** accrued more GIDPs than extra-base hits and ended the season with an OPS+ of 2. ⊘ Led by **Chad Tracy**, the Nationals' reserves held a season-long campaign to rebrand themselves the new cast of "Living Single." No member of the Punch-and-Judy bench eclipsed a .400 slugging percentage.

PITCHERS

PLAYER	TEAM	LVL	AGE	W	L	SV	IP	H	HR	BB	SO	BB9	SO9	GB%	BABIP	WHIP	ERA	FIP	FRA	WARP
A. Barrett	HAR	AA	25	1	1	26	50^1	40	2	15	69	2.7	12.3	54%	.325	1.09	2.15	1.99	2.55	1.5
X. Cedeno	SYR	AAA	26	2	0	4	34^1	23	2	16	45	4.2	11.8	51%	.276	1.14	1.31	2.83	3.43	0.6
	HOU	MLB	26	0	0	0	6^1	10	0	7	3	9.9	4.3	56%	.400	2.68	11.37	6.39	7.31	-0.2
	WAS	MLB	26	0	0	0	6	5	0	1	6	1.5	9.0	69%	.312	1.00	1.50	1.52	2.94	0.1
E. Davis	SYR	AAA	26	3	7	15	52^1	55	4	20	54	3.4	9.3	58%	.333	1.43	3.10	3.28	4.08	0.7
	WAS	MLB	26	1	0	0	8^2	10	0	1	12	1.0	12.5	56%	.391	1.27	3.12	0.60	1.63	0.4
C. Kimball	SYR	AAA	27	0	0	1	25^2	31	4	14	25	4.9	8.8	35%	.370	1.75	8.06	4.92	6.59	-0.4
Y. Maya	SYR	AAA	31	8	8	0	146^1	157	10	31	99	1.9	6.1	53%	.307	1.28	3.87	3.44	4.52	0.9
	WAS	MLB	31	0	1	0	0^1	2	1	0	0	0.0	0.0	%	.500	6.00	54.00	42.02	37.30	-0.2
B. Mooneyham	HAG	A	23	10	3	0	93	50	5	41	79	4.0	7.6	50%	.189	0.98	1.94	3.93	4.71	0.4
	POT	A+	23	0	3	0	11^1	17	2	13	6	10.3	4.8	33%	.366	2.65	13.50	8.03	10.76	-0.4
T. Robertson	ROC	AAA	25	2	0	1	20^2	22	0	16	20	7.0	8.7	49%	.373	1.84	3.05	3.59	3.24	0.5
	SYR	AAA	25	2	2	1	26^2	33	2	8	24	2.7	8.1	57%	.365	1.54	3.04	3.28	6.44	0.0
	MIN	MLB	25	0	0	0	1	1	1	0	2	0.0	18.0	50%	.000	1.00	9.00	12.08	21.92	-0.2
B. Treinen	HAR	AA	25	6	7	0	118^2	125	9	33	86	2.5	6.5	58%	.312	1.33	3.64	3.79	4.33	1.3

Serving as closer at Double-A Harrisburg, **Aaron Barrett** posted elite strikeout numbers thanks to a solid fastball and slider that causes batters to sell out. Until his promotion, he'll be some small pond's real big fish.   Despite throwing only 12 innings between two teams, **Xavier Cedeno** managed to pull off two distinct seasons, posting a 1.50 ERA with Washington compared to an 11.37 ERA in Houston.   A strong season at Triple-A earned **Erik Davis** a brief call-up in June; he'll be in the mix for a long call-up with a strong spring.   **Cole Kimball**'s return from a torn rotator cuff went quickly out of control at Triple-A. If he can regroup, he'll be reunited with an old friend: his 1.93 career ERA in the majors.   At 32 years old, **Yunesky Maya** cemented himself as the less-famous, more-Cuban version of Hideki Irabu. His 2013 big-league campaign: lineout, single, homer.   **Brett Mooneyham** was drafted three times before signing, and he still trails his father in that category by two. With the ceiling of a mid-rotation starter, the big lefty has size, bloodlines and underwhelming stuff.   A soft-tossing lefty with a solid curveball and the upside of a LOOGY, **Tyler Robertson** was snapped off waivers from Minnesota, which should tell you everything you need to know.   **Jefry Rodriguez**'s stateside debut was largely a success, as the lanky right-hander improved on both his strikeout and walk rates.   Acquired as part of the trade that sent Michael Morse to Seattle, **Blake Treinen** has the upside of a back-end starter but, realistically, the future of a middle reliever.

MANAGER: MATT WILLIAMS

Davey Johnson heads out to pasture as the all-time greatest opponent of the intentional walk. Last year was the seventh time a Johnson-run squad finished last in IBBs per inning pitched. It happened once with every team he managed, except Baltimore.

He always liked leaning on his main players, and 2013 was no different. Washington's main eight position players accounted for 70.5 of the team's PA. That ranks third in the NL. Washington has finished in the top four each year that Johnson ran the team for the entire season.

Replacement Matt Williams will be 48 years old in 2014. By that age, Johnson had already been fired from the Mets after six-plus seasons and nearly 600 wins. People tend to break into the managerial ranks a little older these days.

The Unwritten Essay

By Grant Brisbee

On June 10th, Matt Joyce hit a long foul ball against John Lackey. The Rays outfielder crushed an inside pitch, but it was obviously foul—the kind of drama-free fly ball that's pretty to look at, even if it was clear before the ball left the infield that it was going to be wide by plenty.

Joyce got caught between the split-second of hope and reality, and he did an odd dance, part bat flip and part aw-dangit pirouette. When he grounded out to end the inning, Lackey barked at Joyce. Then he turned and barked at the Rays' dugout. The message was clear: *Don't do some weird bat-flip-aw-dangit pirouette when* I'm *on the mound, pal.*

Somewhere, on another plane, a diligent, slow-moving, elderly man got up from his seat and shuffled over to an enormous, hide-covered ledger. He dipped his quill in the ink of the ages, and he wrote the transgression down in impeccable penmanship. *Unwritten rule, MCLVI: Don't react too fantastically to long foul balls.* It took him two hands to close the book, and the dull thud echoed through the halls.

Here, in this existence, the rule wasn't written down. Because it wasn't a rule, really. Lackey made it up on the spot. But it was now an unwritten rule, and it fell under the subheading of "Don't show up the opponent." Later in the game, Lackey hit Joyce with a pitch. Benches cleared. Relievers sprinted in from both bullpens. Guys in pajamas pushed each other and said naughty words. The unwritten rule that didn't specifically exist before the pitch was now unwritten in stone. If Joyce does it again, it'll be another plunking. And how. Baseball loves its unwritten rules.

Baseball isn't the only sport with unwritten rules. It's just the only sport that devotes so much time to the mythology and enforcement of them. A comparison of the unwritten rules and their punishments across different sports:

Basketball

Transgression: Jacking up a three-point shot with a big lead in the last minute of the game, possibly to accomplish an individual achievement, like 50 points or a triple-double

Punishment: Everyone shakes their head at the offending player and makes fun of him

Football

Transgression: Aggressively trying to force a fumble when the opposing team is kneeling down and running out the clock

Punishment: Everyone shakes their head at the offending coach and makes fun of him

Baseball

Transgression: Going first-to-third on a single with a nine-run lead in the eighth inning

Punishment: A rock-hard projectile is fired at the offender's person at speeds upward of 90 mph, which can cause serious injury and/or death

Seems fair. There's no way of definitively explaining why baseball takes these things more seriously than other sports. One explanation might be that baseball is a sport that allows the players to stand around, inactive, for large swaths of the game, thinking, "Did he disrespect my teammate? Wait, did he just disrespect *me*?"

Another explanation might be that baseball spends more time scribbling "♥♥♥America's Pastime♥♥♥" in the margins of its homework than the other sports do. If you had to guess which sport gazes at itself in the mirror most often, it's clearly baseball. With that self-importance comes the right way, and actually writing down the *right way* is gauche because everyone should know it by now. Everyone played the game as a child, after all. For it is America's Pastime, and playing it the right way is important.

Which means there are unwritten rules. Glorious, glorious unwritten rules that some people take seriously and others don't. Did you know that someone peed in a baseball pool in 2013? Someone peed in a baseball pool. You'd better believe that's against some unwritten rules. And possibly Arizona state law. Also, as a reminder, there's a baseball-related pool now.

For the most part, though, the unwritten rules of 2013 weren't too unusual. There was no Mo Vaughn or George Foster hanging out in the dugout during a fight, and there was no Alex Rodriguez jogging across another man's dirt. Bat flips, dinger stare-downs, and you-hit-our-guys-so-we'll-hit-yours were the biggest unwritten-rule related happenings. It almost sounds boring, except it was a pretty cool year for unwritten rules.

Let's hand out some awards for the 2013 season, then. Here are some special achievements in the genre of unwritten rules last year, both in the infractions and sanctions categories.

Home run stare-down of the year

It's probably against the unwritten rules to give a pitcher this award, but I'm not scared of a little retaliation. On September 11th, Jose Fernandez of the Miami Marlins had the best homer stare-down of the season. He had one of the best stare-downs you'll ever see. It was an all-timer, bat flipped, mouth agape, looking up at the ball like it morphed into the star child at the end of 2001: *A Space Odyssey mid-flight*.

There's a backstory, of course. There always is. Evan Gattis hit a homer earlier in the game and pretty much had the same reaction, dialed down to about a 6 or 7. Chris Johnson had some weird jawing match with Fernandez throughout the game, and he also made McKayla faces after several Fernandez fastballs. So, yeah, there was youthful brashness behind the stare-down, but there was also in-game context.

The youthful brashness doesn't hurt, though. Fernandez is 20 and better at throwing baseballs than almost anyone reading this will be at anything in their lives. Then he *hit* a baseball better than almost anyone alive can, and he got to watch it arc and sail into that teal goodnight, a feeling that none of us will never know. I can't imagine what I would do if I did something like that now. I certainly can't imagine what I would have done when I was 20. A 20-year-old should be praised if he avoids riding his bat around the bases like a small horse. And that's before noting the context in the previous paragraph.

Fernandez also spit at Johnson's feet while rounding third. Seems like that one should be written down.

Most pointless invocation of unwritten rules

On June 11th, Gerrit Cole hit Gregor Blanco with a pitch. Later in the game, Marco Scutaro was hit on the hand by a Tony Watson pitch, breaking his pinky. Nothing about those last two sentences should seem off to you. They should seem like a partial account of a baseball game.

There's an unwritten stipulation to the unwritten rules, though. And it's that you know unwritten rules are broken when you know unwritten rules are broken. Basically, the unwritten rules are a priggish Calvinball, and everyone gets to make it up as they go along. For Giants manager Bruce Bochy, two players accidentally hit in the same game is probably acceptable, but only when both of those players are uninjured. When one of the hit batsmen is injured, as Scutaro was, that meant an unwritten rule was broken. And the only way to punish the breaking of an unwritten rule is to wing a baseball at another man's butt.

So reliever George Kontos hit Andrew McCutchen in the butt with a baseball.

Andrew *McCutchen*, people. Hitting him on purpose is like being angry at crosswalks. Who would do that? Bruce Bochy, apparently. Because it's all fun and games until somebody gets hurt, at which point it becomes an unwritten travesty.

Unwritten Cy Young

Zack Greinke is an unassuming fellow. He's a little odd, but mostly quiet. For whatever reason, though, he was at the center of several unwritten rules in 2013.

The first is when he hit Carlos Quentin in April, violating Quentin's unwritten rule of "stop hitting me so damned much." Quentin went out and broke Greinke's clavicle. That was more of a standard brawl than an unwritten-rules violation, but it was some good foreshadowing.

On June 11th, Cody Ross wasn't hit by Greinke's pitch. He convinced home-plate umpire Clint Fagan that he was hit, though, and he would score on a Jason Kubel homer. Several innings later, Greinke's teammate Yasiel Puig was (actually) hit by a pitch. The combination of the two made Greinke a little annoyed, so he chucked one at Miguel Montero.

Does that read like a he-said-she-said account of a middle-school argument? Good, it should. It's stupid. But fascinating. To this point, there weren't really any unwritten rules being mocked. Just a lot of dudes winging baseballs at other dudes for no good reason.

In retaliation, though, Ian Kennedy threw at Greinke's head. That's a written rule, mind you. It's also serious enough to be unwritten and double-secret written in addition to being written. Don't throw at people's heads. Don't ignore the careers of Dickie Thon and Tony Conigliaro. Don't forget about Ray Chapman. Don't throw at heads. If you think you're going to miss, don't throw at people on purpose.

The ensuing fight was a doozy, with Alan Trammell, Mark McGwire, Don Mattingly, Kirk Gibson, and Matt Williams all mixing it up on the field in addition to the players. It was like someone put a can filled with Starting Lineup figures in a paint mixer. Punches were thrown, obscenities were uttered. For the second time that season, Greinke was involved in one of the best/worst fights in the league. The biggest unwritten-rule violations didn't come from him, but was rather directed at him. It doesn't matter who did what; if you're involved in a collarbone-breaking fight just months before you cause a scuffle between the front page of my baseball-card binder from the '80s, you're the Unwritten Cy Young.

Then after the brawl, Greinke took out Didi Gregorious on a fielder's choice that had no chance to be a double play. Gregorious laughed and shook his head in disgust. There was almost certainly an unwritten rule violated there. But everyone already gave at the office. There was only so much caring for unwritten rules on that day.

Unwritten MVP

Yasiel Puig plays baseball as if he's scared the baseball will run out, as if at any second the sky will open up and the baseball gods will descend and take baseball away. He's right, in a way. That's exactly what happened to Ted Williams, Barry Bonds and Mickey Mantle. It's going to happen to

Mike Trout and Bryce Harper. One day, the baseball will run out for everyone.

Puig also plays like he's being chased by the thing that crawled out of the TV in *The Ring*. He plays like he sat in a pile of baby gators, like he's wearing electric underwear, like there was habanero paste on his loofah, like …

You get the idea. Puig plays hard. And that brings us to a surprise unwritten rule: Dude, calm down. Puig is constantly whirling around the bases, trying to turn second basemen into liquid and attempting to make other players look foolish. He'll miss cutoff men because he's above the unwritten rules of how to win baseball games, too, and danged if he isn't right some of the time.

But if Puig's only transgression was playing like a freak, he wouldn't receive consideration for the Unwritten MVP. Luckily, though, he excels in several other areas, like bat-flipping, homer stare-downs and glaring at any teammates who dare to cut off one of his throws. Yet even though he's an excellent stare-down artist, he also has one of the very fastest times around the bases this year—16.91 seconds on a June 4th homer, according to Larry Granillo of TaterTrotTracker.com. That's just two seconds slower than Angel Pagan's inside-the-park homer a month earlier.

Puig doesn't make sense. He's reminiscent of the Kris Kristofferson lyrics—"He's a walking contradiction/partly truth and partly fiction/partly insane, probably standing behind you/run, go, get help/for the love of all that is holy, get help." More importantly, he's *fascinating*. If the purpose of the unwritten rules is to make people like him snap into shape, then the unwritten rules aren't really making baseball as fun as it could be. There needs to be one Puig at all times. We didn't even know this until there was our first Puig.

There isn't a runner-up. Puig made more stodgy people upset in a week than the rest of baseball did all year.

Unwritten Team of the Year

The Dodgers had both the Unwritten Cy Young and Unwritten MVP, and they also peed in a pool. True story: The whole reason there are unwritten rules in the first place is because when Cap Anson and John McGraw sat down to write them down, a bunch of clubhouse jokers kept shouting nonsense suggestions at them. "Don't keep a parrot on your shoulder during an at-bat." "Don't wink at the pitcher three times in less than five seconds." "Don't pee in the pool just past the outfield fence." Finally they gave up and

figured everyone would know the rules even if they weren't written down.

Yet the Dodgers are not the Unwritten Team of the Year. No, it was close, but no team did more to advance the unwritten rule than the Atlanta Braves, bless their curmudgeonly hearts. The Braves are filled with players who play the game the right way, or think they do, or at least get annoyed super-easy. Brian McCann hasn't seen a movie in three years because he's too busy looking out for people checking their phones in the theater.

That's the reputation, anyway, and it was forged by the Braves being in the middle of seemingly every unwritten-rules maelstrom within a two-month period. Bryce Harper hit a long homer, followed by a stare-down? Braves are plunkin'. Jose Fernandez watched his homer until the center-field sculpture stopped its show? Braves are plunkin'. Carlos Gomez staring at the pitcher from the on-deck circle, walking halfway down the line after a home run, and yelling at people? Oh, you'd better believe the Braves are plunkin'.

Except, hold on, is that really fair? There isn't a team in baseball that wouldn't bristle at what Gomez and Fernandez did. The unwritten indiscretion might be in the eye of the beholder, but those two did amazing work in the field of annoying the other team on purpose. Sure, McCann blocking home plate so Gomez couldn't cross after his homer was … unexpected. And a little extreme. But the idea that the Braves are self-appointed guardians of the unwritten rule is a little much. They just got caught in the middle of a couple amazing stare-downs.

Still, the Braves were in the middle of the unwritten storm several times. They did not ask for this duty; this duty asked for them. They're the Unwritten Team of the Year.

The award winners will all win a beautiful untrophy that I will never mail to them. Congratulations, all. And thanks to everyone for taking themselves and the game of baseball so danged seriously. If everyone watched their home runs and flipped their bats, baseball would be that much more boring. It takes the unwritten rules to make the scofflaws stand out.

And baseball's better for it. Baseball's more exciting when the occasional unwritten rule gets broken. The anger comes and goes quickly, like a meteor burning up in the atmosphere, and it's brilliant, violent and beautiful in moderation. All hail the unwritten rules, the mavericks who break them, and the short-tempered heroes who are forever seeking unwritten justice.

Grant Brisbee is a writer for SB Nation at McCovey Chronicles and Baseball Nation.

N=1

By Russell A. Carleton

Pick a player. What do you know about him? No, I don't mean the lovely human interest stories about the quirky hobbies or his tastes in steak or the story about that one time at band camp. What do you know about what makes him tick as a baseball player? How does he make decisions? Are there patterns that he falls into? Are there weaknesses that can be exploited in his game?

Well?

When you have a hammer, everything looks like a nail, and when you have a big data set, everything looks like a question that can be answered with a large N database query. Sure, there are lots of nails out there that have been pounded down and are still left to pound down, but for those of us who research baseball, I worry that we've grown a little too attached to our hammers. Just about every piece of Sabermetric research contains some variation of the line "I looked for *all* players who…" When you want to tell a story about all players, that's a perfectly reasonable place to start. What's concerning is that they all seem to start there, particularly when it doesn't have to.

Often, I'll be listening to interviews with people who know the game well, and the interviewer will ask a question that starts with "When is the proper time to…" or "How can you tell if a player is…" The answer usually starts with some form of "Well, it depends a lot on the player…" No one thinks this is a strange answer. Yes, sometimes saying "It depends…" is a polite way of saying "I have no idea," but there's a general understanding that players differ from one another. Maybe they differ in ways that are complex and hard to pin down in regressions, but they differ. The folks who research baseball, myself included, will acknowledge this, but then we rarely adjust our research methods to address the issue. Figuring out the best pitch to throw early in the count and the best pitch to throw to *Smith* early in the count are two separate questions, and knowing the answer to the first may not help you very much with the second. Not only that, but there are situations when the answer to the second question would be much more important.

Like when Smith is in the batter's box.

Large N database queries tell you how "baseball players" or some sub-group of them (pitchers, hitters, guys with more than seven letters in their last names) perform. They can reveal larger truths about how human beings—or at least baseball players—behave given a certain set of conditions. Left-handed hitters, as a group, fare worse against left-handed pitching than right-handed pitching. There's a certain geometry to the game, and the angle that a left-handed pitcher throws from is harder to pick up than that of a right-handed pitcher. Looking at all players as a collective tells us something bigger about the game of baseball. Some guys have bigger platoon splits than others, but the platoon effect usually (but, not always!) points the same way. Large N works great in situations like that.

Let's play with the possibilities a bit. What happens when there is some variable that makes some hitters better, some worse, and for some it just doesn't have an effect. In a large N database model, a standard ordinary least squares (OLS) regression might find that there's no overall effect for that variable, because the good and bad wash each other out. A researcher might come across that regression and think that there's nothing to be gained from looking at the matter further. In doing so, he's missed a variable that moves the needle quite a bit, just not in a consistent manner across all players. Large N models are good at discovering large, aggregate truths in baseball (and the rest of life), and those can be good to know about. But when it comes to setting a strategy, teams do not send an amalgamation of all MLB hitters to the plate. They send a guy with a specific last name stitched onto the back of his jersey. Is he one of the hitters who tends to get better, worse, or stay the same in this situation? Large N won't help us here.

What if, instead of running an analysis with all players, we limited ourselves to just looking at plate appearances featuring only David Ortiz or just John Jay or strictly Nick Swisher. Sure, the data set would be smaller, but suddenly, a lot of those issues about players differing significantly from one another disappear. Big data isn't always the best answer. Sometimes, smaller, more personal data is better. Interestingly enough, this sort of design isn't completely foreign to baseball analysis. Announcers will often quote a player's splits (e.g., how he fared against lefties vs. righties) in describing a player or in discussing whether the manager is either brilliant or silly to bring in a lefty to face him. The problem with a lot of splits is that for a hitter who has 600 plate appearances, the announcer might be quoting his on-base percentage against righties based on a 350 PA sample, and against lefties based on 250 PA. I've done research on how many plate appearances it takes before a statistic becomes a reliable estimate of true talent. OBP, for example, takes about 460 PA before it reaches a point of reliability. In some sense, the announcer is comparing one unreliably small sample to another. But he is comparing one man against himself. While there may be concerns about measure reliability, there's little concern about the two samples being biased in some hidden way based on the people in each group. It's the same guy 600 times over.

But suppose that we could have the best of both worlds: the purity of a sample composed of a single player and enough statistical power that we could confidently draw conclusions. And on top of it, we could actually do something useful with it. A moment ago, I mentioned research that I had done on when various stats become reliable enough to be considered a true reflection of a hitter's talent level. For big-ticket numbers such as OBP or SLG, the answer is that it can take a few hundred plate appearances. The problem with OBP is that while the batter certainly has a say in whether he can draw a walk or hit the ball hard, there are other factors out there that might get in the way. Sometimes a player will hit the ball hard, but right at someone. Sometimes the defender makes a fantastic diving catch leaving the batter with a really loud out. When we come down to things that are much more within a batter's control, such as the decision of whether or not to swing, things are easier to estimate. For example, I've found that an estimate of a player's swing rate can become reliable within about 50 PA.

But what might affect a hitter's decision of whether or not to swing? Well, maybe he's feeling a little jumpy because the game is on the line. He might the kind of guy who gets nervous and starts hacking. He might be the kind of guy who gets nervous and gets super cautious because it really matters here. He might be the kind of guy for whom it doesn't matter. As the opposing pitcher (or manager), I might like to know that information. If I know a hitter won't swing at all, I can groove one down the middle for a strike. If I know for sure that he will swing, I can bounce a curve two feet in front of home plate and catch a nice breeze as the batter flails away.

Warning! Gory Mathematical Details Ahead!

Let's put together some data sets. Plural. I selected all players (see, I just did it…) who had more than 500 plate appearances (excluding intentional walks) in 2013. There were 139 such players. For each player, I created a data set of what he did in each plate appearance on the first pitch. Using just pitches on an 0–0 count controls for any count-related tendencies to swing (e.g., taking all the way on 3–0, needing to expand the strike zone with 2 strikes, or the fact that some guys have certain pitches that they like to swing on). I coded the pitch as either a swing (foul ball, ball in play, or swinging strike) or a take (ball, called strike). Since we know we have at least 500 observations per player, that should be plenty to power a regression.

(Side note: For the super-initiated, you are probably already mouthing abbreviations like GLM or HLM or MLM. Yes, we could go there, but not today.)

I used game leverage as a proxy for the importance of the situation. Leverage is a concept developed by researcher Tom Tango. It assigns a scalar value (1 is average, 2 is twice as important as the average situation, 0.5 is half as important) to each situation in a game, based on the inning, score, number of outs, and placement of any runners. It measures how much the probabilities of each team winning might shift as a result of what happens in this next at bat. Not surprisingly, situations that take place in the late innings of close games, particularly with runners on, have higher leverage values. Situations in 15–3 games have low leverage values because we already know who's going to win the game.

For each player, I ran a binary logistic regression (swing vs. no swing) as predicted by the leverage of the plate appearance. Each player gets his own regression, so it's the same overall tendency to swing on all the data points. The regression just tells us which way to tilt it for leverage. The results had a few surprises in them. Most players became more patient as the game becomes more tense, but not everyone. In fact, of the 139 players, 37 showed a significant tendency toward swinging more often in higher leverage situations, relative to how often they normally swing. No one had a statistically significant effect in the other direction (although a couple of hitters came close).

Below, we see the more extreme cases from 2013, again with a minimum of 500 PA, and in parentheses, their expected swing rate at a leverage index of 1 (a situation of average importance) and a leverage index of 2 (a situation twice as important as average).

Top 5 Hitters Who Become More Likely to Swing in High Leverage	Top 5 Hitters Who Become Less Likely to Swing in High Leverage	Top 5 Hitters Who Were Most Unaffected by Leverage
Justin Upton (32%, 48%)	Nate Schierholtz (28%, 23%)	Mitch Moreland (14%, 14%)
Kyle Seager (23%, 38%)	Nolan Arrenado (30%, 26%)	Adam Laroche (24%, 24%)
Matt Dominguez (23%, 37%)	Dan Uggla (32%, 28%)	Ben Zobrist (26%, 26%)
Adam Jones (42%, 55%)	Carlos Gomez (52%, 48%)	Jonathan Lucroy (14%, 14%)
Will Venable (29%, 42%)	Prince Fielder (29%, 25%)	Josh Hamilton (41%, 41%)

Justin Upton gets jumpy when faced with the first pitch of a big at bat. Nate Schierholtz gets more passive. Mitch Moreland apparently doesn't notice. But now, when setting a game plan against Justin Upton, a team has a little bit of extra information about how he changes with the game.

To make sure that these weren't just random fluctuations, I found all players who had at least 500 PA in 2012 and ran the same analyses. There were 87 players in both the 2012 and 2013 data sets. I calculated the predicted swing rates for both seasons in all 87 cases at a leverage value of 0.5, 1.0, and 2.0. Across those 87 players, the rates from 2012 and 2013 correlated at .89 for a leverage of 0.5, .88 for a leverage of 1.0, and .71 for a leverage of 2.0. These effects are rather consistent from year to year.

Little Data, Big Possibilities

We've just discovered some interesting things about some players. The kicker is that we only looked at one influencing variable (leverage) and its effect on one decision (whether or not to swing on a 0–0 pitch). Imagine if we looked at other variables and outcomes using this same N = 1 paradigm. Do certain hitters change their approach when facing certain types of pitchers? Do these same basic patterns hold for other counts? Is contact rate affected? Are there certain players who seem to show the same patterns across several of these types of analyses? Now, we can start to build a profile of a player, not just based on his splits, but on how the situation around him affects him. Our analyses will only be applicable to a single hitter (or pitcher… or manager) but they hold the potential to reveal a greater truth about him. Call it Saber-scouting, if you like.

I prefer to think of it in a different way. Maybe it's because of the emphasis on large N research that's been so prevalent across the discipline of Sabermetrics for so long, but the field has marginalized these types of individual differences. Maybe it's the fact that a lot of what Sabermetrics has set out to combat has been narrative-driven pseudo-research that relied on "just trust me" or sample sizes that are laughably small to make a point about a player. But we've come to ignore, or worse, dismiss the thought that players might react to situations in different ways. The point of Sabermetrics shouldn't be to destroy anything which smells of narrative, but to promote good, solid research methods in the study of baseball. There are perfectly good, methodologically sound ways to look at individual players and to find interesting things about them. This sort of research is something that Sabermetrics should already naturally be doing.

I'm often asked what I think "the next big thing" in Sabermetrics will be. It's an awful question, because there are about ten "next big things" and if I pick one, it makes me look as though I'm denying the power of the other nine. I think people who ask this are expecting some sort of major strategic response ("Look for guys with high OBPs, because they'll be underpriced!") I often answer that the next big thing is understanding how each player works, and instead of strategies that can be applied across entire organizations or in every situation, understanding the nuances of each player on a case-by-case basis. The applications from the team's point of view are obvious, and for those who wish to write publicly, it makes for some great long-form profile work analyzing a single player. So, if you're looking for a way to make your mark, maybe the best thing to do would be to brush up on some good ideographic research methodology, and shorten your data set to the smallest sample of all. N = 1.

The Metagame is Far From Solved

By Dan Brooks

"I laugh when I hear guys my dad's age: 'You guys got to shorten up and go to right.'
Well, okay, but you guys used to score 690 runs a year. We're scoring 800.
So somebody's doing something different." — Terry Francona, 2013

Prologue

As of this writing, Googling "Three True Outcomes" produces 27,000 results. On the first page are several articles that contain definitions of the term from Baseball-Reference, Baseball Prospectus and FanGraphs. Each of those pages will define the Three True Outcomes as the Strikeout, the Walk, and the Home Run—the three batter-pitcher confrontations that involve no fielders.

Also on the front page of results are articles from *The Hardball Times* (Alex Connors), *Sports Illustrated* (Joe Lemire) and *Baseball Nation* (Rob Neyer). The titles: "Are the three true outcomes too common?", "Early results show rate of Three True Outcomes on record pace" and "Three true outcomes are up: should something be done?"

Whether something should be done is much more complicated than whether we would like something to be done. This essay, instigated by those articles about the preponderance of certain player traits, explores the dynamics of choices in a strategic game. Baseball's relative balance—between the strategies that teams utilize to build their teams—happened neither by chance nor by fiat.

The Game of Building a Baseball Team

Baseball is an odd game. Despite being colloquially described as "the thinking man's game," it is fundamentally programmatic and instinctual. There is reaction and action, but not much calculation or creativity. There is little diversity in the arrangement of infielders, or in the construction of a lineup, or in the repertoire of most pitchers. There are strategies, and there are plays, but they are mostly common to the game of baseball and not really specific to particular teams. Players can be removed from one lineup and put in another with little thought to strategic consequence, in the sense that Miguel Cabrera or Mike Trout would almost certainly be similarly effective if they switched teams midseason.

On the other hand, building a baseball team is an incredibly creative and calculating game. It has been for decades, since Branch Rickey and Cy Slapnicka, through to Billy Beane and Theo Epstein. It has been played with varying strategies and levels of success. This hierarchically larger game—of fitting players into positions, projecting talent, signing players and finding efficiency—is antithetical to baseball's roots as a pastoral game with no clock and little violence. It is a frequently ruthless enterprise.

If you look at baseball history, and start in the relatively recent past—say, 50 or 60 years ago—the game has undergone change, but the most fundamental changes have occurred not on the field, but off. A good argument could be made that the game of designing baseball teams has changed much more than the game of baseball. These changes have affected the quality and kind of competition, but have not really affected the basic rules by which the game is played.

Baseball as a Competitive Game

Abstract away from baseball, and you'll find that game design is actually a notoriously difficult problem. There are thousands of games, with rulesets ranging from very simple to very complicated. There is a relatively simple truth to competitive game design: gamers (i.e., those people who play the game competitively) will, over time, identify and abuse every available mechanic and imbalance to win. Gamers will gravitate toward drafting the best players, playing the best characters, using the best plays.

This notion doesn't apply to all games or all kinds of players of competitive games. There are plenty of games that are meant to be played simply to be played, and the goal is the enjoyment derived from playing. Candyland and Pictionary can be played "just for fun." On the field, so can baseball. There is an intractable pull toward the game with a group of neighborhood kids, a stick and a pile of sunflower seeds. But major league baseball isn't that.

Even for those games with a rich competitive history, there are players who either aren't interested in playing competitively (not everyone aspires to be a chess champion) or don't find competitive play much fun to watch or participate in, players who consider certain effective strategies "cheap" or "lame" or not aesthetically pleasing. Major league baseball isn't this either—Rickey and Beane have more interest in winning than in playing with style, in making the game fun, in playing "fair."

Players in team design should naturally gravitate toward the strategies that abuse the rules. The goal is to win, and keep winning, at all costs. As the rules of the game become more clear and the conditions for winning more apparent, players should naturally drift toward emulating a specific set of strategies that have better results than other strategies.

Local Maxima

We'll call those advantageous points in the strategy space "local maxima": they increase the likelihood that the player will win, but do not guarantee victory. At any time, several local maxima may exist for any given player. Around these local maxima will emerge what is known as a "metagame": the "game of choosing available strategies to play within a game." The metagame evolves as new strategies or variations on old strategies are discovered and incorporated into the pool of available strategies, so what a player does reflects not only his own skill but his understanding of the current metagame (i.e., what his opponent is likely to do).

A baseball example of metagaming is the concept of designing a lineup to alternate hitter handedness to counter the availability of particularly dominant platoon pitchers in the opponent's bullpen. That might not be important in a game without LOOGYs, but since many teams employ a specialist reliever, you want to minimize the damage he can do late in a game. This concept has been around for some time—Rickey (in a challenge of baseball wits) once asked a scout why championship teams rarely have a lefty-hitting shortstop; the answer being that it is impossible to pinch-hit late in the game when the opposition brings in a lefty reliever because his defense is irreplaceable.

If games are left alone, metagames (and with them, balance) develop and change over the course of time as various play styles emerge. There is constant tension between local strategic maxima and metagaming. If you choose a strategy that beats 99 percent of other strategies but loses to one, other players adjust and you will be forced to vary your strategic choices. If you fill your roster with left-handed power hitters, opposing teams will choose left-handed pitchers to counter your strength. If you find a group of hitters that consistently hit hard groundballs through the infield, teams will shift their defense and force your hitters away from their comfort zones. Although you might have chosen objectively good players or constructed your roster with objectively good talent, the counters for those talents will dominate in the matchups you play.

Balance and the Metagame

The critical assumption at the beginning of this piece was that roster building and player development in baseball are a kind of game played with a set of pieces across a series of contests. In a sense, baseball is a deck-building game, in which players continually choose from a common pool of pieces that they will use in play. It's just an extraordinarily slow one. There is a recycling pool of players that turns over every 10 to 15 years. Your goal is to spend resources trying

to acquire players who you think are the best or who will complement each other best. There are a variety of strategies for doing so, and these strategies cost different kinds and amounts of resources. Teams choose different mixes of statistical analysis, scouting and player development in the quest to identify, acquire and maximize players.

Because of the way the amateur draft works and because of the inequality of resources spread among the players in this game, teams are often locked into a particular strategy or particular model of valuation for a long time, so there can be lag between taking over a seat at the table and acquiring the best pieces (look no further than the Houston Astros). A team might decide that patience is a skill they want to maximize, but it takes three or four years before they acquire a pool of available players who walk a lot. Or a team that decides to maximize stealing bases might currently lack speed.

Additionally, because of uncertainty around player attributes (is this guy a speed guy or a patience guy?) and those attributes' actual contributions to winning (is speed or patience more valuable?), and because attributes vary in cost (patience was once an afterthought; now it is very expensive), the game of roster building is immensely complex. The skill ceiling for designing a baseball roster is extraordinarily high.

Because players with different resources (e.g. salary, scouting and analysis budgets) are competing for the same thing, it makes objective sense for each organization to identify ways to build a deck that maximizes efficiency (wins or championships or star players developed per dollar). Rickey did so by signing dozens of players to participate in a vast minor-league system and illegally tearing up the contracts of those who couldn't cut it. Beane did it by signing dozens of players who were systematically undervalued by teams that did not embrace statistical analysis. George Steinbrenner did it by spending more money than anyone else to acquire exceptional talent. There is a diversity of strategies, and intelligent players will shift around the strategy space attempting to find a local maximum of efficient play while also keeping a close eye on how other teams are acting, either to copy or counter their strategies.

The Rational Player

Although this all seems perfectly obvious to everyone who accepts the "baseball roster construction is a game" metaphor, the game has undergone serious changes over the last 15 years. Before that, players had identified sustainable local maxima and a dynamic metagame had evolved around them, but the strategies they identified were far from the best strategies. This is not to say that current strategies are the best, but they are better than their predecessors. This is, at its heart, why we call these places in the strategy space local, not global, maxima.

Let's be honest—compared to today's team building, historical players in the game of roster construction did a poor job, including at identifying the true rules of the game (i.e. how to score and prevent runs), how to spend resources efficiently, how to determine which players were good and how to determine which attributes of players were important. In recent years, as baseball has incorporated more rigorous statistical analysis, player evaluation, scouting methods and player development systems, particular strategies have become more popular. Teams have begun to play the game of roster building more rationally.

Some of these strategies produce teams that are aesthetically pleasing. Others do not. But there are a number of teams playing the game more effectively than their predecessors—they identify previously unknown local maxima and metagame strategies and attempt to rationally maximize their chances of winning. And, as this new knowledge infiltrates almost every front office, the game will continue to change.

The baseball metagame has reached an interesting place. There is an arms race for scouting and analytics. Teams are building rosters in strange, almost unimaginable ways. They're picking players who on the surface might seem poor at skills that poorly informed observers consider important (e.g. collecting RBIs, pitcher wins or saves). They're more aggressively scouting professional and amateur leagues so they can acquire players with what they perceive to be undervalued attributes. Teams like the Astros aren't spending all of their available resources each turn, instead saving some for next time. Things have turned weird.

Does this make for good baseball?

What I have described about strategy and metagaming is a sort of inevitable truth about complex, evolving systems. As games are often such complex systems, there is an inescapability to all of this. Teams with strong incentives will explore new strategies in the space and identify new maxima, around which new metagames will emerge. But as teams find these new pockets of undiscovered territory—by chance or by insight—the game on the field will evolve to reflect their new choices.

This is particularly relevant for today's game because a strategy has recently emerged that seems to favor aesthetically unpleasing baseball players. Broadly, these can be thought of as Three True Outcomes players—hitters who walk, hit home runs and strike out. Certain independent factors have favored these outcomes on both the offensive and defensive sides of the ball. Because they are kind of boring events, people suggest that baseball should do something about the increase in TTOs: real baseball, fun baseball—as it was intended to be played by the designers (!)—involves people running around on a grassy field chasing a ball around, not simply watching it sail over their heads or into the catcher's glove.

This is a dangerous place for any game designer. There are rules and conditions for winning. The game is essentially "balanced"—although teams invest vastly different amounts of resources, they putatively have the same possible set of strategies at their disposal (the Astros could shrug their shoulders and decide to be the Yankees of the southwest for the foreseeable future, while the Yankees could decide to sell the majority of their payroll and rebuild through the draft). The problem is aesthetics. This is tricky ground, because aesthetics are essentially at the heart of the business model that surrounds the game—no matter how complex or unsolved or interesting the game is, it isn't going to survive if people don't enjoy watching it.

It is a trivial argument to say that personal preferences do not apply to everyone watching. It is also trivial to point out that we have no particular ability to divine the intent of baseball's designers. For the sake of argument, suppose that the TTOs are an aesthetic problem, and that fans will leave the game because they find them boring, and that the original intent of the designers of baseball was not to have these outcomes dominate play.

Back to the Strategy Space

If we've accepted that we want to change the game to minimize the TTOs, we're admitting that the strategies teams are using to win are undesirable. Proposed solutions exist: deadening the ball (to reduce home run rates), shrinking the strike zone (to reduce strikeout rates, though at the cost of increased walk rates) or lowering the mound (presumably to lower strikeout rates). All of these proposed solutions to the game—which I think are the only ones we should seriously consider—would not fundamentally alter the rules, but adjust them at the margins. Although more dramatic solutions could certainly be proposed, most would strain credulity.

Blake Murphy has shown the trends in the TTOs through history at *Beyond the Box Score*. Interestingly, despite the recent recognition of on-base ability as a critical offensive weapon, the two outcomes that have risen most steadily are strikeouts and home runs.

Suppose that, suddenly, strikeout rates dropped because the strike zone was tightened. (This is not an absurd proposal; the zone has repeatedly been "corrected" throughout baseball's history.) It is near-certain that the new zone would differentially affect classes of hitters and pitchers. For example, power pitchers who rely on overwhelming the hitter with hard fastballs or changes in speed might be much less affected than finesse pitchers who rely on deception and command of the zone. Assuming walks increase as a corollary result, are patient hitters now extremely valuable where they were only very valuable before? Is their value decreased because now anybody can work a walk? Are speedy players more valuable because they will get more stolen base attempts? Do power hitters or contact hitters benefit more from more hittable pitches?

In short, the strategy space will change. Previously good strategies might become less advantageous than before or become exceptionally good. As teams struggle to identify the new optimal strategies, the metagame breaks. How are you sure which players to draft if you're uncertain of the path to success? How do you know which players to trade? Are the ones you've spent three years acquiring suddenly worthless?

Suppose a team like the Astros that had spent several seasons compiling top draft talent suddenly found themselves in a position where the players they drafted were suboptimal players. Suppose a budget-bound team like the Mariners, who made a large splash when they signed Robinson Cano, suddenly found themselves with a far less valuable asset for the next 10 years. What happens if the terms of the Wil Myers-for-James Shields trade retroactively shift and hamstring either the Rays or the Royals, neither of whom can spend their way out of problems? This "unfair" outcome of changing the rules isn't just possible, it's essentially inevitable. Just as we've started to reward teams for pushing the limits of team construction and maximizing efficiency, we're going to do a hard pivot on all the players they've been collecting. Is this really how we want to help baseball develop?

Finally, what change will this really have on the game overall, regardless of how fair it might be to the players? I see three possibilities (or ranges of possibility, really):

There's the "optimistic" answer—that we'll make a small balance change, that TTOs will fall, and we'll come away with better, livelier baseball. This is essentially the best we can hope for, though even with this outcome, the unfairness described above still plays a major role.

There's also the possibility of short-term instability followed by a long-term return to a similarly frustrating area of the strategy space. Perhaps strikeouts will be down for a time, while finesse pitchers are still pitching in the majors, but with power pitching at a premium, maybe teams stop caring about guys who can throw a solid five-pitch mix and start caring exclusively about guys who throw 95 mph. If strikeouts are the true path to success, teams will shift their strategies to achieve that outcome in different ways. Ten years later, we might be back where we started, because although the player valuation model changed, the fundamental strategy ("get guys who can strike people out") did not.

Last, there's the most dangerous possibility of all: that the game is fundamentally changed in some dramatic way beyond what we intended. By changing the structure of baseball, even in what we think is such a simple, straightforward and harmless way, we might upset part of the delicate balance that makes the game so entertaining.

The Skill Ceiling

Baseball is a game of high stakes and huge money and limited information. It's like poker that plays out over multiple years per hand. And although organizations have begun to identify good ways to play, they always thought they had good ways to play. Teams are still innovating. We're still learning about baseball. The sabermetric revolution is just beginning, not ending. The metagame is far from solved. Baseball roster construction is a game with an extraordinarily high skill ceiling. It takes exceptional dedication and brilliance to do it right. We're probably not very close to finding the best strategies yet, and the search is fun. We should let it play out for a few more rounds before we upset the balance.

When he isn't watching his Red Sox clinch the World Series, Dan Brooks designs and programs BrooksBaseball.net, a PITCHf/x resource.

The Baseball Prospectus Top 101 Prospects

By Jason Parks

1. Byron Buxton, OF, Minnesota Twins

The premier talent in the minor leagues, Buxton has the type of impact tools to develop into a franchise player at the major-league level. With elite speed, well above-average potential with the glove in center, a plus arm, a plus-plus potential hit tool complemented by an advanced approach, and power potential that he is only scratching the surface of, Buxton has the highest tool-based ceiling of any player in the minors. If everything comes together, he could change the Twins' fortunes.

2. Xander Bogaerts, SS, Boston Red Sox

The 21-year-old shortstop showed the world his mettle in October, flashing the type of big-game coolness that helped define him as a prospect in the minors. Now a prospect in name and eligibility only, Bogaerts is perhaps the safest bet on the 101 to develop into a frontline player, a shortstop with a middle-of-the-order bat and the type of feel for the game to take him above his tool-based ceiling. If everything clicks, he's a perennial all-star and one of the most valuable players in the game.

3. Oscar Taveras, OF, St. Louis Cardinals

In what was supposed to be his spotlight season in the upper minors and his major-league arrival, Taveras suffered through an ankle injury that limited his effectiveness in the field and eventually put him on the shelf. When healthy, Taveras has one of the most dangerous bats in the minors, a swing with the controlled violence of a Vlad Guerrero or Gary Sheffield, the type of hit/power combination that could lead to future batting titles and Most Valuable Player consideration. Assuming the lingering ankle injury is a thing of the past, Taveras won't be long for the minors, and is likely to blossom into an impact bat at the major-league level right out of the gate.

4. Javier Baez, SS, Chicago Cubs

Often labeled a boom-or-bust prospect, 2013 saw Baez boom, hitting his way to Double-A with the type of game power his elite bat speed always suggested was possible. Unlike most top-tier prospects, Baez still comes with considerable risk, mostly because of his ultra-aggressive approach on both sides of the ball. At the plate, Baez is very fastball-happy and can be susceptible to off-speed offerings. In the field, he can play too fast and rush his actions despite easy plus hands and arm. The ultimate profile is an all-star, a borderline-elite player who can stick at shortstop and hit in the middle of a lineup.

5. Carlos Correa, SS, Houston Astros

With some of the best instincts of any prospect, and a unique blend of high-ceiling tools and feel for the game, Correa could be sitting atop this list next year. He has above-average actions in the field, a very big arm, a very advanced approach at the plate and highly projectable pop in the stick. The former first overall pick in the draft looks like a future cornerstone.

6. Francisco Lindor, SS, Cleveland Indians

With a plus-plus glove at a premium position, Lindor could justify his lofty prospect status with his defensive profile alone. But the 20-year-old can swing the bat as well, working himself into favorable hitting conditions with a discerning eye while using a contact-heavy swing to spray hits to all fields. With only 21 Double-A games under his belt, it might seem premature to project Lindor for major-league service in 2014, but the precocious talent has the tools and the makeup to hold his own at the highest level if given a chance to break camp with the major-league team.

7. Addison Russell, SS, Oakland Athletics

Russell is the rare middle infielder who projects to hit for both average and power at the plate. Despite concerns in his amateur days about his long-term defensive home, the 20-year-old has removed doubts as a professional by showing well above-average actions and enough range to stick at the position for a long time. Despite his age and limited professional experience, Russell could reach the major leagues at some point in the 2014 season, a highly aggressive yet completely justifiable projection.

8. Taijuan Walker, RHP, Seattle Mariners

Across three levels (including a three-game spot in the majors), Walker flashed his top-of-the-rotation potential, highlighted by an electric plus-plus fastball, criminally dangerous low-90s cutter and low-70s curve with big depth. Once the command refines and the changeup continues in the maturation process, Walker is going to be one of the better young arms in the game, a long and lively pitcher with knockout stuff and feel for his craft. Dangerous combination.

9. Archie Bradley, RHP, Arizona Diamondbacks

Bradley has all the characteristics of a true power pitcher, with workhorse size, a high-impact arsenal that includes a heavy plus-plus fastball and a violent power curve, and the type of approach and work ethic that scouts champion at every available opportunity. With 21 Double-A starts already under his belt, the 21-year-old righty is primed for a rotation spot in 2014, and it shouldn't take long for him to establish himself as one of the premier young starters in the National League.

10. Kevin Gausman, RHP, Baltimore Orioles

A dominating run in the minors was overshadowed by mixed results in his sporadic major-league spots, as Gausman's command wasn't sharp and his fastball found too many barrels. The former fourth overall pick in the 2012 draft, the idiosyncratic righty can work comfortably in the mid-90s, ratcheting up for more when necessary, and backing up the heater with two distinct change pieces, including one with fall-off-the-table action that is effective against both righties and lefties and can be deployed in any sequence. The refinement of the breaking ball and the transition from good control to good command could be the difference between a solid-average major leaguer and a frontline starter and perennial all-star.

11. Noah Syndergaard, RHP, New York Mets

Not much separates Syndergaard from the top arms in the minors, as the 21-year-old righty shares all the characteristics of a prototypical power arm like Archie Bradley, complete with size, strength, fluidity and athleticism in the delivery, a heavy plus-plus fastball, a breaking ball that has well above-average potential and an overall feel for pitching. Syndergaard's underdeveloped changeup is still a work in progress, but when all the parts come together, the Mets might be able to boast the best young rotation trio in baseball.

12. Yordano Ventura, RHP, Kansas City Royals

My early pick to be this year's AL Rookie of the Year, Ventura is a perfect fit for the reliever box, but with a starter's arsenal and the ability to hold velocity deep into games the slight righty is going to defy the stereotype and emerge as a frontline starter. Durability will be an early concern, as will fastball command and utility of the secondary arsenal,

but the near-elite fastball gives the 23-year-old more wiggle room than the average pitcher, and any step forward with the curveball and changeup could finally give the Royals a homegrown arm worthy of the hype.

13. Lucas Giolito, RHP, Washington Nationals

You can make a case that Giolito has the highest ceiling of any arm in the minors, a distinction he can wear despite a limited professional record and a Tommy John surgery already on his resume. With exceptional size and a frontline arsenal—which includes a fastball and curveball with elite potential and a highly projectable changeup that is still in its infancy—Giolito is ready to explode in 2014. Barring any setback, the 19-year-old could challenge the likes of Buxton and Correa for prospect supremacy in 2015.

14. Miguel Sano, 3B, Minnesota Twins

Sano is a physical beast with 80-grade raw power and the type of athleticism you would expect from an NFL tight end. The swing-and-miss in his game was exploited at Double-A, as he was more prone to expand his zone and chase spin down and away. But the game power still found a way to play—despite the poor contact—and his defensive chops at third, long a subject of scouting debate, improved to the point where some scouts suggest he could end up above average at the position. There is still risk involved with his profile, but the payoff is enormous, a legit middle-of-the-order bat capable of hitting 35-plus bombs from the left side of the infield.

15. Dylan Bundy, RHP, Baltimore Orioles

2013 was a lost year for Bundy, as he hit the shelf after Tommy John surgery and didn't resume a throwing program until December. When fully healthy, Bundy is one of the top young arms in baseball, a power pitcher with a power arsenal, complete with a near-elite fastball that he can manipulate, a big up-and-down curveball with depth and a highly projectable changeup. The arsenal—in combination with his advanced pitchability, hyper-competitiveness and legendary work ethic—will eventually make Bundy a frontline arm in the Orioles' rotation and half of one of the best one-two rotation punches in baseball, along with Gausman.

16. Jonathan Gray, RHP, Colorado Rockies

Selected third overall in the 2013 draft, Gray exploded into a legit 1:1 candidate while at Oklahoma, and he didn't lose a step in his transition to professional ball, shoving it in his brief nine-start run in the minors. With excellent size, strength, dominating fastball/slider combination and developing changeup, Gray fits the mold of a future no. 1 starter. Although some scouts have concerns about the stiff front leg in his delivery and his command profile, most industry sources seem to agree that Gray will develop into a high-end starter, the only debate being whether he blossoms into a legit ace or falls a bit short.

17. Kris Bryant, 3B, Chicago Cubs

The best college bat available in the 2013 draft, Bryant didn't mess around in his professional debut, hitting his way to the Florida State League and then putting on a show in the Arizona Fall League, where the now-22-year-old slugged .727 in 20 games. You can debate his defensive profile at third and the projected utility of his hit tool—both of which could limit his ultimate value—but what isn't up for discussion is his plus-plus power potential, which could easily make him a middle-of-the-order threat for the Cubs as early as 2015.

18. Austin Hedges, C, San Diego Padres

When it comes to catching prospects, you won't find a young player with a more complete defensive package than Hedges, a future Gold Glove-level backstop with an easy plus arm, plus-plus glove, excellent balance and footwork, and the necessary intangibles to develop into a general on the field. The bat is probably more down-the-lineup than one with impact potential, but the swing is simple and easy, so he should be able to make solid contact; the bat speed and strength are present, so some gap and even over-the-fence power could add to the offensive profile. If Hedges can muster a .260 average with some pop, he's a first-division talent. If the bat plays above projection, Hedges could be a perennial All-Star and one of the best all-around catchers in the game. Don't discount the value of an elite defensive catcher, even if the bat fails to impress.

19. Jameson Taillon, RHP, Pittsburgh Pirates

Taillon reached Triple-A Indianapolis last summer as a 21-year-old, holding his own over six starts. The arsenal is loud, headlined by a plus to plus-plus fastball that can climb to triple digits and a low-80s power curve that plays both in the zone and as a bury pitch. The changeup remains his third-best offering, but it took a step forward in 2013, earning more consistent 5 grades (on the 2-to-8 scouting scale) from evaluators. He'll also mix in an average slider from time to time, which serves to keep barrels off his fastball. A half-grade improvement in command could mean a big jump in production, and he figures to arrive in Pittsburgh for good in 2014.

20. George Springer, OF, Houston Astros

After starting the 2013 season with a strong return trip to the Texas League, Springer exploded after moving up a level to Triple-A, hitting for average and power and stealing bases at a healthy clip while playing above-average defense at an up-the-middle position. The former 11th overall pick positioned himself as the Astros' center fielder of the future, although some are still pessimistic about his hit tool; specifically, the swing-and-miss tendencies and struggles against quality off-speed offerings. In all likelihood, the 24-year-old will struggle to hit for a high average against major-league pitching, but he will show plus power and speed, to go along with plus defensive chops in center, and that profile should make him a first-division player.

21. Mark Appel, RHP, Houston Astros

Appel stepped into the Houston organization as its top pitching prospect, bringing mid-90s heat to go with a changeup and breaker that can both register as plus offerings. The stuff has a tendency to play down at times due to a lack of deception and consistent execution, and while Appel earns praise for his even demeanor on the mound, critics counter that he is too passive and too often struggles to assert himself. Overall, the former Stanford ace looks the part of a high-floor starter with a chance to grow into a legit front-end arm if it all comes together.

22. Robert Stephenson, RHP, Cincinnati Reds

The former first-round pick took a big developmental step forward in 2013, pitching his way to Double-A and missing a lot of barrels along the way. The 21-year-old righty has one of the best fastballs in the minors, a lively mid-to-upper-90s pitch that he complements with a hard curveball that is already a plus offering. The changeup and command need refinement, but with an athletic delivery and good overall feel for pitching, Stephenson should eventually put the pieces together and develop into an impact arm at the top of the Reds' rotation.

23. Jackie Bradley Jr., CF, Boston Red Sox

Despite a rocky major-league debut, few question Bradley's future as a fixture in Fenway's spacious center field. The defense grades to plus off the strength of his reads and routes, solid speed and a strong and accurate arm that will play to the deep reaches of Fenway's gaps. He is a disciplined hitter who should fit well at the top of the order with a gap-to-gap approach, top-shelf bat speed and enough pop to keep pitchers honest. With an advanced game and the departure of Jacoby Ellsbury, Bradley should have the inside track on the Opening Day job in Boston and figures to hold it for the foreseeable future.

24. Gregory Polanco, CF, Pittsburgh Pirates

Polanco is a potential five-tool talent with a chance to show impact in each aspect of his game. The bat comes with torque and leverage, regularly producing hard contact, particularly from the middle out, where he can get fully extended. There are some holes on the inner half due to swing length and load. The power could play anywhere from average to plus, and a not-unlikely trajectory could be a slow build in pop through his 20s as the body matures, with the speed running counter and ticking down from plus to average. He has the physical tools to project to center, though Andrew McCutchen's presence makes a corner spot the more likely point of entry.

25. Albert Almora, CF, Chicago Cubs

Despite average straight-line speed, Almora profiles easily as a top-tier defensive center fielder due to an almost prescient first step and instinctive routes to the ball. In the box he shows an advanced understanding of the strike zone and impressive bat-to-ball ability, with a chance for a plus hit tool and average-or-better power. Almora saw an uptick in his physicality in 2013, but he also drew some criticism, rightly or wrongly, for missing too many games for "ticky tack" injuries. His feel for the game is elite and should help him to move quickly through the system, with a 2015 debut not unreasonable.

26. Eddie Butler, RHP, Colorado Rockies

Butler carved through three levels in his first taste of full-season ball, arguably improving his stock more than any other prospect in the process. The former supplemental first-rounder showcases three potential plus-or-better offerings, highlighted by a lively 93 to 97 mph fastball thrown with four- and two-seam variations. The changeup carries deception and mirrors Butler's heavy two-seam action, while the slider flashes plus with mid-to-upper-80s velocity. A long arm action and some crossfire can leave his offerings visible and imprecise, though most believe in the package enough to project him as a potential front-end starter.

27. Marcus Stroman, RHP, Toronto Blue Jays

The diminutive former Duke Blue Devil and USA Baseball standout showcases a dynamic arsenal and, with a plus-plus fastball and slider, one of the most explosive one-two combos in the minors. The heater is a low- to mid-90s offering with late giddyup, while the slider comes with sharp wipeout action. He shows excellent feel for the slide piece, with an additional ability to tighten it up to cutter depth with upper-80s to low-90s velocity. He'll also flash a plus changeup with abrupt late fade and good trajectory deception. While pitch plane will be a concern against more advanced bats, Stroman's polish, command and multiple-look finishes on his offerings give him the weapons necessary to remain a starter, and one with true impact potential.

28. Chris Owings, SS, Arizona Diamondbacks

No one tool screams "impact," but the sum of Owings' parts might be a first-division regular with a long and productive career. He lacks premium range or arm strength, but will get the job done at the six spot due to solid hands, good footwork and a quick and clean release. The bat-to-ball ability took a step forward last summer, resulting in regular loud contact as he showed the potential for fringe-average over-the-fence power. He's an instinctive baserunner with the wherewithal to swipe a bag or grab an extra base when the opportunity arises. After crushing the PCL in 2013, Owings should compete for a spot on the 25-man this spring.

29. Raul Mondesi, SS, Kansas City Royals

One of the youngest players to land on the Top 101, Mondesi played most of the year as a 17-year-old in the Sally, showcasing a skill set that belied his age and carried the potential to impact the game in all facets, albeit through unrefined means. The glove, arm and athleticism give him the chance to profile as a plus defender once he's able to slow the game down, and his natural contact ability from both boxes could push the hit tool to plus provided the approach tightens with reps. Given the likelihood the Royals continue to challenge Mondesi via aggressive promotion, it might take some time for the numbers to catch up with the scouting. But the end result should be well worth the wait.

30. Andrew Heaney, LHP, Miami Marlins

Heaney enjoyed a breakout year in his first full professional season, breezing through 12 Florida State League starts before finishing strong at Double-A Jacksonville. The hard-throwing lefty utilizes a loose and easy arm to produce his plus fastball, which he can dial up to 97 mph when he needs it. His best secondary is a true plus slider with hard, late bite and good depth, and he can also drop an average change piece with slot and plane deception. With three future average-to-plus weapons with which to attack advanced bats, and solid command of each, Heaney projects as a mid-rotation arm capable of no. 2 production with continued refinement.

31. Aaron Sanchez, RHP, Toronto Blue Jays

Four seasons into his pro career, the story of Sanchez remains one of immense upside and inconsistent performance. The long and projectable former supplemental first-rounder boasts a loose and whippy arm capable of regularly producing heavy mid-90s heat and a low-80s power breaker. Sanchez can also turn over a plus changeup with disappearing action and arm-speed deception. He has yet to develop the ability to repeat his mechanics and frequently loses his release point, limiting his command and execution. The ceiling remains that of a front-end starter, but it's a high-risk profile that is perhaps more likely to settle in as a solid, if erratic, no. 3 or 4.

32. Alex Meyer, RHP, Minnesota Twins

Evaluators continue to bifurcate along starter/reliever lines when projecting Meyer, though the former Kentucky Wildcat should have an impact regardless of ultimate role. The long and lanky righty utilizes a mid- to upper-90s plus-plus fastball, with premium extension helping the pitch play up even further. While inconsistent at times, the slider gives Meyer a second plus to plus-plus offering, and even the changeup drew the occasional 6 grade from evaluators in the Arizona Fall League this year. While his long limbs help create angles and extension, Meyer regularly struggles to keep them in sync, leading to mechanical inconsistencies and imprecise execution. There's mid-rotation or front-end upside here, with a late-inning safety net.

33. Kolten Wong, 2B, St. Louis Cardinals

Wong is a baseball player in every sense of the phrase, a gamer who makes plays on all sides of the ball despite a cache of tools more solid than special. The baseball instincts allow everything to play up, which remains true despite the World Series mental lapse that had some questioning his readiness for the big stage. Wong is going to put his bat to the ball with consistency, and he's going to show above-average chops at the keystone, but it remains to be seen whether he'll develop into a true up-the-lineup type or settles into a down-the-lineup role on a veteran-laden World Series contender.

34. Kyle Zimmer, RHP, Kansas City Royals

The former San Francisco Don boasts a clean delivery and a potential front-end four-pitch arsenal. The fastball is a plus offering that sits comfortably between 92 and 96 mph with arm-side life, and Zimmer shows the ability to work the quadrants with it. He can bring two distinct breakers in his curve and slider, and he can manipulate the shape and speed of the former, drawing consistent plus to plus-plus grades. The changeup is inconsistent but projects to average, and he has been known to mix in a cutter as an "off-speed" offering if needed. Zimmer could be major-league ready this year, and profiles as a solid no. 3 with no. 2 upside.

35. Julio Urias, LHP, Los Angeles Dodgers

At age 16, Urias averaged more than a strikeout per inning in the Midwest League while showing poise and feel for a three-pitch arsenal, the likes of which you simply don't see from arms at his developmental stage. The three-way fastball (two-seam, four-seam, cut) clocks anywhere from 91 to 96 mph and works well to the bottom "U" of the zone. He can manipulate the speed and depth of his curve, which already grades as plus, and the changeup will flash as well. There's limited projection in the body and we have yet to see if the stuff will play deeper into games, but these are small issues at this point.

36. Clint Frazier, CF, Cleveland Indians

Frazier's swing can be best described as beautifully violent, with quick-twitch actions and strong hands and wrists delivering the barrel with enough force to bring his back foot off the ground at contact. The bat speed is special, producing easy plus power with a chance for plus hit if he can rein in the approach a bit and limit the empty swings. A recent convert to the outfield, Frazier has the raw tools to grow into an average defender in center, and should benefit greatly from reps and pro instruction. The upside is that of a top 10 prospect in the game if everything clicks.

37. Nick Castellanos, 3B, Detroit Tigers

With the departure of Prince Fielder and Miguel Cabrera's shift across the diamond, the door has opened for Castellanos to return to third base, where his defensive profile fits best. The carrying tools, however, reside in the bat, as Castellanos boasts an impressive ability to barrel up balls on the regular. There's little question he has the feel for the craft to hit for average, and the leverage in the swing combined with a projectable and ever-strengthening frame indicate the potential for plus over-the-fence pop as well. He'll compete for a starting job this spring and could produce from day one.

38. Kyle Crick, RHP, San Francisco Giants

Crick's fastball is a plus-plus weapon capable of reaching the upper 90s and sitting 93 to 96 deep into starts. He rolls out three secondaries, with his change and curve both showing above-average potential and the slider projecting just behind. Mechanical quirks, including a short stride and late hand break, have thus far prevented Crick from throwing with precision in the zone, and at times he's clunky enough to visibly lose balance through his finish. Believers point to his age and argue that he'll refine and stick as a potential front-end arm, while more conservative evaluators see a shift to the 'pen, where he could excel as a shutdown closer.

39. Rougned Odor, 2B, Texas Rangers

An intense competitor on both sides of the ball, Odor looks the part of a first-division regular. He squares up velocity with ease and is at his best when he focuses on simply making obnoxiously hard contact with a compact barrel delivery. He can get loose and uphill when trying to lift and drive, which advanced arms will exploit if given the chance. Defensively he's prone to errors of aggression, but the overall production should be a net positive. He could debut in 2014 with a chance to quickly grow into a plus-plus bat capable of wearing out the gaps and notching 14 to 18 home runs a year in hitter-friendly Arlington.

40. Lucas Sims, RHP, Atlanta Braves

Full-season ball didn't slow Sims down, thanks to his 91 to 95 mph fastball and hammer curveball, a pitch that some project to be a plus-plus offering. For those scoring at home, that's two plus pitches at 19 years old, just a year and a half removed from high school. Last year was a breakout season for Sims, and if the changeup takes a step forward the athletic righty could be on the fast track to the majors, where his three-pitch mix and plus command profile could make him a no. 2 or 3 starter.

41. Jorge Alfaro, C, Texas Rangers

As far as tool-based ceilings are concerned, there aren't many prospects who can stand with Alfaro, a true five-tool talent at a premium position. On the merits of his projection alone, he could be a top 10 prospect in baseball, but questions about his approach and the utility of his hit tool keep the risk high and the assessments optimistic but prudent. He could blossom into an all-star if everything clicks, but Double-A will present a good test for the young Colombian backstop.

42. Tyler Glasnow, RHP, Pittsburgh Pirates

The paragon of the Pirates' "draft projectable high school pitchers" strategy, Glasnow blossomed in his first full season of pro ball. At 6-foot-7, there's still some projection remaining. Glasnow sat in the mid-90s with his fastball, but he'll have to command it better against better competition. His curveball flashes plus potential and he could have an average changeup, but that has a long way to go. Glasnow's fastball will get him to the majors, especially in a Pirates system that stresses pounding the zone with fastballs, but his off-speed pitches will determine his future role.

43. Mike Foltynewicz, RHP, Houston Astros

Foltynewicz walks too many batters and lacks a plus secondary offering, but 100 mph fastballs are rare enough that his make him stand out. The past two years have seen the big right-hander take significant steps forward, but if he wants to remain a starter, he'll have to take another step with either his curveball or his changeup. If either can become an average pitch, it might be enough for him to remain a starter. If not, his fastball alone should make him a solid late-inning reliever.

44. Corey Seager, SS, Los Angeles Dodgers

Seager battered the Midwest League over 74 games before running out of steam upon promotion to High-A Rancho Cucamonga. He has an advanced approach at the plate and does a good job of matching swing plane to pitch plane, allowing him to make hard contact across the quadrants and work pole to pole. With a projectable body already maturing, it's only a matter of time before the raw power starts to emerge with regularity. A return to the homer-friendly California League in 2014 could help jump-start a big offensive breakout for Seager, making the likely shift from short to third a non-issue.

45. Jorge Soler, RF, Chicago Cubs

Injury limited Soler to just 55 High-A games in 2013, but even in small doses it was easy to see the huge offensive upside in his game. A physically imposing presence, Soler relies on a strong core and good barrel acceleration to create heavy backspin and carry, aided by natural loft in his swing. He will be tested by advanced arms capable of effectively working east and west, but most evaluators see enough discipline in the approach to believe Soler will be able to find his pitches and punish them. The result could be 30-plus home runs to go with average defense and a plus to plus-plus arm in right.

46. Miguel Almonte, RHP, Kansas City Royals

Behind an advanced changeup and lively plus fastball, Almonte has been able to carve up low-level bats, but the immature breaking ball could stall his progress as he climbs the professional ladder. He shows both a curveball and a slider, but neither offering has stepped up to the standard set by the rest of the arsenal, and sources are mixed as to which pitch projects higher. Almonte is going to shove in the friendly confines of the Carolina League, with the real test looming in Double-A, where his command and breaking ball will need to be sharper to find the same level of success.

47. Matt Wisler, RHP, San Diego Padres

Sitting comfortably between 92 and 94 mph, Wisler pounds the strike zone with a deceptive and repeatable delivery and complements the fastball with what will one day be a plus slider. It's a profile that allowed him to find success at an advanced level at a young age. He profiles as a mid-rotation starter who could continue to move quickly and eventually thrive by generating weak contact in Petco Park. If the crossfire delivery limits his command or the growth of his secondary arsenal, Wisler could still find success as a max-effort reliever in the 'pen.

48. Travis d'Arnaud, C, New York Mets

Most prospects would lose serious points in rankings such as these for being 25, but d'Arnaud is a catcher who can hit, so he gets extra chances. Had he been healthy, d'Arnaud would have left his prospect status behind long ago. Unfortunately, his list of injuries looks like the Declaration of Independence. He's a solid hitter with good power and solid receiving skills. That's a heck of a catcher, if he can stay on the field.

49. Billy Hamilton, CF, Cincinnati Reds

Will he hit? The speed is game-changing, as Hamilton proved in September that even the best catchers in the world will have a hard time throwing him out. He's still learning center field but has the speed to make up for mistakes and will be better than average on defense for the next decade with the potential for more. But will he hit? It's the only question that matters for Hamilton, as his legs will always make things interesting if he can make enough contact for them to matter.

50. Joc Pederson, OF, Los Angeles Dodgers

Pederson broke out with a strong .278/.381/.497 line at Double-A in 2013 and his prospect stock rose with each passing day. With a broad skill set, Pederson can do a little of everything. He projects as an average hitter, though he is currently anemic against same-side arms, and he should have at least average power. His average speed plays well on the bases and in the field, and there are scouts who believe he can handle center field long term. The overall profile lacks impact, but Pederson does have the potential to be a solid major leaguer.

51. Garin Cecchini, 3B, Boston Red Sox

The third baseman from Louisiana made stops at two levels in 2013 and continued to show solid hitting chops. Cecchini unfolds from a balanced left-handed stroke that's driven by quick-firing hands and a strong base. While the bat speed isn't elite, the 23-year-old shows the ability to adjust his swing to the path of the ball and possesses a sharply tuned hitting eye. Questions surround Cecchini's ability to stick at the hot corner, with a move to a corner outfield spot the likely destination. It's the profile of a major leaguer, not an upper-echelon player, but one who can be an average to slightly above-average regular on a contending team.

52. Maikel Franco, 3B, Philadelphia Phillies

Franco is a naturally gifted hitter who does a lot of things wrong, which is a scary combination for scouts who never know how it will translate against better competition. What we do know is that he put up consecutive .900-plus OPS's in the Florida State League and the Eastern League, both tough hitting environments. His plate discipline is all over the map and he's no lock to stick at third base, but there's enough talent there to carve out a career, with the potential for an impact player with just a little refinement.

53. A.J. Cole, RHP, Washington Nationals

Cole has a big-league, mid-90s fastball coming from a prototypical starter's body, a profile that is both highly projectable and risky because of the present utility of the secondary arsenal. The knock on Cole has been his organizational travels, as he is an oft-traded player who carries the stigma of being disposable despite his enticing profile. But after a very strong Double-A debut in 2013, Cole is starting to look the part of a future no. 3 starter, a reality that could come to fruition by 2014.

54. Kohl Stewart, RHP, Minnesota Twins

A strong, athletic build, a plus fastball and a plus slider already give Stewart more to work with than most pitching prospects, and there's the potential for another plus pitch (curveball) in his repertoire, giving him the type of profile that can stand atop a rotation. If he dominates the low minors the way he's expected to do this season, he should quickly put himself among the top tier of pitching prospects in the minors, perhaps emerging as a top 10 prospect in the game.

55. Max Fried, LHP, San Diego Padres

Fried has the potential for as much success as any left-hander on this list, but he also has a considerable distance between his current and future abilities. His low-90s fastball has good life (especially the two-seamer that features late action) and both his curveball and changeup feature plus potential. He needs to finish his pitches and refine his command, but the arsenal is there for future success. The package has yet to come together, and if he takes the mound in the hitter-friendly California League, the stat sheet might not be kind to the young southpaw.

56. Josmil Pinto, C, Minnesota Twins

After a slow marinade that began all the way back in 2006, Pinto took strong steps forward last year and broke out in a major way. The defensive package is highlighted by solid receiving skills behind the plate, coupled with a quick release. The offense is headed up by a no-nonsense swing and some over-the-fence pop. The 25-year-old's overall game isn't flashy, but it can be steady and dependable in a lineup. The time is now for Pinto to put his claim on the Twins' catching spot, with the outcome potentially adding up to a solid-average big leaguer at a premium spot.

57. Jonathan Singleton, 1B, Houston Astros

The big slugger from California lost some of his shine with a drug-of-abuse suspension and a subsequent return in less-than-ideal shape, but the potential for big power at first base remains. The left-handed hitter generates both impressive bat speed and the type of torque to launch high arcing drives deep into the seats. Singleton's defense at first will be adequate at best, but if the hit tool plays at the highest level it will more than carry the overall profile. It comes down to the 22-year-old's desire to maximize his talent into a first-division role, or else drift toward second-division status.

58. Hunter Harvey, RHP, Baltimore Orioles

The Orioles found a big-time arm late in the first round last summer, and Harvey showed his potential immediately. His curveball proved to be far too advanced for Gulf Coast and New York-Penn League hitters, as he struck out 11.7 batters per nine innings between the two. His fastball is no slouch, sitting from 91 to 94 mph, giving him the potential for two plus pitches. Harvey is another arm who could make a big move up prospect lists after a full-season debut this year.

59. Reese McGuire, C, Pittsburgh Pirates

As Austin Hedges and Jorge Alfaro make their way to the majors in the next few years, McGuire has the skill set to develop into the top all-around catching prospect in the game: plus potential glove with a bat that is stronger than you might think. If it weren't for his having only 50 professional games—none in full-season ball—under his belt, he'd be even higher on this list. He comes in where he does because of the inherent risk of developing high school catchers, but once he proves himself in full-season ball, he'll jump.

60. Eddie Rosario, 2B, Minnesota Twins

Rosario's excellent hitting ability gives him a legitimate major-league future, but how the rest of his game plays will determine his impact. Rosario has good power to the gaps, projecting for plenty of doubles and possibly 15 home runs per season. His defense gives scouts pause as he looks uncomfortable at second base and seems a more natural fit for the outfield, where his speed and arm can have more of an impact. If he can find a way to stay on the dirt as a fringe-average defender, Rosario's bat could carry him to an everyday profile.

61. Eduardo Rodriguez, LHP, Baltimore Orioles

This left-hander out of Venezuela has both the size and diversity of arsenal that you look for in a starting pitcher. Featuring a low-90s fastball that touches 95, a biting slider with tilt and a changeup that can fade quickly off the table, Rodriguez uses multiple options to get the upper hand on opponents. While his stuff is more solid-average to plus and he lacks a true wipeout secondary pitch, the 21-year-old shows solid pitchability and a knowledge of how to execute his craft. It's a profile that points toward eating innings at the back of a rotation, with third starter upside.

62. Braden Shipley, RHP, Arizona Diamondbacks

The Diamondbacks drafted the athletic right-hander 15th overall in June, and Shipley used his mid-90s fastball and plus changeup to strike out more than a batter per inning between the Northwest and Midwest leagues. His curveball gives him the potential for another plus pitch and the chance to move quickly through the Diamondbacks' system. His changeup could be a savior as he battles the tough hitting environments of the California League next season.

63. Phillip Ervin, OF, Cincinnati Reds

The 2013 first-round pick out of Samford University blends high contact ability with the potential for up-the-middle defense. Ervin utilizes a short, compact swing that enables the right-handed hitter to rifle the barrel through the zone. The outfielder profiles as a gap-to-gap hitter who can flash consistent extra-base ability. Opinions are mixed on whether the 21-year-old has enough glove to stick in center. There's enough arm for right field, but the pressure on the bat might be too much in a corner. Expect Ervin to hit his way to Double-A quickly, where he'll get his first true test as a professional and bring the projection into clearer focus.

64. Matt Barnes, RHP, Boston Red Sox

A casting call for a big-league pitcher would end up with Barnes at the top of the list. The right-hander possesses the size, stuff and mound presence to play the part of no. 3 starter. Barnes' bread and butter is a fastball that approaches the mid-90s, with the ability to routinely rack up quality strikes within the zone. The inconsistency of the 24-year-old's secondary stuff causes some hesitation, as both the curveball and changeup need to be firing on all cylinders to churn through unforgiving lineups. Barnes is tasked with pushing his arsenal to the next level in the finishing stages of his minor-league development, and with proving he's ready for the chance to cement his spot in Boston's rotation.

65. D.J. Peterson, 3B, Seattle Mariners

The Mariners' top pick in June, Peterson came off the board in the first round almost entirely because of the potential value in his bat. With a ceiling that includes plus hitting ability and plus power, Peterson has the potential to be an impact middle-of-the-order bat. Defensively, he has plenty of work to do at third base and most scouts believe he is destined to move across the infield, a move that will put plenty of pressure on him to maximize his offensive talents.

66. Stephen Piscotty, OF, St. Louis Cardinals

The Stanford product has entered the upper minors after making short work of the lower levels. His calling card continues to be an above-average hit tool accentuated by loose hands that enable the right-handed hitter to explode to the point of contact and control the head of the bat. The results are plenty of hard line drives to all fields and a projection of a high-average hitter in The Show. Drafted as a third baseman in 2012, Piscotty has moved out to the outfield, where his plus-plus arm plays up in right. While the home run power is likely to be modest, the 22-year-old has the chance to develop into a solid-average major league player.

67. Erik Johnson, RHP, Chicago White Sox

Built to log innings, Johnson's future rests in the middle or back of a big-league rotation, where his broad arsenal should allow him to work through lineups multiple times. Johnson's best pitch is a slider that grades plus, and he supports that swing-and-miss offering with a 90–93 mph fastball, average curveball and fringy changeup. With improved command in 2013, Johnson stepped forward as a viable rotation candidate for the White Sox this season, and he could peak as high as a no. 3 starter once he settles in.

68. James Paxton, LHP, Seattle Mariners

Paxton has been a known commodity for a while now, and at 25 he's one of the oldest prospects on this list. He was underwhelming in Triple-A in 2013 but put together four solid starts in the majors toward the end of the season. His mid-90s fastball gives him a solid ceiling, but his inability to repeat his mechanics will likely keep him a no. 3 or 4 starter or reliever. He's ready for the majors and will get a chance to start in 2014, although with the Mariners going for it this season he won't have much slack on the leash.

69. Henry Owens, LHP, Boston Red Sox

Standing 6-foot-6 and on the lanky side, Owens brings a lot of arms, legs and body for opposing hitters to deal with. The 2011 first-round pick isn't just deception, however. The left-handed starter easily delivers a low-90s fastball that will touch up to 94 and get late swings. Owens' best pitch is a bat-missing changeup, which profiles as a true plus weapon. The curveball lags behind, but will show flashes of being a big-league offering when the lefty stays on top of it. The package has third-starter upside and with more near-term polish on pitchability he can begin to challenge for a look in Boston's rotation.

70. Chi Chi Gonzalez, RHP, Texas Rangers

The Rangers grabbed Alex "Chi Chi" Gonzalez 23rd overall in June, and he looked like a steal after finishing the year with five impressive outings in the Carolina League. His best pitch is a naturally cutting low-to-mid-90s fastball, which is essentially a 93 mph cutter generating weak contact. He also has a slider that grades out with plus potential. At 6-foot-3, he's got a solid build to be a mid-rotation starter, but he'll have to refine something off-speed to really bring out his potential. His unique repertoire could allow him to move quickly through the Rangers system this season.

71. Wilmer Flores, 2B/3B, New York Mets

A controversial prospect in scouting circles, Flores' supporters believe he has a chance to be an average hitter with at least average power while playing a position of at least some defensive value. His detractors see an average offensive talent destined to continue sliding down the defensive spectrum until he ultimately lands at first base. The reality likely lies somewhere in between, with Flores settling in as a .270 hitter with 17 to 20 home runs at an unknown defensive home, which should be enough for a lengthy major-league career.

72. Luis Sardinas, SS, Texas Rangers

Sardinas has a plus hit tool and a plus glove up the middle, which alone make him a solid prospect. The fact that he should be able to stay at shortstop bumps it up a notch, and his well above-average speed puts another feather in his cap. Sardinas has well below-average power, but his game is built on speed and defense, and if he can stay healthy and focused, he has a first-division ceiling with an 1980s throwback profile.

73. Blake Swihart, C, Boston Red Sox

A glance at the statistical output won't tip off anything out of the ordinary, but it's the scouting and long-term vision that make Swihart an attractive prospect. The 22-year-old switch-hitter has the type of hit tool to maintain high rates of contact and lace line drives to all fields. The bat can produce high averages with extra-base pop at full utility. Behind the dish, Swihart's athleticism plays up nicely, with a plus arm, quick reflexes and fast feet. If things come together he's a first-division player, but there's still a large enough gap between the present and the vision to keep him lower... for now.

74. Colin Moran, 3B, Miami Marlins

Moran came out of the University of North Carolina as one the most polished hitters in the 2013 draft, and was popped sixth overall by the Marlins. His best tool is his ability to barrel up the ball, but the power potential is the subject of debate, which could limit his ultimate value if the game power doesn't arrive. His hit tool alone is enough to make Moran a solid regular, and if he can stick at third (another scouting debate) and the power steps up, he could develop into a first-division player and occasional all-star. For a polished college bat, the risk is higher than you would expect.

75. Jose Berrios, RHP, Minnesota Twins

The 2012 first-round pick hit the ground running in full-season ball and continued to sharpen an already mature arsenal. Berrios works his lively fastball at 92 to 96 mph, while flashing the ability to dot both sides of the plate. The 20-year-old leans on a hard curveball to miss bats later in counts and also shows the makings of a changeup that can grow into a plus pitch at his disposal. The downside is his size, which draws concerns about future durability, but the Puerto Rico native pitches with both the fortitude and approach of a future major leaguer. The clues point toward a potential mid-rotation arm and a prospect who can rise into the next tier of this list in short order.

76. Alberto Tirado, RHP, Toronto Blue Jays

Though he's yet to reach full-season ball, this is a name to keep an eye on. Tirado flashes a maturing arsenal consisting of a 91–95 mph fastball, disappearing changeup and late-breaking slider. The right-hander also oozes the easiness you love to see. While the command is presently below average due to inconsistent mechanics, Tirado displays an aptitude for his craft and has a body that can develop further to bring more balance to his delivery. With the potential for three plus pitches and large developmental gains, this is a prospect who can explode and push frontline-starter upside.

77. Josh Bell, OF, Pittsburgh Pirates

A solid athlete with a frame designed to pack on muscle, this switch-hitting outfielder possesses big raw power fueled by a loose, easy swing from both sides of the plate. After a knee injury derailed his first professional season, Bell showed that he was healthy in 2013 and made progress polishing his overall tools. The 21-year-old still has questions to answer about his hit tool and pitch recognition, but the ingredients are there for a power-hitting corner outfielder who can rise quickly into the next tier of prospects.

78. Sean Manaea, LHP, Kansas City Royals

Manaea emerged as a candidate to go first overall in the 2013 draft after dominating the prestigious Cape Cod League, but saw a regression in stuff and control over the course of an injury-plagued junior year. Despite the disappointing spring, Kansas City saw enough upside to invest the draft's fifth-highest signing bonus in the southpaw after selecting him in the supplemental first round. At his best, Manaea spits 93 to 96 mph gas from a low slot and tough angle, showing a sharp slider and improving split-change. There's projection in the body, and if Manaea can remain healthy and return to Cape form, he represents a potential mid-rotation starter with a chance to vault into the top tier of prospect arms with further development.

79. Michael Choice, OF, Texas Rangers

A new addition to the Rangers' outfield mix, Choice has the potential to help in left field over the long term. He is an average runner who plays solid defense, but his arm is below average and does not support a long-term future in center or right field. Choice's calling card is his plus-plus raw power, though it plays down a grade because of considerable swing-and-miss issues. Choice has a solid approach and will take some walks, which combined with 25 home runs a year will help buoy what projects to be a .250-ish batting average.

80. Nick Kingham, RHP, Pittsburgh Pirates

Standing 6-foot-5 and 220 pounds, Kingham's physicality stands out the second he steps on the field. He backs up his physical presence with an impressive array of pitches that includes a fastball that can reach 95 to 96 mph and a curveball and changeup that are both promising. With his height and long arms, Kingham's fastball appears harder than radar guns suggest, and his ability to locate the pitch helps it play up even more. Despite his impressive raw stuff, Kingham can struggle to miss bats and profiles as a mid-rotation workhorse rather than a front-of-the-rotation arm.

81. C.J. Edwards, RHP, Chicago Cubs

Edwards has gone from relative obscurity to "on the radar" thanks to the strength of his fastball and the promise of his secondary stuff. A loose thrower with an easy delivery and fast arm, the right-hander currently sits in the low 90s and can touch 94. Edwards also shows feel for both a mid-70s curveball and changeup, though the latter is still a fairly raw offering. The 22-year-old is presently very slender and lean, which highlights the need for added strength so he can maintain his stuff into outings and over the grind of the season. The package points toward a future reliever, but large physical gains can keep the arm on a starter's track.

82. Jonathan Schoop, 2B, Baltimore Orioles

Schoop might be the Orioles' long-term answer at second base, but he desperately needs additional seasoning in Triple-A before being called on to fill a full-time major-league role. Impressive physically and athletically, Schoop has a host of tools that could make him a quality everyday player. He is a potentially average defender with a plus arm at second base. At his best he makes easy contact with at least average power, but his offensive game remains inconsistent because of a raw approach and a lack of experience against upper-level arms.

83. Arismendy Alcantara, 2B, Chicago Cubs

Alcantara had a bit of a coming-out party at the 2013 Futures Game and cemented his breakout status with a very strong season at Double-A as a 21-year-old. Every part of Alcantara's game stepped forward in 2013. His defense at second base now projects to be above average, and his arm is still a plus tool. His feel for the game on offense took a big step forward, allowing him to work deeper counts and drive the ball more consistently. All told, Alcantara has potential as an everyday second baseman.

84. Zach Lee, RHP, Los Angeles Dodgers

Given a massive signing bonus out of a Texas high school in 2010, expectations for Lee were immediately extreme. A gifted athlete, Lee repeats his delivery well and pounds the zone with an average fastball that plays up because of plus sink. His slider and changeup are both average offerings and his curveball can be effective when set up properly. Once projected as a front-of-the-rotation arm, Lee looks the part of a durable third or fourth starter who could help the Dodgers as early as the second half of this year.

85. Gary Sanchez, C, New York Yankees

Possessing big raw power and a swing with excellent extension, Sanchez can drive baseballs with authority to all fields. The 21-year-old catcher typically punishes mistakes. Behind the dish Sanchez shows a plus-plus arm and fluidity with his catch-and-release mechanics, but the receiving skills need refinement to stick long-term. If everything comes together, Sanchez can be a first-division catcher with 25-homer power and an arm to control the run game. But with his level of engagement drifting for stretches and questions about whether there's enough desire to maximize his talent, he might ultimately end up an average regular at first base at his peak.

86. Brian Goodwin, OF, Washington Nationals

Even after posting a pedestrian .252/.355/.407 line in Double-A, Goodwin still has an all-star ceiling thanks to an impressive set of tools. He has the speed to play center field if he can continue to refine his reads and routes, something he made progress with in 2013. The ball jumps off his bat when he makes contact and if he can develop enough consistency with his swing to hit .270 to .280, then he could contribute 25 to 30 doubles and 15-plus home runs to the lineup. Goodwin still carries considerable risk despite reaching Double-A, but the payoff could be an outstanding everyday player.

87. Christian Bethancourt, C, Atlanta Braves

When going through the checklist of desirable defensive attributes in a catcher, this prospect's scores are at the top. The glove is firm when receiving offerings. The footwork is crisp and there's athleticism for his size. To top it all off, the arm grades as an 8 with a hair-trigger release, leaving Bethancourt more than capable of controlling the running game. The defense screams elite, but the potential offensive contributions may very well end up weak thanks to an uneven approach. This is a big leaguer, but a career as a regular will come down to whether Bethancourt can avoid being an automatic out at the bottom of the lineup.

88. Nick Williams, OF, Texas Rangers

There's a distinct sound heard off the bat from players with legit major-league hitting talent. The "crack" always turns heads in its direction. Williams turned those heads not only with explosive sounds but with his innate barrel-to-ball

ability and easy, controlled swing. The hit tool has the potential to round to plus-plus, with natural raw power that can crest toward 20 home runs at peak. Williams still has a ways to go developing the other aspects of his game, including outfield defense that needs work to reach average, but the bat is good enough to potentially carry him as a regular, with All-Star upside if the baseball skills click.

89. Austin Meadows, OF, Pittsburgh Pirates

Sweet left-handed stroke? Check. Frame to hang dreams on? Check. Easy raw power? Check. Pittsburgh selected Meadows ninth overall in 2013 with aspirations of slow-cooking this raw talent into an outfield fixture at PNC Park for years to come. The hit tool and approach are advanced for his age, though Meadows is going to be challenged to make adjustments during his early career. With the potential for continued physical development, the 19-year-old likely slots into a corner spot down the road. The potential is there for a middle-of-the-order threat, and one who can rise quickly up both the ranks of the minors and prospect lists.

90. Enny Romero, LHP, Tampa Bay Rays

Romero has two paths to an impact role in the big leagues: With improved command, he could profile as a third or fourth starter; without improved command he could profile as a high-powered late-inning reliever. In either scenario he attacks hitters with two plus-plus pitches, a fastball that can reach 96 mph and a hard curveball. Romero lacks feel for his changeup and he is generally considered more of a thrower than pitcher, but his overall ceiling remains tantalizing.

91. Pierce Johnson, RHP, Chicago Cubs

Johnson pushed his way to High-A in his first full season of pro ball, posting impressive numbers in the second half with Daytona. At his best he attacks hitters with a low-to-mid-90s fastball, a hard curveball that can be a true swing-and-miss pitch, and a changeup that is making rapid strides. Johnson still has to prove that his thin frame can handle the rigors of starting every five days over a long season, but if he can demonstrate his durability, he could develop into a quality no. 3 starter in short order.

92. Jake Odorizzi, RHP, Tampa Bay Rays

Part of the package that sent James Shields to the Royals, Odorizzi is on the verge of securing a spot in the Rays' rotation. No part of Odorizzi's game truly stands out, but he makes up for that with three pitches that each grade at least average: a fastball that sits in the low 90s, a solid slider and an above-average changeup. While he lacks the profile to miss bats at the major-league level, he carries minimal risk and should become a no. 4 starter very soon.

93. Matt Davidson, 3B, Chicago White Sox

A classic right-handed power hitter, Davidson's long arms are both his strength and vulnerability. The third baseman generates plenty of extension through the hitting zone and is capable of lifting balls out of the park to all fields. The home run power can play into the mid-20s. Davidson also shows a developed idea of his strike zone and a willingness to work himself into favorable counts. The big concern surrounds his ability to consistently hit for average. The 23-year-old's propensity to overextend leaves him prone to stuff above the belt and on the inner third. Davidson has the ingredients to round into a regular at the hot corner for a handful of seasons, but if the hit tool is exposed over the long haul the profile becomes a likely up-and-down player.

94. Jesse Biddle, LHP, Philadelphia Phillies

Biddle made the leap to Double-A in 2013 and more than held his own despite an increased walk rate against more advanced hitters. With a low-90s fastball, plus curveball and developing changeup, Biddle can miss bats and work through lineups with ease. As his command develops—which it should with his clean delivery—Biddle should develop into a workhorse fourth starter, possibly earning a taste of the big leagues in 2014 and getting a full shot in 2015.

95. Joey Gallo, 3B, Texas Rangers

Gallo's raw power is the stuff of legend, and is the most impressive in the minors. He can drive any pitch out of any park, to any field, and that effort does not require square contact. Gallo has work to do at the plate however, as his hit tool projects well below average and might never reach the heights necessary for his raw power to play. He has improved enough to now project as a solid third baseman with a 70-grade arm. Gallo's future depends entirely on his ability to make contact, and if he improves enough he could be a monster talent.

96. Hunter Dozier, SS, Kansas City Royals

Dozier was the eighth overall selection in the 2013 draft, signing for below slot and allowing the Royals to push the savings to supplemental first rounder Sean Manaea. The former Stephen F. Austin State standout is a fundamental player with power serving as his carrying tool. Well put together and boasting a leveraged swing with natural lift, he could grow into a threat to hit 25 home runs annually and should provide good defensive value once he completes the likely transition from short to the hot corner. The ceiling is limited, but the overall profile could provide lots of surplus value for the Royals in the form of a solid everyday contributor who does everything pretty well.

97. Raimel Tapia, OF, Colorado Rockies

A potential breakout prospect for 2014, Tapia has the type of raw tools that cause prospects to explode onto the national scene. A gifted hitter, he has the potential to develop into an easy plus at the plate, and possibly better, at his peak. He backs up his hitting ability with impressive raw power that could max out in the 20-25 home run range. Defensively, he fits well in right field as an above-average defender with at least a plus arm. Tapia turns 20 before spring training and he could be in line for a monster full-season debut.

98. Alexander Reyes, RHP, St. Louis Cardinals

Reyes arrived on the scene in 2013 and showed well in the Appalachian League after an unusual path to professional baseball. An excellent prep pitcher, Reyes moved to the Dominican Republic to avoid the draft and signed in December 2012 for nearly $1 million. Armed with a 93–95 mph fastball that peaks around 97-98 and a curveball that earns plus grades, Reyes has the raw stuff to dominate the lower levels as he continues to develop his changeup and command. It remains early in the developmental process but Reyes has high-end potential that could make him a no. 2 or 3 starter.

99. Jorge Bonifacio, OF, Kansas City Royals

The Royals' major-league roster is slowly heading in the right direction, and Bonifacio could be part of the future of that roster if he continues to develop the way he did in 2013. A classic right fielder with a big arm and solid defensive skills, Bonifacio has the raw power at the plate to fulfill the other side of the profile as well. A natural hitter, Bonifacio could hit .280 at the highest level, and his power could play in the 20 home run range if he can begin applying more power in game action.

100. David Dahl, OF, Colorado Rockies

A year after Dahl went 10th overall, injuries turned 2013 into a lost season. When healthy, he displays the type of natural hitting ability rarely found in prospects. He demonstrates a quality approach in his at-bats, uses the whole field well and his above-average raw power should arrive in games as he matures. Dahl's supporters stand behind his ability to play center field and believe he can be an above-average defender down the line. While his first full season was a lost one, Dahl still maintains considerable potential as a middle-of-the-order hitter at a premium position.

101. Lewis Thorpe, LHP, Minnesota Twins

Signed out of Australia in 2012, Thorpe's professional debut was nothing short of a rousing success. Not only did he perform exceptionally well, but his stuff took a substantial step forward as well. Armed with an arsenal that could include a plus-plus fastball, plus curveball and plus changeup at his peak, Thorpe also shows an excellent feel for his craft and a promising command profile. He must still adjust to his remaining physical development and the demands of a heavier workload, but Thorpe's future is as promising as any arm in the Twins system.

Team Name Codes

CODE	TEAM	LEAGUE	AFFILIATION	Name	CODE	TEAM	LEAGUE	AFFILIATION	Name
ABE	Aberdeen	NYP	Orioles	IronBirds	CIN	Cincinnati	NL	-	Reds
ABQ	Albuquerque	PCL	Dodgers	Isotopes	CLE	Cleveland	AL	-	Indians
AKR	Akron	EAS	Indians	Aeros	CLE	AZL Indians	AZL	Indians	-
ALT	Altoona	EAS	Pirates	Curve	CLN	Clinton	MID	Mariners	LumberKings
ANA	Los Angeles	AL	-	Angels	CLR	Clearwater	FSL	Phillies	Threshers
ANG	AZL Angels	AZL	Angels	-	COH	Columbus	INT	Indians	Clippers
ARI	Arizona	NL	-	D-backs	COL	Colorado	NL	-	Rockies
ARK	Arkansas	TEX	Angels	Travelers	CRD	GCL Cardinals	GCL	Cardinals	GCL Cardinals
ART	Artemisa	CNS	-		CSC	Charleston	SAL	Yankees	RiverDogs
ASH	Asheville	SAL	Rockies	Tourists	CSP	Colorado Springs	PCL	Rockies	Sky Sox
AST	GCL Astros	GCL	Astros	GCL Astros	CUB	AZL Cubs	AZL	Cubs	-
ATH	AZL Athletics	AZL	Athletics	-	DAC	DSL D-backs/Reds	DSL	-	-
ATL	Atlanta	NL	-	Braves	DAN	DSL Angels	DSL	Angels	-
AUB	Auburn	NYP	Nationals	Doubledays	DAS	DSL Astros	DSL	Astros	-
AUG	Augusta	SAL	Giants	GreenJackets	DAT	DSL Athletics	DSL	Athletics	-
BAK	Bakersfield	CAL	Reds	Blaze	DAY	Daytona	FSL	Cubs	Cubs
BAL	Baltimore	AL	-	Orioles	DBL	DSL Blue Jays	DSL	Blue Jays	-
BAT	Batavia	NYP	Marlins	Muckdogs	DBR	DSL Braves	DSL	Braves	-
BGR	Bowling Green	MID	Rays	Hot Rods	DBW	DSL Brewers	DSL	Brewers	-
BIL	Billings	PIO	Reds	Mustangs	DCA	DSL Cardinals	DSL	Cardinals	-
BIN	Binghamton	EAS	Mets	Mets	DCH	DSL Cubs2	DSL	Cubs	-
BIR	Birmingham	SOU	White Sox	Barons	DCU	DSL Cubs1	DSL	Cubs	-
BLJ	GCL Blue Jays	GCL	Blue Jays	GCL Blue Jays	DDI	DSL D-backs	DSL	D-backs	-
BLT	Beloit	MID	Athletics	Snappers	DDO	DSL Dodgers	DSL	Dodgers	-
BLU	Bluefield	APP	Blue Jays	Blue Jays	DDR	DSL Rays	DSL	Rays	-
BNC	Burlington	APP	Royals	Royals	DEL	Delmarva	SAL	Orioles	Shorebirds
BOI	Boise	NOR	Cubs	Hawks	DET	Detroit	AL	-	Tigers
BOS	Boston	AL	-	Red Sox	DGI	DSL Giants	DSL	Giants	-
BOW	Bowie	EAS	Orioles	Baysox	DIA	AZL D-backs	AZL	D-backs	-
BRA	GCL Braves	GCL	Braves	GCL Braves	DIN	DSL Indians	DSL	Indians	-
BRD	Bradenton	FSL	Pirates	Marauders	DME	DSL Mets1	DSL	Mets	-
BRI	Bristol	APP	White Sox	White Sox	DML	DSL Marlins	DSL	Marlins	-
BRO	Brooklyn	NYP	Mets	Cyclones	DMR	DSL Mariners	DSL	Mariners	-
BRR	AZL Brewers	AZL	Brewers	-	DNV	Danville	APP	Braves	Braves
BRV	Brevard County	FSL	Brewers	Manatees	DOD	AZL Dodgers	AZL	Dodgers	-
BUF	Buffalo	INT	Blue Jays	Bisons	DOR	DSL Orioles	DSL	Orioles	-
BUR	Burlington	MID	Angels	Bees	DPA	DSL Padres	DSL	Padres	-
CAR	Carolina	CAR	Indians	Mudcats	DPH	DSL Phillies	DSL	Phillies	-
CCH	Corpus Christi	TEX	Astros	Hooks	DPI	DSL Pirates1	DSL	Pirates	-
CDR	Cedar Rapids	MID	Twins	Kernels	DPT	DSL Pirates2	DSL	Pirates	-
CFG	Cienfuegos	CNS	-		DRD	DSL Reds	DSL	Reds	-
CHA	Chicago	AL	-	White Sox	DRG	DSL Rangers	DSL	Rangers	-
CHB	Chiba Lotte	NPB	-	Marines	DRO	DSL Rockies	DSL	Rockies	-
CHN	Chicago	NL	-	Cubs	DRS	DSL Red Sox	DSL	Red Sox	-
CHR	Charlotte	INT	White Sox	Knights	DRY	DSL Royals	DSL	Royals	-
CHT	Chattanooga	SOU	Dodgers	Lookouts	DTI	DSL Tigers	DSL	Tigers	-
CHU	Chunichi	NPB	-	Dragons	DTW	DSL Twins	DSL	Twins	-
CIN	AZL Reds	AZL	Reds	-	DUN	Dunedin	FSL	Blue Jays	Blue Jays

CODE	TEAM	LEAGUE	AFFILIATION	Name	CODE	TEAM	LEAGUE	AFFILIATION	Name
DUR	Durham	INT	Rays	Bulls	LOW	Lowell	NYP	Red Sox	Spinners
DWA	DSL Nationals	DSL	Nationals	-	LTU	Las Tunas	CNS	-	
DWS	DSL White Sox	DSL	White Sox	-	LVG	Las Vegas	PCL	Mets	51s
DYA	DSL Yankees1	DSL	Yankees	-	LWD	Lakewood	SAL	Phillies	BlueClaws
DYN	DSL Yankees2	DSL	Yankees	-	LYN	Lynchburg	CAR	Braves	Hillcats
DYT	Dayton	MID	Reds	Dragons	MEM	Memphis	PCL	Cardinals	Redbirds
ELZ	Elizabethton	APP	Twins	Twins	MET	DSL Mets2	DSL	Mets	-
ERI	Erie	EAS	Tigers	SeaWolves	MHV	Mahoning Valley	NYP	Indians	Scrappers
EUG	Eugene	NOR	Padres	Emeralds	MIA	Miami	NL	-	Marlins
EVE	Everett	NOR	Mariners	AquaSox	MID	Midland	TEX	Athletics	RockHounds
FKU	Fukuoka	NPB	-	Hawks	MIL	Milwaukee	NL	-	Brewers
FRD	Frederick	CAR	Orioles	Keys	MIN	Minnesota	AL	-	Twins
FRE	Fresno	PCL	Giants	Grizzlies	MIS	Mississippi	SOU	Braves	Braves
FRI	Frisco	TEX	Rangers	RoughRiders	MNT	Montgomery	SOU	Rays	Biscuits
FTM	Fort Myers	FSL	Twins	Miracle	MOB	Mobile	SOU	D-backs	BayBears
FTW	Fort Wayne	MID	Padres	TinCaps	MOD	Modesto	CAL	Rockies	Nuts
GIA	AZL Giants	AZL	Giants	-	MRL	GCL Marlins	GCL	Marlins	GCL Marlins
GJR	Grand Junction	PIO	Rockies	Rockies	MRN	AZL Mariners	AZL	Mariners	-
GRB	Greensboro	SAL	Marlins	Grasshoppers	MSO	Missoula	PIO	D-backs	Osprey
GRF	Great Falls	PIO	White Sox	Voyagers	MTS	GCL Mets	GCL	Mets	GCL Mets
GRL	Great Lakes	MID	Dodgers	Loons	MYR	Myrtle Beach	CAR	Rangers	Pelicans
GRN	Greenville	SAL	Red Sox	Drive	NAS	Nashville	PCL	Brewers	Sounds
GRV	Greeneville	APP	Astros	Astros	NAT	GCL Nationals	GCL	Nationals	GCL Nationals
GWN	Gwinnett	INT	Braves	Braves	NBR	New Britain	EAS	Twins	Rock Cats
HAB	La Habana	CNS	-		NHP	New Hampshire	EAS	Blue Jays	Fisher Cats
HAG	Hagerstown	SAL	Nationals	Suns	NIP	Nippon Ham	NPB	-	Fighters
HAR	Harrisburg	EAS	Nationals	Senators	NOR	Norfolk	INT	Orioles	Tides
HDS	High Desert	CAL	Mariners	Mavericks	NWA	NW Arkansas	TEX	Royals	Naturals
HEL	Helena	PIO	Brewers	Brewers	NWO	New Orleans	PCL	Marlins	Zephyrs
HIC	Hickory	SAL	Rangers	Crawdads	NYA	New York	AL	-	Yankees
HNS	Hanshin	NPB	-	Tigers	NYN	New York	NL	-	Mets
HOU	Houston	AL	-	Astros	OAK	Oakland	AL	-	Athletics
HRO	Hiroshima Toyo	NPB	-	Carp	OGD	Ogden	PIO	Dodgers	Raptors
HUD	Hudson Valley	NYP	Rays	Renegades	OKL	Oklahoma City	PCL	Astros	RedHawks
HUN	Huntsville	SOU	Brewers	Stars	OMA	Omaha	PCL	Royals	Storm Chasers
IDA	Idaho Falls	PIO	Royals	Chukars	ONE	Connecticut	NYP	Tigers	Tigers
IND	Indianapolis	INT	Pirates	Indians	ORI	GCL Orioles	GCL	Orioles	GCL Orioles
IOW	Iowa	PCL	Cubs	Cubs	ORM	Orem	PIO	Angels	Owlz
JAM	Jamestown	NYP	Pirates	Jammers	ORX	Orix	NPB	-	Buffaloes
JAX	Jacksonville	SOU	Marlins	Suns	PAW	Pawtucket	INT	Red Sox	Red Sox
JCY	Johnson City	APP	Cardinals	Cardinals	PCH	Charlotte	FSL	Rays	Stone Crabs
JUP	Jupiter	FSL	Marlins	Hammerheads	PDR	AZL Padres	AZL	Padres	-
KAN	Kannapolis	SAL	White Sox	Intimidators	PEN	Pensacola	SOU	Reds	Blue Wahoos
KCA	Kansas City	AL	-	Royals	PEO	Peoria	MID	Cardinals	Chiefs
KNC	Kane County	MID	Cubs	Cougars	PHI	Philadelphia	NL	-	Phillies
KNG	Kingsport	APP	Mets	Mets	PHL	GCL Phillies	GCL	Phillies	GCL Phillies
LAK	Lakeland	FSL	Tigers	Flying Tigers	PIR	GCL Pirates	GCL	Pirates	GCL Pirates
LAN	Los Angeles	NL	-	Dodgers	PIT	Pittsburgh	NL	-	Pirates
LEH	Lehigh Valley	INT	Phillies	IronPigs	PMB	Palm Beach	FSL	Cardinals	Cardinals
LEL	Lake Elsinore	CAL	Padres	Storm	PME	Portland	EAS	Red Sox	Sea Dogs
LEX	Lexington	SAL	Royals	Legends	POT	Potomac	CAR	Nationals	Nationals
LKC	Lake County	MID	Indians	Captains	PRI	Princeton	APP	Rays	Rays
LNC	Lancaster	CAL	Astros	JetHawks	PUL	Pulaski	APP	Mariners	Mariners
LNS	Lansing	MID	Blue Jays	Lugnuts	QUD	Quad Cities	MID	Astros	River Bandits
LOU	Louisville	INT	Reds	Bats	RAK	Rakuten	NPB	-	Golden Eagles

CODE	TEAM	LEAGUE	AFFILIATION	Name	CODE	TEAM	LEAGUE	AFFILIATION	Name
RAY	GCL Rays	GCL	Rays	GCL Rays	TAM	Tampa	FSL	Yankees	Yankees
RCU	Rancho Cucamonga	CAL	Dodgers	Quakes	TBA	Tampa Bay	AL	-	Rays
REA	Reading	EAS	Phillies	Fightin Phils	TCV	Tri-City	NYP	Astros	ValleyCats
RIC	Richmond	EAS	Giants	Flying Squirrels	TEN	Tennessee	SOU	Cubs	Smokies
RNG	AZL Rangers	AZL	Rangers	-	TEX	Texas	AL	-	Rangers
RNO	Reno	PCL	D-backs	Aces	TGR	GCL Tigers	GCL	Tigers	GCL Tigers
ROC	Rochester	INT	Twins	Red Wings	TOL	Toledo	INT	Tigers	Mud Hens
ROM	Rome	SAL	Braves	Braves	TOR	Toronto	AL	-	Blue Jays
ROU	Round Rock	PCL	Rangers	Express	TRI	Tri-City	NOR	Rockies	Dust Devils
ROY	AZL Royals	AZL	Royals	-	TRN	Trenton	EAS	Yankees	Thunder
RSX	GCL Red Sox	GCL	Red Sox	GCL Red Sox	TUC	Tucson	PCL	Padres	Padres
SAC	Sacramento	PCL	Athletics	River Cats	TUL	Tulsa	TEX	Rockies	Drillers
SAN	San Antonio	TEX	Padres	Missions	TWI	GCL Twins	GCL	Twins	GCL Twins
SAV	Savannah	SAL	Mets	Sand Gnats	VAN	Vancouver	NOR	Blue Jays	Canadians
SBN	South Bend	MID	D-backs	Silver Hawks	VER	Vermont	NYP	Athletics	Lake Monsters
SBR	Inland Empire	CAL	Angels	66ers	VIS	Visalia	CAL	D-backs	Rawhide
SCO	State College	NYP	Cardinals	Spikes	VPH	VSL PHI	VSL	Phillies	-
SDN	San Diego	NL	-	Padres	VSE	VSL SEA	VSL	Mariners	-
SEA	Seattle	AL	-	Mariners	VTB	VSL TB	VSL	Rays	-
SEI	Seibu	NPB	-	Lions	VTI	VSL DET	VSL	Tigers	-
SFD	Springfield	TEX	Cardinals	Cardinals	WAS	Washington	NL	-	Nationals
SFN	San Francisco	NL	-	Giants	WIL	Wilmington	CAR	Royals	Blue Rocks
SJO	San Jose	CAL	Giants	Giants	WIS	Wisconsin	MID	Brewers	Timber Rattlers
SLC	Salt Lake	PCL	Angels	Bees	WMI	West Michigan	MID	Tigers	Whitecaps
SLM	Salem	CAR	Red Sox	Red Sox	WNS	Winston-Salem	CAR	White Sox	Dash
SLN	St. Louis	NL	-	Cardinals	WPT	Williamsport	NYP	Phillies	Crosscutters
SLO	Salem-Keizer	NOR	Giants	Volcanoes	WTN	Jackson	SOU	Mariners	Generals
SLU	St. Lucie	FSL	Mets	Mets	WVA	West Virginia	SAL	Pirates	Power
SPO	Spokane	NOR	Rangers	Indians	YAK	Hillsboro	NOR	D-backs	Hops
STA	Staten Island	NYP	Yankees	Yankees	YAN	GCL Yankees1	GCL	Yankees	GCL Yankees
STO	Stockton	CAL	Athletics	Ports	YAT	GCL Yankees2	GCL	Yankees	GCL Yankees2
SWB	Scranton/WB	INT	Yankees	RailRiders	YKL	Yakult	NPB	-	Swallows
SYR	Syracuse	INT	Nationals	Chiefs	YKO	Yokohama DeNa	NPB	-	BayStars
TAC	Tacoma	PCL	Mariners	Rainiers	YOM	Yomiuri	NPB	-	Giants

PECOTA Leaderboards

HITTERS

Home Runs

RANK	NAME	TEAM	HR
1	Miguel Cabrera	DET	32
2	Mark Trumbo	ARI	31
3	Jay Bruce	CIN	30
3	Chris Davis	BAL	30
5	Prince Fielder	TEX	29
5	Paul Goldschmidt	ARI	29
7	Adam Dunn	CHA	28
7	Edwin Encarnacion	TOR	28
7	Giancarlo Stanton	MIA	28
10	Jose Bautista	TOR	27
10	Anthony Rizzo	CHN	27
12	Alfonso Soriano	NYA	26
12	Adam Jones	BAL	26
14	Adrian Beltre	TEX	25
14	Joey Votto	CIN	25
14	Chris Carter	HOU	25
14	Evan Longoria	TBA	25
14	Pedro Alvarez	PIT	25
19	Mark Reynolds	NYA	24
19	Mike Trout	ANA	24
19	Josh Hamilton	ANA	24

Runs Batted In

RANK	NAME	TEAM	RBI
1	Miguel Cabrera	DET	104
2	Prince Fielder	TEX	99
3	Mark Trumbo	ARI	94
3	Paul Goldschmidt	ARI	94
5	Jay Bruce	CIN	93
6	Joey Votto	CIN	92
6	Chris Davis	BAL	92
8	Adrian Beltre	TEX	91
9	Edwin Encarnacion	TOR	88
9	Adam Jones	BAL	88
9	Anthony Rizzo	CHN	88
12	Robinson Cano	SEA	87
13	Adrian Gonzalez	LAN	85
14	Evan Longoria	TBA	84
15	Adam Dunn	CHA	83
15	Josh Hamilton	ANA	83
15	Mike Trout	ANA	83
18	Kendrys Morales	SEA	82
18	Hunter Pence	SFN	82
18	Ryan Zimmerman	WAS	82

Runs

RANK	NAME	TEAM	R
1	Mike Trout	ANA	109
2	Shin-Soo Choo	TEX	96
3	Miguel Cabrera	DET	93
4	Prince Fielder	TEX	92
5	Joey Votto	CIN	90
5	Paul Goldschmidt	ARI	90
7	Alex Gordon	KCA	87
8	Jason Kipnis	CLE	86
9	Andrew McCutchen	PIT	85
10	Jay Bruce	CIN	83
11	Ian Kinsler	DET	82
12	Jimmy Rollins	PHI	81
12	Adam Jones	BAL	81
12	Alejandro De Aza	CHA	81
12	Elvis Andrus	TEX	81
16	Edwin Encarnacion	TOR	80
17	Mark Trumbo	ARI	79
17	Justin Upton	ATL	79
17	Jose Altuve	HOU	79
20	Starlin Castro	CHN	78
20	Anthony Rizzo	CHN	78
20	Chris Davis	BAL	78

Stolen Bases

RANK	NAME	TEAM	SB
1	Rajai Davis	DET	38
1	Mike Trout	ANA	38
1	Billy Hamilton	CIN	38
4	Eric Young	NYN	37
5	Michael Bourn	CLE	36
6	Jacoby Ellsbury	NYA	35
6	Carlos Gomez	MIL	35
6	Jean Segura	MIL	35
9	Everth Cabrera	SDN	34
10	Coco Crisp	OAK	33
10	Jose Altuve	HOU	33
12	Elvis Andrus	TEX	32
13	Desmond Jennings	TBA	29
14	Alex Rios	TEX	28
14	Brett Gardner	NYA	28
14	Jason Kipnis	CLE	28
17	Jarrod Dyson	KCA	27
17	Starling Marte	PIT	27
19	Emilio Bonifacio	KCA	26
20	Alcides Escobar	KCA	25

Batting Average

RANK	NAME	TEAM	AVG
1	Miguel Cabrera	DET	.322
2	Joe Mauer	MIN	.312
3	Mike Trout	ANA	.305
4	Ryan Braun	MIL	.303
5	Joey Votto	CIN	.299
6	Robinson Cano	SEA	.297
7	Troy Tulowitzki	COL	.296
7	Buster Posey	SFN	.296
9	Billy Butler	KCA	.295
10	Victor Martinez	DET	.294
10	Carlos Gonzalez	COL	.294
10	Salvador Perez	KCA	.294
13	Adrian Beltre	TEX	.293
14	Yadier Molina	SLN	.291
14	Adrian Gonzalez	LAN	.291
14	Matt Carpenter	SLN	.291
17	Pablo Sandoval	SFN	.290
17	Allen Craig	SLN	.290
19	Jose Reyes	TOR	.289
19	Yasiel Puig	LAN	.289
19	Matt Holliday	SLN	.289

On Base Percentage

RANK	NAME	TEAM	OBP
1	Joey Votto	CIN	.413
2	Miguel Cabrera	DET	.407
3	Mike Trout	ANA	.394
4	Joe Mauer	MIN	.393
5	Prince Fielder	TEX	.390
6	Shin-Soo Choo	TEX	.382
7	Mike O'Neill	SLN	.376
8	Jose Bautista	TOR	.375
9	Buster Posey	SFN	.372
10	Matt Holliday	SLN	.371
10	Ryan Braun	MIL	.371
12	Matt Carpenter	SLN	.370
13	Andrew McCutchen	PIT	.369
13	Troy Tulowitzki	COL	.369
15	Albert Pujols	ANA	.368
15	Carlos Santana	CLE	.368
17	Lance Berkman	TEX	.367
17	Paul Goldschmidt	ARI	.367
19	Billy Butler	KCA	.364
20	Adrian Gonzalez	LAN	.363

Slugging Percentage

RANK	NAME	TEAM	SLG
1	Miguel Cabrera	DET	.566
2	Giancarlo Stanton	MIA	.523
3	Ryan Braun	MIL	.522
4	Troy Tulowitzki	COL	.521
5	Carlos Gonzalez	COL	.519
6	Albert Pujols	ANA	.516
6	Jose Bautista	TOR	.516
8	Joey Votto	CIN	.512
8	Mike Trout	ANA	.512
10	Paul Goldschmidt	ARI	.499
11	Prince Fielder	TEX	.493
12	Yasiel Puig	LAN	.488
13	Matt Kemp	LAN	.486
14	Matt Adams	SLN	.483
15	David Ortiz	BOS	.482
15	Robinson Cano	SEA	.482
15	Evan Longoria	TBA	.482
18	Evan Gattis	ATL	.481
19	Corey Dickerson	COL	.480
20	Edwin Encarnacion	TOR	.479
20	Adrian Beltre	TEX	.479

Isolated Slugging Percentage

RANK	NAME	TEAM	ISO
1	Giancarlo Stanton	MIA	.262
2	Jose Bautista	TOR	.260
3	Joey Gallo	TEX	.255
4	Miguel Cabrera	DET	.244
5	Miguel Sano	MIN	.232
5	Javier Baez	CHN	.232
7	Albert Pujols	ANA	.23
8	Evan Gattis	ATL	.228
9	Troy Tulowitzki	COL	.225
9	Carlos Gonzalez	COL	.225
11	Mike Napoli	BOS	.222
11	Mark Trumbo	ARI	.222
13	Ryan Howard	PHI	.221
13	Paul Goldschmidt	ARI	.221
15	Edwin Encarnacion	TOR	.220
16	Ryan Braun	MIL	.219
16	Chris Davis	BAL	.219
18	Jay Bruce	CIN	.217
18	Mike Hessman	DET	.217
18	Mark Reynolds	NYA	.217

True Average

RANK	NAME	TEAM	TAV
1	Miguel Cabrera	DET	.341
2	Joey Votto	CIN	.332
3	Mike Trout	ANA	.330
4	Jose Bautista	TOR	.318
4	Ryan Braun	MIL	.318
6	Albert Pujols	ANA	.317
7	Prince Fielder	TEX	.316
8	Giancarlo Stanton	MIA	.315
9	Paul Goldschmidt	ARI	.309
10	Andrew McCutchen	PIT	.308
10	Buster Posey	SFN	.308
12	Robinson Cano	SEA	.307
12	Matt Holliday	SLN	.307
12	Troy Tulowitzki	COL	.307
12	Yasiel Puig	LAN	.307
16	Joe Mauer	MIN	.306

17	Evan Longoria	TBA	.305
18	Adrian Gonzalez	LAN	.304
19	Matt Kemp	LAN	.302
20	Carlos Gonzalez	COL	.300

Wins Above Replacement Player, American League

RANK	NAME	TEAM	WARP
1	Mike Trout	ANA	7.3
2	Robinson Cano	SEA	5.4
3	Miguel Cabrera	DET	5.0
4	Evan Longoria	TBA	4.6
5	Albert Pujols	ANA	4.0
5	Prince Fielder	TEX	4.0
7	Adrian Beltre	TEX	3.9
8	Ben Zobrist	TBA	3.8
9	Ian Kinsler	DET	3.7
9	Alex Gordon	KCA	3.7
9	Dustin Pedroia	BOS	3.7

Wins Above Replacement Player, National League

RANK	NAME	TEAM	WARP
1	Joey Votto	CIN	5.9
2	Buster Posey	SFN	4.9
3	Andrelton Simmons	ATL	4.7
4	Andrew McCutchen	PIT	4.3
4	Matt Carpenter	SLN	4.3
6	Jean Segura	MIL	4.2
6	Giancarlo Stanton	MIA	4.2
6	Paul Goldschmidt	ARI	4.2
9	Adrian Gonzalez	LAN	4.0
10	Troy Tulowitzki	COL	3.9

Catcher WARP

RANK	NAME	TEAM	WARP
1	Buster Posey	SFN	4.9
2	Yadier Molina	SLN	3.5
3	Miguel Montero	ARI	3.0
4	Brian McCann	NYA	2.9
5	Matt Wieters	BAL	2.8
6	Salvador Perez	KCA	2.6
7	Jonathan Lucroy	MIL	2.4
8	Carlos Ruiz	PHI	2.3
9	Russell Martin	PIT	2.2
9	Wilin Rosario	COL	2.2
9	A.J. Ellis	LAN	2.2

First Base WARP

RANK	NAME	TEAM	WARP
1	Joey Votto	CIN	5.9
2	Miguel Cabrera	DET	5.0
3	Paul Goldschmidt	ARI	4.2
4	Albert Pujols	ANA	4.0
4	Prince Fielder	TEX	4.0
4	Adrian Gonzalez	LAN	4.0
7	Carlos Santana	CLE	3.3

8	Billy Butler	KCA	3.1
8	Anthony Rizzo	CHN	3.1
10	Joe Mauer	MIN	3.0
10	Mike Napoli	BOS	3.0

Second Base WARP

RANK	NAME	TEAM	WARP
1	Robinson Cano	SEA	5.4
2	Ben Zobrist	TBA	3.8
3	Ian Kinsler	DET	3.7
3	Dustin Pedroia	BOS	3.7
5	Chase Utley	PHI	3.5
6	Jason Kipnis	CLE	3.2
7	Omar Infante	KCA	2.5
8	Howie Kendrick	ANA	2.4
9	Daniel Murphy	NYN	2.2
9	Jedd Gyorko	SDN	2.2
9	Jose Altuve	HOU	2.2

Third Base WARP

RANK	NAME	TEAM	WARP
1	Evan Longoria	TBA	4.6
2	Matt Carpenter	SLN	4.3
3	Adrian Beltre	TEX	3.9
4	Ryan Zimmerman	WAS	3.5
5	Josh Donaldson	OAK	3.4
6	Manny Machado	BAL	3.3
7	Brett Lawrie	TOR	3.2
8	Pablo Sandoval	SFN	2.9
9	David Wright	NYN	2.8
10	Kyle Seager	SEA	2.7

Shortstop WARP

RANK	NAME	TEAM	WARP
1	Andrelton Simmons	ATL	4.7
2	Jean Segura	MIL	4.2
3	Troy Tulowitzki	COL	3.9
4	Starlin Castro	CHN	3.1
5	Elvis Andrus	TEX	2.7
6	Jose Reyes	TOR	2.6
7	Jed Lowrie	OAK	2.5
7	Yunel Escobar	TBA	2.5
9	J.J. Hardy	BAL	2.4
9	Alexei Ramirez	CHA	2.4
9	Ian Desmond	WAS	2.4

Left Field WARP

RANK	NAME	TEAM	WARP
1	Alex Gordon	KCA	3.7
2	Shin-Soo Choo	TEX	3.5
3	Matt Holliday	SLN	3.4
4	Mark Trumbo	ARI	2.9
5	Bryce Harper	WAS	2.7
6	Alejandro De Aza	CHA	2.5
6	Yoenis Cespedes	OAK	2.5

8	Brett Gardner	NYA	2.3
9	Josh Willingham	MIN	2.0
9	Starling Marte	PIT	2.0

Center Field WARP

RANK	NAME	TEAM	WARP
1	Mike Trout	ANA	7.3
2	Andrew McCutchen	PIT	4.3
3	Adam Jones	BAL	3.6
4	Shane Victorino	BOS	3.4
5	Carlos Gonzalez	COL	3.3
6	Jacoby Ellsbury	NYA	3.1
7	Coco Crisp	OAK	2.8
7	Denard Span	WAS	2.8
9	Desmond Jennings	TBA	2.7
10	Jon Jay	SLN	2.5
10	Carlos Gomez	MIL	2.5

Right Field WARP

RANK	NAME	TEAM	WARP
1	Giancarlo Stanton	MIA	4.2
2	Justin Upton	ATL	3.9
3	Jay Bruce	CIN	3.6
4	Josh Hamilton	ANA	3.3
5	Jose Bautista	TOR	3.2
6	Hunter Pence	SFN	3.0
6	Jason Heyward	ATL	3.0
8	Nick Swisher	CLE	2.9
9	Jayson Werth	WAS	2.8
10	Nelson Cruz	TEX	2.7

American League Rookie WARP

RANK	NAME	TEAM	WARP
1	Brandon Guyer	TBA	1.4
2	Xander Bogaerts	BOS	1.2
3	Kevin Kiermaier	TBA	1.1
3	Jackie Bradley	BOS	1.1
5	Antoan Richardson	NYA	1.0
5	Josmil Pinto	MIN	1.0
7	Luke Montz	OAK	0.9
7	Corban Joseph	NYA	0.9
7	Marcus Semien	CHA	0.9
10	Corey Brown	OAK	0.8

National League Rookie WARP

RANK	NAME	TEAM	WARP
1	Billy Hamilton	CIN	1.5
2	Travis d'Arnaud	NYN	1.4
3	Mike Olt	CHN	1.1
3	Kolten Wong	SLN	1.1
5	Tommy Medica	SDN	1.0
6	Thomas Neal	CHN	0.8
6	Tony Sanchez	PIT	0.8
6	Jake Marisnick	MIA	0.8
6	Zach Walters	WAS	0.8
10	Mauro Gomez	WAS	0.7

| 10 | Joey Butler | SLN | 0.7 |
| 10 | Juan Perez | SFN | 0.7 |

WARP Declines

RANK	NAME	TEAM	WARP 2013	WARP 2014	WARP DIFF
1	Chris Davis	BAL	7.0	2.0	-5.0
2	Carlos Gomez	MIL	6.0	2.5	-3.5
3	Paul Goldschmidt	ARI	7.5	4.2	-3.3
4	Mike Trout	ANA	10.4	7.3	-3.1
5	David Wright	NYN	5.8	2.8	-3.0
5	Matt Carpenter	SLN	7.3	4.3	-3.0
7	Miguel Cabrera	DET	7.9	5.0	-2.9
7	Colby Rasmus	TOR	4.1	1.2	-2.9
9	Josh Donaldson	OAK	6.2	3.4	-2.8
9	Shin-Soo Choo	TEX	6.3	3.5	-2.8

WARP Improvements

RANK	NAME	TEAM	WARP 2013	WARP 2014	WARP DIFF
1	B.J. Upton	ATL	-2.1	1.0	3.1
1	Starlin Castro	CHN	-0.0	3.1	3.1
3	Dan Uggla	ATL	-0.9	2.0	2.9
4	Adeiny Hechavarria	MIA	-2.3	0.5	2.8
5	Darwin Barney	CHN	-1.8	0.8	2.6
6	Paul Konerko	CHA	-1.0	1.5	2.5
6	Pablo Sandoval	SFN	0.4	2.9	2.5
8	Jose Altuve	HOU	-0.1	2.2	2.3
9	Jason Kubel	MIN	-1.6	0.6	2.2
9	Rickie Weeks	MIL	-0.7	1.5	2.2

PITCHERS

Wins

RANK	NAME	TEAM	W
1	James Shields	KCA	14
1	CC Sabathia	NYA	14
3	Justin Verlander	DET	13
3	Yu Darvish	TEX	13
3	Clayton Kershaw	LAN	13
3	Adam Wainwright	SLN	13
7	C.J. Wilson	ANA	12
7	Jon Lester	BOS	12
7	Ervin Santana	KCA	12
7	Jeremy Guthrie	KCA	12
7	Hiroki Kuroda	NYA	12
7	Felix Hernandez	SEA	12
7	Derek Holland	TEX	12
7	Cliff Lee	PHI	12
15	Chris Sale	CHA	11
15	Max Scherzer	DET	11
15	R.A. Dickey	TOR	11
15	David Price	TBA	11

| 15 | Mat Latos | CIN | 11 |
| 15 | Patrick Corbin | ARI | 11 |

Strikeouts

RANK	NAME	TEAM	SO
1	Yu Darvish	TEX	218
2	Justin Verlander	DET	203
3	Chris Sale	CHA	198
4	Clayton Kershaw	LAN	196
5	Max Scherzer	DET	182
6	Adam Wainwright	SLN	180
7	Jon Lester	BOS	177
8	Cliff Lee	PHI	176
9	Felix Hernandez	SEA	175
9	Cole Hamels	PHI	175
9	Stephen Strasburg	WAS	175
12	Tim Lincecum	SFN	174
13	Mat Latos	CIN	168
14	C.J. Wilson	ANA	165
14	CC Sabathia	NYA	165
16	James Shields	KCA	164
16	Jeff Samardzija	CHN	164
18	Gio Gonzalez	WAS	162
19	Lance Lynn	SLN	157
20	Mike Minor	ATL	156

Earned Run Average (min. 125 IP)

RANK	NAME	TEAM	ERA
1	Clayton Kershaw	LAN	2.35
2	Jose Fernandez	MIA	2.38
3	Stephen Strasburg	WAS	2.54
4	Chris Sale	CHA	2.70
5	Justin Verlander	DET	2.81
6	Matt Harvey	NYN	2.82
7	Felix Hernandez	SEA	2.86
8	Yu Darvish	TEX	2.92
9	Zack Greinke	LAN	2.94
9	Adam Wainwright	SLN	2.94
11	David Price	TBA	3.02
11	Kris Medlen	ATL	3.02
11	Cliff Lee	PHI	3.02
14	Jered Weaver	ANA	3.03
15	Matt Cain	SFN	3.04
16	Madison Bumgarner	SFN	3.07
17	Mat Latos	CIN	3.10
18	Andrew Cashner	SDN	3.19
19	Rafael Montero	NYN	3.20
20	A.J. Griffin	OAK	3.23

Walks plus Hits Per Innings Pitched (min. 125 IP)

RANK	NAME	TEAM	WHIP
1	Clayton Kershaw	LAN	1.01
2	Stephen Strasburg	WAS	1.02
3	Cliff Lee	PHI	1.04
4	Jose Fernandez	MIA	1.05
5	Chris Sale	CHA	1.08
5	Zack Greinke	LAN	1.08
5	Matt Harvey	NYN	1.08
5	Adam Wainwright	SLN	1.08
9	Kris Medlen	ATL	1.09
10	Dan Haren	LAN	1.10
10	Cole Hamels	PHI	1.10
10	Matt Cain	SFN	1.10
13	Mat Latos	CIN	1.11
13	Madison Bumgarner	SFN	1.11
15	Justin Verlander	DET	1.13
15	Felix Hernandez	SEA	1.13
15	Jordan Zimmermann	WAS	1.13
18	Jered Weaver	ANA	1.14
18	A.J. Griffin	OAK	1.14
20	Mike Minor	ATL	1.15
20	Rafael Montero	NYN	1.15
20	David Price	TBA	1.15

Saves

RANK	NAME	TEAM	SV
1	Craig Kimbrel	ATL	47
2	Jim Johnson	OAK	46
3	Rafael Soriano	WAS	43
4	Mariano Rivera	NYA	39
5	Fernando Rodney	TBA	36
6	Joe Nathan	DET	33
7	Chris Perez	LAN	32
8	Addison Reed	ARI	30
9	Jonathan Papelbon	PHI	29
10	Jason Motte	SLN	28
11	Huston Street	SDN	26
12	Aroldis Chapman	CIN	23
12	Rafael Betancourt	COL	23
14	Ernesto Frieri	ANA	21
14	Kenley Jansen	LAN	21
16	Joel Hanrahan	BOS	20
16	Grant Balfour	OAK	20
16	Sergio Romo	SFN	20
19	Greg Holland	KCA	19
20	Jose Valverde	DET	16

Strikeouts Per Nine (min. 125 IP)

RANK	NAME	TEAM	SO9
1	Yu Darvish	TEX	11.1
2	Stephen Strasburg	WAS	10.1
3	Jose Fernandez	MIA	9.7
3	Chris Sale	CHA	9.7
5	Matt Moore	TBA	9.6
6	Max Scherzer	DET	9.5
7	Matt Harvey	NYN	9.3
8	Justin Verlander	DET	9.2
8	Tim Lincecum	SFN	9.2

10	Francisco Liriano	PIT	9.0
10	Clayton Kershaw	LAN	9.0
12	Shelby Miller	SLN	8.8
13	Felix Hernandez	SEA	8.7
13	Gio Gonzalez	WAS	8.7
15	Yovani Gallardo	MIL	8.6
15	Ubaldo Jimenez	CLE	8.6
17	Trevor May	MIN	8.5
17	Jon Lester	BOS	8.5
17	Zack Greinke	LAN	8.5
20	Cole Hamels	PHI	8.4

Wins Above Replacement Player

RANK	NAME	TEAM	WARP
1	Clayton Kershaw	LAN	5.1
2	Justin Verlander	DET	4.6
3	Chris Sale	CHA	4.4
4	Stephen Strasburg	WAS	4.2
5	Yu Darvish	TEX	3.7
5	Adam Wainwright	SLN	3.7
7	Jose Fernandez	MIA	3.6
8	Cliff Lee	PHI	3.4
8	Felix Hernandez	SEA	3.4
10	Mat Latos	CIN	3.1
11	Zack Greinke	LAN	2.9
11	David Price	TBA	2.9
13	Matt Harvey	NYN	2.8
13	Kris Medlen	ATL	2.8
15	Madison Bumgarner	SFN	2.7
16	Max Scherzer	DET	2.6
16	CC Sabathia	NYA	2.6
16	Jon Lester	BOS	2.6
16	Matt Cain	SFN	2.6
20	Jered Weaver	ANA	2.5

National League Rookie WARP

RANK	NAME	TEAM	WARP
1	Burch Smith	SDN	1.0
2	Nate Karns	WAS	0.9
3	Heath Hembree	SFN	0.7
4	Rob Wooten	MIL	0.6
4	Vic Black	NYN	0.6
4	Carlos Martinez	SLN	0.6
7	Christian Garcia	WAS	0.5
7	Kyuji Fujikawa	CHN	0.5
7	Steven Ames	MIA	0.5
7	Jose De La Torre	MIL	0.5

American League Rookie WARP

RANK	NAME	TEAM	WARP
1	Kevin Gausman	BAL	1.0
2	Jake Odorizzi	TBA	1.0
3	Erik Johnson	CHA	0.9
3	James Paxton	SEA	0.9
5	Yordano Ventura	KCA	0.7
5	Steven Geltz	TBA	0.7
7	Mickey Storey	TOR	0.6
7	Donnie Joseph	KCA	0.6
7	Bruce Billings	OAK	0.6
7	Taijuan Walker	SEA	0.6

WARP Decline

RANK	NAME	TEAM	WARP 2013	WARP 2014	WARP DIFF
1	Bud Norris	BAL	2.9	0.1	-2.8
2	Anibal Sanchez	DET	4.6	1.9	-2.7
2	Scott Kazmir	OAK	2.5	-0.1	-2.7
4	Mike Pelfrey	MIN	2.0	-0.3	-2.3
5	Ryan Raburn	CLE	2.4	0.2	-2.2
6	Lance Lynn	SLN	3.5	1.4	-2.0
6	A.J. Burnett	PIT	2.7	0.6	-2.0
6	Corey Kluber	CLE	2.0	0.0	-2.0
6	Kyle Kendrick	PHI	2.2	0.1	-2.0
10	Max Scherzer	DET	4.6	2.6	-1.9
10	Tyler Chatwood	COL	1.8	-0.1	-1.9

WARP Improvements

RANK	NAME	TEAM	WARP 2013	WARP 2014	WARP DIFF
1	A.J. Griffin	OAK	-0.4	2.4	2.7
2	Stephen Strasburg	WAS	1.7	4.1	2.5
3	CC Sabathia	NYA	0.2	2.6	2.4
4	Roy Halladay	PHI	-0.9	1.3	2.2
5	Matt Cain	SFN	1.0	2.6	1.7
6	Huston Street	SDN	-0.4	1.1	1.6
7	Jarrod Parker	OAK	-0.0	1.5	1.5
7	Jered Weaver	ANA	1.0	2.5	1.5
9	Jason Marquis	SDN	-1.8	-0.4	1.4
9	Ian Kennedy	SDN	0.1	1.5	1.4
9	John Danks	CHA	-0.5	0.9	1.4

Contributors

The BP Team

R.J. Anderson lives in Florida and joined Prospectus in 2011. In the past, Anderson's work has appeared on ESPN, SLAM and Wired, as well as in the Wall Street Journal and USA Today. His nightmares include Wil Myers' hair.

Bill Baer is a Philly-based writer who has authored a book, contributed to ESPN and currently writes for NBC's HardballTalk and Rotoworld. He is on Twitter way too much. You can follow him @CrashburnAlley.

Craig Brown is co-founder of Royals Authority and currently the managing editor of Royals Review. His work has appeared at ESPN and Baseball Prospectus and other places deep in the internet. He lives in Kansas City with his wife and daughters. He doesn't feel like his team won the World Series.

Ken Funck contributes the very occasional "Changing Speeds" column to Baseball Prospectus, focusing on issues both absurd and sublime, and has written for the Baseball Prospectus Annual each year since 2009. Ken spends his days managing Business Intelligence systems and lives outside Madison, Wisconsin with his ever-supportive wife Stephanie, their children Max and Abby, one cat, two dogs, and hair that can flash plus with good arm-side run.

Ryan Ghan lives in Portland, Oregon with his wife, Sarah, and twin girls, Cleo and Annabel. He coaxes teenagers into solving for 'x' by day, and coaxes toddlers into eating their veggies by night. He spends his remaining time watching, thinking and writing about minor-league baseball.

Craig Goldstein joined Baseball Prospectus in August 2013. He lives and works in Washington, DC. His writing has appeared on SB Nation's Fake Teams, and he currently writes for SB Nation's MLB Newsdesk, MLB Draft Insider and The Dynasty Guru, in addition to BP. In his spare time he talks to strangers on the internet about baseball.

Chris Jaffe (manager comments) is a history professor in the suburbs of Chicago. He wrote a book—*Evaluating Baseball's Managers*—that won The Sporting News-SABR Baseball Research Award in 2010.

Andrew Koo is an intern at Baseball Prospectus. He fancies television, clean notebooks and, of course, baseball.

Pursuing his undergraduate degree in mathematics, he's commonly found studying in the campus library resisting the urge to load MLB.com At Bat. As a lifelong Torontonian, he wishes Canada and the United States would agree on the same spelling conventions. This is his first year contributing to the BP Annual.

Ben Lindbergh is the editor-in-chief of Baseball Prospectus, a contributor to Grantland and MLB Network's Clubhouse Confidential, and the co-host of Effectively Wild, the BP daily podcast. This is his fifth appearance in the annual, and he still hasn't thought of anything funny to put on this page.

SABR member **Rob McQuown** is a lifelong Cubs fan who was inspired by a Bill James Abstract to join STATS, Inc., where he was first published in The Scouting Report, 1993. Since then, neither starting up multiple dot-coms or years in big corporate life could pull him convincingly away from his first love, baseball. Getting restarted in the industry in 2006 with Baseball Daily Digest, he was welcomed to the Baseball Prospectus team when BDD became a subsidiary of BP—as a programmer and writer, where he has contributed both extensive web content (both words and programs) and has supported the back-end data provision.

Ian Miller lives in Oakland with his loving wife and indifferent cat. He plays bass in some bands you haven't heard and attends as many Cal League games as possible. With partner-in-crime Riley Breckenridge, he runs the Productive Outs blog/twitter feed/podcast/t-shirt empire.

Sam Miller is a staff writer and editor for Baseball Prospectus, the co-host of the daily BP podcast Effectively Wild and a contributor to ESPN the Magazine. He lives in Northern California with his wife, daughter and French press.

Jack Moore is a freelance sports writer living in Minneapolis. His greatest baseball achievement was probably getting hit in the leg by an 88 MPH fastball.

Adam J. Morris is a divorce lawyer in Houston who founded and still manages Lone Star Ball on the Sports Blog Nation network. He has a wife, Bethany, who tolerates his baseball obsession because it keeps him out of her hair, and two children, Seth and Rowan, who tell people that daddy's favorite thing is the Texas Rangers. He's still very sad Ian Kinsler was traded.

Marc Normandin is the Deputy Editor of SB Nation's MLB hub, the managing editor of Red Sox site Over the Monster, and a former Baseball Prospectus author. His work appears weekly at Sports on Earth, and he has previously written for ESPN, Sports Illustrated, and more. When not at his desk in Portland, ME, engrossed in the above, Marc is absorbed in video games, professional wrestling, and his cats. He is going to pour himself a glass of Scotch after hitting send on the email that brought you this bio.

Tommy Rancel has written for Bloomberg Sports, FanGraphs, Gammons Daily and ESPN.com. He lives in the Tampa Bay area with his wife (Jamie) and their three children (Alexis, Vincent and Jarek).

Daniel Rathman is a graduate student in urban planning at New York University, where he also works as a research assistant. He was born and raised in San Francisco, studied economics at Tufts University, and served as a teacher's assistant for Andy Andres' Sabermetrics course. After the World Series, Daniel morphs into a diehard Green Bay Packers fan and watches Seinfeld reruns virtually every night.

Bret Sayre is the Fantasy Manager at Baseball Prospectus and can also be found running his own website, TheDynastyGuru.com. He's known to be a bit verbose, so he's really trying to keep this brief. By day, he is quite adept at counting other people's trillions of pennies. By night, he is a full-time family man, part-time cook, part-time nurse, full-time baseball writer and part-time musician. As an eight-year old, he was knocked over by a man in his thirties as he tried to catch a dead ball thrown by Kevin Mitchell at Shea Stadium. Now, he lives in New Jersey with his wife, Carolyn, his son, Joshua, and his daughter, Alyson, who thinks every sport with a round ball is golf, despite his repeated attempts to correct her.

Adam Sobsey has been writing for Baseball Prospectus since 2011. He is the featured writer in Bull City Summer, a documentary book project about the Durham Bulls, published by Daylight Books in 2014.

Paul Sporer began writing for Baseball Prospectus in 2012. His work can be found at various outlets on the internet including his new pitching-focused endeavor, PaintTheBlack.com, which launched last fall. His primary outlet, PaulSporer.com, has been around since 2006 and still houses his work, including the well-known Starting Pitcher Guide released annually in the winter. He and his beloved beagle Curtis (named after former Detroit Tiger Granderson) spend their summers enjoying the blistering Texas heat glued to the MLB At Bat app on the computer, iPhone, and iPad watching or listening to as many games as possible, including every Tigers one.

Matt Sussman is an unlicensed Internet joke practitioner who contributes to BP's Hit List power rankings. He currently lives in Toledo, Ohio and is eagerly awaiting someone to launch Curling Prospectus.

Doug Thorburn writes the "Raising Aces" column at Baseball Prospectus, a series which is dedicated to the art and science of pitching, and he is the co-host of a pitching-centric podcast with the self-contradicting title of T.I.N.S.T.A.A.P.P. ("There Is No Such Thing As A Pitching Podcast"). He cut his teeth in the front office of the Sacramento River Cats, earned an M.B.A. in Sports Business Management and spearheaded the motion analysis program at the National Pitching Association. He also co-authored a book about pitching ("Arm Action, Arm Path, and the Perfect Pitch"), and wrote for Baseball Daily Digest prior to joining the BP staff. Thorburn resides in Morgan Hill, California, with his ever-supportive wife, Caitlin, and their two mischievous huskies.

Jason Wojciechowski is a union lawyer in Los Angeles with a fondness for labor history, bow ties and yelling. He lives with his wife, Austen Rachlis, and an ever-growing pile of cats.

Will Woods is a copywriter in New York City. He is less concerned with the game itself than the quality of the announcing. He is a Mets fan, but let's keep that between us. It's just not a great look.

Geoff Young founded Ducksnorts, publishing online content and three books about the Padres under that title from 1997 to 2011. He currently writes for PadresPublic.com, and has previously written for Baseball Prospectus, The Hardball Times, ESPN.com and others. This is his third appearance in the BP annual. He has also contributed to other books, including Best of Baseball Prospectus: 1996-2011. Geoff lives in San Diego with his patient wife, Sandra.

Acknowledgments

Bill Baer: Eric Longenhagen for imparting his knowledge on the Phillies' minor-league system.

Craig Brown: Charles Edward Jones, Joe Hamrahi, Jason Parks, Marc Normandin, Cecilia Tan, Sam Miller, Jason Wojciechowski, Matt Besler, Greg Schaum, David Lesky, Michael Engel, Clint Scoles, Clark Fosler, Josh Duggan, Max Rieper, Jeff Zimmerman, Connor Moylan, Evan Brunell, Rob Neyer, Graham Zusi

Ken Funck: Buddy Bell, Leni DePoister, Zach Eveland, Jim Grant, Joe Hamrahi, Jill Jokela, Doug Laumann, Ben Lindbergh, Dan McCarthy, Sam Miller, Dave Pease, Scott Reifert, Doug Ross, Jason Wojciechowski

Ryan Ghan: Bobby Scales, Angels Director of Player Development, for insight into the next wave of talent.

Craig Goldstein: Laurie Gross, Harvey Goldstein, Alexis Goldstein, Katherine Pappas, Doug Harris, Jason Wojciechowski, Sam Miller, Bret Sayre, Ian Miller, Riley Breckenridge, Jason Parks, BP Prospect Team, Jay Jaffe, Marc Normandin, R.J. Anderson, Chris Crawford, Ray Guilfoyle, Mauricio Rubio, Ben Carsley, Jacob Raim

Andrew Koo: Joe Hamrahi, Ben Lindbergh, Rob McQuown, Sam Miller, Jason Wojciechowski, Doug Gray, the BP Prospect Team led by Jason Parks, and multiple front office sources.

Ian Miller: The following people for their knowledge and insight, which were invaluable: Grant Brisbee, Jason Parks, Jason Cole, Roger Munter, Andrew Koo, Kevin Goldstein, David Stearns, Bobby Evans, and Tracy Miller.

Jack Moore: Thanks to Jim Breen, Ryan Topp and the rest of the crew who has kept my first Brewers blog, Disciples of Uecker, alive in my absence, and who I credit for maintaining a strong discourse in the Brewers online community

Marc Normandin: Steven Goldman, Tyler Bleszinski, Kevin Lockland, Emma Span, Chris Mellen, Mark Anderson, Chris Crawford, Ben Buchanan, Brian MacPherson, Alex Speier, Tim Britton, Evan Drellich, Rob Bradford, Alfredo Aceves, Bradley Ankrom, Neil deMause, Rob Neyer, Justin Bopp, Kevin Goldstein, John Coppolella, Dan Turkenkopf.

Tommy Rancel: R.J. Anderson, Adam Sobsey, Bradley Ankrom, Jonah Keri, Keith Law, Sam Miller, Jason Wojciechowski, Erik Hahmann, Jason Collette, Chaim Bloom, Erik Neander, James Click, Cornell Haynes Jr. James E. Jones, Jamie, Alexis, Vincent and Jarek

Daniel Rathman: Jason Parks, Jason Cole, Zach Mortimer, Joe Hamrahi at BP, and Carter Hawkins and Keith Woolner from the Indians.

Bret Sayre: Carolyn, for being my biggest inspiration both in life and on the page. Alyson and Joshua, for always making me smile. Lynn and Peter Sayre. Joe Hamrahi. Marc Normandin. Ray Guilfoyle. The entire BP Fantasy team. Ryan Westmoreland. Finn Zumsen. Josh Denton. Dan Vogelbach. Brock Landers. Kevin Goldstein. Jason Parks. John Roderick. Howard Johnson. Jack Johnson (the boxer). The Arthur Young Rotisserie League. All of my friends and family not mentioned above. Sam, Jason and editors everywhere for making me look better than I am.

Adam Sobsey: Mitch Lukevics, Heather Mallory, BP Prospect Staff, Weymouth Center for the Arts and Humanities.

Paul Sporer: Curtis the Beagle, Sean Forman, Joe Hamrahi, Jennifer Lawrence, Doug Thorburn, Sam Miller, Jason Wojciechowski, Dan Brooks, Jordan Gorosh, Melissa Parks, Cody Sporer, Dorothy Sporer, Paul Sporer Sr., Gino Barrica, Chandler Parks, and Ellie Goulding whose music underscored all of my writing sessions for the annual.

Doug Thorburn: Joe Hamrahi, Tom House, Ryan Sienko, Eric Andrews, Paul Sporer, Nick Faleris, Jason Cole, Mike Ferrin, Dan Brooks, Harry Pavlidis, anyone who is dedicated to life on the mound.

Will Woods: Ben Lindbergh, without whom I would never have contributed to Baseball Prospectus in the first place; Sam Miller and Jason Wojciechowski, the editors whose style guide made this process less intimidating and more fun; Jason Parks, whose prospect profiles put players' progress into perspective.

Geoff Young: Steve Adler, Corey Brock, Bill Center, Jason Cole, John Conniff, Mike Couzens, Jeff Creps, Scott Dunsmore, Matthew Eddy, Nick Faleris, A.J. Hinch, David Jay, Tom Krasovic, David Laurila, Wayne McBrayer, Howard Megdal, Mike Metzger, Ian Miller, Sam Miller, Zach Mortimer, John Nolan, Michael Palin, Jason Parks, Bernie Pleskoff, Eno Sarris, Randy Smith, Didi Tanadjaja, Doug Thorburn, Sandra Tokashiki, Mike Underhill, Jason Wojciechowski, and anyone else inadvertently missed.

Index

Baseball Prospectus Premium